Eastern Europe
and the Commonwealth
of Independent States
1992

Eastern Europe and the Commonwealth of Independent States 1992

FIRST EDITION

EUROPA PUBLICATIONS LIMITED

First published 1992

© **Europa Publications Limited 1992**
18 Bedford Square, London, WC1B 3JN, England

Australia and New Zealand
James Bennett (Collaroy) Pty Ltd, 4 Collaroy Street,
Collaroy, NSW 2097, Australia

Japan
Maruzen Co Ltd, POB 5050, Tokyo International 100-31

British Library Cataloguing in Publication Data
Eastern Europe and the Commonwealth of
Independent States—1992

ISBN 0-946653-77-1
ISSN 0962-1040

Printed and bound in England by
Staples Printers Rochester Limited
Neptune Close, Medway City Estate, Frindsbury, Rochester, Kent ME2 4LT

FOREWORD

The first edition of EASTERN EUROPE AND THE COMMONWEALTH OF INDEPENDENT STATES was prepared during a year of dramatic changes, as the post-Communist order developed in the region. Albania finally introduced political and economic reforms. Bulgaria introduced a new Constitution. In Yugoslavia, divergent reform programmes and aspirations exacerbated ethnic tensions until civil war broke out over the secession of Croatia and Slovenia. An increasing variety of conflicts and problems emerged in the other Communist federation, and there too the military failed to preserve the Union. The coup attempt of August 1991 catalysed the dissolution of the Union of Soviet Socialist Republics, after almost 70 years of existence, forcing the recognition of Baltic independence and ending with the establishment of a new association of sovereign nations.

More than 30 specialist writers have contributed to this comprehensive description and analysis of the countries of the region, placing them in their international and historical context. The introductory essays provide a general background and assessment of a range of regional issues; most of them focus on the countries of Eastern Europe, covering the former USSR as a regional superpower. There is also an essay on the former East German state. The section remains an invaluable evaluation of many matters common to the whole region.

There are seven chapters on the countries of Eastern Europe, an area defined more by its political experience than its geography. In addition to a chronology for each country, there are political and economic narratives, and geographies, maps and detailed statistical and directory sections. These last include information on government and state institutions, religion, the media, finance and business, environmental organizations and culture, to list but a few. The original plan to include surveys of the constituent republics of the federal countries took on greater significance as the work progressed, not only in the former USSR and Yugoslavia, but also, less tumultuously, in Czechoslovakia. The book therefore contains valuable, and often unique, information on the history, governments and institutions of the newly independent countries.

In Part Three, on the USSR and its Successor States, there are 12 political and economic essays on the 15 former Soviet republics, as a group—despite their recent independence, they remain linked by their common history as a Union and by their interdependent economies. Among the essays is an account of the August coup attempt and its consequences. The series of economic essays consists of sectoral and regional surveys. The section includes the texts of the founding documents of the new Commonwealth and the most recent political developments, in the histories of the republics. The chapters on the 15 republics, like any country chapter, include accounts of the geography, history, and economy, statistics and a directory.

Part Four is an up-to-date Political Profiles section, with biographical outlines of more than 170 men and women prominent in the political life of the region.

The Editor is grateful to all the contributors for their articles and help and to the numerous governments and organizations which have returned questionnaires and provided statistical and other information.

January 1992

ACKNOWLEDGEMENTS

The editors gratefully acknowledge the co-operation, interest and advice of all the authors who contributed to this volume. We are also indebted to many organizations connected with the region, particularly the national statistical offices and the ministries of information, whose help is greatly appreciated. We are especially grateful to Prof. Philip Hanson, Pavlina Popissakova of the Sofia-Press Agency (Bulgaria), the Armenia Encyclopedia Publishers, the *Svaboda* newspaper of Minsk (Byelorussia), the Ministries of Information of Croatia, Serbia and Slovenia, Tanjug Data-Bank (Yugoslavia) and to a number of ministries of social affairs and of the environment. In addition, we are grateful to Edward Oliver, who prepared the maps which are included in this volume.

We are most grateful for permission to make extensive use of material from the following sources: the United Nations' *Demographic Yearbook, Statistical Yearbook, Yearbook of Industrial Statistics* and *Yearbook of National Accounts Statistics*; the Food and Agriculture Organization of the UN's *Yearbook of Fishery Statistics, Production Yearbook* and *Yearbook of Forestry Products*; UNESCO's *Statistical Yearbook*; and *The Military Balance, 1991–92*, published by the International Institute for Strategic Studies, 23 Tavistock Street, London WC2E 7NQ, United Kingdom.

The following publications have been of special use in providing regular coverage of the affairs of the region: *Summary of World Broadcasts: Part 1, USSR* (now *Part 1, former USSR*) and *Summary of World Broadcasts: Part 2, Eastern Europe*, from the BBC, Reading; and *Report on Eastern Europe* and *Report on the USSR*, now combined as *RFE/RL Research Report*, from Radio Free Europe/Radio Liberty Research Institute, Oettingenstraße 67, W-8000 Munich 22, Germany.

EXPLANATORY NOTE ON THE DIRECTORY SECTION

The Directory section of each chapter is arranged under the following headings, where they apply:

THE CONSTITUTION

THE GOVERNMENT
   HEAD OF STATE
   CABINET/COUNCIL OF MINISTERS
   MINISTRIES

LEGISLATURE

LOCAL GOVERNMENT

POLITICAL ORGANIZATIONS

DIPLOMATIC REPRESENTATION

JUDICIAL SYSTEM

RELIGION

THE PRESS

PUBLISHERS

RADIO AND TELEVISION

FINANCE
   CENTRAL BANK
   STATE BANKS
   DEVELOPMENT BANKS
   COMMERCIAL BANKS
   FOREIGN BANKS
   STOCK EXCHANGE
   INSURANCE

TRADE AND INDUSTRY
   PUBLIC CORPORATIONS
   CHAMBERS OF COMMERCE AND INDUSTRY
   COMMERCIAL AND INDUSTRIAL ORGANIZATIONS

EMPLOYERS' ORGANIZATIONS
TRADE UNIONS
CO-OPERATIVES
MAJOR INDUSTRIAL COMPANIES

TRANSPORT
   RAILWAYS
   ROADS
   INLAND WATERWAYS
   SHIPPING
   CIVIL AVIATION

TOURISM

ATOMIC ENERGY

CULTURE
   NATIONAL/REPUBLICAN ORGANIZATIONS
   CULTURAL HERITAGE
   SPORTING ORGANIZATIONS
   PERFORMING ARTS
   ASSOCIATIONS

EDUCATION
   UNIVERSITIES

SOCIAL WELFARE
   NATIONAL AGENCIES
   HEALTH AND WELFARE ORGANIZATIONS

ENVIRONMENT
   GOVERNMENT/REPUBLICAN ORGANIZATIONS
   ACADEMIC INSTITUTIONS
   NON-GOVERNMENTAL ORGANIZATIONS
   REGIONAL ORGANIZATIONS

DEFENCE

CONTENTS

CONTENTS

THE CONTRIBUTORS

Tom Adshead. St Antony's College, University of Oxford.

John Allcock. University of Bradford.

Timothy Ash. Soviet Agriculture Research Group, University of Exeter.

Richard Ross Berry. University of Glasgow.

Rev. Canon Michael Bourdeaux. Keston College.

Michael J. Bradshaw. University of Birmingham.

David H. Childs. Professor at University of Nottingham.

Richard J. Crampton. St Edmund Hall, University of Oxford.

Bob Deacon. Leeds Polytechnic.

Dennis Deletant. University of London.

David Dyker. University of Sussex.

Jonathan Eyal. Director of Studies at Royal United Services Institute.

Philip Hanson. Professor at University of Birmingham.

Don Hinrichsen. Freelance writer.

Keith Howe. Soviet Agriculture Research Group, University of Exeter.

Raymond Hutchings. Freelance writer.

Robert Lewis. Soviet Agriculture Research Group, University of Exeter.

Margot Light. London School of Economics.

Branka Magaš. Historian.

Anthony Marcham. Polytechnic of the South Bank.

Gur Ofer. Professor at Hebrew University of Jerusalem.

Bert Pockney. Professor at University of Surrey.

Martyn Rady. University of London.

Myles Robertson. University of St Andrews.

Angus Roxburgh. Journalist.

Peter Rutland. Professor at Wesleyan University, Connecticut, USA.

George Schöpflin. University of London.

Michael Sheehan. University of Aberdeen.

Alan Smith. University of London.

Keith Sword. University of London.

Miranda Vickers. Freelance writer.

Stephen White. University of Glasgow.

Gordon Wightman. University of Liverpool.

ABBREVIATIONS

Acad.	Academician; Academy
Adm.	Admiral
admin.	administration
a.i.	ad interim
AID	(US) Agency for International Development
AIDS	Acquired Immunodeficiency Syndrome
Al.	Aleja (Alley, Avenue)
AL	Alabama
Alt.	Alternate
AM	Amplitude Modulation
amalg.	amalgamated
AO	Autonomous Oblast
AOk	Autonomous Okrug
approx.	approximately
ASEAN	Association of South East Asian Nations
asscn	association
assoc.	associate
ASSR	Autonomous Soviet Socialist Republic
asst	assistant
Aug.	August
auth.	authorized
Ave	Avenue
b.	born
Bd	Board
Bd.	Bulevardi
b/d	barrels per day
Bldg	Building
br.(s)	branch(es)
Brig.	Brigadier
bul.	bulvar (boulevard)
C	Centigrade
c.	circa
cap.	capital
Capt.	Captain
Cdre	Commodore
Cen.	Central
CEO	Chief Executive Officer
CFE	Conventional Forces in Europe
Chair.	Chairman/woman
c.i.f.	cost, insurance and freight
CIS	Commonwealth of Independent States
C-in-C	Commander-in-Chief
circ.	circulation
cm	centimetre(s)
CMEA	Council for Mutual Economic Assistance
Co	Company; County
Col	Colonel
Commdr	Commander
Commdt	Commandant
Commr	Commissioner
Corpn	Corporation
CP	Communist Party
CPSU	Communist Party of the Soviet Union
CSCE	Conference on Security and Co-operation in Europe
Cttee	Committee
cu	cubic
cwt	hundredweight
DDR	Deutsche Democratische Republik (German Democratic Republic)
Dec.	December
Dep.	Deputy
dep.	deposits
Dept	Department
devt	development
Dir	Director
DM	Deutsche Mark
Dr	Doctor
dwt	dead weight tons

E	East; Eastern
EBRD	European Bank for Reconstruction and Development
EC	European Communities
ECE	(United Nations) Economic Commission for Europe
Econ.	Economist; Economics
ECOSOC	(United Nations) Economic and Social Council
edn	edition
EEC	European Economic Community
EFTA	European Free Trade Association
e.g.	exempli gratia (for example)
eKv	electron kilovolt
eMv	electron megavolt
Eng.	Engineer; Engineering
est.	established; estimate; estimated
etc.	etcetera
excl.	excluding
exec.	executive
F	Fahrenheit
f.	founded
FAO	Food and Agriculture Organization
Feb.	February
FM	frequency modulation
fmrly	formerly
f.o.b.	free on board
Fr	Father
FRG	Federal Republic of Germany
Fri.	Friday
ft	foot (feet)
g	gram(s)
GATT	General Agreement on Tariffs and Trade
GDP	gross domestic product
GDR	German Democratic Republic
Gen.	General
GNP	gross national product
Gov.	Governor
Govt	Government
grt	gross registered tons
GWh	gigawatt hours
ha	hectares
HE	His (or Her) Eminence; His (or Her) Excellency
hl	hectolitre(s)
HM	His (or Her) Majesty
Hon.	Honorary (or Honourable)
hp	horsepower
HQ	Headquarters
HRH	His (or Her) Royal Highness
IAEA	International Atomic Energy Agency
IBRD	International Bank for Reconstruction and Development (World Bank)
ICC	International Chamber of Commerce
ICFTU	International Confederation of Free Trade Unions
IDA	International Development Association
i.e.	id est (that is to say)
ILO	International Labour Organisation/Office
IMF	International Monetary Fund
in (ins)	inch (inches)
Inc, Incorp., Incd	Incorporated
incl.	including
Ind.	Independent
INF	Intermediate-range Nuclear Forces
Ing.	Engineer
Insp.	Inspector
Int.	International
IRF	International Road Federation
irreg.	irregular
Is	Islands
IUCN	International Union for the Conservation of Nature and Natural Reserves

ABBREVIATIONS

Jan.	January		q.v.	quod vide (to which refer)
Jr	Junior			
Jt	Joint		Rd	Road
			reg., regd	register; registered
kg	kilogram(s)		reorg.	reorganized
kHz	kilohertz		res	reserve(s)
km	kilometre(s)		retd	retired
kv.	kvartira (apartment)		Rev.	Reverend
kW	kilowatt(s)		RSFSR	Russian Soviet Federative Socialist Republic
kWh	kilowatt hours			
			S	South; Southern; San
lb	pound(s)		SDR(s)	Special Drawing Right(s)
Lt, Lieut	Lieutenant		Sec.	Secretary
Ltd	Limited		Secr.	Secretariat
			Sen.	Senior
m	metre(s)		Sept.	September
m.	million		SFRY	Socialist Federal Republic of Yugoslavia
Maj.	Major		Soc.	Society
Man.	Manager; managing		Sq.	Square
mem.	member		sq	square (in measurements)
MEV	mega electron volts		SSR	Soviet Socialist Republic
mfrs	manufacturers		St	Saint; Street
Mgr	Monseigneur; Monsignor		START	Strategic Arms' Reduction Treaty
MHz	megahertz		Str.	Strada (street)
Mil.	Military		Sun.	Sunday
mm	millimetre(s)		Supt	Superintendent
Mon.	Monday			
MP	Member of Parliament		tech., techn.	technical
MSS	Manuscripts		tel.	telephone
MW	megawatt(s); medium wave		Thurs.	Thursday
MWh	megawatt hour(s)		Tř	třída (avenue)
			Treas.	Treasurer
N	North; Northern		Tues.	Tuesday
n.a.	not available		TV	television
nab.	naberezhnaya (embankment, quai)			
nám.	náměstí (square)		u.	utca (street)
Nat.	National		u/a	unit of account
NATO	North Atlantic Treaty Organization		UK	United Kingdom
NCO	Non-Commissioned Officer		ul.	ulitsa, ulica (street)
NMP	net material product		UN	United Nations
no.	number		UNCTAD	United Nations Conference on Trade and Development
Nov.	November		UNDP	United Nations Development Programme
nr	near		UNESCO	United Nations Educational, Scientific and Cultural Organization
nrt	net registered tons		UNHCR	United Nations High Commissioner for Refugees
Obl.	Oblast (region)		Univ.	University
Oct.	October		USA	United States of America
OECD	Organisation for Economic Co-operation and Development		USAID	United States Agency for International Development
OIC	Organization of the Islamic Conference		USSR	Union of Soviet Socialist Republics
Ok	okrug (district)			
OPEC	Organization of Petroleum Exporting Countries		VAT	Value Added Tax
opp.	opposite		Ven.	Venerable
Org.	Organization		VHF	Very High Frequency
			viz.	videlicet (namely)
p.	page		vol.(s)	volume(s)
p.a.	per annum		Vul.	vulitsa (street)
Parl.	Parliament(ary)			
per.	pereulok (lane, alley)		W	West; Western
Perm. Rep.	Permanent Representative		WCL	World Confederation of Labour
pl.	ploshchad (square)		Wed.	Wednesday
PLC	Public Limited Company		WFTU	World Federation of Trade Unions
PLO	Palestine Liberation Organization		WHO	World Health Organization
POB	Post Office Box			
pr.	prospekt, praspekt (avenue)		yr	year
Pres.	President			
Prin.	Principal			
Prof.	Professor			
Pte	Private			
p.u.	paid up			
publ.	publication; published			
Publr	Publisher			

LATE INFORMATION

Note: Following the dissolution of the USSR, in December 1991, the Russian Federation assumed control of all Soviet embassies and became the base country of the press agencies IAN and TASS. Any embassies or press agencies still designated as USSR should now read Russia.

ALBANIA (p. 88)
Interim Government
(December 1991)

An interim coalition composed of non-party members, intellectuals and specialists.

Chairman (Prime Minister): VILSON AHMETI.

Deputy Chairman and Minister of Mineral Resources and Energy: ABDYL XHAJA.

Deputy Chairman and Minister of Agriculture: ZYDI PEPA.

Minister of Foreign Affairs: ILIR BOCKA.

Minister of the Economy: GJERGJI KONDO.

Minister of Defence: ALFRED MOISIU.

Minister of Public Order: VLADIMIR HYSI.

Minister of Justice: KUDRET CELA.

Minister of Finance: ROBERT CEKU.

Minister of Light and Food Industry: ILIAZ MEHMETI.

Minister of Foreign Economic Relations: YLLI CABIRI.

Minister of Domestic Trade and Tourism: ROBERT GJINI.

Minister of Construction: LUIGJ ALEKSI.

Minister of Transport: ILIR MATAJ.

Minister of Education: ALFRED PEMA.

Minister of Culture, Youth and Sport: VATH KORRESHI.

Minister of Health: KRISTO PANO.

Chairman of the State Control Commission: YLLI MEMISHA.

Chairman of the Science and Technology Committee: PETRIT SKENDO.

BULGARIA (p. 119)
Presidential Elections
(January 1992)

Dr ZHELIU ZHELEV was re-elected as President of the Republic, and BLAGA NIKOLOVA DIMITROVA as Vice-President, with 52.9% of the votes cast, in a second round of elections, on 19 January 1992.

Chairman of the National Assembly: STEFAN SAVOV.

YUGOSLAVIA (p. 342)
Montenegro—Government Changes
(January 1992)

On 17 January 1992 the Montenegrin Assembly accepted the resignations of the Minister of Finance, BOŽIDAR GOZIVODA, and a Minister without Portfolio, BREDRAG GORANOVIĆ, and approved the appointments of four new ministers:

Minister of Energy, Mining and Industry: MIODRAG GOMILANOVIĆ.

Minister of Ecology: MIHAIL BURIĆ.

Ministers without Portfolio: BRANKO RADOVIĆ, MILADIN VUKOTIĆ.

POLITICAL PROFILES (p. 582)
New Estonian Prime Minister
(January 1992)

VÄHI, Tiit: Prime Minister of Estonia. *Career:* he first joined the Government in 1989, as head of the transport committee, and became Minister of Transport and Communications under Edgar Savisaar (q.v.). He was considered politically unaffiliated and, in January 1992, was the surprising successor of Savisaar as Prime Minister. *Address:* Uus 28, 2001001 Tallinn, Estonia.

PART ONE

Introductory Essays

POLITICAL PERSPECTIVES ON EASTERN EUROPE

JONATHAN EYAL

After the euphoria of 1989, the year of revolutions, Eastern Europe began the task of economic and political reconstruction. The removal of the Communist regimes exposed not only deep-seated ethnic and social divisions, it also delineated the two tiers of Eastern Europe. In the northern tier were the central European countries of Poland, Czechoslovakia and Hungary; in the south, were the peoples of the Balkans (including Romania). This division, which roughly coincides with the old division between the Austro-Hungarian and Ottoman territories, was reinforced by political and economic factors, and, after 1989, swiftly became very apparent. The Balkans witnessed bitterly-contested elections, massive social dislocation and great political strife. Poland, Czechoslovakia and Hungary, however, conducted fair elections, eschewed violence and produced governments which, initially, appeared very stable. In reality, of course, there are more nuances. In all three northern-tier states of Eastern Europe, deeper divisions are barely concealed. Disputes about the pace of economic reforms, state institutions, a new constitutional contract and a new foreign policy are coming to the fore. They may not prove as disruptive as in the Balkans; state institutions are functioning, well-organized parties do exist and venues for a peaceful political debate are present. However the potential for instability is clearly there.

POLITICAL STABILITY IN THE NORTHERN TIER
Poland

In early 1990 Poland began its dramatic programme towards the creation of a market economy. The experiment was remarkable in two respects. At the time when other states in Eastern Europe were contemplating the merits of a sudden (or 'shock therapy') move to market mechanisms or a gradual transition, Poland's Government opted for an 'all-or-nothing' approach: the Minister of Finance, Leszek Balcerowicz, introduced a nearly-balanced budget, abolished most subsidies and price controls and devalued the złoty to a realistic rate of exchange. Real incomes fell by as much as one-third in the first four months of the reform and unemployment started to increase rapidly. In January 1990 inflation rose considerably, to a monthly rate of 80%, as producers passed on the increased costs to consumers. However, as most Polish families had to spend at least two-thirds of their incomes on food, potential customers could no longer afford to buy at any price and inflation slowed dramatically. Although unemployment continued to rise well beyond the Government's expectation, the reform succeeded: throughout 1990 the monthly inflation rate was less than 10%; and Poland developed a sizeable, and quite unexpected, trade surplus. Much to the surprise of many observers, the Poles appeared to bear the reform's privations patiently. There were no major demonstrations, and one strike on the railways was defused with the help of Lech Wałęsa, who, at that time, was still the unchallenged leader of Solidarność. A debt of US $40,000m. provided more of a psychological than a real burden; there was immense international support for the Polish reforms, so most of the country's debts to foreign banks were rescheduled and those owed to foreign governments were cancelled. By mid-1990 a vast privatization programme was announced, offering workers the opportunity to buy up to 20% of the stock in their own factories, with the help of low-interest loans.

However, behind the encouraging statistics, the troubles of Poland remain: the division between the countryside and towns, and between intellectuals and workers. High prices and interest rates were making the cost of machinery and fertilizers prohibitively expensive, and the collapse of state-owned distribution systems caused even more hardship for the farmers. Solidarność's rural counterpart complained about the neglect of the rural sector by the central government, but was unable to impress its case on Balcerowicz's technocrats, who assumed that Poland's private-sector farmers did not require much immediate attention. More importantly, by mid-1990, there were obvious divisions between the intellectuals, who supported Prime Minister Tadeusz Mazowiecki, and the Solidarność activists behind Wałęsa. The conflict should not be viewed as one between 'left' and 'right', although Wałęsa supporters, described as right-wing by Mazowiecki, did emphasize the elimination of the Communist nomenklatura and the imperative of hastening political reforms. In essence, the split within Solidarność went much deeper. Wałęsa, the man responsible for Mazowiecki's appointment to the premiership, complained of a lack of consultation and of general neglect of workers' needs. Mazowiecki, in return, accused Wałęsa of mentioning populist ideas and betraying the Government at a critical moment. The conflict led to the dismissal of several prominent Solidarność leaders, such as Bujak, Michnik and Turowich and, ultimately, to an open split within Solidarność and Wałęsa's challenge for Poland's presidency.

The two rounds of voting for the presidential election, held in November and December 1990, revealed the entire array of Poland's existing and latent difficulties. The electoral campaign was not conducted by political parties (the development of which into cohesive forces is still in its infancy), but remained dominated by personalities. Furthermore, it was a campaign which blurred the allocation of powers in the state even further. Throughout his stewardship, Prime Minister Mazowiecki consolidated the parliamentary rule of the National Assembly. There was no other alternative: because of the peculiar process which brought Solidarność to power, President Jaruzelski remained a figure-head, a man who had little credibility. A direct election for the presidency would immediately raise the crucial question: was Poland a parliamentary or a presidential democracy? As a new constitution was drafted, Mazowiecki and many of the intellectuals wanted presidential elections postponed until late in 1991. Wałęsa's challenge precluded that.

Mazowiecki was then persuaded, against his better judgement, to confront Wałęsa. Neither candidate, however, had reckoned on the sudden appearance of Stanisław Tymiński, an emigré entrepreneur, who had made his money in Peru and Canada. Nobody knew much about this candidate whose political manifesto was contained in a book, which he had had published himself, entitled *Holy Dogs*. Many, however, were attracted to his promise that Poland should be 'transformed into America'. This was to occur within months, a feat which could be achieved through the attainment of 'spiritual, telepathic ability'. Tymiński also suggested that Poland should acquire a nuclear bomb, which he proposed to call the 'Z-bomb', from *Zydzi*, the Polish word for Jews. The fact that such a character managed to defeat Mazowiecki in the first round of the presidential elections was ample proof of the frustration of many Poles and the volatile foundations of their politics. Lech Wałęsa, who called his unexpected opponent an 'accident of democracy', then went on to win the second round and to become Poland's first democratically-elected President for over 50 years.

The sheer shock of the electoral campaign had a sobering effect on all political groups. Mazowiecki tendered his resignation; Wałęsa appointed Jan Krzysztof Bielecki as his successor. Continuity was emphasized by the retention, for instance, of Balcerowicz in the Ministry of Finance (thereby appeasing international creditors and financial institutions). Wałęsa also proved himself to be a shrewd political operator: he intervened little in parliamentary affairs and allowed the cabinet, the Council of Ministers, to continue with most of its activities. Nevertheless, political conflicts were unavoidable.

The foremost conflict was between the institutions of the presidency and the parliament, a difficult issue in all Eastern European states. Secondly, Wałęsa's most trusted advisers were unlikely to remain silent for long. The President's extensive personal office duplicated many government responsibilities. Finally, Prime Minister Bielecki, himself an economist, was unlikely to allow Balcerowicz to continue deciding future reforms. Soon, all these disputes came to the fore. Poland's unrepresentative National Assembly clashed with the country's democratically-elected President, on the contents of the electoral law and the timing of the general election. With little regard to constitutional niceties, Wałęsa was quick to threaten the imposition of presidential rule and the dissolution of parliament. He was eventually persuaded against such a move, mainly because of its international repercussions. The election in October 1991 of a new, if fragmented, Sejm, and the subsequent appointment of a Government headed by Jan Olszewski, reduced the risk of presidential intervention.

Hungary

As expected, the one-party system dismantled itself gracefully in Hungary. In a fitting gesture, the Communist regime's last act was to rehabilitate the victims of 45 years of Party rule. In March 1990 no less than 60 parties contested the first round of the parliamentary elections, including one called the Winnie-the-Pooh Party. Only 10 were of political significance, and the divide was very similar to that in Poland or elsewhere in Eastern Europe, between intellectuals and populists. In Hungary's case, the populists were the Hungarian Democratic Forum (HDF), a centre-right alliance of politicians, who have been described in the West as social-democrats. They had worked with the Communists in the past. The HDF wanted economic reform to come more slowly than it would under 'shock therapy' and, especially, to avoid unemployment in the transition to a market economy. Most importantly, the HDF supported notions of 'Hungarianness', of the unity of the Hungarian (Magyar) nation wherever it resides. As such, the HDF's policies appeared threatening to neighbouring Czechoslovakia and Romania, two nations which incorporate, between them, no less than 3m. ethnic Hungarians. The HDF's most serious opponents were the liberal Alliance of Free Democrats (AFD), a party of intellectuals and students, many of them Budapest-based and, as the HDF told voters, of Jewish extraction. The AFD promised Hungary's 'return to Europe', a massive and immediate shift to a market economy and the removal of all Communist supporters from state affairs. Straddling between these two was the

Independent Smallholders' Party (ISP), a party with a glorious past but with no appealing solutions for Hungary's current problems. There were also the parties of the left (particularly the main successor of the old ruling Party, now called the Hungarian Socialist Party—HSP), who most commentators believed had few electoral prospects.

The campaign proceeded with great gusto and no significant disturbances; the authorities vigorously dealt with the slightest manifestation of anti-Semitism. The first round of the elections, held on 25 March 1990, produced no surprises: the HDF obtained 24.73% of the votes cast; the AFD 21.39%; the ISP 11.73%; and the HSP a relatively respectable 10.89%. In the second round of the elections, held on 8 April, the HDF won almost one-half of the votes and finally obtained 165 seats in the 386-seat parliament. Its main opponent, the AFD, ultimately obtained 92 seats, while the ISP and the HSP claimed 43 and 33 deputies respectively.

The great maturity of the political debate in Hungary was, indeed, striking. Out of the 60 parties which took part in the campaign, only seven major parties gained parliamentary representation. The fact that no party obtained an overall majority in the first free election since 1947 was hardly surprising. Nevertheless, some 78% of parliamentary seats were controlled by the three largest parties, thereby creating a sense of stability and allowing for the relatively swift creation of a coalition. Thus, although the HDF's leader, József Antall, excluded the possibility of any grand coalition with the AFD, an alliance with the ISP and other small parties assured him of a comfortable parliamentary majority. The political transition was smooth: the division of the parliamentary committees, the legislative timetable and many of the tasks of the new National Assembly were already decided after the first round of the election.

However, as the year progressed, economic difficulties created a state of tension within the ruling coalition. The first dispute related to the speed of economic reform: Prime Minister Antall promised a gradual transition to a market economy, but circumstances beyond his control (including an inflation rate of 30%) tended to force a more rapid pace of change. The next contentious issue was the privatization of agriculture and, especially, the restoration to the original owners of land confiscated by the Communists, a principle on which the ISP continued to insist. Both disputes were resolved in a classic Hungarian manner. State enterprises were either sold or privatized themselves, with the help of one of the most liberal foreign investment policies in Eastern Europe. The fact that a small free market, in the services and retail sectors, already existed helped the process and limited the growth in unemployment. As for the land distribution issue, it became the subject of various legal disputes, ultimately resulting in court rulings against the ISP. The appearance of calm and the obviously smooth transfer of power increased Hungary's reputation in the West. No less than two-thirds of all Western investment in Eastern Europe continued to prefer Hungary.

The apparent stability of the Government, however, does hide some serious and potentially disruptive factors. The first is Hungarian nationalism. The fate of the Hungarians abroad, in territories which fervent nationalists still call 'amputated Hungarian lands', has plagued all governments since 1920. Prime Minister Antall, himself a historian of these problems, passionately believed in his duty to defend all his co-nationals, wherever they may be. Although from mid-1991 there was some tension with Yugoslavia, over the Hungarians of Vojvodina (in the territory of Serbia), inevitably the most serious tension is with Romania, where more than 2m. ethnic Hungarians reside. No serious politicians now advocate territorial revision. Nevertheless, Antall appeared determined to gain some leverage over the Romanian government, in order to improve the position of his fellow-Hungarians in the neighbouring state. Diplomacy and reasoning alone do not seem to work: Romania's ruling Front for National Salvation has been accused of being determined to exploit ethnic divisions in order to consolidate its power. The authorities in Bucharest have encouraged the formation of an ultra-nationalist movement, the Vatra Românească (Romanian Hearth, or Romanian Cradle) and have steadfastly refused to grant any group rights to Transylvanian Hungarians. After some failed attempts to negotiate with the Romanians, Antall's Government has decided on a new approach: Hungary will concentrate on enshrining the rights of ethnic minorities in every international treaty and will ensure that Romania's acceptance into any European institution will be made conditional on respect for these rights. Since Hungary is already a full member of the Council of Europe and well advanced towards a treaty of association with the European Community (EC), the policy will increase Hungary's ability to influence Romania. Whether it will improve matters for the Transylvanian Hungarians is uncertain, but relations between the two states are likely to remain extremely strained.

Antall's second difficulty is the economy. Although the process of reform has proceeded better than expected, the Government has avoided abolishing all subsidies or imposing a strict monetary policy. An attempt to raise petrol prices dramatically was quickly rescinded, when there was the threat of a national strike. Relations with the trade unions remain sensitive. Ultimately, however, Hungary's prospects for 1992 were good, provided Antall's personal health improved and the coalition remained united. The country was particularly adept at removing the Soviet military presence and at forging new security relations with other central and Western European states. Hungary's relative stability, together with its small size, great political vitality and solid reputation in the West will continue to serve Antall. Much, however, depends on the course of events inside Romania, the former USSR, Czechoslovakia and Yugoslavia. As Hungary's alleged involvement in supplying arms to the rebel republics in Yugoslavia illustrates, Hungarian internal stability remains connected to the internal stability of most of its neighbours.

Czechoslovakia

The huge popularity of Czechoslovakia's 'Velvet Revolution', augmented by President Václav Havel's personal standing in the West, continued to serve the country in good stead throughout 1990. Czechoslovakia now had a leader who was widely known and admired before the year of the revolutions. Havel's plays were performed throughout the continent and Czechoslovak leaders, from the dissidents of the 1968 'Prague Spring' uprising to the student activists of 1989, were fêted in every Western capital. Yet this favourable international image hides a much more ambiguous reality and a multitude of potential difficulties.

The transition from the Communist dictatorship was orderly, well-controlled from above and entirely in the hands of intellectuals. Civic Forum and its Slovak counterpart, Public Against Violence (PAV), the umbrella organizations which led the opposition to the old regime, remained amorphous associations of disparate interest groups, which, more often than not, excluded the country's large industrial working class. Most of the debate about Czechoslovakia's future political and economic options was conducted, therefore, within Civic Forum and PAV, thereby imparting an impression of a national consensus which, in reality, does not exist.

Before the June 1990 elections, the dispute within the Forum was essentially concerned with the transition to a market economy. Its main protagonists were the Deputy Prime Minister, Valtr Komarek, who advocated a slow transition, and the Minister of Finance, Dr Václav Klaus, who supported a 'shock therapy'. Nevertheless, solidarity between the various factions prevailed in the electoral campaign, and Civic Forum and PAV triumphed. The electoral campaign, acknowledged by all observers as the cleanest and fairest in Eastern Europe during 1990, was only marred by one bomb explosion, in central Prague on 2 June (initially blamed on elements within Czechoslovakia's former security services).

Voters elected representatives to both the Federal Assembly and to the National Councils of the Czech and Slovak Republics. There are 150 seats in each of the two constituent houses of the Federal Assembly, the House of the People and the House of the Nations. In the former, the Czech Lands elect 101 of the members, but, in the House of the Nations there is equal representation for the Czech and Slovak Republics. Civic Forum and PAV won 170 seats (57% of the total number of seats in the Federal Assembly), followed by the Communists (47 seats), the coalition of three parties in the Christian Democratic Union (40 seats), the Movement for Autonomous Democracy-Society for Moravia and Silesia (16 seats), the Slovak National Party (15 seats) and the Hungarian ethnic movement, Soužití (12 seats). The results revealed some interesting factors about Czechoslovak politics. First, while the Forum and PAV gained an absolute majority in the federal parliament, their strength in Slovakia was only one-half of that gained in the Czech Lands. Secondly, while the Christian Democratic Union (CDU) gained only 8% of the votes in elections to the Czech National Council, the alliance's support in Slovakia was almost double that amount. Finally, the relative success of the Communists was particularly important. Given their recent history in government, and their association with the USSR, the Communists did not expect to perform very well. In fact they repeated the feat of their pre-Second World War predecessors by becoming the second-largest party in the country (although far behind the Forum and PAV) and, more significantly, retained exactly the same support in both the Czech and Slovak Republics. This probably indicates that the party's strength transcends national divisions; it also points to a solid future for the Communists.

Despite these results, which clearly pointed to further political divisions, President Havel persisted in his desire for consensus and reappointed as Prime Minister Marián Čalfa, the former Communist who had formed the 'government for national understanding', in December 1989. The divisions, however, were not thus removed. There are two constitutional issues, decentralization and economic reform, which remain areas of major disagreement: that is, the federal structure of the country and the methods of transition to a market economy.

Relations between the Czechs and Slovaks had been difficult ever since the country's foundation at the end of the First World War. The situation is not without its ironies. Just as since 1989, so before the Second World War, Czechoslovakia's leaders enjoyed great international prestige. At home, however, they failed to understand or solve the simmering dispute between their two nations. The Slovaks, devout Catholics and traditionally an agrarian society, were subjected to the rule of the relatively well-developed and industrious Czechs. Prague's inability to cope with this conflict led to a Slovak secessionist movement in the late 1930s, a disaster which the present leaders of the country are determined to avoid. Federalists were encouraged by the Slovak nationalists gaining comparatively few votes in their National Council. This is only part of the picture, for Slovak nationalism also involves Czechoslovakia in a wider dispute with neighbouring Hungary. PAV was forced to yield to Slovak nationalist pressure and restrict the language rights of the Hungarian minority. The dispute with the Hungarians, which is fundamental to the Slovak process of national redefinition, will continue for the foreseeable future. The division between Slovakia and the Czech Lands also has an economic dimension. Throughout the years of Communist rule (and especially during the last 20 years), Slovakia benefited from large investments, intended to lessen the economic disparities in the country. Many of the industrial plants now in Slovakia are scheduled to close, according to the federal economic reform plan, but each closure is deeply resented by the Slovaks, who suspect that the Government in Prague does not care about their plight. An open conflict has already erupted over the central Government's decision to restrict the export of arms. Slovakia, a large weapons producer, has vowed to defy these restrictions, in order to safeguard thousands of jobs. The dispute hampers the federal Government's ability to function and ultimately led to the dismissal of Vladimír Mečiar, Slovakia's Prime Minister. A serious debate continued, during 1991, about the country's Constitution and federal institutions, and the Slovak national movement was gaining ground.

Czechoslovakia's second significant problem was Civic Forum itself. In a sense, the June 1990 elections merely postponed the creation of proper political parties and preserved the air of national unanimity born during the revolution. At its Congress in Prague, during January 1991, the Forum adopted a new programme, which still sought to maintain cohesion. A 17-member executive committee was elected, and the Minister of Finance, Václav Klaus, was reconfirmed as the Front's leader. Klaus, however, was not appeased. He had always argued that the Forum could no longer behave as a revolutionary 'action committee' and must transform itself into a proper political party. Less than one month after the Congress, members of the Forum accepted the inevitable and agreed on a split, between those dedicated to quick market reforms and capitalism (led by Klaus) and more 'moderate' elements, who still advocated a mixed economy or a 'social market'. The behaviour of these two wings, and other parties subsequently created, will ultimately decide the future stability of Czechoslovakia. PAV has been through a similar split. Although the country is still stable, tremendous potential for discord still exists. The Communists, encouraged by their good electoral performance, are striving to maintain control over trade unions and the support of industrial workers. Once economic reforms start to have serious affect, and once the split within the Forum leads to the creation of properly organized political parties, President Havel's talents of mediating political disputes will be sorely tested. The reality is that Havel's performance has not always been very sensitive. The President expressed irritation at the Slovaks' demands for autonomy, initially underestimating the depth of feeling among his citizens on this issue. Furthermore, when faced with increased tension and divisions within the Government, he sought to obtain special presidential powers from the Federal Assembly, in order to manage the transition. On both occasions, he was rebuffed by a parliament whose own powers, although still ill-defined, are nevertheless jealously defended. That, in a sense, is Czechoslovakia's best hope: a tradition of parliamentary democracy, coupled with an abhorrence of any violence and a healthy mistrust of all politicians. Thus, although the country's immediate future promises more, rather than less, instability, Czechoslovakia's integration into Europe looks assured.

THE SOUTHERN TIER'S INSTABILITY

Yugoslavia's disintegration appears to confirm the worst fears about the Balkans: that is, endemic instability brought on by old historical and territorial disputes, laced with economic and social decay. Fundamentally, the problem is one of a clash between Western European ideals and Balkan realities.

The creation of the nation-state as the only viable and desirable political unit was largely a Western idea, which created havoc in the Balkans. At the meeting point of three multinational empires and residing on Europe's strategic waterways, the people of the Balkans could never be neatly separated into homogeneous national entities. An emasculated Turkey still contained large Kurdish and Christian minorities; Greece and Bulgaria incorporated Muslims; Yugoslavia was, from the beginning, a mosaic of nationalities; and no less than one-third of Romania's population, at the end of the First World War, did not belong to the majority nation. All Balkan states, however, remained determined to mould fiction into reality, by regarding themselves as unitary nation-states. The result was a particularly dangerous combination of conflicts, as mutually exclusive territorial demands clashed with historical claims and ideologies. In an area where frontiers changed frequently and historical justifications depended on one's starting point, every one of these nationalist claims entailed an injury to another nation. The situation is complicated even further by the tendency of every Balkan nation to change arguments according to circumstances. In 1990 Serb leaders justified their incorporation of the Kosovo region (overwhelmingly populated by ethnic Albanians) as a historical necessity, since Kosovo was the cradle of Serbian nationhood. The same leaders later justified the annexation of further territory, which never belonged to Serbia, on the principle of defending their co-nationals.

The Balkan experience has had two further effects. First, it created an obsession with history, a discipline which was regarded as an instrument of politics, to be practised by government officials. Every historic episode is reinterpreted or falsified according to the prevailing official need. Tito (Josip Broz), the ruler of modern Yugoslavia, acknowledged a Macedonian nation, an entity whose very existence is denied by neighbouring Bulgarians and Greeks (nor is the separate Macedonian identity fully accepted by Serbia—the Serbian Orthodox Church refuses to recognize the Macedonian Church, for example). Greece continues to deny the existence of a Slav minority; Turkey claimed for decades that it had no Kurds and Bulgaria reclassified its Turkish minority as 'Bulgarians of Muslim faith'.

The second effect of the Balkan experience is an obsession with national unity. This, again, is the result of history: Balkan states are the product of the failure of multinational empires. It therefore remains pointless to suggest that these states should create autonomous regions for their ethnic minorities; their own national movements started with such demands in the last century, only to lead to the disintegration of empires. Nevertheless, post-Second World War Eastern Europe did have such autonomous regions: Romania created one for the Magyars of Transylvania; and, even during the 1980s, Serbia had two autonomous provinces. All these experiments eventually failed because, in the Balkans, decentralization of government control is equated with weakness, and autonomous regions are regarded as the first step towards national disintegration.

The Communist regimes in the Balkans had harnessed nationalism in order to legitimize their rule. Throughout the region, fuelling old nationalist disputes became a mechanism for deflecting public attention from economic difficulties, a vehicle for mass mobilization. Xenophobia therefore reached new heights under the Communists' rule. Furthermore, Communist policies of 'social engineering' created new ethnic difficulties. The Romanians who were settled in Transylvania now swell the ranks of virulently anti-Hungarian organizations. A Serbian neo-fascist leader, Vojislav Seselj, has found many adherents among the Serbian immigrant workers in Croatia. The mixture of nationalism and crude collectivist ideas easily survived the Communist collapse and continues to be employed.

The establishment of Communist rule in much of the Balkans, at the end of the Second World War, initially appeared to offer some hope, for it espoused an internationalist ideology which negated national conflicts and promised economic progress. In fact, Communism merely added further complications. Established in overwhelmingly agrarian countries, but claiming to represent an almost non-existent working class, the Communists embarked on a policy of rapid industrialization. This resulted in massive social dislocations and severe problems which are bound to continue for years. The entire structure of the village community was destroyed, and uprooted peasants were forced into massive industrial concerns and bleak housing estates, usually on the edge of towns. Members of this first generation of working-class peasants, however, remain insecure: having renounced their peasant origins, they have yet to establish an urban existence and ethos. It is this factor which accounted for the relative lack of an organized opposition in Bulgaria and Romania, and matters were not helped by the existence of an Orthodox Church with a long tradition of subservience to state authority.

As Communism collapsed in Europe, the magnitude of the disaster became very clear. The overthrow of Nicolae Ceauşescu in Romania and the removal of Todor Zhivkov in Bulgaria were partly caused by dissensions within their respective Parties, and partly owing to street pressure. Yet the revolutions were incomplete, for the masses which poured on to the streets in Bucharest, Sofia or Belgrade may have known what they opposed, but had no idea of what they were promoting. Thus, while young people spoke passionately of 'democracy' and 'market economy', their former Communist leaders changed their parties' names and continued much as before. Many of the restrictions in force under the old dictatorship disappeared: the citizens of all Balkan states are free to travel (provided they can persuade any foreign embassy to give them a visa); they may publish any newspaper (provided they can find the finances and organize its distribution); and may demonstrate their political convictions at will. However, they cannot influence government decisions.

A political impasse therefore prevails. Governments are not strong enough to crush their opposition, but other political parties are still too weak to assume power. A mass of unqualified industrial workers, a lumpenproletariat in the true Marxist sense, holds the key to the political future of these countries. Their alarm at the prospect of unemployment (a necessary feature of any meaningful reform) has already been utilized. These were the workers who assaulted Romanian opposition supporters, in June 1990, at President Ion Iliescu's behest. In Serbia their counterparts are the backbone of President Slobodan Milošević's rule. Market economy is often confused with pure black-market speculation, and a political career is universally regarded as a means of rapid personal enrichment.

Political life in the Balkans still does not amount to a confrontation between different ideas. Instead, it is a struggle between individuals who regard themselves as national saviours. In the absence of any point of reference or venues for dialogue, everything is disputed, from the constitution and parliamentary powers, to the rights of minorities and economic reform. And every dispute threatens to erupt into open violence.

Violence has been characteristic of Yugoslavia's disintegration, partly because that country lies at the fault-line between the traditions of the Austro-Hungarian Empire (in Slovenia and Croatia) and those of the Ottoman domains. But, although these developments represent troubles for an entire continent, they must also be kept in perspective. First, Yugoslavia remains a unique case of a multinational state which never worked. The struggle in Yugoslavia was not about the nature of the state but, rather, about its very existence. Yugoslavia's collapse may not, therefore, have the further effects which everyone expects: neighbouring Romania and Bulgaria do contain large numbers of different ethnic minorities but, in both, the preponderance of Romanians and Bulgarians is not in question. The danger lies in the creation of a strategic vacuum in the wake of Yugoslavia's demise. Bulgaria and Greece contest the existence of the Yugoslav republic of Macedonia; Albania wishes to protect the ethnic Albanians of Kosovo; while Hungary wishes to act for the ethnic Hungarians of Vojvodina.

Yet even here there is some hope. For the first time this century, the Balkans are truly alone. Despite Serbia's dark hints, European powers which sought to establish spheres of influence in the region are no longer interested in doing so. The disintegration of Yugoslavia cannot, therefore, cause another global confrontation. Nevertheless, more strife is to be expected and Europe's efforts are likely to concentrate on managing, rather than 'solving' the Balkans' deep-rooted problems. The task is unlikely to be very coherent, but it will remain the only practical approach, mainly because the continent is no longer embroiled in an East–West problem, but a North–South one.

SECURITY RELATIONS

For almost two years, Eastern Europe continued to exist in a state of suspended animation. The Warsaw Pact, the military organization created by the USSR in 1955 and fashioned according to the Kremlin's strategic priorities, disappeared. The Pact's political co-ordination functions ended, together with the Communist regimes, in the last days of 1989. However the Pact's military structures were only dismantled on 1 April 1991. With little grace, and after a great deal of financial squabbling, the Soviet authorities agreed to withdraw their forces from Hungary, Czechoslovakia and Poland (although the timetable proposed by the Poles for their own country continues to be disputed). Nevertheless, the hopeful mood of the time was well encapsulated by the Conference on Security and Co-operation in Europe (CSCE) summit, in Paris, in November 1990. The Eastern Europeans readily accepted the West's view, according to which security was no longer a matter of military alliances. There were apprehensions about the future policies of the USSR, but as long as Gorbachev remained in power and Soviet foreign policy was controlled by Eduard Shevardnadze, time appeared to be on the side of the Eastern Europeans. Then, in January 1991, there was a series of repressive incidents in Baltic republics and most of the Eastern Europeans' dreams were shattered. The violence in the USSR reminded the countries of the region of their relatively exposed position. It also represented the best example of just how quickly the spirit of East–West co-operation could be reversed.

Eastern Europe's first reaction, therefore, emerged as a rush to sever any remaining institutional ties with the USSR. Czechoslovakia's President, Václav Havel, sought to seize this opportunity to proclaim his country's total withdrawal from the Warsaw Pact. However the Governments of Poland and Hungary prevailed on the Czechoslovak President to postpone a decision on such matters. The countries of the region did not disagree on the need to dissolve the Warsaw Pact finally, but they feared that this would exacerbate tensions with the USSR. It was argued that there was little point in issuing defiant declarations so long as the security situation on the continent remained unclear. Ever since the overthrow of the Communist regimes, the countries of the region had wondered whether to elaborate national defence doctrines. The Hungarians wanted to adopt a posture not dissimilar from that of Austria, and the Poles went further than most in proclaiming their 'armed neutrality'. To a large extent, these doctrines, hastily prepared and never properly debated, were essential interim devices, underlining Eastern Europe's independence from the Soviet military. Once it became clear that such doctrines could provide no answer to the potential Soviet threat, the search for new security arrangements started.

The West, however, continued to display great reticence in evolving new security arrangements and a not inconsiderable amount of irritation at the fact that the liberation of Eastern Europe raised fundamental questions about the entire continent. Owing to national considerations, France remained the notable opponent to any widening in the membership of major European institutions. Furthermore, the USA and the United Kingdom, determined to preserve NATO and to eschew any confrontation with the USSR, refused to suggest any other alternatives. The result was that the Eastern Europeans remained in exactly the same position they occupied at the end of the 1980s: free, but dependent on Soviet petroleum and trade; without military responsibilities, but also without security structures. In a sense, they were neither East nor West.

Having spent most of 1990 competing for the West's attention, Poland, Czechoslovakia and Hungary impelled themselves towards greater military co-operation. This was the background to the summit, in February 1991, held between their leaders in the Hungarian city of Visegrad. The meeting had two purposes: to emphasize the distinction between the North and the South of Eastern Europe; and, secondly, to present the West with a joint approach towards the elaboration of real security structures. Even before Visegrad, military officials from the three countries co-ordinated practical details, such as advance notification of troop movements and communication lines. The desire for mutual help was also responsible for Czechoslovakia's decision to spurn offers of German financial aid, in return for which it was to abandon its support for Polish demands that all Soviet troops should be withdrawn from Poland's soil. The February meeting in Visegrad (of what is sometimes referred to as the 'trilateral group') was intended to enlarge on this co-operation, by placing it on a more permanent footing and, as such, was received with great relief by Western states, who hoped that it represented the first indication of the creation of a new, regional security arrangement. Such hopes remain misplaced.

Plans for Eastern European alliances are as old as the region. They were usually concocted either by those who sought to prove that Eastern Europe had a special character, which was neither Russian nor Western, or by left-wing intellectuals, who continued to dream about the fam-

ous 'Third Way', of capitalist prosperity coupled with 'socialist welfare'. All such schemes proved to be total failures. Plans for the creation of a 'Danubian Federation', so frequent after the First World War, sought to maintain the free-trade zone operated by the Austro-Hungarian Empire in the heart of the continent. They failed because the newly-independent states had little time for nostalgic reminiscences about the Habsburg domains. The 'Little Entente', a military alliance created by France before the Second World War, essentially in order to contain the influence of Germany in Europe, disintegrated as each member state sought to further its own needs and France proved unable to appease their mutual fears.

Any regional alliance created today is likely to have a similar fate, for exactly the same reasons. Eastern Europe is composed of relatively small states, which cannot defend themselves against all potential threats, but which labour under a long tradition of reciprocal enmity. Furthermore, the countries of the region operate economies which are not compatible. All depend on imports of raw materials, all have to run down decrepit industrial capacities, all have a surplus of labour and all need Western capital.

For many Western states, at least until the dissolution of the USSR, the creation of a regional security arrangement in Eastern Europe remained superficially attractive: it avoided any confrontation with the USSR; and it postponed serious decisions about Europe's integration. In reality, however, such a regional arrangement will prove positively dangerous. It would reinforce the idea that Eastern Europe remains a buffer zone between the USSR and the West. Thus, it would increase, rather than alleviate, the region's problems. Current co-operation between Poland, Czechoslovakia and Hungary is based on this realization. All three central European states have understood that the West's enthusiasm for their liberation is still not matched by deeds. Aware of the gap between promises and reality, Western states initially sought to encourage the role of the CSCE, as the forum which could serve the needs of all European states. The Eastern Europeans quickly realized that the CSCE represented, at best, ersatz security. Nor were they reassured by the fact that Western states, having offered the CSCE as the framework for security co-ordination, proceeded to ignore this institution altogether, in favour of revamping their own military arrangements within the EC and NATO. Poland, Czechoslovakia and Hungary continue to co-operate, mainly because they do not foresee any practical alternative, at least for the moment. Nevertheless, they are determined that their military co-operation should be limited to the very basics, precisely in order not to absolve the West of explicit obligations in the heart of the continent.

Within the USSR itself, the fate of the Eastern Europeans was a subject of acute interest. Early in 1991 the International Department in the Central Committee of the Communist Party of the Soviet Union (CPSU) published a study on the USSR's future policy in the region. The study suggested that the authorities should strive to create a 'cordon sanitaire' across the middle of the continent, should continue co-operating with 'progressive' and 'revolutionary' movements in Europe, and should not hesitate in using economic power in order to coerce the Eastern Europeans into compliance. Although the Foreign Ministry in Moscow viewed matters quite differently, all Soviet decision-makers remained convinced that their country should strive to retain great influence in Eastern Europe, mainly by preventing the West from gaining a foothold in the region.

For more than one year, the USSR insisted that new treaties of 'non-aggression and good neighbourhood' with the countries of the region should replace former military relations. The Eastern Europeans readily agreed, hoping that such treaties might put relations with their powerful neighbour on a more secure basis. They were less enthusiastic about what followed. The USSR insisted on two points. First, it forbade the Eastern Europeans from revealing the security arrangements which operated under the Warsaw Pact. Nevertheless, these arrangements, which included attack procedures in central Europe, were leaked by Eastern government officials to the West. They tended to confirm NATO's pre-1989 strategic contingency planning. Thus, the mission of the Hungarian armed forces, in case of a war, was to violate Austria's neutrality and to outflank German troops in the south. More importantly, the USSR insisted that the new treaties should include a clause forbidding parties from joining in alliances with countries deemed to be 'hostile' by either state. The adoption of such a clause would grant the USSR a veto over Eastern European security arrangements for at least one decade.

For Czechoslovakia, Poland and Hungary, such a clause was unacceptable. Their calculations were not simply related to the fact that such treaties might destroy their chances of joining Western defence structures. Crucially, the USSR's demands threatened to consign them, yet again, to a new sphere of Soviet influence. The USSR anticipated this opposition, by both cajoling and threatening. Soviet officials rushed to sign a treaty with Romania's leaders, who are ideologically closer to Gorbachev's *perestroika*. The treaty with the Romanians made sense for both sides: it neutralized the Soviet Republic of Moldova (largely populated by ethnic Romanians), by guaranteeing that existing frontiers could not be changed, and, at the same time, offered security guarantees to this isolated state. Once concluded, the Soviet negotiators then went to all other Eastern European capitals, offering the treaty as an example of what they meant by 'good neighbourly relations'. Pressure was exerted by veiled threats of difficulties in economic relations, especially in the supplies of much-needed Soviet markets and petroleum, natural gas and other raw materials. Yet these attempts also failed, for the Eastern Europeans considered that they had little to lose and everything to gain by refusing to be rushed into new security arrangements with the USSR. Owing to the collapse of the Soviet economy, deliveries of petroleum and purchasing orders from Eastern Europe have already vanished. Furthermore, the Eastern Europeans assume that their integration into Western security structures is only a matter of time. They suspect that they also know the reason: turmoil in the former USSR. Thus, paradoxically, the development which the Eastern Europeans feared most, also provided an escape from their immediate security predicament.

REFUGEES

One of the most serious problems facing the European continent during the 1990s will be that of controlling movements of people across frontiers. Since the revolutions of 1989, Western states, which spent most of the time after the Second World War advocating that freedom of movement is an 'inherent' right of every citizen, found it hard to refuse entry to people who, after 40 years, suddenly found themselves in possession of a passport. Discouragement, however, was attempted by imposing large visa fees (which usually amount to one-half of the average annual earnings in Eastern Europe) and unrealistic conditions for granting visas (such as demands for possession of large quantities of foreign currency from people who legally had no right to obtain such sums). This swiftly transformed the West's tactics into a sad farce, deeply resented by the citizens of Eastern Europe. More importantly, however, the West

realized that the problem of potential migration was not the same throughout Eastern Europe.

The Hungarians and the Czechoslovaks travel in great numbers. Yet, on the whole, they are mostly bona fide tourists, with every intention of returning to their home state. Poles, Romanians and Bulgarians, however, often travel with the intention of finding work, if only for a temporary period. The differences are not purely economic: after all, the now-defunct East German state, the German Democratic Republic (GDR), enjoyed one of the highest standards of living in the area, but still suffered from significant emigration. Rather, it appears to be more connected to Eastern European trust in their future opportunities at home. Hungarians and Czechoslovaks still believe that their revolutions resulted in genuine changes and, as a consequence, offer hope of a better life. Romanians or Bulgarians have no such hopes. The outflow of Romanians intensified after the government-inspired violence on the streets of Bucharest, in June 1990, and the same happened in Bulgaria, as political turmoil in the Balkans continued. Western states drew the appropriate conclusions: they abolished visa requirements for Hungarians, Czechoslovaks and Poles (the latter at Germany's behest), but retained them for Romanians, Bulgarians and other Balkan nations. A single policy for the former bloc of nations was, therefore, replaced by a more sophisticated approach, which could also be justified on the basis of necessity.

Unfortunately, however, migration patterns are not so neat. First, many Western governments still suspect that, when economic reforms really start to affect Czechoslovakia and Hungary, a flow of people from these countries could still start, mirroring the one fuelled by Poland's shock therapy in 1990. Secondly, some ethnic groups in the region present particular problems. This is especially the case with an estimated population of 5m. Roma (Gypsies), but it also applies to other ethnic minorities in Romania, Slovakia and the Yugoslav republics. Hungary is already the unwilling host of more than 100,000 of its co-nationals from neighbouring countries.

Ultimately, however, the policy of placing a quarantine on the Balkans and opening borders for the central Europeans could have worked, had it not been for the prospect of further trouble in the USSR. Soviet emigration has risen considerably since Mikhail Gorbachev came to power: 108,000 left the USSR in 1988, 235,400 in 1989, and no less than 452,000 in 1990. Over 90% of these legal migrants, however, were ethnic Germans and Jews, and they were absorbed by two states: Germany and Israel. The situation may change radically. As a result of US pressure, linked to the trading provisions and additional aid packages, the Soviet parliament, the all-Union Supreme Soviet, adopted legislation which would allow all citizens of the USSR the right to a passport from the end of 1992. Should such legislation come into force, the rate of emigration may increase dramatically. When the average monthly Soviet salary was equivalent to US $12, at unofficial rates, and even doctors or scientists earned no more than $50, Soviet parliamentarians estimated that no less than 6m. citizens would wish to seek employment overseas, where the illegal earnings in one month could surpass an annual salary at home.

These alarmist predictions may not be justified. First, as the citizens of the Balkans are finding out, possession of a passport is hardly a guarantee of travel. Western visa procedures are likely to be lengthy and extremely strict. Secondly, overseas travel (either by train or air) has to be paid in advance and in convertible ('hard') currency, which is not affordable to the average citizen of the former USSR.

Furthermore, the Soviet authorities had already raised the fees for issuing passports drastically. Thirdly, transport capacity is already over-stretched and is unlikely to be expanded soon. Additionally, these citizens do not usually speak commonly-used languages (as many North Africans and Eastern European migrants do) and are therefore unlikely to be employed in even the most menial work in the West. Finally, the need for illegal employment in Western Europe is disappearing, partly because of the tightening of controls in countries such as Italy and Greece, and partly because of soaring unemployment in Germany, the traditional venue for such activities.

The danger of a vast tide of emigration remains real, for it is dependent on the pattern of disintegration within the old Soviet empire. The intermingling of nationalities, together with the the competing agendas of Communist conservatives or 'hardliners', the reformists, the security forces and the bureaucracy seem to suggest that greater violence is almost inevitable. When this happens, the former USSR will experience not one, but three different migrations. The first will be of ethnic Russians, currently residing in other republics. The USSR had estimated that there were more than 1m. such displaced people who, in the event of a military confrontation, may choose to flee westward, rather than within Russia. The second wave could embrace the citizens of the outlying republics, such as the Balts, Ukrainians, Azerbaidzhanis and Armenians. Finally, the third category will include those citizens who have a nation-state outside the former USSR. Apart from Jews and Germans, there are no less than 700,000 ethnic Hungarians, 1m. Poles and 3m. Romanians, who reside on the former USSR's borders with Eastern Europe. These people, incorporated against their will by Stalin, at the end of the Second World War, will have very little incentive to remain in a disintegrated USSR.

The implications of this migration on Eastern Europe are enormous. It is obvious that most of the potential refugees from the former USSR are likely to travel overland. Their first point of exit will be into Eastern Europe (especially Poland, Czechoslovakia and Hungary). They will have no travel documents, few possessions and little idea where they would like to go. It would be very difficult to turn them back. The Eastern Europeans are preparing themselves for this flood. For the first time since the inception of Commu-nist rule, the countries of the region are likely to have a problem of immigration rather than emigration. They have tended to enact legislation which mirrors the provisions of the 1951 UN Geneva Convention on the Status of Refugees, the most reliable international document regulating treat-ment of such eventualities. In November 1990 Poland opened a special office for refugee affairs in its interior ministry. Headed by Lt-Col Zbigniew Skoczylas, it already handles more than 70,000 registered applicants. Poland has also started moving some its troops from the west, towards its eastern border with Byelorussia and Ukraine, but meas-ures to strengthen frontier controls are extremely expens-ive: according to Polish calculations, the permanent transfer of one brigade absorbs almost US $100m. Czechoslovakia's new law on refugees came into force at the beginning of 1991 and the country has appointed Michaela Freiova as its special commissioner for refugee affairs. A special refugee section also exists within the Hungarian interior ministry. However these three countries are aware that their contin-gency plans will hardly be able to cope with the sheer scale of the potential problem; Freiova estimates that facilities at her disposal can process a maximum of 12,000 people per year, a figure exceeded in the first few months of 1991 alone. In short, a large influx of former Soviet citizens will ruin the already fragile Eastern European economies.

Western European states have preferred to ignore the problem. They have refused to participate in the contin-gency plans of the Eastern Europeans and retained almost complete silence on the entire problem. This policy is unlikely to be maintained for long, for the arrival of refu-gees ultimately raises political and security issues of the first order. In confidential negotiations with Western Euro-pean governments, the Eastern Europeans have made their position quite clear. They are happy to act as the West's buffer zone and absorb migrants fleeing instability in the former USSR. They are even prepared to turn them back at the West's behest. For their services, however, they are demanding a price: their integration into Western economic and security arrangements. In reality, the beginning of an exodus will also mark the end of the period of transition in Europe. The continent will be redefined and its structures re-established. In the process a certain amount of additional instability and strife is unavoidable. The task remains how to manage this as peacefully and as skilfully as possible.

NATIONALISM AND NATIONAL MINORITIES

GEORGE SCHÖPFLIN

Some 20 nationalities live in eastern and central Europe, most of whom have their own nation-state (or constituent republic of a federal state), either in the region or in other parts of Europe (such as Germans, Byelorussians, Ukrainians, Turks, Greeks or Italians). In Eastern Europe, the Roma (Gypsies) are the only group without a national polity (there are the Lusatian Sorbs in what was the German Democratic Republic). None of the groups lives entirely within the borders of its nominal territory, and none of the territories is ethnically homogeneous. In the USSR there were between 60 and 70 nationalities with varying degrees of political recognition, but only 15 were accorded the status of a full union republic. There are perhaps over 100 other minority groups throughout the territories of the former USSR. Traditional ethnic tensions have been added to by Stalin's policies of forced migrations, which complicated the demographic mosaic. The USSR and Yugoslavia have had the most critical nationalist problems (see relevant chapters), but no Eastern European state is without some such tension.

One of the great puzzles of the 20th century concerns the survival of nations and nationhood. Both Marxists and liberals have dismissed nationalism repeatedly over the past 200 years, and yet it survives. Indeed, with the collapse of Communism in Europe, it is very much an ideology with a future. From the conventional Marxist standpoint, this is something that should not happen, given that the individual's class interests must transcend all others[1]. The liberal view, though not as extreme, is similarly uncomfortable with nationalism, because the ultimate assumptions of liberalism are too closely bound to material interests for it to be able to cope adequately with a set of ideas which regularly places non-material interests above the material. Most explanations for the resurgence of nationalism, which constantly surprises liberals and Marxists, ultimately depend on its dismissal as 'irrational' or as 'tribal' or something that other, less 'civilized' countries suffer from. Usually the question of *why* nationalism survives is ignored[2].

There are, however, perfectly good reasons why nationalism not only survives, but actually flourishes. Eastern Europe and the USSR provide particularly good examples, but, first, the theoretical background must be established; material-economic explanations must be placed into an appropriate context and a different set of assumptions be taken into consideration. The essence of the argument to be put forward here is that nationalism and nationhood operate by their own criteria and impose their own rationality on events, separate and at variance from those of liberalism and Marxism.

These criteria are best approached by asking what the purpose of nationhood is. The main point about nationhood is that it is a political category, but one that derives not from economic concerns, but from cultural ones: the rules and perceptions of collectivities, a sense of a shared past and a shared future, and a community's socially-constructed picture of the world.

THE MORAL–CULTURAL UNIVERSE

The ultimate proposition of nationhood is that a community is defined by, and defines itself by, its cultural traits, and that these transcend all other definitions such as religion, dynasty or economic interests. If the nation is to be the fundamental basis of organization, then this not only entails cultural consequences, but also political ones, given that questions of political power are necessarily involved. In this sense, nationalism is the politicization of a community's culture, a claim that these cultural characteristics take precedence over all other claims and that they should receive political protection[3].

Culture is accorded this precedence because of its functions and the particular challenges that cultures have had to face in the modern world. A community's culture provides its moral precepts, the set of rules by which it determines its moral universe and defines what is right and what is wrong, what are acceptable forms of behaviour and what are not[4].

Furthermore, these rules also mould a community's shared values and common prejudices and preferences, the affective dimension. Those who share in this affective dimension, the members of the community, are therefore bound together and understand these bonds as a part of their identity. This is the function of nationhood that is most widely understood. The definitions of this identity can be constructed from a vast array of socially-determined elements (language, history, territory, religion, etc.) and they are expressed in the rituals and symbols that are continuously celebrated, as often as not in unconscious ways. These demarcate both the internal and external boundaries that communities establish for their existence.

The external boundaries, however, are permeable and, as a result, communities feel themselves to be challenged, if not actually threatened. The most serious of these challenges derives from the real or perceived claims of other communities. As a result, such collectivities will go a long way to protect these boundaries by whatever means are available. Thus the nationalist agendas of the Georgians and Serbians have included strong measures directed against their own minorities, such as the South Ossetians and the Albanians of Kosovo. The politicization of culture necessarily involves devising political instruments of protection. This is the function of the nation-state, which is a much stronger and more effective organization than the pre-national state. The nation-state has been invested with the function of protecting the nation, and thus the moral order and identity of a community, and it must supply the most effective protection possible.

At the same time, cultures are also threatened by change, particularly economic and technological change, because these reshape the fabric of everyday life, affect the nature of relations between members of the community and oblige it to evolve new codes of conduct to deal with the transformation. In Romania, under Ceauşescu, the authorities attempted to manipulate this phenomenon for the creation of a 'socialist' Romanian culture with the proposed destruction of thousands of village communities. Such conscious social engineering or, more usually, factors such as the operation of the global market can fundamentally alter the character of, for instance, an agrarian way of life, and this is deeply threatening to those affected. From the viewpoint of the collectivity affected, these changes will often appear to be external and uncontrollable; they will certainly be resisted by some, though not necessarily by all, of the members; and they will inevitably bring a far-reaching recasting of social relations.

The crucial point of this is that the collectivity affected in this way can do little, or nothing, about such threats, other than to try and isolate itself from the rest of the world. This option is not only difficult, but, ultimately, merely postpones the problem to a later date, as the experience of Eastern Europe in the aftermath of Communist rule has shown. Only a relatively open, economically secure and politically integrated community can readily find the self-confidence that is needed to absorb changes of the magnitude that the world is currently experiencing. In this connection, therefore, there is indeed a relationship between material factors and cultural ones. In real terms, however, neither can fully determine the values and precepts by which communities are constituted; rather, the interaction between these factors will be fundamental to how change is integrated and absorbed. The changes in economic conditions in Eastern Europe and the USSR, therefore, contributed directly to the re-emergence of nationalist issues.

CONSTITUTIONAL AND EVERYDAY POLITICS

In essence, a distinction should be made between everyday politics, which is primarily concerned with material issues, and constitutional politics, which is not only about the form of the constitution, but also about identity, moral issues and the norms and codes of conduct determining social interaction. When it comes to constitutional politics, issues of nationhood are important, but they are irrelevant, if not actually misleading, in deciding questions affecting everyday events[5].

The difficulty is that the different functions of the nation, as outlined above, are inevitably intertwined; challenges in one area, therefore, can be interpreted as threats to the totality of the moral order (abortion became a particularly contentious issue in Poland, during 1990 and 1991, because it raised the question of how much the national Church should influence the basic laws of the state). The normal bargaining processes found within a polity are made much more complex when ethno-national issues are involved. When questions of identity are on the agenda, and boundaries appear to be threatened, neither individuals nor groups can make concessions easily and the interactions can become infused with the emotional resources that a community is able to call upon (through appeals to loyalty and the like). The common ground that is essential for negotiations simply disappears. Whenever two communities are in conflict over issues of identity, the bargaining becomes virtually impossible. The situation in Yugoslavia, particularly in 1991, has proved to be an example of this.

This kind of reductionism, therefore, should be avoided and questions of identity excluded from the consideration of political issues. Something approximating this has been achieved in the liberal democracies, where, with one or two exceptions, issues of nationhood do not form a staple part of politics. In effect, questions of ethno-national identity, for the time being at least, have been settled. The most persuasive way of understanding the role of nationhood and nationalism in politics is to see it as only one particular set of interests and identities possessed by groups and individuals. Cleavages along the lines of class, religion, consumption, production, gender, status, concern for the environment, generation, etc., contribute to the complex of factors from which political identities are constructed in these societies. This suggests that much of the emotional impetus of nationhood has been mitigated by an emphasis on material issues. By and large, this is what has taken place in Western Europe, where questions of nationalism have been transformed into questions of ethnicity, which do not usually call into question the basic distribution of power, but are primarily concerned with culture and local-level politics.

The success of this method, which is by no means guaranteed, requires two factors. One is that a sufficiently large section of the society concerned should be committed to democracy as the most effective safeguard of all their interests and aspirations. In particular, where national minorities are concerned, both the majority and the minority must perceive their democratic system to be fair and the best solution for their relationship. Where this has not been achieved, however, a process of reductionism takes place and everything is viewed through the prism of nationhood. The democratic methods of negotiation and bargaining cannot work well until the ethno-national issues are resolved to the satisfaction of all the parties involved, thus fulfilling the second requirement for a successful neutralization of questions of nationalism. This state of affairs can require many years of patient and painful endurance. Northern Ireland or the Basque country offer examples of what happens when mobilization into reductionist nationalism makes bargaining virtually impossible; Yugoslavia and Nagorny Karabakh (an Armenian enclave in Azerbaidzhan) threaten to become similar examples. Moderates are radicalized or marginalized and emotional loyalties protect extremists.

MULTI-NATIONAL STATES

There is a particular difficulty associated with multi-national states, defined here as states which are expressly constituted of more than one ethno-national group. States of this kind are bound to be especially complex, because of the friction that may occur between the communities. The best solution is to attempt to construct an overarching, legitimating ideology that leaves the various cultures intact and, at the same time, offers a further tier of loyalty at the state level. Federal arrangements may contribute towards such a solution, but are not an automatic guarantee of success, because, if the legitimating ideology is eroded, the state as a whole is endangered.

In situations of this kind, it is advisable for the largest group in the state to treat the other groups generously and, indeed, to abandon some of its own agendas for the sake of preserving the state as a whole—always assuming that this is what the largest group actually wants. The ideal solution is when loyalty to the state transcends the local cultures and political identities are defined at this higher level, leaving the lower tier or tiers intact. By and large, this can be seen in Switzerland, where there is an overarching Swiss identity that transcends, but does not threaten, German, French or Italian cultural codes at the state level. In Belgium, the solution has been much less effective and Belgian identity is weak. Few other experiments in dealing with the problem of multi-national state formations have been as successful. The Communist attempts, as practised in Yugoslavia and the USSR, have in fact failed. This failure must be ascribed to the fact that in both these states, the integrity of the state was tied to an anti-national legitimating ideology, Marxism-Leninism in the Soviet Union and the neo-Leninist Titoism in Yugoslavia. Neither of these could offer a successful moral–cultural universe, with the result that when Leninism frayed, the national question returned to the agenda with considerable urgency.

NATIONAL MINORITIES

It is against this background that the question of national minorities should be scrutinized. These ethno-national groups are essentially collectivities that have found themselves dominated by the moral–cultural agendas of other groups, by having been included in nation-state formations where their weight is small. There are many such minorities in Eastern Europe, where nation-states were formed relatively recently, to replace the imperial hegemony over a wide diversity of peoples. Likewise, the USSR inherited an empire of a multitude of ethnic groups, who do not necessarily live in compact geographical units.

Various possibilities for dealing with national minorities can be envisaged, from repression to integration. The problem for democratic systems is that while a range of legal, and even constitutional, provision can be made for ethno-national minorities, these do not altogether solve all the attendant difficulties. If mobilization along the ethno-national cleavage begins, a process of reductionism will ensue, making meaningful negotiation virtually impossible (as argued above). This particular problem has been exacerbated by post-Communist conditions. As the severe restraints of Communism vanished, all ethno-national collectivities began to mobilize, to identify the new limits of political action and, in the process, to encounter other, similar groups. The added difficulty is that during the Communist period, most forms of identity other than the national one were weakened, leaving nationhood with functions that it is not necessarily well placed to meet.

Nationhood cannot be the repository of all positive values, as nationalists will argue. It has little to say about freedom, justice, prosperity, etc., although these ideas can be readily, if mistakenly, associated with it. Many in the Baltic Republics, and in Slovenia and Croatia, have too readily associated political independence with economic progress, for example. The danger in the existing situation is that too many processes will be viewed from an ethno-national perspective, with far-reaching consequences for the stability of the post-Communist political order.

All societies and polities are faced with the complex task of balancing collective and individual rights. This task is much more difficult in the case of ethno-national minorities than with economic groups, for example, because of the very particular moral–cultural role with which ethno-national identity has been invested. The task can be discharged, but requires extra care and the danger of majority domination must be avoided. If the aim is to integrate the minority and preserve a democratic system, policy should be governed by two broad principles: in all cases the spirit as well as the letter of the law should be observed; and provision should actually go beyond what the minority may demand at any one time.

This clearly implies that the agendas of the majority, its particular moral and affective imperatives, will have to be restrained in favour of the minority, notably through the creation of a state identity that includes elements of the minority's culture. (Tito attempted to develop the Yugoslav state in this way, with the creation of a decentralized federation and a rotating presidency, but with a unifying Communist Party and—Serb-dominated—Army.) Members of the majority may baulk at this renunciation of their advantage and insist that the minority should be treated less generously, because the state is the political expression of the majority and, in this argument, the minority lives there on sufferance. However the minority did not choose to live in a state in which its moral–cultural characteristics were compromised. Furthermore, the majority has gained benefit, in terms of territory and power, through having attached other areas to its state.

The autonomy of the state over society can, likewise, complicate matters. The modern state is increasingly entrusted with an ever-widening range of functions. It is a well known phenomenon that, as the role of the state widens, its detachment from its ostensible purposes increases and it will tend to subordinate its formal tasks to its own interests as an organization[6]. The remedies are complex and not always particularly effective. From the standpoint of national minorities, however, their situation can be seriously compromised if, in the pursuit of its autonomy, the state is guided by a different set of moral-cultural precepts, which will be potentially damaging to the minority.

There is also an argument which claims that if the minority has been granted educational, cultural and linguistic rights, it should then accept agendas of the majority in other matters. This is not persuasive. Schooling, the establishment of cultural groups and basic language rights are no more than the starting-point from which minority rights, and decision-making, begin. In education, for example, once minority-language schools have been established, there still remain the questions of which languages are taught for which subjects; the curriculum of such subjects as history; whether technical subjects should be summarized in the majority language or not (if not, members of the minority may have their mobility and, hence, their opportunities severely curtailed), etc. This open-ended nature of the issue can be exaggerated by the majority group, hence the Romanian abolition of Hungarian-language education and the Soviet emphasis on Russian. Tertiary education poses further problems: how large does a minority have to be before it can claim entitlement to a university, and who is to fund it? There are answers to these questions and to problems in other areas: through joint commissions, inspectorates, the localization of politics—subsidiarity is a favoured concept at present. This declares that all decisions should be taken at the level most appropriate for that decision. Problems also arise with the official language of administration. Bilingualism, when strictly adhered to, however, is costly, cumbersome and tends to favour the minority; members of a majority are usually reluctant to learn a minority language.

Matters become still more complex when it comes to economic activity. Clearly the bilingual operation of an enterprise incurs expenditure and the private sector would be reluctant to subsidize it. If there is no provision for the use of the minority language, however, there will be discrimination on economic grounds. The most vexed question of all is territory. Should there be free right of movement for all citizens of the state throughout the territory of that state? An answer may seem self-evident, but, if this threatens the compactness of a minority community, then grounds for serious friction will be present, because the minority will be fearful that its ability to effect its own cultural reproduction will be undermined. In Yugoslavia, free movement has contributed towards the decline of the Serb population in Kosovo and, also, an increase in the proportion of Serbs in Vojvodina, at the expense of the Hungarian population.

CONSOCIATIONALISM

Finally, mention should be made of consociationalism as a means of governing deeply segmented polities. Deep divisions exist, to a greater or lesser extent, in all the countries of Eastern Europe, and even within many of the successor states of the USSR (Poland and Hungary probably suffer least and Romania the Czech and Slovak republics, Yugoslavia and the former USSR the most). In states where there are such major and long-established divisions (ethno-national, religious, racial, linguistic), majoritarian politics will clearly be a recipe for disruption. Indeed, if relations between two ethno-national communities deteriorate and reductionist mobilization takes place (as argued above), separation and, possibly, territorial realignment will be the only solution. But, short of that, the techniques of consociationalism are worth discussing, as well as their application in Eastern Europe, especially as they have been fairly successful in several multi-national states in sustaining democratic order.

The key aspect of consociationalism is that it seeks to draw all the different segments of the polity into the decision-making process, through élite representation, a kind of grand coalition. Other institutional forms can also be envisaged, such as regular consultation with all groups by the president. The basic elements necessary for the establishment, and successful maintenance, of a consociational system must begin with consultation between all groups, in order to build support for constitutional change, and then include: a veto by all groups over major issues affecting them; a proportionate sharing of state expenditure and patronage; and substantial autonomy for each group to regulate and control its supporters. Furthermore, the bureaucracy should develop an ethos of ensuring that policies are implemented accordingly; the government should conduct its negotiations discreetly, even in camera, to prevent popular mobilization around any issue which could be related to group identity; and, a set of tacit rules on how to conduct affairs should be adopted[7].

Consociationalism, however, imposes two essential conditions in order for it to work. The first is that all the groups concerned must be willing to compromise and to make creative use of both substantive and procedural solutions, to help all the parties. In other words, they must avoid an impasse and the onset of a reductionist process, even at the risk of ambiguity. Above all, there must be no major winners or losers. Secondly, the leaders of a group must be able to secure the support of their followers in honouring the consociational bargains. The success of this depends on the confidence of the members of the group in the system as a whole—a recognition that their interests have been taken into consideration in the bargaining. Thus the leadership of the group must be able to convince the membership to support the solutions they have negotiated. Society, as well as its leadership, must be sophisticated for consociational solutions to work well.

Other factors important to the success of consociationalism include a readiness to delegate as much as possible to the groups themselves, that is to allow extensive self-government. This is complicated in modern societies by the erosion of the territorial principle (although sometimes, as with the Roma, this does not apply anyway). On the whole, in dynamic societies, members of different segments will tend to be dispersed throughout the entire area of the state; it would be fatal to consociationalism to base devolution of power solely on territory. Next, the principle of proportionality should be observed rigorously. If anything, there should be an over-representation of smaller groups; the minority veto is, of course, the ultimate resource for the protection of small communities. Over-representation, however, should not be confused with positive discrimination, or affirmative action strategies, which have the different objective of promoting the equality, not the stability, of minorities.

There are various helpful, though not essential, preconditions for the success of consociationalism. These include: the relative equality of the groups and the absence of one with a majority; and, a relatively small total population, for this means a fairly small élite in which it is likely that members of the élite, although from different ethno-national groups, may share values through similar, or identical, educational and other experiences. There should be an

overarching loyalty to a legitimating ideology of the state, and a corresponding moral–cultural outward boundary with other states (the failure of this can be seen in Soviet Moldavia—Moldova—where loyalty to the USSR never achieved a sufficient sense of separateness from Romania). In addition, a tradition of political accommodation can be very useful indeed. It should be emphasized that these preconditions are neither necessary nor sufficient for the success of consociationalism, but they are useful.

What, then, are the chances of introducing consociational practices into post-Communist systems? The countries that would be involved include Czechoslovakia, Yugoslavia, Romania and Bulgaria; recognition of some of these practices would be valuable in Poland and Hungary as well. In Albania, the introduction of democracy is too recent to allow for much speculation on the future of relations with the Greek community, while in the emerging democracies of the USSR successor states nationalist conflicts seem more likely to follow a reductionist course, apart from in the Baltic Republics, where an accommodation seems to have been achieved between the Balts and the Russian communities. For the moment, Romania and Bulgaria can be effectively ruled out, though for different reasons. In Romania the problem of national minorities is particularly acute and the country cannot yet be considered a democracy. In Bulgaria, since 1989, although the representation of the Turkish minority has not been a major difficulty, the basis of anything resembling a stable democratic order has so far eluded the élites.

In Yugoslavia, the events of 1991 (such as the Slovenian and Croation declarations of 'dissociation', in June, and the ensuing violence) led inexorably towards the disintegration of the state and the failure of the rather pallid attempt at Communist consociationalism. Accommodation of the different segments was compromised in favour of the majority principle, with the result that the smaller segments began to consider opting out of the state entirely.

In Czechoslovakia, on the other hand, both the Czech and the Slovak élites have sought to find agreement to keep the state in being; the limited support for the Slovak National Party in local elections, in November 1990, is at least a short-term indicator of their success. However, two problems remain. Neither the Czech nor the Slovak leaderships can be fully secure in having the support of their followers, especially when the economic reforms begin to cause hardship. Secondly, the Czech–Slovak accommodation largely excludes the Hungarian minority and downgrades the significance of the Moravians (Bohemia is the more dominant of the Czech lands). Ethno-national stability can only be assured if the Hungarians and the Moravians are fully integrated in the various ways outlined above.

In Poland, the discovery that a sizeable German minority, which had no cultural rights at all during the Communist period, still exists on the territory of the state (together with Byelorussian, Ukrainian and Lithuanian groups) surprised Polish opinion. The Poles had believed the myth that Poland was an ethnically homogeneous country. This is not a good beginning for the cause of recognition of the rights of minorities, let alone consociationalism. In Hungary, on the other hand, there is little support for consociationalism, but there is strong verbal and some substantive support for the acceptance of minority rights, albeit that the Romany people are only now being accepted as a minority at all. However the precondition for the success of all these experiments is that the democratic systems introduced in 1990 should survive; the success of democracy in Central and Eastern Europe is far from guaranteed.

FOOTNOTES

1. This is the organizing principle behind Hobsbawm, E., and Ranger, T. (Eds). *The Invention of Tradition*. Cambridge, Cambridge University Press, 1983. See also Connor, W. *The National Question in Marxist-Leninist Theory and Strategy*. Princeton, NJ, Princeton University Press, 1984.

2. Isaacs, H. R.. *Idols of the Tribe: Group Identity and Political Change*. Cambridge, Ma, Harvard University Press, 1989.

3. Orridge, A. 'Varieties of Nationalism', in Tivey, L. (Ed.). *The Nation-State: the Formation of Modern Politics.* Oxford, Martin Robertson, 1981 (pp. 39–58).

4. Douglas, M. *How Institutions Think*. Syracuse, NY, Syracuse University Press, 1986. Also, Edwards, J. *Language, Society and Identity*. Oxford, Blackwell, 1985.

5. Dahrendorf, R. *Reflections on the Revolution In Europe*. London, Chatto and Windus, 1990.

6. Nordlinger, E. A. *On the Autonomy of the Democratic State*. Cambridge, Ma, Harvard University Press, 1981. Also, Andreski, S. 'Society, Bureaucrats and Businessmen', in *Survey*, 25:4, Autumn 1980 (pp. 112–126).

7. The classic exposition of consociationalism is Lijphart, A. *Democracy in Plural Societies: a Comparative Explanation*. New Haven, Ct, Yale University Press, 1977. Also, Powell, Jr, G. B. *Contemporary Democracies: Participation, Stability and Violence*. Cambridge, Ma, Harvard University Press, 1982 (pp. 212–218).

RELIGION IN THE REGION

Rev. Canon MICHAEL BOURDEAUX

STALINIST POLICIES TOWARDS RELIGION

For over 30 years before the collapse of the Soviet empire, it was not possible to define a single, coherent Communist policy towards religion. Indeed, if has ever been possible since the Second World War, the period would be limited to approximately 1948–56. Stalin, who had already attempted to eliminate the Church in the USSR, gained vast new territories at the end of the Second World War. He had also acquired by conquest even stronger churches. As soon as the new governments were established and stabilized, Stalin's supporters attempted to break the power of the Church by removing church leaders, abolishing all religious institutions and privileges and intimidating the faithful. This was a first step towards fulfilling the eventual Marxist-Leninist requirement of eliminating religion.

This was a policy which Lenin had instituted during his lifetime and which Stalin had faithfully continued. By this time, however, Stalin had already abandoned such a policy in his own country. When the war against Hitler seemed lost, Stalin had asked the leaders of the Russian Orthodox Church for their moral support in defence of the homeland. In return, they would receive the right to repossess church buildings, to reinstate 'loyal' clergy into parishes and even to reopen a small number of theological seminaries. Only in those parts of the USSR which had been newly incorporated, following the conquests of the Red Army (Soviet Moldavia, the Western Ukraine, Western Byelorussia and the Baltic Republics), were the the same policies to apply as in Poland, Czechoslovakia and other recently subjugated countries.

In the RSFSR, the Russian Federation, on the other hand, Stalin soon discovered the benefits of a malleable church leadership, still intimidated by the horrors of the 1930s. An Orthodox Church which had visibly improved its status, was a useful tool for propaganda in the new Europe of the time.

There was one major exception to these generalizations: the Uniate or 'Greek Catholic' Church (see below). In its major centres (the Western Ukraine, Transcarpathia, Romania and Eastern Slovakia), the Uniate Church was liquidated and required to merge with the Orthodox Church. It was an attempt to divert the loyalty of millions of the faithful from the Vatican to Moscow. Ostensibly, this seemed to have a good chance of success. The Uniate Church (see Appendix below) had, originally, been imposed on the people as a way of securing their loyalty to Rome, and their new Roman Catholic rulers (whether Poles, Germans or Hungarians), without depriving them of their beloved Slavonic liturgy. Thus they seemed more like the Orthodox than the Roman Catholics of the Latin rite, but, in every instance, as soon as it became possible (1968 for the Slovaks, 1989 for most of the others), the majority reverted to Rome. In Poland, Hungary and Bulgaria, where fewer people were affected, this liquidation did not take place.

After Khrushchev's denunciation of Stalin, in 1956, each country of the Communist bloc formulated its own, less rigid, policy towards religion. These were as varied and contrasting as the religious and social histories of those countries themselves. Their formulation was governed more by the practical and the possible than by the application of theory. The policies varied from a move towards religious liberty in Poland to a sustained attempt at eliminating both Christianity and Islam from Albania. Even this latter policy collapsed, in 1991, more than 20 years after its introduction.

Thus, at no time since the Second World War has there been a single Communist policy towards religion. Nevertheless, it would be equally true that, until the accession of Gorbachev, the ultimate goal of Communist theory remained the eradication of religion. The Soviet *perestroika* programme, however, necessitated a complete re-evaluation of the role of religion in society, and the advent of democracy inaugurated religious liberty elsewhere.

The very existence of religion within a Marxist society could be used as a powerful symbol demonstrating that totalitarianism had yet to take complete hold. Apart from one or two minor sects, not even the most complaisant of groups preached Communism. While religion maintained any presence at all in society, it represented a set of alternative values. It could, therefore, be said to undermine the dogmatic unity proclaimed by the state. As time went on, the Church became bolder in proclaiming these values, creating mental, and sometimes even physical, space for their discussion. Likewise, the resurgence of Islamic fundamentalism (marked by the Iranian revolution), emphasized the existence of an ethos that not only challenged, but often rejected, the atheistic Communist state.

This did not happen uniformly. Although developments were different under each regime, there was no country in which the Church did not play some role in the overthrow of the Communist systems, and nowhere in a more decisive manner than in Poland.

POLAND

From the outset, it was clear that the Stalinist policy of brutal oppression was doomed to failure in Poland, short of the incarceration of one-half of the population. The country contained perhaps the most powerful Roman Catholic Church and one of the most homogeneous populations in the world. In fact, by the end of 1953 (the year of Stalin's death), Cardinal Wyszyński, eight other bishops, 900 priests and about 1,000 lay activists were in prison. Even this formidable total, however, formed no more than a few empty rows in the multitude, and served to harden the resolve of the millions of faithful who remained at liberty. After 1970 this policy of repression gradually softened to accommodation, although the state continued to attempt to sever the Church's links with the expanding democratic movement.

In October 1978 a conclave of the Roman Catholic Church's College of Cardinals elected Karol Wojtyła of Kraków as the first Slav Pope. It was clearly seeking spiritual strength from where the Church had its greatest reserves; what the cardinals did not envisage was that they were also contributing to the beginning of a process which would, in barely more than one decade, overthrow Communism itself. Christians throughout the region, even some Protestant groups in Siberia, could draw inspiration from this unprecedented event. Wojtyła's first visit to Poland as Pope John Paul II, in mid-1979, stimulated massive popular demonstrations. This was followed by widespread labour unrest, in 1980, and the foundation of Solidarność (Solidarity), the first anti-Communist, and specifically Christian, trade union in the bloc. Its repression and the imposition of martial law, in December 1981, did no more than harden the opposition. In April–May 1989 the Church, or at least its 'political wing' in the form of Solidarność, was strong enough to bring about a 'round-table' conference between government and opposition. This introduced a limited democratic process and the eventual representation of anti-Communist forces in government. By the end of 1990 a Roman Catholic prime minister (Tadeusz Mazowiecki) and a Roman Catholic president (Lech Wałęsa) had been elected, and the virtually bloodless collapse of Communism was complete.

Polish church leaders, after decades in the forefront of the political struggle, wished then to withdraw quietly to the huge work of social and moral reconstruction. Although the decay of traditional morality was not perceived to have eaten as deeply as in other Communist countries, the years since 1948 had had some effect (the controversy over abortion indicates the conflict between church and secular values). The Church wishes to counter this and has massive tasks ahead in education and the rebuilding of social institutions. Beyond this, there is the old problem of endemic anti-Semitism, which is re-emerging again; this emphasizes that the Church must be wary of impeding or harassing minorities, that is those who wish to belong to a different denomination or religion or to profess no religion at all. This is not psychologically easy for a Church which continues to command such massive support. Furthermore the Pope, during his visit in June 1991, appealed for toleration within the Church, between the majority followers of the Latin rite and the Uniate minority of the east.

HUNGARY

The Roman Catholic Church played a major role in the abortive counter-revolution in Hungary in 1956. Cardinal József Mindszenty was one of the best known and, from the moral point of view, most vigorously defended, of all the hierarchs who suffered indignities under Stalin. When the Hungarians briefly regained their freedom he was released from prison and his words, broadcast over the radio, became a classic Christian defence against Communism. Not even implied criticism later on, or his removal from office by the Vatican itself (while he was, from 1956 to 1974, a refugee in the American legation in Budapest and the church authorities were pursuing an accord with the government), could ever eradicate his example. This was demonstrated by the crowds who attended the reinterrment of his remains at Esztergom, in 1991.

The Catholic Church in Hungary is not monolithic, as it is in Poland. The total population of Hungary is some 10m., of whom an estimated 63% were baptized Roman Catholics (at the beginning of 1989), but there is much nominalism and the Church receives solid support only in some country areas. The Reformed Church (Calvinist) has almost 2m. members and the Lutherans about 350,000. In each instance, however, probably only about 10% attend church regularly.

Following the Mindszenty drama and the state's similar neutralization of the best Protestant leaders, none of the main churches was able to supply charismatic leadership comparable to Poland's. Indeed in both main Protestant churches, with the active intervention of the authorities, a leadership emerged which proclaimed that believers should be servants of the state (the Lutherans refer to the theology of *diakonia* or service). This was assisted by the seeming tolerance practised by the government, which not only applied to the Christian churches but to the country's small Jewish community (the only rabbinical seminary in the Communist Eastern European bloc was in Hungary).

As Hungarian society moved away from the repressions following the 1956 uprising, criticism of the church leadership by their followers became more insistent. The Vatican, too, had appointed new bishops after the state had agreed the names. As a counterweight, however, 'base communities' were quietly encouraged and they developed into a strong movement. At its peak there were some 5,000 groups, and 100,000 members. In the late 1970s and early 1980s, however, the Base Communities proved to be a source of tension within the Church as they clashed with the bishops; the movement threatened the relationship with the secular authorities by their pacifism and challenge to Communism.

No single Christian leader emerged to galvanize believers as democracy became more of a real possibility. From 1988, however, the Roman Catholic bishops became increasingly insistent in their questioning of the political leadership. The Prime Minister, Károly Grósz, heard from Cardinal Paskai that youth work was increasing. Grósz replied: 'We agree that only a church that is capable of functioning can fruitfully assist the realization of our social objectives.' But the days when the Church could help any Hungarian government achieve social, in the sense of Marxist, objectives were now numbered. With a majority of 304 to 1 the democratic National Assembly passed a law on 23 January 1990 guaranteeing complete freedom of religion. Now it is up to the churches to rebuild both their structures and confidence in the leadership, as new people take up key positions.

CZECHOSLOVAKIA

Christians in Czechoslovakia were much more openly engaged in an active struggle for freedom. The policy of the regime virtually ensured that this would be so, because it remained repressive during the 1970s and 1980s, while, in nearby Hungary, the government was gradually relaxing restrictions. After the 'Prague Spring' and the Soviet invasion of 1968, Christian activists were systematically removed from the professions and forced to take more menial jobs. They did not succeed in eventually moving back into their old jobs, so their reinstatement was all the more dramatic when it did occur, after the events of late 1989.

The churches lost nearly two-thirds of their members under Communism, but the remainder (over 3m. Roman Catholics and some 1.3m. Protestants) were a substantial minority. Gradually they regained their self-confidence, following the trauma of 1968. For example, the human-rights movement, Charter 77, contained Christian activists from its foundation. Czechoslovak Protestants were very active in nurturing foreign contacts before 1968 and these links were never entirely broken. The Roman Catholic Church, as an international organization, also enjoys such links, which are, indeed, stronger and more public than for the Protestants. Perhaps most influential of all, was the way in which the aged Roman Catholic primate, František Tomášek (from 1978 the Archbishop of Prague), became more outspoken and seemingly tougher with his declining years. He was already in his mid-70s when he became a cardinal in 1976 (the appointment was not announced immediately), and he fiercely opposed the 'peace priests' of the Pacem in Terris organization, a group which the state had persuaded to endorse its political propaganda. Later, after the decline in their influence, his public statements became a rallying call; he acted as though his venerable years rendered him inviolable.

Cardinal Tomášek lived to see the collapse of Communism, in 1989, and retired at the age of 91. His successor, Miloslav Vlk (who was made a cardinal in May 1991), was a man with a double doctorate, who had nevertheless spent many years as a window cleaner. No other of the new Eastern European democracies saw quite such dramatic transformations (as happened with President Havel himself); dozens of other demoted churchmen found themselves, often overnight, back in leading roles.

The Vatican and the hierarchy did achieve some return from the authorities by their accommodating *Ostpolitik*. Although most of the dioceses continued to lack resident bishops under the Communist government, the authorities did allow some appointments (including Tomášek's) and the creation of a separate Slovak ecclesiastical province (previously dependent upon the Hungarian Church). The Uniate Church, in Eastern Slovakia, retained the legal status it had regained in 1968, but without much of its rightful property and with no possibility of reopening a theological seminary. For it, too, 1990 was a period of major restoration. The dramatic return of Christianity to public life in Czechoslovakia suggests that it will have a high profile in the future.

THE GERMAN DEMOCRATIC REPUBLIC

Among all the upheavals of 1989, it was probably in the GDR that the church played the most decisive public role in the political process. This had been the heartland of the Reformation, Luther's land, but the Evangelische Kirche (EKD) declined under the Marxist regime to probably not more than 3m. members, out of a population of 17m. The psychology of the country, after the defeat of the Second World War, was different to that of other Eastern European countries: there was never a purge of the church leadership, such as occurred elsewhere in the socialist bloc. The clergy never compromised with the political system under duress. Nor did the church leaders adopt an anti-Communist stance, as in Poland; rather, they described themselves as 'the Church in Socialism' and reserved the right to criticize if the regime clearly contradicted Christian morality or did something opposed to the interests of the Church.

In the 1980s, however, this gradually began to change. Young people began to challenge Marxism more openly. The Church, often literally, provided space and protection for them. Political opposition began to congregate in and around Protestant churches. In a dilemma, the leadership took a principled stand and decided it could not expel these people from church premises. The state, fearful of causing a scandal, treated them as though they had gained the medieval right of sanctuary.

In April 1989 a state official warned an ecumenical conference, in Dresden, to end the protection, but this served only to harden the determination of both Protestants and the minority Roman Catholics alike. The much smaller Roman Catholic Church (only about 8% of the population were adherents) had kept itself largely isolated from civic affairs. It had opposed the legalization of abortion in 1972, causing votes of dissent and abstention to be registered in the People's Chamber (Volkskammer) for the first time in its history, and had become more involved in the peace movement from the early 1980s. Like the Protestant churches, it too became more outspoken from 1989.

On Monday evenings, in St Nicholas Church in Leipzig, there had been prayer services for peace since 1982. Increasingly these began to accommodate young activists who had an agenda other than a purely Christian one. In mid-1989 the state security service (Staatssicherheitsdienst or, colloquially, the Stasi) planned to arrest some 1,500 clergy and activists, and remove them to remote castles in Thuringia. Their resolve, however, failed before they proceeded. In September and early October some 6,000 people were attending the meetings and three times as many again were marching around the city at night, chanting slogans. By now the clergy were powerless to restrain the demonstrations.

It seemed as though a bloody confrontation was inevitable. Yet, once again, the Stasi failed to intervene. The huge crowd would sing Luther's hymn, *Ein' feste Burg*. The political events acquired their own momentum, which resulted in the breaching of the Berlin Wall on 9 November. The leading role of the Church, however, was indicated by four of the 23 ministers in the new government being clergy, with several others being Christian laymen. The demise of the German Democratic Republic as an independent state, therefore, brings to an end a remarkable chapter in 20th century church history.

YUGOSLAVIA

As the dissolution of the Yugoslav federation became more likely during the late 1980s and early 1990s, so it became harder to categorize the role of religion there. From the days of Tito's rupture with Stalin, the non-aligned status of the country was reflected in the comparative religious liberty which the government permitted. Earlier, persecution had been as severe as elsewhere. Much of this was because some prominent Roman Catholics, such as Archbishop Sarić of Sarajevo, collaborated with the Nazis during the Second World War and the Fascist Ustaša state of Croatia (1941–44) identified itself with Roman Catholicism. Thus, in 1946, Aloysius Stepinac, Archbishop of Zagreb (who had supported a Croat state but deplored Ustaša atrocities), was tried and imprisoned. During the 1950s Party control gradually eased; this process accelerated after 1966 and the removal of Aleksandar Ranković, head of the secret police, and the conclusion of a concordat between the Vatican and the Yugoslav authorities.

However the Church did not gain as much strength as might have been expected, because the two main denominations, Eastern Orthodoxy and Roman Catholicism, were identified with different forms of nationalism. The Serbian and Macedonian Orthodox Churches have themselves been in dispute since 1967, over the autocephaly of the latter. Slovenia and Croatia are mainly Roman Catholic, while Islam predominates in Bosnia-Herzegovina and in the ethnic Albanian region of Kosovo, which is administratively part of Serbia. The fact that there are strong, but threatened, minorities (for example, of Croats in Serbia) underlines the danger of too close an alliance between religion and nationalism.

From the late 1960s the Roman Catholic Church in Croatia began to act with considerable independence, in no sphere more notably than in the founding of an uncensored weekly newspaper, *Glas Koncila* (Voice of the Council). No such publication, at this time, existed in any other Communist country. By contrast, 80% of the Serbian Orthodox priests joined 'regime-friendly' associations after the Second World War. The Orthodox Church was harassed by the Communist authorities, but enjoyed considerable prestige because of its persecution by the Nazis. From 1958 it was headed by Patriarch German, who did not encourage any criticism of the status quo. He did object to the restoration of the ancient bishopric of Ohrid, with its seat in Skopje (Macedonia), regarding it as an attempt by the authorities to fragment the Church. In 1967, with the backing of the federal government, three dioceses became independent of the Serbian Church, which continues to refuse its recognition to the Macedonian Orthodox Church which was thereby established. After the death of Tito, in 1980, the Serbian Orthodox Church began to identify itself much more strongly with the Serbian nationalist and separatist movement and gained popular support. Patriarch Pavle, elected in 1990, in place of the ailing German, has shown himself acutely aware of the many problems facing his Church, but it is too early yet to forecast how he will cope with them. Popular Roman Catholic faith, meanwhile, has received stimulus from the alleged apparitions of the Virgin Mary at Medjugorje, although the Vatican has yet to make an official pronouncement on their authenticity.

Yugoslavia is home to Eastern Europe's largest Muslim population (to which about 10% of the 23m. population belong). Most live in Bosnia-Herzegovina and Kosovo. Muslims were persecuted after the Second World War (many had fought against Tito's partisans), but, for foreign and traditional domestic policy reasons, they were treated with increasing generosity by the Tito regime. In 1971 legislation even acknowledged the Bosnian Muslims (descendants of Slavs, Serbo-Croats, who had converted under the Ottomans) as a distinct ethnic group. The other Muslims are the Albanians of Kosovo and some Turks. Allowing Muslims to study abroad, however, exposed Yugoslavia to the import of fundamentalist sentiments. In the late 1970s and early 1980s the Communist authorities reacted against any signs of an Islamic revival or Islamic separatism. The greater freedom for religion is bound to give the Muslims greater prominence in a world where Islam in general is a rising force.

ROMANIA

Religion played a decisive role in the displacement of the old system, though the significance of this could easily be exaggerated. In December 1989 the authorities, with the support of the bishop, attempted to evict Father László Tőkés, an outspoken Protestant pastor of the Hungarian Reformed Church, from his parish house in Timişoara. His resistance inspired street protests in Timişoara, bringing opposition into the open, and stimulated riots elsewhere in the country. This movement rapidly crossed ethnic borders, although the relations between the Transylvanian Hungarian community (to which Fr Tőkés belongs) and the majority Romanians are not usually easy.

What is less known, and has been very little reported, is that before this, religion had been playing a role in the development of civic consciousness, in a country where the suppression of opposition was widespread and effective. The Romanian Orthodox Church has at least 17m. adherents (some 75% of the population), lulled into political quiescence by its bishops, who had long since become active or passive supporters of the regime. The Church remained the state church after 1945 (nationalism and religion are closely connected in Romania), co-operated with the Communist regime and became dependent upon the Moscow Patriarchate, but did not entirely escape persecution or harassment. Despite the compliance of the bishops, there have been individuals still prepared to speak out. In the mid-1970s a Christian Committee for the Defence of Religious Freedom and Freedom of Conscience emerged, in which a few Orthodox and Baptists joined forces. The state neutralized this by forcing the leading activists to emigrate. Then Fr Gheorghe Calciu-Dumitreasa attracted the ire of the regime and of his own church hierarchy by teaching courses critical of socialism at the Bucharest Theological Academy. His imprisonment, in 1979, caused international protests, as did Ceauşescu's plans for building his palace and for replacing old villages by apartment blocks, both of which entailed considerable destruction of church property. None of this, however, elicited any official protest from the Romanian Orthodox Church. Patriarch Teoctist was supporting the regime in public virtually up to the day Ceauşescu died. He did resign shortly after, only to be reinstated because his fellow bishops took the view that there was no one yet spiritually ready to succeed him.

There are approximately 1.3m. Roman Catholics in Romania, including the Uniates, who have re-emerged following their abolition and forcible incorporation into the Romanian Orthodox Church in 1948. In May 1991 the Vatican appointed the head of the Uniates, Archbishop Todea, a cardinal. As the Orthodox Church had acquiesced in the suppression of the Uniates, relations between the two are now extremely strained. The fact that most of the Latin-rite Roman Catholics are of the minority ethnic Hungarian and German communities is a further source of tension, and most of the Latin dioceses were also without bishops during the Communist regime.

In recent decades the Baptist Church has rapidly gained converts, numbering between 300,000 and 500,000 adherents by 1990. Over many years, both in Bucharest and Transylvania, it defied state pressure, not only preaching the Gospel with great boldness, but also keeping open major lines of communication with other Christians in Western Europe and the USA. It has now devised a new education programme and seems certain to play a growing public role in the country. The main established Protestant churches are the Reformed Church (almost 800,000 members—a Calvinist denomination, mainly of ethnic Hungarians) and the Lutheran Church (over 200,000 members—Germans), but there are also some Pentecostal and Seventh-day Adventist congregations.

There are only small communities of non-Christian religions, Muslims and Jews, the latter being the smaller, but more controversial, group. The traditional anti-Semitism in Romanian society was exacerbated under the old regime by the coincidence that some of the Communists in the pro-Soviet ('internationalist') faction ousted by Gheorghiu-Dej, from 1952, were Jewish. Throughout the 1950s Jews were persecuted and forced to emigrate. There was some relaxation in the 1960s, but, from the 1970s, there were signs of a general anti-Semitism re-emerging. This has been linked to the extreme nationalism associated with the Ceauşescu regime and which, it is alleged, is now being used for political purposes, despite the negligible size of the Jewish community. Anti-Semitism became very evident in 1990 and 1991. The Chief Rabbi, Moses Rosen, criticized anti-Semitic publications and nationalist attempts to minimize the genocidal massacres of Jews during the Second World War. In June Rosen threatened the mass emigration of the remaining Jewish population from Romania to Israel and criticized the authorities, but he was still heckled by anti-Semitic revisionists at a memorial service later that month. The Muslims, by contrast, do not suffer prejudice to the same degree.

BULGARIA

Politically passive though Bulgaria had seemed to be for many decades, the protests of the Muslim communities at forcible 'bulgarization' added a major impetus to the process of reform, and individual churchmen have played an important part in the progress of democratization. The most influential was the Bulgarian Orthodox monk (and Moscow-trained former scientist) Hristofor Subev, who established an Independent Association for the Defence of Human Rights in Bulgaria, in January 1988. Its membership included representatives of both the Muslim and the Protestant minorities. Persecuted by the state and pressurized by his own Church, Fr Subev nevertheless supported Muslim cultural and religious rights when protests and hunger strikes began in May 1989. His imprisonment for about 10 weeks, in mid-1989, only served to harden the opposition. Up to this time the Orthodox Church (2m. of the 9m.

population, with many more baptized, but inactive, members) had been among the most passive of all within the Communist bloc. It had endured a widespread campaign of persecution and intimidation during the l950s, but enjoyed the benefits of being a national church. As an organization it was not critical of the regime and discouraged its priests, like Fr Subev, from being so. In December 1989, however, agitating with the support of other emerging human rights groups, the Independent Committee was granted legal status. In July l990 the Holy Synod of the Bulgarian Orthodox Church made public an act of repentance, in which they declared they were in error to have criticized Fr Subev in the way they did.

After the Second World War the leaders of the Protestant and Roman Catholic minorities also suffered severely. The Communist authorities did resume contacts with the Vatican after the death of Stalin, particularly in connection with celebrations in honour of St Cyril (Constantine) and St Methodius, and allowed the appointment of bishops. The alleged Bulgarian involvement in the attempted assassination of the Pope, in 1981, marred relations in the mid- and late 1980s.

A new law on religion drafted by the Grand National Assembly, in October 1990, promised to accord full rights to the Muslim faith, as well as to the Christian minorities. With the moral stature of religion in general having been considerably enhanced in the upheavals from l989 onwards, it will probably play a more important role in the evolution of the democratic process than had ever seemed possible a few years ago.

ALBANIA

The most dramatic transformation in the status of religion has occurred in Albania. In 1967 Enver Hoxha's regime went further than any other Communist state in banning religion totally. Even in the People's Republic of China, which provided Albania's ideological model, a nominal church leadership was retained during the Cultural Revolution of that time.

The religious orientation of this country of 3m. people was then estimated to be about 70% Muslims, 20% Eastern Orthodox Christian (mostly in the south, adjacent to Greece) and 10% Roman Catholics (in the north). Although the smallest of the main groups, Roman Catholicism became strongly linked with Albanian nationalism from the late 19th century. After the ban, not only was every church and mosque closed, but many of the buildings were destroyed and all the most active clergy removed to prison camps. There was evidence for the clandestine observance of religious practices, such as Muslim burial customs, the celebration of Easter and fasting in Ramadan or Lent. The authorities campaigned relentlessly against religion.

The ideological structure seemed to remain intact following Hoxha's death, in 1985. Albania's imperviousness to the fall of Communism in 1989, however, was only apparent. The northern city of Shkodër became the first focus for riots of growing intensity, beginning in January 1990, and some of the activists were known to be Roman Catholics. On 8 May 1990 the Government announced to the parliament that the ban on religious propaganda was ended. By January 1991 the Orthodox of the southern town of Korçë were demanding the restoration of their right to worship and the return of their property.

Now clearly on the defensive, the Government permitted public Easter celebrations, with the service in Tirana attended by the best-known Albanian of all, Mother Teresa, on her first visit. In Shkodër Fr Simon Jubani, released from prison two years earlier, reopened the cathedral and later gave extended interviews to a British television

reporter, the first time that anyone from inside the country had been able to speak openly of religious persecution. The same film showed Muslims attending the mosques, as well as Christians in church. In July 1991 the Pope and the Albanian premier agreed that diplomatic relations should be established between the Holy See and Albania.

With the devastation of all religious institutions, it is not easy to forecast how easily believers will begin to play a significant role in public life again. In June 1991, however, the collapse of the Government elected only two months previously and the manifest desire of people to return to their faiths indicate that the new profile of religion will be higher than anyone could have imagined in the 1980s. There is certain, too, to be an influence of Islamic fundamentalism from abroad.

THE USSR

It was Lenin who inaugurated Soviet atheism and Gorbachev who dismantled it. Before its dissolution the USSR had ceased to be an 'atheist state'. However the future of had ceased to be an 'atheist state'. However the future of religion is not therefore secure, because of the manifest instability of society in general. All religions experienced the Second World War, and despite the accommodating passivity of the hierarchy, the Russian Orthodox Church has still endured much repression, particularly of those who criticized the silence of the Church. It has, however, benefited from Soviet attempts at 'russification'. The Moscow Patriarchate has increased its influence at the expense of the local Orthodox Churches in Georgia (there was no separate seminary for Georgian clergy), Moldavia and the Ukraine. The Russian Orthodox Church was also used to absorb the 'internationalist' Roman Catholic Uniates, who were rigorously persecuted and only scantly supported by the Vatican until the pontificate of John Paul II. The Roman Catholic Church of the Latin rite consists mainly of Lithuanians, Latvians and Poles; it was forbidden a central ecclesiastical authority, although a diocesan structure did emerge in Lithuania and Latvia (jurisdiction is exercised over western Byelorussia and the western Ukraine from here). Lithuania witnessed a strong movement of Roman Catholic criticism of the regime, particularly in the 1970s, and in the Ukraine a catacomb or underground Uniate church was established. Protestant sects are smaller and the main victims of persecution were the Pentecostal congregations who refused to register with the forced amalgamation of the All-Union Council of Evangelical Christians and Baptists. The Muslims suffered mainly in the late 1920s and in the 1930s; in 1946 the central government established four Spiritual Directorates for Muslim affairs and allowed a restricted growth in religious observances. The Soviet authorities were particularly concerned to prevent the rise of pan-Islamic sentiments of a fundamentalist nature. Fortunately for these policies, clandestine Muslim activity, although conservative and anti-Soviet, has been conducted by the intellectual Sufi fraternities.

As early as 1988 Gorbachev appeared to realize that his *perestroika* programme was in trouble. When, on 29 April, he summoned a group of leading Russian Orthodox bishops, it was to tell them that the rebuilding of Soviet society was as much their responsiblity as that of the Communists. He had already released most of the religious prisoners, the remaining exceptions consisting of about 30 Christian conscientious objectors. Doubtless mindful of the fact that well over one-third of the population still counted themselves as having religious belief (perhaps 50m. Eastern Orthodox, 40m. Muslims, 10m. Roman Catholics and 2m. Protestant Christians, with substantial minorities of the Armenian Apostolic Church, Jews and Buddhists), Gorbachev referred to the building of socialism as 'our common cause' and criticized the rigid state controls of the past as a deformation of Marx's original ideals. He acknowledged the existing laws to be unjust, and promised that there would be new legislation.

Against opposition, this took almost three years. However, in the meantime, the Church acted as if it had formally gained its freedom. The Russian Orthodox Church had access to the media for the first time during its millennium celebrations, of June 1988, and, thereafter, religious programmes became a feature of Soviet television. Hospitals, psychiatric clinics, orphanages and even prisons opened their doors to the ministrations of teams of Christians of all denominations, who were originally supposed to be covering for the deficiencies of the system and carrying out the most menial tasks, but soon were offering consolation to the suffering and even openly preaching the Gospel. At one time children of families which had the reputation of being religious zealots were being removed to state institutions; now directors of these sometimes sought Christian families who would adopt institutionalized children. Most controversial of all, head teachers began to invite clergy to speak about their faith and teach moral precepts to the children. According to the statute book, this was still an offence carrying a long prison sentence. Furthermore, complaining of the favour being shown to Christianity, particularly Orthodox Christianity, the Muslims too began to claim their rights in religious education and the choice of muftis. In July 1991 the Dalai Lama was allowed to visit the Buddhists of Buryatia (Russian Federation), on the 250th anniversary of the recognition of Buddhism in Russia.

Now was the time to begin to rectify some of the gravest injustices which had been perpetrated against the institution of religion. *Perestroika* and the continuing ban on the Ukrainian Catholic (Uniate) Church were clearly incompatible; so this largest 'underground' church, with perhaps 4m. adherents, became legal again on 1 December 1989, the day the Pope received Gorbachev. Other banned groups, such as Hare Krishna and the Jehovah's Witnesses, could also begin to operate unhindered. This is not to say that there was no opposition to these changes, by local Communist Party officials, but there was no concerted rearguard action.

This was all happening while Soviet power was beginning to lose its grip on Eastern Europe, and was clearly part of the same process. There is no doubt that Gorbachev was personally involved in the decision to give religion a new role in society, but he did not follow up his meeting of April 1988 by providing any public rationale for this.

The new law, scheduled to be enacted in September or October 1991, was complicated by the fact that the republics passed their own legislation, with significant differences. For example, the Lithuanian parliament decreed the return of all church property, soon after its independence declaration of March 1990. The Russian Federation made a firmer provision for the teaching of religion in state schools than did the all-Union law. Nevertheless, in broad outline, the position was now clear: all the activities mentioned above became legal and the USSR now enjoyed religious liberty,

at least in theory. Some vestigial state control remained in the continuing obligation of religious communities to register, though this was allegedly to guarantee their legal rights. The Council for Religious Affairs, the government body established by Stalin to ensure state control, remained in the all-Union legislation (but not the Russian) until it was disbanded, in late 1991, as part of the dissolution of the USSR as a whole.

The emphasis is now passing from persecution to potential or actual inter-religious disputes. The Russian Orthodox Church complains that it is losing property illegitimately to the resurgent Ukrainian Uniates. Furthermore, within the Orthodox Church, the Moscow Patriarchate is losing its influence, as is witnessed by the establishment of an Autocephalous Ukrainian Orthodox Church, or the less dramatic reassertion of liturgies in the local vernacular (as in Moldavia, for instance). There is a growth of anti-Semitism and the Church has not been especially vocal in condemning this. The biggest question of all concerns the massive presence of Islam in the Central Asian republics and Azerbaidzhan. Azerbaidzhani persecution of the Armenian minority clearly has religious overtones. Muslims in the Central Asian Republics are tolerant of the mixed racial minorities, representing Roman Catholics, Baptists, Mennonites, Lutherans and, most numerously, Russian Orthodox, but, if the political situation becomes more unstable, this could change.

However, at least for the moment, it is true to say that all religious communities have the opportunity of rebuilding the ruins of the past and of developing pastoral and teaching programmes which promise to help reform the morality of society and thus, incidentally, respond to Gorbachev's 1988 appeal in the deepest sense.

BIBLIOGRAPHY

Beeson, T. *Discretion and Valour: Religious Conditions in Russia and Eastern Europe.* London, Fontana, 1974.

Bourdeaux, M. *Gorbachev, Glasnost and the Gospel.* London, Hodder and Stoughton, 1990.

Land of Crosses: The struggle for religious freedom in Lithuania, 1939–78. Chulmleigh, Devon, Augustine Publishing House, 1979.

Corley, F., and Eibner, J. *In the Eye of the Romanian Storm: the heroic story of Pastor Laszlo Tokes.* New Jersey, Fleming H. Revell Co, 1990.

Ellis, J. *The Russian Orthodox Church: A Contemporary History.* Beckenham, Kent, Croom Helm, 1986.

Frontier. Two-monthly magazine. Oxford, Keston Research.

Religion, State and Society: the Keston Journal. Quarterly academic journal. Oxford, Keston Research.

Sawatsky, W. *Soviet Evangelicals since World War II.* Ontario, Herald Press, 1981.

Sikorska, G. *Light and Life.* London, Fount Paperbacks, 1989.

Walters, P. (Ed.). *Eastern Europe: World Christianity Series.* California, Marc Europe International and World Vision International, 1988.

Appendix: The Religions of the Region

There is a vast range of religions, denominations and sects in the region, from the many Christian churches, through Islam to the religions of Asia, such as Buddhism. A brief survey of the main groups follows.

CHRISTIANITY

The Christian religion is a monotheistic faith, which evolved from Judaism in the first century AD. Christianity is based on a belief in the divinity and teachings of Jesus Christ, the Messiah or Son of God, through whom salvation (life after death) can be obtained. His followers established the institution of a single Church, originally based on the four leading cities of the Roman Empire: Antioch, Alexandria, Rome itself and Constantinople (from 330 AD, the capital). Four distinct traditions emerged: the Syrian or Jacobite Church was based on Antioch; the Coptic Church was based on Alexandria; the western, or Latin, Church was based on Rome and became known as the Roman Catholic Church (the Protestants sprang from this tradition too); and the eastern, or Greek, Orthodox Church became centred on Constantinople (this is the tradition of most of the region's Orthodox Churches). Later divisions resulted in the emergence of the Armenian (Gregorian) Church and the Nestorian Church.

The Church also established the Christian era (a calendar of years denoted by *Anno Domini*), a reckoning which is now the most widely-used international system and is in official use throughout Eastern Europe and the former USSR. Likewise, it was the Church that preserved the use of the ancient Roman, Julian calendar, which was used in the Russian Empire until the Revolution. In 1582 a reformed Gregorian calendar (in normal use now) was first introduced, but by Pope Gregory XIII, so its adoption was initially resisted by non-Roman Catholic countries. For religious purposes the Eastern Orthodox Church still uses a version of the old Julian calendar. (The Muslims and Buddhists use a lunar calendar, which is about 10 days shorter than the solar calendar of the Gregorian reckoning. Islam dates its years from the date of the *Hijra*, so the year 1413 AH begins in early July 1992 AD. The Buddhist era is dated from the death of Gautama Buddha, reckoned to be 544 BC, making 1992 AD equivalent to 2519.)

The Eastern Orthodox Church

In 1054 the split (schism) in the Church that had become established in the old Roman Empire, became formal. The bishops of what had been the Latin-speaking West supported the authority of the Pope, the Roman patriarch, and the insertion of the *filioque* clause into the standard Nicene Creed. (This claimed that the Holy Spirit, a constituent part of the triune deity, was a product of both the Father and the Son (*Logos*), not merely of the Father.) The bishops of the Greek-speaking Eastern Roman Empire, dominated by the Byzantine Patriarch of Constantinople (today still regarded as the Ecumenical Patriarch), rejected this and so formalized a division of Europe into East and West. The Eastern, or Greek, Orthodox Church continued to use the Greek alphabet, but had also added to the success of its missionary work among the 'barbarian' peoples, on the Byzantine borders, by the introduction of the Cyrillic alphabet and a Slavonic liturgy. This powerful formative influence of the Church, particularly on culture, education and national identity, is still most relevant today. The Romanian

Orthodox are unique among the Orthodox in the use of the Latin alphabet (in Soviet Moldavia, the authorities forced the adoption of a Cyrillic alphabet to replace the traditional Latin one, although this has since been reversed in secular use). The other Orthodox churches use the Cyrillic alphabet, the invention of which is attributed to the Byzantine missionaries, St Cyril (Constantine) and St Methodius, in the ninth century.

The Eastern Orthodox churches now have a membership of over 170m., most of them in Eastern Europe and the Russian Federation. There are some Greek Orthodox in southern Albania, who fall under the jurisdiction of the Greek Church. The Russian Orthodox Church is the largest denomination and also assumed jurisdiction over the Orthodox of Soviet Moldavia, Trans-Carpathian Ukraine and Galicia. The main autocephalous (autonomous) Orthodox churches of Eastern Europe are in Bulgaria, Romania and Yugoslavia (the Serbian Orthodox Church does not acknowledge the separate existence of the Macedonian Orthodox Church). All the countries of the region have at least some Orthodox Christians.

Within the former USSR, there are missions of the Eastern Orthodox Patriarchs of Antioch and Alexandria, but the other main Orthodox Church is the Georgian. The Primate of the Georgian Orthodox Church, the Catholicos-Patriarch, also enjoys jurisdiction over several Russian and Greek communities, but, under the Communists, the Church was restricted by the lack of its own seminary and instruction in Georgian devotional literature and liturgical traditions.

With the liberalization of religion, however, such groups are likely to demand greater autonomy and a reversal of 'russification', as with the Ukrainian Autocephalous Orthodox Church. There is also the return of those Orthodox who went into exile after the Communists came to power, and often formed rival hierarchies abroad, and the secession of the Uniates who were forcibly amalgamated with the Orthodox.

The Roman Catholic Church

The western, or Roman Catholic Church, was the Church of Poland and the Baltic peoples, and the peoples of the central European empires of the Germans, Austrians and Hungarians (though, after the Reformation, a significant number became Protestant). The importance of this original divide continues to be relevant in Yugoslavia: the Slovenes are Roman Catholic; so too are the Croats, who speak the same language as the Serbs, but write it in the Latin script. The Roman Catholics were distinguished by their use of a liturgy in Latin, which is still referred to as the Latin rite, although most services are now conducted in the vernacular.

The Latin rite is not used by the adherents of the Uniate or 'Greek Catholic' Church. This denomination is part of the Roman Catholic Church, but uses the Eastern or 'Byzantine' rite; their Orthodox predecessors had acknowledged the primacy of the Roman pontiff, the Pope (also the existence of Purgatory, the doctrine of the *filioque* and the use of unleavened bread for communion), but retained their traditional liturgies and ecclesiastical organization. This first occured in the late 15th century, as an attempt to consolidate Polish (Roman Catholic) power, in a traditionally Orthodox area. A similar process took place in Transylvania, at the end of the 17th century. Not all Uniates use the Byzantine rite; there are Uniates from non-Orthodox traditions. In the region there are the Armenian Catholics and some Chaldean (Nestorian) Catholics, who also retain their Oriental customs and rites (the remaining Uniates are the Maronites, the Syrian Catholics and the Coptic Catholics).

Protestant Churches

In the Reformation period of the 16th and 17th centuries some of the western, or Catholic, Christians protested against the authority of the Roman pontiff, the Pope, and formed separate ('Protestant') sects. Most of these groups relied more on the authority of the Bible and rejected the episcopal organization of the Church (the Lutherans and some others retain bishops in the hierarchy, but reject the 'apostolic' nature of their authority). The main denominations are Lutheran Evangelical (who define their faith by the Augsburg Confession of 1530); the more fundamentalist Calvinists and Presbyterians (the Reformed Church of Hungary, etc.); Baptists; Pentecostalists; and Unitarians. There are also communities of Seventh-day Adventists (distinguished among Christians by their observance of the Sabbath on Saturday), Methodists, Mennonites (mainly of German descent, combine characteristics of the Baptists and the Society of Friends—Quakers), Molokans (pacifist fundamentalists in the Caucasus) and many others.

Other Christian Churches

The Armenian Apostolic, or Gregorian, Church is one of the Monophysite churches, like the Coptic and Syrian Jacobite Churches. It separated from the rest of the Church when it rejected the authority of the Council of Chalcedon, in 451. (The Monophysites maintain that there is a single, divine nature in the person of the incarnate Christ, whereas Chalcedon decreed that Christ had two natures, both human and divine.) There are significant Armenian communities in the region and abroad, apart from in Armenia itself. Another ancient Christian sect which differed from the orthodox on the nature of Christ, were the Nestorians (followers of a fifth century Patriarch of Constantinople), some communities of whom live in the former USSR.

The major split in the western Church was the Protestant defection from Rome. However there were some precursors of this movement in the 15th century, notably the Hussites of Bohemia and Moravia, who adapted the teachings of English Lollardy. Several sects which sprang from the Hussite factions still exist, mainly in Czechoslovakia: there is the Hussite Church and the Brethren churches, notably the Moravian Church, which has a significant worldwide presence, owing to its extensive missionary activity.

Both the Roman Catholic and the Orthodox Churches lost some members when they underwent reformation. There are Old Catholic communities in many of the countries of Eastern Europe (formed in the 19th century). The Old Believers (Raskolniki) of the Russian Orthodox tradition, who rejected reforms of the 18th century, have long had an eminent role in Russian cultural and spiritual life. The main Old Believer group, those of the Belokrinitsky Concord, recently elected their own patriarch, the Metropolitan of Moscow and All-Russia.

ISLAM

Islam means 'submission' or surrender to God. It is the preferred name for the monotheistic religion founded by Muhammed, the Prophet (570–632 AD), in Arabia. The unparalleled spread of the religion in its first centuries can be attributed to concept of holy war (*jihad*).

The Five Pillars of the practice of Islam are: the Witness that 'there is no god but God' (*Allah*) and that 'Muhammed is His Prophet'; Prayer, which takes place five times daily and includes prostration in the direction of the holy city of Mecca and recitation of set verses, and is also performed in congregational worship at a mosque on Fridays, the Muslim holy day; Almsgiving; Fasting, which must take place during the hours of daylight for the whole of the ninth month of Ramadan (some exceptions are allowed); finally, the Pilgrimage (*hajj*) to Mecca, which is incumbent at least once in the lifetime of a Muslim. The heart of Islam is contained in the Koran, which is considered above criticism as the very Word of God as uttered to his Prophet. This authority is supplemented by various traditions (*hadith*). To interpret the application of Islamic law (*shari'a*) into normal activity, four main schools of thought emerged, the main one in the region being the Hanafi. An ideal of the Islamic community (*umma*) is that the brotherhood of Muslims is its basis and that the religion is international and beyond tribal division. However there has not been an unchallenged Muslim leader since the Prophet, and the last of the caliphs (*khalifas* or 'successors' of Muhammed), who resided in Constantinople (Istanbul), had his office abolished by the Turkish Government in 1924.

The USSR had the largest Muslim population in the region, about three-quarters of them located in Central Asia and of Turkic ethnicity. There are Turkish Muslims in Bulgaria, Romania, Albania and Yugoslavia. The Caucasus is another important Muslim region, and there are small Tatar communities in Poland and Lithuania. In central Russia and Siberia there are large numbers of Volga Tatars, Chuvash and Bashkirs. In Eastern Europe the main Muslim groups are either Albanian or Slavic Muslims, the latter mainly being the Bosnian Muslims of Yugoslavia and the Pomaks of Bulgaria. There are a large number of Muslim Roma (Gypsies), mainly in Central Asia, some Chinese Muslims (Dungans) and a small number of Muslim Semites (the Arabs of Samarkand and the Chalas, Bokharan Jews who converted to Islam, but remained Jewish secretly).

Sunni Muslims

Some 80% of the world's Muslims are Sunni or followers of 'the path' or customary way. They acknowledge the first four Caliphs as successors of Muhammed—Abu Bakr, 'Umar (Omar), 'Uthman (Othman) and 'Ali—and follow one of the four main schools of law. Other Muslims differ only in the interpretation of the true tradition (*sunna*). Except in the Iranian (Persian) influenced area of Azerbaidzhan, most of the region's Muslims are Sunni and of the Hanafi sect. The so-called Wahhabi sect (with no known links to the Saudi Arabian group) are an ascetic, fundamentalist movement based mainly in Uzbekistan. Although small in numbers, they are of increasing influence.

Shi'a Muslims

The Shi'a, or 'followers' of 'Ali (cousin of Muhammed and husband of Fatima, the Prophet's daughter), reject the first three Caliphs of Sunni Islam, and assert that the fourth Caliph was the rightful successor. 'Ali's son, Husain, is the great Shi'ite martyr. 'Ali's name is added after Muhammed's in the confession of faith, otherwise their beliefs are similar to the Sunnis. They instituted an *imam*, rather than a caliph, as their spiritual 'leader'. Most Shi'ites are 'Twelvers' and recognize a succession of 12 Imams, the last disappearing in 878 AD; this occluded or hidden Imam, it is believed, will return as the *Mahdi* ('guided one').

Some Shi'ites, however, the Isma'ilis, are known as 'Seveners', because they believe that Isma'il, or one of his sons, was the seventh and last Imam, and disappeared in

765 AD. There were also political reasons for the schism, but the Isma'ilis do have a more mystical faith. There are several sects. The main group in the region is in Gorno-Badakhshan (Tadzhikistan), and they are Pamiris, followers of the Aga Khan (some Pamiris are Sunni).

Sufis

The Sufis are mystics, found in all branches of Islam, since very early in the religion's history. Named for their woollen (*suf*), monastic robes, the Sufis tempered orthodox formalism and deism, with a quest for complete identification with the Supreme Being and annhilation of the self (the existence of the latter is known as polytheism—*shirk*), although this sometimes approached pantheism. The Sufis verged on the edge of acceptability for some time, but became an important influence. They are organized into what are loosely known as 'brotherhoods' (*turuq* or, singular, *tariqa*). In Central Asia clandestine Sufi groups have been responsible for bolstering the officially-tolerated Islamic institutions; they are fiercely anti-Communist. In Albania, a Sufi dervish sect, the liberal Bektashis, enjoyed strong support before the suppression of religion.

BUDDHISM

The number of Buddhists in Russia is uncertain, but there have been reports of up to 1m., mostly among the Buryats and Tuvinians of Siberia. There are only small groups of Buddhist converts in Eastern Europe. The founder of the faith, sometimes referred to as 'the Buddha', was a north Indian of the warrior caste, Siddhartha Gautama (usually ascribed the dates 563–483 BC). He renounced his privileges in the search for enlightenment, which he found under the Bo or Bodhi-tree and understood the cycle of existence, the cause of suffering and the way to Nirvana. He had become a Buddha or 'enlightened one' and, with the support of a monastic following, taught his *Dharma* (law, virtue, right, religion or truth), which must be followed on a Middle Way between the extremes of sensuality and asceticsm. Gautama taught a scheme of moral and spiritual improvement by which the endless round of existence could be escaped and Nirvana or oblivion obtained. Sometimes described as agnostic, or even atheistic, this ignores the adoration of the Buddha himself. Furthermore, northern Buddhism, as practised in Siberia, has particularly retained and developed the hosts of celestial beings who can help. There are not only many Buddhas, but countless Bodhisattvas ('beings of enlightenment'), who have deferred their own salvation. The northern Buddhists describe themselves as *Mahayana*, followers of the 'great vehicle' to salvation.

OTHER RELIGIONS

Judaism is the oldest of the major monotheistic religions, and also advocates a code of morality and civil and religious duties. Its holy book (the Old Testament of the Christian Bible) is supported by traditions, which are expounded by the rabbis, who are doctors of the law and leaders of the Jewish congregations which meet in synagogues. There are two main Jewish communities, which observe distinct rituals but have no doctrinal differences. The predominant European group is the Ashkenazim; the Sephardim of the region are mainly found in the Balkans, with some in Caucasian and Central Asian Republics. Although both Christianity and Islam claim descent from, or to be the fulfilment of, Judaism, the Jews, as a race as well as a religion, have long been the victims of prejudice. Anti-Semitism has a long history in the Christian Church and, in Islam, the more recent Arab–Israeli conflict of the 20th century has bolstered the prejudice. The Jews are widespread throughout Eastern Europe and the Russian Federation. Their numbers, however, were seriously reduced during the Second World War, particularly in areas dominated by the Nazis. This holocaust of the Jewish people was the most extreme manifestation of the anti-Semitism, which was endemic in central and eastern Europe and in the Russian Empire. These traditional prejudices were not completely rejected by the Communist regimes, but, since the fall of these governments, anti-Semitism has re-emerged strongly in some areas, despite the often small number of Jews. Emigration, usually to Israel, has also reduced numbers.

There are few Hindus in the region, but missionary work has been conducted by one such sect, the Hare Krishna (named for their chant) or Krishna Consciousness. They worship the Hindu pantheon and advocate a harmonious lifestyle, are vegetarian, and distinguished by the orange robes of their devotees. The Communist authorities displayed an ambivalent attitude to them and, in the USSR, they continued to have difficulties in the early 1990s.

Some traditional beliefs persist in parts of the former USSR, including some shamanistic practices and ancestor-worship. There are also some small Zoroastrian communities, to the north of Iran. This ancient religion is sometimes described as dualistic, but believes in the ultimate triumph of the principle of good. It is thought to have influenced both Judaism and Christianity and was once the state religion of Persia (Iran). Some of the Kurdish people are Yazidis, most of whom live in Armenia and Georgia. They are sometimes known as 'Devil-worshippers', owing to a mistaken understanding of their belief in the redemption of Lucifer, the fallen angel or evil principle of Zoroastrian and Christian cosmology. The Yazidi beliefs are a synthesis of Zoroastrian, Nestorian Christian, Jewish and Muslim traditions. In August 1991 it was reported that they had formed a national congress, and were attempting to register as a separate ethnic group and to establish a Yazidi Ziyaret or church.

HUMAN RIGHTS IN THE REGION

Dr ANTHONY MARCHAM

INTRODUCTION

A useful classification of human rights, originally proposed by the jurist, Karel Vasak, relates rights to the slogans of the French Revolution: *liberté*, *égalité* and *fraternité*. The watchword of 'first generation' rights is freedom, from the oppressive powers of Church or state; they are the civil and political rights of the individual, gradually won in 16th, 17th and 18th century Europe, and proclaimed in the *Déclaration des Droits de l'Homme et du Citoyen* (August 1789). 'Second generation' rights are the collective rights of social groups or classes, advanced against the dehumanizing process of industrialization in 19th century Europe; thus they are socio-economic rights, based on the desire for equality. 'Third generation' rights emerged in the 20th century, advanced against the alien power of colonial regimes. They are the rights of peoples to self-determination and to autonomous development, centred upon the concept of fraternity, or, in 20th century parlance, national solidarity. Although first, second and third generation rights had diverse origins they are cumulative, and not sequential. Vasak's classification may be overschematic, but it has the merit of clarity, and will be employed in this discussion.

ATTITUDES TO RIGHTS IN COMMUNIST REGIMES

Communist attitudes to rights have been shaped by the ideas of Karl Marx, whose essay, *On the Jewish Question* (1843), condemned the French Declaration and its individualism: 'None of the so-called rights of man goes beyond egoistic ... man ..., an individual separated from the community', wholly preoccupied with his own private interest. According to Marx, individual rights were a cloak for the interests of the bourgeoisie. Civil and political freedoms enabled the capitalists to deprive the proletariat of socio-economic rights. In this way there arose a theoretical divide between the Lockean championship of individual civil and political rights, and the Marxian championship of collective socio-economic rights.

A second contrast between attitudes to rights in Western liberal democracies and Eastern Communist regimes arose from their different historical development. Whereas liberal democratic systems were established by limiting state power, Communist systems were established by capturing, transforming and then enhancing state power, as after the October Revolution, and in Eastern Europe after 1945. Communists saw these revolutions as a means of transforming the state from an engine of class oppression to an embodiment of popular will. If the post-revolutionary state represented the aspirations of the working class, then, by definition, it could not be oppressive, and must secure rather than threaten rights. It followed that rights are best guaranteed by increasing, not limiting, the power of the state; and, further, that the opponents of the Communist state must be undermining rights by criticizing a regime which vindicates them.

The Communist states of Eastern Europe, established after the Second World War, followed the Soviet model: all were based upon the leading role of the Communist Party, and the principle of 'democratic centralism'; that is, debates on Party policy from the grassroots upwards, but acceptance of the decisions of central Party bodies once they had been made. Centralism was more apparent than democracy, for the supremacy of higher over lower Party bodies was assured. The Party controlled the courts, the media and the trade unions. Dissent was associated with treachery, and hence 'dissidents' were criminalized. However, even in the 'Soviet bloc', in Eastern Europe, there were divergences from the Soviet model. The Communist Party was not always the sole party, as it was in the USSR until March 1990; for instance, the existence of other political parties was tolerated in Poland and the German Democratic Republic (GDR), even though they were under the influence of the Communists. In Poland farming was private, not collectivized.

Moreover, in the USSR itself, attitudes to human rights varied with changes in leadership. After Stalin's death in 1953, Khrushchev's reaction against Stalinism involved some relaxation. Generalizations about human rights policies in the USSR and Eastern Europe may conceal the variations from leader to leader, and from region to region. Nevertheless, it is relevant to recall the longevity of Communist Party leaderships after the Second World War. In the USSR Brezhnev was in office from 1964 to 1982; in Bulgaria, Zhivkov from 1954 to 1989; in Romania, Ceauşescu from 1965 to 1989; in Czechoslovakia, Husák from 1969 to 1987; in the GDR, Honecker from 1971 to 1989; and, in Hungary, Kádár from 1956 to 1988.

SOVIET CONSTITUTIONS AND HUMAN RIGHTS

Soviet Constitutions (and the similar Eastern European ones), even the notorious 'Stalin Constitution' of 1936, set out a panoply of rights, civil and political, socio-economic, and, since the autonomy of the Union Republics was guaranteed, developmental. In Stalin's time the gap between the fine words of the Constitution and the brutality of Soviet practice seemed unbridgeable. Art. 58 of the criminal code on 'counter revolutionary crimes' opened the way for severe penalties against any act which might be construed as opposition. There are some celebrated examples recorded in Solzhenitsyn's *Gulag Archipelago*, which illustrate the working of the criminal code in practice.

The 'Brezhnev Constitution' of 1977 represented no fundamental change in the Soviet attitude to rights. Most of the provisions of 1936 were repeated in an extensive section on the rights and duties of citizens, but they were qualified in various ways. All rights were to be exercised 'in the interests of the people ... and the development of the socialist system', or 'in accordance with the aims of building Communism'. Moreover, all rights were conditional on the fulfilment of duties which were very broadly and vaguely expressed; for example, Art. 59, which imposes the duty of bearing 'with dignity the high calling of a citizen of the USSR', and Art. 62, that of safeguarding 'the interests of the Soviet State', and furthering its 'might and authority'. An official booklet on *The Rights and Obligations of Citizens of the USSR* (1977) declared that, 'Our laws forbid the "freedom" to slander socialist democracy and the Soviet system ... It is forbidden to create anti-Soviet organizations or to use national survivals or religious prejudices for criminal goals'. Until December 1988 the structure of the Soviet state remained, in essence, unchanged from the Constitution of 1936.

In 1948 the USSR abstained from voting in the UN on the Universal Declaration of Human Rights. In 1973, however, in the context of détente with the West, it ratified the two 1966 International Covenants, which had been proclaimed to implement the principles of the Universal Declaration: one on Civil and Political Rights, the other on Economic, Social and Cultural Rights. Moreover, by signing the Helsinki Final Act, in 1975, the USSR and all the Eastern European countries (except Albania) again undertook to respect 'freedom of thought, conscience, religion or belief for all, without distinction of race, sex, language or religion'. Nevertheless, the groups of intellectuals which attempted to monitor these rights in the USSR were systematically suppressed in the late 1970s. The Moscow group, including Anatoly Scharansky, gained international sympathy. In 1978 Yuri Orlov was sentenced to seven years in a hard labour camp, followed by five years in internal exile, while, in 1979, the most celebrated of all dissidents, Andrei Sakharov, was sent into exile in the city of Gorky. During the final years of Brezhnev's leadership the number of 'refuseniks' (would-be emigrants, usually Jews, refused permission to emigrate) increased, and they were often discriminated against for applying to do so. In response to international criticism, the Soviet Government rejected interference in Soviet domestic affairs and asserted the superiority of Soviet socio-economic rights to those in capitalist countries, with their high rates of inflation and unemployment in the late 1970s.

The struggle for rights in the USSR was mirrored in the other countries of Eastern Europe. In January 1977 a group of Czechoslovak writers, including Václav Havel, attempted to circulate 'Charter 77', a human rights manifesto, at the beginning of a year proclaimed as the Year of the Political Prisoners. Supporters of Charter 77 were subjected to repression on the Soviet pattern. Gorbachev's reforms were the catalyst for change in Eastern Europe. In most cases, the observance of human rights in these countries has exceeded the level in the USSR, but the Soviet state remains the best example of the issues and changes.

THE SITUATION IN THE USSR

Gorbachev's Reform Programme

From March 1985, when Mikhail Gorbachev became General Secretary of the Communist Party of the Soviet Union (CPSU), policies towards human rights began to change. This was as essential to changes in Eastern Europe as in the USSR itself. His policies of *perestroika* (restructuring) and *glasnost* (openness or publicity) were essential. *Glasnost* not only allowed, but encouraged, open discussion of the failings of past policies and personalities. Criticisms of the 'years of stagnation' under Brezhnev provided a rationale for reform under Gorbachev, just as condemnation of Stalin's 'cult of personality' had been used as a rationale for reform under Khrushchev. Ideological criticism, however, stopped short at Lenin; to extend criticism to Leninism would have been, in effect, to call into question the whole evolution of Soviet Communism. Needless to say, it was Lenin the pragmatist of the New Economic Policy (1921–23), and not Lenin the ruthless revolutionary, who appealed to the advocates of *perestroika*.

A more relaxed attitude towards critics of official policy was signalled by the release of leading dissidents. Scharansky was allowed to emigrate to Israel, and, in December 1986, Sakharov was invited to return to Moscow. More dramatically, in October 1988, it was announced that all political prisoners would be released by the end of the year. By late 1989 Amnesty International, the international human rights movement, reported a 'dramatic shift' towards greater commitment to human rights in the USSR.

The Rule of Law in the USSR

Perestroika was planned as a legal, as well as an economic, restructuring of the Soviet system. As a lawyer by training, Gorbachev was convinced that democracy could not develop without the rule of law, for, as he wrote in his book, *Perestroika* (1987), 'the law is designed to protect society from abuses of power and guarantee their rights and freedoms'—terminology which, in itself, had the force of novelty in the USSR. Previously, the USSR was not a state based on the rule of law (*pravovoe gosudarstvo*), in the sense understood in the West. In Stalin's time Soviet courts carried posters proclaiming, 'Law is what is good for the Party'. Gorbachev sought to loosen the grip of the Party upon society, as well as on the economy. In June 1988, at the extraordinary 19th Conference of the CPSU, measures were agreed which aimed at securing judicial independence, by giving judges tenure for life, and at prohibiting Party officials from interfering with the work of the courts. It was agreed also to humanize the criminal codes by modifying those articles which, in the past, had been used to suppress freedom of speech and opinion, in particular Art. 70, on 'anti-Soviet agitation and propaganda', and Art. 190 (1), on 'spreading anti-Soviet slander'. These measures were advocated by Gorbachev in order to complete the 'development of Communist legality'.

Electoral Freedom

Until 1990, the foundation of the Soviet system was the leading and guiding role of the CPSU, based upon the principle of 'democratic centralism'. All Communist parties modelled upon the Soviet Communist Party, notably those in Eastern Europe, enshrined in their organization the same supremacy of the Party and 'ban on factions', that is, prohibition of open dissent within the Party, as well as outside it. In his closing speech to the 19th Conference, of 1988, Gorbachev stressed the Party's 'mission as the political vanguard of the working class', and its 'leading role in society'. However the programme of reforms approved by the Conference implied a modification of the structure of the Party and a reinterpretation of its role.

The 19th Conference endorsed the principle of contested elections to party offices, and a new regulation of 1988 limited the holding of any office, including the highest, to two consecutive terms of five years. Gorbachev sought also to demarcate the spheres of responsibility of Party and state, leaving the Party to concentrate upon broad strategy, while withdrawing from intervention in the day-to-day management of Soviet society. The general aim of Gorbachev's policy in this area was described as 'socialist pluralism'; and this was given effect, when a special plenum of the Central Committee, in February 1990, agreed to the removal from the Constitution of Art. 6, which proclaimed the leading and guiding role of the CPSU. In March 1990 the Congress of People's Deputies, meeting in extraordinary session, formally abolished Art. 6. Almost immediately a host of new political parties and trade unions emerged, but most of them were small in size and regional in orientation. In late 1990 a law allowed the creation of political parties, as long as they registered with the Ministry of Justice and did not accept foreign aid.

Gorbachev also set into motion the process of securing political rights in the sphere of state administration. In accordance with a law on elections, adopted in December 1988, competitive elections for the Congress of People's Deputies took place in March 1989. In addition to the 1,500 seats in the Congress, a further 750 were allocated to 'public organizations', 100 of which were chosen by the Party. Gorbachev was nominated for one of the latter seats, so that he did not submit himself to popular election.

Except for the Chairman of the Council of Ministers, those who held government office were excluded from standing for election, thus creating a greater demarcation between the personnel of the executive and the legislature. The elections of March 1989 returned many critics of the old regime, including Boris Yeltsin, previously dismissed from the Politburo and ousted from his position as Party First Secretary in Moscow. Under the revised governmental system, however, it was not the Congress of People's Deputies, but the Supreme Soviet elected from it, which possessed legislative power, and the power to reject edicts and decrees. It was to meet for two continuous sessions, of three to four months, in the spring and autumn of each year. Gorbachev was elected Chairman of the Supreme Soviet, although not without some criticism and demands that he should first resign as General Secretary of the Party. In March 1990 he became an executive president (a post which replaced that of Chairman of the Supreme Soviet as head of state), with power to nominate the Chairman of the Council of Ministers and to exercise general control over the rights and obligations of Soviet citizens, and over the country's Constitution, sovereignty, security and territorial integrity. With the new Supreme Soviet in its infancy there were no effective checks upon the power of the President. Moreover, as the economic and territorial crises became more acute, Gorbachev assumed more and more power in order to deal with them. In September 1990 he was granted extensive powers over the economy: to privatize property; to abolish price controls; and to cut the budget deficit. In December 1990 the Congress of People's Deputies granted him still more power, including direct control over the Government and over a new Security Council, responsible for law and order, whose members included the most important ministers.

The powers assumed by Gorbachev, which made him virtually all-powerful in law, were considered a necessary insurance against the potential disorder arising from the twin challenges of separatism and economic collapse. The USSR had been a centralized system, with the CPSU as its focus of unity. By 1990 it seemed in danger of becoming a system without a centre. In July 1990 Boris Yeltsin, Gavriil Popov and other reformers announced that they were leaving the Party and establishing the so-called Democratic Platform as an independent reform group. The CPSU survived this secession. Gorbachev remained its leader, and Gennady Yanaev, the Vice-President appointed in 1990, was another committed Communist. In these circumstances, reformers feared that presidential powers might be used in an attempt to reimpose control over the republics and uniformity of opinion. However, in July 1991, the leading reformists, including Eduard Shevardnadze (the former Foreign Minister, who had resigned in protest at the increase of presidential powers), announced that they would form a movement (the Movement for Democratic Reforms), which many interpreted as the basis of a new, all-Union party which could challenge the CPSU and even provide support for Gorbachev.

Freedom of Opinion and Belief

Article 19 of the Universal Declaration of Human Rights proclaims freedom of opinion and expression, together with the right to 'seek, receive and impart information and ideas through the media'. Before the introduction of the policies of *glasnost* the articles of the criminal code against 'anti-Soviet agitation and propaganda', and 'circulating anti-Soviet slander' had restrained free expression. Party-state control of the press, radio and television meant that the organs of the media were mouthpieces of official policy. In the 1970s Roy Medvedev, the dissident Soviet historian

observed that 'the overwhelming majority of Soviet Citizens' had 'no means of finding out about domestic or world affairs'. *Glasnost* released an open exchange of ideas and a much more relaxed attitude to the dissemination of information. This change was evident in official attitudes when, after initial hesitation which provoked widespread condemnation, the Soviet Government released details of the Chernobyl disaster of April 1986. The media began to discuss social problems, such as drug abuse and child pornography, the very existence of which had been denied previously. Under Gorbachev new periodicals and newspapers proliferated, some of them, such as the popular *Argumenty i Facty*, outspokenly critical of Soviet society. In July 1989 the constitutional provisions against 'anti-Soviet agitation' and 'circulating anti-Soviet slander' were removed. In August 1990 a new law on the press abolished Party control over the establishment of newspapers and magazines. Under this law any new organization could be registered as long as it did not advocate the forcible overthrow of the Government; and, although the censor's office was not abolished, it could only prevent the publication of state secrets. In August 1991 the office was replaced by the Agency for the Protection of State Secrets, responsible to the newly-founded Ministry of Information and the Press.

Gorbachev was happy to use the media in the service of *perestroika*; however he did not approve of newspaper *glasnost* when it criticized the failures of his own policies. On a number of occasions he criticized *Argumenty i Facty*, and tried to pressure its Editor-in-Chief, Vladislav Starkov, to resign. In January 1991 Leonid Kravchenko, formerly of the official news agency, TASS, was appointed head of the monopolistic State Committee for Television and Radio (renamed the All-Union State Television and Radio Corporation, in February 1991). One of Kravchenko's first decisions was to ban the proposed television discussion of the resignation of Eduard Shevardnadze as Foreign Minister. Infuriated by comparisons of the actions of Soviet troops in Lithuania (January 1991) with the Soviet invasion of Hungary (1956) and the suppression of the 'Prague Spring' reform movement (1968), Gorbachev condemned the Soviet press and argued, unsuccessfully, for a suspension of the press law of 1990. However the Supreme Soviet did authorize the establishment of a *glasnost* commission, to 'ensure objectivity of news'. At the same time Kravchenko ensured that radio and television reports followed the official line that Soviet forces in Lithuania and Latvia had been provoked into action. The Soviet media were also dragooned into advocating support for Gorbachev's new Union Treaty, before the referendum of 17 March 1991. In the first half of 1991 the right to freedom of expression and opinion hung in the balance, a situation neatly encapsulated by the case of Valeriya Novodvorskaya, a leader of the Democratic Union, who had carried a placard accusing Gorbachev of being a 'fascist criminal'. She was tried under a law of 1990, which protected the President's 'honour and dignity', but the case was dismissed, because, although she had protested against army violence in Lithuania, none of her language against the President was obscene. Nevertheless, Novodvorskaya was sentenced to two years hard labour for burning the Soviet flag.

Article 18 of the Universal Declaration of Human Rights lays down 'the right to freedom of thought, conscience and religion or belief in teaching, practice, worship and observance'. However, Soviet laws dating back to 1929, at the height of Stalin's assault upon Russian Orthodox and other faiths, decreed that, although a Soviet citizen might believe what they chose, they could not explain what lay behind their belief. 'Dissidents' who were imprisoned for their religious beliefs were always convicted of spreading 'religious propaganda'. Churches in the USSR gained considerable *de facto* freedom of activity under Gorbachev, especially after 1988, when religious leaders from all over the world were invited to the USSR to celebrate the millennium of Russian Christianity. However, as long as Stalin's laws were in being, repression of religious activity could be renewed. Then, in 1990, a law on freedom of conscience provided a legal basis for freedom of worship. This law separated Church from state, swept away state financing of atheist propaganda, and made all religions equal under the law. This made it possible for church schools to proselytize and even for religious services to be held in the army: previously it was an offence for a soldier to possess a Bible. In 1990 Albania became the last country in the region to abandon its anti-religious policies.

Official anti-Semitism had almost disappeared after July 1988, when it was condemned in a speech by Alexander Yakovlev, a Politburo member, and a close ally of Gorbachev. Officially sanctioned anti-Semitic books and articles stopped appearing. The teaching of Hebrew and Yiddish, and of Jewish history, is no longer taboo. Jewish cultural centres have been established in Moscow and in the Baltic Republics. Ironically, however, the *glasnost* which allowed Soviet Jews to express themselves openly, extended a similar freedom to their opponents. A change in official policy was unable to eliminate ancient prejudices; grassroots anti-Semitism was fostered, especially by the Pamyat nationalist movement, which established branches in many cities of the RSFSR (Russian Federation), and which represented Jews as enemies of the Russian people. Anti-Semitism surfaced, also, in the republics. Likewise, in Eastern Europe, anti-Semitism was officially condemned, but remained a widespread sentiment, particularly in Poland and Romania. It remained a powerfully emotive appeal for politicians wishing to exploit nationalist issues, and was a feature of the Polish election campaign. Both Lech Wałęsa and Stanisław Tymiński were accused of anti-Semitism. In Romania, the ruling National Salvation Front was accused of being reluctant to condemn the anti-Semitic outrages and expressions of opinion which began following the fall of the Ceauşescu regime.

In the areas discussed, and in many others, *glasnost* opened up Soviet society. There have been, on the whole, similar, if not more extensive, improvements in the Eastern European countries. In the sphere of civil and political rights the results have been mainly positive, but the same cannot be said in the areas of socio-economic rights or of national solidarity.

Socio-Economic Rights

Article 25 of the Universal Declaration of Human Rights states that, 'Everyone has the right to a standard of living, adequate for the health and well-being of himself and of his family, including food, clothing, housing, medical care and necessary social services'. The status of socio-economic rights has been more controversial than that of civil and political rights, some authorities maintaining that, because of cultural relativism, socio-economic rights cannot be universal. Most might now agree that the two sets of rights are not sharply divisible, and that both may be derived from the most basic right to life, and from the concept of human dignity. The catalyst of *perestroika* was a steadily deepening economic crisis in the USSR. Both there and in Eastern Europe socialist command economies were stagnating as the inflexibilities of bureaucratic planning were perpetuated from generation to generation. As early as 1957 Khrushchev had proposed some devolution of economic powers, but his policies disappeared after his fall. Both

Hungary's 'New Economic Mechanism' and Edward Gierek's economic reforms in Poland had sought greater flexibility in central planning and price control with only limited success. Initially, Gorbachev's plan for economic *perestroika* was the creation of a decentralized form of socialism, in order to rejuvenate the Soviet economy, whose problems had been compounded by the fall in petroleum prices after 1982, and thus a decline in the revenues available to the world's greatest producer. However *perestroika* proved far more difficult to introduce than *glasnost*.

Just as decentralized socialism failed to work in Eastern Europe, so it failed to work in the USSR. The Law on State Enterprises (1987) reduced the number of centrally-planned targets and allowed enterprises to trade with each other, rather than with their ministries. This reform, however, was frustrated by the dead weight of centralized bureaucratic tradition. In 1988 a law on co-operatives was introduced, to foster the growth of a small business sector, freer from central control. As a result, the number of co-operatives did increase rapidly, but their high prices made them unpopular.

Perhaps it would be inaccurate to assert that *perestroika* failed, for it was never implemented fully. Gorbachev was never wholly convinced that the command economy of state socialism could not be made to work. Most of 1990 was occupied in wrangling over rival plans for economic reform: the radical Shatalin Plan, for the swift introduction of a market economy, the conservative Ryzhkov-Abalkin Plan and the compromise Aganbegyan Plan. In October 1990 Gorbachev opted for a compromise, intended to retain more central control than the Shatalin Plan, in order to phase in price reform and to cushion the effects on pay and pensions. However, while the politicians debated economic policy, the economy descended into increasing chaos, as the central planning system was eroded by the demands of the republics. This resulted in confusion, for the republican economic policies gave priority to their own self-sufficiency, rather than to the economic future of the USSR.

In many areas of the economy production was falling. For instance, the output of petroleum, the USSR's primary source of energy, declined by almost 10% between 1988 and 1990. In March 1991 the State Planning Committee, Gosplan (renamed the Ministry for Economics and Forecasting in 1991), warned that the country was plunging towards a recession as severe as that of the 1930s, and predicted that national income would fall by at least 11%, and perhaps as much as 16%, in 1991.

The effect of increasing economic chaos was to undermine basic socio-economic rights in the USSR. The Soviet citizen was faced not only with the endemic shortage of consumer goods, but with scarcity of food; not only with perpetually poor housing, but with deteriorating health and public services; not only with low wages, but with rapidly rising prices. In these circumstances standards of living fell, and the USSR was reduced to accepting emergency aid from Western governments, in the winter of 1990/91. There had always been shortages in the Soviet economy, but, to some extent, these had been made bearable by the artificial cheapness of heavily subsidized basic necessities, such as food, fuel, rents and transport costs. By 1990, however, the Soviet Government had lost control over prices. Five years of *perestroika* (or talk of *perestroika*) had only produced greater shortages and higher prices. Between December 1990 and March 1991 the price of cooking oil and eggs trebled in the state stores of Moscow, where, according to the traditional Communist claim, prices never rose. During 1991 severe economic measures began to be introduced, including dramatic price rises and the effective confiscation of savings over 1,000 roubles. To add to the misery of

Soviet citizens, health and the environmental problems, particularly in the aftermath of the Chernobyl disaster and the devastation of the Aral Sea area, are approaching a state of crisis. There is a similar situation throughout Eastern Europe. Environmental devastation is widespread, and socio-economic rights are further eroded by economic reforms, whether they are the radical 'shock therapy' or the more gradual transition to a 'social market'.

National Solidarity

Article 1.1 of the International Covenant on Economic, Social and Cultural Rights states that, 'All peoples have the right of self-determination. By virtue of that right they freely determine their political status and freely pursue their economic, social and cultural development'. The USSR was a vast, multi-ethnic state, in which only about one-half of the population was Russian. Nominally, the 15 Union Republics always had the right to secede from the USSR, but the official Soviet theory was that national consciousness would decline, and that the peoples of the Union would draw together, and, finally, amalgamate. Gorbachev abandoned this doctrine and, in 1988, told the 19th Party Conference that, 'The development of our multinational state is naturally accompanied by a growth of national consciousness'. Under Gorbachev the right to self-determination was more freely expressed. However, as the republics, and ethnic groups within the republics, became more self-assertive, the Soviet Government became more determined to limit the demands for the right of self-determination in the interests of preserving the Union. By 1990 the problems of economic reform and national rights had merged; the republics pressed for economic policies which would forward their campaigns for autonomy. In July 1990 Gorbachev proposed a new treaty of union, redefining the powers of the central government and the 15 Union Republics: their sovereignty would be recognized, but they would delegate to the all-Union government powers over foreign policy, defence, transport, telecommunications, monetary policy, taxation, energy and raw materials.

By that time, however, the Baltic Republics, the last to be incorporated into the USSR, had declared their independence. In Lithuania, for example, some 80% of the population is Lithuanian, and supported the national movement, Sajúdis, organized in 1988. The Russian Federation, Moldavia (Moldova) and the Ukraine had passed declarations of sovereignty, proclaiming that their own laws took precedence over Soviet law. The rights and rivalries of the Union Republics in relation to the central government evolved and merged with a further set of issues involving the rights of different ethnic groups within these Republics. Increased insistence upon autonomy for the republics exacerbated conflict between the ethnic groups they contained. From the late 1980s the old dispute between the Christian Armenians and Muslim Azerbaidzhanis degenerated into civil strife in the Armenian enclave of Nagorny Karabakh, within Azerbaidzhan. In 1989 about 100 people were killed in attacks by Uzbeks upon Meskhetian Turks, a minority exiled to Central Asia, from Georgia, by Stalin. In 1990 the Moldavian Republic required the use of Romanian in official business, provoking resistance from Russian speakers in the east of the Republic, and from the Turkic Gagauz people in the south. Similar problems occurred throughout Eastern Europe. For example: in Yugoslavia, in June 1991, Slovenia and Croatia declared their wish to become independent; within the Yugoslav Republics, the Albanians of Kosovo continued to resist the curtailment of their autonomy and the Serbs of Croatia and the Hungarians of Vojvodina began to assert themselves; the Czechoslovak federation became a political issue after 1989, as did

the rights of the minority nationalities, such as the Romany (Gypsy) people and the Hungarians.

The Soviet Government responded both to ethnic conflict and to nationalist defiance with spasmodic severity. In April 1989 about 20 Georgian demonstrators were killed in Tbilisi by Soviet troops. In January 1990 the Army was sent to Baku, capital of Azerbaidzhan, to suppress resistance to central authority. One year later 21 people died when Soviet troops acted against defiant Lithuanians, in Vilnius, and Latvians, in Riga.

Gorbachev's referendum of 17 March 1991, for which he demanded a positive response in a television address, posed the question, 'Do you consider it necessary to preserve the Union of Soviet Socialist Republics as a federation of equal Soviet Republics, in which human rights and freedoms will be guaranteed to persons of any nationality?' The referendum aimed to put pressure on the Republics which wished to stay in the USSR to sign the new Union Treaty, and to force the Republics which demanded independence to observe the law on secession, which required a referendum. However six Union Republics (the Baltic Republics, Georgia, Armenia and Moldavia) boycotted Gorbachev's referendum, to demonstrate their determination for independence. More than 80% of Ukrainian voters declared in favour of additional questions, framed to focus the demand for an independent Ukraine. Thus the results of the referendum, in which only five of the 15 Union Republics posed the question in its original formulation, made Gorbachev's task of preserving the integrity of the USSR no easier, and the outlook for the rights of minorities no more secure. The process of dissolution was accelerated by the failed coup of August 1991. By the end of that year the USSR had ceased to exist and the observance of human rights was likely to vary among the newly-independent republics. The Russian Federation inherited problems similar to those of the USSR, particularly in its internal relations with its Autonomous Republics in the North Caucasus and Tatarstan.

Another issue related to national self-determination is the ecological well-being of the republics, and particularly of the non-Russian areas. A report of 1989 estimated that 16% of the USSR was an ecological disaster area in which some 50m. people, one-quarter of Soviet citizens, suffered from industrial, chemical and nuclear pollution, despite the injunction in the Soviet Constitution 'to protect nature and conserve its riches'. This situation constitutes a further source of protest, that national rights have been violated by years of central planners' obsession with output at the expense of the environment. For instance, after the Chernobyl disaster, there were demands in the Ukraine and the Caucasus that no more nuclear power stations should be built. In Eastern Europe, the environment had provided a focus for opposition to the Communists and there is continuing concern about the legacy of the centrally-planned economies.

CONCLUSION

When Shevardnadze resigned, in December 1990, he did so with a dramatic warning: 'Comrade democrats . . . you have scattered. The reformers have gone to ground. Dictatorship is coming'. He had some reason for concern. Gorbachev's army advisers were threatening the use of the Army to keep the USSR together. The 'liberal' Interior Minister, Vadim Bakatin, who opposed the use of force, had just been replaced by Boris Pugo, the former head of the KGB in Latvia. Vladimir Kryuchkov, the current head of the KGB, had complained on television of 'extremist radical groups', supported from abroad. *Glasnost* was being undermined by Leonid Kravchenko's determination that radio and television should not criticize the state. Although the most visible forces of reaction were removed during 1991, others remained in all of the former USSR republics. At the end of 1991, though largely successful in effect in Eastern Europe, the remarkable achievements of Gorbachev's reforms, in creating a framework in which human rights might be secured in the successor states of the USSR, hung in the balance.

SECURITY AND INTERNATIONAL RELATIONS IN EASTERN EUROPE

Dr MICHAEL SHEEHAN

INTRODUCTION

The revolutions of 1989 in Eastern Europe marked a historical watershed in the post-Second World War history and political development of the region. They were part of a broader process of political evolution in Europe as a whole, and also contributed directly to the dramatic acceleration in the speed of that evolution. Nowhere was this more so than in the area of security and international relations. In the period 1945–89 this subject could be looked at in the context of Soviet military and political domination of the region, and Eastern Europe was quite clearly a political sub-system with clearly defined structures and processes. The democratic regimes that emerged in 1989–90 have chosen to dismantle those structures and institute new processes. While the old, stable pattern has gone, too little time has passed for the states to completely define their new foreign policy orientation; the new security frameworks and alliance patterns are still in the process of being built. Nevertheless, certain patterns of foreign policy and networks of international co-operation have begun to emerge, both within eastern and central Europe and between the countries of that region and those of Western Europe. The new governments emerged from a pre-existing background, however, and it is necessary to review the impact of that background before going on to address the question of what patterns are likely to prevail in the future.

SOVIET DOMINANCE OF EASTERN EUROPEAN SECURITY, 1945–89

The Onset of the Cold War

At the end of the Second World War the armies of the USSR occupied most of eastern and central Europe. These armies gave the Soviet leadership the opportunity to shape the future political development of the region in such a way as to meet the perceived security needs of the USSR. That perception was dominated by the need to constrain Germany in the post-War era and to avoid a repetition of the devastating German invasions of the two World Wars. To this end Stalin was determined to maintain substantial Soviet forces in the eastern part of the divided Germany. To the same end the USSR was determined to ensure that the post-War regimes in eastern and central Europe would not only pose no security threat to the USSR in themselves, but would form a pro-Soviet buffer zone or bloc between Soviet territory and that of a reviving post-War Germany. Given the historical experience of the Russian and succeeding Soviet empires, Churchill and Roosevelt initially accepted this desire as being a reasonable one, an attitude reflected in the concessions made to Soviet concerns at the Yalta negotiations in 1945. Between 1945 and 1947, however, the USSR gradually consolidated its political control over the Eastern European bloc. The onset of the 'Cold War' produced a Soviet desire for fellow-Communist rather than simply 'friendly' governments in Eastern Europe and generated pressures for this development to occur speedily. The speed and completeness of Communist consolidation varied from country to country. In Czechoslovakia the Communist Party benefited from pro-Soviet sentiment generated by the the Red Army's liberation of the country from Nazi occupation, and from substantial, pre-existing

support for the Socialists. Thus, in the free elections of 1946, the Communist Party performed impressively, winning 38% of the votes cast. In Bulgaria the traditional pro-Russian posture of the country made it receptive to a Soviet alliance and to the Soviet ideology. In Poland, by contrast, where national feeling was historically anti-Russian, the opposite occurred and the Communist Party was able to make little progress. An anti-Communist sentiment also prevailed in Hungary. The situation was markedly different in Albania and Yugoslavia, where the indigenous Communist parties had defeated the Axis occupation forces without the support of the Red Army. In these countries an authentic national Communist movement came to power.

As the Cold War intensified, the USSR moved to consolidate its control over Eastern Europe, seeing the region as an essential buffer zone between itself and the political and military threat represented by the West. Andrei Zhadanov's proclamation of the existence of 'two camps', in November 1946, was followed by the foundation of the Cominform (Communist information bureau, which served to co-ordinate the Communist parties internationally), in September 1947, and the autonomy of the Eastern European states was steadily reduced. Non-Communist parties were banned, forcibly merged with the Communists or politically emasculated. In February 1948 the last freely-elected government was overthrown, in Czechoslovakia. The Eastern European Communist parties were henceforth compelled to adhere rigidly to the Soviet model. In October 1949 the Soviet-occupied eastern Zone of Germany was proclaimed as the German Democratic Republic. In Yugoslavia, by contrast, Marshall Tito, the Yugoslav leader, was able to negotiate the withdrawal of Soviet troops from Yugoslav territory as early as March 1945. A mutual assistance treaty was signed with the USSR. Yugoslavia sponsored the idea of a Balkan federation, with Albania and Bulgaria, but this proposal was abandoned in 1948, when Yugoslavia broke with the USSR. Pressure from the USSR to conform to Soviet policy had led to increased tension between the two countries. The absence of Soviet troops from Yugoslavia meant the USSR tried to adopt economic measures to force Tito to accept Soviet demands. This proved to be counter-productive and, in 1949, Yugoslavia cancelled its mutual assistance agreement with the USSR and signed trade agreements with a number of Western countries.

During the 1950s Yugoslavia successfully consolidated its independence. It adopted a Marxist economic system, but one which differed significantly from the Soviet version, tolerating small private enterprises, suspending the collectivization of agriculture and allowing a degree of self-administration in industry. In 1952 the USA began providing economic and military assistance, and, in 1954, Yugoslavia signed the Balkan Pact with Greece and Turkey, two NATO states. During the 1960s and 1970s Yugoslavia pursued a policy of neutral non-alignment with regard to the Cold War confrontation.

By late 1948, therefore, the dynamics of the Cold War had resulted in the creation of a bloc in Eastern Europe. These states were dominated by the Soviet military presence and had political and economic systems modelled upon those of their Soviet mentor.

Although NATO was formed in 1949, the establishment of the Warsaw Treaty Organization (Warsaw Pact or WTO) did not take place until 1955. The trigger for the formation of the Warsaw Pact was the entry of the western Federal Republic of Germany (FRG) into NATO. The USSR feared that, given German territorial claims upon lands which had been incorporated into Poland and the USSR in 1945, by accepting German membership, NATO had transformed itself from a defensive alliance into a potentially offensive one. The establishment of the Warsaw Pact did not really change the military or political realities in Eastern Europe, since the USSR already had bilateral treaties with Poland, Czechoslovakia, Hungary, Romania and Bulgaria, which committed the signatories to providing aid in the event of an attack. However the Warsaw Treaty provided for the establishment of a combined military command and pro-hibited signatories from joining other alliances whose purposes were 'incompatible' with the purposes of the Warsaw Pact. Article 5 of the Warsaw Treaty, which referred to the signatories' need to 'protect the peaceful labour of their peoples' was assumed to be a euphemism for maintenance of the Communist political system within those states. The Treaty was, therefore, to some extent based upon the ideological uniformity of the component states, a factor that would be of significance in the Hung-arian intervention of 1956 and in the new situation that existed after 1989. Neither the bilateral treaties of the late 1940s nor the Warsaw Treaty, however, legitimized the Soviet military presence in Eastern Europe. This was done in 1956–57, through a second series of bilateral treaties.

The Suppression of Reformist Movements

The accession to power of Nikita Khrushchev, in the USSR, was marked by a relaxation of Stalinist controls in Eastern Europe, which was a catalyst for leadership changes and policy evolution. This went furthest in Hungary, which reformed its political and security policies and ultimately declared itself a neutral state, outside the Warsaw Pact. The USSR deemed this an unacceptable breach of its cordon sanitaire; Soviet forces invaded Hungary, in November 1956, reasserting Soviet control over Hungarian policy. However the de-Stalinization of Soviet policy, while not going far enough for Hungary, went too far for Albania. Albania had broken with Yugoslavia in 1948, in protest at Tito's deviation from orthodox Communism and, between 1956 and 1961, the Stalinist Albanian regime of Enver Hoxha became steadily more disillusioned with the USSR. Relations were severed in 1961, though Albania did not formally resign from the Warsaw Pact until September 1968.

Having made clear its determination to maintain its hold on Eastern Europe, the USSR tolerated the emergence of a process of gradual reform in the policies of the Warsaw Pact states over the next 12 years. This process culminated in the 'Prague Spring', of 1968, in which the liberal Commu-nist Government of Alexander Dubček initiated a rapid reform programme that even went so far as to criticize Warsaw Pact military doctrine.

In August 1968 the USSR brought the Czechoslovak political experiment to an end, invading Czechoslovakia, in concert with all the Warsaw Pact states except Romania. In taking this step the USSR promulgated the so-called 'Brezhnev Doctrine', under which the USSR asserted its right to intervene in any socialist (in Western terminology, Communist) state, 'since the sovereignty of individual socialist countries cannot be counterpoised to the interests of world socialism and the world revolutionary movement'.

This was a doctrine of limited sovereignty for the states that comprised the 'socialist commonwealth'.

The USSR did not intervene directly to end the Solidar-ność (Solidarity) led reforms in Poland, in 1980. However Soviet political pressure and troop movements made it clear that intervention would occur unless the movement was suppressed. In order to avoid direct Soviet intervention the Polish armed forces imposed martial law themselves.

The repression of the reform processes in 1956, 1968 and 1980 appears to have been prompted by certain features these crises shared. In each case a divided national Commu-nist party had reacted to severe economic difficulties by starting a reform process while the USSR itself was preoc-cupied with internal affairs. In addition, these national reform programmes produced military and political fears among the other, more conservative, states of the 'socialist commonwealth', but with no agreement on the best way to resolve the situation. This would cause the USSR to inter-vene in order to restore the stability of the Eastern Euro-pean political system.

The difficulty for the USSR, in the period from 1945 to 1985, was that it was trying to maintain a dynamic equili-brium, which balanced conflicting demands. Soviet security needs demanded a cordon of Eastern European states which were internally stable, politically orthodox and exter-nally loyal. In order for these regimes to be internally stable, however, they required a degree of internal legit-imacy which, in turn, demanded that their governments be at least partially responsive to the wishes of their popula-tions. This meant that the USSR was obliged to tolerate change and non-conformity.

Changing Relationships under Gorbachev

The relationship between the USSR and Eastern Europe did not alter during the first 18 months after Mikhail Gorbachev became General Secretary of the CPSU. He had been in power for only one month when the Warsaw Treaty was renewed for a further 20 years, in April 1985. In February 1986, however, at the 27th Party Congress of the CPSU, Gorbachev called for 'unconditional respect in international practice, for the right of every people to choose the paths and forms of its development'. In this period Gorbachev still appears to have seen a stable, Soviet-dominated Eastern Europe as an essential defence even during a period of domestic reform, virtually reaffirming the Brezhnev Doctrine during a visit to Poland, in July 1986.

Soviet attitudes towards Eastern Europe evolved further during 1987–88. In early 1987 Gorbachev began to advocate the Soviet reform programme as a model for other Warsaw Pact states. This was significant given that, as already noted, previous reform efforts in Eastern Europe had developed a momentum which eventually led the USSR to take steps to end them. The decisive changes, however, came in 1988. By then *perestroika* in the USSR was begin-ning to experience grave difficulties. Nationalist unrest increased, while the deterioration of the Soviet economy began to accelerate. Gorbachev began to come under serious criticism from conservative opponents. He reacted by both deepening and hastening the reform process in the USSR. He also accelerated his efforts to defuse the military con-frontation in Europe, following his success in achieving the Intermediate-range Nuclear Forces (INF) Treaty of 1987. In December 1988, at the UN, Gorbachev announced that the USSR would unilaterally reduce its armed forces by 500,000 in number, including 50,000 people and 5,000 tanks based in Eastern Europe. Earlier that year, on a visit to Yugoslavia, Gorbachev emphasized the right of each nation to pursue independent development and declared that, 'the time has passed when a handful of big states made decisions for the whole world and divided it into spheres of influence, according to the law of might is right'. In July 1988 Vadim Medvedev, shortly to become responsible for ideology, stressed the 'unconditional' nature of the principle of sovereignty in bloc relations and suggested that these ties should be no different than relations between states with different social systems. The Brezhnev Doctrine appeared to have been repudiated. The events of 1989 were to confirm that this was so.

The developments that occurred during 1988 were of international significance. As Gorbachev struggled to overcome resistance from Party conservatives at home, it became politically important for *perestroika* to be implemented by the other Warsaw Pact states. As long as it was not, Party opponents could denounce Gorbachev as a political maverick. It was ironic that a leading CPSU conservative, Yegor Ligachev, cautioned the Hungarians against 'slavish imitation' of the Soviet model, in April 1987. As Gorbachev's 'peace offensive' in arms control and the announcement of defence reductions gathered momentum, so the USSR began to lessen its capability militarily to impose its will on Eastern Europe. The rhetorical abandonment of the Brezhnev Doctrine, taken together with these other signs, encouraged the accelerated reform in Eastern Europe. Given Gorbachev's need for a better relationship with the West, it would be difficult for the USSR to halt such reform if it went too far, nor could such repression be justified, if the rhetoric of the 'new thinking' in international relations was to be taken seriously. Gorbachev told the European Parliament, in June 1989, that social change 'is the exclusive affair of the people of that country and is their choice. Any interference in domestic affairs and any attempts to restrict the sovereignty of states, whether friends, allies or any others, is inadmissible'. It was within the context of these new premisses that the revolutions of 1989 took place and within the same context that the new democracies attempted to structure their foreign policies. Between 1988 and 1990 the USSR gradually ceased to define its European security needs in terms of the maintenance of a group of similarly-governed states in Eastern Europe.

Disintegration of the Warsaw Pact

The dramatic political changes that took place in Eastern Europe during 1989 transformed the security situation. While, to an extent, the changes simply confirmed a process that was already happening, that is the transition from an era of confrontation to one of co-operation in Europe, they also radically altered the nature of that transition and also altered the security agenda for the new Europe. Prior to 1989 the prospects were for a continuation of the division of Europe into two blocs, but for the steady evolution of the relationship between the two, in a more co-operative direction, with a dramatic reduction in the armed forces of both sides. This was indicated by the pattern of unilateral arms reductions in the late 1980s, in the 1987 INF Treaty and in the 1990 Conventional Forces in Europe (CFE) Treaty.

The Warsaw Pact was always an alliance based upon the needs of the USSR and, to a lesser extent, a shared perception among the Eastern European leaders of a military–ideological threat represented by the NATO alliance. As the Communist governments fell from power in 1989, so the *raison d'être* of the Warsaw Pact fell with them. That the death-knell of the Pact was not sounded immediately was due only to the political sensitivity of the new democratic governments. They were anxious to reassure the USSR that the political developments of 1989

did not represent a threat to Soviet national security. Nevertheless, having lived for 40 years under the strict tutelage of a hegemonic power, it was inevitable that the Eastern European states would wish to escape from the constraints represented by the Warsaw Treaty as speedily as possible.

The problem for the former Warsaw Pact states was to decide what security posture should replace Pact membership. One possibility was swiftly made clear. For the forseeable future membership of the NATO alliance would not be an option. NATO was quick to declare that it would not consider membership for the former Pact states. Such an action was considered to be unnecessarily provocative to the Soviet authorities and might undermine the domestic political position of the leaders of reform within the USSR.

The second strand of security policy related to diplomatic efforts aimed at the enhancement and institutionalization of the Conference on Security and Co-operation in Europe (CSCE) process. Czechoslovakia, for example, sought to merge the 22-state negotiations on conventional armed forces with the 34-state CSCE talks on confidence and security-building measures. They aimed to institutionalize a Europe-wide security infrastructure that would, at one and the same time, provide the essential reassurance to the USSR that it was more not less secure after the events of 1989 and also embed Eastern European states in what would effectively become a European collective security arrangement. The aim, according to Czechoslovakia, would be, 'to establish firm, all-European security structures that would be based on a low level of armaments and a high level of mutual confidence'. The search by the new democracies for multilateral security frameworks was clearly necessitated by the political realities of their security environment. The option of a 'non-aligned' defence policy, on the model of the heavily-armed Swiss neutrality, was not feasible. All the pressures, domestic and international, were towards reduced defence establishments. Treaties like the 1990 CFE Treaty imposed lower numerical ceilings for equipment, while the need to release funds for socio-economic development, coupled with public disenchantment with conscription and a large visible military presence, meant that national defence effort would contract sharply. Security needs would therefore have to be met through bilateral and multilateral co-operation.

One of the features of the relationship between the USSR and the states of Eastern Europe between 1945 and 1989, was that it was always highly country-specific. Soviet tolerance of the rate of reform and the nature of that reform varied markedly from country to country. This attitude produced variations in the degree to which states attempted to exercise a certain independence in foreign policy and this in turn affected the degree to which the new democratic regimes could build upon foreign policy traditions established by their predecessors. Before 1989 Romania, as the most rigidly Stalinist state of the Warsaw Pact, clearly believed that its ideological reliability allowed it to exercise extreme dissidence in foreign policy terms. Ironically, once ideological conformity disappeared, it proved more cautious than the other new democracies in asserting its independence in the security field.

All the Eastern European states were already engaged in a military reduction process by 1990. Every Warsaw Pact state except Romania was engaged in significant unilateral force reductions. Hungary, for example, announced cuts in the size of the armed forces and of the defence budget in January 1989.

THE NEW PATTERNS OF SECURITY POLICY IN EASTERN EUROPE

Czechoslovakia–Hungary–Poland

The security policies of the Eastern European Warsaw Pact states gradually crystallized into two dominant strategies. The first emphasized disengagement from the embrace of the USSR; it found form in efforts to loosen and eventually end the constraints imposed by membership of the Pact and negotiations to secure the withdrawal of the Soviet garrisons in Eastern Europe. The second involved reaching towards the West for security guarantees and membership of western organizations, such as NATO and the EC. While pursuing these strategies the Eastern Europeans sought to encourage the development of a new security architecture for Europe. This was to supersede the old East–West divide and guarantee mutual security for all European states, including the USSR. The pursuit of these objectives revealed a marked difference in outlook and approach between the states of central Europe and those in the Balkans.

In practice the Eastern Europeans were able to achieve their aims in certain areas far more quickly than in others. Breaking the security linkage with the USSR, paradoxically, proved easier than gaining security guarantees from the West.

Hungary began to assert its own identity even before the revolutions of 1989. Indeed, under Party leader János Kádár, it did so almost continuously from 1956 onwards. Under Kádár a limited degree of dissidence was tolerated and economic policy favoured the provision of consumer goods. In time, both the Hungarian population and the Western states recognized that Hungary 'was exploring the limits of Soviet patience with these reforms'. Hungary's government, internally and externally, was viewed as being as legitimate and as independent as was possible within the constraints imposed by the Soviet domination of Eastern Europe. In spite of a worsening economic position during the 1980s and despite Gorbachev's willingness to accept economic experimentation in Eastern Europe, the Government pursued only minor economic reforms in the late 1980s. This caution ended when Károly Grósz became General Secretary of the Hungarian Socialist Workers' Party in May 1988. The domestic reforms which ensued were to legalize opposition parties and lead to democratic elections in March 1990. These elections produced a non-Communist government. In foreign policy terms, however, it is significant that a new independence in foreign policy was asserted even before the election of a non-Communist government. The term 'Socialist' was dropped from the Republic of Hungary's title; Imre Nagy, Hungary's leader at the time of the 1956 invasion and who had been executed in 1958, was rehabilitated and his body reburied; and Hungary's part in the 1968 invasion of Czechoslovakia was critically re-evaluated. Economic links with the West were energetically promoted and, in July 1988, a special trade status agreement with the European Community (EC) was successfully negotiated. Talks were also held with the European Free Trade Association (EFTA). Hungary began to establish diplomatic relations with states that had long been beyond the pale of the 'socialist commonwealth', such as the Republic of Korea (February 1989) and Israel (September 1989). Hungary also participated in the establishment of a regional co-operation initiative, involving Italy, Austria, Czechoslovakia and Yugoslavia, the so-called 'Pentagonal' group.

In security policy too, the Communist Government anticipated the direction of the foreign policies of the new democratic governments. In early 1989 the 'Iron Curtain' of security fences dividing Austria and Hungary was dismantled. In January 1989 unilateral reductions in Hungary's defence budget and armed forces were announced. Towards the end of that year further financial and numerical reductions were announced (25%, to be implemented in 1990). In January 1990 the still-Communist Government of Hungary emulated Czechoslovakia and asked the USSR to begin negotiations on the complete withdrawal of Soviet forces from the country. As well as being reduced in size, the armed forces of both Hungary and Czechoslovakia were being restructured to give them a more 'defensive' character, primarily by reducing the number of tank regiments. Hungary's force restructuring aimed to replace its tank divisions with mechanized rifle divisions, a process due for completion in 1992. Similarly, Czechoslovakia reduced the number of tanks in its armoured divisions by one-quarter.

These reforms, taken with the cuts necessitated by the CFE process, induced a reduction in the Czechoslovak armed forces from 200,000 to 130,000, and, in Hungary, from 100,000 to 70,000. Reductions in the Balkan states were more cautious. Bulgaria, nervous about pressure from its Turkish minority and instability in Romania and Yugoslavia, stabilized its forces at around 100,000 soldiers, a reduction of some 10%. In Romania the army escaped pressure to reduce significantly, from its already low levels, owing to its crucial political role in underpinning the post-Ceaușescu government.

In 1989 Poland became the first Warsaw Pact country to acquire a non-Communist dominated government. This was both an achievement and a drawback. It was a drawback because, since it was the first, it was unclear both how the USSR would react and how far Poland could go in abandoning Communism. With an economic catastrophe looming, the Polish Communist (PZPR) government engaged in negotiations with Solidarność. This led to an agreement on fundamental political reforms. In the elections, in June 1989, Solidarność won 99% of the seats it contested. The Communists' mandate and self-confidence was completely undermined and, in August 1989, Tadeusz Mazowiecki, a staunch Roman Catholic and Solidarność member, formed a new government. In order to moderate the reaction of the USSR and the other, Communist, Eastern European governments, Mazowiecki left the defence and interior ministries in Communist hands; the new foreign minister was a Solidarność supporter.

Although the new Polish Government moved quickly to reverse decades of Communist economic policy, in the sphere of security and international relations it was far more cautious. Mazowiecki publicly pledged his Government's continuing adherence to the Warsaw Pact. Although Wałęsa called for Soviet troop withdrawals, in January 1990, the Mazowiecki Government did not follow the example of Czechoslovakia and Hungary. A major reason for this was the imminent prospect of German reunification. Until Poland had gained an unequivocal German acceptance of the country's borders and a sense of the likely future direction of German foreign policy, the Solidarność-led Government preferred to maintain a Soviet troop presence in Poland. However, because of the scale of Poland's economic problems, Poland did follow Hungary's example in announcing additional defence cuts, in November 1989, in addition to those announced in January 1989. The planned programme of reductions will eventually reduce the Polish forces from about 400,000 in number, in 1987, to about 250,000 by 1995.

Initially the new democratic governments in Eastern Europe took a cautious attitude towards discontinuing their membership of the Warsaw Pact. They did not wish to alarm the USSR unnecessarily and they were aware that, in 1956, it was Hungary's decision to leave the Pact which had been one of the major factors leading to the Soviet intervention of that year. Nevertheless, in September 1990, the foreign affairs and defence ministers of Poland, Czechoslovakia and Hungary met at Zakopane, in Poland, to consider the role of their armed forces in the light of the political changes in eastern and central Europe. Soviet representatives were not invited, the first time such an event had happened since the formation of the Warsaw Pact. However the Soviet decision to use armed force against the dissident republic of Lithuania, in January 1991, meant that this attitude was reconsidered. The repression brought unwelcome reminders of the events of 1956 and 1968 and led several Pact governments to fear that the Warsaw Treaty might be used as a pretext for intervention against the reformed governments in Eastern Europe. An emergency cabinet meeting in Czechoslovakia, on 13 January 1991, produced a statement which declared that, 'the use of military force . . . mars the process of the consolidation of security, peace and relaxation in Europe, and undermines confidence in the democratic changes which have been taking place in the USSR in the last few years'.

The Czechoslovak Minister of Foreign Affairs, Jiří Dienstbier, was instructed to discuss a possible joint reaction with Hungary and Poland, including a rapid withdrawal from the Warsaw Pact. Until this point, although Hungary had declared its preference for withdrawal from the Pact, Czechoslovakia had been working for the transformation of the Warsaw Pact from a military into a primarily political grouping. Both Czechoslovakia and Hungary had previously supported the efforts of the Baltic Republics to regain full sovereignty. Czechoslovakia established diplomatic representation in the Lithuanian capital, Vilnius, in November 1990.

On 22 January 1991 a meeting of the Polish, Hungarian and Czechoslovakian foreign ministers, held in Budapest (Hungary), led to a joint statement suggesting that the military structure of the Warsaw Pact be abolished by 1 July 1991 and for the organization itself to be dissolved within one year. Géza Jeszensky, the Hungarian Minister of Foreign Affairs, stated that the three governments would prefer agreement with the USSR on the dissolution of the Pact, but, if this was not forthcoming, the necessary action would be taken unilaterally. In order to make this more acceptable to the USSR, they argued that the Warsaw Pact had been rendered obsolete by the moves to set up a collective security system in Europe (this argument could equally well suggest the dissolution of NATO, but this was not suggested). Jeszensky expressed support for the independence of the Baltic republics, but denied that there was a link between the Soviet use of force in Lithuania and the joint decision of the three Eastern European countries to leave the Pact. He insisted that, 'the Warsaw Pact should be abolished as part of an all-European process'. The three Governments also agreed to increase trilateral co-operation in areas such as achieving full political independence and EC membership.

In the event, President Gorbachev surprised the three states by himself suggesting, in early February, the dissolution of the military aspects of the Warsaw Pact; he proposed its military dissolution by April 1991. A joint meeting of Hungary, Poland and Czechoslovakia, held in Visegrad (Hungary) in mid-February, reaffirmed the emergence of a trilateral approach on security and foreign policy issues. Progress was swift. The foreign and defence ministers of the six remaining Warsaw Pact states (the GDR had left the Pact in September 1990, prior to its dissolution and admittance to the Federal Republic) met in Budapest, on 25 February, to end the Pact's military structure. The

agreement took effect on 21 March. The meeting demonstrated continuing differences with the USSR, which wished to maintain the political structure of the Warsaw Pact, for treating as a bloc with NATO at the CFE and CSCE negotiations. The 'trilateral group' re-emphasized their desire to see the remaining functions of the Warsaw Pact ended before the end of 1991. The Hungarian foreign minister, Jeszensky, characterized the Pact as, 'an organization resting on mistaken fundaments, which has outlived itself'. On 1 July 1991, in Prague, the six countries signed a treaty finally dissolving the Warsaw Pact, to take effect upon ratification by the respective legislatures.

A crucial change of emphasis, apparent by late February 1991, was the desire for the continuation of NATO and a closer association with it, in contrast with the earlier emphasis on neutrality. The trilateral states were beginning to move towards bilateral military co-operation agreements with each other, as well as attempting to strengthen their political links with NATO.

The Withdrawal of Soviet Forces

Throughout 1990–91 there was steady progress on securing the withdrawal of the Soviet forces in Eastern Europe. By July 1991 the 73,500 Soviet troops, and their equipment, had completed their withdrawal from Czechoslovakia and the 49,500-strong Soviet force in Hungary had also left. Negotiations on the withdrawal of the 50,000-strong garrison in Poland had only been completed in mid-February, but the first convoys returning to the USSR were underway by 9 April 1991. The process of disengaging from the Soviet military embrace was a difficult one, involving much more than just the withdrawal of the Soviet troop presence. Domestic and international politico-military reforms were required; for example, efforts to reduce the Soviet near-monopoly on arms supplies. Breaking the linkages between the Soviet and Eastern European officer corps was also necessary, involving the retirement or transfer of the most pro-Soviet officers, re-education of the officer corps and efforts to establish links with Western forces. Czechoslovak officers began training courses with the German army, the Bundeswehr, while Romania expressed a desire to send its officers to the United Kingdom, France, Italy and Germany for training. All the former Warsaw Pact states explored the possibility of US training. The intelligence-sharing arrangements with the USSR were also severed.

Withdrawal of weapons from Eastern Europe also took place in this period. Victor Dubinin, the Commander of Soviet forces in Poland, revealed that Soviet nuclear weapons had been based in Poland until 1990. He even asserted that these belonged to Poland, a charge quickly rejected by Poland, which was worried that it might be deemed to be in violation of the nuclear non-proliferation treaty. Hungary's former Communist leader, Grósz, revealed that Soviet nuclear weapons had also been deployed in Hungary until 1988, but had been withdrawn at Grósz's request.

The Search for New Security Arrangements

While the withdrawal of Soviet forces was an entirely welcome development in terms of sovereignty, the central European governments in particular were concerned about the emerging security vacuum in Eastern Europe. The demise of the Warsaw Pact had not been followed by the creation of a new European collective security order, nor had NATO given any security guarantees to the new democracies. President Václav Havel of Czechoslovakia remarked, during a visit to NATO headquarters, that an alliance of countries united by the ideals of freedom 'should not be forever closed to neighbouring countries that are pursuing the same goal'. Hungary and Czechoslovakia, as well as strengthening the trilateral link with Poland, began to show more interest in Italy's proposal for linkages between the 'Pentagonal' group of states which had formed parts of the old Austro-Hungarian Empire: Italy, Austria, Hungary, Czechoslovakia and Yugoslavia. The first meeting of the Pentagonal, held in Venice (Italy), in August 1990, produced a broad agenda similar to that of the CSCE, involving security, economic and human rights issues. The Hungarian foreign minister expressed the hope that the new grouping might have a role to play in regional conflict mediation. In June 1991, when Slovenia and Croatia declared their independence from Yugoslavia, the two 'Western' members, Italy and Austria, were quick to announce that they would not recognize the new states. The Pentagonal was, however, involved in attempts to mediate in the Yugoslav crisis. At the end of July 1991 the forum admitted Poland as a member and became known as the Hexagonal group; Albania was an observer and was considered likely to join in the future.

The search for a new security order has been pursued in the new context created by the successful conclusion of the CFE Treaty. This treaty was designed on a bloc-to-bloc basis, to dramatically reduce the scale of the military confrontation in Eastern Europe. While it will achieve this end, it has largely been overtaken by events. Even so, the CFE Treaty, taken together with the bilateral agreements with the USSR on troop withdrawals and the CSCE agreement of November 1990, represents a tremendous gain for the security of the central and eastern European states. Under the CFE Treaty, NATO and the Warsaw Pact were each required to reduce their forces in Europe to a maximum of 20,000 tanks, 30,000 armoured personnel carriers, 20,000 artillery pieces, 6,800 combat aircraft and 2,000 attack helicopters. This entailed an enormous reduction in Pact forces, most of them Soviet, of 19,200 tanks, 16,500 armoured personnel carriers, 12,000 artillery pieces, 2,100 combat aircraft and 1,700 helicopters. All these had to be destroyed or moved east of the Ural Mountains. Thus the USSR was committed both to withdrawing its garrisons from Eastern Europe, through bilateral agreements, and to dramatically reducing its ability to successfully reintervene, through multilateral agreements. In addition, while for political reasons NATO showed no enthusiasm for Eastern European membership of NATO, the Joint Declaration signed by NATO and the Warsaw Pact, in Paris, in November 1990, specifically reaffirmed the right of any state either to be, or not to be, a party to a treaty or an alliance. During negotiations for a series of bilateral treaties between the USSR and the former Pact members, however, the USSR has attempted to insert a clause which allowed a veto on NATO membership.

The trilateral states of Poland, Czechoslovakia and Hungary have sought, unsuccessfully so far, to have NATO extend its security umbrella as far as the borders of the USSR. Poland's Minister of Foreign Affairs, Krzysztof Skubiszewski, expressed fears of a 'domino effect' of destabilization rippling out from a collapsing USSR, which could only be halted if NATO operated throughout Europe as part of a European security system. The Eastern European states feared that, even with the withdrawal of Soviet forces, Europe would remain divided between a secure West and an insecure East. The East has been left in a security vacuum by NATO. On the one hand, NATO discouraged Eastern applicants, on the grounds that it did not wish to alarm the USSR, and has urged the Eastern states to look to the CSCE process for their security. On the other hand, because they feel that NATO must remain the core of Western security and do not wish to see CSCE emerge as a competitor, NATO states have prevented CSCE from acquiring the structures and competences that would allow it to replace NATO. This satisfies Western objectives, but leaves the former Warsaw Pact states in a limbo, an uncertain situation with which they are deeply dissatisfied, given their unhappy experiences in the late 1930s. They have no wish to be preserved as a 'buffer' between East and West; they wish to be politically and economically 'Western', in a Europe that is undivided in security terms. As with EC membership, incorporation in the Western security framework would both guarantee them against a reassertive Russia and would secure their new political and economic systems within a family of similar regimes. Scepticism about the value of CSCE as an alternative increased markedly when it failed to deter the use of force by Soviet troops in Lithuania, in January 1991.

NATO, like the EC, regards full membership for Eastern European states as premature, but has shown some willingness to begin a process of association through low-level contacts and consultative arrangements. NATO, however, wished to convince the USSR that it was not threatened by the Western alliance. The dissolution of the USSR at the end of 1991 did not stabilize international security, but it lessened the threat to Eastern Europe.

Virtually all the former Warsaw Pact states have expressed a desire to join NATO. In March 1991 the Bulgarian Prime Minister, Dimitur Popov, appealed to NATO to admit Eastern states as associate members, while President Zhelyu Zhelev announced plans to send a delegation to NATO headquarters to plead Bulgaria's case and to join with the trilateral group in seeking associate member status. Poland, with perhaps the greatest desire to be part of NATO, fears that it is least likely to be given membership. Given its unfortunate history, and particularly the events of 1939, Poland sees a need to ensure security from both the East and from Germany. During 1989 and 1990 Poland was the member most reluctant to disband the Warsaw Pact and the last to request its Soviet garrison to leave. This was due to a lingering concern about a unified and resurgent Germany, particularly given that Poland was not convinced that Germany had fully accepted the permanence of Poland's 1945 borders. By early 1991 a combination of factors changed this stance. Soviet repression in the Baltic Republics refocused attention on the eastern frontier. The agreements of 1990 satisfied Poland that Germany had fully accepted the 1945 frontiers. The election of Wałęsa as President produced a more assertively nationalistic leadership, which was less sympathetic to Soviet concerns. Even so, Poland recognized that, given that it bordered the secessionist Soviet republic of Lithuania and straddled the traditional Western invasion route into Russia, the USSR would be peculiarly sensitive regarding Polish security policy. Membership of NATO was out of the question until the USSR dissolved.

Romania has not sought NATO membership, but rather has sought to strengthen Eastern ties. In addition to signing a bilateral treaty with the USSR, in mid-April 1991 it proposed an Eastern version of the Western European Union (WEU—a defensive alliance of nine of the EC states), in which it seemed to envisage a revival of the Warsaw Pact minus the USSR. Romania has also sought to formalize the process of Balkan co-operation, building upon the Balkan foreign ministers conferences, which began in 1988. As with the central European Pentagonal (now Hexagonal) group, Romania sees a need for a structure to pursue regional co-operation in the fields of security, economic development and human rights.

In October 1990 Romania and Hungary initiated a programme of 'confidence-building measures', which were designed to increase trust between the two states and reassure each other that neither posed a threat to the other. The joint border was particularly sensitive, because of the 2m. ethnic Hungarians who live in Romania, which, until the revolution of 1990, denied them economic and political rights.

Unlike the northern-tier states, Romania was willing to sign a bilateral security treaty with the USSR, in which each agreed not to join any alliance hostile to the other party. Czechoslovakia, Poland and Hungary had rejected such an agreement, believing that it would limit their ability to forge closer security ties with the West and, in particular, rule out any possibility of joining NATO. President Havel of Czechoslovakia declared that it was unacceptable in principle, 'as it would restrict our sovereignty for a very long time'. Bulgaria restrained from signing a similar treaty to Romania; it too involved restrictions on the use of territory or airspace for any party in conflict with the USSR, while allowing Soviet forces access to national territory under certain circumstances. Bulgaria did engage in energetic diplomacy designed to improve its relationship with its southern neighbour, Greece.

A clear pattern was developing, in which the trilateral states of central Europe began to evolve similar foreign policies, which distinguished them from their Balkan neighbours. Nervousness towards the USSR (and, to a lesser extent, its successors) remained; a Czechoslovak official declared that, 'our relationship with Poland and Hungary follows positive terms, as to what mutually we want to do for common security, while negotiations with the USSR are defined negatively, by what we're not willing to do'.

A unifying theme of the Eastern European states is the desire to become full members of the EC at the earliest possible date, regardless of the economic and political strains being experienced during the painful transition to a market economy. This desire originates as much from political as from economic motivations. Similar considerations lay behind the successful applications of Hungary, Poland and Czechoslovakia to become members of the Council of Europe. While the Eastern Europeans wish to avoid being dragged down by the collapse of the Soviet economy and the end of the Council for Mutual Economic Assistance (CMEA or Comecon), they wish to join the EC because, like Greece, Spain and Portugal before them, anchoring their sovereignty in the EC is seen as an insurance for the survival of 'Western' political and economic values and systems. The EC is seen as the core of the 'new Europe', of which the Eastern states desperately want to be part. President Havel told the European Parliament, in Brussels, in March 1991, that the political need to be integrated into the EC far outweighed the difficulties posed by the parlous state of the Czechoslovak economy. He suggested Czechoslovak involvement in the EC's discussions on political union and a common foreign and security policy as a way to overcome the disadvantages of being denied NATO membership. He also said Czechoslovakia wanted to have links with the WEU, an idea in which the organization showed no interest.

The trilateral group agreed at their Visegrad summit to co-ordinate their approach to EC matters. In practice, however, there are significant variations between the states. Hungary sees EC membership as an urgent priority and, despite discouraging hints from Brussels, is likely to apply for full membership at the earliest possible date. An application no later than 1992 is likely, with membership envisaged for 1995 or 1996. Hungary's earlier moves towards a market economy and its close links with Austria, which has already applied for membership, are used to justify Budapest's stance. An EC mission in Budapest was opened in December 1990.

Poland and Czechoslovakia are more cautious, wanting more time to adjust their economies to the rigours of EC membership. They see a need for a longer period of political stability before EC membership is feasible, although the Polish President, Wałęsa, has expressed a desire for associate membership by 1992 and full membership as early as possible thereafter. In early 1991 the President of the Commission of the EC, Jacques Delors, cautioned Wałęsa against an early Polish application for membership. However Poland was encouraged by France, which signed an agreement with Poland, in April 1991, as part of which France pledged itself to support Poland's application to join the EC at the earliest possible date. The Polish Ambassador to France was more cautious than President Wałęsa, speaking of a Polish membership application towards the end of the 1990s. In practice, these factors are likely to mean that Hungary will have to wait almost as long as Poland and Czechoslovakia for full membership. In the interim the EC is likely to grant a special form of associate status and a partial customs union to the Eastern states, in order to encourage and support the economic and political reforms already under way. In March 1991 Frans Andriessen, EC external affairs commissioner, visited the Eastern European states. This resulted in the EC looking more favourably upon the regimes in Romania and Bulgaria, who also seek EC membership, though envisaging a more extended timetable than the trilateral group.

CONCLUSIONS

Since the beginning of 1990 a pattern of foreign policy behaviour has begun to emerge in Eastern Europe. One can also distinguish, to some extent, between the groups of states in central Europe (the northern tier) and the Balkan countries and Romania (the southern tier—Romania is not, strictly, a Balkan country). The description 'Eastern Europe' is itself a geographical misnomer, a political, rather than a geographical, description, arising out of the Cold War. Particularly with the disintegration of the Communist bloc, countries like Hungary and Czechoslovakia are more accurately described as central European and their post-1989 foreign policies reflect this. Hence, the initiatives to build co-operative networks with neighbouring states, such as the Hexagonal group, and the sustained efforts to reach out to Western Europe, to rebuild the linkages that were broken by the 45-year division of Europe following the Second World War. Seeing themselves as 'central' (*Mitteleuropa*), these states are also seeking a role as a bridge between the republics of the former USSR and the West and as proponents of a new security order, which could finally overcome the division of Europe.

While the Balkan states and Romania share some of these objectives, they have preoccupations which differentiate them from their northern neighbours. They are conscious that the Warsaw Pact imposed an artificial calm on the region for 45 years. They are also aware of the enormous disruptive potential of the nationalities question within and between their states. Therefore, they have looked for ways to minimize the potential for cross-border tension in a region where the potential for conflict remains high, as the events in Yugoslavia in 1991 clearly demonstrated.

BIBLIOGRAPHY

Brown, A. (Ed.). *The Soviet–East European Relationship in the Gorbachev Era.* Boulder, Co, Westview, 1990.

Dawisha, K. *Eastern Europe, Gorbachev and Reform: The Great Challenge.* Cambridge, Cambridge University Press, 1988.

Dawisha, K. and Valdes, J. 'Socialist Internationalism in Eastern Europe', in *Problems of Communism*, 36:2, March–April 1987.

Holden, G. *The Warsaw Pact: Soviet Security and Bloc Politics*. Oxford, Basil Blackwell, 1989.

Kittrie, N. and Volgyes, I. (Eds). *The Uncertain Future: Gorbachev's Eastern Bloc*. New York, Paragon House, 1988.

Linden, R. H. (Ed.). *Studies in East European Foreign Policy*. New York, Praeger, 1980.

Nelson, D. N. 'Europe's Unstable East', in *Foreign Policy*, 82, Spring 1991.

de Nevers, R. 'The Soviet Union and Eastern Europe: The End of an Era', in *Adelphi Papers*, 249. London, Brasseys and IISS, 1990.

Terry, S. M. *Soviet Policy in Eastern Europe*. New Haven, Ct, Yale University Press, 1984.

Appendix: International Organizations Active in the Region

THE UNITED NATIONS

The United Nations (UN) was founded in 1945, at the end of the Second World War, to maintain international peace and security and to develop co-operation in economic, social, cultural and humanitarian affairs. The UN officially came into existence on 24 October 1945, upon the ratification of the United Nations Charter. In addition to the USSR, two of its constituent Union Republics, the Ukraine and Byelorussia, were also founding members (Stalin, claiming that the USSR was an association of sovereign states, wanted separate membership for all the Union Republics, but the Western Powers would only concede it for the two large, European Republics). As nations associated with the victorious Allied Powers of the Second World War, Czechoslovakia and Yugoslavia were also among the original signatories. Poland, although not represented at the founding conference, became the 51st founding nation. The other Eastern bloc countries, Albania, Bulgaria, Hungary and Romania, joined the UN in 1955. The two German states were admitted as separate members in 1973. The Baltic Republics were admitted in September 1991, and at the end of December Russia was granted the UN seat of the USSR.

The chief administrative officer of the UN is the Secretary-General, who is based at the UN headquarters in: United Nations Plaza, New York, NY 10017, USA; tel. (212) 963-1234. Boutros Boutros Ghali (Egypt) became Secretary-General at the beginning of 1992.

The principal organs of the UN are: the Secretariat, headed by the Secretary-General; the Security Council, which has five Permanent Members (including Russia) and 10 members elected for two-year terms; the General Assembly; the Economic and Social Council (ECOSOC); the Trusteeship Council; and the International Court of Justice (ICJ). All are based in New York, except for the ICJ, which is based in The Hague (Netherlands). The UN has Information Centres in Czechoslovakia (Panská 5, 110 00 Prague 1), Romania (Bucharest, POB 1-701, 16 Aurel Vlaicu St), Yugoslavia (11001 Belgrade, POB 157, Svetozara Markovica 58—also covers Albania) and Russia (121002 Moscow, Ulitsa Lunacharskogo 4/16).

A regional subsidiary of ECOSOC, the Economic Commission for Europe (ECE), includes all the countries of the region, as well as the remaining European countries (including Turkey, Cyprus and Iceland), the USA and Canada. It is based in Switzerland, together with other offices and organizations of the UN, at: Palais des Nations, 1211 Geneva 10; tel. (22) 7346011; telex 412962. Established in 1947, the ECE studies economic, environmental and technological problems and recommends courses of action. It is presided over by Olli Adolf Mennander, and its Executive Secretary is Gerald Hinteregger (Austria).

Another UN body involved in the region is the UN Environment Programme (UNEP—based in Kenya: POB 30552, Nairobi—the Executive Director is Mostafa K. Tolba of Egypt), which has a European Regional Office in Switzerland (Pavillon du Petit Saconnex, 16 ave Jean Trembley, 1209 Geneva; tel. (22) 7999400; telex 28877). Also based in Switzerland is the UN High Commissioner for Refugees (UNHCR—Case postale 2500, 1211 Geneva 2 dépôt; tel. (22) 7398111; telex 41570; fax (22) 7319546), which office is currently occupied by Sadako Ogata (Japan).

Specialized Agencies within the UN System

All the countries of the region are members of the International Atomic Energy Agency (IAEA—Austria, 1400 Vienna, POB 100, Wagramerstrasse 5; tel. (222) 2360; Director-General Hans Blix of Sweden), as they are of the UN Educational, Scientific and Cultural Organization (UNESCO—7 place de Fontenoy, 75700 Paris, France; tel. (1) 45-68-10-00; telex 204461; fax (1) 45-67-16-90). The Director-General of UNESCO is Federico Mayor Zaragoza of Spain. There is a regional office in Romania, the European Centre for Higher Education (CEPES—Bucharest, Stirbei Voda 39, Palatul Kretulescu). Of the other major specialized agencies, all the countries of the region are members of the World Health Organization (WHO—based in Switzerland) and, except for the USSR, were also members of the agencies, the Food and Agriculture Organization (FAO—Italy).

The key financial agency is the International Bank for Reconstruction and Development (IBRD—President: Lewis Preston), which, together with its affiliate, the International Development Association, constitutes the 'World Bank'. The IBRD has two other affiliates: the International Finance Corporation and the Multilateral Investment Guarantee Agency. Only members of the IBRD can become members of the International Monetary Fund (IMF—Managing Director: Michel Camdessus of France). Yugoslavia and Czechoslovakia were among the first members, after the Second World War, but the latter left the Fund in 1954, only to rejoin in 1990. Hungary became a member in 1982 and Poland in 1986 and, since the fall of the Communist regimes, Bulgaria and Romania have also joined. Only Albania and the USSR remained outside the system, although the former applied for membership in January 1991 and the latter, in mid-1991, was promised some form of affiliation. The USSR became a member in October 1991, Russia inheriting its place in December. Both the World

Bank and the IMF are based in the USA. The World Bank is at: 1818 H St, NW, Washington, DC 20433; tel. (202) 477-1234; telex 248423; fax (202) 477-6391. The IMF is at: 700 19th St, NW, Washington, DC 20431; tel. (202) 623-7430; telex 440040; fax (202) 623-4661.

PRINCIPAL ECONOMIC AND FINANCIAL ORGANIZATIONS

Council for Mutual Economic Assistance (CMEA)

The CMEA, or Comecon, was established in 1949 to assist the economic development of the member states. All the countries of the region, except Yugoslavia, joined CMEA, although Albania ceased to participate at the end of 1961. Cuba, Mongolia and Viet-Nam were also members. The fall of the Communist governments of Eastern Europe, in 1989, brought the role and activity of CMEA into question. In June 1991 the nine remaining members agreed to the final dissolution of the organization, to take effect in the following 90 days (that is, before the end of September 1991). There was a continuing dispute about which of its agencies should continue and about what should happen to its assets. The CMEA's headquarters were in the USSR (now Russia—121205 Moscow, Prospekt Kalinina 56; tel. (095) 290-91-11; telex 411141). The head of administration was the Secretary of the Council, Vyacheslav Vladimirovich Sychev.

Among the agencies established by the CMEA were two financial institutions: the International Bank for Economic Co-operation (IBEC Russia, 107078 Moscow, 11 Ul. M. Poryvayevoy; tel. (095) 204-72-20; telex 411391); and the International Investment Bank (Russia, 123557 Moscow, Presnensky Val 17; tel. (095) 253-80-24; telex 411358).

The European Communities (EC)

None of the countries of the region are members of the EC (its main administration is based with the Commission of the EC, in Belgium: 200 rue de la Loi, 1049 Brussels; tel. (2) 235-11-11; telex 21877; fax (2) 235-01-22; the President of the Commission is Jacques Delors of France). However many of the countries of the region are anxious to join, the most likely being Hungary, Czechoslovakia and Poland. In 1991 the three were conducting negotiations on association agreements with the EC, and Bulgaria had been invited to do the same. The EC's economic significance means it is of fundamental importance to the region, not least in terms of development aid. The EC has established various initiatives to assist the political and economic integration of the region, even extending to political mediation in the Yugoslav crisis of 1991.

In 1990 the European Bank for Reconstruction and Development (EBRD) was established by the EC and the World Bank. It is based in the United Kingdom (122 Leadenhall St, London EC3V 4EB; (71) 338-6000; telex 8812161; fax (71) 338-6100; Chairman: Jacques Attali) and is charged with aiding the economic reform of Eastern Europe. An EC European Investment Bank, based in Luxembourg, has also provided financial assistance to the region.

An association of non-EC countries is the European Free Trade Association (EFTA: 9-11 rue de Varembé, 1211 Geneva, Switzerland; tel. (22) 749-1111). These countries negotiated a co-ordinated 'European Economic Area' with the EC (the latter's 'single internal market' comes into effect at the end of 1992; some have applied for EC membership. The Eastern European countries have also held negotiations with EFTA.

POLITICAL AND SECURITY ORGANIZATIONS

The Warsaw Pact

Before the fall of the Communist governments of Eastern Europe, the Warsaw Treaty Organization (Warsaw Pact) was the dominant military alliance, the basis of Soviet authority in the bloc. The Warsaw Treaty of Friendship, Co-operation and Mutual Assistance was signed, in May 1955, by all the countries of the region (including the GDR), except Yugoslavia. Albania ceased to participate in 1961 and formally withdrew in 1968. After 1989 the alliance became increasingly defunct and, on 1 July 1991, representatives of the six remaining members (the USSR, Bulgaria, Czechoslovakia, Hungary, Poland and Romania) agreed to end the political functions of the Pact (military institutions had already been abandoned). Formal dissolution was dependent upon ratification by the respective parliaments.

Despite the dissolution of the Eastern bloc, the former countries of the Warsaw Pact have not been permitted to join the Western bloc's alliance, the North Atlantic Treaty Organization (NATO—based in Belgium). Only the former GDR is in NATO, after the USSR agreed that the united Germany (October 1991) could remain in that organization.

In addition to the bilateral arms reductions treaties between the USSR and the USA (such as the Intermediate-range Nuclear Forces—INF—Treaty of 1987 and the Strategic Arms' Reduction Treaty—START—which was signed in July 1991), the Warsaw Pact negotiated as a bloc. This was what produced the Conventional Forces in Europe (CFE) Treaty, of November 1990.

Conference on Security and Co-operation in Europe (CSCE)

The CSCE process was established to review the Helsinki Final Act of 1975 on East–West relations. This was signed by Canada, the USA and the USSR, as well as every other recognized European country (except Albania—which was admitted as the 35th member of the CSCE, in June 1991). Reluctant to admit Eastern members to NATO, that organization recommended that the CSCE become the basis of a new, continental system of peace and security. In November 1990 the CSCE heads of government met in Paris, to sign the CFE agreement (see above) and the Charter for a New Europe ('Paris Charter'), which undertook to respect democracy and human rights and to settle disputes by peaceful means. By the end of January 1992 all former Soviet Republics (except Georgia) had been granted membership; Slovenia and Croatia had been granted observer status.

At the November 1990 summit, it was agreed to establish a permanent secretariat, in Czechoslovakia (Thunovská 12, Malástrana, 11000 Prague 1; tel. (2) 311-9793; telex 121614; fax (2) 311-6215). The Director is Nils Eliasson (Sweden). The Office of Free Elections was established in Warsaw and a Conflict Prevention Centre in Vienna (Austria).

Other Forums

Since 1989 the Eastern European countries have had to seek new associations with each other. The northern-tier states of Poland, Czechoslovakia and Hungary have had some political and military co-operation since January 1991, and are sometimes referred to as the 'trilateral group'. A more recognized, although uninstitutionalized, forum was established at a summit, in August 1990, in Venice (Italy): this was the so-called 'Pentagonal', of five countries associated by their Austro-Hungarian past. In June 1991 the group became known as the Hexagonal, when Poland joined Italy, Austria, Hungary, Czechoslovakia and Yugoslavia. Albania (and Sweden) attended the latter meeting as an observer. Bulgaria and Romania have applied to join.

Yugoslavia, although a Communist country, was not a member of the Soviet-dominated Warsaw Pact. It is a member of the Non-aligned Movement, which is an association of 102 countries, founded in 1961 by countries rejecting any East–West affiliations. Its Co-ordinating Bureau is based in Yugoslavia (c/o 11000 Belgrade, Ul. Kneza Miloša 24, The Federal Secretariat for Foreign Affairs). Yugoslavia also participates in the Balkan Conference, an informal grouping for that region, which includes Albania, Bulgaria, Romania, Greece and Turkey.

The Council of Europe (BP 431, R6-67006 Strasbourg, France; tel. 88-41-20-00) was founded in 1949, to achieve a greater unity between its members, to facilitate their economic and social progress and to uphold the principles of parliamentary democracy. In 1950 its European Convention on Human Rights led to the creation of the European Court of Human Rights (The Hague, Netherlands). Originally a predominantly Western institution, since 1989 Hungary and Czechoslovakia have become full members, and special guest status has been granted to Bulgaria, Poland, Romania, Yugoslavia and the USSR. Poland was likely to become a full member during 1991 and Bulgaria in early 1992. Albania was likely to be granted special guest status in 1991, which has also been applied for by the Yugoslav Republic of Slovenia and the Soviet Republics of Armenia, Georgia and Moldavia.

However none of the countries of Eastern Europe, in their search for integration into Europe and new security arrangements, has elicited any response from the Western European Union (WEU—based in London, United Kingdom), a defensive alliance of nine EC states (the EC excluding Denmark, Greece and Ireland).

At the dissolution of the USSR in December 1991 11 Republics (omitting Georgia and the Baltics) formed the Commonwealth of Independent States; their level of economic and defence co-operation was still not clear by early 1992.

EASTERN EUROPEAN ECONOMIES

ALAN H. SMITH

INTRODUCTION

Poor economic performance, which had reached crisis proportions by the late 1980s, played a critical role in the collapse of Communist power in Eastern Europe. Economists cannot predict precisely when popular dissatisfaction with economic performance will lead to open confrontation, or how a government will respond. It is clear, however, that growing dissatisfaction with stagnating or even deteriorating living standards and the realization that the difference in those standards, between Eastern and Western Europe, was increasing at an accelerating rate contributed to popular unrest in Eastern Europe. This became widespread dissent in 1989. It was also becoming increasingly apparent to the Eastern European leaderships that attempts to introduce elements of a market economy into a centrally-planned economy had not just failed to bring about a significant improvement in economic performance, but had created new problems. Logically, the economic crisis could only be reversed by a radical change to the economic system, which would also entail a major political and social reform. Furthermore, the Soviet leadership was no longer willing either to bear the costs of supporting an inefficient economic system in Eastern Europe or to provide military support in defence of Communist rule. The majority of Eastern European leaders, therefore, had little alternative to a retreat from power.

THE NATURE OF THE ECONOMIC CRISIS IN 1989

Although the extent of the crisis differed from country to country, a number of common features can be identified. The crisis is most clearly evidenced, on the supply side, by official statistics that show a continued fall in the rate of growth and, in some years, falls in output (negative growth) during the 1980s. This was, in part, a reflection of a long-term trend, apparent since 1945. In each Eastern European country, the rate of growth of industrial output and of national income, in each five-year period (the standard unit of Communist economic planning) since the Second World War (with some exceptions during the mid-1960s) was below that realized in the preceding five-year plan period. However economic performance in the 1980s deteriorated more rapidly than would have been predicted from the previous rate of decline. Furthermore, official output statistics tend to overestimate the real rate of growth (partly by underestimating the effect of unofficial or 'hidden' price increases). Western re-estimates of Eastern European growth rates (Alton, 1989—see Bibliography, p. 50), indicate that the real rate of growth of output, throughout the region, was very low in comparison with both earlier performance and with Western European growth in the 1980s.

The slow growth in output was not the only problem. Terms of trade with the USSR were worsening and there was a need to maintain trade surpluses in convertible ('hard') currency, in order to repay debts accumulated in the 1970s. In the early 1980s these factors resulted in a decline in the volume of resources available to satisfy domestic demand for investment and consumption. Official statistics show that the levels of investment (measured in constant prices) in the majority of Eastern European economies, in the mid- and late 1980s, were below the levels recorded in the late 1970s. Western re-estimates (Alton, 1989) indicate that this decline was severe and has inflicted significant damage to the prospects for long-term economic recovery. Most of the impact of investment cuts has been borne by the industrial sector, resulting in a failure to modernize and, on occasions, even repair industrial plant and equipment. This has contributed to increasing product obsolescence, which, in the early 1980s, was exacerbated by the reduction in imports of Western machinery and equipment. This has damaged the competitiveness of Eastern European products in world markets.

However the major impact of expenditure reductions fell on 'unproductive investment' in transport and communications, education, housing and health. The general neglect of health care in Eastern Europe provides a vivid illustration of problems resulting from economic stagnation and the failure to invest in infrastructure. In 1985, across the region, average life expectancy (at one year of age) was 3.8 years less than the average for Spain, Portugal and Greece, and it actually declined in 1975–85. In 1985 infant mortality, although declining, was 69% higher than the Western European average. The increased incidence in mortality from cardiovascular disease cannot be attributed to levels of health expenditure alone, but also reflects higher levels of smoking, alcohol consumption and general welfare. However it is probable that these factors are in themselves linked to the poor level of economic performance, including poor diet and the non-availability of alternative forms of entertainment, which, together with low levels of investment in safety equipment at the workplace, are symptoms of an economic crisis (Eberstadt, 1990).

The relatively low priority attached to investment in infrastructure has accelerated economic decline. The availability of telephones in Eastern Europe, for instance, ranges from one-eighth to one-quarter of that in Western Europe, and there has been an inability to benefit from the telecommunications and microelectronics revolutions of the 1980s. Housing shortages have not just created major social and family tensions, as growing numbers of adults were forced to stay with their parents, but have hindered labour mobility, which magnifies the social problems associated with the closure of obsolete industries.

The Eastern European authorities attempted to protect the consumer from the full effect of slow or stagnant growth. Personal consumption, however, grew very slowly during the 1980s, with the growth of wages and money incomes being greater than the available supply of consumer goods. Prices in the state retail networks were fixed centrally and did not fluctuate over long periods of time, as part of a deliberate social policy to subsidize basic staple goods to keep prices 'pro-poor'. In state retail markets of virtually all the Eastern European economies, therefore, this resulted in an excess of money demand over the available supply of consumer goods. This was reflected in growing queues for, and shortages of, basic staple goods and the growing problems of 'hidden' and 'repressed' inflation.

An indicator of repressed inflation is the growth of deposits in state savings banks which, in part, represented involuntary savings arising from frustrated purchases. The value of total deposits in state savings banks (excluding cash) grew, on average, by approximately 66%, between 1980 and 1988, in all Eastern European countries, except Poland. Here, savings deposits increased eightfold, but prices also grew ninefold. As these savings are entirely uncapitalized they purely reflect demand that has been deferred from an earlier period to a later period. Excess demand, however, also seeped through into the legal and illegal private markets, where prices were substantially higher than those on state markets, creating new sources of private income and wealth. Hidden inflation chiefly occurred in the state sector, when enterprises charged higher prices for spurious 'new' or 'improved' products. The change would be often largely cosmetic, resulting in a higher price being charged for what was, essentially, the same product. In the 1980s the growth of this phenomenon in Eastern Europe means that official statistics may have seriously overestimated the real growth of consumption and output.

It has been argued (Kolodko, 1989) that, by the late 1980s, all the Eastern European economies were suffering, to varying degrees, from a phenomenon which is sometimes called 'shortageflation', that is, the coexistence of widespread consumer shortages in the state sector with price increases in secondary markets. This resulted in renewed pressures for wage increases, as workers attempted to protect their real incomes. They were being forced to meet a growing proportion of their consumption from private markets, on which prices were both higher and rising. Enterprises were willing to grant wage increases, as they knew that any resulting losses would be subsidized by the state budget, further fuelling the inflationary process.

Finally there was the growth of convertible currency indebtedness, which had originally emerged with the failure of the 'import-led' growth strategy of the 1970s. A factor contributing to the increasing debt, in the second half of the 1980s, was the excess demand for investment and consumption resulting from planners' attempts to accelerate the growth rate. By the end of 1989 three Eastern European countries, Poland, Hungary and Bulgaria, had acute problems of external indebtedness. At the end of 1989 Poland's gross convertible currency debt amounted to US \$41,400m. (or \$38,000m. net, that is excluding Polish assets at Western banks), equivalent to some 550% of the annual value of exports, a debt/export ratio that is as serious as that of the more heavily indebted Latin American countries. Interest payments alone used 33% of convertible currency earnings. In the 1980s most of the growth in debt was caused by the capitalization of unpaid interest, not from the purchase of capital resources. Hungary's gross debt of \$20,700m. (\$19,300m. net) represented the highest debt per head of population in the bloc (just under \$2,000 per head), but its debt/export ratio was relatively low, at 344%. Interest payments absorbed 21% of convertible currency export earnings. Bulgarian gross debt increased threefold, from comparatively safe levels in 1985 to \$9,500m. (\$8,500m. net) at the end of 1989, giving a debt/export ration of 435%, with interest payments taking up 26% of convertible currency export earnings (figures from WEFA, 1991).

The level of convertible currency debt was of less concern in Czechoslovakia, the German Democratic Republic (GDR–'East Germany') and Romania. However the foreign trade relations of these countries did still display signs of systemic weakness. Czechoslovakia, which had pursued a more conservative borrowing strategy in the 1970s, had a relatively modest gross debt of \$7,900m., at the end of 1989, equivalent to 17 months of convertible currency exports, but there were worrying indications that debt was rising quickly, in response to the growing pressure to increase convertible currency imports. East German debt remained reasonable, at \$10,900m., partly as a result of the relatively favourable terms on which it received credit from the then Federal Republic of Germany (FRG–'West

Germany'). Romania had succeeded in eliminating its gross debt entirely during the course of 1989 and, by the end of that year, was a net creditor nation. However this had only been achieved by a drastic reduction in imports, which was continued throughout the 1980s. This policy had imposed draconian restrictions on household consumption of energy and foodstuffs, to the extent that living standards were the lowest in Europe (with the possible exception of Albania). Furthermore, the almost total elimination of imports of machinery, equipment and spare parts has had a devastating impact on that country's economy.

THE CAUSE OF THE ECONOMIC CRISIS

The Origins of the Stalinist Economic System in Eastern Europe

The common nature of the economic problems confronting the Eastern European economies at the end of the 1980s suggests that they originated from a common set of causes. There is widespread agreement among economists, from both Western and Eastern Europe, that these problems were systemic in origin and could be attributed to the imposition of the specific Soviet model of central planning, in each country of the bloc, following the Communist assumption of power in 1948. These problems were aggravated by the introduction of an import-substituting model of industrialization, which was adopted by Stalin in the USSR, in the 1930s, in response to the specific internal and external circumstances facing his country at that time. The policy was singularly inappropriate for the smaller, relatively resource-poor and trade-dependent economies of Eastern Europe in the post-Second World War era.

The Soviet Growth Model and the Redirection of Eastern European Trade

In the 1930s the USSR achieved a high rate of growth in industrial output by maintaining a high rate of growth of inputs (labour, capital and raw materials) to industry. This strategy placed more emphasis on mobilizing resources to meet centrally-determined targets and less emphasis on improving the efficiency with which inputs were used. The strategy also made extensive use of non-indigenous technology, frequently constructing huge new plants that replicated processes which were then in use in Europe and the USA. A high rate of growth of the capital stock was achieved by devoting a relatively large proportion of national income to investment, which was concentrated in the heavy engineering and metallurgical industries. A high rate of growth of the industrial labour force was achieved by the forced transfer of labour from agriculture and by increased female participation in the industrial labour force. The policy of rural collectivization was an essential part of this strategy, as it accelerated the movement of labour from agriculture to industry and facilitated the extraction of a surplus of food and raw materials from the rural sector to the towns. The extraction was at relatively favourable prices, which in turn facilitated the rapid growth of investment. The demand for raw materials created by this policy was met from domestic sources and, in particular, by exploiting the mineral wealth of Siberia, again, often by the use of forced labour.

This economic strategy was transferred to Eastern Europe, in the period from the end of the Second World War to the death of Stalin (in 1953). In 1945–48 the Eastern European countries started to create 'mixed market economies', in which some large-scale industries were nationalized, but small-scale industry, handicrafts, services and agriculture remained in private ownership. During this period the coalition governments advocated a strategy of 'balanced industrialization', involving government policies to stimulate a level of industrialization, but which took into account the comparative advantages of the countries concerned and their natural resource endowment. Following the Communist assumption of power in Eastern Europe, in 1948, each of the Eastern European countries adopted the highly centralized Soviet model of a command economy (the operation of which is analysed below). At the same time the Communist governments accelerated plans to develop an industrial base, increasing the proportion of national income devoted to investment and concentrating a greater share of this in heavy industry. Following the outbreak of the Korean conflict, in 1950, the development of heavy industry in each Eastern European country was revised upwards, under Stalin's instructions. In the 1951–55 plan period each country was instructed to increase its investment in heavy engineering goods. The aim was to double or treble the output of producers' goods and heavy engineering products, in order to meet the Soviet demand for engineering products and weaponry, which was generated by the war in Korea.

The rapid development of heavy industry increased Eastern European demand for energy and raw materials in general, and for iron ore, coal and coking coal, ferrous and non-ferrous metals and crude petroleum in particular. The Eastern European countries are not well-endowed with raw materials and energy. Poland has major deposits of coal, while Romania was a substantial net exporter of petroleum at the end of the Second World War (and continued to be a net exporter until 1977) and also possesses soon-to-be depleted reserves of natural gas. The other major Eastern European sources of primary energy consist of brown coals and lignites, which are low in calorific content, but extremely high in pollutants. Although the Eastern European countries have some mineral deposits (including rich deposits of uranium in Czechoslovakia), the majority are not sufficiently rich to justify commercial exploitation. Nearly 90% of Soviet and Eastern European reserves of fossil fuels, and nearly all of the economically-viable deposits of iron ore, are located in the USSR.

The imposition of Stalinist industrial priorities in Eastern Europe resulted in growing Eastern European dependence on Soviet energy. Meanwhile the excessive development of heavy industry exceeded Eastern, and Western, European demands for these products. Eastern European industry was therefore forced into long-term dependence upon the Soviet market.

The CMEA and trade with the USSR

The foundation of the Council for Mutual Economic Assistance (CMEA—sometimes known as Comecon), in January 1949, formalized the division of Europe into two separate trade blocs. Between the World Wars the Eastern European economies had been largely dependent upon trade in western and central Europe, with Germany in particular, and had conducted a relatively small volume of trade with the USSR. The start of the 'Cold War', in the 1940s, led to Stalin's veto on Eastern European participation in the US-financed European Reconstruction Programme ('Marshall Plan') and the establishment of Western restrictions on the export of strategic goods to Communist countries (administered by COCOM—the Co-ordinating Committee for Multilateral Export Controls). The Eastern European economies, therefore, were forced to reorientate their trade towards the USSR.

Economic integration in the CMEA was hampered by the failure to develop a properly functioning financial and monetary system, which, in turn, is an indication of the underdeveloped role of money and price relations in the domestic economic system (see below). The absence of an adequate means of payments for settling international accounts has meant that the individual Eastern European countries have been reluctant to incur surpluses in their trade with one another. Trade relations between the Eastern European countries have been reduced to a series of cumbersome bilateral barter arrangements. It has been argued (Holzman, 1985) that the CMEA was not just a trade-diverting customs union, but a trade-destroying customs union. That is, although the CMEA countries displayed a preference to conduct trade inside the bloc, even when it would have been advantageous to conduct trade outside the bloc, intra-CMEA trade itself was below optimal levels.

The overexpansion of heavy industry in Eastern Europe placed considerable strain on the Soviet ability to meet Eastern European demands for energy and raw materials. The USSR had abundant reserves of energy (particularly petroleum and gas). The problem is that the major deposits are located in the exceedingly harsh and distant terrains of Siberia, which involves a higher marginal cost of development and transportation to Eastern Europe than alternative sources of supply from world markets. The USSR, however, continued to supply energy to Eastern Europe, until 1990, on terms that were more favourable to Eastern Europe than the latter could have obtained from trading in world markets. The USSR exported petroleum and gas to Eastern Europe at prices that were substantially below world market prices. It also imported manufactured goods from Eastern Europe, at prices which were closer to the world market price for equivalent goods, but which did not reflect their inferior quality. The cost of this arrangement to the USSR grew substantially following the two major increases in world petroleum prices in 1973 and 1979. This pricing arrangement could represent a deliberate subsidy to Eastern Europe (reaching a maximum of US $18,600m., in 1981, according to the estimates of Marrese and Vanous, 1983). In exchange, the USSR received the security benefits offered by the the ability to station troops in Eastern Europe and the allegiance of the Eastern European governments.

Soviet representatives to the CMEA repeatedly expressed their concern at, and attempted to limit, the high costs involved in meeting Eastern European energy needs. From the late 1960s until the late 1980s the USSR principally concentrated on attempts to secure Eastern European co-operation in joint projects to develop Soviet raw materials and energy for bloc consumption. A number of such proposals (the most successful of which included Eastern European participation in the construction of a natural gas pipeline, with repayment in the form of products) were agreed and put into operation during the 1970s. There were, however, major problems concerning the evaluation of participants' contributions and receipts.

Eastern European dependence upon Soviet energy still continued to grow after 1974. By 1987 31% of Eastern European energy consumption was met by imports from the USSR: Bulgaria was dependent on the USSR for 68% of its consumption; Hungary for 46%; and Czechoslovakia for 40%. Although the USSR continued to supply Eastern Europe with energy on relatively favourable terms, the price of Soviet petroleum exports to Eastern Europe increased ninefold between 1974 and 1984 (Dietz, 1986). The volume of Soviet imports from Eastern Europe doubled over the same period, while the volume of Soviet exports to Eastern Europe only increased by 38%, which contributed to Eastern European economic problems in the early 1980s. During the mid-1980s the USSR unsuccessfully sought to increase the volume of Eastern European agricultural products and to improve the quality of Eastern European manufactures, which it imported (Smith, 1991). The Eastern Europeans remained dependent upon the USSR both as a major market for exports and as the source of its most vital import.

Following the collapse of world petroleum prices in 1986 the USSR increased the volume of crude petroleum exported to the West, in order to maintain hard currency earnings, and it came under increasing economic pressure to reduce energy exports to Eastern Europe. During 1989 and 1990 the USSR experienced major difficulties in meeting contracted delivery schedules to Eastern Europe, resulting in further economic dislocation in the region. In December 1989 the Soviet prime minister announced that, from January 1991, trade between the USSR and Eastern Europe would be conducted in convertible currency. This move contributed to the halving of intra-CMEA trade in the first quarter of 1991, resulting in major economic difficulties for the Eastern European economies. Formal proposals to dissolve the CMEA were announced on 18 May 1991 and, in June, the member countries agreed that the organization would be dismantled within 90 days. The future of some CMEA bodies, and the impact of the ending of the USSR and creation of the Commonwealth of Independent States on Eastern European economies, remained uncertain.

THE EASTERN EUROPEAN ECONOMIC SYSTEM, 1948–89

The basic features of the Eastern European economic system were established following the Communist accession to power in 1948. This consisted of the replacement of a market economy with a Soviet-style central planning bureaucracy. It involved the nationalization (normally without compensation) of large-, medium- and small-scale industries and services; the abolition of the majority of private retail and wholesale markets, to be replaced by state-run networks for retail trade and the administration of inter-enterprise supplies (wholesale trade); the abolition of capital and financial markets and their replacement by a single state banking (monobank) system, which involved a greatly enhanced role for the state budget in financial investment; the destruction of existing money wealth by a combination of excessive printing of money, leading to an exceptionally high rate of inflation ('hyperinflation'), and a confiscatory money reform; the establishment of a centrally-administered state monopoly of foreign trade; and the collectivization of agriculture (which was reversed after the death of Stalin, but reimposed in each country, except Poland, after 1957).

The critical distinguishing feature of the economic system that emerged after 1948 was the passive, accountancy function attributed to money and prices, following the destruction of the financial system. Both retail and wholesale prices were fixed by the central authorities and remained unchanged (frequently for several years) and did not respond to changes in supply and demand. Excess demand for a product in the retail market was largely reflected in queues and shortages and did not evoke an increase in supply. Similarly, enterprise production decisions were largely unaffected by the prices of either inputs or outputs.

The broad range of economic decisions about who produces what, where and how, which are normally taken in a market economy by the enterprises responding to price and profit criteria, were taken by central planners. The economy was not so much centrally planned, but centrally administered, in that central planners were responsible for a large number of routine operational decisions. The process of drawing up detailed plans (plan formulation) and putting them into practice (plan implementation) necessitated the creation of a hierarchical administrative planning bureaucracy with its apex at the central planning agency and its base at the productive enterprise.

The principal intermediate agencies in the planning process were industrial ministries. These exercised operational responsibility for an entire industrial sector (such as machine tools, chemicals, electric power) and were further subdivided into departments, which exercised more detailed control over specific products. In addition 'functional' ministries were responsible for administering prices, investment, foreign trade, etc. The system was explicitly designed to ensure that economic control was exercised by people who were politically reliable (the nomenklatura) and who had to be party members.

The enterprise in this system was entirely a creature of the state and had no independent existence. It did not control the prices of its inputs or its outputs, which were fixed by the state. It did not choose its suppliers or the users of its products, which were determined by the state. Similarly it was only entitled to receive such inputs as it had been allocated by the state and could not, legally, buy additional inputs from suppliers. Although the enterprise maintained independent accounts, profits arising from its activity belonged to the state and were returned to the state budget. Similarly, losses from its activity were normally underwritten by state budget subsidies (the 'soft' budget constraint). The enterprise did not own its assets and did not have the right to dispose of them. Investment in the enterprise normally took the form of a state budget grant. The enterprise could be merged or disbanded by the state.

In theory, all decisions concerning the enterprises' inputs and outputs were taken by the state planning apparatus. Perfect centralization of decision-making, however, would have required central planners to possess detailed information about every enterprise, and even workshop, under their jurisdiction and to send out precise instructions, specifying in minute detail what should be produced (and where, when and how). It would also have required the formulation of a system of incentives (or sanctions, or both) to ensure that plan instructions were implemented to the letter, at lower levels in the hierarchy. In practice this remained an impossible task and information had to be aggregated according to a common denominator (normally expressed in physical units, such as tons of steel, numbers of cars, etc.), and then disaggregated as it passed up and down the planning hierarchy. Central planners drew up highly aggregated output instructions, which were then passed down to enterprises, with a greater degree of detail being added at each stage of the process. Enterprises in turn passed up information concerning production possibilities and the levels of inputs that would be required to achieve plan targets. Central planners in Eastern Europe worked with data relating to very basic economic aggregates, while a far greater degree of detail was left to the lower level authorities. In practice this gave enterprise managers a considerable degree of control over their economic environment, which they could use to ensure that they both received plans that could be relatively easily fulfilled, and that they received an adequate supply of inputs to meet plan targets.

ECONOMIC GROWTH AND THE RATCHET PRINCIPLE

Central planning enabled planners to direct resources towards the fulfilment of long-term economic strategies. In the early 1950s the Eastern European planners were principally concerned with the problem of repairing war-damaged economies and creating an industrial base. At that time central direction involved the construction of large new plants (often in 'green-field' sites), together with related workers' hostels, housing and other facilities. During this period central planners could exercise a considerable degree of influence over output and growth rates simply by determining the structure of investment. According to official statistics, in the early 1950s industrial output growth in each of the Eastern European countries exceeded 10% per year. However, as new plants came into use, a greater proportion of output was determined by the production capacity of existing plants. The maintenance of high planned growth rates depended to a greater degree on expanding output from existing plants. Furthermore, the more industrialized central European countries (Czechoslovakia, the GDR and, to a lesser extent, Hungary), which did not have large labour surpluses in agriculture, were finding it increasingly difficult to transfer labour from agriculture into newly-constructed factories. They were starting to experience labour shortages by the late 1950s (W. Brus, 1986). This problem was less severe in the agrarian economies of the Balkans and Romania, where the industrial force continued to grow at a relatively rapid rate until the late 1970s.

In response to political pressures to maintain growth rates, central planners simply 'ratcheted' aggregate plan targets upwards, from the output level that had been achieved in the previous year, in order to obtain the aggregated growth targets that had been established in the five year plan. The new output target was then passed on to industrial ministries, who similarly added a few percentage points to each individual enterprise's output target, in order to arrive at the aggregate target for the industry under its jurisdiction. The desire of central authorities to generate rapid output growth (with a lower priority attached to the efficient use of resources) also led to the preoccupation with gross output targets. Enterprise managers were rewarded for the fulfilment, or overfulfilment, of planned output targets (normally specified in gross physical units) by the payment of money bonuses, which were distributed to both management and workers. Other, non-monetary, material rewards (for example, improved social facilities at the enterprise) were also linked to the overfulfilment of gross output targets. Failure to fulfil gross output targets could also result in sanctions being taken against the manager.

The importance of gross output targets meant that enterprise managers knew that they would always have a guaranteed and rising demand for their output. The enterprise manager's problem, therefore, was the opposite of that which faced a manager in a market economy. The latter's primary problem is finding a market for production (demand constraints). The enterprise manager's problem became one of ensuring that the enterprise could obtain all the supplies necessary to meet centrally-determined output instructions (supply constraints).

The 'ratchet principle' also meant that enterprise managers knew that next year's plan target, and the level of inputs they would receive, depended on output and consumption in the current year. Consequently, they had an incentive to produce below their real production potential and to overindent and overconsume inputs each year. Once an enterprise had obtained an output plan that could be fulfilled easily, it had an incentive to overfulfill the plan by only a small margin, to prevent a sharp increase in subsequent plan targets. Similarly an enterprise had an incentive to accept (and hoard, consume or barter) any inputs offered to it (which were effectively costless), to

ensure it would have adequate supplies for the period when plan targets were increased.

A number of critical problems resulted from the use of gross output indicators for bonus formation. Enterprises were not subject to competitive pressures and had little interest in either the quality of their output or whether the assortment of products (sizes, colours, etc.) corresponded with consumer wishes, provided it met the specifications established in plan targets. Manufactured consumer goods (for which plan targets were frequently specified in volume terms) were frequently faulty and obsolete, in comparison with products in world markets, and might even lack vital components. If output targets were specified in terms of weight, enterprises would concentrate on the production of heavier items in their production range. Another related problem included 'storming'. This was the rush to fulfil a production task before the end of the plan period, in order to achieve a bonus, again at the expense of quality and, sometimes, involving high-cost, short-term measures to overcome supply shortages.

The most critical problem was the bias against innovation and the diffusion of new technology at the enterprise level. Enterprises operating with a guaranteed market for their products and enduring difficulties in obtaining supplies, preferred to maintain existing product ranges, rather than attempt to bring out a new product, as this was likely to incur start-up problems (particularly if it required altering the input mix), which would jeopardize the fulfilment of plan targets and bonuses. The system effectively punished innovation at the enterprise level. Similarly, the absence of competitive pressures meant that new products and processes were diffused through the economy far more slowly than in a market economy.

A Hungarian economist argues that these phenomena result principally from the 'soft' budget constraint (Kornai, 1980). Enterprises in a capitalist market economy face 'hard' budget constraints. If they fail to cover their costs, fail to modernize production or make poor investment decisions, they risk the ultimate prospect of either bankruptcy or take-over. East European enterprises, however, have traditionally had a soft budget constraint. Managers were aware that cost over-runs would be met by state budget subsidies, and, consequently, had no incentive either to produce goods demanded by the markets, or to reduce their costs of production. Similarly, workers who had guaranteed employment at their workplace had no fear of unemployment resulting from poor or shoddy work.

ECONOMIC REFORMS IN EASTERN EUROPE

Despite the rapid rate of growth in industrial output, achieved throughout the region in the early 1950s, living standards deteriorated in the period up to the death of Stalin, in 1953 (Brus, 1986). Most of the gains of industrial growth were either being reinvested in industry or were being directed as exports to the USSR. Living standards did improve slightly, following a transfer of resources towards consumption, during the 'New Course' from 1953–56. It was, however, insufficient to stop open rebellion against the system in Poland and Hungary, in 1956, which surfaced following Khrushchev's de-Stalinization speech in February 1956. While the events of 1956 indicated that radical economic reforms and a change in industrial priorities would be needed to avoid further popular unrest, the Soviet invasion of Hungary, in 1956, revealed the political limits to the reforms acceptable to the Soviet leadership.

A first, cautious attempt to introduce economic reforms was taken in the central European countries of the bloc in the late 1950s. Official reform proposals were published in Poland (1956–57), including an attempt to establish workers' councils as management bodies, and in Czechoslovakia (1958), while economic specialists drafted a quasi-official reform document in Hungary (1957). The first phase of the reforms was largely restricted to measures making prices reflect domestic production costs and giving state enterprises greater powers to determine their own output levels, according to profitability criteria. However they had little practical impact on domestic economic performance and were effectively abandoned by the late 1950s.

A second attempt to introduce economic reforms was undertaken in each of the Eastern European countries in the mid-1960s. This was partly stimulated by growing labour shortages in Czechoslovakia, Hungary and the GDR. These shortages, together with the problem of obtaining supplies of energy and raw materials, were making it increasingly difficult to secure economic growth by the traditional 'extensive' method, of increasing inputs to industry, and implied a greater importance for the efficient use of resources. This, in turn, seemed to require a move away from the development of additional green-field sites. Instead, there was a need for the use of more labour-saving technology and the modernization of machinery and equipment at existing plant, together with closure of obsolete plant, to permit the relocation of labour to modern enterprises.

Equally critically, growing pressure for economic reform in the USSR, initiated by Khrushchev (reflected in the publication of far-reaching proposals by the Soviet economist, E. G. Liberman, in *Pravda*, in September 1962) changed the political environment in which reform discussion took place. Reform proposals in the GDR, Bulgaria, Poland and Romania were relatively cautious, and were similar to those introduced by Kosygin in the USSR in 1965. They involved attempts to preserve the power of central planning organs to determine major economic decisions, while freeing them from day-to-day involvement in routine enterprise decisions. This involved attempts to find new enterprise indicators, which reflected the need to economize on the use of inputs, to replace the old gross output indicator. These varied from country to country, and were frequently altered. Attempts included net output (gross output minus the value of inputs), profit rates (net output minus labour costs, expressed as a proportion of fixed and working capital) and industrial sales (output accepted by another enterprise or wholesale unit).

The reforms also imitated the Soviet reforms by creating a new middle tier of management, between the enterprise and the ministry. This was achieved by amalgamating enterprises into new administrative units, which frequently incorporated a joint research and development unit. The intention was to bring ministerial officials and research and development units closer to production and to simplify co-ordination by increasing vertical and horizontal integration. Enterprise amalgamations, however, tended to strengthen and formalize the already-strong monopolistic tendencies in the economy. Although enterprises (or their parent body) were also granted greater freedom to enter long-term supply contracts with other enterprises, they faced little or no competition and, similarly, had little or no choice over suppliers. They remained essentially supply constrained. Likewise, although the reforms included changes to wholesale prices, this usually involved a single updating of prices to take account of higher energy costs. Where prices were determined by negotiations between enterprises, persistent shortages meant that prices tended to rise to centrally determined ceilings.

Reforms to the system of industrial management in Bulgaria, the GDR, Poland, and Romania left the essential features of the traditional economic system intact. Enter-

prises continued to function as production units and received compulsory output targets (frequently specified in gross outputs) from central authorities, and had little genuine autonomy. Changes in enterprise indicators were primarily intended to provide enterprises with an incentive to economize on the use of resources. Enterprise profits remained the property of the state, and the level of profits to be paid to the state budget, or to be retained by the enterprise (for money bonuses or decentralized investment) was negotiated on a case-by-case basis, not according to fixed rules. Prices remained centrally determined, money remained passive and the state monopoly of foreign trade remained intact.

More far reaching reforms were launched in Czechoslovakia and Hungary. The Hungarian New Economic Mechanism (NEM) was introduced after four years of preparatory discussion, in January 1968. It was intended to reduce the scope of central planning to merely establishing long-term (upwards of five years) macroeconomic targets and to investing in key sectors. Enterprises no longer received annual plans, but were to draw up their own strategies, after considering the general proposals of the Five-Year Plan. The central administration of inter-enterprise supplies was abandoned and enterprises were expected to find their own sources of supply. Planners guided enterprises towards long-term targets by the use of financial instruments, including prices, exchange rates, bank credits and rules on wage determination (Marer, 1986). In principle, enterprises were instructed to maximize profits, which could be used to pay wage increases, to finance new investment, and to establish reserves. The central authorities attempted to influence the use of profits by differentiating taxes according to the use to which profits were put and, in particular, by charging punitive taxes on wage increases above a centrally determined norm. A comprehensive price reform was introduced, which linked prices to production costs.

The Czechoslovak reforms of 1967–69 were even more radical than the Hungarian NEM. They explicitly regarded economic and political reforms as interdependent. Czechoslovak reformers (Sik, 1967) explicitly regarded worker alienation created by the political system as a major factor contributing to poor economic performance in the 1960s. However they argued that the political system itself could not be changed unless central planning was replaced by a market system. Unlike the NEM, market and financial criteria were not considered to be subordinate to plan criteria, but were to become the major determinant of economic activity (Kohoutec, 1968). Enterprises were to become self-managed, with elected workers' councils responsible for major decisions. Enterprises could choose suppliers and markets, and could elect to merge with other enterprises if they wished. Prices, eventually, would be determined by supply and demand. Enterprises would not receive compulsory plan targets, but would attempt to maximize net income, which would be divided between wage payments, investment, social investment, etc. Enterprise taxes were to be differentiated, according to the uses to which enterprise income was to be put. The economy was to be opened to foreign competition. The state would determine long-term economic policy largely through influencing strategic investment decisions, through the medium of an interventionist state banking system.

The attempt to introduce market-orientated reforms in Hungary and Czechoslovakia (and, to a lesser extent, Poland), combined with the limited moves towards economic decentralization in the USSR and Eastern Europe generally, in the mid-1960s, opened the way for the discussion of the use of market forces to stimulate economic integration in the CMEA. These proposals also placed greater emphasis on opening the Eastern European economies to Western competition and on utilizing Western technology. At one extreme, this could have resulted in the development of a form of market-socialist customs union, incorporating Czechoslovakia, Hungary, Poland and, possibly, even Yugoslavia. This prospect, and the perception that successful political and social reform in Czechoslovakia would lead to pressure for political reform in other Eastern European countries and the USSR itself, were major factors contributing to the Warsaw Pact invasion of Czechoslovakia in August 1968. The economic reforms in the majority of socialist (Communist) countries were substantially diluted in the period just before and after the invasion of Czechoslovakia (Smith, 1983).

Although Hungary continued to implement the NEM, reforms were confined to the economic arena and were not allowed to challenge the authority of the Communist party. A major recentralization of economic administration took place in 1972–79, although this did not amount to a formal abandoning of the NEM. This partly indicated the authorities' desire to protect loss-making industries, following the increase in world petroleum prices in 1973, but also revealed anxiety at the widening of income differentials and the growing importance of private sector activity. The period from 1979 to 1990 saw a reaffirmation of the principles of the NEM. Furthermore, there was an extension of the use of financial and market levers, to such a degree that it represented a major departure from the traditional economic system.

The principal changes introduced between 1979 and 1990 included the dismantling of large enterprises and new rules to encourage the development of small enterprises in the state, co-operative and private sectors. It was intended to increase competition and provide a greater incentive to innovation and the development of new products (Hare, 1987). Other reforms included an easing of the restrictions on private sector activity and increased scope for the private sector, such that, by 1989, any private individual or organization could employ up to 500 workers; price reforms, including the gradual abolition of subsidies, which brought domestic relative prices closer to world market prices; the break-up of the monobank system, in 1985, and the development of a Western-type, two-tier banking system, based on a central bank and a series of commercial banks (which became independent in 1987); the establishment of a bond market, whereby local authorities (in 1981) and then enterprises (in 1983) could issue and buy bonds, with the right to buy bonds extended to individuals in 1983; the development of a share market and the reopening of the Budapest Stock Exchange, in 1989, with the possibility of foreign ownership of shares; the decentralization of foreign trade and, in particular, of export rights to all enterprises (1989) and the introduction of a single, unified exchange rate; changes to and experiments with the system of enterprise management and employee relations, including the establishment of workers' councils and the formation of workers' co-operatives and associations within the enterprise, and the election of managers by workers; and, finally, in 1988, the introduction of a non-discriminatory, *ex ante* tax system based on corporation tax, value added tax (sales tax) and a progressive income tax system (Hare, 1987; Marer, 1986; Richet, 1990).

EAST–WEST TRADE

As part of the adoption of the Soviet system of planning, the Eastern European economies also adopted the Soviet foreign trade system, incorporating a state monopoly of foreign trade. The essential features of this system were that all foreign trade relations were conducted by a ministry of foreign trade (or its subordinate bodies) and that enterprises and individuals were not permitted to engage directly in import or export activities. The domestic price system was separated from world market prices, while the domestic currency was nominally linked to world market currencies by an arbitrary, and highly overvalued, official exchange rate. Eastern European currencies were inconvertible, in the sense that the currencies were not traded in international financial markets, residents could not convert the currency into another currency and foreigners could not purchase the currency. Special arrangements and exchange rates were introduced to cover the currency needs of visitors.

Eastern European enterprises were protected from foreign competition by the state monopoly of foreign trade and, as they were provided with a guaranteed domestic market for their products, had no need to compete in foreign markets. They were consequently isolated from international technical developments. Since the Second World War, multinational corporations, seeking foreign markets for their products and cheaper sources of labour, have become a major source of international technology transfer. The Eastern European economies found themselves increasingly unable to compete in world markets, by isolating themselves from the marketing and production activities of multinational corporations.

In the mid-1960s the majority of the Eastern European economies attempted to expand trade links with the West. The more radical reformers in Czechoslovakia and Hungary had envisaged opening their economies to foreign competition as part of a complete reform package designed to stimulate efficiency. However the strategies pursued by the Eastern European economies in the late 1960s and early 1970s were largely seen as a substitute for radical domestic reform. This strategy involved attempts to establish trade relations and co-operation ventures with Western multinational corporations and was intended to enable the Eastern European partner to acquire Western technology. The aim was to modernize industry, but neither to allow the foreign partner to exercise genuine ownership or control over the resulting operation nor to have direct access to the Eastern European market. It was initially hoped that Western corporations would be interested in a number of forms of joint production ventures (whereby the Western partner would supply physical capital, in exchange for repayment in products) and joint ventures, in which the Western partner could have minority participation. However the low level of control offered to potential Western partners (particularly when compared with establishing wholly-owned subsidiaries in newly-industrializing economies in South-East Asia) meant that they were not particularly enthusiastic about this form of co-operation. Consequently the Eastern European economies were forced into greater reliance on direct purchases of Western licences, of Western plant and equipment and of complete installations (turnkey projects), chiefly paid for by credits denominated in convertible currency. It was intended that the Eastern European countries would export a significant proportion of the production of the new plants to Western markets, earning the convertible currency both to service debt (that is, to pay the interest on the loan) and, eventually, to repay the credits. However the Eastern European economies were unable to generate a large enough volume of 'hard' currency exports to both service debt and repay credits.

This problem has been largely attributed to the failure of the Eastern European governments to adopt the systemic reforms that would have been necessary to make Eastern European goods competitive in Western markets. It has been argued (Poznanski, 1986) that Eastern European exports of manufactured goods were no more sophisticated than those emanating from the newly-industrializing economies of South-East Asia, while less sophisticated Eastern European goods were not competitive with exports from these countries, on grounds of price or quality. As a result, the newly-industrializing economies' share of OECD (Organisation for Economic Co-operation and Development—a forum for the industrialized democracies to co-ordinate their economic and social policies) markets for manufactured goods rose, from 2.8% in 1970 to 8.6% in 1983. Meanwhile, the share of Eastern European products actually fell, from 1.2% to 1.1% over the same period.

Furthermore, the maintenance and operation of the imported equipment also necessitated a constant supply of imported components, spare parts and raw materials, placing further strain on the balance of payments. In Poland the problem was further aggravated by the policy of the Gierek Government, which imported consumer goods to increase living standards, following popular unrest in 1968 and 1971. This, in turn, generated popular expectations about the growth of consumption, but this could not be sustained in the long term. A major debt crisis emerged in the late 1970s. In 1976 the Polish authorities first attempted to cut the growth of investment and then, in 1978 and 1979, the growth of consumption. Under conditions of partly controlled and partly free retail prices, this resulted in both inflationary pressures and shortages. These, together with falls in national income, in 1979 and 1980, were major factors in the emergence of the Solidarność movement (Coffin, 1987; Nuti, 1982).

Eastern European convertible currency debt continued to grow throughout the 1970s and reached a peak of US $67,000m., in 1981. Of this, Poland accounted for $25,000m. and Romania $10,000m. In 1981 and 1982 Poland and Romania respectively were forced to reschedule their debts. This contributed to a major re-evaluation by Western banks of the risks involved in lending to Eastern Europe, which, in turn, resulted in the virtual withdrawal of credit facilities. In the early 1980s the Eastern European economies were forced to reduce convertible currency imports, being unable to expand exports and because of the requirement to reduce their convertible currency debt. Eastern European imports from the OECD (excluding trade between the two German states) fell from $20,700m., in 1980, to only $12,000m. in 1984. The major impact of the reduction was on imports of machinery and equipment and food, as the Eastern European economies attempted to sustain imports of industrial components and materials to keep industrial plant in operation. In the 1986–90 period import restraint could not be sustained, as the Eastern European economies attempted to re-expand their economies. There was, therefore, a further growth of indebtedness, to $90,000m., at the end of 1989.

POST-COMMUNIST ECONOMIC POLICIES

Following the collapse of Communist authority in Eastern Europe, in 1989, the post-Communist governments started to construct capitalist market economies based, essentially, on Western European models: having a large private sector; being open to international trade and foreign investment; having a fully convertible currency; and with the long-term goal of full membership of the EC. The speed of the transition to a market economy will vary from country to country for economic, political and social reasons.

The political break with the Communist past was most pronounced in the economies of central Europe. In October 1990, with German reunification, the GDR, the East German state, ceased to exist as a separate country. The

majority of the goals outlined above (including full membership of the EC) were realized without a transitional period. The post-Communist governments of Hungary and Poland have been the strongest in their rejection of the concept of a 'regulated market economy', as both politically undesirable and economically unworkable. Here, progress towards the introduction of market principles was most advanced, and several of the institutions of a market economy had been created, in embryonic form, under socialist governments. Although the political commitment to the introduction of a market economy is strong in both Czechoslovakia and Hungary, the process of transition is being pursued more gradually than in Poland.

The political transition to post-Communist government in the Balkan states is more complicated. In Romania, the National Salvation Front, which included former Communists in its leadership, won the elections by a large majority. Although the new Government included radical reformers, who espoused a strong commitment to the principles of a market economy, the strength of popular support for these policies remained questionable. In Bulgaria, elections were won by the former Communist Party (renamed the Socialist Party), in June 1990. The following November, however, the Government collapsed, because of widespread strikes, which contributed to virtual economic collapse. An interim 'government of experts' was nominated by President Zhelev, prior to further elections, scheduled for the end of 1991. Political uncertainty and social instability in these two countries will delay, and may considerably complicate, the stated intention to introduce a market economy. As for the economic policies of Albania and Yugoslavia, these will be largely determined by political factors whose outcome is extremely difficult to predict.

The features of the transition to a capitalist market economy can by divided into three basic goals: the elimination and control of hyperinflationary pressures, which has major social ramifications, in the form of increased unemployment; the creation of the legal and economic institutions of a properly functioning market economy; and the introduction of widespread private ownership. The methods used to realize these goals raise questions that cannot be answered purely on grounds of economic efficiency. They have widespread implications for the distribution of income and wealth and for the construction of a society built on democratic principles and the rule of law.

The essential features of the transition to a market economy have been identified by Eastern European economists (and their Western European advisers). The following policies have either been introduced in 1990–91, or are under active discussion in the majority of the Eastern European countries: parliamentary procedures for the creation of the legal foundations and institutions of a market economy, including the creation of stock and commodity exchanges, and a conventional Western European type of two-tier banking system; liberalization programmes, which remove the existing legal restrictions on economic activity; programmes for macroeconomic stabilization, to bring the price stability which is considered an essential prerequisite to the proper functioning of a market economy; price and wage deregulation; programmes for the privatization and demonopolization of industry and services (ranging from the development of a private sector *ab initio* in services and small-scale production and the privatization of small-scale state industry and services, to the eventual privatization and dismantling of large-scale state industry); the introduction of a Western-type of tax system, based largely on income taxes and value added taxes, established according to predetermined rules; the creation of a social welfare system to replace the distribution of welfare through the enterprise; measures to open the economy to international competition, to make the currency convertible and to stimulate foreign investment, both through attracting foreign direct investment, from multinational corporations, and opening domestic capital markets to foreign investors.

PROBLEMS AND PROSPECTS FOR THE TRANSITION

The transition to a market economy will be a long and difficult process. At this stage it is not really possible to draw any general conclusions about how successful the process will be. The elimination of potential hyperinflationary pressure is seen as a necessary prerequisite for the efficient functioning of a market economy and will, therefore, have to be implemented in the early stages of the transition. The most rapid and radical transition to a market economy (known as the 'Balcerowicz Plan') has been implemented in Poland, where the economic problems inherited from the previous regime were the most serious. Here, agriculture was already in predominantly private hands and the Government was confronted by the immediate prospect of hyperinflation, following the removal of retail price controls on a large number of goods by the outgoing Communist government. The Balcerowicz Plan, which came into effect in January 1990, consisted of a tight macroeconomic stabilization programme, combined with the use of price levers, rather than quantitative controls, to regulate the economy, and the formulation of institutional measures for the creation of a market economy (Rosati, 1991). The stabilization plan was drawn up with International Monetary Fund (IMF) support and largely followed IMF guidelines. It can be regarded as a model for the other Eastern European countries, the majority of whom will require and receive IMF support on broadly similar terms.

The Polish stabilization plan consisted of the removal of the majority of remaining price controls, to draw out repressed inflationary pressures, combined with a strict monetary policy, involving an attempt to balance the budget (in practice, a surplus was achieved in the first half of 1990) to prevent the re-emergence of inflationary pressures. Budgetary balance was mainly achieved by the withdrawal and elimination of subsidies on basic staple goods (including food and energy) and subsidies to enterprises. In practice, this was combined with the introduction of real interest rates, higher than the rate of inflation, which also discouraged the granting of inter-enterprise credit. Wages were regulated and kept below the growth of inflation by the imposition of progressive tax penalties on enterprises that paid wage increases higher than norms, which were set at proportions of the official inflation rate. The economy was also exposed to foreign competition by the removal of the majority of restrictions on import and export activity and by the introduction of a single, but devalued, exchange rate, which incorporated the 'current account' or 'residents' convertibility. The latter enables residents to exchange the domestic currency freely into convertible currencies, for the purchase of imported goods. This exposed domestic producers to competition from imports and provided a ceiling to domestic price increases, while the devalued exchange rate both offered an incentive to potential exporters and afforded some protection to domestic producers, through prices, instead of quantitative restrictions on imports.

The positive results of the Balcerowicz Plan were that after an immediate increase in open inflation, which rose to a monthly rate of 79.6%, in January 1990, inflation was reduced to 1.8% by the following August. However, by mid-1991, the monthly inflation rate had increased to about 4%–5%, as some aspects of the tight monetary policy were

eased, and the budget moved into deficit in 1991. The economy was transformed from one of shortage to one of demand constraints in a very short period of time. In the retail sector, street trading grew rapidly and has developed into a more sophisticated shop-based economy, following the privatization of a large number of state retail outlets. Exports to convertible currency markets grew by 40% in 1990, leading to a convertible currency trade surplus. On the negative side, the purchasing power of wages (in terms of wages to retail prices) fell more sharply than expected and, in 1990, GDP fell by 12%. Furthermore, open unemployment grew to 7% of the employed labour force, in 1990, and is expected to grow in 1991, while the removal of subsidies on energy and food has badly affected the poorer members of the community.

Polish critics of the programme argue that, although correct in principle, the stabilization plan was too deflationary and had too severe an impact on production and employment. The stabilization programmes conducted in Hungary and Czechoslovakia have, to date, been less deflationary than those of Poland, in part because the open inflationary pressures inherited from the Communist governments were not so severe, but also reflecting a greater degree of hesitancy and political argument.

Stabilization plans elsewhere in the region may prove to be more gradual and will involve less severe, and less competitive, devaluations, with a slower pace of reduction of budget deficits. In all countries, however, the reduction and eventual elimination of budget deficits is being achieved principally by the reduction of subsidies on basic consumer goods (food and energy) and enterprise subsidies, combined with price liberalization, which will allow increases in costs to be passed on in the form of open inflation. In principle, workers will only receive partial compensation for increased prices, in the form of wage increases, which may be expected to stimulate labour unrest. If the authorities yield to pressure in key sectors, this will result in widening income differentials. The removal of enterprise subsidies will also, inevitably, create greater unemployment in the short term, on account of both pressures to reduce overmanning and the closure of unprofitable enterprises. This may stimulate political demands for a relaxation of policy. The size and duration of unemployment will depend to a considerable degree on the ability to attract an inflow of new investment and on labour mobility. The creation of a properly functioning system of unemployment benefits and work-information networks has become an urgent priority in each country.

In Czechoslovakia the reform programme was constrained throughout 1990 by political disagreements and by nationality problems. In September 1990 the Czechoslovak parliament finally approved a more radical reform programme, drawn up by the market-orientated Minister of Finance, Václav Klaus. It resulted in further currency devaluations, in November and January, and price liberalization on 1 January 1991. Some price controls were retained and the devaluation was less severe relative to that of Poland. This should reduce inflationary pressures, but could make Czechoslovak industry less competitive. Similarly, Romania and Bulgaria, although considered to be at the less radical end of the reform spectrum, have both introduced stabilization programmes which combine reduced subsidies and price increases. In the Romanian case, price increases are being phased in gradually. In the Bulgarian case, budget deficits are being reduced more slowly than in Poland.

Progress towards the creation of the economic and financial instruments of a market economy, and towards privatization in particular, has run into far greater difficulties throughout the region than had been anticipated and has been slower than had been expected by many outside observers. This is, in part, a result of major technical problems about how privatization on such a large scale should be conducted and, in part, over debates about the impact of privatization on the distribution of wealth in the long term. Privatization of small-scale services (particularly retail outlets, handicrafts and some elements of small-scale production) proceeded fairly rapidly in most Eastern European countries during 1990. The major problems have been encountered in attempting to privatize large-scale industry. This is viewed by most reformers as an essential part of the strategy to impose external financial discipline on enterprises, in order to stimulate economic efficiency. In Poland, privatization of industry is also intended to create widespread private ownership of industry, with the intent to achieve the largely political goal of 'popular capitalism'.

A critical problem is that, although the level of household savings is high in relation to the available supply of consumer goods, the stock of money balances is low in relation to the stock of capital to be privatized. As a result, the Polish, Czechoslovak and Romanian programmes are introducing schemes which will involve the distribution, to the adult population, of vouchers which will be used for the purchase of shares. The Czechoslovak scheme envisages that citizens will pay a registration fee, entitling them to purchase vouchers at nominal rates. The Polish scheme anticipates free distribution. Hungary and Bulgaria have rejected voucher schemes. They favour proposals based on the development of capital markets and direct sales of enterprises to domestic or foreign businesses and entrepreneurs, which, it is argued, will stimulate greater economic efficiency.

The transition to a market economy is being conducted against the background of a major industrial recession in Eastern Europe. This is affecting those countries that have yet to implement radical reforms, as well as those that are further along the reform process. The collapse of the central authority and guaranteed state orders has left enterprises with major uncertainties about the demand for their products. This problem has been greatly aggravated by the halving of intra-CMEA trade, in the first quarter of 1991, following the move to trade in convertible currency. In 1990 attempts to attract multinational investment were also disappointing. The need to divert trade to Western markets, to substitute for the lost Soviet market, may prove to be the most critical problem confronting the Eastern European economies, if severe economic hardship is to be avoided.

BIBLIOGRAPHY

Alton, T. P. 'East European GNPs, Domestic Final Uses of Gross Product, Rates of Growth, and International Comparisons', in *Pressures for Reform in the East European Economies*, Vol. 1, pp. 77–97. Washington, DC, USGPO (Joint Economic Committee of the US Congress), 1989.

Brus, W. 'The Peak of Stalinism', in Kaser, M. (Ed.). *The Economic History of Eastern Europe 1919–1975*. Oxford, Clarendon Press, 1986.

Coffin, I. 'East European Debt Problems and Prospects for Trade with the Developed West', in *The Economies of Eastern Europe and Their Foreign Economic Relations*, pp. 311–330. Brussels, NATO, 1987.

Dietz, R. 'Advantages and Disadvantages in Soviet Trade with Eastern Europe: The Pricing Dimension', in *Eastern European Economies: Slow Growth in the 1980s*, Vol. 2. Washington, DC, USGPO (Joint Economic Committee of the US Congress), 1986.

Eberstadt, N. 'Health and Mortality in Eastern Europe 1965–85', in *Communist Economies*, 3, pp. 347–372. 1990.

Hare, P. 'Hungary Internal Economic Developments', in *The Economies of Eastern Europe and Their Foreign Economic Relations*. Brussels, NATO, 1987.

'From Central Planning to the Market Economy: Some Microeconomic Issues', in *The Economic Journal*, 1990.

Holzman, F. D. 'Comecon: A 'Trade-Destroying' Customs Union?', in *Journal of Comparative Economics*, 1985 (pp. 410–423.

Kaser, M. C. 'The Technology of Decontrol: Some Macroeconomic Issues', in *The Economic Journal*, 1990.

Kolodko, G. W. 'Economic Reform and Inflation in Socialism: Determinants, Mutual Relationships and Prospects', in *Communist Economies*, 2, pp. 167–182. 1989.

Kohoutec. 'On Problems of the Plan and Market', in *Czechoslovak Economic Papers*, 1968.

Kornai, J. ''Hard' and 'Soft' Budget Constraint', in *Acta Oeconomica*, Vol. 25, pp. 231–245. 1980.

Marer. 'Economic Reform in Hungary: From Central Planning to Regulated Market', in *Eastern European Economies: Slow Growth in the 1980s*, Vol. 2, pp. 223–98. Washington, DC, USGPO (Joint Economic Committee of the US Congress), 1986.

Marrese, M., and Vanous, J. *Soviet Subsidisation of Trade with Eastern Europe: A Soviet Perspective*. Berkeley, Calif, University of California Press, 1983.

Nuti, M. 'The Polish Crisis: Economic Factors and Constraints', in Drewnowski, J. (Ed.). *Crisis in the East European Economy*, pp. 18–64. London, Croom Helm, 1982.

Poznanski. 'Competition Between Eastern Europe and Developing Countries in the Western Markets for Manufactured Goods', in *Eastern European Economies: Slow Growth in the 1980s*, Vol. 2, pp. 62–89. Washington, DC, USGPO (Joint Economic Committee of the US Congress), 1986.

Richet, X. 'Hungary: Reform and Transition towards a Market Economy', in *Communist Economies*, 4, pp. 509–24. 1990.

Rosati, D. K. 'The Polish Road to Capitalism: A Critical Appraisal of the Balcerowicz Plan', in *Thames Papers in Political Economy*, 2. 1991.

Smith, A. H. *The Planned Economies of Eastern Europe*. London, Croom Helm, 1983.

'Soviet Economic Relations with Eastern Europe under Gorbachev', in Pravda, A. (Ed.). *The Soviet Union and Eastern Europe*. 1991.

WEFA. *CPE Outlook for Foreign Trade and Finance*. Pennsylvania, The WEFA Group, 1991.

SOCIAL POLICY IN EASTERN EUROPE AND THE FORMER USSR

BOB DEACON

INTRODUCTION

As the Communist regimes across Eastern Europe were replaced by new economic and political systems more similar to those of Western Europe, and as the USSR embarked, more uncertainly, on the path of democratization and marketization, one of the tests that future historians might use to evaluate the past and the emerging present will be the extent to which these societies met, and will in the future meet, the welfare needs of their populations. This short assessment of the situation is divided into four parts. Firstly, there will be a summary of the social policy of the old regimes and some description of the legacy of social problems which they bequeathed. This will be followed by a survey of the new social problems and the worsening social conditions, consequent upon the transfer to different economic mechanisms and policies. Thirdly, the broad social policy strategies of the new governments of Eastern Europe and the former USSR will be reviewed, as they attempt to manage both the legacy of social problems from the past and the new social problems of the present. Finally, in more detail and in terms of new social policy and provision, developments in five specific fields will be described: poverty; unemployment and social security; health and medical care; housing; and education. In conclusion there will be a few speculative comments on future developments.

THE LEGACY OF THE PAST

Despite the many shortcomings, until 1989 there was a broadly coherent and, in general terms, similar system of welfare policy and provision in operation across the whole of the USSR and Eastern Europe. The old social welfare contract, between the party–state apparatus, the nomenklatura, and the people, consisted of the provision of highly subsidized prices on food, housing, transport and basic necessities, guaranteed employment, and small differentials between the wages of workers, professionals and managers, in return for the political quietude of the population. There were, of course, hidden privileges available to the nomenklatura, but the important point is that they were hidden, because they breached the essential contract.

This system had its achievements and its shortcomings. Thus the advantages of job security for the many did not counter the inadequacy, or absence, of unemployment benefit. Likewise, although workers' wages compared well with average wages, the Party and state bureaucrats benefited from hidden privileges. Health services were free (apart from bribes and 'gifts'), but inefficient and underdeveloped in the preventative approach to health; there were high mortality and morbidity rates. Working women, especially in the German Democratic Republic (GDR) and Hungary, received favourable treatment, such as three-year child-care grants and the right to resume their previous employment; however there was an obligation on women not only to work but to remain responsible for family care, and the division of labour remained sexist. Accommodation was highly subsidized, through cheap rents and mortgages, but it tended to be the better-off who received the most generous subsidies. The state organized a comprehensive system of social security and sick pay, but there was limited index-linking of benefits and a consequent erosion by inflation. A final example: the advantages of a paternalist system involved a converse disadvantage, in the total absence of the right to autonomously articulate social needs from below.

The system of social welfare, with its achievements and shortcomings described above, was part of a total economic and political system which, in general, eschewed both market mechanisms and political democracy. The consequence was a system that was economically inefficient and insensitive to welfare and consumer needs, which, elsewhere, would find expression either through the ballot box or in a free market environment. The work and welfare guarantees coexisted with an egalitarianism of poverty and an inefficient provision of services.

Social Consequences

The legacy of social problems bequeathed to successor regimes are legion. These include extensive poverty among, in particular, the elderly, larger families, and those such as the Gypsies (Roma) living outside the rigid work eligibility requirements of the system. In the case of the USSR, a 1989 estimate suggested that 7%–8% of the 285m. population were in need of help on account of poverty. In the case of Hungary, it has been shown that, between 1977 and 1987, the proportion of the poor among active wage earners increased; it was about 14% of this group in 1987, according to unofficial figures. Another of the most serious of the bequeathed social problems is that of high mortality rates and excessive morbidity. In general, life expectancy within the USSR and across Eastern Europe has been far shorter than that in Western Europe; for a long period during the 1960s and 1970s, and even into the 1980s, the life expectancy of men of working age was actually declining. Hungary showed the most dramatic decline between 1960 and 1979, across all age groups.

The reasons for this were complex and associated with poor and environmentally unsound working conditions, excessive work (not helped by the prevalence of Stakhanovite economics), poor diet and excess alcohol consumption. Particularly following the anti-alcohol campaign in the USSR, there has been some evidence of a recent, localized reversal in the trend of these figures. Thus, according to unofficial figures, male life expectancy at birth in the USSR, moved from 65.3 in 1960, to a nadir of 62.3 in 1980, before rising slowly to 62.9 in 1983 and 65.0 in 1986.

Housing provision, while cheap and increasing in availability, was still far from adequate to meet the needs in all the countries being surveyed. In Poland, during the 1980s, the average waiting time for a flat was 24 years. Furthermore, according to a 1989 estimate, in the towns 22% of houses were without bathrooms. These figures are not untypical for the other countries of the region.

In education the main problem bequeathed by the Communist regimes was that the system was geared too much to the production of academically and professionally qualified people and too little to the needs of industry. Many graduates found themselves in jobs for which they were over-qualified.

In relation to the social situation of women, the double burden of having to work and care has not shifted. This was in spite of the availability of both work and the provision of welfare, in cash and kind, to facilitate child care. Gender relations remain for the most part unreconstructed.

As for the social situation of ethnic minorities, a more complex conclusion must be drawn. On the one hand the living conditions of Romany people, for instance, across Eastern Europe is very poor; until very recently, for example, Communist urban authorities in Hungary were still building segregated streets for the Roma, with no running water and no sewage systems. On the other hand, within the USSR, the Soviet concern to develop the outposts of the old empire led to the comparable improvement of the social situation of, for example, those living in Soviet Central Asia. Life expectancy and literacy rates are higher than those in comparable countries outside the region. One recent study used average life expectancy at birth as an example: in 1979/80 it was 63.2 years for males and 69.8 for females in Soviet Central Asia (in the USSR as a whole, it was 62.2 and 72.5 respectively); in neighbouring Iran, in 1970, average life expectancy at birth was 55.8 for males and 55.0 for females; in Turkey, in 1980–85, it was 60.0 for males and 63.3 for females.

NEW SOCIAL PROBLEMS OF TRANSITION

With varying degrees of speed and conviction all the countries of Eastern Europe and, more slowly, the former USSR are trying to replace their centralized, command economies and their one-party political systems with economies governed by the rules of the market and by political systems that provide for a degree of democracy. This is having an immediate, and in some cases, dramatic impact upon social conditions across the region. Unemployment is being created, or being made explicit where previously it was hidden. Inflation, often initially very rapid, is eroding living standards that were already low. The removal of subsidies has resulted in a dramatic increase in rents. Previously inefficient and underprovided medical-care establishments have found themselves unable to operate in the new cost-accounting frameworks imposed upon them, and some have closed. Some educational institutions, particularly the Academies of Science, find themselves in a similar situation. Women's child-care support systems and other rights and entitlements, for example, to free abortion services, may be under threat. Ethnic minorities, while gaining the freedom to organize autonomously, find that the same freedom gives rise to increased expression of racism and the intolerance of minorities. Foreign workers are being repatriated. However there have been some examples of positive progress in cultural autonomy: Bulgarian Turks have their names back; Hungarians in Romania can be educated in their mother tongue.

Some of the indicators that measure the immediate impact on the well-being of the population (unemployment, decline in living standards, price rises consequent upon the transfer towards a free market economic system), during the period of transition, are summarized here. The only details for Albania concern unemployment; in May 1991 there were between 50,000 and 90,000 people unemployed, of a total working population of some 1.5m. In Bulgaria the unemployment rate was expected to increase from 0.8% in 1990 to 5.0% the following year; in early 1991 a 30% decline in living standards was estimated for the period of transition; in January 1991 the price of bread was increased by 600% and that of other basic foods by 700%. Czechoslovakia's unemployment was 0.7% in 1990, but was predicted to reach 5.0% in 1991; a 20% decline in living standards was predicted for 1991. In Hungary unemployment was only 1.7% in 1990, with an estimated decline in living standards of 20% during the transition; in January 1990 food prices rose by 38%, rents by 35% and mortgages by between 50% and 100%, while in one year later, bread went up by 38% and milk by 20%. In Poland unemployment was 7.5% in 1990; the decline in living standards was 30% in the same year; in January prices for bread rose by 38%, meat by 55% and electricity by 300%. Romanian unemployment was 2.0% in 1990 and was predicted to rise to 10% in 1991; a 30% fall in living standards was predicted for 1991; and price rises of 100% occurred for some goods in November 1990 and for bread and meat in April 1991, with more rises planned for June. In Yugoslavia unemployment was 16.0% in 1990. In the Russian Federation there were massive price rises on most goods in January 1992. Eastern Germany, formerly part of the region as the GDR, could experience unemployment of up to 50% in 1991, compared to 15% in 1990.

It should be noted that in some countries, such as Poland and Hungary, price rises and the consequent decline in living standards began with the so-called 'shock therapy' programme of reforms, early in 1990. Other countries, such as Czechoslovakia, Bulgaria and Romania, only entered this phase in 1991. The USSR had just begun to do so, in April 1991, and the new Albanian Government had yet to make decisions. In Bulgaria, Romania and the former USSR, price rises are sometimes compensated for with rises in pay and benefits. An overall decline in living standards, of around 30%, and an increase in unemployment, to even 10%, appears to be the price for transition from Communism to capitalism, in the short term. In the former GDR the unemployment consequences are worse.

Emerging Social Policy Strategies

In response to the legacy of social problems of the past, and in recognition of the need to develop social policies that both facilitate the move to marketization but compensate those who are paying the highest price for this, each of the governments of Eastern Europe are developing initial policy responses that are broadly similar. These measures and their immediate consequences include:

An *ad hoc* approach to the development of services for the new unemployed and to the compensation of social security recipients and employees for rapid inflation;

appeals to philanthropy and voluntary effort to compensate for any withdrawn state services;

rapid removal of subsidies on many goods and services, including housing, with limited anticipation of the social consequences;

limited privatization of some health and social care services (this may accelerate);

the flourishing of independent social initiatives in the sphere of social care, but there are evident differences in the capacity of citizens to participate;

desecularization of education and pluralization of control over schools and colleges;

erosion of women's rights to some child-care benefits and services and to free legal abortions (although the final outcome is not clear);

deconstruction of state social security system in favour of fully-funded social insurance funds, often differentiated by categories of worker;

many health and recreational facilities provided by enterprises, for their employees, are being abolished or converted into local community or private facilities;

ending of privileged access by the nomenklatura to special clinics and services;

increase of local community control over local social provision, but in an impoverished context;

tension between the limitation of social citizenship rights for certain ethnic minorities (Roma everywhere, Turks in Bulgaria, Hungarians in Romania), on the one hand, and the increased autonomous articulation of ethnic minority needs on the other;

shift in the nature of social inequalities, in the use of and the access to social provision, from those based on bureaucratic or political privilege, to those based on market relations.

There are, however, some obvious differences between countries, even in the initial responses. Commitment to socialist values and the balancing of egalitarianism and efficiency, and social guarantees and autonomy, still seem to apply in the USSR, Romania and Bulgaria, but not in the rest of Eastern Europe, where the old ideology is abandoned and the inequalities and efficiency of capitalism is favoured instead.

The new civil society and democratic politics appear to hold sway in Czechoslovakia and Hungary, whereas authoritarian populism is a much greater tendency in Poland.

The Roman Catholic Church influences abortion policy and contributes to voluntary provision in Poland whereas the Eastern Orthodox Church in Bulgaria has little to say or do in these areas.

The old social democratic infrastructure is, seemingly, being used in Czechoslovakia, whereas this did not exist elsewhere.

The rapid absorption of the GDR, into the Federal Republic of Germany, has led to a different pace of change.

Although it is too early to draw any firm conclusions about the longer-term direction that social policy will take in each of the countries, some initial speculation might provide a framework for thinking about and analysing events as they transpire. It is evident that Hungary, Poland, Czechoslovakia, and parts of Yugoslavia (Slovenia, for example) are likely to develop into one or other variant of the Western welfare state. Western welfare states range in type from those that provide for a minimal state entitlement and act on the subsidiarity principle (liberal welfare states like the USA), through those that conserve and reflect the inequalities of capitalism within their welfare policy by, for example, providing differentiated benefits according to status (conservative, corporatist welfare states like Germany), to social democratic welfare states that are concerned to redistribute from richer to poorer and extend the full range of services to all social classes (such as Sweden). It seems likely that Czechoslovakia, or certainly the Czech lands, will eventually develop social democratic policies, reflective of the social democratic traditions from the period between the First and Second World Wars. Hungary will probably emerge as a liberal welfare regime. The influence of the Roman Catholic Church in Poland and Slovenia is hard to judge, but something more approaching a conservative, corporatist welfare regime may develop. Romania and countries of the Balkans, such as Bulgaria, Albania and the Yugoslav Republic of Serbia, together with large parts of the former USSR, appear, at this stage, to be developing a new historical variant. There is a less than whole-hearted rush to the capitalist market system; property changes are taking place more slowly, the influence of the Communist ideology of equality and protection for workers is higher, the trade unions still appear to be playing a role and many of the old nomenklatura wish to retain something of the past. A post-Communist corporatism may be developing, which strikes a new balance between efficiency and justice. Negotiations are ensuring that some price rises are being partially, or even wholly,

compensated for with agreed wage rises. This is at the clear cost of less efficiency. It might, however, be that this is a temporary phase, before these countries, too, join the leading market-led countries of the region, Hungary and Poland. Some republics of the former USSR would certainly wish to move more quickly in this direction.

NEW POLICY AND PROVISION

Where this information is available, the basic social policy measures taken in each field, by each country, will be summarized below. Recent social welfare policies in Bulgaria, Czechoslovakia, Hungary, Poland and the USSR are dealt with, in the principal fields of: unemployment benefit; retraining measures; price rise compensation measures; housing policy; medical care policy; and education policy. The information is accurate for mid-1991; policy and provision has been changing rapidly, often by the month, in some countries in this period of transition.

Bulgaria

Unemployment benefit has been introduced, although the level and eligibility was unknown, and retraining was being given a high priority. To compensate for price rises, wages are raised every six months, by 70% of the rate of inflation, or monthly, if inflation exceeds 10% (benefits are similarly protected). In medical policy, the state health service is being retained and doctors' salaries have been increased, but private provision was also being encouraged.

Czechoslovakia

Unemployment benefit was set at 50%–60% of the previous level of earnings, for one year, and then it was to be means-tested; small additional earnings were also allowed. Benefit appeared to be dependent upon accepting retraining (benefits are still received during retraining), and there were enterprise allowances for those hoping to start a business. Compensation for price rises was achieved through minimum wages, according to International Labour Organisation (ILO) criteria, and benefits were raised every three months, in line with inflation; pensions appeared likely to be stabilized at 79% of average real wages. Housing policy involves the gradual reduction of state subsidies, the marketization of new housing and supplementary benefits for those unable to meet new costs. The state health service was being retained, but cost accounting was introduced and private and church provision was permitted under local government control; the introduction of insurance funding seemed likely by 1993. Similarly, in education, the state service continued, but with private and religious schools are allowed.

Hungary

Unemployment benefit was to be paid for one year, at a level proportional to the years of previous work (75% of past earnings with 10 years of employment, 65% with two years and nothing for less), and then at a reduced rate; no casual or parallel employment was permitted and disqualification followed the refusal of a job offer. Retraining schemes were being developed and there were enterprise allowances (the equivalent of two years benefit, available in a single payment). Benefit rises were linked to inflation (an independent social security fund was being established), but there was no systematic policy protecting earnings from the effects of price rises. In housing, the subsidy was gradually being reduced; mortgage payments were increased by 100% or 50%, depending on whether the loan originated more or less than 10 years previously; rents could not exceed 20% of a family's income and pensioners were excluded from any rent rises; and state housing was being sold to tenants. In medical-care policy, a state service was retained, but private facilities were being encouraged and insurance funding was planned. State schooling was being diversified in form and religious schools were permitted.

Poland

If unemployed, benefit levels were 70% of past earnings for three months, 50% for the next six months and then 40%, with a maximum payment set by the average public sector wage and a minimum by the minimum wage; registration for work was compulsory; benefits were forfeited if two job offers, retraining or a public works programme were refused. Retraining was available with 80% of previous earnings, for six or 12 months (100% of previous earnings if redundant and 125% of the minimum wage if no previous work experience), and there were loans available for starting businesses. Policy towards price rises was dictated by the need to prevent compensatory wage claims; pensions and benefits were linked to falling real wage levels; there was a voluntary emergency fund. In the housing sector, the rent subsidy was gradually being reduced, with tenants having to meet the real costs by 1993, but benefits were available if rent exceeded 80% of the family income; house building was being transferred to the private sector. Initially, a state health service was retained, but cost accounting has closed some facilities and there were new charges for some services and for pharmaceuticals; a private sector is envisaged eventually. State schooling has been retained, but with private education now allowed; the optional introduction of religious education, by priests, was being contested.

USSR

Unemployment was not offically acknowledged; no new benefits seemed likely, particularly while it was claimed that all redundant workers were found new employment or retrained on full wages. In April 1991 the 66% price rises were compensated for by an 85% increase in benefit levels for pensioners, students and low-earning families; pensions are set at the level of the minimum wage; wage levels that over-compensate were still being met. Rents, then at 3% of household costs, had not been increased, despite cost accounting measures, and the tenants' right to buy their home (in Moscow) was not being implemented. In medical care, an element of cost accounting has been introduced in some areas of the health service and there is a major anti-alcohol campaign. In education there is an attempt to emphasize vocational, rather than academic, training.

Regional Comparisons and Commentary

In the related fields of unemployment benefit, retraining provision and compensation for price rises consequent upon the move to marketization there are several points to note. There is diversity between countries, ranging from those of the former USSR, where measures to compensate the unemployed have hardly begun, to countries like Poland, where detailed schemes are now in operation. Even here, though, it must be noted that the provision, for example, for labour exchanges and retraining is often only formal, as the network of offices is only just being set up and provision is erratic and underfunded. There is also a broad distinction to be drawn between those countries, for example, Bulgaria, Romania (the details for which are not described above) and the USSR, where price rises were being systematically compensated for (in the case of both workers and welfare beneficiaries) by agreements or regulations about wages and prices promulgated at a national

level, and those countries, for example, Poland, where no such all-embracing wage compensation exists. For those dependent on state benefits (pensioners, the ill, children), the compensation situation is variable. Compensation linked to wage levels, as in Poland, means that these people share in the falling living standards. In Czechoslovakia compensation, or valorization, seems to be connected to price rises.

Housing policy, where it is becoming clear, seems to be taking the same direction in all of the countries, but with the former USSR, Bulgaria and Romania adopting their distinctive pace. The goal, certainly in Poland and Hungary and, to a large extent, in Czechoslovakia, is the removal of state subsidy for rent and mortgages over a three-year period. This is to be replaced by specific, targeted housing, or equivalent, benefits for those who cannot afford to pay. There are differences between countries on what is to be regarded as a reasonable percentage of family income to spend on housing costs: Polish policy favours 80% (including heating and lighting); Hungarians prefer 20%. In Czechoslovakia and Hungary whole categories of persons, such as pensioners, are excluded from rent rises. Another, related, policy is to privatize building and construction and to sell, to sitting tenants, the rented state sector. The development of the second of these aims would seem to depend on the capacity of the tenant to purchase.

In medical-care and education policy there is, not surprisingly, a much greater intention, at least in the short term, to retain a prominent role for the state in policy and provision. There are, however, moves towards cost accounting, which is leading to closures, and towards allowing private health and educational facilities to be developed alongside the state sector. Religious organizations are being allowed an increased influence over both medical-care institutions and medical-care policy and educational institutions and policy. Religious education is returning, both as a separate provision and as a part of the curriculum in all schools. Roman Catholic pressure to change the previously freely-available abortion provision is beginning to be experienced. The salaries of doctors and teachers are being raised everywhere.

There are important features of policy, which are not included above. There is pressure to increase the pension age in Hungary and Bulgaria; in both it is 55 years old for women and 60 for men: the cost is regarded as too high. On the other hand, increasing unemployment may lead to a countervailing pressure.

The existing, often generous, provision of child-care grants and allowances for women is under discussion. It is too early to say whether these will be eroded or whether, again, the countervailing pressures of reducing the unemployment total, by removing women from the figures of the unemployed, will work in the opposite direction. Certainly in Poland, when women registered for the new unemployment benefit, the law was rapidly changed to disqualify from receipt of benefit those who had not worked for at least six weeks in the previous 12 months. The likely outcome is the continuation of grants and allowances for the early years of motherhood but the removal of the right to return to work without loss of status or salary.

New services for the care of dependants, for the alleviation of the new poverty and for coping with the increasing homelessness and destitution are being developed within local areas in many of the countries. Often these are new, voluntary initiatives. They exist, however, within or alongside presently under-funded, ill-organized, local social welfare or social aid services. A large part of the social costs of transition is seemingly being placed on local agencies, which themselves are impoverished because of the new rigours of cost accounting. It is evident that in the short term they are often not coping.

CONCLUSION

It is uncertain whether, during this period of transition, the new governments will succeed in transferring to a market economy and whether the populations will allow this to happen with only partial compensation for their impoverishment and unemployment, owing to the present, haphazard welfare measures. In some countries the process may become frozen into a new type of post-Communist regime, which has only a partially marketized economy, perhaps less efficient, but with many more of the old statist welfare policies and provisions in place. In other countries, variations on the theme of developed welfare capitalism will emerge within the next five years.

BIBLIOGRAPHY

Castles, M., and Deacon, B., et al. *Eastern Europe in the 1990s: Past Development in and Future Prospects for Welfare. London, Sage Publication Ltd, 1992.*

Deacon, B. 'Sociopolitics or social policy: Bulgarian welfare in transition', in IJHS, 17:3. 1987.

Deacon, B. (Ed.). *Social Policy, Social Justice and Citizenship in Eastern Europe.* Aldershot, Avebury, 1992.

Deacon, B., and Szalai, J. *Social Policy in the New Eastern Europe.* Aldershot, Avebury, 1990.

Esping-Anderson, G. *The Three Worlds of Welfare Capitalism.* Oxford, Polity, 1990.

McAuley, A. 'The Central Asian Economy in Comparative Perspective', in *The World Congress of Soviet and East European Studies.* Harrogate, 1990.

Mezentseva, E., and Rimachevskaya, N. 'The soviet country profile: health of the USSR population in the '70s and '80s', in *Social Science and Medicine,* 31:8.

Szalai, J. 'Poverty in Hungary during the period of economic crisis', in *Manuscript,* 1990. Budapest.

Tretyakov, V. *Philanthropy in Soviet Society.* Moscow, Novosti Press, 1989.

THE ENVIRONMENT IN THE REGION

DON HINRICHSEN

'Faced with the threat of environmental catastrophe, the dividing lines of the bipolar ideological world are receding. The biosphere recognizes no division into blocs, alliances or systems. All share the same climatic system and no one is in a position to build his own isolated and independent line of environmental defence.' These words were spoken by Eduard Shevardnadze, when he was the Soviet Minister of Foreign Affairs. Since the 1950s serious environmental problems have emerged in Eastern Europe and the USSR, often providing a focus for opposition to the Communist regimes. With the end of the Cold War and the changes of government in Eastern Europe, environmental concerns increasingly occupied the attention of people in the region. Furthermore, the rest of the world became more aware of the environmental problems affecting Eastern Europe.

There are many examples of the consequences of the lack of attention afforded to environment and resource issues. About 2.6m. people in the Silesian industrial zone, in south-west Poland, have had their health seriously endangered by the prevalent industrial waste. The Vistula is so clogged with pollutants that its waters are unfit even for industrial use along some 80% of its total length. It has been estimated that the river empties over 34,000m. cubic metres of agricultural and industrial waste into the Baltic Sea every year. In Hungary, every 17th death and every 24th disability is attributed, directly or indirectly, to atmospheric pollution. Since 1970, in the industrial town of Bratislava (Czechoslovakia), the incidence of cancers has risen by one-third, heart disease by 40%, infant mortality by two-thirds and miscarriages by one-half, on account of the emissions from nearby industries. Over 1.4m. hectares of forestland in eastern Germany (some 50% of the total) are dying from the effects of acid rain and other pollutants, much of it generated by heavy industries and power plants burning lignite (a variety of brown coal which is of even lower calorific value), a notoriously unclean fuel, without filters on the stacks. Bulgaria suffers from severe atmospheric pollution, considerably above European safety levels. The Volga River, which flows through some of the most heavily industrialized regions in Russia, is so full of untreated industrial and municipal effluents that its waters are biologically dead along most of its length.

Pictures which emerged from Romania in the wake of the revolution did much to alert the attention of the world to the environmental plight of Eastern Europe. The pictures showed whole towns and villages, people as well as buildings and roads, to heavily discoloured and dirty from serious atmospheric pollution. However the single incident which heightened global environmental consciousness more than any other event was the serious accident at the Chernobyl nuclear power station in Ukraine. It has been estimated that about 200 people died as a result of the radioactive contamination, and that the total cost of decontaminating the most seriously affected areas, resettling population and reviewing its nuclear power programme could amount to 30,000m. roubles, by 1995. It has to be recognized, however, that any assessment of the little-known subject of radioactive damage could be seriously underestimated. The long-term health and mortality consequences, and the length of the period for which agricultural land in the area will be blighted, will not be known for many years to come. Even then, it may not be fully acknowledged. Environmental damage from the Chernobyl incident was not restricted to Ukraine; it spread across much of Europe within a few days. Sensitivity to the issue of nuclear power stations was evidenced in 1991, when concern was expressed about Bulgaria's only nuclear power station, at Kozloduy, near the Romanian border. In mid-1991 it was decided that the plant would, eventually, be closed.

On the edge of the university town of Pécs, in southern Hungary, there are two, neighbouring thermal power stations. Both plants burn lignite to produce electricity for a part of the country which is lacking in energy resources. There is a stark contrast between the two plants: on one, the main stack gives out clouds of black smoke; the stack of the other plant emits virtually nothing. The clean plant has been fitted with an efficient Swiss filter, which removes most of the particles and dust; the other has no pollution controls at all. Hungary, like the rest of Eastern Europe and the former USSR, is experiencing a period of turbulence. Despite the dramatic, and sudden, political, economic and social changes, the region still has a grim legacy of 40 years of resource exploitation and environmental neglect. The economic system paid little heed to the human and ecological consequences of five-year plans.

Environmentalists and other authorities describe a legacy of ruined forests and water-systems, damaged by acid rain and other pollutants. Rivers and lakes have been fouled by untreated municipal and industrial wastes, often, it is claimed, almost beyond recovery. Croplands are contaminated by the excessive use of agricultural fertilizers. Ground-water has been poisoned with nitrates and trace metals. There are cities with decaying infrastructures, which are polluted by a virulent assortment of airborne chemicals, generated by outdated smoke-stack industries and vehicles. Furthermore, a neglect of basic environmental safeguards, during the rapid industrialization of the region, has seriously affected the health of millions of Eastern European and former Soviet citizens.

A LEGACY OF ENVIRONMENTAL NEGLECT

The basic cause of such problems is the outdated and inefficient industrial system, patterned after the Soviet models of the 1950s. The 'smoke-stack' industries (such as steel works, chemical and petrochemical plants, the metallurgical, food processing and engineering sectors) suffer from a number of inherent problems. Firstly, many heavy industries in the region burn highly polluting coal, notably lignite, which not only has less energy value per kilogram than coal, petroleum or natural gas, but produces much greater emissions of polluting gases and particles. Secondly, these polluting fuels are burnt in very inefficient ways. It has been calculated that these countries use 50%–100% more energy than the USA to produce one unit of gross domestic product, and 100%–300% more than Japan. Thirdly, most industries and power plants are not fitted with equipment to reduce harmful emissions.

Because of these unfortunate circumstances (the use of brown coal, the inefficient combustion of fuel and no pollution controls on factories and power plants) this region has some of the highest levels of sulphur dioxide emissions in the world. Figures from the mid-1980s confirm that, collectively, Bulgaria, the German Democratic Republic

(GDR), Hungary, Czechoslovakia, Poland, Yugoslavia, Romania and the USSR were emitting around 35.6m. metric tons of sulphur dioxide per year. One coal-burning power plant, in eastern Germany (the former GDR), is alleged to produce some 460,000 tons of sulphur dioxide per year, which is more than the combined total for Norway and Denmark.

The transport sector is equally damaging. Most of the vehicles on Eastern European and Soviet roads are manufactured in the region. Of the eight countries listed above (including the former GDR, but excluding Albania), only Hungary and Bulgaria lack an automobile industry, although they do manufacture buses and heavy goods vehicles. None of the vehicles manufactured in Eastern Europe is fitted with catalytic converters or other sophisticated pollution control devices. Most of the lorries and buses have highly-polluting diesel engines and many are in a bad state of repair, therefore being even more of a hazard. Official figures estimated that 35%–40% of Hungary's 2.3m. lorries, buses and cars should be banned from the roads for health and safety reasons.

Despite the fact that there are fewer cars per head in Eastern Europe than in the West, emissions from vehicles, of hydrocarbons, nitrogen oxides, carbon monoxide and lead, remain high. Cities like Budapest, Prague, East Berlin, Bucharest or Sofia are often covered in a pall of photochemical smog, generated mostly by vehicles and home-heating appliances. Two of the cheapest cars available in Eastern Europe were made in the GDR, the Trabant and the Wartburg. Both contain highly polluting two-stroke engines, which emit greater quantities of hydrocarbons, particles, organic chemicals and carbon monoxide, than normal car engines. These two types of car comprise a significant portion of Eastern Europe's car fleet; more than 40% of Hungary's private cars, for example, are Trabants or Wartburgs. The united Germany has halted production of these cars, but many remain on Eastern Europe's roads. Eliminating the use of such cars is now a priority in many Eastern European countries.

Meanwhile, the region's ground-water reservoirs are also deteriorating in quality, owing to pollution. Industrial and agricultural poisons, particularly nitrates from fertilizers, are seeping into surface- and ground-water resources, fouling them beyond recovery. Hungary has some 3,000 main settlements; about 700 of them (with a total population of some 300,000 people) now have to rely on water brought in by tanker or piped in from neighbouring communities. Their own wells are too polluted with nitrates and other chemicals and cannot be used for drinking water.

Vast amounts of untreated sewage and industrial effluents are pumped into the region's waterways each year. This is a serious problem and one that appears to be getting worse. Czechoslovakia treats only 40% of its municipal wastes, Hungary barely 50%, Poland 35% and the former USSR only 30%.

Many rivers, like the Danube (which flows through six Eastern European countries, including Ukraine), the Vistula in Poland, and the Volga (Russia) are environmental disasters by the time they reach the sea. The Danube carries over 1.7m. metric tons of nutrient pollution into the Black Sea each year, mostly from agricultural run-off (that is excess fertilizer seeping into the water system). Large sections of other regional rivers, like the Tisza and the Odra, are biologically dead. It has been estimated that nearly all of Czechoslovakia's rivers are highly polluted with industrial wastes and untreated sewage. In Slovakia, the Hron and Váh rivers transport, respectively, some 100m. cu m and 439m. cu m of industrial and municipal wastes into the Danube every year.

Land degradation is even more serious in many parts of Eastern Europe and the former USSR. Forests are dying over wide areas, killed by the airborne chemical pollutants generated by the region's factories, power plants and vehicles. Forest death surveys, carried out for the Economic Commission for Europe (ECE), in 1989, revealed that damage to total forestland was 71% in Czechoslovakia, 49% in Poland, 44% in the GDR, 43% in Bulgaria, 32% in Yugoslavia and 22% in Hungary—among the highest rates in Europe.

Not only are forests endangered by pollutants, but soils are also deteriorating, from bad management practices and the use of agricultural chemicals. Water erosion now threatens 2.9m. ha of Czechoslovakia (23% of the country's total area). Nearly 25% of Hungary's soils are subject to erosion and another 10% are affected by salinity or alkalinity.

The former USSR is suffering from serious land degradation. At least 1,500m. metric tons of topsoil are lost every year to wind and water erosion. By the early 1990s some 154m. ha of fertile land had been impoverished by poor management, over-use of fertilizers, unsuitable irrigation schemes and erosion. Agricultural production has fallen dramatically, costing the Soviet economy nearly 20,000m. roubles (US $35,000m.) per year. Land degradation has contributed significantly to the critical food shortages, which have troubled the country in recent years.

Among the most well-known environmental disasters in the world is that of the Aral Sea. Once the fourth-largest inland body of water in the world, its total area has shrunk by 40% and it has lost 66% of its water volume. Huge irrigation schemes in the Sea's drainage area radically reduced the amount of fresh water flowing into it. The exposed part of the sea-bed is now a salt-pan desert, with dust storms depositing thousands of metric tons of salt across wide swathes of irrigated cropland in the region. Not only is the Aral Sea dying, but the ruination of once-productive cropland around it is ensuing.

PROSPECTS

There is little doubt that Eastern Europe and the former USSR will have a difficult struggle to modernize their economies while, at the same time, trying to protect the environment from further damage. Environmentalists fear that the governments of the region, in attempts to improve the standard of living, may succumb to the temptation to neglect environmental protection.

Despite the proliferation of 'green' movements in Eastern Europe over the past two years (there are over 200 of them in Poland alone), the majority remain outside the mainstream of political change. The prominence of several green issues in the opposition to the Communist regimes perhaps gave a false impression of the level of convinced support for the environmental movement. The issues were a focus, not the real cause, of opposition. It now seems likely that green movements will be absorbed or divided by the increasing number of groups emerging onto the political landscape of the region. Some may be receptive to green pressure.

It does, however, seem unlikely that environmental issues will be able to significantly affect policy or practice. If the history of industrial development in the West is any comparison, then Eastern Europe is to undergo a period of restructuring, which will still see high pollution levels and a further deterioration of the environment.

The green activists are not without influence, however. For example, there is János Vargha, the founder and director of ISTER, an independent environmental research and lobby group, which is based in Budapest. As one of

Hungary's most outspoken environmentalists, Vargha led the coalition of citizens' action committees and green groups, which successfully halted the construction of a controversial dam on the Danube, at Nagymaros. Acknowledging the public concern, the reconstructed Communist Government decided not to complete the project at Nagymaros, despite the continuing protest of the Czechoslovak Government, which was a partner in the project. Vargha is convinced that any political party in power in Hungary will have to take account of the environmental movement.

It is believed that the younger generation may be less willing to tolerate the polluting consequences of rapid industrial development. Czechoslovakia's Civic Forum has expressed the view that economic growth should be tempered by improvements in health and living standards.

Clearly, the emerging parties in Eastern Europe do not want to repeat the mistakes of the past 40 years. But there are many obstacles ahead. Many Eastern Europeans are most anxious to 'catch up' with the West, to attain the same living standards as in the rest of the continent. It is this pervasive sense of urgency that is driving, in part, the region's pace of change. Furthermore, it remains an imperative for the outdated, and now transitional, economies to modernize as quickly as possible, particularly if social and political stability are to be ensured. Yet the pollution problems of the West are not solved yet, so, even if there is the political will, it will take a great deal of time to deal with the legacy of pollution in Eastern Europe.

For the moment, Eastern European countries do not have to contend with the added burden of burgeoning populations. Birth rates in most of these countries have stagnated. During the 1980s, in Hungary, the death rate consistently exceeded the live birth rate. The tide of emigration at the time of the Eastern European revolutions, and the prospect of further such movements of population in the future, represents a release of population pressure. This may offset the worst effects of the unemployment that will be one of the principal by-products of adjusting the economies from being centrally planned to being market orientated. In some cases, the unemployment may be severe; hundreds of thousands are expected to be out of work in Poland alone over the next few years.

There may be a solution to the unemployment dilemma, which would also counter the damage to the environment. This would involve creating a regional version of the Works Progress Administration or the Civilian Conservation Corps, which were products of the depression in the USA, in the 1930s. Valuable conservation work (such as soil stabilization projects, large-scale afforestation schemes, water management and the protection of vital water catchment areas) could be carried out by such nationally co-ordinated programmes, as well as providing the unemployed with meaningful work and some remuneration.

Many countries in the region seem, at least, to recognize the environmental crises that now exist. They are starting to ensure against further environmental and resource deterioration. The programme to decontaminate and restore the eco-system of Lake Baikal, in Russia, is one example of the changing nature of economic reform and a new-found regard for environmental protection.

Lake Baikal, the world's deepest lake, contains over 23,000 cubic kilometres (23m. million cu m) of fresh water. This one lake accounted for around 80% of the total surface fresh-water resources of the USSR, and nearly one-fifth of the world's reserves. Three hundred and thirty-six rivers and streams flow into this vast lake, which cuts deep into hard rock in southern Siberia. It is home to some 2,600 species of plants and animals, of which three-quarters (including 11 families and 96 genera) are endemic to the lake. Scientists at the Siberian branch (Division V) of the USSR Academy of Sciences, based at the Institute of Limnology at Irkutsk, have been studying the ecology of the lake for decades. Research highlighted the fragile nature of Baikal ecosystems and their complicated interactions with the surrounding land. By the early 1970s it became apparent that the lake was in danger. Industries, especially pulp and paper mills in the lake's catchment area, were flushing thousands of metric tons of untreated effluents into the lake every year. Some of the larger pulping mills were recirculating more than 300,000 cu m of highly polluted water per day. Concerned about the future viability of the lake's ecosystems, scientists from the Irkutsk institute launched a well co-ordinated public education campaign, to inform Soviet citizens of the importance of Lake Baikal and why it should be preserved. At the same time scientists presented their recommendations for saving the lake to the government.

In April 1986, as a result of efforts to change public opinion and alter official policy, the Lake Baikal Region Biosphere Reserve was approved by the 'Man and the Biosphere' bureau of UNESCO, as a new addition to the international network of biosphere reserves. One year later, the Soviet authorities issued a new law, granting special protection to the lake and its surroundings. Most of the pulp and paper plants were scheduled to be phased out over the course of five years. The rescue operation was an example of what can be done when scientists work together with the public and politicians to bring about change.

Other countries are attempting to emulate this type of action. Czechoslovakia has set aside at least US $170m. for urgently needed environmental protection measures. One of the country's top priorities is the afforestation of large tracts of ecologically important watersheds and water catchment areas, currently reduced by air pollution, along the Polish–Czechoslovak border and the Jizerskie Hory Mountains. Hungary plans to invest up to $400m., to combat air pollution alone, particularly in urban areas which suffer from smog. Poland is reportedly seeking external aid to finance resource rehabilitation schemes on a large scale, including the cleansing of the Vistula River, now one of the most polluted rivers in Europe.

Of course, rebuilding the environment takes time and planning. As the economies of the region emerge from their painful restructuring process, many pressure groups are trying to ensure that environmental concerns will not be marginalized. There is an anger that may, just possibly, prevent Eastern Europe and the former USSR from squandering their future to pay for the present.

THE GERMAN DEMOCRATIC REPUBLIC

Professor DAVID CHILDS

Among those who knew the politics of the German Democratic Republic (GDR) well, it was sometimes said that the secret fear of its leaders was that their Soviet masters would betray them. This was especially so in 1952, at the time of Stalin's note to the Western Powers suggesting a neutral, united Germany and, again, in 1953–58, during the post-Stalin easing of relations. There were rumours again in the 1970s, especially in 1978, and this anxiety returned after Mikhail Gorbachev was elected General Secretary of the Communist Party of the Soviet Union (CPSU), in 1985. Throughout the existence of the GDR, fear was one of several factors undermining the regime.

ORIGINS OF THE EAST GERMAN STATE

Germany, ruled by the National Socialist German Workers' Party (Nationalsozialistische Deutsche Arbeiterpartei—NSDAP or Nazis) under Adolf Hitler, was defeated in the Second World War. The country was invaded by the Allies, the Entente Powers, and surrendered in May 1945. The Allies subsequently divided Germany (as defined by its borders at the end of 1937), and Berlin, into four zones of occupation, administered by the United Kingdom, the USA, the USSR and France. Territory east of the Oder and Neisse rivers was, eventually, annexed by Poland; northern East Prussia, around the city of Königsburg (now Kaliningrad), was annexed by the USSR. After the failure of the Occupying Powers to agree on the formation of an all-German government, in 1949 the GDR was established in the eastern, Soviet Zone of occupied Germany. It comprised 24% of the population of 1937 Germany and 23% of its territory. Its Western competitor, the Federal Republic of Germany (FRG), consisted of 62% of the population and 53% of the territory of 1937 Germany (it was established earlier in 1949, in the British, US and French Zones).

In theory the GDR was one of the most modern and productive areas of Europe. Many of pre-Second World War Germany's modern manufacturing industries were strongly represented there. These included: vehicles, office equipment (including calculating machines), chemicals, electrical goods, telecommunications systems, fine optics, scientific instruments, all aspects of light and heavy engineering, as well as textiles, bone china and ceramics, furniture and furnishings, toys, musical instruments, fine printing, sports rifles and camping equipment. Agriculture and forestry were also well-organized and productive, and important deposits of uranium were mined near the Czechoslovak frontier. The Soviet Zone was also an area where distinguished universities (Berlin, Greifswald, Halle, Jena, Leipzig, Rostock) were located, as were such equally distinguished institutions as the mining academy (the world's oldest), in Freiberg, and the art academy at Dresden. The world-famous Bauhaus was at Dessau. Finally, the workforce was highly trained and well disciplined.

Like the other occupation zones, the Soviet Zone had suffered much from the War. Berlin, Dresden, Magdeburg, Rostock and the other large towns suffered heavy punishment from aerial and artillery bombardment, from Hitler's 'scorched earth' policy and from vandalism by the victorious forces. In general, however, physically at least, the eastern Zone was no worse affected than the western Zones. One problem, which soon became apparent, was the loss of population, above all the skilled and active. The US Army had occupied much of the southern part of the Soviet Zone, including Jena, Leipzig, Halle and Magdeburg; the Canadians were in the north. When they left many of the key personnel from the leading firms went with them. Others, both blue- and white-collar employees, fled once they realized that their part of Germany was to be in the Soviet Zone. The Red Army had an unenviable reputation, which did not improve at all after its arrival. The Soviet Zone was further weakened by Soviet removals of both equipment and people as reparations. Such seizures were massive. The Soviet Zone was also in a weak position as a would-be separate state, in that it lacked basic industries, the sinews of economic power in the 1940s: hard coal and iron and steel capacity. Even if the residents had been enthusiastic about the new Republic, it would be difficult to make it economically viable, especially given the Cold War situation.

The early politics of the Soviet Zone were like those of the rest of Germany. From mid-1945, four main parties emerged: the Social Democratic Party of Germany (Sozialdemokratische Partei Deutschlands—SPD); the Communist Party of Germany (Kommunistische Partei Deutschlands—KPD); the Liberal Democratic Party of Germany (Liberal-Demokratische Partei Deutschlands—LDPD); and the Christian Democratic Union (Christlich Demokratische Union Deutschlands—CDU). Given the experience of the Weimar Republic (1919–33), many expected the former two parties to have received most of the votes in an early election. They had been large parties before being banned by the Nazis; they had rightly predicted that Hitler would lead Germany to disaster; and, there was a widespread feeling that the business interests of the right had helped Hitler. At first, the CDU looked as though it might be just another version of the Roman Catholic community's earlier Centre Party. The LDPD had not been very strong in the Weimar era, and seemed irrelevant to some, given the likely SPD–KPD competition. Another reason for opportunists to join the KPD was that the Soviets helped it, without making their intentions immediately clear.

The Soviet authorities, however, became alarmed after the results of the general election in Austria, in November 1945. There the Communists were heavily defeated, with the People's Party (similar to the CDU) winning the most votes, followed closely by the Socialists. They resolved that the SPD and the CDU must be neutralized as rivals to the KPD. In the Soviet Zone the SPD was forced to merge with the KPD, in 1946, to form the Socialist Unity Party of Germany (Sozialistische Einheitspartei Deutschlands—SED). The SED won some 57% of the votes cast in local elections in 1946.

Although the KPD had proclaimed the 'German Road to Socialism', unlike its pre-1933 call for a Soviet Germany, its essential principles became increasingly like those in the USSR. All Communist parties were, at this time, proclaiming their own national paths of socialism, and everywhere the Communists had control, Marxist-Leninist dictatorship was being enforced. The path followed in the Soviet Zone of Germany was similar to those in the other 'people's democracies' of eastern and central Europe. In most cases they were, officially, multi-party systems. In reality, the Communists controlled all real power, aided by the occupying Soviet armed forces. The different aims of the Occupying Powers prevented the re-establishment of a single German republic with which a final peace treaty could be concluded. At first it was disagreement of the USA and the United Kingdom with the USSR and France, but, with the escalation of tension between Communist and Western blocs, the main observable policy differences were between the Soviet Zone and the other three.

THE STALINIST YEARS

In 1949 the GDR emerged from a Communist-dominated People's Congress, backed by the Soviet armed forces and security apparatus. It was headed by the veteran Communist, Wilhelm Pieck (1876–1960), as President, with a government headed by the former Social Democrat, Otto Grotewohl (1894–1964). They were the joint chairmen of the SED. All the parties were represented in the Government. There was a people's parliament, or Volkskammer, in which all the parties and mass organizations (Democratic Women's League—Demokratischer Frauenbund Deutschlands; Free German Youth—Freie Deutsche Jugend or FDJ; Confederation of Free Trade Unions—Freier Deutscher Gewerkschaftsbund; League of Culture—Kulturbund) were represented. In 1948 two new parties were established by the Communists, the National Democratic Party of Germany (National-Demokratische Partei Deutschlands—NDPD), the aim of which was to mobilize former Nazi and nationalist fellow travellers, and the Democratic Peasants Party of Germany (Demokratische Bauernpartei Deutschlands—DBD). With the mass organizations and the two new parties the SED had a majority in the Volkskammer. (In fact, this was less important than it might seem, because parliament was never really very powerful.) In 1950 the SED and the other main parties and 'public organizations' formed a National Front as a ruling 'coalition'. The SED, or rather its leaders, held such power as the Soviets allowed them. Purges had ensured that the only choices were conformity, flight or imprisonment. Thousands were imprisoned, some locally, in prisons like Bautzen, while others were sent to former Nazi concentration camps, like Buchenwald. Conditions were appalling; many people died, others had their health broken. Others, even less fortunate, were sent to the Soviet Gulag. There were executions too, for alleged treason and sabotage. By that time most of the economy was already in the hands of the state. The mass media were all subject to SED and Soviet censorship, even though, officially, there was a diversity of ownership.

In 1952 it was announced that the GDR was 'building socialism'. According to Stalin's theories, the class struggle was to be intensified. This included further purges of unreliable elements, further nationalization measures, a virtual ban on would-be students from 'bourgeois' backgrounds, and the expansion of the armed forces. These last were being established before this time, and this was now formalized as a people's police. Young men were urged and pressured to join this force, which was equipped with tanks, artillery, heavy infantry weapons, fighter aircraft and light naval vessels. The new force helped to seal the frontier with the West German FRG; only the zonal boundaries in Berlin remained open. Massive investments were also made in the steel and other heavy industries. To finance this, new sacrifices were exacted, mainly from the workers. Building socialism also meant a new ideological struggle, which found expression in the imposition of Socialist Realism in the arts and Soviet standards in other things. 'To learn from the USSR, is to learn to be victorious', was the slogan of the time. SED members were urged to read Stalin's works, to the neglect of Marx and Engels. In architecture, the modernism of Bauhaus was replaced by

the ornate, Stalinist 'wedding cake' style, which was wasteful of space and materials. In industry, Stakhanovite norms were introduced, which meant producing more for the same money. Thousands were leaving the GDR each month, for the West. In March 1958 the figure reached a new peak of 58,000 emigrants.

On 6 March 1953 it was announced that Stalin was dead. The Communist world was plunged into uncertainty. Rather than re-evaluating the situation, the SED leaders plodded on with their previous policies; thus, on 28 May, a policy which required 10% more production for the same amount of pay was introduced. By 9 June the New Course was announced, which, in part, was aimed at repairing some of the damage done to the middle classes. No mention was made of concessions to the workers.

There was a strike on the prestigious Stalinallee building project in East Berlin. The strikers called for a lowering of the work norms and the resignation of the Government. This was on 16 June 1953. They appealed for a general strike on the following day. This was well supported. Thousands of workers in Berlin and other towns across the GDR joined the demonstrations. In some places they released prisoners from the local jails. The East German police were unable to cope and the Soviet forces had to assist. Martial law was declared; there was some shooting. The SED and its affiliates were shaken, but the USSR had ensured their survival. The work norms were revised downwards, and the New Course was continued with more emphasis on consumer goods.

CONSOLIDATION OF THE GDR

The SED leader, Walter Ulbricht (1893–1973), a former exile in Moscow who had become Secretary-General (later restyled First Secretary) of the SED in 1950, had survived partly because of the uncertainty in the USSR. The Soviet leaders who had survived Stalin (Malenkov, Molotov, Beria, Bulganin, Khrushchev, etc.) were so busy assessing each other that they did not give their full attention to the sudden explosion in the GDR. They agreed to liquidate their colleague, Beria, a former head of the secret police, who, it was later claimed, had a plan for selling the GDR to the West. Perhaps he did and this was based on a more realistic assessment of the actual situation in Germany. He was executed not for this, however, but because they did not want him as a political rival.

Having secured himself with the Soviet leadership, Ulbricht was able to consolidate his position. He followed the Soviet example as closely as possible and lent ideological support to the new Soviet leadership, when Nikita Khrushchev denounced Stalin at the 20th Congress of the CPSU. The Hungarian uprising and the near-revolution in Poland caused the Soviet leaders to fear democratic experiments among their allies in Eastern Europe. At the Fifth Congress of the SED, in 1958, Ulbricht appeared in total control. He followed the example of the Soviet leader by announcing unreal aims for the GDR. Khrushchev had decreed that the USSR must overtake the USA in basic consumption levels per head by 1961. Ulbricht decreed the same aim for the GDR, in relation to the FRG. The Congress also agreed radical, new socialist measures. What followed was more nationalization of industries, with medium-sized and small businesses being forced into state participation, the collectivization of almost all of the GDR's farms, and the introduction of polytechnic education along the lines of similar educational reforms in the USSR. Changes were also introduced in higher education and cultural policy. Socialist Realism became the favoured and dominant standard; a conference at Bitterfeld, in April

1959, imposed this line for writers. 'Anti-Party' writers, such as Erich Loest, were imprisoned.

It is not entirely clear why Khrushchev decided to create another Berlin crisis (the first was the Soviet blockade of 1948–49). In a note to the Western Powers, on 27 November 1958, he demanded that West Berlin be turned into a 'free city', which involved ending the rights of France, the United Kingdom and the USA as Occupying (and protecting) Powers. He threatened that if the Western Powers did not agree he would conclude a peace treaty with the GDR, which would force them to recognize the East German state. Perhaps Khrushchev felt confident because of his own victories against his opponents in the CPSU. No doubt Ulbricht was pressuring him too, as the SED encountered increasing difficulties. Both agricultural and industrial production were declining and dissatisfaction was mounting. The numbers of people leaving the GDR for the FRG, via West Berlin, were increasing steeply.

Although the frontier between the FRG and the GDR had been closed since 1952, it was still possible for East Germans to escape by going to East Berlin, and then crossing to West Berlin by the urban railway or on foot. The SED regime felt that the country was haemorrhaging, and it asked the USSR to allow it to take action to stop the flow. They agreed and, during the night of 12–13 August 1961, East Berlin was sealed off from the West by armed troops and police. The Berlin Wall was built over the following days. Between 1949 and August 1961 over 2.7m. people, out of a total population of 18m., had fled the GDR to become refugees in the West. Others had left without seeking this status formally; probably about another 1m. had fled in 1945–49.

Ulbricht continued to strengthen his position; he had already assumed the leading posts in the state as well as those in the SED. He was Chairman of the National Defence Council, established in February 1960, and Chairman of the Council of State (the collective head of state), established after the death of President Pieck in September 1960. His position seemed less secure in October 1961, when another series of de-Stalinization measures was announced by Khrushchev, at the 22nd Congress of the CPSU. Ulbricht attempted to align himself with the CPSU by dutifully removing statues of Stalin and eliminating public references to him. He also joined his Soviet colleague in initiating economic reform. In the GDR this was called the New Economic System.

The fact that the SED had stopped the population drain to the West, had embarked upon economic reform and was following the USSR in a moderate cultural policy, augured well for the GDR. Under the economic reform, profit and credit were to be reinstated. There was to be decentralization, a more realistic pricing policy and enterprises were expected to operate more like Western businesses. The reforms were associated with Guenter Mittag, a young technocrat. However, by 1968, many of the reforms had been abandoned. In the USSR, Khrushchev had been overthrown, in 1964, and his successor, Leonid Brezhnev, was more conservative in outlook. In addition, the conservative forces in the Eastern European Communist parties learnt the example of the 'Prague Spring' of 1968, in Czechoslovakia. Led by the Soviet army, the forces of the Warsaw Pact (including units from the GDR) invaded Czechoslovakia in 1968 and overthrew the reformist Communist regime of Alexander Dubček.

Despite the crushing of the 'Prague Spring', Brezhnev was ready for better relations with the West. When the Social Democrats formed a government in Bonn, in 1969, he was ready to negotiate with them. Willy Brandt, the new West German Chancellor, indicated that his Government wanted a better relationship with the USSR and its allies, including the GDR. Brandt announced that his Government would negotiate on equal terms with the GDR. Despite Ulbricht's demand for the full recognition of the GDR before negotiation could begin, Brandt met the GDR head of government, Willi Stoph, in Erfurt, on 19 March 1970. This was the first time a West German leader had visited the GDR and it marked a turning point in post-War German history. On 21 May the two politicians met again at Kassel, in the FRG. In the same year the FRG dramatically improved its relations with the USSR and Poland, by treaties renouncing the use of force. The West Germans were not, however, prepared to accede to Ulbricht's demand that they recognize the GDR as a foreign, independent state, like any other state with which they had relations. They did not regard the GDR as a foreign country, but as a second German state within a single nation.

ERICH HONECKER'S RULE

Because of his obstruction to better relations with Bonn, the USSR forced Ulbricht to resign his position as SED leader on 3 May 1971. He remained head of state until his death in 1973. Erich Honecker, who had been recognized as his likely successor for some time, assumed power as First Secretary (restyled General Secretary in 1976) of the SED. Unlike Ulbricht, who was from Leipzig, Honecker was from the Saarland, which now lay in the FRG. He had been imprisoned by the Nazis for clandestine activities on behalf of the KPD. On his release, in 1945, he had played a leading part in building up the FDJ, serving as its leader until 1955. He was later put in charge of defence and security matters.

Under Honecker the GDR entered into a number of agreements with the FRG, the most important of which was the signing of the Basic Treaty on 21 December 1972. The Treaty obliged the two states to develop good-neighbourly relations on the basis of equality. They accepted the UN Charter and renounced the use of force. They respected each other's independence in internal and external relations. They agreed to co-operate in economics, science and technology, traffic, law, post and telephones, health, culture, sport and the environment. They agreed to exchange representatives. The SED had obtained most of what it had demanded from the FRG since 1949, but it did not get recognition as a *foreign* state. For the FRG this implied that the question of German reunification was still not a question of history. Moreover, the SED was apprehensive of closer relations with the FRG, fearing the effect of these on its people. Because of this fear the SED emphasized its separateness by a policy of *Abgrenzung* (delimiting). Most place-names which reminded East Germans that they were part of the German nation were changed. In 1974 the Constitution of the GDR was amended, deleting the reference to the German nation and proclaiming the alliance of the GDR with the USSR 'for ever and irrevocably'. In cultural policy, the notion of a common German culture was denounced. In a further attempt to cope with the closer relations with the FRG, attempts were made to raise living standards. In 1974 a scientific council to research into the problems of youth was established, headed by Professor Walter Friederich. Such efforts had also been influenced by severe disturbances in Poland in 1970.

The SED also attempted to gain the recognition of its own people and the outside world by building up a sporting élite which would score heavily in international events. By investing vast resources in the GDR's sporting traditions it gained good results. At the Montreal Olympics, in 1976, it won 40 gold medals, compared with the FRG's 10, the

USSR's 47 and the USA's 34. This was achieved by careful selection, strict discipline, high rewards and, allegedly, the use of drugs.

The Basic Treaty enabled a greater degree of international recognition of the GDR. Hitherto, Bonn had always threatened that, if any state outside the Warsaw Pact recognized the GDR, it would end diplomatic relations with that state (as it did in 1957, when Tito's Yugoslavia established diplomatic relations with the GDR). Switzerland recognized the GDR in December 1972, being the first Western state to do so. The United Kingdom and France established formal relations in February 1974, the USA in September. These were among the last states to do so. Both German polities had joined the UN in 1973.

The SED had hoped that the recognition of the GDR, its sporting achievements, some modest improvement in living standards, better relations with the FRG and increased ideological work among the population, would lead its people to gradual acceptance. This was never achieved. The East Germans were never satisfied with their standard of living, which they knew was low, relative to that of the FRG. For them, the only worthwhile comparison was with the FRG, not with Poland and the other Warsaw Pact states. They could make this comparison by what they saw on West German television, which was widely watched in the GDR. Many of them also had the opportunity to talk with their relatives from the West about lifestyles. The Basic Treaty, and associated agreements, had made it easier for West Germans, including those who had formerly lived in the GDR, to visit their relatives. In 1970 there were 1.2m. visits by West Germans to the GDR; by 1976 the figure was 3.1m. In addition, in 1976, there were 3.4m. visits by West Berliners. More East German pensioners (virtually the only group allowed to travel) were going to the FRG. The establishment of 'Intershops' and 'Interhotels' also undermined belief in the success of the SED's Socialism. In these enterprises only 'hard', or convertible, currency could be used to purchase goods and services. Many consumer goods which were unobtainable in normal GDR shops could be bought in these stores. Most East Germans could only look and not buy. This caused resentment as only a privileged few and those with Western family members could get the necessary currency. The Intershops made a nonsense of the claims of the East German media that the GDR had achieved an economic miracle. Many East Germans were also angry because they could only travel in a few Warsaw Pact states, and even then they were treated as the poor relations of the West Germans.

The material situation in the GDR would have been considerably worse had it not been for help from the West. FRG citizens gave millions of marks to their relatives in the GDR, to alleviate their situation. When they visited the GDR they were forced to exchange a minimum sum for every day spent there. The FRG Government paid out large sums of money to improve road and rail communications with Berlin, which benefited the GDR economy. From 1964 onwards the FRG bought the freedom of thousands of East Germans convicted of political offences. They guaranteed credits to the GDR and they attempted to bolster trade between the two German republics. This trade was so organized that the GDR had a considerable interest-free loan most of the time. The FRG also aided GDR pensioners visiting the West.

It would be wrong to suppose that East German grievances were only concerned with living standards. Most people did resent the restrictions placed on their individual liberty. They realized that the official elections which took place every five years were not genuine. They were impressed by the way democratic states such as France, the United Kingdom and, above all, the FRG changed governments after democratic elections. They resented the lack of opportunity to discuss society's problems in the various organizations to which they were often forced to belong. The need to take part in collective hypocrisy and the lack of trust were corrupting influences, which caused resignation, depression and deep dissatisfaction. East Germans also feared the expanding state security service (Staatsicherheitsdienst—SSD or Stasi) of Gen. Erich Mielke, who boasted of the many informers working for him.

The situation in the GDR produced dissidents rather than an underground opposition movement. These dissidents were often individuals who had embraced Marxism-Leninism and grown critical of the practical reality. Often they wanted 'socialism with a human face'. Often, too, they believed in the regime enough to think it could be changed. In the 1970s they were influenced by the emergence of so-called 'Euro-Communism', in the Communist parties of Western Europe. Typical of them was Rudolf Bahro, who was arrested in 1977, after extracts of his book, *The Alternative*, appeared in the FRG weekly *Der Spiegel*. He was later sentenced to eight years' imprisonment. Robert Havemann, another leading Marxist critic of the regime was placed under house arrest, from November 1976 to May 1979. He, and leading Marxist novelist Stefan Heym, were fined for alleged currency offences, in 1979. A favourite tactic of the regime was to expel such dissidents from the GDR or force them to leave under threat of imprisonment. Wolf Biermann, a well-known singer and writer, was deprived of his citizenship while on a tour of the FRG in 1976. Hans Schaedlich, a writer, lost his job after protesting against Biermann's expatriation; he, too, was forced to go to the West, in 1978. Many others in the cultural élite shared this kind of fate.

The churches were also drawn more and more into the struggle to reform the GDR. After attempting to destroy the Church, in the 1950s and early 1960s, the SED tried to reach an accommodation with it. For their part the Church leaderships gave up opposition to the SED regime, as such, and sought to gain concessions on particular issues. At a meeting with the League of Evangelical Churches in the GDR, an association of the traditionally dominant Lutheran churches and the largest Christian organization, on 6 March 1978, Honecker acknowledged the Church as an independent organization, with social relevance in a socialist society. Three months later the Evangelical churches were objecting to the introduction of compulsory military training in schools. This issue, and conscientious objection, were to be key issues of church–state relations; anti-nuclear and 'green' movements in the FRG, in the 1980s, influenced, above all, young people in the GDR to take similar positions. Often they looked to the Church for advice, help and protection.

Many East Germans did not believe the regime was capable of reform and they tried to make the best of their lot by retiring into a kind of inner emigration. Others sought actively to leave, arguing that the Helsinki Final Act, of August 1975, signed by the GDR and virtually all the European states, gave them a right to do so. When they applied to leave they usually lost their jobs and were put under pressure to withdraw their petitions. In desperation some entered foreign embassies, refusing to leave until they had been given permission to go to the West. This became increasingly popular in the 1980s. A few, either foolhardy or very desperate, still tried to cross the frontier or the Berlin Wall illegally, risking their lives in so doing.

In 1985 the elevation of Mikhail Gorbachev to the leadership of the CPSU marked the beginning of the end for the SED regime in the GDR. The SED leadership rejected his reform proposals, either by claiming that they were irrelevant to the GDR or that the GDR had already implemented such reforms years earlier. This was slightly true in so far as the GDR had never completely abolished private enterprise and, after 1976, once again encouraged the private service sector, small retail businesses and the private plots of collective farmers. In other respects the regime remained decidedly conservative. It did, however, give support to the USSR's many international initiatives.

As they saw East–West tensions easing and changes taking place in other Communist states, the people of the GDR became increasingly restless. They had hoped that Honecker's visit to the FRG, in September 1987, would have produced a change for the better. In fact there were only some cosmetic changes, such as the abolition of the (rarely used) death penalty. They also became more frustrated about their living standards. In the latter half of the 1980s the situation appeared to be worsening. This was partly due to the declining ability of the GDR to export successfully to Western markets. Some textiles and consumer goods, which it had previously been able to export, did not fare well against competition from Asian and East European manufacturers. It was also receiving fewer returns for its petroleum products. In 1986, at the SED's 11th Congress, Honecker had ordered that the GDR should invest considerable sums on the new technologies, such as computers, biotechnology and nuclear energy. This policy was then placed at the core of the 1986–91 Five-Year Plan. Thousands of millions of marks were invested, often to the detriment of more traditional industries, in a vain attempt to match the advances of the world market leaders. By 1989 there were increasing shortages. A further factor in the discontent of that year was that the local government election results were allegedly falsified. Encouraged by developments in neighbouring countries, thousands decided to vote against the official list of candidates. The falsification led to open protests. There were also protests about the refusal of the GDR authorities to grant legal recognition to a group called New Forum (Neues Forum), an independent citizens' action movement for the discussion of democratic reforms and social and environmental issues. In Leipzig a series of demonstrations, organized by civil and religious rights activists, about reform and the social problems responsible for continuing emigration, were violently suppressed.

An important turning point was Hungary's decision to open its frontier to Austria, in May 1989. Hungary was one of the few places East Germans could travel to without a visa. From mid-1989 more and more GDR citizens chose this route as their way out of a society from which they were already alienated. Western television interviews with those who had succeeded encouraged others to try. When the GDR tried to prevent its citizens from going to Hungary, Czechoslovakia abandoned the solidarity usual to the countries of the disintegrating Soviet bloc and opened its frontier to the FRG. Thousands of East Germans sought asylum in the FRG embassies in Budapest, Prague and Warsaw. An ageing, sick Honecker was persuaded to let them go.

On 5 October 1989 eight sealed trains took some 10,000 GDR refugees from Prague to the FRG. As the trains passed through Dresden, fighting broke out as police attempted to restrain the crowds trying to join the trains. This was the biggest disorder since 1953. The visit of Gorbachev, to celebrate 40 years of the GDR, on 7 October, gave further impetus to the opposition, with demonstrations

in several towns leading to thousands of arrests. In Leipzig, weekly meetings and demonstrations were organized, centred on the Lutheran church of St Nicholas, which attracted as many as 120,000 people. In Dresden, a series of daily protests began. These actions gained increasing support and, eventually, the police ceased to intervene. (Later reports suggest that the SED Politburo narrowly rejected the use of the armed forces to suppress the unrest.) On 17 October, in a fast-deteriorating situation, the Politburo voted in favour of relieving Honecker of his position and he resigned, ostensibly for health reasons. With him went Mittag and Joachim Herrmann, who had been responsible for media policy.

THE FALL OF THE SED

Egon Krenz, who had replaced Honecker as SED leader and head of state, had little credibility. He was closely associated with the leader he had deposed, and with the Stasi, and was thought not to be sympathetic to Gorbachev. Dialogue with New Forum (which was legalized) and church leaders began and there was some liberalization, but the demonstrations grew and there were demands for free elections. Some 300,000 attended the Leipzig demonstrations in late October and 500,000 were at a demonstration in East Berlin in early November. On 2–3 November most of Honecker's colleagues followed his example and resigned; on 7 November the entire Council of Ministers resigned. A new government and a new travel law failed to ease the crisis or stop the exodus. Over 2,000 East Germans were leaving daily. In these circumstances, the frontiers were opened on 9 November (an estimated 2m. East Germans crossed into West Berlin on the weekend of 10–11 November, and the dismantling of the Berlin Wall began). Free elections were announced for 1990.

An interim government, headed by Hans Modrow, formerly SED First Secretary for the Dresden area, had assumed power on 7 November 1989. Its members were reform-orientated SED members and members of the other, associated parties in the National Front (the CDU, LDPD, DBD and NDPD). These parties had, by that time, expelled their original leaders, who had been subservient to the SED. Civil unrest continued, maintaining pressure on the SED. The Volkskammer removed the SED's constitutional guarantee of power in December. Under a 'round-table' agreement, reached on 6 December, the new Government was to agree all policy with the new opposition groups which had been forming. On 5 February 1990 eight of these groups joined the Government, to shadow the normal ministers. These new groups had originally stood for a reformed, democratic GDR with a socialist, market economy. The first of them was New Forum (founded on 10 September 1989). There were also Democracy Now, Democratic Awakening, United Left, the Greens, the Initiative for Peace and Human Rights, Independent Women's League and, most significantly, the Social Democrats. By this time Krenz was no longer head of state and Honecker and other former SED leaders were under arrest, charged with corruption. The SED itself had reorganized and adopted the new name of the Party of Democratic Socialism (Partei des Demokratischen Sozializmus—PDS); it was preparing to contest general elections, agreed for 18 March, under a system of proportional representation. The Government was dissolving the unpopular Stasi and, under pressure from the other parties, had delayed the establishment of a successor service.

Most in the West had been surprised by the rapid collapse taking place in the GDR and feared a Soviet intervention. FRG and other Western leaders tried to stabilize the situation by lending support to the Modrow Government.

Yet the Bonn politicians could not ignore their compatriots in the GDR, who, by November, were demanding German unity. In response to this the FRG Chancellor, Helmut Kohl, on 28 November 1989, announced a 10-point programme which included 'confederative structures between the two states in Germany', which would lead, eventually, to unity. This rapidly became the main issue leading up to the first democratic election in the GDR.

As the elections approached FRG politicians and parties became more and more involved in the GDR. Undoubtedly most East Germans welcomed this. Without West German help, genuinely free elections would have been impossible. The SED, or, by February 1990, the PDS, still had many advantages. In a matter of weeks its membership had shrunk from 2.3m. to 700,000. However it remained by far the largest party, with a GDR-wide organization, well-run offices, transport, newspapers and printing presses, all of which were in short supply. To a lesser extent, the other four National Front parties also enjoyed similar advantages.

The SPD had originally been considered the most likely to win the March elections, but they had lost support when they advocated a slower pace towards German unity. Their main rivals were the rightist parties of the Alliance for Germany, which consisted of the reformed GDR CDU, which was fully backed by its sister parties in the FRG, and Democratic Awakening. They wanted German unity as soon as possible, by the accession of the GDR to the Federal Republic. The League of Free Democrats was also an alliance, made up of the German Forum Party, the Free Democratic Party (Freie Demokratische Partei—FDP) and the Liberal Democratic Party (which, at the time, was the largest of the three parties, being the reformed LDPD. Alliance '90 comprised New Forum, Democracy Now and Initiative for Peace and Human Rights. The Greens intended to ally with the Independent Women's League. There were a number of other parties standing alone, among them: the old NDPD, the United Left, the Old Democratic Women's League and the Beer Drinkers' Party.

THE DEMISE OF THE EAST GERMAN STATE

The last general election of the GDR was held on 18 March 1990, and 93.4% of the eligible voters participated. The conservative Alliance for Germany was the clear winner, with some 48% of the votes cast (40.8% for the CDU alone), followed by the SPD, with 21.9%, the PDS with 16.4% and the League of Free Democrats with 5.3%. Alliance '90 only managed 2.9% of the votes and the Greens 2%. The Alliance and the old Communists (PDS) had both done better than expected. There had been a strong polarization between those wanting immediate unity, by accession to the FRG, and those totally opposed to it. The PDS had gained the votes of those who feared most for their jobs in the state, military and security apparatus, parts of the educational and cultural élite and the PDS itself. The Alliance had gained 58% of the industrial workers but only 32% of graduates.

Virtually all the parties gained representation in parliament on the basis of proportional representation and a coalition was formed of the Alliance for Germany, the SPD and the League of Free Democrats. Lothar de Maizière (CDU), a lawyer, became premier.

A treaty signed in Bonn, on 18 May 1990, committed the two German states to achieve the unity of Germany as soon as possible 'within a European peace order'. It also committed the GDR to introducing the social market economy and the federal system. FRG law and practice were also to be introduced. On 1 July 1990 the two states were formally joined in a monetary, economic and social union.

The West German Deutsche Mark became the sole legal tender. Later that month the GDR legislature re-established the division of its territory into the five Länder (states) of Brandenburg, Mecklenburg-Vorpommern (Mecklenburg-West Pomerania), Sachsen (Saxony), Sachsen-Anhalt (Saxony-Anhalt) and Thüringen (Thuringia), in preparation for their admittance as constituent members of the Federal Republic. Meanwhile, the so-called 'two-plus-four' negotiations had been taking place, between the two German Governments and the four Second World War Powers, resolving the outstanding issues of the War and other external ramifications of German unity. The most potentially controversial issue was settled in June, when the two German legislatures declared the inviolabilty of the Oder-Neisse border with Poland. (The newly-united Germany signed a treaty with Poland confirming this, on 14 November 1990.)

On 31 August 1990 the representatives of the two states signed the Treaty between the FRG and the GDR on the Establishment of German Unity, in East Berlin. This was then ratified by their respective parliaments. In Bonn, 440 members voted for the Treaty with only 47 Greens voting against and three abstentions. In East Berlin, 299 voted in favour, 80 against (PDS, Alliance '90 and the Greens) and one abstention.

The last major formal act covering the external aspects of German unity was signed on 12 September 1990, in Moscow, by the foreign ministers of France, the USSR, the United Kingdom and the USA and their two German colleagues. Under this agreement Soviet troops would be withdrawn from Germany by 1994. The troops of the three Western Powers would remain in Berlin until that withdrawal. Following the withdrawal, German NATO forces could be garrisoned in the former GDR but not foreign troops or nuclear weapons. The Agreement recognized Germany's right to belong to alliances of its choice: in effect, NATO. On 1 October, in New York (USA), representatives of the four Occupying Powers signed a document recognizing Germany's full sovereignty. German unity was finally restored on 3 October, with the dissolution of the GDR and the accession of the five eastern Länder to the Federal Republic. The new Germany was a member of the EC and NATO. The first free all-German elections since 1933 were held on 2 December and were won by the conservative alliance of Chancellor Kohl.

CONSEQUENCES OF THE UNITING OF GERMANY

The new Germany represented 22.9% of the population of the European Communities (EC). This compared with France's 16.4%, the United Kingdom's 16.7% and Italy's 16.8%. It is by far the strongest economy, in most respects being only behind those of Japan and the USA.

The Western FRG had taken on a massive burden. The former GDR was suffering from severe neglect in every respect. One comparison at least helps to put the financial burden in perspective. In May 1991 it was announced that Yugoslavia (with a population of 24m.) would get, over five years, £500m. of credits from the EC, mainly in loans. Some of this would be German money. On 16 May Bonn announced it would provide a further 36,000m. DM (£12,000m.) in credits to the former GDR (population 16m.). Furthermore, Germany had agreed already to fund the withdrawal of the Soviet forces from Germany and maintain them until 1994. It had also agreed to grant credits to the USSR and aid it in other ways. It once again confirmed its loss of territory to the USSR and Poland. It also committed itself to trade with and aid Poland and Czechoslovakia. No one could really say what the true cost of the rebuilding of German unity would be, but Germany appeared equipped to undertake this task. During 1991, however, there were increasing concerns about the continued strength of the German economy as a result of unity and the restructuring of the eastern German 'colonies'.

The fall of the GDR was significant in a number of ways. The GDR had been an attempt by the SED to build Marxist-Leninist socialism in an advanced industrial society. In this it was a failure. The Soviets, who conceived it, maintained it essentially to serve the Soviet economy, armed forces and diplomacy. The GDR was the USSR's main Warsaw Pact ally but was of declining value to its creator.

Its armed forces would have been of doubtful value in an East–West conflict and its economy could not help the Soviet economy in any fundamental way. The Soviet leadership became convinced that it was better to get aid and trade and genuine goodwill from a united Germany, rather than the official protestations of friendship from the SED. The demise of the GDR marked the final disintegration of the Soviet bloc, and the rise of a new order in central and eastern Europe. Ironically, the USSR itself survived the German Democratic Republic by little more than a year.

PART TWO
Surveys of Eastern European Countries

ETHNIC GROUPS

Albanians	△ Italians	Slovaks
Bulgarians	Macedonians	Slovenes
Czechs	Poles	Turks
Germans	Romanians	Eastern Slavs
Hungarians	Serbs and Croats	

ALBANIA

Geography

PHYSICAL FEATURES

The Republic of Albania (formerly the People's Socialist Republic of Albania) is situated in south-eastern Europe. It is bordered by Greece, in the south, and by three of the Republics of Yugoslavia: Montenegro to the north, Serbia (province of Kosovo) to the north-east and Macedonia to the east. To the west there is a 420-km coastline along the Adriatic Sea and the Strait of Otranto (parts of the Mediterranean Sea). Albania covers an area of 28,748 sq km (11,100 sq miles).

More than three-quarters of Albania's territory is mountain or hill country and nearly one-half is covered by woodland. The Albanian Alps, characterized by tall forests and alpine pastures, dominate the north of the country and rise to a height of 2,693 m at Jezerce. The central mountain region lies between the valley of the River Drin in the north and the central Devoll and lower Osum valleys in the south. It is a less rugged area than the Alps, with wider valleys, dense forests, and large lakes such as the Ohrid and Prespa, but it also has high peaks, reaching 2,751 m at Mt Korab, the highest point in the country. South of the Osum valley the more regular ranges of the southern mountain region continue into northern Greece and extend westwards to the sea. These three mountain areas surround the western coastal lowlands. Communications with the south and east, therefore, are difficult. There are, however, east–west routes along the valleys of the Shkumbini, Devoll and Drin rivers. The western lowlands extend some 200 km from the foothills of the Alps in the north to Vlorë in the south and some 50 km inland. The land is flat and marshy and extensive land reclamation has been necessary to allow previously unused areas to be cultivated.

CLIMATE

The climate is Mediterranean throughout much of the country, although winters in the mountain areas are cold, with snow cover lasting several months. Summers are hot and dry, with average July temperatures of 24°-25°C (75°-77°F). During the winter frequent cyclones make the weather unstable, but it remains relatively mild in the plains, with January temperatures averaging 8°C (47°F) in the coastal town of Durrës, and 4°C (39°F) in the more northerly inland city of Shkodër. Average annual rainfall is 1,300 mm, but regional variations are pronounced; in the Alps it is over 2,000 mm, whereas in the valleys of the interior it is only 650–700 mm.

POPULATION

According to official figures, the total population at the census of April 1989 was 3,182,417, of which approximately 98% were ethnic Albanians. Other nationalities included 58,758 Greeks, the majority of whom live in the south, 4,697 Macedonians, small numbers of Bulgarians and Roma (Gypsies) and about 100 Serbs and Montenegrins. However, all figures for minority groups in Albania are contested by neighbouring countries. Yugoslav sources assert that there are several thousand Serbs and Montenegrins in Albania and 55,000–60,000 Macedonians. Some Greek sources claim that there are more than 300,000 ethnic Greeks living in

Albania. Western sources also mention some 35,000 Vlahs (descendants of the autochthonous Thracians), living in the Korçë region, and more than 5,000 Roma. In 1991 many members of the ethnic minorities were reported to have left the country.

The official ban on religious worship, which was in effect between 1967 and 1990, makes it difficult to assess the religious affiliations of the population. According to the religious census of 1945, 72.8% of the population were Muslims, 17.1% Eastern Orthodox and 10.1% Roman Catholic. Of the Muslim population, an estimated 25% were members of the liberal Bektashi sect. In late 1990 and early 1991 the small community of some 300 Albanian Jews emigrated in its entirety to Israel. The official language is Albanian, the principal dialects being Gheg (spoken north of the River Shkumbin) and Tosk (in the south). The literary language is a fusion of the two dialects, with the phonetic and morphological structure of Tosk prevailing. Ethnic Greeks continue to use their own language.

The majority of the population live on the coastal plains and nearly one-half of the population lives outside major towns. Average population density (persons per sq km), at the 1989 census, was 110.9, but that of the lowland plains was much higher. In 1988 the population density in the coastal province of Lushnjë was 185.7, whereas in the mountain province of Pukë, in the north, it was only 46.6. There are many ethnic Albanians living in other countries, including some 2m. in Yugoslavia, mainly in the neighbouring region of Kosovo (Kosovar Albanians), and in Macedonia. There is a small number of Albanians in northern Greece (the Çam community). The capital, Tirana (Tiranë) is situated in the centre of the country and had an estimated population of 225,700 at mid-1987. Other important towns include Durrës, Albania's largest port (78,700), Elbasan, a major industrial centre (78,300), and Shkodër (76,300).

Chronology

168 BC: Illyria (which included modern-day Albania) was annexed by the Roman Empire.

395 AD: Following a division of the administration of the Roman Empire, Illyria was ruled by the Eastern Roman ('Byzantine') Emperor in Constantinople (Istanbul).

6th–7th centuries: Slavs colonized Albania.

1385: Ottoman (Turkish) forces reached the Albanian coast.

1443: Gjergj Kastrioti (Skënderbeu or Skenderbeg) led Albanians in a revolt against Ottoman rule.

1468: Death of Skënderbeu.

1478: The Ottomans established full control over Albania.

1756: Mehemet of Bushan established an independent principality in northern Albania.

1787: Ali Pasha of Tepelenë (Janina) established an independent principality in southern Albania and neighbouring territories.

1822: Turkish forces overthrew Ali Pasha.

1831: Mustafa Pasha, of the Bushan dynasty, was overthrown.

1878: The Congress of Berlin allotted parts of Albanian territory to Bulgaria, Montenegro, Serbia and Greece. The Albanian League for the Defence of the Rights of the Albanian Nation was established.

1881: The Albanian League was disbanded by the Ottomans.

1910: An uprising against Ottoman rule was suppressed by Turkish forces.

October 1912: The First Balkan War began; Albania was occupied by neighbouring powers.

28 November 1912: A national convention, convened in Vlorë, proclaimed the independence of Albania; Ismail Qemal was appointed President.

July 1913: The London Ambassadors' Conference recognized the principle of Albanian independence, but designated the country a protectorate, under the control of the Great Powers; Kosovo was granted to Serbia; other territories were gained by Greece.

March 1914: Prince William of Wied, who had been appointed ruler of the Albanian protectorate by the Great Powers, arrived in Albania.

August 1914: Italy and Greece occupied southern Albania at the outbreak of the First World War.

September 1914: Prince William of Wied left Albania, following local opposition to his rule.

April 1915: The secret Treaty of London was signed, which provided for much of Albania to be partitioned between Greece, Italy, Serbia and Montenegro.

January 1920: The Congress of Lushnjë reaffirmed Albania's independence and appointed a new Government; Tirana (Tiranë) was declared the capital of Albania.

August 1920: Italy agreed to withdraw its forces from Albania and recognize Albanian independence.

December 1920: Albania was admitted to the League of Nations.

10 June 1924: After an armed uprising, a Government headed by Fan Noli came to power.

24 December 1924: The Government of Fan Noli was overthrown by forces led by Ahmet Zogu.

January 1925: The Republic of Albania was proclaimed; Ahmet Zogu was appointed President.

September 1928: A monarchy was established, with Zogu proclaiming himself King Zog I.

April 1939: Italian troops invaded Albania; King Zog was forced into exile. The union of Albania and Italy under the Italian Crown was subsequently proclaimed.

November 1941: The Communist Party of Albania was founded; Enver Hoxha became its first leader.

September 1942: The National Liberation Front, a Communist-led liberation organization, was established.

September 1943: Italy surrendered to the Allies; Albania was invaded by Nazi German forces.

1943–44: Fierce fighting occurred between Nazi forces and resistance groups, and also between resistance groups of different political persuasions.

24–28 May 1944: The Congress of Përmet established the Anti-Fascist Committee for National Liberation, headed by Enver Hoxha, as a provisional government.

29 November 1944: The National Liberation Front proclaimed the liberation of Albania.

2 December 1945: Elections with only Communist candidates took place; the Communists, as the Democratic Front, won some 90% of the votes cast.

11 January 1946: The People's Republic of Albania was proclaimed; King Zog was declared deposed.

October 1946: Two British warships were damaged in the Corfu Channel (between the Greek island of Corfu and the Albanian coast) by mines, allegedly planted by Albania.

1948: Close relations with Yugoslavia were ended after Yugoslavia was expelled from the Communist Information Bureau (Cominform). Yugoslav personnel in Albania were expelled and economic agreements between the two countries abrogated. The Albanian Communist Party was renamed the Party of Labour of Albania (PLA).

1949: Albania joined the Council for Mutual Economic Assistance (CMEA or Comecon). Koci Xoxe (former Minister of the Interior) and other officials were executed as alleged pro-Yugoslav traitors.

1954: Hoxha resigned as Chairman of the Council of Ministers (head of government), but retained effective power as First Secretary of the PLA. Mehmet Shehu was appointed head of government.

1955: Albania joined the Warsaw Treaty Organization (Warsaw Pact or WTO). The Soviet *rapprochement* with Yugoslavia strained Soviet–Albanian relations.

1959: Khrushchev visited Albania in an attempt to dissuade the Albanians from seeking an alliance with the People's Republic of China.

1961: The USSR denounced Albania and severed diplomatic relations after Hoxha announced his support for the Chinese Communist leader, Mao Zedong, in his ideological conflict with the USSR.

1962: Albania formally left the CMEA.

1967: Religious worship was outlawed and all mosques and churches were closed.

1968: Albania formally left the Warsaw Pact.

1972: Improved US–Chinese relations were denounced by Albania.

1975: Gen. Beqir Balluku, who had been dismissed as Minister of Defence in 1974, was executed as an alleged pro-Chinese traitor.

1976: A new constitution was adopted; the country's name was changed to the People's Socialist Republic of Albania.

1978: Albania declared its support for Viet-Nam, in its conflict with the People's Republic of China; China suspended all military and economic ties.

December 1981: Mehmet Shehu, head of government, died in a shooting incident. There were subsequent allegations that he had been murdered.

November 1982: Ramiz Alia replaced Haxhi Lleshi as Chairman of the Presidium of the People's Assembly (head of state).

April 1985: Death of Enver Hoxha. He was succeeded as First Secretary of the PLA by Ramiz Alia.

March 1986: Nexhmije Hoxha, the widow of Enver Hoxha, was appointed leader of the Communist mass organization, the Democratic Front.

February 1989: Government personnel changes were announced at the Ninth Plenum of the Central Committee.

November 1989: Some political prisoners were released as part of a general amnesty.

December 1989: There were reports of anti-government demonstrations in the northern town of Shkodër.

1990

January

11–14: Anti-government demonstrations were dispersed by police in Shkodër.

March

25: Some 500 football supporters took part in a political demonstration in Kavajë.

April

17: At the 10th Plenum of the PLA Central Committee, Alia announced some relaxation of economic controls and the intention to re-establish relations with the USA and the USSR.

May

7–9: The People's Assembly adopted measures to liberalize the penal code, to end the ban on religious propaganda and to relax the constitutional prohibition on foreign investment.

11–13: Javier Pérez de Cuéllar, Secretary-General of the UN, visited Tirana.

June

6: The Government announced its intention to join the Conference on Security and Co-operation in Europe (CSCE).

12: Restrictions on travel to other countries were relaxed.

July

1: Anti-government demonstrations took place in Tirana.

2: Four Albanians sought asylum in the embassy of the Federal Republic of Germany; over the next few days several thousand people sought refuge in the embassies of foreign countries.

9: Alia dismissed four ministers from the Government.

9–13: Some 5,000 Albanians who had sought asylum at foreign embassies were allowed to leave the country.

30: The USSR and Albania announced that diplomatic relations between them were to be restored.

August

16: Albania signed the Treaty on the Non-Proliferation of Nuclear Weapons.

22: Tian Zengpei, Deputy Foreign Minister of the People's Republic of China, visited Tirana, the first visit by a senior Chinese official since the late 1970s.

29 September: Ramiz Alia visited the USA to address the UN General Assembly.

October

24–25: For the first time, a meeting of the Balkan Conference (the foreign ministers of six Balkan countries) was held in Tirana.

26: Ismail Kadare, Albania's leading novelist, requested political asylum while in France.

November

11: In Shkodër, thousands of people attended the first public celebration of the Roman Catholic Mass since 1967.

19–20: Albania attended the CSCE meeting in Paris as an observer, but was refused membership of the organization.

December

8–9: In Tirana, student protests took place at Enver Hoxha University.

11: The 13th Plenum of the Central Committee of the PLA agreed to the legalization of opposition parties; five full members and two candidate members of the Politburo were dismissed.

12: Opposition activists announced the formation of the Democratic Party of Albania (DPA).

13: Troops were used to disperse rioters in Shkodër; anti-government riots took place in Kavajë.

14: Further riots took place throughout the country.

19: The DPA was officially registered as Albania's first opposition party since the Second World War.

20: Nexhmije Hoxha was replaced as head of the Democratic Front by Adel Çarçani, the Chairman of the Council of Ministers.

22: An estimated 15,000 people demonstrated at Enver Hoxha University, in Tirana.

26: An Extraordinary Party Conference of the PLA drafted a manifesto outlining economic and constitutional reforms.

31: A draft of the new Constitution, guaranteeing multi-party democracy and economic liberalization, was published.

1991

January

5: The first legal opposition newspaper since before the Second World War, *Rilindja Demokratike* (Democratic Revival), was published. The Government announced an amnesty for over 200 political prisoners.

13–14: Konstantinos Mitsotakis, the Prime Minister of Greece, visited Tirana, in an attempt to quell the exodus of ethnic Greeks from Albania.

16: The Government announced that elections, scheduled for 10 February, would be postponed until 31 March, after protests by the newly-formed opposition parties.

18: The first legal Muslim religious service since 1967 took place in Tirana.

23: Legislation which guaranteed the right to strike was adopted by the People's Assembly. Transport workers and dockers ended their strikes.

31: A more reformist government was announced after personnel changes; new members of the Government included Fatos Nano, a reformist economist.

February

6: Student strikes began at Enver Hoxha University, in Tirana.

18: Over 700 students and lecturers started a hunger strike at Enver Hoxha University.

20: Several thousand people demonstrated in Tirana; a statue of Enver Hoxha, in Skënderbeu Square, was pulled down by crowds. Ramiz Alia declared presidential rule.

22: Alia dismissed the Government of Adil Çarçani and appointed a provisional Council of Ministers, headed by Fatos Nano.

25: Tanks were withdrawn from Tirana after several days of rioting, during which several people were reported killed and 54 were arrested.

March

8: The Italian navy was ordered to prevent any more vessels landing at the Italian port of Brindisi, after some 20,000 Albanians had arrived on ships seized in Albanian ports.

12: A general amnesty for all remaining political prisoners was announced.

15: Diplomatic relations were restored with the USA.

31: The PLA won over 60% of the votes cast in Albania's first multi-party election since the 1920s.

April

2: Four people died after security forces fired on rioters in Shkodër; some 3,000 demonstrators in Tirana were dispersed by police and security forces.

10: The new People's Assembly convened; the DPA did not attend its first session.

29: An interim constitutional law was adopted, in which the country was renamed the 'Republic of Albania'.

30: Ramiz Alia was elected to the new post of President of the Republic, by the People's Assembly.

May

16: The Union of Independent Albanian Trade Unions announced a general strike, demanding pay increases and the resignation of the Government.

21: The United Kingdom announced that diplomatic relations with Albania were to be restored.

June

4: The Government led by Fatos Nano resigned.

5: Ylli Bufi, Minister of Food under Fatos Nano, was appointed head of government.

10: The general strike ended after concessions by the Government. The 10th Congress of the PLA opened; the PLA changed its name to the Socialist Party of Albania (SPA).

12: A coalition government, including the first non-Communist ministers since the Second World War, was approved by the People's Assembly.

13: The 10th Congress of the PLA (SPA) ended; nine former Politburo members were expelled from the party; Fatos Nano was elected as President of the party.

19: Albania was admitted as a member of the CSCE.

22: James Baker, the US Secretary of State, visited Albania.

July

4: Albania and the Holy See announced that diplomatic relations would be re-established.

9: Ethnic Albanians from the Yugoslav province of Kosovo attacked border installations on the Yugoslav–Albanian border.

11: The People's Assembly passed a resolution demanding an end to alleged violence against Albanians in the Yugoslav province of Kosovo.

August

8: Thousands of Albanians seized ships, in an attempt to emigrate to Italy. Some vessels were prevented from landing by the Italian authorities, but one ship, with more than 10,000 people on board, reached the port of Bari.

History

MIRANDA VICKERS

THE ESTABLISHMENT OF THE ALBANIAN STATE

On 28 November 1912, after more than 400 years under Ottoman (Turkish) rule, Albania declared its independence under a provisional Government. The Albanians' decision to declare full independence was provoked by the fear that their lands would be divided between Greece, Serbia and Montenegro. In October of that year these states had gained important victories against the Ottoman armies, in the First Balkan War. International recognition followed the declaration of independence, at the London Conference of July 1913. However, the Conference also diminished the territory claimed by the Albanian state, granting the region of Kosovo to Serbia and the area known as Çamëria (Chamouria) to Greece. During the turmoil of the First World War, the armies of Greece, Italy and Austria, and, for a short period, the forces of Serbia and Macedonia, occupied Albanian territory. Italy continued its occupation until 1920, when it agreed to withdraw its forces and Albanian independence was re-established.

In 1920 Albania's first national Government was established at the Congress of Lushnjë, but the limitations of the weakly-constructed constitution were soon evident, as the numerous political forces struggled for power. Until 1924 the country underwent a period of great internal instability, with frequent changes of government. In 1924 there was a short experience of democracy, under Fan Noli, but, being politically inexperienced, he failed to cope with Albania's social and economic disarray.

In December 1924 Ahmed Zogu, who had previously held office as Minister of Internal Affairs, overthrew the Government of Fan Noli and assumed power. In 1925 Albania was declared a republic and Zogu was elected President. Zogu quickly established an autocratic, centralized state and proclaimed himself King Zog I, in 1928. In order to consolidate his regime, Zogu accepted substantial financial subsidies from Italy. Italian economic influence was accompanied by increased political influence in Albania's government. Zogu's need for Italian capital and patronage led to further Italian encroachments into Albania's economy and administration until, eventually, in 1939, Mussolini, the Italian leader, demanded a formal protectorate over Albania. When Zogu objected, the Italians invaded. Although the Albanian armed forces resisted they were soon defeated and Zogu fled into exile. Albania was united with Italy for four years. It was occupied by German forces in 1943. The Germans withdrew after one year, allowing the Communist-led National Liberation Front to take power, in November 1944.

THE ESTABLISHMENT OF COMMUNIST POWER IN ALBANIA

During the 1930s Communist cells were established within Albania. Owing to ideological factionalism no unified Communist organization was established and, by 1941, there were several small Communist groups. In 1941 Tito (Josip Broz), leader of the Communist Party of Yugoslavia (CPY), sent two delegates to Albania. They brought together the Communist leaders and factions that they favoured, and a unified Albanian Communist Party (ACP) was formed in November 1941. In 1942 a National Liberation Movement

(NLM) was established under Yugoslav direction. Although Communists predominated in the NLM, non-Communists were also represented, including some members of Balli Kombëtar (the National Front), a resistance movement which was formed in 1942 by moderately liberal nationalists, who were opposed to the return of Zogu and favoured the re-establishment of a republic.

By the end of 1942 the Albanian partisans had sufficiently impressed representatives of the Allied Powers to be granted military aid. During 1943, however, a fundamental disagreement arose between the Communists and Ballists (members of Balli Kombëtar) over the conduct of the war and over the future of the Kosovo region of Yugoslavia, which was mainly populated by Albanians. Although, initially, they both agreed that a plebiscite should take place in the region, the Communists soon repudiated this, under strong Yugoslav pressure. As distrust intensified, military conflict began between the two groups, despite an attempt at reconciliation in August 1943. Allied support for the Communists in Yugoslavia and Albania allowed the Albanian Communists to defeat their political rivals and occupy Tirana in November 1944. A provisional Government was established, headed by Enver Hoxha, the leader of the ACP. In December 1945 elections took place, with a single list of candidates, all sponsored by the Communists.

ALBANIA UNDER ENVER HOXHA

After 1945 Albania was dominated by the personality of Enver Hoxha, the chief ideologist of Albanian-style socialism. He was born in Gjirokastër, in southern Albania, in 1908. During the early 1930s he studied and worked in France and Belgium. In 1936 he returned to Albania to become a teacher. He became active in the Communist movement and was elected leader of the Provisional Committee of the ACP in 1941.

Under his rule Albania experienced four distinct phases. During the period 1944–48 Albania developed very close relations with Yugoslavia. As the ACP developed and consolidated under Yugoslav tutelage it became virtually a branch of the CPY. Customs and monetary unions were established between the two countries and Albanian sovereignty effectively disappeared as its dependence on Yugoslavia grew. When the Communist Information Bureau (Cominform) was founded, in 1947, Albania was not represented; Yugoslavia acted as its advocate instead. Had it not been for the rupture of relations between Stalin and Tito, in 1948, Albania would probably have become the seventh republic of Yugoslavia.

During the second phase of Hoxha's rule, from 1948–61, Albania's main international ally was the USSR. After the CPY was forced to leave the Cominform, accused of ideological 'revisionism', Albania's leaders, fearing Yugoslav expansionism, relied on the USSR for help. Yugoslav advisers in Albania were replaced by Soviet personnel and, in 1949, Albania joined the Soviet-dominated Council for Mutual Economic Assistance (CMEA). Hoxha studiously imitated the Soviet leader, Stalin, in developing a dictatorship, using widespread purges to eliminate any opposition. To ensure absolute power within the Party of Labour of Albania (PLA—the name was changed from the Albanian Communist Party in 1948), Hoxha frequently replaced members of the Central Committee and the Political Bureau (Politburo) of the PLA. While ensuring political orthodoxy the leadership also continued the transformation of the economy and social system, eliminating private ownership of industry and commerce and forcibly effecting the collectivization of agriculture. Ambitious schemes in social and health policy improved access to educational and medical

facilities and there was great improvement in levels of literacy.

Soviet–Albanian relations began to deteriorate after Stalin's death in March 1953. Khrushchev's *rapprochement* with Tito, in 1955, and his denunciation of Stalin the next year, severely strained Soviet–Albanian relations. Khrushchev's opposition to Albania's plans for large-scale industrialization also contributed to Albanian dissatisfaction with the alliance with the USSR. In 1960 the Albanian leadership declared their support for the People's Republic of China in the Sino–Soviet ideological dispute.

In 1961 the USSR denounced Albania's support for the People's Republic of China and severed relations. Soviet technicians were replaced by Chinese personnel, but the country's precarious economic situation was only partly relieved by Chinese loans, credits and technical expertise. In 1962 Albania ended participation in the CMEA, causing further problems for the economy. For some years Albania was forced to adopt a policy of austerity. Furthermore, in the relentless pursuit of ideological purism, in 1967 the practice of religion was prohibited, and Albania was proclaimed the world's first atheist state. Persecution intensified as Hoxha attempted to imitate the Chinese 'Cultural Revolution' in his own country. Relations with the People's Republic of China deteriorated, however, after the improvement in Chinese relations with the USA, in 1972, and the death of Mao Zedong, in 1976. In 1978 the People's Republic of China suspended all economic and military co-operation with Albania, after Albania had declared its support for Viet-Nam in the Sino-Vietnamese dispute.

During the fourth phase of Hoxha's rule, from 1978 until 1985, Albania's isolationist policies reached their most extreme. Internal political orthodoxy was enforced with the utmost vigour. The internal security police, the Sigurimi, prevented the development of any opposition movements within Albania. Meanwhile, volume after volume of Hoxha's collected works consolidated his 'cult of personality'.

THE POST-HOXHA YEARS

Enver Hoxha died in April 1985 and was succeeded as First Secretary of the PLA by Ramiz Alia. Alia had played an important role in the development of post-1945 Albania, as Secretary for Ideology in the PLA from the 1960s onwards. His rise to the leadership began after the death of Hoxha's expected successor, Mehmet Shehu, in suspicious circumstances, in 1981. (There were allegations that Hoxha had himself shot Shehu, during a meeting.) One year later Alia replaced Haxhi Lleshi as Chairman of the Presidium of the People's Assembly, the nominal head of state. As First Secretary Alia adopted a less rigid style than his predecessor and, during the late 1980s, the Government began to distance itself gradually from the Hoxha legacy. There were cautious attempts at liberalization and decentralization, and a more flexible foreign policy led to improved relations with a number of Western European countries.

Albania's relations with its immediate neighbours, Yugoslavia and Greece, improved during the 1980s, although alleged ill-treatment of the Albanian community in Yugoslavia and the ethnic Greek minority in Albania at times threatened increased co-operation. Relations with Greece improved following bilateral negotiations in 1984. Furthermore, in 1987, Greece decided formally to end the technical state of war with Albania, which had been in existence since 1945. However, the status of the ethnic Greek minority in southern Albania remained a sensitive issue.

In 1988 Albania participated in the Balkan Conference of Foreign Ministers in Belgrade, the first official meeting of all six Balkan states in more than 50 years. By its involvement, Albania accomplished a goodwill gesture, reassuring its neighbours, especially Yugoslavia, of the country's willingness to help establish a general framework of co-operation in the region. Yugoslavia is one of Albania's major trading partners, and any ideological differences between them tended to be exaggerated, involving more rhetoric than reality. This was especially so in the case of the Albanian population in the Yugoslav province of Kosovo. After the violent unrest in Kosovo, in March 1989, which left at least 25 Albanians dead, Albania accused Yugoslavia of brutally oppressing Kosovo's Albanians. The Government in Tirana also warned that Yugoslavian policy in Kosovo would endanger the increased Balkan co-operation that had been painstakingly built up over the previous year.

The Communist victory in Albania had ended any possibility of the country fighting actively for union with Kosovo, and, after 1948, the intended Yugoslav annexation of Albania became impossible. Since then Albania has offered only verbal and written encouragement to the Albanians of Kosovo. After 1948 Yugoslav–Albanian relations were conditioned by the latter's external and domestic insecurity. During the 1940s and 1950s Albanian policy was strongly anti-Yugoslav, in response to the continued threat of Yugoslav interference. In the late 1960s and 1970s the main threat came from the USSR, so a process of reconciliation with Yugoslavia began.

As a result of its acute isolationist position, it was important for Albania to have stability, both in Yugoslavia and in Kosovo. Any attempt by Albania to annex Kosovo would have been a reckless move, considering the strongly contrasting ideo-political systems of the two countries. The overwhelmingly Muslim Kosovars, who could openly practise their religion in Yugoslavia, would not have willingly accepted Albania's enforced atheism. Nor would Albania's agricultural collectivization have appealed to the Kosovar peasants, who owned their own land. Hoxha valued ideological purity above national unity; Albania, therefore, limited its interests in Kosovo to cultural politics. Albania never appealed to international forums on behalf of the Kosovars, and when members of illegal Kosovo groups sought shelter in Albania they were promptly returned to the Yugoslav authorities.

Although the Albanian leadership often used the situation in Kosovo as a way of deflecting discontent at home, several decades of isolation have accentuated the social and psychological differences separating Albanians from Kosovars. Should the two ever unite, a problem of regionalism could arise. The comparatively sophisticated Kosovars are related to Albania's northern, Gheg-speaking people; these groups are divided by cultural, linguistic and historical differences from the southern, Tosk-speaking Albanians. Although Tosk became the predominant dialect after the Second World War, it has not had the unifying affect anticipated, and, with the diffusion of central authority, regionalism is again surfacing.

ALBANIA'S *PERESTROIKA*

Albania embarked on mildly reformist policies, for economic reasons, before the collapse of Communist regimes in Eastern Europe in 1989. However, the example of the 1989 revolutions, and notably the Romanian revolution of December, forced the PLA to consider more fundamental reforms. The impetus for change initially came from within the PLA itself, particularly from its increasingly-educated élite, although large and frequent student protests accelerated the pace of change in 1990.

The first signs of political liberalization appeared in November 1989, when an amnesty was announced for cer-

tain political prisoners. The pace of reform quickened throughout 1990, after a number of demonstrations and strikes in the early part of the year. There were reports of unrest in the northern town of Shkodër, in January 1990, when anti-government demonstrators were violently dispersed by security forces. Further demonstrations were reported during the month, some involving as many as 7,000 people. In late January the Ninth Plenum of the Central Committee of the PLA met to approve a 25-point reform plan, which proposed greater decentralization of the economy and some democratic reform in political institutions. Addressing the Central Committee, Alia proposed bonuses for workers in important industries, pricing changes, and, most significant of all, the prospect of multi-candidate elections. He also proposed some decentralization of Party authority, which would enable local organizations to appoint all but the most senior officials. Increased supplies of food and consumer goods were also promised. Nevertheless, Alia continued to reject the idea of a multi-party system, claiming that such a system was not appropriate for Albania.

In June 1990 Albania made an official request to join the Conference on Security and Co-operation in Europe (CSCE), with an agreement that Albania would adopt all the principles of the 1975 Helsinki Final Act. At the same time the People's Assembly (Albania's legislature) approved further measures of liberalization. The penal code was changed, considerably reducing the number of crimes carrying the death penalty. Religious worship was also to be tolerated, although Albania would remain an atheist state. The Ministry of Justice, which had been abolished in 1965, was re-established, and enterprises were to be allowed to sell some surplus goods on the free market. Albanians were also to be granted the right to a passport, for purposes of foreign travel, and the penalty for attempting to leave the country illegally was considerably reduced.

Despite increasing liberalization, there was further unrest in July 1990, when security forces violently dispersed anti-government demonstrators in Tirana. Immediately following the violence, four Albanians sought asylum in the embassy of the Federal Republic of Germany and, over the next few days, several thousand people sought refuge in foreign embassies. In response to this crisis a meeting of the Central Committee took place, resulting in personnel changes in various ministerial positions, including the dismissal of the leading conservative, Simon Stefani, as Minister of Internal Affairs. However, most of the changes that took place affected the Government, not the real centre of power, the Politburo of the PLA. Stefani, for example, although removed from the Ministry of Internal Affairs, remained a member of the Politburo. The refugee crisis was finally resolved when some 5,000 Albanians were allowed to leave the country, assisted by a multi-national relief operation, co-ordinated by the UN.

In foreign affairs there were significant changes. In July 1990 the restoration of diplomatic links with the USSR was announced. In August talks began in Washington, on the resumption of diplomatic ties with the USA. The US Government showed some reluctance to restore diplomatic relations until multi-party elections were announced; relations were finally re-established in March 1991. Representatives from the United Kingdom and Albania also met to discuss the restoration of diplomatic relations between the two countries. Albania had always insisted on the return of gold seized by the United Kingdom at the end of the Second World War before diplomatic ties could be resumed. The United Kingdom's claim on this gold was agreed by the International Court of Justice as compensation for the sinking, allegedly by Albanian mines, of a

British ship in the Corfu Channel in 1946; the gold was valued at some £20m. in 1991. This was one of Europe's oldest diplomatic disputes, prompting President Alia to accuse consecutive British Governments of remaining 'in a Cold War mentality'. However, both parties agreed that arguments over the confiscated gold should be postponed until after the resumption of diplomatic ties, which were finally restored in May 1991.

The announcement, in May 1990, that the practice of religion was no longer to be an offence was a major reversal of past policy. In November thousands of people attended the first legal Roman Catholic Mass for 23 years in Shkodër. In December celebrations of Christmas were permitted in other towns. In January 1991 Muslims celebrated their first legal service since 1967. During 1991 some churches and mosques were reopened.

In October, as the process of change gathered momentum, the credibility of the Government's reform programme suffered a reverse when Ismail Kadare, the country's foremost author, sought asylum while in Paris. His criticism of the limitations of the reforms being implemented severely embarrassed the Albanian Government, who were hosting the Balkan Conference at the time. In response to popular pressure for more radical reform, Alia announced proposals for reforming the political system, including redefinition of the role of the PLA and a new electoral procedure, requiring the presentation of at least two candidates in every constituency.

THE INTRODUCTION OF A MULTI-PARTY SYSTEM

In early December 1990 there were student demonstrations in Tirana, demanding the introduction of a multi-party system for the elections to the People's Assembly, which were scheduled for February 1991. On 11 December, in response to growing unrest, the Central Committee of the PLA agreed to legalize independent political parties. The formation of the Democratic Party of Albania (DPA), the first legal opposition party since before the Second World War, was announced the next day. The DPA, led by Dr Salih Berisha, a cardiologist, and Gramoz Pashko, an economist, announced that it wished to see the provisions of the Helsinki Final Act as the basis for Albanian society. They demanded that Albania agree to the four principles of the Paris Charter (signed by members of the CSCE—all European countries except Albania—in Paris, in late 1990): a free market economy, self-determination, free elections and the right to own private property. The Council of Ministers granted the DPA 1m. lekë and a loan of US $50,000 to help defray expenses. The first opposition newspaper, *Rilindja Demokratike* (Democratic Revival), which was relatively aggressive in its anti-Communist stance, was published in January 1991, and its first print-run of 50,000 was completely sold within hours. By March 1991 the membership of the DPA had risen to some 60,000, as opposed to the PLA's estimated 130,000 members (a drop from the figure of 147,000 given at the Ninth Congress of the PLA in 1986).

The announcement of the new party came amidst an outbreak of violent unrest in Shkodër. Security forces were sent to quell the trouble, and the leaders of the DPA appeared on television, appealing for restraint and patience from the public, so as not to hinder the pace of reform. The demonstrations seemed to be a spontaneous expression of frustration, by a people who had been promised fundamental reforms, yet were seeing few results. Shortages of consumer goods and the rationing of basic goods had led to bitter discontent and demands for more radical changes. The Government's response was the dismissal of more conservative officials, including Nexhmije Hoxha, Enver Hoxha's widow, who resigned from the presidency of the Democratic Front, a 'mass' organization of the PLA, in charge of organizing elections and maintaining internal security. She was replaced by Adil Çarçani, the Chairman of the Council of Ministers.

Speaking to the Council of Ministers, Alia announced that the PLA must now 'deviate from many of the principles of socialism'. The core of his speech examined the PLA's expressed goal of 'full integration within Europe', with a cautious but significant remark regarding the status of Stalin and people who styled themselves as 'loyal Stalinists'. The Council of Ministers agreed that 'historic circumstances had changed since the time when it was decided to honour J. V. Stalin in our country', and decreed that Stalin's name should be removed from state institutions and places.

In mid-January there were strikes in the mining and public transport sectors; these only ended after increased salaries were agreed and legislation granting the right to strike was adopted by the People's Assembly. The strikes were followed by the second round of government personnel changes in less than six weeks, in which Fatos Nano and Shkelqim Çani, both reformist economists, were appointed deputy premiers. Following threats from the nascent opposition to boycott the forthcoming elections unless they were postponed, the Government announced that the elections would take place on 31 March 1991, instead of on the original date of 10 February.

During January 1991, Greek–Albanian relations had become strained, because of the exodus of more than 5,000 members of Albania's Greek minority, who had begun crossing the border into northern Greece in late December. Although the majority had passports, the Greek embassy in Tirana was reluctant to issue more than a minimum of visas, fearing that Greece might be overwhelmed by large numbers of ethnic Greek Albanians. The Albanian Government estimated the officially-recognized minority in the southern provinces at 50,000, but Greece has long claimed a figure of 300,000 or more (all of whom would be eligible for Greek citizenship if they crossed the border). In mid-January Konstantinos Mitsotakis, the Prime Minister of Greece, was invited to Tirana to discuss the crisis. He sought to discourage further refugees by urging ethnic Greeks to remain in Albania and keep faith in the reform process. When asked, however, most of the refugees appeared to have little confidence in the changes underway in Albania.

The months of February and March 1991 were a time of political crisis in Albania, with many observers predicting military intervention. Demonstrations in early February, by students at the Enver Hoxha University in Tirana, developed into a hunger strike involving some 700 students and lecturers. Their demands included removing the name of Enver Hoxha from the University and an end to the compulsory study of Marxist theory. Several thousand people marched to the centre of Tirana on 20 February and pulled down the statue of Enver Hoxha in the central Skënderbeu Square. There was some violence as security forces attempted to disperse the protesters and an estimated 20 people were injured. Later the same day, in response to the growing unrest, Ramiz Alia declared presidential rule, denouncing the demonstrators as 'vandals' and announcing the formation of a new Government and the establishment of a Presidential Council. The demonstrations continued the next day with protesters publicly burning the works of Enver Hoxha, and there were reports of violence between rival military factions, after 120 reformist officers went on hunger strike to protest at the use of force against demonstrators. At least three people were killed when a crowd tried to enter the Tirana military academy.

Concessions by the authorities, including the removal of Enver Hoxha's name from the University, together with increased force used by the police and security forces, brought an end to the rioting. The underlying tensions, however, remained. Shortly afterwards, a group of officers loyal to Hoxha established a Commission for the Defence of the Homeland and demanded that the statue of Hoxha be re-erected. Groups of 'Enverists', proclaiming loyalty to Hoxha's ideology, staged demonstrations in several towns.

Ramiz Alia was perceived as a strong politician who favoured dialogue and as the motivating force behind the reforms, which were strongly opposed by conservatives in all the state security organizations. Even non-Communists credited Alia with the continuation of reforms, despite pressure from conservatives within the PLA. The DPA was reluctant to stage an open confrontation with Alia, whom they viewed as a pivotal figure in the reform process. Alia seemed to be relatively popular for his reforms and, although he and his fellow leaders had certain obvious privileges (villas, cars, private beaches, foreign travel), there was little evidence of the blatant corruption revealed elsewhere in Eastern Europe. This view was amended somewhat in mid-1991 after several articles in the Albanian press alleged that many leaders in the PLA had enjoyed luxurious life styles earned from illegal activities. For instance, the PLA daily, *Zëri i Popullit*, described the leaders of the Durrës Party Committee as living like 'feudal lords', funding their mansions and hunting reserves from bribery and corruption. Despite the widely-held view of Alia as a positive force in the reform process, in July 1991 Hekuran Isai, Minister of Internal Affairs at the time of the February disturbances in Tirana, claimed that he had refused to carry out orders issued by Alia to shoot at demonstrators. These allegations were strongly denied by Alia himself.

In February 1991, however, the status of Hoxha remained the main focus of the conflict between the youth-led, anti-Communist opposition in the towns and the older, conservative Communists who controlled the security forces and were stronger in the provinces. By the end of February there were reports of serious divisions within the PLA and Alia warned for the first time that his leadership was being questioned.

In early March, a new crisis began, as thousands of Albanians attempted to emigrate to Italy. The would-be emigrants, mostly unemployed young men, commandeered ships in the ports of Vlorë and sailed to the Italian port of Brindisi. The Italian navy was ordered to prevent any more ships from docking and the Albanian authorities placed Durrës under military rule to prevent any more refugees from leaving Albania. There was also violence in Tirana, when security forces prevented Albanians from entering foreign embassies. In all, more than 20,000 people arrived in Brindisi, some of whom subsequently returned to Albania, perhaps disillusioned with the lack of aid offered them by the Italian authorities. Other refugees were moved to camps in southern Italy.

THE ELECTIONS AND THEIR AFTERMATH

Despite the unrest which preceded them, Albania's first multi-party elections for six decades took place peacefully, at the end of March. The elections had originally been scheduled for 10 February, but one of the demands of the DPA had been their postponement, to allow the new parties time to campaign and to enable a more even contest. After talks between the Government and the opposition parties, it was agreed there would be a 'no-strike policy' until 1 May, in exchange for a delaying of the elections until 31 March.

After the establishment of the DPA, in December, other smaller parties were registered, including the Albanian Republican Party, the Agrarian Party, the Ecology Party and the Democratic Union of the Greek Minority (OMONIA). All of these smaller parties nominated candidates for the elections, but the main contenders were the DPA and the PLA. The PLA and its affiliated organizations, such as the Democratic Front, the Union of Working Youth of Albania, the War Veterans' Committee and the Women's Union of Albania nominated 644 of the 1,074 registered candidates. These affiliated groups, once strictly controlled by the PLA, were becoming more independent. The DPA campaign promised a transformation of living standards, to be brought about by EC membership, Western financial aid and jobs in Italian and German factories for the thousands of unemployed. They also advocated privatization of land, a policy which was attacked by the PLA, who claimed it would leave peasants landless.

The most important of the smaller parties was the Republican Party, with a manifesto similar to that of the DPA, but less radical. It advocated a gradual programme of privatization, relying on more foreign investment, in contrast to the DPA's advocacy of rapid privatization and an immediate transition to a free enterprise system. Owing to its relatively moderate stand, the Republican Party was perceived, by some observers, as less hostile towards the PLA than the other opposition parties. The Ecology Party, with its small membership, campaigned for social harmony and environmental protection rather than traditional political and economic issues. OMONIA, while supporting democratic changes, also campaigned on issues specific to the Greek minority. The newest of the opposition groups, the Agrarian Party, which did not have time to develop its proposed programme fully before the elections, promised to raise the living standards of Albania's large rural population.

According to official figures, in the first round of elections, on 31 March 1991, almost 97% of the 1.9m. people eligible to vote did so, the highest level in any multi-party election in Eastern Europe. In the first round of voting, the PLA won 162 of the 250 seats in the Assembly. The DPA won 65 seats, including 17 out of the 19 seats in Tirana, and some 40% of the votes cast. The opposition won all the urban constituencies while the rural areas voted predominantly for the PLA. The fact that the PLA neglected to campaign in the urban centres suggests that they were confident of being able to ignore the results in the towns. Rural Albania consists of a relatively isolated peasantry, comprising almost 60% of the population, who seem to be wary of change and anxious for their security. The PLA successfully gained the support of the rural population with promises of improved standards of living, better housing, increased wages and new free market incentives, thus allaying the fears of many elderly people that they would lose not only their lands if the DPA won, but also their pensions. A crucial factor in the defeat of the DPA was the widespread belief that the DPA would privatize and redistribute the land, whereas the PLA had promised to protect the peasantry from privatization.

On 7 and 14 April 1991 further rounds of voting took place in the 17 electoral districts where no candidate had won an absolute majority in the first round, and in two constituencies where no contest had occurred. In these rounds the DPA won 10 seats, the PLA seven and OMONIA two. Overall, the PLA won a total of 169 of the 250 seats in the People's Assembly, just over the two-thirds majority (167 seats) required to adopt a new Constitution; the DPA won 75 seats and OMONIA won five seats. The most surprising result was the failure of Alia to win a seat in the People's Assembly. He won only 36% of the votes cast in his Tirana constituency, whereas his DPA-supported opponent won 62.5%. Alia apparently misjudged the mood of the capital's population and was a victim of the urban electorate's determination to rid themselves of the PLA. Other leading Communists who were not elected included Spiro Dede, Alia's main ally in the PLA leadership, and Mohamet Kapllani, the Minister of Foreign Affairs. Another surprising outcome of the elections was that the candidates representing the conservatives, or 'hard-liners', within the PLA, including Adil Çarçani, the former premier, and Xhelil Gjoni, a member of the Politburo, fared better than the reformist Communists.

The PLA fared best in the Tosk-inhabited south, where Communist sympathies were strongest, but they also did well in Pezë, just outside Tirana, and Dibra, which borders Macedonia; both regions have a traditionally strong Communist following. The opposition suffered mainly because it was recently formed, and, due to the poor infrastructure throughout Albania, it lacked the transportation and communication necessary to disseminate its views widely and quickly. The DPA complained of a lack of media representation and of psychological pressure to vote for the PLA. They also contradicted the consensus among the 260 international observers by claiming that the elections had been conducted in a 'climate of terror'. Most independent Western observers attested to the overall fairness of the elections, claiming that fraud and manipulation were minimal. They admitted the PLA's control of election scrutineers in some rural areas and domination over the media, but concluded that the PLA's victory was largely the result of the lack of a developed and informed political culture. The results of the elections were, in some respects, similar to those in other, former one-party Balkan states, where many rural voters were wary of change, while the urban population was anxious to see rapid and fundamental reform.

There was a strong reaction to the PLA's victory in the election, especially among the younger urban population. On 2 April 1991, after the first election results had been announced, a demonstration took place in Shkodër, protesting against alleged incidents of fraud and manipulation during the elections. When security forces attempted to disperse the crowd, four people were killed and many injured, allegedly as a result of shots fired by the police. The force used against demonstrators was in contrast to the pre-election tactics of the security forces. At the Presidium of the People's Assembly, Gramoz Rucaj, the Minister of Internal Affairs, described the demonstrators as 'traitors', adding that everyone should 'bow to the will of the people and the actions of the law'. With the elections over and won, it seemed possible that conservative factions within the PLA, including the military, could arrest the process of reform. Indeed, to placate the professional members of the armed forces, it was decided to reintroduce ranks, which had been abolished in the 1960s, into the armed forces.

The Albanian Army, of some 35,000 men with 150,000 reservists, is largely conscripted. It contains a high proportion of students and graduates, who are mainly seconded to menial labour. The army is poorly equipped, relying on outdated Soviet and Chinese armaments, many of which have been rendered inoperative by the lack of spare parts. Much of the small Air Force has been grounded for the same reason. The Army has traditionally wielded less power than the security forces, the Sigurimi, and the PLA has often intervened in military policy by purging and disciplining officers during periods of tension. Despite the opposition of many military leaders to the reforms it is probable that they were dissuaded from attempting to reverse the process by doubts concerning the loyalty of conscripts and junior officers. Divisions within the officer corps had become apparent during the February 1991 disturbances in Tirana.

Following the violence in Shkodër, Alia appealed to the DPA for a 'national salvation coalition government', so as to diffuse 'unnecessary political antagonisms'. His proposal was rejected by the opposition, who insisted that those responsible for the shootings in Shkodër be brought to trial. The new People's Assembly first convened on 10 April, but opposition deputies refused to attend. At this first session, a representative of the DPA announced that opposition deputies would not participate in the legislature until those responsible for the deaths in Shkodër were identified. The Assembly reconvened one week later, when the DPA ended its boycott; a parliamentary commission was established to investigate the events of Shkodër. It reported, within one week, that the police were to blame for provoking violence from initially peaceful demonstrators.

The draft of a new Constitution was presented to the Assembly in late April 1991. The draft Constitution contained many structural changes, including the establishment of political pluralism and the renaming of the country from 'the People's Socialist Republic of Albania' to simply 'the Republic of Albania'. The Constitution made no reference to Marxism-Leninism as an ideology, nor to the 'leading role' of the PLA. However, the opposition objected to the adoption of a new Constitution so soon after the elections; instead, interim legislation was adopted outlining the basic principles of the state. The 'Constitutional Law and its Main Provisions', as this transitional legislation was known, included most of the provisions of the draft Constitution prepared by the PLA. The state was defined as 'democratic and juridical, based on social equality, the defence of freedom and the rights of man'. The right to private property was endorsed and the rights to strike, to demonstrate and to emigrate were guaranteed. In contrast to the previous system (in which the highest organ of state power was the Presidium of the People's Assembly), there was no provision for a collective organ of government. Instead, an executive President of the country was to be elected by two-thirds of the votes cast in the People's Assembly.

On 30 April 1991 there were elections to this new post. Ramiz Alia, still First Secretary of the PLA, and Namik Dokle, also of the PLA, were the only nominations. Alia was elected by an overwhelming majority. Dokle only received two votes; all the opposition deputies abstained. After his election as President, Alia resigned as First Secretary of the PLA, which he had led for six years, in accordance with the new constitutional amendment, which prevented the President from holding office in a political party. He also resigned from the Politburo and the Central Committee of the PLA. In early May the People's Assembly approved a new Government, headed by Fatos Nano, a reform-orientated economist and a member of the PLA. All the new ministers were PLA members, but the programme presented to the Assembly by Nano envisaged fundamental reforms in both political and economic affairs, including extensive privatization and a rapid shift to a market-based economy. The new Government, however, faced immense problems. Nano admitted that the economy was in crisis, industrial and agricultural production having fallen markedly since 1988, while population growth remained high.

THE END OF COMMUNIST RULE

In mid-May 1991 the newly-established independent trade unions organized a general strike, in which more than 300,000 workers were estimated to have participated. The strikers demanded pay rises of up to 100% and a further investigation into the deaths of demonstrators in Shkodër in April. They also sought the right to paid religious holidays and an end to difficult working conditions for women. Workers from all sectors of the economy participated in the strike and, after one week, the independent unions claimed that 90% of the country's enterprises were closed down. In late May miners began a hunger strike, as the Government continued to reject the unions' demands, and further hunger strikes were reported in several cities in support of the fasting miners. In Tirana several people were injured when a rally in support of the miners was dispersed by the police.

The deterioration of the economic and political situation in the country forced the Government and the opposition to agree to the establishment of a new coalition Government. After the March 1991 elections, the DPA had insisted that they would not enter a coalition with the Communists. It seemed that they agreed to do so only in response to the critical situation in the country and on condition that the new Government would merely act as an interim administration until another general election could take place, probably in mid-1992. On 4 June 1991 Nano's Government resigned. The next day Ylli Bufi, previously the Minister for Food under Nano, was appointed Chairman of the Council of Ministers. By mid-June a new 'Government of National Stability', with a total of 12 non-Communist ministers, had been approved by the legislature. The PLA held 12 portfolios, the DPA gained seven, and the Republican Party, the Social Democratic Party and the Agrarian Party shared the other five between them. The general strike, which had lasted more than three weeks and involved an estimated 350,000 workers, had finally ended nearly five decades of exclusive Communist rule. The Government agreed to pay rises of 15%–80% for all state workers and announced a fresh investigation into the Shkodër killings.

The 10th Congress of the PLA also took place in June 1991. The delegates to the Congress approved fundamental changes to the structure and ideology of the party. The PLA was renamed the Socialist Party of Albania (SPA) and Fatos Nano, former Chairman of the Council of Ministers, was elected President of a new Managing Committee, which replaced the Central Committee. Nine former members of the Politburo were expelled from the PLA and others were demoted. The Congress was notable for the criticism of former PLA leaders, including Hoxha and even Alia. Xhelil Gjoni, a former Politburo member who was widely viewed as a conservative, claimed that the grave political and economic situation in the country was the responsibility of the PLA leadership, who should have changed their policies earlier. The ideology of the party was also reformed; the new party manifesto stated that the SPA would be a modern, progressive party, committed to democracy, social justice and economic reform. The Congress was not without controversy, however. Dritëro Agolli, the Chairman of the Writers' Union, severely criticized the past policies of the PLA and, in particular, the policies of Enver Hoxha. Conservative delegates responded by chanting the traditional Communist slogan 'Enver's Party—Always Ready'.

In mid-1991 there were important advances in foreign affairs. In June Albania was finally admitted to the CSCE; diplomatic relations were established with the EC; James Baker, US Secretary of State, was greeted by more than 400,000 people when he visited Tirana in the same month and offered immediate aid of US $6m.; in early July diplomatic relations with the Holy See were restored and the Government confirmed that there were no obstacles to relations being established with the Republic of Korea and South Africa; and in September the European Bank for Reconstruction and Development (EBRD) agreed to admit Albania. However, armed conflict in Yugoslavia did not suggest any development of Balkan co-operation. During 1991 Albanian politicians became increasingly worried about the fate of the Kosovars of Yugoslavia as Serbians continued fighting in Croatia. The Government issued statements containing strong criticism of the policies of the Serbian leadership in Kosovo, and, in August, Albanian armed forces were placed on alert, after reported incidents between Yugoslav and Albanian border guards. In October Albania recognized the 'Republic of Kosovo' as a 'sovereign and independent state'.

In the two months after its formation the National Stability Government introduced important legislation, notably on the privatization of land and the replacement of People's Councils (local administrative organs) by multi-party bodies. This was a belated attempt to prevent further chaos in the countryside, where some collective-farm members were reportedly seizing land on the basis of pre-collectivization boundaries, while others were left without any land to cultivate. The new legislation allowed an equal share for all collective-farm members, but this resolution of the issue was too late to guarantee a good harvest in 1991; many fields had been left untouched until final ownership was established.

In mid-1991 the immediate prospects for Albania seemed poor. The political situation in the Balkans remained highly volatile; demands have been made within Albania for more forthright government action on the issue of Kosovo and Serbian warnings against Albanian involvement in Yugoslavia have become more strident. Despite the introduction of coalition government and the prospect of foreign aid, the economic situation in Albania cannot be expected to improve rapidly. Social unrest may worsen if rising aspirations are not met. In August 1991 a further 10,000 Albanians attempted to emigrate to Italy; many were unemployed and complained of a lack of food at home and administrative dislocation throughout the country (the Italian authorities ordered the forcible repatriation of the refugees). To prevent further emigration Albania required huge amounts of foreign investment and aid. Whether this would suffice to prevent dangerous unrest during Albania's transition to a market economy, depends on the generosity of the West and the political skill of Albania's new leaders.

The Economy

MIRANDA VICKERS

Albania, Europe's poorest country, has remained economically undeveloped for decades. The country is, however, rich in resources, with an estimated US $50,000m.-worth of extractable minerals and $40,000m.-worth of onshore petroleum reserves. Other energy-related minerals include lignite, natural gas and asphalt. Metallic minerals include chromite (chromium ore), nickeliferous iron ore, copper ore and smaller quantities of cobalt and nickel. There are also deposits of phosphorous, bauxite, precious metals, kaolin clay, asbestos and titanomagnetite. Relatively little is known outside the country about Albania's economic performance. In the past statistical data have been highly selective and constantly manipulated in order to conceal the true state of the country's economy.

Until the early 1990s the system was rigidly centralized, with fixed prices, state or co-operative ownership of all means of production and planned regulation of output. The result was a shortage of skilled manpower, a decline in labour productivity due to absenteeism and low morale, outdated, inefficient enterprises and a chronic lack of consumer goods. After Enver Hoxha's death, in 1985, in an attempt to modernize the underdeveloped economy, the leadership experimented with new schemes designed to revitalize the system, without changing its ideological basis. By 1991, however, all the main political parties in Albania were committed to a radical transformation of the economic system, including large-scale privatization and the introduction of a market economy. Such a policy, though necessary, remains fraught with difficulties: the difference in economic performance between Albania and its neighbours, its population's rising expectations, largely obsolete industrial equipment, backward agriculture and inadequate services are just some of the many socio-economic problems facing Albania.

THE ALBANIAN ECONOMY AFTER 1945

Before the Second World War Albania was a largely agricultural country with very little industry. Once the Communists had seized power they nationalized most economic resources and began a programme of rapid industrialization. By 1960, according to official figures, industry accounted for 57.1% of total national income, an increase from 9.8% in 1938. New industrial enterprises included hydroelectric power stations, mineral-processing plants and industrial ventures associated with forestry and agriculture. The increase in industrial production in the 1950s was not, however, matched by a corresponding improvement in agricultural production. Anxiety about this imbalance between agriculture and industry was reflected in the third Five-Year Plan (1961–65), in which the planned growth rate for agriculture was, for the first time, greater than that envisaged for industry. The early 1960s was a period of great difficulty for the Albanian economy, which had suffered serious dislocation after the withdrawal of Soviet assistance in 1961. By the beginning of the fourth Five-Year Plan (1966–70), partly as a result of aid and technical expertise from the People's Republic of China, Albania had largely recovered from the economic crisis of the early 1960s.

During the 'Cultural Revolution' experienced in Albania in the 1960s (a conscious imitation of the policies initiated in the People's Republic of China) there were attempts to minimize differentials between workers in different sectors of the economy and between manual and non-manual workers. During the 1970s measures continued to narrow income differentials, in an attempt to eliminate the possibility of a privileged stratum emerging. Nevertheless, the standard of living gradually increased and there was some progress in the introduction of modern technology, including the opening of Albania's first television station, in 1971, and the completion of an internal telephone system, in 1973. According to Western estimates, annual growth of real gross national product (GNP) was estimated at 4.2% during the 1970s. In 1979 GNP was estimated to be US $2,240m., equivalent to about $840 per head. The 1976 constitutional prohibition on accepting loans and credits from foreign sources severely constrained economic growth and served to keep foreign trade at the barter stage. The ban saved Albania from convertible-currency indebtedness, but also deprived the country of valuable knowledge of foreign markets. The ending of all economic agreements with the People's Republic of China, which, until 1978, accounted for about one-half of all Albania's foreign trade, also had serious consequences for Albania's international trade.

During the 1980s growth rates steadily declined and both industry and agriculture had great difficulty meeting their planned production targets. During the seventh Five-Year Plan (1981–85) net material product (NMP—a similar measure to GNP used in centrally planned economies) increased by 16% against a target of 35%–37%, an average annual growth rate of 3%, only slightly ahead of annual population growth. In November 1986, at the Ninth Congress of the PLA, Ramiz Alia, First Secretary of the PLA, admitted that economic performance during the seventh Five-Year Plan had been much poorer than expected. Agricultural production grew by 27%, instead of the planned 36%–38%, and petroleum extraction reached only about one-half of the expected 58%–60% growth. Alia directed his main criticism at management failures, arguing that 'pre-industrial methods of management can no longer apply'. He then proposed some decentralization of the decision-making process and the linking of salaries to output and quality. Bonuses were paid to workers exceeding targets in important export industries. Such incentives, together with the diffusion of some economic responsibilities to local management and exhortations to the labour force to develop a more competitive spirit, were a response to dire economic necessity, but they produced few results.

Albania persistently struggled to keep pace with rapid population growth during the 1980s. In 1989 the population was 3.18m. and was growing at the rate of 2.1% per year, the highest rate in Europe. At the end of the 1980s almost two-thirds of the population were under the age of 26 and the annual addition to the labour force was around 40,000 people. This demographic boom was not matched by economic growth. The policy of economic autarky pursued by Enver Hoxha, especially after the cessation of Chinese aid in 1978, could not achieve growth rates to match such a rate of population growth.

AGRICULTURE

Agriculture is the principal sector of the Albanian economy. In 1988 the agricultural sector contributed 31.5% of NMP and employed 51.7% of the working population. In 1987 the total cultivated land amounted to 1.111m. ha, equivalent to 39% of the total land area, considerably more than the area cultivated in 1945. This increase has been achieved largely through terracing, irrigation, drainage and desalination projects carried out since the 1950s. There has been considerable investment in afforestation and the construction of reservoirs and irrigation canals. In 1987 some 57% of agricultural land was irrigated, compared to only 10% of a much smaller area of agricultural land in 1938. Terracing continues, though now at a slower pace, with more attention to maximizing yield and minimizing soil loss.

In 1983 there were 420 state and co-operative farms, which were the only legal forms of agricultural landholding, except for small allotments granted to collective-farm members. Private landholdings were merged into collective and state farms in the 1950s and early 1960s. By 1967 collectivization was claimed to be complete. Greater use of agricultural machinery was also introduced, although draught animals are still common, and most machinery is now outdated. Some of the most productive agriculture has been on peasants' private allotments, which, until 1990, were not permitted to exceed 200 sq m.

The development of livestock farming was given the highest priority for the eighth Five-Year Plan (1986–1990). This was prompted by the failure of a previous campaign to herd livestock held on private plots on to collective farms. Farmers reacted to this directive by slaughtering thousands of animals, with dramatic results on the supply of meat and dairy products. In July 1990, in a reversal of the previous policy, it was decided to allow peasants to rear cattle on their own plots, and co-operatives were asked to transfer some of their stock to members for this purpose. It was also recommended that co-operatives in hilly or mountainous regions grant their members 2,000 sq m of land each, in addition to their private plots; co-operative members in lowland areas were permitted to increase their existing landholdings up to a maximum of 2,000 sq m.

The contribution of agriculture to exports has been increased by a substantial investment in glasshouses, for growing tomatoes and cucumbers. Increasing attention has been devoted to producing olives, oranges and tobacco. Tobacco is a major earner of foreign currency, being the third-most important export commodity. Most fruit produced in Albania is exported.

In an attempt to increase food supplies, shortages of which have been one of the major causes of unrest since 1987, and to limit the need to import food, private markets were opened for the first time, in July 1990. Farmers were permitted to set their own prices at markets, and state procurement prices were increased to reflect production costs. This new policy was an extension of reforms introduced in certain districts in 1989, as a result of which substantial improvements in food supplies were reported in these localities. However the 9% increase in agricultural output in 1989 was only in excess of the very poor levels of output in 1988.

The need for reform of the system of co-operative and state farms was one of the main elements in the programme of the Democratic Party of Albania (DPA), the PLA's main contender in the March 1991 general elections. They proposed the privatization of land, giving smallholdings to each member of collective or state farms. Such plans were firmly opposed by the PLA. In January 1991 Fatos Nano, who had been appointed General Secretary of the Council of Ministers in the previous month, visited Budapest, where he learnt of the Hungarian plans to re-establish those profitable co-operatives and state farms which had been partitioned the previous year. Speaking at a meeting of the Council of Ministers on his return, Nano stressed the need not to disband the agricultural co-operatives, but to transform them into major administrators of economic life

in rural areas. Nano continued to oppose private land ownership after his re-election as head of government in April. During April and May, however, there were reports of collective-farm members unilaterally claiming plots of land, sometimes on the basis of pre-collectivization boundaries. The coalition Government, which took office in June, adopted legislation formally allowing private ownership of land, including rights of inheritance.

In 1990 the value of agricultural production fell by some 800m. lekë and, in 1991, the situation worsened considerably. In the first four months of 1991 milk production decreased by 50% compared to the corresponding period in 1990; corn production was about 67% less; the area of cotton sown was 80% less, and of tobacco 50% less. In mid-1991 it was uncertain whether the extension of the nationwide reforms and the de-integration of collective farms would produce the revitalization of agriculture needed to transform the food shortage experienced in that year into a surplus.

INDUSTRY AND MINING

According to official figures, in 1988 industry accounted for 46.3% of NMP and employed 22.9% of the labour force. In the period 1981–85 industrial output increased by 27%; in 1989 production rose by 5.6% in comparison with the previous year. In 1990, however, its value fell by 1,400m. lekë. The five largest industrial sectors, measured by the value of output, are food processing, light industry, engineering, mining and construction materials. In the 1960s Albania began developing a manufacturing base which now produces a fairly wide range of products. The light and food processing industries provided more than 85% of domestic requirements in 1987. In the same year they accounted for 38% of gross industrial production and for 40% of the country's total exports. The production of chemicals was developed as an adjunct to mining and to benefit agriculture. The growth of engineering has been several times faster than that of industry as a whole. Its main focus is on producing spare parts for the many types of foreign-made machines in the country, which were largely the result of the two major changes in Albania's alliance orientation. Production of spare parts increased by more than 25 times between 1960 and 1984.

Energy and Mining

The occurrence of yet another severe drought, in 1990, created an energy crisis, because of Albania's heavy dependence on hydroelectric power sources. Hydroelectric stations, such as the Vau i Dejes (250,000 kW) and the Fierzë (500,000 kW) plants, provided more than 80% of the country's total electricity production in 1988. Albania's largest power station is a 600,000 kW plant at Koman, on the River Drin. As a result of the drought Albania was unable to maintain exports of electricity to Yugoslavia and Greece, thus losing a valuable source of revenue. In 1991 the situation improved considerably, as rainfall returned to normal levels and exports of electricity were resumed.

Petroleum

Albania has been producing petroleum since 1927. There are proven reserves of some 200m. metric tons at existing production sites, but recoverable stocks in 1991 were only 25m. In 1974 production reached 2.5m. metric tons, but, during the 1980s, output steadily declined, as extraction encountered increasing difficulties. One-third of new investments in the ninth Five-Year Plan (1991–95) were allotted to the petroleum industry. In 1990, however, output was only 1.2m. tons and was expected to decrease to 900,000 tons in 1991. Albania's domestic requirements were estimated at 1.1m. tons in 1991, and the Government was forced to consider purchasing petroleum from other countries. In 1990 and 1991, in an attempt to introduce modern technology into the petroleum industry, the Albanian General Petroleum and Gas Directorate was involved in negotiations with a number of foreign firms specializing in onshore and offshore prospecting. In March 1991 Albania signed an agreement, worth US $500m., with Denimex, a German company, to conduct seismological geological studies, drilling of wells and preparation for production. Contracts were also negotiated with the US firms Occidental Petroleum and Chevron, and with Agip of Italy. Little has been done to stabilize or increase production from active petroleum wells and there has been a low extraction coefficient in new wells. At some sites only 12% of the petroleum available is extracted, whereas the introduction of modern technology could allow extraction of up to 40%. The failure of this vital industry has had a marked impact on the performance of the Albanian economy.

Natural Gas

Albania produced about 600m. cu m of natural gas per year during the eighth Five-Year Plan (1986–90). The ninth Five-Year Plan (1991–95) envisaged an increase in production to approximately 1,100m. cu m per year by 1995. In the first three months of 1991, however, production was 22m. cu m less than in the same period in 1990. Proven reserves of natural gas are estimated at 22,500m. cu m. As much as 20% of natural gas production is reinjected, 40% is used as fertilizer feedstock and 15% is consumed in power stations.

Nuclear Power

Work has begun on the construction of a nuclear research reactor, most of which will be funded by the UN. The Albanian Government and the International Atomic Energy Agency will also help finance the project, which includes provision of equipment and laboratories for the production of isotopes, pharmaceuticals and the installation of equipment for the supervision of radioactivity and nuclear medicine.

Coal

Albania is largely self-sufficient in coal, except for some 200,000 metric tons per year imported from Poland. However, the coal produced is mostly low-quality lignite (brown coal of a particularly low calorific value) from small deposits scattered throughout Albania. The industry, which is no longer profitable, produced 2.3m. tons in 1987. The coal is used mainly to generate electricity in power stations and is the major cause of environmental pollution in Albania.

Ore Mining

Albania is well endowed with mineral resources, the most profitable of which (chromite, ferronickle and copper) are located mainly in the north of the country. However, the poor standard of equipment and techniques used has hindered efforts to exploit this mineral wealth. The cost of mining and concentrating iron ore has become so expensive in some places that plants have been forced to close. Similar problems beset copper and nickel mining.

In 1990 Albania was the world's second-largest producer of chromite (chromium ore), producing an estimated 900,000m. metric tons, although unofficial estimates claimed that production might have fallen to about 500,000 tons. In the same year exports of chromium replaced petroleum as the largest source of foreign exchange. In 1991 the mining of chromite was expected to increase by 36%. However, the reduction in power supplies, caused by the 1990 drought, forced the closure of ferrochrome enterprises at

Burrel and Elbasan in 1990. The consequent losses in exports amounted to an estimated $1.8m. Chromite production fell by 65,000 tons in the first quarter of 1991, in comparison with the same period in 1990. In April 1991 workers in the chromite industry went on strike, causing losses estimated at $800,000. Owing to the poor quality of its ore, Albania has lost ground to South Africa in the competition for markets. Chromium production has persistently failed to meet planned targets and the management of the industry was sharply criticized in 1990 and 1991. The poor reputation of Albania's chromium can largely be blamed on mismanagement, poor techniques, antiquated Chinese equipment, a lack of refining and processing plants and inadequate transport facilities.

TRANSPORT

In 1988 there were about 6,700 km of main roads and some 10,000 km of other roads. Road transport now reaches even the most inaccessible parts of the country, although many roads are of poor quality. In the absence of an extensive rail network, roads continue to carry most of the country's freight. Traffic is light, the ownership of private cars having been illegal until 1991, and bicycles and draught animals are common. In July 1990 a protocol was signed by a group of Greek construction companies to build a 200-km motorway across southern Albania. The road is planned to extend from the Albanian–Greek border to the port of Durrës and is expected to take four years to build, at a cost of US $500m.

In 1991 Albania had 509 km of railways. In 1989 the railways carried 48% of freight traffic. The development of new lines is primarily intended to serve mining sites and the coastal plains. The potential for foreign trade was enhanced by the opening, in September 1986, of a line from Shkodër to Titograd in Montenegro (Yugoslavia), which now links Albania with the European railway network. The volume of Albanian goods transported by Yugoslav railways has steadily increased, reaching 174,300 metric tons in the first six months of 1990, an increase of 19.4% over the same period in 1989. A passenger service is being considered between Titograd and Shkodër and a new rail-link is planned with Greece. Albanian railways are standard gauge and thus easily compatible with neighbouring railway networks. No railway lines have yet been electrified. The building of a line from Milot to Klos, in north-central Albania, and an aqueduct near Bulqizë, the main centre of chromium production, should facilitate the transportation of minerals.

Albania has several air links with major European cities and a regular flight between Paris (France) and Tirana was inaugurated in November 1990. France has announced plans to install a radar system at Rinas airport, near Tirana. A freight ferry service between Durrës and Trieste (Italy) began in 1983, and a similar service links Sarandë with the Greek island of Corfu. A regular shipping line has also begun services between Ohrid in Yugoslavia and Pogradec in Albania.

TOURISM

Tourism in Albania was not encouraged until the late 1980s, for fear of contact between Albanians and 'alien ideological influences', but, since 1989, tourism has been viewed as an important potential source of convertible currency. In 1989 and 1990 tourists visited Albania in unprecedented numbers, attracted by an unspoiled coastline and beautiful inland scenery. In 1990 there were some 30,000 foreign visitors, an increase of more than 50% on the previous year. Albtourist, the state tourist agency, is expecting a large increase in the number of visitors and is attempting to develop the necessary infrastructure; in 1991 contracts worth $200m. were being negotiated with various foreign companies to build urgently needed hotels. Development plans announced in 1990 included a US $27m. hotel and business centre in Tirana; a Sheraton hotel complex, also in the capital; and the construction of five tourist villages (10,000 beds in total) near Sarandë, in south-west Albania.

PRICES, WAGES AND RETAIL TRADE

Official figures for retail trade revealed increases in trading of 3.3% in 1987 and 2.7% in 1988. This suggests that the supply of goods is barely keeping pace with the growth of population. Interruptions and shortages in supply have always been common. The draft Plan for 1990 contained a commitment to increase imports of consumer goods and food by 88m. lekë on 1989 figures. In an attempt to satisfy demand for goods not available in state shops, the Government agreed, in July 1990, to the legalization of private handicraft and family trade businesses. These were permitted to set their own prices and find their own suppliers. They were obliged to obtain licences to work and could not employ any person outside the immediate family. By December 1990 there were some 1,500 private entrepreneurs and some 7,000 service units had been privatized, including craft workshops, retail units and restaurants. In 1991 plans were announced for the privatization of state-owned property on a large scale; there will be no limitation on the opening of new trade units. Some of the first items of state property to be privatized will be retail and service units.

Under the centrally-planned system wages were extremely egalitarian for most of the population. In 1983 monthly wages ranged from approximately 400 lekë for the average worker to some 900 lekë for the manager of an enterprise. In September 1990 it was announced that all wages below 450 lekë per month were to be increased by 10%. By April 1991 the average wage was 650–700 lekë. In January 1991 the Government had been forced to grant pay rises of between 30% and 50% to all of the country's 30,000 miners following industrial disputes and, following the general strike, which began in May, it was agreed that wages for all workers were to be increased by 15%–80%. Inevitably, these wage rises had an inflationary affect at a time of severe shortages of goods. The amount of money in circulation increased to finance wage rises; in 1990 the currency in circulation increased by 441m. lekë. In July 1991 the annual rate of inflation was officially estimated to have reached more than 25%.

Until 1991 the existence of unemployment was not officially admitted, yet absenteeism and underemployment were widespread. By 1991 it had been recognized that there were many unprofitable enterprises, which would have to be closed; other industrial plants were overstaffed. The closure of some obsolete plants and the reduction of staff in others were expected to cause very high levels of unemployment. The 1991 Plan stated that new mechanisms of social assistance must be introduced to give workers the time and opportunity to train for other jobs, but little seems to have been done to implement such a proposal. In May 1991 it was announced that 50,000 people were officially unemployed; a further 40,000 were receiving reduced pay, but had no work owing to a lack of raw materials. Unemployment, or the prospect of unemployment, was a major reason for the large numbers of young men attempting to emigrate during 1991.

FOREIGN TRADE

During the 1980s Albania's foreign trade generally recorded a deficit, except in 1981 and 1986, when there was a small trade surplus with member-countries of the International Monetary Fund (IMF). Three-quarters of Albanian exports are industrial, the bulk consisting of petroleum, minerals, ferrochrome, copper wire, nickel and electricity. The remainder consists of products such as alcoholic beverages (raki, brandy), cigarettes (mostly for Eastern Europe), fruit, olives, tomatoes, sardines and anchovies. In 1988, after several years of stagnation, Albania's trade with IMF members grew considerably. In 1990 imports from the West were worth an estimated US $245m., compared with about $165m. in 1989. These imports were predominantly capital goods, such as locomotives, manufacturing machinery, some spare parts and, probably, armaments. In 1991 Albania planned to increase its exports by 33.4%, an optimistic figure given its commitment to increasing domestic consumption. Albania trades with over 50 countries but, according to official figures, over 90% of its exports go to only 18 countries. During the 1980s its major trading partners were Yugoslavia, Italy, Romania, Poland, Germany, Bulgaria and France. In many respects Albania seems to be pursuing a 'regionalist' approach in foreign policy which could stimulate intra-regional trade. It is in this context that Albania has sought to strengthen trade and cultural relations with Greece, Italy, Romania, Yugoslavia and Turkey.

In 1990 goods and services worth $65m. were exchanged with Yugoslavia, which imported chromite, copper wire, bitumen, citrus fruits and medicinal herbs. (Albania is Europe's largest exporter of medicinal herbs.) Albania imported engineering goods, transformer stations, steel products, television sets, concrete, electrical equipment and general consumer goods. In March 1991 Albania and Yugoslavia agreed to transfer the financial basis of their trade to convertible currency. The agreement also included financial details for two projects, which were to involve the construction, by Yugoslav companies, of hotels, blocks of flats, shops and a road around Lake Ohrid, on Albania's eastern border, to link the towns of Ohrid, Pogradec and Struga.

Italy has been particularly committed to aiding Albania's economic reforms since large numbers of refugees began arriving in Italian ports in March 1991, presuming that such attempted emigration on a large scale would only end when Albania's economy showed some sign of recovering. Albania and Italy have agreed to establish a co-ordinating committee to oversee joint projects, particularly in agriculture. Italy has pledged to invest $750m. in Albania in 1991–94. The Italian Government has also provided food and medical aid and, in June 1991, offered a further $50m. in financial assistance. Italy has been active in persuading international organizations to consider Albania as a potential aid recipient. Several Italian companies have announced investment plans in Albania, including the Fiatgari company, which will develop large-scale cultivation of rice and maize, in the Shkodër region. Joint ventures have also been established between Albanian and Italian firms.

After 1985 France increased its economic co-operation with Albania; French engineers assisted in the construction of the hydroelectric dam at Koman, and planned to assist in similar hydroelectric projects in the future. In January 1990 the French company, Cegelec, signed a contract worth $28m., to supply technical equipment for the Banja hydroelectric station, for connecting it to the national grid and for the supply of other power equipment. The contract followed a bilateral agreement with France on co-operation in postal and telecommunications services. France has also provided short-term aid to ensure the continuing availability of food in Albania.

Trade with other countries has also increased. A number of German companies have initiated projects with Albania, incorporating co-production and barter trade. Albania is hoping for German aid in modernizing its chromite and petroleum industries. An agreement between the two countries, on technical and scientific co-operation, was signed in June 1990. In 1990 the United Kingdom had a trade surplus with Albania, although trading was on a modest scale; in the first six months of 1990 the United Kingdom exported £4m.-worth of goods to Albania; Albania exported a more modest £170,000-worth to the United Kingdom. In June 1990, during the first visit by an Albanian premier to Turkey, an economic agreement was signed providing for increased co-operation between the two countries in textiles, petrochemicals and tourism. An Albanian–Bulgarian governmental commission has agreed to increase trade between the two countries, in the areas of copper production, agriculture, tourism, electricity and electronics. In 1989 trade between these two increased by 62% over 1988, and an increase of 75% was planned for 1990. In July 1990 Albania and the People's Republic of China signed a protocol on economic and technical co-operation.

Although foreign investment has been permitted since 1990, trade continues to be constrained by Albania's limited foreign reserves and its small number of export commodities which are able to compete effectively on the international market. In 1990 convertible currency earnings were some $316m. less than the economic plan had projected, and the trade deficit increased from $96m. to $254m. In 1991 Albania asked its foreign creditors for a postponement on debt repayments and was permitted a moratorium on about one-quarter of its outstanding convertible currency obligations. In the short-term Albania received economic aid from Western countries, to enable the Government to continue importing food.

In its efforts to increase exports Albania is constrained by two major factors. Firstly, the move to rationalize production and increase efficiency is hampered by the shortage of technology and skilled personnel. Secondly, the pressure on Albania's export industry is compounded by the Government's commitment to channel more resources into the domestic consumer-goods sector to appease a restless population. Some optimism could be gained from the positive attitude of the Albanian authorities towards foreign investment. In mid-1991 legislation was adopted allowing foreign concerns to lease land and facilities, to repatriate profits and to achieve majority ownership in joint-venture companies. Free economic zones were also planned, along the Adriatic coast, and foreign investors may be eligible for a period of up to five years free of taxes.

BANKING AND FINANCE

Traditionally, the Albanian budget has been based on Soviet-type categories, although the total budget was more centralized. Personal taxes were abolished in 1970, most state revenue coming from economic production. The interim constitutional law, adopted in April 1991, contained provisions committing the state to a return to personal taxation as the main source of state revenue. National revenue fell by 1,300m. lekë in 1990, from a total of 8,558m. lekë in 1989. In May 1991 it was admitted that the budgetary deficit had reached 3,200m. lekë, equivalent to some 30% of total budgeted expenditure.

In June 1990 Albania began negotiations on joining the IMF and, in January 1991, made a formal application for membership. This was a strong indication of Albania's intention to break with central planning and embrace market economics. Albania's application was likely to be accepted if the reform process continued and Albania accepted and complied with the many demands which were expected to be imposed by the IMF. In Albania's case these

would probably include the following measures: extensive liberalization of wholesale and retail prices; unification of the commercial and tourist exchange rates; punitive taxes on wage rises to avoid causing inflation; maintaining a surplus in the government budget; and conducting a tight monetary policy to limit the growth of liquidity in the economy.

Considerable changes are envisaged in the banking sector. The role of the Albanian State Bank has been enlarged to allow it to grant more short- and long-term credits to industry. In addition, in 1990, the Albanian State Bank for Foreign Relations was established, to provide and direct funds for foreign trade. More commercial banks were planned and the savings bank sector was to be restructured. In April 1991 the Illiria Bank, Albania's first private commercial bank, was opened.

The prohibition on receipt of foreign credits, which had been in the 1976 Constitution, was annulled in 1990, thus allowing Albania to receive much-needed credits from abroad. A report issued in January 1991, by the State Bank's foreign exchange and treasury department, concluded that Albania could service a debt of around US $4,000m. However, as Albania's convertible-currency earnings decreased during early 1991, its ability to accommodate such debts seemed less likely, at least in the short term. In early 1991 Albania had short-term debts of about $25m., repayable over 13 years, but it will be forced to borrow much larger amounts to upgrade its existing economic infrastructure. The exchange rate of the lek, which had been maintained at an artificially high level for many years, was expected to be adjusted, with a probable 100% devaluation.

PROBLEMS AND PROSPECTS

Unusually, during the first six months of 1989, Albania allowed its liabilities to exceed its assets, in the first three months by US $17m. and in the second three months by $7m. This has become an established pattern, as Albania has increased expenditure on investment goods and food imports. The country's dependence on imported fuel and materials has been increasing. This is reflected in the higher priority assigned to exports and to import substitution. The more efficient use of materials and energy has been another insistent theme. Imports are needed to replace obsolete machinery; it has been estimated that Albania will need at least $10,000m. during the 1990s to modernize its textile, steel, chromium, mining and petroleum industries.

It would have been surprising if the ambitious and unrealistic targets for the 1990 annual Plan had been fulfilled. Overall industrial production was to be increased by 8.6%, agricultural production was to increase by 15% and exports by 33.4%, yet investment was to increase by a mere 1.4%. As it turned out, in 1990, national revenues fell by 1,300m. lekë, industrial production by 1,400m. lekë and agricultural production by 800m. lekë.

In July 1990 more flexible regulations were introduced in selected enterprises, in an attempt to introduce higher standards of discipline and productivity. Enterprises were to be allowed to fail, were relieved of their obligation to create jobs for new entrants and would also be able to retain a high proportion of their profits for their own use. It was hoped that they would reinvest any profits in the improvement and expansion of their businesses. The new managements were given one or two years to rationalize failing enterprises and, if matters did not improve, the company could be declared bankrupt. However, as the first results from the experimental companies revealed, some serious, if not unpredictable, problems arose: a reluctance to take independent decisions, a tendency to exaggerate difficulties and wait for solutions from above and a lack of self-motivation. It appeared that some managers failed to grasp the fact that the state was no longer prepared to subsidize loss-making enterprises. Inertia and resistance to change were proving difficult to overcome. For too long in Albania there was no debate on the future of the economic system, or an admission that the political ideology was at fault. There was an obvious reluctance to question the wisdom of past economic policies, practices and methods.

Albania's attempts to cope with the problems of its economy developed from these relatively small-scale reforms, announced in mid-1990, to the radical programme, including privatization, proposed by the National Stability Government in mid-1991. The opposition parties established in late 1990 and early 1991 all campaigned strongly for the introduction of a market economy. The DPA, the largest of the opposition groups, advocated a rapid transition to a market-based economy, including privatization of both land and enterprises. Other parties, such as the Republican Party, tended to favour a more gradual transition, but differences were over details rather than the final aims. The PLA moved from its pre-election position of retaining state ownership of most of the economy, while implementing market-orientated changes within a socialist structure, to one of support for privatization and a full market economy. Despite general agreement on the future structure of the Albanian economy, the extent to which Albania can implement any transition programme without external assistance is extremely limited. Since 1990 successive Governments have struggled to ensure that a minimum of goods were available to the population, without being able to indulge in medium- and long-term planning.

Albania was likely to experience severe socio-economic problems in the transition from a centrally-planned economy to one based on market relations. Since the abrupt termination of Albania's barter-trade agreements with CMEA countries, the country has endured unprecedented food shortages, unemployment and demands for pay increases. In 1990 the Government was forced to purchase an additional 7m. kWh of electricity, at a cost of $2m., and 11,000 metric tons of fuel, costing $1.7m. These were expenditures which the economy could hardly afford. The crisis eroded confidence in the reform programme and stimulated the exodus of thousands of refugees. In March 1991 a Committee for Employment and Emigration was established to co-ordinate labour migration, but it is unlikely that many Western governments will be willing to sign an emigration agreement with Albania in the near future.

By mid-1991 Albania was already experiencing widespread food shortages and it was unlikely that the situation would improve in the short term. Shortages of food were mainly the result of a lack of convertible currency, which is required to continue food imports, and chaos in the countryside, which was causing reduced deliveries from collective and state farms. Confusion over the basis for privatization of state and co-operative farms left some areas uncultivated until mid-1991, seriously threatening the harvest prospects for that year. The severe shortages of foodstuffs prompted Western governments and institutions, including the EC, to send emergency food aid.

Speculators were making food shortages worse by selling illegal bulk purchases from state shops at higher prices at the private markets. It has been reported that entire consignments of factory goods have disappeared, only to reappear on sale at markets; even aid shipments have been looted. Albania's immediate economic situation looked rather bleak in mid-1991, with reports of serious food shortages and growing unemployment. There are, however, relatively good investment incentives and a large expatriate community, which has expressed a willingness to invest in light manufacturing, road building and tourist development in Albania. Serbian policies in Kosovo have limited the economic opportunities of the Kosovar Albanians, who are therefore encouraged to trade with Albania. There are also the psychological incentives of nationalism and a long-term interest in unification. Geographically and commercially Albania–Kosovo trade links are practical and are likely to continue to grow.

The technological modernization, which Albania needs to overcome its inefficiencies and economic weakness, is dependent on greater interaction with the rest of the world. Fatos Nano, former head of government, complained of the 'fetish of the principle of self-sufficiency', which has been abandoned, but which resulted in Albania having the most underdeveloped trade network of any European country. This lack of expertise in international trade and the poor quality of Albania's present exports does not allow Albania to earn the foreign currency it requires to improve its infrastructure and production capacity. The future of the Albanian economy is, therefore, dependent on far-sighted Western investment and aid programmes, which, in turn, depend on the ability of Albania's leaders to create an economic environment in which such investment will succeed.

Statistical Survey

Source (unless otherwise stated): Drejtoria e Statistikës, Tirana.

Area and Population

AREA, POPULATION AND DENSITY

Area (sq km)	
Land .	27,398
Inland water .	1,350
Total .	28,748*
Population (census results)	
January 1979 .	2,591,000
2 April 1989 .	3,182,417
Population (official estimates at mid-year)	
1988 .	3,138,100†
1989 .	3,199,000
1990 .	3,250,000
Density (per sq km) at mid-1990	113.1

* 11,100 sq miles.
† Comprising 1,616,100 males and 1,522,000 females.
Ethnic Groups (census of 2 April 1989): Albanian 3,117,601; Greek 58,758; Macedonian 4,697; Montenegrin, Serbian, Croatian, etc. 100; others 1,261.

DISTRICTS (1988)*

	Area (sq km)	Population (annual average)	Density (per sq km)
Berat .	1,027	173,700	169.1
Dibër .	1,568	148,200	94.5
Durrës .	848	242,500	286.0
Elbasan .	1,481	238,600	161.1
Fier .	1,175	239,700	204.0
Gramsh .	695	43,800	63.0
Gjirokastër .	1,137	65,500	57.6
Kolonjë .	805	24,600	30.5
Korçë .	2,181	213,200	97.8
Krujë .	607	105,300	157.2
Kukës .	1,330	99,400	74.7
Lezhë .	479	61,100	127.5
Librazhd .	1,013	70,800	69.9
Lushnjë .	712	132,200	185.7
Mat .	1,028	75,900	73.5
Mirditë .	867	49,700	57.3
Përmet .	929	39,400	42.4
Pogradec .	725	70,500	97.2
Pukë .	1,034	48,200	46.6
Sarandë .	1,097	86,800	78.9
Shkodër .	2,528	233,000	92.2
Skrapar .	775	45,800	59.1
Tepelenë .	817	49,100	60.1
Tiranë .	1,238	363,100	293.3
Tropojë .	1,043	44,200	42.4
Vlorë .	1,609	174,000	108.1
Total .	28,748	3,138,100	109.2

Source: *Statistical Yearbook of the PSR of Albania.*

* In mid-1991 certain changes were made to the administrative-territorial structure of the country, including the creation of the new district of Kavajë.

PRINCIPAL TOWNS (population at mid-1987)

Tiranë (Tirana, the capital)	225,700
Durrës (Durazzo)	78,700
Elbasan	78,300
Shkodër (Scutari)	76,300
Vlorë (Vlonë or Valona)	67,700
Korçë (Koritsa)	61,500
Berat	40,500
Fier	40,300
Lushnjë	26,900
Kavajë	24,200
Gjirokastër	23,800
Qyteti Stalin	20,600

Source: *Statistical Yearbook of the PSR of Albania.*

BIRTHS, MARRIAGES AND DEATHS

	Registered live births		Registered marriages		Registered deaths	
	Number	Rate (per 1,000)	Number	Rate (per 1,000)	Number	Rate (per 1,000)
1985 . .	77,535	26.2	25,271	8.5	17,179	5.8
1986 . .	76,435	25.3	25,718	8.5	17,369	5.7
1987 . .	79,696	25.9	27,370	8.9	17,119	5.6
1988 . .	80,241	25.5	28,174	9.0	17,027	5.4
1989 . .	78,862	24.7	n.a.	n.a.	18,168	5.7

Average Life Expectation (1987/88): 72.0 years (Males 69.4 years, Females 74.9 years).
Source: mainly *Statistical Yearbook of the PSR of Albania.*

ECONOMICALLY ACTIVE POPULATION
(ILO estimates, '000 persons at mid-1980)

	Males	Females	Total
Agriculture, etc. . . .	338	339	677
Industry	237	74	311
Services	144	79	223
Total	719	492	1,211

Source: ILO, *Economically Active Population Estimates and Projections, 1950–2025.*

Mid-1989 (estimates in '000): Agriculture, etc. 746; Total 1,519 (Source: FAO, *Production Yearbook*).

EMPLOYMENT IN THE 'SOCIALIZED' SECTOR
(excluding agricultural co-operatives)

	1986	1987
Industry . . .	272,300	287,000
Construction . . .	78,300	77,800
Agriculture	182,100	190,300
Transport and communications . .	38,000	39,600
Trade	55,400	56,400
Education and culture . .	55,800	57,600
Health service . . .	37,200	37,700
Others	40,300	41,800
Total	759,400	788,200

1988: Total: 811,000.
Source: *Statistical Yearbook of the PSR of Albania.*

ALBANIA

Agriculture

PRINCIPAL CROPS ('000 metric tons)

	1987	1988	1989*
Wheat and spelt	589	633	636
Rice (paddy)	11	9	10
Barley	38*	40*	40
Maize	306	233	280
Rye	10*	10*	10
Oats	30*	30*	30
Sorghum	35*	35*	35
Potatoes	126*	115*	123
Dry beans	25*	25*	26
Sunflower seed . . .	24	18	18
Seed cotton	24	15	15
Cotton seed	6*	8*	8
Olives	41*	57*	57
Vegetables	188*	191*	189
Grapes	20	19	20
Sugar beet	280*	300†	290
Apples	14*	16*	14
Plums	13*	16*	13
Oranges	10*	13*	14
Tobacco (leaves) . . .	20†	29*	20
Cotton (lint)	8*	5*	5

* FAO estimate(s).   † Unofficial estimate.
Source: FAO, *Production Yearbook*.

LIVESTOCK ('000 head, year ending September)

	1987	1988	1989*
Horses	42*	42*	42
Mules	22*	22*	22
Asses	52*	52*	52
Cattle	672	696	705
Pigs	214	197	201
Sheep	1,432	1,525	1,555
Goats	960*	1,076	1,106
Poultry	5,000	5,000	5,000

* FAO estimate(s).
Source: FAO, *Production Yearbook*.

LIVESTOCK PRODUCTS (FAO estimates, metric tons)

	1987	1988	1989
Beef and veal	28,000	28,000	28,000
Mutton and lamb . . .	18,000	19,000	19,000
Goats' meat	8,000	9,000	9,000
Pig meat	9,000	9,000	10,000
Poultry meat	14,000	13,000	14,000
Cows' milk	339,000	340,000	341,000
Sheep's milk	42,000	45,000	45,000
Goats' milk	39,000	42,000	40,000
Cheese	16,100	16,900	17,500
Butter	3,879	3,915	3,915
Hen eggs	13,200	14,000	14,500
Wool:			
greasy	3,000	3,000	3,000
scoured (clean) . . .	1,800	1,800	1,800
Cattle hides	4,026	4,070	4,096
Sheep and lamb skins . .	2,402	2,413	2,427
Goat and kid skins . . .	665	740	743

Source: FAO, *Production Yearbook*.

Forestry

ROUNDWOOD REMOVALS ('000 cubic metres)
Annual total 2,330 (Industrial wood 722, Fuel wood 1,608) in 1976–88 (FAO estimates).

SAWNWOOD PRODUCTION ('000 cubic metres)
Annual total 200 (coniferous 105, broadleaved 95) in 1977–82 (official estimates) and in 1983–88 (FAO estimates).
Source: FAO, *Yearbook of Forest Products*.

Fishing

('000 metric tons, live weight)

	1986	1987	1988
Inland waters	4.9	4.9	6.7
Mediterranean Sea . . .	7.0	8.2	7.9
Total catch	11.9	13.1	14.6

Source: FAO, *Yearbook of Fishery Statistics*.

Mining

PRODUCTION (estimates, '000 metric tons)

	1986	1987	1988
Brown coal (incl. lignite) . .	2,300	2,300	2,400
Crude petroleum . . .	3,000	3,000	3,000
Natural gas (terajoules) . .	15,000	15,000	16,000
Copper*†	15.0	15.5	16.4
Nickel*†	7.5	7.7	8.0
Chromium*‡	245	239	216

* Figures relate to the metal content of ores.
† Estimated by Metallgesellschaft Aktiengesellschaft (Frankfurt).
‡ Estimated by the US Bureau of Mines.
Source: UN, *Industrial Statistics Yearbook*.

Industry

MAIN INDUSTRIAL PRODUCTS
('000 metric tons, unless otherwise indicated)

	1980	1985	1988
Electric energy (million kWh) .	3,717	3,147	3,984
Blister copper	9.8	11	15
Copper wires and cables . .	5.7	9.4	11.6
Carbonic ferrochrome . .	12.2	11.9	38.7
Metallurgical coke . . .	173	250	291
Rolled wrought steel . .	96	107	96
Phosphatic fertilizers . .	150	157	165
Ammonium nitrate . . .	109	95	96
Urea	88	78	77
Sulphuric acid	72	73	81
Caustic soda	25	29	31
Soda ash	23	22	22
Machinery and equipment (million lekë)	350	465	496
Spare parts (million lekë) . .	327	407	493
Cement	826	642	746
Bricks and tiles (million pieces)	294	295	319
Refractory bricks . . .	4.8	28	30
Furniture (million lekë) . .	86	112	131
Heavy cloth (million metres) .	12.5	12.3	11.3
Knitwear (million pieces) . .	9.8	11.0	12.1
Footwear ('000 pairs) . .	4,735	4,800	5,396
Television receivers ('000) .	21	21.3	16.5
Radio receivers ('000) . .	8	16	25
Beer ('000 hectolitres) . .	150	199	237
Cigarettes (million) . . .	4,950	5,348	5,310
Soap and detergent . .	14.7	18.2	21.5

Source: *Statistical Yearbook of the PSR of Albania.*

1989 (FAO estimates, '000 metric tons): Wine 26; Raw sugar 45; Olive oil 8 (Source: FAO, *Production Yearbook*).

Finance

CURRENCY AND EXCHANGE RATES

Monetary Units
100 qindarka (qintars) = 1 new lek.

Denominations
Coins: 5, 10, 20 and 50 qintars; 1 lek.
Notes: 1, 3, 5, 10, 25, 50 and 100 lekë.

Sterling and Dollar Equivalents (30 June 1991)
£1 sterling = 16.19 lekë;
US $1 = 10.00 lekë (non-commercial rates);
1,000 lekë = £61.77 = $100.00.

Exchange Rate
The non-commercial rate, applicable to tourism, was fixed at US $1 = 7.000 lekë between June 1979 and September 1988. A revised rate of $1 = 6.000 lekë was introduced in September 1988 and remained in force until September 1989. The rate was fixed at $1 = 15.000 lekë in November 1990. This remained in effect until June 1991, when the rate was adjusted to $1 = 10.000 lekë. However, in September 1991 it was announced that the rate for all foreign currency transactions would henceforth be linked to the European Currency Unit (ECU). The initial rate was set at ECU 1 = 30 lekë (US $1 = 25 lekë). In October a new rate of $1 = 30 lekë was announced.

STATE BUDGET (million lekë, provisional)

Revenue	1988	1989	1990
National economy	9,140	9,194	9,323
Non-productive sector and other income from the socialist sector	360	356	327
Total revenue	9,500*	9,550	9,650

* Final total: 8,558m. lekë.

Expenditure	1988	1989	1990
National economy . . .	5,120	4,998	4,933
Socio-cultural measures . .	2,747	2,908	3,042
Defence	1,060	1,075	1,030
Administration . . .	161	163	175
Total expenditure (incl. others)	9,450*	9,500	9,600

* Final total: 8,552m. lekë.
Source: *Zëri i Popullit.*

INVESTMENT

Capital investment during the 1986–90 Five-Year Plan was estimated at 24,450 million lekë, 2,800 million more than during the previous Five-Year Plan.
Source: Albanian Telegraphic Agency.

NATIONAL ACCOUNTS

Net Material Product (percentages at 1986 prices)

Activities of the Material Sphere	1987	1988
Industry	45.8	46.3
Agriculture	33.3	31.5
Construction	6.4	6.5
Transport, trade, etc.	14.5	15.7
Total	100.0	100.0

External Trade

(million lekë)

	1985	1987	1988
Imports c.i.f.	2,520	2,650	3,218
Exports f.o.b.	2,236	2,650	2,709

Source: *Statistical Yearbook of the PSR of Albania.* Figures for 1986 are not available.

PRINCIPAL COMMODITIES (%)

Imports	1985	1987	1988
Machinery and equipment . .	25.1	26.2	28.5
Spare parts and bearings . .	5.3	6.7	4.8
Fuels, minerals and metals . .	27.0	28.2	25.2
Chemical and rubber products .	14.1	14.2	13.1
Construction materials . .	1.4	0.1	0.1
Raw materials of plant or animal origin . .	12.8	12.7	14.0
Foodstuffs	8.3	5.4	8.1
Other consumer goods . .	6.0	6.5	6.2
Total	100.0	100.0	100.0

Exports	1985	1987	1988
Fuels	15.1	11.0	7.9
Electricity	7.8	13.1	7.3
Minerals and metals . .	31.2	29.3	39.8
Chemical products . . .	0.7	1.2	0.8
Construction materials . .	1.0	1.3	1.5
Raw materials of plant or animal origin . .	14.6	16.8	16.1
Processed foodstuffs . .	10.8	9.1	8.7
Unprocessed foodstuffs . .	8.1	8.2	8.2
Other consumer goods . .	10.7	10.0	9.7
Total	100.0	100.0	100.0

Source: *Statistical Yearbook of the PSR of Albania.* Figures for 1986 are not available.

PRINCIPAL TRADING PARTNERS (%)

Exports	1986	1987	1988
Austria	1.5	3.5	5.4
Bulgaria	7.5	7.5	9.4
China, People's Republic .	4.9	6.1	5.1
Cuba	1.7	1.0	1.3
Czechoslovakia . . .	12.1	12.4	10.0
Egypt	1.0	1.5	1.2
France	1.9	2.0	1.6
German Democratic Republic .	5.7	6.8	8.2
Germany, Federal Republic .	3.2	4.0	4.2
Greece	6.8	5.5	1.8
Hungary	5.1	6.2	5.9
Italy	3.5	4.4	6.3
Japan	1.2	1.6	1.8
Poland	7.0	6.0	7.5
Romania	9.5	9.3	9.7
Sweden	5.0	3.3	4.6
Switzerland	3.0	4.3	2.5
Yugoslavia	13.9	11.1	7.1
Total (incl. others) . . .	100.0	100.0	100.0

Source: *Statistical Yearbook of the PSR of Albania*. Percentages for imports are not available.

Transport

RAILWAYS (traffic)

	1987	1988
Passengers carried ('000)	10,601	10,966
Passengers-km (million) . . .	661.6	703.0
Freight carried ('000 metric tons) . .	7,666	7,659
Freight ton-km (million)	629	626

Source: *Statistical Yearbook of the PSR of Albania*.

ROAD TRAFFIC

	1987	1988
Passengers carried*	59,210	77,287
Passenger-km (million)*	1,174.0	1,380.2
Freight carried ('000 metric tons) . . .	76,840	76,982
Freight ton-km (million)	1,268	1,269

* Figures refer to operations by the Ministry of Transport only.
Source: *Statistical Yearbook of the PSR of Albania*.

INTERNATIONAL SEA-BORNE SHIPPING
(freight traffic, '000 metric tons)

	1986	1987	1988
Goods loaded	1,061	1,073	1,090
Goods unloaded	995	998	1,020

Source: UN, *Monthly Bulletin of Statistics*.

Communications Media

	1984	1985	1986
Book production:			
Titles*	1,130	939	959
Copies ('000)* . . .	6,506	5,710	6,665
Daily newspapers:			
Number	2	n.a.	2
Average circulation . .	145,000	n.a.	135,000
Radio receivers in use . .	n.a.	493,000	500,000
Television receivers in use . .	n.a.	232,000	250,000

* Figures include pamphlets (158 titles and 494,000 copies in 1984; 95 titles and 300,000 copies in 1985; 52 titles and 380,000 copies in 1986).

1988: Daily newspapers 2 (average circulation 135,000); Radio receivers in use: 525,000; Television receivers in use: 260,000.
Source: UNESCO, *Statistical Yearbook*.

1988: Book production: titles: 1,018; copies: 7,440,000.
Source: *Statistical Yearbook of the PSR of Albania*.

Education

(1988)

	Institutions	Teachers	Pupils
Pre-primary	3,251	5,299	121,000
Primary (8-year) . . .	1,691	27,862	547,000
Secondary:			
general	43	1,783	59,000
vocational	442	7,221	135,000
Higher	8	1,659	25,000

Source: *Statistical Yearbook of the PSR of Albania*.
Pre-primary (1989): Institutions 3,370; Teachers 5,440; Pupils 125,312.

Primary (1989): Institutions 1,700; Teachers 28,440; Pupils 550,656.
Secondary (pupils, 1989): General 63,042; Vocational 139,822.
Source: UNESCO, *Statistical Yearbook*.

Directory

The Constitution

The Constitution adopted on 28 December 1976 was declared invalid in April 1991, following the adoption of interim constitutional legislation. The People's Assembly appointed a commission to draft a new Constitution. On 30 April 1991 the People's Assembly adopted the Law on the Major Constitutional Provisions of the People's Assembly of the Republic of Albania, which was, in effect, an interim Constitution. The following is a summary of the main provisions of that legislation:

THE SOCIAL ORDER

The Political Order

Articles 1–9. The Republic of Albania is a parliamentary republic. The Republic is a juridical and democratic state which observes and defends the rights and freedoms of its citizens.

The fundamental principle of state organization is the separation of legislative, executive and judicial powers. The people exercise their power through their representative organs, which are elected by free, universal, direct and secret ballot.

Legislative power belongs to the People's Assembly; the Head of State is the President of the Republic; the supreme body of executive power is the Council of Ministers; judicial power is exercised by courts, which are independent and guided only by the provisions of the law.

Albania recognizes and guarantees those fundamental rights and freedoms that are proclaimed in international law, including those of national minorities. Judicial norms must be applied equally to all state bodies, political parties and other groups and organizations. All citizens are equal under the law.

Political pluralism is a fundamental condition of democracy in Albania. Political parties are entirely separate from the State and are prohibited from activities in military bodies, state ministries, diplomatic representations abroad, judicial institutions and other state bodies.

Albania is a secular State. The State observes the freedom of religious belief and creates conditions to exercise it.

The Economic Order

Articles 10–14. The country's economy is based on diverse systems of ownership, freedom of economic activity and the regulatory role of the state. All kinds of ownership are protected by law. Foreign persons may gain the right to ownership and are guaranteed the right to carry out independent economic activity in Albania, to form joint economic ventures and to repatriate profits.

All citizens are liable for contributions to state expenditure in relation to their income.

SUPREME BODIES OF STATE POWER

The People's Assembly

Articles 15–23. The People's Assembly is the supreme body of state power and sole law-making body. It defines the main directions of the domestic and foreign policy of the State. It approves and amends the Constitution and is competent to declare war and ratify or annul international treaties. It elects its Presidency which is composed of a Chairman and two Deputy Chairmen. It also elects the President of the Republic of Albania, the Supreme Court, the Attorney-General and his or her deputies. It controls the activity of state radio and television, the state news agency and other official information media.

The People's Assembly is composed of 250 deputies, elected for a period of four years, and meets in regular session no less than four times a year.

The President of the Republic of Albania

Articles 24–32. The President of the Republic is Head of State and is elected by the People's Assembly, in a secret ballot, and by a two-thirds majority of the votes of all the deputies. The term of office is five years. No person is to hold the office of President for more than two successive terms. The President may not occupy any other post while fulfilling the functions of President.

The President guarantees the observation of the Constitution and legislation adopted by the People's Assembly; he appoints the Chairman of the Council of Ministers and accepts his or her resignation; he exercises the duties of the People's Assembly when the legislature is not in session.

The President is Commander-in-Chief of the Armed Forces and Chairman of the Council of Defence. The Council of Defence is responsible for organizing the country's resources to ensure the territorial defence of the Republic. Its members are proposed by the President and approved by the People's Assembly.

The Supreme Organs of State Administration

Articles 33–41. The Council of Ministers is the supreme executive and legislative body. It directs activity for the realization of the domestic and foreign policies of the State and directs and controls the activity of ministries, other central organs of state administration and local organs of administration. It is composed of the Chairman, Vice-Chairmen, Ministers and other persons defined by law. The Chairman of the Council of Ministers is appointed by the President; Ministers are appointed by the President upon the recommendation of the Chairman. The composition of the Council of Ministers is approved by the People's Assembly. Members of the Council of Ministers may not have any other state or professional function.

The Chairman and Vice-Chairmen of the Council of Ministers constitute the Presidency of the Council of Ministers.

FINAL PROVISIONS

Articles 42–46. The creation, organization and activity of the local organs of power, administration, courts and the Attorney-General are made according to existing legal provisions, except those invalidated by the Law on Major Constitutional Provisions. Drafts for amendments to the Law on Major Constitutional Provisions may be proposed by the President of the Republic, the Council of Ministers or one-quarter of the deputies of the People's Assembly. The adoption of amendments requires a two-thirds majority of all deputies. The provisions of the Law on Major Constitutional Provisions operate until the adoption of the Constitution of the Republic of Albania, which will be drafted by the Special Commission appointed by the People's Assembly. The Constitution of the People's Socialist Republic of Albania, adopted on 28 December 1976, is invalidated.

The Government

(November 1991)

HEAD OF STATE

President of the Republic: RAMIZ ALIA (elected 30 April 1991).

COUNCIL OF MINISTERS

An interim coalition of the Socialist Party of Albania (SPA), the Democratic Party of Albania (DPA) and the Agrarian Party (AP), with nine non-party members nominated by the three main parties and by the Social Democratic Party (SDP) and the Albanian Republican Party (ARP). In early December, following the dismissal of ARP-sponsored ministers and the withdrawal of DPA members from the Council of Ministers, the Chairman, Ylli Bufi, offered his resignation (see Late Information for further details).

Chairman (Prime Minister): YLLI BUFI (SPA).

Deputy Chairman and Minister of the Economy: GRAMOZ PASHKO (DPA).

Deputy Chairman: ZYDI PEPA (non-party—nominated by the SPA).

Minister of Agriculture: NEXHMEDIN DUMANI (SPA).

Minister of Construction: EMIN MYSLIU (DPA).

Minister of Culture, Youth and Sport: PREÇ ZOGAJ (DPA).

Minister of Defence: PERIKLI TETA (non-party—DPA).

Minister of Domestic Trade and Tourism: AGIM MERO (DPA).

Minister of Education: Dr MAQO LAKRORI (SPA).

Minister of Finance: GENCI RULI (DPA).

Minister of Food: VILSON AHMETI (non-party—SPA).

Minister of Foreign Affairs: MUHAMET KAPLLANI (SPA).

Minister of Foreign Economic Relations: YLLI CABARI (SPA).

Minister of Health: SABIT BROKAJ (SPA).

Minister of Industry: JORGAN MISJA (non-party—DPA).

Minister of Justice: SHEFQET MUCI (non-party—SDP).

Minister of Mineral Resources and Energy: DRINI MEZINI (SPA).

Minister of Public Order: BAJRAM YZEIRI (non-party—SPA).

Minister of Transport: FATOS BITINCKA (non-party—ARP).

Chairman of the State Control Commission: ALFRED KARAMUKO (non-party—ARP).

Chairman of the Science and Technology Committee: Dr PETRIT SKENDI (non-party—SPA).

Secretary of State for the Economy: LEONTIEV CUCI (SPA).

Secretary of State for Agriculture: RESMI OSMANI (AP).

Secretary of State for Education: Dr PASKAL MILO (SDP).

MINISTRIES

Council of Ministers: Këshilli i Ministrave, Tirana; telex 4201.

Ministry of Agriculture: Ministria e Bujqësisë, Tirana; tel. (42) 26147; telex 4209.

Ministry of Construction: Ministria e Ndertimit, Tirana; telex 4208.

Ministry of Culture, Youth and Sport: Tirana; tel. (42) 27984.

Ministry of Defence: Tirana.

Ministry of Domestic Trade and Tourism: Tirana; telex 4290.

Ministry of Education: Ministria e Arsimit, Tirana; telex 4203.

Ministry of Finance: Ministria e Financave, Tirana; telex 4297.

Ministry of Food: Tirana.

Ministry of Foreign Affairs: Ministria e Punëvet të Jashtme, Tirana; tel. (42) 23338; telex 2164; fax (42) 23791.

Ministry of Foreign Economic Relations: Tirana; telex 2152.

Ministry of Health: Ministria e Shendetesisë, Tirana; telex 4205.

Ministry of Industry: Ministria e Industrisë, Tirana; telex 4204.

Ministry of Justice: Tirana.

Ministry of Mineral Resources and Energy: Tirana; telex 4296.

Ministry of Public Order: Tirana.

Ministry of Transport: Ministria e Transporteve, Tirana; telex 4207.

Legislature

KUVENDI POPULLOR
(People's Assembly)

Presidency: Dr KASTRIOT ISLAMI (Chair.), Dr ALEKSANDR MEKSI, LUSH PERPALI (Deputy Chair.).

General Election, 31 March, 7 and 14 April 1991

Party	Seats
Party of Labour of Albania (PLA)*	169†
Democratic Party of Albania (DPA)	75
Democratic Union of the Greek Minority (OMONIA)	5
National Committee of War Veterans	1
Total	**250**

* Subsequently renamed the Socialist Party of Albania (SPA).

† Including 16 contested jointly with PLA-affiliated organizations, such as the Democratic Front, the Union of Working Youth of Albania, the official trade unions and the Women's Union.

Local Government

Until mid-1991 Albania was divided into 26 districts (rrethe) and 140 communities (lokaliteteve). In July 1991 the Council of Ministers made certain changes to the administrative-territorial structure of the country, including the creation of the new district of Kavajë. Until 1991 administrative affairs in each district were the responsibility of a People's Council. In mid-1991 multi-party executive committees were established to take over the responsibilities of the People's Councils until new elections could take place. (For a full list of districts see Statistical Survey).

Political Organizations

Agrarian Party (AP): Tirana; f. 1991; Leaders MENO GJOLEKA, LLAMBRO BILLA.

Albanian National Democratic Party: Tirana; f. 1991.

Albanian Republican Party—ARP (Partia Republikane Shqiptare): Tirana; f. 1991; Gen. Council of 54 mems, Steering Commission of 21 mems; Chair. SABRI GODO; Dep. Chair. VANGJUSH GAMBETA, ZEF BUSHATI.

Camëria Political and Patriotic Association (Shokata Politike-Patriotike Çamëria): Tirana; supports the rights of the Çam minority (an Albanian people) in northern Greece; f. 1991; Chair. Dr ABAZ DOJAKA.

Democratic Front of Albania (Fronti Demokratik i Shqipërisë): Tirana; tel. (42) 27957; f. 1945 to succeed National Liberation Front (f. 1942); a mass organization, which was affiliated to the former PLA (now the SPA); Gen. Council of 185 mems replaced, in July 1991, by a Managing Council, until a national conference could be convened; Chair. ALEKS LUARASI; Sec. ZEQIR LUSHAJ.

Democratic Party of Albania—DPA (Partia Demokratike të Shqipërisë): Tirana; f. 1990; committed to liberal-democratic ideals and market economics; Chair. of Managing Commission SALI BERISHA; Sec. EDUARD SELAMI.

Democratic Union of the Greek Minority (OMONIA—Bashkimia Demokratik i Minoritet Grek): Tirana; f. 1991; Leaders JANI JANI, PANAJOT BARKA, JANI GJYZELI.

Ecology Party (Partija Ekologjike): Tirana; f. 1990; Chair. NAMIK V. HOTI; Sec.-Gen. IZMINI MECI.

Enver Hoxha Association of Voluntary Union (Shokata e Bashkimit Vullnetar—Enver Hoxha): Tirana; f. 1991; supports the ideals of Enver Hoxha; Chair. HYSNI MILLOSHI.

National Committee of the War Veterans of the Albanian People: Tirana; Chair. (vacant).

Party of National Unity: Tirana; f. 1991; Chair. of Steering Cttee IDAJET BEQIRI.

Social Democratic Party of Albania—SDP (Partia Social Demokratike e Shqipërisë): Tirana; f. 1991; advocates gradual economic reforms and social justice; 11-member Managing Council; Chair. Prof. Dr SKËNDER GJINUSHI.

Socialist Party of Albania—SPA (Partia Socialiste e Shqipërisë): Tirana; telex 4291; f. 1941, renamed Party of Labour of Albania in 1948, adopted present name in 1991; until 1990 the only permitted political party in Albania; now rejects Marxism-Leninism and claims commitment to democracy and a market economy; Managing Cttee of 81 mems, headed by Presidency of 15 mems; 130,000 mems and candidate mems; Pres. FATOS NANO; Vice-Pres ISMAIL LLESHI, SPIRO DEDE, SERVET PELLUMBI.

Women's Union of Albania (Bashkimi të Grave të Shqipërisë): Tirana; tel. (42) 27959; f. 1943 for the ideological, political and social education of women; associated with the PLA (now the SPA); Pres. of General Council LUMTURI REXHA; Sec.-Gen. LEONORA ÇARO.

Diplomatic Representation

EMBASSIES IN ALBANIA

Bulgaria: Rruga Skënderbeu 12, Tirana; tel. (42) 22672; Ambassador: STEFAN NAUMOV.

China, People's Republic: Rruga Skënderbeu 57, Tirana; tel. (42) 22600; telex 2148; Ambassador: GU MAOXUAN.

Cuba: Rruga Kongresi i Përmetit 13, Tirana; tel. (42) 25176; telex 2155; Ambassador: JULIO C. CANCIO FERRER.

Czechoslovakia: Rruga Skënderbeu 10, Tirana; telex 2162; Ambassador: ANTON ŠIMKOVIČ.

Egypt: Rruga Skënderbeu 43, Tirana; tel. (42) 23013; telex 2156; Ambassador: MANZUR AHMAD AL-DALI.

France: Rruga Skënderbeu 14, Tirana; tel. (42) 22804; telex 2150; Ambassador: MICHEL BOULMER.

Germany: Rruga Skënderbeu, Tirana; tel. (42) 23481; telex 2254; Ambassador: FRIEDRICH KRONECK.

Greece: Rruga Frederick Shiroka 3, Tirana; tel. (42) 26850; Ambassador: STILIANIS MALIKURTIS.

Hungary: Rruga Skënderbeu 16, Tirana; tel. (42) 22004; telex 2257; fax (42) 33211; Ambassador: FERENC PÓKA.

Italy: Rruga Labinoti 103, Tirana; tel. (42) 22800; telex 2166; Ambassador: TORQUATO CARDILLI.

Korea, Democratic People's Republic: Rruga Skënderbeu 55, Tirana; tel. (42) 22258; Ambassador: KIM U-CHONG.

Poland: Rruga Kongresi i Përmetit 123, Tirana; Ambassador: WŁADYSŁAW CIASTON.

Romania: Rruga Themistokli Gërmenji 2, Tirana; tel. (42) 22259; Ambassador: GHEORGHE MIKU.

Turkey: Rruga Konferenca e Pezës 31, Tirana; tel. (42) 22449; Ambassador: TEOMAN SÜRENKÖK.

USSR: Tirana; Ambassador: VIKTOR YEFIMOVICH NERUBAYLO.

USA: Tirana; Ambassador: (vacant).

Viet-Nam: Rruga Lek Dukagjini, Tirana; tel. (42) 22556; telex 2253; Ambassador: NGUYEN CHI THANH.

Yugoslavia: Rruga Kongresi i Përmetit 192–196, Tirana; tel. (42) 23042; telex 2167; Ambassador: PREDRAG PJANIĆ.

Judicial System

The judicial system is administered by the Ministry of Justice, re-established in 1990, which supervises the organization and functioning of the Supreme Court, the Territorial Division Courts and the District Courts. The Supreme Court is elected for a four-year term by the People's Assembly.

Extensive reforms of the judicial system were announced in May 1990. In addition to the re-establishment of the Ministry of Justice (the Minister being empowered to overturn court rulings), defendants were guaranteed the right to a defence lawyer. The number of capital offences was reduced from 34 to 11, women being exempt from the death penalty. Further reforms were expected in 1991, in particular at local level, following the replacement of People's Councils (local administrative organs controlled by the PLA) by multi-party institutions in mid-1991. Formerly, Territorial Division Courts were elected for a three-year term by the People's Councils of the districts in which they exercised jurisdiction. The District Courts were elected for a three-year term by all voting citizens through a direct and secret ballot. The Village, City and City Quarter Courts were bodies of a social or unofficial character, operating at the People's Councils, and were elected by the people for a three-year term. Military Tribunals are held at the Supreme Court and at District Courts. Courts of Justice are independent in the exercise of their functions, and are separated from the administration.

A revised Penal Code came into effect in October 1977, followed by a Code of Penal Procedure (1980), a Labour Code (1980), a Civil Code, together with a Code of Civil Procedure (1982) and a Family Code (1982). The penal code was further revised in 1990 and all laws in contradiction to the constitutional legislation adopted in April 1991 were declared invalid. Further revisions were expected in 1991 and 1992. Trials are held in public. The accused is assured the right of defence, and the principle of presumption of innocence is sanctioned by the Code of Penal Procedure. First-degree cases are normally tried by District Courts or, exceptionally, by Territorial Division Courts or the Supreme Court. Second-degree cases are held in the Territorial Division Courts or in the Supreme Court, before three judges and two assistant judges. The verdicts of the lower courts may be altered, within the law, by the higher courts.

The Office of Investigation is a state organ that investigates criminal acts. This department is separated from the organs of internal affairs and from the other administrative organs. The Chairman of the General Department of Investigation and his or her deputies are appointed by the People's Assembly. The chairmen of the district's offices of investigation are appointed by the Chairman of the General Department of Investigation. Attorneys' offices are state organs that control strictly and uniformly the application of the laws from Ministries and other central and local organs, from courts, organs of investigation, enterprises, institutions and citizens' organizations. The Attorney-General and his or her deputies are appointed by the People's Assembly.

President of the Supreme Court: KLEANTHI KOÇO.

Attorney-General: PETRIT SERJANI.

Chairman of the General Department of Investigation: KRISTAQ NGJELA.

Religion

All religious institutions were closed by the Government in 1967 and the practice of religion was prohibited. Many places of worship were converted into museums, sports halls, etc. In 1990, however, the prohibition on religious activities was lifted and religious services were permitted. In 1991 some mosques and churches were reopened. Transitional legislation adopted in April 1991 to replace the 1976 Constitution states that Albania is a secular state which observes 'freedom of religious belief and creates conditions in which to exercise it'. On the basis of declared affiliation in 1945, it is estimated that some 70% of the population are of Muslim background, 20% Eastern Orthodox (mainly in the south) and some 10% Roman Catholic (in the north). In 1991 there were, reportedly, 50 mosques left intact from a pre-1945 total of 700. With financial assistance from Saudi Arabia, some 180 Albanian Muslims were reported to have made the *hajj*, the Muslim pilgrimage to Mecca, in 1991, apparently the first Albanians to do so for some 60 years. During 1991 the small number of Albanians who were adherents of the Jewish faith emigrated to Israel.

CHRISTIANITY
The Roman Catholic Church

Albania formally comprises the archdioceses of Durrës (directly responsible to the Holy See) and Shkodrë (Shkodër), three dioceses, one territorial abbacy and Southern Albania (previously the responsibility of an Apostolic Administrator). After November 1990, when 5,000 Roman Catholics in Shkodër attended the first public service since 1967, several churches were reported to have reopened. In July 1991 diplomatic relations were restored with the Holy See.

Apostolic Administrator of Durrës and Lezhë: NICOLA TROSHANI, Titular Bishop of Cisamo (Cisamus).

Apostolic Administrator of Shkodrë: ERNESTO ÇOBA, Titular Bishop of Mideo (Midaëum).

The Orthodox Church

Kisha Ortodokse Shqiptare (Albanian Orthodox Church): Rruga Kavaja, Tirana; the Albanian Orthodox Church was recognized as autocephalous in 1937, although the Serbian, Macedonian and Greek churches do not recognize its separate existence; during 1991 churches were reopened in at least 10 cities, and the Ecumenical Patriarchate in Istanbul (Constantinople) appointed a Greek bishop as Exarch of the Albanian Church, because there were no longer any Albanian bishops alive; Exarch Bishop ANASTAS JANULATOS.

ISLAM

Bashkesia Islamike Shqiptare (Albanian Islamic Community): c/o Ethem Bay Mosque, Tirana; f. 1991; Chair. HAFIZ SABRI KOCI, Grand Mufti of Albania HAFIZ SALIH TERHAT HOXHA.

Bektashi Sect

World Council of Elders of the Bektashis: Tirana; f. 1991; Chair. RESHAT BABA BARDHI.

The Press

Until 1991 the Press was controlled by the Party of Labour of Albania and adhered to a strongly Marxist-Leninist line. In 1991 several newspapers were established by independent political organizations. The most important publications are the SPA daily, *Zëri i Popullit*, and the journal of the Democratic Party, *Rilindja Demokratike*—the first opposition paper to be established since the Second World War. Other new papers include *Republika*, the Republican Party journal, and *Progresi Agrar*, the publication of the Agrarian Party.

PRINCIPAL DAILIES

Zëri i Popullit (The Voice of the People): Bulevardi Deshmorët e Kombit, Tirana; tel. (42) 27808; telex 4251; fax (42) 27813; f. 1942; daily, except Mon.; organ of the SPA; Editor-in-Chief PERPARIM XHIXHA; circ. 103,800.

Bashkimi (Unity): Bulevardi Deshmorët e Kombit, Tirana; tel. (42) 28110; f. 1943; organ of the Democratic Front; Editor-in-Chief QEMAL SAKAJEVA; circ. 30,000.

PERIODICALS
Tirana

Albania: Tirana; f. 1991; weekly; newspaper; organ of the Ecology Party; environmental issues.

Alternativa SD: Tirana; f. 1991; newspaper; organ of the Social Democratic Party.

Bibliografia Kombëtare e Librit Shqiptar (National Bibliography of Albanian Books): Tirana; 4 a year; publ. by the National Library of Albania.

Bibliografia Kombëtare e Periodikeve Shqip (National Bibliography of Albanian periodicals): Tirana; monthly; publ. by the National Library of Albania.

Bujqësia Socialiste (Socialist Agriculture): Tirana; monthly; publ. by the Ministry of Agriculture; Editor FAIK LABINOTI.

Buletini i Shkencave Bujqësore (Agricultural Sciences Bulletin): Tirana; 4 a year; summaries in French; publ. by the Agricultural Scientific Research Institute; Editor-in-Chief LEFTER VESHI.

Buletini i Shkencave Gjeologjike (Bulletin of Geological Sciences): Tirana; tel. (42) 22511; telex 4204; fax (42) 34031; f. 1965; quarterly; publ. by Geological Research and Designs Institute and Faculty of Geology and Mines of Tirana University; Editor AFAT SERJANI; circ. 650.

Buletini i Shkencave Mjekësore (Medical Sciences Bulletin): Tirana; 4 a year; summaries in French; publ. by the University of Tirana; Editor-in-Chief YLVI VEHBIU.

Buletini i Shkencave të Natyrës (Natural Sciences Bulletin): Tirana; f. 1957; 4 a year; summaries in French; publ. by the University of Tirana; Editor-in-Chief MUHARREM FRASHËRI.

Buletini i Shkencave Teknike (Technical Sciences Bulletin): Tirana; 4 a year; summaries in French; publ. by the University of Tirana.

Çamëria—Vatra Amtare (Çamëria—Maternal Hearth): Tirana; f. 1991; newspaper; organ of the Çamëria Political and Patriotic Association.

Drejtësia Popullore (People's Law): Tirana; f. 1948; 4 a year; publ. of organs of justice; Chief Editor ELENI SELENICA.

Drita (The Light): Rruga Konferenca e Pezës 4, Tirana; tel. (42) 27036; f. 1960; weekly; publ. by Union of Writers and Artists of Albania; Editor-in-Chief BRISEIDA MEMA; circ. 27,000.

Estrada (Variety Shows): Tirana; every 2 months; publ. by the Central House of Popular Creativity.

Fatosi (The Valiant): Tirana; tel. (42) 23024; f. 1959; fortnightly; literary and artistic magazine for children; Editor-in-Chief XHEVAT BEQARAJ; circ. 21,200.

Official Gazette of the Republic of Albania: Kuvendi Popullore, Tirana; tel. (42) 29385; telex 4298; f. 1945; occasional government review.

Gjuha Jonë (Our Language): Rruga Lek Dukagjini, Tirana; tel. (42) 26050; f. 1981; 4 a year; publ. by Academy of Sciences; Editor-in-Chief ALI DHRIMO.

Horizonti (Horizon): Tirana; tel. (42) 29204; f. 1979; monthly; scientific and technical magazine for children; Editor-in-Chief THANAS QERAMA; circ. 18,850.

Hosteni (The Goad): Tirana; f. 1945; fortnightly; political review of humour and satire; publ. by the Union of Journalists; Editor-in-Chief NIKO NIKOLLA.

Iliria (Illyria): Qendra e Kërkimeve Arkeologjike, Bulevardi Dëshmorët e Kombit, Tirana; tel. (42) 26541; telex 2214; f. 1971; 2 a year; summaries in French; publ. by Centre of Archaeological Research at the Academy of Sciences; Chief of Editorial Bd Dr MUZAFER KORKUTI; circ. 750.

Java: Gjirokaster; f. 1991; independent newspaper.

Kënga Jonë (Our Song): Tirana; f. 1960; every 2 months; publ. by the Central House of Popular Creativity.

Kombi (The Nation): Tirana; f. 1991; newspaper; organ of the Party of National Unity.

Kultura Popullore (Folk Culture): Rruga Kont Urani 3, Tirana; tel. (42) 27497; f. 1980; 2 a year; annually in French; publ. by the Institute of Folk Culture at the Academy of Sciences; Editor-in-Chief DALAN SHAPLLO.

Les Lettres Albanaises: Rruga Konferenca e Pezës, Tirana; tel. (42) 22691; 4 a year; in French; literary and artistic review; publ. by Union of Writers and Artists of Albania; Editor DIANA ÇULI.

Luftëtari (The Fighter): Tirana; f. 1945; 2 a week; newspaper; publ. by the Ministry of Defence; Editor-in-Chief DEMOKRAT ANASTASI.

Mbrëmje Tematike (Evening Parties): Tirana; publ. by the Central House of Popular Creativity.

Mësuesi (The Teacher): Tirana; f. 1961; weekly; publ. by the Ministry of Education; Editor-in-Chief THOMA QENDRO.

Monumentet (Monuments): Tirana; f. 1971; 2 a year; summaries in French; publ. by the Institute of Monuments and Culture; Editor-in-Chief SOTIR KOSTA.

Ndërtuesi (The Builder): Tirana; 4 a year; publ. by the Ministry of Construction.

Në shërbim të popullit (In the Service of the People): Tirana; f. 1955; Editor-in-Chief THOMA NAQE.

Në skenën e fëmijëve (On the Children's Stage): Tirana; publ. by the Central House of Popular Creativity.

Nëna dhe Fëmija (Mother and Child): Tirana; 3 a year; publ. by Ministry of Health.

Nëntori (November): Rruga Konferenca e Pezës 4, Tirana; f. 1954; monthly; publ. by the Union of Writers and Artists of Albania; Chief Editor KIÇO BLUSHI.

Për Mbrojtjen e Atdheut (For the Defence of the Fatherland): Tirana; f. 1948; publ. of the Ministry of Defence; Editor-in-Chief BEGE TENA.

Përmbledhje Studimesh (Collection of Studies): Tirana; 4 a year; summaries in French; bulletin of the Ministry of Mineral Resources and Energy.

Pionieri (The Pioneer): Tirana; f. 1944; fortnightly; Editor-in-Chief SKENDER HASKO; circ. 38,000.

Probleme Ekonomike: Tirana; quarterly; organ of Institute for Economic Studies.

Progresi Agrar (Agrarian Progress): Tirana; f. 1991; 2 a week; newspaper; organ of the Agrarian Party.

Pysqyra (The Mirror): Bulevardi Dëshmorët e Kombit, Tirana; f. 1991 to replace *Puna* (Labour—f. 1945); 2 a week; newspaper; also 4 times a year in French; organ of the Confederation of Albanian Trade Unions; Editor-in-Chief KRISTAQ LAKA.

Radio Përhapja: Tirana; fortnightly; organ of Albanian Radio and Television.

Republika: Tirana; f. 1991; 2 a week; newspaper; organ of the Albanian Republican Party; Editor-in-Chief VANGJUSH GAMBETA.

Revista Mjekësore (Medical Review): Tirana; every 2 months; publ. by Ministry of Health.

Revista Pedagogjike: Tirana; 4 a year; organ of the Institute of Pedagogical Studies; Editor SOTIR TEMO.

Rilindja Demokratike (Democratic Revival): Tirana; f. 1991; 2 a week; newspaper; organ of the DPA; Editor-in-Chief NAPOLEON ROSHI; circ. 50,000.

Rruga e Partisë (The Party's Road): Tirana; f. 1954; monthly; theoretical journal; publ. by the SPA; Editor STEFI KOTMILO; circ. 9,000.

Shëndeti (Health): M. Duri 2, Tirana; tel. (42) 27106; f. 1949; monthly; publ. by the National Directorate of Health Education; issues of health and welfare, personal health care; Editor-in-Chief KORNELIA GJATA.

Shkenca dhe Jeta (Science and Life): Tirana; tel. (42) 27609; f. 1969 as the organ of the Union of Working Youth; monthly; Editor-in-Chief KUDRET ISAI; circ. 10,000.

Shqipëria e Re (New Albania): Rruga Asim Vokshi 2, Tirana; f. 1947; published monthly in Albanian; every 2 months in Arabic, English, French, German, Italian, Russian and Spanish; organ of the Committee for Cultural Relations with Foreign Countries; illustrated political and social magazine; Editor YMER MINXHOZI; circ. 170,000.

Shqipëria Sot (Albania Today): Tirana; every 2 months; published in English, French, German, Italian and Spanish; political, cultural and social review; Editor-in-Chief DHIMITER VERLI.

Shqiptarja e Re (The New Albanian Woman): Tirana; f. 1943; monthly; publ. by the Women's Union of Albania; political and socio-cultural review; Editor-in-Chief VALENTINA LESKAJ.

Sindikalisti (Trade Unionists): Tirana; f. 1991; newspaper; organ of the Union of Independent Trade Unions.

Skena dhe Ekrani (Stage and Screen): Tirana; 4 a year; cultural review.

Socio-Political Studies: Tirana; tel. (42) 28395; telex 4291; f. 1981 in Albanian, 1984 in English and French; 2 a year in Albanian, annually in English and French; publ. by Institute of Marxist-Leninist Studies; Chief of Editorial Bd Prof. SOTIR MADHI; circ. 3,000 (Albanian), 1,000 (English and French).

Sot (Today): Tirana; f. 1991; organ of the SPA.

Sporti Popullor (People's Sport): Tirana; f. 1945; weekly; publ. by the Ministry of Culture, Youth and Sport; Editor BESNIK DIZDARI; circ. 60,000.

Studenti (The Student): Tirana; f. 1967; weekly.

Studia Albanica: Rruga Myslym Shyri 7, Tirana; tel. (42) 28290; f. 1964; 2 a year; history and philology; in French; publ. by the Academy of Sciences; Editor-in-Chief LUAN OMARI.

Studime Filologjike (Philological Studies): Rruga Naim Frashëri 7, Tirana; tel. (42) 27251; f. 1964; 4 a year; summaries in French; publ. by the Institute of Language and Literature at the Albanian Academy of Sciences; Editor-in-Chief ANDROKLI KOSTALLARI.

Studime Historike (Historical Studies): Rruga Naim Frashëri 7, Tirana; (42) 25179; f. 1964; 4 a year; summaries in French; publ. by the Institute of History at the Academy of Sciences; historical sciences; Editor-in-Chief STEFANAQ POLLO.

Teknika (Technology): Tirana; f. 1954; 4 a year; publ. by the Ministry of Industry; Editor NATASHA VARFI.

Teatri (Theatre): Tirana; f. 1960; every 2 months; publ. by the Central House of Popular Creativity.

Tirana: Tirana; f. 1987; publ. by Tirana District SPA.

Tregtia e Jashtme Popullore (Albanian Foreign Trade): Rruga Konferenca e Pezës 6, Tirana; tel. (42) 22934; telex 2179; f. 1961; every 2 months; in English and French; organ of the Albanian Chamber of Commerce; Editor AGIM KORBI.

Tribuna e Gazetarit (The Journalist's Tribune): Tirana; every 2 months; publ. by the Union of Journalists of Albania; Editor NAZMI QAMILI.

Vatra e Kulturës (Centre of Culture): Tirana; publ. by the Central House of Popular Creativity.

Ylli (The Star): Tirana; f. 1951; monthly; socio-political and literary review; Editor-in-Chief NEVRUZ TURHANI.

Yllkat (Little Stars): Tirana; monthly; publ. by Institute of Pedagogical Studies.

Zëri i Rinisë (The Voice of Youth): Tirana; f. 1942 as the newspaper of the Union of Albanian Working Youth; 2 a week; Editor-in-Chief REMZI LANI; circ. 53,000.

10 Korriku (10 July): Tirana; f. 1947; monthly; publ. by the Ministry of Defence; Editor-in-Chief SELAMI VEHBIU.

Other Towns

Adriatiku (Adriatic): Durrës; f. 1967; 2 a week.

Drapër e Çekan (Hammer and Sickle): Fier; f. 1967; 2 a week.

Fitorjë (Victory): Sarandë; f. 1971; 2 a week; Editor-in-Chief BELUL KORKUTI.

Jehona e Skraparit (Echo of Skrapar): Skrapar; 2 a week.

Jeta e Re (New Life): Shkodër; f. 1967; 2 a week.

Kastrioti: Krujë; f. 1971; 2 a week.

Kukësi i Ri (New Kukës): Kukës; 2 a week.

Kushtrimi (Clarion Call): Berat; f. 1967; 2 a week.

Laiko Vima (People's Step): Gjirokastër; f. 1945; 2 a week; monthly literary edn; in Greek; Editor-in-Chief VASIL ÇAMI.

Pararoja (Vanguard): Gjirokastër; f. 1967; 2 a week.

Përpara (Forward): Korçë; f. 1967; 2 a week; Editor-in-Chief STRATI MARKO; circ. 4,000.

Shkëndija (The Spark): Lushnjë; f. 1971; 2 a week.

Shkumbimi: Elbasan; 2 a week; Editor-in-Chief MEFAIL PUPULEKU.

Ushtimi i Maleve (Rumble of the Mountains): Peshkopi; 2 a week.

Zëri i Vlorës (The Voice of Vlorë): Vlorë; f. 1967; 2 a week; Editor-in-Chief DASHO METODASHAJ.

NEWS AGENCIES

Albanian Telegraphic Agency (ATA): Bulevardi Marcel Cachin 23, Tirana; tel. (42) 24412; telex 2142; f. 1945; domestic and foreign news; branches in provincial towns; Dir TAQO ZOTO.

Foreign Bureau

Xinhua (New China) News Agency (People's Republic of China): Rruga Skënderbeu 57, Tirana; tel. (42) 33139; fax (42) 33139; Bureau Chief LI JIYU.

PRESS ASSOCIATION

Bashkimi i Gazetarëve të Shqipërisë (Union of Journalists of Albania): Tirana; tel. (42) 27977; f. 1949; Chair. MARASH HAJATI; Sec.-Gen. YMER MINXHOZI.

Publishers

In 1988 a total of 1,018 book titles were published. In the same year 7,446,000 copies were produced. In 1991 several new independent book publishers were established.

Drejtoria Qëndrore e Përhapjes dhe e Propagandimit të Librit (Central Administration for the Dissemination and Propagation of the Book): Tirana; tel. (42) 27841; directed by the Ministry of Education.

Botime të Akademisë së Shkencave të RSH: Tirana; publishing house of the Albanian Academy of Sciences.

Botime të Drejtorisë së Arsimit Shëndetësor dhe të Shtëpisë së Propagandës Bujqësore: Tirana; medicine, sciences and agriculture.

Botime të Institutit të Lartë Bujqësor: Kamzë, Tirana; publishing house of Tirana Agricultural University.

Botime të Shtëpisë Botuese 8 Nëntori: Tirana; tel. (42) 28064; f. 1972; books on Albania and other countries, political and social sciences, translations of Albanian works into foreign languages, technical and scientific books, illustrated albums, etc.; Dir XHEMAL DINI.

Botime të Shtëpisë Botuese të Librit Shkollor: Tirana; f. 1967; educational books; Dir FEJZI KOÇI.

Shtepia Botuese e Librit Universitar: Rruga Dora d'Istria, Tirana; tel. (42) 25659; telex 2211; f. 1988; publishes university textbooks on sciences, engineering, geography, history, literature, foreign languages, economics, etc.; Dir MUSTAFA FEZGA.

Shtëpia Botuese Naim Frashëri: Tirana; tel. (42) 27906; f. 1947; fiction, poetry, drama, criticism, children's literature, translations; Dir GAQO BUSHAKA.

Union of Writers and Artists Publishing House: Tirana; f. 1991; fiction, poetry incl. foreign literature and works by the Albanian diaspora; Dir ZIJA ÇELA.

Government Publishing House

N.I.SH. Shtypshkronjave Mihal Duri (Mihal Duri State Printing House): Tirana; government publications, politics, law, education; Dir HAJRI HOXHA.

WRITERS' UNION

Lidhja e Shkrimtarëve dhe e Artistëve të Shqipërisë (Union of Writers and Artists of Albania): Rruga Konferenca e Pezës 4, Tirana; tel. (42) 29689; f. 1945; 26 branches throughout the country; 1,750 mems; Chair. DRITËRO AGOLLI.

Radio and Television

In 1988 there were an estimated 525,000 radio receivers and 260,000 television sets in use. In 1991 state broadcasting was removed from political control and made subordinate to the People's Assembly.

Radiotelevisioni Shqiptar: Rruga Ismail Qemali, Tirana; tel. (42) 23239; telex 2216; f. 1944; Dir-Gen. SEFEDIN ÇELA; Dir of Domestic Radio THIMI NIKA.

RADIO

Radio Tirana: Tirana; telex 4158; broadcasts more than 24 hours of internal programmes daily from Tirana; regional stations in Berat, Fier, Gjirokastër, Korçë, Kükes, Pukë, Rogozhina, Sarandë and Shkodër; in 1991 radio broadcasts in Macedonian began in the area of Korçë; wire-relay service in Tirana and in factories, mines and clubs all over the country.

External Service: broadcasts for 83 hours daily in Albanian, Arabic, Bulgarian, Chinese, Czech, English, French, German, Greek, Hungarian, Indonesian, Italian, Farsi (Iranian), Polish, Portuguese, Romanian, Russian, Serbo-Croat, Spanish, Swedish and Turkish; Dir NEPALAN GROUCI.

TELEVISION

There are stations at Tirana, Berat, Elbasan, Gjirokastër, Kükes, Peshkopi and Pogradec. Programmes are broadcast for 4 hours daily (9½ hours on Sundays).

Finance

Bank a e Shtëtit Shqiptar (Albanian State Bank): Head Office: Sheshi Skënderbeu 1, Tirana; tel. (42) 22435; telex 2153; f. 1945; bank of issue; branches in 34 towns; Gen. Dir NIKO GJYZARI.

Albanian State Bank for Foreign Relations: Tirana; f. 1990; deals with foreign currency transactions, establishes financial relations with foreign banks; Gen. Dir SHELQIM CANI.

Drejtoria e Përgjithshme e Kursimeve dhe Sigurimeve (Directorate of Savings and Insurance): Tirana; tel. (42) 22542; f. 1949; Dir KOSTAQ POSTOLI.

State Agricultural Bank: Tirana; tel. (42) 27738; f. 1970; gives short- and long-term credits to agricultural co-operatives and enterprises; Dir S. KUÇI.

Commercial and Savings Banks

Iliria Bank: Tirana; f. 1991 as Albania's first private commercial bank since 1945.

In 1990 there were 107 savings banks in operation with 3,800 agencies. In 1987 deposits totalled 1,329m. lekë.

Trade and Industry

CHAMBER OF COMMERCE

Chamber of Commerce of the Republic of Albania: Rruga Konferenca e Pezës 6, Tirana; tel. (42) 27997; telex 2179; f. 1958; Pres. LIGOR DHAMO; Vice-Pres. SIMON POREÇI.

Durrës Chamber of Commerce: Durrës; f. 1988; promotes trade with southern Italy.

Gjirokastër Chamber of Commerce: Gjirokastër; f. 1988; promotes trade with Greek border area; Chair. NAXHI MAMANI; Sec. GENCI SHEHU.

Shkodër Chamber of Commerce: Shkodër; promotes trade with Yugoslav border area; Sec. ENVER DIBRA.

ALBANIA

There are also chambers of commerce in Korçë, Kukës, Peshkopi, Pogradec, Sarandë and Vlorë.

SUPERVISORY ORGANIZATION

Albkontroll: Rruga Skënderbeu 15, Durrës; tel. (52) 22354; telex 2181; fax (52) 22791; f. 1962; brs throughout Albania; independent control body for inspection of goods for import and export, means of transport, etc.; Gen. Man. AGRON KLOSI.

NATIONAL FOREIGN TRADE ORGANIZATIONS

Since 1990 the National Foreign Trade Organizations have no longer been the sole institutions authorized to engage in foreign trade.

Agroeksport: Rruga 4 Shkurti 6, Tirana; tel. (42) 25227; telex 2137; exports vegetables, fruit, canned fish, wine, tobacco, etc.; imports rice, coffee and other foodstuffs, paper products, etc.; Gen. Man. LUAN SHAHU.

Agrokoop: Rruga 4 Shkurti 6, Tirana; telex 2248; specializes in foodstuffs and consumer goods.

Albkoop: Rruga 4 Shkurti 6, Tirana; tel. (42) 24179; telex 2187; f. 1986; import and export of consumer goods, incl. clothing, textiles, handicrafts, stationery, jewellery; Gen. Man. (vacant).

Arteksportimport: Rruga 4 Shkurti 6, Tirana; tel. (42) 24540; telex 2140; fax (42) 24540; f. 1989; exports handicrafts and products of the light industry; imports chemicals, textiles and items required by Albanian industries; Gen. Dir TEFIK KOKONA.

Eksimagra: Rruga Gjon Muzaka, Tirana; tel. (42) 23128; telex 2111; f. 1989; exports fresh vegetables and fruit, figs, pheasants, etc.; imports meat, cereals, edible fats, packaging, etc.; Gen. Man. VIKTOR NUSHI.

Ihtimpeks: Rruga Siri Kodra 32, Tirana; tel. (42) 22287; f. 1990; exports fresh fish, molluscs and mussels, and live eels; imports fishing nets and other equipment.

Industrialimpeks: Rruga 4 Shkurti 6, Tirana; tel. (42) 26123; telex 2112; exports copper wires, furniture, kitchenware, paper, timber, wooden articles, cement, etc.; imports fabrics, cement, chemicals, paper, cardboard, school and office items, etc.; Gen. Man. HAZBI GJIKONDI.

Makinaimpeks: Rruga 4 Shkurti 6, Tirana; tel. (42) 25220; telex 2128; imports vehicles, factory installations, machinery and parts; exports explosives; Gen. Man. THEODHOR DUMA.

Mekalb: Rruga Kongresi i Përmetit, Tirana; tel. (42) 28655; telex 4166; f. 1990; exports spare parts for tractors, agricultural machinery, etc.; imports machine tools, radio and TV components and metal items.

Metalimport: Rruga 4 Shkurti 6, Tirana; tel. (42) 23848; telex 2116; imports ferrous and non-ferrous metals, electrodes, oil lubricants, minerals, etc.; Dir T. BORODNI.

Mineralimpeks: Rruga 4 Shkurti 6, Tirana; tel. (42) 23370; telex 2123; exports chromium ore, ferro-nickel ore, fuels and a wide range of industrial products; imports coal, coke, oils, etc.; Gen. Man. NIQIFOR ALIKAJ.

Minergoimpeks: Rruga Marcel Cachin, Tirana; tel. (42) 22148; telex 2238; f. 1990; exports products of the mining, metallurgical and petroleum industries; imports machinery and equipment, lubricating oils and raw materials; Gen. Man. QAZIM QAZAMI.

Teknoimport: Rruga 4 Shkurti 6, Tirana; tel. (42) 25222; telex 2127; fax (42) 23076; f. 1990; imports industrial and agricultural equipment; Gen. Dir BESNIK KAPO.

Transshqip: Rruga 4 Shkurti 6, Tirana; tel. (42) 27429; telex 2131; fax (42) 23076; f. 1960; transport of foreign trade goods by sea, road and rail; agents in Durrës, Vlorë and Sarandë; Gen. Man. GJOLEK Z. ZENELI.

REGIONAL FOREIGN TRADE ORGANIZATIONS

Dibërimpeks: Peshkopi; f. 1990; handles border trade with Yugoslavia (Kosovo and Macedonia); minerals and agricultural products.

Durrësimpeks: Rruga Skënderbeu 177, Durrës; tel. (52) 22199; telex 2181; f. 1988; handles border trade with southern Italy (Puglia); industrial and agricultural goods; Dir TAQO KOSTA.

Gjirokastërimpeks: Rruga Kombëtare 55, Gjirokastër; tel. 707; f. 1988; handles border trade with Greece; industrial and agricultural goods.

Korçaimpeks: Korçë; handles border trade with Greece.

Kukësimpeks: Kukës; handles trade with Yugoslavia (Kosovo and Macedonia); Dir ASIM BARUTI.

Pogradecimpeks: Pogradec; handles border trade with Yugoslavia (Macedonia).

Sarandaimpeks: Sarandë; handles trade with Corfu and other regions of Southern Greece.

Shkodërimpeks: Shkodër; handles border trade with Yugoslavia (Montenegro); industrial and agricultural goods.

Vloraimpeks: Vlorë; handles trade and economic co-operation with southern Italy; industrial and agricultural goods.

CO-OPERATIVE ORGANIZATIONS

Centrocoop: Sheshi Skënderbeu, Tirana; co-operative import and export organization.

Bashkimi Qëndror i Kooperativave të Artizanatit (Central Union of Handicraft Workers' Co-operatives): Tirana; Pres. KRISTO THEMELKO.

Bashkimi Qëndror i Kooperativave Tregtare (Central Union of Commercial Co-operatives): Tirana.

Bashkimi Qëndror i Kooperativave të Shit-Blerjes (Central Union of Buying and Selling Co-operatives): Tirana.

TRADE UNIONS

Until 1991 independent trade union activities were prohibited. The official trade unions were represented in every work and production centre. They were responsible for improving levels of production and ensuring implementation of the economic production plans of the PLA. They also provided some social and health facilities for their members. During 1991, and especially during the general strike in May, many independent unions were established. The most important organization was the Union of Independent Trade Unions. Other unions were established for workers in the food industry, the defence industry, mineral processing industries and other sectors of the economy.

Bashkimi i Sindikatave të Pavarura të Shqipërisë (Union of Independent Albanian Trade Unions): Tirana; f. 1991; Chair. of Managing Council LUFTI AHMETAJ; Chair. of Central Strike Cttee VALER XHEKA.

Federata Sindikale e Bujqesise (Agricultural Trade Union Federation): Tirana; f. 1991; Leaders ALFRED GJOMO, NAZMI QOKU.

Independent Trade Union of Radio and Television: Tirana; f. 1991; represents interests of media workers.

Konfederate e Sindikatare të Shqipërisë (Confederation of Albanian Trade Unions): Bulevardi Dëshmorët e Kombit, Tirana; f. 1991 to replace the official Central Council of Albanian Trade Unions (f. 1945); includes 14 trade union federations representing workers in different sectors of the economy; Chair. of Managing Council KASTRIOT MUCO; 743,894 mems (1989).

Sindikata e Lire dhe e Pavarur e Minatoreve (Free and Independent Miners' Union): Tirana; f. 1991; Chair. SHYQRI XIBRI.

Trade Union Federation of the Working People of Education and Science: Tirana; f. 1991; represents teachers and academics.

Transport

RAILWAYS

In 1988 there were 509 km of railway track, with lines linking Tirana–Vorë–Durrës, Durrës–Kavajë–Rrogozhinë–Elbasan-Librazhd–Prenjas–Pogradec, Rrogozhinë–Lushnjë–Fier–Ballsh, Milot–Rrëshen, Vorë–Laç–Lezhë–Shkodër and Selenicë–Vlorë. There are also standard-gauge lines between Fier and Selenicë and between Fier and Vlorë. In 1979 Albania and Yugoslavia agreed to construct a 50-km line between Shkodër and Titograd (Montenegro). The line opened to international freight traffic in September 1986.

Drejtoria e Hekurudhave: Tirana; railways administration; Dir QEMAL SINA.

ROADS

In 1988 the road network comprised 6,700 km of main roads and 10,000 km of other roads. All regions are linked by the road network, but many roads in mountainous districts are unsuitable for motor transport. Private cars were banned in Albania until 1991. Bicycles and mules are widely used. Proposals to construct a 200-km motorway between Durrës and the border with Greece, in co-operation with a group of Greek companies, were agreed in 1990.

SHIPPING

Albania's merchant fleet had an estimated total displacement of 56,000 grt in 1982. The chief ports are those in Durrës, Vlorë, Sarandë and Shëngjin. Durrës harbour has been dredged to allow for bigger ships. A ferry service between the Port of Durrës and Trieste (Italy) was inaugurated in November 1983. An agreement to establish a ferry service between Albania and the Greek island of Corfu was confirmed in 1988 and the establishment of a service between Bari (Italy) and Durrës was agreed in June 1991.

Drejtoria e Agjensisë së Vaporave: Port of Durrës; shipping administration.

CIVIL AVIATION

Albania has air links with Athens, Berlin, Bucharest, Budapest, Frankfurt, Paris, Rome, Vienna (summer only) and Zürich. An occasional charter service operates from London. There is a small but modern airport at Rinas, 28 km from Tirana. There is no regular internal air service. There is also no national airline, although a French–Albanian joint-venture company, Adalbanair, began regular flights between Tirana and Bari (Italy) in mid-1991. These were subsequently ruled illegal by the Ministry of Transport.

Albtransport: Rruga Kongresi i Përmetit 202, Tirana; tel. (42) 23026; telex 2154; air agency.

Tourism

In 1990 an estimated 30,000 tourists were permitted to enter Albania, an increase of more than 50% on 1989. The main tourist centres include Tirana, Durrës, Sarandë and Shkodër. The Roman amphitheatre at Durrës is one of the largest in Europe. The ancient towns of Apollonia and Butrint are important archaeological sites, and there are many other towns of historic interest.

Albturist: Bulevardi Dëshmorët e Kombit 6, Tirana; tel. (42) 23860; telex 2148; fax (42) 27956; brs in main towns and all tourist centres; 28 hotels throughout the country; Gen. Man. JETON HAJDARAJ.

Culture

NATIONAL ORGANIZATIONS

Albanian Committee for Cultural Relations with Foreign Countries (Komiteti Shqiptar për Marrëdhënie Kulturore me Botën e Jashtme): Tirana; tel. (42) 23338; telex 2164; fax (42) 23791; attached to the Ministry of Foreign Affairs; manages cultural relations with over 40 countries; Chair. JORGO MELICA.

Ministry of Culture, Art and Sport: see section on The Government (Ministries).

CULTURAL HERITAGE

Centre for Archaeological Research (Qendra e Kërkimeve Arkeologjike): Bulevardi Dëshmorët e Kombit, Tirana; tel. (42) 26541; telex 2214; f. 1948; responsible for research into Albania's archaeological sites and for the **National Museum of Archaeology**; Dir MUZAFER KORKUTI; Curator of Museum ILIR GJIPALI.

Fine Arts Gallery: Tirana; Dir KSENOFON DILO.

Institute of National Culture: Tirana; tel. (42) 27497; f. 1960; includes historical archive of recordings and collection of instruments; responsible for the **Albanian National Culture Museum**; Dir ALI XHIKU.

National Historical Museum: Tirana; f. 1991; history of Albania since Roman times; Dir KSENOFON DILO.

National Library: Tirana; tel. (42) 25887; f. 1922; 1m. vols; over 30,000 items on Albanology; Dir VALDETE SALA.

SPORTING ORGANIZATIONS

Olympic Committee of the Republic of Albania: Rruga Dervish Hima 31, Tirana; tel. (42) 27984; telex 2228; Pres. AGIM ZEKA; Sec.-Gen. LEONIDHA TOSKA.

Bashkimi i Kultures Fizike e Sporteve (Union of Physical Culture and Sports): Tirana; national body responsible for providing sports facilities.

PERFORMING ARTS

There are eight professional theatrical companies in Albania, 15 variety companies and 26 puppet-show groups.

Ensemble of Folk Songs and Dances: Tirana; tel. (42) 27701; f. 1957; Dir RIZO HAJRO.

National Opera and Ballet Theatre (Teatri i Operes e i Baletit): Palace of Culture, Sheshi Skënderbeu, Tirana.

National Theatre: Tirana; Dir ROBERT NDRENIKA.

Film Studio

New Albania Film Studio (Shqipëria e Re): Tirana; tel. (42) 32733; f. 1952; produces 40 documentaries and 12–15 feature films annually; Dir TEODOR LACO.

ASSOCIATION

Union of Writers and Artists of Albania (Lidhja e Shkrimtarëve dhe e Artistëve të Shqipërisë): Rruga Konferenca e Pezës 4, Tirana; tel. (42) 29689; f. 1945; 26 branches throughout the country; 1,750 mems; Chair. DRITËRO AGOLLI.

Education

Education is free and compulsory at primary and secondary level; students in higher education pay a fee related to the family income. Children between the ages of three and six years may attend nursery school (kopshte). Children in the age group of seven to 15 years must attend an 'eight-year school'. There are three main categories of secondary school, namely '12 year schools' (shkollat 12-vjeçare) providing 4-year general courses, secondary technical-professional schools (shkollat e mesme teknik-profesionale), which combine vocational training with a general education, and lower vocational schools (shkollat e ulte profesionale), which train workers in the fields of agriculture and industry.

There are eight institutes of higher education and an Academy of Sciences, which provides facilities for research. Reforms are anticipated in education, including the cessation of compulsory military training in schools and colleges and the teaching of ideologically-orientated subjects. In May 1991 two new universities were established: the Luigj Gurakuji University of Shkodër (formerly the Luigj Gurakuji College of Education); and the Tirana Agricultural University (formerly the Kamze Higher Agricultural College).

UNIVERSITIES

University of Tirana (Universiteti i Tiranës): Bulevardi Deshmorët e Kombit, Tirana; tel. (42) 28258; telex 2211; f. 1957; in 1991 the name was changed from the Enver Hoxha University of Tirana; 8 faculties, 1,051 teachers, 12,000 students; brs in Berat, Elbasan, Korçë, Shkodër. In July 1991 it was announced that Tirana University was to be divided into two higher education institutes, Tirana University and the Polytechnic University; Rector Prof. Dr NIKOLLA KONOMI.

Luigj Gurakuji University of Shkodër: Shkodër; f. 1991 to replace the Luigj Gurakuji College of Education (f. 1957); Dir DHORA LLOJA.

Tirana Agricultural University: Kamzë, Tirana; f. 1991 to replace the Higher Institute of Agriculture; Rector HAXHI ALIKO.

Social Welfare

All medical services are funded by the State. Between 1985 and 1990 expenditure on the health service was to be increased by 17.3%. In 1987 the number of hospitals totalled 158 and there were 12,212 beds available. In the same year there were 5,341 doctors and dentists, the equivalent of one for every 577 persons. Women are entitled to 180 days of maternity leave, receiving 80% of their salary. There is a non-contributory state social insurance system for all workers, with 70%–100% of salary being paid during sick leave. In mid-1991 plans were announced to establish a system of social security payments for the unemployed; previously the existence of unemployment was not officially acknowledged. A pension system provides for the old and disabled. Men retire between the ages of 50 and 60, and women between 45 and 55.

NATIONAL AGENCIES

Ministry of Health: see section on The Government (Ministries).

Committee of Labour, Immigration and Social Support: Tirana; f. 1991; govt. body which provides assistance to unemployed workers.

National Directorate for Health Education: M. Duri 2, Tirana; tel. (42) 27106; est. by the Ministry of Health; fulfils educational role in preventative health.

HEALTH AND WELFARE ORGANIZATIONS

Albanian Association for the Blind: Tirana; f. 1991.

Albanian Red Cross (Kryki i Kuq i Shqipërisë): Tirana; Chair of Presidency CIRIL PISTOLI

Albanians for Albania: Tirana; f. 1991; humanitarian asscn; Chair. MARJETA LJARJA.

Association of Former Political Prisoners and Detainees: Tirana; f. 1991; social and humanitarian organization to give aid to ex-political prisoners; Pres. OSMAN KAZAZI.

Forum for the Protection of Human Rights (Forumi per Mbrojtjen e të Drejtave të Njeriut dhe Lirive Themelore): Tirana;

f. 1990; provides humanitarian assistance to former political prisoners; Chair. Prof. ARBEN PUTO.

The Environment

The Ecology Party, founded in late 1990, was the first unofficial response to environmental problems in Albania. Albania does not have the same concentration of heavy industries as some parts of Eastern Europe, but, nevertheless, there is serious pollution from coal-fired power stations and obsolete factories. In July 1991 the Government of Albania signed a declaration on the ecological protection of the Adriatic Sea, implementing the Adriatic Initiative agreed with Italy, Yugoslavia and Greece in Umag, in 1989. At the same time Albania and Italy agreed to co-operate in environmental and tourist affairs.

GOVERNMENT ORGANIZATIONS

Committee of Public Economy and Protection of the Environment: Tirana; govt. body; Chair. FLAMUR HOXHA.

State Sanitary Inspectorate, Ministry of Health: responsible for environmental health, pollution monitoring, research.

Permanent Commission of the People's Assembly on Health, Protection of the Environment, and Public Services: Kuvendi Popullor, Tirana.

The Ministry of Agriculture is also involved in matters affecting the environment.

ACADEMIC INSTITUTES

Academy of Sciences (Akademia Shkencave): Rruga Myslim Shyri 7, Tirana; tel. (42) 26049; telex 2214; f. 1972; Pres. ALEKS BUDA.

Institute of Hydrometeorology (Instituti Hidrometeorologjik): Rruga Kongresi i Përmitet, Tirana; tel. (42) 22169; f. 1962; responsible for monitoring pollution; Dir JAVER ÇOBANI.

Agricultural Research Institute (Instituti i Kërkimeve Bujqësore): Lushnjë; f. 1947; studies incl. agric. pollution control; Dir XHEVAT SHIMA.

Faculty of Natural Sciences, University of Tirana (Fakulteti Shkencave të Natyrës, Universiteti i Tiranës): Bulevardi Deshmorët e Kombit, Tirana; tel. (42) 26372; telex 2211; f. 1957; Dean of Faculty of Natural Sciences Prof. Dr REXHEP MEJDANI.

Tirana Agricultural University: Kamzë, Tirana; f. 1991 to replace Higher Institute of Agriculture (f. 1951); research incl. water- and land-use problems and forestry; Rector HAXHI ALIKO

NON-GOVERNMENTAL ORGANIZATION

Ecology Party (Partija Ekologjike): see section on Political Organizations.

Defence

In June 1990, according to Western estimates, the total strength of the armed forces was 48,000 (including 22,400 conscripts), comprising 35,000 in the Army, 11,000 in the Air Force and 2,000 in the Navy. The frontier force numbered some 7,000. The interior security force, the Sigurimi, numbered some 5,000, but this was replaced by a National Intelligence Service in mid-1991. Military service is compulsory for all males and lasts for two years in the Army, and three years in the Air Force, Navy and paramilitary forces. Ranks were abolished in the armed forces in the 1960s, but were reintroduced in 1991. Defence expenditure in 1990 was estimated at 1,030m. lekë.

Commander-in-Chief: President of the Republic.

Chief of the General Staff: Gen. KOSTAQ KAROLI.

Bibliography

Altman, F.-L. (Ed.). *Albanien im Umbruch*. Munich, Sudost-Institut, Oldenbourg, 1990.

Artisien, P. 'Albania at the Crossroads', in *The Journal of Communist Studies*, Vol. 3, Sept 1987.

Biberaj, E. *Albania and China: A Study of an Unequal Alliance*. Boulder, Colorado, Westview Press, 1986.

Griffith, W. E. *Albania and the Sino–Soviet Rift*. Cambridge, MA, MIT Press, 1963.

Hibbert, R. *Albania's National Liberation Struggle*. London, Pinter, 1991.

Kaser, M. 'Albania under and after Enver Hoxha' in *East European Economies*, Vol. 3. Washington, DC, USGPO (Joint Economic Committee of the US Congress), 1986.

Logoreci, A. *The Albanians: Europe's Forgotten Survivors*. Boulder, Colorado, Westview Press, 1977.

Marmallaku, R. *Albania and the Albanians*. London, C. Hurst, 1975.

Pano, N. C. *The People's Republic of Albania*. Baltimore, Maryland, Johns Hopkins Press, 1968.

Pipa, A. *Albanian Stalinism*. Colombia, East European Monographs, Columbia University Press, 1990.

Prifti, P. *Socialist Albania since 1944*. Cambridge, MA, MIT Press, 1978.

Skendi, S. *The Albanian National Awakening, 1878–1912*. Princeton, Princeton University Press, 1967.

BULGARIA

Geography

PHYSICAL FEATURES

The Republic of Bulgaria lies in south-eastern Europe, on the east of the Balkan Peninsula. The country is bordered by Romania to the north, by two of the republics of Yugoslavia to the west (Serbia in the north and Macedonia in the south), by Greece to the south and Turkey to the south-east. The country has an eastern coastline along the Black Sea. Its total area is 110,994 sq km (42,855 sq miles).

Central Bulgaria is traversed from west to east by the Balkan Mountains (Stara Planina), which separate the Danubian plains in the north from the Thracian plains of Eastern Rumelia in the south-east. The Rhodope Mountains (Rhodopi Planina) occupy south-west Bulgaria and separate it from Greece and Macedonia. The mountain of Musala (Riladaǧ, in Turkish, and also once known as Stalin Peak) is located in this range, to the south of Sofia, and is Bulgaria's highest point, rising to 2,925 m (9,596 ft). The Sofia depression, in the west of the country, is hill country which separates the Balkan Mountains from the southern mountains and is the main centre of population and communications. The general elevation slopes down from the west towards the Black Sea, and some two-thirds of Bulgaria is less than 500 m above sea level. The River Danube (Dunav) forms most of the length of Bulgaria's northern border, except between the town of Silistra (where the Danube turns north) and the Black Sea (that is, as far east as the Dobrudzha). The fertile Bulgarian plateau, between the Danubian border and the Balkan Mountains, averages some 100 km in width and is traversed by several tributaries of the Danube, the major one being the Iskur. The main rivers running south of the Balkan watershed are the Struma and the Maritza, which flow into the Aegean Sea (part of the Mediterranean Sea). The broad Maritza Valley, which leads on to the Thracian plains, is one of the principal agricultural areas of the country.

CLIMATE

The climate is continental, with hot summers and cold winters. In the south the climate is moderated by the influence of the Mediterranean Sea, which makes winters warmer and wetter. Winters on the Black Sea coast are also slightly milder, although north-easterly winds can bring very cold weather. The mean temperatures in Sofia range between 21°C (69°F) in July and −2°C (28°F) in January. Varna, on the Black Sea, has comparative mean temperatures ranging between 23°C (74°F) and 1°C (34°F). The mean annual rainfall in Sofia is 635 mm (25 in) and 485 mm (19 in) at Varna.

POPULATION

The Bulgars were a Finno-Ugrian people, whose ancestors crossed the Danube in the 7th century AD and merged with the Slavonic population. In 1981, according to official

figures, 85.3% of the total population were ethnic Bulgarians, 8.5% ethnic Turks, 2.6% Roma (Gypsy), 2.5% Macedonian and there were small communities of Karakachani (Vlahs—who speak a language related to Romanian), Albanians, Sarakatsani (a Greek people), Armenians, Russians and other nationalities. Actual numbers of the minority populations are reported to be larger than official figures indicate. At the end of 1990, for instance, a revised figure of 576,926 Roma was reported by local authorities, but this is still claimed to be low. Despite some recognition after the Second World War, the Bulgarian authorities claim that the Macedonians are an ethnic Bulgarian people, not a distinct nationality. Bulgarian, the official language, is one of the Southern Slavonic tongues, closely related to Serbo-Croat and also to Russian, and is written in the Cyrillic alphabet. Minority languages include Turkish, Macedonian (a Slavonic dialect) and Romany. Most of the population are Christian and adhere to the Bulgarian Orthodox Church (some 80%), although there are small communities of Roman Catholics (including Uniates), Armenian Orthodox and Protestants. Of the 13% of the population who are estimated to profess Islam, most are ethnic Turks, but some are ethnic Bulgarians, known as Pomaks, who account for some 3% of the population. Most of the Roma are Muslim. There is also a small Jewish community.

The total population of the country was estimated to be 8,992,316 at the end of 1989, with a population density of 81.0 per sq km (209.8 per sq mile). Sofia, the capital, which is located in the central western part of Bulgaria, is the largest city, with an estimated population of 1,141,537 (1989). Other important cities include Plovdiv (374,004 in 1989), in central Bulgaria, and Varna (311,123) and Burgas (203,093) on the Black Sea coast.

Chronology

865: The Khan of the Bulgars, Boris (852–89), converted to Eastern Orthodox Christianity following the missionary activity of the Eastern Roman (Byzantine) brothers, SS Constantine (Cyril) and Methodius ('the Apostles of the Slavs').

893–927: Reign of Simeon, first Tsar (Caesar) of the Bulgars, who failed in his ambition to take Constantinople (now Istanbul) and the Byzantine throne, but established a powerful empire and the Bulgarian Church as the first new autocephalous Orthodox church.

971: Annexation of eastern Bulgaria as a Byzantine province.

1014: The Bulgar ruler, Samuel, was defeated at the battle of Balathista by the Emperor Basil II ('the Slayer of the Bulgars'), who subsequently made western Bulgaria into a Byzantine province.

1187: A decline in Byzantine power meant that the Emperor in Constantinople recognized the establishment of the second Bulgarian Empire, under the Asen dynasty.

1330: The Bulgars were defeated by Serbian forces at the battle of Küstendil (Velbuzhde).

1396: Bulgaria became a province of the Turkish Ottoman Empire.

1870: Establishment of an autocephalous Exarchate of the Bulgarian Orthodox Church (not recognized by Constantinople until 1945).

1876: Bloody suppression of Bulgarian uprisings by the Ottomans.

1877: Russia declared war on the Turks in support of the Orthodox, Slav subjects of the Ottoman Empire.

1878: The Ottomans recognized an autonomous principality of Bulgaria, at the Congress of Berlin; Eastern Rumelia and Macedonia remained under Turkish rule.

1879: The First Grand National Assembly of Bulgaria, meeting in the town of Turnovo (now Veliko—'Grand'—Turnovo), adopted a liberal constitution (the 'Turnovo Constitution') and invited the nephew of the Russian tsarina, Alexander (Aleksandur) von Battenburg, of the House of Hesse-Darmstadt, to become the ruling prince.

1885: Eastern Rumelia was annexed by Bulgaria. Serbian forces were defeated at the battle of Slivnitsa.

1887: Election of Ferdinand of Saxe-Coburg as Prince of Bulgaria, following the abdication of Alexander.

October 1908: Upheavals in the Ottoman Empire included the proclamation of Tsar (King) Ferdinand I of an independent Bulgarian kingdom.

August 1913: The Peace of Bucharest concluded the Second Balkan War: Bulgaria lost Macedonia and Dobrudzha.

12 October 1915: Bulgaria declared war on Serbia, so entering the First World War on the side of the Central Powers of Germany, Austria-Hungary and the Ottoman Empire.

29 September 1918: Bulgaria surrendered unconditionally to the Entente Powers (consequent abdication of Ferdinand I and accession of Boris III).

29 November 1919: The Treaty of Neuilly was signed: Bulgaria was forced to cede its Thracian territories and Mediterranean coast to Greece; to cede territory on its western frontier to Yugoslavia; and to return the Dobrudzha (which it had regained by the Peace of Bucharest of May 1918) to Romania.

1923: A *putsch* by army officers led to the suppression of the Peasants Party and the Communist Party.

19 May 1934: A coup by two nationalist organizations, Zveno and the Association of the Officers of the Reserve, led to the establishment of the authoritarian regime of Col Georgieff.

January 1935: Resignation of Col Georgieff; authoritarian rule continued by Boris III.

30 August 1940: Second Arbitration Award of Vienna restored Southern Dobrudzha to Bulgaria (confirmed in 1947).

1 March 1941: Bulgaria signed a pact with the Axis Powers of Germany and Italy and, following the outbreak of war in the Balkans, gained western Macedonia from Yugoslavia.

August 1943: Death of Boris III; a regency established for the young Tsar Simeon II.

5 September 1944: The USSR declared war on Bulgaria.

8 September 1944: Bulgaria declared war on Germany.

9 September 1944: Following a coup by the Fatherland Front, a left-wing alliance dominated by the Bulgarian Communist Party (BCP), the Soviet army occupied Bulgaria.

28 October 1944: An armistice was signed with the Allies.

August 1945: The Agrarian and Social Democratic Parties left the Front and the Government.

15 September 1946: The formal deposition of Tsar Simeon II and the declaration of a Republic, following a referendum.

November 1946: Georgi Dimitrov, First Secretary of the BCP, became Chairman of the Council of Ministers.

22 February 1947: A peace treaty was signed with the Allies.

December 1947: A new Constitution abolished all opposition parties and established a system based on the Soviet model. Bulgaria became a People's Republic.

March 1949: Dimitrov was replaced as Chairman of the Council of Ministers by Vasil Kolarov.

July 1949: Vulko Chervenkov became leader of the BCP following Dimitrov's death.

February 1950: Chervenkov became Chairman of the Council of Ministers.

March 1954: Todor Zhivkov became leader of the BCP.

April 1956: Anton Yugov replaced Chervenkov as Chairman of the Council of Ministers.

November 1962: Zhivkov replaced Yugov as Chairman of the Council of Ministers.

1965: An army coup attempt was discovered and suppressed, enabling Zhivkov to consolidate his position.

16 May 1971: A new Constitution was adopted, following a referendum; the Constitution established the Council of State as the supreme executive and legislative body. Zhivkov relinquished his former government posts to become President of the Council of State (*de facto* head of state).

June 1981: Following elections to the National Assembly, Grisha Filipov became Chairman of the Council of Ministers in succession to Stanko Todorov, who had held the post since 1971.

March 1985: Filipov was replaced as Chairman of the Council of Ministers by Georgi Atanasov.

December 1985: A national census was the occasion for accusations of a government policy ('regenerative programme') of forced assimilation of the ethnic Turkish population ('Bulgarian Muslims').

July 1987: Zhivkov promised liberalization and pluralism in his so-called 'July Concept'.

February 1988: A protocol was signed with Turkey to further economic and social relations. The dissident Independent Association for Human Rights was founded and environmental protests in northern areas led to the foundation of Ecoglasnost.

March 1988: Candidates other than those nominated by the BCP were permitted to stand in the local elections.

July 1988: Several prominent proponents of reform were dismissed from office at a plenum of the BCP, including one member of the Politburo.

November 1988: Eighty leading intellectuals founded the Club for the Support of Glasnost and Perestroika.

1989

May

31: Following reports of the violent suppression of protests against the programme for the assimilation of the Bulgarian

Turks, Turkey announced that it would be prepared to receive the entire ethnic Turkish population of Bulgaria.

July

4: The Bulgarian Government issued a decree for civilian mobilization, in order to compensate for the labour shortage caused by Turkish emigration.

August

22: The Turkish Government closed the border with Bulgaria, some 310,000 refugees having arrived.

October

16: An international conference, which was the occasion for several opposition groups to demonstrate against the Government, opened in Sofia.

November

3: Some 4,000 people marched to the National Assembly building with a petition on environmental issues.

10: Zhivkov was forced to resign his post as General Secretary of the BCP and was replaced by the Minister of Foreign Affairs, Petur Mladenov.

16: At a further meeting of the Central Committee, supporters of Zhivkov were removed from BCP posts and many reformists reinstated.

17: The National Assembly elected Mladenov to succeed Zhivkov as President of the Council of State; it also repealed that part of the penal code prohibiting 'anti-state propaganda', granting an amnesty to all those convicted under it.

26: The Government announced the dissolution of the secret police.

December

2: Angel Dimitrov replaced Petur Tanchev as leader of the Bulgarian Agrarian People's Union (BAPU), the BCP's partner in the ruling Fatherland Front and the only other legal political party.

7: Opposition groups, including Ecoglasnost (which achieved legal registration on 11 December), formally established the United Democratic Front (UDF).

8–13: The Central Committee instituted further changes in the BCP hierarchy; it denounced Zhivkov and expelled him from the Party; Mladenov proposed constitutional reform, including the repeal of Article One (which established the BCP's 'leading role' in society) and the holding of free elections.

14–15: The National Assembly introduced legislation to amend Article One and to legalize unofficial demonstrations and other political parties; it declared an immediate amnesty for all political prisoners; it revoked laws used against dissidents and several decrees issued by the former leadership, including the civilian mobilization; and it established a commission to investigate official corruption.

16: The UDF held its first constituent congress in Stara Zagora.

27: A strike by Podkrepa (Support), the independent trade union movement, ensured that the Government agreed to opposition demands, including the dismissal of the Interior Minister and to begin negotiations about convening 'round-table' meetings between the BCP, BAPU and the UDF.

29: The Government approved measures to end discrimination against the Muslim minority in Bulgaria; a vigil by ethnic Turks and Pomaks (ethnic Bulgarian Muslims) then dispersed from outside the National Assembly.

1990

January

8: A 'social council' was formed by the major political and social groups, in reaction to a week of widespread nationalist protests against the restoration of Turkish rights.

12: A declaration by the 'social council' guaranteed the rights of the Turks, but outlawed any attempts to form an independent Turkish state.

15: The National Assembly revoked the leading role of the BCP.

16: Some 60,000 people attended a UDF rally in Sofia, demanding free elections.

18: A warrant was issued for the arrest of Todor Zhivkov on charges of incitement to ethnic hostility and hatred, embezzlement and gross malfeasance.

22: Round-table talks between the major political groups recommenced.

30: The 14th Extraordinary BCP Congress opened.

31: The UDF refused a BCP request to form a coalition government.

February

1: Atanasov and his Government resigned during the BCP Congress, following the failure to form a national coalition.

2: Aleksandur Lilov replaced Petur Mladenov as head of the Supreme Council of the BCP.

3: Andrei Lukanov was elected Chairman of the Council of Ministers by the National Assembly.

8: Lukanov nominated a Government only comprising members of the BCP.

11: Reformers from within the BCP formed the Alternative Socialist Party.

18: The official trade union congress, the Bulgarian Professional Union, completed its renunciation of any party or state affiliations and changed its name to the Confederation of Independent Trade Unions in Bulgaria (CITUB).

25: Some 200,000 people attended an anti-Communist rally in Sofia.

March

5: The National Assembly voted to allow Turks and other Muslims the right to use their own names.

6: The National Assembly legalized the right to strike.

9: Some 50,000 people demonstrated in Sofia against the BCP and in favour of a free press.

12: Agreement was reached for a multi-party system at round-table talks.

18: The Podkrepa Trade Union Confederation was legally recognized and began its first congress.

April

3: Petur Mladenov was elected President of the country by the National Assembly. The BCP changed its name to the Bulgarian Socialist Party (BSP).

5: The dates of the elections were set for 10 and 17 June.

18: The opposition held a massive rally in Sofia.

May

1: There were BSP and opposition rallies in Sofia and throughout the country.

22: The UDF and other opposition parties refused to sign an agreement outlining the provisions to prevent intimidation during the election campaign. Complaints of electoral malpractice were made against the BSP.

June

7: The last pre-election rallies drew crowds of more than 1m. people in Sofia.

10: The first round of voting for seats in the new constituent Grand National Assembly (GNA) took place. The BSP obtained a majority.

11: The UDF refused to form a coalition with the BSP and protested about electoral irregularities.

13: The UDF disassociated itself from threats of civil disobedience, following the elections, as protests over the results continued throughout the country.

17: The second round of voting took place. Widespread allegations of violations and intimidation by the Government and the opposition. The BSP received 211 seats out of 400, the UDF 144. The Muslim Movement for Rights and Freedoms (MRF) won 23. A video tape was released, showing Petur Mladenov outside the National Assembly building, on 14 December 1989, advocating the use of tanks against the demonstrators there.

22: Zheliu Zhelev informed Aleksandur Lilov that the UDF still refused to form a coalition with the BSP.

29: Andrei Lukanov was again approved as Chairman of the Council of Ministers by the GNA.

July

4: A specially-formed commission announced that the video tape showing Mladenov was genuine. Student demonstrators in Sofia demanded Mladenov's resignation.

6: President Mladenov resigned.

7: Students in Sofia ended their 21-day strike.

10: The GNA convened in Veliko Turnovo, seat of the first GNA 111 years previously.

15: The premier, Lukanov, refused to head a one-party government.

18: The GNA announced that Todor Zhivkov would be obliged to appear before it to explain some of the policies of his regime. There was a general strike in Kurdzhali, in opposition to the Turkish-dominated MRF.

19: Nikolai Todorov (BSP) was elected President of the GNA.

21: The Alternative Socialist Party (ASP), a reformist group in the BSP, left the BSP and removed the majority that the BSP had held in the GNA.

23: The Government adopted a decree on public order to control unrest in the provinces.

24: No candidate gained the two-thirds majority required in the GNA to be elected President of the country.

27: The Minister of Internal Affairs, Gen. Atanas Semerdzhiev, resigned.

30: The BSP removed their candidate, Chavdar Kiuranov, from the presidential contest, in order to break the impasse in electing a President. Todor Zhivkov announced that he would not appear before the GNA.

31: After several attempts to elect a President, Zheliu Zhelev, leader of the UDF, decided to stand.

August

1: The BSP announced their support for Zhelev's bid for the presidency. Zhelev was subsequently elected President. Semerdzhiev was elected Vice-President.

3: Dr Petur Beron was elected the new Chairman of the Co-ordinating Council of the UDF.

7: Lukanov's Government submitted its resignation to the GNA, but remained in office in a caretaker role.

22: The Government's resignation was accepted by the GNA, but it was maintained in its caretaker role.

26: The headquarters of the BSP in Sofia was attacked and set ablaze following a demonstration by supporters of the opposition.

30: President Zhelev proposed Andrei Lukanov as Chairman of the Council of Ministers and this proposal was accepted by the GNA.

September

3: The UDF refused to form a coalition government.

5: Pencho Stoyanov Penev was appointed Minister of Internal Affairs.

13: The UDF confirmed that there would be no coalition with the BSP.

18: Food exports were banned to improve domestic supplies.

19: The new all-BSP Government was approved by the GNA.

20: The Council of Ministers was approved in the GNA.

23: Lukanov advocated a purge of the BSP during their Congress.

25: Aleksandur Lilov was re-elected as Chairman of the Supreme Council of the BSP during the BSP Congress.

27: The Government offered to send troops to support the UN-backed forces in the Persian (Arabian) Gulf (during the crisis caused by Iraq's attempted annexation of Kuwait).

October

1: The UDF won a by-election in Velingrad, the first since the general elections (the UDF, therefore, held 145 seats, to the BSP's 210).

6: The Alternative Socialist Party voted to join the UDF.

10: Bulgaria joined the IMF. The Government's reform programme was presented to the GNA.

17: The leader of the Green Party, Aleksandur Karakachanov, was elected mayor of Sofia.

24: The Depoliticization Act (referring to the army, police, security services, judiciary, Ministry of Foreign Affairs and the Presidency) was adopted by the GNA.

November

3: At a UDF rally in Sofia there were demands for a UDF-led government.

9: The BSP lost its majority in the GNA after one of its factions declared itself to be independent.

14: Lukanov threatened to resign as premier unless his economic reform programme was accepted by the GNA. The GNA rejected the programme.

17: The Citizens' Names Act, which had suppressed Turkish customs and language, was revoked.

18: At a UDF rally in Sofia, the resignation of the Government was demanded.

21: It was announced that Todor Zhivkov would go on trial on charges of embezzlement and abuse of power.

22: Armed troops defended members of the GNA from 20,000 demonstrators protesting outside the GNA building. The GNA voted for the country to be renamed the Republic of Bulgaria.

23: The BSP defeated a vote of no-confidence in the Government. The Budget was approved, but only 189 members of the GNA voted for it.

26: The independent union, Podkrepa, called a general strike in an effort to bring down the Government. The strike was supported by CITUB.

28: The strike spread to all sectors of the economy.

29: The Government of Andrei Lukanov resigned, after agreement had been reached on the formation of a multi-party government under a non-party premier.

December

2: Petur Beron resigned as President of the UDF, following allegations that he had been a police informer. The BSP was accused of misusing their access to police files.

7: Dimitur Popov, formerly the Secretary to the Electoral Commission, was appointed to head a caretaker government.

11: Todor Zhivkov was charged with embezzlement and abuse of power.

14: The major political groups signed the 'Agreement Guaranteeing the Peaceful Transition to a Democratic Society', which committed support to the Popov Government, the drafting of a new constitution, the introduction of a market economy and general elections to be held in 1991 (then scheduled for March).

19: The GNA approved Bulgaria's first coalition Government not to be controlled by the Communists since the 1940s.

1991

January

6: The Government, the trade unions and the employers signed a 'Social Agreement', providing for the preservation of 'social peace' during the expected hardships of the transition to a market economy.

31: The GNA approved a comprehensive programme of economic reforms.

February

1: Bulgaria, in response to alleged Soviet repression in Lithuania, reinforced earlier protests by demanding the dissolution of the Warsaw Pact military alliance. The Government raised interest rates and removed the price subsidies on many basic goods and utilities.

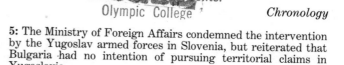

12: The IMF endorsed the economic reforms.

14: The use of the Turkish language in schools was sanctioned, although this occasioned demonstrations by Bulgarian nationalists.

March

1: The GNA adopted the Law on the Ownership and Use of Agricultural Land, which enacted the principle of the restoration of private ownership of land, with priority to be given to the former owners or their heirs.

17: There were violent demonstrations in Sofia, about the lack of progress on constitutional issues in the GNA, the state of the economy and against immigrant workers.

April

15: Demonstrators in Sofia demanded early elections.

19: The Paris Club of nations announced that it had agreed to the rescheduling of Bulgaria's foreign debt.

22: A newspaper published the names of parliamentary deputies alleged to be police informers, causing the Minister of Internal Affairs to threaten legal action over the leaks; the BSP was implicated in the release of the names.

25: The successors of the nomenklatura organizations, including the BSP, were required to repay some 3,500m. leva in state funds.

May

7: Further economic reforms were enacted by the GNA, including laws on trade and foreign investment.

14: A group of 39 UDF deputies walked out of the GNA session, protesting at its delays and demanding elections by July; this action marked the beginning of a split in the UDF.

19: The UDF's third conference endorsed the action of the radicals who withdrew from the GNA on 14 May.

22: President Zhelev secured cross-party agreement to conduct local and parliamentary elections in September, rejecting the practicality of elections in July, although the UDF radicals persisted in their demands.

24–25: There were protests at the proposed treaty with the USSR, which contained security clauses which, it was alleged, limited Bulgaria's sovereignty and ability to enter alliances of its choice.

28: The GNA decided to hold a referendum on whether Bulgaria should become a monarchy again.

29: The GNA approved the first reading of a draft Constitution.

June

2: The Minister of Defence, Col-Gen. Yordan Mutafchiev, denied that a secret agreement had been negotiated with the USSR.

5: The GNA reversed its decision to hold a referendum on the monarchy; protests had been widespread, including some by the monarchists; the former tsar, Simeon II, welcomed the decision.

7: Twenty-one MRF deputies joined the by-now 50 UDF deputies who were boycotting the GNA, in protest at constitutional proposals; this threatened the GNA's ability to adopt any fundamental law.

22: A national UDF conference resolved the divisions in the alliance, by agreeing to many of the demands of the radical 'Group of 39', such as the resolve to contest the elections as a united movement, with a single list of candidates.

26: Bulgaria denied any official recognition of the independence declarations by the Yugoslav Republics of Slovenia and Croatia, but advocated a peaceful resolution of the crisis.

28: An inspection team from the International Atomic Energy Agency (IAEA) declared the nuclear-power plant at Kozlodui to be unsafe and recommended its closure; the Bulgarian Government refused, because of the country's dependence on the station.

July

1: Bulgaria and the other Warsaw Pact countries signed the protocol dissolving the alliance. Tension increased on the Bulgarian–Yugoslav border.

5: The Ministry of Foreign Affairs condemned the intervention by the Yugoslav armed forces in Slovenia, but reiterated that Bulgaria had no intention of pursuing territorial claims in Yugoslavia.

9: The GNA passed the third reading of the proposed Constitution, despite opposition protests, and agreed that it would then continue to function as a normal parliament and no longer as a constituent assembly.

12: The GNA finally ratified the Constitution, which was signed by 309 of the 400 deputies (some 80 UDF and MRF members were continuing their protests, some on hunger strike, at a Constitution enacted by an assembly dominated by the former Communists).

13: The Constitution was formally promulgated and came into effect.

15: The IAEA expressed continued concerns about the Kozlodui power station; the Government agreed to the closure of two of the reactors by mid-September; the EC subsequently agreed to help finance this.

16: The President announced that the general and local elections would take place on 29 September.

18: Parliament rejected a referendum on the Constitution; the MRF deputies resumed their participation in the legislature.

23: The hunger strike already over, the 'Group of 39' (which had numbered almost 50 deputies during the boycott) returned to parliament.

25: A system of proportional representation was agreed for the general elections.

27: Three Agrarian (BAPU) parties united to form BAPU–United. The Clubs for Democracy (formerly the Club for the Support of Glasnost and Perestroika) split into two groups.

29: Romania and Bulgaria discussed solving mutual environmental problems, particularly those in the Ruse–Giurgiu area, which the EC had expressed willingness to help finance. It was reported that two distinct ideological factions had emerged within the UDF: the radical, right-wing 'Dark Blue' faction (UDF–Movement); and the 'central block', moderate 'Light Blues' (UDF–Liberals).

31: Legislation preventing the automatic extension of the Bulgarian–Soviet Friendship Treaty on 5 August was enacted, whether or not a new treaty had been agreed by then.

August

1: Further price rises took effect.

7: The six parties of the UDF–Liberal faction rejected the formation of a UDF Political Consultative Council and distanced themselves from the National Co-ordinating Council.

9: A televised debate between the UDF leader, Filip Dimitrov, and the BSP leader, Aleksandur Lilov, inaugurated the election campaign.

12: The National Assembly election date was postponed, to 13 October, the constitutional deadline, following delays in the electoral law. (The date for the presidential election was later set for 13 January 1992.)

15: The BSP formed an election coalition with five minor parties, most of them of a nationalist orientation: the Bulgarian Liberal Party; the Fatherland Party of Labour; the Christian Women's Movement; the Christian Republican Party; and the Democratic Party in Bulgaria.

17–18: The BSDP–United, the largest party in the UDF, split into two groups, because of its membership of the UDF–Liberals.

19: President Zhelev, the UDF and the BSP all condemned the coup against the Soviet President Gorbachev.

21: Most groups in Bulgaria welcomed the failure of the Soviet coup.

22: There were allegations that the Soviet coup leaders had requested that Bulgaria send a delegation to Moscow, but not all ministers had known of these contacts; the BSP was criticized for its caution in condemning the coup attempt. Agreement to end a miners' strike (begun 14 August) was reached. The new electoral law was passed, rejecting President Zhelev's veto.

24: A Green Party faction elected a rival leadership, rejecting membership of the UDF—Liberal faction.
26: Bulgaria recognized the Baltic states of Lithuania, Latvia and Estonia.
28: The political wing of the MRF, Rights and Freedoms, was refused registration as a party by the Sofia Municipal Court, on the grounds that it was unconstitutionally based on religious and ethnic interests. (Registration was later allowed.)
29: Andrei Lukanov resigned from the BSP, in protest at its minimal response to the Soviet coup attempt. Controversy about BSP and government reactions to, and contacts with, the Soviet coup leaders continued.

History

Prof. RICHARD J. CRAMPTON

BULGARIA BEFORE 10 NOVEMBER 1989

The Bulgarians established an empire in the Balkans during the ninth and tenth centuries AD, mainly at the expense of the Eastern Roman (Byzantine) Empire, from which they received Eastern Orthodox Christianity and a powerful cultural influence. The Bulgarian state eventually succumbed to Byzantine power and, despite a revival in the 13th century, subsequently to the Turkish Ottoman Empire. Modern Bulgaria emerged from the disintegrating Ottoman realm during the 19th century. With Russian assistance, an autonomous Bulgarian principality was established, and, in 1878, recognized by the Congress of Berlin. The following year an assembly adopted the constitution of a limited monarchy. In 1908, with turbulence throughout the Ottoman Empire, the Bulgarian prince was proclaimed tsar (king) of an independent kingdom. Balkan politics inclined Bulgaria to support Germany in both the First and the Second World Wars. Between the Wars the country was headed by an authoritarian regime, which was installed by nationalist forces but continued by Tsar Boris III. He died in 1943 and a regency was established for the young Tsar Simeon II. Despite an attempt to realign itself, Bulgaria was occupied by Soviet troops in September 1944. This resulted in the abolition of the monarchy and the rise of Communist power.

The Bulgarian Communist Party (BCP) was a member of the coalition which came to power on 9 September 1944. By the end of 1947 the BCP had neutralized all other political groups; thenceforth it was the leading force in Bulgarian society and politics. The Communists ostensibly ruled in coalition with the Bulgarian Agrarian People's Union (BAPU), a long-established Bulgarian party, which had been emasculated when its leader, Nikola Petkov, had been executed after a grotesque BCP-engineered trial in 1947.

Communist rule in Bulgaria, in the late 1940s and early 1950s, followed a pattern similar to that elsewhere in Eastern Europe. In 1954 Todor Zhivkov became First Secretary, or leader, of the BCP and, after the failure of an attempted military coup, in 1965, his power was unchallenged. Zhivkov forced Bulgaria through the familiar Communist experiences of collectivization, urbanization and industrialization. His rule was singular in the degree to which it followed the policies of the Soviet Government in Moscow, especially in foreign affairs.

In the 1980s Zhivkov's position was undermined by three main factors. The first was the appointment to the Soviet leadership of Mikhail Gorbachev, to whom the Bulgarian leader epitomized the indulgent, corrupt and inefficient ethos of the Brezhnev years. Zhivkov's enthusiasm for all things Soviet (all Bulgarians were taught Russian and one Soviet television channel was permanently relayed to Bulgaria), however, exposed him to the new, reformist ideas from the USSR: *perestroika* (restructuring) and *glasnost* ('openness'). The second factor was economic decline. Zhiv-kov had already embarked on a form of *perestroika*, economic reform, in the New Economic Mechanism of 1982. However, the initial promises were not fulfilled and the reform programme degenerated into a series of disruptive adjustments to the administration of the economy. Thirdly, there was the disastrous 'regenerative process'.

About 10% of Bulgaria's 9m. inhabitants are Turkish-speaking. In 1984 Zhivkov and some of his colleagues decided that the time had come to 'bulgarize' the Turks. Turkish broadcasts and publications were suspended and the use of the Turkish language in public was banned; most contentious of all was the order that the Turks take Bulgarian or Slavic names. The policy was a disaster. To overcome the resistance of the Turks, the Bulgarian army had to be deployed in what was probably its largest operation since the Second World War, while abroad Bulgaria was excoriated in bodies as diverse as the Islamic Conference and the Council of Europe. The 'regenerative process' also quickened internal opposition and encouraged the growth of human-rights groups. Finally, in mid-1989, some 300,000 Turks fled to Turkey, wreaking havoc with the Bulgarian economy and totally discrediting the Zhivkov regime abroad.

There was further discredit when Bulgarian police treated roughly a number of ecological protesters, amongst whom was a British journalist, on 26 October 1989. If Zhivkov's opponents in the highest levels of the Party did not actually organize this confrontation, they were certainly not slow to make use of it as yet another argument for a change of leadership. At a plenum of the BCP Central Committee, on 10 November 1989, Zhivkov was impelled to resign from office. His successor, as Party leader (General Secretary) and head of state (President of the State Council), was Petur Mladenov, who had served as Minister of Foreign Affairs for 17 years and had taken a leading part in the plot to oust Zhivkov.

CHANGES IN FORM BUT NOT IN STRUCTURE

Todor Zhivkov had been overthrown by his own colleagues in the upper ranks of the Party. Thus, the events of 10 November 1989 were a coup, not a revolution; 'people power' was a consequence, not a cause, of the overthrow of the old regime; revolution was the product of, not the prelude to, the change of leadership.

After this change the BCP was ready to admit that Zhivkov had brought the country close to ruin, not least in amassing a foreign-currency debt which was now revealed to be about US $11,000m. The BCP was also prepared to democratize its own procedures, but that, it seemed, was as far as it was prepared to proceed. However, the process of change had begun. Even before 10 November there had been indications of a revival in independent political activity, with the formation of ecological pressure groups, human rights associations and even of an independent trade union, Podkrepa (Support). After the fall of Zhivkov political parties and civil associations proliferated. Some of them, such as the Bulgarian Social Democratic Party (BSDP), were revivals of suppressed groups; others were adaptations of previous formations, such as the Nikola Petkov Bulgarian Agrarian People's Union (BAPU-NP), established in opposition to the official, coalition BAPU; and other groups, including the Green Party, were entirely new creations. On 14 November some 15 of these bodies came together to form the Union of Democratic Forces (UDF), to which were later added other groups.

By the end of 1989 popular agitation, especially in the cities, was intensifying, the general demand being for an end to the domination of the Communist Party. On 14 December 1989 a massive demonstration outside the parliament building in Sofia demanded an end to the Communist grip on power and for the convocation of 'round-table' negotiations, between the official parties and the opposition, to determine the way to a new, multi-party system. The Government and the Party delayed, but, on 29 December, they did issue a decree revoking the majority of the anti-Turkish legislation passed since 1984. This produced another, but less positive, outburst of popular feeling. On 7 January 1990 a huge crowd, many of them transported to Sofia from outlying, mixed Bulgarian–Turkish areas with local BCP connivance, protested that such an important change could not be introduced without a national referendum. One week later yet another demonstration, this time organized by the UDF, insisted that there could be no going back on the decree of 29 December. The BCP and the UDF both realized that anti-Turkish chauvinism had to be resisted, not least because of Bulgaria's desperate need for financial assistance, some of which could come from the wealthy Arab states.

The common issue discovered at the beginning of January 1990, enabled the BCP and the UDF to begin effective, round-table discussions. At the same time the BCP introduced legislation to modify Article One of the Constitution, which had given it the right to political and social predominance. The appropriate legislation was eventually enacted, but only after further popular demonstrations insisting that the entire Article be removed, including the first clause, which described Bulgaria as a 'socialist state of the working people of the town and the countryside, led by the working class'. After this concession the BCP seemed to be in headlong retreat. It soon conceded the holding of multi-party elections, the rules and procedures for which were made public early in April of that year.

At the beginning of February 1990 the Party assumed sole responsibility for government. Their previous coalition partners, the official Agrarians, had responded to the taunts of the BAPU-NP (accusing them of assisting the heirs of those who had presided over the judicial murder of Nikola Petkov) and resigned from the ruling coalition. Ironically, for the first time in its history, Bulgaria had a purely Communist Government. By that time the BCP had undergone its own restructuring. During the Extraordinary 14th Congress, of 31 January–2 February, the former structures of Central Committee and Political Bureau (Politburo) were replaced by a Supreme Council and its Presidium. There were few members of the old bodies in the new organs. Mladenov relinquished his leadership of the Party to Aleksandur Lilov. On 3 April the BCP changed its name to the Bulgarian Socialist Party (BSP). Meanwhile Mladenov remained President of the country, after the dissolution of the State Council.

By then the Party had, in theory at least, abandoned, or been deprived of, much of its leading role in society. Shortly after 10 November Krustyu Petkov, a professor of sociology, successfully managed to detach the old trades union organization from domination by the Party. The newly-created Confederation of Independent Trade Unions in Bulgaria (CITUB) was to play a vital part in further political reforms. The BCP yielded to further pressure from its opponents and abolished all Party cells in the workplace. The Komsomol or Communist Youth movement, the Fatherland Front, which united various social organizations, and other pillars of the old establishment were also divorced from BCP control.

The concessions made by the BCP/BSP were important, but they could not satisfy its opponents. They would feel secure only when a new Assembly had been convened, to give legal guarantees of political freedom. From April 1990, therefore, the preoccupation of most Bulgarian political activists was with the forthcoming electoral battle.

Under the Turnovo Constitution of 1879, the first in the history of modern Bulgaria, constitutional changes could be enacted only by a Grand National Assembly, which was to be twice the size of an ordinary assembly. In 1990 the round-table parties agreed to follow this precedent. They decided that a new National Assembly should be consituted as a Grand National Assembly (GNA), which would consist of 400 deputies, one-half of whom were to be elected by proportional representation, and one-half in constituencies by a simple majority. Polling was to take place on 10 and 17 June 1990, the second date being for 'run-offs' (that is, a further election for the principal contenders in those single-member constituencies where the candidate who won the most number of votes in the first round had not reached the minimum required percentage of the total vote). There were few restrictions on the political parties, which were free to contest the election. There was, however, one regulation which caused dispute: that no political party could be based upon religious allegiance or ethnic identity.

There is little doubt that the conduct of the voting was, in general, fair. It is also widely accepted that, in the weeks before the election, the BSP exercised considerable intimidation over the electorate, particularly in the rural constituencies, where there were hints that the reformists in Sofia would be incapable of rule and would refuse to pay pensions and other benefits. The leader of the UDF, Zheliu Zhelev, summarized the electoral battle as 'free, but not fair'. The result gave an absolute majority of the seats (211) to the BSP, which had received some 47% of the votes cast. The UDF won about 38% of the votes and gained 144 seats in parliament. The BAPU gained 16 seats, the nationalist Fatherland Party of Labour two, the Bulgarian Social Democratic Party—non-Marxist (subsequently renamed the Liberal Congress Party) one, and there were two independents. The biggest surprise was that the Movement for Rights and Freedoms (MRF), which was primarily concerned with protecting the interests of the Turkish population, gained 23 deputies in the GNA, making it the third-largest party.

THE REVOLUTION STALLED, JULY–NOVEMBER 1990

Before the second round of voting in the general election, in June 1990, considerable controversy was caused by the discovery of a video tape, in which President Mladenov was seen to advocate the use of tanks against demonstrators on 14 December of the previous year. After initial denials of the tape's authenticity, Mladenov resigned on 6 July 1990. On 1 August, after six attempts to elect a successor, Zheliu Zhelev, a former dissident and the leader of the UDF, was elected President of Bulgaria. The Vice-President was a member of the BSP, Col-Gen. Atanas Semerdzhiev.

The Mladenov affair meant that, when the GNA met on 10 July, the political atmosphere was already tense. There were also chauvinist demonstrators, claiming that the MRF was illegal because it was based on ethnic identity; the MRF responded by proving that it had ethnic Bulgarians as well as Turks amongst its members. Further tensions arose from continuing student accusations that evidence of electoral malpractice had been concealed; the students set up 'the city of truth', a tent encampment in the centre of Sofia, in which the capital's intelligentsia formulated a whole series of wide-ranging political demands.

The opening of the GNA did little to restore calm, primarily because the deputies showed a surprising reluctance to begin work. It took a threat of strike action from CITUB to initiate serious political discussions. At the same time there was growing disquiet, especially in the 'city of truth', over the real intentions of the BSP. Its promises to withdraw from its leading role, it was alleged, had been only partially implemented. The Government promised to remove all foreign symbols from public places (a reference to the hammer and sickle, the symbol of the Soviet Communists, and to the Communist accretions to the national coat of arms and flag). These were indeed removed; a number of Soviet and Russian street or town names reverted to their Bulgarian forms; and the body of Georgi Dimitrov, a hero of the Communist International and the first leader of Communist Bulgaria, was removed from its mausoleum in the centre of Sofia. This was not considered enough, however, particularly when, almost opposite the mausoleum, was the BSP headquarters, which was still surmounted by the *petoluchka*, or five-pointed star, the symbol of 45 years of Communist rule. In August 1990 two demonstrators threatened to immolate themselves if the symbol were not removed. Once again tension mounted, but it was the Party headquarters itself which was eventually set on fire, with a considerable portion of it being damaged.

There remains some mystery about the origins of the fire of 26–27 August 1990. The building of the BSP headquarters, previously among the most secure in the country, seemed to have been left virtually unguarded. Members of the BSP made accusations of the return of fascism; their opponents talked of the fire being a provocation, intended to allow the BSP to implement a counter-revolution. In fact, the fire brought about a greater degree of sobriety in Bulgarian politics. The tent encampments in Sofia and other cities were abandoned, in accordance with recently-enacted legislation, and the GNA began serious deliberation on a number of other legislative proposals. There was still little progress, however, over another pressing question: the formation of a new government.

Despite its electoral victory, the BSP under Lukanov was reluctant to form another one-party cabinet. Lukanov believed that the country's economic problems could be rectified only by the most extreme remedies; he argued, therefore, that, to ensure public acceptance of these remedies, all major political forces had to support them, preferably by the formation of a coalition government. The UDF refused, arguing that the BCP/BSP was responsible for the problems and it was its responsibility to resolve them. The UDF did not want to be associated with the unpopularity which the reforms would inevitably bring. Furthermore, it argued, the BSP had a mandate and a programme and should, therefore, carry out the task for which it had been elected. In addition, the UDF insisted that it could not go into government with the BSP until the latter had purged itself of those members of the BCP who the opposition considered had exercised and abused power before 10 November 1989. Not until 20 September 1990 did Lukanov agree to form a single-party government.

By then the chances of public support for that Government had declined sharply, with a persistent suspicion of the real intentions of the BSP. These suspicions were aggravated by the delaying tactics which the Party deployed on a number of issues. A vital proposal for the reform of local government had been debated in the GNA, but had not been formally enacted by 28 August 1990, when the mandates of the existing local-government bodies, People's Councils, expired. Reform of local government was an important issue, not least because it was the locally-elected officials who ran the electoral bureaux which controlled polling during general elections. After 28 August interim local councils were formed, with representation reflecting the distribution of votes in the June general elections. Another occasion for suspicion of the BSP was when a proposal to effect the depoliticization of the army, police, judiciary and diplomatic service was returned to the GNA, from the committee stage, without those clauses mentioning the diplomatic service. They were reinstated after further debate and delay. The BSP also blocked attempts to have BCP party records handed over to public archives, a fact which caused intense disquiet because of the increasingly fierce demands for the punishment of those who, it was said, had brought about 'the third national catastrophe'.

The first and second national catastrophes were the defeats in the Second Balkan War and the First World War, in 1913 and 1918, respectively. By the third such catastrophe was meant the current ruination of the Bulgarian economy. In March 1990 the Lukanov Government had suspended payment on its foreign-debt obligations, a fact which had angered the international financial community and further complicated Bulgaria's position. At home all parties were committed to de-monopolization, decentralization, the decollectivization of agriculture and the transfer to a market economy. The necessary legislation, however, was not passed. Even after forming his cabinet Lukanov refused to enact his reform programme without the support of the opposition, which they were still determined not to give. In this situation the economy became chaotic. Shortages increased, and so also prices on the unregulated and illegal 'black market' or 'parallel economy', which was frequently the only source of supply. Unemployment began to spread rapidly. In the agricultural sector, the uncertainty over land ownership was a disincentive to planting; many producers and traders were already hoarding non-perishable items for when the prices increased; thus, with the lack of foreign currency excluding the Zhivkov expedient of importing agricultural goods, food queues lengthened alarmingly. In industry, production was disrupted by the non-availability of supplies and the collapse of the Council for Mutual Economic Assistance (CMEA or Comecon) trading system, on which Bulgaria had depended. Furthermore, all sectors of the economy were drastically affected by the 1990–91 crisis in the Persian (Arabian) Gulf (brought about by the Iraqi invasion and attempted annexation of Kuwait). Iraq was Bulgaria's biggest foreign-currency debtor, owing some US $1,200m., which, it had been agreed in May 1990, was to be repaid to Bulgaria in the form of crude petroleum, over 600,000 metric tons of which was to be delivered that year alone. All this was lost, as was a further 200,000 tons, which was to come from Iraq via the USSR.

THE REVOLUTION RESUMED

Lukanov's Government had little chance of continuing in office, given the likelihood of economic collapse and the political impasse. It was the students who struck the first blow. For much of October 1990 they had campaigned for university reforms, but they had never neglected their political objectives. On 5 November student leaders decided to occupy the buildings of the University of Sofia, and one of their demands was that the Government resign.

By the end of November 1990, with no prospect of any break in the political deadlock, workers' organizations began to support the students. On 26 November Podkrepa declared a general strike and, three days later, CITUB announced that it would ballot its members on strike action. The strike threats were accompanied by increasing signs of violence and disorder on the streets and even in the debating chamber of the GNA. On 30 November Lukanov's Government resigned, but only after talks arranged by President Zhelev had produced an agreement between the main political factions that a new, multi-party administration would be formed under a non-party premier. The new premier, confirmed by the GNA on 7 December, was Dimitur Popov, who had served as Secretary to the Electoral Commission, in June 1990. His appointment, together with the indictment of Zhivkov and one of his associates on charges of gross embezzlement, did much to calm the political atmosphere. By the middle of December the students and the trade unions had abandoned their actions.

After Popov's nomination the most important political groupings, on 14 December 1990, agreed to sign the 'Agreement Guaranteeing the Peaceful Transition to a Democratic Society'. They resolved to support the Popov Government, which was to hold office until new elections were held, originally scheduled for March 1991. During that time the Government was to devise a new constitution and enact the necessary legislation to create a market economy.

This move towards consensus was followed by general public approval of the cabinet list, which Popov presented on 20 December 1990. He skilfully balanced the existing political forces, not least by appointing an independent to the vital Ministry of Internal Affairs. On 8 January 1991 a further indication of cohesion came with the tripartite 'Social Agreement', signed by the prime minister, representatives from the two major trade union organizations and the chairman of the employers' association. The agreement provided for a suspension of strike activity, sensitive management of the transition to a market system and political support for the necessary economic and social legislation. The Social Agreement was renewed in June 1991.

The conclusion of the Social Agreement allowed the Popov Government to begin real economic restructuring. The reforms to be enacted were, to a considerable degree, determined by the International Monetary Fund (IMF), to which Bulgaria had been admitted in September 1990 and which had agreed to advance a loan, on condition of real economic and fiscal reform. It was in fulfilment of these conditions that the Popov Government raised interest rates from 5% to 45% and, on 1 February 1991, abolished price controls. The latter measure brought hoarded goods into the market and, if prices were initially too high, they did respond to market forces by falling in subsequent weeks, although not to near the level they had been when regulated. The Government also abolished foreign-currency shops, with effect from 1 April. Another important enactment was a law of 1 March, by which land was to be decollectivized and returned, if it was so wished, to the families that had previously owned it.

In the constitutional sphere there was less progress. The GNA was still prone to spend time on procedural matters and, by the end of March 1991, there had been no real debate about a constitution. There was no sign of any local elections being held, and sharp debates were developing as to when the general election should take place and whether it should be conducted simultaneously with the local elections. The BSP were considered reluctant to hold early elections and exploited the divisions in the UDF and other opposition parties. Furthermore, in April, the BSP were accused of still having access to police files, after the publication of embarrassing accusations about opposition politicians. The Minister of Internal Affairs offered his resignation, but the main consequence of the scandal was the realization by the new democratic parties that the old system had to be dismantled. Although some parties wanted to have elections before the enacting of a new constitution, some, such as the MRF, were anxious to resolve the constitutional issues before then. After several months of mounting public, and presidential, pressure the Grand National Assembly finally approved the final reading of the Constitution. It was promulgated, and took effect, on the following day, on 13 July 1991. Transitional arrangements provided for the continuation of the existing state institutions, until such time as the new organs could be established. The Grand National Assembly dissolved itself, but its members continued sessions as the legislature or National Assembly. President Zhelev set the date for national and local elections as 29 September, but, following a delay in enabling legislation, this was changed to 13 October. The UDF became the largest electoral bloc in the new parliament, and formed a Government.

THE PROSPECTS FOR THE FUTURE
External Alignments

An early consequence of the 'palace revolution' of 10 November 1989 was the cessation of the sycophantic attitude to the USSR which had characterized the *Zhivkovshtina*, the period of Zhivkov's rule. The estrangement from the USSR was aided by Soviet insistence that Bulgaria pay market prices for Soviet petroleum and that all trading with Bulgaria, as with other Eastern European states, be paid for in convertible currency, after 1 January 1991. This left the Bulgarians with a particular difficulty, in that they had accumulated a considerable balance of roubles in Soviet banks; these could not to be converted to US dollars and were therefore virtually useless. A further distancing came when Bulgaria, like Czechoslovakia and Hungary, announced that, if the Warsaw Treaty Organization (the Warsaw Pact) were not disbanded, then Bulgaria would withdraw from it. At the same time Soviet action in Lithuania, in January 1991, was thoroughly condemned by all Bulgarian political parties except the BSP, although one faction within that party did join the general condemnation.

With the end of the traditional Communist links with the USSR, Bulgaria needed to establish fresh alignments in its foreign policy. An obvious association was with the other Balkan states. Relations with Greece improved dramatically in 1990, with exchanges of visits and with the Greeks sending large amounts of desperately-needed supplies, particularly medicines, to Bulgaria. Exchanges with Albania intensified after that country emerged from its isolation and there seemed, at mid-1991, to be no cause for contention between the two countries. The atmosphere in official Bulgarian–Turkish exchanges was also warm. The Turkish Government offered to lend Bulgaria money and petroleum, and the Bulgarians were seriously considering Turkish proposals for a 'Black Sea Zone' of economic co-operation. Behind all Bulgarian–Turkish relations, however, lurks the question of the Turkish minority in Bulgaria. Chauvinist elements suspect any improvement in relations with Turkey, even seeing the Black Sea Zone proposals as a Turkish subterfuge by which Turkey would inject capital and even labour into Bulgaria. Bulgaria's relations with its neighbour to the north, Romania, were far from good. The Bulgarians continued to complain that the city of Ruse was being periodically enveloped in poisonous gas leaking from a factory on the Romanian bank of the Danube (such concerns caused the first expressions of opposition to the Communist regime). The Romanians respond with accusations that Bulgaria too is causing environmental damage, not least from its nuclear power complex at Kozlodui (after the International Atomic Energy Agency—IAEA—inspected this plant, in mid-1991, the Bulgarian authorities agreed to close it down). To these aggravations were added disputes over smuggling between the two countries, usually by the universally-unpopular Roma (Gypsies). Towards the end of 1991, however, the real obstacle to a foreign policy based upon Balkan alignments was the fragile nature of the Yugoslav federation and the uncertainty of whether it would survive the civil war, which effectively broke out in June 1991. Should that state finally collapse, the balance of power in the Balkans would be totally destroyed and Bulgaria would have to decide what attitude it was to take towards Macedonia (where, in September 1991, a referendum supported a declaration of independence), upon which some Bulgarian nationalists still cast covetous glances.

It was not to the Balkans, however, but to the developed West that Bulgaria paid most court. President Zhelev's first foreign visit was to the USA, and Bulgaria welcomed advice and advisers in large number from that country. There was a strong faction in favour of Bulgaria becoming a member of NATO; during the Gulf crisis over the Iraqi occupation of Kuwait, in 1990–91, Bulgaria, despite the economic damage it suffered, was unflinching in its support for the international coalition, offering to send medical units to the Persian Gulf and to provide rest and recuperation facilities in Bulgaria for Allied personnel. Bulgaria has also attempted to establish closer relations with the European Community (EC). Application for membership of the Council of Europe was made and Bulgaria also received grants of over 100m. ECUs to help it reconstruct its economy. Full inclusion in the EC, however, can be little more than a distant dream; Bulgaria's economy is far too weak and its potential strengths, particularly in agricultural produce, are those which the EC already enjoys in abundance. In mid-1991, however, the EC did invite Bulgaria to begin negotiations about an association agreement with the Community. For its trading partners, Bulgaria, in all probability, would still have to depend on the USSR, where the need for food imports seems set to continue and upon which Bulgaria is still heavily dependent for energy. Bulgaria has moved from its former subservience to the USSR, however, although there were accusations that members of the establishment had been too ready to negotiate with the leaders of the attempted Communist coup in the USSR, in August 1991. The West, after its initial reluctance, has been more supportive of Bulgaria, following its introduction of a new Constitution (the first of the former bloc to do this) and the radical economic reforms. Bulgaria remains anxious to find a new economic and political partner, to replace the USSR.

Domestic Affairs

Bulgarians proudly describe their political evolution since 10 November 1989 as 'the Gentle Revolution'. This is not unjustifiable; certainly almost no blood had been shed or significant violence occurred in Bulgaria by the time of the elections, in October 1991. However, not all the apparatus of police surveillance and control had been dismantled; suspicions of the BSP sheltering and protecting the old BCP nomenklatura remained, as did fears of KGB (the Soviet security service—after August 1991 apprehension about it was considerably less) penetration of Bulgarian political organizations. The BSP, however, is not the BCP, not least because it allowed internal factionalization and

division to a degree unimaginable in the former ruling Party.

The UDF was committed to continuing its monitoring of BSP activities, although its ability to do so could be impaired by its own internal divisions. The largest of its constituent groups, the Bulgarian Social Democratic Party—United (BSDP), was ambiguous in its attitude towards participation in the Popov Government. There were further rifts over agricultural decollectivization and over the extent of social welfare provision for those affected by the economic reforms. By mid-1991 there were two main factions in the UDF: the 'centre block' or 'Light Blues', led by Dr Petur Dertliev of the BSDP, and including the BAPU-NP (which merged with BAPU and another Agrarian party, in August 1991, to form BAPU—United), the Greens and Ecoglasnost; and the right-wing group, or 'Dark Blues', led by Stoyan Ganev of the United Democratic Centre, which included the increasingly-influential monarchists and the UDF chairman, Filip Dimitrov. Originally, divisions had become apparent when 39 radical UDF deputies had led a protest boycott of the GNA, which even imperilled the adoption of the Constitution. This right-wing group gradually gained the ascendancy in the UDF, favouring a more united movement, with a single list of candidates at the next election (they became known as the UDF—Movement group). In August 1991 the six parties of the UDF—Liberal faction rejected some of the centralizing proposals and formalized the emergence of a split in the UDF. The consequence was the splitting of two UDF—Liberal parties, the BSDP and the Greens. Relations between the UDF and the MRF were also strained, particularly as the UDF was less willing to alienate the potentially-significant anti-Turkish vote in the approach to a general election. The MRF had been anxious about its status, which it considered likely to be ruled illegal under constitutional regulations forbidding ethnic or religious parties. In September the Sofia City Court ruled that it could not register the MRF, but this decision was later reversed.

Should that existing configuration of parties disintegrate, Bulgaria would depend even more upon the skill and sagacity of President Zhelev. He has contributed much to the stability of the country by his unseen activities during times of crisis, and seemed likely to be re-elected at the presidential elections due to be held in early 1992. The Political Consultative Council, which he created and which brings together all the major political forces, has proved a most useful device and could well prove invaluable in future moments of political danger.

Throughout the history of modern Bulgaria the Army has played a significant political role, attempting coups successfully in 1886, 1923 and 1934, and, unsuccessfully, in 1965. At present it does not seem to have any political ambitions and the recently-formed 'Rakovski Legion' has, so far, concentrated on protecting and enhancing the social position and living standards of the military. Another factor, at present outside the political arena, is the Crown. Bulgaria has a vocal monarchist faction whose most valuable asset is its monarch. Tsar Simeon II left Bulgaria in 1946, aged only nine, and, since 10 November 1989, has impressed many Bulgarians. Should President Zhelev be disabled in any way, Simeon's return, either as tsar or as an elected supra-party president, would be a possibility.

Despite the undoubted progress already made towards political plurality and liberty, problems remain. Nationalism is never far from the surface in the Balkans. In Bulgaria, it is most seriously present in the tension between the Bulgarians and the Turkish minority. The excesses of the 'regenerative process' have been abandoned, but further concessions to the Turks have met with some opposition.

In mid-1991 the focus of attention was the agreement that, in Turkish areas, schools should devote four hours per week to teaching Turkish, but this has produced demonstrations and occupations by Bulgarians in the affected areas. For their part, the ethnic Bulgarians fear that the Turkish population is increasing at a faster rate than that of the Bulgarian. This is probably less justified a fear than it was a decade ago, but, given the Bulgarians' low birth-rate and high levels of emigration (the country suffered its first-ever net decrease in population in 1990) this anxiety is not easy to discard. On the other hand, there is no doubt that the rate of increase among the Romany population is faster than in any other group, although precise figures are unobtainable and, in all likelihood, unknown. There are also tensions between Bulgarians and Pomaks (Bulgarian-speaking Muslims), who were subjected to the 'bulgarization' programmes of the 1970s. Many Pomaks have attempted to leave the country and some, it is reported, have sought foreign patronage by trying to become Uniates, or 'Greek Catholics'. Bulgaria also has an immigrant problem. The Zhivkov regime imported over 15,000 Vietnamese labourers, for whom there is now insufficient work and who are often active on the black market, especially that in currency. This has led to occasional clashes, two Vietnamese being killed in one such incident, on 17 March 1991, in Sofia. The Bulgarian authorities have arranged for the repatriation of all Vietnamese, a process hindered late in 1990 and early in 1991 only by the lack of aviation fuel.

The economic problems of Bulgaria are, at least, the equal of those concerning the national groups. Bulgarian industry is uncompetitive and the heavy-industrial sector relies too much upon imported raw materials. Reliance upon external sources of energy is even greater, Bulgaria being more import-dependent in this respect than any other Eastern European state. Meanwhile, agriculture and light industry will have to adapt to the social revolution of privatization.

In addition to these problems there is that of environmental pollution which, as elsewhere in Eastern Europe, is immense. It is hard to avoid the conclusion that, in the long term, almost all the country's available financial resources would have to be devoted to restoring the atmosphere, the waters and the soil. The scale of the problem was indicated by the Government's reluctance to close the Kozlodui nuclear-power station, which was condemned by the IAEA in June 1991. Over 40% of the country's electricity supply is generated there. The Government did decide to implement the closure of the two oldest reactors by September, but used the issue to insist on more aid from the West, particularly in the supply of energy.

Bulgaria will need all its energy, its expertise, and its already much-exercised patience to overcome this and its other problems. In view of the progress so far achieved, however, a degree of optimism would not be unjustified.

The Economy

Dr RAYMOND HUTCHINGS

INTRODUCTION

Following the overthrow of Todor Zhivkov, in November 1989, and the transition to a non-Communist Government, in December 1990, the first one for 46 years, the Bulgarian economy embarked on the difficult process of transition to a market economy. The physical circumstances, much of the organizational structure and many of the attitudes inherited from the socialist (Communist) system remained and all the problems inherent in such a transition were being encountered. These negative factors were aggravated by the previous trend of enlargement of foreign debts, by the Gulf crisis of 1990–91 and by the problems of no longer existing within the framework of the CMEA (the now-defunct economic grouping of the Soviet bloc, of which Bulgaria was one of the founder members and with which it, in particular, traded). Once the economy's basic circumstances and features have been examined, recent intentions and problems must also be surveyed in some detail.

Geography and Transport

Bulgaria is a compact country, roughly rectangular and twice as long from east to west as from north to south. Mountain chains divide it into northern and southern regions, which are of roughly equal size. Bulgaria is mainly bordered on the north by the River Danube, which, besides being a political boundary, is useful for navigation, cooling for industrial plant, irrigation and, to a small extent, for fishing (but scarcely at all for recreation, owing to pollution and the strong current). Navigation is occasionally hindered by low water, while irrigation is complicated by the height of the banks along the Bulgarian side. The Danube is a considerable barrier to north–south traffic, being crossed by only one bridge between Bulgaria and Romania (just east of Ruse), which is the cause of notorious delays. Both water and sea transport primarily serve Bulgaria's external traffic. Bulgaria also lies on the main international road and rail routes between Europe and Asia Minor.

In 1989 Bulgaria had 4,586 km of railway track, of which almost two-thirds was of standard gauge, making Bulgaria slightly better endowed than Romania in terms of railway track per unit of territory. Most railways in Bulgaria are single-track; about one-half their total length was electrified (an unusually high proportion in Eastern Europe). Bulgaria and Romania are about equally provided with roads per unit of territory. In 1990 the total length of roads in Bulgaria was about 37,000 km. Bulgaria's rail and road networks were not being extended, apart from the slow construction of a motorway (ultimately to go completely round the country). Rail-freight traffic has been declining since 1983, while rail-passenger traffic has remained constant. Car ownership per head is average for Eastern Europe, being higher than in Romania and lower than in Czechoslovakia.

Bulgaria's climate is continental, especially in the north and north-east. Bulgaria is the southernmost country in Europe where the average January temperature is 0°C (32°F) or below. However, on the whole, this can be reckoned a warm climate. The soil can be regarded as fertile, since, in the Danubian plain, it includes black earths and grey forest soils; to the south the soil is inferior, but has proved very suitable for tobacco.

As far as water resources are concerned, Bulgaria is one of the least fortunate countries in Europe. Rivers, apart from the Danube, are mostly short and have very uneven flow, which also is least at times when plants' need is greatest. Precipitation is, on the whole, adequate (650 mm annually, for the whole country) and is more suitably timed seasonally. However, it is highest in mountain areas, where it is least needed. Irrigation has, therefore, been greatly expanded: it is concentrated along the Danube, including the Vidin area. Like other Balkan countries, Bulgaria, in recent years (especially from 1985 onwards), has suffered from repeated droughts; these affect hydro-generated electricity as well as crop yields.

Population and Labour Force

The population of Bulgaria is not quite 9m. (8.99m. at the end of 1989). Nine million has become a goal which, perhaps, may never be reached; indeed, the total is likely to decline quite rapidly. (This makes Bulgaria's demographic expectations the opposite of Albania's.) Whereas national policy has been pro-natalist, sentiment among ethnic Bulgarians has strongly favoured small families, whereas the Turkish minority and, doubtless, the Roma (Gypsies), favour larger ones. There are also Bulgarians living in adjacent countries, including, it is claimed, 200,000 in Romania. Bulgaria's population density (81.0 per sq km at the end of 1989) is the lowest in Eastern Europe. The urban population was 66% of the total (in Romania, 53%). The capital city, Sofia, has a population which exceeds 1.1m. people; other cities of more than 150,000 included Plovdiv, Varna, Burgas, Ruse and Stara Zagora. Some 40,000 Bulgarian citizens work in the timber industry in the USSR. About 23,000 Vietnamese were allowed to come to Bulgaria, but have become unpopular with both populace and authorities. Some 13,000 remain but will not stay beyond 1992. Like other Eastern European countries, Bulgaria is now liable to find that many of its skilled and talented workers will emigrate. After years of totalitarian rule, many now have the opportunity to seek what they hope will be a higher standard of living in the West.

Again, as elsewhere, there has been continuous migration from the countryside into the cities, in particular Sofia, where a residence permit is required. This movement tends to result in overcrowding, and housing space in Sofia is admitted to be below the national average. The tendency has been for certain rural areas to become depopulated, though there has been some attempt to reverse this.

In 1989 some 46% of the population was within the workforce, which is a similar proportion to other countries in south-east Europe. Total employment has tended to decline slightly, owing to a long-term fall in the birthrate. Under the Communist regime officially there was no unemployment, but in such circumstances there is invariably under-employment. It is realized that the transition to a market economy will entail a substantial extent of unemployment. In May 1990 some 35,000–40,000 unemployed were forecast by the year's end, with redundancy a real possibility for many Bulgarians; expectations became more pessimistic, and the eventual total reached 70,000. Although this is a small proportion of a workforce of over 4m., it has made a significant psychological impact. A major proportion of the unemployed are university graduates. In mid-June 1991 it was reported that unemployment had reached 205,000, some 5% of the working population.

In 1989 about 22% of the workforce were employed in agriculture and 34% in industry. Both percentages were lower than in Romania, which could imply a higher proportion engaged in services; this can be taken to imply that Bulgarian living standards were superior to those of Romania (a reversal of the situation before the Second World War). After the tribulations experienced by both countries during 1990, it is uncertain whether this is still the case.

Other Factors Affecting the Economy

Bulgaria used to be overwhelmingly an agricultural country. It still remains markedly agricultural, but, according to official figures (which should be treated with caution, as the Communist governments of Eastern Europe tended to overvalue industry and undervalue agriculture), by 1989 agriculture's contribution to the national material product (NMP) had declined to 12.3% of the total, while that of industry had risen to 57.1%. NMP is used as a measure of economic performance in the centrally-planned economies, as gross national or domestic product is used in the West. The agricultural sector normally excludes forestry and the industrial sector consists mainly of manufacturing and utilities.

This measure does not include the activities of the parallel or unofficial economy ('black market'). Given the pervasive shortages, together with quickly-changing legal and administrative arrangements, it is not surprising that the black market is flourishing. A law against speculation was enacted, in December 1990, but was unlikely to cure the problem.

As further background to the transition from a centrally-planned economy to one based on market principles, the shortage of expertise and the social consequences of the changes should be included. Bulgaria was considered to have a serious need for highly-qualified managers, such as experts in marketing, banking, etc. As reported in June 1990, there existed only one Bulgarian management consultancy firm.

The Government hoped to alleviate the worst consequences of the economic transition by its Social Agreements of 1991, but some worsening in living standards seemed inevitable. Draft regulations on the restructuring of health care were published in December 1989. General policy in this sphere was being substantially amended, one of the changes being the introduction of private medical practice, which, it was announced in May 1990, would be permitted on equal terms to state and co-operative practice. Meanwhile, there remained a persistent shortage of medicines. Although the social security system prided itself on its concern for social welfare, pension schemes were considered to be radically outdated and not to reflect the rate of inflation. Leaving a burdensome debt for future generations, pensions were, at the same time, far below subsistence level. In housing construction, as elsewhere in Eastern Europe, it has been built partly by the State, partly by co-operatives and partly by private individuals. Usually about 45% has been built by the State, the remainder, to about an equal extent, by the two other categories. Somewhat more than 4m. sq m of useful space was built annually during the 1970s and early 1980s. However, in the mid-1980s, particularly 1986, state and co-operative construction tended to decline. In 1990 the number of completions in the middle months of the year was much less than normal, perhaps partly owing to factors such as the fall in cement production, by 6.6% in January–August, and the fall in prefabricated production, by 15.6%. By the end of August of that year, 6,841 fewer dwellings had been built than during the same period in 1989.

Finally, Bulgaria must pay for the environmental consequences of the centrally-planned economy. As in other countries of Eastern Europe, the environment in Bulgaria suffered during the Communist period. Awareness of environmental matters developed from the mid-1980s. A more radical ecological policy was discussed in the National Assembly, in March 1990. However, the liveliest environmental issue is that of air pollution above Ruse, which the Bulgarians ascribe to a chemical plant at Giurgiu in

Romania. Morbidity and mortality are claimed to be higher in Ruse than elsewhere in Bulgaria. The Romanians were reluctant to admit responsibility, although they declared themselves ready to help in ascertaining the causes; an international commission examined the problem. In August 1991, partly under pressure from the EC, Romania and Bulgaria agreed to co-operate in environmental matters, to monitor atmospheric pollution in the Ruse–Giurgiu area and to accept aid in improving the area.

SECTORS OF THE ECONOMY

Agriculture

Over one-half (55%) of the total land area, that is, about 61,000 sq km, are farmed. In 1988 just over 10% was farmed as private plots. As in other Communist states, cereals, especially wheat, were grown predominantly by 'socialized units', state and collective farms, but potatoes, meat, eggs, milk and other smaller-scale products mainly in private plots. Some 34% of the total land area of Bulgaria was arable land, compared to 42% in Romania and only 20% in Albania. Bulgaria, therefore, grows less cereals than its northern neighbour, but more tomatoes, grapes (Bulgaria is a major producer and exporter of wine) and tobacco. Bulgaria is famed for the cultivation of roses, and establishes the world standard for rose oil. There were some 1.6m. head of cattle, 4.1m. pigs and 8.6m. sheep. The number of cattle and sheep has been declining, that of pigs rising. On the whole, livestock provides a smaller share of farm products in Bulgaria than in adjacent countries. In the late 1980s, total farm output did not increase. Among the main products, levels of cereal and milk production have been static; the amount of meat and eggs produced has risen very slowly; while wool production has declined. During the 1980s the extent of mechanization of Bulgarian agriculture tended to decrease, although more fertilizer and chemicals have been supplied.

Forestry and Fishing

Like all Balkan countries, Bulgaria has a high proportion of forest and woodland (35%). Afforestation has been on a very considerable scale; however, in recent years, the total area of woodland has scarcely altered. There are both deciduous trees (including oak and beech) and conifers. Only about 15% of the forest has industrial significance. Timber is used for furniture and the manufacture of paper and cellulose. In the summer there is a significant fire risk. Forestry, with agriculture, is among the lowest paid occupations. Fishing seems to have had a low priority. Furthermore, the Iron Gates hydro-electric scheme has, apparently, reduced the catch of fish in the Danube.

Industry

Industrialization took place mainly during the Communist period. According to official statistics, between 40% and 50% of gross fixed capital investments were ordinarily devoted to industry, less than 10% to agriculture. Industrial activity is not evenly distributed throughout the country. One of the main industrial areas is Sofia–Pernik (west-central Bulgaria), which is the most comprehensively developed. Efforts were made to spread industry more widely. Iron and steel industries are concentrated in the Sofia–Pernik region, in two full-cycle integrated works, at Pernik and, on a larger scale, at Kremikovtsi. A third production facility went into operation at Burgas, in 1988. However, the non-Communist Government was likely to reduce sharply investment in these projects. The food-processing industry, while now constituting a smaller proportion of total industrial production than before the Second

World War, has greatly expanded in absolute terms and supplies both internal needs and many products for export. This industry is concentrated in the upper Thracian plains and in the Danube and Sofia basins. In engineering, the main sector is the manufacture of transport equipment, especially fork-lift trucks, electric cars, mopeds and bicycles; shipbuilding is also important. A wide range of electrical equipment (batteries, electric motors, etc.) is manufactured. Another key area is electronics (calculators, robots, etc.), which earns some export revenue in the West. The chemicals industry produces a wide range of items, from fertilizers to pharmaceuticals, including soap and petrochemicals. Ferrous metallurgy, engineering, electrical equipment and chemicals have together absorbed a high proportion of total investment in the economy (for example, in 1987, it was 43.5%). Garments and textiles too are manufactured, while domestic industry includes the making of carpets.

One of Bulgaria's principal export industries, during the late 1970s and the 1980s, was the computer industry. Bulgaria was the CMEA country which specialized in this area. Its advantages here, however, have dissolved with the dissolution of the CMEA and exposure to the more advanced technologies of the West. By mid-1991 the beleaguered computer industry had not yet attracted significant overseas investment or joint-venture deals.

Another industry under threat from the changes since 1989 was the defence industry. This was mainly a political threat, but also a necessity of the restrictions on government spending. The state budget did not itemize defence spending, which was included in an unspecified remainder; this latter rose from 12.2% of actual spending in 1985, to 15.4% in 1988. It was, nevertheless, accepted that military spending ought to be reduced, and a part of the defence industry was to be converted for civilian manufacture. Output of this type was expected to expand almost three-fold in 1989–95.

Mining and Energy

Bulgaria has similar mineral resources to other Balkan countries, but, on the whole, is less well endowed. Available minerals, such as iron ore, are mostly low-grade. Coal is mainly lignite (a low-grade brown coal), which is of much lower calorific value than hard coal (and causes more pollution). Hard coal is imported, both for fuel and for metallurgical purposes. Bulgaria does have some reserves of anthracite (a high-grade hard coal). There are small amounts of petroleum and natural gas, but import-dependence for each of these is over 90%. Ores of lead-zinc, iron, manganese, chrome, tin, cadmium, copper, molybdenum and silver are mined, but statistics of the amounts extracted of several of these are not published. Small quantities of fluorite and sulphur, among others, are also mined.

Like other Communist countries, Bulgaria obeyed, and exceeded, Lenin's injunctions regarding electrification. It is now admitted, for instance, that it was premature to adopt electric street-lighting. Electricity consumption was restricted after the winter of 1984/85. Other drawbacks were that the building of power stations absorbed much labour and resources, the quality of building declined and guaranteed terms of functioning were merely symbolic. Although electricity generation rose, it continued to be insufficient; a shortage of fuel for popular needs intensified the problem.

Furthermore, among the Eastern European countries, Bulgaria is unusually poorly endowed with energy sources. In 1980, for example, some three-quarters of Bulgaria's energy requirements were imported. Local resources were used increasingly, but their proportionate share tended to decrease. This dependence prompted the development of nuclear power; in 1990 Bulgaria, producing about one-third of its electricity from nuclear power, was the country which was the third-most dependent upon nuclear power in the world. The sole nuclear power station is at Kozlodui (on the Danube). It was under discussion for some time whether a second (also riverine) such station should be built at Belene. However, in May 1990, a study group of the Academy of Sciences, reversing the previous opinion of scholars, opposed this and, in mid-1991, the Government confirmed that the project had been finally abandoned. Doubts were raised about safety at Kozlodui and, in 1990, following local and international pressure, an investigatory commission of the IAEA confirmed these doubts and recommended the plant's closure. Romania expressed particular concern at the implications and, although Bulgaria has no immediate alternatives to substantial reliance on nuclear power, in July 1991, the Bulgarian authorities agreed to close two of the five reactors at Kozlodui. This was to be done with EC aid, which Bulgaria had requested.

Banking

In 1987 the Bulgarian State Bank, which previously monopolized domestic banking operations, was restricted to monetary issue and supervisory functions, while an Economic Bank was established to assume an important share of the financing tasks for domestic industry. The Foreign Trade Bank also continued to exist. Other banks, with sectoral and regional titles, were then established, apparently free to function on commercial lines: they could have branches anywhere, while enterprises could choose between them. Interest rates were raised in May 1990 and were entirely market-determined from 1 January 1991. At several times during 1991 the Popov Government reiterated its intention to maintain high interest rates, in order to counter inflation, and this was supported by the IMF. An agricultural credit bank, with ambitious objectives, was founded in early 1990. Legislation in early 1991 provided for the establishment of banks with foreign capital in Bulgaria.

Tourism

Bulgaria's sunshine, scenery (its appreciation aided by a network of marked mountain routes) and coastline are suited to tourism, which makes a significant contribution (about US $400m. annually) to the balance of payments. In 1989 1.6% of the workforce were employed in tourism, which is a relatively low proportion (in Spain it is 5.7%). There are golden sands, with well-arranged facilities, and picturesque monasteries. However, guiding probably needs to be improved and tourist sites may need more sensitive treatment. Since 1988 Bulgarians have been permitted individually to operate hotels and inns, and, in 1991, a new law on tourism was being prepared. Most foreign visitors were from Turkey (in transit), Yugoslavia or former Eastern bloc countries (particularly Poland), and hence did not spend much per head or bring with them convertible currency. From Western countries, the largest number came from the former West German state, and now probably comes from the united Germany. Visits from Norway and Sweden increased substantially. However, the liberalization of travel for Eastern Europeans is sure to mean that less of them holiday within Eastern Europe.

Western participation in the industry is, nevertheless, increasing. Mitsubishi, a Japanese company, in 1990 signed a contract to manage the five-star hotel chain, Vitosha-New Otani. Traditional ties with France were also being strengthened. Already, in 1990, the foreign exchange earned from tourism rose by about 10%, despite a 20% fall in the number of tourists.

ECONOMIC RESULTS IN 1990 AND 1991

The first consequences of the overthrow of the Zhivkov regime, in the field of economics, were not favourable. During the first half of 1990 output fell by 3,400m. leva, that is, by 9.3%, relative to the same period in 1989. Almost one-half of the fall was because of the lack of raw materials, the rest to a variety of causes, including lack of sales contracts and, to a small extent, to the closure of enterprises because they polluted the environment. Industrial production fell by 10.8%, with machine-building, metalworking, chemicals, petroleum refining and food processing being responsible for more than 80% of the decline. Similarly, during the first nine months of 1990, performance was, in almost all respects, significantly less than in the same period of 1989, with heavy industry again being responsible for most of the decline. Retail trade did rise in value terms, but mainly owing to higher prices: between May and the beginning of October, the cost of living increased by one-quarter. Out of 295 items supplied to the domestic market, 193 were supplied in smaller quantities. The decline in housing construction has been mentioned already. During the first 10 months of 1990 a decrease in agricultural produce, such as corn, sugar or tomatoes, was reported; for example, the head of cows declined by 2.8% and that of ewes by 5.6%. The report of the year's first 10 months may be generalized as having depicted irregular work, a continuous and ubiquitous fall in goods production and something approaching chaos in organization and management.

Supply and Demand: Recent Trends

In Bulgaria, as in other centralized economies, stable prices were generally maintained by increasing budget subsidies; incomes, however, increased, producing a combination which caused suppressed inflation and shortages. Monetary emission continued. In March 1990 the state budget envisaged a deficit of 1,200m. leva, but, in November of that year, this was expected to reach 1,600m. leva and might eventually have reached between 2,500m. and 3,000m. leva. At the end of October 1990 an additional 21,000m. leva were in circulation, the total in circulation reaching 44,370m. leva; the volume of goods and services amounted, at best, to one-third as much. Inflation, in practice, was about 10%. The possibility of a monetary reform was mooted.

There were three underlying reasons for the gravely aggravated supply situation. One is Bulgaria's foreign debt situation, which was aggravated over several years, has been revalued and has now become very serious. There have been the travails of changing from one sort of economic system to another. Finally, there were special difficulties resulting from the Gulf crisis, in 1990–91.

The outcome has been severe shortages of almost every commodity. This entailed enormous queues for what goods were obtainable, a black market thriving unchecked and, eventually, rationing being introduced in Sofia, in September 1990. In December the regulations provided for every child in Sofia, aged from four months to three years, to be assured of 30 small jars of fruit purée and four packets of grain-based food. The situation has been aggravated further by financial and fiscal policies. Turnover tax (the mainstay of the fiscal system in every centralized economy) disguised the extent to which supply and demand were out of balance. Price deregulation (in July 1990 over 40% of prices increased), except in certain categories, where prices were hastily frozen (these last, however, did not include milk and dairy products, which are very important to the Bulgarian diet), intensified the chaos. Another result has been a feverish demand for items which might be smuggled into Bulgaria. At one frontier crossing point, in 1990, there were twice as many attempts at illegal crossing as in the previous year, and the motivation had changed from being political to economic. At the Danube bridge and elsewhere customs authorities have seized, for example, pepper, cigarettes and distributor boxes. In one incident, 300 would-be smugglers halted a train and escaped from security forces into Ruse town.

One of the items in shortest supply has been petrol. At first petrol became more expensive, then it disappeared. Traffic came to a standstill. Following the introduction of rationing, queues at filling stations, previously kilometres long, dwindled overnight, but the black market price reached 5 leva per litre. The most significant causes for the shortage were the Soviet decision to sell petroleum products to the Eastern European countries only in return for convertible currency, from 1 January 1991, and the Gulf crisis. Indirect causes include Bulgaria's foreign debts (see below) and poor endowment with energy resources.

Retail Trade

The retail trade amounted, annually, to some 17,000m. leva. According to official sources, the volume of trade consistently rose from year to year, but, in 1990, this was entirely because of price rises. Since both industrial and agricultural output fell, even the previous level of sales is likely to have been maintained only thanks to higher imports. (Imports of certain consumer goods, such as coffee, did in fact rise.) The larger part (63.7% in 1987) of retail trade consists of non-food items, whose share within the total has risen only very slowly.

Foreign Trade

Foreign trade is among the spheres which are greatly affected by the political and economic changes. Under Communist rule, Bulgaria was distinguished among other Eastern bloc countries by the unusually-large proportions of its foreign trade which were conducted with other CMEA countries and with the USSR in particular. Almost 60% of Bulgaria's foreign trade was with the USSR (for Romania the corresponding percentage was only some 20%). The former German Democratic Republic (GDR) was next, but with only 6%. Bulgaria usually had a negative balance in trade with the developed West but a positive one in trade with developing countries. Industrial goods comprised the largest proportion of the items traded, especially of imports where this share exceeded 90%.

The report of the first nine months of 1990 disclosed falls in Bulgarian exports of 24.3%, and of its imports by 17.1%. The biggest drop was in trade with developed countries, although trade with CMEA countries also declined. Over the first 10 months the drop in exports was about 3,000m. leva (29%).

Foreign Debts and Investments

The Communist regime having concealed the extent of Bulgaria's foreign indebtedness, the background to the pronounced fall in foreign trade was a trade situation that was revealed as much worse than was previously thought. This situation had dramatically worsened since 1984. Whereas until 1985 the country's non-socialist trade balance remained under control, the collapse of petroleum prices, in 1986, dealt a severe blow to Bulgaria's exports to the West, which consisted largely of crude or refined petroleum. The demand for Bulgarian products from petroleum-producing developing countries also fell. It was decided, nevertheless, not to reduce investments envisaged to take place

during 1986–90. Furthermore, a severe drought in 1985 compelled Bulgaria to import food, which it normally exported. As a result, between 1985 and 1989, a negative balance of US $7,000m. was accumulated. Loans from abroad also went mainly towards productive and personal consumption, not to specific projects, while even major projects which did obtain funds brought no return to earning foreign exchange. Even in December 1989 the country still had $1,000m., putting Bulgaria in fourth place among CMEA debtors (after the USSR, Hungary and Poland), but without taking into account those countries' larger populations and resources. As reported in July 1990 Bulgaria was owed money by Iran, Iraq, Ethiopia, Syria, Mozambique and Angola, but these either had no intention of paying or, in the case of Iraq, would become unable to do so. Bulgaria's losses because of the UN decision to place a full economic embargo on Iraq were estimated by the Bulgarians to reach $1,388m.; the crisis put an end to Iraqi deliveries of petroleum to Bulgaria, at a time when Iraq was repaying, in petroleum, the $1,300m. which it owed.

In general, the West's response to the election of the Popov Government, replacing that of Lukanov, in November 1990, was favourable and presaged increased readiness to help. Some aid had already been received from abroad. One credit from France was for purchasing imports for babies, in May 1990. Humanitarian aid was supplied by Greece. Turkey too offered help: as agreed in October 1990, a credit of $50m. towards bilateral trade was to be granted and one of $25m. for investments; Turkey was also to lend fuel to Bulgaria, until the end of 1991. The Netherlands were to finance a free delivery of fodder.

The reaction from international bodies was also favourable. Bulgaria was accepted as a member of the International Monetary Fund (IMF) and of the World Bank, on 25 September 1990, and was to receive an initial credit from them of $350m., with further loans under consideration. From a group of European countries, welcoming Bulgaria's commitment to democratization and to the introduction of a market economy, the country was to be granted 25m.–30m. ECUs in aid; also all restrictions on Bulgarian imports were to be phased out by the end of 1990, five years earlier than originally envisaged. In mid-December 1990 the EC voted to extend emergency aid, with Bulgaria to receive roughly $100m. Bulgaria would also be given access to the EC Tempus programme (for training, attendance at seminars, etc.). In January 1991 the president of the EBRD (see p. 39), Jacques Attali, visited Sofia and promised help. Bulgaria has set up a Foreign Aid Agency to co-ordinate and control aid distribution. Limitations on gifts to individuals of foreign exchange have also been lifted, though application has still to be made to the authorities and a gift tax is payable. Further legislation, in May 1991, indicated Bulgaria's willingness to undertake fundamental reform and this encouraged foreign investment, as well as liberalizing the economy.

Joint ventures with foreign firms (mainly German and Austrian) have been launched, especially in engineering, including robotized welding and the manufacture of refrigerators, and in housing construction. Foreign concessions have been granted for petroleum and natural gas prospecting. German companies were taking an active part in furnishing and supplying department stores. Krupp was to study the Bulgarian economy, with a view to helping enterprises to become more competitive.

Restructuring

The Bulgarian economic system used to closely resemble the classic Soviet one, making allowance for Bulgaria's much smaller size; in particular, the republican division was absent. In response to Soviet *perestroika*, complicated revisions of an analogous kind were announced under Zhivkov, but these, however, did not alter its fundamental essence. More fundamental changes were instituted after 1989.

Considerable measures of decentralization and the dismantling of monopolies were undertaken. In November 1990 the four biggest corporations on the home market (concerning industrial goods; car servicing and spare parts; fish and fish products; and packaging materials) ceased to exist, being divided respectively into 68, 45, 14 and 28 separate units. Bulgarplod (producing fruit and vegetables) has been divided into 67 small firms, while Vinprom (the monopoly producer of wine), Bulgartabak (tobacco) and Bulgarsko Pivo (beer) were to be dealt with in like manner.

Land Ownership

A draft law for privatization of land was announced in May 1990: every citizen was to have the right to own land, though priority lay with the previous owners and their heirs. By November 1990 no legislation had been enacted, the proposals only having had their first reading in parliament. Debates centred on the already-set limit of 30 ha in individual regions. The proposals stated three main principles: the right to the inviolable private ownership of land (for the State and the Church as well); non-interference in farming; and virtually no limits on land ownership, between one and 300 ha. The law was finally enacted in March 1991.

Privatization

Two co-ordinated programmes of privatization of the Bulgarian economy were proposed during the first half of 1990. One of these was prepared by US economists, headed by Dr Robert Rahn, at the invitation of the Bulgarian Government. The first programme worked out general principles, while the second dealt with various points of detail. One of the specific proposals was to establish a customs-free zone along much of the Black Sea coast. However, following the fall of the Lukanov Government these proposals and expertise were no longer available.

One of the most prominent problems was income indexation, with the aim of aiding the socially disadvantaged. An agreement between the Government, the trade unions and businessmen was eventually signed and came into effect on 1 September 1990. It was based on the June consumer prices. In the view of the American experts,

however, indexation would hamper the introduction of a market economy. In general, the same dilemma has been encountered in Bulgaria as elsewhere in Eastern Europe: whether to proceed quickly or slowly in the transition to a market system; the issue was not finally settled in mid-1991.

However, privatization was proceeding in various sectors. As indicated above, one of the necessary steps was the dismantling of large corporations. In August 1990 there were reported to be some 30,000 private companies, although many of these were very small, local businesses. Private production was more difficult to encourage. In October 1990 the first private baker in Sofia for decades was established. A new airline, Air Via, for tourist charters and occasional freight flights, was founded by Balkanbank, Interbalkan and several private individuals. A stock market was to be established (originally it was planned for the end of 1990). Bulgaria's first private bank was formed.

Various obstacles to privatization were being encountered. For instance, many managers, especially of profitable enterprises, considered the new policies an opportunity to convert the enterprise they were responsible for into their own property. Some managers, allegedly, sought to make their enterprises not appear profitable, so as to be able to purchase them at a lower price when they were privatized. This relationship probably goes some way to explaining the poor performance of Bulgarian industry during 1990. However, privatization continues.

Conclusions

The drastic economic reforms of the Bulgarian Government, introduced in early 1991, both surprised and were approved by Western countries. These governments and the international institutions have, therefore, responded to Bulgaria's financial needs. This support, and the experience of other Eastern European nations, aided the implementation of the plans. The stabilization measures have, largely, proved successful in restraining the rate of inflation and reducing price subsidies. The process of the transfer of state enterprises to private ownership is not yet fully underway, however, and there remains the problem of Bulgaria's growing foreign debt. It fell to the new UDF Government of Filip Dimitrov, which took office after the elections of October 1991, to continue these economic reforms, while satisfying the demands of both domestic and international audiences.

Statistical Survey

Source (unless otherwise stated): Central Statistical Office at the
Council of Ministers, Sofia, Panayot Volov St 2; tel. 46-01; telex 22001.

Area and Population

AREA, POPULATION AND DENSITY

Area (sq km)*	110,994†
Population (census results)	
2 December 1975	8,727,771
4 December 1985	
Males	4,433,302
Females	4,515,347
Total	8,948,649
Population (official estimates at 31 December)	
1987	8,976,255
1988	8,986,636
1989	8,992,316
Density (per sq km) at 31 December 1989 . . .	81.0

* Including territorial waters of frontier rivers (261.4 sq km).
† 42,855 sq miles.

ADMINISTRATIVE REGIONS (31 December 1989)*

	Area (sq km)	Estimated population	Density (per sq km)
Sofia (capital)†	1,310.8	1,221,436	931.8
Burgas	14,656.7	875,319	59.7
Khaskovo	13,891.6	1,054,442	75.9
Lovech	15,150.0	1,053,895	69.6
Mikhailovgrad	10,606.9	658,284	62.1
Plovdiv	13,628.1	1,279,381	93.9
Razgrad	10,842.4	848,742	78.3
Sofia†	18,978.5	1,013,875	53.4
Varna	11,928.6	986,942	82.7
Total	110,993.6	8,992,316	81.0

* In August 1987 the State Council issued a decree reorganizing Bulgaria's 28 administrative districts (*okruzhi*) into nine regions (*oblasti*). This decree was repealed by the National Assembly in January 1990.
† The city of Sofia, the national capital, had separate regional status. The area and population of the capital region were not included in the neighbouring Sofia region.

PRINCIPAL TOWNS

(estimated population at 31 December 1989)

Sofia (capital) . .	1,141,537	Stara Zagora . .	162,754
Plovdiv . . .	374,004	Pleven . . .	137,964
Varna . . .	311,123	Tolbukhin* . .	114,377
Burgas (Bourgas) .	203,093	Sliven . . .	111,632
Ruse (Roussé) .	192,659	Shumen . . .	109,761

* The town's former name, Dobrich, was restored in September 1990.

BIRTHS, MARRIAGES AND DEATHS

	Registered live births		Registered marriages*		Registered deaths	
	Number	Rate (per 1,000)	Number	Rate (per 1,000)	Number	Rate (per 1,000)
1982 . .	124,166	13.9	67,154	7.5	100,293	11.2
1983 . .	122,993	13.8	67,032	7.5	102,182	11.4
1984 . .	122,303	13.6	65,361	7.3	101,419	11.3
1985 . .	118,955	13.3	66,682	7.4	107,485	12.0
1986 . .	120,078	13.4	64,965	7.3	104,039	11.6
1987 . .	116,672	13.0	64,429	7.2	107,213	12.0
1988 . .	117,440	13.1	62,617	7.0	107,385	12.0
1989 . .	112,289	12.5	63,263	7.0	106,902	11.9

* Including marriages of Bulgarian nationals outside the country but excluding those of aliens in Bulgaria.

Expectation of Life (years at birth, 1978–80): Males 68.35; Females 73.55.

ECONOMICALLY ACTIVE POPULATION
(persons aged 14 years and over, 1985 census)

	Males	Females	Total
Agriculture and hunting . .	392,781	379,081	771,862
Forestry and fishing . .			
Mining and quarrying . .			
Manufacturing . . . }	949,740	828,019	1,777,759
Electricity, gas and water .			
Construction	328,076	78,643	406,719
Trade, restaurants and hotels	120,624	276,807	397,431
Transport, storage and communications . .	234,637	79,870	314,507
Financing, insurance, real estate and business services .	5,285	19,411	24,696
Community, social and personal services . .	419,797	572,814	992,611
Activities not adequately defined	231	324	555
Total labour force . . .	2,451,171	2,234,969	4,686,140

Source: International Labour Office, *Year Book of Labour Statistics*.

EMPLOYEES IN THE 'SOCIALIZED' SECTOR*
(annual averages, '000)

	1987	1988	1989
Agriculture*	824.3	787.8	701.9
Forestry	25.8	26.8	25.2
Industry†	1,437.5	1,451.0	1,570.4
Construction	362.9	354.3	343.7
Commerce	367.7	358.6	346.2
Transport and storage	260.4	255.7	242.4
Communications	43.7	44.2	44.4
Finance and insurance services	23.2	25.2	25.8
Education and culture	315.6	318.7	319.4
Public health, welfare and sports	206.9	210.7	211.9
Administration	57.9	55.3	53.3
Science and scientific institutes	84.6	89.9	98.3
Housing and community services‡	58.5	62.3	63.6
Total (incl. others)	4,108.5	4,077.6	4,085.2

* Excluding agricultural co-operatives (employing more than 280,000 people in 1975) but including state farms and machine-tractor stations.
† Mining, manufacturing and electricity.
‡ Including water supply.

Agriculture

PRINCIPAL CROPS ('000 metric tons)

	1987	1988	1989
Wheat	4,149	4,743	5,402
Rice (paddy)	53	46	50
Barley	1,091	1,313	1,568
Maize	1,858	1,557	2,421
Rye	49	61	51
Oats	41	53	104
Potatoes	316	358	538
Dry beans	30	29	46
Dry peas	35	46	46
Soybeans	33	17	23
Sunflower seed	410	374	447
Seed cotton	20	13	13
Cabbages	117	126	135
Tomatoes	828	806	850
Pumpkins, squash and gourds	66	69	61
Cucumbers and gherkins	165	155	127
Green chillies and peppers	235	245	197
Dry onions	81	96	110
Green beans	17	15	17
Green peas	18	20	21
Water-melons	362	318	79
Grapes	943	922	754
Apples	339	334	398
Pears	74	73	73
Plums	103	139	139
Peaches and nectarines	58	63	97
Apricots	18	35	44
Strawberries	13	15	17
Sugar beets	736	626	912
Tobacco leaves	133	116	125*

* Unofficial figure.
Source: FAO, *Production Yearbook*.

LIVESTOCK ('000 head at 1 January each year)

	1987	1988	1989
Horses	121	123	122
Asses	341	333	329
Cattle	1,678	1,649	1,613
Pigs	4,050	4,034	4,119
Sheep	9,563	8,886	8,609
Goats	441	428	434
Buffaloes	26	24	23
Poultry	39,735	41,424	41,000*

* FAO estimate.

LIVESTOCK PRODUCTS (metric tons)

	1987	1988	1989
Beef and veal	127,000	120,000	121,000
Buffalo meat	2,000	2,000	2,000
Mutton and lamb	74,000	65,000	72,000
Goats' meat	6,000	5,000	6,000
Pigmeat	372,000	394,000	413,000
Poultry meat	169,000	183,000	198,000*
Edible offals	106,000	107,000	112,000
Cow milk	2,181,000	2,168,000	2,126,000
Buffalo milk	19,000	18,000	17,000
Sheep milk	309,000	305,000	285,000
Goat milk	81,000	79,000	64,000
Butter	26,257	23,691	21,420
Cheese (all kinds)	186,594	195,134	192,300
Hen eggs	158,403	153,420	150,000†
Other poultry eggs	2,696	1,156	1,120†
Honey	10,463	10,553	8,645
Raw silk	184	165†	160†
Wool: greasy	31,550	30,654	27,258
scoured	15,332	14,900	13,200
Cattle and buffalo hides†	20,200	19,100	20,900
Sheep skins†	35,800	25,500	26,000

* Unofficial figure.   † FAO estimates.
Source: FAO, mainly *Production Yearbook*.

Forestry

ROUNDWOOD REMOVALS
('000 cubic metres, state forests only)

	1986	1987	1988
Sawlogs, veneer logs and logs for sleepers	1,056	1,040	1,101
Pulpwood	553	575	625
Other industrial wood	1,108	1,059	935
Fuel wood	1,749	1,764	1,810
Total	4,466	4,438	4,471

Source: FAO, *Yearbook of Forest Products*.

SAWNWOOD PRODUCTION ('000 cubic metres, incl. boxboards)

	1986	1987	1988
Coniferous (soft wood)	974	1,097	1,003
Broadleaved (hard wood)	396	372	315
Total	1,370	1,469	1,318

Railway sleepers ('000 cubic metres): 23 in 1986; 21 in 1987; 24 in 1988.
Source: FAO, *Yearbook of Forest Products*.

Fishing

('000 metric tons, live weight)

	1986	1987	1988
Common carp	10.4	10.0	9.5
Southern blue whiting	10.7	7.8	2.2
Patagonian grenadier	0.8	9.6	33.6
Beaked redfish	11.4	12.3	8.8
Cape horse mackerel	48.5	49.4	43.8
European sprat	11.7	11.0	6.2
Other fishes (incl. unspecified)	8.3	7.2	9.0
Total fish	101.7	107.3	113.1
Crustaceans and molluscs	7.6	3.4	4.0
Total catch	109.3	110.7	117.1
Inland waters	14.1	12.9	12.2
Mediterranean and Black Seas	13.0	12.2	8.2
Atlantic Ocean	82.2	85.7	96.6

Source: FAO, *Yearbook of Fishery Statistics.*

Mining

('000 metric tons, unless otherwise indicated)

	1986	1987	1988
Anthracite	80	71	65
Other hard coal	127	127	131
Lignite	29,896	31,401	29,189
Other brown coal	5,119	5,220	4,762
Iron ore*	661	559	528
Copper ore*†	80	80	80
Lead ore*†	97	95	90
Zinc ore*†	70	68	65
Manganese ore*	11.2	10.9	9.9
Salt (refined)	91	92	94
Crude petroleum‡	300	290	290
Natural gas ('000 terajoules)	4	5	5

* Figures relate to the metal content of ores.
† Source: Metallgesellschaft Aktiengesellschaft (Frankfurt am Main).
‡ UN estimate.

Sources: UN, *Industrial Statistics Yearbook; Bulgarian Statistical Yearbook 1989.*

1989 ('000 metric tons): Anthracite 63; Lignite 29,509; Other brown coal 4,596; Iron ore (metal content) 483; Manganese ore (gross weight) 32; Salt (refined) 93. Source: *Bulgarian Statistical Yearbook 1990.*

Industry

SELECTED PRODUCTS
('000 metric tons, unless otherwise indicated)

	1987	1988	1989
Refined sugar	416	361	351
Wine ('000 hectolitres)	3,909	3,468	n.a.
Beer ('000 hectolitres)	6,212.0	6,331.6	6,719.7
Cigarettes and cigars (metric tons)	90,326	89,219	85,750
Cotton yarn (metric tons)[1]	88,094	85,717	82,507
Woven cotton fabrics ('000 metres)[2]	353,418	361,384	357,275
Flax and hemp yarn (metric tons)	8,185	8,225	7,610
Wool yarn (metric tons)[1]	41,002	38,205	35,676
Woven woollen fabrics ('000 metres)[2]	43,773	34,417	33,902
Woven fabrics of man-made fibres ('000 metres)[3]	38,062	32,024	33,410
Leather footwear ('000 pairs)	25,041	26,437	27,468
Rubber footwear ('000 pairs)	8,725	8,606	8,072

—continued	1987	1988	1989
Chemical wood pulp	158.3	168.4	166.6
Paper	366.6	395.9	378.5
Paperboard	68.2	70.9	50.1
Rubber tyres ('000)[4]	1,856.6	1,693.4	1,762.0
Sulphuric acid (100%)	688.5	839.9	846.4
Caustic soda (96%)	108.6	134.2	132.6
Soda ash (98%)	1,070.2	1,100.0	1,153.0
Nitrogenous fertilizers (metric tons)[5]	804,992	956,270	926,046
Phosphate fertilizers (metric tons)[5]	127,962	178,550	168,753
Soap (metric tons)	28,901	26,470	28,005
Coke (gas and coke-oven)	1,314	1,457	1,561
Unworked glass—rectangles ('000 sq metres)	20,273	18,400	16,100
Clay building bricks (million)	1,051	1,049	1,089
Cement	5,494	5,535	5,036
Pig-iron and ferro-alloys	1,706	1,484	1,523
Crude steel	3,045	2,875	2,899
Tractors—10 h.p. and over (number)	4,751	5,309	4,956
Metal-working lathes (number)	4,886	4,953	5,438
Cranes (number)	1,351	1,456	1,688
Fork-lift trucks (number)[6]	85,110	82,485	n.a.
Refrigerators—household (number)	110,530	110,570	101,001
Washing machines—household (number)	171,728	168,923	177,203
Radio receivers (number)	56,090	50,311	52,092
Television receivers (number)	198,592	181,165	185,369
Construction: dwellings completed (number)[7]	63,640	62,785	40,538
Electric energy (million kWh)	43,470	45,036	n.a.

[1] Pure and mixed yarn. Figures for wool include yarn of man-made staple.
[2] Pure and mixed fabrics, after undergoing finishing processes.
[3] Finished fabrics, including fabrics of natural silk.
[4] Tyres for road motor vehicles (passenger cars and commercial vehicles).
[5] Figures for nitrogenous fertilizers are in terms of nitrogen, and for phosphate fertilizers in terms of phosphoric acid. Data for nitrogenous fertilizers include urea.
[6] Including hoisting gears.
[7] Including restorations and conversions.

Finance

CURRENCY AND EXCHANGE RATES

Monetary Units
100 stotinki (singular: stotinka) = 1 lev (plural: leva).

Denominations
Coins: 1, 2, 5, 10, 20 and 50 stotinki; 1, 2 and 5 leva.
Notes: 1, 2, 5, 10 and 20 leva.

Sterling and Dollar Equivalents (30 June 1991)
£1 sterling = 29.63 leva;
US $1 = 18.30 leva;
1,000 leva = £33.75 = $54.64.

Note: The foregoing information refers to non-commercial exchange rates, applicable to tourism. For the purposes of external trade, the average value of the lev was: US $1.1999 in 1988; US $1.1856 in 1989; US $1.2703 in 1990.

STATE BUDGET (million leva)

Revenue	1986	1987*	1988*
National economy . . .	20,384.8	19,011.8	21,109.0
Other receipts	1,622.7	1,661.0	1,843.0
Total	22,007.5	20,672.8	22,952.0

Expenditure	1986	1987*	1988*
National economy . . .	11,377.6	9,590.1	10,842.0
Education, health, science, art and culture	3,736.8	3,884.1	4,304.0
Social security† . . .	3,631.7	3,726.9	3,914.0
Administration . . . }	3,163.6 {	336.9	355.0
Other expenditure . . }		3,124.8	3,537.0
Total	21,909.7	20,662.8	22,952.0

* Approved budget proposals.
† Including the pension fund for agricultural co-operatives.
1989 (forecasts, million leva): Revenue 24,287.8; Expenditure 24,286.3.
1990 (forecasts, million leva): Revenue 24,894; Expenditure 25,851.

COST OF LIVING
(Consumer Price Index; base: 1980 = 100)

	1987	1988	1989
Food	114.6	117.2	119.4
Others	126.7	129.8	142.6
All items	121.2	124.1	132.0

NATIONAL ACCOUNTS
Net Material Product* (million leva at current market prices)

Activities of the Material Sphere	1987	1988	1989
Agriculture and livestock . .	3,712.1	3,712.0	3,798.2
Forestry†	107.9	108.2	90.3
Industry‡	16,649.7	17,088.3	17,624.5
Construction	2,674.7	2,780.3	2,859.1
Trade, restaurants, etc.§ .	2,499.8	2,471.2	2,910.3
Transport and storage . .	1,567.6	2,069.1	2,224.6
Communications . . .	490.6	527.3	570.5
Other activities† . . .	635.6	666.2	762.2
Total	28,338.0	29,422.6	30,839.7

* Defined as the total net value of goods and 'productive' services, including turnover taxes, produced by the economy. This excludes economic activities not contributing directly to material production, such as public administration, defence and personal and professional services.
† Beginning in 1986, forestry includes non-organized hunting and fishing, previously included in other activities.
‡ Principally manufacturing, mining, electricity, gas and water supply. The figures also include the value of hunting, fishing and logging when these activities are organized.
§ Includes material and technical supply.

External Trade

PRINCIPAL COMMODITIES (million foreign exchange leva)

Imports f.o.b.	1986	1987	1988
Machinery and equipment . .	5,371.3	5,582.5	5,794.7
Power and electro-technical machinery	689.0	542.0	478.4
Mining, metallurgical and oil-drilling equipment . .	314.6	436.5	291.4
Tractors and agricultural machinery	334.8	378.3	441.4
Fuels, mineral raw materials and metals	6,306.7	5,701.0	5,108.2
Solid fuels	489.4	445.6	374.4
Ferrous metals . . .	911.3	896.0	854.7
Chemicals, fertilizers and rubber	647.1	704.3	755.1
Chemicals	297.9	351.6	399.3
Agricultural crop and livestock crude materials (except foods)	635.0	663.5	748.7
Timber, cellulose and paper products	231.7	236.8	225.7
Textile raw materials and semi-manufactures . .	180.9	183.3	248.3
Raw materials for food production	471.6	412.4	431.0
Other industrial goods for consumption	580.2	656.4	709.3
Commodities for cultural purposes	165.9	153.9	155.4
Total (incl. others) . . .	14,353.3	14,067.3	13,928.0

1989 (million leva): Machinery and equipment 5,459.1; Fuels, mineral raw materials and metals 4,494.7; Chemicals, fertilizers and rubber 639.1; Agricultural crop and livestock crude materials (except foods) 671.1; Raw materials for food production 510.7; Other industrial goods for consumption 668.8; Total (incl. others) 12,795.8.

Exports f.o.b.*	1986	1987	1988
Machinery and equipment . .	7,719.8	8,359.6	8,723.7
Power and electro-technical machinery	620.2	659.9	627.5
Hoisting and hauling equipment	1,361.3	1,449.8	1,436.6
Agricultural machinery . .	273.0	269.7	244.5
Fuels, mineral raw materials and metals	1,071.3	980.8	1,010.2
Ferrous metals	353.6	367.9	463.7
Chemicals, fertilizers and rubber	443.8	420.5	492.8
Chemicals	278.7	248.8	341.6
Building materials and components	271.0	258.2	273.3
Agricultural crop and livestock crude materials (except foods)	181.9	211.5	234.1
Raw materials for food production (incl. tobacco). .	334.0	346.8	349.2
Foodstuffs, beverages and tobacco products. . .	1,759.7	1,674.6	1,688.6
Meat and dairy products, animal fats and eggs . .	249.0	229.5	251.1
Wine, brandy and spirits. .	306.3	293.5	301.7
Cigarettes	670.8	673.6	672.4
Other industrial goods for consumption	1,434.7	1,460.2	1,541.7
Clothing and underwear . .	313.3	301.4	310.0
Total (incl. others)	13,350.5	13,802.0	14,417.4

* Figures include foreign aid and loans, and exports of ships' stores and bunkers for foreign vessels.

1989 (million leva): Machinery and equipment 8,126.0; Fuels, mineral raw materials and metals 1,048.0; Chemicals, fertilizers and rubber 470.8; Building materials and components 273.3; Agricultural crop and livestock crude materials (except foods) 246.1; Raw materials for food production (incl. tobacco) 302.0; Foodstuffs, beverages and tobacco products 1,592.0; Other industrial goods for consumption 1,517.5; Total (incl. others) 13,672.9.

PRINCIPAL TRADING PARTNERS*
(million foreign exchange leva)

Imports f.o.b.	1987	1988	1989
Austria	218.4	219.5	193.4
Cuba	252.3	172.3	220.0
Czechoslovakia	697.1	751.7	630.2
France	98.7	94.8	131.0
German Democratic Republic	804.2	818.0	738.0
Germany, Federal Republic	694.9	686.1	633.1
Hungary	285.3	265.3	172.4
Italy	164.6	156.3	185.0
Japan	145.1	156.7	167.0
Libya	135.7	92.9	181.5
Poland	669.9	691.6	608.6
Romania	306.5	288.6	240.3
Switzerland	192.7	192.3	212.8
USSR	8,056.1	7,453.8	6,767.0
United Kingdom	161.6	134.8	146.7
USA	91.8	123.8	185.9
Yugoslavia	105.0	136.6	112.4
Total (incl. others)	14,067.3	13,928.0	12,795.8

Exports f.o.b.	1987	1988	1989
Cuba	199.1	258.5	184.5
Czechoslovakia	673.4	665.6	594.2
German Democratic Republic	756.9	749.9	752.4
Germany, Federal Republic	159.7	142.4	184.3
Greece	140.3	136.3	177.2
Hungary	254.0	295.2	187.8
Iraq	394.8	396.2	136.0
Italy	82.5	103.5	88.6
Libya	469.1	328.1	184.0
Poland	598.1	593.0	525.3
Romania	287.5	294.8	276.7
Switzerland	131.8	113.6	141.0
USSR	8,437.3	9,006.5	8,917.9
United Kingdom	75.9	97.4	117.2
Total (incl. others)	13,802.0	14,417.4	13,672.9

* Imports by country of purchase; exports by country of sale.

Transport

RAILWAYS (traffic)

	1987	1988	1989
Passenger-kilometres (million)	8,075	8,143	7,601
Freight ton-kilometres (million)	17,842	17,585	17,034

INLAND WATERWAYS (traffic)

	1987	1988	1989
Passenger-kilometres (million)	17	12	12
Freight ton-kilometres (million)	1,971	2,162	1,946

SEA-BORNE SHIPPING
(international and coastal traffic)

	1987	1988	1989
Passengers carried ('000)	460	464	392
Freight ('000 metric tons)	25,888	24,001	25,517

CIVIL AVIATION (traffic)

	1987	1988	1989
Passenger-kilometres (million)	3,578	3,897	3,876
Freight ton-kilometres (million)	42	45	39

Tourism

VISITORS TO BULGARIA BY COUNTRY OF ORIGIN

	1987	1988	1989
Austria*	53,828	56,082	55,701
Czechoslovakia	398,053	425,934	386,593
France	32,872	34,857	32,760
German Democratic Republic	283,329	309,833	306,133
Germany, Federal Republic*	267,891	276,458	236,887
Greece	149,888	155,313	205,866
Hungary	243,163	246,561	628,329
Iran*	42,887	43,197	37,118
Italy	23,624	25,041	30,614
Poland	746,644	922,352	887,317
Romania	193,034	221,928	265,036
Sweden	28,185	27,549	26,364
Turkey*	2,949,674	3,230,528	2,970,788
USSR	384,054	471,560	552,561
United Kingdom	74,897	89,521	96,592
Yugoslavia	1,436,384	1,454,812	1,221,995
Total (incl. others)	7,593,637	8,294,985	8,220,860

* Mainly visitors in transit, totalling 3,904,816 (of whom 2,946,667 came from Turkey) in 1989.

Communications Media

	1987	1988	1989
Telephone subscribers	2,228,681	2,386,462	2,515,141
Radio licences	1,982,929	1,965,117	1,941,212
Television licences	1,692,411	1,679,777	1,662,558
Book production:			
Titles*	4,583	4,379	4,543
Copies ('000)*	60,078	58,943	57,987

* Figures include pamphlets (797 titles and 9,897,000 copies in 1987; 689 titles and 7,197,000 copies in 1988; 797 titles and 7,950,000 copies in 1989).

1988: Daily newspapers 20 (average circulation 2,396,000 copies); Non-daily newspapers (incl. regional editions) 352 (average circulation 4,335,000 copies); Other periodicals 994 (average circulation 6,091,000 copies). Source: UNESCO, *Statistical Yearbook*.

Education

(1988/89)

	Institutions	Teachers	Students
Kindergartens	4,666	28,897	339,891
Unified secondary polytechnical	3,516	73,794	1,234,851
Special	129	2,404	16,587
Vocational technical	3	50	1,586
Secondary vocational technical	262	7,101	107,964
Technical colleges and schools of arts	265	11,138	124,953
Technical colleges after secondary level	10	512	7,120
Semi-higher institutes (teacher training)	16	868	11,377
Higher educational	30	17,759	126,964

Source: Ministry of Education, Sofia.

Directory

The Constitution

Bulgaria was a monarchy, but, on 15 September 1946, Tsar Simeon II was declared deposed. In 1947 a new Constitution declared Bulgaria to be a People's Republic. The Bulgarian Communist Party was to be the leading force in society and the State. This principle was reiterated in the Constitution of 1971, but abandoned during 1990, when many other amendments were made. In June 1990 the Seventh Grand National Assembly was elected, to draw up a new constitution. The Constitution of the Republic of Bulgaria, summarized below, took effect upon its promulgation, on 13 July 1991, following its enactment the previous day. Transitional arrangements included provision for the interim government of the country and for the constituent Grand National Assembly to act as the legislature until a general election was held.

FUNDAMENTAL PRINCIPLES

Chapter One declares that the Republic of Bulgaria is to have a parliamentary form of government, with all state power derived from the people. The rule of law and the life, dignity and freedom of the individual are guaranteed. The Constitution is the supreme law; the power of the State is shared between the legislative, the executive and the judiciary. The Constitution upholds principles such as political and religious freedom (no party may be formed on separatist, ethnic or religious lines, however), free economic initiative and respect for international law.

FUNDAMENTAL RIGHTS AND OBLIGATIONS OF CITIZENS

Chapter Two establishes the basic provisions for Bulgarian citizenship and fundamental human rights, such as the rights of privacy and movement, the freedoms of expression, assembly and association, and the enfranchisement of Bulgarian citizens aged over 18 years. The Constitution commits the State to the provision of basic social welfare and education and to the encouragement of culture, science and the health of the population. The study and use of the Bulgarian language is required. Other obligations of the citizenry include military service and the payment of taxes.

THE NATIONAL ASSEMBLY

The National Assembly is the legislature of Bulgaria and exercises parliamentary control over the country. It consists of 240 Members, elected for a four-year term. Only Bulgarian citizens aged over 21 years (who do not hold a state post or another citizenship and are not under judicial interdiction or in prison) are eligible for election to parliament. A Member of the National Assembly ceases to serve as a deputy while holding ministerial office. The National Assembly is a permanently-acting body, which is free to determine its own recesses and elects its own Chairman and Vice-Chairmen. The Chairman represents and convenes the National Assembly, organizes its proceedings, attests its enactments and promulgates its resolutions.

The National Assembly may function when more than one-half of its Members are present, and may pass legislation and other acts by a majority of more than one-half of the present Members, except where a qualified majority is required by the Constitution. Ministers are free to, and can be obliged to, attend parliamentary sessions. The most important functions of the legislature are: the enactment of laws; the approval of the state budget; the scheduling of presidential elections; the election and dismissal of the Prime Minister and the Council of Ministers; the declaration of war or conclusion of peace; the foreign deployment of troops; and the ratification of any fundamental international instruments agreed to by the Republic of Bulgaria. The laws and resolutions of the National Assembly are binding on all state bodies and citizens. All enactments must be promulgated in the official gazette, *Durzhaven Vestnik*, within 15 days of their passage through the legislature.

THE PRESIDENT OF THE REPUBLIC

Chapter Four concerns the head of state, the President of the Republic of Bulgaria, who is assisted by a Vice-President. The President and Vice-President are elected jointly, directly by the voters, for a period of five years. A candidate must be eligible for election to the National Assembly, but also aged over 40 years and a resident of the country for the five years previous to the election. To be elected, a candidate must receive more than one-half of the valid votes cast, in an election in which more than one-half of the eligible electorate participated. If necessary, a second ballot must then be conducted, contested by the two candidates who received the most votes. The one who receives more votes becomes President. The President and Vice-President may hold the same office for only two terms and, during this time, may not engage in any unsuitable or potentially compromising activities. If the President resigns, is incapacitated, impeached or dies, the Vice-President carries out the presidential duties. If neither official can perform their duties, the Chairman of the National Assembly assumes the prerogatives of the Presidency, until new elections take place.

The President's main responsibilities include the scheduling of elections and referendums, the conclusion of international treaties and the promulgation of laws. The President is responsible for appointing a Prime Minister-designate (priority must be given to the leaders of the two largest parties represented in the National Assembly), who must then attempt to form a government.

The President is Supreme Commander-in-Chief of the Armed Forces of the Republic of Bulgaria and presides over the Consultative National Security Council. The President has certain emergency powers, usually subject to the later approval of the National Assembly. Many of the President's actions must be approved by the Prime Minister. The President may return legislation to the National Assembly for further consideration, but can be over-ruled.

THE COUNCIL OF MINISTERS

The principal organ of executive government is the Council of Ministers, which supervises the implementation of state policy and the state budget, the administration of the country and the Armed Forces, and the maintenance of law and order. The Council of Ministers is headed and co-ordinated by the Prime Minister, who is responsible for the overall policy of government. The Council of Ministers, which also includes Deputy Prime Ministers and Ministers, must resign upon the death of the Prime Minister or if the National Assembly votes in favour of a motion of 'no confidence' in it or in the Prime Minister.

JUDICIAL POWER

The judicial branch of government is independent. All judicial power is exercised in the name of the people. Individuals and legal entities are guaranteed basic rights, such as the right to contest administrative acts or the right to legal counsel. One of the principal organs is the Supreme Court of Cassation, which exercises supreme judicial responsibility for the precise and equal application of the law by all courts. The Supreme Administrative Court rules on all challenges to the legality of acts of any organ of government. The Chief Prosecutor supervises all other prosecutors and ensures that the law is observed, by initiating court actions and ensuring the enforcement of penalties, etc.

The Supreme Judicial Council is responsible for appointments within the ranks of the justices, prosecutors and investigating magistrates, and recommends to the President of the Republic the appointment or dismissal of the Chairmen of the two Supreme Courts and of the Chief Prosecutor (they are each appointed for a single, seven-year term). These last three officials are, *ex officio*, members of the Supreme Judicial Council, together with 22 others, who must be practising lawyers of high integrity and at least 15 years of professional experience. These members are elected for a term of five years, 11 of them by the National Assembly and 11 by bodies of the judiciary. The Supreme Judicial Council is chaired by the Minister of Justice, who is not entitled to vote.

LOCAL SELF-GOVERNMENT AND LOCAL ADMINISTRATION

Chapter Seven provides for the division of Bulgaria into regions and municipalities. Municipalities are the basic administrative territorial unit at which local self-government is practised; their principal organ is the municipal council, which is elected directly by the population for a term of four years. The council elects the mayor, who is the principal organ of executive power. Bulgaria is also divided into regions (nine in 1991, including the capital). Regional government, which is entrusted to regional governors (appointed by the Council of Ministers) and administrations, is responsible for regional policy, the implementation of state policy at a local level and the harmonization of local and national interests.

THE CONSTITUTIONAL COURT

The Constitutional Court consists of 12 justices, four of whom are elected by the National Assembly, four appointed by the President of the Republic and four elected by the justices of the two

Supreme Courts. Candidates must have the same eligibility as for membership of the Supreme Judicial Council. They serve a single term of nine years, but a part of the membership changes every three years. A Chairman is elected by a secret ballot of the members.

The Constitutional Court provides binding interpretations of the Constitution. It rules on the constitutionality of: laws and decrees; competence suits between organs of government; international agreements; national and presidential elections; and impeachments. A ruling of the Court requires a majority of more than one-half of the votes of all the justices.

CONSTITUTIONAL AMENDMENTS AND THE ADOPTION OF A NEW CONSTITUTION

Chapter Nine provides for constitutional changes. Except for those provisions reserved to the competence of a Grand National Assembly, the National Assembly is empowered to amend the Constitution with a majority of three-quarters of all its Members, in three ballots on three different days. Amendments must be proposed by one-quarter of the parliamentary membership or by the President. In some cases, a majority of two-thirds of all the Members of the National Assembly will suffice.

Grand National Assembly

A Grand National Assembly consists of 400 members, elected by the generally-established procedure. It alone is empowered to adopt a new constitution, to sanction territorial changes to the Republic of Bulgaria, to resolve on any changes in the form of state structure or form of government, and to enact amendments to certain parts of the existing Constitution (concerning the direct application of the Constitution, the domestic application of international agreements, the irrevocable nature of fundamental civil rights and of certain basic individual rights even in times of emergency or war, and amendments to Chapter Nine itself).

Any bill requiring the convening of a Grand National Assembly must be introduced by the President of the Republic or by one-third of the Members of the National Assembly. A decision to hold elections for a Grand National Assembly must be supported by two-thirds of the Members of the National Assembly. Enactments of the Grand National Assembly require a majority of two-thirds of the votes of all the Members, in three ballots on three different days. A Grand National Assembly may resolve only on the proposals for which it was elected, whereupon its prerogatives normally expire.

COAT OF ARMS, SEAL, FLAG, ANTHEM, CAPITAL

The coat of arms of the Republic of Bulgaria depicts a gold lion rampant on a dark gules (red) shield, and this is used on the state seal. The national flag is a tricolour of, from the top, white, green and red, placed horizontally. The use of these symbols is regulated by law. The national anthem is the song *Mila Rodino* and the capital is the City of Sofia.

The Government

(January 1992)

HEAD OF STATE

President: ZHELIU ZHELEV (elected 1 August 1990; re-elected, in direct elections, 19 January 1992).
Vice-President: BLAÇA NIKOLOVA DIMITROVA.

COUNCIL OF MINISTERS

The Council of Ministers is composed of members of the Union of Democratic Forces (UDF) and Independents (Ind.).
Chairman (Prime Minister): FILIP DIMITROV (UDF).
Deputy Chairman (Deputy Prime Minister) and Minister of Foreign Affairs: STOYAN GANEV (UDF).
Deputy Chairman (Deputy Prime Minister) and Minister of Education and Science: NIKOLAI VASILEV (UDF).
Minister of Finance: IVAN KOSTOV (UDF).
Minister of Industry and Technologies: IVAN PUSHKAROV (UDF).
Minister of Transport: ALEKSANDUR ALEKSANDROV (UDF).
Minister of Justice: SVETOSLAV LUCHNIKOV (Ind.).
Minister of Defence: DIMITUR LUDZHEV (UDF).
Minister of Internal Affairs: YORDAN SOKOLOV (Ind.).
Minister of Agriculture: STANISLAV DIMITROV (UDF).
Minister of the Environment: VALENTIN VASILEV (Ind.).
Minister of Labour and Social Affairs: VEKIL VANOV (Ind.).
Minister of Health: NIKOLA VASILEV (Ind.).
Minister of Culture: Dr ELKA KONSTANTINOVA (UDF).

Minister of Regional Development, Housing and Construction: NIKOLA KARADIMOV (Ind.).

MINISTRIES

Council of Ministers: 1000 Sofia, Blvd Dondukov 1; tel. (2) 85-01.
Ministry of Agriculture: 1040 Sofia, Blvd Botev 55; tel. (2) 85-31.
Ministry of Culture: 1000 Sofia, Blvd Stamboliiski 17; tel. (2) 86-111.
Ministry of Defence: 1000 Sofia, Aksakov St 1; tel. (2) 54-60-01.
Ministry of Education and Science: 1540 Sofia, Blvd A. Stamboliiski 18; tel. (2) 84-81; telex 22384; fax (2) 87-12-89.
Ministry of the Environment: 1000 Sofia, ul. William Gladstone 67; tel. (2) 87-61-51; telex 22145; fax (2) 52-16-34.
Ministry of Finance: 1000 Sofia, Rakovski St 102; tel. (2) 87-06-22.
Ministry of Foreign Affairs: 1000 Sofia, Al. Zhendov St 2; tel. (2) 41-441; telex 22530.
Ministry of Health: 1000 Sofia, pl. Sveta Nedelya 5; tel. (2) 86-31.
Ministry of Industry and Technologies: 1000 Sofia, Slavyanska St 8; tel. (2) 87-07-41.
Ministry of Internal Affairs: 1000 Sofia, ul. Shesti Septemvri 11; tel. (2) 82-25-74.
Ministry of Justice: 1000 Sofia, Blvd Dondukov 2; tel. (2) 86-01; telex 23822; fax (2) 767-32-26.
Ministry of Labour and Social Affairs: 1000 Sofia, Triaditza St 2; tel. (2) 86-01; telex 23173.
Ministry of Regional Development, Housing and Construction: Sofia.
Ministry of Science and Higher Education: 1574 Sofia, A. Chapaev St 55; tel. (2) 7-35-41.
Ministry of Transport: 1000 Sofia, Levski St 9–11; tel. (2) 87-10-81; telex 23200; fax (2) 88-50-94.

Legislature

NARODNO SOBRANIYE
(National Assembly)

Chairman: Acad. NIKOLAI TODOROV.
Deputy Chairmen: IVAN GLUSHKOV, GINYO GANEV, NIKODIM POPOV.

General election, 13 October 1991

Parties and Groups	Votes	% of votes	Seats*
Union of Democratic Forces (UDF)	1,903,567	34.36	110
Bulgarian Socialist Party (BSP)†	1,836,050	33.14	106
Movement for Rights and Freedoms (MRF)	418,168	7.55	24
Bulgarian Agrarian Union (BAU)	214,052	3.86	—
Bulgarian Agrarian Union—Nikola Petkov	190,454	3.44	—
UDF—Centre	177,295	3.20	—
UDF—Liberals	155,902	2.81	—
Others	645,349	11.65	—
Total	**5,540,837**	**100.00**	**240**

* Seats were allocated according to the D'Hondt system of proportional representation.
† The BSP contested the election in alliance with the Bulgarian Liberal Party (BLP), the Fatherland Party of Labour (FPL), the Christian Women's Movement (CWM), the Christian Republican Party (CRP) and several other minor parties.

Local Government

The 1991 Constitution provides for the division of Bulgaria into municipalities and regions. At mid-1991 Bulgaria was still divided into nine regions, administered by People's Councils. Temporary executive committees were appointed to conduct regional affairs until local elections could be held (scheduled for October 1991).

Capital People's Council: 1000 Sofia; tel. (2) 85-21; Chair. of Temporary Exec. Cttee ALEKSANDUR KARAKACHANOV.

Burgas Region People's Council: 8000 Burgas; tel. (56) 4-53-31; Chair. NEDELCHO PANDEV.

Haskovo Region People's Council: 6300 Haskovo; tel. (38) 21-21; Chair. IVAN DRAGANOV.

Lovech Region People's Council: 5500 Lovech; tel. (68) 2-22-01; Chair. MLADEN MLADENOV.

Mikhailovgrad Region People's Council: 3400 Mikhailovgrad; tel. (96) 24-31; Chair. GEORGUI MARKOV.

Plovdiv Region People's Council: 4000 Plovdiv; tel. (32) 22-22-05; Chair. TRIFON MIRCHEV.

Razgrad Region People's Council: 7200 Razgrad; tel. (84) 2-68-10; Chair. PETUR ATANASOV.

Sofia Region People's Council: 1000 Sofia; tel. (2) 85-171; Chair. NIKOLAI NIKOLOV.

Varna Region People's Council: 9000 Varna; tel. (52) 2-12-51; Chair. GEORGUI TSENOV.

Political Organizations

Bulgarian Agrarian People's Union—Nikola Petkov (BAPU—NP) (Bulgarski Zemedelski Naroden Soyuz 'Nikola Petkov'—BZNS): 1000 Sofia, Blvd Dondukov 39; tel. (2) 39-01-94; f. 1989; retained name after some mems joined BAPU—United in 1991; left UDF coalition in 1991; Leader MILAN DRENCHEV.

Bulgarian Agrarian People's Union—United (BAPU) (Bulgarski Zemedelski Naroden Soyuz—BZNS): 1000 Sofia, Yanko Zabunov St 1; tel. (2) 88-19-51; telex 23302; fax (2) 80-09-91; f. 1991 by reuniting of three Agrarian parties, the official BAPU (f. 1899; in ruling coalition 1946–89), some mems of the Nikola Petkov BAPU (re-formed 1989, mem. of UDF) and the small BAPU 'Vrabcha 1'; Chair. TSENKO BAREV.

Bulgarian Communist Party (Bulgarska Komunisticheska Partiya): 1404 Sofia, Mladeshki Prokhod Blvd 5B; tel. (2) 59-16-73; f. 1990 by former, conservative mems of the previous, ruling Bulgarian Communist Party (now the Bulgarian Socialist Party); First Sec. of the Central Cttee VLADIMIR SPASSOV.

Bulgarian Socialist Party—BSP (Bulgarska Sotsialisticheska Partiya): Sofia, POB 382, pl. Aleksandur Battenberg; tel. (2) 84-01; fax (2) 87-12-92; f. 1891 as the Bulgarian Social Democratic Party (BSDP); renamed the Bulgarian Communist Party (BCP) in 1919; absorbed the remaining BSDP in 1947; renamed as above in 1990; 560,000 mems (May 1991); Chair. of Supreme Council ALEKSANDUR LILOV; Deputy Chair. ALEKSANDUR TOMOV, CHAVDAR KYURANOV, DIMITUR YONCHEV, LYUBOMIR KIUCHUKOV, APOSTOL DIMITROV; Pres. of the All-Party Control Commission DEYAN RIZOV.

Christian Republican Party: 1606 Sofia, POB 113; tel. (2) 52-24-06; f. 1989; Chair. KONSTANTIN ADZHAROV.

Confederation—Kingdom Bulgaria ('Tsarstvo Bulgaria'): 7000 Ruse, Vassil Kolarov 45; tel. (82) 2-99-64; f. 1990; advocates the restoration of the former Tsar, Simeon II; Chair. GEORGUI BAK-ARDZHIEV.

Fatherland Party of Labour: 1000 Sofia, Slavyanska St 3, Hotel Slavyanska Beseda; tel. (2) 65-83-10; nationalist; Chair. RUMEN POPOV.

Liberal Congress Party: 1000 Sofia, Blvd Dondukov 39; tel. (2) 39-00-18; f. 1989 as the Bulgarian Socialist Party, renamed Bulgarian Social Democratic Party (non-Marxist) in 1990 and as above in 1991; c. 20,000 mems; Chair. YANKO YANKOV.

Movement for Rights and Freedoms (MRF): 1408 Sofia, 'Ivan Vazov', P. Topalov-Schmidt St, Bl. 50, vh. B; tel. (2) 51-98-20; f. 1990; in 1991 it attempted to register a political party, Rights and Freedoms, but this was ruled unconstitutional, in August, because the MRF represents the Muslim minority in Bulgaria; participated in 1991 elections; 140,000 mems; Pres. AHMED DOGAN.

Party of Free Democrats (Centre): 6000 Stara Zagora; tel. (42) 2-70-42; f. 1989; Chair. Asst Prof. KHRISTO SANTULOV.

Union of Democratic Forces—UDF (Soyuz na Demokratichnite Sili): Sofia, Rakovski St 134; f. 1989; alliance of parties, organizations and movements; centre-right after split with Liberal and Centre factions in mid-1991; Chair. of Co-ordination Council FILIP DIMITROV; the following mems are registered as political orgs and parties:

    Alternative Socialist Party: 1000 Sofia, Blvd Levski 10; tel. (2) 44-19-31; f. 1989 as faction of BCP (now BSP); joined UDF in 1990; Chair. NIKOLAI VASILEV.

    Bulgarian Democratic Forum: 1505 Sofia, Rakovski St 82; tel. (2) 89-022-85; Chair. KONSTANTIN TSANEV.

    Bulgarian Social Democratic Party (United—BSDP): 1303 Sofia, Blvd Stamboliiski 87; tel. (2) 39-01-12; f. 1989; in August 1991 a congress rejected the leadership of Dertliev and member-

ship of a centrist faction of the UDF, effectively splitting the party the rest of the BSDP is now in the UDF—Centre (see below).

    Citizens' Initiative Movement: 1000 Sofia, Blvd Dondukov 39; tel. (2) 39-01-93; Chair. LYUBOMIR SOBAZHIYEV.

    Club of Persons Illegally Repressed After 1945: 4000 Plovdiv; tel. (32) 22-70-71; f. 1989; Chair. DIMITUR BAKALOV.

    Democratic Party: 1000 Sofia, Blvd Dondukov 34; tel. (2) 80-01-87; re-formed 1990; Chair. STEFAN SAVOV.

    Ecoglasnost Political Club: 1000 Sofia, Blvd Dondukov 39, Fl. 4, Rm 45; tel. (2) 88-15-30; political wing of the Ecoglasnost Independent Asscn (f. 1989), a founding mem. of the UDF; represented in more than 50 clubs and organizations in Bulgaria; Chair. BORIS KOLEV; Gen. Sec. GEORGI AVRAMOV.

    Federation of the Clubs for Democracy: 1000 Sofia, Blvd Dondukov 39; tel. (2) 39-01-89; f. 1988 as Club for the Support of Glasnost and Perestroika; merged with other groups, as above, 1990; Chair. Assoc. Prof. PETKO SIMEONOV.

    Green Party: 1000 Sofia, Yanko Sakazov St 30; tel. (2) 44-21-85; fax (2) 44-37-80; f. 1989; environmentalist; 10,000 mems; in August 1991 the party split over membership of the UDF—Liberal faction; Pres. ALEKSANDUR KARAKACHANOV.

    New Social Democratic Party: 1504 Sofia, POB 14; tel. (2) 44-99-47; f. 1990; membership of UDF suspended 1991; Chair. VASIL MIKHAILOV.

    Radical Democratic Party: 1000 Sofia, Blvd Dondukov 34, Fl. 3, Rms 6–8; tel. (2) 80-02-69; Chair. Dr ELKA KONSTANTINOVA.

    United Democratic Centre: 1000 Sofia, Blvd Dondukov 34; tel. (2) 80-04-09; Co-Chair. BOZHIDAR DANEV, LYUBOMIR PAVLOV, STOYAN GANEV.

    The UDF also embraces the Podkrepa (Support) Independent Trade Union Federation (see Trade and Industry—Trade Unions), the Committee for the Protection of Religious Rights and Freedoms, the Independent Association for Human Rights in Bulgaria, and the Independent Student League.

Union of Democratic Forces—Centre: 1303 Sofia, Blvd Stamboliiski 87; f. 1991 after split in original UDF coalition and in the Bulgarian Social Democratic Party; Leader Dr PETUR DERTLIEV.

Union of Democratic Forces—Liberals: Sofia, Rakovski St 134; f. 1991 after split in original UDF coalition; its mem. parties incl. factions of parties still in the majority UDF, such as Ecoglasnost and Green Party.

Diplomatic Representation

EMBASSIES IN BULGARIA

Afghanistan: Sofia, L. Karavelov St 34; tel. (2) 66-12-45; Ambassador: MEHRABUDDIN PAKTIAWAL.

Albania: Sofia, Dimitur Polyanov St 10; tel. (2) 44-33-81; Ambassador: BASHKIM RAMA.

Algeria: Sofia, Slavyanska St 16; tel. (2) 87-56-83; telex 22519; Ambassador: ZINE EL-ABIDINE HACHICHI.

Argentina: Sofia, Blvd Klement Gottwald 42; tel. (2) 44-38-21; Ambassador: RAÚL MEDINA MUÑOZ.

Austria: 1000 Sofia, Ruski St 13; tel. (2) 52-28-07; telex 22566; Ambassador: Dr MANFRED KIEPACH.

Belgium: Sofia, ul. Frédéric Joliot-Curie 19; tel. (2) 72-35-27; telex 22455; Ambassador: MICHAEL DOOMS.

Brazil: Sofia, Blvd Ruski 27; tel. (2) 44-36-55; telex 22099; Chargé d'affaires a.i.: SONJA MARIA DE CASTRO.

Cambodia: Sofia, Mladost 1, Blvd S. Aliende, Res. 2; tel. (2) 75-51-35 Chargé d'affaires a.i.: CHUM SOUNRY.

China, People's Republic: Sofia, Blvd Ruski 18; tel. (2) 87-87-24; telex 22545; Ambassador: LI FENLIN.

Colombia: Sofia, Vasil Aprilov 17; tel. (2) 44-61-77; telex 23393; Ambassador: EVELIO RAMÍREZ MARTÍNEZ.

Congo: Sofia, Blvd Klement Gottwald 54; tel. (2) 44-65-18; telex 23828; Chargé d'affaires a.i.: PIERRE ADOUA.

Cuba: Sofia, Mladezhka St 1; tel. (2) 72-09-96; telex 22428; Ambassador: MANUEL PÉREZ HERNÁNDEZ.

Czechoslovakia: Sofia, Blvd Janko Sakazov 9; tel. (2) 44-62-81-6; Ambassador: FRANTIŠEK BARBÍREK.

Denmark: 1000 Sofia, POB 1393, Blvd Ruski 10; tel. and fax (2) 88-17-23; telex 22099; Ambassador: K. O. KAPPEL.

Egypt: 1000 Sofia, ul. Shesti Septemvri 5; tel. (2) 87-02-15; telex 22270; fax (2) 88-14-49; Ambassador: MOHAMED EL-ETREBY.

Ethiopia: Sofia, Vasil Kolarov St 28; tel. (2) 88-39-24; Chargé d'affaires a.i.: AYELLE MAKONEN.

Finland: Sofia, Volokamsko St 57; tel. (2) 68-33-26; telex 23148; Ambassador: PEKKA ARTTURI OINONEN.

France: Sofia, Oborishte St 29; tel. (2) 44-11-71; telex 22336; Ambassador: JACQUES RUMMELHARDT.

Germany: 1113 Sofia, ul. Frédéric Joliot-Curie 25; tel. (2) 65-03-81; telex 22449; fax (2) 65-02-75; Ambassador: CHRISTEL STEFFLER.

Ghana: 1113 Sofia, POB 38, Pierre Degeyter St 9, Apt 37–38; tel. (2) 70-65-09; Chargé d'affaires a.i.: HENRY ANDREW ANUM AMAH.

Greece: Sofia, Blvd Klement Gottwald 68; tel. (2) 44-37-70; telex 22458; Ambassador: GEORGIOS CHRISTOYANNIS.

Hungary: Sofia, ul. Shesti Septemvri 57; tel. (2) 66-20-21; telex 22459; Ambassador: SÁNDOR SIMICS.

India: Sofia, Blvd Patriiarkh Evtimii 31; tel. (2) 87-39-44; telex 22954; Ambassador: GIRISH DHUME.

Indonesia: 1504 Sofia, Veliko Turnovo St 32; tel. (2) 44-23-49; telex 22358; Ambassador: ABDEL KOBIR SASRADIPOERA.

Iran: Sofia, Blvd Klement Gottwald 70; tel. (2) 44-10-13; telex 22303; Ambassador: SAYYED HOMAYUN AMIR-KHALILI.

Iraq: Sofia, Anton Chekhov St 21; tel. (2) 87-00-13; telex 22307; Ambassador: FAWSI DAKIR AL-ANI.

Italy: Sofia, Shipka St 2; tel. (2) 88-17-06; telex 22173; Ambassador: PAOLO TARONI.

Japan: Sofia, ul. Lyulyakova Gradina 14; tel. (2) 72-39-84; telex 22397; fax (2) 72-25-15; Ambassador: TAKASHI TAJIMA.

Korea, Democratic People's Republic: Sofia, Mladost 1, Blvd S. Aliende, Res. 4; tel. (2) 77-53-48; Ambassador: KIM PYONG IL.

Korea, Republic: Sofia, Blvd Anton Ivmon; tel. (2) 624-51; Ambassador: KIM CHOE-SU.

Kuwait: Sofia, Blvd Klement Gottwald 47; tel. (2) 44-19-92; telex 23586; Ambassador: TALIB JALAL AD-DIN AL-NAQIB.

Laos: Sofia, Ovcha Kupel, Buket St 80; tel. (2) 56-55-08; Ambassador: THALEUNE WARRINTRASAK.

Lebanon: Sofia, ul. Frédéric Joliot-Curie 19; tel. (2) 72-04-31; telex 23140; Ambassador: HUSSEIN MOUSSAWI.

Libya: Sofia, Oborishte St 10; tel. (2) 44-19-21; telex 22180; Secretary of People's Bureau: OMAR MUFTAH DALLAL.

Mexico: Sofia, Todor Strashimirov St 1; tel. (2) 44-32-82; telex 22087; Ambassador: JAIME FERNÁNDEZ-MACGREGOR.

Mongolia: Sofia, ul. Frédéric Joliot-Curie 52; tel. (2) 65-84-03; telex 22274; Ambassador: LHAMYN TSERENDONDOG.

Morocco: Sofia, Blvd Klement Gottwald 44; tel. (2) 44-27-94; telex 23515; Ambassador: ABDELHAMID BENNANI.

Mozambique: Sofia; Ambassador: GONÇALVES RAFAEL SENGO.

Netherlands: Sofia, Denkoglu St 19A; tel. (2) 87-41-86; telex 22686; Ambassador: VIVIAN H. MEERTINS.

Nicaragua: Sofia, Mladost 1, Blvd Aliende, Res. 1; tel. (2) 75-41-57; Ambassador: ROGER VÁSQUEZ BARRIOS.

Peru: Sofia, ul. Frédéric Joliot-Curie 19, Apt. 20; tel. (2) 70-32-63; telex 23182; Chargé d'affaires: JULIO VEGA ERAUSQUÍN.

Poland: Sofia, Khan Krum St 46; tel. (2) 88-51-66; telex 22595; Ambassador: WIESŁAW BEK.

Portugal: Sofia, Ivats Voivoda St 6; tel. (2) 44-35-48; telex 22082; fax (2) 46-40-70; Ambassador: LUIZ GONZAGA FERREIRA.

Romania: Sofia, Sitnyakovo St 4; tel. (2) 70-70-47; telex 22321; Ambassador: VASILE PUNGAN.

Spain: Sofia, Oborishte St 47; tel. (2) 43-00-17; telex 22308; Ambassador: JOAQUÍN PÉREZ GÓMEZ.

Sweden: Sofia, pl. Veltchova Zavera 1; tel. (2) 65-10-02; telex 22373; Ambassador: ÅKE BERG.

Switzerland: 1000 Sofia, Shipka St 33; tel. (2) 44-31-98; telex 22792; fax (2) 44-39-47; Ambassador: HARALD BORNER.

Syria: Sofia, Hristo Georgiev 10; tel. (2) 44-15-85; telex 23464; Chargé d'affaires: AHMAD OMRAN.

Turkey: Sofia, Blvd Tolbukhin 23; tel. (2) 87-23-06; telex 22199; Ambassador: YALÇIN ORAL.

USSR: Sofia, Blvd Bulgaro-savetska druzhba 28; tel. (2) 66-88-19; Ambassador: VIKTOR VASILEVICH SHARAPOV.

United Kingdom: Sofia, Blvd Tolbukhin 65–67; tel. (2) 87-95-75; telex 22363; fax (2) 65-60-22; Ambassador: RICHARD THOMAS.

USA: Sofia, Blvd A. Stamboliiski 1; tel. (2) 88-48-01; telex 22690; fax (2) 88-48-06; Ambassador: H. KENNETH HILL.

Uruguay: Sofia, POB 213, Tsar Ivan Asen II St 91; tel. (2) 44-19-57; telex 23087; Ambassador: GUIDO M. YERLAS.

Venezuela: Sofia, ul. Frédéric Joliot-Curie 17; tel. (2) 72-39-77; telex 23495; Ambassador: JOSÉ GREGORIO GONZÁLEZ RODRÍGUEZ.

Viet-Nam: Sofia, Ilya Petrov St 1; tel. (2) 72-08-79; telex 22717; Ambassador: NGUYEN TIEN THONG.

Yemen: Sofia, Blvd S. Aliende, Res. 3; tel. (2) 75-61-63; Ambassador: ALI MUNASSAR MUHAMMAD.

Yugoslavia: Sofia, G. Gheorghiu-Dej St 3; tel. (2) 44-32-37; telex 23537; Ambassador: MILENKO STEFANOVIĆ.

Judicial System

The 1991 Constitution provided for justice to be administered by the Supreme Court of Cassation, the Supreme Administrative Court, courts of appeal, courts of assizes, military courts and district courts. The main legal officials are the justices, or judges, of the higher courts, the prosecutors and investigating magistrates. The Chief Prosecutor is responsible for the precise and equal application of the law. The judicial system is independent, most appointments being made or recommended by the Supreme Judicial Council. The Ministry of Justice co-ordinates the administration of the judicial system and the prisons. There is also the Constitutional Court, which is the final arbiter of constitutional issues. Under transitional arrangements attached to the Constitution, until the new system was enacted and established the existing Supreme Court of Bulgaria was to exercise the prerogatives of the two new Supreme Courts.

Supreme Court: 1000 Sofia, Blvd Vitosha 2; tel. (2) 85-71; Chair. DIMITUR LOZANCHEV.

Office of the Chief Prosecutor: 1000 Sofia, Blvd Vitosha 2; tel. (2) 85-71; fax (2) 80-13-27; Chief Prosecutor EVTIM STOICHKOV; Military Prosecutor MILKO YOTSOV.

Ministry of Justice: see The Government (Ministries).

Religion

Most of the population profess Christianity, the main denomination being the Bulgarian Orthodox Church (some 80% of the population). The 1991 Constitution guarantees freedom of religion, although Eastern Orthodox Christianity is declared to be the 'traditional religion in Bulgaria'. There is a significant Muslim minority (some 13% of the population), most of whom are ethnic Turks, although there are some ethnic Bulgarian Muslims, known as Pomaks. There is a small Jewish community.

Department of Religion: 1000 Sofia, Blvd Dondukov 3; tel. (2) 88-14-88; a dept of the Council of Ministers; conducts relations between govt and religious organizations; Chair. METODI SPASSOV.

CHRISTIANITY

Bulgarian Orthodox Church: 1090 Sofia, Oborishte St 4, Synod Palace; tel. (2) 87-56-11; f. 865; autocephalous Exarchate 1870 (recognized 1945); administered by the Bulgarian Patriarchy; there are 11 dioceses in Bulgaria and two foreign dioceses, each under a Metropolitan; Chair. of the Bulgarian Patriarchy His Holiness Patriarch MAXIM.

Armenian Apostolic Orthodox Church: Sofia, Naitcho Zanov St 31; tel. (2) 88-02-08; some 20,000 adherents (1991); administered by Bishop DIRAYR MARDIKIYAN (resident in Bucharest—Romania); Chair. of the Diocesan Council in Bulgaria GARO DERMESROBIYAN.

The Roman Catholic Church

Bulgarian Catholics may be adherents of either the Latin or the Bulgarian ('Byzantine' or Uniate) Rite. The country comprises two dioceses, both directly responsible to the Holy See.

Latin Rite

Bishop of Nikopol: SAMUIL SERAFIMOV DZHUNDRIN, 7000 Ruse, Rost. Blaskov St 14; tel. (82) 2-81-88; some 20,000 adherents (April 1991).

Diocese of Sofia and Plovdiv: GEORGI IVANOV YOVCHEV (Apostolic Administrator) 4000 Plovdiv, Lilyana Dimitrova St 3; tel. (32) 22-84-30; some 35,000 adherents (April 1991).

Bulgarian Rite

Apostolic Exarch of Sofia: METODI DIMITROV STRATIYEV (Titular Bishop of Diocletianopolis in Thrace), 1606 Sofia, ul. Pashovi 10B; tel. (2) 52-02-97; some 15,000 adherents (May 1991).

The Protestant Churches

Union of Evangelical Baptist Churches: 9000 Varna, Han Krum 35; tel. (52) 22-73-19; Pres. Dr THEODOR ANGELOFF; Gen.-Sec. Rev. BOZHIDAR IGOFF.

Union of the Evangelical Congregational Churches: 1080 Sofia, Vasil Kolarov St 49; tel. (2) 88-05-93; Head Pastor PAVEL IVANOV.

Union of Evangelical Pentecostal Churches: 1557 Sofia, Bacho Kiro St 21; tel. (2) 83-22-33; f. 1928; Head Pastor VICTOR VERCHEV.

Union of Seventh-day Adventist Churches: 1000 Sofia, Vasil Kolarov St 10; tel. (2) 88-12-18; Head Pastor AGOP TACHMISSJAN.

United Methodist Church in Bulgaria: 1000 Sofia, Rakovski St 86; tel. (2) 87-33-58; Gen. Superintendent Rev. ZDRAVKO BEZLOV (1618 Sofia, Bl. 196/52, Krasno selo; tel. (2) 56-13-79).

ISLAM

Supreme Muslim Theological Council: Sofia, Bratya Miladinovi St 27; tel. (2) 87-73-20; adherents estimated at 13% of the actively religious population, with an estimated 800 acting regional imams; Chief Mufti of the Muslims in Bulgaria Dr NEDIM KHAAFUS IBRACHIM GENDZHEV.

JUDAISM

Central Jewish Theological Council: 1000 Sofia, Ekzharkh Yosif St 16; tel. (2) 83-12-73; some 5,000 adherents (May 1991); Head YOSSIF LEVI.

The Press

Prior to the political upheavals which began in late 1989, the press in Bulgaria was largely controlled by the Communist Party (later renamed the Bulgarian Socialist Party—BSP) and by organizations attached to the Fatherland Front. In 1990 the press laws were liberalized, and many publications, hitherto banned, became freely available. Of the new independent dailies established in 1990, the most important was *Demokratsiya*, published by the opposition Union of Democratic Forces, with a circulation of 190,000. At June 1991 other important newspapers included the BSP daily, *Duma* (formerly *Rabotnichesko Delo*), which had the largest circulation (300,000), and *Trud*, the daily of the Confederation of Independent Trade Unions in Bulgaria, with a circulation of 125,000.

PRINCIPAL DAILIES

24 Chasa (24 Hours): 1000 Sofia, Blvd Trakia 47; tel. (2) 43-431; telex 22280; fax (2) 46-32-54; f. 1991; privately-owned; Editor-in-Chief VALLERI NAIDENOV; circ. 85,000.

Bulgarska Armiya (Bulgarian Army): 1080 Sofia, Ivan Vasov St 12, POB 629; tel. (2) 87-91-26; telex 22651; fax (2) 87-43-71; f. 1944; organ of the Ministry of Defence; Editor-in-Chief Col IVAN GANCHEV; circ. 60,000.

Chernomorsky Far (Black Sea Lighthouse): 8000 Burgas, Milin Kamak 9; tel. (56) 4-22-48; telex 83464; fax (56) 4-01-78; f. 1950; independent regional since 1988; Editor-in-Chief MLADEN KARPULSKI; circ. 35,000.

Delo (Cause): 3400 Mikhailovgrad, Blvd G. Dimitrov 76; tel. (96) 2-25-01; f. 1987; fmrly *Septemvriisko Slovo*; independent regional newspaper; Editor-in-Chief BOYAN MLADENOV; circ. 20,000.

Demokratsiya (Democracy): 1000 Sofia, Rakovski St 134; tel. (2) 88-25-01; fax (2) 39-02-12; f. 1990; organ of the Union of Democratic Forces; Editor-in-Chief VOLEN SIDEROV; circ. 190,000.

Duma: 1000 Sofia, Blvd Trakia 47; tel. (2) 43-431; telex 22547; fax (2) 87-50-73; f. 1927; fmrly *Rabotnichesko Delo*; organ of the Bulgarian Socialist Party; Editor-in-Chief STEFAN PRODEV; circ. 300,000.

Faks: 1504 Sofia, Blvd Trakia 47; tel. (2) 44-81-82; fax (2) 65-94-70; f. 1944; formerly *Mladezh*, organ of the Bulgarian Democratic Youth Org.; Editor-in-Chief DIMITUR SHUMNALIEV; circ. 86,000.

Glas (Voice): 4000 Plovdiv, Antonivanovstsi St 2; tel. (32) 22-67-40; telex 44506; fax (32) 22-82-23; f. 1943; fmrly *Otechestven Glas*, an official organ; now independent regional newspaper; Editor-in-Chief MIKHAIL MILCHEV; circ. 90,000.

Isik/Svetlina (Light): 1000 Sofia, Blvd Trakia 47; tel. (2) 44-21-07; telex 22197; f. 1945; formerly *'Eni Isik' Nova Svetlina*; independent newspaper in Turkish and Bulgarian; Editor-in-Chief IVAN BADZHEV; circ. 30,000.

Narodno Delo (People's Cause): 9000 Varna, Khristo Botev St 3; tel. (52) 22-24-37; telex 77377; fax (52) 23-11-16; f. 1944; regional independent; 5 days a week; Editor-in-Chief PETUR TODOROV; circ. 44,000.

Narodno Glas (People's Voice): 5500 Lovech, Regional Council, POB 9; tel. (68) 2-22-42; telex 37429; f. 1988; regional independent; Editor-in-Chief VENETSII GEORGUIEV; circ. 30,500.

Narodno Zemedelsko Zname (People's Agrarian Banner): 1000 Sofia, Dondukov Blvd 39, POB 39; tel. (2) 39-02-16; telex 24536; fax (2) 80-11-31; f. 1945, revived 1982 (in USA); publ. in Bulgaria since 1990; organ of the 'Nikola Petkov' Bulgarian Agrarian People's Union; Editor-in-Chief ISKAR SHUMANOV; circ. 46,000.

Otechestven Vestnik (Fatherland Newspaper): 1040 Sofia, Blvd Trakia 47; tel. (2) 43-431; telex 26300; fax (2) 2-31-06; f. 1942 as *Otechestven Front*; organ of the Fatherland Union; morning and evening editions; Editor-in-Chief LYUBEN GENOV; total circ. 70,000.

Pirinsko Delo (Pirin's Cause): 2700 Blagoevgrad, Assen Khristov St 19; tel. 2-37-36; telex 26300; fax 2-31-06; f. 1945; independent regional daily since 1989; Editor-in-Chief KIRIL AKSHAROV; circ. 20,000.

Shipka: 6300 Haskovo, Georgui Daskslov St 14; tel. (38) 12-52-526; telex 43470; fax (38) 3-76-28; f. 1988; independent regional newspaper; Editor-in-Chief DIMITUR DOBREV; circ. 25,000.

Sport: 1000 Sofia, Blvd Trakia 113A; tel. (2) 77-83-78; telex 22594; fax (2) 77-04-90; f. 1927; 5 a week; independent; Editor-in-Chief NIKOLAI ANDONOV; circ. 50,000.

Svoboden Narod (Free People): 1000 Sofia, Yanko Zabunov 10; tel. and fax (2) 65-74-42; f. 1944; revived 1990; organ of the Bulgarian Social Democratic Party (Unity); Editor-in-Chief OFELIA HADZHIKOLEVA; estimated circ. 50,000–100,000.

Telegraf: 1113 Sofia, Blvd Trakia 72, POB 135; tel. (2) 75-11-22; fax (2) 77-04-11; f. 1991; privately-owned independent newspaper; Editor-in-Chief PLAMEN DIMITROV; circ. 30,000.

Trud (Labour): 1000 Sofia, Blvd Dondukov 82; tel. (2) 80-23-44; telex 22427; fax (2) 65-94-70; f. 1923; organ of the Confederation of Independent Trade Unions in Bulgaria; Editor-in-Chief TOSHO TOSHEV; circ. 125,000.

Vecherni Novini (Evening News): 1000 Sofia, Blvd Trakia 47; tel. (2) 44-14-69; telex 22324; fax 46-73-65; f. 1951; independent newspaper; centre-left; publ. by the Vest Publishing House; Dir GHEORGUI GANCHEV; Editor-in-Chief VASIL GADZHANOV; circ. 120,000.

Zemedelsko Zname (Agrarian Banner): Sofia, Yanko Zabunov St 23; tel. (2) 87-38-51; telex 23303; fax (2) 87-45-35; f. 1902; organ of the Bulgarian Agrarian People's Union; Editor-in-Chief DRAGOMIR SHOPOV; circ. 50,000.

Zemya (Earth): Sofia, 11 August St 18; tel. (2) 88-50-33; telex 23174; fax (2) 83-52-27; f. 1951 as *Kooperativno Selo*; renamed 1990; fmrly an organ of the Ministry of Agriculture, now an independent; Editor-in-Chief KOSTA ANDREEV; circ. 105,000.

PRINCIPAL PERIODICALS

166: 1000 Sofia, G. Dimitrov Blvd 20; tel. (2) 82-30-19; f. 1945; formerly *Naroden Strazh*); weekly; criminal and social issues; Editor-in-Chief VACHO RADULOV; circ. 22,000.

168 Chasa (168 Hours): 1000 Sofia, Blvd Stamboliiski 2; tel. (2) 46-61-17; fax (2) 65-70-79; f. 1990; weekly; business, politics, entertainments; Editor-in-Chief PETYO BLAKOV; circ. 90,000.

ABV (ABC): 1000 Sofia, pl. Slaveikov 11; tel. (2) 87-91-11; fax (2) 80-37-91; f. 1972; weekly; organ of the Books Foundation 'ABV'; Editor-in-Chief DIMITUR ZLATEREV; circ. 11,000.

Az Buki (Alphabet): 1113 Sofia, Blvd Trakia 125; tel. (2) 71-65-73; f. 1991; weekly; education and culture; for schools; organ of the Ministry of Public Education; Editor-in-Chief LYUBOMIR YANKOV; circ. 24,000.

Az i Ti (Me and You): 1000 Sofia, pl. Narodno Sabranie 10; tel. (2) 87-85-66; f. 1990; independent; youth magazine on health and sexual problems; Editor-in-Chief ATANAS TEODOROV; circ. 75,000–110,000.

Avto-moto Svyat (Automobile World): 1000 Sofia, Rakovski St 155, POB 1348; tel. (2) 88-08-08; f. 1957; monthly; illustrated publication on cars; Editor-in-Chief STEFAN STEFANOV; circ. 80,000.

Anteni (Antennae): 1000 Sofia, Khan Krum St 12; tel. (2) 87-48-95; telex 23793; fax (2) 87-30-60; f. 1971; weekly on politics and culture; Editor-in-Chief EVGENI MIKHAILOV; circ. 35,000–40,000.

Balgaria (Bulgaria): 1184 Sofia, Blvd Trakia 113; tel. (2) 74-51-14; f. 1937; every 2 months; in English, French, German and Spanish; illustrated magazine; publ. by Sofia-Press Agency; Editor-in-Chief PETUR GUERASSIMOV; circ. 17,000.

Bulgarski Biznes (Bulgarian Business): 1505 Sofia, Oborishte St 44, POB 15; tel. (2) 46-70-23; telex 22105; fax (2) 44-63-61; weekly; organ of National Union of Employers; Editor-in-Chief DETELIN SERTOV; circ. 10,000–15,000.

Bulgarski Dnevnik (Bulgarian Diary): 1080 Sofia, Vitosha Blvd 18; tel. (2) 88-12-21; f. 1991; weekly independent magazine; Editor-in-Chief DIMITUR EZEKIEV circ. 60,000.

Bulgarski Fermer (Bulgarian Farmer): 1000 Sofia, Neofit Rilski St 19; tel. (2) 52-72-27; f. 1990; 6 a year; independent magazine; Editor-in-Chief VASSIL ASPARUKHOV circ. 50,000.

Computer World: 1000 Sofia, pl. Slaveikov 1; tel. (2) 87-48-69; fax (2) 80-26-52; f. 1991; US–Bulgarian joint venture; computers; Editor-in-Chief SNEZHINA BADZHEVA; circ. 15,000.

Debati (Debates): 1000 Sofia, Blvd Dondukov 2; tel. (2) 887-25-03; f. 1990; weekly; parliamentary issues; independent; Editor-in-Chief PLAMEN DARAKCHIEV; circ. 21,000.

Domashen Maistor (Household Manager): 1000 Sofia, Blvd Tolbukhin 51A; tel. (2) 87-09-14; f. 1991; monthly; magazine for household repairs; Editor-in-Chief GEORGUI BALANSKI; circ. 12,000.

Durzhaven Vestnik (State Gazette): 1123 Sofia; tel. (2) 80-01-27; official organ of the National Assembly; 2 a week; bulletin of parliamentary proceedings and the publication in which all legislation is promulgated; Editor-in-Chief PLAMEN MLADENOV; circ. 60,000.

Ekho (Echo): 1000 Sofia, Serdika St 2; tel. (2) 87-28-42; f. 1957; weekly; tourism publication; organ of the Bulgarian Tourist Union; Editor-in-Chief YASSEN ANTOV; circ. 30,000.

Emigrant: 1000 Sofia, pl. Narodno Sobraniye 12; tel. (2) 87-23-08; fax (2) 87-46-17; f. 1991 (to replace *Kontakti*); every 10 days; magazine for Bulgarians living abroad; Editor-in-Chief MANOL MANOV; circ. 20,000.

Erevan: 1080 Sofia, Naicho Tsanov 31; tel. (2) 87-71-272; f. 1944; weekly; organ of Erevan, the Armenian organization in Bulgaria; Editor-in-Chief GARO KHAIRABEDIAN; circ. 2,100.

Evreiski Vesti (Jewish News): 1303 Sofia, Blvd Stamboliiski 50; tel. (2) 87-03-54; fax (2) 87-01-63; f. 1933; weekly; organ of Shallom, the Jewish organization in Bulgaria; Editor-in-Chief SAMUEL FRANCES; circ. 2,000.

Futbul (Football): 1000 Sofia, Bulgaria Blvd 1, Vassil Levski Stadium; tel. (2) 87-21-05; fax (2) 65-72-57; f. 1988; weekly; independent soccer publication; Editor-in-Chief STOICHO BANCHEV; circ. 85,000.

Ikonomicheski Zhivot (Economic Life): 1000 Sofia, Moskovska St 9; tel. (2) 87-65-60; f. 1970; weekly; independent; Editor-in-Chief VASSIL ALEKSIEV; circ. 20,000.

Klub M (Club M): 1000 Sofia, Blvd Vitosha 18; tel. (2) 80-23-08; f. 1990; monthly; colour magazine of Sofia-Press Agency; Editor-in-Chief KHRISTO PEEV; circ. 40,000.

Kompyutar (Computer): 1000 Sofia, Blvd Tolbukhin 51A; tel. (2) 87-50-45; f. 1985; monthly; hardware and software; Editor-in-Chief GEORGUI BALANSKI; circ. 14,000.

Komunistichesko Delo (Communist Cause): 1000 Sofia, Central Post Office, POB 183; tel. (2) 598-16-73; organ of the Bulgarian Communist Party; Editor-in-Chief VLADIMIR SPASSOV; circ. 15,000–20,000.

Krile (Wings): 1184 Sofia, Blvd Trakia 111; tel. (2) 70-45-73; f. 1911; formerly *Kam Nebeto*, renamed 1991; monthly; civil and military aviation; official organ; Editor-in-Chief TODOR ANDREEV; circ. 20,000.

Kultura (Culture): 1040 Sofia, Sofiiska Komuna St 4; tel. (2) 88-33-22; fax (2) 87-40-27; f. 1957; weekly; newspaper on social, political and cultural affairs; organ of the Committee for Culture; Editor-in-Chief KOPRINKA TCHERVENKOVA; circ. 15,000.

Kurier 5 (Courier 5): 1000 Sofia, Blvd Trakia 47; tel. (2) 70-65-40; f. 1990; weekly; advertizing newspaper; Editor-in-Chief STEPAN EREMYAN.

LIK: Sofia, Blvd Trakia 49; weekly publication of the Bulgarian Telegraph Agency; literature, art and culture; Editor-in-Chief SIRMA VELEVA; circ. 19,000.

Literaturen Forum (Literary Forum): 1040 Sofia, Angel Kanchev St 5; tel. (2) 88-00-31; telex 23635; fax (2) 83-54-11; f. 1944; weekly; organ of the Union of Bulgarian Writers; Editor-in-Chief MARKO GANCHEV; circ. 15,000–20,000.

Lov i Ribolov (Hunting and Fishing): 1000 Sofia, Blvd Vitosha 31–33; tel. (2) 88-42-20; telex 23024; fax (2) 80-36-33; f. 1895; monthly organ of the Hunting and Angling Union; Editor-in-Chief DONCHO TSONCHEV; circ. 15,500.

Makedonia (Macedonia): 1000 Sofia, Pirotska St 5; tel. (2) 87-46-64; f. 1990; weekly; organ of the Inner Macedonian Revolutionary Organization—Union of Macedonian Societies; Editor-in-Chief LUKO ZAKHARIEV; circ. 15,000.

Missul (Thought): 1000 Sofia, Legué St 10; tel. (2) 80-12-71; f. 1990; weekly; politics, economics, culture; organ of the Marxist Alternative Movement; Editor-in-Chief IVAN SPASSOV; circ. 15,000.

Napravi Sam (Do It Yourself): 1000 Sofia, Blvd Tolbukhin 51A; tel. (2) 87-50-45; f. 1981; monthly; Editor-in-Chief GEORGUI BALANSKI; circ. 45,000.

Nauka i Tekhnika (Science and Technology): 1040 Sofia, Blvd Trakia 49; tel. (2) 84-61; f. 1964; weekly of the Bulgarian Telegraph Agency; Editor-in-Chief VESSELIN SEIKOV; circ. 20,000.

Nie Zhenite (We the Women): 1000 Sofia, Patriarch Evtimii Blvd 84; tel. (2) 52-53-18; f. 1990; weekly; organ of the Democratic Union of Women; Editor-in-Chief EVGINIA KIRANOVA; circ. 50,000–70,000.

Nov Den (New Day): 1606 Sofia, Blvd Skobolev 32, 4th Floor; tel. (2) 51-14-84; f. 1990; weekly; organ of the Free Democrats; Editor-in-Chief IVAN KALCHEV; circ. 25,000.

Nova Era (New Era): 1000 Sofia, Blvd Stamboliiski 5; tel. (2) 83-21-15; f. 1990; weekly; organ of the Union of Democratic Parties and Movements ERA-3; Editor-in-Chief DOBRI DOBREV; circ. 45,000–80,000.

Obshestvo i Pravo (Society and Law): 1000 Sofia, Treti April St 7; tel. (2) 83-50-02; fax (2) 87-77-00; f. 1980; monthly of the Ministry of Justice and of the Union of Bulgarian Jurists; Editor-in-Chief Prof. BORIS SPASSOV; circ. 80,000.

Orbita: 1000 Sofia, Tsar Kaloyan St 8; tel. (2) 88-51-68; f. 1969; weekly; science and technology for youth; Editor-in-Chief NIKOLAI KATRANDZHIEV; circ. 50,000.

Paralleli: Sofia, Blvd Trakia 49; tel. (2) 87-40-35; f. 1964; weekly; illustrated publication of the Bulgarian Telegraph Agency; Editor-in-Chief KRASSIMIR DRUMEV; circ. 50,000.

Pardon: 1000 Sofia, Blvd Trakia 47; tel. (2) 43-431; f. 1991; weekly; satirical publication; Editor-in-Chief CHAVDAR SHINOV; circ. 50,000.

Podkrepa (Support): 1000 Sofia, Levski Blvd 10; tel. (2) 46-53-93; fax (2) 46-50-47; f. 1990; weekly; organ of the Podkrepa Independent Trade Union Federation; Editor-in-Chief PLAMEN DARAKCHIEV; circ. 25,000–40,000.

Pogled (Review): 1090 Sofia, 11 August St 6; tel. (2) 87-70-97; fax (2) 65-80-23; f. 1930; weekly; organ of the Union of Bulgarian Journalists; Editor-in-Chief EVGENII STANCHEV; circ. 80,000.

Prava i Svobodi (Rights and Freedoms): 1504 Sofia, Blvd Trakia 47, Alley 1; tel. (2) 43-431; f. 1990; weekly; organ of the Movement for Rights and Freedoms; Editor-in-Chief KAZIM MEMISH; circ. 30,000.

Progres (Progress): 1000 Sofia, Gurko St 16; tel. (2) 89-06-24; fax (2) 89-59-98; f. 1894; formerly *Tekhnichesko Delo*; weekly; organ of the Federation of Scientific and Technical Societies in Bulgaria; Editor-in-Chief PETKO TOMOV; circ. 35,000.

Reporter 7: 1124 Sofia, Khan Omurtag St 4; tel. (2) 44-88-86; fax (2) 46-52-76; f. 1990; weekly; private independent newspaper; Editor-in-Chief BINKA PEEVA; circ. 70,000.

Robinson: 1592 Sofia, Iliia Beshkov St 2; tel. (2) 79-90-23; f. 1990; every 2 months; tourism, business, advertizing; Editor-in-Chief SONIA ALEKSIEVA; circ. 100,000.

Shok Daidzhest (Shock Digest): 1000 Sofia, Blvd Trakia 47; tel. (2) 44-13-37; f. 1991; monthly; digest of the Bulgarian press; Editor-in-Chief VIOLETA BAKALOVA; circ. 20,000.

Sofiiski Vesti (Sofia News): 1184 Sofia, Blvd Trakia 113; tel. (2) 70-20-35; f. 1968; weekly; politics, economics, culture, tourism; in English, French, German, Russian and Spanish also; publ. by Sofia-Press Agency; Editor-in-Chief ZDRAVO DOBREV; circ. 10,000.

Start: 1000 Sofia, Vassil Levski Stadium, POB 797; tel. (2) 87-71-62; telex 22736; fax (2) 87-83-78; weekly; illustrated publication of the Central Council of the Bulgarian Union for Physical Culture and Sports; Editor-in-Chief GEORGUI NIKOLCHEV; circ. 80,000.

Studentska Tribuna (Students' Tribune): 1000 Sofia, pl. Narodno Sabranie 10; tel. (2) 88-33-02; f. 1927; every 2 months; student magazine; independent; Editor-in-Chief ATANAS TEODOROV; circ. 20,000.

Sturshel (Hornet): 1504 Sofia, Blvd Trakia 47; tel. (2) 44-35-50; f. 1946; weekly; humour and satire; Editor-in-Chief YORDAN POPOV; circ. 180,000.

Televiziya i Radio (Television and Radio): 1000 Sofia, ul. Tsar Ivan Shishman 30; tel. (2) 87-10-68; f. 1964; weekly; broadcast listings; Editor-in-Chief DIANA SANDEVA; circ. 107,000.

Tempo: 1184 Sofia, Blvd Trakia 113; tel. (2) 74-54-14; f. 1990; weekly; social and political issues; also in Italian; Editor-in-Chief EKATERINA KONSTANTINOVA; circ. 15,000.

Tsarkoven Vestnik (Church Newspaper): 1000 Sofia, Oborishte St 4; tel. (2) 89-51-15; f. 1900; weekly; organ of the Bulgarian Orthodox Church; Editor-in-Chief DIMITUR KIROV; circ. 4,000.

Uchitelsko Delo (Teachers' Cause): 1113 Sofia, Blvd Trakia 125, Studentski Obshtezhitiya, Blok G; tel. (2) 70-00-12; f. 1905; weekly; organ of the Union of Bulgarian Teachers; Editor-in-Chief YORDAN YORDANOV; circ. 24,000.

Vek 21 (21st Century): 1000 Sofia, Tsar Kaloyan St 10; tel. (2) 46-54-23; fax (2) 46-61-23; f. 1990; weekly; organ of the Radical Democratic Party; Editor-in-Chief ALEKSANDUR YORDANOV; circ. 20,000.

Vesti (News): 1184 Sofia, Blvd Trakia 113; tel. (2) 70-20-35; f. 1991; weekly; politics, culture, society; organ of the Bulgarian Constitutional Forum; Editor-in-Chief BOYAN OBRETENOV; circ. 25,000–40,000.

Weekend: 1592 Sofia, Iliia Beshov St 2; tel. (2) 79-90-23; f. 1990; weekly; Editor-in-Chief PLAMEN STAREV; circ. 80,000.

Zdrave (Health): 1527 Sofia, Byalo More St 8; tel. (2) 44-30-26; fax (2) 44-17-59; f. 1936; monthly; published by Bulgarian Red Cross; Editor-in-Chief YAKOV YANAKIEV; circ. 55,000.

Zhenata Dnes (Women of Today): 1000 Sofia, pl. Narodno Sabranie 12; tel. (2) 89-63-00; f. 1946; monthly organ of the Women's Democratic Union; also in Russian; Editor-in-Chief BOTIO ANGELOV; circ. 120,000.

Zname (Banner): 1184 Sofia, Blvd Dondukov 34; tel. (2) 80-01-83; f. 1894, publ. until 1934 and 1945–49; resumed publishing 1990; weekly; organ of the Democratic Party; Editor-in-Chief BRATISLAV TALEV; circ. 20,000.

Zora (Dawn): 1000 Sofia, Blvd Trakia 77; tel. (2) 71-41-826; f. 1990; weekly; organ of the Bulgarian Democratic Party; Editor-in-Chief MINCHO MINCHEV; circ. 20,000.

NEWS AGENCIES

Bulgarska Telegrafna Agentsia—BTA (Bulgarian Telegraph Agency): 1040 Sofia, Blvd Trakia 49; tel. (2) 84-61; telex 22821; f. 1898; the official news agency, having agreements with the leading foreign agencies and correspondents in all major capitals; publishes weekly surveys of science and technology, international affairs, literature and art; Dir-Gen. IVO INDZHEV.

Sofia-Press Agency: 1040 Sofia, Slavyanska St 29; tel. (2) 88-58-31; telex 22622; fax (2) 88-34-55; f. 1967 by the Union of Bulgarian Writers, the Union of Bulgarian Journalists, the Union of Bulgarian Artists and the Union of Bulgarian Composers; publishes socio-political and scientific literature, fiction, children's and tourist literature, publications on the arts, a newspaper, magazines and bulletins in foreign languages; also operates **Sofia-Press Info** (tel. (2) 87-66-80; Pres. ALEKSANDUR NIKOLOV), which provides up-to-date information on Bulgaria, in print and for broadcast; Dir-Gen. VENTSEL RAICHEV.

Foreign Bureaux

Agence France-Presse (AFP): 1000 Sofia, Blvd Tolbukhin 16; tel. (2) 71-91-71; telex 22572; Correspondent VESSELA SERGEVA-PETROVA.

Agencia EFE (Spain): Sofia; tel. (2) 87-29-63; Correspondent SAMUEL FRANCES.

Allgemeiner Deutscher Nachrichtendienst (ADN) (Germany): 1000 Sofia, Moskovska 27A; tel. (2) 87-82-73; telex 22050; Correspondent HANS-PETKO TEUCHERT.

Československá tisková kancelář (ČSTK) (Czechoslovakia): 1113 Sofia, ul. Gagarin, Bl. 154A, Apt 19; tel. (2) 70-91-36; telex 22537; Correspondent VĚRA IVANOVIČOVÁ.

Deutsche Presse Agentur (dpa) (Germany): Sofia; tel. (2) 72-02-02; Correspondent ELENA LALOVA.

Informatsionnoye Agentstvo Novosti (IAN) (USSR): Sofia, 11 Avgust St 1, Apt 3; tel. (2) 88-13-81; Bureau Man. YEVGENI VOROBYOV.

Magyar Távirati Iroda (MTI) (Hungary): Sofia, ul. Frédéric Joliot-Curie 15, blok 156/3, Apt 28; tel. (2) 70-18-12; telex 22549; Correspondent TIBOR KELLER.

Novinska Agencija Tanjug (Yugoslavia): 1000 Sofia, L. Koshut St 33; tel. (2) 71-90-57; Correspondent PERO RAKOSEVIĆ.

Polska Agencja Prasowa (PAP) (Poland): Sofia; tel. (2) 44-14-39; Correspondent BOGDAN KORNEJUCK.

Prensa Latina (Cuba): 1113 Sofia, ul. Yuri Gagarin 22, Bl. 154B, Apt 22; tel. (2) 71-91-90; telex 22407; Correspondent SUSANA UGARTE SOLER.

Reuters (United Kingdom): Sofia; tel. and fax (2) 54-23-72; Correspondent NIKOLA ANTONOV.

Telegrafnoye Agentstvo Sovetskovo Soyuza (TASS) (USSR): 1000 Sofia, ul. A. Gendov 1, Apt 29; tel. (2) 87-38-03; Correspondent ALEKSANDR STEPANENKO.

United Press International (UPI) (USA): Sofia; tel. (2) 62-24-65; Correspondent GUILLERMO ANGUELOV.

Xinhua (New China) News Agency (People's Republic of China): Sofia, pl. Narodno Sobraniye 3, 2nd Floor; tel. (2) 88-49-41; telex 22539; Correspondent U. SIZIUN.

The following agencies are also represented: SANA (Syria) and Associated Press (USA).

PRESS ASSOCIATIONS

Union of Bulgarian Journalists: Sofia, Graf Ignatiev St 4; tel. (2) 89-53-56; telex 22635; f. 1955; Pres. (vacant); Gen.-Sec. ALEKSANDUR ANGELOV; 4,800 mems.

Publishers

Darzhavno Izdatelstvo 'Khristo G. Danov' ('Khristo G. Danov' State Publishing House): 4000 Plovdiv, ul. Petko Karavelov 17;

tel. (32) 22-52-32; fax (32) 26-33-00; f. 1855; fiction, poetry, literary criticism; Dir YORDAN KOSTURKOV.

Darzhavno Izdatelstvo 'Meditsina i Fizkultura': 1080 Sofia, pl. Slaveikov 11; tel. (2) 87-13-08; f. 1948; medicine, physical culture and tourism; Dir PETUR GOGOV.

Darzhavno Izdatelstvo 'Narodna Kultura': 1000 Sofia, ul. Gavril Genov 4; tel. (2) 87-80-63; f. 1944; foreign fiction and poetry in translation; Dir SERGEI RAIKOV.

Darzhavno Izdatelstvo 'Nauka i Izkustvo': 1080 Sofia, Blvd Ruski 6; tel. (2) 87-57-01; f. 1948; general publishers; Dir ANELIA VASSILEVA.

Darzhavno Izdatelstvo 'Prosveta': Sofia, ul. Vasil Drumev 37; tel. (2) 44-22-11; f. 1948; educational publishing house; Dir TSVETANA POPOVA.

Darzhavno Izdatelstvo 'Tekhnika': 1000 Sofia, pl. Slaveikov 1; tel. (2) 87-12-83; f. 1958; textbooks for technical and higher education and technical literature; Dir NINA DENEVA.

Darzhavno Izdatelstvo 'Zemizdat': 1504 Sofia, Blvd Trakia 47; tel. (2) 44-18-29; f. 1949; specializes in works on agriculture, shooting, fishing, forestry, livestock-breeding, veterinary medicine and popular scientific literature and textbooks; Dir PETUR ANGELOV.

Darzhavno Voyenno Izdatelstvo: 1000 Sofia, ul. Ivan Vazov 12; tel. (2) 88-44-31; military publishing house; Head Col TRENDAFIL VASSILEV.

Izdatelstvo na Bulgarskata Akademiya na Naukite (Publishing House of the Bulgarian Academy of Sciences): 1113 Sofia, Acad. Georgi Bonchev St, blok 6; tel. (2) 72-09-22; telex 23132; f. 1869; scientific works and periodicals of the Bulgarian Academy of Sciences; Dir TODOR RANGELOV.

Izdatelstvo 'Bulgarsky Khudozhnik': 1504 Sofia, Asen Zlatarov St 1; tel. (2) 87-66-57; fax (2) 88-47-49; f. 1952; art books, children's books; Dir STEFAN KURTEV.

Izdatelstvo 'Bulgarsky Pisatel': Sofia, ul. Shesti Septemvri 35; publishing house of the Union of Bulgarian Writers; Bulgarian fiction and poetry, criticism; Dir SIMEON SULTANOV.

Izdatelstvo 'Khristo Botev': 1080 Sofia, Blvd Trakia 47; tel. (2) 43-431; f. 1944; fmrly the Publishing House of the Bulgarian Communist Party; renamed as above 1990; Dir IVAN DINKOV.

Izdatelstvo na CC na DKMS 'Narodna Mladezh' (People's Youth Publishing House): Sofia, ul. Kaloyan 10; politics, history, original and translated fiction, and original and translated poetry for children; Dir ROSEN BOSEV.

Izdatelstvo na Natsionalniya Savet na Otechestveniya Front (Publishing House of the National Council of the Fatherland Front): Sofia, Blvd Dondukov 32; Dir (vacant).

Izdatelstvo 'Profizdat' (Publishing House of the Central Council of Bulgarian Trade Unions): Sofia, Blvd Dondukov 82; specialized literature and fiction; Dir STOYAN POPOV.

Knigoizdatelstvo 'Galaktika': 9000 Varna, pl. Deveti Septemvri 6; tel. (2) 22-50-77; fax (2) 22-50-77; f. 1960; popular science, science fiction, economics, Bulgarian and foreign literature; Dir PANKO ANCHEV.

Missul 90 (Thought): Sofia, Latinka St 7; f. 1990; literature, poetry, criticism; Dir VESSELIN PANAIOTOV.

Sinodalno Izdatelstvo: Sofia; religious publishing house; Dir KIRIL BOINOV.

STATE ORGANIZATION

Jusautor: 1463 Sofia, Ernst Thälmann Ave 17; tel. (2) 87-28-71; telex 23042; fax (2) 87-37-40; state organization of the Council of Ministers; Bulgarian copyright agency; represents Bulgarian authors of literary, scientific, dramatic and musical works, and deals with all formalities connected with the grant of options, authorization for translations, drawing up of contracts for the use of their works by foreign publishers and producers; negotiates for the use of foreign works in Bulgaria; controls the application of copyright legislation; Dir-Gen. YANA MARKOVA.

PUBLISHERS' ASSOCIATION

Union of Publishers in Bulgaria: 1000 Sofia, pl. Slaveikov 11; Chair. VERA GYOREVA.

WRITERS' UNION

Union of Bulgarian Writers: Sofia, Angel Kanchev 5; tel. (2) 88-00-31; f. 1913; Chair. KOLYU GEORGIEV; 400 mems.

Radio and Television

Radio and television are supervised by the Committee for Television and Radio of the Committee for Culture of the Council of Ministers.

There were an estimated 2,007,000 radio receivers in use and about 2,100,000 television receivers in use in 1988. Colour television was introduced in 1977.

Bulgarian Committee for Television and Radio: 1504 Sofia, San Stefano St 29; tel. (2) 46-81; telex 22581; Chair. (vacant).

RADIO

Bulgarsko Radio: 1421 Sofia, Blvd Dragan Tsankov 4; tel. (2) 85-41; telex 22557; there are four Home Service programmes and local stations at Blagoevgrad, Plovdiv, Shumen, Stara Zagora and Varna. The Foreign Service broadcasts in Bulgarian, Turkish, Greek, Serbo-Croat, French, Italian, German, English, Portuguese, Spanish, Albanian and Arabic.

TELEVISION

Bulgarska Televiziya: 1504 Sofia, ul. San Stefano 29; tel. (2) 46-31; telex 22581; programmes are transmitted daily; there are two channels.

Finance

(cap. = capital; dep. = deposits; res = reserves; m. = million; amounts in leva)

BANKING

A major restructuring of the banking system began in 1987. Since then, many commercial banks have been established as self-managing shareholders' societies, legally responsible for their financial dealings. Banking and insurance activities may only be carried out by public limited companies and co-operative organizations. In October 1990 a new monetary, credit and banking system was proposed, as part of a comprehensive reform of the entire economic system. A two-tier banking system, with the Bulgarian National Bank as the central bank, was envisaged. The enactment of the Law on Foreign Investments and the Law on Commerce, in May 1991, provided for the establishment of banks with foreign capital. Reform of the financial sector, at August 1991, awaited the final enactment of the Law on the Bulgarian National Bank and the Law on Banking and Credit. At mid-1991, apart from the major banks, listed below, there were 37 other small commercial banks based in the localities and six based in Sofia.

Central Bank

Bulgarska Narodna Banka (National Bank of Bulgaria): 1000 Sofia, Sofiiska Komuna St 2; tel. (2) 85-51; telex 22392; f. *c.* 1879; bank of issue; Pres. Prof. TODOR VULCHEV; First Deputy Pres. and Exec. Dir EMIL HARSEV.

Other Banks

Bulgarian Foreign Trade Bank: 1040 Sofia, Sofiiska Komuna St 2; tel. (2) 85-51; telex 22031; fax (2) 88-56-81; f. 1964; commercial bank with major shareholders: National Bank of Bulgaria, Ministry of Foreign Economic Relations; cap. 320m.; res 1,091m. (Dec. 1990); Pres. CHAVDAR KANCHEV.

State Savings Bank: 1000 Sofia, Moskovska St 19; tel. (2) 88-10-41; telex 22719; fax (2) 54-13-55; f. 1951; provides general individual banking services; brs throughout country; dep. 16,000m. (1986); Chair. GEORGUI KARAMFILOV.

Postal Bank: 1000 Sofia; resumed operations in 1991 (closed 1951); works in co-operation with post offices (3,000 brs); cap. 60m. (Aug. 1991); Dir VLADIMIR VLADIMIROV.

Agricultural and Co-operative Bank (Zemedelska i kooperativna): 4018 Plovdiv, G. Dimitrov Blvd 37; tel. (32) 23-18-76; telex 44324; fax (32) 22-39-64; f. 1987; supplies credit for reconstruction and modernization, technology transfer and quality improvement; cap. 72.8m. (Dec. 1989); Chair. YANKO MUSURLIEV; 11 brs.

BALKANBANK Commercial Bank: Sofia, Dimo Hadzhidimov St; tel. (2) 54-91-81; fax (2) 58-11-76; cap. 150m. (Dec. 1990); Chair. IVAN MIRONOV.

BIOCHIM Commercial Bank: 1040 Sofia, Ivan Vazov St 1; tel. (2) 54-11-21; telex 23862; fax (2) 54-13-78; f. 1987; cap. 80m., res 27m., dep. 1,498m. (Dec. 1989); Pres. BORIS MITEV; Chair. IVAN DRAGNEVSKI.

Commercial Bank of Burgas: 8000 Burgas; tel. (56) 4-22-31; cap. 25m. (Dec. 1990); Chair. KOUZMAN DACHEV.

Commercial Bank of Karlova: 4300 Karlova, Georgui Dimitrov St 2; tel. (335) 57-24; telex 44278; fax (335) 34-20; cap. 22m. (Dec. 1990); Chair. DONKA SAVOVA.

Commercial Bank of Stara Zagora: 6000 Stara Zagora, G. Dimitrov St 126; tel. (42) 28-02; telex 88518; fax (42) 2-25-22; cap. 35m. (Dec. 1990); Chair. SPASS SPASSOV.

Commercial Bank of Pleven: Pleven; tel. (64) 2-35-63; cap. 32m. (Dec. 1990); Chair. TODOR SAVOV.

Commercial Bank of Plovdiv: 4000 Plovdiv; tel. (32) 22-85-30; cap. 62m. (Dec. 1990); Chair. KOSTADIN STAMATOV.

Commercial Bank of Ruse: 7000 Ruse; tel. (82) 3-91-68; cap. 35m. (Dec. 1990); Chair. IVAN PEICHEV.

Commercial Bank of Varna: 9000 Varna; tel. (52) 22-29-83; cap. 37m. (Dec. 1990); Chair. TODOR VASSILEV.

Commercial Bank of Veliko Turnovo: 5000 Veliko Turnovo, Vassil Levski St 13; tel. (62) 2-68-71; telex 66593; cap. 21m. (Dec. 1990); Chair. SIMEON STPICHEV.

Commercial Bank of Vidin: Vidin; tel. (94) 2-31-82; cap. 121m. (Dec. 1990); Chair. VALO VALOV.

Commercial Bank of Vratsa: Vratsa; tel. (92) 2-35-52; cap. 21m. (Dec. 1990); Chair. IVAN PETROV.

DOBRICH Commercial Bank: Dobrich; tel. (58) 2-20-44; cap. 23m. (Dec. 1990); Chair. VASIL RUSEV.

DOVERIE Commercial Bank: 1040 Sofia, G. Dimitrov Blvd 70; tel. (2) 31-81-92; telex 22413; cap. 42m. (Dec. 1990); Chair. OLEG NEDYALKOV.

Economic Bank (Stopanska Banka): 1000 Sofia, Slavyanska St 8; tel. (2) 87-07-41; telex 23910; fax (2) 88-55-26; f. 1987; cap. 117m. (Dec. 1990); Chair. ZVETAN PETKOV.

ELECTRONIKA Commercial Bank: 1000 Sofia, Blvd Vitosha 6; tel. (2) 65-90-07; telex 23789; fax (2) 88-54-67; f. 1987; cap. 88m., dep. 505m. (1990); Pres. VESSELIN KARADZHOV; 4 brs.

First Private Bank: 1000 Sofia, A. Stamboliiski St 2A; tel. (2) 65-72-76; telex 24540; fax (2) 65-93-88; cap. 100m. (Dec. 1990); Chair. VENTSESLAV YOSIFOV.

HEMUS Commercial Bank: 1505 Sofia, Yanko Sakazov St 25; tel. (2) 44-33-21; telex 22409; fax (2) 43-01-22; cap. 36m. (Dec. 1990); Chair. SIYKA BOICHEVA.

MINERALBANK—Bank for Economic Projects: 1000 Sofia, POB 589, Legué St 17; tel. (2) 80-04-14; telex 23390; f. 1980; cap. 180m., dep. 3,198m., res 457m. (Dec. 1990); Pres. VLADIMIR TASHKOV; 10 brs.

Stroybank Ltd: 1202 Sofia, POB 112, Dunav St 46; tel. 8-38-41; telex 23887; f. 1987; provides funding for construction industry; cap. 50m., dep. 765m. (Dec. 1990); Pres. KHRISTOMIR YORDANOV.

Transport Bank (Transportna Banka): 9000 Varna, Shipka St 5; tel. (52) 22-30-73; telex 77293; fax (52) 23-19-64; f. 1987; commercial bank; cap. 33m. (Dec. 1990); Pres. IVAN KONSTANTINOV; Vice-Pres. MARIA DOLOREVA.

INSURANCE

State Insurance Institute: Sofia, Rakovski St 102; all insurance firms were nationalized during 1947, and were reorganized into one single state insurance company; Chair. TOMA TOMOV.

Bulstrad (Bulgarian Foreign Insurance and Reinsurance Co, Ltd): 1000 Sofia, Dunav St 5; POB 627; tel. (2) 8-51-91; telex 22564; f. 1961; deals with all foreign insurance and reinsurance; Chair. S. DARVINGOV.

Trade and Industry

INTERNATIONAL FREE ZONES

Ruse International Free Zone: 7000 Ruse, Blagoev St 5, POB 107; tel. (82) 722-47; telex 62285; fax (82) 7-84.

Free Zone Svilengrad: Khaskovo, Svilengrad, G. Dimitrov Blvd 60; tel. 26-73; state firm; Gen. Dir DIMITUR MITEV.

CHAMBER OF COMMERCE

Bulgarian Chamber of Commerce and Industry: 1040 Sofia, Blvd A. Stamboliiski 11A; tel. (2) 87-26-31; telex 22374; fax (2) 87-32-09; f. 1895; promotes economic relations and business contacts between Bulgarian and foreign cos and orgs; organizes official participation in internat. fairs and exhibitions and manages the internat. fairs in Plovdiv; publishes economic publs in Bulgarian and foreign languages; patents inventions and registers trade marks and industrial designs; organizes foreign trade advertizing and publicity; provides legal and economic consultations, etc.; registers all Bulgarian cos trading internationally (over 15,000 at mid-1991); Pres. VLADIMIR LAMBREV.

EMPLOYERS' ASSOCIATIONS

Bulgarian Industrial Association (BISA): 1000 Sofia, Alabin St 14; tel. (2) 88-25-01; telex 23523; fax (2) 87-26-04; f. 1980; assists Bulgarian economic enterprises with promotion and foreign contacts; analyses economic situation; assists development of small-

BULGARIA

and medium-sized firms; Pres. IVAN ANDONOV; Vice-Pres. PETUR PAPAZOV.

National Union of Employers: 1505 Sofia, Oborishte St 44, POB 15; f. 1989; federation of businessmen in Bulgaria.

Union of Private Owners in Bulgaria: 1000 Sofia, Graf Ignatiev St 2; f. 1990; Chair. DIMITUR TODOROV.

'Vazrazhdane' Union of Bulgarian Private Manufacturers: 1618 Sofia, Todor Kableshkov Blvd 2; tel. (2) 55-00-16; Chair. DRAGOMIR GUSHTEROV.

FOREIGN TRADE ORGANIZATIONS AND MAJOR COMPANIES

Until 1989, foreign trade was a state monopoly in Bulgaria, and was conducted through foreign trade organizations and various state enterprises and corporations. However, in 1989, Decree 56, on economic activity, was enacted; the *firma* (firm, company) was introduced as a basic structural unit of the economy. After some delay, this law was superseded by legislation of 1991, effecting the move to a market economy, notably the Law on Commerce and the Law on Foreign Investments. The Bulgarian economy was being opened to foreign involvement; the minimum investment was stipulated to be US $50,000, with a 40% tax on any profits (if the investment was over $100,000, the tax on profit was reduced to 30%). In 1991 further reforms began the harmonization of Bulgarian regulations and practices with EC and international norms. A Law on the Protection of Competition signalled a start to the demonopolization of state enterprises (some 90% of fixed assets consisted of state and municipal enterprises) and, in August 1991, further legislative proposals aimed to hasten the transfer of companies to the private sector.

Principal state companies (some are in the process of privatization) include:

Agrocommerce: 1000 Sofia, Blvd Dondukov 86; tel. (2) 80-33-12; telex 23223; fax (2) 87-28-69; export of agricultural products; import and maintenance of industrial equipment; import of consumer products and utilization of waste products; Dir-Gen. PETUR BUDINOV.

Agromachinaimpex: 1040 Sofia, Stoyan Lepoyev St 1; tel. (2) 21-18-81; telex 22563; fax (2) 20-91-29; export and import, maintenance and repair of agricultural equipment; Dir-Gen. TODOR TSONEV.

Arda: 7000 Ruse, Zakhari Stoyanov St 33; tel. (82) 3-59-13; telex 62560; fax (82) 23-641; design, production and trade in women's clothing; Dir-Gen. MARGARITA MINCHEVA.

Balkancarimpex: 1040 Sofia, Kliment Okhridsky Blvd 18; tel. (2) 7-53-01; telex 23431; export of trucks, lorries and other vehicles; construction of vehicle parts; Dir-Gen. NEDYALKO TONEV.

Balkantourist: 1040 Sofia, Blvd Vitosha 1; tel. (2) 43-331; telex 22583; f. 1948; state tourist enterprise and leading firm; Dir ALEKSANDUR SPASSOV.

Banimpex: 1113 Sofia, Acad. G. Bonchev St 4; tel. (2) 70-04-11; telex 23688; fax (2) 71-01-97; import of scientific equipment, electronic components and chemicals; export of scientific equipment and chemicals; Dir-Gen. VIKHAR ANDONOV.

Beroe: Khaskovo, 6000 Stara Zagora, Gerasim Papazchev St; tel. (42) 2-21-86; telex 88565; industrial robots, specialized programme products; Dir-Gen. DINKO DINEV.

Bulgarcoop: 1000 Sofia, Rakovski St 99; tel. (2) 84-41; telex 23429; fax (2) 83-225; export of live snails, live game and game meat; apiarist products; nuts, pulses, medicinal plants, rose hips and rose-hip shells, fruit and vegetables (fresh and processed), essential oil seeds, etc.; onions and mushrooms; natural mineral water; consumer goods; Gen. Man. GEORGUI SOKOLOV.

Bulgariafilm: 1000 Sofia, Rakovski St 96; tel. (2) 87-66-11; telex 22447; fax (2) 88-24-31; export and import of films; participation in international film events; film services; Dir LILI TOSHEVA.

Bulgarplodexport: 1040 Sofia, Blvd A. Stamboliiski 7; tel. (2) 88-59-51; telex 23297; fax (2) 88-48-77; f. 1947; import and export of fresh and preserved fruit and vegetables; Dir-Gen. ALEKSANDUR MIRCHEV.

Bulgartabac: 1000 Sofia, Blvd A. Stamboliiski 14, POB 96; tel. (2) 87-52-11; telex 23288; covers manufacture, import and export of raw and manufactured tobacco; Dir-Gen. DIMITUR YADKOV.

Chimimport: 1000 Sofia, Sofiiska Komuna St 1; tel. (2) 88-38-11; telex 22521; import and export of pharmaceuticals, chemicals, petrochemicals, etc.; Dir-Gen. BELO BELOV.

Corecom: 1000 Sofia, Tsar Kaloyan St 8; tel. (2) 85-131; telex 22811; fax (2) 87-09-13; import and retail sale of imported and local goods for convertible and local currency; Dir-Gen. ORLIN MILEV.

Electroimpex: 1000 Sofia, George Washington St 17; tel. (2) 8-61-81; telex 22076; fax (2) 80-33-09; f. 1960; covers the export and import of electrical and power equipment and components for the electrical engineering industry; Gen. Man. EMIL UZUNOV.

Energoimpex: 1463 Sofia, Ernst Thaelmann Blvd 17A; tel. (2) 51-88-67; telex 22669; fax (2) 52-17-58; import and export of coal, electric power; delivery of machines and power equipment; Dir-Gen. DIMITAR ARNAUDOV.

Hemus: 1000 Sofia, Levski St 7; tel. (2) 80-30-00; telex 22267; fax (2) 80-13-41; import and export of books, periodicals, numismatic items, antique objects, philatelic items, art products, musical instruments, gramophone records, cinematographic equipment and souvenirs; Gen. Man. IVAN ABADZHIYEV.

Hranexport: 1080 Sofia, Alabin St 56; tel. (2) 88-22-51; telex 22525; fax (2) 87-74-53; f. 1949; import and export of grain, cocoa, sugar, oils, feed, pulses, vegetable oils, mixtures, etc.; Gen. Dir DIMITAR DJAMBAZOV.

Industrialimport: 1040 Sofia, Pozitano St 3; tel. (2) 87-30-21; telex 22092; fax (2) 66-53-29; import and export of cotton, woollen and silk ready-made garments, knitwear, cotton, woollen and silk textiles, leather goods, china and glassware, sports equipment; Gen. Man. NEDKO NEDKOV.

Inflot: 1504 Sofia, Blvd Vl. Zaimov 88; 1000 Sofia, POB 634; tel. (2) 87-25-34; telex 22376; fax (2) 44-21-18; agency for foreign and Bulgarian shipping, inland and maritime; Dir-Gen. PANAYOT VEZIREV.

Intercommerce: 1040 Sofia, pl. Sveta Nedelya 16, POB 676; tel. (2) 87-93-64; telex 22067; fax (2) 87-45-29; all kinds of multilateral, compensation and barter deals, import and export, participation in foreign firms; Dir-Gen. IVAN DEEV.

Interpred: 1057 Sofia, Blvd Bulgarosavetska Druzhba 16; tel. (2) 71-46-46-46; telex 23284; fax (2) 70-00-06; agency for the representation of foreign firms in Bulgaria; Chair. KHARALAMBI LAMBEV.

Intrasmach: 1618 Sofia, Buckston Blvd 40; tel. (2) 54-30-56; telex 22331; fax (2) 56-71-12; engineering firm; technological transport, etc.; Dir-Gen. GEORGUI TODOROV.

Isotimpex: 1113 Sofia, Chapayev St 51; tel. (2) 70-72-41; telex 22731; fax (2) 70-65-86; import and export of computing and office equipment, electronic components; Pres. LYUBOMIR VITANOV.

Koraboimpex Co Ltd: 9000 Varna, D. Blagoev Blvd 128; tel. (2) 22-81-60; telex 77550; fax (2) 82-33-86; imports and exports ships, marine and port equipment; Dir-Gen. NIKOLAI PARASHKEVOV.

Lessoimpex: 1303 Sofia, Antim I St 17; tel. (2) 87-91-75; telex 23407; fax (2) 87-27-65; import and export of timber, furniture and wooden products; Dir-Gen. ANGEL ANGELOV.

Neftochim: 8014 Burgas; tel. (56) 24-236; telex 83506; fax (56) 24-970; petroleum products, synthetic fabrics, plastics; Dir-Gen. GANCHO NEDELCHEV.

Machinoexport: 1000 Sofia, Aksakov St 5; tel. (2) 88-53-21; telex 23425; fax (2) 87-56-75; export of metal-cutting and wood-working machines, industrial robots, hydraulic and pneumatic products and other equipment, tools and spare parts; Gen. Dir HRISTO ATZEV.

Maimex: 1431 Sofia, D. Nestorov St 15; tel. (2) 59-61-75; telex 22712; fax (2) 59-81-16; import and export of specialized medical equipment, consumables and pharmaceutical products; Dir ILIYA KALKANOV.

Metal Technology: 1574 Sofia, Chapaev St 53; tel. (2) 7-14-21; telex 22903; export and import of machinery and industrial equipment.

Mineralimpex: 1156 Sofia, Blvd Kliment Okhridsky 44, Bl. 1A; tel. (2) 77-95-06; telex 22973; fax (2) 77-13-48; export of mineral raw materials, drilling tools and products; import of machinery, minerals and diamond tools; Dir-Gen. SLAVCHO NAIDENOV.

Mladost: Sofia, Blvd A. Stamboliiski 45; tel. (2) 87-95-52; telex 22168; fax (2) 88-56-58; production of and trade in footwear, sportswear and ready-made dresses; Dir-Gen. NIKOLAI CHERVENOV.

'Petur Karaminchev' State Co: Ruse, Petur Karaminchev Blvd 73; tel. (82) 5-08-89; telex 62511; fax (82) 4-86-09; manufacture of floorings, synthetic leather, accessories, etc.; Dir-Gen. GEORGUI BAIRAKOV.

Pharmachim: 1220 Sofia, Iliyensko chaussée 16; tel. (2) 38-501; telex 22097; fax (2) 38-81-38; import and export of drugs, pharmaceutical, microbiological and veterinary products, essential oils, cosmetics and dental materials; Dir-Gen. KHRISTO DRASHANSKI.

Pirin State Co: 1303 Sofia, Blvd A. Stamboliiski 125-2; tel. (2) 20-67-11; telex 22761; fax (2) 23-01-01; f. 1965; production, export and import of footwear and leather goods; Dir-Gen. SIMEON GEORGUIEV.

Raznoiznos: 1040 Sofia, Tsar Assen St 1; tel. (2) 88-02-11; telex 23244; fax (2) 31-70-12; export and import of industrial and craftsmen's products, timber products, paper products, glassware, kitchen utensils, furniture, carpets, toys, sports equipment, musical instruments, etc.; Dir-Gen. MAXIM SCHWARTZ.

Ribno Stopanstvo: 1000 Sofia, Parchevich St 42; tel. and fax (2) 80-10-01; telex 22796; import and export of fish and fish products; Dir YULIAN YORDANOV.

Rodopaimpex: 1000 Sofia, Gavril Genov St 2; tel. (2) 88-26-61; telex 22541; fax (2) 87-94-95; export of cattle, sheep, breeding animals, meat, meat products; dairy products, poultry, eggs; import of meat, breeding animals, tallow, artificial casing and equipment for the meat industry; Dir-Gen. ALEKSANDUR GORANOV.

Rudmetal: 1000 Sofia, Dobrudzha St 1; tel. (2) 88-12-71; telex 22027; fax (2) 88-450; f. 1952; export and import of metal and metal products, lead, zinc, copper, pure lead, ores, coal, etc.; Dir-Gen. BORIS NISHKOV.

Shevni Machini State Company: Sofia, Kv. 'Ilientse', Rozhen St 60; tel. (2) 38-30-14; maintenance, import and trade in machine parts; Dir KOSYO KOSSEV.

SO MAT: 1738 Sofia, Gorubliane; tel. (2) 77-31-26; telex 22356; fax (2) 75-80-15; international cargo road transport; Dir-Gen. YORDAN ASSENOV.

SPS—Software Products and Systems: Sofia, Panayot Volov St 2; tel. (2) 43-401; telex 23149; fax (2) 46-71-68; production, import and export of information systems, software products and system-engineering services; Dir-Gen. RASHKO ANGELINOV.

Stroyimpex: 1000 Sofia, Triyaditsa St 5; tel. (2) 80-30-47; telex 22385; fax (2) 58-50-18; export of cement, lime, cement slabs, floor tiles, prefabricated wooden houses; etc.; import of building materials, machines and equipment; Dir-Gen. ATANAS VLAKHOV.

Technoexportstroy: 1303 Sofia, Antim I St 11; tel. (2) 87-85-11; telex 22128; design and construction abroad of all types of public, utility, industrial and infrastructural projects; supply of machines and technical assistance; Gen. Man. EMIL PETROV (acting).

Technika: 1113 Sofia, Blvd Trakia 125, Bl. 2; tel. (2) 733-91; telex 23468; fax (2) 70-02-28; import and export of patents and licences; Dir-Gen. IVAN CHORBADJIEV.

Technoimpex: 1000 Sofia, Tsar Kaloyan St 8, POB 932; tel. (2) 88-15-71; telex 22950; fax (2) 88-34-15; scientific and technological assistance abroad in the fields of industry, architecture, construction, transport and communications and education; Dir-Gen. DIMITUR ZDRAKOV.

Techno-import-export: 1113 Sofia, ul. Frédéric Joliot-Curie 20, POB 541; tel. (2) 639-91; telex 23421; fax (2) 65-81-47; import and export of machines and complete plants in the fields of power generation, metallurgy, mining, construction, plastic-processing industries and crane-building; Dir-Gen. STOYAN DRANDAROV.

Telecom: 1309 Sofia, Kiril Pchelinski St 2; tel. (2) 2-13-01; telex 22077; export and import of radioelectronic equipment and technology for the communications industry; Dir-Gen. LYUBOMIR BUTURANOV.

Transimpex: 1606 Sofia, Skobelev Blvd 65; tel. (2) 54-91-61; telex 22123; import and export of railway equipment, wagons, locomotives, boats and shipping parts; Gen. Dir BORIS KHALACHEV.

Vinimpex: 1080 Sofia, Lavele St 19; tel. 80-32-39; telex 224667; fax 80-12-99; import and export of wine and spirits and equipment and spares for the wine industry; Man. Dir MARGARIT TODOROV.

Private, Collective and Partnership Companies

COMCO: 1000 Sofia, Alabin St 34; tel. (2) 65-83-44; telex 24217; fax (2) 65-84-18; internat. transport, production and trade in construction, food and chemical industries; Dir-Gen. IVAN VICHEV.

DIAMEX Ltd: 1000 Sofia, A. Stamboliiski Blvd 49; tel. (2) 87-01-11; telex 24278; fax (2) 88-50-47; import and utilization of natural and industrial diamonds, etc.; export of raw materials, industrial goods, etc.; Dir-Gen. SERGEI PREVANSKI.

DIANA Partnership Co: 1421 Sofia, Khristo Smirnenski Blvd 18; tel. (2) 65-05-98; fax (2) 65-91-46; trade in computers, word processors, computer software; Pres. BORISLAV RALCHEV.

DOLEX Ltd: Sofia, Aleko Konstantinov St 19; tel. (2) 43-28-94; fax (2) 46-28-30; production and trade in drilling tools, etc.; Dir-Gen. SASHKO MIKHAILOV.

INFOSPORT Ltd: Sofia, Levski Blvd 18; tel. (2) 80-16-81; fax (2) 88-54-64; production and trade in computer systems and programmes; Dir-Gen. STEFKO BANEV.

INFOSYSTEMS: 1000 Sofia, Gurko St 38A; tel. (2) 65-03-12; fax (2) 46-35-64; production and trade in computer systems and programmes, esp. for banking systems; Dir ILONA STOILOVA.

Interinvest Engineering Ltd: 1113 Sofia, Zhendov St 6; tel. (2) 71-00-33; fax (2) 71-00-38; engineering, trade and investment services; Dir-Gen. ELIM ALADZHEM.

Isomatic Ltd: 1113 Sofia, Acad. Georgui Bonchev, Bl. 2; tel. (2) 72-93-19; telex 22836; fax (2) 72-23-11; production and trade in machinery for agriculture and industry; Pres. GEORGUI NACHEV.

Novostroy Partnership Co: Sofia, Kompl. 'Strelbishte', Bl. 27, A, Vh. A; tel. and fax (2) 59-70-33; import and export of machinery, etc., for construction industry; Dir-Gen. LAZAR GYUROV.

PRIM Ltd: 1000 Sofia, Stamboliiski St 2A; tel. (2) 80-14-41; telex 24541; fax (2) 65-94-11; foreign trade company; Dir-Gen. IVAN BOYADZHIEV.

PROGRAMA 5 CONTROL Partnership Co: 1113 Sofia, Chekov St 34; tel. (2) 72-88-69; fax (2) 83-28-93; engineering services; design, assembly and servicing of computerized systems and automative machinery; Pres. KHRISTO ABADZHIEV.

PROSOFT: 1233 Sofia, Kharalampi Karastoyanov St 21; tel. (2) 33-40-49; fax (2) 33-40-48; engineering, production and trade in computerized systems; Pres. YULIAN GENOV.

TEKSI: 1504 Sofia, Marin Drinov St 28; tel. (2) 44-00-09; telex 24570; fax (2) 46-70-24; internat. trade, transport services, tourism; Pres. EVGENI VALCHEV.

TRADE UNIONS AND CO-OPERATIVES

Confederation of Independent Trade Unions in Bulgaria (CITUB): Sofia, pl. D. Blagoev 1; tel. (2) 86-61; telex 22446; fax (2) 87-17-87; f. 1904; changed name from Bulgarian Professional Union and declared independence from all parties and state structures in 1990; still the main trade union organization; at mid-1991 there were 75 mem. federations and four associate mems (principal mems listed below); Chair. Prof. Dr KRUSTYU PETKOV; Sec. MILADIN STOYNOV; total mems 3,064,000 (mid-1991).

Edinstvo (Unity) People's Trade Union: 1000 Sofia, Moskovska St 5; tel. (2) 87-96-40; f. 1990; co-operative federation of Clubs, based on professional interests, grouped into Associations and Regional Asscns; there are 84 asscns and 2 prof. asscns, in 14 regional groups; Chair. OGNYAN BONEV; 384,000 mems (mid-1991).

Podkrepa (Support) Trade Union Confederation: 1000 Sofia, Angel Kanchev St 2; tel. (2) 85-61; fax (2) 87-38-42; f. 1989 as an opposition trade union (affiliated to the Union of Democratic Forces); organized into territorial (31 regions) and professional asscns (33 syndicates); Chair. Dr KONSTANTIN TRENCHEV; Gen. Sec. PETUR GANCHEV; 473,000 mems (mid-1991).

Principal CITUB Trade Unions

Federation of Independent Agricultural Trade Unions: 1606 Sofia, ul. Dimo Hadzhidimov 29; tel. (2) 52-15-40; Pres. LYUBEN KHARALAMPIEV; 640,000 mems (mid-1991).

Federation of Independent Trade Unions of Construction Workers: 1000 Sofia, pl. Sveta Nedelya 4; tel. (2) 80-16-003; Chair. NIKOLAI RASHKOV; 220,000 mems (mid-1991).

Federation of the Independent Trade Unions of Employees of the State and Social Organizations: 1000 Sofia, ul. Alabin 52; tel. (2) 87-98-52; Chair. PETUR SUCHKOV; 144,900 mems (mid-1991).

Federation of Independent Trade Unions of Metallurgists, Power Workers and Geologists: 1000 Sofia, pl. Sveta Nedelya 4; tel. (2) 87-80-83; f. 1909; Pres. YORDAN RUSSKOV; 120,000 mems (mid-1991).

Federation of Light Industry Trade Unions: 1000 Sofia, ul. Shesti Septemvri 4; Chair. YORDAN VASSILEV; 217,300 mems (mid-1991).

Federation of Trade Unions of the Biotechnological and Chemical Industries: 1000 Sofia, ul. Alabin 3; tel. (2) 87-09-37; Pres. LYUBEN MAKOV; 79,800 mems (mid-1991).

Federation of Trade Unions of the Forestry and Timber Industries: 1606 Sofia, ul. Dimo Hadzhidimov 29; tel. (2) 52-31-21; Pres. NIKOLA ABADZHIEV; 115,000 mems (mid-1991).

Federation of Trade Unions of Health Workers: 1000 Sofia, pl. Sveta Nedelya 4; tel. (2) 88-20-97; Chair. ALEKSANDUR SABEV; 90,000 mems (mid-1991).

Independent Trade Union Federation of the Co-operatives: 1000 Sofia, Rakovski St 99; tel. (2) 87-36-74; Chair. NIKOLAI NIKOLOV; 96,000 mems (mid-1991).

Independent Trade Union Federation for Trade, Co-operatives, Services and Tourism: 1000 Sofia, ul. Shesti Septemvri 4; tel. (2) 88-02-51; Chair. PETUR TSEKOV; 212,221 mems (mid-1991).

Independent Trade Union of Food Industry Workers: 1606 Sofia, ul. Dimo Hadzhidimov 29; tel. (2) 52-30-72; Pres. SLAVCHO PETROV; 86,000 mems (mid-1991).

'Metal-electro' National Trade Union Federation: 1080 Sofia, POB 543, pl. Sveta Nedelya 4; tel. (2) 87-48-06; telex 24419; Chair. DOICHO DINEV; 180,000 mems (mid-1991).

Trade Union of Transport Workers: 1233 Sofia, G. Dimitrov St 106; tel. (2) 31-00-32; f. 1911; Chair. ILIIA ALEKSIEV; 90,000 mems (mid-1991).

Union of Bulgarian Teachers: 1000 Sofia, pl. Sveta Nedelya 4; tel. (2) 87-78-18; f. 1905; Chair. IVAN YORDANOV; 186,153 mems (mid-1991).

Other Principal Trade Unions

Bulgarian Military Legion 'G. S. Rakovski': 1000 Sofia, Ruski Blvd 9; tel. (2) 87-72-96; Chair. DOICHIN BOYADZHIEV.

BULGARIA

Inner Macedonian Revolutionary Organization–Union of Macedonian Associations: 1000 Sofia, Treti April St 5; tel. (2) 880-56-36; Chair. DIMITUR GOTSEV.

Podkrepa Professional Trade Union for Chemistry, Geology and Metallurgy Workers: 1000 Sofia, Angel Kanchev St 2; Chair. LACHEZAR MINKOV (acting); 15,000 mems (mid-1991).

Podkrepa Professional Trade Union for the Construction Industry: 1000 Sofia, Angel Kanchev St 2; Chair. PETUR DRAGULEV; 15,000 mems (mid-1991).

Podkrepa Professional Trade Union for Doctors and Medical Personnel: 1000 Sofia, Angel Kanchev St 2; Chair. Dr K. KRASTEV; 20,000 mems (mid-1991).

Roma Democratic Union (Gypsies' Union): 1324 Sofia, Dondukov Blvd 39; tel. (2) 39-01-47; Chair. MANUSH ROMANOV.

Union of Bulgarian Architects: 1504 Sofia, Evlogi Georgiev St 1; tel. (2) 46-71-82; Chair. KHRISTO GENCHEV.

Union of Bulgarian Lawyers: 1000 Sofia, Treti April St 7; tel. (2) 87-58-59; Chair. PETUR KORNAZHEV.

Co-operatives

Central Union of Workers' Productive Co-operatives: 1000 Sofia, Dondukov Blvd 41, POB 55; tel. (2) 80-39-38; telex 23229; fax (2) 87-03-20; f. 1988; umbrella organization of 164 workers' productive co-operatives; Pres. PAVEL TSVETANSKY; 75,000 mems.

TRADE FAIR

Plovdiv International Fair: 4018 Plovdiv, Blvd G. Dimitrov 37; tel. (32) 55-31-46; telex 44432; fax (32) 26-54-32; f. 1933; organized by Bulgarian Chamber of Commerce and Industry; Dir-Gen. KIRIL ASPARUKHOV.

Transport

Ministry of Transport and Communications: 1000 Sofia, ul. Levsky 9–11; tel. (2) 87-49-42; telex 23200; fax (2) 88-50-94; directs the state rail, road, water and air transport organizations.

Despred: 1000 Sofia, Slavyanska St 2; tel. (2) 87-60-16; telex 23306; fax (2) 80-14-37; state firm; Dir-Gen. TRAIKO VARGOV.

RAILWAYS

At the beginning of 1990 there were 4,300 km of track in Bulgaria, of which more than 2,069 km were electrified. The international and domestic rail networks are centred on Sofia. Construction of an underground railway system for Sofia began in 1979, and was still in progress in 1991. The system was to have a total length of 112 km.

Bulgarian State Railways (BDZ): 1080 Sofia, Ivan Vazov St 3; tel. (2) 87-30-45; telex 22423; fax (2) 87-71-51; owns and controls all railway transport; Chair. VESELIN PAVLOV.

ROADS

There were 36,935 km of roads in Bulgaria at the beginning of 1990, including 266 km of motorways, 2,935 km of main roads and 3,796 km of secondary roads. Two important international motorways traverse the country and a major motorway runs from Sofia to the coast.

General Road Administration: 1040 Sofia, Blvd D. Blagoev 3; tel. (2) 51-671; telex 22679; fax (2) 87-67-98; f. 1965; Pres. DIMITAR DIMOV.

SHIPPING AND INLAND WATERWAYS

The Danube River is the main waterway, the two main ports being Ruse and Lom. External services link Black Sea ports (the largest being Varna and Burgas) to the USSR, the Mediterranean and Western Europe.

Bulgarian River Shipping Corporation: 7000 Ruse, pl. Otets Paisi 2; tel. (82) 20-81; telex 62403; fax (82) 700-93; f. 1935; shipment of cargo and passengers on the Danube; storage, handling and forwarding of cargo; Dir-Gen. TSONYU UZUNOV.

Navigation Maritime Bulgare: 9000 Varna, Chervenoarmeiska St 1; tel. (52) 22-24-74; telex 77351; fax (52) 22-24-91; f. 1892; sole enterprise in Bulgaria employed in sea transport; owns tankers, bulk carriers and container, ferry and passenger vessels with a displacement of 1,867,857 dwt (1990); Dir-Gen. DIMITAR MAVROV.

Shipping Corporation: 9000 Varna, Panagyurishte St 17; tel. (52) 22-63-16; telex 077524; fax (52) 22-53-94; organization of sea and river transport; carriage of goods and passengers on waterways; controls all aspects of shipping and shipbuilding, also engages in research, design and personnel training; Dir-Gen. ATANAS YONKOV.

CIVIL AVIATION

There are three international airports in Bulgaria, at Sofia, Varna and Burgas, and seven other airports for domestic services. In 1990 the Bulgarian civil aviation company, Balkan Bulgarian Airlines, had 52 aircraft and operated 79 international and seven domestic routes. At the beginning of 1991 civil aviation was divided between three state companies; airport services were carried out by Bul Air Services.

Balkan Bulgarian Airlines: 1540 Sofia, Sofia Airport; tel. (2) 71-201; telex 22299; fax (2) 79-12-06; f. 1947; restructured and split in 1991; state-owned; operates domestic and international routes; also agricultural aviation services; carried about 2.8m. passengers in 1987; fleet of 9 TU-134, 21 TU-154, 22 AN-24, 2 Il-18, 11 Yak-40 and 4 AN-12 (1987); Dir-Gen. KONSTANTIN BOTEV.

Hemus Airlines: 1540 Sofia, Sofia Airport; tel. (2) 70-20-76; telex 22342; fax (2) 79-63-80; f. 1991; Dir-Gen. NIKOLAI BEISKI.

Via Air: 1540 Sofia, Sofia Airport; f. 1990; private airline.

VSAU Helli Airlines: 1540 Sofia, Sofia Airport; tel. and fax (2) 79-11-51; telex 22498; f. 1991; Dir-Gen. GEORGUI SPASSOV.

Tourism

Bulgaria's tourist attractions include the resorts on the Black Sea coast, mountain scenery and historic centres. There were 8,294,985 foreign visitor arrivals in 1988, of which over one-half were stop-over tourists. In 1989 tourism accounted for 10% of total income in convertible currency. Many of the state-owned firms engaged in tourism were likely to be privatized, it was reported in 1991.

Bulgarian Tourist Chamber: Sofia, Triaditza St 5; tel. (2) 87-40-59; some 350 firms are mems, incl. state enterprises; Chair. TSVETAN TONCHEV.

Atomic Energy

A heterogeneous swimming-pool reactor, with a thermal capacity of 2,000 kW, came into operation near Sofia in 1961. The reactor, supplied under a bilateral agreement by the USSR, is used for the production of radioactive isotopes as well as for experimental work.

Bulgaria's first nuclear power station at Kozlodui, which opened in 1974 with an initial generating capacity of 440 MW, was expanded to provide a capacity of 2,585 MW by 1988. The construction, at Belene, of a second nuclear power station, rated at 6,000 MW, was suspended in 1990 and cancelled in 1991, after widespread protests. In 1989 the Kozlodui station was producing 42% of the country's electricity. In June 1991 an international team of experts recommended the closure of the plant. The Bulgarian Government rejected the practicality of this, but, with EC assistance, eventually agreed to shut down the two oldest reactors by September of that year.

Institute for Nuclear Research and Nuclear Energy of the Bulgarian Academy of Sciences: 1784 Sofia, Blvd Trakia 72; tel. (2) 75-80-32; telex 23561; f. 1973; Dir Acad. KHR. KHRISTOV.

Culture

NATIONAL ORGANIZATIONS

Ministry of Culture: see section on The Government (Ministries).

National Commission for UNESCO: 1000 Sofia, Rokovski St 96B; tel. (2) 87-54-49; Vice-Chair. LYUBOMIR DRAMALIEV.

CULTURAL HERITAGE

Amateur Artists' Centre: 1000 Sofia, Ruski Blvd 8; tel. (2) 80-11-30; Man. PETUR GRIGOROV.

National Academy of Arts: 1040 Sofia, Shipka St 1; tel. (2) 88-17-01; Rector BORIS GONDOV.

National Archaeological Museum: 1000 Sofia, Stamboliiski 2; tel. (2) 88-24-05; f. 1892; attached to the Bulgarian Academy of Sciences; Dir I. SOTIROV.

National Art Gallery: 1000 Sofia, Moskovska St 6; tel. (2) 88-35-59; f. 1948; br. in Aleksandur Nevski Cathedral—icons and ecclesiastical art; Dir S. RUSEV.

National Museum of Applied and Decorative Arts: 1000 Sofia, Blvd Tolbukhin 49; tel. (2) 65-41-72; Dir Z. MANOLOV.

National Museum of Bulgarian Literature: 1000 Sofia, G. Rakovski St 138; tel. (2) 88-24-93; Dir G. SVEZHIN.

National Museum of Ecclesiastical History and Archaeology: 1000 Sofia, pl. V. Lenin 19; tel. (2) 88-13-43; Dir ILARION, Bishop of Trazhanopol.

National Museum of History: 1000 Sofia, Blvd Vitosha 2; tel. (2) 54-46-78; Dir R. KATINCHAROV.

SS Cyril and Methodius National Library: 1000 Sofia, Levski Blvd 11; tel. (2) 88-16-00; f. 1878; Dir Prof. Dr ATANAS NATEV.

State Musical Academy: 1504 Sofia, Klement Gottwald Blvd 11; tel. (2) 47-01-81; Rector GEORGUI KOSTOV.

SPORTING ORGANIZATIONS

Olympic Committee of the Republic of Bulgaria: 1000 Sofia, Angel Kanchev St 4; tel. (2) 87-56-95; Chair. IVAN SLAVKOV.

Bulgarian Union of Physical Culture and Sports: 1000 Sofia, Blvd Levski 18; tel. (2) 86-51; national sporting asscn; Chair. GEORGUI KHRISTOV.

Federation of Physical Culture and Sports: 1040 Sofia, pl. Makedonia 1; trade union; associated with CITUB (see Trade and Industry); Chair. PETKO KRASTEV; 200,000 mems (mid-1991).

PERFORMING ARTS

Theatre

Aleko Konstantinov State Satirical Theatre: 1000 Sofia, Stefan Karadzha St 5; tel. (2) 88-54-24; Dir PLAMEN MARKOV.

Central Puppet Theatre: 1000 Sofia, Gurko St 14; tel. (2) 87-72-88; Dir TODOR DIMITROV.

Ivan Vazov National Theatre: 1000 Sofia, Levski St 5; tel. (2) 87-78-00; Dir VASSIL STEFANOV.

N. O. Massalitinov Drama Theatre: 4000 Plovdiv; tel. (32) 22-48-67; Dir BOGOMIL STOILOV.

Salza i Smyakh (Tears and Laughter) Drama Theatre: 1000 Sofia, Slavyanska St 5; tel. (2) 87-33-89; Dir PETUR MARINKOV.

Sofia Drama Theatre: 1000 Sofia, A. Vl. Zaimov Blvd 23; tel. (2) 45-35-12; Dir VILLY TSANKOV.

Opera Houses

Sofia National Opera: 1000 Sofia, Dondukov Blvd 56; tel. (2) 88-58-69; Dir MIKHAIL ANGELOV.

National Opera in Burgas: 8000 Burgas; tel. (56) 4-30-57; Dir IVAN VULPE.

National Opera in Varna: 9000 Varna; tel. (52) 22-22-23; Dir ANTONII KAMBUROV.

ASSOCIATIONS

Bulgarian PEN Centre: 1040 Sofia, Angel Kanchev St 5; tel. (2) 87-47-11; affiliated to internat. writers' org.; Chair. BOGOMIL NOVEV.

Independent Federation of the Bulgarian Circus Community: 1000 Sofia, Iskar St 11; tel. (2) 83-29-22; trade union; mem. of CITUB (see section on Trade and Industry); Chair. CH. CHOHADZHIEV; 480 mems (mid-1991).

International Charity Foundation for the Development of Islamic Culture: 1000 Sofia, Ruski Blvd 8; tel. (2) 87-38-16; Chair. NEDIM HAAFUZ.

Podkrepa Trade Union Confederation: see Trade and Industry; there are Podkrepa Professional Trade Unions for: Actors (160 mems—at mid-1991); Artists (Chair. NIKOLAI RANOV; 250 mems); Culture (150 mems); Journalists (Chair. BOYAN DASKALOV; 400 mems); Musicians (1,500 mems); the Preservation of Cultural and Historical Heritage (400 mems).

Union of Bulgarian Actors: 1000 Sofia, Pop Andrei St 1; tel. (2) 88-04-40; trade union; mem. of CITUB (see section on Trade and Industry); Chair. STEFAN ILIEV; 5,000 mems (mid-1991).

Union of Bulgarian Artists: 1000 Sofia, Shipka St 6; tel. (2) 44-61-21; Chair. IVAN GONGALOV.

Union of Bulgarian Composers: 1000 Sofia, Ivan Vazov St 2; tel. (2) 88-15-60; f. 1947; Chair. PARASHKEV HADZHIEV.

Union of Bulgarian Film Makers: 1000 Sofia, Shesti Septemvri 7; tel. (2) 87-89-56; f. 1934; Chair. GEORGUI STOYANOV.

Union of Bulgarian Journalists: see section on The Press (Press Association).

Union of Bulgarian Musicians: 1000 Sofia, Alabin St 52; tel. (2) 87-73-32; f. 1965; Chair. Prof. G. ROBEV.

Union of Bulgarian Writers: see section on Publishers (Writers' Union).

Education

Education is free and compulsory at primary and secondary level (six to 16 years of age); higher education is also supported by the State. Children between the ages of three and six years may attend kindergartens (in 1988, of this age group, 79.1% of the total attended). Since the late 1980s plans have been under consideration to make attendance compulsory from the age of five. Education from the age of six upwards is organized into unified secondary polytechnical schools, offering an 11-year course of vocational, as well as general secondary, training. There are two types of such schools: secondary vocational-technical schools, which train the executive cadres; and technical colleges (*tekhnikums*), which offer specialized training in areas such as industry, agriculture, transport, trade and public health. Kindergarten and unified-secondary education is administered by the Ministry of Public Education, with the organs of local government. In the 1988/89 school year 339,891 children attended kindergartens and 1,234,851 pupils attended the unified secondary polytechnical schools.

Having completed secondary education, students are entitled to continue their training in semi-higher or higher education institutions. This level is the responsibility of the Ministry of Science and Higher Education. In 1988/89 the number of students in further education was 138,341. At the beginning of 1991 there were three universities, one technical university, and 16 higher institutes of university status. The system was undergoing extensive reorganization and many foundations were being renamed.

UNIVERSITIES

St Clement of Ohrid University of Sofia (Sofiiski Universitet 'Kliment Ohridski'): 1504 Sofia, Ruski Blvd 15; tel. (2) 85-81; telex 23296; f. 1909 as university; state control; 14 faculties, 1,714 teachers, 14,684 students (1990); Rector NIKOLA POPOV.

SS Cyril and Methodius University of Veliko Turnovo (Veliko Tarnovski Universitet 'Kiril i Metodi'): 5000 Veliko Turnovo, T. Tarnovski 2; tel. (62) 26-11; telex 66739; f. 1991 as university; 330 teachers, 5,463 students (1990); Rector Prof. GEORGUI DANCHEV.

University of National and World Economy: 1156 Sofia, Studentski grad. Khristo Botev, tel. (2) 63-381; telex 22040; f. 1990 as a university (formerly Karl Marx Higher Institute of Economics, f. 1920); 5 faculties, 494 teachers, 7,075 students (1989); Rector LALIU RADULOV.

University of Plovdiv (Plovdivski Universitet): 4000 Plovdiv, Car Asen 24; tel. (32) 23-86-61; telex 44251; f. 1961; 6 faculties, 460 teachers, 5,761 students (1989); Rector Prof. N. BALABANOV.

Social Welfare

Since 1951 the State has provided all medical services and treatment free. In post-Communist Bulgaria, this health service has been retained and doctors' salaries increased, but private medical provision was being encouraged also (private medical and dentistry practices were banned between 1972 and November 1989). In 1983 there were 24,000 doctors. In 1988 there were 88,000 hospital beds and 22,000 beds in sanatoriums and health spas. The Ministry of Health is responsible for the health service, with the assistance of local government and the Bulgarian Red Cross.

Other social benefits, such as unemployment and pension payments, were also being retained, and the Government was attempting to ensure some compensation for the price rises, which were a consequence of the economic reforms after 1989. Bulgarian workers enjoyed compensation during sick leave, full paid maternity leave before and after childbirth and non-contributory pensions (this last provision was, in 1991, considered likely to be adjusted). The retirement age varied between 45 and 60 years, depending on the job, and women retired five years earlier than men. State social insurance is directed by the Department of Public Insurance and the Directorate of Pensions.

NATIONAL AGENCIES

Ministry of Health: see section on The Government (Ministries).

Ministry of Labour and Social Welfare: see section on The Government (Ministries).

Department of Public Insurance: Sofia.

Directorate of Pensions: Sofia; responsible for the administration of pensions and the establishment of a pensions fund.

Foreign Aid Agency: 1123 Sofia, Dondukov Blvd 2; tel. (2) 85-01; fax (2) 88-06-47; Dir PETKO SIMEONOV.

HEALTH AND WELFARE ORGANIZATIONS

Bulgarian National Committee for UNICEF: 1000 Sofia, pl. Sveta Nedelya 5; tel. (2) 80-25-04; Chair. The Minister of Health.

Bulgarian Red Cross: 1527 Sofia, Biryukov Blvd 1; tel. (2) 44-14-43; Chair. of Central Cttee KIRIL IGNATOV.

Committee of Human Rights: 1000 Sofia, pl. Narodno Sabranie 12; tel. (2) 88-26-08; Chair. KONSTANTIN TELLALOV.

Foundation Against Cancer: 1000 Sofia, pl. Sveta Nedelya 5; Chair. The Minister of Health.

Union of the Blind: 1393 Sofia, Naicho Tsanov St 172; tel. (2) 21-91-70; Chair. IVAN KRUMOV.

Union of the Deaf: 1000 Sofia, Denkoglu St 12–14; tel. (2) 54-50-92; Chair. VASSIL PANEV.

The Environment

Environmental concerns prompted the formation of one of the first opposition groups to the Communist regime. Ecoglasnost and the Independent Committee for the Protection of the Environment (or Ruse Committee) began the Green Movement in 1989. There are estimated to be at least 20 environmental groups in Bulgaria. The Bulgarian Government is a member of the Danube Commission (based in Hungary), the Joint Danube Fishery Commission (Czechoslovakia), the IUCN (Gland, Switzerland) and participated in the activities of the CMEA (USSR) Co-ordinating Centres on environmental matters. In August 1991 Bulgaria and Romania agreed to fuller co-operation on environmental matters, in accordance with EC conditions for rendering aid to the two countries.

GOVERNMENT ORGANIZATIONS

Ministry of the Environment: see section on The Government (Ministries).

Environmental Research and Information Centre (ERIC): 1202 Sofia, Industrialna St 7; tel. (2) 39-47-25; telex 23894; fax (2) 39-21-96; co-ordinates research, analysis, environmental protection programmes, national standards; Head Assoc. Prof. TSONIO MIKHAILOV KONSTANTINOV.

The Ministry of Agriculture and Forestry is also concerned with environmental matters.

ACADEMIC INSTITUTES

Bulgarian Academy of Sciences: 1000 Sofia, Sedmi Noemvri 1; tel. (2) 841-41; telex 22424; f. 1869; Pres. Acad. BLAGOVEST SENDOV.

Forest Research Institute: 1756 Sofia, Kl. Ohridski Blvd 132; tel. (2) 62-20-52; studies the structure and functioning of forest ecosystems, etc.; Dir Prof. Dr ALEKSANDUR ALEKSANDROV.

Institute of Botany: 1113 Sofia, Acad. G. Bonchev St 23; tel. (2) 79-09-51; monitoring and conservation of rare and threatened plant species; assessment of plant resources; Dir Prof. VELCHO VELCHEV.

Institute of Ecology: 1113 Sofia, Gagarin St 2; tel. (2) 72-04-59; fax (2) 70-54-98; Dir Prof. KHRISTO NIKOLOV.

Institute of Economy: 1040 Sofia, Aksakov St 3; tel. (2) 87-58-79; fax (2) 88-21-08; assesses economic impact of environmental damage and protection; efficiency assessment; Dir Prof. Dr KIRIL TODOROV KIRIAKOV.

Institute of Oceanology: 9000 Varna, POB 152, Asparuhovo Quarter; tel. (52) 77-20-38; telex 77237; fax (52) 77-42-56; marine ecology and research of the Bulgarian Black Sea coastline and shelf; Dir Assoc. Prof. ZDRAVKO BELBEROV.

Institute of Water Problems: 1113 Sofia, Acad. G. Bonchev St 23; tel. (2) 72-25-72; researches the sensible and ecological use of water resources, especially inland waters; Dir Assoc. Prof. NADEZHDA KRUSTEVA NIKOLOVA.

Institute of Zoology: 1000 Sofia, Ruski Blvd 1; tel. (2) 88-31-63; biological monitoring and preparation of the *Red Data* series on animal and bird life in Bulgaria; Dir Prof. Dr VASSIL GRIGOROV GOLEMANSKI.

National Institute of Meteorology and Hydrology: 1184 Sofia, Blvd Trakia 66; tel. and fax (2) 88-03-80; monitors atmospheric and ground water pollution; Dir VASSIL ANDREEV.

Higher Institute of Forestry: 1154 Sofia, Kl. Ohridski Blvd 10; tel. (2) 62-30-68; fax (2) 68-03-35; particular concern is acid rain; landscape restoration; Dir Prof. ANDREI RAICHEV.

Institute of Hygiene and Occupational Health: 1431 Sofia, Dimitur Nestorov Blvd 15; tel. (2) 59-10-06; fax (2) 59-60-71; assesses the impact of environmental damage and pollution on the health of the population; Dir Assoc. Prof. Dr EVGENIA GEORGIEVA DINCHEVA.

N. Pushkarov Research Institute of Soil Science and Agroecology: 1080 Sofia, Shosse Bankya St 7; tel. (2) 24-64-41; telex 22701; fax (2) 24-77-95; monitors the pollution of soils and underground waters; Dir Assoc. Prof. Dr VULYO TENEV VULEV.

NON-GOVERNMENTAL ORGANIZATIONS

Association of Bulgarian Ecologists (ABECOL): 1040 Sofia, Blvd Vitosha 18; tel. and fax (2) 87-24-21; f. 1990; voluntary, independent, scientific and educational organization; Chair. of Board of Dirs Prof. SIMEON NEDIALKOV.

Association Ecoforum: 1113 Sofia, Gagarin St 2; tel. (2) 70-53-79; fax (2) 55-10-67; org. of scientists, businessmen and public workers committed to promoting sustainable development and conservation, particularly in the transition to a market economy; Gen. Sec. Assoc. Prof. PAVEL GEORGIEV.

Bulgarian Society for the Conservation of the Rhodope Mts: 1113 Sofia, Gagarin St 2; tel. (2) 70-51-78; f. 1991; union committed to the conservation of the natural and cultural heritage of a significant proportion of Bulgaria; Chair. Assoc. Prof. YORDAN KIRILOV DANCHEV.

Bulgarian Society of Natural Research: 1421 Sofia, Dragan Tsankov Blvd 8, POB 1136; tel. (2) 66-65-94; f. 1896; scientific and educational society of natural scientists; promotes the study and conservation of the environment; organized into over 20 regional brs and 5 scientific sections, incl. one on ecology; over 1,500 mems; Chair. Prof. Dr VASSIL GOLEMANSKI.

Bulgarian Society for the Protection of Birds: 1421 Sofia, Dragan Tsankov Blvd 8; tel. (2) 72-06-30; fax (2) 70-54-98; f. 1988; independent ornithological assen; over 400 mems; Chair. TANIO MICHEV.

Ecoforum for Peace: Sofia, Dimitur Nestorov St 15; tel. (2) 59-61-23; fax (2) 59-26-91; f. 1986 by 88 scholars from 32 countries and 12 internat. orgs; internat. movement for world peace and environmental protection; 15 brs in other countries; secretariat in Bulgaria; Gen. Sec. (vacant).

Ecoglasnost Independent Association: 1000 Sofia, Blvd Dondukov 39, POB 548; tel. (2) 88-15-30; fax (2) 88-15-30; f. officially in 1989; mem. of the UDF, with political representation (see section on Political Organizations); Chair. DIMITUR KORUDZHIEV; Sec. EDVINA SUGAREV.

ECOS Foundation: 1000 Sofia, A. Stamboliiski 2A, 6th Floor; tel. (2) 71-433-71; fax (2) 87-24-00; educational foundation, intent on promoting ecological awareness; Dir Gen. OGNIAN CHAMPOEV.

Green Party: see section on Political Organizations.

Green Society Foundation: 1040 Sofia, Vitosha Blvd 18; tel. and fax (2) 87-24-21; f. 1991; co-operates in projects and campaigns with other groups; operates 7 programmes on the environment; Pres. Assoc. Prof. PETUR GULUBOV; Exec. Dir RADIANA STANOEVA.

National Ecological Club: 1000 Sofia, POB 1653; tel. (2) 70-52-25; independent public org., committed to the conservation of nature; Corresponding Mems VASSIL SGUREV, Acad. GEORGUI BLIZNAKOV.

Union for Nature Protection: 1040 Sofia, Vitosha Blvd 18; tel. (2) 83-26-72; f. 1928 as Union for Native Nature Protection; restructured 1991; independent public org.; local brs and internat. contacts; Chair. Assoc. Prof. Dr SVETOSLAV GERASIMOV.

Wilderness Fund: 1113 Sofia, Gagarin St 2; fax (2) 70-54-98; f. 1990; attached to the Instit. of Ecology; assesses the best places to establish reserves for the protection of the natural environment; Chair. JEKO SPIRODONOV.

Defence

In June 1990, according to Western estimates, the total strength of the armed forces was 129,000 (including 86,000 conscripts), comprising 97,000 in the Army, 22,000 in the Air Force and 10,000 in the Navy. Paramilitary forces included 13,000 border troops and 5,000 security police (since abolished). There was a voluntary People's Militia of some 150,000. Compulsory military service for all males was 18 months in the Army, two years in the Air Force and three years in the Air Force. Bulgaria was a member of the Warsaw Pact (see p. 39), which was dissolved in 1991, but had no other military alliances. The Bulgarian Government welcomed a Greek proposal, made in August 1991, to have a demilitarized zone on the Bulgarian–Greek–Turkish borders, but no further progress was made that year. In 1990 defence expenditure was estimated to be 1,656m. leva.

Commander-in-Chief: President of the Republic.

Chief of the General Staff: Col-Gen. LYUBEN PETROV.

Bibliography

Crampton, R. J. *Bulgaria 1878–1918: a history*. Eastern European Quarterly, Boulder, Colorado (Distributed by Columbia University Press), 1983.

A Short History of Modern Bulgaria. Cambridge, Cambridge University Press, 1987.

Economic Geography of the Socialist Countries of Europe. Moscow, Progress Publishers, 1985.

Feiwel, G. R., in *Osteuropa Wirtschaft*, Vol. 24, 2. June 1979.

Höpken, W., in Schönfeld, R. (Ed.). *Industrialiserung und Gesellschaftlicher Wandel in Südosteuropa*. Munich, Südosteuropa-Gesellschaft, 1989.

Jackson, M. R., in *Pressures for Reform in the East European Economies*, Vol. 2. Washington, DC, USGPO (Joint Economic Committee of the US Congress), 1986.

Jelavich, B. *History of the Balkans*. Cambridge, Cambridge University Press, 1983.

Kinow D. W., in Schönfeld, R. (Ed.). *Industrialiserung und Gesellschaftlicher Wandel in Südosteuropa*. Munich, Südosteuropa-Gesellschaft, 1989.

Lampe, J. R. *The Bulgarian Economy in the Twentieth Century*. London, Croom Helm, 1986.

Lang, D. M. *The Bulgarians from Pagan Times to the Ottoman Empire*. London, Thames and Hudson, 1976.

MacDermott, M. *A History of Bulgaria*. New York, Praeger Publishers, 1962.

Miller, L. M. *Bulgaria during the Second World War*. Stanford, California, Stanford University Press, 1975.

Wyzan, M. L., in *Pressures for Reform in the East European Economies*, Vol. 2. Washington, DC, USGPO (Joint Economic Committee of the US Congress), 1986.

CZECHOSLOVAKIA

Geography

PHYSICAL FEATURES

The Czech and Slovak Federative Republic (CSFR) is a land-locked state located in central Europe, covering an area of 127,899 sq km (49,369 sq miles). It comprises the Czech Lands of Bohemia, Moravia and part of Silesia, in the west, which together form the Czech Republic, and the Slovak Republic (Slovakia), in the east. The country is bordered by Poland, to the north and north-east, and by Germany, to the west and north-west. In the south Austria borders the Czech Lands, and Hungary borders Slovakia. Since the Second World War and the Soviet annexation of parts of Poland and Carpatho-Ruthenia, the eastern border has been with Ukraine (USSR).

The River Morava divides the country into its two principal geographical regions: Bohemia and west Moravia; and east Moravia and Slovakia. Bohemia covers the region drained by the upper Labe (Elbe) and its tributary, the Vltava (Moldau), on which the capital, Prague (Praha), stands. This region is a plateau (average height 500 m), bordered to the north-west and south-west by low ranges of mountains, which form a natural frontier with Germany. Several important rivers, including the Vltava and the Ohře, rise in the south-western hill country and flow north into the Labe, and hence into the North Sea. The River Morava, which flows south and joins the Danube (Dunaj), marks the easternmost edge of the plateau; beyond it lies the more rugged region of eastern Moravia and the mountainous relief of Slovakia. Two parallel branches of the Carpathian Mountains, the Low and High Tatras, cross Slovakia from east to west. Slovakia's only fertile plains are in the Danubian basin, in the south-west, and in the basin of the Uh river, near the eastern frontier.

CLIMATE

The climate is typically continental, with cold, dry winters and hot, humid summers. The average July temperature in Prague is 19°C (66°F) and the average January temperature is −1°C (30°F). Prague receives an average annual rainfall of 485 mm, which often falls as snow in winter months. There is little climatic variation throughout the country, although in the east precipitation is somewhat greater and temperatures are slightly higher.

POPULATION

At the census of March 1991 the total population was 15,567,666. Of these, 54.1% were Czechs, 31.0% Slovaks and 3.8% Hungarians. Most of the large pre-Second World War German community was deported after the Second World War; in 1991 there were only some 62,000 Germans remaining in Czechoslovakia. There were also some 61,000 Poles, 20,000 Ukrainians, 18,000 Ruthenians and a Romany (Gypsy) community of an estimated 500,000 people. However, only some 109,000 Roma registered as such at the census. Of the total population, 8.7% declared themselves to be Moravians and 0.4% Silesians, although inhabitants of these areas have traditionally been regarded as ethnically Czech. The two official languages are Czech and Slovak, which are mutually-comprehensible members of the Western Slavonic group of languages. Members of ethnic minorities continue to use their own languages. The major religion is Christianity. At the census of 1991, 46.4% of the population were adherents of the Roman Catholic Church. An estimated 15% are nominally Protestant, and there are small numbers of Old Catholics and Eastern Orthodox.

At the census of 1991 the population density (persons per sq km) in the whole country was 121.7, but was higher in the Czech Republic (130.6) than in Slovakia (107.5). The Federal and Czech capital is Prague. It is situated in central Bohemia and had a population of 1,212,000 at the 1991 census. The capital of the Slovak Republic is Bratislava, which is located in western Slovakia, to the north of where the Czechoslovak, Austrian and Hungarian borders meet. It had an estimated population of 444,482 in December 1990. Other important towns are Brno (392,614) and Ostrava (331,504), both situated in Moravia.

Chronology

5th–7th centuries: Slavic tribes migrated to central Europe from the eastern plains.

830: The establishment of the Great Moravian Empire, which comprised Bohemia, Moravia and Slovakia.

907: Following the Battle of Bratislava, the Great Moravian Empire was overthrown and the Kingdom of Bohemia was established.

1041: Bohemia became a fief of the Holy Roman Empire, after the subjugation of Prince Bretislav of Bohemia, by the forces of Henry III, the German Emperor.

11th century: Slovakia was incorporated into the Kingdom of Hungary.

1310: After a four-year struggle over the succession, the Bohemian nobles granted the throne to John of Luxembourg, thus ending the Přemyslid dynasty in Bohemia.

1346–78: The reign of Charles I of Bohemia (Charles IV as Holy Roman Emperor), who encouraged the cultural and commercial development of the Czech Lands.

1419: Following the martyrdom of Jan Hus (1415), the leader of a reformist religious movement centred in Prague, his followers, the Hussites, rebelled against German rule after the 'First Defenestration of Prague'.

1420–33: The Hussite Wars were fought, in which forces loyal to the Holy Roman Empire attempted to supress the Hussite rebellion.

1526: Czech nobles elected the Habsburg Archduke Ferdinand I to the throne.

1620: After a two-year rebellion, which began with the Second Defenestration of Prague, Czech troops were defeated at the Battle of the White Mountain.

1781–85: Serfdom was abolished in both the Czech and Slovak lands.

1848: An unsuccessful uprising against the Habsburgs took place in Prague. The Slovaks rebelled against Hungarian rule.

1861: A National Congress of Slovaks issued the Memorandum of the Slovak Nation, which demanded autonomy for Slovakia.

30 May 1918: The Pittsburgh Agreement, which provided for the creation of a common Czech-Slovak state, was signed between Slovak and Czech exiles.

28 October 1918: The Republic of Czechoslovakia was proclaimed; Tomáš Garrigue Masaryk was elected President.

28 June 1919: The Treaty of Versailles provided international recognition to the Czechoslovak state and confirmed its frontiers.

November 1935: Masaryk resigned as President; he was succeeded by Edvard Beneš.

29 September 1938: The Munich Conference took place between the leaders of the United Kingdom, France, Italy and Germany; an agreement was signed, which permitted the cession of the Czechoslovak territories known as Sudetenland to Germany.

5 October 1938: Beneš resigned as President.

2 November 1938: Hungary annexed parts of southern Slovakia.

15–16 March 1939: Hitler, the German leader, invaded the Czech Lands: Bohemia and Moravia became a German Protectorate; Slovakia was proclaimed an independent state, under the pro-Fascist leadership of Mgr Jozef Tiso.

29 August 1944: An uprising against Nazi rule began in Slovakia. By the end of October it had been suppressed by German troops.

3 April 1945: Beneš and his Government-in-exile returned to Czechoslovakia.

9 May 1945: Soviet troops entered Prague.

16 May 1946: National elections took place; the Czechoslovak Communist Party (CPCz) won 38% of the votes cast; Klement Gottwald, leader of the CPCz, was appointed Prime Minister.

25 February 1948: The Communists seized power, following the resignation of 12 non-Communist ministers.

9 May 1948: A new Constitution was approved, which declared Czechoslovakia a 'people's democracy'.

30 May 1948: Elections took place, with only Communist-approved candidates nominated.

June 1948: Beneš resigned, after refusing to sign the new Constitution.

December 1952: Rudolf Slánský, former Secretary-General of the CPCz, and other prominent Communists were executed after 'show trials'.

March 1953: Klement Gottwald died. Antonín Novotný was appointed First Secretary of the CPCz; Antonín Zápotocký became President; Viliám Široký was appointed Prime Minister.

1957: First Secretary of the CPCz, Antonín Novotný, replaced Zápotocký as President.

July 1960: A new Constitution was enacted; Czechoslovakia was renamed the Czechoslovak Socialist Republic.

1963: Prime Minister Široký was replaced by Jozef Lenárt, who launched the mildly reformist New Economic Model. Rudolf Slánský and other Communists who had been purged in the 1950s were rehabilitated.

October 1967: A student rally was violently dispersed by police.

5 January 1968: Antonín Novotný resigned as First Secretary of the CPCz; he was replaced by Alexander Dubček, leader of the Communist Party of Slovakia (CPS).

March 1968: Censorship of the press was ended.

April 1968: The Central Committee of the CPCz adopted an 'Action Programme', which proposed constitutional and economic reforms. Gen. Ludvík Svoboda was appointed President. Oldřich Černík was appointed Prime Minister.

3 August: Representatives of the Communist Parties of member-countries of the Warsaw Pact (except Romania) met in Bratislava to discuss Czechoslovakia's 'Prague Spring' reforms.

20/21 August 1968: Warsaw Pact troops invaded Czechoslovakia; Dubček and other government and Party leaders were abducted to Moscow.

16 January 1969: A student, Jan Palach, immolated himself and died, in protest at the ending of reforms.

17 April 1969: Gustáv Husák replaced Dubček as First Secretary of the CPCz.

1 January 1969: A federal system of government was introduced.

January 1970: Černík was dismissed as Prime Minister.

11 December 1973: A treaty, signed between the Federal Republic of Germany and Czechoslovakia, normalized relations between the two countries and formally annulled the 1938 Munich Agreement.

May 1975: Svoboda resigned as President and was replaced by Husák.

1 January 1977: A group of dissidents, including Václav Havel, the playwright, published the 'Charter 77' manifesto, which demanded an end to the abuse of civil and political rights.

April 1987: Mikhail Gorbachev, General Secretary of the CPSU, arrived in Prague on an official visit.

December 1987: Miloš Jakeš replaced Gustáv Husák as General Secretary of the CPCz.

21 August 1988: Large anti-government demonstrations took place in Prague, on the 20th anniversary of the 1968 Soviet invasion.

10 October 1988: Lubomír Štrougal resigned as federal Prime Minister; he was replaced by Ladislav Adamec.

28 October 1988: More anti-government demonstrations took place.

1989

January

16: A large demonstration took place to mark the 20th anniversary of the suicide of Jan Palach; Václav Havel and 13 other dissidents were arrested.

February

21: Václav Havel was sentenced to nine months imprisonment.

May

1: The traditional May Day rally was disrupted when police dispersed demonstrators protesting against human rights violations.

17: Václav Havel was released after international protests at his detention.

August

21: Several thousand people took part in demonstrations in Prague, on the 21st anniversary of the Soviet invasion.

October

28: Anti-government demonstrations took place, on the 71st anniversary of the establishment of a Czechoslovak state.

November

15: Prime Minister Ladislav Adamec announced that exit permits were no longer needed to travel to the West.

17: Students participating in an officially-sanctioned demonstration were attacked by riot police; 140 people were injured.

19: Some 300 opposition activists from various non-Communist organizations united to form Civic Forum, a broad anti-government coalition (in Slovakia, Civic Forum's counterpart was known as Public Against Violence—PAV).

20: Protests and strikes took place in Prague and other cities.

21: Adamec began discussions with Civic Forum.

24: Miloš Jakeš resigned as General Secretary of the CPCz, together with all other members of the Presidium of the Central Committee and the Secretariat of the CPCz. Karel Urbanek was elected leader of the CPCz; Alexander Dubček returned to Prague, to speak to some 250,000 people in Wenceslas Square.

26: Adamec continued talks with Civic Forum leaders; an opposition rally of some 500,000 people was addressed by Adamec, Dubček and Václav Havel; the Central Committee of the CPCz held an emergency session and demanded the resignation of František Kincl and Václav Jireček, the federal and Czech interior ministers; the leadership of the People's Party, nominally the partners of the Communists in government, was forced to resign.

27: A two-hour general strike took place; there were large demonstrations in Prague.

28: Civic Forum was officially registered as a legal organization.

29: The Federal Assembly abolished the CPCz's constitutional monopoly of power.

December

3: A new coalition Government was proposed, but rejected by Civic Forum.

4: Demonstrators in Prague protested against the proposed Government. Restrictions on foreign travel were lifted.

7: Adamec resigned as Prime Minister; he was replaced by Marián Čalfa.

10: Čalfa announced a new federal Government, with a majority of non-Communist members. Gustav Husák resigned as President.

28: Dubček was elected Chairman of the Federal Assembly.

29: Václav Havel was elected President of Czechoslovakia by the Federal Assembly.

1990

January

1: President Havel announced an amnesty for some 16,000 prisoners.

February

1: The abolition of the StB (Státni bezpečnost—the secret police) was announced.

6: Petr Pithart was appointed Prime Minister of the Czech Republic.

7: The National Front, the Communists' political organization, was disbanded.

March

2–3: The Revolutionary Trade Union Movement voted to disband itself; it was replaced by the Confederation of Czech and Slovak Trade Unions.

27–28: The Federal Assembly approved new laws guaranteeing freedom of association and freedom of the press, and allowing exiles to reclaim their citizenship.

29: The name of the country was changed to the Czech and Slovak Federative Republic.

May

2: The death penalty was abolished.

12: Some 100,000 people took part in demonstrations in Prague demanding wider investigations into the activities of former CPCz officials.

27: Václav Klaus, federal Minister of Finance, announced a reform-orientated budget.

June

8: Elections to the Federal Assembly took place; a coalition of Civic Forum (in Bohemia and Moravia) and PAV (in Slovakia) won an overall majority.

28: A coalition Government was formed, with participation from all major parties, except the CPCz.

July

5: Havel was re-elected as President, for a transitional two-year period.

October

17: Gen. Miroslav Vacek was dismissed from the post of Minister of Defence.

December

12: The Federal Assembly approved constitutional legislation delimiting the powers of the federal, Czech and Slovak governments.

1991

January

7: The International Monetary Fund (IMF) approved loans worth US $1,780m. to Czechoslovakia.

9: The Federal Assembly approved a Law on Fundamental Rights and Freedoms.

February

23: Civic Forum was formally disbanded; its members formed two new political parties, the conservative Civic Democratic Party and the liberal Civic Movement.

26: Legislation allowing privatization of state-owned enterprises was approved.

March

2: Thousands of people took part in demonstrations in Moravia, demanding autonomous status for their region.

5: Vladimir Mečiar, the Prime Minister of the Slovak Republic, left PAV to form a new political party, the Movement for a Democratic Slovakia (MDS).

10–14: There were large demonstrations in Slovakia, in favour of independence for the Republic; President Havel was attacked by crowds when he visited Bratislava.

April

20: The Civic Democratic Party held its constituent congress.

23: Mečiar, the Prime Minister of Slovakia, and seven members of his cabinet, were dismissed by the Presidium of the republican legislature, the Slovak National Council, because of his defection from the ruling party, PAV; Jan Čarnogurský, leader of the Christain Democratic Movement, was appointed as premier instead.

27: Civic Movement officialy constituted itself as an independent political party.

June

1: Mgr Miloslav Vlk was formally installed as the new Primate of Bohemia and Archbishop of Prague, following the resignation of Cardinal František Tomašek from these posts.

3: Jozef Kučerák, the Chairman of PAV, announced that PAV would become a formal political party.

13: The first phase of the 'large privatization' programme began, with the sale of 50 state-owned enterprises to Western companies.

21: The withdrawal of Soviet forces, which had been stationed in Czechoslovakia since 1968, was completed.

23: Mečiar, former Prime Minister of the Slovak Republic, was elected Chairman of the newly-formed MDS.

July

1: Leaders of the member-countries of the Warsaw Pact met in Prague to complete the dissolution of the organization, by formally ending the work of its Political Consultative Committee.

18: The Federal Assembly approved legislation that authorized a referendum on the future of Czech–Slovak relations.

August

6: Some 700 people were evacuated from the area between the controversial Gabčíkovo–Nagymarós hydroelectric dam and the River Danube because of fears that the dam might break.

29: The Federal Government formally recognized the independence of Estonia, Latvia and Lithuania.

History

GORDON WIGHTMAN

INTRODUCTION

On 28 October 1918, following the collapse of the Austro-Hungarian Empire at the end of the First World War, the Republic of Czechoslovakia was founded. The new state united the historic Czech Kingdom of Bohemia and Moravia, which had been an important power in central Europe until its incorporation into the Austrian Empire in the early 17th century, and Slovak provinces of Hungary, which had been under Magyar (Hungarian) rule for almost 1,000 years. Although created to fulfil the demands for self-determination of two of the western Slavic peoples, the Czechs and the Slovaks, the country has always been more heterogeneous than the name suggests. Before the Second World War some 25% of its population were ethnic Germans, and, even though most of the German population were deported after the War, sizeable national minorities remain. The census of March 1991 revealed that 9.8m. Czechs and 4.8m. Slovaks constituted 94.1% of a population of 15,567,666. There were, however, some 500,000 Hungarians (mostly in southern Slovakia), over 61,000 Poles, 53,000 Germans, 20,000 Ukrainians and 18,000 Ruthenians. Within the total, however, was apparently an estimated 500,000 Roma, only 109,000 of whom registered as such in the census.

Czechoslovakia has the distinction that it was the only country in Eastern Europe where parliamentary democracy survived intact for almost all of the period between the First and Second World Wars. Much of the credit for this success can be attributed to the influence of its first two Presidents, Tomáš Masaryk (1918–35) and Edvard Beneš (1935–38 and 1945–48). Democracy was maintained despite defects in the constitutional system. Ethnic diversity weakened a party system that was also highly fragmented by ethnic and social divisions. The system produced coalition governments of relatively short duration, which failed to provide lasting political stability. A more serious threat to the security of the country, however, was the growing disaffection felt by two of the three major ethnic groups, the Slovaks and the Germans.

Slovak disaffection with the pre-1938 Czechoslovak state (the so-called First Republic) stemmed, in part, from the predominant role played by Czechs in the country's political and economic life. It was aggravated by attempts to propagate the concept of a single Czechoslovak nation, of which Czechs and Slovaks were said to be two distinct but closely related branches. That policy tended to ignore important differences between the two nations. Although their lan-guages are mutually comprehensible, they are as much divided by their history and divergent cultural and economic development as they are linked by linguistic and geographic proximity.

Czechs and Slovaks once shared a common state—the Great Moravian Empire, in the ninth century—but, thereafter, their histories largely diverged. While the Slovaks came under Magyar rule, the Czechs created a kingdom that was a major political and cultural force in medieval times. The first university in central Europe was established in Prague, in 1348, by Charles I of Bohemia, who was crowned Holy Roman Emperor seven years later (as Charles IV). In the early 15th century the Hussite movement (named after Jan Hus, Rector of Charles University, Prague, who was burned at the stake in 1415) established the Czech kingdom as a Protestant power. However, the Czechs were defeated by the Austrians, at the Battle of the White Mountain, in 1620. Despite this defeat and their subsequent incorporation into the Habsburg Empire and enforced conversion to Roman Catholicism, the Protestant legacy was to play an important part in the search for a Czech national identity in the 19th century. Slovakia, on the other hand, remained profoundly Roman Catholic and did not experience the same level of urbanization and industrialization as the Czech Lands. The rapid economic development in the Czech Lands, together with the nationalist emphasis on the Hussite tradition and the association of Roman Catholicism with the Austrian 'oppressors', further diluted attachment to the Roman Catholic Church among the Czechs.

It would, however, be wrong to overstate differences between the Czechs and Slovaks. Links between them were maintained, if sporadically, over the centuries. Individual Slovaks often benefited from the availability of university education and support for their studies in Prague. Indeed, the 19th-century revival of Czech nationalism owed much to the contributions of Slovak intellectuals, such as the poet Jan Kollár and the archaeologist Pavel Josef Šafařík, both of whom helped to revive the Czech literary language. Many Slovaks were as committed as Czechs to the establishment of an independent Czechoslovak state. In the diplomatic and propaganda campaign for Czechoslovak independence, which was conducted in Western Europe during the First World War, no less a role was played by the Slovak, Milan Rostislav Štefánik (Czechoslovakia's first Minister of Defence, who died in an aeroplane accident, in

1919), than by his more famous colleagues, Masaryk and Beneš. Moreover, ordinary Slovaks, exiles or prisoners of war in France, Italy and Russia, were as ready as Czechs to volunteer for the military units that were formed in those countries to fight on the side of the Allied Powers for Czechoslovak independence.

The establishment of Czechoslovakia as a unitary state was one source of increasing Slovak discontentment during the 1920s and 1930s. However, it was the dissatisfaction of the German minority which proved fatal to Czechoslovak democracy and to the survival of the state. Although many of the German inhabitants had come to terms with the Czechoslovak state and some German political parties participated in government, the rise of Nazism encouraged the emergence of an extreme German nationalism. The Sudeten German Party, led by Konrad Henlein, attracted some 67% of the votes cast by Germans in the 1935 parliamentary elections.

The problem might have been successfully contained had not the United Kingdom and France agreed, in the Munich Agreement of 29 September 1938, to Germany's annexation of Czechoslovakia's border regions (the Sudetenland—mainly inhabited by members of the German minority). Less than one week later, on 5 October, Beneš resigned as President, only three years after his election to that post. He left a country that had not only lost territory, but also its strategic defences. Six months later, on 15 March 1939, Nazi armed forces entered Prague and established a German Protectorate of Bohemia and Moravia. In Slovakia, which had been granted self-government in late 1938, a separate Slovak state was formed, ruled by the 'puppet' regime of Jozef Tiso.

CZECHOSLOVAKIA AFTER 1945

Beneš spent the Second World War War campaigning for the restoration of the Czechoslovak Republic, within its pre-1938 frontiers. In 1945, after the country's liberation, he returned to Prague as President. In many other respects, however, the political situation was markedly different to that of the pre-War years. The problem of the German minority was resolved by their deportation, and an attempt was made, albeit grudgingly approved by Beneš, to satisfy Slovak demands for greater autonomy through the establishment of a legislature in Bratislava (the Slovak National Council) and an executive Board of Commissioners.

Recognition that the proliferation of political parties in the pre-War First Republic had been a major source of political instability led Beneš to favour a reduction in the number of parties that would be permitted after 1945. It was a policy, however, that contributed to the curtailment, rather than the strengthening, of parliamentary democracy. It was achieved largely through the prohibition, not only of parties that had collaborated with the Nazis, but the proscription of the Agrarian Party, whose guilt was highly dubious.

As a result of that ban, the first post-War parliamentary elections, which took place in May 1946, were not wholly free, but they were, nevertheless, competitive. Their outcome indicated a marked increase in support for the Communist Party of Czechoslovakia (CPCz). With 38% of the votes cast in the country as a whole (40% in Bohemia and Moravia, but only 30% in Slovakia), it emerged as the largest party in the new Constituent National Assembly, with 114 of the 300 seats. Of the three other parties who nominated candidates in Czech constituencies, the moderate Czechoslovak Socialist Party won 55 seats, the Catholic-orientated Czechoslovak People's Party 46 and the centre-left Czechoslovak Social Democrats 37. In Slovakia, however, the Democratic Party won 62% of the popular vote,

although it gained only 43 seats in the Assembly. (Two other small parties, the Labour Party and the Freedom Party, contested the elections and won two and three seats respectively.)

Before 1939 the Communists had never attracted more than 13% of the vote. However, this changed because of the Party's patriotic stance in the late 1930s, popular disillusionment with pro-Western liberal parties, after the Munich Agreement, and the benefits that accrued from association with the USSR, which had liberated most of Czechoslovakia from German occupation (US forces stopped near the western Bohemian town of Plzeň). Furthermore, Communist participation in the Provisional Government, which had governed the country until the elections, gave them a respectability they had earlier lacked. The CPCz's declared commitment, in 1946, to 'a specific Czechoslovak road to socialism' suggested that it would retain the country's democratic and parliamentary traditions, rather than introduce Stalinist practices.

For two years after the elections this apparent commitment to democracy continued. Czechoslovakia was ruled by an all-party coalition Government, in which Klement Gottwald, leader of the CPCz, the largest party in the National Assembly, was Prime Minister. However, the period of coalition government proved to be short-lived. On 20 February 1948 12 non-Communist ministers resigned, thus providing Gottwald with the opportunity to seize power by ostensibly constitutional means. On 25 February President Beneš was forced to agree to his appointment as head of a new Government, which was dominated by Communists.

During the remaining months of 1948 there was a gradual eradication of democratic practice and an emasculation of opposition to the Communists. On 9 May the National Assembly approved a new Constitution, which declared Czechoslovakia a 'people's democracy'. On 30 May elections took place to the National Assembly, with only a single list of candidates. This allowed some representation of non-Communist parties, but individuals who were unacceptable to the Communists had already been expelled from such parties. On 2 June, following his refusal to ratify the new Constitution, Beneš resigned from the presidency. The completeness of the Communists' victory was demonstrated by the election of Gottwald to that office 12 days later.

In the years that followed political repression was directed, not only at the Communists' opponents, but at members of the CPCz itself, in a series of 'show trials', which were among the most severe in Eastern Europe. They reached their most extreme in November 1952, when 14 senior Party and government officials, including Rudolf Slánský, former Secretary-General of the CPCz, were found guilty on charges of conspiracy against the state. Eleven of them, including Slánský, were subsequently executed.

Gottwald's death, on 14 March 1953, only one week after the death of Stalin, the Soviet leader, was followed by a period of collective leadership in Czechoslovakia. Antonín Zápotocký, who had succeeded Gottwald as Prime Minister in 1948, became President in his place, and Antonín Novotný was appointed head of the CPCz, as First Secretary of its Central Committee. In other respects, there were few changes to the Stalinist policies conducted since 1948. The continuation of 'hardline' policies was demonstrated by the brutal suppression, in June 1953, of workers' demonstrations in Plzeň and other Czech towns. The workers were protesting against price rises and a currency reform that depleted the value of savings. Furthermore, political trials continued, notably those of alleged 'Slovak nationalists', in 1954, which led to the imprisonment of a number of leading Slovak Communists. Among them was

Gustáv Husák, who had organized the Communist *coup d'état* in Slovakia, in 1947–48, and who was later to become General Secretary of the CPCz and President of Czechoslovakia.

The moderation of Stalinist policies in much of Eastern Europe in the 1950s, inspired by the new leadership in the USSR, had little effect in Czechoslovakia. Not even Khrushchev's denunciation of Stalin, at the 20th Congress of the CPSU, in February 1956, had a significant impact on the Stalinist policies still in effect in Czechoslovakia. The worst aspects of the CPCz's repressive policies were discontinued thereafter, but it was not until Khrushchev's renewed criticism of Stalin, at the 22nd Party Congress, in 1961, that genuine de-Stalinization began to be implemented in Czechoslovakia.

Recognition by Novotný (who had continued as First Secretary of the CPCz after assuming the presidency on Zápotocký's death, in 1957) that Czechoslovakia, like its neighbours, had suffered from 'a personality cult' in the 1950s, brought a partial rehabilitation for its victims. It also created the opportunity for the gradual emergence, in the 1960s, of a reform movement within the CPCz. Although Novotný encouraged the introduction of economic, and even some political, reforms, his failure to respond to growing pressure for more radical changes, combined with hostility towards him among Slovak Communists and members of the cultural intelligentsia, resulted in his dismissal as First Secretary, on 5 January 1968. He was replaced by Alexander Dubček, until then leader of the Communist Party of Slovakia (CPS), part of the CPCz. He immediately embarked on a programme of radical political and economic reforms, thus beginning a short period of political tolerance, which came to be known as the 'Prague Spring'.

THE 1968 'PRAGUE SPRING'

The reforms agreed by the new Dubček leadership were presented in an Action Programme, approved by the Central Committee of the CPCz on 6 April 1968. It envisaged the combination of a socialist economy, albeit one in which the market would have a role to play, with a democratization of the political system, which would permit the re-emergence of Czechoslovakia's democratic traditions. Recognizing that the USSR would be unlikely to accept a complete loss of power by the CPCz, Czechoslovak reformers planned to modify its traditional dictatorial role through the introduction of more genuine elections, both to parliamentary bodies and within the CPCz. In addition, greater freedom of expression was to be permitted, a greater degree of separation between Party and State was envisaged, and a federal system of government was to be introduced.

Although the Czechoslovak reforms were, in some respects, carefully controlled by the CPCz, in order to allay the fears of the Soviet leadership, the USSR and its allies were anxious to prevent Czechoslovakia's experimental 'socialism with a human face' spreading to other countries in the region, thus threatening the USSR's perceived security interests. On the night of 20/21 August 1968, troops from the other Warsaw Pact states (except Romania), led by Soviet forces, invaded Czechoslovakia. The Soviet leadership's original intention of replacing Dubček with more orthodox Communists, however, failed, owing to popular resistance and the refusal of President Ludvík Svoboda (who had replaced Novotný in that post in April) to accept pro-Soviet nominees. Nevertheless, the invasion ended the Prague Spring reforms and, eight months later, on 17 April 1969, the USSR was able to force Dubček's resignation.

SUPPRESSION OF REFORM AND THE EMERGENCE OF DISSENT

After Dubček was replaced as First Secretary of the CPCz by Gustáv Husák, all but one of the 1968 reforms were abandoned. The federal system, which had been proposed in the Action Programme and implemented on 1 January 1969, remained in place. Separate Czech and Slovak Republics were established, within a Czechoslovak federation; a Czech National Council and a Czech government were created (to parallel those established in Slovakia in 1945); and the country's legislature was transformed into a bicameral Federal Assembly. However, failure to federalize the CPCz and increasing centralization during the 1970s rendered the changes ineffective as a means of granting the Slovaks the greater autonomy which they sought (and which the 1945 changes had failed to achieve).

In other spheres Husák began reversing the 1968 reforms and attempting to ensure that Czechoslovakia conformed with a model of socialism acceptable to the USSR. In the period 1969–71 the CPCz lost some 25% of its membership, as proponents of reform left or were expelled. Reformers were dismissed from influential posts in other institutions and organizations. Newspapers, journals and organizations such as the Czechoslovak Writers' Union and the Czechoslovak Youth Union, which continued to oppose the new policies, were closed down. Opposition to the new orthodoxy was firmly suppressed. Public demonstrations on the first anniversary of the invasion, in August 1969, resulted in five deaths and the arrest of almost 1,400 people in Prague alone. Initial attempts to establish opposition movements (notably the Movement of Revolutionary Youth, in 1969, and the Socialist Movement of Czechoslovak Citizens, in 1971) failed, as their leaders were arrested and imprisoned for their activities.

It was only in the latter half of the 1970s that more durable dissident movements were established, notably Charter 77 and the Committee for the Defence of the Rights of the Unjustly Prosecuted (VONS). These differed from earlier opposition movements in that they did not propose an alternative political programme to that of the Communist leadership. Instead, they campaigned for the observance of civil and political rights, which the Communist regime ostensibly recognized. In addition, they attempted to pursue those aims in ways that were, in theory, permitted by the Constitution.

The 1975 Helsinki Final Act and Czechoslovakia's subsequent ratification of the UN's International Covenants on Civil and Political Rights and on Economic, Social and Cultural Rights gave members of the opposition greater scope to campaign on those issues. However, the direct stimulus for the creation of the Charter 77 manifesto, a document made public on 1 January 1977, was the arrest and imprisonment, in 1976, of members of The Plastic People of the Universe, a popular 'underground' rock group. One of the leaders of Charter 77 was Václav Havel, a playwright who came to prominence in the early 1960s and whose work had been banned since 1969. He later observed that the manifesto's authors (one of whom was Havel himself) had been inspired, not only by the injustice inflicted on the rock group, but also by the evident solidarity among the diverse groups of people attending the trial.

Charter 77 was initially signed by only 242 people, but, by the late 1980s, the number of signatories had risen to nearly 2,000. Its influence grew, despite a policy of repression conducted towards it by the authorities. A continual campaign was waged against it in the official media. The Charter's signatories were subject to harassment, dismissal from their jobs, arrest, imprisonment and sometimes pressure to leave the country. The sudden death, in

March 1977, of one of the group's first spokesmen, Prof. Jan Patočka, may be linked to the rough treatment he received while under interrogation.

Any assessment of the achievements of Charter 77 has to recognize that it had little success in the advancement of civil rights during the last decade of Communist rule. Nevertheless, it made a positive contribution in a number of ways. It ensured that the issue of civil and political rights was not forgotten and thus preserved the democratic values that had been revived for only a short time during the Prague Spring. Together with VONS, which dealt with wrongful arrests, it became a valued source of information about abuses of civil rights in Czechoslovakia. It sponsored a range of studies, on issues ranging from the environment to education, which remained relevant in the 1990s. As a movement which united people from diverse sections of the political spectrum, including ex-Communists, liberal democrats and members of the Christian opposition, it established a sense of community, co-operation and trust that was to bear fruit in November 1989, when the Communists' power was finally challenged.

THE END OF COMMUNIST RULE

At the time of Gorbachev's election as General Secretary of the CPSU, in March 1985, Czechoslovakia was ruled by a Presidium of the Central Committee of the CPCz. All of its members had been in power since 1971, and, as a result, were closely identified with the suppression of the 1968 reform movement. Some undoubtedly sympathized with the aims of Gorbachev's new programme. However, the leadership as a whole was forced to choose between maintaining their traditional loyalty to the current policy in the USSR and abandoning such emulation of the Soviet example. The latter choice involved the continuation of hardline policy; the former required a new, more sympathetic attitude to reform.

In practice, the leadership adopted a compromise which involved ostensible commitment to a Czechoslovak version of *perestroika* (restructuring), while continuing to condemn the Prague Spring. Largely token gestures were made, which appeared to follow the direction of the USSR's economic and, to a lesser extent, political reforms. Husák resigned as General Secretary of the CPCz in December 1987. However, his replacement by Miloš Jakeš, a man whose hostility to reform in 1968 was well-known and who had been responsible for the purge of the CPCz after the Prague Spring, did not lead to expectations of more radical reforms. The continuing repressive character of the regime was evident in its generally harsh response to the public protests against its policies, which became a more common event from 1988 onwards. Even a peaceful candle-lit vigil, in Bratislava, in March of that year, by several thousand Roman Catholics demanding religious freedom and respect for human rights, was brutally dispersed by the police.

A greater readiness on the part of those outside traditional dissident groups to demonstrate their support for radical changes was shown on 21 August 1988, when several thousand protesters demonstrated in Wenceslas Square, in Prague. A similar protest took place on 28 October, the 70th anniversary of the foundation of Czechoslovakia. On 10 December, UN Human Rights' Day, the authorities for once agreed to an unofficial meeting that was addressed by Václav Havel.

A still more serious challenge to the authorities, however, came in early 1989, when demonstrations took place on 15–20 January, to commemorate the suicide of Jan Palach, in 1969. Palach had set himself on fire in protest at the concessions made by the Dubček leadership to the USSR's demands for the ending of the 1968 reforms. The crowds were brutally dispersed by police, leading dissidents who had been involved in the demonstrations were arrested (including Václav Havel, who was sentenced to nine-months imprisonment) and restrictive legislation was introduced, in an attempt to prevent further protests.

None of these measures, however, seemed to have much effect. Pro-democracy demonstrations took place again, on 1 May, 21 August and 28 October 1989. Furthermore, the police brutality in January had provoked a written protest to Ladislav Adamec, the federal Prime Minister, from Cardinal František Tomášek, the Archbishop of Prague. He observed that, 'Brutal violence cannot suppress our citizens' desire to enjoy the measure of freedom which has become an accepted feature of 20th-century life.' In addition, a petition, which was signed by more than 2,000 people, condemned the police attacks on the demonstrators and demanded the release of those who had been arrested. In June 1989 another petition, entitled *A Few Sentences*, was published. Among other things, it demanded greater political freedom, the release of political prisoners and an end to censorship and to the oppression of independent initiatives.

The Velvet Revolution

Despite increasing public involvement in protest demonstrations, the collapse of Communist rule surprised most observers. It was a brutal police attack on a student demonstration, on 17 November 1989, which began what came to be known as the 'Velvet Revolution'. The march had been arranged, with the approval of the authorities, to commemorate students executed by the Nazis in 1939. After the dispersal of the crowd by security forces and police, a rumour began that one student had been killed. Although the rumour was later proved to be false, over the next few days protest demonstrations spread from Prague throughout the country.

One week after the march, on 24 November 1989, following mass demonstrations in Wenceslas Square, in Prague, the entire membership of the Presidium and Secretariat of the CPCz resigned. Adamec, the federal Prime Minister, was left with the task of negotiating a settlement with the Communists' opponents. Initially, Adamec seemed to expect the CPCz to retain a kind of 'caretaker role' in the transition to a more democratic regime, as had happened in the German Democratic Republic and Hungary. Such expectations were quickly dispelled. On 19 November Civic Forum (Občanské fórum) was founded to represent all democratic forces in the Czech Republic; a similar movement, Public Against Violence (PAV), was established in Slovakia. These two groups, who worked in close co-operation, presented Adamec with formidable opponents. His attempt to reach agreement with Civic Forum and PAV, on the formation of a coalition government, collapsed in early December, and he resigned. On 10 December a new coalition administration, the 'Government of National Understanding', took office, with Marian Čalfa (formerly Adamec's deputy) as Prime Minister. Only 10 of the 21 members of the new Government were Communists (and two of those had been nominated by Civic Forum).

Initially Civic Forum and PAV were given only seven ministerial posts in the new Government; the remaining four went to the Czechoslovak Socialist Party and the Czechoslovak People's Party. Both these parties had been members of the CPCz-dominated National Front since 1948, but had ended their subservience to the Communists after the November 1989 revolution. In early 1990, however, Civic Forum and PAV increased their representation when Prime Minister Čalfa and three other Communist ministers resigned their membership of the CPCz and joined the new political movements. Yet, even in late 1989, it was already evident that Communist rule was ended. On 28 December Alexander Dubček, who had been expelled from the CPCz in 1970, was elected Chairman of the Federal Assembly. The next day Václav Havel, Civic Forum's leading spokesman, was elected President of Czechoslovakia. He replaced Husák, who had resigned from that post on 10 December.

Czechoslovakia thus began 1990 with an almost completely new leadership. Those associated with the suppression of the Prague Spring had been dismissed from office. In many cases they had been replaced by signatories of Charter 77, and Alexander Dubček, the symbol of 1968, had been restored to a position of political prominence. Nevertheless, it was evident that more than a revival of 'socialism with a human face' was envisaged by the new leaders. A multi-party parliamentary democracy was the aim in the political system; in the economy, a transition to a market-based structure, with at least some degree of privatization, was sought by all the non-Communist political forces.

The Return to Parliamentary Democracy

Seven months after the Velvet Revolution, on 8 and 9 June 1990, elections took place to the bicameral Federal Assembly and to the National Councils (legislatures) of the Czech and Slovak Republics. Earlier in the year legislation had been introduced, which stipulated that the elections could be contested by any party, political movement or coalition of parties with 10,000 members, or which submitted a petition containing the signatures of sufficient electors to make up for any shortfall. To win seats in each chamber of the Federal Assembly and the Czech National Council, parties were required to obtain at least 5% of the votes cast, but a lower 3% threshold applied in the case of the Slovak National Council.

The outcome of the elections was an overwhelming vote in support of parliamentary democracy. Of those eligible to vote, 96% took part. The coalition of Civic Forum and PAV won a majority of the 150 seats in each chamber of the Federal Assembly (87 in the House of the People and 83 in the House of Nations). Only eight of the 22 contenders for seats in that parliament, however, passed the 5% threshold. The Communists, one of only two parties which nominated candidates in both the Czech and Slovak Republics, was the second largest party, with 23 seats in the House of the People and 24 in the other chamber. The other party which campaigned in both republics was Coexistence (Soužití). It sought to attract votes from all ethnic groups, including Poles and Ruthenians, as well as Czechs and Slovaks. Its main support, however, came from the Hungarian minority and it won five seats in the House of the People and seven in the House of Nations, all of them in Slovakia. The Slovak Christian Democratic Movement (CDM), as had been expected, proved to be much more successful than its counterpart in the Czech Republic, the Christian Democratic Union (CDU). The CDM won 25 seats in the Federal Assembly, compared to 15 won by the CDU. However, PAV won more than twice as many seats as the CDM in Slovakia.

The 13% share of the votes retained by the CPCz suggested that the Communists might still regain some political influence. However, perhaps more disturbing for the future of the newly-restored democratic system were the appeals to the electorates in both republics which stressed regional autonomy or independence. The success of the Movement for Autonomous Democracy-The Society for Moravia and Silesia (MAD-SMS) was especially surprising. Although few observers had expected it to reach the 5% threshold, it received 8%–9% of the votes cast, which represented over

20% of the votes in the two constituencies of North and South Moravia, where it had presented a full list of candidates. This suggested that a much larger number of people than had been anticipated were attracted by its programme of greater autonomy for the regions of Moravia and Silesia. Yet that result was expected to be a relatively minor complication in the search for a lasting constitutional settlement in comparison with the question of relations between the Czechs and the Slovaks. It was the 8%–10% share of the Slovak vote received by the separatist Slovak National Party (SNP) which was the potential source of serious destabilization.

Czechoslovakia emerged from the elections, nevertheless, with a Federal Assembly which seemed capable of coping with the major tasks it expected to encounter during the two years until new elections were due to be held. By the end of June 1990, the Federal Assembly had re-elected Havel as President, confirmed Dubček as Chairman and approved Čalfa's reappointment as Prime Minister of a new coalition Government, comprising nominees from the CDM, in addition to Civic Forum and PAV.

The elections to the Czech National Council produced an overall majority for Civic Forum. Petr Pithart, Prime Minister of the Czech Republic, formed a broadly-based Government, with Civic Forum leading a coalition with the Czechoslovak People's Party (which campaigned as a part of the CDU in the elections) and the MAD-SMS. In Slovakia the election results were more fragmented. PAV was the largest party in the Slovak National Council, with 38 of the 150 seats. It formed a coalition Government with the CDM, which was the second-largest party, and the small Democratic Party.

CZECHOSLOVAKIA AFTER THE ELECTIONS

The success of Civic Forum and PAV in the June 1990 parliamentary elections reaffirmed the preference of a majority of Czechs and Slovaks for a pluralist parliamentary democracy. However, developments after the elections indicated that the re-establishment of democracy was unlikely to be smooth.

An area of dispute that dominated politics in late 1990, and again in 1991, was Czech–Slovak relations. Most citizens, politicians and parties (apart from the SNP) were agreed that Czechs and Slovaks should continue to live in a common state. There was also general agreement that there was a need to change the over-centralized federal system which had been inherited from the Communist regime. Beyond these two points, however, there was little common ground.

The promise that new federal and republican constitutions would be submitted for parliamentary approval before the general elections, which were due in mid-1992, set a deadline for the resolution of future Czech–Slovak relations. However, the authors of these documents faced almost diametrically opposed views on what the constitutional settlement should be in the two republics. The polemics in 1990 and 1991 indicated that most Czechs favoured a degree of devolution to the two republics that would still leave a relatively strong federal authority. Many Slovaks, however, tended to propose a degree of republican autonomy that seemed closer to a confederacy than a federation. Czechs claimed that too much devolution would inevitably result in the dissolution of Czechoslovakia. Slovaks, however, suspected that too little devolution would prevent their attainment of adequate control over their own affairs. It would, they claimed, end in an effective recentralization of power in Prague, as had happened after 1945, when they had been granted their own parliament, and after 1969, when the federal system was introduced.

The constitutional issue was made even more complicated by divergent views over economic strategy. Federal ministers envisaged a uniform application of radical liberal reform as a prerequisite for Czechoslovakia's successful transition to a market economy. In Slovakia attitudes were rather different. The effects of economic reform were likely to be much more severe in Slovakia than in the Czech Lands and there was, consequently, stronger, though by no means universal, support for continuing state intervention. This divergence from attitudes in Prague reinforced Slovak preferences for extensive devolution of power to the Republics.

Disagreements between Czechs and Slovaks provided one source of repeated, if temporary, crises during late 1990 and 1991. Whether a durable agreement could be reached before the next elections, scheduled for mid-1992, was impossible to predict. Uncertainty about the future shape of Czechoslovak politics was also heightened by political divisions in Civic Forum, in January 1991, and in PAV, in April.

The dissolution of Civic Forum had long been expected, since the movement embraced people from diverse and often incompatible political backgrounds. They had shared a desire to end Communist rule but were far from united on the direction post-Communist politics should take. Those divergent attitudes became public at the end of 1990 and in early 1991. The result was the creation of two new parties: a centre-right party, the Civic Democratic Party (CDP), led by Václav Klaus, who had headed the campaign for a more effectively structured organization, based on individual membership and with a narrower policy focus; and a centrist Civic Movement (CM), led by Minister of Foreign Affairs, Jiří Dienstbier, who had advocated the retention of a more loosely organized movement, which would continue to include small associations and parties as Civic Forum had done.

The split in PAV was much less expected, since it had not appeared as disparate a movement as its Czech counterpart. Vladimír Mečiar, a founding member of PAV, had established himself as a firm defender of Slovak interests and autonomy since his appointment as Slovak Prime Minister, in June 1990. However, PAV's elected officials, and some of their representatives in the Slovak Government, viewed Mečiar's policies and aggressive style of leadership as detrimental to the future of Czech–Slovak relations. On 23 April 1991 Mečiar was dismissed as head of the Slovak Government. In response, he and his allies left PAV and formed a new political group, the Movement for a Democratic Slovakia (MDS). The MDS was committed to a degree of state intervention in the economy, to protect Slovaks against the worst effects of economic liberalization, and supported a weak federation, in which extensive powers would be devolved to the two republican governments. In mid-1991 its programme seemed to attract more popular support in Slovakia than the advocacy by Mečiar's rivals of uniform economic reform throughout Czechoslovakia and their commitment to a somewhat stronger federation.

In mid-1991 it seemed that popular opinion in Slovakia was moving in the opposite direction to that in the Czech Lands. While in Slovakia the more left-wing MDS was recorded in a June opinion poll as having the support of 29% of Slovak voters (much more than the level of support recorded for PAV), in the Czech Republic the centrist CM was favoured by only 6% of Czech voters, in comparison with 17% for the more right-wing CDP.

By September 1991 there remained a degree of uncertainty about Czechoslovakia's future, with Slovakia even proposing to declare its sovereignty. The division of Civic Forum and PAV meant that the broad public consensus expressed in the 1990 elections was unlikely to be repeated in 1992. Indeed, unless an electoral system was adopted which successfully inhibited a proliferation of parties in the next parliament, it would be as fragmented as that of the pre-Second World War First Republic. If divergences between Czechs and Slovaks seemed to have deepened, the prospects for the survival of a single Czechoslovak state seemed to depend even more on the formulation of new constitutions that would somehow satisfy the different aspirations of those two peoples: the Slovak desire for optimal autonomy and the Czech preference for a united, Czechoslovak state, the stability of which would not be threatened by too much devolution from the centre to the two Republics.

The Economy

Dr PETER RUTLAND

After 1968 Czechoslovakia was the most conservative of the central Eastern European states and, unlike Hungary and Poland, did not experiment with economic reforms such as expansion of the small private sector or increased trade with the West. According to Western estimates, the Czechoslovak gross national product (GNP) growth rate was around 5% in the early 1970s, but declined to zero growth in 1981/82, and barely rose above 3% for the remainder of the decade.

The depression of 1981/82 was caused by the rise in petroleum prices in 1979. The USSR's fixed-price policy for energy protected Czechoslovakia from the impact of the 1974 crisis, but a change in Soviet pricing policy (Eastern European countries were charged on the basis of a five-year moving average of world prices) meant that Czechoslovakia was affected by the second serious petroleum price rise. Although the growth rates were sufficient to provide a modest increase in living standards, the economies of Czechoslovakia's Western neighbours were growing more quickly. Czechoslovak national income per head rose by 60%, in 1970–88, while that of the Federal Republic of Germany (FRG) rose by 200% over the same period. Czechoslovak GNP per head, as a proportion of Austria's, fell from 90% in 1960 to 60% in 1985. In 1985 Czechoslovakia had a GNP per head of US $7,400 (47th place in the world), and per head consumption of $3,390 (45th place).

The apparent stability of the Czechoslovak economy disguised more serious structural weaknesses. With a few exceptions, Czechoslovak managers had little experience of competing in Western markets. The technological level of Czechoslovak industries was falling steadily behind that of their global competitors. Northern Bohemia, with a heavy concentration of brown-coal power stations and steelworks, was on the brink of an ecological catastrophe. Several factors nevertheless suggested that Czechoslovakia had the best chance of all the Eastern European countries of creating a viable, internationally competitive market economy (leaving aside the special case of the former German Democratic Republic—GDR).

At the beginning of its reform programme Czechoslovakia had three main advantages in comparison with neighbouring Poland and Hungary. Firstly, the failure of the earlier, partial reform experiments resulted in international debts of $1,000 per head in Poland and $2,000 per head in Hungary. In 1990 Czechoslovakia, by contrast, had external debts of $8,000m. ($500 per head), which were expected to rise to $11,700m. by the end of 1991. Secondly, by Eastern European standards, Czechoslovakia had a fairly developed and diverse economy, with a mixture of heavy and light industry and a lower dependence on agriculture than its neighbours. (In 1989 only 10.4% of the employed labour force worked in farming.) One in three families owned a car and weekend cottage, and a refrigerator and colour television were the norm. In 1990 Czechoslovak families spent 35% of their income on food (double the proportion found in Western European family budgets, but one-half that of Poland or the USSR). Thirdly, after the 1989 revolution, a strong central leadership emerged, and a consensual political culture developed, both of which will be necessary to effect the transition to a market economy. However, this is not to suggest that Czechoslovakia's path to pluralist democracy and a market economy will be assured. As of mid-1991 it was moving, slowly, in the right direction, and seemed to have learned from some of the mistakes of its neighbours.

THE EMERGENCE OF THE REFORM PROGRAMME

In 1990 the most important development in the economy was political in nature: the emergence of a consensus in favour of reform within the Government which was established after the 'Velvet Revolution' of November 1989. In a speech, on 19 August 1990, President Havel proposed a 'second revolution', to establish a market economy. In September 1990, amid fierce debate, the Federal Assembly adopted a Scenario on Economic Reform. The main elements of the proposals were: lifting price controls; introducing currency convertibility by January 1991; developing a programme for the privatization of small- and large-scale industry.

Commentaries on the programme were solicited from five academic institutes. Predictably enough, the five reports criticized the programme, and proposed five different solutions. The Government did not want to get involved in a protracted debate and argued that every month's delay made it more difficult for the programme to succeed. A broad Transformation Act laying out plans to change the ownership structure of large-scale state industry was introduced on 1 November 1990, but, in early 1991, had not been adopted by parliament. However, in October 1990, strong support from the provincial organizations of Civic Forum enabled Václav Klaus, the radical Minister of Finance, to be elected chairman of Civic Forum. His control over the organization was confirmed by the Civic Forum conference in Olomouc, in December, which declared that there was no 'third way' between capitalism and Soviet-style socialism.

In November 1990 a public opinion poll showed 43% of the public supported the economic reform programme, 23% expressed no opinion, 10% expressed concern and 23% voiced opposition. Opponents included pensioners and agricultural workers who were fearful of the loss of farm subsidies. Thus the public did not seem to be completely united behind the reform programme. However, in several respects the situation seemed more promising than in

Poland or Hungary. Firstly, there was a solid core of public support for reform. Reform advocates dominated the national leadership, and their opponents could not offer a plausible alternative programme. Secondly, the Czechoslovak leadership proceeded carefully, and was anxious to avoid the errors of Czechoslovakia's neighbours, such as Poland's over-zealous 'shock therapy', with its harsh side-effects, or the 'spontaneous privatizations' in Hungary, which saw the premature sale of valuable assets to foreigners and former Communist officials at bargain prices.

FINANCE

At the beginning of 1990 Poland and Yugoslavia were facing inflation of 50% per month and administered a so-called shock-therapy policy. By abruptly introducing currency convertibility and a tight monetary policy, they were able, temporarily, to bring inflation under control. Many Eastern Europeans, however, began to worry about the negative social and economic effects of such policies. Ending credit for enterprises resulted in a 20%–30% reduction in the value of production, while the declining value of the currency meant that prices continued to rise. The Czechoslovaks were determined to learn both the positive and negative lessons from the experiments with shock therapy. Czechoslovakia was better placed than its neighbours to avoid 'stagflation' (the combination of recession with inflation), since it did not have a large foreign debt, and the central authorities had not allowed monetary emissions to get out of control. In 1990 retail prices rose a modest 14%, while wages rose only by 3%. (The average wage at the end of 1990 was 3,250 korunas.) However, like all the socialist economies, there was a money 'overhang' of 300,000m. korunas in consumer savings (18,000 korunas per head, equivalent to 17 months' average income). This meant that despite high prices, consumer durables such as washing machines still disappeared from the stores as soon as they were offered for sale. Until around 1980 the government budget had been approximately in balance. Turnover tax, levied on enterprises, was the principal source of revenue and the channel for subsidy distribution. In the 1970s the net outlays through the turnover tax were less than 5,000m. korunas per year, but rose dramatically to 8,800m. korunas in 1981, 22,600m. in 1986 and 49,700m. in 1989. Most of these subsidies went to farms: in 1988 the agricultural complex received 55% of total non-investment subsidies, whereas housing and communal services received only 13%, transport 9% and industry 9%.

In 1990 the complicated structure of the turnover tax was simplified, with the 1,400 different rates applied being reduced to four. There was also a determined effort to reduce the level of subsidies to economic enterprises. The Government revoked the original 1990 budget, which had been introduced on 30 November 1989, in the last days of the old regime. In late March 1990 Klaus persuaded the Federal Assembly to adopt a new, 'tight' budget, with a projected deficit for 1990 of only 5,000m. korunas (down from a deficit of 7,000m. korunas in 1989). Klaus restricted government expenditure, and 1990 ended with a budget surplus of 5,000m. korunas. The budget for 1991 was 117,000m. korunas, apportioned as follows: 28,000m. korunas for the armed forces; 5,000m. korunas on transport subsidies; 27,000m. korunas compensation to consumers for food price rises; 11,000m. korunas agricultural subsidies; 6,000m. korunas compensation for energy price rises; and 1,500m. korunas compensation for former political prisoners. Thus agricultural subsidies were reduced from 40,000m. korunas to 11,000m. korunas (although most of the money saved was used to compensate consumers). The annual payment of 1,200m. korunas to the Communist Party of Czechoslovakia (CPCz) was discontinued and most of its assets were nationalized. The number of civil servants had already been reduced by some 30% in 1988 and 1989, so only another 5% were removed in 1990.

PRICE LIBERALIZATION

The Government's strict monetary and fiscal policy and the maintenance of rigid wage controls in industry ensured that retail prices only rose by 10% in 1990. However, the Government was committed to eliminating subsidies to industry and agriculture. To achieve this, prices would have to be freed, so as to allow supply and demand to determine which enterprises would be profitable and which would go bankrupt. The declared aim was to free 85% of retail prices by the end of 1991. Price controls were ended on food and energy products, but there was reluctance to free the prices of industrial goods before privatization began, since many producers faced little competition and would be able to raise prices to exorbitant levels. On 9 July 1990 subsidies on a wide range of food products were eliminated, leading to an overall 26% price increase for food items. After public opposition, the Government reduced the initial 75% rise in the price of top quality beef to 40%. Over the whole year, meat of all sorts rose 40% in price, bread 53%, vegetables 48%, and dairy products 63%. In July 1990 petrol prices were increased by 50%. An increase in wholesale energy prices by 50%–60% was introduced on 1 December 1990 and passed on to consumers in January 1991.

From 1 January 1991 price controls were relaxed for a broad range of products (although maximum price ceilings were still fixed for most products). Bread, milk and egg prices doubled within one week, and meat prices rose by 20% (in excess of the 40% rise of July 1990). Manufacturers were also allowed to increase prices, subject to governmental approval on a case-by-case basis. For example, the price of the Skoda Favorit automobile rose from 85,000 korunas, in January 1990, to 150,000 korunas, in January 1991.

RETAILING AND SERVICES

In April 1990 a series of laws was approved, which abolished the previous legal prohibitions on private economic activity. The private sector expanded from 86,000 employees at the beginning of 1990 to about 300,000 employees by the end of the year, although most of these persons retained full-time jobs in the state sector. Private entrepreneurs were granted three years of reduced taxes (a reduction of 60% in the first year, falling to 20% in the third year), but still faced many practical barriers, including: cumbersome registration procedures; an acute shortage of premises; and administrative and financial problems when dealing with foreign suppliers. Czechoslovakia is at a disadvantage in comparison with Poland and Hungary, both of whom relaxed controls on small entrepreneurs in the early 1980s.

'Small privatization' legislation was announced by the Government in September, and approved on 25 October 1990. Some 70,000 small businesses and real-estate properties, which were nationalized in 1955–61, were to be returned to their former owners, or their heirs, who were given six months to lodge their claim. Owners would not be compensated for damage to their property and would be liable to repay the State for any investments which had recently been completed. If the former owners did not submit a claim, the properties were to be auctioned. Foreigners and non-residents were not permitted to buy these properties. An additional measure, passed on 16 November, pledged to auction 100,000 other small businesses, currently operated by state enterprises and local councils. Following threats of strike action by the shopworkers' union, the

Government agreed to provide loans equal to 50% of the purchase price for employees who wished to bid for the store in which they worked.

Auctions of small businesses began in January 1991, under the supervision of the newly-created Ministry of Privatization, headed, in the Czech Republic, by Tomáš Ježek. The whole process was planned to be completed by the end of 1991. The federal Government was to gain 70% of the proceeds of the sales, local authorities 30%. The properties were to be sold by auction, with a minimum price of 50% of the estimated value set for the first round, and 20% for properties which had to be offered at a second round. Foreign citizens were to be allowed to participate in second-round auctions. The first auction took place in Prague, on 26 January 1990. Sixteen properties were sold for 22m. korunas. Many of the properties being sold were small, modest retail outlets and, in many cases, the title to the property had not been resolved, so it was two-year leases that were being auctioned.

The pace of small privatization was expected to be increased, after it was revealed that the IMF attached conditions to the US $1,800m. loan, which it granted to Czechoslovakia in January 1991. (The loan was primarily designed to compensate for the rise in the price of petroleum.) The IMF reportedly expected 13,000 small properties to be auctioned by the end of June 1991 and 20,000 more by the end of December. It seemed unlikely that the Czechoslovak Government would be able to achieve these targets. Apart from doubts about the economic viability of the programme, several fundamental legal and political questions remained unresolved.

The small privatization programme was threatened mainly because of continued disagreement over the restitution of properties seized in 1948–55. Initially, the Government hoped to exclude these properties from the programme altogether, on the grounds that including them would seriously complicate the privatization process. An additional complication was that many of the post-1948 owners had occupied the property of some 3m. Jews and Germans, who had been dispossessed, during and after the Second World War. Parliament also wanted to make the 580,000 people who had emigrated since 1948 eligible for the programme.

However, the Federal Assembly rejected the Government's arguments, and, on grounds of equity, insisted on full restitution. On 21 February 1991 it was decided that all property nationalized since 25 February 1948, including both large and small enterprises, would be restored to its owners. It is estimated that 60% of the enterprises in the Czech Republic, and 50% in the Slovak Republic, may be claimed, at a possible cost of 280,000m. korunas. Former owners were granted six months to lodge their claim. *Emigrés* who had registered as residents would also be eligible for participation in the restitution programme.

The whole restitution process seemed in danger of becoming a legal quagmire, and threatened to delay, and possibly derail, the entire privatization programme. It can also be noted that, with the exception of the former GDR, none of the other Eastern European countries are seeking full restitution back to the first years of Communist rule.

AGRICULTURE

Agriculture has been fairly successful in Czechoslovakia, providing 95% of the country's food needs for most of the period since 1945. The farming, forestry and fishing sectors contributed 10.1% of net material product (NMP) in 1989, when 11.0% of the working population were employed in the sector. Under the Communist regime farms were protected by large state subsidies, which continued, although at lower levels, after 1989. It is not clear how many farms would be viable, if they were forced to rely on retail sales alone to cover their costs. It was expected that the country's 245 state farms would probably be converted to joint-stock companies, as part of the 'large privatization' programme (see below), while the 1,660 co-operative farms would remain more or less intact. The unified agricultural marketing organizations, despite criticism of the monopoly position which they enjoy, were expected to be retained for the time being, in the absence of any immediate alternative.

In May 1991 the Federal Assembly approved legislation which allowed for the return of land nationalized between 25 February 1948 (when the Communists seized power) and 1 January 1990. However, to prevent the complete disruption of state and co-operative farms, former owners, or their heirs, will only be permitted to reclaim a maximum of 150 ha. It is estimated that only 34% of the farmland belonging to state or co-operative farms would be eligible for privatization. Even this level of privatization seemed unlikely to occur, however. Agricultural workers were dubious as to the economic viability of private farming, given the elimination of farm subsidies and new worries about the availability of credit and equipment. A poll carried out by the Institute for Agricultural Economics, in October 1990, showed that 52% of farmers doubted whether private farming would be feasible in their village, and a further 41% thought it was definitely impossible. Only 10% thought that owning or renting a private farm could be economically viable.

MANUFACTURING INDUSTRY

In the early 1980s some limited decentralization took place in Czechoslovak industrial management. The central industrial planning ministries were abolished and replaced with collegial boards, consisting of representatives of the major firms in each sector. The task facing the new Government was to devise some procedure for converting these trusts into private ownership.

A number of laws passed in mid-April 1990 empowered the Government to dissolve the existing trusts, and laid the legal foundations for converting enterprises into joint-stock companies. In the first six months of 1990 the 100 large trusts that dominated the economy of the Czech Republic were divided into 4,500 independent enterprises. In addition, the system of central directive planning was abolished. In July the State Planning Commission and the Federal Price Office were abolished. Firms were no longer given output targets, nor did they have to report their production activities to any central office. However, a Price Control Commission was empowered to set maximum prices for a broad range of goods, and a law passed in December 1990 gave the Government broad reserve powers for strategic economic planning.

While these reorganizations were taking place, the economy stagnated. In 1990, according to official figures, industrial output fell 3.7%, nominal wages rose 3% and retail turnover rose 9.7%. Although the country avoided a slump of similar proportions to that in Poland, the value/volume of industrial output fell by some 5%–10% in key sectors, as follows: coal 9.6%, chemicals 4.8%, metallurgy 2.8%, cars 10%, trucks 5%, computers 25%. There are three principal explanations for this decrease in output. Firstly, in 1990, many suppliers and purchasers in the GDR and the USSR broke their contracts or ceased trading altogether. Secondly, many firms were monopoly producers, and exploited their newly-granted freedom by reducing output and raising prices. Thirdly, in the absence of pressure from central planners, there was little incentive for managers to make an effort to increase production or profits, particularly since they were probably uncertain whether they would still be running their plant in a year's time.

The next phase in economic reform was the implementation of the 'large scale' privatization programme. A significant proportion of the 4,500 state enterprises, holding 40%–80% of the nation's total industrial assets of 3,000,000m.–5,000,000m. korunas (US $110,000m.–180,000m.) were to be converted into joint-stock companies by 1996. Only mines, railways and power generation enterprises were expected to remain under direct state ownership.

The programme envisaged approximately 20% of the stock being made available to foreign buyers, 20% being offered for public sale through a voucher system, and the remaining 60% being retained by the newly-created National Property Fund, to be sold after the stock market began operations. The Government rejected union proposals to sell 20% of the stock directly to employees, as was planned in Poland. Each firm was instructed to draft its own privatization project (subject to approval by the Ministry of Privatization), in which a mix of auction, vouchers and direct sale is proposed for the distribution of shares, possibly including foreign purchasers. By mid-1991 some of the projects involving foreign buyers had already been processed, but confusion over the voucher method was delaying most of the projects.

In mid-1991 the details of the voucher system were still being finalized, and its implementation was postponed until July 1992 (or possibly later). Under the scheme each citizen was to be allowed to buy 1,000 points of vouchers for 2,000 korunas ($70). In some firms vouchers would be exchanged directly for stock; in others stock would be sold at 'Dutch auctions' (where the auctioneer works down from a starting price). The validity of the vouchers was expected to be one–two years, the expected duration of the large-scale privatization process.

That was the programme in outline. As a condition of their January 1991 loan, the IMF requested specific proposals for the privatization of 100 large enterprises by June of that year, and 150 more by December. By then they expected 75% of Czechoslovakia's enterprises to be converted to joint-stock companies. This timetable proved unrealistic. There were many practical problems still to be overcome, which could generate political controversy and threaten the implementation of the reform. For example, there were problems of equity. Some enterprises had powerful political connections and received generous investment capital under the old regime. It seemed unfair to simply retain the old managers, transfer the assets to new owners, and expect other enterprises to compete with them. Such accusations were directed, for example, at the highly successful Slusovice agricultural co-operative, which diversified in the 1980s into a range of manufacturing activities, including computer assembly.

The old regime left behind an ambiguous ownership structure which has caused problems for the transformation process. Some workers' councils are powerful enough to try to hinder reorganization plans. Local councils share dual ownership rights over many small industries with central trusts, and have threatened to oppose plant closures planned for their district. Finally, there have been many disputes where subsidiary plants have objected to the privatization package proposed by their controlling trust. Successful plants preferred to become independent, while ailing plants resisted closure plans. For example, in December, workers in the Budvar brewery went on strike in favour of independence from the Southern Bohemia Brewery Trust, while workers in coal mines in Northern

Bohemia threatened to strike against plans to give them economic independence from their former controlling trust. In both these cases, the Government conceded the workers' demands.

LABOUR AND THE UNIONS

Despite their considerable power at plant level, the trade unions played a surprisingly small role in the national reform debates. A National Association of Strike Committees emerged out of the general strike which took place in November 1989. The old Communist union organization, the Revolutionary Trade Union Movement (Revoluční odborové hnuti—ROH), was formally dissolved on 3 March 1990, and a new Confederation of Czech and Slovak Trade Unions (Česká a Slovenská konfederace odborových svazů—ČSKOS) was formed. ROH's 17 industrial unions were replaced by 50 new unions, and its regional councils abolished. A new set of leaders was chosen in competitive elections: only 20% had previously held office in ROH unions. In 1991 the ČSKOS-affiliated unions included 95% of the labour force. In 1990, Civic Forum's strong electoral performance increased the Government's confidence, and the unions adopted a more conciliatory position to try to prevent their exclusion from the economic reform process. The unions were widely seen as a 'hold-over' from the old regime, and still under the influence of former ROH officials. Few politicians were willing to articulate their interests in public, and privatization plans did not grant any consultative role to the unions.

In September 1990 a Council of Social and Economic Understanding was created to provide a framework for tripartite negotiations, consisting of 10 representatives from the unions, seven from the employers and seven from the Government. By January 1991 the outline of a corporatist arrangement had emerged. In return for the opportunity to influence the reform process, the unions accepted, in principle, the idea of privatization and the creation of a market economy. More specifically, the unions agreed to restrict wage increases to 6% for 1991, with partial adjustment for retail price inflation. In the first six months of 1991 prices rose 50%, while wages increased by only 15%. In return for accepting this decrease in real pay, the unions won a raise in the minimum guaranteed social income and minimum wage (1,500 korunas and 2,000 korunas respectively), and the introduction of an unemployment benefit system. The new minimum wage may cause problems as a result of the compression of wage differentials; the average wage is only 2,900 korunas per month. Dismissed workers will receive between two and five months severance pay, and unemployed workers who show a willingness to work will receive benefits for one year (60% of their former wage, falling to 50% after six months). The number of unemployed is expected to reach 3%–4% of the working population in the Czech Lands, by the end of 1991, and 8% in Slovakia. According to some estimates, 80,000 of the 350,000 steel workers and coal miners may face redundancy. The jobs of many of the 200,000 workers in the armaments industry were also expected to be at risk. A new Labour Code was introduced, which, among other things, removed the previous role of works councils in the selection of managers. In December 1990 new legislation was agreed, which introduced a system of binding collective contracts, with pay-related strikes only allowed during the contract negotiation period. Thus, despite widespread worker agitation, and many short work stoppages or strike threats, a *modus vivendi* between organized labour and the pro-reform Government seemed to be emerging. This was a much more positive result than the situation in neighbouring Poland and Hungary, where worker opposition to market reform seemed more entrenched.

FOREIGN ECONOMIC RELATIONS

Those countries which experienced significant economic successes after 1945 were examples of export-led growth (for example, the Federal Republic of Germany, the Republic of China—Taiwan). Eastern Europe, unfortunately, is not likely to replicate this pattern. The Council of Mutual Economic Assistance (CMEA or Comecon—dissolved in 1991) functioned as a trade-restricting union, which hindered the international integration of the region's economies. Czechoslovakia's foreign trade is only one-sixth of the level of comparable Western countries (measured as a proportion of GNP). Czechoslovakia's total external trade in 1988 was US $30,000m., placing it 31st in the world. This amounted to $3,031 of trade per head, compared to $8,907 for neighbouring Austria. In addition to these past distortions and missed opportunities, in 1990 Czechoslovakia was seriously affected by the sudden collapse of markets in CMEA and the rise in the price of petroleum following the invasion of Kuwait by Iraq, in August.

Trade with the East

In 1989 more than 60% of Czechoslovakia's trade was conducted with member-countries of CMEA, and more than 60% of its trade within CMEA was with the USSR. Only 18% of trade was with the EC. This amounted to $5,500m. of exports to the West and, nominally, $16,000m. to CMEA.

The purpose of the CMEA organization was to provide for the needs of the Soviet economy, and the system of trade balancing in non-transferable 'convertible roubles' inhibited horizontal trade between CMEA partners in Eastern Europe. Some 57% of Czechoslovakia's exports to CMEA countries were raw materials, and only 24% consumer goods. Czechoslovakia accumulated a nominal 44,000m. koruna non-convertible currency surplus with the USSR, although it traded at a deficit with the other CMEA members.

In 1990 this traditional trade pattern started to change. Most Czechoslovak imports from the USSR consisted of petroleum, natural gas and petrochemical products. In 1989 the USSR had been selling petroleum at $7.40 per barrel, when the world price was $19. In 1990 Soviet petroleum and natural gas deliveries were reduced by 15%, and contracted by another 20% in 1991. Furthermore, from 1 January 1991, the USSR began to demand payment for its petroleum in convertible currency, equivalent to a 300% price increase. This required additional expenditure of $2,000m. on imports for 1991, and meant that approximately 80% of Czechoslovakia's export earnings would have to be spent on energy imports (assuming demand stayed at the previous level). At the end of 1990 Czechoslovakia had a $550m. deficit on the current account of the balance of payments. In 1990 the 'transferable rouble' system of handling intra-CMEA trade was ended. Exports to member-countries of CMEA fell 20% in 1990, while imports fell 8%. The largest reductions were in trade with Poland (40%) and Yugoslavia (34%). Despite these problems with financing trade, Czechoslovakia expected 25% of its trade in 1991 to be with the USSR. Although there have been protracted trade negotiations, no new payments system has emerged to replace the transferable rouble. In 1990 and 1991 most of the trade with the USSR was proceeding through barter deals. These were negotiated at three levels: with national, republican and local authorities within the USSR. In December 1990 the first convertible-currency agreement was signed, by ČKD Locomotiva, for the export of railway engines to the USSR. In December 1990 the Soviet and

Czechoslovak Ministers of Foreign Trade signed an agreement whereby the USSR was to repay the old Soviet debt to Czechoslovakia at a ratio of one US dollar to one rouble (that is, on terms quite favourable for the Czechoslovaks). In March 1991, during a visit to Moscow, Petr Pithart, Czech Prime Minister, established a clearing system to co-ordinate the barter deals.

Trade with the West

Trade with the West rose 4.5% in 1990, mostly as a result of an increase in purchases of Western consumer goods. The Czechoslovak federal Government began to limit the increase in foreign imports, which threatened to undermine domestic producers and have an inflationary effect. In January 1991 the former strict system of import licences was replaced by a 20% tariff on imports of consumer goods. (Neo-classical economists are, of course, unanimous in the opinion that if protectionist measures are to be retained, tariffs are more efficient than quotas.)

Western nations have taken measures to lower barriers to trade with Czechoslovakia. In May 1990 COCOM (the Co-ordinating Committee for Multilateral Export Controls—a voluntary, non-treaty organization, consisting of all member-countries of NATO, except Iceland, plus Australia and Japan, which was established to prevent the sale of items with potential military use to Communist countries) relaxed restrictions for exports to Czechoslovakia. The granting of 'most-favoured-nation' status to Czechoslovakia by the USA, in December 1990, meant duty on exports to the USA decreased (for example, the duty on beer was reduced from 13% to 1.6%, on glass 60% to 20%, on tyres 10% to 4%), and on imports from the USA (for example, the duty on wheat fell from 30% to 7%, on computers from 15% to 5%). In January 1991 it was announced that Czechoslovakia was to receive the largest share ($1,800m.) of the $5,000m. in loans which the IMF proposed to grant to Eastern Europe in 1991. Czechoslovakia was also to receive $1,500m. of the $9,000m., which the International Bank for Reconstruction and Development (IBRD—see p. 39) planned to allocate to the region in 1991–94. The USA itself was to give $120m. to Czechoslovakia as emergency aid, and to provide capital for small businesses.

It is hard to predict which areas of trade will grow most rapidly. Apart from the public demand for Western clothing and consumer durables, Czechoslovakia has acute needs for Western technology to re-equip its machine-tool industries and to rebuild its telecommunications system, which is on the level of that of the USA of the 1950s. The problem is finding sectors in which Czechoslovakia can generate the convertible-currency earnings to pay for these items. Tourism seemed likely to show rapid growth, since Czechoslovakia only earned $36 per head in 1988, compared to $200–$800 in Western countries. There is, however, an acute shortage of hotel accommodation, and road connections with the West are poor. In terms of classic trade theory, Czechoslovakia and the other Eastern European countries probably have a comparative advantage in food production, but this is of little relevance, given the protectionist policies of the EC.

Moves towards Currency Convertibility

The Government accepted, in principle, the idea that Czechoslovak industry should expect to take world market prices as a measure of their performance, and moved the koruna steadily towards full convertibility over the course of 1990. In January 1990 there was a 20% devaluation bringing the rate to 16 korunas to the US dollar. In October it was devalued again, by 55%, from 16 to 24 korunas to the dollar. In December 1990 there was a further 17%

devaluation, and a fusion of the business and tourist rates at 28 korunas to the dollar. (Previously the tourist rate had been 50% above the business rate.) While businesses can now freely convert currency, there are limits on the ability of private citizens to exchange korunas for convertible currency. In early 1990 Austrians bought large amounts of food in Czechoslovakia, which was selling at 20% of the price in the West. In March 1990, the Government responded by introducing a ban on tourist exports of food and alcohol. It was expected that, following increases in the price of food, these restrictions would be lifted.

Joint Ventures

Czechoslovakia has been slower and more cautious than its Eastern European neighbours in developing joint ventures with Western partners. The Government's philosophy was to liberalize domestic prices and de-monopolize the industrial structure before encouraging investment by Western partners. Legislation was adopted, in April 1990, which created the legal framework for joint ventures. Another law granted any Czechoslovak enterprise the right to engage in foreign trade (subject to the deposit of a $50,000 bond, a significant disincentive for small companies). Foreigners are not allowed to buy land or property directly, but must operate through joint ventures.

As was true elsewhere in Eastern Europe, co-operation with foreign firms was hampered by the acute shortage of accommodation in Prague. The city authorities maintained tight control over the allocation of business premises, and office rents had already reached Western levels by 1991. Rules governing the repatriation of profits were still in flux in mid-1991: initially, firms were expected to reinvest 30% of their profits within Czechoslovakia.

Nevertheless, foreign firms have shown considerable interest in entering the Czechoslovak market and in acquiring Czechoslovak manufacturing capacity. As of December 1990, there were 1,168 joint ventures (907 in the Czech Republic and 259 in the Slovak Republic), with capital of 4,600m. korunas. The countries of origin of the principal partners were as follows: Austria (348); Germany (330); Switzerland (93); USA (49); Italy (45); United Kingdom (35); Netherlands (34); France (27). In the automobile industry, for example, Volkswagen acquired 25% of the Skoda works in Mladá Boleslav, defeating rival bids from Renault and General Motors. Volkswagen's share was planned to rise to 70% by 1995, as they contribute new investment funds. The plant will produce a modified version of the Skoda Favorit model, plus the Volkswagen Passat. Volkswagen were also negotiating with BAZ, in Bratislava, while Audi were looking seriously at Tatra, in Kopřivnice.

THE SLOVAK QUESTION

The Slovak question, which re-emerged in 1990 and 1991, mostly centred on issues of national pride and political symbolism, but it has also had a strong economic component. Radical Slovak politicians seemed to be manipulating the threat of secession to win more favourable economic terms. Polls and election results showed little evidence of support for complete secession among Slovaks. Czech offers to conduct a referendum on secession were rebuffed by Slovak nationalists, probably because they feared defeat.

Under the old regime resources were channelled into Slovakia to promote its development. In mid-1990, however, Slovakia's share of the federal budget was reduced from 42% to 38%, a proportion closer to its 30% share of the country's population. In a series of meetings between Czech and Slovak leaders, between August and November 1990, the Slovaks demanded economic concessions, such as the creation of a Slovak State Bank, with shared responsibility for federal monetary policy. By December 1990 the two sides had agreed on the proportion of the turnover tax which would be allocated to each Republic; the federal government was to receive 35%, the Czech government 40% and the Slovak government 25%. Also, an independent stock company was created to manage the petroleum and natural gas pipelines which the Slovak Government had claimed as their exclusive property, on the grounds that all the refineries were located in Slovakia.

CONCLUSION

In 1990 and 1991 the issue of Czech–Slovak relations dominated political and economic debate in Czechoslovakia and threatened to distract attention from the problems of a transition to a prosperous market-based economy. However, although many political and constitutional problems remained unsettled in mid-1991, the prospects for a successful transition to a prosperous market economy seemed relatively good. The country has established a high profile in Western financial circles and it can be expected that the 'large privatization' programme will attract considerable interest from Western companies. Nevertheless, the process of transition will entail considerable social and economic costs. Whether the relatively cautious policies of the Czechoslovak leadership will be more able to prevent social unrest than the more rapid programmes begun in Hungary and Poland remains to be seen.

Statistical Survey

Source: mainly Federal Statistical Office, Sokolovská 142, 180 00 Prague 8; tel. (2) 814; telex 121197.

Area and Population

AREA, POPULATION AND DENSITY

Area (sq km)	127,899*
Population (census results)	
December 1985	
Males	7,558,152
Females	7,961,150
Total	15,519,302
1 March 1991	15,567,666
Population (official estimates at 31 December)†	
1988	15,624,254
1989	15,649,765
1990	15,674,753
Density (per sq km) at 1 March 1991	121.7

* 49,382 sq miles.
† Population estimates do not take account of March 1991 census results.

POPULATION BY NATIONALITY
(at 31 December 1989)

	Czech Republic		Slovak Republic		Total	
	'000	%	'000	%	'000	%
Czech . .	9,742	94.0	64	1.2	9,806	62.7
Slovak . .	425	4.1	4,585	86.6	5,010	32.0
Magyar (Hungarian) .	23	0.2	578	10.9	601	3.8
German . .	49	0.5	3	0.1	52	0.3
Polish . .	70	0.7	3	0.1	73	0.5
Ukrainian and Russian .	15	0.1	41	0.8	56	0.4
Others and unspecified .	38	0.4	14	0.3	52	0.3
Total . . .	10,362	100.0	5,288	100.0	15,650	100.0

REGIONS

	Area (sq km)	Population (31 Dec. 1990)	Density (per sq km)
Czech Republic:			
Central Bohemia . . .	10,994	1,114,098	101
Southern Bohemia . .	11,345	701,793	62
Western Bohemia. . .	10,875	869,188	80
Northern Bohemia . .	7,819	1,189,592	152
Eastern Bohemia . .	11,240	1,239,804	110
Southern Moravia. .	15,028	2,059,394	137
Northern Moravia . .	11,067	1,975,654	179
Prague (city) . . .	496	1,215,076	2,450
Total	78,864	10,364,599	131
Slovak Republic:			
Western Slovakia . .	14,492	1,730,786	119
Central Slovakia . . .	17,982	1,622,380	90
Eastern Slovakia . .	16,193	1,512,506	93
Bratislava (city) . .	368	444,482	1,208
Total	49,035	5,310,154	108
Grand total	127,899	15,674,753	123

PRINCIPAL TOWNS
(estimated population at 31 December 1990)

Praha (Prague, capital) . .	1,215,076		Zlín (formerly Gottwaldov) . .	197,737
Bratislava . .	444,482		Žilina . . .	183,469
Brno . . .	392,614		Plzeň (Pilsen). .	174,984
Ostrava . .	331,504		České Budějovice .	174,391
Košice . .	238,343		Hradec Králové .	163,573
Olomouc . .	224,815		Pardubice . .	163,356
Nitra . . .	212,123		Liberec . . .	160,437

BIRTHS, MARRIAGES AND DEATHS

	Registered live births		Registered marriages		Registered deaths	
	Number	Rate (per 1,000)	Number	Rate (per 1,000)	Number	Rate (per 1,000)
1982 . .	234,356	15.2	117,376	7.6	181,158	11.8
1983 . .	229,484	14.9	120,547	7.8	186,907	12.1
1984 . .	227,784	14.7	121,340	7.8	183,927	11.9
1985 . .	226,036	14.6	119,583	7.7	184,105	11.9
1986 . .	220,494	14.2	119,979	7.7	185,718	12.0
1987 . .	214,927	13.8	122,168	7.8	179,224	11.5
1988 . .	215,909	13.8	118,951	7.6	178,169	11.4
1989 . .	208,472	13.3	117,787	7.5	181,649	11.6

1990 (provisional): Live births 210,527 (birth rate 13.4 per 1,000); Deaths 183,710 (death rate 11.7 per 1,000).

CIVILIAN LABOUR FORCE EMPLOYED
('000 persons, excluding apprentices)

	1987	1988	1989
Agriculture . . .	852	839	811
Forestry . . .	94	94	95
Mining, manufacturing, gas and electricity . .	2,939	2,951	2,954
Construction . .	792	797	799
Trade, restaurants, etc. .	708	712	717
Other commerce . .	169	170	169
Transport . . .	400	399	403
Communications . .	106	106	110
Services . . .	293	302	323
Education and culture . .	587	600	604
Science and research . .	179	181	182
Health and social services .	387	397	406
Civil service, jurisdiction .	118	120	115
Others	130	135	137
Total in employment . .	7,754	7,803	7,830
Women on maternity leave .	352	358	376
Total labour force. . .	8,106	8,161	8,206

Agriculture

PRINCIPAL CROPS ('000 metric tons)

	1987	1988	1989
Wheat and spelt . . .	6,154	6,547	6,356
Rye	496	534	708
Barley . . .	3,551	3,411	3,550
Oats* . . .	406	366	330
Maize . . .	1,160	996	1,000
Sugar beet† . .	6,698	5,482	6,390
Potatoes . .	3,072	3,659	3,167
Dry peas . .	175	212	178
Dry broad beans . .	30	22	27
Grapes. . .	102	229	166
Linseed . .	10	12	16
Rapeseed . .	337	380	387
Sunflower seed . .	62	63	70
Hops . . .	12	15	12
Tobacco . .	6	5	5
Carrots . .	170	138	160
Onions . .	146	129	156
Garlic . .	13	13	16
Tomatoes . .	123	124	122
Cabbages . .	296	281	306
Cauliflowers . .	73	69	77
Lettuce . .	20	18	19
Cucumbers and gherkins . .	92	103	63
Apples . . .	308	468	552
Pears . .	32	49	48
Plums . .	21	55	49
Sweet cherries . .	20	23	29
Sour cherries . .	8	10	14
Peaches . .	7	15	27
Apricots . .	8	7	42
Strawberries . .	28	25	33
Currants . .	33	35	38
Walnuts . .	6	8	11
Flax fibre . . .	19	19	25

* Including mixed crops of oats and barley.
† Including sugar beet seed.

LIVESTOCK ('000 head at end of year)

	1987	1988	1989
Cattle	5,044	5,075	5,129
Pigs	7,235	7,384	7,498
Sheep	1,075	1,047	1,051
Goats	50	50	50
Horses. . . .	45	44	42

Chickens (million): 47 in 1987; 46 in 1988; 47 in 1989.

LIVESTOCK PRODUCTS ('000 metric tons)

	1987	1988	1989
Beef and veal . . .	412	405	407
Pig meat . . .	858	915	934
Poultry meat . . .	194	226	233
Edible offals . .	93	94	94
Cows' milk. . .	6,921.4	6,963.4	7,101.1
Sheep's milk . .	42	41	42
Goats' milk . .	19	19	19
Butter . . .	149.2	148.3	156.2
Cheese. . .	215	227	233
Hen eggs . .	277.2	279.8	281.4
Wool:			
greasy . . .	5.7	5.2	5.9
clean . . .	3.4	3.1	3.5
Cattle hides . .	59.3	58.3	57.6

Forestry

ROUNDWOOD REMOVALS
('000 cubic metres, excluding bark)

	1987	1988	1989
Production	18,527	18,125	17,882
Deliveries	18,565	18,271	18,026
of which:			
Industrial	16,946	16,739	16,650
Fuel wood	1,619	1,532	1,376

SAWNWOOD PRODUCTION
('000 cubic metres, including boxboards)

	1987	1988	1989
Coniferous	4,270	4,212	4,112
Broadleaved	798	802	769
Total	5,068	5,014	4,881

Fishing*

(metric tons)

	1987	1988	1989
Carp	16,652	17,240	17,873
Others	4,084	4,007	3,701
Total catch	20,736	21,247	21,574

* Figures refer only to fish caught by the State Fisheries and members of the Czech and Slovak fishing unions.

Mining

('000 metric tons, unless otherwise indicated)

	1987	1988	1989
Hard coal	25,737	25,503	25,071
Brown coal	98,347	96,361	90,915
Lignite	3,639	3,558	3,348
Kaolin	697	686	698
Iron ore:			
gross weight	1,798	1,773	1,780
metal content	483	474	476
Crude petroleum	147	143	144
Salt (refined)	233	243	238
Magnesite	671	631	642
Antimony ore (metric tons)* .	931	947	839
Copper concentrates (metric tons)* .	24,782	23,303	20,895
Lead concentrates (metric tons)* .	5,612	5,429	5,351
Mercury (metric tons) . . .	164	168	131
Tin concentrates (metric tons)* .	545	515	562
Zinc concentrates (metric tons)* .	13,662	13,870	14,137

* Figures refer to the metal content of ores and concentrates.

Industry

SELECTED PRODUCTS
('000 metric tons, unless otherwise indicated)

	1987	1988	1989
Wheat flour	1,384	1,425	1,405
Refined sugar	895	708	878
Margarine (metric tons) . .	37,419	38,937	38,767
Wine ('000 hectolitres) . .	1,403	1,422	1,391
Beer ('000 hectolitres) . .	22,228	22,670	23,333
Cigarettes (million) . .	25,365	25,502	25,428
Cotton yarn—pure and mixed (metric tons)	145,157	147,220	147,079
Woven cotton fabrics ('000 metres)* . .	599,900	591,243	581,845
Wool yarn—pure and mixed (metric tons)	55,397	55,617	56,106
Woven woollen fabrics ('000 metres)*	58,178	58,669	59,106
Chemical fibres . . .	196.5	204.2	208.1
Chemical wood pulp . .	850.9	884.9	889.9
Newsprint	64.7	73.9	74.2
Other paper	917.9	900.1	953.3
Leather footwear ('000 pairs)	53,815	55,320	55,841
Rubber footwear ('000 pairs)	5,163	4,809	4,672
Other footwear ('000 pairs)	60,449	58,959	59,776
Synthetic rubber (metric tons) .	76,488	77,078	75,932
Rubber tyres ('000) . .	5,316	5,519	5,743
Sulphuric acid	1,264	1,249	1,142
Hydrochloric acid . . .	246.4	247.4	237.8
Caustic soda	344.1	337.1	337.1
Soda ash	102.7	112.2	111.9
Nitrogenous fertilizers(a)† .	596.4	596.4	603.8
Phosphate fertilizers(b)† .	277.0	313.0	295.6
Plastics and synthetic resins .	1,150	1,192	1,186
Liquefied petroleum gas . .	142	126	129
Motor spirit (petrol) . .	1,664	1,678	1,647
Kerosene and jet fuel . .	418	416	422
Distillate fuel oils . . .	4,076	4,469	4,495
Residual fuel oils . . .	6,925	6,014	5,745
Petroleum bitumen (asphalt) .	1,057	1,146	1,103
Coke-oven coke . . .	10,586	10,586	10,147
Cement	10,369	10,974	10,888
Pig iron‡	9,788	9,706	9,911
Crude steel	15,416	15,379	15,465
Rolled steel products . .	11,364	11,420	11,395
Aluminium—unwrought (metric tons)	32,366	31,435	32,576
Refined copper—unwrought (metric tons)	27,202	27,076	26,920
Lead—unwrought (metric tons)	26,008	26,045	26,009
Radio receivers (number)§ . .	199,807	183,570	146,545
Television receivers (number) .	506,743	481,897	524,190
Passenger cars (number) .	172,355	163,834	188,611
Goods vehicles (number) .	51,194	50,498	50,570
Motor cycles (number)‖ .	134,573	136,160	118,905
Electric locomotives (number) .	99	132	107
Diesel locomotives (number) .	524	507	500
Trams (number) . . .	950	685	937
Tractors (number) . . .	35,274	37,637	38,575
Electric energy (million kWh) .	85,825	87,430	89,255
Manufactured gas (million cu metres)	7,270	6,782	6,335
Construction:			
New dwellings completed (number)	79,626	82,910	88,510

1990 ('000 metric tons, unless otherwise indicated): Wheat flour 1,418; Beer ('000 hectolitres) 23,527; Woven cotton fabrics ('000 metres)* 580,429; Woven woollen fabrics ('000 metres)* 58,759; Chemical fibres 200.2; Newsprint 74.7; Leather footwear ('000 pairs) 55,101; Sulphuric acid 1,033; Phosphate fertilizers (b)† 256.9; Plastics and synthetic resins 1,174; Coke-oven coke 9,625; Cement 10,215; Crude steel 14,877; Rolled steel products 10,988; Television receivers (number) 504,577; Passenger cars (number) 191,233; Goods vehicles (number) 47,589; Tractors (number) 38,608; Electric energy (million kWh) 86,626.

* After undergoing finishing processes.
† Production of fertilizers is measured in terms of (a) nitrogen or (b) phosphoric acid. The figures for phosphate fertilizers include ground rock phosphate.
‡ Including blast furnace ferro-alloys. § Excluding radiograms.
‖ Engine capacity of 100 cubic centimetres and over.

Finance

CURRENCY AND EXCHANGE RATES

Monetary Units

100 haléřů (singular: halér—heller) = 1 koruna (Czechoslovak crown or Kčs.; plural: koruny).

Denominations

Coins: 5, 10, 20 and 50 haléřů; 1, 2, 5 and 10 Kčs.
Notes: 10, 20, 50, 100, 500 and 1,000 Kčs.

Sterling and Dollar Equivalents (30 June 1991)

£1 sterling = 50.24 Kčs.;
US $1 = 31.03 Kčs.;
1,000 Kčs. = £19.91 = $32.23.

Average Exchange Rate (Kčs. per US $)

1988	14.36
1989	15.05
1990	17.95

BUDGET (million Kčs.)

Revenue	1987	1988	1989
State budget	245,191	258,400	259,607
From socialist economy	276,747	291,387	308,252
Taxes and rates	35,121	36,423	2,159
Other receipts	2,762	3,000	4,412
Less grants and subsidies to local administrative organs	69,439	72,410	55,216
Budgets of local administrative organs	138,541	145,645	155,825
Total	383,732	404,045	415,432

Expenditure	1987	1988	1989
State budget	245,191	258,400	263,107
National economy	94,891	103,638	86,801
Science and technology	9,731	9,754	9,636
Money-order and technical services	6,393	6,740	6,715
Culture and social welfare	101,320	104,447	111,765
Defence	28,496	29,236	43,784
Administration	4,360	4,585	4,406
Budgets of local administrative organs	136,960	142,799	151,839
Total	382,151	401,199	414,946

OFFICIAL RESERVES (US $ million at 31 December)

	1988	1989	1990
Gold*	530	483	252
Foreign exchange	1,583	2,157	1,102
Total	2,113	2,640	1,354

* Valued at market-related prices.

Source: IMF, *International Financial Statistics*.

MONEY SUPPLY ('000 million Kčs. at 31 December)

	1988	1989	1990
Total money	309.46	317.72	290.85

Source: IMF, *International Financial Statistics*.

COST OF LIVING

(Consumer Price Index; base: 1 January 1984 = 100)

	1988	1989	1990
Food	103.9	104.0	115.5
Industrial goods	101.9	104.5	115.5
Public catering	113.5	114.6	124.3
Services	100.6	101.4	108.9
All items	103.5	104.9	115.4

NATIONAL ACCOUNTS

Net Material Product*

('000 million Kčs. at current market prices)

Activities of the material sphere	1987	1988	1989
Agriculture, hunting and fishing	38.7	38.7	56.3
Forestry and logging	4.5	4.2	5.9
Industry†	350.0	362.2	360.0
Construction	62.4	65.0	65.4
Trade, restaurants, etc.	96.2	104.2	100.1
Transport and storage	23.6	23.9	21.9
Communications	5.4	5.6	5.7
Others	2.5	2.6	2.8
Total	583.3	606.4	618.1

* Defined as the total net value of goods and 'productive' services, including turnover taxes, produced by the economy. This excludes economic activities not contributing directly to material production, such as public administration, defence and personal and professional services.

† Principally manufacturing, mining, electricity, gas and water supply.

1990 (million Kčs.): Net material product 649,180.

BALANCE OF PAYMENTS (US $ million)

	1988	1989	1990
Merchandise exports f.o.b.	15,070	14,248	11,721
Merchandise imports f.o.b.	−14,784	−14,073	−13,053
Trade balance	286	175	−1,332
Exports of services	2,846	2,864	2,662
Imports of services	−1,528	−2,093	−2,423
Other income received	357	501	506
Other income paid	−514	−590	−759
Private unrequited transfers (net)	94	130	261
Official unrequited transfers (net)	−29	−23	−52
Current balance	1,512	964	−1,137
Direct investment (net)	—	257	188
Other capital (net)	−908	−558	693
Net errors and omissions	−395	−95	−876
Overall balance	209	568	−1,132

Source: IMF, *International Financial Statistics*.

External Trade

Note: The value of external trade has been recalculated on the basis of the exchange rates for the koruna that took effect on 1 January 1989.

PRINCIPAL COMMODITIES
(distribution by SITC, million Kčs.)

Imports f.o.b.	1987	1988	1989
Food and live animals . .	12,993	14,843	14,906
Vegetables and fruit . .	3,834	4,628	4,507
Crude materials (inedible) except fuels . .	17,090	17,598	18,814
Cotton fibres and waste . .	2,140	2,543	2,798
Metalliferous ores and metal scrap . .	5,315	4,374	4,784
Mineral fuels, lubricants, etc. (incl. electric current) . .	45,539	39,898	37,164
Coal, coke and briquettes . .	2,818	2,487	2,197
Petroleum, petroleum products, etc. . .	29,679	24,830	22,385
Gas (natural and manufactured)	15,986	11,108	10,766
Chemicals and related products. . .	n.a.	n.a.	n.a.
Organic chemicals . .	2,237	3,170	3,565
Manufactured fertilizers . .	1,690	1,640	1,790
Basic manufactures . .	19,680	19,446	22,369
Iron and steel . . .	4,161	3,030	3,357
Non-ferrous metals . .	5,187	6,653	7,508
Machinery and transport equipment . .	71,863	75,835	79,324
Power generating machinery and equipment . .	5,303	3,776	5,747
Machinery specialized for particular industries . .	17,117	21,654	20,942
Agricultural machinery (excl. tractors) and parts. . .	3,698	3,254	2,972
Civil engineering and contractors' plant, equipment and parts . .	5,039	8,123	7,752
Metalworking machinery . .	5,120	5,865	6,184
Machine-tools for working metal . .	3,573	4,294	1,697
General industrial machinery, equipment and parts. .	22,662	21,236	19,790
Office machines and automatic data processing equipment .	6,056	5,699	6,382
Automatic data processing machines and units .	4,868	4,419	4,702
Road vehicles and parts* . .	6,209	6,048	7,088
Parts and accessories for cars, buses, lorries, etc.* .	4,385	4,190	4,220
Miscellaneous manufactured articles . . .	11,321	12,930	13,208
Total (incl. others). . .	203,750	209,554	214,702

* Excluding tyres, engines and electrical parts.

Exports f.o.b.	1987	1988	1989
Food and live animals . .	6,278	7,114	10,076
Crude materials (inedible) except fuels . . .	7,146	6,108	8,000
Mineral fuels, lubricants, etc. (incl. electric current) .	9,327	8,854	11,292
Coal, coke and briquettes . .	3,262	3,552	3,880
Coal, lignite and peat . .	1,759	2,040	2,225
Petroleum, petroleum products, etc. . .	4,566	3,862	5,612
Chemicals and related products. . . .	14,543	17,641	16,434
Organic chemicals . . .	3,376	5,738	5,271
Artificial resins, plastic materials, etc. . . .	2,663	4,754	3,776

Exports f.o.b.—*continued*	1987	1988	1989
Basic manufactures . .	38,921	40,335	48,814
Textile yarn, fabrics, etc. . .	6,436	7,994	8,132
Non-metallic mineral manufactures . . .	5,852	6,017	10,095
Iron and steel . . .	12,921	16,038	18,726
Bars, rods, angles, shapes, etc. . . .	3,724	4,795	3,865
Universals, plates and sheets	2,847	4,436	5,121
Tubes, pipes and fittings . .	3,170	2,315	3,127
Machinery and transport equipment . .	99,574	101,016	96,563
Power generating machinery and equipment . .	7,799	9,344	8,761
Steam power units, steam engines and parts . .	2,534	4,356	3,656
Machinery specialized for particular industries . .	26,829	24,216	24,876
Agricultural machinery (excl. tractors) and parts. .	3,227	2,852	2,688
Civil engineering and contractors' plant, equipment and parts . .	5,765	5,166	6,751
Textile and leather machinery and parts . .	8,504	7,396	6,970
Metalworking machinery . .	7,523	7,032	6,788
Machine-tools for working metal	5,616	5,279	2,197
General industrial machinery, equipment and parts. .	29,358	26,472	22,273
Office machines and automatic data processing equipment .	3,146	2,465	2,055
Telecommunications and sound equipment . .	2,975	2,410	2,969
Other electrical machinery, apparatus, etc. . .	6,417	6,045	6,766
Road vehicles and parts* . .	18,827	16,331	15,854
Motor vehicles for goods transport and special purposes . .	7,740	6,041	5,222
Parts and accessories for cars, buses, lorries, etc.* .	7,540	6,828	6,365
Railway vehicles and associated equipment . .	7,419	5,880	5,442
Miscellaneous manufactured articles . .	22,687	22,829	21,028
Furniture and parts . . .	2,786	2,740	2,537
Footwear	4,847	4,427	4,182
Total (incl. others). . . .	201,558	213,887	217,530

* Excluding tyres, engines and electrical parts.

PRINCIPAL TRADING PARTNERS
(million Kčs., country of consignment)

Imports f.o.b.	1988	1989	1990
Austria	11,102	11,830	23,124
Belgium	1,644	1,593	1,955
Brazil	1,072	1,639	1,932
Bulgaria	5,210	4,808	2,752
China, People's Republic .	5,441	5,902	8,189
Cuba	1,550	1,645	733
France	3,407	3,350	4,203
German Democratic Republic .	17,190	16,797⎱	31,734†
Germany, Federal Republic* .	19,580	19,931⎰	
Hungary	9,282	10,294	8,147
Italy	3,804	3,695	5,436
Japan	1,183	1,113	1,144
Netherlands . . .	2,529	2,184	3,097
Poland	17,280	18,485	20,370
Romania	3,762	3,561	1,732
Switzerland . . .	7,240	7,407	10,048
USSR	65,465	63,792	51,410
United Kingdom . .	4,553	4,731	6,862
Yugoslavia . . .	6,968	7,170	7,588
Total (incl. others). . .	209,554	214,702	238,202

* Excluding imports from West Berlin.
† Figures for 1990 are for the united Germany.

Exports f.o.b.	1988	1989	1990
Austria	8,896	9,938	12,717
Belgium	1,396	1,689	2,236
Bulgaria	5,919	5,073	3,084
China, People's Republic . .	6,225	5,546	3,996
Cuba	1,938	1,699	1,359
France	3,325	3,936	5,662
German Democratic Republic .	14,916	14,257}	
Germany, Federal Republic* .	16,573	17,964}	27,639†
Hungary	9,082	8,641	8,841
Italy	3,751	4,623	6,630
Netherlands	2,854	3,316	4,707
Poland	17,238	18,438	13,394
Romania	3,307	3,938	2,518
Switzerland	3,283	3,805	4,709
Turkey	1,183	1,748	2,385
USSR	71,924	66,439	54,159
United Kingdom . . .	4,413	4,396	5,521
Yugoslavia	6,826	7,095	7,618
Total (incl. others)	213,887	217,530	215,257

* Excluding exports to West Berlin.
† Figures for 1990 are for the united Germany.

Tourism

	1986	1987	1988
Foreign tourist arrivals* .	19,030,469	21,756,306	24,486,814

* Including excursionists and visitors in transit. Visitors spending at least one night in the country totalled 5,330,252 in 1986; 6,263,914 in 1987; 7,054,035 in 1988.
1989: 29.7m. foreign tourist arrivals.

Communications Media

	1987	1988	1989
Telephones in use . . .	3,838,437	3,979,819	4,131,679
Radio receivers (licensed) . .	3,965,689	4,228,991	4,216,838
Television receivers (licensed) .	4,424,529	4,661,775	4,660,543
Book production: titles* . .	7,067	6,977	6,863
Newspapers (dailies) . .	30	30	30
Periodicals	1,080	1,087	1,086

* Figures include pamphlets, and refer to titles produced by centrally managed publishing houses only. The total number of titles produced was: 10,565 in 1987; 9,558 in 1988; 9,294 in 1989.

Transport

	1988	1989	1990
Railway transport:			
Freight ('000 tons) . . .	295,095	283,914	254,343
Passengers (million) . .	415	411	408
Public road transport:			
Freight ('000 tons) . . .	339,458	328,984	256,580
Passengers (million) . .	2,342	2,320	2,296
Waterway transport:			
Freight ('000 tons) . .	15,206	13,524	10,084
Air transport:			
Freight (tons) . . .	28,066	29,123	n.a.
Passengers ('000) . . .	1,449	1,493	1,290

ROAD TRAFFIC (vehicles in use at 30 June)

	1987	1988	1989
Passenger cars	2,903,947	2,999,987	3,122,307
Buses and coaches . . .	36,595	37,720	39,382
Goods vehicles	412,969	422,971	446,725
Motorcycles and scooters . .	555,252	546,576	551,497

Education

(1989/90)

	Institutions	Teachers*	Students
Nursery	11,380	50,519	636,622
Primary (classes 1–8) . .	6,206	98,038	1,961,742
Secondary (classes 9–12)			
Universal	351	10,769	153,179
Special (technical, etc.) .	563	18,630	274,298
Continuation schools . .	957	17,233	465,463
Higher	36	20,317	173,547

* Teachers in full-time employment.

Directory

The Constitution

A new Constitution was proclaimed on 11 July 1960. It was amended in October 1968, July 1971 and May 1975. Following the Revolution of 1989, it was further amended and work was begun on a new Constitution. Adoption of such a document was delayed by continuing disagreements over the delimitation of powers between the federal authorities and the constituent republics. It was expected that a new Constitution would be adopted before the general elections scheduled for mid-1992. The following is a summary of the main provisions of the Constitution remaining in effect, together with laws and amendments that were adopted during 1990 and 1991:

The Czech and Slovak Federative Republic (ČSFR) is a federal state, composed of two republics, the Czech Republic (ČR) and the Slovak Republic (SR), each possessing equal rights.

FUNDAMENTAL RIGHTS AND FREEDOMS*

The State is based on democratic values and can exercise its power only in accordance with the law. Basic liberties and rights are inalienable and cannot be abolished. Fundamental rights and liberties are guaranteed to all Czechoslovak citizens, regardless of their sex, race, ethnic origins or beliefs.

The State guarantees those civil and political rights that are enshrined in international agreements to which Czechoslovakia is a signatory. These include personal freedom, personal integrity and dignity, privacy and property ownership. Freedom of movement, assembly, association, speech and religion is guaranteed to all Czechoslovak citizens. No one may be submitted to cruel or inhuman punishment; the death penalty may not be used.

Each citizen has the right to decide on his or her nationality. Members of national minorities have the right to develop their own culture, publish information in their own language and form their own associations. All ethnic groups have the right to education in their own language and the use of that language in official dealings.

Citizens have the right to freely choose a vocation and to be involved in private business. Everyone has the right to associate with others, in trade unions, to protect his or her economic and social interests. All workers, except members of the armed forces, the security forces and the judiciary, have the right to strike, under conditions stipulated by the law. The State guarantees the provision of basic medical care free of charge. Everyone has the right to education, free of charge, in state-run schools.

FEDERAL ASSEMBLY

The supreme organ of state power in the Republic is the Federal Assembly (Parliament) which is elected for a five-year term and elects the President of the Republic. The President may be relieved of his or her duties by the Assembly in the event of having been unable to fulfil them for over a year. The Federal Assembly consists of two chambers of equal rights: the House of the People and the House of Nations. The composition of the House of the People, which has 150 deputies, corresponds to the composition of the population of the ČSFR. The House of Nations has 150 deputies on parity basis: 75 are elected in the Czech Republic and 75 in the Slovak Republic.

PRESIDENT AND FEDERAL GOVERNMENT

The President, elected by the Federal Assembly, appoints the Federal Government. The Government is the supreme executive organ of state power in Czechoslovakia; it consists of a Prime Minister, four Deputy Prime Ministers and 12 Ministers. The Ministries of Foreign Affairs, of Defence, of Foreign Trade are within the exclusive competence of the Federation, i.e. there are no corresponding portfolios in the governments of the republics. The second group of federal government organs share authority with organs of the two republics, i.e. there are corresponding portfolios in the national governments.

ELECTORAL SYSTEM

All representative bodies are elected, and the right to elect is universal, equal and by secret ballot. Every citizen has the right to vote on reaching the age of 18, and is eligible for election on reaching the age of 21. Deputies must maintain constant contacts with their constituents, heed their suggestions and be accountable to them for their activity. A member of any representative body may be recalled by his or her constituents at any time.

For election purposes, the country is divided into electoral districts; there are 150 electoral districts in the ČSFSR, each represented by one deputy in the House of the People, and 75 electoral districts each in the Czech and Slovak Republics, which send one deputy each to the House of Nations.

The principle of simple majority obtains in the elections: the candidate is elected when he obtains more than 50% of the votes cast, provided that the majority of all voters in his electoral district exercise their right to vote. When either of the two conditions is not met, new elections are held in the electoral district concerned within two weeks. When a seat becomes vacant, the Presidium of the Federal Assembly calls a by-election in the constituency; this is not mandatory in the last year of the deputies' term of office.

NATIONAL COUNCILS

Each of the Republics has its own legislature: the Czech National Council and the Slovak National Council. The members are elected for a five-year term of office. The Czech National Council has 200 deputies, the Slovak National Council 150 deputies. There are also separate Czech and Slovak Governments.

JUDICIAL SYSTEM

The execution of justice is vested in elected and independent courts. Benches are composed of professional judges and of 'associate' judges who carry out their function in addition to their regular employment. Both categories are equal in making decisions. Judges are independent in the discharge of their office and bound solely by the legal order of the State. The supervision of the observance of the laws and other legal regulations by public bodies and by individual citizens rests with the Office of the Procurator. The Procurator-General is appointed and recalled by the President of the Republic and is accountable to the Federal Assembly.

* As stated in the Law on Fundamental Rights and Freedoms, adopted by the Federal Assembly in January 1991.

The Government
(September 1991)

HEAD OF STATE

President of the Republic: VÁCLAV HAVEL (took office 29 December 1989; re-elected 5 July 1990).

FEDERAL GOVERNMENT

A coalition of Civic Movement (CM), Public Against Violence (PAV), the Civic Democratic Party (CDP), the Civic Democratic Alliance (CDA) and the Christian Democratic Movement (CDM).

Prime Minister: MARIÁN ČALFA (PAV).

Deputy Prime Ministers: PAVEL RYCHETSKÝ (CM), JOZEF MIKLOŠKO (CDM), (vacant).

Deputy Prime Minister and Minister of Foreign Affairs: JIŘÍ DIENSTBIER (CM).

Minister of Control: KVĚTOSLAVA KOŘÍNKOVÁ (CM).

Minister of Defence: LUBOŠ DOBROVSKÝ (CM).

Minister, Chairman of the Bureau for Economic Competition: IMRICH FLASSIK.

Minister of the Economy: VLADIMÍR DLOUHÝ (CDA).

Minister of the Environment: JOSEF VAVROUŠEK (CM).

Minister of Finance: Dr VÁCLAV KLAUS (CDP).

Minister of Foreign Trade: JOZEF BAKSAY (PAV).

Minister of the Interior: JÁN LANGOŠ (PAV).

Minister of Labour and Social Affairs: PETR MILLER (CM).

Minister of Strategic Economic Planning: PAVEL HOFFMANN (PAV).

Minister of Telecommunications: EMIL EHRENBERGER (CDM).

Minister of Transport: JIŘÍ NEZVAL (CM).

FEDERAL MINISTRIES

Office of the Presidium of the Federal Government: Nábř. kpt. Jaroše 4, 125 09 Prague 1; tel. (2) 2102; fax (2) 2131424.

Federal Ministry of Control: Jankovcova 63, 170 04 Prague 7; tel. (2) 8734; telex 123118; fax (2) 807730.

Federal Ministry of Defence: Tychonova 1, 161 00 Prague 6; tel. (2) 330802; fax (2) 33041231.

Federal Bureau of Economic Competition: Nám. Slobody 1, 813 70 Bratislava; tel. (7) 415449; fax (7) 415449.

Federal Ministry of the Economy: Nábř. kpt. Jaroše 1000, 170 32 Prague 7; tel. (2) 3891111; telex 121044; fax (2) 7122263.

Federal Committee for the Environment: Slezská 9, 120 29 Prague 2; tel. (2) 2151111; fax (2) 2151111.

Federal Ministry of Finance: Letenská 15, 118 10 Prague 1; tel. (2) 5141111; fax (2) 535759.

Federal Ministry of Foreign Affairs: Loretánské nám. 5, 125 10 Prague 1; tel. (2) 21931111; fax (2) 3110233.

Federal Ministry of Foreign Trade: Politických vězňů 20, 112 49 Prague 1; tel. (2) 21261111; fax (2) 2322868.

Federal Ministry of the Interior: Nad stolou 3, 170 34 Prague 7; tel. (2) 33511111; fax (2) 321123.

Federal Ministry of Labour and Social Affairs: Palackého nám. 4, 128 01 Prague 2; tel. (2) 21181111; fax (2) 297731.

Federal Ministry of Strategic Economic Planning: Nábř. kpt. Jaroše 1000, 170 32 Prague 7; tel. (2) 389111; fax (2) 377637.

Federal Ministry of Telecommunications: Klimentská 27, 125 02 Prague 1; tel. (2) 2323924; fax (2) 2368379.

Federal Ministry of Transport: Nábř. L. Svobody 12, 125 11 Prague 1; tel. (2) 28911111; fax (2) 2321420.

Legislature
FEDERÁLNÍ SHROMÁŽDĚNÍ
(Federal Assembly)

The Federal Assembly consists of 300 deputies elected for a five-year term. The Assembly is bicameral, comprising the House of the People and the House of Nations, each containing 150 members. General elections to both chambers were held on 8–9 June 1990. Deputies were to serve a transitional two-year term of office until the holding of fresh legislative elections in mid-1992.

Chairman: ALEXANDER DUBČEK.

First Deputy Chairman: ZDENEK SIČINSKÝ.

Sněmovna lidu
(House of the People)

This House has 150 members. At the June 1990 elections, 101 were from the Czech Republic, and 49 from the Slovak Republic.

Chairman: RUDOLF BATTEK.

Sněmovna národů
(House of Nations)

This House has 150 members: 75 each from the Czech and Slovak Republics.

Chairman: MILAN SUTOVEC.

General election, 8–9 June 1990

Parties and Groups	House of the People		House of Nations		Total seats in the Federal Assembly
	% of votes	Seats	% of votes	Seats	
Civic Forum/Public Against Violence (PAV)*	46.6	87	45.9	83	170
Communist Party of Czechoslovakia (CPCz)†	13.6	23	13.7	24	47
Christian Democratic Union (CDU)‡ . . .	12.0	20	11.3	20	40
Movement for Autonomous Democracy-Society for Moravia and Silesia (MAD-SMS) .	5.4	9	3.6	7	16
Slovak National Party (SNP)	3.5	6	6.2	9	15
Coexistence (Soužití) .	2.8	5	2.7	7	12
Others	16.1	0	16.6	0	0
Total	**100.0**	**150**	**100.0**	**150**	**300**

* Following the splits in Civic Forum and Public Against Violence, deputies elected under their joint mandate were divided approximately as follows: Civic Movement (42 deputies); Civic Democratic Party (40); Public Against Violence (32); Movement for a Democratic Slovakia (14); Civic Democratic Alliance (9); Association of Social Democrats (8); Czechoslovak Social Democracy (6); Liberal Democratic Party (2); small groups and independents (17).

† Subsequently reorganized as the Federation of the Communist Party of Bohemia and Moravia and the Party of the Democratic Left.

‡ A coalition of the Czechoslovak People's Party (CPP), the Christian Democratic Party (CDP) and the Christian Democratic Movement (CDM). Owing to disagreements between the three parties, the coalition was discontinued after the elections.

Political Organizations

Agrarian Party (Zemědělská strana): Prague; f. 1990; seeks compensation for farmers whose property was confiscated during collectivization; Chair. Dr FRANTIŠEK TRNKA.

Association for the Republic-Republican Party: Prague; extreme right-wing; advocates defederalization of Czechoslovakia and the reincorporation of Carpatho-Ruthenia into the Republic; Chair. MIROSLAV SLADEK.

Christian Democratic Movement (CDM): Zabotova 2, 811 04 Bratislava; tel. (7) 492541; fax (7) 496313; f. 1990; Chair. JÁN ČARNOGURSKÝ.

Christian Democratic Party (CDP): Prague; f. 1989; Leader VÁCLAV BENDA.

Civic Democratic Alliance (CDA): Prague; f. 1991 as a formal political party, following a split in Civic Forum (Občanské fórum—f. 1989); fmrly an informal group within Civic Forum; conservative; Chair. PAVEL BRATINKA.

Civic Democratic Party (CDP): Prague; f. 1991 following a split in Civic Forum (Občanské fórum—f. 1989); conservative; Chair. VÁCLAV KLAUS.

Civic Movement (CM): Prague; f. 1991 as a result of a split in Civic Forum (Občanské fórum—f. 1989); liberal; Chair. of Republican Council JIŘI DIENSTBIER; Dep. Chair. PAVEL RYCHETSKÝ, PETR PITHART.

Civic Party of Slovakia (Občanská strana Slovanska): Bratislava; f. 1991; associated with the CDP; conservative.

Coexistence (Soužití/Együtteles): f. 1990; a coalition of Hungarian, Polish and other ethnic minority groups; Leader MIKLÓS DURAY.

Czechoslovak Green Party: f. 1989; federal body co-ordinating Czech and Slovak branches; Chair. JAN JECMÍNEK.

Czechoslovak People's Party (CPP): Revoluční 5, 110 15 Prague 1; f. 1919; Christian party; 100,000 mems; Chair. JOSEF LUX; Gen. Sec. JIŘÍ ČERNÝ.

Czechoslovak Social Democratic Party (CSDP): Prague; prohibited 1948; re-established 1989; Chair. Prof. JIŘÍ HORÁK.

Czechoslovak Socialist Party (CSP): nám. Republiky 7, 111 49 Prague 1; tel. (2) 2367320; fax (2) 2362980; f. 1897 as the Czechoslovak National Socialist Party; Chair. LADISLAV DVOŘÁK.

Democratic Party (Demokratická strana): Malinovského 70, 812 78 Bratislava; tel. (7) 498020; fax (7) 492273; f. 1944; renamed the Slovak Party of Renewal 1948; original name restored 1989; approx. 12,000 mems; Chair. JÁN HOLČÍK.

Federation of the Communist Party of Bohemia and Moravia and the Party of the Democratic Left: ul. Politických vězňů 911 00 Prague 1; tel. (2) 2199; f. 1991 to replace the Communist Party of Czechoslovakia (CPCz—f. 1921); federal co-ordinating body for the two republican parties (see below); Chair. of Federal Council PAVOL KANIS (to November 1991); Chair.-designate MIROSLAV GREBENÍČEK.

 Communist Party of Bohemia and Moravia (CPBM): Prague; f. 1991 as a result of the reorganization of the CPCz; Leader JIŘI SVOBODA.

 Party of the Democratic Left of Slovakia (PDLS): Mierová 21, 827 05 Bratislava; tel. (7) 231276; telex 92722; fax (7) 235323; f. 1991 to replace the Communist Party of Slovakia; 20,000 mems; Chair. PETER WEISS.

Liberal-Democratic Party: Prague; f. 1990; fmrly a member of the Civic Forum coalition; Chair. BOHUMIL DOLEZAL.

Movement for Autonomous Democracy-Society for Moravia and Silesia (MAD-SMS): Brno; advocates the establishment of a self-administered Republic of Moravia and Silesia, within a Czechoslovak federation; Chair. Dr JAN KRYCER.

Movement for a Democratic Slovakia (MDS): Bratislava; f. 1991 as a result of a split in Public Against Violence; left-wing, advocates further Slovakian autonomy; Chair. VLADIMIR MEČIAR; Chair. of Council RUDOLF FULKUS.

National Social Party: f. 1990; considers itself successor to the Czechoslovak National Socialist Party (f. 1897); Dep. Chair. JOSEF LESÁK.

Public Against Violence—PAV (Verejnosť proti násiliu): Bratislava; f. 1989 as the Slovak counterpart of Civic Forum; Chair. of Slovak Council JOZEF KUČERÁK; Chair of Co-ordination Centre JURAJ FLAMIK.

Slovak Freedom Party (Strana slobody): Obrancov mieru 8, 816 18 Bratislava; f. 1946 as a splinter party from the Slovak Democratic Party; Chair. SILVESTER MINAROVIČ.

Slovak National Party—SNP (Slovenská národná strana): Bratislava; advocates independence for Slovakia; Chair. JOZEF PROKES; Dep. Chair. VILIAM SOJKA.

Slovak National Unification Party: Bratislava; f. 1991; advocates independence for Slovakia; membership limited to ethnic Slovaks; approx. 6,000 mems; Chair. JAN VESELOVSKY.

Slovak Social Democratic Party (Sociálno-demokratická strana na Slovensku): Bratislava; re-established 1990; Chair. BORIS ZÁLA.

Diplomatic Representation

EMBASSIES IN CZECHOSLOVAKIA

Afghanistan: U Vorlíku 17, 125 01 Prague 6; tel. (2) 381532; Ambassador: MOHAMMAD ARAF SAKHRA.

Albania: Pod Kaštany 22, Bubeneč, Prague 6; tel. (2) 379329; fax (2) 379329; Chargé d'affaires a.i.: VANGJEL MITA.

Algeria: Korejská 16, 125 21 Prague; tel. (2) 322021; Ambassador: ABDELHAMID LATRECHE.

Argentina: Washingtonova 25, 125 22 Prague 1; tel. (2) 223803; telex 121847; Ambassador: ABEL PARENTINI POSSE.

Austria: Viktora Huga 10, 125 43 Prague 5; tel. (2) 546550; telex 121849; Ambassador: KARL PETERLIK.

Belgium: Valdštejnská 6, 125 24 Prague 1; tel. (2) 534051; telex 122362; fax (2) 537351; Ambassador: ERIC KOBIA.

Bolivia: Ve Smečkách 25, 125 59 Prague 1; tel. (2) 263209; telex 122402; Ambassador: CARLOS COSTA DU RELS.

Brazil: Bolzanova 5, 125 01 Prague 1; tel. (2) 229254; telex 122292; Ambassador: CARLOS EDUARDO DE AFFONSECA ALVES DE SOUZA.

Bulgaria: Krakovská 6, 125 00 Prague 1; tel. (2) 264310; telex 121381; Ambassador: TONCHO CHAKAROV.

Cambodia: Na Hubálce 1, 169 00 Prague 6; tel. (2) 352603; Ambassador: UNG SEAN.

Canada: Mickiewiczova 6, 125 33 Prague 6; tel. (2) 3120251; telex 121061; fax (2) 3112791; Ambassador: ALAN P. McLAINE.

China, People's Republic: Majakovského 22, 160 00 Prague 6; Ambassador: WANG XINGDA.

Colombia: Příčná 1, 110 00 Prague 1; tel. (2) 291330; Ambassador: CAMILO REYES RODRIGUEZ.

Costa Rica: Dlouhá 36, 110 00 Prague 1; tel. (2) 2619073; telex 121726; fax (2) 2320878; Ambassador: CARLOS E. FERNÁNDEZ GARCÍA.

Cuba: Sibiřské nám. 1, 125 35 Prague 6; tel. (2) 3122246; telex 121163; Ambassador: BENIGNO PÉREZ FERNÁNDEZ.

Denmark: U Havličkových sadů 1, 120 21 Prague 2; tel. (2) 254715; telex 122209; Ambassador: PER POULSEN-HANSEN.

Ecuador: Opletalova 43, 125 01 Prague 1; tel. (2) 261258; telex 123286; Ambassador: OSWALDO RAMÍREZ LANDAZURI.

Egypt: Majakovského 14, 125 46 Prague 6; tel. (2) 341051; telex 123552; fax (2) 3120861; Chargé d'affaires a. i.: Dr KHALED M. EL-KOMY.

Ethiopia: V Průhledu 9, 125 00 Prague 6; tel. (2) 352268; telex 122067; fax (2) 3123464; Ambassador: TEFERRA SHIAWL .

Finland: Dřevná 2, 125 01 Prague 2; tel. (2) 205541; telex 121060; fax (2) 298321; Ambassador: PAULI OPAS.

France: Velkopřevorské nám. 2, 110 00 Prague 1; tel. (2) 533042; fax (2) 539926; Ambassador: JEAN GUÉGUINOU.

Germany: Vlašska 19, 125 60 Prague 1; tel. (2) 532351; telex 122814; Ambassador: HERMANN HUBER.

Ghana: V Tisine 4, 160 00 Prague 6; tel. (2) 373058; telex 122263; Ambassador: MOSES KWASI AHMAD AGYEMAN.

Greece: Na Ořechovce 19, 125 45 Prague 6; tel. (2) 354279; Ambassador: CONSTANTIN POLITIS.

Holy See: Prague; Apostolic Nuncio: Mgr GIOVANNI COPPA.

Hungary: Mičurinova 1, 125 37 Prague 6; tel. (2) 365041; telex 123535; fax (2) 329425; Ambassador: GYÖRGY VARGA.

India: Valdštejnská 6, 125 28 Prague 1; tel. (2) 532642; telex 121901; fax (2) 539495; Ambassador: BHUPATRAY OZA.

Indonesia: Nad Buďánkami II/7, 125 29 Prague 5; tel. (2) 526041; telex 121443; Ambassador: H. R. ENAP SURATMAN.

Iran: Nám. Družby 9, Prague 6; tel. (2) 322745; telex 122732; Ambassador: HAMID REZA HOSSEINI.

Iraq: Na Zátorce 10, 125 01 Prague 6; Ambassador: MUNTHER AHMED AL-MUTLAK.

Israel: Prague; Ambassador: YOEL SHER.

Italy: Nerudova 20, 125 31 Prague 1; tel. (2) 530666; telex 122704; Ambassador: GIOVANNI CASTELLANI PASTORIS.

Japan: Maltézské nám. 6, 125 32 Prague 1; tel. (2) 535751; telex 121199; fax (2) 539997; Ambassador: TISATI CATO.

Korea, Democratic People's Republic: R. Rollanda 10, 160 00 Prague 6; tel. (2) 373953; Ambassador: KIM KWANG SOP.

Korea, Republic: U. Mrázovky 17, 150 00 Prague 5; tel. (2) 542671; fax (2) 530204; Ambassador JOUN YUNG SUN.

Lebanon: Gottwaldovo nábřeží 14, 110 00 Prague 1; tel. (2) 293633; telex 123583; Ambassador: SLEIMAN YOUNES.

Libya: Na baště sv. Jiří 7, 160 00 Prague 6; Secretary of People's Cttee: MUHAMMAD MUSBAH KHALIFA.

Mexico: Nad Kazankou 8, 171 00 Prague 7; tel. (2) 8555554; telex 121947; fax (2) 8550477; Ambassador: JOSÉ CABALLERO BAZÁN.

Mongolia: Korejská 5, 160 00 Prague 6; tel. (2) 328992; telex 121921; Ambassador: DJAMSRAGIYN DULMA.

Morocco: Petrska 24, 124 47 Prague 1; tel. (2) 310935; Ambassador: TAJEDDINE BADDOU.

Myanmar: Romaina Rollanda 3, 125 23 Prague 6; Ambassador: U THAN TUN.

Netherlands: Maltézské nám. 1, 125 40 Prague 1; tel. (2) 531378; telex 122643; fax (2) 531368; Ambassador: HANS J. HEINEMANN.

Nicaragua: Na Baště sv. Jiří 3, 125 46 Prague 6; tel. (2) 324410; telex 123336; Ambassador: MAYRA PASOS MARCIAQ.

Nigeria: Před Bateriemi 18, 160 00 Prague 6; tel. (2) 354294; telex 123575; Ambassador: Prof. S. O. EMEJUAIWE.

Norway: Na Ořechovce 69, 162 00 Prague 6; tel. (2) 354526; telex 122200; Ambassador: KNUT TARALDSET.

Peru: Hradecká 18, 125 01 Prague 3; tel. (2) 742024; telex 123345; Ambassador: IGOR VELÁZQUEZ RODRÍGUEZ.

Poland: Valdštejnská 8, 125 42 Prague 1; tel. (2) 536951; telex 121841; fax (2) 536427; Ambassador: JACEK BALUCH.

Portugal: Bubenská 3, 170 00 Prague 7; tel. (2) 878472; telex 121354; fax (2) 802624; Ambassador: LUÍS QUARTIN.

Romania: Nerudova 5, 125 44 Prague; tel. (2) 533059; Ambassador: ION CIUBOTARU.

Spain: Pevnostní 9, 162 00 Prague 6; tel. (2) 334442; telex 121974; fax (2) 323573; Ambassador: JOSÉ LUIS DICENTA BALLESTER.

Sudan: Malostranské nábřeží 1, 125 01 Prague; tel. (2) 536547; Ambassador: SAYYID ABD AL-MUTASIM.

Sweden: Úvoz 13, 125 52 Prague 1; tel. (2) 533344; telex 121840; Ambassador: L. A. NILSSON.

Switzerland: Pevnostní 7, 162 00 Prague 6; tel. (2) 320406; Ambassador: MAURICE JEANRENAUD.

Syria: Pod Kaštany 16, 125 01 Prague 6; tel. (2) 326231; telex 121532; Ambassador: SUBHI HADDAD.

Tunisia: Nad Kostelem 8, 125 01 Prague 4; tel. (2) 460652; telex 122512; fax (2) 460825; Ambassador: NOUREDDINE BOUJELLABIA.

Turkey: Pevnostní 3, 160 00 Prague 6; tel. (2) 320597; fax (2) 320598; Ambassador: İNAL BATU.

USSR: Pod Kaštany 1, 160 00 Prague 6; tel. (2) 381943; Ambassador: ALEKSANDR LEBEDEV.

United Kingdom: Thunovská 14, 125 50 Prague 1; tel. (2) 533347; telex 121011; fax (2) 539927; Ambassador: DAVID BRIGHTY.

USA: Tržiště 15, 125 48 Prague; tel. (2) 536641; telex 121196; fax (2) 532457; Ambassador SHIRLEY TEMPLE BLACK.

Uruguay: Václavské nám. 64, 111 21 Prague 1; tel. (2) 2351587; telex 121291; Ambassador: ANTONIO L. CAMPS VALGOI.

Venezuela: Janáčkovo nábřeží 49, 150 00 Prague; (2) 536051; telex 122146; Ambassador: JOSÉ DE JESÚS OSÍO.

Viet-Nam: Holečková 6, 125 55 Prague; tel. (2) 536127; telex 121824; Ambassador: NGUYEN PHU SOAI.

Yemen: Washingtonova 17, 125 22 Prague 1; tel. (2) 222411; telex 123300; Ambassador: ABD AL-LATIF MUHAMMAD DHAIF ALLAH.

Yugoslavia: Mostecká 15, 118 00 Prague 1; tel. (2) 531443; telex 123284; Ambassador: STANISLAV STOJANOVIČ.

Judicial System

The judicial system was extensively amended by the Law on Judges and Courts, adopted in July 1991. Under the Communist regime only two types of court, apart from military courts, existed within the judiciary: civil courts and criminal courts. The new law provided for two further types of court: administrative courts and commercial courts. Administrative courts examine the legality of decisions made by state bodies when citizens appeal against such decisions. Commercial courts arbitrate in the case of disputes involving business activities.

As under the previous system, the Supreme Court of the Federation and the military courts are the only federal bodies in the unified judiciary. All other courts are responsible to the republican ministries of justice. These courts are the Supreme Court of the Czech Republic and the Supreme Court of the Slovak Republic, the district courts and the regional courts. The Supreme Court of the Federation and the Supreme Courts of the Republics serve as courts of appeal and interpreters of laws. District courts are courts of first instance. In these courts, most cases are decided by senates, composed of one professional judge and two associate, or lay, judges. Regional courts act as courts of first instance for serious crimes and as courts of appeal that rule on the decisions of district courts. The senates of regional courts are usually composed of two professional judges and three associate judges. Judges of the federal Supreme Court are appointed by the President of the Federation, on the proposal of the Chairman of the federal Supreme Court. Judges presiding over military courts are also appointed by the President, on the proposal of the Minister of Defence. Judges presiding in republican supreme courts, and in district and regional courts are appointed by the Presidium of the National Council of the Republic, acting on the proposal of the republican government. Associate judges do not require formal legal training, but they have equal status in court senates with professional judges.

Military courts continue to be part of the unified judiciary, but are responsible to the Ministry of Defence and cases are adjudicated by professional soldiers.

Chairman of the Supreme Court of the Federation: Dr OTAKAR MOTEJL.

Procurator-General: Dr IVAN GASPAROVIČ.

Religion

Following the adoption of the Church Law, in 1949, the practice of religion was severely restricted. A short period of tolerance, in 1968, was ended by the Soviet invasion. After the 1989 Revolution, the new Government declared a commitment to freedom of worship for all religious groups and many churches, which had been closed after 1949, were reopened. In 1990 legislation was adopted which allowed for the return of property confiscated from religious groups between 1948 and 1989. In July 1991 the Federal Assembly adopted the Law on Freedom of Religion and Churches, which further clarified the nature of Church–State relations and permitted the return of more nationalized property to religious groups.

The principal religion is Christianity. In June 1991 there were 21 registered denominations in Czechoslovakia. The largest is the

Roman Catholic Church, with 7.2m. members, followed by the Hussite Church, with some 400,000 members.

CHRISTIANITY

Ekumenická rada církví v České a Slovenské federativní republice (Czechoslovak Ecumenical Council of Churches): Vítkova 13, 186 00 Prague 8; tel. (2) 227581; f. 1955, present name since 1990; 11 mem. churches; Chair. Rev. Dr JOSEF HROMÁDKA; Vice-Chair. RUDOLF BORSKI; Gen. Sec. Rev. PAVEL VYCHOPEŇ.

The Roman Catholic Church

Czechoslovakia comprises three archdioceses and 10 dioceses, including one (directly responsible to the Holy See) for Catholics of the Slovak (Byzantine) rite (also known as Greek Catholics or Uniates).

Latin Rite

Archbishop of Prague: Mgr Dr MILOSLAV VLK, Hradčanské nám. 16, 119 02 Prague 1; tel. (2) 539548.

Archbishop of Olomouc: (vacant), Wurmova 9, 771 01 Olomouc; tel. (68) 25726.

Archbishop of Trnava: Mgr JÁN SOKOL, Svätoplukovo 3, 917 66 Trnava; tel. (805) 26235.

Slovak Rite

Bishop of Prešov: Mgr JÁN HIRKA, Greckokatolický biskupský úrad, Hlavná ulica 8, Prešov; tel. (91) 34622; 361,060 adherents (December 1988); 201 parishes.

The Orthodox Church

Pravoslavná Církev v ČSFR (Orthodox Church of Czechoslovakia): V Jámě, 6, 111 21 Prague 1; divided into four eparchies: Prague, Olomouc, Prešov, Michalovce; Head of the Orthodox Church, Metropolitan of Prague and of all Czechoslovakia JAN MÍRKO; 100,000 mems; 127 parishes; Theological Faculty in Charles University, Prague.

Protestant Churches

Rada Církve Bratrské (Brethren Church Council): Soukenická 15, 110 00 Prague 1; 10,000 mems, 45 congregations, 190 preaching stations; Pres. JAROSLAV KUBOVÝ; Sec. K. TASCHNER.

Christian Corps: Brno; 3,200 mems; 123 brs; Rep. Ing. PETR ZEMAN.

Baptist Union in Czechoslovakia: Na Topolce 14, 140 00 Prague 4; tel. (2) 430974; f. 1919; 4,000 mems; Gen. Sec. Rev. PAVEL VYCHOPEŇ.

Evangelical Church of the Augsburg Confession in Czechoslovakia (Slovak Lutheran Church): Palisády 46, 811 06 Bratislava; tel. (7) 330827; presided over by the Bishop-General, assisted by bishops of the Western and Eastern districts; 327 parishes in 14 seniorates; 369,000 baptized mems; Bishop-Gen. PAVEL UHORSKAI.

Evangelical Church of Czech Brethren (Presbyterian): Jungmannova 9, 111 21 Prague 1; tel. (2) 2360924; telex 123363; fax (2) 2350521; f. 1781; united since 1918; activities extend over Bohemia, Moravia, and Silesia; 180,000 adherents and 268 parishes; Moderator Rev. PAVEL SMETANA; Gen. Sec. MIROSLAV BROŽ.

Reformed Christian Church of Slovakia: Jókaiho 36, 945 01 Komárno; tel. (819) 2788; 150,000 mems and 310 parishes; Bishop EUGEN MIKÓ; Gen. Sec. BARTOLOMEJ GÖÖZ.

Silesian Evangelical Church of the Augsburg Confession in the Czech Republic (Silesian Lutheran Church): Na Nivách 7, 737 01 Český Těšín; tel. (659) 56656; founded in the 16th century during the Lutheran Reformation, reorganized in 1948; 46,800 mems; Bishop VILÉM STONAWSKI.

Unitarians: Karlova 8, 110 00 Prague 1; tel. (2) 266730; f. 1923; 5,000 mems; 4 parishes; Presiding Officer Dr D. J. KAFKA.

United Methodist Church: Ječná 19, 120 00 Prague 2; tel. (2) 290623; 3,688 mems; 21 parishes; Supt JOSEF ČERVEŇÁK.

Unity of Brethren (Jednota bratrská) (Moravian Church): Hálkova 5, 120 00 Prague 2; tel. (2) 2361340; f. 1457; 5,000 mems; 17 parishes; Pres. Rev. RUDOLF BORSKI.

Other Christian Churches

Apostolic Church: f. 1989; 2,000 mems; Chair. of Central Council of Elders RUDOLF BUBÍK.

Church of the Seventh-day Adventists: Zálesí 50, 142 00 Prague 4; tel. (2) 4723745; 12,000 mems; 106 preaching stations; Pres. KAREL NOWAK.

Czechoslovak Hussite Church: Kujbyševa 5, 166 26 Prague 6; tel. (2) 320041; f. 1920; 400,000 mems; five dioceses divided into 327 parishes; Bishop-Patriarch Dr VRATISLAV STEPANEK.

Old Catholic Church (Byskupský ordinariat a synodní rada Církve starokatolické v ČSFR): Hládkov 3, 160 00 Prague 6; tel. (2) 357051;

f. 1871; 2,000 mems, 6 parishes; Bishop-ordinarius Mgr DUŠAN HEJBAL.

JUDAISM

The present community is estimated at approximately 6,000 people, and is divided under two central organizations:

Council of Jewish Communities in the Czech Republic (Rada židovských náboženských obcí v České republice): Maislova 18, 101 01 Prague 1; tel. (2) 2318559; 6,000 mems; Chair. JIŘI DANIČEK (acting); Sec.-Gen. (vacant); Chief Rabbi of Prague (vacant).

Union of the Jewish Religious Communities in the Slovak Republic (Ústredný zväz židovských náboženských obcí ve Slovenskej republike): Šmeralova ul. 29, 800 00 Bratislava; 3,300 mems; Chair. JURAJ RAIF; Chief Rabbi SAMUEL GROSSMANN (Košice).

The Press

The Czechs and Slovaks far exceed other Eastern European nations in their consumption per head of newspapers and magazines. In early 1991 there were 52 daily and weekly newspapers being published in major towns. In March 1991 there were 14 dailies published in Prague and 12 (two in Hungarian and the remainder in Slovak) in Bratislava. In 1989 there were 1,086 magazines and newspapers published in Czechoslovakia, as well as numerous less frequent periodicals.

In November 1989, during Czechoslovakia's 'Velvet Revolution', the laws on censorship were revoked, and many publications and literary works, hitherto banned, became freely available. In March 1991 the Federal Assembly passed legislation which formally abolished censorship and permitted private citizens to publish periodicals. Among the most influential and widely read of the new independent publications were *Fórum* (a weekly magazine with a circulation of 60,000) and the daily *Občanský deník*, both of which were initially published by Civic Forum. Also important was the daily *Lidové noviny* (formerly an underground publication). *Rudé právo*, formerly the chief organ of the Czechoslovak Communist Party, retained a wide daily circulation (370,000 in 1991). No daily newspaper has a large circulation in both Republics. The titles of principal newspapers and periodicals are listed in the section on the appropriate Republic.

Federal Government Publication

Hospodářské noviny (Economic News): Na Florenci 19, 115 43 Prague 1; tel. (2) 2367481; telex 121435; fax (2) 2327236; federal govt publication; general politics and economics; Editor-in-Chief Dr JIŘÍ SEKERA; circ. 120,000.

Foreign-language Publications

Czechoslovak Foreign Trade: ul. 28 října 13, 112 79 Prague 1; tel. (2) 2139381; telex 121142; fax (2) 2327520; f. 1960; monthly; journal of the Czechoslovak Chamber of Commerce and Industry; published in English, German, Spanish, Russian and French by Rapid, Czechoslovak Advertising Agency; Editor-in-Chief Dr PAVLA PODSKALSKÁ; circ. 15,000.

For You from Czechoslovakia: ul. 28 října 13, 112 79 Prague 1; tel. (2) 139393; telex 121142; quarterly; published by Rapid in English, German, Russian, Spanish and French; Editor-in-Chief MARIE SŮVOVÁ; circ. 15,900.

NEWS AGENCIES

Československá tisková kancelář (ČSTK) (Czechoslovak News Agency): Opletalova 5-7, 111 44 Prague 1; tel. (2) 2147; telex 122841; fax (2) 122841; f. 1918; news and photo exchange service with all international and many national news agencies; maintains wide network of foreign correspondents; English, Russian, French and Spanish news service for foreign countries; publishes daily bulletin in English; publs special economic bulletins in Czech and English and documentation surveys in Czech; Gen. Dir Ing. PETR UHL.

Foreign Bureaux

Agence France-Presse (AFP): Žitná 10, 120 00 Prague 2; tel. (2) 296927; telex 121124; Bureau Chief BERNARD MEIXNER.

Agenzia Nazionale Stampa Associata (ANSA) (Italy): Ve Smečkách 2, 110 00 Prague 1; tel. (2) 2361826; telex 122734; fax (2) 376133; Bureau Chief LUCIO ATTILIO LEANTE.

Allgemeiner Deutscher Nachrichtendienst (ADN) (Germany): Milevská 835, 140 00 Prague 4; tel. (2) 6921911; Bureau Chief WOLFGANG JASINSKI.

Associated Press (AP) (USA): Růžová 7, 110 00 Prague 1; tel. (2) 364838; telex 121987; Correspondent ONDŘEJ HEJMA.

Bulgarska Telegrafna Agentsia (BTA) (Bulgaria): Ždanova 46, 160 00 Prague 6; telex 121066; Bureau Chief LYUBCHO KHRISTOV.

Dan News Agency (Argentina): Dejvická 52, 160 00 Prague 6; tel. (2) 3278594; Correspondent ETIL CHROMOY.

Deutsche Presse-Agentur (dpa) (Germany): Želivského 11/4/13, 130 31 Prague 3; tel. (2) 276595; telex 122706; Bureau Chief THOMAS WOLF.

Informatsionnoye Agentstvo Novosti (IAN) (USSR): Italská 26, 120 00 Prague 3; tel. (2) 2354459; telex 122235; Bureau Chief VLADIMIR FEDOROV; also br. in Bratislava.

Magyar Távirati Iroda (MTI) (Hungary): U Smaltovny 17, 6th Floor, 170 00 Prague 7; tel. (2) 801649; telex 121827; Bureau Chief JÁNOS KÁRPÁTI.

Novinska Agencija Tanjug (Yugoslavia): U Smaltovny 19, 170 00 Prague 7; tel. (2) 806987; Correspondent BRANKO STOŠIĆ.

Polska Agencja Prasowa (PAP) (Poland): Petrské nám. 1, 110 00 Prague 1; tel. (2) 2325223; Correspondent STANISŁAW MAZAN.

Prensa Latina (Cuba): Petrské nám. 1, 110 00 Prague 1; telex 121083; Bureau Chief EDEL SUÁREZ VENEGAS.

Telegrafnoye Agentstvo Sovetskovo Soyuza (TASS) (USSR): Pevnostní 5, 162 00 Prague 6; tel. (2) 327527; Bureau Chief A. P. SHAPOVALOV.

Xinhua (New China) News Agency (People's Republic of China): Majakovského 22, Prague 6; tel. (2) 326144; telex 121561; Correspondent LIU TIENPAI.

PRESS ASSOCIATION

Free Journalists Club: Prague; Chair PETR KELLNER.
See Republic sections for further press associations.

Radio and Television

In 1989 there were 4,216,838 radio receivers and 4,660,543 television receivers licensed.

RADIO

There are eight national networks in Czechoslovakia: Radios Prague and Bratislava (medium wave and VHF), Radio Czechoslovakia (long, medium and VHF—popular and news programmes), Radios Vltava and Děvín (VHF from Prague and Bratislava respectively—programmes on Czech, Slovak and world culture), Regina (medium and VHF—programme of regional studios), Radio FM (VHF from Bratislava), and Interprogramme (medium and VHF—for foreign visitors to Czechoslovakia, in English, German and French).

Local stations broadcast from Prague (Central Bohemian Studio), Banská Bystrica, Bratislava, Brno, České Budějovice, Hradec Králové, Košice, Ostrava, Plzeň, Prešov, Ústí nad Labem and other towns.

Foreign broadcasts are made in English, French, German, Hungarian, Spanish, Ukrainian, and Czech and Slovak.

Československý rozhlas (Czechoslovak Radio): Vinohradská 12, 120 99 Prague 2; tel. (2) 2115111; telex 121100; fax (2) 2321020; f. 1923; Dir-Gen. RICHARD SEEMAN.

Československé zahraniční vysílání (Czechoslovak Foreign Broadcasts): Vinohradská 12, 120 99 Prague 2; tel. (2) 2360823; telex 121189; fax (2) 2321020; Dir Ing. KAREL LÁNSKÝ.

TELEVISION

There are television studios in Prague, Brno, Ostrava, Bratislava and Košice.

Československá televize (Czechoslovak Television): Jindřišská 16, 111 50 Prague 1; tel. (2) 221247; telex 121800; f. 1953; Dir-Gen. JIŘÍ KANTUREK.

For further information see the sections on the Republics.

Finance

(cap. = capital; dep. = deposits; res = reserves; m. = million; Kčs. = korunas)

BANKS

In 1990 and 1991 the Czechoslovak banking system was extensively reorganized. From 1950 until 1989 the State Bank of Czechoslovakia was a monopolistic commercial bank, in addition to being the central bank and sole bank of issue. In January 1990 the State Bank's functions of issue and of credit were separated. Its commercial activities were transferred to the Komerční banka

Praha, the Všeobecná úverova banka Bratislava and the already-existing Investiční banka (Prague), while the State Bank remained as the country's central monetary authority. From 1 January 1991 the establishment of private commercial banks was permitted. For information on republican commercial banks, savings banks and insurance companies see the sections on the Republics.

Central Bank

Státní banka československá (State Bank of Czechoslovakia): Na příkopě 28, 110 03 Prague 1; tel. (2) 2112; telex 121555; fax (2) 2354141; f. 1950; the State Monetary Agency; bank of issue, the central authority of Czechoslovakia in the monetary sphere, legislation and permission, central bank for directing and securing monetary policy, regulation of activities of other banks and savings banks; statutory fund 1,400m. Kčs.; reserve fund 2,033m. Kčs. (Jan. 1991); Chair. Ing. JOSEF TOSOVSKÝ.

Commercial Banks

Agrobanka Praha as: Rumunská 1, 120 00 Prague 2; tel. (2) 295398; fax (2) 263415; f. 1990; functions through a network of independent regional banks; provides a wide range of financial services, participates in privatization programmes; cap. 750m. Kčs. (Jan. 1991); Gen. Man. Ing. JAN KRÁL; 11 brs.

    Agrobanka Haná, as Prostjov: ul. Újezd 12, 796 40 Prostjov 1; tel. (508) 4035; cap. 50m. Kčs. (Jan. 1991); Gen. Man. Ing. JOSEF SEDLÁČEK.

    Agrobanka Hradec Králové as: Nerudova 37, Hradec Králové, 501 01; tel. (49) 38011; telex 194222; fax (49) 34192; f. 1991; provides credit facilities for agricultural enterprises and organizations; cap. 62m. Kčs. (Jan. 1991); Dir Ing. FRANTIŠEK POSPÍŠIL; 3 brs.

    Agrobanka Mladá Boleslav as: Bělská 151, Mladá Boleslav; tel. (326) 21764; fax (326) 23769; f. 1991; cap. 60m. Kčs. (Jan. 1991); Gen. Man. Ing. JAN SULC.

    Agrobanka Olomouc as: Blaniická 1, 772 26 Olomouc; tel. (68) 29512; fax (68) 28285; f. 1991; cap. 50m. Kčs. (Jan. 1991); Gen. Man. Ing. JAROSLAV SNÁSEL.

    Agrobanka Plzeň as: Nerudova 35, 306 29 Plzeň; tel. (19) 295398; fax (19) 263415; f. 1991; cap. 60m. Kčs. (Jan. 1991); Gen. Man. Ing. IVANA KOCOURKOVÁ; 11 brs.

    Ekoagrobanka as: Králova výšina 3132/7, 400 01 Ústi nad Labem; tel. (47) 26019; Gen. Man. Ing. MIROSLAV ADÁMEK.

Československá obchodní banka as (Commercial Bank of Czechoslovakia): Na Příkopě 14, 115 20 Prague 1; tel. (2) 224444; telex 122201; fax (2) 2358416; f. 1965; commercial and foreign exchange transactions; cap. 1,050m. Kčs., res 9,842m. Kčs., dep. 84,599m. Kčs. (1990); Chair. and CEO Ing. ROSTISLAV PETRÁŠ; 11 brs.

Investiční banka: Gorkého nám. 32, 113 03 Prague 1; tel. (2) 2362065; telex 122459; fax (2) 2368945; f. 1989; cap. 1,500m. Kčs., res 89,000m. Kčs., dep. 30,000m. Kčs. (Jan. 1991); Gen. Man. Prof. Ing. MIROSLAV TUČEK; 14 brs.

Joint-Venture Banks

Bankovní dům SKALA (Banking House SKALA): Opletalova 4, Prague 1; tel. (2) 2657419; fax (2) 3115391; cap. 50m. Kčs. (Jan. 1991); Dir Ing. MIROSLAV ROSKOT.

EKO banka, Kroměřiž as: Vejvanovského 384, Kroměřiž; tel. (634) 21788; fax (634) 21788; cap. 51m. Kčs. (Jan. 1991); Gen. Man. Ing. Rudolf Chury.

Poštovní banka as: Plzeňská 139, 150 00 Prague 5; tel. (2) 549549; fax (2) 544949; f. 1991; general financial services supplied through the postal network; cap. 250m. Kčs. (Jan. 1991); Chair. Ing. JAROSLAV VOPÁLECKÝ; 5,200 brs.

SGKB: Vajanského nábr. 5, 811 02 Bratislava; tel. (7) 331351; fax (7) 334656; f. 1990; cap. 400m. Kčs.; Gen. Man. MILAN VRŠOVSKÝ.

Tatra banka: Vajanského nábr. 5, 811 02 Bratislava; tel. (7) 331351; fax (7) 334656; f. 1990; cap. 400m. Kčs. (Jan. 1991); Gen. Man. MILAN VRŠOVSKÝ.

Trade and Industry

CHAMBER OF COMMERCE

Československá obchodní a průmyslová komora (Czechoslovak Chamber of Commerce and Industry): Argentinská 38, 170 05 Prague 7; tel. (2) 8724111; telex 121862; fax (2) 879134; f. 1850; has 1,800 members (foreign trade corporations, industrial enterprises, banks, research institutes and private enterprises); Pres. Ing. Dr VOJTĚCH BUREŠ.

FOREIGN TRADE CORPORATIONS AND MAJOR INDUSTRIAL COMPANIES

Aero Group: Beranovych 130, 199 04 Prague 9; tel. (2) 816; manufactures civil aircraft and aircraft equipment; 23,000 employees.

Artia Ltd: Ve Smečkách 30, 111 27 Prague 1; tel. (2) 2137111; telex 121065; fax (2) 2315206; imports and exports cultural commodities; Gen. Dir EMANUEL PAVLÍČEK.

Barum: 765 31 Otrokovice; tel. (67) 922353; telex 67280; fax (67) 922209; produces motor tyres; Man. Dir. PAVEL PRAVEC; 4,000 employees.

Budejovicky Budvar: Karoliny Svetle 4, 370 54 Česke Budějovice; major brewery, produces the *Budweiser* brand.

Čechofracht: Na Příkopě 8, 111 83 Prague 1; tel. (2) 2129111; telex 122221; fax (2) 2327137; f. 1949; shipping and international forwarding joint-stock co; Gen. Dir Ing. STANISLAV MACH.

Centrotex: nám. Hrdinů 3/1634, 140 61 Prague 4; tel. (2) 415; telex 121232; fax (2) 438771; imports and exports textiles; Gen. Dir Ing. J. CHRBOLKA.

České energeticke zavody (Czech Electricity Works): Jungmannova 29, 111 48 Prague 1; tel. (2) 2119; telex 121151; fax (2) 2368354; energy utilities company in the Czech Republic; Gen. Dir PETR KARAS; 36,000 employees.

Chemapol: Kodaňská 46, 100 10 Prague 10; tel. (2) 715; telex 122021; fax (2) 737007; f. 1948; imports and exports chemical and pharmaceutical products, petroleum and other raw materials; Gen. Dir Ing. VÁCLAV VOLF.

Chirana koncern: 91601 Stara Tura; tel. (834) 963721; telex 71201; fax (834) 963911; production and distribution of medical equipment; Man. Dir KAZIMIR KNET.

Cizkovicka cementarna a vapenice (Ciskovice Cement and Limestone Works): 41112 Ciskovice; tel. (4191) 725100; telex 184313; fax (4191) 725600; cement, mortar and hydraulic lime; Gen. Man. KAREL SIATKA.

ČKD Kombinat: Kolbenky 159, Prague; tel. (2) 8121111; telex 121429; fax (2) 802782; manufactures railway locomotives, ship engines, electric motors.

Colorlak: 68 602 Uherske Hradiste; tel. (632) 471; telex 60360; fax (632) 62141; production and marketing of paints, varnishes and solvents; Gen. Dir ZDENEK TUMA.

Czechoslovak Ceramics: V Jámě 1, 111 91 Prague 1; tel. (2) 214421; telex 121118; fax (2) 267673; exports and imports ceramics; Gen. Dir Ing. MIROSLAV DOBES.

Czechoslovak Filmexport: Václavské nám. 28, 111 45 Prague 1; tel. (2) 2365385; telex 122259; fax (2) 2358432; f. 1957; import and export of films; Gen. Dir JIŘÍ JANOUSEK.

Drevounia: Dr V. Clementisa 10, 826 10 Bratislava; tel. (7) 229962; telex 93291; fax (7) 236164; imports and exports wood and furniture; Gen. Dir Ing. JIŘÍ JIRAVA.

Exico: Panská 9, 111 77 Prague 1; tel. (2) 2124111; telex 122211; fax (2) 2321030; f. 1966; exports and imports leather, shoes, skins; Gen. Dir Ing. FRANTIŠEK FREMUND.

Fatra: 763 61 Napajedla; tel. (67) 942755; telex 67242; fax (67) 942407; manufactures plastic products, incl. pipes, sacks and conveyer belts; Gen. Dir TOUFAR JAROSLAV; 2,500 employees.

Ferromet: Opletalova 27, 111 81 Prague 1; tel. (2) 2141; telex 121411; fax (2) 2360801; imports and exports metallurgical products; Gen. Dir Ing. JIŘÍ FRYBERT.

Gumokov: 500 23 Hradec Kralove; tel. (49) 659; telex 194246; fax (49) 616827; manufactures rubber and metal products; Pres. JAROSLAV BURDA; 1,800 employees.

Gustava Klimenta Factory: 674 83 Trebic, Burovina; tel. (618) 771; telex 62955; fax (618) 7716539; manufactures footwear and clothing; Dir EMIL HEGR; 8,300 employees.

Imex: Revoluční 25, 110 15 Prague 1; tel. (2) 2311000; telex 121977; fax (2) 2317191; f. 1969; imports and exports consumer goods and sales equipment; Gen. Man. J. DANIHELKA.

Inspekta: Olbrachtova 1, 140 00 Prague 4; tel. (2) 6927628; telex 121938; fax (2) 434390; control of goods in foreign trade; Gen. Dir Ing. JAN STRNAD.

Intercoop: Dr V. Clementisa 10, 826 08 Bratislava; tel. (7) 229162; telex 93365; fax (7) 224393; imports and exports toys, fruits, vegetables, honey and wine.

Jablonex Ltd: Palackého 41, 466 37 Jablonec nad Nisou; tel. (428) 510; telex 186238; fax (428) 27362; f. 1949; imports and exports fashion jewellery and decorations; Gen. Dir JAN BERNARD.

Kaucuk: 278 52 Krapuly n Vlt; tel. (205) 510; telex 132237; fax (205) 23566; produces rubber, polystyrene and petroleum products; Gen. Dir MIROSLAV NEVOSAD; 3,100 employees.

Koospol: Leninova 178, 160 67 Prague 6; tel. (2) 3361111; telex 121121; fax (2) 345572; imports and exports foodstuffs; Gen. Dir JAROSLAV ŘÍHA.

Kovo: Jankovcova 2, 170 88 Prague 7; tel. (2) 8741111; telex 121481; fax (2) 800162; imports and exports precision engineering products; Gen. Dir JOSEF KUDRHALT.

Ligna: Vodičkova 41, 112 09 Prague 1; tel. (2) 2134; telex 122066; fax (2) 263525; imports and exports timber, wood products, musical instruments and paper; Gen. Dir Ing. MIROSLAV MRNA.

Martimex Ltd: Červenej armády 1, 036 65 Martin; tel. (842) 33311; telex 75488; fax (842) 39118; f. 1970; imports and exports construction and roadbuilding machinery, fork-lift trucks; Pres. MILAN LAUKO.

Merkuria: Argentinská 38, 170 05 Prague 7; tel. (2) 8724111; telex 121022; fax (2) 802950; exports and imports tools and consumer goods; Gen. Dir Ing. JOSEF CHUCHVALEC.

Metalimex: Štěpánská 34, 112 17 Prague 1; tel. (2) 2359575; telex 121405; fax (2) 2320630; imports and exports non-ferrous metals, electrical power, natural gas and solid fuels; Gen. Dir Ing. JOSEF BULVAS.

Motokov Ltd: Na Strži 63, 140 62 Prague 4; tel. (2) 4141111; telex 121882; fax (2) 434616; imports and exports vehicles, agricultural machinery and light engineering products; Gen. Dir Ing. DALIBOR MOŠOVSKÝ.

Omnipol: Nekázanka 11, 112 21 Prague 1; telex 121299; fax (2) 226792; import and export of sports and civil aircraft; Gen. Dir Ing. FRANTIŠEK HÁVA.

Petrimex: Dr V. Clementisa 10, 826 02 Bratislava; tel. (7) 229962; telex 935259; fax (7) 235622; imports and exports chemicals, raw materials; Man. Dir ANTON RAKICKY.

Pragoexport: Jungmannova 34, 112 59 Prague 1; tel. (2) 2366065; telex 121586; fax (2) 2358964; f. 1948; imports and exports consumer goods; Gen. Dir PAVEL MAJOR.

Pragoinvest: Českomoravská 23, 180 56 Prague 9; tel. (2) 822741; telex 122379; fax (2) 823472; import and export of machinery and complete plant equipment; Gen. Dir Ing. MILOSLAV KOČÁREK.

Severočeské chemicke zavody (North Bohemian Chemical Works): Terezinska 145, 41017 Lovosice; tel. (419) 2541; telex 184231; fax (419) 3472; produces industrial fertilizers; Gen. Man. JOSEF KASPER; 3,000 employees.

Sklo Union: Liben Skolovska 117, Prague 8; tel. (2) 259678; sales US $12m. (1989); produces glass and glass products; due to be privatized in 1991.

Skloexport: tř. 1. máje 52, 461 74 Liberec; tel. (48) 315; telex 186267; fax (48) 421027; exports glass; Gen. Dir Ing. JAROSLAV KŘIVÁNEK.

Škoda AK Ltd: 29301 Mlada Boleslav; tel. (3) 2626512; manufactures motor cars and components; Man. ZDENEK PATOCKA.

Škodaexport: Václavské nám. 56, 113 32 Prague 1; tel. (2) 2131; telex 122413; fax (2) 269563; exports and imports power engineering and metallurgical plants, engineering works, electrical locomotives and trolleybuses, tobacco machines; Pres. JAN RICICA.

Strojexport: POB 662, Václavské nám. 56, 113 26 Prague 1; tel. (2) 2131; telex 121753; fax (2) 2323084; f. 1953; imports and exports machines and machinery equipment, civil engineering works; Gen. Dir JOSEF REGNER.

Strojimport Co Ltd: Vinohradská 184, 130 52 Prague 3; tel. (2) 737141; telex 122241; fax (2) 777554; f. 1953; imports and exports machine tools, tools and gauges, and industrial plants; Pres. IVAN ČAPEK.

Technoexport: Václavské nám. 1, 113 34 Prague 1; tel. (2) 2364325; telex 121268; fax (2) 229024; imports and exports chemical and foodstuff engineering plant; Gen. Dir Ing. OLDŘICH KUCHTA.

Textil a odevy Brno: Nám. Svobody 4, POB 198, 657 98 Brno; tel. (5) 22711; telex 62252; fax (5) 26507; manufactures textiles and yarns; Pres. JOSEF HUBAČEK; 3,500 employees.

Tuzex: Rytířská 13, 113 43 Prague 1; tel. (2) 220292; telex 121012; fax (2) 221808; retail goods for foreign currency; Gen. Dir JIŘI NEMEC.

United Chemical and Metallurgical Works: Revoluční 86, 400 32 Ustí nad Labem; tel. (47) 2181111; telex 184222; fax (47) 24597; produces chemicals and related products; Gen. Dir JOSEF VENCL; 5,000 employees.

Zapadočeské keramicke zavody: 330 12 Horni Briza; tel. (19) 955110; telex 154328; fax (19) 528222; produces ceramic wall tiles, drainage tubes and general stoneware; Gen. Dir JAROSLAV ŠIROKÝ; 3,600 employees.

TRADE UNIONS

Česká a Slovenská konfederace odborových svazů–ČSKOS (Czech and Slovak Confederation of Trade Unions): nám. W. Churchilla 2, 113 59 Prague 3; tel. (2) 2367204; telex 121517; fax (2) 2350784; f. 1990 to replace the Central Council of Trade Unions (f. 1945); embraces 61 trade unions with more than 7m. mems; Pres. ROMAN KOVÁČ.

Federální odborový svaz chemie a příbuzných odvětí (Federal Trade Union of Chemical and Related Industries): nám. W. Churchilla 2, 113 59 Prague 3; tel. (2) 2355489; telex 121517; Pres. VLADIMÍR ŽIŽKA; 180,152 mems.

Federální odborový svaz energetiků (Federal Trade Union of Power Industry Workers): nám. W. Churchilla 2, 113 59 Prague 3; tel. (2) 270081; fax (2) 2352606; f. 1990; Pres. PAVEL HÁJEK; 102,050 mems.

Federální odborový svaz pracovníků hornictví, geologie, naftového průmyslu (Federal Trade Union of Miners, Geologists and Oilmen): nám. W. Churchilla 2, 113 59 Prague 3; tel. (2) 2366260; fax (2) 2369349; Pres. STANISLAV HOŠEK; 257,336 mems.

Federální odborový svaz pracovníků sklářského, keramického, bižuterního průmyslu a porcelánu (Federal Trade Union of Workers in the Glass, Ceramics, Costume Jewellery and Porcelain Industries): nám. W. Churchilla 2, 113 59 Prague 3; tel. (2) 2353561; Pres. JAROSLAV KUCH; 103,294 mems.

Federální odborový svaz pracovníků spojů (Federal Trade Union of Telecommunication Workers): nám W. Churchilla 2, 113 59 Prague 3; tel. (2) 278529; Pres. ZDENĚK KUBĚNA; 146,285 mems.

Federální odborový svaz pracovníků ve stavebnictví a výrobě stavebních hmot, inženýrsko-investorských, projektových a výzkumných organizací (Federal Trade Union of Construction Workers, of Workers in Production of Construction Materials, Civil Engineering and Investments, Design and Research Organizations): Senovážné nám. 23, 112 82 Prague 1; tel. (2) 21142723; Pres. JIŘÍ KOTEN; 637,864 mems.

Konfederace umění a kultury (Confederation of Arts and Culture): Senovážné nám. 23, 112 82 Prague 1; tel. (2) 21142519; f. 1990; independent trade union centre, not affiliated to ČSKOS; Pres. JAN KŘTITEL SÝKORA.

Odborové sdružení železničářů (federální) (Trade Union Association of Railwaymen—Federal): nám. W. Churchilla 2, 113 59 Prague 3; tel. (2) 2353561; telex 124484; Pres. VÁCLAV VANĚK; 324,360 mems.

Odborový svaz kovo v ČSFR (Metalworkers' Federation of the ČSFR): nám. W. Churchilla 2, 113 59 Prague 3; tel. (2) 2368974; telex 121517; fax (2) 2350784; Pres. ALOJZ ENGLIŠ; 1,402,329 mems.

Trade Union Association of Bohemia, Moravia and Slovakia: Prague; f. 1991; critical of economic reform programme.

TRADE FAIR

BVV Trade Fairs and Exhibitions: Výstaviště 1, 602 00 Brno; tel. (5) 3141111; telex 62239; fax (5) 333998; f. 1959; international engineering fair yearly in September; international consumer goods fair yearly in April; Gen. Dir Ing. ANTONÍN SURKA.

Transport

RAILWAYS

At 31 December 1989 the total length of the Czechoslovak railways was 13,106 km; of this total, 3,816 km were electrified, including the connection Prague–Warsaw via Bohumín. The densest section of the network links the north with the south, and there is a direct rail link between the west and east of the country.

Československé státní dráhy (Czechoslovak State Railways): nábř. L. Svobody 12, 110 15 Prague 1; tel. (2) 2891; telex 121096; Dir Ing. IVO MALINA.

Prague Metropolitan Railway: Dopravní podnik hlavního města Prahy, Bubenská 1, 170 26 Prague 7; tel. (2) 878278; telex 122443; fax (2) 878786; the Prague underground railway opened in 1974 and, by Nov. 1990, 38.5 km were operational; there were 41 stations; Gen. Dir Ing. MILAN HAŠEK.

ROADS

In January 1989 there were 73,444 km of roads in Czechoslovakia, including 518 km of motorways. More than 90% of the total road network is hard-surfaced. The Prague–Brno–Bratislava motorway was opened in 1980.

Československá státní automobilová doprava—ČSAD (Czechoslovak State Road Transport): Hybernská 32, 111 21 Prague 1; f. 1949; the organization has 11 regional head offices.

Sdružení československých mezinárodních automobilových dopravců (ČESMAD) (Czechoslovak International Road Transport Enterprises Association): Perucká 5, 120 67 Prague 2; tel. (2)

6911920; telex 122303; fax (2) 256273; f. 1966; Chair. Ing. JOZEF MRÁŽIK; Gen. Sec. Dipl. Ing. JIŘÍ KLADIVA.

INLAND WATERWAYS

The total length of navigable waterways in Czechoslovakia is 480 km. The Elbe (Labe) and its tributary the Vltava connect the country with the North Sea via the port of Hamburg. The Oder provides a connection with the Baltic Sea and the port of Szczecin. The Danube (Dunaj) provides a link with Germany, Austria, Hungary, Yugoslavia, Bulgaria, Romania and the USSR. Czechoslovakia's river ports are Prague Holešovice, Prague Radotín, Kolín, Mělník, Ústí nad Labem and Děčín on the Vltava and Elbe, and Bratislava and Komárno on the Danube.

Československá plavba dunajská (Czechoslovak Danube River Shipping): Červenej armády 35, 815 24 Bratislava; telex 92338; three ships totalling 6,080 grt; Man. Dir Ing. JURAJ PAVELEK.

Československá plavba labsko-oderská (ČSPLO) (Czechoslovak Elbe-Oder River Shipping): K. Čapka 1, 405 91 Děčín; tel. (7) 57271; telex 184241; fax (7) 58801; carries out transport of goods on the Vltava, Elbe and Oder rivers as well as other waterways; transfer and storage of goods in Czechoslovak ports; operates the river ports of Prague, Mělník, Kolín, Ústí nad Labem and Děčín; Man. Dir JIŘÍ ASTR.

SHIPPING

Československá námořní plavba, mezinárodní akciová společnost (Czechoslovak Ocean Shipping, International Joint-Stock Company): Počernická 168, 100 99 Prague 10; tel. (2) 778941; telex 122137; fax (2) 773962; f. 1959; shipping company operating the Czechoslovak sea-going fleet; 18 ships totalling 443,155 dwt; Man. Dir Capt. VLADIMÍR PODLENA.

CIVIL AVIATION

There are civil airports at Prague (Ruzyně), Brno, Bratislava, Karlovy Vary, Košice, Mariánské Lázně, Ostrava, Piešťany, Poprad-Tatry, Sliač (Banská Bystrica) and Zlín, served by ČSA's internal flights. International flights serve Prague, Bratislava, Poprad-Tatry, Ostrava, Brno, Košice and Karlovy Vary.

ČSA (Československé aerolinie) (Czechoslovak Airlines): Head Office: Ruzyně Airport, 160 08 Prague; tel. (2) 341540; telex 120338; fax (2) 3162774; f. 1923; external services to most European capitals, the Near, Middle and Far East, North and Central America and North Africa; Gen. Dir Ing. OLDŘICH CHURAIN; fleet of 2 A310-300, 9 Ilyushin Il-62M, 7 Tupolev TU-134A, 7 Tupolev TU-154-M and 6 Yakovlev Yak-40.

Slov-Air: Ivanka Airport, 823 12 Bratislava; tel. (7) 226172; telex 93270; fax (7) 223621; f. 1969; domestic scheduled and charter services; Dir Dipl. Ing. LUBOMÍR KOVAČIK; fleet of small turboprop aircraft and helicopters including four Let L-410 and two An-2.

Tourism

Czechoslovakia has magnificent scenery, with winter sports facilities. Prague is the best known of the historic cities, and there are famous castles and cathedrals, numerous resorts and 57 spas with natural mineral springs. In 1990 foreign visitor arrivals totalled 46.7m., including excursionists. In the same year income from tourism amounted to US $316m.

Čedok (Travel and Hotels Corporation): Na Příkopě 18, 111 35 Prague 1; tel. (2) 2127111; telex 121109; fax (2) 2321656; f. 1920; the official Czechoslovak Travel Agency; 166 travel offices; 16 branches throughout Europe and in Japan and the USA; Pres. EVA SPAŇÁROVÁ.

Atomic Energy

Nuclear power accounted for 28% of total electricity production in 1989.

Československá komise pro atomovou energii (ČSKAE) (Czechoslovak Atomic Energy Commission): Slezská 9, 120 29 Prague 2; tel. (2) 2151111; responsible for the peaceful utilization of atomic energy and for co-ordinating the atomic energy programme; Chair. Ing. KAREL WAGNER.

Ústav jaderného výzkumu (Institute of Nuclear Research): 250 68 Řež; tel. (2) 6857831; telex 122626; fax (2) 6857567; f. 1955; research on nuclear safety, radioactive waste management, industrial and medical applications of radioactive materials; Dir JAN MRKOS.

Culture

NATIONAL ORGANIZATIONS

Ústav pro kulturně výchovnou činnost (Institute for Culture and Education): Blanická 4, Vinohrady, 120 21 Prague 2; tel. (2) 250161; f. 1906 as the Union of Culture; organizes cultural research and adult education; Dir JOSEF TRNKA.

Československsk komise pro spolupráci s UNESCO (Czechoslovak Commission for Co-operation with UNESCO): Hradčanské nám. 5, Toskán, 125 10 Prague 1; tel. (2) 21933163.

SPORTING ORGANIZATION

Československý olympijský výbor (Czechoslovak Olympic Committee): Národní 33, 110 00 Prague 1; tel. (2) 266976.

ASSOCIATIONS

Svaz československých dramatických umělců (Union of Czechoslovak Dramatic Artists): Pod Nuselskými schodi 3, 120 00 Prague 2; tel. (2) 250682; f. 1978; 3,100 mems.

Svaz československých skladatelů a koncertních umělců (Union of Czechoslovak Composers and Concert Artists): Skroupovo nám. 9, Prague; tel. (2) 6912464; f. 1978; Pres. MILAN NOVÁK.

After 1989 many cultural organizations were reorganized on a republican basis. For further information see the sections on the Republics.

Education

Education is fully funded by the State at all levels. Most children between the ages of three and six attend kindergarten (mateřska škola). Education is compulsory between the ages of six and 16 years, when children attend basic school (základní škola). Most children continue their studies after basic school, either at a secondary grammar school or at a secondary vocational school. In both types of institution students follow four-year courses. There are also apprentice-training centres, at which courses last from two to four years, which prepare young people for workers' professions. In 1990 the establishment of private and religious schools was legalized. In the 1989/90 school year 636,622 children attended kindergarten, 1,961,742 attended basic (elementary) schools, 892,940 the different types of secondary school and there were 173,547 students in higher education.

UNIVERSITIES

Univerzita Karlova (Charles University): Ovocný tř. 5, 116 36 Prague; tel. (2) 228441; f. 1348; 16 faculties; 2,785 teachers; 25,786 students; Rector Prof. Dr RADIM PALOUŠ.

Univerzita Komenského Bratislava (Comenius University of Bratislava): Šafárikova nám. 6, 818 06 Bratislava; tel. (7) 320003; f. 1919; 9 faculties; 2,000 teachers; 12,800 students; Chancellor Prof. Dr LADISLAV MELIORIS.

Univerzita Masarykova (Masaryk University): Burešova 20, 601 77 Brno; tel. (5) 754841; f. 1919; 5 faculties; 971 teachers; 8,824 students; Rector Prof. Dr MILAN JELÍNEK.

Univerzita Palackého v Olomouci (Palacký University): Křížlovského 10, 771 47 Olomouc; tel. (68) 208111; f. 1573, re-opened 1946; 4 faculties; 750 teachers; 7,300 students; Rector Prof. Dr JOSEF JAŘAB.

Univerzita Pavla Jozefa Šafárika (Šafárik University): Šrobárova 57, 041 80 Košice; tel. (95) 22608; telex 77562; fax (95) 66959; f. 1959; 5 faculties; 713 teachers; 4,173 students; Rector Prof. Dr RUDOLF KOREC.

In 1991 the Czech National Council approved plans for the establishment of five new universities in the Czech Republic. They are to be located in Opava, Ostrava, Plžen, České Budějovice and Ústí nad Labem.

Social Welfare

A single and universal social security system was established in Czechoslovakia after the Second World War. Protection of health is stipulated by law, and medical care, treatment, medicines, etc. are, in most cases, available free of charge to the entire population. In 1988 there were 123,000 hospital beds available. In 1989 there were 57,950 physicians, equivalent to one physician per 270 persons, and expenditure on the health service was 38,268m. korunas.

There is a universal pension system, available to women at the age of 60, and to men, at the age of 65.

In 1991 a new system of social security was introduced. The Government planned to guarantee a minimum level of social welfare to all citizens, in an attempt to mitigate the expected consequences of radical economic reform. In addition, benefit was made available to unemployed workers for a maximum period of 12 months, and mandatory redundancy payments, equivalent to two months wages, were introduced. In 1990 a Council of Economic and Social Consensus (the 'Tripartite Council'), composed of representatives of federal and republican governments, employers and the trade unions, was established to discuss welfare issues.

NATIONAL AGENCIES

Federální ministerstvo práce a sociálních věcí (Federal Ministry of Labour and Social Affairs): see section on The Government (Ministries).

HEALTH AND WELFARE ORGANIZATIONS

Arpida—společnost pro rehabilitaci zdravotně postižených (Arpida—Society for the Rehabilitation of Disabled Persons): U Drinopulu 5, 168 00 Prague 6.

Československá rada pro humanitární spolupráci (Czechoslovak Council for Humanitarian Co-operation): 28 října 5, 110 00 Prague 1; tel. (2) 269163; Dir of Secretariat JIŘÍ CHÁRA.

Československy červeny kříž (Czechoslovak Central Committee of the Red Cross): Thunovská 18, 110 00 Prague 1; tel. (2) 532541; Pres. Dr ZDENKO VLK.

For further information see sections on the Republics.

The Environment

Environmental issues caused some of the first expressions of opposition to the Communist regime. Of particular concern is the region of Northern Bohemia, where sulphur dioxide emissions from coal-fired power stations have caused serious air pollution. According to official figures, Czechoslovakia produces more air pollutants per head of population than any other European country. There are estimated to be over 30 environmental groups in Czechoslovakia. The federal Government is a member of the Danube Commission (based in Hungary) and the IUCN (Gland, Switzerland).

FEDERAL GOVERNMENT ORGANIZATIONS

Federal Committee for the Environment: see section on The Government (Ministries).

The Federal Ministry of Agriculture and Food is also concerned with environmental matters.

Regional Organization

Joint Danube Fishery Commission: Šafárikova 20, 011 80 Žilina; eight mem. govts.

ACADEMIC INSTITUTES

Akademie zemědělských věd ČSFR (Czechoslovak Academy of Agriculture): Těšnov 65, 117 05 Prague 1; tel. (2) 2320582; fax (2) 2313161; f. 1924; Pres. Acad. Ing. MIROSLAV ŠPELINA.

Československá Akademie Věd (Czechoslovak Academy of Sciences): Národní tř. 3, 111 42 Prague 1; tel. (2) 266684; telex 121040; fax (2) 265671; f. 1952; Pres. Acad. O. WICHTERLE.

Institute of Experimental Biology and Ecology: Prague; tel. (2) 334595.

Institute of Industrial Landscape Ecology: Chittussiho 10, 710 00 Ostrava 2; tel. (69) 216960; promotes the application of ecology to planning industrial land use.

Institute of Physics of the Atmosphere: Bocni II–1401, 141 31 Prague 4; tel. (2) 766051; monitors atmospheric pollution.

Ustav krajinne ekologie ČSAV (Institute of Landscape Ecology): Na Sadkach 7, 370 05 České Budějovice; tel. (38) 40240; promotes the application of ecology to planning land use.

Czechoslovak Research and Development Centre for Environmental Pollution Control: Laca, Novomestského 2, 816 43 Bratislava.

Výskumný ustav lesného hospodárstva—VULH (Institute of Forestry Research): T. G. Masaryka 22, 960 92 Zvolen; telex 72284; fax (855) 23397; f. 1898; forestry management and ecological research.

NON-GOVERNMENTAL ORGANIZATIONS

Czechoslovak Green Party: See section on Political Organizations.

Green Circle: Prague; a confederation of the three principal environmental groups and some 30 smaller groups; incl.:

Brontosaurus: Prague; national environmental org.; fmrly affiliated to the Communist establishment, now independent.

For further information see the sections on the Republics.

Defence

In June 1990, according to Western estimates, the Army numbered 125,700 (including 100,000 conscripts) and the Air force 44,800 (18,000 conscripts); border troops numbered 13,000. In 1990 changes were made to the system of conscription, which is compulsory for all male citizens: the period of service was reduced from 24 to 18 months, and an alternative of 27 months of non-military duty was introduced. In 1991 it was announced that the period of service was to be reduced to 12 months, beginning in 1993/94. Service with the reserve lasts until 60 years of age. The Czechoslovak Army was to be substantially reduced (by 60,000 men) by 1993. The defence budget for 1991 was 28,000m. korunas. In late June 1991 the last of the 73,500 Soviet troops stationed in Czechoslovakia left the country. Czechoslovakia was a member of the Warsaw Pact (see p. 39), until the dissolution of the alliance in 1991.

Commander-in-Chief: President of the Republic.

Chief of General Staff: Maj.-Gen. KAREL PEZL.

THE CZECH AND SLOVAK REPUBLICS

THE CZECH LANDS

Geography

The Czech Lands of Bohemia and Moravia together comprise the Czech Republic, which is located in the west of Czechoslovakia, and forms a constituent republic of the Czech and Slovak Federative Republic. The territory of the Moravian administrative district also includes part of the historic region known as Silesia, most of which is now in Poland. The Czech Republic is bordered to the east by the Slovak Republic. There are international boundaries with Germany, to the north and west, with Poland, to the north-east, and with Austria, to the south. The Republic covers an area of 78,864 sq km (30,442 sq miles).

Bohemia, the westernmost of the Czech Lands, consists of a plateau, with an average height of 500 m, which is surrounded by low mountain ranges. Most of Bohemia forms the basin of the River Labe (Elbe), which flows across the plateau to the lower-lying regions of the north. The western frontiers are formed by the mountains of the Krušné Hory (Erzgebirge), in the north-west and the Český Les (Böhmerwald) to the west, but there are no high peaks, and there are good communications with Germany. In the north-east the Krkonoše Hory (Riesengebirge) form the highest range of the Sudetic (Sudeten) mountains, rising to 1,603 m (5,259 ft) at Mt Sněžka. The Sudetes extend eastwards along the northern border of Moravia, marking the political boundary between the Czech Lands and Poland. Moravia is a mainly lowland region, which has traditionally been a crossing-point between Poland and south-central Europe. In the east, however, it becomes more rugged and mountainous, with the Little and White Carpathian Mountains separating it from Slovakia.

The Czech Lands are situated in a transitional zone between maritime and continental climates. In Brno the average temperature in January is −2.7°C (27.1°F); the average July temperature is 19.3°C (66.7°F). Average annual rainfall is 527 mm.

At the census of March 1991, the total population of the Republic was 10,298,731. Of these 81.3% were ethnic Czechs and 3% Slovaks. There are also small communities of Poles, Roma (Gypsies) and Germans. At the 1991 census 13.2% of the population declared themselves to be of Moravian ethnicity and 0.6% Silesian. Some 40% of the population live in the administrative districts of Moravia. The principal religion is Christianity. At the 1991 census 39.5% of the population professed themselves to be adherents of the Roman Catholic Church. The second-largest denomination is the Hussite Church, which claimed 400,000 members in 1991. The capital is Prague, which had a population of 1,212,000 in 1991. The administrative capital of Moravia is Brno (population in 1990, 392,614). Other important towns include Ostrava (331,504) and Plzeň (Pilsen—174,984).

History

The Czech Lands have been dominated by the territory of Bohemia since the time of Boleslav I, who ruled in the ninth century, and who incorporated Moravia and Silesia into his realm. Although the territories were subsequently lost, they were soon regained and, under the rule of the Přemysl kings, Bohemia extended its territory as far as the Adriatic Sea. After 1278, however, when Přemysl Otakar II was killed in battle, Bohemia was reduced in size and power. After the succession of the Luxembourg dynasty to the Bohemian throne, in 1310, and in particular during the reign of Charles I, Bohemia was established as an important central European state. The establishment of Prague University, in 1348, by Charles I, was a major factor in the cultural and intellectual renaissance that centred on the Czech Lands in the 14th and 15th centuries.

For much of the 15th century the Czech Lands were divided by religious disputes between Roman Catholics and the Hussites (followers of Jan Hus, who had been martyred for his religious beliefs in 1415). A temporary peace was achieved in 1436, by a compromise agreement which granted Bohemia some degree of religious freedom, but serious divisions remained. Following the Hussite Wars, the succession to the throne was contested until 1526, when Ferdinand I of Austria was installed as monarch, thus establishing Habsburg rule in the Czech Lands, which was to last until 1918. In 1618 religious differences re-emerged, under Ferdinand's descendant, Rudolf II, when Protestant services were prohibited in Prague. Protests against this action culminated in the 'Defenestration of Prague', when two of the King's counsellors were thrown out of a window of Hradčany Castle. This was the beginning of a two-year revolt by the Protestants. It ended in 1620, at the Battle of the White Mountain, when Czech troops were decisively defeated. As a result, the Czech Lands were completely incorporated into the Austrian realm.

The Czech Lands remained part of the Austro-Hungarian Empire of the Habsburgs until the end of the First World War, but there were frequent uprisings against Imperial rule. During the 19th century there was a revival of Czech nationalism, mainly as a result of the movement to re-establish Czech as the language, not only of peasants, but of the intelligentsia and the political élite in Prague (German had been the preferred language until then). The nationalist revival led to demands, firstly for autonomy within the Empire, and then, when it became evident that the Danubian monarchy would not survive the First World War, for complete independence, joining the Slovaks in a unified state.

Although the Slovaks had been promised autonomy by the Czechs, the First Republic (1918–38) was dominated by the Czech Lands and, in particular, by Bohemia. In 1928 Moravia was granted the administrative status of a *Land*, but power remained highly centralized. However, it was the revival of German nationalism among the ethnic German population who inhabited the borderlands of Bohemia (the Sudetenland), that resulted in the dismemberment of the First Republic. As a result of the Munich Agreement of 1938, all territories where more than 50% of the population were ethnic Germans were ceded to Germany, thus leaving Bohemia without its natural defences on its northern, western or southern borders. In addition, Poland seized a small amount of territory near Teschen, on the northern border of Moravia, in 1939. Despite the Czechoslovak territorial concessions, Hitler invaded the Czech Lands, in mid-March 1939, and proclaimed the Protectorate of Bohemia and Moravia.

Following the liberation of Czechoslovakia by Soviet and US troops, in 1945, the new Government attempted to meet Slovak aspirations for genuine autonomy, with a weak regional government and parliament. However, such institutions were not duplicated in the Czech Lands, which was governed solely by the federal authorities. This asymmetrical structure of power was developed by the Communist regime, which came to power in 1948, in imitation of the Soviet example. While a Communist Party of Slovakia (CPS) continued to operate within the Czechoslovak Communist Party (CPCz), there were no corresponding Party organs in the Czech Lands. Even in 1968, when a federal system was introduced, the CPCz only established a Bureau for the Conduct of Party Work in the Czech Lands, rather than a counterpart to the CPS.

The federal system proposed during the Prague Spring of 1968 was implemented in January 1969. The Czech Lands became the Czech Socialist Republic, within the Czechoslovak federation, with its own government and a legislature, the Czech National Council. However, the overthrow of the Dubček Government by Soviet forces, and the subsequent reimposition of centralized Communist control, gave the new institutions little chance to develop. All important decisions were taken by the federal state and Party institutions, leaving the republican bodies merely to implement decisions taken at the centre. Furthermore, even the embryonic Czech Communist Party, in the shape of the 'Bureau', was abolished in 1969.

Following the Revolution of 1989, republican bodies reasserted the rights granted to them in the Constitution. In June 1990 elections were held to the Czech National Council, with Civic Forum winning a large majority of the seats. A coalition Government was established, with Petr Pithart as Prime Minister, which included representatives of all the main political parties, with the exception of the CPCz and the Movement for Autonomous Democracy-Society for Moravia and Silesia (MAD-SMS). The MAD-SMS surprised many observers by the amount of support they had received (gaining 22 seats in the National Council). However, little attention seemed to be paid to the demands of these campaigners for Moravian autonomy by politicians in Prague. In 1991, therefore, the supporters of the MAD-SMS adopted more radical actions, with frequent demonstrations in Brno and other towns in support of their cause.

While the Slovak Government was split, in 1991, by the issue of Czech–Slovak relations, the Czech Government had relatively few internal disagreements and concentrated on implementing an extensive programme of privatization and other economic reforms. Nevertheless, the Czech Government was fully involved in negotiations on the future constitutional form of the Czechoslovak state. Many Czech politicians expressed anxiety that economic reform in the Czech Lands could be delayed by the greater cautiousness displayed by Slovaks towards the programme of economic transformation.

Economy

The Czech Republic contains some of the most prosperous areas of Czechoslovakia. Even before the Second World War Bohemia and Moravia had a well-developed industrial base, although there are few mineral resources. The most important mineral deposits are coking and steam coal, from the Ostrava field, and brown coal from Ostrava and Kladno, which is used in power generation and chemical industries. This causes considerable levels of air pollution. Although from the 1960s there was significant industrialization of the Slovak Republic, Czechoslovakia's most productive indus-

tries are still located in Bohemia and Moravia. The main products of manufacturing industry are heavy machinery, machine tools, electrical equipment, cars and commercial vehicles. There is a wide range of chemical industries, but some plants are threatened with closure since the adoption of stricter environmental legislation. Traditional industries, producing textiles, footwear, pottery, glass and wood-products are also important.

Agriculture remains an important sector of the economy; the main crops are wheat, barley, sugar beets and hops. The latter are used in a well-developed brewing industry, centred on Plzeň (Pilsner beers) and České Budějovice (Budweiser). Other agriculturally-based industries include woollen textiles, shoe-making and food-processing.

Directory
The Government
(September 1991)

GOVERNMENT OF THE CZECH REPUBLIC

Prime Minister: PETR PITHART.

Deputy Prime Ministers: JAN STRASKY, ANTONÍN BAUDYŠ, MILAN LUKEŠ.

Minister of Administration and Privatization of National Wealth: TOMÁŠ JEŽEK.

Minister of Agriculture: BOHUMIL KUBÁT.

Minister of Culture: MILAN UHDE.

Minister, Chairman of the Bureau for Economic Competition: STANISLAV BELEHRADEK.

Minister of Economic Policy and Development: KAREL DYBA.

Minister of Education, Youth and Physical Culture: PETR VOPĚNKA.

Minister of the Environment: IVAN DEJMAL.

Minister of Finance: KAREL ŠPAČEK.

Minister of Health: MARTIN BOJAR.

Minister of Industry: JAN VRBA.

Minister of Internal Affairs: TOMÁŠ SOKOL.

Minister of International Relations and Contacts with the Federal and Slovak Governments: JAROSLAV ŠABATA.

Minister of Justice: LEON RICHTER.

Minister of Labour and Social Affairs: MILAN HORÁLEK.

Minister of State Control: IGOR NEMEC.

Minister of Trade and Tourism: VLASTA ŠTĚPOVÁ.

MINISTRIES

Office of the Government of the Czech Republic: Lazarska 7, 113 48 Prague 1; tel. (2) 2130111; fax (2) 2130484.

Ministry of Administration and Privatization of National Wealth: Senovazne nám. 32, 110 00 Prague 1; tel. (2) 2362065; telex 122900; fax (2) 2362065.

Ministry of Agriculture: Tešnov 17, 117 05 Prague 1; tel. (2) 28621111; telex 121041; fax (2) 2319740.

Ministry of Culture: Valdštejnska 10, 118 11 Prague 1; tel. (2) 5131111; telex 122317; fax (2) 532521.

Bureau of Economic Competition: Brno.

Ministry of Economic Policy and Development: Vršovicka 65, 101 60 Prague 10; tel. (2) 7121111; fax (2) 7122263.

Ministry of Education, Youth and Physical Culture: Karmelitska 8, 118 12 Prague; tel. (2) 531651; fax (2) 531322.

Ministry of the Environment: Vršovicka 65, 100 10 Prague 10; tel. (2) 7121111; fax (2) 2130604.

Ministry of Finance: Letenská 15, 118 10 Prague 1; tel. (2) 530251; telex 122298; fax (2) 5141111.

Ministry of Health: Palackého nám. 4, 128 01 Prague; tel. (2) 21181111; fax (2) 532531.

Ministry of Industry: Na Frantisku 32, 111 80 Prague 1; tel. (2) 2851111; fax (2) 2318544.

Ministry of Internal Affairs: Strojnicka 27/935, 170 89 Prague 7; tel. (2) 33511111; telex 121204.

Ministry of International Relations and Contacts with the Federal and Slovak Governments: Prague.

CZECHOSLOVAKIA

Ministry of Justice: Vysehradská 16, 128 10 Prague 2; tel. (2) 294545; fax (2) 531322.

Ministry of Labour and Social Affairs: Na porincnim pravu 1, 128 00 Prague 2; tel. (2) 2135111; fax (2) 297731.

Ministry of State Control: Za Invalidovnou 144, 186 22 Prague 8; tel. (2) 8141111; fax (2) 2325415.

Ministry of Trade and Tourism: Staromestske nám. 6, 110 01 Prague 1; tel. (2) 2897; telex 123046; fax (2) 2326815.

Legislature
NATIONAL COUNCIL
Chairman: DAGMAR BUREŠOVA.

Elections. 8–9 June 1990

Party	Seats
Civic Forum*	127
Communist Party of Czechoslovakia (CPCz)†	32
Movement for Autonomous Democracy-Society for Moravia and Silesia (MAD-SMS)	22
Christian Democratic Union (CDU)‡	19
Total	200

* Following a split in Civic Forum, deputies formed two main parties, the Civic Democratic Party and the Civic Movement. Other deputies formed smaller groups or remained as independents.
† Subsequently renamed the Communist Party of Bohemia and Moravia.
‡ A coalition of the Czechoslovak People's Party (CPP) and the Christian Democratic Party (CDP). The coalition was discontinued after the elections; deputies operate as members of the CPP or CDP.

Judicial System

All courts in the Czech Lands are within the jurisdiction of the Ministry of Justice of the Czech Republic, with the exception of the Supreme Court of the Federation, which is the final court of appeal.

Chairman of the Supreme Court of the Czech Republic: Dr ANTONÍN MOKRÝ.

Procurator-General: Dr LUDVIK BRUNNER .

The Press
PRINCIPAL DAILIES
Prague

Československý sport (Czechoslovak Sport): Na poříčí 30, 115 23 Prague 1; tel. (2) 2322528; telex 121514; central organ of the Czech Union of Physical Education; Editor JAROMÍR TOMÁNEK; circ. 195,000.

Halo Noviny: Prague; f. 1991; organ of the Communist Party of Bohemia and Moravia.

Lidová demokracie (People's Democracy): Karlovo nám. 5, 120 78 Prague 2; tel. (2) 290451; telex 121179; fax (2) 2322391; f. 1945; morning; official organ of the Czechoslovak People's Party; Editor ZDENĚK ŠEDIVY; circ. 170,000.

Lidové noviny (People's News): Václavské nám. 47, 111 21 Prague 1; tel. (2) 265831; telex 123147; fax (2) 266611; f. 1893, legally re-established 1990; Editor-in-Chief RUDOLF ZEMAN; 170,000.

Mladá fronta dnes (Youth Front Today): Panská 8, 112 22 Prague 1; tel. (2) 224141; telex 122468; fax (2) 2368453; f. 1945; morning; independent; Editor-in-Chief LÍBOR ŠEVČÍK; circ. 450,000.

Občanský deník (Civic Daily): Na Florenci 19, 112 86 Prague 1; tel. (2) 2367487; telex 121856; fax (2) 2320925; f. 1990; first publ. by Civic Forum; Editor-in-Chief JAN VÁVRA; circ. 90,000.

Práce (Labour): Václavské nám. 15, 112 58 Prague 1; tel. (2) 2356594; telex 121134; f. 1945; morning; published by the Czech and Slovak Confederation of Trade Unions; Editor-in-Chief IVAN ČERVENKA; circ. 353,414.

Právo lidu: Hybernská 7, 110 00 Prague 1; tel. (2) 2360432; organ of the Czechoslovak Social Democratic Party; Editor PŘEMYSL JANÝV.

Rudé právo (Red Right): Na Florenci 19, 112 86 Prague 1; tel. (2) 2367487; telex 121184; fax (2) 2321979; f. 1920; morning; fmrly the organ of the Czechoslovak Communist Party; independent; left-wing; Editor-in-Chief ZDENĚK PORYBNÝ; circ. 370,000 (weekdays), 600,000 (Sunday).

Svoboda (Freedom): Na Florenci 3, 113 29 Prague 1; tel. (2) 2321634; telex 121856; Editor-in-Chief JIŘÍ NOVOTNÝ; circ. 61,683.

Svobodné slovo (Free Word): Václavské nám. 36, 112 12 Prague 1; tel. (2) 260341; telex 121432; f. 1907; organ of the Czechoslovak Socialist Party; Editor-in-Chief LUBOMÍR PETRÍK; circ. 220,000.

Večerní Praha (Evening Prague): Na Florenci 19, 112 86 Prague 1; tel. (2) 2327324; telex 121883; f. 1955; evening; Editor-in-Chief Dr JAROSLAV LEMÁK; circ. 170,000.

Zemědělské noviny (Farmer's News): Václavské nám. 47, 113 78 Prague 1; tel. (2) 265951-9; telex 121435; f. 1945; Editor-in-Chief VLADIMÍR KULHÁNEK; circ. 260,000.

Brno

Brněnský večerník (Brno Evening News): Jakubské nám. 7, 658 44 Brno; tel. (5) 228446; f. 1968; Editor-in-Chief Dr DANUŠE ŠKLÍBOVÁ; circ. 33,000.

Rovnost (Equality): Moravské nám. 13, 658 22 Brno; tel. (5) 749000; telex 62342; fax (5) 743832; f. 1885; morning; Editor-in-Chief LUBOMÍR SELINGER; circ. 100,000.

České Budějovice

Deník Jihočeská Pravda (South Bohemia Truth Daily): Vrbenská 23, 370 45 České Budějovice; tel. (38) 22081; fax (38) 22061; published by Vltava České Budějovice; Editor-in-Chief VLADIMÍR DOLEŽAL; circ. 59,500.

Hradec Králové

Pochodeň (Torch): Škroupova 695, 501 72 Hradec Králové; tel. (49) 613511; Editor-in-Chief OLDŘICH ENGE; circ. 74,188.

Ostrava

List občanů Moravy a Slezska—Nova svoboda: Novinářská 3, 709 07 Ostrava 1; tel. (69) 261682; telex 52122; fax (69) 262144; f. 1945; morning; published by the Delta Publishing House; Editor-in-Chief Dr MIROSLAV MRKVICA; circ. 114,000.

Ostravský večerník (Ostrava Evening News): Zeyerova 11, 728 85 Ostrava; tel. (69) 232023; Editor-in-Chief JOSEF ZLOMEK; circ. 28,607.

Plzeň

Deník Nová Pravda (New Truth Daily): Husova 15, 304 83 Plzeň; tel. (19) 551 111; telex 154302; fax (19) 227215; f. 1919; published by Vltava co; Editor-in-Chief STANISLAV NEDVĚD; circ. 75,000.

Ústí nad Labem

Severočeský regionální deník (North Bohemian Regional Daily): Velká hradební 3121/50, 400 90 Ústí nad Labem; tel. (47) 22244-6; telex 184221; fax (47) 23115; f. 1920; published by A. G. Logos; Editor-in-Chief JAROSLAV HAIDLER; circ. 100,000.

PRINCIPAL PERIODICALS

100+1ZZ: Žirovnická 2389, 106 00 Prague 10; tel. (2) 7192248; monthly foreign press digest of the Czechoslovak News Agency (ČTK); Editor-in-Chief JAN BLAŽÍK; circ. 155,000.

Ahoj na sobotu (Hallo Saturday): Václavské nám. 36, 112 12 Prague 1; tel. (2) 264663; illustrated family weekly published by the Czechoslovak Socialist Party; Editor-in-Chief MARIE SOLLEOVÁ; circ. 178,000.

Architekt (Architect): Letenská 5, 118 45 Prague 1; tel. (2) 539768; telex 122064; fax (2) 3114926; f. 1955; fortnightly; Editor Dr JIŘÍ HORSKÝ; circ. 7,500.

Československý život (Czechoslovak Life): Vinohradská 46, 120 41 Prague 2; tel. (2) 257741; telex 122948; fax (2) 254385; f. 1946; illustrated monthly magazine; political, economic, social and cultural; published by Orbis Press Agency in English, French and German; Editor EVA MEISNEROVÁ; circ. 90,000.

Chatař (Weekend House Owner): Václavské nám. 47, 113 11 Prague 1; tel. (2) 264592; monthly; published by State Agricultural Publishing House; Editor-in-Chief Ing. JIŘÍ TRNAVSKÝ; circ. 100,000.

Chovatel (Breeder): Václavské náměstí 47, 113 11 Prague 1; tel. (2) 2351045; monthly; published by the Czech Union of Breeders; Editor-in-Chief Ing. OLGA MAKARIUSOVÁ; circ. 60,000.

Film a doba (Film and Time): Slavíčkova 5, 160 00 Prague 6; tel. (2) 375062; monthly; Editor EVA ZAORALOVÁ; circ. 7,000.

Fórum: Sněmovní 3, 118 00 Prague 1; tel. (2) 518586; fax (2) 539828; f. 1990; weekly; current affairs, economy, culture, ecology; first publ. by Civic Forum; Editor-in-Chief MARTIN MICHALÉK; circ. 60,000.

Fotografie (Photography): Mrštíkova 23, 101 00 Prague 10; tel. (2) 781553; f. 1946; monthly; photographic; Editor (vacant); circ. 57,000.

Hudební rozhledy (Musical Review): Maltézské nám. 1, 118 00 Prague 1; tel. (2) 532931; f. 1948; monthly review; published by the Asscn of Musicians and Musicologists; Editor JAN ŠMOLÍK; circ. 4,200.

Katolický týdeník: Sněmovní 9, 118 01 Prague 1; tel. (2) 533017; fax (2) 533017; weekly; published by Czech Catholic Charity; Editor-in-Chief JOSEF GABRIEL; circ. 128,000.

Kino (Cinema): Slavíčkova 5, 160 00 Prague 6; tel. (2) 375063; an illustrated film magazine published by the Panorama Publishing House; fortnightly; Editor-in-Chief JANA BÍLKOVÁ; circ. 160,000.

Květy (Flowers): Na Florenci 3, 112 86 Prague 1; tel. (2) 2323451; telex 12184; f. 1834; illustrated weekly; Editor-in-Chief Dr MILAN CODR; circ. 130,000.

Magazín Co vás zajímá (What Interests You?): Na Florenci 3, 112 86 Prague 1; tel. (2) 2323451; monthly; published by *Rudé právo* Publishing House; Editor-in-Chief Dr MIROSLAVA PAPEŽOVÁ; circ. 165,000.

Mladý svět (Young World): Panská 8, 112 22 Prague 1; tel. (2) 223726; telex 121510; fax (2) 220039; f. 1956; independent; illustrated weekly; Editor-in-Chief LUBOŠ BENIAK; circ. 250,000.

Motor (Motoring): Jungmannova 24, 113 66 Prague 1; tel. (2) 2362439; f. 1969; monthly; published by State Cttee for Road Traffic Security; Editor-in-Chief PETR DUFEK; circ. 116,000.

Naše rodina (Our Family): Karlovo nám. 5, 120 00 Prague 2; tel. (2) 294196; f. 1968; Christian and cultural weekly published by Czechoslovak People's Party; Editor-in-Chief Dr LIBUŠE DAŇKOVÁ; circ. 179,700.

Nově Knihy: Opatovická 18, 113 81 Prague 1; tel. (2) 297441; weekly; Editor-in-Chief LUDMILA VILDOVÁ; CIRC. 87,786.

Nový dikobraz (New Porcupine): Kubánské nám. 1391, 101 00 Prague 10; tel. (2) 742947; telex 121184; fax (2) 6921392; f. 1945; changed name from *Dikobraz* in 1990; satirical weekly; Editor-in-Chief ZDENĚK ROSENBAUM; circ. 200,000.

Obrana lidu (People's Defence): Jungmannova 24, 113 66 Prague 1; tel. (2) 246886; weekly; published by the Ministry of Defence; Editor-in-Chief MIROSLAV PROCHÁZKA; circ. 87,786.

Odborář (Trade Unionist): Senovážné nám. 23, 112 82 Prague 1; tel. (2) 2363418; fortnightly; Editor-in-Chief Ing. HELENA MANDOVÁ; circ. 121,000.

Ohníček (Little Flame): Radlická 61, 150 02 Prague 5; tel. (2) 536523; fax (2) 536318; f. 1950; fortnightly magazine for children; published by the Mladá fronta Publishing House; Editor-in-Chief Dr EVA VONDRÁŠKOVÁ; circ. 100,000.

Praktická žena (Practical Woman): Na rybníčku 7, 120 00 Prague 2; tel. (2) 224642; f. 1950; monthly; published by Mona Publishing House; Editor-in-Chief MIRKA LÁNSKÁ; circ. 300,000.

Právník (The Lawyer): Národní třída 18, 116 91 Prague 1; tel. (2) 201620; f. 1861; monthly; law; published by Czechoslovak Academy of Sciences (Institute of State and Law); Editor MILAN KINDL; circ. 3,200.

Respekt: Bolzanova 7, 125 01 Prague 1; tel. (2) 221960; fax (2) 222304; f. 1990; weekly; Editor-in-Chief IVAN LAMPEV; circ. 100,000.

Rozhlas (Radio): Na Florenci 3, 112 86 Prague 1; fax (2) 2356467; f. 1923; weekly; cultural and sound radio journal; published by the Delta Publishing House; Editor STANISLAV PSCHEIDT; circ. 270,000.

Sedmička (Seven): Radlická 61, 150 00 Prague 5; tel. (2) 540012; telex 123302; fax (2) 547290; weekly; published by the Mladá fronta Publishing House; Editor-in-Chief SVATAVA HIRSCHOVÁ; circ. 150,000.

Signál (Signal): Jungmannova 24, 113 66 Prague 1; tel. (2) 262367; telex 121572; fax (2) 2362419; f. 1965; weekly; illustrated family magazine; published by Magnet-Press; Editor-in-Chief PAVEL TOUFAR; circ. 150,000.

Sobotni telegraf (Saturday Telegraph): Prague; f. 1991; organ of the Civic Democratic Party.

Stadion (Stadium): Klimentská 1, 115 88 Prague 1; tel. (2) 2312898; weekly; illustrated sport magazine; published by the Czech Central Cttee for Physical Education; Editor-in-Chief MILAN MACHO; circ. 166,000.

Svět (The World): Smetanovo nábř. 18, 110 00 Prague 1; tel. (2) 241216; illustrated weekly; published by the Union of Czechoslovak-Soviet Friendship; Editor-in-Chief MIROSLAV TULEJA; circ. 115,000.

Svět motorů (World of Motors): Jungmannova 24, 113 66 Prague 1; tel. (2) 260651; fax (2) 2368277; f. 1947; weekly; published by Magnet-press; motoring; Editor-in-Chief OTAKAR GREGORA; circ. 100,000.

Svět v obrazech (World in Pictures): Pařížská 9, 110 00 Prague 1; tel. (2) 2324771; f. 1945; illustrated weekly published by the Odeon Publishing House; Editor-in-Chief Dr ZDENĚK HRABICA; circ. 150,000.

Svět práce (The World of Labour): Václavské nám. 15, 112 58 Prague 1; telex 121134; f. 1946, reorganized 1968; political, economic and cultural weekly; published by Czech and Slovak Confederation of Trade Unions; Editor FRANTIŠEK RÍHA; circ. 85,000.

Světová literatura (World Literature): Na Florenci 3, 115 86 Prague 1; tel. (2) 2256774; f. 1956; published by Odeon, bi-monthly; contemporary foreign literature; Editor ANNA KARENINOVÁ-FUREKOVÁ; circ. 10,000.

Tvorba (Creation): Na poříčí 30, 112 86 Prague 1; tel. (2) 2321146; f. 1925; weekly; political, scientific and cultural; published by the Tvorba Foundation ; Editor-in-Chief IVAN MATĚJKA; circ. 10,000.

Týdeník Československé televize (Czechoslovak Television Weekly): nám. Lidových milicí 5, 190 00 Prague 9; tel. (2) 839856; telex 121184; f. 1965; weekly; cultural and television journal; published by *Rudé právo*; Editor-in-Chief JANA KOLÁROVÁ; circ. 510,000.

Vesmír (Universe): Jungmannova 12, 110 00 Prague 1; tel. (2) 2367470; fax (2) 269466; f. 1871; monthly; popular science magazine; published by the Czechoslovak Academy of Science; Editor IVAN M. HAVEL; circ. 31,000.

Vlasta: Jindřišská 5, 116 08 Prague 1; tel. (2) 2357883; f. 1946; weekly; illustrated magazine for women; Editor-in-Chief MARIE FORMÁČKOVÁ; circ. 700,000.

Zahrádkář (Gardener): Čkalova 22, 160 41 Prague 6; tel. (2) 323105; monthly; published by Czech Union of Gardeners; Editor-in-Chief Dr STANISLAV PELEŠKA; circ. 320,000.

Zápisník (Notebook): Vlastina 23, 160 65 Prague 6; tel. (2) 368866; monthly; military topics; published by the Ministry of Defence; Editor-in-Chief Col Ing. MIROSLAV LINKA; circ. 225,000.

Zdraví (Health): Thunovská 18, 118 04 Prague 1; tel. (2) 532342; monthly; published by the Czechoslovak Red Cross; Editor-in-Chief KAREL PRŮSA; circ. 125,000.

Žena a móda (Women and Fashion): Nakázanka 16, 110 00 Prague 1; tel. (2) 221025; monthly; published by the Mona Publishing House; Editor-in-Chief Dr VLADIMÍRA KVĚCHOVÁ; circ. 257,000.

Zlatý máj (Golden May): Na Perštýně 1, 110 01 Prague 1; telex 121605; 10 a year; reviews children's literature; published by Albatros Publishing House; Editor Dr ZDENĚK SLABÝ; circ. 3,500.

Zmena: Prague; weekly; independent.

Zora: Krakovská 21, 115 17 Prague 1; tel. (2) 262783; for the visually handicapped; Editor-in-Chief JIŘÍ REICHEL.

German language

Prager Volkszeitung (Prague People's Newspaper): Helénská 4, 120 00 Prague 2; tel. (2) 242607; weekly; general politics and culture; published by Delta Press and the Union of Germans; Editor UWE MÜLLER; circ. 17,000.

Romany language

Lacho Lav (Good Word): Prague; f. 1990; monthly; general politics and culture and issues specific to the Romany community; Editor-in-Chief VINCENT DANIHEL.

Romano Kurko: Prague; weekly.

PRESS ASSOCIATION

Syndicate of Journalists of the Czech Republic: Pařížská 9, 116 30 Prague 1; tel. (2) 2325109; fax (2) 2326337; f. 1877; reorganized in 1990; 4,800 mems; Chair. RUDOLF ZEMAN.

Publishers

Academia: Vodičkova 40, POB 896, 112 29 Prague 1; tel. (2) 2363065; fax (2) 266022; f. 1953; publishing house of the Czechoslovak Academy of Sciences; scientific books, periodicals; Dir Ing. VÁCLAV ZVĚŘINA.

Albatros: Na Perštýně 1, 110 01 Prague 1; telex 121605; f. 1949; literature for children and young people; Dir MILADA MATJOVICIVÁ.

Artia: Ve Smečkách 30, 111 27 Prague 1; tel. (2) 2137111; telex 121065; fax (2) 2315206; f. 1953; part of the Artia Foreign Trade Corporation; children's books, art books and encyclopedias; Dir RICHARD DAVID.

Avicenum: Malostranské nám. 28, 118 02 Prague 1; tel. (2) 530640; f. 1953; medical books and periodicals; Dir Ing. EVŽEN KADLEC.

Blok: Rooseveltova 4, 657 00 Brno; tel. (5) 27244; f. 1957; regional literature, fiction, general; Dir JAROSLAV NOVÁK.

Československý spisovatel (Czechoslovak Writer): Národní 9, 111 47 Prague 1; tel. (2) 2320924; telex 122645; fax (2) 2328719; publishing house of the Czech Literary Fund; poetry, fiction, literary theory and criticism; Dir Dr MILOŠ POHORSKÝ.

Horizont: Nekázanka 7, 111 21 Prague 1; tel. (2) 268617; f. 1968; publishing house of the Komenský Academy; general; Dir Dr ZDENĚK PERGNER.

Kartografie Praha: Kostelní 42, 170 30 Prague 7; tel. (2) 375555; telex 121471; f. 1954; state map publishing house; Dir Ing. JIŘÍ KUČERA.

Kruh: Dlouhá 108, 500 21 Hradec Králové; tel. (49) 22076; f. 1966; regional literature, fiction and general; Dir Dr JAN DVOŘÁK.

Lidové nakladatelství: Václavské nám. 36, 110 00 Prague 1; tel. (2) 226383; f. 1968; classical and contemporary fiction, general, magazines; Dir Dr KORNEL VAVRINČÍK.

Melantrich: Václavské nám. 36, 112 12 Prague 1; tel. (2) 261372; telex 121432; fax (2) 225012; f. 1919; publishing house of the Czechoslovak Socialist Party; general, fiction, humanities, newspapers and magazines; Dir MILAN HORSKÝ.

Merkur: Gorkého nám. 11, 115 69 Prague 1; tel. (2) 2362891; telex 121648; fax (2) 2362873; commerce, tourism, catering; Dir JIŘÍ LINHART.

Mladá fronta: Panská 8, 112 22 Prague 1; tel. (2) 224121; telex 121510; f. 1945; literature for young people, fiction and non-fiction, newspapers and magazines; Dir MARIE KOŠKOVÁ.

Nakladatelství dopravy a spojů: Hybernská 5, 115 78 Prague 1; tel. (2) 2365774; fax (2) 2356772; state publishing house for transport and communications; Dir Ing. ALOIS HOUDEK.

Nakladatelství Svoboda: Revoluční 15, 113 03 Prague 1; tel. (2) 2317051; f. 1945 as the publishing house of the Communist Party of Czechoslovakia; politics, history, philosophy, fiction, general; Dir STEFAN SZERYŃSKI.

Naše vojsko: Na Děkance 3, 128 12 Prague 1; tel. (2) 299451; fax (2) 294274; f. 1945; publishing house of the Czechoslovak Army; fiction, reference, general; Dir Dr STANISLAV MISTR.

Odeon: Národní tř. 36, 115 87 Prague 1; tel. (2) 260179; telex 123055; f. 1953; literature, poetry, fiction (classical and modern), literary theory, art books, reproductions; Dir (vacant).

Olympia: Klimentská 1, 115 88 Prague 1; tel. (2) 2314861; telex 121717; f. 1954; sports, tourism, illustrated books; Dir Ing. KAREL ZELNÍČEK.

Panorama: Hálkova 1, 120 72 Prague 2; tel. (2) 2361391; Dir Ing. VLADIMÍR NEKOLA.

Panton: Radlická 99, 150 00 Prague 5; tel. (2) 548627; fax (2) 548627; f. 1958; publishing house of the Czech Musical Fund; books on music, sheet music, records; Dir. KAREL ČERNÝ.

Práce: Václavské nám. 17, 112 58 Prague 1; tel. (2) 266151; telex 121134; f. 1945; trade union movement, fiction, general, periodicals; Dir PAVEL LANDA.

Profil: Ciklářská 51, 702 00 Ostrava 1; regional literature, fiction and general; Dir IVAN ŠEINER.

Rapid: ul. 28 října 13, 112 79 Prague 1; tel. (2) 2139111; telex 121142; fax (2) 2327520; advertising; Dir Dr Ing. MIROSLAV HEDBÁVNÝ.

Růže: Žižkovo nám. 5, 370 96 České Budějovice; tel. (38) 38676; f. 1960; regional literature, fiction and general; Dir MIROSLAV HULE.

Severočeské nakladatelství: Prokopa Diviše 5, 400 01 Ústí nad Labem; tel. (47) 28581; regional literature, fiction and general; Dir JIŘÍ ŠVEJDA.

SNTL—Nakladatelství technické literatury: Spálená 51, 113 02 Prague 1; tel. (2) 297670; fax (2) 203774; f. 1953; technology, applied sciences, dictionaries, periodicals; Dir Dr KAREL ČERNÝ (acting).

Státní pedagogické nakladatelství: Ostrovní 30, 113 01 Prague 1; tel. (2) 203787; fax (2) 293883; f. 1775; state publishing house; school and university textbooks, dictionaries, literature; Dir MILAN KOVÁŘ.

Supraphon: Palackého 1, 122 99 Prague 1; tel. (2) 268141; telex 121218; fax (2) 262562; f. 1946; publishing house for music scores; also produces gramophone records, compact discs and musicassettes; Gen. Dir ZDENĚK ČEJKA.

Ústřední církevní nakladatelství: Ječná 2, 120 00 Prague 2; f. 1952; religion; Dir Dr JIŘÍ KAFKA.

Vyšehrad: Karlovo nám. 5, 120 78 Prague 2; tel. (2) 297726; publishing house of the Czechoslovak People's Party; general fiction, newspapers and magazines; Dir JOSEF DANĚK.

Západočeské nakladatelství: B. Smetany 1, 301 35 Plzeň; tel. (19) 34783; f. 1955; regional literature, fiction, general; Dir KATEŘINA RUBÍŠOVÁ.

Zemědělské nakladatelství—Brázda: Václavské nám. 47, 113 11 Prague 1; agricultural publishing house; periodicals; Man. Dir Ing. JAN DIENSTBIER.

Radio

Český rozhlas (Czech Radio): Vinohradská 12, 120 99 Prague 2; tel. (2) 2115111; telex 121100; fax (2) 2321020; Dir JIŘÍ MEJSTŘÍK.

Finance

(cap. = capital; dep. = deposits; res = reserves; m. = million; Kčs. = korunas)

BANKS

Commercial Banks

Banka Bohemia as: Husinecká 11A, 130 00 Prague 3; tel. (2) 6912002; telex 276614; fax (2) 276614; cap. 70m. Kčs. (Jan. 1991); Dir Ing. ARNOŠT KLESLA.

Komerční banka Praha: Na Příkopě 33, 110 05 Prague 1; tel. (2) 2359737; telex 121093; fax (2) 2356158; f. 1990 after the division of the State Bank of Czechoslovakia; state-owned institution; cap. 3,900m. Kčs. (Jan. 1991); Gen. Man. RICHARD SALZMANN; 83 brs, 88 agencies.

Pragobanka as: Jungmannova 32, 112 59 Prague 1; tel. (2) 220128; fax (2) 220128; f. 1990; cap. 60m. Kčs. (Jan. 1991); Gen. Man. Ing. JIŘÍ BEK.

Živnostenská banka: Na příkopě 20, 113 80 Prague 1; tel. (2) 224346; telex 122313; fax (2) 263381; f. 1868; cap. 250m. Kčs., res 374m. Kčs., dep. 12,488m. Kčs. (Dec. 1989); Gen. Man. Ing JIŘÍ KUNERT.

Savings Bank

Česká státní spořitelna (Czech State Savings Bank): Václavské nám. 42, 110 00 Prague 1; tel. (2) 225237; telex 121010; fax (2) 267023; accepts deposits and issues loans; 15,239,363 depositors (June 1990); Gen. Man. Ing. MILOSLAV KOHOUTEK; 1,875 brs.

INSURANCE

Česká pojišťovna (Czech Insurance and Reinsurance Corporation): Spálená 16, 114 00 Prague 1; tel. (2) 2148111; telex 121112; fax (2) 299146; f. 1827; many home brs and some agencies abroad; issues life, accident, fire, aviation and marine policies, all classes of reinsurance; Lloyd's agency; Gen. Man. Dr VLASTIMIL UZEL.

Trade Unions

Českomoravská komora ČSKOS (Czech-Moravian Chamber of the Czech and Slovak Confederation of Trade Unions): nám. W. Churchilla 2, 113 59 Prague 3; tel. (2) 2368426; branch of the Czech and Slovak Confederation of Trade Unions in the Czech Republic; Pres. VLADIMÍR PETRUS.

Českomoravský odborový svaz pracovníků služeb (Czech-Moravian Trade Union of Workers in Services): Senovážné nám. 23, 112 82 Prague 1; tel. (2) 21142726; Pres. RICHARD FALBR; 281,058 mems.

Českomoravský odborový svaz školství (Czech-Moravian Trade Union of Workers in Education): Senovážné nám. 23, 112 82 Prague 1; tel. (2) 2311335; Pres. JAROSLAV RÖSSLER; 280,698 mems.

Odborový svaz pracovníků dřevozpracujícího odvětví, lesního a vodního hospodářství v České republice (Trade Union of Workers in Woodworking Industry, Forestry and Management of Water Supplies in the Czech Republic): nám. W. Churchilla 2, 113 59 Prague 3; tel. (2) 2350848; telex 121484; fax (2) 2365219; Pres. ROBERT ZEDNÍK; 206,391mems.

Odborový svaz pracovníků textilního, oděvního a kožedělného průmyslu Čech a Moravy (Trade Union of Workers in Textile, Clothing and Leather Industry of Bohemia and Moravia): nám. W. Churchilla 2, 113 59 Prague 3; tel. (2) 273589; telex 121517; Pres. MARCEL MÖSTL; 197,769 mems.

Odborový svaz pracovníků zemědělství a výživy Čech a Moravy (Trade Union of Workers in Agriculture and Food Industry of Bohemia and Moravia): nám. W. Churchilla 2, 113 59 Prague 3; tel. (2) 2361915; telex 121484; fax (2) 2369661; Pres. VÁCLAV GUTTENBERG; 295,320 mems.

Odborový svaz zdravotnietví a sociální Péce ČR (Trade Union of Workers in Health Service, of Health Technician Workers and Social Care in the Czech Republic): nám. W. Churchilla 2, 113 59 Prague 3; tel. (2) 2368267; fax (2) 2368267; Pres. JIŘÍ SCHLANGER; 326,000 mems.

Culture

NATIONAL ORGANIZATION

Ministerstvo kultury ČR (Ministry of Culture of the Czech Republic): see section on The Government (Ministries).

CULTURAL HERITAGE

Národní galerie (National Gallery): Hradčanské nám. 15, 110 00 Prague 1; tel. (2) 352441; f. 1796; Dir Prof. Jiří Kotalík.

Národní knihovna v Praze (National Library): Klementinum 190, 110 01 Prague 1; tel. (2) 266541; telex 121207; f. 1348; 6m. vols; Dir Dr Vojtěch Balík.

Národní muzeum (National Museum): Václavské nám., Prague; tel. (2) 269451; f. 1818; Dir Dr Adolf Cejchan.

Historické muzeum (Historical Museum): Vítězného února 74, 110 01 Prague 1; tel. (2) 269450; materials relating to Czech history, ethnography, archaeological collections; Dir Dr Vlasti-mil Vondruška.

Knihovna Národního muzea (National Museum Library): Václavské nám. 68, 115 79 Prague 1; tel. (2) 269451; f. 1818; c. 3m. vols; Dir Dr Helga Turková.

Muzeum české hudby (Museum of Czech Music): Lázeňská 2, tel. (2) 265371; f. 1936; exhibitions on composers and collections of musical instruments; Dir Dr Bohuslav Čížek.

SPORTING ORGANIZATION

Ministerstvo školství, mládeže a tlovýchovy ČR (Ministry of Education, Youth and Sport of the Czech Republic): see section on The Government (Ministries).

PERFORMING ARTS

Central Puppet Theatre: nám. M. Gorkého 28, Prague.

Česka filharmonie (Czech Philharmonic Orchestra): Alšovo nábř 12, 110 00 Prague 1; tel. (2) 2316812.

Národní divadlo (Czech National Theatre): Ostrovní 1, 110 00 Prague; tel. (2) 204341.

Smetana Theatre: Vitězného února 8, Prague.

Tyl Theatre: Zelezná 11.

ASSOCIATIONS

Česká hudební společnost (Czech Music Society): Janačkovo nábř. 59, 150 00 Prague 5; tel. (2) 530868; f. 1973; 17,000 mems; Pres. Jiří Bajer; Sec.-Gen. Dr Radko Rajmon.

Czech Centre for International PEN: Národní tř. 11, 110 00 Prague 1; tel. (2) 533037; f. 1924; 165 mems; Pres. Jiří Mucha.

Matice moravská (Moravian Society of History and Literature): Gorkého 14, 602 00 Brno; tel. (5) 750050; f. 1849; 560 mems; Pres. Dr Jan Janák.

Obec českých spisovatel' (Union of Czech Writers): Národní tř. 11, 110 00 Prague 1; tel. (2) 2320924; f. 1972; 165 mems; reorganized 1990.

Svaz českých architektů (Union of Czech Architects): Letenská 5, tel. (2) 539742; Pres. Ing. arch. Zdeněk Kuna.

Svaz českých skladetelů a koncertních umělců (Union of Czech Composers and Concert Performers): Valdštejnské nám. 1, 110 00 Prague 1; tel. (2) 531814.

Taneční sdružení ČR (Czech Dance Society): Vlasta schneiderová, Gorodcovova 1980, Prague 5; tel. (2) 534841.

Social Welfare

GOVERNMENT AGENCIES

Board of Deputies on Disabled People: Palackého nám. 4, 120 00 Prague 2; tel. (2) 21182196; Chair. Ing. Pavel Dušek.

Česká správa sociálního zabezpečení (Czech Social Security Administration): Křížová 25, 150 00 Prague 5; tel. (2) 541141; Dir Dr Ladislav Antošik.

Committee for Social Policy and Health: Sněmovní 4, 110 00 Prague 1; tel. (2) 2105; parliamentary committee of the Czech National Council; Chair Dr Petr Lom.

Governmental Committee for Disabled People in the Czech Republic: Palackého nám. 4, 120 00 Prague 2; tel. (2) 21182349; First Vice-Chairman Ing. Jaroslav Hrubý.

Ministerstvo práce a sociálních věcí České republiky (Ministry of Labour and Social Affairs of the Czech Republic): see section on The Government (Ministries).

HEALTH AND WELFARE ORGANIZATION

Association of Disabled People in the Czech Republic: Karlínské nám. 12, 186 03 Prague 8; tel. (2) 2350796.

The Environment

Ministry of the Environment of the Czech Republic: see section on The Government (Ministries); incl.:

Statni ustav pamatkove pece a ochrany prirody—SUPPOP (State Institute for the Protection of Monuments and Nature Conservancy): Mala Strana, Waldstejnske nám. 1, 118 01 Prague.

Česky svaz ochrancu prirody—ČSOP (Czech Union of Nature Conservationists): Na Skalce 5, 150 00 Prague; independent asscn of conservation groups in the Czech Republic.

SLOVAKIA

Geography

The Slovak Republic, or Slovakia, forms one of the two constituent republics of the Czech and Slovak Federative Republic. It is bordered to the west by the Czech Republic and has international frontiers with Poland to the north, Ukraine (USSR) to the east, Hungary to the south, and Austria to the south-west. The Republic covers an area of 49,035 sq km (18,934 sq miles).

The terrain is largely mountainous, rising, in the north, to Czechoslovakia's highest point, Gerlach (Gerlachovsky) Peak (2,655 m—8,711 ft), in the High Tatras. The High Tatras (Vysoké Tatry), on the northern border with Poland, and the Low Tatras (Nízké Tatry), in the centre and east of the Republic, are the principal mountain ranges. They form the westernmost branch of the Carpathian mountain chain. The mountains are drained by numerous rivers, flowing south to the lowland areas, including the Váh, the Hron, the Hornád and the Bodrog. Part of the southern border is marked by the River Danube (Dunaj). There are lowland areas in the south-west and south-east of the country. More than two-fifths of the Republic is forested, and only one-third is cultivated land.

The climate is of a more pronounced continental-type than in the Czech Lands. Average temperatures in Bratislava range from −0.7°C (30.7°F) in January to 21.1°C (70.0°F) in July. Average annual rainfall in the capital is 649 mm.

At the census of March 1991, the total population of Slovakia was 5,268,935. Of these, 4,511,679 (85.6%) were ethnic Slovaks, 566,742 Hungarians, 80,627 Roma and 53,422 Czechs. There were also small communities of Ruthenians (16,937), Ukrainians (13,847), Germans (5,629) and Poles (2,969). In 1990 legislation was adopted which declared Slovak to be the official language of the Republic. Slovak is a member of the Western Slavonic group of languages and is closely related to Czech. The Hungarian (Magyar) community use their own language; there are Hungarian-language newspapers and periodicals and Hungarian-language broadcasting. The language law of 1990, however, restricted official use of minority languages to areas where at least 20% of the population were members of an ethnic minority. Christianity is the major religion, the Roman Catholic Church being the largest denomination.

The capital of Slovakia is Bratislava (formerly known as Pressburg), situated in the south of the Republic on the River Danube. In December 1990 it had an estimated population of 440,629. Other important towns include Košice (238,343), in the east, Žilina (183,469), on the River Váh in the north, and Nitra (212,123), the site of the first established Christian church in Czechoslovakia (ninth century), in the south.

History

The territory now known as Slovakia was initially settled by Illyrian, Celtic and then German tribes. Slavic tribes arrived from the east in the sixth or seventh centuries AD. In the ninth century it was part of the Great Moravian Empire, which also included Bohemia and neighbouring territories. Following the dissolution of the Great Moravian Empire, however, in the 10th century, the Czechs and Slovaks were divided, as the latter came under Hungarian rule.

Slovakia remained under Hungarian rule, in different forms, for some 1,000 years. Slovaks were heavily influenced by the Protestant ideas disseminated in Bohemia by the Hussites, but Roman Catholicism was largely restored by the Habsburg rulers, who succeeded to the Hungarian throne in 1526. There was little evidence of significant cultural development in Slovakia until the late 18th century, when a movement of national renaissance began. In the 19th century Slovak nationalists were supported by the Austrian Habsburgs, who were attempting to limit the growing influence of the Hungarians. In 1861 a National Congress, organized by leading Slovak intellectuals, issued a Memorandum, demanding autonomy for Slovakia. However, after the Austro-Hungarian *Ausgleich* (Compromise) of 1867, the Hungarians regained full control over Slovakia and instituted a policy of 'magyarization', which resulted in considerable emigration, in particular to the USA. During the First World War Slovaks joined with Czechs in campaigning for an independent state, composed of the Czech Lands and Slovakia. In 1918, in the USA, the leading campaigners signed the Czech-Slovak Pittsburgh Agreement, in which the Czech and Slovak exile groups agreed to coexistence in a common, democratic state.

The Pittsburgh Agreement envisaged considerable autonomy for Slovakia, but, when Czechoslovakia's first Constitution was promulgated, in 1920, there was no provision for a proper federal system. During the existence of the First Republic (1918–38) the authorities in Prague rejected proposals to grant Slovakia genuine self-government, although, from 1928, the country was divided into four territorial-administrative areas: Bohemia, Moravia-Silesia, Slovakia and Carpatho-Ruthenia. Moreover, although the Czech Lands experienced considerable economic development between the First and Second World Wars, Slovakia remained largely undeveloped.

The centrist policies of the Czechs led to a more radical approach on the part of the Slovaks. The main Slovak national party, the Hlinka Slovak National People's Party (HSNPP), combined elements of Fascism with a fusion of Roman Catholicism and nationalism. In October 1938, following the Munich Agreement and the end of the First Republic, the HSNPP declared autonomy for Slovakia and became the only authorized party in Slovakia, after banning all other political groups. On 14 March 1939, the day before the German occupation of the Czech Lands, Hitler agreed to the establishment of a separate Slovak state, under the leadership of Jozef Tiso.

The wartime Slovak state (March 1939–April 1945) was based on a combination of German and Italian Fascist principles. Any opposition to the Tiso regime was ruthlessly suppressed and the treatment of Jews, especially after the adoption of the Jewish Code in 1941, was particularly severe. Between March and October 1942 an estimated 58,000 Jews were deported to Nazi extermination camps. In August 1944, however, an armed uprising against the Fascist regime began. It lasted two months before being suppressed by German troops, which were invited into Slovakia by Tiso.

Despite the failure of the Slovak National Rising, it did provide legitimacy for Slovak exiles abroad who were opposed to Tiso. The Czechoslovak Government-in-Exile, however, was unwilling to grant genuine autonomy to the Slovaks in a post-War state. There were certain concessions, including the devolution of some powers to the Slovak

National Council and the establishment of a weak governmental structure in Slovakia, the Board of Commissioners. Even this small degree of federalization was largely negated by the seizure of power by the Communists, in Slovakia, in late 1947, and in the whole of the country, in 1948. The Communist *coup d'état* in Slovakia was led by Gustav Husák, later to be General Secretary of the Communist Party of Czechoslovakia (CPCz), on the pretext of preventing the re-emergence of supporters of the Tiso regime.

Husák did not long remain in power in Slovakia. In 1954 he was sentenced to life imprisonment, along with four other Slovak Communists, on charges of Slovak separatism. Under the Communist regime expressions of Slovak nationalism were severely suppressed, and any formal power that Slovak national institutions maintained was nullified by the highly centralized structure of the CPCz.

It was not until the 1960s, with the appointment of Dubček (an ethnic Slovak) as leader of the Communist Party of Slovakia (CPS) and the beginning of the reform movement, that the issue of Slovak autonomy re-emerged in public debate. In 1968 the Government approved plans for the creation of a federal system of two equal republics. Despite the Soviet invasion, in August, the new federal system was introduced on 1 January 1969. Slovakia became the Slovak Socialist Republic, with a Slovak government and a National Council with wide constitutional powers. However, the reimposition of centralized Communist rule, under the leadership of Husák, left these new institutions largely powerless.

Following the Revolution in 1989, Slovaks began to demand real changes in their status within the federation. In November 1989 a coalition of independent groups, called Public Against Violence (PAV), was formed in opposition to the Communist regime. (PAV was the Slovak counterpart to, and ally of, the Czech Civic Forum.) It retained a wide degree of support for the elections to the Slovak National Council, which took place in June 1990, becoming the largest party, with 48 of the 150 seats. However, as debate over the proposed federal Constitution became more polarized, parties such as the Christian Democratic Movement (CDM), which proposed a much looser form of federation, gained in popularity, and separatist groups, notably the Slovak National Party (SNP), also grew in importance.

In 1990 and 1991 the debate over Czech–Slovak relations dominated Slovak politics and was the cause of increasing political turmoil in the Republic. Vladimír Mečiar, who had been elected Prime Minister following the June 1990 elections, was forced to resign over the issue of Czech–Slovak relations. He was accused of harming relations by his advocacy of increased autonomy for Slovakia. He left PAV and formed a new party, the Movement for a Democratic Slovakia (MDS). Controversy continued in mid-1991 when his successor, Jan Čarnogursky, although considered more pro-federal than Mečiar, asserted that Slovakia would probably be an independent member of the EC by 2000. In September, in an attempt to accelerate movement towards independence, and perhaps to forestall a possible referendum on the issue, a group of Slovak politicians, mostly members of the MDS and the SNP, launched the Initiative for a Sovereign Slovakia. The group attempted to persuade the Slovak National Council to adopt a declaration of sovereignty and opposed renewed proposals from President Havel for a referendum to be held on the issue.

Economy

Although the area of cultivated land is relatively small, agriculture is an important sector of the economy. The main crops are wheat, barley, maize, sugar beets, rye, oats and potatoes. The main livestock are cattle, pigs and sheep. There are vineyards on the southern slopes of the Tatras, and tobacco and fruits are grown in the Váh river valley.

There are significant mineral deposits, including copper, manganese, iron ore, lead and zinc. Small deposits of natural gas and petroleum are exploited, and some low-quality brown coal (mainly lignite) is mined. The principal energy source is hydroelectric power, generated by a series of dams on the Váh, Orava, Hornád and Slaná rivers. The controversial Gabčíkovo-Nagymarós dam, which was constructed on the River Danube in the 1980s, will provide considerable energy resources if it begins operation.

In the 1970s and 1980s there was a considerable programme of industrialization in Slovakia. However, owing to inefficient methods of production and the loss of traditional markets in Eastern Europe it was expected that many plants would be forced to close or reduce staffing levels. Such industries are concentrated in eastern Slovakia, in particular at Košice, and around Bratislava. Some 65% of Czechoslovakia's production of armaments is concentrated in Slovakia. The reduction in Czechoslovak exports of armaments has severely affected these plants, and plans for the conversion of the industry to civilian production are expected to cause unemployment of more than 80,000 workers. In 1988 Slovakia produced 20,000m. korunas-worth of armaments and related products; in 1991 the value of production was not expected to exceed 2,000m. korunas.

Directory

The Government

(September 1991)

GOVERNMENT OF THE SLOVAK REPUBLIC

Prime Minister: JÁN ČARNOGURSKÝ.

First Deputy Prime Minister: MARTIN PORUBJAK.

Deputy Prime Ministers: ANTON VAVRO, GÁBOR ZÁSZLÓS.

Minister of Administration and Privatization of National Wealth: IVAN MIKLOS.

Minister of Agriculture and Food: JOZEF KRŠEK.

Minister of Control: MARTIN HVOZDÍK.

Minister of Culture: LADISLAV SNOPKO.

Minister of Economic Strategy: MILAN BUČEK (acting).

Minister of the Economy: JOZEF BELCÁK.

Minister of Education, Science, Youth and Sport: JÁN PIŠÚT.

Minister of the Environment: IVAN TIRPÁK.

Minister of Finance: JOZEF DANCO.

Minister of Forestry and Water Resources: VILIAM OBERHAUSER.

Minister of Health: ALOJZ RAKÚS.

Minister of Housing and Construction: JOZEF BÚTORA.

Minister of Industry: JÁN HOLČÍK.

Minister of Internal Affairs: LADISLAV PITTNER.

Minister of International Relations: Dr PAVEL DEMEŠ.

Minister of Justice: MARIÁN POSLUCH.

Minister of Labour and Social Affairs: HELENA WOLEKOVA.

Minister of Trade and Tourism: JOZEF CHREN.

Minister of Transport and Telecommunications: VLADIMÍR PAVLE.

MINISTRIES

Ministry of Administration and Privatization of National Wealth: Kycerského 1, 812 70 Bratislava; tel. (7) 46395; fax (7) 44571.

Ministry of Agriculture and Food: Suvorovova 12, 812 66 Bratislava; tel. (7) 545815; fax (7) 57834.

Ministry of Control: Štepanovičova 5, 813 14 Bratislava; tel. (7) 498061; fax (7) 491313.

Ministry of Culture: Suvorovova 12, 813 31 Bratislava; tel. (7) 553 81; fax (7) 535 28.

Ministry of the Economy: Mierová 19, 827 15 Bratislava; tel. (7) 232300; fax (7) 230122.

Ministry of Education, Youth and Sports: Hlboká 2, 813 33 Bratislava; tel. (7) 491811; fax (7) 497098.

Ministry of Finance: Štepanovičova 5, 813 25 Bratislava; tel. (7) 48761; fax (7) 43470.

Ministry of Forestry and Water Conservancy: Tř. L. Novomeskeho 2, 842 18 Bratislava; tel. (7) 325303; telex 93385.

Ministry of Housing and Construction: Štepanovičova 5, 813 25 Bratislava; tel. (7) 496951; fax (7) 494727.

Ministry of Industry: Stromová 1, 833 36 Bratislava; tel. (7) 3704111; fax (7) 376364.

Ministry of the Interior: Mierová 19, 827 15 Bratislava; tel. (7) 234062; fax (7) 230122.

Ministry of International Affairs: Udolná 7, POB 87/15, 810 05 Bratislava; tel. (7) 316560; fax (7) 316552.

Ministry of Justice: Oktobrové nám. 13, 813 11 Bratislava; tel. (7) 353111; fax (7) 315952.

Ministry of Labour and Social Welfare: Čs. armady 4, 816 43 Bratislava; tel. (7) 300; telex 92361.

Ministry of Trade and Tourism: Čs. armady 8, 883 15 Bratislava; tel. (7) 300; telex 93192; fax (7) 54093.

Ministry of Transport and Communications: Bratislava.

Commission for the Environment: Hlboká 2, 812 35 Bratislava; tel. (7) 492451; fax (7) 311384.

Legislature

NATIONAL COUNCIL

Chairman: FRANTIŠEK MIKLOŠKO.

Elections, 8–9 June 1990

Party	Seats
Public Against Violence (PAV)*	48
Christian Democratic Movement (CDM)	31
Communist Party of Czechoslovakia (CPCz)†	22
Slovak National Party (SNP)	22
Coexistence	14
Democratic Party	7
Green Party	6
Total	150

* Some deputies subsequently left PAV to form the Movement for a Democratic Slovakia.
† Subsequently renamed the Party of the Democratic Left.

Judicial System

All courts in Slovakia are within the jurisdiction of the Ministry of Justice of the Slovak Republic. The Supreme Court of the Federation, based in Prague, is the final court of appeal.

Chairman of the Supreme Court of the Slovak Republic: Dr KAROL PLANK.

Procurator-General: Dr VOJTECH BACHO.

The Press

PRINCIPAL DAILIES

Bratislava

A Nap (The Sun): Bratislava; f. 1990; independent; associated with Public Against Violence; Hungarian-language.

Čas (Time): Bratislava; f. 1990; circ. 17,000.

Hlas ľudu (Voice of the People): Martanovičova 25, 819 06 Bratislava; tel. (7) 55521; telex 93398; f. 1949; morning; West Slovakia region; Editor-in-Chief PAVOL DINKA; circ. 49,337.

Narodna obroda (National Renewal): Bratislava; f. 1990; published by the Slovak State Government; Editor-in-Chief JURAJ VERES; circ. 95,000.

Práca (Labour): Odborárské nám. 3, 812 71 Bratislava; tel. (7) 64547; telex 93283; fax (7) 212985; f. 1946; published by the Czech and Slovak Confederation of Trade Unions; Editor-in-Chief MILOS NEMEČEK; circ. 230,000.

Pravda (Truth): Martanovičova 25, 819 08 Bratislava; tel. (7) 52503; telex 93386; fax (7) 58305; f. 1920; independent; left-wing; published by the Perex joint-stock co; Editor-in-Chief PETER SITÁNYI; circ. 260,000.

Roľnícke noviny (Farmer's News): Martanovičova 25, 819 11 Bratislava; tel. (7) 54449; telex 93211; fax (7) 51282; f. 1946; organ of the Slovak Ministry of Agriculture; Editor-in-Chief JURAJ ŠESTÁK; circ. 47,000.

Slovensky dennik (Slovak Daily): Bratislava; circ. 40,000.

Smena (Shift): Dostojevského rad 1, 812 84 Bratislava; tel. (7) 54255; telex 93341; f. 1947; Editor-in-Chief LUBOMÍR CHORVATOVIČ; circ. 130,000.

Új Szó (New Word): Martanovičova 25, 819 15 Bratislava; tel. (7) 53220; telex 92308; (7) 50529; f. 1948; midday; independent Hungarian-language paper; fmrly daily of the Communist Party of Slovakia; Editor-in-Chief JOZSEF SZILVÁSSY; circ. 90,000.

Večerník (Evening Paper): Martanovičova 25, 819 16 Bratislava; tel. (7) 55085; telex 92296; fax (7) 2104521; f. 1956; evening; publ. by GAP; Editor-in-Chief Dr RUDOLF MACHALA; circ. 80,400.

Verejnosť (Public): Martanovičova 25, 819 02 Bratislava; tel. (7) 52725; telex 92664; fax (7) 56125; f. 1990; published by Public Against Violence; Editor-in-Chief MILAN RICHTER; circ. 38,000.

Banská Bystrica

Smer (Course): Čs. armády 10, 975 43 Banská Bystrica; tel. 25466; telex 70261; fax 25506; f. 1948; independent; Editor-in-Chief IVAN BAČA; circ. 45,000.

Košice

Východ (East): Šmeralova 18, 042 66 Košice; tel. (95) 33261; Eastern Slovakia region; Editor-in-Chief ŠTEFAN KOČUTA; circ. 58,000.

PRINCIPAL PERIODICALS

Slovak language

Dievča (Girl): Leninovo nám. 12, 815 05 Bratislava; tel. (7) 334171; every 2 months; published by the Slovak Union of Women; Editor-in-Chief Dr ELENA GIRETHOVÁ; circ. 175,000.

EuroTelevízia (Eurotelevision): Martanovičova 25, 819 14 Bratislava; tel. (7) 2104194; telex 92661; fax (7) 50995; weekly; published by Euroscop Inc.; Editor-in-Chief TAŇA LUCKÁ; circ. 290,000.

Eva: Martanovičova 13, 815 85 Bratislava; tel. (7) 52271; every 2 months; magazine for women; Editor-in-Chief Dr GITA PECHOVÁ; circ. 150,000.

Expres: Martanovičova 25, 815 80 Bratislava; tel. (7) 334209; f. 1969; weekly digest of the foreign press; published by the Pravda Publishing House; Editor-in-Chief KAROL HULMAN; circ. 80,000.

Kamarát (Friend): Pražská 11, 812 84 Bratislava; tel. (7) 497218; fax (7) 493305; f. 1950 as Pioneer News; weekly; magazine for teenagers; Editor-in-Chief VLADIMÍR TOPERCER; circ. 60,000.

Katolícke noviny (Catholic News): Kapitulská 20, 815 21 Bratislava; tel. (7) 331717; f. 1849; weekly; published by the St Adalbert Association; Editor-in-Chief LADISLAV BELÁS; circ. 130,000.

Krásy Slovenska (Beauty of Slovakia): Vajnorská 100, 832 58 Bratislava; illustrated monthly; published by Sport, publishing house of the Slovak Physical Culture Organization; Editor Dr MILAN KUBIŠ; circ. 19,000.

Literaturny Tlzdennik (Literary Weekly): Bratislava; weekly; organ of the Slovak Writers' Union; nationalist orientation.

Móda (Fashion): Leninova nám. 12, 815 05 Bratislava; tel. (7) 334172; monthly; Editor-in-Chief EMILIA ŠÁNDOROVÁ; circ. 145,000.

Nové slovo (New Word): Martanovičova 25, 819 07 Bratislava; tel. (7) 50334; f. 1944; weekly; politics, culture, economy; independent; published by the Perex joint-stock co; Editor-in-Chief EMIL POLÁK; circ. 65,000.

Ohník (Little Flame): Dostojevského rad 1, 812 84 Bratislava; tel. (7) 56168; fortnightly; youth; published by the Smena Publishing House; Editor-in-Chief MAGDALÉNA GOCNÍKOVÁ; circ. 130,000.

Roháč (Stag-Beetle): Martanovičova 25, 819 10 Bratislava; tel. (7) 55153; f. 1948; humorous, satirical weekly; published by Slovako-press; Editor-in-Chief MIKULÁŠ SLIACKY; circ. 30,000.

Slovenka (Slovak Woman): Štúrova 12, 814 92 Bratislava; tel. (7) 55061; f. 1949; weekly; illustrated magazine; published by the Slovak Women's Union; Editor-in-Chief LÝDIA BRABCOVÁ; circ. 235,000.

Slovenské národné noviny (Slovak National News): Matica Slovenská, Mudroňova 26, 03652 Martin; tel. 34535; telex 075331; fax 33160; f. 1845; weekly; organ of Matica Slovenská cultural organization; Editor MILOS MAJER.

Slovensky narod (The Slovak Nation): Bratislava; weekly; organ of the Slovak National Party.

Spektr (Spectrum): Sasinkova 5, 815 60 Bratislava; tel. (7) 164551; 10 a year; fmrly Družba (Friendship)—journal of the Union of Czechoslovak–Soviet Friendship; journal of Russian teaching in Czechoslovakia; published by the Slovak Ministry of Education; Editor-in-Chief NATAŠA REPKOVÁ; circ. 15,000.

Svet (World): Bezručova 9, 815 87 Bratislava; tel. (7) 52959; f. 1951; illustrated weekly; Editor-in-Chief VLADO KALINA; circ. 140,000.

Štart (Start): Vajnorská 100/A, 832 58 Bratislava; tel. (7) 69666; f. 1956; illustrated weekly; organ of the Slovak Central Cttee of the Czechoslovak Union of Physical Education; Editor-in-Chief MATEJ SZÉHER; circ. 81,000.

Technické noviny (Technology News): Martanovičova 25, 819 25 Bratislava; tel. (7) 213483; f. 1953; weekly of the Slovak Council of Trade Unions; Editor-in-Chief Ing. EDUARD DROBNÝ; circ. 80,000.

Tip: Vajnorská 32, 832 58 Bratislava; tel. (7) 212100; telex 92650; fax (7) 213778; f. 1969; weekly; football and ice-hockey; published by the Slovak Physical Training Organization; Editor FERDINAND KRÁLOVIČ; circ. 60,000.

Výber (Digest): Októbrové nám. 7, 814 76 Bratislava; tel. (7) 316640; fax (7) 334534; f. 1968; weekly; digest of home and foreign press; in Czech and Slovak; published by the Slovak Syndicate of Journalists; Editor-in-Chief IGOR SLOBODNÍK; circ. 25,000.

Život (Life): Martanovičova 25, 819 17 Bratislava; tel. (7) 54121; fax (7) 59391; f. 1951; illustrated weekly; political, economic, social and cultural matters; published by the Slovakopress Publishing House; Editor-in-Chief MILAN VÁROŠ; circ. 100,000.

Hungarian language

Vasárnap: Martanovičova 25, 819 15 Bratislava; tel. (7) 53220; telex 92308; (7) 50529; f. 1948; weekly; independent Hungarian-language magazine; Editor-in-Chief JOZSEF SZILVÁSSY; circ.

Romany language

Roma: Bratislava; f. 1991; monthly.

Romano L'il: Prešov; f. 1991; publ. by the Cultural Union of the Roma in Slovakia.

PRESS ASSOCIATIONS

Slovak Syndicate of Journalists: Októbrové nám. 7, 815 68 Bratislava; tel. (7) 335071; fax (7) 335434; f. 1968; reorganized in 1990; 2,500 mems; Chair. JÚLIUS GEMBICKÝ .

Hungarian Journalists Association: Bratislava; f. 1990; seeks to promote pluralism in the Hungarian-language press and ensure adequate coverage of ethnic Hungarian events in the media; 300 mems.

Publishers

Alfa: Hurbanovo nám. 3, 815 89 Bratislava; tel. (7) 331441; fax (7) 59443; previously the Slovak Publishing House of Technical Literature; technical and economic literature, dictionaries; Dir MARTIN PARAJKA.

Církevné vydavateľstvo: Palisády 64, 801 00 Bratislava; religious literature; ŠTEFÁNIA HREBÍKOVÁ.

Matica Slovenská: Novomeského 32, 036 52 Martin; tel. (842) 31371; telex 75331; fax (842) 33160; f. 1863; literary science, bibliography, biography and librarianship; literary archives and museums; works on the Slovak diaspora; Chair. Ing. IMRICH SEDLÁK.

Mladé Letá (Young Years); nám. SNP 12, 815 19 Bratislava; tel. (7) 50475; telex 92721; fax (7) 50563; f. 1950; state publishing house; literature for children and young people; Dir Ing. ANTON HYKISCH.

Obzor (Horizon): ul. Čs. armády 35, 815 85 Bratislava; tel. (7) 53021; state publishing house; educational, encyclopedias, popular scientific, fiction, textbooks, law; Dir Ing. RICHARD DAMÉ.

Osveta (Education): Osloboditelov 55, 036 54 Martin; tel. 32921; f. 1953; medical, educational, photographic and regional literature; Editor-in-Chief BOHUSLAV KORTMAN.

Práca: Štefánikova 19, 81271 Bratislava; tel. (7) 333779; fax (7) 330046; f. 1946; publishing house of the Confederation of Slovak Trade Unions; economics, labour, work safety, fiction, etc.; Dir MIROSLAV BERNÁTH.

Pravda: Gunduličova 12, 882 05 Bratislava; f. 1969 as the publishing house of the Communist Party of Slovakia; politics, philosophy, history, economics, fiction, children's literature; Dir JÁN HANZLÍK.

Príroda: Križkova 9, 815 34 Bratislava; tel. (7) 1497598; fax (7) 1497564; agricultural literature, gardening books; Dir Ing. VINCENT ŠUGÁR.

Slovenské pedagogické nakladateľstvo: Sasinková 5, 891 12 Bratislava; pedagogical literature, educational, school texts, dictionaries; Dir Dr SERGEJ TROŠČÁK.

Slovenský spisovateľ: Leningradská 2, 897 28 Bratislava; publishing house of the Union of Slovak Writers; fiction, poetry; Dir VLADIMÍR DUDÁŠ.

Smena: Pražská 11, 812 84 Bratislava; tel. (7) 498018; fax (7) 493305; f. 1949; fiction, literature for young people, newspapers and magazines; Dir Ing. JAROSLAV ŠIŠOLÁK.

Šport: Vajnorská 100/A, 832 58 Bratislava; tel. (7) 69195; telex 93330; publishing house of the Slovak Physical Culture Organization; sport, physical culture, guide books, periodicals; Dir Dr BOHUMIL GOLIAN.

Tatran: Michalská 9, 815 82 Bratislava; tel. (7) 335849; fax (7) 335777; f. 1947; fiction, art books, children's books, literary theory; Dir Dr JÁN VILIKOVSKÝ.

Veda (Science): Klemensova 19, 814 30 Bratislava; tel. (7) 56321; f. 1953; publishing house of the Slovak Academy of Sciences; scientific and popular scientific books and periodicals; Dir JÁN JANKOVIČ.

Východoslovenské vydavateľstvo: Alejová 3, 040 11 Košice; tel. (95) 765710; fax (95) 765204; f. 1960; regional literature, children's literature, fiction, general; Dir Dr IMRICH GOFUS.

Radio and Television

RADIO

Slovenský rozhlas Bratislava (Slovak Radio Bratislava): Mýtna 1, 812 90 Bratislava; tel. (7) 494462; telex 93353; fax (7) 498923; f. 1926; Dir Dr VLADIMÍR ŠTEFKO.

TELEVISION

Slovenská televízia (Slovak Television): Asmolovova 28, 845 45 Bratislava; telex 92277; fax (7) 722341; f. 1956; public broadcasting company; Dir-Gen. RUDOLF ŠIMKO.

Finance

(cap. = capital; dep. = deposits; res = reserves; m. = million; Kčs. = korunas)

BANKS
Commercial Banks

Slovenská polnohospodárska banka: Miletičova 21, 824 82 Bratislava; tel. (7) 61485; fax (7) 61785; f. 1990; joint-stock co; cap. 350m. Kčs. (Jan. 1991); Gen. Man. Ing. LUDOVÍT PÓSA; 15 brs.

Všeobecná úverová banka Bratislava: nám. SNP 19, 818 56 Bratislava; tel. (7) 3191111; telex 93346; fax (7) 51483; f. 1990; state-owned; cap. 2,600m. Kčs. (Dec. 1990); Gen. Man. Ing. JOSEF MUDRÍK; 39 brs.

Savings Bank

Slovenská štátna sporiteľňa (Slovak State Savings Bank): nám. SNP 18, 816 07 Bratislava; tel. (7) 52300; telex 93300; fax (7) 52087; state-owned; foreign currency, credit and deposit services; f. 1967; cap. 1,000m. Kčs. (Jan. 1991); Gen. Man. ALOJZ ONDRA; 323 brs.

INSURANCE

Slovenská štátna poisťovňa (Slovak State Insurance Corporation): Strakova 1, 815 74 Bratislava; telex 93375; fax (7) 827948; Gen. Dir RASTISLAV HAVERLIK.

Trade Unions

Konfederácia odborových zväzov Slovenskej republiky (Confederation of Trade Unions of the Slovak Republic): Vajnorská 1, 815 70 Bratislava; tel. (7) 62265; fax (7) 213303; branch of the Confederation of Czech and Slovak Trade Unions in the Slovak Republic; Pres. SVETOZÁR KORBEĽ.

Odborový zväz pracovníkov drevárského, nábytkárského, papierenského priemyslu, lesného a vodného hodpodárstva (Slovak Trade Union of Workers in Woodworking, Furniture and Paper Industries, in Forests and Management of Water Supplies): Vajnorská 1, 815 70 Bratislava; tel. (7) 213660; Pres. BORISLAV MAJTÁN; 133,626 mems.

Odborový zväz pracovníkov poľnohospodárstva na slovensku (Trade Union of Workers in Agriculture in Slovakia): Vajnorská 1, 815 70 Bratislava; tel. (7) 213942; Pres. EMIL KUČERA; 170,490 mems.

Slovenský odborový zväz pracovníkov textilného, odevného a kožiarského priemyslu (Slovak Trade Union of Workers in Textile, Clothing and Leather Industry): Vajnorská 1, 815 70 Bratislava; tel. (7) 213389; telex 92382; Pres. PAVOL JAKUBIK; 131,679 mems.

Culture

NATIONAL ORGANIZATION

Ministerstvo kultury Slovenskej republiky (Ministry of Culture of the Slovak Republic): see section on The Government (Ministries).

CULTURAL HERITAGE

Galéria hlavného mesta Slovenskej Republiky Bratislavy (Gallery of the Slovak Republic, Bratislava): Mirbachove palač, Dibrovovo nám. 11, 815 35 Bratislava; tel. (7) 332611; Dir Dr MILAN JANKOVSKÝ.

Matica Slovenská: L. Novomeského 32, Martin; tel. (842) 32454; telex 075331; f. 1863; Slovak cultural org.; Chair. Ing. IMRICH SEDLÁCH.

Slovenská národná galéria (Slovak National Gallery): Riečna 1, 800 00 Bratislava; tel. (7) 330437; f. 1948; Dir Dr STEFAN MRUŠKOVIČ.

Slovenské národné múzeum (Slovak National Museum): Vajanského nábr. 2, Bratislava; tel. (2) 330479; f. 1923; Dir Dr BRANISLAV MATOUŠEK.

PERFORMING ARTS

Národné divadlo (Slovak National Theatre): Gorkého 4, 800 00 Bratislava; tel. (2) 53861.

Slovenská filharmónia (Slovak Philharmonic Orchestra): Palackého 2, 800 00 Bratislava; tel. (7) 333351.

ASSOCIATIONS

Asociácia slovenských spisovatelov (Association of Slovak Writers): Štefánikova 14, 815 08 Bratislava; tel. (7) 43615; f. 1949; 350 mems; Pres. JAROSLAV REZNIK; Sec. PETER ANDRUŠKA.

Association of Hungarian Writers: Bratislava; f. 1989.

Spolok architektov Slovenska (Slovak Architects' Society): Nálepkova 15, 811 01 Bratislava; tel. (7) 335711; fax (7) 335744; 1,300 mems; Pres. Ing. arch STEFAN SLACHTA; Sec. PATRIK GULDAN.

Zväz slovenských dramatických umelcov (Union of Slovak Dramatists): Gorkého 4, 812 92 Bratislava; Pres. OSVALD ZAHRADNIK.

Zväz slovenských skladatelov a koncertných umelcov (Union of Slovak Composers and Concert Performers): Sládcovičova 11, Bratislava; tel. (7) 330188; f. 1955; 290 mems; Pres. Prof. Dr OTO FERENCZY; Sec. ALOJZ LUKNÁR.

Social Welfare

GOVERNMENT AGENCIES

Ministerstvo práce a sociálních věci Slovenské republiky (Ministry of Labour and Social Affairs of the Slovak Republic): see section on The Government (Ministries).

Slovenská správa sociálního zabezpečení (Slovak Administration of Social Security): ul. 29 augusta 8, 813 63 Bratislava; tel. (7) 59173.

The Environment

GOVERNMENT ORGANIZATIONS

Commission for the Environment: see section on The Government (Ministries); incl.:

Ústredie štátnej ochrany prírody—UŠOP (State Centre for Nature Conservation): Leninova 11, 031 01 Liptovský Mikuláš.

Slovak Ministry of Culture: see section on The Government (Ministries); incl.:

Ustredie Statnej Pamatkove Pece a Ochrany Prirody—USPPOP (State Institute for the Protection of Monuments and Nature Conservancy): Mostova 6, 811 02 Bratislava.

ACADEMIC INSTITUTES

Slovenská Académia Vied (Slovak Academy of Sciences): ul. Obrancov Mieru 49, 814 38 Bratislava; tel. (7) 42751; telex 93261; fax (7) 496849; f. 1953; Pres. Acad. LADISLAV MACHO.

Botanický ústav (Institute of Botany): Dúbravská cesta 14, 842 38 Bratislava; tel. (7) 372281.

Geografický ústav (Geographical Institute): Štefánikova 49, 814 73 Bratislava; tel. (7) 492751.

Ústav dendrobiológie (Institute of Dendrobiology): 951 52 Vieska nad Žitavou; tel. (814) 94211.

Ústav ekológie lesa (Institute of Forest Ecology): Štúrova 2, 960 53 Zvolen; tel. (855) 27485.

Ústav hydrológie a hydrauliky (Institute of Hydrology and Hydraulics): Trnavská 32, 826 51 Bratislava; tel. (7) 63561.

Ústav krajinnej ekológie (Institute of Landscape Ecology): Štefánikova 3, 814 34 Bratislava; tel. (7) 335435.

Ústav zoológie a ekosozológie (Institute of Zoology and Ecosociology): Mánesovo nám. 2, 851 01 Bratislava; tel. (7) 846184.

Ústav pre životné prostredie-stredisko pre životné prostredie Bratislava (Institute for Living Environment-Centre for Living Environment): tř. L. Novomeského 2, 84242 Bratislava; tel. (7) 726308.

Výskumný ústav vodného hospodárstva (Research Institute of Water Industry): náb. L. Svobodu 5, 811 02 Bratislava.

Výskumný ústav lesného hospodárstva (Research Institute of the Forestry Industry): 960 01 Zvolen; tel. (855) 27311.

NON-GOVERNMENTAL ORGANIZATIONS

Slovensky zväz ochrancov prirody a krajiny—SZOPK (Slovak Union of Nature and Landscape Conservationists): Gorkeho 6, 811 01 Bratislava; tel. (7) 50665.

Strana Zelených na Slovensku (Green Party in Slovakia): Laurinská 1, 811 01 Bratislava; tel. (7) 332604; f. 1990; 4,000 mems.

Strom života (Tree of Life): Pražská ul. 11, 811 04 Bratislava; organizes environmental education for young people; tel. (7) 498473.

Bibliography

Korbel, J. *Twentieth Century Czechoslovakia: The Meaning of Her History.* New York, Columbia University Press, 1977.

Kusin, V. P. *From Dubček to Charter 77. A Study of 'Normalization' in Czechoslovakia, 1968–1978.* Edinburgh, Q Press, 1979.

The Intellectual Origins of the Prague Spring. Cambridge, Cambridge University Press, 1971.

Mamatey, V. S. and Luža, R. (Eds). *A History of the Czechoslovak Republic, 1918–1948.* Princeton, NJ, Princeton University Press, 1973.

Myant, M. *The Czechoslovak Economy.* Cambridge, Cambridge University Press, 1989.

Olivová, V. *The Doomed Democracy. Czechoslovakia in a Disrupted Europe, 1914–1938.* London, Sidgwick and Jackson, 1972.

Paul, D. W. *Czechoslovakia. Profile of a Socialist Republic at the Crossroads of Europe.* Boulder, Colorado, Westview Press, 1981.

Skilling, G. H. *Charter 77 and Human Rights in Czechoslovakia.* London, Allen and Unwin, 1981.

Czechoslovakia's Interrupted Revolution. Princeton, NJ, Princeton University Press, 1976.

Skilling, G. H. and Wilson, P. (Eds). *Civic Freedom in Central Europe. Voices from Czechoslovakia.* London, Macmillan, 1991.

Taborsky, E. *Communism in Czechoslovakia, 1948–1960.* Princeton, NJ, Princeton University Press, 1961.

Ulč, O. *Politics in Czechoslovakia.* San Fransisco, W. H. Freeman, 1974.

Wightman, G. 'The Collapse of Communist Rule in Czechoslovakia and the July 1990 Parliamentary Elections' in *Parliamentary Affairs,* Vol. 44, No. 1, January 1991.

HUNGARY

Geography

PHYSICAL FEATURES

The Republic of Hungary is a land-locked country in central Europe. It is bordered by Austria to the west, the Slovak Republic (Czechoslovakia) to the north and has a short border with Ukraine in the north-east. Romania lies to the east and Hungary's southern border is with three of the republics of Yugoslavia: Serbia (Vojvodina), Croatia and Slovenia. Hungary has a total area of 93,033 sq km (35,920 sq miles) and is one of the smaller countries of Eastern Europe, its territory having been much reduced upon the dissolution of the Habsburg Empire.

The River Danube (Duna) forms Hungary's north-western border with Czechoslovakia and then flows south through Budapest, bisecting the country, which is mostly low-lying and much of it prone to flooding. East of the Danube is the Pannonian or Great Hungarian Plain (*Nagyalföld*), which is also drained by the Tisza, the longest tributary of the Danube. To the west of the Danube the country is hillier, with a spur of the Alps traversing the region from the south-west to the north-east (the Bakony, Vertes and Philis ranges). South-east of these mountains lie Lake Balaton, the largest lake in central Europe, and the downlands of Transdanubia (*Dunántúl*). In the north-west of Hungary, between the mountains and the Danube, are the Little Hungarian Plains (*Kisalföld*). Only some 2% of the total land area of the country is over 400 m, the highest mountain being Kékestetö at 1,014 m, in the Matra range. The Matras lie east of the Danube, along Hungary's northern border, and are foothills of the Carpathian Mountains.

CLIMATE

Hungary has a continental climate, with hot summers and cold winters. In winter the Danube can freeze over for long periods and, in settled weather, fog is frequent. The mean temperatures in Budapest are a maximum of 22°C (71°F) in July and a minimum of −1°C (30°F) in January. Most rainfall is in the spring and early summer, when there are often heavy downpours; in Budapest the annual average is 610 mm. There is little regional variation in the weather.

POPULATION

The Hungarians (Magyars) are a Turkic or Finno-Ugrian people who settled on the Hungarian plains in the 7th century AD. There are still large numbers of ethnic Hungari-

ans outside the borders of the modern state, particularly in areas which once formed part of the old kingdom, such as north-west Romania (Transylvania). In 1984, it was estimated, ethnic Hungarians accounted for 92% of the total population of Hungary. In 1990, however, official figures put the number of Romany (Gypsy) people at over 0.5m. (between 5% and 7% of the total population), Germans at over 2% of the population, Slovaks at about 1%, Southern Slavs at just under 1% and Romanians at about 0.3%. The official language is Hungarian (Magyar), but the various nationalities also speak their own languages. The predominant religion is Christianity, the largest denomination being the Roman Catholic Church (an estimated 67% of the population), followed by Calvinists (20%) and Lutherans (5%). There are also small groups of Eastern Orthodox Christians, Jews and Muslims. The capital of Hungary is Budapest, in the north of the country. The city is located on the Danube, the ancient capital of Buda on the hillier western bank and the commercial centre of Pest on the eastern bank, with an estimated population of 2,016,132 on 1 January 1990. Other major towns include Debrecen (212,247), Miskolc (196,449) and Szeged (175,338) east of the Danube, and Pécs (170,119) to the west. In 1984, it was estimated, some 56% of the population lived in urban areas, compared to 35% in 1945. The total population was estimated at 10,375,300 on 1 January 1991, the population density being 111.5 per sq km.

Chronology

906: The Magyars, under the leadership of Árpád (896–907), migrated to the Hungarian plains.

1001: The coronation of St Stephen I (997–1038), with a crown sent by the Pope, established Hungary as a western Christian kingdom.

1458–90: Reign of Matthias I Corvinus, who prevailed against the rival claims to the throne of the House of Habsburg, extended Hungarian hegemony and moved his capital to Vienna.

1526: The Hungarian army was destroyed by the forces of the Ottoman Empire at the battle of Mohács; with the death of Louis II, the Habsburgs inherited Hungary's Crown of St Stephen.

1533: Hungary was partitioned between the Habsburgs and the Ottomans.

1687: The Imperial Diet of Pressburg (Bratislava) declared the Hungarian Crown to be a hereditary possession of the Austrian House of Habsburg.

1699: The Ottomans ceded Hungary (including Transylvania and Slavonia) to its conqueror, the Habsburg Holy Roman Emperor.

1711: The Peace of Sathmar granted self-administration to Hungary, subject to the laws of the Imperial Diet.

6 August 1806: Francis II, under pressure from Napoleon of France, dissolved the Holy Roman Empire of the German Nation and reigned henceforth as Francis I, having assumed the imperial title for Austria in 1804.

1848: An uprising in Hungary under Louis Kossuth established a national government, but, in December, refused to recognize the new Emperor, Francis Joseph I.

1849: Imperial armies regained control of Hungary.

1867: The Compromise (*Ausgleich*) of 1867 reorganized the Habsburg empire as the Dual Monarchy of Austria (Cisleithania) and Hungary (Transleithania); Emperor Francis Joseph I was crowned as King of Hungary.

28 June 1914: The assassination of the heir to the Dual Monarchy, Archduke Francis Ferdinand, in Sarajevo (Bosnia-Herzegovina) led to the start of the First World War.

21 November 1916: Death of Francis Joseph I and accession of his grand-nephew Charles I.

4 October 1918: Austria-Hungary accepted the same armistice conditions as Germany (to take effect on 3 November).

25 October 1918: Count Mihály Károlyi established a national council following the decision of the Hungarian Diet to recall its troops and the effective dissolution of the Danubian monarchy.

31 October 1918: Károlyi became premier with the backing of Charles I, who then renounced participation in government.

16 November 1918: Hungary was declared a Republic, Karolyi becoming President.

20 December 1918: The Hungarian Communist Party was established by Béla Kun.

21 March 1919: Károlyi resigned in protest at the Allies' territorial demands; Kun formed a coalition government of Communists and Social Democrats.

August 1919: A Romanian counter-offensive, following Hungarian incursions into Slovakia and Transylvania, resulted in the flight of Kun and a brief occupation of Budapest.

March 1920: Admiral Miklós Horthy de Nagybanya restored Hungary as a monarchy, but with a vacant throne and himself as Regent.

4 June 1920: Signature of the Treaty of Trianon concluding peace at the end of the First World War: Hungary ceded Slovakia and Carpatho-Ukraine to Czechoslovakia, Transylvania to Romania, the Banat to Romania and Yugoslavia, Croatia-Slavonia to Yugoslavia and the Burgenland to Austria; the consequent desire of the Hungarians to revise the borders resulted in close relations with Germany.

February 1939: Hungary joined Germany and Italy in the Anti-Comintern Pact.

11 April 1941: Hungary entered the Second World War on the side of Germany.

March 1944: German troops occupied Hungary.

October 1944: Regent Horthy secretly concluded an armistice with the USSR, but was forced to rescind it, was arrested and replaced by the Fascist, Ferenc Szalasi.

20 January 1945: A provisional government signed an armistice with the USSR and agreed to the Hungarian borders of 1937 (as established at Trianon).

November 1945: Following a general election, the Smallholders Party (KGP), the largest party, formed a coalition Government with the Communists.

August 1947: The Communists became the largest single party in the general election, after the discrediting of the KGP.

June 1948: The Communist Party merged with the Social Democratic Party to form the Hungarian Workers' Party (HWP).

May 1949: The Hungarian People's Front for Independence (dominated by the HWP) presented a single list of candidates.

August 1949: A People's Republic was established.

1953 : Imre Nagy became Prime Minister.

April 1955: Nagy was forced to resign by Mátyás Rákosi, the First Secretary of the HWP, and was expelled from the Party.

July 1956: Rákosi was forced to resign and was replaced by Ernő Gerő.

23 October 1956: Demonstrations and rioting broke out in Budapest against the Communist Government.

24 October 1956: Soviet tanks were sent in to quell the rioting.

25 October 1956: The Communist Government was replaced by a reformist regime headed by Imre Nagy; Soviet forces withdrew.

3 November 1956: Nagy established an all-party coalition Government, having already renounced membership of the Warsaw Pact.

4 November 1956: Some 200,000 Soviet troops invaded the country; Nagy was overthrown and János Kádár was installed by the USSR as the new premier in an all-Communist Government.

June 1958: Nagy and four associates were executed for their part in the 1956 uprising. Kádár became leader of the newly-formed Hungarian Socialist Workers' Party (HSWP).

1 January 1968: The New Economic Mechanism, which combined central-planning and market instruments, was introduced.

June 1985: The legislative elections permitted voters a wider choice of candidates under the terms of a new electoral law.

March 1986: Widespread disturbances occurred in Budapest during a protest march by disenchanted young people following violent intervention by the police.

October 1986: A group of academics, supported by Imre Pószgay and other reformers in the HSWP, drew up a paper, 'Change and Reform', which heralded the breakdown in consensus both inside and outside the Party.

June 1987: Károly Grósz was appointed Chairman of the Council of Ministers.

March 1988: Some 10,000 people marched through Budapest, on the 140th anniversary of the 1848 uprising against Austrian rule, demanding the introduction of genuine reforms.

April 1988: Four reformers within the HSWP were expelled from the Party for demanding radical political and economic reform.

May 1988: At a special ideological conference of the HSWP János Kádár was replaced as General Secretary of the Central Committee by Károly Grósz. Kádár also lost his membership of the Politburo.

June 1988: Some 50,000 people demonstrated in Budapest against the Romanian Government's proposed destruction of 7,000 villages, including 1,500 ethnic Hungarian villages.

July 1988: The Central Committee of the HSWP approved an austere economic reform programme which would lead to a reduction in subsidies, a devaluation of the forint and a rapid rise in unemployment.

September 1988: The Hungarian Democratic Forum (HDF) was formally established. Some 20,000 people demonstrated in Budapest against further construction on one of the two dams in the Gabčíkovo-Nagymaros project on the Danube.

21 November 1988: Miklós Németh replaced Károly Grósz as Chairman of the Council of Ministers.

20 December 1988: The National Assembly voted to allow the right to demonstrate and the establishment of independent political organizations.

1989

January

11: The National Assembly approved legislation to legalize independent groups.

February

The historical commission of the HSWP Central Committee published a report which stated that the events of 1956 had been a 'popular uprising against the existing state power' and not a counter-revolution.

12: The HSWP agreed to the establishment of a multi-party system.

20: The Central Committee of the HSWP agreed to abandon the clause in the Constitution guaranteeing the HSWP's leading role in society.

25: Solidarity Workers' Trade Union Alliance, the country's first independent blue-collar trade union, was established.

March

12: The HSWP denounced the errors of Kádár's 32-year rule.

15: Some 100,000 people took part in an anti-Government demonstration in Budapest on the anniversary of the start of the Hungarian uprising against Austria.

29: A new press law was approved allowing any Hungarian to own a media organ.

April

The Communist Youth Union (KISZ) voted to dissolve itself and a new organization, the Hungarian Democratic Youth Federation, was formed in its place, and declared itself independent of the HSWP.

May

Following a reshuffle of the Council of Ministers, the Chairman, Miklós Németh, declared that the Council of Ministers would henceforth be answerable to the National Assembly before the HSWP. János Kádár was relieved of his post as President of the HSWP. Round-table talks between the HSWP and various opposition groups began.

June

1: Hungary applied to join the Council of Europe.

16: Imre Nagy was officially rehabilitated. He was reburied with four associates at a state funeral in Budapest which was attended by 300,000 people.

21: Round-table negotiations between the Government and opposition groups commenced.

July

6: János Kádár died.

23: An opposition deputy was elected to the National Assembly, in a by-election, for the first time since 1947.

August

Two million workers went on strike in protest at planned price increases.

5: The HDF won three more seats in the National Assembly in by-elections.

September

10: The border with Austria was opened allowing the exodus of thousands of East Germans seeking to emigrate to the West.

18: During round-table talks it was decided that the Constitution and electoral law be modified and that the Presidential Council be dissolved.

26: The seven opposition members of the National Assembly formed a parliamentary group.

October

7–8: At the 14th HSWP Congress delegates voted to dissolve the Party and reconstitute it as the Hungarian Socialist Party (HSP). Rezső Nyers was elected Chairman of the new party and Imre Pozsgay was nominated as the party's candidate for the presidential elections.

18: Mátyás Szűrös was elected to the newly-created post of President of the Republic, in an acting capacity.

19: The National Assembly voted to end HSP cells in the workplace.

20: A 15-member Constitutional Court was established. The National Assembly passed legislation disbanding the HSP-controlled Workers' Militia.

23: The Republic of Hungary was proclaimed.

November

The Government decided to end all work on the dam project for the Danube.

1990

January

17: The Minister of the Interior, István Horváth, resigned after it was revealed that his Ministry had received reports on the activities of opposition groups.

29: Some 14,000 demonstrated in Budapest against the Government's austerity policies.

March

1: The National Assembly altered the Constitution to introduce direct presidential elections.

10: An agreement was signed with the USSR for the withdrawal of Soviet troops.

12: The withdrawal of Soviet troops began.

14: The USSR presented the Hungarian Government with a bill of 42,000m. forints for the withdrawal of troops and the handover of Soviet bases in Hungary. The National Assembly rehabilitated all the victims of political repression under the Communist regime and authorized the payment of compensation to those affected.

19: The Government asked the Romanian Government to take measures to ensure the protection of the Hungarian minority in Romania, following anti-Hungarian violence in Tîrgu Mureș.

20: Thousands of people demonstrated in Budapest in support of the Hungarian minority in Romania.

22: The barter-trade agreement with the USSR was ended.

25: The first round of voting in the legislative elections took place.

30: The HDF made an electoral pact with the Christian Democratic People's Party (CDPP) and the Independent Smallholders' Party (ISP).

April

8: The second round of voting in the legislative elections took place.

9: The HDF agreed a coalition Government with the CDPP, the ISP and independents.

May

2: The National Assembly held its constituent session. The HDF and the Alliance of Free Democrats (AFD), the two largest parties in the Assembly, agreed a pact to end their rivalry. Árpád Göncz (AFD) was elected interim President and Speaker of the National Assembly, and was given the backing of the HDF in the presidential election.

3: József Antall (HDF) was appointed Chairman of the Council of Ministers.

9: The AFD, the ISP and the Federation of Young Democrats supported a resolution calling for Hungary's immediate departure from the Warsaw Pact.

16: Antall presented the proposed Council of Ministers to the National Assembly.

22: Premier Antall presented the Government's programme to the National Assembly and announced that entry to the European Communities (EC) would be sought.

23: Antall's cabinet was approved by the National Assembly.

June

8: During a meeting with Soviet Defence Ministry officials, Lajos Für, the Hungarian Minister of Defence, announced that Hungarian troops would not take part in Warsaw Pact exercises in 1990 and would also be removed from the command of the Joint Armed Forces.

12: The National Assembly voted to adopt an amnesty for 3,000 prisoners on the 32nd anniversary of the death of Imre Nagy.

15: The Ibusz travel agency became the first Hungarian company to be privatized.

16: A co-operation agreement was signed with the European Free Trade Association (EFTA).

21: Trading began on the Budapest Stock Exchange after a 42-year break.

26: The National Assembly voted to instruct the Government to start negotiations for the withdrawal from the Warsaw Pact.

29: The Government announced a quickening of its policies on privatization and decentralization.

July

3: Ministers were forced to negotiate with miners striking in protest at the widescale privatizations. Improvements in pay and retirement terms were agreed.

18: The Government took over direct control of the State Property Agency in order to maintain control over its privatizations' policy.

20: The Government demanded that the right to inspect Warsaw Pact forces as well as NATO forces be inserted in the Conventional Forces in Europe Treaty.

August

3: Árpád Göncz was elected President of the Republic by the National Assembly.

10: The AFD announced that the political 'non-aggression' pact made with the HDF in April was over.

September

6: The Government announced that the former heads of the secret police would be put on trial.

26: Some 10,000 students marched through Budapest to protest against rising inflation.

30: Local elections took place across the country.

October

2: Hungary's membership of the Council of Europe was confirmed. The Constitutional Court rejected government plans to return land to its pre-Communist owners.

5: About 100,000 miners went on a 2-hour strike to protest at the worsening economic position.

14: The second round of voting in the local elections took place.

19: The Government offered all state industries for sale.

24: The Constitutional Court abolished the death sentence.

26: Following a government decision to raise petrol prices, protesting transport workers and taxi-drivers blocked roads throughout the country.

28: The Government was forced to halve its earlier 65% rise in petrol prices in order to end the disruption throughout the country.

30: The USSR announced that petroleum supplies on preferential terms would be cut.

November

3: The Warsaw Pact treaty on conventional weapons, detailing the maximum level of armaments, was signed in Budapest.

6: Hungary signed the Charter of the Council of Europe and the European Convention on Human Rights.

9: Imre Pozsgay left the HSP.

16: The Government announced that all its ground-to-ground missiles would be removed from service forthwith.

26: A trade pact was signed with the USSR.

December

4: Antall announced the state budget for 1991.

20: Antall appointed Mihály Kupa as Minister of Finance and Peter Boross as Minister of the Interior.

1991

January

7: The forint was devalued by 15% against convertible currencies.

12: Elemér Gergáta was appointed Minister of Agriculture and Gyula Kiss Minister of Labour.

April

10: The Ambassador to the USA, Peter Zwack, was dismissed after claiming that he had been forced to lie about the sale of Hungarian weapons to Croatia.

22: Talks with the Slovak Government over the Gabčikovo-Nagymarós hydroelectric scheme broke down; Hungary had abandoned the project on environmental grounds in 1989.

24: Legislation on compensating former owners of property nationalized under the Communists was approved by the National Assembly.

May

4: Remains of Cardinal József Mindszenty, previously buried in Austria, reinterred at Esztergom, 16 years after his death.

17: A new political movement, the National Democratic Federation, formed by Imre Pozsgay.

29: Constitutional Court rejects much of property compensation law, objecting to favourable treatment of owners of nationalized land compared to those of property.

31: Agreement signed on bilateral relations with Ukraine, the first such with a Soviet Republic.

June

14: Trade agreement with Republic of Russia concluded; first direct economic arrangement with a Soviet Republic.

19: The USSR claims to have withdrawn all troops from Hungarian soil; however, small numbers of remaining Soviet soldiers were discovered, and detained, in the following days.

26: Revised property compensation law passed by National Assembly, largely removing differentiation between owners of land and of other property.

28: Protocol providing for the dissolution, within 90 days, of the Council for Mutual Economic Assistance (CMEA or Comecon) was signed in Budapest.

July

The first refugees from the fighting in Yugoslavia, mainly ethnic Hungarians, arrived in the country.

15: Hungarian delegate to Conference on Security and Co-operation (CSCE) criticized treatment of Hungarian minorities by Czechoslovakia and Romania.

24: Diplomatic relations were established with South Africa.

August

16–20: Pope John Paul II made his first visit to Hungary.

29: Hungary threatened military retaliation if repeated incursions of its airspace by Yugoslav military aircraft continued.

History

MARTYN RADY

INTRODUCTION

The Kingdom of Hungary was established in the Middle Ages and occupied a territory some three times the size of the present-day Republic of Hungary. In 1526 the King of Hungary, Louis II, was killed by the Ottoman Turks at the Battle of Mohács, and the Kingdom was subsequently partitioned between the Ottoman Empire, the Habsburgs and the principality of Transylvania. In the later 17th century the Habsburg Emperor, Leopold I, expelled the Turks from Hungary and occupied Transylvania, reuniting it with the Hungarian Crown. Although Hungary was permitted a substantial degree of autonomy, particularly after 1867, when it became Austria's partner in the 'Dual Monarchy', the Kingdom remained part of the Habsburg domain until 1918.

Following the collapse of the Austro-Hungarian Empire, in November 1918, Hungary became a fully independent state. However, by the terms of the Treaty of Trianon (1920), Hungary lost two-thirds of its pre-1918 territories and three-fifths of its population. More than 3m. Hungarians (Magyars) were left in the neighbouring states of Austria, Czechoslovakia, Romania and Yugoslavia. The dismemberment of Hungary had a powerful impact on domestic politics in the years between the First and Second World Wars. The major parties advocated revisionist policies and the recovery of Hungary's former lands. As a consequence, Hungary inclined to the support of the of the Axis Powers (receiving some Slovakian territories in 1938), and fought against the Allies during the Second World War.

The boundaries established by the Treaty of Trianon were confirmed in the Treaty of Paris (1947). During the Communist period no Hungarian government expressed an interest in revising the frontier. Nevertheless, during both the Communist and post-Communist periods there has been considerable public disquiet concerning the fate of the Hungarian minorities remaining in Slovakia (Czechoslovakia), Croatia-Slavonia (Yugoslavia) and Transylvania (Romania). Allegations concerning the mistreatment by the Romanian authorities of the 2m. ethnic Hungarians in Transylvania have led to considerable tension between the Governments in Budapest and Bucharest. The civil war in Yugoslavia, from mid-1991, gave rise to further tension. Some senior Hungarian government figures suggested that any redrawing of Yugoslav borders could open the way to a review of the territorial arrangements made in the Treaty of Trianon, although others stressed their desire for a peaceful resolution of Yugoslavia's problems by its transformation into a union of sovereign republics.

In 1919 a Communist Government was installed in Hungary under the leadership of Béla Kun. This proved short-lived, and the country's brief experience under it contributed to the right-wing, authoritarian character of Hungarian politics between the two World Wars. Following the defeat of the Communists the country returned to the uncodified 'royalist' Constitution of the pre-1918 period. The throne, however, was declared to be vacant, so the Head of State carried the title of Regent (*Kormányzó*). Admiral Miklós Horthy de Nagybanya was appointed to this position in 1920, and remained in office until October 1944.

Horthy proved to be an important influence in favour of stability and political conservatism in the inter-war period. The governments which he appointed consisted principally of noblemen. It was not until 1944, under pressure from the Nazis, that Horthy was removed from power and a Fascist Government, headed by the leader of the Arrow Cross organization, Ferenc Szálasi, was established.

THE COMMUNIST TAKE-OVER

In 1944–45 Hungary was occupied by the Soviet army. Thereafter, Communist rule was gradually imposed on the country. Between 1945 and 1947 Hungary was governed by coalitions consisting both of Communists and of representatives from the democratic parties. At elections held in November 1945 the Communists won only 70 of the 409 seats in parliament, while the Small Landowners' Party won 245 seats. However, the Communists, through Imre Nagy, controlled the Ministry of the Interior and had the active support of the occupying Soviet army. With these advantages, they reduced the influence of the other parties by intimidating their leaders and by infiltrating their organizations.

In 1947 new elections were held, following the revelations of 'conspiracies' in the Small Landowners' Party. The Communists only gained 22.7% of the votes cast, but nevertheless became the largest single party, and the left-wing bloc, which they controlled, amassed 60% of the vote. The remnants of the main democratic parties were forced to join a coalition under Communist direction. Over the next year, the surviving non-Communist parties were either dissolved or absorbed into the Communist Party. In June 1948 the ruling party became known as the Hungarian Workers' Party, following the union of the Communist and Social Democratic Parties.

Under its Communist leader, Mátyás Rákosi, Hungary was transformed into a model Soviet satellite. Forced and rapid industrialization and collectivization took place and no political opposition to the regime, either real or imagined, was tolerated. The Department for the Defence of the State (ÁVO) was responsible for internal security, and under it several hundreds of thousands of people were interned in labour camps.

THE UPRISING OF 1956

The oppressive nature of Rákosi's rule led to considerable frustration and discontent, both within the Party and among the population at large. Following the death of Stalin in 1953, a reform wing of the Hungarian Workers' Party received support from members of the Soviet Politburo. The leader of the reformers was Imre Nagy, a Communist since 1918 and a former Minister of Agriculture. The frequent changes in Soviet policy which accompanied the rise of Nikita Khrushchev led to equally rapid shuffling of the composition of the Hungarian Government. In 1953 Rákosi was forced to relinquish the premiership, although remaining First Secretary of the Party, and for the next two years Nagy headed the administration. In March 1955, at the Kremlin's insistence, Nagy was ousted and replaced with András Hegedüs, a close ally of Rákosi. However, in July 1956 Rákosi himself, having lost popularity both within and outside the Party, was dismissed, even though he was succeeded by another Stalinist, Ernő Gerő.

The mood of uncertainty brought about by these changes contributed to the Uprising of 1956. Following increasing demonstrations calling for the return of Nagy, and also supporting Polish resistance to Moscow, a spontaneous rebellion against Soviet domination broke out in Budapest on 23 October and swiftly spread to other parts of the country. A reformist Government, led by Imre Nagy, was installed, and János Kádár took over as the new Party leader. On 4 November, however, Soviet troops occupied Budapest and, after bitter fighting, overthrew the revolutionary Government. Kádár, having previously lauded 'our people's glorious uprising' and given the Communist Party's 'full support for the removal of Soviet forces', now turned to support the Soviet occupiers. On 7 November Kádár was taken by Soviet armoured car to the National Assembly (parliament) building in Budapest.

KÁDÁRISM

Following the Soviet intervention, Kádár became Secretary of the renamed Hungarian Socialist Workers' Party (HSWP). Under Kádár's direction, all remaining traces of opposition to the regime were ruthlessly erased. Some 20,000 participants in the Uprising were arrested, of which 2,000 were subsequently executed, including Imre Nagy, who was hanged in June 1958. Opponents of the regime were deported to the USSR, the precise number involved being unknown. A workers' militia was established, under ÁVO control, and the collectivization of agriculture was vigorously pursued.

In 1961, however, Kádár initiated a new conciliatory policy which was designed to win support for his regime. The new direction was summed up by Kádár's declaration, as printed in the party newspaper, *Népszabadság*, in January 1962, 'Whereas the Rákosiites used to say that those who are not with us are against us, we say that those who are not against us are with us.' In accordance with the principle of *ralliement* (in Hungarian, *Szövetségi politika*), Kádár was willing to enlist non-Party specialists into the bureaucracy and to allow a wider debate within the Party itself over policy. Police surveillance became less obtrusive and there was some attempt to restore 'socialist legality' in the treatment offered to those who had participated in the Uprising. 'Class aliens' who, on account of their background, had been forced to take menial jobs in the countryside were also readmitted to public life.

The *ralliement* was accompanied by a reassessment of economic objectives. Under Rákosi the official policy had been that the country's economic problems had a political solution. Kádár, by contrast, endeavoured to remove political dissatisfaction by pursuing an economic solution. Under the direction of Rezső Nyers, the 'New Economic Mechanism' (NEM) was introduced in 1968, after five years of debate. The NEM partially freed enterprises and collectives from the tutelage of central planning, and devolved initiative from the ministries to managers and farming co-operatives. At the same time the NEM reoriented the economy away from heavy industry towards an expanding consumer sector. By offering higher living standards, Kádár sought to make his regime tolerable to ordinary Hungarians. As he explained in 1985, 'If we do not want to preserve our system by force and the use of arms, which we have no wish to do, then we must prove by other means that our social system is superior.'

THE FAILURE OF KÁDÁRISM

The introduction of the NEM led to a rapid improvement both in industrial production and in living standards. However, the economy faltered in the 1970s, giving way to inflation, declining output and a growing trade deficit. In 1974 Nyers was dismissed from the Politburo and the NEM was modified in order to satisfy conservatives in the Party. A subsequent attempt to reinvigorate the NEM failed to yield the expected dividend. In early 1982 the Party Secretary for Economic Affairs, Ferenc Havasi, admitted publicly that the Hungarian economy was 'clinically dead'.

Between 1979 and 1984 Hungarians suffered a real decline in wages of 10%, and many were forced to seek second and third jobs. Popular resentment was no longer appeased by such palliatives as increasing the availability of salami (1979) or introducing scented soap to the shops (1980). The increase in alcoholism, petty corruption, crime and suicide at this time was widely considered to be a consequence of the country's economic malaise.

The belief that the Party bore special responsibility for the hardship led, in the mid-1980s, to a 20% decline in membership of the KISZ communist youth organization. The level of support for this body was always regarded as a critical barometer of the regime's popularity. Dissatisfaction also expressed itself in the National Assembly. In 1986 a government bill was actually rejected by the deputies, and in the various parliamentary committees there was increased criticism of Party policy. The writers' union (*Magyar Írók Szövetsége*) publicly deplored the failure of the Government to reinvigorate the economy, and the press and other media became increasingly open in their discussion of the country's problems.

Within the Party itself there were growing doubts about the way the Government was managing the economy. Ever since the 1960s the HSWP had been open to reformists as well as to Party dogmatists. In the past, however, the policies of 'democratic centralism' had prevailed; conflicting opinions had been expounded and reconciled so as to yield a consensus behind which the Party might remain unified. By the mid-1980s this sort of consensus was no longer possible. Reformers within the Party advocated market solutions to the economic crisis which were entirely unacceptable to the more doctrinaire Party members. Although the Party Congress of March 1985 recognized the magnitude of the country's economic crisis, its solution was to adjust the existing structure rather than to introduce any major reform. Kádár himself delivered a special appeal for consensus within the Party and criticized the reformers for making their opposition public.

Ignoring Kádár, frustrated groups of reformers began to widen the debate by establishing informal contacts with opposition groups. During the 1970s and 1980s a number of extra-Party movements had emerged in the relatively tolerant atmosphere of Kádár's Hungary. The Party reformers eschewed, however, the 'democratic opposition' which centred upon the *samizdat* publications, *Beszélö* and *Hirmondó*. Instead they forged links with the 'populists', whose programme was more loosely concerned with national identity and traditions, and who were less dogmatically opposed to the Communist regime. In 1986 a meeting of populist writers, economists and historians at Lakitelek was attended by several reformist Party members.

By the mid-1980s, therefore, the Kádárite consensus, or as the Foreign Minister Gyula Horn later called it, 'the charm of the tired compromise', had begun to break down in Hungary. The economy was no longer strong enough to make the regime acceptable to the majority of Hungarians; institutions were beginning to demonstrate their independence of the Party; and sections of the HSWP were no longer inclined to preserve Party unity.

THE REFORMERS TAKE CONTROL

In May 1987 János Kádár celebrated his 75th birthday. By this time it was clear that he would not survive as leader of the HSWP for much longer. Firstly, his age told against him; secondly, he plainly lacked the confidence of the new Soviet leader, the CPSU General Secretary, Mikhail Gorbachev. The collapse of the Kádárite consensus was thus combined with a prolonged leadership crisis inside the HSWP.

Kádár's original choice to succeed him as Party Secretary, the Chairman of the Council of Ministers, György Lázár, had already expressed a wish to retire from politics. Károly Németh, Kádár's deputy as Party leader, was too closely associated with his superior to be acceptable to Moscow. Possibly at the recommendation of Gorbachev, Károly Grósz replaced Lázár as Chairman of the Council of Ministers in June 1987. Németh became President of the Presidential Council (Head of State, but a largely ceremonial post). Grósz had previously been First Secretary of the HSWP Budapest Committee, and had a reputation as a 'pragmatic realist'. He was popular among Party activists on account of his outspoken manner, and at the preceding Party Congress he had warned against the rise of social tension in the country.

Grósz's promotion to the premiership did not, however, represent a victory for the reform wing in the Party. Kádár retained his position as Party leader and, at the same time as Grósz's elevation, conservatives János Berecz and Judit Csehák joined the Politburo. It was considered likely that, should Grósz fail to engineer an economic recovery, then Berecz would be in a good position to succeed Kádár as Party leader.

Anticipating failure, Grósz sought to widen responsibility for economic policy by including the National Assembly in the discussions. In September 1987 he conceded new powers of scrutiny to parliamentary committees, in return for which the deputies agreed to endorse his Consolidation Programme. The Programme imposed a purchase tax on items sold and introduced an income tax on personal salaries. The principal aim behind the Consolidation Programme, which came into effect on 1 January 1988, was to diminish the monetary overhang in the economy.

During 1987 the reform wing of the Party had become increasingly forthright in its criticism of government policy. A major focus of discontent was the Patriotic People's Front (PPF), which was an umbrella organization uniting various social groups and the HSWP. Under its Secretary-General, Imre Pozsgay, the PPF sponsored a discussion paper entitled 'Turn and Reform' (1987), which advocated a thorough overhaul of the economy. Most strikingly, however, the document associated economic reform with a move towards political pluralism. From this time onwards, the debate over the economy became linked to discussion on constitutional issues. It was not until the second half of 1989, however, that the reformists in the Party made an unequivocal commitment to genuine multi-party democracy.

In September 1987 Pozsgay attended a second meeting of the populists at Lakitelek. Under his protection, the populists established the Hungarian Democratic Forum (HDF). During the same month the New March Front was established by Rezső Nyers, the architect of the NEM, and Miklós Vásárhelyi, Imre Nagy's former spokesman. The purpose of this new organization, which involved Party and non-Party members, was to promote the marketization of the economy and the democratization of Hungarian politics.

As Chairman of the Council of Ministers, Grósz was caught between the Politburo, which was still headed by Kádár and had a conservative bias, and the reformers, who were pressing for a more drastic economic solution than the Consolidation Programme and who appeared, additionally, to have the support of Mikhail Gorbachev. As Grósz wavered between the two factions, it became increasingly evident that the regime was losing control. Demonstrations and strikes became more commonplace, and the dissident and populist press flourished. In April 1988 a radical youth party, the Federation of Young Democrats (FYD), was established, while in the following month the various strands of the democratic opposition coalesced into a single confederation called the Network of Free Initiatives. The Network was subsequently renamed the Alliance of Free Democrats (AFD). These various groups joined the HDF in openly demanding the introduction of democratic reforms.

The most severe challenge, however, came from within the Party itself. In the first months of 1988 there was a periodic renewal of Party membership cards. About 45,000 members, some 6% of the total membership, did not reapply for readmission. In March and April party organizations at all levels were canvassed on their views on economic and political reform. The responses received were so critical of the existing policies that the leadership agreed to convene a special Party Conference, to take place in May 1988.

During the early months of 1988 it had seemed that the conservatives within the Party were still in the ascendant. At a meeting of the Central Committee in March, Kádár had obtained the approval for a slowing down of the reform process and for the continued application of democratic centralism to Party discussions. Four Party members closely associated with the HDF were expelled on this occasion. Kádár probably anticipated that he could manage the Party Conference in much the same way as he had the Central Committee, and imagined that he need extend only a few concessions to the reformers.

The 986 conference delegates, however, were more amenable to the wishes of the Party members by whom they had been elected than to the organizing committee, which sought to direct proceedings. The Conference appointed a new Central Committee, rejecting one-third of its existing membership, and dismissed most of the Politburo. Kádár was ousted from the position of General Secretary and given, instead, the honorific and newly-created post of Chairman of the Party; he was among those removed from the Politburo. He was removed as Chairman in May 1989, and died less than three months later. Grósz was appointed General Secretary of the Party in Kádár's place, and also retained the office of Chairman of the Council of Ministers. With Nyers, Pozsgay and several other reformers appointed to the Politburo, the conservatives were now less powerful, although Berecz and Csehák retained their positions. In June 1988 Dr Brunó Ferenc Straub, who was not a member of the HSWP, was appointed as President of the Presidential Council.

During the second half of 1988 the reformers used their ascendancy in the Politburo and Central Committee to install their supporters first in the Party administration and then in the upper levels of the Government. Ernő Lakatos, an ally of János Berecz, was dismissed as head of Party propaganda and appointed ambassador to the German Democratic Republic. Sándor Gáspár, leader of the Hungarian Trade Union Council (SZOT) was obliged to resign. Grósz's commitment to change was considered limited and, in November, he was forced to concede the office of Chairman of the Council of Ministers to the reformist, Miklós Németh. In the same month members of the reform faction were appointed to the deputy premiership and the Ministries of the Interior and Foreign Affairs.

Once established in the principal ministries, the reformers sought to introduce constitutional reform. Ten parliamentary committees, dominated by reformers, were created, with instructions to prepare legislation permitting freedom of association and assembly, the establishment of an independent judiciary and the nomination of parliamentary deputies by non-Party organizations. At the same time a historical commission was established, under the chairmanship of Iván Berend, to investigate and report upon the

Uprising of 1956. There was a relaxation of censorship laws, the HDF achieved legal recognition in September 1988 and an independent trade union (the first in Hungary for 40 years), the Democratic Union of Scientific Workers, was established. In January 1989 rights to strike, demonstrate and form associations and parties outside the HSWP were granted, and in the following month the Central Committee agreed to support the transition to a multi-party democracy.

The response of the conservatives, who had now lost influence in both the Politburo and the Government, was to draw attention to the prevailing 'counter-revolutionary atmosphere' and to hint that the Workers' Militia might be used to restore orthodoxy. Grósz, who was as anxious to conciliate the conservatives as to appease the reformers, joined in the attack in November 1988. In the now-notorious Sportcsarnok speech in Budapest, he talked of an impending 'white terror'. Grósz's intemperate address, together with his failure to obtain concessions from President Nicolae Ceauşescu of Romania over that country's mistreatment of its Hungarian minority in Transylvania, discredited him entirely. Although Grósz remained nominally in charge of the Party, hereafter he became increasingly insulated and played only a minor role in Hungarian politics. In June 1989 Grósz was effectively replaced as Party leader by a four-member Presidium, of which he was a member, along with Miklós Németh, Rezső Nyers and Imre Pozsgay; the Presidium was to direct the Party until its 14th Congress, which was to be held in October. In August Grósz announced that he would resign as General Secretary after the Congress.

THE COLLAPSE OF THE HSWP

By the beginning of 1989 the conservatives within the HSWP were capable of little more than speeches, and they were depressed by the apparent disinterest of the USSR in the fate of the Hungarian regime. In the first months of the year Party organizations in the localities became dominated by reformers and opportunists, who proceeded to remove corrupt and elderly Party officials from office. Nevertheless, at this stage both the Party membership and the reforming leadership believed that the HSWP would survive as the dominant force in Hungarian politics. However, by early 1989 the HSWP had lost about 120,000 members (about one-seventh of its total membership) during the previous 18 months. Party activists looked back to the period immediately after the Second World War, and anticipated forming a 'bogus coalition' with the democratic parties, which would allow them to retain power. In particular, they anticipated negotiating a compromise with the HDF, which was closely linked, through Imre Pozsgay, to the reform wing of the Party.

In February 1989 the HSWP's historical commission published its report, which concluded that the Uprising of 1956 had indeed been a popular uprising (*népfelkelés*), rather than a counter-revolutionary movement. This was an obvious embarrassment to the Party veterans and hard-liners, and also compromised the HSWP's claim to act as the revolutionary instrument of the working class. Imre Nagy was rehabilitated by the HSWP Central Committee, in May; his reburial on 16 June, along with four associates, in the Rákoskeresztúr cemetery was attended by over 250,000 people.

The earliest drafts of a proposed new constitution revealed the Party leadership's limited commitment to a genuine democratic transformation. Hungary was to be 'a free, democratic and *socialist* state'; it was to remain 'a *people's* republic'; and its market economy was to be influenced 'by *socialist* socio-economic goals' (author's italics).

Likewise, the law on associations, passed by the National Assembly in January 1989, postponed the regulation of new political parties (the appropriate legislation was eventually enacted in October). Clearly the Party reformers were hoping to delay the establishment of rival party organizations until as near as possible to the parliamentary elections due in 1990.

During the first months of 1989 it became increasingly evident that the HDF would not respond as the HSWP planned, and that it would be unlikely to enter into an electoral pact with the Communists. Furthermore, the advent of political pluralism, sanctioned by the law on associations, resulted in a proliferation of societies and trade unions determined to make Hungary a genuinely democratic state. New political parties were also set up, despite the still-existing legal limitations on their activity. These circumstances ended any possibility of amending the Constitution so as to allow the HSWP to retain control. A series of serious by-election defeats, in mid-1989, also suggested that unless the Party made a genuine commitment to democracy it would not survive as a political force. Various calculations made by the leadership, however, suggested that, were the Party to pioneer a democratic transformation, then the electorate would reward it with one-third of the votes cast. Given the fragmented character of the opposition, the HSWP hoped thus to obtain the largest single share of seats in a democratically-elected Assembly. It could then retain power as part of a 'genuine coalition'. On the basis of this analysis, on 21 June the leadership of the HSWP entered into talks with the opposition parties on new constitutional proposals to put before the National Assembly.

The outcome of these 'round-table talks', at which the HSWP, HDF, AFD, FYD, PPF and various other Party and non-Party organizations were represented, was a series of legislative proposals which were presented to parliament in September 1989 and rapidly enacted into law. According to this legislation, which amended the Stalinist Constitution of 1949, Hungary became a democracy, where political parties could freely operate (Law XXXI), and where the rule of law was guaranteed by a constitutional court (Law XXXII). A procedure for elections by a combination of party-list and member-constituencies was drawn up (Law XXXIV), and the office of President of the Republic was created (Law XXXI). Perhaps most significantly, the separation of any party from the guidance of the state and its economic structure was formalized. Mátyás Szűrös, then President of the National Assembly, was elected President of the Republic on 18 October, on an acting basis, and on 23 October Hungary formally ceased to be a People's Republic and the red star was removed from public buildings.

In preparation for the parliamentary elections, which were to be held before June 1990, the HSWP called its Party Congress a year early. The Party was anxious to display its democratic credentials: accordingly it renamed itself the Hungarian Socialist Party (HSP), and handed over its property and control of the Workers' Militia to the State.

In the course of negotiations with the opposition, however, the Party had obtained one important concession. It had been agreed between the then HSWP and the HDF that the President of the Republic was to be appointed by the existing Communist-dominated parliament in advance of the 1990 parliamentary elections. The aim of this measure was to ensure the selection of Imre Pozsgay, who was the only candidate acceptable both to the HSP and to the HDF.

The hasty presidential election was resisted by the AFD and the FYD, and the matter was debated in parliament.

At the suggestion of the AFD, premier Miklós Németh agreed to have a national referendum on the issue. On 26 November 1989 the Hungarian electorate voted by a narrow margin to postpone the appointment of the President until after the parliamentary elections of 1990. This verdict represented a defeat for the HSP and the HDF, and established the credibility of the AFD as a major force in Hungarian politics.

THE 1990 ELECTION

On 21 December 1989 the Hungarian parliament voted to dissolve itself in readiness for elections scheduled for 25 March 1990. In the intervening months the Németh Government largely confined itself to the day-to-day management of affairs. Its major achievement was to secure an agreement with the USSR on the evacuation of all Soviet troops from Hungary.

In the extended period of campaigning the HSP was the earliest casualty. It was alleged that the HSP was using the Ministry of the Interior to intercept the telephone conversations of opposition politicians. The HSP Interior Minister, István Horváth, was unable to exonerate himself from the charge of political espionage and was forced to resign on 23 January. The 'Danubegate' scandal deepened when opposition politicians alleged that the Interior Ministry was destroying records of its activities under the Communists. The HSP Minister of State, Imre Pozsgay, was also embarrassed by the accusation that he had sought to influence media coverage of the election campaign by having the head of television news, Endre Aczél, removed from his post.

The opposition parties benefited from the discomfiture of the HSP. Of the 50 parties contesting the election, the principal contenders were the HDF and the AFD. The programmes of these two parties were broadly similar: both advocated political pluralism, genuine multi-party democracy, the restoration of a market economy and a 'return to Europe'. The AFD laid greater stress, however, on individual rights and endorsed a programme of rapid transition to a market economy. By contrast, the HDF espoused a more gradualist approach to the economy and emphasized 'Hungarian' national values.

During the first months of 1990 the HDF defined its policies more exactly. It ceased to be an umbrella movement for disparate groups, united only by their opposition to Communism. Instead, it became a conservative (in the Western European sense of the term) and 'Christian' party. The allies of the HDF were the Christian Democratic People's Party (CDPP) and the Independent Smallholders' Party (ISP), both of which broadly shared the same political outlook as the HDF leadership. The AFD, however, established close links with the anti-Communist youth organization, FYD.

Relations between the HDF and AFD were strained by personal differences. The HDF had evolved under the protection of the reformists in the HSWP; the AFD was led by former dissidents who had suffered harassment at the hands of the old Party apparatus. Moreover, the patriotism espoused by some HDF politicians occasionally gave way to nationalist and anti-Semitic statements. This was resented by the AFD, since a number of its leaders were of Jewish origin. In the election campaign, the posters of both parties were vandalized: those of the AFD in an anti-Semitic fashion, while those of the HDF by associating them with the Communist regime.

The election was held on 25 March 1990. A second round of voting took place on 8 April in those constituencies where no candidate had won an overall majority. Out of 386 seats in the new parliament, 176 were filled by direct

elections in constituencies and 152 from 20 regional party lists. The remaining 58 seats were allocated to parties in accordance with a procedure designed to compensate for the inequities of the 'first-past-the-post' system used in the constituencies.

The HDF obtained 165 seats in the new parliament, the AFD 92, the ISP 43, the HSP 33, and the FYD and CDPP 21 each. Eleven independent and joint party candidates were also elected. The percentages of votes cast in the first round of elections were as follows: HDF 24.7%; AFD 21.4%; ISP 11.8%; HSP 10.9%; FYD 8.9%; CDPP 6.5%; HSWP 3.7%; and others 12.1%. The HDF was the principal beneficiary after the elimination of parties receiving less than 4% of the total votes cast in the first round. The reconstituted HSWP, formed at the end of 1989 by Károly Grósz and János Berecz, was therefore not entitled to any seats in the new legislature.

THE HDF GOVERNMENT

The strength of the HDF vote allowed it to form a ruling coalition with the ISP and the CDPP. This conservative coalition controlled 229 seats in the parliament, giving it a comfortable working majority as far as normal legislation was concerned. The new coalition Government was sworn in on 23 May 1990, under the premiership of Dr József Antall, a historian who had been gaoled for his activities during the Uprising of 1956, and whose father had held high ministerial office between 1939 and 1946. The Foreign Minister was Dr Géza Jeszenszky, another historian, who had cultivated powerful connections in the USA and United Kingdom over the preceding years. Of the 16 other cabinet posts, four were given to the ISP, one to the CDPP and three to 'technocrats', specialists without party affiliation.

According to earlier legislation, a two-thirds majority in parliament was required to alter constitutional laws and to pass the budget. Since the HDF coalition controlled only 59% of the parliamentary seats, the programme of the Government could have been impeded by the opposition. Therefore Antall began discussions with the AFD leadership. The HDF coalition agreed that the AFD spokesman, Árpád Göncz, should be elected acting President of the Republic. In July a national referendum was held to determine the future method of electing the President (whether by direct election or by the National Assembly). However, the result was invalidated as only 14% of the electorate participated, instead of the required minimum of 50%. Consequently, on 3 August 1990 Göncz was elected to a full five-year term; the AFD agreed to restrict the two-thirds majority rule to only the most important constitutional and legislative acts.

The most pressing task facing the new Government was the economic situation, which had not been relieved by the end of Communist rule. On 22 May 1990, Antall presented the Government's programme, the main purpose of which was the creation of a 'social market economy' based on private ownership and enterprise. Antall promised to reduce inflation, then running at an annual rate of between 25% and 30%, to reduce the US $19,500m. foreign debt and to achieve full convertibility for the forint in 1991. Although anticipating some temporary difficulties, Antall envisaged the prospect of an economic growth rate of 3%–4%. Antall's speech was criticized by opposition politicians as implausible and as containing insufficient information on how the promised economic transformation was actually to be achieved. In apparent confirmation of the opposition's charges, the number of unemployed reached 80,000 by the end of the year, the rate of inflation rose above 30%, industrial output declined by 10% and the budget presented in December forecast a record 78,800m.-forint deficit. The forint remained a 'soft currency', with an artificially-high exchange rate. Critics of the HDF-led Government also drew attention to the presence within the bureaucracy of many members of the old Communist nomenklatura. It was argued that this group was deliberately obstructing the process of economic reform.

During the autumn of 1990 the Government parties performed poorly in the municipal elections (held on 30 September and 14 October), taking second place to the AFD–FYD coalition; and in April 1991 the HSP won a parliamentary by-election in Budapest. The Government's confidence was further unsettled by labour unrest. In late October taxi- and lorry-drivers blockaded the centre of Budapest in protest at an increase in petrol prices, and there were suggestions of a general strike. The Government's response was to hasten the pace of privatization and the establishment of a market economy, although its remedies were not as drastic as the so-called 'shock therapy' undertaken in Poland.

The Hungarian transition to democracy was the least violent in all of Eastern Europe. This was mainly because of the contribution made by reforming politicians within the Communist Party. The new democratic parties, among which should be included the HSP, are led by pragmatic politicians who are committed to democracy and eschew dangerous rhetoric. Contrary to reports in the Western press, there is little overt anti-Semitism in Hungary. Those few HDF spokesmen who have made anti-Semitic refer-

ences have been marginalized by the political leadership. In June 1991 the last Soviet troops left Hungary, in accordance with the March 1990 agreement secured by the Communists; Hungary was claiming a sum of 79,000m. forint in compensation for environmental damage caused by the Soviet forces.

Hungarian politicians and people are troubled by the treatment of the ethnic Hungarian minority in Transylvania which, it is claimed, has not improved since the fall of the Ceaușescu Government. Nevertheless, government responses to Romanian policy have not extended to demands for territorial revision. In July 1991 hundreds of ethnic Hungarian schoolchildren and teachers were evacuated from the Serbian autonomous province of Vojvodina, to escape the fighting in Yugoslavia between Serbs and Croats, and by the end of August over 15,000 refugees had entered Hungary. Antall commented at the time that, under the 1920 Treaty of Trianon, Hungarian territory was ceded to Yugoslavia, not to Serbia, and that should the Yugoslav federation break up the situation could be reconsidered.

Given the cohesion of the HDF and its numerical strength in the National Assembly it is likely that the Government will remain in office until the next elections, which are due in 1994. Should the HDF fail to demonstrate that its economic policies have been working, it would then most likely be replaced by a AFD-led coalition.

The Economy
RICHARD ROSS BERRY

INTRODUCTION

The development of the Hungarian economy since the Second World War, focusing as it has on the development of heavy industry, paid little attention to the limits imposed by the country's natural assets. Although up to 70% of Hungary's total area of 93,033 sq km can be used for various agricultural purposes, the country possesses few raw materials in any sizeable quantities. Coal reserves, at 4,500m. metric tons, vary in quality and are often difficult to extract. There are deposits of crude petroleum and natural gas, but imports satisfy the vast bulk of demand for these commodities. However, Hungary does possess up to 12% of the world's total reserves of bauxite. There are also quantities of manganese ore and uranium. In general, the country has a low resource base and has compensated for this by engaging actively in international trade.

At the beginning of the 1990s, in common with the other Eastern European economies, the Hungarian economy was undergoing a profound period of transition to a market economy. In the case of Hungary, however, the adoption of market mechanisms—particularly a reduction in the use of planned indicators and the implementation of a rational price mechanism—took place over a considerable period of time, dating from the promulgation of the New Economic Mechanism (NEM) in 1968.

The erratic progress of the reform of the Hungarian economy throughout the 1970s and 1980s owed as much to political as to economic factors. The deterioration in the country's terms of trade, and continuing balance-of-payments problems, forced reform economics once again on to the agenda. The relative liberalization of the Kádár period and the emergence of Mikhail Gorbachev in the USSR further promoted the cause of reform. However, there were serious political obstacles to the marketization of the

economy, chief among which was the monopoly of power held by the Communist Party. It was clear that the maintenance of this monopoly was a serious obstacle to reform and that further marketization of the economy could only be achieved along with a democratization of the political system. There was, as such, no 'revolution' in Hungary, rather an irrepressible move towards democracy which pre-dated the general period of 'revolutionary' reform in Eastern Europe. However, the latter occurrence certainly accelerated the economic reform process in Hungary.

At the general election held in the spring of 1990 a coalition Government, led by the Hungarian Democratic Forum (HDF), came to power. Relations between the coalition partners have largely determined the pace of economic change. The main issues of the removal of subsidies, the pace and nature of privatization, the level of foreign investment and related questions of property and ownership rights ensured that the first year of the new Government was far from uneventful. Indeed, stormy relations between the HDF and its principal partner, the Independent Smallholders' Party (ISP), have had the effect of slowing down the transformation process. Once again the development of the economy is largely dependent on politics, albeit now in a democratic setting. Low turn-out in recent by-elections and the general apathy of the population present considerable obstacles to the implementation of reform. Regional disputes, such as those between Romania and Hungary and between Slovakia (Czechoslovakia) and Hungary over the issue of the Hungarian ethnic minorities, and the political crisis in Yugoslavia, have serious repercussions for the stability of the region and its economic development.

Since the 1990 general election the economy, or rather its performance, has come to be a prominent feature of

Hungarian life at all levels. The central issues of property rights, privatization, inflation, unemployment and debt have formed the focal points of debate. In the spring of 1991 the Finance Minister, Mihály Kupa, introduced a new four-year economic programme based on the acceleration of privatization, controlling inflation and preparing the groundwork for convertibility of the forint. The programme's aim was to fully integrate Hungary into the world economy on a competitive basis.

However, the scale of the transformation envisaged is enormous; in most OECD countries the state controls or owns enterprises responsible for some 15% of gross domestic product (GDP), while in Hungary the state controlled or owned up to 85% of GDP.

AGRICULTURE

By 1960 Hungarian agriculture was largely collectivized. Up to 90% of farmland and 94% of agricultural workers worked in the socialized sector. In the round of economic reforms in the mid-1960s obligatory targets were removed and, after 1968, co-operative farms became largely autonomous. State farms remained under central control. Prices and subsidies were determined by the government. In 1991 there were over 120 state farms, which cultivated about one-quarter of farmland (2,159,000 hectares) and employed 17% of the 800,000 strong agricultural work-force, while 1,260 co-operatives cultivated about three-quarters of farmland and employed 75% of the agricultural work-force. Most of the co-operative and state farms are heavily indebted to the State, a condition that increased owing to the severe drought of 1990.

In the wake of the Compensation Bill and the fact that an agricultural party, the ISP, forms a part of the governing coalition it was expected that many of the state and co-operative farms would be dismantled. However, the Ministry of Agriculture has proposed that the State should retain control of 20 of the state farms. These 20 cultivate 300,000 ha of farmland out of the total of 8,240,000 ha, and have an annual production value of 100,000m. forint.

Up to two-thirds of the population engage in small-scale agriculture; this includes city dwellers who have weekend plots and the household plots of co-operative workers. Such plots are responsible for up to one-third of agricultural production, including over 50% of pig farming, 75% of vegetables and almost 60% of fruits. In 1990, it was estimated, agriculture and forestry accounted for 20.4% of GDP, and provided the country with 25% of its hard currency exports.

According to the Central Statistical Office, the gross value of agricultural production in 1990 was 6.4% less than in 1989. Total crop production fell by 11.4% and animal husbandry by 1.4%. Soya production fell by 55%, while sugar beet, maize for silage and vegetables fell by 16%, 17% and 12% respectively. Despite a 3% decrease in turnover, earnings from exports of food increased in value by US $200m. compared to 1989, reaching a total of $2,000m. Employment in agriculture fell by 73,000 in 1990 and gross wages increased by 18.4%. The main reasons for the falls in production were severe drought, a fall in domestic demand and a cut-back in rouble exports causing a 30% drop in profitability. Despite the falls in production in some agricultural sectors, domestic supplies are still comfortably met, partly due to falling domestic demand and a reduction in foreign, particularly Soviet, demand.

In 1991 it was likely that Hungary would have 1.5m.–2m. metric tons of surplus wheat, and possibly equal surpluses of maize and barley. Deliveries to the Soviet market have encountered considerable difficulties; there seemed to be little prospect of exporting the hoped for 1.5m.–2m. tons

of wheat, some three-quarters of which were to have been sent to the USSR. Hungarian wheat producers would also encounter difficulties if the Government was to proceed with its planned subsidy review. The world price of wheat of a similar quality to Hungarian wheat is about $70 per metric ton, whereas the producers' price in Hungary is $100, which in turn is supplemented by another 1,000–1,500 forint per ton for exported wheat.

Livestock farming, and particularly pig farming, forms a crucial part of Hungarian agriculture. At the beginning of 1991 farmers had a surplus of 200,000 animals for market. Much of this surplus was accountable to the fall in trade with the USSR. In addition, almost 500m. litres of milk were left unsold in 1990. In 1991 the figure was likely to be in the region of 100m.–200m. litres. Producers are asking for 1,000m. forint to provide for storage for butter and powdered milk. Despite subsidies of over 100m. forint, it was expected that dairy farming would face losses of up to 1,700m. forint during 1991.

In a response to the drought of 1990 the Government was to make loans of 1,000m. forint available to farmers in the form of easy-term loans; these loans have a preferential rate of 22% (compared to the current money-market rate of 32%). The drought of 1990 caused some 28,000m. forint-worth of damage. The latest move comes in addition to 10,000m. forint in the form of preferential loans made in October 1990.

As is the case with many other sectors in the economy, new institutions already familiar to dealers in the West have begun operations in the Hungarian agricultural sector. In the spring of 1991, following negotiations with commodity specialists from Chicago, a meat exchange was established. Pigs and cattle will form the mainstay of trading and the exchange will handle both spot trading and futures. This followed the establishment of a commodity exchange for wheat and maize in August 1989, which had a turnover of 580m. forint in 1990.

According to the Institute of Economic Research and the Ministry of Agriculture, agricultural production was expected to fall by 3.0%–3.5% during 1991. Crop farming was expected to increase slightly, while animal husbandry would decline by some 3.5%. It was estimated that the income of agricultural enterprises would decrease by 7%. It was also expected that there would be a reduction in domestic and foreign demand. Producers' prices were expected to increase by 20%–30%, while inflation was expected to be in the region of 30%–35%. Agricultural input costs were expected to increase by 40%–50%.

The future of many farms will depend on agricultural exports. At present the EC currently accounts for 30% of these and the USSR some 20% The state budget envisages support to the value of 29,000m. forint in 1991 for the export of agricultural produce, though such subsidies may be difficult to maintain. In 1991 overall income from agricultural exports was expected to reach $2,500m.

MINING AND ENERGY

Major restructuring problems are faced by the coal industry. The country's eight colliery enterprises, containing 32 mining units, were expected to incur losses of 2,700m. forint in 1991. In 1991 the debts of the industry amounted to 9,000m. forint. At mid-1991 collieries at Nógrád and Dorog were in danger of imminent closure. In 1990 the country produced 19m. metric tons of coal (principally brown coal), and imported 2.5m. tons. Restructuring is also planned in the aluminium industry. The state aluminium company, MAT, is to be reorganized with a view to privatization. In 1990 the company trust produced 2.3m. metric tons of bauxite, 75,000 metric tons of aluminium ingots and 170,000 metric tons of semi-finished products. In 1990 aluminium-industry exports were valued at US $400m. and imports at only $50m. As is the case with most of the heavy industrial sector, the introduction of hard currency accounting and the rapid fall in trade with the USSR have given rise to considerable fears for the future.

The energy sector accounts for about 20% of total industrial output. Overall energy production fell by 3.9% in 1990, although that of the electrical energy sector rose by 33.8% in the first three months of 1991. Other major sectors undergoing restructuring are the electricity and petroleum industries. As with many industrial sectors, the amounts of money required for the modernization of the Hungarian electricity grid are beyond the available means. As in most of the former CMEA countries there is considerable waste; Hungary inputs about 2.5 times the OECD countries' average number of energy units per unit of production. Energy efficiency has become a major concern for the Government. Some help has been forthcoming from the UN Economic Commission for Europe (see p. 38), which has launched an 'Energy Efficiency Project' and made available a sum of $3.5–$5.5m. Most of the electricity grid remains orientated to the east, with the USSR being a major supplier. At present the country does not have the infrastructural capacity to accept supplementary electricity from Western European countries.

Similar problems are faced in the petroleum industry. Hungary needs to import some two-thirds of its petroleum requirements. In the period 1988–90 crude petroleum production fell from 2m. metric tons to 1.8m. tons. In 1989 the Soviet Union supplied 90% of crude imports, amounting to 7.7m. tons, a figure which fell to 5m. tons in 1990. Securing petroleum supplies from the USSR, which have previously been sold at concessionary rates, will be a major problem in the future. Meanwhile the domestic industry is to be reorganized. The National Oil and Gas Trust, which is responsible for all petroleum and gas production, was to be privatized in a move which would result in a reduction in the work-force from 46,000 to 18,000. Some 50% of the industry was to remain in state hands.

INDUSTRY

The central task of restructuring and privatizing Hungary's industrial base is extremely complex, particularly in the case of the larger heavy industries. It is difficult to make comparisons with privatization in other countries, particularly the United Kingdom, where 'high-tech' profitable industries, amounting to no more than 8% of GDP, were privatized over the course of a decade. Should privatization take place at the same pace in Hungary it would take almost 100 years to arrive at a similar position. In addition, many of the Hungarian plants are in the non-profitable heavy industrial sector and exist on the basis of state subsidies. Thus while the process of transformation may resemble that in the West, the sheer scale of the task has to be taken into consideration. The crisis nature of the transformation process is shown by the fact that, in the course of 1990, GDP in real terms fell by about 5%. Reports of the Central Statistical Office show that, in 1990, output of the principal industries fell by 10%. Manufacturing output, which accounts for nearly two-thirds of industrial production, fell by 8.4%.

The removal of subsidies from uneconomic enterprises is a central, yet controversial point in the Government's programme. It was hoped to cut subsidies from the 1990 level of 115,000m. forint to 101,000m. forint in 1991. Within the budget the level of subsidies remains controversial; by the end of April 1991 retail price subsidies amounted to 42.2% of the planned level of 31,300m. forint for the entire year, and direct state support to enterprises amounted to 8,700m. forint, some 28.5% of the 30,500m. forint planned for 1991. The withdrawal of the level of such subsidies depends on the acceptability of the social consequences of such an action: the price rises, closures and unemployment entailed by this could well result in the moderation of the programme.

The transformation process is complicated by the fact that there are known to be splits not only within the coalition, but also between ministers of the leading party, the HDF. Some ministers favour the 'shock therapy' method of transformation (as employed in Poland) and others, fearing the social consequences of such a move, opt for a more cautious social market approach.

The role of the State in the privatization process remains controversial. The Government has produced a list which states that certain enterprises and industries will remain in majority state control. In some cases, such as broadcasting and the state railways, this merely follows the pattern of many Western European countries. However, in the case of many enterprises, such as the Ikarus bus company and the Csepel automotive works, the Government will promote a restructuring and rationalization plan, designed to avoid making too many workers unemployed. The steel plants at Dunaújváros and Salgótarján are undergoing restructuring and, like many other Hungarian industries, have sought foreign partners in the pursuit of modernization. The declared policy that 50% of the economy will be privatized by 1994 is a mammoth undertaking.

In the course of 1990 some 10% of the total valuation of state property, which was valued at 1,800,000m. forint, was actually privatized, much of it with the help of foreign capital. The largest privatization of this kind took place in March 1991 between the French firm Sanofi, part of the multinational Elf Aquitaine group, and Chinoin, the leading Hungarian pharmaceutical company. The French firm took a 40% stake in the new joint venture at a cost of US $75m. This involvement of foreign capital has become highly controversial and the Government is sensitive to the charge of selling out to foreigners.

Despite the fall in industrial production, in the first two months of 1991 actual sales, totalling 217,000m. forint, were 17,800m. less than the value of output. The accumulation of stocks was most noticeable in the engineering industry, where the value of stocks rose by 5,700m. forint. In the iron and steel industry the value of stocks rose by 1,300m. forint.

The trends of 1990 were repeated in the early part of 1991. In the first three months of 1991 industrial production fell by 8.7% in comparison to the same period in 1990. Output of the building-materials industry fell by almost 30%, and there was some decline in the machine engineering and in the light and food-processing industries. However, the production of the chemical industry rose by 15%.

The downturn in the economy has resulted in the curbing of consumer purchasing power. The 10% fall in production by light industry, in 1990, is clear proof of this. Clothing accounts for 60% of the total production of light industry, but spending on clothing accounted for 5.4% of total national consumption in 1990 compared to 7.8% in 1985. In 1990 sales of clothing fell by 18.5%. Total retail turnover fell in terms of volume by 15.2% in 1990, and was valued at 888,700m. forint. Retail food trade declined by 16.2%. Wholesale trade decreased in value by 0.6% to 299,000m. forint in 1990. Profitability as a whole fell by some 22% in 1990, though there was considerable variation within this; the profitability of financial institutes rose by 30% while that of the production and service sectors fell by 12.4%.

In the course of 1990 there was some growth in the furniture and paper industries, and 300 new companies began operating in the light-industrial sector. Small businesses (those employing less than 50 people) increased in number throughout 1990, rising from 1,913 at the beginning of the year to 4,843 by the end. In general, these businesses are in the services sector and employ an average of 16 people; up to two-thirds of them enjoy trading rights. However, these new businesses employ a relatively small number of people. After the 1988 Associations Act there has been a rapid increase in the number of organizations regarded as companies; in the course of 1990 these doubled to more than 28,000. A company is defined as any venture using double entry bookkeeping with sales of more than 25m. forint a year. However, some 85% of Hungary's value added was produced by companies employing only 20% of all employees.

The rise in environmental problems is directly associated with the pace and nature of Hungarian economic development. The country is characterized by high sulphur-dioxide emissions and high levels of hazardous waste, and consequently by polluted air and water supplies. Many towns have poor sewage facilities. The resolution of such problems has become a highly charged political question.

SERVICES

There has been some retail privatization, although this too has been rather slow moving. Out of the 10,000 outlets, mainly shops and restaurants, only some 100 were sold in the first round of privatization. This was partly owing to the inability to establish ownership and also to the fact that the population as a whole lacks the surplus cash necessary to purchase the outlets. Savings amount to 4% of income as opposed to 10% in the United Kingdom.

The liberalization in Eastern Europe has greatly enhanced the prospects of the tourism industry in the region. The steady improvement in the number of tourists visiting Hungary during the late 1980s accelerated during 1990, to reach a total of 38m. Tourism generated total income of US $2,000m., equivalent to about 10% of GDP.

EMPLOYMENT AND UNEMPLOYMENT

Throughout its recent history the Hungarian economy has been characterized by rapid and concentrated industrial development. In the early 1990s Hungary had 6,889 industrial enterprises, 770 of which had a work-force of over 300. The fall in the production of the large-scale enterprises has entailed a fall in the number of employees. In 1990 industrial organizations employed 1,212,000, some 117,000 down on 1989; this fall was following a gradual decline during the late 1980s. In the basic materials sector the work-force decreased by 12.9% in 1990, mainly owing to a 19% fall in employment in the iron and steel industry. Overall, some 4.8m. of the 10.4m. Hungarian citizens were economically active in 1990, with many having secondary employment.

In January 1991 unemployment stood at 103,278, about 2.2% of the work-force. The rate of unemployment was greatest among unskilled workers, at 6.2%, followed by a 1.5% rate among skilled and qualified workers, while white-collar staff had an unemployment rate of only 1.1%. Widespread unemployment is expected to occur among white-collar workers, however, as the overmanned bureaucracy is rationalized. At the end of 1990 the gross monthly unemployment benefit was 5,886 forint.

Unemployment seemed likely to continue its rise during the course of 1991. The scale of this rise was difficult to predict, although government estimates pointed to a total of at least 300,000. Provisions made in the budget and in the Solidarity Fund—a fund set up to help manage the social effects of unemployment—were clearly insufficient and were certain to require augmentation.

FOREIGN TRADE

Financing

One of the Government's declared aims is that of currency convertibility, though this will rely largely on the state of the economy and access to 'hard' currency sources. A three-year stabilization plan with the IMF will provide some support in this direction. In 1981 a unified exchange rate was introduced and limited convertibility became possible. In addition, the forint was adjusted on a daily basis against a basket of currencies. At present the forint is internally convertible, though the Government is hopeful that full convertibility can be achieved by 1994.

Volume and Direction of Trade

In 1990 Hungary had a hard currency surplus of US $945m., despite having to face an unexpected $400m. bill for petroleum imports, owing largely to the shortfall in supply from the USSR. In addition, the Gulf War resulted in the loss of $500m. worth of exports. Despite this success there has been considerable anxiety about the continuing collapse in Soviet–Hungarian trade, which will be reflected in the the trade figures for 1991. According to the Ministry of International Economic Relations, the export of goods represents some 40% of GDP, tourism 10% and other foreign trade and services a further 1%-2%. Thus the contribution of the external economy to GDP is over 50%.

The most significant aspect in the area of trade has been the demise of the Council for Mutual Economic Assistance (CMEA), and, in particular, the decline in trade between Hungary and the USSR. In reality the CMEA was a largely captive market, producing low-quality goods which could not command a price on the world market. On 1 January 1991 the countries of the CMEA moved over to a system of hard-currency trading, though some calculations in the convertible rouble, the former clearing currency, remained, at least for the first part of 1991. The decline of the CMEA was formalized, during 1991, with the agreement by the member-countries to dissolve the organization.

The domestic difficulties of the Soviet economy and the shortage of hard-currency trading have given rise to a sharp contraction of trade between the Eastern European economies. The petrochemical, iron and steel industries, as well as machine construction and textiles, in this region previously relied on the Soviet market.

It is estimated that Soviet debts to Hungary amount to 2,200m. roubles, and negotiations over these have led to acrimonious debate between the two countries. By mid-1991 few letters of credit had been opened, and stocks of Hungarian enterprises, formerly dependent on Soviet trade, continued to rise. Despite the signing of a trade agreement between the USSR and Hungary, which envisaged a trade turnover of $3,800m. for the whole of 1991, the actual figure was likely to be much less. In June 1991 a trade agreement was signed between the Russian Republic and Hungary, which envisaged an exchange of goods worth $670m. A similar deal was planned with Ukraine. However, the fulfilment of these agreements will depend on the internal situation in the former USSR.

In 1990 the proportion of total Hungarian exports going to the other European countries of the CMEA (including the USSR and the former GDR) fell from 41% in 1989 to 31%, while the share of European CMEA imports decreased from 39% to 34%. At the same time the share of exports to the European Communities (EC) rose to 35% from 27%, while the proportion of imports from the EC rose from

29% to 33%. Exports to EFTA countries rose by about 20%, to reach a total value of $1,777m., while imports from these countries reached a total value of $2,044m., a rise of 27%.

In 1990 the united Germany replaced the USSR as the most important single trading partner. In the course of the year the USSR's share of Hungarian trade declined to 20% (compared to 24% in 1989), while that of the united Germany (or the two German polities together) rose from 20% to 22%.

Trade Organization and Barriers to Trade

In 1988 the Hungarian Government ended its monopoly on foreign trade, although certain restrictions remain, either as a way of protecting certain sectors of the economy or as a means of protecting the balance of payments. However, there has been steady progress towards integration into the world economy. The integration of the Hungarian economy into the modern international economic order began with membership of the GATT (1973) and the IMF (1982).

At the beginning of 1990 the Government implemented changes in the system of tariffs and customs duties. Customs duties on many items were reduced from 16% to 8%. This affected mainly industrial production equipment and accessories. Duties on custom-car parts were reduced from 60% to 10%, while the duty on other electrical items was also significantly reduced. However, the duty on passenger cars was increased, from 10% to 18%. In addition a sales or value added tax (VAT) of 25% is applied.

The Hungarian Government has undertaken such measures with a view to future membership of the EC. Many joint-venture partners who had hoped that Hungarian tariff barriers would act as a protection were disappointed. Further reductions of the system of tariffs and duties will depend on reciprocal arrangements with other countries. Access to many markets remained blocked.

As is the case with Poland and Czechoslovakia, Hungary has been seeking closer co-operation with the EC. A trade and co-operation agreement was signed in June 1988 and, in mid-1991, negotiations took place on the implementation of a free-trade agreement, which, if successful, was to take effect from 1 January 1992. However, there were still considerable tariffs on steel, textiles and agricultural products—three of the most important sectors within the Hungarian economy. Despite attempts by the Hungarians, it is thought unlikely that Hungary will be eligible for EC membership in the short term, and privately EC officials are looking more towards the year 2000. In September 1991 several EC member-countries, including France and Germany, refused to consider allowing ready access to EC markets of Eastern European agricultural goods in particular.

EC aid for the central European countries is available through the PHARE programme, which envisages aid for training, development and the adoption of new technologies.

FINANCE

The Government is determined to pursue a reform course and to this extent has enlisted the help of the IMF. Some US $1,500m. has been allocated by the IMF over a three-year period, much of which is conditional. The overall condition is that the Government must adhere to its economic reform programme. More specific conditions are attached, the most important of which is that the Government must keep to specific financial targets, particularly in respect of the state budget deficit. It has been agreed that the deficit for 1991 should not exceed 78,000m. forint, an agreement which has resulted in across-the-board cuts in expenditure of 12%. The Government had considerable difficulty in persuading parliament to accept such a course. By the end of April 1991 the budget deficit amounted to 22,000m. forint, some 28.2% of the agreed level for the whole year.

Inflation

The problems facing the Government have been compounded by the high level of inflation, which was 30% in 1990 and was expected to rise to 35% in 1991. Prices of essential consumer goods and services, such as food, transport, clothing and consumer durables, housing and lighting were some 30.4% higher than in 1989 and 83.1% higher than in 1987. This has led to clashes with the trade unions. A general strike was only narrowly averted in June 1991 and further unrest was likely in the course of the following few years. The Government instituted central wage regulation in a bid to control inflation. This will affect about 70%–75% of the work-force of over 4m. and almost half of all companies. According to the Central Statistical Office, real wages in the early 1990s were at the same level as in the early 1970s.

Debt

Hungary had a gross debt of $21,270m., in 1990, most of which was contracted under the Communist regime. The repayments on this debt, which currently account for 40% of export revenues, is a considerable source of controversy. This debate intensified in the early part of 1991 following the cancellation of some 50% of the Polish debt of $48,000m. Almost 75% of Hungarian debt is owed to Western commercial banks rather than to governments. It has been suggested that some of the debt could be converted into shares in the course of privatization.

Foreign Investment

After being relatively isolated from many sectors of the world economy, Hungary has sought to accelerate its development by encouraging foreign investment. Considerable tax incentives are available for potential investors. Despite the fact that the Government will retain control over 'strategic industries', in particular certain defence plants, and also over some of the larger public companies (mainly for the purpose of avoiding mass unemployment), foreign investors will be able to invest in the principal sectors of the economy and in many cases will be able to acquire majority control. In the short term the aluminium and pharmaceutical industries will remain under state control, as will some of the larger engineering firms such as Raba, Csepel Auto and Ikarus. The pace of foreign investment will depend on the political agenda, as the Government is sensitive to charges of selling off the country to foreigners.

Liberalization of foreign investment legislation, resulting in the abolition of special licences for joint ventures, and the introduction of limited convertibility, has meant that joint ventures can now use forint to pay for imports. At the end of 1990 some 93,000m. forint ($1,250m.) of foreign capital was invested in joint ventures. This was invested in 5,700 joint ventures, with a total initial capital of 274,000m. forint. The average foreign capital holding was 34%. There were 1,526 joint ventures in industry, including 691 in engineering and 130 in the food industries. In addition, there were 518 in construction, 78 in agriculture, 130 in transport and 1,661 in 'home trade'—mainly service and tourist facilities.

CONCLUSION

Amidst this rather gloomy picture there were some optimistic developments. There has been significant modernization in many areas. After an absence of more than 40 years a stock exchange began operations in May 1990. Though small, initially comprising only a 90-minute trading session under a rather old-fashioned outcry system, and working on an index based on the six leading companies, there were plans to increase the scope of operations and to install a computerized trading system. Hungary was the first socialist (Communist) country to introduce Western-style personal income and value added taxes. A new accounting law, based on Western standards, was to take effect from 1 January 1992. A new bankruptcy law was presented to the National Assembly in mid-1991, replacing the 1986 law, which was flawed and not widely applied. The question remained as to how far this law was to be applied to the large number of uneconomic enterprises and at what pace.

In 1987 a new two-tier banking system was introduced. While the Hungarian National Bank continued to be the main central bank and the bank of issue, it was deprived of its commercial-bank functions. This led to the growth of a healthy commercial-bank sector, much in advance of that in neighbouring countries. Initially, international operations of the banks were still controlled, though this was also reformed and many banks engaged in trade-related activities. Further development of international activities rested on the proposed convertibility of the forint.

In addition, Hungary was taking a more active part in international negotiations, such as those held under the auspices of GATT and the IMF. Plans were being made to have the 1995 EXPO international exhibition in Budapest, and Hungary was also playing an active role in the European Bank for Reconstruction and Development (EBRD—p. 39). However, as is agreed by most observers, the domestic sources of transformation were the most vital.

It was expected that GDP could fall by as much as 5%–6% during 1991. Another 10% fall in industrial production was also expected, although this could be much more should trade with the former USSR fall drastically. Unemployment reached 218,000 by the end of July 1991; the Government expected the total to rise to 300,000 by the end of the year, although OECD economists were predicting a figure of 400,000, or 8% of the total work-force. Inflation was expected to remain at about 30%, while investment would fall overall by 10%, although in many sectors the decrease could be as much as 50%. The number of small businesses was expected to continue to rise, and the Government was hopeful of continuing foreign investment. However, the funds available for small businesses were to be curtailed by a tight monetary policy.

Since such a transformation of the economy has never been attempted previously, it is difficult to state accurately the nature of the transformation process. It can be said, without fear of contradiction, that the early 1990s will be both difficult and crucial for the Hungarian economy. Continuing participation in international trade is vital if the Hungarian economy is to develop. In the 1980s the export of agricultural products allowed the country to import Western technology. Further expansion in this area would depend on the restructuring of agriculture and the removal of subsidies. Considerable barriers, particularly the common agricultural policy of the EC, hamper the further development of agricultural trade. Many Hungarian industrial products are not competitive on the world market and, without mass restructuring, faced an uncertain future. Some restructuring was possible with the aid of foreign capital. In respect of trade financing, the institution of a convertible currency will promote international trade. Hungary's major asset is its position at the heart of Europe. When it joins the EC, trade will play an even more central role in the continuing modernization of the economy.

Statistical Survey

Source (unless otherwise stated): Központi Statisztikai Hivatal (Hungarian Central Statistical Office), 1525 Budapest, Keleti Károly u. 5–7; tel. (1) 202-4011; telex 22-4308.

Area and Population

AREA, POPULATION AND DENSITY

Area (sq km)	93,033*
Population (census results)	
1 January 1980	10,709,463
1 January 1990 (provisional)	
Males	4,987,300
Females	5,388,000
Total	10,375,300
Population (official estimates at 1 January)	
1988	10,604,400
1989	10,588,600
1990	10,375,300
Density (per sq km) at 1 January 1990	111.5

* 35,920 sq miles.

Languages (1980 census): Magyar (Hungarian) 98.8%; German 0.3%; Slovak 0.1%; Romany 0.3%; Croatian 0.2%; Romanian 0.1%.

ADMINISTRATIVE DIVISIONS (1 January 1990)

	Area (sq km)	Resident Popu- lation ('000)	Density (per sq km)	County Town (with population)
Counties:				
Baranya . .	4,487	419	93	Pécs (170,119)
Bács-Kiskun .	8,362	545	65	Kecskemét (102,528)
Békés .	5,632	412	73	Békéscsaba (67,621)
Borsod-Abaúj-Zemplén .	7,247	762	105	Miskolc (196,449)
Csongrád .	4,263	439	103	Szeged (175,338)
Fejér .	4,373	421	96	Székesfehérvár (108,990)
Győr-Moson-Sopron .	4,012	425	106	Győr (129,356)
Hajdú-Bihar .	6,211	549	88	Debrecen (212,247)
Heves .	3,637	335	92	Eger (61,908)
Jász-Nagykun-Szolnok .	5,607	426	76	Szolnok (78,333)
Komárom-Esztergom .	2,251	315	140	Tatabánya (74,271)
Nógrád .	2,544	227	89	Salgótarján (47,826)
Pest . .	6,394	950	149	Budapest* (2,016,132)
Somogy .	6,036	345	57	Kaposvár (71,793)
Szabolcs-Szatmár .	5,938	572	96	Nyíregyháza (114,166)
Tolna .	3,704	254	69	Szekszárd (36,865)
Vas . .	3,337	276	83	Szombathely (85,418)
Veszprém .	4,689	382	81	Veszprém (63,902)
Zala .	3,784	307	81	Zalaegerszeg (62,221)
Capital City				
Budapest* .	525	2,016	3,840	—
Total . .	93,033	10,375	112	—

* Budapest has separate County status. The area and population of the city are not included in the larger County (Pest) which it administers.

PRINCIPAL TOWNS (population at 1 January 1990)

Budapest (capital)	2,016,132	Nyíregyháza . . .	114,166
Debrecen. . . .	212,247	Székesfehérvár .	108,990
Miskolc . . .	196,449	Kecskemét . .	102,528
Szeged . . .	175,338	Szombathely . .	85,418
Pécs	170,119	Szolnok . . .	78,333
Győr	129,356	Tatabánya . . .	74,271

BIRTHS, MARRIAGES AND DEATHS

	Registered live births		Registered marriages		Registered deaths	
	Number	Rate (per 1,000)	Number	Rate (per 1,000)	Number	Rate (per 1,000)
1983 . .	127,258	11.9	75,969	7.1	148,643	13.9
1984 . .	125,359	11.8	74,951	7.0	146,709	13.8
1985 . .	130,200	12.2	73,238	6.9	147,614	13.9
1986 . .	128,204	12.1	72,434	6.8	147,089	13.8
1987 . .	125,840	11.9	66,082	6.2	142,601	13.4
1988 . .	124,296	11.7	65,907	6.2	140,042	13.2
1989 . .	123,304	11.7	66,949	6.3	144,695	13.7
1990 . .	122,251	11.8	66,304	6.4	141,791	13.7

ECONOMICALLY ACTIVE POPULATION*
('000 persons aged 15 years and over at January each year)

	1987	1988	1989
Agriculture and forestry . .	942.7	911.5	887.8
Manufacturing, mining, electricity and water. . .	1,605.4	1,576.8	1,543.9
Construction	341.5	345.4	339.3
Commerce	514.2	519.7	519.3
Transport and communications.	404.3	400.0	400.3
Services (incl. gas and sanitary services).	1,077.1	1,091.4	1,132.1
Total	4,885.2	4,844.8	4,822.7
Males	2,637.2	2,624.0	2,607.4
Females	2,248.0	2,220.8	2,215.3

* Excluding persons seeking work for the first time.

Agriculture

PRINCIPAL CROPS ('000 metric tons)

	1987	1988	1989
Wheat	5,748	7,026	6,540
Rice (paddy)	40	47	28
Barley	794	1,183	1,340
Maize	7,234	6,256	6,996
Rye	186	255	267
Oats	99	138	149
Potatoes	1,077	1,407	1,332
Pulses	272	386	433
Sunflower seed . . .	803	716	699
Rapeseed	108	82	98
Sugar beet. . . .	4,258	4,511	5,301
Grapes	512	736	580
Apples	1,064	1,131	959
Tobacco (leaves) . . .	20	16	15

LIVESTOCK ('000 head at December each year)

	1987	1988	1989
Cattle	1,664	1,690	1,598
Pigs	8,216	8,327	7,660
Sheep	2,336	2,216	2,069
Goats	16	16	n.a.
Horses	88	76	75
Chickens	61,069	56,943	52,821
Ducks	1,906	2,005	1,868
Geese	1,109	1,519	2,125
Turkeys	1,076	1,361	1,750

LIVESTOCK PRODUCTS (metric tons)

	1987	1988	1989
Beef and veal	129,000	110,000	120,000*
Mutton and lamb	5,000	5,000	4,000†
Pig meat	1,037,000	1,022,000	1,010,000†
Poultry meat	463,000	478,000	430,000†
Edible offal	50,000	49,000	47,000
Lard	209,000*	204,000*	n.a.
Cows' milk	2,816,000	2,873,000	2,812,000†
Sheep's milk	8,000	8,000	8,000*
Goats' milk	3,000	3,000	3,000*
Butter	32,788	34,924	37,909
Cheese	91,605	90,657	86,487
Hen eggs	235,376	254,703	236,300†
Honey	15,170	14,400	16,000*
Wool:			
greasy	10,050	9,631	9,000†
clean	4,146	4,027	3,000†
Cattle hides	13,267	9,908	11,000*

* FAO estimate.   † Unofficial figure.

Source: mainly FAO, *Production Yearbook*.

Forestry

ROUNDWOOD REMOVALS ('000 cu metres)

	1987	1988	1989
Industrial wood	3,731	3,581	3,740
Fuel wood	2,936	2,820	2,738
Total	6,667	6,401	6,478

SAWNWOOD PRODUCTION ('000 cu metres)

	1987	1988	1989
Coniferous (soft wood)	361	354	313
Broadleaved (hard wood)	329	335	350
Total	690	689	663

Fishing

(metric tons, live weight)

	1987	1988	1989
Total catch	36,759	38,294	37,517

Mining

('000 metric tons, unless otherwise indicated)

	1988	1989	1990
Hard coal	2,255	2,127	1,736
Brown coal	12,986	12,020	10,373
Lignite	5,634	5,883	5,469
Crude petroleum	1,947	1,966	1,974
Bauxite	2,593	2,644	2,559
Natural gas (million cu metres)	6,272	6,176	4,950

Industry

SELECTED PRODUCTS
('000 metric tons, unless otherwise indicated)

	1988	1989	1990
Pig iron	2,093	1,954	1,693
Crude steel	3,583	3,356	2,809
Rolled steel	2,793	2,539	2,164
Aluminium	74.7	75.2	75.2
Cement	3,873	3,857	3,939
Nitrogenous fertilizers*	574.1	580.8	n.a.
Phosphatic fertilizers†	237.9	215.1	n.a.
Refined sugar	421.5	508.4	505.7
Buses (number)	12,350	11,980	7,949
Cotton fabrics ('000 sq metres)	311,602	262,726	n.a.
Leather footwear ('000 pairs)	35,683	29,528	n.a.
Electric power (million kWh)	29,183	29,580	28,331
Woollen cloth ('000 sq metres)	28,649	32,275	n.a.
Television receivers ('000)	433	502	428
Radio receivers ('000)	129	124	65

* Production in terms of nitrogen.
† Production in terms of phosphoric acid.

Finance

CURRENCY AND EXCHANGE RATES
Monetary Units
    100 fillér = 1 forint.

Denominations
    Coins: 10, 20 and 50 fillér; 1, 2, 5, 10 and 20 forint.
    Notes: 20, 50, 100, 500 and 1,000 forint.

Sterling and Dollar Equivalents (30 June 1991)
    £1 sterling = 125.67 forint;
    US $1 = 77.62 forint;
    1,000 forint = £7.957 = $12.883.

Average Exchange Rate (forint per US dollar)
    1988   50.413
    1989   59.066
    1990   63.206

STATE BUDGET ('000 million forint)

Revenue	1987	1988	1989
Payments made by enterprises (co-operatives) and agricultural co-operatives	469.4	423.6	443.2
Consumers' turnover tax	122.3	210.5	230.7
Payments made by the population	79.3	154.7	209.4
Payments made by organizations financed by state budget	63.7	80.9	138.8
Other receipts	25.9	28.5	41.6
Total revenue	760.6	898.2	1,063.7

Expenditure	1987	1988	1989
Investment	99.9	108.0	115.5
Industrial enterprises (co-operatives) and agricultural co-operatives	150.7	143.8	115.7
Supplement to consumers' prices	66.7	44.5	44.1
Budgetary institutions . .	242.7	304.4	386.5
Health and social welfare .	42.2	55.1	74.7
Culture	73.5	93.0	127.6
Defence	45.4	59.0	62.0
Legal and security order .	3.2	4.6	6.3
Administration . . .	10.5	15.9	23.0
Economic tasks . . .	54.5	64.3	71.2
Others	13.4	12.5	21.7
Social security . . .	154.7	216.6	269.5
Others	80.3	91.1	181.1
Total expenditure . . .	795.0	908.4	1,112.4

1991 (forecasts, '000 million forint): Revenue 852.9; Expenditure 931.7.

INTERNATIONAL RESERVES (US $ million at 31 December)

	1988	1989	1990
Gold*	510	479	97
Foreign exchange . . .	1,467	1,246	1,069
Total	1,977	1,725	1,166

* National valuation.
Source: IMF, *International Financial Statistics*.

MONEY SUPPLY (million forint at 31 December)

	1988	1989	1990
Currency outside banks . .	164,500	180,600	209,800
Demand deposits at commercial and savings banks	129,500	165,800	225,400

Source: IMF, *International Financial Statistics*.

COST OF LIVING (Consumer Price Index; base: 1980 = 100)

	1988	1989	1990
Food	175.0	206.0	278.5
Fuel and light	181.5	202.2	258.0
Clothing	210.7	249.0	307.0
Rent	247.2	264.5	n.a.
All items (incl. others) . .	183.8	215.0	277.1

NATIONAL ACCOUNTS (million forint at current prices)
Expenditure on the Gross Domestic Product

	1987	1988	1989*
Government final consumption expenditure	239,078	289,989	362,650
Private final consumption expenditure	665,723	721,924	840,050
Increase in stocks . . .	23,947	63,375	100,200
Gross fixed capital formation	303,537	295,572	345,000
Total domestic expenditure	1,232,285	1,370,860	1,647,900
Exports of goods and services .	464,391	530,395	621,600
Less Imports of goods and services	470,306	491,738	563,500
GDP in purchasers' values	1,226,370	1,409,517	1,706,000
GDP at constant 1981 prices .	865,726	865,161	863,500

* Figures are provisional.

Gross Domestic Product by Economic Activity

	1986	1987	1988
Agriculture, hunting, forestry and fishing*	182,569	189,222	209,454
Mining and quarrying . .	56,512	56,360	55,446
Manufacturing and gas. . .	275,451	308,902	327,184
Electricity and water* . .	44,750	54,293	64,501
Construction	78,966	92,233	96,775
Trade, restaurants and hotels .	107,977	128,107	125,857
Transport, storage and communications . . .	86,250	94,425	101,170
Finance, insurance, real estate and business services†	59,926	70,275	86,511
Government services (incl. non-profit institutions) . . .	96,538	107,092	131,957
Other community and social services†	8,280	9,430	15,220
Sub-total	997,219	1,110,339	1,214,075
Net taxes on commodities .	79,297	100,826	177,406
Statistical discrepancy‡ . .	12,284	15,205	18,036
Total	1,088,800	1,226,370	1,409,517

* The operation of irrigation systems is included in agriculture and excluded from water. Agriculture also includes veterinary services.
† Sanitary and similar services and personal and household services are included in business services and excluded from community and social services.
‡ This item refers to the difference between subsistence production, valued at approximate basic values, and final consumption of goods from subsistence production, valued at consumer prices.

BALANCE OF PAYMENTS (US $ million)

	1987	1988	1989
Merchandise exports f.o.b. . .	9,967	9,989	10,492
Merchandise imports f.o.b. . .	−9,887	−9,406	−9,449
Trade balance	80	583	1,043
Services (net)	166	−180	−352
Other income received . . .	247	240	232
Other income paid . . .	−1,274	−1,332	−1,625
Private unrequited transfers (net)	105	117	130
Current balance . . .	−676	−572	−571
Capital (net)	239	668	1,134
Net errors and omissions . .	—	—	−2
Overall balance	−437	96	561

Source: IMF, *International Financial Statistics*.

External Trade

PRINCIPAL COMMODITIES
(distribution by SITC, million forint)

Imports c.i.f.	1987	1988	1989
Food and live animals . .	27,535	29,650	32,259
Coffee, tea, cocoa and spices .	7,266	7,300	5,414
Animal feeding-stuff (excl. cereals)	9,355	13,564	15,518
Crude materials (inedible) except fuels .	28,966	32,154	33,201
Cork and wood. . . .	4,858	5,604	5,928
Textile fibres and waste . .	6,235	7,824	7,337
Mineral fuels, lubricants, etc.	70,346	62,804	61,525
Coal, coke and briquettes . .	7,085	7,513	8,229
Petroleum, petroleum products, etc.	38,557	32,150	28,651
Gas (natural and manufactured)	15,184	13,685	14,449

Imports c.i.f.—*continued*	1987	1988	1989
Chemicals and related products.	67,238	74,808	85,075
Organic chemicals	10,766	11,926	14,472
Inorganic chemicals	10,218	11,357	10,977
Artificial resins and plastic materials, etc.	9,995	10,830	12,064
Basic manufactures	73,866	79,355	91,815
Paper, paperboard and manufactures	8,365	8,975	10,888
Textile yarn, fabrics, etc.	15,228	15,474	16,965
Iron and steel	13,742	14,516	17,113
Non-ferrous metals	12,741	14,432	15,591
Other metal manufactures	7,571	8,561	10,792
Machinery and transport equipment	139,769	142,826	175,008
Machinery specialized for particular industries	37,703	35,163	40,797
Metalworking machinery	8,009	7,736	9,797
Road vehicles and parts (excl. tyres, engines and electrical parts)	31,084	31,254	34,514
Miscellaneous manufactured articles	29,415	28,915	36,343
Total (incl. others)	443,956	460,894	523,507

Exports f.o.b.	1987	1988	1989
Food and live animals	70,839	86,625	105,976
Live animals	8,184	10,260	12,618
Meat and meat preparations	25,956	30,318	36,203
Cereals and cereal preparations	9,276	14,680	16,037
Vegetables and fruit	20,300	22,830	27,206
Beverages and tobacco	6,907	6,129	7,650
Crude materials (inedible) except fuels	16,740	20,631	23,663
Mineral fuels, lubricants, etc.	11,028	13,012	16,384
Petroleum, petroleum products, etc.	10,219	11,902	15,036
Chemicals and related products.	49,506	59,136	70,615
Organic chemicals	8,508	9,885	11,580
Medicinal and pharmaceutical products	19,421	20,357	24,639
Basic manufactures	60,417	76,013	97,281
Textile yarn, fabrics, etc.	13,263	14,408	15,729
Iron and steel	14,369	19,865	26,719
Non-ferrous metals	9,999	14,548	20,955
Machinery and transport equipment	151,214	161,347	172,775
Machinery specialized for particular industries	30,917	32,189	33,854
Telecommunications and sound equipment	22,237	23,675	22,075
Other electrical machinery, apparatus, etc.	19,604	22,160	27,671
Road vehicles and parts (excl. tyres, engines and electrical parts)	45,502	45,662	44,734
Miscellaneous manufactured articles	53,959	55,310	60,148
Clothing and accessories (excl. footwear)	17,571	20,028	20,484
Footwear	7,446	6,468	7,020
Professional, scientific and controlling instruments and apparatus	14,356	13,266	13,880
Total (incl. others)	432,609	492,326	571,323

PRINCIPAL TRADING PARTNERS (million forint)*

Imports c.i.f.	1988	1989	1990
Algeria	n.a.	n.a.	10,076
Austria	33,785	44,977	54,233
Belgium and Luxembourg	6,950	8,520	9,243
Brazil	8,179	6,890	8,854
Bulgaria	6,423	4,530	4,197
China, People's Republic	7,829	5,474	3,089
Czechoslovakia	23,695	26,966	25,383
Finland	3,786	4,021	3,642
France	9,323	11,517	11,204
German Democratic Republic	29,553	32,518	32,321
Germany, Federal Republic	64,893	83,917	94,802
Italy	14,518	17,688	22,080
Japan	6,838	8,409	11,429
Netherlands	8,252	10,752	11,414
Poland	19,194	17,222	13,028
Romania	8,189	8,501	4,883
Sweden	6,922	6,915	8,106
Switzerland and Liechtenstein	11,836	15,328	16,767
USSR	115,962	115,513	103,889
United Kingdom	8,494	11,560	11,548
USA	9,858	13,232	14,407
Yugoslavia	13,754	18,222	12,260
Total (incl. others)	460,894	523,507	544,921

Exports f.o.b.	1988	1989	1990
Algeria	3,133	2,309	2,064
Austria	28,202	37,109	45,273
Belgium and Luxembourg	3,982	4,984	6,988
Bulgaria	6,300	4,167	1,822
China, People's Republic	9,256	6,981	5,170
Czechoslovakia	27,020	28,980	25,002
Egypt	2,707	3,152	4,053
Finland	4,534	5,822	5,970
France	9,733	13,655	16,257
German Democratic Republic	26,592	30,880	18,825
Germany, Federal Republic	54,293	68,010	101,861
Greece	3,123	4,772	5,192
Iran	4,718	5,128	7,385
Italy	20,927	26,707	35,435
Japan	4,966	6,605	6,990
Netherlands	5,782	7,584	9,143
Poland	16,650	18,091	10,044
Romania	8,607	8,317	10,730
Sweden	6,021	7,479	8,476
Switzerland and Liechtenstein	9,003	9,449	11,311
Turkey	5,143	5,479	6,600
USSR	137,979	143,587	121,854
United Kingdom	8,814	10,299	12,218
USA	14,686	19,088	21,331
Yugoslavia	13,919	23,560	28,594
Total (incl. others)	492,326	571,323	603,636

* Imports by country of production; exports by country of last consignment.

Transport

RAILWAYS (traffic)

	1987	1988	1989
Passengers carried (million)	332.8	327.9	329.0
Passenger-kilometres (million)	12,262	12,437	12,741
Net ton-kilometres (million)	21,731	21,057	19,820

ROAD TRAFFIC (motor vehicles in use at 31 December)

	1987	1988	1989
Passenger cars	1,660,258	1,789,562	1,732,385
Goods vehicles	191,851	196,105	208,306
Buses	26,893	26,569	23,793
Motor cycles	405,690	412,390	n.a.

INLAND WATERWAYS (traffic)

	1987	1988	1989
Freight carried ('000 metric tons).	3,758	3,942	2,112
Freight ton-km (million) . .	2,046	2,188	2,109

CIVIL AVIATION (traffic)

	1987	1988	1989
Kilometres flown . . .	21,711,900	21,274,980	23,127,000
Passengers carried. . .	1,320,311	1,309,635	1,500,000
Passenger-km ('000) . .	1,285,597	1,344,327	1,576,600
Cargo carried: metric tons .	11,972	10,386	8,000
Cargo ton-km	15,880,000	14,264,000	10,600,000

Tourism

('000 arrivals)

	1987	1988	1989
Foreign tourists . . .	11,826	10,563	14,236
Foreign visitors in transit . .	7,127	7,402	10,683
Total	18,953	17,965	24,919

1990: Total ('000 arrivals) 37,632.

TOURISTS BY COUNTRY OF ORIGIN

('000 arrivals, including visitors in transit)

	1988	1989	1990
Austria	3,844	4,554	5,153
Bulgaria	625	678	924
Czechoslovakia. . .	3,505	3,708	3,920
German Democratic Republic .	1,638	1,573	2,633
Germany, Federal Republic .	1,278	1,612	
Poland	2,820	4,481	3,791
Romania	271	236	9,015
USSR	683	2,066	1,884
Yugoslavia. . . .	2,023	4,416	8,123
Total (incl. others) . . .	17,965	24,919	37,632

Communications Media

	1987	1988	1989
Television receivers* . . .	279	277	279
Radio receivers† . . .	512	n.a.	n.a.
Telephones in use . . .	1,609,465	1,674,139	1,769,889
Books titles (including translations)	7,804	7,562	7,599
Daily newspapers . . .	29	29	31
Average daily circulation. .	3,078,731	3,101,495	2,507,990

* Number of television receivers per 1,000 inhabitants.
† Estimated number of radio receivers per 1,000 inhabitants.

Education

(1989/90)

	Institutions	Teachers	Students
Nursery	4,748	33,835	392,273
Primary	3,527	90,602	1,183,573
Secondary	675	21,425	349,071
Higher	57	16,319	100,868

Directory

The Constitution

A new constitution was introduced on 18 August 1949, and the Hungarian People's Republic was established two days later. The Constitution was amended in April 1972 and December 1983. Further, radical amendments were made in October 1989. Shortly afterwards, the Republic of Hungary was proclaimed.

The following is a summary of the main provisions of the Constitution, as amended in October 1989.

GENERAL PROVISIONS

The Republic of Hungary is an independent, democratic constitutional state in which the values of civil democracy and democratic socialism prevail in equal measures. All power belongs to the people, which they exercise directly and through the elected representatives of popular sovereignty.

Political parties may, under observance of the Constitution, be freely formed and may freely operate in Hungary. Parties may not directly exercise public power. No party has the right to guide any state body. Trade unions and other organizations for the representation of interests safeguard and represent the interests of employees, members of co-operatives and entrepreneurs.

The State safeguards the people's freedom, the independence and territorial integrity of the country as well as the frontiers thereof, as established by international treaties. The Republic of Hungary rejects war as a means of settling disputes between nations and refrains from applying force against the independence or territorial integrity of other states, and from threats of violence.

The Hungarian legal system adopts the universally accepted rules of international law. The order of legislation is regulated by an Act of constitutional force.

The economy of Hungary is a market economy, availing itself also of the advantages of planning, with public and private ownership enjoying equal right and protection. Hungary recognizes and supports the right of undertaking and free competition, limitable only by an Act of constitutional force. State-owned enterprises and organs pursuing economic activities manage their affairs independently, in accordance with the mode and responsibility as provided by law.

The Republic of Hungary protects the institutions of marriage and the family. It provides for the indigent through extensive social measures, and recognizes and enforces the right of each citizen to a healthy environment.

GOVERNMENT

National Assembly

The highest organ of state authority in the Republic of Hungary is the National Assembly which exercises all the rights deriving from the sovereignty of the people and determines the organization, direction and conditions of government. The National Assembly enacts the Constitution and laws, determines the state budget, decides the socio-economic plan, elects the President of the Republic and the Council of Ministers, directs the activities of ministries, decides upon declaring war and concluding peace and exercises the prerogative of amnesty.

The National Assembly is elected for a term of four years and members enjoy immunity from arrest and prosecution without parliamentary consent. It meets at least twice a year and is convened by the President of the Republic or by a written demand of the Council of Ministers or of one-fifth of the Assembly's members. It elects a President, Deputy Presidents and Recorders from among its own members, and it lays down its own rules of procedure and agenda. As a general rule, the sessions of the National Assembly are held in public.

The National Assembly has the right of legislation which can be initiated by the President of the Republic, the Council of Ministers or any committee or member of the National Assembly. Decisions are valid only if at least half of the members are present, and they require a simple majority. Constitutional changes require a two-thirds majority. Acts of the National Assembly are signed by the President of the Republic.

The National Assembly may pronounce its dissolution before the expiry of its term, and in the event of an emergency may prolong its mandate or may be reconvened after dissolution. A new National Assembly must be elected within three months of dissolution and convened within one month of polling day.

Members of the National Assembly are elected on the basis of universal, equal and direct suffrage by secret ballot, and they are accountable to their constituents, who may recall them. All citizens of 18 years and over have the right to vote, with the exception of those who are unsound of mind, and those who are deprived of their civil rights by a court of law.

President of the Republic

The President of the Republic is the Head of State of Hungary. He/she embodies the unity of the nation and supervises the democratic operation of the mechanism of State. The President is also the Commander-in-Chief of the Armed Forces. The President is elected by the National Assembly for a period of four years, and may be re-elected for a second term. Any citizen of Hungary qualified to vote, who has reached 35 years of age before the day of election, may be elected President.

The President may issue the writ for general or local elections, convene the National Assembly, initiate legislation, hold plebiscites, direct local government, conclude international treaties, appoint diplomatic representatives, ratify international treaties, appoint higher civil servants and officers of the armed forces, award orders and titles, and exercise the prerogative of mercy.

Council of Ministers

The highest organ of state administration is the Council of Ministers, responsible to the National Assembly and consisting of a Chairman, Ministers of State and other Ministers who are elected by the National Assembly on the recommendation of the President of the Republic. The Council of Ministers directs the work of the ministries (listed in a special enactment) and ensures the enforcement of laws and the fulfilment of economic plans; it may issue decrees and annul or modify measures taken by any central or local organ of government.

Local Administration

The local organs of state power are the county, town, borough and town precinct councils, whose members are elected for a term of four years by the voters in each area. Local councils direct economic, social and cultural activities in their area, prepare local economic plans and budgets and supervise their fulfilment, enforce laws, supervise subordinate organs, maintain public order, protect public property and individual rights, and direct local economic enterprises. They may issue regulations and annul or modify those of subordinate councils. Local Councils are administered by an Executive Committee elected by and responsible to them.

JUDICATURE

Justice is administered by the Supreme Court of the Republic of Hungary, county and district courts. The Supreme Court exercises the right of supervising in principle the judicial activities and practice of all other courts.

All judicial offices are filled by election; Supreme Court, county and district court judges are all elected for an indefinite period; the President of the Supreme Court is elected by the National Assembly. All court hearings are public unless otherwise prescribed by law, and those accused are guaranteed the right of defence. An accused person must be considered innocent until proved guilty.

Public Prosecutor

The function of the Chief Public Prosecutor is to watch over the observance of the law. He is elected by the National Assembly, to whom he is responsible. The organization of public prosecution is under the control of the Chief Public Prosecutor, who appoints the public prosecutors.

RIGHTS AND DUTIES OF CITIZENS

The Republic of Hungary guarantees for its citizens the right to work and to remuneration, the right of rest and recreation, the right to care in old age, sickness or disability, the right to education, and equality before the law; women enjoy equal rights with men. Discrimination on grounds of sex, religion or nationality is a punishable offence. The State also ensures freedom of conscience, religious worship, speech, the Press and assembly. The right of workers to organize themselves is stressed. The freedom of the individual, and the privacy of the home and of correspondence are inviolable. Freedom for creative work in the sciences and the arts is guaranteed.

The basic freedoms of all workers are guaranteed and foreign citizens enjoy the right of asylum.

Military service (with or without arms) and the defence of their country are the duties of all citizens.

The Government

(December 1991)

HEAD OF STATE

President of the Republic: ÁRPÁD GÖNCZ (elected 3 August 1990).

COUNCIL OF MINISTERS

A coalition of the Hungarian Democratic Forum (HDF), the Independent Smallholders' Party (ISP), the Christian Democratic People's Party (CDPP) and Independents.

Chairman: JÓZSEF ANTALL (HDF).

Minister of the Interior: Dr PÉTER BOROSS (Independent).

Minister of Agriculture: Dr ELEMÉR GERGÁTZ (ISP).

Minister of Defence: LAJOS FÜR (HDF).

Minister of Justice: Dr ISTVÁN BALSAI (HDF).

Minister of Industry and Trade: PÉTER ÁKOS BOD (HDF).

Minister of Environmental Protection and Urban Development: K. SÁNDOR KERESZTES (HDF).

Minister of Transport, Communications and Water Management: CSABA SIKLÓS (HDF).

Minister of Foreign Affairs: Dr GÉZA JESZENSZKY (HDF).

Minister of Labour: Dr GYULA KISS (ISP).

Minister of Culture and Education: Dr BERTALAN ANDRÁSFALVY (HDF).

Minister of International Economic Relations: Dr BÉLA KÁDÁR (Independent).

Minister of Welfare: Dr LÁSZLÓ SURJÁN (CDPP).

Minister of Finance: Dr MIHÁLY KUPA (Independent).

Ministers without Portfolio: Dr FERENC MÁDL (Independent), KATALIN BOTOS (HDF), Dr ANDRÁS GÁLSZÉCSY (Independent), Dr BALÁZS HORVÁTH (HDF), FERENC JÓZSEF NAGY (ISP), ERNŐ PUNGOR (Independent).

MINISTRIES

Council of Ministers (Secretariat): 1055 Budapest, Kossuth Lajos tér 1–3; tel. (1) 112-0600; telex 22-5547; fax (1) 153-3622.

Ministry of Agriculture: 1055 Budapest, Kossuth Lajos tér 11; tel. (1) 153-3000; telex 22-5445; fax (1) 153-0518.

Ministry of Culture and Education: 1055 Budapest, Szalay u. 10–14; tel. (1) 153-0600; telex 22-5935.

Ministry of Defence: 1055 Budapest, Pálffy György u. 7–11; tel. (1) 132-2500; telex 22-5424.

Ministry of Environmental Protection and Urban Development: 1011 Budapest, Fő u. 44-50, POB 351; tel. (1) 115-4840; telex 22-4879; fax (1) 136-2198.

Ministry of Finance: 1051 Budapest, József Nádor tér 2–4; tel. (1) 118-2066.

Ministry of Foreign Affairs: 1027 Budapest, Bem rkp. 47; tel. (1) 156-8000; telex 22-5571.

Ministry of Industry and Trade: 1024 Budapest, Mártírok u. 85; tel. (1) 156-5566; telex 22-5376; fax (1) 175-0219.

Ministry of the Interior: 1051 Budapest, József Attila u. 2–4; tel. (1) 112-1710; telex 22-5216.

Ministry of International Economic Relations: 1055 Budapest, Honvéd u. 13–15; tel. (1) 153-0000; telex 22-5578; fax (1) 153-2794.

Ministry of Justice: 1055 Budapest, Szalay u. 16; tel. (1) 131-8922.

Ministry of Labour: 1051 Budapest, Roosevelt tér 7–8; tel. (1) 132-2100; fax (1) 131-6399.

Ministry of Transport, Communications and Water Management: 1400 Budapest, Dob u. 75–81, POB 87; tel. (1) 122-0220; telex 22-5729; fax (1) 122-8695.

Ministry of Welfare: 1051 Budapest, Arany János u. 6–8; tel. (1) 132-3100; telex 22-4337; fax (1) 153-4955.

Legislature

ORSZÁGGYÜLÉS

(National Assembly)

The unicameral National Assembly consists of 386 deputies, elected for a four-year term. At elections, held in March and April 1990, 176 deputies were elected directly to represent single-member constituencies, 152 according to a system of proportional representation of parties, while the remaining 58 were elected on a national list on the basis of a nationwide summary of surplus votes. An additional eight seats were reportedly to be reserved for one deputy each from Hungary's Romany, Croat, German, Romanian, Serbian, Slovak, Slovene and Jewish minorities.

President of the National Assembly: Dr GYÖRGY SZABAD.

Deputy Presidents: Dr ALAJOS DORNBACH, MÁTYÁS SZŰRÖS, VINCE VÖRÖS.

General election, 25 March and 8 April 1990

	%	Seats
Hungarian Democratic Forum (HDF) . .	42.74	165
Alliance of Free Democrats (AFD) .	23.83	92
Independent Smallholders' Party (ISP) .	11.13	43
Hungarian Socialist Party (HSP) . . .	8.54	33
Federation of Young Democrats (FYD) .	5.44	21
Christian Democratic People's Party (CDPP)	5.44	21
Others	2.88	11
Total	100.00	386

Local Government

In 1990 the National Assembly ratified a law providing for the right of citizens to participate extensively in the government of their local communities, the object being to broaden social co-operation and to prevent local politics becoming the monopoly of élite groups. Hungary is divided into 19 counties (megyei—see Statistical Survey for a complete list). There are, in addition, 168 town authorities (városi), of which 19 larger towns or cities with populations over 50,000 claim separate county status. Larger towns are subdivided into districts; for example, Budapest (with a population almost 10 times that of Debrecen, Hungary's second-biggest town) is divided into 22 districts, which send delegates to the general assembly of the capital. In rural areas villages and large villages (with populations over 5,000) have their own representative bodies. Elections are held every four years for the county, town, district and precinct councils. However, provisions exist for each representative body to hold a public meeting at least once a year, and for referendums to be held on significant local issues. Minimum levels of participation in elections are set, below which a result is invalidated. There is effectively no hierarchical control over local government in Hungary, each tier being regarded as equal and independent. However, the National Assembly may dissolve a local government if it is operating in contravention of the Constitution, and after consultation with the Constitutional Court. Local government decisions may be revised only by the Constitutional Court, or, in cases of illegality, by the courts. Local authorities are free to co-operate in their own representative associations.

Települési Önkormányzatok Országos Szövetsége (National Association of Local Authorities): 1056 Budapest, Váci u. 62–64; tel. (1) 118-1027; Pres. JÓZSEF OTT; Sec.-Gen. Dr FERENC KÖLLNER.

COUNTIES

Bács-Kiskun: 6000 Kecskemét, Május 1 tér 3; tel. (76) 28-788; Pres. of Council MIKLÓS KŐTÖRŐ.

Baranya: 7601 Pécs, Rákóczi út 34; tel. (72) 12-222; Pres. of Council Dr JÓZSEFS SZŰCS.

Békés: 5601 Békéscsaba, Derkovits sor; tel. (66) 21-833; Pres. of Council Dr IMRE SIMON.

Borsod-Abaúj-Zemplén: 3525 Miskolc, Tanácsház tér 1; tel. (46) 16-461; Pres. of Council GYÖRGY SZABÓ.

Csongrád: 6722 Szeged, Rákóczi tér; tel. (62) 21-622; Pres. of Council ISTVÁN LEHMANN.

Fejér: 8000 Székesfehérvár, István tér; tel. (22) 12-312; Pres. of Council HUBA PÁL.

Győ-Moson-Sopron: 9021 Győr, Árpád út 32; tel. (96) 18-122; Pres. of Council GÁBOR BOTOS.

Hajdú-Bihar: 4024 Debrecen, Piac u. 54; tel. (52) 15-255; Pres. of Council ANTAL SZEKERES.

Heves: 3300 Eger, Kossuth L. u. 9; tel. (36) 10-011; Pres. of Council ISTVÁN JAKAB.

Jász-Nagykun-Szolnok: 5000 Szolnok, Kossuth L. u. 2; tel. (56) 39-933; Pres. of Council LAJOS BOROS.

Komárom-Esztergom: 2801 Tatabánya, Felszabadulás tér 4; tel. (34) 11-511; Pres. of Council Dr GYÖRGY ZOLTÁN KOVÁCS.

Nógrád: 3100 Salgótarján, Rákóczi út 192; tel. (32) 10-022; Pres. of Council FERENC KORILL.

Pest: 1052 Budapest, Városház u. 7; tel. (1) 118-0111; Pres. of Council Dr JÁNOS INCZÉDY.

Somogy: 7401 Kaposvár, Csokonai Vitéz M. u. 3; tel. (82) 15-122; Pres. of Council Dr ISTVÁN GYENESEI.

Szabolcs-Szatmár-Bereg: 4400 Nyíregyháza, Tanácsköztársaság tér 5; tel. (42) 14-111; Pres. of Council JÓZSEF MEDGYESI.

Tolna: 7100 Szekszárd, Mártírok tere 11–13; tel. (74) 11-211; Pres. of Council JÓZSEF PROGER.

Vas: 9700 Szombathely, Berzsenyi D. tér 1; tel. (94) 11-211; Pres. of Council GYULA PUSZTAI.

Veszprém: 8200 Veszprém, Lenin tér 3; tel. (80) 21-011; Pres. of Council GÁBOR ZONGOR.

Zala: 8900 Zalaegerszeg, Kosztolányi D. u. 10; tel. (92) 11-010; Pres. of Council Dr DÉNES PÁLFI.

Budapest

Budapest Metropolitan Area Chief Mayor's Office: 1052 Budapest, Városház u. 9–11; tel. (1) 118-6066; Chief Mayor Dr GÁBOR DEMSZKY (AFD); Deputy Chief Mayors Dr MIKLÓS MARSCHALL (AFD), ISTVÁN SCHNELLER (Independent), Dr Gábor Székely (AFD).

Political Organizations

Alliance of Free Democrats—AFD (Szabad Demokraták Szövetsége—SZDSZ): 1051 Budapest, Mérleg u. 6; tel. (1) 117-6911; fax (1) 118-7944; f. 1988; 35,000 mems (1990); Chair. PETER TOLGYESSY.

Christian Democratic People's Party—CDPP (Kereszténydemokrata Néppárt—KDNP): 1126 Budapest, Nagy Jenő u. 5; tel. (1) 156-2897; fax (1) 155-5772; re-formed 1989; Chair. LÁSZLÓ SURJÁN.

Federation of Young Democrats—FYD (Fiatal Demokraták Szövetsége—FIDESZ): 1062 Budapest, Lendvay u. 28 ; tel. (1) 112-1095; fax (1) 131-9673; f. 1988; 12,000 mems; Leader VIKTOR ORBAN.

Green Party (Magyarországi Zöld Párt): 1036 Budapest, Kiskorona u. 3; tel. (1) 168-8800; f. 1989; Chair. LÁSZLÓ BREZOVITS.

Hungarian Democratic Forum—HDF (Magyar Demokrata Fórum—MDF): 1538 Budapest, POB 579; tel. (1) 115-9690; fax (1) 156-8522; f. 1987; 25,000 mems (April 1990); Chair. Dr JÓZSEF ANTALL.

Hungarian People's Party (Magya Néppart—Nemzeti Parasztpért): 1082 Budapest, Baross u. 61; tel. (1) 134-1509; f. 1989; Chair. GYULA FEKETE.

Hungarian Socialist Party—HSP (Magyar Szocialista Párt—MSZP): 1081 Budapest, Köztársaság tér 26; tel. (1) 113-3706; fax (1) 133-5998; f. 1989 to replace the Hungarian Socialist Workers' Party; 67,000 mems (Dec. 1989); Chair. Dr GYULA HORN.

Hungarian Socialist Workers' Party—HSWP (Magyar Szocialista Munkáspárt—MSZMP): 1092 Budapest, Köztelek u. 8; tel. (1) 118-3100; f. 1956; dissolved and replaced by Hungarian Socialist Party in 1989; re-formed in 1989; approx. 80,000 mems (May 1990); Pres. Dr GYULA THÜRMER.

Independent Smallholders' Party—ISP (Független Kisgazda-, Földmunkás- és Polgári Párt—FKgP): 1126 Budapest, Szoboszlai u. 2–4; tel. (1) 155-5333; fax (1) 155-1049; f. 1988; 70,000 mems (April 1990); Chair. Dr FERENC JÓZSEF NAGY.

Social Democratic Party—SDP (Magyarországi Szociáldemokrata Párt—SZDP): 1077 Budapest, Dohány u. 76; tel. (1) 142-2385; f. 1889; absorbed by Communist Party in 1948; revived 1988; 15,000 mems (Nov. 1989); Chair. ANNA PETRASOVITS.

Diplomatic Representation

EMBASSIES IN HUNGARY

Afghanistan: 1062 Budapest, Lendvay u. 23; tel. (1) 132-7187; Ambassador: SHERJAN MAZDOORYAR.

Albania: 1068 Budapest, Bajza u. 26; tel. (1) 122-7251; Ambassador: JANI POLENA.

Algeria: 1014 Budapest, Dísz tér 6; tel. (1) 175-9884; telex 22-6916; Ambassador: BACHIR ROUIS.

Argentina: 1068 Budapest, Rippl-Rónai u. 1; tel. (1) 122-8467; telex 22-4128; Ambassador: GUILLERMO JORGE MCGOUGH.

Australia: 1062 Budapest, Délibáb u. 30; tel. (1) 153-4233; telex 22-7708; fax (1) 153-4866; Ambassador: DOUGLAS TOWNSEND.

Austria: 1068 Budapest, Benczúr u. 16; tel. (1) 121-3213; telex 22-4447; Ambassador: Dr FRANZ SCHMID.

Belgium: 1015 Budapest, Toldy Ferenc u. 13; tel. (1) 201-1571; telex 22-4664; fax (1) 175-1566; Ambassador: WILLEM VERKAMMEN.

Bolivia: 1015 Budapest, Toldy F. u. 60, 1–12; tel. (1) 116-2214; Chargé d'affaires: MACARIO APARICIO BURGOA.

Brazil: 1118 Budapest, Somlói út 3; tel. (1) 166-6044; telex 22-5795; Ambassador: IVAN VELLOSO DA SILVEIRA BATALHA.

Bulgaria: 1124 Budapest, Levendula u. 15–17; tel. (1) 156-6840; telex 22-3032; fax (1) 155-0998; Ambassador: VESSELIN FILEV.

Cambodia: 1121 Budapest, Budakeszi út 55D; tel. (1) 155-1128; Ambassador: UNG SEAN.

Canada: 1121 Budapest, Budakeszi út 32; tel. (1) 176-7686; telex 22-4588; Ambassador: DEREK FRASER.

Chile: 1061 Budapest, Andrássy út 21; tel. (1) 122-4485; Ambassador: MANUEL SANHUEZA CRUZ.

China, People's Republic: 1068 Budapest, Benczúr u. 17; tel. (1) 122-4872; Ambassador: DAI BINGGUO.

Colombia: 1024 Budapest, Mártírok u. 43–45; tel. (1) 201-3448; telex 22-6012; Ambassador: ALBERTO ESTEBAN ROJAS PUYO.

Costa Rica: 1118 Budapest, Iglói u. 2; Ambassador: ARNULFO HERNÁNDEZ.

Cuba: 1021 Budapest, Budakeszi út 55D; Ambassador: FAUSTINO MANUEL BEATO MOREJÓN.

Czechoslovakia: 1143 Budapest, Népstadion út 22; tel. (1) 251-1700; telex 22-4744; Ambassador: RUDOLF CHMEL.

Denmark: 1122 Budapest, Határőr út 37; tel. (1) 155-7320; telex 22-4137; fax (1) 175-3803; Ambassador: OLE KOCH.

Ecuador: 1021 Budapest, Budakeszi út 55D; tel. (1) 176-7593; Ambassador: GALO RIVADENEIRA CUEVA.

Egypt: 1016 Budapest, Bérc u. 16; tel. (1) 166-8060; telex 22-5184; Ambassador: MOHAMED ALI EL-SHEREI.

Finland: 1118 Budapest, Kelenhegyi út 16A; tel. (1) 185-0700; telex 22-4710; fax (1) 185-0772; Ambassador: RISTO HYVÄRINEN.

France: 1062 Budapest, Lendvay u. 27; tel. (1) 132-4980; telex 22-5143; Ambassador: PIERRE BROCHAND.

Germany: 1146 Budapest, Izsó u. 5; tel. (1) 122-3434; telex 22-5951; fax (1) 160-1903; Ambassador: Dr ALEXANDER ARNOT.

Greece: 1063 Budapest, Szegfű u. 3; tel. (1) 122-8004; telex 22-4113; Ambassador: NICOLAS CAPELLARIS.

Holy See: 1021 Budapest, Budakeszi út 55D; tel. (1) 176-3334; Apostolic Nuncio: ANGELO ACERBI.

India: 1025 Budapest, Búzavirág u. 14; tel. (1) 115-5211; telex 22-6374; Ambassador: SURINDER LAL MALIK.

Indonesia: 1068 Budapest, Gorkij fasor 26; tel. (1) 142-8508; telex 22-5263; Ambassador: BUSTANUL ARIFIN.

Iran: 1062 Budapest, Délibáb u. 29; tel. (1) 122-5038; telex 22-4129; Ambassador: KEYVAN IMANI.

Iraq: 1145 Budapest, Szántó Béla u. 13; tel. (1) 122-6418; telex 22-6058; Ambassador: MOHAMMED GHANIM AL-ANAZ.

Israel: 1026 Budapest, Fullánk u. 8; tel. (1) 176-7896; Ambassador: SHLOMO MAROM.

Italy: 1143 Budapest, Népstadion út 95; tel. (1) 121-2450; telex 22-5294; Ambassador: JOSEPH NITTI.

Japan: 1024 Budapest, Rómer Flóris u. 56–58; tel. (1) 156-4533; telex 22-5048; Ambassador: EIJI SEKI.

Korea, Democratic People's Republic: 1068 Budapest, Benczúr u. 31; tel. (1) 142-5174; telex 22-6721; Chargé d'affaires: BANG RYONG GAB.

Korea, Republic: 1125 Budapest, Mátyás király út 14C; tel. (1) 138-3388; Ambassador: HAN TAK-CHAE.

Libya: 1143 Budapest, Népstadion út 111; tel. (1) 122-6076; telex 22-6940; Head of People's Bureau: OMAR IBRAHIM ROKHSY.

Mexico: 1021 Budapest, Budakeszi út 55D; tel. (1) 176-7381; fax (1) 176-7906; Ambassador: LUCIANO JOUBLANC.

Mongolia: 1125 Budapest, Istenhegyi út 59–61; tel. (1) 155-7989; Ambassador: DERGELDALAJN ZSAMBAZSANCAN.

Morocco: 1026 Budapest, Törökvész Lejto 12A; tel. (1) 115-9251; telex 22-3580; Ambassador: MOHAMED CHAHID.

Netherlands: 1146 Budapest, Abonyi u. 31; tel. (1) 122-8432; telex 22-5562; fax (1) 141-6532; Ambassador: HENDRIK JAN VAN OORDT.

Nicaragua: 1021 Budapest, Budakeszi út 55D; tel. (1) 176-7953; Chargé d'affaires a.i.: GUSTAVO CRUZ MORENO.

Norway: 1122 Budapest, Határőr út 35, POB 32; tel. (1) 155-1811; telex 22-5867; fax (1) 156-7928; Ambassador: TORMOD PETTER SVENNEVIG.

Pakistan: 1125 Budapest, Adonisz u. 3A; tel. (1) 155-8017; Ambassador: HAMIDULLAH KHAN.

Peru: 1125 Budapest, Tóth Lörinc u. 5 ; tel. (1) 115-0292; Ambassador: (vacant).

Philippines: 1028 Budapest, Vérhalom u. 12–16; tel. (1) 115-3220; Ambassador: JUANITO P. JARASA.

Poland: 1068 Budapest, Gorkij fasor 16; tel. (1) 142-8135; Ambassador: Dr MACIEJ KOŹMIŃSKI.

Portugal: 1024 Budapest, Mártírok útja 43–45; tel. (1) 201-1855; telex 22-6509; fax (1) 115-4666; Ambassador: ANTÓNIO BAPTISTA MARTINS.

Romania: 1146 Budapest, Thököly út 72; tel. (1) 142-6944; telex 22-5847; Ambassador: SIMION POP.

Russia: 1062 Budapest, Bajza u. 35; tel. (1) 132-0911; Ambassador: IVAN P. ABOIMOV.

Spain: 1067 Budapest, Eötvös u. 11B; tel. (1) 153-1011; telex 22-4130; Ambassador: LUIS DE LA TORRE.

Sweden: 1146 Budapest, Ajtósi Dürer sor 27A; tel. (1) 122-9880; telex 22-5647; Ambassador: STEN STRÖMHOLM.

Switzerland: 1143 Budapest, Népstadion út 107; tel. (1) 122-9491; Ambassador: MAX DAHINDEN.

Syria: 1026 Budapest, Harangvirág u. 3; tel. (1) 176-7186; telex 22-6605; Ambassador: (vacant).

Thailand: 1025 Budapest, Józsefhegyi út 28-30 A/3; tel. (1) 135-4590; telex 20-2706; fax (1) 115-0606; Ambassador: SUTTISWAT KRIDAKON.

Tunisia: 1021 Budapest, Budakeszi út 55D; tel. (1) 176-7595; Ambassador: HABIB AMMAR.

Turkey: 1014 Budapest, Úri u. 45; tel. (1) 155-0737; Ambassador: BEDRETTIN TUNABAS .

United Kingdom: 1051 Budapest, Harmincad u. 6; tel. (1) 118-2888; telex 22-4527; fax (1) 118-0907; Ambassador: JOHN BIRCH.

USA: 1054 Budapest, Szabadság tér 12; tel. (1) 112-6450; telex 22-4222; Ambassador: CHARLES THOMAS.

Uruguay: 1023 Budapest, Vérhalom u. 12–16; tel. (1) 136-8333; Ambassador: JUAN B. ODDONE SILVEIRA.

Venezuela: 1023 Budapest, Vérhalom u. 12–16; tel. (1) 135-3562; telex 22-6666; fax (1) 115-3274; Ambassador: MORITZ EIRIS-VILLEGAS.

Viet-Nam: 1068 Budapest, Benczúr u. 18; tel. (1) 142-9943; Ambassador: NGUYEN VAN QUY.

Yemen: 1025 Budapest, Tömörkény u. 3A; tel. (1) 176-4048; Ambassador: MOHSEN NAGI BIN NAGOI.

Yugoslavia: 1068 Budapest, Dózsa György út 92B; tel. (1) 142-0566; Ambassador: RUDOLF-RUDI SOVA.

Judicial System

The system of court procedure in Hungary is based on an Act that came into effect in 1953 and has since been updated frequently. The system of jurisdiction is based on the local courts (district courts in Budapest, city courts in other cities), labour courts, county courts (or the Metropolitan Court) and the Supreme Court. In the legal remedy system of two instances, appeals against the decisions of city and district courts can be lodged with the competent county court and the Metropolitan Court of Budapest respectively. Against the judgment of first instance of the latter, appeal is to be lodged with the Supreme Court. The Chief Public Prosecutor and the President of the Supreme Court have the right to submit a protest on legal grounds against the final judgment of any court.

By virtue of the 1973 Act, effective 1974 and modified in 1979, the procedure in criminal cases is differentiated for criminal offences and for criminal acts. In the first instance, criminal cases are tried, depending on their character, by a professional judge; where justified by the magnitude of the criminal act, by a council composed of three members, a professional judge and two lay assessors, while in major cases the court consists of five members, two professional judges and three lay assessors. In the Supreme Court, second instance cases are tried only by professional judges. The President of the Supreme Court is elected by the National Assembly. Judges are appointed by the President of the Republic for an indefinite period. Assessors are elected by the local municipal councils.

In the interest of ensuring legality and a uniform application of the Law, the Supreme Court exercises a principled guidance over the jurisdiction of courts. In the Republic of Hungary judges are independent and subject only to the Law and other legal regulations.

The Minister of Justice supervises the general activities of courts. The Chief Public Prosecutor is elected by the National Assembly. The Chief Public Prosecutor and the Prosecutor's Office provide for the consistent prosecution of all acts violating or endangering the legal order of society, the safety and independence of the state, and for the protection of citizens.

The Prosecutors of the independent prosecuting organization exert supervision over the legality of investigations and the implementation of punishments, and assist with specific means in ensuring that legal regulations should be observed by state, economic and other organs and citizens, and they support the legality of court procedures and decisions.

President of the Supreme Court: PÁL SOLT.

Chief Public Prosecutor: KÁLMÁN GYÖRGYI.

Religion

National Council for Religious Affairs: Budapest; f. 1989 to replace State Office for Church Affairs; autonomous body, independent of the State.

CHRISTIANITY

Magyarországi Egyházak Ökuménikus Tanácsa (Ecumenical Council of Churches in Hungary): 1054 Budapest, Szabadság tér 2; tel. (1) 111-4862; f. 1943; member churches: Reformed Church, Evangelical Lutheran, Baptist, Methodist, Hungarian Orthodox, Romanian Orthodox and Council of Free Churches; Pres. Bishop Dr KÁROLY TÓTH; Gen. Sec. Rev. LÁSZLÓ LEHEL.

The Roman Catholic Church

Hungary comprises three archdioceses, eight dioceses (including one for Catholics of the Byzantine rite) and one territorial abbacy (directly responsible to the Holy See). At 31 December 1988 the Church had 6,710,512 adherents in Hungary. There are 3,250 active churches.

Bishops' Conference: Magyar Püspöki Kar Konferenciája, 1053 Budapest, Károlyi M. u. 4–8; tel. (1) 117-4533; f. 1969; Pres. Dr ISTVÁN SEREGÉLY , Archbishop of Eger.

Latin Rite

Archbishop of Eger: Dr ISTVÁN SEREGÉLY, 3301 Eger, Széchenyi u. 1; tel. (36) 13-259.

Archbishop of Esztergom: Cardinal Dr LÁSZLÓ PASKAI, Primate of Hungary, 2500 Esztergom, Berenyi Zsigmond u. 2; tel. (33) 13-690.

Archbishop of Kalocsa: Dr LÁSZLÓ DANKÓ, 6301 Kalocsa, Szabadság tér 1; tel. 155.

Byzantine Rite

Bishop of Hajdudorog: SZILÁRD KERESZTES, 4401 Nyiregyháza, Bethlen u. 5, POB 60; tel. 42-17397; about 250,000 adherents; the Bishop is also Apostolic Administrator of the Apostolic Exarchate of Miskolc, with an estimated 22,800 Catholics of the Byzantine rite (Nov. 1988).

Protestant Churches

Magyarországi Baptista Egyház (Baptist Union of Hungary): 1062 Budapest, Aradi u. 48; tel. (1) 132-2332; f. 1846; 12,250 mems; Pres. Rev. Dr JÁNOS VICZIÁN; Sec. Rev. KORNÉL GYŐRI.

Magyarországi Evangélikus Egyház (Evangelical Church in Hungary—Lutheran): 1085 Budapest, Üllői út 24; tel. (1) 113-0886; 430,000 mems (1985); Presiding Bishop Dr BÉLA HARMATI; Gen. Sec. Dr ÁGOSTON KARNER.

Magyarországi Metodista Egyház (Hungarian Methodist Church): 1068 Budapest, Felsёrdsor u. 5; tel. (1) 122-4723; Superintendent Dr FRIGYES HECKER.

Magyarországi Református Egyház (Reformed Church in Hungary—Presbyterian): 1146 Budapest, Abonyi u. 21; tel. (1) 122-7870; 2m. mems (1987); 1,306 churches; Pres. of Gen. Synod Dr LÓRÁNT HEGEDŰS.

Magyarországi Unitárius Egyház (Hungarian Council of Free Churches—Unitarian): 1055 Budapest, Nagy Ignác u. 4; tel. (1) 111-3094; Bishop JÁNOS HUSZTI.

The Eastern Orthodox Church

Magyar Orthodox Egyház (Hungarian Orthodox Church): 1052 Budapest, Petőfi tér 2.1.2.; tel. (1) 118-4813; Administrator Archpriest Dr FERIZ BERKI.

Görögkeleti Szerb Egyházmegye (Serbian Orthodox Diocese): 2000 Szentendre, Engels u. 5; Parochus DUSÁN VUJICSICS.

Magyarországi Román Ortodox Egyház (Romanian Orthodox Church in Hungary): 5700 Gyula, Groza park 2; tel. (66) 61-281; Bishop PÁL ÁRDELEÁN.

The Russian (6,000 mems) and Bulgarian Orthodox Churches are also represented.

BUDDHISM

Magyarországi Buddhista Misszió (Hungarian Buddhist Mission): 1221 Budapest, Alkotmány u. 83; Representative Dr JÓZSEF HORVÁTH.

Magyarországi Csan Buddhista Közösség Hungarian Zen Buddhist Community): 1092 Budapest, Ráday u. 43–45; Leader FÁRAD LOTFI.

ISLAM

There are about 3,000 Muslims in Hungary. In 1987 it was announced that an Islamic centre was to be built in Budapest, with assistance from the Muslim World League.

Magyar Iszlám Közösség (Hungarian Islamic Community): 1066 Budapest, Teréz krt 65; tel. (1) 177-7602; Leader Dr BALÁZS MIHÁLFFY.

JUDAISM

The Jewish community in Hungary is estimated to number between 80,000 and 100,000 people.

Magyar Izraeliták Országos Képviselete (Central Board of Hungarian Jews): 1075 Budapest, Síp u. 12, Budapesti Izraelita Hitközség (Jewish Community of Budapest); tel. (1) 142-1335; 80,000 mems; 40 active synagogues; Orthodox and Conservative; Pres. of Central Board GUSTÁV ZOLTAI; Chief Rabbi of Budapest RÓBERT DEUTSCH.

The Press

In 1988 the censorship laws were relaxed considerably, and in 1989 private ownership of publications was legalized. By late 1990 most of the former organs of political parties, trade unions, youth and social organizations had been transferred into full or partial private ownership. Most daily newspapers were partially foreign-owned.

In 1989 there were 31 dailies with an average total circulation of 2,507,990. These included more than 20 provincial dailies. Budapest dailies circulate nationally. In order of popularity they are: *Népszabadság*, *Népszava*, the evening *Esti Hirlap* and *Magyar Nemzet*. *Népszabadság*, the most important daily, was formerly the central organ of the Hungarian Socialist Workers' Party, but is now independent. The paper most respected for the quality of its news coverage and commentary is *Magyar Nemzet*.

Among the most popular periodicals are the illustrated weeklies, which include the satirical *Ludas Matyi*, the women's magazine *Nők Lapja*, the illustrated news journal *Képes Újság* and the political paper *Szabad Föld*. A news magazine giving a high standard of reporting and political discussion is *Magyarország*. Specialized periodicals include cultural, medical, scientific, agricultural and religious publications (including *Új Ember*, *Evangélikus Élet* and *Új Élet* for Catholic, Lutheran and Jewish congregations respectively).

PRINCIPAL DAILIES

Békéscsaba

Békés Megyei Népújság: 5601 Békéscsaba, Munkácsy u. 4; tel. (66) 27-844; Editor-in-Chief ZOLTÁN ÁRPÁSI.

Budapest

Daily News: 1016 Budapest, Fém u. 5–7; tel. (1) 175-6722; telex 22-4371; f. 1967; published by the Hungarian News Agency; in English and German; Editor-in-Chief Dr JÁNOS DOBSA; circ. 15,000.

Esti Hirlap (Evening Journal): 1962 Budapest, Blaha Lujza tér 3; tel. (1) 138-2399; telex 22-7040; fax (1) 138-4550; 40% foreign-owned; Editor-in-Chief DÉNES MAROS; circ. 100,000.

Kurír: 1065 Budapest, Hajós u. 30–32; tel. (1) 111-2659; Editor-in-Chief GÁBOR SZŰCS.

Magyar Hírlap (Hungarian Journal): 1087 Budapest, Kerepesi út 29B; tel. (1) 134-3330; telex 22-4268; f. 1968; 40% foreign-owned; Editor-in-Chief PÉTER NÉMETH; circ. 96,000.

Magyar Nemzet (Hungarian Nation): 1073 Budapest, Erzsébet krt 9–11; tel. (1) 141-4320; telex 22-4269; 45% foreign-owned; Editor-in-Chief Tibor Pethő; circ. 160,000.

Mai Nap (Today): 1087 Budapest, Könyves Kálmán Bld 76; tel. (1) 113-0284; telex 22-3634; fax (1) 133-9153; f. 1988; Editor-in-Chief ISTVÁN HORVÁTH; circ. 120,000.

Nemzeti Sport (National Sport): 1981 Budapest, Rökk Szilárd u. 6; tel. (1) 138-4366; telex 22-5245; fax (1) 138-2463; Editor-in-Chief ISTVÁN SZEKERES; circ. 250,000.

Népszabadság (People's Freedom): 1960 Budapest, Blaha Lujza tér 1–3; tel. (1) 138-4300; telex 22-5551; fax (1) 138-4086; f. 1942; independent; Editor-in-Chief PÁL EÖTVÖS; circ. 320,000.

Népszava (Voice of the People): 1964 Budapest, Rákóczi út 54; tel. (1) 122-4810; telex 22-4105; fax (1) 122-2415; f. 1873; trade unions' daily; Editor ANDRÁS DEÁK; circ. 200,000.

Pest Megyei Hírlap: 1446 Budapest, Somogyi Béla u. 6; tel. (1) 138-2399; Editor-in-Chief Dr ANDRÁS BÁRD.

Reggeli Pesti Hírlap (Pest Morning Journal): 1073 Budapest, Osvát u. 8; tel. (1) 111-8007; Editor-in-Chief ANDRÁS BENCSIK.

Üzlet (Business): 1055 Budapest, Bajcsy-Zsilinszky út 78; tel. (1) 111-8260; Editor-in-Chief IVÁN ÉRSEK.

Világgazdaság: 1034 Budapest, Bécsi út 126–128; tel. (1) 180-4310; Editor-in-Chief ISTVÁN GYULAI.

Debrecen

Hajdú-Bihari Napló: 4024 Debrecen, Tóthfalusi tér 10; tel. (52) 12-144; Editor-in-Chief ENDRE BAKÓ.

Dunaújváros

A Hírlap: 2400 Dunaújváros, Városháza tér 1; tel. (25) 16-010; Editor-in-Chief CSABA D. KISS.

Eger

Heves Megyei Hírlap: 3301 Eger, Barkóczy u. 7; tel. (36) 13-644; Editor-in-Chief LEVENTE KAPOSI.

Győr

Kisalföld: 9022 Győr, Szt István út 51; tel. (96) 15-544; Editor-in-Chief Dr ANDOR KLOSS.

Kaposvár

Somogyi Hírlap: 7401 Kaposvár, Latinca Sándor u. 2A; tel. (82) 11-644; Editor-in-Chief Dr IMRE KERCZA.

Kecskemét

Petőfi Népe: 6000 Kecskemét, Szabadság tér 1A; tel. (76) 27-611; Editor-in-Chief Dr SÁNDOR GÁL.

Miskolc

Déli Hírlap: 3527 Miskolc, Bajcsy-Zsilinszky út 15; tel. (46) 42-694; Editor-in-Chief DEZSŐ BEKES.

Ézsak-Magyarország: 3527 Miskolc, Bajcsy-Zsilinszky út 15; tel. (46) 41-888; Editor-in-Chief ZOLTÁN NAGY.

Nyíregyháza

Kelet-Magyarország: 4401 Nyíregyháza, Zrínyi u. 3–5; tel. (42) 11-277; Editor-in-Chief Dr SÁNDOR ANGYAL.

Pécs

Új Dunántúli Napló: 7601 Pécs, Hunyadi út 11; tel. (72) 15-000; Editor-in-Chief JENŐ LOMBOSI.

Salgótarjan

Új Nógrád: 3100 Salgótarján, Palócz Imre tér 4; tel. (32) 10-589; Editor-in-Chief LÁSZLÓ SULYOK.

Szeged

Délvilág: 6740 Szeged, Tanácsköztársaság útja 10; tel. (62) 14-911; Editor-in-Chief ISTVÁN NIKOLÉNYI.

Délmagyarország: 6740 Szeged, Tanácsköztársaság útja 10; tel. (62) 24-633; Editor-in-Chief IMRE DLUSZTUS.

Székesfehérvár

Fejér Megyei Hírlap: 8003 Székesfehérvár, Honvéd u. 8; tel. (22) 12-450; Editor-in-Chief JÁNOS Á. SZABÓ.

Szekszárd

Tolnai Népújság: 7100 Szekszárd, Liszt Ferenc tér 3; tel. (74) 16-211; Editor-in-Chief GYÖRGYNÉ KAMARÁS.

Szolnok

Új Néplap: 5001 Szolnok, Kossuth tér 1, I. Irodaház; tel. (56) 42-211; Editor-in-Chief JÓZSEF HAJNAL.

Szombathely

Vas Népe: 9700 Szombathely, Berzsenyi tér 2; tel. (94) 12-393; Editor-in-Chief SÁNDOR LENGYEL.

Vasvármegye: 9701 Szombathely, Honvéd tér 2; tel. (94) 12-356; Editor-in-Chief LÁSZLÓ BURKON.

Tatabánya

24 Óra: 2801 Tatabánya, Felszabadulás tér 4; tel. (34) 10-053; Editor-in-Chief GÁBOR GOMBKÖTŐ.

Veszprém

Napló: 8201 Veszprém, Szabadság tér 15; tel. (80) 27-444; Editor-in-Chief ELEMÉR BALOGH.

Zalaegerszeg

Zalai Hírlap: 8901 Zalaegerszeg, Ady Endre u. 62; tel. (92) 12-575; Editor-in-Chief József Tarsoly.

WEEKLIES

Élet és Irodalom (Life and Literature): 1054 Budapest, Széchenyi u. 1; tel. (1) 153-3122; fax (1) 111-1087; f. 1957; literary and political; Editor IMRE BATA; circ. 60,000.

Élet és Tudomány (Life and Science): 1073 Budapest, Erzsébet krt 5; tel. (1) 142-0324; telex 22-7040; fax (1) 138-3331; f. 1946; popular science; Editor-in-Chief TAMÁS OLÁH; circ. 42,000.

Evangélikus Élet: 1088 Budapest, Puskin u. 12; tel. (1) 138-2630; f. 1933; Evangelical–Lutheran Church newspaper; Editor MIHÁLY TÓTH-SZÖLLŐS; circ. 12,000.

Film, Szinház, Muzsika (Films, Theatre, Music): 1073 Budapest, Erzsébet krt 9–11; tel. (1) 122-2400; Editor ZOLTÁN ISZLAI; circ. 30,000.

Heti Világgazdaság (World Economics Weekly): 1133 Budapest, Vág u. 13; tel. (1) 140-8776; telex 22-6676; f. 1979; Editor-in-Chief IVÁN LIPOVECZ; circ. 141,000.

Képes Újság (Illustrated News): 1085 Budapest, Gyulai Pál u. 14; tel. (1) 113-7660; f. 1960; Editor MIHALY KOVÁCS; circ. 400,000.

Ludas Matyi: 1077 Budapest, Gyulai Pál u. 14; tel. (1) 133-5718; satirical; Editor JÓZSEF ÁRKUS; circ. 352,000.

L'udové Noviny: 1065 Budapest, Nagymező u. 49; tel. (1) 131-9184; for Slovaks in Hungary; Editor PÁL KONDÁCS; circ. 1,700.

Magyar Ifjúság (Hungarian Youth): 1085 Budapest, Somogyi Béla u. 6; tel. (1) 113-0460; telex 22-6423; Editor LAJOS GUBCSI; circ. 207,000.

Magyar Mezőgazdaság (Hungarian Agriculture): 1355 Budapest, Kossuth Lajos tér 11; tel. (1) 112-2433; telex 22-5445; f. 1946; Editor-in-Chief Dr KÁROLY FEHÉR; circ. 24,000.

Magyar Nők Lapja (Hungarian Women's Journal): 1022 Budapest, Törökvész út 30A; tel. and fax (1) 115-4037; telex 225554; f. 1949; Editor-in-Chief LILI ZÉTÉNYI; circ. 550,000.

Magyarország (Hungary): 1085 Budapest, Gyulai Pál u. 14; tel. (1) 138-4644; telex 22-6351; f. 1964; news magazine; Editor DÉNES GYAPAY; circ. 200,000.

Narodne Novine: 1396 Budapest, POB 495; tel. (1) 112-4869; f. 1945; for Yugoslavs in Hungary; in Serbo-Croat and Slovene; Chief Editor MARKO MARKOVIĆ; circ. 2,800.

Neue Zeitung: 1391 Budapest, Nagymező u. 49, Pf. 224; tel. (1) 132-6334; f. 1957; for Germans in Hungary; Editor PETER LEIPOLD; circ. 4,500.

Ország-Világ (Land and World): 1073 Budapest, Erzsébet krt 9–11; tel. (1) 122-3283; f. 1957; Editor SÁNDOR KÖRÖSPATAKI KISS; circ. 208,000.

Rádió és Televízióújság (Radio and TV News): 1801 Budapest; tel. (1) 138-7210; f. 1956; Editor TAMÁS NÁDOR ; circ. 1,350,000.

Reform: 1443 Budapest, POB 222; tel. and fax (1) 122-4240; telex 22-3333; f. 1988; popular tabloid; 50% foreign-owned; Editor PÉTER TŐKE; circ. 300,000.

Reformátusok Lapja: 1395 Budapest, POB 424; tel. (1) 117-6809; f. 1957; Reformed Church paper for the laity; Editor-in-Chief and Publr ATTILA P. KOMLÓS; circ. 40,000.

Szabad Föld (Free Soil): 1087 Budapest, Könyves Kálmán krt 76; tel. and fax (1) 133-6794; f. 1945; Editor GYULA ECK; circ. 720,000.

Szövetkezet (Co-operative): 1054 Budapest, Szabadság tér 14; tel. (1) 131-3132; National Council of Hungarian Consumer Co-operative Societies; Editor-in-Chief ATTILA KOVÁCS; circ. 85,000.

Tallózó: 1035 Budapest, Miklós tér 1; tel. (1) 180-3420; f. 1989; news digest; Editor-in-Chief GYÖRGY ANDAI; circ. 45,000.

Tőzsde Kurir (Hungarian Stock Market Courier): 1074 Budapest, Rákóczi út 54; tel. (1) 122-3273; fax (1) 142-8356; business; Editor-in-Chief ISTVÁN GÁBOR BENEDEK.

Új Ember (New Man): 1053 Budapest, Kossuth Lajos u. 1; tel. (1) 117-3638; fax (1) 117-3471; f. 1945; religious weekly; Editor LÁSZLÓ RÓNAY; circ. 100,000.

Vasárnapi Hirek (Sunday News): 1979 Budapest, POB 14; tel. (1) 138-4366; telex 22-3174; f. 1984; political; Editor Dr ZOLTÁN LŐKÖS; circ. 300,000.

Világ (World): 1117 Budapest, Kaposvár u. 5–7; f. 1989; survey of political and cultural events; Editor-in-Chief ZOLTÁN ISTVÁN B&RÓ; circ. 50,000.

FORTNIGHTLIES

Foaia Noastra (Our Leaf): 1055 Budapest, Bajcsy Zs. u. 78; for Romanians in Hungary; Editor SÁNDOR HOCOPÁN; circ. 1,500.

Magyar Hirek (Hungarian News): 1068 Budapest, Benczúr u. 15; tel. (1) 122-5616; telex 22-317; fax (1) 122-2421; illustrated magazine primarily for Hungarians living abroad; Editor GYÖRGY HALÁSZ; circ. 70,000.

Pedagógusok Lapja (Teachers' Review): 1068 Budapest, Gorkij fasor 10; tel. (1) 122-8464; f. 1945; published by the Hungarian Union of Teachers; Editor-in-Chief LIEBHARDT ÁGOTA; circ. 15,000.

Szövetkezeti Hírlap (Co-operative Herald): 1052 Budapest, Pesti Barnabás u. 6; tel. (1) 117-0181; National Union of Artisans; Editor MÁRIA DOLEZSÁL; circ. 12,000.

Új Élet (New Life): 1075 Budapest, Síp u. 12; tel. (1) 122-2829; for Hungarian Jews; Editor Dr ISTVÁN DOMÁN; circ. 7,000.

OTHER PERIODICALS

(Published monthly unless otherwise indicated)

Állami Gazdaság (State Farming): General Direction of State Farming, 1054 Budapest, Akadémia u. 1–3; tel. (1) 112-4617; fax (1) 111-4877; f. 1946; Editor Mrs P. GÖRGÉNYI.

Business Partner Hungary: 1051 Budapest, Dorottya u. 6; tel. (1) 117-0850; telex 22-5646; fax (1) 118-6483; f. 1986; quarterly; Hungarian, German, French and English; economic journal published by Institute for Economic, Market Research and Informatics (KOPINT-DATORG).

Cartactual: 1367 Budapest, POB 76; tel. (1) 112-6480; telex 22-4964; f. 1965; every 2 months; map service periodical with supplement *Cartinform* (map bibliography); published in English, French, German and Hungarian; Editor-in-Chief ERNŐ CSÁTI.

Egyházi Krónika (Church Chronicle): 1052 Budapest, Petőfi tér 2.1.2; tel. (1) 118-4813; f. 1952; every 2 months; Eastern Orthodox Church journal; Editor Archpriest Dr FERIZ BERKI.

Elektrotechnika (Electrical Engineering): 1055 Budapest, Kossuth Lajos tér 6–8; tel. (1) 153-0117; telex 22-5792; fax (1) 153-4069; f. 1908; organ of Electrotechnical Association; Editor Dr TIBOR KELEMEN; circ. 3,000.

Élelmezési Ipar (Food Industry): 1361 Budapest, POB 5; tel. (1) 112-2859; f. 1947; Scientific Society for Food Industry; Editor Dr ISTVÁN TÓTH-ZSIGA.

Energia és Atomtechnika (Energy and Nuclear Technology): 1055 Budapest, Kossuth Lajos tér 6–8; tel. (1) 153-2751; telex 22-5792; fax (1) 156-1215; f. 1947; every two months; Scientific Society for Energy Economy; Editor-in-Chief Dr G. BŐKI.

Energiagazdálkodás (Energy Economy): 1055 Budapest, Kossuth Lajos tér 6; tel. (1) 153-2894; Scientific Society for Energetics; Editor Dr TAMÁS RAPP.

Építésügyi Szemle (Building Review): 1054 Budapest, Beloiannisz u. 2–4; tel. (1) 131-3180; building; Editor Dr JÓZSEF KÁDÁR.

Ezermester (The Handyman): 1066 Budapest, Dessewffy u. 34; tel. (1) 132-0542; telex 22-6423; f. 1957; do-it-yourself magazine; Editor J. SZÜCS; circ. 135,000.

Forum: Budapest; f. 1989; periodical of the Hungarian Socialist Party; Editor-in-Chief ISTVÁN SZERDAHELYI.

Gép (Machinery): 1027 Budapest, Fő u. 68; tel. (1) 135-4175; telex 22-5792; fax (1) 153-0818; f. 1949; Scientific Society of Mechanical Engineering; Editor Dr KORNÉL LEHOFER.

Hungarian Book Review: 1051 Budapest, Vörösmarty tér 1.X.1010; tel. (1) 117-6222; f. 1958; quarterly review of Hungarian Publishers' and Booksellers' Asscn; in English, French and German; Editor-in-Chief GYULA KURUCZ.

Hungarian Business Herald: 1087 Budapest, Könyves Kálmán krt 76; tel. (1) 1142-249; f. 1970; quarterly review published in English and German by the Ministry of International Economic Relations; Editor-in-Chief Dr GERD BIRÓ; circ. 4,000.

Hungarian Digest: 1117 Budapest, Bölcső u. 3; tel. (1) 181-1580; f. 1980; illustrated quarterly on political, economic and cultural issues; English; also in French as Revue de Hongrie, and in German as Ungarland; Editor TIBOR ZÁDOR; circ. 50,000.

Hungarian Economy: 1355 Budapest, Alkotmány u. 10; tel. (1) 132-2186; telex 22-6613; fax (1) 132-2990; f. 1972; quarterly; economic and business review; Editor-in-Chief Dr JÁNOS FOLLINUS; circ. 10,000.

Hungarian Trade Union News: 1964 Budapest, Rákóczi út 54; tel. (1) 122-4810; f. 1957; in six languages including English; Editor-in-Chief EMÖKE NÁNDORI.

Hungarian Travel Magazine: 1088 Budapest, Múzeum u. 11; tel. (1) 138-4643; quarterly in English and German; illustrated journal of the Tourist Board for visitors to Hungary; Man. Editor JÚLIA Sz. NAGY.

Ipar-Gazdaság (Industrial Economy): 1371 Budapest, POB 433; tel. (1) 201-8456; f. 1948; Editor Dr TAMÁS MÉSZÁROS; circ. 4,000.

Jogtudományi Közlöny (Law Gazette): 1250 Budapest, Pf. 25, Országház u. 30; tel. (1) 155-6894; f. 1866; law; Editor-in-Chief Dr JÓZSEF HALÁSZ; Editor Dr IMRE VÖRÖS; circ. 2,500.

Kortárs (Contemporary): 1062 Budapest, Bajza u. 18; tel. (1) 142-1168; literary gazette; Editor IMRE KIS PINTÉR; circ. 5,000.

Könyvtáros (The Librarian): 1135 Budapest, Frangepán u. 50-56; tel. (1) 111-3279; f. 1951; Editor LÁSZLÓ BERECZKY; circ. 6,000.

Közgazdasági Szemle (Economic Review): 1112 Budapest, Budaörsi u. 43–45; tel. (1) 185-0777; f. 1954; published by Cttee for Economic Sciences of Academy of Sciences; Editor KATALIN SZABÓ; circ. 15,000.

Look at Hungary: 1906 Budapest, POB 223; tel. (1) 186-0133; f. 1980; quarterly photomagazine in English, Arabic, French and Portuguese; Editor-in-Chief GÁBOR VAJDA.

Made in Hungary: 1426 Budapest, POB 3; economics and business magazine published in English by MTI; Editor GYÖRGY BLASITS.

Magyar Jog (Hungarian Law): 1054 Budapest, Szemere u. 10; tel. (1) 131-4574; fax (1) 111-4013; f. 1953; law; Editor-in-Chief Dr JÁNOS NÉMETH; circ. 3,500.

Magyar Közlöny (Official Gazette): 1055 Budapest, Bajcsy Zs. u. 78; tel. (1) 112-1236; Editor Dr ELEMÉR KISS; circ. 90,000.

Magyar Tudomány (Hungarian Science): Hungarian Academy of Sciences, 1051 Budapest, Nádor u. 7; tel. (1) 117-9524; Editor-in-Chief BÉLA KÖPECZI.

Muzsika: 1073 Budapest, Erzsébet krt 9–11; tel. (1) 121-5440; f. 1958; musical review; Editor-in-Chief MÁRIA FEUER; circ. 7,500.

Nagyvilág (The Great World): 1054 Budapest, Széchenyi u. 1; tel. (1) 132-1160; f. 1956; review of world literature; Editor LÁSZLÓ KÉRY; circ. 6,000.

New Hungarian Quarterly: 1906 Budapest, POB 223; tel. (1) 175-6722; fax (1) 118-8297; f. 1960; illustrated quarterly in English; politics, economics, philosophy, education, culture, poems, short stories, etc.; Editor MIKLÓS VAJDA; circ. 3,500.

Református Egyház: 1146 Budapest, Abonyi u. 21; tel. (1) 122-7870; f. 1949; official journal of the Hungarian Reformed Church; Editor-in-Chief FERENC DUSICZA; circ. 1,600.

Statisztikai Szemle (Statistical Review): 1525 Budapest, POB 51; tel. (1) 202-1291; f. 1923; Editor-in-Chief MARIA VISI LAKATOS; circ. 1,200.

Társadalmi Szemle (Social Review): 1114 Budapest, Villányi ut. 11–13; tel. (1) 166-6300; theoretical-political review; Editor MIHÁLY BIHARI; circ. 10,000.

Technika (Technology): 1428 Budapest, POB 12; tel. (1) 1 67-2148; telex 22-4244; fax (1) 118-0109; f. 1957; official journal of the Hungarian Academy of Engineering; monthly in Hungarian, annually in English, German and Russian; Editor-in-Chief EMIL SZLUKA; circ. 15,000.

Turizmus (Tourism): 1088 Budapest, Múzeum u. 11; tel. (1) 138-4638; telex 22-5297; Editor ZSOLT SZEBENI; circ. 8,000.

Új Technika (New Technology): 1014 Budapest, Szentháromság tér 1; tel. (1) 155-7122; telex 22-6490; f. 1967; popular industrial quarterly; circ. 35,000.

Vigilia: 1364 Budapest, POB 111; tel. (1) 117-7246; fax (1) 117-4895; f. 1935; Catholic; Editor LÁSZLÓ LUKÁCS; circ. 11,500.

Villamosság (Electricity): 1055 Budapest, Kossuth Lajos tér 6–8; tel. (1) 153-0117; organ of Electrotechnical Association; Gen. Editor FERENC KOVÁCS; circ. 3,000.

NEWS AGENCIES

Magyar Távirati Iroda (MTI) (Hungarian News Agency): 1016 Budapest, Naphegy tér 8; tel. (1) 175-6722; telex 22-4371; fax (1) 117-7577; f. 1880; 19 brs in Hungary; 19 bureaux abroad; Gen. Dir OTTÓ OLTVÁNYI.

Foreign Bureaux

Agence France-Presse (AFP): Budapest, Naphegy u. 1; tel. (1) 183-6861; telex 22-3831; Correspondent PAL HERSKOVITS.

Agenzia Nazionale Stampa Associata (ANSA) (Italy): 1024 Budapest, Mártírok u. 43–45; tel. (1) 135-2323; telex 22-4711; Bureau Chief NINO ALIMENTI.

Allgemeiner Deutscher Nachrichtendienst (ADN) (Germany): 1146 Budapest, Zichy Géza u. 5; tel. (1) 121-0810; telex 22-4675; Bureau Chief GERHARD KOWALSKI.

Associated Press (AP) (USA): 1122 Budapest, Maros u. 13; tel. (1) 156-9129; Correspondent ALEX BANDY.

Československá tisková kancelář (ČTK) (Czechoslovakia): 1146 Budapest, Zichy Géza u. 5; tel. (1) 142-7115; telex 22-5367; Correspondent STEFAN NÉMETH.

Informatsionnoye Agentstvo Novosti (IAN) (Russia): 1075 Budapest, Tanács Kőrút 9; tel. (1) 132-0594; telex 61-224792; fax (1) 142-3325; Bureau Chief A. POPOV.

Inter Press Service (IPS) (Italy): 1026 Budapest, Filler u. 26; tel. (1) 136-3903; telex 22-4371; Rep. CATALINA WEINER.

Prensa Latina (Cuba): 1020 Budapest, Budakeszi u. 55D, 7 p.; tel. (1) 176-7474; telex 22-4800; Correspondent MIRIAM CASTRO CASO.

Reuters (UK): c/o Magyar Távirati Iroda, 1426 Budapest, POB 3.

Telegrafnoye Agentstvo Sovetskovo Soyuza (TASS) (Russia): 1023 Budapest, Vérhalom u. 12–16; Correspondent YEVGENI POPOV.

United Press International (UPI) (USA): 1137 Budapest, Pozsonyi u. 14; telex 22-5649; Bureau Chief Dr ANDREW L. SÜMEGHI.

Xinhua (New China) News Agency (People's Republic of China): 1068 Budapest, Benczur u. 39A.1.4; tel. (1) 122-8420; telex 22-5447; Chief Correspondent HOU FENGQING.

PRESS ASSOCIATIONS

Magyar Újságírók Országos Szövetsége (MUOSZ) (National Association of Hungarian Journalists): 1062 Budapest, Andrássy ut 101; tel. (1) 122-1699; telex 22-5045; Chair. LÁSZLÓ ROBERT; Gen. Sec. GÁBOR BENCSIK; 4,700 mems.

Association of Hungarian Newspaper Publishers: Budapest; f. 1986 by four major newspaper publishing companies, MTI and local newspaper publrs; Chair. JÓZSEF BOCZ.

Publishers

PRINCIPAL PUBLISHING HOUSES

Akadémiai Kiadó: 1117 Budapest, Prielle Kornélia u. 19-35; tel. (1) 181-2134; telex 22-6228; fax (1) 166-6466; f. 1828; Publishing House of the Hungarian Academy of Sciences; humanities, social, natural and technical sciences, dictionaries, encyclopaedias, periodicals of the Academy and other institutions, issued partly in foreign languages; Man. Dir FERENC ZÖLD.

Corvina Kiadó: 1051 Budapest, Vörösmarty tér 1; tel. (1) 117-6222; telex 22-4440; fax (1) 118-4410; f. 1955; Hungarian works translated into foreign languages, art and educational books, fiction and non-fiction, tourist guides, cookery books, sport, musicology, juvenile and children's literature; Man. Dir ISTVÁN BART; Editorial Dir BÉLA REVICZKY.

Editio Musica Budapest: 1051 Budapest, Vörösmarty tér 1; tel. (1) 118-4228; telex 22-5500; fax (1) 138-2732; f. 1950; music publishing, engraving and printing, and books on musical subjects; Dir ISTVÁN HOMOLYA.

Európa Könyvkiadó: 1055 Budapest, Kossuth Lajos tér 13–15; tel. (1) 131-2700; telex 22-5645; fax (1) 131-4162; f. 1945; world literature translated into Hungarian; Man. LEVENTE OSZTOVITS.

Gondolat Könyvkiadó Vállalat: 1088 Budapest, Bródy Sándor u. 16; tel. (1) 138-3777; popular scientific publications on natural and social sciences, art, encyclopaedic handbooks; Dir ILDIKÓ LENDVAI.

Helikon Kiadó: 1053 Budapest, Eötvös L. u. 8; tel. (1) 117-4765; telex 22-7100; fax (1) 117-4865; bibliophile books; Dir MAGDA MOLNAR.

Képzőművészeti Kiadó: 1051 Budapest, Vörösmarty tér 1; tel. (1) 118-4981; telex 22-4405; fine arts; Man. PÉTER LÁTKI.

Kossuth Könyvkiadó Vállalat: 1054 Budapest, Steindl u. 6; tel. (1) 111-7440; fax (1) 111-3670; f. 1944; sociological and popular publications; Man. ANDRÁS KOCSIS.

Közgazdasági és Jogi Könyvkiadó: 1054 Budapest, Nagysándor József u. 6; tel. (1) 112-6430; telex 22-6511; fax (1) 131-2327; f. 1955; economics, law, sociology, psychology, history, politics, education, dictionaries; Man. VILMOS DALOS.

Magvető Könyvkiadó: 1806 Budapest, Vörösmarty tér 1; tel. (1) 118-5109; literature; Man. MIKLÓS JOVÁNOVICS.

Medicina Könyvkiadó: 1054 Budapest, Beloiannisz u. 8; tel. (1) 112-2650; f. 1957; books on medicine, sport, tourism; Man. Prof. Dr ISTVÁN ÁRKY.

Mezőgazdasági Könyvkiadó: 1054 Budapest, Báthory u. 10; tel. (1) 111-6650; telex 20-2536; fax (1) 111-7270; ecology, natural sciences, environmental protection, food industry; Man. Dr CSABA GALLYAS.

Móra Ferenc Gyermek és Ifjúsági Könyvkiadó: 1146 Budapest, Május 1 u. 57–59; tel. (1) 121-2390; telex 22-7027; fax (1) 1 22-4276; f. 1950; children's books, science fiction; Man. JÁNOS SZILÁDI.

Müszaki Könyvkiadó: 1014 Budapest, Szentháromság tér 6; tel. (1) 155-7122; telex 22-6490; fax (1) 115-6767; f. 1955; scientific and technical, fiction and non-fiction; Man. PÉTER SZÜCS.

Népszava Lap-és Könyvkiadó Vállalat: 1553 Budapest, Rákóczi u. 54; tel. (1) 122-4810; National Federation of Hungarian Trade Unions; Man. Dr JENŐ KISS.

Statiqum Kiadó és Nyomda Kft: 1033 Budapest, Kaszásdülő u. 2; tel. (1) 180-3311; telex 22-6699; fax (1) 168-8635; f. 1991 as legal successor to Statisztikai Kiadó Vállalat (f. 1954); publications on statistics, system-management and computer science; Dir BENEDEK BELECZ.

Szépirodalmi Könyvkiadó: 1073 Budapest, Erzsébet krt 9–11; tel. (1) 122-1285; telex 22-6754; f. 1950; modern and classical Magyar literature; Man. SÁNDOR Z. SZALAI.

Tankönyvkiadó Vállalat: 1055 Budapest, Szalay u. 10–14; tel. and fax (1) 132-4915; f. 1949; school and university textbooks, pedagogical literature and language books; Man. JÓZSEF VILHELM.

Zrinyi Katonai Kiadó: 1087 Budapest, Kerepesi u. 29; tel. (1) 133-4750; military literature; Man. LÁSZLÓ NÉMETH.

CARTOGRAPHERS

Cartographia (Hungarian Company for Surveying and Mapping): 1443 Budapest, POB 132; tel. (1) 163-4639; telex 22-6218; fax (1) 163-4639; f. 1954; Dir Dr ÁRPÁD PAPP-VÁRY.

Földmérési és Térképészeti Főosztály (Department of Geodesy and Cartography): 1055 Budapest, Kossuth Lajos tér 11; tel. (1) 131-3736; telex 22-5445; fax (1) 153-0518; f. 1954; Man. SÁNDOR ZSÁMBOKI.

PUBLISHERS' ASSOCIATION

Magyar Könyvkiadók és Könyvterjesztők Egyesülése (Hungarian Publishers' and Booksellers' Association): 1051 Budapest, Vörösmarty tér 1; POB 130; tel. (1) 118-4758; f. 1878; most Hungarian publishers are members of the Association; Pres. GYÖRGY FEHÉR; Sec.-Gen. FERENC ZÖLD.

WRITERS' UNION

Magyar Írók Szövetsége (Association of Hungarian Writers): 1062 Budapest, Bajza u. 18; tel. (1) 122-8840; f. 1945; Pres. ANNA JÓKAI; Sec.-Gen. SÁNDOR KOCZKÁS.

Radio and Television

In 1989 there were an estimated 6m. radio receivers and 4.2m. television receivers in use. Cable television systems are expanding, and in early 1985 were operating in 12 cities. In 1986 Hungary completed negotiations to receive TV programmes from a Western European satellite network. By the end of 1987 more than 25,000 homes in the city of Szekesfehervar were able to receive experimental satellite transmissions from the British Sky Channel. Programmes from the British-based Super Channel, the French TV-5 and the USA's CNN-Europe service were also available by 1988. In 1988 more than 40 areas (300,000 homes) were able to receive cable and satellite services.

RADIO

Magyar Rádió: 1800 Budapest, Bródy Sándor u. 5–7; tel. (1) 138-8388; telex 22-5188; fax (1) 138-7004; f. 1924; stations: Radio Kossuth (Budapest); Radio Petőfi (Budapest); Radio Bartók (Budapest, mainly classical music); 6 regional studios; external broadcasts: in English, German, Hungarian, Italian, Romanian, Russian, Slovak, Serbo-Croat, Spanish and Turkish; Pres. CSABA GOMBÁR.

> **Radio Danubius:** f. 1986; commercial station; broadcasts news, music and information in Hungarian 21 hours a day; transmitting stations in Budapest, Lake Balaton region, Sopron, Szeged and Debrecen; Dir GYÖRGY VARGA.

TELEVISION

Magyar Televízió: 1810 Budapest, Szabadság tér 17; tel. (1) 153-3200; telex 22-5568; fax (1) 153-4568; f. 1957; first channel broadcasts about 85 hours a week and the second channel about 63 hours a week, every day, mostly colour transmissions; 100 high-capacity relay stations; Pres. ELEMÉR HANKISS; Head of TV1 GÁBOR BÁNYAI; Head of TV2 TAMÁS VITRAY.

Finance

The Hungarian financial system is being restructured. In January 1985 the functions of issue and credit at the National Bank were separated. Under reforms implemented in January 1987, the central banking and commercial banking functions were separated, and there is now a two-tier banking system. The National Bank of Hungary, as the bank of issue, continues to participate in the formulation of economic policy. The 1987 reforms did not affect the National Bank's foreign exchange authority, nor alter substantially the Bank's total assets. At the second level are the commercial banks. These institutions have general and nation-wide authority, keep the accounts of enterprises, accept their deposits and extend credits to them. The commercial banks may participate in ventures and may provide banking services for their clients. They establish their own business policy and the terms and conditions of their contracts, within the limits of central banking regulations. The commercial banks (established from the units seceding from the National Bank of Hungary, the reorganization of the State Development Bank and the Creditbank of Budapest, and the General Banking and Trust Co Ltd) are: The General Banking and Trust and Co Ltd; Budapest Bank Rt.; Hungarian Creditbank Ltd; Hungarian Foreign Trade Bank; Commercial and Creditbank Ltd. There is a third level to the financial system, which consists of the so-called specialized financial institutions. These small banks may establish deposit and credit links with economic entities, may participate in ventures and may provide banking services. Unlike the commercial banks, the specialized financial institutions may not keep the accounts of their clients.

Like the National Savings Bank (OTP), the Savings Co-operatives (Takarékszövetkezet) function as banks for the use of the general public, operating at the local level. Their main activity is the collection of deposits and the provision of credit to their members. Since January 1985, these co-operatives have been able to maintain accounts for small enterprises and private entrepreneurs, and can extend credit to them. They are also empowered to provide mortgage facilities to individuals. Minimum registered capital is 2.0m. forint at each co-operative. In early 1987 there were 260 such co-operatives in Hungary. Their interests are represented by SZÖVOSZ (National Federation of Consumer Co-operatives—see below).

Financial institutions with foreign capital shares may be founded with government permission. The first bank in Hungary to be founded with foreign capital involvement was the Central European International Bank (CIB), established in 1979. In 1985 a joint Hungarian-US commercial bank was established by the Central Exchange and Credit Bank of Budapest and Citibank of New York. It began operations in 1986, under the supervision of the National Bank of Hungary. Unicbank Rt., founded with 45% foreign capital, commenced operations in January 1987.

The issue of bonds, in order to finance housing and infrastructural projects, is of increasing significance. Offering a higher rate of interest than that of the National Savings Bank, bonds were first issued on a large scale in early 1983, available initially only to enterprises but later also to private individuals. In September 1984 the State Development Bank (now State Development Institution) began repurchasing and reselling bonds, thus giving rise to the existence of a domestic 'bond market'. By mid-1986 local councils and enterprises had issued 130 bonds to a total value of 8,000m. forint (equivalent to almost 3% of total Hungarian investment in 1985), about 70% of which had been purchased by private citizens. The bond market expanded rapidly in 1987, and by December 200 bonds, worth 24,320m. forint, were in circulation. In January 1988 the state guarantee for bonds was terminated, thus rendering the issue of bonds more difficult for less profitable organizations. The State also began to issue treasury bills in order to finance budget deficits. A national securities market opened in Budapest in January 1988, and a stock exchange in May 1990.

BANKING

(cap. = capital; res = reserves; dep. = deposits; m. = million; Ft = forint; brs = branches)

Central Bank

Magyar Nemzeti Bank (National Bank of Hungary): 1850 Budapest, Szabadság tér 8–9; tel. (1) 153-2600; telex 22-5677; fax (1) 132-3913; f. 1924; cap. 10,000m. Ft, res 14,939m. Ft, dep. 1,619,624m. Ft (Dec. 1990); issue of bank notes; transacts international payments business; supervises banking system; 18 brs; Pres. Dr GYÖRGY SURANYI; First Vice-Pres. Dr IMRE TARAFÁS.

Commercial Banks

Általános Értékforgalmi Bank Rt. (General Banking and Trust Co Ltd): 1093 Budapest, Szamuely u. 30-32; tel. (1) 118-8688; telex 22-3578; fax (1) 118-8695; f. 1923; commercial banking activities in Hungarian currency, deposit-taking and account-keeping in foreign currency, services for joint-venture companies; cap. 1,000m. Ft (Dec. 1988); Dir-Gen. ANTAL BESZÉDES.

Budapest Bank Rt.: 1052 Budapest, Deák Ferenc u. 5; tel. (1) 118-1200; telex 22-3013; fax (1) 118-1335; f. 1986; cap. 7,046m. Ft; Dir-Gen. Dr LAJOS BOKROS.

Dunabank Rt.—Duna Befektetési és Forgalmi Bank Rt.: 1054 Budapest, Báthori u. 12; tel. (1) 131-2741; telex 22-5595; fax (1) 131-3786; f. 1987 as Bank for Investment and Transactions; renamed 1989; cap. 1,000m. Ft; Chief Exec. KÁLMÁN DEBRECZENI; Chair. of Supervisory Bd JÓZSEF MARJAI.

Közép-európai Hitelbank Rt. (Central-European Credit Bank Ltd): 1364 Budapest, Váci u. 16; tel. (1) 118-8377; telex 22-6104; fax (1) 117-5657; f. 1988; fully-owned subsidiary of Central-European International Bank Ltd (CIB), for domestic business in the Hungarian market; cap. 659m. Ft, assets 16,738m. Ft (Dec. 1990); Man. Dir GYÖRGY ZDEBORSKY; DEP. MAN. DIR MICHAEL Graf VON MEDEM.

Magyar Hitel Bank Rt. (Hungarian Credit Bank Ltd): 1853 Budapest, Szabadság tér 5–6; tel. (1) 132-7100; telex 20-2505; fax (1) 131-5981; f. 1987; cap. 13,983m. Ft; activities include venture financing, securities trading, real estate investments, joint venture promotion and advisory services; 100 brs; Chief Exec. ÁRPÁD BARTHA.

Magyar Külkereskedelmi Bank Rt. (Hungarian Foreign Trade Bank Ltd): 1821 Budapest, Szt. István tér 11; tel. (1) 132-9360; telex 22-6941; fax (1) 132-2568; f. 1950; cap. 7,125m. Ft (Dec. 1990); 5 brs; Chair. and Man. Dir GÁBOR ERDÉLY.

Merkantil Bank Ltd: 1051 Budapest, József A. u. 24; tel. (1) 118-2688; telex 20-2579; fax (1) 117-2331; f. 1988; affiliated to Commercial and Creditbank Ltd; cap. 1,100m. Ft; Dir ÁDÁM KOLOSSVÁRY.

Országos Kereskedelmi és Hitelbank Rt. (Commercial and Credit Bank Ltd): 1851 Budapest, Arany János u. 24; tel. (1) 112-5200; telex 22-3200; fax (1) 111-3845; f. 1986; cap. 12,107m. Ft (Dec. 1989); Dir Dr GÉZA LENK; First Dep. Chief Exec. MIKLÓS SZIGETHY.

Specialized Financial Institutions

AGROBANK Rt.—Agrár Innovációs Bank Rt. (Agricultural Innovation Bank Ltd): 1052 Budapest, Tanács krt 6; tel. (1) 117-9878; telex 22-3111; fax (1) 117-5650; f. 1984; joint-stock company; cap. 1,500m. Ft; 10 brs; Dir Dr PETER KUNOS.

Általános Vállalkozási Bank Rt. (General Bank for Venture Financing Ltd): 1055 Budapest, Stollár Béla u. 3A; tel. (1) 132-6590; telex 22-3157; fax (1) 131-3181; f. 1985; joint-stock company; cap. 2,200m. Ft; Gen. Man. MIHALY NÉMETH.

Építőipari Innovációs Bank Rt. (Innovation Bank for Construction Industry Ltd): 1063 Budapest, Szív u. 53; tel. (1) 112-9010; telex 22-3743; fax (1) 132-0567; f. 1985; joint stock company; cap. 1,160m. Ft; Man. Dir TAMÁS VARGA.

INNOFINANCE—Általános Innovációs Pénzintézet Rt. (General Financial Institution for Innovation Ltd): 1365 Budapest, POB 718; tel. (1) 138-3366; telex 22-3182; fax (1) 117-7800; f. 1980; joint-stock company; registered cap. 500m. Ft; Man. Dir ERZSÉBET BIRMAN.

Inter-Európa Bank Rt.: 1054 Budapest, Szabadság tér 15; tel. (1) 132-0170; telex 20-7879; fax (1) 153-4850; f. 1980 as INTERINVEST; associated mem. of San Paolo Group; cap. 2,807m. Ft; Man. Dir GYÖRGY IVÁNYI; Dep. Man. Dir ANDRÁS FELKAI.

INVESTBANK Rt. (Bank for Technical Development): 1053 Budapest, Képíró u. 9; tel. (1) 1175-333; telex 22-3250; fax (1) 118-4400; f. 1983; cap. 1,245m. Ft; Dir Dr ANNA TEMESI.

Iparbankház Ltd (Industrial Co-operative Trading Banking House Ltd): 1052 Budapest, Gerlóczy u. 5; tel. (1) 117-6811; telex 22-3042; fax (1) 117-1921; f. 1984; cap. 1,239m. Ft; 7 brs; Gen. Dir ISTVÁN KOLLARIK.

Ipari Fejlesztési Bank Rt. (Industrial Development Bank Ltd): 1054 Budapest, Hold u. 25; tel. (1) 132-0320; telex 22-7351; fax 112-9552; f. 1988 (previously Magyar Iparbank Rt., f. 1987); cap. 3,200m. Ft; Gen. Man. Dr GYULA PÁZMÁNDI.

Kisvállalkozási Bank (Bank for Small Ventures): 1876 Budapest, Nádor u. 16; tel. (1) 131-6940; telex 22-4280; f. 1986; affiliated to NSB; cap. 3,200m. Ft; Dir ÁRPÁD BACSÓKA.

Konzumbank Rt. (Consumers' Co-operative Societies Share Company): 1052 Budapest, Vitkovics M. u. 9; tel. (1) 117-2600; telex 22-3305; fax (1) 117-6721; f. 1986; cap. 1,042m. Ft; Dir Dr GÁBOR PÁL.

Mezőbank (National Bank of Agricultural Co-operatives Corporation): 1025 Budapest, Hold u. 16; tel. (1) 153-1000; telex 22-7615; fax 132-1196; f. 1986; cap. 2,510m. Ft, dep. 11,000m. Ft; 30 brs; Dir Dr GYULA KABAI.

Consortium Banks

Central-European International Bank Ltd (CIB): 1364 Budapest, Váci u. 16, POB 170; tel. (1) 118-8377; telex 22-4759; fax (1) 118-9415; f. 1979; shareholders: National Bank of Hungary (34%), Banca Commerciale Italiana, Bayerische Vereinsbank, Long-Term Credit Bank of Japan, Société Générale, Mitsui Taiyo Kobe Bank (13.2% each); an offshore bank conducting international banking business of all kinds; dep. \$616.9m., total resources \$688.4m. (Dec. 1990); Chair. Dr MARIO ARCARI; Man. Dir GYÖRGY ZDEBORSKY.

Citibank Budapest: 1052 Budapest, Váci u. 19–21; tel. (1) 138-2666; telex 22-7822; f. 1986; joint-stock company; share cap. 1,000m. Ft; Gen. Man. ROBIN M. WINCHESTER.

Creditanstalt: 1363 Budapest, Akademia u. 17; tel. (1) 111-5400; commercial banking and foreign exchange services; owned 75% by Creditanstalt (Austria) and 25% by Budapest Bank Rt.; Man. Dir MATTHIAS KUNSCH.

Unicbank Rt.: 1052 Budapest, Váci u. 19–21; tel. (1) 118-2088; telex 22-3123; fax (1) 138-2836; f. 1986; Shareholders: International Finance Corporation (IFC) (15%); Raiffeisen Zentralbank Österreich AG (RZB), Vienna (30%); Central Bank of Exchange and Credit Ltd, Budapest (20%); National Savings Bank, Budapest (11%); National Federation of Agricultural Co-operators and Producers—MOSZ (6%); Association of Industrial Co-operatives—OKISZ (6%); National Association of General Consumers' Co-operatives—ÁFEOSZ (6%); National Association of Industrial Corporations—IPOSZ (6%); cap. 1,350m. Ft; Man. Dir Dr PÉTER FELCSUTI.

Savings Banks

Országos Takarékpénztár Rt.—OTP Rt. (National Savings and Commercial Bank Ltd—NSB Ltd): 1876 Budapest, Nador u. 16; tel. (1) 153-1444; telex 22-4432; f. 1949; cap. 23,000m. Ft, dep. 376,000m. Ft (Dec. 1990); retail and commercial banking services, foreign exchange and currency transactions, securities; 430 brs; Gen. Man. ELEMÉR TERTÁK .

Postabank és Takarékpénztár Rt. (Post Bank and Savings Bank Corporation): 1920 Budapest, József nádor tér 1; tel. (1) 118-0855; telex 22-3294; fax (1) 117-1369; f. 1988; cap. 4,000m. Ft; Dir GÁBOR PRINCZ.

Financial Development Institution

Állami Fejlesztési Intézet (State Development Institution): 1052 Budapest, Deák F. u. 5; tel. (1) 118-1200; telex 22-5672; fax (1) 166-8643; f. 1987 to succeed the State Development Bank; finance of development projects dealing with company reorganization, privatization and investments; Chief Exec. Dr GUSZTÁVNÉ BÁGER.

Central Corporation

Pénzintézeti Központ (Central Corporation of Banking Companies): 1431 Budapest, Szamuely u. 38; tel. (1) 117-1255; telex 22-6548; f. 1916; banking, property, rights and interests, deposits, securities, and foreign exchange management; cap. 1,000m. Ft; Dir-Gen. MIHÁLY BIRÓ.

STOCK EXCHANGE

Budapesti Értékpapír Tõzsde (Budapest Stock Exchange): 1056 Budapest, Váci u. 19–21; tel. (1) 118-2347; f. 1989, began operations in May 1990; Pres. LAJOS BOKROS; Man. Dir ILONA HARDY.

INSURANCE

In July 1986 the state insurance enterprise was divided into two companies, one of which retained the name of the former Állami Biztosító. Further companies have been founded since 1988.

Állami Biztosító (ÁB) (State Insurance Co): 1813 Budapest, Üllõi u. 1; tel. (1) 118-1866; telex 22-4550; fax (1) 138-4741; f. 1949, reorganized 1986; handles life and property insurance, insurance of agricultural plants, co-operatives, foreign insurance, etc.; Gen. Man. Dr GABOR KEPECS.

Atlasz Utazási Biztosító (Atlasz Travel Insurance Co): 1052 Budapest, Deák F. u. 23; tel. (1) 118-1999; telex 22-6725; fax (1) 117-1529; f. 1988; cap. 1,000m. Ft; Gen. Man. GÁBOR DARVAS.

Garancia Biztosító Rt. (Garancia Insurance Co): 1052 Budapest, Semmelweis u. 17; tel. and fax (1) 117-6226; f. 1988; cap. 1,050m. Ft; Gen. Man. OTTÓ GAÁL.

Hungária Biztosító Rt. (Hungária Insurance, Reinsurance and Export Credit Insurance Co): 1115 Budapest, Bánk bán utca 17B; tel. (1) 175-9211; telex 22-3104; f. 1986; handles international insurance, insurance of state companies and motor-car, marine, life, accident and liability insurance; cap. 3,000m. Ft; Man. Dir TAMÁS UZONYI.

Trade and Industry

CHAMBERS OF COMMERCE AND AGRICULTURE

Magyar Gazdasági Kamara (Hungarian Chamber of Commerce): 1389 Budapest, POB 106; tel. (1) 153-3333; telex 22-4745; fax (1) 153-1285; f. 1848; federation of asscns representing Hungarian cos; develops trade with other countries; mediates between companies, etc.; mems: 45 regional and professional asscns and 4,073 industrial,

agricultural and foreign trade orgs; Pres. LAJOS TOLNAY; Gen. Sec. LÁSZLÓ FODOR.

Budapesti Kereskedelmi és Iparkamara (Budapest Chamber of Industry and Commerce): 1016 Budapest, Krisztina krt 99; tel. (1) 156-9122; Pres. IMRE TÓTH.

Magyar Agrárkamara (Hungarian Chamber of Agriculture): 1055 Budapest, Kossuth L. tér 11; tel. (1) 153-3000; Pres. KÁROLY FARKAS.

SELECTED FOREIGN TRADE ORGANIZATIONS

Since 1980 Hungary's foreign trade organizations have been undergoing modernization. New regulations, introduced in 1988, permitted all business organizations to export products and to conduct business with foreign partners without the involvement of specialized traders. By early 1991 some 90% of all import activities had been liberalized and no special licences were required for foreign trading.

AÉV No 31: 1364 Budapest, POB 83; tel. (1) 118-0511; telex 22-4928; fax (1) 118-4082; f. 1951; state building factory; construction of industrial units, power plants, chemical combines, cement plants, etc.; undertakes building work abroad.

Agrária-Bábolna: 2943 Bábolna; tel. (34) 69-111; telex 22-6555; fax (34) 69-002; f. 1789; turn-key poultry and pig farms with breeding stock and feed premixes; hatching eggs, breeding poultry, pigs, sheep and breeding jumping and riding horses; processed chicken; rodent and insect extermination services, etc.; Gen. Dir LÁSZLÓ PAPOCSI.

Agrikon: 6001 Kecskemét, POB 43; tel. (76) 27-666; telex 26-493; Budapest office: 1364 Budapest, POB 167; tel. (1) 118-9568; telex 22-5517; fax (1) 117-2581; engineering and servicing for agricultural and food processing machines; Man. Dir PÁL HUGYECZ.

Agrimpex Trading Co Ltd: 1392 Budapest, POB 278; tel. (1) 111-3800; telex 22-5751; fax (1) 153-0658; f. 1948; agricultural products; Chair. and Gen. Man. ANDRÁS VERMES.

Agrober: 1518 Budapest, POB 93; tel. (1) 162-0640; fax (1) 161-2469; consulting engineers and contractors for the agriculture and food industry; Gen. Dir IMRE KONCZ.

Agrotek: 1388 Budapest, POB 66; tel. (1) 153-0555; telex 22-6522; fax (1) 153-4316; f. 1961; export and import of agricultural machinery and equipment, and fertilizers; Gen. Man. ÁKOS TAMÁS FEHÉR.

Alkaloida Chemical Company: 4440 Tiszavasvari, Kabay János u. 29; tel. (42) 12-233; telex 73275; fax (42) 15-512; production and export of pharmaceuticals, pesticides, etc.; Gen. Dir LÁSZLÓ HAGYO KOVÁCS.

Artex: 1390 Budapest, POB 167; tel. (1) 153-0222; telex 22-4951; fax (1) 111-1295; f. 1949; furniture, carpets, porcelain, ceramics, gold and silver ware, applied arts, household and sports goods; Gen. Man. Dr ANDRAS BIEBER.

BHG Telecommunication Works: 1509 Budapest, POB 2; tel. (1) 181-3300; telex 22-5933; fax (1) 166-7433; telecommunications; Gen. Dir LÁSZLÓ MIKICS.

Bivimpex Trading Co: 1325 Budapest, POB 55; tel. (1) 169-3522; telex 22-4279; fax (1) 169-4716; f. 1971; raw hide and leather; Dir L. VERMES.

Bõrker: 1391 Budapest, POB 215; tel. (1) 121-0760; telex 22-5543; fax (1) 122-7095; f. 1949; trading company for basic materials and accessories for shoes, fancy leather goods, garments and furniture; Gen. Man. LAJOS ALSÓSZENTIVÁNYI.

BRG: 1300 Budapest, POB 43; tel. (1) 168-2080; telex 22-5928; fax (1) 168-9652; radio engineering.

Buda-Flax: 1113 Budapest, Karolina ut 17; tel. (1) 166-6022; telex 22-5738; fax (1) 166-5486; foreign trading division of the Hungarian linen industry; Man. Dir JUDIT KOLAROVSZKI.

Budapesti Húsipari Vállalat: 1097 Budapest, Gubacsi u. 6; tel. (1) 134-3940; telex 22-4422; fax (1) 133-6868; meat processing factory; Man. Dir GÉZA KISIVÁN.

Budaprint Margareta Trading Co: 1036 Budapest, POB 131; tel. (1) 188-8170; telex 22-6052; fax (1) 168-6205; textiles and textile printing; Pres. and Gen. Dir Dr LÁSZLÓ MOSKOVITS.

Budavox: 1392 Budapest, POB 267; tel. (1) 186-8988; telex 22-5077; fax (1) 161-1288; f. 1956; exports telecommunications equipment and systems; Gen. Man. IKLODY GÁBOR.

BVM Concrete Works: 1117 Budapest, Budafoki út 209; tel. (1) 161-3810; telex 22-4877; fax (1) 161-2018; manufactures and exports concrete and reinforced concrete structures; Gen. Dir SÁNDOR SZIRBIK.

Chemokomplex: 1389 Budapest, POB 141; tel. (1) 132-9980; telex 22-5158; fax (1) 132-8341; machines and equipment for the chemical industry; Man. Dir FERENC NAGY.

Chemolimpex: 1805 Budapest, POB 121; tel. (1) 118-3970; telex 22-4351; fax (1) 117-944; chemicals, agrochemicals, plastics, paints; Gen. Man. Dr PÉTER DOBROVITS.

Chinoin: 1325 Budapest, POB 110; tel. (1) 169-0900; telex 22-4236; pharmaceutical and chemical works; joint venture with Sanofi (France).

CIBINTRA International Trading Company Ltd: 1364 Budapest, Váci u.16, POB 170; tel. (1) 118-8377; telex 22-6102; fax (1) 118-5777; f. 1989; international trading house, with domestic activity also; joint venture between Közep-európai Hitelbank (80%) and Central-European International Bank (20%); Gen. Man. Dr MIKLÓS MARINOV.

Compack: 1441 Budapest, POB 42; tel. (1) 121-1520; telex 22-4846; fax (1) 122-4861; trading, food-processing and packing company.

Csépeli Duna: 1751 Budapest, POB 104; tel. (1) 157-2511; telex 22-6289; fax (1) 158-4523; steel tubes and pipes; Gen. Man. BÉLA SIMON.

Délker: 1051 Budapest, POB 70; tel. (1) 118-5888; telex 22-4428; company for trading of tropical fruits, foodstuffs, cosmetics and household goods.

EMG—Electronic Measuring Gear Works: 1163 Budapest, Cziraky u. 26–32; tel. (1) 183-7751; telex 22-4535; fax (1) 183-7900; electronic measuring equipment; Gen. Man. ZOLTÁN K. SZABO.

Elektroimpex: 1392 Budapest, POB 296; tel. (1) 132-8300; telex 22-5771; fax (1) 131-0526; telecommunication and precision articles.

Elektromodul: 1390 Budapest, POB 158; tel. (1) 149-5340; telex 22-5154; fax (1) 140-2583; electro-technical components; Gen. Man. FERENC KIS KOVÁCS.

ERBE: 1361 Budapest, POB 17; tel. (1) 112-3270; telex 22-3562; fax (1) 153-4158; power plant investment company; Technical Dir ANTAL DOBROSY.

Fékon: 1475 Budapest, POB 67; tel. (1) 157-2447; telex 22-5527; clothing company.

Ferunion: 1051 Budapest, Mérleg u. 4; tel. (1) 117-2611; telex 22-5054; fax (1) 117-2594; tools, glassware, building materials, household articles, hardware, stationery; Gen. Dir LÁSZLÓ KOMPOS.

FMV: 1475 Budapest, POB 215; tel. 252-0666; telex 22-4409; fax (1) 183-5361; precision mechanics.

Folk-art: 1052 Budapest, Régiposta u. 12, POB 20; tel. (1) 117-6138; telex 22-6814; fax (1) 118-2154; f. 1948; foreign trade office of FOLK-ART Trading Corporation; Dir Dr JUDITH LENDVAI.

Foreign Trade Company Ltd for Industrial Co-operation: 1367 Budapest, POB 111; tel. (1) 142-4950; telex 22-4435; fax (1) 132-6371; foreign trade office for co-operation and purchasing of licences in industry.

Gábor Áron Works: 1440 Budapest, POB 39; tel. (1) 133-7970; telex 22-4127; domestic and kitchen appliances; Dir SÁNDOR ANTAL.

Gamma Művek: 1519 Budapest, POB 330; tel. (1) 185-0800; telex 22-4946; fax (1) 166-5632; f. 1920; medical instruments and process control systems, elements for the instrumentation industry; Gen. Dir Dr TIVADAR MASCHEK .

Ganz Danubius Shipyard and Crane Factory: Budapest XIII, Váci u. 202; tel. (1) 149-6370; telex 22-4200; fax (1) 140-1703; f. 1835.

Ganz Electric Works: 1525 Budapest, POB 63; tel. (1) 175-3322; telex 22-5363; fax (1) 156-2989; f. 1878; electric power generators, transformers, switchgear, electrical vehicles.

Ganz-Hunslet Rt.: 1087 Budapest, Vajda P. u. 12; tel. (1) 133-6160; telex 20-2862; fax (1) 114-3481; f. 1844; railway rolling stock, underground trains, trams (light rail rolling stock); Jt CEOs S. F. KOSTYAL, G. MIXNER.

Ganz Measuring Instrument Works: 1191 Budapest, Üllői út 64; tel. (1) 147-0740; telex 22-4395; fax (1) 127-1025; all types of electrical measuring instrument; Gen. Dir ENDRE KADAS.

Generalimpex: 1518 Budapest, POB 168; tel. (1) 162-0200; telex 22-6758; f. 1980; permitted to import or export any product; Dir LÁSZLÓ NAGY.

Geominco: 1525 Budapest, POB 92; tel. (1) 135-4580; telex 22-4442; geological and mining engineering; undertakes exploration and research.

Hajdu-Bihar Megyei Textilfeldolgozo Vállalat: Hajduboszormeny 4220, Petofi u. 1–13; tel. (55) 11-833; telex 72354; fax (55) 11-034; textile and leather clothing factory; Dirs IMRE ELEK, ISTVÁN TOTH, IMRE NAGY.

Herbaria: 1051 Budapest, Arany János u. 29; tel. (1) 131-2900; telex 22-6146; fax (1) 112-1268; medicinal herbs; Gen. Dir JÁZSEF FOGARASSY.

Hungagent Ltd: 1374 Budapest, POB 542; tel. (1) 188-6180; telex 22-4526; fax (1) 188-8769; foreign representations agency; export-import.

Hungarian Aluminium Corporation (HUNGALU): 1387 Budapest, POB 30; tel. (1) 149-4750; telex 22-5471; fax (1) 140-2723; Chair. and Gen. Dir Dr LAJOS DOZSA; Gen. Man. Dr PÉTER KERESZTES.

Hungarocoop: 1370 Budapest, POB 334; tel. (1) 153-1711; telex 22-4858; fax (1) 153-3318; import and export of consumer goods.

Hungarofilm: 1363 Budapest, POB 39; tel. (1) 153-3579; telex 22-5768; fax (1) 153-1850; f. 1956; film distribution; Pres. ISTVÁN VÁRADI.

Hungarofruct: 1394 Budapest, POB 386; tel. (1) 131-7120; telex 22-5351; fax (1) 153-1051; f. 1953; fresh, dehydrated and quick-frozen fruit and vegetables; Gen. Man. TIBOR FODOR.

Hungarotex: 1804 Budapest, POB 100; tel. (1) 117-4555; telex 22-4751; f. 1953; textiles, garments, foodstuffs, etc; Gen. Man. LÁSZLÓ FÖLDVÁRI.

Hungexpo (Hungarian Foreign Trade Company for Fairs and Publicity): 1441 Budapest, POB 44; tel. (1) 157-3555; telex 22-4609; fax (1) 157-2647; advertising, publicity, public relations; printing; fairs, exhibitions; Man. Dir ISTVÁN KOVÁCS.

IDEX Foreign Trading, Contracting and Engineering Co Ltd: 1011 Budapest, Fő u. 14–18; tel. (1) 201-3211; telex 22-4541; fax (1) 201-3128; f. 1953; precision engineering, electronics, construction, oil and gas.

Ikarus: 1630 Budapest, POB 3; tel. 252-9666; telex 22-4766; fax (1) 163-7066; f. 1895; construction and export of buses in complete state or in sets for assembly; Gen. Dir ANDRÁS SEMSEY; Tech. Dir ISTVÁN LEPSÉNYI.

Industria Ltd: 1117 Budapest, POB 272; commercial representation of foreign firms, technical consulting service, market research etc.

Interag Co Ltd: 1390 Budapest, Pannónia u. 11, POB 184; tel. (1) 132-5770; telex 22-4776; fax (1) 153-0736; represents foreign firms; conducts general export-import business, domestic trade.

Intercooperation Co Ltd for Trade Promotion: 1431 Budapest, POB 136; tel. (1) 118-9966; telex 22-4242; fax (1) 118-2161; establishment and carrying out of co-operation agreements, joint ventures and import-export deals.

IPV (Publishing and Promotion Co for Tourism): 1140 Budapest, POB 164; tel. (1) 163-3652; telex 22-6074; fax (1) 183-7320; publishing, publicity, film-making, exhibitions, advertising; Gen. Man ISTVÁN FAZEKAS.

KGyV Metallurgical Engineering Corpn: 1553 Budapest, POB 23; tel. (1) 111-3612; telex 22-5920; fax (1) 111-2274; f. 1951; manufacture of industrial furnaces and steel structures; Gen. Man. Dr SÁNDOR FARKAS.

Komplex Foreign Trade Co: 1807 Budapest, Andrássy ut 10, POB 125; tel. (1) 111-7010; telex 22-5957; fax (1) 111-7450; f. 1953; agricultural machinery, plant and equipment for food industry; Man. Dir ADOLF FÉDERER.

Konsumex: 1446 Budapest, Hungária krt 162 ; tel. (1) 153-0511; telex 22-5151; fax (1) 141-4747; f. 1959; consumer goods, household articles, etc.; Gen. Man. MIHÁLY TEMESI.

Kopint-Datorg Institute for Economic and Market Research and Informatics: 1051 Budapest, Dorottya u. 6; tel. (1) 118-6722; telex 22-5646; fax (1) 118-6483; f. 1964; economic research, information and marketing services, data processing, publishing; Gen. Dir JÁNOS DEÁK.

Kultúra Hungarian Foreign Trading Co: 1389 Budapest, POB 149; tel. (1) 201-4411; telex 22-4441; fax (1) 201-3207; f. 1950; books, periodicals, works of art, sheet music, teaching aids; Gen. Man. JÓZSEF MÉSZÁROS.

Labor Rt: Factory of Laboratory Instruments Co Ltd: 1450 Budapest, POB 33; tel. (1) 133-9708; telex 22-4162; fax (1) 134-0309; f. 1989; scientific instruments, laboratory equipment and engineering; Gen. Dir KÁROLY VARGA.

Lampart: 1475 Budapest, POB 41; tel. (1) 157-0111; telex 22-5365; fax (1) 157-2029; f. 1883; glass-lined processing equipment; Gen. Man. ZOLTÁN RETI.

Lehel Hütőgépgyár: 5101 Jászberény, POB 64; tel. 12611; telex 02-3341; export of domestic refrigerators.

Licencia: 1368 Budapest, POB 207; tel. (1) 118-1111; telex 22-5872; fax (1) 138-2304; f. 1950; purchase and sale of patents and inventions; Gen. Dir LAJOS VEROSZTA.

Lignimpex: 1393 Budapest, POB 323; tel. (1) 112-9850; telex 22-4251; fax (1) 132-2181; timber, paper and fuel.

Magnezitipari Movek: 1475 Budapest, POB 11; tel. (1) 157-5288; telex 22-5644; f. 1892; magnesium industry; Dir B. HAZAI.

Magyar Media Advertising Agency: 1392 Budapest, POB 279; tel. (1) 141-4749; telex 22-3040; direct mail, printing, publicity campaigns, advertising.

MAHIR Hungarian Publicity Company: 1818 Budapest, POB 367; tel. (1) 118-3444; telex 22-5341; fax (1) 117-9032; advertising agency; Commercial Dir MARIA JANCSO.

Masped: 1364 Budapest, Kristóf tér 2, POB 104; tel. (1) 1 18-2922; telex 22-4471; fax (1) 118-8343; international forwarding and carriage; Gen. Man. KÁLMÁN GELENCSÉR.

Mechaniki Művek: 1515 Budapest, POB 64; tel. (1) 166-9400; telex 22-5842; fax (1) 185-0195; electrical equipment; Man. Dir JÁNOS HEINRICH.

Medicor Trading Co Ltd: 1389 Budapest, POB 150; tel. (1) 149-5130; telex 22-5051; fax (1) 149-5957; medical instruments, X-ray apparatus and complete hospital installations; Chair. SZILVIA MÁDAI.

Medimpex: 1808 Budapest; tel. (1) 118-3955; telex 22-5477; export and import of pharmaceutical and biological products, veterinary drugs, laboratory chemicals.

Melyepterv Consulting Engineering: 1051 Budapest, Vigado tér 1; tel. (1) 117-3434; telex 22-4723; fax (1) 117-8623; water supply and environmental planning projects; Gen. Dir FERENC VARGA.

Mertcontrol: 1397 Budapest, POB 542; tel. (1) 132-5300; telex 22-5777; fax (1) 111-6897; f. 1951; quality control of import and export goods.

Metalimpex: 1393 Budapest, POB 330; tel. (1) 118-7611; telex 22-5251; fax (1) 142-9753; metals and metal products; Gen. Dir JÓZSEF BENKO.

Metrimpex: 1391 Budapest, POB 202; tel. (1) 112-5600; telex 22-5451; fax (1) 153-4719; electronic, nuclear and other instruments and equipment.

MIKROMED KFT: 2500 Esztergom, Beke tér 1–11; tel. (33) 13-400; telex 02-7711; fax (33) 12-940; Hungarian-USSR joint venture producing medical equipment; Man. Dir BÉLA BADI.

Mineralimpex: 1062 Budapest, Andrássy ut 64; tel. (1) 1 11-6470; telex 22-4651; fax (1) 153-1779; oils and mining products; Dir-Gen. Dr JÓZSEF TÓTH.

MODEXCO Trading and Servicing Ltd: 1396Budapest, POB 475; tel. (1) 132-9560; telex 22-7620; fax (1) 132-9121; ready-made clothing export, fabric and machine import.

Mogürt: 1391 Budapest, POB 249; tel. (1) 118-6044; telex 22-5357; fax (1) 118-8895; f. 1946; motor vehicles; Gen. Man. PÁL ARDÓ.

MOM: 1525 Budapest, POB 52; tel. (1) 156-4122; telex 22-4151; f. 1876; laboratory and optical instruments; Man. Dir JÓZSEF SEBESFI.

Monimpex Trading House: 1392 Budapest, POB 268; tel. (1) 153-1222; telex 22-5371; fax (1) 112-2072; wines, spirits, paprika, honey, sweets, ornamental plants.

MVMT: 1251 Budapest, POB 34; tel. (1) 201-5455; telex 22-4382; fax (1) 202-1246; Hungarian national electricity company.

Nádex: 1525 Budapest, POB 14; tel. (1) 135-0365; telex 22-6767; reed farming.

National Oil and Gas Trust: Budapest; responsible for all petroleum and national gas production; state enterprise, due to be privatized in 1991.

Nikex Trading Co Ltd: 1016 Budapest, Mészáros u. 48–54; tel. (1) 156-0122; telex 22-4971; fax (1) 175-5131; industrial equipment foreign trading co; Man. Dir MIHÁLY PETRIK.

Novex: 1087 Budapest, Könyves Kálmán Krt. 76; tel. (1) 133-8933; telex 22-3825; foreign trade; Man. Dir JÁNOS KOZMA.

Ofotért: 1917 Budapest; tel. (1) 120-3669; telex 22-4418; f. 1949; optical and photographic articles; Gen. Dir JÁNOS SZILÁGYI.

OMKER: 1476 Budapest, POB 223; tel. (1) 112-3000; telex 22-4683; fax (1) 133-8718; f. 1950; medical instruments; Gen. Dir Dr RÓBERT ZENTAI.

ORION: 1475 Budapest, POB 84; tel. (1) 128-4830; telex 22-5798; fax (1) 127-2490; f. 1913; televisions, satellite receivers, digital microwave and other electrical goods; Gen. Dir CSABA NÉMETH.

Pannonia-Csepel International Trading Co Ltd: 1051 Budapest, POB 354; tel. (1) 132-938; telex 22-5128; fax (1) 132-7318; metallurgical materials, welding electrodes, cast iron fittings, steel tubes and cylinders, bicycles, industrial sewing and pressing machinery and laundry equipment, complete tube manufacturing plants, bottle plants, etc.

Patria Nyomda: Budapest 1088, Szentkiralyi u. 47; tel. (1) 134-0186; telex 22-6271; fax (1) 114-0876; office stationery; Gen. Man. SÁNDOR VASS.

Pharmatrade Hungarian Trading Co: 1367 Budapest, POB 126; tel. (1) 118-5966; telex 22-6650; fax (1) 118-5346; medicinal plants, natural cosmetics, medicinal muds and waters, food and feed additives, seeds, honey and bee products, fruit and vegetables, radioactive products.

Philatelia Hungarica: 1373 Budapest, POB 600; tel. (1) 131-6146; telex 22-6508; fax (1) 111-5421; f. 1950; stamps; wholesale only; Gen. Man. ISTVÁN ZALÁVÁRI.

Phylaxia-Sanofi: 1107 Budapest, Szállás u. 5 ; tel. (1) 127-5418; fax (1) 127-4617; vaccines, veterinary products.

Precision Fittings Factory: 3301 Eger, POB 2; tel. (36) 11911; telex 63-331; fax (36) 11112.

RÁBA (Hungarian Railway Carriage and Machine Works): 9002 Győr, POB 50; tel. (96) 02-4255; telex 02-4255; fax (96) 14311; f. 1896; commercial vehicles, diesel engines, agricultural tractors; Gen. Man. FERENC KÁRPÁTI.

Rekard: 9027 Győr, Kandó Kálmán u. 5–7; tel. (96) 13-122; telex 24-360; farm equipment; Gen. Dir IMRE SZABO.

Sasad: 2040 Budapest, Alsohatar u. 14; tel. (1) 166-9000; telex 22-4789; fax (1) 186-8399; horticultural products, including bulbs, trees, shrubs and cut flowers; Pres. LÁSZLÓ MIHÁLIK.

Skála-Coop: 1092 Budapest, Kinizsi u. 30–36; tel. (1) 118-0100; telex 22-5781; fax (1) 118-7855; national co-operative company for purchase and disposal of goods including fine ceramics and glassware, industrial, agricultural and household metal ware, hand tools, electronic games, rubber and plastic products, cosmetics and chemicals, wood and paper industry products, leather and textile industry products, ready-to-wear clothing, vegetables and other foodstuffs; Chair. and Chief Exec. ISTVÁN IMRE.

Somogyi Erdő és Fafeldolgozo Gazdaság (Somogyi Forestry and Timber Company): 7400 Kaposvar, Bajcsy-Zs. u. 21; tel. (82) 15-022; telex 13348; fax (82) 10-408; wood and wood products, furniture; Man. Dir Dr LÁSZLÓ TAKACS.

Szeged Szalamigyar és Hűsuzem: Szeged 6725, Alsovarosi ff. 64; tel. (62) 26-033; telex 82226; fax (62) 10-643; meat processing factory; Man. Dir VILMOS BIHARI.

Tannimpex: 1395 Budapest, POB 406; tel. (1) 112-3400; telex 22-4557; fax (1) 153-2170; leather, shoes, leather garments, fancy leather goods and furs; Gen. Man. GYÖRGY ENDREFFY.

Tatabánya Mining Co: 2803 Tatabánya, POB 323; tel. (34) 10144; telex 22-6206; fax (34) 11061; f. 1894; production of mining equipment and machinery, preparation of industrial and drinking water, purification of waste waters, dewatering of sludges, tunnelling; Gen. Man. LÁSZLÓ VAS.

Taurus Hungarian Rubber Works: 1965 Budapest, POB 48; tel. (1) 134-0509; telex 22-4201; fax (1) 113-5434; f. 1882; rubber; Chief Exec. Dr LÁSZLÓ PALOTÁS.

Technoimpex: 1390 Budapest, POB 183; tel. (1) 118-4055; telex 22-4171; fax (1) 186-6418; exports machine tools, specialized machinery, equipment for the oil and gas industry, agricultural equipment; imports machine tools, machines for light industry; organizes barter deals, co-operation, leasing and joint ventures; Chair. and CEO ISTVÁN MÁTYÁS.

Temaforg: 1476 Budapest, POB 114; tel. (1) 127-7880; telex 22-3456; fax (1) 147-5777; textile and synthetic wastes, industrial wipers, geotextiles for agriculture, road and railway construction.

Terimpex: 1825 Budapest, POB 251; tel. (1) 117-5011; telex 22-4551; fax (1) 117-3179; cattle and agricultural products; Gen. Man. Dr LÁSZLÓ RÁNKY.

Terta, Telefongyár: 1956 Budapest, POB 16; tel. (1) 252-6949; telex 22-4087; fax (1) 252-9161; f. 1876; telecommunications and data teleprocessing systems.

Tesco: 1367 Budapest, POB 101; tel. (1) 111-0850; telex 22-4642; fax (1) 153-1852; f. 1962; organization for international technical and scientific co-operation; export and import of technical services world-wide; Gen. Man. ISTVÁN BENE.

Transelektro: 1394 Budapest, POB 377; tel. (1) 132-0100; telex 22-4571; fax (1) 153-0162; f. 1957; generators, power stations, cables, lighting, transformers, household appliances, catering equipment, etc.; Dir-Gen. PÁL KERTÉSZ.

Tungsram Co Ltd: 1340 Budapest, Váci út 77; tel. (1) 169-2800; telex 22-5058; fax (1) 169-2868; f. 1896; light sources, lighting systems, lighting machinery ; CEO GEORGE F. VARGA.

Uvaterv: 1051 Budapest, Vigado tér 1; tel. (1) 118-6990; telex 22-5265; fax (1) 117-8575; engineering and consultancy services, building contracting; Gen. Dir Dr MIKLOS LOYKO.

Vasvill: 3520 Miskolc, Setany u. 1; tel. (46) 70-777; telex 62394; fax (46) 79-257; consumer and industrial products; Gen. Man. JENŐ MONOSTORY.

Vegyépszer Co Ltd: 1397 Budapest, POB 540; tel. (1) 135-1125; telex 22-6930; fax (1) 116-9470; building and assembling of chemical plant, supply of complete equipment, engineering, environment protection; Gen. Dir FERENC DERCZY.

VEPEX Ltd: 1370 Budapest, POB 308; tel. (1) 142-5535; telex 22-4208; fax (1) 142-5502; research, development and trading in biotechnology.

Vetomag: 1056 Budapest, Váci u.; tel. (1) 138-2033; telex 22-7126; fax (1) 118-1721; horticultural seeds production; Pres. Dr János Csiszer; Gen. Dir Endre Toth.

Videoton Rt.: 1398 Budapest, POB 557; tel. (1) 121-0520; telex 22-4763; fax (1) 142-1398; consumer electronics, computer technology; Gen. Dir András Gede.

Volánpack Vállalat: 1108 Budapest, Kozma u. 4; tel. (1) 148-4300; telex 22-6935; fax (1) 127-6031; forwarding and transport, packaging, warehousing, etc.; Dir Gábor Pákozdi.

Zalahús: Zalaegerszeg, Balatoni ut.; tel. (92) 11-200; telex 33231; meat-processing factory; Man. Dir Imre Farkas.

TRADE FAIRS

Budapest International Fairs: Hungexpo, 1441 Budapest, POB 44; tel. (1) 157-3555; telex 22-4188; f. 1968; technical goods (spring), consumer goods (autumn), and other specialized exhibitions and fairs.

CO-OPERATIVE ORGANIZATIONS

Általános Fogyasztási Szövetkezetek Országos Szövetsége (ÁFEOSZ) (National Federation of Consumer Co-operatives): 1054 Budapest, Szabadság tér 14; tel. (1) 153-4222; telex 22-4862; fax (1) 111-3647; safeguards interests of Hungarian consumer co-operative societies, co-owner of co-op foreign trading companies and joint ventures; Pres. Dr Pál Szilvasán; Gen. Sec. Dr István Szlamenicky; 3.5m. mems.

Ipari Szövetkezetek Országos Szövetsége (OKISZ) (National Federation of Industrial Co-operatives): 1146 Budapest, Thököly u. 58-60; tel. (1) 141-5140; telex 22-7576; fax (1) 1 41-5521; safeguards interests of over 3,000 member co-operatives; Pres. Lajos Köveskuti.

Országos Szövetkezeti Tanács (OSzT) (National Co-operative Council): 1373 Budapest, Szabadság tér 14; tel. (1) 112-7467; telex 22-4862; Pres. Dr Pál Szilvasán; Sec. Dr József Pál.

Termelőszövetkezetek Országos Tanácsa (TOT) (National Council of Agricultural Co-operatives): 1054 Budapest, Akadémia u. 1-3; tel. (1) 132-8167; telex 22-6810; f. 1967; Pres. István Szabó; Gen. Sec. Dr János Eleki; 1,280 co-operatives with 816,000 mems.

TRADE UNIONS

Since 1988, and particularly after the restructuring of the former Central Council of Hungarian Trade Unions (SZOT) as the National Confederation of Hungarian Trade Unions (MSZOSZ) in 1990, several new union federations have been created. Several unions are affiliated to more than one federation, and others are completely independent.

Trade Union Federations

Autonóm Szakszervezetek (Autonomous Trade Unions): c/o Magyar Vegyipari Dolgozók Szakszervezeti Szövetsége, 1068 Budapest, Benczúr u. 45; tel. (1) 142-1776; Man. Lajos Faiocze.

Principal affiliated unions include:

Magyar Vegyipari Dolgozók Szakszervezeti Szövetsége (Federation of Hungarian Chemical Industry Workers' Unions): 1068 Budapest, Benczúr u. 45; tel. (1) 142-1778; telex 22-3420; fax (1) 142-9975; f. 1897; Gen. Sec. Lajos Főcze; 140,000 mems.

Értelmiségi Szakszervezeti Tömörülés—ÉSZT (Federation of Unions of Intellectual Workers): 1068 Budapest, Gorkij fasor 10; tel. (1) 122-8456; Pres. Dr László Kis; Gen. Sec. Dr Gábor Bánk.

Független Szakszervezetek Demokratikus Ligája—FSZDL (Democratic League of Independent Trade Unions): 1071 Budapest, Gorkij fasor 45; tel. (1) 142-6957; f. 1989; Pres. Pál Forgács; 80,000 mems.

Principal affiliated unions include:

Tudományos Dolgozók Demokratikus Szakszervezete (TDDSZ) (Democratic Trade Union of Scientific Workers): 1064 Budapest, Gorkij fasor 38; tel. (1) 142-8438; f. 1988; Chair. Pál Forgács.

Magyar Szakszervezetek Országos Szövetsége (MSzOSz) (National Confederation of Hungarian Trade Unions): 1415 Budapest, Dózsa György u. 84b; tel. (1) 153-2900; telex 22-5861; fax (1) 141-4342; f. 1898, reorganized 1990; Pres. Dr Sándor Nagy; 3,500,000 mems.

Principal affiliated unions include:

Bányaipari Dolgozók Szakszervezeti Szövetsége (Federation of Mineworkers' Unions): 1068 Budapest, Gorkij fasor 46-48; tel. (1) 122-1226; telex 22-7499; fax (1) 142-1942; f. 1913; Pres. Antal Schalkhammer; Vice-Pres. József Koczi; 126,725 mems.

Bőripari Dolgozók Szakszervezete (Union of Leather Industry Workers): 1062 Budapest, Bajza u. 24; tel. (1) 142-9970; f. 1868; Pres. László Turzo; Gen. Sec. Tibor Tréber; 48,518 mems.

Egészségügyben Dolgozók Szakszervezeteinek Szövetsége (Union of Health Service Workers): 1051 Budapest, Nádor u. 32; tel. (1) 132-7530; f. 1945; Pres. Dr Zoltán Szabó; Gen. Sec. Dr Pálné Kállay; 280,536 mems.

Élelmezésipari Dolgozók Szakszervezetek Szövetsége (Federation of Food Industry Workers' Unions): 1068 Budapest, Gorkij fasor 44; tel. (1) 122-5880; f. 1905; Pres. András Gyenes; Gen. Sec. Béla Vanek; 226,243 mems.

Építő-, Fa- és Építőanyagipari Dolgozók Szakszervezeteinek Szövetsége (Federation of Building, Wood and Building Industry Workers' Unions): 1068 Budapest, Dózsa György u. 84a; tel. (1) 142-5762; f. 1906; Pres. István Gyöngyösi; Gen. Sec. Gyula Somogyi; 365,561 mems.

Helyiipari és Városgazdasági Dolgozók Szakszervégének (Federation of Local Industry and Municipal Workers' Unions): 1068 Budapest, Benczur u. 43; tel. (1) 111-6950; f. 1952; Pres. Józsefné Svever; Gen. Sec. Pál Bakányi; 281,073 mems.

Kereskedelmi Szakszervezetek Szövetségének tagszervezeteiből (Federation of Commercial Workers' Unions): 1066 Budapest, Jókai u. 6; tel. (1) 131-8970; f. 1948; Gen. Sec. Dr János Vágó; 535,834 mems.

Közlekedési Dolgozók Szakszervezeteinek Szövetségé (Federation of Transport Workers' Unions): 1428 Budapest, Köztársaság tér 3; tel. (1) 113-9046; f. 1898; Pres. Gábor Schlembach; Gen. Sec. Gyula Moldovan; 190,464 mems.

Magyar Pedagógusok Szakszervezete (Hungarian Union of Teachers): 1068 Budapest, Gorkij fasor 10; tel. (1) 122-8456; fax (1) 142-8122; f. 1945; Gen. Sec. Istvánné Szöllősi; 240,000 mems.

Magyar Textilipari Dolgozók Szakszervezete (Hungarian Union of Textile Workers): 1068 Budapest, Rippl-Rónai u. 2; tel. (1) 122-5414; f. 1905; Pres. (vacant); Gen. Sec. Tamás Keleti; 100,000 mems.

Mezőgazdasági, Erdészeti és Vizgazdálkodási Dolgozók Szakszervezeteinek Szövetsége tagszervezeteiből (Federation of Agricultural, Forestry and Water Conservancy Workers' Unions): 1066 Budapest, Jókai u. 2-4; tel. (1) 131-4550; telex 22-7535; f. 1906; Pres. (vacant); Gen. Sec. Tibor Czirmay; 389,569 mems.

Müvészeti Szakszervezetek Szövetségé (Federation of Hungarian Artworkers' Unions): 1068 Budapest, Gorkij fasor 38; tel. (1) 121-1120; fax (1) 122-5412; f. 1957; Gen. Sec. Kálmán Pető; 32,000 mems.

Nyomdadaipari Dolgozók Szakszervezete (Printers' Union): 1085 Budapest, Kölcsey u. 2; tel. (1) 114-2413; telex 20-2612; fax (1) 134-2160; f. 1862; Pres. András Bársony; Vice-Pres János Aczél, Zoltán Godzsa; 49,436 mems.

Postai Dolgozók Szakszervezete (Federation of Trade Unions of Postal and Communications Employees): 1146 Budapest, Cházár András u. 13; tel. (1) 142-8777; fax (1) 121-4018; f. 1945; Pres. Enikő Heszky-Gricser; 69,900 mems.

Ruházatipari Dolgozók Szakszervezete (Union of Clothing Workers): 1077 Budapest, Almássy tér 2; tel. (1) 142-2126; f. 1892; Pres. Julianna Tóth; Gen. Sec. Gábor Veres; 37,117 mems.

Vas- és Fémipari Dolgozók Szakszervezeti Szövetsége (Confederation of Iron and Metallurgical Industry Workers' Unions): 1086 Budapest, Magdolna u. 5-7; tel. (1) 113-5200; telex 22-4791; fax (1) 133-8327; f. 1877; Pres. László Paszternák; 535,000 mems.

Vasutasok Szakszervezete (Union of Railway Workers): 1068 Budapest, Benczúr u. 41; tel. (1) 122-1895; telex 22-6819; f. 1945; Pres. Pál Papp; Gen. Sec. Ferenc Koszorus; 196,698 mems.

Szakszervezetek Együttmüködési Fóruma—SZEF (Central Authority of Trade Unions): 1068 Budapest, Gorkij fasor 10; tel. (1) 122-8099; Pres. Istvánné Szöllősi.

Principal affiliated unions include:

Közszolgálati Szakszervezetek Szövetsége (Federation of Public Workers' Unions): 1088 Budapest, Puskin u. 4; tel. (1) 118-8900; fax (1) 118-7360; f. 1945; Pres. Dr Endre Szabó.

Transport

Raabersped: 1531 Budapest, POB 33; tel. (1) 175-1322; telex 22-5919; international forwarding agency (rail, road, air and sea); Dir Klara Cservari Boros.

Other forwarding agencies are Masped and Volánpack (see under Foreign Trade Organizations).

RAILWAYS

Magyar Államvasutak (MÁV) (Hungarian State Railways): 1940 Budapest, Andrássy ut 73-75; tel. (1) 122-0660; telex 22-4342; fax

(1) 142-8596; state-owned since its foundation in 1868; total network 7,600 km, including 2,100 km of electrified lines; Gen Man. János Csárádi.

Győr–Sopron–Ebenfurti-Vasut—Gysev-ROeEE (Railway of Győr–Sopron–Ebenfurt): 9400 Sopron, Matyas Kiraly u. 19; Hungarian-Austrian-owned railway; 84 km in Hungary, 82 km in Austria, all electrified; transport of passengers and goods; Dir-Gen. Dr János Berényi.

There is an underground railway in Budapest, with a network of 23 km in 1989; in that year 296m. passengers were carried.

ROADS

In late December 1988 the road network totalled 105,370 km, including 311 km of motorways, 6,379 km of main or national roads and 23,024 km of secondary roads. Construction of the Budapest ring motorway began in 1987, with financial assistance from the World Bank, and was scheduled for completion in 1990. There are extensive long-distance bus services. Road passenger and freight transport is provided by the state-owned VOLÁN companies and by individual (own account) operators.

Hungarocamion: 1442 Budapest, POB 108; tel. (1) 157-3811; telex 22-5455; international road freight transport company; 17 offices in Europe and the Middle East; fleet of 1,800 lorries; Gen. Man. Imre Torma.

Volán Vállalatok Központja (Centre of Volán Enterprises): 1391 Budapest, Erzsébet krt 96, POB 221; tel. (1) 112-4290; telex 22-5177; centre of 25 Volán enterprises for inland and international road freight and passenger transport, forwarding, tourism; fleet of 17,000 lorries, incl. special tankers for fuel, refrigerators, trailers, 8,000 buses for regular passenger transport; 3 affiliates, offices and joint-ventures in Europe; Head Kálmán Garami.

SHIPPING AND INLAND WATERWAYS

In 1987 the Hungarian merchant fleet comprised 15 vessels totalling 106,710 dwt.

MAHART—Magyar Hajózási Rt. (Hungarian Shipping Co): 1366 Budapest, POB 58; tel. (1) 118-1880; telex 22-5258; fax (1) 118-0733; carries passenger traffic on the Danube and Lake Balaton; cargo services on the Danube and its tributaries, Lake Balaton, and also Mediterranean and ocean-going services; operates port of Budapest (container terminal, loading, storage, warehousing, handling and packaging services); ship-building and ship-repair services; Dir-Gen. András Fáy.

MAFRACHT: 1052 Budapest, Kristóf tér 2, POB 105; tel. (1) 118-5276; telex 22-4471; shipping agency.

CIVIL AVIATION

The Ferihegy international airport is 16 km from the centre of Budapest. An expansion and development programme began in 1977, and the reconstruction work on the runway was completed in 1987. Ferihegy-2 opened in 1985. There are no public internal air services.

Légügyi Főigazgatóság (General Directorate of Civil Aviation): 1400 Budapest, Dob u. 75–81, POB 87; tel. (1) 142-2544; telex 22-5729; controls civil aviation; Dir-Gen. Ödön Skonda.

Légiforgalmi és Repülőtéri Igazgatóság (LRI) (Air Traffic and Airport Administration): 1675 Budapest, POB 53; tel. (1) 157-9123; telex 22-4054; fax (1) 157-6982; f. 1973; controls civil air traffic and operates Ferihegy and Siófok Airports; Dir-Gen. Tamás Erdei.

Magyar Légiközlekedési Vállalat—MALÉV (Hungarian Airlines): 1367 Budapest, Roosevelt tér 2, POB 122; tel. (1) 118-9033; telex 22-4954; fax (1) 117-2417; f. 1946; regular services from Budapest to Europe, North Africa and the Middle East; Gen. Dir Tamás Deri; fleet of 1 Yak-40, 6 TU-134 and 12 TU-154; 3 Boeing 737-200 on lease.

Tourism

Tourism has developed rapidly and is an important source of foreign exchange. In 1990 convertible-currency income from tourism totalled some US $2,000m., 60% more than in 1989. Rouble receipts in 1990 reached 90m., considerably less than in 1989. Lake Balaton is the main holiday centre for boating, bathing and fishing. The cities have great historical and recreational attractions. The annual Budapest Spring Festival is held in March. Budapest has numerous swimming pools watered by thermal springs, which are equipped with modern physiotherapy facilities. The first Budapest Grand Prix, the only Formula-1 motor race to be held in Eastern Europe, took place in August 1986. In 1990 there were 38m.

foreign visitors (including visitors in transit), 25% more than in the previous year. There were 47,317 hotel beds in 1986, and a further 8,000–10,000 were to be created by 1994.

Országos Idegenforgalmi Hivatal (OIH) (Hungarian Tourist Board): 1051 Budapest, Vigadó u. 6; tel. (1) 118-0750; telex 22-5182; fax (1) 118-5241; f. 1968; Head Dr Kazmer Kardos.

Budapest Tourist (Budapest Travel Company): 1051 Budapest, Roosevelt tér 5; tel. (1) 118-6663; telex 22-6448; fax (1) 118-1658; f. 1916; runs tours, congresses and cultural programmes; provides accommodation; Dir Iván Róna.

COOPTOURIST—Co-operative Travel Agency: 1016 Budapest, Derék u. 2; tel. (1) 175-0575; telex 22-5399; general tourism services for groups and individuals; branch offices throughout Hungary; Gen. Dir Dr Sándor Sipos.

DANUBIUS—Danubius Hotels: 1138 Budapest, Margitsziget; tel. (1) 112-1000; telex 22-6850; fax (1) 153-1883; Dir Sándor Betegh.

Express Utazási Iroda (Express Travel Bureau): 1054 Budapest, Szabadság tér 16; tel. (1) 153-0660; telex 22-5384; fax (1) 1 53-1715; f. 1957; package tours, study tours, vacation centres; Gen. Man. Dr Gyula Tarcsi.

HungarHotels—Hungarian Hotel and Restaurant Company: 1052 Budapest, Petőfi Sándor u. 14; tel. (1) 118-2033; telex 22-4209; fax (1) 117-1374; f. 1956; Pres. Tamás Búvári.

IBUSZ—Idegenforgalmi, Beszerzési, Utazási és Szállitási Rt. (Hungarian Travel Agency): 1364 Budapest, Felszabadulás tér 5; tel. (1) 118-1120; telex 22-4976; fax (1) 117-7723; f. 1902; 24-hour service for individual travellers at: 1052 Budapest, Petőfi tér 3; tel. (1) 118-5707; telex 22-4941; IBUSZ has 118 brs throughout Hungary; Gen. Man. Erika Szemenkár.

Locomotiv Tourist: 1536 Budapest, Szilágyi Dezső tér 1, POB 241; tel. (1) 201-1807; telex 22-4249; fax (1) 156-3696; f. 1976; international train and air-travel services; currency exchange services; Dir Dr Ilona Mosonyi.

Malév Air Tours: 1367 Budapest, Roosevelt tér 2, POB 122; tel. (1) 118-3780; telex 22-5370; fax (1) 118-7359; Dir Zsuzsa Vértessy.

Máv Tours (Travel Bureau of Hungarian State Railways): 1378 Budapest, Guszev u. 1, POB 25; tel. (1) 117-3723; telex 22-3251; Dir Thomas Lengyel.

Pannónia Hotels and Restaurants: 1088 Budapest, Puskin u. 6, POB 159; tel. (1) 138-2187; telex 22-4561; fax (1) 118-1344; f. 1949; owns 51 hotels; organizes through its Tourist Service Bureau tours, programmes, conferences etc. in Hungary, and Hungarian gastronomic festivals abroad; Gen. Man. Gyula Harbula.

Pegazus Tours: 1053 Budapest, Károlyi Mihály u. 5; Dir Mausz Gotthard.

Volántourist Vállalat: 1066 Budapest, Teréz krt. 96; tel. (1) 132-2905; telex 22-6722; fax (1) 112-2298; f. 1970; Dir Lajos Csete.

Atomic Energy

Hungary's first nuclear power station at Paks (on the Danube, south of Budapest), built with Soviet assistance, began trial operations in December 1982, and was formally inaugurated in November 1983. Four units, each of 440 MW, were in operation by 1987. In 1988 a record output of 13,420m. kWh was achieved. Hungary has signed agreements for co-operation in the peaceful uses of atomic energy with Bulgaria, Cuba, Czechoslovakia, France, the former German Democratic Republic, India, Italy, Romania and the former USSR. Hungary is a member of the International Atomic Energy Agency (based in Vienna), the Joint Institute for Nuclear Research (at Dubna, near Moscow) and the CMEA Standing Committee on Electricity and Nuclear Power.

Országos Atomenergia Bizottság (National Atomic Energy Commission): 1374 Budapest, POB 565; tel. (1) 132-7172; telex 22-4907; fax (1) 142-7598; f. 1956; Pres. Ernő Pungor.

Budapesti Műszaki Egyetem Nukleáris Technikai Intézet (Institute of Nuclear Techniques of the Technical University of Budapest): 1521 Budapest, POB 91; tel. (1) 181-2564; telex 22-5931; fax (1) 166-6808; f. 1971; Dir Prof. Dr G. Csom.

Kossuth Lajos Tudományegyetem Kisérleti Fizikai Intézete (Institute of Experimental Physics of the Kossuth Lajos University): 4001 Debrecen, POB 105; tel. (52) 15222; telex 72-200; fax (52) 15087; f. 1923; research in low-energy nuclear physics, neutron physics, and application of atomic and nuclear methods; Dir Prof. Dr J. Csikai.

Magyar Tudományos Akadémia Atommag Kutató Intézete—ATOMKI (Institute of Nuclear Research of the Hungarian Academy of Sciences): 4026 Debrecen, Bem tér 18/c; tel. (52) 17266;

telex 72-210; fax (52) 16181; f. 1954; research in nuclear structure, reaction, ion-atom collisions, etc.; Dir Prof. Dr J. PÁLINKÁS.

Magyar Tudományos Akadémia Izotópkutató Intézete (Institute of Isotopes of the Hungarian Academy of Sciences): 1525 Budapest, POB 77, Konkoly Thege u. 29–33; tel. (1) 169-6687; telex 22-5360; fax (1) 156-5045; f. 1959; Dir Gen. Dr G. FÖLDIÁK.

Magyar Tudományos Akadémia Központi Fizikai Kutató Intézete—KFKI (Central Research Institute for Physics of the Hungarian Academy of Sciences): 1525 Budapest, POB 49; tel. (1) 169-8566; telex 22-4722; fax (1) 155-3894; f. 1950; research in computer science, nuclear, particle, reactor and solid state physics; Dir-Gen. ISTVÁN LOVAS.

Országos 'Frédéric Joliot-Curie' Sugárbiológiai és Sugáregészségügyi Kutató Intézet (National Research Institute for Radiobiology and Radiohygiene): 1775 Budapest, POB 101; f. 1957; tel. 226-0026; telex 22-5103; fax 226-6531; research on effects of ionizing and non-ionizing radiations, radiation protection, application of radiation and isotopes for medical purposes; Dir Gen. Dr L. B. SZTANYIK.

Paksi Atomerőmű Vállalat (PAV) (Paks Nuclear Power Plant): 7031 Paks, POB 71; tel. (75) 11-222; telex 14-440; fax (75) 51332; f. 1976; electricity generation, foreign trade in training of nuclear power plant specialists, licences and auxiliary equipment for nuclear power plants; exports spent nuclear fuel; imports fresh nuclear fuel, nuclear power plant mountings; Dir Gen. JÓZSEF PÓNYA.

Villamosenergiaipari Kutató Intézet—VEIKI (Institute for Electrical Power Research) 1368 Budapest, POB 233; tel. (1) 118-3233; telex 22-5744; fax (1) 117-9956; f. 1949; research on technology, safety, structure mechanics, control and instrumentation, water chemistry of nuclear power plants. Scientific divisions; Divisions of Nuclear and Heat Power Engineering, Systemtechnics, Chemical Engineering, Computer Engineering, Electrical Equipment and Combustion Engineering; Dir Dr GYÖRGY VAJDA.

Culture

NATIONAL ORGANIZATIONS

Ministry of Education and Culture: see section on The Government (Ministries).

Nemzetközi Kulturális Intézet (International Cultural Institute): 1051 Budapest, Dorottya u. 8; tel. (1) 118-3899; telex 22-4735; fax (1) 118-5145; co-ordinates non-governmental international cultural, educational, research and scientific relations; Dir-Gen. G. NÁDOR.

CULTURAL HERITAGE

Budapesti Történeti Múzeum (Historical Museum of Budapest): 1014 Budapest, Szent György tér 2; tel. (1) 175-7533; f. 1887; history of Budapest from Roman to modern times; fine arts; Dir-Gen. Dr LÁSZLÓ SELMECZI.

Központi Múzeumi Igazgatóság (National Centre of Museums): 1450 Budapest, Kinizsi u. 39; tel. (1) 117-5950; f. 1961; organizes exhibitions for museums; handles international transportation of *objets d'art* for museums; experimental, documentary and advisory centre for conservationa and museological education; Dir Dr SZATMÁRI SAROLTA.

Magyar Nemzeti Galéria (Hungarian National Gallery): 1250 Budapest, Budavári Palota; tel. (1) 175-7533; telex 223467; f. 1957; collections include Hungarian art from 11th to 20th centuries; Dir Dr LÓRÁND BERECZKY.

Magyar Nemzeti Múzeum (Hungarian National Museum): 1088 Budapest, Múzeum-krt 14–16; tel. (1) 138-2122; f. 1802; Dir-Gen. Dr ISTVÁN FODOR.

Országos Széchényi Könyvtar (National Széchényi Library): 1827 Budapest, Budavári Palota F-épulet; tel. (1) 155-6167; telex 22-4226; f. 1802; 2.4m. books and periodicals, 4.3m. manuscripts, maps, prints, microfilms, etc.; Dir-Gen. Prof. GYULA JUHÁSZ.

Szépművészeti Múzeum (Museum of Fine Arts): 1146 Budapest, Dózsa György ut. 41; tel. (1) 142-9759; fax (1) 122-8298; f. 1896, opened 1906; collections include Egyptian and Greco-Roman antiquities, and foreign paintings, sculptures, drawings and engravings; Dir Dr MIKLÓS MOJZER.

SPORTING ORGANIZATIONS

Olympic Committee of the Republic of Hungary: 1118 Budapest, Balogh Tihamer 4; tel. (1) 186-8000; telex 22-3296; fax (1) 186-9670; f. 1895; Pres. POL SCHMITT; Sec.-Gen. TAMÁS AJAN.

Országos Nestnevélsi és Sporthivatal—OTSH (National Office for Physical Education and Sport): 1054 Budapest, Hold u. 1; tel. (1) 111-9080; dept of the Ministry of Culture and Education; Pres. REZSŐ GALLOV.

PERFORMING ARTS

Budapest Opera House: Budapest, Andrassy u.; f. 1884.

Film Studio

MAFILM—Magyar Filmgyarto Vállalat: Budapest, Rona u. 174; tel. (1) 251-5666; telex 22-6860; fax (1) 251-2896; films, videos, advertisements, management of actors; Gen. Dir LÁSZLÓ VINCZE.

ASSOCIATIONS

Magyar Film- és TV-MŰészek Szövetsége (Federation of Hungarian Film and TV Artists): 1068 Budpaest, Gorkij fasor u. 38; tel. (1) 142-4760.

Magyar Képzőművészek és Iparművészek Szövetsége (Federation of Hungarian Fine and Applied Artists): 1051 Budapest, Vörösmarty tér 1; tel. (1) 117-6222; Pres. Dr LAJOS NÉMETH.

Magyar Kórusok és Zenekarok Szövetsége (Hungarian Choral and Orchestra Federation): 1051 Budapest, Vörösmarty tér 1; tel. (1) 117-9510; Dir JÓZSEF TÓTHPÁL.

Magyar Színházművésti Szövetség (Hungarian Theatrical Artists Federation): 1068 Budapest, Gorkij fasor 38; tel. (1) 142-0146; Mems of Man. Bd LÁSZLÓ BABARCZY, ANDRÁS BÁLINT, PÉTER HUSZTI, TAMÁS KOLTAI, GÁBOR SZÉKELY, LÁSZLÓ VÁMOS.

Education

In 1988 government spending on all levels of education amounted to 85,000m. forint, 8.6% of total public expenditure. Pre-primary education in Hungary is not compulsory, but, in 1986, about 92% of children between the ages of three and six years were attending kindergartens (óvodák). Children under the age of three years attend crèches (bölcsődék). Education is compulsory for children between the ages of six and 16 years, although most continue their schooling beyond that age. Children attend a basic school (általános iskola) until they are 14, studying general subjects together with some practical training; special provision is made in basic schools for talented children, particularly those with notable ability in languages. Of children who left full-time education in 1989, 94% had completed the eight grades of primary education.

Secondary education starts at the age of 14 years. There are three principal types of secondary school: the gymnasium (gimnázium) provides a four-year course of mainly academic studies, although some vocational training is included in the curriculum; the vocational school (technikum) curriculum provides full vocational training, together with general education; and the apprentice training school (ipari tanulók gyakorló iskolai), which are attached to factories, agricultural co-operatives, etc., and provide training leading to full trade qualifications, with general education having a less prominent role. In addition, there are special schools both for children with physical and/or learning difficulties, and for the particularly gifted. Educational reform aimed at revising the curricula and the method of assessing pupils is taking place. In southern Hungary bilingual schools are being established to promote the languages of national minorities. There are 57 higher education institutes, of which 10 are universities and nine technical universities.

UNIVERSITIES

Albert Szent-György Medical University (Szent-György Albert Orvostudománti Egyetem): 6720 Szeged, Dugonics tér 13; tel. (62) 12-729; telex 82441; f. 1872, refounded 1921 as Medical Faculty of Szeged University, independent 1951; 2 faculties, 625 teachers, 2,048 students; Rector Prof. Dr J. SZILÁRD.

Attila József University (József Attila Tudományegyetem): 6701 Szeged, Dugonics tér 13; tel. (62) 24-022; telex 82401; fax (62) 11-988; f. 1872, refounded 1921; 3 faculties, 527 teachers, 3,800 students; Rector Prof. Dr BÉLA CSÁKÁNY.

Budapest University of Economic Sciences (Budapesti Közgazdaságtudományi Egyetem): 1093 Budapest, Dimitrov tér 8; tel. (1) 117-4359; telex 22-4186; f. 1948; 485 teachers, 4300 students; Rector Cs. CSÁKI.

Janus Pannonius University of Pécs (Pécsi Janus Pannonius Tudományegyetem): 7622 Pécs, Rákóczi u. 80; tel. (72) 12-902; telex 12301; f. 1367, refounded 1922; 3 faculties, 531 teachers, 3,989 students; Rector Dr M. ORMOS.

Loránd Eötvös University (Eötvös Loránd Tudomán Yegyetem): 1364 Budapest, Egyetem tér 1–3; tel. (1) 118-0820; telex 22-5467; f. 1635; 4 faculties, 1,353 teachers, 8,748 students; Rector LAJOS VÉKÁS.

Louis Kossuth University (Kossuth Lajos Tudományegyetem): 4101 Debrecen, Egyetem tér 1; tel. (52) 16-666; telex 72200; f. 1912; 2 faculties, 503 teachers, 2,280 students; Rector Dr A. LIPTÁK (acting).

Medical University of Pécs (Pécsi Orvostudományi Egyetem): 7643 Pécs, Szigeti u. 12; tel. (72) 24-122; telex 12311; fax (72) 26-244; f. 1923 as Faculty of Medicine of University of Pécs, independent 1951; 531 teachers, 1,295 students; Rector Prof. Dr M. BAUER.

Postgraduate Medical University (Orvostovábbképző Egyetem): 1135 Budapest, Szabolcs u. 35; tel. (1) 140-8900; telex 22-6595; fax (1) 149-8344; f. 1910, university since 1987; 711 teachers, 9,903 students; Rector Prof. Dr I. FORGÁCS.

Semmelweis University of Medicine (Semmelweis Orvostudományi Egyetem): 1085 Budapest, Üllői u. 26; tel. (1) 113-1244; telex 22-6720; f. 1769 as Medical Faculty of University of Pest, became independent 1951; 3 faculties, 1,237 teachers, 3,590 students; Rector Prof. Dr E. SOMOGYI.

University Medical School of Medicine (Debreceni Orvostudományi Egyetem): 4012 Debrecen, Nagyerdei krt 98; tel. (52) 17-571; telex 72411; fax (52) 13-847; f. 1918 as Faculty of Medicine of Louis Kossuth University, independent 1951; 722 teachers, 1,536 students; Rector Dr A. LEŐVEY.

Technical Universities

Debrecen University of Agrarian Sciences (Debreceni Agrártudományi Egyetem): 4105 Debrecen, POB 36; tel. (52) 17-888; telex 72211; fax (52) 13-385; f. 1868; 1 faculty, 2 colleges, 293 teachers, 1,122 students; Rector Dr A. KOZMA.

Miskolc University (Miskolci Egyetem): 3515 Miskolc, Egyetemváros; tel. (46) 65-111; telex 62-223; fax (46) 69-554; f. 1735 in Selmecbánya, moved to Sopron in 1919 and to Miskolc in 1949; engineering, legal and political sciences, economics; 5 faculites, 557 teachers, 2,481 students; Rector Dr F. KOVÁCS.

Pannon University of Agricultural Sciences (Pannon Agrártudományi Egyetem): 8361 Keszthely, Deák Ferenc u. 16; tel. (82) 12-652; telex 35282; fax (82) 19-105; f. 1797; 3 faculties, 263 teachers, 1,500 students; Rector Prof. PETER HORN.

Technical University of Budapest (Budapesti Műszaki Egyetem): 1521 Budapest, Műegyetem Rkp 3; tel. (1) 166-4011; telex 22-5931; fax (1) 166-6808; f. 1782; 7 faculties, 2,297 teachers, 7,851 students; Rector Prof. Dr LAJOS FODOR.

University of Agricultural Sciences (Agrártudományi Egyetem): 2103 Gödöllő, Páter Károly u. 1; tel. (28) 10-200; telex 22-4892; f. 1945; 3 faculties, 423 teachers, 3,294 students; Rector Dr KÁROLY KOCSIS.

University of Forestry and Wood Science (Erdészeti és Faipari Egyetem): 9400 Sopron, Bajcsy-Zsilinszky u. 4; tel. (99) 11-100; telex 24-9126; fax (99) 12-240; f. 1808; 2 faculties, 1 college, 153 teachers, 1,010 students; Rector Dr ANDRÁS WINKLER.

University of Horticulture and Food Technology (Kertészeti és Élelmiszeripari Egyetem): 1118 Budapest, Villányi ut 35–43; tel. (1) 185-0666; telex 22-6011; f. 1853; 4 faculties, 300 teachers, 1,828 students; Rector Prof. Dr I. TAMÁSSY.

University of Veszprém (Veszprémi Egyetem): 8200 Veszprém, Schönherz Z. u. 10; tel. (80) 22-022; telex 32397; fax (80) 26-016; f. 1949; science; 202 teachers, 771 students; Rector Dr J. LISZI.

University of Veterinary Sciences (Állatorvostudományi Egyetem): 1078 Budapest, Landler Jenő u. 2; tel. (1) 122-2660; telex 224439; fax (1) 142-6518; f. 1787; 108 teachers, 550 students; Rector Prof. Dr F. KOVÁCS.

Social Welfare

In 1989 state expenditure on health and social welfare amounted to 74,700m. forint, with a further 269,500m. forint allocated to social security. Hungary's national insurance scheme is based largely on non-state contributions. Employees contribute 3%–5% of their earnings to the pension fund, while employers usually pay 40% of the earnings of each of their employees. Publicly-financed employers, however, contribute only 10% of employee earnings. The cost of health services and other social services is met by state subsidies and contributions from the place of work.

Men are usually entitled to receive retirement pensions at the age of 60, and women at 55, drawing between 33% and 75% of their earnings, according to length of service. Unemployment benefit was introduced in January 1989. Sickness benefits are provided by social insurance: employees are usually entitled to sick pay for one year, or for two years in cases of tuberculosis, occupational disease or industrial accident. Most medical consultation and treatment is free, although there is a small charge (which rose by 80% in January 1989) for medicines, and one of between 15% and 50% of the cost of medical appliances. Social insurance also covers maternity benefits (women are entitled to 24 weeks maternity leave on full pay), invalidity pensions, widows' pensions and orphans allowances.

At the end of 1989 there were 31,537 doctors in Hungary (2.98 per 1,000 population) and 104,479 hospital beds (9.85 per 1,000). Infant mortality was 15.7 per 1,000 live births in 1989, a slight decline on the previous year. The mortality rate for males was 15.0 per 1,000 population (average life expectancy 64.8), compared to 12.4 per 1,000 for women (average life expectancy 72.2).

NATIONAL AGENCIES

Ministry of Social Welfare: see section on The Government (Ministries).

National Administration of Social Insurance (Országos Társadalombiztosítási Föigazgatóság): 1139 Budapest, Váci út 73; tel. (1) 129-9250; fax (1) 140-9989; finances sickness benefits, medicines and medical appliances, maternity and child-care allowances, pensions, etc.; Dir Dr ALBERT RÁCZ.

National Ambulance Service (Országos Mentöszolgálat): 1395 Budapest, Robert Károly krt 77; Dir Dr LÁSZLÓ ANDICS.

HEALTH AND WELFARE ORGANIZATIONS

'Against Cancer, for the Future of the People' Foundation ('A Rák Ellen, az Emberért, a Holnapért' Társadalmi Alapítvány): 1122 Budapest 1122, Ráth György u. 7–9.

Evangelical Health Care Service (Evangéliumi Gyógyító Szolgálat): 1118 Budapest, Torbágy u. 9; organization for the care and prevention of alcoholics and alcoholism.

Foundation for the Development of Orthopaedics in Hungary (Alapítvány a Magyarországi Ortopédia Fejlesztéséért): 1113 Budapest, Karolina u. 27.

'Heart Sounds' Foundation ('Szól a Szív' Alapítvány): 1146 Budapest, Ajtósi Dürer sor 39; organization for the aid of blind children.

Heart and Vasculary Diseases Foundation (Szív- és Érbetegekért Alapítvány): 1173 Budapest, Kaszáló u. 45.

Hungarian Red Cross (Magyar Vöröskereszt): 1051 Budapest, Arany János u. 31; Pres. Dr LÁSZLÓ PESTA; Sec.-Gen. Dr JÁNOS HANTOS.

LARES Foundation (LARES Alapítvány): Budapest, Károly krt 2; organization of family-help and self-help groups.

National Institute for Health Care (Országos Egészségnevenlési Intézet): 1062 Budapest, Andrássy út 82; tel. (1) 132-7380; Dir Dr JÓZSEF TELKES.

Peter Cerny Foundation for the Treatment of Premature Babies (Peter Cerny Alapítvány a Beteg Koraszülöttek Gyógyításáért): 1066 Budapest, Baross u. 27.

'Shelter' Foundation for Mentally Retarded Children ('Hajlék' Értelmi Fogyatékosokat Segítö Alapítvány): 1051 Budapest, Október 6 u. 22.

S.O.S. Foundation (S.O.S. Alapítvány): Budapest, Attila út 71; organization for the promotion of the welfare of physically handicapped people.

'Stay with Us' Foundation ('Maradj Köztünk' Alapítvány): 1066 Budapest, Dessewffy u. 34; promotes activities to prevent drug abuse.

Transylvania Foundation (Transilvania Alapítvány): 1025 Budapest, Aldás u. 5; refugee organization.

The Environment

Opposition to the Danube Dam project, at Gabčíkovo-Nagymaros, produced an organized environmental movement in Hungary, as well as opposition to the Communist regime. Since the suspension of Hungarian participation in the project, however, the original Danube Circle group has not been evident. The issue continued to place a strain on relations with Czechoslovakia during 1991. There are several small Green parties in Hungary. The Hungarian Government is a member of the Joint Danube Fishery Commission (Czechoslovakia), the IUCN (Gland, Switzerland) and participated in the activities of the CMEA Co-ordinating Centres on environmental matters.

GOVERNMENT ORGANIZATIONS

Ministry of Environmental Protection and Urban Development: see section on The Government (Ministries).

Ministry of Transport, Communications and Water Management: see section on The Government (Ministries).

Environmental Protection Authority (Környezetvédelmi Főfelügyelség): 1054 Budapest, Alkotmány u. 29; tel. (1) 132-9940; Dir Dr GYULA EGERSZEGI.

National Committee for the Protection of Clean Air (National Planning Office): 1370 Budapest, POB 613.

ACADEMIC INSTITUTES

Hungarian Academy of Sciences (Magyar Tudományos Akadémia): 1051 Budapest, Roosevelt-tér 9; tel. (1) 138-2344; telex 224139; f. 1825; Pres. DOMOKOS KOSÁRY; Gen. Sec. ISTVÁN LÁNG.

Forest Research Institute (Erdeszeti Tudomanyos Intezet): 1023 Budapest, Frankel Leo utca 42–44; tel. (1) 115-0624; telex 22-6914; fax (1) 115-1806; f. 1949; general research in forestry and environmental matters.

NON-GOVERNMENTAL ORGANIZATIONS

Hungarian Nature Conservation Federation (Magyar Termeszetvedä Szevelses): 1121 Budapest, Kóltö u. 21; f. 1989; asscn of nine major environmental groups; organizes research.

ISTER (East European Environmental Research Institute): 1056 Budapest, Váci utca 62–64; tel. (1) 119-9057; fax (1) 117-2000; f. 1989; aims to protect the environment through research, advisory work and publications; Pres. JÁNOS VARGHA; Exec. Dir MIKLÓS HEGYI.

REGIONAL ORGANIZATION

Danube Commission: 1068 Budapest, Benczúr utca 25; tel. (1) 122-8083; f. 1948; approves projects for river maintenance; also responsible for navigation issues; mems: Austria, Bulgaria, Czechoslovakia, Hungary, Romania, Ukraine, Yugoslavia; Pres. S. POP (Romania); Sec. R. SOVA (Yugoslavia).

Defence

In June 1990, according to Western estimates, Hungary's regula armed forces numbered 94,000, of which 50,500 were conscripts. The Army had 72,000 forces (including 42,500 conscripts) and the Air Force 22,000 (8,000 conscripts). The armed border force of 18,000 was to be reduced to 9,000 by 1995. In October 1989 legislation to disband the Communist Party-dominated Workers' Militia (60,000 members) was passed. Hungary, a founder member of the Warsaw Pact in 1955, was one of the Eastern European countries most eager for its dissolution in the late 1980s: the Warsaw Pact was finally dismantled in July 1991. The 65,000 troops stationed in Hungary started to be withdrawn in 1989 and the last of them left in June 1991. Hungary's defence budget was estimated at 44,260m. forint in 1990. Plans to reduce the size of the Army and military expenditure were threatened by the civil unrest in Yugoslavia, across Hungary's southern border, in 1991.

Commander-in-Chief: President of the Republic.

Chief of Staff: Maj.-Gen. JÁNOS DEÁK.

Bibliography

Batt, Judy. *Economic Reform and Political Change in Eastern Europe: a Comparison of the Czechoslovak and Hungarian Experiences*. Basingstoke, Hants, Macmillan, 1988.

Berend, Iván. *The Hungarian Economic Reforms 1953-1988*. Cambridge, Cambridge University Press, 1990.

Brada, József C., and Dobozi, István (Eds). *The Hungarian Economy in the 1980s: Reforming the System and Adjusting to External Shocks* (Industrial Development and the Social Fabric series, Vol. 9). London, JAI Press, 1988.

Gati, Charles. *Hungary and the Soviet Bloc*. Durham, NC, Duke University Press, 1986.

Heinrich, Hans-Georg. *Hungary: Politics, Economics and Society* (Marxist Regimes Series). Boulder, CO, Lynne Rienner, 1986.

Hoensch, Jorg K. *A History of Modern Hungary 1867-1986*. Harlow, Longman, 1988.

János, Andrew. *The Politics of Backwardness in Hungary 1825-1945*. Princeton, NJ, Princeton University Press, 1982.

Kovrig, Bennett. *Communism in Hungary: From Kun to Kádár*. Stanford, CA, Hoover Institution Press, 1979.

Lendvai, Paul. *Hungary: The Art of Survival*. London, I. B. Tauris, 1988.

Lomax, Bill. *Hungary 1956*. London, Allison and Busby, 1976.

Macartney, C. A. *October the Fifteenth: A History of Modern Hungary, 1929-45*, 2 vols. Edinburgh, Edinburgh University Press, 1956-57.

Hungary: A Short History. Edinburgh, Edinburgh University Press, 1962.

Molnar, Miklós. *From Béla Kun to János Kádár: Seventy Years of Communism*. Oxford, Berg, 1990.

Révész, Gábor. *Perestroika in Eastern Europe: Hungary's Economic Transformation, 1945-1988*. Boulder, CO, Westview Press, 1990.

Richet, Xavier. *The Hungarian Model: Planning and Market in a Socialist Economy*. Cambridge, Cambridge University Press, 1989.

Schöpflin, George, and Poulton, Hugh. *Romania's Ethnic Hungarians*. London, Minority Rights Group Report, 1990.

Shawcross. *Crime and Compromise: János Kádár and the Politics of Hungary Since the Revolution*. London, Weidenfeld and Nicolson, 1974.

Sugar, Peter (Ed.). *A History of Hungary*. London, I. B. Tauris, 1990.

Vali, Ferenc. *Rift and Reform in Hungary: Nationalism versus Communism*. Cambridge, MA, Harvard University Press, 1961.

POLAND

Geography

PHYSICAL FEATURES

The Republic of Poland is located in north-eastern Europe and is bordered to the west by Germany, to the south by Czechoslovakia and to the north by the Russian Federation enclave around Kaliningrad on the Baltic coast. The eastern frontier is comprised of borders with Lithuania to the north-east, Byelorussia to the east and Ukraine to the south-east. To the north there is a 520-km coastline along the Baltic Sea. After the Second World War Poland lost a considerable amount of territory to the USSR, while gaining the former German provinces of Pomerania and Silesia in the west, and part of East Prussia in the east. Poland's borders are now marked by the Oder (Odra) and Neisse (Nysa) rivers in the west, the River Bug in the east, the Sudetic Mountains in the south-west and the Carpathian range of mountains in the south-east. The country has an area of 312,683 sq km (120,727 sq miles), some 20% less than in 1939.

Poland is a predominantly low-lying country, the average altitude being only 173 m. The most developed and most highly-populated region is the central plain, which covers more than one-third of the country. The plain is crossed by Poland's two major rivers, the Oder and the Vistula (Wisła), which rise in the Sudetic and Carpathian mountains, respectively, along the Polish–Czechoslovak border and flow into the Baltic Sea. South of the plain there is a plateau (average height 700 m) which is drained by the Bug, San and Vistula rivers. On the southern border of Poland, between the Sudetic range in the west and the western reaches of the Carpathians in the east, lies the broad depression of the Moravian Gate, which is the traditional route into central Europe. North of the central plains there are belts of shallow lakes, surrounded by undulating and wooded countryside. North of this lake district are the coastal lowlands, which are most extensive near the estuaries of the Oder and Vistula. Most of the coastline is covered by sand dunes. There are many beaches and lagoons and few natural harbours.

CLIMATE

Poland's climate is largely continental, with hot summers and cold winters, although it is more temperate in the west than in the east. The average July temperature in Warsaw is 18°C (65°F), while the average for January is −4°C (25°F). Warsaw has an average annual rainfall of 560 mm, whereas Kraków, in the south, has an annual average of 745 mm.

POPULATION

Ethnic Poles now constitute some 98% of the total population. Most of the substantial pre-1939 Ukrainian and Jewish populations either fled the country or were killed during the Nazi occupation. There are still minor communities of Byelorussians, Ukrainians and Jews, and small numbers of Greeks, Macedonians, Russians, Lithuanians, Slovaks, Czechs and Roma (Gypsies). Some ethnic Germans remain in the former German territories of Silesia and Pomerania, but most of the Germans living in Poland or in the lands granted to Poland in 1945 were deported after the War. The official language is Polish, a member of the west Slavonic group. Most of the inhabitants profess Christianity, an estimated 95% of the population being adherents of the Roman Catholic Church.

The total population in December 1990 was estimated at 38,183,200; the population density was 122.1 persons per sq km. In December 1989 it was estimated that 1,655,100 people lived in the capital, Warsaw (Warszawa). Other important towns included Łódź (population 851,700), a major industrial centre, and Kraków (population 748,400), an important centre of culture and learning. Since the Second World War there has been a significant movement of the population from rural to urban areas: in 1988 only 38.8% of the population lived in the countryside, compared with 68% in 1946.

Chronology

966: The first historical ruler of Poland, Prince Mieszko I, converted to Latin Christianity.

1320: Lidislav I was crowned King of a reunited Poland.

1386: Vladislav II, Grand Duke of Lithuania, became King of Poland by marriage, founded the Jagiellonian dynasty (1386–1572) and established a personal union with Lithuania.

1493: A two-chamber Sejm (Parliament) was established.

1548–72: Sigismund II established a permanent union with Lithuania which lasted until 1795.

1764: Accession of Stanislav II, who ruled until 1795.

1772: First partition of Poland, between Russia, Prussia and Austria, took place.

1791: Stanislav II created Europe's first modern constitution.

1793: The second partition of Poland.

1795: The third partition of Poland.

1807: The Grand Duchy of Warsaw was established by Napoleon.

1815: The Congress Kingdom of Poland was formed under Russian patronage.

1905–07: Revolution in Russian Poland.

1915: Russian occupation was ended by German victory on the Eastern Front.

1916: Restoration of the Kingdom of Poland by Germany.

3 June 1918: Allied Governments recognized the principle of Polish independence.

11 November 1918: Józef Piłsudski assumed power in Warsaw. Poland was declared an independent Republic.

28 June 1919: The Treaty of Versailles recognized Polish independence.

13–19 August 1920: Soviet forces were defeated at the Battle of Warsaw.

18 March 1921: Signing of the Treaty of Riga by Poland, the Ukraine and Soviet Russia formally concluded the Soviet–Polish war and defined the frontiers in the region.

1922: Stanislav Wojsiechowski was elected Head of State.

12 May 1926: Piłsudski seized power in a *coup d'état*.

25 January 1932: A non-aggression pact was signed with the USSR.

26 January 1934: A non-aggression pact was signed with Germany.

23 March 1935: A new Constitution was enacted.

12 May 1935: Death of Piłsudski.

31 March 1939: France and the United Kingdom announced guarantees of Poland's independence, in response to German territorial demands.

23 August 1939: The Nazi–Soviet Pact was signed, including a secret agreement between the USSR and Germany to partition Poland.

1 September 1939: Germany invaded Poland, which caused the start of the Second World War.

17 September 1939: The USSR invaded Poland.

30 September 1939: A Government-in-Exile was formed in Paris under Gen. Sikorski, moving to London in 1940.

22 June 1941: Germany invaded the USSR; all of Poland was occupied by Nazi forces.

30 July 1941: The Polish Government-in-Exile established diplomatic relations with the USSR.

5 January 1942: The Polish Workers' Party (PWP) was founded.

April 1943: The Warsaw Ghetto uprising was suppressed by German troops.

25 April 1943: German investigators discovered, at Katyn in the USSR, the bodies of 4,000 Polish officers, who had been murdered by Soviet secret police in 1940.

26 April 1943: The USSR severed diplomatic relations with the Polish Government-in-Exile.

4 July 1943: Gen. Sikorski, Prime Minister of the Government-in-Exile, died in an air crash.

23 July 1944: The Polish Committee of National Liberation (Lublin Committee—PKWN) was established under Soviet auspices.

1 August–2 October 1944: The Warsaw Uprising was eventually suppressed by German troops.

February 1945: German forces withdrew from Warsaw. Stalin, Churchill and Roosevelt met at Yalta: the 'Curzon line' was agreed as Poland's eastern border; Stalin promised 'free and unfettered elections' in Poland after the War.

21 April 1945: A Soviet–Polish Treaty of Friendship was signed.

28 June 1945: The USA and the United Kingdom recognized the 'Provisional Government of National Unity', which was dominated by members of the Soviet-backed PKWN, but included Stanisław Mikołajczyk and a few others from the Government-in-Exile.

17 July–2 August 1945: The Potsdam Conference: the Allies agreed to give former German territories east of the Oder–Neisse line to Poland.

19 January 1947: Elections to the Sejm were won by the Democratic Bloc, a grouping dominated by the PWP and led by Władysław Gomułka; the United Kingdom and the USA complained that the elections did not meet the requirements agreed at Yalta.

6 February 1947: The People's Republic of Poland was declared; Bolesław Bierut took office as President.

October 1947: Mikołajczyk fled to London after threats to his life.

September 1948: Gomułka was forced to admit 'political errors' and was dismissed as party leader.

December 1948: The founding congress of the Polish United Workers' Party (PUWP) took place after the PWP merged with the Polish Socialist Party; Bierut was appointed party First Secretary.

1949: Gomułka was arrested, accused of 'rightist and nationalist deviations'.

22 July 1952: A new Soviet-style Constitution was adopted.

1954: Bierut was succeeded by Józef Cyrankiewicz as Chairman of the Council of Ministers.

14 May 1955: The Warsaw Treaty was signed.

March 1956: The First Secretary of the PUWP, Bolesław Bierut, died in Moscow.

28–29 June 1956: Seventy-four people died in riots in Poznań protesting against food price rises.

October 1956: Władysław Gomułka was appointed First Secretary by the 8th Party Plenum and began to introduce some political liberalization.

March 1968: Nation-wide anti-Government student protests took place, followed by a Party-inspired campaign against Jews and intellectuals.

April 1968: Marshal Marian Spychalski was appointed Head of State.

November 1968: Soviet leader Leonid Brezhnev announced the 'Brezhnev Doctrine' (declaring the right of the USSR to intervene in the affairs of its Warsaw Pact allies) in Warsaw.

December 1970: Gomułka and Spychalski resigned after workers were killed when police suppressed strikes and protests in the Baltic ports; Piotr Jaroszewicz replaced Józef Cyrankiewicz, who became Head of State, as Chairman of the Council of Ministers; Edward Gierek was appointed First Secretary.

7 December 1970: A Treaty was signed by Poland and the Federal Republic of Germany confirming the post-war Polish western border.

1972: Gierek launched a 'modernization programme' of large-scale investment funded chiefly by Western banks.

June 1976: Strikes and demonstrations prevented planned food price rises from being implemented.

September 1976: The Workers' Defence Committee (KOR) was formed after striking miners were arrested at Radom.

16 October 1978: Cardinal Karol Wojtyła, Archbishop of Kraków, was elected Pope John Paul II.

June 1979: Pope John Paul II visited Poland.

1980

February
Piotr Jaroszewicz was replaced as Chairman of the Council of Ministers by Edward Babiuch at the Party Congress.

July
Food price rises led to strikes and workers' protests; unofficial strike committees were formed to press for pay increases and, subsequently, for political demands to be met.

August
Babiuch resigned and was replaced by Józef Pińkowski as Chairman of the Council of Ministers.

14: Some 17,000 workers at the Lenin Shipyards in Gdańsk went on strike and issued a list of economic and political demands.

21: The strike spread to Szczecin and now involved over 150,000 workers.

23: Mieczysław Jagielski, a member of the Politburo, met with Lech Wałęsa and other union delegates.

31: The Gdańsk and Szczecin agreements were signed: the Government agreed to the unions' demands, including the right to form free trade unions and the right to strike.

September
5: Gierek was replaced as First Secretary by Stanisław Kania.

17: Representatives from some 35 independent trade union committees met to form the independent trade union, Solidarity (Solidarność).

November
10: Solidarity was officially recognized.

1981

January
1: The Central Council of Trade Unions was dissolved.

February
10–11: Pińkowski was replaced as Chairman of Council of Ministers by Gen. Wojciech Jaruzelski.

March
27: Nation-wide four hour strike.

May
12: Rural Solidarity officially recognized.

July
14–18: Ninth (Extraordinary) Party Congress of PUWP: multi-candidate secret ballots introduced for elections; only four former Politburo members were re-elected.

September
5–10: Solidarity's first National Congress took place.

October
Jaruzelski replaced Kania as Party First Secretary.

December
13: Jaruzelski declared martial law; a Military Council of National Salvation was established; Lech Wałęsa and other Solidarity activists were arrested and imprisoned.

1982

May
1: Anti-Government demonstrations were dispersed by the police.

August
31: Demonstrations took place to mark the second anniversary of the Gdańsk Accords.

October
8: The Trade Union Bill was introduced, outlawing independent union activity.

November
12: Wałęsa was released.

December
13: Martial law was suspended.

1983

July
22: Martial law was formally lifted; the Military Council of National Salvation was dissolved.

October
Lech Wałęsa was awarded the Nobel Peace Prize.

November
Jaruzelski resigned as Minister of Defence to become Chairman of the newly-formed National Defence Committee.

1984

July
An amnesty was proclaimed to mark the Republic's 40th anniversary.

October
Jerzy Popiełuszko, a pro-Solidarity priest, was murdered by security forces.

1985

January
Price rises were introduced, but modified after Solidarity threatened to call a strike.

October
Some multi-candidate ballots were allowed in legislative elections; Solidarity urged a boycott.

November
Jaruzelski resigned as the Chairman of the Council of Ministers, becoming President of the Council of State (Head of State); he was succeeded by Prof. Zbigniew Messner.

1986

February
Wałęsa was put on trial for disputing the voting figures for the elections held in October 1985; the charges were subsequently dropped.

May
Zbigniew Bujak, a leading Solidarity activist, was detained after spending nearly five years in hiding; large demonstrations took place in protest at his arrest.

June
The 10th Congress of the PUWP took place.

July
Legislation was passed to allow the release of political prisoners.

1987

May
Anti-Government protests resulted in 158 arrests.

October
The Government announced plans for radical economic and political reforms, which were to be submitted to popular approval in a referendum.

November
The Government failed to achieve the necessary majority in the referendum, partly due to a Solidarity-backed boycott.

1988

January

30: Price rises were announced; Solidarity protested.

March

Security forces dispersed student demonstrations commemorating the 1968 protests.

April–May

Widespread strikes and demonstrations took place.

June

Only 55% of the electorate participated in local elections after Solidarity urged a boycott.

July

The Government expressed a wish to discuss trade union reform. The Soviet leader, Mikhail Gorbachev, arrived on an official visit.

August

The Government offered round-table talks with labour groups after coal-miners went on strike.

September

19: Prof. Zbigniew Messner's Government resigned; Dr Mieczysław Rakowski became Chairman of a more reformist Council of Ministers.

October

31: Large-scale protests took place after the Government announced the closure of the Lenin shipyards in Gdańsk.

December

21: Six politburo members resigned at a plenum of the PUWP Central Committee as part of wider changes in the Government.

1989

January

18: The Central Committee of the PUWP agreed to negotiate towards the re-legalization of Solidarity.

February

6: 'Round-table' talks between the Government and opposition leaders, headed by Lech Wałęsa, opened in Warsaw.

March

7: The Polish Government for the first time accused the USSR of committing the 1940 Katyn massacre.

April

5: A negotiated agreement was reached at the round-table talks: Solidarity was to be re-legalized; partly-free elections were to be held; economic reforms were promised.

7: Constitutional amendments resulting from the round-table talks were adopted, including the creation of a new bicameral National Assembly.

May

17: Laws were adopted granting full legal status to the Roman Catholic Church and guaranteeing freedom of conscience.

June

4: Elections to the National Assembly took place: Solidarity won 99% of the freely-elected seats.

18: Second round of elections.

July

4: The new National Assembly convened in Warsaw.

17: Full diplomatic relations were re-established with the Holy See.

19: The National Assembly re-elected Jaruzelski as President by a narrow margin.

25: Lech Wałęsa rejected an offer for Solidarity to join a coalition Government.

28–29: Jaruzelski resigned as First Secretary of the PUWP and from the Politburo and Central Committee; he was replaced as First Secretary by Mieczysław Rakowski.

August

2: Lt-Gen. Czesław Kiszczak was elected as Chairman of the Council of Ministers.

7: Solidarity proposed that it should form a Government in alliance with the United Peasants' Party (UPP) and the Democratic Party (DP).

17: Kiszczak resigned after announcing that he was unable to form a Government.

20: Jaruzelski accepted Solidarity's proposal and asked Tadeusz Mazowiecki to form a Government.

24: Mazowiecki was confirmed in office by a vote in the Sejm (lower house).

September

11: Roman Malinowski resigned as the President of the UPP.

12: The Sejm approved Mazowiecki's 23-member cabinet which included ministers from all four major parties.

October

The 'Brezhnev doctrine' was formally renounced by a Warsaw Pact meeting in Warsaw.

December

29–30: The National Assembly approved amendments to the Constitution, including an end to the PUWP's monopoly of power, and the restoration of the official name and flag of pre-war Poland. Finance Minister Leszek Balcerowicz's IMF-approved economic reform plan was approved by the Sejm.

1990

January

2: Sharp price rises and currency devaluation were introduced as part of an austerity programme.

28: The PUWP changed its name to Social Democracy of the Polish Republic at its 11th Congress.

April

13: The USSR admitted liability for the 1940 Katyn massacre.

19–25: Solidarity held its Conference in Gdańsk.

July

13: A Bill was passed by the National Assembly allowing for the sale of state-owned companies to the private sector.

November

Poland's western border was confirmed by the signature of a treaty with the reunified Federal Republic of Germany.

20: Miners held warning strikes in protest at government economic policy.

25: The Presidential election took place: Wałęsa received 40% of the vote, but Chairman of the Council of Ministers Mazowiecki was forced into third place by Stanisław Tymiński.

26: Mazowiecki's Government resigned.

December

9: Wałęsa won the second round of the presidential election with 74% of the vote.

18: Jan Olszewski refused an offer of the Chairmanship of the Council of Ministers.

1991

January

4–5: Jan Bielecki was approved as Chairman of the Council of Ministers by the Sejm, and his proposed membership of a new Council of Ministers was also accepted. The Citizens' Parliamentary Club (OKP—group of Solidarity deputies in the National Assembly) was split by the formation of the Democratic Union.

February

23: Marian Krzaklewski was elected Chairman of Solidarity in succession to Lech Wałęsa.

March

9: The Sejm rejected President Wałęsa's call for immediate parliamentary elections, voting to postpone elections until October.

14: Stanisław Tymiński announced the formation of Party X.

15: The 'Paris Club' of 17 Western countries wrote off 50% of Poland's US $33,000m. foreign debt.

April

4: The first of the 50,000 Soviet troops remaining in Poland were withdrawn; some Soviet troops were to remain until the end of 1993 to support the transit of 380,000 Soviet troops leaving the former German Democratic Republic.

16: Company shares were traded in Warsaw for the first time since before the Second World War.

18: The IMF approved loans totalling $2,500m.

May

12: The Democratic Union party was strengthened by the merger of three groupings of former Solidarity politicians.

16: The Sejm rejected legislation which would have made abortion illegal in virtually all circumstances.

17: The złoty was devalued by 16.8% against the US dollar, and, from 20 May, was to be allowed to float against a basket of currencies.

22: The Solidarity trade union held a day of protest against the Government's economic policies.

June

27: The Government announced plans to transfer ownership of 400 companies (one-quarter of state-owned industry) to every adult citizen through a system of vouchers, starting later in 1991; in October 1991 the programme was reduced to 200 companies (7% of state-owned industry) and postponed until mid-1993.

July

1: President Wałęsa approved an electoral law authorizing Poland's first fully-free parliamentary elections; he had earlier twice vetoed the Sejm's legislation, fearing that it would lead to fragmented governments.

4: Wałęsa announced that parliamentary elections would take place on 27 October.

11: The Sejm rejected Wałęsa's new draft electoral law, intended to replace the law approved on 1 July, which would have entailed voting for party lists rather than for individual candidates.

27: Poland joined Austria, Czechoslovakia, Hungary, Italy and Yugoslavia as a member of the Hexagonal Group (formerly the Pentagonal Group) dealing with regional political issues.

August

11: The Chairman of the National Bank of Poland, Grzegorz Wójtowicz, was suspended in the wake of a financial scandal.

23: A list of 65 parties registered for the October parliamentary elections was published.

27: The Council of Ministers announced plans for the resumption of diplomatic relations with the Baltic states (Estonia, Latvia and Lithuania).

30: The Bielecki Government offered its resignation after repeated obstruction by the Sejm of its policies for economic reform.

31: The Government's resignation was rejected by the Sejm. The Chairman of the National Bank was dismissed by the Sejm.

September

2: Premier Bielecki met with President Wałęsa to discuss the granting of special economic powers to the Government, and later formally requested such powers in the Sejm. Diplomatic relations were re-established with Latvia.

5: Diplomatic relations were re-established with Lithuania.

9: Diplomatic relations were re-established with Estonia.

14: The Governments request for special powers was narrowly rejected by the Sejm.

17: Party X was barred from standing in the October elections in 32 districts following the discovery of falsified candidature documentation.

History
KEITH SWORD

EARLY HISTORY

Present day Poland traces its origins to the unification, in the second half of the 10th century, of a group of Slavic tribes living in the basin of the Warta River. In 966 their King, Mieszko, introduced Christianity, ensuring that henceforth Poland's cultural development would be linked to that of Western Europe. The centre of the country moved gradually southwards to the settlements of the upper Vistula River (Kraków, Sandomierz). Casimir the Great (1333–70), the last of the Piast kings, strengthened state organization through measures such as monetary reform and codified law, and founded the country's first university, at Kraków. In 1386 the Polish Queen, Jadwiga, married Jagiełło, the Grand-Duke of Lithuania. This alliance was eventually to pave the way for full political union (the Union of Lublin, 1569) which was to last until the late 18th century. At its height the combined kingdom stretched from the Baltic to the Black Sea.

In 1572 the last of the Jagiellons died, leaving no heir. For the next 200 years Poland experienced a period of elective monarchy. It was an era marked by numerous wars and military campaigns (against Muscovites, Turks, Tatars, Cossacks and Swedes) but little economic progress. Shaken increasingly by factional conflict and the decline of Royal authority, the Polish Commonwealth began to fragment into a federation of minor states ruled by magnates. The Polish Sejm (parliament) was powerless to prevent a partition of

Polish territory in 1772 by Russia, Prussia and Austria. The last king, Stanisław Poniatowski, attempted to introduce reforms and galvanize the political structure. He created the world's first ministry of education and introduced a liberal Constitution in May 1791. This was not enough to prevent further partitions of the country in 1793 and 1795. The former provoked an unsuccessful insurrection led by Tadeusz Kościuszko, while the latter signalled the disappearance of Poland from the map of Europe.

During the long years of partition (1795–1918) Polish hopes for national rebirth focused initially on Napoleon. His creation of the Duchy of Warsaw (1807–15) encompassed only a small part of Polish territory, however, and this ceased to exist after the French Emperor's downfall. The Kingdom of Poland was formed from an area of the Duchy allocated to Russia at the Congress of Vienna (1815). The harsh policies of Tsarist Russia led to two unsuccessful insurrections, in 1830–31 and in 1863. The incorporation of Polish territories into the three neighbouring empires meant suppression of political and cultural life (less so under Austrian rule) and economic stagnation. One result was the early emigration of many intellectuals and writers (such as Mickiewicz, Słowacki and Norwid), and potential soldiers (to Napoleon's legions). Towards the end of the 19th century emigration from the Polish lands took on a mass character as peasants looked for land and work in the New World.

REBIRTH OF THE POLISH STATE

After the First World War (1914–18) Poland was restored to statehood at the Treaty of Versailles (1919), following the collapse of the three empires which had partitioned it. However, the borders were not finally fixed until a number of plebiscites and further military activity had taken place. The eastern frontier, for example, was only fixed when the Treaty of Riga (1921) marked an end to the Polish–Soviet War of 1919–20. The problems of unifying the three separate partition regions, devastated by the passage of armies, were considerable.

Inter-war Poland was a parliamentary republic, but the dominant figure was Marshal Józef Piłsudski. The country was afflicted with economic problems, experienced difficulty in dealing with its large minority populations, and suffered from political instability. Impatient with the lack of political stability, Piłsudski staged a *coup d'état* in 1926 and became virtually a dictator. Piłsudski died in 1935, but his followers continued to rule in his name.

THE SECOND WORLD WAR (1939–45)

In 1939, with the outbreak of the Second World War, Poland was partitioned once again—this time between Nazi Germany and the USSR. Britain and France declared war in defence of Poland, but could do little to aid it. In June 1941, Germany turned on its Soviet ally, launching an invasion deep into USSR territory, capturing the whole of Poland as it went. During a horrendous six-year period of occupation Poland lost one-sixth of its population, including virtually all of its Jewish community, and 38% of its national wealth. Resistance activity continued throughout the war, and was crowned by the ill-fated Warsaw Rising in 1944, during which 250,000 civilian casualties occurred. Political leadership, in the form of a Government-in-Exile, was organized in Paris and (from 1940) in London, under General Władysław Sikorski. Following Sikorski's death in an air crash at Gibraltar in 1942, he was replaced as premier by the Peasant Party leader, Stanisław Mikołajczyk.

Poland was liberated by the Red Army. In July 1944, when the Red Army units crossed the River Bug, a Committee of National Liberation (PKWN) was established at Lublin. The 'Lublin Committee' consisted of Polish communists subservient to Stalin. They immediately took over the administration of the territory liberated by the Soviet advance and became a *de facto* Government.

The new Poland had a different shape to that of the pre-war Republic. At the conferences of Teheran and Yalta, the Great Power leaders had agreed that Poland should lose almost one-half of its territory to the USSR, but should receive compensation in the north and west at the expense of Germany. These border changes were followed by the expulsion of some 3.5m. Germans from the western territories. At the same time 'repatriation' agreements with the neighbouring Soviet republics provided for the transfer of ethnic Poles from land seized by the USSR in the east. Poland's population was much reduced from its wartime level. It was also homogeneous, because of losses (particularly the wholesale destruction of the Jewish community by the Nazis), border changes and population transfers.

THE IMPOSITION OF COMMUNIST RULE

In January 1945 the PKWN was transformed into a Provisional Government. Stalin had demonstrated that he did not trust the Polish authorities in London and that he was determined to have the dominant voice on how Poland was ruled after the war. As a concession to Western leaders he allowed the Provisional Government to be reconstituted, with the participation of a small group of 'London' politicians headed by Mikołajczyk. Importantly though, the communists retained hold of key ministries such as defence and internal security. This Government—the Provisional Government of National Unity—was recognized by the United Kingdom and the USA on 6 July 1945.

The communists had pledged to hold 'free and unfettered' elections as soon as was possible after the liberation of the country. However, they were aware that their support was thin. (It has been estimated that they could count on the support of only 20,000 Poles in 1944.) They therefore delayed the elections and set about using the Soviet-trained secret police to confuse and terrorize their opponents. The elections were eventually held in February 1947, and they resulted in a victory for the Polish Workers' Party (i.e. communists). There is ample evidence that the results had been manipulated by the communist authorities, but neither the communists' opponents nor the Western powers were able to do anything to remedy the situation. The Peasant Party leader, and main focus of opposition to the communists, Mikołajczyk, fled to the West in October 1947, his attempts to prevent the communist domination of his homeland having failed.

The first post-war Communist leader was Władysław Gomułka, a patriotic Pole and not as subject to Moscow's influence as were some of his colleagues. He was against slavishly imitating the Soviet pattern of social and economic organization in all countries which came under Moscow's influence, and in particular opposed the wholesale collectivization of agriculture, which he feared would alienate the large number of peasant farmers. Unfortunately, his attempt to depart from the orthodox Party line coincided with the 'heresy' of Yugoslavia's Tito in defying Moscow's will. Stalin became determined to crack down on 'nationalist deviationism'. Gomułka's advocacy of a 'Polish road to socialism' earned him rebukes from colleagues and eventually, in 1948, he was dismissed and, in the following year, arrested.

His successor was Bolesław Bierut, a long-term Comintern agent. Bierut took power as the cold war was beginning in earnest, and his period of office marks Poland's darkest period of repressive Stalinism. Bierut's succession was accompanied by a massive expansion of the internal security forces (UB), the beginning of a programme to collectivize agriculture, the development of heavy industry, and expansion of the military–defence sector in line with the wishes of the Warsaw Pact.

On the political front, the Communist Polish Workers' Party was merged with the Socialist Party to form the Polish United Workers' Party (PUWP). The continuing existence of minor parties—a United Peasant Party (UPP) and a Democratic Party (DP)—was window dressing, hinting at continued multi-party democracy. In fact these parties were completely subservient to the Communists; Poland had become a one-party state on the Soviet model.

One centre of recalcitrance which the Communists found it difficult to suppress was the Roman Catholic Church. The Concordat with the Vatican had been renounced in 1945 and a major campaign waged against the Church's influence, with land being seized, church schools being closed, and priests harassed and arrested. In September 1953 the Polish Primate himself, Cardinal Wyszyński, was barred from exercising his functions and compelled to retreat to a monastery. The Church nevertheless grew in stature and became, as it was to remain throughout the period of Communist rule, a source of more enduring national and family values, a haven from the ideological slogans and exhortations of the Communists.

In 1953 Stalin died. Khrushchev's denunciation of Stalin's excesses (in 1956) was quickly followed by the death of Polish Party leader, Bierut. A major crisis in Polish politics developed in the summer of 1956 when workers in a rolling-stock factory in Poznań demonstrated in the city centre. The demonstration developed into a violent display of dissatisfaction with conditions under Communist rule and included an attack on the Party headquarters. It was only finally suppressed when the army was called in. Scores of people died in the violence that resulted.

THE GOMUŁKA PERIOD

An immediate result of the crisis was the political rehabilitation of Władysław Gomułka, and the onset of a period during which, for the first and last time, a Communist leader in Poland enjoyed a measure of popularity. For the next decade there was to be relative stability in Poland—no strikes or popular demonstrations. In the eyes of the people, Communist rule, temporarily at least, ceased to be synonymous with Moscow control; for the first time Poles were able to feel that its leaders were acting in *their* interests. There was also increasing freedom from the attentions of the secret police, with greater tolerance extended towards elements previously characterized as 'reactionary' or 'anti-socialist'. The Church, too, was extended greater freedom of activity and a cautious *modus vivendi* was reached between Church and State. Poles also found it easier to travel abroad—an important consideration for those many Poles who had relatives in the West. There was also greater freedom of expression, with the relaxation of censorship over cultural life.

In the economic sphere Gomułka embarked on his promised 'Polish road' to socialism by abandoning the collectivization of agriculture. His reforms included a partial dismantling of the central planning structure and devolving a large measure of decision-making to local enterprises and workers' councils. By the mid-1960s, however, it had become clear that gains had been at best modest. Despite large investments of capital and labour, productivity remained low. In fact the economy was becoming less, rather than more, efficient. Light industry had been neglected, and there had been only modest progress made in fulfilling promises to accelerate the housing programme. Despite Gomułka's reforms the economy remained over-centralized, bureaucratic and unresponsive both to the demands of the market-place and to those of the workforce. Real wages rose by only 20% during the 1960s—the slowest rate of increase in Eastern Europe.

The later years of the Gomułka period were marked by two shameful episodes: Polish participation in the Warsaw Pact suppression of the 1968 Prague Spring and, in the same year, an 'anti-Zionist' campaign which led to the departure from Poland of most of the country's remaining Jews (only 25,000–30,000). Gomułka, it is true, does not seem to have been implicated in the latter; indeed, it was probably part of a campaign by rivals to discredit and oust him. On the credit side, one major and lasting achievement of the Gomułka period was the *rapprochement* with the Federal Republic of Germany (West Germany), which led to Bonn's recognition of Poland's western border, the Oder–Neisse line.

In December 1970 violent unrest broke out again in Poland, this time on the Baltic coast at Gdańsk. Workers, whose wages had been held down, took to the streets to protest against rises in the price of meat. Gomułka had become out of touch with the situation, and refused to enter into talks with the strikers. Army units were used to quell the protests and once more considerable bloodshed resulted. This unrest highlighted the failure of Gomułka's policies and proved the signal for his removal as Party leader. His successor was Edward Gierek, a former coal-miner from Silesia, who had spent many years working in Western Europe.

THE GIEREK YEARS

Gierek attempted to revitalize the economy—the cornerstone of political stability and prerequisite for the survival of Party leaders. In the atmosphere of détente which characterized the early 1970s, he made use of Western bankers' and governments' readiness to lend money, authorizing massive borrowings to fund investment and the purchase of numerous licences from Western firms. He had a vision of a 'Polish economic miracle' to rival those of the Far East, founded on Poland's availability of, by Western standards, cheap labour. He hoped, moreover, that the borrowings could be repaid from the export earnings that would result from this rapid growth.

In the short term the economy certainly improved. Industrial production rose and living standards improved. A growth in real earnings was accompanied by the appearance of cheap and plentiful food in the shops, and reasonably priced consumer durables. For the first time, Poles could feel that they were part of the 'consumer society' as the number of televisions, washing machines and cars increased rapidly. A number of prestige projects, such as the ultra-modern central station in Warsaw and the Polish capital's urban motorway, added to the aura of progress and modernization. The early decision to rebuild the Royal Castle in Warsaw, destroyed by the Germans in 1944, added to the new regime's popularity.

But Gierek's plan misfired. The Polish economy was incapable of making efficient use of the loans and credits, and producing the surge in exports that the plan required. By the mid-1970s a debt crisis had appeared which was to burden the Polish economy for more than a decade. Ironically, the former emigrant who had seen the salvation of his country in attempting to emulate the West, was now forced to go to Moscow to ask for loans.

The unashamed endorsement of consumerism, together with the widespread corruption that became prevalent within the Communist nomenklatura, alienated many within the Party. Gierek's seeming abandonment of the principles of Communism and of the more ascetic standards which former leaders, such as Gomułka, had exercised was felt to be a betrayal. When his economic 'miracle' began to pale, support for him evaporated. A wave of strikes in protest (once again) against food price rises occurred in 1976, significantly on the 20th anniversary of the Poznań troubles. The authorities' harsh suppression of protest in Ursus and Radom led to the creation of the Committee for Workers' Defence (KOR).

By the end of the decade the Party leadership was demoralized. It had no coherent strategies for finding a way out of the intractable morass of political and economic problems it had helped to generate. The vacuum in moral and spiritual leadership from the Government and Party was highlighted in October 1978 when Cardinal Karol Wojtyła of Kraków was elected to the papacy, as Pope John Paul II—the first Pole to fill that office. His triumphant return to his homeland the following summer brought people out on to the streets in their tens of thousands. It is not difficult to see this as a turning point in post-war Polish history. It was the moment at which the Polish people became confident of their own strength and shared values, in the face of the now enfeebled Communist giant.

A desperate set of economic manoeuvres in late 1979 and early 1980 culminated in yet another attempt to raise meat prices in June. The inevitable strikes followed and Edward Gierek stood down, retiring because of 'ill health'. Stanisław

Kania became leader of a Party which by now had lost all semblance of authority and credibility.

FROM GDAŃSK TO THE 'ROUND TABLE'

The summer of discontent in 1980 led to confrontation between Gdańsk shipyard workers and government officials, and to the birth of Solidarity (Solidarność), the first independent trade union in the Soviet bloc. Its leader, Lech Wałęsa, a shipyard electrician, became a household name around the world. Solidarity was soon claiming 10m. members, including many in the PUWP. In the countryside, Rural Solidarity came into being to represent the interests of the farmers. In the ensuing months, however, Solidarity's demands became more diffuse and its discipline slackened. Strikes broke out randomly as isolated groups of workers sought to take advantage of the Government's weakness to air their grievances.

The first tentative move towards political pluralism ended suddenly in December 1981 when martial law was declared. Gen. Wojciech Jaruzelski attempted to restore the 'leading role' of the Communist Party in political life, seizing the reins of power as leader of a Military Council of National Salvation (WRON). Jaruzelski had been Minister of Defence since 1968, a member of the Politburo since 1971, and had become Chairman of the Council of Ministers in February 1981. The similarities between Jaruzelski's seizure of power and that of Piłsudski in 1926 have been noted by more than one historian (although Party historians took pains to condemn the pre-war regime as repressive and fascist in nature).

In the course of the 1980s the Jaruzelski regime struggled to establish normality on the domestic front and recognition on the international scene. These efforts received a setback in October 1984, when the murder of a pro-Solidarity priest, Father Jerzy Popiełuszko, brought to the world's attention the methods being used by the Interior Ministry to re-establish the Party's authority. In the latter half of the decade there was a softening of official policies. Partly this was due to Poland's deteriorating economic situation and to the recognition by the authorities that while the population could be controlled by force, it could not be forced to co-operate. A further important factor was the accession to power of Mikhail Gorbachev in the USSR. Gradually his more liberal policies permeated the political structures of the Warsaw Pact states.

In 1989 'round table' talks between the Communists and opposition leaders, headed by Lech Wałęsa, led to the legalization of Solidarity and agreement on reform of the political system along more democratic lines. Changes agreed included the creation of a second, upper chamber, the restoration of the presidency, and a gradual return to multi-party, competitive elections. Importantly, restrictions on the freedom of the press were also removed.

SOLIDARITY TAKES POWER

The first election under the new rules was held in June 1989. All 100 seats to the upper chamber (the Senate) were to be freely contested, but 65% of seats in the lower chamber (the Sejm) were reserved for the Communists and their associates. The degree of success that Solidarity candidates enjoyed surprised both Communists and opposition alike. Solidarity won all but one of the seats in the Senate, and all 35% of the seats which they were free to contest in the Sejm. Although in a minority in the lower chamber, they had achieved such a sweeping mandate from the electorate that their moral right to participate in government could not be denied.

Immediately following the elections, parliamentary delegates were asked to vote for a President. The surprising election of Gen. Jaruzelski, the architect of martial law and, less than a decade earlier, the most unpopular man in Poland, can be attributed to two factors; firstly to Solidarity deputies being in a minority, and secondly to worries about the reaction of Moscow to the dramatic political changes taking place. Jaruzelski's election, it was thought, would be a reassuring sign of continuity and stability.

Jaruzelski's initial choice for premier was the former Interior Minister, Czesław Kiszczak. Kiszczak, though, found it impossible to form a government when the Communists' former allies, the Democratic Party (DP) and the United Peasant Party (UPP), turned against them. The way was now clear for the minority Solidarity group to put forward their own candidate. On 24 August Tadeusz Mazowiecki, formerly a Catholic journalist, became the first non-Communist Prime Minister in the Soviet bloc. The Council of Ministers which was formed over the following weeks gave 11 posts to Solidarity, four to the PUWP (Communists), four to the UPP and three to the DP. Among the ministers was Jacek Kuroń (Minister of Labour), who had been a dissident since the 1960s.

Two main tasks faced the Government. One involved carrying out a reform of the political structure and ridding it of those trappings of Communist rule which had become so irksome to the Polish people during the four decades of Communist rule. The other was to tackle the urgent problems on the economic front. An early step was to repeal Article 3 of the Polish Constitution, which guaranteed the 'leading role' of the Communist Party. Work began immediately on drafting a completely new Constitution to serve Poland during its coming period of parliamentary democracy. Further changes included the reversion of the country to being, as it was in pre-war days, a Republic (Rzeczpospolita Polska) rather than a People's Republic. Symbols of Communist rule were erased or torn down, and the country's symbol, the white eagle, had its royal crown restored.

In February 1990 the Polish Communist Party (PUWP) was dissolved at its 11th and final Congress in Warsaw. It was replaced by a new party, called Social Democracy of the Republic of Poland. A breakaway faction named itself the Polish Social Democratic Union. With the demise of the Party, a struggle began for its huge estate. A government commission established that the Communists and their allies (the UPP and the DP) had had in their possession some 5,000 premises, only 86 of which had been legally acquired. In early April the majority of these were reclaimed by the State. (The former Party headquarters were to become transformed into a new Warsaw stock exchange building.)

The economic problems faced by the incoming Polish Government towards the end of 1989 were daunting. A foreign debt of over US $40,000m. and inflation running in excess of 50% per month were the immediate problems that had to be addressed. A radical package of measures was introduced in January 1990 with IMF approval. The measures, named the 'Balcerowicz plan' after the young Finance Minister, Leszek Balcerowicz, aimed at a rapid move from a centrally-planned economy to one run along market lines. A key aim was to free prices from government influence by removing subsidies. At the same time wages would be restrained, in an attempt to ease inflation. It was hoped that by devaluing the złoty and introducing limited convertibility, Polish exporters would be helped. To this end also the Government undertook to adopt responsible monetary policies and to encourage the private sector.

During its 15-month period of office the Mazowiecki Government was subjected to increasing pressures from sectors of the working population, due to the effects of its economic policies. The mood of optimism which had greeted the formation of the Solidarity Government evaporated by the summer of 1990, as productivity and real wages slumped. Unemployment too rose rapidly, and by the autumn the official figure was over one million. The farmers were particularly restive, finding that the free markets in produce for which they had long campaigned were not what they had anticipated, and complaining that the Government's agricultural policies did little to help them.

The strain soon began to show within the Solidarity movement, and criticism of the Government's performance came from none other than the leader of the trade union, Lech Wałęsa. He bemoaned the slow pace of privatization (first sales to the public did not take place until the necessary legislation and administrative mechanisms were in place, in the autumn of 1990). He also criticized the Government's failure to remove members of the former regime (the nomenklatura) more quickly from their positions of privilege. His criticism drew stinging rejoinders from former Solidarity colleagues, and accusations of a tendency towards 'autocratic' behaviour.

When President Jaruzelski offered his resignation in the autumn, the stage was set for a confrontation between Wałęsa and his former adviser, Chairman of the Council of Ministers Mazowiecki, for the vacant presidency. The campaign, seen in advance as a two-horse race, aroused much emotion and confirmed the split in the Solidarity movement. However, the result of the election was unexpected. In the first round, Mazowiecki was eclipsed by a previously unknown Polish-Canadian businessman, Stanisław Tymiński. In the second round, frightened Mazowiecki supporters flocked to vote for Wałęsa, in their eyes the lesser of two evils. Wałęsa triumphed in the second round, but his success was overshadowed by the Tymiński factor. Tymiński had gained 23.1% of the votes in the first round. Although his share of the vote in the second round, after the elimination of the other four candidates, including Mazowiecki, only rose to 25.75%, he had shown how volatile the electorate was and how unpopular the policies of the Solidarity Government (with which, of course, Wałęsa was also associated) had become.

Mazowiecki resigned as premier, unable to carry on under Wałęsa's presidency. His successor was Jan Krzysztof Bielecki, a 39-year old economist and journalist. Of the former Council of Ministers only two were retained: the Finance Minister Leszek Balcerowicz (even though he was the author of the unpopular economic reform package) and the Foreign Minister, Krzysztof Skubiszewski. Their retention was a clear signal of the desire to retain confidence abroad, and particularly in the West from whence much needed investment and loans were being sought.

The development of independent political parties in Poland began in late 1989, but was given greater impetus during the summer of 1990 by the dissolution of the Solidarity movement. (Previously the Solidarity imprimatur had been essential for any candidate who wished to attain office.) Leading parties which emerged by the spring of 1991 included the Centre Accord (Porozumienie Centrum), based upon those Solidarity members who had supported Wałęsa's candidacy for president. This had begun to develop into a right-of-centre Christian Democratic party. In May, the Unia Demokratyczna (Democratic Union) was created, under the leadership of Tadeusz Mazowiecki, by the amalgamation of three groupings of former Solidarity activists: the Ruch Obywatelski-Akcja Demokratyczna—ROAD (Citizen's Movement-Democratic Action), which had been created by Adam Michnik and Jacek Kuroń to back Mazowiecki for the presidency, the Democratic Right Forum and Mazowiecki's own party, also previously known as Democratic

Union. Other parties included PSL (Peasant Party) groupings and the Social Democrats (successors to the Communists), the right-wing Catholic National Christian Union (ZChN), and Party X. The latter was the creation of defeated presidential candidate, Stanisław Tymiński, who had already shown that, as a focus for the votes of the disaffected, he should not be underestimated.

Despite the flourishing of political parties, however, the elections, which many had thought appropriate for the spring of 1991 (to mark the 200th anniversary of the 1791 May Constitution), were delayed. President Wałęsa's wish for them to take place early in the year was defied by a majority in the (still Communist-dominated) Sejm. Further dissension occurred over the method of voting to be adopted in the elections. Wałęsa and the Sejm clashed repeatedly over electoral law legislation to authorize Poland's first fully-free parliamentary elections. The basic disagreement was that the Sejm wanted a system based partly on first-past-the-post voting for individual candidates and partly on proportional representation, while Wałęsa preferred for all voting to be for party lists. Wałęsa feared that the alternative system would lead to a multitude of small parties in parliament, and to fragmented government. In July, Wałęsa called elections for 27 October, even though his final attempts to influence the electoral law met with failure.

At the end of August, the Bielecki Government offered its resignation, exasperated by the constant obstructiveness of a politically-unsympathetic Sejm. However, the Sejm rejected the Government's resignation, but also, in mid-September, rejected its request to be allowed special powers (virtually to rule by decree) in order to pursue its economic reform policies. Contrary to earlier indications that it intended to concentrate on union activities, presenting only a token number of candidates for the general election, Solidarity was eventually represented by a list of over 200 candidates. Only 43% of the electorate participated in the election, of whom 12.3% voted for the Democratic Union (62 Sejm seats) and 12.0% for the Democratic Left Alliance (60 seats, dominated by Social Democracy of the Republic of Poland—the former Communists). Neither party was to form the new Government. Eventually, a coalition of five of the other 27 parties represented in the Sejm nominated Jan Olszewski as Prime Minister, on 5 December, against the wishes of President Wałęsa. The Sejm approved his Government, which relied for support mainly on his own Centre Alliance, the Christian National Union and the Peasant Alliance (the Liberal Democratic Congress and the Confederation for an Independent Poland having left the original coalition), on 23 December.

The role of the Roman Catholic Church continued to be a major issue in Polish politics. Several issues had contributed to this. Controversy flared in May 1990 when it emerged that an administrative decision had been taken to reintroduce religious teaching into schools. A major public debate took place, not only on the move itself, but also on the manner of its introduction. The question had not been discussed in open debate in the Sejm, and Ministry of Education officials admitted that the decision had been taken under Church pressure. Subsequent moves to pass a law outlawing abortion also raised hackles—and fears in some quarters that the Church wished to exercise a dominating role in Polish political life. In the summer of 1990 the Polish episcopate attempted to persuade the Sejm commission, entrusted with drafting the country's new Constitution, that the traditional separation of Church and State should end. It envisaged close co-operation between the two in defence of humanistic and national values.

The result was that by the spring of 1991, on the eve of the Pope's fourth return visit to his homeland (and his first since the collapse of Communism), the Church had, for the first time in many years, lost its position in public opinion surveys as the country's most respected institution—to the Army. In May, despite strong pressure from the Church and from the Pope himself, the Sejm rejected a bill which would have made abortion illegal in virtually all circumstances.

On the foreign relations front, the latter half of 1989 saw the collapse of other Communist regimes in central and Eastern Europe, and growing nationalist ferment in the Soviet republics, particularly in the Baltic states. During 1990 and 1991 the process of withdrawal from Moscow's orbit in these countries continued. Free elections were held in the neighbouring states, the process of German reunification gathered momentum and came to fruition in October 1990, and both the pacts which had bound the Soviet bloc together—the Warsaw Pact (military agreement) and Comecon (trade agreement)—disintegrated. Poland was faced with developing a totally new foreign policy in response to its own changed circumstances, and to the radical reforms taking place around it. Historically, Poland has found itself positioned between two powerful states which have often been enemies, Germany and Russia. It was therefore vital to establish cordial relations with

both. The first success in this field was the signing, in November 1990, by the then premier, Tadeusz Mazowiecki and the German Chancellor, Helmut Kohl, of an Agreement on the legitimacy of the Polish–German border. The Agreement settled the border issue on behalf of the newly-reunified German state.

In the east, the situation was more complex. While it was important to retain a good working relationship with the then USSR, there was an interest in developing contacts with the republics, and particularly with the three on Poland's eastern frontier (Lithuania, Byelorussia and Ukraine). The frontier treaty signed in Kiev during October 1990 by Foreign Minister Skubiszewski was evidence of the desire to encourage bilateral ties. The existing Polish–Ukrainian border was recognized as fixed by both Polish and Ukrainian Governments. While the attempted coup of August 1991 in the USSR posed an immediate and potentially alarming threat to Poland's democracy and security (Poland's defence forces were placed on high alert during its course), the longer-term implications were that the development of closer relations with nearby Soviet republics, which all achieved independence by December, would accelerate. In early September Poland had re-established diplomatic relations with the three Baltic states.

The Economy

KEITH SWORD

Poland is a country of some 312,685 sq km situated in north-central Europe, with a sea border along the Baltic coast. At the end of 1990 it had an estimated 38,183,200 inhabitants. This was an increase of 144,800 (0.4%) over the 1989 figure. While the birth-rate remained constant at 562,000, the mortality rate increased slightly from 381,000 to 385,000. The natural increase in population was, therefore, 177,000—the lowest recorded in the post-war period. The percentage of the total population of productive age (18–59 for women, 18–64 for men) was 57%. For every 100 men in the population there are 105 women.

In the period since the Second World War Poland has been transformed into an industrialized country. Although lagging behind the economies of the West in terms of efficiency and standards of living, gross domestic product (GDP) per head (as estimated by the World Bank) had risen to US $1,860 by 1988. Any economic portrait of the country, however, must take account of two recent historical factors; the calamitous effects of the Second World War and the policies pursued during the resulting four-and-a-half decades of Communist rule.

During the war, Poland's losses were severe; the level of destruction of buildings in many Polish towns ranged between 40% and 80%. Some 353,876 farms (up to 42% of the total in some areas) were destroyed, with large-scale losses of livestock. Its industries had been destroyed by military activity, or else looted by the invaders (from both west and east). Poland's population was reduced by some 11m. people (from 35m. to 24m.) as a result of military losses, population movement and border changes. This included disproportionate losses among the cultural and technical intelligentsia (teachers, engineers, university professors, etc.). The population of Poland did not return to its pre-war levels until 1975.

In 1945, Poland was moved physically to the west, losing almost one-half of its pre-war territory to the USSR and gaining former German territory in the north and west.

Although the changes meant an overall reduction in the area of the country, the territories acquired included superior arable farming land, a longer stretch of coastline (an additional 400 km, including the ports of Gdańsk and Szczecin) and the Silesian coalfields. These advantages more than outweighed the loss of the Drohobycz oilfield and the large expanses of forest in the eastern regions.

The new Communist rulers of Poland set about implementing their economic programme. This involved nationalizing all branches of industry, trade and finance without compensation. Land reform was attempted. Larger estates, including those belonging to the Church and to the aristocracy, were divided up and distributed to landless peasants. A start was made to collectivization along the lines of the Soviet model, but this was abandoned in the 1950s. Education and training was an important part of this programme. Illiteracy rates had been high before the war; the new authorities sought to eliminate illiteracy and to train rapidly a new generation of scientists, engineers, administrators and technicians to carry through the complete economic transformation which they planned.

The Communists sought to transform Poland into a major industrial economy and, following the Stalinist model, great emphasis was placed on engineering and heavy industry. With the help of Soviet investment and technology, several prestige developments were embarked upon. One of the best-known was the giant iron and steel mills complex at Nowa Huta ('New Foundry'), near Kraków. The programme of crash industrialization had the desirable effect, from the Communists' point of view, of drawing in workers from the countryside and creating an industrial proletariat.

The extent of this migration was astonishing. Whereas, in 1946, 68% of the population had lived in the countryside, by 1988 this figure had been reduced to 39%. If one takes into account the fact that Poland had one of the fastest rates of population growth in Europe after the Second World War (between 1947 and 1975 alone its population increased by some 45%), then the true rate of urban growth can be appreciated. Unfortunately, the infrastructure of housing and services was not enough to cope with this speed of rural depopulation; the house-building programme, in particular, could not keep up and housing has remained one of the key areas of inadequacy in the economy. A recent World Bank estimate put the shortage of accommodation at about 1.3m. apartments. What is more, in the final years of the 1980s, the building programme was actually slowing down. In 1987 191,400 dwellings were completed, falling to 189,600 in 1988 and 150,200 in 1989; during 1990 there was a further decline of 14%.

The high rate of economic development over the first three post-war decades due to 'socialist industrialization' was accompanied by other changes. In 1949 Poland joined the Council for Mutual Economic Assistance (CMEA or Comecon), the Soviet bloc's trading organization. Its currency, the złoty, ceased to be convertible, a step which led to a growing black market in Western 'hard' currencies during the ensuing decades. Poland's economic development, and particularly its foreign trade, therefore, became intertwined with that of its Communist partners, and particularly with the dominant partner, the USSR. The overall costs and benefits of this trade are difficult to estimate, since trade was not measured in convertible currency; but the losses which Poland suffered by selling ships and vehicles at below market prices were, to some extent, compensated by receiving manufactured goods and raw materials, particularly energy (petroleum), at prices well below the world level.

National income and per head incomes are estimated to have increased sixfold in the three decades to 1975 although, with priority given to heavy industry and defence spending, there was little availability of consumer goods. In any case, this date marked the high point of the Gierek period, when economic indicators were falsely buoyed by the large-scale borrowing which the Polish administration had made in the early 1970s. The thousands of millions of dollars in credits and loans received by the Gierek administration were eventually to cause his downfall, and also proved to be a millstone around the neck of succeeding governments.

Following the fall of Gierek in 1979, economic activity suffered from the wave of strikes and protests which accompanied the birth of the Solidarity (Solidarność) trade union. The declaration of martial law in December 1981 did little to improve matters, since, with the opposition harried and political dialogue suppressed, the economy became the arena for political struggle. The deteriorating economic situation, while caused by the colossal blunders of the Gierek era, was worsened by industrial stoppages, rising wages, a short working week and the rejection of necessary price increases. Attempts to modify or reform economic policy during the mid- to late 1980s had little effect and, by 1989, had produced not only falling output but inflation that was in three figures and rising.

At the beginning of the 1990s Poland was one of several former Communist states in east-central Europe which were attempting to shake off the legacy of central planning and other elements of Communist control over the economy. However, Poland was not only the largest of these states, it had the most severe economic problems. Its new leaders felt unable to wait for gradual reforms to work and so, with International Monetary Fund (IMF) approval, took the decision to embark upon a series of radical market-oriented reforms. The first moves in this 'shock therapy' were taken in January 1990.

AGRICULTURE

In the four decades from 1946 to 1988, the proportion of the population living in rural areas declined from over 68% to 38.8%. Nevertheless, despite large-scale migration to the cities, and despite an ageing rural population, by 1968 agricultural production was double that of the 1930s. This was the result of the partial reform of the agricultural sector carried out during the early 1950s, notably the creation of state farms, and a major investment of material resources and finance. Post-war investments saw an increase in the level of mechanization. The number of tractors used on the land increased dramatically, from 28,000 in 1950 to 397,000 in 1975, and to 1,101,264 in 1988—although working horses are still a common sight in some regions; the majority of tractors (931,696 in 1988) are used in the private sector. There were also notable increases in the amounts of chemical fertilizer and artificial animal feedstuffs used, in the degree of electrification and in expenditure on farm buildings. However, bare statistics such as these conceal the irregularity of supply (for example, of fertilizers), and the difficulty of obtaining spare parts (for example, for tractors) which has hampered private farmers especially.

Despite the moves made towards collectivization in the 1950s, the state sector has farmed only some 18%–20% of cultivated land in the post-war era. The figure increased slightly as individual plots accrued to the State following death or retirement. In 1989, for example, some 4,068,000 people were employed in private sector agriculture (a significant decline from 4,871,000 in 1960), whereas some 745,000 were employed in the state sector. The large state farms are found in the western territories 'recovered' from Germany in 1945. In the Szczecin, Koszalin, Gorzów, Zielona Góra and Elbląg districts, state farms account for more than 50% of arable land.

A question mark, though, hangs over the future of state farms, which account for no more than one-fifth of total farmland. Their production per hectare of many items (grain, milk and eggs, for example) is higher than on private farms, but they consume more resources and have higher production costs. Moreover, they have become a by-word for mismanagement. There is a lobby arguing for privatization of state farms, but their future will have to be deliberated carefully. The matter is complicated by the claims of former landowners and by the fact that the state sector is of such importance to the Polish food market.

Crops

In 1988 the total area sown with crops was 14,359,000 hectares, or 46% of the area of the country. Crop production generally holds a dominant position in the area under cultivation, but the major source of increase in crop production over the first 25 post-war years was a systematic increase in yields, owing to the use of fertilizers, pesticides and machinery, rather than from any growth in its share of land. Cereals account for about two-fifths of this total and production totals in 1989 included 8.5m. metric tons of wheat, 6.2m. metric tons of rye, 3.9m. metric tons of barley and 2.2m. metric tons of oats. Potatoes and sugar beet saw a gradual decline in production during the 1980s, both in terms of the area sown and in total production. By 1989 the figures for production were 34.4m. metric tons and 14.4m. metric tons respectively.

Livestock

Cattle are kept in Poland both for beef and dairy production. Their numbers doubled in the period between 1950 and 1975, to just over 13m. head, although this number fell back in the 1980s; in 1989 the number stood at 10.7m.

Large numbers of pigs are kept, since pork is very popular with the Poles, whose diet includes a lot of meat. Numbers of pigs reached a high point in 1978 (21.7m. head), after which, like cattle, their numbers began to decline; there were 18.8m. pigs in 1989. Sheep are kept mainly for their wool or hides. Their milk or meat is largely seen as a by-product, neither lamb nor mutton being very popular with the Poles. In 1989 the number of sheep was 4.4m. The greatest concentration of flocks is in the Carpathian-Sudeten highlands to the south.

MINERALS

Poland is one of the world's largest hard coal producers, although production fell from 193m. metric tons in 1988 to 178m. tons in 1989, and to 147m. metric tons in 1990. The Upper Silesian coal basin is one of the richest in the world, resources extending down as far as 1,000 m, and with reserves estimated at 70,000m. metric tons. More modest deposits are found in the Central-Sudetic trough, but these contain valuable coking coal. A third coal-mining region (the Lublin coal basin) began to be developed in the 1970s, centred on the River Wieprz in eastern Poland. Deposits of brown coal (lignite) are of less significance, although since 1960 its production has increased at a faster rate than that of hard coal. In the late 1980s over 70m. metric tons a year was produced, mainly in the regions of Konin and Turoszów; joint reserves in these two areas are estimated at 2,100m. tons. (It is here that Poland's largest thermal power stations have been built.)

The possibilities for coal exports in 1990–91, as labour troubles crippled Soviet coal production, looked promising. Hungary, Czechoslovakia, Germany, Byelorussia and Ukraine already import Polish coal and may be prepared to take more. However, the Polish coal industry itself faces unrest; production has slowed and the Government has been restricting exports to ensure that domestic users (power stations in particular) facing shortages are not forced to import coal.

Rich, natural gas deposits are found in the Lubaczów region (near the Ukrainian frontier), and there are also reserves in the Sudetes region, but Poland's reserves of petroleum are insignificant. Some reserves have been exploited in the Sub-Carpathian depression, east of Kraków, and deposits were also found during the 1970s on the Baltic coast. The bulk of Poland's petroleum, however, is imported and the decline of supplies from the USSR, its main supplier in the post-war period (and, until 1 January 1991, at very favourable prices), has forced Polish leaders to look elsewhere. In 1990 Poland imported just under 2.2m. metric tons of refined products, of which 1.7m. tons came from the West. This figure was likely to rise during 1991, despite the fact that, owing to limited capacity at Polish ports, much of this oil is brought to German ports and then moved onward by road, rail or barge, incurring heavy transportation costs.

The Poles plan to increase their refining capacity by building new plants near the Baltic coast ports, which will be essential if the intention to increase petroleum consumption by the year 2000 is to be fulfilled. Government plans involve reducing the country's dependence upon coal, which in 1990 accounted for 94% of energy produced and 74% of energy consumed. The coal supplies, themselves, are more than adequate for many decades to come, but the environmental costs of burning so much coal are considered prohibitive. Poland's use of energy is, in any case, woefully inefficient. Since its decision in September 1990 to abandon nuclear energy, even more determined efforts will have to be made to increase this efficiency.

Poland is a significant producer of a number of metal ores, but the most important are copper and zinc. In the late 1950s large deposits of copper were found in the Legnica-Głogów region in the west of the country. These have since been exploited and, in 1988, 406,900 metric tons of copper were extracted from the 30m. tons of ore mined. Zinc and lead ores are found in the Bytom-Chrzanów-Olkusz region and output of these two ores reached 5.4m. metric tons in 1988. Iron ore resources are found in the Często-chowa area and near Leczyca, but the iron content is low, barely reaching 30%. More valuable deposits of iron ore in the Suwałki region lie at a considerable depth and are difficult to exploit. Poland's iron ore output (7,400 metric tons in 1989) is, therefore, insufficient for domestic needs and the Polish iron and steel industry has come to rely almost entirely on Soviet imports of raw materials.

Poland also has large reserves of sulphur and rock salt. The sulphur, discovered in the 1950s, is mined in the Tarnobrzeg and Staszów regions. Some 5m. metric tons were exported annually during the 1980s. Large deposits of silver and smaller deposits of bauxite are also exploited, some of the output being exported.

MANUFACTURING INDUSTRY

Under Communist rule Poland became an industrial nation, but consumer goods were given a low priority. By 1988 engineering was the main branch of Polish industry with 25.7% of total output by value and employing 1.4m. workers (this was 31.5% of the 4.3m. workers employed in state sector industry). Foodstuffs accounted for 17.6% of the output but only 9.7% of the work-force. Fuel and energy production accounted for 16% of output and 15.2% of employment (over 11% in the coal industry), while light industry accounted for 10.9% of production, yet 15.3% of employment.

In the early 1980s, following the introduction of martial law, production slumped badly. Although it picked up again in the latter half of the decade, the introduction of the Balcerowicz plan in 1990 was a further set-back. Industrial production in state-owned industry fell 32% during January 1990, and by an estimated 23% during the whole of that year. While this was happening, the private sector's share in industrial output grew from 3.9% to 11% during 1990. The consumer goods sector was hardest hit, with production of washing-machines down by over 40% in 1990 compared with the previous year, of radios down by 42% and of footwear down by over 34%. There were a number of closures of factories and workshops, including those of several textile factories in Łódź, but in general bankruptcies during 1990 were less than anticipated. With the removal of subsidies and central planning, managers in state industries were having to learn about concepts such as profitability and motivation, and to come to terms with skills such as balancing accounts and marketing, before the inevitable privatization of their business took place.

FOREIGN TRADE AND BALANCE OF PAYMENTS

During the early years of the Gierek period (1971–75) there was a sharp rise in imports, especially from the West. In part, these were capital goods (such as machinery) intended as the tools of an export boom which would pay for the cost of loans from the West. When the boom did not materialize, import curbs were introduced and, at the same time, Poland began to reorient its trade towards its socialist partners. In the 1980s, as a result of political and economic factors (the introduction of martial law, leading to US trade sanctions, and the paralysis of the economy at a time of rising indebtedness), this dependency upon Comecon trade continued. In 1989–90, due to the political and economic changes in the region, and particularly to the collapse of the Soviet bloc trading organization, Poland, along with other former Communist states, began once more to orient its trade towards the West.

Terms of trade from the late 1980s onwards have shown a steady improvement; while the value of imports was equivalent to 88.8% of that of exports in 1987, and to 87.7% in 1988, the trade surplus widened so that imports were equivalent to 76.3% of exports in 1989 and to only 59.9% in 1990. The main commodities exported (in 1988 according to value) were engineering products (42.6%), fuel and energy products (11.3%), chemicals (10.7%) and metallurgical products (8.0%). These figures conceal some marked disparities, though, in the direction of exports. Polish engineering products, for example, comprised 58.3% of exports going to socialist countries, but only 23.0% of those going to non-socialist states. Food and agricultural products together made up 10.9% of exports; however, they contributed only 4.1% to the total of exports to socialist countries, in contrast to the 18.9% of exports to non-socialist states.

The shift in the orientation of Poland's trade became immediately clear in 1990. While the principal destination for Poland's exports in 1989 was the USSR (20.8%), followed by West Germany (14.2%), in 1990 the newly-reunited Germany took 25.1% of exports and the USSR only 15.3%. Other major export customers were the United Kingdom (7.1%), Switzerland (4.7%) and Czechoslovakia (4.1%). Imports in 1990 came principally from Germany (20.1%), the USSR (19.8%), Italy (7.5%), Switzerland (6.4%) and Austria and the United Kingdom (both 5.7%). A large proportion of imports from the Soviet Union have traditionally been energy (petroleum and gas) and raw materials (such as iron ore). Poland will have to find either new sources for these materials, or new means of paying the USSR, or its successors, for them, with the termination of favourable pricing to former CMEA countries. More probably, both of the approaches will be necessary.

The level of foreign investment since Poland became more open to Western business has been disappointing. By comparison with Hungary, Poland has fared poorly. By the end of 1990 the Foreign Investment Agency (FIA) in Warsaw had handled only US $230m. worth of investment by overseas partners in joint ventures that were then in operation. Yet the number of applications to the FIA was more than twice that of the previous year, and included such famous names as Philips (electricals) and Pilkington (glass). Germany looks set to dominate the inward investment, with one-third of all applications in 1990. New legislation passing through the Polish parliament is aimed at encouraging foreign interest by, among other things, abolishing minimum capital entry requirements, modifying tax incentives and providing automatic guarantees against nationalization and expropriation.

Poland's foreign debt caused immense problems throughout the 1980s, and provided a major headache for the incoming Solidarity Government in 1989. Although not as large in per head terms as that of Hungary, debt repayment as a proportion of overseas earnings was prohibitively large. In March 1990 the Paris Club of debtor nations (Poland is fortunate in having a greater proportion of its debt owed to foreign governments than to commercial banks) agreed to a suspension of interest payments for 12 months. However, interest was added to the outstanding capital and by the end of 1990 the debt had reached almost $47,000m. In the spring of 1991, following some clever manoeuvring by the Polish Finance Ministry, the USA agreed to write off 70% of the debt owed to them and encouraged its allies to follow this lead. The Paris Club of 17 Western creditor governments had previously agreed

on a 50% reduction of the current value ($33,000m.) of the official debt owed to them.

At about the same time (April 1991) the IMF offered Poland a $2,500m. loan facility, conditional upon government commitment to a path of fiscal and monetary responsibility.

FINANCE

Under Communist rule the złoty was not a freely-convertible currency. In order to conduct foreign trade, a number of devices had to be contrived. In trade with Comecon partners the 'convertible rouble' was concocted as a 'universal measure of value'. However, varying exchange rates came into existence to facilitate trade with the West. An official tourist rate for overseas visitors compelled hapless foreigners to buy złotys at a grossly inflated price. This, in turn, led to a highly-developed 'black market' in goods and currencies.

The Solidarity Government's stabilization plan of January 1990 allowed for a 31.6% devaluation (from 6,500 złotys to 9,500 złotys per US dollar) and, at the same time, provided for the złoty to become internally convertible. Since it was no longer illegal for private citizens to trade in currencies, what had been black market trade moved from the streets into foreign exchange bureaux. The złoty–dollar rate held throughout 1990. However, in May 1991, the rate was increased to 11,100 złotys to the dollar—a further devaluation of 16.8%, and shortly afterwards was allowed to float against a basket of currencies.

A major feature of the new team's economic management was monetary prudence. They promised balanced budgets, control of the money supply and a cutting back of the proportions of government spending directed towards subsidies and defence. Generally they were successful, with state subsidies falling by 60% over a 12 month period. There were also some pleasant surprises; the state budget showed a healthy surplus during 1990 of 900,000m. złotys. A significant change in the source of revenues was the contribution made by a profits tax; it was the largest single contribution to the state treasury, whereas in the previous year tax had provided the dominant contribution. Further changes in the relative weighting of revenue sources can be expected from 1991, since the Polish tax system was due to be reformed. The reforms were to include the introduction of a three-band value added tax (VAT).

Banking

The National Bank of Poland was formed in January 1945 as a central bank with the exclusive right to print currency. For most of the Communist period it was the basic organ of the entire banking system, financing state credit requirements, the needs of other banks, and supplying credit to industry, trade, the construction sector, transport and communications. The Bank Handlowy and the Bank Polska Kasa Opieki (Pekao) acted to finance foreign trade, especially with the non-socialist countries. (Transactions with foreign countries were a state monopoly handled by the three banks mentioned above.)

In 1988 this system began to change. Many of the functions and responsibilities of the National Bank were divided up between new commercial banks and, by the summer of 1990, licences had been granted for more than 50 commercial banks. More than a dozen banks were given foreign exchange licences and a new Export Development Bank (Bank Rozwoju Eksportu) was set up. Despite this, the Bank Handlowy's position in the financing of trade remained strong. In 1990, it financed 90% of Poland's exports and more than 70% of its imports.

PROBLEMS AND PROSPECTS

The Balcerowicz plan introduced in January 1990, after prior consultations with the IMF, involved maintaining a balanced budget and a tight monetary policy—crucial elements in any stabilization plan. The partial freeing of the złoty, and its pegging against the dollar, was seen as a further stabilizing element, and one that introduced a necessary discipline into economic life. (Seventeen countries contributed to a stabilization fund which, by the end of 1990, amounted to more than US $1,000m.) Further moves included the liberalization of trade policy, encouragement of the private sector and reduction of subsidies and defence spending. What have been the effects of this brave attempt to convert the Polish economy from being command-driven to demand-led?

The first achievement was that the hyperinflation inherited from the final months of Communist rule (an annual equivalent rate of 3,900% over the last three months of 1989) was sharply reduced. In the course of 1990 it fell, generally running at 4%–5% per month, with a low of 1.8% in August. It began to gather pace again towards the turn of the year, stoked in part by the increase in world oil prices caused by the Gulf crisis. The Finance Ministry hoped that inflation would be reduced to a monthly figure of less than 2% by 1992.

The removal of subsidies naturally led to substantial price rises. Subsidies on energy, foodstuffs, housing and services (such as transport) have been removed and, in some cases, led to a doubling of prices overnight. But this was an essential measure, since the cost of the subsidies was prohibitive and their effect distorting. In 1989 subsidies accounted for over 50% of budget expenditure and some 15% of GDP. By the following year this had been reduced to around 15% of the budget and 5% of GDP.

Wages were not frozen, but increases in the state sector were limited to 60% of the increases in consumer prices. A prohibitive tax (known as the popiwek) is introduced where the norm is exceeded. This naturally led to a rapid decline in the purchasing power of wages and, therefore, to falling living standards. There have been persistent complaints from groups within the labour force, but the popiwek is a clever incentive towards speedier privatization (since private firms are free from the wage restrictions). Moreover, during the first 18 months of the Balcerowicz plan, the overall impression was one of unusual tolerance and discipline by the general public, especially when compared with the violent protests that so often followed more modest price rises introduced by the Communists.

The freeing of prices and the restraining mechanism imposed on wages have had one more beneficial result. Goods have returned to the shops. Foodstuffs and consumer durables are plentiful, and queues are a thing of the past. Naturally, the change in situation from having plenty of złotys and nothing to spend it on, to not being able to afford items on display, is a major change in itself and is not welcomed by all; but it has largely eliminated the hoarding (born of uncertainty and lack of confidence) which afflicted the previous system and accentuated shortages.

Whereas the Balcerowicz plan had the expected restraining effects on inflation and government spending, there were some surprising side effects. Output by state-owned industry dropped sharply—much more rapidly than had been expected. The index of industrial production fell by 23% between the beginning and end of 1990. Despite some much-publicized factory closures, there were relatively few bankruptcies and profit margins remained high. The reason for this may be that many enterprises are run by workers' councils, and the principle objective of the enterprise is seen as maintaining employment, rather than increasing efficiency, or boosting output or real wages. There is a widespread feeling in government circles that state-run enterprises cannot be reformed; they must be quickly privatized.

Despite this continued hoarding of labour, unemployment rose sharply. It had reached 1,124,000 by the end of 1990 (8.3% of the working population outside agriculture) and was expected to exceed 2m. before the end of 1991. The national average, in any case, conceals wide regional variables; there was least unemployment in Warsaw (2.1%) and in the Kraków and Katowice regions (both 3.4%), and most in the Suwałki region, in north-eastern Poland (11.5%). However, the real unemployment level is much lower. A significant number of those who have registered, either never worked before or else are engaged in the ubiquitous street markets that have mushroomed on the streets of Polish cities.

If these productivity and employment figures are gloomy, there is a gleaming light at the end of the tunnel, and it is the role of the burgeoning private sector. The share of the private sector in industrial output is thought to have grown from 3.9% to 11% between 1988 and 1990. Similarly, employment in the private sector (as a proportion of those employed outside agriculture) rose from 7% of the total in 1988 to 16% in 1990, when it numbered 1.8m. Most of this private enterprise is in the service sector. It is relatively easy to set up a street corner kantor (bureau de change) or a small boutique, and does not require too great an outlay of capital. As the government's privatization plan gathers momentum, the private sector will grow in significance.

The second unforeseen development resulting from the stabilization plan was an improvement in the balance of trade. The recessionary effect of the measures on the domestic economy, combined with the competitive exchange rate at which the złoty had been fixed, created a trade surplus of $3,800m. during 1990. This was achieved due to an increase of 31% in the dollar value of merchandise exports in convertible currencies. However, this healthy performance was not expected to last.

The improvement in Poland's trade position *vis-à-vis* the West is important, given the virtual collapse of its trade with the USSR, formerly its major trading partner. Foreign earnings are important if Poland is to pay for the increased price of its petroleum imports. Two set-backs occurred during the course of 1990. One was the decision of the Soviet authorities to ask its former Comecon partners to pay world market prices (in dollars) for their imports of Soviet petroleum. The second was the sudden rise in the world petroleum prices, due to the Gulf crisis. This led to attempts to reach barter agreements with other, notably Middle Eastern, suppliers.

The Mazowiecki Government had planned to sell off state-owned enterprises in a major privatization campaign. Indeed, it had undertaken to sell one-half of the state enterprises within five years—a considerable undertaking when one considers that Poland had some 8,000 state enterprises of any size. The operation was slow to get under way, however. Indeed, the promise to accelerate the privatization programme was one of the key points of Lech Wałęsa's presidential election campaign during the latter part of 1990. The delay was due partly to problems of getting the appropriate legislation and the administrative mechanisms in place. There were also problems in choosing which enterprises to privatize and in preparing them for this shock treatment. The privatization bill was passed by the Sejm in July 1990, and a Ministry of Ownership Transformation set up to handle the operation.

Essentially, two models or courses for privatization have been created. The first is capital privatization: transforming an enterprise into a joint-stock company totally owned by the Polish Treasury, and then either selling to a foreign buyer, or offering shares to the public. The second method is privatization of smaller companies by liquidation (however good their performance may have been). Their assets are then sold off or leased. The first group of large firms was offered to the public in November 1990. The group of five companies included Exbud (building and construction), Krosno (glassware) and Próchnik (clothing manufacturer). The shares of the newly-privatized firms were the first to be traded on the floor of the new stock exchange which opened in March 1991. The exchange is housed in the imposing Warsaw building which was formerly the seat of the Communist Party's Central Committee. Its operations are run on the lines of the Lyons bourse.

A key problem facing the Government is how to sell shares in state enterprises when there is no capital market and personal savings are relatively modest. One method is to sell an enterprise in its entirety to a trade buyer, most probably a foreign concern. During 1990, Philips (the Netherlands) bought Polam, Poland's largest lighting firm, and the US company Beloit bought Fampa, the largest producer of pulp and paper in central and Eastern Europe. However, the majority of sales will have to be made in piecemeal fashion to the public. In June 1991 it was announced the method to be used would be through vouchers, to which all would be entitled, and that investment would be made indirectly, by way of managed funds. This will obviate the need for cash investment in what are technically, after all, the people's own property, and will spread the risk of investment. At the time of the announcement of the scheme, it was intended that it should extend to 400 companies (amounting to one-quarter of state-owned industry), and that it should be introduced before the end of 1991. However, in October 1991, in order to avoid widespread bankruptcies and unemployment, and in the face of public opposition to the economic reform programme, it was announced that the number of companies involved was to be reduced to 200 (amounting to only 7% of state-owned industry), and that the programme would not be introduced until mid-1993.

The big question concerning the Polish economy is how long it will take for an upturn to occur and for some improvement to filter through to wage-earners and consumers in the form of a rise in living standards. Public opinion soundings indicate that support for the Balcerowicz policies halved over the first 12–14 months of their imposition, and that there was growing pessimism about their chances of success; 92% agreed that their incomes were not keeping up with prices. In an atmosphere of growing militancy, an increasing number of people also felt that strikes were a justified means of securing improved living standards.

With a general election due in October 1991, pressure would grow for a change in course. More than one-half of respondents interviewed felt that some modifications in economic policy were necessary, while almost one-quarter expressed a wish to see a completely new policy introduced. Yet wage controls are an integral part of the Government's attempt to dampen down inflation. Ministers told the IMF in the winter of 1990/91 that restrictions would be introduced if inflation threatened to rise above the predicted 32% level for 1991. With that figure likely to be as high as 55%, the Government was left with even less room to make adjustments which might make its policies more popular.

Statistical Survey

Principal sources: *Rocznik Statystyczny, Biuletyn Statystyczny* and *Concise Statistical Yearbook of Poland*, all published by Główny Urząd Statystyczny (Central Statistical Office), 00-925 Warsaw, Al. Niepodległości 208; tel. (22) 252431; telex 814581.

Area and Population

AREA, POPULATION AND DENSITY

Area (sq km)	
Land .	304,463
Inland water .	8,220
Total .	312,683*
Population (census results)†	
7 December 1978 .	35,061,450
7 December 1988	
Males	18,465,000
Females	19,414,000
Total	37,879,000
Population (official estimates at 31 December)†	
1988 .	37,884,700
1989 .	38,038,400
1990 .	38,183,200
Density (per sq km) at 31 December 1990 .	122.1

* 120,727 sq miles.
† Figures exclude civilian aliens within the country and include civilian nationals temporarily outside the country.

VOIVODSHIPS (estimated population at 31 December 1990)*

	Area (sq km)	Total ('000)	Density (per sq km)	Capital* ('000)
Warszawskie .	3,788	2,421.6	639.3	1,655.1
Bialskopodlaskie . .	5,348	305.3	57.1	52.1
Białostockie . . .	10,055	692.8	68.9	268.1
Bielskie	3,704	900.2	243.0	179.9
Bydgoskie . . .	10,349	1,110.8	107.3	380.4
Chełmskie . . .	3,866	247.2	63.9	64.8
Ciechanowskie . .	6,362	428.4	67.3	43.2
Częstochowskie . .	6,182	776.7	125.6	257.5
Elbląskie . . .	6,103	478.9	78.5	125.2
Gdańskie . . .	7,394	1,431.6	193.6	464.6
Gorzowskie . . .	8,484	500.7	59.0	123.4
Jeleniogórskie . .	4,378	517.9	118.3	93.2
Kaliskie . . .	6,512	710.8	109.2	106.1
Katowickie . . .	6,650	3,988.8	599.8	367.0
Kieleckie . . .	9,211	1,126.7	122.3	212.9
Konińskie . . .	5,139	469.2	91.3	79.7
Koszalińskie. . .	8,470	508.2	60.0	107.6
Krakowskie . . .	3,254	1,231.6	378.5	748.4
Krośnieńskie . .	5,702	495.0	86.8	49.1
Legnickie . . .	4,037	515.8	127.8	104.2
Leszczyńskie . .	4,154	386.8	93.1	57.6
Lubelskie . . .	6,792	1,016.4	149.6	349.6
Łomżyńskie . . .	6,684	346.7	51.9	58.1

—continued

	Area (sq km)	Total ('000)	Density (per sq km)	Capital* ('000)
Łódzkie	1,523	1,139.5	748.2	851.7
Nowosądeckie . . .	5,576	697.9	125.2	76.7
Olsztyńskie . . .	12,327	753.0	61.1	161.2
Opolskie. . . .	8,535	1,018.6	119.3	127.6
Ostrołęckie . . .	6,498	397.3	61.1	49.6
Pilskie	8,205	480.7	58.6	71.5
Piotrkowskie . . .	6,266	642.6	102.6	80.5
Płockie	5,117	516.4	100.9	122.0
Poznańskie . . .	8,151	1,334.1	163.7	588.7
Przemyskie . . .	4,437	406.8	91.7	68.1
Radomskie . . .	7,294	751.1	103.0	226.3
Rzeszowskie . . .	4,397	723.7	164.6	150.7
Siedleckie . . .	8,499	651.4	76.6	70.5
Sieradzkie . . .	4,869	408.2	83.8	42.2
Skierniewickie . .	3,960	419.3	105.9	44.2
Słupskie. . . .	7,453	413.8	55.5	99.5
Suwalskie. . . .	10,490	470.6	44.9	59.6
Szczecińskie. . .	9,981	972.1	97.4	412.1
Tarnobrzeskie . .	6,283	599.1	95.4	45.9
Tarnowskie . . .	4,151	670.3	161.5	120.4
Toruńskie . . .	5,348	659.1	123.2	200.8
Wałbrzyskie. . .	4,168	740.9	177.8	141.1
Włocławskie. . .	4,402	429.4	97.5	120.8
Wrocławskie . .	6,287	1,128.8	179.5	642.3
Zamojskie . . .	6,980	490.4	70.3	60.7
Zielonogórskie . .	8,868	660.0	74.4	113.3
Total	312,683	38,183.2†	122.1	1,655.1

* Each Voivodship is named after the town from which it is administered. The figures for the population of capital towns refer to 31 December 1989.

† Males ('000) 18,606.0; Females ('000) 19,577.2.

PRINCIPAL TOWNS

(estimated population at 31 December 1989)

Warszawa (Warsaw)	1,655,100	Bielsko-Biała . . .	179,900
Łódź	851,700	Ruda Śląska . . .	169,800
Kraków (Cracow).	748,400	Olsztyn . . .	161,200
Wrocław . . .	642,300	Rzeszów . . .	150,700
Poznań . . .	588,700	Rybnik . . .	142,600
Gdańsk . . .	464,600	Wałbrzych . . .	141,100
Szczecin . . .	412,100	Dąbrowa Górnicza .	136,000
Bydgoszcz . . .	380,400	Chorzów . . .	132,700
Katowice. . .	367,000	Opole . . .	127,600
Lublin . . .	349,600	Elbląg . . .	125,200
Białystok. . .	268,100	Gorzów Wielkopolski	123,400
Sosnowiec . .	259,300	Płock . . .	122,000
Częstochowa . .	257,500	Włocławek . . .	120,800
Gdynia . . .	250,900	Tarnów . . .	120,400
Bytom . . .	229,800	Zielona Góra . .	113,300
Radom . . .	226,300	Wodzisław Śląski.	111,300
Gliwice . . .	222,100	Koszalin . . .	107,600
Kielce . . .	212,900	Kalisz . . .	106,100
Zabrze . . .	203,400	Legnica . . .	104,200
Toruń . . .	200,800	Jastrzębie Zdrój .	102,600
Tychy . . .	189,900	Grudziądz . . .	100,900

BIRTHS, MARRIAGES AND DEATHS

	Registered live births		Registered marriages		Registered deaths	
	Number	Rate (per 1,000)	Number	Rate (per 1,000)	Number	Rate (per 1,000)
1982 . .	702,351	19.4	315,767	8.7	334,869	9.2
1983 . .	720,756	19.7	305,907	8.4	349,387	9.5
1984 . .	699,041	18.9	285,258	7.7	364,862	9.9
1985 . .	677,576	18.2	266,816	7.2	381,457	10.2
1986 . .	634,748	17.0	257,887	6.9	376,316	10.1
1987 . .	605,492	16.1	252,819	6.7	378,365	10.1
1988 . .	587,741	15.5	246,791	6.5	370,821	9.8
1989 . .	562,530	14.8	255,643	6.7	381,173	10.0

Average life expectation at birth (1989): Males 66.8 years; Females 75.5 years.

IMMIGRATION AND EMIGRATION*

	1988	1989	1990
Immigrants	2,100	2,230	2,626
Emigrants	36,300	26,645	18,440

* Figures refer to immigrants arriving for permanent residence in Poland and emigrants leaving for permanent residence abroad.

ECONOMICALLY ACTIVE POPULATION (1988 census)

	Males	Females	Total
Agriculture, hunting and forestry* . .	2,772,496	2,361,330	5,133,826
Mining, manufacturing and public utilities† . .	3,650,821	2,002,117	5,652,938
Construction . . .	1,236,934	228,137	1,465,071
Trade (wholesale and retail) and restaurants . .	414,039	1,079,006	1,493,045
Transport, storage and communications . .	740,158	302,680	1,042,838
Other services‡ . .	1,255,557	2,408,955	3,664,512
Total. . .	10,070,005	8,382,225	18,452,230

* Including fishing from inland waters.
† Including sea fishing.
‡ Remaining branches of activity, including hotels.

CIVILIAN LABOUR FORCE EMPLOYED ('000 persons)

	1987	1988	1989
Agriculture, forestry and fishing	4,900.2	4,767.9	4,684.5
Mining and quarrying . . .	572.5	569.0	577.6
Manufacturing	4,196.8	4,177.3	4,173.1
Electricity, gas and water .	182.5	185.3	182.1
Construction	1,341.5	1,352.6	1,320.8
Trade, restaurants and hotels .	1,538.8	1,531.7	1,514.7
Transport, storage and communications . . .	1,290.2	1,279.8	1,221.8
Finance, insurance, property and business services . .	376.8	386.0	380.2
Community, social and personal services . .	2,661.0	2,716.7	2,874.4*
Others	77.6	56.5	200.6*
Total	17,137.9	17,022.8	17,129.8

* Including persons in part-time employment as a proportion of full-time employees (275,700).

Agriculture

PRINCIPAL CROPS ('000 metric tons)

	1987	1988	1989
Wheat	7,942	7,582	8,462
Rye	6,816	5,501	6,216
Barley	4,335	3,804	3,909
Oats	2,428	2,222	2,185
Mixed grain	3,314	3,387	3,466
Millet and buckwheat	62	73	72
Sugar beet	13,989	14,069	14,374
Potatoes	36,252	34,707	34,390
Carrots	771	743	756
Onions (dry)	615	515	564
Beets	485	484	478
Tomatoes	353	527	451
Cabbages	1,793	1,574	1,617
Cauliflowers	235	231	233
Cucumbers	353	496	352
Dry beans and peas	97	108	120
Linseed	11	12	12
Flax fibre	17	18	15
Rapeseed	1,186	1,199	1,586
Tobacco	114	90	56
Hemp fibre	4	3	2
Apples	504	1,393	1,312
Pears	15	56	59
Plums	9	98	75
Sweet cherries	4	21	17
Sour cherries	13	98	88
Strawberries	334	249	269
Raspberries	17	44	43
Currants	102	165	167
Gooseberries	37	40	42

LIVESTOCK (numbers recorded in June)

	1987	1988	1989
Horses	1,141,000	1,051,000	973,000
Cattle	10,523,000	10,322,000	10,733,000
Pigs	18,546,000	19,605,000	18,835,000
Sheep	4,739,000	4,377,000	4,409,000
Chickens	55,667,000	54,735,000	51,037,000
Ducks*	4,390,000	4,812,000	6,466,000
Geese*	966,000	1,008,000	1,434,000
Turkeys*	528,000	548,000	857,000

Beehives: 1,699,000 at 31 December 1988.

* At 31 December.

LIVESTOCK PRODUCTS (metric tons)

	1987	1988	1989
Beef*	750,000	727,000	675,000
Veal*	36,000	33,000	45,000
Mutton and lamb*	42,000	41,000	38,000
Pig meat*	1,714,000	1,808,000	1,819,000
Horse meat*	45,000	29,000	22,000
Poultry meat	325,000	347,000	362,000
Edible offal	197,000	197,000	193,000
Cows' milk	15,531,370	15,632,000	16,404,000
Sheep's milk	8,000	8,000	8,000‡
Butter	264,443	266,847	289,727
Cheese†	450,649	471,298	446,903
Dried milk	204,000	209,000	226,000
Hen eggs	442,556	456,667	446,222
Honey	12,965	14,067	13,500
Wool:			
greasy	17,253	16,406	15,944
clean	10,352†	9,844†	9,600‡
Cattle hides‡	77,000	65,000	63,000

Eggs (million units): 7,966 in 1987; 8,220 in 1988; 8,032 in 1989.

* Figures refer to carcass weight, including slaughter fats.
† Source: FAO.
‡ FAO estimate.

Forestry

('000 cu metres)

	1987	1988	1989
Roundwood removals	23,145	22,695	21,254
Sawnwood production*	5,803	5,799	5,159

* Excluding railway sleepers. Industrial production only.

Fishing

('000 metric tons)

	1987	1988	1989
Sea	639.0	590.0	531.0
Fresh water	42.2	46.9	48.9*
Total catch	681.2	636.9	579.9

* Estimate.

Mining

('000 metric tons, unless otherwise indicated)

	1987	1988	1989
Hard coal	193,011	193,015	177,633
Lignite	73,196	73,489	71,816
Iron ore[1]:			
gross weight	6.3	6.3	7.4
metal content[2]	2	2	n.a.
Crude petroleum	149	163	159
Salt (unrefined)	6,175	6,179	4,670
Native sulphur (per 100%)	4,966	5,000	4,864
Copper ore (metric tons)[2,3]	404,600	406,900	n.a.
Lead ore (metric tons)[2,3,4]	48,800	49,400	n.a.
Magnesite—crude (metric tons)[2,3]	22,300	23,900	n.a.
Silver (metric tons)[3]	831	1,063	1,003
Zinc ore (metric tons)[2,3,4]	185,800	183,400	n.a.
Natural gas (million cu metres)	5,781	5,713	5,368

[1] Including the iron content of iron pyrites.
[2] Source: UN, *Industrial Statistics Yearbook*.
[3] Figures refer to the metal content of ores.
[4] Estimated by Metallgesellschaft Aktiengesellschaft, Frankfurt am Main.

Industry

SELECTED PRODUCTS
(metric tons, unless otherwise indicated)

	1987	1988	1989
Sausages and smoked meat .	777,000	799,000	767,000
Refined sugar ('000 metric tons). . . .	1,671	1,684	1,710
Margarine	204,000	220,000	222,000
Wine and mead ('000 hectolitres) . . .	2,605	2,559	2,560
Beer ('000 hectolitres) . .	11,700	12,200	12,100
Cigarettes (million). . .	98,666	89,681	81,300
Cotton yarn[1] . . .	198,005	205,889	196,000
Woven cotton fabrics ('000 metres)[2] . . .	749,400	783,400	760,000
Flax and hemp yarn[1] . .	28,600	28,200	27,400
Linen and hemp fabrics ('000 metres)[2] . . .	83,800	83,500	75,000
Wool yarn[1] . . .	79,900	83,700	77,200
Woven woollen fabrics ('000 metres)[2] . . .	99,500	101,000	96,800
Cellulosic continuous filaments .	19,300	20,200	18,600
Cellulosic staple and tow .	73,300	74,200	66,700
Leather footwear ('000 pairs) .	65,565	61,902	55,100
Mechanical wood pulp . .	116,000	108,000	105,000
Chemical wood pulp . .	624,000	623,000	582,000
Newsprint	69,100	21,900	8,400
Other paper . . .	1,089,000	1,198,000	1,155,600
Paperboard . . .	221,000	227,100	241,000
Synthetic rubber . .	116,700	127,400	125,000
Rubber tyres ('000)[3] . .	6,020	6,276	6,025
Ethyl alcohol ('000 hectolitres) .	2,733	2,619	2,514
Sulphuric acid—100% ('000 metric tons) . . .	3,149	3,154	3,114
Nitric acid—100% ('000 metric tons). . . .	2,136	2,187	2,175
Caustic soda—96% . . .	440,000	463,000	452,000
Soda ash—98% . . .	930,000	956,000	1,005,000
Nitrogenous fertilizers (a) ('000 metric tons)[4] . . .	1,543.1	1,622.2	1,643
Phosphate fertilizers (b) ('000 metric tons)[4] . . .	942.5	962.1	945
Plastics and synthetic resins .	641,000	723,000	721,000
Motor spirit—Petrol ('000 metric tons)[5] . . .	4,039	4,339	4,407
Distillate fuel oils ('000 metric tons). . . .	4,981	5,172	4,861
Residual fuel oils ('000 metric tons). . . .	2,321	2,457	2,956
Coke-oven coke ('000 metric tons). . . .	16,703	16,795	16,323
Gas coke ('000 metric tons). .	363	276	223
Cement ('000 metric tons) . .	16,090	16,984	17,125
Pig-iron ('000 metric tons)[6] .	10,476	10,264	9,488
Crude steel ('000 metric tons) .	17,145	16,873	15,094
Rolled steel products ('000 metric tons). . . .	12,410	12,424	11,272
Aluminium—unwrought[7] .	47,539	47,720	47,809
Refined copper—unwrought .	390,223	400,560	390,268
Refined lead—unwrought .	89,800	90,700	78,200
Zinc—unwrought[7] . .	176,526	173,566	163,727
Radio receivers ('000) . .	2,833	2,684	2,523
Television receivers ('000) . .	647	749	772

—*continued*	1987	1988	1989
Merchant ships launched (gross reg. tons) . . .	233,000	255,000	139,000
Passenger motor cars (number)	293,000	293,000	285,497
Lorries (number) . . .	45,600	46,800	43,853
Domestic washing machines (number). . . .	779,000	761,000	811,000
Domestic refrigerators (number). . . .	506,000	484,000	516,000
Construction: dwellings completed (number) . . .	191,400	189,600	150,200
Electric energy (million kWh) .	145,835	144,344	145,472
Manufactured gas:			
from gasworks (million cu metres) . . .	176	133	109
from cokeries (million cu metres) . . .	6,468	6,593	6,456

[1] Pure and mixed yarns. Cotton includes tyre cord yarn.
[2] Pure and mixed fabrics, after undergoing finishing processes. Cotton and wool include substitutes.
[3] Tyres for passenger motor cars and commercial vehicles, including inner tubes and tyres for animal-drawn road vehicles, and tyres for non-agricultural machines and equipment.
[4] Fertilizer production is measured in terms of (a) nitrogen or (b) phosphoric acid. Phosphate fertilizers include ground rock phosphate.
[5] Including synthetic products.
[6] Including blast-furnace ferro-alloys.
[7] Figures refer to both primary and secondary metal. Zinc production includes zinc dust and remelted zinc.

Finance

CURRENCY AND EXCHANGE RATES

Monetary Units
100 groszy (singular: grosz) = 1 złoty.

Denominations
Coins: 1, 2, 5, 10, 20 and 50 groszy; 1, 2, 5, 10, 20, 50, 100, 200, 500, 1,000, 2,000 and 10,000 złotys.
Notes: 10, 20, 50, 100, 200, 500, 1,000, 2,000, 5,000, 10,000, 100,000, 200,000, 500,000 and 1,000,000 złotys.

Sterling and Dollar Equivalents (30 June 1991)
£1 sterling = 18,550.5 złotys;
US $1 = 11,458.0 złotys;
100,000 złotys = £5.391 = $8.728.

Average Exchange Rate (złotys per US dollar)
1988   430.5
1988   1,439.2
1989   9,500.0

BUDGET (million złotys)

Revenue	1987	1988	1989
Turnover tax	1,799,009	3,214,587	8,818,288
Share in profits and income tax of state enterprises*. .	2,031,657	3,960,605	12,048,333
Taxes from the private sector .	257,910	470,795	1,490,432
Taxes from population . .	120,353	230,075	970,371
Surplus of financial sector . .	166,300	363,000	2,953,100
Total (incl. others). . .	5,850,497	10,088,700	30,108,500
of which:			
Central government . .	3,928,672	6,702,100	19,394,000
Local authorities . . .	1,921,825	3,386,600	10,759,500

* Including income tax from financial institutions and co-operative organizations.

Expenditure		1987	1988	1989
National economy		2,527,200	4,196,800	11,941,400
Science		10,300	68,600	109,100
Education		607,255	1,010,655	4,342,528
Culture		89,393	164,191	638,779
Public health . . . }		647,651	1,093,259	4,015,807
Social welfare . . .				
Physical culture and tourism .		24,871	51,735	199,492
Social insurance . . .		251,800	432,700	2,344,400
National defence . . .		467,600	742,200	2,118,000
Public administration and jurisdiction		330,300	541,000	1,997,900
Current expenditure (incl. others)		5,030,600	8,430,600	29,617,500
Investment expenditure . .		942,600	1,579,600	4,069,600
Total		5,973,200	10,010,200	33,687,100
of which:				
Central government . . .		3,824,600	6,315,300	20,933,500
Local authorities . . .		2,148,600	3,694,900	12,753,600

INTERNATIONAL RESERVES (US $ million at 31 December)

		1988	1989	1990
Gold*		189.0	189.0	189.0
IMF special drawing rights .		0.1	0.1	0.8
Foreign exchange . . .		2,055.2	2,314.2	4,491.3
Total		2,244.3	2,503.3	4,681.1

* National valuation (US $400 per troy ounce).
Source: IMF, *International Financial Statistics*.

MONEY SUPPLY ('000 million złotys at 31 December)

		1988	1989	1990
Currency outside banks . .		2,523	9,880	39,336
Demand deposits at commercial and savings banks		3,225	9,175	57,240

Source: IMF, *International Financial Statistics*.

COST OF LIVING (Consumer Price Index; base: 1980 = 100)

		1988	1989	1990
Food		985.7	3,945.8	24,984.8
All items		928.7	3,260.7	22,326.0

Source: UN, *Monthly Bulletin of Statistics*.

NATIONAL ACCOUNTS
Net Material Product*
('000 million złotys at current market prices)

Activities of the Material Sphere		1987	1988	1989
Agricultural production† . .		1,453.6	2,890.5	12,610.0
Agricultural services . .		206.7	341.0	1,167.7
Forestry and logging . .		188.9	311.1	1,311.5
Industry‡		6,804.0	12,031.1	52,671.7
Construction§		1,801.0	3,207.1	10,054.9
Trade, restaurants, etc. . .		2,384.7	4,110.6	19,502.3
Transport and storage . .		708.5	1,246.7	4,521.5
Communications . . .		142.7	215.2	662.5
Others		323.1	641.3	2,450.0
Total		14,013.2	24,994.6	104,952.1

* Defined as the total net value of goods and 'productive' services, including turnover taxes, produced by the economy. This excludes economic activities not contributing directly to material production, such as public administration, defence and personal and professional services.
† Including fishing from inland waters.
‡ Principally manufacturing, mining, sea fishing, electricity, gas and water supply.
§ Including geodesy, cartography, geology offices and design offices.

BALANCE OF PAYMENTS (US $ million)

		1987	1988	1989
Merchandise exports f.o.b. . .		12,026	13,846	12,869
Merchandise imports f.o.b. . .		−11,236	−12,757	−12,822
Trade balance		790	1,089	47
Exports of services . . .		2,216	2,472	3,201
Imports of services . . .		−2,028	−2,404	−3,053
Other income received . .		217	271	410
Other income paid . . .		−3,132	−3,226	−3,623
Private unrequited transfers (net)		1,558	1,691	1,521
Official unrequited transfers (net)		—	—	88
Current balance . . .		−379	−107	−1,409
Direct investment (net) . .		4	−7	−7
Other capital (net) . . .		−2,131	−2,921	−1,789
Net errors and omissions . .		91	−267	−110
Overall balance . . .		−2,415	−3,302	−3,315

Source: IMF, *International Financial Statistics*.

External Trade

PRINCIPAL COMMODITIES (million złotys)

Imports f.o.b.	1987	1988	1989
Fuels and power	494,669	781,248	1,882,732
Crude petroleum and natural gas	375,968	596,228	1,011,410
Petroleum products and synthetic liquid fuels . .	93,223	127,964	411,079
Products of basic metal industries*	235,979	431,782	1,298,006
Iron ore (crude and enriched)	43,472	67,767	113,605
Rolled iron and steel products	28,541	53,379	165,779
Steel tubes and pipes . .	21,227	40,057	116,695
Non-ferrous ores and metals .	82,805	163,220	546,618

Imports f.o.b.—*continued*	1987	1988	1989
Products of electro-engineering industries	1,022,620	1,882,366	5,505,261
Products of metal manufacturing	95,732	162,398	470,395
Metal-working machinery and equipment	77,198	143,631	423,619
Machinery and equipment for light industry and food manufacturing	70,092	140,607	543,676
Products of precision instruments industry	105,425	196,849	584,710
Transport equipment	213,587	391,391	1,032,214
Products of electrotechnical and electronics industry	101,992	215,424	755,041
Products of chemical industry*	459,407	837,207	2,237,022
Chemical elements, inorganic products, manufactured fertilizers	66,009	112,326	330,932
Plastics, rubber and synthetic fibres	70,864	145,519	366,754
Products of wood and paper industry	55,930	104,228	285,286
Products of light industry (textiles, clothing and leather)*	157,463	330,510	1,126,930
Textiles	76,434	177,985	505,858
Products of food industry	231,052	468,289	1,349,710
Agricultural products	130,078	266,336	678,228
Cereals	52,569	110,626	281,343
Total (incl. others)	2,875,586	5,272,313	14,864,175

Exports f.o.b.	1987	1988	1989
Fuels and power	362,132	611,571	1,873,686
Hard coal	292,116	478,590	1,294,193
Products of basic metal industries*	274,584	604,828	2,035,384
Rolled iron and steel products	94,017	170,850	606,988
Non-ferrous ores and metals	141,026	303,430	969,961
Products of electro-engineering industries	1,285,534	2,350,480	7,475,108
Products of metal manufacturing	98,900	195,235	694,058
Products of precision instruments industry	104,081	206,999	701,008
Rail transport equipment	34,860	59,038	182,398
Road transport equipment	105,810	196,243	532,779
Water transport equipment	111,822	170,118	687,487
Products of chemical industry*	339,392	655,875	2,050,184
Chemical elements, inorganic products, manufactured fertilizers	123,340	210,922	689,722
Products of wood and paper industry	96,712	198,563	570,865
Products of light industry (textiles, clothing and leather)*	224,599	398,061	1,072,873
Textile clothing and underwear	63,438	104,239	268,477
Products of food industry	287,062	504,471	1,868,635
Meat and meat products	73,705	117,082	397,328
Agricultural products	112,100	210,892	806,082
Total (incl. others)	3,236,528	6,011,745	19,476,174

* Including raw materials.

PRINCIPAL TRADING PARTNERS* (million złotys)

Imports f.o.b.	1988	1989	1990†
Australia	69,461	156,413	290,000
Austria	230,123	886,892	4,403,000
Belgium	71,084	224,203	1,096,000
Brazil	112,556	242,910	383,000
Bulgaria	94,644	186,141	449,000
China, People's Republic	137,128	458,045	1,383,000
Czechoslovakia	335,978	846,166	2,762,000
France	131,295	464,981	2,344,000
German Democratic Republic	264,990	662,884 ⎱	⎰ 15,587,000§
Germany, Federal Republic‡	687,142	2,337,781	
Hungary	118,101	236,580	720,000
Iraq	40,670	212,267	647,000
Italy	174,673	615,761	5,796,000
Japan	83,816	202,397	1,790,000
Netherlands	141,944	444,980	2,038,000
Romania	88,315	153,896	246,000
Sweden	82,497	257,336	1,514,000
Switzerland	239,866	782,392	4,988,000
USSR	1,228,447	2,688,802	15,370,000
United Kingdom	221,728	663,918	4,382,000
USA	103,473	201,193	1,260,000
Yugoslavia	176,234	611,778	1,586,000
Total (incl. others)	5,272,313	14,864,175	77,520,000

Exports f.o.b.	1988	1989	1990†
Austria	183,865	690,865	4,989,000
Belgium	85,296	220,603	2,076,000
Bulgaria	124,689	304,641	986,000
China, People's Republic	144,026	444,935	1,826,000
Czechoslovakia	359,139	1,075,301	5,282,000
Denmark	76,053	266,797	2,271,000
Finland	86,028	354,476	2,031,000
France	135,698	474,767	4,171,000
German Democratic Republic	264,251	815,520 ⎱	⎰ 32,503,000§
Germany, Federal Republic‡	747,156	2,757,736	
Hungary	141,017	312,965	1,271,000
Italy	138,561	448,584	3,810,000
Japan	66,118	274,778	1,050,000
Libya	92,690	262,083	1,022,000
Netherlands	132,006	505,851	4,057,000
Romania	81,633	214,593	1,208,000
Sweden	123,651	421,338	3,393,000
Switzerland	153,738	504,375	6,078,000
Turkey	46,147	165,014	1,581,000
USSR	1,474,580	4,048,255	19,768,000
United Kingdom	301,766	1,262,563	9,227,000
USA	155,639	540,116	3,527,000
Yugoslavia	162,897	582,241	2,021,000
Total (incl. others)	6,011,745	19,476,174	129,455,000

* Imports by country of purchase; exports by country of sale.
† Figures are approximate.
‡ Excluding West Berlin.
§ Figures for 1990 are for the united Germany.

Transport

POLISH STATE RAILWAYS (traffic)

	1987	1988	1989
Paying passengers ('000 journeys)	977,011	983,763	951,544
Freight ('000 metric tons)	428,775	427,956	388,920
Passenger-kilometres (million)	48,285	52,134	55,888
Freight ton-kilometres (million)	121,381	122,204	111,140

ROAD TRAFFIC (motor vehicles registered at 31 December)

	1987	1988	1989
Passenger cars	4,231,700	4,519,094	4,846,411
Goods vehicles* . . .	866,332	919,321	976,986
Buses and coaches	87,336	89,682	91,092
Motor cycles and scooters . .	1,470,128	1,464,130	1,410,859

* Including non-agricultural tractors.

INLAND WATERWAYS (traffic)

	1987	1988	1989
Passengers carried ('000) . .	6,557	6,492	5,770
Freight ('000 metric tons) . .	14,755	15,556	14,040
Passenger-kilometres (million) .	80	76	68
Freight ton-kilometres (million)	1,519	1,394	1,193

SHIPPING FLEET (registered at 31 December)
Number of ships

	1987	1988	1989
Merchant vessels	251	256	249

Displacement ('000 gross registered tons)

	1987	1988	1989
Merchant vessels	3,166	3,177	3,079
Fishing vessels	304	312	337
Total	3,470	3,489	3,416

Source: *Lloyd's Register*, Statistical Tables.

SEA TRANSPORT (Polish merchant ships only)

	1987	1988	1989
Passengers carried ('000) . .	386	453	667
Freight ('000 metric tons) . .	30,213	30,827	28,299
Passenger-kilometres (million) .	234	213	251
Freight ton-kilometres (million)	197,005	227,171	212,259

INTERNATIONAL SEA-BORNE SHIPPING AT POLISH PORTS

	1987	1988	1989
Vessels entered ('000 net reg. tons).	25,594	27,201	27,066
Passengers (number):			
Arrivals	153,668	186,063	274,585
Departures	170,364	192,125	274,918
Cargo* ('000 metric tons):			
Loaded†	31,602	32,038	29,098
Unloaded†	17,390	18,176	17,171

* Including ships' bunkers.   † Including transhipments.

CIVIL AVIATION
Polish Airlines—'LOT' (scheduled and non-scheduled flights)

	1987	1988	1989
Passengers carried. . .	1,858,000	2,018,000	2,305,000
Passenger-kilometres ('000) .	3,340,000	3,947,000	4,887,000
Cargo (metric tons) . .	9,000	11,000	12,000
Cargo ton-kilometres ('000). .	19,000	23,000	40,000

Tourism

FOREIGN TOURIST ARRIVALS (including visitors in transit)

Country of Residence	1987	1988	1989
Austria	38,000	53,000	75,000
Bulgaria	48,000	52,000	55,000
Czechoslovakia. . . .	993,000	1,417,000	1,503,000
Finland	24,000	24,000	33,000
France.	54,000	56,000	75,000
German Democratic Republic .	925,000	1,081,000	1,195,000
Germany, Federal Republic* .	352,000	416,000	596,000
Hungary	470,000	567,000	698,000
Italy	35,000	40,000	60,000
Netherlands	38,000	46,000	56,000
Romania	28,000	22,000	19,000
Sweden	62,000	69,000	115,000
USSR	1,166,000	1,739,000	2,899,000
United Kingdom . . .	33,000	34,000	47,000
USA	51,000	58,000	96,000
Yugoslavia.	187,000	193,000	248,000
Total (incl. others). . . .	4,776,000	6,196,000	8,233,000

* Excluding visitors from West Berlin: 28,000 in 1987; 36,000 in 1988; 53,000 in 1989.

Communications Media

	1987	1988	1989
Radio licences* . . .	10,845,000	11,084,000	11,120,000
Television licences* . . .	9,868,000	10,031,000	10,055,000
Telephones in use*. . .	4,618,000	4,830,000	5,039,000
Book titles produced† . .	10,416	10,728	10,286
Daily newspapers . . .	45	45	48
Non-daily newspapers . .	52	52	63
Newspaper circulation:			
Dailies (average) . . .	7,250,000	6,939,000	6,715,000
Non-dailies (average). . .	3,190,000	3,106,000	3,193,000

* At 31 December.   † Including pamphlets (2,017 in 1987; 2,116 in 1988).

Education*

(1989/90)

	Institutions	Teachers ('000)	Students ('000)
Primary	18,238	293.2	5,229.3
Secondary (General) . . .	1,177	23.3	462.8
Technical, art and vocational .	9,366	85.3	1,755.4
Higher	98	60.3	378.4

* Including part-time courses for workers.

Directory

The Constitution

The Constitution that had been adopted on 22 July 1952 was amended in 1989, to incorporate reforms such as the establishment of an upper legislative chamber, and again in 1990, to permit the holding of direct presidential elections. The following is a summary of the provisions of the 1952 Constitution, as amended:

STATE AUTHORITIES

The Sejm consists of 460 deputies, elected for a four-year term, subject to dissolution. Its prerogatives include the adoption of laws; the adoption of the national socio-economic plans and state financial plans; the appointment and recall of the Chairman of the Council of Ministers (at the motion of the President); the appointment and recall of the members of the Council of Ministers (at the motion of the Chairman presented in conjunction with the President or on the Chairman's own initiative); the appointment of the Civil Rights Ombudsman (with consent of the Senate); the adoption of a resolution concerning a state of war; the expression of consent for prolongation (at most for three months) of a state of emergency imposed by the President (consent for such a decision must also be given by the Senate). The Speaker (Marshal) of the Sejm acts in the capacity of President if this office is vacant.

The Senate is made up of 100 members. Its term coincides with that of the Sejm, subject to dissolution. The Senate reviews the laws adopted by the Sejm; it may proffer its comments and proposals on these laws or even propose their rejection in full. The Senate can be overridden by the Sejm by a qualified majority of two-thirds. Its also reviews drafts of national socio-economic plans and financial plans of the State. It has the right of legislative initiative.

The National Assembly is the combined Sejm and Senate. It should be convened by the Sejm Speaker (Marshal) within two months of elections to the Sejm and the Senate. The National Assembly may be convened in order to declare the permanent incapacity of the President to serve his office and to consider impeaching the President in the Tribunal of State.

The President of the Republic of Poland is the highest representative of the Polish State in domestic and international relations. He is to monitor observance of the Constitution, safeguard the sovereignty and security of the State, inviolability of its territory and observance of political and military alliances entered into by the State. Any Pole aged over 35 years with full electoral rights may stand as a presidential candidate, a minimum of 100,000 signatures being required to secure nomination. The President is directly elected for a five-year term and may be re-elected only once. The President's duties include the calling of elections to the Sejm, Senate and local councils; heading the armed forces; proposing a motion in the Sejm for the appointment or recall of the Chairman of the Council of Ministers; (when necessary) imposing martial law on a segment or the entire territory of the country if such is dictated by defence considerations or an outside threat to state security (the President may announce a partial or general mobilization for the same reasons); (when necessary) introducing a state of emergency on a segment or the entire territory of the country when there is a threat to the domestic security of the State or in case of a natural disaster; the President may introduce it for a period not longer than three months and prolong it (with the consent of the Sejm and the Senate) for another three months.

The Council of Ministers is the supreme executive and managing agency of state authority, serving functions typical of the executive branch and carrying out the decisions adopted by the Sejm. It is appointed by the Sejm which may recall the entire Council of Ministers or its individual members. The Council is responsible to the Sejm and reports to it on its activities. In periods between Sejm terms, this function towards the Council is served by the President. The Council of Ministers co-ordinates actions of the entire state administration.

CONSTITUTIONAL TRIBUNAL AND TRIBUNAL OF STATE

The Constitutional Tribunal pronounces judgment on the consistence with the Constitution of laws and other normative acts issued by the supreme and central state organs. Its decisions are binding. Members of the Tribunal are independent and are subject only to the Constitution.

The Tribunal of State pronounces judgment on the responsibility of persons holding high state positions for violation of the Constitution and laws; it can also pass judgment on penal responsibility of those persons for offences committed in connection with the positions which they have held. Its head is the first president of the Supreme Court. Judges of the Tribunal are independent and subject only to the law.

LOCAL ORGANS OF STATE ADMINISTRATION

Poland comprises 49 voivodships, a government-appointed official supervising state administration in each area. The members of each provincial assembly are elected by local councils. Local councils are directly elected and are completely autonomous, territorial self-government being the basic form of the organization of public life in the rural community.

COURTS AND PUBLIC PROSECUTOR'S OFFICE

The administration of justice is carried out by the Supreme Court, the Supreme Administrative Court, General Courts and Courts Martial. The Supreme Court is the highest judicial organ, and is to be appointed by the Sejm for an unlimited term.

FUNDAMENTAL RIGHTS AND DUTIES OF CITIZENS

The Republic of Poland strengthens and extends the rights and liberties of citizens. Citizens have equal rights, irrespective of sex, origin, education, occupation, nationality, race, religion, descent or social status. Citizens have the right to work and the right to rest; the right to health protection, and the right to education. Women are guaranteed equal rights with men. Freedom of conscience is guaranteed. The Church is separated from the State. Citizens are guaranteed freedom of speech, of the press, of meetings etc.; the right to unite in public organizations; and the inviolability of the person and of the home.

PRINCIPLES OF ELECTORAL LAW

Election to the Sejm and Senate, and to People's Councils, is universal, equal, direct and carried out by secret ballot. At the age of 18 every citizen has the right to vote, and is eligible for election to People's Councils; at the age of 21 every citizen is eligible for election to the Sejm and Senate. Candidates to the Sejm and Senate are nominated by political and social organizations uniting citizens of town and country.

COAT-OF-ARMS, COLOURS AND CAPITAL OF THE REPUBLIC OF POLAND

The coat-of-arms of the Republic of Poland is a white eagle with a golden crown on the head, and with golden beak and claws, on a red field. The National Anthem is the *Mazurek Dabrowskiego*. The capital of the Republic of Poland is Warsaw.

The Government

HEAD OF STATE

President: LECH WAŁĘSA (sworn in 22 December 1990).

COUNCIL OF MINISTERS
(January 1992)

Chairman: JAN OLSZEWSKI

Minister-Head of the Office of the Council of Ministers: WOJCIECH WLODARCYZ.

Minister of Foreign Affairs: KRZYSZTOF SKUBISZWESKI.

Minister of Internal Affairs: ANTONI MACIAREWICZ.

Minister of National Defence: JAN PARYS.

Minister of Justice and Attorney-General: ZBIGNIEW DYKA.

Minister-Head of the Central Planning Office: JERZY EYSYMONTT.

Minister of Finance: KAROL LUTKOWSKI.

Minister of Foreign Economic Relations: ADAM GLAPINSKI.

Minister of Agriculture: GABRIEL JANOWSKI.

Minister of Transport and Maritime Economy: EWARYST WALIGÓRSKI.

Minister of Environmental Protection, Natural Resources and Forestry: STEFAN KOZLOWSKI.

Minister of Labour and Social Policy: JERZY KROPIWNICKI.

Minister of National Education: ANDRZEJ STELMACHOWSKI.

Minister of Culture: ANDRZEJ SICINSKI.

Minister of Health: MARIAN MISKIEWICZ.
Minister without Portfolio: ARTUR BALAZS.

Acting Heads of Ministries to be Dissolved
Ministry of Industry and Trade: ANDRZEJ LIPKO.
Ministry of Land Management and Construction: ANDRZEJ DIAKONOW.
Ministry of Communications: MAREK RUSIN.
Ministry of Ownership Transformation (Privatization): TOMASZ GRUSZECKI.

MINISTRIES

Ministry of Agriculture: 00-930 Warsaw, ul. Wspólna 30; tel. (22) 210251; telex 814597.

Ministry of Culture: 00-071 Warsaw, ul. Krakowskie Przedmieście 15/17; tel. (22) 200231; telex 813762.

Ministry of Communications: 00-928 Warsaw, ul. Chałubińskiego 4; tel. (22) 244303.

Ministry of Environmental Protection, Natural Resources and Forestry: 00-922 Warsaw, ul. Wawelska 52/54; tel. (22) 250001; telex 812816; fax (22) 253355.

Ministry of Finance: 00-916 Warsaw, ul. Świętokrzyska 12; tel. (22) 200311; telex 815592.

Ministry of Foreign Affairs: 00-580 Warsaw, Al. I Armii WP 23; tel. (22) 281678; telex 814301; fax (22) 280906.

Ministry of Foreign Economic Relations: 00-950 Warsaw, Pl. Trzech Krzyży 5; tel. (2) 6935000; telex 814501; fax (22) 286808.

Ministry of Health and Social Welfare: 00-923 Warsaw, ul. Miodowa 15; tel. (22) 312144; telex 813864; fax (2) 6359245.

Ministry of Industry and Trade: 00-926 Warsaw, ul. Wspólna 4; tel. (22) 210351; telex 814261; fax (22) 295043.

Ministry of Internal Affairs: 00-904 Warsaw, ul. Rakowiecka 2B; tel. (22) 210251; telex 813681.

Ministry of Justice: 00-950 Warsaw, Al. Ujazdowskie 11; tel. (2) 6284431; telex 813891; fax (22) 281692.

Ministry of Labour and Social Policy: 00-513 Warsaw, ul. Nowogrodzka 1/3/5; tel. (22) 289041; telex 814710; fax (22) 285700.

Ministry of Land Management and Construction: 00-926 Warsaw, ul. Wspólna 2; tel. (22) 210351; telex 814411; fax (2) 6284030.

Ministry of National Defence: 00-909 Warsaw; tel. (22) 210261.

Ministry of National Education: 00-918 Warsaw, Al. I Armii WP 25; tel. (22) 297241; telex 813523; fax (2) 6283561.

Ministry of Ownership Transformations (Privatization): 00-496 Warsaw, ul. Mysia 5; tel. (22) 283261; fax (22) 213361.

Ministry of Transport and Maritime Economy: 00-928 Warsaw, ul. Chałubińskiego 4; tel. (22) 244000; telex 812315; fax (22) 219968.

Central Planning Office: 00-507 Warsaw, Pl. Trzech Krzyży 5; tel. (2) 6935000; telex 814698.

President and Legislature

PRESIDENT

Presidential elections, 25 November and 9 December 1990

	Votes	
	First ballot	Second ballot
LECH WAŁĘSA	6,569,889	10,622,696 (74.25%)
STANISŁAW TYMIŃSKI	3,797,605	3,683,098 (25.75%)
TADEUSZ MAZOWIECKI	2,973,264	—
WŁODZIMIERZ CIMOSZEWICZ	1,514,025	—
ROMAN BARTOSZCZE	1,176,175	—
LESZEK MOCZULSKI	411,516	—

ZGROMADZENIE NARODOWE
(National Assembly)

The National Assembly consists of an upper chamber (Senat, created in 1989) and a lower chamber (Sejm, the former unicameral legislature).

Senat
Marshal: AUGUST CHELKOWSKI.
Elections, 27 October 1991

Party	Seats
Democratic Union	21
Solidarity Trade Union	11
Catholic Action	9
Centre Citizens' Alliance	9
Polish Peasant Party	8
Peasant Alliance*	7
Liberal Democratic Congress	6
Others†	29
Total	**100**

* A coalition dominated by Rural Solidarity and the Polish Peasants Party—Solidarity.
† Fifteen parties and six independents were also represented.

Sejm
Marshal: Prof. WIESŁAW CHRZANOWSKI.
Elections, 27 October 1991

Party	% of votes cast	Seats
Democratic Union	12.31	62
Democratic Left Alliance*	11.98	60
Catholic Action	8.73	49
Centre Citizens' Alliance	8.71	44
Polish Peasant Party	8.67	48
Confederation for an Independent Poland	7.50	46
Liberal Democratic Congress	7.48	37
Others†	34.62	114
Total	**100.00**	**460**

* Electoral coalition of Social Democracy of the Republic of Poland and the All Poland Trade Unions Alliance.
† Twenty-two other political parties were also represented.

Local Government

A new system of local government was established by a law adopted by the Sejm in March 1990. The lowest tier of local government is the commune, of which there were 2,394 in January 1991. Poland is also divided into 49 voivodships (see Statistical Survey for a complete list), each named after the town from which they are administered. District agencies act as an intermediary tier between local government and the central state administration, through which additional responsibilities may be delegated to communes where requested.

In May 1990 the Competence Act defined the respective functions and areas of competence of local government and the central state administration in 540 specific tasks. Of these tasks, 45% were considered to be the exclusive function of local governments, 17% to be the delegated function of local governments, 35% to be the function of district agencies and only 3% to be the function of the voivodships. Local government operations are financed partly by local taxes and administrative fees, and partly by taxes collected by central government.

Political Organizations

Centre Alliance (Porozumienie Centrum): 00-042 Warsaw, ul. Nowy Świat 58; tel. (22) 264164; telex 813496; fax (22) 263468; f. 1990 by supporters of Lech Wałęsa; Christian democratic party; 50,000 mems; Chair. JAROSŁAW KACZYŃSKI.

Christian National Union—CNU (Zjednoczenie Chrześcijańsko-Narodowe—ZChN): 00-853 Warsaw, ul. Krajowej Rady Narodowej 28; f. 1989; about 4,000 mems; Pres. Prof. WIESŁAW CHRZANOWSKI.

Confederation for an Independent Poland (Konfederacja Polski Niepodległej—KPN): 00-373 Warsaw, ul. Nowy Świat 18/20; tel. (22) 261043; f. 1979; right-wing; Chair. LESZEK MOCZULSKI.

Conservative-Libertarian Party (Konserwatywno-Liberalna Partia 'Unia Polityki Realnej'): 00-042 Warsaw, ul. Nowy Świat 41; tel. (22) 267477; f. 1989, registered 1990; Leader JANUSZ KORWIN-MIKKE.

Democratic Party—DP (Stronnictwo Demokratyczne—SD): 00-021 Warsaw, ul. Chmielna 9; tel. (22) 261001; telex 812502; f. 1939; recruits its members mainly from among progressive intellectuals and craftsmen, inhabitants of towns and cities; 134,737 mems (Dec. 1988); Pres. ALEKSANDER MACKIEWICZ.

Democratic Union (Unia Demokratyczna): 00-024 Warsaw, Al. Jerozolimskie 30; tel. (22) 275047; fax (22) 279741; f. 1991 by merger of Citizens' Movement-Democratic Action (Ruch Obywatelski-Akcja Demokratyczna—ROAD), Democratic Right Forum and the former Democratic Union; Leader TADEUSZ MAZOWIECKI; Gen. Sec. PIOTR NOWINA-KONOPKA.

Labour Party—LP (Stronnictwo Pracy—SP): 00-585 Warsaw, ul. Bagatela 10, m. 7; tel. (22) 291611; f. 1937, reactivated 1989; over 10,000 mems; Pres. WŁADYSŁAW SIŁA-NOWICKI; Sec.-Gen. S. M. GEBHARDT.

Liberal Democratic Congress (Kongres Liberalno-Demokratyczny): 80-306 Gdańsk, ul. Polanski 63; tel. (58) 414073, app. 24; f. 1988; Leader Dr JANUSZ LEWANDOWSKI.

Party X: Komorów; f. 1991 by Stanisław Tymiński; Exec. Mems WANDA BULYCZ, EDWARD STANSZCZAK, ANTONI SZAFRANIEC.

Polish Peasant Party—PPP (Polskie Stronnictwo Ludowe—PSL): 00-131 Warsaw, ul. Gryzbowska 4; tel. (22) 200251; f. 1990 to replace United Peasant Party—UPP (Zjednoczone Stronnictwo Ludowe—ZSL; f. 1949) and Polish Peasant Party—Rebirth (Polskie Stronnictwo Ludowe—Odrodzenie/PSL—Odrodzenie; f. 1989); Pres. ROMAN BARTOSZCZE.

Polish Peasant Party—Solidarity/PPP—Solidarity (Polskie Stronnictwo Ludowe—Solidarność/PSL—Solidarność): 00-020 Warsaw, ul. Rutkowskiego 24, m. 1; tel. (22) 262614; f. 1989; 12,000 mems; Leader JÓZEF ŚLISZ.

Polish Social Democratic Union—PSDU (Polska Unia Socjaldemokratyczna—PUSD): 00-489 Warsaw, ul. Wiejska 4/6; tel. (22) 213286; f. 1990 (as Social Democratic Union of the Republic of Poland, Unia Socjaldemokratyczna Rzeczypospolitej Polskiej—USDRP) by minority reformist group of former PUWP; Chair. TADEUSZ FISZBACH.

Polish Socialist Party (Polska Partia Socjalistyczna—PPS): 00-325 Warsaw, ul. Krakowskie Przedmieście 6; tel. (22) 262054; f. 1987; 3,000 mems; Chair. JAN JÓZEF LIPSKI; Chair. Cen. Exec. Cttee HENRYK MICHALAK.

Social Democracy of the Republic of Poland—SDRP (Socjaldemokracja Rzeczypospolitej Polskiej): 00-419 Warsaw, ul. Rozbrat 44A; tel. (22) 210341; telex 825581; fax (22) 216657; f. 1990 to replace Polish United Workers' Party—PUWP (Polska Zjednoczona Partia Robotnicza—PZPR; f. 1948), which held power until 1989; over 60,000 mems (May 1991); Chair. ALEKSANDER KWAŚNIEWSKI; Gen. Sec. LESZEK MILLER.

Solidarity (Solidarność): the electoral wing of the trade union movement (see p. 240) contested the 1989 legislative elections as the Solidarity Citizens' Cttee; Solidarity representatives to the National Assembly adopted the name of Citizens' Parliamentary Club (OKP); the Citizens' Committee was renamed the National Citizens' Committee (KKO) in Feb. 1991; Chair. ZDZISŁAW NAJDER.

There are numerous other groups. In March 1991 the PPP, CNU and LP announced that they were to form an electoral coalition.

Diplomatic Representation

EMBASSIES IN POLAND

Afghanistan: 02-954 Warsaw, ul. Kubickiego 13; tel. (2) 6423308; Ambassador: KHODAEDAD BASHARMAL.

Albania: 00-789 Warsaw, Słoneczna 15; tel. (22) 498516; Chargé d'affaires a.i.: VIRON TANE.

Algeria: 03-932 Warsaw, Dąbrowiecka 21; tel. (22) 175855; telex 817019; temporarily closed.

Argentina: 03-928 Warsaw, Styki 17/19; tel. (22) 176028; telex 812412; Ambassador: MARIO ENRIQUE BURKUN.

Australia: 03-903 Warsaw, Estońska 3/5; tel. (22) 176081; telex 813032; fax (22) 176756; Ambassador: A. KEVIN.

Austria: 00-748 Warsaw, ul. Gagarina 34; tel. (22) 410081; telex 813629; fax (22) 410085; Ambassador: GERHARD WAGNER.

Bangladesh: 02-516 Warsaw, Rejtana 15, m. 20/21; tel. (22) 497610; telex 816409; Ambassador: KHALEQUZZAMAN CHOWDHURY.

Belgium: 00-095 Warsaw, Senatorska 34; tel. (22) 270233; telex 813340; Ambassador: FRANÇOIS RONSE.

Brazil: 03-931 Warsaw, Poselska 11; tel. (22) 177177; telex 813748; Ambassador: (vacant).

Bulgaria: 00-540 Warsaw, Al. Ujazdowskie 33/35; tel. (22) 294071; Ambassador: (vacant).

Canada: 00-481 Warsaw, Matejki 1/5; tel. (22) 298051; telex 813424; Ambassador: PETER J. ARTHUR HANCOCK.

Chile: 02-932 Warsaw, ul. Morszyńska 71B; tel. (2) 6428155; telex 814542; Ambassador: MAXIMO LIRA ALCAYAGA.

China, People's Republic: 00-203 Warsaw, Bonifraterska 1; tel. (22) 313836; Ambassador: PEI YUANYING.

Colombia: 03-936 Warsaw, Zwycięzców 29; tel. (22) 177157; telex 816496; Ambassador: MANUEL JAIME GUERRERO PAZ.

Costa Rica: 02-516 Warsaw, ul. Starościńska 1A, m. 17; tel. (22) 481478; Ambassador: CARLOS ALBERTO VARGAS.

Cuba: 03-932 Warsaw, ul. Katowicka 22; tel. (22) 178428; telex 813588; Ambassador: ISABEL ALLENDE KARAN.

Czechoslovakia: 00-555 Warsaw, Koszykowa 18; tel. (22) 287221; Ambassador: MARKÉTA FIALKOVÁ.

Denmark: 02-516 Warsaw, Starościńska 5; tel. (22) 490056; telex 813387; Ambassador: NIELS PETER GEORG HELSKOV.

Ecuador: 02-516 Warsaw, ul. Starościńska 1B, m. 21; tel. (22) 480167; telex 817404; Chargé d'affaires: LUIS VIVAR FLORES.

Egypt: 00-570 Warsaw, Al. Wyzwolenia 6; tel. (22) 280133; telex 813605; Ambassador: MAHMOUD HASSAN FARGHAL.

Finland: 00-559 Warsaw, Chopina 4/8; tel. (22) 294091; telex 814286; fax (22) 216010; Ambassador: JYRKI AIMONEN.

France: 00-477 Warsaw, Piękna 1; tel. (22) 288401; Ambassador: ALAIN BRY.

Germany: 03-932 Warsaw, Dąbrowiecka 30; tel. (22) 173011; telex 813455; fax (22) 173582; Ambassador: GÜNTER KNACKSTEDT.

Greece: 01-640 Warsaw, Paska 21; tel. (22) 333488; telex 813692; Ambassador: EFSTRATIOS J. MAVROUDIS.

Holy See: 00-580 Warsaw, Al. I Armii Wojska Polskiego 12 (Apostolic Nunciature); tel. (22) 212337; telex 816493; fax (22) 284556; Apostolic Nuncio: Most Rev. JÓZEF KOWALCZYK, Titular Archbishop of Heraclea.

Hungary: 00-559 Warsaw, Chopina 2; tel. (2) 6284451; fax (22) 218561; Ambassador: ÁKOS ENGELMAYER.

India: 02-516 Warsaw, Rejtana 15; tel. (22) 495470; telex 814891; Ambassador: GURDIP SINGH BEDI.

Indonesia: 00-950 Warsaw, Wąchocka 9, POB 33; tel. (22) 171644; telex 813680; Ambassador: AMBIAR TAMALA.

Iran: 03-928 Warsaw, Królowej Aldony 22; tel. (22) 174293; telex 813823; Ambassador: KIUMARS FOTOUHI-GHIAM.

Iraq: 03-932 Warsaw, Dąbrowiecka 9A; tel. (22) 177065; telex 813918; Ambassador: MOHAMMED FADL HUSSAIN AL-HABBOOBI.

Ireland: 02-614 Warsaw, ul. Lenartowicza 18; Ambassador: RICHARD ANTHONY O'BRIEN.

Israel: 02-078 Warsaw, Krzywickiego 24; tel. (22) 250028; telex 817660; fax (22) 251607; Ambassador: MIRON GORDON.

Italy: 00-055 Warsaw, Plac Dąbrowskiego 6; tel. (22) 263471; telex 813742; Ambassador: VINCENZO MANNO.

Japan: 00-790 Warsaw, Willowa 7; tel. (2) 3523485; telex 813349; fax (22) 498494; Ambassador: SHINTARO YAMASHITA.

Korea, Democratic People's Republic: 00-478 Warsaw, ul. Bobrowiecka 1A; tel. (22) 405813; telex 812707; Ambassador: UI PYO HAN.

Korea, Republic: 02-611 Warsaw, ul. Ignacego Krasickiego 25; tel. (22) 483332; Ambassador: KYUNG CHUL KIM.

Laos: 02-516 Warsaw, Rejtana 15, m. 26; tel. (22) 484786; Chargé d'affaires a.i.: KHOUANEPHET SAYARATH.

Libya: 03-934 Warsaw, Kryniczna 2; tel. (22) 174822; telex 816233; Secretary of People's Bureau: MOHAMED A. NAJAH.

Malaysia: 03-902 Warsaw, ul. Gruzinska 3; tel. (22) 174413; telex 815368; Ambassador: TAN KOON SAN.

Mexico: 02-516 Warsaw, Starościńska 1B, m. 4-5; tel. (22) 495250; telex 814629; fax (22) 487617; Ambassador: JOSÉ LUIS VALLARTA.

Mongolia: 00-478 Warsaw, Al. Ujazdowskie 12; tel. (22) 281651; telex 814399; Ambassador: BAJARCHUGIJN NANZAD.

Morocco: 02-516 Warsaw, Starościńska 1; tel. (22) 496341; telex 813740; Ambassador: ABDELMAJID ALEM.

Netherlands: 02-791 Warsaw, ul. Chocimska 6; tel. (22) 492351; telex 813660; Ambassador: J. W. SEMEIJNS DE VRIES VAN DOESBURGH.

Nigeria: 00-791 Warsaw, Chocimska 18; tel. (22) 486944; telex 814675; Ambassador: GEORGE OCHEKWU AJONYE.

Norway: 00-559 Warsaw, Chopina 2A; tel. (22) 214231; telex 813738; fax (22) 6280938; Ambassador: ARNDT RINDAL.

Pakistan: 02-516 Warsaw, Starościńska 1; tel. (22) 494808; telex 816063; Ambassador: S. M. INAAMULLAH.

Peru: 01-555 Warsaw, Felińskiego 25; tel. (22) 399766; telex 814320; fax (22) 399766; Ambassador: MARÍA SALAZAR CASTELLANOS.

Philippines: 00-484 Warsaw, ul. Górnośląska 22, m. 5; Ambassador: RAFAEL A. GONZALES.

Portugal: 03-910 Warsaw, Dąbrowiecka 19; tel. (22) 176021; telex 815509; Ambassador: RUI FERNANDO MEIRA FERREIRA.

Romania: 00-559 Warsaw, Chopina 10; tel. (22) 283156; telex 813420; Ambassador: IULIU DOBROIU.

Russia: 00-761 Warsaw, Belwederska 49; tel. (22) 213453; telex 813530; Ambassador: YURI KACHLEV.

Spain: 02-516 Warsaw, Starościńska 1B; tel. (22) 499926; telex 814515; Ambassador: JOSÉ ANTONIO LÓPEZ ZATÓN.

Sweden: 00-585 Warsaw, ul. Bagatela 3; tel. (22) 493351; telex 813457; Ambassador: KARL VILHELM WÖHLER.

Switzerland: 00-540 Warsaw, Ujazdowskie 27; tel. (22) 280481; telex 813528; fax (22) 210548; Ambassador: J. RICHARD GAECHTER.

Syria: 02-536 Warsaw, Narbutta 19A; tel. (22) 491454; telex 815465; Ambassador: AHMAD SAKER.

Thailand: 02-516 Warsaw, Starościńska 1B, m. 2–3; tel. (22) 494730; telex 815392; Ambassador: (vacant).

Tunisia: 00-459 Warsaw, Myśliwiecka 14; tel. (22) 286330; telex 812827; Ambassador: MOHAMED FOURATI.

Turkey: 02-622 Warsaw, Malczewskiego 32; tel. (22) 443201; Ambassador: HATAY SAVAŞÇI.

United Kingdom: 00-556 Warsaw, Al. Róż 1; tel. (2) 6281001; telex 813694; fax (22) 217161; Ambassador: MICHAEL LLEWELLYN SMITH.

USA: 00-540 Warsaw, Al. Ujazdowskie 29/31; tel. (2) 6283041; telex 813304; Ambassador: THOMAS W. SIMONS, Jr.

Uruguay: 02-516 Warsaw, Rejtana 15, m. 12; tel. (22) 495040; telex 814647; Ambassador: AUGUSTO H. WILD.

Venezuela: 02-011 Warsaw, Al. Jerozolimskie 101; tel. (2) 6289651; telex 812788; fax (2) 6286740; Ambassador: JORGE DAHER DAHER.

Viet-Nam: 00-468 Warsaw, Kawalerii 5; tel. (22) 413369; Ambassador: NONG THE CAN.

Yemen: 02-954 Warsaw, ul. Marconich 8; tel. (2) 6426743; Ambassador: MANSOOR ABDUL GALIL ABDUL RAB.

Yugoslavia: 00-540 Warsaw, Al. Ujazdowskie 23/25; tel. (22) 285161; Ambassador: MURAT AGOVIĆ.

Zaire: 02-954 Warsaw, Kubickiego 11; tel. (2) 6422367; telex 816015; Ambassador: IPOTO EYEBU-BAKAND 'ASI.

Judicial System

SUPREME COURT

The Supreme Court: 00-958 Warsaw, ul. Ogrodowa 6; tel. (22) 203975; telex 817989; fax (22) 204159; the highest judicial organ; exercises supervision over the decision-making of all other courts; its functions include: the examination of appeals lodged against decisions of other courts; the examination of extraordinary appeals brought against final decisions of other courts and bodies; the adoption of resolutions aimed at providing interpretation of legal provisions that give rise to doubts. Justices of the Supreme Court are appointed by the President of the Republic on motions of the National Council of Judiciary and serve until the age of retirement (life tenure). The First President of the Supreme Court is appointed (and dismissed) from among the Supreme Court Justices by the National Assembly of Poland on the motion of the President of the Republic. The other presidents of the Supreme Court are appointed by the President of the Republic.

First President: Prof. Dr hab. ADAM STRZEMBOSZ.

OTHER COURTS

The Supreme Administrative Court examines, in one procedure, complaints concerning the legality of administrative decisions; it is vested exclusively with the powers of court of cassation.

The General Courts review civil, criminal, family cases and cases of minors, questions of labour and insurance law. They also have the right to try all economic cases.

The office of Prosecutor-General was subordinated to the Ministry of Justice (rather than to the President of Poland) in 1990.

Religion

CHRISTIANITY

The Roman Catholic Church

The Roman Catholic Church was granted full legal status in May 1989, when three laws regulating aspects of relations between the Church and the State were approved by the Sejm. The legislation guaranteed freedom of worship, and permitted the Church to administer its own affairs. The Church was also granted access to the media, and allowed to operate its own schools, hospitals and other charitable organizations.

For ecclesiastical purposes, Poland comprises seven archdioceses (including two covering territory in Lithuania and Ukraine) and 21 dioceses (all but one of which are entirely within Poland). In 1985 an estimated 95% of Poland's inhabitants were adherents of the Roman Catholic Church.

Bishops' Conference: Konferencja Episkopatu Polski, 01-015 Warsaw, Skwer Kardynala Stefana Wyszyńskiego 6; tel. (22) 389251; telex 816550; f. 1969 (statutes approved 1987); Pres. Cardinal JÓZEF GLEMP, Archbishop of Gniezno and of Warsaw.

Archdioceses wholly in Poland:

Archbishop of Gniezno and of Warsaw and Primate of Poland: Cardinal JÓZEF GLEMP, Sekretariat Prymasa Polski, 00-246 Warsaw, ul. Miodowa 17; tel. (22) 312157; telex 817000.

Archbishop of Kraków: Cardinal FRANCISZEK MACHARSKI, 31-004 Kraków, ul. Franciszkańska 3; tel. (12) 211533; telex 0322700.

Archbishop of Poznań: Metropolitan JERZY STROBA, 61-120 Poznań, ul. Mieszka I nr. 2; tel. (61) 524282.

Archbishop of Wrocław: Cardinal HENRYK ROMAN GULBINOWICZ, 50-328 Wrocław, ul. Katedralna 13; tel. (71) 225081.

Archdioceses partly in Poland:

Apostolic Administrator of Lwów (Lvov): Rev. ZYGMUNT ZUCHOWSKI (Administrator of Diocese of Lubaczów), 37-600 Lubaczów, ul. Mickiewicza 85; tel. 211–13.

Apostolic Administrator of Wilno (Vilnius): Mgr EDWARD KISIEL (Bishop of Białystok), 15-087 Białystok, ul. Kościelna 1; tel. (85) 416473.

Old Catholic Churches

Kościół Katolicki Mariawitów (Mariavite Catholic Church): Felicjanów, 09-470 Bodzanów, k. Płocka; tel. Bodzanów 10; f. 1893; 3,012 mems (1989); Archbishop JÓZEF M. RAFAEL WOJCIECHOWSKI.

Kościół Polskokatolicki (Polish Catholic Church): 00-464 Warsaw, ul. Szwoleżerów 4; tel. (22) 416248; f. 1920; 52,400 mems (1989); Prime Bishop Rt Rev. TADEUSZ R. MAJEWSKI.

Starokatolicki Kościół Mariawitów (Old Catholic Mariavite Church): 09-400 Płock, ul. Wieczorka 27; f. 1907; 24,774 mems (1989); Chief Bishop STANISŁAW KOWALSKI.

The Orthodox Church

Polski Autokefaliczny Kościół Prawosławny (Polish Autocephalous Orthodox Church): 03-402 Warsaw, Al. Świerczewskiego 52; tel. (22) 190886; 870,600 mems (1989); Metropolitan BAZYLI (WŁODZIMIERZ DOROSZKIEWICZ); Archbishop of Białystok and Gdańsk SAWA (MICHAŁ HRYCUNIAK); Bishop of Łódź and Poznań SZYMON (SZYMON ROMAŃCZUK); Bishop of Przemyśl and Nowy Sącz ADAM (ALEKSANDER DUBEC); Bishop of Wrocław and Szczecin JEREMIASZ (JAN ANCHIMIUK); Bishop of Lublin and Chełm ABEL (ANDRZEJ POPŁAWSKI).

Protestant Churches

There are approximately 100,000 Protestants in Poland.

Kościół Adwentystów Dnia Siódmego (Seventh-day Adventist Church in Poland): 00-366 Warsaw, ul. Foksal 8; tel. (22) 277611; f. 1921; 9,236 mems, 89 preachers (1989); Pres. WŁADYSŁAW POLOK; Sec. ROMAN R. CHALUPKA.

Kościół Ewangelicko-Augsburski (Evangelical Augsburg Church in Poland): 00-246 Warsaw, ul. Miodowa 21; tel. (22) 315187; c. 100,000 mems (1990); Bishop and Pres. of Synod and Consistory JAN SZAREK.

Kościół Ewangelicko-Reformowany (Evangelical-Reformed Church): 00-145 Warsaw, Al. Świerczewskiego 76A; tel. (22) 312383; f. 16th century; 4,500 mems (1989); Bishop ZDZISŁAW TRANDA; Pres. of the Consistory WŁODZIMIERZ ZUZGA.

Kościół Ewangelicko-Metodystyczny (United Methodist Church): 00-561 Warsaw, ul. Mokotowska 12; tel. (2) 6285328; f. 1921; 5,000 mems; Gen. Supt Rev. EDWARD PUŚLECKI.

Kościół Zielonoświątkowy (Pentecostal Church): 00-825 Warsaw, Sienna 68/70; tel. (22) 248575; f. 1910; 12,000 mems (1991); Pres. MICHAŁ HYDZIK.

Polski Kościół Chrześcijan Baptystów (Baptist Church): 00-865 Warsaw, ul. Waliców 25; tel. (22) 201224; f. 1858; 6,157 baptized mems (1989); Pres. Rev. KONSTANTY WIAZOWSKI; Sec. Rev. IGOR BARNA.

There are also several other small Protestant churches, including the Church of Christ, the Church of Evangelical Christians, the Evangelical Christian Church and the Jehovah's Witnesses.

ISLAM

In 1989 there were about 4,000 Muslims of Tartar origin in Białystok Province (eastern Poland), and smaller communities in Warsaw, Gdańsk and elsewhere.

Muzułmański Związek Religijny (Religious Union of Muslims in Poland): 15-426 Białystok, Rynek Kosciuszki 26, m.2; tel. (85) 414970; Chair. STEFAN MUCHARSKI.

JUDAISM

Związek Religijny Wyznania Mojżeszowego (Religious Union of the Mosaic Faith in Poland): 00-105 Warsaw, ul. Twarda 6; tel. (22) 204324; 21 synagogues and about 3,650 registered Jews; Pres. MOZES FINKELSTEIN.

The Press

Legislation to permit the formal abolition of censorship and to guarantee freedom of expression was approved in April 1990. Many newspapers, however, were in serious financial difficulties, largely owing to the steep increase in the cost of newsprint.

In 1989 there were 48 daily newspapers in Poland with a total circulation of 6,715,000. There were 3,189 periodicals with a combined circulation of 46.5m. copies. Following the political changes of 1989, hundreds of new newspapers were established.

PRINCIPAL DAILIES

Białystok

Gazeta Współczesna: 15-950 Białystok, POB 193, ul. Suraska 1; tel. (85) 20935; f. 1951; Editor ANATOL WAKULUK; circ. 85,000.

Bydgoszcz

Gazeta Pomorska: 85-011 Bydgoszcz, ul. Śniadeckich 1; tel. (52) 221928; telex 056-2386; fax (52) 221542; f. 1948; local independent newspaper for the provinces of Bydgoszcz, Toruń and Włocławek; Editor MACIEJ KAMIŃSKI; circ. 130,000 (weekdays), 300,000 (weekends).

Ilustrowany Kurier Polski: 85-070 Bydgoszcz, ul. Czerwonej Armii 20; tel. (52) 225857; telex 056-2387; f. 1945; regional organ of the Democratic Party (DP); Editor-in-Chief MAREK KWAŚCISZEWSKI; circ. 77,600.

Gdańsk

Dziennik Bałtycki: 80-886 Gdańsk, Targ Drzewny 3/7; tel. (58) 313560; f. 1945; non-party; economic, specializing in Polish maritime affairs; Editor TADEUSZ BOLDUAN; circ. 81,000.

Głos Wybrzeża: 80-886 Gdańsk, Pl. Targ Drzewny 3/7; tel. (58) 315772; f. 1948; local organ of SDRP; Editor-in-Chief ZBIGNIEW ZUKOWSKI; circ. 65,000.

Katowice

Dziennik Zachodni: 40-925 Katowice, ul. Młynska 1; tel. (32) 539984; telex 0315455; f. 1945; non-party; Chief Editor (vacant); circ. 173,600.

Trybuna Śląska: 40-098 Katowice, ul. Młynska 1; tel. (32) 537703; telex 0312432; fax (32) 537997; f. 1945; fmrly Trybuna Robotnicza; independent; Editor JACEK CIESZEWSKI; circ. 266,000 (weekdays), 800,000 (weekends).

Kielce

Słowo Ludu (Word of the People): 25-953 Kielce, Targowa 18; tel. (41) 42480; telex 0612231; f. 1949; local organ of SDRP; Editor JADWIGA KAROLCZAK; circ. 55,400.

Koszalin

Głos Pomorza (Voice of Pomerania): 75-604 Koszalin, ul. Zwycięstwa 137/139; tel. 22693; f. 1952; local organ of SDRP; Editor-in-Chief MIROSŁAW MAREK KROMER; circ. 66,300.

Kraków

Czas Krakowski: 31-072 Kraków, ul. Wielopole 3; tel. (12) 217543; f. 1848, reactivated 1990; independent; Editor (vacant); circ. 60,000.

Echo Krakowa: 31-007 Kraków, ul. Wiślna 2; tel. (12) 224678; f. 1946; independent; evening; Editor JERZY LANGIER; circ. 86,000.

Gazeta Krakowska: 31-072 Kraków, ul. Wielopole 1; tel. (12) 220985; f. 1949; local organ of SDRP; Editor TADEUSZ PIKULICKI; circ. 105,200.

Łódź

Dziennik Łódzki: 90-113 Łódź, ul. Sienkiewicza 9; tel. (42) 364585; telex 886138; fax (42) 322832; f. 1945; non-party; Editor KONRAD TUROWSKI; circ. 75,000.

Głos Poranny: 90-950 Łódź, ul. Sienkiewicza 3/5; tel. (42) 366785; f. 1945; fmrly Głos Robotniczy; local organ of SDRP; Editor GUSTAW ROMANOWSKI; circ. 64,000.

Lublin

Dziennik Lubelski: 20-950 Lublin, Al. Racławickie 1; tel. (81) 23234; f. 1945; fmrly Sztandar Ludu; local organ of SDRP; Editor WIESŁAWA JANKOWSKI; circ. 84,000.

Kurier Lubelski: 20-078 Lublin, ul. 3 Maja 14; tel. (81) 26634; f. 1830; independent; evening; Editor WŁODZIMIERZ WÓJCIKOWSKI; circ. 40,000.

Olsztyn

Gazeta Olsztyńska (Olsztyn Gazette): 10-417 Olsztyn, ul. Towarowa 2; tel. 330277; telex 0526371; f. 1886, renamed 1970; independent; Editor-in-Chief TOMAS ŚRUTKOWSKI; circ. 53,000.

Opole

Trybuna Opolska: 45-086 Opole, ul. Powstańców Śląskich 9; tel. 33870; telex 0732631; f. 1952; local organ of SDRP; Editor MARIAN SZCZUREK; circ. 82,000.

Poznań

Gazeta Poznańska: 60-782 Poznań, ul. Grunwaldzka 19; tel. (61) 665568; f. 1948; local organ of SDRP; Editor KONRAD NAPIERAŁA; circ. 96,100.

Głos Wielkopolski: 60-782 Poznań, ul. Grunwaldzka 19; tel. (61) 45409; telex 0413410; f. 1945; non-party; Editor MAREK PRZYBYLIK; circ. 75,000.

Rzeszów

Nowiny: 35-959 Rzeszów, ul. Lisa-Kuli 19; tel. (17) 34775; telex 0632220; fax (17) 33836; f. 1949; Editor JAN A. STEPEK; circ. 100,000.

Szczecin

Głos Szczeciński (Voice of Szczecin): 70-550 Szczecin, Pl. Hołdu Pruskiego 8; tel. (91) 34864; telex 0422242; fax (91) 45402; f. 1947; Editor-in-Chief MIECZYSŁAW KACZANOWSKI; circ. 100,000.

Warsaw

Codzienna Gazeta Polska: 00-131 Warsaw, ul. Grzybowska 4; tel. (22) 208153; telex 813367; f. 1945; fmrly Dziennik Ludowy, name changed 1990; organ of the Polish Peasant Party (PPP); Editor-in-Chief WIESŁAW M. KORNASIEWICZ; circ. 168,800.

Express Wieczorny: 02-017 Warsaw, Al. Jerozolimskie 125/127; tel. (22) 285231; telex 814461; f. 1946; non-party; evening; Editor ANDRZEJ BUNN; circ. 217,600.

Gazeta Wyborcza: 00-735 Warsaw, ul. Iwicka 19; tel. (22) 411416; telex 825703; fax (22) 413489; f. 1989; non-party; weekend edn: Gazeta Świateczna; Editor ADAM MICHNIK; circ. 430,000 (daily), 550,000 (weekend).

Kurier Polski: 00-018 Warsaw, ul. Hibnera 11; tel. (22) 278081; telex 814725; f. 1957; organ of the Democratic Party (DP); Editor JACEK SNOPKIEWICZ; circ. 130,000.

Polska Zbrojna: 00-950 Warsaw, ul. Grzybowska 77; tel. (22) 202127; f. 1943; fmrly Żolnierz Wolności, name changed 1990; Editor JERZY SLASKI; circ. 60,000.

Przegląd Sportowy: 02-017 Warsaw, Al. Jerozolimskie 125/127, POB 181; tel. (22) 289116; f. 1921; Editor (vacant); circ. 80,000.

Rzeczpospolita (The Republic): 00-921 Warsaw, ul. Krucza 36; tel. (22) 280493; telex 817131; fax (22) 280588; f. 1982; Editor-in-Chief DARIUSZ FIKUS; circ. 240,000.

Słowo Powszechne: 00-551 Warsaw, ul. Mokotowska 43; tel. (22) 297767; telex 814434; f. 1947; organ of the 'Pax' Catholic Association; Editor ANNA BOROWSKA; circ. 150,000.

Sztandar Młodych: 00-687 Warsaw, ul. Wspólna 61; tel. (22) 287661; telex 814767; fax (22) 282049; f. 1950; Editor JERZY DOMAŃSKI; circ. 211,500.

Trybuna: 04-029 Warsaw, Al. Stanów Zjednoczonych 53; tel. (22) 132040; telex 813809; fax (22) 100592; f. 1948; fmrly Trybuna Ludu; organ of the SDRP; Editor MAREK SIWIEC; circ. 248,000.

Życie Warszawy (Warsaw Life): 00-624 Warsaw, ul. Marszałkowska 3/5; tel. (22) 252829; telex 814507; f. 1944; independent; Editor KAZIMIERZ WÓYCICKI; circ. 176,000.

Wrocław

Gazeta Robotnicza: 50-043 Wrocław, ul. Podwale 62; tel. (71) 35756; fax (71) 35756; f. 1948; Editor ANDRZEJ BUŁAT; circ. 150,800.

Zielona Góra

Gazeta Lubuska: 65-042 Zielona Góra, POB 120, ul. Niepodległosci 25; tel. 70955; f. 1952; local organ of SDRP; Editor MIROSŁAW RATAJ; circ. 91,800.

PERIODICALS

Fantastyka: 00-640 Warsaw, ul. Mokotowska 5/6; tel. (22) 253475; f. 1982; monthly; science fiction and fantasy; Editor LECH JĘZMYK; circ. 120,000.

Filipinka: 00-511 Warsaw, Nowogrodzka 31; tel. (22) 282401; f. 1957; fortnightly; illustrated for teenage girls; Editor HANNA JAWOROWSKA-BŁOŃSKA; circ. 126,600.

Film: 02-595 Warsaw, Puławska 61; tel. (22) 455325; fax (22) 454651; f. 1946; weekly; illustrated magazine; Editor MACIEJ PAWLICKI; circ. 100,000.

Forum: 00-656 Warsaw, ul. Śniadeckich 10; tel. (22) 256150; f. 1965; weekly; survey of foreign press; political, social, cultural and economics; Editor-in-Chief BOHDAN HERBICH; circ. 53,400.

Gazeta Bankowa: 00-687 Warsaw, Wspólna 61; tel. (2) 6287272; telex 813439; fax (22) 212653; f. 1988; weekly; finance; Editor ANDRZEJ WROBLEWSKI; circ. 40,000.

Głos Nauczycielski (Teachers' Voice): 00-389 Warsaw, ul. Spasowskiego 6/8; tel. (22) 263420; telex 816896; fax (22) 262112; f. 1917; weekly; organ of the Polish Teachers' Union; Editor WOJCIECH SIERAKOWSKI; circ. 59,900.

Gromada-Rolnik Polski: 00-375 Warsaw, ul. Smolna 12; tel. (22) 278806; telex 814741; f. 1947; 3 a week; agricultural; Editor (vacant); circ. 281,800.

IMT Światowid: 00-695 Warsaw, ul. Nowogrodzka 49; tel. (22) 212376; f. 1952; monthly; illustrated tourist magazine; Editor ROBERT MAKOWSKI; circ. 50,000.

Karuzela (The Merry-Go-Round): 90-113 Łódź, Sienkiewicza 3/5; tel. (42) 331432; telex 886265; f. 1957; fortnightly; satirical; Editor DARIUSZ DOROZYŃSKI; circ. 100,000.

Kobieta i Życie (Women and Life): 00-564 Warsaw, Koszykowa 6A; f. 1946; weekly; women's; Editor ANNA SZYMAŃSKA-KWIATKOWSKA; circ. 471,000.

Literatura: 00-562 Warsaw, Koszykowa 6A; tel. (22) 214856; f. 1972; monthly; literary; Editor JACEK SYSKI; circ. 64,800.

Media Reporter: 00-958 Warsaw, ul. Miedziana 11; tel. (22) 200281, ext. 581; f. 1957; fmrly Ekran; fortnightly; illustrated television and video magazine; Editor ZYGMUNT MARCINCZAK; circ. 100,000.

Morze: 00-024 Warsaw, ul. Widok 10; tel. and fax (22) 273551; f. 1924; illustrated monthly; maritime affairs; Editor-in-Chief JANUSZ WOLNIEWICZ; circ. 50,000.

Nie: Warsaw; satirical weekly; Editor JERZY URBAN; circ. 500,000.

Nie z tej Ziemi (Not from that World): 00-840 Warsaw, Wronia 23; tel. (22) 241485; fax (22) 240657; f. 1990; monthly; para-science, ghost stories, etc.; Editor ADAM HOLLANEK; circ. 220,000.

Nowa Wieś: 00-480 Warsaw, ul. Wiejska 17; tel. (22) 284583; f. 1948; weekly; peasant illustrated magazine; Editor KAZIMIERZ DŁUGOSZ; circ. 100,000.

Panorama: 40-003 Katowice, Rynek 13; tel. (32) 538595; telex 031-5212; f. 1954; weekly; illustrated popular magazine; Editor ANDRZEJ WRAZIDŁO; circ. 165,000.

Państwo i Prawo (State and Law): 00-490 Warsaw, ul. Wiejska 12; tel. (22) 282411; f. 1946; monthly organ of the Polish Academy of Sciences; Editor Dr hab. LESZEK KUBICKI; circ. 5,600.

Po Prostu: 00-921 Warsaw, ul. Krucza 36; tel. (22) 280281; f. 1947, reactivated 1990; weekly; independent; social and political; Editor RYSZARD TURSKI; circ. 40,000.

Poezja: 00-950 Warsaw, ul. Nowy Świat 58; tel. (22) 261096; f. 1965; monthly; poetry, essays and reviews on Polish and foreign poetry; Editor MAREK WAWRZKIEWICZ; circ. 7,500.

Polityka (Politics): 00-182 Warsaw, ul. Dubois 9; tel. (2) 6353491; telex 812546; f. 1957; weekly; political, economic, cultural; Editor JAN BIJAK; circ. 400,000.

Polityka Polska: 00-141 Warsaw, ul. Marchlewskiego 32/11; tel. (22) 241931; f. 1982; monthly; political; Editor MAREK GADZAŁA; circ. 5,000.

Poradnik Gospodarski: 61-816 Poznań, ul. F. Ratajczaka 33; tel. (61) 523342; f. 1889; monthly; agriculture; Editor-in-Chief STANISŁAW BABIARZ; circ. 10,000.

Poznaj Świat: 00-517 Warsaw, ul. Marszałkowska 82/84; f. 1947; monthly; illustrated geographical magazine; Editor Mgr TADEUSZ LENCZOWSKI; circ. 90,000.

Prawo i Życie (Law and Life): 00-028 Warsaw, ul. Bracka 20A; tel. (22) 272466; f. 1956; weekly; legal and social; Editor ANDRZEJ DOBRZYŃSKI; circ. 110,400.

Problemy: 00-537 Warsaw, ul. Krucza 6/14; tel. (22) 282133; f. 1945; monthly; popular science review; Editor HANNA DOBROWOLSKA; circ. 30,000.

Przegląd Tygodniowy: 00-950 Warsaw, POB 992, ul. Bracka 22; tel. (22) 276294; telex 816400; fax (22) 279128; f. 1982; weekly;

political, social, historical, cultural, scientific and artistic; Editor ANDRZEJ NIERYCHŁO; circ. 210,600.

Przekrój: 31-012 Kraków, ul. Reformacka 3; tel. (12) 225954; telex 0322733; fax (12) 214929; f. 1945; weekly; illustrated; Editor-in-Chief MIECZYSŁAW CZUMA; circ. 250,000.

Przyjaciółka (The Friend): 00-490 Warsaw, ul. Wiejska 16; tel. (22) 280583; f. 1948; weekly; women's magazine; Editor EWA ŁUSZCZUK; circ. 1,500,000.

Razem (Together): 00-920 Warsaw, Nowy Świat 18/20; tel. (22) 264253; f. 1976; weekly; illustrated youth magazine; Editor JACEK MARCZYŃSKI; circ. 100,000.

Reporter: 00-585 Warsaw, ul. Bagatela 12; tel. (22) 219376; telex 81-4481; fax (22) 279237; f. 1985; monthly; publ. by Interpress; Editor-in-Chief WOJCIECH PIELECKI; circ. 100,000.

Res Publica: 00-950 Warsaw 1, POB 856, ul. Jasna 26; tel. (22) 262468; fax (22) 264817; f. 1987; monthly; political and cultural; Editor MARCIŃ KRÓL; circ. 5,000.

Sport: 40-953 Katowice, ul. Młynska 1; tel. (32) 637325; f. 1945; 5 a week; Editor ADAM BARTECZKO; circ. 80,000.

Sportowiec (Sportsman): 00-640 Warsaw, ul. Mokotowska 24; tel. (22) 216208; f. 1949; weekly; Chief Editor JACEK ŻEMANTOWSKI; circ. 100,000.

Spotkania: 00-871 Warsaw, ul. Zelazna 67; tel. (22) 204424; telex 817403; fax (22) 241423; f. 1990; weekly; illustrated; political, social, economic, cultural and scientific magazine; Editor MACIEJ IŁOWIECKI; circ. 150,000.

Sprawy Międzynarodowe (International Affairs): 00-950 Warsaw, ul. Warecka 1A; tel. (22) 278888; fax (22) 274738; f. 1948; monthly; published by the Polski Instytut Spraw Międzynarodowych; Editor MICHAŁ DOBROCZYŃSKI; circ. 1,500.

Szpilki: 00-499 Warsaw, Pl. Trzech Krzyży 16A; tel. (22) 280429; f. 1935; weekly; illustrated satirical; Editor (vacant); circ. 78,800.

Teatr: 03-902 Warsaw, ul. Jakubowska 14; tel. (22) 175594; f. 1945; monthly; illustrated; theatrical life; Editor ANDRZEJ WANAT; circ. 6,800.

Twoje Dziecko: 00-519 Warsaw, ul. Wspólna 41, m. 30; tel. (2) 6284412; f. 1951; monthly; women's magazine concerning children's affairs; Editor-in-Chief JANINA SZEWCZYKOWSKA; circ. 150,000.

Tygodnik Demokratyczny: 00-950 Warsaw, ul. Hibnera 11; tel. (22) 272493; f. 1953; weekly; organ of the Democratic Party (SD); political and social; Editor LIDIA SMYCZYŃSKA; circ. 38,500.

Tygodnik Solidarność: 00-950 Warsaw, POB P-6, ul. Czackiego 15/17; tel. (22) 273303; telex 816992; f. 1981, reactivated 1989; weekly; Editor (vacant).

Warsaw Voice: 00-585 Warsaw, ul. Bagatela 12; tel. (22) 211328; telex 814775; fax (22) 284651; f. 1988; weekly; political, social, cultural and economic; in English for foreigners in Poland; Editor ANDRZEJ JONAS; circ. 14,300.

Zielony Sztandar (Green Banner): 00-950 Warsaw, ul. Grzybowska 4; tel. (22) 207554; f. 1931; weekly; main organ of the Polish Peasant Party (PPP); Editor PAWEŁ POPIAK; circ. 195,800.

Żołnierz Polski: 00-950 Warsaw, ul. Grzybowska 77; tel. (22) 201261; f. 1945; weekly; illustrated magazine primarily about the armed forces; Editor Dr WIESŁAW JAN WYSOCKI; circ. 45,000.

Życie Gospodarcze: 00-490 Warsaw, ul. Wiejska 12; tel. (22) 280628; telex 814778; fax (22) 288392; f. 1945; weekly; economic; Editor STANISŁAW CHEŁSTOWSKI; circ. 59,700.

NEWS AGENCIES

Polska Agencja Prasowa—PAP (Polish Press Agency): 00-950 Warsaw, Al. Jerozolimskie 7; tel. (2) 6280001; telex 812509; fax (22) 218518; f. 1944; brs in 28 Polish towns and 21 foreign capitals; 320 journalist and photojournalist mems; information is transmitted abroad in English only; Pres. and Editor-in-Chief IGNACY RUTKIEWICZ.

Polska Agencja Informacyjna (Wydawnictwo Interpress) (Polish Agency Interpress): 00-585 Warsaw, ul. Bagatela 12; tel. (2) 6282221; telex 814481; fax (22) 284651; f. 1967; multi-lingual books, magazines, bulletins and news, television films, feature and photo services on Polish culture, foreign policy and economics; press centre for foreign journalists and publishers; advertising and promotional services; Editor-in-Chief JAN GRZELAK.

Centralna Agencja Fotograficzna—CAF (Press-Photo Agency—CAF): 00-372 Warsaw, ul. Foksal 16; tel. (22) 265221; telex 814801; f. 1951; supplies photographs to Polish press and to foreign press photo agencies; serves photographic publishing houses, and advertising agencies; Editor-in-Chief and Dir CEZARY MAREK LANGDA.

Krajowa Agencja Wydawnicza—KAW (National Publishing Agency—KAW): 00-679 Warsaw, ul. Wilcza 46; tel. (2) 6286481; telex 813487; fax (22) 296807; f. 1974; publishes children's and youths' fiction, popular reference books, postcards, posters and calendars, and audio records, cassettes and compact discs; Dir and Editor-in-Chief JAN WYSOKIŃSKI.

Foreign Bureaux

Allgemeiner Deutscher Nachrichtendienst (ADN) (Germany): 00-116 Warsaw, ul. Świętokrzyska 36, m. 61; tel. (22) 201152; telex 4775.

Agence France-Presse (AFP): 00-672 Warsaw, ul. Piękna 68, p. 305; tel. (22) 216747; telex 813620; Correspondent MICHEL LECLERCQ.

Agencia EFE (Spain): 00-656 Warsaw, Śniadeckich 18, Lokal 16; tel. (2) 6282567; telex 7849; fax (22) 215989; Bureau Chief MANUEL OSTOS.

Agenzia Nazionale Stampa Associata (ANSA) (Italy): 00-672 Warsaw, ul. Piękna 68, p. 301; tel. (22) 298413; telex 813724; fax (22) 299843; Bureau Chiefs MAURIZIO SALVI, WITOLD ZIÓŁKOWSKI.

Associated Press (AP) (USA): 00-057 Warsaw, ul. Filtrowa 45, tel. (22) 252009; telex 813440; fax (22) 253230; Correspondents JOHN DANISZEWSKI, DRUSILLA MENAKER.

Bulgarska Telegrafna Agentsia (BTA) (Bulgaria): 00-019 Warsaw, Kniewskiego 9m. 14; tel. (22) 278059; telex 813720; Correspondent WESELIN JANKOW.

Československá tisková kancelář (ČSTK) (Czechoslovakia): 00-116 Warsaw, ul. Świętokrzyska 36, m. 46; tel. (22) 204504; telex 813746; Correspondent MILAN SYRUČEK.

Deutsche-Presse Agentur (dpa) (Germany): 03-968 Warsaw, ul. Saska 7A; tel. (22) 171058; telex 813374; Correspondent RENATA MARSCH.

Informatsionnoye Agentstvo Novosti (IAN) (Russia): 00-582 Warsaw, Al. I Armii Wojska Polskiego 5; tel. (22) 283092; telex 813355; 6 Correspondents.

Kyodo Tsushin (Japan): 00-679 Warsaw, ul. Wilcza 42, m. 12; tel. (2) 6282045; telex 816997; Chief HIROYASU YAMAZAKI.

Magyar Távirati Iroda (MTI) (Hungary): 02-954 Warsaw, ul. Jakuba Kubickiego 19/22, m. 22; tel. (22) 420089; telex 8144460; Correspondent JÁNOS BARABÁS.

Novinska Agencija Tanjug (Yugoslavia): 00-110 Warsaw, ul. Świętokrzyska 36, m. 38; tel. (22) 240056; telex 813600; Correspondent NIKOLA STANOJEVIĆ.

Prensa Latina (Cuba): 02-301 Warsaw, ul. Grójecka 22/24, m. 46; tel. (22) 226081; telex 814668; Correspondent MIRTA BALEA.

Reuters (UK): 02-057 Warsaw, ul. Filtrowa 45; tel. (22) 250575; telex 813821; fax (22) 253474; Correspondent ANDREW TARNOWSKI.

Telegrafnoye Agentstvo Sovetskovo Soyuza (TASS) (Russia): 00-581 Warsaw, ul. Litewska 10, m. 18; tel. (22) 289745; telex 814425; 4 Correspondents.

United Press International (UPI) (USA): 00-672 Warsaw, ul. Piękna 68, p. 306; tel. (22) 216795; telex 813417; Chief Correspondent PATRICIA KOZA.

Xinhua (New China) News Agency (People's Republic of China): 00-203 Warsaw, ul. Bonifraterska 1; tel. (22) 313876; telex 813357; Correspondents TANG DEQIAO, DONG FUSHENG, MA YUNLIANG.

PRESS ASSOCIATION

Stowarzyszenie Dziennikarzy Polskich—SDP (Polish Journalists' Association): 00-366 Warsaw, ul. Foksal 3/5; tel. (22) 278715; f. 1951, dissolved 1982, legal status restored 1989; over 2,000 mems; Pres. MACIEJ IŁOWIECKI; Gen. Sec. DARIUS FIKUS.

Publishers

A total of 10,286 titles (books and pamphlets) were published in 1989.

AGPOL (Foreign Trade Publicity and Publishing Enterprise): 00-957 Warsaw, ul. Kierbedzia 4, POB 7; tel. (22) 416061; telex 813364; f. 1956; foreign trade publicity services for Polish firms and local advertising for foreign firms; Man. Dir MIECZYSŁAW KROKER.

Instytut Prasy i Wydawnictw 'Novum' Unii Chrześcijansko-Społecznej: 00-580 Warsaw, ul. I. Armii Wojska Polskiego 3; tel. (22) 213413; telex 816721; religious books; Dir KRZYSZTOF BIELECKI.

Instytut Wydawniczy Nasza Księgarnia (Nasza Księgarnia Publishing Institute): 00-580 Warsaw, ul. Spasowskiego 4; tel. (22) 263648; telex 817823; f. 1921; books and periodicals for children and educational publications; Dir and Chief Editor ANNA WĘGRZYN.

Instytut Wydawniczy Pax (Pax Publishing Institute): 00-791 Warsaw, ul. Chocimska 8/10; tel. (22) 499517; telex 813434; f. 1949;

theology, philosophy, religion, history, literature; Editor-in-Chief ANDRZEJ POLKOWSKI.

Instytut Wydawniczy Związków Zawodowych (Trade Unions' Publishing Institute): 00-950 Warsaw, ul. Spasowskiego 1/3; tel. (22) 279011; f. 1950; social, economic, scientific, cultural, labour safety and trade union literature and fiction; Dir and Editor-in-Chief STANISŁAW GRZEŚNIAK.

Księgarnia św. Wojciecha (St Adalbert Printing and Publishing Co): 60-967 Poznań, Pl. Wolności 1; tel. (61) 529186; telex 0414220; f. 1895; textbooks and Catholic publications; Dir Rev. BOLESŁAW JURGA; Editor-in-Chief BOZYSŁAW WALCZAK.

Ludowa Spółdzielnia Wydawnicza (People's Publishing Co-operative): 00-131 Warsaw, ul. Grzybowska 4/8; tel. (22) 205718; f. 1949; fiction and popular science; Chair. and Editor-in-Chief TADEUSZ KISIELEWSKI.

Niezależna Oficyna Wydawnicza NOWA. Wydawnictwo Fundacji NOWEJ (Independent Publishing House NOWA): 00-929 Warsaw, ul. Truskawiecka 1; tel. (22) 423073; belles lettres, recent history, politics; Pres. GRZEGORZ BOGUTA; Editor-in-Chief MIROSŁAW KOWALSKI.

Oficyna Literacka: 30-112 Kraków, ul. Smolénsk 38, m. 12; tel. (12) 218472; f. 1982 clandestinely, 1990 officially; belles lettres, poetry, including débuts, essays; Editor-in-Chief HENRYK KARKOSZA.

Oficyna Wydawnicza Volumen: 02-759 Warsaw, ul. Złotych Piasków 3, m. 10; tel. (22) 425013; f. 1984 (working clandestinely as WERS), 1989 officially; books on social and political subjects and history, albums; Dir ADAM BOROWSKI.

Pallottinum—Wydawnictwo Stowarzyszenia Apostolstwa Katolickiego: 60-959 Poznań, Al. Przybyszewskiego 30; tel. (61) 47212; f. 1947; religious books; Dir Mgr STEFAN DUSZA.

Państwowe Przedsiębiorstwo Wydawnictw Kartograficznych im. E. Romera (Romer State Cartographical Publishing House): 00-410 Warsaw, ul. Solec 18/20; tel. (22) 283251; f. 1951; maps, atlases, books on geodesy and cartography, and a quarterly review; Dir ALINA MELJON.

Państwowe Wydawnictwo Ekonomiczne (State Publishing House for Economic Literature): 00-098 Warsaw, ul. Niecała 4A; tel. (22) 275567; f. 1949; economics books and magazines; Dir and Editor-in-Chief HANNA MALARECKA-SIMBIEROWICZ.

Państwowe Wydawnictwo Iskry (State Publishing Company Iskry): 00-375 Warsaw, ul. Smolna 11/13; tel. (22) 279415; fax (22) 279415; f. 1952; travel, Polish and foreign fiction (poetry and prose), science fiction, essays, popular science, history, memoirs; Dir and Editor-in-Chief Dr WIESŁAW UCHAŃSKI.

Państwowe Wydawnictwo Naukowe—PWN (State Scientific Publishers): 00-251 Warsaw, ul. Miodowa 10; tel. (22) 272544; telex 813763; fax (22) 267163; f. 1951; publications and journals on all sciences except medicine, encyclopaedias, university textbooks; international scientific congresses' proceedings; Dir GRZEGORZ BOGUTA; Editor-in-Chief JAN KOFMAN.

Państwowe Wydawnictwo Rolnicze i Leśne (State Agricultural and Forestry Publishers): 00-950 Warsaw, Al. Jerozolimskie 28; tel. (22) 266451; telex 817509; fax (22) 276338; f. 1947; for professional publications on agriculture and forestry; Dir and Editor-in-Chief MIROSŁAW SOBKOWIAK.

Państwowy Instytut Wydawniczy (State Publishing Institute): 00-950 Warsaw, POB 377, ul. Foksal 17; tel. (22) 260201; f. 1946; Polish and foreign classical and contemporary literature, fiction, literary criticism, biographies, performing arts, culture, history, popular science and fine arts; Dir ANDRZEJ GRUSZECKI; Editor-in-Chief MICHAŁ KABATA.

Państwowy Zakład Wydawnictw Lekarskich (State Medical Publisher): 00-950 Warsaw, POB 379, ul. Długa 38/40; tel. (22) 312161; f. 1945; university textbooks, medical textbooks, monographs, atlases, dictionaries, handbooks for medical personnel, popular medical books; about 45 medical periodicals; Dir and Editor-in-Chief (vacant).

Polska Oficyna Wydawnicza BGW (Polish Publishing House BGW): 02-001 Warsaw, Al. Jerozolimskie 91; tel. (22) 217546; fax (22) 284652; telex 817-965; f. 1990; encyclopaedias, compendia of knowledge, books for children; Pres. ROMAN GÓRSKI.

Polskie Wydawnictwo Muzyczne (PWM—Edition): 31-111 Kraków, Al. Krasińskiego 11A; tel. (12) 227044; telex 813370; f. 1945; music and books on music; Dir JAN BĘTKOWSKI; (see also under Foreign Trade Organizations).

Przedsiębiorstwo Państwowe Wydawnictwo Śląsk (Silesia Publishing House): 40-161 Katowice, Al. W. Korfantego 51; tel. (32) 583221; telex 312326; f. 1954; belles lettres, social and political literature, popular science, juvenile books and regional literature; Dir and Editor-in-Chief TADEUSZ SIERNY.

Spółdzielnia Wydawnicza Czytelnik (Reader Co-operative Publishing House): 00-490 Warsaw, ul. Wiejska 12A; tel. (2) 6281441; fax (2) 6283178; f. 1944; general, especially fiction; Chair. STEFAN BRATKOWSKI; Editor-in-Chief HENRYK CHŁYSTOWSKI.

Społeczny Instytut Wydawniczy Znak (Znak Social Publishing Institute): 30-105 Kraków, ul. Kościuszki 37; tel. (12) 219776; telex 0325707; fax (12) 219814; f. 1959; religion, philosophy, belles-lettres, essays, history; Editor-in-Chief JACEK WOŹNIAKOWSKI.

Wydawnictwa Artystyczne i Filmowe (Art and Film Publications): 02-595 Warsaw, ul. Puławska 61; tel. (22) 455301; fax (22) 455584; f. 1959; theatre, cinema and art publications and reprints; Man. Dir JANUSZ FOGLER.

Wydawnictwa Geologiczne (Geological Publishing House): 00-975 Warsaw, ul. Rakowiecka 4; tel. (22) 495081; f. 1953; geology; Dir ANDRZEJ WACOWSKI.

Wydawnictwa Komunikacji i Łączności (Transport and Communications Publishing House): 02-546 Warsaw, ul. Kazimierzowska 52; tel. and fax (22) 492322; telex 812736; f. 1949; technical books and periodicals on electronics, radio engineering, television and telecommunications, road, rail and air transport; Dir and Editor-in-Chief BOGUMIŁ ZIELIŃSKI.

Wydawnictwa Naukowo-Techniczne (Scientific-Technical Publishers): 00-950 Warsaw, ul. Mazowiecka 2/4, POB 359; tel. (22) 267271; telex 825419; fax (22) 268293; f. 1949; scientific and technical books on mathematics, physics, chemistry, foodstuffs industry, electrical and electronic engineering, computer science, automation, mechanical engineering, light industry; technological encyclopaedias and dictionaries, children's dictionaries; Dir and Editor-in-Chief Dr ANIELA TOPULOS.

Wydawnictwa Normalizacyjne Alfa (Standardization Publishing House): 00-950 Warsaw, ul. Nowogrodzka 22; tel. (22) 216751; telex 812374; f. 1956; standards, catalogues and reference books on standardization, periodicals; popular science for children, science fiction, household directories; Dir and Editor-in-Chief JERZY WYSOKIŃSKI.

Wydawnictwa Szkolne i Pedagogiczne (Publishing House for School and Pedagogical Books): 00-950 Warsaw, POB 480, Pl. Dąbrowskiego 8; tel. (22) 268382; f. 1945; school textbooks and popular science books, scientific literature for teachers, visual teaching aids, periodicals for teachers and youth; Man. Dir JERZY ŁOZIŃSKI; Editor-in-Chief ANDRZEJ CHRZANOWSKI.

Wydawnictwo Arkady: POB 169, 00-950 Warsaw, ul. Sienkiewicza 12/14; tel. (22) 269316; f. 1957; publications on building, town planning, architecture and art; Dir and Editor-in-Chief STEFAN MUSZYŃSKI.

Wydawnictwo Bellora: 00-873 Warsaw, ul. Grzybowska 77; tel. (22) 204291; f. 1947; fiction and military; Dir Col WŁADYSŁAW MIŚ; Editor-in-Chief ANDRZEJ KRZYSZTOF KUNERT.

Wydawnictwo Czasopism i Książek Technicznych Sigma NOT, Spółka z o.o. (Sigma Publishers of Technical Periodicals and Books, Ltd): 00-950 Warsaw, ul. Biała 4, POB 1004; tel. (22) 203118; telex 814550; fax (22) 203116; f. 1949; popular and specialized periodicals and books on general technical subjects; Dir and Editor-in-Chief Dr ANDRZEJ KUSYK.

Wydawnictwo GiG. R. Ginalski i S-ka: 00-050 Warsaw, ul. Świętokrzyska 14, m. 538; tel. (22) 270155; f. 1989; light literature, thrillers, books for children; Dir GRAŻYNA GINALSKA.

Wydawnictwo Interpress (Interpress Publishers): 00-585 Warsaw, ul. Bagatela 12; tel. (22) 219325; telex 814775; fax (22) 284651; Poland past and present, handbooks, monographs, guide-books, albums; publishing co-operation and printing services; Editor-in-Chief BOHDAN GAWROŃSKI; see also under News Agencies.

Wydawnictwo Literackie (Literary Publishing House): 31-147 Kraków, ul. Długa 1; tel. (12) 224644; f. 1953; works of literature and belles-lettres; Dir BOGDAN ROGATKO.

Wydawnictwo Łódzkie: 90-447 Łódź, ul. Piotrkowska 171/173; tel. (42) 360331; fax (42) 368524; f. 1957; contemporary and classical Polish literature, juvenile literature, memoirs, essays, translations, popular science; Dir and Editor-in-Chief JAROSLAV SKOWROŃSKI.

Wydawnictwo Lubelskie (Lublin Publishing House): 20-022 Lublin, ul. Okopowa 7; tel. (81) 27344; f. 1957; social and political literature, memoires, essays, fiction, poetry, translations from Ukrainian literature; Dir and Editor-in-Chief IRENEUSZ CABAN.

Wydawnictwo Morskie (Maritime Publishing House): 80-835 Gdańsk, ul. Szeroka 38/40; tel. (58) 311031; f. 1951; popular science, humanities, maritime economy, belles-lettres, encyclopaedias, dictionaries, children's books; Dir and Editor-in-Chief JOANNA KONOPACKA (acting).

Wydawnictwo Poznańskie (Poznań Publishing House): 61-701 Poznań, ul. Fredry 8; tel. (61) 531901; telex 0413693; f. 1956; fiction, poetry and popular science, translations from Scandinavian and German literature; Dir and Editor-in-Chief KRZYSZTOF LEWANDOWSKI.

Wydawnictwo Prawnicze (Legal Publishing House): 02-520 Warsaw, ul. Wiśniowa 50; tel. (22) 494705; f. 1952; Dir PIOTR SZCZEŚNIEWSKI.

Wydawnictwo Spółdzielcze: 00-013 Warsaw, ul. Jasna 1; tel. (22) 271524; telex 813622; books, periodicals, information bulletins, catalogues, albums; Dir SYLWESTER KOMARNICKI.

Wydawnictwo Sport i Turystyka (State Sport and Tourism Publishers): 00-021 Warsaw, ul. Rutkowskiego 7/9; tel. (22) 262451; telex 816578; fax (22) 274250; f. 1953; publications in the field of tourism, sports, popular topography, and artistic albums; Dir and Editor-in-Chief EUGENIUSZ SKRZYPEK.

Wydawnictwo Spotkania: 00-265 Warsaw, ul. Piwna 44; tel. (22) 313733; telex 817180; f. 1976 (outside Poland), f. 1990 (officially in Poland); memoirs, books on history, including military history, albums, postcards, cassettes, weekly *Spotkania*; Manager JANUSZ KRUPSKI; Propr PIOTR JEGLIŃSKI.

Wydawnictwo Wiedza Powszechna (Popular Knowledge): 00-054 Warsaw, ul. Jasna 26; tel. (22) 269592; fax (22) 269592; f. 1952; popular scientific books, Polish and foreign language dictionaries, teach-yourself handbooks, foreign language textbooks, encyclopaedias and lexicons; Dir JÓZEF CHLABICZ; Editor-in-Chief JANUSZ SIKORSKI.

Zakład Narodowy im. Ossolińskich, Wydawnictwo Polskiej Akademii Nauk (Ossolineum—Publishing House of the Polish Academy of Sciences): 50-106 Wrocław, Rynek 9; tel. (71) 38625; telex 712771; fax (71) 448103; f. 1817; humanities and sciences; Dir EUGENIUSZ ADAMCZAK; Editor-in-Chief JAN MIŚ.

Zakład Wydawnictw Statystycznych (Statistical Publishing Establishment): 00-925 Warsaw, Al. Niepodległości 208; tel. (22) 252724; telex 814581; fax (22) 259545; f. 1971; statistics and theory of statistics, periodicals; Dir ANDRZEJ STASIUN.

Zakłady Wydawniczo-Produkcyjne i Handlowe Epoka: 00-018 Warsaw, ul. Hibernia 11; tel. (22) 278081; telex 814725; f. 1957; newspapers, periodicals, political and social publs of Democratic Party (DP); Pres. ADAM KARAS.

PUBLISHERS' ASSOCIATION

Polskie Towarzystwo Wydawców Książek (Polish Association of Book Publishers): 00-048 Warsaw, ul. Mazowiecka 2/4; tel. (22) 260735; f. 1926; Chair. ANDRZEJ KURZ; 3,000 mems.

WRITERS' ORGANIZATION

Agencja Autorska (Authors' Agency): 00-092 Warsaw, ul. Hipoteczna 2; tel. (22) 278396; telex 812470; f. 1964; represents Polish writers, composers, graphic artists and photographers; publishes monographs on contemporary Polish writers, and periodicals; Pres. ANTONI MARIANOWICZ; Dir EWA MICHAŁSKA.

Radio and Television

At the end of 1989 there were 11.1m. radio and 10.1m. television subscribers. By late 1988 3,500 licences for the reception of satellite television had been issued. Legislation passed by the National Assembly in October 1991 brought to an end the state monopoly over broadcasting; a National Council for Radio and Television Broadcasting was to be established.

Polskie Radio i Telewizja (Polish Radio and Television): Komitet do Spraw Radia i Telewizji, 00-950 Warsaw, ul. Woronicza 17, POB 35; tel. (22) 478501; telex 814825 (radio), 815331 (television); Pres. MARIAN TERLECKI; Dir of International Relations Dr SERGIUSZ MIKULICZ.

RADIO

Home Service: there are four national programmes broadcasting 80 hours per day; one long-wave transmitter (2000 kW) broadcasting on 1,321 m; four medium-wave transmitters and 18 relay stations; six VHF transmitters and 29 relay stations covering all four programmes; Head of Radio JAN MAREK OWSIŃSKI.

Foreign Service: Seven transmitters broadcast on seven frequencies on medium-wave, eight transmitters broadcast on seventeen frequencies on short-wave. Beamed programmes in Polish, English, Esperanto, Finnish, Swedish, Danish, German, French, Spanish, Italian, Russian and Arabic.

TELEVISION

There are two national channels, one broadcasting for twelve-and-a-half hours, the other for seven hours per day via 84 transmitters and 134 relay stations. In addition to the various local programmes, there is a regional programme for Katowice (three hours per day).

Poland's first private (commercial) TV station began operating in Wrocław in early 1990.

Finance

(cap. = capital; res = reserves; dep. = deposits; m. = million; amounts in złotys; brs = branches)

BANKING

A major restructuring of the Polish banking system began in 1987, numerous new banks subsequently being established. The Banking Law of January 1989 allowed the involvement of foreigners in Polish banking.

National Bank

Narodowy Bank Polski (National Bank of Poland): Head Office: 00-950 Warsaw, ul. Świętokrzyska 11/21, POB 10-11; tel. (22) 200321; telex 814681; fax (22) 265645; f. 1945; state central bank; 62 brs throughout Poland; since 1988 nine independent regional banks, two state banks, one state co-operative bank, two foreign banks and 64 commercial banks (joint-stock companies, including six with foreign capital) have been granted licences by the National Bank; Pres. (vacant).

Other Banks

Bank-Agrobank SA: 04-141 Warsaw 44, ul. Grochowska 262, POB 2; tel. (22) 103084; telex 816871; fax (22) 101404; f. 1989; Pres. ALEKSY MISIEJUK.

Bank Depozytowo-Kredytowy w Lublinie (Deposit and Credit Bank in Lublin): 20-928 Lublin, ul. Chopina 6, POB 180; tel. (81) 20081; telex 0643515; fax (81) 24085; f. 1989; Pres. WŁODZIMIERZ KOSACKI.

Bank Gdański: 80-958 Gdańsk, ul. Targ Drzewny 1, POB 436; tel. (58) 311611; telex 0512896; fax (58) 317361; f. 1989; Pres. JAN CESARZ; 47 brs.

Bank Gospodarki Żywnościowej (Bank of Food Economy): 00-916 Warsaw, ul. Świętokrzyska 12; tel. (22) 262830; telex 813869; fax (22) 206112; f. 1975; finances agriculture, forestry and food processing; Pres. JANUSZ CICHOSZ; 95 brs.

Bank Gospodarstwa Krajowego: 00-901 Warsaw, Pałac Kultury i Nauki; tel. (22) 200211; telex 813232; fax (22) 266550; f. 1989; cap. 52,592m., dep. 46,500m.; Pres. CZESŁAW GAWŁOWSKI.

Bank Handlowo-Kredytowy SA: 40-163 Katowice, Plac Gwarków 1, POB 189; tel. (32) 592542; telex 315792; fax (32) 582410; f. 1990; Pres. FRANCISZEK SOBCZAK; brs in Szczecin, Warsaw, Wrocław and Zielona Góra.

Bank Handlowy w Warszawie SA: 00-950 Warsaw, ul. Chałubińskiego 8, POB 129; tel. (22) 303000; telex 814811; fax (22) 300113; f. 1870; authorized foreign exchange bank; cap. 41,000m., res 3,444,386m., dep. 251,410,936m. (Dec. 1989); Pres. CEZARY STYPULKOWSKI; brs throughout Poland; br. in London; offices in New York and Belgrade.

Bank Inicjatyw Gospodarczych SA: 00-950 Warsaw, Al. Jerozolimskie 44, POB 97; tel. (22) 274797; telex 814869; fax (22) 270013; f. 1989; 51% privatized in early 1990; Pres. BOGUSŁAW KOTT.

Bank Polska Kasa Opieki SA (Pekao SA): 00-950 Warsaw, ul. Traugutta 7/9, POB 1008; tel. (22) 269211; telex 817755; fax (22) 261187; f. 1929; state savings bank; domestic and foreign business; cap. 10,000m., res 46,157m., dep. 2,275,052m. (1989); Pres. MARIAN KANTON; Chair. JANUSZ SAWICKI; 21 brs and about 80 offices throughout Poland; also represented in New York, Paris and Tel-Aviv; affiliated companies in USA, Canada, Germany and Australia.

Bank Przemysłowo-Handlowy w Krakowie (Industrial and Commercial Bank in Kraków): 30-960 Kraków, ul. św. Tomasza 43; tel. (12) 223333; telex 0326426; fax (12) 216914; f. 1989; Pres. JANUSZ QUANDT.

Bank Rozwoju Eksportu SA (Export Development Bank SA): 00-950 Warsaw, Al. Jerozolimskie 65/69; tel. (22) 300857; telex 817118; fax (22) 300859; f. 1986; joint-stock co, with Ministry of Foreign Trade as main shareholder; privatization in progress in 1991; provides credit for ventures that promote export growth; cap. 5,000m.; Pres. KRZYSZTOF SZWARC.

Bank Rozwoju Rolnictwa SA: 61-773 Poznań, ul. Stary Rynek 85/86; telex 413218; fax (61) 525194; f. 1990; commercial bank; cap. 100,000m., dep. 153,000m.; Pres. JERZY MAŁECKI; 20 brs.

Bank Rozwoju Rzemiosła, Handlu i Przemysłu Market SA: 61-773 Poznań, Stary Rynek 73/74, POB 72; tel. (61) 528231; telex 0413375; fax (61) 521316; Pres. ERYK WOJCIECHOWSKI.

Bank Śląski w Katowicach (Silesian Bank in Katowice): 40-950 Katowice, ul. Warszawska 14, POB 137; tel. (32) 537281; telex

0312727; fax (32) 537364; f. 1989; commercial bank; cap. 1,992,593m., dep. 8,391,656m.; Pres. MARIAN RAJCZYK; 4 brs.

Bank Turistyki SA: 00-030 Warsaw, Plac Powstancow Warszawy 2; tel. (22) 261452; telex 813915; fax (22) 6256226; commercial bank for tourism industry; Pres. STANISŁAW KOMAN.

Bank Zachódni we Wrocławiu (Western Bank in Wrocław): 50-950 Wrocław, ul. Ofiar Oświęcimskich 41/43, POB 1109; tel. (71) 446621; telex 0715578; fax (71) 34917; f. 1989; Pres. TADEUSZ GŁUSZCZUK.

Bank Ziemi Radomskiej SA: 26-600 Radom, ul. Zeromskiego 75; tel. (48) 455271; telex 067606; Pres. JANUSZ KALOTKA.

Bydgoski Bank Komunalny SA: 85-097 Bydgoszcz, ul. Jagiellońska 34; tel. (52) 229061; telex 0562395; fax (52) 221902; f. 1989; commercial bank; cap. 52,214m., dep. 697,928m. (June 1991); Pres. ROMUALD MEYER; 9 brs.

Łódzki Bank Rozwoju SA: 90-950 Łódź, ul. Piotrkowska 173, POB 465; tel. (42) 365266; telex 885657; fax (42) 375893; f. 1988; Pres. JANUSZ ŁUCKI.

Panstwowy Bank Kredytowy w Warszawie (State Credit Bank in Warsaw): 00-950 Warsaw, ul. Nowogrodzka 35/41, POB 9; tel. (22) 297221; telex 814736; fax (22) 296988; f. 1989; Pres. JANUSZ BIENIEK.

Pomorski Bank Kredytowy w Szczecinie (Pomeranian Credit Bank in Szczecin): 70-952 Szczecin, Pl. Zolnierza 16, POB 613; tel. (91) 400290; telex 0422239; fax (91) 533114; f. 1989; Pres. TADEUSZ ZYWCZAK.

Powszechna Kasa Oszczędności—Bank Państwy (National Savings Bank—State Authority): 00-950 Warsaw, ul. Swietokrzyska 11/21; tel. (22) 200321; telex 814681; fax (22) 263863; f. 1988; Pres. MARIAN KRZAK.

Powszechny Bank Gospodarczy w Łodzi (Universal Economic Bank in Łódź): 90-950 Łódź, ul. Roosevelta 15, POB 12; tel. (42) 329440; telex 885411; fax (42) 365044; f. 1989; Pres. ANDRZEJ SZUKALSKI.

Prosper-Bank SA w Krakowie: 30-960 Kraków, ul. Solskiego 43; tel. (12) 225872; telex 0325403; f. 1990; Pres. ADAM KAWALEC.

Warszawski Bank Zachodni SA: 00-953 Warsaw 37, ul. Ordynacka 11, POB 16; tel. (22) 287261; telex 813438; Agent RYSZARD SLAZAK.

Wielkopolski Bank Kredytowy w Poznaniu (Credit Bank in Poznań): 60-967 Poznań 9, Pl. Wolności 15, POB 516; tel. (61) 521031; telex 0414501; fax (61) 521113; f. 1989; Pres. FRANCISZEK POSPIECH.

Foreign Banks

By the end of 1990 many foreign banks, including Banque Nationale de Paris, Société Générale (France), Deutsche Bank AG, Dresdner Bank AG (Germany), Banca Commerciale Italiana (Italy) and Citibank NA (USA) had opened representative offices in Poland. The Bank Amerykański w Polsce SA (American Bank in Poland) was established in late 1989 with US and Polish capital.

STOCK EXCHANGES

The stock-exchange service was re-established in January 1990. A securities exchange was also planned.

Warsaw Stock Exchange: 00-920 Warsaw, Nowy Świat 6; opened for trading in 1991; Pres. WIESŁAW ROZLUCKI.

INSURANCE

Until 1991 the Polish insurance market was dominated by Polish National Insurance (Państwowy Zakład Ubezpieceń—PZU), which had 60% of business, and Warta Insurance and Reinsurance, which had 30%; the remaining 10% was held by about 20 recently-created private insurance companies. PZU was due to be privatized and replace by smaller, more specialized, companies during 1992.

Państwowy Zakład Ubezpieczeń—PZU (Polish National Insurance): 00-916 Warsaw, ul. Traugutta 5; tel. (22) 269115; telex 814487; fax (22) 269743; f. 1803; state insurance company dealing in all types of insurance; Chair. KRZYSZTOF JARMUSZCZAK; 400 brs.

Towarzystwo Ubezpieczeń i Reasekuracji Warta SA (Warta Insurance and Reinsurance Co Ltd): 00-916 Warsaw, ul. Traugutta 5A; tel. (22) 272625; telex 813549; fax (22) 273312; f. 1920; marine, air, motor, fire, illness, luggage, technical and credit; deals with all foreign business; Pres. JANUSZ STANISZEWSKI; brs in Gdynia, Katowice, Koszalin, Kraków, Łódź, Olsztyn, Poznań, Szczecin and Warsaw; representatives in London and New York.

Trade and Industry

CHAMBERS OF TRADE

Krajowa Izba Gospodarcza (Polish Chamber of Commerce): Head Office: 00-950 Warsaw, Trębacka 4, POB 361; tel. (22) 260221; telex

814361; fax (22) 274673; 21 regional offices; f. 1949; fmrly Polska Izba Handlu Zagranicznego; Pres. ANDRZEJ ARENDARSKI.

The Chamber of Industry and Trade of Foreign Investors and the Economic Chamber of Private Industry were founded in 1989.

FOREIGN TRADE ORGANIZATIONS AND MAJOR COMPANIES

Under new measures introduced in 1982, foreign trade organizations, hitherto operating as state enterprises, began a conversion into joint-stock companies with limited liability, the former Ministry of Foreign Trade holding 51% of the stock and producers and commercial enterprises holding 49%.

Agromet-Motoimport Spółka z o.o.: 00-950 Warsaw, Plac Bankowy 2, POB 990; tel. (22) 285071; telex 813665; fax (22) 284180; import and export of agricultural machinery and equipment; Gen. Dir STANISŁAW RUBAJ.

Agros Spółka z o.o.: 00-950 Warsaw, Chałubińskiego 8, POB P-41; tel. (22) 300614; telex 814391; fax (22) 300791; import of tea, coffee, cocoa beans, tobacco products, citrus fruit, alcoholic drinks, wines, dried fruit and spices; export of vodkas, beer, wines, tobacco, confectionery, fruits, vegetables, etc.

   Agros Holding SA: 00-913 Warsaw, ul. Stawki 2; tel. (2) 6357618; telex 813654; fax (2) 6358428; Gen. Dir ZOFIA GABER-SOBIERALSKA.

Animex Export-Import, Spółka z o.o.: 00-613 Warsaw, Chałubińskiego 8; tel. (22) 300810; telex 814491; fax (22) 300537; imports and exports slaughtering and breeding animals, meat and meat products, poultry, game; Dir WITOLD PERETA.

Ars Polona: 00-068 Warsaw, Krakowskie Przedmieście 7, POB 1001; tel. (22) 261201; telex 813498; fax (22) 266240; import and export of books, newspapers, stamps, coins, musical instruments, records, contemporary works of art and silver jewellery; Dir JANUSZ PALACZ.

AUTOSAN—Sanocka Fabryka Autobusow: 38-500 Sanok, ul. Lipinskiego 109; tel. (137) 50126; telex 065577; fax (137) 50430; manufacture and export of motor buses, and agricultural and goods trailers; Gen. Dir JAN WILK.

Azoty Pulawy—Zakłady Azotowe Pulawy w Pulawach: 24-110 Pulawy, Al. 1000-lecia, Panstwa Polskiego 13; tel. 5555; telex 642316; fax 5444; chemicals, incl. fertilizers, melamine, nitrates and polyethelene; Gen. Dir JOZEF KIJOWSKI.

Baltona SA: 81-963 Gdynia, Pułaskiego 6, POB 365; tel. (58) 202357; telex 054361; fax (58) 203825; f. 1946; import and export of food and industrial goods; supplier to retail shops, ships, airlines, duty-free shops, diplomatic offices; Pres. and Gen. Dir JERZY MROZOWICKI.

Befama: 43-300 Bielsko Biała, Powstańców Śląskich 6; tel. (30) 23061; telex 35333; fax (30) 21293; f. 1851; textile machinery; Man. Dir ANDRZEJ JEREMIENKO.

Bomis Spółka z o.o.: 00-926 Warsaw, ul. Zurawia 6/12; tel. (22) 288181; telex 812773; fax (22) 295354; exports and imports machines, raw and reclaimed materials; co-operation in trade turnover, custom storehouses; Dir ZYGMUNT MAJZEL.

Budex: 42-200 Częstochowa, Sobieskiego 9; tel. (34) 44627; telex 037443; fax (34) 44761; civil and industrial construction; Gen. Dir LECH REGULSKI.

Budimex Spółka z o.o.: 00-926 Warsaw, Marszałkowska 82; tel. (22) 292397; telex 813473; fax (22) 213853; industrial building, civil engineering, housing, assembly works, land reclamation; Dir GRZEGORZ TUDEREK.

Bumar-Labedy: 44-109 Gilwice, ul. Mechanikow 9; tel. (32) 345111; telex 036553; fax (32) 346966; steel machinery and parts for agriculture and construction; Gen. Dir RYSZARD JANKOWSKI.

Bumar Spółka z o.o.: 00-828 Warsaw, Marchlewskiego 11, POB 85; tel. (22) 204661; telex 814805; fax (22) 243670; construction equipment; Dir BOGUSŁAW JARZYŃSKI.

H. Cegielski: 60-965 Poznań, ul. 28 Czerwca 1956 r. 223/229; tel. (61) 333954; telex 0413451; fax (61) 321541; f. 1846; exports power equipment, marine engines, railway locomotives and carriages, etc.; Dir IRENEUSZ PINCZAK.

Centromor SA: 80-819 Gdańsk, ul. Okopowa 7; tel. (58) 312271; telex 512161; fax (58) 319428; f. 1950; import and export of ships and marine equipment; Man. Dir RYSZARD FERWORN.

Centrozap Spółka z o.o.: 40-085 Katowice, ul. Mickiewicza 29; tel. (32) 513401; telex 0315771; fax (32) 598658; imports and exports complete plants, machines and equipment for the metallurgical, foundry and mining industries, air conditioning, etc.; Dir-Gen. HENRYK KALITA.

Cepelia Spółka z o.o.: 00-950 Warsaw, ul. Łucka 11; tel. (22) 205001; telex 813671; fax (22) 204002; export of artistic and folk handicraft articles; Man. Dir WIESŁAW WINIARSKI.

Chemobudowa: 30-104 Kraków, ul. Stachowicza 18, POB 7; tel. (12) 228066; telex 0322371; fax (12) 210333; industrial construction; Dir-Gen. ANDRZEJ LUDWIKOWSKI.

Ciech Spółka z o.o.: 00-950 Warsaw, Jasna 12, POB 271; tel. (22) 269001; telex 814561; fax (22) 266940; imports and exports organic and inorganic chemicals, dyestuffs, fertilizers, paints, varnishes, enamels, cosmetics, petroleum products, rubber and synthetic rubber products, plastics, sulphur and pharmaceutical products; Dir MARIAN MAŁECKI.

Confexim Spółka z o.o.: 90-950 Łódź, ul. Kościuszki 123; tel. (42) 363522; telex 886877; fax (42) 363045; import and export of garments, fabrics and other textile products; Gen. Dir ANDRZEJ KEMP.

Coopexim Spółka z o.o.: 00-975 Warsaw, Puławska 14, POB 215; tel. (22) 494851; telex 814211; import and export of household goods, toys, folk art; Dir PRZEMYSŁAW DELATKIEWICZ.

M. Czarnecki SA: 00-950 Warsaw, ul. Marszałkowska 87, POB 215; tel. (2) 6280296; telex 813278; fax (22) 295943; representation of foreign firms in Poland; Dir TADEUSZ WYZGAL.

Dal SA: 00-683 Warsaw, Al. Jerozolimskie 65/79; tel. (22) 300460; telex 817226; fax (22) 300461; international trading company, barter and compensation transactions, mediation through its affiliated companies all over the world; Dir MAREK PIETKIEWICZ.

Diora: 58-200 Dzierzoniow, ul. Swidnicka 38; tel. (74) 322200; telex 0745231; fax (74) 318561; audio and visual electronic equipment; Chair. and Gen. Dir EUGENIUS NOWAK.

Dromex: 02-105 Warsaw, Trojańska 7; tel. (22) 463901; telex 815473; fax (22) 461319; f. 1967; export of road, bridge, railway and airfield construction work; Gen. Man. JERZY TREPIŃSKI.

Dynamo: 00-950 Warsaw, ul. Stawki 2; tel. (2) 6356864; telex 813428; fax (2) 6356838; import-export and barter business, representation of foreign firms in Poland; Dir HENRYK KOZIARA.

Elana: 87-100 Toruń, Curie-Skłodowskiej 73; tel. (56) 484345; telex 0555161; fax (56) 398406; synthetic fibres; Gen. Dir STANISŁAW CZUSZEL.

Elektrim Spółka z o.o.: 00-950 Warsaw, Chałubińskiego 8, POB 638; tel. (22) 301000; telex 814351; fax (22) 300841; f. 1945; imports and exports power engineering technology, transmission, electrical and telecommunication equipment; Man. Dir ANDRZEJ SKOWROŃSKI.

Elwro: 53-238 Wrocław, Ostrowskiego 30; tel. (71) 610621; telex 0712423; fax (71) 617233; manufacture and export of computer systems, microcomputers, industrial automation and control systems, teleprocessing systems, other computer equipment (hardware and software), calculators, etc.; Man. Dir WŁADYSŁAW KIERZKOWSKI.

Energomontaz-Polnac: 00-950 Warsaw, ul. Nowy Swiat 9; tel. (22) 282392; telex 813429; fax (22) 296324; manufacture and service of power and industrial engineering installations; Man. Dir KAZIMIERZ ZUKOWSKI.

Energopol: 00-950 Warsaw, ul. Nowogrodzka 21, POB 367; tel. (22) 298081; telex 813663; fax (22) 290412; f. 1974; contractors and designers, civil engineering projects, pipelines; Dir JANUSZ GÓRZNY.

Exbud SA: 25-363 Kielce, Wesola 51; tel. (41) 43445; telex 613396; fax (41) 48894; construction company; privatized; Pres. WITOLD ZARASKA.

Eximpol SA: 00-950 Warsaw, Stawki 2, POB 810; tel. (2) 6357641; telex 814640; fax (2) 6353544; representation of foreign firms in Poland; Gen. Dir MAREK DZIUGIEŁŁ.

Expolco Holding SA and Expolco Trading Spółka z o.o.: 01-698 Warsaw, ul. Smoleńska 1/10; tel. (22) 332086; telex 816029; fax (22) 332084; international trade, financial transactions, export of wood, metal and plastic goods, ready-made clothing, knitwear, foodstuffs, technical service; import of consumer goods, materials and instruments; Gen. Dir KRZYSZTOF SRTRZAŁKOWSKI.

Fabryka Samochodow Ciezarowych—FSC: 27-200 Starachowice, ul. Maja 1; tel. 8831; telex 612571; fax 7038; goods vehicles, parts and assemblies; Gen. Dir JANUSZ KROLIKOWSKI.

Fabryka Samochodow Malolitra Zowych—FSM: 43-301 Bielsko-Biala, ul. Komorowicke 79; tel. (30) 20264; telex 0355753; fax (30) 35330; passenger car manufacture (incl. Fiat 126 and Cinquecento).

Fabryka Samochodow Osobowych—FSO: 03-215 Warsaw, ul. Stalingradzka 50; tel. (22) 110211; telex 814571; passenger car manufacture (incl. Fiat 125); Gen. Dir Dr HENRYK OLENIAK.

Film Polski Spółka z o.o.: 00-048 Warsaw, Mazowiecka 6/8; tel. (22) 268455; telex 813640; fax (22) 275784; f. 1964; imports and exports films for television and the cinema, production services, distribution; Gen. Man. LEON WARECKI.

Furnel International Ltd Spółka z o.o.: 00-950 Warsaw, Al. Jerozolimskie 65/69, POB 670; tel. (22) 300467; telex 817543; fax (22) 306525; 8 regional offices; production and export of furniture, wooden goods, electronic and telecommunication equipment; Pres. JAN BANDURSKI.

Gdanska Stocznia Remontowa: Gdańsk 80-958, ul. Ostrowiu 1; tel. (58) 371300; telex 311281; ship repairs and conversions; Gen. Dir PIOTR SOYKA.

Geokart: 00-950 Warsaw, ul. Jasna 2/4; tel. (22) 273278; telex 812770; fax (22) 277629; geodesic and cartographic work and service; Dir JERZY WYSOCKI.

C. Hartwig: 00-950 Warsaw, Poznańska 15, POB 375; tel. (22) 296031; telex 814601; fax (22) 291581; f. 1858; also Katowice, Gdynia, Gdańsk, Szczecin; sole forwarding agent for rail, air, sea, river and road transport; Dir ZYGMUNT KORDECKI.

Hortex: 00-034 Warsaw, ul. Warecka 11A; tel. (22) 277174; telex 816611; fax (22) 270251; exports fresh, frozen and processed fruits and vegetables, forest fruits, mushrooms, honey and flowers, potatoes and potato products, seeds, herbs and snails; imports fresh and processed fruit and vegetables, foodstuffs, manufactured consumer articles, machinery, equipment, etc.; Dir LUDWIK OLEJARZ.

Hortex-Trading Spółka z o.o.: 31-027 Kraków, ul. Legnicka 5; tel. (12) 229801; telex 0322602; export-import and sale of items of food; Dir ADAM BRODOWSKI.

Huta Katowice: 41-303 Dabrowa Gornicza; tel. (32) 622256; telex 0315562; fax (32) 255200; steel mill; Gen. Man. BOHDAN KOLO-MYJSKI.

Huta Sendzimira: 30969 Kraków; tel. (12) 449866; telex 0322441; rolled steel, galvanized steel and steel products.

Huta Stalowa Wola: 37-450 Stalowa Wola, ul. Kwiatkowskiego 1; tel. (16) 435261; telex 062233; fax (16) 425566; heavy construction equipment, steel foundry products; Gen. Dir RYSZARD KAPUSTA.

Impexmetal: 00-842 Warsaw, Łucka 7/9, POB 62; tel. (22) 200201; telex 814371; fax (22) 200544; imports and exports non-ferrous metals, ball and roller bearings; Dir EDWARD WOJTULEWICZ.

Interpegro SA: 03-839 Warsaw, ul. Grochowska 320; tel. (22) 106375; fax (22) 135585; export-import foodstuffs, agricultural products, flowers, fresh and processed fruit and vegetables, electronic, telecommunication equipment and service, etc.; Pres. JAN ZBIG-NIEW HRYNIEWICZ.

Intraco: 00-950 Warsaw, POB 912, ul. Stawki 2; tel. (2) 6356002; telex 812341; fax (2) 6355418; exports building services, interior architecture; imports equipment and spare parts; Dir JERZY PIETRULA.

Kolmex Spółka z o.o.: 00-950 Warsaw, Mokotowska 49, POB 236; tel. (22) 299241; telex 813270; fax (22) 295879; imports and exports railway rolling-stock and containers; Dir ALEKSANDER GUD-ZOWATY.

Kombinat Gorniczo-Hutniczy Miedzi—KGHM: 59-301 Lublin, ul. Curie-Skłodowskiej, m. 48; tel. (81) 461110; telex 782277; fax (81) 461100; mining of copper ore and processing of refined copper; Gen. Dir JAN SADECKI.

Kopex: 40-952 Katowice, Grabowa 1, POB 245; tel. (32) 581631; telex 315681; fax (32) 580040; exports and imports machinery, equipment and appliances for mining, drilling and other engineering industries; consultancy services; Gen. Dir EUGENIUSZ KUCZKA.

Krakowskie Przedsibiorstwo Instalacji Sanitarnych: 31-503 Kraków, ul. Lubicz 27; tel. (12) 211099; telex 0325428; fax (12) 212193; construction of domestic and industrial sanitary installations; Gen. Dir STANISŁAW ZIMNY.

Labimex Spółka z o.o.: 00-950 Warsaw, Krakowskie Przedmieście 79, POB 261; tel. (22) 266431; telex 814230; fax (22) 261941; f. 1973; exports and imports medical, scientific and research apparatus, teaching aids, laboratory equipment, optical and geodetic instruments; Dir-Gen. JERZY RYCHTER.

Mazowieckie Zakłady Rafineryjne i Petrochemiczne: 09-403 Plock, ul. Chemikow 7; tel. (24) 53150; telex 83341; fax (24) 53180; crude petroleum processing and manufacture of petrochemical products; Gen. Dir CZESŁAW DOLASINSKI.

Metalexport Ltd: 00-950 Warsaw, Mokotowska 49, POB 642; tel. (2) 6282291; telex 814241; fax (2) 6286561; f. 1949; exports and imports technological equipment, complete engineering plants, tools and machine tools; Dir Dr JERZY ZIELIŃSKI.

Metronex Spółka z o.o.: 00-950 Warsaw, Mysia 2, POB 198; tel. (22) 291699; fax (2) 6288274; exports and imports measurement instruments, process control devices, nuclear engineering equipment, computers, software, office equipment, etc.; Dir ANDRZEJ ZIAJA.

Minex Spółka z o.o.: 00-950 Warsaw, Chałubińskiego 8, POB 1002; tel. (22) 300500; telex 814401; fax (22) 300448; f. 1949; exports and imports minerals, cement, glass and ceramics; Dir JÓZEF KOSTERA.

Mundial SA: 00-957 Warsaw, Czerniakowska 58, POB 23; tel. (22) 416086; telex 813689; fax (22) 402006; representation of foreign firms in Poland; Dir KAZIMIERZ PISZ.

Navimor Spółka z o.o.: 80-890 Gdańsk, ul. Heweliusza 11, POB 423; tel. (58) 316821; telex 0512453; fax (58) 314497; ship repairs, import and export of shipyard installations, floating docks and pontoons, yachts, river vessels and coasters, fishing vessels, marine equipment, motors for small craft; Dir KRZYSZTOF BANASZAK.

Pagart: 00-078 Warsaw, Pl. Marszałka Józefa Piłsudskiego 9; tel. (22) 260145; telex 813639; fax (22) 275397; f. 1957; represents Polish artists abroad and organizes guest performances of foreign artists in Poland; Gen. Dir WŁODZIMIERZ SANDECKI.

Paged: 00-950 Warsaw, Pl. Trzech Krzyży 18, POB 991; tel. (2) 6238100; telex 814221; fax (2) 6281396; f. 1932; imports machinery and equipment for wood and paper industries, exports furniture, pulp and paper, boards and wooden products; Dir-Gen. MIRON TRZECIAK.

Pewex: 00-697 Warsaw, Al. Jerozolimskie 65/79, POB 240; tel. (22) 300170; telex 815404; fax (22) 300172; import of consumer goods, raw materials, etc.; Dir MARIAN W. ZACHARSKI.

Pezetel Spółka z o.o.: 00-991 Warsaw 44, Al. Stanów Zjedno-czonych 61; tel. (22) 108001; telex 812815; fax (22) 132356; import and export of aircraft, helicopters, sailplanes, turboshaft, jet, and radial-piston aircraft engines, diesel engines, generators, air equipment, electric carts, pneumatics, hydraulics, motor cycles, aviation and agricultural services; Dir JERZY KRĘZLEWICZ.

Polcargo Consulting: 81-963 Gdynia, ul. Żeromskiego 32, POB 223; tel. (58) 205371; telex 054247; fax (58) 216819; f. 1949; international superintendence and testing services; Dir SŁAWOMIR PIĄTKOWSKI.

Polcomex SA: 00-061 Warsaw, Marszałkowska 140, POB 478; tel. (22) 266810; telex 813452; fax (22) 278441; representation of foreign firms in Poland; Dir ANDRZEJ ONACIK.

Polcoop SA: 00-950 Warsaw, Kopernika 30, POB 199; tel. (22) 262363; telex 814451; fax (22) 271053; f. 1957; exports foodstuffs, agricultural products, incl. fruit, vegetables and meat; imports fertilizers, fresh and processed fruit and vegetables, machinery, equipment, spare parts, etc.; Pres. JAN WAGA.

Polexpo: 02-232 Warsaw, Łopuszańska 38, POB 125; tel. (22) 460401; telex 813633; fax (22) 464591; f. 1950; design, construction and display of international fairs, exhibitions; Dir JERZY KARAIM.

Poliglob SA: 00-950 Warsaw, ul. Stawki 2, POB 40; tel. (2) 6353689; telex 813557; fax (2) 6353689; f. 1950; representation of foreign firms in Poland; brs in Gdańsk, Katowice and Łódź; Dir RYSZARD JAROSZYŃSKI.

Polimar SA: 00-950 Warsaw, ul. Stawki 2, POB 151; tel. (2) 6350187; telex 814895; fax (2) 6355154; international trading company; Dir WALERIAN CHRYSZCZANOWICZ.

Polimex-Cekop Spółka z o.o.: 00-950 Warsaw, Czackiego 7/9, POB 815; tel. (22) 268001; telex 814231; fax (22) 260493; f. 1945; exports and imports machines and complete plants; Dir MAZIEJ MĘCLEWSKI.

Polmos: 00-006 Warsaw, ul. Szkolna 2/4, POB 160; tel. (22) 265031; telex 813445; alcoholic beverages.

POL-MOT Co Ltd: 03-370 Warsaw, Stalingradzka 23; tel. (22) 111093; telex 813901; fax (22) 111826; f. 1968; import and export of cars, lorries, buses, service stations, repair equipment, etc.; Gen. Dir ANDRZEJ ZARAJCZYK.

Polservice: 00-613 Warsaw, Chałubinskiego 8; tel. (22) 300522; telex 813539; fax (22) 300076; export and import of consulting and technical services, transfer of technology; Dir JERZY FIJAŁKOWSKI.

Polskie Wydawnictwo Muzyczne: 00-097 Warsaw, ul. Fredry 8; tel. (2) 6353550, Ext. 274; telex 813370; f. 1945; import and export of musical material; Dir ADAM NEUER; see also under Publishers.

PZL-Mielec Wytwornia Sprzetu Komunikacyjnego—WSK-Mielec: 39-300 Mielec, ul. Wojska Polskiego 3; tel. (196) 7819; telex 632293; fax (196) 7451; aircraft manufacturer; Gen. Dir JAN M. SZYMAŃSKI.

Remex Spółka z o.o.: 00-950 Warsaw, Bracka 25; tel. (22) 276021; telex 815387; fax (22) 274472; f. 1977; export of Polish handicraft articles and services; Gen. Dir JÓZEF GŁOWANIA.

Rolimpex: 00-613 Warsaw, ul. Chałubińskiego 8, POB 364; tel. (22) 300636; telex 814341; fax (22) 301867; f. 1951; exports and imports agricultural products of vegetable origin; Dir ROMAN MŁYNIEC.

RYBEX Co Ltd: 70-656 Szczecin, ul. Energetyków 3/4; tel. (91) 624490; telex 0422326; fax (91) 342–47; sole exporter and importer of fish and fish products; exports technical service for fishing and fish processing; Gen. Man. WOJCIECH POLACZEK.

Shipcontrol: 81-334 Gdynia, Polska 21; tel. (58) 207096; telex 054271; fax (58) 210212; f. 1963; tallying, weighing and gauging of cargo, stowage plans and supervision, inspection of containers, etc.; Dir BOGDAN OBSZARSKI.

Skórimpex Spółka z o.o.: 90-950 Łódź, Piotrkowska 148/150, POB 133; tel. (42) 363833; telex 885251; fax (42) 364229; imports skins, hides, leathers, footwear, fur and leather goods, etc.; exports shoes, leather, fur and sheepskin garments, skins, hides, etc.; Dir IRENEUSZ MINTUS.

Spedrapid Spółka z o.o.: 81-361 Gdynia, Zgoda 8, POB 201; tel. (58) 216085; telex 054321; fax (58) 216614; f. 1949; Polish-Czech forwarding company; Chair. PAVEL MÜLLER; Dir WITOLD GÓRSKI.

Stalexport: 40-085 Katowice, Mickiewicza 29, POB 401; tel. (32) 512211; telex 0315751; fax (32) 511941; exports and imports rolled steel products, high quality steel, tubes, ores, pig iron, ferro alloys, power-generating units, ceramic tiles; Gen. Dir RYSZARD HARHALA.

SGS-PTK Supervise Ltd: 81-369 Gdynia, Derdowskiego 7, POB 167; tel. (58) 206001; telex 054446; fax (58) 207975; f. 1947; quality and quantity control, supervisions, appraisals and evaluations for privatizations and joint ventures, environmental services; Dir MAREK SZWAJ.

Textilimpex Spółka z o.o.: 90-950 Łódź, ul. Traugutta 25, POB 320; tel. (42) 361638; telex 886471; fax (42) 788375; import and export of textile goods and raw materials for the textile industry; Dir DONAT ŁAWNICZAK.

Timex SA: 00-193 Warsaw, Stawki 2, POB 268; tel. (2) 6356202; telex 813678; fax (2) 356018; f. 1947; import, export and representation of foreign firms; Dir STANISŁAW LESZKOWICZ.

Torimex Spółka z o.o.: 00-691 Warsaw, ul. Nowogrodzka 35/41, POB 394; tel. (22) 216652; telex 813611; fax (22) 211796; import and export within exchange market, suppliers of stores in Poland and abroad with imported consumer goods, compensatory transactions, rustic restaurant interiors; Dir RYSZARD BACHURA.

Transactor SA: 00-950 Warsaw, Stawki 2, POB 276; tel. (2) 6355221; telex 813288; fax (2) 6357017; representation of foreign firms in Poland; Gen. Dir STANISŁAW JAKUBCZYK.

Tricot Spółka z o.o.: 90-361 Łódź, ul. Piotrkowska 270, POB 278; tel. (42) 810211; telex 884545; fax (42) 817936; became limited liability company in Jan. 1983, continuing activities of former state-owned Textilimpex-Tricot; import and export of textile goods, especially knitwear; Man. Dir ANDRZEJ MORYC.

Unitech: 02-237 Warsaw, ul. Instalatorów 7; tel. (22) 464078; telex 825524; marine service bureau; servicing of equipment on ships in foreign and Polish ports; brs in Gdynia and Szczecin; Man. Dir JERZY JACNIACKI.

Unitex SA: 00-950 Warsaw, Stawki 2, POB 404; tel. (2) 6353619; telex 817478; fax (2) 6356545; Dir CZESŁAW GRAD.

UNITRA Trading and Industrial Corporation: 00-950 Warsaw, ul. Nowogrodzka 50, POB 66; tel. (22) 213382; telex 814878; fax (22) 214761; hi-tech equipment, industrial systems, electronic and other goods; consultancy and promotional services; Dir JAN BRUKSZO.

Universal SA: 00-950 Warsaw, Al. Jerozolimskie 44, POB 370; tel. (2) 6936091; telex 814431; fax (22) 278312; export and import of electrical household appliances, metal, plastic and glass household goods, sports and camping equipment, metal goods, food and agricultural products, chemical goods; Gen. Dir DARIUSZ PRZYWIE-CZERSKI.

> **Universal-Kraktrade SA:** 30-960 Kraków, ul. Floriańska 3, POB 181; tel. (12) 222398; telex 0326335; fax (12) 222398; export and import of commercial articles, building design and consultancy services, etc.; Dir MAREK STRUTYŃSKI.

Ursus: 02-945 Warsaw, Traktorzystów 10; tel. (2) 6626713; telex 813939; fax (2) 6670545; tractor manufacturers; Gen. Dir (vacant).

Varimex: 00-950 Warsaw, Wilcza 50/52, POB 263; tel. (22) 288041; telex 814311; fax (22) 218519; f. 1945; import and export of medical and photographic equipment, valves and fittings, fire-fighting equipment, building hardware, catering and typographic equipment; import of textile machines; Dir ANDRZEJ SOBCZYK.

Węglokoks: 40-185 Katowice, ul. A. Mickiewicza 29; tel. (32) 582431; telex 0315641; fax (32) 515453; imports and exports coal, coke, gas; Dir JAN BARAŃSKI.

Zakłady Włokien Chemicznych Wistom—Chemitex-Wistom: 97-200 Tomaszów Mazowiecki, ul. Zubrzyckiego 103/105; tel. 2301; telex 886214; fax 5248; synthetic fibres; Gen. Man. ANDRZEJ KRZEMIŃSKI.

ZELMER—Zakłady Zmechanizowanego Sprzetu Domwego: 35-016 Rzeszów, ul. Hoffmanowej 19; tel. (17) 37431; telex 0632389; fax (17) 36178; domestic and kitchen appliances.

TRADE UNIONS

In April 1989, after two months of 'round-table' talks, Solidarność and the Government reached agreement on extensive political and economic reforms, as a result of which legal status (removed upon the declaration of martial law in December 1981) was restored to Solidarność and to Rural Solidarity, the independent farmers' union.

Ogólnopolskie Porozumienie Związków Zawodowych—OPZZ (All Poland Trade Unions Alliance): 00-924 Warsaw, Kopernika 36/40; tel. (22) 260231; telex 813834; fax (22) 265102; f. 1984; 5.2m. mems (1990); Chair. (vacant); Vice-Chair. EWA SPYCHALSKA.

Solidarność (Solidarity): 80-855 Gdańsk, Wały Piastowskie 24; tel. (58) 316722; telex 513170; fax (58) 316722; f. 1980; outlawed 1981–89; 2.5m. mems; Chair. MARIAN KRZAKLEWSKI.

> **Rural Solidarity:** Leader GABRIEL JANOWSKI.

TRADE FAIRS

Poznań International Fairs: 60-734 Poznań, ul. Głogowska 14; tel. (61) 692592; telex 413251; fax (61) 665827; f. 1921; international general fair yearly in June, with about 40 countries represented each year; also various specialized national and international fairs in Poznań and Katowice; Gen. Dir STANISŁAW LASKOWSKI.

Transport

RAILWAYS

At the end of 1989 there were 26,644 km of railway lines making up the state network, of which 11,016 km were electrified and 2,357 km were narrow gauge. Substantial modernization, with assistance from the World Bank and other sources, was planned for the 1990s.

Polskie Koleje Państwowe (Polish State Railways): 00-928 Warsaw, ul. Chałubińskiego 4; tel. (22) 244400; telex 813898; fax (22) 212705; f. 1842.

ROADS

In 1989 there were 159,000 km of hard-surfaced, public roads, of which 139,000 km were macadamized.

PKS/Państwowa Komunikacja Samochodowa (Polish Motor Communications): 00-973 Warsaw, ul. Grójecka 17; tel. (22) 220011; telex 816598; f. 1945; state enterprise organizing inland road transport for passengers and goods. Bus routes cover a total of 121,000 km; passengers carried 2,553,968 (1989); freight 7,650m. ton-kilometres (1989).

Pekaes Auto-Transport: 00-950 Warsaw, ul. Świętokrzyska 30; tel. (22) 242813; telex 816201; f. 1958; road transport of goods to all European and Middle East countries.

INLAND WATERWAYS

Poland has 6,850 km of waterways, of which 3,997 km were navigable in 1989. The main rivers are the Vistula (1,047 km), Oder (742 km in Poland), Bug (587 km in Poland), Warta (808 km), San, Narew, Noteć, Pilica, Wieprz and the Dunajec. There are some 5,000 lakes, the largest being the Śniardwy, Mamry, Łebsko, Dąbie and Miedwie. In addition, there is a network of canals (approximately 1,215 km).

About 5,770,000 passengers and 14,040,000 tons of freight were carried on inland water transport in 1989.

Zjednoczenie Żeglugi Śródlądowej (United Inland Navigation and River Shipyards): 50-149 Wrocław 2, Wita Stwosza 28; includes five inland navigation enterprises and eight inland shipyards.

SHIPPING

Poland has three large harbours on the Baltic sea: Gdynia, Gdańsk and Szczecin. The Polish merchant fleet had 249 ships in December 1989, with a total displacement of 3,079,000 grt (excluding fishing vessels).

Principal shipping companies:

Polskie Linie Oceaniczne—PLO (Polish Ocean Lines): 81-364 Gdynia, ul. 10 Lutego 24, POB 265; tel. (58) 201901; telex 054231; fax (58) 278480; f. 1951; 97 ships totalling 920,000 dwt and serving all five continents; Dir-Gen. HENRYK DĄBROWSKI; Exec. Dir ALEKSANDER RUBIN.

Polska Żegluga Morska—PZM (Polish Steamship Co): 70-515 Szczecin, ul. Małopolska 44; tel. (91) 305011; telex 422136; fax (91) 39764; f. 1951; world-wide tramping; fleet of 34 vessels totalling 610,388 dwt (1988); Chair. and Dir-Gen. MIECZYSŁAW ANDRUCZYK.

Przedsiębiorstwo Połowów Dalekomorskich i Usług Rybackich Gryf: 70-952 Szczecin, Port Rybacki, ul. Władysława IV 1; tel. (91) 533772; telex 0425491; fax (91) 47989; deep-sea fishing and fish processing; Man. Dir PIOTR JASNOWSKI.

CIVIL AVIATION

Okęcie international airport is situated near Warsaw. A city terminal was completed in October 1989 under a joint-venture scheme with an Austrian and a US company. A new airport terminal was scheduled for completion in 1992. Domestic flights serve Częstochowa, Gdańsk, Katowice, Koszalin, Kraków, Poznań, Rzeszów, Słupsk, Szczecin, Warsaw and Wrocław. In January 1989 it was announced that a new airport was to be built at Koszalin. A new international airport at Goleniow was due to open in 1991.

Polskie Linie Lotnicze—LOT (Polish Airlines—LOT): 00-697 Warsaw, Al. Jerozolimskie 65/79; tel. (22) 283443; telex 813552; fax (22) 305860; f. 1929; domestic services and international services to the Middle East, Africa, Asia, Canada, USA, Australia and throughout Europe; privatization announced, Feb. 1991; Dir-Gen. BRONISŁAW KLIMASZEWSKI; fleet of 3 Boeing 767, 7 Il-62M, 3 Il-18, 10 An-24, 7 Tu-134A, 14 Tu-154M.

Tourism

The Polish Tourist and Country Lovers' Society is responsible for tourism and itself maintains about 250 tourist hotels and hostels throughout the country. Poland is rich in historic cities, such as Wrocław, Kraków and Warsaw. There are 30 health and climatic resorts, while the mountains, forests and rivers provide splendid scenery and excellent facilities for sporting holidays. In 1989 Poland was visited by 8.2m. foreign tourists, 19% of whom were from Western countries.

Polskie Towarzystwo Turystyczno-Krajoznawcze (Polish Tourist and Country-Lovers' Society): 00-075 Warsaw, ul. Senatorska 11; tel. (22) 265735; telex 812441; fax (22) 262505; f. 1950; Chair. MAREK DĄBROWSKI; the Society has about 260 tourist accommodation establishments; 484,617 mems (1990).

Orbis SA: 00-193 Warsaw, Stawki 2; tel. (2) 6357123; telex 814757; fax (2) 6355621; f. 1923; national tourist enterprise; Gen. Man. RYSZARD CETNARSKI; 180 branch offices and 54 tourist hotels.

Atomic Energy

In 1990 the nuclear power programme was suspended until at least the year 2000. Poland's first nuclear power station was due to open at Zarnowiec in 1991, but construction work was formally abandoned in 1990, owing to financial difficulties. A second station (with a planned generating capacity of 4,000 MW) was to be built at the Warta basin, near Klempicz, but the project was also suspended. Co-operation agreements have been signed with many countries. Poland is a member of the International Atomic Energy Agency, Vienna, and of the Joint Institute for Nuclear Research, Dubna, near Moscow.

Państwowa Agencja Atomistyki (National Atomic Energy Agency): 00-921 Warsaw, ul. Krucza 36; tel. (2) 6280281; telex 816915; fax (22) 290164; Pres. Prof. ROMAN ZELAZNY.

Instytut Energii Atomowej (Institute of Atomic Energy): 05-400 Otwock-Świerk; tel. (22) 793888; telex 813244; fax (22) 793888; f. 1983 (fmrly Institute of Nuclear Research); reactor technology, gas-cooled power reactors, nuclear heating plants, electronic reactor systems, raw materials and fuel for reactor power industry, nuclear safety, waste disposal, etc.; Dir Prof. STEFAN CHWASZCZEWSKI.

Instytut Chemii i Techniki Jądrowej (Institute of Nuclear Chemistry and Technology): 03-195 Warsaw, ul. Dorodna 16; tel. (22) 110656; telex 813027; fax (22) 111532; f. 1983 (fmrly part of Institute of Nuclear Research, f. 1956); nuclear, radiation and analytical chemistry, radiobiology, isotope and radiation techniques and technologies; environmental protection; material and structural studies; Dir Dr LECH WALIŚ.

Instytut Fizyki Jądrowej im. Henryka Niewodniczańskiego (Henryk Niewodniczański Institute of Nuclear Physics): 31-342 Kraków, ul. Radzikowskiego 152; tel. (12) 370222; telex 0322461; f. 1955; department covering high and low energy nuclear physics, structural investigations and applied physics; Dir Prof. ANDRZEJ BUDZANOWSKI.

Instytut Problemów Jądrowych im. A. Sołtana (Sołtan Institute for Nuclear Studies): 05-400 Otwock-Świerk; tel. (22) 798948; telex 813244; fax (22) 793481; f. 1983; nuclear physics, radiation research, etc.; Dir Prof. Dr WOJCIECH RATYŃSKI.

Culture

NATIONAL ORGANIZATIONS

Ministry of Culture: see section on The Government (Ministries); includes:

Institute of Culture (Instytut Kultury): 00-075 Warsaw, ul. Senatorska 13/15; tel. (22) 262477; fax (22) 261069; f. 1974; research centre for Polish culture; Dir Prof. TERESA KOSTYRKO.

Polish Cultural Foundation (Fundacja Kultury Polskiej): 00-252 Warsaw, ul. Podwale 1/3; tel. (2) 6357628; telex 812732; f. 1988; promotes Polish culture of all kinds both in Poland and world-wide; Chair. Prof. STANISŁAW WISŁOCKI; Pres. Dr TADEUSZ POLAK.

CULTURAL HERITAGE

History Museum of the City of Kraków (Muzeum Historyczne m. Krakowa): 31-011 Kraków, Krzysztofory, Rynek Główny 35; tel. (12) 223264; f. 1899; Dir ANDRZEJ SZCZYGIEŁ.

History Museum of the City of Warsaw (Muzeum Historyczne m. st. Warszawy): 00-272 Warsaw, Rynek Starego Miasta 28; tel. (2) 6351625; f. 1947; collections covering the history of Warsaw from the 10th century onwards; Dir JANINA BALCERZAK.

Jagiellonian Library (Biblioteka Jagiellońska): 30-059 Kraków, ul. Mickiewicza 22; tel. (12) 336377; telex 325682; f. 1364; national library for books up to 1800; Dir Dr JAN PIROŻYŃSKI.

National Library (Biblioteka Narodowa): 00-973 Warsaw, Al. Niepodległości 213; tel. (22) 259270); telex 817183; f. 1928; Dir Dr STANISŁAW CZAJKA.

National Museum (Muzeum Narodowe): 00-495 Warsaw, Al. Jerozolimskie 3; tel. (22) 211031; f. 1862; historical and art collections; Dir Dr MARIAN SOŁTYSIAK.

National Museum in Kraków (Muzeum Narodowe w Krakowie): 31-109 Kraków, ul. Manifestu Lipcowego 12; tel. (12) 225434; f. 1879; historical and art collections; Dir KAZIMIERZ NOWACKI.

State Archaeological Museum (Państwowe Muzeum Archeologiczne): 00-950 Warsaw, ul. Długa 52; tel. (22) 313221; f. 1923; Dir Dr JAN JASKANIS.

State Ethnographic Museum in Warsaw (Państwowe Muzeum Etnograficzne w Warszawie): 00-056 Warsaw, ul. Kredytowa 1; tel. (22) 277641; f. 1888; Polish and non-European collections; Dir Dr JAN KRZYSZTOF MAKULSKI.

SPORTING ORGANIZATION

Olympic Committee of the Republic of Poland: 00-483 Warsaw, ul. Frascati 4; tel. (2) 6285038; telex 813522; fax (22) 813522; f. 1918; Pres. ALEKSANDER KWASNIEWSKI; Sec.-Gen. TADEUSZ WROBLEWSKI.

PERFORMING ARTS

Theatre

National Folk Theatre of Kraków (Państwowy Teatr Ludowy w Krakowie): 31-943 Kraków, ul. ós Teatralne 34.

Warsaw Contemporary Theatre (Teatr Współczesny w Warszawie): 00-640 Warsaw, ul. Mokotowska 13.

National Theatre of Poland in Warsaw (Państwowy Teatr Polski w Warszawie): 00-327 Warsaw, ul. Karasia 2.

National Modern Theatre in Warsaw (Państwowy Teatr Nowy w Warszawie): 02-503 Warsaw, ul. Puławska 37/39.

Opera Houses

Kraków Opera and Operatta (Opera i Operetka w Krakowie): 31-002 Kraków, ul Skarbowa 2.

Warsaw National Operetta (Państwowa Operetka w Warszawie): Warsaw, ul. Nowogrodzka 49.

Warsaw Chamber Opera (Warszawska Opera Kameralna): Warsaw, ul. Nowogrodzka 49.

Orchestras

Kraków National Philharmonic (Karol Szymanowski) Orchestra (Państwowa Filharmonia im. Karola Szymanowskiego w Krakowie): 31-103 Kraków, ul. Zwierzyniecka 1.

Warsaw National Philharmonic Orchestra (Filharmonia Narodowa w Warszawie): Warsaw, ul. Jasna 5.

ASSOCIATIONS

Plastic Arts Association of Poland (Związek Polskich Artystów Plastyków): 00-554 Warsaw, ul. Marszałkowska 34/50; tel. (22) 211365; Pres. ZBIGNIEW MAKAREWICZ.

Polish Federation of Photographic Societies (Polska Federacja Stowarzyszeń Fotograficznych): 00-566 Warsaw, ul. Sniadeckich 10; tel. (22) 282862; Pres. ANDRZEJ PROTASIUK.

Polish PEN Club (Polski Klub Literacki PEN): 00-079 Warsaw, ul. Krakowskie Przedmieście 87/89; tel. (22) 26-57-84; Pres. ARTUR MIĘDZYRZECKI.

Polish Society of Graphic Arts and Design (Stowarzyszenie Polskich Artystów Grafików, Projektantów): 00-496 Warsaw, ul. Nowy Świat 7, m. 6; tel. (22) 217819; Pres. STANISŁAW WIECZOREK.

Society of Polish Film Artists (Stowarzyszenie Filmowców Polskich): 00-071 Warsaw, ul. Krakowskie Przedmieście 21/23; tel. (22) 276785; Pres. JAN KIDAWA-BŁOŃSKI.

Society of Polish Musicians (Stowarzyszenie Polskich Artystów Muzyków): 00-526 Warsaw, ul. Krucza 24; tel. (22) 218647; Pres. TADEUSZ TRUGAŁA.

Education

Children up to the age of seven years may attend crèches (złobki) and kindergartens (przedszkola). In 1989 49% of children between the ages of three and six years attended kindergarten, with 96% of all six-year olds attending a pre-school establishment. Education is free and compulsory for all children between the ages of seven and 14 years. Basic schooling begins at the age of seven years with the eight-year school (szkoła podstawowa), for which there is a common curriculum throughout the country.

Four years of free education leading to college or university entrance is available at general secondary schools (liceum ogólnokształcące) to pupils who are successful in the entrance examination. Other pupils, about 75% of those continuing their education beyond the age of 14, attend vocational and technical schools (technika zawodowe) or basic vocational schools (zasadnicze szkoły). Vocational and technical schools provide five-year courses combining vocational and general secondary education, and can lead to qualifications for entry into higher education. Basic vocational schools provide three-year courses consisting of three days' theoretical and three days' practical training per week; in addition, some general secondary education is provided.

There is a small number of private schools, administered under state supervision, and, in 1989, the Roman Catholic Church was granted the right to operate its own schools. There are 97 higher education establishments in Poland, including 11 universities and 19 technical and agricultural universities. In 1989 government expenditure on education amounted to 4,342,528m. złotys, which was 14.7% of total current expenditure.

UNIVERSITIES

Adam Mickiewicz University in Poznań (Uniwersytet im. Adama Mickiewicza w Poznaniu): 61-712 Poznań, ul. Henryka Wieniawskiego 1; tel. (61) 699251; telex 0413260; fax (61) 535535; f. 1919; 9 faculties; 1,705 teachers; 11,891 students; Rector Prof. Dr hab. BOGDÁN MARCINIEC.

Catholic University of Lublin (Katolicki Uniwersytet Lubelski): 20-950 Lublin, al. Racławickie 14; tel. (81) 30426; telex 643235; fax (81) 30433; f. 1918; 5 faculties; 610 teachers; 7,186 students; Rector Rt Rev. Prof STANISŁAW WIELGUS.

Jagiellonian University (Uniwersytet Jagielloński): 31-007 Kraków, Gołębia 24; tel. (12) 221033; telex 322297; fax (12) 226306; f. 1364; 6 faculties; 1,945 teachers; 10,969 students; Rector Prof. Dr hab. ALEKSANDER KOJ.

Marie Curie-Skłodowska University (Uniwersytet Marii Curie-Skłodowskiej): 20-031 Lublin, Plac Marii Curie-Skłodowskiej 5; tel. (81) 375107; f. 1944; 7 faculties, 1 institute; 1,523 teachers; 11,208 students, incl. 3,633 extra-mural students; Rector Prof. Dr hab. ZDZISŁAW CACKOWSKI.

Nicholas Copernicus University of Toruń (Uniwersytet Mikołaja Kopernika w Toruniu): 87-100 Toruń, ul. Gagarina 11; tel. (56) 22694; telex 0552412; fax (56) 24602; f. 1945; 6 faculties; 989 teachers; 7,900 students; Rector Prof. Dr hab. JAN KOPCEWICZ.

Silesian University (Uniwersytet Śląski): 40-007 Katowice, Bankowa 12; tel. (32) 587231; telex 0315584; f. 1968; 10 faculties; 1,590 teachers; 12,000 students; Rector Prof. Dr SĘDZIMIR KLIMASZEWSKI.

Szczecin University (Uniwersytet Szczeciński): 70-540 Szczecin, ul. Korsarzy 1; tel. (91) 42992; telex 0422719; f. 1984; 6 faculties, 1 institute; 874 teachers; 7,816 students; Rector Prof. dr hab. TADEUSZ WIERZBICKI.

University of Gdańsk (Uniwersytet Gdański): 80-952 Gdańsk, ul. Bażyńskiego 1A; tel. (58) 525071; f. 1970; 6 faculties; 1,396 teachers; 10,416 students; Rector Prof. Dr hab. CZESŁAW JACKOWIAK.

University of Łódź (Uniwersytet Łódzki): 90-131 Łódź, Narutowicza 65; tel. (42) 34-98-85; telex 886291; fax (42) 783958; f. 1945; 6 faculties; 311 teachers; 10,972 students; Rector Prof. Dr hab. LESZEK WOJTCZAK.

University of Warsaw (Uniwersytet Warszawski): 00-325 Warsaw, Krakowskie Przedmieście 26/28; tel. (22) 200381; telex 815439; fax (22) 267520; f. 1818; 23 faculties, 1 institute, 1 affiliated college in Białystok; 827 teachers; 25,476 students; Rector Prof. ANDRZEJ WRÓBLEWSKI.

University of Wrocław (Uniwersytet Wrocławski): 50-137 Wrocław, Plac Uniwersytecki 1; tel. (71) 402212; telex 0712791; fax (71) 402800; f. 1702; 6 faculties; 1,650 teachers; 11,840 students; Rector Prof. Dr MIECZYSŁAW KLIMOWICZ.

Technical Universities

Białytstok Technical University (Politechnika Białostocka): 15-351 Białystok, ul. Wiejska 45A; tel. (85) 22393; telex 852424; f. 1949; 4 faculties, 1 institute; 440 teachers; 2,600 students; Rector Prof. Dr KAZIMIERZ PIEŃKOWSKI.

Częstochowa Technical University (Politechnika Częstochowska): 42-201 Częstochowa, ul. Deglera 35; tel. (34) 55211; telex 037341; fax (34) 52385; f. 1949; 4 faculties; 415 teachers; 1,945 students; Rector Prof. Dr hab. Inż. Janusz Elsner.

Hugo Kołłątaja University of Agriculture in Kraków (Akademia Rolnicza im. Hugona Kołłątaja w Krakowie): Kraków, al. Mickiewicza 21; tel. (12) 332355; f. 1890; 8 faculties; 719 teachers; 4,853 students; Rector Prof. Dr WŁADYSŁAW Bala.

Kielce University of Technology (Politechnika Świętokrzyska): 25-314 Kielce, al. Tysiąclecia Państwa Polskiego 7; tel. (41) 24100; f. 1965; 3 faculties; 326 teachers; 2,000 students; Rector Prof Dr hab. Inż. Zbigniew Kowal.

Kraków Technical University (Politechnika Krakowska im. Tadeusza Kościuszki): 31-155 Kraków, Warszawska 24; tel. (12) 330300; telex 0322468; fax (12) 335773; f. 1945; 6 faculties; 1,036 teachers; 3,823 students; Rector Prof. Dr Inż. W. MUSZYŃSKI.

Łódź Technical University (Politechnika Łódzka: 90-924 Łódź, Żwirki 36; tel. (42) 36-55-22; telex 886136; f. 1945; 7 faculties, 2 institutes; 1,350 teachers; 5,700 students; Rector Prof. Dr hab. CZESŁAW STRUMIŁŁO.

Lublin Technical University (Politechnika Lubelska): 20-109 Lublin, ul. Dąbrowskiego 13; tel. (81) 22201; telex 642745; fax (81) 27364; f. 1953; 4 faculties; 391 teachers; 2,441 students; Rector Prof. Dr hab. Inż. WŁODZIMIERZ SITKO.

Poznń Agricultural University (Akademia Rolnicza w Poznaniu): 60-637 Poznań, ul. Wojska Polskiego 28; tel. (61) 40334; telex 0413322; fax (61) 411022; f. 1951; 7 faculties; 729 teachers; 4,549 students; Rector Prof. Dr hab. WŁODZIMIERZ FISZER.

Poznań Technical University (Politechnika Poznańska): 60-965 Poznań, pl. Skłodowskiej-Curie 5; tel. (61) 332581; telex 413250; fax (61) 330217; f. 1919; 5 faculties; 967 teachers; 3,887 students; Rector Prof. Dr hab. Inż. ANDRZEJ RYZYŃSKI.

Rzeszów Technical University (Politechnika Rzeszowska): 35-959 Rzeszow, ul. W. Pola 2; tel. (17) 43281; telex 0632224; f. 1974 as a university; 4 faculties; 380 teachers; 2,000 students; Rector Prof. STANISŁAW KUŚ.

Silesian Technical University (Politechnika Śląska im. W. Pstrowskiego): 44-100 Gliwice, ul. Pstrowskiego 7; tel. (32) 312349; telex 036304; fax (32) 318085; f. 1945; 12 faculties; 1,500 teachers; 8,000 students; Rector Prof. Dr hab. Inż. TADEUSZ CHMIELNIAK.

Stanisław Staszic Academy of Mining and Metallurgy (Akademia Górniczo-Hutnicza im. Stanisława Staszica w Krakowie): 30-059 Kraków, al. Mickiewicza 30; tel. (12) 337600; telex 0322203; fax (12) 331014; f. 1919; 13 faculties; 1,611 teachers; 7,165 students; Rector Prof. Dr hab. Inż. JAN JANOWSKI.

Szczecin Technical University (Politechnika Szczecińska): 70-310 Szczecin, al. Piastów 17; tel. (91) 46751; f. 1946; 4 faculties; 627 teachers; 2,063 students; Rector Prof Dr hab. Inż. WŁADYSŁAW NOWAK.

Technical University of Gdańsk (Politechnika Gdańska): 80-233 Gdańsk, ul. Majakowskiego 11/12; tel. (58) 415791; telex 0512302; f. 1945; 9 faculties, 2 institutes; 1,115 teachers; 5,388 students; Rector Prof. BOLESŁAW MAZURKIEWICZ.

University of Agriculture in Lublin (Akademia Rolnicza w Lublinie): 20-934 Lublin, ul. Akademicka 13; tel. and fax (81) 33549; telex 0643176; f. 1955; 5 faculties; 606 staff; 4,000 students; Rector Prof. Dr hab. Cz. TARKOWSKI.

University of Agriculture and Technology in Olsztyn (Akademia Rolniczo-Technizna w Olsztynie im. Michała Oczapowskiego): 10-957 Olsztyn, Kortowo; tel. 273310; telex 0526419; fax 273908; f. 1950; 9 faculties; 4,713 students; Rector Prof. Dr hab. JERZY STRZEŻEK.

Warsaw Agricultural University (Szkoła Główna Gospodarstwa Wiejskiego—Akademia Rolnicza w Warszawie): 02-766 Warsaw, ul. Nowoursynowska 166; tel. (22) 439041; telex 816238; fax (22) 471562; f. 1816, refounded 1906; 11 faculties; 1,186 teachers; 6,674 students; Rector Prof. Dr WIESŁAW BAREJ.

Warsaw Technical University (Politechnika Warszawska): 00-661 Warsaw, Plac Jedności Robotniczej 1; tel. (22) 210070; f. 1826; 17 faculties; 2,501 teachers; 13,500 students; Rector Prof. Dr Inż. MAREK ROMAN.

Wrocław Technical University (Politechnika Wrocławska): 50-370 Wrocław, Wybrzeże Wyspiańskiego 27; tel. (71) 227336; telex 0712559; fax (71) 223664; f. 1945; 11 faculties; 1,998 teachers; 6,841 students; Rector Prof. JAN KMITA.

Social Welfare

The Polish social welfare system is controlled by the Ministry of Health and Social Welfare. Locally, the system is administered by the Health and Social Welfare Departments of the Presidiums of the National Councils. Medical care is provided free for all workers and rural population. Radical reforms to the health insurance scheme have been under consideration since 1989. The 1989 central government budget allocated a total of 4,015,807m. złotys, which was 13.6% of total current expenditure, to public health and social welfare, and a further 2,344,400m. złotys (7.9% of current expenditure) to social insurance.

At the end of 1989 there were 79,247 physicians and 17,952 dental surgeons in practice. There were 216,807 general hospital beds and a total of 3,321 health centres in operation. The Polish Red Cross organizes and undertakes the care of the sick at home and general home assistance to those who are incapacitated through ill health, etc. Alimony is assured by law to single mothers. Welfare benefits are available to the unemployed. Pensions are organized and managed by the Union of Pensioners, Invalids and Retired Persons.

NATIONAL AGENCY

Ministry of Health and Social Welfare: see section on The Government (Ministries).

HEALTH AND WELFARE ORGANIZATIONS

Institute of Labour and Social Affairs (Instytut Pracy i Spraw Wocjalnych): 00-496 Warsaw, ul. Mysia 2; tel. (22) 219334; f. 1963; Dir LYDIA BESKID.

Marie Skłodowska-Curie Memorial Cancer Centre and Institute of Oncology (Centrum Onkologii, Instytut im. Marii Skłodowskiej-Curie): 00-973 Warsaw, ul. Wawelska 15; tel. (22) 221276; telex 812704; fax (22) 222429; f. 1932; Dir Prof. J. A. STEFFEN.

National Institute of Cardiology (Instytut Kardiologii): 04-628 Warsaw, ul. Alpejska 42; tel. (22) 153011; telex 816052; Dir Prof. SŁAWOMIR PAWELSKI.

Tuberculosis and Pulmonary Diseases Institute (Instytut Gruźlicy i Chorób Płuc): 01-138 Warsaw, ul. Płocka 26; tel. (22) 324451; f. 1948; Dir Prof. Dr hab. med. LILIA PAWLICKA.

The Environment

The environmental movement in Poland became of significance in the early 1980s, with several groups emerging from within the Solidarity trade union movement. There are more than 40 major ecological groups and several Green parties. The Polish Government maintains membership of the IUCN (based in Gland, Switzerland), the Baltic Marine Environment Protection Committee (Helsinki, Finland) and participated in the activities of the environmental Co-ordinating Centres of the CMEA (based in the USSR).

GOVERNMENT ORGANIZATIONS

Ministry of Environmental Protection, Natural Resources and Forestry (Ministerstwo Ochrony Srodowiska, Zasobow Naturalnych i Leśnictwa): 00-922 Warsaw, ul. Wawelska 52/54; tel. (22) 250001; telex 812816; fax (22) 253355; incl.:

Forestry Research Institute (Instytut Badawczy Leśnictwa): 00-973 Warsaw, ul. Bitwy Warszawskiej 1920 r. 3; tel. (22) 223201; telex 812476; fax (22) 224935; f. 1930; comprises 23 scientific sections, incl. environment; Dir Prof. Dr Eng. ANDRZEJ KLOCEK.

Institute of Physical Planning and Municipal Economy (Instytut Gospodarki Przestrzennej i Komunalnej): 02-078 Warsaw, Krzywickiego 9; tel. and fax (22) 250937; telex 813493; f. 1949; research on physical planning, municipal economy and architecture; Dir Prof. Dr ZYGMUNT NIEWIADOMSKI.

National Council for the Protection of Nature (Państwowa Rada Ochrony Przyrody): advises the Government on environmental matters.

Ministry of Agriculture and Food Economy (Ministerstwo Rolnictwa i Gospodarki Zywnosciowej): 00-930 Warsaw, ul. Wspólna 30; tel. (22) 210251; telex 814597; also involved in environmental matters.

Regional Organization

International Baltic Sea Fishery Commission: 00-950 Warsaw, ul. Hoza 20; tel. (22) 288647; telex 817421; six mems.

ACADEMIC INSTITUTES

Polish Academy of Sciences—PAN (Polska Akademia Nauk—PAN): 00-901 Warsaw, POB 24, Palac Kultury i Nauki; tel. (22) 200211; telex 813929; fax (22) 207651; f. 1952; Pres. Prof. ALEKSANDER GIEYSZTOR; attached research insts incl.:

Institute of Ecology (Instytut Ekologii PAN): 05-092 Łomianki, Dziekanów Lesny; tel. (22) 343053; telex 817378; f. 1952; Dir Prof. Dr KAZIMIERZ DOBROWOLSKI.

Institute of Environmental Engineering (Instytut Podstaw Inżynierii Srodowiska PAN): 41-800 Zabrze, ul. M. Skłodowskiej-Curie 34; tel. (22) 716481; telex 036401; f. 1961; air and water pollution control; Dir Assoc. Prof. JAN KAPALA (acting).

Institute of Environmental Protection (Instytut Ochrony Srodowiska—IOS): 00-548 Warsaw, ul. Krucza 5/11; tel. (22) 299254; telex 813493; research centre into major environmental issues.

Institute of State and Law, Research Group on Environmental Law (Instytut Państwa i Prawa PAN, Zespół Prawnych Problemow Ochrony i Kształtowania Srodowiska): 00-330 Warsaw, Nowy Swiat 72 (Palac Staszica); tel. (22) 267853; Dir Prof. JANUSZ ŁETOWSKI.

Nature and Natural Resources Protection Centre (Zakład Ochrony Przyrody i Zasobów Naturalnych PAN): 31-512 Kraków, ul. Lubicz 46; tel. (12) 215637; f. 1920; research centre; headquarters of the Nature Protection Cttee; Dir Prof. Dr KAZIMIERZ KLIMEK.

Research Centre for Agricultural and Forest Environmental Studies PAN (Zakład Badan Srodowiska Rolniczego i Leśnego PAN): 60-479 Poznań, ul. Bukowska 19; tel. (61) 45601; fax (61) 43668; f. 1979; Dir Prof. Dr hab. LECH RYSZKOWSKI.

Silesian Technical University, Faculty of Environmental Protection: 44-100 Gliwice, ul. Pstrowskiego 7, Politechnika Śląska im. W. Pstrowskiego; tel. (32) 312349; telex 036304; fax (32) 318085; Faculty Dean Prof. Dr hab. Inż. MARIA ZDYBIEWSKA.

NON-GOVERNMENTAL ORGANIZATIONS

Ecological Library: Poznań, ul. Ryboki 6A; affiliated to the Green Library (USA); stocks environmental literature.

Nature Conservation League (Liga Ochrony Przyrody—LOP): 02-067 Warsaw, ul. Wawelska 52/54, Zarzad Glowny; f. 1928; official nature conservation asscn.

Polish Ecological Clubs (Polski Kluby Ekologiczne—PKE): 31-010 Kraków, Rynek Glowny 27; f. early 1980s as part of Solidarity; major independent asscn, affiliated to Friends of the Earth Internat.; federation of regional groups.

Polish Green Party: 30-960 Kraków, POB 783; f. 1988; environmental issues.

Polish Tourist-Patriotic Society, Commission for Nature Conservation: 00-075 Warsaw, ul. Senatorska 11; tel. (22) 265735; telex 812441; aims to increase public awareness of the role of conservation in tourism and recreation.

Defence

In June 1990, according to Western estimates, Poland's armed forces numbered 312,800 people, of which 204,000 were conscripts. Of the total, 206,600 were in the army, 20,000 in the navy and 86,200 in the air force. In addition, the internal defence troops numbered 10,000, the border troops and coast guard 15,500 and the prevention units of the citizens' militia 18,000. Military service normally lasts for 12 months in the army, internal security services and air force, and for two years (to be reduced to 18 months from October 1991) in the navy and special services. Since 1988 conscientious objectors have been permitted to perform an alternative community service. The defence budget for 1990 totalled 10,083,400m. złotys.

Poland was a member of the Warsaw Pact until its final dissolution in July 1991. However, in mid-1991 some 50,000 Soviet troops remained in the country, and the last of these were not expected to leave until late 1993; a continued military presence was considered necessary by the then USSR in order to supervise the 380,000 of its troops which were to be withdrawn, through Poland, from the former German Democratic Republic. In July 1991 Poland became a member of the Hexagonal Group, a forum for regional foreign policy interests, to which Austria, Czechoslovakia, Hungary, Italy and Yugoslavia already belonged.

Commander-in-Chief: President of the Republic.

Chief of Staff of the Defence Forces: Vice-Adm. PIOTR KOLOVZIEJCZYK.

Bibliography

Ascherson, N. *The Polish August: the self-limiting revolution.* Harmondsworth, Penguin, 1981.

The Struggles for Poland. London, Michael Joseph, 1987.

Brock, P. de Beauvoir. *Nationalism and Populism in Partitioned Poland.* London, Orbis, 1973.

Bromke, A. *Poland's Politics: idealism vs. realism* (Russian Research Center Studies). Cambridge, MA, Harvard University Press, 1967.

Davies, N. *God's Playground: a history of Poland*, 2 vols. Oxford, Oxford University Press, 1982.

Dziewanowski, M. K. *The Communist Party of Poland: an outline history* (Russian Research Center Studies). Cambridge, MA, Harvard University Press, 1967.

Garlinski, J. *Poland in the Second World War.* Basingstoke, Macmillan, 1985.

Garton Ash, T. *The Polish Revolution: Solidarity 1980-82* (revised edn). London, Granta (in asscn with Penguin), 1991.

Gomułka, S. and Polansky, A. (Eds). *Polish Paradoxes.* London, Routledge, 1990.

Kolankiewicz, G. and Lewis, P. *Poland. Politics, Economics, Society* (Marxist regimes series). London, Pinter, 1988.

Landau, Z. and Tomaszewski, J. *The Polish Economy in the Twentieth Century.* London, Croom Helm, 1985.

Lane, D. and Kolankiewicz, G. (Eds). *Social Groups in Polish Society.* London, Macmillan, 1973.

Majkowski, W. *People's Poland: patterns of social inequality and conflict.* Westport, CN, Greenwood, 1985.

Miłosz, C. *The Captive Mind* (translated by Jane Zielomko, new edn). Harmondsworth, Penguin, 1980.

Polonsky, A. *Politics in Independent Poland: the crisis of constitutional government, 1921-39.* Oxford, Clarendon Press, 1972.

The Great Powers and the Polish Question, 1941-45: a documentary study in Cold War origins. London, London School of Economics, 1976.

Roos, H. *A History of Modern Poland: from the foundation of the State in the First World War to the present day* (translated by J. R. Foster). London, Eyre and Spottiswoode, 1966.

Sanford, G. *Military Rule in Poland: the Rebuilding of Communist Power, 1981-83.* London, Croom Helm, 1986.

Staniszkis, J. *Poland's Self-Limiting Revolution* (edited by Jan. T. Gross). Princeton, NJ, Princeton University Press, 1984.

Swidlicki, A. *Political Trials in Poland, 1981-86.* London, Croom Helm, 1987.

Szajkowski, B. *Next to God . . . Poland: politics and religion in contemporary Poland.* London, Frances Pinter, 1983.

Wandycz, P. *The Lands of Partitioned Poland, 1795-1918* (A History of East Central Europe, vol. 7). Seattle, WA, University of Washington Press, 1975.

Weydenthal, J. B. de. *The Communists of Poland: an historical outline.* Stanford, CA, Hoover Institution Press, 1986.

Woodall, Jean (Ed.). *Policy and Politics in Contemporary Poland.* London, Frances Pinter, 1982.

ROMANIA

Geography

PHYSICAL FEATURES

Romania (formerly the the Socialist Republic of Romania) is a republic in south-eastern Europe; much of the country forms part of the Balkan Peninsula. In the south-east of the country there is a coastline of about 250 km (150 miles) along the Black Sea. The southern border is with Bulgaria and the south-western border with Yugoslavia (Serbia). Hungary lies to the north-west, Ukraine to the north and Moldavia (Moldova) to the north-east. Romania has a total area of 237,500 sq km (91,699 sq miles). The Carpathian Mountains form a horseshoe through central Romania, running south-east from the northern border and then, as the Transylvanian Alps or Southern Carpathians, traversing central Romania from east to west. The Transylvanian Alps rise to over 2,000 m in places, the mountain of Negoiul being the highest point in Romania, at 2,548 m (8,360 ft). South and east of the mountains lies the fertile Romanian Plain, the lowlands of Wallachia (along the Danube) and Moldavia (along the Siret and Prut Rivers, tributaries of the Danube). Most of the southern confines of Romania are marked by the River Danube (Dunărea). However, in the west of the country, the Banat region has a land border with Yugoslavia (Vojvodina, a part of Serbia). The Iron Gates hydroelectric power and navigation system is on the border with Serbia. In the east, before it reaches the Black Sea, the Danube turns north and flows parallel to the coast before entering the sea at the Delta Dunării (Mouths of the Danube), which forms a border with Ukraine. This area between the Danube and the Black Sea, which forms Romania's only land border with Bulgaria, is the Dobrogea (Dobrudzha). The River Prut defines the north-eastern border and divides Romanian Moldavia from the republic of that name. The plateau-land of north-west Romania, across the Carpathians from the plains, is known as Transylvania and was formerly a province of Hungary.

CLIMATE

The climate is continental, with cold, snowy winters and hot summers. Summers are milder and wetter in the mountains, and the Black Sea moderates the winters on the coast. The north and east suffer from drought if the summer is dry. The average annual rainfall for the whole of Romania is 637 mm (25 in), ranging from 1,000 mm in the mountains to 400 mm in the Danube delta.

POPULATION

Romanian is a Romance language, which evolved from the Latin spoken in central Europe at the time of the Roman Empire, but with many archaic forms and influences from the Slavonic languages, Hungarian, French and Turkish. It is the official language, although Hungarian (Magyar), German and other minority languages are also spoken. In 1987, according to official figures, 89% of the total population were ethnic Romanians, 7.9% were ethnic Hungarians and 1.6% ethnic Germans (however, it was estimated that about one-half of Romania's German population migrated to Germany during 1990). There are also communities of the Romany (Gypsy) people, Ukrainians (Ruthenians), Serbs and Croats, other Slavic peoples, Jews, Turks, Tatars and small groups of Greeks and Armenians. Most of the population profess Christianity and are adherents of the Eastern Orthodox Church, some 66% of believers being members of the Romanian Orthodox Church. About 6% of the population are members of the Roman Catholic Church, using not only the Latin rite, but also Romanian (Uniate) and Armenian rites. Protestant churches are particularly strong among the Hungarian and German populations. There are also communities of the Old-Rite Christian Church (an Orthodox sect) and the Armenian-Gregorian Church. The Turks and Tatars are predominantly Muslim and, despite the decline in numbers caused by emigration, there is still a significant Jewish community.

The principal and capital city is Bucharest (Bucureşti), which is located in the south of the country, in the east of the historic territory of Wallachia. At the end of 1989 it had an estimated population of 2,325,037. Other major cities are: Braşov (estimated population of 352,260 at the end of 1989), in the centre of the country; Iaşi (334,371) in the north-east, near the border with Moldavia; Timişoara (324,651) in the west, in what was known as the Banat; Cluj-Napoca (318,975) in central Transylvania; and the port of Constanţa (312,504) on the Black Sea. The total population of the country was estimated to be 23,190,000 at the end of 1990. At the same time the population density was estimated at 97.6 per sq km. The Bucharest Municipality is the most densely populated region (1,274.1 per sq km at the end of 1989).

Chronology

106: Emperor Trajan made Dacia a province of the Roman Empire.

270: Rome abandoned Dacia to Visigothic invaders, the first of many incursions by peoples from the north and east.

1365: Emergence of independent principalities in Moldavia (now north-east Romania and parts of the Republic of Moldavia and Ukraine) and Wallachia (now south-west Romania), having formerly been Hungarian banates or border lordships.

1394: Wallachia became a dependency of the Ottoman Empire.

1457–1504: Reign of Stephen III ('the Great') of Moldavia.

1512: Moldavia recognized Ottoman overlordship.

April 1856: Under the terms of the Treaty of Paris the principalities of Wallachia and Moldavia were unified, but remained under Turkish suzerainty; the Moldavian Bojar, Cuza, became the ruler.

1866: A prince of the House of Hohenzollern-Sigmaringen replaced the ousted Cuza as Carol I of Romania.

13 July 1878: By the Treaty of Berlin Romania was recognized as an independent state and was ceded part of the Dobrogea.

27 March 1881: Romania was recognized as a kingdom.

1919–20: Following the post-First World War peace treaties, Romania received Bessarabia, the Bukovina, Transylvania, the Banat and Crisana-Maramures.

27 June 1940: Romania ceded Bessarabia and northern Bukovina to the USSR.

August 1940: Romania ceded southern Dobrogea to Bulgaria and northern Transylvania to Hungary.

September 1940: Carol II abdicated in favour of his son, Michael, after having appointed Gen. Ion Antonescu as Prime Minister.

22 June 1941: Romania joined the German invasion of the USSR.

31 August 1944: Soviet troops entered Bucharest.

6 March 1945: The Soviets installed a puppet government under Petru Groza.

November 1946: Elections were held.

30 December 1947: The Romanian People's Republic was proclaimed following the abdication of King Michael under pressure from the ruling Romanian Workers' Party (RWP).

24 September 1952: A new Constitution, based on the Soviet model, was approved by the Grand National Assembly.

30 November 1952: Elections were held for the Grand National Assembly. Gheorghe Gheorghiu-Dej, First Secretary of the RWP, became absolute leader.

March 1965: Following Gheorghiu-Dej's death, Nicolae Ceauşescu was elected First Secretary of the RWP.

June 1965: The RWP changed its name to the Romanian Communist Party (RCP).

August 1965: A new Constitution was adopted. The country's name was changed to the Socialist Republic of Romania.

December 1967: Ceauşescu became President of the State Council.

1971: Romania was admitted to GATT.

1972: Romania was admitted to the IMF and the World Bank.

March 1974: Ceauşescu became President of the Republic.

July 1987: An Amnesty International report condemned the lack of human rights in Romania, particularly for the Hungarian community.

15 November 1987: Thousands of workers in Braşov demonstrated against the Government's economic policy. The local RCP headquarters was sacked.

December 1987: Protests took place in Timişoara and other cities. Following a three-day conference of the RCP, Ceauşescu announced improvements in food supplies and wage increases.

March 1988: Ceauşescu announced plans for the complete 'systematization' of the country by the year 2000.

June 1988: Following a demonstration by 50,000 Hungarians outside the Romanian embassy in Budapest, the Romanian Government ordered the closure of the Hungarian consulate in Cluj-Napoca.

1989

March

In an open letter to the President, six retired RCP officials questioned Ceauşescu's uncompromising policies, accusing him of disregard for the Constitution.

November: Ceauşescu received 67 standing ovations during his speech to the 14th RCP Congress.

December

15: A vigil was mounted outside the home of László Tőkes, an ethnic Hungarian pastor in Timişoara, to prevent his arrest by the police.

16: The vigil protecting Tőkes developed into a demonstration against Ceauşescu and the Communist regime.

17: The demonstrations in Timişoara continued. The army opened fire on the demonstration in order to disperse the protesters.

20: Ceauşescu returned from a visit to Iran.

21: Ceauşescu was interrupted by hostile chanting during a speech in the centre of Bucharest. During a subsequent demonstration the police and army shot dead many of the protesters.

22: Ceauşescu declared a state of emergency after the anti-Communist protests spread around the country. Ceauşescu was forced to escape by helicopter from the roof of the Central Committee Building. The Minister of National Defence, Col-Gen. Vasile Milea, was shot after refusing to order his troops to open fire on demonstrators in Bucharest.

23–25: Revolutionaries seized control of the radio and TV stations. A Council of the National Salvation Front (NSF) was formed. The NSF requested that the USSR intervene militarily to defend the revolution, but the USSR refused to interfere in internal affairs. President Ceauşescu and his wife were captured near the town of Tîrgovişte. There were clashes across the country between revolutionaries and members of the Securitate (secret police).

25: After a summary trial by a military tribunal President Ceauşescu and his wife were executed at the military garrison in Tîrgovişte.

26: An 11-member Executive Bureau was elected from the 145 members of the NSF Council. Ion Iliescu was declared President and Dumitru Mazilu Vice-President; Petre Roman was made Prime Minister of the NSF-appointed Government. The ban on abortion was overturned.

27: A final Securitate assault on the television station was driven back by the army. The NSF issued an ultimatum to members of the Securitate that they either give themselves up or be executed. The death penalty was abolished.

28: The name of the country was changed by decree to Romania.

29: The army withdrew from the streets of Bucharest. Radical constitutional amendments were published by the NSF, including the restructuring of the economy along free-market lines. Gen. Vasile Ionel replaced Gen. Stefan Guze as Chief of Staff. The ideologue of the NSF, Silviu Brucan, announced that the NSF would not become a political party.

1990

January

1: The NSF Council abolished the Securitate. Ion Iliescu announced that food exports had been halted.

3: An NSF Council decree guaranteed freedom of assembly. The prohibition on foreign borrowing was ended.

4: The NSF announced that it would be running in the elections, then scheduled for April.

5: The NSF Council amnestied all people sentenced after 1947 for political offences.

7: Students demonstrated in Bucharest against the policies of the NSF and its alleged links with the RCP. An NSF Council decree established military tribunals to try members of the Securitate.

8: All Romanians over the age of 14 were permitted to receive 10-year passports and to travel freely to and from Romania.

12: 10,000 people demonstrated outside the NSF headquarters and shouted down President Iliescu and Prime Minister Roman. The NSF Council met with representatives from the demonstration and announced the banning of the RCP.

13: The decision to ban the RCP was reversed.

23: Silviu Brucan confirmed that the NSF would stand in the elections, which were rescheduled for May 12.

24: Demonstrators in Bucharest protested against the NSF's decision to stand in the elections.

26: Dumitru Mazilu resigned from the NSF.

28: A demonstration in Bucharest, which had been called by several opposition parties and organizations, was involved in clashes with supporters of the NSF who were also marching. Radio and television announcements summoned NSF loyalists to the scene of the trouble, from which the anti-NSF groups were finally forced to retreat.

29: 60,000 supporters of the NSF marched through Bucharest. Corneliu Coposa, leader of the National Peasant's Party, had to be rescued by the army after the crowd besieged his party's headquarters. The headquarters of the Liberal Party were stormed and ransacked.

February

1: Following round-table talks, the representatives of 29 parties agreed to NSF proposals that power be shared in a 180-seat Provisional National Unity Council (PNUC).

3: Silviu Brucan announced that the NSF Executive Bureau would dissolve itself and join the PNUC.

4: Silviu Brucan resigned from the Executive Bureau of the NSF over policy and strategy differences.

5: Four senior RCP officials were found guilty of responsibility for the shootings in Bucharest and Timişoara and sentenced to life imprisonment with hard labour.

9: The NSF agreed to opposition demands that the PNUC be expanded to 253 seats and that political parties be granted only 'observer' status.

12: Officers from the armed forces occupied the NSF headquarters in Bucharest demanding the resignation of the Ministers of the Interior and Defence.

13: The PNUC elected a 21-member Executive Bureau with Ion Iliescu as its President.

16: Ion Iliescu announced the resignation of the Minister of Defence, Gen. Nicolae Militaru, and his replacement by Col-Gen. Victor Stanculescu.

18: Demonstrators in Bucharest demanded the resignation of Ion Iliescu and then attacked the headquarters of the NSF.

19: Following the events of the previous day, miners from the Jiu valley demonstrated in support of the NSF in Bucharest.

March

2: The trial of 21 Securitate officers accused of genocide began in Timişoara.

11: Opposition groups led by George Serban drew up the Timişoara Declaration, which called for the banning of former Communists from office and for democratic reforms.

15: Confrontations took place between ethnic Hungarians attempting to celebrate the Hungarian National Day and Romanian nationalists.

16: There were further confrontations in Tîrgu Mureş between Hungarians and nationalist Romanians.

17: The PNUC adopted a new electoral law and set the date for the elections as 20 May.

18: A joint Hungarian-Romanian demonstration was held in Cluj-Napoca to demand an end to the inter-racial conflict.

19: Romanian nationalists stormed the headquarters of the Hungarian Democratic Union of Romania (HDUR) in Tîrgu Mureş.

20: A state of emergency was declared in Tîrgu Mureş following an attack by armed Romanian nationalists on a peaceful march by 5,000 Hungarians; 70,000 ethnic Hungarians demonstrated in Bucharest.

22: Talks between the HDUR and the nationalist Vatra Românească (Romanian Hearth) movement began.

24: The Vatra Românească–HDUR talks called for the respect of rights of nationalists and minorities and for the right of education in the mother tongue. Romanian nationalists demonstrated in Tîrgu Mureş.

April

7–8: The NSF held its first national conference and endorsed Ion Iliescu as its leader and presidential candidate.

22: Opposition supporters began an occupation of University Square in Bucharest.

May

5: Opposition leader Radu Câmpeanu was attacked in Braila while attempting to address an election rally.

11: Opposition leader Ion Raţiu was prevented from addressing an election rally in Oradea.

20: The NSF won decisively in the first free elections since 1937. Ion Iliescu was elected President with over 85% of the vote.

June

13: Police forcibly cleared the opposition supporters who had been occupying University Square. During ensuing violence the police headquarters was set on fire and demonstrators attempted to take over the television station. President Iliescu appealed on the radio to factory workers to take to the streets and defend the revolution.

14: Miners, who had been transported to the capital by the Government, attacked anyone in Bucharest suspected of being an anti-Government sympathizer. At least six people died during these attacks. Marian Munteanu, the President of the League of Students, was severely beaten and then arrested by the police.

15: The miners were congratulated on their efforts by President Iliescu.

18: Following the withdrawal of the miners, anti-Government protesters again occupied University Square and were granted talks with the Minister of the Interior.

20: Ion Iliescu was sworn in as President and called on Petre Roman to head a new Government.

28: Petre Roman presented the Government to the Grand National Assembly.

July

6: President Iliescu resigned as head of the NSF in accordance with the terms of the electoral law.

23: The National Liberal Party split.

25: The Grand National Assembly approved a bill reorganizing state economic enterprises into autonomous units and commercial companies.

31: A privatization law was passed by the Grand National Assembly.

August

22: Anti-Government demonstrations resumed in University Square; 30,000 people demonstrated in Braşov about the shortage of raw materials which was hindering industrial production.

28: The mayor of Bucharest declared an indefinite ban on meetings and demonstrations in Bucharest's squares.

September

9: Intellectuals and workers staged a joint demonstration against the Government in Braşov.

10: Former Securitate chief Col-Gen. Iulian Vlad went on trial charged with being an accomplice to mass murder.

17: Dockers, seamen and lorry drivers went on strike. A mass anti-Government demonstration was held in Timişoara.

19: The Minister of Reform, Adrian Severin, announced the implementation of free-market measures.

21: Nicu Ceauşescu, son of the former President, was sentenced to 20-years imprisonment for instigating 'extremely grave murder'.

October

3: The Alliance of Democratic Union was established.

18: Petre Roman announced emergency measures to deal with the disastrous state of the economy. These included devaluation and convertibility of the currency, privatizations and the removal of price controls.

19: The mass murder charges against former Securitate chief Col-Gen. Iulian Vlad were dropped.

November

1: The Government's economic reforms were implemented. Workers demonstrated in University Square against these reforms.

4: Demonstrations were held in Cluj-Napoca and Bucharest demanding the reunification of Soviet Moldavia with Romania.

5: Petre Roman met trade union leaders in an attempt to end the protests against his economic reforms.

8: Protests against the Government's economic programme were held in Timişoara and other cities.

12: The Prime Minister was granted special powers by the Grand National Assembly to rule by decree and speed up the reforms for the free-market economy.

15: More than 100,000 people demanded the resignation of the Government at a rally in Bucharest called by the newly-formed Civic Alliance.

16: The RCP re-emerged as the Socialist Party of Labour.

19: A demonstration was held in Bucharest to protest at the launch of the revamped RCP.

20: The NSF held its first rally in Bucharest since May.

27: New charges, of illegal arrest and detention of demonstrators, were made against former Securitate chief Col-Gen. Iulian Vlad.

December

10: Lorry drivers blocked Bucharest's Aviator Square in protest at the Government's economic policies.

11: President Iliescu met union leaders in an attempt to avoid a general strike being called over worsening living conditions. The Government agreed to demands that the second stage of its price liberalization programme be postponed until 1 June 1991 (but it was later brought forward to 1 April 1991).

15: The National Convention for the Restoration of Democracy was established.

16: During a demonstration in Timişoara to mark the first anniversary of the protests that brought about Ceauşescu's downfall, László Tőkés called for a second revolution to bring down the Government.

17: The Government began talks with opposition groups on the possible formation of a coalition government.

21: Thousands of Romanians demonstrated to commemorate the victims of the 1989 revolution. The demonstration in Bucharest became an anti-Government protest.

26: The former sovereign, King Michael, was expelled from the country during a 24-hour visit.

1991

January

30: Group of 24 countries admit Romania to their Eastern Europe aid programme, having initially excluded it after the violent suppression of the demonstrations in Bucharest in June 1990.

February

6: The Government announced the temporary closure of nearly 200 industrial units and factories during February and March in order to conserve energy; the 247,000 workers temporarily made redundant were to receive 60% of their wages.

8: A strike by 20,000 railway workers in north-eastern Romania began, over wages and conditions; railway workers in Timişoara joined the strike on 11 February.

18: Trading in foreign currencies commenced at six authorized Romanian banks.

20: Land reform law came into effect returning between 0.5 and 10 hectares of arable land to agricultural workers, according to the size of the family plot nationalized by the Communists.

21: The railway workers' strike ended after the resolution of their claims in negotiations with the Government.

March

16–17: A national convention of the NSF approved a programme by its leader, Prime Minister Petre Roman, which would reshape the NSF as a social democratic party.

18: Former Securitate chief Col-Gen. Iulian Vlad was sentenced to three-and-a-half years in prison.

20: The Finance Minister, Theodor Stolojan, and two other ministers submitted their resignations in protest at the Government's decision to introduce price-rise ceilings and wages indexation; the resignations were withdrawn the following day.

25: The trial of 21 former politburo members ended with 13 sentenced to between two and five-and-a-half years imprisonment, two to lesser sentences, and six acquitted on mass murder charges.

April

1: The second stage of the Government's price liberalization programme was introduced; prices of essential foodstuffs rose by up to 125%; individual income tax was introduced, with rates between 6% and 45%; the leu was devalued against the US dollar by 72%.

4–6: President Iliescu visited the USSR to sign a Romanian–Soviet friendship treaty.

8: The National Assembly passed legislation allowing direct foreign investment in Romanian enterprises.

11: The International Monetary Fund (IMF) approved a 12-month loan package valued at US $748m.

18–20: The French President, François Mitterrand, visited Romania, becoming the first Western head of state to do so since the revolution.

29: Nine ministers were dismissed in a reshuffle of the Council of Ministers; three non-NSF members were appointed ministers.

30: The National Assembly vetoed the appointment of two radical ministers, including one non-NSF member.

May

20: Anti-Government demonstrations took place in Bucharest and other towns on the anniversary of the first post-Communist elections.

June

10: Talks between the NSF and the opposition parties to form a coalition government broke down.

18: Miners demonstrated against the Government in Bucharest.

July

5: The Civic Alliance movement of extra-parliamentary opposition groupings voted to form a political party parallel to the existing organization.

9: Romania's draft constitution was presented to the Constituent Assembly (the combined chambers of parliament).

22: Col-Gen. Iulian Vlad, former chief of the Securitate, sentenced to nine years' imprisonment for supporting mass murder.

August

6: The Industry Minister, Victor Stanculescu, a former army general, in defending the use of firearms against demonstrators, made allegations in the Bucharest Supreme Court that 'certain neighbouring states' had been involved in the Timișoara uprising of December 1989.

14: The Privatization Law was approved, providing for the distribution of 30% of the capital of state commercial companies by voucher to the general public, and for the sale of the remaining 70%; overall, some 47% of state capital was to remain under government control.

27: The Government announced its recognition of Moldavia immediately after the republic's parliament had declared its independence from the USSR.

28: President Iliescu referred to the inevitability of Moldavia and Romania being reunited. The Party of the Civic Alliance declared its intention to join the National Convention for Establishing Democracy, ruling out the possibility of making an alliance with the NSF.

September

1: The Government doubled the price of motor fuel, bringing it into line with international prices.

3: The Government introduced price ceilings for some foodstuffs; meat prices fell by up to 50%.

13: Romania re-established diplomatic relations with Estonia, Latvia and Lithuania.

23: Coal-miners in the Jiu valley went on strike over pay and conditions.

25: The coal-miners hijacked trains and travelled to Bucharest, attacked government buildings and fought with police, and demanded the resignations of the Government and President Iliescu.

26: More coal-miners arrived by train in Bucharest; the demonstrators again fought their way to the government buildings. Prime Minister Roman and his Government resigned to enable the creation of a government of 'national opening', but vowed to continue in office in the current climate of unrest. On 1 October President Iliescu asked Theodor Stolojan (former Finance Minister and President of the National Privatization Agency) to form a new Government.

History

DENIS DELETANT

Just as the course of Romania's history from the end of the Second World War to the overthrow of Nicolae Ceaușescu in December 1989 was set by the entry of Soviet troops into the capital, Bucharest, on 31 August 1944 and the consequent imposition of Soviet Communist authority, so withdrawal of that authority after 1985 by the Soviet leader, Mikhail Gorbachev, sent a signal to the Romanian population that they could now challenge the legitimacy of their local Communist master, Nicolae Ceaușescu, without fear of Soviet intervention. When they did so, successfully, in late December 1989, a leading Romanian writer declared that, for the Romanians, the Second World War had finally come to an end.

THE ARRIVAL OF COMMUNISM

Although the Soviet forces arrived in 1944, after the young King Michael had firstly courageously arrested the pro-German dictator Marshal Ion Antonescu, and then ordered Romanian troops to side with the Soviet forces, Stalin lost little time in imposing his will on the country. In March 1945, he forced the King to appoint a 'Popular Front' Government under Petru Groza, in which the real power lay with the Communists and whose authority rested on the presence of the Red Army. This Government soon made clear its complexion by abolishing the freedoms of the press and of political assembly, and by arresting almost all of its political opponents. A Soviet army of occupation, the last divisions of which only left the country in 1958, took over the policing of the country, and most of the Romanian army was demobilized. Elections were only held, in November 1946, at the insistence of the United Kingdom and the USA. However, the results, which gave comprehensive victory to the Groza Government, were widely believed to have been falsified. On 30 December 1947 King Michael was forced to abdicate and the Romanian People's Republic was proclaimed.

Between 1948 and 1950 the framework for a Communist Romania was put in place. A new Constitution was adopted in 1948, vesting power in the people through a Grand National Assembly, the Country's new parliament, and, later in the year, industry, the banks and transport companies were nationalized. In March 1949, a land reform was passed, expropriating all agricultural property over 50 hec-

tares, without compensation, and the land was turned into state or collective farms. As an underdeveloped country, Romania could not experience a Communist revolution, as envisaged by Marx, without creating the necessary economic preconditions of industrialization and the political force of a working class. For this reason, the Marxist-Leninist concept of 'building socialism', applied by Stalin in the USSR, dictated the policies of the Communists whom he imposed upon Romania. Initially, under Gheorghe Gheorghiu-Dej, General Secretary of the Romanian Communist Party (RCP, known as the the Romanian Workers' Party—RWP from 1947 until 1965) between 1945 and 1954, and First Secretary from 1955 until his death in 1965, economic development through industrialization was focused upon towns with an established industrial base. In the late 1950s, Gheorghiu-Dej's economic policy of intensive industrialization, in contravention of the USSR's preference for it to be developed as a major supplier of agricultural goods in the Council for Mutual Economic Assistance (CMEA or Comecon), was an early indication of Romania's independence and waywardness within the Eastern Bloc. Romania's desire to develop the economy sufficiently to give it a considerable degree of political autonomy from the USSR resulted in a rapid urbanization of the population. The proportion of people employed in agriculture fell from 75% in 1950 to under 30% in the late 1980s, while the percentage of those working in industry rose from 11% in 1950 to 37% in 1988.

The RWP's rejection, in February 1963, of Khrushchev's plans to give Comecon a supranational economic planning role marked the beginnings of an effective independent Romanian line in economic and foreign policy. Had Romania accepted the Soviet scheme, it would have been obliged to remain a supplier of raw materials to its industrialized partners, and to abandon its own plans for rapid and intensive industrialization. The Romanian Party interpreted the Soviet proposals as a threat to Romania's sovereignty and right to decide its own future, and by rejecting them Gheorghiu-Dej could claim to be defending the national interest. This identification with the national interest and defiance of the USSR also served to increase the Party's popularity in Romania and enabled it to claim greater legitimacy.

ROMANIA UNDER CEAUŞESCU

These policies were continued by Gheorghiu-Dej's successor, Nicolae Ceauşescu, who was elected First Secretary of the Party in March 1965. The RWP reverted to being the Romanian Communist Party in June of that year, Ceauşescu's title of First Secretary was restyled as General Secretary and, under the new Constitution adopted in August the country became known as the Socialist Republic of Romania. As well as in its economic policy, Romania also often defied the USSR and the Warsaw Pact in the international arena. In 1967 Romania became the first Eastern Bloc country to establish diplomatic relations with West Germany and, in the same year, defied its Communist allies by not severing relations with Israel after the Six Day War. On 21 August 1968 Ceauşescu had the temerity to criticize the Soviet-led Warsaw Pact intervention in Czechoslovakia. Romania's 'rewards' from the West for its defiance of the USSR included state visits to and from the USA and the United Kingdom, admission to GATT (General Agreement on Trade and Tariffs) in 1971, and to the International Monetary Fund (IMF) and the World Bank in 1972, and the accordance of preferential trading status with the European Communities in 1973 and 'Most Favoured Nation' status with the USA in 1975.

Lavish international recognition of Ceauşescu obscured the emergence of worrying signs in the country's economic performance. The financing of Romania's industrialization programme through loans from the West led to massive indebtedness. By late 1981 the foreign debt had risen to US $10,200m., and Ceauşescu was obliged to ask for its rescheduling. In part these problems were caused by over-optimistic forecasts of Romania's ability to finance loan repayments from export income, and the quality of Romania's goods was never good enough to generate this in sufficient quantities. The sharp increase in petroleum prices in 1978, and an interruption of petroleum supplies from Iran after its revolution in 1979, left the country's economy exposed, as the rapid industrialization and growth in energy consumption had forced Romania to become an importer of crude petroleum in 1976. Other factors, such as a severe earthquake in 1977 and flooding in 1980 and 1981, also affected the economy, although their effects were largely beyond the control of the Government.

The debt position was a severe humiliation for Ceauşescu. He attempted to restore his image by vowing to repay the entire foreign debt by 1990, and proceeded to follow zealously an appropriate course, requiring Romania to restrict imports, including those of food, and to concentrate on exporting, from the early 1980s. The hardships inflicted on the citizens of Romania can only have contributed to an intense dislike for Ceauşescu, which was only contained by the fear of imprisonment or other punishment. The reduction of food imports from the West from almost $1,000m. in 1981 to a mere $27m. in 1984, while exports of meat to the USSR continued, forced the rationing of food to be introduced, and those rations became progressively smaller through the 1980s. Energy shortages and rationing led to very cold conditions in homes and offices, particularly during the severe winters of 1984/85 and 1986/87.

Ceauşescu's remaining political value to the West was undermined by the adoption of several of the Romanian leader's policies in the foreign policy and defence arena, such as the withdrawal of Soviet troops from Afghanistan and reductions in the numbers of nuclear weapons, in the USSR by Mikhail Gorbachev from 1985 onwards. Furthermore, Ceauşescu continued to follow a path of ultra-Stalinism in his domestic policies. On 15 November 1987 Ceauşescu rejected the idea of introducing Gorbachev-style reforms in Romania, but on the same day the first major manifestation of public opposition to the regime occurred when thousands of people demonstrated in the country's second-largest city, Braşov. The Communist Party headquarters were attacked, and hundreds arrested and beaten as the security forces dispersed the demonstration. Further displays of opposition took place in Timişoara and other cities during December.

Relations with the European Communities, the USA and with neighbouring Hungary remained strained over alleged human rights violations, arising from the President's application of the 'systematization' or rural resettlement programme and from his attempts to silence domestic dissent. Ceauşescu's programme to complete, by the year 2000, the urbanization or 'systematization' of about one-half of Romania's 13,000 villages, which was revived in March 1988, provoked international criticism. The coercive application of this policy, initially involving the bulldozing at short notice of villagers' private houses and the destruction of their plots of land in order to force them into small blocks of apartments in new 'agro-industrial' complexes, focused attention upon the wider issue of Romania's failure to honour its commitments under the Helsinki process relating to human rights. International concern led not only to harsh condemnation from the West, echoed in the European Communities' decision, in April 1989, to break off trade negotiations with Romania, and reiterated at the Paris Conference on the Human Dimension held in June, but also to criticism from its Eastern Bloc allies. In March 1989, the UN Human Rights Commission in Geneva adopted a resolution to investigate alleged human rights violations by Romania; the USSR, Bulgaria and the German Democratic Republic abstained in the voting, but Hungary joined the resolution's sponsors.

In the same month, concern about the situation in Romania was expressed in an open letter to the President from six retired senior figures in the Romanian Communist Party, among them Gheorghe Apostol, a former Party Secretary, and Professor Silviu Brucan, formerly both Ambassador to the USA and editor of the Party daily, *Scînteia*. The signatories called upon Ceauşescu to relax his demands for increased exports, to release more food for internal consumption, to invest in new technology for outmoded industries, to halt the vastly expensive programme of prestige projects of doubtful economic value, and to end systematization because it had seriously damaged the country's international prestige. The President responded by first placing the signatories under house arrest and then relocating them to primitive dwellings.

Against this background of increasing pressure upon her husband, both from within Communist Party circles and from leading intellectuals such as Doina Cornea and Mircea Dinescu, Elena Ceauşescu made increasing efforts to advance her political credentials. Vice-President in all but name (her positions included membership of the Politburo and First Deputy Prime Minister), she was given greater prominence in the Romanian media throughout the year. The 14th Party Congress, held on 20–25 November 1989, when Ceauşescu received 67 standing ovations, seemed to confirm the dominant position of the presidential couple. However, the misleading nature of such staged demonstrations of support was to become fully apparent within weeks.

THE OVERTHROW OF CEAUŞESCU

The tumultuous events in Romania since December 1989, first in Timişoara and then in Bucharest and the rest of the country, might give the impression that the overthrow of Ceauşescu was simply a spontaneous uprising against years of economic hardship and political repression. Certainly the vast majority of demonstrators, who may genuinely be described as revolutionaries, were acting without any carefully formulated plan and, largely, without leadership. However, alongside this movement there was, apparently, already in existence an agenda among disaffected Communists to dispose of Ceauşescu and introduce reforms. The open letter of Silviu Brucan, and others, referred to above, was perhaps an opening gambit in an attempted coup against Ceauşescu. Unsuccessful though their initial moves were, Brucan later claimed that the group had already selected Ion Iliescu as their successor to Ceauşescu. Further demands for reform were circulated during the autumn of 1990 by what was already calling itself the 'National Salvation Front'. In this context, the disappointment of many Romanians at the speed of progress towards reform in the years immediately after the December revolution, particularly compared to that in several of their Eastern European neighbours, can be better understood.

Nevertheless, the sequence of events in the Romanian revolution of December 1989 is worth recording. On 15 December the congregation of an ethnic Hungarian pastor, László Tőkés, an outspoken critic of the Government's policies, particularly the systematization of villages, maintained a vigil outside his house, following attempts to evict him from his church and to detain him for questioning. On the following day, thousands of Romanians joined the Hungarian parishioners in a more general demonstration against living conditions and Ceauşescu himself. The demonstrators were dispersed by baton-wielding militiamen, although no shots were fired, despite orders from Ceauşescu to the army and the Securitate (security police) to open fire on the demonstrators. However, on 17 December the army did open fire against a further demonstration in Timişoara, leaving an estimated 200 people dead or injured.

On 20 December, on his return from a brief visit to Iran, Ceauşescu made a televised address to the nation, in which he blamed the events in Timişoara on 'fascists', 'hooligans' and 'Hungarian irredentists'; no sympathy was shown for the victims of the violence. A public rally of support for Ceauşescu was arranged for the following morning. (These rallies were quite regular events, and 'supporters' were bused in from surrounding areas, and even paid for their attendance.) However, a short while into Ceauşescu's speech, the usual chants and slogans of support were replaced with heckling against Ceauşescu and in support of the Timişoara demonstrators. Visibly shocked, Ceauşescu attempted to quell the opposition by announcing increases in salaries and pensions, but the hostile chanting continued. The President, literally left speechless, was led away from the platform and the live television and radio broadcast was interrupted. The rally quickly developed into a demonstration, with the army and security police opening fire, killing and wounding many people. The Minister of National Defence, Col-Gen. Vasile Milea, was shot by a member of the Securitate for refusing to order his troops to open fire on the demonstrators.

On the following morning, with demonstrators again on the streets in Bucharest, Nicolae and Elena Ceauşescu fled by helicopter, eventually being taken into custody in Tîrgovişte, where, on 25 December, Christmas Day, they were summarily tried by a military tribunal, and executed. A prominent organizer of the military tribunal was Gen. Victor Stanculescu, a Deputy Minister of National Defence under Ceauşescu, and an early convert to the National Salvation Front.

THE NATIONAL SALVATION FRONT (NSF)

Early in the uprising in Bucharest, attention became focused on the television station, which was the scene of bitter fighting. Inside the building, the Council of the National Salvation Front, initially with 145 members, assumed control of the country. On 26 December Ion Iliescu was appointed interim President, Dumitru Mazilu Vice-President and Petre Roman Prime Minister. Although the National Salvation Front (NSF) started with widespread support from reform-minded Communists and dissidents, it was not long before the latter started to become disillusioned; Doinea Cornea, a prominent dissident, resigned from the NSF Council on 24 January 1990, calling it 'demagogic' after an announcement that the NSF would stand as a political party in the forthcoming elections. This contradicted a pronouncement, made on 29 December 1989, by the NSF's chief theorist, Silviu Brucan, that there was no need for the NSF to become a political party. Divisions within the Front became more apparent when both Brucan and Mazilu resigned their positions. A large anti-NSF demonstration, organized by three opposition groups, the National Peasant Party, the National Liberal Party and the Social Democratic Party, was followed by a pro-NSF demonstration exhibiting worrying signs of pre-revolution Communist rallies, including the busing-in of supporters and the threat and use of violence.

To counter these signs of opposition the NSF moved to replace the NSF Council with a Provisional National Unity Council (PNUC) on 1 February. This had 241 members, 105 from the NSF, three each from the then 35 registered parties and 27 representing the nine national minorities. On 10 February the size of the PNUC was raised to 253 members to accommodate two newly-registered parties and more NSF representatives. In March the PNUC adopted an electoral law providing for a bicameral legislature; elections were to be held on 20 May. The combined chambers, sitting as the Constituent Assembly, would be responsible for drawing up a new Constitution.

The presidential and parliamentary elections resulted in landslide victories for the NSF. Ion Iliescu won 85% of the valid votes cast in the ballot for President, with Radu Câmpeanu of the National Liberal Party receiving 11% and Ion Raţiu of the Christian Democratic National Peasants' Party 4%. In the parliamentary voting the NSF won 65% of the vote, giving them 263 of the 387 seats in the Assembly of Deputies, and 91 of the 119 seats in the Senate. Foreign observers considered the conduct of the election to have been generally fair, although there were instances of irregularities, particularly in rural areas where, either because of intimidation or lack of organization, opposition parties were not represented at polling stations. However, the NSF had dealt itself an enormous advantage by inheriting much of the apparatus of the Communist Party, including two mass-circulation newspapers, and not to mention many of its experienced politicians. By contrast, the opposition parties had to prepare themselves for the elections, from a standing start, in less than five months. Furthermore, the NSF was still benefiting from an initial surge of support for its role in the overthrow of Ceauşescu, while certain sections of society saw their futures as being most secure with the NSF, at least keeping some continuity with Romania's immediate political past.

PROBLEMS FACING THE NEW GOVERNMENT

In the periods both before and after the elections, the two principal problems which would determine the NSF's long-term ability to hold on to power were the economy and the handling of Romania's ethnic minorities.

Addressing the NSF Council on 4 January 1990, Prime Minister Petre Roman described the Romanian economy as having been left in 'profound crisis' by the ousted Communist regime. Economic planning and targets had been lacking in reality, particularly in view of the country's resources and technological backwardness; no new technology had been imported for 10 years owing to the restrictions on imports associated with the debt-repayment programme. For similar reasons, health, education and transport services were in a parlous state. Several of Ceauşescu's prestige projects, including the canal linking Bucharest to the Danube, were abandoned, although his Palace was to be completed as a new location for the Assembly of Deputies and the Senate.

The restrictions on the domestic consumption of energy which had been imposed under Ceauşescu were removed from the beginning of 1990, but the additional demand thus created left industry short of energy and adversely affected production. To the energy supply problems must be added a relaxation of discipline in working habits, understandable after decades in which production was regimented along military lines. Together, these difficulties help to explain why, during 1990, industrial production fell by about 20%. The Government's objective was to reorganize the economy along market lines, although there were many differences of opinion among ministers as to how, and the speed at which, this should be achieved. Unwillingness to abandon the ideas and structures of the Communist past plagued the efforts of the young reformers in the NSF Government to implement their bold policy of economic reform. Although a land reform allowing private citizens to reclaim up to 10 hectares (24 acres) of land which had been nationalized by the Communist state was adopted by the National Assembly in February 1991, in many areas of the country the local authorities failed to issue titles to the land. The Romanian currency, the leu, was devalued on 18 October 1990 by 60% and, from 1 November, subsidies were removed from all goods except for bread, meat, heating, electricity and rent, leading to increases of between 100% and 120%. On 15 November, the third anniversary of the anti-Ceauşescu revolt in the industrial centre of Braşov, an estimated 200,000 people took part in a peaceful protest in Bucharest against the price rises. President Iliescu intervened and persuaded the Government to postpone the second stage of price 'liberalization', involving the removal of subsidies from the essential items not included in the first round of price increases, from 1 January 1991 to 1 July 1991. However, reformers in the Government later insisted that this latter date be brought forward to 1 April. Previously exempted items, such as bread, milk, butter, cheese and sugar, more than doubled in price on this date, and the official rate of the Romanian currency, the leu, was further devalued, by 58%, to 60 lei per US dollar. Inflation, according to official figures, was running at 23% in November 1990, but it was not clear how far the drastic price rises implemented in November 1990 had been entered into the calculation. Unemployment in 1990 was estimated by Eugen Dijmărescu, the Minister of State in charge of Economy and Finance, to be 'about 10% of the total labour force', but was predicted to fall to 462,000 (4% of the working population) in 1991. This figure contrasts with the official Romanian news agency, Rompres, forecast on 7 January 1991 that a number of unemployed 'between one and one-and-a-half million seems unavoidable'. This would represent an unemployment rate of 10%–15%. Considerable numbers of workers were laid off during 1990 and 1991 while continuing to receive between 50% and 75% of their wages.

Recognition that firm progress towards economic reform was being made in Romania was met with recognition in the international arena. Accordingly, on 1 February 1991, Romania was granted guest status by the Council of Europe, being the last East European country, with the exception of Albania, to be admitted. The British 'Know-How Fund', set up in June 1989 to assist the countries of Eastern Europe to move towards democracy and a free-market economy, was extended to Romania on 9 May. The US Government remained cautious about Romania's commitment to apply the principles and practice of democracy, and withheld the granting of 'Most-Favoured Nation' status. The US view that the Romanian leadership needed to do more to demonstrate that it had irrevocably abandoned the Communist mentality was regarded by many as fully justified following the sudden announcement that, during a visit to Moscow on 5 April, President Iliescu had signed a treaty of friendship and co-operation with the USSR. Surprise and dismay were expressed in opposition circles in Romania, especially as the treaty recognized the Soviet occupation of the former Romanian territory of Bessarabia, which is largely coterminous with the Moldavian republic.

Ethnic disturbances in Transylvania, which had contributed to the overthrow of Ceauşescu, did not cease with his overthrow. The ethnic Hungarians sought to use their new-found freedom and confidence to achieve a greater degree of cultural autonomy, and in particular the restoration of secondary and university teaching in Hungarian. Although the requests of the Hungarian community initially met with sympathy from the Provisional National Unity Council, a backlash among Romanians resident in Transylvania led to the creation of an ultra-nationalist organization, Vatra Românească (Romanian Hearth or Romanian Cradle). This organization rapidly attracted such a large membership that the NSF could not afford to incur its anger. In March 1990, peaceful demonstrations in the town of Tîrgu Mureş by ethnic Hungarians met with violent ripostes from Romanian crowds, and the attacks were also extended to opposition party buildings. In the same month the Timişoara Proclamation was drawn up, which demanded that all people with active connections to the Communist Party and the security forces should be disqualified from standing in the May elections.

Although the elections provided popular mandates for Iliescu and the Front, it did not give them legitimacy in the eyes of many students, professional people and intellectuals. The continued occupation of Bucharest's University Square by representatives of such groups in support of the Timişoara Proclamation, showed that Iliescu and the Front leadership, despite disavowing their Communist past, had failed to convince everybody. After waiting to see whether the protest would run out of steam in the wake of his landslide electoral success, Iliescu ordered the police to clear the Square, which they did on the morning of 13 June, beating and arresting demonstrators. Groups of people gathered in the afternoon of 13 June to protest against the police action. Several cars and a police van were set on fire and the protesters attacked the police headquarters, the offices of Romanian Television and the Foreign Ministry, where Iliescu and the Government were based.

The failure of the police to disperse the rioters prompted Iliescu, on the evening of 13 June, to appeal to miners from the Jiu valley, and other workers from the area, to defend the Government. Their response was immediate. Special trains were arranged and some 7,000 miners arrived in Bucharest the following morning, armed with wooden staves and iron bars. They were joined by vigilantes, some of whom were later identified in the press as having been members of the Securitate. For two days they terrorized the population of the capital attacking, under the direction of unknown persons, the headquarters of the National Liberal Party and the Christian Democratic National Peasants' Party, which they ransacked, the offices of opposition newspapers, where they threatened the staff, and the University, where they beat students. On the following day President Iliescu, in an address ridden with Ceauşescu-like clichés, thanked the miners for having shown 'workers' solidarity' in the face of a plot which had 'been hatched' by those who were of the view that 'right-wing forces should come to power in all East European countries'. Iliescu's appeal to the miners and his condonement of their violence was to have fateful repercussions in September 1991.

Most Western governments delivered strong protests at Iliescu's behaviour and his inauguration as President was boycotted by the US ambassador. The failure of the NSF Government either to arrest those suspected of perpetrating the violence of 13–15 June, or to take action against those responsible for the deaths in Tîrgu Mureş, tarnished its image, weakened its electoral legitimacy and compromised chances of dialogue with the opposition. Thousands of young, educated Romanians left the country during the summer of 1990, while the forces of the parliamentary opposition attempted to form a united front under the collective banner of 'The Democratic Antitotalitarian Forum' (DAF), which was proclaimed at Cluj-Napoca on 9 August. Extra-parliamentary groups, such as trade unions and student bodies, joined the Group for Social Dialogue, an organization of the intellectual élite, to form the Alianţa Civică (Civic Alliance) in September. In July 1991 the Civic Alliance created the Party of the Civic Alliance to parallel the existing organization.

Threatened with exclusion from privilege and power, former Communists joined forces with retired Securitate officers in exploiting the crisis of authority which was evident in the failure even of certain ministers to take responsibility for their own decisions. Persistent attacks of a virulently xenophobic nature in the ultra-nationalist sections of the press on government policies and personalities, especially those of Jewish descent or connections (even though the Jewish population of Romania stood at only 18,000), not only damaged the credibility of individuals, but also weakened the institutions of democracy which they represented. Particular targets included Silviu Brucan and Petre Roman, even though the latter's Jewish connections were no more than tenuous. The interests of these officers converged with those of elements in the Socialist Party of Labour (essentially a relaunched Romanian Communist Party), and with sections of the governing National Salvation Front which were opposed to the pace of reform, in undermining and seeking to bring down the Government of Petre Roman. It was the grievances of the coal-miners from the Jiu valley which provided the catalyst for these opposition forces to react, but the opportunity for their reaction was created by the Government's insensitivity to a series of long-standing demands by the miners.

THE RESIGNATION OF ROMAN

On 23 September 1991, miners in the Jiu valley coalfield began a strike in protest at what they regarded as the Government's failure to address their grievances. The miners were angered at the growing discrepancy between soaring food prices and their wages, the taxing of their dangerous-work benefit, their dangerous working conditions, the absence of adequate medical centres in the mines, the poor housing conditions in the Jiu valley, where many families lacked cooking facilities, and the low quality

of bread and the difficulty of obtaining it. Although the Jiu Valley Miners' Free Trade Union League had called off a general strike planned for that day in the wake of negotiations with the Government, miners at the Vulcan mine refused to go down the pit, complaining that their wage claim had not been fully settled. Representatives of the striking miners read out two principal demands: the indexing of salaries to prices, and the exemption from tax of their risk benefit. They further demanded that a Government team led by Prime Minister Petre Roman, and a parliamentary team composed of representatives of all political parties, come to meet them.

The miners then marched 12 kilometres from the Vulcan mine to the town of Petroşani, where a protest rally was held. On their way into Petroşani they were reported to have ransacked private shops, attacked peasants selling food and to have assaulted private taxi-drivers. Miron Cosma, the miners' leader, read out a government communiqué replying to the miners' demands, which announced that the Public Coal Corporation would renegotiate wages in keeping with its cash limits, and that the Government would propose to parliament an amendment to the tax law exempting risk benefit from taxation. What many miners appeared to find unacceptable in the communiqué was the failure of the Prime Minister to agree to visit the Jiu valley and so, in their own words, they decided that 'if the Prime Minister won't come to us, we'll go to him'.

Several thousand miners, reports put the numbers at between 4,000 and 8,000, commandeered two trains at Petroşani and forced the drivers to take them to Bucharest. They arrived on the morning of 25 September and marched to the government building. There they demanded to see the Prime Minister, and when he failed to appear they attempted to storm the building. Driven back by militia using tear gas, they eventually dispersed. Three people died and 25 were injured during the clashes. On the morning of 26 September Prime Minister Roman offered his, and the Government's, resignation on the grounds that he had been unable to maintain public order. His resignation was accepted by President Iliescu, despite subsequent indications that it may have been offered as a gesture intended to appease the demonstrators, and that Roman had expected to emerge with his position reaffirmed. The miners, however, urged on by civilians, who appear, from their language and demeanour, to have been representatives from the Ceauşescu order, broke into the parliament building, demanding that the deputies dismiss the President. On being told that the parliament had no such powers, the miners, in concert with several hundred civilians, made their way to the television station, which they attacked with petrol bombs. They were eventually repulsed by troops and militia. On the morning of 27 September, President Iliescu bowed to some of the miners' demands and signed a communiqué with Miron Cosma, in which he agreed to visit the Jiu valley on 30 September. Hearing this, most of the miners boarded specially-provided trains and returned home. Some 500 stragglers were rounded up by the police on the following day and sent home.

If the aim of the miners was to bring down Petre Roman, then they obviously succeeded. But if by doing so they, and the civilians who joined them in Bucharest, hoped to slow down the pace of reform, they are likely to have failed. President Iliescu cancelled his visit to the Jiu valley, and another reformer, Theodor Stolojan, was appointed Prime Minister on 1 October. On 16 October Stolojan's new Government of 'national openness' was confirmed in office by the Assembly of Deputies; it was a four-party coalition, including members from the National Liberal Party, the Agrarian Democratic Party (widely regarded as a NSF satellite) and the Romanian Ecological Movement, but was still dominated by the NSF.

The miners may, indeed, have accelerated the process of reform by giving the pro-Western members of the NSF the excuse which they needed to remove from positions of authority the old conservative, Communist-minded, figures, who had used every opportunity to publicly denounce the rapidity of economic change, and who have encouraged undemocratic forces to undermine the authority of the Government. By pointing to the identity of interest between the miners and opponents of change, and to the violent methods used by the miners to impose their unconstitutional will on the elected Government, the NSF and, in particular, Petre Roman, can claim to be the defenders of democracy, thereby deflecting the charges of neo-Communism which have been levelled at them by their critics since they were voted into office in May 1990, and erasing the memory of their condonement of the miners' violence in June 1990. These events may also demonstrate the lack of any convincing leader outside of NSF circles. While demonstrations have been aimed against Iliescu, Roman and the Government, and have even successfully removed their targets, they have not been in support of a believable alternative. The miners may have chanted for Miron Cosma as President, and other demonstrators may have supported the return of ex-King Michael as a constitutional monarch, whose visit to the country over Christmas 1990 ended in his deportation, but in doing so they merely highlight the absence of a genuine figure behind whom the disaffected might rally.

The Economy

ALAN H. SMITH

INTRODUCTION

Romanian economic policy from the end of the Second World War until the overthrow of the Ceauşescu regime in December 1989 can be interpreted as an extreme version of the pursuit of the traditional Stalinist model of economic development. This involved the rapid construction of a heavy industrial base in a relatively backward agrarian economy, by means of a highly-centralized system of economic management. The major features which differentiate Romanian economic policy from that of the other East European economies during this period were the high degree of concentration of economic power and authority in the hands of the leadership, and the virtual absence of any attempts to reform the economy that would have involved a genuine decentralization of economic decision-making to either enterprises or non-party organizations.

DOMESTIC DEVELOPMENT POLICIES 1950–1980: THE SEEDS OF CRISIS

The policy of economic development in Romania virtually replicated the Stalinist growth model of the 1930s and 1940s, and involved an extremely rapid growth of the industrial capital stock and the industrial labour force. This was not entirely imposed from outside, but reflected the economic priorities of the Romanian Communist Party, which in turn were influenced by the theories of protectionist and nationalist-minded Romanian economists from the inter-war period, who had rejected the idea that Romania should remain a predominantly agrarian country. The most notable of these was Manoilescu (Montias, 1967—see Bibliography, p. 276), who argued that Romania should pursue a deliberate strategy of industrialization, with the domestic consumer market protected by a tariff wall, while imports were concentrated on machinery and equipment to bring about industrial modernization. In practice, however, the pace of Romanian industrial development in the inter-war period was relatively slow and was not sufficient to have any significant impact on the proportion of the population employed outside agriculture (Ronnas, 1984).

The strategy of Romanian industrialization in the Communist era was motivated by the desire to create a form of economic independence by reducing the demand for imported manufactured goods and generating exports of manufactures in place of food and raw materials which, it was argued, would result in a long-term improvement in the terms of trade. This policy was extended beyond a policy of industrialization, viewed as an end in itself under Gheorghiu-Dej (who died in 1965), to embrace a policy of import substitution (described as 'a many-sided industrialization') by Ceauşescu, which involved the domestic production of a wide range of industrial products to minimize dependence on imports. Ironically, this pattern of industrialization, which both neglected the country's traditional comparative advantage in agriculture and drastically increased domestic consumption of energy and raw materials, ultimately made Romania more dependent on imported raw materials and foodstuffs.

The growth of the industrial capital stock was achieved by the traditional Stalinist technique of allocating a large (and growing) proportion of national income to investment, over 85% of which was devoted to what is described in Marxist terminology as 'productive investment', with a relatively low priority attached to investment in infrastructure and social and cultural facilities, including housing, health and scientific research. Furthermore, according to official statistics (*Anuarul Statistic*, various years), over 80% of total investment in the economy was allocated to the creation of additional production capacities, divided approximately equally between construction projects and new machinery and equipment. About 50% of all investment was concentrated in industry, four-fifths of which were devoted to industrial producers' goods. A further 10% of total investment was allocated to transport. In the 1950s and 1960s, industrial investment was largely concentrated on the development of the energy sector (including petroleum) and of the iron and steel, machine tool and chemical industries. When Ceauşescu came to power in 1965, a growing share of industrial investment was concentrated on the development of the machine tool and chemical industries (including petrochemicals), while the energy sector received a smaller proportion of total investment.

According to official statistics, the industrial labour force increased from 800,000 in 1950 to 4.2m. in 1989. In the initial stage of industrialization (before the beginning of the collectivization of agriculture in 1956), the growth in industrial employment was largely achieved by utilizing unemployed urban labour (Ronnas, 1984). From 1956 onwards, the growth of the industrial labour force was largely achieved by the movement of labour from rural areas to the towns, a policy that was drastically accelerated in the Ceauşescu era. This also coincided with a shift in industrial location policy away from traditional industrial regions towards the construction of large greenfield sites, to provide employment accommodation for workers migrating from rural areas (Ronnas, 1991). A major consequence of this policy is that Romania currently has a high proportion of workers of first (or second) generation peasant origin in its industrial labour force.

Romanian economic policy during the Ceauşescu era was increasingly dominated by the tendency to set over-ambitious central plan targets, which reflected the personal preferences of Ceauşescu himself, and which ignored the strains thus imposed on other sectors of the economy, assuming that these could be overcome by exhortation and human will-power alone. The strong impression is that the Ceauşescu leadership simply ignored the strains and bottle-necks which the pursuit of central objectives had created in the economy until these had become critical, whereupon the leadership responded by changing the central priorities, which were then pursued with equal ruthlessness.

Until the late 1970s the major objective was to maximize the rate of industrial growth, which was achieved by devoting a growing proportion of national income to investment in order to compensate for declining investment efficiency. Total investment in the 1976–80 plan period was planned to grow by 83% compared with the preceding five-year plan period, and to consume over one-third of national income produced during that period. In practice, the 1976–80 plan was badly affected by internal and external problems which destroyed the viability of what was already an over-ambitious plan, and pushed the economy closer to crisis. A major earthquake on 4 March 1977, with its epicentre in the oilfields of Ploieşti, badly affected the country's major industrial areas around Bucharest and, more significantly, contributed to a longer-term decline in crude petroleum output from a peak of 14.7m. metric tons in 1976 to 11.5m. tons in 1980, and to below 10m. tons by the late 1980s (*Anuarul Statistic*, various years). The fall in crude petroleum production, combined with the expansion of the oil refining and petrochemicals sectors, was sufficient to turn Romania into a net petroleum importer (in value terms) from 1977 onwards.

The already over-ambitious plan targets for the 1976–80 five-year plan were again revised upwards in October 1977 (industrial output was planned to grow at just under 12% per year), despite the damage the earthquake had inflicted on both the industrial capital stock and domestic energy production, not to mention popular morale, which was reflected in strikes and riots in the principal coal-mining regions in the Jiu valley in the summer of 1977. The planned expansion of industrial output placed further strain on domestic energy production, and on electric power generation in particular, and further aggravated existing shortages and bottle-necks. The planners' response to energy shortages was to increase targets for coal production (including low-quality and highly-polluting brown coal and lignite), despite the disturbances in the mining regions, and to launch a series of unattainable proposals for the expansion of hydroelectric power and the construction of nuclear power. In practice, targets for coal-fired power generation could not be realized, and petroleum and natural gas had to be diverted from exports to power generation (Smith, 1982 and 1987).

The causes of the crisis which overtook the Romanian economy in the 1980s can be largely dated to the response to the problems of the late 1970s. From 1977–80, the domestic imbalances created by unattainable plan targets were partly relieved by increasing imports of not only machinery and equipment, to meet investment targets, but also by increased imports of energy, raw materials (including iron ore) and even food. Partly as a result of Romania's

isolation within the Council for Mutual Economic Assistance (CMEA), all of these imports had to be paid for in hard currency. This was a major factor contributing to the debt crisis of 1981–82 which, in turn, lead to Ceauşescu's decision to repay hard-currency debt in the 1980s (see below). Domestic economic performance was also badly affected by over-taut planning, however. Official statistics (which greatly exaggerate real performance) indicate a decline in the rate of industrial growth after 1977. More critically, the degree of fulfilment of plan targets declined noticeably after 1977, with only two of the 25 plan targets for industrial output established for 1980 actually being fulfilled. The degree of underfulfilment of plan targets was highest in the priority sectors—energy, petrochemicals and metallurgy.

ROMANIAN FOREIGN ECONOMIC RELATIONS

The rift with the CMEA

Romanian foreign economic relations in the Communist period were strongly influenced by the policy of national independence, which was frequently interpreted in the West (to Romania's undoubted advantage) as a desire for independence from the USSR. In practice, Romania's 'independent line' in economic policy was more the result of a dispute with the more-industrialized East European nations, over the economic role that Romania should play within the CMEA (in which the USSR initially took a neutral stance, before siding with the industrialized nations), than a reflection of a conscious desire to improve economic relations with the West.

Romania, in common with the other CMEA economies, was initially forced to accelerate its plans for the development of heavy industry following the outbreak of the Korean War in 1950. Following the death of Stalin in 1953, the new Soviet Government, headed by Malenkov, scaled down the priority attached to heavy industrial production in the CMEA region in favour of increased production of consumer goods (the 'New Course'). Romania responded to the lower level of Eastern Bloc demand for iron and steel and engineering products by reducing its imports of capital goods from CMEA partners and increasing the proportion of investment that was met from domestic production, thereby reducing its trade levels with the other CMEA economies. This resulted in a major conflict with the more-industrialized members of the CMEA, who felt that the less-industrialized Balkan economies should concentrate on the production of food and agrarian products, and meet a greater proportion of their demand for machinery and engineering goods by importing from the central East European countries, which were now faced with excess capacity for industrial products (Montias, 1967).

Similar concerns were expressed by the Soviet authorities, who were becoming increasingly preoccupied with the cost to the Soviet economy of meeting East European demand for energy and raw materials, which had been generated by the pursuit of the Stalinist priority of investment in heavy industry throughout Eastern Europe, but which were now placing considerable strain on Soviet supply capabilities, as the more accessible and cheaper sources of supply became exhausted. Soviet concerns were reflected in a series of proposals for specialization agreements in the late 1950s and early 1960s, which were intended to limit East European production of steel and engineering goods to countries which either had a clear comparative advantage in these industries, or had adequate sources of iron ore and coking coal, in order to limit the demand for Soviet sources. The Soviet proposals received a reasonably enthusiastic response from the German Democratic Republic and Czechoslovakia, who interpreted them as support for the policy of restricting industrial production in the agrarian CMEA economies, which would provide them with a guaranteed market for their products. The proposals were greeted with far less enthusiasm by the Balkan economies, who interpreted the policies as a deliberate attempt to restrict their plans to industrialize, and which would commit them to a permanent agrarian status. Romania, in particular, was reluctant to abandon proposals to build a major metallurgical complex at Galaţi, with Soviet assistance, close to the mouth of the Danube, which would have relied on iron ore imported from the USSR.

Although it can be argued that Romanian policy was largely determined by the desire to pursue an irrational policy of rapid industrialization, which paid little regard to the country's natural comparative advantage or resource endowment, Romania's dispute with the industrialized central East European economies was aggravated by the unwillingness of the latter to give up the production of relatively unsophisticated, labour-intensive manufactured goods which could have been produced more cheaply in the labour abundant agrarian economies. In the absence of competitive market pressures, the more-industrialized economies could simply refuse to import these goods from the agrarian economies, while similarly, the latter refused to import machinery and equipment from the former. In the final analysis, therefore, this dispute could not be resolved without either introducing market forces into the operation of the CMEA economies and their mutual trade, or by giving CMEA organs supranational powers to determine investment plans in the individual economies. The dispute became crystallized in November 1962. The USSR indicated its unwillingness to assist in the production of the Galaţi steel mill while Khrushchev, the Soviet leader, on 19 November 1962, at the end of a speech which included a bitter denunciation of 'metal eaters' (the policy of excess steel production), proposed the establishment of a 'common planning organ' which would be empowered to draw up common plans for the CMEA and to co-ordinate the development of the CMEA economies on a bloc basis. The Romanian delegation withdrew from the plenum, and a special Central Committee plenum was convened on 21–23 November, following which it was announced that the construction of the Galaţi metallurgical combine would now go ahead on the basis of assistance provided by an Anglo-French consortium. The supranational implications of Khrushchev's proposal for a common planning organ were too strong, even for those countries that might have secured economic benefits from it, and Khrushchev, already weakened by the Cuban missile crisis, was forced to backtrack (Fischer-Galati, 1967 and Smith, 1983).

The Romanian rift with the CMEA was accentuated following Ceauşescu's accession to power in 1965. In the latter half of that year, Romania reduced its imports from CMEA partners (particularly of machinery and equipment) by 20%, which marked the beginning of a long-term decline in the importance of trade with CMEA partners. In the late 1960s Romania continued to oppose Soviet proposals to improve economic co-operation and plan co-ordination in the CMEA, and did not participate (or only partially participated) in a number of CMEA investment projects, which were designed to provide East European assistance in the development of Soviet natural resources for bloc consumption. Ironically, this economic 'independence' was achieved at a substantial cost to the Romanian economy. Romania's isolation from the CMEA meant that, unlike the other East European economies, it did not benefit from preferential terms of trade with the USSR, which enabled the other East European economies to import Soviet crude oil in exchange for exports of relatively low-quality exports of manufactured goods, but was forced to import crude oil from hard currency sources and to export manufactured goods to the more demanding hard currency markets.

The Diversion of Trade to the West: the Import-Led Growth Strategy

Romania's trade per head with the West was insignificant in the early 1960s, the lowest of the European CMEA countries, and, despite the rift with the CMEA and the import of Western machinery and equipment for the construction of the Galaţi steel mill, Romanian trade with the West only grew modestly until 1967. In 1967 Romania became the first East European country to embark on the strategy of 'import-led growth', which involved making relatively costless political concessions to the West (including the recognition of the Federal Republic of Germany and taking a neutral stance on the Arab–Israeli conflict of that year) in exchange for improved economic relations. In this sense, the strategy bore a strong similarity to the policy of détente which was subsequently pursued by Leonid Brezhnev in the USSR. The economic goal of the strategy was the modernization of the industrial capital stock, which involved a combination of direct imports of Western machinery and equipment (largely supplied on credit) and the encouragement of a number of different types of 'co-operation ventures' with Western multinational corporations, whereby it was hoped that the latter would provide Romania with technology embodied in machinery and equipment, together with technical documentation and know-how in exchange for repayment in products which would (at least theoretically) be produced by the newly-installed plant and equipment, and by the new industrial processes.

In 1971 Romania became the first CMEA country to enact joint-venture legislation, which enabled Western multinationals to take a minority (up to 49%) equity holding in ventures on Romanian territory. At the same time, in part motivated by the desire to appear open to the West, and in part to avail itself of additional hard-currency credits and to acquire improved access to Western markets, Romania joined GATT (the General Agreement on Tariffs and Trade) in 1971, and the IMF (International Monetary Fund) and the World Bank in 1972. The Federal Republic of Germany has traditionally been the most active Western exporter to Romania, accounting for about one-half of Romania's imports from the West, and, in 1974, overtook the USSR as Romania's largest foreign supplier, according to official statistics.

The strategy of the acquisition of foreign technology, within the framework of a highly centralized system of economic administration, suffered from a number of basic flaws which contributed to its failure in the early 1970s. Firstly, the strategy placed excessive emphasis on building up a technological base in engineering industries, in which Romania had little or no experience or expertise (for example, aerospace and car production), rather than building on Romania's traditional strengths in agriculture, textiles, furniture and footwear. More critically, however, Romania offered Western multinationals a far less attractive economic environment than the newly-industrializing economies of South-East Asia in particular. Central government controls were maintained over a myriad of enterprise decisions, including manning levels, wage and price policy and quality control. As a result, co-operation ventures and joint ventures proved to be far less attractive to Western multinationals than the Romanian authorities had anticipated (only five joint ventures were established), and the Romanians were forced to rely on straightforward purchases of industrial licences and machinery and equipment to a far greater degree than intended.

More crucially, Romanian exports to the West also failed to reach planned levels. Romania was unable to generate a sufficient volume of hard-currency exports to finance either a continued flow of imports of machinery and equipment, or the increased demand for energy, raw materials and components and spare parts required to keep imported plants in operation. Thus the country was unable to meet interest payments and repayments of principal on existing debt.

The first indications that debt was becoming a major cause of concern to Western investors came as early as 1971, when Romania became the most indebted CMEA country, even including the USSR, with a net debt of US $1,200m. Romania was, however, a net petroleum exporter at the time of the first world petroleum-price shock of 1973–74, and benefited slightly from the increase in world petroleum prices; Romanian net debt stabilized at about $2,500m. from 1974 to 1976. The fall in crude petroleum output in 1977, following the earthquake, turned Romania into a net petroleum importer and created a new set of balance-of-payments problems, which was further aggravated by the second world petroleum-price crisis in 1979–80 and by the collapse of a bilateral deal with Iran (which provided for Iranian deliveries of crude petroleum in exchange for Romanian manufactured goods), following the ousting of the Shah. Crude petroleum imports reached 16m. metric tons in 1980, costing Romania $3,800m. in hard currency, which, together with rising interest rates on existing debt, pushed the Romanian current account deficit in its balance of payments in convertible currencies to $2,400m. Despite cuts in imports of $1,000m. in 1981, which resulted in a trade surplus in that year, interest charges pushed the current account further into deficit by $800,000, and gross debt rose to $10,500m. at the end of 1981, with payments arrears of $1,100m. Romania was forced to make a formal request for the rescheduling of its debt and the suspension of interest payments in 1982 (Jackson, 1986 and Smith, 1983 and 1987).

THE DEBT REPAYMENT PROGRAMME

The need to reschedule debt resulted in an abrupt change in Romanian economic policy in the 1980s. The goal of the maximization of industrial output, with little or no regard to balance-of-payments constraint, was suddenly replaced by the goal of the elimination of hard-currency debt, this time with little or no regard to the impact that this policy was having on either domestic living standards, which were reduced to the lowest levels in Europe (except Albania), or on investment in industry and infrastructure, which had long term effects on economic efficiency. Unlike the other East European countries, which were forced to reduce both their borrowing from the West and their gross debt, as repayments of principal became due in the early 1980s, but then increased their debt in the second half of the 1980s, Romania continued with the debt repayment programme in the late 1980s until all outstanding debt had been repaid.

The poor quality of much Romanian manufactured produce, and the low level of competitiveness of Romanian exports in Western markets, meant that surpluses in the balances of trade and payments could only be achieved by a drastic reduction in imports, followed by the export of items with a low level of processing, such as food and energy, which were in high domestic demand. Hard-currency imports were cut from $8,000m. in 1980 to $4,700m. in 1982, and to only $3,400m. (in current prices) in 1989. Imports from the industrialized West were reduced from a peak of $3,900m. in 1980 to $1,300m. in 1983, reaching

their lowest in 1989, at $1,200m. The major burden of the reduction in imports from the industrialized West was borne by machinery and equipment, imports of which fell from just under $1,000m. in 1980 to only $300,000 a year from 1983 onwards. Imports of foodstuffs from the West were cut from a peak of $900,000 in 1981 to $27m. in 1984, and those of crude petroleum were cut from $3,800m. to $2,500m. between 1980 and 1982 (Smith, 1987).

The net effect of import cuts was that a hard-currency trade deficit of $2,400m. in 1980 had been turned into trade surpluses in the region of $2,000m. a year in the mid-1980s, climbing to $2,500m. in 1988 and permitting Ceauşescu to announce, in April 1989, that Romanian debt had been eliminated. Although this claim may have been some months premature, Western data shows that Romanian assets held in Western banks exceeded their liabilities by over $1,000m. at the time of the December revolution. In addition, Romania was owed $3,000m. by developing countries, particularly Iraq, which owed $1,600m.

The repayment of debt was only accomplished at an enormous human and economic cost. In 1982 Romania was transformed from being a net importer of foods and in trade with the industrialized West (although it was a net exporter in trade with socialist countries and in trade in total), into a major net exporter. Despite food price increases in February 1982 (which were officially stated to be 35% but, in practice, appear to have been nearer 70%), severe food shortages and food queues appeared in major cities. Bread, sugar and cooking oil were rationed (and, furthermore, not always available), and meat, apart from occasional items of poultry, was virtually unobtainable. Despite legislation requiring peasants to make compulsory deliveries to the State, according to the size of their land-holdings, and attempts to centralize food supplies to concentrate deliveries to mining regions and tourist areas, widespread shortages of food still occurred in the latter (Jackson, 1986).

The position with energy supplies was even more acute and became critical in the severe winter of 1984/85, when temperatures in some parts of the country were reported to have fallen below −25°C. Communal heating systems were switched off for most of each day, while gas pressures were too low for heating or cooking; electric power supplies were frequently interrupted and the use of electric heaters, refrigerators and vacuum cleaners was banned and household electricity consumption was virtually reduced to the equivalent of a single 40-watt light bulb per household. These regulations were enforced by squads of apparatchiki, loyal to Ceauşescu. The use of private cars was banned for three months, while the public transportation networks collapsed, forcing workers to trudge many miles to work in deep snow. In addition, a virtual ban on public lighting and lighting in stairways of apartments was imposed; offices and shops were required to operate during daylight hours only and, even in tourist areas, bars and cafés had to close at 9 p.m. Hospitals were frequently without heating, adequate lighting or power for operations, and deaths from hypothermia were reported. Indoor temperatures approached freezing-point, and even senior government officials worked in their offices in gloves and overcoats. Several Western embassies evacuated all but their most essential staff. Similar restrictions were imposed in the following winters although, fortunately, weather conditions were not so severe (Smith, 1987).

Although Western attention has largely concentrated on the human costs of the debt repayment policy, the efficiency and competitiveness of Romanian industry was also seriously affected. Cuts in imports of machinery and equipment have resulted in the failure to modernize industry, inadequate investment in infrastructure, including transport and telecommunications, while valuable resources allocated to investment were squandered on grandiose 'prestige' investment projects such as the Presidential Palace in Bucharest and the Danube–Black Sea Canal. Similarly, industrial investment that did take place appears to have been directed towards obsolete industries. As a result, after the revolution the new Prime Minister, Petre Roman, claimed that the majority of industrial plants were using technology that was, in some cases, 30 to 40 years old, and that the technological level of Romanian industry was 15 to 20 years behind that of the West (Smith, 1991).

THE ECONOMY AFTER THE REVOLUTION

The first priority of the National Salvation Front, which took power following the December 1989 revolution, was to win some measure of popular support by bringing an immediate improvement in living standards. This was initially achieved by cutting exports of food and energy, and increasing imports of the most urgent deficit items. At the same time, many of the harshest measures of factory discipline that had been imposed in the 1980s were relaxed. Basic goods remained heavily subsidized by the state budget, while employment was virtually guaranteed, the working week was reduced and many older workers benefited from early retirement. The Front indicated in its election programme that the transition to a market economy would be gradual. Following the election on 20 May, however, the Prime Minister, Petre Roman, nominated a young, essentially meritocratic, cabinet and awarded the principal economic portfolios to economists who supported a rapid transition to a market economy and whose views appeared to conflict with those of President Iliescu.

The combined effect of the relaxation of factory discipline and the continuation of a high level of enterprise subsidies funded by budget deficits was to bring about a rapid collapse of production, and to stimulate inflationary pressures and balance-of-payments problems. Industrial output fell by nearly 30% in the first nine months of 1990, while wages continued to grow by more than 11% and working hours fell by over 16%. This contributed to a widening gap between demand and supply, which was reflected in a growing hard-currency trade deficit which reached $1,500m. in 1990, and in growing indications of domestic shortages.

In the autumn of 1990, Roman argued that the economic problems had become so serious that it was now essential to accelerate the process of economic reform and put a rapid transition to a market economy into effect. He introduced a detailed package of reforms which involved the transition to a West European style of market economy within a two-year period. This would involve measures (ultimately) to make the currency fully convertible, and to expose domestic enterprises to international competition; the introduction of a two-tier banking system incorporating a central national bank and independent commercial banks; liberalization of both wholesale and retail prices; the restructuring of industry away from smoke-stack industries to modern light industry; the removal of existing restrictions on small-scale private enterprises and the privatization of state industry; land reform; tax reform; and the creation of a state welfare system (Roman, 1990).

The level of excess demand in the economy meant that these reforms would have to be accompanied (or preceded) by a severe 'deflationary' (macrostabilization) package, designed to equilibrate supply and demand on domestic markets and to draw out repressed inflationary pressures. This would be achieved by gradually allowing prices to rise to market clearing levels, and then reducing and eliminating the budget deficit by removing subsidies to industrial enterprises and to food, rents, etc. The macroeconomic stabilization programme came into effect in November 1990 and initially involved the removal of state subsidies to virtually all consumer goods, except basic foodstuffs, housing and heating, which resulted in price rises for the affected goods which ranged between 100% and 300%. Further price increases, which affected the majority of food products, were introduced in April 1991, and subsidies on heating and rents were scheduled to be removed in early 1992. Wages and salaries however, were only partially indexed, to prevent a hyperinflationary wage-price spiral.

Not surprisingly, these measures provoked popular opposition which threatened not only the implementation of the reform programme, but also popular support for the Front itself and the social cohesion of the country. Petre Roman and his Government fell, political victims of these policies, in September 1991. The new Prime Minister, Theodor Stolojan, was committed to the programme of economic reforms, and had even threatened to resign from his then position as Finance Minister in March 1991 in protest at a planned relaxation of the speed of its introduction. The resolution of these problems will be the critical factor for Romanian economic development in the 1990s.

Statistical Survey

Source (unless otherwise stated): *Romanian Statistical Yearbook*, published by the Comisia Naţională de Statistică (National Statistics Commission), Bucharest, Str. Stavropoleos 6; tel. (0) 158200; telex 111153.

Area and Population

AREA, POPULATION AND DENSITY

Area (sq km)

Land	229,077
Inland water	8,423
Total	237,500*

Population (census results)

15 March 1966	19,103,163
5 January 1977	
Males	10,626,055
Females	10,933,855
Total	21,559,910

Population (official estimates at mid-year)

1986	22,823,479
1987	22,940,430
1989†	23,152,000

Population (official estimates)

31 December 1988	23,112,000
31 December 1989	23,211,000
31 December 1990	23,190,000
Density (per sq km) at December 1990	97.6

*91,699 sq miles.

† A figure for 1988 is not available.

ADMINISTRATIVE DIVISIONS

	Area (sq km)	Population ('000, at 31 Dec. 1989)	Density (per sq km)	Administrative capital (with population at 31 Dec. 1989)
Alba	6,231	430	68.7	Alba Iulia (73,743)
Arad	7,652	507	66.2	Arad (193,766)
Argeş	6,801	678	99.5	Piteti (162,802)
Bacău	6,606	736	110.7	Bacău (195,763)
Bihor	7,535	663	87.6	Oradea (228,258)
Bistriţa-Năsăud	5,305	330	61.7	Bistriţa (86,880)
Botoşani	4,965	470	94.2	Botoşani (121,351)
Braşov	5,351	695	129.8	Braşov (352,260)
Brăila	4,724	403	85.3	Brăila (238,516)
Buzău	6,072	526	86.4	Buzău (146,224)
Caraş-Severin	8,503	409	48.0	Reşiţa (110,902)
Călăraşi	5,074	351	6.24	Călăraşi (76,792)
Cluj	6,650	744	111.7	Cluj-Napoca (318,975)
Constanţa	7,055	735	104.4	Constanţa (312,504)
Covasna	3,705	239	64.2	Sfîntu Gheorghe (72,820)
Dîmboviţa	4,036	571	141.2	Tîrgovişte (101,332)
Dolj	7,413	775	104.2	Craiova (297,585)
Galaţi	4,425	644	145.1	Galaţi (305,065)
Giurgiu	3,511	325	92.5	Giurgiu (73,416)
Gorj	5,641	389	68.7	Tîrgu Jiu (94,126)
Harghita	6,610	364	54.3	Miercurea-Ciuc (49,304)
Hunedoara	7,016	568	80.9	Deva (80,797)
Ialomiţa	4,449	310	69.5	Slobozia (51,780)
Iaşi	5,469	816	149.2	Iaşi (334,371)
Maramureş	6,215	560	89.5	Baia Mare (152,129)
Mehedinţi	4,900	330	67.1	Drobeta-Turnu Severin (107,982)

—*continued*	Area (sq km)	Population ('000, at 31 Dec. 1989)	Density (per sq km)	Administrative capital (with population at 31 Dec. 1989)
Mureş	6,696	624	92.8	Tîrgu Mureş (166,029)
Neamţ	5,890	584	98.5	Piatra-Neamţ (117,325)
Olt	5,507	536	97.1	Slatina (87,377)
Prahova	4,694	880	186.9	Ploieşti (248,739)
Satu Mare	4,405	418	94.6	Satu Mare (137,936)
Sălaj	3,850	270	69.9	Zalău (66,612)
Sibiu	5,422	509	93.8	Sibiu (182,580)
Suceava	8,555	704	81.7	Suceava (106,905)
Teleorman	5,760	504	87.4	Alexandria (59,033)
Timiş	8,692	715	83.5	Timişoara (324,651)
Tulcea	8,430	276	32.6	Tulcea (94,774)
Vaslui	5,297	472	88.4	Vaslui (76,641)
Vîlcea	5,705	433	75.4	Rîmnicu Vîlcea (105,810)
Vrancea	4,863	397	81.0	Focşani (98,203)
Bucharest Municipality	1,820	2,325	1,274.1	Bucharest (2,325,037)
Total	**237,500**	**23,211**	**97.7**	

PRINCIPAL TOWNS

(estimated population at 31 December 1989)

București (Bucharest, the capital)	2,325,037	Sibiu	182,580
Braşov	352,260	Tîrgu Mureş	166,029
Iaşi	334,371	Piteşti	162,802
Timişoara	324,651	Baia Mare	152,129
Cluj-Napoca	318,975	Buzău	146,224
Constanţa	312,504	Satu Mare	137,936
Galaţi	305,065	Botoşani	121,351
Craiova	297,585	Piatra-Neamţ	117,325
Ploieşti	248,739	Reşiţa	110,902
Brăila	238,516	Drobeta-Turnu-Severin	107,982
Oradea	228,258	Suceava	106,905
Bacău	195,763	Rîmnicu-Vîlcea	105,810
Arad	193,766	Tîrgovişte	101,332

BIRTHS, MARRIAGES AND DEATHS

	Registered live births		Registered marriages		Registered deaths	
	Number	Rate (per 1,000)	Number	Rate (per 1,000)	Number	Rate (per 1,000)
1982	344,369	15.3	174,448	7.8	224,120	10.0
1983	321,498	14.3	163,826	7.3	233,892	10.4
1984	350,741	15.5	164,110	7.3	233,699	10.3
1985	358,797	15.8	161,094	7.1	246,670	10.9
1986	376,896	16.5	167,254	7.3	242,330	10.6
1987	383,196	16.7	168,079	7.3	254,286	11.1
1988	380,043	16.5	172,527	7.5	253,370	11.0
1989	369,544	16.0	177,943	7.7	247,306	10.7

ECONOMICALLY ACTIVE POPULATION*
(Census of 5 January 1977)

	Males	Females	Total
Agriculture and forestry . .	1,497,380	2,478,249	3,975,629
Industry†	2,306,488	1,196,070	3,502,558
Construction	620,090	77,147	697,237
Electricity, gas, water and sanitary services. . .	89,037	26,523	115,560
Commerce	252,531	322,665	575,196
Transport, storage and communications . . .	468,666	87,839	556,505
Services	607,322	716,235	1,323,557
Other activities (not adequately described) . .	25,369	21,991	47,360
Total	5,866,883	4,926,719	10,793,602

* Excluding persons seeking work for the first time.
† Manufacturing, mining, quarrying, hunting and fishing.

CIVILIAN LABOUR FORCE EMPLOYED (official estimates)

	1987	1988	1989
Industry*	4,008,800	4,064,600	4,169,000
Agriculture and forestry . .	3,022,600	3,066,900	3,056,300
Construction	793,200	771,800	766,700
Transport and communications.	739,600	750,500	757,100
Trade	632,400	635,400	648,900
Housing, communal and other services	482,300	503,700	533,600
Public education, culture and arts	364,400	370,900	372,800
Science and science services .	139,300	140,800	141,200
Public health, social welfare and physical culture . .	289,400	288,900	292,300
State and local administration .	53,600	56,300	53,800
Total (incl. others) . . .	10,718,600	10,805,400	10,945,700

* Manufacturing, mining, quarrying, electricity, gas, water and sanitary services.

Agriculture

PRINCIPAL CROPS ('000 metric tons)

	1987	1988	1989
Wheat*	6,000	9,000	6,000
Rice (paddy)*	154	160	175
Barley*	1,800	2,200	1,800
Maize	10,500*	10,000*	11,800†
Rye	55	60*	63†
Oats*	100	160	140
Potatoes	7,572	8,000†	7,200†
Sunflower seed . . .	1,102	1,190†	1,100†
Cabbages	1,400*	1,300†	1,200†
Tomatoes	2,420*	2,300†	2,200†
Onions (dry) . . .	470*	435†	420†
Grapes	1,800†	2,245	2,000†
Sugar beet	7,149	6,500*	6,650†
Apples	716	800†	780†
Pears	125	130†	128†
Peaches	49	86†	82†
Plums	727	800†	765†
Apricots	37	45†	42†
Strawberries	32	39†	36†
Walnuts	37	47†	45†

* Unofficial estimates.   † FAO estimates.
Source: FAO, Production Yearbook.

LIVESTOCK ('000 head at 1 January)

	1987	1988	1989
Horses.	686	693	700†
Cattle*	7,017	7,182	7,170
Pigs	14,711	15,224	15,400*
Sheep	18,762	18,793	18,800*
Poultry	130,941	135,956	142,000†

* Unofficial estimates.   † FAO estimates.
Source: FAO, Production Yearbook.

LIVESTOCK PRODUCTS

	1987	1988	1989
Meat ('000 metric tons). .	1,656	1,549	1,628
Cow milk ('000 metric tons)* .	4,275	4,300	4,350
Cheese (metric tons) . .	92,692	95,800†	98,860†
Butter (metric tons) . .	37,805	44,000*	41,000*
Hen eggs (metric tons) . .	430,600	400,000*	380,000*
Honey (metric tons) . .	15,285	17,000†	17,000†
Wool:			
greasy	43,460	44,000*	44,000*
clean	25,640	28,000†	28,000†

* Unofficial estimates.   † FAO estimates.
Source: FAO, Production Yearbook.

Forestry

ROUNDWOOD REMOVALS
('000 cubic metres, excluding bark)

	1986	1987	1988
Sawlogs, veneer logs and logs for sleepers . . .	5,000	5,000	4,650
Pulpwood	5,485	5,485*	5,485*
Other industrial wood* . .	5,659	5,659	5,659
Fuel wood	4,569	4,569*	4,575*
Total	20,713	20,713	20,369

* FAO estimates.
Source: FAO, Yearbook of Forest Products.

SAWNWOOD PRODUCTION
('000 cubic metres, incl. boxboards)

	1986	1987	1988
Coniferous (soft wood) . . .	1,380	1,300	1,250
Broadleaved (hard wood) . .	2,100	1,500	1,450
Total	3,480	2,800	2,700

Railway sleepers ('000 cubic metres): 58 per year in 1986–88 (FAO estimates).
Source: FAO, Yearbook of Forest Products.

Fishing

('000 metric tons, live weight)

	1986	1987	1988
Common carp	19.6	17.8	17.0
Goldfish	17.7	14.3	20.1
Silver carp. . . .	10.9	13.0	21.0
Other freshwater fishes .	16.8	20.8	17.9
Cape horse mackerel . .	97.6	66.7	46.7
Other jack and horse mackerels . . .	43.3	65.4	45.4
Round sardinella . . .	10.0	11.8	19.0
European pilchard (sardine) .	8.4	16.8	28.1
Chub mackerel . . .	6.3	6.5	16.7
Other fishes	40.5	31.2	35.7
Other aquatic animals . .	0.1	0.0	—
Total catch . . .	271.1	264.4	267.6
Inland waters . . .	65.8	66.9	77.3
Mediterranean and Black Sea .	15.8	14.0	14.0
Atlantic Ocean. . . .	189.5	183.5	176.4

Source: FAO, *Yearbook of Fishery Statistics.*

Mining

	1988	1989	1990
Hard coal ('000 metric tons) .	9,142	8,300	3,826
Brown coal ('000 metric tons) .	58,754	61,343	38,183
Crude petroleum ('000 metric tons). . . .	9,389	9,173	7,928
Iron ore ('000 metric tons)* . .	2,252	2,482	n.a.
Salt ('000 metric tons) . .	5,353	5,038	n.a.
Methane gas (million cu metres)	25,195	22,222	28,336

* Figures refer to gross weight. The estimated metal content is 26%.

Industry

SELECTED PRODUCTS
('000 metric tons, unless otherwise indicated)

	1988	1989	1990
Canned fish	12	8	57
Canned vegetables. . .	370	343	n.a.
Canned fruits	171	190	n.a.
Refined sugar	580	693	n.a.
Margarine	46	48	n.a.
Wine ('000 hectolitres) . .	6,425	4,632	4,356
Beer ('000 hectolitres) . .	10,655	10,573	12,511
Tobacco products . . .	33	33	n.a.
Cotton yarn—pure and mixed .	165	157	n.a.
Cotton fabrics—pure and mixed (million sq metres) .	689	688	544
Woollen yarn—pure and mixed.	76	70	n.a.
Woollen fabrics—pure and mixed (million sq metres) .	133	133	115
Silk fabrics—pure and mixed (million sq metres)* . .	140	137	n.a.
Flax and hemp yarn—pure and mixed	36	35	n.a.
Linen and hemp fabrics—pure and mixed (million sq metres)	140	151	n.a.
Chemical filaments and fibres .	297	273	105
Footwear ('000 pairs) . . .	109,000	111,000	74,279
Chemical wood pulp . .	612	592	n.a.
Paper and paperboard . .	730	709	n.a.
Synthetic rubber . . .	161	149	102
Rubber tyres ('000) . . .	6,940	6,838	3,703
Sulphuric acid	1,825	1,687	1,112

—continued	1988	1989	1990
Caustic soda	821	763	556
Soda ash	918	889	640
Chemical fertilizers . .	2,295	2,805	1,742
Insecticides, fungicides, etc. .	39	33	12
Plastics and resins . . .	653	640	n.a.
Motor spirit (Petrol) . .	6,594	6,074	4,667
Distillate fuel oils . . .	8,471	8,435	6,232
Residual fuel oils . . .	9,954	10,172	8,121
Lubricating oils . . .	544	516	368
Coke	5,751	5,870	n.a.
Cement	14,447	13,265	10,383
Unworked glass ('000 sq metres)	76,379	76,199	56,649
Pig-iron	8,941	9,052	n.a.
Crude steel	14,314	14,415	9,687
Rolled steel products . .	10,355	10,263	6,788
Steel tubes. . . .	1,569	1,360	1,059
Aluminium—unwrought . .	266	269	178
Electric motors ('000 kilowatts) .	8,231	6,351	5,231
Electric generators ('000 kilovoltamperes) . .	869	720	800
Radio receivers ('000) . .	623	590	478
Television receivers ('000) . .	511	511	401
Merchant ships launched ('000 deadweight tons) . .	104	502	n.a.
Passenger motor cars (number)	120,000	123,000	84,161
Motor buses and lorries (number). . . .	16,556	13,515	8,531
Tractors (number) . . .	32,150	17,124	25,556
Sewing machines (number). .	17,763	12,410	n.a.
Combine harvester-threshers (number). . . .	6,705	5,649	n.a.
Freight wagons (number) .	11,485	11,274	6,888
Domestic refrigerators ('000) .	442	470	364
Domestic washing machines ('000)	236	204	n.a.
Gas cookers ('000) . . .	524	518	n.a.
Construction: new dwellings completed ('000) . .	103	60	n.a.
Electric energy (million kWh) .	75,322	75,851	64,161

* Including fabrics of artificial silk.

Finance

CURRENCY AND EXCHANGE RATES

Monetary Units
100 bani (singular: ban) = 1 leu (plural: lei).

Denominations
Coins: 5, 15 and 25 bani; 1, 3 and 5 lei.
Notes: 10, 25, 50, 100, 500 and 1,000 lei.

Sterling and Dollar Equivalents (30 June 1991)
£1 sterling = 100.46 lei;
US $1 = 62.05 lei (commercial rates);
1,000 lei = £9.954 = $16.116.

Average Exchange Rate (lei per US $, commercial rate)
1988   14.277
1989   14.922
1990   22.432

STATE BUDGET ('000 million lei)

Revenue	1987	1988	1989
Tax revenue	86.87	89.46	94.88
Social security contributions .	49.15	50.67	53.94
Taxes on payroll and workforce	37.72	38.79	40.94
Entrepreneurial and property income	280.17	244.21	255.37
Share of gross sales . .	48.72	144.71	150.61
Share of enterprise profits .	93.17	74.12	83.11
Other receipts from social units	17.32	16.28	16.49
Share of net production . .	116.30	34.18	—
Administrative fees, charges and non-industrial sales . .	0.16	0.24	1.02
Fines and forfeits . . .	1.01	2.40	1.54
Other non-tax revenue . . .	35.64	27.77	33.52
Total	**403.85**	**364.08**	**386.33**

Expenditure	1987	1988	1989
General public services, incl. public order	1.87	1.88	1.90
Defence	25.28	27.54	29.33
Education	15.48	15.31	16.08
Health	14.80	15.09	16.20
Social security and welfare .	66.89	69.82	75.40
Housing and community amenities	22.80	26.09	25.10
Recreational, cultural and religious affairs and services .	1.27	1.08	0.28
Economic affairs and services .	192.54	154.38	153.29
Fuel and energy	29.39	27.29	26.51
Agriculture, forestry, fishing and hunting	22.89	19.88	18.60
Mining, manufacturing and construction . . .	34.10	36.85	35.94
Transportation and communication	12.63	19.78	19.51
Other purposes . . .	93.53	50.58	52.73
Total	**343.79**	**314.09**	**320.55**

Source: IMF, *Government Finance Statistics Yearbook*.
1990: a deficit of 3,800m. lei was recorded.

BALANCE OF PAYMENTS (US $ million)

	1984	1985	1986
Merchandise exports f.o.b. . .	12,646	12,167	12,543
Merchandise imports f.o.b. . .	−10,334	−10,432	−10,590
Trade balance . . .	**2,312**	**1,735**	**1,953**
Exports of services* . .	957	849	928
Imports of services* . .	−1,550	−1,345	−1,392
Current balance . . .	**1,719**	**1,239**	**1,489**
Long-term capital (net) . .	−1,183	−1,189	−1,041
Short-term capital (net) . .	−508	−359	132
Net errors and omissions . .	104	1	−437
Total (net monetary movements) . .	132	−308	143
Valuation changes (net) . .	62	−107	379
Changes in reserves . .	**194**	**−415**	**522**

* Including unrequited transfers.
Source: IMF, *International Financial Statistics*.

External Trade

PRINCIPAL COMMODITIES (million lei)

Imports c.i.f.	1987	1988	1989
Fuel, mineral raw materials and metals . . .	75,540	65,244	75,633
Industrial equipment and means of transportation . .	33,603	32,284	34,361
Chemicals, fertilizers and rubber	6,892	7,611	7,471
Raw materials (other than foodstuffs	5,286	5,964	7,329
Manufactured consumer goods .	4,888	5,514	4,613
Foodstuffs	1,771	1,268	1,981
Total (incl. others) . . .	**132,984**	**122,263**	**134,982**

1990: Total imports 209,912m. lei.

Exports f.o.b.	1987	1988	1989
Industrial equipment and means of transportation . .	56,551	57,508	49,067
Fuels, mineral raw materials and metals . . .	45,181	51,164	53,922
Manufactured consumer goods .	29,800	33,819	30,401
Chemicals, fertilizers and rubber	14,808	19,233	15,933
Foodstuffs	9,379	8,289	7,163
Raw materials (other than foodstuffs) . . .	7,583	7,464	6,929
Total (incl. others) . . .	**167,850**	**182,258**	**167,780**

1990: Total exports 135,191m. lei.

PRINCIPAL TRADING PARTNERS (million lei)

Imports c.i.f.	1984	1985	1989*
Austria	1,567.9	1,206.0	879.2
Brazil	1,105.9	1,297.2	406.6
Bulgaria	3,710.5	4,504.0	3,451.9
China, People's Republic . .	5,702.5	5,487.0	5,148.0
Cuba	1,896.6	2,152.9	1,875.3
Czechoslovakia . . .	4,184.9	4,917.7	6,172.9
Egypt	13,287.3	15,468.9	2,447.2
France	2,658.2	1,996.6	786.3
German Democratic Republic .	8,751.0	8,573.6	9,935.7
Germany, Federal Republic .	6,495.8	5,046.5	2,933.3
Hungary	3,832.8	4,110.6	4,379.5
India	1,621.0	1,304.5	614.4
Iran	14,956.5	12,693.3	16,216.6
Iraq	1,246.6	2,555.4	908.4
Italy	2,159.1	2,501.7	834.0
Japan	1,540.7	1,577.3	714.3
Libya	3,010.6	1,153.6	184.3
Netherlands . . .	1,487.8	760.7	707.7
Poland	9,172.0	8,137.4	5,395.6
Saudi Arabia . . .	2,480.1	256.1	8,463.2
Switzerland . . .	1,153.6	1,075.1	663.4
Syria	10,531.7	6,310.3	2,246.1
Turkey	1,117.1	781.9	774.4
USSR	31,886.6	33,262.8	42,493.3
United Kingdom . . .	3,406.7	2,692.8	1,146.4
USA	5,748.8	4,549.6	2,735.8
Yugoslavia . . .	2,687.6	2,387.3	2,452.7
Total (incl. others) . . .	**160,816.3**	**148,361.4**	**134,982.3**

* Figures for 1986–88 are not available.

Exports f.o.b.	1984	1985	1989*
Austria	4,034.8	3,311.4	2,689.2
Brazil	286.7	1,246.4	198.2
Bulgaria	3,721.9	3,256.9	2,791.8
Canada	844.3	1,086.2	1,043.1
China, People's Republic	9,424.7	7,762.7	5,657.7
Cuba	2,405.1	1,440.7	2,224.7
Czechoslovakia	4,924.5	4,992.2	5,234.4
Egypt	6,065.1	6,835.3	3,092.8
France	6,398.6	4,956.4	3,997.9
German Democratic Republic	9,295.9	8,163.5	8,990.0
Germany, Federal Republic	16,059.4	14,439.1	10,928.8
Greece	3,999.9	1,861.1	2,616.9
Hungary	4,336.7	4,581.9	4,516.6
India	2,223.9	2,191.6	1,141.5
Iran	3,873.9	4,064.9	5,009.3
Iraq	8,939.7	7,003.1	2,168.2
Italy	19,887.4	14,364.0	15,980.6
Japan	1,751.7	1,065.4	2,754.8
Lebanon	3,026.0	1,212.4	955.9
Libya	2,131.2	632.9	187.2
Netherlands	5,334.3	3,444.9	2,385.9
Poland	8,064.8	6,818.2	5,079.2
Switzerland	1,674.9	1,057.9	1,393.6
Syria	2,385.6	2,050.9	744.2
Turkey	2,317.5	1,394.7	4,968.3
USSR	35,305.4	41,069.9	37,981.8
United Kingdom	5,115.3	5,176.6	4,050.1
USA	14,969.2	11,094.9	9,127.7
Yugoslavia	2,254.0	2,132.6	2,814.8
Total (incl. others)	228,122.9	192,295.2	167,779.5

* Figures for 1986–88 are not available.

Transport

RAILWAYS (traffic)

	1987	1988	1989
Passenger-km (million)	33,520	34,643	35,456
Freight ton-km (million)	78,074	80,607	81,131

INLAND WATERWAYS (traffic)

	1987	1988	1989
Passenger-km (million)	73	78	72
Freight ton-km (million)	2,656	3,318	3,366

INTERNATIONAL SEA-BORNE SHIPPING
(freight traffic, '000 metric tons)

	1986	1987	1988
Goods loaded	13,589	13,728	13,800
Goods unloaded	31,998	33,262	33,300

Source: UN, *Monthly Bulletin of Statistics.*

CIVIL AVIATION (traffic)

	1987	1988	1989
Passenger-km (million)	3,851	4,019	3,842
Freight ton-km (million)	73	63	78

Tourism

FOREIGN TOURIST ARRIVALS BY COUNTRY OF ORIGIN
('000)

Country of origin	1979	1980	1981
Bulgaria	824.6	1,007.0	890.0
Czechoslovakia	748.5	796.6	833.6
France	53.1	53.4	43.6
German Democratic Republic	312.4	372.6	400.6
Germany, Federal Republic	247.1	226.9	208.5
Greece	90.7	82.1	68.8
Hungary	701.0	904.5	1,265.6
Italy	43.5	39.6	33.0
Poland	803.5	718.4	638.5
USSR	518.4	540.5	532.8
United Kingdom	66.5	84.2	50.1
Yugoslavia	1,226.8	1,531.4	1,685.8
Total (incl. others)	6,034.8	6,742.0	7,002.3

Total arrivals ('000): 4,535 in 1986; 5,142 in 1987; 5,514 in 1988.
Source: UN, *Statistical Yearbook.*

Communications Media

	1987	1988	1989
Radio licences	2,533,000	3,112,000	3,073,000
Television receivers	3,801,000	3,740,000	3,696,000
Telephone subscribers	n.a.	n.a.	2,287,868
Book production:			
Titles	n.a.	2,478	2,159
Copies ('000)	n.a.	60,095	62,399
Daily newspapers	36	36	36
Annual circulation ('000)	1,143,708	1,145,603	1,138,684
Weeklies	24	24	24
Annual circulation ('000)	n.a.	39,863	42,218

Telephone subscribers: 2,287,800 (Dec. 1989).

Education

(1989/90)

	Institutions	Pupils	Teachers
Kindergartens	12,108	835,890	31,293
Primary and gymnasium schools	13,357	2,891,810	141,732
Secondary schools	981	1,346,315	42,519
Vocational schools	798	304,533	1,898
Higher education	101*	164,507	11,696

* Number of faculties.

Directory

The Constitution

Following its assumption of power in December 1989, the National Salvation Front (NSF) decreed radical changes to the Constitution of 1965. This had enshrined the leading role in society of the Romanian Communist Party, and provided for a unicameral Grand National Assembly, with powers to elect and recall the President, State Council, Council of Ministers and other state bodies. The NSF decrees changed the name of the country from the 'Socialist Republic of Romania' to 'Romania'. The leading role of a single political party was abolished, a democratic and pluralist system of government being established. Free elections were to be held in April (subsequently postponed to May) 1990.

In March 1990 a new electoral law was adopted by the Provisional National Unity Council (PNUC). Political power in Romania belongs to the people and is exercised according to the principles of democracy, freedom and human dignity, of inviolability and inalienability of basic human rights. Romania is governed on the basis of a multi-party democratic system and of the separation of the legal, executive and judicial powers. Romania's legislature, consisting of the Assembly of Deputies (with 387 seats) and the Senate (with 119 seats), and Romania's President are elected by universal, free, direct and secret vote, the President serving a maximum of two terms. Citizens have the right to vote at the age of 18, and may be elected at the age of 21 to the Assembly of Deputies and at the age of 30 to the Senate, with no upper age limit. Those ineligible for election include former members of the Securitate (the secret police of President Ceauşescu) and other former officials guilty of repression and abuses. Independent candidates are eligible for election to the Assembly of Deputies and to the Senate if supported by at least 251 electors and to the Presidency if supported by 100,000 electors. Once elected, the President may not remain a member of any political party.

The combined chambers of the legislature elected in May 1990, working as the Constituent Assembly, were to be responsible for drafting a new Constitution, to replace that of 1965. Instalments of the draft were published from December 1990, until the complete draft was presented in July 1991. The Constituent Assembly passed the final version (based on the Constitution of France's Fifth Republic) on 21 November. On 8 December the Constitution was approved by 76% of the votes cast in a referendum (in which 66% of the electorate had participated).

The Government

(December 1991)

HEAD OF STATE

President: ION ILIESCU (assumed power as President of the National Salvation Front 26 December 1989, confirmed as President of Provisional National Unity Council 13 February 1990, elected by direct popular vote 20 May 1990).

COUNCIL OF MINISTERS

A coalition of the National Salvation Front (NSF), the National Liberal Party (NLP), the Agrarian Democratic Party (ADP) and the Romanian Ecological Movement (REM).

Prime Minister: THEODOR STOLOJAN (NSF).

Minister for Relations with the Legislature: ION AUREL STOICA (NSF).

Minister of Economy and Finance: GEORGE DANIELESCU (NLP).

Minister of Trade and Tourism: CONSTANTIN FOTA (NSF).

Minister of Foreign Affairs: ADRIAN NĂSTASE (NSF).

Minister of National Defence: Lt-Gen. CONSTANTIN NICOLAE SPIROIU (NSF).

Minister of the Interior: VICTOR BABIUC (NSF).

Minister of Industry: DAN CONSTANTINESCU (NSF).

Minister of Public Works and Physical Planning: DAN NICOLAE (NSF).

Minister of Transport: TRAIAN BĂSESCU (NSF).

Minister of Communications: ANDREI CHIRICĂ (NSF).

Minister of Agriculture and Food Industry: PETRE MARCULESCU (ADP).

Minister of Labour and Social Protection: DAN MIRCEA POPESCU (NSF).

Minister of Education and Science: MIHAI GOLU (NSF).

Minister of Health: MIRCEA MAIORESCU (NSF).

Minister of Justice: MIRCEA IONESCU-QUINTUS (NLP).

Minister of the Environment: MARCIAN BLEAHU (REM).

Minister of Youth and Sports: IOAN MOLDOVAN (NSF).

Minister of Culture: LUDOVIC SPIESS (NSF).

Minister in charge of the Budget within the Ministry of Economy and Finance: FLORIAN BERCEA (NSF).

Secretary of State at the Ministry of Education and Science: EMIL TOKACS (NLP).

MINISTRIES

Office of the Prime Minister: Bucharest, Palatul Victoria, Piaţa Victoriei 1; tel. (0) 143400; fax (0) 176160.

Ministry of Agriculture and Food Industry: 70030 Bucharest, Bd. Republicii 24; tel. (0) 144020; telex 11217.

Ministry of Communications: Bucharest.

Ministry of Culture: 71341 Bucharest, Piaţa Presei Libere 1, Sector 1; tel. (0) 170906; fax (0) 594781.

Ministry of Economy and Finance: Bucharest, Calea Victoriei 152; tel. (0) 505020; telex 11109.

Ministry of Education and Science: Bucharest, Str. Gral Berthelot 30; tel. (0) 142680; telex 11637; fax (0) 157736.

Ministry of the Environment: 70005 Bucharest, Bd. Libertatii 12; tel. (0) 316104; telex 11457; fax (0) 316486.

Ministry of Foreign Affairs: Bucharest, Piaţa Victoriei 1; tel. (0) 166850; telex 11220.

Ministry of Health: 70052 Bucharest, Str. Ministerului 2–4, Sector 1; tel. (0) 134230; telex 11982; fax (0) 156192.

Ministry of Industry: Bucharest.

Ministry of the Interior: Bucharest, Str. Eforie 3; tel. (0) 160080.

Ministry of Justice: Bucharest, Bd. Gheorghe Gheorghiu-Dej 33; tel. (0) 144400.

Ministry of Labour and Social Protection: Bucharest, Str. Demetru I. Dobrescu 2; tel. (0) 156563; fax (0) 131010.

Ministry of National Defence: Bucharest, Intrarea Drumul Taberei 9; tel. (0) 314150.

Ministry of Public Works and Physical Planning: Bucharest.

Ministry of Trade and Tourism: Bucharest, Str. Apolodor 17; tel. (0) 310289; telex 11278; fax (0) 314907.

Ministry of Transport: Bucharest, Bd. Dinicu Golescu 38; tel. (0) 177140; telex 11372.

Ministry of Youth and Sports: Bucharest.

President

Presidential Election, 20 May 1990

Candidates	Valid votes cast	
	Number	%
ION ILIESCU (National Salvation Front) . .	12,232,498	85.07
RADU CÂMPEANU (National Liberal Party) .	1,529,188	10.64
ION RAŢIU (Christian Democratic National Peasants' Party)	617,007	4.29
Total	14,378,693	100.00

In addition, a total of 447,923 invalid votes were cast.

Legislature

Speaker of the Assembly of Deputies: DAN MARŢIAN.

Speaker of the Senate: ALEXANDRU BÎRLĂDEANU.

General Election, 20 May 1990

	Seats	
	Assembly of Deputies	Senate
National Salvation Front	263	91
Hungarian Democratic Union of Romania .	29	12
National Liberal Party	29	10
Romanian Ecological Movement. . . .	12	1
Christian Democratic National Peasants' Party.	12	1
Romanian Unity Alliance—AUR. . . .	9	2
Agrarian Democratic Party	9	—
Romanian Ecological Party	8	1
Romanian Socialist Democratic Party . .	5	—
Romanian Social Democratic Party . . .	2	—
Centrist Democratic Group	2	—
Others	7	1
Total	**387**	**119**

Note: Twelve of Romania's minorities were to be represented in the new legislature, three of which won a seat at the ballot. The remaining nine were to be given a seat each at the Assembly of Deputies, in accordance with the Electoral Law.

Local Government

The system of local government in Romania was to be reformed under the terms of the new Constitution, which was approved by referendum on 8 December 1991. According to the Constitution, the basic principle of local government was to be local autonomy and the decentralization of public services. The lowest tier of local government was to be the local council of a city or commune; these were to have mayors and council members elected by constituents in each relevant area. The activities of local councils were to be co-ordinated by county councils, which were also to be elected by their constituents. A prefect for each county was to be appointed by the central Government as its representative at the local level, and would have the power to challenge acts of all tiers of local government. Romania has 40 administrative divisions (counties), and the municipality of Bucharest, the capital city, which is itself divided into administrative sectors.

Political Organizations

Following the downfall of President Ceauşescu in December 1989, numerous political parties were formed or re-established in preparation for the holding of free elections. By April 1990 more than 80 parties had been registered by the Bucharest Municipal Court. Numerous additional parties were formed in 1990–91. The financing of political parties from abroad is not permitted.

Agrarian Democratic Party: Bucharest; supported by agricultural workers; advocates defence of the Romanian villagers' way of life; Leader VALERIU PESCARU.

Christian Democratic National Peasants' Party/Partidul Naţional Ţărănesc-Creştin şi Democrat: 70433 Bucharest, Bd. Carol 34; tel. (0) 147819; fax (0) 154533; f. 1990 by merger of centre-right Christian Democratic Party and traditional National Peasant Party (f. 1869, banned 1947, revived Dec. 1989; original party re-established in Aug. 1990 by separate group); supports pluralist democracy; advocates a return to a market economy and the restoration of peasant property, the reorganization of education, the separation of powers in the State, the free election of management bodies and the equality of all nationalities and religious beliefs; supports Christian morals; 615,000 mems; Pres. CORNELIU COPOSU.

Civic Alliance: Bucharest; f. 1990; alliance of opposition groupings outside legislature; voted, in July 1991, to create a parallel political party, the Party of the Civic Alliance; Pres. IOAN MANUCU .

Hungarian Democratic Union of Romania (HDUR): supports the rights of ethnic minorities; Hon. Pres. LÁSZLÓ TÖKES; Pres. GEZA DOMOKOS; Vice-Pres. GEZA SZÖCS.

Liberal Monarchist Party: Bucharest; advocates the restoration of the monarchy.

Liberal Union: f. 1990 following split in National Liberal Party; Chair. ION I. BRATIANU.

National Liberal Party/Partidul Naţional Liberal: Bucharest, Bd. Bălcescu 21; f. 1869, banned 1947; merged with Socialist Liberal Party in 1990; (breakaway youth wing f. 1990); advocates

separation of powers in the State, restoration of democracy, freedom of expression and religion, observance of the equal rights of all minorities, the abolition of collectivization and nationalization in agriculture, the gradual privatization of enterprises, trade union freedom and the right to strike, and Romania's observance of its obligations towards the Warsaw Treaty; Chair. RADU CÂMPEANU.

National Salvation Front (NSF): Bucharest, Al. Modrogan 1; f. Dec. 1989 following downfall of President Ceauşescu, with aim of establishing democracy, liberty and national dignity; formed first provisional Government pending elections of May 1990; centre-left; supports political pluralism, separation of the legislative, executive and judicial powers in the State; advocates a free-market economy, privatization of state property, encouragement of foreign investment, reorganization of education, freedom of the press and of religion, respect for the rights and freedoms of the national minorities, curbing of pollution and Romania's observance of international agreements; 500,000 mems; National Leader of NSF PETRE ROMAN; Exec. Chair. of NSF Steering Collegium ION AUREL STOICA.

Party of the Civic Alliance (PCA): Bucharest; f. 1991; set up by the Civic Alliance to contest elections; Pres. NICOLAE MANOLESCU.

Romanian Ecological Movement/Mişcarea Ecologistă din Romania: Bucharest, Str. Alexandru Phillippide 11; f. 1990; advocates protection of the environment and the pursuit of democratic, pacifist and humanist values; Chair. TOMA GEORGE MAIORESCU.

Romanian Ecological Party/Partidul Ecologist Român: Bucharest, Bd. Leontin Salăjăn 55; tel. (0) 744384; supports protection of the environment; Chair. OTTO WEBER.

Greater Romania/Romania Máre: Bucharest; nationalist; Leaders EUGEN BARBU, CORNELIU VADIM TUDOR.

Romanian National Unity Party: 4300 Tîrgu Mureş, Piaţa Trandafirilor 34; tel. (54) 37200; f. 1990; political wing of the nationalist Romanian movement, Vatra Românească; Leader RADU CEONTEA.

Romanian Social Democratic Party/Partidul Social-Democrat Român: Bucharest, Bd. Dr Petru Groza 12; tel. (0) 377036; f. 1893; centre-left; Exec. Pres. SERGIU CUNESCU.

Romanian Socialist Democratic Party/Partidul Socialist Democratic Român: Pucioasa; tel. (27) 60005; Pres. MARIAN CIRCIUMARU.

Socialist Labour Party: Bucharest; f. 1990 by Romanian Communist Party members and left-wing Democratic Labour Party; Exec. Pres. ILIE VERDEŢ.

Prior to the elections of May 1990, the National Liberal Party, the Christian Democratic National Peasants' Party and the small Social Democratic Party announced that they were forming an alliance in order to challenge the National Salvation Front. In August 1990 the Democratic Antitotalitarian Forum (DAF) was formed by political groupings inside and outside parliament, and in December the National Convention on Establishing Democracy was founded by the following six parliamentary opposition groups: the Christian Democratic National Peasants' Party, the Hungarian Democratic Union of Romania, the National Liberal Party, the Romanian Ecological Movement, the Romanian Ecological Party and the Romanian Social Democratic Party.

Diplomatic Representation

EMBASSIES IN ROMANIA

Albania: Bucharest, Str. Ştefan Gheorghiu 4; Ambassador: PIRO VITO.

Algeria: Bucharest, Bd. Ana Ipătescu 29; Ambassador: LIAMINE ZEROUAL.

Argentina: Bucharest, Str. Drobeta 11; telex 11412; Ambassador: (vacant).

Austria: 70254 Bucharest, Str. Dumbrava Roşie 7; tel. (0) 119377; telex 11333; fax (0) 117653; Ambassador: CHRISTOPH PARISINI.

Bangladesh: Bucharest, Bd. Kiseleff 55; tel. (0) 171544; telex 10197; Ambassador: M. ANWAR HASHIM.

Belgium: 79359 Bucharest, Bd. Dacia 32; tel. (0) 114212; telex 11482; Ambassador: JAN HELLEMANS.

Brazil: Bucharest, Str. Praga 11; tel. (0) 331110; telex 11307; Ambassador: MARCEL DEZON COSTA HASLOCHER.

Bulgaria: Bucharest, Str. Rabat 5; tel. (0) 332150; telex 11329; Ambassador: TVETAN DIMITROV NIKOLOV.

Canada: 71118 Bucharest, Str. N. Iorga 36; tel. (0) 506580; telex 10690; Ambassador: SAUL GREY.

Chile: Bucharest, Bd. Ana Ipătescu 8; tel. (0) 115691; telex 11197; Ambassador: SERGIO MIMICA BEZMALINOVIC.

China, People's Republic: Bucharest, Şos. Nordului 2; tel. (0) 331925; Ambassador: WANG JINQING.

Colombia: Bucharest, Str. Polonă 35; tel. (0) 115108; Ambassador: Víctor Alberto Delgado Mallarino.

Congo: Bucharest, Str. Pictor Mirea 18; tel. (0) 170343; Ambassador: (vacant).

Costa Rica: Bucharest, Str. Lt. Dumitru Lemnea 3-5, Et. 1, Apt. 4; tel. (0) 592008; telex 11939; Chargé d'affaires: Elizabeth Segura Hernández.

Cuba: Bucharest, Al. Alexandru 33; tel. (0) 796895; telex 11305; Ambassador: Niel Ruíz Guerra.

Czechoslovakia: Bucharest, Str. Ion Ghica 11; tel. (0) 159141; Ambassador: Milan Resutik.

Denmark: Bucharest, Str. Atena 28; tel. (0) 796380; telex 11325; Ambassador: Ulrik Helweg-Larsen.

Ecuador: Bucharest, Str. Polonă 35; tel. (0) 110503; telex 10836; Ambassador: Marcelo Fernández de Córdova.

Egypt: Bucharest, Bd. Dacia 21; tel. (0) 110138; telex 11549; Ambassador: Saad Abou el-Kheir.

Finland: Bucharest, Str. Atena 2 bis; tel. (0) 335440; telex 11293; Ambassador: Bo Adahl.

France: Bucharest, Str. Biserica Amzei 13-15; tel. (0) 110540; telex 11320; fax (0) 506576; Ambassador: Renaud Vignal.

Germany: 79449 Bucharest, Str. Rabat 21; tel. (0) 792580; telex 11292; fax (0) 796854; Ambassador: Dr Klaus Terfloth.

Greece: Bucharest, Str. Orlando 6; tel. (0) 503988; telex 11321; Ambassador: Giorgios Linardos.

Guinea: Bucharest, Str. Bocşa 4; tel. (0) 111893; telex 10255; Ambassador: Abel Niouma Sandouno.

Holy See: 70764 Bucharest, Str. Pictor C. Stahi 5-7 (Apostolic Nunciature); tel. (0) 139490; Apostolic Nuncio: Most Rev. John Bukovsky, Titular Archbishop of Tabalta.

Hungary: Bucharest, Str. J. L. Calderon 63; tel. (0) 146621; telex 11323; fax (0) 142846; Ambassador: Ernő Rudas.

India: 71274 Bucharest, Str. Brîncuţei 11; tel. (0) 797630; telex 11619; Ambassador: J. F. Ribeiro.

Indonesia: Bucharest, Orlando 10; tel. (0) 507720; telex 11258; Ambassador: Lamtiur Andaliah Panggabean.

Iran: Bucharest, Bd. Ana Ipătescu 39; tel. (0) 334471; telex 11507; Ambassador: Abdoul Rasoul Mohager Hegeazi.

Iraq: Bucharest, Str. Polonă 8; tel. (0) 110835; Ambassador: Sultan Ibrahim Shuja.

Israel: 73102 Bucharest, Str. Dr Burghelea 5; tel. (0) 132634; telex 11685; fax (0) 132633; Ambassador: Zvi Mazel.

Italy: Bucharest, Str. I. C. Frimu 7-9; tel. (0) 505110; telex 11602; Ambassador: Luigi Amaduzzi.

Japan: Bucharest, Str. Polonă 4, Sector 1; tel. (0) 118527; telex 11322; fax (0) 113658; Ambassador: Kiyoshi Furukawa.

Jordan: Bucharest, Str. Dumbrava Roşie 1; tel. (0) 104705; telex 11477; Ambassador: Yasin Istanbuli.

Korea, Democratic People's Republic: Bucharest, Şos. Nordului 6; tel. (0) 331926; Ambassador: Mun Biong Rok.

Korea, Republic: 70412 Bucharest, Calea Victoriei 2; tel. (0) 137941; Ambassador: Yi Hyun-Hong.

Lebanon: Bucharest, Str. Atena 28; tel. (0) 113942; telex 11645; Ambassador: Emile Bedran.

Liberia: Bucharest, Str. Mihai Eminescu 82-88; tel. (0) 193029; telex 11375; Chargé d'affaires: G. Marcus Kelley.

Libya: Bucharest, Bd. Ana Ipătescu 15; tel. (0) 505511; telex 10290; Secretary of People's Bureau: Muhammad al-Baruni.

Malaysia: Bucharest, Bd. Dacia 30; tel. (0) 113801; Ambassador: Zainuddin bin Abdul Rahman.

Mauritania: Bucharest, Str. Duiliu Zamfirescu 7; tel. (0) 592305; telex 10595; Ambassador: Kane Cheikh Mohamed Fadhel.

Mongolia: Bucharest, Str. Făgăraş 6; tel. (0) 507237; telex 11504; Ambassador: Dosoryn Ghenden.

Morocco: Bucharest, Bd. Dacia 25; tel. (0) 192945; telex 11687; Ambassador: Mohamed Halim.

Netherlands: 71271 Bucharest, Str. Atena 18; tel. (0) 332292; telex 11474; Ambassador: Coenraad Frederik Stork.

Nigeria: Bucharest, Str. Orlando 9; tel. (0) 504050; telex 10478; Ambassador: L. E. Okogun.

Pakistan: Bucharest, Str. Barbu Delavrancea 22; tel. (0) 177402; Ambassador: Rasheed Ahmad.

Peru: Bucharest, Str. Paris 45A; tel. (0) 331124; telex 11566; Ambassador: Guillermo Gerdau O'Connor.

Philippines: Bucharest, Stirbei Voda 87; tel. (0) 137643; telex 10237; Ambassador: Alicia C. Ramos.

Poland: Bucharest, Al. Alexandru 23; tel. (0) 794530; telex 11302; Ambassador: Zygmunt Komorowski.

Russia: Bucharest, Şos. Kiseleff 6; tel. (0) 170120; Ambassador: Felix P. Bogdanov.

Somalia: Bucharest, Str. Galaţi 52; tel. (0) 110472; Ambassador: Mohamed Ahmed Abdi Tafadal.

Spain: Bucharest, Str. Tirana 1; tel. (0) 335730; telex 11508; Ambassador: Antonio Núñez García-Sauco.

Sudan: Bucharest, Bd. Dacia 35; tel. (0) 118352; telex 10855; Ambassador: Lawrence Mode Tombe.

Sweden: Bucharest, Str. Sofia 5; tel. (0) 173184; telex 11313; Ambassador: Nils G. Rosenberg.

Switzerland: 79324 Bucharest 1, Str. Pitar Moş 12; tel. (0) 106585; telex 11579; Ambassador: Sven Beat Meili.

Syria: Bucharest, Bd. Ana Ipătescu 50; tel. (0) 503195; telex 10061; Ambassador: Hicham Kahaleh.

Thailand: Bucharest, Str. Mihai Eminescu 44-48; tel. (0) 114686; telex 10247; Ambassador: Praphot Narithrangura.

Tunisia: Bucharest, Str. Mihai Eminescu 50-54; tel. (0) 111895; telex 11829; Ambassador: Rauf Said.

Turkey: Bucharest, Calea Dorobanţilor 72; tel. (0) 193625; Ambassador: Tugay Ulucevik.

United Kingdom: 70154 Bucharest, Str. Jules Michelet 24; tel. (0) 111634; telex 11295; fax (0) 595090; Ambassador: Michael W. Atkinson.

USA: Bucharest, Str. Tudor Arghezi 7-9; tel. (0) 104040; telex 11416; fax (0) 861669; Ambassador: Alan Green, Jr.

Uruguay: Bucharest, Str. Polonă 35; tel. (0) 118212; telex 10475; Ambassador: Domingo Schipani.

Venezuela: Bucharest, Str. Mihai Eminescu 124, Apt. 4; tel. (0) 113215; telex 10470; Ambassador: Milos Alcalay Mirkovich.

Viet-Nam: Bucharest, Str. Gr. Alexandrescu 86; tel. (0) 116120; telex 11604; Ambassador: Nguyen Trong Lieu.

Yemen: Bucharest, Str. Mihai Eminescu 124A; tel. (0) 114896; Ambassador: Ali Abdallah as-Sallal.

Yugoslavia: Bucharest, Calea Dorobanţilor 34; tel. (0) 119871; telex 92535; fax (0) 191752; Ambassador: Dr Desimir Jevtić.

Zaire: Bucharest, Al. Alexandru 41; tel. (0) 795717; telex 11503; Ambassador: Musungayi Nkuembe Mampuya.

Zimbabwe: Bucharest, Str. Nicolae Iorga 11; tel. (0) 502833; telex 10637; Ambassador: Dzingai C. Chigiga.

Judicial System

The judicial system was to be reorganized and reformed under the terms of the new Constitution, which was approved by referendum in December 1991.

SUPREME COURT

The Supreme Court of Justice exercises control over the judicial activity of all courts. It ensures the correct and uniform application of the law. The members of the Supreme Court are appointed by the President of Romania, with the agreement of the Senate.

Chief Justice: Dr Teofil Pop; 70503 Bucharest, Calea Rahovei 4; tel. (0) 133736; telex 11165.

COUNTY COURTS AND LOCAL COURTS

In every county there is a county court and two or three local courts. The county courts act as appeal courts against sentences passed by local courts, which are generally considered courts of first instance. In certain complex litigation cases, county courts act as courts of first instance, appeal to the Supreme Court being possible. In both county courts and local courts the panel of judges consists of professional magistrates and, under certain circumstances, people's jurors.

MILITARY COURTS

Military courts judge contraventions of the law by servicemen and, in certain circumstances, by civilians. The panel consists of professional military judges and, under certain circumstances, of military people's jurors (officers who are not magistrates).

Military Prosecutor: Col Mircea Levanovici.

ORGANS OF THE PROSECUTOR'S OFFICE

The organs of the Prosecutor's office are: the Prosecutor-General's office and the county, local and military prosecutor's offices. The Prosecutor-General's office supervises the activity of the subordinate organs. It submits to the Supreme Court extraordinary appeals against final decisions containing judicial errors. As part of a reorganization, the organs of the Prosecutor's Office were to pass under the authority of the Ministry of Justice.

Prosecutor-General: Mihai Ulpian Popa Cherecheanu; tel. (0) 812727.

Religion

A State Secretariat for Religious Affairs was established in 1990. There are numerous churches and denominations, with 66% of believers belonging to the Romanian Orthodox Church.

CHRISTIANITY
The Romanian Orthodox Church

The Romanian Orthodox Church is the major religious organization in Romania and is organized as an autocephalous patriarchate, being led by the Holy Synod, headed by a patriarch. The Patriarchate consists of six metropolitanates. The archbishoprics and bishoprics were in the process of reorganization in 1990.

Holy Synod: 70666 Bucharest, Str. Antim 29; tel. (0) 313413; Sec. Nifon Ploieşteanul.

Patriarhia Română: 70526 Bucharest, Str. Patriarhiei 2; tel. (0) 163435.

Patriarch, Metropolitan of Wallachia and Dobrogea and Archbishop of Bucharest: Teoctist Arăpaşu.

Metropolitan of Moldova and Bukovina and Archbishop of Iaşi: Dr Daniel Ciobotea (resident in Iaşi).

Metropolitan of Transylvania and Archbishop of Sibiu: Dr Antonie Plămădeală (resident in Sibiu).

Metropolitan of Oltenia and Archbishop of Craiova: Dr Nestor Vornicescu (resident in Craiova).

Metropolitan of Banat and Archbishop of Timişoara and Caransebeş: Dr Nicolae Corneanu (resident in Timişoara).

Metropolitan of the Lower Danube: post created in 1990; fmrly the Bishopric of Galaţi.

Archbishop of Tomis: Lucian Tomitanul (resident in Galaţi).

Archbishop of Vad, Feleac and Cluj-Napoca: Teofil Herineanu (resident in Cluj-Napoca).

The Archbishoprics of Tîrgovişte and of Suceava and Radauti (with seats in Tîrgovişte and Suceava respectively) were re-established in 1990.

The Roman Catholic Church

Catholics in Romania number 1.35m., and include adherents of the Armenian, Latin and Romanian (Byzantine) rites.

Latin Rite

There is one archdiocese and five dioceses (Alba Iulia, Iaşi, Satu Mare, Oradea and Timişoara).

Archdiocese of Bucharest: 70749 Bucharest, Str. Gral Berthelot 19; tel. (0) 133936; Archbishop Most Rev. Ioan Robu.

Romanian Rite

There is one archdiocese and four dioceses.

Archbishop of Făgăraş and Alba Iulia: Cardinal Alexandru Todea, 3175 Blaj, Str. P. P. Aroni 2.

Protestant Churches

Baptist Church (Union) of Romania: 78152 Bucharest, Bd. N. Titulescu 56/1; tel. (0) 173705; 1,100 churches; Gen. Sec. Rev. Ion Rincu; Pres. Rev. Traian Grec.

The Evangelical Church of the Augsburg Confession: founded in the 16th century, comprises some 40,000 mems, mainly of German nationality; Bishop of Sibiu Dr Christoph Klein, 2400 Sibiu, Str. General Magheru 4; tel. (24) 33680.

The Reformed (Calvinist) Church: 700,000 mems; two bishoprics:

Bishop of Cluj-Napoca: Dr Kálmán Ciha, 3400 Cluj-Napoca, Str. 23 August 51; tel. (51) 12453.

Bishop of Oradea: László Tőkes, 3700 Oradea, Str. Craiovei 1; tel. (91) 31710.

The Synodo-Presbyterian Evangelical Church: comprises about 25,000 mems of Hungarian, 4,000 mems of Slovak and 150 mems of Romanian nationality; Superintendent Paul Szedressy, 3400 Cluj-Napoca, Bd. 22 Decembrie 1; tel. (51) 16614.

The Unitarian Church: comprises about 70,000 mems of Hungarian nationality; Bishop Lajos Kovács, 3400 Cluj-Napoca, Bd. 22 Decembrie 1.

Other Christian Churches

The Armenian-Gregorian Church: 70334 Bucharest, Str. Armenească 9; tel. (0) 140208; 2,000 mems.; Archbishop Dirayr Mardichian.

The Old-Rite Christian Church: 6100 Brăila, Str. Zidari 1; 48,000 mems. of Russian nationality; Metropolitan Timon Gavrila.

Other Christian churches include the Pentecostal Church (Pres. Rev. Pavel Bochian), the Seventh-day Adventist Church (Pres. Rev. Dumitru Popa), Christians according to the Gospel and the Open Brethren Church (Head Meliton Lazarovici).

ISLAM

The Muslim Community comprises some 52,000 members of Turkish-Tatar nationality.

Grand Mufti: Yacub Mehmet Septar, 8700 Constanţa, Bd. Tomis 41.

JUDAISM

In 1990 there were about 18,000 Jews, organized in 68 communities, in Romania.

Federation of Jewish Communities: Chief Rabbi Dr Moses Rosen, 70478 Bucharest, Str. Sf. Vinieri 9–11; tel. (0) 132538; telex 10798; fax (0) 130911.

The Press

The Romanian press is highly regionalized, with newspapers and periodicals appearing in all of the administrative districts (as listed below). In 1990 a total of 1,700 newspapers and magazines were published, with a total circulation of 1,245m. copies. Many newspapers and periodicals are published in the languages of co-inhabiting nationalities in Romania, including Hungarian, German, Serbian, Ukrainian, Armenian and Yiddish. The Ministry of Culture relinquished control of the press in June 1990. As a result of rapidly increasing prices for newsprint and distribution in March and April 1991, many newspapers and periodicals ceased publication.

PRINCIPAL NEWSPAPERS

Adevărul (Truth): 71341 Bucharest, Piaţa Presei Libere 1; tel. (0) 180608; telex 11342; fax (0) 175540; f. 1989; daily except Sun. and Mon.; independent.

Alianta Civica: Bucharest; f. 1991; daily; organ ofthe Civic Alliance.

Azi (Today): Bucharest; f. 1990; daily; organ of National Salvation Front; Hon. Dir Alexandru Bîrladeǎnu.

Dreptatea: ; Bucharest; f. 1990; daily evening newspaper published by Christian Democratic National Peasants' Party.

Gazeta Sporturilor (Sports Gazette): 79773 Bucharest, Str. Vasile Conta 16, Sector 6; tel. (0) 116033; telex 10350; fax (0) 113459; f. 1924; daily except Sun.; independent; Editor-in-Chief Constantin Macovei; circ. 450,000.

Libertatea (Freedom): Bucharest, Str. Brezoianu 23–25; tel. (0) 132777; telex 10169; fax (0) 137895; f. 1989; daily except Sun.; evening paper; Editor-in-Chief Octavian Andronic; circ. 250,000.

Neuer Weg (New Way): 71341 Bucharest, Piaţa Presei Libere 1; tel. (0) 181723; telex 11618; fax (0) 183758; f. 1949; daily except Sun. and Mon.; political, economic, social and cultural news; in German; Editor-in-Chief Emmerich Reichrath; circ. 30,000.

România Liberă (Free Romania): 71341 Bucharest, Piaţa Presei Libere 1; tel. (0) 177849; telex 11179; fax (0) 174205; f. 1943; daily except Sat. and Sun.; independent; Editors-in-Chief Anton Uncu, Mihai Creanga; circ. 300,000–350,000.

Romániai Magyar Szó (Hungarian Word from Romania): 79776 Bucharest, Piaţa Presei Libere 1; f. 1947; daily except Sun. and Mon.; in Hungarian; Editor-in-Chief Gyarmath János; circ. 50,000.

Tineretul Liber (Free Youth): 71341 Bucharest, Piaţa Presei Libere 1; tel. (0) 176736; fax (0) 177876; f. 1989; daily except Sun. and Mon.; Editor-in-Chief Stefan Mitroi; circ. 300,000.

Viitorul Romanesc (Future of Romania): Bucharest; organ of the National Liberal Party's youth wing.

DISTRICT NEWSPAPERS

Until December 1989 the following newspapers were published by the respective District Committees of the Romanian Communist Party in conjunction with the District People's Councils. These newspapers were undergoing reorganization in 1990–91.

Alba

Unirea (The Union): Alba Iulia, Piaţa 23 August 1; f. 1968; daily except Mon.; Editor-in-Chief TRUŢĂ SEBASTIAN; circ. 32,000.

Arad

Flacăra Roşie (Red Flame): 2900 Arad, Bd. Revoluţiei 81; f. 1944; daily except Mon.; Editor-in-Chief CRĂCIUN BONTA; circ. 43,000.

Jelen (Present): 2900 Arad, Bd. Revoluţiei 81; tel. (66) 12414; telex 76373; f. 1989; fmrly Vörös Lobogó; daily except Sun. and Mon.; independent; in Hungarian; Editor-in-Chief LAJOS NÓTÁROS; circ. 12,000.

Argeş

Secera şi ciocanul (Sickle and Hammer): Piteşti, Bd. R.S.R. 88; f. 1951; weekly; Editor-in-Chief NICOLAE OANŢĂ; circ. 40,000.

Bacău

Steagul Roşu (Red Flag): Bacău, Str. Eliberării 63; f. 1946; weekly; Editor-in-Chief PETREA FILIOREANU; circ. 55,000.

Bihor

Crişana: Oradea, Str. Romană 3; f. 1946; daily except Mon.; Editor-in-Chief POP AUREL; circ. 33,000.

Fáklya (The Torch): Oradea, Str. Romană 3; f. 1946; daily except Mon.; in Hungarian; Editor-in-Chief ILLÉS FRANCISC; circ. 28,000.

Bistriţa-Năsăud

Ecoul (The Echo): Bistriţa, Str. Parcului 3; f. 1968; weekly; Editor-in-Chief IOAN BURCUŞEL; circ. 24,000.

Botoşani

Clopotul (The Bell): Botoşani, Bd. Lenin 91; f. 1933; weekly; Editor-in-Chief ION MAXIMIUC; circ. 45,000.

Brăila

Libertatea (Freedom): Brăila, Piaţa Independenţei 1; tel. (46) 35946; f. 1989; daily; Editor-in-Chief OANĂ RODICA; circ. 20,000.

Braşov

Brassói Lapok (Braşov Gazette): 2200 Braşov, Str. M. Sadoveanu 3; tel. (21) 42029; telex 61224; f. 1849; weekly; in Hungarian; Editor-in-Chief MADARAS LÁZÁR; circ. 15,000.

Gazeta de Transilvania: 2200 Braşov, Str. M. Sadoveanu 3; tel. (21) 42029; telex 61224; f. 1838, ceased publication 1946, re-established 1989; daily except Mon.; independent; Editor-in-Chief EDUARD HUIDAN.

Karpatenrundschau (Carpathian Panorama): 2200 Braşov, Str. M. Sadoveanu 3; tel. and fax (21) 43624; f. 1968; weekly; in German; Editor-in-Chief DIETER DROTLEFF; circ. 3,000.

Buzău

Viaţa Buzăului (Life of Buzău): Buzău, Str. Chiristigii 3; f. 1968; weekly; Editor-in-Chief MIHAIL BÂZU; circ. 40,000.

Călăraşi

Vremuri Noi (The New Time): Călăraşi; weekly; Editor-in-Chief RODICA-MARIA SIMIONESCU; circ. 23,000.

Caraş-Severin

Timpul (The Times): Reşiţa, Piaţa Republicii 7; tel. (64) 12739; telex 74235; f. 1990; daily; Editor-in-Chief GHEORGHE JURMA; circ. 25,000.

Cluj

Făclia (The Torch): 3400 Cluj-Napoca, Str. Napoca 16; f. 1945; daily except Mon.; Editor-in-Chief LIVIU RÎUREANU; circ. 35,000.

Szabadság: 3400 Cluj-Napoca, Str. Napoca 16, POB 340; tel. (51) 18985; telex 31447; fax (51) 17206; f. 1989; daily except Sun. and Mon.; in Hungarian; Editor-in-Chief ZOLTÁN TIBORI SZABÓ; circ. 35,000.

Constanţa

Dobrogea Nouă (New Dobrogea): Constanţa, Şos. Filimon Sîrbu 5; f. 1948; daily except Mon.; Editor-in-Chief AURELIA BERARIU; circ. 40,000.

Litoral: Constanţa, Şos. Filimon Sîrbu 5; f. 1970; daily except Mon., 1 June–30 Sept.; Editor-in-Chief AURELIA BERARIU; circ. 40,000.

Covasna

Cuvîntul nou (The New World): Sfîntu Gheorghe, Str. Presei 8; f. 1968; daily except Mon.; Editor-in-Chief GABRIEL FLORESCU; circ. 10,000.

Megyei Tükör (County Glass): Sfîntu Gheorghe, Str. Presei 8; f. 1968; daily except Mon.; in Hungarian; Editor-in-Chief FERENC VASAS; circ. 24,000.

Dîmboviţa

Dîmboviţa: Tîrgovişte, Str. Mierlei 32; f. 1968; weekly; Editor-in-Chief FLOREA RADU; circ. 34,000.

Dolj

Cuvîntul Libertăţii (The Word of Liberty): Craiova, Str. Olteţului 8; tel. (41) 12457; fax (41) 13833; f. 1989; daily except Mon.; Editor-in-Chief DAN LUPESCU; circ. 60,000.

Galaţi

Viaţa Nouă (New Life): Galaţi, Str. Primăverii 1; f. 1944; daily except Mon.; Editor-in-Chief TUDOREL OANCEA; circ. 28,000.

Giurgiu

Cuvintul Liber (Free World): 8375 Giurgiu, Str. 1 Dec. 1918 60A; tel. (12) 21227; f. 1990; weekly; Editor-in-Chief ION GAGHII; circ. 10,000.

Gorj

Gazeta Gorjului (The Gorj Journal): Tîrgu-Jiu, Str. Victoriei 4; f. 1968; daily except Mon.; Editor-in-Chief XENOFON IACOB; circ. 22,000.

Harghita

Hargita Népe: Miercurea-Ciuc, Str. Lelicëni 45; tel. (58) 11322; f. 1968; daily except Mon.; in Hungarian; Editor-in-Chief LADISLAU BORBÉLY (acting); circ. 40,000.

Informaţia Harghitei (Harghita Information): Miercurea-Ciuc, Str. 7 Nov. 45; f. 1968; daily except Mon.; Editor-in-Chief TEODOR VANCU; circ. 8,500.

Hunedoara

Cuvîntul liber (The Free World): 2700 Deva, Str. 1 Decembrie 35; tel. 11275; telex 72288; fax 18061; f. 1949; daily except Mon.; Editor-in-Chief NICOLAE TÎRCOB; circ. 30,000.

Steagul Rosu (Red Flag): Petroşani, 90 Str. Republicii; f. 1944; daily except Sun.; Editor-in-Chief SIMION POP; circ. 15,000.

Ialomiţa

Tribuna Ialomiţei (The Ialomiţa Tribune): Slobozia, Str. Dobrogeanu-Gherea 2; f. 1968; weekly; Editor-in-Chief TITUS NIŢU; circ. 25,000.

Iaşi

Flacăra Iaşului (The Flame of Iaşi): 6600 Iaşi, Str. V. Alecsandri 8; tel. (81) 45105; telex 22233; f. 1944; daily except Mon.; Editor-in-Chief GHEORGHE MIHALACHE; circ. 57,000.

Maramureş

Bányavidéki Új Szó (Miner's New Word): Baia Mare, Bd. Bucureşti 25; tel. (94) 32585; f. 1989; weekly; in Hungarian; Editor-in-Chief KLACSMÁNYI ALEXANDRU; circ. 7,000.

Pentru Socialism (For Socialism): Baia Mare, Bd. Bucureşti 25; f. 1958; daily except Mon.; Editor-in-Chief MIHAI GRIGORESCU; circ. 30,000.

Mehedinţi

Viitorul (The Future): Drobeta-Turnu Severin, Str. Traian 89; f. 1968; weekly; Editor-in-Chief ION DĂESCU; circ. 22,000.

Mureş

Steaua Roşie (The Red Star): Tîrgu-Mureş, Str. Gheorghe Doja 9; f. 1949; daily except Mon.; Editor-in-Chief IOAN POP; circ. 24,000.

Vörös Zászló: Tîrgu-Mureş, Str. Gheorghe Doja 9; f. 1949; daily; in Hungarian; Editor-in-Chief GIDOFALVI ILDIKO; circ. 32,000.

Neamţ

Ceahlăul: Piatra Neamţ, Al. Tiparului 14; f. 1968; weekly; Editor-in-Chief VASILE OROŞANU; circ. 60,000.

Olt

Oltul: Slatina, Str. Al. I. Cuza 54; f. 1968; weekly; Editor-in-Chief EMILIAN ROUĂ; circ. 29,000.

Prahova

Flamura Prahovei (The Prahova Banner): Ploieşti, Bd. Republicii 2; f. 1948; weekly; Editor-in-Chief NECULAI STOIAN; circ. 66,000.

Sălaj

Năzuinţa (The Aspiration): Zalău, Piaţa 1 Decembrie 7; f. 1968; weekly; Editor-in-Chief IOAN CHIOREANU; circ. 26,000.

Satu Mare

Cronica Sătmăreană (The Chronicle of Satu Mare): Satu Mare, Calea Traian 1; f. 1968; daily except Mon.; Editor-in-Chief ION RAŢIU; circ. 20,000.

Szatmári Hirlap (Satu Mare Journal): Satu Mare, Calea Traian 1; f. 1968; daily except Mon.; in Hungarian; Editor-in-Chief STEFAN IOSIF STHAL; circ. 16,000.

Sibiu

Hermannstädter Zeitung: 2400 Sibiu, Str. Dr I. Raţiu 7; tel. (24) 11176; f. 1968; fmrly *Die Woche*; weekly; in German; Editor-in-Chief GEORG SCHERER; circ. 3,000.

Tribuna Sibiului: Sibiu, Str. George Coşbuc 38; tel. (24) 12810; telex 69247; fax (24) 12026; Bd. Victoriei 8; f. 1884; daily; independent; Editor-in-Chief OCTAVIAN RUSU; circ. 40,000.

Suceava

Zori noi (New Dawn): Suceava, Str. Tipografiei 1; f. 1946; daily except Mon.; Editor-in-Chief ION PARANICI; circ. 25,000.

Teleorman

Teleormanul: Alexandria, Str. Dunării 178; f. 1968; weekly; Editor-in-Chief MARIN LEOVEANU; circ. 35,000.

Timiş

Banatske Novine: Timişoara, Bd. Revoluţiei din Decembrie 1989 8; f. 1957; weekly; in Serbian; Editor-in-Chief IVAN MUNCIAN; circ. 3,000.

Neue Banater Zeitung: 1900 Timişoara, Bd. Revoluţiei din Decembrie 1989 8; tel. (61) 15586; fax (61) 15586; f. 1957; daily except Sun. and Mon.; in German; Editor-in-Chief GERHARD BINDER; circ. 5,000.

Renaşterea bănăţeană (Romanian Renaissance): Timişoara, Bd. Revoluţiei din Decembrie 1989 8; tel. (61) 19176; fax (61) 33112; f. 1944; daily; Editor-in-Chief GEORGE BOIERU; circ. 70,000.

Szabad Szó: Timişoara, Bd. Revoluţiei din Decembrie 1989 8; f. 1944; daily except Mon.; in Hungarian; Editor-in-Chief ANNA MARIA POP; circ. 9,000.

Tulcea

Delta (The Delta): 8800 Tulcea, Str. Spitalului 4; tel. (15) 12406; telex 52235; f. 1885; daily except Mon.; Editor-in-Chief NECULAI AMIHULESEI; circ. 26,000.

Vaslui

Vremea Nouă (New Times): Vaslui, Str. Ştefan cel Mare 79; f. 1968; weekly; Editor-in-Chief VASILE AVRAM; circ. 25,000.

Vîlcea

Orizont (Horizon): Rîmnicu Vîlcea, Str. Lenin 201; f. 1968; weekly; Editor-in-Chief CONSTANTIN BULACU; circ. 27,000.

Vrancea

Milcovul: Focşani, 13 Bd. Unirii; f. 1968; weekly; Editor-in-Chief IONEL NISTOR; circ. 29,000.

PRINCIPAL PERIODICALS

Many of the publications founded prior to the revolution of December 1989 were undergoing reorganization in 1990–91. Numerous new periodicals were subsequently established.

Bucharest

22: Bucharest; weekly; published by the Group for Social Dialogue.

Agricultura României (Agriculture of Romania): 71341 Bucharest, Piaţa Presei Libere 1; tel. (0) 176020; f. 1974; weekly; published by the Ministry of Agriculture and Food Industry; Editor-in-Chief LUCIAN ROŞCA; circ. 70,000.

A Hét (The Week): 79776 Bucharest, Piaţa Presei Libere 1; tel. (0) 184939; f. 1970; weekly; in Hungarian; social, cultural, scientific and ecological review; Editor-in-Chief GÁFALVI ZSOLT; circ. 4,000.

Albina (The Bee): 71341 Bucharest, Piaţa Presei Libere 1; tel. (0) 173487; f. 1897; monthly; social and cultural review; Editor-in-Chief VLADIMIR PANĂ; circ. 80,000.

Anticipaţia: 79781 Bucharest, Piaţa Presei Libere 1; f. 1990; monthly; science-fiction literature; Editor-in-Chief VIORICA PODINĂ; circ. 50,000.

Apărarea Patriei (The Defence of the Country): Bucharest, Str. Izvor 137; f. 1945; weekly; published by the Ministry of National Defence; Editor-in-Chief Col RADU OLARU; circ. 75,000.

Arhitectura (Architecture): Bucharest, Str. Academiei 18–20; f. 1906; every 2 months; review of the Union of Architects; Editor-in-Chief Arch. ŞTEFAN RADU IONESCU; circ. 3,000.

Arta (Art): 70205 Bucharest, Str. C. A. Rosetti 39; tel. (0) 131380; f. 1953; monthly; Editor-in-Chief CĂLIN DAN; circ. 5,000.

Basarabia si Bucovina: Bucharest; f. 1990; historical and cultural journal on Bessarabia and Moldavia.

Biserica ortodoxă română (The Romanian Orthodox Church): Bucharest, Intrarea Patriarhiei 9; tel. (0) 234449; f. 1822; monthly; official bulletin of the Romanian Patriarchate; Editor Rev. DUMITRU SOARE; circ. 10,000.

Cimbora (Friend): 71341 Bucharest, Piaţa Presei Libere 1; tel. (0) 176010; f. 1922; monthly; in Hungarian; for children; Editor-in-Chief GABRIELLA CSIRE; circ. 25,000.

Cîntarea României: 71341 Bucharest, Piaţa Presei Libere 1; f. 1980; monthly; appears both in Romanian-Hungarian and Romanian-German edns; Editor-in-Chief MIHAIL NEGULESCU; circ. 15,000.

Contemporanul Ideea Europeană: 71341 Bucharest, Piaţa Presei Libere 1; tel. (0) 177413; f. 1881; weekly; cultural, political and scientific review, published by the Ministry of Culture; Chief Editor NICOLAE BREBAN; circ. 10,000.

Curierul Comercial: f. 1898, re-established Dec. 1989; weekly trade journal.

Curierul românesc: 71273 Bucharest, Al. Alexandru 38; tel. (0) 797510; fax (0) 796530; f. Dec. 1989 to replace Tribuna României; fortnightly; cultural and social; published by the Romanian Cultural Foundation; circulated internationally; Pres. AUGUSTIN BUZURA; circ. 15,000.

Cutezătorii (The Bold): 71341 Bucharest, Piaţa Presei Libere 1; tel. (0) 176948; f. 1967; weekly; Editor-in-Chief ION IONAŞCU; circ. 280,000.

Democratia (Democracy): f. 1990; independent periodical; supports National Salvation Front.

Era Socialistă (Socialist Age): 71341 Bucharest, Piaţa Presei Libere 1; tel. (0) 176010; f. 1920; fortnightly; theoretical and political review of the RCP Central Committee until Dec. 1989; Editor-in-Chief ION MITRAN; circ. 50,000.

Falvak Dolgozo Népe (Village World): 71341 Bucharest, Piaţa Presei Libere 1; f. 1945; weekly; in Hungarian; review published by Ministry of Agriculture and Food Industry, the National Union of Producer Co-operative Farms and the Central Union of Production, Procurement and Goods Distribution Co-operatives; Editor-in-Chief NICOLAE SIMIONESCU; circ. 5,500.

Fapta (The Deed): f. 1990; weekly; published by Democratic Labour Party.

Femeia (Woman): 71341 Bucharest, Piaţa Presei Libere 1; f. 1948; monthly; published by National Women's Council; Editor-in-Chief CONSTANŢA NICULESCU; circ. 475,000.

Filatelia: 70100 Bucharest, POB 1-870; tel. (0) 131007; f. 1950; monthly; published by Philatelists' Federation; Editor-in-Chief AURELIAN DÂRNU; circ. 8,000.

Flacăra (The Flame): 71341 Bucharest, Piaţa Presei Libere 1; f. 1952; weekly; Editor-in-Chief (vacant); circ. 385,000.

Foresta: Bucharest, Bd. N. Bălcescu 22; f. 1969; quarterly; in English, French and German; wood, furniture and building materials review published by Chamber of Commerce and Industry; circ. 3,000.

Gazeta cooperaţiei: 71341 Bucharest, Piaţa Presei Libere 1; tel. (0) 176020; weekly; published by Centrocoop; Editor-in-Chief GHEORGHE ANGELESCU; circ. 50,000.

Holidays in Romania: 70148 Bucharest, Str. Gabriel Péri 8; tel. (0) 597893; telex 11724; f. 1958; monthly; in English, French and German; published by Ministry of Trade and Tourism; Editor-in-Chief SIMION POP; circ. 22,000.

Ifjúmunkás (Young Workman): 71341 Bucharest, Piaţa Presei Libere 1; f. 1957; weekly; in Hungarian; Editor-in-Chief JÓZSEF VARGA; circ. 22,000.

Infoclub: 79781 Bucharest, Piaţa Presei Libere 1; f. 1990; every 2 months; computing magazine; Editor-in-Chief MIHAELA GORODCOV; circ. 30,000.

Közoktatás (Public Education): 71341 Bucharest, Piaţa Presei Libere 1; f. 1957, known as *Tanügyi Ujság* until 1989; monthly; published by Ministry of Education and Science; in Hungarian; Editor STEFAN BANTO; circ. 4,000.

Luceafărul (The Morning Star): 71341 Bucharest, Piaţa Presei Libere 1; f. 1958; weekly; published by the Writers' Union; Editor-in-Chief NICOLAE DAN FRUNTELATĂ; circ. 7,000.

Lumea (The World): 71341 Bucharest, Piaţa Presei Libere 1; tel. (0) 185081; telex 11272; f. 1963; weekly; review of international affairs; Dir DARIE NOVĂCEANU ; circ. 50,000.

Luminiţa (The Little Light): 71341 Bucharest, Piaţa Presei Libere 1; tel. (0) 176010; f. 1949; monthly; Editor-in-Chief ION IONAŞCU; circ. 265,000.

Lupta CFR (Romanian Railway Workers' Struggle): Bucharest, Bd. Dinicu Golescu 38; f. 1932; weekly; Editor-in-Chief IONEL CHIRU; circ. 150,000.

Magazin: 71341 Bucharest, Piaţa Presei Libere 1; f. 1957; weekly; for the popularization of science; Editor-in-Chief MARIA COSTACHE; circ. 520,000.

Magazin istoric (Historical Magazine): 70100 Bucharest, Intrarea Ministerului 2; tel. (0) 150991; f. 1967; monthly; review of historical culture; Chief Editor CRISTIAN POPIŞTEANU; circ. 120,000.

Manuscriptum: Bucharest, Str. Fundaţiei 4; tel. (0) 502096; telex 10376; f. 1970; quarterly; published by the Ministry of Culture; Editor-in-Chief PETRU CREŢIA; circ. 5,000.

Modelism—International: 71341 Bucharest, Piaţa Presei Libere 1; quarterly; hobbies; Editor-in-Chief Dr CRISTIAN CRĂCIUNOIU; circ. 60,000.

Munca (Labour): Bucharest, Str. Stefan Gheorghiu 14; f. 1944; weekly; trade union interests; Editor-in-Chief AUREL MOJA; circ. 170,000.

Munkásélet (Labour Life): 71341 Bucharest, Piaţa Presei Libere 1; tel. (0) 185795; f. 1957; weekly; trade union interests; in Hungarian; Editor-in-Chief AUREL MOJA; circ. 12,000.

Neamul Romanesc (Serie Nouă) (The Romanian Nation—New Series): f. 1990; Iaşi; weekly; political, scientific and cultural review published by the National Salvation Front.

Noul Cinema: 41917 Bucharest, Piaţa Presei Libere 1; f. 1963; monthly; Editor-in-Chief ADINA DARIAN; circ. 150,000.

Novîi vik (New Age): 71341 Bucharest, Piaţa Presei Libere 1; f. 1949; fortnightly; social, political and cultural journal for the Ukrainian population; Editor-in-Chief ION COLESNIC; circ. 1,600.

Oblio: f. 1990; monthly; magazine of the National Democratic Party; Romanian, European and international affairs, incl. cultural and economic issues.

Panoramic Radio-TV: Bucharest, Str. Gral Berthelot 60–62; fax (0) 156992; weekly; circ. 300,000.

Pentru patrie (For the Motherland): 70622 Bucharest, Sector 5, Str. Mihai Vodă 17; tel. (0) 143795; telex 88810; f. 1949; monthly; illustrated; published by Ministry of the Interior; Editor-in-Chief OLIMPIAN UNGHEREA; circ. 300,000.

Psihologia: 79781 Bucharest, Piaţa Presei Libere 1; f. 1991; quarterly; psychology; Editor-in-Chief ADINA CHELCEA; circ. 30,000.

Revista Cultului Mozaic (Review of the Mosaic Creed): 70478 Bucharest, Str. Sf. Vineri 9–11; tel. (0) 132538; telex 10798; fax (0) 130911; f. 1956; fortnightly; English, Romanian, Hebrew and Yiddish; published by Federation of Jewish Communities; Pres. Dr MOSES ROSEN; circ. 9,800.

Revista de statistică (Review of Statistics): Bucharest, Str. Stavropoleos 6; f. 1952; monthly; organ of the National Statistics Commission; Editor-in-Chief (vacant); circ. 8,500.

Revue roumaine des sciences sociales: Bucharest, Str. Oneşti 11; quarterly; philosophy and logic series; articles in French, English, Russian and German; published by the Academy of Social and Political Sciences; Editor-in-Chief Prof. DUMITRU GHIŞE; circ. 500.

România apicolă (Apicultural Romania): 70231 Bucharest, Str. I. Fuçik 17; tel. (0) 137877; telex 11205; f. 1926; monthly; review of apiculture published by the Beekeepers' Association; Editor ELISEI TARŢA; circ. 25,000.

România Literară (Literary Romania): 71341 Bucharest, Piaţa Presei Libere 1; tel. (0) 176190; f. 1968 as successor to *Gazeta Literară*; weekly; literary, artistic and political magazine; published by the Writers' Union; Chief Editor NICOLAE MANOLESCU; circ. 25,000.

România Máre: Bucharest; weekly; nationalist; Editor-in-Chief CORNELIU VADIM TUDOR; circ. 500,000.

Romania—Pages of History: 71341 Bucharest, Piaţa Presei Libere 1, POB 33–22; tel. (0) 173836; telex 11272; f. 1976; quarterly; in English, French, German, Russian and Spanish; academic studies, biographies, book reviews, etc.; published by the Foreign Languages Press Group 'Romania'; Editor-in-Chief GEORGE G. POTRA.

România pitorească (Picturesque Romania): 70148 Bucharest, Str. Gabriel Péri 8; tel. (0) 597893; telex 11724; f. 1972; monthly; published by the Ministry of Trade and Tourism; Editor-in-Chief POP SIMION; circ. 32,000.

Romanian Books: 71341 Bucharest, Piaţa Presei Libere 1; tel. (0) 173306; f. 1972; in English, French, German and Russian; Editor-in-Chief PAUL DUGNEANU; circ. 6,500.

Romanian Engineering: Bd. N. Bălcescu 22; f. 1966; quarterly; in English, French, Spanish and German; technical and commercial review published by Chamber of Commerce and Industry; circ. 3,500.

Romanian Foreign Trade: Bucharest, Chamber of Commerce and Industry, Bd. Nicolae Bălcescu 22; f. 1952; quarterly; in English, French, German, Russian and Spanish; circ. 2,000.

Romanian Journal of Chemistry: Bucharest, Chamber of Commerce and Industry, Bd. Nicolae Bălcescu 22; f. 1952; quarterly; in English, French, German and Russian; circ. 6,000.

Romanian Orthodox Church News: 71341 Bucharest, Piaţa Presei Libere 1; quarterly; in English and French; circ. 2,000.

Romanian Panorama: 71341 Bucharest, Piaţa Presei Libere 1, Corp B, POB 33–38; tel. (0) 173836; telex 11272; f. 1955; monthly; in Chinese, English, French, German, Russian and Spanish; economy, politics, social questions, science, history, culture, sport, etc.; published by the Foreign Languages Press Group; Editor-in-Chief N. SARAMBEI; circ. 10,000.

Romanian Review: 71341 Bucharest, Piaţa Presei Libere 1; tel. (0) 173836; telex 11272; f. 1946; monthly; in English, French, German and Russian; literature, the arts, history, philosophy, sociology, etc.; published by Foreign Languages Press Group; Editor-in-Chief N. SARAMBEI; circ. 5,000.

Satul românesc (Romanian Village): 71341 Bucharest, Piaţa Presei Libere 1; tel. (0) 170304; weekly; publ. by Federation of Agricultural Cos of Romania; Editor-in-Chief TITU CONSTANTIN; circ. 80,000.

Sănătatea (Health): Bucharest, Str. Biserica Amzei 29; f. 1952; monthly; published by the National Council of the Red Cross; Editor-in-Chief GHEORGHE M. GEORGE; circ. 140,000.

Secolul 20 (20th Century): Bucharest, Calea Victoriei 115; f. 1961; monthly; published by the Writers' Union; Editor-in-Chief DAN HĂULICĂ; circ. 8,000.

Şoimii Patriei: 71341 Bucharest, Piaţa Presei Libere 1; tel. (0) 176010; f. 1979; monthly; Editor-in-Chief ION IONAŞCU; circ. 220,000.

Sportul Ilustrat: Bucharest, Str. Vasile Conta 16; tel. (0) 116033; telex 10350; fax (0) 113459; f. 1947; monthly; illustrated magazine; Editor-in-Chief CONSTANTIN MACOVEI; circ. 120,000.

Start 2001: 71341 Bucharest, Piaţa Presei Libere 1; tel. (0) 181361; f. 1990; monthly review; Editor-in-Chief IOAN VOICU; circ. 95,000.

Steaua Dunării (Danube Star): published by the National Liberal Party; Dir PAUL PACURARU.

Ştiinţă şi Tehnică (Science and Technology): 79781 Bucharest, Piaţa Presei Libere 1; f. 1949; monthly; Editor-in-Chief TITI TUDORANCEA; circ. 60,000.

Studentimea Democrata: f. 1990; independent students' weekly.

Tehnium: 79784 Bucharest, Piaţa Presei Libere 1; tel. (0) 183566; f. 1970; monthly; science review; Editor-in-Chief Ing. ILIE MIHAESCU; circ. 150,000.

Tribuna economică (Economic Tribune): 70159 Bucharest, Bd. Magheru 28–30; tel. (0) 595158; f. 1886; weekly; Editor-in-Chief BOGDAN PADURE; circ. 50,000.

Tribuna învăţămîntului (Education's Tribune): 71341 Bucharest, Piaţa Presei Libere 1; tel. (0) 181508; f. 1990; weekly; guide to schools and colleges; published by the Ministry of Education and Science; Editor-in-Chief RECEAN DUMITRU MIRCEA; circ. 70,000.

Urzica (Stinging Nettle): 79751 Bucharest, Str. Brezoianu 23–25, Sector 1; f. 1949; monthly; humour and satire; Editor-in-Chief TUDOR POPESCU; circ. 225,000.

Viaţa (The Life): Bucharest, Brezoianu 23; tel. and fax (0) 135617; f. 1990 to replace *Săptămîna culturală a capitalei*; weekly socio-cultural review; Editor-in-Chief MIRCEA MICU.

Viaţa Armatei (Army Life): 70768 Bucharest, Str. Cobălcescu 28A, Sector 1; tel. (0) 142012; f. 1947; fmrly *Viaţa Militară*; monthly illustrated review of the Ministry of National Defence; Editor-in-Chief ION JIANU; circ. 30,000.

Viaţa cooperaţiei meşteşugăreşti (News from the Handicrafts Cooperatives): Bucharest, Calea Plevnei 46; f. 1953; monthly; Editor-in-Chief MARIN PETRE; circ. 65,000.

Vînătorul şi Pescarul Român (The Romanian Hunter and Angler): Bucharest, Calea Moşilor 128; tel. (0) 136698; f. 1948; monthly review; published by the Association of Hunters and Anglers; Editor-in-Chief VICTOR ŢARUŞ; circ. 25,000.

Bacău

Ateneu (Atheneum): Bacău, Str. Eliberării 63; f. 1964; monthly; cultural review; Editor-in-Chief GEORGE GENOIU; circ. 7,000.

Braşov

Astra: 2200 Braşov, Str. M. Sadoveanu 3; tel. 43179; f. 1966; monthly; literature, art, culture, philosophy; Editor-in-Chief AUREL ION BRUMARU; circ. 15,000.

Cluj-Napoca

Dolgozo Nö (Working Woman): Cluj-Napoca, Str. Napoca 16; f. 1945; monthly; published by the National Women's Council; in Hungarian; Editor-in-Chief (vacant); circ. 106,000.

Helikon: 3400 Cluj-Napoca, Str. Eroilor 2; tel. (51) 12420; weekly; organ of the Writers' Union; in Hungarian; Editor-in-Chief ISTVÁN SZILÁGYI; circ. 4,000.

Korunk (Our Time): 3400 Cluj-Napoca, Calea Moţilor 3; tel. (51) 17836; f. 1926; monthly; social review; in Hungarian; Dirs PÉTER CSEKE, SÁNDOR KERESKÉNYI, LEVENTE SALAT, ANDRÁS VISKY; circ. 4,500.

Napsugár (Sun Ray): 3400 Cluj-Napoca, Piaţa Păcii 1–3; tel. (51) 11184; f. 1957; monthly; in Hungarian; Editor-in-Chief KÁROLY TAR; circ. 40,000.

Steaua (Star): 3400 Cluj-Napoca, Piaţa Libertăţii 1; tel. (51) 12852; f. 1949; monthly review of the Writers' Union; Editor-in-Chief AUREL RĂU; circ. 3,500.

Tribuna: Cluj-Napoca, Str. Universităţii 1; f. 1884; weekly; cultural review; Editor-in-Chief VASILE SALĂJAN; circ. 6,000.

Constanţa

Tomis: Constanţa, Şos. Filimon Sîrbu 5; f. 1966; monthly review; Chief Editor CONSTANTIN NOVAC; circ. 6,000.

Craiova

Ramuri (Branches): Craiova, bis Str. Săvineşti 3; f. 1964; monthly; review of culture; Editor-in-Chief MARIN SORESCU; circ. 4,000.

Iaşi

Convorbiri literare (Literary Conversations): Iaşi, Str. Dimitrov 1; f. 1867, new series 1972; monthly; review of literature; published by the Writers' Union, Iaşi branch; Editor-in-Chief CORNELIU STURZU; circ. 3,000.

Cronica: Iaşi, Str. Vasile Alecsandri 8; f. 1966; weekly; political, social and cultural review; Editor-in-Chief ION ŢARANU; circ. 8,000.

Oradea

Familia (Family): 3700 Oradea, Str. Romană 3; tel. (91) 14129; f. 1865, new series 1965; monthly; social and cultural review; Editor-in-Chief IOAN MOLDOVAN; circ. 4,000.

Piteşti

Argeş: Piteşti, Bd. R.S.R. 88; f. 1966; monthly; social and cultural review; Editor-in-Chief SERGIU NICOLAESCU; circ. 3,000.

Sibiu

Transilvania: Sibiu, Bd. Victoriei 11; f. 1868; monthly; political, social and cultural; Editor-in-Chief MIRCEA TOMUŞ; circ. 2,000.

Tribuna Sporturilor: 2400 Sibiu, Str. George Coşbuc 38; tel. (24) 12810; telex 69247; fax (24) 12026; f. 1990; weekly; sports magazine; Editor-in-Chief MIRCEA BIŢU; circ. 20,000.

Timişoara

Orizont (Horizon): Timişoara, Piaţa Sf. Gheorghe 3; tel. (61) f. 1949; weekly; review of the Writers' Union (Timişoara branch); Editor-in-Chief MIRCEA MIHAIES; circ. 5,000.

Tîrgu Mureş

Erdélyi Figyelő (Transylvanian Observer): 4300 Tîrgu-Mureces, Str. Primăriei 1; tel. (54) 26780; f. 1958, known as *Új Élet* until 1989; fortnightly; illustrated magazine; Editor-in-Chief ÉLTETŐ JÓZSEF; circ. 15,000.

Lató (Visionary): 4300 Tîrgu Mureş, Str. Primăriei 1; tel. (54) 26610; f. 1953; fmrly *Igaz Szó*; monthly; in Hungarian; literature; Editor-in-Chief BÉLA MARKÓ; circ. 5,000.

Vatra (Home): 4300 Tîrgu Mureş, Str. Primăriei 1; tel. (54) 35005; f. 1894, 1971; monthly; review of literature, sociology; published by the Writers' Union, Mureş branch; Editor-in-Chief CORNEL MORARU; circ. 5,000.

NEWS AGENCY

Rompres (Romanian News Agency): 71341 Bucharest, Piaţa Presei Libere 1; tel. (0) 176061; telex 11272; f. 1949; fmrly Agerpres; co-operates with, and provides news and photo services to, 64 overseas news agencies; daily news released in English, French, Russian and Spanish; publs news and feature bulletins in English, French, German, Russian and Spanish, and one in Arabic; Dir-Gen. NEAGU UDROIU.

Foreign Bureaux

Agence France-Presse (AFP): Bucharest, Bd. Nicolae Bălcescu 22; tel. (0) 135226; Correspondent MICHEL CONRADH.

Agenzia Nazionale Stampa Associata (ANSA) (Italy): 70185 Bucharest, Bd. Dacia 9A, Apt. 2; tel. (0) 335325; telex 11642; Correspondent GIAN MARCO VENIER.

Allgemeiner Deutscher Nachrichtendienst (ADN) (Germany): 70256 Bucharest, Bd. Dacia 37B, Apt. 3; tel. (0) 111214; telex 11327; Correspondent JOACHIM SUNNENBERG.

Bulgarska Telegrafna Agentsia (BTA) (Bulgaria): Bucharest, Str. Mihai Eminescu 124; tel. (0) 191880; Correspondent PETIO PETKOV.

Československá tisková kancelář (ČTK) (Czechoslovakia): Bucharest, Str. Drobeta 4–10, Apt. 12, Sector 2; tel. (0) 114473; telex 11301; Correspondent JAN KOKES.

Informatsionnoye Agentstvo Novosti (IAN) (Russia): Bucharest, Al. Alexandru 40; tel. (0) 795648; telex 11300; Correspondent VYACHESLAV SAMOSHIN.

Magyar Távirati Iroda (MTI) (Hungary): 72263 Bucharest, Al. Alexandru 10, Apt. 1; tel. (0) 792436; telex 11211; Correspondent P. LÁSZLÓ.

Novinska Agencija Tanjug (Yugoslavia): Bucharest, Str. Drobeta 4–10; tel. (0) 116208; telex 11304; Correspondent PETAR TOMICI.

Polska Agencja Prasowa (PAP) (Poland): Bucharest, Str. Mircea Vodă 14; tel. (0) 206870; telex 11298; Correspondent STANISŁAW WOJNAROWICH.

Telegrafnoye Agentstvo Sovetskovo Soyuza (TASS) (Russia): Bucharest, Str. General Praporgescu 33; tel. (0) 134802; telex 11317; Chief Correspondent DMITRII DIAKOV.

Xinhua (New China) News Agency (People's Republic of China): Bucharest, Şos. Nordului 2; tel. (0) 331927; telex 11308; Correspondent ZHANG HANWEN.

PRESS ASSOCIATIONS

Societatea Ziariştilor din România-Federaţia Sindicatelor din Întreaga Presă (Society of Romanian Journalists-Federation of All Press Unions): Bucharest, Piaţa Presei Libere 1; tel. (0) 184293; telex 11272; fax (0) 170487; f. 1990; affiliated to International Organization of Journalists; Pres. SERGIU ANDON; 6,000 mems.

The **Union of Professional Journalists** (Pres. STEFAN MITROI) was established in 1990, as was the **Democratic Journalists' Union** (Pres. P. M. BACANU).

Publishers

In 1990 some 1,529 book titles (61m. copies) were published.

Editura Academiei Române (Publishing House of the Romanian Academy): 79717 Bucharest, Calea Victoriei 125; tel. (0) 502130; f. 1948; important books and periodicals on original scientific work, 66 periodicals in Romanian and foreign languages; Dir CONSTANTIN BUSUIOCEANU.

Editura Albatros: 71341 Bucharest, Piaţa Presei Libere 1; tel. (0) 180448; f. 1971; general; Dir MIHAI SIN.

Editura Cartea Românescă (Publishing House of The Romanian Book): 79721 Bucharest, Str. Gral Berthelot 41; tel. (0) 149352; f. 1969; Romanian contemporary literature; Dir GEORGE BĂLĂIŢĂ.

Editura Ceres: 79722 Bucharest, Piaţa Presei Libere 1; tel. (0) 180174; f. 1953; books on agriculture and forestry; Dir Eng. ECATERINA MOŞU.

Editura Ion Creangă (Ion Creangă Publishing House): 79725 Bucharest, Piaţa Presei Libere 1; tel. (0) 182525; f. 1969; children's books; Dir DANIELA CRĂSNARU.

Editura Dacia (Dacia Publishing House): 3400 Cluj-Napoca, Str. Emil Isac 23; tel. (51) 18912; telex 31347; f. 1969; classical and contemporary Romanian literature, art books, literary, and scientific books in Romanian, Hungarian and German; Dir VASILE IGNA.

Editura Didactică şi Pedagogica (Educational Publishing House): 79724 Bucharest, Str. Spiru Haret 12; tel. (0) 152455; telex 011352; f. 1951; school, university, technical and vocational textbooks; pedagogic literature and methodology; teaching materials; Dir CONSTANTIN FLORICEL.

Editura Mihai Eminescu (Mihai Eminescu Publishing House): 79731 Bucharest, Piaţa Presei Libere 1; tel. (0) 177380; f. 1969; contemporary original literary works and translations of world literature; Dir EUGEN NEGRICI.

Editura Enciclopedică (Encyclopaedic Publishing House): 71341 Bucharest, Piaţa Presei Libere 1; tel. (0) 175168; f. 1968; merged with Scientific Publishing House, as Editura Ştiinţifică şi Enciclopedică, 1974–90; encyclopaedias, dictionaries, bibliographies, chronologies and reference books; popular and informational literature; provides photographs and encyclopaedic and statistical data about Romania for publishing houses abroad; Dir MARCEL POPA.

Editura Humanitas (Humanitas Publishing House): 70734 Bucharest, Piaţa Presei Libere 1; tel. (0) 172987; fax (0) 181455; philosophy, religion, political and social sciences, economics, history, fiction.

Editura Junimea (Junimea Publishing House): 6600 Iaşi, O. P. 1, POB 28; tel. (81) 17290; f. 1970; Romanian literature, art books, translations, scientific and technical books; Dir NICOLAE CREŢU.

Editura Kriterion (Kriterion Publishing House): 71341 Bucharest, Piaţa Presei Libere 1; tel. (0) 174060; f. 1969; classical and contemporary literature, reference books in science and art in Hungarian, German, Romanian, Russian, Serbian, Slovak, Tatar, Turkish, Ukrainian and Yiddish; translations in Romanian, Hungarian and German; Dir GYULA H. SZABÓ.

Editura Litera (The Letter Publishing House): 79727 Bucharest, Piaţa Presei Libere 1; tel. (0) 182471; 1969; original literature; Dir VIORICA OANCEA.

Editura Medicală (Medical Publishing House): 79728 Bucharest, Str. Smîrdan 5; tel. (0) 143252; f. 1954; medical literature; Dir VALENTIN STROESCU.

Editura Meridiane (Meridiane Publishing House): 79729 Bucharest, Piaţa Presei Libere 1; tel. (0) 181087; f. 1952; fine arts, theatre, cinema, architecture; art history, theory and criticism; picture art books, monographs, postcards; Dir DANIEL BARBU.

Editura Militară (Military Publishing House): 79735 Bucharest, Str. Cobălescu 28A; tel. (0) 133601; f. 1950; military history, theory, science, technics and medicine, and fiction; Dir CORNEL BARBULESCU.

Editura Minerva (Minerva Publishing House): 79732 Bucharest, Piaţa Presei Libere 1; tel. (0) 184464; f. 1969; Romanian classical literature, world literature, original literary works, literary criticism and history; Dir DUMITRU MICU.

Editura Muzicală (Musical Publishing House): 70718 Bucharest, Str. Poiana Narciselor 6; tel. (0) 138743; f. 1957; books on music, musicology and musical scores; Dir VLAD ULPIU.

Editura Presa Libera (Free Press Publishing House): 71341 Bucharest, Piaţa Presei Libere 1; f. 1954; newspapers, magazines; Dir (vacant).

Editura Scrisul românesc (Romanian Writing Publishing House): 1100 Craiova, Str. Mihai Viteazul 4; tel. (41) 13763; f. 1972; socio-political, technical, scientific and literary works; Dir MARIN SORESCU.

Editura Sport-Turism (Sport-Tourism Publishing House): 79736 Bucharest, Str. Vasile Conta 16; tel. (0) 107480; f. 1968; sport, tourism, monographs, translations, postcards, children's books; Dir MIHAI CAZIMIR.

Editura Ştiinţifică (Scientific Publishing House): 71341 Bucharest, Piaţa Presei Libere 1; tel. (0) 176689; f. 1990; fmrly Editura Ştiinţifică şi Enciclopedică; language dictionaries, bibliographies, monographs, chronologies, reference books, popular and informational literature; Dir DINU GRAMA.

Editura Tehnică (Technical Publishing House): 79738 Bucharest, Piaţa Presei Libere 1; tel. (0) 180630; f. 1950; technical and scientific books, technical dictionaries; Dir Dr Eng. IOAN GANEA.

Editura Univers: 79739 Bucharest, Piaţa Presei Libere 1; tel. (0) 181762; f. 1961; translations from world literature; Dir Prof. Dr MIRCEA MARTIN.

Editura de Vest (West Publishing House): 1900 Timişoara, Str. Rodnei 1; tel. (61) 18218; fax (0) 14212; f. 1972 as Editura Facla; socio-political, technical, scientific and literary works in Romanian, Hungarian, German and Serbian; Dir VASILE POPOVICI.

Întreprinderea de Stat pentru Imprimate şi Administrarea Publicaţiilor (State Enterprise for Printed Matter and Periodicals): 71341 Bucharest, Piaţa Presei Libere 1; f. 1951; general publications; Dir NICOLAE BAZAC.

Tribuna Press and Publishing House: 2400 Sibiu, Str. George Coşbuc 38; tel. (24) 12810; telex 69247; fax (24) 12026; f. 1991; Dir EMIL DAVID.

PUBLISHERS' ASSOCIATION

Romlibri: 79715 Bucharest, Piaţa Presei Libere 1; tel. (0) 181255; f. 1962 as Centrala Editorială; a state organization which co-ordinates book production and distribution throughout Romania as well as the economic and financial activities of the publishing houses; organizes the import and export of books and other cultural goods; Man. Dir MIRCEA VICTOR.

WRITERS' UNION

Uniunea Scriitorilor din România (Romanian Writers' Union): Bucharest, Calea Victoriei 133; tel. (0) 507245; telex 11796; fax (0) 505594; f. 1949; Pres. MIRCEA DINESCU.

Radio and Television

In March 1991 there were 2,355,800 radio subscribers and 3,640,791 television subscribers. Romania's first regional TV station (at Timişoara) was registered in December 1989. Plans for the reception of satellite TV in Romania were also under way.

Radioteleviziunea Română (Romanian Radio and Television): Bucharest, Calea Dorobanţilor 191, POB 63–1200; tel. (0) 334710; telex 11251; fax (0) 337544; Pres. Prof. Dr RĂZVAN THEODORESCU.

RADIO

Radiodifuziunea Română: Bucharest, Str. Gral Berthelot 60–62; tel. (0) 503055; telex 11252; fax (0) 156992; f. 1928; 39 transmitters on medium-wave, 69 transmitters on VHF. First, Second, Third and Fourth Programme.

Foreign broadcasts on one medium-wave and eight short-wave transmitters in Arabic, English, French, German, Greek, Italian, Persian, Portuguese, Romanian, Russian, Serbian, Spanish and Turkish.

TELEVISION

Televiziunea Română—Telecentrul Bucureşti (Romanian Television—Bucharest TV Centre): Bucharest, Calea Dorobanţilor 191, POB 63–1200; tel. (0) 334710; telex 11251; 39 transmitters; daily transmissions (some in colour since 1983).

Finance

(cap. = capital; dep. = deposits; m. = million; amounts in lei)

BANKING
Central Bank

Banca Naţională (National Bank of Romania): Bucharest, Str. Lipscani 25; tel. (0) 130410; telex 11136; f. 1880; until 1947 was the Banca Naţională a României; from 1947–65 was the Banca Republicii Populare Române; central bank; the only bank of issue; manages monetary policy; supervises commercial banks and credit business; Gov. MUGUR ISĂRESCU.

Other Banks

Banca Agricolă (Agriculture Bank): 70006 Bucharest, Str. Smîrdan 3; tel. (0) 144260; telex 11622; f. 1968; accepts deposits; grants short-, medium- and long-term loans; all kinds of banking transactions in domestic and foreign currency for private, state and co-operative cos and individuals, irrespective of their field of activity; Pres. GHEORGHE BĂRBULESCU.

Banca Română de Comerţ Exterior (Romanian Bank for Foreign Trade): 70012 Bucharest, Calea Victoriei 22–24; tel. (0) 149190; telex 11703; fax (0) 141598; f. 1968, reorganized 1991; provides complete range of banking services and financial operations, in lei and foreign currency, for domestic and foreign customers; cap. 7,500m.; dep. 24,378m.; Pres. DAN PASCARIU; 8 brs.

Bankcoop: Bucharest, Str. Ion Ghica 13; tel. (0) 147618; Pres. Mr DINULESCU.

Casa de Economii şi Consemnaţiuni—CEC (Savings and Consignation Bank): Bucharest, Calea Victoriei 13; tel. (0) 154810; f. 1864; handles private savings and other operations for individuals and institutions as established by law; Pres. NICOLAE EREMIA.

Romanian Commercial Bank SA: 70348 Bucharest, Bd. Republicii 14; telex 10893; f. 1990; commercial banking services for domestic and foreign customers; subscribed cap. 12,000m.; Pres. ION GHICA; 35 brs and agencies.

Romanian Development Bank: Bucharest, Str. Doamnei 4; tel. (0) 134640; telex 11238; f. 1990 to replace Investment Bank (f. 1948); grants credits in lei and convertible currency; banking services for investment, production and commercial activities, etc.; cap. 5,000m.; Pres. MARIAN CRISAN.

A private bank, The Bank for Small Industry and Free Initiative, was established in 1990, with capital of 1,500m. lei.

INSURANCE

Asigurarea Românească SA (Asirom): 79118 Bucharest, Str. Smîrdan 5; tel. (0) 147748; telex 11269; all types of insurance, including life insurance; Gen. Man. GHEORGHE PARASCHIV.

Insurance and Reinsurance Company SA (Aatra): 79118 Bucharest, Str. Smîrdan 5; tel. (0) 150986; telex 11209; fax (0) 139306; all types of insurance, including commercial insurance; Gen. Man. EMIL BOLDUŞ.

Trade and Industry

There are chambers of commerce throughout Romania.

CHAMBER OF COMMERCE AND INDUSTRY

Chamber of Commerce and Industry of Romania: 79502 Bucharest, Bd. Nicolae Bălcescu 22; tel. (0) 154707; telex 11374; fax (0) 130091; f. 1868; Pres. AUREL GHIBUTIU.

FOREIGN TRADE ORGANIZATIONS AND MAJOR COMPANIES

Arcif: 70448 Bucharest, Str. Scaune 1–3; tel. (0) 155040; telex 92504; f. 1982; export of land reclamation work, water course regulation works, water supply and treatment plants, sewerage works, agricultural and civil construction works, studies, surveys, etc.; Dir VIOREL GIHAC.

Arcom International SA: Bucharest, Str. Scaune 1–3; tel. (0) 153632; telex 11490; f. 1969; civil and industrial constructions, mechanical and electrical installations, engineering and technical assistance services; Pres. and Dir-Gen. MARCEL FLORESCU.

Arpimex Trading SA: Bucharest, Str. Lipscani 19, Sector 3, POB 1–130; tel. (0) 144140; telex 11472; fax (0) 145464; f. 1970; export of footwear, leather goods, leather and fur garments, gloves; import of raw hides, organic dyes, chemical auxiliaries; Gen. Dir MIRCEA STADOLEANU.

Auto-Dacia SA: Pitești, Str. Mircea Vodă 42; tel. (76) 34978; telex 18296; fax (76) 36762; manufacture, export and import of road vehicles, vehicle parts and special purpose vehicles; Dir CONSTANTIN STROE.

Confex: Bucharest, Bd. Armata Poporului 5–7; tel. (0) 814450; telex 011195; fax (0) 316170; exports ready-made clothes and knitwear.

Contransimex: 77115 Bucharest, Bd. Dinicu Golescu 38, POB 2006; tel. (0) 180042; telex 11606; fax (0) 180042; civil engineering and construction projects; import and export of transport and telecommunication equipment and installations; Gen. Man. ALFONS IRINESCU.

Electroexportimport: Bucharest, Calea Victoriei 216, POB 22; tel. (0) 502175; telex 11388; fax (0) 502870; electrical and electrotechnical products, medical equipment, automotive parts; Gen. Dir P. TUDOR.

Electronum: Bucharest, Bd. Magheru 28–30; tel. (0) 137081; telex 11547; fax (0) 506940; exports and imports computer parts and accessories, telecommunication equipment, radio receivers, TV sets, components, etc.; Dir M. TUDOR.

Fructexport-Agroexport: 70714 Bucharest, Str. Brezoianu 43, POB 790; tel. (0) 136563; telex 10963; fax (0) 149747; f. 1950; exports fruit and vegetable produce, wine, spirits, medicinal herbs, aromatic seeds, technical assistance; imports agricultural products, veterinary supplies, etc.; Gen. Dir VICTOR STOICULESCU.

Ilexim: Bucharest, Str. 13 Decembrie 3, POB 1–136; tel. (0) 148530; telex 11226; exports carpets, toys, furniture, handicrafts, ready-made clothes, metal and rubber goods, wooden articles, foodstuffs, agricultural goods, cultural goods; Dir BUJOR URSULESCU.

Industrialexport SA: Bucharest, Bd. Dacia 13, Sector 1; tel. (0) 118905; telex 10052; fax (0) 116218; exports and imports oilfield and mining equipment, complete chemical, petro-chemical oil refining and food industry plants and equipment, grain silos, pumps and industrial valves and fittings; barter operations; Pres. and Gen. Man. Eng. GEORGES CONSTANTIN.

Mașinexportimport: 70033 Bucharest, Bd. Republicii 32, Sector 3, POB 113; tel. (0) 137596; telex 11206; fax (0) 136963; exporter and importer of machine tools for metal-working; also exports woodworking and textiles machinery; Gen. Dir TRAIAN CRUCERU.

Mecanoexportimport SA: 79522 Bucharest, Bd.Dacia 30, POB 22–107; tel. (0) 119855; telex 10269; fax (0) 116650; imports and exports road construction equipment, metal railway sleepers, diesel and electric railway engines, rolling stock, air compressors, lifting and conveying equipment; Gen. Dir CORNEL ANGHEL.

Mercur Trading SA: Bucharest, Calea Victoriei St, Sector 1; tel. (0) 503784; telex 11368; fax (0) 506375; importer and exporter of food and consumer goods; barter trade; Gen. Man. SERBAN ALTANGIU.

Metalexportimport: Bucharest, Str. Mendeleev 21–25; tel. (0) 593850; telex 11515; fax (0) 507922; exports and imports rolled steel products, welded and seamless tubes, ferro-alloys, non-ferrous metals; Gen. Man. CONSTANTIN GHITA.

Mineralimportexport SA: Bucharest, Bd. Republicii 16; tel. (0) 139167; telex 11873; fax (0) 126927; f. 1962; exports coal-tar, graphite electrodes, abrasives, etc.; imports iron ore, manganese ore, pyrite, bauxite, coal, coke, anthracite, potassium fertilizers, refractory materials, abrasive materials, etc.; Dir DAN GEORMANEANU.

Mondexim SA: 70701 Bucharest, Str. Constantin Mille 17; tel. (0) 149548; telex 11496; fax (0) 149404; exports metallurgical products, chemicals, wood products; imports raw materials for metallurgical industry, electronics, spare parts, etc.

Navlomar SA: Bucharest, Bd. Republicii 16, POB 851; tel. (0) 132279; telex 11783; fax (0) 144071; f. 1969; shipbrokers, Danube River chartering agents, cargo transit and transhipment, ship agents, ship-chandlers, consultancy and legal assistance; Gen. Dir VIOREL COVRIG.

Petrolexportimport: Bucharest, Bd. Magheru 1–3; tel. (0) 133045; telex 11519; fax (0) 156550; export of petroleum products; import of raw materials for petrochemical industry; Dir GHEORGHE ALBU.

Prodexport: Bucharest, Str. Valter Mărăcineanu; tel. (0) 384940; telex 11527; fax (0) 152107; f. 1948; exports and imports livestock, meat, sugar, vegetable oils, tobacco, spices, food additives, etc.; Dir N. DAVID.

Românoexport: 70014 Bucharest, Str. Doamnei 17–19, POB 594; tel. (0) 133699; telex 11186; fax (0) 131841; f. 1948; exports: fabrics, knitwear, carpets, and blankets; imports: wool, cotton, jute, dye-stuffs, felts, etc.; Man. Dir. PETRU CRIȘAN.

Romelectro: Bucharest, Calea Dorobanților 60; tel. (0) 112170; telex 10449; fax (0) 116932; export and import of power equipment, electrical appliances, spare parts, etc.; Dir CORNELIU LAZĂR.

Romenergo SA: 71101 Bucharest, Calea Victoriei 91-93, POB 22–153; tel. (0) 506682; telex 11525; fax (0) 506682; import and export of power generation equipment for hydro, thermal and nuclear power projects, boilers, turbines, generators; studies, training, service, etc.; Gen. Man. ALEXANDRU PÂRVESCU.

Romferchim SA: Bucharest, Splaiul Independenței 202A, POB 12–226; tel. (0) 384715; telex 11489; fax (0) 385820; exports fertilizers, pharmaceuticals, cosmetics, cellulose, fibres, chemical products, etc.; imports phosphorites, apatite, acids, etc.; Man. Dir MIHAIIONESCU.

Rompetrol: 70176 Bucharest, Calea Victoriei 109; tel. (0) 594325; telex 10155; fax (0) 595405; provides geological survey and geophysical prospecting, drilling works, construction of pipelines and storage tanks for crude oil, LPG and petroleum products, technical assistance; Gen. Man. NELU IONESCU.

Romproiect SA: 70704 Bucharest 1, Str. Matei Millo 13; tel. (0) 154237; telex 11785; fax (0) 158523; f. 1969; exports design and drafting services, technical assistance for building and irrigation works, mass housing programmes, construction management; Dir DOREL RĂDULESCU.

Romsit: 70418 Bucharest, Str. Doamnei 15–17, Sector 3; tel. (0) 156821; telex 11836; f. 1972; export of glassware, lead crystal, tableware and ornamental porcelain, hotel porcelainware, ornamental earthenware, clear sheet glass; Man. Dir I. SPIRIDON.

Romtrans SA: 75260 Bucharest, Calea Rahovei 196; tel. (0) 236040; telex 11346; fax (0) 413516; f. 1952; international forwarding agency; Dir EUGEN BÂR.

Tehnoforestexport: Bucharest, Piața Rosetti 4; tel. (0) 136717; telex 10330; fax (0) 154020; exports furniture, wooden prefabricated houses and other finished wooden products; Dir CONSTANTIN POPA.

Tehnoimportexport: Bucharest, Str. Doamnei 2, POB 110; tel. (0) 152653; telex 10254; fax (0) 132526; imports and exports bearings and technical goods, aircraft, helicopters, spare parts, etc.; Gen. Dir MIRCEA BORTEȘ.

Terra SA: Bucharest, Bd. Republicii 16, POB 86; tel. (0) 153043; telex 11571; fax (0) 138483; imports and exports various commodities; co-operation ventures, etc.; technical assistance; Gen. Man. FLORIN CASPRUF.

Universal-Trading SA: 2200 Brașov, Str. Turnului 5; tel. (21) 62661; telex 61335; exports tractors and farming machinery, lorries, buses; Dir SAVA RADU BASARAB.

Uzinexportimport SA: 70033 Bucharest, Bd. Republicii 32; tel. (0) 132959; telex 11214; fax (0) 139389; f. 1966; export and import of complex installations and basic equipment for the machine-building industry and ships and shipbuilding industry and cement industries, metallurgical and iron and steel plants; Man. Dir MATACHE NICOLAIDE.

Vitrocim SA: Bucharest, Str. Blănari 18; tel. (0) 131638; telex 11330; fax (0) 142412; f. 1970; import and export of building materials and machinery for the building industry; Gen. Dir CONSTANTIN MĂRGINEANU.

CO-OPERATIVE ORGANIZATIONS

Uniunea centrală a cooperativelor de consum si de credit—Centrocoop (Central Union of Consumer and Credit Co-operatives): Bucharest, Str. Brezoianu 31; tel. (0) 144800; telex 11591; f. 1950; 2,577 producer and 822 credit co-operatives were affiliated to the Central Union in 1989.

Uniunea centrală a cooperativelor mesteşugăresti—UCECOM (Central Union of Handicrafts Co-operatives): Bucharest, Calea Plevnei 46; tel. (0) 151810; Chair. Ing. DUMITRU DANGA.

Uniunea cooperatiei agricole (Union of Farming Co-operatives): 70111 Bucharest, Bd. Nicolae Bălcescu 17–19, Sector 1; tel. (0) 131869; f. 1989; represents 4,000 farming co-operatives and 41 district unions; Pres. AUREL STIRBU.

TRADE UNIONS

The regulations governing trade unions were liberalized in early 1990. The Uniunea Generală a Sindicatelor din România (UGSR) was dissolved. By early 1991 seven new trade union organizations had been established.

Confederaţia Naţională a Sindicatelor Libere din România—CNSLR (National Free Trade Union Confederation of Romania): 70109 Bucharest, Str. Ministerului 1–3; tel. (0) 136579; telex 10844; fax (0) 133883; f. 1990; 3.5m. mems (1991); 16 professional or branch federations, in all sectors of the economy, and 39 territorial leagues; Pres. VICTOR CIORBEA.

Frăţia (Brotherhood): Bucharest; f. Dec. 1989; includes 49 trade unions and federations; 1m. mems; Leader MIRON MITREA.

Other organizations include Infratirea, Alfa, the Justice and Brotherhood Union and the Convention of Non-Affiliated Trade Unions of Romania.

TRADE FAIRS

The Fairs and Exhibitions Co: 71331 Bucharest, POB 32; tel. (0) 183160; telex 11108; f. 1970; Man. Dir MIRCEA PERJU.

Transport

RAILWAYS

At the end of 1989 there were 11,343 km of track, of which 3,654 km were electrified lines.

The first phase of the Bucharest underground railway network opened in 1979, and the 27-km East–West line was completed in 1983. The first section of the North–South line was opened in January 1986 and the second section in October 1987. The third section opened in August 1989, bringing the total network to 60 km.

Căile Ferate Române-CFR (Departamentul Căilor Ferate) (Romanian Railways Board—Department of Railways): Bucharest 1, Bd. Dinicu Golescu 38; tel. (0) 172160; Gen. Dir OVIDIU RADU.

ROADS

In December 1989 there were 72,816 km of roads, of which 113 km were motorways, 14,570 km were main roads and 26,967 km were secondary roads. Under the 1991–95 road development programme, more than 3,000 km of motorways were to be built and existing roads were to be modernized.

Direcţia Drumurilor (Directorate of Roads): Ministerul Transporturilor, Bucharest 1, Bd. Dinicu Golescu 38; tel. (0) 173914; telex 10835; Man. Dr Ing. MIHAI BOICU.

INLAND AND OCEAN SHIPPING

Navigation on the River Danube is open to shipping of all nations. The Danube–Black Sea Canal was officially opened to traffic in May 1984, and has an annual handling capacity of 80m. metric tons. Work on the 85-km Danube–Bucharest Canal was abandoned in early 1990. A new port was planned at Bucharest. The first joint Romanian-Yugoslav Iron Gates (Porţile de Fier) power and navigation system on the Danube was completed in 1972, and Iron Gates-2 opened to navigation in December 1984. Romania's principal seaports are Constanţa (on the Black Sea), Tulcea, Galaţi, Brăila and Giurgiu (on the Danube). In 1985 Romania's merchant fleet had 252 ships, with a total capacity of 4.2m. dwt.

NAVROM (Romanian Shipping Co): 8700 Constanţa; telex 14327; organizes sea transport; lines: Mediterranean, North West Europe and West Africa, Persian Gulf, Far East.

CIVIL AVIATION

There are four international airports in Romania: Bucharest-Otopeni, M. Kogălniceanu-Constanţa, Timişoara and Arad.

Transporturile Aeriene Române—TAROM (Romanian Air Transport): Bucharest, Otopeni Airport; tel. (0) 333137; telex 11491; f. 1954; services throughout Europe, the Middle East, Africa, Asia and the USA and extensive internal flights; Dir-Gen. LORIN DUMITRESCU; fleet of 32 An-24, 12 An-26, 11 Tu-154, 11 Il-18 V/D, 3 Il-62, 2 Il-62M, 6 BAe 1-11 500, 2 BAe 1-11 400, 4 Rombac 1-11 500, 4 Boeing 707-320C; 2 Airbus 310-300 to be delivered in 1992.

Liniile Aeriene Române—LAR: Bucharest, Baneasa Airport; tel. (0) 793830; telex 11379; f. 1975 by TAROM to operate passenger charter services; re-established 1990; Man. Dir C. RADUT; fleet of 3 BAe 1-11 400.

Tourism

The Carpathian mountains, the Danube delta and the Black Sea resorts (Mamaia, Eforie, Mangalia and others) are the principal attractions. The Danube delta development programme, instigated in 1983, is to affect only half the total area of the delta, the remainder being designated a nature reserve. In 1988 there were 5.5m. tourist arrivals; receipts totalled US $176m.

Ministry of Trade and Tourism: Bucharest 5, Str. Apolodor 17; tel. (0) 310289; telex 11278; fax (0) 314907.

National Tourist Office, Carpaţi: Bucharest 1, Bd. Magheru 7; telex 11270; Gen. Man. ORESTE UNGUREANU.

National Tourist Office, Litoral: Mamaia Constanţa, Bucureşti Hotel; Gen. Man. PETRE ARITON.

Postavaural—Tourism Trade Co: 2200 Braşov, Str. Mureşenilor 12; tel. (21) 42840; telex 61228; fax (21) 44286; f. 1990; fmrly National Tourist Office; Gen. Man. LUCIAN CAPRARIN.

Atomic Energy

Construction of Romania's first nuclear power station at Cernavoda, in south-eastern Romania, began in 1981. Built with Canadian assistance, the station was to comprise five generating units, each of 625 MW. Under the 1986–90 Five-Year Plan, a similar station was to be built in Transylvania, and a third station with three 1,000-MW units was to be constructed in Moldavia. In January 1986 it was announced that the site of a nuclear power plant to be built with Soviet help had been selected. The construction programme has been delayed, however, and the first unit of the Cernavoda station was not expected to commence generating until 1994. Romania is a member of the Joint Institute for Nuclear Research, Dubna (Ukraine), and of the International Atomic Energy Agency, Vienna (Austria).

National Commission for the Control of Nuclear Activities: Bucharest, Bd Libertăţii 12, Sector 5; f. 1990; dept of the Ministry of the Environment; Chair. Dr PETRU POPA.

Culture

NATIONAL ORGANIZATIONS

Ministry of Culture: see section on The Government (Ministries).

Romanian Cultural Foundation (Fundaţia Culturală Română): Bucharest, Al. Alexandru 38; f. 1990; aims to promote Romanian culture world-wide; Pres. AUGUSTIN BUZURA; Sec. TUDOR PACURARU.

Romanian National Commission for UNESCO (Comisia Naţională a României pentru UNESCU): Bucharest, Str. Cehov 8, Sector 1; tel. (0) 174249; f. 1956; Pres. Prof. MIHAI GOLU; Sec. GEORGE VAIDEANU.

CULTURAL HERITAGE

Historical Museum of Bucharest (Muzeul de Istorie şi Artă al Municipiuli Bucureşti): Bucharest, Bd. 1848 2; tel. (0) 132154; f. 1984; 10 affiliated museums; Dir Dr VASILE BORONEANŢ.

Library of the Romanian Academy (Biblioteca Academiei Române): 71102 Bucharest, Calea Victoriei 125; f. 1867; 9.3m. items; Dir Prof. VICTOR SAHINI.

Museum of Romanian Literature (Muzeul Literaturii Române): Bucharest, Str. Fundaţiei 4; tel. (0) 503395; f. 1957; Dir DAN PETRESCU.

National Art Museum (Muzeul Naţional de Artă): Bucharest, Calea Victoriei 49–53; tel. (0) 133030; f. 1950; 4 affiliated galleries; Dir THEODOR ENESCU.

National History Museum of Romania (Muzeul Naţional de Istorie a României): Bucharest, Calea Victoriei 12; tel. (0) 157055; f. 1968; Dir LUCIA MARINESCU.

National Library (Biblioteca Naţională): Bucharest, Str. Ion Ghica 4; f. 1955; 8.3m. items; Dir GHEORGHE-IOSIF BERCAN.

State Archives (Arhivele Statului): Bucharest, Bd. M. Kogălniceanu 29; tel. (0) 152446; f. 1831; Gen. Dir VASILE MOISE.

Village Museum (Muzeul Satului): 71321 Bucharest; tel. (0) 171732; f. 1936; ethnographic open-air museum, folk art, rural architecture, agricultural machinery, etc.; Dir Dr IOAN GODEA.

SPORTING ORGANIZATION

Olympic Committee of Romania: Bucharest, Str. Vasile Conta 16, Sector 1; tel. (0) 119787; telex 11180; fax (0) 120450; f. 1914; Pres. LIA MANOLIU; Sec.-Gen. ALEXANDRU MOGOS.

PERFORMING ARTS

Theatre

Caragiale National Theatre: Bucharest, Bd. Nicolae Bălcescu 2.

Comedy Theatre: Bucharest, Str. Mandinești.

Romanian Athenaeum: Bucharest, Str. Franklin 1.

Tandarica Puppet Theatre: Bucharest, Calea Victoriei 50.

Opera Houses

Opera House: Bucharest, Bd. Gheorghiu-Dej 70.

Operetta House: Bucharest, Piața Natiunile Unite 1.

ASSOCIATIONS

Architects' Union of Romania (Uniunea Arhitecților din România): 79182 Bucharest, Str. Academiei 18–20; tel. (0) 158472; f. 1952; Prs. Prof. DAMIAN ASCANIO.

Bessarabia and Bucovina Cultural Association (Asociația culturală 'Pro Basarabia și Bucovina'): 70238 Bucharest, Str. Alexandru Donici 32; tel. (0) 193126; f. 1983; Pres. NICOLAE LUPAN; Gen. Sec. VALERIU GRAUR.

Cinema Workers' Union of Romania (Uniunea Cineaștilor din România): 70169 Bucharest, Str. Mendeleev 28–30; tel. (0) 505741; f. 1963, reorganized 1990; Pres. HIHNEA GHEORGHIU; Dir CONSTANTIN PIVNICIERU.

Composers' and Musicologists' Union of Romania (Uniunea Compozitorilor și Musicologilor din România): 70140 Bucharest, Str. Constantin Exarhu 12; tel. (0) 138159; f. 1920, reorganized 1949; Pres. PASCAL BENTOU.

Ethnology Society of Romania (Societatea de Etnologie din România): 70714 Bucharest, Str. Zalomit; tel. (0) 535846; f. 1990; Pres. Dr ROMULUS VULCĂNESCU; Sec. ION MOANȚA.

European Centre of Culture (Centrul European de Cultură): 71268 Bucharest, Șos. Kiseleff 47; tel. (0) 185462; Pres. RĂZVAN THEODORESCU.

PEN Club: Bucharest, Casa Scriitorilor Mihail Sadoveanu, Calea Victoriei 115.

Photographers' Association of Romania (Asociația Fotografilor din România): 70711 Bucharest, Str. Brezoianu 23; tel. (0) 149558; f. 1952; Co-ordinator NICOLAE HANU.

Romanian Union of Fine Arts (Uniunea Artiștilor Plastici din România): 71118 Bucharest, Str. Nicolae Iorga 21; tel. (0) 507380; f. 1950; Pres. MIHAI MĂNESCU.

Romanian Writers' Union: see section on Publishers (Writers' Union).

Education

Education is free and compulsory between the ages of six and 16 years. Before reaching the age of six years, children may attend crèches (creșe) and kindergartens (grădinițe de copii); in 1985 77.6% of pre-school age children were attending kindergarten. Between the ages of six and 16 years children attend the general education school (școală de cultură generală de zece ani).

There are five types of secondary school. The general secondary school (școala medie de cultură generală), for which there is an entrance examination, provides a specialized education suitable for preparation of students for admission to university or college. Vocational secondary schools (școli profesionale de ucenici), where training is given for careers in, for example, industry or agriculture, along with some general education. (Courses in these schools are also available to adults requiring retraining.) Secondary art schools (școală medie de artă) provide a general secondary education, but with an emphasis on music, art and the theatre. Secondary physical education schools (școala medie de educație fizică) also provide a general secondary education, but with an emphasis on physical fitness and training. Finally, teacher training secondary schools (școala pedagogică de învățători and școală pedagogică de educatoare) provide courses to prepare students for work as kindergarten and general education teachers.

Tuition in minority languages, particularly Hungarian and German, is available. There are 44 higher educational institutes in Romania, with 101 faculties, including seven universities and four technological universities. In 1989 spending of 16,080m. lei, or 5.0% of the state budget, was allocated to education. Following the revolution of 1989, education was to be reorganized, including the elimination of ideological training.

UNIVERSITIES

Bucharest University (Universitatea București): Bucharest, Bd. M. Kogălniceanu 64; tel. (0) 157187; f. 1864; 6 faculties; 857 teachers; 5,801 students; Rector Dr I. IOVIT POPESCU.

Cluj-Napoca University (Universitatea Cluj-Napoca): 3400 Cluj-Napoca, Str. M. Kogălniceanu 1; tel. (51) 16101; fax (51) 11905; f. 1919; 8 faculties; 600 teachers; 6,000 students; Rector Prof. Dr IONEL HAIDUC.

Iași University 'Al. I. Cuza' (Universitatea 'Al. I. Cuza' Iași): Iași, Calea 23 August 11; tel. (81) 47540; f. 1860; 9 faculties; 430 teachers; 4,526 students; Rector Prof. Dr CĂLIN IGNAT.

University of Brașov (Universitatea din Brașov): 2200 Brasov, Bd. Gh. Gheorghiu-Dej 29; tel. (21) 41580; f. 1971; 4 faculties; 400 teachers; 8,000 students; Rector Prof. Dr Eng. FILOFTEIA NEGRUȚIU.

University of Craiova (Universitatea din Craiova): 1100 Craiova, Str. 'Al. I. Cuza' 13; tel. (41) 16574; f. 1966; 7 faculties; 612 teachers; 10,000 students; Rector Prof. Dr TIBERIU NICOLA.

University of Galați (Universitatea din Galați): 6200 Galați, Bd. Republicii 47; tel. (34) 14112; f. 1974 as university; 6 faculties; 412 teachers; 7,000 students; Rector Prof. MIHAI JĂSCANU.

University of Timișoara (Universitatea din Timișoara): 1900 Timisoara, V. Pârvan 4; tel. (61) 12805; f. 1962; 6 faculties; 305 teachers; 5,800 students; Rector E. TODORAN.

Technological Universities

Bucharest Polytechnic Institute (Institutul Politehnic București): 77206 Bucharest, Splaiul Independenței 313; tel. (0) 314010; telex 10252; f. 1819; 11 faculties; 1,540 teachers; 26,000 students; Rector Prof. Dr VIRGIL N. CONSTANTINESCU.

Cluj-Napoca Polytechnic Institute (Institutul Politehnic Cluj-Napoca): Cluj-Napoca, Str. Emil Isac 15; tel. (51) 34565; f. 1948; 3 faculties; 420 teachers; 8,150 students; Rector Dr Eng. HORIA COLAN.

'Gheorghe Asachi' Polytechnic Institute (Institutul Politehnic 'Gheorghe Asachi'): Iași, Calea 23 August 22; tel. (81) 46577; telex 22368; f. 1912; 10 faculties; 951 teachers; 16,600 students; Rector Prof Dr Ing. VITALIE BELOUSOV.

'Traian Vuia' Polytechnic Institute Timișoara (Institutul Politehnic 'Traian Vuia' Timișoara): Timisoara, Piața Operei 2; tel. (61) 34717; f. 1920; 8 faculties; 740 teachers; 13,423 students; Rector Prof Dr Ing. RADU VLADEA.

Social Welfare

Romania has a comprehensive state insurance scheme, premiums being paid by enterprises and institutions on behalf of their employees. A new law on unemployment allowance was adopted in January 1991. In addition, funds are allotted to sickness benefits, children's allowances, pensions and the provision of health resorts. There were 215,000 hospital beds in service, and 41,600 doctors and 7,200 dentists in practice, in 1988. Spending of 16,200m. lei (5.0% of the state budget) was allocated to health in 1989, and a further 75,400m. lei (23.5%) to social security and welfare.

Following the revolution of December 1989, international attention was focused on the orphanages in Romania housing large numbers of unwanted and neglected children (contraception and abortion having been illegal during the Ceaușescu years), many of whom were found to be suffering from AIDS, hepatitis and other serious illnesses, due to poor medical treatment. Owing to persistent shortages of foodstuffs and high levels of pollution, many Romanians were believed to be suffering from malnutrition and other serious conditions. Numerous cases of cholera were reported in 1990 and 1991.

NATIONAL AGENCIES

Ministry of Health: see section on The Government (Ministries).

Ministry of Labour and Social Protection: see section on The Government (Ministries).

Department of Labour: Bucharest, Str. Onești 2, Sector 1; Secretary of State OCTAVIAN PARTENIE.

Department of Social Protection: Bucharest, Str. Onești 2, Sector 1; Secretary of State MIHU BIJI.

HEALTH AND WELFARE ORGANIZATIONS

Institute of Hygiene and Public Health (Institutul de Igienă și Sănătate Publică): 79636 Bucharest, Str. Dr Leonte 1–3; telex 11468; f. 1927; Dir Dr MANOLE CUCU.

Institute of Research for the Quality of Life (Institutul de Cercetare a Calității Vieții): Splaiul Independenței 202A, Sector 6; Dir CĂTĂLIN ZAMFIR.

Research Institute for Labour Safety (Institutul de Cercetări pentru Protecţia Muncii): 70744 Bucharest, Str. Gral. Budişteanu 15, Sector 1; tel. (0) 131720; f. 1951; Dir Dr Ing. ALEXANDRU DARABONT.

Union of Societies of Medical Sciences of Romania (Uniunea Societăţilor de Ştiinţe Medicale din România): 70754 Bucharest, Str. Progresului 10; tel. (0) 141817; f. 1877; Pres. Prof. Dr ZOREL FILIPESCU; Sec.-Gen. Prof. Dr EMANOIL POPESCU.

The Environment

Environmental problems caused some concern under the Communist regime, but the most controversial issue was the threatened destruction of traditional villages (see History). The extent of heavy pollution and environmental damage in Romania became apparent after the revolution of December 1989. The many examples included the town of Copsa Mica, where lead and cadmium pollution was 10 times the internationally accepted level, and surfaces and inhabitants were covered in black soot. Estimates have claimed as many as 112 local environmental groups in existence, with some 100,000 members, in Romania. The Romanian Government is a member of the Danube Commission (based in Hungary), the Joint Danube Fishery Commission (Czechoslovakia), the IUCN (Gland, Switzerland) and participated in the activities of the environmental co-ordinating centres of the CMEA (based in the USSR) Co-ordinating Centres on environmental matters. Romania's Danube Delta Project is considered to be the most important bird preservation scheme in Europe. In August 1991 Romania and Bulgaria agreed to fuller co-operation on environmental matters, in accordance with EC conditions for rendering aid to the two countries.

GOVERNMENT ORGANIZATIONS

Ministry of the Environment: see section on The Government (Ministries).

National Council for Environmental Protection: Bucharest, Piaţa Victoriei 1; tel. (0) 143400; incl. Commissions for Air Protection and Noise Abatement, Water Protection, Soil and Subsoil Protection, the Protection of Flora, Fauna and the Monuments of Nature and the Protection of Human Settlements.

ACADEMIC INSTITUTES

Academy of Agricultural and Forest Sciences (Academia de Ştiinţe Agricole şi Silvice): Bucharest, Bd. Mărăşti 61; tel. (0) 180699; telex 11394; f. 1969; Pres. TIBERIU MUREŞAN; particularly involved in environmental matters through the activities of:

Central Research Station for Soil Erosion Control (Staţiunea Centrală de Cercetări pentru Combatarea Eroziunii Solului): Perieni; Dir Eng. GH. STOIAN.

Danube Delta Institute (Institutul Delta Dunării) 8800 Tulcea, Str. Babadag 165; tel. (15) 24242; fax (15) 24547; f. 1970; conser-

vation of the diverse ecology of the Danube delta, monitoring of the wetlands, fish ecology, tourism research; Dir Eng. GRIGORE BABOIANU.

Forest Research and Design Institute (Institutul de Cercetări şi Amenajări Silvice—ICAS): Bucharest, Şos. Stefăneşti 128, Sector 2; f. 1933; Dir Eng. M. IANCULESCU.

Romanian Marine Research Institute (Institutul Român de Cercetări Marine): 8700 Constanţa 3, Bd. Mamaia 300; f. 1970; studies Black Sea hydrology, ecosystems and pollution; biochemistry, extraction and utilization of aquatic living resources; aquaculture; fishery resources; marine technology; Dir Dr Eng. S. NICOLAEV.

Energy Information and Documentation Office (Oficiul de Informare Documentară pentru Energetică): 79619 Bucharest, Bd. Energeticienilor 8, Sector 3; tel. (0) 206730; telex 10783; f. 1966; Dir V. PLEŞCA.

National Institute of Metrology (Institutul Naţional de Metrologie): Bucharest, Şos. Vitan-Bîrzeşti 11, Sector 4; tel. (0) 343520; telex 11871; f. 1951; Dir I. ISCRULESCU.

Romanian Academy (Academia Romana): Bucharest, Calea Victoriei 125; tel. (0) 507680; telex 11907; f. 1866 as Societatea Literară Română, present name 1948; concerned with protection of both natural and human environments; Pres. MIHAI DRĂGĂNESCU.

NON-GOVERNMENTAL ORGANIZATIONS

The **Romanian Ecological Movement** (Mişcarea Ecologistă din România) and the **Romanian Ecological Party** (Partidul Ecologist Român) (see section on Political Organizations) are members of the National Convention on Establishing Democracy. There are several other small Green parties.

Defence

Prior to its dissolution in 1991, Romania was a member of the Warsaw Pact, although it allowed no Pact troops on to its soil and did not participate in military exercises. Military service is compulsory and lasts for 12 months in the army and air force, and for 24 months in the navy. In June 1990, according to Western estimates, regular forces totalled 163,000 (including 107,500 conscripts); of these, 126,000 were in the army, 28,000 in the air force and 9,000 in the navy. In addition, there were 75,000 paramilitary forces, comprising 15,000 border guards and 30,000 security troops (both under Ministry of National Defence control), and the Patriotic Guard of 30,000. Spending of 21,062m. lei was allocated to defence in the 1990 state budget.

Commander-in-Chief of the Armed Forces: President of Romania.

Chief of Staff of the Army: Maj.-Gen. DUMITRU IOAN CIOFLINA.

Bibliography

Behr, Edward. *Kiss the Hand You Cannot Bite: the rise and fall of the Ceauşescus.* London, Hamish Hamilton, 1991.

Fischer, Mary Ellen. *Nicolae Ceauşescu: a study in political leadership.* Boulder, CO, Lynne Rienner Publishers, Inc, 1989.

Fischer-Galati, S. *The New Rumania.* Cambridge, MA, MIT Press, 1967.

Fischer-Galati, S., Florescu, R. R. and Ursu, G. R. (Eds). *Romania between East and West: historical essays in memory of Constantin C. Giurescu.* Boulder, CO, East European Monographs, 1982.

Georgescu, Vlad. *The History of the Romanians.* London, I. B. Tauris, 1991.

Graham, Lawrence S. *Romania: a developing socialist state.* Boulder, CO, Westview Press, 1982.

Jackson, M. *Romania's Debt Crisis: its causes and consequences,* Vol. 3 of East European Economies: Slow Growth in the 1980s. Washington, DC, USGPO (Joint Economic Committee of the US Congress), 1986.

Montias, J. M. *Economic Development in Communist Romania.* Cambridge, MA, MIT Press, 1967.

Otetea, Andrei (Ed.). *A Concise History of Romania.* London, Hale, 1985.

Roman, P. 'Report on the Stage of Implementation of Economic Reform and the Demand to Step up its Pace'. Copy of speech of 18 October 1990.

Ronnas, P. *Urbanization in Romania.* Stockholm, Economic Research Institute, Stockholm School of Economics, 1984.

'The Economic Legacy of Ceauşescu' in *Economic Change in the Balkan States,* Orjan Sjoberg and Michael L. Wyzan (Eds). London, Pinter, 1991.

Shafir, Michael. *Romania: Politics, Economics and Society.* London, Frances Pinter, 1985.

Smith, A. H. 'Is There a Romanian Crisis? The Problems of Energy and Indebtedness' in *Crisis in the East European Economy,* J. Drewnowski (Ed.). Beckenham, Croom Helm, 1982.

The Planned Economies of Eastern Europe. Beckenham, Croom Helm, 1983.

'Romania: international economic developments and foreign economic relations' in *The Economies of Eastern Europe and their Foreign Economic Relations,* P. Joseph (Ed.). Brussels, NATO, 1987.

'The Romanian Economy: policy and prospects for the 1990s' in *The Central and East European Economies in the 1990s: prospects and constraints,* R. Weichardt (Ed.). Brussels, NATO, 1991.

Sweeney, John. *The Life and Evil Times of Nicolae Ceauşescu.* London, Hutchinson, 1991.

YUGOSLAVIA

Geography

PHYSICAL FEATURES

The Socialist Federal Republic of Yugoslavia was established in south-eastern Europe, much of it on the Balkan Peninsula, with a western coastline along the Adriatic Sea (part of the Mediterranean), as a federation of six Republics: Slovenia (the most northerly) and Croatia in the north-west; Bosnia-Herzegovina in the centre, with Montenegro to its south on the Adriatic coast; and, inland, occupying the east of the country, lie Serbia and Macedonia.

In the far north-west Yugoslavia has a short land border with Italy, which also faces the country to the south-west, across the Adriatic. The northern border is with Austria and, further east, Hungary. To the east lie Romania and Bulgaria; the Macedonian Republic, the southernmost territory of Yugoslavia, not only has Bulgaria to the east, but Greece to the south and Albania to its west. Albania juts into Yugoslavia from the south, along the Adriatic.

The north-west of the country is occupied by the Julian Alps (Julijske Alpe) and the more easterly Karawanken Alps (Karavanke). Yugoslavia's highest peak, Triglav (2,863 m—9,394 ft), is in the Julian Alps. From the Julian Alps, the Dinaric Alps (Dinara Planina) run south-east, parallel to the Dalmatian coast, which is fringed with many islands. The entire south of the country is mountainous. There are fertile plains in the north and north-east of the country, drained by the Danube, Tisa (Tisza), Sava (the longest river totally in Yugoslavia) and Drava rivers. The highlands of the south are cleft by deep river valleys, notably those of the Morava (a tributary of the Danube) and the Vardar (Axiós), which flows south to the Aegean Sea. Much of the country is forested (37% of the total area, in 1989, according to the FAO) and there are several large lakes on the southern border, including Scutari (Skadarsko), Prespa (where the Yugoslav, Albanian and Greek borders all meet) and Ohrid.

CLIMATE

The climate is Mediterranean on the coast and continental inland. The highlands have a colder climate with heavy snow in winter, but in summer it can be very hot, particularly in Macedonia. The average summer temperature in Belgrade, in July, is 22°C (71°F) and in winter, in January, the average temperature is 0°C (32°F). Rainfall is fairly constant throughout the year, although summer is the wettest season in the north. The north-western plains are prone to drought. The average annual rainfall is 635 mm (25 in) in Belgrade, 890 mm (35 in) in Zagreb, which is nearer the northern mountains, and 510 mm (20 in) in Skopje, which is in the far south.

POPULATION

Yugoslavia, as its name denotes, is dominated by Southern Slavic peoples, predominantly the Serbo-Croats. The Serbs (36% of the total population, according to the census of 1981) and Croats (20%) are closely related, divided mainly by religion and the consequent divergence in cultural development. Likewise, the Slavs who adopted Islam (mainly in Bosnia-Herzegovina) are regarded as a separate ethnic group. The Slav Muslims accounted for some 9% of the total Yugoslav population in 1981. The Montenegrins (3%) are a Serb people. The Slovenes (8%) and Macedonians (6%) are also Southern Slavs, and there are small communities of Slovaks, Czechs, Bulgarians and Ruthenians. The main non-Slavic ethnic groups are the Albanians (8% in 1981) and the Hungarians (Magyars—2%), but there are small communities of Romanians, Turks, Roma (Gypsies) and Italians as well. The principal language, and the lingua franca of Yugoslavia, is Serbo-Croat. Although there is a single spoken language, it has two written forms: Croatian, which uses the Latin script; and Serbian (also used in Montenegro and Bosnia-Herzegovina), which uses the Cyrillic script. Some difference in dialect is also acknowledged by the Novi Sad Agreement of 1954, which settled the language question. Particularly in 1991, however, there has been an increasing tendency of the Croats and, to a lesser extent, the Bosnians to reject this agreement and to emphasize the distinctness of their language. Of the other two languages of the Southern Slavonic group, Slovene uses the Latin alphabet and Macedonian the Cyrillic. The other nationalities use their own languages, all being constitutionally equal, except in the Armed Forces, in which Serbo-Croat is compulsory.

The majority of Yugoslavs profess Christianity, but there is a substantial Muslim population, comprising 12% of the population in 1981. Some 41% of the population adhered to the Eastern Orthodox Church (which introduced the Cyrillic alphabet), as represented by the Serbian and Macedonian Orthodox Churches. The Roman Catholic Church (which also sanctions the use of a 'Byzantine' rite for Uniates) has 32% of the population, mainly in the north and west. There are some Protestant churches, but they account for less than 1% of the population, as does the Jewish community.

According to the census of March 1991, the total population of Yugoslavia was 23,462,976. This was an increase of 4.6% on the population of the 1981 census, the largest increase being in Kosovo. In 1991, therefore, the population density was 91.7 per sq km. The capital and largest city is Belgrade (Beograd), in Serbia, which had a population of 1,553,854, according to the 1991 census. Other large towns include the Croatian towns of Split, Osijek, Zagreb and Rijeka, and the Macedonian capital, Skopje or Skoplje.

Chronology

168 BC: Illyria (which included modern-day Yugoslavia) was annexed by the Roman Empire and Macedonia was finally defeated.

395 AD: Following a division of the administration of the Roman Empire, Illyria was ruled by the Eastern Roman ('Byzantine') Emperor in Constantinople (Istanbul).

5th century: Southern Slav peoples began to move from Pannonia into Illyria and the Balkans.

7th–8th centuries: Western Christian missionaries, from Aquileia (Trieste) and Salzburg, were active among the Croats and the Slovenes, respectively, introducing the Latin script and a Western cultural orientation.

812: By the Treaty of Aix-la-Chapelle (Aachen), the Byzantine Emperor, Michael I, acknowledged the Frankish (German) ruler, Charles ('the Great'—Charlemagne), as Emperor in the West; Byzantine suzerainty over Istria and Dalmatia was confirmed and German influence over the Slovene-inhabited areas of Carinthia and Carniola was established.

863: The missionary activity of the Byzantine brothers, SS Constantine (Cyril) and Methodius, led to the conversion of the Serbs (including the ancestors of the Bosnians and Montenegrins) and the Bulgars (and Macedonians) to Eastern Orthodox Christianity; a Slavonic liturgy (based on a Macedonian dialect) was introduced with a written language, in the Cyrillic script, which remains common to all the East and Balkan Slavic peoples.

1014: Final defeat of the western Bulgarian, or Macedonian, realm under Samuel by the Byzantine Emperor, Basil II.

1076: Coronation, by the Pope, of Dimitar Zvonimir, who had rejected Byzantine overlordship of the Croatian kingdom established in the 10th century.

1082: Venice was granted trading privileges in the Eastern Empire, securing their independence and their growing influence along the formerly Byzantine Dalmatian coast.

1102: Croatia's personal union with Hungary effectively, if not finally, linked it to the Hungarian Crown, together with parts of Dalmatia.

1151: Accession of Stjepan (Stephen) I Nemanja as Grand Zhupan; he united the Serb tribes and established the Serbian Empire.

1187: The Emperor in Constantinople acknowledged Hungarian conquests in Croatia and Bosnia, Serbian independence and the establishment of the second Bulgarian Empire (which was to include much of Macedonia and the surrounding territories).

1219: St Sava, brother of the Serbian king, Stjepan II, was consecrated the first autocephalous archbishop of the Serbian Orthodox Church, at Nicasa.

1330: The Serbs defeated the Bulgarians and the Greek Byzantines at the Battle of Velbuzhde (Küstendil).

1335: Carniola and Carinthia became hereditary possessions of the Austrian House of Habsburg, within the Holy Roman Empire.

1346: Establishment of a Serbian patriarchate and the coronation of Uroš IV (Stjepan Dušan of Raška, who reigned 1331–55) as Tsar of the Serbs and Greeks, at Skopje; however, he failed in his ambition to conquer Constantinople (Zarigrad).

1377: Stjepan Trvtko (1353–91) proclaimed himself King of the Bosnians and Serbs, ruling a Bosnia which was now dominated by the dualist Christian heresy of the Bogomils.

1389: The Turkish Ottoman Empire, which had already conquered Macedonia, destroyed the Serbian nobility at a battle on the plain of Kosovo Polje, 'the Field of Blackbirds'.

1459–83: The Ottomans finally incorporated the rest of Serbia into the Empire and completed the subjugation of Bosnia and Herzegovina; the Montenegrins (Serbs of the principality of Zeta) maintained a semi-independence.

1490: Death of the Hungarian King, Matthias I Corvinus, who had secured modern Croatia and the Vojvodina (Slavonia and the Banat) for Hungary and, temporarily, conquered the Habsburg lands.

1526: Louis II and the Hungarian forces were destroyed by the Ottomans at the Battle of Mohács; the Hungarian Crown was claimed as a hereditary possession of the House of Habsburg, but the kingdom itself was subsequently partitioned between the Habsburgs (Croatia) and the Ottomans (Slavonia).

1599: The Counter-Reformation secured the Slovenes for Roman Catholicism by the final extinction of the Protestant (Calvinist) Church of Carniola, the writings of which, however, provided the basis of Slovene literature.

1690: Serbs ('the 30,000 Families', led by Patriarch Arsenije III Crnojević), retreating with Habsburg armies, first settled in the Vojvodina.

1718: The Peace of Passarowitz confirmed the Habsburg liberation of Hungary, including Croatia and Slavonia; the Ottomans ceded the Banat and northern Serbia (but the latter was held only until 1739).

1796: Montenegro, never completely subdued by the Ottomans, was acknowledged as an independent principality.

1804–12: A revolt of the Serbian peasantry against the local Turkish garrison became a popular revolt for autonomy, led by Kara Djordje ('Black George') Petrović.

1815: The Congress of Vienna confirmed Austrian rule over Istria and Dalmatia, which were formerly Venetian.

1817: Serbia became an autonomous principality, after a second uprising under Miloš Obrenović, whose house was, from then on, in constant rivalry with the Karadjordjević dynasty.

1848: At a time of revolution in Habsburg and other territories, the Croatian assembly, in Agram (Zagreb), was forced to end consideration of a Southern Slav state.

1868: Croatia, united with Slavonia, was granted autonomy by Hungary, which, since the *Ausgleich* or Compromise of the previous year, was now a partner in the Habsburg 'Dual Monarchy'.

March 1878: The Treaty of San Stefano concluded the war between Russia, in support of the Orthodox Slavs, and the Ottomans, but the Great Powers rejected the settlement.

July 1878: At the Congress of Berlin, Bulgaria was denied the annexation of Macedonia, Montenegro's independence was confirmed, Serbia's tributary status was ended and it was awarded territory around Niš, and Austria-Hungary secured administration rights in Bosnia and Herzegovina and ensured that the Ottomans remained in the Sandzak of Novi Pazar (the Sandjak) and Kosovo, as a restraint on Serbian expansion.

1881: Final abolition of the 'Military Frontier' or Krajina, in which, since the 17th century, the Habsburgs had allowed some autonomy to Serb settlers defending the borders against the Ottomans.

1882: Serbia was proclaimed a kingdom under Milan Obrenović, whose regime was conservative and pro-Habsburg.

1903: Assassination of King Aleksandar I of Serbia; accession of Petar I Karadjordjević, leader of the Radical party, who was anti-Habsburg and saw the rise of the Southern Slav movement ('Yugoslavism'—its champion in Croatia-Slavonia was Bishop Strossmayer).

1908: The 'Young Turk' uprising in the Ottoman Empire led to disturbances in the Balkans; Austria-Hungary annexed Bosnia-Herzegovina, despite international objections, but its ally, Germany, prevented war against Serbia.

1910: Nikita I of Montenegro proclaimed himself king. The secret, Greater Serb society, Union or Death (the 'Black Hand'), was founded by Col Dimitrijević-Apis.

May 1913: The Peace of London concluded the First Balkan War, in which a league of Bulgaria, Greece, Montenegro and Serbia succeeded in removing the Turks from the bulk of their European possessions.

June 1913: Bulgaria attacked Serbia, which was supported by Greece, Montenegro, Romania and the Turks.

August 1913: The Peace of Bucharest concluded the Second Balkan War; Bulgaria lost Macedonia, which was divided between Serbia and Greece; the Sandjak was divided between Serbia and Montenegro; but Austria-Hungary and Italy succeeded in preventing Serbia gaining access to the Adriatic, notably by the recognition of Albanian independence.

28 June 1914: The heir to the Habsburg throne, Archduke Francis Ferdinand, and his wife were assassinated in Sarajevo, by a Bosnian student acting for the Serb Black Hand group.

28 July 1914: Austria-Hungary declared war on Serbia, which started the First World War between the Central Powers, of Austria-Hungary and Germany, and the Entente Powers, of France, Russia, Serbia and the United Kingdom.

1915: Serbia, including Macedonia, was conquered by the Central Powers and Bulgaria.

1916: Habsburg troops invaded Montenegro.

July 1917: Serbia and the other Southern Slavs (excluding the Bulgarians) declared their intention to form a unitary state, under the Serbian monarchy.

29 October 1918: Following the defeat and dissolution of the Danubian Monarchy, the Southern Slav (Yugoslav) peoples separated from the Austro-Hungarian system of states (a Southern Slav republic was established on 15 October); Dalmatia, Croatia-Slavonia, Bosnia-Herzegovina, parts of Carinthia, Carniola and the Banat were, subsequently, ceded formally to the new state.

4 December 1918: Proclamation of the Kingdom of Serbs, Croats and Slovenes, which united Serbia and Montenegro with the former Habsburg lands.

August 1921: Prince Aleksandar, Regent of Serbia since 1914 and of the new Kingdom since its formation, became King, upon the ratification of the 'Vidovdan' Constitution.

August 1928: A separatist Croatian assembly convened in Zagreb.

3 October 1929: Following the imposition of a royal dictatorship, the country was formally named Yugoslavia.

1931: The dictatorship was suspended by the introduction of a new Constitution, although this did not prevent Croat unrest and the rise of the Fascist Ustaša ('Rebel') movement.

October 1934: King Aleksandar I of Yugoslavia was assassinated in France by Croatian extremists; his brother, Prince Paul, became Regent, on behalf of the young King Petar II.

1937: Josip Broz (Tito) became General-Secretary of the Communist Party of Yugoslavia (CPY), which was to become the main partner in the Partisan (National Liberation Army) resistance to the German invasion.

March 1941: A *coup d'état*, by air-force officers, ousted the Regent and installed King Petar II, who reversed previous policies and aligned himself with the Allied Powers of the Second World War.

April 1941: German and Italian forces invaded Yugoslavia: Germany annexed Lower Styria and parts of Carinthia; Italy annexed Ljubljana (Laibach) and Dalmatia, and the nominally independent Montenegro became its client; Albania (in personal union with the Italian Crown) annexed Kosovo; part of the Vojvodina (eastern Slavonia) was annexed by Hungary; Macedonia was occupied by Bulgaria; the remainder of Serbia was placed under German military administration; and, on 10 April, an Independent State of Croatia was established (including much of Bosnia-Herzegovina), with the Italian, Duke Aimone of Spoleto (Split), as King, and an Ustaša Government under Ante Pavelić.

29 November 1943: In the Bosnian town of Jejce, following fierce resistance and civil conflict with the royalist Četniks (Yugoslav Army of the Fatherland) of western Serbia and with the Ustaša regime, Gen. (later Marshal) Tito's Partisans proclaimed their own government for liberated areas (mainly in Bosnia, Croatia and Montenegro); Tito's leadership was subsequently acknowledged by the Allies and the royal Government-in-Exile.

1944: King Petar II was declared deposed.

29 November 1945: Following elections for a Provisional Assembly, the Federative People's Republic of Yugoslavia was proclaimed, with Tito as prime minister.

January 1946: A Soviet-style Constitution, establishing a federation of six republics and two autonomous regions, was adopted.

June 1948: Yugoslavia was expelled from the Soviet-dominated Cominform; the break with the USSR ended Yugoslav ambitions for a Balkan federation with Albania and Bulgaria.

November 1952: The Communist Party was renamed the League of Communists of Yugoslavia (LCY) and several liberal reforms were adopted.

January 1953: A new Constitution was adopted, with Tito becoming President of the Republic.

1954: Istria was partitioned between Italy, which gained the city of Trieste, and Yugoslavia. The so-called Novi Sad Agreement proclaimed Serbo-Croat to be one language with two scripts.

1955: Relations with the USSR were normalized.

April 1963: A new Constitution changed the country's name to the Socialist Federal Republic of Yugoslavia (SFRY).

1966: Monetary reform and economic liberalization were introduced; later in the year the reformists secured the fall of Vice-President Aleksandar Ranković, the head of the secret police and an advocate of strong central government.

July 1971: Following the granting of the rights of autonomy to the federal units, Tito introduced a system of collective leadership and the regular rotation of posts; a collective State Presidency for Yugoslavia was established, with Tito as its head.

November 1971: Tito criticized the reformist Croatian leadership, causing them to resign; the suppression of the Croatian 'mass movement', or *Maspok*, and a purge of liberals throughout Yugoslavia followed.

February 1974: A new Constitution was adopted.

May 1979: The principle of rotating leadership was extended to the secretaryship of the LCY.

4 May 1980: Tito died; his responsibilities were transferred to the collective State Presidency and to the Presidium of the LCY.

1981: Protests by students in Priština led to demonstrations by Albanian nationalists throughout Kosovo; a state of emergency was declared after rioting broke out in the Province.

March 1982: Further demonstrations took place in Kosovo.

December 1985: Demonstrations again took place in Kosovo.

March 1987: There was widespread strike action throughout Yugoslavia, following the implementation of a government policy refusing to grant any wage increases.

April 1987: Thousands of Serbs and Montenegrins, who had gathered at Kosovo Polje to protest at harassment by the Albanian population, clashed with police.

August 1987: The credibility of the Federal Government was undermined by a financial scandal involving Agrokomerc, a major agro-industrial enterprise.

October 1987: Emergency security measures were introduced in Kosovo.

June 1988: Widespread strike action was initiated by workers protesting against the decline in living standards.

July 1988: Protesting workers forced their way into the Federal Assembly building in Belgrade.

October 1988: The Presidium of the League of Communists of Vojvodina resigned, following protests in Novi Sad.

November 1988: Some 100,000 ethnic Albanians demonstrated in Priština, demanding the reinstatement of two Kosovo Party leaders who had been pressured into resigning. An estimated 1m. people demonstrated in Belgrade, against alleged discrimination by the Albanian population of Kosovo. Public demonstrations were banned in Kosovo.

December 1988: Branko Mikulić, the President of the Federal Executive Council (Yugoslav prime minister), and his Government were forced to resign following the Federal Assembly's rejection of the proposed state budget for 1989.

January 1989: In Montenegro, the State Presidency and the Presidium of the local League of Communists resigned as a result of public pressure.

February 1989: Azem Vlasi, a prominent Albanian from Kosovo, was dismissed from the LCY Central Committee, provoking protests in Kosovo, during which federal troops intervened.

March 1989: A new Federal Government, under Ante Marković, was appointed. Azem Vlasi and other Albanian leaders were arrested on suspicion of inciting unrest; a curfew was imposed in Kosovo.

May 1989: Slobodan Milošević was elected President of the Serbian State Presidency (re-elected, in direct elections, in November).

September 1989: The Slovenian Assembly reaffirmed the sovereignty of their Republic and declared its right to secede from the SFRY; thousands demonstrated in Serbia and Montenegro against the perceived threat to the unity of the SFRY.

October 1989: Renewed rioting took place in Kosovo following the opening of the trial of Azem Vlasi and other Albanian leaders.

November 1989: The first direct, secret ballot in Serbia since before the Second World War was held for local, parliamentary and presidential elections, although the Communists continued to dominate the electoral and candidate lists.

December 1989: Serbian enterprises were instructed to sever all links with Slovenia, which retaliated by closing its border with Serbia and implementing reciprocal economic sanctions.

18 December 1989: The federal prime minister, Ante Marković, introduced a series of IMF-backed economic austerity measures.

26 December 1989: Yugoslavia's first stock exchange was established in Ljubljana.

1990

January

2: The new, fully convertible dinar, worth 10,000 old dinars, was introduced.

20–23: At its 14th (Extraordinary) Congress, in Belgrade, the LCY voted to abolish its leading role in society, but rejected Slovenian proposals to restructure the federal Party; the Slovenian delegation withdrew from the Congress and the League of Communists of Slovenia suspended its links with the LCY; the Congress adjourned following its decision not to continue without the Slovenian delegation.

27: At least nine Albanians were killed by the police in Kosovo, following several days of rioting.

30: After the escalation of the unrest in Kosovo, there was direct confrontation between Albanians and Serbs in the village of Kosovska Vitina.

31: The federal State Presidency ordered 'special measures' to end the violence in Kosovo; demonstrators in Belgrade and Titograd demanded that the Yugoslav People's Army (YPA) be used to quell the disturbances.

February

1: Troops were deployed in Kosovo for the first time.

4: A conference of the League of Communists of Slovenia renounced its links with the LCY and decided to change its name to the Party of Democratic Reform. Slovenia withdrew its police contingent from Kosovo.

5: Milošević, the Serbian Presidency President, proclaimed a 'mobilization for Kosovo', requesting that Serbs move to settle in Kosovo.

20: The federal State Presidency approved any action by the YPA needed to maintain the status quo in Kosovo; a curfew was imposed in Priština.

March

8: The Slovenian Assembly dispensed with the word 'Socialist' from their Republic's title.

22: There was considerable anxiety among the ethnic Albanian population of Kosovo following a case of mass poisoning, involving 400 students.

24: Troops were sent to Kosovo, to stop the rioting and to arrest the leaders of the Albanian community.

30: The LCY failed to achieve a quorum for its plenary session, intended to reconvene the 14th Congress.

April

3: Yusuf Zehjnulahu, the Chairman of the Executive Council (Premier) of Kosovo, resigned his post in protest at the excessive force used against the ethnic Albanians in the Province.

8: The opposition DEMOS coalition won the direct elections to the Slovenian Assembly's main Socio-Political Chamber (gaining 47 of the 80 seats); there were also the first-round elections to the Chamber of Municipalities, to the Chamber of Associated Labour (on a non-party basis) and for the President of the republican State Presidency.

11: The Federal Assembly voted to extend its mandate, and that of the Government, until the end of 1990 (this was subsequently extended again).

17: Milošević announced that the Serbian internal affairs ministry had assumed the federal ministry's responsibility for security in Kosovo.

18: The federal State Presidency ended the special measures imposed in Kosovo.

22: In Slovenia, the second round of voting for the parliamentary and presidential elections was held: Milan Kučan, the leader of the former Communists, was elected as President of the republican Presidency; DEMOS emerged as the winner in the Chamber of Municipalities. In Croatia, the first-round elections to the three chambers of the Croatian Assembly (for a maximum of 356 seats) were held.

24: Azem Vlasi, the former Party leader of Kosovo, was released from custody.

May

6–7: A second round of voting took place in Croatia; in the final results, the nationalist opposition party, the Croatian Democratic Union (CDU), gained 205 of the eventual 351 seats in the Assembly.

15: Borisav Jović (Serbia) took over as President of the federal State Presidency.

16: Lojze Peterle, Chairman of the Slovene Christian Democratic Party (a member of DEMOS), was elected President of the Executive Council (Premier) of Slovenia.

23: The provincial Assembly in Kosovo refused to accept the resignation of the Premier, Zehjnulahu.

26: The final session of the 14th Congress of the LCY resumed, despite the absence of the Slovenian, Croatian and Macedonian delegations.

30: The Assembly of Croatia elected Franjo Tudjman, leader of the CDU, as President of the Republic; Stjepan (Stipe) Mesić was elected President of the Executive Council (Premier) of Croatia.

June

13: Anti-Communist demonstrators in Belgrade demanded the holding of early elections in Serbia.

26: The Kosovo Assembly was suspended and its responsibilities assumed by the Serbian Assembly.

30: The Federal Government introduced a second set of austerity measures.

July

2: The Slovenian Assembly proclaimed the full sovereignty of the Republic. In a referendum, a majority of Serbians approved the proposed new republican Constitution, which, among other matters, effectively removed the distinct status of the Autonomous Provinces of Kosovo and Vojvodina; 114 deputies of the 180-member Kosovo Assembly declared that Kosovo was, thenceforth, independent of Serbia and a constituent republic of the SFRY.

5: The Serbian Assembly voted to dissolve the Kosovo Assembly permanently.

17: The League of Communists of Serbia merged with the republican Socialist Alliance of the Working People (a Communist mass organization), to form the Socialist Party of Serbia (SPS); Slobodan Milošević was elected leader.

25: The Croatian Assembly approved constitutional changes, including: the removal of the word 'Socialist' from the Republic's title; the redesignation of the republican Executive Council as a 'Government'; the replacement of the republican Presidency with a President and six Vice-Presidents; and the downgrading of the use of the Cyrillic alphabet. The leaders of the Serb minority in Croatia, who had formed a 'Serb National Council', proclaimed the right to sovereignty and autonomy for all Croatian Serbs.

29: Ante Marković formed the Alliance of Reform Forces (ARF), an all-Yugoslav party which supported his Government and advocated Western-style reforms.

31: The Serb National Council denounced the amendments to the Croatian Constitution, and demanded a referendum on immediate cultural autonomy.

August

8: The Federal Assembly finalized their approval of constitutional amendments establishing a multi-party system.

19: The Croatian Serbs began their referendum on autonomy (which continued until 2 September), despite the ban by the republican authorities and the violence in support of it.

24: The Croatian Assembly dismissed the Republic's member of the federal State Presidency, a Communist, and nominated the Croatian Premier, Mesić, instead; Josip Manolić was elected Premier; the Assembly also outlawed 'parallel' government bodies and voluntary armed formations.

26: At least 170 miners died in an explosion at the Kreka coal mine Dobrnja, Bosnia-Herzegovina.

September

3: In Kosovo, a strike advocated by the Independent Trade Union Organization of Kosovo was widely observed; the Serbian authorities subsequently refused to allow any strikers employed in state-owned enterprises to return to work.

13: The 111 members of the Kosovo Assembly, who, at a secret session in Kačanik on 7 September, had declared the Assembly to have been re-formed, proclaimed a 'Constitution of the Republic of Kosovo'.

28: Serbia's new Constitution formally took effect: the word 'Socialist' was removed from the Republic's title; a multi-party system was established; the independence of the institutions of the Autonomous Provinces was effectively removed; and Kosovo was renamed Kosovo and Metohija. The Slovenian Assembly asserted its jurisdiction over the Slovenian Territorial Defence Force, which move was denounced by the federal authorities.

October

1: The Serb National Council announced the results of their autonomy referendum, proclaiming autonomy for the Serb-dominated Krajina (borderland) areas of Croatia (the 'Serb Autonomous Region—SAR—of Krajina', was based in Knin).

3: Following sometimes-violent inter-ethnic tension and a directive from the federal State Presidency, Croatian police units were withdrawn from the troubled Serb areas.

4: The YPA occupied the headquarters of the Slovenian Territorial Defence Force.

19: Stipe Mesić was endorsed, by the Federal Assembly, as the Croatian member of the State Presidency and Vice-President of the collective body.

November

8: The Croatian Assembly placed the Territorial Defence Force under republican control.

11: The first round of elections to a new, unicameral Assembly was held in Macedonia.

18: Elections to the collective State Presidency of Bosnia-Herzegovina were held (the three nationalist parties—representing the main Bosnian Muslim, Serb and Croat ethnic groups—secured all seven seats); the first round of voting for the new, bicameral Assembly also took place.

23: The Serbian opposition parties refused to participate in the republican elections, following the Serbian Assembly's rejection of five demands designed to prevent electoral fraud.

25: The second round of voting in the Macedonian parliamentary elections took place.

December

2: The second round of the elections to the Assembly was held in Bosnia-Herzegovina.

6: Croatia and Slovenia (threatened with the use of force by the Federal Secretary for National Defence, Col-Gen. Veljko Kadijević) signed an agreement of friendship.

9: The final round of voting in Bosnia-Herzegovina took place; the three nationalist parties won most of the seats in the Assembly. The final round of voting in Macedonia also produced an inconclusive result, with the nationalist opposition, the Internal Macedonian Revolutionary Organization-Democratic Party for Macedonian National Unity (IMRO-DPMNU) winning the largest number of seats (37) in the Assembly. In Serbia, a presidential election was won by Milošević, with 65% of the votes cast; the first round of the elections to the Assembly was held. The first-round elections to the presidency and to a new, unicameral Assembly were also held in Montenegro.

16: The final round of voting in the Montenegrin Assembly elections took place; the ruling League of Communists of Montenegro won 83 of the 125 seats.

20: The three nationalist parties of Bosnia-Herzegovina announced their coalition agreement: Dr Alija Izetbegović, the leader of the predominantly Muslim Party of Democratic Action (PDA), was to be President of the republican State Presidency; Jure Pelivan of the Croatian Democratic Union of Bosnia-Herzegovina (CDU-BH), the Premier; and Momčilo Krajišnik of the Serb Democratic Party (SDP), President of the Assembly.

21: The Croatian Assembly promulgated a new Constitution, which proclaimed the Republic's full sovereignty and its right to secede from Yugoslavia.

23: A referendum, in which an overwhelming majority voted in favour of secession, was held in Slovenia, despite federal warnings of unconstitutionality and economic sanctions. No candidate having won an overall majority in the Montenegrin presidential election, a second round was held and won by Momir Bulatović, of the League of Communists. The second round of elections to the Serbian Assembly was held; the final results gave 194 of the 250 seats to the ruling SPS.

1991

January

1: The new dinar was devalued.

7: In Macedonia the IMRO-DPMNU, the League of Communists-Party of Democratic Reform (LCM-PDR) and the Macedonian ARF agreed to form a coalition administration (subsequently Stojan Andov of the ARF was elected President of the Assembly and, eventually, Kiro Gligorov of the LCM-PDR President of the Republic, with Ljupčo Georgievski of the IMRO-DPMNU as Vice-President).

8: Yugoslavia's international financial reputation was damaged by revelations that the Serbian National Bank had issued an unauthorized 18,300m. dinars to the Serbian Government.

9: The federal State Presidency ordered that all 'unauthorized' armed units should surrender their weapons, causing tension between the YPA and forces controlled by the Croatian and Slovenian Republics.

10: Inter-republican negotiations about Yugoslavia's future constitutional structure convened, but immediately adjourned because of the crisis between the federal authorities and Croatia and Slovenia; meetings were resumed, intermittently, over the following months.

15: The Serbian Assembly elected Dragutin Zelenović, until then the Vojvodina member of the federal State Presidency, as the republican Premier (he resigned in December).

16: Milo Djukanović was elected Premier of Macedonia.

20: Croatia and Slovenia concluded a mutual defence pact, amid rising tension between the republican authorities and the YPA.

25: The Macedonian Assembly unanimously adopted a declaration of the Republic's sovereignty, including a statement of its right to secede from the federation. Imminent conflict in Yugoslavia was averted, following a meeting of the federal State Presidency and the Croatian leadership; the YPA agreed to end its state of alert and the Croatians agreed to demobilize, if not disband, the new paramilitary special police reserve (*specijalci*).

30: The YPA ordered the arrest of Croatia's Minister of Defence, Col-Gen. Martin Spegelj, on sedition charges, following the broadcast of an apparently incriminating videotape; the republican authorities refused to co-operate with the YPA.

February

2: The Hungarian Government first admitted that a small consignment of weapons had been delivered by a Hungarian firm to Yugoslavia (later acknowledged to be to Croatia).

14: The Presidency of Vojvodina nominated its President, Jugoslav Kostić, to act as its member of the federal State Presidency.

20: The Slovenian Assembly overwhelmingly adopted a resolution initiating its process of 'dissociation' from Yugoslavia, although it declared its willingness to negotiate on the federation's future as well as the details of secession.

21: Croatia asserted the primacy of its Constitution and laws over those of the federation and declared its conditions for participation in a confederation of sovereign states.

26: The Military Prosecutor in Zagreb formally indicted Col-Gen. Spegelj, who was in hiding, on a charge of armed rebellion.

28: The self-proclaimed SAR of Krajina declared its separation from Croatia and its desire to unite with Serbia (on 16 March it formally resolved on its separation from Croatia and adherence to the Yugoslav federation).

March

1–3: The YPA rebutted attempts by the Croatian police to reimpose their authority in the Serb town of Pakrac (part of the SAR of Krajina), which had been the cause of civil disturbances.

9: Massive demonstrations in Belgrade, demanding less confrontational policies by the SPS and resignations from the Serbian Government, were opposed by riot police; many opposition leaders were among those arrested, notably Vuk Drasković of the nationalist Serbian Renaissance Movement.

12: Drasković was released from custody, but rioting continued in Belgrade.

15: Dr Borisav Jović of Serbia, President of the federal State Presidency, resigned after the body refused to order the YPA to impose a state of emergency.

16: In what was alleged to be an attempt by President Milošević of Serbia to render the federal State Presidency inquorate and force the intervention of the YPA, the Montenegrin member of the Presidency resigned, the Serbian Assembly dismissed the ethnic Albanian member for Kosovo-Metohija and the Vojvodina member, Kostić, refused to attend meetings.

19: The General Staff of the YPA rejected political involvements and, effectively, acknowledged the legitimacy of the federal State Presidency.

20: The Serbian Assembly rejected Dr Jović's resignation and voted to restore all Serbian representation of the federal Presidency. The Macedonian Assembly elected Nikola Kljusev to be Premier in a new Government.

21: Dr Jović withdrew his resignation as President of the federal State Presidency; Kostić of Vojvodina resumed his attendance at the Presidency; Bulatović, President of the republican Presidency, acted as the Montenegrin member; and Sejdo Bajramović was appointed as the member for Kosovo-Metohija (the Serbian Assembly restored the functions of the Kosovo-Metohija Presidency, which it had abolished on 18 March).

28: The republican presidents replaced the federal State Presidency as the leading negotiators of Yugoslavia's future, with the first of a series of weekly 'summit' meetings.

April

1: The SAR of Krajina, in Croatia, decided to unite with Serbia.

2: The Serbian Assembly did not endorse the unity decision of the SAR of Krajina. Croatian police agreed to YPA demands that they withdraw from the Plitviče National Park, which had been the scene of violence between forces of the Krajina Serbs and the YPA and the Croatians.

8: There were anti-Serb and anti-YPA incidents in Croatia, particularly in Split.

10: The Serbian Assembly accepted the resignation of the interior minister, over the rioting of the previous month, but three votes of 'no confidence' in members of the Serbian Government were defeated.

11: The summit of republican presidents, meeting in Brdo kod Kranja, Slovenia, agreed that a national referendum on Yugoslavia's future should be held (the options consisted of a community of independent states, a united federal state or a compromise suggested by Bosnia-Herzegovina and Macedonia). Croatia established an army, the Croatian National Guard Corps, after increasing anxieties about the intentions of the YPA.

16: The Serbian Government agreed to many of the demands of textile, leather and metallurgical workers, who staged Yugoslavia's biggest strike since the Second World War.

18: The trial of the absent Col-Gen. Spegelj, and seven other Croats charged with armed rebellion, resumed (it had been postponed on 8 April, because of demonstrations).

19: The Federal Government devalued the dinar.

26: Serb-dominated districts in north-west Bosnia-Herzegovina unilaterally announced the formation of the 'Municipal Community of Bosanska (Bosnian) Krajina'; the move was repudiated by the republican authorities.

29: The summit of republican presidents, in Cetinje, Montenegro, failed to agree on the details of the proposed referendum on Yugoslavia's future.

30: The SAR of Krajina's self-proclaimed government or executive council announced the formation of a Krajina Assembly.

May

6: The USA suspended all economic aid to Yugoslavia, because of alleged human rights abuses in Kosovo-Metohija and for the 'destabilization' of the State Presidency.

8: Slovenia announced that it would secede from Yugoslavia by 26 June; increasing tension between its Territorial Defence Force and the YPA followed.

9: The federal State Presidency refused to impose a state of emergency in Croatia (as favoured by Serbia and Montenegro), following a series of increasingly violent clashes between Serbs and Croats, but granted wider powers to the YPA.

10: The Croatian opposition parties rejected the federal Presidency's plan, saying Croatia was at war; President Tudjman refused to disarm the police reservists.

15: Dr Jović's term of office as President of the federal State Presidency ended; under the system of rotating leadership, Stipe Mesić of Croatia was scheduled to become the first non-Communist President of Yugoslavia, but the Presidency members for Serbia, Kosovo-Metohija and Vojvodina voted against him, and the Montenegrin member abstained.

16: The Krajina Assembly confirmed that it considered the SAR to be an integral part of Serbia, following a referendum decision to this effect on 12 May.

17: Serbia, Kosovo-Metohija, Vojvodina and Montenegro again voted against Mesić's accession, effectively leaving Yugoslavia without a head of state.

19: In a referendum in Croatia, some 93% voted in favour of an independent Republic (possibly as part of a confederation of sovereign states).

27: Marković persuaded the republican presidents to end all internal trade barriers, which had been the subject of dispute since the end of 1989.

29: The SAR of Krajina announced that its basic statute was a constitution law; its Assembly enacted a series of measures and appointed a government, led by Milan Babić.

June

6: A summit of the republican presidents considered a proposal to make Yugoslavia an alliance of states; by this time Slovenia had enacted legislation enabling its eventual assumption of independent power and had formed a new Slovenian Territorial Army.

7: The Macedonian Assembly removed the word 'Socialist' from the Republic's title; it also provided that it alone could authorize a state of emergency in the Republic, among other constitutional amendments.

12: A delegation from the Federal Government met Slovenian representatives and condemned the continuing moves towards secession; a dispute about receipt of customs duties subsequently soured relations between the Slovenian and Federal Governments.

18: The Croatian Assembly convened for a permanent session, intended to enact all legislation necessary for the assumption of independence.

19: The Slovenian Constitutional Commission presented a draft decree, which would effect the transfer of federal competencies to the Republic, for the consideration of the Slovenian Assembly.

22: Macedonia announced its proposed course if it were to begin a process of dissociation from the federation.

24: Marković visited Zagreb and addressed the Croatian Assembly, supporting the continuation of the federation and the necessary measures which would be required to maintain it.

25: The Croatian and Slovenian Assemblies declared the independence and sovereignty of their Republics, beginning the process of dissociation from the federation.

27: The YPA began military operations, mainly in Slovenia, mobilizing (with the support of the Federal Government, in the absence of the State Presidency) to secure the international borders of the SFRY and bombing Ljubljana airport (Belgrade traffic control closed all Slovenian airports). The union of the two Krajinas was announced: the SAR in Croatia; and Bosanska (Bosnian) Krajina in Bosnia-Herzegovina.

28: Fighting continued in Slovenia until the afternoon; the YPA then claimed to have achieved its objectives. A 'troika' of foreign ministers from three EC countries (Luxembourg, the Netherlands and Italy) met federal and republican leaders in Belgrade and Zagreb, securing agreement to a short-lived cease-fire.

30: Following continued fighting, mainly in Slovenia, the three EC foreign ministers returned to Yugoslavia and secured agreement to the cease-fire with the threat of EC sanctions; one condition was implemented forthwith—the proclamation of Stipe Mesić as President of the federal State Presidency.

July

1–5: The emergency committee of senior officials of the Conference on Security and Co-operation in Europe (CSCE) and the CSCE Conflict Prevention Centre met for the first time, to discuss the situation in Yugoslavia; the CSCE meetings supported the EC's peace efforts, which continued with agreement on an arms embargo (endorsed by the USA on 8 July), a decision to send in cease-fire observers and the suspension of financial aid to Yugoslavia.

2: Fighting continued mainly in Slovenia, including an aerial bombardment of Ljubljana, but there were also the first incidents in Zagreb, Croatia. The Slovenian Government agreed to begin the implementation of the cease-fire proposals (YPA troops were able to begin their withdrawal from Slovenia late the next day).

4: The federal State Presidency, excluding the Slovenian member, met for the first time under Mesić's Presidency and demanded Slovenian observance of the cease-fire.

5: Slovenia rejected the federal Presidency's imposed deadlines, but announced a partial demobilization and began to free captured troops. Conflict between Croatian armed units, Serbian fighters and the YPA continued to escalate in Croatia, particularly the Slavonia region.

7–8: The EC troika and representatives of the State Presidency, Croatia and Slovenia met on the Adriatic island of Brioni; their final agreement included: all fighting should cease immediately; Slovenia and Croatia should have a three-month moratorium on further implementation of their declarations of dissociation.

11: The Federal Government secured the passage of an emergency budget, designed to maintain the administration and prevent the complete collapse of the economy.

12: The federal State Presidency endorsed the Brioni agreement, although it added extra conditions, which had already been accepted by the Croatian and Slovenian parliaments.

18: The federal State Presidency convened, in Belgrade, following the earlier refusal of the Serbian bloc of members to participate; agreement was reached to order the withdrawal of the YPA from Slovenia within three months. In Croatia, the Premier (Prime Minister), Josip Manolić, was appointed the head of a new war cabinet or state council, being replaced by his deputy, Franjo Gregurić (there had been an earlier reallocation of portfolios on 3 July).

22: The federal State Presidency and the republican presidents attended negotiations on the future of Yugoslavia at Ohrid, in Macedonia; President Tudjman of Croatia refused to sign the agreed peace plan, warning of imminent war as the worst day of fighting in eastern Croatia claimed 21 lives.

26–27: The Pentagonal group of countries, including Yugoslavia, met for their second annual meeting, in Dubrovnik; they were joined by Poland, hence becoming known as the Hexagonal (or the Central European Initiative). Fighting in Croatia continued to escalate; Serb–Croat encounters cost between 40 and 100 lives during these days.

29: The EC offered to increase the number of observers in Yugoslavia, if their safety was guaranteed; the WEU and the CSCE continued to support the EC efforts.

30: As Serbian fighters, with the tacit and active support of the YPA, occupied tracts of Slavonia, in eastern Croatia, President Tudjman refused to attend a meeting of the federal Presidency; Mesić withdrew from the meeting, in protest at the appointment of the Montenegrin member, Kostić, as head of the commission to supervise the cease-fire in Croatia.

31: Following secret negotiations with Serb leaders in Croatia, Tudjman announced legislative proposals offering some political autonomy, including their own police force, to the so-called SAR of Krajina. The Serbian Government was reorganized.

August

1: President Tudjman reorganized the Croatian Government, forming an administration of 'democratic unity', with 16 of the 27 posts being filled by opposition parties.

4: Macedonia declared a state of emergency and, subsequently, decided to hold a referendum on independence.

6: The first of many cease-fires in eastern Croatia was declared by the federal State Presidency, but failed to take effect. EC foreign ministers, meeting after the failure of further mediation attempts by the troika, agreed to consider restoring aid selectively, by republic.

13: An SAR of Western Slavonia was declared (later an SAR of Slavonia, Baranja and Western Srem was also declared). The official news agency reported that nearly 90,000 people were refugees from the fighting in eastern Croatia.

16: Gunfire forced an EC cease-fire monitoring helicopter to land, as widespread fighting resumed in Croatia. Dr Izetbegović, President of the Presidency of Bosnia-Herzegovina, announced that a referendum on the Republic's future would be held; he repudiated a recent claim by the Serbians, Montenegrins and other Serbs to have reached an accommodation between them and the Slav Muslims. The Democratic Alliance of Kosovo announced that a referendum on the future of the

Province would be held, following further Serbian restrictions on provincial autonomy.

21: The federal State Presidency and the republican authorities reached an agreement that provided for the basic economic and political operation of the federation for three months, but only after controversy was caused by a Serbian claim to the Serb territories of Croatia.

22: Following two days of intense fighting around Osijek, the main town of eastern Croatia, President Tudjman demanded an end to Serb aggression and the withdrawal of YPA troops from the Republic.

23: The Macedonian Assembly approved a new draft constitution, amid cabinet reshuffles.

25: The Croatian-held towns of Vukovar and Vinkovci, south of Osijek, were severely bombarded; fighting also continued around Knin, where the self-proclaimed authorities of Krajina ordered a general mobilization.

26: The presidential cease-fire commission collapsed with the resignation of its secretary, who stated that the Brioni agreement of August had been breached some 200 times and that more than 70 people had been killed.

27: Condemnation of Serbia, as the aggressor in the Yugoslav conflict, was general at an EC meeting (a view echoed by the USA on 29 August); the EC proposed new peace measures, but Milošević refused to endorse them. Another cease-fire was arranged between Croatia and the YPA, but renewed fighting in Vukovar soon breached it; Kijevo, a symbol of Croat resistance in the Serb areas of western Croatia, was taken by Serb irregulars and the YPA.

September

2: The six Republics accepted the EC cease-fire plan, which provided for EC monitors and a peace conference on the future of Yugoslavia.

5: Heavy fighting continued in Croatia, particularly around Osijek, despite cease-fire attempts; Croatian forces attempted to retake Okučani, the loss of which had closed the main Zagreb–Belgrade highway and severed the Croatian capital's links with eastern Croatia.

7: The peace conference opened in The Hague (Netherlands), chaired by the former British foreign minister and NATO Secretary-General, Lord Carrington; the federal State Presidency met with all eight members for the last time.

8: In Macedonia, some 95% of the two-thirds of eligible voters who participated in the referendum were in favour of an independent and sovereign Republic; the large ethnic Albanian minority boycotted the poll.

12: The fighting, which remained heavy in eastern Croatia, around Osijek, Vukovar and Vinkovci, had also spread westward in Slavonia and along the Bosnian border; Serb and federal troops attempted to sever links between Zagreb and the Dalmatian coast (official figures put casualties in Croatia, since 2 August, at 84 dead and 214 wounded). The YPA and the Serbian Presidency member denied that the federal State Presidency President, Mesić, had the authority to order federal troops alone, asserting that he could only do so as part of the Presidency (the previous week Mesić said that a refusal by the YPA to return to barracks would constitute a coup). In Bosnia-Herzegovina, six Serb-dominated municipalities in the far south of the Republic and two on the eastern border with Serbia proclaimed an 'Autonomous Region', or SAR, of Eastern and Old Herzegovina.

16: In Bosnia-Herzegovina, the Serbs of the 18 municipalities of Bosanska Krajina proclaimed an 'Autonomous Region', or SAR, in the north-west of the Republic (excluding the far north-west); similar proclamations were made, on 18 September, in three municipalities near Sarajevo (SAR of Romanija) and, on 20 September, in three municipalities of North-Eastern Bosnia (an SAR of Northern Bosnia was proclaimed on 4 November).

22: The sixth cease-fire agreement between the YPA and Croatia took effect, following a major YPA offensive to liberate its blockaded barracks in Croatia, starting on 20 September. Bosnia-Herzegovina ordered a mobilization of its reserves,

alleging that attempts were being made to involve the Republic in the conflict.

25: The UN Security Council unanimously ordered an arms embargo on Yugoslavia. The federal defence minister, Serbia and Croatia agreed to strengthen the terms of the cease-fire, despite continued sporadic fighting. In the SAR of Slavonia, Baranja and Western Srem, its 'Grand National Assembly' enacted a constitutional law.

26: A referendum on independence for Kosovo, announced by the provincial Assembly-in-Exile (based in Zagreb), began, despite Serbian determination to prevent it; it lasted until 30 September and the result was reported to be an overwhelming endorsement of independence. In Bosnia-Herzegovina, ethnic tensions resulted in shooting incidents along the borders with Croatia and Montenegro.

28: The International Red Cross suspended its activities in Croatia until such time as all sides in the conflict respected its work and neutrality. Fighting resumed in eastern Croatia, particularly around Pakrac, and on the Dalmatian coast, around YPA bases. The YPA announced that all images of Tito (of Croat parentage) were to be removed from their facilities.

30: At the EC peace conference, three committees were formed, to begin negotiations on national minorities, the economy and general institutional frameworks. The YPA threatened that, for every YPA facility attacked or taken, a facility of 'vital importance' to Croatia would be destroyed: the siege of Vukovar was intensified; Dubrovnik was isolated; and parts of historic Zadar were bombarded.

October

1: A major YPA offensive in eastern Croatia and on Dubrovnik began, although peace efforts continued in The Hague. Hungary made further allegations of Yugoslav violations of its territory.

2: The Slovenian Assembly resolved to end all involvement in Yugoslavia from 7 October, the last day of the EC-negotiated moratorium. The YPA rejected a Croatian offer to end the blockade of army bases if it halted its offensive (the Yugoslav navy reimposed a blockade of Croatian ports the following day).

3: The Serbian bloc on the federal State Presidency announced that, because of the imminent threat of war, Serbia was to assume certain powers of the Federal Assembly; the other four Presidency members were not present and repudiated the decision of this 'rump' Presidency and refused to participate in further activities of the body (Macedonia and Bosnia-Herzegovina became increasingly estranged from Serbia and its allies).

7: The EC moratorium on the Croatian and Slovenian processes of dissociation expired at midnight. Earlier in the day Zagreb suffered a rocket attack, allegedly by federal aircraft; Mesić, Marković and Tudjman narrowly escaped injury in the presidential residence, Banski Dvori (Ban's Palace); the parliament building was also damaged; the YPA and Serbia were widely condemned internationally, including by the USSR. Prince Aleksandar Karadjordjević, the claimant to the Yugoslav ('Aleksandar II') and Serbian thrones, but a British citizen, ended his visit to Belgrade.

8: The Croatian Assembly declared all federal laws null and void. Slovenia's independence declaration took effect, it introduced its own currency, the tolar, and recalled all its citizens in federal institutions. The State Presidency of Bosnia-Herzegovina endorsed its President's declaration of the Republic's neutrality.

9: As part of another short-lived cease-fire agreement, the federal naval blockade of Rijeka and Zadar ended and the Croatian forces withdrew from around some YPA barracks; the siege of Dubrovnik, a World Heritage site, with no significant Serb minority, continued.

13: In Slovenia, the ruling DEMOS became a coalition of seven, rather than six, parties, following a split in the Slovenian Democratic Union (the coalition split in December).

15: The Assembly of Bosnia-Herzegovina declared the Republic's sovereignty, emphasizing the inviolability of its borders and its willingness to consider a form of Yugoslav association. Presidents Tudjman and Milošević met, in Moscow, with President Gorbachev of the USSR, and agreed to peace talks; another ineffective cease-fire was signed.

16: The SAR of Krajina, in Croatia, and Bosanska Krajina, in Bosnia-Herzegovina, announced their unification; Babić, leader of the former, was authorized to represent the areas at The Hague conference (Babić was subsequently proclaimed President of a 'Republic of Serbian Krajina', which also claimed to include Western Slavonia). Other Serb 'Autonomous Regions' in Bosnia-Herzegovina rejected the sovereignty declaration and were to subject themselves only to the federation.

17: The EC was reported to be ready to recognize the independence of Croatia and Slovenia if a settlement was not reached (its member states recognized the two Republics on 15 January 1992). Croatia agreed that it would evacuate its town of Ilok, on the Danube border with Serbia, and surrender it to the YPA.

18: In order to end the civil war, Montenegro agreed to consider an EC proposal for a Yugoslav confederacy; the Montenegrin Assembly declared the Republic's sovereignty.

19: Serbia was isolated when the other five Republics accepted the proposal for a Yugoslav association of sovereign states (with rights guaranteed for minorities) as the basis of negotiations; the USA and the USSR supported acceptance of the plan. In Croatia, the 10th cease-fire since the June declaration of independence failed to end fighting around Dubrovnik. The Kosovo Assembly-in-Exile, citing their referendum results, declared Kosovo to be an independent and sovereign Republic; the Assembly appointed a provisional coalition government.

23: In Macedonia, the IMRO-DPMNU announced that it was to leave the Government, following the resignation of the IMRO-DPMNU republican Vice-President the previous day.

24: A cease-fire between the federal and Croatian authorities was agreed in Zagreb (violated by a renewed YPA assault on Dubrovnik the following day). In Serbia, local elections, scheduled for 10 November, were postponed (assembly elections in Vojvodina, due on the same day, were also later postponed). In Bosnia-Herzegovina, the Serb deputies announced the formation of an 'Assembly of the Serb Nation of Bosnia-Herzegovina', which then proposed a referendum on a common Serb state, to be held on 9–10 November (there was overwhelming support for remaining in a common Serb state). The SAR of Slavonia, Baranja and Western Srem, in Croatia, announced its union with the Krajina regions.

26: The last YPA troops left Slovenia by sea. In the Sandjak (mainly in Serbia, but partly in Montenegro), the Slav Muslims voted for autonomy in a referendum banned by the Serbian authorities.

27: The village of Barcs, in Hungary, was bombed; the Hungarian Government accused Yugoslav aircraft of the raid, and tension between the two countries increased. The Croatian authorities rejected a YPA ultimatum to surrender Dubrovnik; they also estimated that some 5,000 people had been killed, since 25 June, 10,000 wounded and 350,000 made homeless by the civil war.

28: The EC demanded that Serbia accept its peace proposals by 5 November, or trade sanctions would be imposed (Serbia rejected the ultimatum). Hungary protested about a Yugoslav air attack on one of its border towns. Macedonia announced that more than 60% of federal bases in the Republic had been evacuated, without explanation. With international attention on Dubrovnik, YPA activities continued in Bosnia-Herzegovina, threatening Croatian control of the Dubrovnik coast; Vukovar was subjected to intense bombardment (the Croatian forces formally surrendered on 18 November); the YPA and Serb irregulars launched attacks on the central coastal area of Croatia, and elsewhere in Slavonia, notably a new front in the north, near Podraska Slatina, and to the south of Zagreb.

Note: The UN subsequently arranged the 15th cease-fire and secured some agreement, except from Krajina, on the introduction of a peace-keeping force, in early 1992.

Recent Political History of Yugoslavia

BRANKA MAGAŠ

During the 1980s and early 1990s, Yugoslavia experienced a process of tumultuous change, in the course of which the main parameters of its internal politics became substantially modified. To understand the nature of this change, it is necessary to begin by measuring it against the basic laws organizing the country's life, enshrined in the Constitution of 1974.

THE ROAD TO CONSTITUTIONAL CRISIS

The Yugoslav Constitution of 1974 gave Tito (Josip Broz) the position of President-for-Life, in which capacity he chaired the meetings of a federal State Presidency. This comprised representatives of Yugoslavia's eight federal units: six republics (Bosnia-Herzegovina, Croatia, Macedonia, Montenegro, Serbia, Slovenia) and two provinces of Serbia (Kosovo and Vojvodina). The members of the State Presidency were elected for a four-year term, by a secret vote in the respective republican or provincial assemblies, to which they remained directly responsible. After Tito's death, in May 1980, the State Presidency became the collective head of state. To facilitate its functioning, a position of President of the Presidency was created. This post was filled by the representatives of the federal units, on the basis of a strict annual rotation between them. Thus, on 9 May 1989, the post of President of the Presidency went to Slovenia (Janez Drnovsek), then, on 9 May 1990, to Serbia (Dr Borisav Jović), and, on 9 May 1991, it was due to go to Croatia (Stjepan 'Stipe' Mesić). However, Serbia, supported by the votes of the previously autonomous provinces of Kosovo and Vojvodina and the abstention of Montenegro, refused to ratify Mesić's appointment and the country became involved in a major constitutional crisis.

Duties of the President of the Presidency involved receiving representatives of foreign states and, in turn, representing the country on official occasions abroad. The President also convened meetings of the State Presidency, the functions of which included: the appointment of the Federal Executive Council (Federal Government); the signing of laws passed by the Federal Assembly (comprised of the Federal Chamber and the Chamber of Republics and Provinces); and the performance of the duties of Commander-in-Chief of the Yugoslav People's Army. In the performance of this last function, the State Presidency was empowered to introduce a state of emergency in the country, in response to a possible external threat. Its ability to do this in response to a domestic crisis, however, was limited by the principle of consensus: that is, it required unanimity among all the representatives on the Presidency. The 1974 Constitution thus combined confederal and federal elements; it attempted to balance a substantial autonomy of the individual federal units with a centralism inscribed in the supremacy of the federal over the republican and provincial legislatures.

Until early 1990 the country's supreme legislative body was the Yugoslav Federal Assembly. Of its two Chambers, the Chamber of Republics and Provinces (whose members were appointed by republican and provincial assemblies) was the more powerful, for it had the right to veto decisions of the Federal Government. If supported by the State Presidency, the Federal Government could implement a controversial decision as an emergency measure, but only for a period of up to one year. In the course of 1989–91 this emergency procedure became the norm, indicating the emergence of deep divisions between federal units. At first, these divisions were mainly of an economic nature, related to the size and financing of the federal state budget, but they soon acquired political significance as well.

The political aspect of intra-Yugoslav differences was greatly increased during the period 1989–91. Several important changes occurred during this time, altering the relationship between the federal units and undermining the 1974 Constitution and, thus, the authority of the federal State. In regard to Yugoslavia's future, the mechanism of change proved to be, if anything, more important than its final outcome. The process involved factionalization within the ruling League of Communists of Yugoslavia (LCY). By the end of the 1980s a broad alliance had emerged between Party conservatives (strongly represented in the LCY organization in the Army) and the leadership of the Republic of Serbia, with the aim of recentralizing Yugoslavia, by removing the confederal aspects of the 1974 Constitution. Against them stood Party reformists, strongly represented within the leaderships of the Republics of Slovenia and Croatia, who not only resisted the attempt to recentralize, but also wished to strengthen political pluralism and civil liberties within the country. The final outcome of this polarization was the disintegration of the post-Second World War system and growing civil strife.

The initiative which led to the collapse of the status quo came from Serbia, seeking to strengthen its weight within the federation. In 1989, following a prolonged campaign, the Serbian Assembly enacted several amendments to the republican Constitution, which removed key aspects of the autonomy of Kosovo and Vojvodina. Under the 1974 Constitution, these two regions were Autonomous Provinces, which, though part of Serbia, were also federal units in their own right. The amendments ended the right of the Provinces to: make their own laws (within the framework of federal laws); run their own security services; to make their own economic decisions; act independently of Serbia within the federal institutions. These decisions, described as a 'reunification of Serbia', were unprecedented in the country's post-1944 history. It was not only the effect, the erasure of two federal units, but also that the amendments were proposed and implemented unilaterally, in open defiance of the federal Constitution. Serbia's expansion caused the federal structure to become unbalanced.

Although these amendments abolished any basis for the Provinces' separate representation in the federation, Serbia did not proceed towards their *de jure* removal from federal bodies. Serbia claimed that it was merely an administrative reorganization of its internal affairs. The other Republics, although they did not wish to sanction the new situation, were unable to reverse the process and meekly complied with it. This seeming consensus was never likely to last, however, because the incorporation of the two Provinces substantially increased Serbia's influence in the federal institutions. Thus, on the State Presidency, Serbia acquired three representatives in place of the previous one. Serbia's constitutional amendments therefore altered the national balance in Yugoslavia, by redistributing the federation's legislative and executive powers in its own favour. In mid-1990 these amendments were incorporated into the new republican Constitution, but not into the federal one.

By exposing the fragility of the constitutional order, these developments pointed also to the advanced state of decomposition of the ruling Party, which alone controlled the instruments of discipline and coercion at the federal level (most notably the Army). Furthermore, met by a lack of support in much of Yugoslavia for its changes, Serbia was forced to act outside the legal institutions of the system. Between 1987 and 1990 the League of Communists of Serbia used the republican state machinery and mass media to organize many demonstrations by Serb nationals throughout the Republic; they denounced the Party and state leaders of Vojvodina and Kosovo and demanded Serbia's 'reunification'. This campaign displayed a resurgent nationalism, but was also reminiscent of the Chinese Cultural Revolution, in that it was officially described as an 'anti-bureaucratic revolution'. This 'anti-bureaucratic revolution' targeted not only the provincial leaders, but also politicians from other parts of Yugoslavia who were unwilling to endorse Serbia's actions. What is more, the campaign soon went beyond the borders of Serbia, to involve the Serb minorities living in Croatia and Bosnia-Herzegovina. It engulfed also Montenegro, linked to Serbia by history and tradition. In mid-1989 the Serbian Party leader, Slobodan Milošević, openly endorsed non-constitutional forms of action where Serb national interests were concerned.

By the end of 1989 Serbia's campaign could be judged a success. The Governments of Vojvodina and Montenegro had fallen and been replaced by new ones, loyal to the Serbian leadership. In Kosovo, however, with its predominantly Albanian population, the campaign had encountered stiff resistance. In the winter of 1988/89 mass demonstrations and two general strikes, involving hundreds of thousands of Albanians, articulated a general determination not to accept the obliteration of Kosovo's autonomy. This opposition was finally broken by the intervention of the Army (with considerable loss of life). The federal State Presidency approved this action, although not unanimously, since Slovenia voted against it. Acting under military and other coercion, the Kosovo Assembly eventually ratified Serbia's constitutional amendments. In mid-1990, however, it refused to approve the new Serbian Constitution. This act of defiance led to the Assembly's summary dissolution by the Serbian authorities, creating a constitutional crisis for the entire country. Without a functioning Assembly, the representatives of Kosovo in the federal bodies became illegitimate and, with them, also the work of these bodies as a whole.

For a time, however, this crisis of the Yugoslav state order was overshadowed by another. This crisis was intimately linked to the other, but would prove even more portentous for Yugoslavia's future. It was a crisis, which was to be terminal, within the ruling Party. The situation had been becoming increasingly problematic since the mid-1980s, but it became critical with the decision of the Slovenian Assembly, in September 1989, to amend the republican Constitution and allow multi-party elections to take place in the following year.

Slovenia thus became the second Republic formally to defy a major provision of the 1974 Constitution. It replaced 45 years of one-party rule with a multi-party system. Slovenia was soon followed by Croatia. In both these Republics the change was approved by the republican branches of the LCY, without the approval of the central leadership and in advance of the all-Yugoslav Party Congress. However, when the Congress was convened, in late February 1990, no agreement regarding the need for drastic political or economic reform could be reached. As a result, the LCY, which had governed the country ever since the Second World War, fell apart. The consequences of its collapse were somewhat mitigated by the fact that the Federal Government, headed by Ante Marković, was itself already committed to the introduction of a full market economy and a multi-party political system.

The democratic tide had by now swept through nearly all of Eastern Europe, leaving Party conservatives isolated. Multi-party elections in Slovenia and Croatia (April and May 1990) were followed by similar elections in Bosnia-Herzegovina (October 1990), Macedonia (November 1990) and, finally, Serbia and Montenegro (December 1990). In Kosovo, however, the elections were massively boycotted and no legitimate order restored. These significant political changes involved an enormous amount of legislative work, including the writing of new republican constitutions. It was characteristic of the new situation in Yugoslavia that this work was localized; the new electoral laws and constitutional provisions differed widely from republic to republic. Since the election results also varied considerably, by the end of 1990 the earlier inter-republican divisions had deepened dramatically. In Slovenia, the elections were won by a nationalist coalition, the Democratic Opposition of Slovenia (DEMOS). In Croatia, a Croat nationalist party, the Croatian Democratic Union (CDU), won an overall majority of seats (though not of votes). In Bosnia-Herzegovina, three nationalist parties, the Serb Democratic Party (representing the Serb population), the Croat Democratic Union (representing the Croat population) and the Party of Democratic Action (representing the Muslim population), formed a coalition government. In Macedonia, the nationalist party, the Internal Macedonian Revolutionary Organization-Democratic Party for Macedonian National Unity, or IMRO-DPMNU, won most votes, but not enough to allow it to rule alone, given the strong performance of the erstwhile Communists (known as the Party of Democratic Reform and subsequently renamed the Social Democratic Alliance). In Serbia and Montenegro, however, the Communists (in the former, renamed the Socialist Party of Serbia) won large majorities.

The electoral and legal-constitutional discord produced by the autonomous activity of the six Yugoslav Republics was enhanced by new republican laws, which not only conflicted with the federal Constitution, but were also designed to maximize republican independence. This was particularly true of Slovenia, Croatia and Serbia. The possibility of harmonization by way of federal elections was excluded, at least until such time as the Republics could agree on a new form for the joint state. Judicial chaos now paralysed the work of the federal institutions, expressing fundamental differences affecting all aspects of organization of the Yugoslav state and economy.

The republican elections also altered the membership of those federal bodies that were under the direct jurisdiction of the Republics (the Chamber of Republics and Provinces, and the State Presidency), but not that of the second chamber of the Federal Assembly, which was constituted by all-Yugoslav elections. Such elections were scheduled to have taken place in 1989, but were postponed. The mandate of this chamber was consequently extended, by agreement of the Republics, but in violation of the federal Constitution. This placed the Federal Government in a difficult position, since it no longer had either the constitutional right or the practical instruments to impose its will upon the federal member states. The final blow came in May 1991, with Serbia's refusal to allow the Croatian representative to become the country's President (President of the Presidency). The State Presidency consequently broke up, leaving Yugoslavia without a head of state and its Army without a Commander-in-Chief. Without the Presidency, moreover, the Federal Government could not resort to rule

by decree. The work of the Federal Assembly too became totally blocked, since its decisions required formal approval by the State Presidency before they became law. The country thus entered a state of seemingly permanent constitutional limbo.

THE POLITICAL RUPTURE

Until 1990 Yugoslav political life was structured by the ruling Communist Party, the LCY. In many important respects, the organization of the Party mirrored the organization of the State. Its republican and provincial branches enjoyed a considerable degree of autonomy, symbolized by the fact that their local congresses took place before the all-Yugoslav Party Congress. Formally, however, the LCY and its component parts were organized on the principle of 'democratic centralism', that is, with authority emanating from the top down. The high Party leadership would make decisions, these would then be adopted by the Party Congress, after which they would become mandatory for all lower Party organizations and members. The federalization of the LCY, however, diluted the rigid centralism of the Party, in that all important decisions, however contentious, were made by consensus. This was of crucial importance for the country's internal stability, since the Party leaderships operated not only their Party organizations but also the State and the economy.

At the apex of the Party structure was the LCY Presidency, composed of the presidents of republican and provincial parties (thus ensuring a balanced national representation) and the representative of the LCY organization in the Army. At this level, the Party administrative bodies were also composed on a parity basis. This equitable distribution of power, however, did not correspond to the size of the Party membership in the different federal units; this varied considerably, being, proportionally, smallest in Slovenia and largest in Montenegro. This created a potential problem in that, theoretically, the all-Yugoslav Congress was the body which decided Party policy, but the number of delegates attending the Congress was a direct function of the absolute number of Party members in each federal unit. A simple arithmetic calculation of representation would have left the influence of the Serb component as decisive. To prevent such national 'majorization', congress attendance was bolstered by invitations to other Party members, in order to bring about a more balanced national distribution.

Although the federalization of the LCY pre-dated the Second World War, for the first 20 years of its rule, the Party was much more centralized than in the 1970s and 1980s. All-Yugoslav congresses would take place before local ones, while the composition of the high leadership did not follow the parity principle. The change resulted from internal struggles in the LCY, reflecting both the country's national composition and what became known as the 'Yugoslav road to socialism'. Two crucial events determined its ultimate organizational form. In 1966 Aleksandar Ranković, the Federal Secretary (Minister) of Internal Affairs and Tito's second-in-command, and his mainly conservative allies were purged from the Party. This action was used to break the growing power of the central state bureaucracy, rooted in the state security service, and as a necessary step towards the adoption of market mechanisms within the system of workers' self-management in the economic system. This produced new rules of Party organization, including the parity principle. In 1971–72, however, there was a reaction against this. Party leaders (now also generationally renewed), in several key republics, had used their newly won autonomy to encourage further reliance upon market mechanisms and more liberal internal politics. This trend, if it had been allowed to proceed, would, ultimately, have weakened substantially, if not eliminated outright, the Party monopoly over the decision-making process.

An extensive purge of the Party was conducted to put a stop to this. Decentralization of the State did continue (resulting in the semi-confederal Constitution of 1974). The autonomy of federal LCY units was also retained and, with it, the parity principle in appointments to federal Party bodies. However, 'democratic centralism' was reinforced in ideological matters, symbolized by the Party branch in the Army acquiring the right to representation on the LCY Presidency.

The emergence of the Yugoslav People's Army as an autonomous factor in the political life of the country reflected its role in the purges of the early 1970s. The Army was organized on strict hierarchical principles, was centralized and insisted upon the use of Serbo-Croat as its official language (despite the constitutional equality of national languages in every other sphere). In an important sense, this counter-balanced the decentralization of the civilian state security services (including intelligence) and the introduction, in the early 1970s, of Territorial Defence units under the control of the republican leaderships, which could have been used to make the Republics (and, to a lesser extent, the Provinces) near-independent states. There was no doubting the Army's complete loyalty to Tito, its Commander-in-Chief. After his death, however, its loyalty was no longer automatic, so that it became of paramount importance for any aspiring Yugoslav LCY leader to win Army support. The Army high command showed few liberal propensities and, as a rule, supported the conservative wing of the Party. Furthermore, throughout the 1970s and 1980s, the proportion of officers of Serb and Montenegrin nationality grew well beyond their proportion in the population as a whole. This fact was also to influence the role of the Army in the political crisis from 1987 onwards.

At the final Congress of the LCY, from late February to early March 1990, the fissures that were revealed indicated not only the usual division between reformers and conservatives, but also growing national divisions. The Serbian Party leaders, supported by their Montenegrin counterparts and Army representatives, urged a recentralization of the Party structure, as a prelude to recentralization of the Yugoslav State. In both cases, the organizational changes would have involved an end to the principle of national parity in the composition of the federal bodies, a strengthening of the authority of federal over republican institutions and a redefinition of internal borders as merely administrative. This, therefore, entailed not merely a return to the centralism prevailing before the fall of Ranković, but, in many ways, to the situation pertaining before the Second World War (for instance, in the insistence that the internal Yugoslav borders, of the Republics and Provinces, were just administrative). This was, essentially, an effort to achieve Serb national supremacy. It was overlaid, however, with a rhetoric appealing to Yugoslav unity, patriotism and working-class rule. The enemies were identified as Albanian, Slovene and Croat 'separatists' and all those who advocated a multi-party system. This offensive resulted in a common front being forged to resist, between those who supported political and economic reforms and those who defended the principle of national equality, as enshrined in the Constitution of 1974. The Congress, moreover, had convened at a time when Slovenia and Croatia were already in the throes of election campaigns, with the greatest challenge to the local Communists coming from the nationalists. The sense of crisis was heightened by regional factors, such as the fall of Ceauşescu, only two months earlier, and the outcome could not but be destructive. At this Congress,

the LCY split along lines that have remained permanent in the political life of the country. On one side were the Party organizations in Slovenia, Croatia, Macedonia, Bosnia-Herzegovina and Kosovo (what remained in of it). On the other side were the Party organizations in Serbia, Montenegro, Vojvodina and the Army. The split was not completely clear-cut, in that there were also national divisions within some of the republican and provincial organizations. For example, certain ethnic-Serb members of the parties in Croatia and Bosnia-Herzegovina voted with the Serbian group and certain ethnic Montenegrins voted with the reformers. What was clear, however, was that the country had divided into two factions. The results of the 1990 elections only exacerbated already existing divisions.

THE GROWING CHAOS

The political climate in the immediate aftermath of the elections of 1990 indicated also the extent of continuity and discontinuity within each of the Republics. In four of them (Slovenia, Croatia, Macedonia and Bosnia-Herzegovina), the left bloc included not only the previous Communist parties (renamed Parties of Democratic Reform), but also parties emerging out of the transformation of other quasi-political Communist institutions. Thus, the various Socialist Alliances of Working People (SAWP) spawned socialist or social-democratic parties, and the Alliances of Socialist Youth (ASY) either joined the socialists and social democrats or constituted themselves as autonomous parties with a liberal-democratic prefix. This decomposition of the previous ruling apparatus was conducive both to a marginalization of its conservative wing and to the separation into distinct parliamentary political parties of different opinions.

Exactly the opposite happened in Serbia and Montenegro. There, the Communists simply absorbed the apparatus and property of the SAWP and ASY, boosting enormously their own material power and ensuring the dominance within them of the conservative factions. Furthermore, the Communists' already-high nationalist profile prevented any clear distinction between the nationalists and their political opponents. One result of this was to be the emergence of an extreme-nationalist right-wing in Serbian and Montenegrin politics, with a propensity towards extra-institutional forms of action. In Kosovo, meanwhile, the Albanian population, having boycotted Serbian elections, created strong national organizations, which were completely outside official political activity.

This reorganization of republican and provincial politics was not matched by similar changes at the federal level. An exception was provided by the Army. The collapse of the LCY removed the Army from direct representation in the political life of the country, while multi-party elections in Slovenia and Croatia brought to power anti-Communist administrations. This only confirmed the Army high command in its determination not to recognize the election results as legitimate. Its response was articulated at several levels.

To begin with, in May 1990, the Army confiscated weapons held by the Territorial Defence units of Slovenia and Croatia. Subsequently, with less urgency, the same was done in Bosnia-Herzegovina and Macedonia. The action was in clear contravention of constitutional provisions and without authorization from the federal State Presidency. Since the Army also banned the sale of weapons from its munitions factories for the use of the police forces in these Republics, the new Governments in Slovenia and Croatia, fearing a military coup, began to create their own paramilitary organizations and import weapons from abroad. The conflict between the Army and the two western Republics escalated throughout 1990 and the first half of 1991, eventually dissolving into civil war.

The second move made by the Army was to create its own successor to the now-defunct Communist party. In November 1990 the League of Communists-Movement for Yugoslavia formally replaced the LCY, founded by a group of active and retired generals (including the Federal Secretary for National Defence, the Federal Secretary for Internal Affairs and the Army Chief of Staff), with the aim of enlisting in it the whole of the officer corps. It soon became clear, however, that the new party would not be a success.

Finally, the Army used its own institutions and its control over the federal ministry of defence to press for direct participation in the on-going political discussions, and, at the same time, to legitimize its various interventions against the new administrations in Croatia and Slovenia. Its policy of active non-cooperation with, and destabilization of, these two Governments found support in the Serbian leadership, which was already implicated in fomenting armed rebellion among Serbs in Croatia and Bosnia-Herzegovina. During 1990–91, under the pretext of preventing civil war in Croatia, the Army did, in fact, establish direct control over a considerable part of that Republic. The facts that the Communists had remained in power in Serbia (as the Socialist Party of Serbia) and that a substantial proportion of Army officers were of Serb ethnicity made the co-operation between Serbia and the Army much easier. It was helped also by the State Presidency, the Army's Commander-in-Chief, now being hopelessly split: Slovenia, Croatia, Macedonia and Bosnia-Herzegovina voted regularly one way, and Serbia, Montenegro, Kosovo and Vojvodina the other.

However, in early March 1991, the Army–Serbian alliance appeared to weaken, under the impact of a dramatic series of events. Mass anti-Government demonstrations erupted in Belgrade, and the republican leadership sought an immediate military intervention against the demonstrators. It also demanded that the whole country be placed under a state of emergency. The federal State Presidency did agree to the first demand, but it refused to sanction the second. Upon this occasion the Kosovo representative voted with Slovenia, Croatia, Macedonia and Bosnia-Herzegovina. Serbia promptly recalled its own and the two provincial representatives from the Presidency, and Montenegro followed suit. Within days, these resignations were in fact rescinded; nevertheless, the Army moved closer to the federal prime minister, Ante Marković, as the person representing the country as a whole. This provided Marković with additional authority, as he struggled to keep federal institutions working. Marković's prestige was further strengthened by the support his efforts in keeping Yugoslavia together gained, both in the West and in the USSR. Keen to preserve the status quo in Europe, the outside world rallied around Marković, and also condemned Slovenian and Croatian plans to 'dissociate' themselves from the rest of Yugoslavia, unless a new agreement could be found regarding the organization of the common state.

The Serbian leadership, keen to increase internal political chaos and, hence, the chances of the military taking even more power at the federal level, proceeded to deliver another constitutional coup. They refused to respect the procedure for electing the President of the State Presidency. The consequent disintegration of the presidential system created a political vacuum at the very heart of the Yugoslav state.

TOWARDS THE BREAK-UP OF YUGOSLAVIA

In April 1991 Croatia and Slovenia submitted to the other Yugoslav Republics a proposal for the transformation of Yugoslavia into a loose union of sovereign states. The basis for such a confederation was derived from the actual organization of the European Communities (EC), with some variations designed to meet Yugoslavia's specific needs. Thus a common currency, market, foreign policy, transport and defence were to be retained, and possibly also a common parliament, but the prerogatives of all central institutions were to be considerably reduced. Serbia and Montenegro, on the other hand, rejected this model in favour of a federation more centralized than that prescribed by the Constitution of 1974. The bicameral parliament was to be retained, but the composition of both chambers modified. Instead of the Republics having an identical number of deputies, their number in the second chamber would depend on the numerical size of the nationalities, while the Provinces (hence, the national minorities) were to lose their direct representation in both chambers. Furthermore, according to this model, the power of the federal centre would be enlarged, especially in the economic sphere. The two Republics also declared their intention, in the event of their proposal being rejected, to seek a redrawing of internal borders, in a way that would ensure that all Serbs and Montenegrins lived within the same state. In June 1991 Macedonia and Bosnia-Herzegovina proposed a third model, which sought to combine features of the first two, though it inclined more to the Slovenian–Croatian proposal in its affirmation of republican sovereignty.

Serbia's threat to Yugoslavia's internal borders was perceived by the non-Serb nationalities (including many Montenegrins) as a first step in the creation of a 'Greater Serbia'. The existing internal borders were not ethnic, and could not be so, given the territorial intermingling of the national groups, especially in Bosnia-Herzegovina, where no nationality could claim a majority. Thus any attempt to create a state of all Yugoslav Serbs threatened not only the integrity of the Republics of Croatia and Bosnia-Herzegovina, but also involved the incorporation of hundreds of thousands of Croats and Bosnian Muslims. A Greater Serbia could, consequently, come into being only as a result of civil war.

Serbia's declaration of intent was accompanied by action. In mid-1990, it gave its support to the creation of a so-called 'Serbian Autonomous Region of Krajina', within Croatia. Since Krajina does not border with Serbia, the Army intervened, to defend it from any counter-action by the Croatian authorities. This sparsely populated and mountainous area, mostly but not exclusively inhabited by Serbs, is vital to Croatia in that it is traversed by the main transport routes connecting the ports of Dalmatia with the north. In the spring of 1991 Krajina formally declared its secession from Croatia. The creation and secession of this entity was buttressed by an armed body of men, supplied and maintained by Serbia, with the connivance of the Army. This allowed Krajina to block the movement of people and goods through much of Croatia. In the course of 1991 similar 'no-go' areas were established in some Serb-inhabited villages of eastern Slavonia, close to the Serbian border. This enabled the Serbs and the Army to secure control of much of eastern Slavonia during the fighting from August onwards, even threatening Croatian control of Osijek. A similar approach was also used in Bosnia-Herzegovina, where, initially, two such 'Krajinas' involving the Serb population were created, one in the north and the other in the south. This time the Montenegrin Government too helped. The idea was that these 'Krajinas' would merge together, obliterating the borders between Croatia, Bosnia-Herzegovina, Serbia and Montenegro, and, at a suitable moment, the Serbian Assembly could proclaim their adhesion to the 'motherland'.

The manifest reluctance of most of the Yugoslav population to fight each other delayed the onset of civil war and encouraged the negotiation of cease-fire agreements, whether for reasons of political pressure or because of the logistical problems of desertion by troops. However, a consequence of the political ploys and rhetoric was a massive arming of the population, leading to the erosion of state authority over large parts of Yugoslavia and an increase in banditry and all kinds of organized crime. This visible militarization of everyday life proceeded alongside a growing economic crisis, including a steep rise in the number of unemployed, as the work of republican and federal bodies became preoccupied with continuous emergencies or blocked outright. Unable to reach an agreement, on 25 June 1991, Slovenia and Croatia declared themselves independent states, in the process of 'dissociation' from the rest of Yugoslavia. The Macedonian parliament responded by declaring its intention to move in the same direction (endorsed by a referendum in September), while the creation of the two 'Krajinas' in Bosnia-Herzegovina threatened the collapse of central government institutions in that Republic; in October Bosnia-Herzegovina declared its sovereignty, and even Montenegro did the same.

CONCLUSION

The period of Yugoslav history that opened with Tito's death, in May 1980, and ended with Slovenia's and Croatia's declarations of independence, in June 1991, is characterized by a deep polarization between Serbia, and its ally, Montenegro, and the rest of the federation. The issue at the centre of the intense political battles fought during these years was Serbia's desire to control the Yugoslav state as a whole and the resistance which this engendered among Yugoslavia's non-Serb nationalities. The problem of finding an equitable balance between different national interests has been endemic to Yugoslav history ever since the state was created, in 1918, under Serbian domination. During the civil war of 1941–45 a new international settlement was forged, leading to the transformation of the previously unitary state structure into a federation of national republics. This arrangement permanently weakened Serbia's chances of regaining its pre-Second World War status. From the mid-1980s Serbia was able to mount a challenge to this post-War settlement because it found support in the Yugoslav People's Army. By the mid-1970s the Army had become the main bastion of political conservatism in the country, following the purge of reform-minded Communist leaders in Croatia and Serbia, in 1971–72. The sharpening of the political struggle and its escalation into armed hostilities, after June 1991, suggested that neither side was able to secure a purely political solution; recourse to outright war, by Serbia and its allies, became the increasingly likely option. By the beginning of 1992 it seemed that only international pressure had any chance of securing peace.

Nationalism and Politics in Yugoslavia

JOHN B. ALLCOCK

A key difference between Yugoslavia and most, if not all, of the other countries of eastern and central Europe, is that everybody in Yugoslavia is a member of a national minority. Only the USSR is comparably complex in the mosaic of nationalities which comprise it. There, however, the manner in which nationality enters into politics has a great deal to do with the unquestionable numerical superiority of the Russians. The principal groups are South Slavs, after which the Yugoslav federation is named; they consist of Croats, Macedonians, Montenegrins, Muslims, Serbs and Slovenes. These groups are the officially recognized 'nations of Yugoslavia', each with their national home based in the federation. The Muslims were recognized as a distinct ethnic group in 1971; the term actually refers to the Slavic Muslims, most of whom speak Serbo-Croat and are often known as Bosnian Muslims, but some of whom speak Macedonian—or Bulgarian—and are known as Pomaks. The official designation excludes Albanians and Roma (Gypsies), most of whom are adherents of Islam, and Turks, all of whom are. In addition to these six nations, there are very substantial numbers of Albanians and Hungarians (Magyars). Furthermore, the census records no fewer than 16 other nationalities, which are sufficiently numerous to merit separate counting, to which should be added the substantial numbers who declare themselves to be 'Yugoslavs'. Apart from the six nations, there are 10 officially recognized 'nationalities of Yugoslavia', which enjoy a variety of language and cultural rights: Albanians, Hungarians, Bulgarians, Czechs, Italians, Roma, Romanians, Ruthenians, Slovaks and Turks. The final official category is that of 'other nationalities and ethnic groups', and includes the remaining minorities, such as Austrians, Germans, Greeks, Jews, Poles, Russians, Ukrainians, Vlahs and those who classify themselves as 'Yugoslavs'.

Taking the federation as a whole, there is no single group which finds itself in the position of providing a demographic nucleus around which other nationalities are arranged as satellites. In relation to this central fact, several important points emerge, which can be illustrated by reference to the census results of 1981 (see Statistical Survey below).

The census of 31 March 1981 recorded that, of the total population of Yugoslavia of 22.4m., 36.3% or some 8.1m. were Serbs. The Croats constituted 19.7% of the population, Muslims 8.9%, Slovenes 7.8%, Albanians 7.7%, Macedonians 6.0%, Yugoslavs 5.4%, Montenegrins 2.6% and Hungarians 1.9% (with some 427,000 people). Other groups totalled 3.7% of the population.

Within each Republic, the situation varies considerably. In Bosnia-Herzegovina, in 1981, the ethnic Muslims constituted 39.5% of the republican population, the Serbs 32.0% and the Croats 18.4%. The Republic is the official 'home' Republic of the Slav Muslims, in that 81.5% of all Yugoslavia's ethnic Muslims resided there. In Croatia, the Croats accounted for 75.1% of the population and 78% of all Yugoslav Croats were within its borders. The Serbs constituted 11.6% of the republican population. In Macedonia, 67.0% of the population were ethnic Macedonians and 19.8% Albanian, but 95.5% of all Yugoslavia's Macedonians were found within the Republic. In Montenegro, 68.5% of the population were Montenegrin and they, in turn, constituted 69.2% of Yugoslavia's total Montenegrin population. Also, 13.4% of the population was Muslim and 6.5% Albanian. In Slovenia, the most homogeneous part of Yugoslavia, 90.5% of the population of the Republic was Slovene and 91.7% of all Yugoslav Slovenes resided there.

In the Republic of Serbia, according to the 1981 census, Serbs constituted 66.4% of the total population, Albanians 14.0%, Yugoslavs 4.7% and Hungarians 4.3%. Of all Yugoslavia's Serbs, 75.9% lived within the borders of the 'home' Republic. Within inner Serbia or Serbia proper (that is, excluding the Autonomous Provinces of Kosovo and Vojvodina), the Serbs constituted 85.4% of the population and accounted for 59.8% of all Serbs. In Vojvodina, too, Serbs were the major ethnic group, accounting for 54.4% of the provincial population (and 13.6% of all Serbs); since the Second World War the Hungarian population has declined and only accounted for 18.9% of the population. In Kosovo, however, Albanians were the main ethnic group, constituting 77.4% of the population, and they formed 70.9% of the total population of Yugoslav Albanians. The Serbs provided 13.2% of the population of Kosovo.

Thus, considering the situation of the Serbs as a starting point for consideration of the nationality question in Yugoslavia, it can be seen that, although the Serbs are clearly the largest ethnic group within the Yugoslav federation, they are far from constituting an overall majority. Furthermore, Serbs, more than any other group, are scattered in significant numbers throughout the federation. In particular, there are significant Serb minorities in the Republics of Bosnia-Herzegovina, where they make up nearly one-third, and Croatia, where they constitute roughly one-eighth of the total.

Even within the Republic of Serbia itself, the Serbs provide only about two-thirds of the total population. The importance of large minorities of Albanians and Hungarians was recognized by the existence of the two 'Autonomous Provinces', of Kosovo and the Vojvodina, until the revision of the republican Constitution in 1990 (the principle remained established in the federal Constitution). Within Kosovo, Serbs are a rather small minority in relation to the Albanian majority; in the Vojvodina, the extreme diversity of the ethnic groups leaves Serbs with little over one-half of the total population.

The diaspora of the Serbs throughout the federation contrasts strongly with the spatial concentration of Slovenes and Macedonians, the preponderant majority of which are found within their 'home' Republics. As indicated above, around 95% of all the Macedonians who live in Yugoslavia, and 92% of all the Slovenes, actually reside in the Republics of Macedonia and Slovenia, respectively. Neither of these groups, therefore, can be found as a significant minority in any of the other Republics of the federation.

The situation is very different in the Republic of Bosnia-Herzegovina. In this case, there is no nationality which forms a majority within the Republic. The Serb population accounted for less than one-third of the republican total and the Croat minority for less than one-fifth. Even the dominant Bosnian Muslims (South Slavs who adopted Islam under the Ottomans) amounted to less than 40% of the population of the Republic. Bosnia-Herzegovina is certainly the 'home' Republic of the Slav Muslims, containing more than 80% of their number. However, it cannot be considered a 'Muslim republic' in anything like the way in which Macedonia is a 'Macedonian republic'.

The situation outlined in the information above has certainly changed since the census of 1981, both through natural increases and decreases and through migration. It is known that, on the whole, Slovenes and Croats tend to have somewhat lower rates of natural increase than the federal average, and Albanians and Muslims (particularly the former) somewhat higher rates. Consequently, it was expected that the census of 1991 would confirm that there are now more Albanians in Yugoslavia than Slovenes. Most significantly, the differential migration of other nationalities from the Kosovo region will probably have greatly increased the Albanian demographic advantage there.

There have been continuing pressures which are expected to erode the numbers of the minor national groups, both absolutely and relatively, throughout the federation. The most important of the problems is that these nationalities are more prone than larger groups to marry outside their own members. Their children are likely to abandon the minority ethnic identity, preferring either to be assimilated with the locally dominant nationality or to adopt a neutral 'Yugoslav' designation.

SOME BACKGROUND CONSIDERATIONS

It would be inappropriate in this context to attempt a full account of the historical dimension to the nationality issue. Nevertheless, a full understanding of this complex matter and the capacity to make any sense of how the politics of nationality are likely to develop in the future demand an awareness of some important historical background.

The most important factor to shape the pattern of ethnic dispersion in the Balkans was the division of the Peninsula, from the Middle Ages to the end of the First World War, between two great multi-national empires. As it affected Yugoslavia, the area now composed by Slovenia, Croatia and the Vojvodina was incorporated into the Habsburgs' Austro-Hungarian Empire and most of the remainder (Bosnia-Herzegovina, Macedonia and the greater part of Serbia) was part of the Turkish Ottoman Empire. Although retaining a degree of nominal independence throughout, the Kingdom of Montenegro was, to some extent, part of the Turkish 'sphere of influence'. Following a successful uprising against the Ottoman Government, the 'Sublime Porte', in 1815, the Serbs also steadily expanded their own independence during the 19th century. This division was reinforced by, and partly related to, an earlier division of east and west. The Ottomans expanded their European empire at the expense of the East Roman or Byzantine Empire, from whom the Serbs, Macedonians and Montenegrins received Eastern Orthodox Christianity and culture. The Habsburgs were the Roman Catholic power to defend the West against the Muslim advance, and they ruled over the Slovenes, Croats and Hungarians, who were adherents of Latin Christianity.

Throughout this imperial phase of their history, however, the South Slav lands were subject to numerous forces which stimulated the migration of their peoples. War and rebellion resulted in repeated and, occasionally, massive migrations of threatened or defeated populations. On the lands which these migrants vacated, the imperial powers settled other groups to till the soil, pay taxes and provide military manpower. Administrators, soldiers, religious functionaries, traders and groups of specialized artisans migrated throughout the Peninsula, to wherever they were sent by the State or Church, or to wherever their services found a profitable welcome. Thus, the Banat (of which the Vojvodina was a part) gained its name from being a border territory, a march, of the Hungarian realm. The Serb areas along the Croatian-Bosnian border owe their origin to the settlement policies of the Habsburgs, which aimed to bolster defences against the Turks.

The struggles for independence did not end this process, but, rather, complicated it, as new states sought to 'rectify' patterns of settlement to their own advantage. Indeed, the process of nation-building (or 'ethnogenesis') might be considered to be one of the most important undertakings of the Communist regime, installed after 1945. Three of the Yugoslav nations (Macedonians, Montenegrins and Slav Muslims) can be regarded as being, in large measure, the fruit of that effort. A discussion of the politics of nationality in Yugoslavia, therefore, has to contend not only with complex patterns of dispersion rooted in history, but also with continuing and very active processes of ethnogenesis.

When a united South Slav ('Yugoslav'—the name of the country was changed from the Kingdom of Serbs, Croats and Slovenes to Yugoslavia in 1929) state was established at the end of the First World War, the difficulty of reconciling the aspirations of different nationalities within the state soon became apparent. In particular, there was an obvious clash between the long-cherished Serb ambition to unite into one state all Serbs ('Greater Serbia'), and the historical memories of a struggle to protect the autonomy of the nation from the imperial powers, which shaped Slovene and Croat perceptions of what the new state should be. The manner in which the Kingdom of Serbs, Croats and Slovenes was created, however, ensured effective Serb dominance. A heavily centralized, unitary state was imposed, under the 'Vidovdan' Constitution, despite the vigorous demands for a federal structure advanced by the smaller nationalities. Only the former Serbian Kingdom brought into the new state an effective army, which had fought on the side of the victorious Allies or Entente Powers of the First World War, and the Crown was taken by the Serbian dynasty of Karadjordjević.

The inter-war political history of the country can be viewed as an attempt to secure a more acceptable constitutional settlement for non-Serbs. The unhappy, and largely unsuccessful, character of that struggle can be regarded as one of the most significant factors to facilitate the collapse of 'the first Yugoslavia' under the impact of the Second World War and the invasion by the Axis powers, in 1941. This inter-War experience also gave rise to the appallingly bloody civil war between Serbian Royalist and Communist forces, which followed the invasion, and which overlaid the fight for liberation from the occupier.

Consequently, there was extreme sensitivity to everything relating to nationality and the political autonomy of nations. Therefore, great care went into the construction of the new Yugoslavia, following the defeat of Nazism. Even as early as November 1942, when the Communists organized the first meeting of an Anti-Fascist Council for the National Liberation of Yugoslavia (usually known by its Yugoslav acronym, AVNOJ), the aspirant post-War rulers had declared themselves firmly in favour of a federal Constitution. The form of that federation was carefully worked out in the three years leading up to the promulgation of the new Constitution, in January 1946.

Two Theories of the Yugoslav State

In spite of the care which went into the construction of the new Yugoslav federation, or perhaps because of it, contradictory theories have emerged regarding the principle intentions underlying it. In considering the current situation, it does not matter which, if either, of these theories is correct. The matter could only be resolved by more historical research than is available at present. The important fact is that the result has been a highly ambiguous structure, for which there are two main interpretations. This ambiguity posed such questions as whether the purpose of the federal structure adopted for Yugoslavia, in 1946, was to contain Serbia or to give adequate weight to the interests of Serbia? Some claim that the federation was constructed so as to make impossible the kind of hegemony enjoyed by one nation over the others in the pre-War period, by ensuring that those units which were principally settled by Serbs were outnumbered by those in which Serbs were either largely absent or reduced to a minority status. The alternative view was that the Constitution was framed in such a way as to ensure that, as the most numerous nation and the group which had been forced to

abandon its central historical aspiration by assimilating to a Yugoslav state, Serb sensitivities would be respected by ensuring that their interests were always given adequate weight.

According to the first theory, that of containment, the two Autonomous Provinces were a device to divide the historic Serb lands. Two areas were thus created in which other nationalities were sufficiently numerous to ensure that their voices would always be heard. The fact that Serbs are not a majority of the population of Bosnia-Herzegovina could also be interpreted as an attempt to neutralize Serbs living there, so placing Bosnia-Herzegovina with the 'non-Serb' interests (Croatia, Macedonia and Slovenia).

Alternatively, according to the second theory, that of adequate weight, the creation of the Autonomous Provinces was a device to ensure that Serbs were effectively given three votes in federal institutions, in place of the one which they would have if all Serbs were simply contained in a single republic. By this theory also, Bosnia-Herzegovina was viewed as 'pro-Serb', as the Serb minority is sufficiently numerous there to ensure that any representative coming from the Republic would always need to give voice to Serb interests. Furthermore, Serbia was always assured of the support it traditionally received from the Serb Montenegrins.

This discussion intensified during 1990–91, with the debates about the need for constitutional reform. It serves to emphasize one very important feature of the nationalities problem in the country. The unit of account in Yugoslav post-Second World War politics was the nation: that is to say, the key element in these calculations is the nation, and not individuals who happen to have national identities. The entire manner in which the problem has been conceptualized and discussed in Yugoslavia, focuses upon the need to protect notional rights of nations and to balance their interests. On this point hang many of the most distinctive features of Yugoslavia's post-War political history, and many of its current problems.

Whatever the intentions of the original framers of the Constitution, with respect to the two theories of the Yugoslav state mentioned above, these are now, to all intents and purposes, irrelevant. However, their insistence on taking the nation as the basic unit of political account, has had at least two important results.

Possibly the most significant consequence of this way of looking at things was that a group simply did not figure in the determination of the key political decisions unless it was a nation. Consequently, three substantial groups were constituted as nations, during the post-War period: Macedonians, Montenegrins and Slav Muslims. These had no clearly developed identity as nations before the Second World War. Although the Macedonians had a nascent national movement, which emerged during the last quarter of the 19th century, the Karadjordjević state always insisted that Macedonians were really 'South Serbians' and attempted to enforce that identity with every means of political and economic coercion at its disposal. Montenegrins often thought of themselves (and were so identified by others) as Serbs, although they enjoyed a history of distinct, if precarious, independence. The term 'Muslim' was not previously regarded as conveying anything other than a specifically religious allegiance. The federalization of Yugoslavia after 1945, in conjunction with the predominance of the view that the political unit of account was the nation, resulted in a rapid process of ethnogenesis in each of these cases (varying to some extent in its effectiveness). Whether or not it was the case before, three new nations now exist in Yugoslavia.

A second important consequence of this view of politics was that the structure of Yugoslav politics moved from a position of *de facto* balance, with respect to Serbia, to one of containment. Particularly important in this process was the growth in the numbers of ethnic Albanians within the federation, especially within Kosovo, and their growing political self-awareness. This is entirely understandable. If the rules of Yugoslav politics specify that the protagonists must be 'nations', then a precondition for the political existence of nearly 2m. Albanians becomes their recognition as a nation. This meant that, before the effective abolition of the Autonomous Provinces in the revised Serbian Constitution of 1990, Kosovo was in the process of moving to the non-Serb group from the pro-Serb one.

The Position of Serbia

In many respects, the position of Serbia within Yugoslavia is central to an understanding of the entire nationality problem in the country. That is not to say, of course, that Serbs are to be blamed for problems of this kind. However, Serbs have increasingly come to see themselves as politically isolated within the federation and as systematically disadvantaged. Social-scientific investigation does not support this view. A survey of the patterns of conflict and cohesion in Yugoslavia after 1966 showed that, in the principal instances of inter-republican conflict during that time, there was no single configuration of interest groups which could be detected (S. Burg—see Bibliography, p. 361). A more recent investigation, of the composition of Yugoslav élites, revealed that Serbs were systematically over-represented in almost every institutional area (L. Cohen). If the gibes of the more extreme Serb nationalists regarding Tito's Croatian background and Kardelj's Slovene origins are fundamentally misplaced, however, why do Serbs persist in adopting what generally appears to outsiders to be a rather paranoid view of their situation as a nation within the Yugoslav federation?

The answer to this question can be found at two levels. Possibly the more important is the dispersion of the Serbs. The 24% (according to the 1981 census) of their number who reside in republics other than the Serbian Republic have come to feel more and more that they have no rights in the state. If Croatia, for example, is primarily a Croat republic (a homeland above all for Croats and legitimately run by and for Croats) then Serbs are, at best, permanently marginalized and, at worst, live under a constant threat. Even discounting the more sensational interpretations put about by the Milošević faction in Serbia, concerning the character of the Croatian regime elected in 1990 (that it was a restoration of the war-time Ustaša regime), it is hard to avoid the suggestion that any who are not Croats are second-class citizens. The Serbs of Croatia may live in Croatia, but there is a real sense in which it can never be 'their' Republic.

In addition to this, the growth of regional autonomy under the 1974 Constitution meant that the Autonomous Provinces became republics, in all but name. Consequently, even within the Republic of Serbia itself ('their' Republic), Serbs felt themselves to be disadvantaged, to the benefit of other nationalities. At the end of the 1980s central Serbian control was no longer assured in Vojvodina and was fast becoming, at best, nominal in Kosovo.

Instead of a situation in which Serbian interests could rely on the effective representation of a balanced half of the federal units, it seemed that only in one out of the eight units did Serbs feel their rights as a nation were likely to be regarded at all. Whether or not this description of the situation is an exaggeration is irrelevant. With some exceptions and qualifications, increasing regional autonomy

(seen as desirable and welcomed elsewhere) was perceived as a definite threat by Serbs.

The Serb response came in two forms. The revision of the republican Constitution, finally enacted in 1990, aimed to reassert the control of the Republic over its constituent Autonomous Provinces, effectively eliminating their autonomy. In addition, Serbs constantly sought to buttress the power of the federation as an effective counterweight to that of the republics. Federal authority was regarded as the sole instrument at the Serbs' disposal by which force could be brought to bear on the other Republics, in order to defend the interests of the Serb minorities.

This assessment of political priorities is, to some extent, shared by other, similarly dispersed nations within Yugoslavia, especially the Montenegrins and Bosnian Muslims. However, it became the fundamental of Serb politics during the 1980s.

'PLAYING THE NATIONALIST CARD'

The federal programme of reforms, introduced under the leadership of Ante Marković after 1989, was seen, both inside Yugoslavia and abroad, as offering a way out of the deep-seated economic problems which beset the country (for details, see the essay below and the Bibliography—particularly H. Lydall, D. Dyker, and Allcock, Milivojević and Horton). Even so, progress towards the implementation of this programme was entirely obstructed by the inability of Yugoslavia's politicians to move towards any solution to the constitutional problem of the proper relationship between republics within the federation. Without a framework for legitimate government, there could be no effective enforcement of economic reform.

For as long as the Party, the League of Communists of Yugoslavia (LCY), was strong enough to impose some form of socialist rhetoric on Yugoslav politics and to retain its hold on power, the fissiparous tendencies within the system were contained and containable. As Yugoslavia participated in the general collapse of Stalinism, however, and control from the centre was eroded, the logic of its internal contradictions (and especially those relating to the ethnic diversity of the country) began to emerge. Socialist politics was replaced by nationalist politics as the more or less natural medium for the expression of political differences (for a consideration of the conditions under which nationalist rhetoric might be considered as 'natural' in contemporary Yugoslav politics, see the Bibliography—Allcock, Milivojević and Horton).

Under these conditions, many insisted that the problems of Yugoslavia were inherently insoluble and that the only way forward was to recognize that Yugoslavia, as it was constituted, was not a workable system. The rational response to the situation was to allow as peaceable a movement as possible towards the disintegration of the Yugoslav state. This leads to consideration of the relevance of the metaphor of 'playing the nationalist card' for the understanding of Yugoslav politics.

In many card games, play continues until somebody produces the unbeatable card. The holder of this card determines the course of the game; once it is played the outcome is a foregone conclusion. It has become a commonplace, in the discussion of the Yugoslav situation, to treat nationalist definitions of the nature of political problems as just such a natural determinant of the shape of politics in Yugoslavia.

The problem which any sociologist would have with this definition of the situation, is that it presupposes that the underlying reality of Yugoslav society is constituted by its pattern of national differences. It assumes that these have been temporarily overlaid by economic or ideological surface forms, and postulates that these have now been stripped away, revealing the underlying and irresistibly determining factor of nationality. The appeal to nationality in politics, the playing of 'the nationalist card', means that the 'game' will have to come to its end. There will have to be a new dealing of hands, a new political and economic arrangement.

The use of metaphors in the sociological analysis of politics has its limitations and can sometimes mislead. The central argument here is that the limitations of this particular metaphor, which, although it is both popular and compelling as an image of the future of Yugoslav politics, is potentially thoroughly inept. There are two grounds upon which the metaphor of 'playing the nationalist card' can be challenged. One can do so by reference to the underlying continuity of problems and processes in the Balkans and by reference to the unstable nature of national identities. The first of these challenges is best considered by republic, on the general premiss that, if the 'nationalist card' has been played and the 'game' of federal Yugoslavia must end, the newly independent states cannot begin a completely new game. All the principal nationalities will continue to confront the same long-term historical problems which they confronted in the past, and may even fare worse than in the post-1945 confederal Yugoslavia. Finally, after the assessment of the situation in each of the six Republics, the unstable nature of national identities must be considered.

Slovenia

Slovenia has generally been thought to be the prime candidate for easy separation from the Yugoslav federation. There are no large Slovene minorities living elsewhere in Yugoslavia and relatively few of the Republic's inhabitants are of other nationalities. This assumption seemed to be confirmed by the readier acceptance of a withdrawal from Slovenia by the Yugoslav People's Army, in July 1991, than from Croatia. The manifesto on which the Democratic Opposition of Slovenia (DEMOS) coalition won the republican elections of April 1990 assumed a gradual and relatively painless separation of the Republic from its neighbours. Following the referendum on independence, conducted in the Republic in December 1990, the new Slovenian Government began to prepare contingency plans, which anticipated eventual disengagement from the federation at the end of June 1991. As time passed, however, it became clear that Slovenian independence could not offer a clean break with the past. At least two of the region's long-term problems came to demand attention, even in advance of the attempted separation.

The first of these relates problems centrally to the issue of nationality. The Slovene national movement of the 19th century encountered, as its central task, the need to resist pressure towards Germanization. For as long as Slovenes were incorporated into the Austro-Hungarian Empire, this pressure affected strongly the entire conduct of politics and economic life. It went well beyond simple linguistic domination. At the heart of Slovene political culture, for over one century, has been the effort to create a vigorous 'civil society'. That is, to create a network of institutions, below the level of the state, which would constitute a tissue of specifically Slovene mediums for co-operative action. In large measure, it is this insistence upon the vital importance of civil society which has been Slovenia's most significant contribution to the recent restructuring of Yugoslav politics.

The Slovenes have, in part, based their recent movement towards independence upon the desire to escape from the domination of the Serbo-Croat language. However, it is unquestionably the case that it has been easier for Slovenes to secure a place for their own culture within a Slav state than within a predominantly German state. The severing of the links between Slovenia and the rest of Yugoslavia would, in all probability, reverse that process. As economic liberalization was encouraged, under the Marković reforms, the new group to become most evident in Ljubljana business circles was the Austrians. Under these circumstances, some Slovene intellectuals have had cause to reflect upon the steady decline of Slovene communities in both Italy and Austria, which have been compelled to face, without protection, the threat of larger and more powerful linguistic groups.

If, at the level of national identity, Slovenian independence would mean the revival of an older and long-term problem, at the level of politics it would pose a new one. The ethnic homogeneity of the Slovenian Republic has facilitated the creation of a political myth, that of a politically homogeneous nation. For as long as Slovenia has been lodged securely within Yugoslavia, the nationalist movement has been able to feed upon the need for a united voice. This proved to be extremely effective, giving rise to the DEMOS coalition of six parties, which installed the first non-Communist government to be elected in Yugoslavia since the Second World War. The drive towards independence, however, successfully masked some deep divisions between the parties to that coalition, regarding the kind of society which should be the goal of Slovenian independence. By May 1991 DEMOS had begun to show the fragility of a unity which was based solely upon the issue of constitutional change (in December the coalition finally split). Beyond independence itself, there is no Slovenian consensus about the direction of change for Slovenian society.

The coherence created by the independence movement, however, concealed a society which is deeply differentiated. This is not surprising from a sociological point of view. Slovenia is the economically most developed region of Yugoslavia; and development, typically, coincides with structural complexity. A politics which is appropriate to the state of Slovenian society will be one which gives place to the articulation of a wide variety of interests. For all its small size, the Slovenian economy is a remarkably diverse one, ranging from high-tech industry to peasant agriculture. Independence will mean the rapid rediscovery of problems which hitherto have been concealed within the managerial apparatus of Communist politics, but which suddenly require recognition, redefinition and the creation of new institutional mediums.

Croatia

The other leading contender for secession from the Yugoslav federation was Croatia. If anything, Croatian criticism of Yugoslavia has been more sustained and radical than that voiced by the Slovenes. Between the World Wars Yugoslav politics was fraught by Serb–Croat rivalry, occasioned by the undoubted Serb hegemony under the Vidovdan Constitution. For all the discredit which attached to its collaboration with the invader and with fascism, the wartime Ustaša regime held out the possibility that there could be an Independent State of Croatia. Since the reconstitution of Yugoslavia along federal lines, the Croats also found repeated cause for dissatisfaction over the degree of autonomy allowed to the Republics. This was particularly, and most memorably, the case during the *Maspok* period, which was suppressed in 1971–72.

During the post-war years the form in which Croat dissatisfaction has been most typically expressed, has been the sense of economic grievance. Croat politicians have not tired of noting the fact that as one of the more economically developed regions of the federation, they have carried a disproportionate burden of taxation, extracted in order to support the underdeveloped regions. The recipients of this federal largesse, they have alleged, have not been distinguished by the efficiency with which they have used it. In short, Croatian wealth has been wasted in order to finance egalitarian gestures which have been of dubious economic value.

As the Tudjman regime flirted openly with secession and then declared independence, in June 1991, however, these accusations lost their force. Croatia was immediately, and rather savagely, hit by the consequences of the rising civil disorder and, eventually, conflict, which followed the threat of secession. During the summer season, in mid-1991, foreign tourists abandoned the Adriatic littoral. The alternative to access to only a share of foreign currency income within the federation, therefore, may not be (in the short term, at least) unrestricted access to 'Croatian earnings' in an independent Croatia, but the collapse of the Adriatic tourist market. This would mean no earnings at all. The physical damage and disruption of the civil war further affected the economic situation and prospects of Croatia.

The extent of the economic integration into a wider Yugoslav economic system of several large, Croatian-based enterprises, such as the petroleum and chemicals conglomerate, INA, and the engineering firm Rade Koncar, caused great concern. A Government which came to power upon an economic platform of rapid and radical privatization suddenly found itself advocating measures to ensure the effective state protection of a 'Croatian' economy. Economic autarky increasingly seemed to be a chimera.

Even the notion that independence would provide relief from the drain of resources into the underdeveloped areas is now exposed as severely problematic. The ethnic unrest among the Serb minority, along Croatia's Bosnian border, which was important in the drift towards civil war, drew attention not only to their demographic distinctiveness, but also to their poverty. Assuming that the Serbian 'Krajina' could be brought into an independent Croatian state, the result would be the need to deal with a permanent 'Croatian Kosovo', and not only in the sense that the new state would harbour within it an area of constant ethnic dissent. Many of these communes, in their bleak *karst* wildernesses, far from the comfortable tourist zones of the coast or from the sophistication of Zagreb, suffer levels of poverty little removed from that endured by the Albanians of Kosovo. Under conditions of independence, their development, as well as their discipline, would become an exclusively Croatian responsibility (the intra-republican dimension of the situation in Yugoslavia is often neglected—see J. Allcock, 1983).

Montenegro

Montenegro is a part of Yugoslavia generally neglected by outside observers, possibly because it is often taken for granted as no more than an extension of Serbia. In fact, its situation is very interesting; and developments there can, by no means, be related directly to those in Serbia. In relation to the possible disintegration of the federation, Montenegrin interests should be recognized as quite specific.

The tendency to reduce Montenegro to an outpost of Serbia is understandable, especially as Montenegrins are the most dispersed of the nations in the federation, with only some 69% of them resident in the Republic itself. Consequently, they have shared the Serbian preference for a strong centre in relation to the republics. Before 1918 the Montenegrins had their own state and had long been an independent kingdom; even so, they have always been torn between a political leaning towards Serbia and an economic orientation on the Adriatic. The dilemma became pronounced during the 1980s because of the rapid development of the Montenegrin economy, especially through the means of international tourism. The importance of this regional economic identity is suggested by the observer status which the Republic secured at the 'Alpe-Adria' discussions of countries in the region. It would certainly be strengthened by current plans to improve the international communications network along the Adriatic coast. These developments would become particularly significant if current changes in Albania permit a substantial reintegration of the Albanian economy into wider regional and world economic exchanges.

The often-supposed, and frequently exaggerated, cultural ties between Serbs and Montenegrins, then, are by no means the only incentives which might lead the Republic to be a strong advocate of its continuing integration into some kind of Yugoslav grouping.

Bosnia and Herzegovina

The future for Bosnia-Herzegovina is problematic either within a continuing Yugoslavia or after its dissolution. Should something like the present federation remain in being, as the ethnically most diverse of the Republics, Bosnia-Herzegovina would remain the subject of pressure from others, anxious to assert control over or to support the interests of their co-nationals. In a divided Yugoslavia, the primary issue to be determined would be the fate of Bosnia-Herzegovina. The geographical distribution of the various ethnic groups within the Republic is such that no simple territorial division is possible; also, Muslims do not see their best interests as served by their reduction to the status of second class citizens within anybody else's 'home' republic. There is no doubt that Bosnia-Herzegovina could only be divided as the consequence of war.

The hard choices facing Bosnians, and their ambivalent position in relation to the outcomes sought by Serbs and Croats in particular, is clearly illustrated by their political behaviour. Elaborate attempts have been made within the Republic's Constitution to preserve the delicate ethnic balance within the organs of representation and government. Only Bosnia-Herzegovina has preserved at the republican level the complex mechanism of a collective presidency, filled according to a fixed ethnic key, which characterized the federation as a whole. Within the bargaining process which stood at the centre of the attempt to break the constitutional deadlock of May 1991, the representatives of Bosnia-Herzegovina were in favour of a continuing Yugoslav federation (suggesting support for the Serbian position on the Constitution), but highly critical of the way in which military intervention was advocated by the Serbs in order to secure order. By the end of 1991, however, consensus had broken down and the Serbs were isolated.

Macedonia

The Macedonians find themselves still with a continuation of their age-old dilemma. They find themselves threatened by both Serbian expansionist ambitions (the more radical Serb nationalists still regard them as 'South Serbians') and by Bulgarian aspirations for the restoration of the 'San Stefano' boundaries (the 1878 Treaty of San Stefano, superseded by the resolutions of the Congress of Berlin, endowed Bulgaria with most of Macedonia). Both parties are likely to deny Macedonian claims to a proper national identity. Greece, too, has traditional claims in the area and also denies the existence of a distinct Macedonian nationality. During the civil war of 1991, and after Macedonia's September declaration of sovereignty, Greece, alone among the

EC countries, tended to support Serbia. Macedonians, therefore, had an incentive to support the status quo.

If the dissolution of Yugoslavia left Macedonia in a federation dominated by Serbia, Macedonians would run the risk of a return to their pre-War situation. This is already threatened very explicitly in some Serb nationalist propaganda, which pointedly includes maps of the 14th-century empire of Car Dušan Nemanja. Alternatively, to claim independence, would leave the Macedonians without allies against both Bulgarian territorial ambitions and, which is more immediately problematic, the pressure from a growing Albanian population in the west of the Republic. Faced with these unpalatable choices, Macedonian politicians tended to reveal their relative risk assessments as a fairly consistent backing for the Serb position on the future of federation. However, in September 1991, with Slovenia and Croatia asserting their own separation from the Yugoslav state and the rise of 'Great Serb' nationalism, a referendum in Macedonia overwhelmingly supported independence for the Republic. In January 1992, however, although Bulgaria gave the Republic recognition, Greece ensured that the EC did not.

Serbia

Assessment of the Serbian view of the future of Yugoslavia is often obscured by the personalization of issues in the media of mass communication. Following the death of Tito, Slobodan Milošević was rapidly identified as a potential 'strong man' to take over the reins of power. Even though subsequent events worked consistently to ensure that it would be difficult for him to develop a political career outside Serbia, the legacy of this early perception has remained implicit in any discussion of Serb politics in the Western press. Abandoning this impression was not made easier by the fact that this portrayal of his political ambition serves the interests of politicians elsewhere in Yugoslavia, who stand to gain from exaggerating the dangers of Serbian 'hegemonism'. Clientelism is, generally, an important feature of Yugoslav politics, but it is important to realize that the phenomenon is by no means confined to the Milošević coterie.

It is essential to recognize that there are solid structural reasons why the Serbian approach to politics, and to the nature of any Yugoslav state, is at odds with the position taken by several other groups. As has already been indicated, the dispersal of Serbs throughout the federation, and the size and local concentration of these Serb minorities, ensures that Serb politicians have a natural and continuing interest in the fate of their compatriots, regardless of any particular constitutional arrangements which may be devised for regulating the relationship between republics. This interventionist stance is reinforced by the tendency, which has been noted already, to treat nations, rather than individuals, as the subjects of politics in Yugoslavia, since the Second World War. It is not necessary to consent to the rather paranoid version of Yugoslav politics, espoused by Serb nationalists, which portrays the Yugoslav state as a mechanism for the 'containment' of the Serbian nation. Nevertheless, it is undoubtedly the case that the AVNOJ concept of Yugoslavia as a union of peoples does, inevitably, tend to turn Serbia into a victim of the system.

The tragic truth for the Serbs is that Yugoslavia offers the only means by which it might be possible to unite into one state the majority, if not all, Serbs. However, the disposition of Serbia's neighbours is certainly not towards the enhancement of Serbia's position within the federation. Furthermore, several aspects of the demographic and political situation point strongly towards a weakening of it, especially in Kosovo. The abrasively confrontational conduct of the Milošević regime, repeatedly pushing the entire federation to the brink, and beyond, of civil war, is based upon the perception that only through the retention of a strong Party and a strong Army at the centre, would it be possible to protect the Serb diaspora from the *de facto* disenfranchisement, which the move towards confederation threatened.

The Instability of National Identity

Surveying the several regions of Yugoslavia, therefore, it is evident that any attempt to 'play the nationalist card' and bring to an end the federation and the existing rules of Yugoslav politics would not result in a new deal, in which those involved would improve their positions. Any new arrangement is likely to involve similar problems and advantages to those which existed before, by virtue of underlying structural continuities which must re-emerge. For several of the nationalities, their position would almost certainly be weakened. The bleakest view, which was increasingly realistic after mid-1991, was that the only likely alternative to something resembling the existing federal arrangement was war.

The metaphor of 'playing the nationalist card', of terminating the game of Yugoslav politics by confronting the old order with the unanswerable, basic reality of ethnicity, can be misleading for another reason. The image presupposes that nationalities are fixed, natural components of the political landscape, along the lines of Durkheimian 'social facts'. Nationalities do not, however, exist in that way. They are plastic, fluid and dynamic.

It is the case that an unrecognized element of impermanence hangs over every one of Yugoslavia's national groups. They have not always been what they think they are; and there is no reason to suppose that the identities which they possess today are any more immutable. No nationality in Yugoslavia, in the modern sociological sense of that word, is more than 200 years old. Montenegro had a tribal organization up until the 19th century. Macedonians and the Slav Muslims have only been recognized as 'nations' during the post-Second World War period. There is no evidence that the process of ethnogenesis is completed in any of these cases. The different Muslim groups, for example, whether Bosnian Muslims, Albanians, Turks, Pomaks or Muslim Roma, are not always distinct from each other. Sometimes the political and social situation favoured one registration or the other, and sometimes the dominant nationality of a region absorbs a minority. Furthermore, as another example of the acuteness of nationalist sensibilities in the Balkans, many of the Roma of Macedonia and Kosovo now claim to be Egyptians, 'descendants of the Pharaohs', and were registered as such, in Macedonia, for the census of 1991. Even with the supposedly more firmly established groups, it is possible to show that the criteria of identification are not fixed and static. One illustration of the factors involved will serve to make this general point in the present context.

The essential components of national identity are typically drawn from language, religion and a sense of a common cultural heritage. These combine in varying degrees of salience in the several Yugoslav nationalities. It is instructive to ask what might happen in the Balkans if, for one reason or another, the religious component of nationality became dominant. What would be the consequence of the enhancement of the specifically confessional element of 'Muslim' identity, so that membership of the community of belief became more important than, say, a common language? Two currently very distinct ethnic groups share a general identification with Islam: the Bosnian or Slav Muslim and the Albanian. The suggestion is not that 'Muslim' and 'Albanian' might cease altogether to be clearly distinct designators of identity, but that under the circumstances being hypothesized for the moment, it might well become less easy to insist upon the community of cultural heritage which now links 'Muslims' with a wider Serbo-Croat cultural heritage. At the same time, the sharing of a religious faith could become more significant as the frame in which common interests were perceived and more important as the basis of common political action.

Another, equally possible, scenario is that Balkan society might gradually undergo a process of secularization, and the specifically religious connotations of 'Muslim' identity become even more attenuated than they are today. Under these circumstances, it might become progressively more difficult to sustain the claim that Bosnian 'Muslims' are anything more than 'Croats of the Islamic persuasion'. The embryonic ties of political interest which can now be detected between Croats and Muslims could become far more significant as a factor shaping the alignment of ethnic groupings in Yugoslav politics.

These two scenarios are not sociological predictions. Their function is to illustrate forcefully the important claim that ethnogenesis is still a very active and open-ended process in the Balkans as a whole, and in Yugoslavia in particular.

The future of ethnic politics in the region can not be said to be permanently inscribed in the current definitions and distribution of 'nations'.

CONCLUSION

It is not that things never change in the politics of nationality in Yugoslavia. By the beginning of 1991, however, popular wisdom seemed to be giving too great a weight to the idea of the necessary disintegration of the Yugoslav federation. This outcome is not altogether unlikely and, indeed, was seeming increasingly possible, by October 1991, so volatile was the situation in that country. Nevertheless, two things, which are emphasized here, were certain.

For as long as there is a Yugoslavia everybody there will remain a member of a national minority, for the foreseeable future. Furthermore, there is no way in which the playing of 'the nationalist card' can end the issues and problems of Yugoslav politics. Should the Yugoslav federation disappear, its successor states would still perpetuate within themselves problems relating to the nature and relationship of nationalities which would be very similar to those upon which the post-War settlement is widely expected to founder.

The Economy
Dr DAVID A. DYKER

INTRODUCTION

By 1991 Yugoslavia was confronting its deepest crisis since the Nazi German invasion of 1941. The crisis was not only political, but economic in nature. On the economic side, there has been continuous crisis since the breaking of the external debt-service shock of 1982. However, the origins of that shock must be sought in earlier periods and, to a degree, in the whole pattern of the economic development of the country since the formation of Communist Yugoslavia, in 1945.

The Yugoslav Communist Party was independent of the Communist Party of the Soviet Union (CPSU) and enjoyed considerable popular support among the Yugoslav population, on account of its leadership of the Second World War partisan movement. However, over the initial post-War period of 1945–48, it was distinguished by a passion for imitating all things Soviet, including grossly over-centralized five-year planning exercises. When Stalin denounced Tito, in 1948, and declared an economic blockade of Yugoslavia, following a period of worsening relations, he cited Tito's revisionism as a root cause of the rift. It is difficult to take this charge seriously, certainly on the economic side, and, indeed, the Yugoslav leadership initially reacted by even closer adherence to the Soviet model. The disastrous collectivization campaign of 1949, which brought the Yugoslav peasantry to the brink of insurrection, was the result. It was towards the end of that year that a process of reappraisal began, which eventually produced a complete rejection of the Soviet economic-planning style. By 1953 directive planning had been abandoned. Astonishingly, for a Communist government in the early 1950s, the Yugoslav Communists publicly proclaimed the need to abandon target planning completely, and to reinstate the market as the focal point of economic activity. To reinforce the socialist credentials of all this, workers' councils were created in each enterprise, with the prerogative, theoretically at least, of making all major decisions of business strategy.

While the break with the Soviet economic system was complete, however, that with Soviet development strategy was not. The Soviet-Marxist tendency to overemphasize industrial development, in particular, heavy industrial development, was almost as marked in Yugoslavia, in the 1950s and early 1960s, as it had been in the USSR, in the 1930s. However, this was more dangerous in the Yugoslav case, in that the weight of comparative advantage for Yugoslavia clearly lay with agriculture and services. Nevertheless, market-socialist Yugoslavia performed very impressively, in growth terms, in 1953–65. A certain element of political enthusiasm apart, however, that growth performance was based largely on the massive transfer of unskilled labour, from the over-populated countryside into the towns, and the virtually unlimited support which US aid afforded the Yugoslav balance of payments, up to 1961. This latter factor, in turn, made it possible for Yugoslavia to import food, petroleum and equipment at a very low real cost. By the early 1960s the process of indiscriminate transfer of labour from the countryside was clearly approaching its natural limits, while US aid stopped altogether in 1962. The growth strategy based on cheap labour, cheap food and cheap energy was over. Further growth would have to be based on high productivity performance and efficient assimilation of technology.

Yugoslavia was already a market economy, of sorts, by the early 1960s. Theoretically, the reforms of 1965 heralded a transition to a much more 'full-blooded' form of market socialism. The capital-investment sector and, implicitly, growth strategy were now also to be subordinated to the market mechanism, through the development of an autonomous banking system. In this context it is striking that Yugoslavia's failure to make the transition from 'extensive' to 'intensive' growth was almost as complete as that of the Soviet bloc countries, the majority of which continued to struggle with some variant of the central-planning model. The explanation for this is to be found in a complex of interrelated factors, with the political dimension playing a key role. The attempt to extend the market principle into the area of capital formation exacerbated nationality tensions, which, previously, had been, to a degree, repressed or subdued. By the early 1970s this had provoked a reaction which increasingly subordinated the market principle to the principle of the 'planning agreement'. This latter tended to produce a peculiarly Yugoslav pattern of cartelization. At the same time the central Communist leadership placed its faith in regional League of Communists activists, as the cement that would bind multi-national Yugoslavia together. In the event, it was precisely these regional élites who were primarily to blame for the progressive disintegration of central economic policy-making in Yugoslavia, in the 1970s, as they sought to consolidate their own prerogatives. The planning-agreement system proved to be particularly vulnerable in this connection.

The 1970s was a period of faltering growth, which indicated stagnating labour productivity, a loss of technological dynamism and increasing wastefulness in the utilization of material inputs. Behind these unsatisfactory trends lay: failures of industrial policy, as import-substitution programmes, often promoted by regional leaderships, simply created new import needs; failures of foreign trade policy, as plans to transfer resources to 'assured' exports achieved nothing; and failures of regional policy, as development funds were wasted on prestige projects. It was against this background that Yugoslavia had to face the challenges of the 'Oil Crises', significant increases in international petroleum prices, of the 1970s.

The huge escalation in the price of petroleum posed challenges to the efficiency of the Yugoslav economy which it was ill-equipped to meet. More insidiously, the excess supply of petro-dollars in the international banking system, which the Oil Crises produced, made it too easy for medium-developed countries, like Yugoslavia, to ignore underlying structural problems and simply to borrow in order to remain viable. One of the crucial areas that the central authorities lost control of, in the mid-1970s, was the balance of payments. The National Bank of Yugoslavia was unable to prevent enterprises and regional governments continuously borrowing from international bankers, who paid little heed to the likely efficiency with which the funds lent would be used. In 1979 the current-account deficit reached a new record level of US $3,700m.

It was the sharp increase in international interest rates, in 1980, which finally condemned Yugoslavia to international insolvency. Though the current-account deficit was reduced, in the early 1980s, the rapidly growing burden of interest and amortization payments forced the Yugoslav Government to seek rescheduling of the debt, at the end of 1982. The rescheduling was not, in itself, difficult to negotiate and, indeed, Yugoslavia managed to achieve a surplus on the current account of its balance of payments as early as 1983, which was maintained until 1989. In this respect the Yugoslav case differed sharply from the typical Eastern European scenario of the 1980s, in which initial debt-service crisis was followed by pronounced failure to remove current-account deficits, so that total debt continued to grow. In Yugoslavia, by contrast, net debt was reduced by a total of some $3,000m., between 1983 and 1989. This re-establishment of a degree of international financial equilibrium was not, however, without its negative consequences. The improvement in the current account was dependent upon the reduction of imports, including imports of raw materials and equipment, and this was connected to an almost complete cessation of economic growth in Yugoslavia. The failure of the economy to generate any significant new exporting dynamic, following the 'Debt-Shock' period,

indicated a continuing failure to address underlying structural problems, which, in turn, reflected a deepening tendency for the old Titoist one-party system to fragment and lose impetus. Those political trends were also partly responsible for a rapid escalation in the problem of inflation, as regional leaderships used their 'decentralized' prerogative to create primary money as a way of shoring up existing structures. By the end of 1989 the annual rate of inflation had reached 2,500%.

THE MARKOVIĆ PLAN: THE PRINCIPLES

Ante Marković succeeded Branko Mikulić as the Yugoslav prime minister, the President of the Federal Executive Council, at the beginning of 1989. He came to the premiership with a reputation as a highly efficient technocrat, and quickly made it clear that he intended to remain largely aloof from the political and ethnic tensions that were becoming critical in that year. Then, at the end of 1989, he announced a programme of radical economic reforms, to be implemented from 1 January 1990. The key measures, which were influenced by the Polish experience and the ideas of the economist, Geoffrey Sachs, are summarized below (including a number of details, which were subsequent to, but augmented the original proposals):

A new dinar was introduced, to exchange for the old one at the rate of 10,000 old to 1 new;

the new dinar was linked or 'pegged' to the Deutsche Mark at a rate of 7:1;

the new dinar was to be internally convertible, that is, Yugoslav citizens were to be allowed to convert unlimited amounts of dinars into convertible or 'hard' currency, for current-transaction purposes;

imports would be liberalized, although foreign-exchange quotas for broad bands of imports (such as consumer goods) were retained;

a process of deregulation and privatization was initiated, which was to increase the share of the private sector in the Yugoslav economy to some 35%, by 1995, leaving the socialized sector with a reduced, but still substantial, share of the economy. Agencies for restructuring and development, modelled on the German Treuhandanstalt (the government agency responsible for privatization in the former German Democratic Republic—GDR), were to be established at the republican level, to implement privatization plans and restructuring programmes within the socialized sector. There were to be two main models of privatization. According to the first, shares would be sold to employees and former employees of the enterprise to be privatized, at a discount of 30% on nominal value (with an additional percentage point of discount for each year of work service, up to a maximum of 70%). Pension funds and private citizens with no connection with the firm would be permitted to buy shares at a discount of 30%. In order to protect the liquidity of the enterprises concerned, it was stipulated that, while shareholders would have up to 10 years to pay for their shares, they would not receive full dividends until the shares were fully paid for. The alternative model would involve the sale of whole enterprises, normally by public auction, to Yugoslav or foreign individuals or organizations. The proceeds from such sales were to go to regional development funds (distinct from the restructuring agencies), which could then, however, re-invest the money in the privatized firms;

joint-venture regulations were liberalized and it became possible, for the first time, for foreigners to own 100% of Yugoslav companies. These changes represented the main policy of a strategy designed to open the Yugoslav economy to foreign private capital.

Behind these six key points lay a seventh, which was less explicitly iterated, but was, ultimately, the most important of them. As with Chancellor Nigel Lawson of the United Kingdom, some years earlier, for Ante Marković, the significance of 'shadowing the Deutsche Mark' lay in the fact that it provided an automatic and accurate guideline on which to base domestic macroeconomic policy. The parity of seven new dinars to the Deutsche Mark would only remain tenable if the value of the dinar remained at least as stable as that of the German currency. If not, against a background of liberalization of import controls, the balance of trade would start to fall into critical disequilibrium. Thus, the enemy that Marković was really countering, with his internal convertibility proposals, was domestic inflation. This could only be controlled, however, if the National Bank was able to reclaim the authority over vital, 'high-powered', monetary emissions, which it had lost during the 1970s, and finally to stop the process of politically-inspired accommodation of inflationary pressures.

THE MARKOVIĆ PLAN: OUTCOMES AND PROBLEMS

Domestic Macroeconomic Balance

The internal convertibility strategy was remarkably successful in its attack on inflation. Within six months the annual rate of inflation had been reduced from 2,500% to under zero. It was equally successful in restoring confidence in the dinar, which, in turn, induced a massive conversion of private hard-currency holdings into dinars, and a substantial resultant increase in national hard-currency reserves (see below). All of this enabled Yugoslavia to improve relations with the IMF. A new stand-by arrangement was concluded, in early 1990, and this facilitated the extension of substantial new World Bank credits.

However, success at the macroeconomic level was not matched at the microeconomic level. The sharp downward trend in output, particularly industrial output, during 1990, in itself was no particular cause for anxiety. The new monetary rigour was precisely calculated to force firms to restructure, to eliminate loss-making activities and, in some cases, to force entire firms, or even sub-sectors, to close down. In the event, most enterprises reacted to the January 1990 programme by reducing output in all areas, including exports, while largely maintaining employment levels. Between August 1989 and August 1990 employment in the still-dominant socialized sector fell by just 4.1%.

Firms were able to do this without going bankrupt because they received substantial and, essentially, unlimited support from the commercial banks. In particular, the banks showed a willingness, throughout the first part of 1990, to capitalize unpaid interest on loans. In effect, then, they simply assumed the role that the National Bank of Yugoslavia had previously fulfilled. This was to give general support to all enterprises of the socialized sector which wanted to continue in their traditional manner, rather than addressing the priorities of the future.

This did not solve the problem of insolvency. Rather, it shifted it from the level of the enterprise to that of the commercial banking system. By the end of 1990 the banking system faced collapse. Bad debts were estimated at three times the value of capital, and 57.8% of total deposits. This put tremendous pressure on the National Bank to relax its tight monetary policy.

The whole issue became more controversial following a bizarre development, at the end of November 1990, which was dubbed the 'Great Bank Robbery'. The republican Government of the Socialist Party of Serbia (SPS—formerly the League of Communists) prevailed upon the National Bank of Serbia to rediscount bank loans to the value of 18,000m. dinars (US $1,700m.). This, effectively, created new, 'high-powered' money, equivalent to some 10% of the total Yugoslav stock of money at that time. This enabled the Serbian President, Slobodan Milošević, to pay salaries and pensions to millions of state employees, retirees, invalids, etc., for the first time for months, just a few days before Serbia's first democratic election since the Second World War. The operation was in direct contravention of the new monetary regime, under which republican national banks were only allowed to rediscount loans with the express approval of the Board of Governors of the National Bank of Yugoslavia. It was, however, only too clearly in the tradition of a pre-1990 Yugoslav system which had effectively given regional leaderships a licence to print their own money. A few months later the Government of Montenegro gained finance in exactly the same way, to compensate for federal funds which it should have received (for the payment of such things as pensions, hard-currency obligations and export support), but had not. Meanwhile a number of commercial banks, mainly in Slovenia and Croatia, had borrowed hard currency from the National Bank of Yugoslavia, purportedly to meet external payments commitments, in order to expand domestic credit. This was dangerously reminiscent of the practices of the late 1970s.

The National Bank of Yugoslavia is the Federal Government's banker. Furthermore, there is not really a money market in Yugoslavia (it was an aim of the Federal Government to establish money markets). Therefore, a particularly close link exists between fiscal policy and monetary policy. This is not only true of Yugoslavia, but of every other Eastern European country. Thus, however commendable the intentions of the Federal Government, with respect to the money supply, and no matter how closely it tried to align the dinar with the Deutsche Mark, if government expenditure exceeded tax revenue, the Federal Government had no other recourse but to ask the National Bank to print money to cover the deficit. Previously, budget deficits in Yugoslavia were 'hidden' in the notorious 'extra-budgetary balance'. Thus, although public expenditure increased rapidly during the first half of 1990, tax increases ensured that no major budgetary shortfalls appeared, but only on paper. The reality was that many insolvent enterprises were unable to pay increased tax demands. Also, the Republics of Croatia and Slovenia withheld their contributions to the maintenance of the Yugoslav People's Army, in response to what they viewed as an unacceptable *rapprochement* between the Army and the Serbian populism of Milošević, which was increasingly expressing itself in anti-Croat and anti-Slovene terms. Here again, Yugoslavia was reverting to a familiar problem of tending to spend money before it was received. In an attempt to sort out these problems, the 1990 budgetary year was extended to the end of April 1991. Between 31 December 1990 and 28 March 1991 the revenue shortfall was reduced from 12,500m. dinars to 1,100m. dinars, out of a total budget of 88,000m. dinars. However, a total of 3,700m. dinars had already been borrowed from the National Bank of Yugoslavia, for the Army, and the impact of this must have been directly inflationary.

It was inevitable that these developments should compromise Yugoslavia's new-found macroeconomic equilibrium. From July 1990 the National Bank again started to increase the supply of primary money. After the extraordinary 0.6% inflation rate recorded for June 1990, the monthly rate of increase in the retail price index once more began to escalate. It was already 8.2% in October and, although it then fell again (as low as 2.7% in December), it had increased to 9.2% by February 1991. Considering the pressures they were under, the Federal Government and the National Bank had, at February 1991, done well to keep the inflation rate still well below the hyperinflationary threshold. It was a major, if unexpected, achievement when the monthly inflation rate reduced to 3.2% in March 1991. Even before the onset of civil war, in mid-1991, however, all the signs were that the situation would get worse rather than better in the immediate future. A massive labour strike in Serbia, in April, in protest at another period of unpaid wages and salaries, was only ended when President Milošević promised that all claims would be settled. While new National Bank of Yugoslavia procedures make it unlikely that another 'Great Bank Robbery', as such, could take place, it was quite clear that the inflationary emission of currency was the only way Milošević could keep his promise. A preliminary look at the budget situation for the first three months of 1991 reveals a similar picture, with only 30.1% of 'invoiced' revenues actually received. Here again, even before the Slovenian and Croatian declarations of independence, inter-republican politics had made matters that much more difficult for the federal authorities. At the end of 1990, for instance, the Croatian Government decided to remove the import duty on foreign cars, in order to reduce the dependence of the Croatian market on the Serbian Zastava car firm. This was a reprisal against the imposition, by the Serbian Government, of deposit requirements on Croatian (and Slovenian) goods which amounted to 'import' duties. The Croatian Government had no constitutional right to pre-empt a federal prerogative in this way. The fact is, however, that another 'legitimate' source of revenue has been lost to the federal authorities.

Towards the end of April 1991 there were rumours that the federal prime minister, Marković, would resign. In the event, Marković decided to continue his efforts with the republican leaders. It was considered that as long as Marković remained in power the cause of 'sound' money and balanced budgets was not altogether lost. There was little indication, however, that the republican governments intended to observe such restrictions. By October, with civil war raising the political pressures and damaging economic activity and infrastructure, and with Marković's administration becoming increasingly powerless, federal economic objectives had been rendered irrelevant until the resolution of the political situation. On 19 December Marković finally resigned, with the federation dissolving and some 80% of the federal budget allocated to the Yugoslav People's Army.

The Balance of Payments

The history of Yugoslavia's external balance of payments, during the span of the Marković Plan, closely mirrors that of the domestic macroeconomic balance. That is, early policy successes were succeeded by a more sombre scenario in the middle of 1990. Then, by mid-1991, the situation was finely poised, with the downward trends predominant. The increasing violence of inter-republican and inter-ethnic relations, however, seemed likely to secure the failure of federal economic efforts, for the immediate future.

In external financial matters, the Marković Plan was based on an audacious gamble. It was assumed that the internal convertibility measures, however modified by vestiges of exchange control, would inevitably produce a sharp increase in imports, particularly in imports of consumer goods. Restructuring, if it did begin to take effect, could only be expected to have a substantial positive impact on exports in the medium term. However, it was reckoned, if confidence in the new dinar could be firmly established, there would be a massive inflow of hard currency into the Yugoslav banking system, as Yugoslavs, including Yugoslav expatriate workers in Germany and elsewhere, transferred their hard-currency savings into the Yugoslav banking system. Thus, while the hard-currency balance of trade would inevitably worsen in the short term, it was hoped that improvements on the 'invisible' balance (that is, from services) would ensure that there was a surplus on the overall current account.

For the first seven months of 1990 this gamble seemed to be succeeding. Net inflows of foreign exchange into the Yugoslav banking system, in January–July 1990, totalled more than US $1,900m. The impact of this on the current account of the balance of payments was amplified by a strong tendency, over the first six months of 1990, for Yugoslavia to export for cash and import on credit. As a result, in January–August 1990, foreign exchange reserves grew by about 80%, to reach some $10,000m., or approximately two-thirds of the annual value of hard-currency imports.

From August 1990, however, contrary pressures began to nullify the effects of results in the earlier part of the year. The original policy proposals, as announced at the end of 1989, had envisaged that, after six months of strict pegging to the Deutsche Mark (at the 7:1 parity), the dinar would be allowed to float (that is, to become freely convertible). In the event, at the end of June, Marković decided to maintain the 7:1 parity. This was despite the fact that the residual inflation of January arch 1990 had been enough to ensure that that this parity (which had been reasonable enough in January) was substantially too high by the beginning of July. However, Marković remained intent on maintaining the parity of what had become an overvalued dinar because he was worried that a devaluation would intensify cost-inflationary pressures, just at a time when federal control of the money supply was not secure. The problem with this policy was that it invited speculation against the dinar. This is exactly what happened. In the last four months of 1990 there were massive withdrawals of hard currency from the Yugoslav banking system, in anticipation of a devaluation of the dinar, but also as a way of maintaining living standards in an environment of falling real wages. By December 1990 all the balance-of-payments gains made by hard currency deposited over the first seven months of the year had been lost. At 31 December hard-currency reserves were $6,700m., which was only a little more than at December 1989. With the hard-currency balance of trade for 1990 recording a deficit of nearly $5,000m., and the balance of cash and credits on imports and exports now level, the current account went into deficit for the first time since 1982. In the last days of 1990 the dinar was finally devalued, to a parity of 9:1 against the Deutsche Mark. At this stage, it was not sufficient and, in April 1991, a further devaluation brought the parity to 13:1. This rate had been widely canvassed by economists as the appropriate one for August 1990.

These developments raised fundamental questions about the sustainability of internal convertibility measures based on fixed exchange rates. As the old Bretton Woods system showed on a world scale, fixed-exchange-rate systems are always vulnerable to speculative pressure, and even limited convertibility is bound to increase the scope for speculation. At the same time, the original 7:1 parity had enormous psychological importance in the domestic fight against hyperinflationary psychosis. It is difficult to see how Marković could have won public confidence in the new dinar if he had not effectively enlisted the help of the German central bank, the Bundesbank. A devaluation on 30 June 1990 which was big enough to leave the dinar undervalued might have maintained confidence (on the basis that no further devaluations would be required for some time) and forestalled the negative balance-of-payments movements of late 1990. However, this would have had to be accompanied by further restrictions on the money supply, to keep down inflation, which might have gone beyond the bounds of political feasibility.

At mid-1991 prospects for the Yugoslav external balance were not good. Although Yugoslavia was not a member, the collapse of the CMEA in Eastern Europe has had a generally depressing effect on trade with the USSR, while the crisis in the Persian Gulf, in 1990–91, removed Yugoslavia's significant exports of construction services to Iraq. (In both these cases Serbia has suffered proportionately more than the other Yugoslav Republics.) The continued failure to set in motion a powerful restructuring impetus meant that there was limited scope for increased hard-currency exports. Internal political tensions and then, in mid-1991, the outbreak of civil war had a catastrophic effect on earnings from foreign tourism, which had already fallen substantially in 1990. If the Yugoslav Government had been able to establish firmly the new dinar parity, it was possible that there may have been a renewed inflow of hard currency into the domestic banking system. Again, economic progress must await the resolution of the now-dominant political troubles. On balance, it seems likely that Yugoslavia will suffer severe payments problems through 1991 and 1992, and that this will inevitably mean a new growth in gross external debt. The problems of the internal conflicts apart, it seemed unlikely that Yugoslavia would receive significant further financial support from the IMF or the World Bank immediately, apart, perhaps, from some project-specific funding from the Bank.

PROSPECTS FOR A NEW YUGOSLAV COMMUNITY

Against the background of the powerful fissiparous tendencies, which dominated the internal politics of Yugoslavia from the beginning of democratization, a considerable debate developed over the possibility of a complete redesign of the system. If the old federal system was untenable (which the events of June 1991 onwards almost definitely proved), was it possible to construct some new system which would yet maintain, or even deepen, the unity of Yugoslav economic space? One of the most striking proposals to emerge was one for a confederal Yugoslavia, based on the model of the European Community. From a political point of view, the confederal proposal suffered from its association with the Croatian and Slovenian regimes, which the Governments of Serbia and Montenegro were bound to oppose. Although the civil war of 1991 made a negotiated settlement more difficult, it also increases the pressure for an eventual settlement, which seems unlikely to leave Yugoslavia unaltered. Even if some kind of consensus was reached within Yugoslavia, on transition to a confederal system, it is not clear that the EC model is

really appropriate. The EC, for example, managed very well without a common currency, and it was this success which encouraged the prospect of a transition to a single European currency. But that degree of monetary harmony was only achieved because of a very high degree of underlying consensus between member states on the general orientation of macroeconomic policy, making it possible to keep inflation rates broadly similar. In a Yugoslavia consisting of at least six sovereign states, each with its own currency and running its own fiscal and monetary policy, such a consensus is difficult to imagine. In the Yugoslav case there do, indeed, seem to be but two macroeconomic scenarios. One is the 'Bundesbank model', in which the National Bank of Yugoslavia maintains tight grip on the money supply and, implicitly, on the budgetary situation for Yugoslavia as a whole, on the basis of a single Yugoslav currency. This is essentially an optimal version of the Marković Plan. The other is the 'free-for-all model', in which each Republic has its own free-floating currency, unmediated by any kind of 'Yugoslav Monetary System'. Both scenarios are feasible, but neither is compatible with an EC-type confederacy.

CONCLUSION

Before the Slovenian and Croatian declarations of independence, in June 1991, and the consequent onset of civil war, Yugoslavia's economic prospects seemed sombre in hue, but not altogether black. A beleaguered federal prime minister, Marković, was making little progress with basic economic restructuring, but was just about controlling inflation. Externally, the trends were not promising, although there seemed little danger of Yugoslavia's external financial situation deteriorating to the level of, for example, Hungary or Bulgaria. The one great advantage that Yugoslavia retains over all the other Eastern European countries is that it has operated a form of market economy for some 40 years, after an interval of Stalinist central planning that was so brief as to leave little imprint on mass consciousness. In the crucial dimension of business–market culture, then, Yugoslavia was perhaps better placed than any other country in the region. The political obstacles to the transition to a rational economic system, based on the principle of a fully-fledged market for capital and labour as well as for goods, and on that of the unity of Yugoslav economic space, were immense. These problems were exacerbated enormously by the increasing bitterness of the internal strife and the spread of armed conflict. Added problems came from the Slovenian introduction of a new currency (the 'tolar', in October 1991) and the inflationary consequences of the federal authorities' printing money to cover the costs of the war. If these political obstacles could be overcome, however, there is reason to believe that the economic restructuring of Yugoslavia or its successor states is feasible within a timespan of around five years.

Statistical Survey

Source: *Statistički godišnjak Jugoslavije* (Statistical Yearbook of Yugoslavia), published by Savezni zavod za statistiku (Federal Statistical Office), 11000 Belgrade, Kneza Miloša 20; tel. (11) 681999; telex 11317; fax (11) 642368.

Area and Population

AREA, POPULATION AND DENSITY

Area (sq km)	255,804*
Population (census results)	
31 March 1981	
Males	11,083,778
Females	11,340,933
Total	22,424,711
31 March 1991	23,462,976
Population (official estimates at mid-year)	
1988	23,565,746
1989	23,695,000
1990	23,809,000†
Density (per sq km) at census of 31 March 1991 .	91.7

* 98,766 sq miles.   † Provisional figure.

REPUBLICS (Census of 31 March 1981)

Republic	Area (sq km)	Population	Density (per sq km)	Capital (with population)
Serbia . .	88,361	9,313,676	105	Belgrade (1,470,073)
Vojvodina* .	21,506	2,034,772	95	Novi Sad (257,685)
Kosovo* . .	10,887	1,584,441	145	Priština (210,040)
Croatia . .	56,538	4,601,469	81	Zagreb (768,700)
Slovenia .	20,251	1,891,864	93	Ljubljana (305,211)
Bosnia and				
Herzegovina	51,129	4,124,256	81	Sarajevo (448,519)
Macedonia .	25,713	1,909,136	74	Skopje (506,547)
Montenegro .	13,812	584,310	42	Titograd (132,290)
Total . . .	255,804	22,424,711	88	—

* Provinces within Serbia.

PRINCIPAL TOWNS (population at 1981 census)*

Beograd (Belgrade,		Ljubljana . .	305,211
the capital) . .	1,470,073	Novi Sad . .	257,685
Split . . .	882,050	Niš . . .	230,711
Osijek . . .	867,646	Priština . .	210,040
Zagreb . . .	855,568	Maribor . .	185,699
Rijeka . . .	540,485	Banja Luka .	183,618
Skoplje (Skopje) .	504,932	Subotica . .	154,611
Sarajevo . .	448,519	Kraljevo . .	121,622

* Figures refer to districts, each including rural areas as well as an urban centre.

POPULATION BY ETHNIC GROUP (1981 census)

Ethnic Group	Population ('000)	%
Serbs	8,140	36.3
Croats	4,428	19.7
Muslims	2,000	8.9
Slovenes	1,754	7.8
Albanians	1,730	7.7
Macedonians	1,340	6.0
Yugoslavs	1,219	5.4
Montenegrins	579	2.6
Hungarians	427	1.9
Total (incl. others)	22,425	100.0

BIRTHS, MARRIAGES AND DEATHS

	Registered live births		Registered marriages		Registered deaths	
	Number	Rate (per 1,000)	Number	Rate (per 1,000)	Number	Rate (per 1,000)
1983 . .	374,610	16.4	171,909	7.3	218,980	9.6
1984 . .	377,383	16.4	167,789	7.3	214,725	9.3
1985 . .	366,629	15.9	163,022	7.0	212,883	9.2
1986 . .	359,626	15.5	160,277	6.9	213,149	9.2
1987 . .	359,338	15.3	163,469	7.0	214,666	9.2
1988 . .	356,268	15.1	160,419	6.8	213,466	9.1
1989* .	335,914	14.2	159,269	6.7	215,540	9.1
1990* .	333,746	14.0	n.a.	6.3	213,841	9.0

* Provisional.

ECONOMICALLY ACTIVE POPULATION
(persons aged 10 years and over, 1981 census)

	Males	Females	Total
Agriculture, hunting, forestry and fishing	1,464,710	1,218,118	2,682,828
Mining and quarrying . . .			
Manufacturing	}1,441,223	768,470	2,209,693
Electricity, gas and water . .			
Construction	630,846	58,445	689,291
Trade, restaurants and hotels .	409,491	418,084	827,575
Transport, storage and communications . . .	385,277	60,085	445,362
Financing, insurance, real estate and business services . . .	102,985	101,881	204,866
Community, social and personal services	876,180	709,025	1,585,205
Activities not adequately defined	98,798	36,061	134,859
Total employed	5,409,510	3,370,169	8,779,679
Unemployed	331,150	247,842	578,992
Total labour force	5,740,660	3,618,011	9,358,671

Mid-1989 (estimates, '000 persons): Agriculture, etc. 2,428; Total 10,733 (Source: FAO, *Production Yearbook*).

EMPLOYMENT IN THE 'SOCIALIZED' SECTOR
('000 employees, average of March and September each year)

	1986	1987	1988
Agriculture, forestry and fishing	335	341	338
Mining and quarrying . .	148	146	147
Manufacturing	2,508	2,588	2,595
Electricity, gas and water . .	136	140	143
Construction	596	593	563
Trade, restaurants and hotels .	898	911	922
Transport, storage and communications	509	515	522
Financing, insurance, real estate and business services	206	209	208
Community, social and personal services . . .	1,230	1,260	1,277
Total	6,566	6,703	6,715
Males	4,053	4,100	4,073
Females	2,513	2,603	2,642

1989 ('000 employees): Total 6,697.

Agriculture

PRINCIPAL CROPS ('000 metric tons)

	1987	1988	1989
Wheat .	5,272	6,300	5,599
Rice (paddy) .	49	36	27
Barley .	504	615	702
Maize .	8,863	7,697	9,415
Rye .	69	76	75
Oats .	232	253	279
Potatoes .	2,210	1,935	2,359
Dry beans .	131	104	136
Other pulses .	59	58	64
Soybeans (Soya beans) .	237	180	209
Sunflower seed .	486	410	420
Rapeseed .	88	68	64
Cabbages* .	660	496	678
Tomatoes .	480	402	434
Cucumbers and gherkins .	137	114	106
Chillies and peppers (green) .	376	305	263
Onions (dry) .	273	269	339
Garlic .	54	55	65
Carrots .	107	105	118
Watermelons and melons .	436	391	396
Grapes .	1,325	1,186	1,022
Sugar beet .	6,238	4,558	6,797
Apples .	423	518	546
Pears .	147	173	177
Peaches and nectarines .	78	77	91
Plums .	757	765	819
Apricots .	21	28	46
Strawberries* .	36	43	47
Raspberries .	36	53	61
Tree nuts .	31	26	43
Tobacco (leaves) .	76	52	57

* Unofficial estimates (Source: FAO, *Production Yearbook*).

LIVESTOCK ('000 head)

	1987	1988	1989*
Cattle .	5,030	4,881	4,759
Pigs .	8,459	8,323	7,396
Sheep .	7,819	7,824	7,564
Horses .	384	362	340
Poultry .	79,696	78,589	74,872

* Preliminary figures.

LIVESTOCK PRODUCTS

	1987*	1988*	1989
Beef ('000 metric tons) .	317	301	309
Pork ('000 metric tons) .	557	546	528
Poultry meat ('000 metric tons)	323	329	310
Crude fats ('000 metric tons) .	305	296	285
Milk (million litres) .	4,748	4,638	4,069
Wool: greasy (metric tons) .	10,188	10,209	10,103
Eggs (million) .	4,922	4,491	4,612

* Preliminary figures.

Forestry

ROUNDWOOD REMOVALS ('000 cubic metres)*

	1987	1988	1989
Sawlogs and veneer logs .	7,039	6,983	6,876
Pitprops (mine timber) .	527	467	549
Pulpwood .	1,863	1,938	1,774
Other industrial wood .	2,080	2,049	2,390
Fuel wood .	4,226	4,301	3,804
Total .	15,735	15,738	15,393

* From socially-owned forests only.

SAWNWOOD PRODUCTION ('000 cubic metres)

	1987	1988	1989
Coniferous (soft wood) .	2,381	2,290	2,176
Non-coniferous (hard wood) .	2,206	2,287	2,305
Total .	4,587	4,577	4,481

Fishing

('000 metric tons, live weight)

	1987	1988*	1989
Freshwater fishes .	25.2	26.4	25.0
Marine fishes .	56.2	45.3	40.4
Crustaceans and molluscs .	2.4	3.1	6.3
Total catch .	83.8	74.8	71.7

* Preliminary figures.

Mining

('000 metric tons)

	1987	1988	1989
Coal .	71,873	72,590	74,631
Crude petroleum .	3,867	3,681	3,392
Iron ore* .	5,983	5,545	5,080
Copper ore* .	27,745	30,056	30,078
Lead and zinc ore* .	3,908	3,847	3,885
Bauxite .	3,394	3,034	3,252
Natural gas ('000 cu m) .	2,887	3,015	3,871

* Figures refer to gross weight of ores. The metal content (in '000 metric tons) was: Iron 1,764 in 1987, 1,844 in 1988; Copper 130.5 in 1987, 103.5 in 1988; Lead 106.7 in 1987, 103.3 in 1988; Zinc 87.4 in 1987, 91.2 in 1988.

Industry

SELECTED PRODUCTS
('000 metric tons, unless otherwise indicated)

	1987	1988	1989
Electric energy (million kWh) .	80,791	83,651	82,775
Motor spirit (petrol) . . .	4,009	4,168	4,053
Distillate fuel oils . . .	3,622	3,834	3,407
Residual fuel oil . . .	4,867	6,122	6,038
Pig iron	2,867	2,916	2,899
Steel	4,367	4,485	4,500
Electrolytic copper . . .	139	145	151
Refined lead	112	110	97
Zinc	108	116	107
Aluminium	281	313	332
Iron castings . . .	472	433	430
Construction machinery . .	47	42	41
Industrial machinery . .	57	60	55
Agricultural machinery . .	114	114	106
Tractors (number) . .	60,426	58,267	55,376
Lorries (number) . .	13,723	13,747	11,194
Motor cars (number)* . .	312,000	305,000	n.a.
Wagons (number) . .	1,333	643	651
Bicycles ('000) . .	819	808	806
Rotating machines ('000 kW)	5,417	5,543	6,682
Power transformers ('000 kVA)	10,597	7,771	8,054
Thermal apparatus (metric tons)	76,322	63,315	n.a.
Sulphuric acid	11,610	1,731	1,634
Calcined soda	202	214	204
Clay building bricks (million) .	4,062	4,047	4,048
Roofing tiles (million) . .	455	487	483
Cement	8,963	8,840	8,560
Mechanical woodpulp . .	132	129	131
Chemical woodpulp . .	546	582	580
Semi-chemical woodpulp .	122	132	131
Stationery and newsprint .	319	320	307
Cotton yarn . . .	140	136	125
Woollen yarn . . .	53	50	48
Woven cotton fabrics (million sq metres)† . . .	366	351	339
Sole leather (metric tons) . .	2,581	2,081	1,650
Upper leather . . .	20,316	19,477	21,103
Footwear (excl. rubber) ('000 pairs)	93,594	86,336	91,616
Radio receivers ('000) . . .	198	130	86
Television receivers ('000) .	591	549	503
Sugar	872	636	960
Canned vegetables (metric tons)	150,000	112,000	133,000
Canned meat (metric tons) .	89,000	83,000	77,000
Canned fish (metric tons) .	31,000	33,000	33,000
Edible oil (metric tons) .	251,000	256,000	253,000
Wine ('000 hectolitres) . .	3,864	3,665	3,593
Beer ('000 hectolitres) . .	12,054	11,970	11,286
Cigarettes (million) . .	55,817	59,698	59,698

* Including cars assembled from imported parts.
† Including cellulosic fabrics.

Finance

CURRENCY AND EXCHANGE RATES

Monetary Unit
100 para = 1 new Yugoslav dinar.

Denominations
Coins: 1, 2, 5, 10, 20 and 50 new dinars.
Notes: 50, 100, 200, 500, 20,000, 50,000 new dinars.

Sterling and Dollar Equivalents (30 June 1991)
£1 sterling = 37.91 new dinars;
US $1 = 23.41 new dinars;
1,000 new Yugoslav dinars = £26.38 = $42.71.

Average Exchange Rate (new dinars per US $)
1988   0.252
1988   2.876
1989   11.318

Note: On 1 January 1990 the new dinar, equivalent to 10,000 old dinars, was introduced. Some figures in this survey may still be in terms of old dinars. On 8 October 1991 Slovenia introduced its own currency, the tolar (SLT). On 23 December Croatia introduced a Croatian dinar (see republican Finance sections).

BUDGETS (million new dinars)

	Federal budget		Other budgets*	
Revenue	1988	1989	1988	1989
Total receipts .	813.1	11,376.5	745.9	8,782.3

	Federal budget		Other budgets*	
Expenditure	1988	1989	1988	1989
Schools . .	—	—	12.7	155.2
Science and culture .	—	—	4.4	39.3
Public health and social welfare .	118.4	1,105.7	33.4	308.9
National defence .	524.7	6,112.4	5.0	37.2
Non-economic investment .	1.5	44.1	19.7	154.8
Government . .	45.4	1,163.4	323.4	5,140.4
Investment and interventions in the economy .	—	1,579.1	95.6	351.9
Other . . .	69.6	822.1	220.4	2,487.9
Total . .	**759.7**	**10,826.9**	**714.9**	**8,675.6**

* Republican, Provincial (Vojvodina and Kosovo) and Communal Budgets.

INTERNATIONAL RESERVES (US $ million at 31 December)

	1988	1989	1990
Gold*	80	80	81
Foreign exchange . .	2,298	4,136	5,461
Total	**2,378**	**4,216**	**5,542**

* Valued at US $42.22 per troy ounce.
Source: IMF, *International Financial Statistics.*

MONEY SUPPLY (million new dinars at 31 December)

	1988	1989	1990
Notes in circulation . .	585	12,375	52,517
Private-sector deposits at national banks . .	24	896	175
Deposit money at basic and associated banks . .	1,798	37,759	73,591
Total money	**2,407**	**51,030**	**126,283**

Source: IMF, *International Financial Statistics.*

NATIONAL ACCOUNTS (million old dinars at current prices)
Gross Material Product by Activities of the Material Sphere*

	1987	1988	1989†
Manufacturing, mining and quarrying	22,296,701	70,988,799	109,928
Agriculture and fishing .	5,252,180	15,198,420	23,500
Forestry	432,937	1,273,969	1,937
Operation of irrigation systems and kindred activities . .	130,845	323,025	423
Construction	3,299,510	8,672,268	13,713
Transport and communications	3,496,776	10,445,395	15,099
Trade	8,326,493	24,484,450	33,085
Catering and tourism . .	1,673,637	5,075,733	6,278
Arts and crafts (productive) .	1,976,277	5,652,843	7,746
Public utilities (productive) .	538,770	1,511,205	2,094
Other productive economic activities	1,788,300	4,696,149	7,556
Sub-total	49,212,426	148,322,256	221,430
Statistical discrepancy . .	52,226	238,484	433
Total	49,264,652	148,560,740	221,862

* By establishment principle.
† Million new dinars.

BALANCE OF PAYMENTS (US $ million)

	1987	1988	1989
Merchandise exports f.o.b. .	11,425	12,779	13,560
Merchandise imports f.o.b.. .	11,343	12,000	13,502
Trade balance	82	779	58
Exports of services . .	4,312	4,712	5,441
Imports of services . .	−5,715	−6,076	−8,245
Other income received . .	153	190	403
Other income paid . . .	−1,863	−1,987	−1,872
Private unrequited transfers (net)	4,281	4,871	6,645
Official unrequited transfers (net)	−2	−2	−3
Current balance . . .	1,248	2,487	2,427
Other capital (net) . . .	−758	−683	−697
Net errors and omissions . .	−252	149	201
Overall balance . . .	238	1,953	1,931

Source: IMF, *International Financial Statistics.*

External Trade

PRINCIPAL COMMODITIES
(distribution by SITC, million old dinars)

Imports c.i.f.	1986	1987	1988
Food and live animals . .	296,139	529,400	2,125,856
Cereals and cereal preparations	32,029	70,757	77,145
Fruit and vegetables . . .	31,559	89,446	294,705
Coffee, tea, cocoa and spices .	125,318	161,090	568,110
Beverages and tobacco . .	12,750	21,667	72,892
Crude materials (inedible) except fuels . . .	482,599	876,506	3,764,686
Hides, skins and fur skins, undressed	39,481	54,045	243,887
Wood, lumber and cork . .	35,699	57,806	143,761
Pulp and waste paper . .	44,471	95,353	366,583
Textile fibres and waste . .	139,093	217,179	873,421
Crude fertilizers and crude minerals	74,067	143,680	677,585
Metalliferous ores and metal scrap	63,722	120,651	693,929
Mineral fuels, lubricants, etc.	925,259	1,659,010	6,054,645
Animal and vegetable oils and fats	22,158	13,922	71,112
Chemicals	706,704	1,553,181	5,958,031
Chemical elements and compounds	284,828	645,353	2,622,220
Dyeing, tanning and colouring materials	68,706	146,054	545,525
Medicinal and pharmaceutical products	51,664	114,654	393,476
Fertilizers, manufactured . .	44,647	77,333	349,140
Basic manufactures . .	793,838	1,580,560	5,486,850
Textile yarn, fabrics, etc. .	151,539	362,721	1,087,009
Non-metallic mineral manufactures	52,485	125,513	447,545
Iron and steel	292,156	507,980	1,650,110
Non-ferrous metals . . .	86,301	157,862	632,959
Other metal manufactures . .	84,848	174,839	645,153
Machinery and transport equipment . . .	1,483,139	2,904,431	9,340,017
Non-electric machinery . .	837,069	1,572,859	4,783,381
Electrical machinery, apparatus, etc. . . .	344,381	697,014	1,815,388
Transport equipment . . .	301,688	634,558	2,103,003
Miscellaneous manufactured articles	176,921	382,562	1,497,188
Other commodities and transactions . . .	3,235	2,834	5,406
Total	4,902,741	9,524,073	34,376,683

Exports f.o.b.	1987	1988	1989
Food and live animals . .	679,670	2,454,546	29,487,049
Live animals . . .	121,906	444,168	3,731,531
Meat and meat preparations .	156,515	508,089	5,653,619
Cereals and cereal preparations . . .	85,070	273,001	5,223,020
Fruit and vegetables . .	193,354	767,254	8,659,991
Beverages and tobacco .	87,666	319,037	4,263,389
Crude materials (inedible) except fuels . .	434,706	1,801,114	27,140,843
Wood, lumber and cork . .	191,707	735,689	8,700,013
Textile fibres and waste .	63,649	231,067	2,956,194
Crude fertilizers and crude minerals	12,198	58,972	655,684
Metalliferous ores and metal scrap	71,943	344,349	9,012,051
Mineral fuels, lubricants, etc.	169,980	519,940	6,339,528
Animal and vegetable oils and fats . . .	8,374	86,354	275,534
Chemicals . . .	996,378	2,982,490	56,527,979
Chemical elements and compounds . . .	252,819	832,623	n.a.
Dyeing, tanning and colouring materials . . .	47,397	211,947	5,326,418
Basic manufactures . .	2,327,112	9,412,563	n.a.
Wood and cork manufactures (excl. furniture) . . .	116,532	405,710	4,665,106
Textile yarn, fabrics, etc. . .	326,415	1,326,045	2,456,194
Non-metallic mineral manufactures . . .	156,507	618,628	n.a.
Iron and steel . . .	523,809	2,013,810	19,226,681
Non-ferrous metals . .	519,312	2,113,076	24,188,880
Other metal manufactures .	299,641	1,468,439	n.a.
Machinery and transport equipment . . .	2,682,996	10,113,354	115,101,133
Non-electric machinery .	1,019,731	4,132,719	n.a.
Electrical machinery, apparatus, etc. . .	817,203	2,701,642	26,673,347
Transport equipment . .	846,062	3,187,076	19,601,335
Miscellaneous manufactured articles . . .	1,408,612	5,127,293	67,056,100
Furniture . . .	325,091	1,241,155	14,801,471
Clothing (excl. footwear) .	439,286	1,354,533	14,670,417
Footwear . . .	392,517	1,304,208	23,791,856
Other commodities and transactions . .	23,954	64,352	816,164
Total	8,819,448	32,881,044	510,531,574

PRINCIPAL TRADING PARTNERS (million new dinars)

Imports c.i.f.	1987	1988	1989
Austria	42.6	156.9	1,994
Czechoslovakia . . .	40.6	118.3	1,533
France	43.3	145.0	1,886
German Democratic Republic .	24.9	92.2	n.a.
Germany, Federal Republic .	174.0	589.8	7,815
Hungary . . .	18.7	77.2	1,184
Iran	11.9	52.1	264
Iraq	32.4	164.2	1,790
Italy	97.8	358.2	4,896
Japan	13.2	45.3	573
Libya	13.2	73.6	675
Netherlands . . .	15.8	61.9	1,173
Poland	30.7	113.4	1,653
Romania . . .	10.0	41.6	449
Sweden	13.1	51.8	527
Switzerland . . .	23.9	71.0	796
USSR	145.5	456.9	6,734
United Kingdom . .	24.4	77.7	816
USA	54.1	190.1	2,223
Total (incl. others) . .	952.4	3,437.7	n.a.

Exports f.o.b.	1987	1988	1989
Algeria	7.2	33.7	348
Austria	31.9	112.7	1,284
Bulgaria	10.8	37.8	466
Czechoslovakia	32.5	138.0	1,307
Egypt	17.3	43.6	523
France	32.2	128.1	1,410
German Democratic Republic .	25.9	85.3	n.a.
Germany, Federal Republic .	102.7	372.8	4,748
Greece	13.5	44.4	597
Hungary	18.3	66.7	810
Iran	7.6	28.5	344
Iraq	25.1	103.4	1,116
Italy	115.0	492.2	6,257
Liberia	2.2	24.4	380
Libya	9.9	26.8	176
Netherlands	1.3	27.0	134
Poland	31.6	128.3	1,325
Romania	8.8	27.6	410
Switzerland	8.4	26.6	1,122
USSR	171.5	614.5	8,983
United Kingdom . . .	20.8	83.9	1,139
USA	56.6	189.2	1,931
Total (incl. others) . . .	881.9	3,288.1	51,053

Transport

RAILWAYS (traffic)

	1987	1988	1989
Passenger journeys (million) .	120.0	116.0	117.0
Passenger-kilometres ('000 million) . . .	11.8	11.4	11.6
Freight carried (million metric tons)	84.2	83.6	84.8
Freight ton-kilometres ('000 million)	26.1	25.4	26.0

ROAD TRAFFIC (registered motor vehicles at 31 December)

	1987	1988	1989
Motor cycles (up to 50 cc) . .	96,198	88,288	89,950
Passenger cars . . .	3,023,693	3,089,605	3,323,940
Buses	29,241	28,575	29,407
Lorries	207,283	206,202	217,639
Special vehicles . . .	53,942	54,786	58,601
Tractors	531,114	546,454	575,268

INLAND WATERWAYS

Fleet (number of vessels)

	1987	1988	1989
Tugs	282	284	280
Motor barges	81	83	83
Barges	614	602	595
Tankers	149	149	149
Passenger vessels . . .	30	31	37

Traffic

	1987	1988	1989
Passengers ('000) . . .	20	31	29
Goods unloaded (million metric tons)	16.5	16.2	16

SEA-BORNE SHIPPING (international freight traffic)

	1987	1988	1989
Vessels entered (million net reg. tons) .	51.1	60.5	60.0
Goods loaded (million metric tons) . .	6.1	7.1	6.2
Goods unloaded (million metric tons). .	19.5	21.9	20.1
Goods in transit (million metric tons) .	5.2	5.1	5.5

CIVIL AVIATION*

	1987	1988	1989
Passengers carried ('000) . .	6,871	6,517	5,585
Passenger-kilometres (million) .	8,342	8,688	7,985
Cargo carried (tons) . .	42,708	47,601	49,009
Ton-kilometres ('000) . . .	112,167	138,855	154,205
Kilometres flown ('000) . . .	73,145	75,040	73,656

* Data include JAT, Inex and Aviogenex.

Tourism

FOREIGN TOURIST ARRIVALS (by country of origin)

	1987	1988	1989
Austria	799,000	804,000	746,000
Czechoslovakia . . .	342,000	272,000	245,000
France	407,000	371,000	315,000
Germany, Federal Republic .	2,786,000	2,749,000	2,462,000
Hungary	195,000	200,000	202,000
Italy	1,125,000	1,238,000	1,424,000
Netherlands . . .	444,000	524,000	381,000
USSR	247,000	303,000	408,000
United Kingdom . .	700,000	673,000	650,000
USA	232,000	295,000	258,000
Total (incl. others) . . .	8,907,000	9,018,000	8,644,000

Communications Media

	1987	1988	1989
Telephone subscribers . . .	3,909,000	4,243,000	4,550,000
Radio licences	4,772,000	4,735,000*	4,703,000
Television licences . . .	4,089,000	4,092,000*	4,074,000
Books (titles published) . .	10,619	12,100*	11,339
Daily newspapers . . .	28	28*	28
Average circulation ('000) .	2,857	2,354*	2,011
Newspapers (all frequencies) .	2,825	2,723*	n.a.
Average circulation ('000) .	26,817	24,172*	26,631
Periodicals	1,659	1,719*	1,453
Average circulation ('000) .	4,127	4,485*	n.a.

* Provisional figure.

Education

(1988/89)

	Institutions	Students	Teachers
First level	11,907	1,422,162	62,534
Second level (first stage) . .	4,856	1,402,789	79,050
Second level (second stage) .	1,217	958,743	59,409
General secondary (public general)	n.a.	167,100	n.a.
Teacher training . . .	n.a.	27,609	n.a.
Technical and vocational . .	n.a.	762,269	n.a.
Religion and theology (private)	18	1,738	324
Institutions for higher education	310	341,341	26,301

Directory

The Constitution

It was expected that a new constitution would be introduced in the early 1990s. The Constitution adopted on 21 February 1974 and subsequently amended was still in force, despite the moves towards independence by several republics during 1991, and is summarized below.

INTRODUCTION

The introductory section of the Yugoslav Constitution contains 10 chapters dealing with basic principles. The first chapter states:

'The nations of Yugoslavia, taking as their point of departure the right of every nation to self-determination, including the right of secession; on the basis of their will freely expressed in the common struggle in the National Liberation War and socialist revolution; and in line with their historical aspirations, aware that the further consolidation of their fraternity and unity is in the common interest, have, together with the nationalities with whom they live side by side, united into a federal republic of free and equal peoples and nationalities and created a socialist federal community of working people—the Socialist Federal Republic of Yugoslavia (SFRY), in which, in the interest of each nation and nationality individually and collectively, they are implementing and assuring:

socialist social relationships based on self-management by the working people and the protection of the socialist system of self-management;

national freedom and independence;

the fraternity and unity of the nations and nationalities; the integral interests of the working class and the solidarity of the workers and all working people;

the possibility and freedom for the comprehensive development of the human personality and for rapprochement among men, nations and nationalities, in line with their interests and aspirations along the road of creating a richer culture and civilization for the socialist society; the unification and co-ordination of efforts to develop the material foundations of socialist society and prosperity for the people;

the system of socio-economic relationships and the integral foundations of the political system for the purpose of pursuing the joint interests and assuring the equality of the nations and nationalities, and the working people; the integration of their own aspirations with the progressive aspirations of mankind.

The working people, the nations and nationalities exercise their sovereign rights in the socialist republics and in the socialist autonomous provinces in line with their constitutional rights, and in the Socialist Federal Republic of Yugoslavia where this is established by the Constitution of the SFRY as being in the common interest.

The working people, the nations and nationalities make their decisions at federal level in line with the principles of agreement between the republics and autonomous provinces; solidarity and mutuality; equitable participation by the republics and autonomous provinces in federal organs in accordance with this Constitution; and the responsibility of the republics and autonomous provinces for their own development and for the development of the socialist community as a whole'.

It is stated in the second chapter that the inviolable foundation for the position and role of man is social ownership of the means of production; the emancipation of labour and the transcendence of historically conditioned socio-economic inequalities and dependence of people in labour; the right to self-management; the right of the working man to enjoy the fruits of his labour and the material progress of the social community; the economic, social and personal security of man; democratic political relationships, etc. The third chapter deals with social ownership, as a reflection of socialist socio-economic relationships among people; the fourth chapter with the working class and working people as the bearers of power and management of social affairs; the fifth chapter with the liberties, rights, duties and responsibilities of individuals and citizens; the sixth chapter with the determination of the working people and citizens, the nations and nationalities of Yugoslavia consistently to pursue a policy of peace and against war and aggressive pressures of any kind whatsoever; the seventh chapter with the international position and foreign policy of Yugoslavia inspired by peaceful coexistence and the principles of non-alignment; the eighth chapter with the League of Communists of Yugoslavia which, by its guiding ideological and political activity in conditions of socialist democracy and social self-management, represents the basic moving force and vehicle of political activity, and also with the role and activities of other socio-political organizations; the ninth chapter with the socio-economic and political system and the tenth chapter with the basic principles as a 'component part of the Constitution and the basis and direction for interpreting the Constitution and the laws and for the activity of one and all'.

THE SOCIALIST FEDERAL REPUBLIC OF YUGOSLAVIA

Part one, with nine articles, is devoted to the Socialist Federal Republic of Yugoslavia as a 'federal state, a state community of voluntarily united peoples and their socialist republics and the socialist autonomous provinces of Kosovo and Vojvodina which are part of the Socialist Republic of Serbia, based on the government and self-management of the working-class and all working people and on the socialist, self-management, democratic community of working people and citizens and equal nations and nationalities'.

THE SOCIAL SYSTEM

Part two is devoted to the social order. Chapter I (comprising Articles 10 to 87) deals with the socio-economic position of man in associated labour, the integration of labour and the means of social reproduction, the self-managed communities of interest, social planning, information systems, socio-economic status and association of farmers, independent personal labour with means owned by citizens, legal property relations, goods of general interest and the protection of the human environment.

Chapter II (Articles 88 to 152) deals with the foundations of the socio-economic system and regulates the position of the working people in the socio-political system, self-management in the organizations of associated labour, self-management in the self-managed communities of interest, self-management in the local communities, the position of the commune as a self-managed and basic socio-political community founded on the power and self-management of the working class and all working people, self-management agreements and social compacts, the protection by society of the rights of self-management and social property, the foundations of the assembly system which rests on the principle of delegates as a new form of direct participation by the working people in the management of society's affairs from the local communities to the federation. Each socio-political body (i.e. the communes, Autonomous Provinces, Republics and the Federation) has an assembly as its supreme organ of power and self-management. Working people in self-managing organizations and communities form delegations, elected for a four-year term by secret ballot from members of those bodies, to exercise their responsibilities in the assemblies. Each assembly has an executive council.

Chapter III (Articles 153 to 203) deals with the liberties, rights, duties and responsibilities of man and citizen, pursued 'in mutual solidarity and through the fulfilment of the duties and discharge of responsibilities of each toward all and all toward each'.

Chapter IV (Articles 204 to 216) is dedicated to constitutionality and legality. Constitutionality and the rule of law are the concern of the courts, self-managed judicial organs, organs of the socio-political communities, organizations of associated labour and other self-managed organizations and communities and the bearers of self-management, public and other social functions.

Chapter V (Articles 217 to 236) deals with the judiciary and public prosecutor.

Chapter VI (Articles 237 to 243) covers national defence. Article 237 states: 'It is the inviolable and inalienable right and duty of the nations and nationalities of Yugoslavia, of the working people and citizens, to protect and defend the independence, sovereignty, territorial integrity and socio-political system of the SFRY, the latter having been established by the Constitution of the SFRY'. Article 238 states that 'no one has the right to recognize or sign capitulation, or to accept or recognize the occupation of the SFRY or any of its parts'. The armed forces of the SFRY are an integral entity and consist of the Yugoslav People's Army, as the joint armed force of all the nations and nationalities and all working people and citizens; and of the territorial defence forces as the broadest form of organized armed resistance by the people.

RELATIONS IN THE FEDERATION AND THE RIGHTS AND DUTIES OF THE FEDERATION

Part three, from Articles 244 to 281, deals with relationships at federal level. 'In the SFRY, the nations and nationalities and the working people and citizens exercise and assure: sovereignty, equality and national freedom, independence, territorial integrity, security and social self-defence, the defence of the country and the international position and relations of the country with other states and inter-state organizations, the system of socialist self-management of socio-economic relationships, the integral foundations of the political system, the fundamental democratic freedoms and rights of men and citizens, solidarity and the social security of the working people and citizens and the integral market, and co-ordinate their joint economic and social development and other of their common interests.' These common interests are pursued through the organs and organizations of the federation with the equitable participation and responsibility of the republics and autonomous provinces; through direct co-operation and agreement between the republics, autonomous provinces, communes and other socio-political communities, by self-management agreement, social compact and integration of organizations of associated labour and other organizations and self-managed communities of interest; through the activities of socio-political and other organizations and through free and multifaceted activities by the citizens.

THE ORGANIZATION OF THE FEDERATION

Part four, dealing with the rights and duties, and the organization, of the federation, comprises Articles 282 to 397. Chapter I deals with the rights and duties of the SFRY Assembly, defined as 'a body of self-management and the supreme organ of power within the framework of federal rights and duties'. The Assembly comprises two chambers: the Federal Chamber and the Chamber of Republics and Provinces. The Federal Chamber has 220 members (30 from each of the six republics and 20 from each of the two provinces) who 'lay down the fundamentals of internal and foreign policy', 'decide on war and peace' and ratify international treaties. The Chamber of Republics and Provinces has 88 members (12 from each Republican Assembly and eight from each Provincial Assembly) who are responsible for the adoption of a Social Plan, the formulation of economic policy and the determination of the Federal Budget.

Chapter II deals with the Presidency of the SFRY which 'represents the SFRY at home and abroad and discharges other rights and duties as established by the Constitution', and Chapter III with the President of the Republic and contains the express formulation that 'in view of the historic role of Josip Broz Tito in the National Liberation War and socialist revolution, in the creation and development of the SFRY, in the advancement of the Yugoslav socialist society of self-management of the Yugoslav socialist society of self-management, in the achievement of fraternity and unity among the nations and nationalities of Yugoslavia, in the consolidation of the country's independence and its position in international relations, in the struggle for peace in the world, and in line with the expressed will of the working people and citizens, nations and nationalities of Yugoslavia—the SFRY. Assembly may, on the proposal of the Assemblies of the Republics and Autonomous Provinces, elect Josip Broz Tito President of the Republic for an unlimited term of office'.*

Chapter IV deals with the Federal Executive Council (elected by the SFRY Assembly for a four-year term); Chapter V with the federal administrative organs; Chapter VI with federal judicial organs, and Chapter VII with the Constitutional Court of Yugoslavia.

Part five (Articles 398 to 403) deals with the procedure of amending the Constitution; and Part six (Articles 404 to 406), with transitional and terminal provisions.

* Upon the death of President Tito in May 1980, the function of President of the Republic was terminated. The rights and duties of this office are exercised henceforth by the SFRY Presidency. The Vice-President of the Presidency became President until the expiry of the term for which he was elected Vice-President.

AMENDMENTS

The following amendments were promulgated in 1981:

Amendment I establishes equality of all the members of a collective organ, particularly in the process of decision-making.

Amendment II sets the upper limit of the duration of term of office of the elected and appointed officials and holders of public and self-management functions. The term of office is limited to four years' duration.

Amendment III specifies the tenure of office for the highest-placed officials of the SFRY Assembly. The President, Vice-President, and President of both Chambers shall be elected to one-year terms of office, every time from some other Republic or Province. The highest post in the League of Communists of Yugoslavia also has a one-year tenure.

Amendment IV alters the relevant Constitutional provision, so that instead of President of the League of Communists of Yugoslavia (LCY) a member of the SFRY Presidency shall, by virtue of office, be president of an LCY organ as established by the LCY Statute.

Amendment V, which pertains to the Federal Executive Council, introduces the following changes: the preliminary procedure of nominating the candidates for the election of President and members of the Federal Executive Council shall take place within the Socialist Alliance; one person may not be elected Council President for two consecutive terms; Council members may be re-elected only once to the same function; two years following its election, the Council submits to the SFRY Assembly a progress report.

Under Amendment VI, the officials who manage Federal Organs of Administration, and others nominated by the SFRY Assembly, may be appointed to the same function for no more than two consecutive terms.

Amendment VII pertains to the Constitutional Court of Yugoslavia whose judges are elected to terms of eight years, without the right to re-election, whereas the President is elected from among the judges for one year's term, every year from some other Republic or Province.

Amendment VIII drafts the basis for enacting the Constitutional Law on the Promulgation of the Amendments.

The following amendments were promulgated in 1988:

Amendments IX–XVIII pertain to the socio-economic order, and envisage the development of social ownership and improved production and management, in addition to the participation of the Yugoslav economy in joint ventures with foreign concerns; constitutional guarantees are extended to foreign investors in Yugoslavia. The independence of economic and banking organizations with respect to the State is stressed, as is their joint responsibility for decisions. The basis of the internal market is to be broadened, and the introduction of uniform systems of credit and taxation is also proposed. Changes in property rights include an increase in the maximum land holding to more than 15 ha.

Amendments XIX–XXIII, which pertain to the political system, provide a more adequate definition of the role of the State, and are intended to establish a greater rationality and efficiency within the political system. The role of workers' councils is to be strengthened; the assembly system and the principle of delegates are to be developed further; and the electoral system is to be revised, on the basis of establishing direct, general and secret elections for all assemblies of socio-political communities.

Amendments XXIV–XXXVII pertain to relations within the Federation, and to the rights, duties and organization of the Federation, with particular reference to the functioning of the integral Yugoslav market and the social plan; the operation of the Yugoslav National Bank; the uniform implementation of federal laws; the financing of the Yugoslav People's Army; and the strengthening of the role of associated labour.

Note: In August 1990 the Federal Chamber approved 24 draft amendments to the Constitution, permitting pluralism of ownership and a multi-party system. Freedom of political organization is guaranteed, but this freedom is restricted if the activity of individual parties is directed at a violent change of the constitutional order, threat to the territorial integrity of the SFRY and of the Republics or involves the dissemination of national or religious hatred.

The Government

HEAD OF STATE

President of the Collective Presidency: (vacant)*.

COLLECTIVE STATE PRESIDENCY*
(May 1991–May 1992)

The functions of President and Vice-President are carried out for a period of one year by members of the Presidency in the following sequence: Macedonia, Bosnia-Herzegovina, Slovenia, Serbia, Croatia, Montenegro, Vojvodina and Kosovo.

President: (vacant).

Vice-President: Dr BRANKO KOSTIĆ (Montenegro).

Members: JUGOSLAV KOSTIĆ (Vojvodina), SEJDO BAJRAMOVIĆ (Kosovo-Metohija), BOGIĆ BOGICEVIĆ (Bosnia-Herzegovina), Dr BORISAV JOVIĆ (Serbia).

* The other members of the federal Presidency were STJEPAN (STIPE) MESIĆ (Croatia—resigned December 1991), JANEZ DRNOVSEK (Slovenia—resigned October) and VASIL TUPURKOVSKI (Macedonia—resigned January 1992). Upon the expiry of Dr Borisav Jović's term of office on 15 May 1991, Mesić was due to assume the Presidency. Branko Kostić was to have become Vice-President. The members for Serbia, Montenegro, Vojvodina and Kosovo ('the Serbian bloc'), however, did not endorse the appointment of Mesić. Nevertheless, Mesić declared himself to be the rightful President and, on 30 June, this was officially proclaimed. In early October the Serbian bloc on the Presidency, chaired by the Vice-President, conducted meetings without Mesić or the representatives of Bosnia-Herzegovina, Macedonia and Slovenia, who repudiated their authority. In November Croatia followed Slovenia in declaring that all its citizens should discontinue their participation in federal institutions. Mesić formally resigned on 5 December.

FEDERAL EXECUTIVE COUNCIL
(January 1992)

President: (vacant).

Vice-President: ALEKSANDAR MITROVIĆ.

Federal Secretary for Foreign Affairs: (vacant).

Federal Secretary for National Defence: (vacant).

Federal Secretary for Internal Affairs: PETAR GRAČANIN.

Federal Secretary for Finance: (vacant).

Federal Secretary for Foreign Economic Relations: (vacant).

Federal Secretary for Trade: NAZMI MUSTAFA.

Federal Secretary for Development: (vacant).

Federal Secretary for Energy and Industry and for Transport and Communications: STEVAN SANTO.

Federal Secretary for Agriculture: Dr STEVO MIRJANIĆ.

Federal Secretary for Labour, Health, Veterans' Affairs and Social Policy: RADISA GAČIĆ.

Federal Secretary for Justice and Administration: Dr VLADO KAMBOVSKI.

Members without Portfolio: SABRIJA POJSKIĆ, NIKOLA GASOVSKI.

Note: The withdrawal of Croatian and Slovenian members of the Government, during 1991, meant that many of the Federal Secretariats were controlled by deputy Ministers.

FEDERAL SECRETARIATS

Office of the Federal Executive Council: 11070 Belgrade, bul. Leninja 2; tel. (11) 334281.

Federal Secretariat for Agriculture: 11070 Belgrade, bul. AVNOJ-a 104; tel. (11) 602555; telex 11062; fax (11) 195244.

Federal Secretariat for Development: 11070 Belgrade, Omladinskih brigada 1; tel. (11) 2223550; telex 11062; fax (11) 195244.

Federal Secretariat for Energy and Industry: 11070 Belgrade, bul. AVNOJ-a 104; tel. (11) 602555; telex 11062; fax (11) 195244.

Federal Secretariat for Finance: 11070 Belgrade, Omladinskih brigada 1; tel. (11) 2223550; telex 11062; fax (11) 195244.

Federal Secretariat for Foreign Affairs: 11000 Belgrade, Kneza Miloša 24; tel. (11) 682555; telex 11173; fax (11) 682668.

Federal Secretariat for Foreign Economic Relations: 11070 Belgrade, Omladinskih brigada 1; tel. (11) 2223550; telex 11062; fax (11) 195244.

Federal Secretariat for Internal Affairs: 11000 Belgrade, Kneza Miloša 92; tel. (11) 685555; telex 11185; fax (11) 2351005.

Federal Secretariat for Justice and Administration: 11070 Belgrade, bul. AVNOJ-a 104; tel. (11) 602555; telex 11062; fax (11) 195244.

Federal Secretariat for Labour, Health, Veterans' Affairs and Social Policy: 11070 Belgrade, bul. AVNOJ-a 104, SIV-II; tel. (11) 602555; telex 11062; fax (11) 195244.

Federal Secretariat for National Defence: 11000 Belgrade, Kneza Miloša 29; tel. (11) 656122; telex 12216.

Federal Secretariat for Trade: 11070 Belgrade, bul. AVNOJ-a 104; tel. (11) 602555; telex 11062; fax (11) 195244.

Federal Secretariat for Transport and Communications: 11070 Belgrade, bul. AVNOJ-a 104; tel. (11) 602555; telex 12062; fax (11) 2223946.

Legislature
(October 1991)

SAVEZNA SKUPŠTINA (FEDERAL ASSEMBLY)

The SFRY Assembly is composed of two chambers. The Federal Chamber has 220 members (30 from each of the six republics and

20 from each of the two provinces) while the Chamber of Republics and Provinces has 88 members (12 from each Republican Assembly—elected from a multi-party basis—and eight from each Provincial Assembly). During 1991 several republican and provincial delegations discontinued their participation in the Assembly.

President: Dr SLOBODAN GLIGORIJEVIĆ.

Federal Chamber

President: BOGDANA GLUMAC-LEVAKOV (Vojvodina).

Chamber of Republics and Provinces

President: (vacant).

Political Organizations

Following the approval of the introduction of a multi-party system by the ruling League of Communists of Yugoslavia (LCY) in early 1990, numerous new parties and groups were founded or re-established. By early 1991 a total of 269 parties were operating. The following (most of which have republican branches or affiliates) were among the more prominent of the federal parties:

NATIONAL PARTIES

Alliance of Yugoslav Reform Forces (Savez Reformskih Snaga Jugoslavije): Belgrade; f. 1990 by ANTE MARKOVIĆ.

Association for a Yugoslav Democratic Initiative: f. 1989 as nationwide alternative to the League of Communists of Yugoslavia (now the League of Communists-Movement for Yugoslavia).

League of Communists-Movement for Yugoslavia (LC-MY) (Savez Komunista-Pokret za Jugoslaviju—SK-PJ): Novi Beograd (Belgrade), bul. Lenjina 6; f. 1919 as Socialist Workers' Party of Yugoslavia; renamed Communist Party of Yugoslavia 1920, League of Communists of Yugoslavia 1952; present name adopted Nov. 1990; 200,000 mems; ceased to be sole authorized party in early 1990; Leader DRAGAN ATANASOVSKI.

People's Radical Party (Narodna Radikalna Stranka): Belgrade; f. 1881, re-est. 1990; advocates a federation that would have jurisdiction over defence, security, foreign policy and a unified economy.

Social Democratic Alliance of Yugoslavia: f. 1990; supports a federal state of equal citizens and federal units.

Workers' Party of Yugoslavia (Radnicka Partija): Belgrade; f. 1990; opposes any change in Yugoslavia's borders; supports Serbia's right to resolve independently the conflict in Kosovo; Pres. MILOŠ JOVANOVIĆ.

Yugoslav Democratic Party: f. 1990; supports federative system and implementation of Federal Government's measures; advocates abolition of SFRY Presidency and Presidencies of the Republics and Provinces, proposing instead the introduction of one President to be popularly elected in free elections.

Yugoslav Green Party: Belgrade; f. 1990; open to all citizens regardless of national, religious or racial affiliation.

Diplomatic Representation

EMBASSIES IN YUGOSLAVIA

Afghanistan: 11000 Belgrade, Njegoševa 56/1; tel. (11) 4448716; Ambassador: SARWAR MANGAL.

Albania: 11000 Belgrade, Kneza Miloša 56; tel. (11) 646864; telex 12294; Ambassador: KUJTIM HYSENAJ.

Algeria: 11000 Belgrade, Maglajska 26B; tel. (11) 668211; telex 12343; Ambassador: AHMED ATTAF.

Angola: 11000 Belgrade, Tolstojeva 51; tel. (11) 663199; telex 11841; Ambassador: EVARISTO DOMINGOS.

Argentina: 11000 Belgrade, Knez Mihajlova 24/I; tel. (11) 621550; telex 12182; Ambassador: FEDERICO CARLOS BARTTFELD.

Australia: 11000 Belgrade, Čika Ljubina 13; tel. (11) 624655; telex 11206; fax (11) 624029; Ambassador: FRANCIS W. MILNE.

Austria: 11000 Belgrade, Kneza Sime Markovića 2; tel. (11) 635955; telex 11456; fax (11) 638215; Ambassador: (vacant).

Bangladesh: 11000 Belgrade, Dragorska 4; tel. (11) 666153; telex 12459; Ambassador: HARUN AHMED CHOWDHURY.

Belgium: 11000 Belgrade, Proleterskih brigada 18; tel. (11) 330016; telex 11747; fax (11) 330016; Ambassador: Baron ALAIN GUILLAUME.

Bolivia: 11000 Belgrade, Romena Rolana 60; tel. (11) 781576; Ambassador: RAÚL ŽELADA COVARRUBIAS.

Brazil: 11000 Belgrade, Proleterskih brigada 14; tel. (11) 339781; telex 11100; Ambassador: JOSÉ OLYMPIO RACHE DE ALMEIDA.

Bulgaria: 11000 Belgrade, Birčaninova 26; tel. (11) 646222; telex 11665; Ambassador: MARKO MARKOV.

Cambodia: 11000 Belgrade, Gospodar Jovanova 67; tel. (11) 631151; Ambassador: RENE VANHON.

Canada: 11000 Belgrade, Kneza Miloša 75; tel. (11) 644666; telex 11137; fax (11) 641480; Ambassador: JAMES B. BISSETT.

Chile: 11000 Belgrade, Vasilija Gaćeše 9A; tel. (11) 648340; Ambassador: LUIS JEREZ RAMÍREZ.

China, People's Republic: 11000 Belgrade, Kralja Milutina 6; tel. (11) 331484; telex 11146; Ambassador: ZHANG DAKE.

Colombia: 11000 Belgrade, Njegoševa 54/II–5; tel. (11) 457246; telex 12530; fax (11) 457120; Ambassador: (vacant).

Cuba: 11000 Belgrade, Kneza Miloša 14; tel. (11) 657694; Ambassador: ZOILA ROSALES BRITO.

Cyprus: 11040 Belgrade, Diplomatska Kolonija 9; tel. (11) 663725; telex 12729; fax (11) 665348; Ambassador: ANDRESTINOS N. PAPADOPOULOS.

Czechoslovakia: 11000 Belgrade, bul. Revolucije 22; tel. (11) 330134; Ambassador: FRANTIŠEK LIPKA.

Denmark: 11000 Belgrade, Neznanog Junaka 9A; tel. (11) 667826; telex 11219; Ambassador: HANS JESPERSEN.

Ecuador: 11000 Belgrade, Kneza Miloša 16; tel. (11) 684876; telex 12751; Ambassador: FRANCISCO PROAÑO ARANDI.

Egypt: 11000 Belgrade, Andre Nikolića 12; tel. (11) 651225; telex 12074; Ambassador: Dr HUSSEIN HASSOUNA.

Ethiopia: 11000 Belgrade, Knez Mihajlova 6/IV; tel. (11) 628666; telex 11818; Ambassador: MAKONNEN GIZAW.

Finland: 11001 Belgrade, Birčaninova 29; tel. (11) 646322; telex 11707; fax (11) 683365; Ambassador: MAUNO CASTRÉN.

France: 11000 Belgrade, Pariska 11; tel. (11) 636555; telex 11496; Ambassador: MICHEL CHATELAIS.

Gabon: 11000 Belgrade, Dragorska 3; tel. (11) 669683; telex 12019; Ambassador: EMMANUEL MENDOUME-NZE.

Germany: 11000 Belgrade, Kneza Miloša 74–76; tel. (11) 645755; telex 11107; fax (11) 686989; Ambassador: Dr HANSJÖRG EIFF.

Ghana: 11000 Belgrade, Ognjena Price 50; tel. (11) 4442445; telex 11720; fax (11) 436314; Ambassador: THOMAS BENJAMIN SAM.

Greece: 11000 Belgrade, Francuska 33; tel. (11) 621443; telex 11361; Ambassador: ELEFTHERIOS KARAYANNIS.

Guinea: 11000 Belgrade, Ohridska 4; tel. (11) 431830; telex 11963; Ambassador: MOROU BALDE.

Holy See: 11000 Belgrade, Svetog Save 24; tel. (11) 432822; Apostolic Pro-Nuncio: GABRIEL MONTALVO.

Hungary: 11000 Belgrade, Proleterskih brigada 72; tel. (11) 4440472; Ambassador: ÖSZI ISTVÁN.

India: 11070 Belgrade, B-06/07 Genex International Centre, Vladimira Popovića 6; tel. (11) 2223325; telex 71127; fax (11) 2223357; Ambassador: ADITYA NARAYAN DHAIRYASHEEL HAKSAR.

Indonesia: 11000 Belgrade, bul. Oktobarske Revolucije br. 18; tel. (11) 662122; telex 11129; Ambassador: ATWAR NURHADI.

Iran: 11000 Belgrade, Proleterskih brigada 9; tel. (11) 338782; telex 11726; fax (11) 338784; Ambassador: NASROLLAH KAZEMI KAMYAB.

Iraq: 11000 Belgrade, Proleterskih brigada 69; tel. (11) 434688; telex 12325; Ambassador: Dr WAHBI AL-QARAGULI.

Italy: 11000 Belgrade, Birčaninova 11; tel. (11) 659722; telex 12082; Ambassador: SERGIO VENTO.

Japan: 11000 Belgrade, Ilirska 5; tel. (11) 768255; telex 11263; fax (11) 762934; Ambassador: TAIZO NAKAMURA.

Jordan: 11000 Belgrade, Kablarska 28; tel. (11) 651642; telex 12904; Ambassador: HANI B. TABBARA.

Korea, Democratic People's Republic: 11000 Belgrade, Dr Milutina Ivkovića 9; tel. (11) 668739; telex 11577; Ambassador: CHI JAE RYONG.

Korea, Republic: 11070 Belgrade, Genex International Centre, Vladimira Popovića 6; tel. (11) 2223531; Ambassador: DOO BYONG SHIN.

Kuwait: 11000 Belgrade, Čakorska 2; tel. (11) 664961; telex 12774; Ambassador: ISSA AHMAD AL-HAMMAD.

Lebanon: 11000 Belgrade, Vase Pelagića 38; tel. (11) 651290; telex 11049; Ambassador: Dr WILLIAM HABIB.

Libya: 11000 Belgrade, Generala Ždanova 42; tel. (11) 644782; telex 11787; Secretary of People's Committee: ASSUR MUHAMED KARKUM.

Malaysia: 11000 Belgrade, Čakorska 8; tel. (11) 660823; telex 12129; Ambassador: ZAINUDDIN A. RAHMAN.

Mali: 11000 Belgrade, Generala Hanrisa 1; tel. (11) 493774; telex 11052; Ambassador: N'Tji Laico Traore (designate).

Mexico: 11000 Belgrade, trg Republike 5/IV; tel. (11) 638111; telex 12141; fax (11) 629566; Ambassador: Agustín García-López Santaolalla.

Mongolia: 11000 Belgrade, Generala Vasića 5; tel. (11) 668536; telex 12253; Ambassador: Ludevdorjyn Khashbat.

Morocco: 11000 Belgrade, Sanje Živanović 4; tel. (11) 651775; Ambassador: Hassan Fassi Fihri (designate).

Myanmar: 11000 Belgrade, Kneza Miloša 72; tel. (11) 645420; telex 72769; Ambassador: Ü Hla Maung.

Netherlands: 11000 Belgrade, Simina 29; tel. (11) 626699; telex 11556; fax (11) 628986; Ambassador: J. H. W. Fietelaars.

Nigeria: 11000 Belgrade, Geršićeva 14a; tel. (11) 413411; telex 12875; Ambassador: Ezekiel Gotom Dimka (designate).

Norway: 11000 Belgrade, Kablarska 30; tel. (11) 651626; telex 11668; fax (11) 651754; Ambassador: Georg Krane.

Pakistan: 11000 Belgrade, bul. Oktobarske Revolucije 62; tel. (11) 661676; Ambassador: Saidulla Khan Dehlavi.

Panama: 11000 Belgrade, Strahinjića Baua 51/II-5; tel. (11) 620374; telex 11451; Ambassador: Ricardo T. Pezet H.

Peru: 11000 Belgrade, Baba Višnjina 26/II-10; tel. (11) 454943; telex 12272; Ambassador: Eduardo Llosa.

Philippines: 11040 Belgrade, Tolstojeva 49; tel. (11) 661442; telex 12052; Ambassador: José U. Fernandez.

Poland: 11000 Belgrade, Kneza Miloša 38; tel. (11) 644866; telex 72006; fax (11) 646275; Ambassador: Jerzy Chmielewski.

Portugal: 11110 Belgrade, Stojana Novakovića 19; tel. (11) 750358; telex 11648; fax (11) 754421; Ambassador: João Morais da Cunha Matos.

Romania: 11000 Belgrade, Kneza Miloša 70; tel. (11) 646071; telex 11316; Ambassador: Ionel Stanculescu.

Russia: 11000 Belgrade, Deligradska 32; tel. (11) 657533; Ambassador: Vadim Loginov.

Spain: 11000 Belgrade, Njegoševa 54/I Apt. 1–3; tel. (11) 454777; telex 12864; fax (11) 4440614; Ambassador: José Manuel Allendesalazar.

Sri Lanka: 11000 Belgrade, Lepenička 10; tel. (11) 460661; telex 12475; Ambassador: Razik Zarook (designate).

Sudan: 11000 Belgrade, Nemaujina 4/V; tel. (11) 657960; telex 12479; Ambassador: Ibrahim A. Hamra.

Sweden: 11000 Belgrade, Pariska 7; tel. (11) 626422; telex 11595; fax (11) 626492; Ambassador: Jan Af Sillen.

Switzerland: 11000 Belgrade, Birčaninova 27; tel. (11) 646899; telex 11383; fax (11) 657253; Ambassador: Jean-Jacques Indermühle.

Syria: 11000 Belgrade, Mlade Bosne 31; tel. (11) 4449985; telex 11889; fax (11) 453367; Ambassador: Ismail al-Kadi.

Thailand: 11000 Belgrade, Molerova 11/V; tel. (11) 454053; telex 12657; Ambassador: Ukirt Durayaprama.

Tunisia: 11000 Belgrade, Vase Pelagića 19; tel. (11) 652966; telex 11461; Ambassador: Raouf Said.

Turkey: 11000 Belgrade, Proleterskih brigada 1; tel. (11) 335431; telex 12081; Ambassador: Berhan Ekinci.

United Kingdom: 11000 Belgrade, Generala Ždanova 46; tel. (11) 645055; telex 11468; fax (11) 659651; Ambassador: Peter E. Hall.

USA: 11000 Belgrade, Kneza Miloša 50; tel. (11) 645655; telex 11529; fax (11) 645221; Ambassador: Warren Zimmermann.

Uruguay: 11000 Belgrade, Vasina 14; tel. (11) 620994; telex 12650; Ambassador: Dr Fernando Gómez Fyns.

Venezuela: 11000 Terazije 45/II; tel. (11) 331604; telex 12856; Ambassador: Freddy Christians.

Viet-Nam: 11000 Belgrade, Lackovićeva 6; tel. (11) 663527; telex 11292; Ambassador: Vo Anh Tuan.

Yemen: 11000 Belgrade, Vasilija Gaćeše 9c; Ambassador: Mohamed Mahmood Hassan al-Baihi.

Zaire: 11000 Belgrade, Oktobarske revolucije 47; tel. (11) 668931; telex 11491; Ambassador: Lundunge Kadahi Chiri-Mwami.

Zambia: 11000 Belgrade, Simina 17; tel. (11) 637955; telex 12152; Ambassador: Anderson Henry Kaluya.

Zimbabwe: 11000 Belgrade, Perside Milenković 9; tel. (11) 647047; Ambassador: Chimbidzayi E. C. Sanyangare.

Judicial System

The Yugoslav Constitution states that judicial functions are to be discharged within a uniform system and that the jurisdiction of the courts shall be established and altered only by law. In general, court proceedings are conducted in public (exceptionally the public may be excluded to preserve professional secrets, public order or morals) in the national language of the region in which the court is situated. Citizens who do not know the language in which the proceedings are being conducted may use their own language.

The judicial system comprises courts of general jurisdiction, i.e. communal courts, county courts and republican supreme courts. The courts of general jurisdiction are organized in accordance with individual republican legislation. In general, the courts are entitled to proceed in criminal, civil and administrative matters. Military courts, headed by the Supreme Military Court, proceed in criminal and administrative matters connected with military service or national defence.

Self-management courts decide specific disputes as laid down by the Constitution or Statute (labour disputes, conciliation between citizens or organizations; courts of arbitration).

Economic or trade matters are heard in some Republics (Serbia, Macedonia, Croatia) by economic courts. They proceed also in penal-economic matters.

Judges are elected or relieved by the assembly of the particular socio-political community (local, republican or federal assembly).

The basic principles of regulation of the judicial system are set out in the Constitution of the SFRY and further elaborated by federal and republican legislation.

CONSTITUTIONAL COURT

This court decides on the conformity of statutes with the federal Constitution, whether or not a republic statute or regulation is contrary to federal statute and on the conformity of enactments of federal agencies with the Constitution and federal statute. The court has 14 members (the President and 13 judges).

President of the Constitutional Court: Milovan Buzadzić.

FEDERAL COURT

This is the highest organ of justice in Yugoslavia. It decides on extraordinary legal remedies against decisions of supreme courts of the Republics and the Supreme Military Court, and on the legality of finally binding administrative acts of federal government agencies, based on federal statutes. The Court also decides property disputes between Federation and Republics, and reviews, in the final instance, sentences in which the death penalty for a criminal offence, defined by federal statute, has been passed. Judges are elected or dismissed by the Federal Chamber of the SFRY Assembly. The Court comprises the President and 13 judges.

President of the Federal Court of Yugoslavia: Dr Rafael Cijan, 11000 Belgrade, Svetozara Markovića 21; tel. (11) 333911.

OFFICE OF THE PUBLIC PROSECUTOR

The Federal Public Prosecutor is elected or dismissed by the Federal Assembly. Public prosecutors of the various republics are nominated by the Federal Public Prosecutor with the approval of the Executive Council of the particular Republic. All other public prosecutors are appointed by the public prosecutor of the Republic.

Federal Public Prosecutor: Ljubo Prljeta.

OFFICE OF THE PUBLIC ATTORNEY

Represents proprietary interests of the federation, republics, districts and communities. There is a Federal Office, and in addition there are six republican offices, two offices in the autonomous regions, five town offices and 228 communal offices.

Federal Attorney-General: Sašo Ivanovski.

Federal Social Attorney of Self-Management: carries out his or her function within the framework of federal rights and duties.

Social Attorney of Self-Management: Ivica Čačić.

Religion

The principle of the complete separation of Church and State is incorporated in the Constitution, which also states that religious confession shall in no way be restricted and makes other provisions for the welfare of religious bodies. The Republic safeguards the freedom of faith and of religious assembly, provided the state laws are respected, and ensures full equality for each religious community, as well as the freedom of its activity. Most of the inhabitants of the SFRY are, at least nominally, Christian, but there is a significant Muslim minority. The main Christian denomination is Eastern Orthodox, but the Roman Catholic Church is dominant in the north, in Croatia and Slovenia. There are small minorities of Old Catholics, Protestants and Jews throughout Yugoslavia.

CHRISTIANITY
The Eastern Orthodox Church

Serbian Orthodox Church: Headquarters: 11001 Belgrade, 7 jula 5, POB 182; tel. (11) 638161; fax (11) 182780; 9m. adherents throughout Yugoslavia (mainly in Serbia and Montenegro); Patriarch of Serbia: His Holiness PAVLE, Archbishop of Peć and Metropolitan of Belgrade-Karlovci; Sec. Archdeacon MOMIR LEČIĆ.

The Macedonian Orthodox Church is separate from, although not recognized by, the Serbian Church; there are communities of Greek, Albanian, Romanian and Bulgarian Orthodox in Yugoslavia. In June 1991 it was reported that the Free Serbian Orthodox Church of Australia and New Zealand (the main denomination of the Serb diaspora, which had split from the mother Church in 1963, alleging Communist domination) was ready for reconciliation with Belgrade.

The Roman Catholic Church

Yugoslavia comprises eight archdioceses (including two directly responsible to the Holy See) and 15 dioceses (including one for Catholics of the Byzantine rite).

The majority of the 7m. adherents in Yugoslavia are resident in Croatia and Slovenia.

Bishops' Conference: Biskupska konferencija Jugoslavije, 41000 Zagreb, Kaptol 22; tel. (41) 275449; fax (41) 431529; f. 1918; Pres. Cardinal FRANJO KUHARIĆ, Archbishop of Zagreb.

Latin Rite

Archbishop of Bar: PETAR PERKOLIĆ, Nadbiskupski Ordinarijat, 85000 Bar, Popovići 98; tel. (85) 21705.

Archbishop of Belgrade: Dr FRANC PERKO, Nadbiskupski Ordinarijat, 11000 Belgrade, ul. Svetozara Markovića 20; tel. (11) 334846.

Archbishop of Ljubljana: Dr ALOJZIJ ŠUŠTAR, 61001 Ljubljana, pp 121/III, Ciril-Metodov trg 4; tel. (61) 310673; fax (61) 314169.

Archbishop of Rijeka-Senj: Dr ANTUN TAMARUT, Nadbiskupski Ordinarijat, 51000 Rijeka, Slaviše Vajnera Čiče 2; tel. (51) 37999.

Archbishop of Split-Makarska: ANTE JURIĆ, 58001 Split, pp 142, ul. Zrinjsko-Frankopanska 14; tel. (58) 46755.

Archbishop of Vrhbosna-Sarajevo: VINKO PULJIĆ, Nadbiskupski Ordinarijat Vrhbosanski, 71001 Sarajevo, pp 362, Radojke Lakić 7; tel. (71) 39239.

Archbishop of Zadar: MARIJAN OBLAK, Nadbiskupski Ordinarijat, 57000 Zadar, Zeleni trg 1; tel. (57) 22395; fax (57) 25399.

Archbishop of Zagreb: Cardinal FRANJO KUHARIĆ, 41000 Zagreb, pp 553, Kaptol 31; tel. (41) 275132.

Byzantine Rite

Bishop of Križevci: SLAVOMIR MIKLOVŠ, Ordinarijat Križevačke Eparhije, 41000 Zagreb, Kaptol 20; tel. (41) 270767; 48,715 adherents in all Yugoslavia (1986).

There are Old Catholic Churches, which split with Rome during the 19th century (and are now in communion with the Anglican Churches), in Croatia, Serbia and Slovenia.

Protestant Churches

Baptist Union of Yugoslavia: 21000 Novi Sad, Koruška 24; tel. (21) 623273; f. 1922; Sec. ŽELIMIR SRNEC.

Christian Assemblies—Church of Christ's Brethren: 21470 Bački Petrovac, Janka Kralja 4; tel. (21) 780153; Pres. of Elders SAMUEL RYBAR.

Christian Church Jehovah's Witnesses: 11000 Belgrade, Milorada Mitrovića 4; tel. (11) 450383.

Christian Nazarene Community: Hrišćanska nazarenska zajednica, 21000 Novi Sad, Vodnikova br. 12; tel. (21) 57998; Pres. KAROL HRUBIK VLADIMIR.

Christian Reformed Church: 24323 Feketic, ul. Bratsva 26; tel. (11) 738070; f. 1919; 22,000 mems; Bishop IMRE HODOSY.

Evangelical Church of Republic of Croatia, Republic of Bosnia and Herzegovina and SAP Vojvodina: 41000 Zagreb, Gundulićeva 28; tel. (41) 420685; 4,950 mems; Pres. Dr VLADO L. DEUTSCH.

Evangelical Hungarian Church: Subotica, Brace Radiča 17; Pastor DANNY NOVÁK.

Evangelical Lutheran Church of Slovenia: Headquarters: 69000 Murska Sobota, Titova 9, Slovenia; tel. (69) 22304; f. 1561; 20,000 mems; Chair. LUDVIK NOVAK.

Seventh-Day Adventist Church: Hrišćanska adventistička crkva, 11000 Belgrade, Božidara Adzije 4; tel. (11) 453842; telex 72645; fax (11) 458604; Pres. JOVAN LORENCIN; Sec. NEDELJKO KAČAVENDA.

Slovak Evangelical Church of the Augsburg Confession: 21000 Novi Sad, Karadžićeva 2; tel. (21) 611882; Lutheran; 51,500 mems (1990); Bishop Dr ANDREJ BEREDI.

United Methodist Church: 21000 Novi Sad, L. Mušičkoga 7; tel. (21) 610377; f. 1898; 3,000 mems; Superintendent MARTIN HOVAN.

ISLAM

Islamic Community: Rijaset Islamske Zajednice, 71000 Sarajevo, Save Kovačevića 2; tel. (71) 214546; fax (71) 211035; f. 1882; *c.* 4.5m. adherents, in four administrative Regions: Sarajevo, Priština, Skopje and Titograd; the Reis-ul-ulema is the spiritual leader of the Islamic Community of Yugoslavia and the Supreme Assembly is the chief judicial and representative body.

Reis-ul-ulema (Supreme Head): Hadži JAKUB SELIMOVSKI.

President of the Supreme Assembly: Hadži MUSTAFA PLICARIĆ.

JUDAISM

Federation of Jewish Communities in Yugoslavia: Belgrade, 7 jula 71A/III, POB 841; tel. (11) 624359; fax (11) 626674; f. 1919, revived 1944; 6,000 mems in 30 communities; Pres. of Federation of Jewish Communities in Yugoslavia Dr LAVOSLAV KADELBURG.

The Press

Since 1956 the Yugoslav press has enjoyed an organizational freedom that has enabled it to establish a position of independence and individuality. In that year, ownership of Yugoslav newspapers was transferred to societies controlled by their employees, who share in the profits. The Constitution guarantees newspaper publishers the right to exercise self-management, which includes the appointment of directors, editors and a board comprising a large number of people from public and political life, as well as representatives of the workers. This board has an important role in shaping the newspapers' policy. Censorship is not imposed, editors being aware of their responsibilities and of the flexibility of the Press Law in force since 1960. This lays down the usual restrictions regarding the publication of false and distorted news, confidential information, and items harmful to foreign relations, to the Government or to representatives of other countries. The republican authorities are increasingly influential in the control of press legislation.

About 30 dailies are published in Yugoslavia, printed in Serbian (Cyrillic alphabet), Croatian (Roman), Slovene, Macedonian, Hungarian, Italian, English and Albanian. In 1987 there were 204 weekly newspapers and periodicals, 293 fortnightly publications and 953 monthlies. In 1989 the circulation of all daily newspapers in Yugoslavia had fallen to 2.0m., having stood at 2.9m., in 1987. The most influential are those published in Belgrade and the capitals of the Republics. Important newspapers include *Borba* and *Politika* (Belgrade, Serbia), *Vijesnik* (Zagreb, Croatia), *Delo* (Ljubljana, Slovenia), *Oslobodjenje* (Sarajevo, Bosnia-Herzegovina), *Nova Makedonija* (Skopje, Macedonia) and *Pobjeda* (Titograd, Montenegro). Evening papers are also popular, notably *Večernje novosti* (Belgrade).

The daily papers are listed in the sections on the individual Republics, but the principal periodicals, wherever they are published in Yugoslavia, are listed below:

PERIODICALS

4. Jul.: Belgrade, trg bratstva i jedinstva 9/III–IV; weekly; organ of Federation of Veterans of the People's Liberation War of Yugoslavia; Dir and Editor-in-Chief RAJKO PAVIČEVIĆ; circ. 10,000.

21: 71000 Skopje, Bul. Ilinden bb; 2 a month; organ of the Social Democratic Alliance of Macedonia.

Arena: 41000 Zagreb, Ljubice Gerovac br. 1; f. 1957; Yugoslav illustrated weekly; Editor MILIVOJ PAŠIĆEK; circ. 224,000.

Auto magazin: 61000 Ljubljana, Titova 35; tel. (61) 319180; telex 31255; f. 1967; review for motorists and pedestrians; Slovene and Serbo-Croat editions; Editor MARKO SPAZZAPAN; circ. 80,000.

Danas: Zagreb; weekly; news magazine; Chief and Exec. Editor MLADEN MALOCA.

Duga: Belgrade; news magazine; Editor-in-Chief ILIJA REPAIĆ.

Ekonomist: Belgrade, Nušićeva 6/III; f. 1948; quarterly; journal of the Yugoslav Association of Economists; Editor Dr HASAN HADŽIOMEROVIĆ.

Ekonomska Politika: 11000 Belgrade, trg Marksa i Engelsa 7; tel. (11) 335355; telex 11410; f. 1952; weekly; Editor-in-Chief SLOBODAN VUJICA.

Finansije: Belgrade, Jovana Ristića 1; f. 1945; every 2 months; organ of the Federal Secretariat of Finance; Editor BOGOLJUB LAZAREVIĆ.

Front: Belgrade, Proleterskih brigada 13; f. 1945; 2 a month; illustrated review; Editor-in-Chief STEVAN KORDA; circ. 263,000.

Gospodarski vestnik: 61000 Ljubljana, Titova 35; tel. (61) 318389; fax (61) 311871; Slovenian; business weekly.

Hrvatska Riječ: Subotica, Vase Stajica 13; weekly; Editor JOSIP KUJUNDZIĆ.

Ilustrovana Politika: Belgrade, Makedonska 29; tel. (11) 326938; telex 11099; f. 1958; weekly illustrated review; Editor MIRKO BOJIĆ; circ. 250,000.

Informativni tednik Dela-TELEKS: Ljubljana, Titova 35; tel. (61) 319280; telex 31255; f. 1977; weekly news magazine; Slovene language; Editor VILKO NOVAK; circ. 40,000.

Informator: 41000 Zagreb, Masarykova 1, POB 794; tel. (41) 429333; telex 21264; fax (41) 426247; f. 1952; 2 a week; economic and legal matters; Editor DUBRAVKO ABRAMOVIĆ.

Intervju: Belgrade; news magazine; Editor-in-Chief PETAR ILIĆ.

Jeta e Re: Priština, Beogradska 22; Albanian; Editor MEKULI HASAN.

Jež: Belgrade, Nušićeva 6/IV; f. 1935; humorous weekly; Editor RADIVOJE IVANOVIĆ; circ. 50,000.

Književnè Novine: Belgrade, Francuska 7; f. 1948; fortnightly; review of literature, arts and social studies; Editor-in-Chief (vacant); circ. 7,500.

Književnost: Belgrade, Čika Ljubina 1; tel. (11) 620130; fax (11) 182581; f. 1946; monthly; literary review; Editor VUK KRNJEVIĆ; circ. 1,800.

Komunist: 11000 Belgrade, trg Marksa i Engelsa 11; tel. (11) 335061; telex 12337; f. 1925; weekly; organ of League of Communists-Movement for Yugoslavia; Dir and Editor-in-Chief MILIVOJE TOMASEVIĆ; circ. 520,000.

Letopis Matice Srpske: Novi Sad, Matice srpske 1; f. 1825; monthly literary review; Editor BOŠKO IVKOV.

Medjunarodna Politika (Review of International Affairs): Belgrade, Nemanjina 34, POB 413; f. 1950 by the Federation of Yugoslav Journalists; every 2 weeks; published in English, French, Russian, German, Spanish and Serbo-Croat; Dir and Editor-in-Chief Dr RANKO PETKOVIĆ.

Medjunarodni Problemi: Belgrade, Makedonska 25; tel. (11) 321433; fax (11) 324013; f. 1949; every 3 months; review of the Institute of International Politics and Economics; Editor B. MARKOVIĆ; circ. 1,000.

Mladina: 61000 Ljubljana; news magazine; Slovene; Editor-in-Chief FRANC ZAVRL.

Mladost: Belgrade, Maršala Tita 2/II; weekly; organ of People's Youth organization of Yugoslavia; literary review; Editor-in-Chief SENAD AVDIĆ; circ. 96,000.

Narodna Armija: Belgrade, Proleterskih brig. 13; f. 1945; weekly; Yugoslav People's Army organ; Dir MILAN KAVGIĆ; Editor-in-Chief GAJA PETROVIĆ.

Naši Razgledi: 61001 Ljubljana, Titova 35, POB 188; tel. (61) 318445; telex 31255; fax (61) 311871; f. 1952; political and cultural fortnightly; Editor SLAVKO FRAS.

Nedeljski Dnevnik: 61000 Ljubljana, Kopitarjeva 2; tel. (61) 325261; telex 31177; fax (61) 312775; f. 1961; weekly; popular; in Slovene; Exec. Editor ZLATKO ŠETINC; circ. 220,000.

NIN (Nedeljne informativne novine): Belgrade, Cetinjska 1, POB 208; tel. (11) 324410; telex 12000; fax (11) 633368; f. 1935; weekly; Editor TEODOR ANDJELIĆ; circ. 140,000.

Nova Proizvodnja: Ljubljana, Erjavceva 15; tel. (61) 212139; f. 1949; bi-monthly; technics and economics; organ of the Association of Engineers and Technicians of the Republic of Slovenia; Editor MARJAN LAČIĆ.

Official Gazette of the SFR of Yugoslavia: 11000 Belgrade, Jovana Ristića 1; f. 1945; editions in Serbo-Croat, Slovene, Albanian, Hungarian and Macedonian; Dir VELJKO TADIĆ; circ. 73,000.

Politikin Zabavnik: Belgrade, Makedonska 29; f. 1939; weekly; comic; Editor RADOMIR SOŠKIĆ; circ. 260,000.

Pravoslavlje: 11000 Belgrade, 7 Jula 5; tel. (11) 635699; fax (11) 630865; 2 a month; religious; published by the Serbian Orthodox Church; Editor Dr SLOBODAN MILEUSNIĆ; circ. 22,500.

Privredni vjesnik: 41000 Zagreb, Rooseveltov trg 2; tel. (41) 453422; telex 21524; fax (41) 446428; f. 1953; weekly; economic; Serbo-Croat; Man. ANTE GAVRANOVIĆ; Editor-in-Chief FRANJO ŽILIĆ.

Rad: Belgrade, trg Marksa i Engelsa 5; tel. (11) 330927; telex 11121; weekly; organ of the Confederation of Trade Unions; Dir RADOSLAV ROSO; Editor-in-Chief STANISLAV MARINKOVIĆ; circ. 70,000.

Radna i Društvena Zajednica: Belgrade 25, Lenjinov bul., SIV Building; f. 1946; formerly *Nova administracija*; monthly; publ. by Federal Institute of Public Administration; Editor Dr NIKOLA BALOG.

Republika: Zagreb, Frankopanska 26; f. 1945; monthly; published by Društvo književnika Hrvatske; literary review; Editor-in-Chief VELIMIR VISKOVIĆ.

Review: Belgrade, Terazije 31; tel. (11) 345541; telex 12954; fax (11) 333091; f. 1963; illustrated monthly on life in Yugoslavia; in French, English, German, Russian, Spanish; Dir and Editor-in-Chief RAJKO BOBOT.

Socialist Thought and Practice: 11000 Belgrade, trg Marksa i Engelsa 11, POB 576; monthly review covering current theoretical aspects and practical problems of socialist development in Yugoslavia; also in Russian and Spanish.

Socijalistička Izgradnja: Sarajevo; monthly.

Socijalizam: Belgrade, trg Marksa i Engelsa 11; f. 1957; 6 a year; ideological, political and theoretical questions of socialism; Editor-in-Chief Dr STIPE ŠUVAR.

Stop: Ljubljana, Titova 35; tel. (61) 215660; telex 31255; f. 1967; weekly magazine of film, theatre and pop music, radio and television programmes; Editor MIRAN SATTLER; circ. 100,000.

Student: Belgrade, Balkanska 4; f. 1937; Editor-in-Chief ŠIME CICKOVIĆ; circ. 10,000.

Stvaranje: Titograd, bul. Revolucije 11; f. 1946; monthly literary review; publ. by the Literary Asscn of Montenegro; Man. SRETEN ASANOVIĆ.

Svijet: Sarajevo; illustrated; weekly; Editor-in-Chief JELA JEVREMOVIĆ; circ. 115,000.

Tehničke novine: 11000 Belgrade, Vojvode Stepe 89; tel. (11) 468596; fax (11) 473442; monthly; technical; Chief Editor SAŠA IMPERL; circ. 70,000.

Trudbenik: Skopje, Udarna brigada 12; weekly; organ of Macedonian Trade Unions; Editor SIMO IVANOVSKI.

Yugoslav Echo: 61000 Ljubljana, Titova 35; tel. (61) 318389; telex 31255; fax (61) 311871; quarterly; in English; economy, finance, trade.

Yugoslav Information Bulletin: 11000 Belgrade, trg Marksa i Engelsa 11, POB 576; monthly; also in French and Spanish; Editor-in-Chief JOVAN LAKIĆEVIĆ.

Yugoslav Law (1975–): Belgrade, Terazije 41; tel. (11) 333213; fax (11) 329; 3 a year in English and French; publ. by the Instit. of Comparative Law and the Union of Jurists Asscn; Editor Dr VLADIMIR JOVANOVIĆ.

Yugoslav Life: 11000 Belgrade, Obilićev Venac 2, POB 439; tel. (11) 636715; telex 11220; fax (11) 183946; f. 1956; monthly paper describing social and political events and culture in Yugoslavia, in English, French, Russian and Spanish; published by Tanjug news agency; Exec. Editor DRAGAN MILENKOVIĆ; circ. 30,000.

Yugoslav Survey: Belgrade, Moše Pijade 8/1 (POB 677); tel. (11) 333610; fax (11) 332295; f. 1960; quarterly general reference publication of basic documentary information about Yugoslavia in English; Editor-in-Chief IKA BOROVNJAK (acting); circ. 3,000.

Zadrugar: Sarajevo, Omladinska 1; f. 1945; weekly; journal for farmers; Editor-in-Chief FADIL ADEMOVIĆ; circ. 34,000.

Zeri: Priština; political weekly; Albanian; Editor-in-Chief BLERIM SHALA.

NEWS AGENCY

Novinska Agencija Tanjug: 11001 Belgrade, Obilićev Venac 2, POB 439; tel. (11) 332230; telex 11220; f. 1943; 90 correspondents in Yugoslavia and 50 offices abroad; press and information agency governed by self-management; news service for Yugoslavia press, radio and television; news and features service for abroad in English, French, Spanish, Russian and German; also features service in Arabic; photo and telephoto service; economic and financial services for home and abroad; publishes EITI, service for trade, industry and banking in Serbo-Croat, English, French, German and Spanish; computerized commodity service for Yugoslav businesses and banks; Dir RISTO LAZAROV; Editor-in-Chief MLADEN ARNAUTOVIĆ.

Foreign Bureaux

Agence France-Presse (AFP): 11000 Belgrade, trg Marksa i Engelsa 2; tel. (11) 332622; telex 11262; Correspondent NICOLAS MILETITCH.

Agenzia Nazionale Stampa Associata (ANSA) (Italy): 11000 Belgrade, Braće Jugovića 5; tel. (11) 620221; telex 11680; Bureau Chief MARIO MARTELLI.

Allgemeiner Deutscher Nachrichtendienst (ADN) (Germany): 11000 Belgrade, Siva Stena 1A; tel. (11) 461752; telex 11338; Correspondent Dr WILLFRIED MUCH.

Associated Press (AP) (USA): 11000 Belgrade, Dositejeva 12; tel. (11) 631553; telex 11264; Correspondent IVAN STEFANOVIĆ.

Bulgarska Telegrafna Agentsia (BTA) (Bulgaria): Belgrade, Gospodar Jevremova 41; tel. (11) 636361; fax (11) 636361; Correspondent NIKOLA KITSEVSKI.

Československá tisková kancelář (ČSTK) (Czechoslovakia): 11070 Belgrade, III Bulevar 190/Stan. 6, Blok 37; tel. (11) 134892; telex 11657; Correspondent MIROSLAV JILEK.

Deutsche Presse-Agentur (dpa) (Germany): 11000 Belgrade, Osogovska 21; tel. (11) 556884; telex 11885; Correspondent Dr THOMAS BREY.

Informatsionnoye Agentstvo Novosti (IAN) (Russia): Belgrade, Strahinjića Bana 50; tel. (11) 629419; Bureau Chief SERGEY GRIZUNOV.

Korean Central News Agency (KCNA) (Democratic People's Republic of Korea): Belgrade, Dr Milutina Ivkovića 9; tel. (11) 668426; telex 11577; Bureau Chief KIM ZONG SE.

Magyar Távirati Iroda (MTI) (Hungary): 11000 Belgrade, Ivana Milutinovića 64/1/5; tel. (11) 4447201; telex 11783; Correspondent GYULA MÁRKUS.

Middle East News Agency (MENA) (Egypt): Belgrade, Vladete Kovačevića 16; tel. (11) 651486; Correspondent RAGAA ABU-SHAHIBA.

Prensa Latina (Cuba): 11000 Belgrade, Morauska 5; tel. (11) 438215; telex 11352; Correspondent HÉCTOR DANILO RODRÍGUEZ RODRÍGUEZ.

Reuters (UK): 11000 Belgrade, Brankova 13–15, 6th Floor; tel. (11) 626330; telex 11475.

Telegrafnoye Agentstvo Sovetskovo Soyuza (TASS) (Russia): 11000 Belgrade, Ognjena Price 17; tel. (11) 4446928; Correspondent MIKHAIL ABELEV.

United Press International (UPI) (USA): 11000 Belgrade, Generala Zdanova 19; tel. (11) 342490; telex 11250; Correspondent NESHO DJURIĆ.

Xinhua (New China) News Agency (People's Republic of China): Belgrade, Bože Jankovica 23; tel. (11) 493789; telex 11375; Correspondent YANG DAZHOU.

PRESS ASSOCIATIONS

Savez Novinara Jugoslavije (Federation of Yugoslav Journalists): Belgrade, Trg Republike 5/III; tel. (11) 624993; f. 1945; 11,500 mems; Pres. MILISAV MILIĆ.

Yugoslav Newspaper Publishers' Association: Belgrade; Dir RASTKO GUZINA.

Publishing

Publishers are listed in the section on the relevant Republics.

PUBLISHERS' ASSOCIATION

Udruženje izdavača i knjižara Jugoslavije (Association of Yugoslav Publishers and Booksellers): 11000 Belgrade, Kneza Miloša 25, POB 883; tel. (11) 642533; fax (11) 646339; f. 1954; organizes Belgrade International Book Fair; Dir OGNJEN LAKIĆEVIĆ; 101 mem. organizations.

Radio and Television

In 1990 there were 4,552,717 radio licences and 3,942,629 television licences issued. In 1989 some 200,000 homes were receiving cable television. Yugoslavia's first satellite, Yugo-Sat, was due to be launched in 1995, for the transmission of domestic television programmes.

Jugoslovenska Radiotelevizija (JRT) (Association of Yugoslav Radio and Television Organizations): 11000 Belgrade, Generala Ždanova 28; tel. (11) 330194; telex 12158; fax (11) 434023; f. 1952; Exec. Dir ALEKSANDAR TODOROVIĆ.

Radio-Jugoslavija: 11000 Belgrade, Hilandarska 2/IV, POB 200; tel. (11) 346884; telex 12432; fax (11) 332014; f. 1951; foreign service; broadcasts in Albanian, Arabic, Bulgarian, English, French, German, Greek, Italian, Russian and Spanish; Dir Dr DRAGAN MARKOVIĆ.

An independent television station, YUTEL, secured agreement from all six Republics, in 1990, to broadcast programmes throughout Yugoslavia. However, by mid-1991, it was subject to increasing restrictions.

Finance

The National Bank of Yugoslavia is the country's central bank, its powers and obligations being determined by law. Its functions include the issue of money, provision of credit to banks and government authorities, control of credits and bank activities,

recommendation of legislation relating to the activities, recommendation of legislation relating to the foreign exchange system and its implementation, management of gold and foreign exchange reserves, control of foreign exchange operations and other special activities. The National Bank of Yugoslavia and the national banks of the Republics and Provinces operated within the framework of a single monetary system. However, on 8 October 1991, as part of its declared process of dissociation from the federation, Slovenia introduced a new currency (tolar—initially at par with the dinar), which introduced new uncertainties into the financial situation of the Yugoslav territories. On 23 December 1991 Croatia introduced its own currency, initially a Croatian dinar, and then proposed a kruna or crown.

In 1988 there were 148 basic banks and nine associated banks in Yugoslavia. With the adoption of new legislation in mid-1989, a radical reorganization of the banking sector commenced, the system of basic and associated banks being abolished. Henceforth, banks were to be independent financial organizations, their resources comprising the invested capital funds of the shareholders and deposits. By March 1990 the number of banks reorganized in accordance with the new regulations totalled 68. Most banks are listed in the sections on the Republics in which they are based. Also listed under the Republics are the stock exchanges of Belgrade, Ljubljana and Zagreb.

BANKING

Central Bank

Narodna banka Jugoslavije (National Bank of Yugoslavia): 11001 Belgrade, Bul. revolucije 15, POB 1010; tel. (11) 332001; telex 72000; f. 1883 as Banque Nationale Priviliégiée du Royaume du Serbie; in 1920, name changed to Banque Nationale du Royaume des Serbes, Croates et Slovenes and in 1929 to Banque Nationale du Royaume de Yougoslavie; in 1946 name changed to Banque Nationale de la République Fédérative Populaire de Yougoslavie; received its present name 1963; the Bank has the sole right of issuing notes and performs the usual functions of a central bank; the National Bank of Slovenia has assumed the performance of these functions in that Republic; Gov. DUŠAN VLATKOVIĆ.

Bank for International Economic Co-operation

Jugoslovenska Banka Za Medjunarodnu Ekonomsku Saradnju—JUBMES (Yugoslav Bank for International Economic Co-operation): Head Office: 11070 Belgrade, Bul. AVNOJ-a 121, POB 219; tel. (11) 143004; telex 11710; fax (11) 131457; f. 1979; replaced the Export Credit and Insurance Fund and assumed the assets and liabilities of the Fund; established by a special Law; grants export credits; underwrites insurance of exports against non-commercial risks, etc.; total assets 2,556,604m. dinars (1988); Pres. IVAN STAMBOLIĆ; Deputy Pres. MOMČILO PEJIĆ.

Banking Association

Udruženje banaka Jugoslavije (Association of Yugoslav Banks): 11001 Belgrade, Masarikova 5/IX; tel. (11) 684797; telex 11767; fax (11) 684947; f. 1955; association of Yugoslav business banks; works on improving inter-bank co-operation, organizes agreements of mutual interest for banks, gives expert assistance, establishes co-operation with foreign banks, other financial institutions and their associations, represents banks in relations with the Yugoslav Government and the National Bank of Yugoslavia; Pres. DJORDJE ZARIĆ; Sec.-Gen. MILOVAN MILUTINOVIĆ.

INSURANCE

'DUNAV' Deoničko Društvo za Osiguranje (Dunav Insurance Company): 11000 Belgrade, Makedonska 4, POB 624; tel. (11) 324001; telex 11359; f. 1974; all types of insurance.

Trade and Industry

CHAMBER OF COMMERCE

Privredna Komora Jugoslavije (Yugoslav Chamber of Economy): 11000 Belgrade, Terazije 23, POB 1003; tel. (11) 339461; telex 11638; fax (11) 631928; independent organization affiliating all Yugoslav economic organizations; promotes economic and commercial relations with foreign countries; the Presidency of the eight-member Presidium rotates annually.

The **Yugoslav Chamber of Commerce** was established in December 1990.

FOREIGN TRADE INSTITUTE

Institut za Spoljnu Trgovinu: 11000 Belgrade, Moše Pijade 8; tel. (11) 339041; telex 12214; Dir Dr SLOBODAN MRKŠA.

TRADE UNIONS

Veće Saveza sindikata Jugoslavije (Council of Confederation of Trade Unions of Yugoslavia): 11000 Belgrade, trg Marksa i Engelsa 5 (Dom sindikata); tel. (11) 330481; telex 11121; 6,348,858 mems.

Trade unions forming the Confederation of Trade Unions of Yugoslavia (address, telephone and telex number as above unless otherwise stated):

Sindikat radnika delatnosti vaspitanja, obrazovanja, nauke i kulture (Education, Science and Culture Workers): Pres. Federal Cttee BORIS LIPUŽIĆ; 430,000 mems.

Sindikat radnika delatnosti zdravstva i socijalne zaštite (Health and Social Care Workers): Pres. Federal Cttee LJILJANA MILOŠEVIĆ; 421,000 mems.

Sindikat radnika državne uprave i finansijskih organa (State Administration and Finance Workers): Pres. Federal Cttee RAM BUĆAJ; 520,000 mems.

Sindikat radnika energetike (Energy Workers): Pres. Federal Cttee VASKRSIJE SAVIČIĆ; 180,000 mems.

Sindikat radnika gradjevinarstva (Building Workers): Pres. Federal Cttee MILOŠ ŽORIĆ; 680,000 mems.

Sindikat radnika grafičke, novinsko-izdavačke i informativne delatnosti (Printing, Newspaper, Publishing and Information Workers): Pres. Federal Cttee BORIS BIŠĆAN; 130,000 mems.

Sindikat radnika hemije i nemetala (Chemistry and Non-Metallic Industry Workers): Pres. Federal Cttee STOJMIR DOMAZETOVSKI; 255,000 mems.

Sindikat radnika industrije tekstila, kože i obuće (Textile, Leather, and Footwear Workers): Pres. Federal Cttee JOZEFINA MUSA; 600,000 mems.

Sindikat radnika u komunalnoj privredi i zanatstvu (Public Utilities and Handicrafts Workers): Pres. Federal Cttee JOSIP KOLAR; 300,000 mems.

Sindikat radnika poljprivrede, prehrambene i duvanske industrije (Agricultural, Food and Tobacco Industry Workers): Pres. Federal Cttee ERNE KIČI; 525,000 mems.

Sindikat radnika proizvodnje i prerade metala (Metal Production and Manufacturing Workers): Pres. Federal Cttee SLAVKO URŠIĆ; 980,000 mems.

Sindikat radnika saobraćaja i veza (Transport and Communications Workers): 11000 Belgrade, Miloša Pocerca 10; tel. (11) 646321; Pres. Federal Cttee HASAN HRNJIĆ; 520,000 mems.

Sindikat radnika šumarstva i prerade drveta (Forestry and Wood Industry Workers): Pres. Federal Cttee DRAGOLJUB OBRADOVIĆ; 320,000 mems.

Sindikat radnika u trgovini (Commerce Workers): Pres. Federal Cttee LJUBICA BRAČKO; 650,000 mems.

Sindikat radnika u ugostiteljstvu i turizmu (Catering and Tourism Workers): Pres. Federal Cttee MILAN FRKOVIĆ; 250,000 mems.

Federation of Independent Trade Unions of Yugoslavia: Pres. MOMO COLAKOVIĆ.

Transport

RAILWAYS

Railways in Yugoslavia are owned by eight self-managing enterprises, one in each republic and autonomous province. The Community of Yugoslav Railways is the co-ordinating body. In 1991 the Croatia and Slovenia withdrew from this system. The total length of track was 9,270 km in 1987, 3,771 km of which was electrified.

Construction of a new double-track railway between Rijeka and Zagreb was scheduled for completion in 1990. The 25-km Yugoslav section of a railway linking Titograd with Shkodër, in Albania, was completed in late 1985 but services were discontinued in 1988, owing to economic difficulties. In the 1986–90 period a total of 500,000m. dinars was to be invested in the railways. The civil war, which began in June 1991, however, caused considerable disruption to rail traffic and serious physical damage to the railway infrastructure.

Zajednica Jugoslovenskih Železnica (Community of Yugoslav Railways): 11000 Belgrade, Nemanjina 6, POB 553; tel. (11) 685822; telex 12495; Gen. Man. N. ZURKOVIĆ.

ROADS

The road network totalled 122,062 km, including 871 km of motorways, in 1988. The most important roads are the main inland route through Ljubljana, Zagreb, Belgrade, Niš and Skopje to the Greek frontier, the Adriatic highway linking Rijeka, Split, Dubrovnik and Titograd, and a number of intermediate roads. Work on the 7,840-metre Karavanke road tunnel (of which 3,540m is in Yugoslavia), linking Slovenia with Rosenbach in Austria, began in 1986. The tunnel opened to traffic in June 1991. In 1987 the European Investment Bank approved a loan of 550m. ECUs to improve road links with Greece and other EEC countries. In 1986 the World Bank granted a long-term credit of US $121.5m. for the building of sections of the 1,813-km Bratstvo-Jedinstvo (Brotherhood and Unity) motorway through Yugoslavia and by late 1987 600 km had been completed. The World Bank granted a loan in 1987 towards various road projects, which included a new 1,000 km motorway to be constructed along the Adriatic coast, running from Trieste, in Italy, to Skopje via Rijeka, and a further loan of $292m. in 1991.

INLAND WATERWAYS

Navigable waterways are: the Danube (Dunav), 588 km; Sava, 593 km; Tisa, 164 km; Drava, 51 km (for vessels up to 1,500 tons-capacity); Begej, 77 km (vessels up to 650 tons-capacity); the and the Danube-Tisa canal system, 321 km (vessels up to 650 tons-capacity). Completion of the Danube–Sava canal was scheduled for 1990. Inland waterways are supervised by the Federal Committee for Transport and Communications.

SHIPPING

In December 1990 the merchant fleet had 399 vessels, with capacity totalling 3.8m. grt. The principal ports are Rijeka (formerly Fiume—in Croatia) and Koper (Slovenia) in the north, Sibenik, Split and Ploče (formerly Kardeljevo) along the central Dalmatian coast (Croatia), Dubrovnik (Croatia) and Bar (Montenegro) in the south. All ports have good road and railway connections.

Jadrolinija (Adriatic Shipping Line): 51000 Rijeka, Obala Jugoslovenske Mornarice 16; tel. (51) 30899; telex 24195; fax (51) 213116; f. 1947; regular passenger and car-ferry services between Italian, Greek and Yugoslav ports; cruises in the Mediterranean, northern Europe, etc.; Man. Dir Capt. ANTON LENAC.

Jugolinija (Yugoslav Shipping Line): 51000 Rijeka, Obala Jugoslavenske Mornarice 8, POB 379; tel. (51) 205111; telex 24218; fax (51) 211309; f. 1947; cargo and passenger services from the Adriatic to North and South America, the Near and Middle East, the Indian sub-continent, People's Republic of China and the Far East; tramp service; Man. Dir MILIVOJ BROZINA; fleet of 51 vessels totalling 970,000 dwt.

Jugoslovenska Oceanska Plovidba (Yugoslav Ocean Lines): 85330 Kotor; tel. 25011; telex 61116; regular service every 30 days between Yugoslav ports and Tampico (Mexico), USA, Italy; Pres. ANTON MOŠKOV.

Jugoslovenska Pomorska Agencija (Yugoslav Shipping Agency): Belgrade, Bul. Lenjina 165A, POB 210; tel. (11) 130004; telex 11140; f. 1947; charter services, liner and container transport, port agency, passenger service, air cargo service; Gen. Man. STEVAN OBRADOVIĆ.

CIVIL AVIATION

In 1987 there were 20 international airports, including Belgrade and all the republican capitals. There are also several domestic airports, including Niš (Serbia) and Banja Luka (Bosnia-Herzegovina). In January 1992, following international recognition of Slovenian independence, Austria announced that it would assume responsibility for traffic control in Slovenian airspace.

Jugoslovenski Aerotransport (JAT) (Yugoslav Airlines): 11070 Belgrade (Novi Beograd), Ho Si Minova 16; tel. (11) 2224222; telex 12035; fax (11) 2221082; f. 1947; mem of IATA; scheduled and charter services to Europe, Africa, Asia, Australia and North America; internal services; Dir ZIVKO MARKIČEVIĆ (acting); fleet of 4 DC-10, 8 Boeing 727-200, 9 Boeing 737-300, 9 DC-9, 3 ATR-72.

There were 18 smaller operators in Yugoslavia, in mid-1991, incl.:

Adria Airways: 61001 Ljubljana, Kuzmičeva 7; tel. (61) 313366; telex 31268; fax (61) 323356; f. 1961; after June 1991 operations were based in Klagenfurt (Austria); in Oct. 1991 operations were suspended completely, following moves by the internationally recognized Yugoslav aviation authorities; services resumed in Jan. 1992; internat. scheduled services between Ljubljana, Klagenfurt, Larnaca, Frankfurt, Munich, Moscow, London, Paris, Vienna and Tel Aviv; domestic scheduled services between all major Yugoslav cities; domestic and international charter services (passenger and cargo); Pres. JANEZ KOCIJANČIĆ; fleet of 5 MD 81/82, 2 DC-9-32, 1 DC-9-33, 2 DHC Dash-7, 3 A320.

Air Jugoslavia: 11000 Belgrade, Moše Pijade 1/III; tel. (11) 338812; telex 12125; f. 1969; wholly-owned subsidiary of JAT; overseas passenger and cargo charter flights to Australia, USA, etc.; Gen. Man. MARKOVIĆ ZORAN; JAT aircraft chartered as required.

Aviogenex: 11070 Belgrade, Milentija Popovića 9; tel. (11) 149729; telex 11711; fax (11) 2222439; f. 1968; passenger and cargo flights within Europe, the Mediterranean and the Middle East; Gen. Man. MIROSLAV SPASIĆ; fleet of 3 Boeing 727-200, 4 Boeing 737-200.

Several new airlines were established in 1990–91. These included Air Commerce (charter flights from Sarajevo to Istanbul and Cairo; scheduled service to Switzerland began in Dec. 1991—fleet of 1 Boeing 727 and 1 DC-9; Dir MOHAMED ABADZIĆ); Bonanca Air (based in Dubrovnik); Croatian Airlines (domestic services; Dir-Gen. MATIJA KATIČIĆ); and Palair-Macedonian Airlines (domestic services and flights to USA, Canada and Australia).

Tourism

Tourist attractions include the Adriatic resorts, the mountains, the great lakes of Scutari, Prespa and Ohrid in the south, and historic cities such as Dubrovnik. Tourism is an important source of foreign currency (receipts estimated at US $2,700m. in 1990). In 1989 about 8.6m. tourist arrivals were recorded. During 1991 the increasing tension and then the outbreak of hostilities within Yugoslavia virtually ended tourist activity.

Turistički savez Jugoslavije (Tourist Association of Yugoslavia): 11001 Belgrade, Moše Pijade 8/IV, Poštanski fah 595; tel. (11) 339041; telex 11863; fax (11) 634677; f. 1953; mem. World Travel Organization; publs tourist leaflets, folders, brochures, etc., in foreign languages; Pres. (vacant); Sec.-Gen. GEORGI GOŠEV.

Apart from the Tourist Association of Yugoslavia, there are specialist tourist organizations in many regions.

Atlas: 50000 Dubrovnik, Pile 1; tel. (50) 27333; telex 27515; fax (50) 28359; travel agency; f. 1923; 52 branch offices; 1 overseas office.

Autotehna: 11000 Belgrade, Bul. Revolucije 94; tel. (11) 433323; telex 11713; AVIS licensee; car hire services; 17 branch offices.

Dalmacijaturist: 58000 Split, Titova obala 5; tel. (58) 44666; telex 26145; fax (58) 591404; f. 1923; more than 40 branch offices; 3 offices abroad.

Emona Globtour: 61000 Ljubljana, Šmartinska 130/X; tel. (61) 444177; telex 39606; fax (61) 441325; 41 branch offices, 2 foreign offices.

Generalturist: 41000 Zagreb, Praška 5; tel. (41) 450888; telex 21467; fax (41) 422633; f. 1923, renamed 1963; 40 branch offices, 3 representatives abroad.

Inex Turist: 11000 Belgrade, trg Republike 5/VIII; tel. (11) 622360; telex 12990; fax (11) 634263; f. 1968; 10 branch offices.

Jugotanker-Turisthotel: 57000 Zadar, I. L. Ribara bb; tel. (57) 24255; telex 27136.

Kvarner Express: 51410 Opatija, M. Tita 186–192; tel. (51) 271111;' telex 24379; fax (51) 271741; f. 1952; arranges accommodations, tours, conventions, etc.; 40 branch offices, 1 foreign office.

Putnik: 11000 Belgrade, Dragoslava Jovanovića 1; tel. (11) 332591; telex 11324; fax (11) 344505; f. 1923; 120 branch offices.

Srbijaturist: 18000 Niš, Voždova 12; tel. (18) 25249; telex 16256; fax (18) 23663; f. 1951; hotels and tourism enterprise.

Vojvodina Tours: 21000 Novi Sad, Ivana Milutinoviča 3; tel. (21) 622854; telex 14478; fax (21) 622578; f. 1960; 12 branch offices.

Yugotours: 11000 Belgrade, Djure Djakovića 31; tel. (11) 764622; telex 11000; fax (11) 766447; f. 1957; organizes travel and accommodation arrangements for foreign and domestic tourists; 9 branch offices, 26 European and overseas offices; Man. Dir DANILO TODOROVIĆ.

Atomic Energy

Yugoslavia's first nuclear power plant (installed capacity 664 MW) was constructed at Krško, 40 km west of Zagreb in Slovenia, and began operations in late 1981. A second station was to be built at Prevlaka (Croatia), 40 km east of Zagreb. Further nuclear power stations were planned, with total output expected to reach 3,000–4,000 MW by the year 2000, and invitations for bids were issued in October 1985. These projects were postponed in 1986, however, following the nuclear power station accident at Chernobyl, in the USSR, and in November 1987 a moratorium until the year 2000 on the construction of further nuclear stations was declared. In mid-1989 legislation banning the construction of further nuclear plants was adopted. Nuclear generation accounted for 5.3% of electricity output in 1990. Yugoslavia is a member of the International Atomic Energy Agency (IAEA) and is an observer at the European Organization for Nuclear Research (CERN).

Federal Secretariat for Energy and Industry: 11070 Belgrade, bul. AVNOJ-a 104; tel. (11) 602555; telex 11062; fax (11) 195244; Pres. Dr ANDREJ OCVIRK.

Komisija Saveznog izvršnog veća za nuklearnu energiju (Nuclear Energy Commission of the Federal Executive Council): 11070 Belgrade, Palata Federacije; tel. (11) 636797; telex 11448; Sec. MILAN PAVIĆEVIĆ.

Elektrotehnički Institut Rade Končar (Rade Končar Institute of Electrical Engineering): 41001 Zagreb; tel. (41) 327999; telex 21104; research includes nuclear energy field; Dir DIMITAR MANDJUROV.

Energoinvest-ITEN (Institute for Thermal and Nuclear Technologies): 71000 Sarajevo, Stup, Tvornička 3; tel. (71) 542969; telex 41826; fax (71) 629681; f. 1961; research organization; Dir Dr ALIJA LEKIĆ.

GEOINSTITUT: 11000 Belgrade, Rovinjska 12; tel. (11) 4889966; telex 11903; fax (11) 4885296; f. 1948; research organization for geological, geophysical and mining exploration of nuclear and other mineral raw materials, exploratory drilling, engineering geology and hydrogeology; Dir PREDRAG SRBLJANOVIĆ.

Geološki zavod (Geological Survey): 61000 Ljubljana, Parmova 37; tel. (61) 344261; telex 31448; research in geology, geophysics and geo-engineering; operates uranium mine with annual production of 120 tons of concentrate; Dir AVGUST ČEBULJ.

JUGEL (Union of Yugoslav Electric Power Industry): 11000 Belgrade, Balkanska 13; tel. (11) 686337; telex 11876; Head of Nuclear Power Dept MILAN GAVRILOVIĆ.

JUMEL (Business Association of Yugoslav Machine Industry): 11070 Belgrade, bul. Lenjina 143; tel. (11) 130195; telex 11076; Sec. DUŠAN RADOJKOVIĆ.

NUKLIN: 11001 Belgrade, POB 522; tel. (11) 455663; telex 11563; f. 1977; association of nuclear research institutes; Dir Prof. NAIM AFGAN.

Institut Rudjer Bošković (Rudjer Bošković Institute): 41001 Zagreb, Bijenička 54, POB 1016; tel. (41) 435111; telex 21383; fax (41) 425497; f. 1950; research in nuclear and atomic physics, etc.; Dir Dr KRUNOSLAV PISK.

Institut za nuklearne nauke Boris Kidrič (Boris Kidrič Institute of Nuclear Sciences): 11001 Belgrade, POB 522; tel. (11) 4440871; telex 11563; f. 1948; Dir Dr DJORDJE JOVIĆ.

Institut Jožef Stefan (Jožef Stefan Institute): University of Ljubljana, 61111 Ljubljana, Jamova 39; tel. (61) 159199; telex 31296; fax (61) 219385; f. 1949; Dir Prof. Dr TOMAŽ KALIN.

Culture

Cultural affairs are the responsibility of the Republics (for details, see the sections on those Republics). Federal budget allocations, therefore, are not significant and artistic and cultural activities and monuments are financed at the republican and local level. State or social funding accounts for some 70%–80% of financing, the balance being obtained from fees and private sources.

Federal Administration for International Scientific, Educational, Cultural and Technical Co-operation: 11000 Belgrade, Kosančićev venac 29; tel. (11) 626661; fax (11) 629785; Dir Dr MARIJAN STRBAŠIĆ.

Yugoslav Olympic Committee: 11030 Belgrade, ada Čiganlija 10; tel. (11) 543568; telex 11984; fax (11) 543171; during 1991 Slovenia and Croatia declared that they would apply for separate entry in the Olympic Games; Pres. ALEKSANDER BAKOČEVIĆ; Sec.-Gen. CASLAV VELJIĆ.

Education

The entire educational system is organized at the republican and municipal level. Primary education is free and compulsory for all children aged between the ages of seven (six in Croatia) and 15 years—the so-called eight-year school. There are various types of secondary education, available to all who qualify, but the technical and vocational schools are the most popular. Alternatively, children may attend a general secondary school (gymnasium); the four-year course here can be in preparation for university entrance. In 1988/89 the total enrolment at the primary level was 97.4% of the school-age population and 91.2% at the secondary level.

Until 1987 higher education was available to all who could qualify, but, for the 1987/88 academic year, the student intake was cut by 7% and the number of courses reduced. There are 19 universities, a theological college of university status, schools of higher learning for teachers and two-year post-secondary schools for those who had attended the technical schools (these last were created in response to the needs of industry and the social services).

UNIVERSITIES

Bitola University (Univerzitet Bitolj): 97000 Bitola, bul. 1 Maj bb; tel. (97) 23788; f. 1979; Rector Prof. Dr DAME NESTOROVSKI.

Cyril and Methodius University of Skopje (Univerzitet 'Kiril I Metódij' vo Skopje): 91000 Skopje, POB 576, bul. Krste Misirkov bb; tel. (91) 237712; f. 1949; language of instruction: Macedonian; 18 faculties; 980 teachers; 28,822 students; Rector Prof. Dr DRAGI DANEV.

Džemal Bijedić University of Mostar (Univerzitet 'Džemal Bijedić' u Mostaru): 88000 Mostar, trg 14 Februar bb; tel. (88) 39140; fax (88) 39141; f. 1977; language of instruction: Serbo-Croat; 6 faculties; 250 teachers; 5,500 students; Rector Prof. Dr BERISLAV BLAZEVIĆ.

Edvard Kardelj University of Ljubljana (Univerza 'Edvarda Kardelja' v Ljubljani): Ljubljana, trg Osvoboditve 11; tel. (61) 331716; fax (61) 311734; f. 1595; language of instruction: Slovene; 21 faculties and institutes; 1,330 teachers; 23,420 students; Rector Prof. Dr BORIS SKET.

Faculty of Theology in Ljubljana: 61000 Ljubljana, Poljanska 4; tel. (61) 312593; f. 1919 as part of Ljubljana University, separate status since 1952; theological college; 42 teachers; 198 students; Dean Dr METOD BENEDIK.

Kosovo University of Priština (Universiteti Kosovës në Prishtinë/Univerzitet Kosova u Prištini): 38000 Priština, M. Tito 53; tel. (38) 24970; fax (83) 27628; f. 1970; languages of instruction: Albanian and Serbo-Croat; 13 faculties; 2,000 teachers; 26,000 students; Rector Prof. Dr SKENDER KARAHODA.

Svetozar Marković University of Kragujevac (Univerzitet 'Svetozar Marković' u Kragujevcu): 34000 Kragujevac, trg AVNOJ-a 1; tel. (34) 65424; f. 1976; language of instruction: Serbo-Croat; 7 faculties; 480 teachers; 4,755 full- time students, 2,717 part-time students; Rector Prof. Dr ILIJA ROSIĆ.

University of Arts in Belgrade (Univerzitet Umetnosti u Beogradu): 11000 Belgrade, Vuka Karadžića 12; tel. (11) 624020; f. 1973 as university; language of instruction: Serbo-Croat; 4 faculties; 352 teachers; 1,600 students; Rector Prof NANDOR GLID.

University of Banja Luka (Univerzitet 'Duro Pucar Stari' u Banja Luci): 78000 Banja Luka, trg Palih Boraca 2/II; tel. (78) 35018; f. 1975; language of instruction: Serbo-Croat; 6 faculties; 3 institutes; 158 teachers; 7,000 students; Rector Prof Dr. RAJKO KUZMANOVIĆ.

University of Belgrade (Univerzitet u Beogradu): 11001 Belgrade 6, Studentski trg 1; tel. (11) 635153; f. 1863; language of instruction: Serbo-Croat; 24 faculties; 3,702 teachers; 57,200 students; Rector Prof Dr SLOBODAN UNKOVIĆ.

University of Maribor (Univerza v Mariboru): 62000 Maribor, Krekova ul. 2; tel. (62) 212281; telex 33334; fax (62) 212013; f. 1975; language of instruction: Slovene; 6 faculties; 351 full-time teachers, 146 part-time teachers; 7,008 full-time students, 4,234 external students; Rector Dr ALOJZ KRIZMAN.

University of Niš (Univerzitet u Nišu): 18000 Niš, trg Bratstva i Jedinstva 2; tel. (18) 25544; telex 16362; fax (18) 24488; f. 1965; language of instruction: Serbo-Croat; 9 faculties; 888 teachers; 12,978 students; Rector Prof. Dr BRANIMIR DJORDJEVIĆ.

University of Novi Sad (Universitet u Novom Sadu): 21000 Novi Sad, Veljka Vlahovića 3, Post. fah; tel. (21) 55622; f. 1960; language of instruction: Serbo-Croat; 12 faculties; 1,819 teachers; 28,946 students; Rector Prof. Dr ZORAN STOJANOVIĆ.

University of Osijek (Sveučilište u Osijeku): 54000 Osijek, Brace Radića 15; tel. (54) 31822; f. 1975; language of instruction: Serbo-Croat; 8 faculties; 600 teachers; 7,177 students; Rector Prof. IVAN MECANOVIĆ.

University of Sarajevo (Univerzitet u Sarajevu): 71000 Sarajevo, Obala Vojvode Stepe 7/II, Post. fah 186; tel. (71) 211216; f. 1949; language of instruction: Serbo-Croat; 21 faculties; 1,225 teachers; 24,000 full-time students, 9,000 part-time students; Rector Prof. Dr NENAD KECMANOVIĆ.

University of Split (Sveučilište u Splitu): 58000 Split, Livanjska 5/I; tel. (58) 49966; f. 1974; language of instruction: Croatian; 7 faculties; 618 teachers; 11,646 students; Rector Prof. STJEPAN LIPANOVIĆ.

University of Tuzla (Univerzitet u Tuzli): 75000 Tuzla, M. Fizovića-Fiska 6; tel. (75) 34650; f. 1976; 465 teachers; 15,000 students; Rector Prof. IBRO PASIĆ.

University of Zagreb (Sveučilište u Zagrebu): 41000 Zagreb, POB 815, trg Maršala Tita 14; tel. (41) 272411; f. 1669; language of instruction: Croatian; 16 faculties; 3,666 teachers; 41,164 students.

Veljko Vlahović University of Titograd (Univerzitet 'Veljko Vlahović' u Titogradu): 81000 Titograd, POB 105, Cetinjski put bb; tel. (81) 14484; f. 1974; language of instruction: Serbo-Croat; 11 faculties; 833 teachers; 8,000 students; Rector Prof Dr MILOS RADULOVIĆ.

Vladimir Bakarović University of Rijeka (Sveučilište 'Vladimir Bakarić' u Rijeci): 51000 Rijeka, trg Rijecke Rezolucije 7/I; tel. (51) 25682; f. 1973; language of instruction: Croatian literary language; 12 faculties; 718 teachers; 6,350 full-time students, 2,873 part-time students; Rector Prof. Dr PETER SARCEVIĆ.

Social Welfare

There are obligatory social insurance schemes for anyone in employment and their families. These provide for health insurance, money payments and grants in kind, in the case of sickness, accidents, disability and old age; the schemes also have life insurance elements. The state retirement pension makes payments which are usually equivalent to 85%–87% of average monthly income during the last five years of employment. All workers are entitled to annual leave, which varies between 18 and 36 days. Working women are entitled to paid maternity leave and shorter working hours for child-care. Women and young children enjoy special protection under the health-insurance scheme.

In 1985 there were 7,903 clinics and 4,174 dental clinics in Yugoslavia. In early 1990 there were about 280 hospitals, with 145,000 beds. There were more than 45,000 practising physicians. During the 1980s primary health care was developed through the establishement and use of a network of health centres (out-patient clinics—of which there were about 450 in 1988) and health stations (some 2,550). The Republics have increasingly assumed responsibility for social welfare, particularly with the collapse of federal authority and institutions in 1991; towards the end of that year the situation in Yugoslavia remained unclear. The outbreak of war in the country created new welfare problems, not in terms of casualties alone, but with the problems of refugees, the damage to facilities such as hospitals and water systems, and the economic consequences of sanctions. Although the international community imposed an arms embargo and other financial and econmic restrictions, humanitarian activity increased (such as the presence of the French-based medical organization, Médecins sans Frontières).

FEDERAL AGENCIES

Federal Secretariat for Labour, Health, Veterans' Affairs and Social Policy: see section on The Government (Federal Secretariats).

Red Cross of Yugoslavia: 11000 Belgrade; national federation of republican societies; in 1991 the Slovenian and Croatian Red Crosses withdrew their participation.

The Environment

Environmental concerns are not as widespread in Yugoslavia as in other countries of Eastern Europe, although the Citizens' Green Party of Slovenia was among the first registered opposition to the then-ruling League of Communists. There are numerous national and local environmental groups, however, and the Yugoslav Government has membership of the IUCN (based in Gland, Switzerland). In July 1991 Yugoslavia signed a declaration on the ecological protection of the Adriatic, implementing the Adriatic Initiative agreed by Italy, Yugoslavia, Greece and Albania in Umag, in 1989. The civil war, which began in 1991, however, was a cause of considerable concern. International attention was most attracted by the assault on the medieval city of Dubrovnik (formerly Ragusa), from September.

GOVERNMENT ORGANIZATIONS

Federal Agency for the Human Environment (Savez za Zastitu Covekoves Sredine): 11000 Belgrade, bul. Leninja 2; federal org. responsible for the environment.

The republican authorities are responsible for environmental matters (the relevant government and political bodies are listed in the sections on the Republics).

ACADEMIC INSTITUTES

Yugoslav Academy of Sciences and Arts (Jugoslavenska Akademija Znanosti i Umjetnosti): 41000 Zagreb, Zrinski trg 11; tel. (41) 433661; f. 1866; some of the mems and the 18 institutes are involved in environmental research, as are the affiliated Academies of Croatia, Kosovo, Macedonia, Montenegro, Serbia, Slovenia and Vojvodina; Pres. Dr JAKOV SIROTKOVIĆ; Gen.-Sec. Dr HRVOJE POŽAR.

Association of Scientific Unions: 41000 Zagreb, POB 327, trg Maršala Tita 3, Sveučlšte u Zagrebu (University of Zagreb), Referral Centre; tel. (41) 422965; telex 22486.

Marine Research Institute (Centar za Istrazivanje Mora): 41000 Zagreb, Bijenicka 54; concentrates on environmental concerns in the Adriatic Sea.

NON-GOVERNMENTAL ORGANIZATIONS

Ekoloski Zbor (Ecological Assembly): 64274 Zirovnića, Moste 34; environmental group.

Yugoslav Clean Air Society (Jugoslovensko Društve za Čistocu Važduha): 71001 Sarajevo, Mašinski Fakultet.

Yugoslav Green Party: see section on Political Organizations.

Defence

Yugoslavia has no defensive alliances (it is host to the headquarters of the Non-aligned Movement). Its armed forces, the Yugoslav People's Army (YPA), are responsible for the defence of the country and the maintenance of the federation. Military service is compulsory for men and is for 12 months (since 1983 there has been voluntary military service for women). In June 1990, it was estimated, the total strength of the YPA was 180,000 (including 101,400 conscripts), comprising land forces of 138,000, a navy of 10,000 and an air force of 32,000. There were 15,000 Frontier Guards and a civil defence force of some 2m., upon mobilization. During 1991 the Republics not only began to assume control of their Territorial Defence Forces and to limit the conscription and deployment of their nationals with the YPA, but also to establish formal armies of their own.

Commander-in-Chief: President of the State Presidency of the SFRY.

Acting Federal Secretary for National Defence and Chief of the General Staff: Col-Gen. BLAGOJE ADŽIĆ.

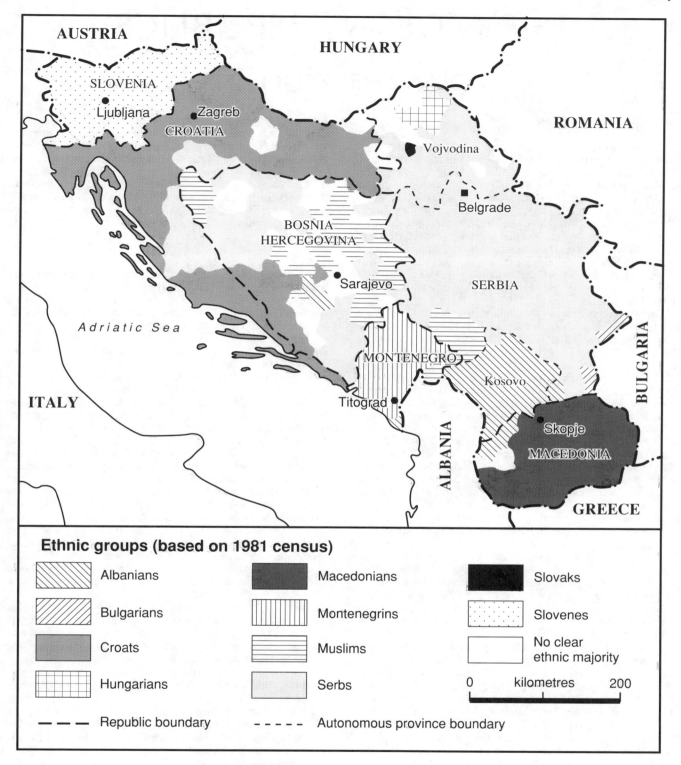

AUSTRIA

HUNGARY

ROMANIA

SLOVENIA

Ljubljana

Zagreb

CROATIA

Vojvodina

Belgrade

BOSNIA
HERCEGOVINA

Sarajevo

SERBIA

Adriatic Sea

MONTENEGRO

Kosovo

ITALY

Titograd

ALBANIA

BULGARIA

Skopje

MACEDONIA

GREECE

Ethnic groups (based on 1981 census)

Albanians	Macedonians	Slovaks
Bulgarians	Montenegrins	Slovenes
Croats	Muslims	No clear ethnic majority
Hungarians	Serbs	0 kilometres 200

- – – Republic boundary   - - - - Autonomous province boundary

THE FEDERAL REPUBLICS

BOSNIA-HERZEGOVINA

Geography

The Socialist Republic of Bosnia and Herzegovina is a constituent partner in the Socialist Federal Republic of Yugoslavia, although it declared its sovereignty in October 1991. It lies in the centre of the country, with only about 20 km (12 miles) of coastline, which is of little maritime significance, and is largely a mountainous territory. Roughly triangular in shape, the Republic juts into Croatia, which forms its western border (running from north-west to south-east, along the Dinaric Alps) and its northern border. Serbia lies to the east (there is a short border with the Serbian territory of the Vojvodina in the north-east) and Montenegro to the south-east. The total area of the Republic is 51,129 sq km.

The ancient province of Bosnia is roughly the territory bounded by the Sava, Drina and Una rivers. Along the Sava, which forms the northern border, there are fertile lowlands. The chief town, and the capital of the Republic, is Sarajevo, which is in the south, near the headwaters of the River Bosna (from which the province acquired its name). Sarajevo is the largest city in the Republic, with a population of 525,980 in 1991. The second city of the Republic is Banja Luka, in the north, with a population of 195,139 in 1991. The smaller province of Herzegovina (only 18.0% of the total area) occupies the south of the Republic, with the Dalmatian coastal strip (Croatia) to the south-west and Montenegro to the south-east. Its chief town is Mostar, which had a population of 126,067 in 1991. Most of Herzegovina is mountainous and infertile, but there are fruitful valleys.

The population, according to the preliminary results of the census of 1991, totalled 4,365,639, with a density of 85.4 per sq km. No single ethnic group constitutes an overall majority. The Bosnians were a Serbo-Croat-speaking people, originally Roman Catholic, who adopted Islam during the Ottoman occupation. In 1971 they were accorded separate status as a Yugoslav national unit (the term 'Muslim' not only includes the Bosnian Muslims, however, but other Slav Muslims), and they are the largest single group in the Republic. In 1991 they comprised 43.7% of the total population. (More than 80% of the ethnic Muslims in Yugoslavia live in Bosnia-Herzegovina.) The Serbs accounted for 31.3% of the population and the Croats 17.3%. Religious affiliation is roughly equated with ethnicity. Most of the Bosnian Muslims are Sunni, although a few are members of a Dervish order, introduced in 1974. The Croats are Roman Catholic, while the Serbs and Montenegrins adhere to the Serbian Orthodox Church. The principal language is Serbo-Croat; the Muslims use the Latin script, like the Croats, while the Serbs use the Cyrillic.

During 1991, within the borders of the Republic, certain Serb-dominated areas declared themselves to be 'Autonomous Regions': Bosanska Krajina ('Bosnian borderland') in the north-west, with its headquarters in Banja Luka; Romanija, to the east of Sarajevo, which city is claimed as the seat of its headquarters; Eastern and Old Herzegovina in the south, with its headquarters in Trebinje (two of the eight municipalities are physically separate from the bulk of the region, being further north and east, on the border with Serbia); and North-East Bosnia, with its base in

Ugljevik. Together they account for about one-third of the Republic's territory, but they are not officially recognized nor accepted by other ethnic groups in the areas. These Serb areas, in their turn, did not acknowledge the validity of the Republic's declaration of sovereignty, in October 1991. In November another such region was established in Northern Bosnia; it was based in Doboj, between Bosanska Krajina and North-East Bosnia, but the area did not have a Serb majority.

History

The territory that now constitutes Bosnia-Herzegovina was settled by Southern Slavs during the Dark Ages, in the sixth century AD. The ancestors of the Bosnians spoke Serbo-Croat, but their exact ethnic identification is obscured by political controversy and their long existence on the borders of the various Eastern and Western blocs. The original Bosnian principality, Rama, which emerged in the 11th century, is often identified with the related principalities of Zeta (the original Montenegrin state) and Raška (Serbia). However, the Bosnians were also Roman Catholics, which associates them with the Croats. On the borders of the surviving Roman Empire, the Eastern Empire ruled from Constantinople, Bosnia eventually fell under Hungarian domination in the 12th century. Bosnia remained a subject of dispute and rivalry between the powers, however, and was fought over by the Hungarians, the Eastern Romans or Byzantines, Serbs, Croats and Venetians. All these peoples did have the pursuit of one policy in common though, with their crusades against the Bogomil heresy (an ascetic, radical dualistic sect, influenced by the Manichees). The heresy, nevertheless, established itself and, in 1353, the territory gained its independence from Hungary, under Stjepan Tvrtko, who styled himself as the King of the Bosnians and the Serbs. Bosnia maintained a precarious independence until its final conquest by the Ottoman Turks, in 1463. Meanwhile, the territory now known as Herzegovina had become part of the Serbian Empire of Stjepan Dušan (Uroš IV). This Empire disintegrated in the latter half of the 14th century, the power of the Serbian princes finally being defeated by the Ottomans, in 1389. Herzegovina became an Austrian border duchy (hence its name, from the Serbo-Croat for 'duke', *herceg*), in 1448, but was itself incorporated into the Ottoman Empire, in 1483.

From the end of the 15th century, therefore, Bosnia and Herzegovina fell under the same occupying power. During the centuries of Ottoman rule, many of the Slavs of Bosnia converted to Islam, and the Bosnian nobility enjoyed a favoured status in the region. Generally, however, the normal administration of the Ottoman Empire was based on confessional grounds. The *millet* system grouped people according to their religion, making the religious leaders responsible for the civil obedience of their followers. This was an effective means of governing the area, with its complicated ethnic and religious divisions, but it also preserved those divisions.

The Habsburg Empire, which was to the north of Bosnia, settled Serbs in the borderlands (Krajina), to defend against the Turks. With the disintegration of Ottoman power and the increasing unrest in the Balkans, the Austro-Hungarian Empire gained administration rights in Bosnia-Herzegovina by the agreements of the Congress of Berlin, in 1878. The province was formally annexed to the Habsburg Crown, on 5 October 1908, in response to the Turkish revolution of that year. This caused the so-called Bosnian Crisis, which was among the first of the Great-Power confrontations preceding the First World War. Germany sided with Austria-Hungary, which was concerned to limit Serbian expansionism, against Russia and, to an extent, the United Kingdom. Serbian nationalist activity continued to trouble the province, despite the Trialist proposals to transform the Dual Monarchy of Austria-Hungary into a 'Triple Monarchy', with the Southern Slavs as a partner. On 28 June 1914 the heir to the Habsburg throne, Archduke Francis Ferdinand, and his wife were assassinated in Sarajevo, while on a visit to Bosnia-Herzegovina. Their murderer, Gavril Princip, was a Bosnian student acting for a radical Serb nationalist group. The Serbian Government was not involved, but Austria-Hungary decided to use the opportunity to end the threat it perceived from Serbia. One month after the assassination the Empire declared war on Serbia and this conflict escalated into the First World War. During the War, the Serbs and Croats were among the parties to an agreement to form a common state under the Serbian monarchy. At the end of the War, therefore, Bosnia-Herzegovina became part of the Kingdom of Serbs, Croats and Slovenes, which was proclaimed on 4 December 1918 (it was renamed Yugoslavia in 1929).

With the decline of Ottoman power during the 19th century the Muslim Slavs, notably the Bosnian élite, formed the National Muslim Organization to protect their political, religious and cultural rights. It developed the policy of maximizing its influence by supporting either the Serbs or the Croats. These two ethnic groups competed for dominance in Bosnia-Herzegovina and sometimes tried to reclaim the Bosnian Muslims as their own ethnic group. Under the Habsburgs, particularly Governor Benjamin Kallay, between 1882 and 1903, the Muslims had little political influence. However, Mehmet Spaho succeeded in influencing the royal regime of the unitary Southern Slav state, after the First World War. During the Second World War some Muslims supported the Axis Powers, but many others were members of Tito's Partisans, who were dominant in most of Bosnia-Herzegovina. The province experienced the most savage strife of the civil war, which raged at the same time as the resistance to the Nazi occupation and the Ustaša Croatian regime, owing to the ethnic complexity of the area.

After the War Bosnia-Herzegovina was made a constituent Republic of the Yugoslav federation (despite Serbian pressure to make it a province, like Kosovo or the Vojvodina) and, during the 1960s, it was Tito who truly established Muslim power. This was to help counter the growing ethnic tension between the Serbs and Croats of the Republic. The federal authorities were attempting to create a Muslim power-base independent of, but equal to, the Serbs and Croats. This policy led to the Slav Muslims being granted a distinct ethnic status, as a nation of Yugoslavia, for the 1971 census. The politicians of Bosnia-Herzegovina became adept at coalition politics and, following the changes in Yugoslavia during 1990, remained committed to the institution of a collective Presidency.

Rising ethnic tensions in Bosnia-Herzegovina, potentially the most dangerous in the mosaic of ethnic groups of Yugoslavia, were exemplified in September 1990. Followers of the Party of Democratic Action (PDA), the principal Muslim party of the Republic, demonstrated in the neighbouring Sandjak area of Serbia. They were supporting Muslim rights in the Novi Pazar district, but clashed with Serb nationalists. Furthermore, in the November–December republican elections, the electorate was motivated by ethnic loyalties. There were three rounds of elections for a newly-reorganized Assembly of 240 seats, on 18 November, 2 December and 9 December. The ruling League of Communists of Bosnia-Herzegovina were convincingly ousted, gaining only 19 seats, five of which were in alliance with the Socialist Alliance, which also won one seat separately. The new, liberal, all-Yugoslav party, the Alliance of Reform Forces gained 13 seats. The three main parties to emerge, however, were all nationalist: the Muslim PDA, with 86 seats; the Serb Democratic Party (SDP), with 72 seats; and the Croatian Democratic Union of Bosnia-Herzegovina (CDU-BH—an affiliate of the ruling CDU party of Croatia), with 44 seats. Four other parties shared the five remaining seats. The three nationalist parties also took all seven seats on the directly elected collective Presidency, to which separate elections took place on 18 November (three seats for the PDA and two each for the SDP and the CDU-BH). These three parties formed a coalition administration for the Republic. On 20 December they announced that Dr Alija Izetbegović of the PDA was to be President of the Presidency, Jure Pelivan of the CDU-BH was to be President of the Executive Council (Premier), and Momčilo Krajišnik of the SDP was to be President of the Assembly.

In 1991 the politics of Bosnia-Herzegovina were increasingly dominated by the Serb–Croat conflict. Early in June Dr Izetbegović, President of the Presidency, rejected suggestions that he had discussed the partition or cantonization of the Republic with the leaders of Serbia and Croatia. Following the June declarations of independence by Slovenia and Croatia, he, together with the Macedonian leader, suggested a looser federation, but civil conflict continued. Furthermore, Serb-dominated territories in Bosnia-Herzegovina also declared their intent to remain within the Yugoslav federation (or in a 'Greater Serbia'). On 27 June the self-proclaimed Serb 'Municipal Community of Bosanska Krajina' announced its unification with the 'Serbian Autonomous Region (SAR) of Krajina', in Croatia (the leaders of the Autonomous Region of Bosnian or Bosanska Krajina and the SAR of Krajina held joint sessions, in October; later that month the SAR of Slavonia, Baranja and Western Srem announced its unification with the Krajinas). An SAR of Bosanska Krajina was proclaimed on 16 September. The republican Government rejected these moves and declared the inviolability of the internal boundaries of Yugoslavia. Armed incidents contributed to the rising tension, throughout mid-1991, and many Serb areas announced the formation of other 'Autonomous Regions': Eastern and Old Herzegovina (12 September), Romanija (18 September) and North-Eastern Bosnia (20 September). Other ethnic groups accused the Serbs, with the backing of the Yugoslav People's Army (YPA), of planning a Greater Serbia. In October the YPA assumed effective control of Mostar, to the north-west of the Serb 'Old' Herzegovina, and began a siege of the Croatian city of Dubrovnik, which was reported to be the favoured capital of the same territory.

However, a federation dominated by Serbia was not an attractive proposition to the Muslims and Croats of Bosnia-Herzegovina. In October 1991 both the republican Presidency (with the dissenting votes of the Serb members) and the PDA proposed to the Assembly that the Republic declare its independence (Macedonia had already done so in September). The proposals did favour a renewed federation, but only one in which the Republic had equal relations with both Serbia and Croatia. On 14 October, during the debate in the Assembly, the Serbs (mainly the SDP) rejected any such declaration as a move towards secession. They claimed that Serbs should live in one state. No compromise was reached and Krajišnik, the President of the Assembly and a member of the SDP, ruled an end to the debate and closed the session; the Serb representatives, mainly the SDP, then withdrew from the chamber. However, the other deputies, dominated by the members of the PDA and the CDU-BH, continued the session; on 15 October the 'rump' Assembly declared that the Republic of Bosnia-Herzegovina was a sovereign state within its existing borders.

The deputies of the three main parties continued to negotiate, but the PDA condemned what it described as the threats of the SDP leader, Radovan Karadžić. The 'Autonomous Regions' of the Serbs rejected the republican Assembly's resolution and declared that only the federal laws and Constitution would apply on their territory; Bosanska Krajina considered that the Republic of Bosnia-Herzegovina had dissolved itself. On 24 October the Serb deputies of the Bosnia-Herzegovina Assembly constituted an 'Assembly of the Serb Nation'. This body then resolved to hold a referendum on whether the Serbs of Bosnia-Herzegovina should stay in a common Yugoslav state or not and nominated Karadžić as its representative for the federal State Presidency. On 4 November another SAR was proclaimed, consisting of the Serbs of Northern Bosnia, with an Assembly based in Doboj (this area did not have a Serb majority). On 9–10 November the referendum of the Republic's Serbs overwhelmingly supported staying in a Yugoslav or Serb state.

Economy

The economy of Bosnia-Herzegovina is overwhelmingly agricultural. It produces tobacco, fruit and livestock. Sheep are grazed in the mountainous terrain, where timber reserves are also exploited. There are extensive mineral resources, the Republic being a major source of copper, lead, zinc and gold. Iron ore is mined and there are reserves of lignite (a poor-quality brown coal). Federal government policy favoured the development of Bosnia-Herzegovina and the other poorer regions, but industrialization has not become a significant feature of the local economy. There are some light industries and, during the 1970s and 1980s, the Sava Valley (along the northern border of the Republic) became the favoured development area for some heavy industries. There are iron and steel plants at Zenica. The armaments manufacturing industry is also important. Service industries, notably tourism, are not well developed, relative to Croatia (Dalmatia) and Slovenia. The Republic was dependent on transfers from central government. Its economy was adversely affected by the civil war, which began in June 1991. The naval blockade of the Croatian ports, through which Bosnia-Herzegovina's petroleum supplies are delivered, was particularly serious. This added to the Republic's economic difficulties and, by September 1991, the number of unemployed had reached 320,000, the highest number since soon after the Second World War.

Directory
The Constitution

The Constitution of the Socialist Republic of Bosnia and Herzegovina was promulgated in 1990, under the rule of the League of Communists. In 1991 the Assembly planned to draft a new Constitution, on the basis of consensus, but a deterioration in relations between the three main parties, in October, delayed any implementation of this process. The Assembly did declare the sovereignty and inviolability of the borders of Bosnia-Herzegovina, without actually seceding from the Yugoslav federation. The existing constitutional provisions were for: a seven-member, collective State Presidency (the members elected a President from among their own number); an Executive Council or Government, presided over by a Premier (all members of and responsible to the Assembly); and a legislative, bicameral Assembly, with 240 deputies in total. Bosnia-Herzegovina is a multi-party, democratic state, which guarantees basic human rights and freedoms. The principles of rotating leaderships and balanced ethnic representation were preserved in the Republic, the constitutional arrangements for which were similar to those of the federation itself (thus, there is a republican Supreme Court and Constitutional Court).

The Government
(September 1991)

The administration of the Socialist Republic of Bosnia-Herzegovina is conducted by a coalition of three nationalist parties: the Party of Democratic Action (PDA—representing the Muslims); the Serb Democratic Party (SDP); and the Croatian Democratic Union (CDU).

STATE PRESIDENCY

Elections to the republican collective State Presidency were held on 18 November 1990; all seven seats were won by the three coalition parties above; on 20 December they announced that the PDA leader would be elected President of the Presidency.

President of the Presidency: Dr ALIJA IZETBEGOVIĆ (PDA).

Other Members: Dr EJUP GANIĆ (PDA), FIKRET ABDIĆ (PDA), NIKOLA KOLJEVIĆ (SDP), BILJANA PLAVŠIĆ (SDP), STJEPAN KLJUIĆ (CDU), FRANJO BORAS (CDU).

EXECUTIVE COUNCIL

Premier: JURE PELIVAN (CDU).

Minister of National Defence: JERKO DOKO (CDU).

Minister of Internal Affairs: ALIJA DELIMUSTAFIĆ (PDA).

Minister of Finance: MOMČILO PEJIĆ (SDP).

Minister of the Economy: Dr REŠID BEGTIĆ (PDA).

Minister of International Co-operation: Dr HARIS SILAJDŽIĆ (PDA).

Minister of Agriculture, Forestry and Water Resources Management: Dr MILIVOJE NADAŽDIN (SDP).

Minister of Territorial Management and Environmental Protection: Dr MUNIR JAHIĆ (PDA).

Minister of Transport and Communications: TOMISLAV KRSTIĆEVIĆ (CDU).

Minister of Information: VELIBOR OSTOJIĆ (SDP).

Minister of Justice and Administration: BRANKO NIKOLIĆ (SDP).

Minister of Education, Science, Culture and Physical Culture: Dr NIHAD HASIĆ (PDA).

Minister of Health, Labour and Social Security: Dr ISMET LIPA (PDA).

Minister of Veterans and Disabled Veterans Affairs: DAVID BALABAN (SDP).

Ministers without Portfolio: BOŽIDAR ANTIĆ (SDP), IBRAHIM ČOLAKHODŽIĆ (PDA), Dr ISMET KASUMAGIĆ (PDA), VITOMIR MIRO LASIĆ (CDU), Dr BRANKO DERIĆ.

MINISTRIES

Office of the Executive Council: 71000 Sarajevo, vojvode Putnika 3; tel. (71) 213777; fax (71) 272877.

Ministry of Agriculture, Forestry and Water Resources Management: 71000 Sarajevo, Vojvode Putnika 3; tel. (71) 213777; fax (71) 653592.

Ministry of the Economy: 71000 Sarajevo, Vojvode Putnika 3; tel. (71) 213777; fax (71) 653592.

Ministry of Education, Science, Culture and Physical Culture: 71000 Sarajevo, Vojvode Putnika 3; tel. (71) 213777; fax (71) 653592.

Ministry of Finance: 71000 Sarajevo, Vojvode Putnika 3; tel. (71) 213777; fax (71) 653592.

Ministry of Health, Labour and Social Security: 71000 Sarajevo, Vojvode Putnika 3; tel. (71) 213777; fax (71) 653592.

Ministry of Information: 71000 Sarajevo, Vojvode Putnika 3; tel. (71) 213777; fax (71) 213350.

Ministry of Internal Affairs: 71000 Sarajevo, Boriše Kovačevića 7; tel. (71) 512877; fax (71) 653592.

Ministry of International Co-operation: 71000 Sarajevo, Vojvode Putnika 3; tel. (71) 213777; fax (71) 653592.

Ministry of Justice and Administration: 71000 Sarajevo, Vojvode Putnika 3; tel. (71) 213777; fax (71) 653592.

Ministry of National Defence: 71000 Sarajevo, Vojvode Putnika 3A; tel. (71) 35427; fax (71) 653592.

Ministry of Territorial Management and Environmental Protection: 71000 Sarajevo, Vojvode Putnika 3; tel. (71) 213777; fax (71) 653592.

Ministry of Transport and Communications: 71000 Sarajevo, Vojvode Putnika 3; tel. (71) 213777; fax (71) 653592.

Ministry of Veterans and Disabled Persons Affairs: 71000 Sarajevo, Vojvode Putnika 3; tel. (71) 213777; fax (71) 653592.

Legislature

ASSEMBLY

President: MOMČILO KRAJIŠNIK, 71000 Sarajevo, trg Dure Pucara; tel. (71) 615355; fax (71) 217583.

Elections, 18 November, 2 and 9 December 1990

Party	Seats
Party of Democratic Action (PDA)	86
Serbian Democratic Party (SDP) . . .	72
Croatian Democratic Union (CDU-BH) . .	44
League of Communists (LC-BH)†/Socialist Alliance (SA)	20*
Alliance of Reform Forces (ARF)	13
Others	5
Total	240

* The LC-BH won 14 seats alone and five in alliance with the SA; the SA gained one seat alone.
† The LC-BH was renamed the Socialist Democratic Party.

Local Government

Local government is based on the municipality, of which there are 109 in the Republic (Sarajevo is divided into 10 communities). Each municipality has a local assembly. During 1991, as part of an alleged move towards the cantonization of Bosnia-Herzegovina, four areas with ethnic Serb majorities constituted themselves as 'Autonomous Regions' (*Autonomna Oblast*) or, as in Croatia, 'Serb Autonomous Regions' (SAR—*Srpska Autonomna Oblast*). In November the Serbs of the municipalities between Krajina and North-East Bosnia constituted themselves as an SAR. Later in the month, in the south of the Republic, a Croatian Community of Herzeg-Bosna (Pres. MATE BOBAN) was formed, although it did not claim autonomy. These polities were not recognized by the republican authorities or by the other ethnic groups.

'AUTONOMOUS REGIONS'

Bosanska Krajina: Banja Luka; Municipal Community of Bosanska (Bosnian) Krajina declared in April 1991, union with Croatian Krajina announced in June, and autonomy proclaimed 16 October; 18 municipalities in north and west Bosnia; Pres. of the Assembly VOJO KUPRESANIN.

Herzegovina: Trebinje; autonomy unilaterally declared on 12 October 1991, as Eastern and Old Herzegovina; eight municipalities in the south of the Republic; Premier/Prime Minister MILORAD BOJOVIĆ.

North-East Bosnia: Ugljevik; autonomy unilaterally declared on 20 October 1991; three municipalities; assembly of 35 deputies; Pres. of Assembly MILADIN STJEPANOVIĆ.

Northern Bosnia: Doboj; autonomy unilaterally declared on 4 November 1991; the minority Serbs of 16 municipalities; Pres. of Assembly NIKOLA PERIŠIĆ.

Romanija: Sarajevo; autonomy unilaterally declared on 18 October 1991; three municipalities, two communities of Sarajevo and several villages.

Political Organizations

Croatian Democratic Union of Bosnia-Herzegovina (CDU-BH) (Hrvatska Demokratska Zajednika—HDZ): c/o 71000 Sarajevo, trg Dure Pucara bb; f. 1990; affiliate of the CDU in Croatia; Croat nationalist party; Pres. STJEPAN KLJUIĆ.

Muslim Bosniak Organization: 71000 Sarajevo; f. 1990, after split in PDA; secular Muslim party; Leader MUHAMMED FILIPOVIĆ.

Party of Democratic Action (PDA) (Stranka Demokratske Akcije—SDA): c/o 71000 Sarajevo, trg Dure Pucara bb; leading Muslim nationalist party; has brs in Serbia; Leader Dr ALIJA IZETBEGOVIĆ; Sec. IRFAN AJANOVIĆ.

Serb Democratic Party (SDP) (Srpska Demokratska Stranka—SDS): c/o 71000 Sarajevo, trg Dure Pucara bb; f. 1990; allied to SDP of Croatia; Serb nationalist party; Pres. Dr RADOVAN KARADŽIĆ.

Socialist Alliance: c/o 71000 Sarajevo, trg Dure Pucara bb; former Communist mass organization; allies of Socialist Democratic Party; left-wing.

Socialist Democratic Party (Sokijalisticka Demokratska Partija): c/o 71000 Sarajevo, trg Dure Pucara bb; registered as political party in republican Higher Court March 1990; formerly the ruling League of Communists of Bosnia-Herzegovina; Pres. Dr NIJAZ DURAKOVIĆ.

The all-Yugoslav party, the Alliance of Reform Forces (see above, in the Directory for federal Yugoslavia), is also represented in the republican Assembly, as are five other, minor parties.

Judicial System

The courts in Bosnia-Herzegovina are supervised by the Ministry of Justice and Administration (see section on The Government—Ministries). The highest courts in the republican judicial system are the Supreme Court and the Constitutional Court. Final appeal lies to the Federal Court and, in constitutional matters, to the Yugoslav Constitutional Court, both of which are based in Belgrade.

Constitutional Court of the SR of Bosnia-Herzegovina: 71000 Sarajevo, Save Kovačevića 6; tel. (71) 214555; Pres. Dr KASIM TRNKA.

Supreme Court: 71000 Sarajevo, Valtera Perića 11; tel. (71) 213577; Pres. MARTIN RAGUZ.

Office of the Public Prosecutor: 71000 Sarajevo, Valtera Perića 11; tel. (71) 214990; Public Prosecutor SLOBODAN KOVAČ.

Religion

Bosnia-Herzegovina has a diversity of religious allegiances. Just over one-half of the inhabitants are nominally Christian, but these are divided between the Serbian Orthodox Church (Metropolitan VLADISLAV of Dabrobosna is the republican religious leader) and the Roman Catholic Church (the Archbishop of Vrhbosna-Sarajevo is the responsible prelate). The dominant single religion is Islam; the Republic comprises the Sarajevo Region of Islam in Yugoslavia (it also covers the few Muslims of Croatia and Slovenia). The Reis-ul-ulema, the head of the Yugoslav Muslims, is resident in Sarajevo (see above, in the Directory for federal Yugoslavia). Most of the Muslims are also ethnic Muslims, or Bosnian Muslims (Slavs who converted to Islam under the Ottomans). There are, however, some ethnic Albanian and Turkish Muslims. Virtually all are adherents of the Sunni sect.

Islamic Community of the Sarajevo Region: 71000 Sarajevo, Save Kovačevića 2; Pres. of Massahat SALIH EFENDIJA COLAKOVIĆ.

The Press

PRINCIPAL DAILIES

Oslobodjenje: 71000 Sarajevo, Džemala Bijedića 185; tel. (71) 454144; telex 41136; f. 1943; morning; Editor-in-Chief IVICA MISIĆ; circ. 49,577.

Sarajevske novine: Sarajevo, Boriše Kovačevića 22; evening; Editor-in-Chief IVICA BANUŠIĆ; circ. 15,671.

Večernje novine: Sarajevo, Pavla Goranina 13; tel. (71) 33603; telex 41732; fax (71) 33205; f. 1964; Editor-in-Chief PREDRAG NIKOLIĆ; circ. 85,000.

Večernje novosti: Sarajevo, Maršala Tita 13; evening; Editor Dr AZIS HADŽIHASANOVIĆ; circ. 20,000.

Publishers

Glas: 78000 Banja Luka, Borisa Kidriča 1; tel. (78) 37978; f. 1973.

Svjetlost: 71000 Sarajevo, Petra Preradovića 3; tel. (71) 512144; telex 41326; f. 1945; textbooks and literature; Dir SAVO ZIROJEVIĆ.

Veselin Masleša: 71000 Sarajevo, Obala 4; tel. (71) 214633; telex 41154; fax (71) 272369; f. 1950; school and university textbooks, general literature; Dir RADOSLAV MIJATOVIĆ.

Radio and Television

Radio-Televizija (RTV) Sarajevo: 71000 Sarajevo, VI Proleterske brigade 4; tel. (71) 455107; telex 41124 (Radio); fax (71) 455166; tel. (71) 652333; telex 41122; fax (71) 461569 (TV); f. 1945 (Radio), 1969 (TV); 4 radio and 2 TV programmes; broadcasts in Serbo-Croat; Dir-Gen. NEDJELJKO MILJANOVIĆ; Dir of Radio NADJA PAŠIĆ; Dir of TV BESIM CERIĆ.

Finance

(d.d. = dioničko društvo (joint-stock company); dep. = deposits; res = reserves; m. = million; amounts in dinars; brs = branches)

BANKS

Republican National Bank

National Bank of Bosnia-Herzegovina: 71000 Sarajevo, Maršala Tita 25; tel. (71) 33326; Gov. JADRANKO PRLIĆ.

Selected Banks

Privredna Banka Sarajevo (Credit Bank, Shareholding Company): 71000 Sarajevo, JNA 52; tel. (71) 533688; telex 41235; fax (71) 214087; f. Dec. 1989, succeeding Privredna banka Sarajevo-Osnovna banka Sarajevo; deals with deposits, credits and other banking activities in the country and abroad; total assets 88,402,536m., dep. 31,572,486m. (Dec. 1989); Gen. Man. VOJISLAV MILIJAŠ (acting).

Privredna Banka Sarajevo d.d., Sarajevo: 71000 Sarajevo, Vojvode Stepe Obala 19, POB 160; tel. (71) 213144; telex 41280; fax (71) 219517; f. 1971; Gen. Dir DJORDJE ZARIĆ; 13 brs.

Trade and Industry

Chamber of Economy of Bosnia-Herzegovina: 71000 Sarajevo, Mis Irbina 13; tel. (71) 211777; Pres. MENSUR SMAILOVIĆ.

MAJOR ENTERPRISES AND COMPANIES

ALHOS Export-Import: 71000 Sarajevo, Tesanjska 24A; tel. (71) 39481; telex 21436; fax (71) 215999; clothing manufacturer; Dir. of Manufacture KEMAL HUJIĆ; 1,400 employees.

Aluminij: 88000 Mostar, 25 Novembra BB; tel. (88) 411333; telex 46241; fax (88) 33951; produces alumina, etc.; Gen. Man. Mijo Brajković; 4,500 employees.

Boris Kidrić Coking and Chemical Works, Lukavać (Boris Kidrić Lukavać): 75300 Lukavać, Zeljeznicka 1; tel. (75) 215151; telex 44139; production of coke, fertilizers, synthetic organic products; 5,821 employees.

Bratstvo: 72290 Pućarevo, Borisa Kidrića 1; tel. (72) 791022; telex 43139; fax (72) 791018; manufactures parts for and assembles automobiles and tractors; Gen. Dir JOZO KRIŽANOVIĆ; 11,000 employees.

Energoinvest: 71000 Sarajevo, Bratstva Jedinstva; tel. (71) 654177; telex 41221; fax (71) 656877; production, design and development of power systems; Chair. Dr BOŽIDAR MATIĆ; 47,000 employees.

Feroelektro: 71000 Sarajevo, Maršala Tita 48; tel. (71) 219611; telex 41133; fax (71) 217649; import and export of goods and services; Gen. Dir Dr MIRKO PULJIĆ; 450 employees.

Krivaja: 72220 Zavidovici; tel. (72) 871220; telex 43140; fax (72) 874341; timber industry, construction industry and metals industry; 13,000 employees.

Kula: Gradačac, Pere Bošića 23; tel. (76) 817229; telex 44726; fax (76) 818366; clothing manufacturer; Gen. Man. ŠESTAN FABIJAN; 1,570 employees.

Medic: 77226 Coraliči; tel. (77) 514222; fax (77) 511350; manufactures medical instruments and equipment; Gen. Dir ZLATKO JUŠIĆ; 530 employees.

RMK Zenica: 72000 Zenica, bul. Lenjina 1; tel. (72) 33322; telex 43129; fax (72) 419088; engineering, metal processing, casting, metallurgy and mining; Pres. MILAN MALBASIĆ.

Ro Rafinerija Ulja, Modrica: 74480 Modrica, Vjekoslava Bakulica 49; tel. (74) 880160; telex 445588; fax (74) 882541; production of base oils, paraffin waxes, special mineral oils, etc; Gen. Man. STEVO DOKIĆ; 930 employees.

Sipad Export-Import: 71000 Sarajevo, POB 56, Maršala Tita 15; tel. (71) 213188; telex 41212; fax (71) 218667; foreign trade org. dealing in forestry, industrial production, foreign trading, scientific research and internat. forwarding; Gen. Dir MORIS PAPO; 307 employees.

Sodaso: 75001 Tuzla, Bratstva i Jedinstva 17; tel. (75) 211111; telex 44141; fax (75) 212172; salt and mineral products; Gen. Man. ANTO RAOS; 6,927 employees.

Unis: 71000 Sarajevo, Trscanska 7; tel. (71) 215522; telex 41570; fax (71) 219319; a variety of businesses, incl. cars and motor accessories; 52,000 employees.

UPI Sarajevo—Associated Agriculture, Trade and Industry: 71000 Sarajevo, JNA 20; tel. (71) 518574; telex 41321; primary agriculture on socially owned land and land of co-operating farmers (246,000 ha in total); 36,000 employees.

Culture

REPUBLICAN ORGANIZATIONS

Ministry of Education, Science, Culture and Physical Culture: see section on The Government (Ministries).

Republican Agency for Cultural and Artistic Activities (Republicka Poslovnica za Kulturno-umjetnicke Priredbe): 71000 Sarajevo, Radićeva 15; tel. (71) 273664; Dir PUNISA RAKOCEVIĆ.

CULTURAL HERITAGE

Art Gallery of Bosnia and Herzegovina (Umjetnička galerija BiH): 71000 Sarajevo, JNA 38; tel. (71) 218644; f. 1946; Dir VEFIK HADŽISMAJLOVIĆ.

'Collegium Artisticum' Gallery: 71000 Sarajevo, Skenderija; tel. (71) 35903.

Museum of Bosanska Krajina (Muzej Bosanske Krajine): 78000 Banja Luka, V. Karadžića bb; tel. (71) 35486; f. 1930; Dir AHMET ČEJVAN.

National Museum of Bosnia and Herzegovina (Zemaljski Muzej BiH): 71000 Sarajevo, Vojvode Putnika 7; tel. (71) 35322; f. 1888; Dir ALMAZ DAUTLEGOVIĆ.

PERFORMING ARTS

'55 Chambre' Theatre: 71000 Sarajevo, Marsala Tita 56/II; tel. (71) 39031.

National Theatre (Narodno Pozoriste): 71000 Sarajevo, Obala 9; tel. (71) 518795; Ballet and Opera Dir TEODOR ROMANIĆ.

Open Theatre 'Obala': 71000 Sarajevo, Vojvode Stepe Obala 13; tel. (71) 213692.

Music

Mostar Symphony Orchestra (Simfonijski Orkestar Mostar): 79000 Mostar, Rade Bitange 16; tel. (88) 38608; Dir/Conductor TIBOR BAUER.

Sarajevo Philharmonic Orchestra (Sarajevska Filharmonija): c/o Narodno Pozoriste, 71000 Sarajevo, Obala 9; tel. (71) 511197; Chief Conductor MIROSLAV HOMEN.

Symphony Orchestra RTV Sarajevo (Simfonijski Orkestra RTV Sarajevo): 71000 Sarajevo, VI Proleterske brigade 4; tel. (71) 461101; Chief Conductor JULIO MARIĆ.

ASSOCIATIONS

Association of Composers (Udruženje Kompozitora): 71000 Sarajevo, Radićeva 15.

Association of Musicians (Udruženje Muzičkih Umjetnika): Muzička akademija, 71000 Sarajevo, Svetozara Markovića 1; tel. (71) 25007.

Association of Writers (Udruženje Književnika): 71000 Sarajevo, Preradovićeva 3; tel. (71) 516400; f. 1945; Pres. ABDULLAH SIDRAN.

Historical Society (Društvo Istoričara): Filozofski fakultet, 71000 Sarajevo, Račkog 1.

Society of Music Lovers and Young Musicians (Musička Omladina): Muzička akademija, 71000 Sarajevo, Sv. Markovića 1; tel. (71) 25007; f. 1958; Sec. BORISLAV CURIĆ.

The Environment

GOVERNMENT ORGANIZATIONS

Ministry of Territorial Management and Environmental Protection: see section on The Government (Ministries); incl.:

Institute for the Preservation of Natural and Cultural Heritage in Bosnia-Herzegovina (Zavod za Zastitu Spomenika Kulture i Prirode BiH): 71001 Sarajevo, POB 650, Obala 27 Jula 11A; f. 1947; Dir DZEMAL CELIĆ.

Most environmental activity by research bodies and the 'Green' movement takes place at the federal level (see p. 317).

Defence

Bosnia-Herzegovina is defended by the Yugoslav People's Army (YPA), which is also responsible for the republican Territorial

Defence Force. Since December 1991 and a reorganization of the YPA, Sarajevo has been the headquarters of the Second Military District. There are a great number of firearms in civilian hands in the Republic (officially, 271,000 citizens have registered some 323,000 weapons, but it is feared that the actual number may be three times that) and consequent fears about paramilitary groups and the capability of the Republic to defend itself. The republican

Assembly declared Bosnia-Herzegovina neutral on several occasions during 1991.

Commander of the Second District of the YPA: Col-Gen. MILU-TIN KUKANJAC.

Chief of Staff of the Territorial Defence: Maj.-Gen. FIKRET JAKIĆ.

CROATIA

Geography

The Republic of Croatia is a constituent partner in the Socialist Federal Republic of Yugoslavia, although it declared itself to be in a process of 'dissociation' from the federation on 25 June 1991, and then, on 8 October, adopted an act of independence. It lies in the north-west of Yugoslavia, with Slovenia further north-west, the Vojvodina area of Serbia to the east and Bosnia-Herzegovina abutting into it, forming a southern border, along the Sava River, and an eastern one, inland from the Dalmatian coast which stretches southwards. At the southern tip of this narrowing stretch of Croatia, beyond a short coastal strip of Bosnia-Herzegovina, is the territory of Dubrovnik (once known as Ragusa), which has a short border with Montenegro. There is an international border with Hungary, in the north-east.

Croatia, which has a total area of 56,538 sq km, consists of two principal parts: there is a long coastal region, narrowing as it goes south, extending from the Istrian peninsula, down the Dalmatian coast to the area of the former city state of Dubrovnik; the north of this coastal region is attached, by a narrow bridge of territory, to eastern Croatia, which extends inland. Beyond the 'waist' attaching it to the coast, the Republic widens out into Croatia proper, beyond the mountains, and stretches eastwards. Slovenia juts into this 'waist' from the north-west and Bosnia from the south-east. To the north-east of the waist of the Republic lies the capital, Zagreb (Agram), in the heart of old Croatia. Eastwards, is the fertile territory of Slavonia, an ancient province that lies between the Drava and the Sava rivers. The chief town of Slavonia is Osijek. Western or coastal Croatia is defined by the mountains running parallel to the littoral, which is fringed with more than 1,100 islets and islands. The most populous towns of Dalmatia are Split, in the central coastal area, and Rijeka (Fiume), in the north. The main town of Slavonia is Osijek, in the east of the territory. These towns, and Zagreb, are among the largest in Yugoslavia.

The total population of Croatia was 4,763,941, in 1991, and the Republic had a population density of 84.3 sq km. According to the provisional results of the census of 1991 ethnic Croats comprised 77.9% of the total population of the Republic (in 1981 some 78% of all Croats lived within the borders of the Republic). There was, in 1991, a significant Serb minority, of 12.2%; they were concentrated in certain areas, mainly along the border with Bosnia-Herzegovina. (The Habsburgs settled many Serbs along the frontier with its Muslim rival, the Ottoman Empire, in an area known as the Krajina—borderlands.) Both peoples speak versions of Serbo-Croat (or Croato-Serb), but the largely Roman Catholic Croats use the Latin script and the Eastern Orthodox Serbs use the Cyrillic script. The Roman Catholic Church is the largest religious denomination. Since 1991 the Croatians have rejected the 1954 Novi Sad Agreement (see Chronology), and now claim the distinctness of a Croatian language. In 1981 there was also a significant number classing themselves as ethnically neutral Yugoslavs (8.2%), but this was considerably less at the 1991 census (only 2.2%).

In 1991 three 'Serb Autonomous Regions (SARs)' were established: Krajina, along those borders where Bosnia juts into Croatia; Western Slavonia, to the south-east of Zagreb; and Slavonia, Baranja and Western Srem, nearer the border with Serbia. The SARs are fragmented territories. Krajina,

most of which has a Serb-majority, consists of the districts of: Eastern Dalmatia and Lika (inland from Zadar and northwards along the border with Bosnia-Herzegovina, which lies to the east); Kordun (which straddles the apex of Bosnia—the SAR is divided by and excludes the Croat-dominated municipality of Slunj); and Banija (which lies between the Una and Kupa rivers, with Bosnia-Herzegovina to the south). There is an overwhelming Serb majority in the district of Eastern Dalmatia and Lika, but in the northern areas of Krajina there remain significant Croat minorities.

In the SAR of Western Slavonia (three municipalities in the centre of eastern Croatia, stretching between, but not contiguous with, the borders of Hungary and Bosnia-Herzegovina) there was a Serb majority, but they only accounted for some 38% of the population, compared to the 36% of Croats, in 1991. This area was physically isolated from other Serb-dominated areas, largely occupied by Croatian forces and declared united with Krajina in December 1991. In the SAR of Slavonia, Baranja and Western Srem there were no districts in which the Serbs constituted an overall majority (according to the census of 1991, the largest proportion of Serbs was in Pakrac, where they accounted for 46% of the population, compared to the 36% of Croats). Baranja is in the north-east of the Republic of Croatia, bordering on Hungary and Vojvodina. Some of Baranja lies in Hungary, and the whole area was, historically, administered as the Hungarian province of Serbian Vojvodina. In 1918 Yugoslav Baranja declared itself to be part of Serbia, and, in 1920, it was formally ceded to the new state, together with Vojvodina. Baranja became part of Croatia in 1945, partly on ethnic considerations and partly as compensation for the loss of Eastern Syrmia (Srem). Although Baranja (Beli Minastir) is administered by an SAR, there was a Croat majority by 1991. In Western Syrmia (Western Srem to the Serbs), there was an overall Croat majority in 1991, and this is a likely explanation of the ferocity of the fighting in this area (Srem includes Vukovar and Vinkovci and claims Osijek), during the civil war of 1991.

History

From the fifth century AD the Croats (*Čorvats* or 'mountaineers') began to settle in Illyria (a Province of the Eastern Roman, or Byzantine, Empire since the fourth century). Despite the usually nominal overlordship of the Roman Emperor in Constantinople (Istanbul), the Croats were more influenced by Western Europe. Missionaries from Aquileia (Trieste) first attached them to Christianity and their allegiance remained to the Roman Church. An independent kingdom was established, in the 10th century, between the river Drava and the Adriatic Sea. The realm controlled much of Bosnia, the inhabitants of which were also Roman Catholic. To varying degrees, Byzantine influence remained along the Dalmatian coast and in Istria, thus establishing the Croatian heartland to be inland, in the mountains and around Agram (Zagreb). In 1074 Dimitar Zvonimir succeeded to the throne; he was crowned by the Pope, in 1076, having finally rejected the sovereignty of the Eastern, Byzantine Emperor. He died in 1089 and was replaced by the Hungarian king, László I. His successor, Coloman I, formalized the personal union with Hungary under the *Pacta Conventa;* he became King of Croatia, which was administered by a ban (frontier commander or marcher lord). In the late 12th century Bela III finally expelled Byzantine influence and consolidated Hungarian control of Croatia and Bosnia. Under the pressure of the Mongol invasions, particularly after the defeats of 1241, the Hungarian kingdom disintegrated. Venice consolidated its possession of the former Byzantine strongholds in Istria and along the Dalmatian coast, but, by the reign of Matthias I Corvinus (1485–90), Hungarian rule in the rest of Croatia had been re-established.

The Hungarians were defeated by the forces of the Ottoman Empire at the battle of Mohács, in 1526, and Croatia became a border territory between the Islamic world and the Christian West. The Habsburgs, who were the Holy Roman Emperors, had a claim to the Hungarian Crown (their hereditary possession of it was confirmed by the 1687 Imperial Diet of Pressburg). In 1529 the Habsburgs and the Ottomans divided the Hungarian territories. Northern Croatia became part of the Habsburg Kingdom of Hungary, while southern Croatia and most of Slavonia became part of the Ottoman Empire. In the 17th century the Turkish advance ended and, by 1699, the Habsburgs had secured all of modern Croatia, except for the Venetian territories of Dalmatia and Istria and the city-state of Ragusa (Dubrovnik). The Habsburg authorities settled Serbs on the borderlands with the Ottomans, in areas of Croatia known as Krajina. Although part of the Habsburgs' Hungarian patrimony, Croatia, like the rest of the Empire, was more under Austrian influence during the 18th century. Between 1809 and 1813 the Croatian coast and immediate hinterland was united with Dalmatia, Istria, Ragusa and neighbouring territories to the north in French-ruled Illyria, a province created by the French Emperor, Napoleon I Bonaparte. Slavonia remained in the Austrian Empire (the Habsburg Emperor had taken the imperial title for Austria and the Holy Roman Empire had been dissolved).

The Habsburg territories were restored at the 1815 Congress of Vienna, which also bestowed Dalmatia and Istria on Austria. As a consequence of the Hungarian revolution of 1848–49 Croatia and Slavonia were made Austrian crownlands. In 1868, after the Habsburg Empire had become the Dual Monarchy of Austria-Hungary under the *Ausgleich* or Compromise of the previous year, Croatia and Slavonia were restored to the Hungarian Crown. Croatia gained its autonomy and was formally joined with Slavonia in 1881. However, the central Hungarian authorities pursued policies of 'Magyarization', particularly after 1875. Together with the anti-Serbian commercial practices of the Habsburgs, from 1904, this transformed traditional Croat–Serb rivalries into Southern Slav ('Yugoslav') solidarity. During the First World War representatives of the Croats met with delegates of the other Southern Slavic peoples and, in the Corfu Declaration, announced their intention to form a unitary, democratic state under the Serbian monarchy. In October 1918 the Habsburg Danubian Monarchy collapsed and the Southern Slav territories declared themselves a republic, their separation from the Austro-Hungarian Empire and, on 4 December, were proclaimed to be united with Serbia and Montenegro in the new Kingdom of Serbs, Croats and Slovenes.

The new Kingdom, however, was dominated by the Serbs, and the Croats, the second most populous ethnic group, sought a greater share of power. They led the dissatisfaction of the non-Serb peoples against the regime. The increasing unrest within the Kingdom, which included the meeting of a separatist assembly in Zagreb, in 1928, led King Aleksandar to impose a royal dictatorship, in 1929, when the country's name formally became Yugoslavia. In

1934 he was assassinated, while in France, by Croatian extremists. At the same time the Fascist Ustaša movement was gaining support among the discontented Croat peasantry. They were not placated by the inclusion of Croats in the Government, in 1939. When the Germans and Italians invaded, in 1941, many Croats welcomed their support for the establishment of an Independent State of Croatia, on 9 April.

The new Croatian state invited an Italian duke, Aimone of Spoleto (Split), to be the nominal sovereign, but government was conducted by the leader of the Ustaša, the 'Poglavnik' Ante Pavelić. His territory included most of Bosnia-Herzegovina and parts of Serbia, as well as the modern Republic (Istria was annexed to Italy, which also continued to hold the coastal enclave of Zara, or Zadar, until 1947). The Ustaša regime was notorious for its policies towards its minorities: a vast number of Jews, Serbs, Roma (Gypsies) and the politically 'unreliable' were murdered in extermination camps. At the same time a vicious civil war was being waged against the resistance forces, particularly Tito's Partisans. By 1943 Tito's forces were able to proclaim a provisional government in areas under their control and the Fascist regime was beginning to lose control. The Ustaša state collapsed in 1944 and Croatia was restored to Yugoslavia as one unit of a federal Communist republic.

The legacy of the Ustaša regime was the official hostility of the Communists to any expression of Croat nationalism. It was equated with Fascism. At the same time the development of the tourist industry along Croatia's Dalmatian coast added to the wealth of the Republic, and the Croatians resented their effective subsidy of the poorer parts of Yugoslavia, which was considered to be Serb-dominated. However, during the 1960s, there was an increase of nationalism in Croatia. This 'mass movement' (*Maspok*), which was led by organizations such as the ostensibly cultural association, Matica Hrvatska, was supported by members of the ruling League of Communists, as well as by non-Communists. The movement encouraged the local Communist leadership, which was associated with the reform wing of the Party, to defy central policy in certain areas. In December 1971 Tito committed himself to opposing the tendency: the Croatian Communist leadership was obliged to resign and they, and others prominent in the *Maspok*, were arrested. A purge of the League of Communists of Croatia followed. During 1972 many people were charged with crimes 'against the People and the State', some 427 being convicted in Croatia that year. The central authorities also moved against liberals in other republics, notably Serbia, thus avoiding the charge of being anti-Croat. In 1974, however, Tito introduced a new Constitution, which enshrined the federal (almost confederal) and collective nature of the Yugoslav state. The Constitution was designed to placate nationalist sentiments, particularly in Croatia, and also to restrain those tendencies within a unifying framework. Any manifestations of Croatian nationalism, however, continued to be prosecuted, even after the death of Tito, in 1980.

An added impetus to Croatian nationalism and the perception that the Yugoslav federation was Serb-dominated, was that the League of Communists of Croatia contained a high proportion of Serbs. Any reaction against the Communists was readily associated with Croatian nationalism. When Communist power began to decline, from 1989 particularly, Croatian nationalism re-emerged as a significant force. Dissidents of the 1970s and 1980s were the main beneficiaries. Dr Franjo Tudjman, for example, a historian and former Partisan general, had been imprisoned in 1972 and 1981. In 1990 he formed the Croatian Democratic Union (CDU—Hrvatska Demokratska Zajednica). This rapidly became a mass party and the main challenger to the ruling Party, which had changed its name to the League of Communists of Croatia-Party of Democratic Reform (LCC-PDR). The Communists introduced a 'first-past-the-post' voting system (the candidate with more votes than any other single candidate wins the constituency seat—to the main Socio-Political Chamber) for the multi-party elections to the republican legislature, in April 1990. Tudjman campaigned as a nationalist, causing controversy by advocating a 'Greater Croatia' (that is, including Bosnia) and complaining of Serb domination, although he did promise the Croatian Serbs cultural autonomy. This rhetoric caused considerable anxiety among the Serbs, however, and there were demonstrations protesting against the CDU and accusations of reviving the Ustaša. On 18 March 1990 there was an assassination attempt made against Tudjman, which heightened ethnic tensions.

In the elections to the tricameral republican Assembly (Sabor), which took place in two rounds, on 24 April and 6–7 May 1990, the CDU gained from the voting system, taking a majority of the seats, despite only winning some 42% of the votes cast in the second round (in both the Socio-Political Chamber and the Chamber of Municipalities). In the Socio-Political Chamber the CDU gained 54 of the 80 seats; in the Chamber of Municipalities the CDU gained 68 of the 115 seats filled; in the Chamber of Associated Labour the CDU gained 83 of the 156 seats filled. Of the 351 seats of all three chambers of the Sabor (a maximum of 356 could have been filled), the CDU won 205. The next-largest party was the LCC-PDR, with a total of 73 seats. Both the leading parties won further seats in alliance with other parties. Tudjman was elected President of Croatia, but he attempted to allay Serb fears by offering the vice-presidency of the Sabor to Dr Jovan Rasković, the leader of the Serb Democratic Party (SDP). Rasković eventually refused the post, but another Serb was appointed to it.

Serb-dominated areas were alienated by Tudjman's Croat nationalism and the Republic's adoption of a new flag (the traditional Croatian chequerboard symbol was used; although subtly altered, to the Serbs this remained balefully like the Ustaša emblem) and new police uniforms. The Serb stronghold of Knin, in the eastern hinterland of that arm of Croatia which lay along the coast, was the centre of resistance. A 'Serb National Council', based in Knin (the chief town of the Krajina area on the Bosnian border), was formed in July. This group organized a referendum on autonomy for the Croatian Serbs, which was banned by the Croatian authorities. Amid virtual insurrection in some areas, the referendum was held between 19 August and 2 September. The results of the referendum, announced on 1 October, overwhelmingly endorsed the move for an ill-defined autonomy. By December Serbian areas were issuing declarations of autonomy, the extent of which expanded as Croatia itself moved further from acceptance of the federal Yugoslav state. By October 1991 there were three 'Serb Autonomous Regions' (SARs) in Croatia: Krajina, with its headquarters in Knin (which had declared its unity with the Autonomous Region of Krajina in neighbouring Bosnia-Herzegovina); Slavonia, Baranja and Western Srem, with its temporary headquarters in Dalj; and Western Slavonia, most of which the Croats held. The three regions stated their determination to remain in a federal Yugoslavia or in a Greater Serbian state. In October the SARs rejected the Croatian declaration of independence and claimed representation on the federal State Presidency and at The Hague peace conference.

Meanwhile, the new Croatian Government was intent on the dismantling of the structures of Communist power. In August 1990 the Socialist Republic of Croatia became the Republic of Croatia. In the same month the Sabor voted to dismiss the republican member of the federal State Presidency, Dr Stipe Šuvar, and replace him with Stjepan (Stipe) Mesić, then President of the Government (Premier) of Croatia. His appointment was confirmed in October. In December the Croatian Assembly enacted a new republican Constitution, which declared the Republic's sovereignty, its authority over its own armed forces and its right to secede from the federation. Tensions increased when, in January 1991, the federal State Presidency ordered the disarming of all paramilitary groups and the Croatian authorities refused to comply. The Croatian Minister of Defence was then indicted on a charge of plotting armed rebellion, but the Croatian Government refused to arrest him and boycotted negotiations on the future of the federation. In March the Sabor resolved that republican legislation took precedence over federal legislation; the SAR of Krajina announced its unilateral secession from the Republic. In the negotiations about the future of Yugoslavia, Croatia favoured a looser federation of sovereign states and, like Slovenia, warned that it intended to end its membership of the federation by mid-1991 if no agreement was forthcoming. On 19 May some 94% of the votes cast in a referendum in Croatia (84% of the registered electorate voted) favoured the Republic becoming a sovereign entity, possibly within a confederal Yugoslavia (the referendum was largely boycotted by the Serb population) and 92% rejected a federal Yugoslavia. The refusal of Serbia and its allies to endorse the election of Stipe Mesić as President of the federal Presidency added to Croat anxieties. Constitutional proposals made by the Presidencies of Bosnia-Herzegovina and Macedonia did not achieve general acceptance and, on 26 June, Croatia and Slovenia declared their independence and the beginning of their process of dissociation from the federation.

The YPA's first actions against the recalcitrant Republics took place in Slovenia, but the local defence force maintained a successful guerrilla resistance and a policy of isolating military barracks. The EC mediated a cease-fire (for details, see Chronology) and the YPA began its withdrawal from Slovenia. However, the federal and Serbian authorities were less prepared to accept the loss of Croatia, where a significant Serb minority feared for itself under an independent, Croat-dominated state. During July 1991, despite the continuing EC peace efforts and the Serbian agreement to the election of Mesić as President of the Yugoslav State Presidency, civil war effectively began in Croatia. By November 1991 the YPA, supported by Serb irregulars, had secured about one-third of Croatian territory. The initial successes of the YPA had been checked, during August and September, when the Croatians adopted the tactics of besieging army and naval bases (this strategy had proved successful in Slovenia). The YPA also encountered problems of desertion and organization, particularly because of its multi-ethnic character (although it was Serb-dominated).

In October the YPA was able to mount a counter-offensive and to extend its operations beyond the neighbourhood of the military bases and the main battlefields of Slavonia. Thus, the city of Dubrovnik, which contained neither a YPA barracks nor a significant Serb minority (6.7% in 1991), came under attack. The threat to this medieval city, a UNESCO-listed World Heritage site, caused international consternation, but this did not abate the YPA siege. It was alleged that the city and its environs, which the YPA claimed were a base for Croatian military activities into Bosnia-Herzegovina, were intended for outright annexation, either to Montenegro (although that Republic withdrew its reservists from the attack) or to the 'SAR' of Herzegovina.

A large Adriatic port would be needed for the navy of the 'rump' Yugoslavia (or Greater Serbia), for which the Montenegrin ports were insufficient. The Serb and YPA attacks were also concentrated on the port of Zadar, in central Dalmatia, to the west of Knin. The main theatre of war, however, remained in Slavonia, eastern Croatia. There was conflict even in areas without a Serb majority, again leading to accusations that the YPA was attempting to secure the borders of a Greater Serbian state. Among the main obstacles to this ambition of linking the Krajina territories to Serbia proper were the eastern Slavonian cities of Osijek, capital of the region, Vinkovci and Vukovar. The last of these was a particular symbol of Croatian resistance. However, the city, on the Danube border with Serbia, finally surrendered on 18 November, after the 13th cease-fire arranged by the EC, which supervised the subsequent civilian evacuation. In the same week Western nations agreed that they would be prepared to send naval detachments to ensure the safe implementation of the work of the International Red Cross and both Croatia and Serbia indicated readiness to accept a UN peace-keeping force. Military action did continue, while negotiations on the terms for such a force were conducted. One problem was that the Croatians favoured a UN force guaranteeing the established borders, but the YPA was unwilling to withdraw from territory it had occupied. The 14th cease-fire, therefore, involved the UN, although it did not end all the fighting (mainly continued YPA and Serb pressure on Osijek, Vinkovci, Dubrovnik and Zadar, and Croatian counter-attacks on Pakrac). However, on 15 December, the UN Security Council resolved to send observers to Yugoslavia and a small team of civilian and military personnel to prepare for a possible peace-keeping force.

President Tudjman's administration was under domestic as well as military pressure. He was criticized for indecisiveness and for his dependence on the advice of former exiles and their unfulfilled hopes of Western military support. On 1 August 1991 Tudjman appointed a coalition Government of Democratic Unity, which was confirmed by the Sabor on 3 August. Nearly all the parties in the legislature participated, although the CDU remained the dominant partner. The SDP was not involved. The new Government continued to seek international recognition and to pursue negotiations at The Hague (Netherlands) peace conference, even after the declaration of independence, in October, following the expiry of the EC-mediated moratorium on the process of dissociation. The Hague conference was dissolved on 8 November, although its chairman, Lord Carrington, a former British foreign minister, continued his efforts to secure peace. In November, in accordance with the principles formulated at The Hague, the Sabor was ready to enact legislation guaranteeing minority rights, to allay the anxieties of the Serbs. However, there were increasing numbers of tales of atrocities on both sides and suspicion was becoming heightened. The CDU was certainly under pressure from its own right wing and more extreme groups. One of the most prominent of the nationalist parties was the Croatian Party of Rights (CPR—or Croatian Party of Justice; its Croatian acronym was HSP). Its armed wing,

the Croatian Defence Association (CDA, or HOS), was active in the fighting and was implicated in other anti-Serb incidents (there was also a worrying increase in anti-Semitic activities). Tudjman's ban on political activity in the armed forces was believed to be directed at the CDA, which denied accusations that it was plotting a coup. On 22 November the leader of the CPR, Dobroslav Paraga, was arrested and accused of co-operating with Croatia's enemies.

These domestic and military pressures cast doubt on the credibility of any international recognition of Croatian independence, although such a move was likely (Germany, particularly, favoured recognition of Croatia and Slovenia, but was anxious to secure general EC agreement first). However, the Croatian Government continued the process of dissociation. It proposed a new currency (kruna or crown), to be introduced in 1992. On 19 November 1991 the Supreme Council ordered all Croatians to vacate any federal offices they held and to place their services at the disposal of the Croatian state. On 5 December Mesić, Yugoslavia's nominal head of state, resigned and, on 19 December, so did Ante Marković, the federal prime minister. On 23 December an interim Croatian dinar was introduced and, on 15 January 1992, the EC initiated general international recognition of Croatia.

Economy

Croatia was one of the richer Republics of Yugoslavia, producing some 25% of the country's gross national product (GNP), according to Western estimates. In the late 1980s some 82% of Yugoslavia's total tourist trade was in Croatia, mainly on the Dalmatian coast. From mid-1991 the industry, already in decline because of the increasing troubles, was virtually eliminated by the onset of civil conflict. Tourism officials estimated, in July 1991, that losses to the Republic could total US $1,200m. Croatia's foreign-currency reserves were reckoned to total some $2,000m. for 1991, or 50% of the 1990 level. The civil war could also cause some lasting, physical damage to the environment and to the tourist infrastructure, with popular tourist destinations, such as Dubrovnik, coming under heavy bombardment and hotels suffering destruction and despoilation. In early October 1991 the Croatian premier informed the Sabor that war damage was estimated at some $15,000m.

Other sectors of the Croatian economy were suffering, even before the outbreak of war. The Government claimed this was an inevitable consequence of privatization and the transition to a market-orientated economy, but the opposition accused it of lacking a coherent economic policy and providing insufficient social protection. In 1990 some 500 state enterprises were declared bankrupt, which was four times as many as in 1989. This figure was considered likely to double in 1991; in the first three months of 1991 industrial output declined by 12%, compared to the same period in 1990. Furthermore, federal economic policy was likely to continue to affect Croatia; for example, during 1991 the printing of money was predicted to cause an annual inflation rate of up to 500% by mid-1991.

Directory

The Constitution

The Constitution of the Republic of Croatia was promulgated in December 1990. It declared Croatia to be a sovereign, democratic state, which guaranteed basic human rights and the rights of minority populations. The Republic was to be governed as a parliamentary democracy, although the existing Assembly (Sabor) was elected under the previous, amended Constitution. This provided for the tricameral parliament and had replaced the collective State Presidency with a single President at the head of the state. The President was elected by the Sabor and empowered to appoint and dismiss the Government (formerly known as the Executive Council). The republican Premier, or Prime Minister, headed the Government. During the civil war, which began with the declaration of dissociation, on 25 June 1991 (formal independence was proclaimed on 8 October 1991), a special war cabinet, or Supreme Council, was formed, chaired by the President of the Republic. The legislature, the Sabor, consists of three chambers, separately elected in two rounds of voting: the Socio-Political Chamber, with a maximum of 80 seats; the Chamber of Municipalities, with 116 seats; and the Chamber of Associated Labour, with 160 seats. The maximum total seats in the combined Chambers of the Sabor, therefore, amounts to 356. The independence of Croatia received a degree of international recognition in January 1992.

The Government

(December 1991)

HEAD OF STATE

The republican Assembly (Sabor) elected the leader of the largest party represented there, the Croatian Democratic Union (CDU), as President of Croatia, following the elections.

President of the Republic: Dr FRANJO TUDJMAN (elected by the Sabor on 30 May 1990).

Office of the President: 41000 Zagreb, Banski Dvori.

GOVERNMENT

On 3 August 1991 the Sabor confirmed in office the 'Government of Democratic Unity', appointed by President Tudjman. The CDU formed this coalition with the Party of Democratic Reform (former Communists, now the Social Democratic Party-Party of Democratic Reform—SDP-PDR), the Social Democratic Party of Croatia (SDPC), the Croatian Christian Democratic Party (CCDP), the Croatian People's Party (CPP), the Croatian Social Liberal Party (CSLP), the Socialist Party (SP) and inidviduals with no party affiliations. The Croatian Democratic Party (CDP) left the coalition in December 1991.

Premier (Prime Minister): Dr FRANJO GREGURIĆ (CDU).

Deputy Premiers: Dr MATO GRANIĆ (CDU), Dr ZDRAVKO TOMAĆ (SDP-PDR), Dr MILAN RAMLJAK.

Minister of Energy, Industry, Mining and Crafts: Dr ENCO TIRELLI (SDP-PDR).

Minister of Finance: Dr JOZO MARTINOVIĆ.

Minister of Information: BRANKO SALAJ.

Minister of Foreign Affairs: Dr ZVONIMIR ŠEPAROVIĆ (CDU).

Minister of National Defence: GOJKO SUŠAK (CDU).

Minister of Justice and Administration: BOSILJKO MIŠETIĆ (CPP).

Minister of Transport and Communications: JOSIP BOŽIČEVIĆ.

Minister of Maritime Affairs: Dr DAVORIN RUDOLF.

Minister of Agriculture and Forestry: IVAN TARNAJ (CDU).

Minister of Education, Culture and Physical and Technical Culture: Dr VLATKO PAVLETIĆ.

Minister of Labour and Social Security: BERNARDO JURLINA (CDU).

Minister of Trade: PETAR KRISTE (CDU).

Minister of Tourism: MARCELO POPOVIĆ.

Minister of the Interior: IVAN VEKIĆ (CDU).

Minister of Environmental Protection, Territorial Management and Construction: Dr IVAN CIFRIĆ (SP).

Minister of Health: ANDRIJA HEBRANG (CDU).

Minister of Science, Technology and Informatics: Dr ANTE ČOVIĆ (SDPC).

Minister of Veterans and Disabled Persons Affairs: MARIN CRNJA.

Minister of Water Resources Management: BRANKO BERGMAN.

Ministers without Portfolio: Dr ZVONIMIR BALETIĆ (SDPC), DRAZEN BUDIŠA (CSLP), Dr IVAN CESAR (CCDP), ŽIVKO JUZBAŠIĆ, Dr STJEPAN ZDUNIĆ, MUHAMED ZULIĆ (CDU).

MINISTRIES

Office of the Executive Council: Government of the Republic of Croatia, 41000 Zagreb, Opatička 2; tel. (41) 444000.

Ministry of Agriculture and Forestry: 41000 Zagreb, trg Drage Iblera 9; tel. (41) 412055; fax (41) 446722.

Ministry of Education, Culture and Physical and Technical Culture: 41000 Zagreb, trg Joze Vlahovića 6; tel. (41) 411122; fax (41) 446134.

Ministry of Energy, Industry, Mining and Crafts: 41000 Zagreb, trg Drage Iblera 9; tel. (41) 452055; fax (41) 446722.

Ministry of Environmental Protection, Territorial Management and Construction: 41000 Zagreb, Marulićev trg 16/III; tel. (41) 447811.

Ministry of Finance: 41000 Zagreb, Katanićeva 5; tel. (41) 445639.

Ministry of Foreign Relations: 41000 Zagreb, Radićev trg 3; tel. (41) 444666.

Ministry of Health: 41000 Zagreb, ul. 8. maja 1945 br. 42; tel. (41) 440809.

Ministry of Information: 41000 Zagreb, Radićev trg 3; tel. (41) 444666.

Ministry of the Interior: 41000 Zagreb, Savska Cesta 39; tel. (41) 444000; fax (41) 443715.

Ministry of Justice and Administration: 41000 Zagreb, Savska Cesta 41; tel. (41) 519022; fax (41) 536321.

Ministry of Labour and Social Security: 41000 Zagreb, Gruška 22; tel. (41) 518155; fax (41) 518113.

Ministry of Maritime Affairs: 41000 Zagreb, Gruška 22; tel. (41) 518155; fax (41) 518113.

Ministry of National Defence: 41000 Zagreb, Opatička 1; tel. (41) 444000; fax (41) 278483.

Ministry of Science, Technology and Informatics: 41000 Zagreb, Amruševa 4; tel. (41) 423686; fax (41) 428897.

Ministry of Tourism: 41000 Zagreb, trg Drage Iblera 9; tel. (41) 412055; fax (41) 446722.

Ministry of Trade: 41000 Zagreb, trg Drage Iblera 9; tel. (41) 412055; fax (41) 446722.

Ministry of Transport and Communications: 41000 Zagreb, Gruška 22; tel. (41) 518155; fax (41) 518113.

Ministry of Veterans and Disabled Persons Affairs: 41000 Zagreb, ul. 8. maja 1945 br. 42; tel. (41) 446611.

Ministry of Water Resources Management: 41000 Zagreb, Proleterskih brig. 220; tel. (41) 510522.

Legislature

SABOR

(Assembly)

President: Dr ŽARKO DOMLJAN; 41000 Zagreb, Radićev trg 6; tel. (41) 444000.

The Sabor consists of three Chambers, which sometimes sit separately for debate and the amendment of legislation, but as one body for enacting laws and other important resolutions. The maximum number of seats for the assembled Sabor is 356, of which only 351 were filled in the 1990 elections: all 80 in the Socio-Political Chamber; 115 of the 116 in the Chamber of Municipalities; and 156 of the 160 in the Chamber of Associated Labour.

President of the Socio-Political Chamber: VICE VUKOJEVIĆ (CDU).

President of the Chamber of Municipalities: LUKA BEBIĆ (CDU).

President of the Chamber of Associated Labour: IVAN MATIDA (SDP-PDR).

Elections, 22 April and 6–7 May 1990

Party	Seats
Croatian Democratic Union (CDU)	209*
League of Communists of Croatia-Party of Democratic Reform (LCC-PDR)†	96‡
Coalition of National Agreement (CNA)‖	11
Croatian Democratic Party (CDP)	10
Serb Democratic Party (SDP)	5
Independents	13
Other parties	11¶
Total	351

* The CDU won 205 seats alone, two seats in alliance with the Croatian Peasant Party (CPP) and two with the Croatian Social-Liberal Party (CSLP).

† In October 1991 the LCC-PDR was renamed the Social Democratic Party-Party of Democratic Reform (SDP-PDR), despite the protests of the existing Social Democratic Party of Croatia (SDPC).

‡ The LC-PDR won 73 seats alone and 23 seats in alliance with other parties: 17 with the Socialist Party (SP); three with the SP and the League of Socialist Youth of Croatia (LSYC); two with the SP, the LSYC and the League of War Veterans of Croatia; and one seat with Green Action of Split.

‖ The CNA consisted of the CPP, the CSLP, the SDPC, the Croatian Democratic Party (CDP—which also won 10 seats alone), the Croatian Christian Democratic Party and some minor parties; the alliance dissolved itself soon after the elections, leaving the named parties represented.

¶ The SP won four seats alone; the LSYC one; the CPP one; and the Association of Independent Businessmen one.

Note: Of the 205 seats won by the CDU alone, 54 were in the Socio-Political Chamber, 68 in the Chamber of Municipalities and 83 in the Chamber of Associated Labour; of the LCC-PDR's 73 seats, 12 were in the Socio-Political Chamber, 23 in the Chamber of Municipalities and 38 in the Chamber of Associated Labour.

Local Government

Local government is based on the municipality or commune, of which there are 102 in the Republic. Each municipality has a local assembly. During 1991 the so-called Krajina ('borderlands') areas of Croatia, most of them with ethnic Serb majorities, constituted themselves as 'Serb Autonomous Regions' (SAR—*Srpska Autonomna Oblast*), together with the Croatian parts of the historic territories of Baranja and Syrmia (Srem). These polities were not recognized by the republican authorities, but claimed representation at The Hague peace conference and on the federal State Presidency.

'SERB AUTONOMOUS REGIONS'

Krajina: Knin; Krajina declared its autonomy on 1 October 1990, its separation from Croatia on 16 March 1991 and its union with Bosnian (Bosanska) Krajina in June and with the other Croatian SARs in Oct.; a 'Republic of Serbian Krajina' was proclaimed in December; consists of 12 of the 13 municipalities of Krajina (i.e. excl. Croat Slunj); Pres. MILAN BABIĆ; Interior Minister MILAN MARTIĆ.

Slavonia, Baranja and Western Srem: Vukovar; autonomy unilaterally declared in Aug. 1991 and union with Krajina in Oct.; consists of the municipality of Beli Minastir (Baranja) and claims 4 municipalities in Western Syrmia or Srem, incl. Osijek; Pres. of Grand Assembly ILIJA KONČAREVIĆ; Premier GORAN HADŽIĆ.

Western Slavonia: the 3 municipalities of this area were largely in Croatian control; autonomy declared in Aug. and union with Krajina in Dec.; Pres. of Assembly VELJKO VUKELIĆ.

Political Organizations

Croatian Christian Democratic Party (CCDP) (HKDS): 41000 Zagreb, Vlahovića 2, Park V; tel. (41) 327233; fax (41) 325190; Pres. IVAN CESAR.

Croatian Democratic Party (CDP) (Hrvatski Demokratski Stranka—HDS): 41000 Zagreb, Tkalčićeva 4; tel. (41) 422062; fax (41) 421969; Pres. MARKO VESELICA.

Croatian Democratic Union (CDU) (Hrvatska Demokratska Zajednica—HDZ): 41000 Zagreb, trg hrvatskih velikana 4/III; tel. (41) 450338; fax (41) 426934; f. 1989; nationalist; Leader Dr FRANJO TUDJMAN; Pres. of Exec. Cttee SLAVKO DEGORICIJA.

Croatian Party of Rights (CPR) (HSP): 41000 Zagreb, Šenoina 13; tel. (41) 424368; fax (41) 423929; right-wing, nationalist; armed br. is the Croatian Defence Asscn or HOS; Pres. DOBROSLAV PARAGA; Chair. of Military Cttee of HOS IVAN DZAPIĆ.

Croatian Peasants Party (CPP) (HSS): 41000 Zagreb, Gundulićeva 21A; tel. (41) 433830; Pres. DRAGO STIPAC.

Croatian People's Party (Hrvatska Narodna Stranka—HNS): 41000 Zagreb, Gajeva 12/II; tel. and fax (41) 425332; Pres. SAVKA DABČEVIĆ-KUČAR.

Croatian Social-Liberal Party (CSLP) (HSLS): 41000 Zagreb, Šubićeva 29; tel. (41) 417093; Pres. DRAŽEN BUDIŠA.

Green Action—Split (Zelena akeija—Split): 58000 Split, Zrtava fašizma 8; tel. (58) 44421; Pres. ZORAN POKROVAC.

Serb Democratic Party (SDP) (Srpska Demokratska Stranka—SDS): 59300 Knin, Jove Miodragovića 22; tel. (59) 22499; f. 1990; seeks equality with Croats for Serbs in Croatia; Pres. Dr JOVAN RAŠKOVIĆ, 41000 Zagreb, Preradovićeva 18/I; tel. (41) 423583.

Social Democratic Party of Croatia (SDPC) (SDSH): 41000 Zagreb, Setalište Karla Marxa 14; tel. (41) 537604; fax (41) 534432; f. 1990; Pres. ANTUN VUJIĆ.

Social Democratic Party-Party of Democratic Reform of Croatia: 41000 Zagreb, Setalište Karla Marxa 14; tel. (41) 517000; fax (41) 518249; present name adopted 1991; formerly the ruling League of Communists of Croatia-Party of Democratic Reform; Pres. IVICA RAČAN.

Socialist Party of Croatia (SPC) (SSH): 41000 Zagreb, Kruge 48; tel. (41) 512861; fax (41) 510422; Pres. ŽELJKO MAŽAR.

At November 1991 there were 35 other registered political parties in Croatia, including branches of federal or other republican parties, such as: the Alliance of Reformation Forces (the Croatian, Zagreb and Istrian brs); the Party of Yugoslavs; the Party of Democratic Action—Branch for Croatia; the Serbian People's Party and other minority representatives (for Albanians, Bosnians, Istrians, Hungarians and Roma—Gypsies).

Judicial System

The judicial system of Croatia is administered by the Ministry of Justice and Administration (see republican section on The Government—Ministries). The highest courts are the Supreme Court of Croatia and the Constitutional Court of Croatia. The Republic's process of dissociation from the Yugoslav federation, initiated in June 1991, ended futher appeal to the Yugoslav Constitutional and Federal Courts.

Constitutional Court of Croatia: 41000 Zagreb, Radićev trg 4; tel. (41) 444822; Pres. Dr JADRANKO CRNIĆ.

Supreme Court: 41000 Zagreb, trg Nikole Zrinjskog 3; tel. (41) 257787; Pres. VJEKOSLAV VIDOVIĆ.

Office of the Public Prosecutor: 41000 Zagreb, Proleterskih brig. 84; tel. (41) 515422; Public Prosecutor ZELJKO OLUJIĆ.

Religion

Most of the population are Christian, the largest denomination being the Roman Catholic Church, of which most ethnic Croats are adherents. The Archbishop of Zagreb is the most senior Roman Catholic prelate in Yugoslavia (for details, see Directory for federal Yugoslavia, above). A Croatian Old Catholic Church does not acknowledge the authority of Rome or the papal reforms of the 19th century. There is a significant Serbian Orthodox minority (at mid-1991 Bishop LUKIJAN of Slavonia was the senior Orthodox cleric in the Republic). According to the 1991 census 76.5% of the population of Croatia were Roman Catholic, 11.1% were Orthodox, 1.2% Muslim and there were small communities of Protestant Christians and Jews.

Old Catholic Church

Croatian Catholic Church: Hrvatska Katolička Crkva Ordinariat, 41000 Zagreb, ul. Kneza Branimirova 11; tel. (41) 275224; f. 894, re-established 1923; Archbishop MIHOVIL DUBRAVČIĆ.

The Press

PRINCIPAL DAILIES

Osijek

Glas Slavonije: Osijek, Prolaz Vitomira Sukića 2; tel. (54) 126722; telex 28276; fax (54) 26751; morning; independent; Editor DRAGO HEDL; circ. 21,735.

Pula

Glas Istre: 52000 Pula, Obala Maršala Tita br. 10; tel. (52) 23577; telex 25248; fax (52) 41434; morning; Dir ŽELJKO ŽMAK; circ. 25,000.

Rijeka

Novi List: Rijeka, bul. Marksa i Englesa 20, POB 130; tel. (51) 32122; telex 24236; morning; Dir ZDENKO MANCE; circ. 59,000.

La Voce del Popolo: Rijeka, bul. Marksa i Engelsa 20; f. 1944; morning; Italian; Editor MARIO BONITA; circ. 2,970.

Split

Nedjeljna Dalmacija: 58000 Split, Splitskog odreda 4; tel. (58) 513888; telex 26124; weekly; Editor DUŠKO MAŽIBRADA; circ. 55,000.

Slobodna Dalmacija: 58000 Split, Splitskog odreda 4; tel. (58) 513888; telex 26124; morning; Pres. DEJAN KRUZIĆ; circ. 100,000.

Zagreb

Sportske novosti: 41000 Zagreb, Lj. Gerovac br. 1; circ. 174,000.

Večernji list: 41000 Zagreb, Av. bratstva i jedinstva 4; tel. (41) 333333; telex 21121; fax (41) 341850; evening; Editor IVO LAJTMAN; circ. 255,403.

Vjesnik: 41000 Zagreb, Avenija bratstva i jedinstva 4; tel. (41) 515555; telex 21121; f. 1940; morning; Chair. of Bd VJEKOSLAV KOPRIVNJAK; Editor STEVO MAODUS; circ. 68,519.

Publishers

August Cesarec: 41000 Zagreb, Prilaz JA 57; tel. (41) 571038; fax (41) 577267; Yugoslav and foreign literature.

Informator IRO: Novinsko-izdavačko, štamparski i birotehnički zavod, 41000 Zagreb, Masarykova 1; tel. (41) 429333; telex 21264; newspapers, periodicals, books, forms, etc.; Dir Dr IVO BURIĆ.

Jugoslavenska Akademija Znanosti i Umjetnosti: 41000 Zagreb, Zrinski trg 11; tel. (41) 433504; fax (41) 433383; f. 1866; publishing dept of the Yugoslav Academy of Sciences and Arts; Pres. Dr JAKOV SIROTKOVIĆ.

Leksikografski zavod 'Miroslav Krleža': 41000 Zagreb, Frankopanska 26; tel. (41) 456244; telex 21297; fax (41) 434948; f. 1951; encyclopaedias, bibliographies and dictionaries; Dir Dr DALIBOR BROZOVIĆ.

Mladost: 41000 Zagreb, Ilica 30; tel. (41) 453222; telex 21263; fax (41) 434878; f. 1947; fiction, science, art, children's books; Gen. Dir BRANKO VUKOVIĆ.

Motovun: 51424 Motovun, V. Nazora 1; tel. (53) 81722; fax (53) 81642; photomonographs and international co-productions.

Muzička naklada: 41000 Zagreb, Nicole Tesle 10/I; tel. (41) 424099; telex 22430; f. 1952; musical editions, scores; Dir RAJKO LATINOVIĆ.

Nakladni zavod Matice hrvatske: 41000 Zagreb, Ulica Matice hrvatske 2, POB 515; tel. (41) 275522; fax (41) 432430; f. 1960; fiction, popular science, politics, economics, sociology, history; Dir MARIJA PEAKIĆ-MIKULJAN.

Nakladni zavod Znanje: 41000 Zagreb, Zvonimirova 17; tel. (41) 411500; f. 1946; popular science, agriculture, fiction, poetry, essays; Dir STIPAN MEDAK; Editor-in-Chief ZLATKO CRNKOVIĆ.

Naprijed: 41000 Zagreb, POB 1029, Palmotićeva 30; tel. (41) 420666; fax (41) 430927; f. 1946; philosophy, psychology, religion, sociology, medicine, dictionaries, children's books, art, politics, economics, etc.; Dir GOJKO ŠTEKOVIĆ.

Naša Djeca: 41000 Zagreb, Gajeva 7; tel. (41) 423550; picture books, postcards, etc.; Dir Prof. DRAGO KOZINA.

Školska Knjiga: 41001 Zagreb, Masarykora 28, POB 1039; tel. (41) 420784; telex 21894; education, textbooks; Dir ANTUN ZIRAR.

Stvarnost (Izdavačka kuća): 41000 Zagreb, Frankopanska 11/3; tel. (41) 413808; telex 21365; Yugoslav and translated books on journalism, philosophical thought; Yugoslav and foreign literature, monographs and textbooks; Dir MILAN OSMAK.

Tehnička Knjiga: 41000 Zagreb, Jurišićeva 10; tel. (41) 278172; fax (41) 423611; technical literature, popular science, reference books; Dir ZVONIMIR VISTRIČKA.

Radio and Television

Hrvatska Radiotelevizija: 41000 Zagreb, Jurišićeva 4; govt-owned; Dir-Gen. ANTUN VRDOLJAK.

Croatian Radio: 41000 Zagreb, Jurišićeva 4; tel. (41) 426333; telex 21154; fax (41) 434369; f. 1926; 4 radio stations; broadcasts in Serbo-Croat/Croato-Serb; Dir of Radio TOMISLAV BAKARIĆ.

Croatian Television: 41000 Zagreb, Šetalište Karla Marksa bb; tel. (41) 618855; telex 21427; fax (41) 537921; f. 1956; 3 channels; broadcasts in Croato-Serb/Serbo-Croat; Dir of TV BRANKO LENTIĆ.

The so-called SAR of Krajina has established a separate radio and television service, based at the studios in Knin.

Finance

(d.d. = dioničko društvo (joint-stock company); cap. = capital; dep. = deposits; res = reserves; m. = million; amounts in dinars; * denotes figures in convertible dinars; brs = branches)

BANKS

Republican National Bank

National Bank of Croatia: 41000 Zagreb, trg Račkogo 5; tel. (41) 451899; in 1991 it assumed the responsibilities of a central bank and was to be empowered as the Republic's bank of issue (a new currency was not expected to be introduced until early 1992—a Croatian dinar, and then the kruna or crown); Gov. Dr ANTE CIČIN-SAIN.

Selected Banks

Dalmatinska Banka d.d., Zadar: 57000 Zadar, trg Sv. Stošije 3; tel. (57) 311311; telex 27224; fax (57) 437867; f. 1957; dep. 1,868m.* (Dec. 1990); Gen. Man. NEVEN DOBROVIĆ.

Dubrovačka Banka d.d., Dubrovnik (Bank of Dubrovnik): 50000 Dubrovnik, Put Republike 5; tel. (50) 32366; telex 27540; fax (50) 32939; f. 1956; total assets 1,774m.* (Jan. 1990); Gen. Man. NIKOLA SAMBRAILO.

Istarska Banka d.d., Pula (Bank of Istria): 52000 Pula, Premanturska 2; tel. (52) 33966; telex 25241; fax (52) 41498; Gen. Man. MARIO FLORIČIĆ.

Privredna Banka Zagreb d.d.: 41000 Zagreb, Račkoga 6; tel. (41) 450822; telex 21120; fax (41) 447234; f. 1966; commercial bank; total assets 37,984.4m.*, cap. 3,415.4m.*, dep. 11,549.3m.* (Dec. 1990); Man. Dir JOZO MARTINOVIĆ; 19 brs.

Samoborska Banka d.d., Samobor (Bank of Samobor): 41430 Samobor, Tomislavov trg 8; tel. (41) 782530; telex 21811; fax (41) 781523; f. 1873; total assets 2,956.4m.* (Dec. 1990); Gen. Man. MARIJAN TRUSK.

Slavonska Banka d.d., Osijek (Bank of Slavonia): 54000 Osijek, Bul. JNA 29; tel. (54) 125022; telex 28090; fax (54) 124846; f. 1989; total assets 14,372,094m., dep. 7,681,057m. (Dec. 1989); Gen. Man. IVAN PATARČIĆ.

Zagrebačka Banka Zagreb d.d. (Bank of Zagreb): 41000 Zagreb, Paromlinska 2; tel. (41) 630444; telex 21463; fax (41) 536626; f. 1978; total assets 27,976.0m.*, cap. and res 2,626.0m.*, dep. 15,323.9m.* (June 1990); Gen. Man. JOSIP PRIBANIĆ.

STOCK EXCHANGE

Zagreb Stock Exchange: Zagreb; f. 1990.

Trade and Industry

Chamber of Economy of Croatia: 41000 Zagreb, Ruzveltov trg 1; tel. (41) 453422; Pres. IVICA GAŽI.

Association of Independent Businessmen (Udruženje samostalnih privrednika): 41000 Zagreb; has representation in the Chamber of Associated Labour of the Croatian Assembly.

Zagreb Trade Fair: Zagrebački Velesajam, 41020 Zagreb, Dubrovačka cesta 2, POB 41020–16; tel. (41) 623111; telex 21385; fax (41) 520643; f. 1909; International Spring Fair, annually in April; International Autumn Fair, annually in September; International Leather and Footwear Week; and numerous specialized fairs; the civil war, which began in 1991, caused some disruption to these events.

MAJOR ENTERPRISES AND COMPANIES

ASTRA Foreign Trade Co Ltd: 41000 Zagreb, Varsavska 9; tel. (41) 457111; telex 21254; fax (41) 426296; foreign trade network incl. 29 foreign enterprises and representatve agencies for the import and export of various goods; Pres. S. R. B. VJEKOSLAV; 1,500 employees.

Auto-Hrvatska: 41000 Zagreb, Proleterskih brig. 37B; tel. (41) 533622; telex 21133; fax (41) 533810; wholesale and retail trade in vehicles, spare parts, etc; 1,000 employees.

Brodokomerc, Export-Import: 51000 Rijeka, Mijekarski trg 2; tel. (51) 21133; telex 24245; fax (51) 212249; Dir MIRKO PAVICIĆ; 1,700 employees.

Brodomaterijal: 51000 Rijeka, Josipa Kraša 12; tel. (51) 211211; telex 24203; 1,300 employees.

Brodomerkur: 58000 Split, Rade Končara bb; tel. (58) 44655; telex 21136; fax (58) 42893; 1,200 employees.

Chromos Zagreb: 41000 Zagreb, Proleterskih brig. 271; tel. (41) 334400; telex 21358; fax (41) 448814; production of paints and varnishes; Pres. VLADIMIR KONIĆ; 5,000 employees.

Belje: 54326 Darda; tel. (54) 41026; telex 18210; primary agriculture and industrial processing of agricultual produce; 8,000 employees.

Dubrovkinja: 50000 Dubrovnik, Put Republike 26; tel. (50) 27777; telex 27511; Man. of Agency Dept: DAMIR BULIĆ; 2,800 employees.

Duro Daković: 55000 Slavonski Brod, Njegoševa 1; tel. (55) 231011; telex 28615; fax (55) 232007; manufactures equipment for the construction industry, etc.; Pres. ZVONKO MIROSAVLJEVIĆ; 13,000 employees.

Duro Salaj: 54550 Valpovo, Bratstva Jedinstva 9; tel. (54) 81519; telex 28355; fax (54) 81274; manufactures food products and plastic products; Gen. Dir ANTUN SAUER; 2,800 employees.

Elektrokontakt: Zagreb, Radnicka c. bb; tel. (41) 230866; telex 21258; fax (41) 220847; manufactures signal lights, etc.; Gen. Dir ZVONKO ORINCIĆ; 1,600 employees.

Gavrilović: 44250 Petrinja, 29 Slavonske Udarne Divižije 59; tel. (44) 81126; telex 23631; fax (44) 40844; food processing; the largest enterprise of its field in Yugoslavia; 6,000 employees.

INA-Oki Oour Rotoform: 41000 Zagreb, Zitnjak bb; tel. (41) 231666; telex 21226; fax (41) 231975; petrochemical production; mem. co of the INA Group; Gen. Man. VLADO RADIĆ; 3,500 employees.

INA Zajednica Poduzeća: 41000 Zagreb, Proleterskih brig. 78; tel. (41) 539444; telex 21223; fax (41) 538982; petroleum and gas exploration and production; mem. co of the INA Group; 36,000 employees.

Industrijsko Poljoprivredni Kombinat, Osijek—IPK Osijek: 54000 Osijek, ul. Republike 45; tel. (54) 25455; telex 28088; agricultural industry; 16,000 employees.

Jadrolinija: Rijeka, Obala Jugoslavenska Mornarice 16; tel. (51) 30899; telex 24225; fax (51) 213116; fleet of 50 ships, providing cruise and ferry services; Gen. Man. ANTON LENAĆ; 2,300 employees.

Jedinstvo: 41230 Krapina, Mihaljekov Jarek 33; tel. (49) 71202; telex 23134; fax (49) 71429; manufactures trapezoid aluminium and galvanized plate sections; Gen. Dir ZVONIMIR BUCONJIĆ; 740 employees.

Jozo Lozovina Mosor: 58000, Radnicki put 16; tel. (58) 882500; telex 26244; fax (58) 881881; a mem. of the Jadranbrod Shipbuilding Asscn; builds and repairs maritime vessels; Pres. ANTE ROZIĆ; 2,770 employees.

Jugoturbina: 47000 Karlovac, 8 Kordunaske uderne divije 10; tel. (47) 31533; telex 23745; fax (47) 26011; designs, manufactures and services power equipment; Marketing Dir. KATUNAR BISERKA; 7,500 employees.

Jugovonil: 58213 Kastel Sučurac; tel. (58) 41999; telex 26106; production of PVC powder, in particular the production of PVC flooring and battery parts; 3,292 employees.

Koka: 42000 Varaždin, Millice Pavlić-Kate 2; tel. (42) 49244; telex 23240; fax (42) 51432; integrated poultry organization covering all stages of broiler-meat production; Gen. Dir ANA SELEĆ.

Nikola Tesla Company—Telecom Systems and Equipment Co: 41000 Zagreb, Krapinska 45; tel. (41) 334433; telex 21416; fax (41) 328540; manufactures, installs and maintains telecommunications equipment; Gen. Man. MARIJAN CRNJAK; 4,953 employees.

Pazinka—Pazinka Kemijsko-tekstilna industrija: 51400 Pazin, Valici 1; tel. (53) 22022; telex 25137; fax (53) 22601; chemical-textile industry, manufacturing cotton bed-linen, cotton yarns, woollen and acrylic mixtures, etc; Gen. Dir BOGDAN MEDANCIĆ; 1,500 employees.

Pik Vrbobec Co: 43216 Vrbovec, Zagrebacka 148; tel. (43) 751024; telex 23327; fax (43) 751863; exports meat and canned meat to Western Europe and the USA; Dir FRANJO DONCEVIĆ; 2,571 employees.

Pliva: 41000 Zagreb, Ive Lola Ribara 89; tel. (41) 571666; telex; 21246; fax (41) 576690; manufacture of pharmaceuticals, veterinary products, food products and cosmetics; 6,950 employees.

Podravka: 43300 Koprivnica, Ive Marinkovica 32; tel. (43) 827144; telex 23348; fax (43) 827169; agri-business, food processing, pharmaceuticals and cosmetics; 10,231 employees.

Poduzec Pamucna Industrija 'Duga Resa', Duga Resa: 47250 Duga Resa, Jurkas Dragutina 8; tel. (47) 8122; telex 23722; fax (47) 81904; textile production; Gen. Dir GABRIJEL PRSTEĆ; 3,806 employees.

Poslovna Zajednica Exportdrvo: 41000 Zagreb, trg Mazuranića 6; tel. (41) 446066; telex 22490; forestry, timber processing, furniture manufacture, paper production and processing and ancillary activities; 85,000 employees.

Rade Koncar: 41000 Zagreb, Fallerovo Setalliste 22; tel. (41) 336666; telex 21159; electrical industry; 23,713 employees.

Regeneracija: POB Zabok 41210, K. S. Dalskog 4; tel. (49) 23255; telex 23119; fax (49) 21418; textiles; Gen. Dir PETAR JAKOPEĆ; 1,403 employees.

Shipbuilding Industry, Split: 58000 Split, Put udarnika 19: tel. (58) 521222; telex 26125; fax (58) 42474; contracting, designing and construction of all types of vessels; Pres. IGNACIJE STIPOLJEV; 7,000 employees.

Varteks: 42000 Varaždin, Maršala Tita 94; tel. (42) 44444; telex 23238; manufacture and sale of textiles and clothing; also manufacture of disc brakes for the motor industry, fishing tackle, etc.; graphic design services; 9,600 employees.

Viktor Lenać Shipyard: 51001 Rijeka, POB 210; tel. (51) 442255; telex 24305; fax (51) 442433; shipbuilding, ship repairs and ship conversions; Pres. DAMIR VRHOVNIK; 1,650 employees.

Zeljezara Sisak (Sisak Ironworks): 44105 Sisak, Božidara Adzije 2; tel. (44) 30444; telex 23017; fax (44) 30284; manufacture of coke, iron and steel; metal products.

'Zletovo' Battery Factory: 92210 Probistip; tel. (92) 83006; fax (92) 83656; telex 53666; production of starter batteries for motor vehicles, etc.; Gen. Dir BONA SPASOVSKA; 1,500 employees.

Culture

REPUBLICAN ORGANIZATIONS

Ministry of Education, Culture and Physical and Technical Culture: see section on The Government (Ministries).

Institute for the Preservation of Historical and Cultural Monuments: 41000 Zagreb, Ilica 44; f. 1910; Dir Prof. VLADO UKRAINČIK.

Institute for the Preservation and Scientific Study of Historical Monuments in Dalmatia: 58000 Split, Topuska 4/I, pp 40; tel. (58) 42327; f. 1854; Dir Prof. DAVOR DOMANČIĆ.

CULTURAL HERITAGE

Archives of Croatia (Arhiv Hrvatske): 41000 Zagreb, Marulićev trg 21; tel. (41) 446325; f. 1643; Dir PETAR STRČIĆ.

Gallery of Modern Art (Moderna Galerija): 41000 Zagreb, Braće Kavurića 1; tel. (41) 433802; f. 1905; Dir Prof. IGOR ZIDIĆ.

Historical Museum of Croatia (Povijesni musej Hrvatske): 41000 Zagreb, Matoševa 9; tel. (41) 277991; f. 1846; Dir Prof. JASNA TOMIČIĆ.

Museum and Gallery Centre: 41000 Zagreb, Jezuitski trg 4; tel. (41) 433274.

Strossmayer Gallery of Old Masters (Strossmayerova gallerija starih majstora): 41000 Zagreb, Zrinski trg 11/II; f. 1884; Dir Prof. VINKO ZLAMALIK.

Zagreb City Galleries (Galerije grada Zagreba): 41000 Zagreb, Katarinin trg 2; tel. (41) 425227; f. 1961; controls five galleries: Contemporary Art; Benko Horvat Gallery (antique and Renaissance art); Primitive Art; Ivan Meštrović Gallery (exhibits of the sculptor); Photography, Film and Television Centre; Dir MARIJAN SUSOVSKI.

SPORTING ORGANIZATION

Croatian Olympic Committee: 41000 Zagreb, trg Jože Vlahovića 6; f. 1991; Pres. ANTUN VRDOLJAC.

PERFORMING ARTS

Croatian National Theatre (Hrvatsko narodno kazalište): 41000 Zagreb, trg Maršala Tita 15; tel. (41) 449311; Dir (vacant); Opera and Ballet: tel. (41) 447644; Dir of Opera VLADIMIR BENIĆ; Dir of Ballet LEO STIPANIČIĆ.

Croatian National Theatre—Ivan Zajc (Hrvatsko narodno kazalište 'Ivan Zajc'): 51000 Rijeka, Aldo Negri 1/I; tel. (51) 424679.

Croatian National Theatre—Osijek (Hrvatsko narodno kazalište—Osijek): 54000 Osijek, A. Cesarca 9; tel. (54) 32182.

Croatian National Theatre—Split (Hrvatsko narodno kazalište—Split): 58000 Split, trg Gaje Bulata 1; tel. (58) 585999.

Jazavac Satirical Theatre: 41000 Zagreb, Ilica 31; tel. (41) 412069.

Komedija—Zagreb Municipal Theatre of Comedy: 41000 Zagreb, Kaptola 9; tel. (41) 275027.

Marin Držić Theatre: 50000 Dubrovnik, Ispred Dvora; tel. (50) 26437.

Theatre Etcetera: 41000 Zagreb, Šavska 25; tel. (41) 278068.

Visiting Theatre: 41000 Zagreb, Varšavka 16; tel. (41) 424528.

Music

Croatian Television Choir (Zbor HTV): 41000 Zagreb, Teslina 7; Chief Conductor IGOR KULJERIĆ.

Croatian Television Big Band (Plesni Orkestar HTV): 41000 Zagreb, Teslina 7; dance band; Chief Conductor MILJENKO PROHASKA.

Dubrovnik Symphony Orchestra (Dubrovački simfonijski orkestar): 50000 Dubrovnik, Kovačka 3/II; tel. (50) 26316; Chief Conductor IVO DRUŽINIĆ.

Pro-Arte String Quartet ('Pro Arte' gudački kvartet): 41000 Zagreb, Mikulićeva 22; tel. (41) 445174.

Zagreb Concert Management (Koncertna direkcija Zagreb): 41000 Zagreb, Trnjanska bb; tel. (41) 539995; impresarios and concert promoters; Dir MIROSLAV POLJANEC.

Zagreb Philharmonic Orchestra (Zagrebačka filharmonija): 41000 Zagreb, Trnjanska bb; tel. (41) 539699; Chief Conductor KAZUSHY ONO; Permanent Conductor PAVLE DEŠPALJ.

Zagreb Soloists (Zagrebački solisti): 41000 Zagreb, Dalmatinska 5; Sec. TONKO NINČIĆ.

Zagreb Symphony Players (Zagrebački sinfoničari): c/o HTV, 41000 Zagreb, Teslina 7; Conductor VLADIMIR KRANJČEVIĆ.

ASSOCIATIONS

Croatian Society (Matica Hrvatska): 41000 Zagreb, Matice hrvatske ul. 2; f. 1842, banned 1971, re-formed 1990; Pres. VLADO GOTOVAC.

Federation of Museum Associations of Croatia (Savez muzejskih društava hrvatske): 41000 Zagreb, Mesnička 5; tel. (41) 426534; f. 1945; Sec. JADRANKA VINTERHALTER.

Italian Union of Croatia: Pula; cultural and social org. of ethnic Italians in Istria; Pres. MAURIZIO TREMUL.

The Environment

Ministry of Environmental Protection, Territorial Management and Construction: see section on The Government (Ministries); incl.:

> **Bureau for the Conservation of the Environment, Nature and Natural Heritage (Dept for the Conservation of Nature and Natural Heritage):** 41000 Zagreb, Ilica 44/II; tel. (41) 432022; f. 1961 as Instit. for Nature Preservation; Dir Ing. MIHO MILJANIĆ.

Croatian Society of Natural Sciences, Section for the Protection of Nature: Hrvatsko Prirodoslovno Društvo, 41000 Zagreb, Ilica 16/III; Pres. Prof. Dr DIONIS SUNKO; Sec. Dr HRVOJ VANČIK.

Hydro-Meteorological Institute of Croatia (Hidrometeoroloski Zavod Hrvatske): 41000 Zagreb, Grič 3; tel. (41) 421222; telex 21356; f. 1947; responsibilities incl. ecological studies, pollution monitoring; Dir Dipl. Eng. TOMISLAV VUČETIĆ.

NON-GOVERNMENTAL ORGANIZATIONS

Green Action Ecological Movement (Šibenik): 59000 Šibenik, Roberta Vissiania 3; tel. (59) 29097; fax (59) 29097; Pres. PAVLE ČALA.

Green Action (Split) (Zelena akeija—Split): see republican section on Political Organizations.

Green Party (Rijeka): 51000 Rijeka, Ivana Rendića 8; Pres. DANKO HOLJEVIĆ.

Defence

The Fifth Military District of the Yugoslav People's Army (YPA) includes most of Croatia (and Slovenia) and was headquartered in Zagreb. Eastern Slavonia lies within the jurisdiction of the First Military District, which was responsible for the campaigns against cities such as Osijek and Vukovar. The YPA Districts were, however, reorganized in December 1991. The Croatian coastline, with its many harbours, is important for the bases of the Yugoslav navy. The process of forming a distinct Croatian armed force began in November 1990, when the Croatian Assembly decreed that the Territorial Defence Force, which had previously fallen under the jurisdiction of the YPA, was to be placed under republican control. In January 1991 Croatia formed a mutual defence pact with Slovenia and a special armed police reserve (*specijalci*). The YPA resisted such moves and attempted to limit the acquisition of weaponry by the groups. The Croatian National Guard Corps was formed on 11 April 1991. In mid-1991 civil war began in Croatia.

It was not just the regular forces which engaged in combat during the civil war. The so-called Territorial Defence Force of the SAR of Krajina was commanded by Lt-Col-Gen. Ilija Djujić with the approval of the Federal Defence Secretariat. On 9 October the SAR of Slavonia, Baranja and Western Srem formally integrated its Territorial Defence with the YPA. The Serb irregulars also seemed to be under the co-ordination of the YPA and the Serbian authorities. One of the most prominent commanders, based in Knin, was a 'Capt. Dragan', which was the *nom de guerre* of an ethnic Serb and former mercenary of Australian citizenship. The main Croatian paramilitary force, which was prominent in the defence of Slavonia, was the Croatian Defence Association (HOS—led by Ivan Dzapić), the armed wing of the extremist, nationalist Croatian Party of Rights (HSP—led by Dobroslav Paraga). The President of the Republic of Croatia was declared the Commander-in-Chief of the armed forces.

Chief of Staff of the Croatian National Guard Corps: Col-Gen. ANTON TUS.

Fifth Military District of the YPA: Commander Col-Gen. ZIVOTA ABRAMOVIČ; Deputy Commander Col-Gen. ANDREJA RASETA.

MACEDONIA

Geography

The Republic of Macedonia is a constituent partner in the Socialist Federal Republic of Yugoslavia. Roughly rectangular in shape, Macedonia lies in the southernmost part of Yugoslavia, having a northern border with the Republic of Serbia (Kosovo to the north-west and 'Inner' Serbia to the north-east). To the west lies Albania, to the south Greece and to the east Bulgaria.

The historical region of Macedonia is divided between the Yugoslav Republic, Greece and Bulgaria. The Republic of Macedonia, which is sometimes known as Vardar Macedonia (Pirin Macedonia is that part of the territory in Bulgaria and Aegean Macedonia in Greece), has a total area of 25,713 sq km. The Republic is mountainous. It is bisected by the Vardar (Axiós) river, which flows from north-west to south-east, across the centre of the Republic and in to Greece, where it enters the Aegean Sea. Agriculture is the chief occupation, especially dairy farming, but there are also some mineral reserves in the territory.

According to the census of 1991 the total population of the Republic of Macedonia was 2,033,964, which gave a population density of 79.1 sq km. The capital is Skopje (Skoplje or, in Turkish, Usküb), which is located on the Vardar, in the central north of the Republic. The district of Skopje, anciently a capital of the Serbs, had a population of some 563,000 in 1991. Other principal towns include Ohrid and Bitola, in south-west Macedonia, Titov Veles, in the centre, and Tetovo, west of Skopje, the centre of Albanian settlement.

According to the census of 1991, ethnic Macedonians accounted for 64.6% of the republican population (compared to some 67% in 1981) and ethnic Albanians for some 21%. Most Albanians are concentrated in the west of the Republic, particularly the north-west, where they tend to live in distinct communities, mostly in the countryside. The official language of the Republic, under the Constitution of November 1991, is Macedonian, but provision is made for the use of minority languages (notably Albanian) at the local level. Most of the population is nominally Christian and of the Eastern Orthodox faith. The Macedonians are adherents of the Macedonian Orthodox Church, which is autocephalous or independent, but is not recognized by the other Orthodox. Most of the Albanians are Muslim, although there are some Roman Catholics in Skopje (immigrants from the Prizen area of Kosovo) and some Orthodox near Ohrid. Most of the remaining minority groups are also Muslim. In 1991 some 4.8% of the population were ethnic Turks (most of Yugoslavia's Turkish community), 2.7% Roma (Gypsies—for the 1991 census a separate category of 'Egipcani', or 'Egyptians', was allowed for those Roma renouncing their previous ethnicity and claiming to be 'descendants of the Pharaohs'), 2.1% Serbs, mostly in Skopje and Kumanovo, and a few less Slav Muslims (known as Torbeshes, Poturs or Pomaks). In 1981 there were also some 7,190 Vlahs (Koutsovlahs, Aromani, Cincari), Macedonia being the main Yugoslav territory of this traditionally nomadic, Romanian-speaking people.

History

Macedonia is an ancient territory, covering areas in northern Greece and south-west Bulgaria, as well as the modern Yugoslav Republic. The ancient kingdom of Macedonia, or Macedon, is believed to have been established in the sixth century BC; its ancient capitals, Aigai (Edessa) and Pella, are both now in Greece. Its most famous king was Alexander III ('the Great'), who succeeded to the throne in 336 BC, consolidated Macedonian rule in Greece and then campaigned against the Persian Empire, conquering Asia Minor, the Levant, Egypt, Mesopotamia, Persia and parts of India. Alexander the Great died in 323 and his empire dissolved during wars between his successors. Eventually three monarchies were established, one of which was a Macedonian state, under the Antigonids. Macedonia, however, declined in power and was finally defeated by Rome, in 168 BC, being made a province of the Roman Empire in 148.

Slavic settlers moved into the province during the sixth century AD and the Turkic ancestors of the Bulgarians moved south of the Danube in the seventh century. These peoples merged with the original population, although the predominant language was Slavonic. In the ninth century, the Eastern Roman (Byzantine) missionaries took a Macedonian dialect as the basis of a written Slavonic language (Old Church Slavonic), using the new Cyrillic script. At the time, Macedonia was dominated by the Bulgarians (who still claim the Macedonians to be a Bulgarian people). The Bulgarian resistance to the Byzantine reconquest was led, from a base near Lake Ohrid, by a tsar, Samuil (Samuel), of a western Bulgarian or Macedonian realm (the exact identification of this regime remains a matter of nationalist dispute between modern Bulgaria and the Macedonian Republic). This survived against the Emperor Basil II until 1014, after which the territory was reabsorbed into the Eastern Empire. At this time the Orthodox bishopric of Ochrida (Ohrid) was established as a metropolitan see. From the 12th century control of Macedonia was contested between the Byzantine Empire, the Bulgarians and the Serbs. These last established the first patriarchate of the autocephalous Serbian Orthodox Church at Skopje (Skoplje), in the 14th century. In 1371, however, the Serbs were unable to prevent the Muslim Ottomans from conquering Macedonia. The territory then remained under Ottoman rule until the 19th century.

The disintegration of the Ottoman Empire and the rise of nationalism, during the 19th century, made the fate of Macedonia and the identification of its Slavic population a matter of some political controversy. The Ottoman administration was based on the *millet* system, or confessional divisions, which effectively subordinated all the Orthodox populations to the authority of the Ecumenical Patriarch of Constantinople and the use of the Greek liturgy. In 1870 the Bulgarians declared an Exarchate church (that is, independent from Constantinople and using a Slavonic liturgy), which contested the Greeks for the allegiance of the Macedonians. The Greeks continue to claim that the Macedonians are 'Slavophone Greeks'. In 1878 the Congress of Berlin thwarted the 'Greater Bulgaria' of the Treaty of San Stefano. The Bulgarian state, therefore, retained its ambitions to annex Macedonia. Meanwhile, the expansion of Austria-Hungary limited the Serbian state's ambitions to the north and west and, after defeat by the Bulgarians, in 1885, the Serbs too pressed their claims to Macedonia, describing it as 'South Serbia'. Both the Serbs and the Greeks formed nationalist societies, intent on promoting their cause in Macedonia (Society of St Sava and Ethnike Hetairia, respectively). In 1895 the Greeks claimed to have retained control of 1,400 schools in Macedonia. Also in the 1890s the Bulgarians, mainly under the aegis of their Exarchate, claimed between 600 and 700 schools, while the Serbs claimed 100. Even the Romanians were subsidizing about 30 schools, by 1912, based on the presence of the Vlah population in western Macedonia. The resident population, therefore, endured the competing and often violent attentions of the different claimants, as well as the depredations of their own nationalists.

In 1893 the Internal Macedonian Revolutionary Organization (its Macedonian acronym is VMRO) was founded, opposing the partition of Macedonia and supporting the idea of a Southern Slav federation of Macedonians, Bulgarians and Serbs. However, the unity of the nationalists was fatally distracted by a rival sentiment in favour of the incorporation of Macedonia within Bulgaria. This was advocated by the External Organization of Supremacists, founded in 1895 and based in Sofia, where there were considerable numbers of Macedonian refugees, following the failure of the San Stefano agreement. The so-called Ilinden Uprising against the Ottomans, in August 1903, led by Gotse Delchev, is commemorated as a national anniversary by both the Bulgarians and the Macedonians. The fate of the territory was to be partitioned after the Balkan Wars of 1912–13, mainly between Serbia and Greece, the ultimate victors. After the First World War, during which Macedonia was occupied by the Bulgarians and the Central Powers, Vardar Macedonia became part of the new Kingdom of Serbs, Croats and Slovenes (Yugoslavia from 1929). Macedonia was placed under the authority of the Serbian Church and Serbian was made the official language, which policies helped foster pro-Bulgarian sentiments.

In the Second World War the Bulgarian occupation of 1941–44 (Nazi Germany would not sanction formal annexation) disillusioned many Yugoslav Macedonians. From 1943 Tito's Partisans began to increase their support in the region. Since the rise of the Nazis and other Fascist parties as the leading revisionists, the Communists had rejected the idea of a united Macedonia under Bulgaria. The new Yugoslav state and its Communist rulers resolved to include a Macedonian nation as a federal partner. Furthermore, Tito regarded a Macedonian nationality as a useful link with Communist Bulgaria (the leader of which, Georgi Dimitrov, was of Macedonian parentage), with which he hoped to unite Yugoslavia in a Balkan federation. The death of Dimitrov, in 1949, following Tito's split with the Soviet Communist bloc began a period of tension between Bulgaria and the new Macedonian Republic.

Following the Second World War the new Communist regime began to consolidate a distinct Macedonian identity, particularly as a counter to any residual pro-Bulgarian sentiments among the population. A written language was necessary and this was, first of all, based on a northern dialect. This was not sufficiently distinct from Serbian, however, and the more southerly dialects of Bitola-Veles became the standard. These were closer to the Bulgarian literary language, but standard Bulgarian was based on its eastern dialects, which distinguished it enough from Macedonian. The alphabet and orthography were prepared and accepted in 1945 and, since then, Macedonian has been encouraged and standardized by the educational and official establishment. Macedonian shares with Bulgarian most of the same distinguishing characteristics from other Slavonic languages (such as the preservation of the simple verbal forms for the perfect and imperfect tenses and the lack of cases), and whether they are separate languages can be debated. However, differences have been fostered and the obvious Serbian and Bulgarian influences among the

dialects of older people are less common now. Certainly this linguistic policy and the fostering of a historical and cultural tradition increased Macedonian self-awareness. The authorities also utilized the fundamental cultural expression of the Orthodox Slavs, the Church. In 1958 the archdiocese of Ohrid was re-established. The Serbian Orthodox Church bitterly contested this move towards separation and the loss of its jurisdiction. It refused to acknowledge the final declaration of Macedonian autocephaly, on 18 July 1967, and succeeded in persuading Constantinople and the other Orthodox from granting recognition of this status (the Greek and Bulgarian Churches are influenced by the political considerations of their governments). This Macedonian nationalism, surrounded by countries which deny its legitimacy, has encouraged the Republic's ambivalence towards the Yugoslav federation. Membership of Yugoslavia gave Macedonia a protected identity, but it feared resurgent Serbian nationalism in a federation without the balancing influence of Croatia and Slovenia.

There was also the perceived insecurity of a large ethnic Albanian minority (20% of the population, according to the 1981 census) in western Macedonia. Demands for the creation of a seventh Yugoslav republic, in the Albanian areas of western Macedonia, were first expressed in 1968, following demonstrations in neighbouring Kosovo, after the fall of Ranković. The Macedonian authorities were particularly active against Albanian nationalism from 1981, mainly in the field of education and language, which was what provoked the most reaction from the Albanian community. There had been attempts to ban personal names of an 'Albanian-nationalist' nature and to discourage the rate of births. The campaign in the education system merely exacerbated the problem of Albanians not being able to use the Macedonian language. In 1988 there were demonstrations, in which young Albanian students were prominent, and tension continued into the early 1990s. Most Albanian political activity, however, was centred on Kosovo. Indeed, the main ethnic Albanian party in Macedonia, the Party for Democratic Prosperity (PDP), is accused of being an appendage of the Democratic Alliance of Kosovo, although the PDP has reiterated its commitment to the territorial integrity and sovereignty of the Republic. Macedonian nationalism has reacted to the threat of a 'Greater Albania': in 1989 the ruling Communists amended the republican Constitution, declaring Macedonia to be a 'nation-state' of the ethnic Macedonians, excluding mention of the 'Albanian and Turkish minorities'; the new Constitution of 1991 also refused to specify the Republic as a 'homeland' of the Albanians as well as the Macedonians, although it was enacted only by avoiding the specific mention of official languages. Support for the PDP and the smaller People's Democratic Party is predominantly among the Albanian community, although other Muslim groups also vote for them.

In mid-1989 the Macedonian Communist regime conceded the introduction of a multi-party system in the Republic and amended the Constitution accordingly. In February 1990 the Movement for All-Macedonian Action (MAMA—its Macedonian acronym is MAAK) was founded by a group of intellectuals. It renounced any territorial claims, but discussed co-operation with the Macedonian-nationalist Ilinden movement in Bulgaria and held several large demonstrations protesting at the oppression of fellow nationals in Albania, Bulgaria and Greece. In June a more nationalist party was founded, in the Internal Macedonian Revolutionary Organization-Democratic Party for Macedonian National Unity (IMRO-DPMNU or VMRO-DPMNE). There were delegates from the Macedonian diaspora at the founding congress, which elected Ljupčo Georgievski, a 26-year-old unemployed university graduate, as leader. The congress declared its party's intention to seek the return of territories then within Serbia. The Communist authorities suspected the IMRO-DPMNU of favouring the Bulgarian cause (the movement was not without its factions) and of fostering inter-ethnic tension with the Serbs. However, the republican Communist leader, Petar Gosev, president of what was now named the League of Communists of Macedonia-Party for Democratic Reform (LCM-PDR), also condemned the threat of Serbian nationalism, which made explicit claims later in the year. Serbia's main opposition leader, Vuk Drasković, revived the concept of 'South Serbia' and proposed a partition of Macedonia between a 'Greater Serbia' and Bulgaria.

In November and December 1990 elections to a new, unicameral republican Assembly (Sobranje) were held in Macedonia. The MAMA and the IMRO-DPMNU formed an electoral alliance, the Front for Macedonian National Unity, to counter the strong support of the ruling LCM-PDR. The first round of the elections was held on 11 November and the nationalist Front alleged irregularities after it failed to win any seats. The Front did not boycott the subsequent rounds of voting (25 November and 9 December) and the IMRO-DPMNU emerged as the single party with the most seats in the new Sobranje (37), against all expectations. The LCM-PDR gained 31 seats and the two predominantly Albanian parties a total of 25. The republican branch of the federal Alliance of Reform Forces (ARF) won 19 seats. These results were inconclusive, the uncertainty being added to by a split in the IMRO-DPMNU, when Vladimir Golubovski challenged Georgievski for the leadership (the IMRO-DPMNU factions continued to vote as a single bloc in the Sobranje). A coalition administration for Macedonia was finally agreed in January 1991: Stojan Andov of the ARF was elected President of the republican Sobranje; Kiro Gligorov of the LCM-PDR was eventually elected President of Macedonia; and Georgievski of the IMRO-DPMNU was elected Vice-President. Following some dispute over the allocation of portfolios the three parties agreed to support a Government largely consisting of independent members, without political affiliation. On 20 March the Sobranje approved a new Government, headed by an independent, Nikola Kljusev. This 'Government of experts' committed itself to concentrating on the economic problems of Macedonia, which had been exacerbated by the Sobranje's inactivity in this area over the previous months.

The Macedonians were active in attempts to mediate in the growing crisis in Yugoslavia, during 1991. The Republic's interests were best served by the preservation of the federation, although, on 25 January, the Sobranje had unanimously adopted a motion declaring the Republic a sovereign territory. However, after the June declarations of Croatian and Slovenian 'dissociation' and the later escalation into civil war, Macedonia became wary of Serbian domination of the 'rump' federal institutions. It declared its neutrality and emphasized its sovereign status. On 8 September a referendum vote, boycotted by the Albanian population, overwhelmingly supported the sovereignty of Macedonia, which was again declared by the Sobranje. With war in the north of Yugoslavia, there was little federal reaction to this and, in October, the evacuation of some 60% of the military bases in the Republic was reported. The Macedonian authorities had received no official explanation, but it was believed that the forces were to be used in Croatia.

In October 1991 the coalition collapsed. Georgievski resigned the Vice-Presidency on 22 October and, the following day, his party, the IMRO-DPMNU, announced that it had joined the opposition. The party complained that,

although it had the largest representation in the Assembly, it was being excluded from the decision-making process. However, the IMRO-DPMNU did participate in the passage of the new Constitution. The party proposed an introductory nationalist statement, which was strongly opposed by the predominantly Albanian parties, causing a delay in the passage of the document. The Government supported the exclusion of continual nationalist references, but did not support PDP demands to include educational and linguistic rights in the Constitution. The final version did not declare Macedonia to be the 'motherland' of the Macedonian people, but nor did it grant the Albanian language official equality with Macedonian. On 17 November the Constitution was passed by 96 of the 120 Assembly members; the majority of Albanian deputies and three IMRO-DPMNU deputies did not support its enactment. Although an EC commission did not view the new Constitution as a bar to recognition, Greece ensured that no EC country recognized the Republic, in January 1992 (Bulgaria did).

Economy

Macedonia was famed for its gold and silver mines, later for its petroleum, and for its wine. In the 20th century, however, it has found itself poor in resources and, after the Second World War, was very dependent upon federal grants for its economic development. With the possible exception of Montenegro, it is Yugoslavia's poorest Republic. It has an overwhelmingly agricultural economy; dairy farming is the most important sector. Activity is concentrated along the Vardar and in the lowlands around other river valleys. There is some mining, Macedonia having moderate mineral reserves, such as chrome, near Skopje. Metallurgy is a major industrial activity. The Republic had severe economic problems by 1991, however. At the end of January 1991, of the 823 firms incurring losses, 66 had declared themselves bankrupt.

The Yugoslav civil war and the new regime in Albania encouraged the Macedonian Government to seek closer economic co-operation with Albania during 1991, although this did not significantly offset the problems of the internal Yugoslav situation. Between 50% and 60% of Macedonia's trade was conducted with the internal Yugoslav market. The Government did seek to reduce dependence on its traditional sources for energy supplies, securing agreement to the construction of a pipeline from the Bulgarian border for Soviet natural gas. The civil war, and the accompanying economic sanctions by the Western economies, compounded Macedonia's problems. These had already been exacerbated by the long drought affecting agriculture, the consequences of the crisis in the Persian (Arabian) Gulf (caused by the Iraqi occupation of Kuwait), the problems in other Eastern European economies and the tardy implementation of free-market reforms by the republican authorities. In 1990 the volume of industrial output in Macedonia declined by 10.6% (in January 1991 it was 20.9% lower than in the previous January); total exports decreased by 11.8% and imports increased by 20.7%. The average annual rate of inflation in 1990 was 120%. At the beginning of 1991 more than 20% of the labour force were unemployed. In October 1991 a total of 477,238 were officially reported to be in employment in the Republic (18.3% in public administration).

Directory

The Government

(November 1991)

In January 1991 the League of Communists of Macedonia-Party of Democratic Reform (now the Social Democratic Alliance of

Macedonia—SDAM), the Alliance of Reform Forces (ARF) and the Internal Macedonian Revolutionary Organization-Democratic Party for Macedonian National Unity (IMRO-DPMNU) formed a coalition administration, although most members of the Executive Council were not to be affiliated to any party. The Communist leader, Kiro Gligorov, was elected President of the Republic by the Sobranje. On 23 October 1991, however, the IMRO-DPMNU announced that it was formally to join the opposition.

STATE PRESIDENT

President of Macedonia: KIRO GLIGOROV (elected by the Assembly on 27 January 1991).

GOVERNMENT OF THE REPUBLIC OF MACEDONIA

Premier: Dr NIKOLA KLJUSEV.

Deputy Premiers: Dr BLAŽE RISTOVSKI, JOVAN ANDONOV, Dr BEĆIR ŽUTA.

Minister of Internal Affairs: Dr LJUBOMIR FRČKOVSKI.

Minister of Defence: TRAJAN GOČEVSKI.

Minister of Justice and Administration: DORDI NAUMOV.

Minister of Finance: METODIJA TOŠEVSKI.

Minister of the Economy: STOJAN TRAJANOVSKI.

Minister of Foreign Relations: Dr DENKO MALESKI.

Minister of Information: MARTIN TRENEVSKI.

Minister of Development: Dr GOCE PETRESKI.

Minister of Agriculture, Forestry and Water Resources Management: Dr IVAN ANGELOV.

Minister of Urban Planning, Construction, Transport and Environmental Protection: Dr ALEKSANDAR LEPAVČEV (IMRO-DPMNU).

Minister of Public Health: Dr PERKO KOLEVSKI.

Minister of Labour and Social Policy: ILIJAZ SABRIU.

Minister of Culture: Dr CVETAN GROZDANOV.

Minister of Science: Dr DORDI EFREMOV.

Minister of Education and Physical Culture: DIMITAR BAJALDŽIEV.

Ministers without Portfolio: TOSKA ALAJDIN, ILIJA ANDONOV ČENTO, Dr RISTO DAMJANOVSKI, Dr JANE MILJKOVSKI.

MINISTRIES

Office of the Executive Council: 91000 Skopje, Dame Grueva 6; tel. (91) 201211; fax (91) 211393.

Ministry of Agriculture, Forestry and Water Resources Management: 91000 Skopje, Vasil Glavinov bb; tel. (91) 231812.

Ministry of Culture: 91000 Skopje, Veljka Vlahovića bb; tel. (91) 223574.

Ministry of Development: 91000 Skopje, Tiranska 2; tel. (91) 220678.

Ministry of the Economy: 91000 Skopje, Bihačka bb; tel. (91) 231259.

Ministry of Education and Physical Culture: 91000 Skopje, Veljka Vlahovića bb; tel. (91) 223548.

Ministry of Finance: 91000 Skopje, Dame Grueva 14; tel. (91) 228411.

Ministry of Foreign Relations: 91000 Skopje, Dame Grueva bb; tel. (91) 236311.

Ministry of Information: 91000 Skopje, 11 Oktomvri 25; tel. (91) 221913.

Ministry of Justice and Administration: 91000 Skopje, Veljka Vlahovića bb; tel. (91) 223065.

Ministry of Labour and Social Policy: 91000 Skopje, Dame Grueva 14; tel. (91) 228411.

Ministry of National Defence: 91000 Skopje, Dimče Mirčeva bb; tel. (91) 237373.

Ministry of Public Health: 91000 Skopje, Dame Grueva 14; tel. (91) 228411.

Ministry of Science: 91000 Skopje, Veljka Vlahovića bb; tel. (91) 223574.

Ministry of Urban Planning, Construction, Transport and Environment Protection: 91000 Skopje, Nikole Vapčarova bb; tel. (91) 239521.

Legislature

SOBRANJE
(Assembly)

President: STOJAN ANDOV (ARF), 91000 Skopje, 11 Octomvri bb; tel. (91) 227111.

Elections, 11 and 25 November and 9 December 1990

Party	Seats
Internal Macedonian Revolutionary Organization-Democratic Party for Macedonian National Unity (IMRO-DPMNU)	37
League of Communists of Macedonia-Party for Democratic Reform (LCM-PDR)*	31
Party of Democratic Prosperity (PDP)	25†
Alliance of Reform Forces (ARF)	19‡
Socialist Party of Macedonia‖	4
Party of Yugoslavs	1
Independents	3
Total	**120**

* The LCM-PDR subsequently was renamed the Social Democratic Alliance of Macedonia (SDAM).
† The PDP gained 18 seats alone and seven in alliance with the People's Democratic Party.
‡ The ARF won 11 seats alone, six in alliance with the Young Democratic Progressive Party (YDPP) and two in alliance with the YDPP, the Socialist Party (which also won four alone) and the Roma Party.
‖ The Socialist Party of Macedonia subsequently was renamed the Socialist Alliance-Socialist Party of Macedonia.

Political Organizations

Internal Macedonian Revolutionary Organization—Democratic Party for Macedonian National Unity (IMRO-DPMNU) (VMRO-DPMNE): 91000 Skopje, 11 Oktomvri bb; nationalist; Leader LJUPČO GEORGIEVSKI; breakaway faction led by VLADIMIR GOLUBOVSKI.

Party of Democratic Prosperity (Partija za Demokratski Prosperitet): Tetovo; f. 1990; predominantly ethnic Albanian and Muslim party; Chair. NEVZAT HALILI; Gen. Sec. MITHAT EMINI.

Party of Yugoslavs—Branch for Macedonia: Skopje; favours the continued federation and supports the rights of ethnic Yugoslavs.

People's Democratic Party: Tetovo; f. 1990; predominantly ethnic Albanian and Muslim party; Gen.-Sec. JUSUF REDZEPI.

Social Democratic Alliance of Macedonia (SDAM) (Socijaldemokratski Savez Makedonije—SDSM): 91000 Skopje, bul. Ilinden bb; tel. (91) 233610; fax (91) 231777; f. 1943; name changed from League of Communists of Macedonia-Party of Democratic Reform in 1991; Chair. BRANKO CRVENKOVSKI; Sec. NIKOLA POPOVSKI.

Socialist Alliance-Socialist Party of Macedonia (SA-SPM): 91000 Skopje, 11 Oktomvri bb; formerly Socialist Party of Macedonia; left-wing.

Young Democratic Progressive Party (YDPP): 91000 Skopje, 11 Oktomvri bb; party of Yugoslav orientation.

Judicial System

All courts in Macedonia are within the jurisdiction of the Ministry of Justice and Administration of the Republic. Final appeal lies to the Yugoslav Federal Court or, in constitutional matters, to the Constitutional Court, both of which are based in Belgrade.

Constitutional Court of the Republic of Macedonia: 91000 Skopje, 12 Udarnas brig. bb; tel. (91) 233063; Pres. JORDAN ARSOV.

Supreme Court: 91000 Skopje, Borisa Kidriča bb; tel. (91) 234111; Pres. TIHOMIR VELKOVSKI.

Office of the Public Prosecutor: 91000 Skopje, bul. Krste Misirkova bb; tel. (91) 229314; Public Prosecutor MARKO BUNDALEVSKI.

Religion

Most ethnic Macedonians are adherents of the Eastern Orthodox Church and, since 1967, there has been an autocephalous Macedonian Orthodox Church. However, the Serbian Church refuses to recognize it and has persuaded the Ecumenical Patriarch and other Orthodox Churches not to do so either. There are some adherents of other Orthodox rites in the Republic. Those Macedonian (and Bulgarian) Slavs who converted to Islam during the Ottoman era are known as Pomaks and are included as an ethnic group of Muslims. The substantial Albanian population is mostly Muslim (mainly Sunni, but some adherents of a Dervish sect); there are a few Roman Catholic Christians and some Jews (see Directory for federal Yugoslavia).

CHRISTIANITY

Macedonian Orthodox Church: Skopje, POB 69; Metropolitan See of Ochrid revived in 1958; autocephaly declared 18 July 1967; 1m. mems; Head of Church and Archbishop of Ochrid and Macedonia: Metropolitan GAVRILO (DJORDJI MILOŠEVSKI) of Debar and Kičevo—reported to have resigned in Jan. 1992.

ISLAM

Islamic Community: Skopje; headquarters of the Skopje Region, one of the four administrative divisions of the Yugoslav Muslims.

The Press

PRINCIPAL NEWSPAPERS

Birlik: 91000 Skopje; Turkish-language newspaper.

Flaka e Vellazerimit: 91000 Skopje; Albanian-language newspaper.

Nova Makedonija: 91000 Skopje, ul. Mito Hadživasilev bb; tel. (91) 235455; telex 51154; f. 1944; daily; morning; in Macedonian; Editor-in-Chief GEORGI AJANOVSKI; circ. 25,000.

Večer: 91000 Skopje, Mito Hadživasilev bb; tel. (91) 220858; telex 51154; fax (91) 224453; f. 1963; daily; evening; in Macedonian; Editor-in-Chief ALEKSANDAR IVANOVSKI (acting); circ. 29,200.

Publishers

Kultura: 91000 Skopje, bul. JNA 68A; tel. (91) 220821; fax (91) 239772; f. 1945; history, philosophy, art, poetry, children's literature and fiction; in Macedonian; Dir DIMITAR BAŠEVSKI.

Makedonska knjiga: 91000 Skopje, ul. 11 oktomvri bb; tel. (91) 224055; telex 51637; arts, non-fiction, novels, children's books; Editor KOSTA BOJADZIEVSKI.

Misla: 91000 Skopje, Partizanski odredi 1; tel. (91) 237238; modern and classic Macedonian and translated literature; Dir BOŽIN PAVLOVSKI.

Prosvetno Delo: 91000 Skopje, Veljko Vlahović 15; tel. (91) 228022; f. 1945; works of domestic writers and textbooks in Macedonian for elementary, professional and high schools; fiction and scientific works; Dir Dr KRSTE ANGELOVSKI.

Radio and Television

Radiotelevizija Skopje: 91000 Skopje, Goce Delčev bb; tel. (91) 227711; telex 51157; fax (91) 236856; f. 1944 (Radio), 1964 (TV); 3 radio and 2 TV programmes; broadcasts in Macedonian, Albanian and Turkish; Dir-Gen. TIHOMIR ILIEVSKI; Dir of Radio SLOBODAN ČAŠULE; Dir of TV SLOBODAN TRAJKOVSKI.

Finance

(a.d. = joint-stock company; cap. = capital; dep. = deposits; res = reserves; m. = million; amounts in dinars; * denotes figures in convertible dinars; brs = branches)

BANKS

National Bank

National Bank of Macedonia: 91000 Skopje, Kompleks banki bb; tel. (91) 230111; Gov. BORKO STANOEVSKI.

Selected Banks

Komercijalna Banka a.d.—Skopje: 91000 Skopje, Kej Dimitar Vlahov 4; tel. (91) 236111; telex 51162; fax (91) 211344; f. 1955; total assets 11,050m.* (Dec. 1990); Gen. Man. Dr ALEKSANDAR MANEVSKI.

Stopanska Banka a.d.—Skopje: 91000 Skopje, 11 Oktomvri 7; tel. (91) 235111; telex 51140; fax (91) 239321; f. 1944; cap. and res 1,678m.*, dep. 11,228m.* (June 1991); Gen. Man. and Chief Exec. LJUBOMIR POPOVSKI; 24 brs.

Trade and Industry

Chamber of Economy of Macedonia: 91000 Skopje, Ivo R. Lola 25; tel. (91) 229211; Pres. DUŠAN PETRESKI.

MAJOR ENTERPRISES AND COMPANIES

Alumina: 91000 Skopje, Ivo R. Lola 164; tel. (91) 229111; telex 51149; fax (91) 230805; aluminium products; Gen. Dir VASIL KOSTOJČINOSKI; 1,595 employees.

Biljana: 97500 Prilep, Krusevski pat bb; tel. (98) 21140; telex 53165; fax (98) 24107; carded yarn, sanitary products, absorbent cotton, knitwear and ready-made clothing; Gen. Dir BLAGOJA PORJAZOVSKI; 1,800 employees.

Brako: 91400 Tito-Veles, Novi Veles 12; tel. (93) 26655; telex 53449; fax (93) 23210; main areas of activity incl. caravans, boat trailers, beekeepers' trailers, etc.; Dir DORDI MANČEVSKI; 650 employees.

Bucim Co—Enterprise for Mining and Metallurgy of Copper: 92420 Radovis; tel. (902) 61113; telex 53661; fax (902) 61119; mining of copper, gold and silver; manufacture of gold and silver jewellery: Gen. Man. VANCO CIFLIGANEE.

Hemteks: 91000 Skopje, Gorno Lisiće 8; tel. (91) 234711; telex 51489; fax (91) 213320; social enterprise engaged in the production of polyester fibre; Gen. Man. IVANCO PANCEVSKI; 750 employees.

Jugotutun: 91000 Skopje, Makedonska Udarna brig., bl. 111; tel. (91) 237133; telex 51462; fax (91) 231114; responsible for a group of 31 mem. enterprises engaged in the tobacco industry.

Karpos: 91330 Kriva Palanka, Maršal Tito 7; tel. (901) 75201; telex 51245; fax (901) 74335; decorative upholstery products and taffeta fabrics; Gen. Dir RUSE DIMOVSKI.

Makpetrol Co: 91000 Skopje, POB 537, Mito Hadživasilev-Jasmin str. 4; tel. (91) 230311; telex 51129; fax (91) 213377; import and export of petroleum products; Gen. Dir GAVRILO GAVRILSKI; 2,203 employees.

Metalski Zavod 'Tito': 91000 Skopje, ul. Pero Nakov bb; tel. (91) 223111; telex 51151; fax (91) 233252; mechanical engineering industry; 9,114 employees.

Organsko Hemijska Industrija—OHIS: 91000 Skopje, Provmajska bb; tel. (91) 233111; telex 51487; fax (91) 211489; manufactures polyacrylonitrillic fibre, PVC powder, etc.; Man. Dir JORGO ČUKA; 5,774 employees.

Pelister-Bitola: 97000 Bitola, Devejani 13; tel. (97) 34544; telex 53146; fax (97) 38209; manufactures clothing; Gen. Dir DIMITAR STOJANOVSKI; 900 employees.

Rafinerija na Nafte, Skopje: 91000 Skopje, p. fah 66; tel. (91) 239511; telex 51366; fax (91) 236920; production of gasoline, diesel fuel, fuel oil, automobile gasoline and LPG; Gen. Dir VANGEL ARANUTOV; 1,432 employees.

Rik Sileks: Kratovo, ul. Goce Delcev; tel. (901) 81188; telex 51345; fax (901) 81700; mining, industry, agriculture, construction, trade, tourism and hotel management; Gen. Man. LJUPČO IVANOVSKI; 3,160 employees.

Rudnici i Zelezarnica Skopje (Skopje Mines and Iron Works): 91000 Skopje, POB 54; tel. (91) 221076; telex 51136; fax (91) 221257; engaged in all stages, from iron ore mining to production of steel sheets and related products; 11,000 employees.

Ruen—Pos Industrija za Avtomobilski Delovi i Traktori: Kočani, 29 Novembri 32; tel. (903) 21600; telex 53644; fax (903) 21223; clutches, etc., for all types of vehicles; Dir IVAN IVANOV.

Technometal-Vardar: 91000 Skopje, Velijka Vlahovića 11; tel. (91) 229411; telex 51453; fax (91) 211696; exports and imports metals, metal products and chemical products; 1,600 employees.

Toranica: Palanka; tel. (901) 75478; telex 51343; fax (901) 74280; manufactures lead-zinc concentrate; Gen. Dir DUSKO ARSOVSKI.

Treska: 91000 Skopje, ul. Ive Lole Ribara 130; tel. (91) 223222; telex 54481; timber industry and wood-working; 10,000 employees.

Zletovo—Sasa: 91000 Skopje, Partizanski odredi 18; tel. (91) 230322; telex 51199; fax (91) 211730; trading co founded by a group of zinc-mining companies; Gen. Dir TITO TRENESKI.

Culture

REPUBLICAN ORGANIZATIONS

Ministry of Culture: see section on The Government (Ministries).

Committee for Education, Culture and Physical Culture: 91000 Skopje, Veljka Vlahoviča 9; tel. (91) 223411; fax (91) 220859.

Cultural and Information Centre (Kulturno-Informativni Centar): 91000 Skopje, Moše Pijade bb; tel. (91) 236724; Dir OLGA POPOVSKA.

Republican Institute for the Protection of Cultural Monuments of Macedonia (Republički Zavod za Zaštita na Spomenicite na Kulturata): 91000 Skopje, Maršal Tito bb, Gorče Petrov; f. 1949; Dir DIMITAR KORNAKOV.

CULTURAL HERITAGE

Archaeological Museum of Macedonia (Arheološki muzej na Makedonija): 91000 Skopje, Kuršumli An; f. 1924; Dir SARŽO SARŽOSKI.

Art Gallery: 91000 Skopje, POB 278, Daut Pašin Amam; tel. (91) 233904; f. 1948; Dir DRAGAN BOŠNAKOVSKI.

Institute of Folklore (Institut za Folklor): 91000 Skopje, Ruzveltova 3; f. 1950; Dr BLAŽE PETROVSKI.

Museum of Modern Arts: 91000 Skopje, Samuilova bb; tel. (91) 235244.

PERFORMING ARTS

Drama Theatre: 91000 Skopje, Šekspirova 15; tel. (91) 250005.

Macedonian National Theatre (Makedonski Naroden Teater—Drama): 91000 Skopje, Dimitar Vlahov bb; tel. (91) 230755.

Macedonian National Theatre (Opera and Ballet): 91000 Skopje, Bitpazarska bb; tel. (91) 222133; Dir LJUPČO PETRUŠEVSKI.

Pralipe Drama Group: 91000 Skopje, Kej Dimitar Vlahov bb; tel. (91) 230041.

Music

Macedonian Philharmonic Orchestra (Makedonska Filharmonija): 91000 Skopje, bul. JNA bb; tel. (91) 220139; Chief Conductor FIMCO MURATOVSKI; Dir MELPOMENI KORNETI.

Skopje RTV Big Band (Plesni Orkestar RTV Skopje): 91000 Skopje, Nov dom na RTV; tel. (91) 227205; Chief Conductor ALEKSANDAR DZAMBAZOV.

Skopje RTV Chamber Orchestra (Kamerni Orkestar RTV Skopje): 91000 Skopje, Nov dom na RTV; tel. (91) 227205.

Skopje RTV Choir (Hor RTV Skopje): 91000 Skopje, Nov dom na RTV; tel. (91) 227205; Chief Conductor DRAGAN SUPLEVSKI.

ASSOCIATIONS

Albanian Cultural Association: Tetovo; aims to preserve and foster language and culture of ethnic Albanians in Macedonia.

Association of Macedonian Muslims: 91000 Skopje; f. 1970; supports rights for Slav Muslims (Pomaks/Poturs/Torbeshes) *vis à vis* Orthodox Macedonians and the dominant Albanian Muslims; Chair. Dr RIZA MEMEDOVSKI.

Egyptian Association of Citizens: Ohrid; f. 1990; group who reject Roma ethnicity and claim to be Egipcani or Egyptians; allowed separate registration in Macedonian census of 1991; Leader NAZIM ARIFI.

Phralipe (Brotherhood—Roma Union of Macedonia): 91000 Skopje, Suto Orizari; f. 1948; cultural asscn of the Roma (Gypsies).

Pitu Guli Cultural Association: 91000 Skopje; cultural asscn of the Vlahs.

Society of Composers of Macedonia (Društvo na Kompozitorite na Makedonija): 91000 Skopje, Maksim Gorki 18; f. 1950; Sec. SOTIR GOLABOSKI.

Society of Plastic Arts of Macedonia (Društvo na Likovnite Umetnike na Makedonija): Umetnička galerija, 91000 Skopje, Krusevska 1A; f. 1944; Sec. NASO BEKAROSKI.

Society of Writers of Macedonia (Društvo na Pisatelite na Makedonija): 91000 Skopje, Maksim Gorki 18; tel. (91) 236205; f. 1951; Secs TRAJAN PETROVSKI, RADE SILJAN.

Union of Associations for Macedonian Language and Literature (Sojuz na Društvata za Makedonski Jakiz i Literatura): Filoški fakultet, 91000 Skopje, bul. Krste Misirkov bb; f. 1954; Sec. VANČO TUŠEVSKI.

The Environment

GOVERNMENT ORGANIZATIONS

Ministry of Urban Planning, Construction, Transport and Environmental Protection: see section on The Government (Ministries).

Most environmental activity by research bodies and the 'Green' movement takes place at the federal level (see Directory for federal Yugoslavia).

Defence

Macedonia is defended by the Yugoslav People's Army, although, during 1991, many of its military bases were reported to be empty and the forces involved in the civil war in Croatia. The YPA's Third Military District covers Macedonia and was headquartered in Skopje. Under legislation of 1991 and the new republican Constitution of that year, the Assembly (Sobranje) withdrew its citizens from service in the civil war and reserved to itself the power to declare a state of emergency and control over the Territorial Defence Forces. During 1991 the Republic declared itself neutral.

Commander of the Third Military District of the YPA: Col-Gen. NIKOLA UZELAC.

Commander of the Territorial Defence: Lt-Gen. TOMISLAV TRAJČEVSKI.

MONTENEGRO

Geography

The Republic of Montenegro is part of the Socialist Federal Republic of Yugoslavia. It lies on the Adriatic Sea, next to Albania, which juts into it from the south, forming an international border to the east and south. Northwards, up the Adriatic coast, is Croatia; in south-west Montenegro the Republic has a short border with Croatia's Dubrovnik (formerly the city-state of Ragusa) territory. During 1991 this border emerged as the subject of dispute between Montenegro and Croatia. Inland, the main north-western border is with the Republic of Bosnia-Herzegovina. To the east is the Republic of Serbia, the Kosovo province on the eastern border and 'Inner' Serbia on the north-east. Montenegro is the smallest of the Yugoslav Republics, both in terms of area (13,812 sq km) and population.

Most of Montenegro has a rugged mountainous terrain, with some fertile river valleys traversing it towards the south of the Republic and the lowlands around Lake Scutari (Skadarsko Jezero). There are some coastal lowlands around the harbour of Kotor (formerly Cattaro—on the Boka Kotorska bay) and to the south of the Adriatic city of Bar and Lake Scutari. The capital, Titograd (formerly Podgorića), is located to the north of Scutari, at the head of the lacustrine plain. According to the census of 1991, the population of the Titograd municipal district was 152,288. The old royal capital, in the highlands above the Adriatic, is Cetinje. Other major cities include: the industrial city of Nikšić (74,821), to the north-west of Titograd; Bijelo Polje (55,145) and Ivangrad (45,662) in the west of the Republic; Pljevlja (39,628) in the north; and Bar (37,331) in the south.

In 1981 some 68% of the ethnic Montenegrins of Yugoslavia lived in the Republic of Montenegro. Montenegrins accounted for 2.6% of the total population of the federation. The Montenegrins speak a Serbo-Croat dialect, use the Cyrillic script and are a Serb people. They are mostly adherents of the Serbian Orthodox Church; there are also some Roman Catholic Christians and a significant Muslim minority (Slav Muslims and most of the ethnic Albanian population). According to the 1991 census, the population density was 44.6 per sq km. The total population of the Republic was 616,327, of which 61.8% were Montenegrin, 14.6% Slav Muslims, 9.3% Serbs, 6.6% Albanian and 4.2% ethnic Yugoslavs. The dominant language is Serbo-Croat, although the Albanian population uses its own language.

History

Montenegro is a Serb territory, first settled by the Slavs in the sixth century AD. The Serbs converted to Eastern Orthodox Christianity in the ninth century. Despite this cultural and political reinforcement of Eastern Roman (Byzantine) claims to overlordship, the Serbs did maintain a degree of internecine independence. The main Serb principality, and the original Serbian state, was Raška, but it was Mihajlo (Michael) of Zeta who first united the Serbs in one kingdom, in the 11th century. The principality of Zeta was the original Montenegrin state, consisting of the Southern Slav tribes in the inaccessible mountains of the modern Montenegro ('Black Mountain'). Zeta shared the fate of the Serbs generally for the rest of the Middle Ages, falling under Byzantine and Serbian rule. Following the Ottoman

destruction of Serbian power in the 14th and 15th centuries, the Montenegrins maintained a precarious independence, emerging as an identifiable political entity by the 15th century. The Montenegrins resisted complete domination by the Venetians or, from the 16th century, by the Turks, although they were, initially, nominally tributary to the Sublime Porte, the government of the Ottoman Empire. The Montenegrin tribes were often engaged in warfare, therefore, and became a noted military people. They remained faithful to the Serbian Orthodox Church, but did not establish a unitary state, being ruled by a succession of different dynasties. The modern principality emerged during the 19th century, its independence being acknowledged in 1796 and confirmed in 1878.

With the revival of a Serbian principality, Montenegrin policy was guided by its ethnic-Serb roots and an alignment with its co-religionists. Austria-Hungary, which had occupied neighbouring Bosnia-Herzegovina, was determined to preserve the physical separation of Serbia and Montenegro and supported the continued Ottoman administration of its Sandzak of Novi Pazar (the Sandjak). In 1910 Montenegro was proclaimed a kingdom, under Nikita I. Shortly after this Montenegro supported Serbia in the Balkan Wars of 1912–13 and gained part of the Sandjak, on its north-eastern borders. Montenegro also supported Serbia, and the Entente Powers, in the First World War. It was invaded and occupied by Habsburg troops in 1916. During the War the Montenegrins joined in negotiations to form a common Southern Slav state. The Montenegrin royal family acquiesced in the loss of its power and the Serbian dynasty occupied the new throne of the Kingdom of Serbs, Croats and Slovenes (from 1929, Yugoslavia). In the Second World War Montenegro regained a nominal independence, as a client of Fascist Italy, but support for Tito's Partisan resistance was strong in the mountains of the territory. After the War Montenegro, with the additional territory of the city-state of Cattaro (now Kotor), became a Republic of federal Yugoslavia.

The Montenegrins were well represented in the ruling Communist party and in the Yugoslav People's Army (YPA). During the 1980s, following the death of Tito, Montenegro's traditional alliance with Serbia once more became evident. In 1988 this was ensured by allegedly Serbian-organized demonstrations, which brought about the replacement of the Montenegrin Communist leadership with conservatives in sympathy with the Serbian leader, Milošević. Similarity to the Serbian situation was further demonstrated by the elections of 1990. The ruling Communists amended the republican Constitution, which then provided for a unicameral Assembly, with 125 seats, and a directly-elected State President, replacing the previous collective Presidency. The first rounds of voting for both the legislative and presidential elections were held on 9 December. One week later the second round of elections to the Assembly took place: the ruling League of Communists of Montenegro (subsequently renamed the Democratic Party of Socialists—DPS) won 83 of the 125 seats; the republican branch of the Alliance of Reform Forces (ARF) won 17 seats; the predominantly ethnic Muslim and Albanian Democratic Coalition (consisting of the Equality Party, the Democratic Action Party and the Democratic Alliance) a total of 13 seats; and the Popular Party 12 seats. The Communist candidate to be President of Montenegro,

Momir Bulatović, defeated the ARF candidate in a second round of voting, on 23 December.

The Communists (that is, the DPS), as in Serbia, could therefore form a single-party administration. During 1991 Montenegro loyally supported Serbia in the political crises of Yugoslavia. In March the Montenegrin member of the federal State Presidency resigned, when the Serbian request for a state of emergency was not granted. The new member, Dr Branko Kostić, was considered to be strongly pro-Serb. He became Vice-President of the federal head of state organ, at the end of June, after being party to the 'Serbian bloc' on the State Presidency, which had refused to endorse the normal succession of its rotating leadership. In this capacity he chaired meetings of the 'rump' Presidency (that is, Montenegro, Serbia, Kosovo-Metohija and Vojvodina), which first convened without the other representatives in October. It was declared illegitimate and the instrument of an effective coup by the authorities of Bosnia-Herzegovina, Croatia, Macedonia and Slovenia.

Bulatović, the President of Montenegro, did cause some surprise when he accepted the EC peace proposals formulated at The Hague (Montenegro was strongly influenced by Italy in this), also in October 1991. Serbia, alone of the Yugoslav republics, had rejected the plan. There was some tension in relations between Montenegro and Serbia, following this action and a declaration of sovereignty by the Montenegrin Assembly, on 18 October. Furthermore, the Montenegrin Government objected to the use of YPA reservists of Montenegrin citizenship in the civil war. Some of the YPA pressure on Dubrovnik, particularly, was relieved by the order for all Montenegrin reservists to be withdrawn to their own Republic (over 600 joined the Croatian forces). The assertion of republican over federal law, however, was prompted by uneasiness with the civil war and, it was believed, as a pragmatic response to the disintegration of Yugoslavia. It was a formality, intended to ensure proper representation at any future negotiations on the federation, more than a symptom of a distinct Montenegrin nationalism. The Republic remained in line with Serbian policy in attempting to prevent the referendum on autonomy by the Sandjak Muslims (which, according to the organizers, gave an overwhelming endorsement to autonomy).

Economy

Montenegro, one of the poorest of the Yugoslav Republics, has an agricultural economy, dominated by stock-raising activities, mainly of pigs, sheep and goats. Some cereals and tobacco plants are cultivated in river valleys and on the coastal lowlands, but arable farming is primitive. During the 1980s the Republic began to develop tourism along its Adriatic coast and, until the civil war of 1991, this was becoming the main source of foreign, convertible currency. The inhospitable mountain terrain excludes the possibility of extensive industrial development, although federal policy has ensured the basing of some industry in the larger cities.

Directory
The Government
(November 1991)

STATE PRESIDENCY

President of the Presidency: MOMIR BULATOVIĆ (elected by popular vote on 23 December 1990).

Office of the Presidency: Titograd; fax (81) 42329.

GOVERNMENT OF THE REPUBLIC OF MONTENEGRO

President (Premier): MILO DJUKANOVIĆ.
Vice-Presidents (Deputy Premiers): BLAGOJE LUKIĆ, VUK OGNJANOVIĆ, ZORAN ŽIŽIĆ.
Minister of Internal Affairs: PAVLE BULATOVIĆ.
Minister of the Economy: VOJIN DUKANOVIĆ.
Minister of Finance: BOŽIDAR GAZIVODA.
Minister of Foreign Affairs: NIKOLA SAMARDŽIĆ.
Minister of National Defence: Col BOŽIDAR BABIĆ.
Minister of Justice: MOMĆILO KNEŽEVIĆ.
Minister of Labour and Social Protection: MILIVOJE JAUKOVIĆ.
Minister of Agriculture, Forestry and Water Resources Management: BRANKO ABRAMOVIĆ.
Minister of Culture and Physical Culture: LLIJA LAKUŠIĆ.
Minister of Health and the Environment: Dr MOMIR MUGOŠA.
Minister of Education and Science: Dr PREDRAG OBRADOVIĆ.
Minister of Urbanism, Construction and Housing-Communal Affairs: DORDIJE PRIBILOVIĆ.
Minister of Tourism and Trade: NEBOJŠA ZEKOVIĆ.
Ministers without Portfolio: BREDRAG GORANOVIĆ, DRAGO ŠOFRANAC.

MINISTRIES

Office of the Executive Council: Government of the Republic of Montenegro, Titograd, Jovana Tomaševića bb; tel. (81) 52833; fax (81) 52246.
Ministry of Agriculture, Forestry and Water Resources Management: Titograd, Omladinskih brig. 2; tel. (81) 31287; fax (81) 52935.
Ministry of Culture and Physical Culture: Titograd, Vuka Karadžića 3; tel. (81) 51355; fax (81) 42028.
Ministry of the Economy: Titograd, Stanka Dragojevića 2; tel. (81) 42104; fax (81) 42028.
Ministry of Education and Science: Titograd, Ulica slobode bb; fax (81) 612780.
Ministry of Finance: Titograd, bul. Blaža Jovanovića 2; tel. (81) 42835; fax (81) 42028.
Ministry of Foreign Affairs: Titograd, Stanka Dragojevića 2; tel. (81) 52821; fax (81) 45752.
Ministry of Health and the Environment: Titograd, Stanka Dragojevića 2; fax (81) 42028.
Ministry of Internal Affairs: Titograd, bul. Lenjina 6; tel. (81) 5223; fax (81) 52919.
Ministry of Justice: Titograd, Vuka Karadžića 3; tel. (81) 51355; fax (81) 612780.
Ministry of Labour, Social Protection and Protection of Veterans and Disabled Persons: Titograd, Vuka Karadžića 3; tel. (81) 51255; fax (81) 612912.
Ministry of National Defence: Titograd, bul. Blaža Jovanovića 4; tel. (81) 42396; fax (81) 45431.
Ministry of Urbanism, Construction and Housing-Communal Affairs: Titograd, Pete proleterske brig. 36; tel. (81) 2142; fax (81) 52246.
Ministry of Tourism and Trade: Titograd; fax (81) 42028.

Legislature
ASSEMBLY

President: RISTO VUKČEVIĆ, 81000 Titograd, bul. Blaža Jovanovića 5; tel. (81) 42034; fax (81) 42641.

Elections, 9 and 16 December 1990

Party	Seats
League of Communists of Montenegro*	83
Alliance of Reform Forces (ARF)	17
Democratic Coalition†	13
People's Party	12
Total	**125**

* The League of Communists of Montenegro subsequently renamed itself the Democratic Party of Socialists.
† This alliance consisted of the Equality Party, Democratic Action Party and the Democratic Alliance.

Political Organizations

Alliance of Reform Forces for Montenegro: Titograd; republican branch of federal, pro-Yugoslav party; favours free-market economic reform.

Democratic Action Party: Titograd; mem. of Democratic Coalition of Muslims and Albanians in Montenegro.

Democratic Alliance: Titograd; mem. of Democratic Coalition of Muslims and Albanians in Montenegro.

Democratic Party of Socialists (DPS) (Demokratska Partija Socijalista): Titograd; name changed from League of Communists of Montenegro in 1991; supports continued federation; Chair. MOMIR BULATOVIĆ; Gen. Sec. SVETOZAR MAROVIĆ.

Equality Party: Titograd; mem. of Democratic Coalition of Muslims and Albanians in Montenegro.

Party of Democratic Action—Montenegro: Rozaj; Slav Muslim party, affiliated to PDA of Bosnia-Herzegovina; support mainly in Sandjak region; Leader HARUN HADŽIĆ.

People's Party (PP) (Narodna Stranka—NS): Titograd; advocates the union of Montenegro and Serbia; Leader NOVAK KILIBARDA.

Other parties include the Montenegro Social Democratic Party, the Montenegrin Liberal Alliance, the Yugoslav National Party, the Party of Socialists of Montenegro and the Independent Organization of Communists.

Judicial System

The courts in Montenegro are supervised by the republican Ministry of Justice (see section on The Government—Ministries). The highest courts in the republican judicial system are the Supreme Court and the Constitutional Court. Final appeal lies to the Yugoslav Federal Court and, in constitutional matters, to the Constitutional Court, both of which are based in Belgrade.

Constitutional Court of the Republic of Montenegro: 81000 Titograd, bul. Lenjina 3; tel. (81) 41846; Pres. LJUBOMIR SPASOJEVIĆ.

Supreme Court: 81000 Titograd, Njegoševa 6; tel. (81) 43070; Pres. MARKO MARKOVIĆ.

Office of the Public Prosecutor: 81000 Titograd, Njegoševa 6; tel. (81) 43053; Public Prosecutor VLADIMIR SUŠOVIĆ.

Religion

Most ethnic Montenegrins are adherents of the Serbian Orthodox Church, which is based in Serbia. There was an autocephalous Montenegrin Orthodox Church, between 1855 and 1920, and, in August 1990, there was a petition to re-establish this, but there seemed to be little general support for such a move. There are a few Roman Catholics on the coast, around Kotor, and among the Albanian population (the leading Roman Catholic prelate in the Republic is the Archbishop of Bar). Almost 20% of the population profess Islam as their faith, many being ethnic Muslims of the Sandjak area (which was partitioned between Montenegro and Serbia in 1913). One of the four administrative Regions of Yugoslav Islam is headquartered in Titograd.

The Press

Koha (Time): Titograd; f. 1978; Albanian-language magazine; circ. 2,000 (estimated).

Pobjeda: Titograd, Marka Milanova 7; daily; morning; Editor-in-Chief VIDOJE KONTAR (acting); circ. 17,959.

Publisher

Pobjeda: 81000 Titograd, Južni bul. bb; tel. (81) 44433; f. 1974; poetry, fiction, lexicography and scientific works.

Radio and Television

Radiotelevizija Crne Gore: 81000 Titograd, Cetinjski put bb; tel. (81) 41800; telex 61133; fax (81) 43640; f. 1944 (Radio), 1971 (TV); 2 radio and 2 TV programmes; broadcasts in Serbo-Croat; Dir-Gen. BRANIMIR BOJANIĆ; Dir of Radio ZORAN JOCOVIĆ; Dir of TV MILUTIN RADULOVIĆ (acting).

Finance

(m. = million; amounts in dinars)

BANKS

National Bank of Montenegro: 81000 Titograd, bul. Blaža Jovanovića 7; tel. (81) 43381; Gov. KRUNISLAV VUKČEVIĆ.

Investiciona Banka Titograd: 81000 Titograd, bul. Revolucije 1; tel. (81) 42922; telex 61118; f. 1966; total assets 1,606,826m. (Dec. 1987); in process of reorganization.

Trade and Industry

Chamber of Economy of Montenegro: 81000 Titograd, Novaka Miloševa 29/II; tel. (81) 31071; fax (81) 34926.

MAJOR ENTERPRISES AND COMPANIES

Industriaimpex: 81000 Titograd, Marka Miljanova 17; tel. (81) 32811; telex 61132; fax (81) 22152; foreign trading co; 350 employees.

Industriaimport: 81000 Titograd, Vuka Karadžića 41; tel. (81) 31322; telex 61138; import-export trading; 3,500 employees.

Jadran: 85336 Boka Kotorska, Obala Marka, Martinovića bb Perast; tel. (82) 25003; telex 61392; fax (82) 14799; manufactures heavy garments; Gen. Dir VLADIMIR POCANIĆ; 700 employees.

Kombinat Aluminijuma, Titograd: 81000 Titograd, POB 22; tel. (81) 53011; telex 61114; metal processing; 4,948 employees.

Metallurgical and Metalworking Corporation (MMK): Nikšić; tel. (83) 41422; telex 61120; fax (83) 44750; manufacture of crude steel, steel castings, etc.; Pres. ZARKO MIJUSKOVIĆ; 6,500 employees.

Metalursko Metalski Kombinat, Nikšić: 81400 Nikšić; tel. (83) 31422; telex 61120; metallurgy and foreign work, processing and provision of related services.

Rudnici Boksita Nikšić Oour Prerada (Nikšić Bauxite Mines): 81000 Nikšić, bul. var 13 Jula 30; tel. (83) 24122; telex 61216; non-ferrous metallurgy; 1,600 employees.

Rudnik Olova i Činka, Mojkovac: 84205 Mojkovac, Vojvode Scepanovića bb; tel. (84) 72137; telex 61351; manufacture of lead, zinc and pyrites concentrates; Gen. Dir MILIJA ZEJAK.

Veljko Vlahović: 85343 Bijela; tel. (82) 81122; telex 61179; fax (82) 82303; shipyard, providing building and repair services for vessels of various sizes; Gen. Dir ILIC VASILIJE; 1,100 employees.

Culture

REPUBLICAN ORGANIZATIONS

Ministry of Culture and Physical Culture: see section on The Government (Ministries).

Republican Centre for Cultural and Artistic Activities (Republički Centar za Kulturno-umjetničke Delatnosti): 81000 Titograd, Vasa Raičkovića 27; tel. (81) 44270; Dir MILAN POPOVIĆ; Programme Organizer: VESELIN RADUNOVIĆ.

Republican Institute for the Protection of Cultural Monuments (Republički Zavod za Zaštitu Spomenika Kulture): 81205 Cetinje, Bajova 150; tel. (86) 21182; f. 1948; Dir CEDOMIR MARKOVIĆ.

CULTURAL HERITAGE

Historical Institute of Montenegro (Istoriski Institut Crne Gore): 81000 Titograd, Naselje Kruševac; f. 1948.

Maritime Museum (Pomorski muzej): 81330 Kotor; f. 1900; Dir JOVAN MARTINOVIĆ.

State Museum (Državni muzej): 81250 Cetinje, Titov trg; Dir STANISLAV-RAKO VUJOŠEVIĆ.

PERFORMING ARTS

National Theatre of Montenegro (Crnogorsko Narodno Pozoriste): 81000 Titograd, Stanka Dragojevića 12; tel. (81) 43293; drama, ballet, opera; Dir BLAGOTA ERAKOVIĆ.

Symphony Orchestra of Montenegro RTV (Simfonijski orkestar Crnogorske RTV): 81000 Titograd, Cetinjski put bb; Chief Conductor RADOVAN PAPOVIĆ.

The Environment

GOVERNMENT ORGANIZATIONS

Ministry of Health and the Environment: see section on The Government (Ministries).

Most environmental activity by research bodies and the 'Green' movement takes place at the federal level (see Directory for federal Yugoslavia).

Defence

Montenegro is defended by the Yugoslav People's Army (YPA), in which many Montenegrins serve. The Fourth Military District is headquartered in Titograd and the Federal Navy is based at Kumbor (Boka Kotorska). The Territorial Defence is under the command of the YPA. In October 1991 the republican authorities refused to sanction the use of their reservists beyond the borders of Montenegro, although they remained committed to the federal Yugoslav state.

Commander of the Fourth Military District of the YPA: Col-Gen. PAVLE STRUGAR.

SERBIA

Geography

The Republic of Serbia (formerly the Socialist Republic of Serbia) is a constituent partner in the Socialist Federal Republic of Yugoslavia (SFRY). The Republic also includes the Autonomous Province of Kosovo and Metohija (formerly known as Kosovo) and the Autonomous Province of Vojvodina, both of which are federal units of the SFRY. Kosovo-Metohija occupies the south-west corner of the Republic and Vojvodina comprises the northern part. The Republic has international borders with Hungary to the north, Romania to the north-east, Bulgaria to the east and a short border with Albania in the south-west. The Yugoslav Republic of Macedonia lies to the south of Serbia, Montenegro to the south-west and Bosnia-Herzegovina and Croatia to the west.

The terrain is mountainous, except in the north, where the Pannonian plains begin. These fertile plains of Vojvodina and northern Serbia are watered by the Danube (Dunav), Tisa, Sava and Drava rivers. Another river to join the Danube on these plains is the Morava, which clefts through a deep valley from the mountains of the south. The climate is barely mitigated by the Mediterranean and is hot in summer and severe in winter.

The capital of the Republic of Serbia is the federal capital, Belgrade (Beograd), which lies in the very north of 'Inner' Serbia. Other important towns of Inner Serbia, which had a population of 5,753,825, in 1991, include Niš, Kragujevac and Leskovac. Inner Serbia is administered as nine regions, including the city of Belgrade, Yugoslavia's largest city.

Kosovo-Metohija lies on plateau-land in the south-east of the Republic, bordering Macedonia and Albania. Its population, which, according to the preliminary results of the 1991 census, was 1,954,747 (an increase of some 23% on 1981, the highest rate of population growth in Yugoslavia), is now predominantly Muslim and ethnic Albanian. The Province has a western border with Montenegro, mainly with the south of its Sandjak region; the Serbian Sandjak lies to the north-west. The provincial capital is Priština; other important towns include Prizren, Peć and Kosovska Mitrovica.

The other Autonomous Province, Vojvodina, is a fertile plain, bordering Hungary and Romania. It lies just to the north of Belgrade and its western border, with Croatia, is defined by the Danube. Formerly part of the Banat, a border territory of the Habsburg realm, it is an area of very mixed ethnic composition, originally with a large Hungarian (Magyar) population, but now dominated by Serbs. In 1991 the population of Vojvodina was 2,012,605, a slight decline since 1981. The provincial capital is Novi Sad, and other important towns include Subotica and Zrenjanin.

At the census of March 1991, the total population of the Republic was 9,721,177. The Serbs are the dominant ethnic group; in 1981 they constituted some 66% of the total population (76% of all Yugoslavia's Serbs lived within the borders of the Republic), with minorities of Albanians (14%), Yugoslavs (5%) and Hungarians (4%). Within Inner Serbia the Serbs accounted for 85% of the population and 60% of all Serbs. In Kosovo-Metohija (then Kosovo) some 77% were Albanian and only 13% Serb. About 71% of the Albanians of Yugoslavia lived in Kosovo-Metohija. Albanian and Serbo-Croat are the most common languages in use. In 1981

Vojvodina's population was 54% Serb and only 19% Hungarian. Also in the Vojvodina are the majority of Yugoslavia's Slovak, Romanian and Ruthenian (or Ukrainian) populations, and the languages of these minorities are in widespread official use in the Province, together with Hungarian and Serbo-Croat. There are other minority communities in Serbia. There are Slav Muslims, mainly in the Sandjak region, on the border with Montenegro and to the north of Kosovo-Metohija, Roma (Gypsies), Vlahs, Bulgarians and Czechs. The main language is Serbo-Croat, written in the Cyrillic script. Another reflection of the Serb majority is the predominance of Orthodox Christianity, the Serbian Orthodox Church being the largest denomination. There are followers of other Orthodox rites, some Roman Catholics (in the Vojvodina and among the Albanian and Croat minorities) and a few Protestants. Islam is the religion of a significant minority, mainly in the south of the Republic, and there are some Jews.

History

Serbs settled in the Roman province of Illyria in the sixth century AD. Their conversion to Eastern Orthodox Christianity strengthened the claims of the Eastern Roman (Byzantine) Empire to suzerainty, although the Serb tribes did maintain varying degrees of independence, which included a 10th-century state under the leadership of the principality of Zeta (the original Montenegrin state). However, in the ninth and 10th centuries, the main Southern Slav power was the Bulgarian Empire. Despite Bulgarian, Byzantine and Hungarian pressures, a Serbian kingdom was established in the 12th century. It did not include the northern parts of modern Serbia; the territories of the Serbs were in southern and central Serbia, based on the principality of Raška (Rascia), but including the principalities of Zeta and Rama or Bosnia. Stjepan (Stephen) I of the Nemanjid dynasty was able to end Byzantine rule and, in 1187, Serbian independence was acknowledged by the Emperor. In the next century the Ecumenical Patriarch, also based in Constantinople, acknowledged the autocephaly of the Serbian Church. This Orthodox denomination was established by St Sava, who opposed the pro-Western policies of his brother, Car (Tsar) Stjepan II, who, in 1217, had received the royal dignity by grant of the Pope. In 1219 St Sava was consecrated the autocephalous archbishop of the Serbs. The Serbian Orthodox Church was to become the repository of national culture and identity, particularly following the destruction of the medieval empires.

The Serbian state of the Nemanjids declined, but a period of Balkan pre-eminence was secured by the destruction of the Bulgarian and Byzantine armies at Velbuzhde (Küstendil), in 1330. The following year Stjepan Dušan succeeded to the principality of Raška and he led the Serbs in campaigns against the other Orthodox powers for dominance in the Balkans. In 1346, as Uroš IV, he was crowned Tsar of the Serbs and Greeks and established a Serbian patriarchate. His capital was at Skopje, although he hoped to conquer Constantinople and inherit the legitimate claims of the Roman Empire. Uroš IV was succeeded by Uroš V (1355–67), under whom the kingdom disintegrated into feudal 'despotates'. One of the more powerful of the ruling noblemen, Lazar of Raška, attempted to unite the despotates against the advance of the Ottoman Turks, but the power of the Serbs was crushed on the plains of Kosovo Polje ('the Field of Blackbirds'), in 1389. By 1396 Serbia was a vassal of the Ottoman Empire. Djordje (George) Branković (1427–56) moved the main Serbian centre north to Smederevo, but, despite his efforts to resist, in 1459 Serbia was finally absorbed by the Ottoman Empire. During the following centuries the Serbs preserved their Orthodox Christian culture and proved to be valuable recruits against the Turks, even for the Roman Catholic Habsburgs (Vojvodina became a Habsburg territory, as was, in the early 18th century, northern Serbia).

The modern Serbian state was established during the 19th century. A peasant uprising, which began in 1804, escalated into a popular revolt by the Serbs against the Turks. The revolt was led by Kara Djordje ('Black George') Petrović, who demanded autonomy for the Serbs. By 1812 the uprising had been crushed, but the dynasty of Karadjordje, the Karadjordjević, had become recognized heroes of the Serbian independence movement. It was, however, Miloš Obrenović who led the successful revolt against the Ottomans and became ruler of the autonomous Serbian principality recognized in 1817 (the new Serbian state did not include Vojvodina; its capital was Belgrade, near its northern border, and it consisted of the northern part of what is now Inner Serbia). The Obrenović and the Karadjordjević were in constant, and often bloody, rivalry from then on.

In 1878, at the Congress of Berlin, the Great Powers agreed to grant Serbia some territory around Niš. The principality's independence was also acknowledged by the Ottomans. However, the Habsburgs of Austria-Hungary were suspicious of Serbian expansionism and were determined to contain it, although they had attempted to placate the nationalism of their own Serb population by the creation of the province of Serbian Vojvodina. The Habsburg Government resolved to prevent the union of Serbia and Montenegro and, thence, Serbian access to the Adriatic. Thus Austria-Hungary wished to maintain the Ottoman administration in Kosovo and in the sandzaks south of Bosnia-Herzegovina (which was to be administered by the Habsburgs). The Sandzak of Novi Pazar (the Sandjak), which was dominated by Serbo-Croat-speaking Muslims, separated Serbia from Montenegro. Serbian ambition was, therefore, constrained and its only outlet was to the south. This was reinforced by the conservative, pro-Habsburg policies of Milan Obrenović, under whose rule Serbia was proclaimed a kingdom in 1882.

In 1903 King Aleksandar I Obrenović was assassinated and the Karadjordjević dynasty ascended the throne of Serbia, under Petar I. King Petar I was leader of the Radicals, who were anti-Habsburg, and resentful of appeasing Austria-Hungary. His regime also witnessed the rise of the Southern Slav movement ('Yugoslavism'). This increasing nationalism was accompanied by growing turbulence in the Ottoman Empire and the involvement of Great-Power politics in the Balkans. In 1908 Austria-Hungary formally annexed Bosnia-Herzegovina, although its ally, Germany, prevented it going to war with Serbia. Serbia, for its part, confined its ambition to the south, against the disintegrating Turkish power. With the other Orthodox states of Montenegro, Bulgaria and Greece, Serbia removed the Turks from most of their remaining European possessions in the First Balkan War, of 1912–13. In June 1913 Bulgaria attacked Serbia, starting the Second Balkan War. Serbia, however, was supported by Montenegro, Greece, Romania and the Turks. Bulgaria's defeat was formalized at the Peace of Bucharest, in August. Serbia, therefore, partitioned Macedonia with Greece alone and the Sandjak

with Montenegro. Its direct access to the Adriatic, however, was still prevented by Austria-Hungary and Italy insisting on the recognition of an Albanian state.

In June 1914 the Archduke Francis Ferdinand, the Habsburg heir, and his wife were assassinated by a Serb nationalist. Although the Serbian Government had no involvement with the assassination, Austria-Hungary was determined to stifle the newly-expanded Serbian Kingdom. On 28 July 1914 Austria-Hungary declared war on Serbia; this was the start of the First World War, between the Central Powers of Austria-Hungary and Germany and the Entente Powers or Allied Powers of France, Russia, Serbia and the United Kingdom. Serbia itself was occupied by Habsburg troops for most of the War, being invaded in 1915. The Bulgarians assisted Austria-Hungary and satisfied their own ambitions by the occupation of Macedonia ('South Serbia'). Meanwhile, the Serbian authorities in exile met with representatives of the Montenegrins and the Habsburg-ruled Southern Slavs and agreed the Corfu Declaration, of July 1917. This envisaged the formation of a common state, under the Serbian monarchy. This came closer with the collapse of the Habsburg monarchy, in October 1918, and, on 4 December, a Kingdom of Serbs, Croats and Slovenes was proclaimed. It united Serbia, including Macedonia and Kosovo, with Montenegro and the Habsburg lands (modern Croatia, Slovenia and Vojvodina). The Serbian Regent since 1914, Prince Aleksandar Karadjordjević, was declared Regent of the Southern Slav ('Yugoslav') realm. In August 1921, upon the agreement and ratification of the Constitution, he became King Aleksandar I of a Serb-dominated state.

The other nationalities resented Serbian domination of the Kingdom (known as Yugoslavia from 1929) and this added to the violence of the civil war, which erupted after the German invasion of 1941, during the Second World War. The royal family and the Government fled into exile and Serbia was partitioned between the Fascist Croatian state, Hungary and Bulgaria; the 'rump' Serbia was placed under German military administration. The occupation was fiercely resisted, however, the main Serbian group being the royalist Četniks (Yugoslav Army of the Fatherland). The Allied Powers finally gave their support to the Communist-dominated Partisans of Josip Broz (Tito). They declared King Petar II deposed, in 1944, and, after the War, Serbia became part of a federal Yugoslav state. Serbia was one of the constituent Republics of Communist Yugoslavia, but it included two autonomous regions, Kosovo and Vojvodina, which were also distinct units of the federation. Serbian territory was further restricted by the creation of a Macedonian Republic.

Serbia remained dissatisfied with the federal arrangement, as the two Autonomous Provinces were *de facto* republics, particularly after the adoption of a new Constitution in 1974. Serb nationalists complained that they did not receive their due weight of influence in Yugoslavia. Tito had supported the gradual decentralization of Yugoslavia, but Serb aspirations were placated by their domination of the Yugoslav People's Army (YPA) and of the Communist Party. After Tito's death, in 1981, and with rising tension in Kosovo, the Serbian authorities began to seek a rearrangement of the balance of power within the Republic and in the federation (for events in the Autonomous Provinces, see below). In May 1989 Slobodan Milošević became President of the republican State Presidency. A conservative Communist, he appealed to Serbian nationalism and granted some constitutional reforms. Thus, in November 1989, he secured his position by being re-elected President of the Presidency, in the first direct, secret ballot in Serbia since before the Second World War. On 9 December 1990 he was elected, with over 65% of the votes cast, as the sole President of Serbia, under the new Serbian Constitution. This Constitution made Serbia a Republic, rather than a Socialist Republic, and effectively removed the autonomy of Kosovo (which was renamed Kosovo-Metohija) and Vojvodina. It was approved by referendum in July 1990. The Constitution (which effectively gave Serbia control of three votes, instead of one, in the federal institutions) was not entirely in accordance with the federal Constitution, but Milošević was not challenged. Croatia and Slovenia pressed more urgently for a looser federation, but Serbia continued to veto proposals for reform and, instead, advocated more centralization. With the threat to the federation and the disintegration of the ruling League of Communists of Yugoslavia (LCY), co-operation between the Serbian leadership and the YPA increased. Ethnic tension increased and there were allegations that Milošević was in contact with the Serb minorities of Croatia and Bosnia-Herzegovina. Certainly this alliance of allegedly 'Greater Serbian' interests was evidenced during the civil war, which began in June 1991. The YPA's campaigns in Croatia and its manoeuvres in Bosnia-Herzegovina were cited as evidence of a conspiracy to secure the borders of a new state. Furthermore, with the support of the State Presidency members for Kosovo-Metohija, Vojvodina and Montenegro, Serbia took effective control of the 'rump' federal Presidency. By the end of 1991, however, there were signs that the YPA was not entirely satisfied with its role and the power of Milošević (there were proposals to transform the YPA into a Serbian national army).

Milošević and his Socialist Party of Serbia (founded in 1990 by the merging of the republican League of Communists and a Communist mass organization) had secured 194 of the 250 seats in the Serbian Assembly, in the elections of December 1990. The SPS had exploited nationalist sentiments, but their main opposition, the Serbian Renaissance Movement (SRM), was even more nationalist. In early 1991 the SRM leader, Vuk Drasković, emerged as the main figure in an anti-Communist alliance of opposition parties, which found increasing support on the streets of Belgrade. The initial demands concerned SPS control of the media, but these escalated during the course of the demonstrations. The riots and demonstrations, in March, caused a crisis in the federal Presidency, when it refused to endorse the imposition of a state of emergency. Serbia relented and the immediate pressure of the opposition abated and, with the onset of civil war, the SPS was again able to exploit the nationalism engendered by the conflict, although opposition criticism did not cease completely. Most of the major Serbian parties rejected the EC's peace proposals, tabled at The Hague, and dismissed threats of sanctions, which were imposed on Yugoslavia in October. In the international arena Serbia was widely to be primarily responsible for the civil war and, in December 1991, the EC sanctions were ended for all the Republics other than Serbia and Montenegro.

In domestic political affairs, the civil war of 1991 caused the postponement of local elections and a growing dissatisfaction with the SPS. Expressions of opposition remained difficult, with the press and broadcasting media under pressure from the ruling SPS, and allegations of intimidation against opponents. Some opposition figures were drafted and sent to the war front and, in November, there were raids by unidentified vandals on the offices of the anti-war movement, the independent television station and the Serbian branch of the Alliance of Reform Forces (federal prime minister Ante Marković's party). Economic problems were increasing, not helped by the EC sanctions, although the opposition remained divided and hindered by its own nationalist sympathies. A lack of leadership in the opposition was exemplified among the resurgent royalists, who had two claimants to the Karadjordjević throne (both of whom visited Belgrade in October). Milošević was also under pressure from his allies: the Serbs of Croatia and, to a lesser extent, of Bosnia-Herzegovina were less willing to compromise on plans for a Greater Serbia, demanding the escalation of the war; meanwhile, Montenegro was increasingly reluctant in its support, particularly following the imposition of EC sanctions.

The situation in Kosovo-Metohija (see below) continued to demand a massive commitment of policing resources and, in the Sandjak, the Muslims were increasingly dissatisfied at the erosion of minority security. On 26 October 1991, in a referendum, a majority of the Sandjak Muslims was claimed to have endorsed proposals for autonomy, despite the ballot being declared illegal by the republican authorities. In December a new Government was formed.

Recent Events in the Autonomous Provinces

The Autonomous Province of Kosovo-Metohija is populated by a large Albanian majority. The region is important historically to the Serbs and to the Albanians (the Albanian national revival began here, in 1878, with the foundation of the League of Prizren). The Serbs remain suspicious of ambitions for a 'Greater Albania' and have seldom tolerated nationalist aspirations. Between the First and Second World Wars the Serbian-dominated Yugoslav Kingdom encouraged settlement by Serb and Montenegrin peasants, but the Serb population has declined since then. Between 1971 and 1981 over 30,000 Serbs left the Province (then known simply as Kosovo), and there was further net emigration of Serbs in the 1980s. Under President Milošević, the Serbian Government again implemented policies designed to encourage resettlement of Kosovo-Metohija by ethnic Serbs, although there was little evidence to suggest that this was countering the effects of continuing Serb and Montenegrin emigration or the high birth rate among the Albanians.

The Albanians did achieve some national rights under the federal state, but Serbs and Montenegrins continued to dominate the provincial administration and the Communist apparatus until the fall of the Serb head of the security services, Aleksandar Ranković, in 1966. There were then demands for a Kosovo republic, and some concessions were granted to both the Autonomous Provinces by the federal authorities, in 1968. These rights were confirmed in the new Yugoslav Constitution of 1974. Dissatisfaction continued in Kosovo during the 1970s. The federal and Serbian authorities remained repressive of nationalist groups, accusing them of separatist sympathies. Certainly the Albanians of Kosovo were not culturally threatened and the leadership of the local League of Communists and provincial administration was predominantly ethnic Albanian. The main demand of the nationalists was for republican status.

In March and April 1981 there were nationalist riots in Kosovo, mainly in Priština, which were vigorously repressed after a state of emergency had been declared. The Communist authorities instituted a policy of 'differentiation', which involved the purging of any Party member or official who did not actively denounce the campaign for a seventh republic. During the early 1980s the main opposition groups were underground formations, advocating Albanian nationalist aims and an ostensibly Marxist-Leninist ideology. Between 1981 and 1990, according to the human-rights group, Amnesty International, over 7,000 Albanians were arrested and imprisoned in Kosovo, for nationalist activities.

This environment did not alleviate ethnic tensions and, from the mid-1980s, the rise of Serb nationalism caused a reaction. From 1985 the issue of Serb and Montenegrin emigration became of note in the Serbian media, with allegations of harassment by the Albanians. Kosovo, where demonstrations by the Kosovar Albanians continued throughout the early 1980s, was to be a major issue in the re-emergence of nationalist sentiment among the Serbs. In 1986 a large group of prominent Belgrade intellectuals petitioned the authorities about the situation in Kosovo and, by 1987, Serbian nationalists were regularly citing incidents of what was increasingly described as 'genocide'. A change in the leadership of the League of Communists of Serbia, notably the rise of Slobodan Milošević, was indicative of the increasingly nationalist mood of the Serbs. The 1974 Constitution was now perceived to be against Serbian interests and the new leadership sought to reduce the autonomy of the two Provinces. This alienated the ethnic Albanian Communist leadership of Kosovo, which had supported the 1974 settlement against demands for republican status, but would not support the destruction of that settlement.

In November 1988, under pressure from Serbia, the prominent Albanian politician, Azem Vlasi, resigned from the Kosovo politburo, causing widespread protests in the Province. In February 1989 he was dismissed from the Central Committee of the LCY, causing further protests in Kosovo. In March he was arrested, together with other Albanian leaders, and charged with 'counter-revolutionary' activities; their trial became a source of continuing tension, until their release, in April 1990. From February 1989 the YPA were policing the Albanian demonstrations, which were beginning to come into contact with Serb counter-demonstrations. The situation deteriorated in 1990 and, in March, Serbia assumed direct control of the Kosovo police force, causing the resignation of the Premier of Kosovo and, by May, of every ethnic Albanian member of the provincial Government. Despite some placatory gestures in April, the Serbians continued to take control of the key institutions from ethnic Albanians. In February the Slovenian Government ordered the withdrawal of its police contingents from Kosovo and, in April, the Croatians did likewise. Even Macedonia moved towards the withdrawal of its militia forces. The Kosovo Assembly's functioning was hindered by the inability of the Kosovars and the Serbs and Montenegrins to co-operate and by the interventions of the Serbian authorities.

The new Serbian Constitution of 1990 removed the remaining vestiges of autonomy from the two Provinces. On 20 June 1990 a large group of ethnic Albanian deputies in the Provincial Assembly (which consisted of 183 members) tried to hinder the passage of the proposed Constitution. Instead, they proposed a new provincial constitution, separating Kosovo from Serbia. The Serb President of the Assembly adjourned the session, giving a date of reconvening as 2 July, subsequently postponing it to 5 July and ordering the Assembly building to be locked until then. A Republic-wide referendum on the new Serbian Constitution, largely boycotted by the Albanians, was conducted on 1–2 July (it was formally promulgated on 28 September, from when Kosovo was known as the Autonomous Province of Kosovo and Metohija). On 2 July, however, the referendum result was rejected by 114 of the 123 ethnic Albanian deputies (an Assembly quorum was 111) and the alternative constitutional proposal adopted instead. On 5 July the Serbian authorities dissolved the provincial Assembly and Government. The Kosovo Presidency resigned in protest and Serbia introduced a special administration. By September some 15,000 ethnic Albanian officials had been dismissed

and measures limiting the number of Albanians in the education system had been implemented.

On 7 September 1990 about two-thirds of the deputies of the Kosovo Assembly met in secret in the town of Kačanik, in the south of the Province. They again declared Kosovo to be a Republic and adopted a constitution, but the outraged reaction of the Serbian authorities caused most of the participants to flee Serbia. The dependence of the provincial administration on central Serbian authority, however, was demonstrated in the federal constitutional crisis of March 1991. The Albanian member for Kosovo-Metohija on the federal State Presidency was dismissed by the Serbian Assembly on 16 March, to ensure the paralysis of the federal head of state, and, on 18 March, the functions of the Kosovo-Metohija Presidency were suspended. On 21 March, the crisis having been resolved, the Serbian Assembly restored the Kosovo-Metohija Presidency and appointed a new member of the federal Presidency. This action by Serbia, and alleged rights abuses in Kosovo-Metohija, however, was what the USA used to justify its termination of economic aid to Yugoslavia. Meanwhile the Kosovo Assembly-in-Exile, based in Zagreb, organized a referendum on independence, on 26–30 September, although it was banned by Serbia. On 19 October, citing overwhelming support for this in the referendum, the Assembly-in-Exile declared Kosovo to be a sovereign Republic. This was declared to be illegal by the Serbian authorities.

The other Autonomous Province, Vojvodina, was also affected by the changes in Serbia, although the ethnic Serb majority there made them less controversial. Vojvodina had originally been a Hungarian marcher territory or banate, in which the Habsburgs had settled other ethnic groups to defend Christendom against the Ottomans. In the 19th century the Habsburgs had created a province of Serbian Vojvodina, hoping to satisfy the aspirations of the Serb nationalists. Serbs had first settled there in 1690, when the so-called 30,000 Families, led by Patriarch Arsenije III Crnojević, had retreated from the Ottomans with the Habsburg armies, from Kosovo and Serbia proper. More Serbs had settled there at the end of the Second World War and they became the dominant ethnic group.

Until the late 1980s Vojvodina retained some provincial independence. In late 1989 demonstrations allegedly organized by the Milošević faction secured a Communist leadership sympathetic to the new Serbian leadership. The Hungarian Government expressed concern for the rights of the ethnic Hungarian minority, during 1990 and 1991. There are a great number of ethnic minorities in Vojvodina, all of which have political or social organizations to represent them. The largest is the Democratic Community of Vojvodina Hungarians (DCVH), which, unlike the Albanian parties of Kosovo, did not boycott the Serbian elections of December 1990 and secured representation in the new parliament. The former Communists remain in power, as in Inner Serbia.

Economy

The north of the Republic, particularly Vojvodina, is a rich agricultural region, where cereal crops are grown and livestock kept. Even in the more mountainous south there are forestry resources and good pasture-land. Vines are cultivated in the valleys. There are extensive mineral reserves, which are partially developed. Valuable deposits include copper, chrome, antimony, coal, lead and silver. Petroleum extraction, mainly in Vojvodina, satisfies some

20% of domestic demand. Industry has been developed since the Second World War, Belgrade and the Vojvodina being the main areas. The civil war, which began in June 1991, seriously affected the Serbian economy, with the average annual inflation reaching some 150%, wages being irregularly paid and severe shortages of goods. With the imposition of EC sanctions, in October (only on Serbia and Montenegro from December), the situation was unlikely to improve, although some economic results for the first nine months of the year were good: exports to the convertible-currency markets increased by 9.7%, compared to the same period in the year before; imports declined by about 2%; and there was a record harvest, some 20% larger than in the previous year. Economic losses totalled almost 24,000m. dinars, in the first six months of 1991, and industrial output declined by some 15%.

Directory
The Government
(January 1992)

STATE PRESIDENT

President of Serbia: SLOBODAN MILOŠEVIĆ (took office as President of the collective Presidency in May 1989 and re-elected, by direct ballot, in November 1989; elected as sole President on 9 December 1990).

Office of the President: 11000 Belgrade, Nemanjina 11.

EXECUTIVE COUNCIL

The Government consisted of members of the Socialist Party of Serbia and of those with no political affiliation.

President: Dr RADOMAN BOŽOVIĆ.

Vice-Presidents: SRBOLJUB VASOVIĆ, Dr ZORAN ARANDJELOVIĆ, Dr NEBOJSA MALKJOVIĆ.

Vice-President and Minister of Finance: JOVAN ZEBIĆ.

Vice-President and Minister of Mining and Energy: NIKOLA SAJNOVIČ.

Minister of Defence: Col-Gen. MARKO NOGOVANOVIĆ.

Minister of Internal Affairs: ZORAN SOKOLOVIĆ.

Minister of Foreign Affairs: VLADISLAV JOVANOVIĆ.

Minister of Foreign Economic Relations and Economic Development: SRDJAN SAVIĆ.

Minister of Justice: ZORAN CELKOVIĆ.

Minister of Agriculture, Forestry and Water Resources Management: Dr JAN KISGECI.

Minister of Urbanism, Housing-Communal Affairs and Construction: UROŠ BANJANIN.

Minister of Trade and Tourism: SAVA VLAJKOVIĆ.

Minister of Labour, Veterans and Social Security Affairs: BRANKA JEŠIĆ.

Minister of Science and Technology: Dr DIVNA TRAJKOVIĆ.

Minister of Education: DANILO Z. MARKOVIĆ.

Minister of Culture: MIODRAG DJUKIĆ.

Minister of Religious Affairs: DRAGAN DRAGOJLOVIĆ.

Minister of Information: MILIVEJO PAVLOVIĆ.

Minister of Health: NIKOLA MITROVIĆ.

Minister of Environmental Protection: Dr PAVLE TODOROVIĆ.

Minister of Youth Affairs and Sport: DRAGAN KIĆANOVIĆ.

Minister responsible for liaison with Serbs outside Serbia: STANKO CVIJAN.

MINISTRIES

Office of the Executive Council: Government of the Republic of Serbia, 1000 Belgrade, Nemanjina 11; tel. (11) 683166; fax (11) 682167.

Ministry of Agriculture, Forestry and Water Resources Management: 11000 Belgrade, Nemanjina 26; tel. (11) 658755; fax (11) 659146.

Ministry of Culture: 11000 Belgrade, Kneza Miloša 101; tel. (11) 645086; fax (11) 683854.

Ministry of Defence: 11000 Belgrade, Nemanjina 11; tel. (11) 685240; fax (11) 682167.

Ministry of Education: 11000 Belgrade, Nemanjina 22–26; tel. (11) 658324; fax (11) 683724.

Ministry of Environmental Protection: 11000 Belgrade Nemanjina 26; (11) 659547; fax (11) 642242.

Ministry of Finance: 11000 Belgrade, Nemanjina 11; tel. (11) 658883; fax (11) 6464363.

Ministry of Foreign Affairs: 11000 Belgrade, Nemanjina 22–26; tel. (11) 658755; fax (11) 683041.

Ministry of Foreign Economic Relations and Economic Development: 11000 Belgrade, Nemanjina 11; tel. (11) 683166; fax (11) 684793.

Ministry of Health: 11000 Belgrade, Nemanjina 22–26; tel. (11) 658755; fax (11) 642634.

Ministry of Industry: 11000 Belgrade, Nemanjina 22–26; (11) 658334; fax (11) 642681.

Ministry of Information: 11000 Belgrade, Nemanjina 26; tel. (11) 685755; fax (11) 685937.

Ministry of Internal Affairs: 11000 Belgrade, Kneza Miloša 103; tel. (11) 684266; fax (11) 641867.

Ministry of Justice: 11000 Belgrade, Nemanjina 26; tel. (11) 685755; fax (11) 659146.

Ministry of Labour, Veteran and Social Security Affairs: 11000 Belgrade, Nemanjina 22–26; tel. (11) 659547; fax (11) 682758.

Ministry of Mining and Energy: 11000 Belgrade, Nemanjina 22–26; tel. (11) 658755.

Ministry of Religious Affairs: 11000 Belgrade, Nemanjina 11; tel. (11) 682185; fax (11) 688841.

Ministry of Science and Technology: 11000 Belgrade, Nemanjina 26; tel. (11) 658324.

Ministry of Trade and Tourism: 11000 Belgrade, Nemanjina 22–26; tel. (11) 658755; fax (11) 642148.

Ministry of Traffic and Communications: 11000 Belgrade, Nemanjina 26; tel. (11) 661666; fax (11) 659379.

Ministry of Urbanism, Housing-Communal Affairs and Construction: 11000 Belgrade, Nemanjina 22–26; tel. (11) 659087; fax (11) 659055.

Ministry of Youth Affairs and Sport: 11000 Belgrade, Nemanjina 11; tel. (11) 659699; fax (11) 682167.

Ministry responsible for liaison with Serbs outside Serbia: 11000 Belgrade, Nemanjina 11; tel. (11) 683845.

Legislature
NATIONAL ASSEMBLY

President: ALEKSANDAR BAKOČEVIĆ; 11000 Belgrade, Maršala Tita 14; tel. (11) 322001; fax (11) 682850.

Elections, 9 and 23 December 1990

Party	Seats
Socialist Party of Serbia (SPS)	194
Serbian Renaissance Movement (SRM)	19
Democratic Community of Vojvodina Hungarians	8
Democratic Party	7
Party of Democratic Action of Serbia	3
Alliance of Reform Forces of Vojvodina	2
Serbian Alliance of Peasants Party	2
Others	15
Total	**250**

Note: The Constitution also provided for provincial Assemblies in the Autonomous Provinces of Kosovo-Metohija (dissolved in July 1990) and Vojvodina (Pres. DAMNJAN RADENKOVIĆ).

Local Government

Local government is based on the municipality or commune. Those in Inner Serbia are, in turn, grouped into nine administrative Districts, including the city of Belgrade. There are also two Autonomous Provinces, which are federal units of Yugoslavia. In 1990 between 110 and 120 deputies of the Kosovo (now Kosovo-Metohija) provincial Assembly rejected the Serbian constitutional reforms and their own body's dissolution and formed a 'Kosovo Assembly-in-Exile', which proclaimed Kosovo a Republic and formed its own interim Government. It was based in Zagreb. In

October 1991 the Slav Muslims of the Sandjak area voted for autonomy in a banned referendum.

AUTONOMOUS PROVINCES

Kosovo-Metohija: Priština; Presidency and Govt suspended by the Serbian Assembly.

Vojvodina: Novi Sad; Pres. of the Presidency JUGOSLAV KOSTIĆ; Pres. of the Provincial Govt (vacant).

'KOSOVO ASSEMBLY-IN-EXILE'

President of the Assembly: ILJAZ RAMAJLI.

President of the Provisional Government: Dr BUJAR BUKOSHI.

Political Organizations

Democratic Alliance of Kosovo (Demokratski Savez Kosovo—DSK): 38000 Priština; f. 1990 by dissidents and take-over of provincial brs of the Socialist Alliance of Working People; ethnic Albanian grouping; Chair. Dr IBRAHIM RUGOVA.

Democratic Community of Vojvodina Hungarians (VDMK): 21000 Novi Sad; f. 1990; supports interests of ethnic Hungarian minority in the Vojvodina; c. 20,000 mems; Pres. ANDRAS AGOSTAN.

Democratic Party (Demokratska stranka): 11000 Belgrade, Maršala Tita 14; nationalist; Leader DRAGOLJUB MIČUNOVIĆ.

Liberal Party: 11000 Belgrade; favours a free-market economy; Leader NIKOLA MILOŠEVIĆ.

Muslim Party of Democratic Reform: 11000 Belgrade; party of ethnic Muslims; left-wing.

Party of Democratic Action of Kosovo-Metohija (PDA-KM): Vitomirića; party of ethnic Muslims; affiliated to the PDA of Bosnia-Herzegovina; Chair. NUMAN BALIĆ.

Party of Democratic Action of the Sandjak (PDA-S): Novi Pazar; party of ethnic Muslims; affiliated to the PDA of Bosnia-Herzegovina; advocates autonomy for the Sandjak region; Chair. SULEJMAN UGLJANIN.

Serbian Alliance of Peasants' Party: 11000 Belgrade, Maršala Tita 14; Leader DRAGAN VESELINOV.

People's Party (Narodna Stranka): 11000 Belgrade, Maršala Tita 14; Leaders MILAN PAROSKI, DRAGOSLAV PETROVIČ.

Serbian Radical Party (Srpska Radikalna Stranka—SRS): 11000 Belgrade, Maršala Tita 14; right-wing; nationalist; armed br. supported war in Croatia in 1991; Leader Dr VOJISLAV SESELJ.

Serbian Renaissance Movement (SRM) (Srpski Pokret Obnove—SPO): 11000 Belgrade, Maršala Tita 14; right-wing; nationalist; Leader VUK DRASKOVIĆ.

Socialist Party of Serbia (SPS) (Socijalisticka Partija Srbije): 11000 Belgrade, Maršala Tita 14; f. 1990 by merger of League of Communists of Serbia and Socialist Alliance of the Working People (SAWP) of Serbia; Gen. Sec. PETAR SKUNDRIĆ.

Other political parties include the federal Alliance of Reform Forces (Vojvodina, Serbia and Kosovo branches), Social Democratic Party, the Peasant Democratic Party of Kosovo, the Albanian Democratic Christian Party and the Yugoslav Alliance of Ruthenians and Ukrainians.

Judicial System

All courts in Serbia are within the jurisdiction of the Ministry of Justice of the Republic. The Federal Court, also based in Belgrade, is the final court of appeal from the Supreme Courts of Serbia, Kosovo-Metohija and Vojvodina and the Supreme Military Court. Serbia also provides for economic courts, in certain cases.

Constitutional Court of the Republic of Serbia: 11000 Belgrade, Nemanjina 22–26; tel. (11) 658755; Pres. Dr BALŠA SPADIJER.

Supreme Court of Serbia: 11000 Belgrade, Nemanjina 22–26; tel. (11) 658755; Pres. CASLAV IGNJATOVIĆ.

Office of the Public Prosecutor of the Republic of Serbia: 11000 Belgrade, Nemanjina 22–26; tel. (11) 658755; Public Prosecutor MILOMIR JAKOVLJEVIĆ.

Provincial Secretariat of Justice for the AP of Kosovo-Metohija: 38000 Priština, ul. Zejnel Salihu br. 4; fax (38) 31929.

Provincial Secretariat of Justice for the AP of Vojvodina: 21000 Novi Sad, ul. bul. Maršala Tita br. 16; fax (21) 56672.

Religion

Most Serbs are adherents of the Serbian Orthodox Church (see federal Directory—Religion), and there are some other Orthodox groups. There is a Roman Catholic minority (mainly ethnic Albanians, but also some Croats and Hungarians) and some Protestant sects. Most Muslims of Serbia and its two Provinces are in Kosovo-Metohija and are ethnic Albanians. Most of the ethnic Slav Muslims are those of the Sandjak, in south-west Serbia. Serbian Islam is predominantly Sunni, although a Dervish sect, introduced in 1974, is popular among the Albanians (some 50,000 adherents, mainly in Kosovo-Metohija). The Republic constitutes the Priština Region of Yugoslav Islam. There are also some Jews.

Old Catholic Church in Serbia and Vojvodina: 11000 Belgrade; Dir of Bishop's Diocese JOVAN AJHINGER.

Islamic Community in the Republic of Serbia: 38000 Priština; Pres. of the Mesihat Dr REDZEP BOJE.

The Press

PRINCIPAL DAILIES
(In Serbo-Croat except where otherwise stated)

Belgrade

Borba: Belgrade, trg Marksa i Engelsa 7; tel. (11) 334531; telex 11104; fax (11) 344913; f. 1922; morning; Cyrillic/Roman; Dir MILAN RAKAS; circ. 59,800.

Newsday: 11001 Belgrade, Obiličev Venac 2, POB 439; f. 1983; Mon.–Fri; published in English by Tanjug and *Privredni Pregled*.

Politika: 11000 Belgrade, Makedonska 29; f. 1904; morning; non-party; Dir-Gen. ZIVORAD MINOVIĆ; Editor-in-Chief ALEXANDAR PRLJA; circ. 202,875.

Politika Ekspres: 11000 Belgrade, Makedonska 29; tel. (11) 325630; telex 11852; evening; Chief Editor SLOBODAN JOVANOVIĆ; circ. 219,542.

Privredni Pregled: 11000 Belgrade, M. Birjuzova 3; tel. (11) 182888; telex 11509; fax (11) 627591; f. 1950; the only economic daily in Yugoslavia; Dir and Chief Editor DUŠAN DJORDJEVIĆ; circ. 14,000.

Sport: 11000 Belgrade, trg Marksa i Engelsa 7; tel. (11) 333429; telex 12022; fax (11) 455862; f. 1945; Editor SLAVOLJUB VUKOVIĆ; circ. 100,000.

Večernje novosti: 11000 Belgrade, trg Marksa i Engelsa 7; tel. (11) 334531; telex 12200; fax (11) 344913; f. 1953; evening; Chief and Executive Editor RADISAV BRAJOVIĆ; circ. 312,000.

Niš

Narodne Novine: 18000 Niš, Vojvode Gojka 14; morning; Chief Editor LJUBIŠA SOKOLOVIĆ (acting); circ. 7,210.

Novi Sad

Dnevnik: 21000 Novi Sad, bul. 23; f. 1942 as *Slobodna Vojvodina*; morning; Editor-in-Chief DRAGAN RADEVIĆ; circ. 61,000.

Magyar Szó: 21000 Novi Sad, V. Mišića 1; f. 1944; morning; in Hungarian; Editor-in-Chief (vacant); circ. 25,590.

Priština

Jedinstvo: 38000 Priština, Maršala Tita 41; morning; Editor-in-Chief MILENKO JEVTOVIĆ; circ. 2,465.

Rilindja: 38000 Priština, Druga Zejnel Salihi 1; morning; in Albanian; Editor-in-Chief HILMI SULJA; circ. 32,512; banned by Serbian authorities, 1990.

Publishers

BIGZ—Beogradski izdavačko-grafički zavod: 11000 Belgrade, bul. vojvode Mišića 17; tel. (11) 651666; telex 11855; fax (11) 651841; f. 1831; literature and criticism, children's books, pocket books, popular science, philosophy, politics; Gen. Dir ILIJA RAPAIĆ.

Dečje novine: 32300 Gornji Milanovac, T. Matijevića 4; tel. (32) 711195; telex 13731; fax (32) 711248; general literature, children's books, science, science fiction, textbooks; Gen. Dir MIROSLAV PETROVIĆ.

Forum: Novinsko-izdavačka i štamparska radna organizacija, 21000 Novi Sad, Vojvode Mišića 1, POB 200; tel. (21) 611300; telex 14199; f. 1957; newspapers, periodicals and books in Hungarian; Dir BORDAS DEZE.

Gradjevinska Knjiga: 11000 Belgrade, trg Marksa i Engelsa 8/II; tel. (11) 333565; fax (11) 333565; f. 1948; technical, scientific and educational textbooks; Dir MILAN VIŠNJIĆ.

IP Matice Srpske: 21000 Novi Sad, trg heroja Toze Markovića 2; tel. (21) 615599; Yugoslav and foreign fiction and humanities; Dir DRAGOLJUB GAVARIĆ.

Medicinska knjiga: 11001 Belgrade, Mata Vidakovića 24–26; tel. (11) 458135; f. 1947; medicine, pharmacology, stomatology, veterinary; Dir MILE MEDIĆ.

Minerva: Izdavačko-štamparsko preduzeće, 24000 Subotica, trg 29 novembra 3; tel. (24) 25701; novels and general; Dir LADISLAV ŠEBEK.

Narodna Knjiga: 11000 Belgrade, Šafarikova 11; tel. (11) 328610; f. 1950; economics, scientific and popular literature, reference books, dictionaries; Dir RADOMIR NIKOLIĆ.

Naučna knjiga: 11000 Belgrade, Uzun Mirkova 5; tel. (11) 637230; f. 1947; school, college and university textbooks, publications of scientific bodies; Dir Dr BLAŽO PEROVIĆ.

Nolit: 11000 Belgrade, Terazije 27/II; tel. (11) 345017; fax (11) 627285; f. 1929; Yugoslav and other belles-lettres, philosophy and fine art; scientific and popular literature; Dir-Gen. RADIVOJE NEŠIĆ; Editor-in-Chief MILOS STAMBOLIĆ.

Proex: 11000 Belgrade, Terazije 16; tel. (11) 688563; fax (11) 641052; editorial and typographic co-productions; export and import of books and periodicals.

Prosveta: 11000 Belgrade, Čika Ljubina 1/I; tel. (11) 629843; f. 1944; general literature, art books, dictionaries, encyclopaedias, science, music; Dir BRANKA RISTIĆ.

Rad: 11000 Belgrade, M. Pijade 12; tel. (11) 339998; f. 1949; labour and labour relations, politics and economics, sociology, psychology, literature, biographies, science fiction; Man. Dir MILOVAN VLAHOVIĆ; Editor-in-Chief DRAGAN LAKIĆEVIĆ.

Rilindja: 38000 Priština, Dom štampe; tel. (38) 23868; telex 18163; popular science, literature, children's fiction and travel books, textbooks in Albanian; Dir NAZMI RRAHMANI.

Savremena administracija: 11000 Belgrade, Crnotravska 7–9; tel. (11) 663824; telex 11233; fax (11) 624095; f. 1954; economy, law, science university textbooks; Dir MILUTIN SRDIĆ.

Sportska Knjiga—IGRO: 11000 Belgrade, Makedonska 19; tel. (11) 320226; f. 1949; sport, chess, hobbies; Dir BORISLAV PETROVIĆ.

Srpska Književna Zadruga: 11000 Belgrade, Maršala Tita 19/I; tel. (11) 330305; f. 1892; works of classical and modern Yugoslav writers, and translations of works of foreign writers; Pres. RADOVAN SAMARDŽIĆ; Editor RADOVAN RADOVANAC.

Svetovi: 21000 Novi Sad, Arse Teodorovića 11; tel. (21) 28036; general; Dir JOVAN ZIVLAK.

Tehnička Knjiga: 11000 Belgrade, Vojvode Stepe 89; tel. (11) 468596; fax (11) 473442; f. 1948; technical works, popular science, reference books, 'how to' books, hobbies; Dir RADIVOJE GRBOVIĆ.

Vuk Karadžič: 11000 Belgrade, Kraljevića Marka 9, POB 762; tel. (11) 628066; fax (11) 623150; scientific literature, popular science, children's books, general; Gen. Man. VOJIN ANČIĆ.

Zavod za udžbenike i nastavna sredstva: 11000 Belgrade, Obilićev Venac 5/I; tel. (11) 335337; fax (11) 344075; f. 1958; textbooks and teaching aids; Dir TOMISLAV BOGAVAC.

Radio and Television

Radiotelevizija Beograd: 11000 Belgrade, Hilandarska 2; tel. (11) 346801; telex 11727; fax (11) 326768 (Radio); 11000 Belgrade, Takovska 10; tel. (11) 342001; telex 11884; fax (11) 543178 (TV); f. 1929 (Radio), 1958 (TV); 5 radio programmes, plus 1 experimental, and 3 TV programmes in Serbo-Croat; Dir-Gen. and Dir of TV DOBROSLAV BJELETIĆ; Dir of Radio NIKOLA MIRKOV.

Radiotelevizija Novi Sad: 21000 Novi Sad, Žarka Zrenjanina 3; tel. (21) 611588; telex 14127; fax (21) 26624 (Radio); 21000 Novi Sad, Kamenički put 45; tel. (21) 56855; telex 14303; fax (21) 52079 (TV); f. 1949 (Radio), 1975 (TV); 6 radio and 1 TV programme; broadcasts in Serbo-Croat, Slovak, Romanian, Hungarian and Ruthenian; Dir-Gen. and Dir of Radio MILAN LUČIĆ (acting); Dir of TV PETAR LJUBOJEV.

Radiotelevizija Priština: 38000 Priština, Maršala Tita bb; tel. (38) 26255; telex 18134; fax (38) 25355 (Radio); 38000 Priština, Zejnel Ajdini 12; tel. (38) 31211; telex 18186; fax (38) 32073 (TV); f. 1944 (Radio), 1975 (TV); 3 radio and 1 TV programme; broadcasts in Albanian, Serbo-Croat, Romany and Turkish; Dir-Gen. PETAR JAKŠIĆ; Dir of Radio MILORAD VUJOVIĆ; Dir of TV NIKOLA SARIĆ.

In November 1991 there were proposals to unite the three companies as a single RTV Serbia.

Finance

(d.d. = dioničko društvo (joint-stock company); cap. = capital; dep. = deposits; res = reserves; m. = million; amounts in dinars; * denotes figures in convertible dinars; br. = branch)

BANKS
National Bank

National Bank of Serbia: 11000 Belgrade, 7 jula 12; tel. (11) 625555; Gov. BORISLAV ATANACKOVIĆ.

Selected Banks

Beogradska Banka d.d., Beograd: 11001 Belgrade, Knez Mihajlova 2–4; tel. (11) 624455; telex 11712; f. 1978; total assets 264,439,882* (Sept. 1989); Man. Dir and Chief Exec. LJUBISA IGIĆ (acting).

Glavna filijala Beobanka, Beograd: 11000 Belgrade, Zeleni Venac 16; tel. (11) 629455; telex 11802; f. 1978; main br. within Beogradska Banka d.d., Belgrade; total assets 60,597.1m.* (Sept. 1989); Man. Dir and Chief Exec. PETAR VASILJEVIĆ (acting).

Glavna filijala Investbanka, Beograd: 11000 Belgrade, Terazije 7–9; tel. (11) 335201; telex 11147; f. 1862; main br. within Beogradska Banka d.d., Belgrade; total assets 83,499,532* (Sept. 1989); Man. Dir and Chief Exec. Dr STOJAN DABIĆ (acting).

Jugobanka d.d., Beograd: 11000 Belgrade, 7 Jula 19–21; tel. (11) 630022; telex 11610; fax (11) 635085; f. 1955 as Yugoslav Bank for Foreign Trade; name changed 1971; total assets 31,382,455m. (Dec. 1988); Gen. Man. and Pres. of Board MILOŠ MILOSAVLJEVIĆ.

Jugobanka d.d., Beograd, Jugobanka Beograd: 11000 Belgrade, Maršala Tita 11; tel. (11) 334931; telex 11280; f. 1956; total assets 4,019,740m. (Dec. 1988); Gen. Man. LJUBOMIR POTKONJAK.

Jugobanka d.d., Beograd, Jugobanka k.b. Beograd: 11000 Belgrade, Radivoja Koraća 6; tel. (11) 455666; telex 12133; fax (11) 458396; f. 1970 as br. of Sremska banka, joined Jugobanka 1977; total assets 3,500m.* (March 1991); Gen. Man. LJUBOMIR POTKONJAK.

Jugoslovenska izvozna i kreditna banka d.d. (Yugoslav Export & Credit Bank Inc.): 11000 Belgrade, Knez Mihailova 42, POB 234; tel. (11) 632822; telex 11350; fax (11) 430197; f. 1946; total assets 6,817.6m.* (Dec. 1990); Pres. MIODRAG PRICA.

Kosovo

Udružena Kosovska Banka (Kosovo Associated Bank): 38000 Priština, Maršala Tita 4; tel. (38) 34111; telex 18149; cap. 316,474.8m., res 112,184.5m., dep. 6,300,309.9m. (Dec. 1988); Pres. MUHAREM ISMAILJI.

Vojvodina

Privredna Banka d.d., Novi Sad: 21001 Novi Sad, Grčkoškolska broj 2; tel. (21) 26333; telex 14132; fax (21) 623025; f. 1956; total assets 34,563,604m. (Dec. 1989); Gen. Man. GOJKO BJELICA.

Vojvodjanska Banka, d.d.: 21001 Novi Sad, POB 391, bul. Maršala Tita 14; tel. (21) 57222; telex 14129; fax (21) 624940; f. 1978; cap. 22,008,375.3m., res 23,683,206.5m., dep. 248,572,989.8m. (Dec. 1989); Gen. Dir ZIVOTA MIHAJLOVIĆ.

STOCK EXCHANGE

Belgrade Stock Exchange: Belgrade; f. 1886, ceased operation 1941, reopened 1990.

Trade and Industry

Chamber of Economy of Serbia: 11000 Belgrade, Gen. Zdanova 13–15; tel. (11) 340611; fax (11) 330949; Pres. Dr MIHAJLO MILOJEVIĆ.

TRADE FAIRS

Belgrade Fair: Belgrade, Bulevar Vojvode Mišića 14, POB 408; tel. (11) 655555; telex 11306; fax (11) 688173; Internat. Technical Fair, annually in May; Internat. Motor Show, annually in April; Internat. Chemical Fair, annually in May; Internat. Clothing Fair 'Fashions in the World', annually in October; Internat. Book Fair, annually in October; Internat. Furniture Fair, annually in November; and other fairs; Pres. SINIŠA ZARIĆ.

Novi Sad: Novosadski Sajam, Novi Sad, Hajduk Veljkova 11; tel. (21) 25155; telex 14180; fax (21) 616121; Novi Sad Internat. Agricultural Fair, annually in May; Internat. Fair of Hunting, Fishing, Sports and Tourism, annually in October; Internat. Autumn Fair, annually in October; and other fairs; Dir-Gen. JOVAN NEŠIN.

MAJOR ENTERPRISES AND COMPANIES

Agrooprema: 11000 Belgrade, Balkanska 44; tel. (11) 658655; telex 11124; fax (11) 684842; manufacture of agricultural machinery, vehicles and chemicals, etc.; 1,100 employees.

Agrovojvodina: 21000 Novi Sad, bul. M. 17 Tita 6 VI; tel. (21) 21661; telex 14150; fax (21) 52068; wholesale and retail trade of agricultural machinery, construction equipment, chemicals, tools, etc.; Dir of Trade PETKO SEKULIĆ; 5,500 employees.

Beko: 11000 Belgrade, Donjogradski bul. 6–8; tel. (11) 620122; telex 11403; fax (11) 620847; produces and exports clothing; Gen Man. TOMAS ZUGIĆ; 5,058 employees.

Beocinaska Fabrika Cementa: 21300 Beocin, trg Ive Lole Ribara 1; tel. (21) 870030; telex 14161; f. 1839; cement manufacturer.

BIP—Unified Beer, Malt and Soft Drinks Industry: 11000 Belgrade, Bulevar Vojvode Putnika 5; tel. (11) 652322; telex 11880; brewing and soft drinks manufacture; 2,600 employees.

Centroprom: 11000 Belgrade, Knez Mihailova 20; tel. (11) 622730; telex 11971; fax (11) 624630; wholesale and retail trading; 7,322 employees.

Centrotextil: 11000 Belgrade, Knez Mihailova 1-3; tel. (11) 185333; telex 11150; fax (11) 630565; design, manufacture and sale of textiles, clothing, leather goods and footwear; 2,600 employees.

DMB—Dvadesetprvi Maj: 11090 Rakovica, Oslobodenja 1; tel. (11) 592111; telex 72718; fax (11) 593967; production of engines, transmissions and equipment; Dir-Gen. ALEKSANDAR LAKOVIĆ; 5,500 employees.

Fabrika Vagona-Kraljevo (FVK): 36000 Kraljevo, Industriska 27; tel. (36) 333455; telex 17625; fax (36) 339919; manufactures all types of freight wagons, tanks for transport of acids, etc; Gen. Dir TOMISLAV SIMOVIĆ; 3,100 employees.

F-KA Pumpi Jastrebac, Niš: 18000 Niš, 12 februara br. 82; tel. (18) 42047; telex 16237; fax (18) 42362; manufacture of pumps for all types of liquids and operations; Gen. Dir DRAGOSLAV MILUTINOVIĆ; 1,700 employees.

Galenika-Oour—Galenika Farmaceutsko-Hemijska Industrija: 11080 Zemun, Batajnicki Drum bb; tel. (11) 190810; telex 11289; fax (11) 199424; pharmaceutical and chemical production; 6,000 employees.

Genex—Generalexport: 11070 Belgrade, ul. Narodnih Heroja br. 43; tel. (11) 696992; telex 11228; fax (11) 609228; general trading internationally and in the execution of export-import business on a large scale; Gen. Dir MILORAD SAVICEVIĆ; 5,228 employees.

Gosa: 11420 Smederevska Palanka, Industrijska 70; tel. (26) 32022; telex 11684; design, production and assembly of vehicles and engineering equipment; 13,000 employees.

Gosa-Commerce: 11000 Belgrade, Kolarceva 8; tel. (11) 628337; telex 11568; fax (11) 650773; Pres. MOMIR PAVLICEVIĆ; 8,500 employees.

Hemijska Industrija, Pancevo (Pancevo Chemical Industry): 26000 Pancevo, Spoljnostarcevacka 80; tel. (13) 44122; telex 13124; engaged in the production of petrochemicals, inorganic chemicals, fine and special chemicals, etc.; 11,700 employees.

IHP Prahovo: 19330 Prahovo; tel. (19) 512551; telex 19138; fax (19) 513885; production of mineral fertilizers; Gen. Dir RADOMIR SLADOJEVIĆ; 3,400 employees.

Industrija Masina i Traktora—IMT: 11000 Belgrade, Novi Beograd, Tosin Bunar 268; tel. (11) 150747; telex 11518; manufacture of agricultural machinery; 13,500 employees.

Industrija Stakla, Pancevo: 26000 Pancevo, Prvomajska 10; tel. (13) 47255; telex 13266; fax (13) 47993; production of flat glass; Gen. Man. Dr VIDOMIR J. PAREŽANIN; 2,400 employees.

Industrija Kablova Svetozarevo Yugoslavia (Cables Manufacturing Industry of Svetozarevo): 35000 Svetozarevo; tel. (35) 221102; telex 17845; fax (35) 231446; Yugoslavia's largest cables manufacturer; 9,038 employees.

Industrija Kotrljajucih Lezaja—IKL: 11000 Belgrade, Kneza Danila 23-25; tel. (11) 331472; telex 12105; fax (11) 339417; manufacture of ball bearings; 2,400 employees.

Inex: 11000 Belgrade, Marta 69 ul. 27: tel. (11) 621149; telex 72963; import and export, manufacturing, tourism and transportation.

Istra—Fabrika Armatura Istra Deonicarsko Drustvo: 25230 Kula, ul. Ise Sekičkog 30; tel. (25) 722122; telex 15346; fax (25) 722173; manufactures sanitary fittings; Gen. Dir ROMODA DJORDJE; 1,500 employees.

Ites Lola Ribar: 25250 Odžaci, POB 5, Lola Ribar str. 40; tel. (25) 742113; telex 15336; fax (25) 742419; manufactures hemp yarn, twines, cordage and polypropylene products; Gen. Man. METODIJE KOSTIĆ; 1,500 employees.

Ivo Lola Ribar: 11000 Belgrade, bul. Revolucije 84; tel. (11) 4440884; telex 72788; fax (11) 431494; designs and manufactures drilling and milling machinery, industrial cranes and computers, etc; Gen. Dir STANOJE KONSTANTINOVIĆ; 9,500 employees.

Jugodent: 21000 Novi Sad, Futoski put 10; tel. (21) 394566; telex 14423; fax (21) 396365; produces dental equipment; Gen. Dir BRANKO ZMUKIĆ; 930 employees.

Jugopetrol: 11070 Belgrade, Milentija Popovića 66; tel. (11) 2223311; telex 12311; sale and distribution of petroleum derivatives.

Kolor Konfekcija Drustveno Preduzeće Konfekcija Kolor: 31230 Arile, Svetolika Lazarevića 22; tel. (31) 892461; telex 13665; fax (31) 891970; manufactures and exports clothing; Gen. Man. SLAVKO PAVLOVIĆ; 1,100 employees.

Komgrap—DP Komgrap Gradevinski Kombinat: 11000 Belgrade, Terazije 4; tel. (11) 688155; telex 118185; 7,858 employees.

Krusik Metalopreradjivacka Industrija: 14000 Valjevo, Beogradski put bb; tel. (14) 23121; telex 10232; manufactures textile machinery; 16,000 employees.

Lece: 16240 Medvedja, B. Stojanovića br. 1; tel. (16) 84020; telex 19745; fax (16) 84047; Gen. Dir RADOVAN MILLIOEVIĆ.

Leskoteks: 16000 Leskovac, AVNOJ-a 95; tel. (16) 43042; telex 19648; fax (16) 53364; manufacture of woollen fabrics and garments; Gen. Dir JELICA KOCIĆ; 9,550 employees.

Metalservis: 11000 Belgrade, POB 337, Karadjordjeva 65; tel. (11) 186333; telex 11546; fax (11) 626325; supplies tools, machines and equipment, building materials, electrical meterials, chemical products; Gen. Dir MILOVAN MILOŠEVIĆ; 1,140 employees.

Metalurski Kombinat Smederevo: 11300 Smederevo, Goranska 12; tel. (26) 23413; telex 11621; production of iron and steel; 10,300 employees.

Milan Blagojević: 32240 Lucani, Radnicka bb; tel. (32) 817100; telex 13715; fax (32) 818916; f. 1948 as manufacturer of defence products, has developed a chemical industry with a wide product assortment; Gen. Dir MILIJA JANKOVIĆ; 3,700 employees.

Miloje Zakić: 37000 Krusevac, Maršala Tita bb; tel. (37) 22328; telex 17454; fax (37) 23517; rubber processing, manufacture of industrial explosives and production of environmental protection equipment; 7,000 employees.

Minel: 11000 Belgrade, Cara Lazara br. 3; tel. (11) 181181; telex 11643; fax (11) 623566; produces thermal power equipment, electrical power equipment and food-processing facilities; Pres. MILOSAV FILIPOVIĆ; 13,000 employees.

Naftagas-Hip-Jugopetrol: 21000 Novi Sad, Sutjeska 1; tel. (21) 615144; telex 14196; f. 1990 by merger of 42 social enterprises, previously affiliated to 3 composite orgs of associated labour; petroleum and natural gas exploration and production in Yugoslavia and abroad; refines crude petroleum and natural gas, producing a variety of petroleum derivatives and associated products, incl. mineral fertilizers and synthetic rubber; also operates petrochemical and chemical plants; 36,000 employees.

Naftagas Promet: Novi Sad, bul. 23 Oktobra 27; tel. (21) 29682; telex 14130; fax (21) 614692; wholesale and retail distribution of petroleum products; Gen. Man. MLADEN MARKOVIĆ; 2,956 employees.

Pik-Bicej: 21220 Becej, Mose Pijade 2; tel. (21) 811180; fax (21) 812049; telex 14101; agricultural production, being one of Yugoslavia's largest producers of milk and meat; 4,500 employees.

PKB–Belgrade Agricultural Combine: Belgrade, 11213 Padinska Skela; tel. (11) 769181; telex 11457; fax (11) 754426; agricultural production, industrial production, catering and tourism; 36,000 employees.

Proleter: 23000 Zrenjanin, Temisvarski drum bb; tel. (23) 44210; telex 15518; fax (23) 49138; produces machine-woven carpets, machine-tufted carpets and yarn; Gen. Dir JOKO IVANCEVIĆ; 1,500 employees.

Prvi Maj: 18300 Pirot; tel. (10) 32255; telex 16810; fax (10) 35116; produces clothing and knitwear; Gen. Man. HRISTIVOJE KOSTIĆ; 6,000 employees.

Ratko Mitrović: 11000 Belgrade, Koste Glavinića 8; tel. (11) 650522; telex 11649; fax (11) 650356; design, construction, civil engineering and manufacture of building materials; 7,000 employees.

Reik Kolubara: 14220 Lazarevac, Slobonana Kozareva bb; tel. (11) 810226; telex 12840; mining of lignite coal (estimated production of 33m. metric tons in 1992); 15,500 employees.

Rudarsko Topionicarski Basen, Bor: 19210 Bor, Maršala Tita 29; tel. (30) 230252; telex 19204; fax (30) 34462; extraction and processing of copper, precious metals and minerals; manufacture of chemicals and provision of engineering services; 24,000 employees.

Servo Mihalj IPK: 23000 Zrenjanin, Petra Drapšina 1; tel. (23) 44410; telex 15511; primary agricultural production, food processing, chemicals and services; 21,893 employees.

Simpo: 17500 Vranje, Radnicka 6; tel. (17) 22280; telex 16766; fax (17) 24136; manufacturer and exporter of furniture, mattresses and decorative upholstery fabrics; Gen. Man. DRAGAN TOMIĆ; 5,000 employees.

Sintelon: 21400 Backa Palanka, Salas 1; tel. (21) 742012; telex 14122; fax (21) 742677; manufacture of PVC floor coverings and machine-woven carpets; 2,330 employees.

Sirmium: 22000 Sremska Mitrovića, trg Brace Radica 4; tel. (22) 221122; telex 15721; primary agriculture, food processing, trade, catering and tourism services; 21,000 employees.

Sloboda: 25230 Kula, Josipa Kramera 27; tel. (25) 722444; telex 15360; fax (25) 723620; produces textiles; Gen. Dir BORISA CALA-SAN; 1,100 employees.

Sport—Jugoslovenski Kombinat 'Sport': 11060 Belgrade, Visnijicka 84; tel. (11) 771333; telex 11850; fax (11) 782882; produces and sells sporting goods; Gen. Man. DRAGAN VOSTINIĆ; 1,950 employees.

Srbocoop: 11000 Belgrade, Sredacka 2A; tel. (11) 431657; telex 11702; meat processing; 1,200 employees.

Tamis: 26000 Pancevo, POB 116, trg Borisa Kidrića 6; tel. (13) 44999; telex 13113; primary agriculture and food processing; 13,000 employees.

Valjaonića Bakra i Aluminijuma 'Slobodan Penezić' (Krcun—Copper and Aluminium Rolling Mill): 31205 Sevojno; tel. (31) 21015; telex 13611; processing metal into products; 7,870 employees.

Viskoza Loznića: 15300 Loznića, Gradiliste bb; tel. (15) 82411; telex 101718; fax (15) 82047; production and processing of viscose fibres and foils; Pres. PAVLE DJOKIĆ; 10,386 employees.

Vojvodina: 22000 Sremska Mitrovića, Parobrodska ul. 2/I; tel. (22) 222284; telex 15701; forestry, processing of timber; manufacture of furniture, cellulose, paper; foreign trade; 14,000 employees.

Vrbas: 21460 Titov Vrbas, Maršala Tita 89; tel. (21) 701045; telex 14181; primary agricultural production, food processing, chemicals and trade; 14,780 employees.

Zastava SDP: 34000 Kragujevac, Spanskih boraca br. 4; tel. (34) 224011; telex (34) 215542; manufacture, sales and maintenance of passenger vehicles, lorries and firearms for hunting and sports use; Gen. Dir RADOLJUB MICIĆ; 52,161 employees.

Zavarivac: 11000 Belgrade, str. Brankova 23; tel. (11) 633125; telex 12247; fax (11) 620560; manufactures load-bearing steel structures, steel locks and specialist processing equipment for the petrochemical, chemical and food industries; Gen. Dir NOVIĆA JANKOVIĆ; 2,400 employees.

Zmaj Co: 11080 Zemun-Belgrade, Autoput 18; tel. (11) 600452; telex 11579; fax (11) 676867; production and development of agricultural machinery and equipment; Gen. Man. RADOSLAV MITROVIĆ; 4,200 employees.

Culture

REPUBLICAN ORGANIZATIONS

Ministry of Culture: see section on The Government (Ministries).

Cultural Centre of Novi Sad (Kulturni Centar grada Novog Sada): 21000 Novi Sad, Katolička porta 5; tel. (21) 25539; Dir DJORDJE KAĆANSKI.

CULTURAL HERITAGE

Art Gallery: 38000 Priština, POB 267; tel. (38) 27833.

Cvijeta Zuzorić Gallery: 11000 Belgrade, Mali Kalemegdan 1; tel. (11) 621585.

Ethnological Museum: 11000 Belgrade, Uzun Mirkova 2; tel. (11) 181888.

Museum of Applied Arts: 11000 Belgrade, Vuka Karadžića 18; tel. (11) 626494.

Museum of Contemporary Art: 11070 Belgrade, Novi Beograd, Ušće Save; tel. (11) 145500.

Museum of Vojvodina: 21000 Novi Sad, Dunavska 35; tel. (21) 26766.

National Museum: 11000 Belgrade, trg Republike 1A; tel. (11) 624734.

Serbian Society Gallery ('Matica Srpska' Galerija): 21000 Novi Sad, trg Proleterskih brig. 1; tel. (21) 24155.

PERFORMING ARTS

'Atelier 212' Theatre: 11000 Belgrade, Lole Ribara 21; tel. (11) 346731.

Belgrade Drama Theatre: 11000 Belgrade, Save Kovačevića 64A; tel. (11) 423183.

Bitef Theatre: 11000 Belgrade, Terazije 29/I; tel. (11) 343109.

National Theatre (Narodno Pozorište): 11000 Belgrade, Francuska 3; tel. (11) 622469; Dir of Drama (vacant); Dir of Opera KONSTANTIN VINAVER; Dir of Ballet BORE MARKOVIĆ.

National Theatre—Subotica: 24000 Subotica, Ive Vojnovića 2; tel. (24) 25507.

Provincial National Theatre (Pokrajinsko Narodno Pozorište): 38000 Priština, Maršala Tita 21; tel. (38) 22396.

Serbian National Theatre (Srpsko Narodno Pozorište): 21000 Novi Sad, Pozorišni trg 1; Drama: tel. (21) 621411; Opera and Ballet: tel. (21) 52399; Opera and Ballet Dir MLADEN SABLJIĆ.

Terazije Theatre: 11000 Belgrade, trg Marksa i Engelsa 3; tel. (11) 334037.

Ujvideki Szinhaz Theatre of Novi Sad: 21000 Novi Sad, Jovana Subotica 3–5; tel. (21) 622306.

Yugoslav Drama Theatre: 11000 Belgrade, Maršala Tita 50; tel. (11) 657766.

Zvezdara Theatre: 11000 Belgrade, bul. Revolucije 77A; tel. (11) 422170.

Music

Belgrade Opera Orchestra (Orkestar Beogradske opere): 11000 Belgrade, trg Republike 1; tel. (11) 615085; Conductors ANTON KOLAR, NIKOLAJ ŽLIČAR.

Belgrade Philharmonic Orchestra (Beogradska Filharmonija): 11000 Belgrade, Studentski trg 11; tel. (11) 635518; Chief Conductor VASILIJ SINAIJSKI.

Collegium Musicum Choir ('Collegium Musicum' hor): c/o Fakultet muzičke umetnosti, 11000 Belgrade, Maršala Tita 50; tel. (11) 642414; Chief Conductor DARINKA MATIĆ MAROVIĆ.

Dušan Skovran Chamber Orchestra (Kamerni orkestar 'Dušan Skovran'): c/o Jugokoncert, 11000 Belgrade, Terazije 4/I; tel. (11) 339916; Chief Conductor ALEKSANDAR PAVLOVIĆ.

Jugokoncert: 11000 Belgrade, Terazije 41/I; tel. (11) 339916; Dir EDUARD ILLE.

Marković Jazz Sextet (Jazz sekstet Marković/Gut): c/o RTV Beograd, 11000 Belgrade, Hilandarska 2; tel. (11) 346801.

Niš Symphony Orchestra (Niški Sinfonijski Orkestar): 18000 Niš, Stanka Paunovića 16a; tel. (18) 23047; Chief Conductor DEJAN SAVIĆ.

Pro Musica Chamber Orchestra (Kamerni Orkestar 'Pro Musica'): c/o Djura Jakšić, 11000 Belgrade, Požeška 92; tel. (11) 552580; Conductor DJURA JAKŠIĆ.

Radio-television Belgrade (RTV Belgrade) Jazz Band (Jazz orkestar RTV Beograd): 11000 Belgrade, Hilandarska 2; tel. (11) 346801; Conductors VOJISLAV SIMIĆ, ŽVONIMIR SKERL.

RTV Belgrade Mixed Choir (Mešoviti hor RTV Beograd): 11000 Belgrade, Hilandarska 2, tel. (11) 346801; Chief Conductor VLADIMIR KRANJČEVIĆ.

RTV Belgrade Symphony Orchestra (Simfonijski orkestar RTV Beograd): 11000 Belgrade, Hilandarska 2; tel. (11) 346801; Conductor VANCO CAVDARSKI.

RTV Novi Sad Big Band (Plesni orkestar RTV Novi Sad): 21000 Novi Sad, Žarka Žrenjanina 3; tel. (21) 611588; Chief Conductor RUDOLF TOMŠIĆ.

Renaissance Ensemble of Ancient Music (Ansambl stare muzike 'Renesans'): c/o Zorž Grujić, 11000 Belgrade, Kneza od Semberije 16; tel. (11) 440476.

Yugoslav People's Army (YPA) Choir (Hor JNA): Dom JNA, 11000 Belgrade, Braće Jugovića 19; tel. (11) 339551; Conductor DJORDJE MINOV.

YPA Symphony Orchestra (Sinfonijski orkestar umetničkog ansambla JNA): Dom JNA, 11000 Belgrade, Braće Jugovića 19; tel. (11) 339551; Chief Conductor MAJOR ILIJA ILIJEVSKI.

ASSOCIATIONS

Historical Society of Serbia: Faculty of Philosophy, 11000 Belgrade, Čika Ljubina 18–20; f. 1948; Pres. Prof. Dr LJUMBOMIR MAKSIMOVIĆ.

Roma Union of Serbia (Društva Rom Srpska): 11000 Belgrade; f. 1930; federation of some 60 local asscns; Pres. SAIT BALIĆ.

Serbian Literary Association (Srpska književna zadruga): 11000 Belgrade, Maršala Tita 19/I; tel. (11) 330305; f. 1892; Sec.-Gen. RADIVOJE KONSTANTINOVIĆ.

Serbian PEN Centre: 11000 Belgrade, Francuska 7; f. 1926, reformed 1962; Sec. KOSTA ČAVOŠKI.

Serbian Society (Matica srpska): 21000 Novi Sad, ul. Matice srpske 1; f. 1826; Sec. DUŠAN POPOV.

Society of Serbian Language and Literature (Društvo za srpski jezik i književnost): Belgrade University, 11000 Belgrade, Studentski trg 1; f. 1910; Sec. D. PAVLOVIĆ.

The Environment

GOVERNMENT ORGANIZATIONS

Ministry of Environmental Protection: see section on The Government (Ministries).

Hydro-Meteorological Institute of Serbia (Hidrometeoroloski zavod Srbije): 11000 Belgrade, Kneza Visleslava 66; responsibilities incl. ecological studies, pollution monitoring; Dir NIKOLA DUTINA.

Most environmental bodies are listed in the federal Directory section.

Defence

The Yugoslav People's Army (YPA) is responsible for the defence of the Republic of Serbia. The First Military District of the YPA is based in Belgrade. The officer corps is dominated by those of Serb ethnicity. In other of the Yugoslav Republics there have been allegations that the YPA was being used, during 1991, as a Serbian army. The YPA, however, is constitutionally charged with the preservation of the federation and there have been Serbian proposals to create a Serbian national army. The Serbians and other Serbs, and the Montenegrins, have been the most loyal supporters of the YPA.

SLOVENIA

Geography

The Republic of Slovenia is a constituent partner in the Socialist Federal Republic of Yugoslavia. The Republic lies in the north-west of that country. On 25 June 1991 Slovenia announced that it had begun a process of dissociation from the federation and, on 8 June, independence was declared. It assumed control of its borders, declaring them all to be international borders, although previously it had only had such frontiers with Italy in the west, Austria to the north and, along a short border in the east, with Hungary. Its southern border is with Croatia. In the south-west of the Republic there is a short coastal strip, on the Istrian Peninsular, to the south of the Italian city of Trieste, around the port of Koper.

Slovenia is an Alpine area, being dominated by the Julian and Karawanken Alps. Most of the territory is mountainous, the main areas of lower land being in the south-west, near the coast, in the central southern areas, along the Sava river, and in the east, where Slovenia reaches a narrowing strip of territory towards the Pannonian plains. The river valleys and *karst* lands of the Adriatic contribute to the agricultural territory and there is considerable woodland.

At the census of March 1991, the total population of Slovenia was 1,974,839, which gave it a population density of 97.5 per sq km. Most of the population were ethnic Slovenes (90.5% in 1981) and most of Yugoslavia's Slovenes (91.7%) reside in the Republic. There are also Slovene communities in Austria and Italy. The official language is Slovene, a Southern Slavonic tongue, related to but distinct from Serbo-Croat. The traditional religion of the Slovenes is Christianity, as practised by the Roman Catholic Church, to which most of the population adhere. There are small communities of other Christian denominations, including Eastern Orthodox Christians, of Muslims (mainly guest workers) and Jews. The capital of Slovenia is Ljubljana, the five communes which comprise it having a total population of 323,291, according to the 1991 census. It is located in the centre-west of the Republic. Other important towns include Maribor (153,053 in 1991), Kranj (72,814), Ptuj (68,846) and Celje (66,443).

History

The Slovenes settled in the area of the modern Republic during the fifth century AD. Their territory was, nominally, part of the Roman Empire, although actual jurisdiction had been variously exercised by the Western and Eastern Emperors or the 'barbarian' kingdoms, such as that of the Ostrogoths. The ascendancy of Western influence was established by the conversion of the Slovenes to Christianity after the missionary activity of the Church in Salzburg, which owed allegiance to the Roman pontiff. In political terms this was confirmed by the Treaty of Aix-la-Chapelle (Aachen), in 812. By this agreement, the Eastern Roman Emperor, Michael I, acknowledged the Frankish ruler, Charles the Great, or Charlemagne, as Emperor in the West. The German-dominated Holy Roman Empire became the main power in the Slovene lands (Frankish rule had been established first in the eighth century, with the marches of Friuli and Carinthia), although Byzantine influence remained in Istria and along the Adriatic coast to the south. The Slovenes were ruled by the dukes of Carinthia (based to the north, mainly in Austria) and Carniola, with some of the western regions remaining under the overlordship of Aquileia (Trieste). The territories had some independence in the ninth century, but were within the traditional borders of the Holy Roman Empire until its demise in the 19th century. They then remained part of the Habsburg Austrian Empire, having become hereditary possessions of the House of Habsburg, in the 14th century. The main interruptions to this domination were: in the late 15th century, when the Hungarian kingdom temporarily conquered the Habsburg lands; in the Reformation when, at the end of the 16th century, Calvinist sects were established in Carinthia and Carniola (they were suppressed, but their use of the vernacular laid the basis of the Slovene literary language); and in the Napoleonic wars, at the beginning of the 19th century, when there was a period of French rule over the Slovenes.

From 1867 the Habsburg realm was organized as the Dual Monarchy of Austria-Hungary. The Slovenes fell, therefore, under the jurisdiction of the Austrian Crown, in Cisleithania. They did not have a single territory, but were found in four of the 15 crownlands: Carniola, where they constituted a majority; Carinthia; Styria; and the Coastal Lands around Trieste. They were sympathetic to the 'Trialist' demands for a Slav element to be added to the division of power in the Dual Monarchy, but increasingly sympathized with the Southern Slav movement. Thus, during the First World War, the Slovenes were represented at the 1917 meeting which resolved on a Southern Slav state under the Serbian monarchy. Habsburg rule collapsed in October 1918 and, on 4 December, the Kingdom of Serbs, Croats and Slovenes was proclaimed. Carniola and parts of Carinthia, Styria and the Coastal Lands were subsequently ceded to the new state (known as Yugoslavia from 1929). These ancient borders did not lose their significance, however: during the Second World War, Germany claimed and annexed Lower Styria and Yugoslav Carinthia, while Italy annexed Istria and the territory around Ljubljana (Laibach); after the War, there was a continuing dispute with Italy over Istria (in 1954 Italy was awarded the city of Trieste and Yugoslavia the remainder of the territory—it is this settlement that gave Slovenia a coast); and, in 1991, the Austrian province of Carinthia protested at Slovenia's adoption, as a symbol on its new currency, of the coronation stone of the dukes of Carinthia. After the Second World War Slovenia became one of the constituent Republics of federal Yugoslavia.

Suspicion of Serb domination, common to most of the other Yugoslav ethnic groups, was exacerbated for the Slovenes by the prosperity of their Republic in relation to the rest of Yugoslavia. Separatist sympathies were reinforced by the resurgence of Serbian nationalism, particularly the situation in Kosovo. The ruling Communists in Slovenia were liberal, had a good human-rights record and supported the move towards the assertion of Slovenian nationalism. On 27 September 1989 the Slovenian Assembly overwhelmingly adopted a resolution confirming the Republic's sovereignty and explicitly declaring its right to secede. This act and Slovenian sympathy for the Kosovars caused the Serbian leader, Slobodan Milošević, to attempt to arrange demonstrations against the leadership of Slovenia (as he had done in Vojvodina and Montenegro). The demonstration, planned for December, was banned in November. Milošević retaliated by urging an economic boycott of Slovenian enterprises. Furthermore, the disintegration of the Communist system was witnessing the rise of opposition parties. Six of the main parties formed a coalition called the Democratic Opposition of Slovenia (DEMOS), in December, proposing economic sovereignty. The republican League of Communists retained some popular support, however, by advocating nationalist policies as well. In January 1990 the Slovenian delegation withdrew from the Extraordinary Congress of the League of Communists of Yugoslavia (LCY), after the rejection of their proposals to reform the federal Party. The League of Communists of Slovenia suspended its links with the LCY, withdrawing in February and changing its name to the League of Communists of Slovenia-Party of Democratic Reform (LCS-PDR). In March the formal designation of Slovenia was changed from 'Socialist Republic' to 'Republic'. Thus, at the elections of April 1990, despite DEMOS winning a majority in the republican Assembly, the leader of the LCS-PDR, Milan Kučan, was elected President of the State Presidency (defeating the DEMOS leader in the second round of voting). DEMOS formed a coalition Government.

On 2 July 1990 the Slovenian Assembly, by 187 votes to three (out of a total of 240), declared the sovereignty of the Republic and resolved that republican laws should take precedence over federal laws. The Assembly confirmed this by an amendment to the republican Constitution, on 27 September, and assumed control over the local Territorial Defence. This brought Slovenia into direct confrontation with the Serb-dominated Yugoslav People's Army (YPA), which considered itself the preserver of the federal order and had been concerned at Slovenia's earlier actions. The YPA attempted to reassert its authority by the confiscation of weapons and the seizure of the Territorial Defence headquarters. Slovenian and Croatian proposals to reform the Yugoslav federation were rejected and Serbia imposed economic barriers to the Republics' goods. Slovenia continued its secessionist course, however, conducting a plebiscite on whether the Republic should be an independent state. On 23 December such a move was supported by some 89% of the votes cast, in a referendum in which almost 94% of the population of Slovenia participated.

In 1991 tensions between the YPA and the Slovenian authorities continued, although a Slovenian armed unit was formed and trained. Friendship and military co-operation treaties were concluded with Croatia. However, the Republic expressed willingness to consider a looser federation, even after approving a programme for 'dissociation' from the federation, in February. Following the Serbian-led crisis in the federal State Presidency, in March, the Slovenian Government became more resolved on separation from the Yugoslav state. In May Slovenia declared its intention to secede before the end of June that year. Serbia and its allies then effectively blocked the election of a Croat as President of the federal Presidency and Slovenia adopted legislation enabling its eventual assumption of independence, including the establishment of a Slovenian Territorial Army. Slovenia attempted to take control of the collection of customs, which increased friction with the federal authorities, and refused to discontinue its programme towards dissociation.

On 25 June 1991 the Slovenian Assembly declared the sovereignty and independence of the Republic. Croatia also made a similar move, but the immediate federal reaction was against Slovenia. On 27 June the YPA mobilized, with the support of the Federal Government, in the absence of the State Presidency. The YPA declared its intention to

be in accordance with its constitutional duty to secure the international borders and the observance of internal peace. All the Slovenian airports were closed. There was some sporadic fighting, which attracted the intervention of the EC which attempted to arrange a cease-fire. On 2 July there was an aerial bombardment of Ljubljana, the first of a European city since the Second World War. However, on the same day, the Slovenian Government agreed to the implementation of the EC cease-fire and the YPA, which had not fared well in the fighting, began its withdrawal from Slovenia on 3 July. The Slovenian forces had adopted guerrilla tactics and a strategy of besieging YPA barracks (the Croatians achieved some success with such policies, but not until much later in the civil war). By 26 October all YPA units had withdrawn from the territory of Slovenia, which had proclaimed its full independence on 8 October (following the expiry of the EC-agreed moratorium on dissociation). The federal authorities had seemingly accepted the secession of the homogeneous border Republic. Furthermore, although Slovenia took part in The Hague peace conference, the republican leadership was less willing to participate in any future Yugoslav structure, preferring to foster its links with Austria and Germany.

On 8 October 1991, Slovenia's Independence Day, the Republic introduced its new currency, the tolar, and recalled all its citizens in federal institutions. The coalition Government, however, was experiencing increasing problems in functioning as the struggle for independence became less of a unifying factor. Later in October the Slovenian Democratic Union, one of the larger and most influential of the DEMOS parties, split into two factions, both of which remained in the coalition. The SDU was the first opposition party in Slovenia since the Second World War and, therefore, contained a disparate membership with often conflicting political views. A minority liberal wing remained loyal to the Minister of Foreign Affairs, Dr Dimitrij Rupel, who was elected leader of the new Democratic Party of Slovenia. The majority of the parliamentary delegates supported a more right-wing programme, adding the name of the National Democratic Party, and electing the Minister of Justice and Administration, Dr Rajko Pirnat, as leader. The continued stability of the Government was consequently undermined, and, at the end of December, the coalition acknowledged its split and scheduled elections for April or May 1992.

Economy

Slovenia was the wealthiest of the Yugoslav Republics, accounting for some 20% of the SFRY's gross national product (GNP) and almost 30% of exports, although it has only 8.4% of the population. The economy was, however, severely affected by Serbian sanctions and the civil war of 1991. Disruption was compounded by the process of dissociation (federal government controlled some 80% of the economy) and moves such as the introduction of the Slovenian currency, the tolar (SLT). The Republic has a balanced economy, with a varied agricultural sector (producing cereals, sugar beets, potatoes and timber, and raising livestock), exploitable mineral resources (lignite, lead, mercury), an established industrial base (including a textile industry and manufacturing of motor vehicles, steel, etc.) and a strong services sector (tourism, banking, trade). However, most sectors were undergoing severe problems. There is need for fundamental agrarian reform. The Communist legacy of central planning has been blamed for many of the economic woes, particularly in industry. Financial services were complicated by the new tolar (although the

Government claimed that this would protect Slovenia from the worst excesses of the Yugoslav inflation rate) and the lack of international recognition for Slovenia. This problem was also evident in the transport sector; the national carrier, Adria Airways, which had operated from Klagenfurt, in Austria, after the declaration of independence, was prevented from operating by the internationally recognized federal aviation authorities, in October 1991. Tourism, which accounted for an estimated 12% of GNP in 1990, virtually ceased to function following the crises of 1991. Considerable resources were likely to be necessary to restore and then reform the Slovenian economy, which had been flourishing until 1989. Unemployment had risen by 80%, to over 50,000, even by November 1990 and, of the working population, over 40% were reported to be employed in loss-making enterprises. By October 1991 the total of registered unemployed had risen to some 80,000, and the number was expected to double over the next two years.

Directory
The Constitution

Slovenia, then the Socialist Republic of Slovenia, first affirmed its sovereignty and its right to secede from the SFRY in September 1989. The Assembly proclaimed the full sovereignty of the Republic in July 1990 and, in December, a referendum endorsed independence proposals. On 20 February 1991 the Assembly initiated a programme of disengagement from the SFRY and, on 25 June, declared the Republic to be a sovereign state, in the process of 'dissociation' from the Yugoslav federation. On 8 October independence was declared to have taken effect. Recognition from the international community was accorded in January 1992.

A new Constitution for the Republic of Slovenia was enacted by the Assembly in December 1991. It provided for a bicameral legislature, to which elections were scheduled for April or May 1992. The previous Constitution, with its amendments and subsidiary legislation, provided for a tricameral, 240-seat legislative Assembly, to which the Executive Council or Government was responsible. Basic human rights and the independence of the judiciary were assured. The Assembly consisted of three Chambers, each with 80 members: the Socio-Political Chamber, in which parties were accorded seats according to the proportion of votes received in an election; the Chamber of Communes or Municipalities, to which members were elected by a majority of votes in a territorial constituency (two rounds of voting); and the Chamber of Associated Labour, to which working people elected representatives of different economic branches and organizations (the highest percentage of votes, in two rounds of voting). The three Chambers must all review and agree to legislative proposals before they are enacted, although sometimes the members of the three Chambers sit as a single Assembly in order to pass laws. The Executive Council or Government of the Republic of Slovenia, presided over by the republican Premier or Prime Minister, is responsible to the Assembly and nominated by the State Presidency. The State Presidency, the republican head of state, is an elective body, with five members, including the President of the Presidency. If one candidate does not win an overall majority of the valid votes cast, the two candidates with the most votes contest a second round of elections.

The Government
(January 1992)

The Republic of Slovenia is governed by a coalition, dominated by members of the Democratic Opposition of Slovenia (DEMOS) electoral alliance, which, since October 1991, has consisted of seven parties: two factions of the Slovenian Democratic Union, the National Democratic Party (NDP) and the Democratic Party of Slovenia (DPS); the Social Democratic Party of Slovenia (SDPS); the Slovenian Christian Democrats (SCD); the Slovenian Farmers' Association-People's Party (SFA-PP); the Greens of Slovenia; and the Liberal Party (LP). In December DEMOS was dissolved, although the existing Government was expected to continue until the 1992 elections. Although DEMOS won the parliamentary elections, in April 1990, it was the leader of the Party of Democratic Reform (PDR—former Communists) who was elected President of

the State Presidency, and the PDR also has members in the Government. There are also several independent members.

STATE PRESIDENCY

President of the Presidency: MILAN KUČAN (PDR).

Other Members: Dr MATJAŽ KMECI (PDR), IVAN OMAN (SFA-PP), Dr DUŠAN PLUT (Greens), CIRIL ZLOBEC (Socialist Party of Slovenia).

Office of the Presidency: 61000 Ljubljana, Erjavčeva 17; tel. (61) 224250.

EXECUTIVE COUNCIL

President (Premier): LOJZE PETERLE (SCD).

Vice-President responsible for Social Services: MATIJA MALESIČ.

Vice-President responsible for the Economy: ANDREJ OCVIRK (SDPS).

Vice-President responsible for Environmental Protection and Regional Development: LEO SEŠERKO (Greens).

Minister of Finance: DUŠAN ŠEŠOK.

Minister of Defence: JANEZ JANŠA (NDP).

Minister of Interior Affairs: IGOR BAVČAR (DPS).

Minister of Justice and Administration: RAJKO PIRNAT (NDP).

Minister of Labour: JOŽICA PUHAR.

Minister of Planning: IGOR UMEK.

Minister of Information: JELKO KACIN.

Minister of Legislation: LOJZE JANKO.

Minister of Environmental Protection and Physical Planning: MIHA JAZBINŠEK (Greens).

Minister of Foreign Affairs: DIMITRIJ RUPEL (DPS).

Minister of Energy: MIHA TOMŠIČ (PDR).

Minister of Industry and the Construction Industry: IZIDOR REJC (SCD).

Minister of Trade: MAKS BASTL (SCD).

Minister of Tourism and Catering: INGO PAŠ (LP).

Minister of Small-Scale Industry: VIKTOR BREZAR (LP).

Minister of Agriculture, Forestry and Foods: JOŽE OSTERC (SFA-PP).

Minister of Transport and Communications: MARJAN KRAJNC (SDPS).

Minister of Veterans and Disabled Veterans: FRANC GODEŠA (PDR).

Minister of Health, Family Affairs and Social Security: Dr VOLC.

Minister of Education and Sports: PETER VENCELJ (SCD).

Minister of Culture: ANDREJ CAPUDER (SCD).

Minister of Science and Technology: PETER TANCIG (Greens).

Minister responsible for Slovenes in the Diaspora and for Minorities in Slovenia: Dr JANEZ DULAR.

MINISTRIES

Office of the Executive Council: 61000 Ljubljana, Prešemova st. 8; tel. (61) 210552.

Ministry of Agriculture, Forestry and Foods: 61000 Ljubljana, Parmova st. 33; tel. (61) 323643.

Ministry of Culture: 61000 Ljubljana, Vankarjeva st. 5; tel. (61) 214122; fax (61) 210872.

Ministry of Defence: 61000 Ljubljana, Županvičeva st. 3; tel. (61) 223112; fax (61) 213839.

Ministry of Education and Sports: 61000 Ljubljana, Župančičeva st. 6; tel. 331411.

Ministry of Energy: 61000 Ljubljana, Gregorčičeva st. 25; tel. (61) 224141.

Ministry of Environmental Protection and Physical Planning: 61000 Ljubljana, Župančičeva st. 19; tel. (61) 331411.

Ministry of Finance: 61000 Ljubljana, Župančičeva st. 3; tel. (61) 223112.

Ministry of Foreign Affairs: 61000 Ljubljana, Gregorčičeva st. 25; tel. (61) 224141.

Ministry of Health, Family Affairs and Social Security: 61000 Ljubljana, Kidričeva st. 5; tel. (61) 211628.

Ministry of Industry and the Construction Industry: 61000 Ljubljana, Gregorčičeva st. 25; tel. (61) 224141.

Ministry of Information: 61000 Ljubljana, Levstikova st. 10; tel. (61) 215611; fax (61) 212312.

Ministry of Interior Affairs: 61000 Ljubljana, Kidričeva st. 2; tel. (61) 325361.

Ministry of Justice and Administration: 61000 Ljubljana, Župančičeva st. 3; tel. (61) 223113; fax (61) 210200.

Ministry of Labour: 61000 Ljubljana, Levstikova st. 15; tel. (61) 224844.

Ministry of Legislation: 61000 Ljubljana, Kardeljeva cesta st. 25; tel. (61) 217611.

Ministry of Planning: 61000 Ljubljana, Gregorčičeva st. 25; tel. (61) 224114.

Ministry of Science and Technology: 61000 Ljubljana, Cankarjeva st. 5; tel. (61) 210978.

Ministry of Small-Scale Industry: 61000 Ljubljana, Kidričeva st. 5; tel. (61) 218872.

Ministry of Tourism and Catering: 61000 Ljubljana, Prežihova st. 3; tel. (61) 221643; fax (61) 219401.

Ministry of Trade: 61000 Ljubljana, Prešemova st. 27; tel. (61) 224313.

Ministry of Transport and Communications: 61000 Ljubljana, Prešemova st. 23; tel. (61) 218712.

Ministry of Veterans and Disabled Veterans: 61000 Ljubljana, Župančičeva st. 6; tel. (61) 221120.

Ministry responsible for Slovenes in the Diaspora and Minorities in Slovenia: 61000 Ljubljana, Gregorčičeva st. 27; tel. (61) 224352.

Legislature

NATIONAL ASSEMBLY

President: Dr FRANCE BUČAR (SDU); 61000 Ljubljana, Šubičeva st. 4; tel. (61) 217123.

The Assembly consists of three Chambers, each with 80 members: the Socio-Political Chamber; the Chamber of Communes; and the Chamber of Associated Labour.

Elections, 8 and 22 April 1990

Party	Seats
Liberal Democratic Party (LDP)	40
Party of Democratic Reform (PDR)	34
Slovenian Farmers' Assen-People's Party (SFA-PP)*	34
Slovenian Christian Democrats (SCD)*	29
Slovenian Democratic Union (SDU)*†	27
Social Democratic Party of Slovenia (SDPS)*	17
Greens of Slovenia*	17
Socialist Party of Slovenia (SPS)	14
Liberal Party*	4
Independents, etc.‡	24
Total	240

* Member parties of the ruling DEMOS coalition; the combined strength of DEMOS, including the support of three members elected as independents, is 131.

† In October 1991 the SDU split into two factions: the minority liberal wing was renamed the Democratic Party of Slovenia; the majority right-wing faction became the Slovenian Democratic Union-National Democratic Party.

‡ Three independents support DEMOS and a few generally do so.

Political Organizations

DEMOS—Democratic Opposition of Slovenia: 61000 Ljubljana, Šubičeva st. 4; f. 1989; electoral alliance of seven parties (six until Oct. 1991); its dissolution was agreed in Dec. 1991; Pres. JOŽE PUČNIK; Parliamentary Group Leader FRANC ZAGOŽEN.

   Democratic Party of Slovenia: f. 1991 after split in Slovenian Democratic Union (SDU—f. 1989, first opposition party to Communists); minority faction, but retained SDU leadership and liberal orientation; centrist party; Leader Dr DIMITRIJ RUPEL.

   Greens of Slovenia (Zelena Slovenije—ZS): f. 1989 as one of first opposition groups to Communists; advocates protection of the environment and demilitarization of an independent Slovenia; Pres. Dr DUŠAN PLUT; Parl. Group Leader Dr BOŽIDAR VOLČ.

   Liberal Party: f. 1989 as the Slovenian Artisans' Party; changed name 1990; supports a free market economy; right-wing; Pres. and Parl. Leader FRANC GOLIJA.

   Slovenian Christian Democrats: f. 1989; centrist, conservative party; mem. of European Union of Christian Democrats; Pres. LOJZE PETERLE; Parl. Group Leader IGNAC POLAJNAR.

Slovenian Democratic Union-National Democratic Party (SDU-NDP): f. 1991 by majority faction of SDU (f. 1989, first opposition party to Communists); became more populist and right-wing; Leader Dr RAJKO PIRNAT.

Slovenian Farmers' Association-People's Party (SFA-PP) (SKZ-LS): f. 1989 as a farmers' trade union; agricultural concerns; Pres. IVAN OMAN; Parl. Group Leader MARJAN PODOBNIK.

Social Democratic Party of Slovenia (SDPS) (SDSS): f. 1989; workers' party of nationalist orientation; centre-left; Pres. Dr JOŽE PUČNIK; Parl. Group Leader MATJAŽ ŠINKOVEC.

Liberal Democratic Party (LDP) (LDS): former Union of Socialist Youth, a Communist youth org., it changed its name and renounced its previous character in 1990; centre-left party; Pres. and Parl. Group Leader JOŽE ŠKOLČ.

New Social Democracy: 61000 Ljubljana; f. 1990; Pres. MILAN BALAŽIC.

Party of Christian Socialists: 61000 Ljubljana; f. 1990; Pres. Dr MATIJA KOVAŽIC.

Party of Democratic Reform (PDR) (Stranka Democratskih Reformi—SDP): 61000 Ljubljana, Šubičeva st. 4; former League of Communists of Slovenia, disaffiliated from LCY and changed name in 1990; left-wing; Pres. CIRIL RIBIČIČ; Parl. Group Leader MIRAN POTIČ.

Social Democratic Union: 61000 Ljubljana; f. 1990; Pres. Dr RASTKO MOČNIK.

Socialist Party of Slovenia (SPS) (SSS): 61000 Ljubljana, Šubičeva st. 4; former Communist org., the Socialist Alliance of Slovenia, changed name and became independent party in 1990; left-wing; Pres. VIKTOR ŽAKELJ; Parl. Group Leader DUŠAN SEMOLIČ.

Workers Party of Slovenia: 61000 Ljubljana; f. 1990; Pres. VLADIMIR RANČIGAJ.

Judicial System

All courts in Slovenia are within the jurisdiction of the Ministry of Justice and Administration (see section on The Government—Ministries). The Republic renounced the authority and jurisdiction of the Yugoslav Federal Court (formerly the final court of appeal) and Constitutional Court (which has declared Slovenia's moves towards independence as unconstitutional), both of which are based in Belgrade.

Constitutional Court of Slovenia: 61000 Ljubljana.

Supreme Court: 61000 Ljubljana, Tavčarjeva 9; Pres. FRANCKA STRNOLE-HLASTEC.

Office of the Public Prosecutor: 61000 Ljubljana, Tavčarjeva 9; Public Prosecutor ANTON DROBNIČ.

Office of the Public Attorney: 61000 Ljubljana, Cankarjeva 5; Public Prosecutor JOŽE MAG. GREGORIČ.

Religion

Most of the population are Christian, predominantly adherents of the creeds of the Roman Catholic Church. The Archbishop of Ljubljana is the most senior Roman Catholic prelate in Slovenia (for details, see Directory for federal Yugoslavia). There is also a Slovene Old Catholic Church, but there are few Protestant Christians, despite the importance of a Calvinist sect (Church of Carniola) to the development of Slovene literature, in the 16th century. There are some members of the Eastern Orthodox Church and some who profess Islam and a small Jewish community.

Old Catholic Church

Slovene Old Catholic Church: Ljubljana, trg Francoske revolucije 1/I; Maribor, Vita Kraigherja 2; f. 1948; Bishop Rev. JOSIP KVOČIĆ.

The Press

PRINCIPAL DAILIES

Delo: 61000 Ljubljana, Titova 35; tel. (61) 315366; telex 31255; fax (61) 311871; f. 1959; morning; in Slovene; Editor TIT DOBERŠEK; circ. 100,000.

Neodvisni Dnevnik: 61000 Ljubljana, Kopitarjeva 2; tel. (61) 325261; telex 31177; fax (61) 312775; f. 1951; evening; independent; in Slovene; Chief Editor MILAN MEDEN; Exec. Editor ROBERT MECILOŠEK; circ. 74,000.

Večer: Maribor, Svetozarevska 14; tel. (61) 26951; telex 33183; f. 1945; evening; in Slovene; Editor DRAGO SIMONČIĆ; circ. 55,395.

PRESS AGENCY

Slovenska Tiskovna Agencija (STA): 61000 Ljubljana; f. June 1991.

Publishers

Cankarjeva založba: 61000 Ljubljana, Kopitarjeva 2; tel. (61) 323841; telex 31821; fax (61) 318782; f. 1945; philosophy, science and popular science; dictionaries and reference books; Yugoslav and translated literature; import and export; international co-productions; Dir-Gen. JANEZ STANIČ.

Državna založba Slovenije: 61000 Ljubljana, Mestni trg 26; tel. (61) 332111; fax (61) 215675; f. 1945; Slovenian textbooks, Yugoslav authors, world classics, natural sciences, art books, dictionaries; import and export; Man. UROŠ ISTENIČ.

Mladinska knjiga: 61000 Ljubljana, Titova 3; tel. (61) 221233; telex 31345; fax (61) 215320; f. 1945; books for youth and children, including general, fiction, science, travel and school books; international co-operation; Dir BORUT INGOLIČ.

Slovenska Matica: 61000 Ljubljana, trg Osvoboditve 7; tel. (61) 214200; f. 1864; poetry, science, philosophy; Pres. Prof. Dr PRIMOŽ SIMONITI.

Založba Lipa: 66000 Koper, Muzejski trg 7; tel. (66) 23291; fiction; Dir MITJA LOGAR.

Založba Obzorja: 62000 Maribor, Partizanska 3–5; tel. (62) 28971; telex 33255; fax (62) 26696; f. 1950; popular science, general literature, periodicals, etc.; Man. Dir FRANC FILIPIČ.

Radio and Television

Radiotelevizija Slovenija: 61000 Ljubljana, Tavčarjeva 17; tel. (61) 322390; telex 31118; fax (61) 317066 (Radio); 61000 Ljubljana, Moše Pijadejeva 10; tel. (61) 311922; telex 32283; fax (61) 319971 (TV); f. 1928 (Radio), 1958 (TV); 3 radio and 2 TV programmes; main MW stations at Ljubljana, Koper and Maribor; TV studios at Ljubljana and Koper; broadcasts in Slovene and Italian languages; transmissions for tourists; Dir-Gen. JANEZ JEROVŠEK; Dir of Radio BORIS DOLNIČAR; Dir of TV BORUT ŠUKLJE.

Finance

Following Slovenia's declaration of dissociation from the Yugoslav federation, on 25 June 1991, the Assembly began to assume control over the financial affairs of the Republic. Independence Day was celebrated on 8 October 1991 and a new Slovenian currency, the tolar (SLT), became legal tender on the same day, although it did not appear in circulation until 9 October. The currency was to be represented by coupons until coins and notes were ready. The tolar (one tolar consists of 100 stotins) was exchanged at a rate of 1:1 with the Yugoslav dinar, until 11 October, then at a rate of 1: 0.85, until 31 October, and thereafter at a rate determined by the financial markets. It was reported that 1 DM was worth 32 SLT and US $1 was worth 53.7 SLT, on 8 October 1991.

BANKS

(d.d. = dioničko društvo (joint-stock company); dep. = deposits; m. = million; amounts in dinars; * denotes figures in convertible dinars; brs = branches)

National Bank

Bank of Slovenia: 61000 Ljubljana, Titova 11; tel. (61) 157333; fax (61) 215448; formerly National Bank of Slovenia, as part of the Yugoslav banking system; assumed central bank functions in 1991; bank of issue since Oct. 1991; Gov. Dr FRANC ARHAR.

Selected Banks

Abanka d.d. Ljubljana (Abanka Joint-Stock Company): 61000 Ljubljana, Titova 32; tel. (61) 310388; telex 31228; fax (61) 314535; total assets 32,237.151m.; Gen. Dir MIROSLAV KERT.

Komercialna In Hipotekarna Banka, d.d., Ljubljana (Commercial and Mortgage Bank, Joint-Stock Company, Ljubljana): 61000 Ljubljana, Titova 38; tel. (61) 319166; telex 32255; fax (61) 328256; Dir LOJZE SKOK.

Ljubljanska Banka—Kreditna Banka, Maribor d.d. (Ljubljana Bank—Credit Bank, Maribor): 62000 Maribor, Vita Kraigherja 4; tel. (62) 27441; telex 33167; fax (62) 29207; total assets 963,536,000* (Dec. 1989); Gen. Man. FRANC HVALEC.

Ljubljanska Banka d.d., Ljubljana: 61000 Ljubljana, trg Revolucije 2; tel. (61) 215511; telex 31256; fax (61) 222422; f. 1955; total

assets 97,205m.*, dep. 49,362m.* (Dec. 1990); Man. Dir and Chief Exec. A. SLAPERNIK; 383 brs.

Ljubljanska Banka—Posavska Banka d.d.: 68270 Krško, trg Matije Gubca 1; tel. (608) 31650; telex 35775; fax (608) 33135; total assets 8,813,296.7m.; Dir Dr DEJAN AVSEC.

SKB—Stanovanjsko komunalna banka Ljubljana d.d.: 61000 Ljubljana, trg Ajdovščina 1; tel. (61) 216644; telex 31606; fax (61) 314549; total assets 886,103m. (Dec. 1988); Dir IVAN NERAD.

STOCK EXCHANGE

Ljubljana Stock Exchange: Ljubljana; f. 1989.

Trade and Industry

Chamber of Economy of Slovenia: 61000 Ljubljana, Titova 19; tel. (61) 150122; fax (61) 219536; Pres. FRANC HORVAT.

Federation of Slovenian Free Trade Unions: 61000 Ljubljana; Pres. DUŠAN SEMOLIČ.

MAJOR ENTERPRISES AND COMPANIES

ABC Pomurka: 69000 Murska Sobota, POB 127, Lendavska c. 9; tel. (69) 21176; fax (69) 25570; telex 35219; federation of 39 work orgs and 4,000 co-operating agricultural producers; largest food producer in Slovenia; 12,000 employees.

Aero: 63000 Celje, Copova 24; tel. (63) 33301; fax (63) 37610; telex 33853; paper, printing and chemical industries; 2,637 employees.

Almira: 64240 Radovljica, Jalnova 2; tel. (64) 75460; telex 34569; fax (64) 74170; knitted clothing, using natural materials; Gen. Dir ALES SMIT; 700 employees.

Alpos & Co: 63230 Sentjur, Leona Dobrotinska ul. 2; tel. (63) 741411; telex 33565; fax (63) 741619; manufactures tools for industry, agricultural equipment, etc.; Gen. Man. MIRJAN BEVC; 730 employees.

Audio Video Inzeniring: 61000 Ljubljana, Trzaska 118; tel. (61) 273465; engaged in advice, engineering and design in the fields of sound, light and electronics; Dir DARE STOJAN.

Donit, Kemicna Industrija: 61215 Medvode, Česta Komandanta Staneta 38; tel. (61) 613121; telex 31365; fax (61) 612030; manufactures asbestos and non-asbestos jointing sheet, gaskets, filters, etc; Gen. Man. JOŽE ZAGORČ; 1,457 employees.

Giposs: 61101 Ljubljana, Dvorzakova 5; tel. (61) 315544; telex 32232; fax (61) 326641; major construction firm; 11,000 employees.

Gostol: 65001 Nova Gorica, Prvomajska 37; tel. (65) 23411; telex 34346; fax (65) 23495; production and sale of machines and equipment for bakeries, foundries, and associated technology; Gen. Dir DRAGAN MOŽETIĆ; 1,050 employees.

Iskra: 61000 Ljubljana, Trg revolucije 3; tel. (61) 213213; telex 31356; fax (61) 214162; manufacturer and supplier of optical electronic products, electrical automotive parts, etc.; 35,000 employees.

Iskra Avtoelectrika Nova Gorica: 65290 Sempeter pri Novi Gorici, Vrtojbenska 62; tel. (65) 31211; telex 34317; fax (65) 32371; manufactures electric motors and parts; Chair. of the Board NEMEČ ALES; 2,500 employees.

Kamnik Co: 61241 Kamnik, Fužine 9; tel. (61) 831011; telex 31264; fax (61) 832735; produces aluminium pastes and powders, explosives, other plastics, etc.; Gen. Dir PETAR SKUFČA; 850 employees.

KLI, Logateč: 61370 Logateč, Tovarniska 36; tel. (61) 741711; telex 31656; fax (61) 741279; manufactures furniture and machinery; Gen. Man. ALOJZ SALJOVEČ; 1,187 employees.

Konus: 63210 Slovenska Konjiče, Titov trg 17; tel. (63) 751212; telex 33526; fax (63) 751331; produces natural and artificial leather, engineering plastics, conveyer and driving units; Gen. Dir JURIJ POKORN; 1,600 employees.

Lek Ljubljana: 61000 Ljubljana, Verouskova 57; tel. (61) 340161; telex 31171; fax (61) 348820; pharmaceuticals and medical products; 2,750 employees.

Liv Postojna: 66230 Postojna, pp 77; tel. (67) 21741; telex 34231; fax (67) 23723; Gen. Dir MIRKO KALUŽA; 1,000 employees.

LTH: 64220 Skofja Loka, Kidričeva 66; tel. (64) 632451; telex 34519; fax (64) 632881; cooling equipment for the food-service industry, shops and domestic use; Dir of Production GASPER POLJANEČ; 1,130 employees.

Mehano: 66310 Izola, Polje 9; tel. (66) 62121; telex 34134; fax (66) 62983; manufacturer of battery-operated toys; Gen. Dir MARJAN STARČ; 1,300 employees.

Mercator Kmetijstvo Industrija Trgovina (Mercator KIT): 61000 Ljubljana, Titova 137; tel. (61) 371282; telex 31174; wholesale and retail trade, manufacturing, agribusiness; 19,800 employees.

Metalflex Tolmin: 65220 Tolmin, Poljubinj 89E; tel. (65) 81711; telex 34373; fax (65) 81161; components for household appliances and industrial equipment; Gen. Man. FON IGOR; 850 employees.

Mura—European Fashion Design: 69000 Murska Sobota, Bijedičeva 2; tel. (69) 21535; telex 35215; fax (69) 25510; production of ready-made garments and fashion design; Gen. Man. BOZO KUHARIČ; 6,500 employees.

Saturnus: 61000 Ljubljana, Letaliska 17; tel. (61) 442577; telex 31208; fax (61) 444866; produces metal packaging, lighting and signalling equipment, tools and machinery; Gen. Dir JOZKO CUK; 1,860 employees.

Skupina Emona R.O.: 61000 Ljubljana, Smartinska 130; tel. (61) 441944; telex 31205; fax (61) 445707; production, trading, tourism, catering and engineering; 6,000 employees.

Slovenijales: 61000 Ljubljana, Titova 52; tel. (61) 326961; telex 31314; fax (61) 326158; wood-processing industry; 14,500 employees.

TAM—Tovarna Automobilov In Motorjev, Maribor: 62000 Maribor, Ptujska 184; tel. (62) 411321; telex 33482; fax (62) 412112; manufactures buses, trucks, other motor vehicles and components; Gen. Dir MAKSIMILJAN SENIČA; 6,600 employees.

Tekstilna Industrija PO: 68000 Metlika, Tovarniska 2; tel. (68) 58133; telex 35719; fax (68) 58390; produces synthetic yarn, manufactures knitted goods and leisure clothing; Gen. Dir MIROSLAV STIMAČ; 1,925 employees.

Tobacna Tovarna: 61000 Ljubljana, Tobacna ul. 5; tel. (61) 331111; telex 31250; tobacco products and manufacture of leather accessories; 2,100 employees.

Tovarna Dusika Ruse: 62342 Ruse, Tovarniska c. 51; tel. (62) 661108; telex 33112; fax (62) 511504; manufacture of metallurgical products, chemical products, fertilizers, etc.; Gen. Man. MARJAN HRIBERŠEK; 2,100 employees.

TVT Boris Kidrič—Tovarna Vozil in Toplotne Tehnike 'Boris Kidrič', Maribor: 62101 Maribor, Leningrajska c. 27; tel. (62) 302321; telex 33161; fax (62) 303990; manufactures railway and other vehicles; has a heating-technology programme; Gen. Dir POTOČNIK SRECKO; 2,800 employees.

Unior: 63214 Zrece, Kovaska c. 10; tel. (63) 761122; telex 33527; fax (63) 761643; producer of hand tools, etc.; other activities incl. machine manufacture and tourism; 2,300 employees.

Zelezarna Ravne: 62390 Ravne na Koroskem, Koroska česta 14; tel. (602) 21596; telex 33114; fax (602) 23013; produces machines, tools and steel castings; Pres. JOZE ZUNEČ; 5,500 employees.

Zlatarna, Celje: 63000 Celje, Kersnikova 19; tel. (63) 31711; telex 33597; fax (63) 31570; precious-metal processing, design, jewellery and coin production; Chair. STANE SENIČAR; 690 employees.

Tourism

Centre of Tourist and Economic Promotion (Chamber of Economy): 61000 Ljubljana, Cesta VII, korpusa 1; tel. (61) 302984; fax (61) 315944; Dir RUDI TAVČAR.

Tourist Association of Slovenia: 61000 Ljubljana, Milošičeva 38; tel. (61) 120141; fax (61) 301570; Pres. Dr MARJAN ROŽIČ.

Culture

REPUBLICAN ORGANIZATIONS

Ministry of Culture: see section on The Government (Ministries).

Festival Ljubljana: 61000 Ljubljana, trg Francoske revolucije 1–2; tel. (61) 221948; annual cultural event; Dir VLADIMIR VAJDA.

Cankarjev dom: 61000 Ljubljana, Kidričev park 1; tel. (61) 221121; impresarios and sponsors of cultural events; Dir MITJA ROTOVNIK.

CULTURAL HERITAGE

Archives of the Republic of Slovenia (Arhiv Republike Slovenije): 61000 Ljubljana, Zevezdarska 1; tel. (61) 216551; f. 1945; Chief MARIJA OBLAK-ČARNI.

International Graphic Arts Centre (Mednarodni Grafični Likovni Center): 61000 Ljubljana, Grad Tivoli, Pod turnom 3; tel. (61) 219744; f. 1986; Dir Prof. ZORAN KRIŽIŠNIK.

Modern Art Gallery (Moderna galerija): 61000 Ljubljana, Tomšičeva 14; tel. (61) 214085; f. 1947; Dir Dr JURE MIKUŽ.

National Art Gallery (Narodna galerija): 61000 Ljubljana, Prežihova 1; tel. (61) 219740; f. 1918; Dir Dr ANICA CEVC.

National Museum (Narodni muzej): 61000 Ljubljana, POB 529-X, Prešernova ul. 20; f. 1821; Dir BORIS GOMBAČ.

PERFORMING ARTS

City Theatre of Ljubljana: 61000 Ljubljana, Čopova 14; tel. (61) 214111.

Slovenian National Theatre (Slovensko narodno gledališče): 61000 Ljubljana, Erjavčeva 1; tel. (61) 221492.

Slovenian National Theatre—Maribor: 62000 Maribor, Slovenska 27; tel. (62) 21215; Dir JURI KISLINGER.

Slovenian National Theatre—Opera and Ballet: 61000 Ljubljana, Zupančičeva 1; tel. (61) 214148; Dir of Opera KRISTIJAN UKMAR; Dir of Ballet NEBOJŠA ZUPA.

Slovenian Youth Theatre: 61000 Ljubljana, trg V.II kongresa SKJ 1; tel. (61) 310610.

Music

Slovenian Philharmonic Orchestra (Slovenska filharmonija): 61000 Ljubljana, trg Osvoboditve 9; tel. (61) 22093; Chief Conductor UROŠ LAJOVIC.

Slovenian RTV Big Band (Plesni orkestar RTV Slovenija): 61000 Ljubljana, Tavčarjeva 17; tel. (61) 311922; Chief Conductor JOŽE PRIVŠEK.

Slovenian RTV Chamber Orchestra (Komorni orkestar RTV Slovenija): 61000 Ljubljana, Tavčarjeva 17; tel. (61) 311922.

Slovenian RTV Symphony Orchestra (Simfonijski orkestar RTV Slovenija): 61000 Ljubljana, Tavčarjeva 17; tel. (61) 311922; Chief Conductor ANTUN NANUT.

ASSOCIATIONS

Historical Association of Slovenia (Zveza zgodovinskih društev Slovenije): 61000 Ljubljana, Aškerčeva 12; tel. (61) 332611; fax (61) 332659; f. 1839; Pres. Dr DARJA MIHELIČ.

Slovenian Society (Slovenska matica): 61000 Ljubljana, trg Osvoboditve 7; tel. (61) 214200; f. 1864; Pres. Prof. Dr PRIMOŽ SIMONITI; Sec. DRAGO JANČAR.

Society for Slavic Studies of Slovenia (Slavistično društvo Slovenije): 61000 Ljubljana, Aškerčeva 12/II; f. 1935; Chair. Dr JOŽE TOPORIŠIC.

Society for Slovene Composers (Društvo Slovenskih skladateljev): 61000 Ljubljana, trg Francoske revolucije 6; f. 1945; Sec. MAKS STRMČNIK.

Defence

By early December 1991, with no international recognition, Slovenia did not have any military alliances with other nations. However, it had concluded a friendship treaty with Croatia, in December 1990, and agreed to military co-operation, in January 1991, following an attempt by the Yugoslav People's Army (YPA) to disarm the republican forces. During 1990 and 1991 the Slovenian Government had assumed control of and formed a national army, trained it and prepared its tactics against the YPA.

On 28 September 1990 the Assembly of Slovenia asserted its command over the republican Territorial Defence Force. These reservists had previously fallen under the jurisdiction of the Yugoslav People's Army (YPA—Slovenia was part of the Fifth Military District, based in Zagreb) and the federal authorities condemned the Slovenian move. By early June 1991 a Slovenian Territorial Army had been formed. The State Presidency was the Commander-in-Chief of the armed forces. It engaged in conflict with the YPA, in late June and early July, but agreed to the EC-brokered cease-fire. The YPA agreed to withdraw. Independence was proclaimed on 8 October and, by 11 October, the last YPA forces had left the territory of the Republic of Slovenia.

Chief of Staff of the Slovenian Territorial Army: Maj.-Gen. JANEZ SLAPAR.

Headquarters of the Territorial Defence: 61000 Ljubljana, Prežihova 4; tel. (61) 219748; fax (61) 219764.

Bibliography of Yugoslavia

Allcock, J. B. 'Tourism and Social Change in Dalmatia' in *Journal of Development Studies*, Vol. 20, No. 1, 1983.

Auty, P. *Tito: A Biography*. Harmondsworth, Penguin, 1974.

Berg, S. *Conflict and Cohesion in Socialist Yugoslavia: political decision making since 1966*. Princeton, Princeton University Press, 1983.

Biberaj, E. 'Kosovo: the Struggle for Recognition' in *Conflict Studies*, No. 137/138, 1982.

Bićanić, R. *Economic Policy in Socialist Yugoslavia*. Cambridge, Cambridge University Press, 1973.

Cohen, L. J. *The Socialist Pyramid: Elites and Power in Yugoslavia*. London, Tri-Service Press, 1989.

Djilas, M. *Tito: the Story from Inside*. London, Weidenfeld and Nicolson, 1981.

Dyker, D. *Yugoslavia: Socialism, Development and Debt*. London, Routledge, 1990.

Gruenwald, O. *The Yugoslav Search for Man: Marxist Humanism in Contemporary Yugoslavia*. South Hadley, MA, J. F. Bergin, 1983.

Kardelj, E. *Reminiscences: the Struggle for Recognition and Independence: the New Yugoslavia 1944–57*. London, Blond and Briggs, 1984.

Lydall, H. *Yugoslav Socialism: Theory and Practice*. Oxford, Clarendon Press, 1984.

Yugoslavia in Crisis. Oxford, Clarendon Press, 1989.

Pavlowitch, S. K. *Yugoslavia*. London, Ernest Benn, 1971.

'Kosovo: an Analysis of Yugoslavia's Albanian Problem' in *Conflict Studies*, No. 137/138, 1982.

The Improbable Survivor: Yugoslavia and its Problems 1918–1988. London, C. Hurst, 1988.

Shoup, P., Palmer, S. and King, R. *Yugoslav Communism and the Macedonian Question*. Hamden, CN, Archon Books, 1971.

Singleton, F. *A Short History of the Yugoslav Peoples*. Cambridge, Cambridge University Press, 1985.

Singleton, F. and Carter, B. *The Economy of Yugoslavia*. London and Canberra, Croom Helm, 1982.

Tudjman, F. *Nationalism in Contemporary Europe*. Boulder, CO, East European Monographs, 1981.

Wilson, D. *Tito's Yugoslavia*. Cambridge, Cambridge University Press, 1979.

World Directory of Minorities. London, Longman (for Minority Rights Group), 1989.

PART THREE
The USSR and its Successor States

Successor States of the USSR

Political Boundaries of the former USSR

Russian Federation

The Western Republics

The Caucasus

Central Asia

Geography

TERRITORIES AND BOUNDARIES

The Union of Soviet Socialist Republics (USSR), when it was established in 1922, consisted of the main territories which had comprised the Russian Empire until 1917, with the exception of the Baltic States and Finland, which gained their independence, and Bessarabia, which reunited with Romania. The Baltic States and Bessarabia were regained in 1940. During and after the Second World War further territories, including parts of Germany, Poland, Czechoslovakia, Romania and Finland in the west, the Republic of Tannu-Tuva, on the Soviet–Mongolian border, and the Kurile Islands and southern Sakhalin in the east, were annexed. This collection of territories was the largest state in the world, stretching 9,600 km (6,000 miles) from the Baltic Sea to the Pacific Ocean, and 4,800 km (3,000 miles) from north to south. The total area of the USSR was 22,402,000 sq km. To the north-west it was bordered by Norway and Finland, to the west by Poland, Czechoslovakia, Hungary and Romania, and to the south by Turkey (much of this border being through the Black Sea), Iran and Afghanistan. The People's Republic of China had a long border with the USSR to the east of the Central Asian republics and again in the Far East along the Amur River. Southern Siberia borders Mongolia, and the Far Eastern Region of the Russian Federation has a short border with the Democratic People's Republic of Korea, to the south of Vladivostok. The dissolution of the USSR, which began with the secession of the Baltic Republics (Estonia, Latvia and Lithuania), in September 1991, was finalized by the agreement, signed by 11 former Soviet Republics on 21 December 1991, to create a Commonwealth of Independent States (CIS).

The Republics which formed the USSR cover a huge landmass, extending over much of two continents. Geographically, the territories covered by the Republics may be divided into two main zones: an area consisting mainly of lowland or hill country west of the River Yenisei, and an area of mountains and plateaus to the east. The western region is further divided by the Ural Mountains, which traditionally mark the eastern edge of Europe. To the west of the Urals is the European region of the Russian Federation, with its broad lowlands and intermittent hill country, the flat, swampy plains of Byelorussia and the fertile lands of Ukraine. The Russian Federation extends east of the Urals in the Western Siberian Lowland, a marshy area of tundra and prairie, which extends eastwards to the River Yenisei. The region beyond the Yenisei consists of the Mid-Siberian Plateau in the west, which varies in height between 300 m and 1,000 m above sea-level and is crossed by many large rivers, and the mountainous areas of the Far East and southern Siberia, which extend into the Pacific Ocean and the Sea of Okhotsk as peninsulas and archipelagos. The whole region of Siberia and the Far East is within the Russian Federation.

South of the West Siberian Lowland is the varied landscape of Central Asia. The two main features are the Kazakh plateau and the lowlands around the Aral Sea, much of which is desert. The Republics of Central Asia (Kazakhstan, in the north, Uzbekistan, which covers the central regions, Turkmenistan, in the remote south-west, and Tadzhikistan and Kyrgyzstan, in the south-east) are flanked by mountainous border areas such as the Pamirs, to the south and east, and by the Caspian Sea, to the west. To the west of the Caspian Sea, and extending to the eastern coast of the Black Sea, is the geologically disturbed area of Transcaucasia, occupied by the Republics of Armenia, Georgia and Azerbaidzhan, and physically dominated by the Greater and Lesser Caucasus ranges. On the northern side of the Greater Caucasus are several small autonomous formations, which are part of the Russian Federation.

POPULATION

At the census of January 1989 the total population of the USSR was 286,717,000. The Eastern Slavs (Russians, Byelorussians, Ukrainians) together constituted nearly 70% of the total population, but their low rates of population growth relative to those among Turkic and other groups meant that they formed a declining percentage of the population after 1945. In total there were more than 100 distinct nationalities registered at the 1989 census. The major nationalities were: Russians (145.2m), Ukrainians (44.2m), Uzbeks (16.7m), Byelorussians (10.0m.), Kazakhs (8.1m.), Azerbaidzhanis (6.8m.), Tatars (6.6m.), Armenians (4.6m.), Tadzhiks (4.2m.), Georgians (4.0m.), Moldavians (3.4m.), Lithuanians (3.1m.), Turkmen (2.7m.), Kirghiz (2.5m.), Germans (2.0m.), Chuvash (1.8m.), Latvians (1.5m.), Bashkirs (1.4m.), Jews (1.4m.), Mordovians (1.2m.), Poles (1.1m.) and Estonians (1.0m.).

Under the provisions of the 1977 Constitution more than 50 nationalities were recognized politically in administrative units ranked according to size as union republics (Soviet Socialist Republics—SSR), autonomous republics (Autonomous Soviet Socialist Republic—ASSR), autonomous oblast (region—AO) or autonomous okrug (area—AOk). In 1990 and 1991 many of these territories adopted declarations of sovereignty or independence.

Large areas of Siberia, the Far East and the Far North are very sparsely inhabited. In 1989 the average population density (persons per sq km) of the USSR was 12.8, but the population density of the vast Yakut Autonomous Republic in north-east Siberia was only 0.3, whereas that of Ukraine was 85.7. There was still a considerable rural population, although there had been considerable rural–urban drift since the 1920s. In 1989 66% of the population lived in urban areas.

At the 1989 census there were more than 112 languages spoken. Only three of the languages, however, were spoken by more than 10m. people: Russian, Ukrainian and Uzbek. Some languages, such as that spoken by the Yentsy, were known by less than 500 people. Russian was taught throughout the USSR as a second language, although mastery of it varied from Republic to Republic. In 1989 only 23.8% of ethnic Uzbeks claimed to speak Russian fluently, in comparison with 60.4% of ethnic Kazakhs. In 1989 Russian was the first language of 163.5m. people in the USSR, and a further 69m. were fluent in Russian as a second language.

All the world's major religions have adherents in the 15 former Soviet Republics. The major religion is Christianity, but there are many other religious communities, often identified with particular ethnic groups. The Russian Orthodox Church is the largest Christian denomination. The majority of the population of the Central Asian Republics are Muslims, and there are adherents of Buddhism among the Buryats and other Siberian peoples. During the 1970s and 1980s many Jews left the USSR, but new synagogues were opened as a result of increasing toleration towards religion by the authorities in the late 1980s.

Chronology

RUSSIA AND THE RUSSIAN EMPIRE

c. 878: Kievan Rus, the first unified state of the Eastern Slavs, was founded, with Kiev as its capital.

c. 988: Vladimir, ruler of Kievan Rus, converted to Christianity.

1237–40: The Russian principalities were invaded and conquered by the Mongol Tatars.

1462–1505: Reign of Ivan III of Muscovy (Moscow), who consolidated the independent Russian domains into a centralized state.

1480: Renunciation of Tatar suzerainty.

1533–84: Reign of Ivan IV ('the Terrible'), who began the eastern expansion of Russian territory.

1547: Ivan IV was crowned 'Tsar of Muscovy and all Russia'.

1552: Subjugation of the Khanate of Kazan.

1556: Subjugation of the Khanate of Astrakhan.

1581: The Russian adventurer, Yermak, led an expedition to Siberia, pioneering Russian expansion beyond the Ural Mountains.

1645: A Russian settlement was established on the Sea of Okhotsk, on the coast of eastern Asia.

1654: Eastern Ukraine came under Russian rule as a result of the Treaty of Pereyaslavl.

1679: Russian pioneers reached the Kamchatka peninsula and the Pacific Ocean.

1682–1725: Reign of Peter I ('the Great'), who established Russia as a European Power, expanded its empire, and modernized the civil and military institutions of the state.

1703: St Petersburg (Petrograd 1914–24, Leningrad 1924–91) was founded at the mouth of the River Neva, in north-west Russia.

1721: The Treaty of Nystad with Sweden ended the Great Northern War and brought Estonia and Livonia (now Latvia and parts of Estonia) under Russian rule. Peter I, who was declared the 'Tsar of all the Russias', proclaimed the Russian Empire.

1762–96: Reign of Catherine II ('the Great'—Princess Sophia of Anhaldt-Zerbst), who expanded the Empire in the south, after wars with the Turks, and in the west, by the partition of Poland.

1772: Parts of Byelorussia were incorporated into the Russian Empire at the First Partition of Poland.

1774: As a result of the Treaty of Kuchuk Kainardji with the Turks, the Black Sea port of Azov was annexed and Russia became protector of Orthodox Christians in the Balkans.

1783: Annexation of the Khanate of Crimea.

1793: Second Partition of Poland; acquisition of western Ukraine and Byelorussia.

1795: Third Partition of Poland.

1801–25: Reign of Alexander I.

1801: Annexation of Georgia.

1809: Finland became a possession of the Russian Crown.

1812: Bessarabia was acquired from the Turks. Napoleon I of France invaded Russia.

1815: The Congress Of Vienna established 'Congress Poland' as a Russian dependency (annexed 1831).

1825: On the death of Alexander I, a group of young officers, the 'Decembrists', attempted to seize power. The attempted *coup d'état* was suppressed by troops loyal to the new Tsar, Nicholas I.

1853–56: The Crimean War was fought, in which the United Kingdom and France aided Turkey against Russia, after the latter had invaded the Ottoman tributaries of Moldavia and Wallachia. The War was concluded by the Congress of Paris.

1825–55: Reign of Nicholas I.

1855–81: Reign of Alexander II, who introduced economic and legal reforms.

1859: The conquest of the Caucasus was completed, following the surrender of rebel forces.

1860: Acquisition of provinces on the Sea of Japan from China and the establishment of Vladivostok.

1861: Emancipation of the serfs.

1867: The North American territory of Alaska was sold to the USA for US $7m.

1868: Subjugation of the Khanates of Samarkand and Bukhara.

1873: Annexation of the Khanate of Khiva.

1875: Acquisition of Sakhalin from Japan in exchange for the Kurile Islands.

1876: Subjugation of the Khanate of Kokand.

1881: Assassination of Alexander II.

1881–94: Reign of Alexander III, who re-established autocratic principles of government.

1891: Construction of the Trans-Siberian railway was begun.

1894–1917: Reign of Nicholas II, the last Tsar.

1898: The All-Russian Social Democratic Labour Party (RSDLP), a Marxist party, held a founding congress in Minsk (Byelorussia). In 1903, at the Second Congress in London, the party split into 'Bolsheviks' (led by Vladimir Ilych Ulyanov–Lenin) and 'Mensheviks'.

WAR AND REVOLUTION

1904–05: Russia was defeated in the Russo–Japanese War.

22 January 1905: Some 150 demonstrators were killed by the Tsar's troops, in what came to be known as 'Bloody Sunday'.

17 October 1905: Strikes and demonstrations in the capital, St Petersburg, and other cities forced the Tsar to introduce limited political reforms, including the holding of elections to a Duma (parliament).

January 1912: At the Sixth Congress of the RSDLP the Bolsheviks formally established a separate party, the RSDLP (Bolsheviks).

1 August 1914: Russia entered the First World War against Germany, Turkey and Austria (the Central Powers).

2 March (New Style: 15 March) 1917: Abdication of Tsar Nicholas II after demonstrations and strikes in Petrograd (St Petersburg was renamed in 1914); a Provisional Government, led by Prince Lvov, took power.

9 July (22 July) 1917: In response to widespread public disorder, Prince Lvov resigned; he was replaced as prime minister by Aleksandr Kerensky, a moderate socialist.

25 October (7 November) 1917: The Bolsheviks, led by Lenin, staged a *coup d'état* and overthrew Kerensky's Provisional Government; the Russian Soviet Federative Socialist Republic (RSFSR or Russian Federation) was proclaimed.

6 January (19 January) 1918: The Constituent Assembly, which had been elected in November 1917, was dissolved on Lenin's orders.

14 February (Old Style: 1 February) 1918: First day upon which the Gregorian Calender took effect in Russia.

1918–21: The Civil War was fought between the Bolshevik Red Army and various anti-Communist leaders ('the Whites'), who received support from German and Allied forces.

3 March 1918: Treaty of Brest-Litovsk: the Bolsheviks ceded large areas of western territory to Germany, including the Baltic regions, and recognized the independence of Finland and Ukraine. Byelorussia, Georgia, Armenia and Azerbaidzhan subsequently proclaimed their independence.

6–8 March 1918: The RSDLP (Bolsheviks) was renamed the Russian Communist Party (Bolsheviks)—RCP (B).

10 July 1918: The first Constitution of the RSFSR was adopted by the Fifth All-Russian Congress of Soviets.

18 July 1918: Tsar Nicholas II and his family were murdered in Yekaterinburg (Sverdlovsk 1924–91) by Bolshevik troops.

11 November 1918: The Allied Armistice with Germany (which was denied its gains at Brest-Litovsk) ended the First World War.

4 March 1919: Establishment of the Third Communist International (Comintern).

8–16 March 1921: At the 10th Party Congress of the RCP (B), the harsh policy of 'War Communism' was replaced by the New Economic Policy (NEP), which allowed peasants and traders some economic freedom.

18 March 1921: A rebellion by Russian sailors in the island garrison of Kronstadt was suppressed by the Red Army. Signing of the Treaty of Riga between Russia, Ukraine and Poland, which formally concluded the 1919–20 Soviet–Polish War, with territorial gains for Poland.

3 April 1922: Stalin (Josef V. Dzhugashvili) was elected General Secretary of the RCP (B).

18 April 1922: The Soviet–German 'Treaty of Rapallo' was signed, which established diplomatic relations between the two powers.

THE UNION OF SOVIET SOCIALIST REPUBLICS

30 December 1922: The Union of Soviet Socialist Republics (USSR) was formed at the 10th All-Russian (first All-Union) Congress of Soviets by the RSFSR, the Transcaucasian Soviet Federative Socialist Republic (TSFSR), the Ukrainian SSR (Soviet Socialist Republic) and the Byelorussian SSR.

6 July 1923: Promulgation of the first Constitution of the USSR.

21 January 1924: Death of Lenin.

31 January 1924: The first Constitution of the USSR was ratified by the Second All-Union Congress of Soviets.

October 1927: Expulsion of Trotsky (Lev Bronstein) and other opponents of Stalin from the Communist Party.

1928: The NEP was abandoned; beginning of the First Five-Year Plan and forced collectivization of agriculture, which resulted in widespread famine, particularly in Ukraine.

November 1933: Recognition of the USSR by the USA.

18 September 1934: The USSR was admitted to the League of Nations.

1 December 1934: Sergey Kirov, a leading member of the Political Bureau (Politburo) of the Communist Party, was shot in Leningrad, allegedly on the orders of Stalin; following the shooting, Stalin initiated a new campaign of repression.

25 November 1936: The anti-Comintern Pact was signed between Japan and Germany.

26 September 1936: Nikolay Yezhov replaced Genrikh Yagoda as head of the NKVD (People's Commissariat for Internal Affairs—security police); a series of mass arrests and executions, which came to be known as the 'Great Purge' or the 'Yezhovshchina', began.

5 December 1936: The second Constitution of the USSR (the 'Stalin' Constitution) was adopted; two new Union Republics (the Kirghiz and Kazakh SSRs) were created, and the TSFSR was dissolved into the Georgian, Armenian and Azerbaidzhani SSRs.

March 1938: Nikolay Bukharin, Aleksey Rykov and other prominent Bolsheviks were sentenced to death at the Moscow 'Show' Trials.

23 August 1939: Signing of the Treaty of Non-Aggression with Germany (the Nazi–Soviet Pact), including the 'Secret Protocols' which sanctioned territorial gains for the USSR in Eastern Poland, the Baltic States and Bessarabia (Romania).

17 September 1939: Soviet forces invaded Eastern Poland.

28 September 1939: The Treaty on Friendship and Existing Borders was signed by Germany and the USSR, by which the two powers agreed that the USSR should annex Lithuania.

30 November 1939: The USSR invaded Finland.

14 December 1939: The USSR was expelled from the League of Nations.

June 1940: The Baltic States and Bessarabia were annexed by the USSR.

21 August 1940: Trotsky was murdered in Mexico by a Soviet agent.

22 June 1941: Germany invaded the USSR.

2 February 1943: German forces surrendered at Stalingrad (now Volgograd), marking the first reverse for the German Army. Soviet forces began to regain territory.

15 May 1943: The Comintern was dissolved.

8 May 1945: German forces surrendered to the USSR in Berlin and Germany subsequently capitulated; most of eastern and central Europe had come under Soviet control.

26 June 1945: The USSR, the USA, the United Kingdom, China and 46 other countries, including the Byelorussian and Ukrainian SSRs, signed the Charter of the United Nations.

8 August 1945: The USSR declared war on Japan and occupied Sakhalin and the Kurile Islands.

September 1947: The Communist Information Bureau (Cominform) was established, to control and co-ordinate Communist Parties that were allied to the USSR.

25 January 1949: The Council for Mutual Economic Assistance (the CMEA or Comecon) was established, as an economic alliance between the USSR and its Eastern European allies.

14 July 1949: The USSR exploded its first atomic bomb.

5 March 1953: Death of Stalin; he was replaced by a collective leadership, which included Georgy Malenkov and Nikita Khrushchev.

17 June 1953: Soviet troops suppressed demonstrations in Berlin.

September 1953: Khrushchev was elected First Secretary of the Central Committee of the Communist Party of the Soviet Union (CPSU).

14 May 1955: The Warsaw Treaty of Friendship, Co-operation and Mutual Assistance was signed by Albania, Bulgaria, Czechoslovakia, the German Democratic Republic (GDR), Hungary, Romania, Poland and the USSR. The Treaty established a military alliance between these countries, known as the Warsaw Treaty Organization (or the Warsaw Pact).

14–25 February 1956: At the 20th Party Congress Khrushchev denounced Stalin in the 'secret speech'.

17 April 1956: The Cominform was abolished.

26 August 1956: The first Soviet inter-continental ballistic missile (ICBM) was launched.

4 November 1956: Soviet forces invaded Hungary to overthrow Imre Nagy's reformist Government.

June 1957: Malenkov, Molotov and Kaganovich (the so-called 'Anti-Party' group) were expelled from the CPSU leadership after attempting to depose Khrushchev.

4 October 1957: The USSR placed the first man-made satellite (Sputnik I) in orbit around the earth.

March 1958: Khrushchev consolidated his position in the leadership by being elected Chairman of the Council of Ministers (premier), while retaining the office of CPSU First Secretary.

August 1960: Soviet technicians were recalled from the People's Republic of China, as part of the growing dispute between the two countries.

12 April 1961: The first manned space flight was undertaken by Maj. Yury Gagarin on the Vostok I spacecraft.

3–4 June 1961: US President John F. Kennedy met Khrushchev for official talks in Vienna.

30 October 1961: Stalin's body was removed from its place of honour in the mausoleum in Red Square, in Moscow.

18–28 October 1962: The discovery of Soviet nuclear missiles in Cuba by the USA led to the 'Cuban Missile Crisis'; tension eased when Khrushchev announced the withdrawal of the missiles, following a US blockade of the island.

5 August 1963: The USSR signed the Partial Nuclear Test Ban Treaty.

13–14 October 1964: Khrushchev was deposed from the leadership of the CPSU and the USSR and replaced by Leonid

Brezhnev (as First Secretary) and Aleksey Kosygin (as premier).

20–21 August 1968: Soviet and other Warsaw Pact forces invaded Czechoslovakia to overthrow the reformist Government of Alexander Dubček.

12 August 1970: A non-aggression treaty was signed with the Federal Republic of Germany.

May 1972: US President Richard Nixon visited Moscow, thus marking a relaxation in US–Soviet relations, a process which came to be known as *détente*.

1 August 1975: Signing of the Helsinki Final Act by 32 European countries, plus the USA and Canada, committing all signatories to approve the post-1945 frontiers in Europe and to respect basic human rights.

16 June 1977: Brezhnev became Chairman of the Presidium of the Supreme Soviet (titular head of state).

7 October 1977: The third Constitution of the USSR was adopted.

24 December 1979: Soviet forces invaded Afghanistan.

October 1980: Kosygin was replaced as premier by Nikolay Tikhonov.

10 November 1982: Death of Leonid Brezhnev; Yury Andropov, former head of the Committee for State Security (KGB), succeeded him as General Secretary of the CPSU.

1 September 1983: A South Korean airliner, which had strayed into Soviet airspace, was shot down by Soviet Air Force planes, killing all 269 people on board.

9 February 1984: Death of Andropov; Konstantin Chernenko succeeded him as General Secretary.

THE GORBACHEV ERA

10 March 1985: Death of Chernenko; he was succeeded as General Secretary by Mikhail Gorbachev.

2 July 1985: Andrei Gromyko was replaced as Minister of Foreign Affairs by Eduard Shevardnadze; Gromyko became Chairman of the Presidium of the Supreme Soviet.

27 September 1985: Nikolay Ryzhkov replaced Tikhonov as Chairman of the Council of Ministers.

November 1985: Gorbachev and US President Reagan met for official talks in Geneva.

24 February–6 March 1986: At the 27th Congress of the CPSU Gorbachev proposed radical economic and political reforms and 'new thinking' in foreign policy; emergence of the policy of *glasnost* (meaning a greater degree of freedom of expression).

26 April 1986: An explosion occurred at a nuclear reactor in Chernobyl (Ukraine), which resulted in discharges of radioactive material.

December 1986: Andrei Sakharov, the prominent human rights campaigner, returned from internal exile in Gorky (now Nizhny Novgorod, Russian Federation). Rioting occurred in Alma-Ata (Kazakhstan) after the ethnic Kazakh First Secretary of the Communist Party of Kazakhstan was replaced by an ethnic Russian.

January 1987: At a meeting of the CPSU Central Committee Gorbachev proposed plans for the restructuring (*perestroika*) of the economy and some democratization of local government and the CPSU.

21 June 1987: At local elections the CPSU nominated more than one candidate in some constituencies.

21 October 1987: Boris Yeltsin, who had been appointed First Secretary of the Moscow City Party Committee in 1985, resigned from the Politburo in a speech to the Central Committee which criticized the slow pace of change and warned of a growing 'personality cult' around Gorbachev.

7 November 1987: Gorbachev rehabilitated many of the victims of Stalin's purges.

8 December 1987: In Washington, DC (USA) Gorbachev and Reagan signed a treaty to eliminate all intermediate-range nuclear forces (INF) in Europe.

27–29 February 1988: In the first serious inter-ethnic conflict under Gorbachev, 32 people died in attacks on Armenians in Sumgait (Azerbaidzhan).

29 May 1988: Gorbachev and Reagan began official talks in Moscow.

5–17 June 1988: A millennium of Christianity in Russia was celebrated with official approval.

1 July 1988: The 19th Party Conference of the CPSU ended, after approving extensive political and legal reforms, including partly-free elections to a new legislature, the Congress of People's Deputies.

September 1988: At a meeting of the Central Committee, Gorbachev announced a radical restructuring of the central administrative organs of the CPSU, which resulted in the demotion of the leading conservative in the Politburo, Yegor Ligachev.

October 1988: Andrei Gromyko resigned as Chairman of the Presidium of the Supreme Soviet; he was succeeded by Gorbachev.

1 December 1988: The all-Union Supreme Soviet approved constitutional amendments creating a new legislative system, consisting of the Congress of People's Deputies and a full-time Supreme Soviet.

6 December 1988: In a speech at the UN, Gorbachev outlined his 'new thinking' on foreign policy and announced troop withdrawals from Eastern Europe.

7 December 1988: A severe earthquake struck Armenia, causing an estimated 25,000 deaths.

1989

February

14: The last Soviet troops were withdrawn from Afghanistan.

March

25: Multi-party elections to the newly-established Congress of People's Deputies took place; several prominent 'hardliners' were defeated by radical candidates.

April

9: Twenty people were killed in Tbilisi (Georgia) when soldiers dispersed a demonstration using toxic gas and sharpened shovels.

25: Seventy-four voting members of the Central Committee of the CPSU resigned.

May

15: Gorbachev arrived in Beijing on an official visit to the People's Republic of China.

18: The Lithuanian Supreme Soviet issued declarations of political and economic sovereignty.

25: The Congress of People's Deputies convened for the first time; Gorbachev was elected Chairman of the Presidium of the Supreme Soviet.

27: Congress elected an all-Union Supreme Soviet, which would act as a full-time legislature, but there were protests when only a few radicals managed to gain seats.

July

10–19: Miners in Siberia and Ukraine went on strike in protest at their living conditions.

September

28: Vladimir Shcherbitsky, an opponent of reform, resigned as First Secretary of the Communist Party of Ukraine after being dismissed from the Politburo; he was replaced by Vladimir Ivashko.

October

9: The Supreme Soviet adopted legislation which granted the right to strike; this right was suspended in certain key industries.

December

6: The Supreme Soviet of Lithuania abolished the CPSU's constitutional right to power, thus establishing the first multi-party system in the USSR.

1990

January

7: Elections to the Supreme Soviet of Turkmenistan took place.

11: President Gorbachev visited Lithuania. The Supreme Soviet of Latvia voted to abolish the CPSU's constitutional right to a monopoly of power.

19: A state of emergency was declared in Baku (Azerbaidzhan), following widespread disturbances, which included attacks on Armenians and on government and Party buildings. Soviet troops were sent into the capital, Baku, causing more than 100 deaths.

20–21: Democratic Platform, a reformist faction within the CPSU, held its founding conference.

February

4: Some 150,000 people joined a pro-reform march in the centre of Moscow.

7: The CPSU Central Committee approved draft proposals to abolish Article 6 of the Constitution, which had guaranteed the CPSU's monopoly of power.

18: Elections to the Supreme Soviet of Uzbekistan took place.

24: The Lithuanian Restructuring Movement (Sąjūdis) won an overall majority in elections to the Lithuanian Supreme Soviet.

25: Elections to the Supreme Soviets of Kirghizia, Moldavia and Tadzhikistan took place; in Moldavia supporters of the local Popular Front won the largest number of seats. Pro-reform rallies were organized in cities throughout the Russian Federation.

March

4: Elections took place to the local and republican soviets of Byelorussia, Ukraine and the Russian Federation; reformists made substantial gains in the larger cities, notably Moscow, Leningrad and Kiev.

11: The Supreme Soviet of Lithuania declared the re-establishment of Lithuanian independence.

15: Congress approved the establishment of the post of President of the USSR and elected Mikhail Gorbachev to that office. Congress resolved that the declaration of Lithuanian independence was unlawful.

18: Nationalist groups won majorities in elections to the Supreme Soviets of Estonia and Latvia.

25: Elections to the Supreme Soviet of Kazakhstan took place.

April

6–7: The Communist Party of Latvia held an extraordinary congress, at which it divided into a separatist party and a party which continued its affiliation with the CPSU.

19: Moscow ended petroleum and natural gas supplies to Lithuania as part of an economic blockade of the Republic.

May

5: Opposition protests took place during traditional May Day parades.

29: Boris Yeltsin was elected as Chairman of the Supreme Soviet of the Russian Federation.

June

5: More than 500 people were killed when ethnic Kirghiz attacked Uzbeks in the town of Uzgen in the Osh region of Kirghizia, and three-quarters of the town was destroyed by fire.

July

2–13: At the 28th Party Congress Gorbachev was re-elected as General Secretary despite some criticism of his reforms.

16: The Supreme Soviet of Ukraine declared Ukraine to be a sovereign state, with the right to maintain its own armed forces.

23: Leonid Kravchuk, formerly Second Secretary of the Communist Party of Ukraine, was elected Chairman of the Ukrainian Supreme Soviet.

August

2: The USSR condemned the invasion of Kuwait by Iraq, a Soviet ally.

22: Turkmenistan declared itself to be a sovereign state.

23–26: Rioting took place in Chelyabinsk (RSFSR) to protest against food shortages.

24: Tadzhikistan declared itself to be a sovereign state.

September

3: Boris Yeltsin announced a 500-day programme of economic reform to the Supreme Soviet of the Russian Federation.

30: The Communist Party of Azerbaidzhan gained an overall majority in the first round of elections to the Supreme Soviet of Azerbaidzhan.

October

1: The all-Union Supreme Soviet enacted legislation which guaranteed freedom of conscience and religious belief and ended state teaching of atheism.

9: Legislation allowing the existence of other political parties, apart from the CPSU, was adopted by the all-Union Supreme Soviet.

17: Vitaly Masol, prime minister of Ukraine, was forced to resign after hunger strikes and protest marches by students in Kiev.

19: The all-Union Supreme Soviet approved a reform programme designed to establish a market economy.

25: Kazakhstan declared itself to be a sovereign state and outlawed the storing or testing of nuclear weapons on its territory.

28: The Round Table-Free Georgia coalition of pro-independence parties won an overall majority in the first round of elections to the Georgian Supreme Soviet.

30: Kirghizia declared itself a sovereign state.

November

7: Two gunshots were fired near President Gorbachev during the October Revolution celebrations in Red Square.

14: Zviad Gamsakhurdia, a former dissident, was elected as Chairman of the Supreme Soviet of Georgia.

17: Gorbachev announced constitutional changes, including an enhanced role for the Council of the Federation.

23: A draft of the proposed new Union Treaty was published.

December

1: Gorbachev issued a decree ordering compliance in the Republics with the military draft.

21: Eduard Shevardnadze resigned as Minister of Foreign Affairs, claiming that the country was moving towards dictatorship.

25: Congress approved a constitutional amendment granting Gorbachev extended presidential powers. Nikolay Ryzhkov, the Soviet premier, suffered a heart attack and did not resume his duties; he was succeeded by Valentin Pavlov.

27: Congress initially rejected Gorbachev's choice of Vice-President, Gennady Yanayev, before accepting him on a second ballot.

1991

January

13: Thirteen people died and some 500 were injured when Soviet troops occupied radio and television buildings in Vilnius (Lithuania).

20: Four people died in Riga (Latvia) when Soviet troops occupied government buildings.

22: A presidential decree announced that high denomination banknotes would no longer be legal tender; there were protests from many people who lost savings.

26: The KGB and the police were granted extra powers to search and inspect enterprises and institutions, apparently in an attempt to combat a growing 'black' market.

February

1: The Army began street patrols in major cities and towns throughout the country, despite protests from liberal politicians.

9: A national referendum on the issue of independence was held in Lithuania; over 90% of voters favoured independence.

12: Prime Minister Pavlov claimed that the withdrawal of high-denomination banknotes in January was prompted by discovery of a Western plot to destabilize the Soviet economy.

19: Yeltsin demanded Gorbachev's resignation in a live television broadcast.

22: Some 400,000 people demonstrated in Moscow, in support of Yeltsin and reform.

March

7: The all-Union Supreme Soviet approved Gorbachev's nominations to the new Security Council, which had been formed in December 1990. They were: Vadim Bakatin, Gennady Yanayev, Valentin Pavlov, Aleksandr Bessmertnykh, Gen. Vladimir Kryuchkov, Yevgeny Primakov, Boris Pugo, Marshall Dmitry Yazov.

17: In an all-Union referendum on the issue of the future state of the USSR, some 75% approved Gorbachev's concept of a 'renewed federation'.

April

23: Gorbachev and the leaders of nine Union Republics, including Yeltsin, signed the 'Nine-Plus-One Agreement', a five-point statement on measures to stabilize the crisis situation in the country.

25: Gorbachev offered to resign at a meeting of the Central Committee of the CPSU. An emergency Politburo meeting gave him unanimous support.

May

5: Vladimir Kryuchkov, Chairman of the KGB, agreed to the establishment of a branch of the KGB to operate under the jurisdiction of the Government of the Russian Federation.

15: Jiang Zemin, General Secretary of the Chinese Communist Party, arrived in Moscow on an official visit, the first visit by a Chinese Party leader since 1957.

21: Mircea Druc, the Moldavian Prime Minister, resigned after losing a vote of 'no confidence' in the Supreme Soviet of Moldavia.

26: Zviad Gamsakhurdia was elected President of Georgia in direct elections.

June

12: Yeltsin was elected President of the Russian Federation in direct elections; Anatoly Sobchak was elected Mayor of Leningrad; Gavriil Popov was elected Mayor of Moscow; residents of Leningrad voted to change the city's name back to St Petersburg.

21: A request by Prime Minister Pavlov for executive powers similar to those held by President Gorbachev was rejected by the Supreme Soviet.

July

1: The USSR, together with the other member-countries of the Warsaw Pact, signed a protocol which formalized the dissolution of the alliance. Eduard Shevardnadze and Aleksandr Yakovlev, together with other reformists, announced the formation of a new reformist movement, later known as the Movement for Democratic Reforms.

17: Gorbachev requested aid at a meeting of the 'Group of Seven' (an economic grouping, comprising the USA, the United Kingdom, France, Germany, Japan, Italy and Canada).

20: President Yeltsin issued a decree prohibiting activity by political parties in state institutions and enterprises, effective from 4 August.

23: The conservative newspaper *Sovetskaya Rossiya* published a manifesto, signed by 12 leading hardliners, which demanded a *coup d'état* and emergency rule.

25: Gorbachev announced that agreement had been reached on the substance of a new Union Treaty.

26–27: The Central Committee approved a new Party Programme, which effectively abandoned Marxism-Leninism.

31: Eight Lithuanians were killed at a customs post, allegedly by troops of the Soviet Ministry of Internal Affairs, while US President Bush held official talks with Gorbachev.

August

16: Yakovlev resigned from the CPSU, warning of the possibility of a coup against Gorbachev.

18: Gorbachev was placed under house arrest in his Crimean *dacha*, following his refusal to declare a state of emergency and transfer power to Vice-President Gennady Yanayev, as demanded by a delegation from the self-proclaimed State Committee for the State of Emergency in the USSR (SCSE).

19: It was announced that Yanayev had assumed power as acting president, owing to the inability of Gorbachev to continue in office as a result of 'ill health'; an eight-member SCSE was announced, which included Yanayev and the ministers of Defence (Dmitry Yazov) and Internal Affairs (Boris Pugo) and the head of the KGB (Vladimir Kryuchkov); the SCSE decreed that strikes, rallies, demonstrations and all newspapers, with the exception of a limited list of conservative publications, were banned; the Soviet Cabinet of Ministers met and approved the new leadership; military vehicles moved into the centre of Moscow; Yeltsin issued a decree, which declared the SCSE illegal and its members guilty of treason; thousands of people demonstrated against the coup in Leningrad; in Moscow, despite a state of emergency, some 5,000 people gathered to support Yeltsin at the building of the Russian Federation Government.

20: Yeltsin issued an ultimatum demanding the restoration of Gorbachev to power; some 200,000 people demonstrated in Moscow; some members of the SCSE were rumoured to have resigned; a curfew was imposed in Moscow; three demonstrators were killed by armoured vehicles in Moscow. Estonia declared independence.

21: The *coup d'état* collapsed: some members of the SCSE travelled to the Crimea to try and negotiate with Gorbachev; an emergency session of the Russian Federation Supreme Soviet was convened; a delegation of Russian leaders travelled to the Crimea to free Gorbachev; the Presidium of the all-Union Supreme Soviet declared the seizure of power by Yanayev illegal and formally reinstated Gorbachev as President. Latvia declared independence.

23: Gorbachev addressed the Supreme Soviet of the Russian Federation; Yeltsin suspended the activities of the Russian Communist Party; Gorbachev appointed Vadim Bakatin Chairman of the KGB, Gen. Yevgeny Shaposhnikov Minister of Defence and Viktor Barannikov Minister of Internal Affairs. Aleksandr Bessmertnykh was dismissed as Minister of Foreign Affairs. Yeltsin suspended six CPSU newspapers, including *Pravda*.

24: Gorbachev resigned as General Secretary of the CPSU, nationalized the Party's property, demanded the dissolution of the Central Committee and banned party cells in the Armed Forces, the KGB and the police. The Supreme Soviet of Ukraine adopted a declaration of independence, pending approval by referendum on 1 December.

25: Gorbachev established an interim government, the Committee for the Operational Management of the National Economy, headed by Ivan Silayev, with Yury Luzhkov, Arkady Volsky and Grigory Yavlinsky as deputy chairmen. The Supreme Soviet of Byelorussia adopted a declaration of independence.

26: The all-Union Supreme Soviet convened.

27: The Supreme Soviet of Moldavia proclaimed the Republic's independence.

30: The Supreme Soviet of Azerbaidzhan voted to 're-establish' the independent status it had enjoyed until 1920.

31: The Supreme Soviets of Uzbekistan and Kyrgyzstan (Kirghizia had been renamed in December 1990) adopted declarations of independence.

September

4: The newly-formed State Council, which comprised the supreme officials of Union Republics, recognized the independence of Estonia, Latvia and Lithuania.

5: The session of the Congress of People's Deputies, which had convened on 1 September, ended; it had approved a number of constitutional changes, including the creation of a new bicameral all-Union Supreme Soviet and a State Council.

8: Ayaz Mutalibov won a large majority in unopposed, direct elections to the presidency of Azerbaidzhan.

9: The Supreme Soviet of Tadzhikistan adopted a declaration of independence.

11: Gorbachev announced that 11,000 Soviet troops were to be withdrawn from Cuba.

17: Estonia, Latvia and Lithuania were admitted to the UN.

18: Stanislau Shushkevich replaced Mikalai Dzemtyantsei (Nikolai Dementei) as Chairman of the Supreme Soviet of Byelorussia.

23: The leaders of Armenia, Azerbaidzhan, the Russian Federation and Kazakhstan signed an agreement to begin peace negotiations over the disputed territory of Nagorny Karabkh. The Armenian Supreme Soviet declared the independence of Armenia, following a referendum on the issue on 21 September, in which some 94% of the electorate voted for independence.

25: Gorbachev established a new Political Consultative Council to advise him on policy. The members were all identified as pro-reform politicians; they were: Eduard Shevardnadze, Aleksandr Yakovlev, Gavriil Popov, Anatoly Sobchak, Yegor Yakovlev, Nikolai Petrakov, a former adviser on economic policy, Yevgeny Velikhov, an academician, Vadim Bakatin, Chairman of the KGB and Yury Ryzhkov, an expert on security issues.

27: Ivan Silayev officially resigned as Prime Minister of the Russian Federation, following his appointment as Soviet Prime Minister.

28: The Leninist Young Communist League of the Soviet Union (Komsomol) voted to disband itself.

30: Yevgeny Primakov was appointed head of KGB foreign intelligence and KGB first deputy chairman. The Supreme Soviet of Turkmenistan voted to hold a referendum on independence on 26 October.

October

5: The USSR was officially admitted as an associate member of the International Monetary Fund.

7: After two weeks of protests in Dushanbe (Tadzhikistan) Rakhmon Nabiyev, the hardline Communist leader elected in September, resigned.

9: The USSR established diplomatic relations with Lithuania and Estonia.

12: In Alma-Ata (Kazakhstan) 12 of 13 Republics participating in talks on the future of the USSR declared a willingness to sign an economic agreement. President Akayev was confirmed as President of Kyrgyzstan in direct elections, winning some 95% of the votes cast.

14: It was announced that the system of *propiska*, which controlled the movement of citizens from one city to another, would be abolished.

16: Levon Ter-Petrosyan was elected President of Armenia in direct elections.

18: The representatives of Armenia, Byelorussia, Kazakhstan, Kyrgyzstan, the Russian Federation, Tadzhikistan, Turkmenistan and Uzbekistan signed a treaty, which established an Economic Community between the signatories. The USSR restored diplomatic relations with Israel.

19: The First Congress of Soviet Germans advocated the restoration of the Volga German autonomous republic.

21: The first session of the newly-established all-Union Supreme Soviet was attended by delegates of Byelorussia, Kazakhstan, Kyrgyzstan, the Russian Federation, Tadzhikistan, Turkmenistan and Uzbekistan. Representatives of Azerbaidzhan and Ukraine attended as observers.

26: In Turkmenistan some 94% of the electorate voted for the independence of the Republic in a referendum.

28: At a session of the Russian Federation Congress of People's Deputies Yeltsin proposed a programme of radical economic reform for Russia and offered to act as prime minister while reforms were being implemented.

November

6: President Yeltsin announced the formation of a new Russian Government, with himself as Chairman and Gennady Burbulis as First Deputy Chairman.

11: The RSFSR Supreme Soviet refused to endorse a decree issued by President Yeltsin, which proclaimed a state of emergency in Chechen-Ingushetia, following unrest in the Autonomous Republic.

19: Eduard Shevardnadze was appointed USSR Minister of External Relations.

24: Rakhmon Nabiyev, former First Secretary of the Communist Party of Tadzhikistan, was elected President of the Republic in direct elections.

29: Nasirdin Isanov, Prime Minister of Kyrgyzstan, was killed in an automobile accident.

December

1: In Ukraine some 90% of voters in a referendum approved the declaration of independence adopted by the Ukrainian Supreme Soviet in August 1991. Nursultan Nazarbayev was confirmed in office as President of Kazakhstan in direct elections to that post; he was the sole candidate.

8: The leaders of Byelorussia, the Russian Federation and Ukraine met in Brest (Byelorussia) and agreed to form a Commonwealth of Independent States to replace the USSR. Mircea Snegur was confirmed in office as President of Moldavia after direct elections to that post were held; he was the sole candidate.

13: Leaders of the five Central Asian Republics (Kazakhstan, Kyrgyzstan, Tadzhikistan, Turkmenistan and Uzbekistan) met in Ashkhabad (Turkmenistan) and agreed to join the Commonwealth of Independent States.

21: At a meeting in Alma-Ata the leaders of 11 former Union Republics of the USSR signed a protocol on the formation of the new Commonwealth of Independent States (CIS). Georgia did not sign, but sent observers to the meeting.

25: Mikhail Gorbachev formally resigned as President of the USSR.

26: At its final meeting the Supreme Soviet of the USSR dissolved itself.

30: The 11 members of the CIS agreed, in Minsk (Byelorussia), to establish a joint command for armed forces, although several member states were also to establish independent armies; use of nuclear weapons was to be under the control of the Russian Federation's President, after consultation with other Commonwealth leaders and the agreement of the Presidents of Byelorussia, Kazakhstan and Ukraine.

Recent Political History

ANGUS ROXBURGH

After Mikhail Gorbachev became General Secretary of the Communist Party of the Soviet Union (CPSU), in March 1985, fundamental changes took place in the USSR, which affected both the domestic situation in the country and the position of USSR in the world. Even before the revolutionary events of August 1991, a one-party Communist system had been replaced by a multi-party parliamentary and presidential system of government. The Government had decided, in principle, to abandon the centrally planned economy in favour of a mixed, market-orientated system, allowing private and foreign investment and various forms of ownership. Other fundamentals of the Communist system, such as a controlled press, the difficulty of foreign travel for most citizens, restrictions on religious and political activity, and the absence of an independent legal system had also been abandoned. The basic structure of the USSR, as a federation of 15 Union Republics and more than 100 peoples, was changing rapidly, with several Republics striving to leave the USSR altogether, while others were negotiating a new treaty of union with the all-Union Government to satisfy their aspirations for greater self-determination. After August 1991 the whole structure effectively collapsed, with the Baltic States achieving international recognition as independent nations, and the other Republics (with the exception, at least initially, of Georgia) declaring their independence and agreeing to dissolve the USSR by creating a Commonwealth of Independent States.

In foreign affairs, the USSR withdrew its troops from Afghanistan, lessened its support for socialist or socialist-orientated (or, in the terminology of the West, Communist or Marxist) governments and liberation movements in developing countries, and negotiated far-reaching arms-reduction agreements with the USA. Most dramatically, in 1989, the USSR did not intervene to prevent the overthrow of Communist governments in Eastern Europe, and the Warsaw Pact, the USSR's military alliance in the region, was dissolved.

THE LEGACY

Leonid Brezhnev's years as First (later General) Secretary of the CPSU (1964–82), particularly from the mid-1970s onwards, were later termed 'the period of stagnation'. Economic growth rates steadily declined. The system of rigid central planning and social control, which under Stalin had enabled the industrialization of the country in about one decade, appeared to be unsuited for the development of a modern economy. As Western economies entered a 'post-industrial' phase, concentrating on consumer industries, public services and computerized technology, the USSR still regarded high levels of steel and coal production as the criteria of economic success. The Soviet people were becoming better educated and more sophisticated, despite attempts to isolate them from the West by preventing reception of foreign radio broadcasts, and by prohibiting most foreign travel and the import of Western publications. However, their standard of living was falling further and further below that of the West. By the early 1980s it was evident that reform was essential if the USSR was to retain its position as a leading political and economic power in the world.

The political system, however, was unsuited to change. The control of all decision-making by the CPSU hindered effective management of the economy. Although the bicam-

eral legislature, the Supreme Soviet, was formally the highest organ of state power, it only convened infrequently to pass legislation adopted by the Party organs. The Political Bureau (Politburo) of the Central Committee was the real leading power in the country. The Central Committee (elected by the Party Congress, the CPSU's supreme decision-making institution, which normally took place every five years) directed both Party and state policy. Members of the Council of Ministers, formally the executive and administrative branch of government, were subordinate to corresponding departments and secretariats in the Central Committee. In the same way, local and republican government was also directed by parallel organs of the CPSU. Thus policies which were formally adopted by local soviets (councils) were actually the responsibility of local Party Committees, and the first secretaries of these committees were often also chairmen of the local soviets. This system hindered effective decision-making, especially in industrial sectors, where decisions made by the director of an enterprise could be reversed by the chairman of the enterprise's Party committee.

Changes in the system required a new generation of leaders: in 1982 the average age of the Soviet leadership was over 70. When Brezhnev died, in November of that year, Yury Andropov was chosen as his successor. Andropov, who was 68 when appointed, had been Chairman of the Committee for State Security (KGB) for 15 years before rising to the unofficial position of 'second secretary' in the CPSU, six months before Brezhnev's death. (The second secretary was responsible for fulfilling the duties of the General Secretary during his absence and overseeing the activities of the Central Committee apparatus. The second secretary also held the important 'ideology' portfolio.) Perhaps as a result of his experience in the KGB, Andropov recognized the need for change and initiated limited reforms, including an experimental decentralization of management in some industries. In the absence of more radical measures, he launched a campaign against indiscipline and corruption. Police patrolled public places in an attempt to prevent absenteeism from work, while a series of investigations into bribery resulted in the arrest of several senior colleagues of Brezhnev and thousands of lesser officials. Perhaps Andropov's main achievement was to appoint many younger officials to important posts in the CPSU and the Government. He appointed Mikhail Gorbachev, the Central Committee Secretary for Agriculture and, at 51 years of age, the youngest member of the Politburo, as his effective deputy. He gave Gorbachev two main responsibilities: to research methods of improving the economy (in this he was helped by Nikolai Ryzhkov, who had been appointed Secretary for the Economy); and to make new appointments to all important posts (in this he was aided by Yegor Ligachev, who was promoted by Andropov from being First Secretary of the Tomsk oblast (region) to head the Central Committee's organization department).

On 9 February 1984, before his limited reforms could produce any results, Andropov died, having suffered a long illness. Conservatives in the CPSU, worried even by Andropov's moderate attempts at reform, rejected Andropov's favoured successor, Gorbachev. In December 1983 Andropov had tried to ensure that Gorbachev would succeed him by requesting the Central Committee to entrust Gorbachev with the day-to-day management of the Politburo and Secretariat of the CPSU. Andropov himself was too ill to make the request in person, at a plenum of the Central Committee. Gorbachev's opponents deleted the paragraph containing the proposal from the printed version of Andropov's speech, which was distributed to members of the Central Committee. Instead, Konstantin Chernenko, formerly Leonid Brezhnev's closest aide and second secretary under Andropov, was chosen to be the new General Secretary.

As General Secretary, Chernenko all but ended the limited reforms that Andropov had introduced. There were few new appointments (Andropov had replaced about one-fifth of government ministers and provincial first secretaries). The campaigns against indiscipline in industry and corruption also ended, and there was a general return to the complacency of the Brezhnev years. Chernenko did, however, insist that Gorbachev be second secretary in the CPSU, thereby making his eventual succession to the general secretaryship more likely. Other conservative members of the Politburo, notably Nikolai Tikhonov, another protégé of Brezhnev, opposed Gorbachev's promotion, but were overruled.

After only 13 months in power, and much of that time spent in hospital, Chernenko died. Within hours of Chernenko's death, on the evening of 10 March 1985, the Politburo met and chose Gorbachev to succeed him. Although there were subsequent rumours of a fierce argument at that meeting over the succession, in fact Gorbachev's appointment was almost a formality. He had already fulfilled many of the duties of the General Secretary as second secretary under Chernenko and he had the support of the influential Minister of Foreign Affairs, Andrei Gromyko, who formally proposed him for the post. The First Secretary of Moscow, Viktor Grishin, may have desired to succeed Chernenko, but he had little support within the Politburo; his candidature was not even proposed. There appears to have been a strong feeling among the leadership that the country could not afford to have another elderly and frail General Secretary. As the youngest and clearly the most capable member of the Politburo, Gorbachev was a natural choice.

Few of the older members of the Politburo, and probably not even Gorbachev himself, could have imagined the kind of revolutionary reforms he would eventually introduce. His early career suggested an intelligent reformer, cautiously trying to make the Communist system function better. He was born in 1931, the son of a peasant, near Stavropol, in the south of the RSFSR (Russian Federation). Gorbachev's most remarkable early achievement was to win entry to Moscow University's Law Faculty. It was not as a lawyer, however, but in the Komsomol (Leninist Young Communist League of the Soviet Union—a political organization for students and young people controlled by the CPSU) and the CPSU that Gorbachev made his career, rising to become First Secretary of his native Stavropol kray (province) in 1970.

His administrative abilities and his reform of agriculture in the region attracted the attention of Politburo members, and he was appointed Agriculture Secretary in the Central Committee of the CPSU in 1978. In 1980 he became a full member of the Politburo and, after Brezhnev's death, began to demonstrate his understanding of the importance of personal incentives and social justice in society. He developed these themes in a speech shortly before he became General Secretary, in December 1984. In it he placed unusual emphasis on the social sciences, on 'commodity–money relations' (a Soviet euphemism for market forces) and on 'openness' (*glasnost*), which he described as an 'inalienable part of socialist democracy'.

GLASNOST AND PERESTROIKA

The policies of Gorbachev's first year or so in office were characterized by a similar openness of mind and cautious experimentation. The period began with a careful re-examination of the situation which he had inherited. Meanwhile, Gorbachev resumed Andropov's campaigns against corruption and indiscipline in the economy. In May 1985 he announced campaigns against official corruption and excess consumption of alcohol. The campaign against alcoholism was typical of Gorbachev's early approach to social problems, and caused considerable public dissatisfaction. In the 1970s and early 1980s the consumption of alcohol in the USSR had increased markedly. Absences from work due to alcohol consumption rose; the effect on levels of productivity in industry was considerable. Gorbachev planned to reduce alcohol consumption by raising prices, reducing production and limiting the places and times at which alcohol could be sold. Although levels of consumption initially fell, the establishment of private production facilities and unofficial distribution networks soon replaced the shortfall in official supplies. By 1988 it was realized that the campaign was having a serious affect on the Government's income, which depended heavily on sales of alcohol, and that the level of consumption was scarcely affected by the campaign.

As part of Gorbachev's campaign against corruption and mismanagement the press was encouraged to be more open about shortcomings in the economy and to investigate cases of malpractice. This new policy of *glasnost* (literally meaning 'publicity', but currently used to mean greater freedom of expression) suffered a reverse when a massive explosion took place in one of the reactors at the Chernobyl nuclear power station in Ukraine, in April 1986. As a result of the accident a considerable amount of radioactive material was released, affecting large areas of the western USSR and spreading into other European countries. The first reaction of the authorities in Ukraine and in Moscow was to prevent any information on the incident being released, either to the Soviet people or to foreign countries that were affected.

However, the subsequent negative reaction to the suppression of information about Chernobyl may have encouraged a relaxation of the limits of *glasnost* to allow accurate coverage of natural and man-made disasters and other negative aspects of life in the USSR. Editors supportive of the new approach to journalism were appointed to many of the main newspapers and magazines. The weeklies *Moscow News* and *Ogonek* were particularly noted for a critical approach to Soviet history, and, in particular, the policies of repression under Stalin.

In official discussion of economic affairs, the word 'reform' was not used until the 27th Congress of the CPSU, in February 1986, when Gorbachev began to advocate more fundamental changes. At first, *uskoreniye* (acceleration), not *perestroika* (restructuring), was the watchword. Two things distinguished this from the later, more radical reforms: firstly, the belief that changes could, indeed must, be carried out by the CPSU; secondly, that the system of central planning was essentially correct and merely had to be made to function efficiently. This could be achieved, it was believed, by increasing discipline, by introducing material incentives and by the modernization of industry, especially through investment in automated and computerized machinery. At this stage, nobody in the Soviet leadership discussed the possibility of introducing a Western-style market economy; indeed, Gorbachev explicitly rejected such an idea. The major reform of the early years of reform was the Law on State Enterprises, adopted in

June 1987. It aimed to make enterprises self-financing (that is, losses should no longer be covered by transfers of state finance to the enterprise, and the enterprise would have more control over the use of any profits) and to decrease the control of the central planners over enterprises' inputs, production quotas and trade. In theory, state enterprises became free to choose their own customers. In practice, however, the state had priority, and the orders placed with enterprises by the state were little different to the central planning of the past.

There was one small-scale reform, however, which hinted at changes beyond the limits of the centralized, command economy. Under legislation which was approved in November 1986 and which came into effect in May 1987, small individual and co-operative businesses were made legal. The phrase 'private enterprise' was still not used, and restrictions were placed on the types of activity that could be engaged in, but the reform did represent the first move towards private enterprise since the 1920s.

PERSONNEL CHANGES

To ensure support for his reforms Gorbachev had to work within the limits of the collective Politburo leadership. His freedom to introduce changes depended on his success in promoting like-minded colleagues and dismissing or demoting those who opposed reform. In one of his first major speeches, made in Leningrad, in May 1985, Gorbachev had warned that those who opposed reforms would be dismissed. However, the rate at which conservatives in the leadership of the CPSU were replaced was slow, amounting to only one or two per year. First to be dismissed was Grigory Romanov, First Secretary of the Leningrad oblast, who may have aspired to Gorbachev's position himself. In September 1985 Nikolai Tikhonov, the 80-year-old Chairman of the Council of Ministers, who had been a close friend of Brezhnev and showed no desire to change his policies, was persuaded to resign. Three months later Viktor Grishin, the 70-year-old First Secretary of Moscow, also reluctantly resigned, after what he described as an orchestrated campaign to discredit him. It was another year before a further prominent colleague of Brezhnev, Dinmukhamed Kunayev, First Secretary of the Communist Party of Kazakhstan (CPK), was dismissed. In so doing, Gorbachev seriously misjudged the situation in Kazakhstan. In December 1987, without consulting the CPK, he appointed Gennady Kolbin, an ethnic Russian with no connection to the Republic, as the new First Secretary. In protest at the appointment, some 3,000 people took part in anti-Russian demonstrations in the Kazakh capital, Alma-Ata.

It was not until October 1987 that Gorbachev felt secure enough to dismiss another conservative Politburo member, Geidar Aliyev. Even after that, the Politburo still included three men opposed to radical reforms: Andrei Gromyko, who had been appointed Chairman of the Presidium of the Supreme Soviet (titular head of state) in July 1985; Vladimir Shcherbitsky, First Secretary of the Communist Party of Ukraine, and Mikhail Solomentsev, the head of the CPSU's Control Commission.

While Gorbachev dismissed opponents, he also gradually promoted his allies. In April 1985 Nikolai Ryzhkov and Yegor Ligachev, who had both worked closely with Gorbachev during Andropov's rule, became full members of the Politburo. In September Ryzhkov was appointed Chairman of the Council of Ministers, replacing Tikhonov. Ligachev assumed the unofficial post of second secretary, overseeing the everyday work of the Central Committee apparatus, reviewing important personnel appointments and having responsibility for ideological matters. Eduard Shevard-

nadze, First Secretary of the Communist Party of Georgia, was one of the few men with whom Gorbachev had privately discussed the state of the country before becoming General Secretary. In July 1985 he was promoted from candidate to full membership of the Politburo and simultaneously became Minister of Foreign Affairs, replacing Gromyko.

Another significant early promotion was that of Boris Yeltsin, the robust and aggressive First Secretary of the Sverdlovsk oblast. Within one month of Gorbachev's accession to the leadership Yeltsin was transferred to Moscow, to head the Central Committee's construction department. In December 1985 he was appointed First Secretary of Moscow (replacing Grishin), and, in February 1986, he was appointed a candidate member of the Politburo.

It was not surprising, given the continuing dominance of conservatives in the leadership, that it took much longer for Gorbachev's liberal ally, Aleksandr Yakovlev, to be appointed to the Politburo. In 1973 he had lost favour with the CPSU leadership and was sent to Canada as Soviet ambassador. In 1983 Gorbachev met him, during a visit to Canada, and immediately arranged for his return to Moscow as director of the prestigious research institute, IMEMO (Institute of the World Economy and International Relations). Even at this stage they met almost every day and, on becoming General Secretary, Gorbachev appointed Yakovlev head of the Central Committee's propaganda department. However, unlike Ryzhkov and Ligachev, who quickly became full members of the Politburo without a period as candidate members, Yakovlev's promotion took some time. He became a Central Committee secretary in March 1986, a candidate member of the Politburo in January 1987 and a full member only in June of that year.

Yakovlev and Shevardnadze were largely responsible for the changes in foreign policy which were among the most significant achievements of Gorbachev's first years in power. They diversified Soviet diplomacy, ending the obsession with US–Soviet relations which had been a feature of foreign policy under Gromyko; relations were improved with the People's Republic of China; Soviet troops were withdrawn from Afghanistan; several arms-control agreements were signed with the USA, including the Intermediate-range Nuclear Forces Treaty in 1987. The new policy was represented by the phrase 'new thinking', by which was meant, in particular, the abandonment of a commitment to the class struggle as the basis of international relations and the recognition of 'common human interests' as being more important. The priority given to human over class values was strongly disputed in the leadership; Yegor Ligachev, for one, found the new approach unacceptable.

DEMOCRATIZATION AND THE CONSERVATIVE REACTION

The first changes in domestic policy that really distinguished Gorbachev from his predecessors took place in early 1987. The leadership had concluded that economic reforms would not be successful unless accompanied by political reforms that would give people a greater sense of involvement in the management of society and the economy. Previous attempts to reform the economy, under Khrushchev and Brezhnev, had failed, they believed, precisely because of the lack of concomitant democratization.

In January 1987, at a plenum of the Central Committee, Gorbachev proposed a measure of democratization in three areas: industry; local government; and the CPSU itself. Not all of his ideas were accepted by the plenum. The concept of democracy in factories was adopted and soon it became obligatory for directors of enterprises to be elected by their labour forces. The plenum also agreed to introduce an element of competition into the Soviet election system: instead of being given a ballot paper with only one name on it, voters could have a choice of candidates, though these would still be officially nominated and the innovation would apply only at local levels. The first multi-candidate elections, for local and municipal councils, took place on 21 June 1987. The most controversial of Gorbachev's proposals was for secret, multi-candidate elections of all officials in the CPSU. The Central Committee, composed largely of officials who would have to face such elections, did not endorse this idea.

The defiance of the leadership at the plenum of the Central Committee in January 1987 was the first public sign of an increasing polarization of views within the CPSU. For his part, Gorbachev urged that the proposals (including that for the election of CPSU officials) be implemented immediately, at least on an experimental basis. The press began demanding more democracy, and other moves towards liberalization seemed to mark a break with the past: Andrei Sakharov and hundreds of other political prisoners were released, and the Soviet Minister of Justice promised the repeal or amendment of anti-dissident laws; 'jamming' (the disruption of broadcasts by emitting signals of similar wavelength) of foreign radio stations ended; more Soviet Jews were permitted to emigrate; articles began to appear in the press which were highly critical of the Brezhnev period; and banned books and films were released, including an acclaimed Georgian film called *Repentance*, which, in allegorical form, condemned the legacy of Stalinism and demanded that the truth be told about Soviet history.

The growing perception that the system itself must inevitably be changed produced a conservative reaction. Ideological purists perceived the reforms as an attack on traditional Marxism-Leninism. Ligachev had supported Gorbachev's policies while they did not extend beyond the campaigns against corruption and indiscipline begun by their mentor Andropov (he had been a strong supporter of the anti-alcohol campaign, for example). In 1987 he emerged as the conservatives' chief spokesman. He criticized attempts to portray Soviet history as a 'chain of mistakes' and even described the Stalin period as a 'time of new heights in arts and literature'. As *glasnost* extended throughout the media, Ligachev, responsible for ideology, attempted to reverse the process. In September 1987 he demanded the resignation of Yegor Yakovlev, editor of *Moscow News*, for printing an obituary of Viktor Nekrasov, a Soviet novelist who had emigrated to France. Yakovlev avoided dismissal only by appealing directly to Gorbachev.

Within the Politburo, Gorbachev attempted to maintain a balance, appeasing the conservatives, led by Ligachev, while apparently inclining more to the positions held by the liberal Aleksandr Yakovlev. Since Yakovlev, in charge of propaganda, and Ligachev, in charge of ideology, shared responsibility for the press, they began to personify the debate about the limits of *glasnost*. Newspaper editors received conflicting instructions from the two men.

While the debate between Yakovlev and Ligachev was rather restrained and intellectual, Boris Yeltsin criticized Ligachev in a much more personal way. Yeltsin had quickly become well known as a reformist in Moscow. He dismissed many officials associated with the Brezhnev regime; he travelled on public transport and inspected food shops (and had hundreds of corrupt managers arrested); and he made speeches in which he attacked official malpractices and privileges. He also relaxed many restrictions in the capital, allowing fairs (*yarmarki*) to be established, to which collective farms could deliver their produce direct, thus circumventing the inefficient and notoriously corrupt trade

system. He also allowed a greater degree of cultural freedom than had previously been acceptable; the Arbat, an old street near the centre of Moscow, was turned into a pedestrian precinct where street entertainers could perform.

Within the Politburo there were frequent arguments over policy between Yeltsin and Ligachev. In September 1987 Ligachev, who was chairing the Politburo while Gorbachev was away, rebuked Yeltsin for permitting political demonstrations in Moscow and established a commission of inquiry into his conduct of affairs in the capital. Yeltsin at once wrote to Gorbachev. He complained of Ligachev's 'persecution' and offered his resignation. Gorbachev asked Yeltsin not to act hastily and promised to deal with the matter after the celebrations of the 70th anniversary of the October Revolution.

Yeltsin did not wait, however, and caused the first major crisis of Gorbachev's period in office. At a plenum of the Central Committee, on 21 October 1987, he offered his resignation in a speech criticizing what he regarded as the slow pace and mistaken strategy of *perestroika* and even warning of a growing 'personality cult' around Gorbachev. The Central Committee declared Yeltsin's speech to have been 'politically mistaken', but postponed a decision on his resignation until after the Revolution celebrations. The authorities tried to suppress information about what had happened, but it soon became known, causing sporadic demonstrations in Yeltsin's support. He was dismissed from his post as First Secretary of Moscow at a plenum of the Moscow City Party Committee three weeks later, when he was strongly criticized by his subordinates, who accused him of 'stabbing the Party in the back' and placing his personal interests above those of the Party. The abusive speeches made at this meeting were published in full, but the proceedings at the Central Committee plenum remained secret, leaving the public unsure as to the reasons for Yeltsin's sudden dismissal. Yeltsin's outspoken criticisms forced Gorbachev to take the side of the conservatives. From then on Gorbachev criticized not only conservative opponents, but also the radicals who shared Yeltsin's views, whom he termed 'ultra-leftists' and 'pseudo-revolutionaries'. The affair was, therefore, perceived as a victory for the conservatives. Their leader, Ligachev, was at his most powerful for the next six months.

In March 1988, however, Ligachev became associated with an apparent attempt to reverse the policies of *perestroika* and, in particular, *glasnost*. One of the most conservative newspapers, *Sovetskaya Rossiya*, an organ of the Central Committee, published a full-page article by Nina Andreyeva, a chemistry lecturer from Leningrad, which defended Stalin, criticized the 'blackening' of Soviet history, and complained that *perestroika* was in the hands of 'left-wing liberal intellectuals'. The following day, when both Gorbachev and Yakovlev were out of the country, Ligachev called a meeting of leading editors, and recommended that they reprint Nina Andreyeva's article. The article appeared in dozens of provincial newspapers, giving the impression that it represented the new official policy of the CPSU. Gorbachev considered the matter to be so serious that, upon his return from abroad, the Politburo devoted two entire days to consideration of the article and its implications. At Gorbachev's insistence a decision was taken to print an official rebuttal, drafted by Yakovlev, in *Pravda*. Ligachev denied any connection with the affair and retained his post as second secretary, but Yakovlev was given sole responsibility for the press.

POLITICAL REFORMS

Ligachev's attempt to reverse the reforms by ending the policy of *glasnost* came at a crucial moment, just three months before the 19th Conference of the CPSU, which was scheduled for June 1988. This was to be a highly important event, at which Gorbachev planned to introduce major policy changes and, if possible, have new members elected to the Central Committee.

In the weeks before the Conference political debate widened to cover every possible alternative to the existing system, including multi-party democracy, presidential government and market economics. As the selection of 5,000 delegates to the Conference proceeded, unauthorized demonstrations took place throughout the country, especially in places where conservative Party committees chose anti-reform delegates.

The debate in the media over the country's political future reflected discussions within the leadership. At this stage Gorbachev and his most liberal advisers were already planning to introduce democratic structures of government, which would give the electorate a genuine choice. It was also their intention to reform the CPSU, transforming it into a truly popular organization capable of winning in fair elections.

However, nothing in the leadership's public speeches prepared the public for the far-reaching reforms that Gorbachev proposed to the Conference, on 28 June 1988. The proposals involved limiting the control of the CPSU over the management of the economy and other aspects of public life by instituting a new all-Union Supreme Soviet, with real legislative powers. This new legislature was to assume the functions of government hitherto exercised without public scrutiny by the Politburo and Central Committee of the CPSU.

The old Supreme Soviet, which had met for two or three days each year to automatically pass decisions taken by the Politburo or the Central Committee, was to be replaced by a new working legislature, which would meet for up to eight months in the year. This body would have 400–500 (later revised to 542) members, chosen from a new assembly with ultimate authority, the Congress of People's Deputies. Two-thirds of the Congress's 2,250 members were to be elected directly by citizens, the remaining 750 by 'public organizations', including the CPSU and its affiliated bodies, such as trade unions, women's and youth organizations.

The head of state, the Chairman of the Presidium of the Supreme Soviet, who had previously fulfilled a largely ceremonial role, was to formally fulfil all those non-Party functions that were previously the responsibility of the General Secretary of the CPSU. These included overall control of law-making, social and economic programmes, foreign policy, defence and security, chairmanship of the Defence Council and the right to nominate the head of government. It was agreed, though not formally specified, that normally this post would be combined with that of General Secretary of the CPSU.

Gorbachev's proposals were greeted with little enthusiasm by the delegates, the majority of whom were conservatives. Gorbachev persuaded them, however, to vote for the reforms, and even for a timetable which envisaged elections to the new Congress of People's Deputies being held in early 1989.

Gorbachev was unable to replace any of the members of the Central Committee at the Conference. However, his reforms were destined to reduce the importance of the Central Committee by transferring to the elected Congress and Supreme Soviet many of the legislative functions which it had assumed. Having secured the support of the CPSU

in principle, Gorbachev proceeded with the necessary state legislation and reforms within the CPSU.

In September 1988, at a plenum of the Central Committee, Gorbachev announced a radical reform of the central administrative organs of the CPSU. The number of Central Committee departments, which had previously supervised the work of government ministries, was reduced from 20 to nine. They would no longer be subordinate to the Party Secretariat, which was effectively abolished, but to six new commissions. These were to cover 'party development' and personnel, ideology, social and economic policy, agrarian policy, international policies and legal policy. The creation of the commissions and the accompanying reduction in the Central Committee's staff were designed to end interference in the work of government bodies by the bureaucracy of the CPSU.

The changes also brought short-term political gain for Gorbachev by severely diminishing Ligachev's power, which, as second secretary, depended on his control of the Secretariat. The six commissions were approximately equal in status, and all were answerable directly to the Politburo, rather than to the Secretariat as the old departments had been. Moreover, Ligachev was deprived of the once-predominant ideology portfolio and appointed head of the agriculture department. The decision to demote Ligachev may have been prompted by his uncompromising public statements, in August 1988, in which he contradicted Gorbachev by insisting on the class nature of international relations and attacked the market economy as 'fundamentally unacceptable for the socialist system'. At the September plenum the new international affairs commission was entrusted to Yakovlev, while a centrist, Vadim Medvedev, was placed in charge of ideology.

The personnel changes allowed Gorbachev to proceed with his plans for a new legislature. In October 1988 drafts of constitutional amendments and an election law were published, which gave more details of the proposals Gorbachev had made at the Party Conference in June. Although the plans represented a significant move towards democracy, many radicals criticized the proposals, especially the system of elections from public organizations, which, they claimed, provided too many advantages for the CPSU.

Nationalists in some areas, notably Georgia and the Baltic Republics of Estonia, Latvia and Lithuania, alleged that the new Supreme Soviet gave the all-Union authorities even greater powers with respect to the Republics than under the previous Constitution. In response to large demonstrations in these Republics, Gorbachev promised further reforms to widen regional autonomy.

On 1 December 1988 the old-style Supreme Soviet met for the last time, to vote itself out of existence by enacting legislation which would enable the election of its more democratic successor.

CIVIL SOCIETY

The political reforms aimed to make the CPSU operate through democratic structures rather than as a 'state within the state'. Under the previous system, the CPSU, as a result of its constitutionally guaranteed 'leading role' in society, had dominated not just politics, but every area of life. It controlled industry, trade unions, all public organizations and even the Church. The establishment, from about 1987, of organizations outside the control of the CPSU, represented the first stage in the creation of a 'civil society' in the USSR (that is, a society in which citizens, through public organizations, exercise control over the state rather than being mere objects of control by the state).

The first so-called 'informal associations' (*neformaly*) were mostly environmental, cultural or conservationist groups. Some campaigned for the preservation of historic buildings, others for the closure of polluting factories. Hundreds of small political groups were established. A group called Club Perestroika held twice-weekly seminars in a Moscow institute, aiming to encourage free discussion. Other groups, like the Club for Social Initiatives, were embryonic political parties. One of the most important pressure groups to be founded was Memorial, an anti-Stalinist organization supported by prominent writers and human-rights campaigners.

In some of the non-Russian regions, particularly the Western-orientated Baltic Republics, the preservation of local culture and language inevitably implied opposition to the 'russification' that had taken place under Soviet rule. Environmental groups began to argue that much of the ecological damage in the Baltic Republics was due to the industrial policies of all-Union ministries. The informal organizations in these Republics thus developed beyond purely environmental or cultural issues and became the focus for a revival of national self-awareness. In Estonia, and then in Latvia and Lithuania, 'popular fronts' were established to campaign for national rights. They soon became mass movements, and included both non-Communists and liberal members of the CPSU. Initially the popular fronts did not openly demand independence from the USSR; they campaigned for greater economic autonomy, the recognition of their national languages and flags, and for greater political decentralization within the USSR. In all three Republics Gorbachev appointed new Communist Party leaders who were more sympathetic to the aims of the popular fronts. One by one, the Baltic Communist Parties adapted their policies to retain nationalist support, but they never matched the public appeal of the popular fronts.

In other parts of the USSR the upsurge of national sentiment presented Gorbachev with seemingly insoluble problems, which would eventually bring about the destruction of the Soviet state. In February 1988 Armenians began campaigning for the incorporation into their Republic of Nagorny Karabakh, an autonomous oblast, which was populated mainly by Armenians, but was within Azerbaidzhan. In most of the Union Republics popular fronts were established to campaign for greater sovereignty. Crimean Tatars, who had been exiled *en masse* from their homeland, by Stalin, demanded to be allowed to return. Territorial and ethnic disputes emerged in several areas.

These were problems which Gorbachev apparently never expected. In his speech to mark the anniversary of the October Revolution, in 1987, he had claimed that the solution of the nationalities problem in the USSR was one of the great achievements of Soviet power. Now the 'friendship of Soviet peoples' was revealed to have been little more than a policy enforced from above, which had repressed signs of nationalism, rather than solving complex inter-ethnic disputes.

Gorbachev responded to the challenge with a mixture of concessions and suppression. On three occasions (in Tbilisi—Georgia—in April 1989, in Baku—Azerbaidzhan—in January 1990 and in the Baltic Republics, in January 1991) Soviet troops were used to impose order. In such incidents, and in many inter-ethnic clashes from 1988 onwards, hundreds of Soviet citizens were killed.

THE CONGRESS

The first elections to the Congress of People's Deputies, in March 1989, produced remarkable results, despite the ability of CPSU officials to control the registration of candidates and dominate the mass media during the campaign. In the initial stages some 8,000 candidates were nominated, but most of them were rejected at pre-election registration meetings, usually controlled by the CPSU. In the end, 2,850 candidates stood for the 1,500 constituency seats in the Congress. The other 750 deputies were elected by approved public organizations. Radicals had expressed fears that these organizations would only elect orthodox Communist candidates, but many of the most radical deputies in the Congress were elected by the Union of Cinematographers, the Union of Writers, the Academy of Sciences, and even the CPSU itself. In the Baltic Republics and Armenia, candidates supported by the new national movements won convincing victories over the official Communist candidates. The most significant victory for the radicals occurred in the Moscow City constituency, where Boris Yeltsin, standing against an official CPSU candidate, won 89% of the votes cast and entered the Congress with a larger popular mandate than any other deputy. Gorbachev and most other members of the Politburo, by contrast, were elected only by the Central Committee, in an election with no choice of candidates.

When the Congress convened, on 26 May 1989, some 400 of the elected deputies showed themselves to be committed to radical political and economic reform. The radicals (who later formed a parliamentary faction known as the Inter-Regional Group of Deputies) aimed to turn the Congress into a real legislature, rather than a mere electoral college to choose the 542-member Supreme Soviet and its Chairman. In some ways they succeeded: the Congress lasted longer than the authorities had intended, and became a twice-yearly institution rather than an annual one. The radicals succeeded in using the Congress as a forum to air unofficial views to a huge audience watching the proceedings on television. There was unprecedented criticism of all features of the Soviet system, including the KGB, Lenin and personal criticism directed at members of the Politburo. Nikolai Ryzhkov was appointed Chairman of the Council of Ministers only after thorough questioning by Congress, and it became normal practice for government ministers to be appointed only after similar hearings in the new Supreme Soviet. Special commissions were established to investigate the killings in Tbilisi, the privileges enjoyed by CPSU officials and the existence of the so-called 'Secret Protocols' to the 1939 Nazi–Soviet Pact, which had agreed the annexation of the Baltic States by the USSR.

The proceedings were not dominated, as in the past, by the members of the Politburo, but by a new generation of politicians, such as Anatoly Sobchak, Sergei Stankevich, Yury Afanasyev and Gavriil Popov. The dissident physicist Andrei Sakharov repeatedly spoke. He was heckled by conservative deputies, but an opinion poll conducted after the Congress found Sakharov to be the most popular deputy. The Congress had a dramatic effect on public opinion. Huge demonstrations in Moscow and other cities during the Congress protested against the attitude of the conservative majority. In July 1989 miners staged the first organized strikes since the Revolution. During a two-week period some 500,000 miners went on strike, mainly in Siberia and Ukraine; the strike only ended when the Government granted the miners considerable concessions. Most worryingly for the authorities, the miners' demands were not only economic, but political. When the strikes ended, some of the strike committees became independent trade unions. From then on, strikes became a constant feature of Soviet political life.

THE END OF THE COMMUNIST PARTY MONOPOLY

Towards the end of 1989 public demands increased for a fundamental change in the Soviet political system: an end to the CPSU's monopoly on power and the establishment of a multi-party system. The dominance of political life by the CPSU was defined by Article Six of the 1977 Constitution, which described the CPSU as the 'leading and guiding force of Soviet society and the nucleus of its political system'. Radicals had long advocated the abolition of Article Six to allow the development of a multi-party system, but towards the end of 1989 three factors ensured widespread public support for democratic reform.

Firstly, in 1989, there were revolutions in almost every country in Eastern Europe, as Communist regimes were overthrown or forced to abandon their monopoly on power. Secondly, travel to the West had been made much easier, and many Soviet citizens took the opportunity to compare life there with conditions in the USSR. This undoubtedly had a demoralizing effect inside the country, compounded by the publication of dozens of overtly anti-Soviet books and films. Thirdly, the economic situation was sharply deteriorating, and many newspapers had openly begun to blame the CPSU, which still refused to contemplate a radical shift away from central planning to the market economy.

It was not until February 1990 that Gorbachev was able to persuade the Central Committee, against a background of unprecedented demonstrations in Moscow, to accept that the 'leading role' of the CPSU must be abolished. A new Article Six, passed by the Congress of People's Deputies, on 13 March 1990, still named the CPSU (at the conservatives' insistence), but gave 'other parties' the right to operate for the first time in 70 years.

At the same time, Gorbachev persuaded the Congress to establish a new post of executive president. In the past, the CPSU, with its strong vertical structures and discipline, had ensured implementation of its decisions. However, as a result of Gorbachev's political reforms, the role of the CPSU in government had been much diminished, leaving a vacuum of executive power which the presidency was designed to fill. The move was opposed by those who suspected that Gorbachev simply wanted more personal power, but, after three days of debate, the new post was established. Gorbachev was elected to it by the Congress, by 1,329 votes to 495, with 54 abstentions, in a secret ballot. Thereafter, the constitutional amendment provided for popular elections to the post.

THE 'WAR OF LAWS'

In early 1990 elections to republican legislatures and local soviets in most parts of the country introduced a new element of confusion into the political picture. In many places the CPSU was no longer in power. They were in opposition in the legislatures of Lithuania, Latvia, Estonia, Moldavia, Armenia and, from October, Georgia; radicals took control of the municipal soviets of Moscow and Leningrad; several regions of the western Ukraine elected anti-Communist councils headed by former political prisoners. The Supreme Soviet of the Russian Federation, the largest Union Republic, was balanced between orthodox Communists and radicals, and narrowly elected Boris Yeltsin as its Chairman, against the advice of President Gorbachev.

The result was a situation described in the Soviet press at the time as a 'paralysis of power'. On the one hand, there was conflict between the new democratically-elected state organs and the CPSU bureaucracy, whose functionaries still controlled the economy. On the other hand, a 'war of laws' developed between the centre, with its Communist-dominated Supreme Soviet, and the non-Communist Republics, many of which immediately passed declarations of sovereignty or, in the case of Lithuania, outright independence. Most declarations of sovereignty asserted the validity only of legislation adopted by the republican legislature;

this was strongly disputed by the all-Union authorities who claimed that legislation adopted by all-Union bodies was valid throughout the USSR. All-Union laws and Gorbachev's presidential decrees were simply ignored or vetoed in many areas of the country. Gorbachev himself was in a difficult situation, obliged to accept the outcome of democratic elections, but also determined to maintain central control. He was committed to reform, but also determined that the CPSU should be at the forefront of change.

In July 1990, at the 28th Congress of the CPSU, Gorbachev was strongly criticized by conservative delegates, who condemned his tolerance of the revolutions in Eastern Europe and his moves towards a market economy. Delegates called for 'personal assessment' of each member of the leadership, tantamount to a 'vote of no confidence', and the foremost conservative, Yegor Ligachev, defied Gorbachev's wishes by allowing himself to be nominated for the post of Deputy General Secretary. Both attempts failed, but the majority of delegates clearly did not accept Gorbachev's view that 'everything in the past is largely outmoded and unacceptable'.

As a result of the Congress the powers of the CPSU and of the state were separated further. Although Gorbachev himself remained General Secretary of the CPSU as well as President, all the other members of his Government left the Politburo, which became responsible only for the policy of the CPSU, not for governing the state. The new members of the CPSU leadership were little known to the general public. Yegor Ligachev, having tried and failed to be elected Deputy General Secretary, was left with no political post at all.

During the next month or so, Gorbachev appeared to feel free to take decisions which may have been impossible while he was beholden to the conservatives. He ended the monopoly of the CPSU over broadcasting. He ordered the 'political organs' of the army to take orders from the state, not the CPSU. He agreed to the unification of Germany. He rehabilitated all of Stalin's victims and restored Soviet citizenship to a group of dissidents. A new law on the press was adopted which abolished censorship and allowed hundreds of independent newspapers to be established.

Most significantly, Gorbachev ended months of indecision over the pace of economic reform, and, at the same time, ended three years of hostility towards Boris Yeltsin. In August 1990 the two men brought together a group of economists, headed by Stanislav Shatalin, a member of the Presidential Council (a body appointed and headed by the executive President of the USSR, which was to advise on domestic and foreign policy and ensure the country's security), to draft a programme which envisaged widespread privatization and a transfer to a decentralized market-orientated economic system in just 500 days (the so-called 'Shatalin Plan').

REACTION OF THE OLD ORDER

By late 1990 almost every section of the Soviet 'establishment' had reason for dissatisfaction. The Soviet political élite had lost many of its privileges and in many places had been voted out of power. The Party apparatus had been reduced in size and forbidden to interfere in the running of the country. The decision to introduce a market economy threatened the livelihoods of the bureaucrats who ran the centralized economy. The KGB had lost its ability to control society. The military had lost its 'buffer zone' in Eastern Europe, and faced immense problems in housing thousands of returning soldiers and officers. Several Republics were threatening to establish their own armies, and many young men were refusing to serve in the Soviet Armed Forces. Most importantly, the military-industrial complex, which remained highly centralized, with enterprises in every Republic, had strong objections to any attempts to federalize the country and introduce a market economy.

The Soviet Government, headed by Nikolai Ryzhkov, argued that the Shatalin Plan would lead to the disintegration of the USSR. This argument was supported by an influential new conservative parliamentary faction known as Soyuz (Union), which included many representatives of the military and its associated industries. Gorbachev, who had often warned of the adverse social consequences of the market and of the dangers of allowing the Union to disintegrate, appears to have been persuaded by their arguments. He reneged on his commitment to the Shatalin Plan and adopted instead a set of 'guidelines' for a much more cautious transition to the market economy. Critics claimed that the new plan would perpetuate the domination of the all-Union authorities and the planned economy.

In November 1990 Gorbachev surprised everyone, including even the Chairman of the Council of Ministers, Ryzhkov, and his closest liberal ally, Aleksandr Yakovlev, by announcing another reorganization of the structures of state power. The presidency acquired greatly increased executive powers, including the right to rule by decree. The Presidential Council was abolished, and the Federation Council, established as a consultative body in March and comprising the presidents or parliamentary chairmen of all the Union Republics and Autonomous Republics, was transformed into the President's chief executive organ. The Council of Ministers was replaced by a slightly smaller Cabinet of Ministers, headed by a Prime Minister, who was directly responsible to the President rather than to the Supreme Soviet. A new Security Council, including representatives of the Armed Forces, the KGB and the Ministry of Internal Affairs, as well as some of Gorbachev's personal advisers, was also established. In December Eduard Shevardnadze, the liberal Minister of Foreign Affairs, who had increasingly come under pressure from conservatives, suddenly resigned, warning of an 'impending dictatorship'.

In January 1991 Valentin Pavlov, formerly Minister of Finance, was appointed Prime Minister, following the retiral of Ryzhkov, who had suffered a serious heart attack. The appointment of Pavlov was not welcomed by economic reformers, who criticized his record as Minister of Finance, when he had permitted the budget deficit to increase sharply. In January an attempt was made to reduce the amount of excess cash in the monetary system by withdrawing high-denomination banknotes from circulation. However, the measure caused chaos, owing to the short period of time allowed for exchange of the notes. In February, however, Pavlov asserted that the withdrawal of the banknotes had been necessary to prevent the success of attempts by financial and banking institutions in the West to undermine the stability of the Soviet economy by introducing millions of roubles, thus causing hyperinflation. His accusation was rejected by most observers.

Many of Gorbachev's actions over the first few months of 1991 were widely interpreted as denoting a return to more conservative or authoritarian policies. After intensive pressure from the Soyuz group, Gorbachev dismissed his liberal Minister of Internal Affairs, Vadim Bakatin (though he later appointed him to the Security Council). He appointed a conservative, Leonid Kravchenko, as head of Soviet television and radio. In January 1991, after Gorbachev accused the leaders of Lithuania of attempting to restore the 'bourgeois' system, Soviet interior ministry troops stormed the television centre in the capital, Vilnius, killing 13 people. The troops appear not to have acted on Gorbachev's direct orders, but at the behest of a 'national salvation committee' supported by pro-Moscow Lithuanian Communists. There were also allegations that the KGB had been involved. The fact that Gorbachev did nothing to punish those who acted in this way suggested that he was no longer fully in control.

As the 'war of laws' continued, food supplies dwindled (despite a record harvest in 1990), and industrial production slumped. The central government faced a massive budget deficit, partly because several Republics refused to pay their full contribution to the all-Union budget.

The search for a political solution to the crisis concentrated on the drafting of a new Union Treaty, which would redefine relations between the all-Union authorities and the Union Republics. Six Republics declared that they did not wish to sign such a treaty at all, and others, notably the Russian Federation, led by Yeltsin, and Ukraine, led by Leonid Kravchuk, demanded far greater republican autonomy than Gorbachev was prepared to concede. In March 1991, in a referendum on the future of the Union, some three-quarters of voters in those Republics which participated favoured a 'renewed federation', but in several Republics voters also indicated a strong desire for greater autonomy.

Despite disagreements between the Republics, the increasing crisis in the economy encouraged agreement on the new Union Treaty. In April 1991 Gorbachev announced that agreement had been reached on the main elements of a new treaty, with the powers of the all-Union Government much diminished. His agreement with the Republics, and notably a renewed alliance with Yeltsin, seemed to give Gorbachev more confidence to oppose the conservatives. On 26 April he shocked the Central Committee by offering to resign as General Secretary. A clearly worried Politburo unanimously declared its full support for the leader.

Gorbachev's apparent move away from conservative policies prompted a response from the hardliners. In late June Prime Minister Pavlov, apparently supported by leaders of the KGB and the military, requested executive powers from the Supreme Soviet, which would have allowed him to circumvent the presidency. Although this attempt at a 'constitutional *coup d'état*' was easily defeated by Gorbachev, it demonstrated the growing pressure from the conservatives.

On 24 July 1991 Gorbachev announced that a Union Treaty would be signed by nine Republics. The new draft of the treaty further diminished the powers of the centre from that proposed in April, and the implication of the agreement was that those Republics who did not sign would not be forced to join the new union. The new agreement was fiercely opposed by conservatives, who were dedicated to preserving the territorial integrity of the USSR. As Gorbachev's critics within the CPSU became more vocal, liberal members of the CPSU prepared to establish a new democratic movement outside the structures of the Party, asserting that no further democratization was possible through the CPSU. Two of the most respected liberals still in the CPSU, Yakovlev and Shevardnadze, both resigned their Party membership. Yakovlev resigned in mid-August, warning that 'an influential Stalinist clique has been formed within the leading nucleus of the Party . . . and is preparing for social revenge and for a Party and state coup.'

The August Revolution and its Consequences

ANGUS ROXBURGH

The period of evolutionary change initiated by Mikhail Gorbachev in 1985 came to a sudden climax in August 1991. An attempt by hardline Communists and military leaders to overthrow Gorbachev failed spectacularly. The collapse of the *coup d'état* precipitated a revolution that within days removed the CPSU from power and was swiftly followed by the disintegration of the USSR itself.

On the morning of 19 August 1991 a self-proclaimed State Committee for the State of Emergency in the USSR (SCSE) announced that 'in view of Gorbachev's inability, for health reasons, to perform the duties of USSR President', his powers had been transferred to Vice-President Gennady Yanayev. The SCSE tried to legitimize the transfer of power by reference to the Soviet Constitution (paragraph seven, article 127), but it quickly became clear that their actions were unconstitutional, and that the aim, far from being to 'continue with Gorbachev's policies', as Yanayev claimed at a press conference, was to put an abrupt end to them.

The SCSE's first statement, entitled An Appeal to the Soviet People, declared that the policies of *perestroika* had 'come to a dead end'. It spoke of a 'mortal danger' hanging over the country, which had 'become ungovernable'. It criticized almost every result of Gorbachev's reforms: the 'chaotic and uncontrolled slide towards the market economy'; the 'war of laws' between the centre and the republics; the 'inevitable' prospect of famine; the 'unbridled personal dictatorships' of some elected leaders (apparently a reference chiefly to Boris Yeltsin, the President of the Russian Federation); the growth of crime and the 'propaganda of sex and violence'; and, above all, the impending disintegration of the USSR itself.

Indeed, the timing of the *coup d'état* appeared to be dictated by the imminent signing of a new Union Treaty, which was planned for 20 August 1991. The Treaty would have effectively ended the old USSR. Six union republics (the Baltic Republics, Moldavia, Georgia and Armenia) would be permitted to secede from the Union, while the remaining nine would be united in a loose federation, in which the federal authorities would not even have the right to raise taxes. The SCSE's Appeal to the Soviet People claimed that the results of the referendum held in March 1991 on the unity of the USSR (which had in fact produced a highly ambiguous result) had been 'scorned', and promised to reopen the debate on the Union Treaty. They evidently intended to ensure the retention of the USSR as a unitary state.

BACKGROUND TO THE COUP

In late 1990 and throughout 1991 the prospect of the disintegration of the USSR had aroused strident criticism from an informal coalition of conservatives in the Armed Forces, the military–industrial complex and the CPSU. These interest groups were all represented in the composition of the eight-man SCSE. Apart from Vice-President Yanayev, it included Valentin Pavlov, the Prime Minister; Vladimir Kryuchkov, the Chairman of the KGB; Boris Pugo, Minister of Internal Affairs; Dmitry Yazov, Minister of Defence; Oleg Baklanov, Deputy Chairman of the Defence Council; and two representatives of the centralized, state-run economy, Aleksandr Tizyakov, President of the Association of State Enterprises, and Vasily Starodubtsev, Chairman of the USSR Peasants' Union.

Towards the end of 1990 President Gorbachev submitted to intense pressure from the conservatives. He abandoned his plans for a swift transfer to a market-based economy and replaced some moderate or liberal ministers with hardliners. It was then that Yanayev, Pavlov and Pugo, among the leaders of the August coup, were appointed to their positions.

Gorbachev's adviser Aleksandr Yakovlev described the concessions as part of a 'major tactical manoeuvre'. However, Gorbachev seemed to have allowed his policy options to be severely restricted. In January 1991 the conservatives staged what in retrospect appears to have been a 'dress-rehearsal' for a *coup d'état*. It involved military repression in the Baltic Republics, in which several civilians were killed in Vilnius and Riga, and the establishment of 'national salvation committees', which consisted of members of the military and of the pro-Moscow Communist Parties. These committees apparently aimed to supplant the democratically-elected Governments in the Baltic Republics. Despite the deaths of innocent civilians and the obvious unconstitutionality of the national salvation committees, Gorbachev did not condemn the events and did not attempt to punish the culprits. When he tried to justify their actions, in a speech in the Supreme Soviet, it seemed as if the hardliners had finally regained control.

However, in March and April 1991 Gorbachev recovered his position somewhat and initiated a number of more liberal policies. At a series of meetings with the leaders of nine of the 15 Republics at his Novo-Ogarevo country house near Moscow, Gorbachev drafted the principles of an entirely new USSR. This 'Nine-Plus-One Agreement' effectively recognized the right of the other six republics (Lithuania, Latvia, Estonia, Moldavia, Georgia and Armenia) to secede from the Union. In economic affairs, Gorbachev agreed to the so-called 'Grand Bargain', a plan which requested massive Western aid in return for extensive Soviet reforms, drafted by the radical economist Grigory Yavlinsky together with US economists. In July 1991, at a plenum of the Central Committee, Gorbachev forced the CPSU to accept a new Programme, which entirely abandoned Marxism-Leninism. He even suggested that it ought to rename itself a 'socialist' or 'social-democratic' party.

These more liberal policies brought Gorbachev into almost open confrontation with the hardliners. The Soyuz (Union) group had become the most influential faction in the Supreme Soviet, campaigning for the retention of a unitary state with a strong centre. The position of its members was supported by leaders of the military–industrial complex, which itself was highly centralized and enjoyed plentiful resources, and by conservatives in the CPSU and in the military. Throughout the months preceding the coup, the conservatives repeatedly tried to embarrass or undermine Gorbachev.

When President Gorbachev flew to Norway to receive the Nobel Peace Prize, the Soviet prosecutor issued a report exonerating the troops who had killed civilians in Vilnius (Lithuania), in January 1991. Then, in July, as Western leaders were discussing whether to invite Gorbachev to the meeting of the 'Group of Seven' to be held in London later that month, the Armed Forces staged a show of force in Vilnius. In late July, when President Bush arrived in Moscow, eight Lithuanian customs officials were shot dead by interior ministry troops.

In June, an attempt at a 'constitutional *coup d'état*' was made when Prime Minister Pavlov asked the Supreme Soviet to grant him emergency powers, similar to those of the President. Gorbachev angrily opposed the suggestion, but the idea was supported by three of the future plotters: Yazov, Kryuchkov and Pugo.

The conservatives' arguments were becoming increasingly desperate. In Febuary 1991 Pavlov had claimed that there was a plot by Western banks to import huge amounts of roubles into the USSR, causing hyperinflation and destabilizing the economy. Kryuchkov alleged that offers of Western economic aid were all part of a decades-old plot by the US Central Intelligence Agency (CIA) to weaken the USSR. The 'ideological preparations' for the coup were completed with the publication, in the right-wing newspaper, *Sovetskaya Rossiya*, of a 'patriotic' appeal entitled *Word to the People*. It appeared on 23 July, only three days after Boris Yeltsin outlawed Party activities in workplaces throughout the Russian Federation. It described Gorbachev's rule as 'six tragic years', during which the CPSU, 'being destroyed by its own leaders', had ceded power to 'frivolous and clumsy parliamentarians who have set us against each other and brought into effect thousands of stillborn laws, of which the only ones that function are those which enslave people and divide the tormented body of the country into pieces.'

The *Word to the People* was signed by 12 leading conservatives, including two future leaders of the August *putsch*: Starodubtsev, who campaigned for the retention of the collective-farm system, and Tizyakov, who had led a delegation of representatives of the military–industrial complex to Gorbachev, in late 1990, and virtually demanded that he reject plans for a market economy. Also among the signatories were Boris Gromov, the hardline Deputy Minister of Internal Affairs, whose OMON riot police (the 'Black Berets') had been involved in the bloodshed in the Baltic Republics, and Valentin Varennikov, Deputy Minister of Defence, who would play a crucial role during the coup, travelling, for instance, to Kiev to attempt to persuade the leadership of Ukraine to implement the orders of the SCSE.

THE LAUNCH OF THE COUP

On 18 August, the plotters, probably led by Kryuchkov and Pugo, despatched four representatives to deliver an ultimatum to Gorbachev, who was on holiday at his *dacha* in Foros, in the Crimea. Gorbachev later described how he discovered that all his telephone communications were disconnected as the four arrived. Only one of them, Baklanov, was a member of the SCSE. The others were Varennikov, Oleg Shenin, secretary of the CPSU Central Committee, and Valery Boldin, the chief of Gorbachev's own presidential staff. (Conspicuously absent from the list of those involved was Anatoly Lukyanov, the Chairman of the Supreme Soviet and Gorbachev's friend from university. He was later described as the 'chief ideologist' of the coup and must have been closely involved throughout. His own statement, highly critical of the Union Treaty which was to be signed on 20 August, was circulated and broadcast alternately with the very first statements issued by the SCSE.)

The delegation demanded that Gorbachev declare a state of emergency and approve the transfer of power to Yanayev. When he refused he was placed under house arrest. The leaders of the coup proceeded with their plans for a reversal of *perestroika* and a nation-wide suppression of all dissent and of democratically-elected bodies and leaders.

On their return to Moscow, on the night of 18/19 August, Boldin, Shenin and Baklanov reportedly held a secret meeting in the Kremlin with Yanayev, Pavlov, Kryuchkov, Pugo and Yazov (who had all joined the SCSE) plus Lukyanov (who remained outside the SCSE) and Aleksandr Bessmertnykh, the Minister of Foreign Affairs, (who apparently declined to join the SCSE) and told them that Gorbachev was so ill that 'he doesn't understand a word'. Meanwhile, Kryuchkov intimidated them into supporting the coup by claiming that an armed revolt was under way, that 'gangs of thugs' were already surrounding vital installations and that their names were on 'death lists' found by the KGB on two detainees.

During the same night, Lev Spiridonov, the Director-General of TASS (the official Soviet news agency) and Leonid Kravchenko, the head of the All-Union State Television and Radio Corporation, were summoned to the Kremlin and told to distribute the SCSE's first statements and decrees. The Ministry of Foreign Affairs was ordered to inform foreign governments. Instructions on implementing the state of emergency were sent to all parts of the USSR. (After the coup collapsed, the compliance or non-compliance of various officials would be used as a test of their 'suitability' to continue in office.) Most ominously, lists were drawn up of people to be arrested, including Boris Yeltsin, the President of the Russian Federation. Blank forms were printed for mass arrests and deportations, and a factory in Pskov was even ordered to produce 250,000 pairs of handcuffs. With the exception of seven CPSU newspapers, plus *Trud*, the official trade union newspaper, and the more liberal government daily, *Izvestiya*, all newspapers and periodicals were temporarily banned. The radical Russian radio and television stations were closed down.

THE COLLAPSE OF THE COUP

Despite months of preparation, however, the members of the SCSE and their allies proved to be inept in executing the attempted coup. They misjudged the mood of the people, especially in Moscow, who simply did not believe their cynical promises of abundant food, price reductions and higher wages. For some reason (perhaps because they wanted their actions to be seen as constitutional rather than as a straightforward *coup d'état*), they failed to arrest Boris Yeltsin or to impose a complete news black-out. As a result, Yeltsin was able to install himself in the Russian Federation government building ('the White House'), and to organize opposition on the streets through his own radio transmitters, operating from within the building, and via foreign radio broadcasts. He immediately declared the coup leaders guilty of treason and challenged them to allow independent medical doctors to examine Gorbachev to establish whether he was really ill. As columns of tanks entered Moscow, tens of thousands of people gathered to defend the White House from attack, setting up barricades of trolleybuses and construction materials.

The coup quickly began to disintegrate. The leaders found their pronouncements ridiculed by foreign leaders. They argued among themselves over how to proceed and, in some cases, apparently took crucial decisions in a state of drunkenness. Some of the most important units of the Army and the KGB refused to act against Yeltsin. The KGB's élite Alpha anti-terrorist force, for example, refused to obey orders to storm the White House. A curfew introduced in Moscow on the night of 20/21 August was never implemented.

After three young men were killed by tanks during the night of 20/21 August, the leaders of the coup seemed to lose their confidence. By the next afternoon they were attempting to escape via the government airport at Vnukovo, near Moscow. Yazov, Kryuchkov, Lukyanov, Baklanov and Vladimir Ivashko, Deputy General Secretary of the CPSU, flew to the Crimea, apparently to ask for pardon from Gorbachev. Meanwhile, a delegation from the Russian Supreme Soviet flew to the Crimea to free Gorbachev. Gorbachev returned to Moscow in the early morning of 22 August. The members of the SCSE and their accomplices were arrested and were charged with treason (apart from Pugo, who committed suicide).

FROM COUP TO REVOLUTION

The situation in the USSR was dramatically changed by the events surrounding the failed coup. The old system quickly collapsed. Within one week the CPSU, discredited by the involvement of so many of its leaders in the coup attempt, was suspended, and its offices throughout the country were sealed. Within two weeks an emergency session of the Congress of People's Deputies had effectively voted itself out of existence and established an entirely new system of state structures for a transitional period, pending the establishment of a new 'union of sovereign states', in which former Soviet Republics could choose their form of participation. The future union would be mainly an economic one, perhaps based on the model of the European Communities, possibly with a military and strategic alliance, but only the most limited political ties. The Baltic Republics were recognized by the USSR as independent states on 6 September.

The impetus for these momentous changes came not from Gorbachev, however, but from Yeltsin. Initially Gorbachev did not seem to have grasped the fundamental changes that were in process. When he returned to Moscow after the coup he continued to talk about 'reforming' the CPSU and ridding it of conservatives so that it could 'lead' the reform process. He was also beholden to Yeltsin, the man who had effectively saved him and defeated the *putsch*.

During the three days of the coup Yeltsin had asserted himself as sole legitimate leader in Moscow, and was recognized as such by Western leaders. The Government of the Russian Federation took over most of the functions of the all-Union Government and retained them even after Gorbachev's return. It was the Russian KGB that arrested the coup leaders. It was Yeltsin who dismissed the heads of Soviet television and the TASS and Novosti news agencies, all ostensibly Soviet, not Russian, organizations.

By 23 August, two days after the coup collapsed, Yeltsin was in full control. In the Russian Supreme Soviet he forced Gorbachev, on live television, to read out the minutes of a meeting of the Soviet Cabinet of Ministers on 19 August, at which the majority of ministers had supported the coup. As Gorbachev still protested the innocence of ordinary members of the CPSU, Yeltsin signed a decree suspending the activities of the Russian Communist Party, literally leaving Gorbachev speechless. Yeltsin proceeded to suspend temporarily all the CPSU-controlled newspapers which had been allowed to function during the coup. He banned political organs in the Armed Forces, took control of all Soviet government communications, sealed the buildings of the Russian Communist Party and transferred its archives, and those of the KGB, to Russian jurisdiction.

All Soviet government appointments were now made only in consultation with Yeltsin (and, nominally, the leaders of the other Republics). Vadim Bakatin, the liberal dismissed as Minister of Internal Affairs at the conservatives' insist-

ence in December 1990, was made Chairman of the KGB, with instructions to reform the organization completely.

Gorbachev followed most of Yeltsin's moves, one step behind. It was only on 24 August, apparently after his old colleague Aleksandr Yakovlev had enlightened him on the unsustainability of his position, that he finally abandoned his allegiance to the CPSU. In a momentous series of decrees that revolutionized the politics of the USSR, he resigned as General Secretary of the CPSU, demanded that the Central Committee disband itself, and nationalized the CPSU's property and assets. From that moment, the CPSU, with all its offices closed and its assets seized, was no longer capable of running the country. A few days later the Supreme Soviet suspended its activities altogether.

The Supreme Soviet, which met for one week at the end of August, spent most of its time deliberating how and why the coup had occurred and questioning the role of its own members. The Congress of People's Deputies, by contrast, was more forward-looking, searching for structures to govern the country through its transition to a new non-Communist future. It established a State Council, comprising the USSR President and the leaders of participating Republics, as the leading organ to establish domestic and foreign policy. A new Supreme Soviet, in which each Republic would have greater influence, became the supreme legislative body. And a new Inter-republican Economic Council was set up to co-ordinate economic policy during the transition period.

The dramatic political changes of these August days were accompanied by the symbols of revolution: the toppling of statues of Communist heroes, notably the statue of Feliks Dzherzhinsky, the founder of the KGB, opposite the KGB's headquarters in Moscow, and the raising of national flags in every Republic. The USSR finally caught up with the rest of Eastern Europe, two years after their anti-Communist revolutions.

THE END OF THE USSR

All the old problems remained, of course: economic chaos and the possibility of famine; inter-ethnic strife; fears of a nascent Russian chauvinism; arguments over what kind of country or alliance should replace the USSR. The latter issue continued to dominate politics until the end of the year. The first attempt to create some new inter-republican structure emerged from talks held between the Republics in Alma-Ata (Kazakhstan) on 12 October. Twelve Republics expressed a willingness to sign an inter-republican agreement and, on 18 October, eight Republics (the five Central Asian Republics, Armenia, Byelorussia and the Russian Federation) signed a treaty establishing an Economic Community. The Treaty of the Economic Community, which was also signed by Ukraine and Moldavia in early November, envisaged the preservation of a common economic space between the member-states and a significant degree of co-ordination of economic policy, managed by an Interstate Economic Committee. However, the Economic Community did not specify any political or military relations between the Republics. To address such issues President Gorbachev proposed the establishment of a new Union of Sovereign States (USS) as the successor to the USSR. On 14 November seven Republics (the Russian Federation, Byelorussia, Azerbaidzhan, Kazakhstan, Kyrgyzstan, Tadzhikistan and Turkmenistan) announced a willingness to join such a Union. A draft treaty defined the new union as a confederative state, which would preserve centralized control of the armed forces and nuclear weapons, and have its own citizenship, government and presidency. The seven Republics (together with Uzbekistan, which had not attended the 14 November meeting) were to sign the Treaty on 25 November, but, at the meeting of the State Council where the signing was to take place, Yeltsin announced that he did not agree that the future union should be a state, but that it should only be a loose confederation. The other Republics apparently concurred, since all the Republics announced that the draft agreement would have to be ratified by republican legislatures before they could sign.

On 1 December Gorbachev's plans to re-establish a common state on the territory of the old USSR received a setback when Ukraine's declaration of independence received overwhelming endorsement in a referendum. The Ukrainian leader, Leonid Kravchuk, who was elected President the same day, had already refused to join any new political union, but the level of support demonstrated for an independent Ukraine effectively precluded any Ukrainian involvement in a new state. On 5 December Yeltsin met Gorbachev and informed him that there was no prospect for the creation of the USS if Ukraine did not participate. Two days later Yeltsin met Kravchuk and the Byelorussian leader, Stanislav Shushkevich, for talks near Brest, in Byelorussia. On 8 December the three leaders announced that they had agreed to form a Commonwealth of Independent States (CIS), which would not be a state, but merely an interstate agreement to preserve some measure of economic co-ordination between the Republics and ensure the maintenance of a united command over a 'common military-strategic space' and unified control over military weapons. Above all, the agreement announced that the USSR had 'ceased to exist as a subject of international law and a geopolitical reality'. The three Republics invited other former Soviet Republics to join the new Commonwealth and, on 21 December, 11 Republics (Georgia did not sign) agreed to establish the new Commonwealth and to dissolve the USSR. No central government was envisaged for the CIS, the supreme interstate body being a Council of Heads of State of the members. The Soviet seat in the UN Security Council was to be occupied by the Russian Federation.

The establishment of the CIS meant an end to the USSR's 70-year history. In the last weeks of December Yeltsin asserted control over all the remaining Soviet institutions, including the symbolic centre of Soviet power, the Kremlin. It was the end of Gorbachev's attempt to reform the USSR, to create a more humane state and an economic, as well as a military, superpower. Instead, the USSR was disbanded and Yeltsin's Russia began to emerge as a new and largely unknown entity in world politics.

Nationalism in the USSR

Dr STEPHEN WHITE

By the end of 1991 15 independent states had emerged from what had been the Union of Soviet Socialist Republics, 11 of them loosely united in a Commonwealth of Independent States. As constituent republics of the USSR they had been united on a supposedly voluntary basis, forming an 'integral, federal, multinational state', according to the 1977 Constitution. Under that Constitution they enjoyed an extensive range of formal powers, including the right to enter into diplomatic relations with other states (Art. 80) and to determine all matters of purely local significance (Art. 76). Under the previous Constitution, from 1944 onwards, the Union Republics had even enjoyed a nominal right to maintain their own armed forces. Emphasizing the point that this was a 'voluntary association of equal Soviet Socialist Republics', each of the Union Republics had a nominal right to secede from the USSR (Art. 72). To provide some basis for this purely fictional right, each Union Republic occupied a territory with an international boundary, within which a particular nationality was predominant: Uzbeks in Uzbekistan, Byelorussians in Byelorussia, and Russians in the Russian Federation, which was by far the largest Republic.

Under the Soviet federal system some 60 smaller nationalities were also granted various levels of territorial-administrative autonomy. There were 20 Autonomous Soviet Socialist Republics (ASSRs) and eight Autonomous oblasts (regions) listed in the 1977 Constitution. A further 10 Autonomous okrugs (areas), all within the Russian Federation, were also established. ASSRs had the right to their own constitutions and to participation in decision-making at both union republic and all-Union levels. The Constitution did not offer any formal rights to autonomous oblasts or to autonomous okrugs, since they were subordinate to the union republic (in the case of oblasts) or the administrative area (okrugs) in which they were situated. In practice their autonomy was largely nominal, although some were granted a measure of cultural and administrative independence.

Many nationalities were granted no territorial autonomy, including over 1m. Poles and large communities of Koreans, Meskhetian Turks, Bulgarians, Kurds and Greeks. Other nationalities, such as the Crimean Tatars and the Volga Germans, were dispossessed of their autonomous territories during the Second World War.

The complicated administrative structure established in the USSR reflected the various and changing ethnic composition of its peoples. At the census of 1989, Russians constituted just over one-half (50.8%) of the total population; the balance was accounted for by 100 or more different national groups (the 1989 census recorded 128), ranging from a few hundred Negidals, in the Far East, to the other major Slavic nations (Byelorussians and Ukrainians) in the European Republics, and the Turkic Muslim groups of Central Asia, the Caucasus and the Russian Federation. More inclusive counts than those of the census recorded as many as 400, or even 800, ethnic groups in the USSR. The histories and cultures of these various nationalities are often very different, affecting language, religion and social customs of all kinds. The largest group of nationalities is the Slavs (Russians, Ukrainians and Byelorussians), who share a common linguistic and religious inheritance and together constituted about two-thirds of the total Soviet population. The traditionally Muslim peoples of Central Asia accounted for a further 15% and the larger national groups in Transcaucasia and the Baltic Republics were the other major contingents.

THE MAJOR NATIONALITIES

Russians dominated the USSR not only in numbers, but in their predominance in the central institutions of power. Russians are a Christian people (the millennium of the Russian Orthodox Church was celebrated in 1988), speaking an Eastern Slavonic language, and they have represented the core of the Russian or Soviet state since early medieval times. The overwhelming majority of Russians (some 83%

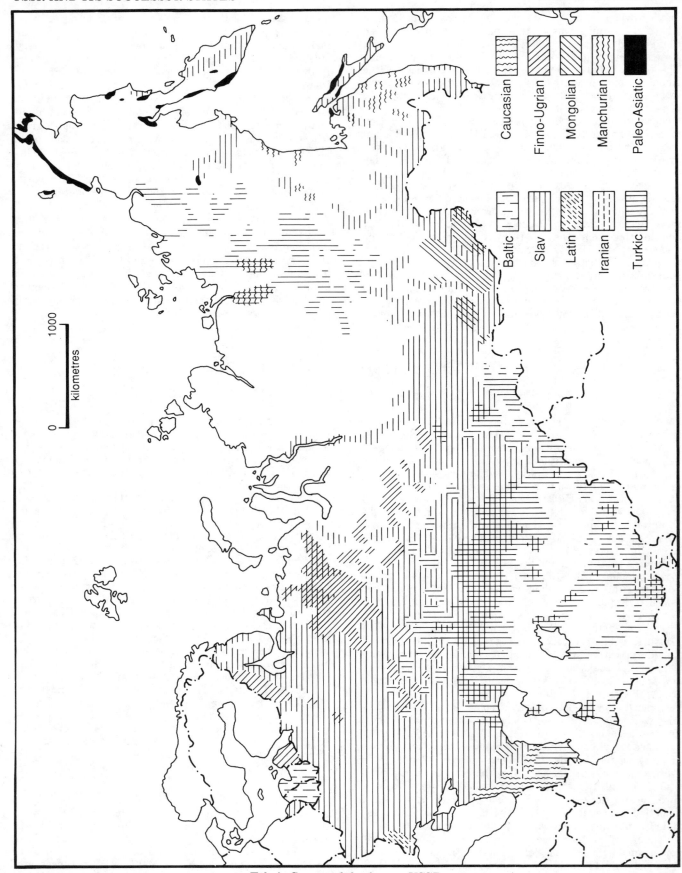

Ethnic Groups of the former USSR

in the 1989 census) live in the Russian Federation, where they account for the same percentage of the local population. About 11m. live in Ukraine, and there are millions more in other Republics (in Kazakhstan, Russians almost outnumber the Kazakhs). Although not challenged by the numbers of any other national groups, Russians constituted a steadily diminishing proportion of the total population of the USSR after the Second World War. Furthermore, many areas of the Russian Federation were relatively underdeveloped in comparison with other republics, which created at least an impression that it subsidized developments in more prosperous, non-Russian areas. For such reasons national self-consciousness steadily increased from the 1960s onwards. It was expressed particularly in a movement to protect ancient monuments and churches and also by a group of writers and film-makers who tried to express the honesty, simplicity and even patterns of speech of traditional village life.

The Ukrainians, the second most numerous nationality in the former USSR, are more than 40m. strong, with a distinct language (also Eastern Slavonic) and a culture of their own. Ukraine is predominantly Orthodox Christian by religion, although with a Uniate (part of the Roman Catholic Church) minority. Both the Russians and Ukrainians claim Kievan Rus, in the ninth century AD, as the origin of their states. In reality, the Eastern Slavs did not form distinct nationalities until about the 13th century, when they became identifiable as Russians, Ukrainians and Byelorussians. The Kievan principalities, in what is now Ukraine, enjoyed an extended period of independence, but then came under Lithuanian, Polish and, from the 17th century, Russian control.

Ukraine became one of the constituent republics of the USSR in 1922. It suffered particularly during the 1930s: there was a devastating and, it is now accepted, largely man-made famine during the early part of the decade. In the late 1930s many members of the republican leadership were imprisoned or executed after being accused of 'nationalism' (in practice, pointing out the likely outcomes of central policies). There were more heavy losses, of both population and resources, during the Second World War, in which a substantial volunteer detachment fought on the German side. As a consequence of the War, much of western Ukraine (where most of the Uniates live) was annexed from Poland and other neighbouring countries. Ukraine was an important element in the Soviet economy, including about one-third of the USSR's most important industries (coal, iron and steel) and some of its richest agricultural land. It was the home of some of the USSR's strongest political dynasties; the best known is, perhaps, the so-called 'Dnepropetrovsk mafia', which included Leonid Brezhnev. There has, however, been resistance to what was seen as 'russification' since at least the 1960s and, in the 1980s, the development of nuclear power, particularly after the accident at Chernobyl in 1986, became a new and very potent source of public disenchantment.

The Byelorussians (about 10m. in 1989) also speak a distinct Eastern Slavonic language and are, traditionally, mainly Orthodox Christian by religion. Formerly a part of Kievan Rus, Byelorussia also came under Lithuanian and Polish control, until it passed to the Russian Empire under the partitions of the late 18th century. A generally swampy land without significant natural resources, Byelorussia suffered greatly during the wars between Russia and Poland in the 16th and 17th centuries, and then again during the Napoleonic invasion and the First and Second World Wars. After a brief period of independence, Soviet rule was established in 1919 and the larger part of historic Byelorussia joined the USSR in 1922. Western Byelorussia, under Polish rule between the World Wars, was incorporated in 1939.

Moldavia, which was also a part of Kievan Rus, is home to a Latin rather than a Slavic community and had originally constituted part of the Roman province of Dacia. The people of Moldavia and Wallachia, therefore, were known as Romanians. After some centuries of independence Moldavia became part of the Ottoman Empire and then came under Russian influence from the early 19th century. Bessarabia, a part of historic Moldavia between the Prut and Dniester rivers, was part of the Romanian state in 1918–40 and again in 1941–44. It was then incorporated into the USSR, together with other Moldavian territories, as a constituent republic.

Of the major non-Slavic groups, the Baltic nations have a particularly distinctive inheritance, having come under strong German, Polish and Swedish influence from early medieval times. The Baltic peoples are Christian by religion, but generally Lutheran (Estonians and Latvians) or Roman Catholic (Lithuanians) rather than Orthodox. They were under Soviet rule for a much shorter period of time than most other nationalities, having been annexed in 1940 rather than during the immediate post-revolutionary period (when Communist-led governments were briefly established in all three countries). The Baltic States had an extended experience of representative government, which was not the case in other parts of what became the USSR. There was also a thriving commercial capitalism, particularly around the ports of Riga and Reval (now Tallinn). Reflecting these influences, the way of life in the Baltic Republics was demonstrably more 'Western', even during Soviet rule, than in the other Soviet Republics, and they were always among those most exposed to outside cultural influences. Thus it was not surprising that the Baltics were the first of the USSR's Republics to demand restoration of their independence. In September 1991 their independence was recognized by the USSR and they were accepted as members of the United Nations (UN).

The Caucasian peoples (Georgians, Armenians and Azerbaidzhanis are the major nationalities of the region) are also very different in their history, religion, language and culture from the Slavic nations. They have, historically, been no less conscious of these differences than the Baltic peoples. The Caucasian peoples are renowned for the Mediterranean climate of the areas in which they live, for their fruit and wine, for their feuds and corruption, for their longevity, and for their paternalistic attitude towards women. However, the peoples of these Republics, particularly the Georgians and Armenians, are also celebrated for their high levels of educational and cultural achievement, especially in theatre, film and painting. Tengiz Abuladze's celebrated anti-Stalinist film *Repentance*, released in 1988, was produced in Georgia; the same Republic's Rustaveli Theatre, under its director Robert Sturua, enjoys an international reputation. Prominent Armenians have included the composer Aram Khachaturyan, the painter Arshile Gorky and the writer William Saroyan. Both Georgians and Armenians have their own independent churches and have been Christian since the fourth century, long before any of the Slavic peoples; their distinctive languages and alphabets also date from the fourth century. The Azerbaidzhanis, by contrast, are a Shi'ite Muslim community of Persian (Iranian) culture; their language, however, is Turkic in origin. The territory that presently constitutes their Republic came under Russian control in the early 19th century and entered the USSR, together with Georgia and Armenia, in 1922.

The greatest cultural division of all is between the Slavs and other European peoples and the predominantly Muslim nationalities of Central Asia. (Central Asia is used here in the Western sense; Soviet geographers exclude Kazakhstan from the term.) The peoples of these Republics (Uzbeks, Kazakhs, Kirghiz, Tadzhiks and Turkmen are the main nationalities) are the descendants of the great Mongol empires of medieval times. Most of them speak languages that are of Turkic origin, with the notable exception of the Tadzhiks, whose language is of Iranian origin. The territories which they inhabit are largely inhospitable, with large expanses of desert and some of the world's highest mountains. Levels of literacy traditionally have been low (some of the nationalities concerned had no written language at the time of their incorporation into the USSR). Industry is relatively little developed (although there are important iron and coal deposits in Kazakhstan) and there is a heavy emphasis upon 'cash crops' of various kinds, mostly cotton. The peoples of these Republics are overwhelmingly Muslim (mostly Sunni) by religion, and their traditional customs and values, with which their religion is inextricably bound up, have been altered relatively little by the experience of Russian and Soviet rule, which has lasted for no more than about one century (most of Central Asia only came under Russian control in the second half of the 19th century).

THE NATIONAL QUESTION UNDER GORBACHEV

The first significant expression of nationalist discontent after Mikhail Gorbachev's accession as Soviet leader was in the Central Asian Republic of Kazakhstan, in December 1986. It followed the nomination of an ethnic Russian, Gennady Kolbin, to replace the ethnic Kazakh incumbent as First Secretary of the Communist Party of Kazakhstan. Kazakhs, although less than a majority of the population, had always held the leading posts in their own Republic. The appointment led to demonstrations in which some 3,000 people took part.

Then, in mid-1987, a group of about 700 Crimean Tatars staged an unprecedented demonstration in Red Square, Moscow. The Tatars had been expelled from their traditional homelands in the Crimea in 1944, following allegations that they had collaborated with the Nazis. They were not exonerated until 1967, which was much later than other nationalities who had suffered a similar fate, and they were given no general right to return to the Crimea (a part of Ukraine since 1954). The Tatars' public protests were allowed to take place without police harassment, and a government commission was established to examine the merits of their case. It reported in June 1988, recommending the removal of any restrictions upon the right of individual Tatars to return to their native land, but also rejecting the Tatars' demand that their autonomous republic be re-established. Pressure for change continued nevertheless, and, in February 1991, a Crimean Autonomous Republic was finally restored, but with the overwhelming Russian population remaining largely opposed to a mass return by the Tatars to their homeland.

Other nationalities who were deported during or after the Second World War were often exiled to Central Asia, causing resentment in a region with growing unemployment. In both Uzbekistan and Kazakhstan economic hardship and high levels of unemployment among young people were thought to have contributed to the inter-ethnic conflict which occurred there in the late 1980s and early 1990s. Meskhetian Turks, deported from Georgia in 1944, were the victims of violent attacks in the Fergana region of Uzbekistan in mid-1989. The violence began in early June and swiftly became the bloodiest in Soviet peacetime history, with at least 100 deaths and over 1,000 injuries during a two-week period. The riots appear to have been precipitated by an apparently casual incident, when a

Meskhetian tipped over a table of strawberries being sold by an Uzbek. This provoked disorders in which one person died and 60 were injured. A much more serious incident began on 3–4 June when gangs of armed youths in search of Meskhetians appeared on the streets of Fergana and other towns. In the nearby village of Tashlak over 400 houses and several public buildings were destroyed. In June and September 1989 inter-ethnic disturbances, leading to seven deaths, were reported in Kazakhstan, as ethnic Kazakhs expressed their resentment at settlers from Transcaucasia. In February 1990 there were also disturbances in Dushanbe, the capital of Tadzhikistan, following rumours that Armenian refugees were to be given scarce housing accommodation.

In mid-1987 what was, in many ways, the most significant of all the nationality disputes in the USSR began to acquire open form in the Baltic Republics. Lithuania, Latvia and Estonia had been incorporated into the USSR after agreement with Germany in the 'Secret Protocols' of the 1939 Nazi–Soviet Pact. In 1940 the Republics were occupied by Soviet forces and were proclaimed constituent republics of the USSR. In June 1987 demonstrations occurred in Latvia to commemorate those who had been deported from the Republic by the Soviet authorities in 1941. On 23 August, the anniversary of the signature of the Pact, several thousand Estonians and Latvians were reported to have taken part in demonstrations. The Secret Protocols, the existence of which had previously been denied by the Soviet authorities, were finally published in the Baltic press in August 1988 and in the all-Union press the following year. However, far from resolving the issue, the public acknowledgement that the Protocols existed cast doubt upon the legality of the incorporation of these Republics into the USSR.

In 1988 developments such as these encouraged the formation of 'popular fronts', ostensibly in support of *perestroika* but, in practice, in support of a greater degree of national self-government. Inter-ethnic relations in the USSR entered an entirely new stage when, in February 1990, supporters of the Lithuanian nationalist movement, Sąjūdis, won a majority of seats in the republican Supreme Soviet, which then, on 11 March, formally declared the Republic independent, on the basis of its pre-1940 Constitution. Gorbachev, addressing the all-Union Congress of People's Deputies, described the Lithuanian action as 'illegitimate and invalid' and refused to negotiate with what remained, in his view, an integral part of the USSR. The central authorities demanded that the declaration of independence be rescinded; after the Lithuanians refused to comply with this ultimatum an economic blockade was imposed, on 18 April. Estonia and Latvia adopted more cautious declarations of independence on 30 March and 4 May respectively, despite threats of similar action against them.

The situation eased somewhat when the Lithuanian declaration of independence was suspended, on 29 June 1990, allowing the blockade to be lifted and discussions to begin. Gorbachev, on a visit to Lithuania in January 1990, had promised that a law would be adopted allowing republics to become fully independent. However, the new law, approved on 3 April, specified a two-thirds majority in a referendum on the issue and then a transitional period of up to five years in which territorial, proprietorial and other issues would be resolved. Only the Lithuanians accounted for so large a proportion of the population of their own republic, and the measure was widely seen as impeding rather than facilitating a transition to full independence. The resolution of differences in this or any other way became still more unlikely when, in January 1991, military force was used in an apparent attempt to restore central authority in Latvia and Lithuania, on the pretext that the Constitution of the USSR was being violated. Thirteen people died when troops stormed the television centre in Vilnius (Lithuania); four died in a battle for government buildings in Riga (Latvia).

The actions of the central authorities rallied local opinion more closely around the republican leaderships. Thus, at republican referendums, in early 1991, the demand for full independence received overwhelming endorsement. In Lithuania, over 75% of the electorate voted for independence. In Latvia and Estonia, in March, over 60% of those eligible to vote endorsed the independence proposals. The referendums had little constitutional force, but they strengthened the authority of the republican leaderships as they gradually extended their control over local affairs. All three Republics withdrew from the work of all-Union institutions, and suspended contributions to the all-Union budget. They established their own customs services and, despite a continuing lack of recognition by most other countries, issued their own stamps and passports.

When it was announced, on 19 August 1991, that power had been seized by an eight-man committee of hardliners, the Baltics immediately suspected that they would be among the first areas to be subjected to military suppression. Interior ministry troops, who had conducted a campaign of violence against the Baltic Governments since late 1990, seized media and communications facilities in Latvia and Lithuania and the Baltic leaderships prepared to establish governments-in-exile in the event of full military suppression. In defiance of the new Soviet leaders the Supreme Councils of Estonia and Latvia met to declare the full independence of their Republics. However, the feared military action did not take place, as the coup collapsed within three days. The prospect of renewed repression was replaced by that of formal independence, as political pressure increased for Western countries to extend diplomatic recognition to the Baltic States. There was a sudden rush of support from previously reluctant foreign ministries, and by the end of August more than 30 countries had recognized the three states. In September the USA and, most importantly, the USSR itself extended recognition, and Estonia, Latvia and Lithuania were all admitted to the UN on 17 September.

Whereas the three Baltic Republics co-operated closely in their attempts to achieve independence, conflict in Transcaucasia was as evident between neighbouring nationalities as between republican and all-Union authorities. Nationalist tensions took a particularly violent and intractable form in the case of Nagorny Karabakh, an autonomous oblast which, since 1923, had formed a part of the Azerbaidzhan SSR. According to the census of 1979, its population of about 162,000 was 75.9% Armenian and only 22.9% Azerbaidzhani, and there had been pressure for some years for the transfer of the region to Armenia. The conflict began in early 1988, after the central authorities of the CPSU rejected an appeal for Nagorny Karabakh to become part of Armenia. In early February, following demonstrations in Stepanakert, the oblast's capital, a resolution was adopted by the regional soviet, demanding the transfer of Nagorny Karabakh to Armenia. Further demonstrations took place in the Armenian capital, Yerevan, to support the campaign for the incorporation of Nagorny Karabakh into the Republic. The demonstrations temporarily ended after a personal appeal by Gorbachev, but they began again after 26 Armenians were killed in an anti-Armenian riot in Azerbaidzhan, in the town of Sumgait.

In January 1989, in response to continued tension in the area, the Soviet Government established a 'special commission' to govern Nagorny Karabakh, effectively introducing direct rule from Moscow. Demonstrations and disorders persisted nevertheless; the decision of the Congress of People's Deputies to elect an Azerbaidzhani, as well as an Armenian, to represent the region in the new all-Union Supreme Soviet aroused particular indignation. Further disorders were precipitated by the decision to abolish the special commission, in November 1989, and return Nagorny Karabakh to Azerbaidzhani rule. In January 1990 the dispute extended into intercommunal violence across both Republics, precipitated by an Armenian decision to extend the provisions of their republican budget and electoral law to the enclave. Tens of thousands took to the streets in Baku, the capital of Azerbaidzhan, and in other cities, and up to 60 people lost their lives in anti-Armenian pogroms. On 19–20 January troops were used to restore order in Baku and other towns where the Azerbaidzhani Popular Front was in control. Over 100 people lost their lives in the first days of fighting. Despite the increased use of Soviet troops in the area, the underlying tensions remained and inter-ethnic violence continued throughout 1990 and 1991. Indeed, in mid-1991 the use of Soviet troops was criticized by the Armenian leadership, who claimed that they were siding with Azerbaidzhani forces and attempting to deport the Armenian population of Nagorny Karabakh. This alleged bias of the military seemed to have ended after the August coup, and hopes for peace rose after a cease-fire was agreed, in September, at talks arranged by Boris Yeltsin, President of the Russian Federation, and Nursultan Nazarbayev, President of Kazakhstan. However, negotiations collapsed after Azerbaidzhan alleged that Armenians had shot down an aircraft carrying leading Azerbaidzhani officials. Violence flared again at the end of December when Azerbaidzhani forces bombarded Stepanakert.

Long-standing tensions also emerged in the Georgian Republic in the late 1980s, inspired in part by nationalist pressures for republican autonomy or independence, and, in part, by differences of a social and ethnic character within Georgia itself. The 1989 census showed the Georgians to be one of the most 'patriotic' of the major nationalities of the USSR, as measured by the proportion that lived in their own Republic, and their share of the republican population had been steadily increasing during the 1970s and 1980s, unlike the position in the Baltic Republics. There were public disturbances in 1956, shortly after Khrushchev's denunciation of Stalin, and in 1978, when the status of the republican language appeared to be under threat. As in the Baltic Republics, there was public opposition to apparently centralizing constitutional amendments, which were published in 1988. An unprecedented hunger strike took place in Tbilisi, the Georgian capital, and there were strikes and demonstrations in other large towns.

In February 1989, on the anniversary of the incorporation of the Republic into the USSR, further protests took place. In April there were even larger demonstrations in Tbilisi; more than 100,000 people gathered in front of the headquarters of the Communist Party and the Republic's Government. They were demanding both the secession of Georgia from the USSR and the full integration of the Abkhazian Autonomous Republic, which was itself seeking to secede from Georgia. On the night of 9/10 April these demonstrators were attacked by Soviet troops; at least 20 were killed, according to official sources, and a curfew was introduced.

In October 1990 tensions became still greater when Round Table–Free Georgia, a coalition of nationalist parties, won a majority of seats in the republican Supreme Soviet. The Supreme Soviet then adopted a resolution calling for a gradual transition to independence. Following a referendum in favour of independence, the republican Supreme Soviet declared Georgia fully independent in April 1991. The previous December, however, the South Ossetian Autonomous Oblast, which had existed within Georgian boundaries since 1922, had been abolished by the new Georgian Government. Gorbachev overruled the decision by decree, but, by March 1991, inter-ethnic violence in South Ossetia had caused at least 51 deaths, and some 13,000 people had left the area. The violence continued throughout 1991, with the South Ossetians seeking to secede from Georgia and unite with their neighbouring co-nationals in the North Ossetian Autonomous Republic, in the Russian Federation.

There were strong pressures from other nationalities for a greater degree of control over their own affairs. In late 1988 a popular front was established in Ukraine, influenced by concerns about the environment as well as by enduring linguistic and other cultural issues. The Front, known as Rukh (Movement), held its founding congress in September 1989. The republican leadership, meanwhile, began to address one of its central concerns by making Ukrainian the official language in the Republic. A declaration of sovereignty, in July 1990, asserted the Republic's right to its own armed forces and control over its natural resources. The strength of Ukrainian nationalism grew rapidly in 1991, with the leadership being forced by public pressure to adopt an increasingly independent policy in negotiations for a new Union Treaty. On 24 August 1991 the Supreme Soviet adopted a declaration of independence, subject to approval by a referendum due to take place in December. Independence was overwhelmingly approved in the referendum, with some 90% of participants in the referendum voting for an independent Ukraine.

In Moldavia, ethnic Romanian inhabitants demonstrated in favour of greater control over local affairs, and, in May 1990, a non-Communist, nationalist Government was formed. Non-Moldavian inhabitants (mainly Slavs to the east of the Dniester river and Gagauz Turks in the south) responded by establishing their own 'autonomous republics' and electing their own 'supreme soviets'. Inter-ethnic violence was reported when the Moldavian Government attempted to reassert its control throughout the Republic. Moldavia also declared independence following the August coup, but ethnic strife continued when the Government arrested leaders of the non-Moldavian areas, allegedly for supporting the coup.

In mid-1990 national assertiveness reached the largest and most populous of the USSR's republics, the Russian Federation. In May 1990 elections took place to the republican Congress of People's Deputies, in which radical candidates won about one-third of the votes cast. After several ballots Boris Yeltsin, the former First Secretary of Moscow, was elected Chairman of the republican Supreme Soviet. Yeltsin's programme combined demands for radical political reform with a strong appeal for increased sovereignty for the Russian Federation, including ownership of all the Republic's natural resources, an independent foreign policy and the primacy of republican legislation over all-Union legislation. The Russian Congress of People's Deputies adopted such a programme on 12 June 1990. In a separate development, a Russian Communist Party was established, and Ivan Polozkov, the conservative First Secretary of Krasnodar, was elected as its leader. Other republican institutions, including a trade union organization, a union of journalists and a national symphony orchestra, were established later in the year. In 1991 a republican Academy of Sciences and a Committee of State Security (KGB) were established, and a Russian radio and television service began to operate. In June 1991 there was a popular election for an executive presidency of the Russian Federation. The elections were won by Yeltsin, who pledged to implement a programme of economic and political reforms.

The opposition of Yeltsin to the failed *coup d'état* of August 1991 and the subsequent dissolution of central administrative organs greatly enhanced the power of the Russian Federation. Immediately after the coup collapsed Yeltsin asserted control over many all-Union bodies and all economic enterprises on Russian territory. The Russian KGB took over some parts of the all-Union KGB, expanding from a force of some 300 officers to one numbering some 20,000. Other all-Union bodies, such as the USSR Academy of Sciences, also reverted to Russian jurisdiction. By the end of 1991, with the creation of the Commonwealth of Independent States as the replacement for the USSR, the Russian Federation took control over all Soviet institutions in Russia and, indeed, in other countries, including Soviet embassies and the Soviet seat in the UN Security Council.

During 1990 many autonomous republics, oblasts and okrugs within the Russian Federation adopted declarations of sovereignty, and some unilaterally upgraded their status. In late 1990 both the Tatar ASSR (Tatarstan) and the Bashkir ASSR claimed the status of union republics and complained of exploitation of their plentiful resources by all-Union and Russian ministries. There were also frequent protests from many of the smaller nationalities of the USSR about decreasing populations and the use of their territories for unrestricted industrial activity, particularly in Siberia. The declarations of sovereignty were aimed as much at the newly-elected Government of the Russian Federation as at the all-Union authorities. The decision to allow autonomous republics to sign the protocol to a new Union Treaty, in March 1991, was challenged by the Government of the Russian Federation, which was worried about the threat to its own federal system. In late 1991, as the Russian leadership developed its power *vis-à-vis* the all-Union authorities, there was unrest in several autonomous formations, notably in Tatarstan and Chechen-Ingushetia, where local nationalists advocated full independence from Russia. Several nationalities, such as the Ingush and the Karachai, further developed their campaigns to re-establish autonomous territories that had been abolished after they were deported during the Second World War.

Conservatives predominated in the leaderships of many of these autonomous territories, and some seemed to being using declarations of sovereignty as a way to preserve their privileged status and weaken the democratic Russian leadership. The independence of former Union Republics bordering the Russian Federation offered further prospects for the dissolution of Russia by secessionist autonomous republics. The Russian Government opposed any prospect of independence for its autonomous territories, since none of them, with the exception of the Tuva ASSR (the Republic of Tuva—until 1944 a nominally independent country between the USSR and Mongolia) and the Buryat ASSR (Buryatia) had an international border. By October 1991, however, the four Autonomous Republics in the northern Caucasus (Kabardino-Balkaria, North Ossetia, Chechen-Ingushetia and Daghestan) had frontiers with Republics which had proclaimed their independence.

NATIONALITIES POLICY AND THE END OF THE UNION

The Soviet leadership, under Gorbachev, was relatively slow to respond to the challenge of national assertiveness. It was not until September 1989 that a plenary meeting of the CPSU Central Committee was held to deal with the deepening crisis. The meeting approved a 'platform' on the national question which acknowledged the harm that had been done to inter-ethnic relations by the repression of the

Stalinist years and by later attempts to accelerate the natural convergence of different nationalities. The document suggested that in future there should be radical changes in the state structure, leading to a 'renewed federation'. This was to involve greater devolved powers for the republics, including a greater degree of economic autonomy. National languages were to be encouraged, but Russian was to remain the language of inter-ethnic communication and all languages were to have equality of status. Gorbachev insisted that there could not be any retreat from the 'internationalist inheritance' of the October Revolution; the CPSU stood for a 'powerful federal state, convinced that this corresponded to the interests of all the people that (made up) the USSR'.

The plenum, however, had little influence upon subsequent events and, from 1990 onwards, the emphasis shifted to a new Union Treaty, which would regulate relations between the Republics and which would also guarantee the position of national groups in whatever Republic they were resident. The draft of a treaty of this kind was published in November 1990 and then, with some modifications, in March 1991. According to the revised draft, all the Republics that agreed to sign the treaty were to constitute a 'federal democratic state' in which they would have the right to choose their own forms of property and government. The central government would be responsible for defence and foreign policy, law enforcement and the all-Union budget. Other responsibilities, including socio-economic development, energy, education and science, would be regulated jointly by the central and republican governments. In December 1990 Gorbachev proposed that a referendum should take place to determine the attitude of the peoples of the USSR towards a new federal structure, and an exercise of this kind (the first in Soviet history) took place on 26 March 1991. Some 80% of the total eligible electorate took part, with 76% of these voting in favour. Six of the 15 Republics (the three Baltic Republics, Georgia, Armenia and Moldavia) refused to participate, and in several of the big cities (such as Moscow and Leningrad) the majority in favour was small. Following the referendum, the nine republics which had participated signed an agreement with Gorbachev (the 'Nine-plus-One Agreement') designed to prevent further economic decline and to resolve the conflict between the all-Union and republican Governments. A revised draft of the Union Treaty was agreed in July, with the powers of the centre yet further reduced, prompting conservatives to renew their efforts to preserve the unity of the USSR.

It was no coincidence that the attempted *coup d' état* in August 1991 took place the day before the nine republics were due to sign the revised Union Treaty. There is little doubt that the coup leaders would have used military force, if necessary, to prevent the secession of any of the Republics. In the event, the failure of the coup only served to hasten the dissolution of the Union. During the coup Estonia and Latvia declared independence, followed by Azerbaidzhan, Uzbekistan and Moldavia. Ukraine also declared independence, subject to a referendum to be held in December, and in Turkmenistan independence was declared after approval in a referendum. This *de facto* devolution of power to the Republics was formalized by the all-Union Congress of People's Deputies on 5 September. All-Union institutions were to be reduced to a minimum, and a new State Council, which consisted of the heads of each republic, plus President Gorbachev, was established as the foremost executive power in the country. In addition, a new Supreme Soviet was created, which consisted of delegations from each participating Republic. However, despite an economic agreement between eight of the former Union Republics, signed on 18 October, there seemed little prospect of anything more than minimal political union between the erstwhile constituent members of the USSR, with only seven of the Republics participating in the first session of the new Supreme Soviet. When the Russian Federation leadership rejected Gorbachev's proposal to establish a loose confederal state, the Union of Sovereign States, as the successor to the USSR, the prospects for any new state emerging from the collapse of the Soviet state were effectively ended. Instead, on 21 December 1991, 11 of the former Union Republics agreed to dissolve the USSR and create the Commonwealth of Independent States.

Perhaps the clearest lesson of these developments was that earlier Soviet perceptions of the national question were gravely inadequate. In line with at least a part of the Marxist tradition, nationality differences were seen as having no real social basis, unlike the divisions that existed between classes (for theoretical background see essay on *Nationalism and National Minorities*, pp. 11–15). Under Stalin, and to some extent under Khrushchev, it was argued that nationality differences would lose their importance until eventually the different nationalities 'fused' into a single Soviet nation. During the 1970s and early 1980s it began to be accepted that fusion (*sliyanie*) was probably unattainable, at least in the short-term, and the emphasis shifted to 'convergence' (*sblizhenie*). Under Gorbachev it became clearer that nationality differences could no longer be attributed to vestiges of capitalism or external influences, nor was there any solution to them within the framework of Marxism. Indeed, Soviet rule worsened rather than solved the nationality problem and, with its policies of arbitrary deportation and encouragement of Russian emigration to the non-Russian Republics, ensured that it would remain a problem for the successor states to the USSR for years to come.

The Armed Forces, the KGB and Gorbachev

Dr MYLES ROBERTSON

Although very different institutions, serving different purposes and with varied functions, both the Soviet Armed Forces and the Committee of State Security (KGB) were central all-Union organs with overlapping responsibilities for aspects of domestic security and external affairs. Both had vital associations, in their own ways, to the pre-August 1991 central political apparatus. At their most basic, *perestroika* and *glasnost* redesigned the structures and mechanics by which each organization carried out its duties and exerted influence.

Mikhail Gorbachev's approach to administrative reform emphasized streamlining, co-ordination and 'specific tasking' whereby 'objective-orientated' groups were established. This usually involved a distinct change from the rigid structures of the past, and often these new groupings did not follow formalized lines of authority. When applied to the highest levels of national security policy, what Gorbachev tried to establish was an overall framework, which was empowered to oversee, extend and regularize the entire process. This had fundamental consequences for the role, status and influence of the Armed Forces, the KGB, the Ministry of Internal Affairs (MVD) and the Ministry of Foreign Affairs (MID). Their position to influence policy, to act as recipients of large shares of central resources and their ability to function as 'lobby groups', was in some cases strengthened, in others weakened. As part of the establishment of a 'constitutional base' for policy, both domestic and foreign, these groups became responsible to parliamentary committees of the Congress of People's Deputies and the Supreme Soviet.

This increase in formal accountability to state institutions was the primary impact of the democratization of the Soviet political system as it affected both groups. At the time of the August coup it seemed that the Armed Forces had been more substantially affected than the KGB. The constraint of genuine parliamentary accountability was yet to be applied to the KGB.

Under Gorbachev, both organizations were accused of, at the least, hindering reform and, in many cases, actively and brutally opposing it. Their stance was attributed to many causes: protection of deeply entrenched interests, political affiliation to the old order, the continuing subversive influence of the remnants of the CPSU, innate conservatism on the part of personnel and, simply, inertia. Evidence to support this view was to be found in examples provided by the use of troops (apparently sanctioned by the all-Union authorities), especially in the Baltic Republics, to suppress democracy; the prominence and anti-reform activity of military conservatives—the so-called 'Black Colonels' in the Supreme Soviet; allegations of KGB interference to discredit liberal reformers; and harassment campaigns against prominent reform-minded individuals.

More realistically, the motives of participants, the cohesiveness of political platforms and the lines of authority and command were not so clearly delineated. There was genuine confusion, uncertainty and hesitation on the part of decision-makers. Republican authorities in all branches of government had, in practice, considerable latitude in interpreting or enforcing instructions or policies issued by the all-Union authorities. To portray recent and current issues in terms of 'reform' versus 'stagnation', and groups as 'liberals', 'radical reformers', 'conservatives' and 'hardliners', is a simplistic and misleading labelling. All institutions undertook reform and most individuals viewed reform as inevitable and irreversible. For the majority of participants, the real debate was over how far and how quickly reform should proceed and what should be sacrificed in the process. As with other groups, the Army and the KGB had their own views; some coincided with those of others, some did not.

THE SOVIET ARMED FORCES AND GORBACHEV

Both *perestroika* and *glasnost* affected the military in a number of major ways. Though the Army seemed to have avoided significant upheaval in the early years of Gorbachev's period of office (partly due to resistance from within the higher ranks), by 1987–88 the reform programme was beginning to have notable impact.

One of the fundamental themes of the restructuring of the Soviet system concerned the reallocation of economic resources, particularly from the military to civil sectors. Justifying such a radical shift required changes in the ideological justification of various groups and policies as they pertained to Soviet society. Aside from the command economy, the military represented the single most important of such groups where economic allocation was concerned. The ideological justification for the high priority afforded to military expenditure was dependent upon the Marxist-Leninist view of international relations, which emphasized the conflictual nature of international relations with capitalist states. However, the rejection of such traditional class-based analyses of both domestic and international politics permitted a radical reappraisal of the role of the military in Soviet foreign policy and their relationship to the political leadership of the Soviet, or any future Russian, state.

Proposals from Gorbachev and his fellow reformers instituted a re-examination of the traditional role of the military in foreign policy. New emphases and new objectives for policy resulted in a decrease in the influence of the military factor in external relations. Although the majority of the military were clearly relieved to complete the withdrawal from Afghanistan, in early 1989, the retrenchment from overseas bases and allied countries further afield (such as the former People's Democratic Republic of Yemen, Viet-Nam, Angola and Mozambique) was not welcomed by sections of the Soviet High Command.

Despite initial resistance and continuing discontent, shown by the reluctance to implement the Conventional Forces in Europe (CFE) arms reduction agreement, signed in November 1990, the Soviet High Command grudgingly accepted unilateral reductions and the advantages of further arms-control measures. Although it was a great psychological shock, the withdrawal from Eastern European countries was accepted as a *fait accompli*. The scale of military change achieved under Gorbachev was made possible by a variety of factors. Firstly, the appointment of some new personnel to leading positions, including the promotion of Dmitry Yazov to Minister of Defence, in May 1985, and Mikhail Moiseyev to Chief of the General Staff, in 1988. Both men were reputed to be reformers of a sort and very competent officers. The replacement of senior personnel was made easier for the political leadership by fortuitous circumstances. A series of embarrassing incidents occurred, highlighting widespread military incompetence (notably, the event which resulted in Yazov's appointment, when Matthias Rust, a young West German, flew a private aircraft from Helsinki to Moscow, without alerting air defences, and landed in Red Square) and thereby provided the leadership with legitimate reason to engage in wholesale dismissals of recalcitrant personnel. Thirdly, the exploitation of divisions within the ranks of the military prevented the senior ranks from forming a coherent opposition to strategic withdrawal and overall retrenchment. Fourthly, the political leadership often succeeded in distancing itself from controversial military action within the country. Thus they were able to use the military's growing unpopularity against itself.

The withdrawal from Eastern Europe was the most troublesome issue. This proved difficult not so much because of resistance to the idea of withdrawal *per se*, though in some quarters that was significant, but because of the practical consequences of too hurried a withdrawal. The rapid nature of the withdrawal caused organizational disruption which worsened morale problems. The Soviet withdrawal from Czechoslovakia and Hungary was completed by mid-1991, less than 18 months after the terms of withdrawal were agreed with the new non-Communist leaders. Withdrawal also began of Soviet troops in Poland, which numbered some 50,000 in mid-1991, and the 380,000 troops stationed in the former German Democratic Republic were to leave by the end of 1994. In addition, by late 1991, the newly-independent Baltic States were demanding that some 400,000 Soviet forces leave by the end of the year; the military claimed that no withdrawal could be completed before 1994. This geographic restructuring and redeployment of Soviet forces, combined with other factors (see below), gave greater urgency to the debate on the need for a review of military doctrines and strategies, especially as they pertained to the European theatre of operations. This, in turn, also had implications for the future size and structure of the Armed Forces.

Paralleling the reorganization of the military and its role in policy, decision-making structures were also reformed. The result of these reforms was to confine the participation and influence of the military in the decision-making process to defence-orientated areas. The remit of the Defence Council was restricted to solely defence matters, while a new structure, the Security Council, was created in November 1990, to advise (it had no legal authority) the Soviet President on matters of national security. The Minister of Defence was a member of this body.

The Soviet Army represented the last vestiges of the Russian imperial system; the principles under which it operated and its bases of recruitment made it the institutional embodiment of the Soviet empire. Despite its multinational representation, it remained formally subordinate to the all-Union authorities. In the early 1990s more than 90% of the officer corps were ethnic Slavs and 80% were ethnic Russians. The Russians dominated the élite combat units and technical services. This basic structure of the Army was the source of the second major crisis to afflict it in the Gorbachev era, the severe problems caused by ethnic and nationalist disturbance and the demands for political and economic decentralization.

As an almost entirely conscript multi-national force, the Army was placed in a position of deep internal schism as a result of the breakdown of social cohesion and law and order in many of the Union Republics. As the demands for genuine autonomy and decentralization of authority increased, the previously subsumed ethnic allegiances asserted themselves and the delicate inter-ethnic balance within the Army was disturbed. Although groupings by nationality had become prevalent within the ranks, there were also quite notable divisions within the officer corps

itself, not simply between 'reformers' and 'conservatives' but between higher and junior officer ranks. These divisions reflected not merely disputes over the nature and extent of political or economic reform but also divergence over the structure and nature of future Soviet armed forces. These disputes focused on proposals for a smaller, more technically professional army and also the evolution of new military doctrines compatible with changed military balances, new force structures and the exploitation of high technology for military purposes.

As an organization which was always utilized as a force for social cohesion and one perceived, by the population and by itself, as defender of the people and their values, the domestic disarray had a severe effect on the Army. The role played by the Army in repressing civil discontent, particularly in the killing of civilians in Tbilisi (Georgia) in April 1989, and in Baku (Azerbaidzhan) in 1990, the stories of brutality in Afghanistan, the revelations of the years of mismanagement within the forces, the emergence of previously hidden statistics detailing the very high numbers of conscript fatalities as a result of accident and negligence during peacetime service (15,000 in 1985–90) and widespread reports of bullying within the ranks, all contributed to a drastic decline in public respect for the military. In the pro-independence Republics and among radical liberal reformers respect for the Army was negligible.

Consequently, the military as a vocation and career lost much of its attractiveness. Previously a privileged claimant on economic resources and a means of secure employment, the status of the Armed Forces changed. Levels of pay became comparatively less favourable, job security was lessened as a result of retrenchment and reductions in resources, and the rapid retreat from Eastern Europe resulted in at least 200,000 servicemen being relocated to sub-standard housing. At officer corps level, it became very difficult to recruit and retain personnel, while at conscript level, the 1990/91 drafts were the worst on record, with hundreds of thousands of young men evading the call-up. The half-hearted and heavy-handed attempts at remedial measures by the authorities to enforce conscription merely served to illustrate the weakness of the military and foster further discontent with its methods.

The general dislocation of the economy affected the military–industrial sector, resulting in supply and labour disruption and raising costs. Despite intentions to convert military production to civilian use, much of this sector remained intact. A transition to a market-orientated system for the entire economy would inevitably raise yet further the procurement price of military equipment from its artificially low levels. This will have a disruptive effect on defence budgeting. Procurement will be reduced, unbalancing certain sections compared with others and affording greater importance to the necessity of efficient use of equipment, stricter management and professionalization of the military system.

Overall, in 1991, it was too early to gauge the full impact of this expected decrease in expenditure. Though reductions in expenditure had already been implemented, these were largely accommodated by the reduction of commitment overseas and by unilateral and negotiated reductions in manning and equipment levels. By mid-1991 approximately 500,000 troops had been demobilized, there had been a complete withdrawal from Mongolia, in addition to withdrawals from Eastern European countries, and thousands of tanks and other items of equipment had been destroyed under the terms of the CFE agreement.

However, these reductions did not substantially affect the basic capability of Soviet forces. Major procurement programmes and core military components were spared drastic change (for example, the procurement of major Soviet naval units remained at high pre-Gorbachev levels). However, the partial discrediting of the military and the economic crisis affecting the country in 1991 made it inevitable that much more radical reductions would have to be made. The loss of any all-Union centre, with tax-gathering powers made any unified Armed Forces dependent upon contributions from individual Republics. The Republics may decline to continue high levels of contribution towards defence when there are more politically important demands on their expenditure budgets.

The broader re-evaluation of Soviet society and its values placed the Army in a very difficult and ambivalent role. In general, it is true that its officers were of the opinion that reform brought instability, pacifism, separatism and hostility towards the Armed Forces. However, military dissatisfaction and criticism should not be portrayed as hostility to reform *per se*. Military motivations and beliefs were at best mixed. The officer corps was divided on the issue of rapid reform but, equally, the large majority were against being used by the political leadership to maintain public order. The more astute officers voiced publicly the need to have legal prohibitions against the military ever being deployed in such a cause. The result of the coup of August 1991 demonstrated where the basic loyalty of the military lay.

The combination of many of the disruptive factors outlined above with the concurrent debate over military doctrine, the necessity for a force of highly trained manpower to fight a high technology war and the events of the August coup are powerful arguments for the creation of a professional, rather than conscript, army. In 1991 the Soviet Navy had already begun the transition to an all-volunteer force. After the coup the most likely model suggested for the future seemed to be that of a 'Russian' army, supported when necessary by national or regional territorial units.

The scale of civil disturbance, growing economic disruption, political instability and the politicization of the officer corps, inevitably produced frequent rumours of a military coup against Gorbachev from 1989 onwards. All available evidence indicated that such an event seemed unlikely to occur. The reasons why most thought any military involvement in a coup was not likely are various. Firstly, it has not been a traditional role for the military in Russian or Soviet history. Secondly, the military leadership seemed to be aware of the immense problems it would encounter by assuming 'control' of the country (even the assumption that they could actually do the latter was highly questionable). It seemed to be accepted that national difficulties were such that it was doubtful if anyone could govern any better than Gorbachev. Unlike a political leadership, a military government would never be supported by more than a small minority of the population. Beyond that, it was highly questionable that the military would wish to intervene in politics. Such actions would have transgressed the professional military ethic.

The Military and the August Coup

However, the reasons outlined above were not enough to prevent partial involvement in the coup of August 1991. They do, however, seem to account for the fact that the military failed to participate fully and very quickly declared its support for the constitutionally elected authority.

The difficulties experienced by the military under Gorbachev provided the general background to the military's partial participation in the August coup attempt. There were, however, more immediate reasons for the military's involvement: a threat to 'traditional values' perceived by some elements in the military; a hasty decision by leaders to participate without a full consideration of the issues; and a feeling of desperation that 'something must be done' to prevent further 'chaos' in the country. Resentment at the effects of reform on the Soviet Armed Forces did not seem to feature highly as a motive. Indeed, as events showed, a huge majority of the military (certainly the rank and file, mid-ranking officers too, with the High Command being divided) were in favour of reform, if not Gorbachev personally.

In practice, prior to the coup, when the military was used to maintain public order it had been élite units such as airborne forces that were used. However, these were very limited in numbers and were neither specifically equipped nor trained for an internal security role such as, for example, riot control. Therefore, despite the general impression, in practice the burden of maintaining order and of carrying the responsibility for domestic intervention fell not upon the military, but upon USSR Ministry of the Interior (MVD) troops. Even among MVD troops specialized units were used, in co-operation with those of the KGB.

THE KGB AND GORBACHEV

The relationship between Gorbachev, the political leadership and the KGB, was much more complex than that with the Armed Forces. The KGB and its predecessors (the internal security forces or 'secret police' have had various structures and names, beginning with the *Cheka*, in 1917, headed by Feliks Dzherzhinsky) always served as the 'second pillar' of Soviet power, as the 'action arm' of the Party. As a result they were always closely connected with the leadership. Many commentators have depicted an 'independent' KGB apparatus; this is a misrepresentation of the true state of affairs. At all levels the political leadership exerted its influence throughout the KGB, such that all major KGB actions and policies were sanctioned by the political authorities.

In one sense, therefore, the KGB was very much a politicized organization. However, as an organization with professional responsibilities which it sought to protect and gain influence from, it tried to follow an apolitical course even within a one-Party state. It was always aware of the need to balance these two tendencies. Because of this, beyond agreement over fundamentals, there is a spectrum of opinion as to the exact role and influence of the KGB in the pre-coup Soviet state. Similarly, there is disagreement over the degree of emphasis placed on its internal, as opposed to its external, responsibilities. A common view stresses the primacy of its internal role as the guardian of the political system, with its overseas activities taking second place. There is also an approach which depicts a broader picture and a KGB participation in the Soviet polity resultant from its various roles, political influence and status as a large government bureaucracy.

As a result of the policies of *perestroika* and *glasnost*, in some ways this picture became clearer, but in other ways more complex. For example, prior to the coup attempt, the implications for the future KGB role, given the evolution of a genuine multi-party parliamentary system in the USSR or 'Russia' were already being considered. Already the move to a separate Russian Federation KGB was under way with the establishment of such an organization with a staff of some 300. Though still reliant upon the all-Union KGB, such a move could not entirely be dismissed as a cosmetic publicity gesture.

In the early years of Gorbachev's leadership, the KGB had supported the movement for reform. By 1987–88, however, its support had become less than enthusiastic. At the 27th Congress of the CPSU Gorbachev made it clear that he expected the KGB itself to reformed. After that, many

KGB personnel, particularly in the higher echelons of the organization, were replaced. Three other important consequences became apparent. Firstly, KGB operations and powers were placed on a comparatively more open legal basis. Secondly, although opinions as to its motivations and objectives may have differed, the KGB was, despite elements of resistance, inextricably involved in the reform programme (events of the August coup were to substantiate this). Thirdly, commitment to this process, the unpredictability of its own domestic involvement and the perception of a weakened USSR all combined to bestow greater importance on KGB activities overseas. These circumstances increased its influence internally.

Externally, KGB activity continued much as before, but with some new emphases. There was greater stress on the production of high quality analytical assessment of world affairs for the new Soviet national security planning structures that had been established. The weakened position of the Soviet state and the radical realignments in Eastern Europe generated an immediate necessity for greater attention to information as it pertained to potential threats overall and to unfavourable European regional developments. Economic intelligence was viewed as increasingly important, as the viability of the state became increasingly dependent on success in the world economy. This remit was also extended to the provision of KGB-gathered economic information to new Russian firms to minimize their disadvantageous position in a highly competitive international market. In addition, the protection of economic and commercial information, relating to both state and private trade, became a major concern for the KGB.

Internally, the KGB assumed a wide range of responsibilities. KGB officers and ex-officials were used to support a weakened state administration. In circumstances of domestic disturbance, loss of credibility and authority by the CPSU, inefficiency and bureaucratic upheaval, the KGB provided a resource of highly-trained administrative manpower. Though not necessarily actively sought, the overall influence of the KGB became more pervasive, reflected in, for example, the increase in KGB and MVD representation among deputies in the all-Union Congress of People's Deputies from 1.4% in 1989 to 4.9% in 1990.

Aside from continuing its standard duties of internal security, handled by its renamed Directorate for the Protection of the Soviet Constitution, the KGB assumed responsibility for investigating 'economic sabotage' and organized crime. These were crucial tasks as both economic and organized crime became significant subversive phenomena with international dimensions. The KGB also played a major role in combating nationalist unrest. In these cases it mainly concentrated on co-ordination of other state bodies, the elaboration of effective policies and the gathering of intelligence and information. It had the primary responsibility for combating the rising trend in terrorism and developed, and increasingly deployed, special anti-terrorist resources.

The KGB's principal role became one of a co-ordinating central authority in coping with these various sources and symptoms of discontent. It achieved this position, in part, by design, but also by default. Except for a few specific exceptions, the KGB was the only all-Union institution capable of at least attempting to fulfil such a role. The military was unwilling and unable to tackle civil or politicized issues; the MVD, although it had some specially trained high profile troops, notably the Otrady militsii osobovo naznacheniya (Special Purpose Police Detachments—OMON, also known as 'Black Berets'), was generally undermanned, underfunded, massively underequipped and staffed by underpaid personnel of questionable quality and training.

Steps were taken to rectify these deficiencies, but improvement was not expected in the short term.

Before the coup there were an estimated 380,000 troops under KGB control. Together with the MVD troops, internal security organs controlled approximately 1m. troops, but many of these were already committed to routine or comparatively low-priority tasks, such as border monitoring and protection work. Actual numbers of operationally deployable troops were far smaller. The numbers of forces with special training and equipment were far smaller. In 1991 the controversial OMON units, thought to have been formed in July 1988, only numbered 8,000 men, deployed in 30 units nationally.

In order to maximize the use of limited resources, much of the KGB effort, via its intelligence-gathering function, was put into preventative measures to contain the problem. This was more desirable than more costly and disruptive 'after-the-event' activity. In many senses, the KGB was the primary organization granted the task of 'holding the line'.

As an organization, the KGB made great efforts to be seen publicly to embrace democratization, to the extent that it agreed to remain accountable to guidelines established by the Supreme Soviet. The appointment as its Chairman of Gen. Vladimir Kryuchkov, in October 1988, was 'ratified' by parliamentary committee, and the size of the KGB budget for 1991 was made public: 4,900m. roubles (including expenditure on KGB Border Troops). However, this outward commitment to constitutional norms did not necessarily reduce the power of the KGB. The long-awaited Law on State Security, which was adopted in May 1991 by the Supreme Soviet, although formally and publicly codifying KGB powers, actually extended KGB authority in some areas.

Prior to the August coup, the question of division within the KGB concerning the desirability of certain developments in the USSR was problematic for outside observers. Information to substantiate significant differences of opinion was scant. Unlike the military, if dispute had taken place, it remained internal. Former KGB officers, most prominently Gen. Oleg Kalugin, had assumed the status of dissenters and took the view that the progress and support for reform within the KGB, in any meaningful sense, was minimal. To an extent, the KGB involvement in the coup validated this point of view. However, it became apparent that many KGB rank and file officers, as opposed to its ruling body, the KGB Collegium, did not want to be involved in an attempt to overturn the constitutional order. Regional KGB chiefs, notably in Leningrad, similarly rejected the actions of the plotters.

Some seven years after reforms were begun in the military and KGB by Andropov, the reform programme had had a significant impact on traditional Soviet institutions. The Soviet Armed Forces and the KGB each reacted in their own way when confronted by reform. The KGB had accepted publicly the *perestroika* programme, though doubts remained as to whether change had genuinely affected some of the central premises of the organization. Nevertheless, it proved more adaptable and flexible than the military, at least in the short term.

PROBLEMS AND PROSPECTS

In late 1991 the future of both the military and the security and intelligence organizations in a dissolved Soviet empire remained undecided. Following the coup the KGB was the organization most severely affected. The prominent role of its chairman, Kryuchkov, and, apparently of many of the members of the Collegium, in the coup forced the Russian and Soviet leadership to instigate a full review of its personnel and its involvement and role in society, in the political apparatus and in the military. Vadim Bakatin, the former Minister of the Interior, was appointed as the organization's new chairman. He immediately began investigations into the organization's role in the coup and how it could be adapted to meet the needs of the new political structures emerging from the confusion which followed the August coup. Although Bakatin and the newly-appointed Minister of Defence, Yevgeny Shaposhnikov, emphasized the need for a continued federal security agency and unified military forces, it was not evident that either body could easily continue without some political agreement between the Republics. In October 1991 the newly-created State Council agreed to replace the KGB with an inter-republican co-ordinating committee, the Inter-Republican Security Service, to complement the increasingly-independent republican state security committees. The KGB's intelligence and counter-intelligence functions were transferred to a new institution, the USSR Central Intelligence Service, headed by Yevgeny Primakov. KGB border troops were delegated to a new body, the Committee for Guarding the USSR State Border, which was headed by the former chief of staff of KGB Border Troops, Ilya Kalinichenko.

The new structures which replaced the KGB still faced considerable problems, including the status of an unknown number of KGB informers of various sorts (estimates range from 3m. to 20m.). Although Bakatin emphasized that records pertaining to such people would not be released, it seemed unlikely that full control could be maintained over such sensitive documents, especially in an organization that seemed likely to contain a large number of disaffected employees. Both the military and the KGB expressed concern about a situation in which they would be dependent only on republican governments for income; Bakatin claimed that the financial situation for the KGB was 'catastrophic' in late 1991. It will remain difficult for governments to justify military and security forces expenditure if the economic situation worsens.

However, these immediate problems should not obscure the fact that any future Russian state will need internal security and external intelligence organizations, as well as strong military forces. It seems very likely that many of the centralized departments and directorates of the KGB will continue to function as before, probably with only nominal changes in top level personnel, but under the jurisdiction of the Russian Federation; meanwhile, the newly-independent Republics were expected to form their own security and intelligence organizations, also drawing from the infrastructure of the former KGB. Despite the attempt by the new Commonwealth of Independent States (CIS) to assert centralized control over conventional armed forces, at a meeting held in Minsk on 30 December, several Republics (including Russia, Ukraine, Byelorussia, Azerbaidzhan, Moldavia and Turkmenistan) also announced the formation of 'national guards' or other nascent military formations. Some Republics, notably Azerbaidzhan and Ukraine, asserted republican control over former Soviet forces on their territory. Ukraine was the most serious aspirant towards its own military establishment, proposing to form an army of some 250,000 men, and disputes between Ukraine and Russia over the division of military personnel and hardware proved an early threat to harmony within the CIS. The fear in many of the non-Russian republics was of a Russian dominated security network throughout the new CIS, with Russia becoming effectively the military successor to the USSR.

Foreign Policy

Dr MARGOT LIGHT

When Mikhail Gorbachev became General Secretary of the CPSU, in 1985, Soviet foreign policy seemed, superficially at least, to be highly successful. The USSR had achieved military parity with the USA; a number of developing countries had declared themselves to be socialist-orientated; Eastern Europe had been relatively calm since 1981; and, although Leonid Brezhnev had been unable to normalize relations with the People's Republic of China, the Sino–Soviet dispute was no longer acute.

What prompted Gorbachev to embark on a fundamental transformation of Soviet foreign policy? Firstly, the foreign policy problems which confronted the leadership in 1985 must be examined, before considering why a shift in foreign policy was the *sine qua non* of domestic economic reform. The nature of the changes must then be analysed by looking at the transformation of the foreign policy decision-making apparatus, before turning to the new concepts which were adopted by Soviet foreign policy officials and examining how they were reflected in new policies. Finally, there will be an interim assessment of the relative successes and failures of Gorbachev's foreign policy and of the position of the USSR and its successor states in world affairs in the early 1990s.

THE IMPETUS FOR CHANGE

The most intractable foreign policy problem facing the Soviet leadership in 1985 was the war in Afghanistan. The decision to send Soviet troops into Afghanistan, in December 1979, had limited and quite specific aims: to replace Hafizullah Amin, the Afghan leader, with Babrak Karmal, a more moderate Communist, and to help Karmal defeat the rebel forces that were destabilizing the country. Once law and order had been restored, the Soviet Army would withdraw. By 1985, however, this aim had not been achieved. The Afghan Government was still unstable, the rebel forces were better armed than they had been when the invasion took place, Soviet casualties were high, and the war had become very unpopular in the USSR. The new Soviet leadership had to extricate itself from an expensive mistake.

The costs of the Afghan war were high, not only in financial terms, but also because of the damage caused to other aspects of Soviet foreign policy. For example, many developing countries objected to the invasion of a non-aligned country, and voted against the USSR at the United Nations (UN) and in meetings of the Non-Aligned Movement. Moreover, when Brezhnev tried to improve relations with the People's Republic of China, in 1982, the Chinese Government made the withdrawal of the Soviet army from Afghanistan a condition for normalizing relations. However, the most significant reverse for the USSR was the end of East–West *détente*, one of the USSR's most important foreign-policy achievements in the 1970s. Relations with the USA, already strained in 1979, deteriorated almost to the level of hostility that had been characteristic of the 1950s and early 1960s.

One reason why East–West relations were already in decline in 1979 was Western apprehension about Soviet defence policy. In the 1970s the level of Soviet conventional forces in Europe had steadily increased. Moreover, the USSR had replaced its intermediate-range nuclear weapons with mobile multiple-warhead SS-20 missiles. Although the Brezhnev leadership argued that this modernization did not contravene existing arms-control treaties, NATO responded by deploying US cruise and Pershing II missiles in Europe. In protest, the Soviet Government ended all arms-control negotiations. As a result, not only was Soviet security seriously diminished (particularly because of the short flight time of the Pershing II missiles), but dialogue ended between the USA and the USSR. US President Ronald Reagan's decision to proceed with the Strategic Defense Initiative (SDI) was perceived as an even more serious threat to Soviet security. In 1985 it was clear that, unless East–West relations were improved, the USSR would be drawn into another costly escalation of the arms race.

The West was also alarmed by increased Soviet influence in Africa, Asia and Latin America in the 1970s. Soviet and Cuban military aid to Angola and Ethiopia caused particular concern. However, Soviet policy towards developing countries was more expensive and less successful than the West perceived. A number of the USSR's allies faced insurgencies, requiring ever greater quantities of military aid, and increasingly exposing the USSR to the danger of becoming involved more directly in distant conflicts. Economic relations with developing countries offered no benefits to the ailing Soviet economy. Indeed, the prevailing poverty in developing countries seemed to affect socialist-orientated regimes more severely than those which had adopted the capitalist economic model. The famine in Ethiopia, in 1984–85, was a stark example, and it also demonstrated how little the Communist states could offer in aid.

By 1985 economic decline was evident throughout Eastern Europe and plans for greater economic integration in the Council for Mutual Economic Assistance (CMEA or Comecon) had not progressed. Solidarność (Solidarity), the independent trade union in Poland, had been suppressed, but it continued to operate illegally, and there were dissident movements in many other Eastern European countries. Thus, when the new leadership considered the position of the USSR in the international system, Brezhnev's claim that the 'correlation of forces' (a Soviet term for the international balance of power, incorporating economic and political factors, as well as military) had shifted in favour of socialism seemed no more than an empty boast.

The initial impetus for a new foreign policy arose from the domestic situation, however, and not from foreign policy failures. The long-standing decline in the Soviet economy had become an acute problem. It could not, it seemed, be reversed without economic reform, and the restructuring programme proposed by the leadership (*perestroika*) envisaged the modernization of industry and agriculture. There were immediate implications for Soviet foreign policy. One way to acquire the capital to invest in modernization was to decrease defence expenditure. However, that implied an improvement in Soviet foreign relations to reduce the threats to the USSR's security, and the adoption of a more positive approach to arms control. Another way was to make Soviet foreign policy less expensive, by reducing military and economic aid to the socialist-orientated developing countries, and ensuring that relations with these countries and Eastern Europe became more economically beneficial.

However, the economic reform programme also made direct demands on Soviet foreign policy. The technology for modernization, for example, had to be imported from the West. That required better East–West relations, because the West embargoed the export to member-countries of the Warsaw Pact of technology which had a potential military application. During the 1970s it had become clear that the West's embargo was less strictly applied in periods of *détente*. The reform programme also presupposed an increase in Soviet foreign trade to generate the convertible currency to pay for imported technology. Moreover, Soviet reformers hoped that foreign capital would be invested in the USSR through joint-venture companies, which would not only increase Soviet production but also promote the transfer of technology and expertise. Unless economic sanctions (imposed in response to the invasion of Afghanistan and the suppression of Solidarność in Poland) were ended, trade would not increase and foreign capitalists would not risk investing in the USSR. Thus it was evident that domestic *perestroika* could only succeed if it was accompanied by changes in Soviet foreign policy.

For analytical purposes it is useful to distinguish between the transformation that occurred in the decision-making apparatus after Gorbachev's accession to power and the accompanying conceptual and policy changes, although there are obvious causal and temporal connections between different aspects of change.

PERSONNEL AND INSTITUTIONAL CHANGES

The promotions and structural alterations in the Ministry of Foreign Affairs (MID) and the apparatus of the Central Committee of the CPSU seemed, at first, to signify no more than the natural desire of a new leader to promote supporters and to ensure that the decision-making institutions reflected the changing interests of Soviet foreign policy. Andrei Gromyko, for example, Minister of Foreign Affairs since 1957, was replaced by Eduard Shevardnadze, formerly First Secretary of the Communist Party of Georgia. A number of new deputy foreign ministers were appointed and, within 18 months, nearly two-thirds of Soviet ambassadors had been replaced. The heads of the two foreign departments of the Central Committee apparatus were also replaced and new departments were created in both the MID and the Central Committee apparatus.

In terms of the impact of Soviet policy abroad, perhaps the most significant new department was the Information Department of the MID, which immediately displayed great skill in using the media and public relations to publicize Soviet policies. The effect on the style of Soviet foreign policy was dramatic. The stereotypical grey and faceless bureaucrats who defended intransigent Soviet positions were replaced by younger, more flexible and outgoing diplomats, seemingly more willing and able to negotiate.

It soon became apparent that what was happening represented more than a new style. The structural changes marked a distinct shift in the locus of foreign policy decision-making. Until 1985 the MID implemented foreign policy, but policy decisions were pre-eminently the responsibility of the Politburo and the Secretariat of the CPSU. Gorbachev maintained a high level of involvement in foreign affairs after 1985, but at first he worked through the CPSU. (He had no constitutional powers in foreign policy until 1988, when he became the formal head of state.) Gradually, however, a combination of new personnel, new departments, constitutional changes and the steady loss of power by the CPSU ensured that foreign policy was both made and implemented by the MID with the Central Committee apparatus having less and less influence. Moreover, the all-Union Supreme Soviet that was elected in 1989 had proper legislative powers and began to exert some influence on foreign policy.

In March 1990, when Gorbachev acquired extensive executive powers as the USSR's first President and appointed a Presidential Council (which included Shevardnadze) to advise him, the locus of foreign policy decision-making shifted almost entirely to the presidency and the MID. The enlarged, but much less powerful, Politburo lost virtually all control over Soviet foreign policy. By the end of 1990 the presidency had acquired even more control, thereby lessening the influence of the MID. This loss of power over policy-making was one reason for the resignation of Shevardnadze, in December 1990, and his replacement by Aleksandr Bessmertnykh, a career diplomat with little political influence, reduced still further the policy-making role of the MID. In November 1990 Gorbachev disbanded his Presidential Council, transferring its functions to a Security Council. However, by this time some of the Union Republics of the USSR had begun to practise *de facto* separate foreign policies; assurances were given that a new Union Treaty, which was being negotiated, would devolve some foreign policy power to individual Republics. The coup in August and the subsequent events provided the Baltic Republics with full independence, including UN membership, and the remaining Republics further developed their own foreign policies. In December 1991 the Soviet Ministry of External Affairs, which replaced the MID in November, was taken over by the Russian Ministry of Foreign Affairs and, with the creation of the Commonwealth of Independent States, it was envisaged that all the former Soviet Republics would achieve international recognition and, for the most part, take over responsibility for their own foreign relations.

CONCEPTUAL AND POLICY CHANGES

The organizational changes were aimed, in part, at promoting people who believed in the 'new political thinking' (*novoye politicheskoye myshleniye*), the name given to the concepts which would form the philosophical basis for future Soviet foreign policy, and who could translate them into practical policies. Gorbachev and his colleagues hoped that the new political thinking would replace the old principles on which Soviet foreign policy had been based and also affect the way Soviet policy was perceived abroad. Four important aspects of the new political thinking must be examined, and how Soviet foreign policy changed to reflect them.

Security

Perhaps the most significant change in Soviet theory concerned the nature of security. Absolute security had previously seemed unobtainable to Soviet theorists, given the conflictual nature of international relations as long as there were antagonistic classes. The best that could be achieved before the establishment of the classless world of international socialism was the precarious, temporary security offered by defence preparedness and deterrence. In other words, it was believed that if the Communist countries lessened their military preparedness, capitalist countries would be tempted to attack them. According to this view of international relations, security was 'zero-sum' (that is, potential gains are fixed, so what one side achieves the other side loses); if one country enjoyed more security, its adversaries necessarily became more insecure.

The new political thinkers understood the security dilemma: efforts by one state to increase security at the expense of another were invariably perceived as hostile, with a consequent reduction in the security of both countries. Recognizing that security is 'positive sum' (for one side to feel safe, its adversaries must also feel secure), they began to talk of mutual, indivisible, interdependent security. It was also recognized that security could not be achieved by military means alone: security was essentially a political problem and therefore had to be addressed by political means. This implied responding to the insecurities of other countries, adopting flexible foreign policies and being prepared to negotiate and compromise.

The new political thinking about security was reflected in Soviet–US relations and particularly in the stance taken by the USSR in the arms-control negotiations that were reopened in 1985. When, for example, Soviet attempts to link an agreement on the curtailment of intermediate-range nuclear weapons with an undertaking to curtail research on SDI proved to be unacceptable to the US administration, Soviet negotiators displayed unusual flexibility by separating the two issues. Gorbachev also withdrew the long-standing Soviet objection to intrusive on-site verification of arms agreements. This made possible the signing, in December 1987, of the Intermediate-range Nuclear Forces (INF) Treaty, an agreement to remove all such weapons from Europe. At the same time the USA and the USSR agreed, in principle, to negotiate a reduction of 50% in strategic nuclear weapons. The details of this Strategic Arms Reduction Treaty (START) proved more difficult but, at the end of July 1991, a treaty agreeing a reduction of 30% in strategic nuclear arms was signed. This was followed, after the August coup, by a series of unilateral announcements by both sides, including the destruction of tactical nuclear weapons by both sides, the removal of tactical nuclear weapons from surface ships, the removal from alert of nuclear-armed strategic bombers and proposals for reductions in strategic weapons to levels far below those agreed under START. The whole nature of relations between the two powers had changed, as hostile rhetoric and confrontation were replaced by negotiation and co-operation.

A further demonstration of the new political thinking was Gorbachev's announcement at the UN, in December 1988, of a unilateral decrease in Soviet conventional forces by 500,000 soldiers, concentrating particularly on those units that could be used for a surprise attack. In the previous three years Gorbachev had developed good bilateral relations with the European members of NATO, and he appeared to understand that Soviet deployments in Europe had threatened Western European security. Soon after his speech at the UN, multilateral Warsaw Pact–NATO negotiations began, aiming to reduce conventional forces in Europe even further. The result was the Conventional Forces in Europe (CFE) agreement, signed in Paris, in November 1990. Underlying these arms agreements were efforts in Moscow to work out new military doctrines and strategies, based on the principles of reasonable sufficiency (that is, the possession of armaments sufficient to defend the USSR, but insufficient to launch an offensive) and defensive defence.

However, the new ideas about security were not accepted without opposition in the USSR. Civilian and military strategists disagreed about the level of armaments that would be 'sufficient', and whether a reliable defence strategy could completely eschew the ability to take the offensive. Conservative politicians and military officers expressed their disapproval of Gorbachev's readiness to make concessions and the scale of arms reductions to which he agreed. Ratification of the CFE agreement was delayed when the USSR circumvented the treaty by transferring some troops and arms from the Army to the Navy, which was excluded from the treaty. Other military units were moved east of the Ural Mountains, beyond the area covered by the treaty.

Conflict

Marxist-Leninists have always believed that conflict is an inherent feature of the relations between states representing different classes, primarily between capitalist and socialist states and between capitalist states and national liberation movements. The theorists maintained that capitalism was invariably the source of conflict and that conflict was potentially beneficial to the future of international revolution, since it weakened capitalist states. Socialists should, therefore, not only aid socialist and socialist-orientated states that were under attack, but also struggles for national liberation. This was the explanation for socialist intervention in conflicts in developing countries. However, civil wars in Afghanistan, Ethiopia and Angola and the insurgencies in other allied states prompted Soviet theorists to re-evaluate the effects of conflict. They began to point to inherent dangers rather than benefits: the propensity of conflict to spread from one area to another and from one issue to others, and its tendency to escalate. In a bipolar world there was a risk that the two main power blocs could be drawn into a local conflict, turning it into a nuclear confrontation. Far from supporting opposing sides in a local conflict, theorists now maintained that the USA and the USSR should co-operate to find a political settlement. This would involve encouraging the conflicting parties to adopt policies of reconciliation, compromise and coalition and, if necessary, underwriting a settlement with military guarantees.

The earliest attempt to translate these ideas into practice occurred in Afghanistan. The Afghan Government was persuaded to modify its economic and social policies, Babrak Karmal resigned in favour of a more acceptable leader, non-Communists were co-opted into central and local government, and offers of cease-fires, amnesties and coalition government were made to the rebels. When the civil war continued despite all this, the decision was made to withdraw Soviet troops, leaving the disputing parties to settle matters themselves. By February 1989 the last Soviet soldiers had left Afghanistan, but both the USSR and the USA continued to supply military aid to their respective clients.

Soviet–US co-operation was more fruitful in the negotiations to end the war in Angola. However, here too it proved easier to negotiate the withdrawal of foreign troops from Angola and the independence of neighbouring Namibia than to resolve the civil conflict. The Soviet role in the Cambodian negotiations was less direct, although pressure was put on the Vietnamese Government to withdraw its troops. Once again, the withdrawal of the Vietnamese did not produce immediate reconciliation. With regard to Ethiopia, international pressure and the curtailment of Soviet military aid eventually persuaded the Government to negotiate, but it was too late; the anti-government forces were too close to winning the war to need to compromise.

The most striking example of direct Soviet–US co-operation in dealing with regional conflict occurred after Iraq invaded Kuwait, in August 1990. The Soviet Government supported the imposition of international economic sanctions against Iraq (despite a Soviet–Iraqi Treaty of Friendship) and, later, reluctantly agreed to the use of force. However, throughout the crisis Gorbachev tried to negotiate a political settlement to the dispute.

There are, therefore, many examples of how the new political thinking about conflict was translated into policy, but there are few examples of the successful application of the theory. Soviet withdrawal from conflict situations in developing countries is evident, however, and national liberation movements can no longer depend on Soviet support.

East–West relations benefited as a consequence and regional conflict became a prominent subject of discussion at meetings between Soviet and Western officials.

Economic Development

Soviet disillusion with the economic progress made by socialist-orientated states in the developing world predated the new political thinking. In the 1960s it was assumed by Soviet theorists that wars of national liberation would develop into socialist revolution, and that desperately underdeveloped states that adopted a non-capitalist economic model would advance from feudalism to socialism without an intervening capitalist phase. It had become clear in the 1970s that such optimistic Marxist-Leninist assumptions were simplistic. There was, therefore, nothing original about the pessimism expressed by the new political thinkers concerning the economic predicament of socialist-orientated developing countries. Nor was the Gorbachev leadership the first to advocate mutually advantageous economic relations with developing countries. However, the 'old thinkers' denied the existence of a North–South divide and thought that poverty in the developing countries was the unique responsibility of the industrialized capitalist states, since, according to Marxist theory, capitalist exploitation was the original cause of underdevelopment.

According to the new political thinkers, problems such as the North–South divide and the depletion of natural resources were global problems that required interdependent solutions. They began to doubt whether socialist-orientated states could advance to socialism without building capitalism first. Moreover, many of them rejected the idea that socialist states had a special responsibility to socialist-orientated states, and some even doubted the whole concept of socialist orientation. They proposed that the USSR should diversify its relations in developing countries to seek diplomatic and economic ties with richer capitalist and newly industrialized countries.

The new political thinking about development was reflected in policy in three distinct ways: the USSR diversified its relations with developing countries; it reduced its aid budget; and it urged socialist-orientated states to adopt reforms similar to *perestroika*.

Diversification had positive results. Between 1986 and 1991 the USSR established or renewed diplomatic relations with Albania, Bahrain, Chile, Honduras, Kiribati, Namibia, Oman, Qatar, Saudi Arabia, the Republic of Korea, the United Arab Emirates and Vanuatu. In some cases, such as the Republic of Korea, the Soviet leadership was prepared to pursue new relations even at the risk of offending traditional allies. (The re-establishment of diplomatic relations with Israel and informal contacts with South Africa, neither of them really developing countries, also fall into this category.) However, few economic gains have followed, in part because the USSR and most developing countries (whether rich or poor) do not complement each other economically and, in part, because of the virtual collapse of the Soviet domestic economy.

The collapse of the economy and the massive budget deficit also contributed to the second change in Soviet relations with developing countries: the curtailment of aid. In 1989 12,500m. roubles were allocated to aid. In 1990 the amount was reduced to 9,300m. roubles, and only 400m. roubles were projected for 1991. However, it proved impossible to cancel all subsidies to developing socialist states. Both Cuba and Viet-Nam, for example, continued to buy petroleum at subsidized prices, although they received smaller quantities than they needed. Even this level of aid seemed unlikely to continue beyond the end of 1991, as the USSR faced a serious decline in petroleum production.

Ironically, while most pro-Soviet states among the developing countries responded to Soviet insistence on political and economic reform by introducing market reforms and abolishing one-party political systems, it proved difficult to persuade the Cubans and the Vietnamese to modify their economic and political systems.

Socialist Internationalism

In the past, Soviet theorists maintained that relations between socialist states were based on the principle of socialist internationalism. In using this term they assumed that because socialist states shared common interests and did not contain antagonistic classes, conflict was impossible between them. Moreover, they imagined that all socialist states would place the international interests of socialism (as interpreted by the USSR) above their separate national interests. Consequently, no institutions were ever established to manage or mediate inter-socialist conflict and whenever conflicts occurred, as they often did, they were interpreted as the result of internal or external counter-revolution. Furthermore, although socialist internationalism was said to include respect for sovereignty and non-interference in one another's domestic affairs, the 'Brezhnev Doctrine', articulated after the intervention in Czechoslovakia in 1968, asserted that socialist sovereignty was limited and would be ignored if socialism was deemed to be threatened in any way.

The new political thinkers took a very different view of inter-socialist relations. Accepting that national distinctions were natural and could lead to conflicting national interests, they began to realize that the unquestioning acceptance of the precedence of the interests of international socialism had in itself been the cause of conflict. They also recognized that there had been little respect for sovereignty and non-interference within the socialist system and that no thought had been given to achieving genuine equality among socialist states. They proposed that the principles of socialist internationalism should, in future, be put into proper practice.

As far as Sino–Soviet relations were concerned, the new thinking about inter-socialist relations, combined with new security definitions and the new approach to conflict, made it possible to end the long-standing dispute. Bilateral trade increased, cultural relations were resumed and serious negotiations began about border issues. Gorbachev's visit to Beijing, in May 1989, was to have been both symbol and climax of this process of 'normalization'. However, the Sino–Soviet summit was overshadowed by student protests while he was there, and by the massacre in Tian An Men Square soon after he left.

When the new thinkers called for non-interference in domestic affairs and respect for sovereignty, they clearly did not envisage that the consequences would be the dismantling of socialism in Eastern Europe. At first, when *perestroika* began in the USSR, Gorbachev encouraged his Eastern European allies to adopt similar policies, but was reluctant to impose reform on those who did not wish to change. Soviet *glasnost*, however, served to inspire popular protests against the more conservative governments of Eastern Europe in 1989. Gorbachev then made it clear that if the 'old guard' would not reform, Soviet troops would not be sent to support them. He probably hoped that they would be replaced by reformist socialists. When socialism itself was rejected, however, he did not attempt to revive the Brezhnev Doctrine. He agreed to withdraw Soviet troops from Eastern Europe and, a few months later, he reluctantly agreed to the unification of Germany. By mid-1991 both the Warsaw Pact and the CMEA had been dissolved. The Cold War was over and the 'socialist commonwealth' had ceased to exist. Of all the foreign policy modifications that took place under Gorbachev, none more dramatically illustrated the fundamental nature of the changes.

THE PARADOXES OF GORBACHEV'S FOREIGN POLICY

In evaluating the relative successes and failures of Gorbachev's foreign policy two ironic paradoxes are striking. Firstly, there can be no doubt that the dismantling of the Soviet bloc, the reduction in conventional and nuclear arms and, above all, the public exposure of the poor state of the Soviet economy led to a tremendous loss of traditional influence and power. The economic chaos that accompanied *perestroika* weakened Soviet power even further. A few discerning Western analysts had long described the USSR as a one-dimensional or 'flawed superpower'. Blinded by Soviet military prowess, however, many Western politicians and analysts accepted the Soviet claim that the correlation of forces had shifted in favour of socialism. It is now generally accepted that, notwithstanding the vast military forces which the USSR had acquired, in all the other dimensions which contribute to the power of a state, Soviet performance had always fallen well below that of many other countries.

The first paradox is that, until the end of 1990 at least (when, first, domestic opposition to Gorbachev became more vocal, and second, some of the international problems of the future began to emerge), there was an enormous increase in Soviet prestige in the international system. The Cuban, Vietnamese, North Korean and even Chinese governments may well have been horrified at Soviet foreign policy; national liberation leaders probably decried Soviet defection from their cause; and leaders of the developing countries certainly regretted the reduction in aid. Nevertheless, Soviet standing in the international system had never been higher. Gorbachev was credited with ending the Cold War and making a new international order possible. The symbol of his prestige was the award of the Nobel Peace Prize. If his domestic critics who opposed the diminution of Soviet power had thought about it, they might have recognized that Gorbachev had succeeded in achieving one of the most elusive post-1945 aims of Soviet foreign policy: the acceptance of the USSR as an important and equal member of the international system.

The second paradox concerns Soviet security. The most important foreign policy task in any country is to ensure national security. With respect to Soviet security, Gorbachev's foreign policy can be rated very highly, for the USSR was certainly more secure from external attack by the early 1990s than it had been since the Second World War. At the same time, however, the USSR had probably never been less secure. The threat was not from external attack but from internal implosion. It was more serious than any of the worst-case scenarios that the military used in the past to evaluate Soviet security requirements, precisely because military power, as the failure of the August coup demonstrated, cannot alleviate demands for national independence and it probably cannot even prevent inter-ethnic hostility.

THE AUGUST COUP AND THE DE-INTEGRATION OF FOREIGN POLICY

It is worth noting that the participants in the attempted *coup d'état* of August 1991 were careful to emphasize their commitment to the USSR's international agreements. They must surely have realized that, even if they managed to preserve the USSR as a unitary state and reverse domestic *perestroika*, it was unlikely that they would be able to revert to the previous aims and methods of Soviet foreign policy. They could not, for example, reverse the changes that had taken place in Eastern Europe, despite the anxiety felt in former Warsaw Pact countries during Gennady Yanayev's three days in power. They were preoccupied with restoring domestic order and attempting to control the economy. Using or threatening to use nuclear weapons could not restore the status quo ante, nor achieve any other foreign or domestic policy aims, and they had neither a credible ideology to export, nor the ability to project power beyond the borders of the USSR.

The response of many Soviet diplomatic personnel to the coup demonstrated that the new thinking had not been adopted by all members of the foreign policy establishment. The Soviet media named 12 ambassadors who had demonstrated their support for the coup, including those to the United Kingdom, the USA, France and Germany. Subsequently several ambassadors were recalled. Aleksandr Bessmertnykh was replaced as Minister of Foreign Affairs by Boris Pankin, who had strongly opposed the coup as Ambassador to Czechoslovakia. Plans for significant reductions in staffing levels were also reported, perhaps by more than 50%. It was expected that among the first dismissals would be a large proportion of the KGB officials who were present in all Soviet embassies.

Alongside personnel changes, structural changes within the MID were also announced. The Council of the Ministries of Foreign Affairs of the Union and Republics, which originally had only a consultative role, was expected to acquire a more formal and prominent role, with Pankin claiming that it should become 'the supreme diplomatic organ of the Soviet Union'. Republics were also offered greater representation among diplomatic personnel, which has always been dominated by ethnic Slavs.

For many Republics, however, structural changes in the MID were not enough. The increasing political dissolution of the USSR, which eventually led to its demise in December 1991, made an end to a 'Soviet' foreign policy inevitable. Although the newly-established Commonwealth of Independent States advocated co-operation in the sphere of foreign policy, more formal structures to co-ordinate policy were not envisaged. The successor states to the former USSR will probably have a number of different foreign policies. It seems likely that the Republics with the greatest potential for international influence, such as Byelorussia and Ukraine, will probably concentrate on developing relations with central European states and the European Community. Meanwhile other Republics will develop regional ties, such as those which the Turkic-speaking Republics have developed with their neighbours and the Baltic States plan with other countries bordering the Baltic. During 1991 Turkey and Iran were actively competing for influence in the Caucasus and Central Asia. The Russian Federation, however, seemed destined to accept the world role which had been developed by the USSR, having persuaded other Republics to agree to it taking over from the USSR as a permanent member of the UN Security Council.

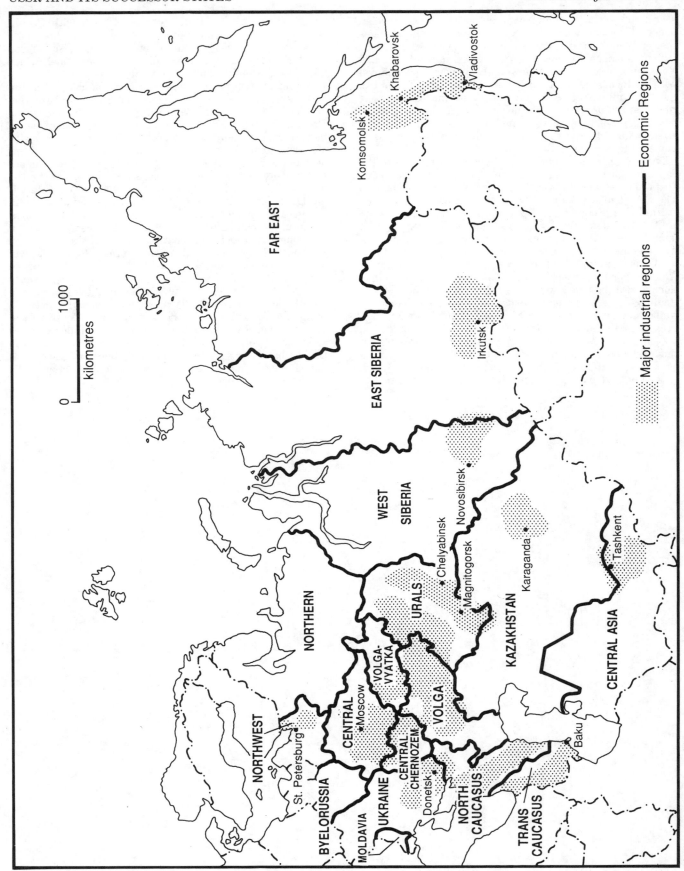

Economic and Industrial Regions of the former USSR

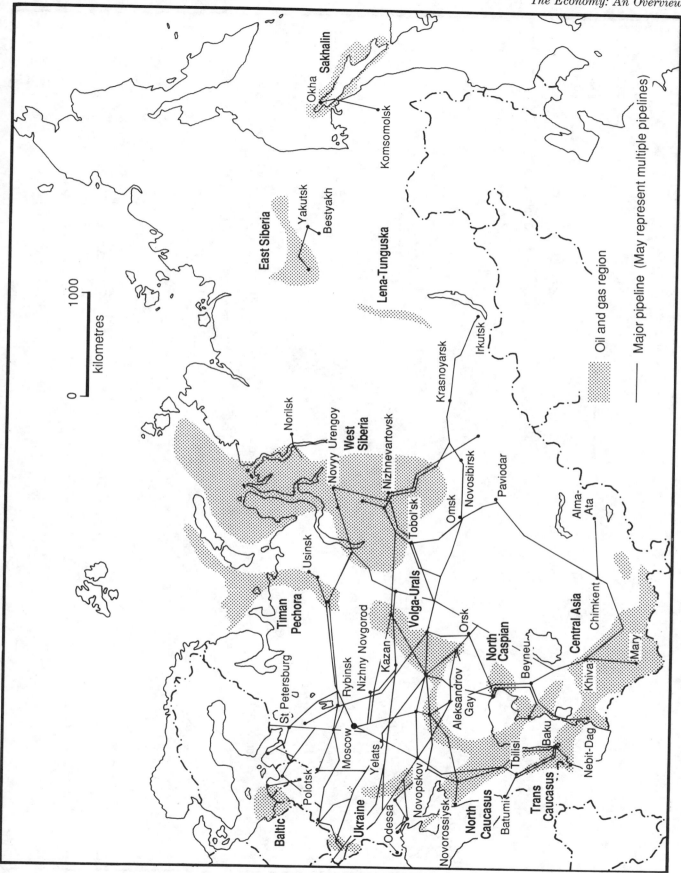

Oil and Gas Regions and Pipelines

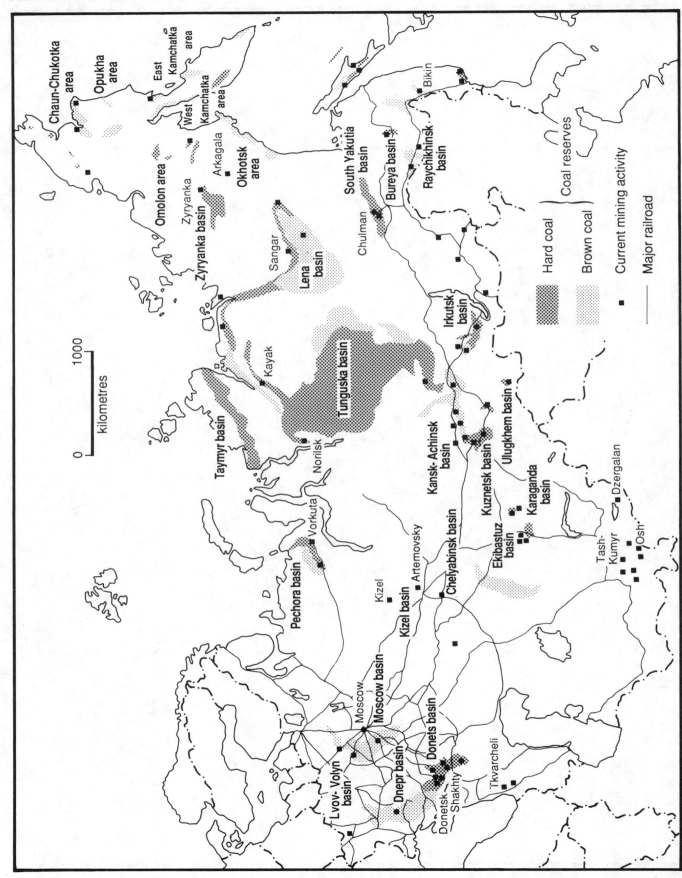

Mining and Railways

The Economy: An Overview

Prof. PHILIP HANSON

Despite covering nearly one-sixth of the world's land surface, spanning 13 time-zones, and possessing vast natural resources and a population, at the end of 1990, of 290m., throughout its existence the USSR remained only potentially, and not actually, a major economic power.

The level of development of the Soviet economy was always exceptionally difficult to assess. The composition of economic activity was unusual, with the service sector underdeveloped in relation to industry and as much as 20% of the labour force still engaged in a high-cost, low-productivity farming sector. The structure of prices was quite unlike that of other countries, since Soviet prices were always centrally-controlled and insulated, by state trading and a non-convertible currency, from the influence of the world market. International comparisons were further complicated by the traditional Soviet statistical reporting system, with its non-standard definitions of industrial, agricultural and (until recently) total output, plus what are now acknowledged to be severe deficiencies in both the collection and the processing of economic data.

For all these reasons, assessments of the size of the Soviet economy were always controversial. The US Central Intelligence Agency (CIA), which has been the source of the most systematic efforts at comparative measurement, estimated Soviet gross domestic product (GDP), in 1990, at about one-half that of the USA, and GDP and consumption per head at about 40% and 30%, respectively, of US levels. These estimates placed Soviet economic performance per head approximately equal with Portugal and Mexico. In 1990 one experimental assessment by the Soviet State Statistics Committee was even less flattering to the USSR, as are most other Western estimates.

After growing rapidly, by international standards, in the 1950s, the Soviet economy slowed down considerably. The slow-down in Soviet output and productivity growth started some 10–15 years before that of the developed West, and there has been no clear sign yet of a change in trend. Indeed, macro-economic performance deteriorated sharply after 1988. Real GDP decreased by 2%–4% in 1990 and by 12% in the first nine months of 1991. Since medium-developed countries usually grow faster than highly-developed countries, and since the USSR was, by the 1970s, a political and military superpower, the growth slow-down assumed an exceptional importance for the nation's policy-makers.

In 1983 under Yury Andropov, and from March 1985 under Mikhail Gorbachev, there were serious and increasingly radical efforts by these policy-makers to transform the performance of the Soviet economy. For some time there was no consensus about the reasons why the USSR increasingly lagged behind its capitalist rivals. Various explanations were suggested, with some degree of plausibility: major policy errors; an erosion of discipline in a centrally-managed system; an excessive military burden; semi-isolation from the Western world of commerce and technology.

By 1987, however, it was quite widely accepted among Soviet leaders that the centrally-administered economic system was the chief reason for economic decline, and that a major reform of the economic system, from a command-type economy to a market economy, was therefore needed. For some time the policy-makers aimed to establish a 'semi-market' economy, in which product markets would be largely de-controlled, but land and capital would remain in state ownership, thus preventing the development of a capital market. From about 1989, however, the idea of a shift to a Western type of mixed economy became more accepted. This was reflected in a large volume of legislation designed to create the legal framework of a full market economy, with various forms of private enterprise, stock exchanges, anti-monopoly measures, a convertible currency and so on.

The rapid evolution of reform ideas, however, was not matched by a rapid shift to a functioning market economy. Such an unprecedented systemic transformation was bound to take time and encounter obstacles. However, it was hindered by policy errors, by resistance from potential losers from change and, increasingly, by political turmoil.

The situation in late 1991 was one of steeply declining output, accelerating inflation and political and economic fragmentation. Price controls and centralized output allocation were still important, though less so than before. The all-Union budget deficit was running at about 8% of gross national product (GNP) and it was possible that the total state deficit (all-Union plus republic budgets plus special off-budget Union funds) was as much as 20% of GNP. The deficits were exacerbated by fiscal conflict between all Republics and the all-Union authorities, with the former withholding tax revenue from the latter, and all authorities refusing to take responsibility for financial stabilization. Regional trade barriers increased as Republics, cities and other regional authorities gave priority to feeding and supplying their own populations. The failure of the attempted coup of August 1991 precipitated a political transition to non-Communist governments in most Republics, and left the centre severely weakened. The secession of the Baltic States (2.8% of Soviet population and 3.5% of GDP) was one result. An accelerated shift of power from the Union to the Republics was another. The signing of an Economic Community agreement by 10 of the remaining 12 Republics (in November 1991 Azerbaidzhan and Georgia were refusing to sign the agreement) was only a statement of intent and its annulment by the agreement to establish a Commonwealth of Independent States made economic co-ordination between the Republics even more difficult.

GROSS DOMESTIC PRODUCT

The broad structure of Soviet national output could not be altered rapidly. Neither installed capacity nor the location of the labour force can change by large amounts in a short time, especially as geographical labour mobility is impeded by the absence of a housing market. (One exception is the new phenomenon of enforced internal migration as a result of ethnic conflicts. In mid-April 1991, according to official Soviet estimates, there were 673,255 internal refugees in the USSR, mostly Azerbaidzhanis and Armenians.)

The 1988 sectoral composition of GDP was therefore a reasonable guide to the structure in 1991. According to Soviet official estimates, it was divided as follows: industry 34%, agriculture 18%, construction 10%, transport and communications 6%, distribution 12% and other services 20%. The sectoral distribution of employment, as officially reported, was broadly in line with these figures. The true importance of agriculture was somewhat understated, because of price distortions and a low evaluation of labour inputs into agriculture. The service sector was dominated by state health, education and research and development (R. & D.) provision, with other consumer and business services underdeveloped by Western standards.

By the late 1980s the Soviet authorities were also providing estimates of GNP by end-use. In 1989 the breakdown was as follows: household consumption 48%, state provision of services to the population 7%, gross fixed and inventory investment 31%, state administration, defence, R. & D. and other 14%. In these figures the importance of defence expenditure is understated even though it was already increasing at a lower rate in 1989; the emphasis on investment at the expense of private and public consumption, however, is reflected in the Soviet figures.

In 1990–91 there was a shift of these shares towards consumption at the expense of investment and defence. The policy of 'conversion' in the defence industry (converting defence factories to civilian production) was probably only a minor factor in this shift. A deliberate reduction of centrally-planned investment and defence procurement by the policy-makers was reinforced by the decline in central control and the associated efforts by state industrial enterprises to protect their workers by producing consumer items or bartering output for consumer goods for them. In early 1991, while this relative shift continued, the overall reduction in economic activity was such that the absolute volume of food and consumer-goods output began to fall. The rise of a new legal private sector (including the new co-operatives) to about 7%–10% of GDP, probably did not contribute greatly to the shift towards the production of consumer goods. The new co-operatives were most visible in the form of cafés and restaurants in some of the big cities, but most of them in fact operate in the sphere of business services, and are attached to state industrial enterprises.

AGRICULTURE

In the early 1990s Soviet agriculture was still dominated by huge collective and state farms. At the beginning of 1990 there were 27,900 collective and 23,300 state farms. The average collective farm had 6,000 ha of land, and the average state farm 15,600 ha. Collective farms had an average labour force of 423 and state farms averaged 481 employees. The household smallholdings of rural (and some urban) residents were numerous (over 30m.) but tiny; the allocation of land on long-lease or restricted-conditions sale to family farms became possible in 1990, but by late 1991 very little land had been reallocated to private farming. The private sector of agriculture, consisting predominantly of the long-established household plots, may nevertheless have provided about one-third of farm output by value in 1990. The private sector in this form, however, was very labour-intensive and concentrated on livestock products, fruit and vegetables.

The low productivity of the Soviet farm sector as a whole is indicated by the fact that it employed as much as 20% of the labour force, but still could not feed the population of the USSR, even though agricultural self-sufficiency was a Soviet objective for a long time, and a very large share of investment has gone to agriculture. In the early 1980s about 10% of the population's calorie intake was derived from imports. Reform attempts under Gorbachev made no significant difference to this situation.

Soviet farm output grew quite strongly from the mid-1950s, after the death of Stalin, when its priority was increased, to the late 1970s. This growth was achieved by a massive and costly injection of capital. In the 1980s, however, output barely kept pace with population growth. In 1990 output, as officially reported, included 218m. metric tons of grain, 81.2m. tons of sugar-beet, 8.3m. tons of

raw cotton, 63.7m. tons of potatoes, 26.4m. tons of other vegetables, 14.1m. tons (carcase weight) of meat, 77.0m. tons of dairy products and 51,600m. eggs. Though achieved at very high cost, by international standards, these figures suggest that the farm sector was not so far from producing a reasonable food supply for the Soviet population, albeit a food supply that is stronger on meat, bread and potatoes than on vegetables and fruit. However, losses in transport and storage are high, and heavily subsidized retail prices have long contributed to chronic shortages in food stores.

Moreover, in 1990, output, apart from grain, was generally less than in 1989; money incomes were rising rapidly, and a proliferation of local rationing schemes in cities, favouring local residents, led to retaliatory reductions in deliveries through state channels from the countryside. In 1991 the decline in production accelerated.

Owing to its low levels of output, the USSR was a major food-importing nation, and had negligible food exports. In 1990 32m. tons of grain were imported. In 1989 imports were: grain, flour and rice 38m. tons; meat 700,000 tons; butter 250,000 tons; vegetables 500,000 tons; fruit 850,000 tons; raw sugar 5.0m. tons; coffee 113,000 tons; cocoa beans 179 tons; tea 215,000 tons; oil-seeds and oil-seed meal 4.4m. tons.

INDUSTRY

Soviet statisticians defined industry to include mining, petroleum and gas extraction, and electricity supply as well as manufacturing. The abundant natural resources of petroleum, natural gas, coal, metals and minerals (see the essays on Energy and Industry) necessarily make the extractive sector of industry, thus defined, very large. Of 36.4m. people employed as production personnel in industry in 1989 (average over the year), 2.6m. were in the fuel and energy sector and 2.1m. were in the extraction and processing of metals. Otherwise the distribution of employment by broad industrial sector is not in any obvious way unusual. However, about 20% of industrial workers were employed in enterprises that came under the Government's Military–Industrial Commission (Voenno-promyshlennaya komissiya—VPK). Not all were engaged in weapons production, for VPK plants had long had extensive side-lines in civilian production, including television sets, refrigerators and other consumer durables. Since, however, it is also the case that many non-VPK plants have some military-orientated production (usually equipment and components for VPK military production), the figure of one-fifth may be a fair approximation of the weight of military production, so far as total industrial employment is concerned. In addition, since the military sector has been better-equipped and better-supplied with materials than the civilian sector, there is no doubt that the burden of military requirements on Soviet industry has been heavy. Moreover, with military programmes probably accounting for more than one-half of all R. & D., the overall importance of military objectives for the industrial sector has been very large indeed.

From 1988 this pressure of military requirements was reduced by international arms agreements, a general easing of East–West relations, reductions in Soviet weapons procurement and the associated Soviet policy of conversion of some military production facilities to civilian purposes. Conversion, however, has been a rather confused process. In 1991 many VPK factories remained largely unaffected by it. Those plants which had been involved in the programme were often set civilian output targets that were either impractical or that failed to make good use of the technical skills and equipment available.

Despite the long-established Soviet priorities for defence and 'heavy' industry, the share of industrial employment in other industry sectors was not low by international standards. In 1989 the chemicals, timber and paper-and-pulp industries employed 4.4m. production personnel; textiles, clothing and footwear about 4.8m., and food-processing some 3.0m. Past priorities are more obvious in the relatively poor equipment and productivity levels of those sectors, although almost all Soviet industries lagged technologically behind their Western European, Japanese and US counterparts. Soviet manufacturers' market share in OECD countries, always small, declined from the mid-1960s, while the newly-industrializing countries' (NICs') share increased. Only in the export of armaments was any major branch of Soviet industry internationally competitive.

The other distinctive feature of Soviet industry, apart from the prominence of resource-based industries and military production, was its extremely high concentration (see the essay on Regional Economic Activity). One indicator of this is the very small number of administratively and managerially separate industrial enterprises. The total was just under 46,000 at the end of 1989. (The United Kingdom's much smaller industrial sector, in manufacturing alone, has about twice as many firms.) The typical state enterprise, moreover, is a single-plant enterprise, located at one site. Therefore, the typical factory is several times larger than its Western counterpart and there are few small or medium-sized factories.

The typical factory is more self-sufficient than its Western counterpart, often manufacturing on its own premises specialized equipment for its own use, and components and sub-assemblies that would, in the West, be bought in from specialist outside suppliers. This tendency is the result of enterprise managers' desire to protect themselves from the uncertainties of the centralized supply system and the lack of suppliers' motivation to meet customers' requirements. It means that the real degree of monopoly power in industry is less than it would seem to be from data on inter-enterprise deliveries. However, it also means that industrial restructuring as a result of market reform will be especially complicated.

FOREIGN TRADE AND PAYMENTS

Traditionally, Soviet planners sought to minimize Soviet dependence on the outside world. The large size and rich natural resource endowment of the USSR would, in any case, have ensured that foreign trade was less important to the USSR than it would be to a small or medium-sized, industrially-developed country. The effect of the traditional economic system and policies, however, was to make the USSR a country that is semi-isolated from the rest of the world economy (see the essay on Foreign Trade).

This semi-isolation arose in part from an adversarial relationship with the developed West, and in part from the economic logic of a centrally-administered system: a non-convertible currency; separation of domestic and foreign prices; central planning and control of imports and exports, which insulated Soviet enterprises from contact with foreign firms and made quid pro quo negotiations over tariffs and quotas with the governments of Western and developing countries virtually impossible; prohibition on foreign direct investment in the USSR, and virtual absence of labour migration between the USSR and other countries.

Soviet involvement in trade was nevertheless increasing even before the Gorbachev leadership adopted new policies of economic reform. After the extreme isolation of the period between the First and Second World Wars, the establishment of Communist regimes in Eastern Europe provided a set of trade partners, without the accompanying 'risks' of trade with capitalist countries. Under Nikita Khrushchev, the USSR began an active policy of trade with,

and aid to, the developing world. Also under Khrushchev, domestic pressures were for the first time resolved by importing on a large scale from the West. Harvest failures were remedied by large grain imports, and, increasingly, technological lags were reduced by the purchase of advanced equipment from Western suppliers. In the 1970s this tendency to cope with acute systemic weaknesses in agriculture and technological innovation by importing from other countries was made considerably easier by increases in the USSR's international purchasing power, as a result of increases in the price of petroleum from 1973 onwards. Even though the East–West *détente* of the early 1970s was succeeded by more conflictual relations in the late 1970s and early 1980s, by that time the USSR had become more than marginally dependent on Western supplies of food and advanced equipment. Policy, however, remained cautious with respect to borrowing from Western banks and governments. The USSR was therefore able to cope with losses of purchasing power in the mid-1980s without immediately experiencing acute external debt problems (see the essay on Foreign Trade).

Initially, the Gorbachev leadership found itself in an apparently anomalous position: on the one hand, reforming the Soviet foreign trade system to promote greater openness while, on the other hand, reducing imports and selling gold to maintain a modest debt-service ratio in convertible-currency transactions and a high credit rating among Western lenders.

From 1989, however, the Soviet external financial position deteriorated. Production difficulties, including 'bottlenecks' arising from import reductions, impeded exports from the supply side. The decentralization of import decisions, although limited, was apparently enough to generate arrears in payments to Western suppliers. This, together with the rapid decline in Soviet deposits with Western banks and the rise in gross and net external debt, caused the sovereign credit rating of the USSR to fall very sharply indeed in 1989–91. Private lending without government guarantees of at least 95% largely ended.

Precise assessment of this situation was impeded by the continued secrecy surrounding Soviet gold production, gold reserves and balance-of-payments statistics. If, as some analysts suggested, Soviet gold production was closer to 180 tons than to 280 tons a year during the 1980s, the Soviet reserve position was considerably weaker than had usually been assumed. Neither officials from the International Monetary Fund (IMF) nor representatives of the European Commission, who both prepared detailed studies of the Soviet economy in 1990, could obtain official data on gold production and reserves (or on several other traditionally-sensitive matters). Confusion over the extent of Soviet gold reserves continued in late 1991, with Grigory Yavlinsky, Deputy Chairman of the Committee for the Management of the National Economy, claiming that reserves totalled only 240 tons, considerably less than most Western estimates. This figure was confirmed, in November, by the publication of official statistics, which showed a decline in gold reserves from 850.4 tons in 1989 to some 240 tons in late 1991.

In December 1990 the IMF projected a US $16,000m. financing gap for the Soviet balance of payments in 1991. Later assessments by Soviet Ministry of Foreign Economic Relations officials were broadly in line with this. Much depended on how the transfer to convertible-currency settlement with Eastern European trade partners would work out. It was quite widely expected that Moscow would be a beneficiary in convertible currency from this change; in the event, trade flows between the USSR and Eastern Europe fell so sharply that this effect did not materialize.

BUDGET AND FINANCES

Like other sectors, in 1991 the financial sector of the Soviet economy was in a state of confused transition. The traditional banking system, known to Western specialists as the 'monobank system', was really a monolithic system of accounting and financial control, complementing the central administration of output and supply allocation, and not a banking system in the Western sense.

USSR Gosbank, the state bank, combined central and commercial bank functions in that it was both the banker to the Government and the sole source of cash emission, on the one hand, and its numerous branches housed the accounts of state enterprises, on the other. Specialist foreign trade, savings and investment banks were also effectively branches of Gosbank. At the same time, the role of money in the traditional system was passive. Gosbank branches were not profit-seeking financial intermediaries but agencies monitoring compliance with centrally-planned goods deliveries and cash payment of planned wages. Gosbank as a central bank had no independent influence on the money supply, but lent to the Government and printed money as the latter required.

Correspondingly, budget deficits were financed chiefly by printing money. There was no bond or treasury bill market and no means of funding budget deficits. The household sector could hold only rouble cash or savings-bank accounts. The only alternative liquid asset was illegal or semi-legal holdings of foreign currency. Otherwise, with some loss of liquidity, households could resort to holding gold and jewellery.

In 1989–91 there were some very limited developments towards a financial system appropriate to a market economy. Two laws of December 1990 created a formal separation between central and commercial banks, and there were by that time some 1,400 new 'commercial' banks. However, these changes were accompanied by a loss of central financial control, an acceleration of growth of inflationary pressure and a shift from 'repressed' towards 'open' inflation, while an effective financial system was still not in place. The de-integration of the Soviet economy in late 1991 and the aspirations of some Republics towards separate monetary policies and separate currencies made the continuation of a single monetary authority, even for the 11 Commonwealth of Independent States members, unlikely.

Traditionally, the state budget was highly centralized. In theory, republics and local authorities had quite substantial tax-collection and expenditure functions, but they fulfilled them strictly in accordance with directives from the centre. The budget revenue came principally from a turnover tax levied mainly on consumer goods and from state appropriation of most enterprise profit. The budget revenue was also boosted by large differences between domestic prices and the official rouble equivalent of foreign prices, for example, on petroleum exports and butter imports. Budgetary expenditure, by comparison with budgets in Western countries, was heavily concentrated on investment finance, subsidies to producers and subsidies to retail food prices.

Until 1988 it was always claimed that the Soviet budget had a small overall surplus. In late 1988, however, it was admitted that there was a large and growing deficit. This deficit was minor until the mid-1980s, but it increased rapidly after that. Officially, the 1990 overall budget deficit was 58,000m. roubles. The true figure may have been closer to 100,000m. roubles, or about 10% of GNP. In January–April 1991 the all-Union budget deficit was running at an annual rate of 125,000m. roubles, and the situation worsened throughout the year. By October, with the deficit still being funded by printing more money, the forecast for the all-Union deficit for the year had grown to 200,000m. roubles; one estimate put the combined budget deficit of the all-Union Government and the Republics at an annual rate of 328,000m. roubles. By November President Gorbachev had confirmed the most pessimistic estimates by admitting to the Supreme Soviet that the deficit would exceed 300,000m. roubles.

In these circumstances, it was not surprising that the money supply and money incomes were growing much faster than real output. In 1990, when total output fell by 2%–4%, household money incomes rose by 17% and household holdings of cash increased by 27%. Increasingly, inflation became open. In the first three months of 1991 the uncontrolled prices on peasant markets were rising at an annual rate of 310%, but even in state stores prices were rising at an annual rate approaching 100%.

On 2 April 1991 the Soviet Government introduced an administrative increase in what were still, nominally, controlled retail prices. This was supposed to be accompanied by compensatory increases in money incomes. However, the actual price rise was considered by almost all commentators to have been greater than that officially announced, and the income compensation appeared to have been less than announced. This adjustment of controlled prices was probably of the order of a 100% increase. Some observers judged subsequently that the 'overhang' of purchasing power (cash savings in excess of goods available for purchase) in the hands of the population had been largely eliminated. Availability of goods in the shops increased at the new prices. The underlying inflationary process, however, remained out of control.

The origins of the post-1985 inflation were various: over-ambitious investment plans in 1986–87; the reductions in official alcohol production, as a result of the anti-alcohol campaign of 1985–88; the decline in world energy prices; reduced central control over enterprise profits, wage payments, product prices and the composition of output. In 1990–91 these problems were compounded by a shrinking tax base as output fell, and fiscal conflict between the all-Union authorities and the Republics.

PROBLEMS AND PROSPECTS

The major problems of the Soviet economy in the early 1990s have been indicated above. External circumstances (falling real energy prices) and Soviet policy errors contributed to them. However, they were largely the result of the reduction of central economic and political control that accompanied a radical but confused attempt at transforming the entire Soviet social system.

Soviet liberal reformers believed that successful transformation of the economy into a mixed, market economy required financial stabilization, the de-control of most prices, extensive privatization and a fuller 'opening-up' to the world economy. These changes needed to be accompanied by the creation of a social security system, which would be able to cope with the unemployment that will follow from the structural adjustment necessary for market reform. This very general view was shared by most Western observers.

There remained, however, many differences of opinion about the pace and sequence of desirable changes, and about society's ability to cope with such a large-scale transformation. Above all, as the USSR disintegrated into its constituent parts, the debate shifted to the issue of how to retain some inter-republican links in an economic union. The highly integrated nature of the Soviet economy persuaded many observers that the lack of any central institutions could only lead to economic collapse. Other views, however, stressed the increased legitimacy gained by the more popular governments of the Republics and their consequent ability to effect economic reforms which would inevitably cause hardship and lower most people's standard of living. Republics such as Ukraine seemed likely, in the end, to reject any central economic controls for political reasons, seeing economic union as an encroachment on political sovereignty and likely to delay, rather than attract, international recognition. Moreover, the leadership of the Russian Federation, while launching its own radical reform programme at the end of October 1991, continued to assert its claims as the effective successor to the all-Union Government, making partnership in equal terms with other Republics extremely difficult.

The developments that favour a successful transition include: the avoidance so far of violence in most regions of the former USSR; the emergence of an embryonic new business class in most Republics, including many young would-be entrepreneurs as well as enterprising members of the old Party–state apparatus ready to convert political into commercial assets; and the emergence of democratically-elected reformist leaderships in several cities, including Moscow, St Petersburg (formerly Leningrad) and Yekaterinburg (formerly Sverdlovsk). However, given the existing conflicts, and the deteriorating state of the economy, less encouraging prospects were quite easy, in late 1991, to imagine.

Agriculture

Dr ROBERT LEWIS, TIMOTHY ASH and Dr KEITH HOWE

In 1990 the USSR had 558m. ha of agricultural land, the largest area of any country. However, this represented only one-quarter of its total land area, whereas in the USA, by comparison, agricultural land covers one-half of the country. Furthermore, in terms of geography and climate, the land is much less favourably endowed than that of the USA. Two-thirds of Soviet farmland was north of the 49th parallel, which marks the border between the USA and Canada west of the Great Lakes.

As a result of this northerly latitude and the huge continental landmass of which it is a part, some 40% of the former Soviet lands are under permafrost; the vast majority of those lands are in the Russian Federation. The growing season is short, with frost a possibility even in summer over much of the country; 60% of arable land is in areas with an annual average temperature of no more than 5°C (41°F). While some areas, such as the black-earth region of Ukraine and the adjoining area of the Russian Federation, are renowned for the quality and depth of their soils, the northern regions have poorer-quality acidic soils deficient in many essential nutrients. In the areas with good soils, however, the annual level of precipitation is comparatively low. Some 40% of arable land receives, on average, less than 400 mm of rainfall and suffers from severe drought once every three years.

There is considerable variation in the agriculture of the former constituent republics of the USSR. Much of the Russian Federation is unsuited for agriculture, so that while it comprised three-quarters of the land area, it only produced approximately one-half of Soviet agricultural output. The northern areas are largely dominated by livestock farming, while the southern parts of European Russia and western Siberia produce grain. Ukraine contains some of the most fertile soils and provides a wide range of agricultural products. While covering less than 3% of the former USSR it produced some 20% of its total agricultural output. In the other Republics the pattern of farming tends to be more specialized. The Baltic Republics concentrate on livestock rearing and over 65% of their output consists of meat and milk products. As well as being a livestock area, Byelorussia is a major potato producer. Moldavia and the Republics of the Caucasus are important sources of fruit and vegetables. In the case of Georgia this includes subtropical products such as tea. In Central Asia fruit and vegetables are again a substantial part of the agricultural sector, but Uzbekistan, in particular, has concentrated on

the production of cotton. Kazakhstan differs from the rest of the region by its degree of specialization in grain.

THE DEVELOPMENT OF SOVIET AGRICULTURE

Before the Revolution of 1917, the Russian Empire was still a largely agrarian economy. Agriculture comprised a mixture of large estates and small-scale peasant farming. During and immediately after the Revolution, the large estates were expropriated and almost totally divided among the peasantry. In November 1917, however, the land was nationalized, so the peasants themselves did not become landowners. Some co-operative farms (*kolkhozy*) were established and other farms were run directly by the state (*sovkhozy*). On the former the means of production were owned by the co-operative, and peasant incomes depended on the farm's performance. Workers on state farms were employed as wage labourers by the state at guaranteed wages.

The co-operatives were to form the basis for the mass collectivization of agriculture which began in late 1929, which was to shape the future structure of Soviet agriculture and to provide the means for the state to exercise economic and political control over the sector. Initially there were substantial differences between the collective farms and the small number of state farms. This was particularly the case as regards their relationship to the central planning and administrative authorities. While state farms owned their own tractors and machinery, the collectives bought in activities such as ploughing and combining from the machine-tractor stations which had also been established in the early 1930s.

After the Second World War, however, a process began whereby collective farms were reformed into state farms, and at the same time the internal structures and the central control mechanisms of collective and state farms began to converge. In 1958 the machine-tractor stations were abolished. There was also a continuing policy of merging farms. At the time of Stalin's death, in 1953, there were over 90,000 collective farms and less than 5,000 state farms. In 1989 there were 27,900 collective farms and 23,300 state farms. Both types of farm are large in terms of the world agricultural system. At the beginning of 1990 the former had an average size of some 6,000 ha and an average workforce of 423; the latter averaged over 15,000 ha with 481 workers.

Early in the collectivization process it became established that each household which was a member of a collective farm would have an individual allotment for its use, and would be able to keep a small number of personal livestock. In the hard years of the 1930s these plots enabled the peasants to survive. They also provided fresh foodstuffs for the urban population as peasants sold their surplus produce through the network of collective farm markets, which became a feature of all Soviet towns and cities. In the late 1980s urban dwellers were also encouraged to cultivate such allotments. In 1990 there were some 40m. of these personal subsidiary holdings. While less than one-half of the plot-holders owned any cattle, 25% of all cattle and 30% of cows were tended by these households. They remain a major source of fruit and vegetables. In 1990 they provided an estimated 59% of potatoes and 58% of fruit and berries. In 1986–90 these holdings produced 25% of total agricultural output, while covering only some 3% of the agricultural land. When making this comparison, however, it needs to be noted that private plots tend to specialize in labour-intensive products with a high value added, and they utilize a considerable amount of resources originating in the collective and state farms. In fact, milk yields on subsidiary plots have been estimated at only 80% of yields on the collective and state farms.

In the early 1990s a small-scale independent farming sector was re-emerging. Legislation approved in 1990 gave individuals the right to lease land for a farm, either for life or for a fixed period. In early 1991 there were 40,600 such farms working a total of 700,000 hectares. These farms were very unevenly distributed, being largely concentrated in the Baltic Republics and the Caucasus. In 1991 there were three times as many individual farms in Latvia as in the whole of the Russian Federation.

Until the mid-1950s agriculture remained largely neglected and lacked resources. In order to meet the rising expectations of the population and as a consequence of a growing awareness of the backwardness of the sector, Nikita Khrushchev (First Secretary of the CPSU 1953–64) committed more funds to agriculture and adopted a series of policies aimed at improving performance. An important part of this policy was the 'Virgin Lands' campaign. Large areas of previously fallow land were ploughed up for growing spring wheat in northern Kazakhstan and south-western Siberia. In 1954–62 the area of arable land increased by about one-third. However, the variability of the climate in this area meant that good harvests were irregular. As a consequence, in the mid-1960s, in order to maintain the attempt to meet the rising demand for food and, in particular, for the higher quality foodstuffs produced by the livestock sector, a decision was taken to import agricultural products. In particular, this involved the purchase of grain when the harvest did not match the growing demands for livestock feed. In 1970–90 about 50% of Soviet grain was fed to livestock. After the mid-1960s, with Leonid Brezhnev as Soviet leader, agriculture attracted further attention, to the extent that it received approximately 25% of investment funds during his period in office. However, while agricultural production continued to grow, this growth was largely a reflection of extra resources invested, rather than a consequence of the productivity growth which was a feature of agriculture in the developed market economies at this time. For example, it has been estimated that in 1964–76, the first 12 years of Brezhnev's rule, labour productivity in Soviet agriculture grew at only 60% of the rate of labour productivity in the USA.

AGRICULTURAL REFORMS IN THE 1980s

In 1982, in a further attempt to improve performance, a new policy known as the 'Food Programme' was announced. Although the Programme appeared as Brezhnev's last major policy initiative, Mikhail Gorbachev, who had been appointed Central Committee Secretary for Agriculture in 1978, played a major part in its formulation. There were three major features of this new package. Firstly, attempts were made to simplify the decision-making structure in agriculture. In addition, the aim was to attend more to the food chain or agro-industrial complex, as it was called in the USSR, rather than to deal with agriculture in isolation. Administrative developments concentrated on the integration of production, input supply and marketing. Initially these changes were made at the local level and developed on the basis of existing inter-farm links in such areas as food-processing. In 1985, however, a 'super-ministry', Gosagroprom (the State Agro-Industrial Committee), was established, in an attempt to provide strong and coherent planning and management at the all-Union level.

A second theme of the policy was concerned with raising productivity through the provision of incentives for farmers. Initially, this was to be implemented by giving the individual more control over his or her work through the formation of autonomous work teams, which were to sign contracts with farms under which they would be assigned land, equipment and inputs. The members of the team received an income according to the quality and quantity of their work. Later, there was increasing emphasis on the possibility of long-term leasing of land and the means of production to work the land.

The third aim of the Food Programme was to improve yields and productivity by the application of improved technology. Farms were to be provided with better equipment and materials, more and better fertilizers and improved varieties of seeds and livestock.

As with previous reforms in agriculture these policy measures did not produce the desired response. Agricultural output, which had grown at 1.3% per year in 1970–82, only increased at the same rate in 1983–89. There was no marked rise in productivity, and yields remained generally, although not consistently, low by international standards. Soviet wheat yields per hectare remained at only two-thirds of the levels of the USA; nevertheless they almost matched the levels achieved in Canada, where the climatic conditions are more similar. The performance of the large poultry farms which were developed in the 1970s and 1980s also did not fall far short of their Western equivalents. However, the average milk yield per cow was less than 40% of that in the USA.

Meanwhile, the continuing policy of cheap food for the consumer meant that the state had to pay ever increasing amounts to subsidize retail food prices. In the period 1980–90 these subsidies increased from some 24m. roubles to an estimated 115m. roubles. While the prices paid to the farms for produce increased, they failed to match increases in costs. Soviet farms were not receiving the degree of support which the high commitment of central investment resources to agriculture might suggest. This fact, when coupled with the poor performance of many farms, resulted in escalating indebtedness of both collective and state farms. Imports continued to play an important role. Firstly, they provided foodstuffs directly to the consumer; Soviet butter imports in the late 1980s were the equivalent of 15% of domestic production. Secondly, imports of animal feedstuffs were just as vital, in that they enabled the improvement of livestock production. In the 1980s grain imports were, on average, equal to 19% of production, and almost 50% of the supply of maize was imported. Soybeans and other oilseeds were other products purchased abroad in large quantities for feed. Whereas in the late 1960s and 1970s imports were used to overcome temporary 'bottlenecks' in supply, by the late 1980s they had become an essential feature of the agriculture system.

DISTRIBUTION, INPUTS AND PROCESSING

Since the establishment of the USSR the distribution sector has been one of the weakest links in the economy. In the case of foodstuffs, where the objective is the supply of a wide range of products which originate in a variety of different areas to individual households spread across a vast landmass, good distribution is vital. Distance is a major problem. The average distance for grain consignments to travel is over 1,000 km; the average Soviet farm was located some 300–400 km from a grain storage facility and 200–250 km from a meat-processing plant. It is commonly suggested that some 20%–30% of food products are wasted during harvesting, storage, transport and distribution. For the more perishable crops, such as fruit, losses in some cases may be as high as 70%. Meat losses could be as large as meat imports.

Food distribution in the USSR was handicapped by a shortage of refrigerated transport and by a lack of adequate refrigeration within shops and stores. In addition, the climatic conditions of most of the USSR meant that frost-free facilities were equally important for winter storage. The lack of good quality rural roads was also a problem; many Soviet farms were not served by metalled roads. There are shortages of packaging, and much of that which is available is of poor quality. Frequently the handling of goods is careless. The increase in investment in agriculture was not matched by related expenditures in these other parts of the food chain. In 1988 only 6.4% of the investment in the agro-industrial complex went to industries processing agricultural products and only 7.3% to those providing agriculture with inputs. The ratio of the number of people employed in agricultural supply and agro-business to the agricultural work-force is many times lower than in the USA and Western Europe.

The supply of essential inputs, such as fertilizers, is a further cause for concern. During most of the 1970s and 1980s the USSR was the world's largest producer of mineral fertilizers. However, 10%–15% of production was lost during storage and transportation. The Soviet fertilizer industry produced an insufficient supply of phosphate fertilizers, which are vital since 40% of all cultivated land is deficient in phosphorous. As a result of failings in the range and scale of production of plant-protection agents, the USSR was forced to import between 20% and 30% of domestic consumption. Moreover, the supply of machinery for applying fertilizer and plant-protection agents to fields did not keep pace with the availability of these chemicals.

AGRICULTURE IN THE EARLY 1990s

It was soon evident that Gosagroprom was not the answer to the problems of co-ordinating and managing the production and processing of Soviet food supplies. This overly large and bureaucratic organization was abolished in 1989, although its republican equivalents continued in existence.

In 1990 Soviet agricultural production fell by 2.3%. It had appeared at one time that the USSR would have a record harvest, but the final figure for the grain harvest was 218m. metric tons. This was below the record, and considerably less than the 250m.–255m. tons which was the planned harvest for 1990 in the Food Programme. Nevertheless, it exceeded the average level for the 1980s by 20%. There were also problems with other products. Poor weather conditions in the autumn created problems in the harvesting of essential winter vegetables.

These difficulties were compounded by the breakdown of the long-existing practice of mobilizing students and workers from the urban areas to provide the necessary extra manpower. The potato harvest declined by 12% from its 1989 level. The growing disruption in economic relationships affected those sectors of agriculture such as egg production and poultry meat, where large specialized facilities had been established which relied on the shipment of high protein feed additives from other parts of the country. Meat imports were identified as a priority for 1991 and it was envisaged that they would increase by approximately 50% on their level of 1990, when imports showed a similar increase over 1989. This was likely to represent about 10% of total supply.

The agricultural situation in 1990 was not helped by the performance of the agricultural input industries. Fertilizer production was down by 8%, the output of tractors fell by 7% and production of many other kinds of agricultural equipment declined by a similar amount. This was despite the well-publicized conversion of some capacity in the military industries to the production of plant and equipment for agriculture and other parts of the food chain. Production continued to decline in 1991, with fertilizer output down by 8% in the first six months of the year. Future prospects were not helped by the general failure to reach the desired levels in the construction and commissioning of new food-processing and agricultural engineering plants.

Prices on the free collective farm markets rose in 1990. In July they were, on average, 29% higher in urban markets than a year previously. In April 1991 the first sizeable increase in official state food prices for nearly 30 years occurred as part of a general round of price increases. Beef prices were raised by 350%, best quality flour by 300%, bread by between 240% and 400%. There was an increase of 250% in the cost of butter, while sunflower oil and eggs doubled in price.

The 1990s will be critical years. In the early 1990s the old system for managing agriculture was breaking down and a new system had not been established. With the apparent end of central direction, the only alternative seemed to be the price mechanism. A dynamic agricultural sector is dependent on efficiently functioning markets for inputs and outputs. While prices of food products were raised in April 1991, it was not until after the August coup that there was any sign that there would be complete deregulation of agricultural prices. In October 1991 Boris Yeltsin, President of the Russian Federation, announced plans to deregulate almost all prices, and price increases of between 300% and 500% were introduced for most basic products in Russia and Ukraine at the beginning of 1992.

In 1991 discussion continued on the issue of land ownership. Perhaps the most controversial issue was the extent to which market principles should be applied to land. The future system of land tenure was a matter of intense continuing debate. The success of policies such as leasing, which decentralize farm decision-making and enable farm workers to operate to a large extent independently within a farm, were severely limited by the still considerable power of the agricultural bureaucracy. The new legislation aimed at encouraging the development of peasant farms may increase the power of the bureaucrats by giving them control over the distribution of land to new prospective peasant farmers. The assertion of republican control over economic reform after the events of August seemed to offer greater scope for implementation of nascent land-reform policies, but, especially in the Russian Federation, opposition by local authorities and the agricultural bureaucracy remained a formidable obstacle. Two crucial issues in the land reform debate are whether the collective farms should be dissolved into individual peasant farms and who should have the right to purchase land if large-scale privatization is implemented.

Questions of privatization reach further than simply the land. Agriculture also involves farm structures, machinery and housing. In addition, there are the processing facilities which are attached to farms. Equally important will be the policies which affect those industries which supply machinery and products to the farms and the food-processing sector. The situation will have to be avoided in which small-scale farms are faced by monopoly suppliers of services and inputs. In these fields the giants of Western agri-business could have a leading role to play. Their participation could either be through joint enterprises or through wholly-owned subsidiaries.

With any substantial growth in individual peasant farms the failure of agricultural supply industries to meet the needs of small-scale farming will be even more of a handicap. Less than 1% of fertilizer is produced in small bags suitable for the small farmer. For a long time there has been a lack of suitable machinery for the peasants' subsidiary holdings. In particular, Soviet industry has not manufactured low horsepower tractors. Agricultural credit will have a key role to play, but the existing system is geared to the needs of the large farms.

The vital question which faces agriculture in all the former Soviet Republics is the extent to which it can be revitalized without completely destroying its current institutional structure. It is possible to envisage a radical scenario in which the existing system is totally removed and the sector, newly based largely on individual peasant farms, has to start virtually from scratch building the mechanisms of supply, marketing and co-operation which exist in the developed economies. In this case, there is likely to be a lengthy transition period before a new growth path is achieved and, without large-scale food imports, the consumer may face, even in the medium term, continuously rising prices.

Industry and Mining

TOM ADSHEAD

Under Soviet classification the term industry (*promyshlennost*) included not just manufacturing industry, but also mining and energy-generating industries, as well as food processing. The term is therefore broader than that used in the West, with the result that, in the USSR, industrial output as a fraction of national income was high relative to Western economies. According to Soviet statistics, in 1987, industry produced 61% of the gross social product (GSP—a measure of economic activity, which includes the gross value of output of material goods in agriculture, industry, mining and other productive activities, plus the values of material services, such as trade communications, transport and other infrastructural services, but excludes non-material services such as education, defence, health and social welfare, which are classified as consumption), employed 32% of the labour force, used 33% of the capital stock (*osnovniye fondy*) and generated 58% of total profits in the economy. However, using more conventional Western definitions, the US Central Intelligence Agency (CIA) estimated the share of industrial output in gross national product (GNP) at 34%.

GROWTH PERFORMANCE

This problem of comparison is compounded by the unreliable nature of Soviet statistics. There is a high level of disparity between official Soviet figures of industrial growth and estimates produced by the CIA. Although the two sources provide different magnitudes of growth, both sets of data show the same declining trend. Before the advent of *glasnost* Soviet propaganda claimed that the speed at which the economy had industrialized was one of the triumphs of Soviet power, and that the transformation of a semi-rural economy into a major industrial power, capable of putting the first man in space and matching the USA in weapons production, was a vindication of the planning mechanism.

The truthfulness of this picture is a matter of controversy, with Western analysts agreeing that Soviet statistics overstate the industrial growth that took place, but disagreeing over the extent of this overstatement. There are problems with the weights that can be used in constructing a growth index, as well as with the prices that are used in their construction, and according to one analyst, 'any output or national income series with a pre-1950 base is almost bound to be highly exaggerated'.

The same analyst states that industrial output in 1937 was at least 300% that of 1928 (against an official Soviet figure of 551%), indicating an annual growth rate of 13%. This was the first period of accelerated industrialization, and one of the reasons for the rapidity was that the economy was starting from a small base, given the relative backwardness of Tsarist Russia, and the damage suffered during the First World War, the Revolution and subsequent Civil War.

The next period of growth came immediately after the Second World War, when, despite the low levels of consumption then enjoyed by Soviet citizens, economic policy allocated resources towards the development of heavy industry, at a time when most Western European economies were attempting to restore the consumption levels of their populations. The result was the rapid growth of the 1950s, concentrated on the armaments sector. Towards the end of the 1950s, Khrushchev ordered a shift in resources towards consumption and was the first leader to recognize the need to rely not on increased inputs of raw materials, labour and land, but on efficiency gains through better use of these inputs. The late 1950s also saw the first attempt to make the centrally-planned system more efficient, by devolving decision-making powers.

The decline in economic growth rates of 1960–75 was caused in part by diminishing returns in the extractive industries during the period, requiring an ever increasing allocation of resources to this sector (with little effect, because depletion of stocks made extraction more costly). There was also a general decline in the growth of labour and capital inputs which compounded the failure to increase productivity.

Industrial decline after 1976 was far more marked and was partly due to shortages of key raw materials, and transport problems, together causing 'bottlenecks' within the planning process, but also due to policy changes, particularly a slowdown in industrial investment, and a diversion of investment resources to agriculture as part of the Food Programme. The 10th Five-Year Plan (1976–80) envisaged a slowdown in industrial output, intending that less ambitious plans could be more easily achieved, without any reduction in output quality. Finally, increased requirements for military spending, arising from the war in Afghanistan, from 1979, caused a further drain on resources.

In the late 1980s, industry particularly suffered from the effects of economic reform and inter-republican tension, and especially from the strikes of mid-1989 and early 1991. The breakdown in the planning mechanism, compounded by the inadequacy of past investment, as well as the failure to complete projects on time, if at all, and worsening shortages of supplies and logistical problems with transport, resulted in decreased output in 1990 and 1991.

INDUSTRIAL STRUCTURE

According to official Soviet statistics the share of industrial output in GDP increased from 23.8% in 1917 to 58.8% in 1987. The greater part of this increase in industrial output was the result of a massive increase in that part of industry producing means of production (usually termed group A), rather than that which produces objects of final consumption (group B). It should be noted that the distinction between groups A and B is not the same as that between heavy and light industry, since enterprises from the former sector produce group-B items such as fuel, household tools and furniture.

Growth in group-A industries exceeded that in group-B industries by a considerable amount, owing to the high priority given to the former sector throughout the Soviet period. The tendency to prefer heavy industry at the expense of light industry is demonstrated by the fact that the share of group A increased, from 61% in 1940 to 74% in 1989, and by the fact that the share of heavy industry grew from 60.0% in 1970 to 69.9% in 1989. Of this relative growth, the sector to benefit most was machine-building, which increased from producing 16.3% of total output in 1970 to 29.3% in 1989, which is partly accounted for by the expansion of military production.

SECTORAL ANALYSIS

Soviet industry was dominated by heavy industry, particularly military production, and the production of consumer goods; the USSR was the only major industrial nation to be self-sufficient in energy.

In 1989 19% of all electricity generating capacity was hydroelectric, but this form of generation produced only 13% of total electricity output, the remainder being produced by the thermal generating sector. Within the thermal sector 14% of both capacity and production was atomic, having rapidly grown from 0.1% in 1965. The trend towards increasing reliance on nuclear generation was halted following the explosion at the Chernobyl nuclear power station, in 1986. The environmental consciousness that developed after the Chernobyl disaster also led to the construction of some conventional thermal and hydroelectric power stations being abandoned.

The fuel sector was a vital part of the Soviet economy, generating 40% of its convertible-currency earnings. It comprised huge proven reserves, including the world's biggest natural gas field, in Urengoy (Tyumen oblast, in the north of the Russian Federation). It showed the most marked productivity decline of any industrial sector, with material expended per rouble's worth of output rising by 3.6% per year during the 1980s, despite the fact that the fuel sector's capital stock grew faster than any other branch of industry during the period.

Metallurgical output was dominated by ferrous metals; iron ore output reached a plateau of 250m. metric tons per year in the mid-1980s. In 1987 the USSR was the world's leading producer of manganese ore, tungsten ore, rolled steel, refined nickel, refined copper, primary aluminium, and in addition, was believed to be second in the world in the production of gold, magnesium, cobalt and chromite (official data on these were not published). Its inefficiency in processing this huge wealth is shown by the fact that while it mined 28% of the world's iron ore in 1987, it produced only 22.4% of the world's crude steel with it.

The machine-building and metal-working sector was the fastest growing branch in the industrial sector in the late 1980s, reflecting the priority that continued to be given to producer goods output. It also produced the largest share of industrial output of any of the branches listed here, although its share of exports was low, reflecting the low competitiveness of its output on world markets. It concentrated on producer goods for other branches of industry, for example electricity generators, robots and metal-working tools. The dominance of this branch was partly explained by the fact that it contained many enterprises that produced for the military. Its output grew fastest during the 1980s, by 53% in the period 1980–87, in comparison with the sector average of 31%.

PRIVATIZATION

Privatization became part of the economic policy agenda in late 1989, although the need for pluralism of ownership forms had been accepted since the liberalization of the operating regime of co-operatives in 1987–88. Privatization was a central part of the unsuccessful '500-days programme', proposed in mid-1990, and was officially accepted by being included in President Gorbachev's 'Basic Directions for Economic Stabilization and the Transition to a Market Economy'.

The Law on Privatization was passed in mid-1991, but little was done towards actually transferring state-owned property into private hands, although local and republican authorities were more advanced than all-Union bodies in promoting this process. One tendency which had become marked by 1991 was that many enterprises were transforming themselves into joint-stock companies, subsequently to be bought out either by individual workers, or by the work collective as a group, with the state, in the form of the ministry to which the enterprise was subordinated, retaining a 51% stake in the enterprise. In early 1991 the Ministry of the Machine Tool and Instrument Making Industry (Minstankoprom) and other machine-building ministries turned themselves into state-owned joint-stock companies, which were independent of the state administrative apparatus, allowing their ministerial structures to survive privatization by forming a cartel-type structure.

MILITARY INDUSTRY

Soviet figures for defence spending were criticized in the West as incomplete for a long time. In 1989 it was admitted by the Soviet authorities themselves that they had been misleading, when the figure for defence spending, previously stable at around 18,000m. roubles, was revised to 77,000m. roubles. This increase was explained by the previous inclusion of much defence spending under other headings of state expenditure, such as science and the economy. That this statistical 'juggling' was possible is an indication of the close connections that existed between civilian and military production in the USSR, which affected the debate about the role of the defence–industrial complex in the industrial sector. From official employment data for 1985, it appeared that about one-fifth of industrial employment was in the industrial branches co-ordinated by the Military–Industrial Commission.

This lack of data made the actual size of the Soviet defence burden hard to estimate, but some calculations, taking into account the full cost of maintaining Soviet defence capability, rather than the more narrow measures used by the CIA, put the burden in the mid-1980s at 20%–30% of GDP, contrasted with the 15%–17% estimated by the CIA, and the Soviet figure of 8.4%. The equivalent figure for the USA is 6.5%. The defence industry was more efficient and successful than the rest of Soviet industry. The production efficiency in the industry is explained by the high priority given to it since the Second World War. Much of post-War industrial growth was a result of increased military expenditure, culminating in the production of a hydrogen bomb in the early 1950s. During the Khrushchev period there was a change in priorities towards consumer output, with a resurgence in military production in the early period of Brezhnev's rule, followed by a stagnation in the late 1970s and early 1980s, when leaders were unwilling to sacrifice consumption for the sake of defence.

During the Gorbachev era changes in Soviet foreign policy meant that the pre-eminence of military production in terms of plan priority was ended. With the shift in emphasis towards production of consumption goods at the end of the 1980s, much hope was placed on conversion of military capacity as a source of growth in this field. The Western aid programmes of the early 1990s made technical and financial assistance for the conversion of military industry a priority.

Conversion was seen as a means to take advantage of the 'new world order' to use high-quality military capacity to produce high-quality consumer goods. However, the expected gains in civilian production did not occur, largely because many directors in the defence industry resisted conversion, because of the loss of prestige and plan priority that this entailed. There was evidence that the gains that did accrue from conversion came from parallel, but separate, production lines at military enterprises, rather than from actual conversion of military production lines to civilian use.

EXPORT PERFORMANCE

In 1989 energy exports accounted for 39.9% of total Soviet exports, while machines and equipment accounted for 38.5% of imports. Many of the latter came from the former member-countries of the Council for Mutual Economic Assistance (CMEA or Comecon). The switch to convertible-currency trading for trade within the CMEA in 1990, combined with the shortage of convertible currency, was a contributing factor to the industrial slowdown at that time, as much of Soviet industry relied on machinery and spare parts from Eastern Europe to maintain production.

The poor performance on export markets of the industrial sector is demonstrated by the fact that in 1987 no product had more than 20% of its total output exported, apart from such isolated instances as timber-working tools (36.5%), passenger cars (25.5%), potash fertilizers (29.3%), newsprint (21.9%), cameras (37.5%) and watches (21.3%). While this is partly attributable to domestic demand, it is evidence of the inward-looking nature of Soviet industry, despite active policies in the early part of the Gorbachev period to encourage manufactures exports.

MONOPOLIZATION

The monopoly structure of the Soviet economy was a result of the centralized planning mechanism that had been in place since the 1930s, under which there was a tendency for production to be concentrated in single units because of the informational and production economies that were expected to result.

In 1990 Gossnab, (the State Supply Commission, subsequently renamed the Ministry of Material Resources, which was responsible within the planning system for ensuring that producers received necessary supplies) estimated that about 2,000 enterprises were monopoly suppliers to the state supply network (out of a total of 45,900 industrial enterprises). However, many enterprises had acquired the capability to produce their own inputs, without actually delivering these to the supply network or the open market. In 1990 for 87.0% of goods produced by the machine-building industry a single producer accounted for all deliveries to Gossnab, with only 0.8% of goods produced by more than 21 enterprises. The Gossnab figures clearly demonstrated how production in Soviet industry was concentrated in one or a few units, with only the construction and social sectors having a few goods with a relatively large number of producers. In the construction sector 53.3% of goods were produced by more than one enterprise; in the social sphere the equivalent figure was 55.1%. Figures from *A Study of the Soviet Economy*, prepared by the IMF, the IBRD, the OECD and the EBRD in 1991, showed the percentage share of an industrial product group held by the largest producer. In 36.6% of a total of 344 industrial product groups the largest producer produced 75%–100% of the total output of that product group. The figures showed a trend for consumer goods to have less monopolized production than producer goods, and for a large proportion of non-tradable goods to have their largest producer producing well over 50% of total output.

The Energy Industries

Prof. BERTRAM POCKNEY

Within their borders the Republics of the former USSR, and especially the Russian Federation, contain great reserves of petroleum, coal, natural gas, uranium and hydro-electric power. Some of this potential has been developed, but most has not yet been harnessed and known reserves (although still officially state secrets) are known to be sufficient for many decades to come. Some recent estimates have suggested that proven and probable reserves are 58,000m. barrels of petroleum, 52,000,000m. cu m of natural gas and 240,000m. metric tons of coal. The territories of the former USSR have enough coal to last for several centuries at present rates of extraction. The USSR also announced that its uranium reserves were estimated at 2m. metric tons. Over 40% of the world's known natural gas reserves are in the former USSR, as well as some 20% of the world's petroleum reserves. However, these figures are provisional as huge new deposits are still being found and prepared for future development.

One of the major problems in developing these great reserves is that most of the population (over 200m. out of a total population of some 290m.) live to the west of the Ural mountains, while most of the energy reserves are to the east. This adds greatly to the cost of moving the coal, petroleum and gas over distances of thousands of kilometres. It was estimated that, by 1991, fuel transport accounted for some 40% of railway freight traffic. Vitaly F. Konovalov, former Soviet Minister for Nuclear Power, claimed that the average distance for coal transport was 4,000 km in 1991. One of the world's largest petroleum fields is in western Siberia and produces about 1m. metric tons per day. However, it is located in a climatically harsh region and most of the petroleum has to be pumped through main-line pipelines over distances of 1,000 km or more to refineries and the inhabited regions of the country.

An alternative to moving large amounts of coal by railway to the electricity-generating power stations, which provide electricity for the industrial and domestic consumers in the European regions, is to locate the power stations in the coalfields and then transmit the electricity along overhead power-lines. However, electricity 'leaks' from power-lines; the further it travels, the greater the leakage. The solution to this problem is to greatly enhance the voltage. The USSR was a world leader in super-high voltage transmission and claimed to have introduced one power-line of 1,150 kilovolts. Experiments at shifting coal by pipeline have been tried, but the method, which involves making a slurry out of the coal and sending the liquid mass to its destination, has not yet been pronounced a success.

NUCLEAR ENERGY

In the 1970s the Soviet leadership initiated a programme of rapid construction of nuclear power stations in the European regions of the USSR. The distance between reserves and consumers of fuel was one of the important factors which encouraged this programme; local nuclear power stations would not only help to solve the problem of generating assured supplies of electricity, but would ease the acute 'bottlenecks' in rail transport. The decision was also influenced by the rapid increase in the price of petroleum following the 1973 Arab–Israeli War. The intention was to build a chain of huge nuclear power stations in the European regions, which would supply 25% of the region's electricity by 1990 (and in Ukraine would provide up to 40%). It was also intended that increased supplies of electricity would be provided to the USSR's partners in the Council for Mutual Economic Assistance (CMEA).

An immense programme of construction of nuclear power stations was in progress by the late 1970s. By 1990 there were 16 nuclear power stations equipped with 45 reactors which generated 2,115,000m. kWh (12.5% of the country's total production of electric energy). This was only one-half of the planned amount and two factors were responsible for the shortfall. The long-term factor was the systemic inability of the power engineering industry to manufacture the reactors in the planned times and in the quantities demanded. A huge factory, 'Atommash', was built to manufacture eight nuclear reactors per year, each of 1,000-MW capacity, but it was located on soft foundations and work was delayed for years while the ground was reinforced. There was also a non-nuclear explosion at the factory in the early 1980s. However, the more dramatic factor was the accident at a nuclear reactor in Chernobyl (Ukraine), when the USSR's newest reactor, Number Four, of 1,000-MW capacity, exploded, causing the world's worst nuclear accident. The radioactive discharge spread well beyond the borders of the USSR and within the country it contaminated large expanses of agricultural land as well as resulting in the illness and death of countless people. The explosion had one positive effect: it was largely responsible for ending the obsessive secrecy of the authorities and extending the policy of *glasnost*.

A powerful anti-nuclear movement developed, combined in some regions with a nationalist movement. As a result, work ended at various stages on the construction of 100,000-MW of nuclear capacity. Following the Armenian earthquake in December 1988 the Armenian nuclear station (which was located on a line of seismic activity) was closed. Power shortages and failures became the norm in many regions.

HYDROELECTRICITY

The Long-Term Energy Programme, which was launched in 1982, envisaged an increase in the number of hydroelectric power stations. From the point of view of the power engineer with responsibility for maintaining electricity supplies to the population, a combination of nuclear and hydroelectric power is ideal, as the inflexible nuclear station can provide the base load, while the hydroelectric station can respond quickly to changes in demand. Most of the potential hydroelectric power in the European regions has been harnessed, and future developments will be concentrated to the east of the Ural mountains. It had seemed to the planners that many of the problems would be solved by the complementarity of the hydroelectric and nuclear stations. However, one of the earlier results of *glasnost* was that a furious argument began in the specialist press about the merits and demerits of hydroelectric power stations. Opposition to hydroelectric power resulted in the abandonment of work on most of the big dams under construction. Only the smaller dams, in mountainous regions to the south and east of the Urals, were to be continued. The opponents of hydroelectric power argued that the dams and reservoirs upset the ecological balance, causing great damage to the soil and to crops. In addition, hydroelectric projects absorbed huge volumes of capital in the early stages of a long construction period before generating any electricity and beginning to recover costs. Thus two of the main features of the Long-Term Energy Programme, the rapid development of nuclear and hydro-electric power, were severely disrupted by the growth of public awareness in the USSR in the late 1980s.

PETROLEUM AND GAS

These developments ensured a continual increase in the extent to which petroleum and gas were used in electricity generation. However, not only was this exactly contrary to the stated aim of the Long-Term Energy Programme (to preserve petroleum and gas, and in particular to reduce significantly the volumes of petroleum burned at the power stations), it also coincided with a period when great difficulties were being experienced in maintaining petroleum output. In 1984/85 output declined from 603m. metric tons to 595m. tons, the first year in peacetime during which output had declined.

Emergency measures were adopted and huge extra investments were directed to the oilfields. There was an improvement in output to 615m. tons in 1986 and 624m. tons in 1987. In 1989, however, output fell to 607m. tons and in 1990 declined to 570m. tons. Output for the first three months of 1991, 132m. tons, was 9% below the level of the first three months of 1990. There was no improvement later in the year, and it was estimated that total output for 1991 would not exceed 500m. tons. However, the fall in petroleum output was merely the result of a complex set of problems, some of which were specific to the petroleum industry while others were general to the whole economy.

The cost of extracting petroleum grew rapidly in the 1980s and was still increasing in the early 1990s. In 1991 it seemed likely that the real costs of raising petroleum would rise by 50%–80% in the 1990s and then increase by a further 100%–150% in the first decade of the 21st century. The result of this would be that the petroleum industry would require massive investments which would draw scarce capital away, not only from the other fuel industries, such as coal and gas, and from the building or renovation of electricity stations, but also away from the engineering and other sectors. Of course, the yield of petroleum could be improved with a reduction in cost if modern machinery were available. However, to achieve production of such machinery, engineering enterprises would need large capital investments and a market structure which would reward them for supplying equipment which met the requirements of the petroleum industry, rather than what is considered necessary by central planners.

Statistical data and authoritative estimates of the quality of Soviet oil drilling equipment vary, but it is likely that only 15%–20% is of international standard. Some 80% or more is outdated and this has negative effects on yields and labour productivity. The energy industries (that is petroleum plus gas, coal and electricity) already absorb some 40% of the investment funds allocated to industry but, apart from gas and electricity, output declined during the 1980s.

COAL

In the coal industry the targets for the three Five-Year Plans of 1976–80, 1981–85 and 1986–90, were not achieved. Again, one of the critical problems was the lack of sufficient investment in modern machinery. Despite the apparently large sums invested in coal-mining each year, there was little visible improvement in output or yield.

Some of the coalfields have particular problems. At the beginning of the 1990s the Don field (Donbass, in Ukraine) remained the premier field in the USSR, yielding some 190m.–200m. metric tons of good quality coal per year during the 1980s. However, by the end of the 1980s it had been mined for over 200 years; current mine shafts were over 1 km in depth, and many of the seams were fractured, narrow in width and ran at a variety of angles. Such conditions do not easily allow a high degree of mechanization. In the huge Kuznetsk field (Kuzbass, in southern Siberia) working conditions were still relatively good, and a considerable amount of coal was mined by open-cast methods. In the giant fields of Ekibastuz (Kazakhstan) and Kansk-Achinsk (in the Krasnoyarsk kray, in western Siberia—the Kansk-Achinsk field, although not the largest, was planned to grow to 22,000 sq km of open-cast mining) the coal is in huge seams, some of which are 50 m or more in depth, and is often close to the surface, thus making open-cast the preferred method of extraction. Reserves of coal at these sites have been measured in hundreds of millions of tons, but it is mostly low-quality fuel, which is liable to self-ignition when exposed to the air and can clog the boilers of power stations when burned in them.

Thus, although these fields have huge reserves of coal, the low cost of extraction is counter-balanced by the low calorific value of the coal and the extra costs of building power stations near the coalfields and then transmitting the electricity over long distances. Coal from the Kuzbass is mainly transported to the Urals for power generation and for industry, while the long-term aim was to direct much of the Donbass coal to the iron and steel industry. There are other fields, but the four discussed above are the main fields likely to be used during the 1990s. Of course, long-term plans for the integration of fuel extraction, power generation and electricity transmission depend on the level of political and economic co-operation between the Republics. The position of the main coalfields, in the Republics of Ukraine, Kazakhstan and the Russian Federation, means that increasing demands by local industries and consumers, perhaps especially in Ukraine, could severely disrupt the integrated energy network.

LABOUR DISPUTES

As the old 'administrative-command' system disintegrated during the late 1980s, and as the rouble lost its value and basic consumer goods became rare objects in the shops, the social circumstances of the miners deteriorated. In 1989 strikes began, mainly in the Kuzbass and Donbass, with support from the Vorkuta field, in the far north of the Russian Federation. The miners went on strike not only for increased pay to keep pace with the increasing inflation, but also for provision of the basic necessities of life. They wanted guaranteed supplies of soap and medicines, as well as improved working and safety conditions. By early 1991 they considered that the Government had failed to keep its promises. A new union, independent of the 'official' miners' union, was formed and a continuous strike, which included many individual pits, but not whole fields, lasted for over two months. Settlement was finally reached by a big wage increase. While the miners' salaries were already considerably higher than the national average level for industrial workers (for example, in 1989 miners were paid an average of 445 roubles per month, while the average for industry was 255 roubles, medical personnel were paid 165 roubles and educational personnel 175 roubles, but urban bus drivers received 510 roubles per month), the settlement of May 1991 gave the coal-miners a wage of some 1,000 roubles per month.

Many of the strikers' demands acquired a strongly political note and demands were made for the resignation of President Gorbachev and, in the case of the Donbass miners, for their pits to be subordinate to the Ukrainian

Government in Kiev and not to the All-Union Ministry of the Coal Industry in Moscow. By April 1991 the general economic and political situation had deteriorated so rapidly that the authorities were threatened with simultaneous strikes by the oil workers.

After the financial concessions to the coal-miners in May and June 1991, similar large increases were granted to oil and rail workers. Although the immediate danger of a strike was averted, the inflationary pressures were increased and added to the general debility of the economy.

THE EFFECTS OF ENERGY PROBLEMS ON INDUSTRY

The threat of a strike by workers in the petroleum industry was particularly ominous for the authorities, as the decline in output was leading to serious interruptions in the supply of refined products to key sectors of the economy, and to a loss of considerable export markets. During 1990 hundreds of flights by the Soviet airline, Aeroflot, were cancelled owing to a lack of aviation fuel, and this problem was again acute in late 1991. The record harvest of 1990 could not be fully gathered in as the tractors and other machinery also lacked fuel. The refineries were operating at less than full capacity and the fuel shortage was disrupting many other sectors of industry.

By mid-1991 the disintegration of the administrative-command system was so advanced that the problems in transport, engineering supplies and the provision of basic foodstuffs were having a very debilitating effect on the energy sector, and only gas output was slightly above the level of the previous year. However, the problems in the energy industries were having a retarding effect on the whole of industry and society.

TRADE IN ENERGY PRODUCTS

The serious decline in petroleum output in 1990 coincided with the collapse of the CMEA trading system in Eastern Europe and the transition of the former member-countries of the CMEA to multi-party market-orientated societies. Until 1989 high proportions of these countries' imports of petroleum and gas were from the USSR, and the general economic crisis of the Soviet economy was accompanied by the severe 'crisis of transition' in Eastern Europe. Soviet exports of petroleum in 1990 to former allies were well below the contracted levels, and this created complications in several countries. From 1 January 1991 the countries of Eastern Europe attempted to trade with each other 'at world prices in convertible currencies' but, lacking adequate reserves of convertible currencies and having non-convertible currencies themselves, the result was that relatively little petroleum was traded in this way. Instead, it was reported that barter deals were being concluded.

The position was even more confused because of lack of reliable data, and also because of confusion about who was actually selling Soviet petroleum abroad. In the first three months of 1991 the central Soviet authorities reported 20m. metric tons of crude petroleum and other petroleum products being exported, but OECD preliminary data claimed that 27m. tons were exported. This difference of 35% was too great to be the result of methodological differences and may have been a result of sales for currency and barter by enterprises in the USSR, or by Republics within the USSR acting independently of the all-Union authorities, and not reporting to them.

The difficulties in the Soviet petroleum industry resulted in a decline in Soviet exports of petroleum not only to Eastern Europe but also to some 40 other countries in the world. In 1988 exports of petroleum and products were 205m. tons, but these fell to 184m. tons in 1989 and close

to 100m. tons in 1990. Some authoritative sources suggested that the petroleum-producing Republics would be unable to supply demand from their former USSR markets by the mid-or late 1990s. If this should happen, the consequences for the petroleum-producing Republics, would be very serious, as petroleum exports earned about one-half of the USSR's convertible-currency earnings during the 1970s and 1980s. In early 1991 a number of measures were enacted by presidential decree which attempted to give oil workers an incentive to increase output. However, while these may have had some beneficial effects, the fundamental problem remained the failure to establish a new market-orientated system in sufficient breadth and depth to replace the old administrative-command system, which had all but collapsed.

ENERGY PRICES

A crucial problem if the economy was to be transferred to a market system was that of energy prices. Until late 1991 the prices for all fuels were established by the central authorities and had no relation to supply and demand, relative scarcity or value. Prices were mainly viewed as an accounting device, and enterprises were not responsible for generating profits in such a manner as to accumulate capital for renovation or expansion of capital equipment. Furthermore, the prices of the fuels to consumers were frequently less than the costs of production and large subsidies were required. There was a complex system of cross-subsidies and taxes within the energy sector. The result of this system was that there was virtually no efficient correlation of supply and demand; consumers, finding that fuel was 'cheap', tended to use it wastefully. Thus, at the domestic level, a Soviet television set consumed three times as much electricity as a Japanese set and comparatively few apartments had domestic meters to inform the occupant how much gas or electricity had been used. The costs were included within an already subsidized rent.

Prices of fuels to industrial consumers and farms were also subsidized. Such a system generated and encouraged inefficiency. Usually there were three different prices for each fuel or energy product: prices for the producer, wholesale prices (that is, those used between enterprises) and retail prices to the consumer. However, the construction of the price lists was different for each product. In 1990 wholesale prices were in the region of 26–28 roubles per metric ton for coal, 25 roubles per thousand cu m for gas, 30 roubles per metric ton for petroleum and 1–4 kopeks per kWh for electricity (as reported in *The Economy of the USSR*, by the IMF, IBRD, OECD, EBRD.)

These prices were revised upwards on 1 January 1991, but were exempted from the huge increases in retail prices which became operative from 2 April 1991. In the whole post-1945 period prices for energy were revised only in 1947, 1969 and 1982. As a consequence, in 1991 Soviet internal energy prices remained very different from world prices; this remained a complicating factor in the attempt by the USSR to integrate its economy into the world system, as energy exports were the most important element in Soviet foreign trade. From 1989–91 arguments continued in the Soviet energy ministries, government circles and the specialist press on pricing policy and on how to convert to a market economy and integrate with the world economy. In October 1991 some advance was made when the Russian Federation Government announced plans to raise the price of petroleum from the 1991 level of 70 roubles per ton to 300–350 roubles per ton, as part of a gradual transition to world prices. In addition, enterprises would be permitted to sell 30% of their output at free market prices. Household energy prices rose from sharply the beginning of 1992, along with the prices for most other basic commodities.

All these arguments were greatly complicated by the dissolution of the USSR in late 1991. Despite the creation by 11 Republics of the Commonwealth of Independent States, in December 1991, it seemed unlikely that there would be any significant role for the centralized authorities in the energy industries. Lithuania and Moldavia have no petroleum, gas or coal reserves; 91% of the petroleum reserves are within the Russian Federation. The independent Baltic States, and other independent Republics, may, therefore, be forced to pay world prices in convertible currency for fuel. By the end of 1991 the Soviet Ministry of the Oil and Gas Industry had been disbanded and its responsibilities were being transferred to republican-owned petroleum corporations, including the newly-established Russian Oil and Gas Corporation.

PROBLEMS AND PROSPECTS

The problems faced by the energy sector in the 1980s and 1990s were similar to the problems of the whole economy.

The rapid rate of industrialization of a very backward society, exhausted by the First World War and the Civil War, was associated with the development of a command-style economy, similar in many respects to a wartime economy, in which costs, values and other economic concepts were of little importance.

This rapid, forced development over 60 years resulted in the creation of the world's largest energy complex in the USSR. However, by the 1980's, that system of economic management had exhausted itself and was counter-productive; it could not generate the resources for renovation, resisted the introduction and application of modern science and technology, and gave the illusion to consumers of cheap and abundant fuels. Gorbachev's *perestroika* was an attempt to solve these economic problems, within a socialist-style system. The problems turned out to be too severe to be solved in the short term and within existing Soviet structures. By late 1991 most elements of the old system, even the USSR itself, had been abandoned and new structures were being sought in which the former Soviet Republics could fully exploit their huge energy resources.

The Service Sector

GUR OFER

A low level of activity in the service sector was always a characteristic of the Soviet economy. This was manifested in the low shares of the service sector in total employment, capital stock and in the gross national product (GNP), as compared with other countries at similar levels of development. Although this appears to have been merely a single structural indicator of the Soviet economy, it is in fact a reflection of the many problems of the old economic system and its development strategy. Changes in the size and role of services have been, and will continue to be, indicators of the direction and success of economic reform.

THE LEVEL OF ACTIVITY IN SERVICES

The service sector includes transportation and communications, domestic trade, public services, education and culture, health services and public administration, housing, communal, domestic and personal services. In addition to the division according to the type of service, services can also be divided functionally in ways which facilitate the characterization of the Soviet system. One division is between intermediate and final services. The intermediate services (i.e. services for goods and enterprises, most transportation and communications services, as well as most trade and other services for enterprises) are considered 'productive' services and were included under the Soviet concept of net material product (NMP). Services for final use, whether for the Government or for households, such as passenger transportation, public services and personal services, as well as banking, insurance and public administration (the latter even when providing services to the production sector, including the military sector), are considered 'non-productive' and are not included in NMP. Only recently did the Soviet statistical authorities start to compute and release national income data in line with the Western concept of gross national product (GNP), which includes 'non-productive' services in national accounts.

A second distinction is made between services purchased directly by households, such as passenger transportation, personal services and entertainment, and those usually provided free of charge to households by the Government,

such as most education and health services. Some of the directly-purchased services, such as public transportation and cultural services, are, nevertheless, heavily subsidized. In the USSR, unlike in the other former socialist countries, almost all services (and, indeed, most other goods) were, until the late 1980s, provided exclusively by government-owned enterprises and organizations. There was only limited legal private service activity, even in the sphere of personal services, such as retail trade and restaurants. Most activity in services was managed by different levels of local governments.

The relative importance of an economic branch is measured by the share of the labour force employed, the proportion of capital invested and the percentage of total output produced by the branch. In the Soviet economy, most of the above shares did rise over time for the service sector, as expected in a normal process of modernization, but both the levels and rates of growth at any point in time were typically below those of other countries. During the period 1950–89, the share of the civilian labour force employed in services rose from 23.1% to 42%. The corresponding changes in the subsectors were as follows: transportation from 5.1% to 7.7%; communications from 0.7% to 1.2%; domestic trade and restaurants from 4.2% to 7.1%; housing, communal and personal services from 2.7% to 4.6%; health services from 2.5% to 4.8%; and education, science and culture from 5.2% to 11.6%. The only branches which registered a decline were banking, insurance and public administration, from 2.6% in 1950 to 2.2% in 1989. The share of total investment in services (not including housing construction) which stood at 26.9% during 1976–80, went down slightly to 24.6% in 1989. Investment in the so-called non-productive services (which includes trade) remained stable at around 15%, of which investment in trade stood at 2.5%–3.0%; the entire decline was accounted for in transportation and communications.

In the period 1960–85 the share of services in Soviet GNP rose from 33% to 40% when measured in constant prices. Most of this increase in the share of GNP came in transportation, up from 5% in 1960 to 10% in 1985, and in trade, up from 5% to 7%. The GNP shares of public and personal services, pooled together, stayed constant at 19%, while that of communications remained at 1%. The consumption of final services by the population rose during the 1980s from 13% of GNP and 21.6% of total private consumption, to 13.4% and 23.5% respectively. The share of paid-for services remained constant at 4.1% of GNP, but rose from 6.8% to 7.5% of private consumption. The value of public services consumed by households rose only very slightly over the period, and accounted for 8.9% of GNP in 1960 and 9.2% in 1985, and for 14.8% of private consumption in 1960 and 16.0% in 1985.

Despite the general rise in most branches, the comparative levels of activity remained low. In 1985 the proportion of labour employed in services was lower by almost 11 percentage points than the 'normal' level in other countries at a similar level of development (39% as compared with 50%), and the share of services in GNP was lower by almost 17 points (40% as compared with 57%). These extreme differences are not distributed evenly among the different service industries. The relative size of the Soviet trade industry is about 50% of those in comparable countries, and there is a very small business service sector. The relative size of the transportation and communications sectors is about equal with those in comparable countries. This is also the case with respect to education, science and cultural services. The size of the health services is also smaller than those in comparable countries, but to a lesser degree.

According to the official data, the public administration sector is very small by comparison. Part of this difference may be explained by a higher proportion of bureaucrats and executives in the production sector. However, an examination of the occupational structure of the labour force in the production sector does not reveal a higher proportion of bureaucrats and executives, of service-type workers, information and decision-making personnel, or 'professional and technical' employees ('specialists' in Soviet parlance), who provide management and intermediate type services. All available inter-country comparisons show that there was a significantly lower proportion of these groups in the USSR, including the proportion of white collar employees. Still, Soviet economists mentioned the need to eliminate some 18m. jobs connected to various planning and administrative control tasks, upon shifting the Soviet economy to a market system.

Finally, the inter-country comparisons reveal that, in 1955–85, there was no convergence of the relative size of the Soviet service sector, even when the differences in the rates of growth are taken into account. Despite an increase in the share of services, the structure of the Soviet economy remained largely unchanged.

THE ROLE AND SIZE OF SERVICES

There are a number of factors that were responsible for the low level of activity in the services sector in the USSR. They were related to the nature of the economic system and its institutional organization, economic development strategy and underlying doctrine and ideology.

A general explanation for the limited role of services is the particular interpretation of the Marxist doctrine that defined 'non-material production' as non-productive. In addition, the return on capital, and interest payments in general, were considered a form of exploitation and thus illegitimate; hence, the bias against banking, money and other business services, and any other income that is defined as 'non-earned'. To this should be added the historical Russian tradition against 'speculation' and trade. It is true that services that serve goods, as distinct from people,

such as transportation and even trade, are considered productive by this doctrine, but are not treated as such in practice. It is also true that, despite being non-productive, investments and expenditures on education and, to some degree, health, were considered very important and were encouraged; the same is true with respect to military expenditures. There was a clear Marxist preference in favour of goods production and a long-term bias, not only against the provision of services, but against 'white collar' work within the production sector as well.

The distinction between 'productive' and 'non-productive' activities also existed for capital investment and, partly as a result, service industries were not allocated capital to the extent that production sectors were. Also, within goods production, there was a clear preference towards goods investment in the production process itself, rather than in surrounding ancillary services. In addition to doctrine, which was based on the scientific reasoning of Marxist economic theory, the low level of investment in services and in infrastructure was also motivated by a growth maximization strategy which had a strong bias towards military build-up and heavy industry.

Transportation

Over the relatively short term, the concentration of capital in direct production, and the postponement of investments in infrastructure, may produce benefits. The outcome is an extremely overloaded infrastructure in transportation and communications, in storage and refrigeration, in warehousing and trade bases, as well as in urban services and environmental protection. In transportation the USSR depended primarily on a very extensive railway network, which was unable to meet the demand for movement of goods. One of its main problems was the lack of computerized control and co-ordinating equipment. The movement of passengers over long distances was far behind Western levels. This was also true of road transport for all uses. One exception is the excellent Metro (underground railway) services in Moscow and some other cities.

Communications

The situation in the sphere of communications is even worse. The number of telephone lines is about one-quarter of the Western standard, and the communications technology and, therefore, quality, is even further behind. Availability of data transmission capability is very limited, as is the capacity of international lines. The limited capacity and backward technology in civilian communications is also explained by the norms of utmost secrecy imposed by the military, and by the restrictions on free exchange of information and views in the civilian sector which was an integral part of the totalitarian regime. Even in the early 1990s there were no ordinary public telephone books for users.

Education, Health and Research and Development

Investments in education, research and development (R. & D.) and, to a lesser extent, health services were always high from the beginning of the Soviet regime. As a result, in terms of levels of literacy and schooling, the number of technically trained professionals and the development of R. & D. infrastructure, the USSR moved ahead of many countries at a similar or even higher level of development. In the case of health services, there was a substantial rise in the number of medical doctors (at 4.3 per '000 people in 1986 it is one of the highest in the world relative to the population), but investments in hospitals and other medical facilities, and especially in medical equipment and in the production of medicines, was low and inadequate. During the 1970s and 1980s the health status of the population deteriorated. There was an increasing rate of infant mortality and a decline in life expectancy. In addition, there was a bias towards serving the working-age population.

Investments in human capital served the goal of rapid growth in the health and education services, but were also intended to achieve military objectives. During the 1970s and 1980s other countries more than caught up in the level of investment in educational and health services and in infrastructure, and increasing military expenditure and declining economic growth rates caused a deterioration even in the levels of these services, especially health care.

Consumer Services

A number of factors contributed, beyond those listed above, to the low level of private consumer services, including retail trade. Firstly, consumer services suffered, together with private consumption as a whole, from being a low priority target of the system. This was manifested in low wages, inadequate provision of capital equipment and inputs, and low priority claim on supplies. Compared with the overall average monthly wage of 240.4 roubles per month in 1989, the average wage in trade was 187.1 roubles, in housing, communal and personal services 180.6 roubles, in health services 163.3 roubles and in education services 175.5 roubles. In comparison, average wages in manufacturing were 263.7 roubles. Only some 3% of total investment was devoted to trade. A low level of private consumption also implies less trade services.

Secondly, within consumption, many services were given low priority. Some consumer service activities in the spheres of information and social organizations were restricted on political grounds. The decision not to develop the private automobile sector eliminated, until quite recently, the development of supporting services.

Thirdly, there was a clear policy of merging the supply of services from the market to the household (i.e. eliminating intermediary stages between the producer and consumer). This created a heavy burden on labour within households, since there was little help in the form of household appliances, processed and pre-prepared food and other amenities, and since it occurred under conditions of near 90% participation of working-age women in the labour force.

The situation in the sphere of retail trade, even before the reforms, illustrates most of these points, though they are common to other areas of personal services as well. With the exception of the free 'collective-farm markets', where farmers were always allowed to sell their products at market prices, all other trade, both retail and wholesale (about 98% of the entire volume) was run by two major organizations, a state network and a seemingly 'co-operative' network. All trade employees were employed by these two organizations. Trade was conducted almost exclusively at constant prices determined by the state, a fact that reduced the flexibility of operation both when shortages developed, which was the common case, and when there were surpluses. It is generally assumed that the perennial long queues in front of stores, and the lengthy periods spent by Soviet citizens shopping, was caused by the general state of shortage under which the Soviet economy operated. It should be emphasized that part of this burden on the population was due to the small amount of investment in stores, equipment, distribution infrastructure, poor preparation and packaging of goods, low level of technology, conservative mode of selling and the relatively few poorly-paid employees.

In addition to the information mentioned above concerning the share of employment and investment, the following further illustrates the point: in the USSR there were 20 retail outlets per 10,000 population, compared to between 60 and over 100 in a sample of developed market economies. There were 177 trade employees per 10,000 population compared to between 300 and 500 elsewhere. Stores are somewhat larger on average, and therefore further apart from each other, and have much higher ratios of labour to capital and labour to store area than in the developed market economies. This is partly a result of the low level of equipment and poor preparation of the goods, and partly of the time-consuming (to both employees and customers) 'three lines' mode of selling (select the goods, pay, go back to fetch the goods), which is still very common. Self-service was introduced only in a small proportion of stores, but had to be abolished as shortages became acute in the late 1980s. Despite all this, sales per employee and per unit of wages, in 1985, were still higher in the USSR by a factor of 10 when compared to most market economies and the average mark-up of trade over wholesale prices was about 11%, only 20%–25% of the level typical in market economies. Clearly, these features are not the result of high operational efficiency, but of limited provision of retail services. Some of the services that are usually included under retail trade in the West have not traditionally been offered at all, while others have been shifted to the free time of the customers, as explained above.

Finally, the low efficiency and poor performance of the trade industry and of other personal services, including restaurants, is also the result of the monopoly on provision held by public bureaucracies and the exclusion of private operators from provision of these services. It is very difficult to plan centrally for the provision of consumer services and to deal with a multitude of small units and a diversity of tastes. Bureaucratic provision also lacks the flexibility, the personal attention to the client and the personal incentives of the providers.

One outcome of the above is the development of 'underground' economic activities as substitutes. They are supplied both by the people employed by the state in retail trade and services, by workers in other branches and by independent workers. Estimates of the supply of private services such as maintenance, repair and personal services show that the amount provided privately is at least as high as that supplied by the state. In addition, there is a substantial private activity in retail trade, mostly inside the state system, in transportation, in health services and similar areas. The relatively low wages paid in the service industries encourage employees to supplement their income in this way. Wage rates per hour for the private worker are at least three times higher than state wages and, in many cases, much higher than that. In some cases, such as medical services and communal services, earnings from private work may be greater than those from legitimate earnings. In addition, trade employees can earn substantial incomes by selling 'under the counter'.

The third gap found in the Soviet service sector was that of 'intermediate and producers' services'. This category included, in addition to transportation and communications, distribution, planning, money and banking services, business, professional and legal services, and other similar services. The main explanation for the persistent gap in intermediate services is the replacement of the market by central planning and the replacement of most market-type services by various kinds of administrative ones. The absence of a market, together with the permanent state of shortage, eliminated the need for marketing and advertisement services. Similarly, public ownership of productive assets eliminated the need for a capital market. Banking and financial services were a passive reflection of the planning process. Financial services to enterprises were automatic and, for the most part, carried out administrative directives. In the consumer sector there were very limited consumer credit services and the entire household sector conducted its business on a cash basis. Western-style personal bank accounts, credit cards and other banking services were not available. People used bank accounts only as personal saving accounts.

Under the Soviet system, there was also a strong tendency against specialization and towards self-sufficiency and internal enterprise autarky. This was largely the result of the difficulty of establishing dependable horizontal connections, due to the hierarchical planning procedure. Within enterprises, there was constant pressure to restrict the number of people providing services and, like most services, business services were not adequately equipped with modern data-processing and communications equipment. The underground economy could provide only partial relief in the sphere of business services. In order to improve the supply of raw materials and other inputs, however, enterprise managers used various kinds of 'expediters' and other non-official channels.

Finally, there was only a limited service sector connected with international trade. The above provides ample explanation for why the USSR was not an important exporter of services. The exceptions were maritime transportation and technical aid to developing countries. The monopolistic form of organization of foreign trade, and the high proportion of trade in inter-government barter deals and with other socialist countries, reduced the need for an elaborate business infrastructure. The lack of support services for the export of goods, especially to the West, negatively affected the demand for these goods and, in many cases, the servicing of the goods was transferred to local import agents.

REFORMS AND SERVICES: DEVELOPMENTS, CONSTRAINTS AND PROSPECTS

The major reforms of the former Soviet economic system, the intended shift in social goals, the changes in property relations and ideological principles, and the declared shift toward an open economy were expected to change the parameters and constraints of the operation and level of activity of the service sector in several ways. The changes were, however, constrained by the legacy of the low level of activity and the inefficiency of services under the old system, and by their nature and mode of operation. Some changes in the service sector took place as part of Gorbachev's *perestroika*. Quantitatively, however, the changes in 1985–91 were only marginal, which is not surprising in such a short period of time. A discussion of the changes and their significance, and an attempt to describe their most recent quantitative expression, follows below.

Five major changes in the Soviet system necessitated and allowed correspondingly major changes in the nature of the service sector.

Firstly, a shift from central planning and a command economy to a market system as the main economic mechanism. An important element of this shift is the opening up of the Soviet economy to a world market operating by these same market principles.

Secondly, the legalization of alternative kinds of property ownership to that of public ownership, including private property and individual, co-operative and corporate entrepreneurship, encouraged by an active public policy to privatize most of the public production sector.

Thirdly, a shift of the social welfare function from an emphasis on investments, heavy industry and military development to emphasis on private and public consumption and the welfare of the population.

Fourthly, a shift towards democracy and personal and political freedoms.

Fifthly, a shift away from Marxist ideology, including the bias against services.

The transition from central planning to the market system is the most difficult. Some 18m. people would have to move from bureaucratic jobs to market-orientated ones, and many more will have to change their mode of operation. The old, virtually passive, wholesale, distribution and banking systems will have to shift to operating as businesses which will include, for example, active marketing and providing economically-sound credit. In addition, a long list of completely new business services used in a market environment, such as marketing, advertising, consulting, information services, financial management and legal services will have to be created. An idea of the difficulty involved can be obtained from the great strain imposed on the distribution system, at all levels, as a result of only initial market liberalization steps during 1989–91. Substitute channels of distribution, direct supply to places of work, a shift to barter deals and a rise in the volume of trade in the underground economy all increased substantially; and, as a result of difficulties faced by the banking system, a much-too-large expansion of credit occurred. Difficulties also arose from the lack of an adequate legal system, the slow process of price liberalization and the continued government control over input markets.

From 1987 onwards a few hundred private firms were established, which provided a variety of business services, such as exchange of goods, wholesale, banking, computer and consulting services, training services, and information and consulting services to domestic and foreign investors and businesses. In 1991 the number of such firms was increasing at a rapid rate. Some of these new companies were based on units that moved out of larger public enterprises, or government offices, and became private. In the early 1990s a capital market was just beginning, which will demand a large variety of supporting services. Given the relative lack of experience in the provision of business services, there is an increasing volume of import of such services, mostly in the form of branches of Western companies being established in the former USSR, either independently or as joint ventures with domestic partners. A major problem faced by the Soviet economy was that while there was a great need to develop modern business capital and financial services with assistance from abroad, such services did not provide the foreign exchange demanded by the investors in the short term.

The most significant reform for the consumer in the short term is the legalization and privatization of personal services, including taxis, restaurants, house maintenance and repair, some medical services, and, not least important, cultural, news-media and entertainment services. Legalization of small-scale, co-operative trade was followed by permission to engage in all kinds of trade. In addition, the government programme envisaged the privatization of two-thirds of all small-scale enterprise, including most services, by the end of 1993.

A major privatization of the retail and wholesale networks had still not begun in late 1991. Full privatization of services for final consumption could improve the supply, quality and variety of such services and raise both the standard of living and the general welfare of the population with a relatively small amount of effort and inputs, as was shown in Hungary. In 1991 the private service sector was still small, but its rate of growth was very high. By the end of 1989, there were 4.3m. members of private co-operatives and self-employed (1.2m. of them also held a public job)—

about 3.2% of the Soviet labour force, and 2.4% of those holding public jobs. In 1989 the number of people employed in the public sector declined for the first time, as people moved to co-operatives and individual employment. The numbers increased very rapidly after that. The emerging private service sector still suffered, as could be expected, from a multitude of difficulties, including problems in the supply of inputs, bureaucratic harassment, unclear legal status and legal protection. There is also resentment against high prices, large incomes made and probably the attitudes of some of the operators.

Despite the long tradition of high investment in education services and health care, both sectors, and particularly the latter, suffered from an increasing shortage of budget resources during the 1980s and remained in need of improvements, both material and organizational, in order to adjust to a free and democratic society. To these, one should add the need to reorganize the sector of welfare and support services, including the establishment of new services required in a market economy, such as employment placement and social security for the unemployed. Efforts to increase allocations to these services created heavy pressure on the state budget and contributed to its rising deficits from 1988 onwards.

Foreign Trade

Dr MICHAEL J. BRADSHAW

As a result of the size of the Soviet domestic economy, its substantial resource wealth and a long-standing policy of economic self-sufficiency, the USSR was never a major actor in the international economic system. It was only after the early 1970s that foreign trade became an important factor in Soviet economic development strategy. In 1970, according to the International Monetary Fund (IMF), the USSR's share of world exports was 4.2% and its share of imports 3.7%; the total value of trade turnover was US $24,500m. By 1988 the USSR's share of world exports had fallen slightly to 3.9% and its share of imports to 3.6%. In 1985, however, before the decline in petroleum prices took effect, the value of turnover had increased to $168,900m., with a trade surplus of $3,900m. Thus, while in the 1970s and the 1980s there was a substantial increase in the value of Soviet foreign trade, this growth in Soviet trade did not match the growth in international trade and the USSR's relative position in the world economy declined. By comparison, in 1988, Canada accounted for 4.0% of world exports and 3.8% of imports; and, in 1985, the total value of Japanese trade turnover was $307,700m. and Japan's trade surplus was $467,000m.

The increase in the value of Soviet foreign trade turnover was the consequence of increased profits from resource exports, rather than an increase in the volume of goods traded. According to Soviet trade statistics, in the period 1970–85 the value of trade turnover increased sevenfold, but the volume of trade barely doubled. Soviet purchasing power in convertible currency benefited from the increases in energy prices in 1974 and 1979, and, conversely, was damaged by the depression of energy prices after 1984. The importance of foreign trade lies not so much in its value, but in the role it played in a stagnating Soviet economy. The complexities of the Soviet pricing system made it very difficult to evaluate the importance of foreign trade to the Soviet economy. The Soviet economists, Shmelev and Popov, suggested that, in 1970, foreign trade accounted for 8% of national income (4% of gross national product—GNP—using Western methods); by the mid-1980s the share of trade had increased to 25% of Soviet national income (12%–15% of GNP). However, such measures must be treated with caution; firstly, because the Soviet pricing system made it very difficult to calculate the value of Soviet foreign trade; and secondly, because the calculation of Soviet GNP was also very problematic. In reality, there is no accurate evaluation of the value and importance of foreign trade to the Soviet economy. Western analyses of the role of Western technology in Soviet investment suggested that the share of Western imports as a percentage of total equipment reached its highest point at 8% in 1976, and averaged 7.2% in 1980–84. During the early 1980s food imports accounted for about 10% of total calorific intake in the USSR. Against a backdrop of domestic economic stagnation, increases in the value of Soviet foreign trade and its share of national income suggest that, during the 1970s and 1980s, foreign trade became an increasingly important factor in Soviet economic performance.

FOREIGN TRADE AND CENTRAL PLANNING

The dominance of central planning and the absence of a convertible currency required the Soviet economic system to isolate enterprises from the international market. Prior to 1987 foreign trade transactions took place predominantly through the Ministry of Foreign Trade and its foreign trade organizations (FTOs). The Ministry of Foreign Trade and related organizations served to integrate the foreign trade policy dictated by the CPSU and the State Planning Committee (Gosplan) with the operations of various industrial ministries and their subordinate enterprises. Since the Soviet pricing system differed substantially from prices in the world market, it was also necessary to devise a very complex set of foreign exchange coefficients to calculate the domestic value of goods imported and exported. The non-convertibility of the rouble meant that, when dealing on international markets, Soviet traders had to use a convertible currency, a situation which continued in the early 1990s. Thus, to a large degree, the level of Soviet imports from convertible currency partners was determined by the value of exports earning convertible currency. In situations where export revenues were reduced by falling resource prices, the response of the central planners was to reduce the level of imports. Such control of the trade deficit was made possible by the central monopoly over foreign trade activity. In the case of trade between member-countries of the Council for Mutual Economic Assistance (CMEA or Comecon), a convertible rouble was created as an accounting unit for clearing arrangements to enable trade between partners. As of 1 January 1991 the convertible rouble was abolished and trade within CMEA was conducted, in theory at least, using convertible currency. In June 1991, however, the CMEA itself was formally dissolved, making the whole system redundant. While the foreign trade monopoly enabled the central planners to use foreign economic relations to address specific economic problems, such as the failings of the agricultural system, it also isolated Soviet industry from the competitive pressures of the international market. When Soviet enterprises were granted greater freedom to engage in foreign trade in the late 1980s they found themselves to be ill-equipped to face international competition.

THE GEOGRAPHICAL DISTRIBUTION OF FOREIGN TRADE

The foreign trade handbooks published by the Ministry of Foreign Economic Relations (previously the Ministry of Foreign Trade), which was dissolved in November 1991, traditionally divided the countries of the world into three main groups: socialist countries (subdivided into member-countries of the CMEA and non-member-countries); the industrially developed capitalist countries; and the developing countries. This division reflected the different financial systems used to regulate trade: the convertible roubles accounting system for intra-CMEA trade; convertible currency for trade with the industrialized West; and a combination of barter, convertible currency and foreign aid for trade with the developing world. Traditionally, about 70% of Soviet foreign trade was conducted on the basis of clearing arrangements, a further 5% on a barter basis and only 20%–25% based on convertible currencies.

Changes after 1989 made this classification redundant, as almost all Soviet trade moved towards a convertible-currency basis. At the same time foreign aid was reduced and there was increasing international pressure to reduce the level of armaments sales to developing countries. During the early 1980s the USSR had a sizeable surplus in its trade with Western Europe, sufficient to cover the cost of grain imports from the USA and Canada, and imports of machinery and equipment from Japan. Similarly, until the mid-1980s, as a result of the value of energy exports, the USSR was able to balance its trade with Eastern Europe.

After the mid-1980s, however, the decline in energy prices severely eroded Soviet terms of trade. In 1989 Soviet trade with other CMEA members accounted for 55.8% of total trade turnover, trade with the industrially developed capitalist countries 26.1% and with the developing countries 12.1%. Overall, the USSR registered a deficit of 3,300m. foreign trade roubles. The trade deficit with CMEA members was 2,600m. roubles and with the developed capitalist countries 4,100m. roubles

In 1990, when trade with the former German Democratic Republic (GDR) was reclassified as trade with the West, Soviet trade with other socialist countries accounted for 50.4% of total trade turnover. Trade with the industrially developed capitalist countries accounted for 38.8% and trade with the developing countries 10.8%. In the same year the USSR registered an overall foreign trade deficit of US $16,800m. The trade deficit with the socialist countries was $9,600m. and with the developed capitalist countries $9,900m. By the end of 1990 the USSR's aggregate debt to Eastern Europe was 8,000m.–10,000m. roubles. In early 1991 the Soviet Minister of Finance declared the USSR's total foreign debt to be 39,000m. roubles ($62,400m.). By October 1991 total foreign debt had reached an estimated $65,000m. and, by the the end of the year, was expected to reach $70,000m.–75,000m.

THE STRUCTURE OF FOREIGN TRADE

Soviet exports were dominated by trade in energy resources and raw materials. According to OECD statistics, in 1980–85 exports of mineral fuels and energy accounted for an average of 78.4% of Soviet exports to the West. When exports of cork and wood, diamonds and non-ferrous metals are included, raw materials comprised an average of 86% of exports to the West. In 1989, according to Soviet trade statistics, fuels and electricity accounted for 41.1%

of exports to socialist countries and 55.1% of exports to non-socialist countries. Machinery and equipment exports are more important in trade with the socialist and developing countries because most Soviet manufactured goods cannot compete successfully on Western markets. In 1989 exports of crude petroleum accounted for 21% of total Soviet petroleum production (13.6% to socialist countries and 6.3% to non-socialist developed countries). In the case of natural gas, exports accounted for 12.7% of total production.

The structure of Soviet imports was rather different, with the most important items being machinery and equipment, and food products. The USSR imported most of its machinery from other members of the CMEA. In the 1970s the developed capitalist countries accounted for about 30% of Soviet machinery imports, but during the 1980s their share fell to about 23%. However, these summary figures hide some important sectoral differences. Imports of Western equipment have been particularly important to the automotive, chemical and forestry sectors, and imports of large-diameter pipe were essential to development of the petroleum and gas industry in Siberia. After the late 1970s imports of food, predominantly grain, from the developed capitalist countries increased at the expense of machinery and equipment imports. In 1980–85 machinery, equipment and pipe imports accounted for an average of 37.3% of Soviet convertible-currency imports, while food products accounted for 40.2% of imports. In 1989 the domestic grain harvest was 211.1m. metric tons and the USSR imported a further 36m. tons, equivalent to 17% of domestic production.

The commodity structure of Soviet imports suggests that there were three roles for foreign trade. Firstly, imports of manufactured goods from Eastern Europe compensated for inadequate domestic production of consumer goods; secondly, imports of machinery and equipment assisted the domestic innovation process and helped to develop important sectors of the economy; and, thirdly, imports of agricultural products improved the diet of the population and compensated for the inefficiencies of Soviet agriculture.

A combined classification based on major trading blocs and the commodity composition of trade resulted in three broad types of trading partner. Firstly, the countries of Europe (Eastern and Western), together with Japan, to which the USSR traditionally supplied fuel and raw materials in return for manufactures; secondly, the developing countries, to which the USSR mainly exported manufactured goods in return for agricultural products, raw materials and small amounts of petroleum; and, thirdly, the USA, Canada, Australia and Argentina, which supplied the USSR with agricultural products, but imported little in return. The dominant trade relationship was the export of energy and raw materials in return for manufactures, with surpluses with Western Europe financing deficits with North America, Japan and Australia.

DYNAMICS OF FOREIGN TRADE

The reliance upon exports of energy resources and raw materials meant that the dynamics of Soviet foreign trade reflected changes in world resource prices. As already noted, during the 1970s increases in energy prices funded an expansion of Soviet foreign trade. After 1985 the situation became more complicated. During 1986 the price of petroleum fell from US $30 per barrel to around $10 per barrel. As a consequence the USSR's revenue from petroleum exports fell from $16,100m. in 1984 to $7,070m. in 1986. During 1985 production problems made it difficult to increase the volume of petroleum available for export. In 1985–87, however, the volume of Soviet petroleum exports to countries of the Organization of Economic Co-operation and Development (OECD) increased by 22%, but revenue from those exports still decreased by 38.8%. In 1989 the strategy of increasing the volume of exports was further complicated by problems in the petroleum industry, which resulted in a 3% decrease in production and a decline of 18.8% in petroleum and petroleum product exports to the OECD. In 1990 the problems continued and petroleum production fell a further 5.5%, exports to the West declined by 15% and exports to Eastern Europe by 27%.

In 1990 the USSR sought to transfer exports from Eastern Europe towards convertible-currency markets. This resulted in a record deficit in Soviet trade with Eastern Europe and the virtual collapse of intra-CMEA trade. In the first six months of 1991 petroleum production was down by 9% on the same period in 1990, and production for the whole year was not expected to exceed 500m. metric tons. This decline in production, together with lower petroleum prices, further eroded Soviet export revenue.

In an attempt to compensate for declining petroleum revenues the USSR increased sales of gold: in 1989 sales generated $4,000m., in 1990 $5,000m. and, in 1991, they were expected to reach $6,000m. In July 1990 the USSR signed an agreement with the South African mining group De Beers to sell $5,000m. worth of diamonds in 1990–94. Despite protests from the Government of the Russian Federation (all Soviet diamond mines are in the Russian Federation) this deal proceeded and, in 1991, the USSR was making deliveries on time. Faced with declining trade revenues, increasing demands for imports and repayment of outstanding debts, Soviet foreign trade was facing a crisis in late 1991. The USSR's external debt increased from $16,000m. in 1985 to over $55,000m. by the end of 1990. By late July 1991 it had reached some $62,000m., against reserves of only $5,000m., while commercial arrears totalled some $4,000m. In mid-1991 the debt ratio (ratio of net foreign debt to annual convertible-currency revenue) was estimated at over 200%, and the USSR was facing increasing liquidity problems. By October the situation was grave, with the 'Group of Seven' leading industrialized countries prepared to extend an emergency loan to the USSR, to prevent it defaulting on its debts. Furthermore, the disintegration of the USSR into its constituent Republics raised the issue of the responsibility for repaying the Soviet debt.

REFORM OF THE FOREIGN TRADE SYSTEM

The reform of the Soviet foreign trade system began in August 1986, and continued as part of the general reform process. Numerous new laws dealing with joint-venture companies (involving collaboration between Soviet enterprises and Western businesses), foreign currency transactions, foreign investment and other aspects of foreign trade were enacted. In addition, many of the domestic economic reform measures that were introduced, such as the Law on Enterprise, had implications for foreign companies operating in the USSR. The result of all this activity was confusion and the lack of a clear legal environment for foreign investment in the USSR. The situation was further complicated by the introduction of legislation at the republican level that contradicted all-Union legislation.

Decentralization

On 1 January 1987 the Ministry of Foreign Trade lost the monopoly over foreign trade that it had enjoyed since the 1930s. Twenty-two ministries and 77 associations, enterprises and organizations were granted the right to carry out export-import transactions. In late 1988 the right to conduct foreign trade was extended to most ministries and more than 100 enterprises, inter-sectoral scientific technical complexes and other organizations. In December 1988 the Council of Ministers decreed that, as of 1 April 1989, the right to carry out export-import operations would be extended to all enterprises, associations and production co-operatives and other organizations with products which would be competitive on the international market. In all instances enterprises were to register with the Ministry of Foreign Economic Relations. By 1990 more than 20,000 organizations had registered. Thus, in a relatively short period of time, the right to engage in foreign trade was decentralized. Nevertheless, until late 1991 the all-Union authorities retained control over the bulk of export revenue and also controlled the legal environment in which trade was conducted. The virtual collapse of central power in the latter half of 1991 allowed republican authorities to formulate, and, for the first time, implement, their own rules regarding the administration of foreign trade.

As part of the reorganization of the foreign trade system, the Ministry of Foreign Trade and the State Committee for Foreign Economic Relations were amalgamated to form the Ministry of Foreign Economic Relations. A 'super-ministry', entitled the State Commission for Foreign Economic Relations, was established to oversee the country's foreign economic strategy, but this was abolished in mid-1991. A number of the FTOs subordinate to the former Ministry of Foreign Trade were transferred to the appropriate industrial ministries (for example Exportles, which was responsible for exporting products of the forestry industry, was transferred to Minlesprom—the Ministry for the Forestry Industry), while other ministries created their own FTOs. Prior to the introduction of the reforms the Ministry of Foreign Trade had 47 FTOs; by the end of 1988 it retained control over 25 FTOs which traded in raw materials, food and certain types of machinery. Previously the FTOs of the Ministry of Foreign Trade controlled 95% of imports from the West; by the end of 1988 their share had fallen to 40%. However, even in 1991, the FTOs of the Ministry of Foreign Economic Relations retained responsibility for over 70% of Soviet exports. While the decentralization of foreign trade rights enabled enterprises to engage in trade, the central authorities retained control over the revenue necessary to finance trade. Many of the late-payment problems that occurred from 1989 onwards were due to enterprises making purchases without access to their own sources of foreign currency, a situation aggravated by the selective decentralization of foreign trade rights.

In 1987, in addition to the reorganization of the foreign trade management system, a system of financial incentives was introduced to encourage enterprises to engage in foreign trade. The aim of the foreign trade retention scheme was to reward enterprises by allowing them to retain a proportion of their export revenue for their own use. Previously, all export revenue had been received by the appropriate ministry. Initially, the retention quotas did not include exports of raw materials and thus excluded over 70% of Soviet exports. The reason was that the scheme was intended to promote the export of finished products. In 1990, however, the retention quotas were revised and extended to include some raw materials. Significantly, petroleum, natural gas, gold and diamonds remained outside the system. Also in 1990, a presidential tax of 40% on all export revenues was introduced to generate revenue to manage the convertible-currency balance of payments. In 1991 a Union-Republic Currency Committee was established to manage the convertible-currency revenue collected by the central authorities. A related measure outlawed most forms of barter trade as such arrangements avoided taxes. When the 40% presidential tax was combined with claims by the industrial ministries and republican and local authorities, an enterprise seldom received more than 10% of its export revenue (the balance was converted into roubles at the commercial exchange rates). The fact that joint ventures were excluded from many of these measures encouraged Soviet enterprises to seek foreign partners.

Joint Ventures

In January 1987 two decrees were introduced on joint ventures with partners from member-countries of CMEA and from Western countries. These decrees, and subsequent amendments to them, formed the legal basis for the establishment of joint ventures in the USSR. The first joint venture was registered in early 1987; by early 1990 over 3,000 joint ventures had been registered with the Soviet Ministry of Finance. However, joint ventures failed to fulfil the expectations of both Soviet politicians and Western companies. For the USSR the principal goals for joint ventures were technology transfer, improvement of the structure of exports and import substitution. Access to the USSR's resource wealth and a potential market of some 290m. people attracted Western companies. The limiting factor was that potential Soviet customers could only pay for goods in non-convertible roubles, thus making profit repatriation difficult.

After 1987 there were numerous amendments to the legal framework governing joint ventures. It was a requirement of the initial legislation that the Soviet partner had a majority share in the joint venture, but this limitation was waived (indeed, 100% foreign ownership became possible), various tax concessions were introduced (including a reduced level of taxation for joint ventures in the Soviet Far East) and joint ventures were declared exempt from the presidential export tax and the foreign currency retention scheme. However, the constant revision of the laws affecting joint ventures and conflict between all-Union, republican and local governments had a negative affect on Western interest in joint ventures. In 1987 only 23 joint ventures were created. By the end of 1988 a further 168 had been registered. Major revisions to the joint venture legislation in late 1988 resulted in a substantial increase in activity and, between December 1988 and December 1989, 1,076 joint ventures were registered. However, official registration of a joint venture did not mean that it was operational. The State Committee for Statistics (Goskomstat) estimated that of the 2,905 joint ventures registered by early 1991, only 1,027 were actually in operation, 35% of the total.

In October 1990 the most important joint venture partners were: Germany (263), the USA (214), Finland (179), Italy (120) and the United Kingdom (101). Most of these joint ventures were small operations; 63% had a capitalization of less than 1m. roubles and 90% less than 5m. roubles. By early 1991 the total capitalization of joint ventures was about 7,000m. roubles, with foreign partners owning 38%. The small scale of investment is explained by the type of activities in which joint ventures were involved. The single most popular activity was production of personal computers and computer programming, followed by consulting services, consumer goods production and construction activity. This spectrum of activities is very different from the traditional structure of East–West technology, which favoured heavy industry and manufacturing. The Russian Federation accounted for 74.4% of all the joint ventures registered, and 50.5% of all joint ventures were in Moscow (the Russian Federation's share of all Soviet imports in 1988 was 68.9%). At the end of 1990 there were 1,715 joint ventures in the Russian Federation and they accounted for 0.27% of exports (worth US $63m.) and 1.7% of imports (worth $400m.).

The Baltic Republics were also active in the creation of joint ventures: at the end of 1990 Estonia had 105, Latvia 46 and Lithuania 18 (in 1988 the three Baltic Republics accounted for 2.7% of Soviet imports; by late 1990 they accounted for 9% of the joint ventures registered). In the four years after joint ventures were introduced they attracted a great deal of attention, yet, in 1990, they only employed 103,700 workers (including 1,000 foreigners) and were estimated to contribute only 0.2% of Soviet GNP. By 1991 they had not achieved the success expected of them. Nevertheless, in 1991, some very ambitious resource-oriented joint ventures were still under negotiation. However, many of these agreements were disrupted by all-Union-republican disputes and by the collapse of the Soviet economy. The virtual economic independence gained by the Republics after the August coup, enhanced by the replacement of the USSR by the Commonwealth of Independent States, offered some hope that joint ventures would no longer be hindered by the central authorities. However, the lack of coherent economic legislation in most of the Republics, the difficulties faced in establishing any inter-republican economic agreement and, above all, the continuing political turmoil, suggested that foreign companies would continue to be wary of a rapid increase in investment in the former Soviet Republics. The exception might be the Baltic States, where proposals were made for the establishment of liberal tax regimes for potential investors. Companies from the Scandinavian countries were expected to greatly increase their involvement.

CONCLUSION: THE REGIONALIZATION OF FOREIGN TRADE

The reform measures introduced after 1986 introduced a rapid decentralization of foreign trade rights, but did not result in a growth in trade activity. Indeed, in 1991 there was a significant reduction in Soviet foreign trade. The failure to introduce radical market reform lessened the ability of Soviet enterprises to compete internationally and increased demand for imported goods. At the same time neglect of the western Siberian petroleum industry, together with low petroleum prices, severely reduced export earnings.

Until 1991 the reform of the foreign trade system was conducted by the all-Union authorities. During 1991 the regions and republics of the USSR were seeking to gain greater control over their foreign trade activities. The Russian Federation, which accounted for 70% of Soviet exports and 68.9% of imports in 1988, created its own foreign trade bank and had gained full control over its export revenue. In July 1990 the Supreme Soviet of the Russian Federation approved the creation of 'Free Economic Zones' to promote foreign trade. Foreign investment would be exempt from some or all taxes in such regions. In 1991 the list of potential zones included: Primorsky Kray, Altay Kray, St Petersburg and Leningrad oblast, Kaliningrad, Chita, Sakhalin, Kemerovo and Novgorod oblasts, Zelenograd and the Yeversky Autonomous oblast. Approval was granted for the establishment of the Nakhodka Free Economic Zone in Primorsky Kray and, in June 1991, the proposed zone in Sakhalin was approved.

Regional commodity exchanges were also established. These exchanges sought to provide an alternative to the disintegrating state supply system; however, they may also provide a conduit for foreign trade. In June 1991 the Tyumen Commodity Exchange opened and was permitted to dispose of 10% of the petroleum produced in the Tyumen region, about 30m. metric tons per year. Much of this petroleum will be sold for convertible currency, bringing substantial revenue direct to the Tyumen region.

This process of regionalization was largely formalized after the revolutionary events of August 1991. Republics took control of enterprises on their territories and established their own 'central' banks. Some, such as Ukraine, planned to issue their own currencies and the IMF demonstrated a willingness to deal with Republics on a 'case-by-case' basis. Nevertheless, eight Republics signed an initial Treaty of an Economic Community in October, and were joined by two others in November, but the Community was replaced, in December, by the even looser arrangements envisaged in the Commonwealth of Independent States. The low level of co-ordination envisaged in the Commonwealth meant that foreign trade would become exclusively the responsibility of individual Republics. In all of the Republics the supply of convertible currency was dangerously low and the prospects for foreign trade in late 1991 looked poor. Without Western aid, it seemed, foreign trade might only be conducted by primitive bartering.

Regional Economic Activity

Dr MICHAEL J. BRADSHAW

With the replacement of the USSR by the Commonwealth of Independent States in December 1991, analysis of the Soviet economy threatened to become analysis of 15 separate economies. However, this apparently sudden collapse of the integrated Soviet economy was only partly the result of the failed coup of August 1991 and the subsequent declarations of independence by the Republics. Pressures had been increasing since 1988 for the Republics and, indeed, smaller territorial formations, such as the autonomous republics and the large cities, to achieve greater control over their own economic resources and policies.

With a total area of 22,402,200 sq km the USSR was by far the largest state in the world, occupying 15% of the earth's land surface. From its borders in the west to the Bering Strait, in the east, the USSR spanned 9,600 km. From the Arctic Ocean, in the north, to the borders of Afghanistan, in the south, it covered a distance of almost 4,800 km. The size and relative position of the USSR bestowed both advantages and disadvantages upon its population of, in 1990, some 290m. people. Its vast size provided access to a wide array of the natural resources required by a modern industrial state, but the increasing geographical separation of resource-producing and resource-consuming regions placed considerable stress upon the transportation system.

The fact that most of the USSR occupied northerly latitudes also influenced economic development. The interaction of physical geography, hydrology, latitude, soil and climate restricts the areas available for comfortable human settlement and agriculture. Only 10% of the territory of the USSR was viable for arable farming and a further 15% for grazing. In simple terms, the northern regions receive adequate water, but insufficient heat, while the southern regions receive sufficient heat, but insufficient water. It is only in the mid-latitudes that there is sufficient water and heat, and even here some regions are prone to drought. It was within this relatively fertile mid-latitudinal belt that the majority of the population of the USSR resided.

THE OLD REGIME

With over 100 indigenous nationalities, the USSR was one of the most ethnically diverse states in the world. Russians predominated, comprising, at the 1989 census, some 145m. people or 50.8% of the total population. Together with the Ukrainians and the Byelorussians, the Slavic nationalities accounted for 69.8% of the total population. The largest non-Slavic group, the Turkic Muslim peoples, numbered over 50m. people or 17.5% of the population in 1989.

As a result of its size and ethnic diversity the USSR was structured as a federal state. For most of its history, however, it was federal in name only; the concentration of political power within the organs of the all-Union Government and the CPSU meant that decision-making was not devolved to the republican governments. Not until the early 1990s did the process of reform begin to transfer real decision-making authority to the republican governments.

When the USSR was formed, in 1922, it comprised four Republics: the Russian Soviet Federative Socialist Republic (RSFSR—now the Russian Federation), which included much of Central Asia, the Byelorussian SSR, the Ukrainian SSR and the Transcaucasian Soviet Federative Socialist Republic (TSFSR). The latter was disbanded in 1936 to form the Georgian, Armenian and Azerbaidzhani SSRs and Central Asia was divided into five Republics, the Kazakh, Kirghiz, Tadzhik, Turkmen and Uzbek SSRs. In addition, in 1940 the previously independent states of Estonia, Latvia and Lithuania were incorporated into the USSR and Bessarabia, also annexed in 1940, formed part of a Moldavian SSR. Thus, according to the 1977 Constitution, the USSR was divided into 15 Union Republics.

The name of each republic was normally taken from that of the dominant nationality group within the republic. Thus, for example, in Armenia, Armenians comprised 93.3% of the population in 1989, and, in the same year, in Ukraine, Ukrainians were 72.7% of the population. Below the level of the Union Republic a number of other administrative units were created that gave territorial expression to nationality. The 1977 Constitution listed 20 Autonomous Soviet Socialist Republics (ASSR), which represented the larger nationality groups within some of the Union Republics. There are 16 of these autonomous republics within the Russian Federation, which itself has a federal structure (it was expected that the former Volga German Autonomous Republic would be re-established in 1992), two in Georgia, one in Uzbekistan and one in Azerbaidzhan. At the next level 8 Autonomous Oblasts and 10 Autonomous Okrugs were established. The remaining territory was organized into administrative oblasts, usually carrying the name of the largest city within their boundaries. Within the Russian Federation there are also five large administrative districts known as krays, such as the Maritime (Primorsky) Kray in the Soviet Far East. During 1990 and 1991 many autonomous territories adopted declarations of sovereignty and unilaterally upgraded their status. In other regions minority groups proclaimed new autonomous formations, such as the Russian-populated 'Dniester SSR', in Moldavia. In 1991 the Crimean Autonomous Republic was re-established.

REGIONAL PLANNING

In addition to the federal administrative structure discussed above, the State Planning Committee (Gosplan—renamed the Ministry of Economics and Forecasting in 1991 and later disbanded) devised a system of economic regions. These regions had no institutional status of their own, but were designed for use in planning and have been particularly important within the Russian Federation, where they have often formed the basis for policy and economic analysis. Since their inception in the 1920s there have been many versions of the economic planning regions. In 1991 there were 19 regions, plus Moldavia, which was outside the system. The three Baltic Republics were combined into the 'Baltic' region; similarly Georgia, Armenia and Azerbaidzhan were combined to form the 'Transcaucasus' region. The Russian Federation was divided into 11 economic regions. Regions such as 'West Siberia' were thus economic regions within the Russian Federation.

Despite the complexity of the federal structure and the existence of economic regions, the USSR was planned and managed principally by industrial sector, rather than by republic or region. The principal actors in the planning process, the CPSU, the all-Union Government and Gosplan, produced Five-Year Plans on the basis of major industrial sectors. The most important sectors of the economy were controlled by All-Union Ministries in Moscow. Some sectors of the economy were controlled by Union-Republic Ministries which had a 'dual-subordination' to the all-Union and republican governments. Finally, a limited amount of activity was the direct responsibility of republican and local governments. The result of this system was that in any particular region or city the amount of local control was strongly influenced by industrial structure. A high reliance upon heavy industry or defence-related industry would result in a high level of central control. For example, in Sverdlovsk (now Yekaterinburg), a major defence-orientated industrial city in the Urals Economic Region of the Russian Federation, 80% of industry was controlled by All-Union Ministries in Moscow.

The national importance of a particular region was, therefore, the consequence of the national priority afforded the industries within that region. Thus, it is misleading to talk of coherent republican economies because the key sectors of the Soviet economy have been planned on an all-Union rather than republican basis. The central planning system produced a highly specialized and interdependent set of republican and regional economies. It was only in the early 1990s, with the pressure to decentralize, that republican governments had to devise economic strategies for their own regions. One of the problems they faced was the absence of an institutional framework for devising and implementing regional economic strategy and managing inter-republican economic relations.

DEMOGRAPHIC VARIATIONS

Regional economic analysis of the USSR has been hampered by a lack of information on the regional distribution of economic activity. Although the situation is improving, with increased information available from republican bodies, the majority of data is still only available at republican level. However, the results of the 1989 census provided some information on levels of economic development.

The census results revealed that the average annual population growth rate in the USSR, in the period 1979–89, was 0.9% and that, in 1989, 66% of the population resided in urban areas. However, this aggregate figure disguised considerable regional variation. In the European regions of the USSR population growth rates were lower than average (0.7% in the Baltic, 0.4% in Ukraine and 0.6% in Byelorussia); levels of urbanization in these regions reflected the all-Union average. In the southern Muslim-dominated Republics the population growth rates have been considerably higher than the national average: 2.0% in Kirghizia (Kyrgyzstan), 3.0% in Tadzhikistan, 2.5% in Turkmenistan and 2.6% in Uzbekistan. The levels of urbanization there

are lower than the national average: 38% in Kirghizia, 33% in Tadzhikistan, 45% in Turkmenistan and 41% in Uzbekistan.

The variations in population growth rates are even greater when examining rural populations: in Ukraine, for example, the average annual rate of rural population change in 1979–89 was −1.2%, while in Tadzhikistan it was 3.4%. Aggregate figures for the Russian Federation reflect the all-Union average, but within the Federation there is some variation. The European regions of the Russian Federation have low population growth rates, are experiencing rural depopulation and have high levels of urbanization. In Siberia and the Soviet Far East population growth rates have been above the all-Union average, with Tyumen oblast, the centre of the Western Siberian petroleum industry, recording a growth rate of 5.0%; levels of urbanization have also been above the all-Union level. In general these figures reflect the contrast between the highly urbanized and industrialized population of the European regions which, in common with the rest of Europe, are experiencing very low rates of population growth, and the predominantly rural population of Central Asia which is experiencing high rates of population growth. These high rates of natural increase are due to declining death rates combined with high birth rates, a demographic pattern common to many developing countries.

As a consequence of these regional variations in population growth, together with the ageing of the population in the European regions and the wasteful use of labour, there is a relative shortage of labour in the industrial regions of the European Republics. The population of Central Asia has shown little willingness to migrate northwards to realize employment opportunities in the 'industrialized north'. In the 1980s there was an increase in out-migration from Central Asia, but this was predominantly in the form of Russians moving northwards.

THE REGIONAL DISTRIBUTION OF ECONOMIC ACTIVITY

Any discussion of investment in the USSR must be wary of the distortions caused by the Soviet pricing system. Assessments of regional investment productivity are susceptible to price distortions that undervalue resources and, in some instances, overvalue the cost of industrial inputs. Economists in Siberia have consistently argued that Siberian development only appears 'uneconomic' because of the distortions of the price system, which undervalue the region's resource production. Whether this is the case or not, the important point is that precise measures of efficiency and productivity based on the Soviet pricing system, or conversions to so-called world price for that matter, should be treated with considerable suspicion.

Production

However it is measured, the Russian Federation dominated the Soviet economy. In 1988 the Russian Federation accounted for 61.1% of net material product (NMP), and, together with the other Slavic Republics, Ukraine and Byelorussia, accounted for 81.5% of NMP (their share of total population, in 1989, was 72.8%). By comparison, the four Republics of Central Asia (Kirghizia, Uzbekistan, Tadzhikistan and Turkmenia—traditionally the Soviet view of Central Asia has not included Kazakhstan) accounted for 5.7% of NMP (their share of the population was 11.6%). If net output by industry is examined the level of concentration is even greater, with the share of the Slavic regions being 85.1% and that of Central Asia 4.1%. It is only in the agricultural sphere that Central Asia's share of 9.5% of output approaches that of its share of population.

However, analysis of the republican distribution of agricultural production reveals that Central Asian agriculture is highly specialized. For example, the Central Asian Republics supplied 2.3% of the USSR's grain, 13.8% of its vegetables and 88.3% of its cotton. Central Asian leaders have complained that their limited agricultural areas are given over to the production of 'cash crops' rather than to producing food for local consumption. It is worth noting that, in 1989, the Slavic Republics produced 80.6% of the USSR's cotton cloth. Measures of industrial output per head show a similar pattern, mainly higher than all-Union averages in the European Republics and lower than average measures in the Central Asian Republics. There was a wide range between the highest relative measure of 119 in the Russian Federation (using as a base the USSR = 100) and the lowest of 43 in Tadzhikistan. In sum, the share of industrial output in the Central Asian Republics rarely exceeded their share of population, while the European Republics typically have a more than proportionate share of industrial output relative to their population.

In 1985 the Russian Federation accounted for 60.6% of total employment in industry. The European regions of the Russian Federation accounted for 49.9% of total industrial employment, with the Central (14.2%), Urals (10.0%) and Volga (7.1%) regions being of particular importance. When the European part of the Russian Federation is combined with the European republics, the total share for the European USSR was 74.5%. The European regions have an even greater share of heavy (78.8%) and defence-related (81.4%) industrial employment. By contrast, Central Asia only accounted for 4.0% of total industrial employment in 1985.

Investment

Because Soviet investment strategy traditionally favoured investment in the so-called 'productive' sphere, it is not surprising that the Russian Federation was the major beneficiary of capital investment. At the end of 1990 the Russian Federation accounted for 61.8% of fixed assets in the material sphere of production, and the combined share for the Slavic Republics was 80.4%; meanwhile, for Central Asia it was 5.7%. The Russian Federation's share of total investment increased from 59.4% in 1970, to 63.3% in 1988. After 1970 the only Republics with consistent above-average rates of investment growth were the Russian Federation and Byelorussia. At certain times Uzbekistan, Azerbaidzhan and Turkmenistan also experienced above average rates of investment growth. Not only were the European regions the major beneficiaries of capital investment, but investment in those regions has been far more productive than in Central Asia. In most instances above-average rates of growth can be explained by large investment projects; in the Russian Federation, for example, the rapid development of the Western Siberian petroleum and natural gas complex had a significant impact on the distribution of capital investment within the Republic. Data on the regional distribution of capital investment within the Russian Federation show that Western Siberia's share of total Russian Federation investment increased from 10.6% in 1970 to 16.3% in 1980, reaching 22.4% in 1989.

Since no Republic had a clear picture of its relative role in the all-Union economy, it is impossible to assess the costs and benefits of their being incorporated in the USSR. All the Republics claim to have been exploited by the Soviet system. Analysis of income flows by Western specialists suggests that the Russian Federation, Ukraine, Byelorussia and Azerbaidzhan were long-term donors to the all-Union economy, consuming less than they produced. At the same time, Uzbekistan, Kazakhstan and Tadzhikistan were long-term recipients, consuming more than they produced. These conclusions are compatible with the general pattern of republican economic development discussed so far. However, to gain an understanding of inter-republican dependencies it is necessary to examine specific industrial sectors.

Energy Resources

Over 90% of the USSR's energy resources were located in the Russian Federation. The USSR accounted for 20% of the world's petroleum production, 40% of natural gas production and 15% of coal production. Nevertheless, despite this obvious resource wealth, as a consequence of the changing geography of energy production and a failure to manage efficiently the exploitation of resources, at the beginning of the 1990s the USSR was experiencing an energy crisis. While somewhat delayed, in common with other industrialized nations, the USSR experienced a shift in the structure of energy production away from coal to petroleum and, more recently, to natural gas. This change in energy use-mix, together with the depletion of the most accessible deposits, brought dramatic changes in the geography of energy resource production.

In the immediate post-1945 period the energy base of the USSR centred on the coalfields of the European USSR and the petroleum resources of the Volga-Urals and Baku (Azerbaidzhan) regions. Today coal production is concentrated in the Russian Federation, Ukraine and Kazakhstan. Many smaller fields served local needs, but the most important coal basins were the Donbass, in Ukraine, the Kuzbass, in Western Siberia, and Karaganda, in Kazakhstan. Since the early 1970s there was a general drift eastward as new open-pit mines, such as Ekibastuz, in Kazakhstan and Kansk-Achinsk, in western Siberia, were developed. The share of open-cast or strip mining increased from 26.7% of total production in 1970 to 44.3% in 1988. Coal production from deep mines in the older fields, such as the Donbass, has become increasing costly and is unlikely to be profitable under market conditions.

In 1940 petroleum accounted for 18.7% of Soviet energy resource production; by 1960 that figure had risen to 30.5%. The depletion of fields in the European regions forced the USSR to exploit the resources of Siberia and Central Asia. In the 1960s the Volga-Urals region accounted for 70% of the USSR's petroleum production; in 1990 the region's share was estimated to have fallen to 20%. Until the late 1980s, the relative decline of the Volga-Urals fields was more than matched by the development of petroleum and gas production in Western Siberia. In 1970 the Western Siberian economic region produced 8.9% of the USSR's petroleum; by 1980 that figure had risen to 51.8%. In 1990 the share was estimated at 66.5%. However, over-reliance upon Siberian production proved costly, as the ill-planned rapid development of the Western Siberian petroleum fields led to production problems. Soviet petroleum production fell from 606.3m. metric tons in 1989 to an estimated 570m. tons in 1990, a decline of 6.0%. During the same period production in western Siberia fell by 6.7%. A rapid investment programme was begun, but, by the end of the first six months of 1991, production had fallen a further 9.0% and total production for the whole year was not expected to exceed 500m. tons.

From the late 1970s Soviet energy policy stressed the need to substitute natural gas for petroleum, particularly in thermal power stations. Siberia was also the major centre for natural gas production. The region's share of national production rose from 5% in 1970 to 68% in 1989. The Central Asian Republics of Turkmenistan and Uzbekistan were also important centres of production. Further development of the natural gas sector has been hampered by a lack of sufficient pipeline capacity to deliver gas to its markets, as well as the high cost and environmental problems associated with development above the Arctic Circle. The development of petroleum and gas fields remote from the major centres of energy consumption required a massive investment in the construction of transcontinental pipelines. The average distance of transportation by pipeline increased from 80 km in 1970 to 1,910 km in 1980 and 2,350 km in 1988.

As a consequence of the concentration of energy resource production in the eastern regions of the Russian Federation, only the Russian Federation, Azerbaidzhan and Turkmenistan had a positive inter-republican trade balance in petroleum and gas. It therefore was no surprise that the control of energy resources and the pipeline system became important issues in negotiations between the Republics.

Industrial Activity

Analysis of general patterns of investment and production have already revealed the dominance of Byelorussia, Ukraine and the Russian Federation. This pattern was repeated throughout the industrial sectors of the economy. The iron and steel industries were concentrated in the Russian Federation and Ukraine. Despite the changes in petroleum and gas production, the European USSR was still producing over 80% of the gross output of the chemical industry in 1989. In the case of the forestry industry, the Russian Federation alone accounted for over 80% of lumber and paper production. The automotive industry was also concentrated in the European regions of the Russian Federation, in centres such as Moscow, Nizhny Novgorod (formerly Gorky), Toliyatti and Naberezhnye Chelny (formerly Brezhnev). The only non-Russian automotive centres were Zaporozhye (Ukraine) and Minsk (Byelorussia).

In the light industrial sectors there was a wider distribution of production, with the Baltic Republics being important producers of some types of consumer goods. Regional specialization was also promoted by the dominance of industrial ministries, their desire to achieve economies of scale and the high degree of concentration and monopoly that existed in Soviet industry. For example, in 1990, for 87% of the 5,885 products produced by the machine-building industry, a single producer accounted for all of the deliveries to Gossnab (the State Supply Commission). Similarly, it was estimated that 30%–40% of Soviet industrial output was composed of goods produced at a single location. Further evidence of this high level of concentration is provided by the size structure of Soviet enterprises. In 1988 enterprises employing more than 1,000 people accounted for only 16.6% of Soviet enterprises, but accounted for 73.3% of the labour force. This high level of monopolization will make the economic survival of republics, independent from any far-reaching inter-republican economic union, extremely difficult.

INTER-REPUBLICAN TRADE

The geographical distribution of natural resource wealth, together with the dominance of sectoral planning, resulted in a high degree of regional specialization within the Soviet economy. This high level of specialization inevitably produced high levels of trade between the constituent republics of the USSR. The distortions of the domestic pricing system make it very difficult to assess the contribution made by inter-republican trade to individual republics and the balance between imports and exports.

In domestic prices, in 1988, inter-republican trade amounted to 21% of gross domestic product. Ratios of the value of inter-republican exports to republican NMP, in 1988, show the Russian Federation (18%) and Ukraine (39%) to be the most self-sufficient, while Byelorussia (70%) and the Baltic Republics (60%) are the most export-orientated. Inter-republican trade balances were particularly susceptible to price distortions which undervalued energy resources and heavy industrial products, and overvalued consumer goods. On the basis of domestic prices, in 1988 all Republics recorded a deficit in inter-republican trade. However, recalculating these trade values using world prices there is general improvement for all Republics, and the Russian Federation registers a sizeable surplus. This change in fortunes results from an increase in the value of energy exports from the Russian Federation. This type of analysis suggests that the shift to trading in market prices will favour the Russian Federation. It will, however, also force all Republics to reassess their trading relations with one another. Clearly an important factor in shaping the composition and value of inter-republican trade is the structure of republican economies. Under the Soviet economic system individual Republics had very little control over their own economies. One of the most immediate problems for Republics attempting to establish their economic independence is dealing with the high levels of specialization and interdependence inherited from the central planning system.

CONCLUSION: REGIONAL DE-INTEGRATION

Over 70 years of central planning produced a highly specialized and interdependent pattern of regional economic activity. Despite ideological claims to have reduced the level of inter-republican economic inequality, there remained a considerable gap between the richest and poorest republics. The result was that the former constituent republics of the USSR seemed ill-prepared to take over their own economic development. The Baltic States were widely perceived as the most developed of the former Republics, while the Central Asian Republics seemed likely to be clear 'losers' following de-integration. However, in the short term at least, all Republics, regardless of their resource base, will remain tied to each other by existing economic relationships. In the longer term they will seek to reorientate their economies to better meet the needs of their populations, and in doing so will establish more conventional trading relations with each other.

Statistical Survey

Source (unless otherwise stated): State Committee of Statistics of the USSR, Moscow, ul. Kirova 39; tel. (095) 228-16-33.

Note: Unless otherwise indicated, all the figures in this Survey refer to the 15 republics of the USSR, prior to the secession of Estonia, Latvia and Lithuania, in September 1991, and to the dissolution of the Union itself, in December 1991.

Area and Population

AREA, POPULATION AND DENSITY

Area (sq km)	22,402,200*
Population (census results)	
17 January 1979	262,436,227
12 January 1989	
Males	135,361,000†
Females	151,370,000†
Total	286,730,817
Population (official estimates at 1 January)	
1990	288,624,000
1991	290,077,000
Density (per sq km) at 1 January 1991 . . .	12.9

* 8,649,540 sq miles. The total includes two areas of ocean, the White Sea (90,000 sq km) and the Sea of Azov (37,300 sq km).
† Figuires are rounded to the nearest 1,000.

UNION REPUBLICS (official estimates at 1 January 1991)

Union Republic	Area ('000 sq km)	Popu-lation ('000)	Capital	Population of capital ('000) at census of 12 January 1989
Armenia . .	29.8	3,376	Yerevan	1,215†
Azerbaidzhan .	86.6	7,137	Baku	1,757†
Byelorussia .	207.6	10,260	Minsk	1,612†
Estonia . .	45.1	1,582	Tallinn	503†
Georgia . .	69.7	5,464	Tbilisi	1,264†
Kazakhstan .	2,717.3	16,793	Alma-Ata	1,132†
Kyrgyzstan .	198.5	4,422	Frunze‡	626†
Latvia . .	64.6	2,681	Riga	915
Lithuania .	65.2	3,728	Vilnius	582
Moldavia . .	33.7	4,367	Kishinev	720†
Russia . .	17,075.4	148,543	Moskva (Moscow)	8,967†
Tadzhikstan .	143.1	5,358	Dushanbe	604†
Turkmenistan .	488.1	3,714	Ashkhabad	402†
Ukraine . .	603.7	51,944	Kiev	2,602†
Uzbekistan . .	447.4	20,708	Tashkent	2,079†
Total USSR .	22,402.2*	290,077		—

* Including areas of the White Sea (90,000 sq km) and the Sea of Azov (37,300 sq km), which are not part of the territories of adjacent Union Republics.
† Including communities under the authority of the town council.
‡ Reverted to its former name of Bishkek in February 1991.

AUTONOMOUS REPUBLICS (census of 12 January 1989)

Autonomous Republic	Area (sq km)	Popu-lation ('000)	Capital	Population of capital ('000)
Within RSFSR:				
Bashkir . . .	143,600	3,952	Ufa	1,083
Buryat . . .	351,300	1,042	Ulan-Ude	353
Chechen-Ingush . .	19,300	1,277	Grozny	401
Chuvash . . .	18,300	1,336	Cheboksary	420
Daghestan . . .	50,300	1,792	Makhachkala	315
Kabardino-Balkar .	12,500	760	Nalchik	235
Kalmyk . . .	75,900	322	Elista	120
Karelian . . .	172,400	792	Petrozavodsk	270
Komi . . .	415,900	1,263	Syktyvkar	233
Mari . . .	23,200	750	Yoshkar-Ola	242
Mordovian . .	26,200	964	Saransk	312
North Ossetian . .	8,000	634	Ordzhonikidze†	300
Tatar . . .	68,000	3,640	Kazan	1,094
Tuva . . .	170,500	309	Kyzyl-Orda	153
Udmurt . . .	42,100	1,609	Izhevsk (Ustinov)	635
Yakut . . .	3,103,200	1,081	Yakutsk	187
Within Azerbaidzhan:				
Nakhichevan .	5,500	295	Nakhichevan	37*
Within Georgia:				
Abkhazian . .	8,600	537	Sukhumi	121
Adzhar . .	3,000	393	Batumi	136
Within Uzbekistan:				
Karkalpak . .	165,600	1,214	Nukus	169

* At 1 January 1976.
† Reverted to its previous name of Vladikavkaz in October 1990.

AUTONOMOUS REGIONS (census of 12 January 1989)

Region	Area (sq km)	Popu-lation ('000)	Capital	Population of capital ('000)
Within RSFSR:				
Adygei	7,600	432	Maikop	149
Gorno-Altai . .	92,600	192	Gorno-Altaisk	40*
Jewish . . .	36,000	216	Birobidzhan	78†
Kharachayevo-Cherkess . .	14,100	418	Cherkessk	113
Khakass . . .	61,900	569	Abakan	154
Within Azerbaidzhan:				
Nagorny Karabakh .	4,400	188	Stepanakert	35*
Within Georgia:				
South Ossetian . .	3,900	99	Tskhinvali	34*
Within Tadzhikistan:				
Gorno-Badakhshan .	63,700	161	Khorog	15*

* At 1 January 1976.   † At 1 January 1985.

PRINCIPAL TOWNS
(population, in '000, at census of 12 January 1989)

Moskva (Moscow, the capital) . . .	8,967*	Krivoy Rog . . .	713
Leningrad† . . .	5,020*	Vladivostok . . .	648
Kiev	2,602*	Izhevsk (formerly	
Tashkent . . .	2,079*	Ustinov) . . .	635
Baku	1,757*	Yaroslavl . . .	633
Minsk	1,612*	Tolyatti . . .	630
Kharkov . . .	1,611	Irkutsk . . .	626
Gorky†	1,438	Frunze† . . .	626*
Novosibirsk . . .	1,436	Ulyanovsk . . .	625
Sverdlovsk† . .	1,367	Krasnodar . . .	620
Tbilisi	1,264*	Karaganda . . .	614
Kuybyshev† . .	1,257	Dushanbe . . .	604*
Yerevan	1,215*	Barnaul . . .	602
Dnepropetrovsk . .	1,179	Khabarovsk . .	601
Omsk	1,148	Novokuznetsk . .	600
Chelyabinsk . .	1,143	Vilnius . . .	582
Alma-Ata . . .	1,132*	Orenburg . . .	547
Odessa	1,115	Penza . . .	543
Donetsk	1,110	Tula	540
Kazan	1,094	Kemerovo . . .	520
Perm	1,091	Mariupol (formerly	
Ufa	1,083	Zhdanov) . . .	517
Rostov-on-Don . .	1,020	Ryazan	515
Volgograd . . .	999	Astrakhan . . .	509
Riga	915	Nikolayev . . .	503
Krasnoyarsk . .	912	Tallinn	503*
Saratov	905	Tomsk	502
Voronezh . . .	887	Naberezhniye Chelny	
Zaporozhye . .	884	(formerly Brezhnev)	501
Lvov	790	Gomel	500
Kishinev . . .	720*	Voroshilovgrad† . .	497
		Ivanovo . . .	481

* Including communities under the authority of the town council. The population of the city proper (in '000) was: Moscow 8,769; Leningrad† 4,456; Kiev 2,587; Tashkent 2,073; Baku 1,150; Minsk 1,589; Tbilisi 1,260; Yerevan 1,199; Alma-Ata 1,128; Kishinev 665; Frunze† 616; Dushanbe 595; Tallinn 482.

† These towns subsequently reverted to their former names: Leningrad became Sankt Peterburg (St Petersburg) in September 1991; Gorky became Nizhny Novgorod (October 1990); Kuybyshev became Samara (January 1991); Frunze became Bishkek (February 1991); Voroshilovgrad became Lugansk (November 1989). In September 1991 the town council of Sverdlovsk voted to adopt the city's former name of Yekaterinburg.

BIRTHS, MARRIAGES AND DEATHS

	Registered live births		Registered marriages		Registered deaths	
	Number	Rate (per 1,000)	Number	Rate (per 1,000)	Number	Rate (per 1,000)
1982 .	5,100,282	18.9	2,769,234	10.3	2,723,596	10.1
1983 .	5,391,869	19.8	2,834,806	10.4	2,822,649	10.4
1984 .	5,386,893	19.6	2,634,144	9.6	2,964,921	10.8
1985 .	5,374,393	19.4	2,717,805	9.8	2,947,068	10.6
1986 .	5,610,769	20.0	2,753,075	9.8	2,737,351	9.8
1987 .	5,599,195	19.8	2,776,568	9.8	2,804,785	9.9
1988 .	5,381,056	18.9	2,673,056	9.4	2,888,753	10.1
1989 .	5,062,231	17.6	2,711,040	9.4	2,874,535	10.0

ECONOMICALLY ACTIVE POPULATION
(persons aged 15 years and over, 1989 census)

	Males	Females	Total
Agriculture . . .	16,303,351	11,345,441	27,648,792
Industry, construction, transport and communications	40,784,158	24,933,826	65,717,984
Trade, public catering, material and technical supply, sales and state purchases	2,879,596	7,666,093	10,545,689
Public health, sports, social security, public education, arts, science and scientific services	13,068,914	24,076,218	37,145,132
Other non-productive branches of activity	1,083,791	1,182,605	2,266,396
Total	74,119,810	69,204,183	143,323,993

Source: International Labour Office, *Year Book of Labour Statistics.*

EMPLOYMENT (annual averages, '000 employees)

	1988	1989	1990
Agriculture	23,351	22,790}	22,761
Forestry	423	393}	
Industry*	37,376	36,414	35,400
Printing and publishing . .	2,128	2,156	2,090
Construction	12,746	13,184	12,550
Trade, restaurants and hotels .	10,088	9,877	9,800
Transport, storage and communications . . .	11,066	10,223	10,225
Financing, insurance, real estate and business services .	676	689	720
Community, social and personal services . .	31,049	31,331	31,425
Total	128,903	127,057	124,971

* Comprising manufacturing (except printing and publishing), mining and quarrying, electricity, gas, water, logging and fishing.

Source: mainly International Labour Office, *Year Book of Labour Statistics.*

Agriculture

PRINCIPAL CROPS ('000 metric tons)

	1987	1988	1989
Wheat .	83,312	84,445	92,307
Rice (paddy)	2,683	2,866	2,560
Barley .	58,409	44,463	48,509
Maize	14,808	16,030	15,305
Rye	18,082	18,546	20,057
Oats	18,495	15,287	16,828
Millet†	3,926	3,171	4,108
Sorghum	238	148	159
Buckwheat.	1,297	1,073	1,347
Other cereals	239	154	130
Potatoes	75,908	62,705	72,205
Dry beans .	72	82	78
Dry peas .	8,407	7,571	8,088
Lentils.	36	38	57
Other pulses	1,437	1,224	1,385
Soybeans	712	884	956
Castor beans .	66	60	62
Sunflower seed	6,120	6,164	7,070
Rapeseed	296	420	424
Linseed	228	220	226
Flax fibre .	433	324	345
Cottonseed.	4,950†	5,300†	5,225
Cotton (lint)	2,460	2,760	2,690
Hempseed .	7	5	6
Hemp fibre	21	24	24
Cabbages† .	9,550	9,700	9,300
Tomatoes† .	7,400	7,300	7,100
Cucumbers and gherkins† .	1,460	1,470	1,400
Onions (dry)†	2,750	2,640	2,500
Carrots†	2,600	2,550	2,400
Watermelons‡ .	4,751	5,243	5,300*
Grapes.	5,964	5,581	4,984
Sugar beet.	90,405	87,855	97,414
Apples .	5,496	5,700	6,300†
Plums*	850	1,000	1,050
Tea (made).	156	123	143*
Tobacco (leaves)	303	245	233
Kenaf (Mesta)*.	45	47	47

* FAO estimates.   † Unofficial figures.
‡ Including melons (about 18%) and pumpkins and squash (about 30%).
Sources: State Committee for Statistics of the USSR, and FAO, *Production Yearbook* and *Quarterly Bulletin of Statistics.*
1990 ('000 metric tons, official estimates): Maize 9,800; Potatoes 63,700; Grapes 5,600; Sugar beet 81,200; Sunflower seed 6,500; Flax fibre 245.

LIVESTOCK ('000 head at 1 January)

	1987	1988	1989
Cattle .	122,103	120,593	119,580
Pigs	79,501	77,403	78,143
Sheep .	142,210	140,783	140,678
Goats .	6,491	6,560	6,815
Buffaloes* .	320	320	315
Horses.	5,912	5,885	5,904
Asses .	300	300*	300*
Camels.	260	265*	270*
Chickens	1,125,000	1,130,000	1,154,000*
Turkeys	49,000	48,000*	47,000*

* FAO estimates.   † Unofficial figures.
Sources: State Committee for Statistics of the USSR, and FAO, *Production Yearbook.*
1990 ('000 head at 1 January): Cattle 118,429; Pigs 79,033; Sheep 138,443; Goats 6,974; Horses 5,920; Poultry 1,213,819.
1991 ('000 head at 1 January, official estimates): Cattle 116,200; Pigs 76,800; Sheep and Goats 141,100.

LIVESTOCK PRODUCTS ('000 metric tons)

	1987	1988	1989
Beef and veal .	8,281	8,616	8,800*
Mutton and lamb† .	870	840	850
Goats' meat*	30	25	28
Pig meat .	6,315	6,595	6,750*
Poultry meat .	3,127	3,235	3,250*
Other meat .	277	287	292
Cows' milk.	102,880	105,950	107,600†
Sheep's milk	90†	86*	87*
Goats' milk	350†	360†	364*
Butter .	1,755	1,794	1,780*
Cheese.	1,903.0	1,979.5*	2,090.0*
Hen eggs	4,587	4,714	4,680
Other poultry eggs*	86	88	90
Honey .	219	222*	230*
Wool and other animal hair:			
greasy	455.0	478.0	474.0
clean .	273.0	286.8	284.4
Cattle and buffalo hides* .	794.2	818.9	822.7
Sheep skins* .	129.2	130.0	130.8

* FAO estimates.   † Unofficial figures.
Note: Meat production is in terms of slaughter weight, i.e. including offals and slaughter fats.
1990: Butter 1,710,000 metric tons.
Source: State Committee for Statistics of the USSR, and FAO, *Production Yearbook.*
Lard (FAO estimates, '000 metric tons): 813 in 1987; 842 in 1988.
Tallow (FAO estimates, '000 metric tons): 383 in 1987; 388 in 1988.

Forestry

ROUNDWOOD REMOVALS
(FAO estimates, '000 cubic metres, excluding bark)

	1986	1987	1988
Sawlogs, veneer logs and logs for sleepers .	164,600	169,000	170,000
Pulpwood .	41,000	42,000	42,300
Other industrial wood .	90,400	92,000	92,700
Fuel wood* .	86,800	86,800	86,800
Total .	382,800	389,800	391,800

* Assumed to be unchanged since 1985.
Source: FAO, *Yearbook of Forest Products.*

SAWNWOOD PRODUCTION
('000 cubic metres, incl. railway sleepers)

	1986	1987	1988
Coniferous (soft wood) .	88,500	89,400	90,300
Broadleaved (hard wood) .	12,500	12,600	12,700
Total .	101,000	102,000	103,000

Source: FAO, *Yearbook of Forest Products.*

Fishing

('000 metric tons, live weight)

	1986	1987	1988
Common carp	232.2	246.9	252.9
Other carps, barbels, etc. . .	151.1	164.3	183.0
Other freshwater fishes .	182.0	160.8	183.5
Pink (Humpback) salmon .	40.4	97.7	37.8
Azov tyulka	360.6	403.7	304.3
Other diadromous fishes .	108.5	110.1	110.8
Flounders, halibuts, soles, etc. .	142.5	132.8	130.0
Atlantic cod	205.3	244.9	200.9
Pacific cod	168.4	175.3	148.4
Alaska pollack	3,584.1	3,421.7	3,369.9
Blue whiting (Poutassou) .	284.0	278.2	179.3
Cape hakes	153.9	82.9	116.9
Blue grenadiers . . .	13.2	66.2	103.3
Atlantic redfishes . . .	143.0	129.3	107.3
Capelin	99.2	51.3	22.9
Chilean jack mackerel . .	673.0	818.6	938.3
Cape horse mackerel . .	169.4	282.7	241.8
Greenback horse mackerel .	105.5	107.3	58.8
Other jack and horse mackerels . . .	311.8	344.4	343.1
Atlantic herring . . .	142.5	133.1	145.6
Pacific herring . . .	168.4	220.7	189.5
Round sardinella . . .	118.8	162.7	161.3
Other sardinellas . . .	145.8	100.7	111.6
Japanese pilchard (sardine) .	820.8	764.7	794.6
European pilchard (sardine) .	169.3	338.7	425.9
European sprat . . .	79.6	90.2	98.3
European anchovy . . .	262.9	151.1	364.1
Chub mackerel . . .	363.9	229.9	325.3
Other marine fishes (incl. unspecified)	1,285.6	1,174.0	1,197.8
Total fish	**10,685.8**	**10,684.8**	**10,847.1**
Antarctic krill . . .	379.3	290.4	284.9
Other crustaceans . . .	49.5	51.8	58.5
Squids	114.9	103.0	118.9
Other molluscs	24.2	23.6	18.0
Sea-urchins	6.3	6.0	4.7
Total catch* . . .	**11,260.0**	**11,159.6**	**11,332.1**
Inland waters . . .	926.9	988.4	995.6
Arctic Sea . . . }			
Atlantic Ocean . . . . }	3,155.5	3,348.3	3,575.7
Mediterranean and Black Sea .	390.6	261.3	347.3
Indian Ocean	74.3	81.5	54.1
Pacific Ocean	6,712.7	6,480.2	6,359.4

* Figures exclude aquatic plants and aquatic mammals, including whales (see below) and seals. The harvest of aquatic plants (in '000 metric tons) was: 178.2 in 1986; 166.4 in 1987; 194.0 in 1988. The number of Northern fur seals caught was 7,262 in 1985.

WHALING*

	1986	1987	1988
Number of whales caught . .	3,375	3,220	158

* Figures include whales caught during the Antarctic summer season beginning in the year prior to the year stated.

Source: FAO, *Yearbook of Fishery Statistics*.

Mining

('000 metric tons, unless otherwise indicated)

	1986	1987	1988
Hard coal*	588,000	595,000	599,000
Brown coal (incl. lignite)* . .	163,000	165,000	171,600
Peat[1]	19,480	11,445	17,500
Iron ore:			
gross weight	249,959	250,874	249,737
metal content . . .	137,252	138,216	137,000
Bauxite[2]	4,600	4,600	4,600
Chromium ore[2,3] . . .	920	910	930
Copper ore[3,4]	1,030	1,010	990
Ilmenite concentrates[2] . .	450	454	460
Lead ore[2,3]	440	440	440
Magnesite ('000 short tons)[2] .	2,375	2,425	2,375
Manganese ore[2,3] . . .	2,831	2,812	2,722
Zinc ore[2,3]	810	810	810
Fluorspar (excl. precious stones)[2,5]	560	560	560
Gypsum (crude)[2] . . .	4,599	4,781	4,800
Salt (unrefined)[2] . . .	15,347	15,438	14,822
Phosphate rock[2] . . .	33,900	34,100	34,400
Potash salts[6]	10,228	10,888	11,301
Native sulphur[2] . . .	1,900	1,900	1,900
Asbestos[2]	2,400	2,552	2,600
Crude petroleum[7] . . .	614,753	624,177	624,323
Antimony ore (metric tons)[2,3] .	9,500	9,600	9,600
Cobalt ore (metric tons)[2,3] .	2,800	2,900	3,000
Molybdenum ore (metric tons)[2,3] .	11,400	11,500	11,500
Nickel ore (metric tons)[2,3] .	195,000	205,000	215,000
Rutile concentrates (metric tons)[2] .	10,000	10,000	n.a.
Tin concentrates (metric tons)[3,4] .	16,000	15,000	15,000
Tungsten concentrates (metric tons)[2,3] .	9,200	9,200	9,200
Mercury (incl. secondary) (76 lb flasks)[2,3] .	66,000	67,000	67,000
Gold (metric tons)[2,3] . .	275.3	275.3	279.9
Silver (metric tons)[2,3] . .	1,499	1,499	1,493
Diamonds ('000 metric carats)[2] .	10,800	10,800	11,000
Natural gas (million cu metres)	684,620	730,750	757,250

* Figures refer to gross weight. Excluding waste, the totals (in '000 metric tons) were: Hard coal 512,896 in 1986, 519,085 in 1987, 523,040 in 1988; Brown coal 159,807 in 1986, 161,214 in 1987, 168,000 in 1988.

[1] Peat for fuel, excluding peat gathered for agricultural use.
[2] Estimated data (Source: Bureau of Mines, US Department of the Interior).
[3] Figures refer to the metal content of ores and concentrates.
[4] Estimated data (Source: Metallgesellschaft Aktiengesellschaft, Frankfurt am Main, Germany).
[5] Acid and metallurgical grade.
[6] Figures refer to the potassium oxide content of salts.
[7] Including gas condensates.

1989 ('000 metric tons, unless otherwise indicated): Hard coal 575,300 (gross weight); Brown coal 163,500 (gross weight); Iron ore 241,350 (gross weight); Crude petroleum 607,180; Natural gas 746,580 million cu m.
1990 ('000 metric tons, unless otherwise indicated): Hard coal 471,600 (gross weight); Brown coal 156,500 (gross weight); Iron ore 236,150 (gross weight); Crude petroleum 570,430; Natural gas 703,000 million cu m.

Sources: United Nations, *Industrial Statistics Yearbook* and *Monthly Bulletin of Statistics*; R. Levine (US Bureau of Mines); USSR State Committee for Statistics.

Industry

SELECTED PRODUCTS ('000 metric tons, unless otherwise indicated)

	1987	1988	1989†
Refined sugar	13,680	12,056	13,300
Margarine	1,534.8	1,493.5	1,503
Wine ('000 hectolitres)	14,692	17,883	19,300
Beer ('000 hectolitres)	50,711	55,811	60,200
Cigarettes (million)	378,475	358,218	343,000
Cotton yarn (pure and mixed)	1,725.1	1,764.4	1,760
Woven cotton fabrics—pure and mixed (million sq metres)[1]	8,721	8,670	n.a.
Flax yarn	216.7	220.3	216.0
Linen fabrics ('000 sq metres)	868,500	882,900	n.a.
Jute fabrics ('000 sq metres)	118,100	116,100	n.a.
Woven fabrics of natural silk ('000 sq metres)[1]	62,222	63,907	n.a.
Wool yarn—pure and mixed (metric tons)	427,700	439,400	n.a.
Woven woollen fabrics—pure and mixed ('000 sq metres)	853,900	875,900	n.a.
Rayon and acetate continuous filaments (metric tons)	224,500	216,000	n.a.
Rayon and acetate discontinuous fibres (metric tons)	388,400	385,000	n.a.
Woven rayon and acetate fabrics (million sq metres)[1]	1,111.8	1,071.9	n.a.
Non-cellulosic continuous filaments (metric tons)	509,800	541,000	n.a.
Non-cellulosic discontinuous fibres (metric tons)	394,400	412,200	n.a.
Woven fabrics of non-cellulosic fibres ('000 sq metres)	878,100	943,800	n.a.
Leather footwear ('000 pairs)[2]	808,993	819,050	827,000
Mechanical wood pulp	2,033*	2,177	2,149
Chemical and semi-chemical wood pulp	7,446*	8,749	8,509
Newsprint	1,663	1,694	1,719
Other printing and writing paper	1,310*	1,394	1,571
Other paper and paperboard	7,156*	7,733	7,364
Rubber tyres ('000)[3]	67,802	69,125	69,700
Rubber footwear ('000 pairs)	232,552	236,776	230,000
Synthetic rubber[4]	2,366	2,485	n.a.
Acetylene (Ethine)	265	277	n.a.
Ethylene (Ethene)	2,977	3,175	3,137
Propylene (Propene)	1,353	1,420	1,447
Methyl alcohol (Wood alcohol)	3,824	3,211	3,331
Xylenes (Xylol)	1,048.1	1,022.8	n.a.
Benzene (Benzol)	2,168	2,245	n.a.
Sulphuric acid (100%)	28,531	29,372	28,276
Caustic soda (Sodium hydroxide)	3,288	3,323	3,185
Soda ash (Sodium carbonate)	5,162	5,098	n.a.
Nitrogenous fertilizers (a)[5]	15,743	15,815	14,400
Phosphate fertilizers (b)[5]	9,693	10,013	9,700
Potash fertilizers (c)[5]	10,888	11,300	10,233
Insecticides, fungicides, disinfectants, etc. (metric tons)	326,900	317,000	276,000
Soap	1,484.4	1,570.0†	1,037
Plastics and resins	5,500	n.a.	4,700
Motor spirit (petrol)	80,000	80,200	n.a.
Kerosene and jet fuel	36,600	36,700	n.a.
Distillate fuel oils	109,500	109,500	n.a.
Residual fuel oils	185,000	195,000	n.a.
Lubricating oils	8,700	8,800	n.a.
Petroleum bitumen (asphalt)	28,000	28,500	n.a.
Liquefied petroleum gas†:			
(a)[6]	1,100	1,200	n.a.
(b)[6]	8,400	8,500	n.a.
Coke†[7]	86,000	86,000	n.a.
Clay building bricks (million)	27,815	28,996	30,000
Cement	137,404	139,499	140,436
Concrete blocks, bricks, pipes, etc. ('000 cu metres)	149,121	153,432	152,000
Unworked glass—rectangles ('000 sq metres)	251,829	250,323	243,000
Pig-iron (incl. ferro-alloys)	113,877	114,558	113,930
Crude steel	161,887	163,037	160,096
Rolled steel products	114,081	115,958	115,550
Steel tubes (seamless and welded)	20,346	20,839	20,600
Aluminium (unwrought)†[8]	2,400	2,400	n.a.
Refined copper (unwrought)†[9]	1,430	1,380	n.a.
Refined lead (unwrought)[8]	780	785	n.a.
Magnesium—unwrought[10]	90	91	n.a.
Tin—unwrought (metric tons)[11]	18,000	17,000	n.a.
Zinc (unwrought)†[8]	1,000	963	n.a.
Electric motors—alternating current ('000 kilowatts)	54,631	55,507	48,400
Generators for hydraulic turbines ('000 kilowatts)	} 12,573	13,745	12,600
Generators for steam and gas turbines ('000 kilowatts)			
Radio receivers ('000)	8,143	8,025	8,561
Television receivers ('000)	9,081	9,637	9,938

—continued

	1987	1988	1989†
Cameras: photographic ('000)[1][2]	2,415	2,722	2,856
Watches and clocks ('000)	70,552	73,507	74,700
Passenger motor cars ('000)	1,332	1,262	1,217
Motor cycles, scooters, etc. ('000)	1,047	1,068	1,076
Bicycles ('000)	5,550	5,647	5,605
Tractors (number)[1][3]	567,493	559,197	532,000
Tractor-drawn ploughs (number)	207,976	191,104	185,000
Combine harvester-threshers (number)	96,225	71,316	62,200
Domestic refrigerators and freezers ('000)	5,984	6,231	6,465
Domestic washing machines ('000)	5,779	6,104	6,698
Electric energy (million kWh)	1,664,924	1,698,400	1,722,000
Manufactured gas:			
from gas works (terajoules)†	6,000	6,000	} 550,600
from cokeries (terajoules)†[1][4]	556,000	560,000	

* FAO estimate.   † Provisional estimates.
[1] After undergoing finishing processes.
[2] Including sporting footwear (of all types) and orthopaedic shoes.
[3] Tyres for road motor vehicles (excluding motor cycles) and for agricultural and other off-the-road vehicles.
[4] Estimated production (Source: International Rubber Study Group).
[5] Production of fertilizers is in terms of (a) nitrogen; (b) phosphoric acid; and (c) potassium oxide. The figures for nitrogenous fertilizers include an unspecified amount of technical nitrogen.
[6] Production from (a) natural gas plants; and (b) petroleum refineries.
[7] Gas coke and coke-oven coke (humidity 6%).
[8] Estimated primary metal production (Source: Bureau of Mines, US Department of the Interior).
[9] Estimated primary and secondary metal production (Source: Metallgesellschaft Aktiengesellschaft, Frankfurt am Main, Germany).
[10] Estimated metal production, incl. secondary (Source: Bureau of Mines, US Department of the Interior).
[11] Estimated primary metal production (Source: Metallgesellschaft Aktiengesellschaft, Frankfurt am Main, Germany).
[12] Excluding industrial still cameras.
[13] Tractors of 10 horse-power and over, excluding industrial tractors and road tractors for tractor-trailer combinations.
[14] Excluding gas used for the gasification of coal.

1990: Refined sugar 12.2m. metric tons; Margarine 1,400,000 metric tons; Cotton yarn 1,704,000 metric tons; Flax yarn 200,300 metric tons; Leather footwear 820m. pairs; Paper 6.2m. metric tons; Chemical fertilizers 31.7m. metric tons; Cement 137,330,000 metric tons; Pig-iron 110,170,000 metric tons; Crude steel 154,414,000m. metric tons; Rolled steel products 112m. metric tons; Steel tubes 19.5m. metric tons; Radio receivers 9.2m.; Television receivers 10.5m.; Passenger motor cars 1,259,000; Motor cycles, etc. 1,014,000; Domestic refrigerators and freezers 6.5m.; Domestic washing machines 7.9m.; Electric energy 1,727,900m. kWh.

Finance

CURRENCY AND EXCHANGE RATES

Monetary Units
100 kopeks = 1 rubl (ruble or rouble).

Denominations
Coins: 1, 2, 3, 5, 10, 15, 20 and 50 kopeks; 1 rouble.
Notes: 1, 3, 5, 10, 25, 50, 100 and 200 roubles.

Sterling and Dollar Equivalents (30 June 1991)
£1 sterling = 99.4 kopeks;
US $1 = 61.4 kopeks;
100 roubles = £100.60 = $162.87.

Average Exchange Rate (US $ per rouble)
1988   1.648
1989   1.588
1990   1.710

Note: The foregoing information refers to official rates of exchange. At 30 June 1991 the commercial exchange rate was US $1 = 1.80 roubles.

STATE BUDGET (million roubles)

Revenue	1984	1985	1989*
Turnover tax	102,700	101,000	111,100
Profits tax paid by state enterprises and organizations	115,600	117,800	121,200
Personal income tax	28,800	29,700	39,400
Total (incl. others)	376,700	397,400	458,400

Expenditure	1984	1985	1989*
National economy	211,700	228,300	172,700
Social and cultural programmes } Science	119,700	125,100	163,500
Defence	17,100	19,060	70,300
Total (incl. others)	371,200	397,000	494,700

* Complete figures for 1986, 1987 and 1988 are not available.

1988 (million roubles): Revenue 443,500; Expenditure 443,500, of which: National economy 240,820; Education 61,300; Defence 20,401.

1990 (million roubles): Revenue 429,914; Expenditure 489,914 (Defence 70,975).

UNION-REPUBLICAN BUDGET TOTALS (million roubles)

	1982	1983	1984
RSFSR	72,740.0	74,318.6	88,855.1
Ukrainian SSR	23,929.0	24,102.3	27,786.6
Byelorussian SSR	5,705.8	5,736.7	6,697.4
Uzbek SSR	6,043.8	6,551.3	7,255.9
Kazakh SSR	9,232.8	9,351.1	10,486.7
Georgian SSR	2,367.4	2,387.3	2,781.1
Azerbaidzhan SSR	2,261.8	2,428.3	2,550.8
Lithuanian SSR	2,613.8	2,703.6	3,237.1
Moldavian SSR	1,789.9	1,952.5	2,264.5
Latvian SSR	1,723.8	1,861.6	2,154.0
Kirghiz SSR	1,582.6	1,647.3	1,788.9
Tadzhik SSR	1,319.1	1,369.7	1,512.3
Armenian SSR	1,595.2	1,624.9	1,773.0
Turkmen SSR	1,152.6	1,193.4	1,346.0
Estonian SSR	1,174.3	1,259.5	1,447.1

NATIONAL ACCOUNTS ('000 million roubles in current prices)

	1987	1988	1989
Total consumption . . .	441.9	465.7	501.6
Accumulation of stocks and reserves	143.9	153.4	150.3
Losses	} 13.8	11.7	4.9
Net exports of goods and services			
Net material product . .	599.6	630.8	656.8
of which:			
Industry	268.6	269.5	277.1
Agriculture	122.6	143.3	150.0
Construction	74.7	80.6	83.0
Transport and communications . .	36.6	38.7	39.5
Distribution and supply . .	97.1	98.7	107.2

Note: Net material product is defined as the total net value of goods and 'productive' services, produced by the economy. This excludes economic activities not contributing directly to material production, such as public administration, defence and personal and professional services.

External Trade

PRINCIPAL COMMODITIES
('000 metric tons, unless otherwise indicated)

Imports	1987	1988	1989
Machines and equipment ('000 roubles) . . .	25,155,825	26,583,761	27,743,042
Cast iron ('000 roubles) . .	2,572	7,289	n.a.
Rolled stock ('000 roubles) .	1,351,874	n.a.	n.a.
Tin plate ('000 roubles) . .	264	2,806	3,432
Cement	901	1,083	826
Timber ('000 cu metres) . .	203.2	196.5	186.1
Plywood ('000 cu metres) .	30.2	26.6	28.0
Pulp	224.5	253.2	236.8
Paper	470.8	506.8	604.8
Cardboard	84.2	95.0	105.1
Cotton fibre . . .	74.6	89.8	77.1
Furs ('000 roubles) . . .	2,299	1,642	5,373
Wool	134.0	114.3	128.4
Tobacco ('000 roubles) . .	149.4	136.2	99.4
Flour	218.6	170.3	179.8
Grain	30,385	35,042	36,969
Cocoa beans	148.0	138.5	179.4
Coffee beans . . .	57.9	49.5	112.9
Tea	135.0	133.6	214.9
Meat and meat products .	858.0	719.1	695.6
Vegetable oils . . .	824.6	341.6	1,065.1
Sugar	5,035	4,094	370.7
Cotton fabrics ('000 metres)	251,226	227,130	188,599
Cameras ('000) . . .	n.a.	n.a.	n.a.
Knitted wear ('000 roubles) .	699,993	715,277	847,523
Furniture ('000 roubles) .	534,472	586,838	539,904
Pipes	5,167	4,743	3,486
Crude petroleum . . .	13,990	19,845	13,336
Chemical products ('000 roubles)	1,547,448	1,655,775	2,070,586
Medical supplies ('000 roubles)	1,249,374	1,316,929	1,847,359

Total imports (million roubles): 60,741 in 1987; 65,040 in 1988; 72,137 in 1989; 70,728 in 1990.

Source: 'Vneshniye ekonomicheskiye svyazi SSSR' of the Ministry of Foreign Economic Relations of the USSR.

Exports	1987	1988	1989
Machines and equipment ('000 roubles) . . .	10,583,089	10,848,115	11,303,386
Petroleum and petroleum products ('000 roubles)	22,826,291	19,708,375	18,634,832
Iron ore	34,567	32,171	29,281
Manganese ore . . .	714	982	895
Cast iron ('000 roubles) .	450,156	474,617	524,922
Rolled stock ('000 roubles)	1,773,532	n.a.	n.a.
Tin plate ('000 roubles) .	39,513	45,873	45,349
Cement	2,423	2,223	1,762
Ammonium sulphate . .	765	687	812
Timber ('000 cu metres) .	19,345	20,486	18,986
Plywood ('000 cu metres)	485.3	416.2	418.8
Pulp	1,087.8	1,055.0	1,020.4
Paper	763.0	695.2	667.9
Cardboard	488.6	404.1	352.5
Cotton fibre . . .	783.2	731.2	790.7
Flax fibre	6.1	6.4	4.3
Furs ('000 roubles) . .	143,388	102,547	73,833
Wool	27.5	18.8	19.3
Tobacco ('000 roubles) . .	2,167	2,198	7,106
Flour	249.7	202.2	208.5
Tea	4.8	5.1	4.3
Meat and meat products .	34.9	30.4	25.8
Vegetable oils . . .	118.2	140.0	138.7
Sugar	158.9	212.9	170.6
Cotton fabrics ('000 metres) .	311,752	376,083	441,755
Clocks and watches ('000)	18,554	16,990	15,670
Cameras ('000) . . .	905.0	832.0	797.0
Knitted wear ('000 roubles) .	5,950	7,713	8,124
Furniture ('000 roubles) .	30,199	33,067	40,295
Chemical products ('000 roubles)	1,052,973	1,219,522	1,255,397

Total exports (million roubles): 68,142 in 1987; 67,115 in 1988; 68,741 in 1989; 60,757 in 1990.

Source: 'Vneshniye ekonomicheskiye svyazi SSSR' of the Ministry of Foreign Economic Relations of the USSR.

PRINCIPAL TRADING PARTNERS (million roubles)

	1988		1989	
	Imports	Exports	Imports	Exports
Afghanistan	184.8	478.4	79.3	504.5
Algeria	223.5	145.4	98.9	188.6
Argentina	546.5	23.9	626.6	69.3
Australia	350.0	13.9	587.4	17.7
Austria	711.7	454.9	1,004.5	429.6
Belgium	376.0	771.3	509.5	817.2
Brazil	151.4	17.0	245.9	22.3
Bulgaria	6,873.1	6,093.7	7,307.1	6,170.5
Canada	535.0	16.4	412.9	38.5
China, People's Republic .	844.9	1,005.2	1,083.5	1,328.5
Cuba	3,836.8	3,726.8	3,867.0	3,833.5
Czechoslovakia . . .	6,817.3	6,384.6	6,609.8	6,255.4
Denmark	105.2	119.9	145.2	175.0
Egypt	314.2	271.2	329.3	306.0
Finland	2,188.3	1,528.7	2,126.8	1,758.8
France	1,189.9	1,578.9	1,218.4	1,348.6
German Democratic Republic	7,024.4	7,193.2	7,175.4	6,662.5
Germany, Federal Republic	3,231.3	2,397.2	4,076.4	2,478.3
Greece	92.4	309.5	125.6	289.9
Hungary	4,943.2	4,484.3	4,813.3	4,187.7
India	1,123.3	1,128.7	1,770.6	1,147.2
Iran	77.0	119.2	61.2	125.4
Iraq	961.4	309.1	975.9	255.4
Italy	1,343.1	1,691.2	1,606.3	1,920.1
Japan	1,950.9	1,184.2	2,138.0	1,343.0
Korea, Democratic People's Republic . .	539.5	1,062.2	561.5	940.5
Libya	459.2	20.6	93.5	33.6
Mongolia	406.2	1,130.8	397.3	1,005.2
Netherlands . . .	227.9	656.8	438.5	971.7
Nicaragua	2.2	247.1	7.6	180.4
Norway	83.0	82.1	112.2	134.6

—continued	1988 Imports	1988 Exports	1989 Imports	1989 Exports
Poland	7,109.3	6,298.0	7,409.8	5,770.6
Romania	2,431.2	2,344.1	2,488.7	2,681.3
Spain	154.0	627.2	216.4	598.1
Sweden	246.0	462.6	434.8	559.9
Switzerland . . .	772.6	404.9	988.1	416.1
Syria	239.1	170.5	704.6	207.9
Turkey	178.3	216.8	495.6	349.0
United Kingdom . .	623.1	1,794.1	1,009.1	2,208.7
USA	1,772.6	2,865.2	2,865.2	529.9
Viet-Nam	388.6	1,393.6	519.7	1,390.9
Yugoslavia . . .	2,147.4	1,693.8	2,405.5	1,926.4
Total (incl. others) . .	65,040.1	67,115.4	72,137.0	68,741.6

Source: 'Vneshniye ekonomicheskiye svyazi SSSR' of the Ministry of Foreign Economic Relations of the USSR.

Transport

FREIGHT TRAFFIC ('000 million ton-kilometres)

	1987	1988	1989
Railways	3,824.7	3,924.8	3,851.7
Roads	492.0	508.0	502.1
Inland waterways . . .	252.7	251.2	239.6
Pipelines (oil and oil products) .	1,450.1	1,466.4	1,422.2
Pipelines (gas)	1,343.4	1,451.2	1,522.2

ROAD TRAFFIC ('000 motor vehicles in use at 31 December)

	1985	1986	1987
Passenger cars	12,590.1	13,456.6	14,343.9
Buses and coaches . . .	302.6	308.7	309.8

PASSENGER TRAFFIC ('000 million passenger-kilometres)

	1987	1988	1989
Railways	402.2	413.8	410.7
Roads	470.6	480.3	480.4
Inland waterways . . .	5.7	5.4	5.4

OCEAN SHIPPING

	1987	1988	1989
Cargo carried (million metric tons)	252	257	245
Freight ton-km (million) .	972,100	1,011,400	991,200
Passengers (million) . .	50	49	45
Passenger-km (million) . .	2,300	2,000	2,000

CIVIL AVIATION

	1985	1986	1987
Passengers carried (million) .	112.3	115.8	118.3
Passenger-km (million) . .	187,611	194,349	200,123
Freight (million ton-km) .	26,883	26,504	28,272

Source: UN, *Statistical Yearbook*.

Tourism*

(Visitors by country of origin)

	1986	1987
Bulgaria	272,500	302,900
Czechoslovakia	336,600	360,900
Finland	727,200	893,900
France	73,200	77,600
German Democratic Republic . .	588,300	620,400
Germany, Federal Republic . .	166,100	203,300
Hungary	190,800	215,500
Poland	900,100	1,242,000
Romania	127,900	148,500
United Kingdom	62,600	77,400
USA	84,400	125,800
Yugoslavia	86,900	97,600

* Excluding visits of less than 24 hours.

Total arrivals (estimates, '000 visitors): 4,309 in 1986; 5,246 in 1987; 6,007 in 1988 (Sources: UN, *Statistical Yearbook;* Intourist).

Communications Media

	1986	1987	1988
Telephones in use ('000) .	26,210	28,184	30,234
Radio receivers (million) .	185.0	192.1	193.9
Television receivers (million) .	n.a.	88.0	90.0
Books published (number of titles)* . . .	83,472	83,011	n.a.
Books published (million copies)* . . .	2,234.4	2,276.2	n.a.
Number of newspapers† .	8,515	8,532	8,622
Daily circulation (million copies) . . .	198.1	207.9	217.4
Periodicals	5,275	5,295	5,413
Annual circulation (million copies) . .	3,690.8	3,885.2	4,260.6

* Figures refer to the production of both books and pamphlets. Books accounted for 55,002 titles (1,599.2 million copies) in 1986, and for 55,069 titles (1,640.1 million copies) in 1987.
† Daily and non-daily newspapers.

Education

STUDENTS ('000)

	1985/86	1986/87	1988/89†
General schools . . .	44,446	43,852	44,106
Professional and technical schools	4,174	4,269	4,048
Secondary specialized schools* .	4,498	4,485	4,502
Higher educational establishments* . . .	5,147	5,088	5,178
Professional courses . . .	50,383	52,455	47,300
Total	108,648	110,149	105,134

* Including evening and correspondence courses.
† Figures for 1987/88 are not available.

THE COMMONWEALTH OF INDEPENDENT STATES

THE MINSK AGREEMENT

The Minsk Agreement establishing a Commonwealth of Independent States was signed by the heads of state of Byelorussia, the Russian Federation and Ukraine on 8 December 1991. The text is as follows:

PREAMBLE

We, the Republic of Byelorussia, the Russian Federation and the Republic of Ukraine, as founder states of the Union of Soviet Socialist Republics (USSR), which signed the 1922 Union Treaty, further described as the high contracting parties, conclude that the USSR has ceased to exist as a subject of international law and a geopolitical reality.

Taking as our basis the historic community of our peoples and the ties which have been established between them, taking into account the bilateral treaties concluded between the high contracting parties;

striving to build democratic law-governed states; intending to develop our relations on the basis of mutual recognition and respect for state sovereignty, the inalienable right to self-determination, the principles of equality and non-interference in internal affairs, repudiation of the use of force and of economic or any other methods of coercion, settlement of contentious problems by means of mediation and other generally-recognized principles and norms of international law;

considering that further development and strengthening of relations of friendship, good-neighbourliness and mutually beneficial co-operation between our states correspond to the vital national interests of their peoples and serve the cause of peace and security;

confirming our adherence to the goals and principles of the United Nations Charter, the Helsinki Final Act and other documents of the Conference on Security and Co-operation in Europe;

and committing ourselves to observe the generally recognized internal norms on human rights and the rights of peoples, we have agreed the following:

ARTICLE 1

The high contracting parties form the Commonwealth of Independent States.

ARTICLE 2

The high contracting parties guarantee their citizens equal rights and freedoms regardless of nationality or other distinctions. Each of the high contracting parties guarantees the citizens of the other parties, and also persons without citizenship that live on its territory, civil, political, social, economic and cultural rights and freedoms in accordance with generally recognized international norms of human rights, regardless of national allegiance or other distinctions.

ARTICLE 3

The high contracting parties, desiring to promote the expression, preservation and development of the ethnic, cultural, linguistic and religious individuality of the national minorities resident on their territories, and that of the unique ethno-cultural regions that have come into being, take them under their protection.

ARTICLE 4

The high contracting parties will develop the equal and mutually beneficial co-operation of their peoples and states in the spheres of politics, the economy, culture, education, public health, protection of the environment, science and trade and in the humanitarian and other spheres, will promote the broad exchange of information and will conscientiously and unconditionally observe reciprocal obligations.

The parties consider it a necessity to conclude agreements on co-operation in the above spheres.

ARTICLE 5

The high contracting parties recognize and respect one another's territorial integrity and the inviolability of existing borders within the Commonwealth.

They guarantee openness of borders, freedom of movement for citizens and of transmission of information within the Commonwealth.

ARTICLE 6

The member-states of the Commonwealth will co-operate in safeguarding international peace and security and in implementing effective measures for reducing weapons and military spending. They seek the elimination of all nuclear weapons and universal total disarmament under strict international control.

The parties will respect one another's aspiration to attain the status of a non-nuclear zone and a neutral state.

The member-states of the community will preserve and maintain under united command a common military-strategic space, including unified control over nuclear weapons, the procedure for implementing which is regulated by a special agreement.

They also jointly guarantee the necessary conditions for the stationing and functioning of and for material and social provision for the strategic armed forces. The parties contract to pursue a harmonized policy on questions of social protection and pension provision for members of the services and their families.

ARTICLE 7

The high contracting parties recognize that within the sphere of their activities, implemented on the equal basis through the common co-ordinating institutions of the Commonwealth, will be the following:

co-operation in the sphere of foreign policy;

co-operation in forming and developing the united economic area, the common European and Eurasian markets, in the area of customs policy;

co-operation in developing transport and communication systems;

co-operation in preservation of the environment, and participation in creating a comprehensive international system of ecological safety;

migration policy issues;

and fighting organized crime.

ARTICLE 8

The parties realize the planetary character of the Chernobyl catastrophe and pledge themselves to unite and co-ordinate their efforts in minimizing and overcoming its consequences.

To these ends they have decided to conclude a special agreement which will take consider the gravity of the consequences of this catastrophe.

ARTICLE 9

The disputes regarding interpretation and application of the norms of this agreement are to be solved by way of negotiations between the appropriate bodies, and, when necessary, at the level of heads of the governments and states.

ARTICLE 10

Each of the high contracting parties reserves the right to suspend the validity of the present agreement or individual articles thereof, after informing the parties to the agreement of this a year in advance.

The clauses of the present agreement may be addended to or amended with the common consent of the high contracting parties.

ARTICLE 11

From the moment that the present agreement is signed, the norms of third states, including the former USSR, are not permitted to be implemented on the territories of the signatory states.

ARTICLE 12

The high contracting parties guarantee the fulfilment of the international obligations binding upon them from the treaties and agreements of the former USSR.

ARTICLE 13

The present agreement does not affect the obligations of the high contracting parties in regard to third states.

The present agreement is open for all member-states of the former USSR to join, and also for other states which share the goals and principles of the present agreement.

ARTICLE 14

The city of Minsk is the official location of the co-ordinating bodies of the Commonwealth.

The activities of bodies of the former USSR are discontinued on the territories of the member-states of the Commonwealth.

The Alma-Ata Declaration

The Alma-Ata Declaration was signed by 11 heads of state on 21 December 1991.

PREAMBLE

The independent states:

The Republic of Armenia, the Republic of Azerbaidzhan, the Republic of Byelorussia, the Republic of Kazakhstan, the Republic of Kyrgyzstan, the Republic of Moldavia, the Russian Federation, the Republic of Tadzhikistan, the Republic of Turkmenistan, the Republic of Ukraine and the Republic of Uzbekistan;

seeking to build democratic law-governed states, the relations between which will develop on the basis of mutual recognition and respect for state sovereignty and sovereign equality, the inalienable right to self-determination, principles of equality and non-interference in the internal affairs, the rejection of the use of force, the threat of force and economic and any other methods of pressure, a peaceful settlement of disputes, respect for human rights and freedoms, including the rights of national minorities, a conscientious fulfilment of commitments and other generally recognized principles and standards of international law;

recognizing and respecting each other's territorial integrity and the inviolability of the existing borders;

believing that the strengthening of the relations of friendship, good neighbourliness and mutually advantageous co-operation, which has deep historic roots, meets the basic interests of nations and promotes the cause of peace and security;

being aware of their responsibility for the preservation of civilian peace and inter-ethnic accord;

being loyal to the objectives and principles of the agreement on the creation of the Commonwealth of Independent States;

are making the following statement:

THE DECLARATION

Co-operation between members of the Commonwealth will be carried out in accordance with the principle of equality through co-ordinating institutions formed on a parity basis and operating in the way established by the agreements between members of the Commonwealth, which is neither a state, nor a super-state structure.

In order to ensure international strategic stability and security, allied command of the military-strategic forces and a single control over nuclear weapons will be preserved, the sides will respect each other's desire to attain the status of a non-nuclear and (or) neutral state.

The Commonwealth of Independent States is open, with the agreement of all its participants, to the states—members of the former USSR, as well as other states—sharing the goals and principles of the Commonwealth.

The allegiance to co-operation in the formation and development of the common economic space, and all-European and Eurasian markets, is being confirmed.

With the formation of the Commonwealth of Independent States the USSR ceases to exist. Member states of the Commonwealth guarantee, in accordance with their constitutional procedures, the fulfilment of international obligations, stemming from the treaties and agreements of the former USSR.

Member states of the Commonwealth pledge to observe strictly the principles of this declaration.

Agreement on Councils of Heads of State and Government

A provisional agreement on the membership and conduct of Councils of Heads of State and Government was concluded between the members of the Commonwealth of Independent States on 30 December 1991.

PREAMBLE

The member states of this agreement, guided by the aims and principles of the agreement on the creation of a Commonwealth of Independent States of 8 December 1991 and the protocol to the agreement of 21 December 1991, taking into consideration the desire of the Commonwealth states to pursue joint activity through the Commonwealth's common co-ordinating institutions, and deeming it essential to establish, for the consistent implementation of the provisions of the said agreement, the appropriate inter-state and inter-governmental institutions capable of ensuring effective co-ordination, and of promoting the development of equal and mutually advantageous co-operation, have agreed on the following:

ARTICLE 1

The Council of Heads of State is the supreme body, on which all the member-states of the Commonwealth are represented at the level of head of state, for discussion of fundamental issues connected with co-ordinating the activity of the Commonwealth states in the sphere of their common interests.

The Council of Heads of State is empowered to discuss issues provided for by the Minsk Agreement on the creation of a Commonwealth of Independent States and other documents for the development of the said Agreement, including the problems of legal succession, which have arisen as a result of ending the existence of the USSR and the abolition of Union structures.

The activities of the Council of Heads of State and of the Council of Heads of Government are pursued on the basis of mutual recognition of and respect for the state sovereignty and sovereign equality of the member-states of the Agreement, their inalienable right to self-determination, the principles of equality and non-interference in internal affairs, the renunciation of the use of force and the threat of force, territorial integrity and the inviolability of existing borders, the peaceful settlement of disputes, respect for human rights and liberties, including the rights of national minorities, conscientious fulfilment of obligations and other commonly accepted principles and norms of international law.

ARTICLE 2

The activities of the Council of Heads of State and the Council of Heads of Government are regulated by the Minsk Agreement on setting up the Commonwealth of Independent States, the present agreement and agreements adopted in development of them, and also by the rules of procedure of these institutes.

Each state in the council has one vote. The decisions of the council are taken by common consent.

The official languages of the Councils are the state languages of the Commonwealth states.

The working language is the Russian language.

ARTICLE 3

The Council of Heads of State and the Council of Heads of Government discuss and where necessary take decisions on the more important domestic and external issues.

Any state may declare its having no interest in a particular issue or issues.

ARTICLE 4

The Council of Heads of State convenes for meetings no less than twice a year. The decision on the time for holding and the provisional agenda of each successive meeting of the Council is taken at the routine meeting of the Council, unless the Council agrees otherwise. Extraordinary meetings of the Council of Heads of State are convened on the initiative of the majority of Commonwealth heads of state.

The heads of state chair the meetings of the Council in turn, according to the Russian alphabetical order of the names of the Commonwealth states.

Sittings of the Council of the Heads of State are generally to be held in Minsk. A sitting of the Council may be held in another of the Commonwealth states by agreement among those taking part.

ARTICLE 5

The Council of Heads of Government convenes for meetings no less frequently than once every three months. The decision concerning the scheduling of and preliminary agenda for each subsequent sitting is to be made at a routine session of the Council, unless the Council arranges otherwise.

Extraordinary sittings of the Council of Heads of Government may be convened at the initiative of a majority of heads of government of the Commonwealth states.

The heads of government chair meetings of the Council in turn, according to the Russian alphabetical order of the names of the Commonwealth states.

Sittings of the Council of Heads of Government are generally to be held in Minsk. A sitting of the Council may be held in another of the Commonwealth states by agreement among the heads of government.

ARTICLE 6

The Council of Heads of State and the Council of Heads of Government of the Commonwealth states may hold joint sittings.

ARTICLE 7

Working and auxiliary bodies may be set up on both a permanent and interim basis on the decision of the Council of the Heads of State and the Council of the Heads of Government of the Commonwealth states.

These are composed of authorized representatives of the participating states. Experts and consultants may be invited to take part in their sittings.

Agreement on Strategic Forces

The Agreement on Strategic Forces was concluded between the 11 members of the Commonwealth of Independent States on 30 December 1991.

PREAMBLE

Guided by the necessity for a co-ordinated and organized solution to issues in the sphere of the control of the strategic forces and the single control over nuclear weapons, the Republic of Armenia, the Republic of Azerbaidzhan, the Republic of Byelorussia, the Republic of Kazakhstan, the Republic of Kyrgyzstan, the Republic of Moldavia, the Russian Federation, the Republic of Tadzhikistan, the Republic of Turkmenistan, the Republic of Ukraine and the Republic of Uzbekistan, subsequently referred to as 'the member-states of the Commonwealth', have agreed on the following:

ARTICLE 1

The term 'strategic forces' means: groupings, formations, units, institutions, the military training institutes for the strategic missile troops, for the air force, for the navy and for the air defences; the directorates of the Space Command and of the airborne troops, and of strategic and operational intelligence, and the nuclear technical units and also the forces, equipment and other military facilities designed for the control and maintenance of the strategic forces of the former USSR (the schedule is to be determined for each state participating in the Commonwealth in a separate protocol).

ARTICLE 2

The member-states of the Commonwealth undertake to observe the international treaties of the former USSR, to pursue a co-ordinated policy in the area of international security, disarmament and arms control, and to participate in the preparation and implementation of programmes for reductions in arms and armed forces. The member-states of the Commonwealth are immediately entering into negotiations with one another and also with other states which were formerly part of the USSR, but which have not joined the commonwealth, with the aim of ensuring guarantees and developing mechanisms for implementing the aforementioned treaties.

ARTICLE 3

The member-states of the Commonwealth recognize the need for joint command of strategic forces and for maintaining unified control of nuclear weapons, and other types of weapons of mass destruction, of the armed forces of the former USSR.

ARTICLE 4

Until the complete elimination of nuclear weapons, the decision on the need for their use is taken by the president of the Russian Federation in agreement with the heads of the Republic of Byelorussia, the Republic of Kazakhstan and the Republic of Ukraine, and in consultation with the heads of the other member-states of the Commonwealth.

Until their destruction in full, nuclear weapons located on the territory of the Republic of Ukraine shall be under the control of the Combined Strategic Forces Command, with the aim that they not be used and be dismantled by the end of 1994, including tactical nuclear weapons by 1 July 1992.

The process of destruction of nuclear weapons located on the territory of the Republic of Byelorussia and the Republic of Ukraine shall take place with the participation of the Republic of Byelorussia, the Russian Federation and the Republic of Ukraine under the joint control of the Commonwealth states.

ARTICLE 5

The status of strategic forces and the procedure for service in them shall be defined in a special agreement.

ARTICLE 6

This agreement shall enter into force from the moment of its signing and shall be terminated by decision of the signatory states or the Council of Heads of State of the Commonwealth.

This agreement shall cease to apply to a signatory state from whose territory strategic forces or nuclear weapons are withdrawn.

Agreement on Armed Forces and Border Troops

The Agreement of Armed Forces and Border Troops was concluded between the members of the Commonwealth of Independent States on 30 December 1991.

PREAMBLE

Proceeding from the need for a mutually-acceptable settlement of matters of defence and security, including guarding the borders of the Commonwealth member-states, the member-states of the Commonwealth of Independent States have agreed the following:

THE AGREEMENT

The commonwealth member-states confirm their legitimate right to set up their own armed forces;

jointly with the Commander-in-Chief of the armed forces, to examine and settle, within two months of the date of this agreement, the issue of the procedure for controlling general purpose forces, taking account of the national legislations of the Commonwealth states and also the issue of the consistent implementation by the Commonwealth states of their right to set up their own armed forces. For the Republic of Ukraine, this will be from 3 January 1992;

to appoint I. Ya. Kalinichenko Commander-in-Chief of Border Troops;

to instruct the Commander-in-Chief of Border Troops to work out, within two months and in conjunction with the leaders of the Commonwealth member-states, a mechanism for the activity of the Border Troops, taking account of the national legislations of the Commonwealth states, with the exception of states with which a mechanism for the activity of Border Troops has already been agreed.

Note: In addition, Marshal Yevgeny Shaposhnikov was confirmed as acting Commander-in-Chief of the Armed Forces of the Commonwealth of Independent States.

The Council of Heads of State

(January 1992)

MEMBERS

Armenia: Levon H. Ter-Petrosyan.
Azerbaidzhan: Ayaz Niyaz ogly Mutalibov.
Byelorussia: Stanislau Shushkevich.
Kazakhstan: Nursultan A. Nazarbayev.
Kyrgyzstan: Askar Akayev.
Moldavia: Mircea Ion Snegur.
Russia: Boris N. Yeltsin.
Tadzhikistan: Rakhmon Nabiyev.
Turkmenistan: Saparmuryad A. Niyazov.
Ukraine: Leonid M. Kravchuk.
Uzbekistan: Islam A. Karimov.

The Council of Heads of Government

(January 1992)

MEMBERS

Armenia: Gagik Arutyunyan.
Azerbaidzhan: Hasan Aziz ogly Hasanov.
Byelorussia: Vyacheslau F. Kebich.
Kazakhstan: Sergey Tereshchenko.
Kyrgyzstan: (vacant).
Moldavia: Valeriu Muravschi.
Russia: Boris N. Yeltsin.
Tadzhikistan: Akbar Mirzoyev.
Turkmenistan: Khan A. Akhmedov.
Ukraine: Vitold P. Fokin.
Uzbekistan: Abdulkhashim Mutalov.

ARMENIA

Geography

The Republic of Armenia (formerly the Armenian Soviet Socialist Republic) is situated in south-west Transcaucasia, on the north-eastern border of Turkey. Its other borders are with Iran to the south, Azerbaidzhan to the east, and Georgia to the north. The Nakhichevan Autonomous Republic, an Azerbaidzhani territory, is an enclave within Armenian territory. The Armenian Republic, which today covers 29,800 sq km (11,506 sq miles), is the remnant of a much larger area of Armenian settlement which existed before the First World War and included many areas of eastern Turkey and other regions of the Caucasus.

The central physical feature of Armenia is Lake Sevan, a mountainous lake at an altitude of 1,924 m, which is surrounded by high mountain ranges, reaching 4,090 m at Mt Aragats. The mountains are drained by numerous streams and rivers flowing into the River Araks, which empties into the Caspian Sea. The Araks marks the south-western border of the Republic and its basin forms a fertile lowland to the south of Yerevan called the Ararat Plain.

The climate is typically continental: dry, with strong temperature variations. Winters are cold, the average January temperature in Yerevan being −3°C (26°F), but summers can be very warm, with August temperatures averaging 25°C (77°F), although high altitude moderates the heat in much of the country. Precipitation is low in the Yerevan area (annual average, 322 mm), but much higher in the mountains.

At the 1989 census, 93.3% of the total population of 3,283,000 were Armenians, 1.7% Kurds and 1.5% Russians. Other ethnic groups included Ukrainians (8,341), Assyrians (5,963), Greeks (4,650), Georgians (1,364). As a result of inter-ethnic tension, almost the entire Azerbaidzhani population was reported to have left Armenia after the census was conducted, and Armenian refugees entered Armenia from Azerbaidzhan. There are many Armenians in other Republics, notably in Georgia and in Azerbaidzhan, although numbers in the latter Republic have fallen since the recent inter-ethnic conflict. There are also important Armenian communities abroad, particularly in the USA and France. The official language is Armenian, the sole member of a distinct Indo-European language group. It is written in the Armenian script. Most of the population are taught Russian as a second language, and Kurdish is used in broadcasting and publishing for some 56,000 Kurds living in the Republic. Most of the population are adherents of Christianity, the largest denomination being the Armenian Apostolic Church. There are also Russian Orthodox, Protestant, Islamic and Yazidi communities.

The estimated total population at 1 January 1991 was 3,376,000. The capital is Yerevan, which had a population of 1,218,000 in 1989. Other important towns include Kirovakan and Kumayri (formerly Leninakan), which suffered considerable damage in the earthquake of 1988.

History

Although Armenia was an important power in ancient times, for much of its history it has been ruled by foreign states. In 1639 Armenia was partitioned, with the larger, western part being annexed by Turkey and the eastern region becoming part of the Persian Empire. In 1828, after a period of Russo–Persian conflict, eastern Armenia was ceded to the Russian Empire by the Treaty of Turkmenchai and subsequently became a province of the Empire.

At the beginning of the 20th century Armenians living in western, or Anatolian, Armenia, under Ottoman rule, were subject to increasing persecution by the Turks. By the end of the First World War, as a result of brutal massacres and deportations, particularly in 1915, the Anatolian lands were largely emptied of their Armenian population. After the collapse of Russian imperial power in 1917, Russian Armenia joined the anti-Bolshevik Transcaucasian Federation, which included Georgia and Azerbaidzhan. This collapsed when threatened by Turkish forces and, on 28 May 1918, Armenia was forced to establish an independent state. Without Russian protection, however, the newly-formed Republic was almost defenceless against Turkish expansionism and was forced to cede the province of Kars and other Armenian lands to Turkey. Armenia was recognized as an independent state by the Allied Powers, and by Turkey in the Treaty of Sèvres, signed on 10 August 1920. However, the rejection of the Treaty by the new Turkish ruler, Mustafa Kemal, left Armenia vulnerable to renewed Turkish threats.

In September 1920 Turkish troops attacked Armenia. The Turks were only prevented from establishing full control over the country by the invasion of Armenia, from the east, by Russian Bolshevik troops, and the establishment, on 29 November 1920, of a Soviet Republic of Armenia. In December 1922 the Republic became a member, together with Georgia and Azerbaidzhan, of the Transcaucasian Soviet Federative Socialist Republic (TSFSR), which, in turn, became a constituent republic of the USSR. In 1936 the TSFSR was dissolved and Armenia became a full Union Republic of the USSR.

Although many Armenians suffered under Communist rule, advances were made in economic and social development. Under Tsarist rule Russian Armenia had been an underdeveloped region of the Empire, with very little infrastructure, but under Soviet rule a policy of forced modernization was carried out, which expanded communications and introduced industrial plants. Literacy and education were also improved.

Soviet leader Mikhail Gorbachev's policies of *perestroika* and *glasnost* had little initial impact in Armenia. The first manifestations of the new policies were campaigns against corruption in the higher echelons of the Communist Party of Armenia (CPA). On a more public level, ecological problems became a focus for popular protest. The first demonstrations against ecological degradation took place in September 1987, but the demands of protesters soon began to include historical and political problems.

Among the historical and ethnic issues discussed in late 1987 and early 1988 the status of Nagorny Karabakh, an autonomous oblast within Azerbaidzhan, but largely populated by Armenians, was the most significant. Demands for the incorporation of Nagorny Karabakh into the Armenian Republic began within the enclave itself in early 1988. In February 1988 crowds of up to one million people took part in demonstrations in Yerevan supporting their demands. The demonstrations were organized by a group of Yerevan intellectuals, who formed a group known as the Karabakh Committee.

In response to increased unrest within Armenia, many Azerbaidzhanis began to leave the Republic. Rumours of ill-treatment of the refugees led to anti-Armenian riots in

Sumgait (Azerbaidzhan) in late February 1988, in which 26 Armenians died. This event provoked further Armenian anger, which was compounded by the decision of the Presidium of the all-Union Supreme Soviet not to transfer Nagorny Karabakh to Armenia. This official decision on the future of Nagorny Karabakh was a serious disappointment to many Armenians, who had expected a favourable response from the Gorbachev administration. Strikes and rallies continued under the leadership of the officially-outlawed Karabakh Committee, and the inability of the local authorities to control the unrest led to the dismissal, in May, of the First Secretary of the Communist Party of Armenia (CPA). In December, however, the issue of Nagorny Karabakh was temporarily subordinated to the problems of overcoming the effects of a severe earthquake which had struck northern Armenia. The city of Leninakan (now Kumayri) was seriously damaged and the village of Spitak was completely destroyed. Some 25,000 people were reported to have been killed. Thousands more were made homeless.

In the chaos following the earthquake the members of the Karabakh Committee were arrested, ostensibly for interfering in relief work. They were only released in May 1989 after huge demonstrations took place protesting against their continued internment. Meanwhile, in January 1989, the Soviet Government had formed a Special Administration Committee of the Council of Ministers to administer Nagorny Karabakh, although the enclave remained under formal Azerbaidzhani jurisdiction.

Throughout 1989 unrest continued both in Armenia and within Nagorny Karabakh, but there were other significant political developments within the Republic. *Glasnost* allowed a much fuller examination of Armenian history and culture and a number of unofficial groups, concerned with both cultural and political issues, were formed. In May the *yerakuyn*, the national flag of independent Armenia, was flown again, and 28 May, the anniversary of the establishment of independent Armenia, was declared a national day. However, all internal politics continued to be dominated by events in Nagorny Karabakh. Following a general strike in Azerbaidzhan, an economic blockade was implemented against Armenia, seriously affecting the reconstruction programme required after the 1988 earthquake. In November 1989 the Special Administration Committee was disbanded and Azerbaidzhan resumed control over the region. This prompted the Armenian Supreme Soviet to declare the enclave part of a 'unified Armenian Republic'. In January 1990 this declaration was declared unconstitutional by the all-Union Supreme Soviet. The Armenian Supreme Soviet responded by granting itself the power to veto any legislation approved by the central authorities.

The increasing disillusionment among Armenians with the Soviet Government was apparently responsible for the low turn-out in the elections to the Armenian Supreme Soviet, which took place in May–July 1990. No party achieved an overall majority, but the Armenian Pan-National Movement (APM), the successor to the Karabakh Committee, was the largest single party, with some 35% of the seats in parliament. Supported by other non-Communist groups, Levon Ter-Petrosyan, the leader of the APM, defeated Vladimir Movsisyan, the First Secretary of the CPA, in elections to the chairmanship of the Supreme Soviet. Vazgen Manyukan, also a leader of the APM, was appointed Chairman of the Council of Ministers (head of government). On 23 August 1990 the Armenian Supreme Soviet adopted a declaration of sovereignty, including the right to maintain armed forces and a demand for international recognition that Turkish massacres of Armenians in 1915 constituted genocide. The Armenian SSR was renamed the Republic of Armenia. The new Government began to establish political and commercial links with the Armenian diaspora and several prominent exiles returned to the Republic. In late November the CPA, after heated debate, voted to become an independent organization within the CPSU. Stepan Pogosyan was elected First Secretary, replacing Movsisyan.

The Armenian Government refused to enter into the negotiations on a new Treaty of Union which took place in late 1990 and early 1991, and officially boycotted the referendum on the renewal of the Union which took place in March 1991 in nine of the other Republics. Instead, the Supreme Soviet decided to conduct a referendum on Armenian secession from the USSR on 21 September 1991. Initially, it was planned that the referendum would be carried out within the provisions of the Soviet law on succession, adopted in April by the all-Union Supreme Soviet. This entailed a transitional period of at least five years before full independence could be achieved.

The moderate policies of the new Government, especially in developing relations with Turkey, attracted internal criticism from more extreme nationalist groups, notably the Union for National Self-Determination (UNS), which continued to seek the recovery of lands lost to Turkey after the First World War. The CPA also attacked the Government for its willingness to develop relations with Turkey, as did the Armenian Revolutionary Federation (ARF—in Armenian, Dashnaktsutyun, which had formed the Government of independent Armenia from 1918–20). Nevertheless, the Government insisted that good relations with Turkey were essential to Armenia if it were to survive outside the USSR. The CPA strongly opposed the idea of secession, while the ARF advocated a more gradual process towards independence. The acceptance by the Government of the principles of the Soviet law on secession was criticized by the UNS, which campaigned for immediate secession in breach of the constitutional procedure.

The attempted coup in Moscow, and subsequent events of August 1991, forced the Government to accelerate the moves towards independence. The response of the Armenian leadership to the overthrow of Soviet President Mikhail Gorbachev on 19 August was initially cautious, with Ter-Petrosyan stressing the need for maximum restraint. He was, it seems, anxious not to provoke further action by Soviet troops in Nagorny Karabakh, or even in Armenia proper. The events of August provided further support for those who advocated complete independence for Armenia. The referendum on independence took place as scheduled, on 21 September. According to official returns, 94.4% of the electorate took part, of which 99.3% voted in favour of Armenia being 'an independent, democratic state outside the Union'. Instead of conforming to the Soviet law on secession, on 23 September the Supreme Soviet declared Armenia to be an independent state.

The independence declaration was followed, on 16 October 1991, by elections to the post of President of the Republic. There were six candidates in the election, but it was won overwhelmingly by the incumbent, Ter-Petrosyan. He continued to demand international recognition of Armenia, but also signed the Treaty of the Economic Community on 19 October, stressing, however, that it did not encroach on Armenia's political independence, and refusing to sign a new treaty on political union. The Armenian leadership did, however, join the Commonwealth of Independent States, and signed the founding Alma-Ata Declaration, on 21 December.

Economy

Armenia developed a limited industrial base under Soviet rule. Non-ferrous metallurgy is a leading industrial sector, with electrical equipment, instruments, machinery and computers other major products. The chemical industry is also important. Light industries concentrate on textiles and leather footwear.

Products from the agricultural sector include wines and brandies, but the wine industry suffered as a result of Gorbachev's campaign against alcoholism in the mid-1980s. Other agricultural goods include a wide variety of fruit, grapes, tobacco, industrial crops, vegetables and melons.

In 1988 Armenia accounted for 0.9% of total Soviet net material product (NMP), including 1.2% of total production value in industry and 0.7% in agriculture. Armenia is heavily dependent on inter-republican trade, with 63.7% of NMP deriving from exports to other Republics in 1988, but only 1.4% from exports abroad. Armenia is also dependent on imports from other Republics, with some 60%–65% of foodstuffs being imported, including over 70% of bread and 66% of dairy products.

Armenia's economic infrastructure was seriously affected by the earthquake of 1988. Factories and power stations were destroyed and considerable resources were required for reconstruction and for humanitarian relief. The economy was also affected by the severing of trade links with Azerbaidzhan and the general decline in the Soviet economy. In 1990 national income decreased by 6.9% compared with 1989, the volume of industrial production fell by 7.3% and labour productivity by 8.4%.

Statistical Survey

Population

BIRTHS AND DEATHS (per 1,000)

	1987	1988	1989
Birth rate	22.9	25.3	21.6
Death rate	5.7	10.3	6.0

Agriculture

PRINCIPAL CROPS ('000 metric tons)

	1988	1989	1990
Grain	373.5	192.1	270.9
Sugar beet	117.3	n.a.	n.a.
Potatoes	207.2	256.3	212.3
Other vegetables . . .	567.3	466.4	377.5
Grapes	214.0	118.4	143.7
Other fruit	241.1	148.4	155.4

LIVESTOCK ('000 head at 1 January)

	1989	1990	1991
Cattle	742.0	478.5	428.9
Pigs	319.4	187.2	170.0
Sheep	1,450.1	812.3	686.5
Poultry	n.a.	9,067.0	6,731.2

LIVESTOCK PRODUCTS ('000 metric tons)

	1988	1989	1990
Meat (slaughter weight) . .	113.2	113.7	99.3
Milk	565.9	319.1	270.6
Eggs (million)	618.1	382.2	345.1
Wool (greasy)	4.0	3.3	n.a.

Mining and Industry

Production (1990): Caustic soda 40,700 metric tons, Cement 1,465,500 metric tons, Tyres 1,008,700, Electric energy 10,433 million kWh, Clinker 1,242,500 metric tons.

Education

(1990/91)

	Institutions	Students
Secondary schools	1,397	608,800
Secondary specialized institutions . .	70	45,900
Higher schools (incl. universities) . .	14	68,400

Directory

The Government

(January 1992)

HEAD OF STATE

President of the Republic: LEVON H. TER-PETROSYAN (elected 16 October 1991).

Vice-President and Chairman of the Council of Ministers: GAGIK G. ARUTYUNYAN.

COUNCIL OF MINISTERS

Chairman of the Council of Ministers: GAGIK ARUTYUNYAN.

First Deputy Chairmen: GRANT BAGRATYAN, GEVORG A. VARDANYAN, RUBEN CHIFTALARYAN.

Deputy Chairmen: VARDAN AMIRBEKYAN, MIKHAIL GRIGORYAN, KTRICH SARDANYAN.

Minister of Agriculture: YURY DZHAVADYAN.

Minister of Communications: ROBERT ABOYAN.

Minister of Construction: GAGIK MARTIROSYAN.

Minister of Culture: PERCH ZEYTUNTSYAN.

Minister of Education: AREG GRIGORYAN.

Minister of Finance: DZHANIK DZHANOYAN.

Minister of the Food Industry: ROBERT MEGRABYAN.

Minister of Grain Products: RAFIK SHAKHBAZYAN.

Minister of Foreign Affairs: RAFFI HOVANNISYAN.

Minister of Foreign Economic Relations: YESAI STEPANAYAN.

Minister of Health: MIGRAN NAZARETYAN.

Minister of Internal Affairs: ASHOT MANUCHARYAN (acting).

Minister of Justice: VAGE STENANYAN.

Minister of Labour and Social Security: ASHOT ESAYAN.

Minister of Light Industry: ROBERT MKRTCHYAN.

Minister of Motor Transport: GENRIK KOCHINYAN.

Minister of Power Engineering and Fuel: SEPUKH TASHCHYAN.

Minister of Trade: NINA ASMARYAN (acting).

Chairmen of State Committees

Chairman of the State Committee for the Economy: GRANT BAGRATYAN.

Chairman of the State Commitee for Higher Education and Science: VILIK ARUTYUNYAN.

Chairman of the State Security Committee: USIK ARUTYUNYAN.

MINISTRIES AND STATE COMMITTEES

Ministry of Agriculture: 375010 Yerevan, pl. Respubliki, Dom pravitelstva 2; tel. (885) 52-46-41; telex 243369; fax (885) 52-37-93.

Ministry of Communications: 373002 Yerevan, ul. M. Saryana 22; tel. (885) 52-66-32; telex 243311; fax (885) 53-86-45.

Ministry of Construction: 375010 Yerevan, pl. Respubliki, Dom pravitelstva 3; tel. (885) 58-90-80.

Ministry of Culture: 375001 Yerevan, ul. Tumanyana 5A; tel. (885) 56-19-20; telex 243366; fax (885) 52-39-22.

Ministry of Education: 375010 Yerevan, ul. Marksa 13; tel. (885) 52-47-49.

Ministry of Finance: 375010 Yerevan, ul. Melik Adamyana 1; tel. (885) 52-70-82.

Ministry of the Food Industry: 374010 Yerevan, pl. Respubliki, Dom pravitelstva 2; tel. (885) 52-19-64; telex 243369; fax (885) 52-37-93.

Ministry of Foreign Affairs: 375019 Yerevan, ul. Antarain 188; tel. (885) 52-35-31; telex 243313; fax (885) 56-56-16.

Ministry of Grain Products: 375010 Yerevan, ul. Nalbandyana 48; tel. (885) 52-96-11; telex 243338.

Ministry of Foreign Economic Relations: 375010 Yerevan, pl. Respubliki 2; tel. (885) 52-05-79.

Ministry of Health: 375001 Yerevan, ul. Tumanyana 8; tel. (885) 58-24-13; telex 243347; fax (885) 56-41-59.

Ministry of Internal Affairs: 375025 Yerevan, ul. Halbandyana 130; tel. (885) 56-09-08; fax (885) 57-84-40.

Ministry of Justice: 375010 Yerevan, ul. Shaumyana 8; tel. (885) 58-21-57.

Ministry of Labour and Social Security: 375025 Yerevan, ul. Isaakyana 18; tel. (885) 56-53-21; telex 243306; fax (885) 56-30-75.

Ministry of Light Industry: 375033 Yerevan, ul. R. Kochara 4; tel. (885) 22-65-00.

Ministry of Motor Transport: 375015 Yerevan, ul. Zakiyana 10; tel. (885) 56-33-91; fax (885) 52-52-68.

Ministry of Power Engineering and Fuel: Yerevan.

Ministry of Trade: 375009 Yerevan, ul. V. Teryana 69; tel. (885) 56-25-91.

State Committees

Committee for State Security: 375001 Yerevan, ul. Nalbandyana 104; tel. (885) 52-97-33.

State Committee for the Economy: 375010 Yerevan, pl. Respubliki, Dom pravitelstva 2; tel. (885) 52-73-42.

State Committee for Higher Education and Science: 375010 Yerevan, ul. Marksa 13; tel. (885) 52-66-02.

Legislature

SUPREME SOVIET

The supreme legislative body in the Republic is the Supreme Soviet (or Supreme Council). It consists of 260 deputies. Elections to the Supreme Council were held in May–July 1990.

Chairman: BABKEN ARARKTSYAN.

In mid-1991 deputies in the Supreme Council were divided approximately as follows: Armenian Pan-National Movement 110; Republic Group of Deputies 69; Communist Party of Armenia 25; Armenian Revolutionary Federation 10; independents and other parties 31.

Political Organizations

In September 1991 a Congress of the Communist Party of Armenia (CPA) voted to dissolve the party. In the same month the Presidium of the Armenian Supreme Council decided to nationalize the property and funds of the CPA.

Armenian Pan-National Movement (APM): 375019 Yerevan, pr. Marshala Bagramyana 14; f. 1989; dedicated to the preservation of Armenia's culture and environment and to greater sovereignty for Armenia; Chair. VANO S. SIRADEGYAN.

Armenian Revolutionary Federation—ARF (Hai Heghapokhakan Dashnaktsutyun): 375025 Yerevan, pr. Myasnyaka 2; f. 1891; formed the ruling party in independent Armenia, 1918–20; prohibited under Soviet rule, but continued its activities in other countries; permitted to operate legally in Armenia from 1991; Chair. PUBEN OVSEPYAN, GRAYR KARAPETYAN.

Democratic Party of Armenia: Yerevan; f. 1991 as the successor to the Communist Party of Armenia; Chair. ARAM SARKISYAN.

National Democratic Union: Yerevan; f. 1991 as a splinter party from the APM; Leader VAZGEN MANUKYAN.

Party of Democratic Freedom (Partiya Ramkavar Azatakan): 375010 Yerevan, ul. Anrapetutyun 47; Chair. of Founding Council PUBEN MIRZAKHANYAN.

Republican Party of Armenia: Yerevan; f. 1990 following a split in the Union for National Self-Determination; Chair. ASHOT NAVASRDYAN.

Union for National Self-Determination: Yerevan; advocated complete independence of Armenia; Chair. PARUIR AIRIKIAN.

Judicial System

Chairman of the Supreme Court: T. K. BARSEGYAN.
General Procurator: A. A. GEVORGYAN.

Religion

The major religion is Christianity. The Armenian Apostolic Church is the leading denomination and has been widely identified with the movement for national independence. There are also Russian Orthodox and Islamic communities, although the latter have lost adherents as a result of the large numbers of Muslim Azerbaidzhanis who have left the Republic. However, most Kurds are also adherents of Islam.

GOVERNMENT AGENCY

Council for the Affairs of the Armenian Church: 375001 Yerevan, ul. Abovyana 3; tel. (885) 56-46-34; fax (885) 56-41-81; Chair. LYUDVIG KHATCHATRYAN.

CHRISTIANITY

Armenian Apostolic Church: Echmiadzin; tel. 52-24-77; four dioceses in Armenia, three in other Republics and 20 bishoprics in the rest of the world; 4m. members; there are 13 monasteries and one theological seminary; main following is in Armenia and Georgia; Supreme Patriarch VAZGEN I, Catholicos of All Armenians.

The Press

At 1 January 1991 there were 45 national newspaper titles being published in Armenia and 60 periodicals. There were also 37 local newspapers.

PRINCIPAL NEWSPAPERS

(In Armenian except where otherwise stated.)

Avangard: 375023 Yerevan, pr. Ordzhonikdze 2; f. 1923; 3 a week; organ of the Youth League of Armenia; Editor M. K. ZOHRABYAN.

Epokha (Epoch): 375023 Yerevan, pr. Ordzhonikidze 2; f. 1938; fmrly *Komsomolets*; weekly; in Russian; organ of the Youth League of Armenia; Editor V. S. GRIGORYAN.

Golos Armenii (The Voice of Armenia): 375023 Yerevan, pr. Ordzhonikidze 2; f. 1934 as *Kommunist*; 6 a week; fmrly organ of the Central Committee of the Communist Party of Armenia; in Russian; Editor B. M. MKRTCHYAN.

Grakan Tert (Literary Paper): 375019 Yerevan, ul. Marshala Bagramyana 3; tel. (885) 52-05-94; f. 1932; weekly; organ of the Union of Writers; Editor F. H. MELOYAN.

Hayastan (Armenia): 375023 Yerevan, pr. Ordzhonikidze 2; f. 1920; fmrly organ of the Communist Party of Armenia, as *Sovetakan Hayastan* (Soviet Armenia); 6 a week; Editor G. ABRAMYAN.

Hayastani Hanrapetutyun (Republic of Armenia): 375023 Yerevan, pr. Ordzhonikidze 2; f. 1990; 6 a week; organ of the Supreme Council of the Republic of Armenia; also in Russian (as *Respublika Armeniya*); Editor A. MORIKYAN; Editor responsible for the Russian edition T. AKOPYAN.

Hayk (Armenia): 375019 Yerevan, ul. Bagramyana 14; tel. (885) 56-34-56; weekly; organ of the Armenian Pan-National Movement; Editor S. GUEVORKIAN; circ. 30,000.

Hazatamart (The Battle for Freedom): 375070 Yerevan, Atarbekyan 181; organ of the Armenian Revolutionary Federation; Editor M. MIKAYELYAN.

Hazg (Nation): 375010 Yerevan, ul. Hanrapetutyan 47; organ of the Party of Democratic Freedom; Editor A. AVETIKYAN.

Ria Taze (New Way): Yerevan; 2 a week; in Kurdish.

Yerokoyan Yerevan (Evening Yerevan): 375023 Yerevan, pr. Ordzhonokidze 2; organ of Yerevan City Council; Editor N. YENGIBARYAN.

PRINCIPAL PERIODICALS

Aghbiur (Source): Yerevan; f. 1923, fmrly *Pioner;* monthly; for teenagers; Editor T. V. TONOYAN.

Angakhutyun: Yerevan; journal of the Union for National Self-Determination.

Aroghchapakutyun (Health): Yerevan; f. 1956; monthly; journal of the Ministry of Health; illustrated; Editor M. A. MURADYAN.

Arvest (Art): Yerevan; f. 1932, fmrly *Sovetakan Arvest* (Soviet Art); monthly; publ. by the Ministry of Culture; aspects of Armenian national art; Editor G. A. AZAKELYAN.

Dprutyun (Education): Yerevan; f. 1926; 2 a week; organ of the Ministry of Education; Editor L. H. KARAPETYAN.

Garun (Spring): 375015 Yerevan-15, ul. Karmira Banaki 15; tel. (885) 56-29-56; f. 1967; independent; fiction and sociopolitical issues; Editor L. Z. ANANYAN.

Gitutyun ev Tekhnica (Science and Technology): Yerevan; f. 1963; monthly; journal of the Research Institute of Scientific-Technical Information and of Technological and Economic Research; illustrated.

Hayastani Ashkhatavoruhi (Working Women of Armenia): Yerevan; f. 1924; monthly; for women; illustrated; Editor A. G. CHILINGARYAN.

Hayastani Zhoghovrdakan Tntesutyun (People's Economy of Armenia): Yerevan; f. 1957; monthly; organ of the State Committee for the Economy and the Academy of Sciences of Armenia; Editor R. H. SHAKHKULYAN.

Hayreniky Dzayn (Voice of the Motherland): Yerevan; f. 1965; weekly; organ of the Armenian Committee for Cultural Relations with Compatriots Abroad; Editor L. H. ZAKARYAN.

Literaturnaya Armeniya (Literature of Armenia): 375019 Yerevan, ul. Marshala Bagramyana 3; tel. (885) 56-36-57; f. 1958; monthly; journal of the Union of Writers; fiction; in Russian; Editor A. M. NALBAUDYAN.

Nork: Yerevan; f. 1934; fmrly *Sovetakan Grakanutyun* (Soviet Literature); monthly; journal of the Union of Writers; fiction; Editor R. G. HOVSEPYAN.

Veratsnvats Hayastan (Reborn Armenia): Yerevan; f. 1945 as *Sovetakan Hayastan* (Soviet Armenia); monthly; journal of the Armenian Committee for Cultural Relations with Compatriots Abroad; fiction; illustrated; Editor V. A. DAVTYAN.

Vozni (Hedgehog): Yerevan; f. 1954; 3 a month; satirical; Editor A. A. SAHAKYAN.

NEWS AGENCY

Armenpress (Armenian Press Agency): Yerevan; state information agency; Dir G. OGANESYAN.

Publishers

In 1989 a total of 1,003 titles (books and pamphlets) were published, of which 699 were in Armenian.

Anait: Yerevan; art publishing.

Arevik (Sun Publishing House): Yerevan, ul. Isaakyana 28; political, scientific, fiction for children; Dir V. S. KALANTARYAN.

Hayastan (Armenia Publishing House): 375009 Yerevan, Isaakyan St 91; tel. (885) 52-85-20; f. 1921; political and fiction; Dir D. SARGSYAN.

Haykakan Hanragitaran (Armenian Encyclopaedia): 375001 Yerevan 1, Tumanyana 17; tel. (885) 52-43-41; f. 1967; encyclopaedias and other reference books; Editor K. S. KHOUDAVERDYAN.

Luys (Enlightenment Publishing House): Yerevan, ul. Kirova 19A; textbooks; Dir S. M. MOVSISYAN.

Nairi: Yerevan, ul. Teryana 91; fiction; Dir H. H. FELEKHYAN.

Academy of Sciences Publishing House: Yerevan, pr. Marshala Bagramyana 24G; Dir KH. H. BARSEGHIAN.

Radio and Television

State Committee for Television and Radio Broadcasting of the Armenian Republic: 375025 Yerevan, ul. Mravyana 5; Chair. H. V. HOVHANNISYAN.

> **Radio Yerevan:** 3 programmes; broadcasts inside the Republic in Armenian, Russian and Kurdish; external broadcasts in

Armenian, Russian, Kurdish, Turkish, Arabic, English, French, Spanish and Persian (Farsi).

> **Armenian Television:** broadcasts in Armenian and Russian.

Finance

BANKING

State Banks

National Bank of the Republic of Armenia: 375010 Yerevan, ul. Nalbandyana 6; Dir ISAAK I. ISAAKYAN.

Armenian Foreign Trade Bank: Yerevan; Chair. of Bd S. A. CHZMACHYAN.

Commercial and Co-operative Banks

Anelik Commercial Bank: Yerevan, ul. G. Kochara 4.

Gaik Co-op Bank: Yerevan, pr. Oktemberyana 1; tel. (885) 52-41-80.

Prometei-MNGS-Yerevan Commercial Bank: 375000 Yerevan, Marshal Bagramyana 85; tel. (885) 27-16-50.

Yerevan Co-op Bank: Yerevan, ul. Avetisyana 74; tel. (885) 22-02-23.

COMMODITY EXCHANGE

Yerevan Commodity and Raw Materials Exchange: 375051 Yerevan, 31/1 Arama Hachaturyana; tel. (885) 25-26-00; fax (885) 25-09-93; f. 1991; authorized capital 5m. roubles; Gen. Man. ARA ARZUMANAYAN.

Trade and Industry

CHAMBER OF COMMERCE

Chamber of Commerce and Industry of the Republic of Armenia: 375033 Yerevan, ul. Alevardyana 39; tel. (885) 56-53-58; telex 243322; Chair. ASHOT L. SARKISYAN.

FOREIGN TRADE ORGANIZATION

Armentorg: 375010 Yerevan, pl. Respublika, Dom pravitelstva; import and export of all types of goods; Gen. Dir R. A. SARKISYAN.

MAJOR INDUSTRIAL ENTERPRISES

Airumsky Cannery: 377100 Noemberyansky, Poc. Airum; tel. 22447; produces fruit juices, canned and frozen food; Dir GEORGY MAMAJANYAN; 1,115 employees.

Armenian Scientific-Production Electronic Machinery Association—Armelektromash: Yerevan; Dir MARTUNIK ARUTYUNYAN.

Luys Production Association: Yerevan; Dir BENIAMIN TUMASYAN.

Vector: 375062 Yerevan, Knunyants 8; tel. (885) 57-03-25; clothing and textiles; Chair. KAREN GRIGORIYAN.

Yerevan Automobile Factory—Yeraz: Yerevan; Dir EDVARD BABADZHYAN; 2,000 employees.

Zakavkazkabel: 375061 Yerevan, Tamantsineri 55; tel. (885) 44-12-50; production of cables and wires; Gen. Dir EDUARD SASUNTSIAN; 2,200 employees.

TRADE UNIONS

Council of Armenian Trade Unions: 375010 Yerevan, ul. Nalbandyana 26; Chair. MARTIN ARUTYUNYAN.

Transport

RAILWAYS

In 1989 there were 820 km of railway track in use. There are international lines to Turkey and Iran. There are also lines to Georgia and Azerbaidzhan.

ROADS

In 1989 the road network comprised 10,200 km of roads, of which 9,500 were hard-surfaced.

CIVIL AVIATION

In 1991 the Armenian Airlines Company, which was an integral part of the USSR Ministry of Civil Aviation, was restructured as the State Airlines Company of Armenia.

State Airlines Company of Armenia: Yerevan; f. 1991; Chair. VALENTIN V. NAZARYAN.

Culture

NATIONAL ORGANIZATION

Ministry of Culture: see section on The Government (Ministries).

CULTURAL HERITAGE

Armenian State Picture Gallery: 375010 Yerevan, ul. Spandaryana 1; tel. (885) 58-07-65; f. 1921; Western European, Armenian, Russian and oriental art; Dir TER-GABRIELYAN.

Museum of Armenian History: Yerevan, pl. Respubliki; 160,000 exhibits tracing the history of the Armenian people; Dir M. S. ASRATYAN.

Matenadaran Institute of Ancient Armenian Manuscripts: Yerevan, pr. Lenina 111; tel. (885) 58-32-92; f. 1920; manuscripts and archival documents on Armenian history; Dir S. AREVSHATIAN.

State Library of the Republic of Armenia: 375009 Yerevan, ul. Teryana 72; tel. (885) 56-58-45; f. 1921; over 6.4m. vols; Dir A. M. TIRABYAN.

PERFORMING ARTS

Alexander Spendiarov Opera and Ballet Theatre: Yerevan, ul. Tumanyana 36.

Tumanyan Puppet Theatre: Yerevan, pr. Savat-Novy 4.

Yerevan Drama Theatre: Yerevan, ul. Isaakyana 28.

Yerevan Institute of Fine Arts and Theatre: 375009, Yerevan, ul. Isaakyana 36; tel. (885) 56-07-26; f. 1944; training in all aspects of theatre and fine arts.

ASSOCIATIONS

Armenian Committee for Cultural Relations with Compatriots in Other Countries: Yerevan; develops links with the Armenian disapora.

Union of Writers of Armenia: 375019 Yerevan, ul. Marshala Bagramyana 3; tel. (885) 56-38-11.

Education

Education is free and compulsory at primary and secondary levels. Until the early 1990s the general education system conformed to that of the centralized Soviet system. Extensive changes were made, with more emphasis placed on Armenian history and culture. In 1989 58% of the population over 15 years had completed secondary education and 14% had completed higher education. In 1984/85 ethnic Armenians formed 98% of all students in higher education in the Republic, hence most instruction is in Armenian, although Russian is widely taught as a second language. In 1988, in general day schools, 80.5% of all pupils were taught in Armenian, 15.1% in Russian and 4.4% in Azerbaidzhani. In addition to Yerevan State University and the newly-established State Engineering University, higher eduation is provided at seven other institutes of higher education.

UNIVERSITIES

Yerevan State University: 375049 Yerevan, ul. Mravyana 1; tel. (885) 55-46-29; telex 243575; f. 1920; languages of instruction: Armenian and Russian; 17 faculties; 910 teachers; 8,241 students; Rector S. A. AMBARTSUMIAN.

State Engineering University of Armenia: 375009 Yerevan, ul. Teryana 105; tel. (885) 56-59-82; f. 1991; fmrly Yerevan Polytechnic Institute (f. 1930); 13 faculties; 1,650 teachers; 21,000 students; brs in Goris, Kumayri and Kirovakan; Rector Y. L. SARKISIAN.

Social Welfare

Much of Armenia's expenditure on health and welfare services has been directed towards the victims of the 1988 earthquake, which caused an estimated 25,000 deaths and 8,500m. roubles-worth of damage. As in other Republics, all medical and social services are provided by the state, and a full range of basic services is available. In 1986/87 average life expectancy at birth was 73.9 years, considerably higher than the average for the USSR, partly perhaps because Armenia had the lowest rate of alcoholism in the USSR, with 175 recorded cases per 100,000 of the population in 1988. In that year 400,000 people were in receipt of state pensions, 75% of which were provided on account of old age.

GOVERNMENT AGENCIES

Ministry of Labour and Social Welfare: see section on The Government (Ministries).

Armenian Pension Fund: 375025 Yerevan, ul. Moskovyan 35; branch of the USSR Pension Fund; Chair. Z. NUNUSHYAN.

The Environment

As in other Republics environmental problems were among the major political issues of the late 1980s. Yerevan experiences particularly severe pollution as a result of its high concentration of industrial enterprises and the surrounding mountains, which can confine the pollution.

ACADEMIC INSTITUTES

Academy of Sciences of the Republic of Armenia: 375019 Yerevan, pr. Marshala Bagramayana 24; tel. (885) 52-07-04; f. 1943; Pres. V. A. AMBARTSUMYAN.

Armenian Botanical Society; Yerevan; Chair. V. O. KAZARYAN.

Armenian Geographical Society: Yerevan; Chair. L. A. VALESYAN.

Council on Problems of the Biosphere: Yerevan; Chair. G. A. BAGRAMYAN.

AZERBAIDZHAN

Geography

The Republic of Azerbaidzhan (formerly the Azerbaidzhan Soviet Socialist Republic) is situated in eastern Transcaucasia, on the western coast of the Caspian Sea. It has an international border to the south with Iran. To the west it borders the Republic of Armenia, to the north-west the Republic of Georgia and, to the north, the Daghestan Autonomous Republic (Republic of Daghestan) in the Russian Federation. The Nakhichevan Autonomous Republic (ASSR) is part of Azerbaidzhan, although it is separated from the rest of Azerbaidzhan by Armenian territory. Azerbaidzhan also includes the Nagorno-Karabakh Autonomous Oblast, which is largely populated by Armenians, but does not legally constitute part of Armenia. The historical region of Azerbaidzhan also includes northern regions of Iran, where there is a significant Azerbaidzhani minority. The Republic covers an area of 86,600 sq km (33,436 sq miles), 10% of which is forested.

The greater part of Azerbaidzhan is dominated by the lowlands around two rivers; the River Kura flows from the north-west into the Caspian Sea, and its tributary, the Araks, runs along the border with Iran. North of the Kura lies the main axis of the Greater Caucasus mountain range (Bolshoy Kavkaz), the traditional boundary between Asia and Europe. This mountain range extends along the northern border of the Republic into north-east Azerbaidzhan and ends in the Apsheron Peninsula, a promontory in the Caspian Sea which has significant petroleum reserves. Numerous mountain rivers flow into the Kura basin from the mountains of the Lesser Caucasus in the south-west. South of the mouth of the Kura, the Caspian littoral around the town of Lenkoran forms the Lenkoran plain, an area noted for its subtropical climate.

The Kura plain has a hot, dry, temperate climate with an average July temperature of 27°C (80°F) and an average January temperature of 1°C (34°F). Average annual rainfall on the lowlands is 200–300 mm, but the Lenkoran plain normally receives between 1,000 mm and 1,750 mm.

According to the 1989 census, at which the total population was 7,029,000, Azerbaidzhanis form the largest ethnic group (82.7% of the total population), followed by Russians and Armenians (each 5.6%) and Lezghis (2.4%); there are also small numbers of Avars (44,072), Ukrainians (32,345), Tatars (28,019), Jews (25,190), Talysh (21,169), Turks (17,705), Georgians (14,197), Kurds (12,226), Udins (6,125) and others. The official language is Azerbaidzhani, one of the South Turkic group of languages; since 1939 it has been written in the Cyrillic script. In 1989, only 27% of Azerbaidzhanis claimed to have a good knowledge of Russian and less than 2% of Russians and less than 1% of Armenians in the Republic claimed fluency in Azerbaidzhani. Armenians predominate in Nagorny Karabakh (75.9% in 1979) and ethnic Azerbaidzhanis in Nakhichevan. Religious adherence corresponds largely to ethnic origins: almost all ethnic Azerbaidzhanis are Muslims, some 70% being Shi'ite and 30% Sunni. There are also Christian communities, mainly representatives of the Russian Orthodox and Armenian Apostolic denominations.

At 1 January 1991 the total estimated population was 7,137,000. The capital is Baku, which had a population of 1,779,500 in January 1990. It is located on the coast of the Caspian Sea, near the southern shore of the Apsheron Peninsula. Other major cities include Sumgait, a port on the Caspian Sea to the north of Baku, and Gyanzha (formerly Kirovabad), an industrial town in the foothills of the Lesser Caucasus.

History

The Azerbaidzhanis, or Azeris as they are also known, are probably descendants of the area's indigenous inhabitants, although linguistically influenced by Turkish settlers. An independent state was first established in the region in the fourth century BC by Atropates, a vassal of Alexander III of Macedonia. From Atropates came the name Azerbaidzhan. The Persian Sasanian dynasty took control of the region in the third century AD and it remained part of their empire until the Muslim Arab conquest of the area in the seventh century. From the 11th century the Iranian-speaking indigenous inhabitants began to be assimilated by the increasing numbers of Turkic settlers, who migrated to the region from the east. In the early 16th century Azerbaidzhan again came under Persian domination, but there were frequent incursions into the area by the Ottoman Turks and, in 1728, their control over the region was confirmed by the Treaty of Constantinople. After a short reassertion of Persian supremacy from 1735, local khanates established a degree of independence from both the Ottomans and the Persians. Meanwhile, Russia was increasing its influence in Transcaucasia and by 1805 several of the khanates had become Russian protectorates. In 1828, after a period of Russo–Persian conflict, Azerbaidzhan was divided, with the River Araks as the border, between Persia (which was granted southern Azerbaidzhan) and Russia (northern Azerbaidzhan) by the Treaty of Turkmenchai. During the latter half of the 19th century petroleum was discovered in Azerbaidzhan and, by 1900, the region had become one of the world's leading petroleum producers. Immigrant Slavs began to dominate Baku and other urban areas.

After the October Revolution of 1917 in Russia, there was a short period of pro-Bolshevik rule in Baku before a nationalist Government took power and established an independent state, with Gyandzha as the capital. Azerbaidzhan was occupied by both Allied and Central Power troops during its two years of independence; after their withdrawal Azerbaidzhan was invaded by the Red Army in April 1920 and a Soviet Republic of Azerbaidzhan was established (28 April 1920). In December 1922 the Republic became a member of the Transcaucasian Soviet Federative Socialist Republic (TSFSR), which entered the USSR as a constituent republic on 31 December 1922. The TSFSR was disbanded in 1936 and Azerbaidzhan became a full Union Republic.

Following the Soviet seizure of power in 1920, many nationalist and religious leaders and their followers were persecuted or killed. Religious persecution was particularly severe in the 1930s and many mosques and religious sites were destroyed. In 1930–31 forced collectivization led to peasant uprisings which were suppressed by Soviet troops. Many members of the Communist Party of Azerbaidzhan (CPA) were executed or imprisoned in the purges of 1937–38, including Sultan Medzhit Efendiev, the Republic's leader, and two republican premiers. In 1945 the Soviet Government attempted to unite the Azerbaidzhani population of northern Iran with the Azerbaidzhan SSR, by supporting a local 'puppet' Government in Iran with military forces. Soviet troops were forced to withdraw by Anglo-American opposition.

The most important of Azerbaidzhan's post-war leaders was Geidar Aliyev, installed as First Secretary of the CPA in 1969. He vastly increased the all-Union sector of the economy at the expense of local industry, while retaining popularity with his liberal attitude to local corruption. It was this corruption in the CPA which was the first target of Soviet leader Mikhail Gorbachev when he came to power. Aliyev was dismissed in October 1987, but popular dissatisfaction with the poor state of the economy and the Party élite became more vocal. Unlike most Republics Azerbaidzhan had an annual trade surplus with the rest of the USSR and yet its income per-head was the lowest outside Central Asia. Economic grievances were expressed at demonstrations in November 1988, which were initially concerned with the problem of Nagorny Karabakh, but rapidly turned to issues of economic mismanagement and privileges enjoyed by the Party leadership. Demonstrators occupied Baku's main square for 10 days before being dispersed by troops, who arrested the leaders of the demonstrations.

The initial impetus for the demonstrations was the debate on the status of Nagorny Karabakh and Nakhichevan. Both territories were claimed by Armenia, on historical grounds, and Nagorny Karabakh still had a majority Armenian population. Nakhichevan, despite an apparent surrender of Azerbaidzhan's claims to the territory in 1920, never became part of Soviet Armenia. The Soviet–Turkish Treaty of March 1921 included a clause guaranteeing Azerbaidzhani jurisdiction over Nakhichevan. During the next 70 years the 45%–50% of the region's population which had been ethnically Armenian in 1919 was reduced to less than 5% by 1989. Nagorny Karabakh had been a disputed territory during the period of Armenian and Azerbaidzhani independence (1918–1920) but, in June 1921, the Bureau for Caucasian Affairs (the Kavburo) voted to unite Nagorny Karabakh with Armenia. However, some days after the original Kavburo decision, following an intervention by Stalin, the decision was reversed. In 1923 it was declared an autonomous oblast within the Azerbaidzhan SSR. There were attempts to challenge Azerbaidzhan's jurisdiction over the region, including two petitions from the inhabitants of Nagorny Karabakh in the 1960s, but they were strongly opposed by the all-Union and Azerbaidzhani authorities.

Conflict over the territory began again in February 1988, when the Nagorny Karabakh regional soviet requested the Armenian and Azerbaidzhani Supreme Soviets to agree to the transfer of the territory to Armenia. The all-Union and Azerbaidzhani authorities rejected the request, thus provoking huge demonstrations by Armenians, not only in Nagorny Karabakh, but also in the Armenian capital, Yerevan. Azerbaidzhanis began leaving Armenia, and rumours that refugees had been attacked led to three days of anti-Armenian violence, on 27–29 February, in the Azerbaidzhani town of Sumgait. According to official figures, 32 people died, 26 of whom were Armenians.

Demands for the transfer of Nagorny Karabakh to Armenian jurisdiction continued throughout 1988, but they were strongly opposed both by the Azerbaidzhani and the Soviet leadership. In November thousands of people protested when an Azerbaidzhani was sentenced to death for his part in the Sumgait massacre, and a curfew was imposed in Baku. Some 14,000 Armenians left Azerbaidzhan during the month as rallies and demonstrations spread to Kirovabad (now Gyandzha) and other towns. Meanwhile, inter-ethnic tension in Armenia forced some 80,000 Azerbaidzhanis to leave Armenia during the same period.

In January 1989, in an attempt to end the violence, the Soviet Government suspended the activities of the local authorities in Nagorny Karabakh and established a Special Administration Committee (SAC), responsible to the USSR Council of Ministers. Although it was stressed that the region would formally retain its status as an autonomous region within Azerbaidzhan, the decision was widely viewed by Azerbaidzhanis as an infringement on Azerbaidzhan's territorial integrity. This imposition of 'direct rule' from Moscow and the dispatch of some 5,000 interior ministry troops did little to reduce tensions within Nagorny Karabakh, where Armenians went on strike in May and did not resume work until September.

In mid-1989 the Popular Front of Azerbaidzhan (PFA) was established. Following sporadic strikes and demonstrations throughout August 1989, the PFA organized a national strike in early September and demanded discussion on the issue of sovereignty, the situation in Nagorny Karabakh, the release of political prisoners and official recognition of the PFA. After a week of the general strike the Azerbaidzhan Supreme Soviet agreed to concessions to the PFA, including official recognition. In addition, draft laws on economic and political sovereignty were published and, on 23 September, the Supreme Soviet adopted the 'Constitutional Law on the Sovereignty of the Azerbaidzhan SSR', effectively a declaration of sovereignty. The conflict with Armenia continued, with the imposition of an economic blockade of Armenia, the effect of which was only partially lessened by the use of Soviet troops to run the Baku–Yerevan railway.

In November 1989 the Soviet Government transferred control of Nagorny Karabakh from the SAC to an Organizing Committee, which was dominated by ethnic Azerbaidzhanis. This decision was denounced on 1 December by the Armenian Supreme Soviet, which declared Nagorny Karabakh to be part of a 'unified Armenian republic'. This pronouncement prompted a week-long resumption of the Azerbaidzhani economic blockade and further outbreaks of violence in Nagorny Karabakh and along the Armenian–Azerbaidzhani border. Growing unrest within Azerbaidzhan, exacerbated by the return of refugees from Armenia to Baku, was directed both at the local Communist regime and at ethnic Armenians.

In January 1990 there were serious disturbances which threatened to overthrow Soviet power in Azerbaidzhan. Radical members of the PFA led attacks on Party and government buildings in Baku and other towns. Border posts were attacked on the Soviet–Iranian border, which separates Soviet Azerbaidzhanis from their co-nationals in Iran, and local nationalists seized Party buildings in the enclave of Nakhichevan and declared its secession from the USSR. In addition, there was renewed violence against Armenians, with some 60 Armenians killed in rioting in Baku. There was a hasty evacuation of the remaining non-Azerbaidzhanis, including ethnic Russians, from the city.

On 19 January 1990 a state of emergency was declared in Azerbaidzhan and Soviet troops were ordered into Baku, where the PFA was in control and had established barricades and other makeshift defences. In the military action which ensued, lightly-armed Azerbaidzhanis were no match for Soviet troops, who soon controlled most of the city. Officially, 124 people were killed during the Soviet intervention; unofficial sources assert that the real figure was much higher. The inability of the CPA to ensure order in the Republic led to the dismissal of Abdul Vezirov as First Secretary of the CPA; he was replaced by Ayaz Niyaz ogly Mutalibov. Order was restored in Azerbaidzhan by the end of January, after leading members of the PFA had been arrested, other radical nationalist organizations outlawed, and decrees issued banning all strikes, rallies and demonstrations.

The continuing unrest caused the elections to the Republic's Supreme Soviet (held in most other Republics in February) to be postponed. When they did take place, on 30 September 1990, with further rounds in October, the CPA won an overall majority. In the first round alone they won 220 of the 260 seats decided. Indeed, the Democratic Alliance, which included the PFA, could only nominate 218 candidates in 350 constituencies. The CPA victory was attributed to an increasingly firm stance on the issue of Nagorny Karabakh, which attracted nationalist support, combined with a willingness to compromise with Moscow to avoid further bloodshed. Opposition figures, however, contested the validity of the elections, complaining of electoral irregularities. In addition, the continuing state of emergency, which did not permit large meetings of people, severely disrupted campaigning by the Democratic Alliance and the PFA. When the new Supreme Soviet convened in February 1991, some 80% of the deputies were members of the CPA. The small group of opposition deputies united as the Democratic Bloc of Azerbaidzhan.

Unlike the other Caucasian Republics, Azerbaidzhan declared a willingness to sign a new Union Treaty and participated in the all-Union referendum concerning the preservation of the USSR which took place in March 1991. Official results of the referendum demonstrated a qualified support for the preservation of the USSR, with 75.1% of eligible voters participating, of whom 93.3% voted for a 'renewed federation'. In Nakhichevan, however, only some 20% of eligible voters approved President Gorbachev's question. Opposition politicians also contested the results of the referendum claiming that only 15%–20% of voters had actually participated.

In August 1991, when the State Committee for the State of Emergency (SCSE) seized power in Moscow, Mutalibov issued a statement which seemed to demonstrate support for the coup. Mutalibov denied that he had supported the SCSE, but there were large demonstrations in the last week of August, demanding his resignation, the declaration of Azerbaidzhan's independence, the lifting of the state of emergency, which had been imposed in January 1990, and the postponement of the presidential elections, scheduled for 8 September. The opposition was supported by Geidar Aliyev, the former First Secretary of the CPA, and the Chairman of the Supreme Majlis (parliament) of Nakhichevan, who had become increasingly critical of Mutalibov's leadership. Mutalibov responded to some of the protesters' demands by ending the state of emergency and resigning as First Secretary of the CPA, and, on 30 August, the Azerbaidzhani Supreme Soviet voted to 'restore the independent status of Azerbaidzhan'.

Despite continued protests from the PFA, which called a poorly-supported general strike on 3 September 1991, the elections to the presidency proceeded, although they were boycotted by the opposition, with the result that Mutalibov was the only candidate. According to official results, he won 84% of the vote.

Independence was formally restored on 18 October 1991, when the Supreme Soviet adopted legislation putting into effect the declaration of independence of 30 August. The Supreme Soviet also voted not to sign the Treaty on the Economic Community, which was signed by eight other Republics on the same day. In a further move towards full independence, legislation was adopted allowing for the creation of national armed forces, and Azerbaidzhan began to take over the military facilities of the Soviet Army in the Republic. Azerbaidzhan did join the Commonwealth of Independent States, however, signing the Alma-Ata Declaration, on 21 December 1991, although it reserved its right to form a national guard rather than participate in the unified command structure agreed by most of the other Republics.

During early 1991 there was further inter-ethnic violence in the region around Nagorny Karabakh, with allegations that Soviet interior ministry troops co-operated with Azerbaidzhani forces to deport Armenians from villages near the Armenian–Azerbaidzhani border. There was some progress, however, in September 1991, when Boris Yeltsin, President of the Russian Federation, and Nursultan Nazarbayev, President of Kazakhstan, arranged a peace agreement between the two Republics, signed in Zheleznovodsk (Russian Federation), on 23 September. The agreement provided for considerable autonomy for Armenians in Nagorny Karabakh, in exchange for a renunciation by Armenia of any territorial claim to the region. However, some inter-ethnic violence was reported immediately after the agreement was signed, and the PFA organized demonstrations to protest against the agreement. The negotiations received a serious set-back when an aircraft carrying leading Azerbaidzhani negotiators crashed, killing all the passengers. The Azerbaidzhani leadership alleged that the aircraft had been shot down by Armenians, and relations between the two Republics worsened. By the end of 1991 there were increasingly violent conflicts between the Republics, and particularly within Nagorny Karabakh. In late December the regional capital, Stepanakert, was bombarded.

In 1991 Azerbaidzhan attempted to develop economic and political relations with other countries, notably with its traditional ally, Turkey, and with its neighbour Iran. In November 1991 Turkey became the first country to recognize Azerbaidzhan's declaration of independence. Relations with Iran have also been developed, and informal links between Azerbaidzhanis on both sides of the border were increased.

Economy

Industry and mining are the most important sectors in the economy. Petroleum is extracted from the Apsheron Peninsula and around Siyar, Neftechala and Ali-Bayramli. The largest unexploited reserves are off shore, in the Caspian Sea; foreign companies have been encouraged to invest in offshore exploration, where high technology is required. Petroleum is refined in Baku; there is, however, also a pipeline to Batumi (Georgia), on the Black Sea. Azerbaidzhan produces some 60% of the required extraction and production machinery and spare parts for the entire Soviet petroleum industry. Other heavy industries include chemical processing, construction and machine building. Azerbaidzhan relies heavily on hydroelectric power, mostly produced by plants on the River Kura. Light industries include food processing, textiles and viniculture. Most arable land requires extensive irrigation, but there are large pasture-lands, which are used by cattle, goats and sheep. The main crops are cotton, tea, tobacco, wheat, fruit, nuts and wine grapes.

Azerbaidzhan provided 1.7% of total Soviet net material product (NMP) in 1988, including 1.7% of total industrial NMP and 2.2% of total agricultural NMP. Exports to other countries constituted 3.7% of Azerbaidzhan's NMP, while exports to other Republics made up 58.7% of NMP.

Statistical Survey
Population

BIRTHS AND DEATHS (per 1,000)

	1987	1988	1989
Birth rate	26.8	26.5	26.0
Death rate	6.7	6.8	6.5

Agriculture

PRINCIPAL CROPS ('000 metric tons)

	1987	1988	1989
Grain	1,117.6	1,417.3	860.8
Seed cotton . . .	702.3	616.1	581.9
Potatoes . . .	201.9	165.1	179.8
Other vegetables . . .	855.0	879.7	912.9
Grapes	1,549.9	1,249.7	1,024.4
Other fruit	431.3	429.1	454.2
Tea (green)	34.2	34.5	32.7

LIVESTOCK ('000 head at 1 January)

	1988	1989	1990
Cattle	2,013.0	1,979.0	1,934.8
Pigs	225.6	213.4	190.6
Sheep and goats . . .	5,697.0	5,747.7	5,258.2

LIVESTOCK PRODUCTS ('000 metric tons)

	1987	1988	1989
Meat (slaughter weight) . .	183.9	184.7	185.6
Milk	1,062.1	1,067.0	1,071.7
Eggs (million)	1,055.3	1,076.7	1,051.2
Wool (greasy)	11.4	11.7	10.2

Mining and Industry

Production (1989, unless otherwise indicated): Crude petroleum 13.2m. tons, Natural gas 11.1m. tons, Steel 819,700 tons, Iron ore 772,300 tons (1987), Steel pipes 575,000 tons, Mineral fertilizers 274,900 tons, Refrigerators 354,200, Deep-water pumps 92,100 (1987), Pump rods 323,100 (1987), Footwear 17.6m. pairs, Carpets and rugs 2,710,000 sq m, Tinned goods 710.4m. cans, Electric energy 23,200m. kWh.

Education

(1990/91)

	Institutions	Students
Secondary schools	4,441	1,379,000
Secondary specialized institutions . .	80	70,000
Higher schools (incl. universities) . .	17	105,000

Directory
The Government
(December 1991)

HEAD OF STATE

President: AYAZ NIYAZ OGLY MUTALIBOV (took office 18 May 1990, elected 8 September 1991).

STATE COUNCIL

Counsellor for Economic Policy: VAID JUMSHUD OGLY AKHUNDOV.

Counsellor for Humanitarian Issues: KYAMRAN ENVER OGLY RUSTAMOV.

Counsellor for Legal Policy: SABIR KAMAL OGLY GADZHIYEV.

Counsellor for Work with Regional and Local Bodies of Power and Government: ADIL KHANBAB OGLY GADZHIYEV.

COUNCIL OF MINISTERS

Chairman: HASAN AZIZ OGLY HASANOV.

Minister of Automobile Transport: FUAD KARA-OGLY RUSTAMOV.

Minister of Communications: BAGADUR MAMED OGLY AKHYNDOV.

Minister of the Construction Materials Industry: ARIF E. MANSUROV.

Minister of Culture: BYUL-BYUL OGLY POLAD.

Minister of Defence: Maj.-Gen. TADZHADDIN MEKHTIYEV.

Minister of Education: RAFIK BABASH OGLY FEYZULLAYEV.

Minister of Finance: BADIR DZHAMIL KARAYEV.

Minister of Foreign Affairs: MUSA G. SADYKOV.

Minister of Grain Products: RAGIM DZHALIL DZHAMILOV.

Minister of Health: ALI TALYAT KASUMOV.

Minister of Housing: VENIAMIN STEPANOVICH MAYOROV.

Minister of Internal Affairs: AIDYN ISRAFIL MAMEDOV.

Minister of Justice: ALISAAB SAFTAR OGLY ORUDZHEV.

Minister of Light Industry: AKHMED MIRZA MUSTAFAEV.

Minister of Local Industry: AGABBA IMAN OGLY YABDULLAYEV.

Minister of National Security: ILGUSEYN PIRGUSEYN OGLY GUSEYNOV.

Minister of Public Services: NAILYA AGADADASH BAGIROVA.

Minister of Social Security: LIDIYA KHUDAT KYZY RASULOVA.

Minister of Trade: AGASALIM YAGUB OGLY BAGIROV.

Minister of Water Resources: SALEKH GILAL GADZHIEV.

MINISTRIES

Ministry of Automobile Transport: 370602 Baku, Tbilissky pr., kvartal 1054; tel. (892) 31-91-11.

Ministry of Communications: 370139 Baku, pr. Azerbaidzhana 33; tel. (892) 93-00-04.

Ministry of the Construction Materials Industry: 370122 Baku, Tbilissky pr. 57; tel. (892) 31-31-61.

Ministry of Culture: 370016 Baku, Dom pravitelstva; tel. (892) 93-42-98.

Ministry of Defence: Baku, pr. Azerbaidzhana.

Ministry of Education: 270016 Baku, Dom pravitelstva; tel. (892) 93-72-66.

Ministry of Finance: 370601 Baku, ul. Sameda Burguna 6; tel. (892) 93-30-12.

Ministry of Foreign Affairs: 370005 Baku, Kontrolny per. 2; tel. (892) 93-82-31.

Ministry of Grain Products: 370033 Baku, ul. A. Geydarova 13; tel. (892) 66-74-51.

Ministry of Health: 370014 Baku, ul. Todorskovo 4; tel. (892) 93-29-77.

Ministry of Housing: 370016 Baku, Dom pravitelstva; tel. (892) 93-34-67.

Ministry of Internal Affairs: 370005 Baku, ul. Gusi Gadzhiyeva 7; tel. (892) 92-57-54.

Ministry of Justice: 370601 Baku, pr. Kirova 13; tel. (892) 93-97-85.

Ministry of Light Industry: 370016 Baku, Dom pravitelstva; tel. (892) 93-54-07.

Ministry of Local Industry: 370016 Baku, Dom pravitelstva; tel. (892) 98-53-25.

Ministry of National Security: Baku.

Ministry of Public Services: 370016 Baku, Dom pravitelstva; tel. (892) 93-56-00.

Ministry of Social Security: 370016 Baku, Dom pravitelstva; tel. (892) 93-05-42.

Ministry of Trade: 370016 Baku, Dom pravitelstva; tel. (892) 98-50-74.

Ministry of Water Resources: 370016 Baku, Dom pravitelstva; tel. (892) 93-61-54.

Legislature

The Supreme Soviet is the highest representative body in the Republic. Elections were held to the Supreme Soviet on 30 September and 14 October 1990. It formally consists of 360 deputies, but polling did not take place in 11 constituencies in Nagorny Karabakh and Shaumyan rayon because of security concerns. In October 1991 the Supreme Soviet voted to establish a new standing legislative body, the National Council, which was to include some 20% of the members of the Supreme Soviet.

Chairman of the Supreme Soviet: ELMIRA M. GAFAROVA.

Deputy Chairmen: TAMERLAN KARAYEV, GEIDAR ALIYEV.

Local Government

Azerbaidzhan includes one autonomous oblast and one autonomous republic. The status of Nagorny Karabakh is disputed.

NAGORNY KARABAKH AUTONOMOUS OBLAST

Chairman of the Nagorny Karabakh Supreme Soviet: ARTUR MKRTCHYAN.

On 10 December 1991 a referendum took place, in which residents voted overwhelmingly for independence.

NAKHICHEVAN AUTONOMOUS REPUBLIC:

Chairman of the Supreme Majlis: GEIDAR ALIYEV.

Chairman of the Council of Ministers: BEDZHAN FARZILIYEV.

Political Organizations

On 14 September 1991, at an extraordinary congress of the Communist Party of Azerbaidzhan, delegates voted to disband the Party.

Popular Front of Azerbaidzhan (PFA): Baku; f. 1989; Pres. of Council TAMERLAN KARAYEV; Chair. I. GAMBAROV.

Social Democratic Group: Baku; f. 1990; 2,000 mems (1990); Leader ZARDUSHT ALI-ZADE.

Other political groups include the Green Party of Azerbaidzhan and the United Democratic Intelligentsia.

Judicial System

Chairman of the Supreme Court: G. G. TALIBOV.

Procurator-General: (vacant).

Religion

ISLAM

The majority (some 70%) of Azerbaidzhanis are Shi'ite Muslims; most of the remainder are Sunni (Hanafi school). The Muslim Board of Transcaucasia is based in Baku. It has spiritual jurisdiction over the Muslims of Armenia, Georgia and Azerbaidzhan. The Chairman of the Directorate is normally a Shi'ite, while the Deputy Chairman is usually a Sunni.

Muslim Board of Transcaucasia: Baku; Chair. (vacant).

The Press

In 1989 there were 151 officially-registered newspaper titles being published in Azerbaidzhan, including 133 in Azerbaidzhani, and 95 periodicals, including 55 in Azerbaidzhani.

PRINCIPAL NEWSPAPERS

(In Azerbaidzhani except where otherwise stated.)

Adabiyat ve Indzhisenet: 370146 Baku, ul. B. Avakyana, kv. 529; tel. (892) 39-50-37; organ of the Union of Writers of Azerbaidzhan.

Azadlyg (Liberty): Baku, Akademik Sh. Azizbeyov St 62; f. 1989; weekly; organ of the Popular Front of Azerbaidzhan; in Azerbaidzhani and Russian; Editor-in-Chief N. A. NADZAFOV; circ. 142,000.

Azerbaidzhan: Baku, 28 Aprel by St 4; f. 1989; weekly; publ. by the People's Committee for Relief to Karabakh; in Azerbaidzhani and Russian; Editor-in-Chief S. H. RUSTAMHANLI; circ. 124,000.

Azerbaidzhan Gandzhlyari (Youth of Azerbaidzhan): Baku; f. 1919; 3 a week; fmrly organ of the Cen. Cttee of the Communist Union of Youth for the Progress of Azerbaidzhan; Editor YU. A. KERIMOV; circ. 161,000.

Bakinsky Rabochy (The Baku Worker): 370146 Baku, Metbuat pr., kv. 529; tel. (892) 32-11-10; f. 1906; 6 a week; fmrly organ of the Communist Party of Azerbaidzhan; in Russian; Editor GENNADI G. GLUSHKOV; circ. 68,000.

Hayat (Life): 370146 Baku, Metbuat pr., kv. 529; f. 1991; 5 a week; publ. by the Supreme Soviet of Azerbaidzhan; Editor-in-Chief A. H. ASKEROV; circ. 40,000.

Istiglal (Independence): Baku; organ of the Azerbaidzhan Social Democratic Group; Editor Z. ALI-ZADE.

Khalg Gazeti: Baku; f. 1919; fmrly *Kommunist* (Communist); fmrly an organ of the Communist Party of Azerbaidzhan; 6 a week; Editor T. T. RUSTAMOV; circ. 254,000.

Molodezh Azerbaidzhana (Youth of Azerbaidzhan): Baku; f. 1919; 3 a week; fmrly organ of the Communist Union of Youth for the Progress of Azerbaidzhan; in Russian; Editor V. EFENDIEV; circ. 22,700.

Respublika (Republic): 370146 Baku, Metbuat pr., kv. 529; f. 1990; weekly; government newspaper; Editor-in-Chief A. M. ISAYEV; circ. 57,000.

Sovet kendi (Soviet Village): 370146 Baku, Metbuat pr, kv. 529; f. 1923; 5 a week; fmrly publ. by the Communist Party of Azerbaidzhan; Editor R. M. NAGIYEV; circ. 40,000.

Veten Sesi (The Voice of the Motherland): 370146 Baku, Metbuat pr., kv. 529; f. 1990; weekly; publ. by the Society of Refugees of Azerbaidzhan; in Azerbaidzhani and Russian; Editor-in-Chief T. A. AHMEDOV; circ. 47,000.

Vyshka (The Tower): 370146 Baku, Metbuat pr., kv. 529; tel. (892) 39-85-65; f. 1928; 5 a week; fmrly publ. by the Cen. Cttee of the Communist Party of Azerbaidzhan; in Russian; Editor Y. M. IVANOV; circ. 70,000.

PRINCIPAL PERIODICALS

Azerbaidzhan: 370001 Baku, ul. Kommunisticheskaya 31; tel. (892) 92-59-63; f. 1923; monthly; publ. by the Union of Writers of Azerbaidzhan; recent works by Azerbaidzhani authors; Editor-in-Chief YUSIF SAMEDOGLU.

Azerbaidzhan Gadyny (Woman of Azerbaidzhan): Baku; f. 1923; monthly; popular, for women; illustrated; Editor H. M. HASILOVA.

Azerbaidzhan Kommunisti (Communist of Azerbaidzhan): 370066 Baku, ul. Kommunisticheskaya 19; tel. (892) 92-19-29; f. 1920; monthly; fmrly publ. by the Publishing House of the Cen. Cttee of the Azerbaidzhan Communist Party; theoretical and political; in Azerbaidzhani and Russian; Editor-in-Chief K. I. RAHIMOV; circ. 30,000.

Dialog (Dialogue): Baku; f. 1989; fortnightly; fmrly publ. by the Communist Party of Azerbaidzhan; in Azerbaidzhani and Russian; Editor R. A. ALEKPEROV.

Grakan Adrbedzhan: 370001 Baku, ul. Kommunisticheskaya 31; tel. (892) 92-64-93; 6 a year; organ of the Union of Writers of Azerbaidzhan; in Armenian.

Kend Khayaty (Country Life): Baku; f. 1952; monthly; journal of the Ministry of Agriculture; advanced methods of work in agriculture; in Azerbaidzhani and Russian; Editor D. A. DAMIRLI.

Kirpi (Hedgehog): Baku; f. 1952; fortnightly; satirical; Editor A. M. AIVAZOV.

Literaturny Azerbaidzhan (Literature of Azerbaidzhan): 370001 Baku, ul. Kommunisticheskaya 31; tel. (892) 92-39-31; f. 1931; monthly; journal of the Union of Writers of Azerbaidzhan; fiction; in Russian; Editor-in-Chief I. P. TRETYAKOV.

Ulduz: 370001 Baku, ul. Kommunisticheskaya 31; tel. (892) 92-27-43; 12 a year; organ of the Union of Writers of Azerbaidzhan.

NEWS AGENCY

Azerinform (Azerbaidzhan Information Agency): Baku; Dir A. A. SHARIFOV.

Publishers

Azerbaidzhan Ensiklopediyasy (Azerbaidzhan Encyclopaedia): 370004 Baku, Boyuk Gala St 41; tel. (892) 92-87-11; f. 1965; Editor-in-Chief I. O. VELIYEV (acting).

Azerneshr (State Publishing House): Baku, Huzi Hajiyev St 4; tel. (892) 92-50-15; f. 1924; various; Dir A. A. MUSTAFAZADE.

Elm (Azerbaidzhani Academy of Sciences Publishing House): 370073 Baku, pr. Narimanova 37; scientific books and journals; Dir (vacant).

Gyandzhlik (Youth): 370005 Baku, Husi Hajiyev St 4; books for children and young people; Dir E. T. ALIYEV.

Ishyg (Light): 370601 Baku, ul. Gogolya 6; posters, illustrated publs; Dir G. N. ISMAILOV.

Maarif (Education): 370122 Baku, Tagizade St 4; educational books.

Yazychy (The Writer): 370005 Baku, Natavan St 1; fiction; Dir F. M. MELIKOV.

Radio and Television

State Committee for Television and Radio: 370011 Baku, ul. Mekhti Huseina 1; tel. (892) 92-71-55; HEISAR OGLY KHALILOV.

Radio Baku: f. 1926; broadcasts in Azerbaidzhani, Russian, Arabic, Persian (Farsi) and Turkish.

Baku Television: f. 1956; programmes in Azerbaidzhani and Russian; Dir G. W. HALILOV.

Finance

BANKING

State Banks

National Bank of Azerbaidzhan: Baku; First Deputy Chair. N. I. KADYROV.

Bank of Azerbaidzhan for Foreign Economic Activity: Baku; fmrly br of USSR Vneshekonombank; Chair. of Bd V. K. AKHMEDOV.

Other Banks

Azeri Co-op Bank: 370000 Baku, ul. Naftyanikov 127; tel. (892) 93-59-50.

Baku Co-op Bank: 370025 Baku, ul. Barinova 12; tel. (892) 67-45-46.

Commercial Bank (Universal): 370001 Baku, ul. Ostrovskovo 39/11; tel. (892) 92-76-56.

Deka-Bank: 370141 Baku-141, ul. Alekpera Alekporova 82/83; tel. (892) 39-84-30.

Vostochny Co-op Bank: 370070 Baku, pr. Kirova 19; tel. (892) 93-22-47; co-operative bank; Pres. AZIK RAGULMOV.

Trade and Industry

CHAMBER OF COMMERCE

Chamber of Commerce and Industry of the Republic of Azerbaidzhan: 370601 Baku, ul. Kommunisticheskaya 31/33; tel. (892) 39-85-03; Chair. KAMRAN ASAD OGLY GUSEYON.

FOREIGN TRADE ORGANIZATION

Azerbintorg: 370004 Baku, ul. Nekrasova 7; tel. (892) 93-71-69; telex 212183; imports and exports a wide range of goods; Dir E. M. GUREJNOV.

MAJOR INDUSTRIAL ENTERPRISES

Azinmash: 370603 Baku, Volodarsky St 4; tel. (892) 67-28-88; telex 142188; manufactures equipment for petroleum and natural gas industries; Dir VALERY A. ALIYEV.

Bakinsky Rabochy Engineering: 370034 Baku; tel. (892) 25-93-91; telex 142445; equipment for the petroleum industry, including pumping units and pipe transporters; Dir MAMED VELIEV; 1,200 employees.

Transport

RAILWAYS

Railways connect Baku with Tbilisi (Georgia), Makhachkala (Daghestan) and Yerevan (Armenia). The rail link with Armenia runs through the autonomous republic of Nakhichevan. From Nakhichevan an international line links Azerbaidzhan with Tabriz (Iran). In 1991 plans were agreed with the Iranian Government for the construction of a rail line between Azerbaidzhan and Nakhichevan, which would pass through Iranian territory, thus bypassing Armenia.

ROADS

At 31 December 1989 the total length of roads in Azerbaidzhan was 30,400 km, of which 28,600 km were hard-surfaced.

SHIPPING

Shipping services on the Caspian Sea link Baku with Krasnovodsk (Turkmenistan) and the Iranian ports of Bandar Anzali and Bandar Nowshar.

Shipowning Company

Caspian Shipping Company: 370005 Baku, ul. Dzhaparidze 3; telex 142102; nationalized by the Azerbaidzhani Govt in 1991; Pres. T. K. AKHMEDOV.

Culture

NATIONAL ORGANIZATION

Ministry of Culture: see section on The Government (Ministries).

CULTURAL HERITAGE

Azerbaidzhan State Art Museum: Baku, ul. Chkalova 9; 7,000 exhibits; Dir Z. M. KYAZIM.

Museum of the History of Azerbaidzhan of the Academy of Sciences: 370005 Baku, ul. Malygina 4; tel. (892) 93-36-48; f. 1920; 120,000 exhibits on the history of the Azeris; Dir P. A. AZIZBEKOVA.

State Library of Azerbaidzhan: 375009 Baku, ul. Khagani 29; tel. (892) 93-68-01; f. 1923; 3,122,000 vols; Dir K. A. SULEYMAN ZADE.

State Museum of Azerbaidzhan: 370001 Baku, ul. Kommunisticheskaya 53; tel. (892) 92-18-64; f. 1939; 75,000 exhibits on the history of Azerbaidzhani literature; Dir H. A. ALLAHYAROGLU.

Stepanakert Museum of History of Nagorny Karabakh: Nagorny Karabakh AO, Stepanakert, ul. Gorkovo 4; collection on the history of the Armenian people of Nagorny Karabakh (Arthakh).

PERFORMING ARTS

Mirza Akhundov Opera and Ballet Theatre: Baku, ul. 28 Oktabrya 8.

Muslim Magomayev Philharmonia: Baku, ul. Kommunisticheskaya 2; Azerbaidzhan's leading orchestra.

Samed Vurgun Russian Drama Theatre: Baku, ul. Hagani 7.

State Puppet Theatre: Baku, pr. Neftyanikov 36.

ASSOCIATIONS

Union of Writers of Azerbaidzhan: 370000 Baku, ul. Khagani 25; tel. (892) 93-66-40.

Veten: Baku; f. 1987; cultural organization for developing contacts with Azerbaidzhanis in other countries; Chair. V. ELCHIN.

Education

Before 1920 Azerbaidzhan was an important centre of learning among Muslims of the Russian Empire. Under Soviet rule, a much more extensive education system was introduced and the level of literacy was greatly increased from 8.1% in 1926 to over 99% in 1970. The main language of instruction is Azerbaidzhani, but there are also Russian-language schools and some teaching in Georgian and Armenian. In 1988 79.5% of pupils in general day schools were taught in Azerbaidzhani, 18.5% in Russian and 1.9% in Armenian. Two schools used Georgian as the language of instruction. In higher education technical subjects are often taught in Russian, but there have been demands that there should be greater use of Azerbaidzhani. In 1990/91 there were 105,000 students in higher education. There are a number of specialized institutes, which prepare experts for work in the major industries of the Republic. There is one university, in Baku, founded by the nationalist government of independent Azerbaidzhan, in 1919.

UNIVERSITY

Baku State University: 370073 Baku, ul. Patrisa Lumumby 23; tel. (892) 39-01-86; f. 1919; 14 faculties; 1,093 teachers; 12,500 students; Rector M. G. GASYMOV.

Social Welfare

NATIONAL AGENCIES

Ministry of Health: see section on The Government (Ministries).

Ministry of Social Security: see section on the Government (Ministries).

HEALTH AND WELFARE ORGANIZATIONS

People's Committee for Relief to Karabakh: Baku; f. 1987; Chair. B. BAIRAMOV.

Society of Refugees of Azerbaidzhan: Baku; humanitarian organization; aids refugees from Armenia and other regions of interethnic conflict.

The Environment

Considerable environmental damage has resulted from exploitation of the petroleum and gas resources of the Caspian Sea, and from the industrial areas in the east of the Republic.

ACADEMIC INSTITUTES

Academy of Sciences: 370001 Baku, ul. Kommunisticheskaya 10; Pres. E. Yu. SALAYEV; institutes incl.:

Commission on the Caspian Sea: Baku, ul. Narimanova 31; in the Dept of Earth Sciences; Chair. A. A. GYUL (acting).

Commission on Nature Conservation: 370001 Baku, ul. Kommunisticheskaya 10; in the Dept of Biological Sciences; Chair. (vacant).

Institute for the Study of Natural Resources from Space: Baku, Novaya ketskhoveli 9; in the Dept of Earth Sciences; researches on space and on the ground in environmental protection and information; Dir T. K. ISMAILOV.

BYELORUSSIA

Geography

The Republic of Byelorussia (Byelarus or Belarus, formerly the Byelorussian Soviet Socialist Republic—BSSR), is situated in north-eastern Europe. It is also referred to as White Russia or White Ruthenia. It is bounded by Lithuania and Latvia to the north-west, by Ukraine to the south, and by the Russian Federation to the east. There is an international frontier with Poland to the west. It covers an area of 207,600 sq km (80,154 sq miles).

The land is a plain with numerous lakes, swamps and marshes. There is an area of low hill country north of Minsk, but the highest point is only 350 m above sea-level. The southern part of the Republic is a low, flat marshland. Forests cover some 30% of the territory. The main rivers are the Dniepr, which flows south to the Black Sea, and the Pripyat, which flows eastwards, to the Dniepr, through a forested, swampy area, known as the Pripyat Marshes.

The climate is of a continental type, with an average January temperature, in Minsk, of −5°C (23°F) and an average for July of 19°C (67°F). Average annual precipitation is between 560 mm and 660 mm.

Of a total population at the 1989 census of 10,200,000, 79.4% were Byelorussians, 11.9% Russians, 4.2% Poles, 2.4% Ukrainians and 1.4% Jews. There were also small numbers of Tatars (12,436), Roma (10,762), Lithuanians (7,606) and other ethnic groups. Since 1990 the official language of the Republic has been Byelorussian, an Eastern Slavonic language written in the Cyrillic script. However, at the 1989 census, only 80.2% of Byelorussians considered Byelorussian to be their native language. The remainder spoke Russian as their first language, although 48% of these claimed fluency in Byelorussian as a second language. Some 64% of ethnic Poles claimed Byelorussian as their first language, while only some 13% knew Polish. The major religion is Christianity, the Roman Catholic Church and the Eastern Orthodox Church being the largest denominations. There are also small Muslim and Jewish communities.

At 1 January 1991 the total population was estimated to be 10,260,000. The capital is Minsk (Mensk), which is situated in the centre of the Republic. Minsk was also declared to be the headquarters of the Commonwealth of Independent States. It had a population of 1,612,000 in 1989. Other important towns are Gomel (Homel—500,000), in the south-east of the Republic, and Mahilou (Mogilev).

History

The first Eastern Slavic tribes appeared in modern-day Byelorussia in the seventh century and, by the ninth century, they had settled throughout the area. Following the Mongol invasions of Kievan Rus, in the 13th and 14th centuries, Byelorussia became a part of the Grand Duchy of Lithuania, in which an early version of Byelorussian was the official language. The Grand Duchy of Lithuania was united with Poland in the 16th century and the Byelorussian lands came under the control of the Polish-Lithuanian nobility. As a result of the partitions of Poland (1772–95) Byelorussia became a part of the Russian Empire.

In the 19th century there was a growth of national consciousness in Byelorussia and, as a result of industrialization, a significant movement of people from rural areas to the towns. After the February Revolution of 1917 in Russia, Byelorussian nationalists and socialists formed a Rada (council), which sought a degree of autonomy from the Provisional Government in Petrograd (St Petersburg). In November, after the Bolsheviks had seized power in Petrograd, Soviet troops were dispatched to Minsk and the Rada was dissolved. However, the Bolsheviks were forced to withdraw by approaching German troops. The Treaty of Brest-Litovsk, signed in March 1918, assigned most of Byelorussia to the Germans and they duly occupied the country. On 25 March 1918 Byelorussian nationalists convened to proclaim a Byelorussian National Republic, but it had little real power. Once the Germans had withdrawn, the Bolsheviks easily reoccupied Minsk, and a Byelorussian Soviet Socialist Republic was declared on 1 January 1919.

In February 1919 the Byelorussian Republic was merged with Lithuania in a Lithuanian-Byelorussian Soviet Republic (known as 'Litbel'). In April 1919, however, Polish armed forces entered Lithuania and Byelorussia and both were declared part of Poland. It was only in July 1920 that the Bolsheviks recaptured Minsk and, in August, the Soviet Republic of Byelorussia was re-established; Lithuania became an independent state. However, the Byelorussian SSR contained only the eastern half of the lands populated by Byelorussians. Western Byelorussia was granted to Poland by the Treaty of Riga, signed on 18 March 1921. The Treaty of Riga also assigned Byelorussia's eastern regions to the Russian Federation, but they were returned to the Byelorussian SSR in 1924 and 1926.

During the 1920s the Byelorussian SSR developed both culturally and economically. The New Economic Policy, which provided some liberalization of the economy, brought a measure of prosperity, and there was significant cultural and linguistic development, with the use of the Byelorussian language officially encouraged. This period ended in 1929 with the beginning of Stalin's collectivization campaign, which was strongly resisted by the peasantry. There were frequent riots and rebellions in rural areas and many peasants were deported or imprisoned. The purges of the early 1930s were particularly targeted against Byelorussian nationalists and intellectuals, but, by 1936–38, they had widened to include all sectors of the population.

After the Soviet invasion of Poland, in September 1939, the Byelorussian SSR was enlarged by the inclusion of the lands it had lost to Poland and Lithuania in 1921. Between 1941 and 1944 Byelorussia was occupied by German forces; an estimated 1,300,000 people died during the occupation, including most of the Republic's large Jewish population. At the Yalta conference, in February 1945, the Allies agreed to recognize the 'Curzon line' as the western border of Byelorussia, thus endorsing the unification of western and eastern Byelorussia. As a result of the Soviet demand for more voting powers in the United Nations (UN), the Western powers permitted Byelorussia to become a member of the UN in April 1945.

The immediate post-War period was dominated by the need for reconstruction of the Republic's infrastructure. The reconstruction programme and the local labour shortage increased Russian immigration into the Republic, thus further discouraging use of the Byelorussian language. During the 1960s and 1970s the process of 'russification' continued; there was a decrease in the use of Byelorussian in schools and in publishing and other media. The Republic was, however, one of the most prosperous in the USSR, with a wider variety of consumer goods available than in most other Republics.

This relative prosperity was one reason why the Communist Party of Byelorussia (CPB) was initially able to resist implementing economic and political reforms proposed by Soviet leader Mikhail Gorbachev from 1985 onwards. By 1987, however, the CPB was being criticized in the press for its stance on cultural and ecological issues. Intellectuals and writers campaigned for the greater use of Byelorussian in education, pointing out that there were no Byelorussian-language schools operating in any urban areas in the Republic. Campaigners also demanded more information about the consequences of the explosion at the Chernobyl nuclear power station, in Ukraine, in April 1986, which had affected large areas of southern Byelorussia. Not surprisingly, the two most important unofficial groups that developed in the late 1980s were the Byelorussian Language Association and the Byelorussian Ecological Union.

There was, however, little opportunity for overt political opposition. In October 1988 riot police were used to disperse a public commemoration of All Saints' Day, an action which was condemned even in the conservative newspaper of the CPSU, *Pravda*. A Byelorussian Popular Front (BPF—also known as Adradzhenne—Rebirth) was established in October 1988, but the CPB did not permit the republican media to report its activities and refused to allow rallies or public meetings to take place. The BPF did have some success in the elections to the all-Union Congress of People's Deputies, which took place in March 1989, persuading voters to reject several leading officials of the CPB. However, the inaugural congress of the BPF took place in Vilnius (Lithuania), in June 1989, the Front having been refused permission to meet in Minsk.

In early 1990, in anticipation of the elections to the republican Supreme Soviet, the CPB did adopt some of the BPF's policies towards the Byelorussian language. On 26 January 1990 a law was passed declaring Byelorussian to be the state language, effective from 1 September 1990. However, the period of the transfer from Russian was to be as long as 10 years in some institutions.

The BPF was not officially permitted to participate in the elections to the Byelorussian Supreme Soviet which took place on 4 March 1990. Instead, its members joined other pro-reform groups in a coalition known as the Byelorussian Democratic Bloc (BDB). The BDB won about one-quarter of the 310 seats available for popular election; most of the remainder were won by CPB members loyal to the republican leadership. The opposition won most seats in the large cities, notably Gomel and Minsk, where Zenyon Paznyak, the leader of the BPF, was elected.

When the new Supreme Soviet first convened, on 15 May 1990, the deputies belonging to the BDB immediately demanded the adoption of a declaration of sovereignty. The CPB initially opposed such a move, but, on 27 July 1990, apparently after consultations with the CPSU leadership in Moscow, a Declaration of the State Sovereignty of the Byelorussian SSR was adopted unanimously by the Supreme Soviet. The declaration asserted the Republic's right to maintain armed forces, to establish a national currency and to have full control over its domestic and foreign policies. On the insistence of the opposition, a clause was included which claimed the right of the Republic to compensation for the damage caused by the accident at the Chernobyl nuclear power station.

The issue of Chernobyl was one that united both Communist and opposition deputies. The Byelorussian Government asked the all-Union Government for a minimum of 17,000m. roubles to overcome the consequences of the disaster, but were offered only 3,000m. roubles compensation. Moreover, in June 1990, Soviet President Mikhail Gorbachev declined an invitation to visit Minsk to discuss the problem, an action that was badly received in the Republic. He eventually visited the BSSR in February 1991, but promised little further assistance. Gennady Buravkin, the Byelorussian representative at the UN, used his position to ask other countries for aid to pay for decontamination of the area and treatment of affected civilians.

The 31st Congress of the CPB, which took place in November 1990, was notable for the criticisms voiced by delegates of Soviet President Mikhail Gorbachev's reforms, notably of his foreign policy towards Eastern Europe. Yefrem Sokolov (Sakalau), who had led the CPB since 1987, did not stand for re-election as First Secretary. He was replaced by Anatoly Malofeev (Malafeyeu), who only narrowly defeated an outspoken critic of Gorbachev, Vladimir Brovikov.

The Byelorussian Government took part in the negotiation of a new treaty of union and signed the protocol to the draft of such a treaty on 3 March 1991. The all-Union referendum on the preservation of the union took place in Byelorussia on 17 March 1991; the ballot paper in Byelorussia did not include any additional questions on sovereignty, unlike in neighbouring Ukraine. The results did not demonstrate any widespread support for independence. Of the 83% who took part, 83% voted in favour of Gorbachev's proposals for a 'renewed federation of equal sovereign republics', the highest percentage in any Republic outside Central Asia. Members of the BPF conducted a campaign advocating a vote against Gorbachev's proposals, but complained that they were denied the opportunity to present their views to the general public.

Byelorussia's reputation as the most stable of the European Republics was challenged by a series of strikes in April 1991 which threatened the continued power of the CPB. In early April, in response to price rises, workers went on strike in Minsk and held protest meetings in the city. Demonstrators demanded higher wages and the cancellation of the 5% sales tax introduced in January 1991, but also announced political demands, including the resignation of the Byelorussian Government and the depoliticization of republican institutions. As the Government continued to reject most of the strikers' demands strikes and demonstrations took place in other cities, and on 10 April a general strike took place, and an estimated 100,000 people attended a demonstration in Minsk. The strike continued the next day, but was suspended by the newly-formed Minsk Strike Committee (MSC) when the Government agreed to negotiate with workers' representatives. Certain economic concessions were agreed by the Government, including high wage rises, but the strikers' political demands were rejected. Among these was the proposal that the Supreme Soviet should convene in emergency session to discuss the strikers' demands. Some 200,000 workers were estimated to have taken part in a second general strike on 23 April in protest at the refusal to recall the Byelorussian Supreme Soviet.

The Supreme Soviet, which was still dominated by members of the CPB, eventually convened in May 1991. Although it rejected the workers' political demands, the power of the conservative CPB was threatened by increased dissent within the Party. In June 33 deputies joined the opposition as a 'Communists for Democracy' faction.

The Byelorussian leadership did not strongly oppose the attempted coup of August 1991. The Presidium of the Supreme Soviet issued a neutral statement, on the last day of the coup, but the Central Committee of the CPB issued a statement unequivocally supporting the coup. After the coup collapsed an extraordinary session of the Supreme Soviet was convened. Nikolai Dementei (Mikolai Dzemyantsei), the Chairman of the Supreme Soviet and republican head of state, was forced to resign. He was replaced by Stanislau Shushkevich, a respected centrist politician, until elections to the office could be held. In addition, the Supreme Soviet agreed to nationalize all Party property, to prohibit Party activities in law-enforcement agencies, and to suspend the CPB, pending an investigation into its role in the coup. On 25 August the parliament voted to grant constitutional status to the Declaration of State Sovereignty, adopted in July 1990, and declared the political and economic independence of Byelorussia.

On 19 September 1991 the Supreme Soviet voted to rename the Byelorussian SSR the Republic of Byelarus. The Supreme Soviet also elected Stanislau Shushkevich as Chairman of the Supreme Soviet, after several rounds of voting. In October Shushkevich demonstrated his strong support for the continuation of some type of union, by signing the Treaty of the Economic Community, on 19 October, and, in November, by agreeing to the first draft of the Treaty on the Union of Sovereign States. However, his moderate approach was criticized by many opposition deputies, who demanded the resignation of the Government, which was still dominated by CPB members, new elections to the Supreme Soviet and the holding of presidential elections in the near future. On 8 December 1991 Shushkevich signed the Minsk Agreement, with the Russian and Ukrainian Presidents, establishing a new Commonwealth of Independent States (CIS). On 21 December the leaders of 11 former Soviet Republics, including the original signatories of the Slavic Republics, confirmed this decision by the Alma-Ata Declaration. The proposal that the capital of the CIS should be in Minsk was widely welcomed in the Republic as a means of attracting Western political and economic interest in Byelorussia.

Economy

Byelorussia has relatively few natural resources, although there are small deposits of petroleum and coal and important peat reserves. Machine-building and metal-working are the most important industries. Products include automobiles, heavy-duty vehicles, tractors, and industrial and agricultural machinery. Light industry concentrates on textiles and the production of consumer goods, including radio and television receivers.

The most important agricultural crops are potatoes, rye, wheat, barley, oats and sugar beet. Large areas of agricultural land are still unused after being contaminated as a consequence of the accident at the Chernobyl nuclear power station.

In 1988 Byelorussian net material product (NMP) amounted to 4.2% of total Soviet NMP, including 4.0% of total Soviet industrial NMP and 4.9% of total agricultural NMP. In that year 69.6% of Byelorussian NMP derived from exports to other Republics, the highest proportion of any Republic, while 6.5% of NMP came from exports to other countries. A programme of economic reform was being drawn up in late 1991, including extensive price liberalization and privatization. A national monetary unit, to be known as the Taler, was expected to be introduced during 1992.

Statistical Survey
Population

BIRTHS AND DEATHS (per 1,000)

	1987	1988	1989
Birth rate	16.1	16.1	15.0
Death rate	9.9	10.1	10.1

Agriculture

PRINCIPAL CROPS ('000 metric tons)

	1987	1988	1989
Grain	9,281	6,922	8,509
Sugar beet.	1,484	1,585	1,810
Flax fibre	126	86	87
Potatoes	11,755	7,708	11,097
Other vegetables . . .	927	880	894
Fruit (incl. grapes). . .	178	261	494

LIVESTOCK ('000 head at 1 January)

	1988	1989	1990
Cattle	7,364	7,271	7,176
Pigs	5,095	5,134	5,204
Sheep and goats . . .	615	570	510
Poultry	45,100	47,471	50,000

LIVESTOCK PRODUCTS ('000 metric tons)

	1987	1988	1989
Meat (slaughter weight) . .	1,108	1,180	1,195
Milk	7,254	7,460	7,419
Eggs (million)	3,495	3,572	3,651

Mining and Industry

Production (1989, unless otherwise stated): Peat 2,341,000 tons, Crude petroleum 1,500,000 tons, Natural gas 300m. cu m, Synthetic fibres 450,000 tons, Paper 204,000 tons, Cement 2,283,000 tons, Crude steel 1,105,000 metric tons, Metal-cutting lathes 14,800, Lorries 35,419 (1975), Tractors 101,300, Television receivers 1,102,000, Electric energy 38,500m. kWh.

Education

(1989/90)

	Institutions	Students
Secondary schools	2,611	1,331,200
Secondary specialized institutions . .	145	147,100
Higher schools (incl. universities) . .	33	189,400

Directory
The Government
(December 1991)

HEAD OF STATE
Chairman of the Supreme Soviet: STANISLAU SHUSHKEVICH.

COUNCIL OF MINISTERS

Chairman: VYACHESLAU F. KEBICH.

First Deputy Prime Minister: MIKHAIL MYASNIKOVICH.

Deputy Prime Minister (with responsibility for construction): STANISLAU BRYL.

Deputy Prime Minister (with responsibility for science, education, culture and social issues): MIKHAIL DZIAMCHUK.

Deputy Prime Minister (with responsibility for trade): ULADZIMIER ZALAMAY.

Deputy Prime Minister (with responsibility for agriculture): ALAKSEY SHAKOVICH.

Deputy Prime Minister (with responsibility for the economy and planning): SIARHEY LINH.

Minister of Agriculture and Food: FIODAR MIRACHYTSKY.

Minister of Communications: IVAN HRYTSUK.

Minister of Construction: MIKALAI NAVITSKI.

Minister of Construction and Utilization of Roads: STANISLAU YAKUTA.

Minister of Culture: YAUHEN VAYTOVICH.

Minister of Defence: Col-Gen. PETR CHAUS.

Minister of External Economic Relations: ULADZIMIER YAHORAY.

Minister of Finance: STSYAPAN YANCHUK.

Minister of Foreign Affairs: PYATRO KRAUCHANKA.

Minister of Health: VASIL KAZAKOU.

Minister of Housing: BARYS BATURA.

Minister of Internal Affairs: ULADZMIER YAHORAU.

Minister of Light Industry: MIKALAY HULIYEU.

Minister of Transport: ULADZIMIER BARODZIC.

Chairmen of State Committees

Chairman of the State Committee on the Aftermath of the Chernobyl Nuclear Power Station Disaster: IVAN KENIK.

Chairman of the State Committee for Ecology: ANATOL DARAFIEIEU.

Chairman of the State Committee for Labour and Social Protection: HEORHY BADZIEY.

Chairman of the State Committee for the Press: ANATOL BUTEVICH.

Chairman of the State Committee for Privatization: VALERY MATSIUSHEUSKY.

Chairman of the State Committee for Sport: ULADZIMIER RYZHANKOU.

Chairman of the State Security Committee: EDUARD SHYRKOUSKY.

MINISTRIES AND STATE COMMITTEES

Ministries

The Council of Ministers of the Republic of Byelarus: 220010 Minsk, Government House.

Ministry of Agriculture and Food: Minsk, vul. Kirava 15; tel. (0172) 27-37-51.

Ministry of Communications: Minsk, Leninsky pr. 10; tel. (0172) 27-21-57.

Ministry of Construction: Minsk, vul. Myasnikova 39; tel. (0172) 27-26-42.

Ministry of Construction and Utilization of Roads: Minsk, vul. Myasnikova 29; tel. (0172) 20-86-94.

Ministry of Culture: Minsk, vul. Savietskaya 9; tel. (0172) 29-68-90.

Ministry of Defence: Minsk.

Ministry of External Economic Relations: 220010 Minsk, vul. Lenina 14; tel. (0172) 24-17-58.

Ministry of Finance: 220010 Minsk, Government House; tel. (0172) 29-61-37.

Ministry of Foreign Affairs: Minsk, Leninsky pr. 8; tel. (0172) 27-29-22.

Ministry of Health: Minsk, vul. Myasnikova 39; tel. (0172) 29-60-33.

Ministry of Housing: Minsk, vul. Bersana 16; tel. (0172) 20-15-45.

Ministry of Internal Affairs: Minsk, vul. Uryckaha 5; tel. (0172) 29-78-08.

Ministry of Light Industry: Minsk, vul K. Tsetkin 16; tel. (0172) 20-30-65.

Ministry of Transport: Minsk, vul. Valadarskaha 8; tel. (0172) 27-16-42.

State Committees

State Committee on the Aftermath of the Chernobyl Nuclear Power Station Disaster: 220010 Minsk, Government House; tel. (0172) 29-64-60.

State Committee for Ecology: Minsk, vul. Kalektarnaya 10; tel. (0172) 20-66-91.

State Committee for Labour and Social Protection: Minsk, pr. Masherava 23; tel. (0172) 23-45-21.

State Committee for the Press: Minsk, pr. Masherava 11; tel. (0172) 23-75-74.

State Committee for Privatization: Minsk, vul. Bersana 1; tel. (0172) 29-62-16.

State Committee for Sport: Minsk, vul. Kirava 8/2; tel. (0172) 27-72-37.

State Security Committee: Minsk, Leninsky pr. 17; tel. (0172) 29-94-01.

Legislature

SUPREME SOVIET

The Supreme Soviet is composed of 360 deputies. Its Chairman is the head of state, the *de facto* President of Byelorussia. Elections were held to the Supreme Soviet in March 1990. The majority of deputies elected were members of the Byelorussian Communist Party, but 27 members of the Byelorussian Popular Front were also elected. In June 1991 33 Communist deputies formed an opposition faction, Communists of Byelorussia for Democracy.

Supreme Soviet of the Republic of Byelarus: 220010 Minsk, Dom Urada; tel. (0172) 29-60-12.

Chairman: STANISLAU SHUSHKEVICH.

First Deputy Chairman: (vacant).

Political Organizations

The Communist Party of Byelorussia was suspended temporarily in August 1991, pending investigation into its role in the August coup.

Byelorussian Christian-Democratic Union (Byelaruskaya Khrystsiyanska-Demakratychnaya Zluchnasts): 220065, Minsk-65, POB 24; tel. (0172) 23-21-18.

Byelorussian Popular Front 'Adradzhenye'—BNF (Byelarusky Narodny Front 'Adradzhenye'): 220040 Minsk, POB 208; tel. (0172) 31-48-93; f. 1988; Sec. SERGEY NAUMCHIK; Chair. ZENYON PAZNYAK; 500,000 mems.

Byelorussian Peasant Party (Byelaruskaya Syalanskaya Partiya): 220108 Minsk-108, POB 333; tel. (0172) 77-96-31; f. 1990; advocates agricultural reforms; Leader YAIGEN M. LUGIN.

Byelorussian Social Democratic Group (Byelaruskaya Satsiyaldemokratychnaya Hramada): 220095 Minsk-95, POB 34; tel. (0172) 27-22-14; f. 1991; Leader MIKHAS TKACHOU.

National Democratic Party of Byelorussia (Natsyianal-Demokratychnaya Partiya Byelarusi): Minsk; tel. (0172) 36-99-72; Leader MIKOLA MIKHNOUSKI.

United Democratic Party of Byelorussia (Abyadnanaya Demokratychnaya Partiya Byelarusi): 220060 Minsk-60, POB 74; tel. (0172) 56-11-21; f. 1990; Leader MIKHAIL PLISKO.

Judicial System

Chairman of the Supreme Court: ULADZIMIER S. KARAVAY.

Procurator-General: MIKALAI IHNATOVICH.

Religion

CHRISTIANITY

The major denomination is the Orthodox Church, but there are an estimated 2m. adherents of the Roman Catholic Church. Of these, some 25% were ethnic Poles and there were a significant number of Uniates or 'Greek Catholics'. There is also a growing number of Baptist Churches. In 1990 there were 195 associated with the All-Union Council and 24 independent chapels.

The Roman Catholic Church

Although five Roman Catholic dioceses, embracing 455 parishes, had officially existed since the Second World War, none of them had a bishop. In 1989 a major reorganization of the structure of the Roman Catholic Church in Byelorussia took place. The dioceses of Minsk and Mogilev were merged to create an archdiocese, and two new dioceses were formed in Grodno and Pinsk. The Eastern-rite, or Uniate, Church was abolished in Byelorussia in 1839, but appeals have been made to the Pope for it to be re-established.

Archdiocese of Minsk and Mogilev: 231011 Grodno, vul. Krasnopartizanskaya 1, kv. 2; tel. (01522) 23-267; Archbishop KAZIMIERZ SWIATEK.

The Eastern Orthodox Church

In 1990 Byelorussia was designated an exarchate of the Russian Orthodox Church, thus creating the Byelorussian Orthodox Church.

ISLAM

There are small communities of ethnic Tatars, who are adherents of Islam.

The Press

In 1989 there were 216 officially-registered newspapers being published in Byelorussia, 131 of which were in Byelorussian. There were also 134 periodicals, 36 of which were in Byelorussian. In 1991 publications belonging to the Communist Party of Byelorussia were transferred to state control.

GOVERNMENT AGENCY

State Committee for the Press: see section on The Government (State Committees).

PRINCIPAL NEWSPAPERS

In Byelorussian except where otherwise stated.

Belorusskaya Niva (Byelorussian Cornfield): 220041 Minsk, Leninsky pr. 77; tel. (0172) 32-15-04; f. 1921; 5 a week; fmrly organ of the Cen. Cttee of the Byelorussian Communist Party and the Byelorussian Union of Agrarian Workers; in Russian; Editor L. K. TOLKACH.

Chyrvonaya Zmena (Red Rising Generation): 220041 Minsk, Leninsky pr. 77; tel. (0172) 32-13-54; f. 1921; weekly; fmrly organ of the Cen. Cttee of the Leninist Young Communist League of Byelorussia; Editor V. P. BELSKY.

Golas Radzimy (Voice of the Motherland): 220600 Minsk, Leninsky pr. 44; tel. (0172) 33-01-97; f. 1955; weekly; articles of interest to Byelorussians in other countries; Editor-in-Chief VASLAV G. MATSKEVICH.

Litaratura i Mastatstva (Literature and Art): 220600 Minsk, vul. Zakharova 19; tel. (0172) 33-24-61; f. 1932; weekly; publ. by the Ministry of Culture and the Union of Writers of Byelorussia; Editor MIKOLA S. GIL.

Narodnaya Hazeta (The People's Newspaper): 220010 Minsk, Dom Urada; tel. (0172) 29-65-50; f. 1990; organ of the Byelorussian Supreme Soviet; in Byelorussian and Russian; Editor I. P. SEREDICH.

Nabat: 220034 Minsk, vul. Frunze 5; tel. (0172) 20-39-04; f. 1990; publ. by the Byelorussian Socio-Ecological Union 'Chernobyl'; inter-republican newspaper; Editor VASIL YAKOVENKO.

Naviny (News): 220050 Minsk, vul. K. Marksa 25–79; tel. (0172) 27-06-04; f. 1990; organ of the Byelorussian Popular Front; Editor ALES SUSHA.

Sovetskaya Belorussiya (Soviet Byelorussia): 220041 Minsk, Leninsky pr. 77; tel. (0172) 32-02-64; f. 1927; 5 a week; fmrly organ of the Central Committee of the Byelorussian Communist Party, Supreme Soviet and Council of Ministers; in Russian; Editor ZINOVY K. PRIGODICH; circ. 595,000.

Svaboda (Freedom): 220045 Minsk, POB 17; tel. (0172) 34-22-95; fax (0172) 34-22-95; f. 1902; publ. restored 1990; weekly; independent; Editor-in-chief IHAR HERMYANCHUK.

Znamya Yunosti (Banner of Youth): 220041 Minsk, Leninsky pr. 79; tel. (0172) 32-81-11; f. 1938; 5 a week; fmrly organ of the Leninist Young Communist League of Byelorussia; in Russian; Editor A. V. KLASKOVSKY.

Zvyazda (Star): 220041 Minsk, Leninsky pr. 77; tel. (0172) 32-51-05; f. 1917 as *Zvezda*; 6 a week; organ of the Supreme Soviet and Council of Ministers; Editor V. B. NARKEVICH.

PRINCIPAL PERIODICALS

Byelarus (Byelorussia): 220034 Minsk, vul. Zakharova 19, tel. (0172) 33-20-01; f. 1930; monthly; publ. by the Polymya (Flame)

Publishing House; journal of the Union of Writers of Byelorussia; fiction and political essays; Editor-in-Chief A. A. SHABALIN.

Byarozka (Birch-tree): 220041 Minsk, Leninsky pr. 79; tel. (0172) 32-94-66; f. 1924; monthly; fmrly journal of the Leninist Young Communist League (Komsomol) and the Republican Council of the V. I. Lenin Pioneer Organization of Byelorussia; fiction; illustrated; for 10–15-year-olds; Editor-in-Chief V. V. ADAMCHIK.

Krynitsa (Spring): 220807 Minsk, vul. Kiseleva 11; tel. (0172) 36-61-42; f. 1988; monthly; fmrly publ. by the Leninist Young Communist League of Byelorussia; political and literary; in Byelorussian and Russian; Editor V. P. NEKLYAEV.

Maladosts (Youth): 220041 Minsk, Leninsky pr. 79; tel. (0172) 31-85-43; f. 1953; monthly; journal of the Union of Writers of Byelorussia; novels, short stories, essays, translations, etc., for young people; Editor-in-Chief A. S. GRACHANIKOV.

Mastatstva Byelarusi (Art of Byelorussia): Minsk 220600 Minsk, vul. Frantsyshka Skaryny 15A; monthly; illustrated; tel. (0172) 39-59-37; Editor-in-chief ANATOL SMOLSKI.

Narodnaya Asveta (People's Education): 220023 Minsk, Makaenka 12; tel. (0172) 64-62-68; f. 1924; publ. by the Ministry of Education; Editor-in-chief N. I. KALESNIK.

Neman (The River Nieman): 220005 Minsk, Leninsky pr. 39; tel. (0172) 33-14-61; f. 1960; monthly; publ. by the Polymya (Flame) Publishing House; journal of the Union of Writers of Byelorussia; fiction; in Russian; Editor-in-Chief A. P. KUDRAVETS.

Politichesky Sobesednik (Political Speaker): 220041 Minsk, Leninsky pr. 79; tel. (0172) 32-35-94; f. 1932; monthly; fmrly publ. by the Communist Party of Byelorussia; political; in Russian; Editor NIKOLAI D. ASTANEVICH; circ. 20,000.

Polymya (Flame): 220600 Minsk, vul. Zakharova 19; tel. (0172) 33-20-12; f. 1922; monthly; publ. by the Polymya (Flame) Publishing House; journal of the Union of Writers of Byelorussia; fiction; Editor-in-Chief S. I. ZAKONNIKOV.

Rabotnitsa i Syalyanka (Woman Worker and Woman Peasant): 220041 Minsk, Leninsky pr. 77; tel. (0172) 32-38-14; f. 1924; monthly; fmrly journal of the Cen. Cttee of the Byelorussian Communist Party; popular political and literary journal for women; Editor-in-Chief M. I. KARPENKO.

Vozhyk (Hedgehog): 220041 Minsk, Leninsky pr. 79; tel. (0172) 32-01-23; f. 1941; fortnightly; fmrly publ. by the Cen. Cttee of the Byelorussian Communist Party; satirical; Editor-in-Chief VALENTIN B. BOLTAN.

Vyaselka (Rainbow): 220048 Minsk, vul. Kollektornaya 10; tel. (0172) 20-92-61; f. 1957; monthly; fmrly journal of the Cen. Cttee of the Leninist Young Communist League and the Republican Council of the V. I. Lenin Pioneer Organization of Byelorussia; popular, for 5–10-year-olds; Editor-in-Chief V. S. LIPSKY; circ. 115,000.

NEWS AGENCY

BelTA (Byelorussian News Agency): Minsk, vul. Kirava 26; tel. (0172) 27-19-92; fax (0172) 27-13-46; Dir YAKAU ALAKSEYCHYK.

Publishers

In 1989 there were 2,980 titles (books and pamphlets) published in Byelorussia (59m. copies), of which 439 (9.4m. copies) were in Byelorussian.

Byelarus (Byelorussia Publishing House): 220600 Minsk, pr. Masherova 11; tel. (0172) 23-77-34; telex 252964; fax (0172) 20-91-25; f. 1921; political, medical and musical literature, art reproductions; Dir V. L. DUBOVSKY.

Belorusskaya Sovetskaya Entsiklopediya (Byelorussian Soviet Encyclopaedia): 220072 Minsk, vul. F. Skaryny 15A; tel. (0172) 39-47-67; f. 1967; encyclopaedias, dictionaries and reference books; Editor-in-Chief I. P. SHAMYAKIN.

Izdatelstvo Tsentralnovo Komiteta Kommunisticheskoi Partii Belorussii (Publishing House of the Byelorussian Communist Party): 220041 Minsk, Leninsky pr. 79; tel. (0172) 32-21-18; telex 252182; fax (0172) 31-91-15; f. 1950; transferred to state control in 1991; Dir B. A. KUTOVOY.

Mastatskaya Litaratura (Fiction Publishing House): 220600 Minsk, pr. Masherova 11; tel. (0172) 23-48-09; f. 1972; Dir V. GRISHANOVICH.

Narodnaya Asveta (People's Education Publishing House): 220600 Minsk, pr. Masherova 11; tel. (0172) 23-48-09; f. 1972; school textbooks and teaching aids; Dir V. N. GRISHANOVICH.

Navuka i Tekhnika (Science and Technology Publishing House): 220067 Minsk, Zhodinskaya 18; tel. (0172) 63-76-18; f. 1924; books on science and technology; in Byelorussian and Russian; Dir F. I. SAVITSKY.

Polymya (Flame Publishing House): 220600 Minsk, pr. Masherova 11; tel. (0172) 23-52-85; f. 1950; books on domestic science, sport, leisure activities, cars and radios, catalogues, calendars and magazines; Dir M. A. IVANOVICH.

Universitetskae (University Publishing House): 220048 Minsk, pr. Masherova 11; tel. (0172) 23-58-51; f. 1967; general scientific and reference; Dir V. K. KASKO.

Uradzhai (Harvest Publishing House): 220600 Minsk, pr. Masherova 11; tel. (0172) 23-64-94; f. 1961; books and booklets on agriculture; in Byelorussian and Russian; Dir G. P. ZDANOVICH.

Vysheyshaya Shkola (Higher School Publishing House): 220048 Minsk, pr. Masherova 11; tel. (0172) 23-54-15; f. 1954; textbooks and science books for higher educational institutions; Dir A. A. ZHADAN.

Yunatstva (Youth Publishing House): 220600 Minsk, pr. Masherova 11; tel. (0172) 23-24-30; fax (0172) 26-66-16; f. 1981; children's books; Dir V. A. LUKSHA.

Radio and Television

Byelorussian Television: 220807 Minsk, vul. A. Makayenka 9; tel. (0172) 33-45-01; telex 152267; fax (0172) 64-81-82; f. 1956; Chair. A. G. STOLYAROV.

Radio Minsk: 220807 Minsk, vul. Krasnaya 4; tel. (0172) 33-88-75; fax (0172) 36-66-43.

Finance

(cap. = capital)

BANKING

State Bank

National Bank of the Republic of Byelarus: 220010 Minsk, Leninsky pr. 20; tel. (0172) 27-09-46; Chair. ULADZIMIER BAHDAN-KEVICH; First Dep. Chair. NIKOLAY A. KUZMICH.

Other Banks

Byelorussian Industrial Innovation Bank: 220048 Minsk, vul. Khoruzhey 31A; tel. (0172) 34-63-52; telex 252268; fax (0172) 34-01-35; wide range of financial services to small businesses and joint-ventures; subsidiaries in Gomel, Vitebsk, Soligorsk and Obninsk; Chair. SERGEY A. KOSTYUCHENKO.

Commercial Bank of Byelorussia: 22050 Minsk, vul. Bersana 16; tel. (0172) 20-35-38; fax (0172) 20-35-38.

Minsk Commercial Bank (Micobank): 220121 Minsk, vul. Pritytskovo 56; tel. (0172) 575-57.

Minsk Innovation Bank: 220678 Minsk, B. Lunacharskovo 6; tel. (0172) 33-09-84.

Minskbusinessbank: Minsk, Kiselevskaya vul. 61A; tel. (0172) 34-98-93; f. 1990 by Minsk City Council; cap. 50m. roubles; Chair KAZIMIR TARUTA.

COMMODITY EXCHANGES

Gomel Regional Commodity & Raw Materials Exchange (GCME): 246000 Gomel, 16 vul. Sovetskaya; tel. (0232) 55-73-28; fax (0232) 55-70-07; f. 1991; Gen. Man. ANATOLY KUZILEVICH.

Belagroprambirzha (Byelorussian Agro-Industrial Exchange): Minsk, vul. Kazintsa 86, kor. 2; tel. (0172) 77-07-26; telex 25-22-96; fax (0172) 77-30-80; trade in agricultural products, supplies and equipment.

Byelorussian Universal Exchange (BUE): 220099 Minsk, Kazintsa vul. 4; tel. (0172) 78-11-21; fax (0172) 78-85-16; f. 1991; Pres. VLADIMIR SHEPEL.

Trade and Industry

CHAMBER OF COMMERCE

Chamber of Commerce and Industry of the Republic of Byelarus: 220843 Minsk, vul. Ya. Kolasa 65; tel. (0172) 66-04-60; brs in Brest and Gomel; Chair. ULADZIMIER K. LESUN.

AGRICULTURAL AND INDUSTRIAL ORGANIZATIONS

Byelorussian Peasants' Union (Syalansky Sayuz): 220199 Minsk, vul. Brestskaya 64/327; tel. (0172) 77-99-93; Chair. KASTUS YARMOLENKA.

Union of Enterpreneurs and Farmers: 200079 Minsk, POB 257; tel. (0172) 20-16-16; Pres. MARK KUNIAUSKY.

Union of Small Ventures: Minsk, vul. Bersana 1; tel. (0172) 20-92-70; Chair. VIKTAR DROZD.

FOREIGN TRADE ORGANIZATION

Byelorusintorg: 220084 Minsk, vul. Kollektornaya 10; tel. (0172) 29-63-08; telex 220010; import and export of consumer goods; Gen. Dir VIKTOR V. ANDRYUSHIN.

MAJOR INDUSTRIAL ENTERPRISES

Bobruiskshinaeksport: 213824 Bobruisk, Minskoe shosse; tel. (02251) 35-065; telex 252167; fax (02251) 35-068; manufactures tyres for domestic and industrial use; Dir VIKTAR V. ALEKSEYEV; 1,000 employees.

Boridovdrev: 222120 Borisov, 1840 Let Vlksm; tel. (01777) 3-16-53; telex 252299; wood products; Gen. Dir ALAKSEY G. LIVSHITS; 4,000 employees.

Brest Electric Lamp Co: Brest, Moskovskaya vul. 204; tel. (01622) 20-530; telex 229113; manufactures electric incandescent lamps for automobiles and medical use; Dir ANATOLY M. SOLOGUB; 4,500 employees.

Brest Gas Apparatus Factory: 224663 Brest, Ordzhonikidze 22; tel. (01622) 64-152; telex 229114; design and manufacture of domestic gas appliances; Dir MIKHAIL F. IOFFE; 2,014 employees.

Dolomit Industrial Association: 211321 Vitebsk, ul. Tsentralnaya 23; tel. 91-52-36; produces dolomite fertilizer; Gen. Dir M. YA. CHUMANIKHINA.

Dormash: 220736 Minsk, vul. Ponomarenko 7; tel. (0172) 51-02-00; telex 252196; fax (0172) 51-64-55; manufactures road construction machinery, including front loaders and road rollers; Gen. Dir VASILY M. SHLYNDIKOV; 4,500 employees.

Eleventh State Bearing Plant: 220830 Minsk, vul. Yelunovich 2; tel. (0172) 451052; telex 252176; fax (0172) 45-15-14; production of ball and roller bearings; Man. ANATOLY V. ZINKEVICH; 9,000 employees.

Gomel Machine Tool Production Group: 246640 Gomel, vul. Internatsionalnoy 10; tel. (0232) 52-32-62; telex 252117; fax (0232) 53-04-98; production of metal-cutting machine tools; Gen. Dir G. KAZAKOV; 2,600 employees.

Kamerton Plant: 225710 Pinsk, Brestskaya vul. 137; tel. (01653) 415-80; telex 229662; manufactures electronic wrist-watches and pedometers; Gen. Dir NIKOLAI S. PASS; 2,500 employees.

Minsk Chemical Plant: 220600 Minsk, vul. Serova 8; tel. (0172) 77-19-14; produces a wide range of chemicals; Dir V. P. KORSHUNOV.

Minsk Motor Factory: 220829 Minsk-70, Vaupshasov vul. 4; tel. (0172) 44-11-24; telex 252282; fax (0172) 44-31-88; design and manufacture of diesel engines; Gen. Dir IVAN YA. VOROBEV; 8,000 employees.

Minsk Motorcycle and Bicycle Factory: 220765 Minsk, Partizansky pr. 8; tel. (0172) 21-68-18; telex 252964; fax (0172) 21-68-06; design and manufacture of small motorcycles and a range of bicycles; Gen. Dir KONSTANTIN A. USTYMCHUK; 6,500 employees.

Mogilev Textile Factory: 212781 Mogilev, vul. Grishina 87; tel. (0222) 23-13-12; telex 252263; produces a wide range of textiles; Gen. Dir VLADIMIR SEMYONOV; 60,000 employees.

Mogilevselmash (Mogilev Agricultural Machinery Plant): 212030 Mogilev; tel. (0222) 24-38-31; telex 252207; agricultural machinery, including front-end loaders and trailers; Dir VALERY CHERTKOV; 4,000 employees.

Spinning and Knitting Production Association: Brest obl., 225710 Pinsk, Pervomaiskaya vul. 159; tel. (01653) 2-32-39; telex 229660; knitted products, wool and acrylic yarn; Gen. Dir V. A. NAIDENKO; 7,800 employees.

Pinskdrev Industrial Woodworking Association: Brest obl., 225710 Pinsk, Chuklaya vul. 1; tel. (01653) 2-50-34; telex 229110; fax (01653) 2-50-34; produces industrial and domestic furniture, matches; Gen. Dir LORAN S. ARINICH; 4,200 employees.

Vitebsk Grinding Machines' Works: 210618 Vitebsk, pr. Frunze 83; tel. 4-10-37; manufactures specialized machines for grinding metal-cutting tools; produces spare parts and consumer goods; Man. Dir YEVGENY KISELEV; 3,000 employees.

Transport

RAILWAYS

At 31 December 1989 the total length of rail lines in use was 5,590 km. There is an underground railway in Minsk, the Minsk Metro.

In 1991 plans were announced for the expansion of the Metro, beginning in 1993.

ROADS

At 31 December 1989 the total length of roads in Byelorussia was 265,600 km, of which 227,000 km were hard-surfaced.

Culture

NATIONAL ORGANIZATION

Ministry of Culture: see section on The Government (Ministries).

CULTURAL HERITAGE

Byelorussian Humanities Centre: 220050 Minsk, vul. Karala 16A; f. 1990; promotes the study of Byelorussian culture and language.

Byelorussian State Art Museum: Minsk, vul. Lenina 20; f. 1939; 20,000 exhibits; Dir YURY A. KARACHUN.

Byelorussian State Museum: Minsk, vul. Marksa 12; over 250,000 exhibits on the history of the Byelorussian people; library; Dir I. P. ZAGRISHEV.

Grodno State Historical Museum: Grodno, vul. Zamkovaya 22; 90,000 exhibits.

State Public Library of Byelorussia: 220636 Minsk, Krasnoarmeiskaya vul. 9; tel. (0172) 22-54-63; telex 252316; f. 1922; over 7m. vols; Dir G. N. OLEINIK.

SPORTING ORGANIZATION

State Committee for Sport: see section on The Government (State Committees).

PERFORMING ARTS

Byelorussian Bolshoy Opera and Ballet Theatre: Minsk, pl. Parizhskoy Komuny.

Byelorussian State Theatrical and Art Institute: 220012 Minsk, Leninsky pr. 81; tel. (0172) 32-15-42; f. 1945; training in drama, arts and applied arts; Rector E. P. GERASIMOVICH.

Gorky Russian Drama Theatre: Minsk, vul. Volodarskovo 5.

Kupala Byelorussian Drama Theatre: Minsk, vul. Engelsa 7.

Byelorussian Philharmonia: Minsk, Leninsky pr. 60.

Byelorussian State Puppet Theatre: Minsk, Leninsky pr. 23.

ASSOCIATIONS

Byelorussian Cultural Fund: 220030 Minsk, vul. Yanki Kupaly 17/30; tel. (0172) 29-34-30; Pres. IVAN CHYHRYNAY.

Byelorussian Rerykhau Fund: 220050 Minsk-50, POB 177; tel. (0172) 23-07-40.

Byelorussian World Association—Batskaushchyna (Fatherland): 220048 Minsk, vul. Sukhaya 4; tel. (0172) 23-66-21; develops contacts with the Byelorussian diaspora.

Francis Skaryna Byelorussian Language Society: 220005 Minsk, vul. Rumyantsava 13; tel. (0172) 33-25-11.

Theatrical Union: Minsk, vul. Kisyalova 13/6; tel. (0172) 36-69-82; Chair. MIKALAI YAROMENKA.

Union of Artists: Minsk, vul. K. Marksa 8; tel. (0172) 27-37-23; Chair. HIENADZ BURALKIN.

Union of Cinematographers: Minsk, vul. K. Marksa 5; tel. (0172) 27-04-61.

Union of Composers: Minsk, plats Svabody 5; tel. (0172) 23-45-47; Chair. IHAR LUCHANOK.

Union of Journalists: 220034 Minsk, vul. Rumyantsava 3; tel. (0172) 36-51-95; Chair. LAVON YEKEL.

Union of Writers of Byelorussia: 220034 Minsk, vul. Frunze 5; tel. (0172) 36-00-12; Chair. VASIL ZUYONAK.

Education

In response to public demand, in the early 1990s the Government began to introduce greater provision for education in the Byelorussian language and more emphasis on Byelorussian, rather than Soviet or Russian, history and literature. Following the adoption of Byelorussian as the official language, all pupils were to be taught Byelorussian from primary school level onwards. In 1988 79.2% of pupils were taught in Russian, compared with 65.0% in 1980. In 1989/90 there were 189,400 students studying at 33

higher education institutions, including three universities, four Polytechnic Institutes and several colleges specializing in technical or agricultural sciences. Research is co-ordinated by the Byelorussian Academy of Sciences (see section on Environment, below).

UNIVERSITIES

Byelorussian State University: 220080 Minsk, Leninsky pr. 4; tel. (0172) 20-94-15; f. 1921; 13 faculties, 4 institutes; 1,370 teachers; 17,600 undergraduate students, 1,000 postgraduate students; Rector L. I. KISELEVSKY.

Gomel State University: 246699 Gomel, Sovetskaya vul. 104; tel. (0232) 57-11-15; f. 1969; 8 faculties; 500 teachers; 7,000 students; Rector B. V. BOKUT.

Grodno State University: 230023 Grodno, vul. Ozheshko 22; tel. (01522) 70-173; f. 1978; 7 faculties; 6,200 students.

Social Welfare

GOVERNMENT AGENCIES

Byelorussian Children's Fund: Minsk, vul. Kamunistychnaya 2; tel. (0172) 36-62-67; Chair. ULADZIMIER LIPSKY.

Ministry of Health: see section on The Government (Ministries).

State Committee on Labour and Social Protection: see section on The Government (State Committees).

HEALTH AND WELFARE ORGANIZATIONS

Chernobyl Children's Fund: Minsk, vul. Staravilenskaya 14; tel. (0172) 34-21-53; fax (0172) 34-34-58; charity fund to aid the victims of the Chernobyl disaster; Chair. HYENADZ HRUSHAVY.

Children of Chernobyl: 220082 Minsk, pr. Pushkina 47/89; tel. (0172) 55-01-13; fax (0172) 55-01-13; aids children affected by Chernobyl disaster, by supplying medicines, medical equipment and funding treatment in other countries; Chair. VALERY BUYVAL.

The Environment

In 1990 Byelorussia declared itself an ecological disaster area and claimed that 2m. people lived in areas contaminated by radioactive matter, released as a result of the Chernobyl disaster. The Chernobyl nuclear power station is situated in Ukraine, very close to the Byelorussian border. When an explosion occurred, in April 1986, the radioactive discharge was carried by the prevailing winds across southern and western Byelorussia. In 1990 700m. roubles were assigned to overcoming the consequences of the disaster and more than 50,000 people were resettled.

GOVERNMENT ORGANIZATIONS

State Committee on the Aftermath of the Chernobyl Nuclear Power Station Disaster: see section on The Government (State Committees).

State Committee on Ecology: see section on The Government (State Committees).

ACADEMIC INSTITUTES

Academy of Sciences: 220041 Minsk, Leninsky pr. 66; tel. (0172) 39-48-01; telex 252277; f. 1929; Pres. ULADZIMIER P. PLATONAU; institutes incl.:

Institute of the Problems of the Use of Natural Resources and Ecology: 220114 Minsk, Staroborisovsky trakt 10; tel. (0172) 64-26-31; f. 1932; in the Dept of Chemical and Geological Sciences; environmental research; Dir I. I. LISHTVAN.

NON-GOVERNMENTAL ORGANIZATIONS

'Belovezhskaya Pushcha' Museum: Brest obl., Belovezhskaya Puscha Game Preserve; works to preserve the almost extinct European bison; Dir V. S. ROMANOV.

Byelorussian Ecological Union: 220030 Minsk, vul. Lenina 15A; tel. (0172) 27-87-96; unites various groups concerned with environmental issues.

Green Party of Byelorussia: Minsk; active environmentalist political party.

Socio-Ecological Union 'Chernobyl': Minsk, 220034 Minsk, vul. Frunze 5; tel. (0172) 20-39-04; campaigns on ecological issues; Chair. VASIL YAKORENKO.

KAZAKHSTAN

Geography

The Republic of Kazakhstan (until December 1991, the Kazakh SSR) is the second largest of the former Soviet Republics, extending some 1,900 km (1,200 miles) from the Volga river in the west to the Altai mountains in the east, and about 1,300 km (800 miles) from the Siberian plain in the north to the Central Asian deserts in the south. Western geographers consider Kazakhstan to be the northernmost of five Central Asian republics, but Soviet geographers, for historical reasons, do not include it in their concept of Central Asia. To the south it borders the Republics of Turkmenistan, Uzbekistan and Kyrgyzstan. To the east there is an international frontier with the People's Republic of China. There is a long border in the north with the Russian Federation and a 2,320 km coastline on the Caspian Sea in the south-west. The total area is 2,717,300 sq km (1,049,155 sq miles), over four-fifths the size of India (but with only 2% of the population).

The relief is extremely varied. Lowlands account for more than one-third of the territory, mountainous regions cover nearly one-fifth and hilly plains and plateaus occupy the rest of the Republic. The Western regions are dominated by the lowlands of the Caspian Depression, which is drained by the River Ural. To the east of the western lowlands is the vast Turan plain, much of which is sparsely inhabited desert. The flat north-central regions are the beginning of the West Siberian plain; to the south of the plain are the hilly uplands of central Kazakhstan. On the eastern and south-eastern borders there are high mountain ranges. The major rivers are the Irtysh, which rises in the north-east of the Republic and flows north, across Siberia, and empties into the Arctic Ocean; the Ural, in the west, which flows south into the Caspian Sea; and the Syr-Dar'ya, which rises in the Tien Shan mountain range and empties into the Aral Sea. The waters of the Syr-Dar'ya have been extensively used for irrigation, causing serious desiccation of the Aral Sea, the northern part of which is in Kazakhstan.

The climate is of a strongly continental type but there are wide variations throughout the territory. Average temperatures in January range from −18°C (0°F) in the north to −3°C (27°F) in the south. In July average temperatures are 19°C (66°F) in the north and 28°–30°C (82°–86°F) in the south. Levels of precipitation are equally varied. Average annual rainfall in mountainous regions reaches 1,600 mm, whereas in the central desert areas it is less then 100 mm.

According to the census of 1989, at which the total population was 16,538,000, Kazakhs formed the largest ethnic group in the Republic, with 39.7% of the population, but they were only slightly more numerous than the Russians (37.8%), who had formed a majority of the population at the 1979 census. Other major ethnic groups are Germans (5.8%) and Ukrainians (5.4%). There are also Tatars and small numbers of Uighurs, Koreans (deported from the Soviet Far East in the late 1930s) and Dungans (Chinese Muslims who migrated to Russian-held territory after the anti-Manzhou Muslim uprising of 1862–77). Kazakh, a member of the Central Turkic group of languages, replaced Russian as the official language in September 1989. Since 1940 it has been written in the Cyrillic script. A Latin script was used until 1940, the traditional Arabic script having been replaced in 1929. The predominant religion is Islam; most Kazakhs are Sunni Muslims of the Hanafi school. Other ethnic groups have their own religious communities, notably the (Christian) Eastern Orthodox Church, which is attended mainly by Slavs.

The total population at 1 January 1991 was estimated to be 16,793,000. The large areas of desert account for the low population density of 6.2 persons per sq km in 1991. In 1989 57% of the population lived in urban areas. The capital, Alma-Ata, had an estimated population of 1,151,300 in January 1990. It is situated in the extreme south-east of the Republic, near the border with Kyrgyzstan. Other important towns include Petropavlovsk, near the border with the Russian Federation, and Karaganda, an industrial city in central Kazakhstan.

History

The Kazakhs are descended from Mongol and Turkic tribes which settled in the area in about the first century BC. They emerged as a distinct ethnic group from a tribal confederation known as Kazakh Orda, which was formed in the late 15th century AD. Following the dissolution of the Kazakh Orda, in the early 17th century, the Kazakhs split into smaller nomadic groups, which were united in three large federations, or Hordes, known as the Larger, Middle and Lesser Hordes. In the first half of the 18th century, as a result of invasions from the east by the Oirot Mongols, the three Hordes sought protection from the Russian Tsar. Although the threat from the Oirots was ended, after they were conquered by the Manzhous (Manchus) in 1758, the Russians retained control over the Kazakhs, and deposed the Khans (leaders) of the Hordes. Following the abolition of serfdom in Russia, in 1861, many Russian and Ukrainian peasants moved to Kazakhstan and were granted Kazakh lands. Resentment against Russian immigration led to disaffection with Russian rule, and in 1916 a major rebellion against Russian rule was brutally repressed, with some 150,000 people killed.

After the February Revolution and the Bolshevik *coup d'etat* in 1917, there was civil war throughout Kazakhstan, Bolshevik forces finally overcame those of the anti-Bolshevik White Army (led by Denikin), foreign interventionists and local nationalists (led by the Alash Orda party). On 26 August 1920 the Kirghiz Autonomous Soviet Socialist Republic (ASSR—until the mid-1920s the Kazakhs were known to the Russians as Kirghiz, to distinguish them from the unrelated Cossacks) was created within the Russian Soviet Federative Socialist Republic (RSFSR—the Russian Federation). As a result of the National Delimitation of Central Asia, in 1924–25, the Kirghiz ASSR was enlarged by the inclusion of certain Kazakh-populated territories originally belonging to the Turkestan Republic (Turkestan covered much of the area now occupied by the four other Central Asian Republics). In 1925 the Kirghiz ASSR was renamed the Kazakh ASSR. The Karakalpak region was detached from the Kazakh ASSR in 1932; it became an Autonomous Republic within the Uzbek SSR in 1936. On 5 December 1936 the Kazakh ASSR became a full Union Republic, the Kazakh Soviet Socialist Republic (SSR).

Under Soviet rule, parts of Kazakhstan were heavily industrialized, and communications and infrastructure were greatly improved. However, Kazakhstan was one of the worst affected regions during the campaign to collectivize agriculture and settle nomadic peoples in the early 1930s. More than 1m. people are estimated to have died as a result of starvation. There was also severe repression from the 1930s onwards and Russian immigration was greatly increased. Peoples deported from the war-zone, during the Second World War (including Germans, Crimean Tatars and Caucasian peoples), were often sent to Kazakhstan, causing some resentment among the local inhabitants.

During Nikita Khrushchev's period in office large areas of previously uncultivated land in Kazakhstan were transformed into arable land under the 'Virgin Lands' scheme, a policy which resulted in serious ecological problems. Schemes such as the Virgin Lands, the nuclear testing sites in eastern Kazakhstan, the Baikonur space centre at Leninsk and the huge industrial sites in the north and east of Kazakhstan all attracted large numbers of ethnic Russians to the Republic; the ethnic Russian proportion of the population rose from 19.7% in 1926 to 42.7% in 1959.

Mikhail Gorbachev's accession to power, in 1985, and his subsequent campaign against corruption, which involved replacing prominent allies of the late Soviet President Leonid Brezhnev with a new generation of officials, had serious consequences in Kazakhstan. In mid-December 1986 some 3,000 people took part in protests in Alma-Ata after Gennady Kolbin, an ethnic Russian, was appointed First Secretary of the Communist Party of Kazakhstan (CPK), replacing the prominent, if corrupt, Dinmukhamed Kunayev, an ethnic Kazakh. At least two people died and 200 were injured when the protesters were dispersed by police. Despite the protests Kolbin remained in office and dismissed many of Kunayev's former associates on charges of nepotism and bribe-taking.

As in other Republics, linguistic and environmental issues were the main subjects of public debate after the introduction of Gorbachev's policy of *glasnost*. Complaints about the lack of school instruction in the Kazakh language led to a decree issued in March 1987 which advocated improvements in the teaching of both Kazakh and Russian. In September 1989 the Supreme Soviet adopted legislation which established Kazakh as the official language of the Republic, while Russian remained a language of inter-ethnic communication. However, all officials dealing with the general public were to know both languages.

As a result of the intensive development of Kazakhstan's economy, the Republic suffered from serious environmental problems. Many of the unofficial groups which were established in the late 1980s were concerned with such issues as the effects of nuclear testing near Semipalatinsk, industrial pollution (particularly from Kazakhstan's chemical works) and the degradation of arable land as a result of over-intensive farming. The effects of nuclear tests at Semipalatinsk, in eastern Kazakhstan, caused particular anxiety; local residents complained of medical problems normally caused by exposure to excess radiation. The campaign to end nuclear testing was led by one of Kazakhstan's largest unofficial groups, Nevada-Semipalatinsk, which regularly organized large demonstrations in Alma-Ata. In 1991 the Kazakh President Nursultan Nazarbayev, announced that nuclear testing would not continue in Semipalatinsk after the end of the year. In mid-September 1990 an explosion in a factory making nuclear fuel in Ulba, in eastern Kazakhstan, led to the contamination of a large area by toxic gases, including the city of Ust-Kamenogorsk. Official estimates stated that up to 120,000 people could have been affected by the incident. Demonstrators demanded the closure of the plant and stricter controls on the city's many non-ferrous metallurgical works. Nazarbayev demanded that the area be declared an ecological disaster zone.

The introduction of Kazakh as the official language was opposed by many non-Kazakh residents. A local branch of the Russian nationalist organization, Yedinstvo, was established, and some members campaigned for annexation of Kazakhstan's northern regions by the Russian Federation. The publication, in September 1990, of the Russian author and ex-dissident Alexander Solzhenitsyn's proposal for the transfer of territory to Russia led to demonstrations by ethnic Kazakhs demanding the preservation of Kazakhstan's boundaries. Other instances of inter-ethnic conflict arose between Kazakhs and other national groups apparently as a result of high unemployment and economic hardship. In June 1989 a gang of Kazakh youths rioted in Novy Uzen, in south-western Kazakhstan, demanding that immigrant Lezghins and other Caucasian settlers in the area be expelled and their jobs given to locals. Five people were reported killed and 118 injured after several days of rioting and some 3,500 people fled the region. There were reports of further inter-ethnic violence in the region later in the year.

The elections to the all-Union Congress of People's Deputies, in March 1989, were conducted in traditional Soviet style, with only one candidate standing in most constituencies. In June 1989 Kolbin was transferred to Moscow and Nursultan Nazarbayev, an ethnic Kazakh, was appointed First Secretary of the CPK. Nazarbayev quickly established himself as a prominent politician in republican and all-Union affairs, who strongly supported economic reform while emphasizing the need for political stability. In September 1989 the political and administrative system in Kazakhstan was reformed: a full-time Supreme Soviet was to be established and elections were to be conducted on a multi-candidate basis. In addition, the state duties which were the responsibility of the First Secretary of the CPK were transferred to the office of Chairman of the Supreme Soviet. In February 1990 Nazarbayev was elected to this post. Elections to the new Supreme Soviet took place on 25 March 1990. Many candidates stood unopposed, the system of reserved seats for CPK-affiliated organizations was retained and the result was an overwhelming Communist majority when the Supreme Soviet first convened in April. Nazarbayev was elected to the newly-established post of President of Kazakhstan by the Supreme Soviet in the same month.

On 25 October 1990 a declaration of sovereignty was adopted by the Supreme Soviet, which asserted republican control over natural resources and the economy, but stressed the equality of all nationalities living in the Republic. Nevertheless, there were protests against the legislation in the predominantly Slav-populated town of Ust-Kamenogorsk; Kazakh nationalist groups considered the declaration too weak and also expressed their disapproval. Nazarbayev strongly supported the concept of a new Union Treaty and the Kazakh Government participated in the discussions on the Union Treaty in early 1991. However, Nazarbayev was also a strong advocate of economic sovereignty for Kazakhstan, where some 90% of enterprises were under all-Union control. When miners went on strike in Karaganda, in March 1991, demanding higher living conditions and more control over profits from their mines, Nazarbayev persuaded the all-Union authorities to transfer control of enterprises in Kazakhstan to the jurisdiction of the Kazakh Government, in order to satisfy the miners' demands.

Kazakhstan took part in the referendum on the future of the Union in March 1991, although Nazarbayev insisted that the republican referendum should be on the basis of a different question to that in other participating Republics. Voters were asked 'Do you consider it necessary to preserve the Union of Soviet Socialist Republics as a union of sovereign states with equal rights?'. Of those eligible to vote 88.2% did so, and 94.1% voted in favour of the proposal. In June 1991 the Kazakh Supreme Soviet voted to adopt a draft Union Treaty in principle, although Nazarbayev expressed reservations about certain aspects of the proposed federation.

Kazakhstan was to sign the new Union Treaty on 20 August 1991, but the event was forestalled by the attempted *coup d'état* in Moscow. Nazarbayev was initially cautious, advocating calm, without openly condemning the coup. On 20 August, however, he issued a statement which denounced the State Committee for the State of Emergency (SCSE) as illegal and harmful to economic and political progress. As the coup collapsed, Nazarbayev resigned from the Politburo and Central Committee of the CPSU, complaining of the open support granted to the SCSE leaders by the Party leadership. The same day the CPK was ordered to cease activities in state and government organs. Following the coup, Nazarbayev consolidated his position as the foremost non-Slav leader in the USSR, frequently meeting foreign leaders and playing a crucial role in the negotiations on establishing new relations between the former Soviet Republics.

Kazakhstan signed the Treaty of the Economic Community on 19 October 1991, and, in November, Nazarbayev agreed to a draft treaty of a new Union of Sovereign States. When these agreements were largely nullified by the proposed Commonwealth of Independent States, agreed by the three leaders of the Slavic Republics in December, Nazarbayev expressed an initial reluctance to participate in a new political formation which he had not been invited to negotiate. Nevertheless, on 13 December, together with the other Central Asian Republics, Kazakhstan agreed to join the new Commonwealth. It was formally recognized as a co-founder of the Commonwealth at the Alma-Ata meeting of 11 Republics, on 21 December.

Until December, when a declaration of independence was finally adopted (16 December) and the Republic finally changed its name to the Republic of Kazakhstan, dropping the 'Soviet' and 'Socialist' from the official title, Kazakhstan remained one of only two Republics which had not declared its independence from the USSR. Partly, Nazarbayev seemed intent on preserving the delicate inter-ethnic balance between Russians and Kazakhs and preventing further discussion of the cession of Kazakhstan's northern territories to the Russian Federation. Above all, it was seen as evidence, along with his determination to retain many of the personnel and structures of the CPK (although reformed as the Socialist Party of Kazakhstan) as the channel for economic policy in the Republic, of his view of economic reform as far more important than political reform. There was little political opposition to his policies, however, and he also gained popularity by finally being able to ban nuclear tests at the Semipalatinsk site, on 29 August (following the failure of the coup attempt). On 1 December 1991 he was the only candidate in elections to the presidency. He won 98.8% of the votes cast. Some 87.4% of the electorate took part.

In 1990 and 1991 Nazarbayev was active in establishing links with other Union Republics and with foreign states. In June 1990, at a meeting of the heads of all five Central Asian Republics in Alma-Ata, he outlined a proposal to increase economic, political and cultural co-operation in the region. The five Republics signed a co-operation agreement, which was reaffirmed at a further meeting in August 1991, at which an inter-republican council was established to oversee the implementation of agreements between the five Republics. Kazakhstan concluded a number of bilateral agreements with Union Republics outside Central Asia, including the Russian Federation and Ukraine. In 1990 and 1991 Nazarbayev visited the USA, Canada, the Republic of Korea, Turkey, the United Kingdom and other countries to attract foreign investment and establish direct economic and political contacts with foreign partners, and several foreign leaders and officials visited Kazakhstan.

Economy

Kazakhstan has a rich variety of natural resources, including major reserves of coal, iron ores, lead, zinc, copper and petroleum; their are also several rare metals and phosphates. The major coalfields are in the Karaganda, Turgay, Ekibastuz and Maykuben basins, while petroleum and natural gas reserves are found in the Caspian Depression and the Mangyshlak Peninsula. There are large areas of land available for agriculture. Principal crops include fruit, sugar beet, vegetables, potatoes, cotton and, most importantly, grain. However, in 1991 a severe drought affected the production of grain and other crops. The Republic is an important producer of meat for the region; sheep are also raised for their wool, and fishing is highly developed. Parts of the Republic are highly industrialized. Major industries are associated with the processing of raw materials, including metal-processing, fuel, power, chemical, machine-building, textiles and food-processing industries.

In 1988 Kazakhstan provided 4.3% of total Soviet net material product (NMP), including 2.5% of total industrial NMP and 6.1% of total agricultural NMP. Kazakhstan is relatively self-sufficient, with only 30.9% of its NMP derived from exports to other Republics, in 1988. In the same year 3.0% of NMP was earned from exports abroad.

In late 1990 President Nursultan Nazarbayev invited economists to prepare a radical economic reform programme for Kazakhstan. In October 1990 the Government announced a proposal for transition to a market economy, which included large-scale 'destatization' and privatization. A Supreme Economic Council, chaired by Nazarbayev and including prominent economists from other Republics and from the USA, was established to produce a detailed programme of privatization. In June 1991 the Supreme Soviet approved a draft of such a programme. Privatization was to proceed by distributing vouchers to citizens to enable them to purchase state property. It was also expected that a Kazakh currency would be introduced in 1992, to operate alongside the rouble. Such reforms gained added urgency, following the dramatic price reforms in the Russian Federation, in January 1992.

Statistical Survey

Source: Kazakh Soviet Encyclopaedia, Alma-Ata.

Population

BIRTHS AND DEATHS (per 1,000)

	1987	1988	1989
Birth rate	25.5	24.6	23.0
Death rate	7.5	7.7	7.6

Agriculture

PRINCIPAL CROPS ('000 metric tons)

	1987	1988	1989
Grain	27,444	22,560	20,356
Seed cotton	312	325	315.2
Sugar beet	1,804	1,312	1,118
Sunflower seed . . .	117	139	105
Potatoes	2,066	2,260	1,783
Other vegetables . . .	1,190	1,354	1,254
Grapes	141	94	48.2
Other fruit	209	276	118.2

LIVESTOCK ('000 head at 1 January)

	1988	1989	1990
Cattle	9,672.4	9,751.5	9,818.0
Pigs	3,237.2	3,187.9	3,264.2
Sheep and goats . . .	36,388.2	36,498.0	36,222.0

LIVESTOCK PRODUCTS ('000 metric tons)

	1987	1988	1989
Meat (slaughter weight) . .	1,399.2	1,493.1	1,573
Milk	5,185.2	5,321.0	5,562
Eggs (million)	4,189.3	4,201.8	4,253
Wool (greasy)	106.4	108.4	109.9

Mining and Industry

PRODUCTION

	1987	1988	1989
Electric power (million kWh) .	88,490	88,417	89,700
Petroleum (incl. gas condensate, '000 metric tons)	24,500	25,500	25,400
Coal ('000 metric tons) . .	142,100	143,000	138,400
Rolled ferrous metals ('000 metric tons) .	4,580	4,874	5,013
Iron ore ('000 metric tons) .	24,224	24,342	23,764
Mineral fertilizers ('000 metric tons) .	1,603	1,737	1,705
Plastics ('000 metric tons) .	194	182	203
Chemical fibres and thread ('000 metric tons) . .	23	22	21
Excavators (number) . . .	1,054	570	528
Bulldozers (number) . .	15,220	14,810	15,308

Education

(1989/90)

	Institutions	Students
Secondary schools	8,064	3,021,070
Secondary specialized schools . .	244	255,400
Higher schools (incl. universities) . .	55	285,600

Kazakhstan

Directory

The Government

(December 1991)

PRESIDENCY

President of the Republic of Kazakhstan: NURSULTAN A. NAZARBAYEV (elected 1 December 1991).

Vice-President: YERIK M. ASANBAYEV.

COUNCIL OF MINISTERS

Prime Minister: SERGEY TERESHCHENKO.

First Deputy Prime Minister: YE. G. YEZHIKOV-BABAKHANOV.

Deputy Prime Ministers: KALYK ABDULLAYEV, DAULET KH. SEMBAYEV.

Minister of Agriculture and Foodstuffs: VALENTIN I. DVURECHENSKY.

Minister of Education: SHAYSULTAN SHAYAKHMETOV.

Minister of Energy and Electrification: BULAT G. NURZHANOV.

Minister of External Economic Relations: SYZDYK ZH. ABISHEV.

Minister of Finance: TULEYBEK ABDIKADIROV.

Minister of Foreign Affairs: TOLEUBAI SULEIMENOV.

Minister of the Forestry Industry: ALEKSANDR K. AMANBAYEV.

Minister of Health: AKSULTAN AMANBAYEV.

Minister of Industry: VIKTOR I. VLASOV.

Minister of Internal Affairs: MIKHAIL T. BERSENEV.

Minister of Justice: GALIKHAN N. YERZHANOV.

Minister of Roads: SHAMIL KH. BEKBULATOV.

Minister of Social Welfare: ZAURE ZH. KADYROVA.

Minister of Trade: OKTYABR I. ZHELTIKOV.

Minister of Transport: NIGMATSHAN K. ISINGARIN.

Chairmen of Principal State Committees

Chairman of the State Committee for Architecture and Construction: AKSAR A. KULIBAYEV.

Chairman of the State Committee for Defence: Lt-Gen. SAGADAT K. NURMAGAMBETOV.

Chairman of the State Committee for the Economy: TILEUKHAN S. KABDIRAKHMANOV.

Chairman of the State Committee for the Support of New Economic Structures and the Limitation of Monopolization: KHRISTIAN D. DRILLER.

Chairman of the State Committee for Material-Technical Procurement: AMANGELDY I. BEKTEMISOV.

Chairman of the State Committee for State Property: KYLYMBEK S. IZBASKHANOV.

Chairman of the State Committee for Statistics and Analysis: TULEYBAY ZHUMASULTANOV.

Chairman of the State Security Committee: BOLAT A. BAYKENOV.

MINISTRIES

Ministry of Agriculture and Foodstuffs: Alma-Ata, pl. Respubliki 15; tel. (3272) 63-44-44.

Ministry of Communications: Alma-Ata, ul. Kirova 134; tel. (3272) 62-31-94.

Ministry of Education: Alma-Ata, ul. Dzhambula 25; tel. (3272) 61-03-09.

Ministry of Energy and Electrification: Alma-Ata, ul. Kirova 142; tel. (3272) 62-64-10.

Ministry of External Economic Relations: Alma-Ata, pr. Kommunistichesky 77; tel. (3272) 62-40-57.

Ministry of Finance: Alma-Ata, pr. Kommunistichesky 97; tel. (3272) 62-40-75.

Ministry of Foreign Affairs: Alma-Ata, ul. Mira 167; tel. (3272) 63-25-38.

Ministry of the Forestry Industry: Alma-Ata, ul. Mira 112; tel. (3272) 62-63-20.

Ministry of Health: Alma-Ata, pr. Kommunistichesky 63; tel. (3272) 33-46-11.

Ministry of Industry: Alma-Ata, pr. Kommunistichesky 93/95; tel. (3272) 62-06-03.

Ministry of Internal Affairs: Alma-Ata, ul. Kalinina 95; tel. (3272) 62-84-57.

Ministry of Justice: Alma-Ata, ul. Sovetskaya 66; tel. (3272) 62-64-01.

Ministry of Roads: Alma-Ata, ul. Gogolya 86; tel. (3272) 32-39-29.

Ministry of Social Welfare: Alma-Ata, ul. Karla Marksa 122; tel. (3272) 63-67-78.

Ministry of Trade: Alma-Ata, pr. Kommunistichesky 93/95; tel. (3272) 62-38-12.

Ministry of Transport: Alma-Ata, ul. Panfilova 110; tel. (3272) 60-40-40.

Principal State Committees

State Committee for Architecture and Construction: Alma-Ata, pr. Kommunistichesky 93; tel. (3272) 62-91-00.

State Committee for Defence: Alma-Ata.

State Committee for the Economy: Alma-Ata, ul. Mira 115; tel. (3272) 62-65-00.

State Committee for the Support of New Economic Structures and the Limitation of Monopolization: Alma-Ata; tel. (3272) 62-50-13.

State Committee for Material-Technical Procurement: Alma-Ata, ul. Sovetskaya 65; tel. (3272) 62-70-21.

State Committee for State Property: Alma-Ata, pr. Kommunistichesky 93/95; tel. (3272) 62-85-62.

State Committee for Statistics and Analysis: Alma-Ata, pr. Abaya 125; tel. (3272) 62-14-61.

State Security Committee: Alma-Ata; tel. (3272) 69-35-28.

Legislature

SUPREME SOVIET

The Supreme Soviet comprises 360 deputies. Elections were held in March 1990.

Chairman: Serikbolsyn Abdildin.

Political Organizations

Party of Islamic Renaissance: Alma-Ata; f. 1991; advocates the establishment of a united Muslim state.

Popular Congress of Kazakhstan: Alma-Ata; f. 1991; unites progressive and democratic groups; Co-chair. Olzhas Suleimenov, Muktar Shakhanov; incl., among others, the Nevada-Semipalatinsk Movement, the Kazakh Language Society and the following groups:

Azat (Freedom): Alma-Ata; advocates full sovereignty for Kazakhstan within a renewed federation of union republics; Co-Chair. M. Isanaliyev.

Jeltoqsan (December): Alma-Ata; f. 1989; advocates full political independenceof Kazakhstan.

Yedinstvo (Unity): Alma-Ata; represents the Russian minority in Kazakhstan.

Socialist Party of Kazakhstan: Alma-Ata; f. 1991 to replace Kazakh Communist Party; Chair. (vacant).

Turkestan Party: Alma-Ata; f. 1991; advocates unification of the Central Asian Republics.

Judicial System

Chairman of the Supreme Court: Tamaz K. Aitmukhambetov.

Procurator-General: Zh. A. Tuyakbayev.

Religion

The major religion of the Kazakhs is Islam. They are almost exclusively Sunni (Hanafi school). The Russian Orthodox Church is the dominant Christian denomination; it is attended mainly by Slavs. There are also Protestant Churches (mainly Baptists).

ISLAM

The Kazakhs were only converted to Islam in the early 19th century and for many years there remained elements of animist practices among them. In 1985–90 the number of mosques in Kazakhstan increased from 25 to 60, 12 of which were newly-built. By 1991 there were an estimated 230 Muslim religious communities functioning in Kazkahstan, an Islamic institute had been opened in Alma-Ata and several translations of the Koran into Kazakh had been made. Until 1990 the Muslims of Kazakhstan were under the spiritual jurisdiction of the muftiate of Central Asia and Kazakhstan, which is based in Tashkent (Uzbekistan). In 1990 the Muslim authorities in Kazakhstan established an independent muftiate.

Mufti of Kazakhstan: Ratbek-haji Nysanbai-uly.

The Press

In 1989 there were 453 officially-registered newspaper titles being published in Kazakhstan, of which 160 were in the Kazakh language. Newspapers were also published in Russian, Uighur, German and Korean. There were 94 periodicals, including 31 in Kazakh.

GOVERNMENT AGENCY

State Committee on the Press: Alma-Ata, ul. Mechnikova 64; tel. (3272) 67-27-56; Chair. Kalit Zakiryanov.

PRINCIPAL DAILY NEWSPAPERS

Freundschaft (Friendship): Alma-Ata; f. 1966; 5 a week; in German.

Kazakhstanskaya Pravda (Pravda of Kazakhstan): Alma-Ata, ul. Gogolya 39; tel. (3272) 63-03-98; f. 1920; 6 a week; sponsored by the Council of Ministers; independent; in Russian; Editor Vyatcheslav M. Srybnyh..

Kommunizm Tugi: Alma-Ata; f. 1957; 5 a week; in Uighur.

Lenin Kichi: Alma-Ata; f. 1938; 5 a week; in Korean.

Leninshil Zhas (Leninist Youth): Alma-Ata, pr. Zhibek zholy 50; tel. (3272) 33-02-19; f. 1921; 5 a week; in Kazakh; Editor U. Kalizhanov; circ. 270,000.

Leninskaya Smena (Leninist Rising Generation): 480044 Alma-Ata, pr. Zhibek zholy 50; tel. (3272) 33-44-81; telex 251349; f. 1922; 5 a week; in Russian; Editor O. Nikanov; circ. 300,000.

Sotsialistik Kazakhstan (Socialist Kazakhstan): Alma-Ata, ul. Gogolya 39; tel. (3272) 63-25-46; f. 1919; 6 a week; organ of the Supreme Soviet and Council of Ministers; in Kazakh; Chief Editor Sh. Murtasayev.

OTHER PUBLICATIONS

Amanat (Voter): Alma-Ata, pr. Zhibek zholy 50; tel. (3272) 33-71-71; f. 1990; weekly; publ. by the Nevada-Semipalatinsk movement; articles on disarmament and environmental protection; in Kazakh and Russian; Chief Editor E. Tursunov; circ. 50,000.

Ana Tili: Alma-Ata, ul. Pushkina 118; tel. (3272) 63-15-39; f. 1990; weekly; publ. by the Kazakh Tili society; in Kazakh; Chief Editor G. Beisenbayuly; circ. 110,000.

Ara-Shmel (Bumble-bee): Alma-Ata, ul. Gogolya 39; tel. (3272) 63-59-46; f. 1956; monthly; satirical; in Kazakh and Russian; Chief Editor K. Mukamedzhanov; circ. 53,799.

Arai-Zaria (Dawn): Alma-Ata, ul. Furmanova 53; tel. (3272) 32-29-45; f. 1987; monthly; socio-political; Chief Editor A. Kopishev.

Baldyrgan (Sprout): 480044 Alma-Ata, pr. Zhibek zholy 50; tel. (3272) 33-16-73; f. 1958; monthly; illustrated; for pre-school and first grades of school; in Kazakh; Editor T. Moldagaliyev; circ. 150,000.

Densaulik (Health): Alma-Ata; f. 1990; organ of the Ministry of Health; medicine; in Kazakh.

Ekonomika i Zhizn (Economics and Life): Alma-Ata, pr. Mira 115; tel. (3272) 62-96-22; f. 1990; monthly; journal of the Council of Ministers; theory and practice of economic reform and managment of the economy; in Russian; Chief Editor M. Dzhanguzhin; circ. 5,706.

Kazakh Adebieti: 480091 Alma-Ata, pr. Kommunistichesky 105; tel. (3272) 69-54-62; f. 1934; weekly; organ of the Union of Writers of Kazakhstan; weekly; in Kazakh; Chief Editor T. Abdikov.

Kazakhstan Aielderi (Women of Kazakhstan): Alma-Ata, Zhibek zholy 50; f. 1929; monthly; popular women's magazine; in Kazakh; Chief Editor A. Dzhaganova; circ. 332,952.

Kazakhstan Kommunisi (Communist of Kazakhstan): Alma-Ata, ul. Gogolya 39; tel. (3272) 63-94-19; f. 1921; monthly; fmrly publ. by the Publishing House of the Cen. Cttee of the Communist Party of Kazakhstan; in Kazakh; Chief Editor K. Smailov; circ. 53,099.

Kazakhstan Mektebi (Kazakh School): 480091 Alma-Ata, pr. Kommunistichesky 34; f. 1925; monthly; journal of the Ministry of Education; organization of public education; in Kazakh; Chief Editor S. Abisheva; circ. 40,033.

Kazakhstan Mugalimi: 480091 Alma-Ata, pr. Kommunistichesky 34; f. 1952; weekly; publ. by the Ministry of Education; in Kazakh; Editor M. Sermagambetov; circ. 71,602.

Kazakstannyn Auyl Sharuashylygy (Agriculture of Kazakhstan): Alma-Ata; f. 1936; monthly; agricultural news; in Kazakh and Russian.

Parasat (Intellect): 480044 Alma-Ata, pr. Zhibek zholy 50; tel. (3272) 33-51-16; f. 1958; 2 a year; publ. by the Kazakhstan Publishing House; socio-political, literary, illustrated; in Kazakh; Chief Editor B. NURZHEKEYEV; circ. 210,000.

Partiinaya Zhizn Kazakhstana (Party Life of Kazakhstan): Alma-Ata, ul. Gogolya 39; tel. (3272) 63-32-79; f. 1920; monthly; fmrly publ. by the Communist Party of Kazakhstan; political; in Russian; Chief Editor G. M. SHESTAKOV; circ. 25,000.

Podrostok (Teenager): 480083 Alma-Ata, ul. Pastera 186/37; tel. (3272) 32-25-43; fortnightly; in Russian; Editor L. BALAYAN; circ. 10,000.

Pozitsia (Position): Alma-Ata, ul. Gogolya 49; tel. (3272) 63-28-68; f. 1990; fortnightly; Editor V. A. PARAMONOV.

Prostor (Wide Horizons): 480091 Alma-Ata, pr. Kommunistichesky 105; tel. (3272) 69-63-19; f. 1933; monthly; journal of the Union of Writers of Kazakhstan; fiction; in Russian; Editor G. I. TOLMACHEV; circ. 127,063.

Russky Yazyk i Literatura v Kazakhskoy Shkole (Russian Language and Literature in the Kazakh School): 480091 Alma-Ata, pr. Kommunistichesky 34; tel. (3272) 39-76-68; f. 1962; monthly; journal of the Ministry of Education; linguistic problems; in Russian; Chief Editor B. S. MUKANOV; circ. 17,465.

Shalkar: Alma-Ata, pr. Zhibek zholy 50; f. 1976; publ. by the Kazakhstan Society; in Kazakh; Editor U. KYDYRKHANOV.

Sovieti Kazakhstana (Councils of Kazakhstan): Alma-Ata; tel. (3272) 63-89-44; weekly; publ. by the Supreme Soviet of Kazakhstan; Editors S. AKTAYEV, YU. A. TARAKOV; circ. 30,000.

Sport: Alma-Ata, pr. Zhibek zholy 50; tel. (3272) 33-92-90; f. 1959; publ. by the State Committee for Youth Affairs, Physical Culture and Sport; in Kazakh and Russian; Editor A. ZHAKSYBEKOV; circ. 137,684.

Uchitel Kazakhstana (Teacher of Kazakhstan): Alma-Ata; f. 1952; weekly.

Ulan: Alma-Ata, pr. Zhibek zholy 50; tel. (3272) 33-80-03; f. 1930; 2 a week; fmrly publ. by the Leninist Young Communist League of Kazakhstan (Komsomol); Editor G. DOSKENOV; circ. 183,014.

Vestnik Selskokhozyaistvennoy Nauki Kazakhstana (Chronicle of Agricultural Science of Kazakhstan): Alma-Ata, ul. Dzhanosova 51; tel. (3272) 21-48-57; f. 1958; monthly; publ. by the Kazakh Agricultural Academy; problems of agriculture in different areas of Kazakhstan; in Russian; Chief Editor K. B. IMANGALIYEV; circ. 2,235.

Zerde (Intellect): Alma-Ata, pr. Zhibek zholy 50; tel. (3272) 33-83-81; f. 1960; monthly; popular, scientific, technical; Editor E. RAUSHANOV; circ. 68,629.

Zhalyn: 480124 Alma-Ata, pr. Abaya 143; tel. (3272) 42-44-22; 6 a year.

Zhuldyz (Star): 480091 Alma-Ata, pr. Kommunistichesky 105; tel. (3272) 62-51-37; f. 1928; monthly; journal of the Union of Writers of Kazakhstan; literary, artistic, socio-political; Editor-in-Chief MUKHTAR MAGAUÌN; circ. 134,206.

Zhurnal Mod (Fashion Magazine): Alma-Ata; f. 1958; 2 a year; publ. by the Dom Modely Ödezhdy (Fashion House) Publishing House; everyday fashions; in Kazakh and Russian.

NEWS AGENCY

KazTAG (Kazakh Telegraph Agency): Alma-Ata, pr. Kommunistichesky 75; tel. (3272) 62-50-37; Dir AMANGELDY AKHMETALITOV.

Publishers

Gylym (Science): 480100 Alma-Ata, ul. Pushkina 111–113; tel. (3272) 61-18-77; f. 1946; books on the natural sciences, the humanities and scientific research journals; Dir S. G. BAIMENOV; Editor-in-Chief M. A. AIMBETOV.

Kainar (Spring Publishing House): 480124 Alma-Ata, pr. Abaya 143; tel. (3272) 42-66-67; f. 1962; agriculture; Dir KH. A. TLEMISOV; Chief Editor I. I. ISKUZHIN.

Kazakhskaya Sovetskaya Entsiklopediya (Kazakh Soviet Encyclopaedia): Alma-Ata, ul. Kommunisticheskaya 93/95; tel. (3272) 62-55-66; f. 1968; Chief Editor R. N. NURGALIEV.

Kazakhstan Publishing House: 480124 Alma-Ata, pr. Abaya 143; tel. (3272) 42-29-29; political and popular edns; Dir E. KH. SYZDYKOV; Chief Editor N. D. SITKO.

Oner (Art): 480124 Alma-Ata, pr. Abaya 143; tel. (3272) 42-08-88; f. 1980; books on art; Dir S. S. ORAZALINOV; Chief Editor A. A. ASKAROV.

Rauan (Science): 480124 Alma-Ata, pr. Abaya 143; tel. (3272) 42-25-37; f. 1947; fiction by young writers; Dir ZH. H. NUSKABAYEV; Editor-in-Chief K. KURMANOV.

Zhazushy (Writer Publishing House): 480124 Alma-Ata, pr. Abaya 143; tel. (3272) 42-28-49; fiction; Dir KALDARBEK NAIMANBAYEV.

Radio and Television

State Committee for Television and Radio: 480013 Alma-Ata, ul. Mira 175; tel. (3272) 63-37-16; Chair. SAGAT ASHIBAYEV.

Kazakh Radio: f. 1923; broadcasts in Kazakh, Russian, Uighur, German and Korean.

Kazakh Television: f. 1959; broadcasts in Kazakh, Uighur, Russian and German.

Finance

(cap. = capital)

BANKING

State Banks

National State Bank: Alma-Ata, mkr. Kokteli-3 21; tel. (3272) 47-37-97; Chair. of Bd BORIS D. RYABOV.

Kazakh Republican Foreign Trade Bank: Alma-Ata, pr. Lenina 39; tel. (3272) 61-83-82; fmrly br. of Vneshekonombank USSR; Chair. of Bd BERLIN K. IRSHIYEV.

Other Banks

Chimkent Co-op Bank (Soyuzbank): 486018 Chimkent, pl. Lenina 2A; tel. 3-56-91; f. 1988; cap. 1m. roubles (1988); commercial bank; Chair. B. BEKTAYEV.

Commercial Innovation Bank (Kramos Bank): 480046 Alma-Ata, ul. 16-ya Liniya 160; tel. (3272) 44-08-58; commercial bank; Pres. LEONID ABLOTEY.

Co-op Bank of the Alma-Ata Union of Co-operatives (Centre Bank): 480091 Alma-Ata, ul. Panfilova 98; tel. (3272) 33-69-96; co-operative bank.

Kazdorbank: Alma-Ata; tel. (3272) 32-48-61; commercial bank.

COMMODITY EXCHANGE

Karaganda Regional Commodity Exchange: 470074 Karaganda, pr. Stroiteley 28; tel. (372) 74-04-82; telex 251338; fax (372) 74-43-25; f. 1991; authorized cap. 15m. roubles; Gen. Man. GEORGY REVAZOV.

Trade and Industry

CHAMBER OF COMMERCE

Chamber of Commerce and Industry of Kazakhstan: 480091 Alma-Ata, pr. Kommunistichesky 93/95; tel. (3272) 62-14-46; telex 25-12-28; fax (3272) 62-05-94; Chair. A. M. KYRBASOV.

FOREIGN TRADE ORGANIZATION

Kazakhintorg: 480091 Alma-Ata, ul. Gogolya 11; tel. (3272) 32-83-81; telex 251238; import and export; subsidiary of Ministry of External Economic Relations; Gen. Dir SAKEN SEYDUALIYEV.

MAJOR INDUSTRIAL ENTERPRISES

Capacitor Plant: 492029 Vostochny Kazakhstan obl., Ust-Kamenogorsk; tel. 66-02-91; produces complete capacitor installations; Dir VLADIMIR A. NAKONETSHYJ; 2,800 employees.

Chimkent Industrial Amalgamation: 486008 Chimkent, ul. Ordzhonikidze 28; tel. 12-29-43; telex 184112; specializes in the production of press-forging equipment; Dir-Gen. EDUARD DAVIDZHAN; 4,110 employees.

Dzhambul Industrial Corporation (Khimprom): 484026 Dzhambul; tel. (326) 3-25-69; telex 251282; fax (326) 3-28-73; production of phosphorus and its derivatives; Gen. Dir MUKHAN D. ATABAYEV; 6,000 employees.

CO-OPERATIVE ORGANIZATION

Kazakhtrebsoyuz: Alma-Ata, ul. Komsomolskaya 57; tel. (3272) 62-34-94; union of co-operative entrepreneurs; Chair. UMIRZAK SARSENOV.

Transport

RAILWAYS

At 31 December 1989 the total length of rail track in use was 14,460 km. The rail network is concentrated in the north of the Republic, where it joins the rail lines of the Russian Federation. From the capital, Alma-Ata, lines run north-east, to join the Trans-Siberian Railway, and west, to Chimkent, and then north-west along the Syr-Dar'ya river, to Orenburg in European Russia. In June 1991 an international line was opened between Druzhba, on the eastern border of Kazakhstan, and Alataw Shankou, in the Xinjiang Uygur (Sinkiand Uighur) Autonomous Republic of the the People's Republic of China. A passenger service was due to begin on this line in mid-1992.

ROADS

At 31 December 1989 there was a total of 164,900 km of roads, of which 99,000 km were hard-surfaced.

Culture

NATIONAL ORGANIZATION

State Committee for Culture: Alma-Ata, ul. Gogolya 35; tel. (3272) 30-63-18; Chair. KANAT B. SAUDBAYEV.

CULTURAL HERITAGE

A. Kasteyev Kazakh State Art Museum: 480070 Alma-Ata, ul. Satpayeva 30A; tel. (3272) 67-99-62; f. 1976; 20,000 exhibits; library of 30,000 vols; Dir. ERMEK T. ZHANGELDIN.

State Public Library of Kazakhstan: 480021 Alma-Ata, pr. Abaya 14; f. 1931; over 3,458,700 vols; Dir. N. K. DAULETOVA.

Central State Museum of Kazakhstan: Alma-Ata, Park 28 Panfilovtsev; 90,000 exhibits; Dir. R. K. KOSHAMBEKOVA.

SPORTING ORGANIZATION

State Committee for Youth Affairs, Physical Culture and Sport: Alma-Ata, pr. Abaya 48; tel. (3272) 67-39-86; Chair. IMANGALY TASMAGANBETOV.

PERFORMING ARTS

Abay Opera and Ballet Theatre: Alma-Ata, 112 ul. Kalinina.

Auezov Drama Theatre: Alma-Ata, 55 pr. Abaya.

Lermontov Russian Drama Theatre: Alma-Ata, 43 pr. Abaya.

Uighur and Korean Theatre of Music and Drama: Alma-Ata, ul. Dzherzhinskovo.

ASSOCIATION

Union of Writers of Kazakhstan: Alma-Ata, Kommunistichesky pr. 105; tel. (3272) 62-62-95; subsidiary Writers' Organizations in Karaganda, Semipalatinsk, Uralsk, Tselinograd and Chimkent.

Education

Education is fully funded by the state at primary and secondary level. Most pupils are taught in Russian, although, since the adoption of Kazakh as the state language, there have been attempts to extend the provision of Kazakh-language education. In 1988 64.2% of all pupils at general day schools were taught in Russian, 33.0% in Kazakh, 1.9% in Uzbek, 0.4% in Uighur and 0.1% in Tadzhik. Higher education is conducted in 55 institutions of higher education, including three universities. In 1991 plans were announced for the establishment of a new university in Turkestan. Ethnic Kazakhs form a greater proportion of students in higher education than in primary and secondary education, since many ethnic Russians choose to study at universities outside the Republic. In 1984/85 Kazakhs formed 46% of students in specialized secondary education, but 54% of students in higher education.

UNIVERSITIES

Karaganda State University: 470074 Karaganda, Universitetskaya ul. 28; tel. (3272) 74-49-50; f. 1972; 10 faculties; 8,436 students.

Kazakh State University: 480121 Alma-Ata, ul. Timiryazeva 46; tel. (3272) 62-41-42; f. 1934; languages of instruction: Russian and Kazakh; 12 faculties; 1,003 teachers; 13,000 students; Rector Prof. M. ABDILDIN.

Technical University at Karaganda Metallurgical Combine: 472300 Temirtau, pr. Lenina 34; tel. 3-65-82; telex 251234; f. 1964; 3 faculties; Rector YU. A. MINAYEV.

Social Welfare

NATIONAL AGENCIES

Ministry of Health: see section on The Government (Ministries).

Ministry of Social Security: see section on The Government (Ministries).

Committee of the Supreme Soviet of Kazakhstan on Health and Social Security: 480091 Alma-Ata, Dom pravitelstva; tel. (3272) 62-78-30; Chair. TANIRBERGEN T. TOKHTAROV.

Committee of the Supreme Soviet of Kazakhstan on War Veterans, Invalids and Servicemen: 480091 Alma-Ata, Dom pravitelstva; tel. (3272) 62-52-26; Chair. SAGADAT K. NURMAGAMBETOV.

Kazakh Republican Branch of the USSR Pension Fund: 480100 Alma-Ata, ul. K. Marksa 122; tel. (3272) 63-67-37; Dir TEMIRKAN N. NURTAYEV.

State Committee for Labour: 480091 Alma-Ata, pr. Kommunistichesky 93/95; tel. (3272) 62-11-68; Chair. SAYAT D. BEYSENOV.

State Committee for Supervision of Safe Working Practices in Industry and Mining: Alma-Ata, ul. Proletarskaya 80/84, ug. Dzhambula; tel. (3272) 61-13-91; Chair. ORYNBASAR MULKIBAYEV.

Social Insurance Fund: 480003 Alma-Ata, ul. Mira 37/41; tel. (3272) 62-28-95; Dir MAKSUT S. NARIKBAYEV.

State Employment Fund: 480091 Alma-Ata, pr. Kommunistichesky 93/95; tel. (3272) 62-11-68; Chair. SAYAT D. BEYSENOV.

HEALTH AND WELFARE ORGANIZATIONS

Central Committee of the Red Crescent and Red Cross of Kazakhstan: 480100 Alma-Ata, ul. Karla Marksa 86; tel. (3272) 61-62-91; Pres. ASYLBEK U. KONAKBAYEV.

Charity and Health Fund of Kazakhstan: 480100 Alma-Ata, ul. Karla Marksa 86; tel. (3272) 62-41-62.

Kazakh Republican Branch of the Soviet Children's Fund: 480064 Alma-Ata, ul. Furmanova 162; tel. (3272) 62-24-02; Chair. KOZHAKHMET B. BALAKHMETOV.

Voluntary Society of Invalids of Kazakhstan: 480100 Alma-Ata, ul. Karla Marksa 122; tel. (3272) 63-75-87; Chair. SEYDALIM N. TANIKEYEV.

The Environment

GOVERNMENT ORGANIZATIONS

State Committee for Ecology and Land Use: Alma-Ata, ul. Panfilova 106; tel. (3272) 63-12-73; Chair. ANATOLY M. DUBITSKY.

State Committee for Geology and Conservation of Resources: Alma-Ata, ul. Kirova 115; tel. (3272) 61-60-87; Chair. MUKHTAR M. BAKENOV.

State Committee for Water Resources: ul. Mira 118; tel. (3272) 63-76-01; Chair. NARIMAN KIPSHAKBAYEV.

ACADEMIC INSTITUTE

Academy of Sciences of Kazakhstan: 480021 Alma-Ata, ul. Shevchenko 28; several attached institutes involved in environmental research; Pres. U. M. SULTANGIZIN.

NON-GOVERNMENTAL ORGANIZATION

Nevada-Semipalatinsk Movement: 480021 Alma-Ata, pr. Lenina 85; fax (3272) 63-12-07; f. 1989; environmental group opposed to nuclear testing; Chair. OLZHAS SULEIMENOV.

KYRGYZSTAN

Geography

The Republic of Kyrgyzstan, or Kirghizia (formerly the Kirghiz Soviet Socialist Republic), is a small, land-locked state situated in eastern Central Asia. It borders Kazakhstan to the north, Uzbekistan to the west and Tadzhikistan to the south. There is an international frontier to the east with the People's Republic of China. It covers an area of 198,500 sq km (76,640 sq miles).

The terrain is largely mountainous, dominated by the western reaches of the Tian-Shan mountain range in the north-east and the Pamir-Alay range in the south-west. The highest mountain is Pik Pobeda (Victory Peak, 7,439 m), in the Tian-Shan range on the border with China. Much of the mountain region is permanently covered with ice and snow and there are many glaciers. The Fergana mountain range, running from south-west to north-east across the centre of the Republic, separates the eastern and central mountain regions from the Fergana valley in the south-west. Other lowland areas include the Chu and Talas valleys near the northern border with Kazakhstan. The most important rivers are the Naryn river, which flows through the central regions and eventually joins the Syr-Dar'ya, and the Chu river, which forms part of the northern border with Kazakhstan.

There are distinct variations in climate between low-lying and high-altitude areas. In the valleys the mean July temperature is 28°C (82°F), whereas in January it falls to an average of −18°C (−0.5°F). Annual precipitation ranges from 180 mm in the eastern Tian-Shan mountains to 750–1,000 mm in the Fergana mountains. In the settled valleys the annual average varies between 100 mm and 500 mm.

At the census of 1989, at which the total population was 4,291,000, 52.4% of the population were ethnic Kirghiz (Kyrgyz), 21.5% Russians, 12.9% Uzbeks, 2.5% Ukrainians, 2.4% Germans and 1.6% Tatars. There were also small numbers of Kazakhs (37,318), Dungans (36,928), Uighurs (36,779), Tadzhiks (33,518), Turks (21,294), Koreans (18,355) and others. Kirghiz replaced Russian as the official language in September 1989. It is a member of the south Turkic group of languages and is written in the Cyrillic script. The Arabic script was in use until 1928 when it was replaced by a Latin script. The Latin script was replaced by Cyrillic in 1940. In 1991 it was proposed to reintroduce the use of the Latin script. The major religion is Islam. Kirghiz and Uzbeks are traditionally Sunni Muslims of the Hanafi school.

The total population at 1 January 1991 was estimated to be 4,222,000. The average population density (persons per sq km) was 21.3. Bishkek (known as Frunze, 1926–91), the capital, is situated in the Chu valley in the north of the Republic. It had an estimated population of 626,900 in January 1990.

History

The ancestors of the Kirghiz were probably settled on the upper reaches of the Yenisei until about the 10th century. From there they migrated south to the Tian-Shan region, a movement hastened by the rise of the Mongol Empire, in the 13th century. The Kirghiz were ruled by various Turkic peoples until 1685, when they came under the control of the Mongol Oirots. The defeat of the Oirots by the Manzhous (Manchus), in 1758, left the Kirghiz as nominal Chinese subjects, but the Chinese did not interfere with their independent nomadic life styles. They came under the suzerainty of the Khanate of Kokand in the early 19th century and were formally incorporated into the Russian Empire, as part of the Khanate, in 1876. The suppression of the 1916 rebellion in Central Asia caused a major migration of the Kirghiz to China.

Following the October Revolution of 1917 in Russia, there was a period of civil war, with anti-Bolshevik forces, including the Russian 'White' Army, and local *basmachi* armed groups, fighting against the Bolshevik Red Army. Soviet power was established in the region by 1919. In 1918 the Turkestan ASSR was established within the Russian Soviet Federative Socialist Republic (RSFSR, or Russian Federation) and included Kirghizia until 1924, when the Kara-Kirghiz Autonomous Oblast was created, also within the RSFSR (the Russians used the term Kara-Kirghiz for the Kirghiz until the mid-1920s to distinguish them from the Kazakhs, who at that time were also known as Kirghiz by the Russians). In 1925 it was renamed the Kirghiz Autonomous Oblast and it became the Kirghiz Autonomous Soviet Socialist Republic (ASSR) in February 1926. On 5 December 1936 the Kirghiz Soviet Socialist Republic (SSR) was established as a full Union Republic of the USSR.

During the 1920s Kirghizia developed considerably in cultural, educational and social life. Literacy was greatly improved and a standard literary language was introduced. Economic and social development was also notable. Land reforms were carried out in 1920–21 and 1927–28, which resulted in the settlement of many of the nomadic Kirghiz. Land reforms were followed by the collectivization programme of the early 1930s, which was strongly opposed by many Kirghiz, and prompted a partial revival of the *basmachi* movement, which had been largely suppressed by the mid-1920s.

Leading members of the Kirghiz Communist Party (KCP) attempted to increase the role of ethnic Kirghiz in the government of the Republic, but these so-called 'national Communists' were expelled from the KCP and often exiled or imprisoned, particularly during the late 1930s. Despite the suppression of nationalism during the Stalin era, many aspects of Kirghiz national culture were retained, and tensions with the all-Union authorities were evident in the post-1945 period. There were allegations that the murder of Sultan Ibraimov, the Chairman of the Kirghiz Council of Ministers, in 1980, was a result of his support for greater republican autonomy.

The first evidence of Soviet leader Mikhail Gorbachev's new policies came with the resignation of Turdakan Usubaliyev, the First Secretary of the KCP, in November 1985. His replacement, Absamat Masaliyev, accused Usubaliyev of corruption and nepotism and dismissed many of his closest allies from office. However, Masaliyev's commitment to *perestroika* did not extend beyond correcting the excesses of his predecessor. The policy of *glasnost*, which permitted greater openness in the press, was frequently criticized by Masaliyev. Nevertheless, by 1988 the Republic's press had begun to adopt a more liberal stance, notably *Literaturny Kirghistan*, the newspaper of the Union of Writers. The conservative leadership also opposed the development of unofficial political groups, but several groups were established in 1989 with the intention of alleviating the acute housing crisis in the Republic, by seizing vacant land and building houses on it. One of these groups, Ashar, was partially tolerated by the authorities and soon developed a wider political role. Osh Aymaghi, a similar organization to Ashar, but based in Osh oblast, where a majority of the population are ethnic Uzbeks, attempted to obtain land and homes for the ethnic Kirghiz in the region.

Disputes over land and housing provision in the crowded Fergana valley region of Osh oblast precipitated violent confrontation between Kirghiz and Uzbeks in 1990. Osh had been incorporated into Kirghizia in 1924, although Uzbeks formed a majority of the population, and Uzbeks had begun to demand the establishment of an Uzbek autonomous region in Osh oblast. On 4 June 1990 at least 11 people died and more than 200 were injured as a result of conflict between Uzbeks and Kirghiz. A state of emergency and a curfew were introduced, and the border between Uzbekistan and Kirghizia was closed, but the violence escalated. Order was not restored until August. According to official reports, 230 people died in the violence, but unofficial sources claimed that over 1,000 people had been killed. The state of emergency was not lifted until November. The republican and regional leadership blamed Osh Aymaghi and other informal groups for initiating the violence, but the opposition movement criticized Masaliyev and the local KCP leadership for not responding to social and economic problems in the area. In August Renat Kulmatov, the First Secretary of Osh oblast, was forced to resign, and the republican leadership was increasingly criticized for its role in the violence.

Despite an increase in the influence of the nascent democratic movement, the elections to the Supreme Soviet of Kirghizia, in February 1990, were conducted in traditional Soviet style, with KCP candidates winning most seats unopposed. In April 1990 the Supreme Soviet elected Masaliyev to the newly-instituted office of Chairman of the Supreme Soviet. He favoured the introduction of an executive presidency, as had been effected in other Republics. Election to the post was to be by the Supreme Soviet, and the overwhelming KCP majority in the Supreme Soviet seemed to guarantee the election of Masaliyev to the post. However, by October, when an extraordinary Supreme Soviet session was convened to elect the president, Masaliyev had been seriously discredited by the violence in Osh, and the democratic movement, which had united as the Kyrgyzstan Democratic Movement (KDM), had developed into a significant political force. In the first round of voting in the Supreme Soviet, Masaliyev failed to achieve the necessary percentage of votes to be elected as President and he was refused permission to be renominated. In a further round of voting, Askar Akayev, the liberal President of the Kirghiz Academy of Sciences, was elected to the presidency. Akayev quickly allied himself with reformist politicians and economists, including leaders of the KDM, which had been influential in turning public opinion against Masaliyev following the events in Osh. Economic reformists were appointed to a State Commission on Economic Reform, and plans were announced for a programme of privatization.

In December 1990 Masaliyev resigned as Chairman of the Supreme Soviet, and was replaced by Medetkan Sherimkulov. In January 1991 Akayev introduced new government structures, replacing the unwieldy Council of Ministers by a smaller Cabinet of Ministers, and appointed a new Government, comprised mainly of younger reformist politicians. Despite opposition from the KCP, and Masaliyev in particular, in mid-December 1990 the Supreme Soviet had voted to change the name of the Republic from the Kirghiz SSR to the Republic of Kyrgyzstan, and, in Febru-

ary 1991, the capital, Frunze, named after the Red Army commander who had conquered much of Central Asia in the Civil War, reverted to its original name of Bishkek.

Although Kyrgyzstan was one of the most democratic of the Central Asian Republics, economic realities seemed to prevail against secession from the USSR. In the referendum on the preservation of the USSR, in March 1991, an overwhelming majority (87.7% of those eligible to vote) approved the proposal to retain the USSR as a 'renewed federation'.

Akayev's programme of political and economic reform had many opponents in the KCP and the security forces. In April, apparently as a result of differences with President Akayev, Masaliyev resigned as First Secretary of the KCP. He was replaced by Dzhumgalbek Amanbayev. Although Amanbayev seemed to be more enthusiastic about Akayev's reform programme than his predecessor had been, there was much opposition in the KCP leadership to controversial plans which would lead to the 'de-partyization' (removal of Party cells from workplaces) of government and the security forces.

On 19 August 1991, when a State Committee for the State of Emergency (SCSE) announced that it had assumed power in Moscow, there was an attempt to depose Akayev in Kyrgyzstan. The KCP declared its support for the coup leaders, and the commander of Turkestan military district threatened to dispatch troops and tanks to the Republic. To pre-empt military action against him, Akayev dismissed Gen. Asasankulov, the Chairman of the republican KGB, and ordered interior ministry troops to guard strategic buildings in Bishkek. Despite warnings from Vladimir Kryuchkov, Chairman of the all-Union KGB and a member of the SCSE, Akayev established contact with Boris Yeltsin, President of the Russian Federation, and broadcast Yeltsin's opposition to the SCSE on republican television. On 20 August 1991 Akayev publicly denounced the coup and issued a decree prohibiting activity by any political party in government or state bodies. The next day Akayev ordered all military units in the Republic to remain in their barracks. On 26 August, after the coup had collapsed in Moscow, Akayev and Vice-President German Kuznetsov announced their resignation from the CPSU, and the entire bureau and secretariat of the KCP resigned. Following the coup, Akayev continued with his policies of seeking more independence for Kyrgyzstan and the implementation of ambitious economic reforms. On 31 August the Supreme Soviet of Kyrgyzstan voted to declare independence from the USSR. With the dissolution of the KCP and the CPSU there was little remaining opposition to Akayev and his policies. On 12 October 1991 Akayev was elected President with 95% of the votes cast; no other candidate was nominated.

Kyrgyzstan participated in meetings of the five Central Asian Republics in 1990 and 1991 and developed relations with the European Republics of the former USSR. Together with the representatives of seven other Republics, Akayev signed the Treaty of the new Economic Community on 18 October 1991 and the republican Government also approved the draft treaty of the proposed Union of Sovereign States. When Russia, Byelorussia and Ukraine proposed a new Commonwealth of Independent States to replace the USSR, Akayev was quick to announce his approval of the proposal. On 13 December all five Central Asian Republics formally agreed to join the new Commonwealth and, on 21 December, a total of 11 Republics agreed to its formation.

Economy

Kyrgyzstan has major deposits of antimony, mercury, uranium and coal. There is also natural gas, petroleum, lead, zinc and other minerals. Mountain rivers (notably the Naryn, Talass and Chu) provide a source of hydro-electric energy. Industries are chiefly associated with the extraction and processing of the region's raw materials, including coal, natural gas and petroleum extraction, power generation and the mining and processing of non-ferrous metals. Cement and other building materials are also produced; light industries include footwear, textiles and food-processing. Grain, sugar beet, tobacco and cotton are the main agricultural crops. There is some excellent land for stock breeding, notably of sheep and pigs.

Kyrgyzstan has one of the smallest economies of the former Soviet Republics, contributing only 0.8% of Soviet net material product (NMP) in 1988. Of total Soviet industrial NMP, Kyrgyzstan provided 0.6%, and of agricultural NMP, 1.2%. In 1988 50.2% of NMP was derived from exports to other Republics, and 1.2%, the lowest of any Republic, came from exports to other countries.

Statistical Survey

Source: State Committee of the Republic of Kyrgyzstan, 720084 Bishkek.

Population

BIRTHS AND DEATHS (per 1,000)

	1987	1988	1989
Birth rate	32.6	31.2	30.4
Death rate	7.3	7.4	7.2

Agriculture

PRINCIPAL CROPS ('000 metric tons)

	1987	1988	1989
Grain	1,909	1,758	1,654.8
Seed cotton	73	79	74
Potatoes	287	332	324.3
Other vegetables . . .	491	553	585.3
Grapes	36	28	33.3
Other fruit	89	145	79.4

LIVESTOCK ('000 head at 1 January)

	1988	1989	1990
Cattle	1,161.0	1,190.1	1,213.9
Pigs	387.6	416.4	440.5
Sheep and goats . . .	10,389.8	10,404.9	10,485.9

LIVESTOCK PRODUCTS ('000 metric tons)

	1987	1988	1989
Meat (slaughter weight) . .	203.6	222.5	239.4
Milk	997.5	1,063.2	1,148.0
Eggs (million)	612.1	665.8	699.7
Wool (greasy)	37.4	38.0	38.2

Mining and Industry

Production (1989, unless otherwise stated): Coal 3,997,000 metric tons, Crude petroleum 230,000 tons (1975), Natural gas 1.05m. tons, Cement 1,165,900 tons, Crude steel 8,900 tons (1975), Motor cars 17,700 (1975), Electric energy 14,903m. kWh.

Education

(1988/89)

	Institutions	Students
Secondary schools	1,752	928,200
Secondary specialized schools . . .	47	49,152
Professional/Technical Schools . .	109	38,923
Higher schools (incl. universities) . .	10	57,109

Directory

The Government

(December 1991)

PRESIDENCY

President of the Republic of Kyrgyzstan: ASKAR AKAYEV (elected 12 October 1991).

Vice-President: GERMAN S. KUZNETSOV.

CABINET OF MINISTERS

Chairman: (vacant).

Minister of Agriculture: (vacant)

Minister of Communications: EMIL BEKPETOV.

Minister of Culture: DANIEL NAZARMASHEV.

Minister of Education: (vacant).

Minister of Finance: KERIMZHAN KUNAKUNOV.

Minister of Foreign Affairs: MURAT INOMALIYEV.

Minister of Health: NAKEN KASIYEV.

Minister of Internal Affairs: FELIKS KULOV.

Minister of Justice: USUP MUKUMBAYEV.

Minister of Tourism: (vacant).

Minister of Trade: ALEKSANDR N. ZHELEZNOV.

Minister, Chairman of the State Committee for National Security: ANARBEK BAKAYEV.

MINISTRIES

Ministry of Agriculture: Bishkek, ul. Pervomayskaya, Gosagroprom Bldg.

Ministry of Communications: 720000 Bishkek, Leninsky pr. 96; tel. (3312) 22-20-34.

Ministry of Culture: 720003 Bishkek, ul. Kirova 205; tel. (3312) 22-25-32.

Ministry of Education: Bishkek, ul. Krasnooktyabrskaya 157; tel. (3312) 72-08-88.

Ministry of Finance: 720505 Bishkek, ul. Kirova 207; tel. (3312) 22-34-35.

Ministry of Foreign Affairs: 720003 Bishkek, ul. Kirova 205; tel. (3312) 22-59-14.

Ministry of Health: 720005 Bishkek, ul. Moskovskaya 148; tel. (3312) 22-86-97.

Ministry of Internal Affairs: Bishkek, ul. Frunze 469; tel. (3312) 22-54-90.

Ministry of Justice: 720505 Bishkek, ul. Orazekova 37; tel. (3312) 26-47-92.

Ministry of Tourism: Bishkek, pr. Dzerzhinskovo 5; tel. (3312) 72-08-74.

Ministry of Trade: Bishkek; tel. (3312) 26-46-76.

Legislature

SUPREME SOVIET

Elections to the Supreme Soviet were held on 25 February 1990, the Communist candidates mostly being elected unopposed. The Party subsequently became split into factions and, following the coup attempt of August 1991, it was formally banned.

Chairman: M. SHERIMKULOV.

Deputy Chairman: RENAT KULMATOV.

Local Government

The system of local government was reorganized in 1990 with the creation of two new oblasts, Chu oblast and Dzhalal-Abad oblast.

Bishkek City Soviet of People's Deputies: Bishkek; Chair. ABDYBEK ASANKULOVICH SUTALINOV.

Chu Oblast Soviet of People's Deputies: Bishkek; Chair. APAS DZHUMAGALUVICH DZHUMAGULOV.

Dzhalal-Abad Oblast Soviet of People's Deputies: Dzhalal-Abad; Chair. BEKMAMAT OSMONOVICH OSMONOV.

Issyk-Kul Oblast Soviet of People's Deputies: Przhevalsk; Chair. TEMPI DUYSHEYEVICH OROZBAYEV.

Naryn Oblast Soviet of People's Deputies: Naryn; Chair. KEMEL ZHAKESHOVICH ASHIRILAYEV.

Osh Oblast Soviet of People's Deputies: Osh; Chair. BATYRALI SYDYKOVICH SYDYKOV.

Talas Oblast Soviet of People's Deputies: Talas; Chair. DASTAN ISLAMOVICH SARYGULOV.

Political Organizations

On 31 August 1991 the Communist Party of Kyrgyzstan was disbanded.

Erkin Kyrgyzstan (ErK): Bishkek; advocates economic system based on private ownership; Chair. OMURBEK TEKEBAYEV.

Kyrgyzstan Democratic Movement: Bishkek; f. 1990; co-ordinating body for democratic groups; Pres QAZAT AKHMATOV, TOPCHUBEK TURGUNALY KOZHOMBERDITEGIN.

  Ashar: Bishkek; f. 1989; concerned with provision of land and homes for Kirghiz.

  Aqiqat (Truth): Bishkek; student political organization.

Osh Aymaghi (Osh Region): Osh; concerned with allocation of land in Osh region.

Kirghiz Democratic Wing: Osh; f. 1990; works for greater religious tolerance and the construction of mosques and religious schools.

National Unity: Bishkek; f. 1991; moderate democratic party, seeks to unite different ethnic groups; Leader GERMAN KUZNETSOV.

The Slavic Association: Bishkek; represents Slavic minority in Kyrgyzstan; Vice-Pres. ANATOLY BULGAKOV.

Uzbek Adalet (Uzbek Justice): Osh; f. 1989; advocates autonomy for the Uzbeks in Osh and use of Uzbek as a state language in the region; 400,000 mems.

Judicial System

Chairman of the Supreme Court: K. D. BOOBEKOV.

Procurator-General: GENNADY I. IVANTSOV.

Religion

ISLAM

The majority of Kirghiz are Sunni Muslims (Hanafi school), as are some other groups living in the Republic, such as Uzbeks and Tadzhiks. In 1991 there were 60 mosques operating in the Republic (18 of which opened in 1991). Under Soviet rule, only small, selected groups were permitted to travel on the Muslim pilgrimage, the *hajj*, but in 1991 some 500 Muslims were reported to have made the journey. Muslims in Kyrgyzstan are officially under the jurisdication of the Spiritual Directorate of Central Asia, based in Uzbekistan. The directorate is represented in the Republic by a *kazi*.

Pres. of the Islamic Centre of Kyrgyzstan: SADYKZHAN-HAJI KAMALOV.

The Press

In 1990 there were 114 newspapers published in Kyrgyzstan, including 42 published in Kirghiz. The daily circulation was 1,529,000 copies (862,000 in Kirghiz). There were 42 periodicals, including 16 in Kirghiz, with a total circulation of 35.4m. copies (10.2m. in Kirghiz).

PRINCIPAL NEWSPAPERS

Bishkek Shamy (Bishkek Evening Newspaper): Bishkek; f. 1989; 4 a week; official organ of the Bishkek City Soviet of People's Deputies; in Kirghiz; Editor M. AIDARKULOV; circ. 115,000.

Komsomolets Kyrgyzstan (Member of the Leninist Young Communist League of Kyrgyzstan): Bishkek; f. 1938; weekly.

Kyrgyz Tuusu: Bishkek; f. 1924; 6 a week; fmrly *Sovettik Kyrgyzstan* (Soviet Kyrgyzstan), organ of the Kirghiz Communist Party; organ of the Council of Ministers; in Kirghiz; Chief Editor T. ISHEMKULOV; circ. 180,000.

Slovo Kyrgyzstana (Word of Kyrgyzstan): Bishkek.

Vecherny Bishkek (Bishkek Evening Newspaper): Bishkek; f. 1974; 5 a week; official organ of the Bishkek Soviet of People's Deputies; in Russian; Editor K. Y. MUSTAFAYEV; circ. 118,500.

Zhashtyk Zharchysy (Youth Herald): Bishkek; f. 1926; 3 a week; in Kirghiz; Chief Editor A. RYSKULOV; circ. 148,800.

PRINCIPAL PERIODICALS

Monthly unless otherwise indicated.

Ala Too (Ala Too Mountains): 720300 Bishkek, ul. Kirova 205; tel. (3312) 26-88-75; f. 1931; monthly; publ. by the Ala Too Publishing House; journal of the Union of Writers; politics, novels, short stories, plays, poems of Kirghiz authors and translations into Kirghiz; in Kirghiz; Editor-in-Chief K. DZHUSUPOV; circ. 30,000.

Chalkan (Stinging-nettle): Bishkek; f. 1955; satirical; in Kirghiz; Editor-in-Chief A. STAMOV; circ. 111,700.

Den Cooluk (Health): Bishkek; f. 1955; journal of the Ministry of Health; popular science; in Kirghiz; Editor-in-Chief M. ALIYEV; circ. 125,500.

Kirghizstan Kommunisti (Kirghiz Communist): Bishkek; f. 1926; fmrly publ. by the Kirghiz Communist Party Publishing House; political; in Kirghiz and Russian; Editor-in-Chief U. CHOTONOV; circ. 16,900.

Kyrgyz Zheri (Land of Kyrgyzstan): Bishkek; f. 1955; problems of agriculture; in Kirghiz and Russian; Editor-in-Chief T. NASIRIDINOV; circ. 14,850.

Kyrgyzstan Ayaldary (Women of Kyrgyzstan): Bishkek; f. 1951; popular; in Kirghiz; Editor-in-Chief D. MUKAMBETOVA; circ. 79,500.

Kyrgyzstan Madaniyaty (Culture in Kyrgyzstan): 729301 Bishkek, ul. Bokonbayeva 99; tel. (3312) 26-14-06; f. 1967; weekly; organ of the Union of Writers and the Ministry of Culture; Editor-in-Chief D. SADYKOV; circ. 87,600.

Literaturny Kirghizstan (Literature of Kyrgyzstan): 720301 Bishkek, ul. Pushkina 70; tel. (3312) 26-14-63; f. 1955; monthly; publ. by the Ala Too Publishing House; journal of the Union of Writers; fiction, literary criticism, journalism; in Russian; Editor-in-Chief A. I. IVANOV; circ. 45,000.

Zaman Dzharchisi (Herald of Time): Bishkek; f. 1944 as the journal of the Kirghiz Communist Party; socio-political; in Kirghiz and Russian; Editor-in-Chief L. B. DZHOLMUKAMEDOVA; circ. 14,050.

Zdravookhraneniye Kirgizii (Public Health System of Kyrgyzstan): Bishkek; f. 1938; 6 a year; publ. by the Ala Too Publishing House; journal of the Ministry of Health; medical experimental work; in Russian; Editor-in-Chief B. I. ISMAILOV; circ. 6,300.

NEWS AGENCY

KirTAG (Kirghiz Telegraph Agency): Bishkek.

Publishers

Adabiyat (Literature): Bishkek, ul. Sovetskaya 170; f. 1988; fiction; in Russian, Kirghiz, Dungan and English; Dir S. D. DZHETIMISHEV.

Ilim (Science): Bishkek, ul. Pushkina 144; scientific and science fiction; Dir L. V. TARASOVA.

Kirghizskaya Sovetskaya Entsiklopediya (Kirghiz Soviet Encyclopedia): Bishkek, pr. Dzerdzhinskova 56; dictionaries and encyclopaedias; Editor-in-Chief M. B. BORBUGULOV.

Kyrghyzstan (Kyrgyzstan Publishing House): 720737 Bishkek, ul. Sovetskaya 170; tel. (3312) 26-79-80; politics, science, economics, agriculture and fiction; Dir A. D. IMANKULOV.

Mektep (School): Bishkek, ul. Sovetskaya 170; popular for children; Dir. S. N. NAMATBAEV.

Radio

Dom Radio: 720885 Bishkek 10, pr. Molodoy gvardii 63; broadcasts in Kirghiz, German, Dungan and Russian.

Finance

BANKING

State Banks

State Bank of Kyrgyzstan: Bishkek, ul. Sverdlova 101; Chair. of Bd. S. A. BORONBAYEV; First Deputy Chair. of Bd. LYUDMILA V. PISMENNAYA.

Republican Foreign Trade Bank of Kyrgyzstan: Bishkek; fmrly br. of USSR Vneshekonombank; Man. O. B. ABDYRAZAKOV.

COMMODITY EXCHANGE

Kyrgyzstan Commodity and Raw Materials Exchange (KICME): 720010 Bishkek, ul. Kievskaya 43; tel. (3312) 28-55-91; fax (3312) 28-52-31; f. 1990; authorized cap. 6m. roubles; Gen. Dir TEMIR SARIYEV.

Trade and Industry

CHAMBER OF COMMERCE

Chamber of Commerce and Industry of the Republic of Kyrgyzstan: 720300 Bishkek, ul. Kirova 205; tel. (3312) 26-49-42; telex 251239; Chair. KARCHINB Y. IVANOVICH.

Culture

NATIONAL ORGANIZATION

Ministry of Culture: see section on The Government (Ministries).

CULTURAL HERITAGE

Chernyshevsky State Public Library of Kyrgyzstan: 720873 Bishkek, ul. Ogonbayeva 242; tel. (3312) 6-25-70; over 3,514,700 vols; Dir. A. S. SAGIMBAYEVA.

State Historical Museum of Kyrgyzstan: Bishkek, Krasnooktyabrskaya ul. 236; 20,000 items; Dir. N. M. SEITKAZIYEVA.

State Museum of Fine Art of Kyrgyzstan: Bishkek, ul. Pervomaiskaya 90; 4,000 modern exhibits; Dir. K. N. UZUBALIYEVA.

PERFORMING ARTS

State Drama Theatre: Bishkek, ul. Panfilova 273.
State Opera and Ballet Theatre: Bishkek, ul. Sovetskaya 167.
State Philharmonia: Bishkek, pr. Lenina.

ASSOCIATION

Union of Writers of Kyrgyzstan: 720301 Bishkek, ul. Pushkina 70; tel. (3312) 22-26-53.

Education

Until the 1920s there was little provision for education in Kyrgyzstan, although there were some Islamic schools and colleges and Russian-language schools were provided for the Slav population. The first Soviet schools were established in 1923; by 1988/89 there were 1,908 institutions of secondary education in the Republic. There were also 10 institutions of higher education, including one university. In 1988 52.4% of pupils in general education dayschools were taught in Kirghiz, 34.0% were taught in Russian, 13.1% in Uzbek and 0.2% in Tadzhik.

UNIVERSITY

State University of Kyrgyzstan: 720024 Bishkek, ul. Frunze 537; tel. (3312) 26-26-34; f. 1951; 15 faculties; 600 teachers; 13,000 students; Rector M. Z. ZAKIROV.

The Environment

As a result of its low level of industrialization and its distance from the ecological problems of the Aral Sea, Kyrgyzstan has been less affected than some other Republics by environmental problems. Nevertheless, the climate of the entire Central Asian region is affected by the climatic changes engendered by the dessication of the Aral Sea.

ACADEMIC INSTITUTE

Academy of Sciences of the Republic of Kyrgyzstan: 720071 Bishkek, Leninsky pr. 265A; tel. (3312) 26-45-41; telex 251245; f. 1954; several attached institutes involved in environmental research; Pres. Acad. I. T. AITMATOV.

MOLDAVIA

Geography

The Republic of Moldavia, or Moldova (formerly the Moldavian Soviet Socialist Republic, a constituent Union Republic of the USSR), is situated in south-eastern Europe. It includes only a small proportion of the historical territories of Moldavia, most of which are in Romania, while others (southern Bessarabia and Northern Bukovina) are in Ukraine. The Republic is bounded to the north, east and south by Ukraine. To the west there is an international frontier with Romania. It covers an area of 33,700 sq km (13,010 sq miles).

Moldavia is a fertile plain with small areas of hill country in the centre and north of the Republic. The main rivers are the Dniestr (Dniester), which flows through the eastern regions into the Black Sea, and the Prut (Prutul), which marks the western border with Romania. The climate is very favourable for agriculture, with long, warm summers and relatively mild winters. Average temperatures in Kishinev (Chişinău) range from 21°C (70°F) in July to −4°C (24°F) in January.

At the census of 1989, at which the total population was 4,341,000, 64.5% of the population were Moldavians (ethnic Romanians), 13.8% Ukrainians, 13.0% Russians, 3.5% Gagauz, 2.0% Jews and 1.5% Bulgarians. Romanian, a Romance language, replaced Russian as the official language in 1989. It is now mostly written in the Latin alphabet; in 1940 the Cyrillic script had been introduced and the language referred to as 'Moldavian'. Ethnic minorities continue to use their own languages; only some 12% of non-Romanians in the Republic are fluent in Romanian, whereas most of them speak Russian. The Gagauz speak a Turkic language, written in the Cyrillic script, but 71% of them claim fluency in Russian; only 4.4% are fluent in Romanian. Most of the inhabitants of Moldavia profess Christianity, the largest denomination being the Eastern Orthodox Church. The Gagauz, despite their Turkish origins, are adherents of Orthodox Christianity. The Russian Orthodox Church (Moscow Patriarchy) has jurisdiction in the Republic, but there are Romanian and Turkish liturgies.

The total population at January 1991 was 4,367,000. The capital is Kishinev (Chişinău), which was situated in the central region of the Republic. It had a population of 720,000 in 1989. Other important centres are the northern town of Beltsy (Bălţi—population in 1989, 159,000) and Tiraspol (182,000), which is situated on the east bank of the River Dniestr, where a majority of the population are ethnic Slavs. The Gagauz mostly inhabit the southern districts, especially the region around the town of Komrat (Comrat).

History

The medieval principality of Moldavia was, for much of its history, under Hungarian and, briefly, Lithuanian suzerainty. During the 16th century, however, Eastern Moldavia (or Bessarabia—the portion of Moldavia east of the River Prut) came under Turkish control, and in 1812 it was annexed by Russia. In 1856, as a result of the Crimean War, Russia lost southern Bessarabia (now part of Ukraine) to Romanian Moldavia, but recovered it at the Congress of Berlin in 1878. In March 1918, after the collapse of the Russian Empire, Bessarabia became part of Romania, but the USSR refused to recognize Romania's claims to the territory, and, on 12 October 1924, formed a Moldavian

Autonomous Soviet Socialist Republic (ASSR) on the eastern side of the Dniestr, in an area largely populated by Ukrainians. In June 1940 Romania was forced to cede Bessarabia and northern Bukovina to the USSR, the annexation having been agreed with Germany in the 1939 Nazi-Soviet Pact. Northern Bukovina, southern Bessarabia and the Kotovsk-Balta region of the Moldavian ASSR were incorporated into the Ukrainian SSR. The remaining parts of the Moldavian ASSR and of Bessarabia were merged to form a new Union Republic, the Moldavian Soviet Socialist Republic, which formally joined the USSR on 2 August 1940.

Between July 1941 and August 1944 the Moldavian SSR was reunited with Romania. However, the Soviet Army reannexed the region in 1944, and the Moldavian SSR was re-established. Soviet policy in Moldavia concentrated on isolating the region from its historical links with Romania: cross-border traffic virtually ceased; the Cyrillic script was imposed on the Romanian language (which was referred to as Moldavian); and Russian and Ukrainian immigration was encouraged. In the 1950s thousands of ethnic Romanians were deported to Central Asia.

The policy of *glasnost*, introduced by Soviet leader Mikhail Gorbachev, in 1986, allowed the expression of opposition to this process of 'russification'. Although the Communist Party of Moldavia (CPM) issued a decree, in May 1987, which increased provision for the teaching of Romanian in schools, this did little to satisfy public opinion. In 1988 there were demands for an immediate halt to immigration, for the restoration of the Latin alphabet and for Romanian to be declared the official language of the Republic.

In May 1989 a number of independent cultural and political groups, which had emerged in 1988–89, but were denied legal status by the authorities, joined together to form the Popular Front of Moldavia. In June some 70,000 people attended a protest demonstration, organized by the Popular Front, on the anniversary of the Soviet annexation of Bessarabia in 1940. This was followed, in August, by large demonstrations in Kishinev, to support legislation in the Supreme Soviet which proposed to make Romanian the official language of the Republic. Following protests from the non-Romanians and a strike, on 29 August, by ethnic Russians and Ukrainians, the proposals were amended. On 1 September a law was enacted, which provided for Russian to be retained as a language of inter-ethnic communication, but the official language was to be Romanian and the Latin script reintroduced.

Disturbances during the Revolution Day celebrations in Kishinev, on 7 November 1989, and rioting three days later led to the dismissal of the First Secretary of the CPM, Semyon Grossu. He was replaced by Petr Luchinsky (Lucinschi), a younger man and an ethnic Romanian considered to be more supportive of Gorbachev's reforms.

The increasing influence of the Romanian-speaking population was strongly opposed by the other inhabitants of the Republic. In the areas east of the Dniestr, where Russians and Ukrainians predominated, the local authorities refused to implement the language law. Opposition to growing Moldavian nationalism was led by Intermovement 'Yedinstvo' (Unity), a group dominated by leading CPM members, and the United Work Collectives, an organization based among the working-class Slavs of the towns east of the Dniestr. These two organizations acted in close co-operation, and had strong links with Gagauz Halky (Gagauz People), the most prominent of the political groups representing the Gagauz minority. On 28 January 1990 a referendum took place in Tiraspol, in which the predominantly Russian-speaking population voted overwhelmingly to seek greater autonomy for the region beyond the Dniestr (Transdniestria).

None of the independent political groups were officially allowed to support candidates in the elections to the Moldavian Supreme Soviet, which took place on 25 February 1990, but individual candidates made clear where their sympathies lay. Although some 80% of the 380 deputies elected were members of the CPM, many were also sympathetic to the aims of the Popular Front. Approximately 40% of the new deputies were supported by the Front and a further 30% were estimated to be broadly in favour of its main aims. The remaining 30% were mostly representatives of the non-Romanian population. When the new Supreme Soviet convened in April, Mircea Snegur, a CPM member supported by the Popular Front, was elected Chairman of the Supreme Soviet. (In September he was elected to the newly-instituted post of President of the Republic and the Chairman of the Supreme Soviet became solely a parliamentary speaker.) Another of the nationalists' proposals, the adoption of the red, yellow and blue tricolour of Romania as the Republic's official flag (although with a Moldavian coat of arms to distinguish it from that of the Romanian state) was also approved.

On 24 May 1990 the Government of Petr Paskar resigned after losing a vote of 'no confidence'. A leading reformist economist, Mircea Druc, was appointed Chairman of a Council of Ministers dominated by radical reformers. The new Government carried out far-reaching changes to political life in Moldavia. The CPM's constitutional right to power was revoked and interference by any political party in the management of state institutions, the media and law-enforcement agencies was forbidden. Printing presses, newspapers and radio stations belonging to the CPM were transferred to state control. On 23 June 1990 the Moldavian Supreme Soviet passed a declaration of sovereignty which asserted the supremacy of Moldavia's Constitution and laws throughout the Republic. The Supreme Soviet also declared the 1940 annexation of Bessarabia to have been illegal and, on 24 June, thousands of Moldavians and Romanians met on the border for a ceremony to mark the 50th anniversary of the annexation.

The actions of the increasingly radical Romanian majority in parliament provoked further anxiety among the minorities during 1990. The Gagauz, on 19 August, and then the east-bank Slavs, on 2 September, proclaimed 'Autonomous Soviet Socialist Republics'. The 'Gagauz Soviet Socialist Republic' was proclaimed in the southern region, around Komrat, where most of the Gagauz live. The 'Dniestr Soviet Socialist Republic' consisted of Moldavian territory east of the Dniestr and had its headquarters in Tiraspol. Both declarations were immediately annulled by the Moldavian Supreme Soviet.

On 25 October 1990 the Gagauz held elections to a 'Republic of Gagauzia' Supreme Soviet. Moldavian nationalists sought to prevent this by sending some 50,000 armed volunteers to the area. Violence was only prevented by the dispatch of Soviet troops to the region. The elections proceeded and, on 31 October, the new 'Gagauz Supreme Soviet' convened in Komrat. Stepan Topal was elected as its president.

In November 1990 further inter-ethnic violence occurred in the predominantly Russian-speaking areas east of the Dniestr, when elections were announced to a 'Transdniestr Supreme Soviet'. Four people were killed and at least 16 injured when Moldavian police attempted to regain control of the east-bank town of Dubossary, where the local authorities had announced a state of emergency. Talks held in Moscow, between the Moldavian Government, the east-bank Slavs and the Gagauz failed to resolve the crisis, but the elections proceeded without further violence.

The Moldavian leadership refused to attend further tripartite talks, proposed in December 1990. Instead, on 16 December, an estimated 800,000 people, attending a 'Grand National Assembly' (the previous Grand National Assembly, in August 1989, had demanded Romanian as the official language), voted by acclamation to reject any new Union Treaty. Furthermore, on 19 February 1991, the Moldavian Supreme Soviet resolved not to carry out the all-Union referendum on the future of the Union, which was scheduled for 17 March, and to endorse the idea of a confederation of states without central control as the preferred replacement for the USSR. Despite the official boycott, some 650,000 people did take part in the referendum, mostly Russians, Ukrainians and Gagauz: they voted almost unanimously for the preservation of the Union.

Despite opposition to Moldavian secession from the Republic's ethnic minorities, the Moldavian-dominated Government and parliament continued the process of *de facto* secession from the USSR. All-Union enterprises were placed under republican jurisdiction, a Moldavian State Bank was established, independent of the USSR Gosbank, the Communist Party was prohibited from activities in state and government organs, the military draft to the USSR Armed Forces was not implemented and the Government announced its intention to form a national guard, the *carabinieri*.

Following the seizure of power by an eight-man emergency committee in Moscow, on 19 August 1991, the commanders of the South-Western Military District attempted to impose a state of emergency in Moldavia. Their demands were rejected by the republican leadership, which immediately announced their support for Russian President Boris Yeltsin's opposition to the coup and demanded the reinstatement of Gorbachev as President of the USSR. On 27 August, after the coup had collapsed, the Moldavian Parliament and a Grand National Assembly proclaimed Moldavia's independence from the USSR. The independence proclamation committed Moldavia to adhere to international agreements on human rights, declared the exclusive validity of Moldavian legislation in the Republic, and demanded the withdrawal of Soviet troops from Moldavian territory.

The declaration of independence was followed by practical measures to implement Moldavian secession from the USSR. The Moldavian Government asserted its jurisdiction over the border with Romania, including all customs installations. Customs posts were also introduced on the border with Ukraine. In September President Snegur ordered the creation of national Armed Forces and took control of the republican KGB, transforming it into a Ministry of National Security. In the same month the Government announced that it would no longer participate in any all-Union structures or in negotiations for a new political union. However, in November the leadership did sign the Treaty of the Economic Community. When a Commonwealth of Independent States was proposed as the replacement for the USSR, in December, Moldavia expressed a willingness to participate, on the condition that the Commonwealth did not impinge on Moldavian independence. Support for independence was further demonstrated when elections were held to the republican presidency on 8 December. Mircea Snegur was the only candidate and received 98.2% of the votes cast. On 21 December Moldavia agreed to membership of the Commonwealth of Independent States, by the Alma-Ata Declaration of 11 Republics. Subsequent negotiations over a continued unified command for Commonwealth armed forces allowed Moldavia (and other Republics) to have a national guard.

Following the revolution in Romania, in December 1989, some members of the Popular Front advocated reunification with Romania. Although subsequent events in Romania lessened some of the support for such a policy it continued to be advocated by some of the more extreme nationalist groups. In January 1990 the Romanian–Moldavian border was reopened for private travel and cultural and educational contacts were quickly developed. Economic links were proposed but the problems of both economies limited the development of cross-border trade. Consular links were established and, in August 1991, Romania recognized the independence of Moldavia and established diplomatic relations. In late 1991 there was an increase in support for reunification, prompted by the establishment, in December, of the National Council for Reunification, which aimed to achieve a united Romanian state in the near future. President Snegur rejected such ambitions, in an attempt to allay the fears of the ethnic minorities. Moldavia had difficulty establishing developed political or economic relations with other countries, many of which cited inter-ethnic tension within the Republic as reasons for delaying recognition of independent Moldavia. However, following the formation of the Commonwealth of Independent States and the effective dissolution of the USSR, Moldavia was one of the first Republics to be recognized by the international community.

Economy

The economy is concentrated on agriculture and related industries. Important crops include fruit, wine grapes, vegetables, tobacco and grain. In 1990, according to official estimates, Moldavia produced 25% of Soviet fruit and vegetables, 23% of its tobacco and 10% of its meat. Viniculture is well established, and exports of wines earn important convertible currency revenue. The industry was, however, seriously disrupted by the anti-alcohol campaign of the mid-1980s, when some vineyards were replaced by other crops.

There has been some development of light industry, but it is still largely dominated by food-processing plants, wine distilleries and tobacco production. Textiles, chemicals and consumer goods are also important products. In 1988 Moldavia provided 1.2% of total Soviet net material product (NMP), including 1.0% of total industrial NMP and 1.8% of total agricultural NMP. In that year 62.1% of NMP was derived from exports to other Republics, while 3.4% came from exports to other countries.

Statistical Survey
Population

BIRTHS AND DEATHS (per 1,000)

	1985	1986	1987
Birth rate	21.9	22.7	21.8
Death rate	11.2	9.7	9.6

Agriculture

PRINCIPAL CROPS ('000 metric tons)

	1985	1986	1987
Grain	2,373	2,044	2,011
Sugar beet	2,365	2,413	2,155
Sunflower seed . . .	244	253	209
Potatoes	408	449	304
Other vegetables . .	1,253	1,438	1,282
Grapes	n.a.	1,222	1,040
Other fruit	999	1,202	1,074

LIVESTOCK ('000 head at 1 January)

	1986	1987	1988
Cattle	1,259	1,214	1,162
Pigs	1,962	1,892	1,703
Sheep and goats . .	1,257	1,253	1,258
Poultry	22,631	20,927	21,485

LIVESTOCK PRODUCTS ('000 metric tons)

	1985	1986	1987
Meat (slaughter weight) . .	303	328	331
Milk	1,402	1,398	1,421
Eggs (million) . . .	1,082	1,119	1,116
Wool (greasy)	2.6	2.8	2.7

Industry

SELECTED PRODUCTS

	1985	1986	1987
Pumps (number) . . .	107,000	106,300	92,000
Tractors (number) . .	11,200	11,600	11,800
Refrigerators (number) . .	200,000	194,300	n.a.
Electric energy (million kWh) .	16,800	17,700	17,400

Education

(1987/88)

	Institutions	Students
Secondary schools	1,617	731,000
Secondary specialized institutions . .	52	52,084
Higher schools (incl. universities) . .	9	58,970

Directory
The Government
(December 1991)

HEAD OF STATE

President: MIRCEA ION SNEGUR (elected 8 December 1991).

COUNCIL OF MINISTERS

Chairman: VALERIU MURAVSCHI.

First Deputy Chairman: CONSTANTIN OBOROC.

Deputy Chairman and Minister of Finance and the National Economy: CONSTANTIN TAMPIZA.

Deputy Chairman and Minister of Agriculture and the Food Industry: ANDREY N. SANGELI.

Minister of Construction: GEORGIU G. KELUGERU.

Minister of Culture and Religion: ION S. UNGURIANU.

Minister of Foreign Affairs: NIKOLAE A. TSYU.

Minister of Health: GEORGE P. GIDIRIM.

Minister of Information and Communications: TIMOFEY I. ANDROS.

Minister of Industry and Energy: DUMITRU N. LESHENKO.

Minister of Internal Affairs: ION G. KOSTASH.

Minister of Justice: ALEXEI A. BARBENIAGRE.

Minister of Labour and Social Security: GEORGE A. SPINEY.

Minister of Material Resources: CONSTANTIN N. YAVORSKY.

Minister of National Security: ANATOL T. PLUGARU.

Minister of Science and Education: NIKOLAE G. MATKASH.

Minister of Trade: VALERIU BOBUTSAK.

Minister of Transport: VALERIU G. KOZLOV.

Minister, Director-General of the State Department for Military Affairs: Col NICOLAE CHIRTOACA.

MINISTRIES

Ministry of Agriculture and the Food Industry: Kishinev, Bd. Ştefan cel Mare; tel. (0422) 23-35-36.

Ministry of Construction: Kishinev; tel. (0422) 23-35-17.

Ministry of Culture and Religion: Kishinev, pl. Maria Adonari Natsionale, Government House; tel. (0422) 23-39-86.

Ministry of Finance: Kishinev, ul. Kosmonavtov 7; tel. (0422) 23-35-75.

Ministry of Foreign Affairs: Kishinev, pl. Maria Adonari Natsionale, Government House; tel. (0422) 23-37-28.

Ministry of Health: Kishinev, Str. Hînceşti 1; tel. (0422) 72-10-10.

Ministry of Information and Communications: Kishinev, Bd. Ştefan cel Mare; tel. (0422) 24-27-47.

Ministry of Industry and Energy: Kishinev, Bd. Ştefan cel Mare 67; tel. (0422) 23-35-56.

Ministry of Internal Affairs: Kishinev, Bd. Ştefan cel Mare 67; tel. (0422) 23-35-69.

Ministry of Justice: Kishinev; tel. (0422) 23-33-79.

Ministry of Labour and Social Security: Kishinev, Str. Hînceşti 1; tel. (0422) 73-75-72.

Ministry of Material Resources: Kishinev, Bd. Ştefan cel Mare; tel. (0422) 23-33-34; fax (0422) 22-44-47.

Ministry of the National Economy: Kishinev, pl. Maria Adonari Natsionale, Government House; tel. (0422) 23-35-31.

Ministry of National Security: Kishinev, Bd. Ştefan cel Mare 166; tel. (0422) 23-93-09.

Ministry of Science and Education: Kishinev, ul. Mitropolit G. Benulecku-Bodoni; tel. (0422) 22-61-89; fax (0422) 22-61-89.

Ministry of Trade: Kishinev, Bd. Ştefan cel Mare 77; tel. (0422) 23-35-82.

Ministry of Transport: Kishinev; tel. (0422) 62-07-50.

State Department

State Department for Military Affairs: Kishinev.

Legislature

MOLDAVIAN PARLIAMENT

The Parliament comprises 366 deputies. Elections were held in February 1990 to the Supreme Soviet (renamed the Moldavian Parliament in May 1991), with the Communist Party as the only officially recognized party. Of those elected an estimated 122 had the support of the Popular Front of Moldavia.

Chairman: ALEXANDRU MOŞANU.

First Deputy Chairman: ION HADIRCA.

Local Government

In August 1991 the mainly Russian-speaking inhabitants of the region of Moldavia east of the Dniestr river unilaterally declared the independence of the 'Dniestrian Soviet Socialist Republic'. Igor Smirnov, the 'premier' of the Republic, was arrested in August, charged with supporting the coup attempt of 19 August. In the south of Moldavia, around the town of Komrat, the Gagauz also established an autonomous 'Gagauz Soviet Socialist Republic'. On 1 December 1991 the two regions conducted referendums on

independence and presidential elections were held. The referendums and elections were declared unconstitutional by the Moldavian authorities.

'President of the Dniestr SSR': IGOR N. SMIRNOV.

'President of the Gagauz SSR': STEPAN TOPOL.

Political Organizations

In August 1991 the Moldavian Parliament voted to ban the Communist Party of Moldavia.

Gagauz Halky: Komrat; represents the ethnic Gagauz population.

National Alliance for Independence: Kishinev; f. 1991 as a coalition of 12 pro-independence parties; incl.:

Moldavian Democratic Movement: Kishinev; Chair. YURY BOGDANOV.

National Christian Party: Kishinev; f.1990.

Popular Front of Moldavia: Kishinev; f. 1989 as a co-ordinating body for various unoffical groups, incl. the Alexei Mateevici Cultural Club and the Moldavian Democratic Movement in Support of Perestroika; Chair. of Executive Cttee IURIE ROSCA.

Social Democratic Party: Kishinev; f. 1990.

Yedinstvo: Kishinev; supported mainly by ethnic Slavs, opposed to an independent Moldavia.

In 1991 several small political groups, which represented ethnic minorities, but supported Moldavian indepedence, were established. They included **Democratic Moldavia** (leader, YELENA BARTASHEVICH), a movement of ethnic Russians in support of independence, the **Society for Ukrainian Culture** (MIKHAILO REPCHINSKY) and the **Jewish Cultural Society** (ALEKSANDR BRODSKY).

Judicial System

Chairman of the Supreme Court: V. S. PUŞCAŞ.

Procurator: M. DEMIDENCO.

The Press

In 1989 there were 200 officially-registered newspapers being published in Moldavia, including 85 published in Romanian (Moldavian), and 65 periodicals, including 30 in Romanian. In 1990 the number of Romanian-language newspapers and periodicals increased, and most publications began using the Latin script.

PRINCIPAL NEWSPAPERS

Glasul (The Voice): Kishinev.

Moldova Suverană (Sovereign Moldavia): 277612 Kishinev; f. 1924; 6 a week; organ of the Government of Moldavia; in Romanian; Editor TUDOR TSOPA; circ. 200,000.

Rabochy Tiraspol (Working Tiraspol): Tiraspol; main newspaper of the east-bank Slavs; anti-government; in Russian; Editor VALENTIN LESNICHENKO.

Nezavisimaya Moldova (Independent Moldavia): 277612 Kishinev, Str. Puşkin 22; tel. (0422) 23-36-05; f. 1925; 5 a week; independent; in Russian; Editor YELENA ZAMURA.

Tinerimya Moldovei/Molodezh Moldovy (Youth of Moldavia): Kishinev; f. 1928; 3 a week; fmrly organ of the Cen. Cttee of the Leninist Young Communist League of Moldova; editions in Romanian (circ. 130,000) and Russian (circ. 30,000); Editor V. BOTNARU.

Vyatsa Satului (Life of the Village): Kishinev, Str. Puşkin 22, Casa presei, et. 4; tel. (0422) 23-30-68; f. 1945; 3 a week; govt publication; in Romanian; Editor V. S. SPINEY; circ. 112,000.

PRINCIPAL PERIODICALS

Femeya Moldovei (Moldavian Woman): Kishinev; f. 1951; monthly; popular, for women; in Romanian; circ. 304,000.

Chiparuşul (Peppercorn): 277612 Kishinev, Str. Puşkin 22; tel. (0422) 23-38-16; f. 1958; fortnightly; satirical; in Romanian; circ. 40,000; Editor-in-Chief ION VIKOL.

Literatura şi Arte: 277612 Kishinev, ul. 31 Augusta, Dom pisatelei; tel. (0422) 24-92-96; f. 1954; weekly; organ of the Union of Writers of Moldavia; literary; Editor NICOLAE DABIJA; circ. 100,000.

Nistru (The River Dniestr): Kishinev; f. 1931; monthly; journal of the Union of Writers of Moldavia; fiction; in Romanian; Editor-in-Chief D. MATKOVSKY; circ. 6,600.

Moldova (Moldova): Kishinev; f. 1966; monthly; illustrated popular and fiction; in Romanian; circ. 98,000.

Politica (Politics): 277033 Kishinev, Bd. Ştefan cel Mare 105; tel. (0422) 23-36-69; f. 1991; monthly; political; in Romanian and Russian; Editor-in-Chief Boris M. Stratulat; circ. 12,000.

Scînteia Leninista (Leninist Spark): Kishinev; f. 1930; monthly; fiction; for 10–15-year-olds; in Romanian; circ. 60,000.

Tribuna (Tribune): Kishinev; f. 1945; monthly; fmrly organ of the Cen. Cttee of the Moldavian Communist Party; in Romanian and Russian; Editor-in-Chief F. G. Tsopa; circ. 31,000.

NEWS AGENCY

Moldavian Information Agency—Moldovapres: 277012 Kishinev, Str. Puşkin 22; tel. (0422) 23-34-95; telex 163140; fax (0422) 23-43-71; f. 1990.

Publishers

In 1989 there were 1,479 titles (books and pamphlets) published in Moldavia (21.3m. copies), of which 522 titles were in Romanian (9.5m. copies).

Cartea Moldoveneasca (Moldavian Book Publishing House): Kishinev, Bd. Ştefan cel Mare; political and fiction; in Romanian, Russian, Ukrainian, Gagauz and Bulgarian; Dir N. N. Mumzhi.

Hyperion: 277004 Kishinev, Bd. Ştefan cel Mare; tel. (0422) 24-64-14; f. 1977; fiction, non-fiction, poetry, art books; in Romanian, Russian, English, French, Spanish, Gagauz and Bulgarian; Dir Ion M. Ciocanu.

Lumina (Light): Kishinev, Bd. Ştefan cel Mare 180; tel. (0422) 24-63-95; f. 1977; educational textbooks; Man. V. I. Kistruga; Editor-in-Chief Kiril F. Vakulovsky.

Moldavskaya Entsiklopediya (Moldavian Encyclopaedia): 277612 Kishinev, Str. Zhukovsky 42; tel. (0422) 22-31-86; Editor-in-Chief Ion Grosu.

Shtiintsa: Kishinev, ul. Grosul 3; tel. (0422) 21-74-21; f. 1959; scientific literature; in Romanian and Russian; Dir G. N. Prini.

GOVERNMENT AGENCY

State Department for Publishers, Polygraphy and the Book Trade: Kishinev; tel. (0422) 24-65-25; Chair. Vasily I. Bakhnaru.

Radio and Television

Radio Kishinev: 277028 Kishinev, Str. Prerezhnikov 1; broadcasts in Romanian and Russian.

Kishinev Television: 277028 Kishinev, Str. Prerezhnikov 1.

Finance

BANKING

State Banks

National Bank of Moldavia: 277006 Kishinev, Molodeji Bd. 7; Chair. of Bd L. P. Talmachov.

Bank of Foreign Economic Activity: Kishinev; tel. (0422) 26-07-48; Dir Vili A. Strashulat.

Commercial Bank

Victoriobank Moldavian Commercial Bank: Kishinev, Bd. Ştefan cel Mare 54; tel. (0422) 24-45-12; Pres. Viktor Tsurkan.

Trade and Industry

CHAMBER OF COMMERCE

Chamber of Commerce and Industry of the Republic of Moldavia: 277012 Kishinev, ul. Komsomolskaya 28; tel. (0422) 22-15-52; Chair. Vasily D. Gandrabura.

FOREIGN TRADE ORGANIZATION

Moldimpex: 277018 Kishinev, Botanicheskaya ul. 15; tel. (0422) 55-70-36; Gen. Dir V. D. Volodin.

CO-OPERATIVES' ORGANIZATION

Moldavpotrebsoyuz (Union of Co-operative Managers): Kishinev; tel. (0422) 23-35-95; Chair. Pavel. G. Dubalar.

Tourism

State Department for Tourism: Kishinev; tel. (0422) 23-33-38; Chair. Vladimir G. Dobrya.

Culture

NATIONAL ORGANIZATIONS

Ministry of Culture and Religion: see section on The Government (Ministries).

State Department for Architecture and Town Planning: Kishinev; tel. (0422) 23-39-20; Chair. Alexei G. Paladi.

CULTURAL HERITAGE

Moldavian State Art Museum: Kishinev, ul. Lenina 115; 22,000 exhibits; Dir T. V. Stavila.

National Library of the Moldavian Republic: 277612 Kishinev, Kievskaya ul. 78a; tel. (0422) 22-14-75; f. 1832; 3,500,000 vols; Dir T. M. Levandovskaya.

SPORTING ORGANIZATION

State Department for Youth Affairs and Sport: Kishinev; tel. (0422) 22-60-61; Chair. Grigore D. Popovich.

PERFORMING ARTS

Chekhov Russian Drama Theatre: Kishinev, ul. 28-vo Iyunya 75.

Opera and Ballet Theatre: Kishinev, Bd. Ştefan cel Mare 180.

Likurich Puppet Theatre: Kishinev, ul. Kievskaya 121.

State Philharmonia: Kishinev, ul. 25-vo Oktyabrya.

ASSOCIATION

Union of Writers of Moldavia: 277612 Kishinev, ul. Kievskaya 98; tel. (0422) 22-73-73.

Education

Until the late 1980s the system of education was an integral part of the Soviet system, with most education in the Russian language. In 1990 and 1991 there were extensive changes to the education system, with Romanian literature and history added to the curriculum. In the period 1980–88 the percentage of pupils in general day-schools taught in Russian increased from 36.9% to 40.9%; this trend was reversed in 1990 and 1991.

UNIVERSITIES

Moldavian State University: 277014 Kishinev, ul. Livezilor 60; tel. (0422) 24-00-41; telex 163645; languages of instruction; Russian and Romanian; f. 1945; 13 faculties; 950 teachers; 11,800 students; Rector B. E. Melnik.

State University of Komrat: Komrat; f. 1991 to provide higher educational facilities for the Gagauz and Bulgarian minorities.

Social Welfare

The social security and health systems provide a comprehensive service, which is fully funded by the state. Social security provides allowances for families, especially those with low incomes, pensioners and invalids. Pensions and invalid allowances are funded by the Moldavian Social Fund, established in 1991, which collects taxes from enterprises, organizations and institutions to fund the social security system. In 1990 the amount collected in this way was was more than 2,000m. roubles. In the same year more than 800,000 people were in receipt of pensions.

NATIONAL AGENCIES

Ministry of Health: see section on The Government (Ministries).

Department of Pensions and Social Welfare: Kishinev, Str. Hînceşti 1; tel. (0422) 72-99-85; Dir Alexei A. Sîci.

Moldavian Social Fund: Kishinev, Str. Hînceşti 1; tel. (0422) 72-99-55; Dir Gheorghe A. Ciumak.

HEALTH AND WELFARE ORGANIZATIONS

Invalids' Society of Moldavia: Kishinev; tel. (0422) 72-80-63; Pres. Maricica P. Levitskaya.

Moldavian Charity and Health Fund: Kishinev; tel. (0422) 72-96-89; Ion P. Cuzuioc.

Organization of the Red Cross in Moldavia: Kishinev; tel. (0422) 72-97-00; Pres. ION P. DUMITRAŞ.

The Environment

GOVERNMENT ORGANIZATION

State Department for the Environment and Nature Resources: Kishinev; tel. (0422) 22-22-35; Chair. ION I. DEDIU.

ACADEMIC INSTITUTES

Academy of Sciences of the Republic of Moldavia: 277612 Kishinev, Bd. Ştefan cel Mare 1; tel. (0422) 26-14-78; f. 1961; Pres. A. A. ZHUCHENKO; attached institutes incl.:

Commission on Nature Conservation: 277612 Kishinev, Bd. Ştefan cel Mare 1; attached to the Presidium of the Academy; Chair. S. I. TOMA.

NON-GOVERNMENTAL ORGANIZATION

Ecological Movement of Moldavia: Kishinev; f. 1990; local Green movement and political party.

THE RUSSIAN FEDERATION

Geography

The Russian Federation (until 25 December 1991, officially known as the Russian Soviet Federative Socialist Republic—RSFSR) constituted the major part of the USSR, providing some 76% of its area and some 51% of its population in 1990. It is bounded by Norway, Finland, Estonia and Latvia to the north-west and by Byelorussia and Ukraine to the west. The southern borders of European Russia are with the Black Sea, Georgia, Azerbaidzhan, the Caspian Sea and Kazakhstan. The Siberian and Far Eastern regions have southern frontiers with the People's Republic of China, Mongolia and the People's Democratic Republic of Korea. The eastern coastline is on the Sea of Japan, the Sea of Okhotsk, the Pacific Ocean and the Barents Sea. The northern coastline is on the Arctic Ocean. The region around Kaliningrad (formerly Königsberg in East Prussia), on the Baltic Sea, became part of the Russian Federation in 1945. It is separated from the rest of the Russian Federation by Lithuania and Byelorussia. It borders Poland to the south, Lithuania to the north and east and has a coastline on the Baltic Sea. The Russian Federation covers an area of 17,075,400 sq km (6,592,819 sq miles), making it by far the largest country in the world. Within its territory there are 16 Autonomous Republics, five Autonomous Oblasts (regions) and 10 Autonomous Okrugs (areas).

The territory includes a wide variety of physical features. European Russia (traditionally meaning that part of Russia to the west of the Ural Mountains) and western Siberia form a vast plain, interrupted only by occasional outbreaks of hill-country and wide river-valleys. In the south, between the Black and Caspian Seas, the territory is more undulating, until it reaches the foothills of the Caucasus mountain range in the far south. The Ural Mountains provide only a symbolic barrier between Siberia and European Russia, their mean altitude being only 500 m. Beyond them the Great Russian Plain extends for some 2,000 km, before reaching the Mid-Siberian Plateau and high mountain ranges on the southern border with Mongolia. The territory of Eastern Siberia and the Far East is dominated by several mountain ranges (notably the Verkhoyansk, Chersky and Anadyr mountains) which extend off shore in a series of islands and peninsulas. The Kamchatka peninsula, which extends 1,200 km south to the northernmost of the Kurile Islands, has 100 active volcanoes, the highest being Klyuchevskaya Sopka at 4,800 m. Only the basins of the Amur and Ussuri rivers in the south of the Far Eastern Region can support any significant population. The northern regions of both Asian and European Russia are inhospitable areas, much of the territory being covered by permafrost.

The climate of Russia is extremely varied. The central regions experience the climatic conditions characteristic of central and eastern Europe, although in a more extreme form. There are wide temperature differences between summer and winter, and there is considerable snow in winter. The average temperature in Moscow in July is 19°C (66°F); the average for January is −9°C (15°F). Average annual precipitation in the capital is 575 mm. Further south the climate is more temperate, especially along the Black Sea coastline. Average temperatures in Rostov-on-Don range from −5.3°C (22.5°F) in January to 23.5°C (74.3°F) in July. In the northern areas of Russia and in much of Siberia the climate is severe, with Arctic winters and short, hot summers. Only the northern fringe is under the polar ice-cap; the zone of permafrost is, however, extensive. Average temperatures in the southern Siberian town of Irkutsk range from −20.8°C (−5.4°F) in January to 17.9°C (64.2°F) in July. Average annual rainfall is 458 mm, most of which falls in the summer months. In Verkhoyansk, in the far north of Siberia, the average January temperature is −46.8°C (−52.2°F). The Far East region combines the extreme temperatures of Siberia with monsoon-type conditions common elsewhere in Asia, although they are not so pronounced, owing to the protection of mountain ranges on the Pacific coast. The mean temperature in January in the eastern port of Vladivostok is −14°C (7°F); in August the average is 21°C (70°F).

At the 1989 census, Russians formed the largest ethnic group in the Republic, accounting for 82.6% of the population. Other important ethnic groups included Tatars (3.6%), Ukrainians (2.7%) and Chuvash (1.2%). There are also Byelorussians, Bashkirs, Jews, Mordovians, Mari, Chechens, Kazakhs and Uzbeks. Religious adherence is equally varied, with many religions closely connected with particular ethnic groups. Christianity is the major religion, mostly adhered to by ethnic Russians and other Slavs. The Russian Orthodox Church is the largest denomination. The main concentrations of adherents of Islam are among Volga Tatars, Chuvash and Bashkirs, and the peoples of the northern Caucasus, including the Chechen, Ingush, Ossetians, Kabardinians and the peoples of Daghestan. Buddhism is the main religion of the Buryats, the Tuvans and the Kalmyks. The large pre-1917 Jewish population has been depleted by war and emigration, but there remain some 2m. Jews in the Russian Federation.

The official language in the Russian Federation is Russian, but a large number of other languages are in daily use. The majority of the population live in European Russia, the population of Siberia and the Far East being only some 32m., in 1989, approximately 22% of the total. In 1989 some 74% of the population lived in urban areas, although there were substantial regional differences, with 83% of the inhabitants of central Russia living in towns, compared with only 57% in the North Caucasus region. The capital of the Russian Federation is Moscow (formerly the capital of the USSR), which had a population of 8,967,000 in 1989. The second city is St Petersburg (Leningrad, 1924–91, with a population of 5,020,000), the former capital of the Russian Empire. Other important regional centres are Nizhny Novgorod (previously Gorky—1,438,000), the Siberian cities of Novosibirsk (1,436,000) and Omsk (1,148,000), the industrialized Ural towns of Yekaterinburg (1,367,000) and Chelyabinsk (1,143,000), the regional centre of Siberia, Irkutsk (626,000), and the Far Eastern towns of Khabarovsk (601,000) and Vladivostok (648,000). As a result of political events in the USSR many places in the Russian Federation have reverted to their previous names. In 1991 these included: St Petersburg (previously Leningrad), Yekaterinburg (Sverdlovsk), Sergiev Posad (Zagorsk), Samara (Kuybyshev), Tver (Kalinin), Lisky (Georgiu-Dezh), Ryabinsk (Andropov), Naberezhniye Chelny (Brezhnev), Sharyopovo (Chernenko), Vladikavkaz (Ordzhonikidze) and Lugansk (Voroshilovgrad).

History

The Slavs first settled in the Russian plain in about the sixth century, having migrated eastwards from the Carpathian Mountains. The Eastern Slavs—forerunners of the Great Russians (now known simply as Russians), Ukrainians (Little Russians) and Byelorussians (White Russians)—formed a disparate area of settlement between the Dniepr and Volga rivers. Probably as a result of invasion by the Varangian ruler, Rurik, in 842, the Eastern Slavs were united in a state known as Kievan Rus. Rus developed contacts with the rest of Europe, aided by the adoption of Eastern Orthodox Christianity by Vladimir, in 988. In the 11th century, however, the power of Rus declined, and it was easily subjugated by the Mongols, who arrived from the east in 1233; by 1240 they had conquered all the Slav principalities.

It was not until the reign of Ivan III of Muscovy (1462–1505) that the Russians (by now the distinct branches of the Eastern Slavs were apparent) were able to renounce Mongol suzerainty. Ivan united the Russian princes around his own principality of Muscovy and formed a centralized Russian state which extended far to the east and north, and some way to the west, of the small state of Muscovy which he had inherited. With the fall of Constantinople to the Turks, in 1453, Moscow could lay claim to being the 'Third Rome' and the capital of the most pre-eminent Orthodox state. By 1582, when Ivan IV ('the Terrible'), the first Tsar (Caesar or Emperor), died, Russia controlled a huge area east of Smolensk, extending as far as the Caspian Sea in the south and the Ural Mountains in the east.

The death of Ivan IV was followed by a period of great instability, the 'Time of Troubles', when the succession was disputed. Several 'false Tsars' attempted to seize the throne, and the Poles and Swedes invaded Russia. In 1613, however, representatives of the aristocracy, clergy and gentry convened an Assembly of the Land to elect a new Tsar, Mikhail Romanov. With the re-establishment of centralized rule, the expansion of Russia's borders continued throughout the 17th century, notably under Tsar Alexis (1645–76). He acquired much of Ukraine, including Kiev, by the Treaty of Pereyaslavl, in 1654. Peter I ('the Great', 1682–1725) increased relations with the West, developed a navy, introduced Western military technology and modernized many of the state's most backward institutions. His orientation towards the West was symbolized by the construction of St Petersburg as the capital city. Access to northern Europe was improved by the incorporation of Baltic territories, after the Great Northern War with Sweden, but Russia also became an Asian power during his reign, through the conquest of Siberia. The Russian Empire was formally proclaimed in 1721.

Under Catherine II ('the Great') the Empire continued to expand. This was mainly as a result of the partitions of Poland, in the late 18th century, by which it gained Western Ukraine, Byelorussia and Courland, and the treaties of Kuchuk-Kainardji (1774) and Iaşi with the Turks, by which the Russian Empire gained the northern coastline of the Black Sea, the Crimea and the Sea of Azov.

In the 18th and 19th centuries Russian involvement in European politics and its contacts with the West increased, but its political and economic institutions did not evolve to match those of Western Europe and North America. The system of government was autocracy, and agriculture remained in a state of feudalism even after the formal emancipation of the serfs in 1861. The influx of Western ideas into Russia produced intellectual and political opposition to the Tsarist system of government. The 'Decembrist' revolt of 1825, when young officers attempted to seize power on the death of Alexander I, was easily suppressed, but the more liberal reign of Alexander II (1855–81) allowed a growth of political societies and groups, opposed to the perceived injustices of the Russian political

system. As European Russia became more industrialized in the late 19th century and urban areas attracted more peasants to work in the new industries, socialist ideas became more prevalent. One of the many left-wing groups established was the Russian Social Democratic Labour Party (RSDLP), a small Marxist group founded in 1898, which included Vladimir Ilych Ulyanov, known in revolutionary circles as 'Lenin'.

Growing dissatisfaction in urban areas with economic conditions, combined with the shock of defeats in the Russo–Japanese War (1904–05), culminated in street demonstrations against the regime in early 1905. The brutal repression of a demonstration in January, and the final capitulation of Russia in the war with Japan forced the Tsar, Nicholas II, to issue a manifesto in October 1905, which promised respect for civil liberties and the introduction of some constitutional order in Russia.

The attempt at reforms which followed, under Prime Ministers Sergei Witte (1905–06) and Petr Stolypin (1906–11), did not effect the transformations necessary to placate the increasingly restive workers and peasants. In 1917, again while Russia was being defeated in war, this time the First World War, strikes and demonstrations took place in Petrograd (the new name for St Petersburg since 1914). By February the Tsar had been forced to resign and the Empire was ruled by a Provisional Government, composed mainly of liberal landowners. However, most real power lay with the Petrograd and other *soviets* (councils), which were composed largely of workers and soldiers, and were attracted to socialist ideas.

The inability of the Provisional Government, first under Prince Lvov, and then under Aleksandr Kerensky, a moderate socialist, to fulfil the expectations of the peasants with regard to land reform, or to effect a withdrawal from the War, allowed more extreme groups, such as Lenin's 'Bolshevik' faction of the RSDLP (the party had split into 'Bolsheviks' and 'Mensheviks' in 1903), to develop support among disaffected soldiers and workers. In October the Bolsheviks, who had come to dominate the Petrograd Soviet, seized power in the capital, with minimal use of force. On the same day, 7 November 1917 (25 October, Old Style), the Russian Soviet Federative Socialist Republic (RSFSR or Russian Federation) was proclaimed.

Initially, the Russian Federation was presented as the territorial successor to the Russian Empire, but the Bolsheviks also claimed that they would respect the self-determination of the Empire's many nations. Finland and the Baltic States were granted independence, but other independent states which had been established in 1917–18 were forced, by military means, to proclaim themselves Soviet Republics. These were proclaimed as 'independent' socialist republics, in alliance with the Russian Federation, but the laws, Constitution and Government of the Russian Federation were supreme in all the republics. In accordance with the Bolshevik promises of self-determination, 17 autonomous territories had been formed within the Russian Federation by 1923, including all the territories of Central Asia. However, these territories were normally formed not by agreement between the local leaders and the Russian Federation, but by administrative decree of the Russian Government. This recentralization of Russian power, with the Russian Federation controlling all but the newly-independent Baltic territories, was recognized as politically damaging by the Bolsheviks. Thus, in 1922, the Russian Federation joined the Byelorussian, Ukrainian and Transcaucasian Republics as constitutionally equal partners in a Union of Soviet Socialist Republics (USSR), and institutions of the RSFSR were reformed as institutions of the new Union.

The Russian Federation, as in the other Republics, experienced considerable hardship as a result of the collectivization campaign of the early 1930s and the widespread repression under Stalin. The centralized Five-Year Plans, introduced in the late 1920s, concentrated on the Russian Federation, but with considerable investment directed towards the previously neglected eastern regions. This relocation of the industrial 'heartland' of Russia was reinforced by the removal of strategic industries from the west of the Republic to the Ural regions during the Second World War or 'Great Patriotic War' (1941–1945). Victory over Germany and Japan in the Second World War led to territorial gains for the Russian Federation. In the west it gained part of East Prussia around Königsberg (now Kaliningrad) from Germany, a small amount of territory from Estonia and those parts of Finland that had been annexed during the Soviet–Finnish War (1939–40). In the east it gained the strategically important Kurile Islands from Japan. In addition, the nominally independent Republic of Tuva, situated between the USSR and Mongolia, was annexed in 1944, and subsequently became an Autonomous Republic within the Russian Federation. The territorial extent of the Russian Federation in 1991 was achieved in 1954, when the Crimea was ceded to the Ukrainian SSR.

The position of the Russian Federation within the Soviet federal system was paradoxical. It was clearly the predominant Union Republic, both economically and politically, and ethnic Russians dominated the Soviet élite. This dominant position within the USSR, however, meant that Russia developed few institutions of its own. Thus all Republics had an Academy of Sciences, cultural institutions, trade unions, and above all Communist Parties, except the Russian Federation. This asymmetry in the federal system continued until the beginning of the 1990s.

The Russian Federation, and particularly its larger cities, was profoundly affected by the changes that took place under the Soviet leader Mikhail Gorbachev. *Glasnost* allowed freer discussion of all aspects of Russian history and the status of Russians in the USSR. This allowed the open development of different strains of Russian nationalism, which, though previously evident, had not been permitted open form. Right-wing groups such as Pamyat (Memory), while stressing their concern for the preservation of Russian culture, represented extreme, chauvinistic views and were accused of attacks on non-Russians and especially Jews.

This violent aspect of Russian nationalism was also accompanied by a peaceful process of achieving sovereignty from all-Union institutions. In May 1990 Boris Yeltsin was elected as Chairman of the Russian Supreme Soviet. He pledged to implement radical reforms in the economic and political structure of the Russian Federation, including full sovereignty for the Republic over its resources. On 12 June 1990 the Russian Congress of People's Deputies adopted a declaration of sovereignty, which declared the primacy of republican legislation over all-Union laws, and full sovereignty over the natural resources of the Republic. This led to increased conflict with the all-Union Government and President, but the process of creating republican institutions continued. In September 1989 the all-Union Government had outlined plans for the creation of new political and economic structures for the Russian Federation and, in December, the Communist Party of the Soviet Union (CPSU) announced the establishment of a Central Committee Russian Bureau. In mid-1990 a Russian Communist Party was established, led by Ivan Polozkov, a conservative Communist opposed to Yeltsin. The institutions which Russia had lacked, including a trade union organization, a journalists' union, an academy of sciences and national cultural organizations, began to be established. In 1991 a radio and television broadcasting network, controlled by the Russian Government, and largely supportive of Boris Yeltsin in its political stance, began broadcasting, and the the all-Union Committee of State Security (KGB) permitted the establishment of a republican branch of the KGB, under the jurisdiction of the Russian Federation.

Although these were all important developments in the process of creating a Russian sovereign state, Yeltsin himself had little power to effect the policies which he announced. Only after his direct election to the new post of President of the Russian Federation, in June 1991, did he have a sufficient popular mandate to challenge the jurisdiction of the all-Union Government. He immediately began implementing radical reforms, including a reorganization of the system of government, with the creation of a State Council responsible directly to the President, and the beginnings of economic reform, with a programme similar to the 'Shatalin plan', which had been rejected by Gorbachev in late 1990 (see p. xxx).

The failure of the coup of August 1991 further enhanced Yeltsin's power, both as a result of his role in opposing the *putsch*, and owing to the virtual collapse of all-Union institutions after the coup had ended. Yeltsin asserted his control over all-Union bodies, dismissing the head of the all-Union television and radio company and appointing Russian Federation ministers to head central economic ministries and institutions. Although some of these decrees were subsequently annulled, the power of the centre was sharply diminished. Immediately after the coup, Yeltsin had banned the Russian Communist Party and, with the suspension of the CPSU, formal political opposition to Yeltsin was largely removed. Yeltsin's approach to the establishment of new union structures after the coup was initially ambiguous. He agreed to the creation of an Economic Community, which was founded by eight Republics, on 8 October, and seemed to favour Gorbachev's proposed Union of Sovereign States. However, in November, Yeltsin reorganized the Russian Government, appointing himself as head of the new Council of Ministers, and Gennady Burbulis as First Deputy Chairman. Burbulis and his allies in the new Government were strongly opposed to the creation of a new union and were reported to have been influential in the proposal for a Commonwealth of Independent States (CIS), agreed between Byelorussia, Russia and Ukraine, on 8 December. Within days a further eight Republics had expressed their intention to join the CIS, leaving only Georgia and the Baltic States, among former Soviet Republics, outside the new formation. The Alma-Ata Declaration, of 21 December, formally established a Commonwealth of 11 states, although the stability and longevity of the CIS was doubted. On 25 December the Russian Supreme Soviet formally changed the name of the RSFSR to the Russian Federation.

Russian domination of the CIS was to be expected, due to the size of its territory, and its greater potential economic and military power. The Russian President was to have control over the Commonwealth's nuclear forces, but only after consultation with the three former Soviet Republics that had nuclear weapons stationed on their territories (Byelorussia, Kazakhstan and Ukraine). Conventional forces were to fall under a centralized command, although three states, Azerbaidzhan, Moldavia and Ukraine were also to establish independent national armies. The immediate prospects for political security in the Russian Federation, in early 1992, appeared to rest on public reaction to Boris Yeltsin's planned price liberalization, which saw the cost of most basic commodities increase three- to fivefold on 2 January. Vice-President Aleksandr Rutskoy was among those to voice strong opposition to these increases.

During 1990 and 1991 the Russian Federation faced similar problems to the USSR as a whole in attempting to satisfy the aspirations of its many nationalities for self-determination. Autonomous territories within the Russian Federation adopted declarations of sovereignty and attempted to exert greater influence over local affairs. In some regions, notably Tatarstan and Chechen-Ingushetia, there was considerable support for secession from the Russian Federation. Other nationalities, notably the Karachai and the Ingush, whose separate autonomous territories had been abolished after the Second World War and incorporated into other autonomous formations, began campaigns for the restoration of separate territories. Germans in the Russian Federation campaigned for the restoration of the Volga Autonomous Republic, which had been an autonomous territory for ethnic Germans until the Second World War.

Economy

The Russian Federation, as a result of its its vast resource base, always dominated the Soviet economy. Its main industries are involved in the extraction and processing of raw materials, notably petroleum, coal and natural gas. There are extensive deposits of ferrous and non-ferrous metals, such as gold, manganese, molybdenum, iron and aluminium. However, European Russia is largely devoid of resources; most mineral deposits are in Siberia, where adverse topographic and climatic conditions make access difficult.

Agriculture is limited to the southern regions, the north being climatically unsuited for cultivation, although some animal husbandry is practised. The most fertile regions are in southern Russia, in such regions as Stavropol kray. In late 1990 the Government of the Russian Federation began a process of land reform, which was aimed at creating independent peasant farms in the place of the inefficient collective and state farms. By May 1991 20,144 independent farms had been established, but most were of small size averaging only 41 ha in area. In 1988 the Russian Federation provided 48.0% of total Soviet agricultural net material product (NMP).

In 1988, according to official estimates, the NMP of the Russian Federation totalled 381,250m. roubles, 61.1% of the total Soviet NMP. Of total Soviet industrial NMP, 61.9% was contributed by the Russian Federation. The size of the Russian economy makes it less dependent on exports than other Republics; 18.0% of its NMP in 1988 was derived from such goods. In that year the value of exports to other countries amounted to 8.6% of NMP.

Statistical Survey
Population

BIRTHS AND DEATHS (per 1,000)

	1982	1983	1984
Birth rate	18.9	20.1	16.9
Death rate	10.1	10.3	11.6

Agriculture

PRINCIPAL CROPS ('000 metric tons)

	1986	1987
Grain	118,000	109,000
Sugar beet	29,200	33,900
Flax fibre	156	135
Sunflower	2,400	3,000
Potatoes	43,100	38,000
Other vegetables	11,700	11,100
Grapes	780	763
Other fruit	2,900	2,300

LIVESTOCK ('000 head at 1 January)

	1984	1987*	1988
Cattle	59,500	60,500	59,800
Pigs	39,100	40,200	39,200
Sheep and goats	66,200	64,100	62,800

* Figures for 1985 and 1986 are not available.

LIVESTOCK PRODUCTS ('000 metric tons)

	1983	1986*	1987
Meat (slaughter weight)	8,000	8,900	9,300
Milk	50,200	52,200	52,800
Eggs (million)	43,400	46,200	47,100
Wool (greasy)	219	226	212

* Figures for 1984 and 1985 are not available.

Mining and Industry

Production (1987, unless otherwise stated): Coal 415,000,000 tons, Crude petroleum 569,000,000 tons, Natural gas 544,000m. cu m, Woven cotton fabrics 6,101.6m. sq m (1975), Woven woollen fabrics 390.8m. sq m (1975), Paper 4,700,000 tons (1983), Cement 84,518,000 tons (1989), Iron ore 95,700,000 tons (1983), Steel pipes 11,100,000 tons (1983), Metal-cutting lathes 93,000 (1981), Motor cars 1,200,000 (1983), Lorries 652,000 (1982), Tractors 253,000 (1981), Electric energy 1,049m. kWh.

Education

(1981/82)

	Institutions	Students
Secondary schools	73,100	20,152,000
Secondary specialized institutions	2,520	2,543,000
Higher schools (incl. universities)	500	3,073,000

Directory

The Government

(January 1992)

PRESIDENCY

President of the Russian Federation and Chairman of the Government: BORIS N. YELTSIN (elected President 12 June 1991).
Vice-President: ALEKSANDR V. RUTSKOY.

As part of the reorganization of the Russian government, which took place in November 1991, a Centre for the Operational Supervision of the Progress of Reforms was established, within the structure of the presidency. This institution was to be headed by the Vice-President. The other members were: the Chairman of the presidential committee for ecology, public health and epidemiological supervision, supervision of safety of work in industry, mining supervision and radiation safety; the Chairman of the presidential committee for the protection of economic interests; the Chairman of the presidential committee for conversion affairs; the Chairman of the presidential customs committee; the Chairman of the state tax inspectorate; the Chairman of the state insurance supervision.

GOVERNMENT

Chairman (responsible for security and defence): BORIS N. YELTSIN.

First Deputy Chairman (responsible for foreign, media and judicial affairs): GENNADY E. BURBULIS.

Deputy Chairman (responsible for economic policy) and Minister of the Economy and Finance: YEGOR T. GAYDAR.

Deputy Chairman (responsible for social policy) and Minister of Labour and Employment of the Population: ALEKSANDR N. SHOKHIN.

Deputy Chairman (responsible for legal policy): SERGEY SHAKRAY.

Minister of Agriculture and Food Production: VIKTOR N. KHLYSTUN.

Minister of Communications: VLADIMIR B. BULGAK.

Minister of Culture: (vacant).

Minister of Ecology and the Use of Natural Resources: VIKTOR I. DANILOV-DANILYAN.

Minister of Education: EDUARD D. DNEPROV.

Minister of Foreign Affairs: ANDREY V. KOZYREV.

Minister of Fuel and Power Engineering: VLADIMIR M. LAPUKHIN.

Minister of Health: ANDREY I. VOROBYEV.

Minister of Industry: ALEKSANDR A. KIPKIN.

Minister of Internal Affairs: VIKTOR YERIN.

Minister of Justice: NIKOLAY V. FEDOROV.

Minister of Nucler Energy: (vacant).

Minister of the Press and Mass Media: MIKHAIL N. POLTORANIN.

Minister of Science and Technical Policy: BORIS G. SALTYKOV.

Minister of Security: VIKTOR P. BARANNIKOV.

Minister of Social Protection of the Population: ELLA A. PANFILOVA.

Minister of Trade and Material Resources: STANISLAV KH. ANISIMOV.

Minister of Transport: VITALY B. YEFIMOV.

Minister, Chairman of the State Committee for Anti-monopoly Policy and Support for New Economic Structures: (vacant).

Minister, Chairman of the State Committee for Civil Defence, Emergencies and the Elimination of Consequences of Natural Disasters: SERGEY K. SHOYGA.

Minister, Chairman of the State Committee for Defence Issues: PAVEL S. GRACHEV.

Minister, Chairman of the State Committee for the Management of State Property: ANATOLY B. CHUBAYIS.

Minister, Chairman of the State Committee for the Social and Economic Development of the North: (vacant).

MINISTRIES

Council of Ministers: Moscow, Staraya pl. 4; tel. (095) 206-25-11.

Ministry of Agriculture and Food Production: 107802 Moscow, Orlikov per. 3; tel. (095) 204-43-07.

Ministry of Communications: 103091 Moscow, Delegatskaya ul. 5; tel. (095) 292-70-70.

Ministry of Culture: 103693 Moscow, Kitaysky proezd 7; (095) 925-11-95.

Ministry of Ecology and Use of Natural Resources: Moscow.

Ministry of the Economy and Finance: 103381 Moscow, Neglinnaya ul. 23; tel. (095) 200-38-48.

Ministry of Education: Moscow, Chistoprudny bul. 6; tel. (095) 924-71-12.

Ministry of Foreign Affairs: Moscow, pr. Mira 49A; tel. (095) 281-10-11.

Ministry of Fuel and Power Engineering: Moscow.

Ministry of Health: 101474 Moscow, Vadkovsky per. 18–20; tel. (095) 289-30-65.

Ministry of Industry: 103655 Moscow, ul. Petrovka 14; tel. (095) 200-45-35.

Ministry of Internal Affairs: Moscow, ul. Ogareva 6.

Ministry of Justice: 103051 Moscow, ul. Yermolovoy 10A; tel. (095) 209-61-73.

Ministry of Labour and Employment of the Population: 107078 Moscow, 1-y Basmanny per. 3; tel. (095) 261-20-30.

Ministry of Nuclear Energy: Moscow.

Ministry of the Press and Mass Media: 121811 Moscow, ul. Kachalovo 12; tel. (095) 290-53-66.

Ministry of Science and Technical Policy: Moscow.

Ministry of Security: Moscow, ul. B. Lubyanka 2; tel. (095) 221-07-62.

Ministry of Social Protection of the Population: 117934 Moscow, ul. Shabolovka 4; tel. (095) 236-44-82; telex 412127; fax (095) 236-42-62.

Ministry of Trade and Material Resources: Moscow, ul. Myasnitskaya 47; tel. (095) 207-70-00.

Ministry of Transport: 129301 Moscow, Sadovo-Samotechnaya ul. 10; tel. (095) 200-08-09.

State Committees

State Committee for Anti-monopoly Policy and Support for New Economic Structures: Moscow.

State Committee for Civil Defence, Emergencies and the Elimination of Consequences of Natural Disasters: Moscow.

State Committee for Defence Affairs: Moscow.

State Committee for the Management of State Property: Moscow.

State Committee for the Social and Economic Development of the North: Moscow.

President and Legislature

PRESIDENT

Election, 12 June 1991

Candidate	Votes	% of total
BORIS N. YELTSIN	45,552,041	57.30
NIKOLAI RYZHKOV	13,395,335	16.85
VLADIMIR ZHIRINOVSKY	6,211,007	7.81
AMAN-GELDY TULEYEV	5,417,464	6.81
VADIM BAKATIN	2,719,757	3.42
ALBERT MAKASHOV	11,136	0.7

CONGRESS OF PEOPLE'S DEPUTIES

The Congress of People's Deputies is the supreme legislative body in the Russian Federation. It comprises 1,068 deputies, who were elected on 4 and 18 March 1990.

SUPREME SOVIET

The Supreme Soviet was elected from among the deputies of the Congress of People's Deputies on 9 June 1990. It is a bicameral legislature, composed of the Council of Nationalities and the Council of the Republic.

Supreme Soviet: 103724 Moscow, Krasnopresenskaya nab. 2; tel. (095) 205-61-71.

Chairman: RUSLAN I. KHASBULATOV.

First Deputy Chairman: SERGEY FILATOV.

Deputy Chairmen: YURY YAROV, VLADIMIR SHUMEIKO, YURY VORONIN.

Council of the Republic

Chairman: N. T. RYABOV.

Council of Nationalities

Chairman: ROMAZAN G. ABDULATIPOV.

Local Government

The Russian Federation embraces 49 administrative oblasts (regions) and six krays (provinces). There are also 16 Autonomous Republics, five Autonomous Oblasts and 10 Autonomous Okrugs. The cities of Moscow and St Petersburg (known as Leningrad until October 1991) have been granted considerable autonomy, particularly in economic policy. In June 1991 both cities elected mayors.

MOSCOW

Moscow City Council: 103032 Moscow, ul Tverskaya 13; tel. (095) 924-09-90.

Mayor of Moscow: GAVRIIL POPOV (elected 12 June 1991).

ST PETERSBURG

St Petersburg City Council: St Petersburg, City Soviet.

Mayor of St Petersburg: ANATOLY SOBCHAK (elected 12 June 1991).

AUTONOMOUS REPUBLICS

In 1990–91 most autonomous formations in the Russian Federation unilaterally upgraded their status from that of an Autonomous Soviet Socialist Republic (ASSR) to that of a Soviet Socialist Republic (SSR). The formal name in current use is given here.

Bashkir SSR (Bashkortostan)

Bashkiria was annexed by Russia in 1557. The Bashkir Autonomous Soviet Republic was established on 23 March 1919. The Republic declared sovereignty on 11 October 1990. Bashkiria covers an area of 143,600 sq km. The capital is Ufa. In 1989 the population was 3,952,000, of which 21.9% were Bashkirs and 39.3% Russians.

Chairman of the Supreme Soviet: MURTAZA RAKHIMOV.

Chairman of the Government: MARAT MIRGAZYAMOV.

Buryat SSR (Buryatia)

Russian influence reached Buryatia in the 17th century but possession was contested with China until 1727. An Autonomous Soviet Republic was established on 1 March 1920. The Republic is situated in southern Siberia, on the southern shores of Lake Baikal. It covers an area of 351,300 sq km. The capital is Ulan-Ude. In 1989 the population was 1,042,000, of which 24.0% were Buryats and 70.0% were Russians.

Chairman of the Supreme Soviet SERGEY N. BULDAYEV.

Chechen-Ingush ASSR (Chechen Republic)

The Chechens and Ingush were conquered by Russia in the late 1850s. A Chechen Autonomous Oblast was established on 30 November 1922. An Ingush Autonomous Oblast was established on 7 July 1924. In 1934 the two regions were combined, and, in 1936 constituted as an Autonomous Republic. The Chechen and Ingush were deported to Central Asia in 1944 and their Autonomous Republic was dissolved. On 9 January 1957 the Autonomous Republic was reconstituted, but certain Ingush territories, which had been absorbed by North Ossetia, were not included in the reconstituted Republic. In 1991 an All-National Congress of the Chechen People gradually seized effective power in the territory and, on 27 October, held elections to the presidency of a 'Chechen Republic'. The Chechen and Ingush peoples are closely related and known collectively as Vainakhs; they speak Nakh dialects and are Sunni Muslims. The Republic is situated in the northern Caucasus region. It covers an area of 19,300 sq km. The capital is Grozny. In 1989 the total population was 1,277,000, of which 57.8% were Chechens, 12.9% were Ingushi and 23.1% were Russians.

President of the Chechen Republic: Gen. DZHOKAR DUDAYEV.

Chuvash ASSR (Republic of Chuvash'en)

Russia annexed Chuvash lands in the 16th century. A Chuvash Autonomous Oblast was established on 24 June 1920 and was subsequently upgraded to the status of an Autonomous Republic. The Republic is situated in the central regions of Russia. It covers an area of 18,300 sq km. The capital is Cheboksary. In 1989 the total population was 1,336,000, of which 67.8% were Chuvash and 26.7% Russians. Presidential elections were held on 8 December 1991, but there was no outright winner. Further rounds of voting were to take place.

Chairman of the Supreme Soviet: ANATOLY M. LEONTYEV.

Daghestan SSR (Republic of Daghestan)

Daghestan came under Russian rule in 1723 when it was annexed from Persia. A Daghestan Autonomous Republic was established on 20 January 1920. The Republic is situated in the northern Caucasus region, on the western coast of the Caspian Sea. It covers an area of 50,300 sq km. The capital is Makhachkala. In 1989 the total population was 1,792,000, of which 27.5% were Avars, 15.6% Darghins, 12.9% Kumyks, 11.3% Lezghis, 5.1% Laks, 1.6% Nogays, 0.8% Rutuls, 0.8% Aguls, 4.3% Tabasarans, 0.3% Tsakhurs and 9.2% Russians.

Chairman of the Supreme Soviet: M. MAGOMEDOV.

Chairman of the Government: ABDUL RAZAK MIRZABEKOV.

Kabardino-Balkar ASSR

Kabardinians came under Russian rule in the 16th century. The Kabardino-Balkar ASSR was established on 5 December 1936. On 18 November 1991 the first congress of the National Council of the Balkar People declared the sovereignty of Balkaria and the formation of a Republic of Balkaria within the Russian Federation. This formation, and many of the Russian and Cossack population, opposed the presidential elections for the whole region, the second round of which was held on 5 January 1992 and were won by the former Chairman of the Supreme Soviet. The Republic is situated in the northern Caucasus region. It covers an area of 12,500 sq km. The capital is Nalchik. In 1989 the total population was 760,000, of which 48.2% were Kabardians, 9.4% Balkars and 32.0% Russians.

President of Kabardin-Balkaria: VALERY KOKOV.

Chairman of the National Balkar Council: B. K. CHABADAROV.

Kalmyk SSR (Kalmyk Republic)

A Kalmyk Autonomous Oblast was established on 4 November 1920. Its status was upgraded to that of an Autonomous Republic in 1935, which was dissolved in 1943, when the Kalmyks were deported to Central Asia. A Kalmyk Autonomous Oblast was reconstituted in 1957 and an Autonomous Republic in 1958. A declaration of sovereignty was adopted on 18 October 1990. The Republic is situated on the western shores of the Caspian Sea, to the north of Daghestan. It covers an area of 75,900 sq km. The capital is Elista. In 1989 the total population was 322,000, of which 45.4% were Kalmyks and 37.7% Russians.

Chairman of the Supreme Soviet: VLADIMIR M. BASANOV.

Republic of Karelia

A Karelian Labour Commune was formed in June 1920 and became an autonomous republic in July 1923. A Karelo-Finnish SSR, including territory annexed from Finland, was created in 1940 as a Union Republic of the USSR. However, part of its territory was ceded to the Russian Federation, in 1946, and Karelia resumed its status of an Autonomous Republic. The Republic declared sovereignty on 10 August 1990. It was renamed on 13 November 1991 as the Republic of Karelia. The Republic is situated in the north-west of the Russian Federation, on the border with Finland. It covers an area of 172,400 sq km. The capital is Petrozavodsk. In 1989 the total population was 792,000, of which 10.0% were Karelians (Finnish) and 73.6% Russians.

Chairman of the Supreme Soviet: V. STEPANOV.

Komi SSR

The territory of the Komi Autonomous Republic has been under Russian rule since the 14th century. A Komi Autonomous Oblast was established in 1921 and an Autonomous Republic in 1936. The Republic declared sovereignty on 30 August 1990. It is situated in the north of the Russian Federation and covers an area of 415,900 sq km. The capital is Syktyvar. In 1989 the total population was 1,263,000, of which 23.3% were Komis and 57.7% were Russians.

Chairman of the Supreme Soviet: YURY A. SPRIDONOV.

Mari SSR (Republic of Mari-el)

The Mari were under the suzerainty of the Khanate of Kazan until it was annexed by Russia in 1552. A Mari Autonomous Oblast was established in 1920. On 5 December 1936 the territory became the Mari ASSR. The Republic declared sovereignty on 22 October 1990. Presidential elections were held on 14 December 1991. The Mari SSR is situated in the central regions of the Russian Federation and covers an area of 23,200 sq km. The capital is Yoshkar-Ola. In 1989 the total population was 415,900, of which 43.3% were Maris (also known as Cheremiss) and 47.5% Russians.

President: VLADISLAV M. ZOTIN.

Mordovian SSR

The Mordovian territories have been under Russian rule since the 13th century. A Mordovian Autonomous Oblast was established in 1930 and the territory became the Mordovian ASSR in 1934. Presidential elections were held on 15 December 1991, but there was no outright winner. A further round of voting took place on 22 December, the Chairman of the Supreme Soviet being defeated by the local leader of the Democratic Russia movement. The Republic is situated in central Russia and covers an area of 26,200 sq km. The capital is Saransk. In 1989 the total population was 964,000, of which 32.5% were Mordovians and 60.8% Russians.

President of Mordovia: VASILY GUSLYANNIKOV.

North Ossetian ASSR

Ossetia was ceded to Russia by Turkey at the Treaty of Kuchuk-Kainardji in 1792. An Autonomous Oblast was established in 1924, which became an Autonomous Republic on 5 December 1936. In 1944 its territory was expanded to the east by the inclusion of former Ingush territories. During 1991 there was considerable debate about some form of unification with South Ossetia, in Georgia, as well as Ingush claims to land. The Republic is situated in the northern Caucausus region and covers an area of 8,000 sq km. The capital is Vladikavkaz (formerly Ordzhonikidze). In 1989 the total population was 634,000, of which 53.0% were Ossetians and 29.9% Russians.

Chairman of the Supreme Soviet: AKHSARBEK KH. GALAZOV.

Tatar SSR (Republic of Tatarstan)

After the dissolution of the Mongol Empire the region became the Khanate of Kazan. It was conquered by Russia in 1552. A Tatar Autonomous Republic was established on 27 May 1920. The Republic declared sovereignty on 31 August 1990. The Tatar SSR is situated in the central regions of Russia, to the west of Bashkiria. It covers an area of 68,000 sq km. The capital is Kazan. In 1989 the total population was 3,640,000, of which 48.5% were Tatars and 43.3% Russians.

President of Tatarstan: MINTIMER SHAYMIYEV.

Republic of Tuva

The Republic of Tannu-Tuva was a nominally independent state until 1944, when it was incorporated into the USSR. It became an Autonomous Republic on 10 October 1961, prior to which it had been an Autonomous Oblast. It is situated in southern Siberia, on the Russian border with Mongolia. The Republic covers an area of 170,500 sq km. The capital is Kyzyl-Orda. In 1989 the total population was 309,000, of which 64.3% were Tuvans and 32.0% Russians.

Chairman of the Supreme Soviet: CHIMIT-DORZHU B. ONDAR.

Udmurt ASSR (Udmurt Republic)

The territories inhabited by Votyaks (the former name for the Udmurts) came under Russian rule in the 15th century. A Votyak Autonomus Oblast was established on 4 November 1920. In 1934 it became the Udmurt Autonomous Republic. The Republic declared sovereignty on 19 September 1990. It is situated in the north-central region of Russia and covers an area of 42,100 sq km. The capital is Izhevsk. In 1989 the total population was 1,609,000, of which 30.9% were Udmurts and 58.9% were Russian.

Chairman of the Supreme Soviet: VALENTIN K. TUBYLOV.

Yakut-Sakha SSR

The Yakuts came under Russian rule in the late 17th century. A Yakut Autonomous Republic was established on 27 April 1922. The Yakut ASSR declared its sovereignty on 27 September 1990 and changed its name to the Yakut-Sakha SSR. On 22 December 1991 elections for an executive presidency were held, and won by the former Chairman of the Supreme Soviet. The Republic is situated in the north-eastern region of Siberia and covers an area of 3,103,200 sq km. The capital is Yakutsk. In 1989 the total population was 1,081,000, of which 33.4% were Yakuts and 50.3% were Russians.

President of the Yakut-Sakha SSR: MIKHAIL YEFIMOVICH NIKOLAYEV.

Political Organizations

In September 1989 the Government outlined plans for the establishment of new political and economic structures for the Russian Federation, and in December the Communist Party created a Central Committee Russian Bureau to oversee the ensuing decentralization of power from Moscow. A Russian Communist Party was established in June 1991, but it was banned following the coup of August 1991. The Russian President also prohibited the activities of the CPSU on the territory of the Russian Federation and confiscated its property and financial assets. Numerous non-Communist political movements emerged in 1988–91, the most important of which was the Democratic Russia movement which supported Boris Yeltsin.

Democratic Party of Russia: Moscow; f. 1990 by the radical wing of the Democratic Platform in the CPSU and the Moscow Society of Electors; liberal-conservative; advocated retention of some union structures and a united Russia; Chair. NIKOLAY TRAVKIN; 45,000 mems.

People's Party of Free Russia: Moscow; f. 1991 as the Democratic Party of Communists of Russia within the CPSU; Chair. ALEKSANDR RUTSKOY; 2.5m. mems.

People's Party of Russia: Moscow; f. 1991; democratic, liberal; Chair. TELMAN GDLYAN.

Republican Party of the Russian Federation: Moscow; f. 1990 by former members of the Democratic Platform within the CPSU; advocates a mixed economy, defence of the sovereignty of Russia; Co-chair. VLADIMIR LYSENKO, VLADISLAV SHOSTAKOVSKY, STEPAN SULASHKIN; c. 6,000 mems.

Russian Conservative Party: Moscow; f. 1990; right-wing; Chair. LEV UBOZHKO.

Russian Christian-Democratic Movement: Moscow; f. 1990; favours parliamentary democracy; advocates a monarchist system and religious education; Co-Chair. VIKTOR AKSYUSHITS, VYACHESLAV POLOSSIN, GLEB ANISHCHENKO; 15,000 mems.

Russian Green Party: St Petersburg; f. 1991 by a conference of ecological movements; Leader ALEKSANDR DONIN.

Russian National Party: Moscow; f. 1990; advocates restoration of Grand Duke Vladimir Romanov to the throne; Pres. ALEKSEY BRUMEL.

Social Democratic Party of the Russian Federation: Moscow; f. 1990; advocates the creation of a democratic society, social forms of privatization, national-cultural autonomy for minorities; Co-chair OLEG RUMYANTSEV, BORIS ORLOV, LEONID VOLKOV; 5,000 mems.

Diplomatic Representation

EMBASSIES IN RUSSIA

Afghanistan: Moscow, Sverchkov per. 3/2; tel. (095) 928-50-44; telex 413270; fax (095) 924-04-78; Ambassador: MUHAMMAD DAOUD RAZMYAR.

Albania: Moscow, ul. Mytnaya 3, kv. 23; tel. (095) 230-78-75; Chargé d'affaires a.i. PERTEF HASAMATAJ.

Algeria: Moscow, Krapivinsky per. 1A; tel. (095) 200-66-42; telex 413273; Ambassador: HADJ MUHAMMAD YALA.

Angola: ul. Olof Palme 6; tel. (095) 143-63-24; telex 413402; Ambassador: MANUEL BERNARDO DE SOUZA.

Argentina: Moscow, ul. Sadovo-Triumfalnaya 4/10; tel. (095) 299-03-67; telex 413259; Ambassador: GASTON DE PRAT GAY.

Australia: Moscow, Kropotkinsky per. 13; tel. (095) 246-50-12; telex 413474; fax 230-26-06; Ambassador: CAVAN O. HOGUE.

Austria: Moscow, Starokonyushenny per. 1; tel. (095) 201-73-17; telex 413398; fax (095) 230-23-65; Ambassador: FRIEDRICH BAUER.

Bangladesh: Moscow, Zemledelchesky per. 6; tel. (095) 246-79-00; telex 413196; fax (095) 248-31-85; Ambassador: MUSTAFIZUR RAHMAN.

Belgium: Moscow, ul. Malaya Molchanovka 7; tel. (095) 291-60-27; telex 413471; fax (095) 291-60-05; Ambassador: Baron THIERRY DE GRUBEN.

Benin: Moscow, Uspensky per. 4A; tel. (095) 299-23-60; telex 413645; fax (095) 200-02-26; Ambassador: BABATOUNDÉ CONSTANT KOUKOUI.

Bolivia: Moscow, Lopukhinsky per. 5; tel. (095) 201-25-08; telex 413356; Ambassador: Dr JAVIER MURILLO DE LA ROCHA.

Brazil: Moscow, ul. Gertsena 54; tel. (095) 290-40-22; telex 413476; Ambassador: SEBASTIÃO DO REGO BARROS NETTO.

Bulgaria: Moscow, ul. Mosfilmovskaya 66; tel. (095) 143-90-27; Ambassador: VLADIMIR VELCHEV.

Burkina Faso: 129090 Moscow, Meshchanskaya ul. 17; tel. (095) 971-37-49; telex 413284; Ambassador HANITAN JONAS YÉ.

Burundi: Moscow, Uspensky per. 7; tel. (095) 299-72-00; telex 413316; Ambassador: ILDEPHONSE NKERAMIHIGO.

Cambodia: Moscow, Starokonyushenny per. 16; tel. (095) 201-47-36; telex 413261; fax (095) 201-76-68; Ambassador: BO RASY.

Cameroon: Moscow, ul. Vorovskovo 40; tel. (095) 290-65-49; telex 413445; Ambassador: Alhadji YÉRIMA SOUAIBOU HAYATOU.

Canada: Moscow, Starokonyushenny per. 23; tel. (095) 241-58-82; telex 413401; fax (095) 241-44-00; Ambassador: MICHAEL R. BELL.

Cape Verde: Moscow, Bolshaya Spasskaya ul. 9; tel. (095) 208-08-56; telex 413929; Chargé d'affaires a.i.: PEDRO LOPES.

Central African Republic: Moscow, ul. 26-Bakinskikh-Kommissarov 9, kv. 124–125; tel. (095) 434-45-20; Ambassador: CLAUDE BERNARD BELOUM.

Chad: Moscow, Rublevskoye Chaussée 26, kor. 1, kv. 20–21; tel. (095) 415-41-39; telex 413623; Chargé d'affaires a.i.: BRAHIM DJIDAH.

Chile: Moscow, ul. Yunosti 11; tel. (095) 373-9176; telex 413751; Ambassador: CLODOMIRO ALMEYDA MEDINA.

China, People's Republic: Moscow, Leninskiye Gory, ul. Druzhby 6; tel. (095) 143-15-40; telex 413981; Ambassador: WANG JINQING.

Colombia: Moscow, ul. Burdenko 20; tel. (095) 248-30-42; telex 413206; fax (095) 248-30-25; Ambassador: RICARDO EASTMAN DE LA CUESTA.

Congo: Moscow, Kropotkinsky per. 12; tel. (095) 246-02-34; telex 413487; Ambassador: GABRIEL EMOUENGUÉ.

Costa Rica: Moscow, Rublevskoye shosse 26, kv. 58–59; tel. (095) 415-40-42; telex 413963; Ambassador: ARTURO ROBLES ARIAS.

Côte d'Ivoire: Moscow, Molochny per. 9/14; tel. (095) 201-24-00; telex 413091; Ambassador: MOÏSE AKA.

Cuba: Moscow, ul. Mosfilmovskaya 40; tel. (095) 147-43-12; Ambassador: JOSÉ RAMÓN BALAGUER CABRERA.

Cyprus: 121069 Moscow, ul. Gertsena 51; tel. (095) 290-21-54; telex 413477; fax (095) 200-12-54; Ambassador: CHARALAMBOS CHRISTO-FOROU.

Czechoslovakia: Moscow, ul. Yuliusa Fuchika 12/14; tel. (095) 251-05-40; Ambassador: RUDOLF SLÁNSKY.

Denmark: Moscow, per. Ostrovskovo 9; tel. (095) 201-78-60; telex 413378; fax (095) 201-78-60; Ambassador: VAGN EGEBJERG.

Ecuador: Moscow, Gorokhovsky per. 12; tel. (095) 261-55-44; telex 413174; Ambassador: PEDRO ANTONIO SAAD HERRERÍA.

Egypt: Moscow, Skatertny per. 25; tel. (095) 291-32-09; telex 413276; fax (095) 291-46-09; Ambassador: AHMED MAHIR AL-SAYYID.

Equatorial Guinea: Moscow, Kutuzovsky pr. 7/4, kor. 5, kv. 37; tel. (095) 243-96-11; Ambassador: POLICARPO MENSUY MBA.

Estonia: Moscow; Sobinovsky per. 5; tel. (095) 290-50-13.

Ethiopia: Moscow, Orlovo-Davydovsky per. 6; tel. (095) 230-20-36; telex 413980; Ambassador: GIRMA YILMA.

Finland: Moscow, Kropotkinsky per. 15/17; tel. (095) 246-40-27; telex 413405; fax (095) 230-27-21; Ambassador: HEIKKI TALVITIE.

France: Moscow, ul. Dimitrova 45/47; tel. (095) 236-00-03; telex 413290; fax (095) 230-21-69; Ambassador: BERNARD DUFOURCQ.

Gabon: Moscow, ul. Vesnina 16; tel. (095) 241-00-80; telex 413245; Ambassador: MARCEL ONDONGUI-BONNARD.

Germany: Moscow, ul. Bolshaya Gruzinskaya 17; tel. (095) 252-55-21; telex 413412; fax (095) 253-92-76; Ambassador: Dr KLAUS BLECH.

Ghana: Moscow, Skatertny per. 14; tel. (095) 202-18-70; telex 413475; Ambassador: CHRIS HESSE.

Greece: Moscow, ul. Stanislavskovo 4; tel. (095) 290-22-74; telex 413472; fax (095) 200-12-52; Ambassador: ELIAS GOUNARIS.

Guinea: Moscow, Pomerantsev per. 6; tel. (095) 201-36-01; telex 413404; Ambassador: CHERIF DIALLO.

Guinea-Bissau: Moscow, ul. Bolshaya Ordynka 35; tel. (095) 231-79-28; telex 413055; Ambassador: CHÉRIF TURÉ.

Guyana: Moscow, 2-Kazachy per. 7; tel. (095) 230-00-13; telex 413071; Ambassador: RANJI CHANDISINGH.

Hungary: Moscow, ul. Mosfilmovskaya 62; tel. (095) 143-86-11; telex 414428; fax (095) 143-46-25; Ambassador: SÁNDOR GYÖRKE.

Iceland: Moscow, Khlebny per. 28; tel. (095) 290-47-42; telex 413181; fax (095) 200-12-64; Ambassador: ÓLAFUR EGILSSON.

India: Moscow, ul. Obukha 6–8; tel. (095) 297-08-20; telex 413409; Ambassador: Prof. ALFRED S. GONSALVES.

Indonesia: Moscow, ul. Novokuznetskaya 12; tel. (095) 231-95-49; telex 413444; fax (095) 230-22-13; Ambassador: JANWAR MARAH DJANI.

Iran: 109028 Moscow, Pokrovsky bul. 7; tel. (095) 227-57-88; telex 413493; Ambassador: NEMATOLLAH IZADI.

Iraq: Moscow, Pogodinskaya ul. 12; tel. (095) 246-55-06; telex 413184; fax (095) 230-29-22; Ambassador: GHAFIL JASSIM HUSSAIN.

Ireland: Moscow, Grokholsky per. 5; tel. (095) 288-41-01; telex 413204; Ambassador: PATRICK MCCABE.

Israel: Moscow, ul. Bolshaya Ordynka 56; tel. (095) 238-27-32; fax (095) 238-13-46; Ambassador: ARIEH LEVIN.

Italy: Moscow, ul. Vesnina 5; tel. (095) 241-15-33; telex 413453; fax (095) 253-92-89; Ambassador: FERDINANDO SALLEO.

Jamaica: Moscow, Korovy val 7, kv. 70–71; tel. (095) 237-23-20; telex 413358; Ambassador: ARTHUR HENRY THOMPSON.

Japan: Moscow, Kalashny per. 12; tel. (095) 291-85-00; telex 413141; Ambassador: SUMIO EDAMURA.

Jordan: Moscow, per. Sadovskikh 3; tel. (095) 299-95-64; telex 413447; fax (095) 299-43-54; Ambassador: Dr MOHAMMED ADWAN.

Kenya: Moscow, ul. Bolshaya Ordynka 70; tel. (095) 237-47-02; telex 413495; fax (095) 230-23-40; Ambassador: (vacant).

Korea, Democratic People's Republic: Moscow, ul. Mosfilmov-skaya 72; tel. (095) 143-62-49; telex 413272; Ambassador: SON SONG-PIL.

Korea, Republic: 119121 Moscow, ul. Gubkina 14; tel. (095) 938-28-02; Ambassador: RO-MYUNG GONG.

Kuwait: Moscow, 3-Neopalimovsky per. 13/5; tel. (095) 248-50-01; telex 413353; fax (095) 230-24-23; Ambassador: ABDULMOHSIN Y. AL-DUAIJ.

Latvia: Moscow, ul. Chaplygina 3; tel. (095) 925-27-07.

Laos: Moscow, ul. Bolshaya Ordynka 18/1; tel. (095) 233-20-35; telex 413101; Ambassador: KHAMPHONG PHANHVONGSA.

Lebanon: Moscow, Sadovo-Samotechnaya ul. 14; tel. (095) 200-00-22; telex 413120; fax (095) 200-32-22; Ambassador: SELIM TADMOURY.

Libya: Moscow, ul. Mosfilmovskaya 38; tel. (095) 143-03-54; telex 413443; fax (095) 143-76-44; Secretary (Ambassador): AHMED MOHAMED RHAIM.

Lithuania: Moscow, ul. Pisemskovo 10; tel. (095) 291-66-98.

Luxembourg: Moscow, Khrushchevsky per. 3; tel. (095) 202-53-81; telex 413131; fax (095) 200-52-43; Ambassador: HUBERT WURTH.

Madagascar: Moscow, Kursovoy per. 5; tel. (095) 290-02-14; telex 413370; Ambassador: SIMON RABOARA RABE.

Malaysia: Moscow, ul. Mosfilmovskaya 50; tel. (095) 147-15-14; telex 413478; fax (095) 147-15-26; Ambassador: MOHAMED HARON.

Mali: Moscow, Novokuznetskaya ul. 11; tel. (095) 231-06-55; telex 413396; Ambassador: CHEICK A. T. CISSÉ.

Malta: Moscow, Korovy val 7, kv. 219; tel. (095) 237-19-39; telex 413919; fax (095) 237-21-58; Ambassador: MAURICE LUBRANO.

Mauritania: Moscow, ul. Bolshaya Ordynka 66; tel. (095) 237-37-92; telex 413439; Ambassador: ALY GUELADIO KAMARA.

Mexico: Moscow, ul. Shchukina 4; tel. (095) 201-25-53; telex 413125; fax (095) 230-20-42; Ambassador: CARLOS TELLO.

Mongolia: Moscow, ul. Pisemskovo 11; tel. (095) 290-30-61; Ambassador: NYAMYN MISHIGDORJ.

Morocco: Moscow, per. Ostrovskovo 8; tel. (095) 201-73-51; telex 413446; fax (095) 230-20-67; Ambassador: (vacant).

Mozambique: Moscow, ul. Gilyarovskovo 20; tel. (095) 284-40-07; telex 413369; Ambassador: JOSÉ RUI MOTA DO AMARAL.

Myanmar: Moscow, ul. Gertsena 41; tel. (095) 291-05-34; telex 413403; fax (095) 291-01-63; Ambassador: U TIN TUN.

Namibia: Moscow, ul. Konyushkovskaya 28, kv. 10; tel. (095) 252-24-71; telex 413567; fax (095) 253-96-10; Ambassador: N. NASHANDI.

Nepal: Moscow, 2-Neopalimovsky per. 14/7; tel. (095) 244-02-15; telex 413292; Ambassador: (vacant).

Netherlands: Moscow, Kalashny per. 6; tel. (095) 291-29-99; telex 413442; fax (095) 200-52-64; Ambassador: JORIS M. VOS.

New Zealand: 121069 Moscow, ul. Vorovskovo 44; tel. (095) 290-34-85; telex 413187; fax (095) 290-46-66; Ambassador: GERALD MCGHIE.

Nicaragua: Moscow, Mosfilmovskaya ul. 50, kor. 1; tel. (095) 938-27-01; telex 413264; Ambassador: ADOLFO EVERTZ VÉLEZ.

Niger: Moscow, Kursovoy per. 7/31; tel. (095) 290-01-01; telex 413180; fax (095) 200-42-51; Ambassador: MOUTARI OUSMANE.

Nigeria: Moscow, ul. Kachalova 13; tel. (095) 290-37-83; telex 413489; Ambassador: JIBRIN D. CHINADE.

Norway: Moscow, ul. Vorovskovo 7; tel. (095) 290-38-72; telex 413488; fax (095) 200-12-21; Ambassador: DAGFINN STENSETH.

Oman: Moscow, per. Obukha 6; tel. (095) 928-56-30; telex 411432; fax (095) 975-21-74; Chargé d'affaires a.i.: AHMED MOHAMMAD AL-RIYAMI.

Pakistan: Moscow, Sadovo-Kudrinskaya ul. 17; tel. (095) 254-97-91; telex 413194; Ambassador: ASHRAF JAHANGIR QAZI.

Peru: Moscow, Smolensky bul. 22/14, kv. 15; tel. (095) 248-77-38; telex 413400; fax (095) 230-20-00; Ambassador: Dr ARMANDO LECAROS DE COSSÍO.

Philippines: Moscow, Karmanitsky per. 6; tel. (095) 241-38-70; telex 413156; fax (095) 230-25-34; Ambassador: (vacant).

Poland: Moscow, ul. Klimashkina 4; tel. (095) 255-00-17; telex 414362; fax (095) 254-22-86; Ambassador: STANISŁAW CIOSEK.

Portugal: Moscow, Botanichesky per. 1; tel. (095) 230-24-35; telex 413221; fax (095) 280-31-34; Ambassador: ANTÓNIO COSTA LOBO.

Qatar: Moscow, Korovy val 7, kv. 197–198; tel. (095) 230-15-77; telex 413728; fax (095) 230-22-40; Ambassador: FAHD AL-KHATER.

Romania: Moscow, ul. Mosfilmovskaya 64; tel. (095) 143-04-24; telex 414355; Ambassador: VASILE SANDRU.

Rwanda: Moscow, ul. Bolshaya Ordynka 72; tel. (095) 237-32-22; telex 413213; Ambassador: ANASTASE NTEZILYAYO.

Senegal: Moscow, ul. Donskaya 12; tel. (095) 236-20-40; telex 413438; Ambassador: PASCAL-ANTOINE SANÉ.

Sierra Leone: Moscow, ul. Paliashvili 4; tel. (095) 203-62-00; telex 413461; Ambassador: OLU WILLIAM HARDING.

Singapore: Moscow, per. Voyevodina 5; tel. (095) 241-37-02; telex 413128; fax (095) 230-29-37; Ambassador: JOSEPH FRANCIS CONCEICAO.

Somalia: Moscow, Spasopeskovskaya pl. 8; tel. (095) 241-96-24; telex 413164; Ambassador: ABDULLAHI EGAL NUR.

Spain: Moscow, ul. Gertsena 50/8; tel. (095) 202-21-61; telex 413220; fax (095) 200-12-30; Ambassador: JOSÉ CUENCA ANAYA.

Sri Lanka: Moscow, ul. Shchepkina 24; tel. (095) 288-16-51; telex 413140; Ambassador: NISSANKA PARAKRAMA WIJEYERATNE.

Sudan: Moscow, ul. Vorovskovo 9; tel. (095) 290-39-93; telex 413448; Ambassador: IBRAHIM MOHAMMED ALI.

Sweden: Moscow, ul. Mosfilmovskaya 60; tel. (095) 147-90-09; telex 413410; fax (095) 147-87-88; Ambassador: ÖRJAN BERNER.

Switzerland: Moscow, per. Stopani 2/5; tel. (095) 925-53-22; telex 413418; fax (095) 200-17-28; Ambassador: JEAN-PIERRE RITTER.

Syria: Moscow, Mansurovsky per. 4; tel. (095) 203-15-21; telex 413145; Ambassador: MUHAMMAD ISSAM NAEB.

Tanzania: Moscow, ul. Pyatnitskaya 33; tel. (095) 231-81-46; telex 413352; fax (095) 230-29-68; Ambassador: WILSON TIBAIJUKA.

Thailand: Moscow, Eropkinsky per. 3; tel. (095) 201-48-93; telex 413309; Ambassador: KASIT PIROMYA.

Togo: 103001 Moscow, ul. Shchuseva 1; tel. (095) 290-65-99; telex 413967; Ambassador: EGOULIA KPANZOU.

Tunisia: Moscow, ul. Kachalova 28/1; tel. (095) 291-28-58; telex 413449; Ambassador: SLAHEDDINE ABDELLAH.

Turkey: Moscow, Vadkovsky per. 7/37; tel. (095) 972-69-00; telex 413731; fax (095) 200-22-23; Ambassador: VOLKAN VURAL.

Uganda: Moscow, per. Sadovskikh 5; tel. (095) 251-00-60; telex 413473; fax (095) 200-42-00; Ambassador: FELIX OKOBOI.

United Arab Emirates: Moscow, Olof Palme ul. 4; tel. (095) 147-62-86; telex 413547; Ambassador: NASSER SALMAN AL-ABOODI.

United Kingdom: Moscow, nab. Morisa Toreza 14; tel. (095) 231-85-11; telex 413341; fax (095) 233-35-63; Ambassador: Sir RODRIC BRAITHWAITE.

USA: Moscow, Novinsky bul. 19/23; tel. (095) 252-24-51; telex 413160; Ambassador: ROBERT S. STRAUSS.

Uruguay: Moscow, Lomonosovsky pr. 38; tel. (095) 143-04-01; telex 413238; fax (095) 938-20-45; Ambassador: JUAN JOSÉ REAL.

Venezuela: Moscow, ul. Ermolovoi 13–15; tel. (095) 299-96-21; telex 413119; fax (095) 200-02-48; Ambassador: RAFAEL LEON MORALES.

Viet-Nam: Moscow, Bolshaya Pirogovskaya ul. 13; tel. (095) 247-02-12; Ambassador: NGUYÊN MANH CÂM.

Yemen: Moscow, 2-Neopalimovsky per. 6; tel. (095) 246-15-31; telex 413214; Ambassador: ALI ABDULLA AL-BUGERY.

Yugoslavia: Moscow, ul. Mosfilmovskaya 46; tel. (095) 147-41-06; Ambassador: ANJELKO RUNIC.

Zaire: Moscow, per. N. Ostrovskovo 10; tel. (095) 201-76-64; telex 413479; fax (095) 201-79-48; Ambassador: MITIMA K. MURAIRI.

Zambia: Moscow, pr. Mira 52A; tel. (095) 288-50-01; telex 413462; Ambassador: OBINO RICHARD HAAMBOTE.

Zimbabwe: Moscow, Serpov per. 6; tel. (095) 248-43-67; telex 413029; fax (095) 230-24-97; Ambassador: Dr MISHECK J. M. SIBANDA.

PERMANENT REPRESENTATIVES OF COMMONWEALTH OF INDEPENDENT STATES MEMBERS

Armenia: Moscow, Armyansky per. 2; tel. (095) 925-57-58; Permanent Representative: FELIKS MAMIKONYAN.

Azerbaidzhan: Moscow, ul. Stanislavskovo 16; tel. (095) 229-16-49; Permanent Representative: V. R. VERDIYEV.

Byelorussia: Moscow, ul. Maroseika 17/6; tel. (095) 924-70-31.

Kazakhstan: Moscow, Chistoprudny bul. 3A; tel. (095) 208-26-49; Permanent Representative: K. B. SAUDABAYEV.

Kyrgyzstan: Moscow, ul. Bolshaya Ordynka 64; tel. (095) 237-48-82.

Moldavia: Moscow, Kuznetsky most 18; tel. (095) 928-54-05.

Tadzhikistan: Moscow, Skatertny per. 19; tel. (095) 290-61-02; Permanent Representative: S. K. NASRETDINOV.

Turkmenistan: Moscow, ul. Aksakova 22; tel. (095) 291-66-36.

Ukraine: Moscow, ul. Stanislavskovo 18; tel. (095) 229-28-04; Permanent Representative: V. G. FEODOROV.

Uzbekistan: Moscow, Pogorelsky per. 12; tel. (095) 230-00-78.

PERMANENT REPRESENTATIVE OF GEORGIA

Georgia: Moscow, ul. Paliashvili 6; tel. (095) 291-21-36; Permanent Representative: P. P. CHKHEIDZE.

Judicial System

Supreme Court of the Russian Federation: 103289 Moscow, ul. Ilyinka 3/7; tel. (095) 921-36-24; Chairman of the Supreme Court: VYACHESLAV M. LEBEDEV.

Office of the Procurator-General: 103760 Moscow, Kuznetsky most 13; tel. (095) 928-90-43; Procurator-General: VALENTIN STEPANKOV.

In October 1991 the first judges were appointed by the Congress of People's Deputies to a new Russian Constitutional Court (Chair. Prof. VALERY D. ZORKIN).

Religion

The majority of the population of the Russian Federation are adherents of Christianity, but there are significant Islamic, Buddhist and Jewish minorities.

CHRISTIANITY

The Russian Orthodox Church

The Russian Orthodox Church is the dominant religious organization in the Russian Federation. In May 1991 the Russian Orthodox Church announced plans to begin building 542 churches in the Republic.

Moscow Patriarchate: 113191 Moscow, Danilov Monastery, Danilovsky val 22; tel. (095) 235-04-54; fax (095) 230-26-19; Patriarch ALEKSEY II.

The Roman Catholic Church

In May 1991 Tadeusz Kondrusiewicz became the first Roman Catholic Archbishop of Moscow for more than 50 years. In February 1991 the Russian 'Greek Catholic' Church (Uniate) was re-established.

Protestant Churches

Society of Evangelical Christians-Baptists: Moscow, 3 Vuzovsky pr.; tel. (095) 297-89-47.

Other Christian Churches

Armenian Apostolic Church: Moscow, ul. Sergeya Makeyeva 10; tel. (095) 255-50-19.

Old Believers (The Old Faith): Moscow, Rogozhovsky pos. 29; tel. (095) 361-51-92; divided into three branches: the Belokrinitsky Concord, under the Metropolitan of Moscow and All-Russia, the Bezpopovtsy Concord and the Beglopopovtsy Concord; Metropolitan of Moscow and All-Russia: Bishop ALIMPI.

ISLAM

Most Muslims in the Russian Federation are adherents of the Sunni sect. Muslims in the Russian Federation come under the spiritual jurisdiction of the Muslim Board of the European USSR and Siberia and the Muslim Board of the North Caucasus.

JUDAISM

There are many independent Jewish communities in the Russian Federation, Ukraine and Byelorussia, particularly in the larger cities, such as Moscow, Minsk and Kiev. There are a small number of Jews in the Jewish Autonomous Region, in the Far East region of the Russian Federation. There is an Orthodox Jewish Seminary (yeshiva) in Moscow. In the Jewish Autonomous Oblast the teaching of Yiddish has begun in schools and institutes.

Chief Rabbi of Moscow: ADOLF SHAYEVICH.

BUDDHISM

Buddhism is most widespread in the Buryat Autonomous Republic, where the Central Spiritual Department of Buddhists for the former USSR territories has its seat, the Kalmyk and Tuva Autonomous Republics and in some districts of the Irkutsk and Chita Regions. There are also newly established communities in Moscow and St Petersburg. Before 1917 there were more than 40 datsans (monasteries) in Buryatia, but by 1990 only two of these remained in use. The number of Buddhist communities increased from one, in 1988, to five, in 1989. Estimates of the number of Buddhists range from Soviet estimates of some 200,000 to Western estimates of more than 600,000. In July 1991 the Dalai Lama, the spiritual leader of the Buddhists, visited Buryatia to attend the celebrations marking the 250th anniversary of the recognition of Buddhism as an official religion in Russia.

Chairman of the Central Spiritual Department of Buddhists: Bandido Hambo Lama MUNKO TSYBIKOV.

The Press

In 1989 there were 4,772 officially-registered newspaper titles published in the Russian Federation, of which 4,471 were in Russian. There were also 3,781 periodicals, including 3,504 in Russian. Many newspapers and periodicals based in the Russian Federation were undergoing a process of transformation to realign themselves with the new structure and orientation of their sponsoring organizations.

PRINCIPAL NEWSPAPERS

Moscow

Argumenty i Fakty (Arguments and Facts): 103104 Moscow, ul. Malaya Bronnaya 12; tel. (095) 290-59-65; telex 411630; fax (095) 200-22-52; f. 1978; weekly; Editor VLADISLAV A. STARKOV; circ. 31,517,100.

Gudok (Whistle): Moscow, ul. Gertsena, Khlynovsky tupik 8; f. 1917; organ of the Ministry of Communications and the Railway and Transport Construction Workers' Union; Editor G. I. LAPTEV; circ. 500,000.

Izvestiya (News): 103791 Moscow, Pushkinskaya pl. 5; tel. (095) 209-91-00; telex 411121; fax (095) 230-23-03; f. 1917; fmrly organ of the Presidium of the Supreme Soviet of the USSR; independent; Editor I. GOLEMBIOVSKY; circ. 4,700,000.

Komsomolskaya Pravda (Komsomol Pravda): 125865 Moscow, ul. Pravdy 24; tel. (095) 257-21-39; telex 111551; fax (095) 200-22-93; f. 1925; fmrly organ of the Leninist Young Communist League (Komsomol); independent; Editor V. A. FRONIN; circ. 17,600,000.

Krasnaya Zvezda (Red Star): 123826 Moscow, Khoroshevskoye shosse 38; tel. (095) 941-21-58; f. 1924; fmrly organ of the USSR Ministry of Defence; Editor I. M. PANOV; circ. 2,500,000.

Leninskoye Znamya (Banner of Lenin): 123847 Moscow, D-22, ul. 1905 goda; tel. (095) 259-48-97; f. 1918; fmrly organ of the Moscow city committee of the CPSU; Editor L. V. GUSEV; circ. 400,000.

Moskovskaya Pravda (Moscow Pravda): 123846 Moscow, ul. 1905 goda 7; tel. (095) 259-82-33; fax (095) 259-64-11; f. 1918; fmrly organ of the Moscow city committee of the CPSU and the Moscow City Soviet; independent; Editor A. K. VISHNEVETSKY; circ. 500,000 (1991).

Moskovsky Komsomolets (Member of the Leninist Young Communist League of Moscow): 107143 Moscow, ul. 1905 goda 7; tel. (095) 259-50-36; fax (095) 259-43-58; f. 1919; 5 a week; independent; Editor-in-Chief PAVEL GUSEV; circ. 1,559,836.

Nezavisimaya Gazeta (The Independent Newspaper): Moscow, ul. Myasnitskaya 13; tel. (095) 924-47-06; f. 1990; independent; Editor-in-Chief VITALY TRETYAKOV.

Pravda (Truth): 125867 Moscow, ul. Pravdy 24; tel. (095) 257-37-86; telex 111164; f. 1912; fmrly organ of the Cen. Cttee of the CPSU; independent; left-wing; Editor-in-Chief GENNADY N. SELEZNEV.

Pravitelstvenny Vestnik (Government Bulletin): 103012 Rybny per. 3; tel. (095) 924-28-18; f. 1989; fmrly organ of the USSR Cabinet of Ministers; fmrly official organ of the Committee for the Operational Management of the National Economy (interim govt); Editors V. P. VOLKOV, G. K. LOMANOV; circ. 250,000.

Rabochaya Tribuna (Workers' Tribune): Moscow, ul. Pravdy 24; tel. (095) 257-27-51; telex 114040; f. 1969; fmrly organ of the Cen. Cttee of the CPSU; organ of the Federation of Independent Trade Unions of the Russian Federation; Editor-in-Chief ANATOLY YURKOV; circ. 932,000 (1991).

Rossiskaya Gazeta: Moscow; organ of the govt of the Russian Federation.

Selskaya Zhizn (Country Life): 125869 Moscow, ul. Pravdy 24; tel. (095) 257-29-36; fax (095) 200-22-94; f. 1918; fmrly organ of the Cen. Cttee of the CPSU; independent; Editor-in-Chief A. P. KHARLAMOV; circ. 3,850,000 (1991).

Sovetskaya Rossiya (Soviet Russia): 125868 Moscow, ul. Pravdy 24; tel. (095) 257-28-84; fax (095) 200-22-90; f. 1956; fmrly organ of the Cen. Cttee of the CPSU and the Russian Federation Supreme Soviet and Council of Ministers; 5 a week; independent; Editor V. V. CHIKIN; circ. 1,770,000 (1991).

Sovetsky Sport (Soviet Sport): 101913 Moscow, ul. Arkhipova 8; tel. (095) 924-74-28; telex 411271; f. 1924; fmrly organ of the USSR State Cttee for Physical Culture and Sport and the General Confederation of Trade Unions; Editor V. G. KUDRYAVTSEV; circ. 5,200,000; Sunday supplement—*Football*, circ. 3,900,000.

Trud (Labour): 103792 Moscow, Nastasyinsky per. 4; tel. (095) 299-42-00; f. 1921; 6 a week; organ of the CIS Labour Union Federation; Editor A. S. POTAPOV; circ. 19,800,000.

Vechernyaya Moskva (Moscow Evening): 123846 Moscow, ul. 1905 goda 7; tel. (095) 259-33-33; f. 1923; organ of the Moscow City Council; Editor S. INDURSKY; circ. 630,000.

St Petersburg

Sankt-Peterburgskiye Vedomosti (St Petersburg News): 191023 St Petersburg, Fontanka 59; tel. (812) 314-71-76; f. 1918; fmrly *Leningradskaya Pravda* (Leningrad Truth); organ of the St Petersburg Mayoralty; Editor O. KUZIN; circ. 350,000.

Vecherny Sankt Petersburg (St Petersburg Evening): St Petersburg, Fontanka 59; f. 1946; organ of the St Petersburg City Council; Editor G. F. KONDRASHEV.

Vladivostok

Krasnoye Znamya (Red Banner): 690600 Vladivostok, Leninskaya 43, Krasnoye Znamya pr. 10; tel. (423) 5-06-68; f. 1917; fmrly organ of the Primorye regional committee of the CPSU, the Vladivostok city committee and the regional Soviet of Working People's Deputies; Editor V. P. SHKRABOV; circ. 400,000.

PRINCIPAL PERIODICALS

Agriculture, Forestry, etc.

Agrokhimiya (Agricultural Chemistry): Moscow, Podsosensky per. 21; f. 1964; monthly; publ. by the Nauka (Science) Publishing House; journal of the Russian Academy of Sciences; results of theoretical and experimental research work; Editor N. N. MELNIKOV; circ. 5,900.

Doklady Vsesoyuznoy ordena Lenina i ordena Trudovovo Krasnovo Znameni Akademii Selskokhozaistvennykh Nauk im. V. I. Lenina (Reports of the V. I. Lenin All-Union Academy of Agricultural Sciences): 107807 Moscow, Sadovaya-Spasskaya ul. 18; f. 1936; monthly; the latest issues in agriculture; Editor-in-Chief N. Z. MILASHCHENKO; circ. 2,430.

Ekonomika Selskokhozaistvennykh i Pererabatyvayushchikh Predpriyatiyakh (Economics of Agricultural and Processing Enterprises): Moscow, Sadovaya-Spasskaya 18; f. 1926; monthly; Editor V. A. ORLOV; circ. 78,740.

Lesnaya Promyshlennost (Forest Industry): 125047 Moscow, Bokzal pl. 3; tel. (095) 250-46-23; f. 1926; 3 a week; fmrly organ of the USSR State Committee for Forestry and the Cen. Cttee of the Timber, Paper and Wood Workers' Union of the USSR; Editor V. A. ALEKSEYEV; circ. 250,000.

Mekhanizatsiya i Elektrifikatsiya Selskovo Khozyaista (Mechanization and Electrification of Agriculture): 107807 Moscow, Sadovaya-Spasskaya ul. 18; f. 1930; monthly; Editor I. E. CHESNOKOV; circ. 27,890.

Mezhdunarodny Selsko-Khozhiaistveni Zhurnal (International Agricultural Journal): 107807 Moscow, Sadovaya-Spasskaya ul. 18; tel. (095) 207-16-56; monthly.

Molochnoye i Myasnoye Skotovodstvo (Dairy and Meat Cattle Breeding): Moscow, Sadovaya-Spasskaya ul. 18; tel. (095) 207-21-20; f. 1956; 6 a year; Editor V. V. KORGENEVSKY; circ. 39,800.

Selskokhozaistvennaya Biologiya (Agricultural Biology): Moscow, Sadovaya-Spasskaya ul. 18; f. 1966; every 2 months; publ. by the V. I. Lenin All-Union Academy of Agricultural Sciences; Editor V. M. ANANINA; circ. 1,980.

Svinovodstvo (Pig Breeding): Moscow, Sadovaya-Spasskaya ul. 18; f. 1930; 6 a year; Editor K. D. BAYEV; circ. 37,830.

Tekhnika v Selskom Khozyaistve (Agricultural Technology): 107807 Moscow, Sadovaya-Spasskaya ul. 18; f. 1941; every 2 months; journal of the V. I. Lenin All-Union Academy of Agricultural Sciences; Deputy Editor P. S. POPOV; circ. 42,730.

Vestnik Selskokhozyaistvennoy Nauki (Agricultural Scientific Bulletin): Moscow, Sadovaya-Spasskaya ul. 18; f. 1956; monthly; journal of the V. I. Lenin All-Union Academy of Agricultural Sciences; Editor-in-Chief A. A. NIKONOV; circ. 6,460.

Veterinariya (Veterinary Science): Moscow, Sadovaya-Spasskaya ul. 18; tel. (095) 207-10-60; f. 1924; monthly; Editor V. A. GARKAVTSEV; circ. 76,000.

Zashchita Rastenii (Plant Protection): 107807 Moscow, Sadovaya-Spasskaya ul. 18; tel. (095) 207-21-30; f. 1932; monthly; Editor V. E. SAVZDARG; circ. 62,000.

Zemledeliye (Farming): Moscow, Sadovaya-Spasskaya ul. 18; f. 1939; monthly; Editor V. IVANOV; circ. 53,000.

Zhivotnovodstvo (Cattle Breeding): Moscow, Sadovaya-Spasskaya ul. 18; f. 1928; monthly; Editor A. T. MYSIK; circ. 106,870.

For Children

Koster (Campfire): 193024 St Petersburg, Mytninskaya ul. 1/20; tel. (812) 274-15-72; telex 321584; f. 1936; monthly; fmrly journal of the Union of Pioneer Organizations (Federation of Children's Organizations) of the USSR; fiction, poetry, sport, reports and popular science; for 10–14 years; Editor-in-Chief O. A. TSAKUNOV; circ. 800,000 (1991).

Murzilka: 125015 Moscow, Novodmitrovskaya ul. 5A; tel. (095) 285-18-81; f. 1924; monthly; publ. by the Molodaya Gvardiya (Young

Guard) Publishing House; fmrly journal of the Union of Pioneer Organizations (Federation of Children's Organizations) of the USSR; illustrated; for first grades of school; Editor T. ANDROSENKO; circ. 2,960,000.

Pioner (Pioneer): 101459 Moscow, Bumazhny proyezd 14; tel. (095) 212-14-17; f. 1924; monthly; fmrly journal of the Cen. Cttee of the Leninist Young Communist League; fiction; illustrated; for children of fourth–eigth grades; Editor A. S. MOROZ; circ. 1,770,000.

Pionerskaya Pravda (Pioneer Pravda): 101502 Moscow, Sushchevskaya ul. 21; tel. (095) 972-22-38; f. 1925; 3 a week; fmrly organ of the Union of Pioneer Organizations (Federation of Children's Organizations) of the USSR; Editor O. I. GREKOVA; circ. 3,600,000.

Veselye Kartinki (Merry Pictures): 125015 Moscow, Novodmitrovskaya ul. 5A; tel. (095) 285-80-90; f. 1956; monthly; publ. by the Molodaya Gvardiya (Young Guard) Publishing House; humorous; for pre-school and first grades; Editor R. A. VARSHAMOV; circ. 9,350,000.

Yuny Naturalist (Young Naturalist): Moscow, Novodmitrovskaya ul. 5A; f. 1928; monthly; publ. by the Molodaya Gvardiya (Young Guard) Publishing House; fmrly journal of the Union of Pioneer Organizations (Federation of Children's Organizations) of the USSR; popular science for children of fourth–10th grades who are interested in biology; Editor A. G. ROGOZHKIN; circ. 1,500,000.

Yuny Tekhnik (Young Technologist): 125015 Moscow, Novodmitrovskaya ul. 5A; tel. (095) 285-80-81; f. 1956; monthly; publ. by the Molodaya Gvardiya (Young Guard) Publishing House; popular science for schoolchildren; Editor BORIS CHEREMISINOV; circ. 1,095,000.

Culture and Arts

Avrora (Aurora): 191065 St Petersburg, Khalturina ul. 4; tel. (095) 312-13-23; f. 1969; monthly; journal of the USSR and Russian Federation Unions of Writers; fiction; Editor-in-Chief E. SHEVELYOV; circ. 1,090,000.

Biblioteka 'V Pomoshch Khudozhestvennoy Samodeyatelnosti' (Amateur Art): Moscow; f. 1945; 2 a month; publ. by the Sovetskaya Rossiya (Soviet Russia) Publishing House; songs, plays and articles by leading actors; Editor N. M. SERGOVANTSEV; circ. 72,000.

Dekorativnoye Iskusstvo SSSR (Decorative Art of the USSR): 103009 Moscow, ul. Tverskaya 9; tel. (095) 229-19-10; fax (095) 200-42-44; f. 1957; monthly; publ. by the Sovetsky Khudozhnik (Soviet Artist) Publishing House; journal of the Union of Artists of the USSR; Editor S. B. BAZAZIANTS; circ. 28,000.

Govorit i Pokazyvayet Moskva: Programmy Tsentralnovo Televideniya i Radioveshchaniya (Moscow Speaks and Shows: Central Television and Radio Programmes): Moscow, Vtoroy Troitsky per. 4; f. 1967; Editor N. F. IVANKOVICH; circ. 1,650,000.

Iskusstvo (Art): Moscow, Vorotnikovsky per. 11; f. 1933; monthly; publ. by the Iskusstvo (Art) Publishing House; journal of the Union of Artists of the USSR and the USSR Academy of Arts; fine arts; Editor V. ZIMENKO; circ. 18,500.

Iskusstvo Kino (Cinema Art): 125319 Moscow, Usievicha 9; tel. (095) 151-02-72; telex 411939; fax (095) 200-42-84; f. 1931; monthly; journal of the Confederation of Soviet Film-makers Unions; Editor K. A. SHCHERBAKOV; circ. 53,000.

Knizhnoye Obozreniye (Book Review): 129272 Moscow, Sushchevsky val 64; tel. (095) 281-62-66; f. 1966; weekly; summaries of newly published books; Editor E. S. AVERIN; circ. 280,000–300,000.

Kultura (Culture): 101484 Moscow, ul. Novoslobodskaya 73; tel. (095) 285-78-02; f. 1929; fmrly *Sovetskaya Kultura* (Soviet Culture); weekly; Editor A. A. BELYAYEV; circ. 385,000.

Kultura i Zhizn (Culture and Life): 103674 Moscow, proyezd Sapunova 13–15; tel. (095) 921-35-60; f. 1957; monthly; Russian, English, French, Spanish and German; publ. by the Union of Soviet Societies for Cultural and Friendly Relations with Foreign Countries; Editor ADO KUKANOV; circ. 130,000.

Literaturnaya Gazeta (Literary Newspaper): 103654 Moscow, Kostyansky per. 13; tel. (095) 200-24-17; telex 411294; fax (095) 200-02-38; f. 1830; publ. restored 1929; weekly; independent; fmrly organ of the USSR Writers' Union; Editor-in-Chief ARKADY UDALTSOV; circ. 1,200,000.

Literaturnaya Rossiya (Literature of Russia): 103662 Moscow, Tsvetnoy bul. 30; tel. (095) 200-40-05; fax (095) 200-27-55; f. 1958; weekly; organ of the Russian Federation Union of Writers; essays, verse, literary criticism; Editor ERNST I. SAFONOV.

Moskva (Moscow): 121918 Moscow, Arbat 20; tel. (095) 291-71-10; f. 1957; monthly; journal of the Russian Federation Union of Writers and its Moscow branch; fiction; Editor-in-Chief MIKHAIL N. ALEKSEYEV; circ. 800,000.

Muzykalnaya Akademiya (Musical Academy): 103009 Moscow, ul. Ogareva 13; tel. (095) 229-81-66; f. 1933; fmrly *Sovetskaya Muzyka* (Soviet Music); monthly; publ. by the Sovetsky Kompozitor (Soviet

Composer) Publishing House; journal of the Union of Composers of the USSR and the Ministry of Culture; Editor YU. S. KOREV; circ. 10,650.

Muzykalnaya Zhizn (Musical Life): 103006 Moscow, Sadovaya-Triumfalnaya ul. 14-12; tel. (095) 209-75-24; f. 1957; fortnightly; publ. by the Sovetsky Kompozitor (Soviet Composer) Publishing House; journal of the Union of Composers of the USSR and the Ministry of Culture; development of music; Editor INNOKENTI YE. POPOV; circ. 131,000.

Neva (The River Neva): 191065 St Petersburg, Nevsky pr. 3; tel. (812) 312-65-37; f. 1955; monthly; journal of the St Petersburg Writers' Organization; fiction, literary criticism; Editor B. NIKOLSKY; circ. 255,000 (1991).

Oktyabr (October): Moscow, ul. Pravdy 11; tel. (095) 214-62-05; f. 1924; monthly; fmrly journal of the Russian Federation Union of Writers; published by the Pravda (Truth) Publishing House; independent literary journal; new fiction and essays by Russian and foreign writers; Editor A. A. ANANIYEV.

Sovetskoye Foto (Soviet Photography): Moscow, ul. Malaya Lubyanka 16; f. 1926; monthly; journal of the Union of Journalists of the USSR; Editor G. M. CHUDAKOV; circ. 142,000.

Sovetsky Ekran (Soviet Screen): Moscow, ul. Chasovaya 5; f. 1925; fortnightly; publ. by the Pravda (Truth) Publishing House; journal of the Confederation of Soviet Film-makers' Unions; achievements of Soviet cinema; Editor Y. S. RYBAKOV; circ. 1,700,000.

Sovetsky Film (Soviet Film): 103009 Moscow, B. Gnezdnikovsky per. 9; tel. (095) 229-06-43; telex 411143; fax (095) 200-12-56; f. 1957; monthly; Russian, English, French, German and Spanish; illustrated; Soviet and foreign films; Editor VALERY S. KICHIN; circ. 130,000.

Teatr (Theatre): 121069 Moscow, ul. Gertsena 49; tel. (095) 291-57-88; monthly; publ. by the Izvestiya (News) Publishing House; journal of the Theatrical Workers' Union and the Union of Writers of the USSR; new plays by Soviet and foreign playwrights; Editor A. SALYNSKY; circ. 50,000.

Televideniye i Radioveshchaniye (Television and Radio Broadcasting): 113326 Moscow, Pyatnitskaya ul. 25; tel. (095) 292-82-68; f. 1952; monthly; Editor-in-Chief N. S. BIRYUKOV; circ. 50,000.

Economics, Finance

Dengi i Kredit (Money and Credit): 103016 Moscow, Neglinnaya ul. 12; tel. (095) 221-50-23; f. 1927; monthly; publ. by the Finansy (Finances) Publishing House; all aspects of banking and money circulation; Editor Y. G. DMITRIEV; circ. 69,860.

Ekonomicheskiye Nauki (Economic Sciences): 103009 Moscow, pr. Marksa 18; tel. (095) 203-31-54; f. 1958; monthly; publ. by the Vysshaya Shkola (Higher School) Publishing House; fmrly journal of the State Committee of Public Education; articles on theory and methodology of economic sciences; Editor A. D. SMIRNOV; circ. 24,326.

Ekonomika i Matematicheskiye Metody (Economics and Mathematical Methods): 117418 Moscow, ul. Krasikova 32; f. 1965; 6 a year; publ. by the Nauka (Science) Publishing House; journal of the Central Institute of Economics and Mathematics of the Russian Academy of Sciences; development of mathematical methods in economics, applicability of computers, systems of optimal planning, etc.; Editor V. L. MAKAROV; circ. 3,500.

Ekonomika u Zhizn (Economics and Life): 101462 Moscow, Bumazhny proyezd 14; f. 1918; weekly; fmrly organ of the Cen. Cttee of the CPSU; Editor B. G. VLADIMIROV; circ. 750,000.

Finansy SSSR (Finances of the USSR): 103050 Moscow, ul. Tverskaya 22B; tel. (095) 299-43-33; f. 1926; monthly; publ. by the Finansy (Finances) Publishing House; fmrly journal of the Ministry of Finance; theory and information on finances; compiling and execution of the state budget, insurance, crediting, etc.; Editor YU. M. ARTEMOV; circ. 45,000.

Kommersant: Moscow, Khoroshovskoye Shosse 41; tel. (095) 941-09-00; f. 1989; independent; economics, business and politics; Editor VLADIMIR YAKOVLEV.

Mir Daidzhest Pressi (Business World Press Digest): 191180 St Petersburg, POB 55; f. 1989; 8 a year; publ. by St Petersburg branch of Union of Journalists; all aspects of finance; Editors YAN STRUGACH, SERGEI GRACHEV.

Mirovaya Ekonomika i Mezhdunarodniye Otnosheniya (World Economy and International Relations): Moscow, Profsoyuznaya ul. 23; tel. (095) 128-08-83; telex 411687; fax (095) 31-07-27; f. 1957; monthly; publ. by the Nauka (Science) Publishing House; journal of the Institute of the World Economy and International Relations of the Russian Academy of Sciences; problems of theory and practice of world socio-economic development, international policies, international economic co-operation, economic and political situation in different countries of the world, etc.; Editor Prof. G. G. DILIGENSKY; circ. 26,000.

Voprosy Ekonomiki (Problems of Economics): 117218 Moscow, ul. Krasikova 27; tel. (095) 129-04-54; f. 1929; monthly; published by the Pravda (Truth) Publishing House; journal of the Institute of Economics of the Russian Academy of Sciences; theoretical probelems of economic develoment, market relations, social aspects of transition to a market economy, international economics, etc.; Editor (vacant); circ. 47,000.

Education

Professionalno-tekhnicheskoye Obrazovaniye (Vocational and Technical Education): 125319 Moscow, ul. Chernyakhovskovo 9; tel. (095) 152-75-41; f. 1941; monthly; Editor-in-Chief VLADIMIR G. CHERNYKH; circ. 35,000 (1991).

Russky Yazyk v SSSR (The Russian Language in the USSR): 119034 Moscow, Smolensky bul. 4; tel. (095) 971-15-63; f. 1957; monthly; publ. by Academy of Pedagogical Sciences; Editor M. I. ISAYEV; circ. 15,000.

Semya (Family): Moscow; f. 1988; weekly; publ. by Soviet Children's Fund; Editor-in-Chief SERGEI A. ABRAMOV; circ. 4,600,000.

Semya i Shkola (Family and School): 129278 Moscow, ul. Pavla Korchagina 7; tel. (095) 283-80-09; f. 1946; monthly; publ. by Academy of Pedagogical Sciences; Editor V. F. SMIRNOV; circ. 1,140,000.

Shkola i Proizvodstvo (School and Production): 107847 Moscow, Lefortovsky per. 8; tel. (095) 246-65-91; f. 1957; monthly; publ. by the Pedagogika (Pedagogics) Publishing House; fmrly journal of the State Cttee for National Education; Editor YU. YE. RIVES-KOROBKOV; circ. 205,000.

Sovetskaya Pedagogika (Soviet Pedagogics): 119034 Moscow, Smolensky bul. 4; tel. (095) 248-51-49; f. 1937; monthly; publ. by Academy of Pedagogical Sciences; Chief Editor G. N. FILONOV; circ. 46,500.

Uchitelskaya Gazeta (Teachers' Gazette): 103635 Moscow, proyezd Sapunova 13/15; tel. (095) 928-82-53; f. 1924; fmrly organ of the Union of Educational and Scientific Workers of the USSR; weekly; independent; Editor P. POLOZHEVETZ; circ. 520,000.

Vestnik Vysshey Shkoly (Higher Schools' Review): 103031 Moscow, ul. Rozhdestvenka 11; tel. (095) 924-73-43; f. 1940; monthly; fmrly organ of the State Cttee for National Education; Editor O. V. DOLZHENKO; circ. 17,000.

Vospitaniye Shkolnikov (The Upbringing of Schoolchildren): Moscow, Lefortovsky per. 8; f. 1966; 6 a year; publ. by Pedagogika (Pedagogics) Publishing House; Editor L. V. KUZNETSOVA; circ. 733,230.

International Affairs

Ekho Planety (Echo of the Planet): Moscow; tel. (095) 290-66-45; fax (095) 203-30-49; f. 1988; weekly; Russian; publ. by TASS; international affairs, economic, social and cultural; Editor-in-Chief NIKOLAI SETUNSKY; circ. 750,000.

Mezhdunarodnaya Zhizn (International Life): 103064 Moscow, Gorokhovsky per. 14; tel. (095) 265-37-81; f. 1954; monthly; Russian, English and French; publ. by the Pravda (Truth) Publishing House; journal of the USSR Society Znaniye (Knowledge); problems of foreign policy and diplomacy of the USSR and other countries; Editor B. D. PYADYSHEV; circ. 71,620.

Novoye Vremya (New Times): 103782 Moscow, pl. Pushkina 5; tel. (095) 229-88-72; telex 411164; fax (095) 200-41-92; f. 1943; weekly; Russian, English, French, German, Spanish, Portuguese, Italian, Polish, Greek and Czech; publ. by the Moskovskaya Pravda Publishing House; foreign affairs; Editor V. IGNATENKO; circ. 500,000.

Vek XX i Mir (20th Century and Peace): 103009 Moscow, ul. Tverskaya 16/2; tel. (095) 200-38-07; telex 411426; f. 1958; monthly; Russian, English, German, Spanish and French; journal of the Soviet Peace Committee; Russian and foreign writers and journalists on the most important developments in international relations and disarmament; Editor A. BELAYEV; circ. 101,000.

Za Rubezhom (Abroad): 125865 Moscow, ul. Pravdy 24; tel. (095) 257-23-87; telex 411421; fax (095) 200-22-96; f. 1960; weekly; publ. by the Pravda Independent Publishing House; review of foreign press; Editor-in-Chief S. MOROZOV; circ. 650,000.

Language, Literature

Filologicheskiye Nauki (Philological Sciences): Moscow, prospekt Marksa 18; f. 1958; 6 a year; publ. by the Vysshaya Shkola (Higher School) Publishing House; reports of institutions of higher learning on the most important problems of literary studies and linguistics; Editor P. A. NIKOLAYEV; circ. 2,960.

Russkaya Literatura (Russian Literature): 199164 St Petersburg, nab. Makarova 4; f. 1958; quarterly; journal of the Institute of Russian Literature of the Russian Academy of Sciences; development of Russian literature from its appearance up to the present day; Editor V. V. SKATOV; circ. 13,149.

Russkaya Rech (Russian Speech): Moscow, ul. Volkhonka 18/2; f. 1967; 6 a year; publ. by the Nauka (Science) Publishing House; journal of the Institute of Russian Language of the Academy of Sciences; popular; history of the development of the literary Russian language; Editor V. P. VOMPENSKY; circ. 30,000.

Russky Yazyk za Rubezhom (The Russian Language Abroad): 117485 Moscow, ul. Volgina 6; tel. (095) 336-66-47; f. 1967; 6 a year; publ. by the Russky Yazyk (Russian Language) Publishing House; journal of the Pushkin Institute of the Russian Language; current problems of methodology of teaching the Russian language to foreigners; Editor A. V. ABRAMOVICH; circ. 44,300.

Sovetskaya Literatura (Soviet Literature): 121248 Moscow, Kutuzovsky pr. 1/7; tel. (095) 243-38-78; f. 1931; monthly; English and Russian journal of the Union of Writers of the USSR; novels, short stories, verses, poems, literary criticism by Soviet authors, non-fiction and topical articles; Editor ALEXEI BARKHATOV; circ. 70,000.

Voprosy Literatury (Questions of Literature): 103009 Moscow, Bolshoy Gnezdnikovsky per. 10; tel. (095) 229-49-77; f. 1957; monthly; publ. by the Izvestiya (News) Publishing House; joint edition of the Union of Writers of the USSR and the Institute of World Literature of the Academy of Sciences; theory and history of modern literature and aesthetics; Editor D. M. URNOV; circ. 20,000.

Voprosy Yazykoznaniya (Questions of Linguistics): 121019 Moscow, Volkhonka 18/2; tel. (095) 203-00-78; f. 1952; 6 a year; publ. by the Nauka (Science) Publishing House; journal of the Department of Literature and Language of the Russian Academy of Sciences; actual problems of general linguistics on the basis of different languages; Editor T. V. GAMKRELIDZE; circ. 3,770.

Leisure, Physical Culture and Sport

Filateliya SSSR (Philately in the USSR): 121069 Moscow, Khlebny per. 8; f. 1966; monthly; journal of the All-Union Philatelic Society; Editor-in-Chief J. G. BEKHTEREV; circ. 70,000.

Fizkultura i Sport (Physical Culture and Sport): Moscow, Kalyayevskaya ul. 27; f. 1922; monthly; publ. by the Fizkultura i Sport (Physical Culture and Sport) Publishing House; fmrly journal of the USSR State Committee for Physical Culture and Sport; activities and development of Soviet sport; Editor A. CHAIKOVSKY; circ. 717,000.

Mir puteshestvy (World of Travels): 107078 Moscow, Bolshoi Kharitonyevsky per. 14; tel. (095) 921-13-90; telex 111777; f. 1929, fmrly *Turist*; journal of the CIS Labour Union Federation; monthly; publ. by the Profizdat (Trade Union Literature) Publishing House; articles, photo-essays, information, recommendations about routes and hotels for tourists, natural, cultural and historical places of interest; Editor BORIS V. MOSKVIN; circ. 32,800.

Shakhmaty v SSSR (Chess in the USSR): 121019 Moscow, POB 10, Gogolevsky bul. 14; tel. (095) 291-87-70; f. 1921; monthly; publ. by the Fizkultura i Sport (Physical Culture and Sport) Publishing House; journal of the USSR Chess Federation; Editor Y. AVERBAKH; circ. 30,000.

Sportivnye Igry (Sports): 101421 Moscow, Kalyayevskaya ul. 27; tel. (095) 258-06-56; fax (095) 200-12-17; f. 1955; monthly; publ. by the Fizkultura i Sport (Physical Culture and Sport) Publishing House; fmrly journal of the USSR State Committee for Physical Culture and Sport; Editor D. L. RYZHKOV; circ. 160,000.

Sport v SSSR (Sport in the USSR): 103772 Moscow, ul. Moskvina 8; tel. (095) 229-46-59; f. 1963; monthly; Russian, English, Spanish, and Hindi; publ. by Voskresenye Publishing Corporation; illustrated; Editor O. D. SPASSKY.

Teoriya i Praktika Fizicheskoy Kultury (Theory and Practice of Physical Culture): Moscow, Kalyayevskaya ul. 27; f. 1925; monthly; publ. by the Fizkultura i Sport (Physical Culture and Sport) Publishing House; fmrly journal of the USSR State Committee for Physical Culture and Sport; Editor A. V. SEDOV; circ. 16,200.

Politics and Military Affairs

Ekspress-Khronika (Express-Chronicle): 601010 Kirzhach-1, a/ya 14; tel. (8-09237) 22052; f. 1987; weekly; independent chronicle of events throughout the former USSR; also an edition in English; Editor ALEKSANDR PODRABINEK.

Moskovskiye Novosti (Moscow News): 103829 Moscow, ul. Tverskaya 16/2; tel. (095) 209-17-28; fax (095) 200-02-78; f. 1930; weekly; Russian, English, French and Spanish; monthly edition in German; independent; Editor-in-Chief LEN KARPINSKY; circ. 2,100,000.

Politicheskoye Obrazovaniye (Political Education): Moscow, ul. Pravdy 24; f. 1957; monthly; publ. by the Pravda (Truth) Publishing House; fmrly journal of the Cen. Cttee of the CPSU; Editor N. Y. KLEPACH; circ. 1,862,000.

Sovetsky Voin (Soviet Soldier): 123831 Moscow, 32A/3 Khoroshevskoye Shosse; tel. (095) 198-55-63; f. 1990; fortnightly in Russian, monthly in English and German; fmrly publ. by the USSR Ministry of Defence; Editor-in-Chief LEONID GOLOVNYOV; circ. 1,000,000.

Svobodnaya Mysl (Free Thought): 119875 Moscow, ul. Marksa i Engelsa 5; tel. (095) 291-60-67; f. 1924; fmrly *Kommunist* (Communist), the theoretical journal of the Cen. Cttee of the CPSU; 18 a year; problems of political theory, philosophy, economy, etc.; Editor-in-Chief N. B. BIKKENIN; circ. 995,000.

Syn Otechestva (Son of the Fatherland): Moscow; f. 1990; military and civilian problems in society, articles on ethics, culture and education; Editor Col NIKOLAY VELIKANOV.

Voprosy Istorii KPSS (Questions of History of the CPSU): 129256 Moscow, ul. Vilgelma Pika 4; tel. (095) 181-15-79; f. 1957; monthly; fmrly publ. by the Pravda (Truth) Publishing House; fmrly journal of the Institute of Marxism-Leninism under the Cen. Cttee of the CPSU; history of the CPSU, international Communist and labour movements; Editor V. I. KASYANENKO; circ. 35,000.

Popular, Fiction and General

Druzhba Narodov (Friendship of Peoples): Moscow, ul. Vorovskovo 52; tel. (095) 291-62-27; f. 1938; monthly; publ. by the Izvestiya (News) Publishing House; independent; works of writers, poets and critics from all the Republics of the former USSR; Editor A. RUDENKO-DESNYAK; circ. 250,000.

Inostrannaya Literatura (Foreign Literature): Moscow, Pyatnitskaya ul. 41; tel. (095) 233-51-47; fax (095) 230-23-03; f. 1955; monthly; publ. by the Izvestiya (News) Publishing House; independent; Russian translations of modern foreign authors; Editor-in-Chief VLADIMIR LAKSHIN; circ. 200,000.

Moskva (Moscow): Moscow, ul. Arbat 20; f. 1957; monthly; publ. by the Khudozhestvennaya Literatura (Fiction) Publishing House; Editor M. N. ALEKSEYEV; circ. 760,000.

Nash Sovremennik (Our Contemporary): Moscow, Tsvetnoi bul. 30; f. 1933; monthly; publ. by the Literaturnaya Gazeta (Literary Gazette) Publishing House; Editor STANISLAV KUNAYEV; circ. 270,000.

Novy Mir (New World): 103806 Moscow, Maly Putinkovsky per. 1/2; tel. (095) 200-08-29; f. 1925; monthly; publ. by the Izvestiya (News) Publishing House; journal of the Union of Writers of the USSR; new fiction and essays; Editor SERGEI P. ZALYGIN; circ. 1,560,000.

Ogonek (Beacon): 101456 Moscow, Bumazhny per. 14; tel. (095) 212-23-27; fax (095) 943-00-70; f. 1923; weekly; independent; popular illustrated; Editor LEV GUSHCHIN; circ. 3,200,000.

Oktyabr (October): Moscow, ul. Pravdy 11; tel. (095) 214-62-05; f. 1924; monthly; publ. by the Pravda (Truth) Publishing House; circ. 380,000.

Rodina (Motherland): Moscow; f. 1989; monthly; publ. by Pravda (Truth) Publishing House; social, political and scientific; illustrated.

Roman-Gazeta (Novels): Moscow, Novo-Basmannaya ul. 19; tel. 261-49-29; f. 1927; fortnightly; publ. by the Khudozhestvennaya Literatura (Fiction) Publishing House; the most widespread periodical of fiction and best works previously published in journals, including translations into Russian; Editor V. GANICHEV; circ. 3,500,000.

Sovetsky Soyuz (Soviet Union): 103772 Moscow, ul. Moskvina 8; tel. (095) 924-56-89; telex 411721; f. 1930; monthly; 14 languages including Russian, Arabic, Bengali, Chinese, English, Finnish, French, German, Hindi, Italian, Spanish, Tamil, Urdu and Vietnamese; publ. by Voskresenye Publishing Corporation; illustrated; Editor A. N. MISHARIN.

Zakon (Law): 103798 Moscow, Pushkinskaya pl. 5; tel. (095) 299-74-55; f. 1991; publ. by the Izvestiya printing house; publishes legislation relating to business and commerce; legal issues for businessmen; Editor YURY FEOFANOV.

Znamya (Banner): Moscow, ul. Nikolskaya 8/1; f. 1931; monthly; independent; novels, poetry, essays; Editor-in-Chief GRIGORY YA. BAKLANOV; circ. 970,000.

Zvezda (Star): St Petersburg, Mokhovaya 20; f. 1924; monthly; publ. by the Khudozhestvennaya Literatura (Fiction) Publishing House; journal of the Union of Writers of the USSR; novels, short stories, poetry, art and literary criticism; Editor G. KHOLOPOV; circ. 215,000.

Popular Scientific

Meditsinskaya Gazeta (Medical Gazette): 129010 Moscow, Sukharevskaya pl. 1/2; tel. (095) 208-86-95; f. 1938; 2 a week; organ of the Union of Medical Workers of the USSR; Editor K. V. SHEGLOV; circ. 1,430,000.

Modelist-Konstruktor (Modelling-Designing): 125015 Moscow, Novodmitrovskaya ul. 5A; tel. (095) 285-17-04; f. 1962; monthly; publ. by the Molodaya Gvardiya (Young Guard) Publishing House;

designs and descriptions of technical models; Editor Y. STOLYAROV; circ. 1,200,000.

Nauka i Religiya (Science and Religion): 109004 Moscow, Ulyanovskaya 43; f. 1959; monthly; journal of the USSR Society Znaniye (Knowledge); Editor V. F. PRAVOTVOROV; circ. 480,000.

Nauka i Zhizn (Science and Life): 101877 Moscow, ul. Myasnitskaya 24; tel. (095) 923-21-22; fax (095) 200-22-59; f. 1934; monthly; publ. by the Pravda (Truth) Publishing House; popular; recent developments in all branches of science and technology; Chief Editor I. K. LAGOVSKY; circ. 1,313,000.

Priroda (Nature): 117069 Moscow, Maronovsky per. 26; tel. (095) 238-26-33; f. 1912; monthly; publ. by the Nauka (Science) Publishing House; journal of the Presidium of the Academy of Sciences; popular; natural sciences; Editor N. G. BASOV; circ. 54,000.

Radio: 103045 Moscow, Seliverstov per. 10; tel. (095) 207-68-89; f. 1924; monthly; fmrly joint edition of the Ministry of Communications and the USSR Voluntary Society of Assistance to the Army, Air Force and Navy (DOSAAF); popular radio-engineering; Editor A. V. GOROKHOVSKY; circ. 1,500,000.

Tekhnika-Molodezhi (Engineering—For Youth): 125015 Moscow, Novodmitrovskaya ul. 5A; tel. (095) 285-89-81; f. 1933; monthly; publ. by the Molodaya Gvardiya (Young Guard) Publishing House; fmrly journal of the Cen. Cttee of the Leninist Young Communist League; popular; engineering and science; Editor S. V. CHUMAKOV; circ. 1,819,000.

Vokrug Sveta (Around the World): 125015 Moscow, Novodmitrovskaya ul. 5A; tel. (095) 285-88-83; f. 1861; monthly, including the supplement *Iskatel* (Seeker) in alternate issues; publ. by the Molodaya Gvardiya (Young Guard) Publishing House; fmrly journal of the Cen. Cttee of the Leninist Young Communist League; geographical, travel, adventure and science fiction, detective stories; illustrated; Editor A. A. POLESHCHUK; circ. 2,800,000.

Vrach (Physician): Moscow; f. 1990; monthly; publ. by Meditsina Publs.; popular scientific and socio-political; illustrated; circ. 100,000.

Zdorovye (Health): Moscow, Bumazhny per. 24; f. 1955; monthly; publ. by the Pravda (Truth) Publishing House; publ. by the Russian Federation Ministry of Health; popular scientific; medicine and hygiene; Editor M. D. PIRADOVA; circ. 16,800,000.

Zemlya i Vselennaya (Earth and Universe): Moscow, Maronovsky per. 26; tel. (095) 238-42-32; f. 1965; 6 a year; publ. by the Nauka (Science) Publishing House; joint edition of the Academy of Sciences and the USSR Society of Astronomy and Geodesy; popular; current hypotheses of the origin and development of the earth and universe; astronomy, geophysics and space research; Editor V. K. ABALAKIN; circ. 49,000.

Znaniye-Sila (Knowledge is Strength): 113114 Moscow, Kozhevnicheskaya ul. 19; tel. (095) 235-89-35; f. 1926; monthly; publ. by the Znaniye (Knowledge) Publishing House; journal of the USSR Society Znaniye (Knowledge); general scientific; Editor G. A. ZELENKO; circ. 350,000.

The Press, Printing and Bibliography

Knizhnaya Letopis (Book Chronicle): 127018 Moscow, Oktyabrskaya ul. 4; tel. (095) 288-92-38; f. 1907; weekly; publ. by the Knizhnaya palata (Book Chamber) Publishing House; registration of all books published in the former USSR, with description of books; Editors V. N. TYURICHEVA, G. N. DMITRIYENKO; circ. 3,751.

Notnaya Letopis (Chronicle of Music): 127018 Moscow, Oktyabrskaya ul. 4; tel. (095) 288-92-38; f. 1931; monthly; publ. by the Knizhnaya palata (Book Chamber) Publishing House; registration of issues of music in the former USSR; Editors N. A. ROSTOVSKAYA, G. N. DMITRIYENKO; circ. 776.

Poligrafiya (Printing): 117071 Moscow, Leninsky prospekt 15; equipment and technology of the printing industry; Dir A. I. OVSYANNIKOV; circ. 18,500.

Sovetskaya Bibliografiya (Soviet Bibliography): 129272 Moscow, Sushchevsky val 64; tel. (095) 284-57-65; f. 1929; 6 a year; publ. by the Knizhnaya Palata (Book Chamber) Publishing House; theoretical, practical and historical aspects of bibliography; Editor E. S. NURIDZHANOV; circ. 10,000.

V Mire Knig (In the World of Books): 129272 Moscow, Sushchevsky val 64; tel. (095) 281-50-98; f. 1936; monthly; publ. by the Knizhnaya Palata (Book Chamber) Publishing House; reviews of new books, theoretical problems of literature, historical and religious; Editor A. V. LARIONOV; circ. 147,000.

Zhurnalist (Journalist): 101453 Moscow, Bumazhny proyezd 14; tel. (095) 212-20-58; f. 1920; monthly; journal of the Union of Journalists of the USSR; problems of professionalism, journalistic ethics and the life of journalists; Editor D. S. AVRAAMOV; circ. 30,000.

Religion

Bratsky Vestnik (Herald of the Brethren): 101000 Moscow, POB 520, Maly Vuzovsky per. 3; tel. (095) 297-96-26; f. 1945; 6 a year; organ of the All-Union Council of Evangelical Christian Baptists of the USSR; Chief Editor A. M. BICHKOV.

Pravoslavnaya Beseda (Orthodox Discussion): Moscow; f. 1991; publ. by the Orthodox Brotherhood.

Religiya v SSSR (Religion in the USSR): Moscow, M. Zubovsky bul. 4; f. 1987; monthly; Russian, English, Arabic, Spanish, German and Portuguese; fmrly publ. by the Informatsionnoye Agentstvo Novosti (Novosti Press Agency) Publishing House; articles on churches and religious associations in the former USSR; Editor I. A. TROYANOVSKY.

Zhurnal Moskovskoy Patriarkhii (Journal of the Moscow Patriarchate): 119435 Moscow, Pogodinskaya 20; tel. (095) 246-98-48 (Russian), (095) 245-14-41 (English); fax (095) 230-27-35; f. 1931; monthly; publ. by the Patriarchate in Russian and English; Editor Metropolitan PITIRIM (K. V. NECHAEV); circ. 40,000.

Satirical

Krokodil (Crocodile): 101455 Moscow, Bumazhny proyezd 14; tel. (095) 250-10-86; f. 1922; 3 a month; publ. by the Pravda (Truth) Publishing House; Editor A. S. PYANOV; circ. 2,200,000.

Trade, Trade Unions, Labour and Social Security

Sotsialistichesky Trud (Socialist Labour): Moscow, ul. Solyanka 3; f. 1956; monthly; Editor S. M. SEMYONOV; circ. 73,618.

Sotsialnoye Obespecheniye (Social Security): Moscow, ul. Shabolovka 14; f. 1926; monthly; journal of the Ministry of Social Protection of the Population; Editor L. S. MALANCHEV.

Sovetskaya Torgovlya (Soviet Trade): Moscow, Berezhkovskaya nab. 6; tel. (095) 240-48-37; f. 1927; monthly; fmrly organ of the USSR Ministry of Trade; Editor M. M. LYSOV; circ. 50,000.

Sovetskiye Profsoyuzy (Soviet Trade Unions): Moscow, ul. Myasnitskaya 13; f. 1917; 2 a month; fmrly publ. by the General Confederation of Trade Unions of the USSR; Editor M. P. MUDROV; circ. 452,424.

Vneshnyaya Torgovlya (Foreign Trade): 121108 Moscow, ul. Minskaya 11; tel. (095) 145-68-94; fax (095) 145-51-92; f. 1921; monthly; Russian, English, French, and German; fmrly organ of the Ministry of Foreign Economic Relations; Editor-in-Chief V. N. DUSHENKIN; circ. 25,000.

Transport and Communication

Avtomatika, Telemekhanika i Svyaz (Automation, Telemechanics and Communication): Moscow, Krasnovorotsky proyezd 3B; f. 1923; monthly; publ. by the Transport Publishing House; fmrly journal of the USSR Ministry of Railway Transport; utilization of new equipment in rail transport; Editor L. P. SLOBODYANYUK; circ. 27,780.

Grazhdanskaya Aviyatsiya (Civil Aviation): Moscow; f. 1931; monthly; journal of the Union of Civil Aviation Workers of the USSR; development of air transport; utilization of aviation in construction, agriculture and forestry; Editor A. M. TROSHIN.

Radiotekhnika (Radio Engineering): Moscow, Kuznetsky most 20; f. 1937; monthly; publ. by the Svyaz (Communication) Publishing House; journal of the A. S. Popov Scientific and Technical Society of Radio Engineering, Electronics and Electrical Communication; theoretical and technical problems of radio engineering; Editor A. L. MIKAELYAN.

Radiotekhnika i Elektronika (Radio Engineering and Electronics): Moscow, pr. Karla-Marksa 18; f. 1956; monthly; journal of the Russian Academy of Sciences; theory of radio engineering; Editor N. D. DEVYATKOV; circ. 8,098.

Vestnik Svyazi (Herald of Communication): Moscow, ul. Kazakova 8A; tel. (095) 261-05-55; f. 1917; monthly; publ. by the Svyaz (Communication) Publishing House; joint edition of the Union of Communication Workers of the USSR; mechanization and automation of production; Editor E. B. KONSTANTINOV; circ. 63,000.

For Women

Krestyanka (Peasant Woman): 101460 Moscow, Bumazhny per. 14; tel. (095) 212-20-63; f. 1922; monthly; publ. by the Pravda (Truth) Publishing House; popular; Editor G. V. SEMENOVA; circ. 20,500,000.

Moda i Mir (Fashion and the World): 103031 Moscow, Kuznetsky Most 7/9; tel. (095) 921-73-93; annually; Editor USSR Fashion Centre; circ. 250,000.

Modeli Sezona (Models of the Season): Moscow, Kuznetsky Most 7/9; tel. (095) 921-73-93; f. 1945; 4 a year; Editor USSR Fashion Centre; circ. 600,000.

Rabotnitsa (Working Woman): 101460 Moscow, Bumazhny per. 14; f. 1914; monthly; publ. by the Pravda (Truth) Publishing House; popular; Editor Z. P. KRYLOVA; circ. 20,500,000.

Sovetskaya Zhenshchina (Soviet Woman): 103764 Moscow, Kuznetsky Most 22; tel. (095) 221-04-81; f. 1945; monthly; Russian, Chinese, English, French, German, Hindi, Hungarian, Japanese, Korean, Bengali, Arabic, Spanish, Portuguese, Finnish and Vietnamese; fmrly publ. by the Soviet Women's Committee and the General Confederation of Trade Unions; popular; illustrated; Editor-in-Chief V. I. FEDOTOVA.

Zhurnal Mod (Fashion Journal): 103031 Moscow, Kuznetsky Most 7/9; tel. (095) 921-73-93; f. 1945; 4 a year; Editor USSR Fashion Centre; circ. 1,000,000.

Youth

Molodaya Gvardiya (Young Guard): 125015 Moscow, Novodmitrovskaya ul. 5A; tel. (095) 285-88-58; f. 1922; monthly; publ. by the Molodaya Gvardiya (Young Guard) Publishing House; fiction, criticism, popular science; Editor A. IVANOV; circ. 640,000.

Molodoy Kommunist (Young Communist): 125015 Moscow, Novodmitrovskaya ul. 5A; tel. (095) 285-88-05; f. 1918; monthly; publ. by the Molodaya Gvardiya (Young Guard) Publishing House; fmrly journal of the Cen. Cttee of the Leninist Young Communist League; political indoctrination of the young; Editor Z. G. APRESYAN; circ. 630,000.

Rovesnik (Contemporary): 125015 Moscow, Novodmitrovskaya ul. 5A; tel. (095) 285-89-20; f. 1962; publ. by the Molodaya Gvardiya (Young Guard) Publishing House; fmrly journal of the Cen. Cttee of the Leninist Young Communist League and the Publishing-Printing Unit of Molodaya Gvardiya; popular illustrated monthly of politics, fiction, verses, songs, etc.; Editor A. A. NODIYA; circ. 2,050,000.

Selskaya Molodezh (Rural Youth): Moscow, Novodmitrovskaya ul. 5A; f. 1925; monthly; publ. by the Molodaya Gvardiya (Young Guard) Publishing House; fmrly journal of the Cen. Cttee of the Leninist Young Communist League; popular illustrated, fiction, verses, problems of rural youth; Editor O. POPTSOV; circ. 1,450,000.

Smena (Rising Generation): 101457 Moscow, Bumazhny proyezd 14; tel. (095) 212-15-07; f. 1924; monthly; publ. by the Pravda (Truth) Publishing House; popular illustrated, short stories, essays and problems of youth; Editor-in-Chief M. G. KIZILOV; circ. 1,900,000.

Vozhaty (Pioneer Leader): Moscow, Novoslobodskaya ul. 5A; tel. (095) 285-39-29; f. 1924; monthly; publ. by the Molodaya Gvardiya (Young Guard) Publishing House; fmrly organ of the Cen. Cttee of the Leninist Young Communist League and the Central Council of the V. I. Lenin Pioneer Organization; activities of pioneer units; Editor S. V. TUPICHENKOV; circ. 215,000.

Yunost (Youth): Moscow, ul. Tverskaya 32/1; f. 1955; monthly; publ. by the Pravda (Truth) Publishing House; journal of the Union of Writers of the USSR; novels, short stories, essays and poems by beginners; Editor A. DEMENTEV; circ. 3,300,000.

NEWS AGENCIES

Informatsionnoye Agentstvo Novosti (IAN) (Novosti Press Agency): Moscow, Zubovsky bul. 4; tel. (095) 201-24-24; telex 411321; fax (095) 201-21-19; f. 1961; collaborates by arrangement with foreign press and publishing organizations in 110 countries of the world; Chair. ALBERT I. VLASOV.

Russian Information Agency: subsidiary information agency of IAN.

Interfax: Moscow; tel. (095) 250-92-57; independent news agency.

Postfactum: Moscow; f. 1990; independent news agency.

Telegrafnoye Agentstvo Sovetskovo Soyuza—TASS (Telegraphic Agency of the Soviet Union): Moscow, Tverskoy bul. 10; tel. (095) 290-32-14; telex 411186; f. 1925; state information agency; Dir-Gen. VITALY IGNATENKO.

Foreign Bureaux

Agence France-Presse (AFP): Moscow, Sadovaya-Samotechnaya ul. 12–24, kv. 67–68; tel. (095) 200-12-44; telex 413321; fax (095) 200-19-46; Dir BERNARD ESTRADE.

Agencia EFE (Spain): 103051 Moscow, Sadovaya-Samotechnaya ul. 12–24, kv. 23; tel. (095) 200-15-32; telex 413114; fax (095) 200-02-19; Bureau Chief SILVIA ODORIZ GONZÁLEZ.

Agenzia Nazionale Stampa Associata (ANSA) (Italy): Moscow, Kutuzovsky pr. 9, kv. 12–14; tel. (095) 243-73-93; telex 413451; fax (095) 243-06-37; Bureau Chief ALESSANDRO SERPIERI.

Anatolian News Agency (Turkey): Moscow, Rublevskoe Chausée 26, kor. 1, kv. 279; tel. (095) 415-29-34; telex 413641; Correspondent MUSTAFA KEMAL ERICH.

Associated Press (AP) (USA): Moscow, Kutuzovsky pr. 7/4, kor. 5, kv. 33; tel. (095) 243-51-53; telex 413422; fax (095) 230-2845; Bureau Chief BRYAN BRUMLEY.

Bulgarska Telegrafna Agentsia (BTA): Moscow, Kutuzovsky pr. 9, kor. 2, kv. 64–65; tel. (095) 243-65-80; telex 414494; Correspondent NACHO HALACHEV.

Československá tisková kancelář (ČSTK) (Czechoslovakia): 121069 Moscow, Novinsky bul. 28, kv. 4; tel. (095) 203-04-24; telex 414463; Correspondent VACLAV FRANK.

Dan News Agency (Argentina): Moscow, pl. Vosstaniya 1, kv. 371; tel. (095) 255-47-21; telex 413361; Correspondent ILDA RANDI.

Deutsche Presse-Agentur (DPA) (Germany): Moscow, Kutuzovsky pr. 7/4, kv. 210; tel. (095) 243-97-90; telex 413122; Correspondent Dr FRANZ SMETS.

Excelsior (Mexico): 123056 Moscow, Bolshoy Gruzinsky per. 3, kv. 266; tel. (095) 250-41-65; telex 413013; Correspondent MIGUEL ANGEL BARBERENA.

Interpress (Poland): 121248 Moscow, Kutuzovsky prospekt 7/4, Kor. 6, kv. 63; tel. (095) 243-75-23; telex 414376; Bureau Chief TOMAS PIVOVARUN.

Iraqi News Agency: Moscow, Simferopolsky bul. 7, kv. 119–120; tel. (095) 316-94-92; telex 413484; Correspondent AHMED SAKRAN KDEP.

Jiji Press (Japan): Moscow, Sadovaya-Samotechnaya ul. 12/24, kv. 21; tel. (095) 200-10-17; telex 413137; fax (095) 200-02-31; Bureau Chief KENRO NAGOSHI.

Korea Central News Agency (Democratic People's Republic of Korea): Moscow, ul. Mosfilmovskaya 72; tel. (095) 143-90-71; Bureau Chief CHAN KON SOB.

Kuwait News Agency (KUNA): Moscow, Korovy val 7, kv. 52; tel. (095) 237-49-32; telex 413463; fax (095) 230-25-10; Correspondent ADIB AL-SAYYED.

Kyodo News Service (Japan): 121248 Moscow, Kutuzovsky pr. 14, kv. 13; tel. (095) 243-62-70; telex 413382; fax (095) 243-52-67; Bureau Chief KAZUHIRO EZAWA.

Magyar Távirati Iroda (MTI) (Hungary): Moscow, Bolshaya Spasskaya ul. 12, kv. 46; tel. (095) 280-04-21; telex 414419; fax (095) 280-04-21; Bureau Chief SÁNDOR DOROGI.

Middle East News Agency (MENA) (Egypt): Moscow, Sokolnichesky val 24, kor. 2, kv. 176; tel. (095) 264-82-76; fax (095) 288-95-27; Correspondent Dr MAMDOUH MUSTAFA.

Mongol Tsahilgaan Medeeniy Agentlag (Montsame) (Mongolia): Moscow, ul. Gilyarovskovo 8, kv. 81–82; tel. (095) 284-48-14; Bureau Chief CH. TUMENDELGER.

News Agency of Nigeria (NAN) (Nigeria): Moscow, Leninsky pr. 148, kv. 231; tel (095) 434-73-07; telex 413914; Correspondent VICTOR A. UDOM.

News Agencies of Sweden, Norway, Denmark and Finland: Moscow, Kutuzovsky pr. 7/4, 196; tel. (095) 243-06-74; telex 413469; Correspondents THOMAS HAMBURG, BERIT HAMBURG.

Novinska Agencija Tanjug (Yugoslavia): Moscow, pr. Mira 74, kv. 125; tel. (095) 971-19-21; Bureau Chief MIHAILO SARANOVIĆ.

Polska Agencja Prasowa (PAP) (Poland): Moscow, Leninsky pr. 45, kv. 411; tel. (095) 135-78-75; telex 414367; Bureau Chief JERZY MALCZYK.

Prensa Latina (Cuba): 103031 Moscow, ul. Petrovka 15, kv. 22; tel. (095) 208-10-51; telex 414476; fax (095) 921-76-98; Chief Correspondent MIGUEL LOZANO.

Press Trust of India: 129041 Moscow, Bolshaya Pereyaslavskaya ul. 7, kv. 133–134; tel. (095) 280-27-49; telex 413319; Correspondent V. S. KARNIC.

Reuters (United Kingdom): Moscow, Sadovo-Samotechnaya ul. 12/24, kv. 55, 58–60; tel. (095) 200-39-48; telex 413342; Bureau Chief OLIVER WATES.

Rompres (Romania): Moscow, Kutuzovsky pr. 14, kv. 21; tel. (095) 243-67-96; Bureau Chief NICOLAE CRETU.

Syrian Arab News Agency (SANA): Moscow, Kutuzovsky pr. 7/4, kv. 184–185; tel. (095) 243-13-00; Dir SULEIMAN ABU DIAB.

United Press International (UPI) (USA): Moscow, Kutuzovsky pr. 7/4, kv. 67; tel. (095) 243-68-29; telex 413424; Bureau Chief GERALD NADLER.

Viet-Nam News Agency (VNA): Moscow, Leninsky pr. 45, kv. 326–327; tel. (095) 137-38-67; telex 414490; Correspondent PHAM QUE LAM.

Xinhua (New China) News Agency (People's Republic of China): Moscow, ul. Druzhby 6, kor. 4, kv. 118; tel. (095) 143-15-64; telex 413983; fax (095) 938-20-07; Chief Correspondent TANG XIUZHE.

Publishers

Following the failure of the coup attempt in the USSR, all publishing houses affiliated to the Communist Party of the Soviet Union (CPSU) were transferred to the jurisdiction of the Russian Federation Government and were to be privatized by 1993, until which time they were to receive financial support from the Ministry of the Press and Mass Media.

Agropromizdat (Agricultural Industry Publishing House): 107807 Moscow, Sadovaya-Spasskaya ul. 18; tel. (095) 207-29-92; f. 1985; all aspects of agricultural production; Dir (vacant).

Avrora (Aurora): 191065 St Petersburg, Nevsky pr. 7/9; tel. (095) 312-37-53; telex 121562; fax (095) 312-54-70; f. 1969; fine arts; published in foreign languages; Pres. BORIS PIDEMSKY; Dir BORIS KHOLMYANSKY.

Detskaya Entsiklopediya: 107042 Moscow, Bakuninskaya ul. 55; tel. (095) 269-52-76; f. 1933; science fiction, literature, poetry, biographical and historical novels.

Detskaya Literatura (Children's Literature): Moscow, Maly Cherkassky per. 1; tel. (095) 928-08-03; f. 1933; State Publishing House of Children's Literature (other than school books); Dir T. M. SHATUNOVA.

Ekonomika (Economy): 121864 Moscow, Berezhkovskaya nab. 6; tel. (095) 240-48-77; fax (095) 240-48-69; f. 1963; various aspects of economics and economic planning; Dir I. D. TROTSENKO.

Energoatomizdat: 113114 Moscow, Shluzovaya nab. 10; tel. (095) 925-99-93; f. 1981; different kinds of energy, nuclear science and technology; Dir A. P. ALESHKIN.

Epokha (Epoch): Moscow, Miusskaya pl. 7, A-47; tel. (095) 251-45-94; fax (095) 200-22-54; f. 1918; fmrly *Politizdat* (Political Publishing House); books on politics, human rights, philosophy, history, economics, religion, fiction, children's literature; Dir A. P. POLYAKOV.

Finansy i Statistika (Finances and Statistics): 101000 Moscow, ul. Chernishevskovo 7; tel. (095) 925-47-08; f. 1924; banking, taxation, accountancy, etc.; Dir A. N. ZVONOVA.

Fizkultura i Sport (Physical Culture and Sport): 101421 Moscow, Kalyayevskaya ul. 27; tel. (095) 258-26-90; fax (095) 200-12-17; f. 1923; books and periodicals relating to all forms of sport, chess and draughts, etc.; Dir V. A. ZHILTSOV; Editor-in-Chief V. I. VINOKUROV.

Iskusstvo (Art): 103009 Moscow, Sobinovsky per. 3; tel. (095) 203-58-72; f. 1938; fine arts, architecture, cinema, photography, television and radio, theatre; Dir O. A. MAKAROV.

Izdatelstvo Novosti (Novosti Publishers): 107082 Moscow, Bolshaya Pochtovaya ul. 7; tel. (095) 265-63-35; telex 411323; fax (095) 230-21-19; f. 1964; fmrly *Izdatelstvo Informatsionnoye Agentstvo Novosti* (Novosti Press Agency Publishing House); politics, economics and history; guidebooks, reference materials, children's literature; pamphlets on current affairs, in English, French, German and Spanish; Man. Dir ALEKSEY V. PUSHKOV.

Izobrazitelnoye Iskusstvo (Fine Art): Moscow, Sushchevsky val 64; tel. (095) 281-65-48; reproductions of pictures, pictorial art, books on art, albums, postcards; Dir V. S. KUZYAKOV.

Izvestiya (News): 103798 Moscow, Pushkinskaya pl. 5; tel. (095) 209-91-00; publishes the newspaper *Izvestiya* (News) with weekly supplement *Nedelya* (Week), and other publications and journals; Dir Y. I. BALANENKO.

Khimiya (Chemistry): Moscow B-76, ul. Strominka 21, kor. 2; tel. (095) 268-29-76; f. 1963; chemistry and the chemical industry; Dir BORIS S. KRASNOPEVTSEV.

Khudozhestvennaya Literatura (Fiction): Moscow, Novo-Basmannaya ul. 19; tel. (095) 261-88-65; telex 412162; fax (095) 261-83-00; fiction and works of literary criticism, history of literature, etc.; Dir G. A. ANDJAPARIDZE.

Kniga (Book): 125047 Moscow, ul. 1-Tverskaya-Yamskaya 50; tel. (095) 251-60-03; telex 411871; fax (095) 250-04-89; books on publishing, printing and bookselling; facsimiles and reprints of literary classics; fiction and biographies and criticism of popular writers and their works; historical works, guidebooks; Dir VIKTOR N. ADAMOV.

Legprombytizdat (Light Industry and Consumer Services Literature): 113035 Moscow, 1 Kadashevsky per. 12; tel. (095) 233-09-47; f. 1932; scientific and technical publishing house on light industry (clothing, footwear, sewing, etc.; welfare services, domestic science); Dir T. G. GROMOVA.

Lesnaya Promyshlennost (Forest Industry): 101000 Moscow, ul. Myasnitskaya 40A; tel. (095) 228-78-60; publications about forestry, wood and paper products, game management, nature conservation; Dir P. P. TIZENGAUZEN.

Malysh (Little One): 121352 Moscow, Davydkovskaya ul. 5; tel. (095) 443-06-54; fax (095) 443-06-55; f. 1958; books, booklets and posters for children aged between 3–10 years; Dir V. M. MAYBORODA.

Mashinostroyeniye (Machine Building): 107076 Moscow, Stromynsky per. 4; tel. (095) 268-38-58; fax (095) 269-48-97; f. 1931; books and journals on mechanical engineering, aerospace technology; Dir MAXIM A. KOVALEVSKY.

Meditsina (Medicine): Moscow K-142, Petroverigsky per. 6/8; tel. (095) 924-87-85; telex 412282; fax (095) 928-60-03; f. 1918; medical and health literature; Dir E. A. LEPALSKY.

Metallurgiya (Metallurgy): 119034 Moscow, 2 Obydensky per. 14; tel. (095) 202-55-32; f. 1939; metallurgical literature; Dir I. I. OSADCHY.

Mezhdunarodnye Otnosheniya (International Relations): 107078 Moscow, Sadovaya-Spasskaya ul. 20; tel. (095) 207-67-93; fax (095) 200-22-04; international questions, economics and politics of foreign countries, foreign trade, international law, foreign language textbooks and dictionaries, translations and publications for UN and other international organizations; Dir B. P. LIKHACHEV.

Mir (Peace): 129820 Moscow, Pervy Rizhsky per. 2; tel. (095) 286-17-83; telex 411466; fax (095) 288-95-22; f. 1946; Russian translations of foreign scientific, technical and science fiction books; translations of Soviet books on science and technology into foreign languages; Dir G. B. KURGANOV.

Molodaya Gvardiya (Young Guard): 103030 Moscow, Sushchevskaya ul. 21; tel. (095) 972-05-46; telex 411261; fax (095) 972-05-82; f. 1922; fmrly publishing and printing combine of the Leninist Young Communist League; joint-stock co; books and magazines, newspaper for children and for adolescents; Gen. Dir V. F. YURKIN.

Moscow University Press: 103009 Moscow, ul. Gertsena 5/7; tel. (095) 229-50-91; telex 411483; f. 1756; more than 200 titles of scientific, educational and reference literature annually, 19 scientific journals; Dir N. S. TIMOFEYEV.

Moskovsky Rabochy (Moscow Worker): 101854 Moscow, Chistoprudny bul. 8; tel. (095) 921-07-35; f. 1922; publishing house of the Moscow city and regional soviets; all types of work, including fiction; Dir D. V. YEVDOKIMOV.

Muzyka (Music): 103031 Moscow, Neglinnaya ul. 14; tel. (095) 923-04-97; fax (095) 200-52-48; f. 1861; sheet music, music scores and related literature; Dir LEONID S. SIDELNIKOV.

Mysl (Idea): Moscow, Leninsky pr. 15; tel. (095) 234-07-22; f. 1964; science, popular science, economics, philosophy, demography, history, geography; Dir V. M. VODOLAGIN.

Nauka (Science): 117864 Moscow, Profsoyuznaya ul. 90; tel. (095) 336-02-66; telex 411612; fax (095) 420-22-20; f. 1964; publishing house of the Academy of Sciences; general and social science, mathematics, physics, chemistry, biology, earth sciences, oriental studies, books in foreign languages, university textbooks, scientific journals, translation, typesetting and printing services; Dir S. A. CHIBIRYAYEV.

Nedra (Natural Resources): 125047 Moscow, Tverskaya zastava 3; tel. (095) 250-52-55; fax (095) 250-48-56; f. 1963; geology, natural resources, mining and coal industry, petroleum and gas industry; Dir YU. B. KUPRIYANOV.

Pedagogika (Pedagogics): 100034 Moscow, Smolensky 4; tel. (095) 246-59-69; f. 1969; scientific and popular books on pedagogics, didactics, psychology, developmental physiology; young people's encyclopaedia, dictionaries and magazines; 18 periodicals; Dir V. S. KHELEMENDIK.

Planeta (Planet): Moscow, ul. Petrovka 8/11; tel. (095) 923-04-70; telex 411733; fax (095) 200-52-46; f. 1969; postcards, calendars, guidebooks, brochures, illustrated books; co-editions with foreign partners; Dir V. G. SEREDIN.

Pravda (Truth): Moscow, ul. Pravdy 24; tel. (095) 257-53-11; publishes booklets, books and many newspapers and periodicals; Dir V. P. LEONTEV.

Profizdat (Trade Union Literature): 101000 Moscow, ul. Myasnitskaya 13; tel. (095) 924-57-40; f. 1930; publishing house of the CIS Labour Union Federation; economic, legal and other matters; Dir ALEXANDER GAVRILOV.

Progress (Progress): 119847 Moscow, Zubovsky bul. 17; tel. (095) 246-90-32; telex 411800; f. 1931; translations of Russian and other former USSR language books into foreign languages and of foreign language books into languages of the former USSR; political and scientific; Dir A. K. AVELICHEV.

Prosveshcheniye (Education): 129846 Moscow, proyezd Marinoy Roshchi 41/3D; tel. (095) 289-14-05; telex 111999; fax (095) 200-42-66; f. 1969; textbooks; Dir D. D. ZUEV; Editor-in-Chief A. P. SUDAKOV.

Radio i Svyaz (Radio and Communication): 101000 Moscow, ul. Myasnitskaya 40; tel. 258-53-51; telex 411665; f. 1981; radio engineering, electronics, communications, computer science; Dir YE. N. SALNIKOV; Editor-in-Chief I. K. KALUGIN

Raduga (Rainbow): 121019 Moscow, Sivtsev Vrazhek 43; tel. (095) 241-68-15; telex 411826; fax (095) 230-24-03; f. 1982; translations of Russian fiction into foreign languages and of foreign authors into Russian; Dir NINA S. LITVINETS.

Russky Yazyk (Russian Language): 103009 Moscow, Pushkinskaya ul. 23; tel. (095) 229-10-79; f. 1974; textbooks, reference, dictionaries; Dir V. I. NAZAROV.

Sovetskaya Entsiklopediya (Soviet Encyclopaedia): 109817 Moscow, Pokrovsky bul. 8; tel. (095) 297-74-83; f. 1925; universal and special encyclopaedias; Dir V. G. PANOV.

Sovetskaya Rossiya (Soviet Russia): Moscow, proyezd Sapunova 13/15; Dir YE. A. PETROV.

Sovetsky Khudozhnik (Soviet Artist): 125319 Moscow, ul. Chernyakhovskovo 4; tel. (095) 151-25-02; f. 1969; art reproduction, art history and criticism; Dir V. V. GORYAINOV.

Sovetsky Kompozitor (Soviet Composer): 103006 Moscow, Sadovaya-Triumfalnaya ul. 12-14; tel. (095) 209-23-84; f. 1957; established by the Union of Composers of the USSR; music and music criticism; Dir Y. Y. BELAYEV.

Sovetsky Pisatel (Soviet Writer): 121069 Moscow, ul. Vorovskovo 11; tel. (095) 202-50-51; f. 1935; fiction and literary criticism, history, biography; established by the Union of Writers of the USSR; Dir A.N. ZHUKOV.

Stroyizdat (Construction Literature): 101442 Moscow, Kalyayevskaya ul. 23A; tel. (095) 251-69-67; f. 1932; building, architecture, environmental protection, fire protection and building materials; Dir V. A. KASATKIN.

Sudostroyeniye (Shipbuilding): 191065 St Petersburg, ul. Gogolya 8; tel. (095) 312-44-79; f. 1940; shipbuilding, navigation, underwater exploration; Dir A. A. ANDREYEV.

Transport (Transport): 107174 Moscow, Basmanny tupik 6A; tel. (095) 262-67-73; f. 1923; publishes works on all forms of transport; Dir V. P. TITOV.

Vneshtorgizdat (The Foreign Trade Economic Printing and Publishing Association): 125047 Moscow, ul. Fadeyev 1; tel. (095) 250-51-62; telex 411238; fax (095) 253-97-94; f. 1925; publishes foreign technical material translated into Russian, and information on export goods, import and export firms, joint ventures; in several foreign languages; Dir Gen. V. I. PROKOPOV.

Voyenizdat (Military Literature): Moscow K-160, Voyennoye Izdatelstvo; tel. (095) 495-01-54; military theory and history; all books (including fiction) intended for Army use; Dir B. V. PENDYUR.

Vysshaya Shkola (Higher School): Moscow, Neglinnaya ul. 29/14; tel. (095) 200-14-95; f. 1939; textbooks for higher-education institutions; Dir M. I. KISELEV.

Yuridicheskaya Literatura (Law Literature): 121069 Moscow, ul. Kachalova 14; tel. (095) 202-83-84; f. 1917; law subjects; Dir E. I. MACHULSKY.

Znaniye (Knowledge): 101835 Moscow, proyezd Serova 4; tel. (095) 928-15-31; f. 1951; popular books and brochures on politics and science; USSR Society Znaniye (Knowledge); Dir V. K. BELYAKOV.

Radio and Television

Ostankino—All-Russian State Television and Radio Broadcasting Company: Moscow; f. 1991; Dir Gen. ANATOLY LYSENKO; Chair. OLEG POPTSOV.

Finance

BANKING

State Bank of the Russian Federation: Moscow, 4 Zhitnaya ul.; tel. (095) 237-30-65; Chair. GEORGY MATYUKHIN; Dep. Chair. VLADIMIR P. RASSKAZOV.

Rosvneshtorgbank (Bank for Foreign Trade of the Russian Federation): 103031 Moscow, Kuznetsky most 16; tel. (095) 925-52-31; telex 414726; fax (095) 973-20-96; Chair. VALERY M. TELEGUIN.

Commercial and Co-operative Banks

Commercial Bank Industriaservis: Moscow, Z. & A. Kosmodemyanskikh 35; tel. (095) 459-32-51.

Commercial Credobank: 113035 Moscow, Osipenko 15, kor. 2, podyezd 4; tel. (095) 220-34-35.

Commercial Conversion Bank (Conversbank): 109017 Moscow, Bolshaya Ordynka 24/26; tel. (095) 239-26-20; fax (095) 233-25-40; telex 411001; specializes in financing conversion programmes for the mining and defence industry; Pres. NIKOLAY G. PISEMSKY.

Commercial Innovation Bank (Stroisedzapbank): Moscow, ul. Stroiteley 8, kor. 8; tel. (095) 930-71-55.

Co-operative Bank Stolichny (Stocoopbank): 113005 Moscow, Pyatnitskaya ul. 72; tel. (095) 928-76-83; provides finance for small manufacturing companies; Dir-Gen. ANATOLY I. SHABALOV.

International Moscow Bank: 103009 Moscow, ul. Pushkinskaya 5/6; tel. (095) 292-96-32; telex 412284; fax (095) 975-22-14; f. 1989 and opened for operations 1990; joint venture between Banca Commerciale Italiana (12%), Bayerische Vereinsbank (12%), Creditanstalt-Bankverein (12%), Credit Lyonnais (12%), Kansallis-Osake-Pankii (12%) and three former credit banks of the USSR banking system, Vneshekonombank (20%), Promstroibank (10%) and Sberbank (10%); specializing in the financing of joint ventures, investments and projects of domestic and foreign customers and international trade deals; cap. 275m. roubles (80% foreign currency and 20% roubles); Chair. Y. MOSKOVSKY.

St Petersburg Innovation Bank: 191194 St Petersburg, ul. Chaykovskovo 24; tel. (812) 279-03-33.

St Petersburg Industrial and Construction Bank: 191011 St Petersburg, Nevsky pr. 38; tel. (812) 110-46-38; fax (812) 310-61-73; telex 121345; Chair. of Bd of Founders GEORGY HIZHA.

Stroynovatsia Commercial Bank: 103655 Moscow, ul. Petrovka 14; tel. (095) 200-45-14; telex 411191; full range of commercial banking services including credits, factoring and leasing; Chair. of Bd ALEKSANDR V. KOVYZHENKO.

Zolotobank: 103211 Moscow, ul. Novy Arbat 19; tel. (095) 291-43-61.

INSURANCE

Ingosstrakh Insurance Co. Ltd: 113805 Moscow, Pyatnitskaya ul. 12; tel. (095) 231-16-77; telex 411144; fax (095) 230-25-18; f. 1947; undertakes all kinds of insurance and reinsurance; Chair. MIKHAIL A. SAFRONOV.

COMMODITY EXCHANGES

Baikal Commodity Exchange (BCE): 670000 Ulan-Ude, 23 ul. Sovetskaya, kom. 37; tel. (30122) 2-26-81; fax (30122) 2-26-81; f. 1991; Chair. ANDREY FIRSOV.

Commodity and Raw Materials Exchange 'Konversia': 140056 Moscow, 6 ul. Sovetskaya; tel. (095) 551-01-88; fax (095) 175-24-94; f. 1991; Gen. Dir VADIM IVANOV.

Khabarovsk Commodity Exchange (KHCE): 680037 Khabarovsk, 66 Karl Marx Street; tel. (81422) 33-65-60; fax (81422) 33-65-60; f. 1991; Pres. GEORGE GAPONENKO.

Komi Commodity Exchange (KOCE): 167610 Syktyvkar, Komi SSR, 16 October Prospekt; tel. (82122) 2-32-86; fax (82122) 3-84-43; f. 1991; Pres. MIKHAIL GLUZMAN.

Kuzbass Commodity and Raw Materials Exchange (KECME): 650043 Kemerovo, 7 ul. Yermaka; tel. 26-85-02; f. 1991; Gen. Man. FEDOR MYASIPOV.

Kuznetsk Commodity and Raw Materials Exchange (KCME): 650079 Novokuznetsk, 2 ul. Nevskovo; tel. (83843) 42-15-29; fax (83843) 42-22-75; f. 1991; Gen. Man. YURY POLYAKOV.

Moscow Commodity Exchange (MCE): 129223 Moscow, pr. Mira, VDNKh USSR, Pavilion 4; tel. (095) 188-95-38; fax (095) 188-95-83; f. 1990; Pres. GENNADY POLESHUK.

Moscow Exchange of Building Materials (ALISA): 117334 Moscow, 45 Leninsky pr.; tel. (095) 137-00-06; fax (095) 137-67-23; f. 1990; Chair. of Exchange Cttee GERMAN STERLIGOV.

Petrozavodsk Commodity Exchange (PCE): 185028 Petrozavodsk, 31 Krasnaya ul.; tel. 7-80-57; fax 7-80-57; f. 1991; Gen. Man. VALERY SAKHAROV.

Russian Commodity and Raw Materials Exchange (RCME): 103070 Moscow, ul. Myasnitskaya 26; tel. (095) 262-80-80; fax (095) 262-57-57; f. 1990; Gen. Man. KONSTANTIN BOROVOY.

Russian Commodity Exchange of the Agro-Industrial Complex (ROSAGROBIRZHA): Moscow, 11 Volokolamskoye shosse; tel. (095) 209-52-25; f. 1990; Chairman of Exchange Committee: ALEXANDR KHOLOSTOV.

St Petersburg Commodity Exchange (SCE): 198147 St Petersburg, 32 Bronnitskaya ul.; tel. (812) 217-59-04; fax (812) 292-47-57; f. 1990; Chair. of Exchange Cttee VIKTOR NIKOLAYEV.

Siberia Commodity Exchange (SCE): 630106 Novosibirsk, 25 Krasny pr.; tel. (8383-2) 22-30-95; fax (8383-2) 22-03-90; f. 1991; Chair. OLEG FILCHENKO.

Surgut Commodity and Raw Materials Exchange (SCME): 626400 Surgut, ul. Let Pobedi 30; tel. (34561) 2-05-69; tel. (Moscow) (095) 315-09-56; telex 412 547; f. 1991.

Tyumen Commodity Exchange (TCE): 625016 Tyumen, 106 Melnikaytskaya ul.; tel. (3452) 24-04-75; fax (3452) 22-34-96; f. 1991; Pres. SERGEY DENISSOV.

Udmurt Commodity Universal Exchange (UCUE): 426000 Izhevsk, tel. (3412) 69-64-87; f. 1991; Pres. YURY UTEKHIN.

Ural Commodity Exchange (UCE): 620012 Yekterinburg, 23 pr. Kosmonavtov; tel. (3432) 55-69-61; fax (3432) 51-53-64; f. 1991; Chair. of Exchange Cttee KONSTANTIN ZHUZHLOV.

Trade and Industry

CHAMBER OF COMMERCE

Chamber of Commerce and Industry of the Russian Federation: 103684 Moscow, ul. Ilyinka 6; tel. (095) 923-43-23; telex 411126; fax (095) 230-24-55; f. 1991.

FOREIGN TRADE ENTERPRISES

AKP Sovkomflot: 121002 Moscow, Kaloshin per. 10/12; telex 411170; leasing, purchase and sales of vessels, international commercial operations; Pres. I. S. OSMININ.

Almazyuvelireksport: 119021 Moscow, Zubovsky bul. 25, kor. 1; tel. (095) 245-34-10; telex 411115; fax (095) 200-52-67; exports jewellery, gems, precious metals and stones; imports equipment for diamond cutting and polishing; Chair. I. V. GORBUNOV.

Atomenergoexport: 113324 Moscow, Ovchinnikovskaya nab. 18/1; tel. (095) 220-14-36; telex 411397; fax (095) 233-21-84; export and import of equipment for nuclear power generation and research; undertakes projects and services in the field of nuclear science and technology; Chair. V. V. KOZLOV.

Aviyaeksport: 121355 Moscow, ul. Ivana Franko 48; tel. (095) 417-00-55; telex 411929; fax (095) 417-03-85; export and import of aircraft, air navigational aids and other civil aviation equipment; Chair. V. S. STUDENIKIN.

Avtotraktoroeksport: 119902 Moscow, ul. Marx-Engels 8; tel. (095) 202-85-35; telex 411135; fax (095) 202-60-75; f. 1990; joint stock holding company; has three subsidiary joint stock companies, Avtoeksport, Avtoimport and Traktoroeksport; Dir-Gen. E. N. LYUBINSKY.

Avtoeksport: renders services on publicity and promotion of sales, engineering, marketing and after-sale servicing of motor vehicles and equipment; Dir-Gen. I. A. AKSENOV.

Avtoimport: imports motor vehicles and equipment and sets up and develops commodity circulation networks, and organizes after-sale service; Dir-Gen. N. V. CHUMAKOV.

Traktoroeksport: offers same services as Avtoeksport with regard to tractors and agricultural machinery and equipment; Dir-Gen. V. A. TSUKANOV.

Dalintorg: 692900 Nakhodka (Primorsky Kray), Nakhodkinsky pr. 16A; tel. 4-48-77; telex 213814; Eastern Siberian and Far Eastern Trade with Japan, Australia, China and North and South Korea; Dir E. A. BILIM.

Eksportkhleb: 121200 Moscow, Smolenskaya-Sennaya pl. 32/34; tel. (095) 244-47-01; telex 411145; fax (095) 253-90-69; f. 1923; exports and imports wheat, rye, barley, oats, maize, rice, pulses, flour, oil seeds and other grain and fodder products; Chair. O. A. KLIMOV.

Eksportles: 121803 Moscow, Trubnikovsky per. 19; tel. (095) 291-61-16; telex 411229; fax (095) 200-12-19; f. 1926; exports and imports sawn and round timber, wooden articles, cellulose, paper and cardboard; imports machines and equipment for timber enterprises; sets up joint-ventures, carries import and export operations under compensation agreements; Dir Gen. V. A. RADZISHEVSKY.

Elektronorgtekhnika: 121099 Moscow, Novinsky bul. 11A; tel. (095) 205-00-33; telex 411385; fax (095) 205-3901; imports computer hardware, software and associated equipment; exports computer software, advertising services; Gen. Dir J. V. TRIFONOV.

Energomasheksport: 129010 Moscow, Bezbozhny per. 25A; tel. (095) 288-84-56; telex 411965; fax (095) 288-79-90; f. 1966; exports metallurgical and mining equipment, equipment for thermal and hydroelectric power stations and industrial utilities, diesel engines, generators, railway equipment; Chair. MIKHAIL V. NOSANOV.

Gammachim: 121200 Moscow, Smolenskaya-Sennaya pl. 32/34; tel. (095) 244-18-14; telex 411297; fax (095) 244-21-81; f. 1990 as a foreign trade stock corporation to replace Soyuzkhimeksport; exports and imports chemical and other products; imports machinery and equipment for industry; Gen. Dir IGOR S. VOROBIEV.

Lenfintorg: 196084 St Petersburg, Moskovsky pr. 98; tel. (812) 292-56-33; telex 121518; fax (812) 298-99-18; f. 1960; export and import trade in consumer goods, timber goods and semi-finished goods of the timber industry including paper and packing materials, building and finishing materials, feeds and foodstuffs, chemicals, wines and spirits with Denmark, Finland, Norway and Sweden, and between the Baltic States and the north-west of the Russian Federation; Dir V. N. GLADKOV.

Litsenzintorg: 121108 Moscow, Minskaya ul. 11; tel. (095) 145-11-11; telex 411415; fax (095) 142-59-02; export and import of patents; Chair. V. V. IGNATOV.

Mashinoeksport: 117330 Moscow, ul. Mosfilmovskaya 35; tel. (095) 143-84-68; telex 411207; fax (095) 938-21-15; f. 1952; exports mining and construction equipment, equipment and tools for geological and geophysical prospecting; equipment for the steel industry, the non-ferrous metals industry, pipeline construction; railway carriages and trolley-buses; Chair. V. V. ZASEDATELEV.

Mashinoimport: 121200 Moscow, Smolenskaya-Sennaya pl. 32/34; tel. (095) 244-33-09; telex 411231; fax (095) 244-38-07; imports power engineering and electrical engineering equipment, extracting equipment for the petroleum and natural gas industries, industrial fittings; Chair. A. G. YUSHKIN.

Mashpriborintorg: 117909 Moscow, 2 Spasonalivkovsky per. 6; tel. (095) 238-81-31; telex 411235; fax (095) 230-21-26; exports and imports wire and wireless communication equipment, control and automation instruments, material testing equipment, complete laboratories, physical and hydro-meteorological instruments; import of geophysical equipment; Chair. G. LOZHNIKOV.

Medeksport: 113461 Moscow, ul. Kakhovka 31, kor. 2; tel. (095) 331-82-00; telex 411247; fax (095) 331-89-88; exports and imports medicines, pharmaceutical raw materials, medical equipment and instruments, serums, vaccines and medicines; Chair. I. N. FILIMONOV.

Metallurgimport: 117393 Moscow, ul. Arkhitektora Vlasova 33; tel. (095) 128-09-32; telex 411388; imports mining and ore-dressing equipment, metallurgical and foundry equipment, iron and steel works machinery and equipment, rotor excavators; Gen. Dir N. P. MAKSIMOV.

Mezhdunarodnaya Kniga: 113095 Moscow, ul. Dimitrova 39; tel. (095) 238-46-00; telex 411160; fax (095) 230-21-17; exports and imports books, periodicals, newspapers, pictures, maps, gramophone records, postage stamps, slides and film-strips; Chair. Y. B. LEONOV.

V/O Morsvyazsputnik: 103759 Moscow, ul. Rozhdestvenka 1/4; tel. (095) 258-70-45; telex 411197; fax (095) 253-99-10; communications and navigational aids; Pres. V. A. BOGDANOV.

Novoeksport: 117393 Moscow, ul. Arkhitektora Vlasova 33; tel. (095) 218-07-86; telex 411204; export and import of handicrafts, antiques, furs, textiles, sculpture, jewellry and raw materials; Dir Gen. V. K. SLOVTSOV.

Obschemasheksport: 101444 Moscow, Krasnoproletarskaya ul. 9; tel. (095) 258-86-40; telex 411836; exports tractors, medical and domestic appliances; imports accessories, equipment for developing new technologies.

Prodintorg: 121200 Moscow, Smolenskaya-Sennaya pl. 32/34; tel. (095) 244-26-29; telex 411206; fax (095) 244-26-29; exports and imports meat, fish, animal by-products, sugar, vegetable oil, grease; horses, pedigree cattle and animals for zoos; Chair. V. YE. GOLANOV.

Prommashimport: 121200 Moscow, Smolenskaya-Sennaya pl. 32/34; tel. (095) 244-43-57; telex 411261; imports equipment for the pulp and paper, woodworking and timber and electrical industries; Chair. G. F. RAKHIMBAYEV.

Promsyrioimport: 121834 Moscow, Novinsky bul. 13; tel. (095) 203-06-46; telex 411151; fax (095) 203-61-77; exports and imports pig iron and ferro alloys, steel wire and metal prodcuts; Chair. G. S. AFANASIYEV.

Radioeksport: 101959 Moscow, ul. Myasnitskaya 35; tel. (095) 923-79-49; telex 411376; export and import of computers and technical maintenance.

Raznoeksport: 107896 Moscow, ul. Verkhnaya Krasnoselskaya 15; tel. (095) 264-56-56; telex 411408; fax (095) 288-95-39; exports and imports light industrial and consumer goods; Chair. YURY KOSTROV.

Raznoimport: 113324 Moscow, Ovchinnikovskaya nab. 18/1; tel. (095) 233-22-79; telex 411118; fax (095) 200-32-18; imports and exports non-ferrous metal and alloys, rolled iron and rare-earth metals; Chair. I. A. RUSSOV.

Russian Independent Oil Co: 121200 Moscow, Smolenskaya-Sennaya pl. 32/34; tel. (095) 253-94-88; telex 411148; fax (095) 244-22-91; fmrly Soyuznefteksport; exports and imports petroleum, petroleum products; declared itself a private co 1991; Chair. VLADIMIR A. ARUTUNYAN.

Selkhozpromeksport: 113324 Moscow, Ovchinnikovskaya nab. 18/1; tel. (095) 220-16-92; telex 411933; fax (095) 921-93-64; assists in construction of hydrotechnical and irrigation facilities, storage plants and the other agricultural projects; Chair Yu. A. BORISOV.

Skotoimport: Moscow, Skatertny per. 8; tel. (095) 290-24-07; telex 411645; imports slaughtered livestock, exports racehorses and breeding stock of cattle, horses, sheep and goats.

Soveksportfilm: 103009 Moscow, Kalashny per. 14; tel. (095) 290-50-09; telex 411143; fax (095) 200-12-56; imports and exports films; joint film production; Chair. V. Y. MAYATSKY.

Sovbunker: 103030 Moscow, ul. Novoslobodskaya 14/19, kor. 7; tel. (095) 258-91-22; telex 411134; fax (095) 288-95-69; export, import and bunkering operations; Pres. Y. P. DROBININ.

Sovfrakht: 103759 Moscow, ul. Rozhdestvenka 1/4; tel. (095) 926-11-18; telex 411168; fax (095) 230-26-40; chartering and broking of tanker, cargo and other ships; trading and intermediary services; legal and consultative services; Gen. Dir V. L. SHUTOV.

Soyuzagrochimexport: 119900 Moscow, ul. Gritsevetskaya 2; tel. (095) 202-51-58; telex 411678; fax (095) 200-12-16; f. 1987; joint-stock co; exports and imports nitrogen and potassium fertilizers, phosphate fertilizers, raw materials; Dir-Gen. YURY A. ORLOV.

Soyuzgazeksport: 117071 Moscow, Leninsky pr.20; tel. (095) 244-22-84; telex 411987; exports and imports natural gas, liquefied petroleum gas, inert and other gases; Chair. Y. V. BARANOVSKY.

Soyuzkinoservice: 121069 Moscow, Skatertny per. 20; tel. (095) 290-10-00; telex 411114; fax (095) 200-12-86; establishes and coordinates commercial ties between film studios and foreign firms; Chair. A. K. SURIKOV.

Soyuzkoopvneshtorg: 103626 Moscow, Bolshoy Cherkassky per. 15; tel. (095) 924-81-71; telex 411127; exports fruit and vegetables, household appliances; imports clothing, footwear, etc.; Chair. A. N. STARYH.

Soyuzplodoimport: 121200 Moscow, Smolenskaya-Sennaya pl. 32/34; tel. (095) 244-22-58; telex 411262; fax (095) 244-36-36; f. 1961; exports and imports fruit, vegetables, foodstuffs and beverages, incl. Pepsi-Cola; Chair. E. F. SOROCHKIN.

Soyuzpromeksport: 121200 Moscow, Smolenskaya-Sennaya pl. 32/34; tel. (095) 244-19-79; telex 411268; fax (095) 244-37-93; exports coal and coal by-products, manganese, chrome and iron ore, asbestos and other mineral and semi-finished products; Chair. B. K. KOSOLAPOV.

Soyuzpushnina: 103012 Moscow, ul. Ilyinka 6; tel. (095) 923-09-23; telex 411150; exports and imports furs, bristles, animal hair, hides, skins and casings, casein products, oils, etc.; organizes fur auctions in St. Petersburg, concludes long-term agreements for deliveries of fur goods to foreign firms; Chair. V. M. IVANOV.

Soyuzregion: 117218 Moscow, ul. 2-Lesnoy per.10; tel. (095) 258-04-16; telex 411126; fax (095) 124-30-42; exports joint venture and regional products, imports raw materials and equipment.

Soyuztransit: 121200 Moscow, Smolenskaya-Sennaya pl. 32/34; tel. (095) 244-39-51; telex 411266; fax (095) 230-28-50; f. 1963; reorganized as an indepdendent organization 1980; handles transit of goods through former USSR, incl. Europe–Japan Trans-Siberian Container Service; Man. Dir S. G. MELNIK.

Soyuzvneshstroyimport: 103009 Moscow, Tverskoy bul. 6; tel. (095) 290-07-36; telex 411434; fax (095) 291-79-61; f. 1974; arranges joint construction projects with foreign firms; Chair. G. T. GRIGORYAN.

Soyuzvneshtrans: 121019 Moscow, Gogolevsky bul. 17/16; tel. (095) 203-11-79; telex 411441; fax (095) 201-28-70; handles transport and forwarding of imports and exports; Pres. V. I. ALISSEYCHIK.

Stankoimport: 117342 Moscow, ul. Obrucheva 34/63; tel. (095) 333-51-01; telex 411991; fax (095) 310-70-19; f. 1930; exports and imports machine tools and precision instruments; Dir-Gen. V. I. MARININ.

Stroydormasheksport: 121019 Moscow, Suvorovsky bul. 7; tel. (095) 291-49-31; telex 411063; fax (095) 202-90-56; f. 1988; exports and imports construction and road-building machinery; Gen. Dir Yu. A. MALYSHEV.

Stroymaterialintorg: 121059 Moscow, ul. Kievskaya 19; tel. (095) 243-71-86; telex 411887; fax (095) 243-90-86; export and import of cement, glass, asbestos and other building materials; Chair. V. V. DEVYATOV.

Sudoeksport: 123231 Moscow, Novinsky bul. 11; tel. (095) 255-18-13; telex 411116; fax (095) 200-22-50; exports ships.

Sudoimport: 103006 Moscow, Uspensky per. 10; tel. (095) 299-68-49; telex 411383; fax (095) 209-13-31; exports and imports all kinds of ships; import and export of rigs and equipment for offshore petroleum exploration and extraction; ship-repairing abroad; Chair. O. S. KROPOTOV.

Tekhmasheksport: 101850 Moscow, Mosfilmovskaya ul. 35; tel. (095) 202-48-00; telex 411068; fax (095) 291-58-08; exports machinery and equipment for the textile industries; Dir-Gen. V. F. FADEYEV.

Tekhmashimport: 121819 Moscow, Trubnikovsky per. 19; tel. (095) 290-48-53; telex 411194; fax (095) 291-58-09; f. 1959; imports and exports refrigeration equipment and machinery for chemical and textile plants; completes projects for the petroleum, petrochemical, pulp-and-paper and microbiological industries; Chair. V. I. GRIB.

Tekhnoeksport: 121200 Moscow, Ovchinnikovskaya nab. 18/1; tel. (095) 220-17-82; telex 411338; assists in petroleum production; construction of industrial plants, pharmaceutical plants, hospitals, schools; Chair. Y. V. CHUGUNOV.

Tekhnointorg: 113836 Moscow, ul. Pyatnitskaya 64; tel. (095) 231-26-22; telex 411200; export and import of mountain-rescue equipment, lasers, electronic and video equipment, and electrical household appliances; Chair. M. S. KOZIN.

Tekhnopromeksport: 113324 Moscow, Ovchinnikovskaya nab. 18/1; tel. (095) 220-15-23; telex 411158; fax (095) 233-33-73; assists construction of thermal and diesel power stations; Chair. A. S. POSTOVALOV.

Tekhnopromimport: 113324 Moscow, Ovchinnikovskaya nab. 18/1; tel. (095) 231-82-42; telex 411233; fax (095) 230-21-11; import of equipment for the light, food, electro-technical and electronics industries; polygraphic enterprises, cable- and glass-producing plants, plants for the production of building materials; Chair. G. A. KONOPLEV.

Tekhnostroieksport: 113324 Moscow, Ovchinnikovskaya nab. 18/1; tel. (095) 220-14-48; telex 411474; assists construction of plants producing building materials; Chair. D. M. SHPILEV.

Tekhsnabeksport: 109180 Moscow, Staromonetny per. 26; tel. (095) 233-48-60; telex 411328; fax (095) 230-26-38; f. 1963; export and import of isotopes, ionising radiation sources; export of heat-producing elements for various types of atomic reactors, components and parts for nuclear power stations, rare and rare-earth metals, nuclear physics equipment, consumer goods; Dir-Gen. A. A. SHISHKIN.

Tekhvneshtrans: 113324 Moscow, Ovchinnikovskaya nab. 18/1; tel. (095) 220-19-53; telex 411110; organizes transportation of foreign trade freight turnover connected with the construction of industrial projects overseas and in Russia; Chair. A. P. SOBOLEV.

Tsvetmetpromeksport: 113324 Moscow, Ovchinnikovskaya nab. 18/1; tel. (095) 220-18-61; telex 411983; assists construction of non-ferrous metallurgy projects, mines, quarries, metallurgical works; Chair. R. I. KUPREVICH.

Tyazhpromeksport: 113324 Moscow, Ovchinnikovskaya nab. 18/1; tel. (095) 220-16-10; telex 411931; assists construction and extension of integrated iron and steel mining complexes and hardware plants; Chair. Y. N. KALASHNIKOV.

Vneshposyltorg: 109147 Moscow, Marksistskaya ul. 5; tel. (095) 271-90-12; telex 411250; exports and imports foodstuffs, industrial and household consumer goods including sanitary goods and equipment; their sale abroad in small wholesale lots to diplomatic missions, foreign companies and individuals with payment in freely convertible currencies; Dir-Gen. YU. G. BULAKH.

Vnestorgreklama: 113461 Moscow, ul. Kakhovka 31, kor. 2; tel. (095) 331-83-11; telex 411265; export and import of advertising services; Dir.-Gen. Y. M. DEOMIDOV.

Vostokintorg: 121200 Moscow, Smolenskaya-Sennaya pl. 32/34; tel. (095) 205-60-55; telex 411123; fax (095) 253-92-75; exports and imports all goods except machinery, industrial equipment, petroleum products and medicines in trade with Mongolia, Afghanistan, Iran, Turkey and Yemen; Chair. A. A. ALEKPEROV.

MAJOR INDUSTRIAL ENTERPRISES

10th State Ball-Bearing Factory: 344717 Rostov-na-Donu, ul. Peskova 1; tel. (8632) 22-56-72; telex 123122; fax (8632) 22-56-71; production of bearings; Gen. Dir IGOR O. SHCHERBINA; 8,500 employees.

23rd State Bearing Factory: 160028 Vologda, Okruzhnoe shosse 13; tel. (81722) 2-23-91; fax (81722) 3-43-93; manufactures ball-bearings; Gen. Dir ALEKSANDR I. YELPERIN.

Agrovod: 125040 Moscow, Leningradsky pr. 22/2; tel. (095) 213-40-36; telex 411614; fax (095) 213-02-56; design and construction of irrigational systems, roads, dams and agricultural equipment; Pres. GEORGY G. GULYUK; 150,240 employees.

Almetyevsk Electrical Submersible Pumps Plant (Alnas): Tatarstan, 423400 Azpen, Almetyevsk 11; tel. 8-43-12; telex 224843; fax 2-73-64; produces electrical pumps; Dir-Gen. PAUL R. SHOTTER; 2,600 employees.

Altai Tractor Factory: 658212 Altay kray, Rubtsovsk, ul. Tractornaya 17; tel. 2-86-45; telex 233515; fax 3-74-72; design and production of 'Crawler' tractors; Gen. Dir ARTHUR A. DERFLER; 23,000 employees.

Altai Motorworks: 656023 Altay kray, Barnaul, pr. Kosmonavtov 8; tel. 77-01-17; telex 133145; manufactures diesel engines, fuel pumps, etc.; Gen. Dir VLADIMIR ZAKHAROV; 18,000 employees.

Altaiselmash Production Association: 658204 Altay kray, Rubtsovsk, ul. Krasnaya 100; tel. 2-26-65; telex 233129; fax 2-76-72; design and manufacture of all types of agricultural machinery and hand tools; Gen. Dir VICTOR K. TOLSTOV; 7,000 employees.

Automobile and Tractor Electrical Equipment Plant: 309530 Belgorod obl., Stary Oskol, ul. Vatutina 54; tel. (075) 22-09-65; fax (075) 241015; produces spare and assembly parts for automobiles, etc.; Plant Man. ANATOLY M. MAMONOV; 4,500 employees.

Automobile and Tractor Electrical Equipment Plant: 625630 Tyumen, Chiolkovsky 1; tel. 26-15-90; telex 235151; produces components for ignition systems, etc.; Plant Dir. VLADISLAV P. ZAGVAZDIN.

Carburettor and Fittings Factory: 192102 St Petersburg, Samoilovoy 5; tel. (812) 166-48-05; telex 321245; design, development and manufacture of carburettors for automobiles; Dir GENNADY B. ORLOV.

Chapayevsk Chemical Fertilizer Factory: 446100 Samara obl., Chapayevsk, ul. Ordzhonikidze 1; tel. 2-39-09; fax 21-40-13; produces chemical fertilizers; Factory Dir E. MORKOVKIN.

Cheboksary Tractor Works: 428033 Cheboksary, pr. Tractorostroiteley; tel. (095-8350) 23-37-48; telex 412627; fax (095-8350) 23-76-36; production of heavy-duty tractors and their maintenance and repair; Gen. Dir HANIF H. MINGAZOV; 25,000 employees.

Chelyabinsk Tractor Plant: 454007 Chelyabinsk, pr. Lenina 3; tel. 77-14-51; fax 73-07-65; telex 124886; design and manufacture of caterpillar tractors; Chief Dir NICOLAI R. LOSHENENKO.

Chemistry Research Production Association: 197198 St Petersburg, Dobvlyubov pr. 14; tel. (812) 238-55-36; fax (812) 233-89-89; telex 121345; research and development of chemical products, etc.; Gen. Dir GENNADY TERESCHENKO; 10,000 employees.

Dzerzhinsky Tractor Plant: 400061 Volgograd; tel. (844) 77-26-22; produces agricultural machinery and equipment; Dir N. M. BUDKO; 35,000 employees.

Electropribor Production Association: 428000 Cheboksary, Yakovlevsky pr. 3; tel. 22-25-73; fax 20-50-02; produces electronic measuring instruments, microprocessor controllers and analog-digital converters; Gen. Dir LEONID V. YAKOVLEV; 5,300 employees.

Fifth State Bearing Plant Productive Amalgamation: 634006 Tomsk-6, Severny Gorodok GPZ-5; tel. 75-15-01; produces all types of bearings; Gen. Dir YURY GALVAS; 6,500 employees.

First State Bearing Plant: 109088 Moscow, Sharikopodshipnikovskaya ul. 13; tel. (095) 275-08-29; design and manufacture of over 2,000 types of bearings; Gen. Dir VALERY B. NOSOV; 20,000 employees.

Gidromash: 129626 Moscow, 2-aya Mytischinskaya ul. 2; tel. (095) 287-78-20; fax (095) 287-11-81; development and manufacture of pumps and other products; Pres. VLADIMIR KARAKHANYAN; 21,000 employees.

Kabardino-Balkarian Diamond Tool Factory: 361200 Terek, Yubileinaya ul. 1; tel. 9-11-76; produces diamond-boring tools, diamond drills, etc; Factory Dir VLADIMIR SH. KHAZHUYEV; 2,880 employees.

Kamaz: 423808 Naberzhnyye Chelny, pr. Musy Dzhalilya 29; tel. (855) 42-20-16; manufactures and distributes heavy trucks; Gen. Dir NIKOLAY H. BEKH; 150,000 employees.

Kaskad: 125047 Moscow, 1-aya Brestskaya ul. 35; tel. (095) 250-38-87; fax (095) 973-20-48; telex 412310; research, development and manufacture of electronic and cybernetic systems; Dir-Gen. ANATOLY V. MYSCHLEZOV; 40,000 employees.

Kazanresinotekhnika: 420026 Tatarstan, Kazan, Tekhnicheskaya 2; tel. 37-28-84; manufactures rubber products; Dir VENIAMIN GRIGORIEV; 5,000 employees.

Krasny Proletary Machine-Tool Building Factory: 117071 Moscow, Malaya Kaluzhskaya ul. 15; tel. (095) 232-27-66; fax (095) 310-70-03; telex 411017; manufactures lathes, and loading and production-processing robots; Gen. Man. YURY I. KIRILLOV; 6,000 employees.

Kzame Production Association: 248631 Kaluga, Azarovskaya 18; tel. (0842) 2-53-09; fax (0842) 2-75-16; telex 412691; design and manufacture of a wide range of electronic motors and control units for the automobile industry; 8,500 employees.

Moskvich Production Association: 109316 Moscow, Volgogradsky pr. 42; tel. (095) 276-32-96; telex 411333; fax (095) 274-00-49; design and manufacture of automobiles, consumer goods, hand tools and machine tools; Gen. Dir VALENTIN P. KOLOMNIKOV; 25,000 employees.

Ninth State Bearings Factory: 443008 Samara, GPZ-9; tel. (846) 56-36-04; design and manufacture of roller bearings; Gen. Dir IGOR SHVIDAK.

Nizhny Novgorod Automobile Plant: 603046 Nizhny Novgorod, Leninsky pr.; tel. (831) 256-42-06; telex 412521; fax (831) 253-05-57; manufacture of cars, trucks and related parts and accessories; Dir-Gen. B. P. VIDYAYEV; 120,000 employees.

Pervouralsky Novotrubny Zavod (First Ural Tube Manufacturing Plant): Yekaterinburg, 623112 Pervouralsk, Torgovaya ul. 1; tel. (343) 7-56-56; telex 348715; fax (343) 2-44-78; production of steel piping and steel cylinders; Dir V. N. DUYEV; 25,000 employees.

Pressmash Taganrog Production Association: 347927 Taganrog, Polyakovskaya ul.; tel. (863) 4-91-23; telex 123249; manufacture of sheet stamping presses and smelting machinery; Gen. Dir ANATOLY FILIPPOV; 10,075 employees.

Second Watch Factory: 125040 Moscow, Leningradsky pr. 8; tel (095) 251-29-37; fax (095) 257-15-02; produces mechanical and electronic watches and clocks; Gen. Dir VLADIMIR M. KOROLEV; 10,000 employees.

Sixth State Bearings Plant: 620075 Yekaterinburg, Shartashskaya ul. 13; tel. (343) 55-21-48; telex 221153: manufactures roller bearings; Plant Dir VLADIMIR B. TERESHENKO.

Stalkonstruktsiya: 103001 Moscow, Sadovaya Kudrinskaya 8/12; tel. (095) 209-95-60; fax (095) 975-22-17; manufacture and erection of steel structures; Pres. VICTOR K. VOROBIOV; 50,000 employees.

Stroytechstecklo: 117036 Moscow, ul. Kedrova 15; tel. (095) 129-09-09; telex 411737; produces glassware, crystalware and patterned tiles; Gen. Dir NIKOLAY V. FEDULOV; 30,000 employees.

Ufa Electric Lamp Factory: Bashkiria, 450029 Ufa, Yubileynaya ul. 1; tel. 42-52-11; fax 42-52-30; produces electric light bulbs and lamps; Plant Man. TIMERBAY A. GASHIMOV.

Vladimir Tractor Factory: 600005 Vladimir, Traktornaya ul. 43; tel. 3-84-86; telex 412528; design and manufacture of tractors; Gen. Man. ANATOLY V. GRISHIN.

Volgokhemmash United Enterprises: 445621 Tolyatti, ul. M. Gorgovo 96; tel. (848) 23-51-21; telex 214137; manufactures crushing equipment for construction-materials and ore-mining industries; Dir-Gen. VIKTOR A. KOPIN; 12,000 employees.

ZIL: 109280 Moscow, Avtozavodskaya ul. 23; tel. (095) 275-33-28; telex 411006; fax (095) 274-00-78; manufactures trucks, engines, industrial ovens and washing machines; also automobiles, particularly luxury limousines; Dir-Gen. YEVGENY A. BRAKOV.

TRADE UNIONS

It was expected that the trade union structure of the former USSR would become increasingly decentralized, as economic policy was devolved to the new national governments.

CIS Labour Union Federation: 117119 Moscow, Leninsky pr. 42; tel. (095) 938-70-00; telex 411010; fax (095) 938-21-55; f. 1990; fmrly the General Confederation of Trade Unions of the USSR; Pres. VLADIMIR I. SHCHERBAKOV.

Federation of Independent Trade Unions of the Russian Federation: Moscow; Chair. IGOR KLOCHKOV.

Aircraft Engineering Workers' Union: Moscow, Leninsky pr. 42; Pres. G. K. ALBOV.

All-Union Federation of Timber and Related Industries Workers' Unions: 117119 Moscow, Leninsky pr. 42; tel. 938-82-02; Pres. VIKTOR P. KARNIUSHIN.

All-Union Federation of Trade Unions 'Electrounion': 117119 Moscow, Leninsky pr. 42; tel. (095) 938-86-80; telex 411010; fax (095) 938-83-14; f. 1905; electrical workers; Pres. NIKOLAI A. PUGACHEV.

Association of Free Trade Unions: Moscow; Chair. BORIS M. FEDEROV.

Association of Socialist Trade Unions: Moscow; independent union dedicated to ensuring maximum wages for its members and optimum working conditions; Chair. Co-ordinating Council A. KHRAMOV; 20,000 mems.

Automobile, Tractor and Farm Machinery Industries Workers' Union: Moscow, Leninsky pr. 42; Pres. A. P. KASHIRIN.

Automobile Transport and Highway Workers' Union: Moscow V-218, ul. Krzhizhanovskovo 20/30, kv. 5; Pres. LEV A. YAKOVLEV.

Civil Aviation Workers' Union: Moscow V-218, ul. Krzhizhanovskovo 20/30, kor. 5; Pres. A. G. GRIDIN.

Coal Mining Industry Workers' Union: Moscow, Zemlyanoy val 64, kor. 1; Pres. M. A. SREBNY.

Construction and Building Materials Industry Workers' Union: 117119 Moscow, Leninsky pr. 42; f. 1957; tel. (095) 938-76-62; Pres. G. D. ARJANOV.

Educational and Scientific Workers' Union: Moscow, Leninsky pr. 42; f. 1919; Pres. R. M. PAPILOV.

Engineering and Instrument-Making Industries Workers' Union: 117119 Moscow, Leninsky pr. 42; tel. (095) 930-85-25; fax (095) 930-80-25; Pres. ANATOLI Y. RYBAKOV.

Federation of the Agroindustrial Unions of the USSR: 117119 Moscow, Leninsky pr. 42; tel. (095) 938-75-95; f. 1919, merged with Food Workers' Union in 1986; Pres. M. B. RYZHIKOV; 37m. mems.

Federation of Chemical Industries Workers' Unions of the USSR: 117119 Moscow, Leninsky pr. 42; tel. (095) 938-83-70; Pres. V. K. BORODIN.

Federation of Communication Workers' Unions of the USSR: 117119 Moscow, Leninsky pr. 42; tel. (095) 930-84-58; fax (095) 938-21-63; f. 1905; Pres. ANATOLY NAZEYKIN.

Federation of Cultural Workers' Unions: 109004 Moscow, Zemlyanoy val 64, kor. 1; tel. (095) 297-86-12; fax (095) 925-85-17; Pres. I. A. NAUMENKO.

Federation of State Employees' Union: 117119 Moscow, Leninsky pr. 42; tel. (095) 938-80-53; telex 411010; fax (095) 938-21-55; f. 1918; Pres. I. L. GREBENSHIKOV.

Fishing Industry Workers' Union: 117119 Moscow, Leninsky pr. 42; tel. (095) 938-77-82; fax (095) 930-77-31; f. 1986; Pres. V. A. ZYRIANOV.

Geological Survey Workers' Union: Moscow V-218, Leninsky pr. 42; Pres. M. GOUBKIN.

Heavy Engineering Workers' Union: Moscow, Leninsky pr. 42; Pres. N. I. ZINOVIYEV.

Independent Trade Union of Railwaymen and Transport Construction Workers: 107217 Moscow, Sadovo-Spasskaya ul. 21; tel. (095) 262-58-73; Pres. I. A. SHINKEVICH.

Local Industries and Public Services Workers' Union Federation: 117119 Moscow, Leninsky pr. 42; tel. (095) 938-85-12; f. 1957; Pres. Y. Y. ABRAMOV.

Medical Workers' Union: Moscow, Leninsky pr. 42; Pres. L. I. NOVAK.

Metallurgical Industry Workers' Union: Moscow, Pushkinskaya ul. 5/6; Pres. I. I. KOSTYUKOV.

Moscow Federation of Trade Unions: Moscow; Chair. MIKHAIL V. SHMAKOV.

Oil and Gas Workers' Union: Moscow, Leninsky pr. 42; Pres. V. T. SEDENKO.

Radio and Electronics Industry Workers' Union: Moscow, Pervy Golutvinsky per. 3; Pres. V. N. TUZOV.

Sea and River Workers' Union: 109004 Moscow, Zemlyanoy val 64, kor. 1; tel. (095) 227-29-96; Pres. K. YU. MATSKYAVICHYUS.

Shipbuilding Workers' Union: Moscow, Leninsky pr. 42; Pres. A. G. BURIMOVICH.

State Trade and Consumer Co-operative Workers' Union: Moscow, Leninsky pr. 42; Pres. G. N. ZAMYTSKAYA.

Textile and Light Industry Workers' Union: Moscow, Leninsky pr. 42; tel. (095) 938-74-70; Pres. M. V. IKHARLOVA.

Transport

RAILWAYS

In 1989 the total length of railway track in use was 87,090 km. The railway network is of great importance, owing to the poor road system and relatively few private vehicles. The Trans-Siberian Railway provides the main route connecting European Russia with Siberia and the Far East.

ROADS

At 31 December 1989 the total length of roads was 854,000 km, of which 624,100 km were hard-surfaced. The road network is of most importance in European Russia; in Siberia and the Far East there are few roads, and they are often impassable in winter.

SHIPPING

The sea ports of the Russian Federation provide access to the Pacific Ocean, in the east, the Baltic Sea and the Atlantic Ocean, in the west, and the Black Sea, in the south. Major eastern ports are at Vladivostok, Nakhodka, Magadan and Petropavlovsk. In the west St Petersburg and Kaliningrad provide access to the Baltic Sea, and the northern port of Murmansk has access to the Atlantic Ocean, via the Barents Sea. Novorossiysk and Sochi are the principal Russian ports on the Black Sea. In May 1991 plans were announced for the construction of a major new port facility near Ust-Luga, near St Petersburg. In addition, facilties at St Petersburg, Vyborg and Kaliningrad were being upgraded, with assistance from foreign companies.

Principal Shipowning Companies

Baltic Shipping Co: 198035 St Petersburg, Mezhevoy kanal 5; tel. (812) 251-07-42; telex 121051; freight and passenger services; Pres. V. I. KHARCHENKO; 30,000 employees.

Far Eastern Shipping Company: 690019 Vladivostok, ul. 25 Oktyabrya 15; telex 213115; Pres. V. M. MISKOV.

Kamchatka Shipping Company: 683000 Petropavlovsk-Kamchatsky, ul. Radiosvyazi 65; tel. 2-22-63; telex 244112; fax 2-19-60; f. 1949; freight services; Pres. V. G. KULAGIN.

Murmansk Shipping Company: 183636 Murmansk, ul. Kominterna 15; tel. 5-54-78; telex (478) 554495; f. 1939; shipping and icebreaking services; Pres. V. V. BELETSKY.

Northern Shipping Company: 163061 Arkhangelsk, nab. Lenina 36; telex 242111; Pres. A. N. GAGARIN.

Novorossiysk Shipping Company: 353900 Novorossiysk, ul. Svobody 1; tel. 5-12-76; telex 279113; Pres. LEONID I. LOZA.

Primorsk Shipping Company: 692900 Nakhodka, ul. Pogranichnaya 6; tel. (42366) 5-53-09; telex 213812; fax (42366) 5-60-78; f. 1972; Pres. P. K. CHERNYSH.

Sakhalin Shipping Company: 694620 Sakhalin, Kholmsk, ul. Pobedy 16; telex 412613; Pres. M. A. ROMANOVSKY.

CIVIL AVIATION

In 1991 the establishment of a Russian transcontinental airline, Air Rossiya, was announced. The airline was to be a joint venture between British Airways and the Russian Government and was expected to commence services, based at Domodedovo airport in Moscow, by 1994. Assets of the former monopoly air carrier of the USSR were to be devolved to Russia and the other former Republics.

Aeroflot: 125167 Moscow, Leningradsky pr. 37; tel. (095) 155-55-98; telex 411182; fax 155-66-47; f. 1923 as Dobrolet, restyled Aeroflot in 1932; the world's largest airline and the operator of all kinds of air services in the former USSR, which, apart from scheduled flights, include agricultural, survey and ambulance services and the maintenance of airfields and navigation aids. Its extensive domestic network, which covers more than 1m. km, serves the capitals of all the former Republics of the USSR and over 3,600 other towns, while international flights, covering about 250,000 km, serve 134 destinations in 102 countries in Europe, Africa, Asia and the Americas. In 1990 Aeroflot transported 137m. passengers and 2,548,000 metric tons of freight. There are no official figures published for the size of the Aeroflot fleet; the following estimates for 1986 appeared in *Flight International*, April 1989: more than 50 An-2, 150 An-12, 350 An-24/26, 150 Il-18, up to 180 Il-62M, up to 100 Il-76, 100 Il-86, more than 400 Tu-134, 450 Tu-154, 300 Yak-40, up to 200 Yak-42, 600 Let 410 and various helicopters and aircraft for special purposes.

Tourism

Intourist: 103009 Moscow, ul. Mokhovaya 16; tel. (095) 292-22-60; telex 411211; fax (095) 203-52-67; f. 1929; branches in the former Republics of the USSR and other countries; organizes tours in most cities of the former USSR and has contracts with more than 700 foreign companies; Chair. VLADIMIR MALININ.

Intourist Holdings: 103009 Moscow, ul. Mokhovaya 16; tel. (095) 292-25-77; telex 411211; fax (095) 203-52-67; f. 1991 as a result of reorganization within Intourist; manages tourist facilties throughout the former USSR, incl. hotels, with capacity for 56,000 tourists, and catering facilties; Chair. IGOR KONOVALOV.

Culture

NATIONAL ORGANIZATIONS

Ministry of Culture: see section on The Government (Ministries).

Cultural Foundation: 121019 Moscow, 6 Gogolevsky bul.; tel. (095) 291-27-48; telex 411071; fax (095) 200-12-38; f. 1986 as Cultural Foundation of the former USSR; encourages interest in and study of cultural heritage, especially architecture, literature, music and education; Chair. DMITRY LIKHACHEV; Deputy Chair. GEORGY MYASNIKOV.

Union of Soviet Societies for Friendship and Cultural Relations with Foreign Countries: 103885 Moscow, ul. Vozdvizhenka 14; tel. (095) 290-69-32; telex 411286; fax (095) 200-12-20; f. 1958; unites 86 societies of friendship and cultural relations with other countries; Chair. V. V. TERESHKOVA; 65,000 mems;

INTERNATIONAL ORGANIZATION

National Commission of the United Nations Educational, Scientific and Cultural Organization (UNESCO): Moscow, ul. Vozdvizhenka 9; tel. (095) 290-08-53; telex 411587; fax (095) 202-10-83.

CULTURAL HERITAGE

Moscow

A. V. Shchusev State Research Architectural Museum: 121019 Moscow, ul. Novy Arbat 5; tel. (095) 291-21-09; f. 1934; over 70,000 sheets of architectural drawings; over 300,000 negatives and 400,000 photographs of architectural monuments; Dir V. I. BALDIN.

Andrei Rublev Museum of Ancient Russian Art: 107120 Moscow, ul. Pryamikova 10; tel. (095) 278-14-89; f. 1947; important collection of Russian icons; library of 22,000 vols; Dir S. V. VASHLAYEVA.

Central State Archives of the Russian Federation: 121059 Moscow, Berezhkovskaya nab. 26; tel. (095) 240-32-54; f. 1920; library of 1,281,757 vols; Dir V. V. NIKANOROVA.

Central State Theatrical Museum: 113054 Moscow, ul. Bakhrushina 31/12; tel. (095) 233-44-18; telex 412101; f. 1894; over 1m. exhibits; library of 100,000 vols; Dir T. B. BONILYA.

Folk-Art Museum: 103009 Moscow, ul. Stanislavskovo 7; tel. (095) 290-52-22; f. 1885; about 50,000 exhibits; Dir G. A. YAKOVLEVA.

Kremlin Museums: 103073 Moscow, Kremlin; tel. (095) 928-44-56; Dir I. A. RODIMTSEVA.

M. I. Glinka State Central Museum of Musical Culture: 125047 Moscow, ul. Fadeyeva 4; tel. (095) 251-31-43; f. 1943; some 700,000 items; Dir R. N. ŽDOBNOV.

Novodevichy Monastery Museum: 119435 Moscow, Novodevichy pr. 1; tel. (095) 245-29-54; Russian fine and decorative art; Dir V. G. VERZHBITSKY.

Obraztsov's Central State Puppet Theatre Museum: Moscow, Sadovo-Samotechnaya ul. 3; f. 1937; over 2,600 dolls from 50 countries; library of over 5,300 books; Dir N. KOSTROVA.

State Central Theatrical Library: 103031 Moscow, Pushkinskaya ul. 8/1; tel. (095) 292-48-92; f. 1922; over 1.7m. items; Dir T. I. SILINA.

State Historical Museum: 103012 Moscow, Krasnaya pl. 1/2; tel. (095) 921-43-11; f. 1872; 4,226,000 exhibits on Russian and Soviet history; Dir K. G. LEVIKIN.

State Literature Museum: 103051 Moscow, ul. Petrovka 28; tel. (095) 221-38-57; f. 1934; library of 250,000 vols; 6 brs; Dir N. V. SHAKHALOVA.

State Museum of Ceramics: 111402 Moscow, stantsiya Kuskovo, Yunosti ul. 2; tel. (095) 370-01-60; large collection of Russian art; Dir E. S. ERITSAN.

State Museum of Oriental Art: 121019 Moscow, Suvorovsky bul. 12A; tel. (095) 291-03-41; f. 1918; large collection of Middle and Far Eastern art; Dir V. S. MANIN.

State Pushkin Museum of Fine Arts: 121019 Moscow, Volkhonka 12; tel. (095) 203-69-74; f. 1912; some 550,000 items of ancient Eastern, Graeco-Roman, Byzantine, European and American art; library of 200,000 vols; Dir I. A. ANTONOVA.

State Tretyakov Gallery: 117049 Moscow, Krymsky val 10–14; tel. (095) 231-13-62; f. 1856; collection of 40,000 Russian icons and works of Russian painters, sculptors and graphic artists; Dir P. I. LEBEDEV.

State Russian Library: 10100 Moscow, ul. Novy Arbat 3; tel. (095) 202-40-56; telex 411167; f. 1862 as the Rumyantsev Library; reorganized in 1925; fmrly State V. I. Lenin Library; over 30m. books, periodicals and serials; Dir Dr N. S. KARTASHOV.

Tolstoy State Museum: 119034 Moscow, ul. Prechistenka 11; tel. (095) 201-58-11; f. 1911; library of 71,000 works by or about Tolstoy; over 42,000 exhibits; Dir L. M. LUBIMOVA.

St Petersburg

Central Music Library, attached to the State Academic Theatre of Opera and Ballet: St Petersburg, ul. Zodchevo Rossi 2; contains one of the largest collections in the world of Russian music; Dir S. O. BROG.

Literary Museum of the Institute of Russian Literature: 199034 St Petersburg, Pushkinsky dom, nab. Makarova 4; tel. (812) 218-05-02; 95,000 exhibits and over 120,000 items of reference material; Dir T. A. KOMAROVA.

Museum of the Academic Maly Theatre of Opera and Ballet: St Petersburg, pl. Iskusstv 1; f. 1935; collection of materials depicting the history of the theatre and its work; Dir V. LIPHART.

Peter the Great Museum of Anthropology and Ethnography: St Petersburg B-034, Universitetskaya nab. 3; tel. (812) 218-14-12; f. 1714; 900,000 items; Dir Prof. R. F. ITS.

Pushkin Museum: 191186 St Petersburg, nab. Moiki 12; tel. (812) 311-38-01; f. 1938; 45,000 exhibits; Dir M. N. PETY.

State Circus Museum: 191011 St Petersburg, ul. Fontanka 3; tel. (812) 210-44-13; telex 121285; f. 1928; some 80,000 exhibits; library of about 4,000 items; Dir NATALYA KUZNETSOVA.

State Ethnographical Museum of the Peoples of the USSR: St Petersburg, Inzhenernaya ul. 4/1; 300,000 exhibits; Dir D. A. SERGEYEV.

State Hermitage Museum: St Petersburg, Dvortsovaya nab. 34; f. 1764 as a court museum; richest collection in Russia of the art of pre-historic, ancient Eastern, Graeco-Roman and mediaeval times; Dir B. B. PIOTROVSKY.

State Russian Museum: St Petersburg, Inzhenernaya ul. 4; f. 1898; 360,000 exhibits of Russian art; Dir V. A. LENYASHIN.

State Theatrical and Musical Museum: 191011 St Petersburg, pl. Ostrovskovo 6; f. 1918; over 380,000 exhibits; library of 5,000 vols; 3 brs; Dir I. V. EVSTIGNEYEVA.

Other Regions

Arkhangelsk State Museum: 163061 Arkhangelsk, pl. Lenina 2; tel. 3-66-79; telex 02242518; f. 1859; 150,000 items; library of 25,000 vols, 8,000 journals; Dir YU. P. PROKOPEV.

North-Ossetian K. L. Khetagurov Memorial Museum: North Ossetia, Vladikavkaz, pr. Mira 12; collection of materials on Caucasian poetry and literature.

Sergiev Posad State History and Art Museum: Moscow obl., Sergiev Posad, Lavra; tel. 4-13-58; f. 1920; 10,000 items dealing with the development of Russian art; library of 17,000 vols; Dir A. I. REDKIN.

Stalsky Memorial Museum: Daghestan, Kasumkentsky raion, Ashaga-stal; exhibits on the history of Daghestani literature; library of 20,000 vols.

State Museum of Tatarstan: Tatar Autonomous Republic, Kazan, ul. Lenina 2; f. 1894; over 500,000 exhibits; library of 5,000 vols; Dir V. M. DYAKONOV.

Tolstoy Museum Estate: Tulskaya obl., Shchekinsky raion, Yasnaya Polyana; f. 1921; 27,695 exhibits; Dir S. YU. BUNIN.

Yaroslavl State Historical Museum: 150000 Yaroslavl, pl. Podbelskovo 25; tel. 22-02-72; f. 1864; over 370,000 exhibits; library of 35,000 vols; Dir V. I. LEBEDEV.

SPORTING ASSOCATIONS

National Olympic Committee of the Russian Federation: 103064 Moscow, Kazakova ul. 18; tel. (095) 263-08-41; telex 411287; fax (095) 265-32-26; Chair. VLADIMIR VASIN.

Russian Republican Council of the Voluntary Physical Culture and Sport Society of Trade Unions: 109017 Moscow, M. Tolmachevsky per. 4; tel. (095) 238-91-66.

PERFORMING ARTS

Bolshoy Theatre: Moscow, Teatralnaya pl. (095) 928-40-91; f. 1824; opera and ballet company; Dir YURY N. GRIGORIYEVICH.

Leninsky Komsomol Theatre: Moscow, ul. Chekova 6; tel. (095) 299-96-68.

Maly Drama Theatre: Moscow, Teatralnaya 1/6; tel. (095) 925-98-68.

Mayakovsky Theatre: Moscow, ul. Gertsena 19; tel. (095) 290-62-41.

Sovremenik Theatre: Moscow, Chistoprudny bul. 19A; tel. (095) 921-17-90.

State Conservatoire: Moscow, ul. Gertsena 13; tel. (095) 229-81-83.

State Kirov Academic Ballet: St Petersburg, Teatralnaya pl. 2; Dir O. VINOGRADOV.

Taganka Comedy and Drama Theatre: Zemlyanoy Val 76; tel. (095) 271-28-26; Dir YURY LYUBIMOV.

Teatr-Studio na Yugo-Zapade (Theatre-Studio of the South-West): Moscow, pr. Vernadskovo 125; tel. (095) 434-74-83.

ASSOCIATIONS

All-Russian Culture Fund: 103051 Moscow, ul. Petrovka 28/2; tel. (095) 924-63-73.

All-Russian Musical Society: 103009 Moscow, Sobinovsky per. 9; tel. (095) 290-56-47.

Russian Branch of the All-Union Znanie Society: 101814 Moscow, Novaya pl. 3/4; tel. (095) 921-90-58.

Russian PEN Centre: Moscow, Ivanovskaya 34-32; f. 1989; Pres. ANATOLY RYBAKOV; Sec. VLADIMIR STABNIKOV.

Theatre Union of the Russian Federation: 103009 Moscow, ul. Tverskaya 16/2; tel. (095) 229-91-52; telex 411030; f. 1986; fmrly All-Russia Theatrical Society; 30,124 mems; library of 300,000 vols; Chair. M. A. ULYANOV.

> **Theatrical Fund of the Russian Federation:** 103031 Moscow, Pushkinskaya 34/10; tel. (095) 200-13-56.

Union of Architects of the Russian Federation: 103001 Moscow, ul. Shchuseva 22; tel. (095) 291-55-79.

Union of Artists of the Russian Federation: 103062 Moscow, ul. Chernyshevskovo 37; tel. (095) 297-56-52.

Artistic Fund: 103726 Moscow, Tverskoy bul. 26/5; tel. (095) 229-90-50.

Union of Composers of the Russian Federation: 103009 Moscow, ul. Nezhdanovoy 8/10, kor. 2; tel. (095) 229-52-18.

> **Musical Fund of the Russian Federation:** 103006 Moscow, Sadovaya-Tirumfalnaya 14/12; tel. (095) 200-19-14.

Union of Independent Journalists of the USSR: Moscow; f. 1988; represents unofficial magazines and journals; Chair. SERGEI GRIGORYANTS; 60 mems.

Union of Journalists of the USSR: 119021 Moscow, Zubovsky bul. 4; tel. (095) 201-77-70; telex 411421; fax (095) 200-42-37; f. 1959; Chair. EDUARD SAGALAYEV; 80,000 mems.

Union of Russian Writers (Soyuz Rossiiskikh Pisateley): Moscow; f. 1991 as an alternative to the Union of Writers of the Russian Federation; 1,300 mems.

Union of Writers of the Russian Federation: 119087 Moscow, Komsomolsky pr. 13; tel. (095) 246-75-65; Chair. YURY BONDAREV.

Union of Writers of the USSR: 121069 Moscow, ul. Vorovskovo 52; tel. (095) 291-63-50; telex 950411; f. 1934; Chair. of Bd YURY CHERNICHENKO; First Sec. of Bd YEVEGENY YEVTUSHENKO; 10,000 mems.

USSR Press Association: Moscow; f. 1991; Chair. ALEKSANDR GRKOVLYUK; 500 mems.

Education

The level of education in the Russian Federation is relatively high. In 1989 11.3% of the population over the age of 15 years had completed higher education, compared with an average for the USSR of 10.8%. In the early 1990s there were extensive changes to the curriculum, with particular emphasis on changes in the approach to Soviet history, and the introduction of study of literary works which had previously been banned. At the start of the academic year 1988/89, 98.2% of pupils in general education day schools were taught in Russian. However, there were also 10 other languages in use in secondary education, including Tatar (0.5%), Yakut (0.3%), Chuvash (0.2%) and Bashkir (0.2%).

UNIVERSITIES

Altai State University: 656099 Barnaul, ul. Dimitrova 66; tel. 2-53-80; f. 1973; 10 faculties; 4,700 students.

Bashkir State University: 450074 Bashkir ASSR, Ufa, ul. Frunze 32; tel. 22-63-70; telex 1629560; f. 1957; 10 faculties; 525 teachers; 8,336 students; Rector R. N. GUIMAYEV.

Chechen-Ingush State University: 364907 Checheno-Ingush ASSR, Grozny, ul. Sheripova 32; tel. 3-40-89; f. 1972; 10 faculties; 5,600 students; Rector M. P. PAVLOV.

Chelyabinsk State University: 454136 Chelyabinsk, ul. Br. Kashirinykh 129; tel. 42-09-25; f. 1975; 6 faculties; 2,100 students.

Chuvash I. N. Ulyanov State University: 428015 Chuvash ASSR, Cheboksary, Moskovsky pr. 15; tel. 24-11-67; f. 1967; 13 faculties; 800 teachers; 11,000 students; Rector Prof. Dr P. A. SIDOROV.

Daghestan V. I. Lenin State University: 367025 Daghestan ASSR, Makhachkala, Sovetskaya ul. 8; tel. 7-29-50; telex 175333; f. 1957; 13 faculties; 515 teachers; 8,000 students; Rector Prof A. M. MAGOMEDOV.

Far Eastern State University: 690600 Vladivostok, ul. Sukhanova 8; tel. (423) 2-47-00; telex 213218; f. 1920; 10 faculties; 600 teachers; 10,000 students; Rector Prof V. GLUSHCHENKO.

Irkutsk State University: 664003 Irkutsk, ul. K. Marksa 1; tel. 4-44-30; f. 1918; 12 faculties; 500 teachers; 9,000 students; Rector Dr N. F. LOSEV.

Ivanovo State University: 153377 Ivanovo, ul. Yermaka 39; tel. 4-02-16; f. 1974; 10 faculties; 5,000 students.

Kabardino-Balkar State University: 360004 Kabardino-Balkar ASSR, Nalchik, ul. Chernyshevskovo 173; tel. 2-52-54; f. 1957; 12 faculties; 500 teachers; 9,000 students; Rector Prof. K. N. KEREFOV.

Kaliningrad State University: 236041 Kaliningrad, ul. A. Nevskovo 14; tel. 3-49-41; f. 1967; 11 faculties; 200 teachers; 5,000 students; Rector Prof. A. A. BORISOV.

Kalmyk State University: 358000 Kalmyk ASSR, Elista, ul. Pushkina 11; tel. 2-50-60; f. 1970; 9 faculties; 5,000 students; Rector N. P. KRASAVCHENKO.

Kazan State University: 320008 Tatar ASSR, Kazan, ul. Lenina 18; tel. 32-88-75; f. 1804; 11 faculties; 700 teachers; 11,000 students; Rector Prof. A. I. KONOVALOV.

Kemerovo State University: 650043 Kemerovo, Krasnaya ul. 6; tel. 23-12-26; telex 215350; f. 1974; 10 faculties; 400 teachers; 6,500 students; Rector U. A. ZAKHAROV.

Krasnoyarsk State University: 660062 Krasnoyarsk, pr. Svobodny 79; tel. 25-64-00; telex 288020; f. 1969; 416 teachers; 3,561 students; Rector N. D. PODUPHALOV.

Kuban State University: 350751 Krasnodar, ul. Karla Libknekhta 149; tel (861) 33-75-37; f. 1970; 14 faculties; 9,800 students; Rector K. A. NOVIKOV.

Mari University: 424001 Mari ASSR, Yoshkar-Ola, pl. Lenina 1; tel. 6-20-90; f. 1972; 5 faculties; 3,400 students; Rector V. I. KOLLA.

Mordovian N. P. Ogarev State University: 430000 Mordovian ASSR, Saransk, Bolshevistskaya ul. 68; tel. 4-45-63; f. 1957; 18 faculties; 16,000 students; Rector A. I. SUKHAREV.

Moscow M. V. Lomonosov State University: 117234 Moscow, Leninskiye gory; tel. (095) 939-53-40; f. 1755; 17 faculties, 1 institute; 8,000 teachers; 28,000 students; Rector VIKTOR SADOVNICHY.

Nizhny Novgorod N. I. Lobachevsky State University: 603600 Nizhny Novgorod, pr. Gagarina 23; tel. 65-84-90; telex 224846; f. 1918; 9 faculties; 800 teachers; 9,500 students; Rector Prof. A. F. KHOKLOV.

North-Ossetian K. L. Khetagurov State University: 362000 North-Ossetian ASSR, Vladikavkaz, ul. Vatutina 46; tel. 3-98-24; f. 1969; 11 faculties; 7,000 students; Rector A. K. GUDEV.

Novosibirsk State University: 630090 Novosibirsk, ul. Pirogova 2; tel. (383) 35-35-60; f. 1959; 6 faculties; 600 teachers; 3,700 students; Rector Prof. YU. L. ERSHOV.

Omsk State University: 644077 Omsk, pr. Mira 55A; tel. 64-17-01; f. 1974; 9 faculties; 3,000 students.

Patrice Lumumba People's Friendship University: 117302 Moscow, ul. Ordzhonikidze 3; tel. (095) 234-00-11; f. 1960; 7 faculties; 1,500 teachers; 6,700 students; Rector V. F. STANIS.

Perm A. M. Gorky State University: 614600 Perm, ul. Bukireva 15; tel. 33-61-83; f. 1916; 12 faculties; 660 teachers; 9,300 students; Rector V. V. MALANIN.

Petrozavodsk O. V. Kuusinen State University: 185640 Karelian ASSR, Petrozavodsk, pr. Lenina 33; tel. 7-17-91; f. 1940; 10 faculties; 450 teachers; 7,000 students; Rector V. V. STEPHANIKHIN.

Rostov State University: 344066 Rostov-on-Don, ul. Fridrikha Engelsa 105; tel. (863) 65-95-30; telex 123228; f. 1915; 12 faculties; 850 teachers; 9,600 students; Rector Prof. A. V. BELOKON.

St Petersburg State University: 199034 St Petersburg, Universitetskaya nab. 7/9; tel. (812) 218-76-31; fax (812) 218-13-46; f. 1724; 17 faculties; 2,150 teachers; 20,000 students; Rector Prof S. P. MERKUREV.

Samara State University: 443086 Samara, ul. Akademika Pavlova 1; tel. (846) 34-54-02; f. 1969; 8 faculties; 4,500 students; Rector A. I. MEDVEDEV.

Saratov N. G. Chernyshevsky State University: 410600 Saratov, Astrakhanskaya ul. 83; tel. 21-16-96; f. 1909; 10 faculties; 700 teachers; 10,000 students; Rector Prof. V. N. SHEVCHIK.

Syktyvkar State University: 167001 Komi ASSR, Syktyvkar, Oktyabrsky pr. 55; tel. 3-68-20; f. 1972; 7 faculties; 3,000 students.

Tomsk State University: 634010 Tomsk, pr. Lenina 36; tel. 3-30-60; f. 1888; 11 faculties; 700 teachers; 9,000 students; Rector Prof A. P. BYCHKOV.

Tver State University: 170000 Tver, ul. Zhelyabova 33; tel. 3-15-50; f. 1971; 12 faculties; 600 teachers; 8,000 students; Rector A. N. KUDINOV.

Tyumen State University: 625610 Tyumen 3, ul. Semakova 10; tel. 6-19-30; 9 faculties; 6,000 students.

Udmurt State University: 426037 Udmurt ASSR, Izhevsk, Krasnogeroiskaya ul. 71; tel. 75-16-10; telex 255154; f. 1972; 10 faculties; 470 teachers; 3,200 students; Rector V. A. ZHURAVLEV.

Urals A. M. Gorky State University: 620083 Yekaterinburg, pr. Lenina 51; tel. (343) 55-74-20; f. 1920; 9 faculties; 1,000 teachers; 7,000 students; Rector Prof. P. E. SUETIN.

Volgograd State University: 400062 Volgograd, 2-ya Prodolnaya ul. 30; tel. (844) 43-81-24; f. 1978; 6 faculties; 1,000 students.

Voronezh State University: 294693 Voronezh, Universitetskaya pl. 1; tel. 5-29-83; f. 1918; 15 faculties; 800 teachers; 12,500 students; Rector Prof. B. I. MIKHANTEV.

Yakutsk State University: 677891 Yakut ASSR, Yakutsk, ul. Belinskovo 58; tel. 4-38-22; f. 1956; 11 faculties; 400 teachers; 8,000 students; Rector I. G. POPOV.

Yaroslavl State University: 150000 Yaroslavl, Sovetskaya ul. 14; tel. 22-82-10; f. 1970; 6 faculties; 3,000 students; Rector L. V. SRETENSKY.

Social Welfare

GOVERNMENT AGENCIES

Ministry of Social Protection of the Population: see section on The Government (Ministries).

Pension Fund of the Russian Federation: 117934 Moscow, ul. Shabolovka 4; tel. (095) 236-45-78; br. of the former USSR Pension fund; Chair. A. V. KURTIN.

HEALTH AND WELFARE ORGANIZATIONS

All-Russian Society of the Blind: 103672 Moscow, Novaya pl. 14; tel. (095) 925-24-28; Chair. A. YA. NEUMYVAKIN.

All-Russian Society of the Deaf: 123022 Moscow, ul. 1905 goda 10A; tel. (095) 252-10-43; Chair. V. A. KORABLINOV.

All-Russian Society of Invalids: 121099 Moscow, 2-Smolensky per. 3/4; tel. (095) 241-22-86; Chair. A. V. Deryugin.

Central Committee of the Russian Federation Red Cross: 103031 Moscow, Kuznetsky most 18/7; tel. (095) 925-58-48; fax (095) 928-20-74; Chair. of Central Committee O. M. SUDOROV.

Russian Charity and Health Fund: 100062 Moscow, ul. Chernyshevskovo 22; tel. (095) 227-18-88; fax (095) 975-22-45; Chair. A. K. KISILEV.

The Environment

GOVERNMENT ORGANIZATIONS

Ministry of Ecology and the Use of Natural Resources: see section on The Government (Ministries).

RUSSIAN ACADEMY OF SCIENCES

Russian Academy of Sciences: 117901 Moscow, Leninsky pr. 14; tel. (095) 234-21-53; telex 411964; f. 1725; renamed Academy of Sciences of the USSR 1925; original name reinstated 1991; Pres. YURY S. OSIPOV; a Commission on Problems of Ecology is attached to the Presidium of the Academy; the principal sections and institutes involved in environmental matters incl.:

Vsesoyuzny Nauchno-issledovatelsky Institut Okhrany Prirody i Zapovednovo Dela (All-Union Scientific Research Institute for Nature Conservation and Reserves): Moskovskaya obl. M-628, Leninsky raion, 142790 P/O VILR, Znamenskoye-Sadki; applied research inst.; major repository of research material.

Section of Chemical, Technological and Biological Sciences

Institut evolyutsionnoi morfologii i ekologii zhivotnykh imeni A. N. Severtsova (A. N. Severtsov Institute of Evolutionary Morphology and Animal Ecology): 117071 Moscow, Leninsky pr. 33; tel. (095) 234-75-53; in the Dept of General Biology; incl. research on protection of natural environment; Dir Acad. V. E. SOKOLOV.

Institute of the Biology of Inland Waters: Yaroslavskaya oblast, P/O Borok; in the Dept of General Biology; incl. Commission on the Conservation of Natural Waters; Dir N. V. BUTORIN.

Institute of Soil Science and Photosynthesis: 142292 Moscow oblast, Serpukhovsky raion, Pushchino; in the Dept of Biochemistry, Biophysics and Physiological Chemistry; research incl. soil conservation and land reclamation; Dir V. I. KEFELYA.

Institute of the Ecology of the Volga River Basin: Samara oblast, 445003 Toglyatti, ul. Komzina 10; tel. 23-56-85; f. 1983; in the Dept of General Biology; monitors the environment of the lower Volga; Dirs G. P. KRASNOSHCHEKOV, G. S. ROZENBURG.

Section of Earth Sciences

Institute of Water Problems: 103064 Moscow, Sadovaya-Chernogryazskaya 13/3; tel. (095) 208-46-11; in the Dept of Oceanology, Atmospheric Physics and Geography; Dir M. G. KHUBLARYAN.

Laboratory for the Monitoring of the Environment and Climate: c/o Dept of Oceanology, Atmospheric Physics and Geography, 117901 Moscow, Leninsky pr. 14; tel. (095) 234-14-24; Dir (vacant).

Research Co-ordination Centre 'Aral': c/o Dept of Oceanology, Atmospheric Physics and Geography, 117901 Moscow, Leninsky pr. 14; tel. (095) 234-14-24; responsible for researching the environmental spoilation of the Aral Sea region; Dir V. M. KOTLYAKOV.

The Section of Earth Sciences also includes the Institiue of Lake Conservation and the Scientific Council on Study of the Caspian Sea.

Section of Social Sciences

Institute of State and Law, Sector on Environmental Law: 119841 Moscow, ul. Znamenka 10; tel. (095) 291-87-56; f. 1925; research into Soviet and Russian environmental law; in the Dept of Philosophy and Law; Dir BORIS N. TOPORNIN.

Siberian Division

630090 Novosibirsk, pr. Akademika Lavrenteva 17; tel. (383) 35-05-67; Chair. Acad. V. A. KOTYUG; institutes involved in environmental matters incl:

Chita Institute of Natural Resources: 672014 Chita 14, ul. Nedorezova 16; tel. 1-24-81; f. 1981; scientific research into the region's ecosystems; Dir O. A. VOTAKH; Scientific Sec. ALEKSANDR P. CHECHEL.

Institute of Limnology: 666016 Irkutsk oblast, pos. Listvenichnoe; tel. 46-05-64; studies the ecology of lakes; particularly concerned with the conservation programme in Lake Baikal; Dir M. A. GRACHEV.

Institute of Water and Ecological Problems (IWEP): 656009 Barnaul 99, ul. Papaninzeva 105; tel. (3852) 25-21-25; fax (3852) 24-03-96; f. 1987; research into water-resource use, land reclamation and environmental protection in Siberia; environmental assessment of large-scale engineering projects; Dir Prof. OLEG F. VASILIYEV.

Far Eastern Division

690600 Vladivostok, ul. Leninskaya 50; tel. (423) 2-25-28; Chair. V. I. ILICHEV; environmental research by:

Institute of Biological Problems of the North: 685000 Magadan, ul. K. Marksa 24; Dir A. A. AIDARALIYEV.

Institute of Water and Ecological Problems: 680063 Khabarovsk, ul. Kim Yu Chena 65; tel. 33-39-48; telex 141359; f. 1968; research into use and management of water resources; Dir I. P. DRUZHININ; Vice-Dir V. A. VORONOV.

Urals Division

620219 Yekaterinburg, ul. 1-vo Maiskaya 91; tel. (343) 44-02-23; Chair. G. A. MESYATS; attached institutes incl.:

Institute of Ecological Problems of the North: environmental research; Dir (vacant).

Institute of Plant and Animal Ecology: 620219 Yekaterinburg, ul. 8-vo Marta 202; tel. (343) 22-41-61; environmental research; Dir V. N. BOLSHAKOV.

GOVERNMENT ORGANIZATIONS

Arctic and Antarctic Research Unit: 199226 St Petersburg, ul. Bering 38; tel. (812) 352-03-19; telex 121423; fax (812) 352-26-88; f. 1920; research into ecology of the Arctic and Antarctic; responsible for the Soviet Antarctic Expedition; Dir Dr B. A. KRUTSKIKH.

NON-GOVERNMENTAL ORGANIZATIONS

All-Russian Society for Nature Conservation (Vserossiiskoe Obshchestvo Okhrany Prirody): 103012 Moscow L-12, Kuibyshevsky pr. 3; f. 1924; civilian asscn focusing on environmental education; mems mainly in the Russian Federation.

Association for the Support of Ecological Issues: Moscow, Lomonosovsky pr. 111–119; co-ordinating group.

International Foundation for the Survival and Development of Humanity (IF): c/o Yevgeny Velikhov, Vice-President of the Academy of Sciences: 117901 Moscow, Leninsky pr. 14; tel. (095) 232-29-10; f. 1988; international environmental asscn; Dir YE. P. VELIKHOV.

Krasnoyarsk Green World (Krasnoyarsky Zeleny Svet): Krasnoyarsk; local environmental group opposed to nuclear power and weapons.

Moscow Society of Naturalists: 103009 Moscow, ul. Gertsena 6; tel. (095) 203-67-04; f. 1805; 2,700 mems; library of 500,000 vols; Chair. A. L. YANSHIN.

Movement for a Nuclear-Free North: Murmansk; advocates demilitarization of the Kola peninsula and an end to nuclear testing on Novaya Zemlya.

Social-Ecological Union: Moscow, POB 273; tel. (095) 945-40-94; fax (095) 292-65-11; f. 1988; asscn of groups; monitors the environment and breaches of environmental law; Chair. MARIYA CHERKASOVA.

TADZHIKISTAN

Geography

The Republic of Tadzhikistan (formerly the Tadzhik Soviet Socialist Republic) is situated in the south-east of Central Asia. To the north and west it is bounded by Uzbekistan, and to the north-east by Kyrgyzstan. Its eastern boundary forms an international frontier with the People's Republic of China. To the south there is an international boundary with Afghanistan. Its territory includes the Gorno-Badakhshan Autonomous Oblast (of which the capital is Khorog). The Republic covers an area of 143,100 sq km (55,250 sq miles).

The terrain is almost entirely mountainous, with more than one-half of the country above 3,000 m. The major mountain ranges are the western Tien Shan in the north, the southern Tien Shan in the central region and the Pamirs in the south-east. The highest mountains of the former USSR, Lenin Peak (7,134 m) and Communism Peak (7,495 m), are situated in the northern Pamirs. There is a dense river network, which is extensively used to provide hydroelectric power. The major rivers are the upper reaches of the Syr-Dar'ya and the Amu-Dar'ya, which forms the southern border with Afghanistan, as the Pyandzh. The Zeravshen river flows through the centre of the Republic. Most settlement is in the valleys of the south-west and the northern areas around Khodzhent (formerly Leninabad) in the Fergana Valley.

The climate varies considerably according to altitude. The average temperature in January in Khodzhent (lowland) is −0.9°C (30.4°F); in July the average is 27.4°C (81.3°F). In the southern lowlands the temperature variation is somewhat more extreme. Precipitation is low in the valleys ranging from 150–250 mm per year. In mountain areas winter temperatures can fall below −45°C (−51°F); the average January temperature in Murgab, in the mountains of south-east Gorno-Badakhshan, is −19.6°C (−3.3°F). Levels of rainfall are very low in mountain regions and seldom exceed 60–80 mm per year.

At 1 January 1991 the total population was estimated to be 5,358,000. The largest ethnic group is the Tadzhiks (62.3% of the population in 1989), followed by Uzbeks (23.5%), Russians (7.6%) and Tatars (1.4%). In the 1989 census the Pamiri Peoples (also known as Mountain Tadzhiks or Galchaks), who inhabit the Gorno-Badakhshan Autonomous Oblast, were counted as Tadzhiks, although they have distinct languages and cultural traditions. Other ethnic minorities include Kirghiz (63,832), Ukrainians (41,375), Germans (32,671), Turkmen (20,487) and Koreans (13,431). In 1989 Tadzhik replaced Russian as the official language of the Republic. Tadzhik belongs to the south-west Iranian group of languages and is closely related to Farsi (Persian). Since 1940 the Cyrillic script has been used. The major religion is Islam. Most Tadzhiks and Uzbeks follow the Sunni tradition, but the Pamiris are mostly of the Isma'ili sect. There are also representatives of the Russian Orthodox Church. There is a small Jewish community, which, in 1989, included 9,701 European Jews and 4,879 Central Asian Jews. The capital is Dushanbe (Stalinabad 1929–61), which is situated in the west of the Republic, and had an estimated population of 602,000 in 1990. Khodzhent (formerly Leninabad), in the north, is Tadzhikistan's second largest city.

History

The Tadzhiks were probably a distinct ethnic group by about the eighth century AD. They were distinguished from their Turkic neighbours by their sedentary life style and Iranian language. They formed several semi-independent territories under Uzbek suzerainty, but as the Russian Empire expanded southwards in the 19th century, the northern Tadzhik principalities came under Russian rule. The southern regions were annexed by the expanding Emirate of Bukhara.

In 1918 the Bolsheviks re-established control over northern Tadzhikistan, which was incorporated into the Turkmenistan ASSR, but did not conquer Dushanbe and the other territories subject to Bukhara until 1921. Opposition to Soviet rule was led by the *basmachis* (local guerrilla fighters) and foreign interventionists. Full Soviet control was not established in the remote south-east of Tadzhikistan until 1925. In 1924 the Tadzhik ASSR was established as a part of the Uzbek SSR and, on 2 January 1925, the south-east of Tadzhikistan was designated a Special Pamir Region (later renamed the Gorno-Badakhshan Autonomous Oblast) within the Tadzhik ASSR. On 16 October 1929 the Tadzhik ASSR became a full Union Republic of the USSR (the Tadzhik Soviet Socialist Republic) and was slightly enlarged by the addition of the Khodzhent okrug (district) from the Uzbek SSR.

Soviet power brought economic and social benefits to Tadzhikistan, but living standards remained low even by Soviet standards. Cattle breeding, the main occupation in the uplands, was severely disrupted by collectivization. During the repressions of the 1930s almost all Tadzhiks in the republican government were removed and replaced by Russians, sent from Moscow.

During the 1970s there were reports of increased Islamic influence and violence towards non-indigenous nationalities. In 1978 there were reports of an anti-Russian riot, involving some 13,000 people, and, after 1979, there were arrests of some activists opposed to Soviet intervention in Afghanistan.

As in other Central Asian Republics, the first manifestation of Soviet leader Mikhail Gorbachev's new policies was a campaign against corruption. Rakhmon Nabiyev, who had been First Secretary of the Communist Party of Tadzhikistan (CPT) since 1982, was replaced by Kakhar Makkhamov, who accused his predecessor of tolerating nepotism and corruption. Makkhamov was also openly critical of the economic situation in the Republic, admitting that there were high levels of unemployment and that many people lived in poverty. Censorship was also relaxed and there was increased discussion of perceived injustices, such as alleged discrimination against Tadzhiks in Uzbekistan. In June 1989 there were violent confrontations between villagers on the Kirghiz–Tadzhik border and there were discussions in the media about the fairness of the Uzbek–Tadzhik boundary.

Increased freedom of expression allowed discussion of Tadzhik culture and language, and greater interest in Iranian cultures in other countries. Links with Iran had been limited since the 1979 Iranian Revolution, but the pro-Soviet regime in Afghanistan developed cultural contacts with Tadzhikistan, and many Tadzhiks served in Afghanistan as interpreters. Tadzhik was declared the state language in 1989, and the teaching of the Arabic script (used by Tadzhiks prior to sovietization) was begun in schools.

In February 1990 rioting occurred in Dushanbe, after rumours that Armenian refugees were to be settled there. The scarcity of housing and work seemed to be the cause of the protests, which were directed against the Communist authorities in the Republic. Demonstrators demanded democratic reforms and more radical economic reform. Violence broke out at a protest rally of about 3,000 people, when demonstrators clashed with police, overturned cars and looted shops. A state of emergency was declared and a night-time curfew was imposed in Dushanbe. Makkhamov requested aid from the all-Union authorities and some 5,000 Soviet interior ministry troops were dispatched to the city. In conjunction with 'civilian militia' units, they suppressed the demonstrations; 22 people were reported dead and 565 injured.

The events of February 1990 prompted a more inflexible attitude towards political pluralism from the Republic's leadership. The state of emergency was not lifted during 1990 and two nascent opposition parties, Rastokhez, which was involved in the February demonstrations, and the Democratic Party of Tadzhikistan (DPT), were refused official registration. In addition, the Islamic Renaissance Party was refused permission to hold a founding congress in Dushanbe, but all three groups continued to attract popular support. In the elections to the Supreme Soviet, held in March 1990, opposition politicians were refused permission to participate and 94% of the deputies elected were members of the CPT.

In an apparent concession to growing Tadzhik nationalism, the Tadzhik Supreme Soviet adopted a declaration of sovereignty, on 25 August 1990. Although the declaration emphasized the equality of all nationalities living in Tadzhikistan, the growth in Islamic influence, the rediscovery of the Tadzhiks' Iranian heritage and language and the uncertain political situation all contributed to an increase in emigration from the Republic, mainly by Europeans and educated Tadzhiks. In November 1990 Makkhamov was elected President of the Republic by the Supreme Soviet. His only opponent was former Party leader Rakhmon Nabiyev.

The Tadzhik Government, possibly anxious about increased Turkic dominance in Central Asia, displayed great enthusiasm for a new Union Treaty and Tadzhikistan was the first Republic to declare its willingness to sign such a treaty. Tadzhiks voted overwhelmingly for preservation of the USSR in the all-Union referendum in March 1991. According to official figures, 90% of the electorate voted to preserve the USSR.

In August 1991, before the new Union Treaty could be signed, conservative leaders of the CPSU and the security forces staged a *coup d'état* in Moscow. Makkhamov did not oppose the coup, and, on 31 August, after the attempted coup had collapsed, he resigned as President. His resignation had been forced by mass demonstrations, which continued throughout much of September. They were organized by the three main opposition parties (the Democratic Party, the Islamic Renaissance Party and Rastokhez). On 9 September, following Uzbekistan's declaration of independence, the Tadzhik Supreme Soviet voted to proclaim Tadzhikistan an independent state, based on democratic principles and the rule of law. The name of the Republic was changed to the Republic of Tadzhikistan. This did not, however, satisfy the demonstrators, who demanded the dissolution of the CPT and new, multi-party elections. Kadriddin Aslonov, the Chairman of the Supreme Soviet and acting President, issued a decree which banned the CPT and nationalized its assets (earlier in September the CPT had reorganized as the Socialist Party of Tadzhikistan, but the original name was reinstated in January 1992). In response, the Communist majority in the Supreme Soviet demanded Aslonov's resignation, declared a state of emergency in the Republic and rescinded the prohibition of the Communist Party. Aslonov resigned and was replaced by former CPT leader, Rakhmon Nabiyev.

The Communist majority appeared to have suffered a set-back, when, in response to growing popular protest, the Supreme Soviet rescinded the state of emergency, suspended the CPT and legalized the Islamic Renaissance Party, which had previously been banned under legislation which prohibited the formation of religious parties. On 6 October 1991 Nabiyev resigned as acting President, in advance of the presidential elections.

There were seven candidates in the presidential elections, which took place on 24 November 1991. The main contenders were Nabiyev and Davlat Khudonazarov, the liberal Chairman of the USSR Cinematographers' Union, who was supported by the main opposition parties. Mostly as a result of strong support in rural areas, Nabiyev won 57% of the votes cast, compared with 30% for Khudonazarov. The latter claimed that there were electoral malpractices, but his complaints were not upheld and Nabiyev took office in early December. In early January 1992 a new premier, Akbar Mirzoyev, was appointed to head the Government, replacing Izatullo Khayeyev, who resigned for reasons of health.

The Republic's leadership participated in meetings of the five Central Asian leaders in 1990 and 1991, although relations with Uzbekistan were strained by disputes over borders and the treatment of minorities in each Republic. In foreign affairs, Tadzhikistan began to develop relations with Middle Eastern states, notably with Iran, with which the Tadzhiks have strong ethnic and cultural ties. In late 1991 Iran and Tadzhikistan agreed to establish consulates-general in each other's territory, and to introduce direct economic links between the two states. The continuation of the civil war in Afghanistan prevented any significant development of Afghan–Tadzhik economic relations and the effects of the demise of the USSR on the situation remained uncertain at the beginning of 1992.

Tadzhikistan, as was expected, signed the Treaty on the Economic Community, on 19 October 1991, and demonstrated its willingness to join the proposed Union of Sovereign States. When a Commonwealth of Independent States was suggested in December, initially by the three Slav republics, Tadzhikistan expressed its desire to become a co-founder, along with the other Central Asian Republics. The Republic was a signatory of the Alma-Ata Declaration, on 21 December.

Economy

Tadzhikistan has considerable mineral deposits including gold, iron, lead, mercury and tin. There are important coal deposits and small reserves of petroleum and natural gas. The mountain river system is widely used for hydroelectric power generation. There is little heavy industry except for mineral exploitation. Light industry concentrates on textiles, carpet-making and food-processing. There are some engineering plants producing agricultural equipment and machinery for power stations. Cotton is the main agricultural crop. Cattle-raising and horticulture are also significant and dried apricots, nuts and grapes are important exports. Most areas require extensive irrigation, which is provided by a network of canals and reservoirs.

Tadzhikistan's role in the overall Soviet economy has been limited. In 1988 it provided only 0.8% of total Soviet net material product (NMP), including only 0.4% of industrial NMP and 1.2% of agricultural NMP. However, in comparison with some other republics it is relatively self-sufficient, with 41.8% of its NMP derived from exports to other republics. Exports to other countries constituted 6.9% of NMP.

Statistical Survey

Population

BIRTHS AND DEATHS (per 1,000)

	1987	1988	1989
Birth rate	41.9	40.2	38.7
Death rate	6.9	7.0	6.5

Agriculture

PRINCIPAL CROPS ('000 metric tons)

	1988	1989	1990
Grain	381.3	306.1	318
Seed cotton . . .	963.8	922.5	842.1
Potatoes	182.7	217.3	207.0
Other vegetables . .	555.5	567.9	528.3
Grapes	178.5	174.1	189.5
Other fruit	215.0	196.6	220.2

LIVESTOCK ('000 head at 1 January)

	1988	1989	1990
Cattle	1,347.3	1,363.2	1,349.2
Pigs	231.9	216.9	210.0
Sheep and goats . . .	3,223.3	3,340.3	3,358.9

LIVESTOCK PRODUCTS ('000 metric tons)

	1987	1988	1989
Meat (slaughter weight) . .	114.5	113.2	112.4
Milk	567.3	574.4	579.7
Eggs (million)	585.4	632.3	618.5
Wool (greasy)	5.2	5.3	5.4

Mining and Industry

Production (1989, unless otherwise stated): Coal 515,000 metric tons, Crude petroleum 190,000 tons, Natural gas 303 million cu m, Mineral fertilizers 88,100 tons, Domestic refrigerators 170,500, Copper cable (by copper weight) 16,200 tons, Technical lighting equipment 8.9 million roubles, Cotton yarn 129,000 tons, Woven cotton fabrics 125 million m, Knitted garments 13,200,000 (1986), Hosiery 36.1 million pairs (1986), Leather footwear 10.8 million pairs, Carpets and rugs 10.8 million sq m, Vegetable oil 93,200 tons, Tinned goods 374 million cans, Cement 1,111,0000 tons, Reinforced concrete 1,169,000 cu m, Bricks 320.0 million, Electric energy 15,277 million kWh.

Education

(1989/90)

	Institutions	Students
Secondary schools	3,101	1,258,800
Secondary specialized schools . . .	42	41,694
Higher schools (incl. universities) . .	10	65,586

Directory

The Government

(January 1992)

HEAD OF STATE

President of the Republic of Tadzhikistan: RAKHMON NABIYEV (elected 24 November 1991).
Vice-President: NARZULLO DUSTOV.

COUNCIL OF MINISTERS

Prime Minister: AKBAR MIRZOYEV.
First Deputy Prime Minister: DZHAMSHED KH. KARIMOV.
Deputy Prime Minister: ABDUZHALIL SAMADOV.
Minister of Internal Affairs: MAMADAEZ NAVZHUVANOV.
Minister of Finance: N. A. YUNUSOV.
Chair of State Economic Committee: G. KOSHLAKOV.
Chair of Committee for National Security: Major-Gen. ANATOLY STROYKIN.

MINISTRIES

All Ministries are in Dushanbe.
Secretariat of the Council of Ministers: Dushanbe; tel. (3772) 23-27-93.

President and Legislature

PRESIDENT

Presidential Election, 24 November 1991*

Candidate	% of Votes Cast
RAKHMON NABIYEV	56.92
DAVLAT KHUDONAZAROV	30.07
TURAYEV	5.03
NASRADINOV	1.28
HALIMOV	0.53
SHOYEV	0.37
MAKSUMOV	0.23

* Preliminary results.

SUPREME SOVIET

Elections to the Supreme Soviet were held in March 1990. Of those deputies elected, 94% were members of the CPT.
Chairman: SAFARALI KENDZHAYEV.

Local Government

Tadzhikistan contains three oblasts (Kulyab, Kurgan-Tyubinsk and Khodzhent) and one autonomous oblast (Gorno-Badakhshan).

AUTONOMOUS OBLAST

Gorno-Badakhshan:

The Gorno-Badakhshan Autonomous Oblast is situated in the south-east corner of Tadzhikistan. It has international frontiers with the People's Republic of China in the east and Afghanistan in the south.

Political Organizations

Communist Party of Tadzhikistan: Dushanbe; First Sec. of Cen. Cttee SHODI SHABDOLLOV.

Democratic Party of Tadzhikistan: Dushanbe; f. 1990; advocates full sovereignty for Tadzhikistan within a confederation of independent states; First Sec. of Cen. Cttee SHADMAN YUSUPOV; *c.*15,000 mems (1991).

Islamic Renaissance Party (IRP): Dushanbe; branch of what was the all-Union IRP; 10,000 mems (1990).

Rastokhez (Rebirth): Dushanbe; Leader TAKHIR ABDULDZHABOROV.

Judicial System

Chairman of the Supreme Court: S. MAKHMUDOV.
Procurator: N. KHUVAYDULLAYEV.

Religion

The majority of Tadzhiks are adherents of Islam and are mainly Sunnis (Hanafi school). Some of the Pamiri peoples, however, are of the Shi'a sect. The Muslims of Tadzhikistan come under the spiritual jurisdiction of the Muslim Board of Central Asia, which is represented in the Republic by a kazi.

Chief Kazi: Hajji AKBAR TURADZHONZODA.

The Press

In 1990, according to official statistics, there were 74 newspaper titles being published in Tadzhikistan, including 66 published in Tadzhik. The daily circulation was 1,598,000 copies (1,239,000 in Tadzhik). There were 48 periodicals being published, including 13 in Tadzhik, with a total annual circulation of 16.2m. copies (9.2m. in Tadzhik).

PRINCIPAL NEWSPAPERS

Adabiyet va Sanat (Literature and Art): Dushanbe, ul. Putovskovo 8; tel. (3772) 24-57-39; f. 1959; weekly; organ of the Union of Writers and Ministry of Culture; in Tadzhik; Editor A. KHAKIMOV.

Djavononi Todjikiston (Tadzhik Youth): Dushanbe; f. 1930; 5 a week; fmrly organ of the Cen. Cttee of the Leninist Young Communist League of Tadzhikistan; in Tadzhik; Editor O. FAKHRIEV.

Komsomolets Tadzhikistana (Member of the Leninist Young Communist League of Tadzhikistan): Dushanbe; f. 1938; 5 a week; fmrly organ of the Cen. Cttee of the Leninist Young Communist League of Tadzhikistan; in Russian; Editor V. V. KRASOCHIN.

Narodnaya Gazeta: Dushanbe; f. 1929; fmrly *Kommunist Tadzhikistana* (Tadzhik Communist), the organ of the Communist Party of Tadzhikistan; 5 a week; in Russian; Editor N. N. KUZMIN.

Omuzgor (Teacher): Dushanbe; f. 1932; weekly; organ of the Ministry of Education; in Tadzhik; Editor B. NASRIDDINOV.

Sadoi mardum (The Voice of the People): Dushanbe; f. 1991; 5 a week; organ of the Supreme Soviet; in Tadzhik; Editor MURODULLO SHERALIYEV.

Sovet Tochikistoni (Soviet Tadzhikistan): Dushanbe; f. 1929; 5 a week; organ of the Supreme Soviet; in Uzbek; Editor T. A. DJURABOYEV.

Tochikistoni (Tadzhikistan): Dushanbe; f. 1925; 5 a week; fmrly organ of the Communist Party of Tadzhikistan; in Tadzhik; Editor M. MUHABBATSHOYEV.

PRINCIPAL PERIODICALS

Monthly unless otherwise indicated.

Hajoti dehot (Village Life): 734025 Dushanbe, pr. Lenina 46; tel. (3772) 22-82-68; f. 1947; journal of the Ministry of Agriculture; problems of agriculture; in Tadzhik; Editor-in-Chief K. YA. AFZALI.

Khorpushtak (Hedgehog): Dushanbe; f. 1953; fortnightly; satirical; in Tadzhik.

Maktabi Soveti (Soviet School): Dushanbe; f. 1930; journal of the Ministry of Education; theory of pedagogical science; in Tadzhik; Editor-in-Chief O. BOZOROV.

Mashal (Torch): Dushanbe, Rudaki 33; tel. (3772) 24-83-17; f. 1952; fmrly journal of the Cen. Cttee of the Leninist Young Communist League and Republican Council of the Pioneer Organization of

the Tadzhikistan; juvenile fiction; in Tadzhik; Editor-in-Chief T. NIGOROVA; circ. 120,000.

Pamir: 734001 Dushanbe, ul. Putovskovo 8; tel. (3772) 24-56-56; f. 1949; journal of the Union of Writers of Tadzhikistan; fiction; in Russian; Editor-in-Chief MASUD MULLODZHONOV.

Sadoi Shark (Voice of the East): 734001 Dushanbe, ul. Putovskovo 8; tel. (3772) 24-56-79; f. 1924; journal of the Union of Writers; fiction; in Tadzhik; Editor-in-Chief (vacant).

Selskaya Zhizn (Agriculture): Dushanbe; in Russian.

Tochikiston (Tadzhikistan): Dushanbe; f. 1938; social and political; in Tadzhik and Russian; Editor-in-Chief (vacant).

Zanoni Tochikiston (Women of Tadzhikistan): Dushanbe; f. 1954; popular; in Tadzhik; Editor-in-Chief M. KHAKIMOVA.

Zdravookhraneniye Tadzhikistana (Tadzhikistan Public Health System): Dushanbe; f. 1924; 6 a year; journal of the Ministry of Health; medical research; in Russian; Editor-in-Chief YA. T. TADZHIYEV.

NEWS AGENCY

Khovar (East): Dushanbe, pr. Lenina 37; f. 1991 to replace TadzhikTA (Tadzhik Telegraph Agency); govt information agency; Dir Z. NASRIDDINOV.

Publishers

Adib (Literary Publishing House): Dushanbe, kuchai Ayni 126; f. 1987; juvenile and adult fiction; Dir K. MIRZOYEV.

Entsiklopediyai Sovetii Todzik (Encyclopaedia Publishing House): Dushanbe, kuchai Ayni 126; tel. (3772) 25-18-41; f. 1969; Editor-in-Chief J. AZIZQULOV.

Irfon (Light of Knowledge Publishing House): Dushanbe, kuchai Ayni 126; politics, science, economics and agriculture; Dir A. SANGINOV.

Maorif (Education Publishing House): Dushanbe, kuchai Ayni 126; educational; Dir A. GHAFUROV.

Radio and Television

State Television and Radio Corporation: 734013 Dushanbe, ul. Bekhzod 7A; f. 1992, to replace the State Television and Radio Committee for the Republic of Tadzhikistan; Chair. SAYFULLOYEV ATAKHAN SAYFULLOYEVICH.

Tadzhik Radio: 734025 Dushanbe, kuchai Chapayev 25; broadcasts in Russian, Tadzhik, Farsi (Persian) and Uzbek.

Tadzhik Television: 734013 Dushanbe, ul. Bekhzod 7A; broadcasts on four channels in Tadzhik, Russian and Uzbek.

Finance

BANKING

State Banks

National Bank of Tadzhikistan: 734004 Dushanbe, pr. Lenina 24; Chair. of Board T. A. GAFAROV; Dep. Chair. TAMARA D. ZAPROMETOVA.

Bank for Foreign Economic Activity: Dushanbe; fmrly br. of USSR Vneshekonombank; Chair. I. L. LALBEKOV.

COMMODITY EXCHANGES

Tadzhik Republican Commodity Exchange (NAVRUZ): 374001 Dushanbe, 37 ul. Ordzhonikidze; tel. (3772) 23-48-74; telex 116249; fax (3772) 27-03-91; f. 1991; Chair. SULEYMAN CHULEBAYEV.

Vostok-Mercury Torgovy Dom: 734026 Dushanbe, ul. Lomonosova 162; tel. (3772) 24-60-61; fax (3772) 24-60-61; f. 1991; trades in a wide range of goods.

Trade and Industry

CHAMBER OF COMMERCE

Chamber of Commerce and Industry: 734012 Dushanbe, ul. Mazayeva 21; tel. (3772) 27-95-19; Chair. S. K. SUFIEVICH.

INDUSTRIAL ORGANIZATIONS

Tadzhikvneshtorg: 734051 Dushanbe, pr. Lenina 42; tel. (3772) 23-29-03; co-ordinates foreign trade in a wide range of goods; Gen. Dir YU. G. GAYTSGORI.

Tadzhikvneshtorg Industrial Association: 734025 Dushanbe, POB 48; tel. (3772) 23-29-03; telex 116119; fax (3772) 22-81-20; est. by Council of Ministers to encourage trade and economic relations with foreign countries; Gen. Dir ABDURAKHMON MUKHTASHOV.

Culture

CULTURAL HERITAGE

Firdousi State Public Library of the Republic of Tadzhikistan: 734610 Dushanbe, pr. Lenina 34; tel. (3772) 22-33-16; 2,839,329 vols; Dir S. GOIBNAZAROV.

Tadzhik Historical State Museum: Dushanbe, ul. Ayni 31; 90,000 items; library of over 200,000 vols.

ASSOCIATION

Union of Writers of Tadzhikistan: 734001 Dushanbe, ul. Putovskovo 8; tel. (3772) 24-57-37.

Education

Education is controlled by the Ministry of Education of Tadzhikistan and is fully funded by the state at all levels. The majority of pupils receive their education in Tadzhik (66.0% of pupils in general day schools in 1988); other languages used included Uzbek (22.9%), Russian (9.7%), Kirghiz (1.1%) and Turkmen (0.3%). Following the adoption of Tadzhik as the state language pupils in Russian-language schools were to learn Tadzhik from the first to 11th grades. Greater emphasis has been made in the curriculum on Tadzhik language and literature, including classical Persian literature. In 1991 a new university was established in Khodzhent.

UNIVERSITIES

Khodzhent State University: Khodzhent; f. 1991; fmrly Khodzhent Pedagological Institute; 12 faculties.

Tadzhik State University: 734016 Dushanbe, pr. Lenina 17; tel. (3772) 27-35-17; f. 1948; languages of instruction: Tadzhik and Russian; 16 faculties; 750 teachers; 6,500 full-time, 2,225 evening and 3,576 extra-mural students; Rector Prof. I. D. DAVLYATOV.

The Environment

Tadzhikistan has been less affected than other Central Asian Republics by the consequences of over-irrigation, which have caused major environmental problems in other regions. However, there is anxiety about the effect on the extensive glaciers of the Pamir mountains of wind-borne pesticides and other chemicals from the Aral region.

ACADEMIC INSTITUTES

Academy of Sciences of the Republic of Tadzhikistan: 734025 Dushanbe, pr. Lenina 33; tel. (3772) 22-50-83; f. 1951; Pres. S. K. NEGMATULLAYEV; INSTITUTES INCL.:

  Department of Conservation and the Rational Use of Natural Resources: 734025 Dushanbe, Kommunisticheskaya 42; in the Dept of Biological Sciences; Dir K. A. NASREDDINOV.

TURKMENISTAN

Geography

The Republic of Turkmenistan, or Turkmenia, (formerly the Turkmen Soviet Socialist Republic) is situated in the south-west of Central Asia. It is bordered on the north by Uzbekistan, on the north-west by Kazakhstan and on the west by the Caspian Sea. To the south there is an international frontier with Iran and, to the south-east, with Afghanistan. The Republic has an area of 488,100 sq km (188,455 sq miles).

The Kara-Kum (Black Sand) desert, one of the largest sand deserts in the world, covers four-fifths of Turkmenistan, occupying the entire central region. There are mountainous areas along the southern and north-western borders, including the Kopet-Dag range, along the frontier with Afghanistan, which is prone to earthquakes. The major rivers are the Amu-Dar'ya (Oxus), which flows through the eastern regions of the Republic and empties into the Aral Sea, and the Murghab river, which flows south into Afghanistan. The central and western regions have no significant natural waterways. The Kara-Kum Canal, which was begun in 1954, carries water from the Amu-Dar'ya to these arid regions. The existence of this canal is one of the main factors contributing to the desiccation of the Aral Sea.

The climate is severely continental, with extremely hot summers and cold winters. The average temperature in January is −4°C (25°F), but winter temperatures can fall as low as −33°C (−27°F). In summer temperatures often reach 50°C (122°F) in the south-east Kara-Kum; the average temperature in July is 28°C (82°F). Precipitation is slight throughout much of the region. Average annual rainfall ranges from only 80 mm in the north-west to about 300 mm per year in mountainous regions.

The largest ethnic group is the Turkmen (72.0% of the total population, in 1989). Minority groups include Russians (9.5%), Uzbeks (9.0%) and Kazakhs (2.5%). Other ethnic groups include Tatars (39,245), Ukrainians (35,578), Azerbaidzhanis (33,365), Armenians (31,829) and Baluchis (an Iranian people, most of whom live in Pakistan and Iran—28,280). Among the Turkmen there remains a strong sense of tribal loyalty, reinforced by dialect. The largest tribes are the Tekke in central Turkmenistan, the Ersary in the south-east, and the Yomud in the west of the Republic. In 1990 Turkmen was declared the official language of the Republic. Russian is also used, but, in 1989, only some 25% of Turkmen claimed fluency in Russian. Turkmen is a member of the Southern Turkic group; in 1929 the traditional Arabic script was replaced by a Latin script, which was, in turn, replaced by the Cyrillic script in 1940. Most of the population are Sunni Muslims. Islam in Turkmenistan has traditionally featured elements of Sufi mysticism and shamanism, and pilgrimages to local religious sites are reported to be common.

The total estimated population at 1 January 1990 was 3,622,100. Most non-Turkmen live in urban areas: 41% of the population of Ashkhabad (Ašhabad) are Russian. The capital, Ashkhabad, is in the south of the Republic, near the border with Iran. In 1990 it had an estimated population of 407,200. Chardzou (Čaržou—161,000), situated on the Amu-Dar'ya river, is the second largest city.

History

The Turkmen are descendants of the Oghuz tribes who migrated to Central Asia in about the 10th century AD. By the 15th century, they had emerged as a distinct ethnic group, but were divided by tribal loyalties and territorial division between neighbouring powers. From the 15th to the 17th centuries the southern tribes were under Persian rule, while the north was under the suzerainty of the (Uzbek) Khanates of Khiva and Bukhara. In the early 18th century the Persians annexed Khivan and Bukharan territories, but Bukhara regained its power in the latter half of the century and retook Merv (now Mary) and deported its entire population to Bukhara. Meanwhile, the Russians had begun their expansion into Central Asia and, during the 19th century, they gradually reduced the Khanates to the status of protectorates. In 1877 the Russians began a campaign against the Turkmen, which culminated in the battle of Gök Tepe, in 1881, at which some 150,000 Turkmen are estimated to have been killed. In 1895 the Russian conquest was confirmed by agreement with the British; the international boundary thus established divided some Turkmen under Russian rule from others in the British sphere of influence.

In 1917 the Bolsheviks attempted to take power in the region, but there was little support for them among the local population. An anti-Bolshevik Russian Provisional Government of Transcaspia was formed and a Turkmen Congress was also established. Soviet forces were sent to Ashkhabad, and a Turkestan ASSR, which included Transcaspia, was declared on 30 April 1918. In July, however, nationalists, aided by British forces, overthrew the Bolshevik Government and established an independent Government in Ashkhabad protected by a British garrison. After the British withdrew, however, the Government was soon overthrown and, by 1920, the Red Army, under the control of Frunze, was in control of Ashkhabad. As part of the National Delimitation of Central Asia, the Turkmen SSR was established on 27 October 1924.

After the establishment of a Soviet Republic in Turkestan, resistance to Soviet forces continued for some years. The collectivization programme, which was begun in 1929 and entailed the forced settlement of traditionally nomadic people in collective farms, provoked further military resistance; guerrilla warfare against Soviet power continued until 1936. In 1928 a campaign against the practice of religion in Turkmenistan was launched: almost all Muslim institutions were closed, including schools, courts and mosques. In 1917 an estimated 500 mosques were functioning in the region; by 1979 only four were still operating. In the early 1930s there was a campaign among the Turkmen intelligentsia for greater political autonomy for Turkmenistan. As a result many Turkmen intellectuals were imprisoned or executed. The scope of the 'purges' widened, in the late 1930s, to include government and Party officials.

Despite the repressions, advances were made in the provision of social and health facilities among the Turkmen. Campaigns against illiteracy had a high rate of success, despite two changes in the written script of the Turkmen language. According to official figures, the level of literacy rose from 2.3% of the population, in 1926, to 99%, in 1970.

There was some small-scale industrialization of the Republic in the 1920s, but after the early 1930s there was little development in the industrial sector. Agriculture was encouraged and irrigation extended, although with little regard for the possible ecological effects. Irrigation projects such as the Kara-Kum Canal, the largest irrigation project in the USSR, enabled rapid development of cotton-growing, especially after 1945. However, the ecological consequences for the Aral Sea, to the north of the Republic, were catastrophic.

The immigration of Russians into the urban areas of Turkmenistan, during and after the 1920s, gradually diminished the proportion of Turkmen in leading posts in the Republic. In 1958 the First Secretary of the Communist Party of Turkmenistan (CPT), Babayev, proposed that Turkmen should occupy more leading positions. He was dismissed, together with many of his colleagues in government.

The major issues in Turkmenistan in the late 1980s were economic, environmental and cultural. Turkmenistan's position as a provider of raw materials (mainly natural gas and cotton) to more developed Republics, in the European parts of the USSR, provoked strong criticism of the relationship between Turkmenistan and the all-Union authorities. The environmental and health hazards connected with over-intensive agriculture, notably the cultivation of cotton, were also widely discussed in the republican media. These issues, combined with those of language and history, all provoked dissatisfaction with the relationship with the Union. However, the geographical remoteness of the Republic and its poor level of communications with other parts of the USSR inhibited its involvement in the political changes occurring in other Soviet Republics. Moreover, the lack of any history of a unified nation, together with the continuing tribal divisions, did not engender any mass movement for national autonomy, as occurred elsewhere.

In the absence of any significant democratic movement, the CPT dominated elections to the Congress of People's Deputies, in early 1989. However, in September 1989, Turkmen intellectuals met to form Agzybirlik, a popular-front style organization concerned with the status of the Turkmen language, indigenous arts in the Republic, environmental matters and economic issues. In October 1989 it was officially registered with some reluctance, but, after support for the movement had increased, it was banned in January 1990. Nevertheless, Agzybirlik's founding congress took place in February 1990. As a result of the official animosity towards the nascent democratic movement, the CPT was the only party permitted to participate in elections to the republican Supreme Soviet and local soviets in the Republic, which took place on 7 January 1990. Communist Party members won most of the seats. When the new Supreme Soviet convened Saparmuryad Niyazov was elected Chairman of the Supreme Soviet, the highest government office in the Republic.

Despite the continuing dominance of the CPT, some concessions were made to popular pressure. In May 1990 the Turkmen language was introduced as the state language; Turkmenistan was the last Republic to introduce such legislation. On 22 August 1990 the Turkmen Supreme Soviet adopted a declaration of sovereignty, which declared the Republic a zone free of nuclear and chemical weapons, and asserted the right of the Republic to determine its own political and social system and to secede from the USSR. On 27 October 1990 Niyazov was elected, by direct ballot, as President of Turkmenistan. He was unopposed in the election and received 98.3% of the votes cast.

In late 1990 and early 1991 Turkmenistan participated in negotiations towards a new Union Treaty. The backward state of the economy and the Republic's dependence on the central Government for subsidies ensured that the Republic's leadership was one of the most enthusiastic proponents for retaining the Union. When the all-Union referendum on the status of the USSR was conducted in Turkmenistan, 95.7% of all eligible voters approved the preservation of the USSR as a 'renewed federation', the highest proportion of any Soviet Republic.

There was little response in Turkmenistan to the attempted conservative coup of August 1991. President Niyazov made no public announcements either opposing or supporting the self-proclaimed 'Emergency Committee' in Moscow. The two small opposition groups, Agzybirlik and the Democratic Party, publicly opposed the coup, but when democratic groups attempted to form a coalition opposed to the coup, some opposition leaders were arrested.

Following the coup attempt, Niyazov remained in power and announced that the Communist Party would be retained as the ruling party, unlike in other Republics, where it had been suspended or dissolved (in December 1991 it changed its name to the Democrat Party of Turkmenistan). On 26 October 1991 a national referendum took place, on the issue of independence. According to the official results, 94.1% of the electorate voted for independence. On 27 October the Turkmen Supreme Soviet adopted a law on independence and declared 27 October to be Independence Day. The name of the Republic was changed from the Turkmen SSR to the Republic of Turkmenistan, and a new state emblem, flag and national anthem were adopted. On 19 October 1991 the Republic's representatives signed the Treaty on the Economic Community and the Turkmen leadership agreed to the draft proposals for a new political union, the Union of Sovereign States, in November. However, when this plan was superseded by the Commonwealth of Independent States, initially proposed by the Slav Republics, Turkmenistan indicated its wish to become a founder member. On 21 December it became a signatory of the Alma-Ata Declaration, which decision was subsequently ratified by the Supreme Soviet.

In 1991 Turkmenistan began to develop political and economic relations with several foreign countries. It has concentrated on developing contacts with its neighbour, Iran, and, in October, it was announced that Iran would establish a consulate in Ashkhabad. The Republic has attempted to retain its economic links with other former Soviet Republics, signing several bilateral trade agreements, and participating in meetings of Central Asian leaders. In common with the other Turkic Republics, it has been anxious to develop economic, cultural and political relations with Turkey (the Turkmen are related to the Turks). President Niyazov visited Turkey in late 1991.

Economy

The major sectors of the economy are petroleum and natural gas extraction and the cultivation of cotton. Petroleum and gas deposits are concentrated in western Turkmenistan and off shore, under the Caspian Sea. There are also significant deposits of potassium, sulphur and sodium chloride. The level of industrialization is low, but there are large chemical plants in Chardzou and traditional industries, such as textile production and cotton-ginning, are still of importance. Cotton is by far the most important agricultural crop, although fruit and melons are grown and also cereal and fodder crops. Karakul sheep, with their distinctive soft, curled hair, horses (Turkoman horses) and camels are bred.

The Turkmen economy is one of the the least productive of the former Soviet Republics, producing only 0.6% of total Soviet net material product (NMP) in 1988. It provided the lowest proportion of total Soviet industrial NMP (0.4%), but its extensive cotton crop forms a considerable part

(1.2%) of total Soviet agricultural NMP. In 1988 50.7% of Turkmenistan's NMP was derived from exports to other Republics and 4.2% from exports to other countries. The rate of unemployment is high, with estimates ranging from 18.8% to 40% in 1990.

Statistical Survey

Source: Academy of Sciences of Turkmenistan, Ashkhabad.

Population

BIRTHS AND DEATHS (per 1,000)

	1987	1988
Birth rate .	37.2	36.6
Death rate.	7.9	7.8

Agriculture

PRINCIPAL CROPS ('000 metric tons)

	1987	1988	1989
Grain .	354	435.3	391.8
Seed cotton	1,272	1,341	1,381
Potatoes .	n.a.	38	37
Other vegetables .	347	372	405
Grapes.	155	165	176
Other fruit .	46	50	49

LIVESTOCK ('000 head at 1 January)

	1987	1988	1989
Cattle .	776	778	807
Pigs .	229	243	268
Sheep and goats .	4,816	4,754	5,083

LIVESTOCK PRODUCTS ('000 metric tons)

	1986	1987	1989*
Meat (slaughter weight) .	90	95	101
Milk .	373	392	448
Eggs (million) .	301	318	332
Wool (greasy) .	16.0	16.0	15.3

* Figures for 1988 are not available.

Mining and Industry

Production (1989, unless otherwise stated): Oil 5,812,000 metric tons, Mineral fertilizers 204,400 metric tons, Sulphur 5,547,000 metric tons, Sodium sulphate 261,000 metric tons, Electric energy 14,460m. kWh.

Education

(1984/85)

	Institutions	Students
Secondary schools .	1,900	800,000
Secondary specialized schools .	35	36,900
Higher schools (incl. universities) .	9	38,900

Directory

The Government

(December 1991)

HEAD OF STATE

President of Turkmenistan: SAPARMURYAD A. NIYAZOV.

COUNCIL OF MINISTERS

Chairman: KHAN A. AKHMEDOV.
Deputy Chairmen: DZHORAKULY BABAKULYYEV, MERED B. ORAZOV, MATKARIM RAZHAPOV, NAZAR T. SUYUNOV, ATA CHARYYEV.
Minister of Defence: DANATAR KOPEKOV.
Minister of Foreign Affairs: AVDY KULIYEV.
Minister of Internal Affairs: V. GRININ.

MINISTRIES

All ministries are in Ashkhabad.

SUPREME SOVIET

The Supreme Soviet is the highest legislative organ in the Republic. Elections were held in February 1990 and were contested only by the Communist Party (now the Democrat Party) and its approved organizations.

Chairman: SAKHAT N. MURADOV.
Deputy Chairman: ALEKSANDR D. DODONOV.

Local Government

Turkmenistan contains five oblasts, named for the chief towns: Ashkhabad (Ašhabad); Chardzhou (Čhardžou); Krasnovodsk; Mary; and Tashauz (Tašauz).

Political Organizations

Agzybirlik: Ashkhabad; f. 1989; advocates a democratic, independent Turkmenistan.
Democrat Party of Turkmenistan: Ashkhabad; name changed from Communist Party of Turkmenistan in 1991; First Sec. of the Cen. Cttee SAPARMURYAD A. NIYAZOV; 116,000 mems (1991).
Democratic Party of Turkmenistan: Ashkhabad; f. 1990; participates in the Congress of Democratic Parties of Central Asia.
Party of Islamic Renaissance: Ashkhabad; advocates the establishment of a Muslim state; br. of what was an all-Union party.
Turkestan Party: Ashkhabad; f. 1991; advocates unification of the Central Asian Republics.

Judicial System

Chairman of the Supreme Court: N. M. YUSUPOV.
Procurator: V. M. VASILIUK.

Religion

The majority of the population are adherents of Islam. In June 1991 the Turkmen Supreme Soviet adopted a Law on Freedom of Conscience and Religious Organizations.

ISLAM

Turkmen are traditionally Sunni Muslims, but with a tradition of Sufism. Until July 1989 Ashkhabad was the only Central Asian capital without a functioning mosque. The Muslims of the Republic are officially under the jurisdiction of the Muslim Board of Central Asia, based in Uzbekistan. The Board is represented in Turkmenistan by a kazi.

Kazi of Turkmenistan: NASRULLO IBADULLAYEV.

The Press

In 1989, according to official statistics, 66 newspaper titles were being published in Turkmenistan, including 49 published in Turkmen. There were 34 periodicals, including 16 in Turkmen. All publications are in Turkmen except where otherwise stated.

PRINCIPAL NEWSPAPERS

Edebiyat ve Sungat (Literature and Art): 744604 Ashkhabad, ul. Atabayeva 20; tel. (3662) 5-30-34; f. 1958; 2 a week; publ. by the Ministry of Culture and the Union of Writers of Turkmenistan; Editor TIRKISH DZHUMAGELDIYEV.

Komsomolets Turkmenistana (Member of the Leninist Young Communist League of Turkmenia): Ashkhabad; f. 1938; 3 a week; fmrly organ of the Cen. Cttee of the Leninist Young Communist League of Turkmenistan; in Russian; Editor B. BERDIYEV.

Sovet Turkmenistani (Soviet Turkmenistan): Ashkhabad; f. 1920; 6 a week; organ of the Supreme Soviet and Council of Ministers; Editor K. ILYASOV.

Turkmenskaya Iskra (Turkmen Spark): Ashkhabad; f. 1924; 6 a week; organ of the Supreme Soviet and Council of Ministers; in Russian; Editor V. V. SLUSHNIK.

Vsegda gotov (Always Ready): Ashkhabad; in Russian.

Yash Kommunist (Young Communist): Ashkhabad; f. 1925; 3 a week; fmrly organ of the Cen. Cttee of the Young Communist League of Turkmenistan; Editor S. HANOV.

PRINCIPAL PERIODICALS

Monthly unless otherwise indicated.

Ashkhabad (City of Ashkhabad): 744000 Ashkhabad, ul. Makhtumkuli 5; tel. (3662) 09-65-44; journal of the Union of Writers of Turkmenistan; popular; in Russian; Editor V. N. POU; circ. 6,000.

Ovadan: Ashkhabad; f. 1952; for women; Editor A. B. SEITKU-LIYEVA.

Pioner (Pioneer): Ashkhabad; f. 1926; fmrly journal of the Republican Council of the Pioneer Organization of Turkmenistan; juvenile fiction; Editor A. RAKHMANOV.

Sovet Edebiyaty: 744000 Ashkhabad, ul. Makhtumkuli 5; tel. (3662) 5-14-33; journal of the Union of Writers of Turkmenistan; fiction and literary criticism; .

Tokmak (Beetle): 744000 Ashkhabad, ul. Atabayeva 20; tel. (3662) 25-10-39; f. 1925; satirical; Editor TACHMAMED DZHURDEKOV.

Turkmenistan Kommunisti (Communist of Turkmenia): Ashkhabad; f. 1925; fmrly publ. by the Cen. Cttee of the Turkmen Communist Party; Editor DZH. HODZHAYEV.

Turkmenistanyn oba Khozhalygy (Agriculture of Turkmenia): Ashkhabad; f. 1957; journal of the Ministry of Agriculture; Editor B. POLLIKOV.

NEWS AGENCY

Turkmen Press: Ashkhabad; Dir MURAD KARANOV.

Publishers

Magaryf Publishing House: Ashkhabad; Dir N. ATAYEV.

Turkmenistan Publishing House: Ashkhabad, ul. Gogolya 17A; politics and fiction; Dir A. M. DZHANMURADOV.

Ylym Publishing House: 744000 Ashkhabad, 6 ul. Engelsa; tel. (3662) 9-04-84; f. 1952; science; Dir B. M. AKMAMEDOV.

Radio and Television

State Committee for Television and Radio Broadcasting: 744024 Ashkhabad, Kurortnaya III; Pres. S. S. RAKHIMOV.

Turkmen Radio: broadcasts local programmes and relays from Moscow in Turkmen and Russian.

Turkmen Television: Ashkhabad; broadcasts local programmes and relays from Moscow in Turkmen and Russian.

Finance

BANKING

State Bank of the Republic of Turkmenistan: Ashkhabad; Chair. of Bd A. B. BORDZHAKOV.

Trade and Industry

CHAMBER OF COMMERCE

Chamber of Commerce and Industry: 744000 Ashkhabad, ul. Lakhuti 17; tel. (3662) 5-57-56; Chair. LIDIA N. OSIPOVA.

Transport

RAILWAYS

The main rail line in the Republic runs from Krasnovodsk, on the Caspian Sea, in the west, via Ashkhabad, to Chardzhou in the east. From Chardzhou one line runs to the east, to the other Central Asian Republics, while another runs north-west to join the rail network of the Russian Federation. In 1989 the total length of rail track in use was 2,120 km. In 1991 plans were approved for a rail link with Iran on the route Tedzhen–Serakhs–Mashhad. From the Iranian town of Mashhad, the railway would be able to join the Iranian rail network and thus provide the possibility of rail travel between Turkmenistan and Istanbul (Turkey).

ROADS

At 31 December 1989 there was a total of 22,600 km of roads, of which 17,800 km were hard-surfaced. In November 1991 a 600-km road was opened between Ashkhabad and Tashauz.

SHIPPING

Shipping services link Krasnovodsk with Baku (Azerbaidzhan) and the major Iranian ports on the Caspian Sea. The Amu-Dar'ya is an important inland waterway.

Shipowning Company

Middle-Asia Shipping Company: 746100 Chardzhou, Flotilskaya ul. 8; Pres. N. B. BAZAROV.

Culture

CULTURAL HERITAGE

Karl Marx State Public Library of the Republic of Turkmenistan: 744000 Ashkhabad, pl. K. Marksa; f. 1895; 4m. vols; Dir P. E. ELLYDZHEV.

Turkmen State Museum of Fine Art: 744000 Ashkhabad, ul. Pushkina 9; tel. (3662) 25-63-71; f. 1938; 60 mems; library of 6,100 vols; Dir N. SHABUNTS.

Turkmen State United Museum of History and Ethnography: Ashkhabad, ul. Shevchenko 1; tel. (3662) 5-58-16; f. 1899; 200,000 exhibits; library of 3,000 vols; Dir A. TADYEV.

PERFORMING ARTS

Makhtumkuli Opera and Ballet Theatre: Ashkhabad, ul. Engelsa 9.

Turkmen Drama Theatre: Ashkhabad, ul. Kemineh 42.

Pushkin Russian Drama Theatre: Ashkhabad, ul. 1-ovo Maya 15.

State Philharmonia of Turkmenistan: Ashkhabad, ul. Oktyabrskaya 13.

ASSOCIATION

Union of Writers of Turkmenistan: 744000 Ashkhabad, ul. Makhtumkuli 5; (3662) 5-51-78; brs in Mary, Tashauz and Chardzhou.

Education

There were few educational establishments in pre-revolutionary Turkmenistan, but a state-funded education system was introduced under Soviet rule. Most school education is conducted in Turkmen (76.9% of all pupils at general day-schools in 1988), but there are also schools using Russian (16.0%), Uzbek (6.1%) and Kazakh (1.0%). Until the early 1990s most institutions of higher education used Russian, but there have been attempts to increase the provision of Turkmen-language courses. In 1989 8.3% of the population over 15 years of age had completed courses of higher education.

UNIVERSITY

Turkmen A. M. Gorky State University: 744014 Ashkhabad, pr. Lenina 31; tel. (3662) 5-11-59; f. 1950; 10 faculties; 11,000 students; Rector Prof. S. N. MURADOV.

Social Welfare

In 1988 the average life expectancy at birth was 65.9 years, considerably less than the all-Union average of 69.5 years. In 1989 the rate of infant mortality reached 54.2 per 1,000 live births, the highest rate of any Soviet Republic. However, under-reporting of mortality rates is widespread and it is estimated that true figures may be 50%–100% higher than offically reported. A basic, state-funded health system was introduced under Soviet rule, but the system is of low quality and underfunded. The high levels of disease in Turkmenistan (among adults as well as children) are attributed to poor overall medical and sanitary conditions, and the critical state of the environment.

The Environment

Turkmenistan has experienced severe ecological problems as a result of the desiccation of the Aral Sea. From the dehydrated sea-bed of the Aral Sea large amounts of salted dust and sand are blown onto fertile areas in northern Turkmenistan, particularly in Tashauz Oblast. Excessive use of chemical pesticides and herbicides in cotton-growing areas has also caused severe problems. The chemicals enter the soil and the water supply, and, since only 13% of the population is provided with piped water, most water for domestic use is drawn directly from polluted water channels.

ACADEMIC INSTITUTES

Academy of Sciences of the Republic of Turkmenistan: 744000 Ashkhabad, ul. Gogolya 15; tel. (3662) 25-49-49; telex 228164; Pres. A. G. BABAYEV; institutes incl.:

Commission on Nature Conservation: 744000 Ashkhabad, ul. Gogolya 15; attached to the Presidium; Chair. A. O. TASHILIYEV.

Desert Research Institute: 744000 Ashkhabad, ul. Gogolya 15; tel. (3662) 29-54-27; programme incl. research into desert resources and environment; incl. International Centre for Research and Training in the Problems of Desertification; Dir A. G. BABAYEV.

Scientific Consultative Ecological Centre (EKOTSENTR): Ashkhabad, ul. Gogolya 15; Chair. A. G. BABAYEV.

UKRAINE

Geography

The Republic of Ukraine (formerly the Ukrainian Soviet Socialist Republic) is situated in east-central Europe. It is bordered by Poland, Czechoslovakia, Hungary, Romania and Moldavia to the west, by Byelorussia to the north and by the Russian Federation to the north-east and east. To the south lie the Black Sea and the Sea of Azov. Ukraine covers an area of 603,700 sq km (233,089 sq miles), greater than any other European country, except the Russian Federation.

The relief consists of a steppe lowland, bordered by uplands on the west and south-west, and by the Crimean mountains in the south. The main rivers are the Dniepr (Dnieper), which drains the central regions of the Republic and flows into the Black Sea, and the Dniestr (Dniester), which flows through Western Ukraine and Moldavia before entering the Black Sea near Odessa.

The climate is temperate, especially in the south. The north and north-west share many of the continental climate features of Poland or Byelorussia, but the Black Sea coast is noted for its mild winters. Droughts are not infrequent in southern areas. Average temperatures in Kiev range from −6.1°C (21°F) in January to 20.4°C (69°F) in July. Average annual rainfall in Kiev is 615 mm.

According to official estimates, the total population at 1 January 1991 was 51,944,000. At the 1989 census Ukrainians formed the largest ethnic group, forming 72.7% of the total population, while 22.1% were Russians. There were also significant minorities of Byelorussians, Moldavians and Poles. The official state language is Ukrainian, an Eastern Slavonic language written in the Cyrillic script. Most of the population are adherents of Christianity, the major denominations being the Ukrainian Orthodox Church (an Exarchate of the Russian Orthodox Church), the Ukrainian Autocephalous Orthodox Church and the Roman Catholic Church (mostly Greek Catholics, followers of the Uniate or Eastern rite). There are also a number of Protestant churches, and small communities of Jews and Muslims.

The capital is Kiev, which had a population of 2,602,000 in 1989, making it the third largest city in the then USSR. It is situated in the north of the country, on the River Dniepr. Other important towns include Kharkov (Kharkiv, population 1,611,000 in 1989), Dnepropetrovsk (Dnipropetrovske, 1,179,000), Odessa (Odesa, 1,115,000), Donetsk (Donetske, 1,110,000) and Lvov (Lviv, 790,000).

History

The original Russian state, Kievan Rus, was based in what is now Ukraine, and is claimed as the precursor of Russia, Byelorussia and Ukraine. Following the fall of the Rus principalities, in the 13th and 14th centuries, during the Mongol invasions, the Ukrainians (sometimes known as Little Russians or Ruthenians) developed distinctively from the other Eastern Slavs, mainly under Polish and Lithuanian rulers. Ukrainians first entered the Russian Empire in 1654, when a Cossack state east of the Dniepr sought Russian protection from Polish invasion. In 1667 Ukraine was divided: the regions east of the Dniepr became part of Russia, while Western Ukraine was annexed by Poland. Russia gained more Ukrainian lands as a result of subsequent partitions of Poland (1793 and 1795); the western regions were acquired by Austria.

When the Russian Empire collapsed, in 1917, Ukrainian nationalists set up a Central Rada (council or soviet) in Kiev and demanded Ukrainian autonomy from the Provisional Government in Petrograd (St Petersburg). After the Bolshevik coup, in October 1917, the Rada proclaimed a Ukrainian People's Republic. Although they initially recognized the new Republic, in December the Bolsheviks established a rival Government in Kharkov and, by February 1918, after a two-month military offensive, almost the whole of Ukraine was occupied by Soviet forces. One month later, however, the Bolsheviks were forced to cede Ukraine to Germany, under the terms of the Treaty of Brest-Litovsk. Ukraine was the battleground for much of the fighting in the Civil War over the next two years, but, in December 1920, a Ukrainian Socialist Soviet Republic was established.

The Treaty of Riga, which formally ended the Soviet–Polish War, in 1921, assigned Western Ukraine to Poland, Czechoslovakia and Romania, while eastern and central lands formed the Ukrainian Soviet Socialist Republic (SSR). The Ukrainian SSR was one of the founding members of the USSR, in December 1922. The 1920s were a period of national development for Ukrainians: the use of the Ukrainian language was encouraged, literacy improved and the New Economic Policy (NEP) gave the peasants a certain measure of prosperity. However, the end of the NEP, in 1928, and the introduction of collectivization of agriculture, had severe consequences for the Republic. Collectivization resulted in famine, in which an estimated 7m. Ukrainians died (although figures are disputed). The repressive policies of Stalin were also particularly severe in Ukraine. The initial aim of Stalin's policies was to end the Ukrainian national revival, which had occurred in the 1920s. Advocates of greater use of the Ukrainian language, or of more autonomy for the Republic, were labelled 'bourgeois nationalists' and arrested. By the late 1930s almost the entire Ukrainian cultural and political élite had been imprisoned, killed or exiled. Later the repressions widened to include people from all sectors of society.

The Second World War brought further suffering to Ukraine. Some 6m. Ukrainians are estimated to have died during the War and material losses were great. Soviet victory in the War did, however, unite the western and eastern areas of Ukraine and, in 1954, the territory was further expanded by the inclusion of the Crimea (formerly part of the Russian Federation), whose Tatar inhabitants had been deported *en masse* to Central Asia, in 1944.

During the 1960s there was an increase in covert opposition to the regime, manifested in the production of independent publications, known as *samizdat* (self-publishing). In 1972, however, there was widespread repression of dissidents and a purge of the membership of the Communist Party of Ukraine (CPU). In 1973 Petr Shelest, First Secretary of the CPU, who had been accused of tolerating dissent in the Republic, was replaced by Vladimir Shcherbitsky, a loyal ally of Soviet leader Leonid Brezhnev. He remained in power until 1989.

The accession of Mikhail Gorbachev to the Soviet leadership, in 1985, had little initial effect in Ukraine. The reforms which he advocated were seldom implemented in Ukraine during Shcherbitsky's rule, despite his avowed support for *perestroika*. Dissidents were still harassed by the police, independent political and cultural groups were refused legal status, and the republican media remained under the strict control of the CPU.

On 26 April 1986 a serious explosion occurred at the Chernobyl nuclear power station, in northern Ukraine. Large amounts of radioactivity leaked into the atmosphere, but information on the accident and its consequences was strictly controlled by the authorities. Only after foreign scientists reported the unusually high levels of radiation in other European countries did Soviet officials admit the full extent of the damage. Thirty-one people were killed in the initial explosion and perhaps thousands more died from acute radiation sickness. A 50-km (30-mile) exclusion zone was created around Chernobyl, from which 135,000 people were evacuated, but other affected areas were not evacuated and increased numbers of cancers and other related illnesses were reported throughout a large area.

Reaction to the secrecy surrounding the Chernobyl accident led to greater public support for opposition movements in Ukraine, which were also inspired by events elsewhere in the USSR, notably the success of the Popular Fronts in the Baltic Republics. In November 1988 the Ukrainian People's Movement for Restructuring (known as Rukh) was founded in Kiev by a group of prominent writers and intellectuals. Despite official opposition, Rukh's manifesto was published, in February 1989, and local branches were established throughout the Republic. Other independent organizations were also established in late 1988 and early 1989, including the environmental group Zeleny Svit (Green World), the Ukrainian 'Memorial' Society and the Ukrainian Democratic Union.

In 1989 the other major political force opposing the Government was the independent workers' movement, based in the mining communities of the Donbass area. Problems of housing, working conditions and food supply all contributed to a growing militancy, which produced 11 strikes in the first three months of 1989. In July miners in the Donbass joined the country-wide miners' strike which had begun in western Siberia. The miners included political issues in their list of demands, including the removal of Article 6 from the Constitution, which guaranteed the Communist Party exclusive political power, and the resignation of Shcherbitsky as leader of the CPU.

Opposition also came from religious groups. The Ukrainian Catholic Church (Uniate) and the Ukrainian Autocephalous Orthodox Church began campaigns for official recognition in 1989. In May Ukrainian Catholics began a hunger strike in Moscow; in September 150,000 Catholics marched through Lvov demanding legalization; in late October Catholics took over the Church of the Transfiguration in Lvov and held public services. Legalization was eventually granted when Soviet leader Mikhail Gorbachev met Pope John Paul II, in December.

The failure of Shcherbitsky to control the growing influence of Rukh, or to cope with the outbreak of worker unrest in mid-1989 led to his dismissal in September. Volodymyr Ivashko was elected as his replacement. Although the new leadership of the CPU began negotiations towards legalizing Rukh in late 1989, it was not registered until February 1990, after the date for nominations for the local and republican elections scheduled for 4 March. Nevertheless, candidates supported by the Democratic Bloc, a coalition of Rukh and other groups with similar aims, won 108 of the 450 seats in the Ukrainian Supreme Soviet. Independents supported by the Bloc won about 60 seats, giving the opposition parties up to 170 votes in the new Supreme Soviet, with an estimated 280 supporting the CPU leadership. The Bloc was particularly successful in western Ukraine and in urban areas (Rukh supporters took control of the city soviets of Lvov and Kiev), but performed poorly in the Russian-speaking communities of eastern Ukraine and in rural regions.

In June 1990 Vladimir Ivashko was elected Chairman of the Supreme Soviet (the highest state post in the Republic). In response to protests by deputies of the Democratic Bloc, who asserted that the Chairman of the Supreme Soviet should not also be the Party leader, he resigned later in the month as First Secretary of the CPU and was replaced by his former deputy Stanislav Hurenko. Vitaly Masol, the Chairman of the Council of Ministers, was re-elected to that office after four attempts to choose a replacement failed.

On 16 July 1990 the Ukrainian Supreme Soviet adopted a declaration of sovereignty, which asserted the right of Ukraine to have a national army and security forces, and proclaimed the supremacy of republican authority on the territory of the Republic. Also in July Volodymyr Ivashko resigned as Chairman of the Supreme Soviet, after his appointment as Deputy General Secretary of the CPSU. The new Chairman of the Supreme Soviet was Leonid Kravchuk, formerly Second Secretary of the CPU.

In October 1990 Masol was forced to resign as premier after protest marches by up to 100,000 students in Kiev, some of whom were also on hunger strike. The Supreme Soviet also agreed to meet many of the students' political demands. In November Vitold Fokin was elected to succeed Masol as Chairman of the Council of Ministers. He was seen as a compromise candidate who could unite the opposition and liberal Communists behind a programme of economic reforms.

The student protests of October 1990 and increased dissatisfaction with the progress of *perestroika* in the Republic gave an impetus to the more radical wing of Rukh. At the movement's second Congress, which took place in late October, delegates adopted complete independence of Ukraine as their main policy objective, instead of the former policy of seeking state sovereignty within a reformed USSR. Despite Rukh's support for independence, the Government participated in negotiations on a new Union Treaty and signed the protocol to a draft Treaty, in March 1991. The Government also agreed to conduct the all-Union referendum on the future of the USSR, but added an additional question to the ballot paper, asking voters if they agreed that Ukraine's 1990 declaration of sovereignty should form the basis for participation in a renewed federation. Of those eligible to vote, 84% participated in the referendum, 70% of whom approved Gorbachev's proposal to preserve the USSR as a 'renewed federation'. However, Ukraine's own question received greater support (80%), and an additional question in Western Ukraine (Lvov, Ternopol and Ivano-Frankovsk Oblasts), which asked voters if they supported a fully independent Ukraine, gained the support of 90% of those voting.

Despite the apparent support for the preservation of some sort of union demonstrated in the March referendum, demands for full implementation of Ukraine's declaration of sovereignty increased during the next few months. Separatist parties such as the Ukrainian Republican Party and the Ukrainian Peasant Democratic Party advocated full independence, acquired by parliamentary means. More radical groups, many of which united in the Ukrainian Interparty Assembly, denied the legality of Ukraine's incorporation into the USSR and advocated the restoration of the Ukrainian National Republic of 1918–19. Its parties did not recognize Soviet institutions; instead they recognized the Ukrainian Government-in-Exile, based in the USA. Meanwhile, within the CPU signs of growing differences emerged between the so-called 'National Communists', who supported moves towards more independence, and the 'Imperial Communists', who remained committed to the Union.

When the State Committee for the State of Emergency (SCSE) took power in Moscow, on 19 August 1991, there was an initially cautious response from the Ukrainian leadership. A declaration, which effectively denounced the SCSE, was adopted by the Presidium of the Supreme Soviet, on 20 August, but opposition leaders protested that the leadership had been indecisive in its response. The collapse of the coup and the subsequent banning of the CPU led to significant changes in the politics of Ukraine. On 24 August the Supreme Soviet adopted a declaration of independence, pending confirmation by a referendum on 1 December, when presidential elections were also scheduled.

Despite his past record as a loyal Communist official, Kravchuk's experience and support for Ukrainian independence ensured his election as President of the Republic on 1 December. He was aided by the divided opposition, which nominated five candidates from the different factions. Kravchuk won 62% of the votes cast. His closest rival, with 23%, was Vyacheslav Chornovil, a former dissident and the leader of the radical Lvov regional council. The declaration of independence was overwhelmingly approved. Some 84% of the electorate took part in the referendum, of which 90% voted in favour of independence.

Although Ukraine did not experience the inter-ethnic violence experienced in some other Republics, in the late 1980s and early 1990s, the ethnic diversity of the population caused serious political problems. In the Crimea, which was part of the Russian federation until 1954 and has a significant Russian majority, there was considerable opposition to Ukrainian independence. The situation was further complicated by the desire of the Crimean Tatars to return to their homeland, from which they had been forcibly deported in 1944. In a referendum, on 20 January 1991, residents of the Crimea voted to restore the region to the status of an Autonomous Republic. The decision, although it had no legal basis in current Soviet law, was ratified by the Ukrainian Supreme Soviet. The referendum was opposed by the Crimean Tatars, who claimed an exclusive right for the indigenous peoples to vote, and viewed the movement for autonomy as led by the local Russian-dominated Communist Party, which sought the status to prevent 'ukrainianization' and the influx of Tatars.

Other problems were experienced in the eastern Donbass region, where Russians were also dominant. Although there was no strong movement for secession, there was support for some autonomy for the region, with discussion on the reinstatement of the short-lived Donetsk-Krivoy Rog Republic of 1918. In the western region of Transcarpathia, which had formed parts of Czechoslovakia and Hungary before the Second World War, the independence referendum of 1 December 1991 included a separate question on the introduction of autonomous status for the region. In the Hungarian-dominated Beregovo rayon there was an additional question concerning the establishment of a Hungarian autonomous district. Although, at the census of 1989, Ukrainians formed 78.4% of the population in Transcarpathia, there was also a significant Hungarian minority (12.5%). Demands for the establishment of a Transcarpathian Autonomous Oblast have been made especially strongly by the Society of Carpathian Ruthenians (Rusyns), who consider themselves ethnically distinct from Ukrainians.

Even before the independence referendum, on 1 December 1991, Ukraine had begun establishing political and economic links with other countries. The leadership concentrated on relations with neighbouring countries, especially Hungary and Poland, and countries in which there are significant Ukrainian minorities, such as the USA and Canada. Following the approval of independence in the December referendum, many countries indicated that they would recognize Ukraine as an independent country and establish diplomatic relations. Poland, Hungary and Canada were the first countries to do so; other states, including the USA, expressed reluctance to extend recognition until the Ukrainian Government could clarify its policies on nuclear weapons and on its ethnic minorities. Ukraine's cause was helped by its existing membership of the UN (granted after the Second World War, effectively to allow the USSR more voting rights). Relations with Romania were complicated by Romania's continued territorial claims to Northern Bukovina (now Chernovtsy Oblast) and Southern Bessarabia (the southern part of Odessa Oblast, between Moldavia and the Black Sea), which were annexed from Romania in 1940. These claims were also popular in Moldavia.

The Ukrainian leadership was reluctant to sign any union agreement with the other former Soviet Republics which might compromise its declaration of independence. Although Ukraine eventually signed the Treaty of the Economic Community, on 6 November 1991, it refused to enter any new political union, such as the proposed Union of Sovereign States. Instead, on 8 December, in Minsk, together with the leaders of the Russian Federation and Byelorussia, President Kravchuk agreed to establish a Commonwealth of Independent States, which would have very limited central powers. On 21 December 11 of the former Republics of the USSR formally committed themselves to membership of the new Commonwealth. However, there were considerable difficulties over the details of the agreements, particularly in relation to the armed forces. Ukraine had reluctantly agreed to a unified command for a Commonwealth successor to the Soviet armed forces, but had reserved the right to form its own national guard. The size of this force caused some controversy, particularly with the Russian Federation, which had been generally acknowledged internationally as the successor state to the USSR. In January 1992 the main dispute was over control of the Black Sea fleet; it was eventually decided to split the fleet, despite the reservations of its commanders.

Economy

According to Western estimates, in 1989 Ukrainian gross national product (GNP) was US $240,000m. Ukraine was a major source of economic resources and production within both the Russian Empire and the USSR. Its mineral resources include large deposits of coal (mainly in the huge Donbass coalfield), high grade iron ore, manganese, lignite peat and mercury. Unlike Russian resources in Siberia, Ukraine's mineral deposits are favourably located and easily accessible. The chemical industry is important for the production of acids, soda, alkaline dyes and fertilizers. More than 25% of Soviet machinery was produced in Ukraine. Products include locomotives, railway equipment, tractors and other heavy-duty vehicles, automobiles and machine tools.

Ukraine is an important agricultural producer, providing 17.1% of total Soviet agricultural net material product (NMP) in 1988. In 1986 the area of cultivated land was 48.6m. ha. Major crops include wheat, sugar beet, cotton, flax, tobacco, soya, fruit and vegetables. Cattle and pig breeding are also important. In 1987 there were 2,466 state farms and 7,452 collective farms.

In 1988 Ukraine provided 16.3% of total Soviet NMP, including 16.7% of total industrial NMP. Deliveries to other Republics provided 39.1% of Ukrainian NMP in 1988. In the same year exports to other countries contributed 7.4% of Ukrainian NMP.

Statistical Survey

Source: State Committee of Ukraine for Statistics, Kiev.

Population

BIRTHS AND DEATHS (per 1,000)

	1988	1989	1990*
Birth rate	14.4	13.3	12.7
Death rate	11.6	11.6	12.1

* Figures are provisional.

Agriculture

PRINCIPAL CROPS ('000 metric tons)

	1988	1989	1990
Sugar beet.	42,112	51,917	44,264
Grain	47,388	53,186	53,167
Flax fibre	91	111	108
Sunflower seed . . .	2,775	2,885	2,725
Potatoes	13,510	19,308	16,732
Other vegetables . . .	7,292	7,443	6,666
Grapes.	662	789	836
Other fruit. . . .	2,225	2,500	2,902

LIVESTOCK ('000 head at 1 January)

	1989	1990	1991
Cattle	25,621	25,195	24,636
Pigs	19,471	19,947	19,392
Sheep and goats . . .	9,243	9,003	8,400

LIVESTOCK PRODUCTS ('000 metric tons)

	1988	1989	1990
Meat (slaughter weight) . .	4,395	4,430	4,306
Milk	24,229	24,377	24,535
Eggs (million)	17,672	17,393	16,414
Wool (greasy)	30.2	30.1	29.6

Mining and Industry

Production (1990): Hard coal 155,532,000 metric tons, Brown coal 9,280,000 tons, Crude petroleum 5,252,100 tons, Natural gas 28,082,100m. cu m, Paper 369,208 tons, Cement 22,729,000 tons, Iron ore 104,982,400 tons, Rolled steel products 38,610,129 tons, Motor cars 195,421, Tractors 106,221, Electric energy 294,800m. kWh.

Education

(1990/91)

	Institutions	Students
Secondary schools	21,825	7,131,800
Secondary specialized institutions . .	742	757,000
Higher schools (incl. universities) . .	149	881,300

Directory

The Government

(December 1991)

HEAD OF STATE

President: LEONID M. KRAVCHUK (elected 1 December 1991).

CABINET OF MINISTERS

Chairman: VITOLD P. FOKIN.

First Deputy Chairman: KONSTANTIN MASYK.

Deputy Chairman: OLEKSANDR MASELSKYY.

Minister of Agricultural Construction: VIKTOR LEMESH.

Minister of Communications: VOLODYMYR DELIKATNY.

Minister of Culture: LARYSA KHOROLETS.

Minister of Defence: KONSTANTIN MOROZOV.

Minister of the Defence Complex and Military Conversion: VIKTOR ANTONOV.

Minister for Destatization of Property and the Demonopolization of Production: VIKTOR SALNIKOV.

Minister of State for the Economy: ANATOLY MINCENKO.

Minister for the Elimination of the Consequences of the Chernobyl Disaster: HRYHORIY HOTOVCHYTS.

Minister of External Affairs: A. M. ZLENKO.

Minister of External Economic Relations: VALERY KRAVCHENKO.

Minister of Finance: O. M. KOVALENKO.

Minister of Forests: V. I. SAMOPLAVSKY.

Minister of Health Protection: YU. P. SPIZHENKO.

Minister of Higher Education: PETR TALANCHUK.

Minister of State for Questians of Humanitarian Policy: NIKOLAY ZHULINSKY.

Minister of State for Matters of Industry and Transport: VIKTOR D. HLADUSH.

Minister of Internal Affairs: ANATOLIY VASYLYSHYN.

Minister of State for Issues of Investment Policy: VOLODOMYR BORYSOVSKY.

Minister of Justice: V. F. BOYKO.

Minister of Light Industry: GRIGORY NIMITENKO.

Minister of National Education: IVAN ZYAZYUN.

Minister of Power Engineering and Electrification: V. F. SKLYAROV.

Minister of State for Issues of Property and Entrepreneurship: VOLODYMYR LANOVYY.

Minister for the Protection of the Environment: YURY SHCHERBAK.

Minister of Statistics: M. I. BORYSENKO.

Minister of Trade: O. I. SLEPICHEV.

Minister for Youth and Sports Affairs: VALERIY BORZOVA.

Minister, Chair of National Security Service: YEVGENY MARCHUK.

MINISTRIES

Cabinet of Ministers: 252008 Kiev, vul. Kirova 42/2; tel. (044) 293-52-27.

Ministry of Agricultural Construction: c/o State Committee for Agriculture, 252601 Kiev, vul. Kreshchatik 24; tel. (044) 228-00-10.

Ministry of Communications: Kiev, vul. Kreshchatik 22; tel. (044) 226-21-40.

Ministry of Culture: Kiev, vul. Franka 19; tel. (044) 226-25-23.

Ministry of Defence: Kiev.

Ministry of the Defence Complex and Military Conversion: Kiev.

Ministry of External Affairs: Kiev, vul. Karla Libknikhta 15/1; tel. (044) 226-33-79; fax (044) 293-44-88.

Ministry of External Economic Relations: Kiev, vul. Pushkinska 4; tel. (044) 212-29-51; fax (044) 212-52-71.

Ministry of Finance: Kiev, vul. Kirova 12/2; tel. (044) 293-53-63.

Ministry of Forests: Kiev, vul. Kreshchatik 34; tel. (044) 226-32-53.

Ministry of Health Protection: Kiev, vul. Kirova 7; tel. (044) 226-22-05.

Ministry of Higher Education: Kiev, vul. Kreshchatik 34; tel. (044) 226-32-31.

Ministry of Internal Affairs: Kiev, vul. Bogomoltsa 10; tel. (044) 291-33-33.

Ministry of Justice: Kiev, vul. Katsubsinskovo 12; tel. (044) 226-24-16.

Ministry of Light Industry: Kiev.

Ministry of National Education: Kiev, vul. K. Marksa 13; tel. (044) 226-26-61.

Ministry of Power Engineering and Electrification: Kiev, vul. Kreshchatik 30; tel. (044) 226-30-27.

Ministry for the Protection of the Environment: Kiev.

Ministry of Trade: Kiev, Lvovskaya pl. 8; tel. (044) 212-52-02.

Ministry for Youth and Sports Affairs: Kiev.

Service of National Security of Ukraine: Kiev.

President and Legislature

PRESIDENT

Election, 1 December 1991

Candidate				Votes	% of total
Leonid M. Kravchuk	.	.	.	19,643,481	61.59
Vyacheslav M. Chornovil	.	.	.	7,420,727	23.27
Levko G. Lukyanenko	.	.	.	1,432,556	4.49
Vladimir B. Grinov	.	.	.	1,329,758	4.17
Ihor P. Yukhnovsky	.	.	.	554,719	1.74
Leopold I. Taburyansky	.	.	.	182,713	0.57

SUPREME SOVIET

The Supreme Soviet (or Supreme Council) is the highest legislative body in Ukraine. It comprises 450 deputies, who were elected in March 1990.

Chairman: Ivan Plyushch.

Local Government

Ukraine is divided into 24 oblasts and one Autonomous Republic.

CRIMEAN AUTONOMOUS SOVIET SOCIALIST REPUBLIC

Chairman of the Presidium of the Supreme Soviet: Nikolay Bagrov.

Political Organizations

In August 1991 the Communist Party of Ukraine was suspended.

Green Party: Kiev; Chair. Yury Shcherbak.

People's Party of Ukraine: Kiev; Chair. Leopold I. Taburyansky.

Rukh (People's Movement of Ukraine): Kiev; f. 1989; political movement including several political parties; Chair. Ivan Drach; 632,828 mems (1990).

Ukrainian Peasant Democratic Party: Lvov-58, vul. 700-richya Lvova 63, kv. 213; tel. 59-96-71; f. 1990; Chair. S. Plachynda; Deputy Chair. V. Pleshko; 3,256 mems (1990).

Ukrainian Republican Party: Kiev; f. 1990 as successor to Ukrainian Helsinki Union (f. 1988); advocates independence, democracy and a market economy; Chair. Levko Lukyanenko.

Union of Ukrainian Students: Kiev; f. 1991; Chair. Volodymyr Cheremys.

Judicial System

Chairman of the Supreme Court: A. N. Yakimenko.
Procurator: Viktor Shishkin.

Religion

CHRISTIANITY

Roman Catholicism

Metropolitan See of Lvov (Latin Rite): Lubaczów, Poland; Archbishop Marian Jaworski.

Ukrainian (Uniate) Catholic Church: Lvov, St George's Cathedral; established in 1596 by the Union of Brest, which permitted Orthodox clergymen to retain the Eastern rite, but transferred their allegiance to the Pope; at the 'Lviv Sobor' (Synod of Lvov), in 1946, the Uniates were forcibly integrated into the Russian Orthodox Church, but continued to function in an 'underground' capacity; it uses the Eastern Orthodox liturgies and rites, but acknowledges the primacy of the Pope; recognized in 1990 and its congregations registered in the manner of all other denominations; Hon. Chair. of Synod of Uniate Bishops His Holiness Pope John Paul II; Chair. of Cen. Cttee Josyp Terelya (in Toronto), Ivan Gell (in Ukraine); an estimated 4m.–5m. adherents; Archbishop-Major of Lviv (Lvov) Cardinal Myroslav Lubachivsky.

The Eastern Orthodox Church

Ukrainian Autocephalous Orthodox Church: established in 1921 as part of the wider movement for Ukrainian autonomy, but in 1930 it was forcibly incorporated into the Russian Orthodox Church; it re-emerged in the late 1980s, but remained unrecognized by the Russian Orthodox Church; Patriarch Mstyslav.

Ukrainian Orthodox Church: formerly an Exarchate of the Russian Orthodox Church, still owes ultimate allegiance to the Moscow Patriarchate; Metropolitan of Kiev Filaret.

The Press

In 1989 there were 1,763 officially-registered newspaper titles being published in Ukraine, of which 1,241 were in Ukrainian. There were also 203 periodicals, 96 in Ukrainian.

PRINCIPAL NEWSPAPERS

Democratychna Ukraina (Democratic Ukraine): 252047 Kiev-47, pr. Peremogi 50; tel. (044) 441-85-46; f. 1918; fmrly *Radyanska Ukraina* (Soviet Ukraine); fmrly organ of the Communist Party of Ukraine, the Supreme Soviet and Council of Ministers; 6 a week; independent; in Ukrainian; Editor V. Y. Stadnichenko; circ. 311,300.

Holos Ukrainy (Voice of Ukraine): Kiev; organ of the Supreme Council; in Ukrainian and Russian; supplements in other languages used in Ukraine.

Koza (Goat): Kiev; fmrly *Komsomolskoe Znamya* (Komsomol Banner).

Literaturna Ukraina: 252601 Kiev-601, bul. Lesi Ukrainki 20; tel. (044) 296-36-39; f. 1927; weekly; organ of the Union of Writers of Ukraine; Editor-in-Chief Vasil Plyushch.

Narodnaya Armiya (National Army): Kiev; fmrly *Leninskoe Znamya* (Leninist Banner); organ of the Ministry of Defence.

News from Ukraine: 252055 Kiev, vul. Artema 91; f. 1964; weekly; publ. by the Association for Cultural Relations with Ukrainians Abroad; in English; readership in 70 countries; Editor V. P. Kanash; circ. 20,000.

Pravda Ukrainy (Ukrainian Pravda): Kiev; f. 1938; 6 a week; organ of the Supreme Council; Editor A. T. Zonenko; circ. 358,300.

Rabochaya Gazeta/Robitnycha Hazeta (Workers' Gazette): Kiev-47, pr. Pobedy 50; tel. (044) 441-83-33; fax (044) 446-68-85; f. 1957; 5 a week; Chief Editor E. V. Babenko; publ. by the Cabinet of Ministers; editions in Russian and Ukrainian; Editor N. A. Shibik; circ. 317,700 (1991).

Silski Visti (Rural News): Kiev; f. 1920; 6 a week; fmrly publ. by the Cen. Cttee of the Ukrainian Communist Party; in Ukrainian; Editor I. V. Spodarenko; circ. 2,530,500.

Za Vilnu Ukrainu: Lvov, vul. Timiryazeva 3; tel. 72-25-64; fax 72-95-27; f. 1990; 5 a week; publ. by Lvov Regional Council; Editor-in-Chief Vasil Baziv; circ. 459,470.

Zemlia i Volia (Land and Freedom): Lvov-58, vul. 700-richya Lvova 63, kv. 213; tel. 59-96-71; f. 1991; organ of the Ukrainian Democratic Peasant Party.

PRINCIPAL PERIODICALS

Barvinok (Periwinkle): 252119 Kiev, vul. Parkhomenko 38–44; tel. (044) 211-04-98; f. 1928; 2 a month; publ. by the Molod (Youth) Publishing House; fmrly journal of the Cen. Cttee of the Leninist Young Communist League and the Republican Council of the V. I. Lenin Pioneer Organization of Ukraine; illustrated popular fiction for school-age children; in Ukrainian and Russian; circ. 1,000,000.

Berezil; (March): 310078 Kharkov, bul. Chernyshevskovo 59; tel. (044) 43-41-84; f. 1956; fmrly *Prapor;* monthly; publ. by the Berezil (March) Publishing House; journal of Union of Writers of Ukraine; fiction; in Ukrainian; Editor-in-Chief L. Toma; circ. 10,000.

Dnipro (The Dniepr River): 252119 Kiev, vul. Parkhomenko 38–44; tel. (044) 213-98-79; f. 1927; monthly; publ. by the Molod (Youth) Publishing House; fmrly journal of the Cen. Cttee of the Leninist Young Communist League of Ukraine; novels, short stories, essays, poems by young Ukrainian authors; social and political topics; in Ukrainian; circ. 71,900.

Donbass (The Donets Coal Basin): 340055 Donetsk, vul. Artema 80A; tel. 93-82-26; f. 1923; 12 a year; journal of Union of Writers of Ukraine; fiction; in Ukrainian and Russian; circ. 20,000 (1991).

Dzvin (Bell): 290005 Lvov, vul. Vatutina 6; tel. 72-36-20; f. 1940; monthly; publ. by the Kamenyar Publishing House; journal of Union of Writers of Ukraine; fiction; in Ukrainian; Editor ROMAN FEDORIV; circ. 152,500.

Kiev: 252025 Kiev, vul. Desyatinna 11; tel. (044) 229-02-80; f. 1983; monthly, publ. by the Radyansky Pismennik (Soviet Writer) Publishing House; journal of the Union of Writers of Ukraine and the Kiev Writers' Organization; fiction; in Ukrainian; Editor-in-Chief PETR M. PEREBEINOS; circ. 39,600.

Kommunist Ukrainy (Communist of Ukraine): 252009 Kiev, vul. Ordzhonikidze 8; tel. (044) 291-57-72; f. 1925; monthly; publ. by the Radyanska Ukraina (Soviet Ukraine) Publishing House; political; in Ukrainian and Russian; circ. 21,700 in Ukrainian, 11,200 in Russian.

Lyudina i Svit (Man and World): 254025 Kiev, 10 Rylsky provulok; tel. (044) 228-23-87; f. 1960; monthly; publ. by the Radyanska Ukraina (Soviet Ukraine) Publishing House; journal of the Ukrainian Society Znanye (Knowledge); popular scientific; religious; in Ukrainian; Editor-in-Chief MIKOLA RUBANETS; circ. 46,000.

Malyatko (Child): 252119 Kiev, vul. Parkhomenko 38–44; tel. (044) 213-98-91; f. 1960; monthly; publ. by the Molod (Youth) Publishing House; illustrated; for pre-school children; in Ukrainian; Editor-in-Chief SVETLANA YEFIMENKO; circ. 530,000 (1991).

Muzyka (Music): 252601 Kiev, vul. Yanvarskovo Vosstaniya 21, kor. 20; tel. (044) 290-49-70; f. 1923; 6 a year; organ of the Ministry of Culture, of the Union of Ukrainian Composers and the Musicians' Society of Ukraine; musical culture and aesthetics; in Ukrainian; circ. 8,200.

Nauka i Suspilstvo (Science and Society): 252047 Kiev, pr. Pobedy 50; tel. (044) 441-88-10; f. 1923; monthly; publ. by the Radyanska Ukraina (Soviet Ukraine) Publishing House; journal of the Ukrainian Society Znanye (Knowledge); popular scientific; illustrated; in Ukrainian; Editor-in-Chief YURY ROMANYUK; circ. 48,800.

Novini Kinoekranu (Screen News): 252033 Kiev, vul. Saksaganskovo 6; tel. (044) 227-47-07; f. 1961; monthly; journal of the the Ukrainian Union of Cinematographers; cinema criticism and information; in Ukrainian; circ. 410,000.

Obrazotvorche Mistetstvo (Fine Arts): 252015 Kiev, vul. Yanvarskovo Vosstaniya 21, kor. 20; tel. (044) 290-47-51; f. 1935; 6 a year; publ. by the Mistetstvo (Fine Art) Publishing House; journal of the Ministry of Culture and the Artists' Union of Ukraine; fine arts; in Ukrainian; circ. 5,500.

Odnoklassnnik (Classmate): 252119 Kiev, vul. Parkhomenko 38-44; tel. (044) 211-02-78; f. 1923, fmrly *Pioneriya:* fmrly journal of the Cen. Cttee of the Leninist Young Communist League (Democratic Youth League) of Ukraine; monthly; fiction; for 10–15-year-olds; in Ukrainian and Russian; Editor-in-Chief SERGEI CHIRKOV; circ. 206,050 in Ukrainian, 130,350 in Russian.

Perets (Pepper): 252047 Kiev, vul. P. Nesterova 4; tel. (044) 441-82-14; f. 1927; fortnightly; publ. by the Radyanska Ukraina (Soviet Ukraine) Publishing House; satirical; circ. 1,946,900.

Politika i Chas (Politics and Time): 252009 Kiev, vul. Ordzhonikidze 6-8; tel. (044) 291-52-96; f. 1941, fmrly *Pid Praporom Leninismu;* fortnightly; publ. by the Radyanska Ukraina (Soviet Ukraine) Publishing House; political; in Russian and Ukrainian; circ. 47,000.

Raduga (Rainbow): 252047 Kiev, vul. Pobedy 50; tel. (044) 224-91-98; f. 1950; monthly; publ. by the Radyansky Pismennik (Soviet Writer) Publishing House; journal of the Union of Writers of Ukraine; fiction and politics; in Russian; circ. 51,140.

Radyanska Zhinka (Soviet Woman): 252047 Kiev, pr. Peremogi 50; tel. (044) 441-83-67; f. 1920; monthly; publ. by Radyanska Ukraina (Soviet Ukraine) Publishing House; social and political subjects; fiction; for women; in Ukrainian; circ. 1,000,000.

Ranok (Morning): 252119 Kiev, vul. Parkhomenko 38–42; tel. (044) 213-15-96; f. 1953; monthly; publ. by the Molod (Youth) Publishing House; fmrly journal of the Cen. Cttee of the Leninist Young Communist League of Ukraine; for young people; social, political and fiction; in Ukrainian; circ. 105,000.

Start (Start): 252033 Kiev, vul. Tarasovska 6; tel. (044) 224-71-20; f. 1922; monthly; publ. by the Molod (Youth) Publishing House; organ of the State Cttee for Sports and Physical Culture; sports news; in Ukrainian; circ. 115,000.

Ukraina (Ukraine): 252047 Kiev, Peremohy pr. 50; tel. (044) 441-88-31; f. 1941; weekly; publ. by the Radyanska Ukraina (Soviet Ukraine) Publishing House; social and political life in Ukraine; illustrated; in Ukrainian; Editor-in-Chief ANATOLY MIKHAILENKO; circ. 70,000.

Ukrainsky Teatr (Ukrainian Theatre): Kiev, vul. Yanvarskovo Vosstaniya 21, kor. 20; tel. (044) 290-79-49; f. 1936; 6 a year; publ. by the Mistetstvo (Fine Art) Publishing House; journal of the Ministry of Culture and the Union of Theatrical Workers of Ukraine; in Ukrainian; Editor-in-Chief TAMARA ANUFRIENKO; circ. 4,100.

Visti z Ukrainy (News from Ukraine): Kiev-34, Zoloti Vorota 6; tel. (044) 229-65-71; fax (044) 228-04-28; f. 1932; monthly; aimed at Ukrainian diaspora; Editor VALERY STETSENKO.

Vitchizna (Fatherland): 252021 Kiev, vul. Kirova 34; tel. (044) 293-28-51; f. 1933; monthly; publ. by the Radyansky Pismennik (Soviet Writer) Publishing House; journal of the Union of Writers of Ukraine; Ukrainian prose and poetry; in Ukrainian; circ. 50,100.

Vsesvit (All the World): 252021 Kiev, vul. Kirova 34; tel. (044) 293-13-18; f. 1925; monthly; publ. by the Radyansky Pismennik (Soviet Writer) Publishing House; joint edition of the Union of Writers of Ukraine, the Ukrainian Society of Friendship and Cultural Relations with Foreign Countries and the Ukrainian Peace Council; foreign fiction, critical works and reviews of foreign literature and art; in Ukrainian; Editor-in-Chief OLEG MIKITENKO; circ. 60,000.

Znannya ta Pratsya (Knowledge and Labour): 252047 Kiev, vul. Parkhomenko 38–42; tel. (044) 211-02-51; f. 1929; monthly; publ. by the Molod (Youth) Publishing House; fmrly journal of the Leninist Young Communist League of Ukraine; popular science and technology; in Ukrainian; circ. 28,000.

NEWS AGENCY

RATAU (Ukrainian Telegraph Agency): Kiev.

Ukrainian Press Agency: 252190 Kiev, vul. Sonyachna 14; tel. (044) 449-04-26; fax (044) 449-04-26; independent news agency.

Publishers

In 1989 there were 8,449 book titles (including pamphlets and brochures) published in the Republic (total circulation, 189.5m.), including 1,934 in Ukrainian (95.2m.).

Berezil (March): 310002 Kharkov, vul. Chubarya 11; tel. (044) 47-72-52; fiction and criticism; in Ukrainian and Russian; Dir A. M. KUMAKA.

Budivelnik (Building): 254053 Kiev, Observatorna vul. 25; tel. (044) 212-10-90; f. 1947; books and journals on building and architecture; in Ukrainian and Russian; Dir S. N. BALATSKY.

Carpathy (Carpathian Mountains): 294000 Ushgorod, Radyanska pl. 3; tel. 3-25-13; fiction and criticism; in Ukrainian and Russian; Dir V. I. DANKANICH.

Dnipro (The Dnepr River): 252601 Kiev, Vladimirska vul. 42; tel. (044) 224-31-82; f. 1919; fiction, poetry and critical works; in Ukrainian and Russian; Dir TARAS I. SERGIYCHUK.

Donbass (The Donets Coal Basin): 340002 Donetsk, vul. Khmelnitskovo 102; tel. 93-25-84; fiction and criticism; in Ukrainian and Russian; Dir B. F. KRAVCHENKO.

Kamenyar (Stonecrusher): 290006 Lvov, vul. Pidvalna 3; tel. 72-19-49; fiction and criticism; in Ukrainian; Dir M. V. NECHAY.

Mayak (Lighthouse): 270001 Odessa, vul. Zhukovskovo 14; tel. 22-35-95; fiction and criticism; in Ukrainian and Russian; Dir D. A. BUKHANENKO.

Mistetstvo (Fine Art): 252034 Kiev, vul. Zolotovoritska 11; tel. (044) 225-53-92; fax (044) 229-05-64; f. 1932; fine art criticism, theatre and screen art; in Ukrainian, Russian, English, French and German; Dir VALENTIN M. KUZMENKO.

Molod (Youth): 252119 Kiev, vul. Parkhomenko 38-44; tel. (044) 213-11-60; fmrly publishing house of the Cen. Cttee of the Leninist Young Communist League of Ukraine; books and periodicals; in Ukrainian; Dir A. I. DAVIDOV.

Muzichna Ukraina (Music of Ukraine): 252004 Kiev, Pushkinska vul. 32; tel. (044) 225-63-56; f. 1966; books on music; in Ukrainian; Dir N. P. LINNIK; Chief Editor B. R. VERESHCHAGIN.

Naukova Dumka (Scientific Thought Publishing House): 252601 Kiev, vul. Repina 3; tel. (044) 224-40-68; fax (044) 224-70-60; f. 1922; scientific books and periodicals in all branches of science; research monographs; in Ukrainian, Russian and English; Dir YU. A. KHRAMOV.

Politvidav Ukrainy (Ukraine Publishing House): 254025 Kiev, vul. Desyatinna 4/6; tel. (044) 229-16-92; academic, reference and popular works; law, social and economic issues, religion; calendars, posters, etc.; in Ukrainian, Russian and other European languages; Dir G. F. NEMAZANY.

Radyanska Shkola (Soviet School): 252053 Kiev, Kotsubinskovo vul. 5; tel. (044) 216-58-02; textbooks for secondary schools; Dir A. F. DENISOV.

Radyansky Pismennik (Soviet Writer Publishing House): 252054 Kiev, vul. Chkalova 52; tel. (044) 216-25-92; f. 1933; fiction; in Ukrainian; Dir V. P. SKOMAROVSKI.

Sich: 320070 Dnepropetrovsk, K. Marx pr. 60; tel. 45-22-01; f. 1964; fiction, juvenile, socio-political, criticism; in Ukrainian, English, German, French and Russian; Dir V. A. SIROTA; Editor-in-Chief V. V. LEVCHENKO.

Tavria: 330000 Simferopol, vul. Gorkovo 5; tel. 7-45-66; fiction and criticism; in Ukrainian and in Russian; Dir I. N. KLOSOVSKY.

Tekhnika (Technical Publishing House): 252601 Kiev, vul. Khreshchatik 5; tel. (044) 228-22-43; f. 1930; industry and transport books, popular science, posters and booklets; in Russian and Ukrainian; Dir M. G. PISARENKO.

Ukrainska Radyanska Encyclopedia (Ukrainian Soviet Encyclopaedia): 252030 Kiev, vul. Lenina 51; tel. (044) 224-80-85; encyclopaedias, dictionaries and reference books; Dir A. V. KUDRITSKY.

Urozhai (Crop Publishing House): 252034 Kiev, Yaroslavov val 10; tel. (044) 220-16-26; books and journals about agriculture; Dir V. G. PRIKHODKO.

Veselka (Rainbow Publishing House): 252050 Kiev, vul. Melnikova 63; tel. (044) 213-82-55; f. 1934; books for pre-school and school age children; in Ukrainian and foreign languages; Dir YAREMA HOYAN.

Vyscha Shkola (Higher School): 252054 Kiev, Gogolevska vul. 7; tel. (044) 216-33-05; f. 1968; educational, scientific, reference, etc.; Dir V. P. TARANIK.

Zdorovya (Health Publishing House): 252601 Kiev, vul. Chkalova 65; tel. (044) 216-89-08; books on medicine, physical fitness and sport; in Ukrainian; Dir A. P. RODZIYEVSKY.

Radio and Television

State Committee for Television and Radio: Kiev, vul. Khreshchatik 26; tel. (044) 228-42-08; radio broadcasts in Russian and Ukrainian; also broadcasts to Europe and North America in Ukrainian.

Finance

BANKING
State Banks

National Bank of Ukraine: 252007 Kiev, Zhovtnevoji Revolyutsiji 9; tel. (044) 293-42-64; fax (044) 293-16-98; Chair of Board VOLODYMYR MATVIYENKO; Vice-Chairman Dr OLEKSANDR SAVCHENKO.

Ukrbank: 252001 Kiev-1, vul. Kreshchatik 8; tel. (044) 229-75-52; fmrly br. of USSR Vneshekonombank; deals with foreign firms, joint ventures and import-export associations.

Commercial and Co-operative Banks

Commercial Bank for Development of Construction Materials Industry: Kiev, vul. Artyoma 73; tel. (044) 216-75-95.

Commercial Bank for Development of Light Industry in Ukraine (Ukrlegbank): 252023 Kiev, vul. Kuybysheva 8/10; tel. (044) 220-81-36.

Joint-Stock Commercial 'Personal Computer' Bank (Perkombank): Kiev, vul. Severo-Siretska 1; tel. (044) 449-94-58.

Kiev Narodny Bank: Kiev-1, vul. Sofiyevska 1; tel. (044) 228-39-45.

Kievcoopbank: Kiev-5, vul. Anry Barbyusa 9; tel. 268-32-04.

Ukrainian Commercial Bank (Transformatorbank): 330600 Zaporozhye, Dnepropetrovskoe shosse 11; tel. 59-56-01.

Ukrainian Republican Joint-Stock Innovation Bank (Ukrinnbank): Kiev-1, vul. Malopodavalna 8; tel. (044) 229-38-04.

Zapadkoopbank: Ivano-Frankovsk; tel. 2-32-35; cap. 650,000 roubles; Dep. Chair. NELA POLITIKO.

COMMODITY EXCHANGES

Dnepropetrovsk Commodity Exchange (DCE): 320006 Dnepropetrovsk, 3 Turbinny Spusk; tel. (044) 42-03-14; f. 1991; Gen. Man. VADIM KOMEKO.

Kharkov Commodity and Raw Materials Exchange (KHCME): 310022 Kharkov, Office 307, Gosprom; tel. (0572) 47-82-78; fax (0572) 22-82-01; f. 1991; Chair. of Exchange Cttee: ZAKHAR BRUK.

Kiev Universal Commodity Exchange (KUCE): 252015 Kiev, 1A Leyptsigskaya ul.; tel. (044) 290-27-14; f. 1990; Pres. NIKOLAY DETOCHKA.

Odessa Commodity Exchange (OCE): 270114 Odessa, 43 Leninskoy Iskri proyezd; tel. (044) 44-81-56; f. 1991; Gen. Man. ANATOLY GLUSHKOV.

South Universal Commodity Exchange (SUCE): 327017 Nikolayev, ul. Pushkinskaya 73; tel. (044) 36-91-82; telex 36-08-52; f. 1990; Gen. Dir NIKOLAY KOZHEMYAKIN.

Trade and Industry
CHAMBERS OF COMMERCE

Chamber of Commerce and Industry: 252055 Kiev, ul. Bolshaya Zhitomirskaya 33; tel. (044) 212-29-11; telex 131379; fax (044) 212-33-53; nine brs; Chair. ALEKSEY P. MIKHAILICHENKO.

Congress of Business Circles of Ukraine: 252601 Kiev, vul. Proresnaya 15; tel. (044) 228-64-81; fax (044) 229-63-76; Pres. VALERY G. BABICH.

Lehteks: Kiev, vul. Kuybisheva 8/10; tel. (044) 226-21-05; f. 1991 as successor to the State Cttee for Light Industry; state corporation, uniting manufacturers of light industrial products.

FOREIGN TRADE ORGANIZATION

Ukrimpex: 252054 Kiev, ul. Vorovskovo 22; tel. (044) 216-21-74; telex 131384; fax (044) 216-29-96; imports and exports a wide range of goods; organizes joint ventures, exhibitions; provides marketing expertise and business services; Dir-Gen. STANISLAV I. SOKOLENKO.

MAJOR INDUSTRIAL ENTERPRISES

Avtozaz Production Association: 330063 Zaporozhye, Leninsky pr. 8; tel. 64-36-89; telex 127437; fax 64-54-53; produces small passenger cars; Gen. Dir STEPAN I. KRAVCHUN; 20,000 employees.

Azovmash: 341035 Mariupol, pr. Ilyicha 145/147; tel. 47261; telex 115172; Gen. Dir ANATOLY E. ANTIFEYEV; 37,000 employees.

Belotserkovshina Production Association: 256400 Kiev, Belaya Tserkov, pr. Lenina 91; tel. (044) 5-54-39; telex 131486; manufactures tyres for cars, trucks, etc.; Gen. Dir YURY V. KRASOTKIN; 13,000 employees.

Chemical Reagent Plant: 257036 Cherkassy; tel. 43-21-63; development and manufacture of chemical reagents; Dir VALENTIN V. BYHOV; 3,000 employees.

Dnepropetrovsky Industrial Corporation: 320600 Dnepropetrovsk, vul. Shchepkina 53; tel. (0562) 42-22-10; fax (0562) 59-02-37; manufacture and sale of hydraulics, centrifugal pumps and vacuum cleaners; Dir Gen. VITALY ZAVGORODNY; 7,000 employees.

Donetsk Excavator Plant: 346338 Donetsk; tel. 5-22-32; telex 123235; produces excavators for use in industry, agriculture, etc; Plant Dir ALBERT V. KRUGLOV; 4,000 employees.

Donetskgormash Industrial Association: 340005 Donetsk, 1 vul. Tkachenko 189; tel. 61-45-08; fax 63-14-76; telex 115114; research, design and production of mining equipment; Gen. Man. VLADIMIR F. OSMERIK.

Electric Machine Building Plant: 325000 Kherson, vul. Ushakov 57; tel. 2-62-68; telex 273134; produces starter motors and alternators for car, tractor and motorcycle engines, car engine fans, etc; Dir Z. I. GORLOVSKY; 3,000 employees.

Kamenka Engineering Plant: Cherkasskoy obl., 258450 Kamenka, vul. Lenina 40; tel. 2-14-55; telex 147685; manufactures industrial pumps; Plant Dir ALEKSANDR V. ZHEVCHENKO; 2,500 employees.

Karpatpressmash Production Association: 284023 Ivano-Frankovsk, Yunosti vul. 16; tel. 2-34-83; design and manufacture of metal-plate pressing machinery, washing machines and a wide range of other consumer goods; Gen. Dir NIKOLAY SHINKARENKO; 3,600 employees.

Kharkov Tractor Plant: 310007 Kharkov, Moskovsky pr. 275; tel. (057) 93-00-69; telex 115163; fax (057) 94-17-60; production of all types of tractors; Dir NIKOLAY A. PUGHIN.

Khimprom Industrial Association: Donetsk obl., 343204 Slavyansk, vul. Chubarska 91; tel. (6262) 3-33-49; fax (6262) 2-99-04; production of various chemical products, including detergents, fire extinguishing powders, soda products, etc.; Dir EDVARD E. KRECH; 5,000 employees.

Mayak Kiev Plant: 252073 Kiev, pr. Krasnikh Kozakov 8; tel. (044) 435-12-44; fax (044) 410-26-67; telex 131068; manufacture of audio equipment; Dir NIKOLAY I. PIVEN; 7,100 employees.

Preobrazovatel: 330069 Zaporozhye, Dnepropetrovskoye Shosse; tel. (0612) 52-71-31; fax (0612) 52-03-71; telex 127446; manufacture of power-conversion equipment and electrical household appliances; Gen. Dir MIKHAIL D. KOBLITSKY; 7,000 employees.

Stankiev Machine-Tool Production: 252062 Kiev, pr. Pobedy 67; tel. (044) 449-97-46; fax (044) 443-79-86; telex 131426; production of automatic lathes and other machinery; Chair. YURY E. ZABRODSKY; 7,000 employees.

Ukrelektromash Scientific and Industrial Association: 310005 Kharkov, Iskrinskaya ul. 37; tel. (057) 21-45-50; fax (057) 21-84-92; telex 115170; produces electric motors; Gen-Dir NIKOLAY P. BELOUS.

Vinnitsa Plant of Tractor Units: 287100 Vinnitsa, Kotsubinsky 4; tel. 7-05-15; telex 119173; specializes in the production of hydraulic gear pumps and cylinders, and high-pressure hoses; Gen. Dir VLADIMIR A. BEDENKO.

Yuzhelektromash: Kakhovka obl., 326840 Novaya Kakhovka-3, Pervomaiskaya ul. 35; tel. 4-23-80; design and manufacture of electric motors; Gen. Dir DMITRY I. MOTSYO; 11,000 employees.

Co-ordinating Organizations

Exchange Union of Ukraine (EUU): Ukraine, 252015 Kiev, 1A Leyptsigskaya ul.; tel. (044) 290-27-14; Pres. NIKOLAY DETOCHKA.

Headquarters of Congress of Exchanges in Kiev: Ukraine, 252601 Kiev, 15 Proreznaya ul.; tel. (044) 294-91-38.

Transport

RAILWAYS

In 1989 there were 22,730 km of railway track in use, with lines linking most towns and cities in the Republic. Kiev is linked by rail to all the other Republics, and there are direct international lines to Warsaw (Poland), Budapest (Hungary) and Bucharest (Romania).

ROADS

In 1989 there was a total of 247,300 km of roads, of which 201,900 were hard-surfaced.

SHIPPING

The main ports are Yalta and Yevpatoriya in the Crimea, and Odessa. In addition to international shipping lines, there are services to the Russian ports of Novorossiysk and Sochi, and Batumi and Sukhumi in Georgia. The River Dniepr is the most important inland waterway.

River Authorities

Principal Board of Fishing (Glavrybkhoz): Kiev, ul. Artyoma 45A; tel. (044) 216-62-42.

State Board of River Shipping (Glavrechflot): Kiev, ul. Nizhny Val 51; tel. (044) 226-24-92.

Shipowning Companies

Azov Shipping Company: 341010 Mariupol, pr. Admirala Lunina 89; tel. 5-80-33; telex 115156; Pres. A. I. BANDURA.

Black Sea Shipping Company: 270026 Odessa, ul. Lastochkina 1; telex 232711; Pres. V. V. PILIPENKO.

Danube Shipping Company: 272630 Izmail, pr. Suvorova 2; telex 232817; Pres. A. F. TEKHOV.

CIVIL AVIATION

Ukraine has air links with cities throughout the former USSR and with several major European and North American cities.

Civil Aviation Board: Kiev, ul. Pobedy 14; tel. (044) 226-3163.

Tourism

The Black Sea coast of Ukraine has several popular resorts, including Odessa and Yalta. The Crimean peninsula is a popular tourist centre in both summer and winter, owing to its temperate climate. Kiev and Odessa have important historical attractions. The tourist industry is little developed outside Kiev and the Black Sea resorts, and the number of hotels and other facilities is low.

Association of Foreign Tourism: Kiev, ul. Yroslavov Val 36; tel. (044) 212-55-70; VLADIMIR I. SKRINNIK.

Culture

NATIONAL ORGANIZATION

Ministry of Culture: see section on The Government (Ministries).

CULTURAL HERITAGE

Historical and Architectural State Museum, 'Sofiysky Museum': 252601 Kiev, ul. Vladimirskaya 24; tel. (044) 228-67-06; f. 1934; Curator VALENTINA N. ACHKASOVA.

Kamenets-Podolsk State Historical Museum-Preserve: Khmelnitskaya obl., Kamenets-Podolsk, ul. K. Marksa 20; Dir K. G. MIKOLAIOVICH.

Kiev Lesya Ukrainka State Literature Museum: 252032 Kiev, ul. Saksaganskovo 97; tel. (044) 220-57-52; f. 1962; library of 5,000 vols; Dir IRINA L. VEREMEYEVA.

Kiev-Pechersky State Historical Museum: Kiev, ul. Yanvarskogo Vosstaniya 21; large collection of icons.

Kiev State Historical Museum: Kiev, ul. Vladimirskaya 2; 53,000 exhibits; Dir I. E. DUDNIK.

Kiev State Museum of Russian Art: Kiev, ul. Repina 9; tel. (044) 224-82-88; f. 1922; 10,000 exhibits; library of 17,000 vols; Dir M. N. SOLDATOVA.

Kiev State Museum of Ukrainian Art: Kiev, ul. Kirova 6; 11,000 items; Dir V. F. YATSENKO.

Kiev State Museum of Western and Oriental Art: Kiev, ul. Repina 15; 16,000 items; Dir V. F. OVCHINNIKOV.

Kiev T. G. Shevchenko State Museum: Kiev, bul. Shevchenko 12; 21,000 exhibits; Dir E. P. DOROSHENKO.

Lvov Historical Museum: Lvov, pl. Rynok 4/6; tel. 74-33-04; f. 1893; 300,000 exhibits; Dir B. N. CHAIKOVSKY.

Odessa Archaeological Museum: Odessa, ul. Lastochkina 4; tel. (048) 22-01-71; f. 1825; about 200,000 items; library of some 24,000 vols; Dir V. P. Vantchugov.

State Public Library of the Republic of Ukraine: 252001 Kiev, ul. Kirova 1; f. 1866; 3,391,000 vols; Dir A. P. KORNIENKO.

Ukrainian Museum of Folk and Decorative Art: Kiev, ul. Yanvarskovo Vosstaniya 21; f. 1954; 54,834 exhibits; library of 3,180 vols; Dir V. G. NAGAY.

Ukrainian State Museum of Theatrical, Musical and Cinematographic Art: Kiev 15, Sichnevoho Povstanya 21/24; 190,000 exhibits; Dir V. A. KOZIENKO.

PERFORMING ARTS

Ivan Franko Ukrainian Drama Theatre: Kiev, 3 pl. Franko.

Lesya Ukrainka Russian Drama Theatre: 5 ul. Lenina.

Taras Shevchenko Opera and Ballet Theatre: Kiev, ul. Vladimirskaya 50.

Ukrainian Puppet Theatre: Kiev, 13 ul. Rustaveli.

Ukrainian State Philharmonia: Kiev, 2 Vladimirsky Spusk.

ASSOCIATION

Union of Writers of Ukraine: 252008 Kiev, ul. Ordzhonikidze 2; tel. (044) 93-45-86; incl. 25 regional Writers' Organizations.

Education

The reversal of perceived 'russification' of the education system was one of the prinicipal demands of the opposition movements which emerged in the late 1980s. In the period 1980–88 the proportion of pupils who were taught in Russian increased from 44.5% to 51.8%, while the proportion taught in Ukrainian decreased from 54.6% to 47.5%. After Ukrainian was adopted as the state language, in 1990, policies were adopted to ensure that all pupils were granted the opportunity of tuition in Ukrainian. In 1988 there was also tuition in Romanian (0.6% of all school pupils), Hungarian (0.3%) and a small number of pupils were taught in Polish. In the early 1990s there were significant changes to the curriculum, with more emphasis on Ukrainian history and literature. Some religious and private educational institutions were established in 1990–91, including a private university, the Kiev Mihyla Academy, which had been one of Europe's leading educational establishments before 1917.

UNIVERSITIES

Chernovtsy State University: 274012 Chernovtsy, vul. Kotsyubinskovo 2; tel. 2-62-35; telex 149193; f. 1875; languages of instruction: Russian and Ukrainian; 13 faculties; 585 teachers; 9,750 students; Rector S. S. KOSTYSHIN.

Dnepropetrovsk State University: 320625 Dnepropetrovsk, pr. Gagarina 72; tel. 3-16-71; telex 1280; f. 1918; 12 faculties; 950 teachers; 12,345 students; Rector Prof. V. F. PRISNYAKOV.

Donetsk State University: 340055 Donetsk, vul. Universitetska 24; tel. 93-30-28; telex 115102; f. 1965; languages of instruction: Russian and Ukrainian; 11 faculties; 562 teachers; 12,000 students; Rector V. P. SHEVCHENKO.

Kharkov State University: 310077 Kharkov, pl. Dzerzhinskovo 4; tel. (057) 45-61-96; f. 1805; languages of instruction: Russian, Ukrainian; 15 faculties, research institutes; 1,020 teachers; 12,000 students; Rector I. YE. TARAPOV.

Kiev T. G. Shevchenko State University: 252601 Kiev, Vladimirska vul. 64; tel. (044) 266-54-77; f. 1834; 18 faculties, 12 institutes; 1,700 teachers; 20,000 students; Rector Dr M. U. BELY.

Lvov Ivan Franko State University: 290602 Lvov, Universitetska vul. 1; tel 72-20-68; language of instruction: Ukrainian; f. 1661; 14 faculties; 700 teachers; 13,000 students; Rector N. G. MAKSIMOVICH.

Odessa State University: 270057 Odessa, vul. Petra Velikovo 2; tel. (048) 23-52-54; telex 232229; f. 1865; languages of instruction: Russian and Ukrainian; 10 faculties; 800 teachers; 12,000 students; Rector Prof. I. P. ZELINSKY.

Simferopol State University: 333036 Simferopol, Yaltinska vul. 4; tel. 23-22-80; telex 861; f. 1918; 9 faculties; 500 teachers; 6,600 students; Rector V. G. SIDYAKIN.

Uzhgorod State University: 294000 Uzhgorod, vul. M. Gorkovo 46; tel. 3-42-02; f. 1945; 9 faculties; 8,000 students; Rector V. I. LENGYEL.

Zaporozhe State University: 330600 Zaporozhe, vul. Zhukovskovo 66; tel. 64-45-46; telex 127764; f. 1985; languages of instruction: Russian and Ukrainian; 6 faculties; 301 teachers; 5,000 students; Rector Prof. V. A. TOLOK.

The Environment

An explosion at the Chernobyl nuclear power station in April 1986 resulted in serious contamination of many areas in the Ukraine, as well as in many other European countries. In addition, as well as 31 killed in the initial explosion, many people, possibly thousands, died from radiation sickness and related diseases. The incident, and particularly the secrecy surrounding it and the subsequent decontamination operation, led to the formation of several environmental campaigning and political organizations.

GOVERNMENT ORGANIZATIONS

Ministry for Protection of the Environment: see section on The Government (Ministries).

ACADEMIC INSTITUTES

Ukrainian Academy of Sciences: 252601 Kiev, ul. Vladimirskaya 54; tel. (044) 225-22-39; telex 131376; fax (044) 224-32-43; f. 1918; Pres. B. E. PATON; attached instits incl.:

Ukrainian State Steppe Reservation: Donetsk oblast, Khomutovo, Novoazov rayon; in the Dept of General Biology; has some environmental responsibilities; Dir A. P. GENOV.

NON-GOVERNMENTAL ORGANIZATIONS

Zeleny Svit (Green World): 252137 Kiev, vul. Belgorodska 8, kv. 55; f. 1988; ecological asscn of various Ukrainian groups; affiliated to Rukh and to the Ukrainian Peace Council's campaign against nuclear power; Chair. YURY SCHERBAK.

Ukrainian Green Party: f. 1990 as political wing of Zeleny Svit; advocates the priority of ecology over economy; supports claims for Ukrainian sovereignty and neutrality.

UZBEKISTAN

Geography

The Republic of Uzbekistan (formerly the Uzbek Soviet Socialist Republic) is located in Central Asia. It is bordered by the Republics of Kazakhstan, to the north, Turkmenistan, to the south, Kyrgyzstan, to the east, and Tadzhikistan to the south-east. There is a short international frontier with Afghanistan in the south. Uzbekistan covers an area of 447,400 sq km (172,741 sq miles). The Kara-Kalpak Autonomous Republic forms part of Uzbekistan.

Much of the land is desert, including the south-west part of the Kyzyl Kum desert, but the western reaches of the Tien Shan range extend into the south-east of the Republic. The Syr-Dar'ya and the Amu-Dar'ya are the two major rivers; they flow from the mountainous south-east to the Aral Sea in the north-west and provide most of Uzbekistan's irrigation needs.

The climate is marked by extreme temperatures and low levels of precipitation. Summers are long and hot with average temperatures in July of 32°C (90°F); daytime temperatures often exceed 40°C (104°F). During the short winter there are frequent severe frosts and temperatures can fall as low as −38°C (−36°F).

Uzbeks form the largest ethnic group in the Republic (71.4% of the total population in 1989); the remainder includes Russians (8.3%), Tadzhiks (4.7%), Kazakhs (4.1%) and Tatars (2.4%). Other ethnic groups include Karakalpaks (411,878), most of whom are resident in the Kara-Kalpak Autonomous Republic, Crimean Tatars (188,772), who were deported from their homeland in 1944, Koreans (183,140), Kirghiz (174,907), Ukrainians (153,197), Turkmen (121,578) and Turks (106,302). According to unofficial figures, there were some 200,000 Arabs in Kaskadarin Oblast, in 1990. Islam is the predominant religion. Most Uzbeks are Sunni Muslims (Hanafi school), but there are small communities of Wahhabis, whose influence is reported to be growing. There are also Orthodox Christians among the Slavic communities, and some 65,000 European Jews and 28,000 Central Asian Jews. The official language is Uzbek, a member of the Eastern Turkic language group. Since the 1940s it has been written in Cyrillic and is closely related to modern Uighur. In the early 1990s there was some support for a return to the Latin script (in use 1930–40) or the Arabic script (in use until 1930). Minority communities continued to use their own languages and Russian was still widely used in business and official circles, although, in 1989, only 49% of Uzbeks claimed fluency in Russian.

According to official estimates, the total population at 1 January 1991 was 20,708,000, and the population density was 46.3 persons per sq km. In 1989 41% of the population lived in urban areas. The capital is Tashkent, which was the USSR's fourth largest city in 1990, with an estimated population of 2,093,900. Other important urban centres are the historic towns of Samarkand (366,000 in 1989) and Bukhara (224,000), and Nukus (169,000), the capital of the Kara-Kalpak Autonomous Republic.

History

The Uzbeks are descendants of nomadic Mongol tribes who mixed with the sedentary inhabitants of Central Asia, in the 13th century AD. In the 18th and 19th centuries the most prominent political formations in the territory were the khanates of Bukhara, Samarkand and Kokand. Russian conquest of the region between the Syr-Dar'ya and the Amu-Dar'ya was completed when Russian forces conquered the Khanate of Kokand, in 1876.

Soviet power was first established in Tashkent in November 1917. The Turkestan ASSR was proclaimed, in April 1918, but Soviet forces then withdrew against opposition from the nationalist *basmachi* movement, the White Army and a British expeditionary force. Soviet power was re-established, in September 1919, although armed opposition continued until the early 1920s. Bukhara and Khiva became nominally independent People's Soviet Republics, in 1920, but were incorporated into Turkestan by 1924. On 27 October 1924 the Uzbek Soviet Socialist Republic was established, including, until 1929, the Tadzhik ASSR. In 1936 the Kara-Kalpak ASSR was transferred from the RSFSR (Russian Federation) to the Uzbek SSR, retaining, however, its autonomous status.

The National Delimitation of the Central Asian Republics of 1924–25 created an Uzbek nation-state for the first time. Its formation was accompanied by the creation of corresponding national symbols, including the development of a new literary language (the ancient Uzbek literary language, Chatagai, was accessible only to a small minority of the population). Campaigns promoting literacy were an integral part of the establishment of the Soviet ideology in the region, and the level of literacy rose from 3.8%, at the 1926 census, to 52.5% in 1932. There was an increase in the provision of educational facilities, which formed an important part in the policy of secularization in the region. The campaign against religion, initially promoted by educational means, became a repressive policy against all who admitted their adherence to Islam. Muslim schools, courts and mosques were closed and Muslim clergy were subject to persecution.

There had been little industrial development in Central Asia under the Tsarist regime, although the extraction of raw materials was developed. Under the first two Five-Year Plans (1928–33 and 1933–38), however, there was considerable economic growth, aided by the immigration of skilled workers from the Slavic Republics. Although economic growth continued at quite high rates after the Second World War (when Uzbekistan's industrial base was enlarged by the transfer of industries from the war-zone), most Uzbeks continued to lead a traditional rural life style, affected only by the huge increase in the amount of cotton grown in the Republic.

The policies of *glasnost* and *perestroika* introduced by Soviet leader Mikhail Gorbachev in the 1980s did not result in significant political changes in the short term. The traditional respect for authority and the relatively small intelligentsia in the Republic allowed the leadership to hinder, or actively oppose, attempts at political or economic reform. Nevertheless, there was some greater freedom of the press in the late 1980s, allowing discussion of previously unexamined aspects of Uzbek history and contemporary ecological and economic problems. The poor condition of the environment was one major source of popular dissatisfaction. The over-irrigation of land to water the vast cotton-fields caused both salination of the soil and, most importantly, the desiccation of the Aral Sea, the southern part of which is in the Kara-Kalpak Autonomous Republic, and is a vital element in the ecology of the entire region. By the early 1980s it was evident that excessive drainage of the Amu-Dar'ya and Syr-Dar'ya rivers was resulting in dangerously low levels of water reaching the Aral Sea. The problem was not addressed, however, until the introduction of *glasnost* in the media.

Environmental problems and the status of the Uzbek language were among the issues on which Uzbekistan's first major non-Communist political movement, Birlik (Unity), campaigned. It was formed in late 1989, by a group of intellectuals in Tashkent, but quickly grew to be the main challenger to the ruling Communist Party of Uzbekistan (CPUz). However, the movement was not granted official registration, and its attempts to nominate a candidate in the 1989 elections to the all-Union Congress of People's Deputies were unsuccessful. Nevertheless, its campaign for recognition of Uzbek as the official language of the Republic led to the adoption of legislation, in October 1989, which declared Uzbek to be the state language.

On 18 February 1990 elections were held to the Uzbek Supreme Soviet. Members of Birlik were not permitted to stand as candidates and many leading members of the CPUz stood unopposed, as had been the tradition in old-style Soviet elections. In such constituencies there were isolated protests by opposition groups. The new Supreme Soviet convened in March 1990 and elected Islam Karimov to the newly-created post of executive President. Shak-urulla Mirsaidov was elected Chairman of the Council of Ministers (premier). In November 1990 there was a reorgan-ization of government. The Council of Minsters was abol-ished and replaced by a Cabinet of Ministers, headed by the President of the Republic. The post of Chairman of the Council of Ministers was abolished, and Shakurulla Mirsaidov was appointed to the newly-established post of Vice-President. In early January 1992, however, the post of Vice-President was abolished (Mirsaidov was appointed State Secretary under the President) and the post of pre-mier re-established.

In April 1991 Uzbekistan agreed, together with eight other Republics, to sign a new Union Treaty. However, on 19 August, the day before the signing was to take place, a State Committee for the State of Emergency (SCSE) attempted to stage a *coup d'état* in Moscow. President Karimov did not initially oppose the coup, and some oppo-sition leaders in Uzbekistan were temporarily detained. However, once it was clear that the coup had failed, Kari-mov declared that the orders of the SCSE were invalid. On 31 August, after the coup had collapsed, an extraordinary session of the Supreme Soviet voted to declare the Republic independent and changed its name to the Republic of Uzbekistan.

After its declaration of independence, Uzbekistan attempted to develop relations with other former Soviet Republics and with other countries. Foreign relations con-centrated on developing relations with Turkey, while relations with other Republics were largely limited to ties with the other Central Asian Republics. Uzbekistan signed the Treaty of the Economic Community in October 1991, and, in November, agreed to a draft of the proposed Union of Sovereign States. These agreements were nullified by the agreement between the three Slavic Republics, in early December, to establish a Commonwealth of Independent States (CIS). On 13 December Uzbekistan, together with the other four Central Asian Republics, agreed to join the CIS, providing it would be acknowledged as a co-founder of the Commonwealth. Uzbek membership was formalized at a ceremony in Alma-Ata, on 21 December, when Karimov agreed, together with 10 other republican leaders, to dis-solve the USSR and formally establish the CIS.

In June 1989 inter-ethnic conflict was reported between Uzbeks and the Meskhetian Turk minority. The origins of the conflict were unclear, but seemed to stem from high levels of unemployment and the shortage of housing in the Fergana Oblast. During a two-week period in early June at least 100 people died during rioting, most of them Meskhetians (see also p. 390). In February and March 1990 there was a resurgence of inter-ethnic conflict. On 3 March, in Parkent, near Tashkent, three people died after clashes between demonstrators and the police. There was further inter-ethnic tension in connection with clashes in Osh, a city in Kyrgyzstan with an Uzbek majority, in June 1990. Border crossings were sealed to prevent up to 15,000 armed Uzbek citizens crossing the Kirghiz–Uzbek border to join their co-nationals in Kyrgyzstan. Karimov declared a state of emergency in Andizhan Oblast (which borders Kyr-gyzstan's Osh Oblast).

Economy

Uzbekistan contains considerable mineral wealth, including huge reserves of natural gas, significant deposits of coal, petroleum and several other minerals, including gold, uran-ium, copper, tungsten and aluminium ore. Industry is con-centrated on extraction and processing of these minerals, but also includes machine-building, power-generation, chemical and iron and steel industries. Light industry includes textiles, cotton-ginning, food-processing and con-sumer goods.

Agriculture is dominated by the cultivation of cotton. Other crops include jute, grain, fruits and vegetables, and grapes. Uzbekistan was the USSR's main producer of kanaf, a plant used to make sacking. Pigs and sheep are important; the latter are bred for their astrakhan pelts.

In 1988 Uzbekistan's net material product (NMP) was officially estimated to be 20,625m. roubles, equivalent to 3.3% of the USSR's total NMP. In industry Uzbekistan contributed only 2.3% of total Soviet industrial NMP, but provided 5.2% of total agricultural NMP. Unlike its neigh-bours, Kyrgyzstan and Kazakhstan, Uzbekistan made little effort to implement economic reforms in the early 1990s. However, the expected reduction of subsidy payments from central government, on which Uzbekistan was long depend-ent, made certain changes inevitable.

Statistical Survey

Source: State Committee of Uzbekistan on Publishing, 700000 Tashkent.

Population

BIRTHS AND DEATHS (per 1,000)

	1985	1988	1989
Birth rate	37.2	35.1	33.3
Death rate	7.2	6.8	6.3

Birth rate (per 1,000): 37.8 in 1986; 36.9 in 1987.

Agriculture

PRINCIPAL CROPS ('000 metric tons)

	1987	1988	1989
Grain (except maize and rice) .	1,821.9	607.0	1,640.8
Maize (grain only) . . .	420.5	520.3	460.6
Rice (paddy)	532.5	617.0	483.7
Seed cotton	4,858.0	5,365.2	5,292.3
Potatoes	261.5	308.4	324.6
Other vegetables . . .	2,557.6	2,759.9	2,584.6
Grapes.	637.6	655.0	416.1
Other fruit	595.2	627.5	548.3

LIVESTOCK ('000 head at 1 January)

	1988	1989	1990
Cattle	4,080.3	4,130.3	4,180.2
Pigs	761.2	728.6	742.9
Sheep and goats . . .	8,479.7	8,721.8	8,785.6

LIVESTOCK PRODUCTS ('000 metric tons)

	1987	1988	1989
Meat (slaughter weight) . .	403.0	439.6	477.8
Milk	2,614.5	2,836.6	2,929.3
Eggs (million) . . .	2,186.2	2,333.9	2,429.1
Wool (greasy) . . .	24.3	25.2	24.4

Mining and Industry

Production (1989): Paper 25,700 metric tons, Cardboard 56,100 metric tons, Plastics 158,100 metric tons, Sulphuric acid 2,641,900 metric tons, Mineral fertilizers 1,899,900 metric tons, Coal 2,673,000 metric tons, Gas 41,092m. cu m, Electric energy 55,900m. kWh.

Education

(1989/90)

	Institutions	Students
Secondary schools	8,329	4,649,000
Secondary specialized schools . . .	244	277,300
Higher schools (incl. universities) . .	44	331,600

Directory

The Government

(December 1991)

HEAD OF STATE

President of the Republic: ISLAM (ISLOM) A. KARIMOV.

Presidential elections took place on 29 December 1991 and were won by Karimov, who was uncontested, with 86% of the votes cast. On 8 January 1992 the post of Vice-President was abolished (SHAKURULLA MIRSAIDOV became State Secretary) and that of Chairman of the Cabinet of Ministers (hitherto a function performed by the President) re-established.

CABINET OF MINISTERS

Chairman (Prime Minister): ABDULKHASHIM MUTALOV.
Minister of Communications: KALIMDZHAN RAKHIMOV.

Minister of Construction: KUDRATILLA KH. MAKHAMADALIYEV.
Minister of the Construction-Materials Industry: TAKHIR YA. SHARIPOV.
Minister for Defence Affairs: Maj.-Gen. RUSTAM U. AKHMEDOV.
Minister of Education: KAMEL YUSUPOV.
Minister of Finance: E. D. BAKIBAYEV.
Minister of Foreign Affairs: UBAIDULLA ABDURAZZAKOV.
Minister of Health: SAIDZHALA M. BAKHRAMOV.
Minister of Higher and Specialized Secondary Education: SHAVKAT A. ALIMOV.
Minister of Housing Services: VIKTOR K. MIKHAILOV.
Minister of Internal Affairs: VYACHESLAV M. KAMALOV.
Minister of Justice: MIRZAULUK E. ABDUSALAMOV.
Minister of Light Industry: ANVAR S. IKRAMOV.
Minister of Local Industry: VIKTOR A. CHZHEN.
Minister of Motor Transport: LERIK AKHMETOV.
Minister of Roads: RUSTAM R. YUNUSOV.
Minister of Public Services: (vacant).
Minister of Social Welfare: SANOBAR A. KHODZHAYEVA.
Minister of Special Construction Work: PULAT NUGMANOV.
Minister of Trade: MIRABROR Z. USMANOV.
Minister of Water Resurces: RIM A. GINIYATULLIN.

MINISTRIES

Ministry of Communications: Tashkent, ul. A. Tolstovo 1; tel. (3712) 33-65-03.
Ministry of Construction: Tashkent, ul. Proletarskaya 17; tel. (3712) 33-77-25.
Ministry of the Construction-Materials Industry: Tashkent, ul. 2-ya Akhunbabayeva 68; tel. (3712) 55-49-65.
Ministry of Defence: Tashkent.
Ministry of Education: Tashkent, alleya Paradov 5; tel. (3712) 39-47-38.
Ministry of Finance: Tashkent, alleya Paradov 6; tel. (3712) 33-70-73.
Ministry of Foreign Affairs: Tashkent.
Ministry of Grain Products: Tashkent, ul. Lakhuti 36; tel. (3712) 33-27-25.
Ministry of Health: Tashkent, ul. Navoi 12; tel. (3712) 41-16-80.
Ministry of Higher and Specialized Secondary Education: Tashkent, alleya Paradov 5; tel. (3712) 39-15-00.
Ministry of Housing Services: Tashkent, ul. Uritskovo 1; tel. (3712) 35-80-70.
Ministry of Internal Affairs: Tashkent, ul. Germana Lopatina 1; tel. (3712) 33-95-32.
Ministry of Justice: Tashkent, ul. A. Kadiry 1; tel. (3712) 41-42-33.
Ministry of Light Industry: Tashkent, alleya Paradov 6; tel. (3712) 33-65-37.
Ministry of Local Industry: Tashkent, alleya Paradov 6; tel. (3712) 39-15-19.
Ministry of Motor Transport: Tashkent, ul. Shirokaya 6; tel. (3712) 33-61-48.
Ministry of Roads: Tashkent, ul. Pushkina 68A; tel. (3712) 39-14-06.
Ministry of Public Services: Tashkent, ul. 1-vo Maya 3; tel. (3712) 33-43-66.
Ministry of Social Welfare: Tashkent, ul. Babura 20A; tel. (3712) 53-53-71.
Ministry of Special Construction Work: Tashkent, ul. Engelsa 25; tel. (3712) 34-75-78.
Ministry of Trade: Tashkent, alleya Paradov 6; tel. (3712) 33-49-71.
Ministry of Water Resources: Tashkent, ul. A. Kadiry 5A; tel. (3712) 41-13-53.

State Committees

State Committee for the Economy: Tashkent; Chair. MAKHMUDDOV.
State Committee for Foreign Trade and Relations with Foreign Countries: Chair. SULTONOV.
State Committee for Labour and Social Affairs: Tashkent, ul. Abaya 4; tel. (3712) 33-79-13. Chair. KHAMIDULLA KH. GULYAMOV.
State Committee for Nature Conservation: Tashkent, ul. A. Kadiry 5A; tel. (3712) 41-08-81; Chair. TIMUR A. ALIMOV.

State Planning Committee: Tashkent, Dom pravitelstva; tel. (3712) 39-80-65; Chair. KHAMIDOV BAKHTIYAR.

National Security Service: Tashkent; tel. (3712) 33-56-48; Chair. ANATOLY S. MORGASOV.

Legislature

SUPREME SOVIET

The Supreme Soviet, which is comprised of 550 members, is the supreme legislative organ in the Republic. The majority of deputies elected in 1990 were members of the Communist Party. In late 1991 20 were members of the opposition party Erk; the remainder were mainly members of the newly-formed People's Democratic Party of Uzbekistan.

Chairman: SHAVKAT YULDASHEV.

Local Government

Uzbekistan contains one Autonomous Republic (the Kara-Kalpak Autonomous Republic), 10 oblasts (regions) and 149 rayons. In January 1992 a reorganization of local government provided for the post of khokim to be established; a khokim was to head the executive and representative organs in each oblast, rayon and town, being accountable to the appropriate soviet and to the republican President.

Political Organizations

Birlik (Unity): c/o Union of Writers of Uzbekistan, 700000 Tashkent, ul. Pushkina 1; tel. (3712) 33-79-21; f. 1989; advocated secession from the USSR; Chair. Prof. ABDUL RAHMID PULATOV.

Erk (Freedom): Tashkent; f. 1990; advocates economic and political independence for Uzbekistan within the framework of a renewed federation; Chair. MUHAMMAD SOLIKH; 5,000 mems (1991).

Islamic Democratic Party: Tashkent; f. 1990.

People's Democratic Party of Uzbekistan: Tashkent; f. 1991 to replace Communist Party of Uzbekistan; Leader ISLAM A. KARIMOV.

People's Front of Uzbekistan: Tashkent.

The activities of the following group were banned under legislation adopted in 1991, which prohibited the formation of religious political parties.

Islamic Renaissance Party (IRP): Tashkent; advocates introduction of a political system based on the tenets of Islam; br of all-Union IRP.

Judicial System

Chairman of the Supreme Court: M. IBRAGIMOV.

Procurator: B. MUSTAFAYEV.

Religion

ISLAM

In January 1992 it was reported that Mufti Muhammad-Sadyk Muhammad-Yusuf had resigned. However, it was later reported that he remained in office.

Muslim Religious Board of Central Asia: Tashkent-55, ul. Khamzy 109, Barak Khan Madrasah; Chair. MUHAMMAD-SADYK MUHAMMAD-YUSUF.

The Press

In 1990, according to official statistics, there were 279 newspapers being published in Uzbekistan, including 185 published in Uzbek. The average daily circulation was 5,158,400 copies (4,120,500 in Uzbek). There were 93 periodicals being published, including 33 in Uzbek. Newspapers were also published in Russian, Greek, Tadzhik, Crimean Tatar and Karakalpak.

State Committee for the Press: Tashkent, ul. Navoi 30; tel. (3712) 44-32-87; Chair. UBAIDULLA A. ABDURAZZAKOV.

PRINCIPAL NEWSPAPERS

Khaik suzi (The People's World): Tashkent; f. 1991; 5 a week; organ of the Supreme Soviet of Uzbekistan; Editor N. MUKHTAROV.

Molodets Uzbekistana (Young Person of Uzbekistan): 700083 Tashkent, ul. Leningradskaya 32; tel. (3712) 32-56-51; f. 1926; 5 a week; fmrly organ of the Cen. Cttee of the Leninist Young Communist League of Uzbekistan; in Russian; Editor A. PUKEMOV; circ. 30,000.

Narodnoye Slovo: Tashkent; f. 1990; organ of the Supreme Soviet.

Pravda Vostoka (Eastern Truth): Tashkent; f. 1917; 6 a week; organ of the Supreme Soviet and Council of Ministers; in Russian; Editor R. SAFAROV.

Sovet Uzbekistoni (Soviet Uzbekistan): Tashkent; f. 1918; 6 a week; organ of the Supreme Soviet and Council of Ministers; in Uzbek; Editor R. RAKHMANOV.

Uzbekiston adabieti va sanyati (The Literature and Art of Uzbekistan): 700000 Tashkent, Leningradskaya ul. 32; (3712) 32-54-66; f. 1956; weekly; organ of the Union of Writers of Uzbekistan; Editor N. MELIBAYEV.

Yash Leninchy (Young Leninist): Tashkent; f. 1925; 5 a week; fmrly organ of the Cen. Cttee of the Leninist Young Communist League of Uzbekistan; in Uzbek; Editor ZH. RAZZAKOV.

PRINCIPAL PERIODICALS

Monthly unless otherwise indicated.

Chelovek i politika (Man and Politics): Tashkent; f. 1920; fmrly publ. by the Publishing House of the Cen. Cttee of the Uzbek Communist Party; political; in Uzbek and Russian.

Fan va Turmush (Science and Life): 700000 Tashkent, ul. Gogolya 70; tel. (3712) 33-69-61; f. 1933; publ. by the Fan (Science) Publishing House; journal of the Academy of Sciences of Uzbekistan; popular scientific; in Uzbek.

Gulistan (Flourishing Area): Tashkent; f. 1925; fmrly journal of the Cen. Cttee of the Uzbek Communist Party; fiction; in Uzbek.

Gulkhan (Bonfire): 700083 Tashkent; tel. (3712) 32-78-85; f. 1929; illustrated juvenile fiction; in Uzbek.

Guncha (Small Bud): Tashkent; f. 1958; fmrly journal of the Cen. Cttee of the Leninist Young Communist League of Uzbekistan and the Republican Council of the V. I. Lenin Pioneer Organization of Uzbekistan; juvenile; illustrated; in Uzbek.

Mushtum (Fist): Tashkent; f. 1923; fortnightly; publ. by the *Sovet Uzbekistoni* newspaper; satirical; in Uzbek.

Obshchestvennye Nauki v Uzbekistane (Social Sciences in Uzbekistan): 700000 Tashkent, ul. Gogolya 70; tel. (3712) 33-69-61; f. 1957; publ. by the Fan (Science) Publishing House of the Academy of Sciences of Uzbekistan; history, oriental studies, archaeology, economics, ethnology, etc.; in Russian.

Saodat (Happiness): Tashkent; f. 1925; fmrly journal of the Cen. Cttee of the Uzbek Communist Party; women's popular; in Uzbek.

Shark Yulduzi (Star of the East): 700000 Tashkent, pr. Lenina 41; tel. (3712) 33-21-81; f. 1932; journal of the Union of Writers of Uzbekistan; fiction; in Uzbek.

Sovet Maktabi (Soviet School): Tashkent; f. 1925; publ. by the Uchitel (Teacher) Publishing House; journal of the Ministry of Education; educational issues; in Uzbek.

Sovet Uzbekistan: (Soviet Uzbekistan): 700000 Tashkent, ul. Lenina 41; tel. (3712) 31-11-67; f. 1984; publ. by Uzbek Society for Friendship and Cultural Relations with Foreign Countries; history politics, culture, general interest; in Uzbek, English, Russian, Spanish, French, Arabic, German, Farsi (Persian), Hindi, Dari and Urdu; Editor-in-Chief KAKHAR F. RASHIDOV.

Uzbek Tili va Adabyati (Uzbek Language and Literature): 700000 Tashkent, ul. Gogolya 70; f. 1958; fortnightly; publ. by the Fan (Science) Publishing House; journal of the Academy of Sciences of Uzbekistan; history and modern development of the Uzbek language, folklore, etc.; in Uzbek.

Uzbekiston Kishlok Khuzhaligi (Agriculture of Uzbekistan): Tashkent; f. 1925; journal of the Ministry of Agriculture; cotton-growing, cattle-breeding, forestry; in Uzbek.

Zvezda Vostoka (Star of the East): 700000 Tashkent, ul. gazety Pravda 41; tel. (3712) 33-42-68; f. 1932; monthly; publ. by the Publishing House Gafur Gulyam; journal of the Union of Writers of Uzbekistan; fiction; translations into Russian from Arabic, English, Hindi, Turkish, Japanese, etc.; Editor-in-Chief SABIT MADALIYEV; circ. 82,678.

NEWS AGENCY

UzTAG (Uzbek Telegraph Agency): Tashkent, ul. Khamza 2; tel. (3712) 39-49-82; Dir ERKIN K. KHAITBAYEV.

Publishers

In 1989 there were 2,336 book titles (including pamphlets and brochures) published in Uzbekistan, in a total of 48m. copies, including 929 (28.6m. copies) in Uzbek.

Chulpon (Little Star): Tashkent, ul. Gazety Pravda; Dir N. NORBUTAYEV.

Esh Gvardiya (Young Guard Publishing House): Tashkent, ul. Navoi 30; juvenile books and journals; Dir KH. E. PIRMUKHAMEDOV.

Fan (Science Publishing House): Tashkent, ul. Gogolya 70, k. 105; tel. (3712) 33-69-61; scientific books and journals; Dir N. T. KHATAMOV.

Gafur Gulyam Publishing House: 700129 Tashkent, ul. Navoi 30; tel. (3712) 44-22-53; f. 1957; fiction, the arts; books in Uzbek, Russian and English; Dir B. S. SHARIPOV.

Meditsina (Medicine Publishing House): Tashkent, ul. Navoi 30; tel. (3712) 44-51-72; f. 1958; medical sciences; Editor-in-Chief R. RESKIN.

Ukituvchi (Teacher): Tashkent, ul. Navoi 30; tel. (3712) 44-05-85; f. 1936; literary textbooks and education manuals; Dir M. MIRZAEV.

Uzbekistan Publishing House: Tashkent, ul. Navoi 30; tel. (3712) 44-38-10; f. 1924; socio-political, economic, illustrated; Editor-in-Chief R. SHAGULIYAMOV.

Uzbekskoy Sovetskoy Entsiklopedii (Uzbekistan Soviet Encyclopaedia): Tashkent, ul. Zhukovskovo 52; tel. (3712) 33-50-17; f. 1968; encyclopaedias, dictionaries and reference books; Editor-in-Chief N. TUCHLIYEV.

Radio and Television

State Committee for Television and Radio: Tashkent, yl. Khorezmskaya 49; tel. (3712) 41-05-51; Chair. NAIM YA. GAIBOV.

Radio Tashkent: 700047 Tashkent, ul. Khorezmskaya 49; tel. (3712) 33-02-49; telex 116139; f. 1947; broadcasts in Uzbek, English, Urdu, Hindi, Farsi (Persian), Arabic and Uighur.

Tashkent Television Studio: Tashkent, ul. Navoi 69.

Finance
BANKING
State Banks

State Bank of the Republic of Uzbekistan: 700001 Tashkent, ul. Uzbekistanskaya 6; tel. (3712) 32-72-72; Chair. of Bd F. M. MULLOZHANOV; Dep. Chair. of Bd VALENTINA I. POPOVA.

Uzvneshekonombank (Uzbek Bank for Foreign Economic Activities): 700015 Tashkent, ul. Tarasa Shevchenko 29; tel. (3712) 54-59-01; telex 116194; fax (3712) 55-13-51; fmrly br. of USSR Vneshekonombank; Dir NARIMAN K. KARIMOV.

Other Banks

Uzbek Commercial Bank: 700015 Tashkent, Poltoratskovo ul. 73B, tel. (3712) 54-79-51.

Uzbek Joint-Stock Innovation Bank (Uzinbank): 700027 Tashkent, Massiv Besh-Agach 7; tel. (3712) 45-08-08.

COMMODITY EXCHANGE

Tashkent Commodity Exchange (TACE): 700003 Tashkent, 45 Uzbekistanskaya ul.; tel. (3772) 45-71-41; fax (3772) 45-62-79; Chair. Exchange Cttee KABUL USMANOV.

Trade and Industry
CHAMBER OF COMMERCE

Chamber of Commerce and Industry: 700017 Tashkent, pr. Lenina 16A; tel. (3712) 33-62-82; Chair. DELBART YU. MIRSIAADOVA.

FOREIGN TRADE ORGANIZATION

Uzbekintorg: 700115 Tashkent, pr. Uzbekistani 45; tel. (3712) 45-73-13; imports and exports a wide range of goods; Gen. Dir AL IKRAMOV.

MAJOR INDUSTRIAL ENTERPRISES

Sredazelektroapparat: 700005 Tashkent, Manjara 1; tel. (3712) 291-29-04; engaged in the production of low-voltage equipment, incl. packet-type switches, cam switches, etc; Gen. Dir ALIM ABDURAIMOVICH; 9,000 employees.

Tashkent Industrial Amalgamation: 700090 Tashkent, Barbur 73; tel. (3712) 55-17-23; fax (3712) 44-30-43; produces diamond and elbor grinding wheels, instruments of galvanic binder, etc; Gen. Man. ANATOLY HEGAY; 1,100 employees.

Transport
RAILWAYS

The Tashkent Metro was inaugurated in 1977. In 1991 two new stations were opened. The total length is 31 km with 23 stations.

Culture
CULTURAL HERITAGE

Alisher Navoi State Public Library of Uzbekistan: 700000 Tashkent, alleya Narodov 5; tel. (3712) 33-05-47; f. 1870; 4,157,500 vols; Dir D. TADZHIYEVA.

Karakalpak Historical Museum: Nukus, ul. Rakhmatova 3; contains material on the history of Karakalpakia and the Uzbek people.

Museum of Uzbek History, Culture and Arts: Samarkand, Sovetskaya ul. 51; f. 1874; over 100,000 items; Dir N. S. SADYKOVA.

Tashkent Historical Museum of the People of Uzbekistan: 700047 Tashkent, ul. Kuibysheva 15; tel. (3712) 33-57-32; f. 1876; over 200,000 exhibits; Dir G. R. RASHIDOV.

Uzbek State Museum of Art: 700060 Tashkent, Proletarskaya 16; tel. (3712) 32-34-44; f. 1918; library of 22,700 vols; Dir D. S. RUSIBAYEV.

SPORTING ORGANIZATION

State Committee for Physical Culture and Sport: Tashkent, alleya Paradov 5; tel. (3712) 39-45-59; Chair. ABID NAZIROV.

PERFORMING ARTS

Alisher Navoi Opera and Ballet Theatre: Tashkent, 31 ul. Pravdy Vostoka.

Central Puppet Theatre of Uzbekistan: Tashkent, 1 pr. Kosmonavtov.

Khamza Uzbek Drama Theatre: Tashkent, 34 pr. Navoi.

Maxim Gorky Russian Drama Theatre: Tashkent, 28 ul. K. Marksa.

ASSOCIATION

Union of Writers of Uzbekistan: 700000 Tashkent, ul. Pushkina 1; tel. (3712) 33-79-21; Sec. MUKHAMMAD SOLIKH.

Uzbek Society for Friendship and Cultural Relations with Foreign Countries: 700000 Tashkent, ul. Lenina 41; tel. (3712) 31-11-67; promotes cultural and educational relations with other countries.

Education

Until the early 1990s education was based on the Soviet model, but some changes were introduced, including a greater emphasis on Uzbek history and literature, and study of the Arabic script. In 1988/89 76.8% of pupils at day schools were educated in Uzbek. Other languages used include Russian (15.0%), Kazakh (2.9%), Karakalpak (2.4%), Tadzhik (2.3%), Turkmen (0.4%) and Kirghiz (0.2%). Higher education is provided in several specialized institutes and three universities.

UNIVERSITIES

Nukus State University: 742012 Nukus, Universitetskaya ul. 1; tel. (3712) 2-42-58; f. 1979; 11 faculties; 7,000 students.

Samarkand Alisher Navoi State University: 703004 Samarkand, bul. M. Gorkovo 15; tel. (3712) 5-26-26; f. 1933; 13 faculties; 600 teachers; 11,000 students; Rector Prof. Acad. A. K. ATAKHODZHAEV.

Tashkent State University: 700095 Tashkent, Vozgorodok, Universitetskaya ul. 95; tel. (3712) 46-02-24; f. 1920; 17 faculties; 1,480 teachers; 19,300 students; Rector Dr S. K. SIRAZHDINOV.

Social Welfare
HEALTH AND WELFARE ORGANIZATION

Uzbek Institute of Sanitation and Hygiene: Tashkent, ul. K. Marksa 85.

The Environment

The principal environmental concerns in Uzbekistan revolve around the desiccation of the Aral Sea, to which the extensive use of the Syr-Dar'ya and Amu'-Dar'ya rivers for irrigation purposes is a major contributing factor.

ACADEMIC INSTITUTE

Uzbek Academy of Sciences: 700000 Tashkent, ul. Gogolya 70; fax (3712) 33-49-01; several attached institutes involved in environmental research; Pres. M. S. SALAKHITDINOV.

OTHER FORMER SOVIET REPUBLICS

ESTONIA

Geography

The Republic of Estonia (formerly the Estonian Soviet Socialist Republic) is situated in north-eastern Europe. It is bordered to the south by Latvia, and, to the east, by the Russian Federation. Its northern coastline is on the Gulf of Finland and its territory includes over 1,520 islands, mainly off its western coastline in the Gulf of Riga and the Baltic Sea. Until 1945, when a small amount of territory south of Lake Pihkva (Lake Pskov) was ceded to the Russian Federation, Estonia covered an area of 47,548 sq km. The country now covers an area of 45,215 sq km.

Estonia is situated on the north-western edge of the Great Russian Plain. The land is mainly flat, with some undulating terrain in the south. Forests cover some 36% of the territory. Rivers, the largest of which is the Narva, are mainly short and carry low volumes of water. There are many marshes and bogs, and more than 1,500 lakes, of which the largest are the Estonian parts of the Peipsi (Chudskoye) and Pihkva (Pskov) lakes, on the eastern border with the Russian Federation. The largest of the Republic's many islands are Saaremaa and Hiiumaa, in the Gulf of Riga.

The climate is influenced by Estonia's position between the Eurasian landmass and the Baltic and North Atlantic seas. The mean January temperature in Tallinn is −5.0°C (23.0°F); in July the mean temperature is 17.1°C (62.6°F). Annual precipitation is 568 mm.

At the census of 1989, when the total population was 1,565,662, 61.5% of the population were Estonians, 30.3% Russians, 3.1% Ukrainians, 1.8% Byelorussians and 1.1% Finns. Other nationalities included Jews (4,613), Tatars (4,058) and Germans (3,466). In 1989 Estonian replaced Russian as the official state language. It is a member of the Baltic-Finnic group of the Finno-Ugric languages and is written in the Latin script. It is closely related to Finnish. Many Russian residents do not speak Estonian (85% in 1989) and have protested at its official use. Most of the population are adherents of the Christian religion. By tradition, Estonians are Lutheran. The Russian Orthodox Church and smaller Protestant sects are also represented in the Republic.

At 1 January 1991 the total population was estimated to be 1,582,000. The capital is Tallinn, which is situated in the north of the Republic, on the Gulf of Finland. It had an estimated population of 484,000 in 1990. Other important towns include the university town of Tartu (115,400), and the Russian-dominated industrial towns of Narva (82,300) and Kohtla-Järve (76,800), in the north-east of Estonia.

History

The Estonians, a Finno-Ugric people, have inhabited the north-east coastline of the Baltic Sea for some 5,000 years. At the beginning of the 13th century AD the Estonians, who totalled some 100,000 at this time, were conquered by the German Order of the Teutonic Knights, with the aid of the Danes. The decline of German power in the 16th century allowed Sweden to seize Northern Estonia, in 1561, while Southern Estonia, or Livonia, became part of the Lithuanian-Polish Duchy of Courland. In 1629, after the Swedish–Polish Wars, all of mainland Estonia came under Swedish rule. Russia drove the Swedes out of Estonia in 1710, and Russian annexation was formalized at the Treaty of Nystad, in 1721. During the latter half of the 19th century, as the powers of the dominant Baltic German nobility declined, Estonians experienced a national cultural revival, which culminated in political demands for autonomy during the 1905 Revolution, and for full independence after the beginning of the First World War.

On 30 March 1917 the Provisional Government in Petrograd (St Petersburg), which had taken power after the abdication of Tsar Nicholas II in February, approved autonomy for Estonia. A Land Council was elected as the country's representative body. However, in October the Bolsheviks staged a *coup d'état* in Tallinn, and declared the Estonian Soviet Executive Committee as the sole Government of Estonia. As German forces advanced towards Estonia, in early 1918, the Bolshevik troops were forced to leave. The major Estonian political parties united to form the Estonian Salvation Committee, and, on 24 February 1918, an independent Republic of Estonia was proclaimed. A Provisional Government, headed by Konstantin Päts, was formed, but the Germans refused to recognize Estonia's independence and the country was occupied by German troops until the end of the War. After the capitulation of Germany, in November 1918, the Provisional Government assumed power. After a period of armed conflict between Soviet and Estonian troops, the Republic of Estonia and Soviet Russia signed the Treaty of Tartu, on 2 February 1920. By the terms of the Treaty the Soviet Government recognized Estonian independence and renounced any rights to its territory. Estonian independence was recognized by the major Western Powers, in January 1921, and Estonia was admitted to the League of Nations.

Estonia's independence lasted until 1940. During most of this period the country had a liberal-democratic political system, in which the Riigikogu (parliament) was the dominant political force. Significant social, cultural and economic advances were made in the 1920s, including radical land reform, and important developments in research and scholarship. However, the decline in trade with Russia and the economic depression of the 1930s, combined with the political problems of a divided parliament, caused public dissatisfaction with the regime. On 12 March 1934 Konstantin Päts, the Prime Minister, seized power in a bloodless coup and introduced a period of authoritarian rule. The Rugikogu and political parties were disbanded, but, in 1938, a new Constitution was adopted, which provided for a presidential system of government, with a bicameral parliament. In April 1938 Päts was elected President.

In August 1939 the USSR and Germany signed a Non-Aggression Treaty (the Nazi–Soviet or Molotov–Ribbentrop Pact). The Secret Supplementary Protocol to the Treaty provided for the occupation of Estonia (and Latvia) by the USSR. In September Estonia was forced to sign an agreement which permitted the USSR to base Soviet troops in Estonia. In June 1940 the Government, in accordance with a Soviet ultimatum, resigned, and a new Government was appointed by the Soviet authorities. Johannes Vares-

Barbarus was appointed Prime Minister. In July elections were held, in which only candidates approved by the Soviet authorities were permitted to participate. On 21 July 1940 the Estonian Soviet Socialist Republic was proclaimed by the new parliament, and, on 6 August, the Republic was formally incorporated into the USSR.

Soviet rule in Estonia lasted less than a year, before German forces occupied the country. In that short period Soviet policy resulted in mass deportations of Estonians to Siberia (in one night, on 14 June 1941, more than 10,000 people were arrested and deported), the expropriation of property, severe restrictions on cultural life and the introduction of Soviet-style government in the Republic.

In July 1941 German forces entered Estonia and remained in occupation until September 1944. After a short-lived attempt to reinstate Estonian independence, Soviet troops occupied the whole of the country and the process of 'sovietization' was continued. By the end of 1949 most Estonian farmers had been forced to join collective farms. Heavy industry was expanded, with investment concentrated on electricity generation and the chemical sector. Structural change in the economy was accompanied by increased political repression, with deportations of Estonians continuing until the death of Stalin, in 1953. The most obvious form of opposition to Soviet rule was provided by the 'forest brethren' (*metsavennad*), a 'guerrilla' movement, which continued to conduct armed operations against Soviet personnel and institutions until the mid-1950s. In the late 1960s, as in other Soviet Republics, more traditional forms of dissent appeared, concentrating on cultural issues, provoked by the increasing domination of the Republic by immigrant Russians and other Slavs. Before 1940 ethnic Estonians constituted nearly 90% of the population. Emigration, losses during the War and deportations, combined with in-migration by Russians to occupy political posts and to work in heavy industry, resulted in a steady decline in the proportion of ethnic Estonians in the population. By 1989 only 61.5% of the population were ethnic Estonians.

During the late 1970s and the 1980s the issues of 'russification' and environmental degradation were increasingly subjects of debate in Estonia. The policy of *glasnost*, introduced by Soviet leader Mikhail Gorbachev, in 1986, allowed debate to spread beyond dissident groups. The first major demonstrations of the 1980s protested against plans to greatly increase the scale of open-cast phosphorite mining in north-eastern Estonia. The public opposition to the plans caused the all-Union Government to reconsider its proposals, and this success prompted further protests. On 23 August 1987 a demonstration, attended by some 2,000 people, marked the anniversary of the signing of the Nazi–Soviet Pact. Following the demonstration an Estonian Group for the Publication of the Molotov–Ribbentrop Pact (MRP-AEG) was formed. The growing opposition movement was strongly opposed by the conservative Communist Party of Estonia (CPE) leadership, but reformers within the Party began making proposals allowing more autonomy for Estonia, particularly in economic policy. The most significant document produced by the reformers was the proposal for Economic Self-Management, which advocated full republican jurisdiction over the economy, including the introduction of a convertible currency.

During 1988 the policy of *glasnost* allowed the republican press to discuss previously censored subjects, such as russification, environmental degradation and politically sensitive aspects of Estonian history. The opposition movement also grew in strength and, in April, a Popular Front of Estonia (PFE) was established, which organized mass demonstrations throughout July and August. The campaign led by the MRP-AEG to publish the Nazi–Soviet Pact achieved its aim and the MRP-AEG re-formed as the Estonian National Independence Party (ENIP), proclaiming the restoration of Estonian independence as its political goal. The PFE, which was formally constituted at its first Congress, in October, and included many members of the CPE, was more cautious in its approach, advocating the transformation of the USSR into a confederal system. The CPE itself was forced to adapt its policies to retain a measure of public support. On 16 November the Estonian Supreme Soviet adopted a declaration of sovereignty, which included the right to annul all-Union legislation. The Presidium of the USSR Supreme Soviet declared the sovereignty legislation unconstitutional, but the Estonian Supreme Soviet affirmed its decision in December.

One of the main demands of the opposition, the adoption of Estonian as the state language, was agreed to by the Supreme Soviet in January 1989, and the tricolour of independent Estonia was also reinstated as the official flag. Despite the successes of the opposition, there were serious differences over political tactics between the radical ENIP and the PFE. ENIP refused to nominate candidates for elections to the all-Union Congress of People's Deputies in March 1989. Instead, the ENIP leadership announced plans for the registration of all citizens of the pre-1940 Estonian Republic and their descendants by 'Citizens' Committees'. An electorate registered in this way would elect a 'Congress of Estonia' as the legal successor to the pre-1940 Estonian parliament. The PFE, however, participated in the elections to the Congress of People's Deputies and won 27 of the 36 contested seats. Five seats were won by Intermovement, a political group established in July 1988 to seek to oppose the growing influence of the Estonian opposition movements in the Republic. In August, in response to a new electoral law approved by the Supreme Soviet which required voters in elections to have been resident in the Republic for two years and candidates to have been resident for 10 years, Intermovement organized protest rallies and strikes, in which some 30,000 people were estimated to have taken part. In response to the protests, the legislation was suspended by the Supreme Soviet.

In October, delegates at the second Congress of the PFE, influenced by the growing popularity of the ENIP and the Citizens' Committees, voted to adopt the restoration of Estonian independence as official policy. In November the Supreme Soviet voted to annul the decision of its predecessor in 1940 to enter the USSR, declaring that the decision had been reached under coercion from Soviet armed forces.

On 2 February 1990 a mass rally was held to mark the anniversary of the 1920 Treaty of Tartu. Deputies attending the rally later met to approve a declaration calling on the USSR Supreme Soviet to begin negotiations on restoring Estonia's independence. The declaration was approved by the Estonian Supreme Soviet on 22 February. On 23 February the Estonian Supreme Soviet voted to abolish the constitutional guarantee of power enjoyed by the Communist Party, which was enshrined in Article Six of the Constitution. This formal decision permitted largely free elections to take place to the Estonian Supreme Soviet on 18 March 1990. The PFE won 43 of the 105 seats and 35 were won by the Association for a Free Estonia and other pro-independence groups. The remainder were won by members of Intermovement. Candidates belonging to the CPE, which were represented in all these groups, won 55 seats.

At the first session of the new Supreme Soviet, Arnold Rüütel, previously Chairman of the Presidium of the Supreme Soviet, was elected to the new post of Chairman of the Supreme Soviet, which included those state powers which had previously been the preserve of First Secretaries of the CPE. On 30 March 1990 the Supreme Soviet adopted a declaration, which declared the beginning of a transitional period towards independence and denied the validity of Soviet power in the Republic.

In late February and early March 1990 elections were held to a rival parliament to the Supreme Soviet, the Congress of Estonia. The elections were organized privately by Citizens' Committees and participation was limited to those who had been citizens of the pre-1940 Estonian Republic and their descendants. Some 580,000 people took part. The Congress convened on 11–12 March and declared itself the constitutional representative of the Estonian people. Resolutions were adopted that demanded the restoration of Estonian independence and the withdrawal of Soviet troops from Estonia.

On 26 March 1990 delegates to an extraordinary congress of the CPE adopted a resolution which favoured the principle of its independence from the Communist Party of the Soviet Union (CPSU), but allowed for a transitional period of six months before a final vote on the secession of the Party would be taken. Following the Congress, some deputies, mostly non-Estonians, announced that they were planning to establish a Communist Party which would remain subordinate to the CPSU. Vaino Vaeles, who had been First Secretary of the CPE since 1988, was elected to the newly-created post of party chairman.

On 3 April 1990 the Supreme Soviet (which was renamed the Supreme Council) elected Edgar Savisaar, a leader of the PFE, as Prime Minister. On 8 May the Supreme Council voted to restore the first five articles of the 1938 Constitution, which described Estonia's independent status. The formal name of pre-1940 Estonia, the Republic of Estonia, was also restored, as were the state emblems, flag and anthem of independent Estonia. On 16 May a transitional system of government was approved.

Although formal economic sanctions were not imposed on Estonia, as was the case with Lithuania, the Republic's declaration of independence severely strained relations with the all-Union authorities. On 14 May 1990 Soviet President Mikhail Gorbachev annulled the declaration, declaring that it violated the USSR Constitution. The Estonian leadership's request for negotiations on the status of the Republic was refused by Gorbachev, who insisted that the independence declaration be rescinded before negotiations could begin. There was also opposition within the Republic, mostly from ethnic Russians affiliated to the Intermovement. On 15 May some 2,000 people protested against the declaration and attempted to occupy the Supreme Soviet building. There were also protest strikes in some factories on 21 May, but the response among Russian workers was lower than expected.

When Soviet interior ministry troops attempted military intervention in Latvia and Lithuania in January 1991, the Estonian leadership expected similar actions in Estonia. Barricades and makeshift defences were erected, but military conflict did not occur. However, the military action in the other Baltic Republics strengthened local feeling against Estonian involvement in a new Union, which was being negotiated by other Republics. Consequently, Estonia refused to participate in the all-Union referendum on the future of the USSR, although some 225,000 people did take part in unofficial voting in the Slav-dominated north-eastern regions. Of these, some 95% approved the proposal to preserve the USSR as a 'renewed federation'. The Estonian authorities, however, conducted a poll on the issue of independence on 3 March. Voters were asked 'Do you want the restoration of the state independence of the Estonian

Republic?'. According to the official results, 82.9% of the registered electorate took part, of which 77.8% voted in favour.

When the State Committee for the State of Emergency (SCSE) announced that it had seized power in the USSR, on 19 August 1991, Estonia, together with the other Baltic Republics, expected military intervention to overthrow the pro-independence Governments. Gen. Fedor Kuzmin, Commander of the Baltic Military District, informed Arnold Rüütel, Chairman of the Supreme Council, that he was taking full control of Estonia. On 20 August military vehicles entered Tallinn, and, although military officials agreed that no military force would be used against civilians, troops occupied Tallinn television station the next day. The military command did not prevent a session of the Estonian Supreme Council convening on 20 August. Deputies adopted a resolution declaring full and immediate independence of the Estonian Republic, thus ending the transitional period which had begun in March 1990. Plans were also announced for the formation of a government-in-exile should the Government and the Supreme Council be disbanded by Soviet troops.

After it became evident, on 22 August 1991, that the coup had collapsed, the Government began to take measures against those which it alleged had supported the coup. The anti-government movements, Intermovement and the United Council of Work Collectives, were banned, as was the CPSU. Several directors of all-Union enterprises were dismissed and the KGB was ordered to terminate its activities in Estonia.

As the Estonian Government moved to assert its authority over former Soviet institutions, other countries quickly began to recognize Estonia's independence. By the end of August 1991 more than 30 countries had recognized Estonia and, on 4 September, the USSR State Council finally recognized the re-establishment of the independent Estonian Republic. On 17 September Estonia, together with the other Baltic States, was admitted to the United Nations. During the remainder of 1991 Estonia re-established diplomatic relations with most major states and was offered membership of leading international organizations. In internal politics there was hope for an end to conflict between the radical Congress of Estonia and the Supreme Council, with the establishment of a Constituent Assembly, composed of equal numbers of delegates from each organization, which was to draft a new Constitution. Initially, the Assembly was to finalize a draft Constitution by 15 November, to be submitted to a national referendum. However, procedural disputes between Congress and Supreme Council delegates delayed work in the Assembly and meant that a final draft was not expected until early 1992.

Economy

The Estonian economy was one of the most prosperous in the USSR. Its mineral resources include an estimated 15,000m. metric tons of oil shale (60% of total Soviet deposits) and deposits of peat and phosphorite ore. Oil shale is used in power stations to generate electricity, much of which is exported to the Russian Federation. In 1980 extraction of oil shale reached 31m. tons but decreased to only 23m. tons in 1988. Phosphorite ore is processed to produce phosphates used in agriculture, but development of the industry has been accompanied by increasing environmental problems. The large forests provide resources for important timber-related industries, including wood-working and paper plants.

Industry is dominated by machine-building, electronics and electrical engineering. Other light industries include textiles, fish- and food-processing and consumer goods. Estonia was one of the largest producers of consumer goods in the USSR; production per head of textiles and shoes, for example, was the highest in the country. The services sector was also the most developed in the USSR and is expected to expand in response to increased tourism and Western investment.

The main activity in the agricultural sector is animal husbandry. Estonia produced 1.4% of total Soviet meat production in 1988. Dairy produce, cattle fodder and vegetables are the other main agricultural products.

In 1988, according to Soviet statistics, Estonia recorded a balance of trade deficit of 748m. roubles. Of this, 332m. roubles was with other Soviet Republics and 416m. roubles with foreign countries. The main exports are agricultural products and furniture and other consumer goods. Light industry and the food-processing industry recorded trade surpluses, while heavy industry and the energy sector recorded large deficits. Trade is developing with Western countries, notably with Finland and other Scandinavian countries. In 1988, however, trade remained largely orientated towards the Soviet republics; 92% of exports and 82% of imports went to the rest of the USSR.

Estonia was severely affected by the decline in the Soviet economy in 1990 and 1991. In the first three months of 1991 industrial output decreased by 4.8%, labour productivity declined by 1.6%, while wages increased by 36.5%. The Government has attempted to attract Western investment, especially through the creation of joint-venture companies. At 1 April 1991 Estonia had 97 functioning joint ventures, many of which involved partnership with Finnish companies. It was expected that an Estonian currency, the kroon (crown), would be introduced in 1992.

Statistical Survey

Population

BIRTHS AND DEATHS (per 1,000)

	1987	1988	1989
Birth rate	16.0	15.9	15.4
Death rate	11.7	11.8	11.7

Agriculture

PRINCIPAL CROPS ('000 metric tons)

	1987	1988	1989
Grain	1,257.1	591.2	1,182.6
Potatoes	728.4	715.7	864.2
Other vegetables . . .	116.2	128.9	144.0
Fruit	31.6	21.7	74.9

LIVESTOCK ('000 head at 1 January)

	1987	1988	1989
Cattle	821.2	819.3	806.1
Pigs	1,083.0	1,099.4	1,080.4
Sheep and goats . . .	136.1	135.0	140.2

Poultry: 6,765,200 at 1 January 1987.

LIVESTOCK PRODUCTS ('000 metric tons)

	1987	1988	1989
Meat (slaughter weight) . .	222.0	227.9	228.9
Milk	1,290.2	1,288.6	1,277.2
Eggs (million)	556.7	578.7	600.1

Mining and Industry

SELECTED PRODUCTS

	1987	1988	1989
Peat ('000 metric tons) . . .	169	208	n.a.
Oil-shale ('000 metric tons) . .	24,906	23,307	25,331
Paper ('000 metric tons) . .	90.1	94.6	91.8
Excavators (number) . . .	2,195	2,054	1,645
Electric energy (million kWh) .	17,900	17,627	17,611

Education

(1989/90)

	Institutions	Students
Secondary schools	634	227,500
Vocational schools	42	13,800
Secondary specialized institutions . .	36	19,900
Higher schools (incl. universities) . .	6	26,279

Directory
Constitution

The 1938 Constitution of the Republic of Estonia was annulled after the Soviet annexation. Estonia became a Union Republic of the USSR and had a Soviet-style Constitution. In 1978 a new such Constitution was adopted, but this was amended, in 1988, to ensure accordance with the Declaration of the Sovereignty of the Estonian SSR. The constitutional basis for Estonian membership of the USSR, the Resolution on Estonian Entry into the USSR of 22 July 1940, was declared null and void in November 1989. On 8 May 1990 the Supreme Council (legislature) voted to restore the first six paragraphs of the 1938 Constitution, which describe Estonia as an independent and sovereign state. The Constitution was further amended by the Law on Bases for Provisional Government in Estonia, adopted on 16 May 1990, which ended subordination of Estonian government, judicial and state bodies to those of the USSR. On 7 August 1990 the Supreme Council adopted the Resolution on Relations between the Republic of Estonia and the USSR, which annulled the 1978 Constitution of the Estonian SSR. As part of the declaration of independence of August 1991, an Assembly was to draft a new Constitution.

The Government

(January 1992)

HEAD OF STATE

Chairman of the Supreme Council: ARNOLD F. RÜÜTEL.

COUNCIL OF MINISTERS

Prime Minister: TIIT VÄHI.
Minister of Agriculture: (vacant).
Minister of Construction: OLARI TAAL.
Minister of Culture: MÄRT KUBO.
Minister of the Economy: HEIDO VITSUR.
Minister of Education: REIN LOIK.

Minister of the Environment: Tõnis Kaasik.
Minister of Finance: Rein Miller.
Minister of Foreign Affairs: Lennart Meri.
Minister of Health: Andres Kork.
Minister of Industry and Energy: Aksel Treimann.
Minister of the Interior: Robert Närska.
Minister of Justice: Märt Rask.
Minister of Labour: Arvo Kuddo.
Minister of Social Security: (vacant).
Minister of the State Chancellery: Uno Veering.
Minister of Trade: Aleksandr Sikkal.
Minister of Transport and Communications: Enn Sarap.

MINISTRIES

Ministry of Agriculture: Lai 39/41, Tallinn 200102; tel. (0142) 441-166; telex 173216; fax (0142) 440-601.

Ministry of Construction: Harju 11, Tallinn 200001; tel. (0142) 440-577.

Ministry of Culture: Suur-Karja 23, Tallinn 200001; tel. (0142) 445-077; telex 173260; fax (0142) 440-963.

Ministry of the Economy: Komsomoli 1, Tallinn 200100; tel. (0142) 683-444; telex 173106; fax (0142) 682-097.

Ministry of Education: Kingissepa 60, Tallinn 200103; tel. (0142) 437-760; fax (0142) 437-892.

Ministry of the Environment: Toompuiestee 24, Tallinn 200110; tel. (0142) 452-507; telex 173238; fax (0142) 453-310.

Ministry of Finance: Kohtu 8, Tallinn 200100; tel. (0142) 452-801; fax (0142) 452-992.

Ministry of Foreign Affairs: Lossi plats 1A, Tallinn 200001; tel. (0142) 443-266; telex 173269; fax (0142) 441-713.

Ministry of Health: Lossi plats 7, Tallinn 200100; tel. (0142) 445-123; fax (0142) 440-869.

Ministry of Industry and Energy: Lomonossovi 29, Tallinn 200104; tel. (0142) 423-550; telex 173278; fax (0142) 425-468.

Ministry of the Interior: Pikk 61, Tallinn 200101; tel. (0142) 663-262; fax (0142) 602-785.

Ministry of Justice: Pärnu mnt. 7, Tallinn 200104; tel. (0142) 445-120.

Ministry of Labour: Lomonossovi 29, Tallinn 200104; tel. (0142) 423-434.

Ministry of Social Security: Estonia pst. 15, Tallinn 200001; tel. (0142) 666-930.

Ministry of Trade: Kiriku 2/4, Tallinn 200100; tel. (0142) 421-597; telex 173145; fax (0142) 450-540.

Ministry of Transport and Communications: Viru 9, Tallinn 200100; tel. (0142) 443-842; fax (0142) 449-206.

Legislature

SUPREME COUNCIL

The Supreme Council is the highest legislative body in the country. It consists of 105 deputies. Elections took place on 18 March 1990.

Supreme Council: Lossi plats 1A, Tallinn 200100; tel. (0142) 426-200.

Speaker: Ülo Nugis.

Deputy Speakers: Marju Lauristin, Viktor Andreyev.

Local Government

For administrative purposes, Estonia is divided into 15 counties (maakond) and six towns. The counties are divided into communes (vald), and include 27 towns.

Mayoralty of Tallinn: Vabaduse väljak 7, Tallinn; tel. (0142) 444-955; Mayor Hardo Aasmäe.

Political Organizations

Estonian Christian Democratic Party: POB 3578, 200090 Tallinn; tel. (0142) 609-688; fax (0142) 441-047; f. 1988; Chair. Aivar Kala.

Estonian Christian Democratic Union: Rahukohtu 1-33, 200090 Tallinn; tel. (0142) 444-896; telex 173557; fax (0142) 449-865; f. 1988; Chair. Illar Hallaste.

Estonian Communist Party: Lenini puiestee 9, 200100 Tallinn; tel. (0142) 445-118; f. 1920; declared its independence from the CPSU 1990; Chair. Vaino Väljas; 5,000 mems (1990).

Estonian Entrepreneur Party: Pikk 68, Tallinn 200001; tel. (0142) 609-620; f. 1990; Chair. Tiit Made.

Estonian Green Movement: POB 300, 202400 Tartu; tel. (01434) 32-986; telex 173243; fax (01434) 35-440; f. 1988; campaigns on environmental issues; Chair. Tõnu Oja.

Estonian Liberal Democratic Party: POB 2, Tallinn 200090; tel. (0142) 445-909; telex 173298; fax (0142) 440-963; f. 1990; Chair. Paul-Eerik Rummo.

Estonian National Independence Party (ENIP): Endla 6-4, Tallinn 200001; tel. (0142) 452-472; fax (0142) 452-864; f. 1988; Chair. Lagle Parek.

Estonian Rural Centre Party: Rahukohtu 1-15, Tallinn 200001; fax (0142) 442-835; f. 1990; Chair. Ivar Raig.

Estonian Social Democratic Party: POB 3437, 200090 Tallinn; tel. (0142) 421-150; fax (0142) 444-902; f. 1990; mem. of Socialist International; Chair. Marju Lauristin.

Popular Front of Estonia (Rahvarinne): Uus 28, 200101 Tallinn; tel. (0142) 449-236; fax (0142) 448-442; f. 1988; Chair. Edgar Savisaar.

Following the attempted coup of August 1991 in the USSR, two political groups, the Intermovement of the Working People of the Estonian SSR and the Union of Working Collectives, were suspended, owing to their alleged support for the coup.

Diplomatic Representation

EMBASSIES IN ESTONIA

Denmark: Vana-Viru 4, Tallinn 200101; tel. (0142) 446-836; telex 173134; fax (0142) 601-247; Ambassador: Sven Nordberg.

Finland: Kingissepa 12, Tallinn 200001; tel. (0142) 449-522; fax (0142) 446-392; Ambassador: Jaako Kaurinkoski.

France: Tallinn; Ambassador: Jacques Huntzinger.

Germany: Tallinn; Ambassador: Henning von Wistinghausen.

Italy: Tallinn; Ambassador: Carlo Siano.

Latvia: Tallin; tel. (0142) 237-665; Ambassador: Anna Žigure.

Lithuania: Vabaduse väljak 10, Tallinn 200001; tel. (0142) 448-917; Ambassador: Sigitas Kudarauskas.

Sweden: Endla 4A, Tallinn 200001; tel. (0142) 450-350; telex 173124; fax (0142) 450-676; Ambassador: Lars Arne Grundberg.

United Kingdom: Tallinn; Ambassador: Brian B. Low.

USA: Tallinn; Ambassador-designate: Robert C. Frasure.

Judicial System

Supreme Court: Pärnu mnt. 7, Tallinn 200104; tel. (0142) 442-931; Chair. Jaak Kirikal.

Public Prosecutor's Office: Wismari 7, Tallinn 200100; tel. (0142) 445-226; Prosecutor-General Leo Urge.

Religion

CHRISTIANITY

Protestant Churches

Association of the Estonian Evangelical Christian Baptist Communities: Pargi 9, Tallinn 200016; tel. (0142) 513-005; Chair. Ülo Meriloo.

Consistory of the Evangelical Lutheran Church of Estonia: Kiriku 8, Tallinn 200106; tel. (0142) 451-682; fax (0142) 601-876; Archbishop Kuno Pajula.

Estonian Union of Seventh-day Adventists: Mere pst. 3, Tallinn 200001; tel. (0142) 447-879; Chair. Rein Kalmus.

Methodist Church of Estonia: Apteegi 3, Tallinn 200001; tel. (0142) 449-246; Superintendent Olav Pärnamets.

The Eastern Orthodox Church

Council of the Russian Orthodox Diocese: Pikk 64-4, Tallinn 200001; tel. (0142) 601-747; Bishop Kornelius.

The Press

In 1989 there were 111 officially-registered newspapers being published in Estonia, including 73 published in Estonian, and 161 periodicals, including 109 in Estonian.

PRINCIPAL NEWSPAPERS

In Estonian except where otherwise stated.

Äripäev (Daily Business): Raua 1A, Tallinn 200010; tel. (0142) 431-201; fax (0142) 426-700; f. 1989; business and finance; Editor-in-Chief HALLAR LIND; circ. 20,000.

Eesti Ekspress (Estonian Express): Kentmanni 20, Tallinn 200001; tel. (0142) 666-864; f. 1989; Editor-in-Chief IVO KARLEP; circ. 60,000 (1991).

Eesti Elu (Estonian Life): Närva mnt. 5, Tallinn 200090; tel. (0142) 445-466; (0142) fax 449-558; f. 1989; fortnightly; political and cultural affairs; Editor-in-Chief MADIS JÜRGEN.

The Estonian Independent: Pärnu mnt. 67A, Tallinn 200090; tel. (0142) 683-074; telex 173193; fax (0142) 691-537; f. 1990; weekly; publ. by ETA and the Perioodika (Periodicals) Publishing House; in English; Editor-in-Chief TARMU TAMMERK; circ. 8,000.

Maaleht (Country News): Toompuiestee 16, Tallinn 200106; tel. (0142) 683-074; fax (0142) 452-902; f. 1987; weekly; Editor-in-Chief OLEV ANTON; circ. 169,200 (1990).

Molodezh Estonii (Youth of Estonia): Pärnu mnt. 67A, Tallinn 200090; tel. (0142) 681-431; f. 1950; in Russian; Editor-in-Chief SERGEY SERGEYEV; circ. 75,000.

Õhtuleht (The Evening Gazette): Pärnu mnt. 67A, Tallin 200090; tel. (0142) 681-154; fax (0142) 441-924; f. 1944; daily; in Estonian and Russian; Editor-in-Chief ENDEL LEPISTO; circ. 76,400 (in Estonian), 41,700 (in Russian).

Paevaleht (Daily): Pärnu mnt. 67A, Tallin 200090; tel. (0142) 681-235; fax (0142) 442-762; f. 1905; daily; Editor-in-Chief MARGUS METS; circ. 100,000 (1991).

Postimees (Postman): Gildi 1, Tartu 202400; tel. (01434) 33-353; f. 1857; daily; Editor-in-Chief MART KADASTIK; circ. 120,000 (1991).

Rahva Hääl (The Voice of the People): Parnu mnt. 67A, Tallinn 200090; tel. (0142) 681-202; fax (0142) 448-534; f. 1940; daily; organ of the Supreme Council and Government; Editor-in-Chief TOOMAS LEITO; circ. 160,000 (1991).

Sirp (The Sickle): Toompuiestee 30, Tallinn 200031; tel. (0142) 601-703; fax (0142) 449-900; f. 1940; fmrly *Reede* (Friday); weekly; cultural affairs; Editor-in-Chief TOOMAS KALL.

Vaba-Maa (Free Land): 200001 Tallinn, Uus 28; f. 1985; organ of the Popular Front of Estonia; Editor-in-Chief TEET KALLAS; circ. 20,000.

PRINCIPAL PERIODICALS

Akadeemia: Küütri 1, Tartu 202400; tel. (01434) 31-117; f. 1937, publ. suspended 1940, resumed publ. 1989; journal of the Union of Writers; Editor-in-Chief AIN KAALEP; circ. 6,000 (1991).

Eesti Loodus (Estonian Nature): Veski 4, Tartu 202400; tel. (01434) 32-368; f. 1933; monthly; publ. by the Perioodika (Periodicals) Publishing House; joint edition of the Academy of Sciences and the Ministry of the Environment; popular science; illustrated; Editor-in-Chief AIN RAITVIIR; circ. 31,000 (1991).

Eesti Naine (Estonian Woman): Pärnu mnt. 67A, Tallinn 200106; tel. (0142) 68-13-10; f. 1924; monthly; popular, for women; Editor-in-Chief AIMI PAALANDI; circ. 100,000 (1991).

Horisont (Horizon): Närva mnt. 5, Tallinn 200102; tel. (0142) 444-385; f. 1967; monthly; publ. by the Eesti Press (Estonian Press) Publishing House; popular scientific; Editor-in-Chief INDREK ROHTMETS; circ. 16,500 (1991).

Keel Ja Kirjandus (Language and Literature): Roosikrantsi 6, Tallin 200106; tel. (0142) 449-228; f. 1958; monthly; publ. by the Perioodika (Periodicals) Publishing House; joint edition of the Academy of Sciences and the Union of Writers; linguistic and literary journal; Editor-in-Chief AKSEL TAMM; circ. 2,200 (1991).

Kultuur Ja Elu (Culture and Life): Närva mnt. 5, Tallinn 200090; tel. (0142) 442-900; fax (0142) 449-558; f. 1958; monthly; publ. by the Perioodika (Periodicals) Publishing House; Estonian history, cultural affairs, memoirs, biographies, travel; Editor-in-Chief SIRJE ENDRE; circ. 16,000.

Linguistica Uralica: Roosikrantsi 6, Tallinn 200106; tel. (0142) 440-745; f. 1965; Editor-in-Chief PAUL KOKLA; circ. 1,230.

Looming (Creation): Harju 1, Tallinn 200090; tel. (0142) 443-262; f. 1923; publ. by the Perioodika (Periodicals) Publishing House; journal of the Union of Writers; fiction, poetry, literary criticism; Editor-in-Chief ANDRES LANGEMETS; circ. 12,600.

Loomingu Raamatukogu (Library of Creativity): Harju 1, 200001 Tallinn; tel. (0142) 449-254; f. 1957; publ. by the Perioodika (Periodicals) Publishing House; journal of the Union of Writers; poetry, fiction and non-fiction by Estonian and foreign authors; Editor-in-Chief AGU SISASK; circ. 23,000.

Noorus (Youth): Pärnu mnt. 67A, 200106 Tallinn; tel. (0142) 681-322; f. 1946; monthly; youth issues, contemporary life in Estonia;

short stories, novels, poems, essays, etc.; Editor-in-Chief LINDA JÄRVE; circ. 45,000 (1991).

Oil Shale: Akadeemia tee 15, Tallinn 200108; tel. (0142) 537-084; fax (0142) 536-371; f. 1984; 4 a year; geology, mining; Editor-in-Chief ILMAR ÕPIK; circ. 1,000.

Täheke (Little Star): 200109 Tallinn, Pärnu mnt. 67A; tel. (0142) 681-497; f. 1960; illustrated; for 6–10-year-olds; Chief Editor ELJU MARDI; circ. 51,000.

Teater, Muusika, Kino (Theatre, Music, Cinema): Närva mnt. 5, POB 3200, 200090 Tallinn; tel. (0142) 44-04-72; fax (0142) 43-41-72; f. 1982; monthly; publ. by the Perioodika (Periodicals) Publishing House; joint edition of the Ministry of Culture and of the creative unions; Editor-in-Chief MIHKEL TIKS; circ. 9,000.

Vikerkaar (Rainbow): Toompuies tee 30, Tallinn 200031; tel. (0142) 445-826; fax (0142) 44-24-84; f. 1986; monthly; publ. by the Perioodika (Periodicals) Publishing House; fiction, poetry, critical works; in Estonian and Russian; Editor-in-Chief TOIVO TASA; circ. 53,000.

NEWS AGENCY

ETA (Estonian Telegraph Agency): Pärnu mnt. 67A, 200090 Tallinn; tel. (0142) 681-301; telex 173193; fax (0142) 682-201; f. 1918; Dir AIMAR JUGASTE.

Publishers

Eesti Raamat (Estonian Book): Pärnu mnt. 10, Tallinn 200090; tel. (0142) 443-937; f. 1940; fiction; juvenile and children's literature; Dir ROMAN SIIRAK.

Estonian Encyclopaedia Publishers: Pärnu mnt. 10, Tallinn 200090; tel. (0142) 449-469; fax (0142) 445-720; f. 1991; encyclopaedias and reference; Chair. of Bd ÜLO K. KAEVATS.

Koolibri: Pärnu mnt. 10, Tallinn 200090; tel. (0142) 445-223; f. 1991; textbooks; Dir ANTS LANG.

Kunst (Fine Art): Lai 34, Tallinn 200001; tel. (0142) 602-035; f. 1958; Dir SIRJE HELME.

Kupar: Harju 1, Tallinn 200001; tel. (0142) 446-832; f. 1987; Chair ENN VETEMAA.

Olion: Pikk 2, Tallinn 200090; tel. (0142) 445-403; f. 1989; politics, economics, history, law; Dir HEINO KÄÄN.

Perioodika (Periodicals): Pärnu mnt. 8, Tallinn 200090; tel. (0142) 441-262; f. 1964; newspapers, guidebooks, periodicals, politics, children's books in foreign languages; Dir UNO SILLAJÕE.

Valgus: Pärnu mnt. 10, Tallinn 200090; tel. (0142) 443-702; fax (0142) 445-197; f. 1965; Dir ARVO HEINING.

Radio and Television

Eesti Raadio (Estonian Radio): Gonsior St 21, Tallinn 200100; tel. (0142) 434-115; telex 173271; fax (0142) 434-457; regular broadcasts since 1926; four programmes (three in Estonian, one in Russian); external broadcasts in Estonian, Russian, Finnish, Swedish, English, Ukrainian, Byelorussian and Esperanto; Dir-Gen. PEETER SOOKRUUS.

Eesti Televisioon (Estonian Television): Faehlmanni 12, Tallinn 200100; tel. (0142) 434-113; telex 173271; fax (0142) 434-155; regular transmissions since 1955; four channels; programmes in Estonian and Russian; Dir-Gen. MART SIIMANN.

Finance

(cap. = capital; dep. = deposits)

BANKING
Central Bank

Eesti Pank (Bank of Estonia): 200100 Tallinn, Kentmanni 13; tel. (0142) 445-331; telex 173146; fax (0142) 443-393; f. 1989; cap. 76m. roubles; dep. 474.3m. roubles; Pres. SIIM KALLAS.

Commercial Banks

Bank of Tallinn: Vabaduse väljak 10, Tallinn; tel. (0142) 449-983; f. 1990; Exec. Dir JURI TRUMM.

Commercial Bank of the Estonian Small Business Association (EVEA Bank): Närva mnt. 40, Tallinn 200106; tel. (0142) 422-122; telex 173184; fax (0142) 421-435; f. 1989; Chair. of Bd BORIS SPUNGIN.

Estonian Commercial Bank of Industry: Suur-Karja 7, Tallinn 200001; tel. (0142) 442-410; fax (0142) 440-495; f. 1988; Chair. of Bd ALEKSANDR GELLART.

Estonian Provincial Bank: Estonia pst. 11, Tallinn 200105; tel. (0142) 441-797; fax (0142) 441-797; f. 1990; Exec. Dir HARRY-ELMAR VOLMER.

Estonian Social Bank: Estonia pst. 13, Tallinn 200100; tel. (0142) 446-900; fax (0142) 445-255; f. 1990; Chair. of Bd SAIMA STRENZE.

Esttexpank: Sakala 1, Tallinn 200100; tel. (0142) 666-657; f. 1989; Chair. MART SILD.

South Estonian Development Bank: Kesk 42, Põlva 202600, tel. (01430) 96-239; f. 1990; Man. TOOMAS LEHISTE.

Tartu Commercial Bank: Munga 18, Tartu 202400; tel. (01434) 33-197; telex 173107; fax (01434) 33-593; f. 1988; Chair. of Bd REIN KAAREPERE; 5 brs.

Union Baltic Bank: Tõnismägi 16, Tallinn 200001; tel. (0142) 682-233; fax (0142) 444-778; f. 1990; Chair. VALENTIN PORFIRYEV.

West-Estonian Bank: Karja 27, Haapsalu 203170; tel. (01447) 44-091; fax (01447) 45-076; f. 1990; Dir AARE SOSAAR; 4 brs.

Savings Bank

Estonian Savings Bank: Kinga 1, Tallinn 200100; tel. (0142) 441-758; f. 1920; Chair. RUSLAN DONTSOV.

Trade and Industry

CHAMBER OF COMMERCE

Chamber of Commerce and Industry of the Republic of Estonia: Toom-Kooli 17, Tallinn 200106; f. 1922; tel. (0142) 444-929; telex 173254; fax (0142) 443-656; Pres. PEETER TAMMOJA.

INDUSTRIAL ASSOCIATION

Estonian Small Business Association (EVEA): Kuhlbarsi 1, Tallinn 200104; tel. (0142) 431-577; telex 173254; fax (0142) 771-675; f. 1988; Man. Dir VELLO VELLASTE.

MAJOR INDUSTRIAL COMPANIES

Ahtme Building Materials Plant: Ahtme, Kohtla-Järve 202020; tel. (01433) 22-405; concrete, lime and gypsum building components; Man. Dir ALEKSANDR VOROBYOV.

Aseri Ceramics Works: Tehase 1, Aseri, Ida-Virumaa 202043; tel. 51-382; bricks, roofing tiles and other building materials; Man. Dir IVO TOMERI.

Balti Manufaktuur: Kopli 35, Tallinn 200090; tel. (0142) 493-511; fax (0142) 444-126; cotton yarns, materials and fabrics; Man. Dir JAAGU KURG.

Desintegraator: Leningradi mnt. 71, Tallinn 200104; tel. (0142) 211-001; telex 173214; fax (0142) 211-008; design and production of disintegrators and associated machinery; Man. Dir JURI EELMA.

Eesti Fosforiit: Fosforiidi 4, Maardu 200901; tel. 234-146; phosphorite mining; production of phosphorous and mixed fertilizers; Man. Dir ALEKSANDR REVKUTS.

Eesti Kaabel: Joe 4, Tallinn 200102; tel. (0142) 422-049; fax (0142) 422-049; copper and aluminium wires and cables; Man. Dir VALERY MALYSHKO.

Eesti Põlevkivi Production Association: Lenini 10, Kohtla-Järve 202020; tel. (01433) 26-554; oil-shale mining and refining; Man. Dir OTTO SULLAKATKO; 14,000 employees.

Estel: Telliskivi 6, Tallinn 200110; tel. (0142) 495-410; telex 179234; fax (0142) 495-489; development and manufacture of semiconductors and converters; Man. Dir VLADIMIR MIROSHNICHENKO.

Flora: Tulika 19, Tallinn 200109; tel. (0142) 472-448; telex 173256; fax (0142) 491-021; paints and other household chemicals; Man. Dir ELMAR KRUUSMA.

Ilmarine: Mustamäe tee 5, Tallinn 200108; tel. (0142) 495-000; fax (0142) 496-062; manufacture of equipment for industrial boilers; household goods; Man. Dir TOOMAS TALVING.

Kohtla-Järve Oil-Shale Chemicals Production Association: Närva mnt. 14, Kohtla-Järve 202020; tel. (01433) 44-545; oil-shale gas and oil; Man. Dir NIKOLAY KUTASHOV.

Oru Peat Works: Oru, Ida-Virumaa 202020; tel 27-141; production of peat and peat briquets; Man. Dir ANATOLY LEPETKIN.

Talleks: Mustamäe tee 12, Tallinn 200100; tel. (0142) 449-048; telex 173201; fax (0142) 498-285; produces excavators, cast-iron goods; Man. Dir PAUL TREIER.

Tallinn Engineering Plant: Kopli 68, Tallinn 200110; tel. (0142) 444-621; fax (0142) 444-621; Man. Dir ALEKSEY MOROZ.

Tallinn Pulp and Paper Mill: Masina 20, Tallinn 200104; tel. (0142) 424-477; fax (0142) 424-303; paper, pulp, etc.; Man. Dir ERNST VAHER.

Tootsi Production Association: Tootsi, Pärnumaa 203470; tel. 66-221; fax 43-554; peat, peat briquets; mica, graphite and other mineral-based products; Man. Dir ARVO LUBERG.

Vasar: Pärnu mnt. 139c, Tallinn 200013; tel. (0142) 555-143; telex 173166; fax (0142) 557-596; manufactures cooling equipment and components; boilers and radiators; Man. Dir ANTS VIIGISALU.

Volta: Tööstuse 47, Tallinn 200110; tel. (0142) 446-002; production of electric generators, motors and home appliances; Man. Dir BORIS CHURIKOV.

Võit: Kalmistu 21/23, Tartu 202400; tel. (01434) 32-808; farming and forestry machinery; Man. Dir KALJU KALJUSTE.

Võru Gas Analysers Plant: Kreutzwaldi 59, Võru 202710; tel. (01441) 21-521; monitoring and control equipment; Man. Dir EINAR KUUSE.

Vihur: Kreutzwaldi 4, Tallinn 200102; tel. (0142) 432-880; telex 173187; Man. Dir TAIVO TANDRE.

TRADE UNIONS

Estonian Trade Union Head Office: Tartu mnt. 4, Tallinn 200100; tel. (0142) 425-100; Chair SIIM KALLAS.

Transport

RAILWAYS

In 1989 there were 1,030 km of railway track in use. Main lines link Tallinn with Narva and St Petersburg (Russia), Tartu and Pskov (Russia), and Pärnu and Riga (Latvia).

ROADS

In 1989 the total length of roads was 30,200 km, of which 29,100 km were hard-surfaced.

Roads Administration: Pärnu mnt. 24, Tallinn 200001; tel. (0142) 445-829; fax (0142) 440-357; Gen. Dir JURI RIIMAA.

SHIPPING

Tallinn is the main port for freight transportation. There are regular passenger services between Tallinn and Helsinki (Finland). A service between Tallinn and Stockholm (Sweden) was inaugurated in 1991.

National Maritime Board: Viru 9, Tallinn 200100; tel. (0142) 442-725; fax (0142) 449-206; Gen. Dir NATHAN TÕNNISSON.

Shipowning Company

Estonian Shipping Company: Estonia pst. 3/5, Tallinn 200101; tel. (0142) 443-802; fax (0142) 424-958; f. 1940; Chief Exec. TOIVO NINNAS.

CIVIL AVIATION

Estonia has air links with most cities in the former Soviet Republics and with several Western European destinations.

Department of Aviation: Viru 9, Tallinn 200100; tel. (0142) 441-785; fax (0142) 449-206; Gen. Dir REIN JÄRVA.

Tourism

Estonia has a wide range of attractions for tourists, including the historic towns of Tallinn and Tartu, extensive nature reserves and coastal resorts. In 1990 the National Tourist Board was established to develop facilities for tourism in Estonia. In 1990 there were over 200,000 visitors to Estonia from other countries (not including visitors from the USSR).

Estonian Association of Travel Agents: Pikk 71, Tallinn 200101; tel. (0142) 425-594; fax (0142) 425-594; Pres. DAISI JÄRVA.

Estonian Marine Tourism Association: Regati pst. 1, Tallinn 200103; tel. (0142) 421-003; fax (0142) 450-893; Chair. MART KUTSAR.

National Tourist Board: Suur-Karja 23, Tallinn 200101; tel. (0142) 441-239; fax (0142) 440-963; Gen. Dir TIIA KARING.

Culture

NATIONAL ORGANIZATION

Ministry of Culture: see section on The Government (Ministries).

Department of Language: Roosikrantsi 6, Tallinn 200106; tel. (0142) 446-906; govt agency established to promote use of Estonian language; Gen. Dir MÄRT RANNUT.

CULTURAL HERITAGE

Estonian Historical Archives: Liivi 4, Tartu 202400; tel. (01434) 32-482; f. 1921; Dir ENDEL KUUSIK.

Estonian Museum of Art: Weizenbergi 37, Tallinn 200103; tel. (0142) 426-246; f. 1919; Dir MARIKA VALK.

Estonian National Museum: Veski 32, Tartu 202400; tel. (01434) 34-279; f. 1909; history of the Estonian and other Finno-Ugric peoples; Dir ALEKSEY PETERSON.

Estonian National Library: Tõnismägi 2, Tallinn 200001; tel. (0142) 448-778; f. 1918; 4.1m. items; Dir IVI EENMAA.

Estonian State Archives: Maneeži 4, Tallinn 200107; tel. (0142) 441-118; f. 1921; Dir HEINO VALMSEN.

F. R. Kreutzwald Museum of Literature: Vanemuise 40, Tartu 202400; tel. (01434) 30-035; f. 1940; Dir PEETER OLESK.

Library of The Estonian Academy of Sciences: Lenini pst. 10, Tallinn 200105; tel. (0142) 440-649; f. 1946; Dir MAIVE DOBKEVICH.

SPORTING ORGANIZATIONS

Department of Sports: Regati pst. 1, Tallinn 200103; tel. (0142) 238-059; telex 173236; fax (0142) 238-355; govt agency; Gen. Dir MATI MARK.

Estonian Central Sports Union: Regati pst. 1, Tallinn 200103; tel. (0142) 237-959; telex 173236; fax (0142) 238-355; f. 1922; Chair. TIIT NUUDI; Sec. Gen. TOOMAS TÕNISE.

Estonian Olympic Committee: Regati pst. 1, Tallinn 200103; tel. (0142) 237-277; fax (0142) 238-100; f. 1923; readmitted to International Olympic Movement 1991; Pres. ARNOLD GREEN.

PERFORMING ARTS

Estonian Drama Theatre: Parnü mnt. 5, Tallinn; tel. (0142) 443-378.

Russian Drama Theatre: Vabaduse väljak 5, Tallinn; tel. (0142) 443-716.

Vanalinnstuudio: Sakala 3, Tallinn; tel. (0142) 448-408.

Youth Theatre: Lai 23, Tallinn; tel. (0142) 609-624.

ASSOCIATIONS

Estonian Architects' Union: Lai 29, Tallinn 200110; tel. (0142) 442-337; fax (0142) 441-179; f. 1921; Chair. IKE VOLKOV.

Estonian Artists' Union: Vabaduse väljak 6, Tallinn 200105; tel. (0142) 445-014; f. 1944; Chair. ANDO KESKKÜLA.

Estonian Composers' Union: Lauteri 7, Tallinn 200105; Chair. JAAN RÄÄTS.

Estonian Cultural Foundation: Olevimägi 14, Tallinn 200100; tel. (0142) 449-512; fax (0142) 601-247; f. 1987; Chair. JAAK KANGILASKI.

Estonian Film-Makers' Union: Uus 3, Tallinn 200101; tel. (0142) 445-337; telex 173213; fax (0142) 601-423; f. 1962; Chair. REIN MARAN.

Estonian Heritage Society: POB 3141, 200090 Tallinn; tel. (0142) 449-216; f. 1987; collects Estonian memoirs and documents and restores monuments; Chair. TRIVIMI VELLISTE.

Estonian Journalists' Union: Närva mnt. 30, Tallinn 200010; tel. (0142) 443-889; (0142) fax (0142) 433-585; f. 1919; Chair. MÄRT MÜÜR.

Estonian Music Association: Tõnismägi 10, Tallinn 200001; tel. (0142) 681-679; telex 173260; fax (0142) 449-147; f. 1987; Chair. VENNO LAUL.

Estonian Theatre Union: Uus 5, Tallinn 200001; tel. (0142) 441-519; fax (0142) 443-582; f. 1945; Chair. MIKK MIKIVER.

Estonian Writers' Union: Harju 1, Tallinn 200001; tel. (0142) 444-583; f. 1922; Chair. VLADIMIR BEEKMAN.

Mother Tongue Society: Roosikrantsi 6, Tallinn 200106; tel. (0142) 449-331; f. 1920; promotes use of Estonian; Chair. HENN SAARI.

Society of Estonian Regional Studies: Estonia pst. 7, Tallinn 200101; tel. (0142) 440-475; f. 1990; Chair. VELLO LÕUGAS.

Education

A comprehensive system of primary and secondary education was introduced in Estonia in 1919. Following the occupation of Estonia, in 1940, the Soviet education system was introduced. Estonian-language schools consist of 12 years of education, with nine years in elementary schools and three years in secondary schools. Russian-language schools consist of 11 years of instruction. Special schools are provided for disabled pupils, and for specialized instruction in music, art and sport. Higher education is provided at seven institutes of higher education, including the Lutheran Theological Institute and the Tallinn Conservatoire.

UNIVERSITIES

Tallinn Technical University: Ehitajate tee 5, 200108 Tallinn; f. 1936; 6 faculties; 816 teachers; 9,049 students; Rector Prof. B. TAMM.

Tartu University: Ülikooli 18, 202400 Tartu; tel. (01434) 34-866; telex 173243; fax (01434) 35-440; f. 1632; languages of instruction: Estonian and Russian; 9 faculties; 1,230 teachers; 8,000 students; Rector Prof. JÜRI KÄRNER.

Social Welfare

In pre-1940 Estonia health care was provided by both state and private facilities. A comprehensive state-funded health system was introduced under Soviet rule. There is a relatively high number of physicians, equivalent to 39 per 10,000 inhabitants, but a shortage of auxiliary staff. In 1988 average life expectancy at birth was 71.0 years, one of the highest in the USSR. The rate of infant mortality decreased from 18.2 per 1,000 live births, in 1975, to 12.4 in 1988.

NATIONAL AGENCIES

Ministry of Health: see section on The Government (Ministries).

Ministry of Social Security: see section on The Government (Ministries).

HEALTH AND WELFARE ORGANIZATIONS

Estonian Children's Fund: Sakala 3, Tallinn 200105; tel. (0142) 443-310; f. 1988; Chair REIN AGUR.

Estonian Committee of the Red Cross: Lai 17, Tallinn 200101; tel. (0142) 444-265; f. 1919; Chair. URSEL VAGUR.

Estonian Pensioners' Union: POB 2956, Tallinn 200032; f. 1990; Chair. HARRI KÄRTNER.

Union of Estonian Societies of the Disabled: Tatari 14, Tallinn 200001; tel. (0142) 442-804; f. 1989; Chair. MIHKEL AITSAM.

The Environment

Environmental concerns concentrate on the high level of pollution produced in industrialized north-eastern Estonia. Of particular concern in the 1980s was the proposed expansion of open-cast phosphorite mining. After public protests, the planned expansion was suspended.

GOVERNMENT ORGANIZATION

Ministry of the Environment: see section on The Government.

ACADEMIC INSTITUTES

Estonian Academy of Sciences: Kohtu 6, Tallinn 200106; tel. (0142) 443-116; telex 173257; fax (0142) 442-149; f. 1938; Pres. ARNO KOORNA; incl.:

Institute of Ecology and Marine Research: Paldiski mnt. 1, Tallinn 200031; tel. (0142) 451-634; fax (0142) 453-748; f. 1990; Dir MATI PUNNING.

Institute of Zoology and Botany: Tartu 202400, Vanemuise 21; tel. (0142) 31-331; fax (0142) 33-472; f. 1946; Dir ANDRES KOPPEL.

Tallinn Botanical Gardens: Kloostrimetsa tee 44/52, Tallinn 200019; tel. (0142) 238-913; fax (0142) 238-468; f. 1961; Dir HEIKI TAMM.

Estonian Institute of Forestry: Rõõmu tee 2, Tartu 202400; tel. (01434) 36-381; f. 1969; Dir IVAR ETVERK.

Estonian Institute for Information: Tõnismägi 8, Tallinn 200106; tel. (0142) 440-513; telex 173178; fax (0142) 682-057; f. 1972; collects data on environmental pollution; Dir GUSTAV LAIGNA (acting).

Estonian Research Institute of Agriculture and Land Reclamation: Saku Sjk., Harjumaa 203400; tel. 721-408; f. 1946; Dir VALDEK LOKO.

NON-GOVERNMENTAL ORGANIZATIONS

Baltic Commission for the Study of Bird Migration: Vanemuise 21, Tartu 202400; interests include effects of pollution in the Baltic Sea on migratory birds' habitats; Chair. VILJU LILLELEHT.

Estonian Green Movement: POB 300, Struve 2, Tartu 202400; tel. (0142) 492-087; f. 1988; Chair. TONU OJA.

Estonian Society for Nature Conservation: Koidu 80, Tallinn 200007; f. 1966; Chair. JAAN EILART.

GEORGIA

Geography

The Republic of Georgia (formerly the Georgian Soviet Socialist Republic) is situated in west and central Transcaucasia, on the southern foothills of the Greater Caucasus mountain range. There is a short frontier with Turkey to the south and a western coastline on the Black Sea. The northern border with the Russian Federation follows the axis of the Greater Caucasus, and includes borders with the Daghestan, Chechen-Ingush, North-Ossetian and Kardino-Balkar Autonomous Republics, and the Autonomous Oblast of Karachayevo-Cherkessia, all of which form part of the Russian Federation. To the south lies Armenia, and to the south-east, Azerbaidzhan. Georgia includes two Autonomous Republics (Abkhazia and Adzharia). The status of the South-Ossetian Autonomous Oblast has been disputed since 1990, when its autonomous status was abolished by the Georgian Supreme Soviet. Georgia has an area of 69,700 sq km (26,911 sq miles).

Geographically, Georgia is divided by the Suram mountain range, which runs from north to south between the Lesser and Greater Caucasus mountains. To the west of the Surams lie the Rion plains and the Black Sea littoral; to the east lies the more mountainous Kura basin. The Rion, flowing westwards into the Black Sea, and the Kura, flowing eastwards through Azerbaidzhan into the Caspian Sea, are the Republic's two main rivers.

The Black Sea coast and the Rion plains have a warm, humid subtropical climate, with over 2,000 mm of rain annually and average temperatures of 6°C (42°F) in January and 23°C (73° F) in July. Eastern Georgia has a more continental climate, with cold winters and hot, dry summers.

At the 1989 census, when the total population was 5,449,000, 68.8% of the population were Georgians, 9.0% Armenians, 7.4% Russians, 5.1% Azerbaidzhanis, 3.2% Ossetians (or Ossetes), 1.9% Greeks and 1.7% Abkhazians. Other ethnic groups included Ukrainians (52,443), Kurds (33,331), Georgian Jews (14,314) and European Jews (10,312). After 1989 some non-Georgians left the Republic as a result of inter-ethnic violence, notably Ossetians seeking refuge in North Ossetia, on the other side of the Caucasus, and many Pontian Greeks. Adzharians, who are ethnic Georgians but were forcibly converted to Islam under Turkish rule, have not been counted separately in Soviet censuses since 1926, when Adzharians accounted for less than 4% of the population of Georgia. Until 1944 there were also some 200,000 Meskhetian Turks in Georgia, who are of mixed Turkish and Georgian descent and are predominantly Muslim. In November 1944 they were deported *en masse* to Central Asia and, although they were rehabilitated and granted the right to return to Georgia in 1968, few were actually permitted to leave Central Asia. Many were forced to flee Central Asia following inter-ethnic violence in 1989, but were refused permission by the Georgian authorities to resettle in their homelands.

Most of the population are adherents of Christianity; the principal denomination is the Georgian Orthodox Church. Islam is professed by Adzharians, Azerbaidzhanis, Kurds and some others. Most Ossetians in Georgia are Eastern Orthodox Christians, although their co-nationals in North Ossetia are largely Sunni Muslim. There are also other Christian groups, and a small number of adherents of the Jewish faith (both European and Georgian Jews). The official language is Georgian, a non-Indo-European language, which is written in the Georgian script.

At 1 January 1991 the total estimated population was 5,464,000. In that year the average population density was 78.4 persons per sq km. The capital is Tbilisi, which is situated in the south-east of the Republic, on the River Kura. In 1989 it had a population of 1,264,000. Other important towns include the ports of Batumi (population in 1989, 136,000), which is the capital of the Adzharian Autonomous Republic, and Sukhumi (121,000), which is the capital of the Abkhazian Autonomous Republic. Rustavi (159,000) is an important industrial centre near Tbilisi.

History

The first Georgian state was established in the fourth century BC, following the conquest of the Persian Empire by Alexander III ('the Great'). Christianity was adopted as the state religion in the fourth century AD, but from the sixth century Georgia enjoyed only short periods of independence. Georgia regained its independence and territories under King David II ('the Restorer'), in the 12th century, but was conquered by the Mongols in 1236. Despite frequent attempts to preserve the country's unity and independence, Georgia became divided into principalities, which preserved only nominal independence under either Turkish or Persian suzerainty and were frequently in conflict with each other. Kartlia and Kakhetia, the principalities under Persian rule, were incorporated into the Russian Empire in 1801. During the next three-quarters of a century, the remaining Georgian lands were annexed by Russia from Turkey.

After the collapse of the Russian Empire in 1917, an independent Georgian state was established on 26 May 1918. Independent Georgia was ruled by a Menshevik Socialist Government and received Soviet recognition by treaty in May 1920. However, against the wishes of the Bolshevik leader Lenin, Georgia was invaded by Bolshevik troops, in early 1921, and a Georgian Soviet Socialist Republic was proclaimed on 25 February of that year. In December 1922 it was absorbed into the Transcaucasian Soviet Federative Socialist Republic (TSFSR), which, on 22 December 1922, became a founder member of the USSR. The Georgian SSR became a full Union Republic, in 1936, when the TSFSR was disbanded.

Georgians were particularly subject to persecution during the period when Stalin (Joseph Vissarionovich Djugashvili), an ethnic Georgian, was the Soviet leader. The first victims had been opponents of Stalin during his time as a revolutionary leader in Georgia. Later, in the 1930s, the persecution became more indiscriminate. Most members of the Georgian leadership were dismissed after the death of Stalin, in 1953. There was a further 'purge' in 1972, when Eduard Shevardnadze became First Secretary of the Communist Party of Georgia (CPG) and attempted to remove officials accused of corruption. Despite Soviet policy, Georgians retained a strong national identity. Opposition to a perceived policy of 'russification' was demonstrated in 1956 when anti-Russian riots were suppressed by security forces, and in 1978 when there were mass protests against the weakened status of the Georgian language in the new Constitution.

The increased freedom of expression under Soviet President Mikhail Gorbachev allowed the formation of unofficial groups, which campaigned on linguistic, environmental and ethnic issues. Such groups were prominent in organizing demonstrations in November 1988 against russification in the Republic. In February 1989 Abkhazians renewed a campaign, begun in the 1970s, for secession of their autonomous republic from the Georgian SSR. Counter-demonstrations were staged in Tbilisi by Georgians demanding that Georgia's territorial integrity be preserved. On the night of 8/9 April 1989 demonstrators in Tbilisi, who were demanding that Abkhazia remain within the Republic and advocating the restoration of Georgian independence, were attacked by soldiers using sharp implements and toxic gas. Twenty people were reported killed and many more injured. Despite the resignation of Party and state officials after the incident and the announcement of an official investigation into the deaths, anti-Soviet sentiment and inter-ethnic conflict increased sharply in the Republic.

The public outrage over the April killings and the increasing influence of unofficial groups forced the Communist Party of Georgia (CPG) to adapt its policies to retain some measure of public support. In November 1989 the Georgian Supreme Soviet, at the time still dominated by CPG members, declared the supremacy of Georgian laws over all-Union laws. In February 1990 the same body declared Georgia 'an annexed and occupied country'. In March Article Six of the Georgian Constitution, which ensured that the Communist Party retained a monopoly on power, was abolished, and, in the same month, the CPG's youth wing, the Komsomol, disbanded itself. Pressure from the opposition parties also forced the elections to the Georgian Supreme Soviet, which were scheduled for 25 March, to be postponed to allow time for a more liberal election law to be drafted. Legislation permitting full multi-party elections was finally adopted in August, but only after opposition groups staged a week-long blockade of Georgia's main railway junction.

Despite the success of the opposition in influencing the position of the CPG, there were considerable differences between the many opposition parties. There were attempts to create a united front for the independence movement, notably the formation, in October 1989, of the Main Committee for National Salvation, which collapsed within two months. No other attempts had succeeded either. In early 1990, however, many of the principal political parties united, in the Round Table-Free Georgia coalition. This and other leading parties aimed to achieve independence by parliamentary means and were willing to participate in elections to Soviet institutions such as the Supreme Soviet. The more radical parties refused to recognize the legality of Soviet institutions or elections. Many of them united in the National Forum, headed by Giorgi (Gia) Chanturia, which announced its intention to boycott the elections to the Supreme Soviet and, instead, to elect a rival parliament, the National Congress. The announcement of elections to the Congress, to be held on 30 September 1990, thus pre-empting the elections to the Supreme Soviet, scheduled for 28 October, caused increased tension in relations between parties of the two tendencies. Political rivalry turned to violence in September: a leading member of the Round Table-Free Georgia coalition was kidnapped; exchanges of gunfire were reported between supporters of the two groups; and the offices of pro-Congress parties were attacked, ransacked and set on fire. The elections to the National Congress took place on 30 September, as scheduled, but only 51% of the electorate participated. Many parties did not take part, preferring to participate in elections to the Supreme Soviet.

In the elections to the Supreme Soviet, which took place on 28 October and 11 November 1990, the Round Table-Free Georgia bloc of pro-independence parties won 64% of the votes cast. This was represented by 155 seats in the 250-seat chamber. Fourteen political parties or coalitions of parties were involved in the election campaign; all of them, including the CPG, were united in seeking Georgia's independence. The CPG, despite its nationalist stance, won only 64 seats. The remainder were won by the Georgian Popular Front, smaller coalitions and independents. The elections were boycotted by many non-Georgians, since parties limited to one area of the country were prevented from participating.

The new Supreme Soviet convened for the first time on 14 November 1990 and elected Zviad Gamsakhurdia, a leading intellectual, the leader of the Round Table-Free Georgia group and Chairman of the Georgian Helsinki Union, as Chairman of the Supreme Soviet. Two symbolic gestures of independence were adopted: the territory was to be called the Republic of Georgia, without any reference to 'Soviet' or 'Socialist', and the white, black and plum-coloured flag of independent Georgia was adopted as the official flag. The next day Tengiz Sigua, also a member of the Round Table-Free Georgia coalition, was appointed head of government.

The new Supreme Soviet, dominated by radical nationalists, passed a number of controversial laws in its first session. On 15 November 1990 the Georgian Supreme Soviet declared illegal the conscription of Georgians into the Soviet armed forces. On 1 January 1991 only 10% of those eligible had complied with the military draft; many young men were reported to have joined nationalist paramilitary groups or were ready to join the National Guard, a *de facto* republican army, which the Supreme Soviet established on 30 January 1991.

The Georgian authorities officially boycotted the all-Union referendum on the future of the union, held in nine other Republics, in March 1991, but polling stations were opened in South Ossetia and Abkhazia, and also in local military barracks. In South Ossetia 43,950 people took part in the referendum; of these, only nine voted against the preservation of the USSR. In Abkhazia almost the entire non-Georgian population voted to preserve the Union. The Georgian leadership refused to participate in the negotiations on a new Union Treaty. Instead, on 31 March 1991, the Government conducted a referendum asking whether 'independence should be restored on the basis of the act of independence of 26 May 1918'. Of those eligible to vote, 95% participated in the referendum, 93% of whom voted for independence.

Following the referendum, on 9 April 1991 the Georgian Supreme Soviet (Supreme Council) approved a decree formally restoring Georgia's independence. On 15 April the Supreme Soviet elected Gamsakhurdia to the newly-instituted post of executive President, pending direct elections for the post on 26 May. These elections were duly won by Gamsakhurdia, who received 86.5% of the votes cast. His closest rival was Valerian Advadze, of the Georgian Union for National Accord and Rebirth, who won only 7.6%. None of the other four candidates won more than 2% of the vote. Voting did not take place in South Ossetia or Abkhazia.

Despite the high level of popular support that Gamsakhurdia received from the electorate, there was considerable opposition from other politicians to what was perceived as an authoritarian style of rule. His actions during the failed Soviet coup attempt of August 1991 were also strongly criticized. He allegedly agreed to demands made by the members of the State Committee for the State of Emergency (SCSE) to disarm military formations in Georgia and, initially, refrained from publicly condemning the coup leaders. It was even claimed by opposition politicians that

Murman Omanidze, the Minister of Foreign Affairs, had travelled to Moscow to meet members of the SCSE. After the coup had collapsed the Georgian leadership strongly denied such allegations. However, Tengiz Kitovani, the leader of the Georgian National Guard, who was officially dismissed by Gamsakhurdia, on 19 August, announced that 15,000 of his men had remained loyal to him and were no longer subordinate to Gamsakhurdia. Kitovani was joined in opposition to the President by Tengiz Sigua, the former Prime Minister, who had resigned in mid-August, and Giorgi Khoshtaria, former Minister of Foreign Affairs, who was dismissed by Gamsakhurdia in August. In September 30 opposition parties united to demand the resignation of Gamsakhurdia and organized a series of anti-government demonstrations. Gamsakhurdia imposed a state of emergency and arrested Giorgi Chanturia, the most prominent opposition politician. There were several deaths after violent clashes between the opposition and supporters of Gamsakhurdia. When opposition supporters occupied the television station in Tbilisi, several people were killed after clashes between Kitovani's troops and those forces still loyal to Gamsakhurdia.

Throughout October demonstrations by both supporters and opponents of Gamsakhurdia continued, but the strength of Gamsakhurdia's support among the rural and working-class population, his arrests of prominent opposition leaders and his effective monopoly of the republican media all weakened the position of the opposition. By November Gamsakhurdia seemed to be in a more powerful position. However, continued unrest severely weakened the economy and discouraged political and economic ties with the West.

In December 1991 the opposition to President Gamsakhurdia resorted to force to oust him. Kitovani, leader of the National Guard, and Dzhaba Ioseliani, leader of the paramilitary Mkhedrioni (Horsemen) group, provided the main military forces, but they were joined by other opposition figures and increasing numbers of former Gamsakhurdia supporters. Chanturia and Ioseliani were released from detention early in the fighting, which was mostly confined to central Tbilisi, around the parliament buildings, where Gamsakhurdia was besieged. He escaped, via Azerbaidzhan, to Armenia, on 6 January 1992. A few days previously, on 2 January, the opposition had declared him deposed and formed a Military Council, led by Kitovani and Ioseliani, which appointed Tengiz Sigua acting Prime Minister. Chanturia was reported to have refused membership of the Military Council, which declared its intention of holding power only until the Supreme Soviet could meet, later that month, and appoint an interim administration, to hold office until parliamentary elections had taken place (scheduled for April). The office of President was to be abolished and the functions of head of state were to be exercised by the Chairman of the Supreme Soviet.

The election of Gamsakhurdia's nationalist government in 1990 severely worsened inter-ethnic tensions in the Republic, which had taken open form in 1988–89. The principal areas of dispute were in the autonomous territories of South Ossetia, Abkhazia and Adzharia. The most violent confrontation was in South Ossetia. Georgian animosity towards the Ossetians stemmed partly from their pro-Soviet stance during the existence of the independent Georgian Republic in 1917–20. The current dispute began in early 1989, when leading Ossetians began to demonstrate support for the Abkhazian movement for secession. Tensions increased after the publication, in August, of legislation strengthening the status of the Georgian language in the Republic. The South-Ossetian Popular Front, Adaemon Nykhas, established earlier in the year, complained that the law discriminated against Ossetian-speakers, few of whom know Georgian. Adaemon Nykhas demanded that South Ossetia be upgraded to the status of an Autonomous Republic and eventually reunited with the North Ossetian Autonomous Republic, in the Russian Federation. These demands met with strong opposition from local Georgians and, in December 1989, there were violent clashes between Ossetians and Georgians. Soviet interior ministry troops were dispatched to the region in January 1990. The region was quiet for some months, but, in August, the Georgian Supreme Soviet passed an electoral law which effectively banned Adaemon Nykhas from nominating candidates in elections to the Supreme Soviet. In response to what was viewed as discriminatory legislation, the South Ossetian Supreme Soviet proclaimed the autonomous South Ossetian Soviet Democratic Republic, as a sovereign republic, on 20 September 1990. The next day this decision was declared unconstitutional by the Presidium of the Georgian Supreme Soviet.

Tension in South Ossetia increased when the Georgian Supreme Soviet formally abolished the region's autonomous status, on 11 December 1990. In January 1991 Gorbachev annulled both this decision and South Ossetia's September 1990 declaration of sovereignty, but violence continued between Georgians and Ossetians throughout 1991. By late 1991 an estimated 83,000 Ossetians had fled to North Ossetia and some 10,000 Georgians had left for other parts of Georgia. By October 1991, according to Western estimates, some 300 Ossetians had died as a result of the conflict. Tensions in the area eased, in January 1992, following the deposition and flight of President Gamsakhurdia. The Military Council ordered the release from detention of the South Ossetian leader, Torez Kulumbekov.

Abkhazians, who constituted only 17% of the population of their autonomous republic in 1989, began a campaign in the late 1980s for secession from Georgia, which was strongly opposed by nationalist Georgians. (Abkhazians were influenced by the Greek Eastern Roman or Byzantine Empire, before falling under the influence of Georgia, particularly from the 10th century.) In July 1989 there were violent clashes between ethnic Georgians and Abkhazians in Sukhumi, the Abkhazian capital. At Sukhumi University 16 people were killed during fighting between students, after Georgian students had attempted to reduce the autonomy of the university by making it a branch of Tbilisi University. A state of emergency and a curfew were imposed in Sukhumi, but troops did not manage to prevent further intermittent violence throughout August.

On 25 August 1990 the Supreme Soviet of the Abkhazian ASSR voted to declare independence from Georgia and adopt the status of a full union republic. On the following day the declaration was pronounced invalid by the Presidium of the Georgian Supreme Soviet, and Georgians living in Abkhazia staged protests and began a rail blockade of the capital, Sukhumi. On 31 August Georgian deputies in the Abkhaz Supreme Soviet reversed its previous decision and rescinded the independence declaration. During 1991 further tensions were reported as a result of Abkhazian participation in the Confederation of Mountain Peoples of the Caucasus, which unites the small ethnic groups of the Northern Caucasus. The support of the Confederation for Abkhazian independence was criticized by the Georgian Government as interference in the internal affairs of Georgia. In January 1992 the new regime of the Military Council made overtures to the Abkhazian leadership, in an attempt to forestall any further moves towards secession.

Despite being of ethnic Georgian origin, the Adzhars, whose autonomous status was the result of a Soviet–Turkish Treaty of Friendship, seem to have retained a sense of separate identity, owing to their adherence to

Islam. Some Christian Georgians considered the Muslim Adzhars a threat to a unified Georgian nation. Before the elections to the Supreme Soviet in October 1990, Gamsakhurdia, leader of the Round Table-Free Georgia bloc, announced that he intended to abolish the autonomous status of Adzharia. Although he did not do so, tensions between Muslims and Christians increased in 1991, after the Georgian Supreme Soviet ruled as unconstitutional an election law for the Adzhar Supreme Soviet, which restricted nominations for the forthcoming elections to permanent residents of Adzharia. In April there were several days of demonstrations to protest against proposals to abolish Adzhar autonomy and against perceived 'christianization' of the Muslim population. Elections took place to the Adzhar Supreme Soviet in June 1991, in which Round Table-Free Georgia won the largest number of seats, but with far less support than in other regions of Georgia.

Gamsakhurdia's Government had little success in 1991 in developing relations with foreign countries or with other former Soviet Republics. Georgia refused to sign either the Economic Community Treaty or the proposed treaty of political union, for the establishment of a new Union of Sovereign States. The policies of the Government towards ethnic minorities and towards its political opponents gave it little support in the West, and several Western countries announced that recognition of Georgian independence would be dependent on its observance of human rights. Recognition was further delayed by the outbreak of civil war in Georgia, in December 1991, and the ousting of President Gamsakhurdia. The new regime did express some interest in joining the new Commonwealth of Independent States (Georgia and the Baltic States were the only Union Republics of the USSR not to have joined the new community).

Economy

The climate experienced in Georgia allows the cultivation of subtropical crops, such as tea and citrus fruits. Non-citrus fruits, flowers, wine grapes, tobacco and almonds are also produced, and some grain and sugar beet is grown. The mountain pastures are used for sheep and goat farming.

Resources include important deposits of manganese. Power generation is based on coal deposits and hydro-electric power stations. There are oil refineries in Batumi, which process petroleum from Baku (Azerbaidzhan), although there have been frequent interruptions in supply as a result of unrest in the region.

There was some industrialization under Soviet rule, including the development of metallurgy, machine-building and the construction-materials industry. In August 1991 legislation permitting the privatization of state enterprises and organizations was adopted and it was expected that similar plans for the privatization of land and housing would also be introduced.

In 1988 Georgia provided 1.6% of total Soviet net material product (NMP), including 1.4% of total industrial NMP and 2.1% of agricultural NMP. In the same year 3.9% of Georgia's NMP came from exports abroad and 53.7% from deliveries to other Republics.

Statistical Survey

Source: Georgian National Encyclopaedia, Tbilisi.

Population

BIRTHS AND DEATHS (per 1,000)

	1987	1988	1989
Birth rate	17.9	17.0	16.7
Death rate	8.8	8.8	8.6

Agriculture

PRINCIPAL CROPS ('000 metric tons)

	1988	1989	1990
Grain	714.2	484.2	647.6
Sugar beet.	51.2	39.3	32.3
Sunflower seed . . .	16.9	2.6	8.5
Potatoes	326.2	332.4	284.4
Other vegetables . .	640.9	515.4	443.7
Grapes.	619.7	514.1	631.4
Other fruit. . . .	733.2	644.1	636.5
Tea (green)	458.7	497.5	501.7

LIVESTOCK ('000 head at 1 January)

	1988	1989	1990
Cattle	1,585	1,548	1,427
Pigs	1,118	1,099	1,028
Sheep and goats . . .	1,920	1,894	1,834
Poultry	23,916.5	25,171.1	24,002.1

LIVESTOCK PRODUCTS ('000 metric tons)

	1988	1989	1990
Meat (slaughter weight) . .	172.1	178.8	163.3
Milk	730.5	711.4	702.5
Eggs (million)	890.2	860.8	810.2
Wool (greasy)	6.2	6.1	6.1

Mining and Industry

Production (1990, unless otherwise stated): Steel tubes 499,000 metric tons, Manganese ore 1,316,000 tons, Mineral fertilizers 130,000 tons, Synthetic fibres 32,300 tons, Plastics 36,500 tons (1987), Paper 28,200 tons, Electric energy 14,200m. kWh.

Education

(1989/90)

	Institutions	Students
Secondary schools	3,700	880,600
Secondary specialized institutions . .	88	44,100
Higher schools (incl. universities) . .	19	93,100

* 1980/81 figure.

Directory

The Government

(January 1992)

HEAD OF STATE

On 2 January 1992 opposition forces proclaimed a Military Council and the deposition of President Zviad Gamsakhurdia (elected 26 May 1991), who fled the country on 6 January. The Military Council appointed an acting Government and was to exercise authority until the Supreme Soviet (legislature) could meet and appoint a Provisional Government, pending general elections (scheduled for April). The Presidency was likely to be abolished and the Chairman of the Supreme Soviet to act as the head of state.

Leaders of the Military Council: TENGIZ KITOVANI, DZHABA IOSELIANI.

Office of the Head of State: 380018 Tbilisi, pr. Rustaveli 8; tel. (8832) 99-97-20; fax (8832) 98-97-97.

COUNCIL OF MINISTERS

Following the deposition of President Gamsakhurdia, the members of the Council of Ministers were dismissed and a new Provisional Government was formed. The Military Council took direct control of four ministries of the Provisional Government: defence, security, internal affairs and the procuracy. The remaining ministries were under the control of the acting premier, Tengiz Sigua.

Chairman: TENGIZ SIGUA.

First Deputy Chairman: OTAR KVILITAYA.

Minister of Defence: Lt-Gen. LEVAN SHARASHENIDZE.

Minister of Internal Affairs: ROMAN GVENTSADZE.

Minister of Justice: DZHONI KHETSURIANI.

POLITICAL-CONSULTATIVE COUNCIL

On 19 January 1992 the Provisional Government created a temporary political-consultative council attached to the office of the acting premier, comprising members of the Military Council, the Chairman of the Supreme Soviet and representatives of leading political parties and parliamentary factions. The Council was to meet, together with the Council of Ministers, to discuss political, economic and social policies. Members of the Council included the following:

VAZHA ADAMIA, MURMAN ALEKSIDZE, AKAKI ASATIANI, IRAKLI BATIASHVILI, AKAKI BAKRADZE, DAVID BERDZHENISHVILI, KONSTANTINE GABASHVILI, TAMAZ GAMKHRELIDZE, GURAM GEGESHIDZE, ARCHIL GEGELIA, ROMAN GOTSIRIDZE, DZHABA IOSELIANI, ALEKSANDR KAVSADZE, TENGIZ KITOVANI, GIORGI MAYSURADZE, NODAR NATADZE, MIKHAIL NANAISHVILI, TEDO PAATASHVILI, ZURAB ZHVANIA, TEIMURAZ ZHORZHOLIANI, TEIMURAZ KHUTIA, NODAR SHAISHVILI, GIORGI SHENGELAIA, ELDAR SHENGELAIA, IRAKLI SHENGELAIA, TAMAR CHKHEIDZE, IRAKLI TSERETELI, GIORGI CHANTURIA, GIORGI KHAINDRAVA, ILYA KHAINDRAVA, TAMAZ DZHANELIDZE.

MINISTRIES

Office of the Chairman of the Council of Ministers: 380034 Tbilisi, ul. Ingorokva.

Ministry of Agriculture, Fisheries and Forestry: 380079 Tbilisi, Kostava 41; tel. (8832) 99-62-61.

Ministry of Architecture and Construction: 380095 Tbilisi, pr. Vazha Pshavela 16; tel. (8832) 37-42-63.

Ministry of Communications: 380004 Tbilisi, pr. Rustaveli 12; tel. (8832) 99-94-24.

Ministry of Culture: 380008 Tbilisi, pr. Rustaveli 35; tel. (8832) 93-22-55.

Ministry of Defence: Tbilisi.

Ministry of Ecology and Nature Conservation: 380071 Tbilisi, ul. Mindeli 9; tel. (8832) 38-58-39.

Ministry of Economics and Finance: 380008 Tbilisi, pr. Rustaveli 8; tel. (8832) 99-97-58.

Ministry of Education: 380002 Tbilisi, ul. Uznadze 52; tel. (8832) 95-88-86.

Ministry of Electric Energy: 380026 Tbilisi, ul. V. Vekua 1; tel. (8832) 99-95-46.

Ministry of Foreign Affairs: 380008 Tbilisi, ul. Chitadze 4; tel. (8832) 99-72-49.

Ministry of Health and Social Security: 380060 Tbilisi, ul. K. Gamsakhurdia 30; tel. (8832) 38-70-71.

Ministry of Industry: 38060 Tbilisi, ul. K. Gamsakhurdia 28; tel. (8832) 38-47-79.

Ministry of Internal Affairs: 380014 Tbilisi, ul. Bolsaya alleya 10; tel. (8832) 99-62-33.

Ministry of Justice: 380026 Tbilisi, pr. Rustaveli 30; tel. (8832) 93-27-21.

Ministry of Labour, Social Security and Demography: 380007 Tbilisi, ul. Leonidze 2; tel. (8832) 93-62-36.

Ministry of Materials and Equipment Supply: 380079 Tbilisi, ul. Kazbegskaya 42; tel. (8832) 38-30-98.

Ministry of Science and Technology: 380008 Tbilisi, ul. Dzhordzhiashvili 12; tel. (8832) 98-70-08.

Ministry of Sport and Tourism: 380062 Tbilisi, pr. Chavchavadze 49; tel. (8832) 23-02-03.

Ministry of Trade: 380062 Tbilisi, pr. Chavchavadze 64; tel. (8832) 29-30-61.

Ministry of Transport: 380060 Tbilisi, pr. A. Kazbegi 12; tel. (8832) 36-45-27.

State Department

Department of National Security: Tbilisi; responsible directly to the head of state.

President and Legislature

PRESIDENT

Presidential Election, 26 May 1991

Candidates	% of Votes Cast
ZVIAD K. GAMSAKHURDIA (Round Table-Free Georgia)	86.5
VALERIAN ADVADZE (Georgian Union for National Accord and Rebirth)	7.6
DZHEMAL MIKELADZE (CPG)	1.6
NOTAR NOTADZE (GPF)	1.2
IRAKLY SHENGELAYA	0.9
TAMAZ KVACHANTIRADZE	0.3

Note: After street fighting in Tbilisi, on 6 January 1992 President Gamsakhurdia fled from Georgia. On 2 January the opposition had formed a Military Council and declared him deposed. The Military Council announced that the office of President was to be abolished. Gamsakhurdia refused to acknowledge the legitimacy of the new regime.

SUPREME SOVIET

Chairman: AKAKI T. ASATIANI.

Deputy Chairman: NEMO BURCHULADZE.

Elections, 28 October and 11 November 1990

Party	Seats
Round Table-Free Georgia	155
Communist Party of Georgia (CPG)*	64
Others	31
Total	250

* In August 1991, following the dissolution of the CPG, Communist Party deputies in the Supreme Soviet (Supreme Council) were removed from office.

Local Government

Georgia contains two autonomous republics and one disputed autonomous oblast. In January 1991 a system of prefectures was introduced, appointed by and responsible directly to the President of the Republic. In January 1992 the Military Council abolished the prefectures and appointed its own representatives in the regions.

AUTONOMOUS REPUBLICS

Abkhazia

The Abkhazian Soviet Socialist Republic was established in February 1922, in union with Georgia, but in 1930 its status was reduced to that of an Autonomous Soviet Socialist Republic (ASSR) within Georgia. It is situated in the north-west of Georgia and covers an area of 8,600 sq km. In 1989 the total population was 537,000. In

1979 17.1% of the population were Abkhazians, most of the remainder being ethnic Georgians. The capital is Sukhumi. Formerly a colony of the Eastern Roman or Byzantine Empire, Abkhazia was an important power in the ninth and 10th centuries, but it was later dominated by Georgian, Turkish and Russian rulers. The language is Abkhazian, a member of the north-western group of Caucasian languages.

Chairman of the Supreme Soviet: VLADISLAV G. ARDZINBA.

Adzharia

The Adzhar ASSR was established on 16 July 1922. It is situated in the south-west of Georgia, on the border with Turkey, and covers an area of 3,000 sq km. In 1989 the population was 393,000. The capital is Batumi. The Adzhars are a Georgian people, who adopted Islam while Adzharia was under Ottoman rule. The Adzhars have an unwritten language, Adzhar, which is closely related to Georgian, but has been strongly influenced by Turkish.

Chairman of the Supreme Soviet: ASLAN ABASHIDZE.

AUTONOMOUS OBLAST
South Ossetia

The South Ossetian Autonomous Oblast (Region) was established on 20 April 1922. It is situated in the north of Georgia and borders the North Ossetian Autonomous Republic (within Russia) to the north. It covers an area of 3,900 sq km. In 1989 the population was 99,000. In 1979 66.4% of the population were Ossetians and 28.8% Georgians. The capital is Tshkhinvali. The Regional Council (oblast soviet) adopted a declaration of sovereignty in September 1990 and proclaimed the territory the South Ossetian Soviet Democratic Republic. The region's autonomous status was abolished by the Georgian Supreme Soviet, in December 1990, and it was merged with adjoining areas to form an administrative region known as Shidi Kartli. The Ossetians are an Iranian (Persian) people, some of whom adopted Islam from the Kabardinians. The national language is Ossetian, a member of the north-eastern group of Iranian languages. Jurisdiction in the region was disputed between the 'Supreme Soviet' and a Presidential Representative for Shidi Kartli. Following the ousting of President Gamsakhurdia, the Military Council released the South Ossetian leader and tension in the area eased.

Chairman of the Supreme Soviet of South Ossetia: TOREZ KULUMBEKOV.

Chairman of the Council of Ministers: ZANAUR N. GASSIEV.

Political Organizations

In March 1990 the Georgian Supreme Soviet amended Article Six of the Republic's Constitution, which had guaranteed the Communist Party's monopoly of power. In August 1991 the Communist Party of Georgia was disbanded. In October 1991 the Law on Political Parties, which permitted a multi-party system to function, was temporarily suspended.

All-Georgian Rustaveli Society: Tbilisi; Chair. TENGIZ SIGUA.

All-Georgian Society of St Ilya the Righteous: Tbilisi; left the Round Table-Free Georgia coalition in September 1991; Chair. TADO PAATASHVILI.

Georgian Monarchists' Party: Tbilisi; advocates independent kingdom of Georgia; Chair. TEYMUR ZHORZHOLIANI.

Georgian Popular Front: Tbilisi; f. 1989 to seek a greater political and economic sovereignty for Georgia; Chair. Prof. NODAR NOTADZE; 50,000 mems.

Ilya Chavchavadze Society: Tbilisi; Chair. IVIKO CHAVCHAVADZE.

National Democratic Party: 380008 Tbilisi, pr. Rustaveli 21, Tbilisi; tel. (8832) 98-31-86; fax (8832) 98-31-88; f. 1981; pro-independence; Leader GEORGI CHANTURIA; Political Sec. MAMUKA GIORGADZE.

National Independence Party: Tbilisi; Chair. IRAKLI TSERETELI.

Round Table-Free Georgia includes the following organizations:

All-Georgian Merab Kostava Society: Tbilisi; f.1990; Chair. VAZHA ADAMIA.

Georgian Helsinki Union: Tbilisi; f. 1977; Chair. ZVIAD K. GAMSAKHURDIA.

Georgian National Christian Party: Tbilisi; Chair. EMZAR GOGUADZE.

Georgian National Front—Radical Union: Tbilisi; Chair. RUSLAN GONGADZE.

Georgian National Liberal Union: Tbilisi; Chair. GEORGE MARJANISHVILI.

Union of Georgian Traditionalists: Tbilisi; left the Georgian Monarchist Party, but is committed to restoration of the Bagration monarchy; Chair. AKAKI ASATIANI.

Social-Democratic Party: Tbilisi; f. 1893, dissolved 1921, re-established 1990; Sec.-Gen. GURAM MUCHAIDZE.

Judicial System

Chairman of the Supreme Court: M. UGREKHELIDZE.
Procurator-General: VAKHTANG RAZMADZE (acting).

Religion
CHRISTIANITY
The Georgian Orthodox Church

The Georgian Orthodox Church is divided into 15 dioceses, and includes not only Georgian parishes, but also several Russian and Greek Orthodox communities, which are under the jurisdiction of the Primate of the Georgian Orthodox Church. There are eight monasteries, a theological academy and a seminary. In 1986 there were an estimated 5m. members.

Patriarchate: 380005 Tbilisi, 4 Sioni St; tel. (8832) 72-27-18; Catholicos-Patriarch of All Georgia ILIYA II.

ISLAM

There are Islamic communities among the Adzhars, Abkhazians, Azerbaidzhanis, Kurds and some Ossetians. The country falls under the jurisdiction of the muftiate based in Baku (Azerbaidzhan).

The Press

In 1989 there were 149 officially-registered newspaper titles being published in Georgia, including 128 published in Georgian, and 75 periodicals, 61 in Georgian. Newspapers are also published in Russian, Armenian, Azerbaidzhani, Abkhazian and Ossetian.

Department of the Press: 380008 Tbilisi, ul. Dzordzhiashvili 12; tel. (8832) 98-70-08; govt regulatory body; Dir REVAZ M. GLONTI.

PRINCIPAL NEWSPAPERS

In Georgian except where otherwise stated.

Akhalgazrda Iverieli (Young Iberian): Tbilisi; 3 a week; organ of the Supreme Soviet; Editor M. BALARJISHVILI.

Eri (Nation): Tbilisi; weekly; organ of the Supreme Soviet; Editor A. SILAGADZE.

Literaturuli Sakartvelo (Literary Georgia): 380004 Tbilisi, pr. Rustaveli 7; tel. (8832) 99-84-04; weekly; organ of the Union of Writers of Georgia; Editor E. DZHAVELIDZE.

Mamuli (Native Land): Tbilisi; fortnightly; organ of the Rustaveli Society; Editor T. CHANTURIA.

Respublika (Republic): Tbilisi; weekly; organ of the Council of Ministers; Editor J. NINUA.

Sakartvelos Respublika (The Republic of Georgia): Tbilisi; 5 a week; organ of the Supreme Soviet; Editor M. PACHUASHVILI.

Tavisupali Sakartvelo (Free Georgia): Tbilisi; 2 a week; organ of Round Table-Free Georgia.

Vestnik Gruzii (Georgian Herald): Tbilisi; 5 a week; organ of the Supreme Soviet; in Russian; Editor V. KESHELAVA.

PRINCIPAL PERIODICALS

Alashara: 394981 Sukhumi, Dom pravitelstva, kor. 1; tel. (88300) 2-35-40; organ of Abkhazian Writers' Organization of the Union of Writers of Georgia; in Abkhazian.

Dila (Morning): 380096 Tbilisi, ul. Lenina 14; tel. (8832) 99-41-30; f. 1904; monthly; illustrated; for 5–10-year-olds; Editor-in-Chief REVAZ INANISHVILI; circ. 168,000.

Drosha (Banner): Tbilisi; f. 1923; monthly; fmrly publ. by the Communist Party of Georgia; politics and fiction; Editor O. KINKLADZE.

Fidiyag: Tskhinvali, ul. Lenina 3; tel. 2-22-65; organ of the South Ossetian Writers' Organization of the Union of Writers of Georgia; in Ossetian.

Khelovneba (Art): Tbilisi; f. 1953, fmrly *Sabchota Khelovneba*; monthly; journal of the Ministry of Culture; art; Editor N. GURABANIDZE.

Kritika (Criticism): 380008 Tbilisi, pr. Rustaveli 42; tel. (8832) 93-22-85; f. 1972; every 2 months; publ. by Merani Publishing House; journal of the Union of Writers of Georgia; literature, miscellaneous; Editor J. GVINJILIA.

Literaturnaya Gruziya (Literary Georgia): 380008 Tbilisi, ul. Lenina 5; tel. (8832) 93-65-15; f. 1957; monthly; journal of the Union of Writers of Georgia; politics and fiction; in Russian; Editor R. MIMINOSHVILI.

Metsniereba da Tekhnika (Science and Technology): Tbilisi; f. 1949; monthly; publ. by the Metsniereba (Science) Publishing House; journal of the Georgian Academy of Sciences; popular; Editor Z. TSILOSANI.

Mnatobi (Luminary): 380004 Tbilisi, pr. Rustaveli 12; tel. (8832) 93-55-11; f. 1924; monthly; journal of the Union of Writers of Georgia; fiction and politics; Editor A. SULAKAURI.

Nakaduli (Stream): Tbilisi, Kostava 14; tel. (8832) 93-31-81; f. 1926; fmrly *Pioneri*; monthly; journal of the Ministry of Education; illustrated; for 10–15-year-olds; Editor V. GINCHARADZE; circ. 35,000.

Niangi (Crocodile): Tbilisi; f. 1923; fortnightly; satirical; Editor Z. BOLKVADZE.

Politika (Politics): Tbilisi; theoretical, political, social sciences; Editor M. GOGUADZE.

Sakartvelos Kali (Georgian Woman): 380096 Tbilisi, Kostava 14; tel. (8832) 99-98-71; f. 1957; monthly; journal of the Georgian Supreme Soviet; popular, socio-political and literary; for women; Editor-in-Chief NARGIZA MGELADZE; circ. 95,000.

Sakartvelos Metsnierebata Akedemiis Matsne (The Herald of the Georgian Academy of Sciences): Tbilisi; f. 1960; quarterly; journal of the Georgian Academy of Sciences; published in series; scientific; in Georgian and Russian.

Sakartvelos Metsnierebata Akademiis Moambe (Bulletin of Georgian Academy of Sciences): Tbilisi; f. 1940; quarterly; journal of Georgian Academy of Sciences; scientific; in Georgian, Russian and English; Editor E. KHARADZE.

Saundzhe (Treasure): 380007 Tbilisi, ul. Dadiani 2; tel. (8832) 72-47-31; f. 1974; 6 a year; organ of the Union of Writers of Georgia; foreign literature in translation; Editor S. NISHNIANIDZE.

Tsiskari (Dawn): 380007 Tbilisi, ul. Dadiani 2; tel. (8832) 99-85-81; f. 1957; monthly; organ of the Union of Writers of Georgia; fiction; Editor I. KEMERTELIDZE.

NEWS AGENCY

In November 1991 the Council of Ministers disbanded Sakartvelo, the official Georgian news agency. A new government information agency was established.

Georgian News Agency: 380008 Tbilisi, pr. Rustaveli 42; f. 1921; Dir IRAKLY KENCHOSVILI.

Publishers

Ganatleba (Education): 380025 Tbilisi, ul. Ordzhonikidze 50; f. 1957; educational, literature; Dir L. KHUNDADZE.

Georgian National Universal Encyclopaedia: Tbilisi, Tseretely ul. 1; Editor-in-Chief. I. ABASHIDZE.

Khelovneba (Art): 380002 Tbilisi, pr. David the Builder 179; f. 1947; books about art; Dir N. JASHI.

Merani (Writer Publishing House): 380008 Tbilisi, pr. Rustaveli 42; f. 1921; fiction; Dir G. GVERDTSITELI.

Metsniereba (Science): 380060 Tbilisi, Kutuzov 19; f. 1941; publishing house of the Georgian Academy of Sciences; scientific; Editor S. SHENGELIA.

Nakaduli (Stream Publishing House): 380060 Tbilisi, pr. Mshvidoba 28; f. 1938; books for children and youth; Dir V. CHELIDZE.

Publishing House of Tbilisi State University: 380079 Tbilisi, pr. I. Chavchavadze 14; f. 1933; scientific and educational literature; Editor V. GAMKRELIDZE.

Sakartvelo (Georgia): 380002 Tbilisi, ul. Marjanishvili 16; f. 1921; fmrly *Sabchota Sakartvelo* (Soviet Georgia); political, scientific and fiction; Dir D. CHARKVIANI.

Radio and Television

Department of Television and Radio Broadcasting: 380071 Tbilisi, Kostava 68; tel. (8832) 36-24-60; govt body; Chair. TEYMURAZ SH. KVANTALIANI.

Radio Tbilisi: broadcasts in Georgian, Russian, Armenian, Azerbaidzhani, Abkhazian and Ossetian.

Tbilisi Television: broadcasts in Georgian and Russian.

Finance

BANKING

In August 1991 the Supreme Soviet adopted legislation which nationalized all branches of all-Union banks in Georgia. Georgian branches of the USSR State Bank (Gosbank) were transferred to a national state bank, the National Economic and Finanical Bank.

State Banks

National Economic and Financial Bank: Tbilisi, Leonidze 3–5; tel. (8832) 99-55-89; fax (8832) 99-07-38; Chair. BAZHE ZHINZHEN-KHADZE.

Georgian Bank for Foreign Economic Activity: Tbilisi; fmrly br of USSR Vneshekonombank; Chair. of Board M. L. LIKHACHEV.

COMMODITY AND STOCK EXCHANGES

Caucasian Commodity and Raw Materials Exchange: 380020 Tbilisi, Ketevan Tsambuki pr. 71; tel. (8832) 74-35-49; telex 212254; fax (8832) 51-55-29; f. 1991; authorized cap. 30m. roubles.

Caucasus Stock Exchange: 380086 Tbilisi, pr. B. Pshavela 72; tel. (8832) 38-46-90; telex 212313; fax (8832) 38-46-81.

Trade and Industry

CHAMBER OF COMMERCE

Chamber of Commerce and Industry of Georgia: 380079 Tbilisi, pr. I. Chavchavadze 11; tel. (8832) 23-00-45; telex 212183; fax (8832) 23-57-60; brs in Sukhumi and Batumi; Chair. GURAM D. AKHVLEDIANI.

FOREIGN TRADE ORGANIZATION

Gruzimpex: 380018 Tbilisi, pr. Rustaveli 8; tel. (8832) 93-71-69; telex 212183; Gen. Dir D. A. VERULISHVILI.

MAJOR INDUSTRIAL ENTERPRISES

Elektroapparat Industrial Association: 380024 Tbilisi, Tornike Eristavi ul. 8; tel. (8832) 66-80-36; telex 212191 fax (8832) 99-89-08; produces a wide range of low-voltage electrical equipment and goods for general use; Gen. Dir. GURAMI GZIRISHVILI.

Tbilisi Instrumental Production Amalgamation: 380094 Tbilisi, Saburtalo 32; tel. (8832) 38-14-69; fax (8832) 38-20-07; manufactures metal-cutting and wood-processing machinery; Gen. Dir. SHUKURI A. KOIAVA; 1,000 employees.

TRADE UNIONS

Federation of Independent Trade Unions of Georgia: Tbilisi; Chair. L. DZIKURIDZE.

Transport

RAILWAYS

In 1989 there were 1,570 km of railway track. The main rail links are with the Russian Federation, along the Black Sea coast, with Azerbaidzhan and with Armenia. The Georgian–Armenian railway continues into eastern Turkey.

ROADS

At 31 December 1989 the total length of roads in use was 35,100 km, of which 31,200 km were hard-surfaced.

SHIPPING

There are international shipping services with Black Sea and Mediterranean ports. The main ports are at Batumi and Sukhumi.

Shipowning Company

Georgian Shipping Company: 384517 Batumi, ul. Gogebashvili 60; telex 412617; fax (87314) 0-06-44; Pres. D. K. CHIGVARIYA.

Culture

NATIONAL ORGANIZATION

Ministry of Culture: see section on The Government (Ministries).

CULTURAL HERITAGE

Georgian State Art Museum: Tbilisi, Ketskhoveli 1; Dir S. Y. AMIRANISHVILI.

Georgian State Museum of Oriental Art: Tbilisi, ul. Azizbekova 3; large collection of Georgian art, carpets, fabrics, etc.; Dir G. M. GVISHIANI.

Georgian State Picture Gallery: Tbilisi, pr. Rustaveli 11; Dir M. A. KIPIANI.

Kutaissi State Museum of History and Ethnography: Kutaissi, ul. Tbilisi 1; 10,000 items; Dir M. V. NIKOLISHVILI.

State Literary Museum of Georgia: Tbilisi, ul. Dzhiordzhiashivili 8; f. 1929; 150,000 exhibits; library of 19,000 vols; Dir I. K. KAK-ABEDZE.

State Museum of the Abkhazian Autonomous Republic: Sukhumi, ul. Lenina 22; f. 1915; 100,000 exhibits; Dir A. A. ARGUN.

State Museum of the History of Georgia: Tbilisi, pr. Rustaveli 3; f. 1852; library of over 204,000 vols; Dir N. G. CHERKEZISHVILI.

State Public Library of the Republic of Georgia: 380007 Tbilisi, Ketskhoveli 5; tel. (8832) 99-92-86; f. 1946; 8m. vols; Dir A. K. KAVKASIDZE.

Tbilisi State Museum of Anthropology and Ethnography: Tbilisi, Komsomolsky pr. 11; archaeological material; library of over 150,000 vols; Dir A. V. TKESHELASHVILI.

PERFORMING ARTS

Georgian Puppet Theatre: Tbilisi, 103 pr. Plekhanova.

Kote Marjanishvili Drama Theatre: Tbilisi, ul. Mardzhanashvili 8.

Shota Rustaveli Drama Theatre: Tbilisi, pr. Rustaveli 17; Dir ROBERT STURUA.

Zakhary Paliashvili Opera and Ballet Theatre: Tbilisi, pr. Rustaveli 25.

ASSOCIATIONS

Union of Writers of Georgia: 380000 Tbilisi, ul. Machabeli 13; tel. (8832) 99-84-90; includes 5 regional Writers' Organizations.

Abkhazian Writers' Organization: 384000 Sukhumi, ul. Frunze 44; tel. (88300) 2-35-34.

Adzhar Writers' Organization: 384516 Batumi, ul. Engelsa 21; tel. (87314) 3-29-66.

South-Ossetian Writers' Organization: 383570 Tskhinvali, ul. Lenina 3; tel. 2-32-63.

Education

Until the late 1980s the education system was an integrated part of the Soviet system. Considerable changes were made, including the ending of teaching of ideologically-orientated subjects, and more emphasis on Georgian language and history. In 1988 66.6% of all pupils were taught in Georgian-language schools, while 23.6% were taught in Russian-language schools. There was also teaching in Azerbaidzhani, Armenian, Abkhazian and Ossetian. In 1991 there were 19 higher education institutions.

UNIVERSITIES

Abkhazian State University: Abkhaz AR, 384900 Sukhumi, ul. Tsereteli 9; tel. (88300) 2-25-98; f. 1985; 8 faculties; 3,800 students.

Georgian Technical University: 380075 Tbilisi, ul. Kostava 63; tel. (8832) 36-07-62; f. 1990; 14 faculties; 2,042 teachers; 28,000 students; Rector Prof G. G. CHOGOVADZE.

Ivan Dzhavakhiladze University of Tbilisi: 380028 Tbilisi, pr. Chavchavadze 1; tel. (8832) 31-47-92; f. 1918; language of instruction Georgian, with a Russian section in some faculties; 19 faculties; 1,659 teachers; 16,000 students; Rector Prof. DAVID I. CHKHIKVISHVILI.

State University of Batumi: Adzhar AR, Batumi; Rector NURI VERZADZE.

The Environment

GOVERNMENT ORGANIZATIONS

Ministry of Ecology and Nature Conservation: see section on The Government (Ministries).

Department of Geology, Geodesy and Cartography: 380030 Tbilisi, ul. Mosashvili 24; tel. (8832) 22-69-14; Dir VLADIMIR I. GUGUSHVILI.

ACADEMIC INSTITUTES

Georgian Academy of Sciences: 380024 Tbilisi, ul. Dzherzhinskovo 8; Pres. A. N. TAVKHELIDZE; attached institutes incl.:

Commission on Nature Conservation: Tbilisi, ul. Z. Rukhadse 1; attached to the Presidium of the Academy; Chair. L. K. GABUNIA.

NON-GOVERNMENTAL ORGANIZATIONS

Georgia Green Movement: Tbilisi; f. 1988; activist environmental group; non-political; Pres. GIVI TUMANISHVILI; c.6,000 mems.

Mtsvanta Partia (Green Party of Georgia): Tbilisi; f. 1990 by mems of the Georgia Green Movement; ecological party favouring Georgian independence; Leader ZURAB ZHVANIA.

LATVIA

Geography

The Republic of Latvia (formerly the Latvian Soviet Socialist Republic) is situated in north-eastern Europe, on the east coast of the Baltic Sea. It is bounded by Estonia to the north and by Lithuania to the south and south-west. To the east there is a frontier with the Russian Federation and, to the south-east, with Byelorussia. Latvia covers an area of 64,589 sq km. The present territory is essentially that of the pre-1940 Republic, except for the area around Pytalovo (formerly Jaunlatgale), which was transferred to the Russian Federation in 1945.

The country is divided into the Coastal Lowlands and three main inland regions: Western Latvia, Central Latvia and Eastern Latvia. The Coastal Lowlands comprise the low-lying littoral of the Baltic Sea and the Gulf of Riga, along which there are several natural harbours. Western Latvia is also largely flat terrain, interrupted only by the undulating relief of the Western Kursa Upland. Central Latvia offers more varied terrain, ranging from the Zemgale plain in the south-west, part of which is below sea-level, to the Vidzeme Upland, a region of uneven relief, which includes the highest point in Latvia (Gaizinkalns—312 m). Eastern Latvia is dominated by the Latgale Upland, which extends to the south-eastern border with Byelorussia, and includes more than 1,000 lakes. Although there are more than 12,000 rivers in the country, the only major waterways are the Daugava (Dvina), which flows through the centre of the country and empties into the Gulf of Riga, and the Gauja, which rises in the Vidzeme Upland, in the east.

Owing to the influence of maritime factors, the climate is relatively temperate but changeable. Average temperatures in January range from −2.6°C (27.3°F) in the western, coastal town of Liepāja, to −6.6°C (20.1°F) in the inland town of Daugav'pils. Mean temperatures for July range from 16.8°C (62.2°F) in Liepāje to 17.6°C (63.7°F) in Daugav'pils. Average annual precipitation in Riga is 567 mm.

At the census of 12 January 1989, of a total population of 2,681,000, 51.8% were Latvians, 33.8% Russians, 4.5% Byelorussians, 3.4% Ukrainians and 2.3% Poles. There were also small numbers of Lithuanians (34,630), Jews (22,897), Roma (7,044), Tatars (4,828) and Germans (3,783). By comparison, in 1935, 75.5% of the population were ethnic Latvians. There are significant communities of Latvians in other countries, notably in the USA. The proportion of the population living in rural areas declined from 68.2% in 1935 to 28.9% in 1989. Population distribution is quite uneven, with almost 50% of the population living in the region around Riga. The average population density (persons per sq km) was 41 in 1989, but was as low as six in parts of Western Latvia.

Latvian replaced Russian as the official language of the Republic in 1988. It is an Indo-European language, a member of the Baltic group, and is written in the Latin script. At the census of 1989 22.3% of ethnic Russians claimed fluency in Latvian. The major religion is Christianity: most ethnic Latvians are traditionally Lutheran, although smaller Protestant sects have a considerable following among the younger generation, and the Roman Catholic Church is also represented. Adherents of the Russian Orthodox Church in Latvia are mostly ethnic Russians.

At 1 January 1991 the total estimated population was 2,681,000. The capital is Riga (Rīga), which is an important port, situated near the mouth of the River Daugava. In 1990 it had an estimated population of 916,500. Other important cities include Daugav'pils (128,200), Liepāja (114,900) and Jelgava (75,100).

History

In 1290 the German Teutonic Knights conquered Latvia and established the Livonian State. In 1591 Livonia was partitioned. South-western Latvia became the hereditary Duchy of Courland, under the suzerainty of Poland. The other Livonian territories became a dependency of Poland, until they were conquered by Sweden in 1629. They remained under Swedish rule until the Great Northern War between Russia and Sweden. The conclusion of the War by the Treaty of Nystad, in 1721, brought most of Latvia under Russian rule. The eastern region of Latgalia remained under Polish suzerainty until 1772, when it was annexed by Russia at the first Partition of Poland. The Duchy of Courland was absorbed into the Russian Empire at the Third Partition, in 1795. Even under Russian rule, Latvians remained divided. In west-central Latvia (the Duchy of Courland and southern Lifland) the descendants of the Teutonic Order, the Baltic Germans, or *Ritterschaften*, were granted considerable economic and cultural autonomy. Latgalia, however, was absorbed into the Russian province of Vitebsk, where the Latvian peasantry was ruled by Russian and Polish nobility.

During the latter half of the 19th century, the privileges of the Baltic nobility were gradually diminished, and Latvians were permitted to become small landowners. The onset of industrialization encouraged the Latvian peasantry to move to urban areas and an indigenous middle class began to emerge. As a result of these economic and social changes, a Latvian nationalist movement developed in the 1860s, led by groups such as the Young Latvian Movement, which aimed to promote Latvian language and culture. By the early 1900s national-cultural groups had developed into a political movement which advocated territorial autonomy for Latvia within the Russian Empire, a stance which continued until after the February Revolution of 1917 in Russia, when other national groups within the Empire were demanding complete independence. However, in October 1917, representatives of most Latvian political groups, united in the Riga Democratic Bloc, met to establish an independent Latvian state. On 18 November 1917 the independent Republic of Latvia was proclaimed.

The establishment of independence, under the nationalist Government of Kārlis Ulmanis, was only fully achieved after the expulsion of the Bolsheviks from Riga, with the aid of German troops, and from Latgale, with Polish and Estonian assistance. Latvia's first Constitution was adopted in 1922. It introduced a democratic system of government, which, owing to an electoral system based on proportional representation, permitted a large number of small parties to be represented in the 100-member Saeima (parliament). A series of coalition governments, dominated by the Latvian Peasants' Union, concentrated on developing the agrarian base of the economy, introducing agrarian reforms and developing the export of agricultural products to Western Europe. The economic decline of the 1930s, together with the politically fragmented Saeima, prompted a *coup d'état*, in 1934, by the Prime Minister, Kārlis Ulmanis.

He introduced authoritarian rule, headed by a Cabinet of National Unity, and became President in 1936.

Under the Treaty of Non-Aggression (the Nazi–Soviet Pact), signed by Germany and the USSR on 23 August 1939, the incorporation of Latvia into the USSR was agreed by the two powers. A Treaty of Mutual Aid between the USSR and Latvia forced the Government to allow the establishment of Soviet military bases in Latvia. Under military pressure, elections were held to the Saeima, with only the nominations of candidates approved by Soviet officials permitted. The parliament thus produced proclaimed the Latvian Soviet Socialist Republic on 21 July 1940, and requested membership of the USSR. On 5 August 1940 the Latvian SSR was formally admitted to the USSR as a constituent Union Republic.

In 1941 Soviet rule in Latvia was ended by German occupation. Most German troops had withdrawn by 1944, although Courland was retained by Germany until the end of the War. Soviet Latvia was re-established in 1944–45 and the process of 'sovietization', begun in 1940, was continued. Independent political activities were prohibited and exclusive political power was exercised by the Communist Party of Latvia (CPL), headed by Jānis Kalnērziņš (First Secretary 1940–59), which was dominated by the so-called *latovichi*, the term used to describe russified Latvians who had spent the 1920s and 1930s in the USSR. Under Communist rule a process of industrialization was initiated, with the introduction of metal- and machine-working industries, and development of the chemical industry. This forced industrialization encouraged Russian immigration into the Republic.

Rapid development of the industrial sector left the agricultural sector neglected. By the early 1950s almost all of Latvia's privately-owned farms had been merged into collective farms, a policy which was implemented by frequent deportations and arrests of reluctant peasants. The stagnant state of agriculture was addressed as a result of greater powers granted the Latvian authorities as a result of the policy of economic decentralization introduced in the USSR in the mid-1950s. Increased economic independence was paralleled by a movement within the CPL for greater cultural autonomy, which focused on the need to retain the Latvian language as the predominant language in the Republic. In the late 1950s some 2,000 alleged members of this so-called 'nationalist group' were dismissed from leading government and Party positions. Among them was First Secretary of the CPL, Jānis Kalnērziņš. He was replaced by Arvīds Pelše, one of the *latovichi* favoured by the Soviet authorities. Under Pelše, and under his successor Augusts Voss (First Secretary 1966–84), the limited autonomy gained in the 1950s was reversed, and repression of Latvian cultural and literary life was increased.

In the late 1970s and early 1980s there was a significant revival in traditional Latvian cultural activities, such as folk singing, and youth groups began a movement to restore historical monuments and churches. Political groups began to be established, including the Environmental Protection Club, established in 1984 to campaign against environmental degradation, and Helsinki-86, established to monitor Soviet observance of the Helsinki accords. The latter group issued an unofficial journal, *Tevija* (Fatherland), and organized anti-Soviet demonstrations in June and August 1986, which were disrupted by the police. In November 1986 the growing influence of public opinion was demonstrated by the decision to end construction of the Daugav'pils Hydroelectric Station after protests by environmentalists. In 1987 there were further demonstrations on the anniversaries of significant events in Latvian history, such as 23 August (the signing of the Stalin–Hitler Pact) and 18 November

(the establishment of Latvian independence). These nascent opposition movements, engendered by the greater freedom of expression permitted by Soviet leader Mikhail Gorbachev's policy of *glasnost*, were strongly opposed by the conservative republican leadership, headed since 1984 by Boris Pugo as First Secretary of the CPL.

In 1988 the opposition movements began to unite into a significant political force in the Republic. Leading intellectuals, led by Jānis Peters, the Chairman of the Writers' Union, began to criticize the CPL for its attitude to *perestroika* and to advocate more radical political and economic change. In June Latvia's cultural unions issued a joint resolution demanding that Latvian be made the state language, that the Secret Protocols of the Stalin–Hitler Pact be published and that measures be taken to cope with ecological degradation resulting from forced industrialization. Similar demands were made in the Republic's press. In October 1988 representatives of the leading opposition movements, together with radicals from the CPL, organized the inaugural congress of the Latvian Popular Front (LPF). The LPF quickly became the largest and most influential political force in Latvia, with an estimated 250,000 members by the end of 1988. At its inaugural congress it adopted a policy of seeking sovereignty for Latvia within a renewed Soviet federation and elected Dainis Ivans as its first President.

In September 1988 Boris Pugo, who was to be one of the leading participants in the coup of August 1991, was transferred to Moscow, and replaced as First Secretary of the CPL by Jan Vigris. The new Party leadership, which came increasingly under the control of members of the Popular Front (in October 1988 one-third of the Front's 120,000 members were also members of the CPL), was far more sympathetic to the Front's aims than it had been under Pugo. On 29 September 1988 Latvian was designated the state language and the symbols of national independence, such as the Latvian flag and anthem, were no longer considered illegal. During 1989 the nationalist movement began to adopt more radical policies. The National Independence Movement of Latvia (NIML), which had been formed in 1988, held its first congress in February. The NIML's policies advocated full economic and political independence for Latvia, and its influence within the opposition movement (many of its members were also members of the LPF) led to the proposal, in May, by the leadership of the LPF to conduct a referendum on full independence for Latvia.

On 26 March 1989 candidates supported by the LPF won 26 of 34 seats in the elections to the all-Union Congress of People's Deputies. On 28 July, following similar moves by Lithuania and Estonia, the Supreme Soviet adopted a declaration of sovereignty and economic independence. The growing support for full independence outside the USSR was demonstrated at the Second Congress of the LPF (7–8 October 1989), where delegates supported demands for total political and economic independence, and the introduction of a multi-party system and a market-based economy. Despite the establishment of political groups opposed to the LPF (principally Interfront, a group opposed to independence, dominated by Russian-speakers), in December 1989 candidates supported by the Latvian People's Front won some 75% of seats in local elections. The high level of support for the LPF seemed to indicate a degree of indifference rather than opposition to political change among non-Latvians.

In January 1990 the Latvian Supreme Soviet voted to abolish the constitutional provisions which guaranteed the Communist Party its monopoly of political power. On 15 February the Supreme Soviet adopted a declaration condemning the decision of the 1940 parliament to request admission to the USSR, and, in the same month, the Supreme Soviet restored the flag, state emblems and anthem of pre-1940 Latvia to official use. In the elections to the Supreme Soviet, on 18 March 1990, the LPF won a convincing victory. Candidates endorsed by the LPF, who were members of a variety of political parties which supported independence, won 131 of the 201 seats in the Supreme Soviet. Members of the CPL won about 59 seats, and there were 11 independents. In April, at an extraordinary congress, the CPL split into two parties. The majority of delegates rejected a motion to leave the Communist Party of the Soviet Union (CPSU). Instead, they voted to remain an integral part of the CPSU and elected Alfred Rubiks, a hardline opponent of independence, as First Secretary. The pro-independence faction of some 260 delegates left the Congress and established the Independent Communist Party of Latvia. Ivars Kezbers was elected as Chairman of the new party and the demand for Latvian independence outside the USSR was adopted as part of a new party programme.

The new Supreme Soviet (which subsequently changed its name to the Supreme Council) convened on 3 May 1990 and elected Anatolijs Gorbunovs, a member of the CPSU-affiliated Communist Party, as its Chairman (*de facto* president of the Republic). The next day the Supreme Council adopted a resolution which declared the incorporation of Latvia into the USSR in 1940 as unlawful and announced the beginning of a transitional period which was to lead to full political and economic independence. (The resolution reinstated the Constitution of 15 February 1922 and the formal name, the Republic of Latvia. During the transitional period the 1922 Constitution was to be suspended, with the exception of four articles describing Latvia as an independent democratic state and asserting the sovereignty of the Latvian people.) Ivars Godmanis, the Deputy Chairman of the Popular Front, was elected as Prime Minister of a new Government, which was dominated by members of the Popular Front.

On 30 April–1 May 1990 a rival parliament to the Supreme Council, the Congress of Latvia, convened. It had been elected in unofficial elections, in which 700,000 people were estimated to have participated. Only citizens of the pre-1940 Republic and their descendants were permitted to vote. The Congress, in which members of the radical NIML predominated, declared Latvia to be an occupied country and adopted resolutions on independence and the withdrawal of Soviet troops.

The declaration of 4 May, although more cautious than independence declarations adopted in Lithuania and Estonia, severely strained relations with the Soviet authorities. On 14 May President Gorbachev issued a decree, which annulled the Latvian declaration of independence, describing it as in violation of the USSR Constitution. The declaration was also also opposed by some non-Latvians, who organized strikes and demonstrations to protest against the decisions of the Supreme Council. Opposition to the pro-independence Government continued throughout 1990, with the all-Union authorities attempting to persuade Latvia to sign a new Union Treaty, and local anti-government movements, allied with Soviet troops stationed in Latvia, conducting a campaign of propaganda and harassment against the Government. In December a series of explosions were reported in Riga, and the Government claimed that special units of the Soviet Ministry of Internal Affairs (OMON units) were responsible.

In January 1991 hardline forces in the Republic were involved in an apparent attempt to overthrow the Latvian Government and re-establish Soviet rule. On 2 January OMON troops seized the Riga Press House, previously the property of the CPL. On 14 January OMON units tried to occupy a police station and attempted to remove barricades which had been erected by Latvians in anticipation of military intervention. On 20 January a 'Committee of Public Salvation', headed by Alfred Rubiks, the hardline First Secretary of the CPL, declared itself as a rival Government to that led by Godmanis. The same day three people died when OMON troops attacked the building of the Latvian Ministry of Internal Affairs.

The attempted seizure of power by the Committee of Public Salvation reinforced opposition in the Republic to inclusion in the new Union Treaty being prepared by nine Republics. Latvia refused to conduct the all-Union referendum on the future of the Union, which was scheduled for 17 March (some 680,000 people did participate, on an unofficial basis, mostly Russians and Ukrainians). Instead of the official referendum, on 3 March 1991 a referendum on Latvian independence was held. Voters were asked 'Are you for a democratic and independent Latvian Republic?' Of those eligible to vote (members of the Soviet Armed Forces were excluded), 87.6% participated. According to official results, 73.7% of these voters approved an independent Latvia, a higher result than expected, given that ethnic Latvians only constituted 52% of the population.

When the State Committee for the State of Emergency announced that it had taken power in August 1991, military intervention was immediately expected in Latvia. Preparations were made for the establishment of a Government-in-Exile and, despite the presence of troops in Riga, an emergency session of the Supreme Council convened on 21 August. The Supreme Council declared the full independence of Latvia and declared the SCSE unconstitutional. When the coup collapsed the Government quickly began to assert its control over events in the Republic. On 23 August the CPSU was banned in the Republic and Alfred Rubiks, leader of the pro-CPSU Latvian Communists, was arrested.

Other countries quickly recognized Latvian independence and, on 4 September 1991, the USSR State Council formally recognized the independent Latvian Republic. Latvia was admitted to the UN on 17 September. However, difficult internal political issues remained to be resolved. Among the most controversial issues was that of citizenship of the Latvian Republic. On 15 October the Supreme Council adopted legislation on citizenship, which automatically restored the citizenship of those Latvians and their descendants who had been citizens of the pre-1940 Republic. Other residents of Latvia, according to the legislation, would have to apply for naturalization. Many Russians and other Slavs protested against the requirements for naturalization, which included residence of 16 years in Latvia and a knowledge of the Latvian language. The more radical nationalists, including members of the Congress of Latvia, protested that the Supreme Council, which they viewed as a Soviet institution, had no authority to make such decisions.

Economy

In 1989, according to official estimates, Latvia's gross national product (GNP) totalled 16,700m. roubles, equivalent to 6,229 roubles per head. In that year the total labour force was 1,317,000.

Agriculture contributed 20.4% of GNP and employed some 18.8% of the working population in 1989. In that year the total area of cultivated land was 2,570,000 ha. Forced collectivization of agriculture had a serious affect on output. The real value of output increased by only 50% in the period 1939–89. Principal sectors are dairy farming and pig-breeding. Flax, cereals, sugar beets, potatoes and fodder crops are the main crops grown.

Industrial production accounted for 60.9% of GNP and employed 28.4% of the working population in 1989. The major sectors are machine-building, metal-working, and chemical and petrochemical industries.

Latvia has limited natural resources, and is dependent on imported fuels to provide energy. In 1989 total electric energy produced was 5,801m. kWh.

Latvia's trade is mainly with other former Soviet Republics; in 1988 deliveries to other Republics comprised 64.1% of total NMP. In the same year exports to the rest of the world contributed 5.7% of NMP. The liberalization of foreign trade in the late 1980s permitted an increase in contacts with foreign partners and the establishment of joint-venture companies, of which 85 were functioning by 1 April 1991.

In 1990 and 1991 the Latvian Government initiated economic reforms designed to introduce a market economy. It was expected that a Latvian currency, the Lat, would be introduced in 1992.

Statistical Survey

Source: Ministry of Culture, Riga.

Population

BIRTHS AND DEATHS (per 1,000)

	1987	1988	1989
Birth rate	15.8	15.4	15.5
Death rate	12.1	12.1	12.1

Agriculture

PRINCIPAL CROPS ('000 metric tons)

	1987	1988	1989
Grain	2,086	1,413	1,410
Sugar beet	352	455	470
Flax fibre	5.7	4.6	4.7
Potatoes	1,135	1,110	1,127
Other vegetables . .	194	214	210
Fruit (incl. grapes) . . .	32	49	47

LIVESTOCK ('000 head at 1 January)

	1987	1988	1989
Cattle	1,481	1,460	1,467
Pigs	1,718	1,620	1,710
Sheep and goats . . .	170	165	160
Poultry	12,487	12,209	12,197

LIVESTOCK PRODUCTS ('000 metric tons)

	1987	1988	1989
Meat (slaughter weight) . .	338.1	334.4	334.0
Milk	1,987.7	1,974.0	1,976.0
Eggs (million)	920.8	920.0	920.3

Mining and Industry

Production (1990): Steel 499,000 metric tons, Rolled ferrous metal products 681,000 metric tons, Chemical fertilizers 169,000 metric tons, Plastics 31,300 metric tons, Chemical fibres and threads 57,950 metric tons, Paper 99,000 metric tons, Electric energy 5,949m. kWh.

Education

(1990/91)

	Institutions	Students
Secondary schools	787	303,570
Secondary professional schools . . .	83	327,960
Secondary specialized institutions . .	57	38,090
Higher schools (incl. universities) . .	11	44,050

Directory
The Government

(January 1992)

HEAD OF STATE

Chairman of the Supreme Council: ANATOLIJS GORBUNOVS (elected 3 May 1990).

COUNCIL OF MINISTERS

Prime Minister: IVARS GODMANIS.

Minister of Agriculture: DAINIS GEGERIS.

Minister of Architecture and Construction: AIVARS PRŪSIS.

Minister of Culture: RAIMONDS PAULIIS.

Minister of Defence: TALAVS JUNDZIS.

Minister of Economic Reform: AMIS KALNINS.

Minister of Education: ANDRIS PIEBALGS.

Minister of Finance: ELMĀRS SILINŠ.

Minister of Foreign Affairs: JĀNIS JURKĀNS.

Minister of Foreign Trade: EDGARS ZAUSĀJEVS.

Minister of Forestry: KAZIMIRS SLAKOTA.

Minister of Internal Affairs: ZIEDONIS CEVERS.

Minister of Justice: VIKTORS SKUDRA.

Minister of Maritime Affairs: ANDREJS DANDSBERGS.

Minister of Power and Industry: AIVARS MILLERS.

Minister of Social Welfare: TEODORS ENINS.

Minister of State Affairs: JĀNIS DINEVICS.

Minister of Transportation: (vacant).

MINISTRIES

Ministry of Agriculture: Republikas lauk. 2, Riga 226168; tel. (0132) 325-107.

Ministry of Architecture and Construction: Raina bul. 7, Riga 226800; tel. (0132) 227-643.

Ministry of Culture: L. Paegles 2, Riga 226310; tel. (0132) 224-772.

Ministry of Defence: Riga.

Ministry of Economic Reform: Brīvības bul. 36, Riga; tel. (0132) 288-844.

Ministry of Education: Valnu 2, Riga 226050; tel. (0132) 228-482.

Ministry of Finance: Smilšu 1, Riga 226919; tel. (0132) 211-752.

Ministry of Foreign Affairs: Pils 11, Riga 226800; tel. (0132) 220-079.

Ministry of Foreign Trade: kr. Valdemāra 26, Riga 226329; tel. (0132) 286-489.

Ministry of Forestry: Smilšu 1, Riga 226909; tel. (0132) 228-873.

Ministry of Internal Affairs: Raina bul. 6, Riga 226181; tel. (0132) 287-260.

Ministry of Justice: Brīvības bul. 34, Riga 226173; tel. (0132) 282-607.

Ministry of Maritime Affairs: Smilšu 6, Riga 226176; tel. (0132) 322-498.

Ministry of Power and Industry: Riga.

Ministry of Social Welfare: E. Veidenbauma 25, Riga 226305; tel. (0132) 286-720.

Ministry of State Affairs: Riga.

Ministry of Transportation: Brīvības 58, Riga 226305; tel. (0132) 226-922.

Legislature

SUPREME COUNCIL

The highest legislative body in Latvia is the Supreme Council. It is a unicameral parliament, consisting of 201 deputies. Elections were held in March 1990.

First Deputy Chairman: DAINIS IVANS.

Political Organizations

In January 1990 the Latvian Supreme Soviet abolished clauses in Article Six of the Republic's Constitution which had guaranteed the Communist Party's monopoly of power. In August 1991 the Communist Party was banned.

Democratic Inititiative Centre: Riga; f. 1991 by members of the Ravnopravie faction in the Supreme Council; Chair. MIKHAIL GARILOV.

Democratic Labour Party of Latvia: Terbatas 23/25, Riga 226700; tel. (0132) 280-845; fax (0132) 280-846; f. 1990 after a split in the Communist Party of Latvia; Chair. JURIS BOJARS; 20,000 mems.

Interfront of the Working People of the Latvian SSR: Smilšu 12, Riga 226050; tel. (0132) 223-280; f. 1988; unites ethnic Russian inhabitants opposed to independence; 10-mem. presidium; Chair. ANATOLIJS ALEKSEJEVS; 316,000 mems. (1988).

Latvian National Independence Movement: Gertrūdes 19/21, Riga 226050; tel. (0132) 272-220; fax (0132) 272-220; f. 1988; exec. cttee of 40 mems, 15-mem. presidium; Chair. VISVALDIS LĀCIS; 11,700 mems.

Latvian Green Party: Riga; tel. (0132) 323-916; f. 1990; Chair. OLEG BATAREVSKIS; 300 mems.

Latvian Social Democratic Workers' Party: Avotu 11–32, Riga 226011; tel. (0132) 287-783; f. 1904; re-established 1989; Chair. ULDIS BERZINŠ; 740 mems.

Latvijas Tautas Fronte (LTF) (Latvian People's Front): Vecpilsētas 13/15, Riga 226050; tel. (0132) 212-286; telex 161177; fax (0132) 213-978; f. 1988; 157-mem. ruling council, 2,300 brs; Chair. ROMUALDS RAŽUKS; 186,000 mems (1991).

Diplomatic Representation

EMBASSIES IN LATVIA

Belgium: Riga; Chargé d'affaires a.i.: JAN F. MUTTON.

Denmark: Kr. Barona 12, Riga 226400; tel. (0132) 289-994.

Sweden: Lāčplēša 13, Riga 226050; tel. (0132) 286-276.

United Kingdom: Riga; Ambassador: RICHARD SAMUEL.

USA: Ridzēne Hotel, Endrupa 1, Riga; tel. (0132) 324-433; Ambassador-designate: INTS SILINS.

Judicial System

Supreme Court: Brīvības bul. 34, Riga 226616; tel. (0132) 289434; following recognition of Latvian independence the Soviet legal system ceased to be effective on Latvian territory. The Supreme Court is the final arbiter in criminal and civil cases. A complete reorganization of the judicial system was expected.

Chairman: GVIDO ZEMRIBO.

Office of the Procurator-General: Komunāru bul. 6, Riga 226050; tel. (0132) 320085.

Procurator-General: JĀNIS SKRASTINS.

Religion

After 1940, when Latvia was annexed by the USSR, many places of religious worship were closed and clergymen were imprisoned or exiled. In the late 1980s there was a revival of official tolerance of religion.

Department of Religious Affairs: Elizabetes 57, Riga 226050; tel. (0132) 288-879; govt agency; Dir ARNOLDS KUBLINSKIS.

CHRISTIANITY

The Roman Catholic Church

Metropolitan See of Riga: M. Pils 2A, Riga 226047; tel. (0132) 227-226; f. 1918; Metropolitan JĀNIS PUJĀTS.

Orthodox Churches

Latvian Eparchy of the Orthodox Church: M. Pils 11, Riga 226050; tel. (0132) 228-324; f. 1850; the Orthodox Church in Latvia is subordinate to the Moscow Patriarchate, which appoints the Metropolitan; members are mostly ethnic Slavs; Bishop ALEKSANDRS KUDRJAŠOVS.

Latvian Old Believers Pomor Church: Krasta 73, Riga 226003; (0132) 222-981; f. 1760; Head of Central Council IVANS MIROLUBOVS.

Protestant Churches

Consistory of the Evangelical Lutheran Church: Lāčplēša 4, Riga 226010; tel. (0132) 334-194; fax (0132) 334-194; f. 1920; Archbishop KĀRLIS GAILĪTIS.

Union of the Latvian Baptist Church: Matīsa 50B, Riga 226009; tel. (0132) 271-312; Bishop JĀNIS EISĀNS.

Union of the Seventh Day Adventists in Latvia: J. Kupalas 9-1, Riga 226010; tel. (0132) 321-050.

JUDAISM

Hebrew Religious Community of Riga: Peitavas 6/8, Riga 226050; tel. (0132) 224-549; Head MIHAILS ARONS.

OTHER RELIGIOUS GROUP

Dievturi: Dārza 36A–53, Riga 226083; tel. (0132) 450-797; community celebrating the ancient Latvian animist religion; Leader EDUARDS DETLAVS.

The Press

After the incorporation of Latvia into the USSR the entire legal press was operated by the Publishing House of the Latvian Communist Party Central Committee and strict censorship was imposed. The policy of *glasnost* allowed the publication of some unofficial periodicals in the late 1980s, the most influential of which was *Atmoda*, the journal of the Latvian Popular Front. In early 1990 the Party's monopoly of publishing facilities was ended, by the establishment of the Riga Press House, a joint-stock company without political affiliations, but in January 1991 troops of the Soviet Interior Ministry occupied the Press House, preventing publication of the major Latvian newspapers. Control of the Press House was reclaimed after the recognition of independence in August 1991. In 1989 some 290 newspapers and journals were published, with a combined circulation of 516.1m. Of these, 183 publications, with a circulation of 344.3m, were in Latvian.

PRINCIPAL NEWSPAPERS

Atmoda (Awakening): Vecpilsētas 13/15, Riga 226250; tel. (0132) 210-452; fax (0132) 213-978; f. 1988; weekly; organ of the Latvian People's Front; Editor-in-Chief ELITA VEIDEMANE; circ. 100,000.

Diena (The Day): Smilšu 1/3, Riga 226900; tel. (0132) 220-019; fax (0132) 228-826; f. 1990; 5 a week; in Latvian and Russian; Editor-in-Chief VIKTORS DAUGMALIS; circ. 120,000.

Literatūra un Māksla (Literature and Art): Maskava 40/42, Riga 226081; tel. (0132) 222-453; f. 1945; weekly; publ. by the Publishing House Literatūra un Māksla; joint edition of Latvian Cultural Unions; Editor-in-Chief M. ČAKLAIS; circ. 41,000.

Latvijas Jaunatne (Latvian Youth): Riga; tel. (0132) 466-011; f. 1921; 5 a week; fmrly organ of the Young Communists of Latvia; Editor A. CIRULIS; circ. 133,000.

Lauku Avīze (Country Newspaper): Republikas laukums 2, Riga 226081; tel. (0132) 327-606; f. 1988; weekly; publ. by the Publishing House 'Lauku Avīze'; popular agriculture; Editor V. KRUSTIŅŠ; circ. 236,000.

Neatkarīgā Cīņa (Independent Struggle): Balasta dambis 3, Riga 226081; tel. (0132) 462-496; f. 1990; 5 a week; Editor ANDRIS JAKUBĀNS; circ. 183,000.

PRINCIPAL PERIODICALS

Avots (Spring): Riga; tel. (0132) 225-654; f. 1987; monthly; journal of the Ministry of Culture and the Writers' Union; fiction, art, social and political; for young people; in Latvian and Russian; Editor-in-Chief A. KĻAVIS; circ. 23,000.

Dadzis (Thistle): Balasta dambis 3, Riga; tel. (0132) 465-960; f. 1957; fortnightly; satirical; Editor E. STRAUTIŅŠ; circ. 41,000.

Dambrete (Draughts): Centrs, a.k. 55, Riga 226098; tel. (0132) 225-629; f. 1959; monthly; publ. by Chess and Draughts Club of Latvia; in Latvian and Russian; Editor-in-Chief VLADIMIRS VIGMANS.

Draugs (Friend): Riga; f. 1945; monthly; illustrated fiction, art, social and political; for 10–15-year-olds; Editor A. SPROĀGIS; circ. 50,000.

Karogs (Banner): Riga; tel. (0132) 289-875; f. 1940; monthly; publ. by the Publishing House 'Karogs'; journal of the Latvian Writers' Union; fiction, social and political; Editor-in-Chief MĀRA ZĀLITE; circ. 25,000.

Lauku Dzīve (Country Life): Riga; f. 1963; journal of the Ministry of Agriculture; popular agriculture; Editor I. BŪMANE; circ. 39,000.

Liesma (Flame): Riga; f. 1958; monthly; journal of the Cen. Cttee of the Youth Progress Union of Latvia; politics, short stories, poems, etc.; for young people; Editor-in-Chief D. CAUNE; circ. 138,000.

Māksla (Art): Riga; f. 1959; 6 a year; joint edition of the Unions of Artists, Composers, Architects, Cinematographists and Actors; development of art in the Republic; Editor-in-Chief Ē. STRODS; circ. 6,000.

Šahs (Chess): Riga 226050; tel. (0132) 286864; f. 1959; fortnightly; publ. by Joint Republican Chess and Draughts Club of the Latvian Republic; journal of the Physical Culture and Sport State Cttee of the Latvian Republic and Chess Federation of the Latvian Republic; in Latvian and Russian; Editor-in-Chief A. ĢIPSLIS; circ. 800 in Latvian, 3,500 in Russian.

Sieviete (Woman): Riga; f. 1952; monthly; popular, for women; Editor-in-Chief MONIKA ZĪLE; circ. 202,000.

Skola un Ģimene (School and Family): POB 14, Riga 226081; tel. (0132) 22-7021; f. 1964; monthly; journal of the Ministry of Education and the Latvian Children's Foundation; social and educational, illustrated; Editor-in-Chief J. GULBIS; circ. 110,000.

Sociologija un Rēsture (Sociology and History): Riga; tel. (0132) 465887; f. 1940; monthly; fmrly publ. by the Latvian Communist Party Cen. Cttee Publishing House; theoretical and political; in Latvian and Russian; Editor-in-Chief V. BROKĀNS; circ. 1,200.

Zīlīte (Blue Titmouse): Riga; tel. (0132) 225-810; f. 1958; monthly; illustrated; for 5–10-year-olds; Editor-in-Chief DAINA OLIŅA; circ. 90,000.

Zinātne un Mēs (Science and Us): Riga; f. 1960; monthly; popular science and technology; in Latvian and Russian; Editor-in-Chief A. DARZIŅŠ; circ. 7,000 in Latvian, 500 in Russian.

Zvaigzne (Star): 226013 Riga, K. Valdemāra; tel. (0132) 467600; f. 1965; fortnightly; illustrated popular, political and fiction; in Latvian; Editor-in-Chief A. LEDIŅŠ; circ. 41,500.

NEWS AGENCIES

Baltic News Service: Smilšu 1/3, Riga 226900; tel. (0132) 212858; telex 161101; fax (0132) 228826; f. 1990; Dir GINTS VĪNS.

LETA (Latvian Telegraph Agency): Palasta 10, Riga 226947; tel. (0132) 223462; telex 161139; fax (0132) 224502; f. 1920; government information agency; Dir AIVARS BAUMANIS.

Publishers

Avots (Spring Publishing House): Aspazijas bul. 24, Riga; tel. (0132) 225824; political, industrial, agricultural, judicial, tourist, sport, scientific, etc.; Dir KĀRLIS SKRUZIS.

Latvijas Enciklopēdiju Redakcija (Latvian Encyclopedia Publishers): Maskavas 68, Riga 226018; tel. (0132) 220-150; f. 1963; encyclopaedias, terminological reference books; Editor-in-Chief A. VILKS.

Liesma (Flame Publishing House): Aspazijas Blvd 24, Riga 226256; tel. (0132) 223-063; f. 1980; fiction, poetry, literary criticism, fine arts; Dir V. JANSONS.

Sprīdītis: Aldaru 2/4, Riga 226800; tel. (0132) 224-921; fax (0132) 224-921; f. 1989; books for children and adolescents; Dir JĀZEPS OSMANIS.

Vieda: Odesas 17, Riga 226018; tel. (0132) 223-497; f. 1989; ecological issues; Dir-Gen. AIVARS GARDA.

Zinātne (Science Publishing House): Turgeneva 19, Riga 226530; tel. (0132) 212-797; publishing house of the Latvian Academy of Sciences; scientific and scholarly books; Man. I. RIEKSTIŅŠ.

Zvaigzne (Star Publishing House): Kr. Valdemata 105, Riga 226013; tel. (0132) 372-396; textbooks, children's books, medical, books for the blind; Dir GUNTARS VITOLIŅŠ.

Radio and Television

Committee for Television and Radio Broadcasting: Doma lauk. 8, Riga 226935; tel. (0132) 226-304; telex 161188; fax (0132) 200-025; Chair. RIŠARDS LABANOVSKIS.

Latvian Radio: Doma Laukums 8, POB 266, Riga 226935; tel. (0132) 206-722; telex 161188; fax (0132) 200-025; f. 1925; broadcasts in Latvian, Russian, Swedish, English and German.

Finance

BANKING

Central Bank

Bank of the Republic of Latvia: Kr. Valdemāra 2A, Riga 226022; tel. (0132) 323-863; fax (0132) 325-486; Pres. EINARS REPSE; Vice-Pres. ALFREDS BERGS-BERGMANIS.

Commercial Banks

Baltija: Aspazijas bul. 34, Riga 226250; tel. (0132) 323863; fax (0132) 325-486; f. 1988; regional bank; Chair. of Bd ALEKSANDRA STECJUNA.

Riga Commercial Bank: Smilšu 6, Riga 226800; tel. (0132) 323-967; telex 161112; fax (0132) 210-080; Chair. of Bd VLADIMIRS KULIKS.

Savings Bank

Latvian Savings Bank: Palasta 1, Riga 226929; tel. (0132) 222-871; Chair. of Bd EDUARDS GROSS.

INSURANCE

Latva: Vaļņu 1, Riga 226912; tel. (0132) 212-341; fax (0132) 210-134; f. 1940; state insurance co; Chair. JĀNIS MEDENS.

COMMODITY EXCHANGE

Riga Commodity Exchange (RCE): 6 Domskaya Square, 226047 Riga; tel. (0132) 224-515; fax (0132) 224-212; f. 1990; Gen. Man. RIHARD KLUCHANS.

Trade and Industry

CHAMBER OF COMMERCE

Latvian Chamber of Commerce: Bribas bul., Riga 226189; tel. (0132) 228-036; telex 161111; fax (0132) 332-276; f. 1934; re-established 1990; mem. Conference of Baltic Chambers of Commerce, Nordic Chambers of Commerce.

MAJOR INDUSTRIAL COMPANIES

Alfa: Brīvības 372, Riga; tel. (0132) 553-075; production of electronic equipment, incl. measuring and testing instruments; Dir-Gen. JURIJS OSOKINS.

Brocēni Cement and Slate Works: Saldus raj., Brocēni 229451; tel. 65-216; fax 65-067; cement, ceramic tiles, crumbled limestone; Dir JURIS RESSONS.

Daugav'pils Chain Belt Plant: Višķu 17, Daugav'pils 228400; tel. 22-057; manufactures roll-drive chains, double-lined plate chains, children's tricycles; Dir ALEKSANDRS KAREVS.

Laima: Miera 22, Riga 226486; tel. (0132) 372-282; fax (0132) 379-690; produces chocolate confectionery; Dir ELMĀRS GOZITIS.

Latvijas Balzams: A. Čaka 160, Riga 226012; tel. (0132) 277-231; produces beverages, incl. *Riga Black Balsam* vodka; Dir-Gen. LEONS DUKULIS.

Latvijas Stikls: Daugavgrivas 77, Riga 226007; tel. (0132) 459-145; all types of glassware, incl. glass bottles and industrial glassware; Dir-Gen. DMITRIJS LAĻKOVS.

Kompresors: Starta 1, Riga 226026; tel. (0132) 378-066; produces refrigeration equipment for domestic and industrial use; Dir-Gen. ALDIS ZICMANIS.

Radiotehnika: Popova 3, Riga 226067; tel. (0132) 418-088; manufacture of acoustic systems, amplifiers and other audio equipment; Dir-Gen. VLADIMIRS MARTINSONS.

Riga Asphalt-Concrete Plant: Granīta 13, Riga 226065; tel. (0132) 248-828; fax (0132) 248-833; concrete and reinforced concrete; Dir JĀNIS BERTRANDS.

Riga Carriage Building Plant: Brīvības 201, Riga 226098; tel. (0132) 365-440; telex 161124; fax (0132) 555-219; produces railway rolling stock, mostly electric and diesel suburban trains; Dir-Gen. VALENTĪNS SAVINS.

Riga Diesel Plant: Ganību dambis 40, Riga 226005; tel. (0132) 391-662; telex 161198; fax (0132) 381-402; Dir ANDREJS KRASOVSKIS.

Sarkandaugava: Sliežu 6, Riga 2260005; tel. (0132) 392-419; produces sheet glass, window glass; Dir PJOTRS GERAŠČENKOVS.

Sloka Cellulose and Paper Factory: Fabrikas 2, Jūrmala 229070; tel. 32-469; telex 168318; produces paper for specialized uses, including book covers, ice-cream holders, etc.; Dir MIHAILS PISKUNS.

Straume: E. Tēlmaņa 2, Riga 226004; tel. (0132) 627-010; fax (0132) 627-997; manufactures electrical household appliances; Dir-Gen. ANATOLIJS ŠABALOVS.

VEF: Brīvības 214, Riga 226039; tel. (0132) 567-208; telex 161138; fax (0132) 567-208; produces portable radios, telephones, cassette recorders; Dir-Gen. IVARS BRAŽIS.

Transport

Following the recognition of Latvian independence by the USSR, in September 1991, transportation facilities on Latvian territory came under the control of the Latvian Government.

RAILWAYS

In 1989 there were 2,397 km of railways on the territory of Latvia, of which 237 km were electrified. In the same year Latvian railways carried 20.5m. metric tons of freight and 135m. passengers. Until the recognition of Latvian independence by the USSR, the railway network formed apart of the all-Union railway system and it remains orientated towards communication with Moscow.

ROADS

In 1989 there were 20,500 km of motorable roads. In the same year there were 94 cars and 58 motorcycles per 1,000 persons.

SHIPPING

The major Latvian ports are at Riga and Ventspils. The latter is particularly important for the shipping of Russian petroleum exports. In 1989 some 38m. metric tons of freight were transported through Latvian ports, including 32m. tons of petroleum products and 2m. tons of chemicals and fertilizers.

Port Authority

Riga Fishing Seaport: Atlantijas 27, Riga 226020; tel. (0132) 620323; f. 1949; Man. GEORGS ŠEVČUKS.

Shipowning Company

Latvian Shipping Company: bul. Basteja 2, Riga 226807; fax (0132) 325-414; telex 161121; f. 1940; sea transportation of wide variety of goods; Pres. Y. L. PADEROV.

CIVIL AVIATION

In 1990 Riga was connected to 85 cities in the USSR by the services of Aeroflot. Since 1990 international flights have commenced to Helsinki (Finland), Stockholm (Sweden), Copenhagen (Denmark) and Frankfurt (Germany).

Avialat: Pils lauk. 4, Riga 226050; tel. (0132) 225560; telex 161168; f. 1988 as the first independent airline in the USSR; joint venture between Latvian Directorate of Civil Aviation (LAUGA) and Injener risk project management consultancy; destinations include Athens, Belgrade, Copenhagen, Frankfurt, Hamburg, Helsinki, New York, Sofia, Stockholm, Tel Aviv, Vienna and major cities in the former USSR; Dir-Gen. ANATOLIJS BELAIČUKS.

Tourism

Tourism is relatively underdeveloped in Latvia, although there are sites of major historical interest, seaside resorts and beautiful scenery. The Gauja National Park, which stretches east of the historic town of Sigulda for nearly 100 km along the Gauja River, attracts many visitors. Sigulda also offers winter sports facilities. Since the establishment of better communications with Sweden and Finland in the late 1980s there has been an increase in the number of visitors from northern Europe. It was expected that the number of tourists would increase considerably following recognition of Latvian independence.

Riga Travel Agency: Elizabetes, Riga 226185; tel. (0132) 211-755; fax (0132) 283-595; telex 161129; Gen. Man. GEORGY KORSHAK.

Culture

NATIONAL ORGANIZATIONS

Ministry of Culture: see section on The Government (Ministries).

CULTURAL HERITAGE

Central Board of Archives: Šķūņu 11, Riga 226050; tel. (0132) 212-539; Head JĀNIS ŠNEIDERS.

Institute of Bibliography; Anglikānu 5, Riga 226816; tel. (0132) 225-135; f. 1940; research and compilation of a national bibliography, in co-operation with UNESCO; Dir LAIMDOTA PRŪSE.

Latvian State Museum of Foreign Fine Arts: Pils lauk. 3, Riga 266844; tel. (0132) 226-467; f. 1773; library of 15,000 vols; 18,500 exhibits; Dir M. LAPINA.

Museum of the History of Latvia: Pils lauk. 3, Riga 226050; tel. (0132) 223-004; f. 1869; materials on archaeology, history, ethnography; Dir INĀRA BAUMANE.

Museum of the History of Literature and Arts: Basteja bul. 14, Riga 226852; tel. (0132) 220-134; f. 1925; over 500,000 exhibits; materials on Latvian literature, theatre, music, folk art and cinema; Dir P. ZIRNĪTIS.

National Library: Kr. Barona 14, Riga 226437; tel. (0132) 280-851; f. 1919; over 5m. vols; Dir ANDRIS VILKS.

State Museum of Fine Arts: Kr. Valdemāra 10A, Riga 226342; tel. (0132) 325-021; f. 1905; Dir MĀRA LĀCE.

SPORTING ORGANIZATIONS

Committee for Physical Culture and Sports: Tērbatas 4, Riga 226723; tel. (0132) 284-206; govt cttee; Chair. DAINA ŠVEICA.

Latvian Institute of Physical Culture: Brīvības 333, Riga 226037; tel. (0132) 520-595; telex 161172; educational and training establishment; 1,250 students; Rector ULDIS GRĀVĪTIS.

Latvian Olympic Committee: Elizabetes 49, Riga 226050; tel. (0132) 288613; telex 161183; fax (0132) 284-412; f. 1920; readmitted to the Olympic Movement 1991; Pres. VILNIS BALTIŅŠ.

PERFORMING ARTS

Art Theatre: Brīvības 75, Riga 226705; tel. (0132) 279-474; f. 1920; Chief Dir KĀRLIS AUŠKĀPS.

Cinematographers' House: A. Čaka 67/69, Riga 226001; tel. (0132) 297-010; fax (0132) 277-300; f. 1962; Dir JĀNIS SULCS.

Latvian Circus: Merķeļa 4, Riga 226050; tel. (0132) 213-479; f. 1888; Chief Dir and Man. GUNĀRS KATKĒVIČS.

Latvian Puppet Theatre: Kr. Barona 16/18, Riga 226011; tel. (0132) 285-415; Artistic Dir TĪNA HERCBERGA.

National Opera: Aspazijas bul. 3, Riga 226251; tel. (0132) 223-817; telex 161155; fax (0132) 551-542; f. 1919; Artistic Dir KĀRLIS ZARIŅŠ.

National Theatre: Kronvalda bul. 2, Riga 226829; tel. (0132) 332-828; f. 1919; Chief Dir OĻGERTS KRODERS.

Russian Drama Theatre: Kaļķu 16, Riga 226050; tel. (0132) 224-660; Dir LEONĪDS BEĻAVSKIS.

ASSOCIATIONS

Latvian Artists' Union: Kr. Barona 12, Riga 226400; tel. (0132) 287-626; telex 161115; f. 1941; Chair. DŽEMMA SKULME.

Latvian Cinematographers' Union: Brīvības 85, Riga 226250; tel. (0132) 272-715; f. 1962; Chair. IVARS SELECKIS.

Latvian Composers' Union: Kr. Barona 12, Riga 226440; tel. (0132) 287-447; f. 1944; Chair. JURIS KARLSONS.

Latvian Culture Fund: Basteja bul. 12, Riga 226900; tel. (0132) 228-449; f. 1987; promotes Latvian culture, provides scholarships for cultural studies.

Latvian Journalists' Union: Basteja bul. 4, Riga 226050; tel. (0132) 211-433; f. 1957; Chair. AIVARS BAUMANIS.

Latvian Theatrical Society: E. Smiļģa 37/39; tel. (0132) 226-002; tel. (0132) 615-169; fax (0132) 210-368; Chair. ĢIRTS JAKOVĻEVS.

Latvian Writers' Union: Kr. Barona 12, Riga 226400; tel. (0132) 287-629; f. 1940; Chair. IMANTS AUZIŅŠ.

Education

A system of comprehensive elementary education was introduced after 1918. Following the incorporation of Latvia into the USSR, in 1940, the Soviet system of education was introduced. Latvian is the main language of education, although, in 1988, 47.6% of pupils in general schools were taught in Russian. Since the adoption of Latvian as the state language, in 1988, the teaching of Latvian has become a compulsory part of the curriculum for all pupils. In 1990/91 higher education was offered at 11 institutions, including two universities.

UNIVERSITIES

Riga Technical University: Kaļķu 1, Riga 226355; tel. (0132) 225-885; telex 161172; fax (0132) 225-885; f. 1990; 10 faculties; 1,400 teachers; 14,600 students; Rector Prof. Egons Lavandelis.

University of Latvia: Raiņa bul. 19, Riga 226098; tel. (0132) 228-928; f. 1919; languages of instruction: Latvian and Russian; 13 faculties; 850 teachers; 13,000 students; Rector Prof. Dr Juris Zaķis.

Social Welfare

In 1989 expenditure on the health service totalled 265m. roubles, equivalent to 3.6% of national income. In that year there were 202 hospitals with 39,300 beds available (equivalent to 147 beds per 10,000 persons). There were 673 other medical establishments, such as polyclinics, and 13,400 medical doctors (equivalent to one doctor per 200 persons). Social welfare is also funded by the state. In 1989 there were 631,000 people in receipt of pensions, of which 478,000 were on account of old age. In December 1989 the average monthly old-age pension provided by the state amounted to 100.4 roubles.

NATIONAL AGENCIES

Ministry of Social Welfare: see section on The Government (Ministries).

HEALTH AND WELFARE ORGANIZATIONS

Latvian Children's Fund: Brīvības 85, Riga 226450; tel. (0132) 271-662; f. 1987; assists deprived children; Pres. Andris Berziņš.

Latvian Red Cross Society: Skolas 28, Riga 226300; tel. (0132) 275-635; fax (0132) 276-445; f. 1918; Chair. Uldis Laucis.

Society of the Blind: Pāles 14, K-1, Riga 226300; tel. (0132) 532-607; f. 1926; Chair. of Cent. Bd Genrihs Lebedeks.

Society of the Deaf: Jāņa sēta 5, Riga 226350; tel. (0132) 212-485; Chair. Jānis Liepa.

The Environment

Degradation of the environment was one of the principal issues addressed by the political groups which emerged in the 1980s. The emission of untreated sewage and industrial waste into the Daugava, the high levels of harmful effluent from industrial plants and pollution caused by Soviet Armed Forces stationed in Latvia were among the major concerns of environmental groups.

GOVERNMENT ORGANIZATIONS

Committee for Environmental Protection: Peldu 25, Riga 226282; tel. (0132) 226-304; Chair. Indulis Emsis.

ACADEMIC INSTITUTES

Latvian Academy of Sciences: Turgeņeva 19, Riga 226524; tel. (0132) 225-361; fax (0132) 228-784; several instits involved in environmental research; Pres. Jānis Lielpeteris.

NON-GOVERNMENTAL ORGANIZATIONS

Environmental Protection Club: Kalnciema 30, Riga 226046; tel. (0132) 612-850; active environmental group; Pres. Arvīds Ulme.

Latvian Green Party: see section on Political Organizations.

LITHUANIA

Geography

The Republic of Lithuania (formerly the Lithuanian Soviet Socialist Republic) is situated on the eastern coast of the Baltic Sea, in north-eastern Europe. It is bounded by Latvia to the north, Byelorussia to the south-east, Poland to the south-west and by the territory of the Russian Federation around Kaliningrad to the west. It covers an area of 65,200 sq km.

The low-lying littoral along the Baltic coastline, known as the the Pajūrio Lowland, extends some 15–20 km from the sea. To the east of the coastal plain lies the Žemaičių Upland, which rises to a height of 234 m. at Medvġalis. The Upland is separated from the Baltic Highlands of the south and east by a long plain across the central regions, called the Middle Lowland. The highest point in Lithuania is at Juozapinė Hill (294 m.) in the east of the Republic. There is a dense network of waterways, the main river being the Nemunas (Neman), which flows south to north and empties into the Baltic Sea. There are also many lakes, concentrated in the northern regions of the Baltic Highlands.

Lithuania's maritime position moderates an otherwise continental-type climate. Temperatures range from an average in January of −4.9°C (23.2°F) to a July mean of 17.0°C (62.6°F). The level of precipitation varies considerably from region to region. In the far west average annual precipitation is 930 mm, while in the Middle Lowland it is 540 mm.

At the census of 1989, when the total population was 3,674,802, 79.6% of the population were Lithuanians, 9.4% Russians and 7.0% Poles. Other ethnic groups included Byelorussians (63,169), Ukrainians (44,789), Jews (12,314), Tatars (5,135) and Latvians (4,229). In 1989 Lithuanian, a Baltic tongue which uses the Latin alphabet, replaced Russian as the official state language. The predominant religion is Christianity. Most ethnic Lithuanians are Roman Catholics by belief or tradition, but there are small communities of Lutherans and Calvinists, and a growing number of modern Protestant denominations. Adherents of Russian Orthodoxy are almost exclusively ethnic Slavs. Most Tatars have retained an adherence to Islam.

At 1 January 1991 the total estimated population was 3,728,000. The capital is Vilnius, which is situated in the south-east of the Republic and was in Poland until 1939. In 1990 it had an estimated population of 592,500. Other important towns include Kaunas (434,000), situated on the upper reaches of the Nemunas river, Klaipėda (206,000), which is Lithuania's principal port, and Šiauliai (148,000) and Panevėžys (129,000), in the north of the Republic.

History

Lithuanians have inhabited the eastern littoral of the Baltic Sea for over 2,000 years. In the 13th century Duke Mindaugas united the lands inhabited by Lithuanians and formed the Grand Duchy of Lithuania, of which he was crowned King in 1253. Grand Duke Gediminas, who ruled from 1316 to 1341, established a dynasty (the Gediminaičiai) which ruled Lithuania until 1572. The territory of the Lithuanian state expanded to the east during the rule of Grand Duke Algirdas (1345–77), but was frequently under attack from the German Livonian and Teutonic Orders. In 1385, in response to the continued German threat, Grand Duke Jogaila and the Polish Queen Jadvyga agreed the Union of Kreva, which formed an alliance between the two states. As one condition of the Union, Lithunania adopted Christianity, in 1387. Under Jogaila's successor, Grand Duke Vytautas ('the Great'), the territory of the Grand Duchy expanded far to the south, covering what are now Byelorussian and Ukrainian lands and some regions of western Russia. The territories of the Grand Duchy were increasingly threatened by the rise of the Russian state of Muscovy during the 16th century. In 1569, to counter the threat from the east, Lithuania united with Poland in the Union of Lublin, forming a Polish-Lithuanian Commonwealth. In 1795, at the third Partition of Poland, Lithuania was annexed by the Russian Empire. Uprisings against Russian rule were suppressed, in 1830–31 and 1863, and a policy of 'russification' was conducted, including the prohibition of publications in Lithuanian. Nevertheless, a strong nationalist movement was established in the late 19th century.

In 1915, after the outbreak of the First World War, Lithuania was occupied by German troops. Despite the occupation a Lithuanian Conference was convened, in September 1917, which issued a resolution demanding the establishment of an independent Lithuanian state. The Conference elected a Lithuanian Council, headed by Antanas Smetona. It proceeded to declare the independence of Lithunania, on 16 February 1918. The new state survived a Soviet attempt to create a Lithuanian-Byelorussian Soviet Republic and a Polish campaign aimed at reincorporating Lithuania within Poland. At the end of 1920 Poland annexed the region of Vilnius (Wilno), but was forced to recognize the rest of Lithuania as an independent state (with its capital at Kaunas). Soviet Russia recognized Lithuanian independence in the Treaty of Moscow, signed on 12 July 1920.

On 1 August 1922 Lithuania's first Constitution was adopted, which declared Lithuania a parliamentary democracy. However, on 17 December 1926 Antanas Smetona seized power in a military *coup d'état* and established an authoritarian regime, which lasted until 1940. Despite Smetona's coup Lithuania made important advances in the 1920s, introducing a comprehensive system of education and enjoying considerable success in agriculture, owing to the radical land reform of 1922.

According to the 'Secret Protocols' to the Nazi–Soviet Pact, signed on 23 August 1939 by the USSR and Germany, Lithuania was to be part of the German sphere of influence. However, the Treaty on Friendship and Existing Borders, which was agreed between the two states on 28 September, permitted the USSR to take control of Lithuania. On 10 October Lithuania was forced to agree to the stationing of 20,000 Soviet troops on its territory. In return, the USSR granted the city of Vilnius to Lithuania, after it had been seized by Soviet troops in September. In June 1940 the USSR forced the Lithuanian Government to resign and a Soviet-approved 'People's Government' was formed. Elections were held to a 'People's Seim' in July. Only pro-Soviet candidates were permitted. The Seim convened and proclaimed the Lithuanian Soviet Socialist Republic on 21 July. On 3 August Lithuania formally became a Union Republic of the USSR. The establishment of Soviet rule was followed by the arrest and imprisonment of many Lithuanian politicians and government officials. In the period 14–18 June 1941 some 12,000 people were deported to Siberia.

The German invasion in June 1941 ended the process of 'sovietization', but instituted a regime of even greater brutality: some 210,000 people, including 165,000 Jews, were killed during the Nazi occupation. The return of the Soviet Army, in 1944, was not welcomed by most Lithuanians, and anti-Soviet partisan warfare continued until 1952. After the defeat of Germany traditional features of Soviet rule were swiftly introduced: Lithuanian agriculture was forcibly collectivized; rapid industrialization was implemented; some 350,000 people were deported; and leaders and members of the Catholic church were persecuted and imprisoned. Lithuanian political parties were disbanded and exclusive political power became the preserve of the Lithuanian branch of the CPSU, the Communist Party of Lithuania (CPL). The CPL was led by A. Šniečkus (First Secretary 1940–74).

A significant dissident movement was established during the 1960s and 1970s. There were demonstrations in Kaunas, in May 1972, in support of religious and political freedom; one man, Romas Kalenta, burnt himself alive in protest at the persecution of the Church. With the introduction of Soviet leader Mikhail Gorbachev's policy of *glasnost*, in the mid-1980s, a limited discussion of previously censored aspects of Lithuanian history, notably the 1939 Nazi–Soviet Pact which had permitted the Soviet annexation of Lithuania, appeared in the press. Dissident groups sought to take advantage of a more tolerant attitude to political protests by staging a demonstration, in August 1987, which denounced the 1939 Nazi-Soviet Pact. Although this demonstration was tolerated, army and police troops were used in February 1988 to prevent the public celebration of the 70th anniversary of Lithuanian independence. The police repression in February and the dismay among the intelligentsia at the slow pace of reform in the Republic led to the establishment, in June 1988, of the Lithuanian Movement for Reconstruction (Sąjūdis) by a number of intellectuals and writers. Throughout the remainder of 1988 Sąjūdis organized mass demonstrations to protest against environmental pollution, the suppression of national culture and 'russification', and, in August, to condemn the signing of the Nazi–Soviet Pact. The movement held its inaugural congress in October and began to press the CPL to support a declaration of independence and recognition of Lithuanian as the state language. The latter demand was adopted by the Supreme Soviet in November, together with restoration of traditional Lithuanian state symbols, but the parliament failed to adopt a declaration that would declare the supremacy of Lithuania's laws over all-Union legislation.

Despite concessions made by the CPL to Lithuanian public opinion during 1988, including the restoration of Independence Day as a public holiday, the return of church buildings to the Catholic church, and the restoration of Lithuanian as the principal language, Sąjūdis won the greatest number of seats in the elections to the Congress of People's Deputies which took place in March 1989. Of the 42 popularly elected deputies, 36 were members of Sąjūdis. The defeat for the CPL forced it to adopt a more radical position to retain some measure of popular support. On 18 May 1989 the Supreme Soviet, still dominated by CPL members, adopted a declaration of Lithuanian sovereignty which asserted the supremacy of Lithuania's laws over all-Union legislation. This was followed by increased public debate on the legitimacy of Soviet rule in Lithuania: a commission of the Lithuanian Supreme Soviet declared the establishment of Soviet power in 1941 unconstitutional. On the anniversary of the signing of the Pact (23 August) more than 1m. people participated in a 'human chain'

extending from Tallinn in Estonia, through Latvia, to Vilnius.

Despite denunciations of Baltic nationalism by the all-Union authorities, the Lithuanian Supreme Soviet continued to adopt reformist legislation, including the establishment of freedom of religion and the legalization of a multi-party system. In December 1989 the CPL, despite an appeal from Gorbachev, declared itself an independent party, no longer subordinate to the CPSU. It also adopted a new programme which condemned Communist policies of the past and declared support for multi-party democracy and independent statehood. Algirdas Brazauskas, the First Secretary of the CPL, was elected Chairman of the Presidium of the Supreme Soviet, defeating three other candidates, including Romualdas Ozalas, a leading member of Sąjūdis.

Despite the reformist policies adopted by the CPL, Sąjūdis remained the dominant political force in the Republic. It won an overall majority in the elections to the Lithuanian Supreme Soviet which took place in February 1990. This new pro-independence parliament elected Vytautas Landsbergis as its Chairman (*de facto* President of Lithuania) to replace Brazauskas and, on 11 March 1990, declared the restoration of Lithuanian independence. The parliament (which was renamed the Supreme Council) also restored the pre-1940 name of the country (the Republic of Lithuania) and suspended the USSR Constitution on Lithuanian territory. On 17 March Kazimiere Prunskiene was appointed head of government.

The Soviet Government swiftly demonstrated its disapproval of the Lithuanians' actions. The declarations were condemned by a special session of the all-Union Congress of People's Deputies as 'unconstitutional' and Soviet forces seized some Communist Party buildings in Vilnius and took over newspaper printing presses. On 17 April 1990 an economic embargo was introduced, under which vital fuel supplies were suspended. The economic embargo was only lifted on 30 June when Lithuania agreed to a moratorium on the independence declaration for a period of six months, if formal negotiations began between the Soviet Government and Lithuania. In August talks began between the two sides, but were soon ended by the Soviet Government.

In January 1991 Landsbergis announced that the suspension of the declaration of independence was ended, since substantive negotiations on Lithuania's status had not begun in the six-month period agreed. Tension increased in the Republic, when Soviet interior ministry troops (notably the special units, known as OMON or the 'Black Berets') occupied buildings which had previously belonged to the CPSU but had been nationalized by the Lithuanian Government. Meanwhile, there were policy differences within the Lithuanian leadership, and Prunskiene and her cabinet resigned after the Supreme Council refused to support proposed price rises. She was replaced as premier by Gediminas Vagnorius.

After more buildings were seized by OMON troops, Landsbergis appealed to the people to help defend the parliament building, which he believed might be the troops' next target. Thousands of Lithuanians went to the Supreme Council and erected barricades and other makeshift defences. On the night of 13/14 January Soviet troops seized the radio and television centre and the television tower. Thirteen civilians were killed in the attack and some 500 were injured. The troops' actions were supported by a self-proclaimed National Salvation Committee, which demanded that it be granted full power to proclaim a state of emergency in the Republic.

The military intervention in January strengthened popular support for independence. On 9 February 1991 a referendum on Lithuanian independence took place in the Republic. Some 84% of the population took part, of which 90% voted for the re-establishment of an independent Lithuania. Together with five other Republics, Lithuania refused to conduct the all-Union referendum on the future of the USSR, which was held in nine Republics in March. However, there was unofficial voting in predominantly Russian- and Polish-populated areas. Some 500,000 people voted, of which some 99% approved the preservation of the USSR.

There was further harassment and violence against Lithuanian state and government officials. In March Audrius Butkevičius, the head of the Lithuanian Defence Department, was seized by OMON troops, and later in the month OMON troops opened fire on members of the nascent Lithuanian defence force, injuring several people. In May Landsbergis warned that Soviet troops might attempt further military intervention, after a series of attacks by OMON forces on Lithuania's newly-established customs posts on the border with Byelorussia. In July, while US President George Bush was on an official visit to Moscow, seven Lithuanian border guards died after being attacked by OMON troops.

In August 1991 the seizure of power by a State Committee for the State of Emergency (SCSE) in Moscow raised fears in Lithuania that there would be a renewed attempt to overthrow the Government and reimpose Soviet rule. Military vehicles entered Vilnius but did not prevent the convening of an emergency session of the Supreme Council. The Supreme Council condemned the SCSE and issued a statement supporting Boris Yeltsin, President of the Russian Federation. There was sporadic violence in the Republic, when Soviet troops occupied broadcasting facilities and attacked customs posts. One member of the Lithuanian Defence Department was killed by Soviet forces.

As the coup collapsed the Lithuanian Government ordered the withdrawal of Soviet forces from the Republic, banned the pro-CPSU Lithuanian Communist Party and nationalized all its property. It also began to assume effective control of its borders, taking over customs posts at airports and on the Polish frontier. The collapse of the coup prompted the long-awaited recognition of Lithuanian independence by other states. By 30 August more than 40 states had announced the establishment or restoration of diplomatic ties with Lithuania. Throughout the rest of 1991 the Government continued to develop control over former Soviet institutions and entered negotiations with Soviet and Russian representatives on issues related to the restoration of Lithuanian independence. Foremost among these was the issue of Soviet troops still remaining in Lithuania. The Lithuanian Government had requested that troops be withdrawn by 1 December 1991, but Soviet military officials insisted that troops could not be withdrawn until 1994. Other problems faced by the Government included the status of the Polish minority in Lithuania. Leaders of councils in areas dominated by Poles had been dismissed following the August coup in response to their alleged support for the coup. Polish groups complained of alleged cultural discrimination and demanded that a Polish university be established in Vilnius and that current boundaries in the Polish-speaking region should not be changed.

Following its declaration of independence on 11 March 1990, the Lithuanian Government requested recognition from other states. However, until August 1991, only Iceland (in January 1991) had extended recognition. In other countries the response was generally sympathetic, but the USA and Western Europe did not wish to strain relations with the USSR by recognizing Lithuanian independence. Attempts by all three Baltic Republics to gain observer

status at CSCE meetings were prevented by Soviet representatives. However, important links with the Scandinavian countries were established. Following the August coup, these links were further developed, with Sweden being the first state to open an embassy in Vilnius. Relations with Poland were complicated by the issue of the Polish minority in Lithuania. Lithuanian was admitted to the Conference on Security and Co-operation in Europe (CSCE) on 10 September and to the United Nations on 17 September. In December, together with the other Baltic States, Lithuania was granted membership of the European Bank for Reconstruction and Development. Lithuania welcomed the creation of the Commonwealth of Independent States, in succession to the USSR, in December.

Economy

In 1989, according to official estimates, Lithuania's gross national product (GNP) totalled 24,300m. roubles, equivalent to 6,612 roubles per head. In that year the total labour force was 1,544,500.

In 1989 agriculture contributed 22.9% of GNP, and employed 7.9% of the working population. In that year the total area of cultivated land amounted to 4,625,600 ha, of which 3,273,500 ha was occupied by 835 collective farms, 1,208,200 ha by 275 state and other farms, and 20,695 ha by over 1,000 individual farmers. The major agricultural sector is animal husbandry, which accounted for 66% of the value of total agricultural production in 1989. Principal crops grown are cereals, flax, sugar beets, potatoes and vegetables. In 1991 legislation was adopted, which envisaged the privatization of state-owned farms and the reorganization of collective farms.

Industrial production accounted for 56.3% of GNP in 1989, and employed 32.9% of the labour force. Total industrial output in 1989 (in wholesale prices) was 13,700m. roubles, of which 39.7% was contributed by the production of consumer goods. The major industrial sectors are machine-building and metal-working (25.7% of total value of industrial output in 1989), food-processing (21.9%) and light industry (20.8%).

Lithuania is dependent on imported sources of fuel for energy generation, mostly petroleum, coal and natural gas. There is a nuclear power station at Ignalina. In 1989 output of electric energy reached 29,158m. kWh.

The Government has announced plans for a wide range of market-orientated reforms, including privatization and measures to encourage foreign investment. As preparation for transition to a full market economy there were officially-sanctioned price rises in November 1991. In the same month the Supreme Council approved plans to introduce a Lithuanian currency, the Litas, in 1992.

Statistical Survey

Source: Ministry of Culture and Education of the Republic of Lithuania, Vilnius.

Population

BIRTHS AND DEATHS (per 1,000)

	1987	1988	1989
Birth rate	16.2	15.4	15.0
Death rate	10.1	10.2	10.3

Agriculture

PRINCIPAL CROPS ('000 metric tons)

	1987	1988	1989
Grain	3,063.1	2,687.9	3,272.0
Sugar beet.	838.3	1,213.2	1,075.0
Flax fibre	16.3	14.1	15.1
Potatoes	1,397.3	1,850.3	1,926.6
Other vegetables . . .	317.1	370.4	325.7

LIVESTOCK ('000 head at 1 January)

	1987	1988	1989
Cattle	2,488.2	2,493.5	2,434.6
Pigs	2,772.1	2,706.3	2,705.0
Sheep and goats . . .	93.3	90.1	78.6

LIVESTOCK PRODUCTS ('000 metric tons)

	1987	1988	1989
Meat (slaughter weight) . .	530.7	544.6	534.4
Milk	3,119.8	3,208.6	3,234.9
Eggs (million)	1,278.6	1,347.2	1,330.7

Mining and Industry

Production (1989): Paper 117,000 metric tons, Plastics 109,500 metric tons, Chemical fibres and threads 14,400 metric tons, Sulphuric acid 512,000 metric tons, Chemical fertilizers 632,000 metric tons, Electric energy 29,200m. kWh.

Education

(1990/91)

	Institutions	Students
General-education schools*	2,097	518,727
Secondary specialized institutions . .	66	51,717
Higher schools (incl. universities) . .	13	69,547

* General-education schools include secondary schools (646 in 1989/90), elementary schools and incomplete secondary schools.

Directory

The Government

(December 1991)

HEAD OF STATE

Chairman of the Supreme Council: VYTAUTAS Z. LANDSBERGIS.

COUNCIL OF MINISTERS

Prime Minister: GEDIMINAS VAGNORIUS.

Deputy Prime Ministers: VYTAUTAS PAKALNISKIS, ZIGMAS VAISVILA.

Minister of Agriculture: RIMVYDAS RAIMONDAS SURVILA.

Minister of Communications: KOSTAS BIRULIS.

Minister of Culture and Education: DARIUS KUOLYS.

Minister of Defence: AUDRIUS BUTKEVIČIUS.

Minister of Economics: ALBERTAS SIMENAS.

Minister of Energy: LEONAS VAIDOTAS ASMANTAS.

Minister of Finance: ELVYRA KUNEVICIENE.

Minister of Foreign Affairs: ALGIRDAS SAUDARGAS.

Minister of Forestry: VAIDOTAS ANTANAITIS.

Minister of Health Care: JUOZAS OLEKAS.

Minister of Housing and Urban Development: ALGIMANTAS NASVYTIS.

Minister of the Interior: MARIJONAS MISIUKONIS.

Minister of Justice: VYTAUTAS PAKALNISKIS.

Minister of Material Resources: VILIUS ZIDONIS.

Minister of Social Welfare: ALGIS DOBRAVOLSKAS.

Minister of Trade: ALBERTAS AMBRAZIEJUS SINEVICIUS.

Minister of Transportation: JONAS BIRZISKIS.

MINISTRIES

Council of Ministers: Tumo-Vaizganto 2, Vilnius 232039; tel. (0122) 622-101; telex 261105; fax (0122) 619-953.

Ministry of Agriculture: Gedimino pr. 19, Vilnius 232025; tel. (0122) 625-438.

Ministry of Communications: Vilniaus 33, Vilnius 232008; tel. (0122) 620-443.

Ministry of Culture and Education: Volano 2/7, Vilnius 232691; tel. (0122) 622-483.

Ministry of Defence: Gyneju 3, Vilnius 232710; tel. (0122) 624-821.

Ministry of Economics: Gedimino pr. 38/2, Vilnius 232600; tel. (0122) 622-416.

Ministry of Energy: Gedimino pr. 12, Vilnius 232600; tel. (0122) 615-140.

Ministry of Finance: Sermuksniu 9, Vilnius 232600; tel. (0122) 625-172.

Ministry of Foreign Affairs: A. Vienuolio 8, Vilnius 232684; tel. (0122) 621-657; fax (0122) 618-689.

Ministry of Forestry: Gedimino pr. 56, Vilnius 232685; tel. (0122) 626-864.

Ministry of Health Care: Gedimino pr. 27, Vilnius 232682; tel. (0122) 621-625.

Ministry of Housing and Urban Development: Jaksto 4/9, Vilnius 232694; tel. (0122) 610-558.

Ministry of the Interior: Sventaragio 2, Vilnius 232754; tel. (0122) 626-752.

Ministry of Justice: Lentpjuviu 24, Vilnius 232755; tel. (0122) 626-757.

Ministry of Material Resources: Tumo-Vaizganto 8A/2, Vilnius 232640; tel. (0122) 628-830.

Ministry of Social Welfare: Vivulskio 11, Vilnius 232693; tel. (0122) 651-236.

Ministry of Trade: Gedimino pr. 30/1, Vilnius 232695; tel. (0122) 617-007.

Ministry of Transportation: Gedimino pr. 17, Vilnius 232679; tel. (0122) 621-445.

Legislature

SUPREME COUNCIL

Supreme Council: Gedimino pr. 53, 232026 Vilnius; tel. (0122) 628-986; telex 261138; fax (0122) 614-544.

Vice-Chairman: KAZIMIERAS MOTIECKA.

Political Organizations

Christian Democratic Party: Aukštaičių 6, 233000 Kaunas; f. 1917, refounded 1990; Chair. D. KATILIUS; 1,500 mems.

Democratic Labour Party of Lithuania: B. Radvilaitės 1, 232000 Vilnius; tel. (0122) 61-26-56; fax (0122) 61-72-90; f. 1990 following a split in the Communist Party of Lithuania; Chair. ALGIRDAS MYKOLAS BRAZAUSKAS; 20,000 mems.

Independence Party: Vilniaus 39, 232600 Vilnius; tel. (0122) 221-529; f. 1990; Chair. VIRGILIJUS CEPAITIS.

Lithuanian Democratic Party: Gedimino pr. 34/9, 232001 Vilnius; tel. (0122) 626-033; fax (0122) 479-275; f. 1989; Chair. SAULIUS PEČELIŪNAS.

Lithuanian Green Party: B. Radvilaitės 1, 232000 Vilnius; tel. (0122) 618-428; f. 1990; seeks a demilitarized, neutral and ecologically sound Lithuania; Chair. IRENA IGNATAVIČIENE.

Lithuanian Humanism Party: Mykolaičio-Putino 5, 232009 Vilnius; tel. (0122) 735-831; f. 1989; Chair. VYTAUTAS KAZLAUSKAS.

Lithuanian Liberty League: Nemenčinės pl. 68, 232016 Vilnius; tel. (0122) 764-841; f. 1981, achieved legal status 1988; Leader ANTANAS TERLECKAS.

Lithuanian Nationalist Union: Gedimino pr. 22, 232000 Vilnius; f. 1924, refounded 1989; Chair. RIMANTAS SMETONA.

Lithuanian Social Democratic Party: Basanavičiaus 16/5, 232009 Vilnius; tel. (0122) 652-380; fax (0122) 652-157; f. 1896, re-formed 1989; Chair. ALOYZAS SAKALAS; 2,000 mems (1990).

Sąjūdis (Movement): Gedimino pr. 1, 232001 Vilnius; tel. (0122) 224-881; telex 261111; fax (0122) 224-890; f. 1988 as Lithuanian Movement for Restructuring; Chair. JUOZAS TUMELIS; Sec. ANDRIUS KUBILIUS.

Diplomatic Representation

EMBASSIES IN LITHUANIA

Holy See: Vilnius; Papal Nuncio: Mgr JUSTO MULLOR GARCIA.

Italy: Vilnius; Ambassador: FRANCO TEMPESTA.

United Kingdom: Vilnius; Ambassador: MICHAEL PEART.

Judicial System

Supreme Court: Lentpjuviu 24, Vilnius 232725; tel. (0122) 610-560; Chair. MINDAUGAS LOŠYS.

Office of the Prosecutor-General: Smetonos 6, Vilnius 232709; tel. (0122) 610-537; Prosecutor-General ARTURAS PAULAUSKAS.

Religion

CHRISTIANITY

The Roman Catholic Church

The Roman Catholic Church in Lithuania comprises 668 parishes, organized in two archdioceses (Kaunas and Vilnius) and four dioceses (Kaišiadorys, Panevėžys, Vilkaviškis and Telšiai). There are seminaries at Kaunas and Telšiai.

Archbishop of Kaunas: Cardinal VINCENTAS SLADKEVIČIUS, Valančiaus gatvė 6, Kaunas 233000; tel. (0127) 222-197;

Archbishop of Vilnius: JULIJONAS STEPONAVIČIUS, Šv. Mikalojaus 4, Vilnius 232001; tel. (0122) 627-098.

Orthodox Churches

Lithuanian Old Believers Pomor Church: Naujininkų 24, Vilnius 232030; tel. (0122) 752-068; 51 congregations; Chair of Supreme Pomor Old Ritualists' Council IVAN YEGOROV.

Vilnius and Lithuanian Eparchy of the Russian Orthodox Church: Aušros vartų 2, Vilnius 232024; tel. (0122) 625-896; incl. 45 congregations; Archbishop CHRIZOSTOM (Martishkin).

Protestant Churches

Consistory of the Lithuanian Evangelical Lutheran Church: Laisvės 68, Tauragė 235900; tel. 52-345; Bishop JONAS KALVANAS.

Consistory of the Lithuanian Evangelical Reformed Church: Basanavičiaus 17, Biržai 235280; tel. 52-061; Chair. REINHOLDAS MORAS.

JUDAISM

Jewish Community: Vilnius; f. 1992, to replace and expand the role of the Jewish Cultural Society; Chair. GRIGORIJUS KANOVICIUS.

The Press

In 1990 there were 456 newspapers published in Lithuania, including 414 published in Lithuanian, and 104 periodicals, including 100 in Lithuanian.

PRINCIPAL NEWSPAPERS

Ekho Litvy (Echo of Lithuania): Jakšto 7, Vilnius 232600; tel. (0122) 227-404; f. 1940; 5 a week; publ. by the Supreme Council and Council of Ministers; in Russian; Editor VASILY YEMELYANOV; circ. 55,000.

Kurier Wileński (Vilnius Express): Subaciaus 60, Vilnius 232024; tel. (0122) 616-881; fax (0122) 224-246; f. 1953; 5 a week; publ. by the Supreme Council and Council of Ministers; in Polish; Editor ZBIGNIEW BALCEWICZ; circ. 30,000.

Lietuvos aidas (Echo of Lithuania): Gynėju 3, Vilnius 232710; tel. (0122) 615-208; fax (0122) 224-876; f. 1917; re-est. 1990; 5 a week; Editor-in-Chief SAULIUS STOMA; circ. 110,000.

Lietuvos Rytas (Lithuania's Morning): Gedimino pr. 12A, Vilnius 232008; tel. (0122) 622-680; telex 261129; fax (0122) 227-656; f. 1919; 5 a week; publ. by the 'Lietuvos rytas' joint-stock company; weekly Russian edition; Editor GEDVYDAS VAINAUSKAS; circ. 240,000.

Respublika (Republic): Šventaragio 4, Vilnius 232600; tel. (0122) 223-112; fax (0122) 223-538; f. 1989; 7 a week; weekly Russian edition; Editor-in-Chief VITAS TOMKUS; circ. 230,000.

Sportas (Sports): Gedimino pr. 37, Vilnius 232600; tel. (0122) 616-757; f. 1956; 2 a week; Editor ALEKSANDRAS KRUKAUSKAS; circ. 25,500.

Tiesa (Truth): Laisvės pr. 60, Vilnius 232019; tel. (0122) 429-788; f. 1917; 5 a week; publ. by the Lithuanian Democratic Labour Party; Editor DOMAS ŠNIUKAS; circ. 110,100.

Valstiečių laikraštis (Peasants' Newspaper): Laisvės pr. 60, Vilnius 232019; tel. (0122) 429-942; f. 1940; 3 a week; Editor VLADAS BŪTĖNAS; circ. 209,400.

PRINCIPAL PERIODICALS

Aitvaras (Brownie): Laisvės pr. 60, 232019 Vilnius; tel. (0122) 429-462; f. 1989; children's newspaper; Editor LAIMA DRAZDAUSKAITE; circ. 204,860.

Atgimimas (Rebirth): Žigimantu 26, Vilnius 232600; tel. (0122) 224-406; fax (0122) 227-531; f. 1988; weekly; Editor-in-Chief RIMVYDAS VALATKA; circ. 30,000.

Caritas: Vilniaus 29, 233000 Kaunas; tel. (0127) 209-683; f. 1989; monthly; publ. by Women's Catholic Union 'Caritas'; Editor ALBINA PRIBUŠAUSKAITĖ; circ. 30,000.

Genys (Woodpecker): Bernardinų 8, Vilnius 232600; tel. (0122) 616-334; fax (0122) 227-656; f. 1940; monthly; illustrated; for 5–10-year-olds; Editor-in-Chief VYTAUTAS RAČICKAS; circ. 96,500.

Gimtasis kraštas (Native Land): Tilto 8/2, Vilnius 232600; tel. (0122) 623-881; fax (0122) 222-727; f. 1967; weekly; publ. by the Tėviškė (Motherland) Society for Cultural Relations with Lithuanians Living Abroad; Editor-in-Chief ALGIMANTAS ČEKUOLIS; circ. 102,400.

Jaunimo gretos (Ranks of Youth): Bernardinų 8, Vilnius 232600; tel. (0122) 624-818; f. 1944; monthly; publ. by the Publishing House 'Spauda' (Publish); journal of the joint stock company 'Jaunatis'; popular illustrated, problems of youth; short stories and essays by beginners, translations; Editor-in-Chief KAZYS ŽILĖNAS; circ. 100,000.

Kalba Vilnius (Vilnius Calling): Konarskio 49, Vilnius 232674; tel. (0122) 661-022; f. 1956; weekly; Lithuanian TV and Radio programmes; Editor-in-Chief ALGIRDAS KRATULIS; circ. 105,500.

Katalikų Pasaulis (Catholic World): Pylimo 27, Vilnius 232001; tel. (0122) 222-422; fax (0122) 222-122; f. 1989; fortnightly; publ. by the Publishing House of the Episcopalian Conference of the Lithuanian Catholic Church; information about the Catholic Church and its doctrine; Editor-in-Chief VACLOVAS ALIULIS; circ. 50,000.

Krantai (Banks): POB 511, 232000 Vilnius ARP-3; tel. (0122) 224-743; f. 1989; monthly; journal of the Ministry of Culture and Education; general culture, art; Editor-in-Chief VAIDOTAS DAUNYS; circ. 5,000.

Kultūros barai (Domains of Culture): S. Daukanto 3/8, Vilnius 232600; tel. (0122) 610-538; f. 1965; monthly; journal of the Ministry of Culture and Education; culture and arts; Editor-in-Chief VILHELMAS CHADZEVIČIUS; circ. 7,300.

Literatūra ir menas (Literature and Art): Universiteto 4, 232600 Vilnius; tel. (0122) 612-586; f. 1946; weekly; publ. by the Lithuanian Writers' Union; fiction, essays, art; Editor-in-Chief VYTAUTAS RUBAVIČIUS; circ. 17,000.

Magazyn Wileński (Vilnius Journal): Didžioji 40, 232601 Vilnius; tel. (0122) 474-007; f. 1990; fortnightly; political, cultural; in Polish; Editor-in-Chief MICHAŁ MACKIEWICZ; circ. 6,900.

Mažoji Lietuva (Lithuania Minor): H. Manto 2, Klaipėda 235800; tel. 18-074; f. 1932; weekly; independent; politics, social and cultural issues; Editor KĘSTUTIS OGINSKAS; circ. 23,600.

Metai (Tears): Gedimino pr. 37, Vilnius 232600; tel. (0122) 617-344; f. 1991; monthly; journal of the Lithuanian Union of Writers; fiction, criticism; Editor-in-Chief JUOZAS APUTIS; circ. 11,700.

Moteris (Woman): Maironio 1, Vilnius 232600; tel. (0122) 610-169; f. 1952; monthly; popular, for women; Editor-in-Chief REGINA PAULAUSKIENĖ; circ. 350,000.

Mūsų gamta (Our Nature): Rudens 33B, Vilnius 232600; tel. (0122) 696-964; f. 1964; monthly; popular science, nature preservation, tourism; Editor-in-Chief RIMANTAS BUDRYS; circ. 23,000.

Nemunas: Gedimino 45, Kaunas 233000; tel. (0127) 223-066; f. 1967; monthly; journal of the Lithuanian Writers' Union; popular, for youth; Editor-in-Chief ALGIMANTAS MIKUTA; circ. 40,000.

Šluota (Broom): Bernardinų 8/8, Vilnius 232722; tel. (0122) 613-171; f. 1934; fortnightly; satirical; Editor-in-Chief RYTIS TILVYTIS; circ. 70,100.

Soglasiye (Concord): Zygimantu 26, Vilnius 232600; tel. (0122) 226-206; fax (0122) 224-415; f. 1988; weekly; independent; in Russian; Editor LIUBA CIORNAJA; circ. 10,000.

Švyturys (Beacon): Maironio 1, Vilnius 232600; tel. (0122) 627-488; f. 1949; fortnightly; political, fiction; Editor-in-Chief JUOZAS BAUŠYS; circ. 90,000.

Tėvynės šviesa (Light of the Homeland): Antakalnio 31, Vilnius 232055; tel. (0122) 741-571; f. 1953; weekly; publ. by the Ministry of Culture and Education; educational; Editor JUOZAS SUBAČIUS; circ. 11,700.

Žalioji Lietuva (Green Lithuania): Jakšto 9-127, Vilnius 232300; tel. (0122) 627-458; fax (0122) 766-737; f. 1989; weekly; publ. by the Lithuanian Green Movement; ecology, preservation of nature; Editor DAINA KARLONAITĖ; circ. 10,000.

NEWS AGENCY

ELTA (Lithuanian Telegraph Agency): Gedimino pr. 21/2, Vilnius 232750; tel. (0122) 613-667; telex 261196; fax (0122) 619-507; f. 1920; Dir ADOLFAS GUESKIS.

Publishers

Mintis (Idea): Z. Sierakausko 15, Vilnius 232600; tel. (0122) 632-943; political and popular books and booklets; Dir ZIGMAS MALIU-KEVIČIUS; Editor-in-Chief KĘSTUTIS TREČIAKAUSKAS.

Mokslas (Science): Žvaigždžių 23, Vilnius 232050; tel. (0122) 458-525; telex 261107; f. 1975; natural and technical sciences, agricultural, medicine, economics, history, linguistics and literature; dictionaries; Dir ZIGMANTAS POCIUS.

Šviesa (Light): Vytauto pr. 25, Kaunas 233000; tel. (0127) 741-634; f. 1945; textbooks and pedagogical literature; Dir JONAS BARCYS; Editor-in-Chief STANISLOVAS PETRAUSKAS.

Vaga (Furrow): Gedimino pr. 50, 232600 Vilnius; tel. (0122) 626-443; fax (0122) 616-902; f. 1945; fiction; Dir ALGIRDAS PEKELIŪNAS; Editor-in-Chief ALEKSANDRAS KRASNOVAS.

Valstybinė enciklopedijų leidykla (State Encyclopaedia Publishers): Algirdo 31, Vilnius 232600; tel. (0122) 660-349; f. 1957; encyclopaedias, reference books; Editor-in-Chief MYKOLAS MIKA-LAJŪNAS.

Vyturys (Lark): Algirdo 31, Vilnius 232600; tel. (0122) 660-665; fax (0122) 263-449; fiction and non-fiction for children and youth; Dir JUOZAS VAITKUS; Editor-in-Chief LIUDAS PILIUS.

Publishers' Association

Lithuanian Publishers' Association: Algirdo 31, Vilnius 232600; tel. (0122) 660-665; f. 1989; Pres. JUOZAS VAITKUS.

Radio and Television

Lithuanian Radio and Television: Konarskio 49, Vilnius 232674; tel. (0122) 660-637; f. 1940; Dir-Gen. SKIRMANTAS VALIULIS.

Radio Vilnius: f. 1926; broadcasts in Lithuanian, Russian, Polish and English.

TV Vilnius: f. 1957; broadcasts in Lithuanian, Russian and Polish.

Finance

(cap. = capital; dep. = deposits)

BANKING
State Banks

Bank of Lithuania: Gedimino pr. 6, Vilnius 232001; tel. (0122) 224-015; telex 261246; fax (0122) 221-501; f. 1990; Chair. of Bd VILIUS BALDISIUS.

Lithuanian Bank for Foreign Economic Affairs: Totorių 2/8, Vilnius 232629; tel. (0122) 224-790; telex 261123; f. 1988; Chair. of Bd DANUTE TUCKIENE.

Commercial Banks

Agricultural Bank of Lithuania: Totoriu 4, Vilnius 232629; tel. (0122) 628-842; f. 1990; Chair. of Bd PRANAS VILIUNAS.

Joint-Stock Innovation Bank of Lithuania: Šv. Stepono 27, Vilnius 232006; tel. (0122) 261-826; telex 261114; fax (0122) 661-550; f. 1988; Dir ARTURAS BALKEVICIUS.

Okio Bankas: Gruodzio 9, Kaunas 233000; tel. (0127) 203-651; fax (0127) 203-296; f. 1989; Chair. of Bd VALDEMARAS BUTENAS.

Spaudos Bankas: Vrublevskio 6, Vilnius 232671; tel. (0122) 610-723; f. 1990; Chair. JULIUS NIEDVARAS.

Savings Bank

Savings Bank of Lithuania: Vilniaus 16, Vilnius 232736; tel. (0122) 618-409; f. 1988; Chair. of Bd KOSTAS JAKUTIS.

COMMODITY EXCHANGES

Vilnius Commodity Exchange (VICE): 5 Laisves pr., Exhibition Palace, 232600 Vilnius; tel. (0122) 454-866; fax (0122) 454-866; f. 1991; Gen. Dir RIMAS BUTILA.

Headquarters of Congress of Exchanges in Lithuania: 14 Gedimino pr., 232001 Vilnius; tel. (0122) 628-804; arranges contacts with other exchanges in the former Soviet Republics.

Trade and Industry
CHAMBER OF COMMERCE

Chamber of Commerce and Industry of the Republic of Lithuania: Algirdo 31, Vilnius 232600; tel. (0122) 662-480; telex 261114; fax (0122) 661-542; f. 1925, closed 1940, restored 1991; over 180 mems; Pres. JONAS POVILAITIS.

INDUSTRIAL ASSOCIATIONS

Association of Lithuanian Businessmen: Pylimo 4, Vilnius 232001; tel. (0122) 614-963; f. 1989; Pres. ARVYDAS BARAUSKAS.

Lithuanian Manufacturers' Association: Traku 9/1, Vilnius 232001; tel. (0122) 221-323; f. 1989; Pres. ALGIMANTAS MATULE-VICIUS.

TRADE UNIONS

Lithuanian Confederation of Free Trade Unions: Gynėju 3, Vilnius 232710; tel. (0122) 615-260; fax (0122) 226-106; f. 1990; 20 affiliated unions; Chair. MARIJONAS VISAKAVIČIUS; 1,100,100 mems.

Lithuanian Workers' Union: Mykolaičio-Putino 5, Vilnius 232600; tel. (0122) 621-743; fax (0122) 625-092; f. 1988; 37 brs; Chair. ALDONA BALSIENĖ; 100,000 mems.

MAJOR INDUSTRIAL COMPANIES AND FOREIGN TRADE CORPORATIONS

Agrolitas: Latvių 53–54, Vilnius; tel. (0122) 352-919; telex 261113; fax (0122) 352-622; state foreign trade enterprise; Dir V. PECUIKE-VIČIUS.

Alytus Soft Drinks and Champagne Factory: Miškininkų 17, Alytus 234580; tel. (01235) 52-337; telex 269841; fax (01235) 54-467; produces wines, soft drinks, concentrated juices; Dir JUOZAS DAUKŠYS.

Akmenės Cementas: Naujoji, Akmenė 235464; tel. 58-323; telex 296419; f. 1952; produces cement, slate boards, asbestos-cement pipes, etc.; Dir LEOPOLDAS PETRAVIČIUS; 2,500 employees.

Alytus Cotton Fabric Factory: Pramonės 1, Alytus 234580; tel. (01235) 57-357; fax (01235) 35-566; f. 1968; cotton yarn and fabrics; Dir GINTAUTAS ANDRIUŠKEVIČIUS; 5,634 employees.

Astra: Ulonų 33, Alytus 234580; tel. (01235) 52-176; fax (01235) 52-265; f. 1929; washing machines, other household goods; Dir SEMION BONDAREV.

Azotas: Taurosto 26, Jonava 235000; tel. (01219) 56-621; telex 304152; f. 1965; produces chemical fertilizers; Dir-Gen. BRONIS-LAVAS LUBYS; 4,210 employees.

Banga: Draugystės 19, Kaunas 233031; tel. (0127) 756-777; telex 261147; f. 1987; television broadcasting equipment; Dir-Gen. LEONAS JANKAUSKAS; 18,000 employees.

Ekranas: Elektronikos 1, Panevėžys 235300; tel. (01254) 63-450; telex 287424; fax (01254) 23-415; electronic components; f. 1962; Dir EIMUTIS ŽVYBAS; 6,950 employees.

Elfa: Vytenio 50, Vilnius 232654; tel. (0122) 631-531; telex 261226; fax (0122) 662-436; electrical household appliances; f. 1940; Dir-Gen. GINTARAS SAUNORIS; 5,200 employees.

Lietcom: Kauno 3A, Vilnius; tel. (0122) 633-499; fax (0122) 633-589; state foreign trade company; Dir J. KIRIUSHCHENKO.

Lietuvos Prekyba: Gedemino pr. 30–31, Vilnius; tel. (0122) 618-001; telex 261149; fax (0122) 612-820; foreign trade enterprise; Dir P. GROBOVAS.

Litimpex: Verkių 37, Vilnius 232600; tel. (0122) 352-544; telex 261148; fax (0122) 614-194; f. 1987; foreign trade enterprise; arranges export and import of a wide range of goods; provides business services to companies engaged in foreign trade; Dir-Gen. JUSTINAS ANTANAITIS.

Kėdainiai Chemical Plant: Juodkiskio 32, Kėdainiai 235030; tel. (01257) 52-273; fax (01257) 53-241; f. 1963; produces sulphuric acid, amophos fertilizer and other chemical products; Dir KAZYS PIL-KAUSKAS.

Neris: Pramonės 97, Vilnius 232048; tel. (0122) 670-023; telex 261256; f. 1958; agricultural equipment; Dir-Gen. VYTAUTAS ŠUMAKARIS.

Nuklonas: Architektų 1, Šiauliai 235419; tel. (01214) 52-235; telex 296426; fax (01214) 53-504; f. 1968; electronic goods, incl. integrated circuits, household appliances; Dir VYTAUTAS SLANINA.

Panevėžys Glass-Works: Pramonės 10, Panevėžys 235319; tel. (01254) 63-747; telex 287421; fax (01254) 65-703; f. 1965; produces window glass; Dir STASYS STOŠKUS.

Šilkas: Neries kr. 16, Kaunas 233713; tel. (0127) 264-235; fax (0127) 261-293; f. 1956; produces textiles and fabrics; Dir-Gen. JURGIS KELIUOTIS; 3,000 employees.

Snaigė: Pramonės 6, Alytus 234580; tel. (01235) 57-580; telex 269849; fax (01235) 57-612; f. 1964; produces household refrigerators; Dir-Gen. ANTANAS ANDRIULIONIS; 3,200 employees.

Tauras: Pramonės 15, Šiauliai 235419; tel. (01214) 52-220; telex 296126; fax (01214) 27-344; produces colour television sets; f. 1961; Dir RAIMUNDAS VIRBICKAS.

Vilnius Fuel Outfit Company: Kalvarijų 143, Vilnius 232650; tel. (0122) 776-261; telex 261161; fax (0122) 776-569; f. 1959; manufactures components for diesel engines; Dir-Gen. ALGIRDAS DIDŽIULIS; 7,110 employees.

Vilnius Fur Factory: Paupio 28, Vilnius 232600; tel. (0122) 627-803; f. 1964; processes mink, rabbit, fox, musk-rat and astrakhan hides; produces fur clothes; Dir-Gen. JUOZAS MACEVIČIUS.

Vingis: Savanorių 176, Vilnius 232646; tel. (0122) 653-884; f. 1959; components for television and radio sets; Dir-Gen. ALGIRDAS LINARTAS.

Žalgiris: Vilnius 232048, Pramonės 141; tel. (01214) 671-476; telex 261145; f. 1947; metal cutting machines, milling machines, other machine tools; Dir JURIJUS SIVICKIS.

Transport

RAILWAYS

In 1989 there were 2,010 km of railway track in use. Main lines link Vilnius with Riga (Latvia), Minsk (Byelorussia) and Kaliningrad (Russian Federation), and Warsaw (Poland), via the Byelorussian city of Grodno.

ROADS

In 1989 the total length of roads was 43,100 km, of which 34,100 km were hard-surfaced.

SHIPPING

The main port is at Klaipėda.

Shipowning Company

Lithuanian Shipping Company: Yuliusa Yanonisa 24, Klaipėda 235813; telex 278111; Pres. A. A. ANILENIS.

CIVIL AVIATION

Lithuania has air links with most cities in former Soviet Republics and with several Western European destinations.

Tourism

Tourist attractions in Lithuania include the historic city of Vilnius, coastal resorts, such as Palanga and Kuršių Nerija, and picturesque countryside. In 1989 some 70,000 foreign tourists visited Lithuania.

Culture

NATIONAL ORGANIZATION

Ministry of Culture and Education: see section on The Government (Ministries).

CULTURAL HERITAGE

Art Museum of the Republic of Lithuania: Gorkio g. 55, Vilnius 232024; tel. (0122) 628-030; f. 1941; over 297,390 items; library of 19,571 vols; Dir ROMUALDAS BUDRYS.

Institute of Culture and Arts: Tilto 4, Vilnius 232001; tel. (0122) 613-646; f. 1990; Dir ALGIRDAS GAIZUTIS.

Institute of the Lithuanian Language: Antakalnio 6, Vilnius 232055; tel. (0122) 624-726; Dir ALEKSANDRAS VANAGAS.

Kaunas State Historical Museum: Donelaitis 64, Kaunas; f. 1921; 127,459 exhibits; library of 5,510 vols; Dir A. Y. KVEDARAS.

Lithuanian National M. Mazvydas Library: Gedimino pr. 51, Vilnius 232635; tel. (0122) 629-023; f. 1919; 4m. vols; Dir VLADAS BULAVAS.

Museum of History and Ethnography of Lithuania: Vrublevskio 1, Vilnius; tel (0122) 627-774; f. 1855; over 382,000 exhibits; library of over 10,000 vols; Dir E. J. SKRUPSKELIS.

SPORTING ORGANIZATIONS

Department of Physical Training and Sports: Zemaites 6, Vilnius 232600; tel. (0122) 635-363; govt agency; Dir-Gen. ALGIRDAS RASLANAS.

PERFORMING ARTS

Lithuanian Academic Drama Theatre: Gedimino pr. 4, Vilnius; tel. (0122) 629-771.

Lithuanian Academic Opera and Ballet Theatre: Vienuolio 1, Vilnius; tel. (0122) 620-727.

Lithuanian Puppet Theatre: Arlių 5, Vilnius; tel. (0122) 628-678.

National Philharmonic: Didžioji 45, Vilnius; tel. (0122) 627-165.

Russian Drama Theatre: Basanivičiaus 13, Vilnius; tel. (0122) 620-552.

ASSOCIATIONS

Lithuanian Artists' Union: Kosciuškos 28, Vilnius 232600; tel. (0122) 622-935; f. 1935; Chair. BRONIUS LEONAVICIUS; 960 mems.

Lithuanian Cinematographers' Union: Kalvarijų 1; Vilnius 232005; tel. (0122) 731-204; Chair. SKIRMANTAS VALIULIS.

Lithuanian Composers' Union: Mickeviciaus 29, Vilnius 232600; tel. (0122) 752-232; f. 1941; Chair. JULIUS ANDREJEVAS.

Lithuanian Culture Fund: Vienuolio 5/32, Vilnius 232600; tel. (0122) 617-634; fax (0122) 226-036; f. 1989; Chair. JURGIS DVARIONAS.

Lithuanian Journalists' Union: Vilniaus 35, Vilnius 232600; tel. (0122) 611-790; f. 1957; Chair. RIMGAUDAS EILUNAVICIUS.

Lithuanian Folk Art Association: Vytenio 13, Vilnius 232009; tel. (0122) 662-974; f. 1966; Chair. ZILVINAS BAUTRENAS.

Lithuanian Society for Study of Local Lore: Traku 2, Vilnius 232001; tel. (0122) 622-476; f. 1926; Chair. IRENA SELIUKAITE.

Lithuanian Theatre Union: Gedimino pr. 1, Vilnius 232001; tel. (0122) 623-586; f. 1987; Chair. JUOZAS BUDRAITIS.

Lithuanian Writers' Union: Rasytoju 6, Vilnius 232600; tel. (0122) 223-919; f. 1940; Chair. VYTAUTAS MARTINKUS.

Motherland (Teviske): Tilto skg. 8/2, Vilnius 232600; tel. (0122) 613-580; fax (0122) 624-092; f. 1964; Chair. VACLOVAS SAKALAUSKAS.

PEN Centre of Lithuania: Mildos 31/16, 232055 Vilnius; tel. (0122) 358-909; f. 1989; 35 mems; Pres. ROMUALDAS LANKAUSKAS; Sec. GALINA BAUZYTE-CEPINSKIENE.

Polish Union: Didzioji 40, Vilnius 232601; tel. (0122) 223-388; f. 1988; Chair. JAN MINCEWICZ.

Education

The developed education system of pre-1940 Lithuania, which included 2,600 elementary schools, 98 gymnasiums and pro-gymnasiums and 25 other schools in 1938, was replaced by a Soviet-type education system after 1944. Lithuanian is the main language of instruction. In 1988 82.2% of pupils in general day schools were taught in Lithuanian, 15.8% in Russian and 2.0% in Polish. Higher education is provided in 16 institutions of higher education, including four universities.

UNIVERSITIES

Kaunas Technological University: Donelaicio 73, Kaunas 233006; tel. (0127) 227-044; f. 1950; Rector VLADISLAVAS DOMARKAS.

Vilnius Technical University: Sauletekio al. 11, Vilnius 232054; tel. (0122) 769-600; f. 1969; Rector EDMUNDAS KAZIMIERAS ZAVADSKAS.

Vilnius University: Universiteto 3, 232734 Vilnius; tel. (0122) 623-779; telex 261128; fax (0122) 223-563; f. 1579; language of instruction: Lithuanian; 1,291 teachers; 15,800 students; Rector J. KUBILIUS.

Vytautas Magnus University: Daukanto 28, Kaunas 233000; tel. (0127) 206-753; f. 1922, closed 1950, reopened 1989; 5 faculties, 2 institutes; 150 teachers; 425 students; Rector ALGIRDAS AVIZIENIS.

Social Welfare

NATIONAL AGENCIES

Department of Labour Safety: Jaksto 1/25, Vilnius 232600; tel. (0122) 661-854; Dir-Gen. JONAS SIMKUNAS.

Ministry of Social Welfare: see section on The Government (Ministries).

Ministry of Health Care: see section on The Government (Ministries).

HEALTH AND WELFARE ORGANIZATIONS

Children's Fund of Lithuania: Zygimantu 12, Vilnius 232600; tel. (0122) 627-180; f. 1988; Chair. JUOZAS NEKROSIUS.

Lithuanian Invalids Society: Jogailos 9/1, Vilnius 232001; tel. (0122) 226-727; f. 1988; Chair. JONAS MACIUKEVIČIUS.

Lithuanian Red Cross Society: Gedimino pr. 3A, Vilnius 232600; tel. (0122) 619-923; f. 1940; Chair. JUOZAS SAPOKA.

Lithuanian Society of the Deaf: Šv. Kazimiero 3, Vilnius 232600; tel. (0122) 628-115; Chair. ALGIRDAS JAKAITIS.

Lithuanian Union of the Blind: Labdariu 7/11, Vilnius 232001; tel. (0122) 619-691; f. 1944; Chair. JUOZAS DZIDOLIKAS.

The Environment

GOVERNMENT ORGANIZATION

Department of the Environment: Juozapaviciaus 9, Vilnius 232686; tel. (0122) 355-868; Dir-Gen. EVALDAS VEBRA.

ACADEMIC INSTITUTES

Lithuanian Academy of Sciences: Gedimino pr. 3, Vilnius 232600; telex 261141; f. 1941; several attached institutes involved in environmental research; Pres. J. K. POŽELA.

Institute of Ecology: Akademijos 2, Vilnius 232600; tel. (0122) 776-991; f. 1958; research into degradation of water systems and affect of pollution on terrestrial ecosystems; Dir Prof. JUOZAS VIRBICKAS.

NON-GOVERNMENTAL ORGANIZATION

Lithuanian Green Movement: Kalvariju 130–48, Vilnius 232048; tel. (0122) 765-609; fax (0122) 766-737; f. 1988; directed by a Co-ordination Council.

BIBLIOGRAPHY OF THE USSR AND ITS SUCCESSOR STATES

Aganbegyan, A. *The Challenge: Economics of Perestroika.* London, Hutchinson, 1988.

Akiner, S. *Islamic Peoples of the Soviet Union.* London, Kegan Paul International, 1983.

Allworth, E. (Ed.). *The Tatars of the Crimea.* Durham, North Carolina, Duke University Press, 1989.

Central Asia: a Century of Russian Rule. London and New York, Columbia University Press, 1967.

Andrew, C., and Gordievsky, O. *KGB, the Inside Story.* London, Hodder and Stoughton, 1990.

Brown, A. (Ed.). *The Soviet–East European Relationship in the Gorbachev Era.* Boulder, Colorado, Westview, 1990.

Campbell, K. M., and MacFarlane, S. N. (Eds). *Gorbachev's Third World Dilemmas.* London, Routledge, 1989.

Clarke, R. A., and Matko, D. J. I. *Soviet Economic Facts, 1917–81.* London, Macmillan, 1983.

Dawisha, K. *Eastern Europe, Gorbachev and Reform: the Great Challenge,* 2nd Edn. Cambridge, Cambridge University Press, 1988.

Dawisha, K., and Valdes, J. 'Socialist Internationalism in Eastern Europe', in *Problems of Communism,* Vol. 36, No. 2, March/April 1987.

Desai, P. *The Soviet Economy.* Oxford, Basil Blackwell, 1987.

Doder, D., and Branson, L. *Heretic in the Kremlin.* London, Futura, 1990.

Dyker, D. A. *The Future of the Soviet Economic Planning System.* London, Croom Helm, 1985.

Galbraith, J. K., and Menshikov, S. *Capitalism, Communism and Co-existence: from the Bitter Past to a Better Prospect.* Boston, Massachusetts, Houghton Mifflin Co, 1989.

Gorbachev, M. *Perestroika,* 2nd Edn. London, Fontana Collins, 1988.

Grancelli, B. *Soviet Management and Labor Relations.* Boston, Massachusetts, Unwin Hyman, 1988.

Gray, K. R. (Ed.). *Soviet Agriculture: Comparative Perspectives.* Ames, Iowa, Iowa State University Press, 1990.

Hanson, P. *Trade and Technology in Soviet–Western Relations.* London, Macmillan, 1981.

Hedlund, S. *Crisis in Soviet Agriculture.* London, Croom Helm, 1984.

Private Agriculture in the Soviet Union. London, Routledge, 1990.

Hewett, E. A. *Reforming the Soviet Economy: Equality versus Efficiency.* Washington, DC, Brookings Institution, 1989.

Hiden, J., and Salmon, P. *The Baltic Nations and Europe: Estonia, Latvia and Lithuania in the Twentieth Century.* London, Longman, 1991.

Holden, G. *The Warsaw Pact: Soviet Security and Bloc Politics.* Oxford, Basil Blackwell, 1989.

Hudson, G. E. (Ed.). *Soviet National Security Policy under Perestroika,* Mershon Center Series on International Security and Foreign Policy (Vol. IV). Boston, Massachusetts, Unwin Hyman, 1990.

Kittrie, N., and Volgyes, I. (Eds). *The Uncertain Future: Gorbachev's Eastern Bloc.* New York, Paragon House, 1988.

Kochan, L., and Abraham, R. *The Making of Modern Russia,* 2nd Edn. London, Penguin, 1983.

Kozlov, V. I. *The Peoples of the Soviet Union.* London, Hutchinson, 1988.

Laird, R. F., and Hoffmann, E. P. (Eds). *Soviet Foreign Policy in a Changing World.* New York, Aldine de Gruyter, 1986.

Lang, D. *A Modern History of Georgia.* London, Weidenfeld and Nicolson, 1962.

Light, M. *The Soviet Theory of International Relations.* Brighton, Wheatsheaf, 1988.

Linden, R. H. (Ed.). *Studies in East European Foreign Policy.* New York, Praeger, 1980.

Litvin, V. *The Soviet Agro-Industrial Complex.* Boulder, Colorado, Westview, 1987.

Lynch, A. *The Soviet Study of International Relations.* Cambridge, Cambridge University Press, 1988.

McGwire, M. *Perestroika and Soviet National Security.* Washington, DC, Brookings Institution, 1991.

Malcolm, N. *Soviet Policy Perspectives on Western Europe,* Chatham House Paper. London, Routledge (for the Royal Institute of International Affairs), 1989.

Medvedev, Z. A. *Soviet Agriculture.* New York and London, Norton, 1977.

Mellor, R. E. H. *The Soviet Union and its Geographical Problems.* London, Macmillan, 1982.

Menon, R., and Nelson, D. (Eds). *Limits to Soviet Power.* Lexington, Massachusetts, Lexington Books, 1989.

Moskoff, W. (Ed.). *Perestroika in the Countryside: Agricultural Reform in the Gorbachev Era.* Armonk, NY, M. E. Sharpe, 1990.

Nahaylo, B., and Swoboda, B. *Soviet Disunion: a History of the Nationalities Problem in the USSR.* London, Hamish Hamilton, 1990.

Nelson, D. N. 'Europe's Unstable East', in *Foreign Policy,* No. 82 (Spring), 1991.

de Nevers, R. 'The Soviet Union and Eastern Europe: the End of an Era', in *Adelphi Papers,* No. 249. London, Brasseys and International Institute for Strategic Studies, 1990.

Nogee, J. L., and Donaldson, R. H. (Eds). *Soviet Foreign Policy since World War II,* 3rd Edn. Oxford, Pergamon, 1988.

Nove, A. *An Economic History of the USSR,* Revised Edn. Harmondsworth, Penguin, 1982.

Pipes, R. *The Formation of the Soviet Union: Communism and Nationalism, 1917–23.* Cambridge, Massachusetts, Harvard University Press, 1964.

von Rauch, G. *The Baltic States: the Years of Independence, 1917–40.* London, C. Hurst and Co, 1974.

Roxburgh, A. *The Second Russian Revolution.* London, BBC Books, 1991.

Ryan, M. (Ed.). *Contemporary Soviet Society: a Statistical Handbook.* Aldershot, Edward Elgar, 1990.

Saikal, A., and Maley, W. (Eds). *The Soviet Withdrawal from Afghanistan.* Cambridge, Cambridge University Press, 1989.

Smith, G. *The Nationalities Question in the Soviet Union.* London, Longman, 1990.

Smith, H. *The New Russians.* London, Hutchinson, 1990.

Symons, L., and White, C. (Eds). *Russian Transport: an Historical and Geographical Survey.* London, G. Bell and Sons, 1975.

Terry, S. M. *Soviet Policy in Eastern Europe.* New Haven, Connecticut, Yale University Press, 1984.

Turnbull, M. *Soviet Environmental Policies and Practices: the Most Critical Investment.* Aldershot, Dartmouth, 1991.

Wädekin, K.-E. (Ed.). *Communist Agriculture.* London, Routledge, 1990.

White, S. *Gorbachev in Power.* Cambridge, Cambridge University Press, 1990.

White, S., Pravda, A., and Gitelman Z. (Eds). *Developments in Soviet Politics.* London, Macmillan, 1990.

Whiting, A. S. *Siberian Development and East Asia.* Stanford, California, Stanford University Press, 1981.

PART FOUR
Political Profiles of the Region

POLITICAL PROFILES

ADŽIĆ, Col-Gen. Blagoje: Yugoslav Chief of the General Staff and Acting Federal Secretary for National Defence; b. in Croatia; ethnic Serb. *Career:* a conservative Communist and a Serb nationalist, he lost his parents during the Ustaša atrocities of the Second World War. His career has been spent in the Yugoslav People's Army. In 1991 he was one of the main advocates of a hardline policy against Croatia and Slovenia, although he did suffer illness during the year. In January 1992 his political superior, Col-Gen. Kadijević (q.v.), who was considered to be more moderate, resigned and Adžić replaced him, as acting federal defence minister. This was considered to be a victory for the more radical faction, which opposed the proposed deployment of UN forces in Yugoslavia. *Address:* c/o Federal Secretariat for National Defence, Yugoslavia, 11070 Belgrade, Kneza Miloša 29.

AGOSTAN, Andros: Yugoslav (Vojvodina/Serbian) politician; b. in Vojvodina, Republic of Serbia; ethnic Hungarian (Magyar). *Career:* the deputy director of the Forum publishing house, he was elected to the Serbian Assembly as leader of the main ethnic Hungarian party of Yugoslavia, the Democratic Community of Vojvodina Hungarians. This party was founded in August 1990 and is one of the better-organized political opposition groups of Serbia. It has eight seats in the Serbian parliament. Agostan was a prominent opponent of the fighting in Croatia, during 1991. *Address:* VDMK, Yugoslavia, Vojvodina, Ada, trg Oslobodjenja 11.

AHMETI, Vilson: Prime Minister of Albania; b. 1951, in Fieri. *Education:* he graduated in mechanical engineering from Tirana University (1973). *Career:* from 1973 to 1978 he worked at a vehicle factory in Tirana, before joining the Ministry of Food. He became Deputy Minister for the food industry in 1987. He was Minister of Industry in the March 1991 Government of Fatos Nano (q.v.). Although an independent, it was the Socialist Party of Albania (former Communists) which nominated him as Minister of Food in the June Government of Ylli Bufi. Upon Bufi's resignation in December, following the withdrawal of Democratic Party support, Ahmeti was appointed to lead a new, interim Government of 'experts'. *Address:* Këshilli i Ministrave, Albania, Tirana.

AKAYEV, Askar: President of Kyrgyzstan; b. 1944, in Kyrgyzstan. *Career:* he was a mathematics professor who joined the CPSU in 1981 (resigning from it in 1991). He was a member of the Central Committee of the Kirghiz Communist Party, President of the Kirghiz SSR (now Kyrgyzstan) Academy of Sciences in Frunze (now Bishkek), a member of the CPSU Constitutional Compliance Committee and, in 1991, a member of the USSR Supreme Soviet Committee on Economic Reform. A known liberal, he was elected by the republican Supreme Soviet as executive President in October 1990, after the Communist leader (for whom the post had been designed) failed to win a majority. He was a compromise candidate, who favoured reform and was unconnected with the dominant factions, having been in Leningrad (now St Petersburg) for many years of his academic career. He favoured the introduction of economic reform before political changes, although he also achieved some consensus with the opposition and was the first to suggest a 'Commonwealth' successor to the USSR, in mid-1991. He ensured that Kyrgyzstan was one of the most ostensibly liberal of the Central Asian Republics, despite the continued influence of entrenched Communist conservatives. He condemned the coup attempt against President Gorbachev (q.v.) of the USSR, in August 1991, and was himself threatened by Communist putschists. He took precautionary measures, however, and, when the Moscow coup attempt failed, he and the Vice-President, German Kuznetsov (q.v.), resigned from the Communist Party, which was subsequently dissolved. In October Akayev was unopposed in direct presidential elections. *Address:* Office of the President of the Republic, Kyrgyzstan, Bishkek.

AKHMEDOV, Khan A.: Prime Minister of Turkmenistan; b. 1936. *Career:* he joined the CPSU in 1963. A conservative Communist, he was First Deputy Chairman of the Council of Ministers when promoted to Chairman (Prime Minister), in 1989. He was confirmed in office after the elections of November 1990. *Address:* Office of the Council of Ministers, Turkmenistan, Ashkhabad.

AKHTAYEV, Akhmed-kazi: Russian politician; ethnic Avar of Daghestan. *Career:* as chairman (*amir*) of the Islamic Renaissance Party, previously an all-Union organization, he heads one of the principal political vehicles of the Muslims of the former USSR. Most of its support is in Central Asia and, within the Russian Federation, in the North Caucasus.

ALEXSEY II, His Holiness Patriarch: Head of the Russian Orthodox Church, Chairman of the Moscow Patriarchy; b. 23 Feb. 1929, in Tallinn, Estonia; of Baltic German and ethnic Russian descent. *Education:* a graduate of the Leningrad (now St Petersburg) Theological College. *Career:* originally Aleksey M. Ridiger, his early career in the Russian Orthodox Church was in his native Estonia, and he became Bishop of Tallinn and Estonia in 1961. He moved to the Moscow Patriarchate in 1962, where he was Vice-Chairman of the Dept of External Affairs. In 1964 he became an Archbishop, the Administrative Manager of the Patriarchate and a permanent member of the Holy Synod. In 1968 he became Metropolitan of Tallinn and Estonia and, in 1986, Metropolitan of Leningrad (now St Petersburg) and Novgorod. In 1990 he succeeded Patriarch Pimen as Patriarch of Moscow and All Russia. He is considered theologically conservative, but relatively liberal in politics (he condemned the attempted coup of August 1991 and is a supporter of Boris Yeltsin). *Address:* Russian Federation, 113191 Moscow, Danilovsky val 22.

ALIA, Ramiz: President of Albania; b. 1925, in Shkodër. *Career:* he joined the Communist Party (later renamed the Party of Labour of Albania—PLA—and then, in 1991, the Socialist Party of Albania) in 1943 and achieved responsibility in the National Liberation Army and the youth movement before moving into the Party hierarchy. He became a full member of the Politburo in 1961 and, in 1982, head of state. He was responsible for introducing moderate reforms after the death of Enver Hoxha, in 1985, particularly with the increase in popular opposition from 1990. He formally left the PLA in April 1991, upon being elected to the post of President of the Republic. *Address:* Office of the President, Albania, Tirana.

ALIYEV, Geidar Ali Rza ogly: Azerbaidzhani politician, Chairman of the Supreme Majlis of Nakhichevan; b. 1923. *Education:* graduate of Azerbaidzhan State University (1957). *Career:* already active in the administration of his home territory of Nakhichevan, he joined the CPSU in 1945 and was prominent in the republican apparatus by the 1960s. He became First Secretary of the Azerbaidzhan Communist Party in 1969. He was dismissed in 1987, a victim of Mikhail Gorbachev's (q.v.) drive against corruption. He left the Communists in July 1991, alleging their suppression of the democratic movement, and, in September, was elected Chairman of the Supreme Majlis (soviet or parliament) of the Autonomous Republic of Nakhichevan. *Address:* Supreme Majlis, Azerbaidzhan, Nakhichevan.

ANDOV, Stojan: Yugoslav politician, President of the Macedonian Assembly. *Career:* he was in public service, serving as ambassador to Iraq during the late 1980s. He was a supporter of the federal prime minister, Ante Marković's (q.v.), economic reforms and favoured gradual political reform, but the maintenance of a Yugoslav federation. He became leader of the Macedonian branch of the federal party of Ante Marković, the Alliance of Reform Forces, which was one of the major parties in Macedonia, following the parliamentary elections of November–December 1990. Helped by his reputation as a skilled negotiator, and with the need for political compromise in the Assembly apparent, Andov was elected President of the

Assembly (speaker), on 8 January 1991. *Address:* Yugoslavia, Macedonia, 91000 Skopje, 11 Octomvri bb.

ANTALL, Dr Jószef: Prime Minister of Hungary; b. 7 April 1932, in Hungary. *Education:* at the University of Budapest. *Career:* his father was one of the original founders of the Independent Smallholders' Party and, after the failure of the Uprising of 1956, his own political activities barred him from continuing a career as a history teacher. In 1974 he became director of the Semmelweis Museum in Budapest. He was a co-founder of the Hungarian Democratic Forum, in September 1987. He became its Chairman, in October 1989, being re-elected in December 1990. On 3 May 1990 he was appointed as Chairman of the Council of Ministers. He was a popular politician and the coalition Government depended on his leadership. During 1991 there were anxieties about his health. *Address:* Council of Ministers, Hungary, 1055 Budapest, Kossuth Lajos tér 1–3.

ARUTYUNYAN, Gagik Garushevich: Vice-President of Armenia and Chairman of the Council of Ministers; b. 1948, in Soviet Armenia. *Education:* a graduate in economic sciences. *Career:* an economist by profession (a lecturer and writer), he was a head of the Armenian Communist Party's Central Committee. He joined the nationalist opposition and, from August 1990, was a Deputy Chairman of the Armenian Supreme Soviet. In October 1991, with the support of President Levon Ter-Petrosyan (q.v.), he was elected Vice-President of the Republic. On 22 November he was appointed Chairman of the Council of Ministers (Prime Minister). *Address:* Council of Ministers, Armenia, Yerevan.

ASANBAYEV, Erik Magzumovich: Vice-President of Kazakhstan; b. 10 March 1936. *Career:* he joined the CPSU in 1967 and was Chairman of the republican Supreme Soviet from April 1990 until December 1991. A reformist Communist, he was a supporter and deputy of President Nursultan Nazarbayev (q.v.). He was popularly elected as Vice-President of the Republic, in December 1991. *Address:* Office of the Vice-President of the Republic, Kazakhstan, Alma-Ata.

ATANASOVSKI, Dragan: Yugoslav politician; b. 1943, in Macedonia. *Career:* a member of the League of Communist of Yugoslavia since June 1982, he was prominent in the restructuring of the Party, in 1990, and was elected the Chairman of the renamed and reorganized League of Communists-Movement for Yugoslavia, in December. *Address:* League of Communists-Movement for Yugoslavia, Yugoslavia, Belgrade, bul. Lenjina 6.

BABIĆ, Milan: Yugoslav politician, 'President of the Republic of Serbian Krajina', in Croatia; b. in Croatia; ethnic Serb. *Career:* he was leader of the Croatian Serbs who began the formation of an autonomous Serb-controlled area in Croatia, when that Republic began moves towards secession. Trouble in the Krajina region began in mid-1990 and, gradually, allegedly with the support of the federal armed forces, the ethnic Serbs of Croatia established a large measure of effective self-rule in a large part of the Republic. Based in Knin, he became Krajina's head of government, and, at the end of 1991, was declared to be President of the Republic of Serbian Krajina, which claimed membership of the Yugoslav federation and its separation from Croatia. Previously supported by the Serbian authorities, he would not support their agreement to the UN-brokered peace plan, objecting to the presence of peace-keeping forces in Krajina. The split became public in January 1992.

BAJRAMOVIĆ, Sejdo: Yugoslav Collective State Presidency member for Kosovo-Metohija (Republic of Serbia); b. 1928, in Kosovo (now Kosovo-Metohija); ethnic Albanian. *Career:* he was elected by the Serbian Assembly as the federal Presidency's member for Kosovo-Metohija, in May 1991. He was a deputy in the Serbian Assembly, having been elected for the Socialist Party of Serbia (former Communists) in the constituency of Glogovac (Kosovo), with about 100 votes. The Federal Assembly had initially refused to confirm his membership of the State Presidency, because the Slovenian and Croatian representatives had questioned the constitutionality of his

appointment (the Assembly of Kosovo had been suspended). They also cast doubt on his Albanian ethnicity, claiming that he was of the Roma (Gypsy) people and his grandfather had slavicized his surname. He was a member of the State Presidency *de facto*, however, and was co-ordinator of the body, following its failure to elect Stjepan Mesić (Croatia) as its President, in May 1991. *Address:* Office of the Federal Presidency, Yugoslavia, 11070 Belgrade.

BALCEROWICZ, Dr Leszek: Polish politician and economist; b. 19 January 1947, in Lipno; m., with three c. *Education:* graduated from the Main School of Planning and Statistics in Warsaw (1970); studied business administration at St John's University, New York (USA), until 1974. *Career:* staff member at the Institute of International Economy Relations, 1970–80, then worked at the Economic Development Institute. He was a member of the Polish Union of Workers' Party, 1969–81. In 1989–91 he was Minister of Finance and introduced reforms designed to introduce a market economy. *Address:* Ul. Świętokrzyska 12, 00-916 Warsaw, Poland.

BERISHA, Dr Sali: Albanian politician and doctor. *Career:* a cardiologist, he became the leader of the main anti-Communist opposition group, the Democratic Party. In December 1991 he withdrew Democratic Party support from the Bufi Government, in protest at the failure to satisfy opposition demands. The move was also believed to bolster his own authority as head of the radical, more militant wing of the party. *Address:* Partia Demokratike të Shqipërisë, Albania, Tirana.

BIELECKI, Jan Krzysztof: Polish politician; b. 1951, in Poland. *Career:* after training and working as an economist, he was nominated to be Prime Minister by the newly-elected President Wałęsa (q.v.), in December 1990. In December 1991, following his defeat in a general election, he was replaced by Jan Olszewski. *Address:* Warsaw, Poland.

BÎRLADEANU, Alexandru: President of the Romanian Senate; b. 25 January 1911, in Komrat, Moldavia. *Education:* at the University of Iaşi. *Career:* he taught law at the University of Iaşi and held a chair of the Academy of Economic Studies, Bucharest, 1946–51. He was elected a full member of the Romanian Academy in 1955 and subsequently became its Vice-President. He was Minister of Foreign Trade, 1948–54. In May 1990 he was elected a senator for the National Salvation Front, following life-long membership of the Communist Party. *Address:* Senate, Bucharest, Romania.

BOGICEVIĆ, Bogić: Yugoslav Collective State Presidency member for Bosnia-Herzegovina; b. 1953, in Bosnia-Herzegovina; ethnic Serb. *Career:* in January 1989 he was elected to the Central Committee of the League of Communists of Bosnia-Herzegovina. In June he became the member of the federal State Presidency for Bosnia-Herzegovina, following a popular, direct ballot, for a five-year term. Although a loyal Communist, he was a reformist and was retained as the Republic's federal representative by the new Government of the three nationalist parties, after December 1990. During 1991 he tended, increasingly, to support Croatia, Slovenia and Macedonia in the constitutional disputes. *Address:* Office of the Federal Presidency, Yugoslavia, 11070 Belgrade.

BOŽOVIĆ, Dr Radoman: Yugoslav politician, Premier of Serbia; b. 1953, in Serbia; ethnic Serb; m., with two c. *Education:* he graduated in economics, from Belgrade University, later gaining a doctorate in law. *Career:* he worked as an academic, 1976–89, and was then elected as a deputy to the Vojvodina Assembly. He later headed its provincial government. A member of the Socialist Party of Serbia (the former Communists), he was head of its parliamentary group in the Assembly of the Republic of Serbia, having been elected to it as a deputy in December 1990. On 23 December 1991 he was voted into office by the Serbian Assembly. *Address:* Government of Serbia, Yugoslavia, 11000 Belgrade, Nemanjina 11.

BUČAR, Dr France: Yugoslav politician, President of the National Assembly of Slovenia; b. 1923, in Slovenia. *Career:* a doctor of law, he was a respected member of the Slovene

Democratic Union, the oldest and one of the most influential of the original DEMOS opposition parties. When DEMOS won the parliamentary elections of April 1990, he was elected speaker. *Address:* National Assembly, Slovenia, 61000 Ljubljana, Šubičeva st. 4.

BULATOVIĆ, Momir: Yugoslav politician, President of the Presidency of Montenegro; b. 1928, in Montenegro. *Career:* a Communist, he became prominent in the leadership of the League of Communists of Montenegro, following the protests of early 1989, which caused the resignation of the old leadership. Bulatović became leader of the republican Communists (who were renamed the Democratic Party of Socialists in 1991) and secured the Party's nomination for the presidential elections, in December 1990. On 25 December, in the second round of voting, he was elected President of the seven-member State Presidency of Montenegro. Under him, Montenegro has been a loyal supporter of Serbia, in the developing constitutional crises of 1991. However, he also wished to avoid EC economic sanctions and to maintain a distinct Montenegrin identity within the Yugoslav federation. The Montenegrin leadership came to express reservations about the war in Croatia and, in October, supported the peace proposals of the Hague (Netherlands) conference on Yugoslavia's future. This caused some surprise and outrage in Serbia, but was supported by the Montenegrin Assembly. *Address:* Office of the State Presidency of Montenegro, Yugoslavia, Montenegro, 81000 Titograd.

BURBULIS, Gennady: First Deputy Chairman of the Russian Council of Ministers, State Secretary; b. 1945, in Pervouralsk, Sverdlovsk (now Ekaterinburg) region; of mixed Lithuanian and ethnic Russian parentage. *Education:* graduate of Ural State University, in Philosophical Sciences; speaks German. *Career:* a philosopher, he first worked in factories and the Soviet Rocket Forces, before going to the Ural State University. He then lectured on Marxism-Leninism at the Institute of the All-Union Ministry of Non-Ferrous Metallurgy, in Sverdlovsk, until he was elected to the Soviet Congress of People's Deputies. He joined the CPSU in 1970, but, in 1988, he formed a political club in favour of democratization, the Discussion Tribune, in Sverdlovsk. He was elected to Congress in 1989 and was a prominent member of the radical Inter-Regional Group. He became a supporter of Boris Yeltsin (q.v.) and, after Yeltsin's election as Chairman of the Supreme Soviet of the Russian Federation, his chief of staff. A Russian nationalist, Burbulis is the leader of the 'Young Turks' (*Mladoturki*), a radical group of young politicians, who opposed the Union. In 1991 he was appointed State Secretary, the head of the Russian Federation State Council, an advisory body to President Yeltsin. On 6 November 1991 Yeltsin formally formed a new Government of the Russian Federation, with himself as Chairman. Burbulis was appointed First Deputy Chairman and granted additional powers to act for the Chairman. *Address:* Council of Ministers, Russian Federation, Moscow.

BUREŠOVA, Dagmar: Czechoslovak politician, Chairwoman of the Czech National Council; b. 1929, in Kladno. *Education:* graduated in law from Charles University, Prague. *Career:* she worked as a lawyer from 1952 and was an active member of various legal organizations. Following the 'Velvet Revolution', in November 1989, she was made Minister of Justice, and was elected Chairwoman of the republican National Council of the Czech Lands, in June 1990. *Address:* Czech National Council, Prague, Czechoslovakia.

ČALFA, Marián: Prime Minister of the Czechoslovak Federal Government; b. in 1945, in Trebisov, eastern Slovakia. *Education:* studied law, in Prague. *Career:* he was a legal official for the official press agency between 1972 and 1988. In April 1988 he was made a Minister without Portfolio. As a Communist, he aided the Government in its negotiations with the opposition, during the unrest of November 1989. In December he was made Prime Minister. In January 1990 he resigned his membership of the Communist Party of Czechoslovakia and was re-elected to the Federal Assembly, in June 1990, as a member of the Civic Forum/Public Against Violence coalition. It is often considered to be to his credit that he could overcome the disadvantages of his Communist background. *Address:*

Office of the Prime Minister, Nábř. kpt. Jaroše 4, 125 09 Prague 1, Czechoslovakia.

CÂMPEANU, Radu: Romanian politician and Vice-President of the Senate; b. 1922, in Bucharest, Romania. *Career:* educated as a lawyer and economist, he was imprisoned, 1947–56, by the Communists, because of his political activities. Following his later exile in Paris, he returned to Romania in 1990, when he became leader of the National Liberal Party (PNL). *Address:* Bucharest, Romania.

ČARNOGURSKÝ, Ján: Czechoslovak politician, Premier of Slovakia; b. 1944, in Bratislava, Slovakia. *Education:* graduated in law from Charles University, Prague. *Career:* he practised law until he was banned, in 1981, after defending a teacher acccused of sedition. In 1981–87 he worked as a company lawyer, while, at the same time, dealing with human rights cases. He was unemployed for two years and was then detained in prison, from August to November 1989, charged with incitement. In December 1989 he was made Deputy Federal Prime Minister and remained in the Federal Government until June 1990. He was a founder of the Christian Democratic Movement (CDM), a predominantly Slovak party favouring a looser federation, in early 1990. In June 1990 he was invited to join the new coalition Federal Government, but he declined the offer, preferring to take office in the Slovak Republic as First Deputy Premier. He became the republican Premier in April 1991. *Address:* Slovak National Council, Bratislava, Czechoslovakia.

CHANTURIA, Georgi ('Gia'): Georgian politician; b. 1960. *Career:* a member of the nationalist opposition to Communist rule, he was leader of the National Forum (subsequently the National Democratic Party) and one of the most serious political opponents of Zviad Gamsakhurdia (q.v.). He urged the boycott of the 1990 Supreme Soviet elections and the election of a National Congress instead. This was to act as a parliament until Georgia gained its independence. He was arrested by the Gamsakhurdia regime, but released by rebel forces during the civil war, in December 1991. In this conflict he and other radicals were allied with more moderate opposition figures. *Address:* National Democratic Party, Georgia, Tbilisi.

CHORNOVIL, Vyacheslav Maksimovich: Ukrainian politician; b. 1937; m. *Education:* studied journalism at the University of Kiev. *Career:* from 1960 to 1965 he held various editorial jobs in television, radio and the press, all in Ukraine. He engaged in some dissident activity, was dismissed from his posts and was sentenced to prison and hard labour, in 1965. In 1968 he went on hunger strike, was pardoned and released. In 1972 he was again arrested for further dissident activity and, in 1975, despite many protests he was sentenced to the Mordovian camp. He was subsequently released, after numerous petitions and complaints. In the late 1980s he became a leading figure in the radical wing of the Rukh nationalist opposition movement. He was elected as Chairman of Lvov Regional Council, Western Ukraine. In the presidential elections of December 1991 he came second to the victor, Leonid Kravchuk (q.v.), with 23% of the votes cast. *Address:* Lvov Regional Council, Ukraine, Lvov.

CHRZANOWSKI, Wiesław: Polish Minister of Justice, Marshal of the Sejm; b. 20 December 1923, in Warsaw. *Education:* in law at Warsaw University, and in Economics at Poznań University; he graduated in law from the Jagiellonian University in Kráków. *Career:* he was involved with underground publications and was a soldier in the Home Army, during the Second World War. A member of the Labour Party, he was imprisoned from 1948 to 1954, accused of trying to overthrow the regime. In 1980–81 he was an adviser to Solidarity, before becoming a practising lawyer and, in 1989, the Chairman of the Christian National Union, upon its foundation. *Address:* Ul. Krajowej Rady Narodowej 28, 00-853 Warsaw, Poland.

COPOSU, Corneliu: Romanian politician. *Career:* he was initially the leader of the National Peasants' Party, which merged with the Christian Democratic Party, in 1990, to become the Christian Democratic National Peasants' Party, of which he became President. He was a prominent member of the coalition opposed to the ruling National Salvation Front, the Democratic Convention. *Address:* Romania, 70433 Bucharest, Bd. Carol 34.

DEMEŠ, Dr Pavel: Czechoslovak politician, Minister of International Relations for the Slovak Republic. *Address:* Ministry of International Relations, Udolná 7, POB 87/15, 810 05 Bratislava, Czechoslovakia.

DEMSZKY, Dr Gábor: Hungarian politician; b. in 1952. *Education:* he trained as a lawyer. *Career:* formerly a dissident, he was a member of the Alliance of Free Democrats. He was made Mayor of the Budapest Metropolitan Area in late 1990. As Chief Mayor he was prominent in the protracted controversy about the staging of the 1996 Expo, which was meant to be held in both Vienna (Austria) and Budapest—the old Habsburg capitals. *Address:* Chief Mayor's Office, Hungary, 1052 Budapest, Városház u. 9–11.

DIENSTBIER, Jiří: Czechoslovak Deputy Prime Minister and Minister of Foreign Affairs, in the Federal Government; b. 20 April 1937, in Prague. *Education:* graduated in philosophy, from Charles University, Prague. *Career:* he was a journalist and playwright and became a prominent dissident against the Communist regime. From 1959 he was a reporter for the state radio company, spending much of the 1960s abroad, as a foreign correspondent. He was dismissed in 1970. He was a signatory to Charter 77 and was spokesman for the human rights group in 1979, for which he received a three-year prison-sentence. He was spokesman again in 1985. In February 1988 he helped establish the *samizdat* publication, *Lidové Noviny*. He was a co-founder, in November 1989, of the Civic Forum and, in December 1989, became Minister of Foreign Affairs in the Federal Government. He was reappointed following the elections of June 1990. *Address:* Federal Ministry of Foreign Affairs, Loretánské nám. 5, 125 10 Prague, Czechoslovakia.

DIMITROV, Filip: Prime Minister of Bulgaria; b. 31 March 1955, in Sofia. *Education:* graduated in law, in Sofia. *Career:* from a professional, intellectual family, he became a lawyer and was not politically affiliated until the fall of Communism, in November 1989. He was a leader of the Greens and was elected leader of the main opposition coalition, the Union of Democratic Forces (UDF), as a compromise candidate, in December 1990. He was leader of the UDF—Movement, or Dark Blue, faction, which favoured more radical, right-wing policies. His success was confirmed by the departure of the liberal groups in mid-1991 and the main UDF victory in the elections of October 1991. Dimitrov therefore led Bulgaria's first Government without Communist membership since the Second World War. *Address:* Bulgaria, Sofia, Rakovski St 134.

DJUKANOVIĆ, Milo: Yugoslav politician, Premier of Montenegro; b. 15 Feb. 1962, in Nikšić, Montenegro. *Education:* he is a graduate in economics. *Career:* he joined the League of Communists of Yugoslavia in 1979. In early 1989 the Montenegrin Communist leadership was forced to resign and was replaced by a relatively young group of Communists, of whom Djukanović was one. They favoured a Montenegrin renaissance, although they remained loyal allies of Serbia. The new leadership was among the first in Yugoslavia to agree to the holding of multi-party elections. These took place in December 1990 and were won by the League of Communists of Yugoslavia (subsequently renamed the Democratic Party of Socialists), which formed a Government, led by Djukanović, in January 1991. *Address:* Yugoslavia, Montenegro, 81000 Titograd, bul. Lenjina brig. 13.

DOBROVSKÝ, Luboš: Czechoslovak Minister of Defence, in the Federal Government; b. 1930. *Education:* he attended a military secondary school but then decided to study languages (Russian and Czech) at university. *Career:* he was a reporter for state radio, 1968–69, and then briefly worked on *Listy*, until it was closed down, in 1969. An active dissident he signed the human-rights Charter 77. From November 1989 he worked in the Ministry of Foreign Affairs and, in October 1990, was made Minister of Defence. *Address:* Federal Ministry of Defence, Tychonova 1, 161 00 Prague 6, Czechoslovakia.

DOGAN, Ahmed: Bulgarian politician; b. 29 March 1954; ethnic Turk. *Education:* doctorate in philosophy. *Career:* under the Communist regime, he was prosecuted for his championing of ethnic Turkish rights and, in June 1989, he was arrested and sentenced to 10 years in prison for being a founder and leader of an 'anti-state organization', the Movement for Rights and Freedoms. He was amnestied in December of the same year. He was elected as a deputy in June 1990 and, after the October 1991 elections, his party was the third-largest in the National Assembly and agreed to support a Government of the Union of Democratic Forces. *Address:* Bulgaria, 1408 Sofia, j.k. Ivan Vazov, Petar Topalov-Shmid str. 55, bl. 50, vh. B.

DOMLJAN, Dr Žarko: Yugoslav politician and historian, President of the Croatian Assembly; b. 14 September 1932, at Imotski, Croatia. *Education:* he graduated in English and history of art from the University of Zagreb and gained a doctorate in 1973. *Career:* he worked as a musician and a book editor, before becoming employed at the Institute of Historical Sciences (Zagreb) in 1987. Previously unaffiliated to any political organization, he joined the Croatian Democratic Union, in 1989, and was elected as a deputy to the Croatian Assembly, in 1990. In May he was elected to the post of parliamentary speaker. *Address:* Croatia, 41000 Zagreb, Radićev trg. 6.

DRACH, Ivan Fyodorovich: Ukrainian politician and writer; b. 1936, in Telizhentsy, Kiev district. *Education:* studied philology at University of Kiev, then theatre and drama at Moscow State University. *Career:* apart from writing novels and poetry (he has many published works), he has also worked on the *Literaturnaya Ukraina* newspaper, in the Kiev Aleksandr Dovenko Film Studio and on the Kiev newspaper, *Witczyna*. He joined the CPSU in 1959 but resigned his membership in 1990. A Ukrainian nationalist, he was a founding member of the People's Movement (Narodny Rukh) of the Ukraine for Perestroika and was elected leader of Rukh at its inaugural Congress, in September 1989. In 1990 he was elected to the Ukrainian Supreme Soviet. *Address:* Union of Ukrainian Writers, Ukraine, 252008 Kiev, ul. Ordzhonikidze 2.

DRASKOVIĆ, Vuk: Yugoslav (Serbian) politician. *Career:* an ardent nationalist, he was vociferous in demands for resistance to the Croats and the Albanians of Kosovo (now Kosovo-Metohija). He also revived reference to Macedonia as 'South Serbia', but did, during 1991, express some opposition to the war in Croatia. His right-wing tendencies were said to have contributed to his poor showing in the presidential elections of 1990, when he gained only 20% of the votes cast. In March 1991, however, he emerged as the leading opposition figure, during the anti-government demonstrations in Belgrade. His party, the Serbian Renaissance Movement, is the largest opposition group in the Serbian parliament, with 19 seats. *Address:* Srpski Pokret Obnove, Yugoslavia, 11000 Belgrade, Maršala Tita 14.

DRNOVSEK, Janez: Yugoslav (Slovenian) politician, former Yugoslav Collective State Presidency member for Slovenia; b. 1950, in Slovenia. *Education:* he has a doctorate in economics. *Career:* he worked variously as an industrialist, banker and diplomat. In May 1989 he was elected, in a direct popular ballot, as Slovenia's representative on the federal State Presidency. Despite anxieties about his political inexperience, he was elected by the Presidency for Slovenia's turn as President of the federal head of state. He served in this capacity until May 1990. He then remained as a member of the State Presidency until 8 October 1991, when Slovenia formally recalled all its citizens from participation in federal institutions. In January 1992, following international recognition of Slovenia, he was being mentioned as a future prime minister in a new Government. *Address:* c/o Government of Slovenia, Slovenia, 61000 Ljubljana, Prešemova st. 8.

DUBČEK, Alexander: Chairman of the Czechoslovak Federal Assembly and former Communist First Secretary; b. 27 November 1921, in Uhrovice, Slovakia; m., with three c. *Education:* studied at the Communist Party College in Moscow (USSR—now the Russian Federation), and graduated in law at the Comenius University, Bratislava. *Career:* he rose steadily through the ranks of the Communist Party of Czechoslovakia, to become First Secretary in January 1968. His popular attempts at liberal reform were brought to an abrupt end when the USSR sent tanks into Prague, on 21–22 August 1968. Dubček was immediately taken to Moscow and, in October, forced to denounce his own policies. In April 1969 he resigned as First Secretary. Having been Chairman of the Federal Assembly and sent as ambassador to Turkey, he was dismissed from the Party altogether, in the mid-1970s. He worked at the Slovak Forestry Commission until the 'Velvet Revolution' of November 1989, when he returned to politics. He was elected Chairman of the Federal Assembly on 28 December 1989. *Address:* Federal Assembly, Prague 1, Czechoslovakia.

DUDAYEV, Gen. Dzhakar Musayevich: Russian politician, 'President of the Chechen Republic'; b. April/May 1944; ethnic Chechen; m., with three c. *Education:* he graduated as a pilot from the Tambov Higher Military College and later attended Gagarin Air Force Academy. *Career:* his childhood was spent in Kazakhstan, following the deportation of many of the Chechen at the end of the Second World War. He served in the Air Force of the USSR, ending as commander of the Tartu (Estonia) base. In November 1990 he was elected Chairman of the Executive Committee of the All-National Congress of the Chechen People. This became an increasingly dominant force in the Chechen-Ingush Autonomous Republic (where the Chechen formed some 58% of the population, in 1989) and, following the discrediting of the conservative Supreme Soviet after the Moscow coup attempt of August 1991, it effectively replaced the Communist parliament in the territory. On 27 October 1991 he was elected President of the unilaterally proclaimed Chechen Republic, which was not recognized by the Russian authorities. He is one of the most prominent politicians of the Caucasus and has strong support in the North Caucasus and in the Assembly of the Mountain Peoples of the Caucasus. *Address:* Russian Federation, Checheno-Ingushetia, Grozny.

FOKIN, Vitold Pavlovych: Ukrainain Prime Minister; b. 1932; ethnic Russian. *Career:* a Communist since 1957, he was elected Chairman of the Council of Ministers in November 1990, as a compromise candidate, following public demonstrations. A nationalist sympathiser, he was considered able to unite the opposition and the liberal Communists behind a programme of economic reform. By the end of 1991 his position at the head of Government was considered to be less secure. *Address:* Cabinet of Ministers, Ukraine, Kiev.

FÜR, Lajos: Hungarian Minister of Defence; b. in 1930. *Career:* an historian by training, he became a prominent member of the Hungarian Democratic Forum. On the centre-right of the movement, he became joint Chairman, with Jószef Antall (q.v.), in October 1990. He was nominated as the party's presidential candidate, in 1989, but the elections were postponed. In May 1990 he was made Minister of Defence. *Address:* Ministry of Defence, Hungary, 1055 Budapest, Pálffy György u. 7–11.

GAFAROVA, Elmira Mikail kyzy: Chairman of the Supreme Soviet of Azerbaidzhan; b. 1934. *Education:* graduate in Philological Sciences from the Kirov Azerbaidzhani Institute. *Career:* member of the CPSU from 1958, she was already in the Komsomol, of which she was Deputy Chairman between 1955 and 1961. She was then an Instructor at the Central Committee of the Azerbaidzhan Communist Party until 1970, although she retained links with the republican Komsomol. In 1970–80 she held high office in the Azerbaidzhan and Baku City Party committees, before becoming a member of the republican Government. From 1980 she was Minister of Education and then, from 1983, Minister of Foreign Affairs, until she became Deputy Chairman of the Council of Ministers, in 1987. She was elected Chairman of the Supreme Soviet of Azerbaidzhan in 1989, effectively the republican head of state. A nationalist, she was, however, effectively demoted in the government reorganization of May 1990, when her responsibilities were confined to those of a parliamentary speaker. *Address:* Supreme Soviet, Azerbaidzhan, Baku.

GAMSAKHURDIA, Zviad Konstantinovich: Georgian politician and writer and the ousted President; b. 1939. *Career:*

the son of one of the greatest men of Georgian literature and himself an expert and translator of Shakespeare, during the 1970s he became known as an advocate of human rights, greater religious freedom and Georgian nationalism. In 1977 he co-founded the Georgian Helsinki Union, established to monitor the 1975 Helsinki Accords, but was arrested and imprisoned until 1979. In the late 1980s he became a prominent leader of the Georgian independence movement and led the Round Table-Free Georgia coalition, which won the 1990 elections to the Georgian Supreme Soviet. He was elected Chairman of the Georgian Supreme Soviet, in November 1990, and, in May 1991, President of Georgia in direct elections. His extreme nationalism, the detention of political opponents and suppression of press criticism caused allegations of autocratic rule and, in December 1991, civil war broke out in Georgia. At the beginning of January 1992 the opposition forces announced his deposition and the formation of a ruling Military Council; shortly after this he and his family fled to refuge in Armenia. Later in January he was reported to have declared his intention to fight for his position and was based in western Georgia, where his support remained strong.

GAYDAR, Yegor Timurovich: a Deputy Chairman of the Russian Council of Ministers, responsible for economic affairs, and Minister of Economics and Finance; b. 1956; *Education:* gained a doctorate of Economic Sciences at Moscow State University; speaks Serbo-Croat, English and Spanish. *Career:* he worked on the journal Kommunist and the newspaper Pravda, before being appointed Director of the Institute of Economic Policy of the USSR Academy of Sciences. A Russian nationalist, he is the leading economist of the radical 'Young Turks' (*Mladoturki*) group of politicians. He was appointed to the Russian Federation's Government, in November 1991, becoming a Deputy Chairman and co-ordinator of the 13 ministries responsible for economic affairs. He was the primary co-ordinator of the harsh economic programme of reforms, including the removal of price controls at the beginning of 1992, which was the cause of increasing discontent. *Address:* Ministry of Economics and Finance, Russian Federation, Moscow.

GENDZHEV, Dr Nedim Khaafus Ibrachim: Chief Mufti of Bulgaria; b. 1 Oct. 1945, in Glodjevo village, Razgrad region; ethnic Turk; m., with five c. *Education:* graduated in law from Sofia University, he gained a doctorate in theology. *Career:* he became the Chief Mufti of the Turkish Muslims in 1989, and the senior spiritual leader of Islam in Bulgaria. *Address:* Bulgaria, Sofia, Bratya Miladinovi St 27.

GEORGIEVSKI, Ljupčo: Yugoslav (Macedonian) politician; b. 1964, in Macedonia. *Career:* a nationalist, he was elected leader of the Internal Macedonian Revolutionary Organization-Democratic Party for Macedonian National Unity (IMRO-DPMNU), in June 1989. He was a co-founder of this more radical wing of the nationalist movement, which favoured a Macedonian claim to territories outside its existing borders (although, under pressure from the EC conditions for recognition of the Republic, the party did agree to constitutional changes renouncing territorial ambitions). He was an unemployed university graduate and virtually unknown outside Macedonia when his party, surprisingly, became the largest in the Assembly elected in November–December 1990. The more politically experienced former Communists and the Alliance of Reform Forces, however, secured the posts of State President and parliamentary speaker for their candidates. On 1 February 1991 Georgievski was elected State Vice-President. By then his leadership of the IMRO-DPMNU had been challenged by Vladimir Golubovski (ousted as Vice-President of the party in December), who led a breakaway faction, although it continued to vote as a bloc with the main IMRO-DPMNU. The party's factionalism and inexperience, however, contributed to its perception of being excluded from the decision-making process in the Republic and, on 22 October, Georgievski resigned as State Vice-President, to lead his party into opposition. The IMRO-DPMNU had influenced the Macedonian declaration of independence, however, and the new Constitution. *Address:* VMRO-DPMNE, Yugoslavia, Macedonia, 91000 Skopje, 11 Octomvri bb.

GLEMP, Cardinal Archbishop Józef: Roman Catholic primate of Poland; b. 18 December 1929, in Inowrocław. *Education:* in Polish literature at Warsaw and Toruń; he gained a double doctor's degree in canon law and civil law at the Lateran and Gregorianum Universities in Rome (Italy). *Career:* he was ordained in 1956 and studied in Rome, 1958–64. After joining the secretariat of the Polish Primate in 1967, he was appointed Archbishop-Metropolitan of Gniezno and Warsaw and Primate of Poland in 1981, and became a Cardinal in 1983. He has also worked on a government committees and been prominent in the political changes in Poland since the early 1980s. *Address:* Rezydencja Prymasa Polski, ul. Miodowa 17, 00-246 Warsaw, Poland.

GLIGOROV, Kiro: Yugoslav politician and economist, President of Macedonia; b. 3 May 1917, in Štip, Macedonia. *Education:* graduated in law from Belgrade University. *Career:* he fought in the resistance struggle, from 1941, and joined the Communist Party in 1944. He worked in various Party and government positions, most notably as deputy federal prime minister, 1967–69, as federal finance minister and, 1974–78, as President of the Federal Assembly. Following the Macedonian Assembly elections of 1990, the major parties decided to nominate him as State President, although they had failed to elect him, on 19 January 1991, when he was only the Communist candidate. His experience of economic affairs and the support of the other parties eventually persuaded the largest party to vote for him, and he was elected President of Macedonia on 27 January. *Address:* Office of the President of Macedonia, Yugoslavia, Macedonia, 91000 Skopje.

GODMANIS, Ivars: Prime Minister of Latvia; b. 1940. *Career:* he was a university lecturer in mathematics when he became a deputy leader of the Latvian Popular Front, at its founding congress in 1988. The Front won the elections to the Supreme Soviet (subsequently renamed the Supreme Council), in March 1990. In May he was appointed premier of the republican Government. He successfully, and in a conciliatory manner, led Latvia towards full independence (declared on 21 August 1991), remaining respected by ethnic Latvians, Slavs and the two parts of the Popular Front (the main movement and the parliamentary deputies). *Address:* Government of Latvia, Riga, Latvia.

GÖNCZ, Árpád: President of Hungary; b. 1922. *Education:* he studied law at the Pázmány Péter University of Budapest. *Career:* a playwright, he worked for one of the leaders of the Independent Smallholders' Party, until 1947, after which he worked as a welder. He was arrested and sentenced to life imprisonment in 1956, for his part in the anti-Communist Uprising. During the six years that he actually spent in prison, he taught himself English and used this skill to find work as a translator, upon his release. In 1989 he was made president of the writers' union and, in 1990, he gained a seat in the National Assembly, as a deputy for the Alliance of Free Democrats. He was named as interim President, on 2 May 1990, and was elected President by the National Assembly, on 3 August 1990. He was the only presidential candidate. *Address:* Office of the President, Hungary, 1055 Budapest, Kossuth Lajos tér. 1.

GORBACHEV, Mikhail Sergeivich: Russian politician and last President of the USSR; b. 2 March 1931, in Privolnoye, Krasnogvardeisky district; m. (Raisa Gorbacheva, 1956), with one d. *Education:* in law at Moscow State University, and at Stavropol Agricultural Institute. *Career:* he began work as a machine operator, but soon moved to CPSU and Komsomol work. Although one of the youngest members of the Politburo, which he joined as a full member in October 1980, he became a likely successor to the Soviet leadership during the rule of Yuri Andropov, who was also a native of the North Caucasus and advanced his prospects. However, the conservatives were not willing to elect him as Andropov's immediate successor, but, in March 1985, following the death of Konstantin Chernenko, he became General Secretary of the CPSU. He was elected to the position of titular head of state (Chairman of the Presidium of the Supreme Soviet of the USSR) in October 1988. In March 1990 he was elected to the new post of executive President of the USSR. He introduced a new style of leadership and dramatic reforms throughout the USSR, the key ideas being glasnost ('openness'), perestroika ('restructuring') and 'new thinking' in foreign policy. He was credited with ending the Cold War and catalysing the massive changes in Soviet politics and society. However, he was discredited in his own country by the apparent failure of real reform, his continued faith in the use of the Communist Party and advocacy of a strong Union. Particularly following the unsuccessful coup attempt against him, in August 1991, he was unable to maintain the power of the Union in the face of the increasingly assertive republican leaderships. In December 1991 the formation of the Commonwealth of Independent States marked the end of the USSR and of his post; he resigned on 25 December and the USSR was deemed to have ceased to exist. He announced that he would remain involved in politics and, in January 1992, announced the formation of the Social and Political Research Foundation ('Gorbachev Foundation'), which also involved the Shevardnadze, Shatalin and Velikhov foundations. *Address:* Foundation for Socio-Economic and Political Research, Russian Federation, Moscow.

GORBUNOVS, Anatolijs: Chairman of the Supreme Council of Latvia; b. 1942, in Latvia. *Career:* a member of the Communist Party of Latvia, he had a career in the Party apparatus. However, he was also a Latvian nationalist and a supporter of full independence for the Republic. In October 1988 he spoke at the founding congress of the Latvian Popular Front and found favour even as the Communist Chairman of the Presidium of the Supreme Soviet from the same month. He was elected, with the support of the Front, in March 1990, and, although he remained with the Communists loyal to the CPSU after a split in April, the Front also supported his re-election as republican, *de facto*, head of state, now designated Chairman of the Supreme Council. He was prominent in the cautious development of Latvian independence, fully claimed on 21 August 1991, and in the efforts to secure the support of non-Latvian residents (only 52% of the population were ethnic Latvian, in 1989). *Address:* Supreme Council, Riga, Latvia.

GREGURIĆ, Dr Franjo: Yugoslav politician, Premier (Prime Minister) of Croatia; b. 12 October 1939, in Lobor, Zlata Bistrica, Croatia. *Education:* he gained a doctorate at the Faculty of Technology, University of Zagreb. *Career:* he was a member of the Croatian Democratic Union, and a deputy premier in the Government of Josip Manolić. In July he became Prime Minister himself and, from August, then headed a coalition Government. *Address:* Office of the Prime Minister, Croatia, 41000 Zagreb, Opatička 2.

HALILI, Nevzat: Yugoslav (Macedonian) politician; b. in Macedonia; ethnic Albanian. *Career:* an English teacher in Tetovo, the main Albanian area of western Macedonia, he was elected leader of the Party of Democratic Prosperity on 25 August 1990, at its founding congress. In the elections of November–December it emerged as the dominant Albanian and Muslim party, winning 18 seats alone and a further seven with an allied party. He supported equal rights for all ethnic groups, within the existing Republic. However, he and his party opposed the nationalist elements of the 1991 Constitution and threatened the creation of an 'Autonomous Region of Western Macedonia', for the ethnic Albanians. Despite accusations by ethnic Macedonians of separatist ambitions and links with the Kosovo Albanian party, the Democratic Alliance of Kosovo, Halili has expressly denied this and supported the territorial integrity of Macedonia. *Address:* Party of Democratic Prosperity, Yugoslavia, Macedonia, 91000 Skopje, 11 Octomvri bb.

HASANOV, Hasan Aziz ogly: Chairman of the Council of Ministers of Azerbaidzhan; b. 20 October 1940. *Career:* a Communist since 1963 and senior Party official, he was a moderate reformist. He was appointed premier in January 1990, as part of the reorganization of government which was consequent upon the increase of nationalist sentiment and of ethnic violence. He was a contender for the leadership of the Communist Party, but was defeated by Ayaz Mutalibov, whom he replaced as Chairman of the Council of Ministers. *Address:* Council of Ministers, Azerbaidzhan, Baku.

HAVEL, Václav: President of Czechoslovakia; b. 5 October 1936, in Prague; m. (Olga Šplíchalová, 1964). *Education:* studied drama at the Academy of Arts, Prague. He was excluded from further education in the 1950s because of his wealthy background and instead attended evening classes. *Career:* a playwright by profession, he worked at the Theatre on the Balustrade from 1959, and published his first play, *The Garden Party*, to great critical acclaim, in 1963. In 1968 his political activities meant that his theatrical career was blocked and he could only find menial jobs thereafter. He was a co-founder of Charter 77 and its spokesman in 1977, 1978–79 and 1989. In the intervening years he was imprisoned on three separate occasions for his dissident activities. In 1978 he helped set up the Committee for the Defence of the Unjustly Persecuted. He was a co-founder of the samizdat publication *Lidové Noviny,* in February 1988. In November 1989 he helped establish Civic Forum. The Federal Assembly elected him President of the Republic on 29 December 1989. He was re-elected on 5 July 1990, by a very large majority. He has been active in attempting to resolve the constitutional negotiations between the federal and republican authorities. *Address:* Nábř. kpt. Jaroše 4, 125 09 Prague, Czechoslovakia.

HORN, Gyula: Hungarian politician and economist; b. 5 July 1932. *Education:* Rostow Institute of Economics and Political Academy of Budapest. *Career:* he worked in government and the diplomatic service before spending 16 years at the international section of the Hungarian Socialist Workers' Party (now the Hungarian Socialist Party—HSP). He was State Secretary (1985–89) and Minister of Foreign Affairs (1989–90). He became Chairman of the HSP in May 1990. *Address:* Hungarian Socialist Party, Hungary, 1081 Budapest, Köztársaság tér. 26.

ILIESCU, Ion: President of Romania; b. 3 March 1930, in Oltenița, Ilfov district; m. Elena Iliescu. *Education:* studied at the Bucharest Polytechnic Institute, before going to Moscow to study water engineering at the Power Engineering Institute. *Career:* he was elected to the Communist Party Central Committee in 1968, after 22 years of Party membership. From 1971, however, his Party career was considered less promising, as he went from being the chief of propaganda in Timișoara and then First Secretary of the Iași local Party (1974). In 1979 he was made head of the National Water Council and, in 1984, director of a technical publishing house, which position he held until 1989. Following the overthrow of President Nicolae Ceaușescu, Iliescu, as head of the National Salvation Front (NSF), became interim President, in December 1989. His Presidency was confirmed by a direct popular vote, in May 1991. *Address:* R.71341, Piața Victorei 1, Bucharest, Romania.

IOSELIANI, Prof. Dzhaba: Georgian politician and playwright. *Career:* he gained a doctorate in philology and worked as a playwright, although he also spent time in prison, for murder. He opposed the Communists and President Zviad Gamsakhurdia (q.v.) and was a paramilitary commander, the leader of the Mkhedrioni (Horsemen) group, which was established in 1989. He enjoyed significant popular support, but was barred from standing in the presidential elections of 1991 because he had been arrested, in February, and charged with the illegal possession of firearms. He was prominent in the opposition coalition and was released from detention by the anti-Gamsakhurdia forces, in December. He and Tengiz Kitovani (q.v.) were joint heads of the Military Council, which the rebels announced had assumed power, at the beginning of January 1992, declaring the President deposed and his office abolished. *Address:* Georgia, 380024 Tblisi, Ul. Dzerzhinsogo 8.

IZETBEGOVIĆ, Dr Alija: Yugoslav politician, President of the State Presidency of Bosnia-Herzegovina; b. 1925, in Bosnia-Herzegovina; ethnic Muslim. *Career:* a legal advisor, he was a prominent dissident and political prisoner under the Communist regime. He was imprisoned in 1946, for 'pan-Islamic activity', and again in 1983, for 14 years, although he was released in an amnesty of 1988. In 1970 he wrote the *Islamic Declaration,* on the all-inclusive nature of Islam. He is a strict Muslim, but claims not to be a fundamentalist; the party he founded,

in 1990, the Party of Democratic Action, is centrist politically. On 20 December 1990, as the leader of the largest party, he was elected President of the seven-member State Presidency of Bosnia-Herzegovina (*de facto* republican head of state). *Address:* Office of the State Presidency of Bosnia-Herzegovina, Yugoslavia, Bosnia-Herzegovina, 71000 Sarajevo.

JESZENSZKY, Dr Géza: Hungarian Minister of Foreign Affairs; b. 1941; m., with two c. *Education:* he studied history at the Loránd Eötvös University, Budapest. *Career:* having specialized in international relations, he worked on the foreign affairs committee of the anti-Communist opposition movement, the Hungarian Democratic Forum (HDF). He was made Minister of Foreign Affairs in May 1990, by his father-in-law, Prime Minister Jószef Antall (q.v.). In December 1990 he was elected to the presidium of the HDF. He has been anxious to encourage NATO links with Hungary and to orientate Hungary, and the other Central European countries, towards the West. *Address:* Ministry of Foreign Affairs, Hungary, 1027 Budapest, Bem rkp. 47.

JOVIĆ, Dr Borisav: Yugoslav Collective State Presidency member for Serbia; b. in 1928, in Batočins, Serbia. *Education:* he has a doctorate in economics. *Career:* he joined the Communist Party of Yugoslavia (subsequently the League of Communists of Yugoslavia) in 1951. He held several Party posts before being made a federal minister in 1971. In 1975–80 he was the Yugoslav ambassador to Italy and, in 1988–89, he was President of the Presidency of Serbia. In 1989 he became Serbia's member on the Collective State Presidency, being Vice-President of the body from May that year, until May 1990, when he became President of the Presidency. When his term expired, it was the failure of the Presidency to agree the normally automatic succession of the Croatian member that marked the beginning of the moves towards civil war. He remained a member of the State Presidency, serving on the 'rump' Presidency, which continued to function after the withdrawal of the members for Bosnia-Herzegovina, Croatia, Macedonia and Slovenia, during 1991. He is President of the Socialist Party of Serbia (the former Communists), which supports President Slobodan Milošević (q.v.) of Serbia. *Address:* Office of the Federal Presidency, Yugoslavia, 11070 Belgrade.

KACZYNSKI, Jarosław: Polish politician. *Career:* the chief political adviser to Lech Wałęsa (q.v.) since 1989, in that year he was also instrumental in the formation of the coalition which was to support Tadeusz Mazowiecki's (q.v.) Government. In May 1990 he founded and became Chairman of the centre-right Centre Alliance group. By late 1990 he had been made head of the presidential chancellery, holding the rank of a minister of state. He is the twin brother of Lech Kaczynski (q.v.). *Address:* Ul. Nowy Świat 58, 00-042 Warsaw, Poland.

KACZYNSKI, Lech: Polish politician. *Career:* a Solidarity activist, he specializes in labour law. He was elected as a Solidarity senator and was the interim co-chairman of the movement, with Stefan Jurczak, following Lech Wałęsa's (q.v.) election to the Presidency, in December 1990. He is the twin brother of Jarosław Kaczynski (q.v.). *Address:* Warsaw, Poland.

KÁDÁR, Béla: Hungarian Minister of International Economic Relations; b. in 1934. *Career:* an economist, he was director of the Hungarian World Economy Institute. He advised the Communist Government on economic issues and lectured abroad. An independent, he entered the Government as the Minister of International Economic Relations, in May 1990. *Address:* Ministry of Internationl Economic Relations, Hungary, 1055 Budapest, Honvéd u. 13–15.

KADIJEVIĆ, Col-Gen. Veljko Dušan: former Yugoslav Federal Secretary for National Defence; b. in 1925, in Glavin, near Split, Croatia; ethnic Serb. *Education:* he was educated at the Military Academy and the Higher Military Academy in Belgrade. *Career:* he joined Tito's Partisans in 1943. His career was spent in the Yugoslav People's Army (YPA). He served as the assistant of the Federal Secretary for National Defence, 1981–85, and as Deputy, 1985–88, before obtaining the post himself on 15 May 1988. He was leader of the YPA, therefore, at the start of the civil war over the secession of Croatia and Slovenia, in 1991. He was accused of being in league with the Serbian leadership and for using the YPA to secure a 'Greater Serbia', but he claimed to be defending the federation. In the last months of the year it became increasinly apparent that he did not have full control over the YPA hardliners or their Serb militia allies. After a series of unsuccessful cease-fire arrangements, and following the 15th, UN-mediated one, he resigned, in January 1992. *Address:* c/o Federal Secretariat for National Defence, Yugoslavia, 11000 Belgrade, Kneza Miloša 29.

KARADŽIĆ, Dr Radovan: Yugoslav (Bosnia-Herzegovina) politician; b. in Bosnia-Herzegovina; ethnic Serb. *Career:* the leader of the nationalist Serb Democratic Party, he did not accept any government posts, but did agree to a coalition with the main Muslim and Croat parties, after the 1990 elections. However, as the Yugoslav crisis of 1991 escalated, he became less able to agree to consensus decisions. He did not denounce the 'Serbian Autonomous Regions', proclaimed during the year, and helped organize the 'Assembly of the Serb Nation', following the Republic's declaration of sovereignty in October. He articulated the Serb desire to remain in the Yugoslav federation, although he was accused of threatening the other ethnic groups of the mixed Republic. *Address:* Srpska Demokratska Stranka (BiH), Yugoslavia, Bosnia-Herzegovina, 71000 Sarajevo, trg Dure Pucara bb.

KARAYEV, Tamerlan: Azerbaidzhani politician; b. 1953. *Career:* a jurist by profession, he became involved in opposition politics during the late 1980s. A leader of the moderate wing of the Popular Front, he was elected as a deputy to the Supreme Soviet, in the elections of September 1990, and became a Deputy Chairman (the Popular Front has only 40 seats in the 350-seat, Communist-dominated parliament, but a greater degree of influence than the number of seats would indicate). *Address:* Supreme Soviet, Azerbaidzhan, Baku.

KARIMOV, Islam (Islom) Abduganiyevich: President of Uzbekistan; b. 30 Jan. 1938. *Career:* he worked as a mechanical engineer before, in 1966, moving into economic planning. He became a regional Communist Party leader in 1986 and republican Party leader in 1989. He became the Chairman of the Supreme Soviet (President) of Uzbekistan in March 1990. Although he has a reputation as an old-style, conservative Communist (he supported the Moscow coup attempt of August 1991) and for a repressive regime, he did favour a greater degree of republican control over central government. After the coup attempt of August 1991 he banned the Communist Party, but it was succeeded by the People's Democratic Party, with the same personnel. In December he was elected President of the Republic in free elections. Until January 1992 he also acted as Chairman of the Council of Ministers. *Address:* Office of the President, Uzbekistan, Tashkent.

KEBICH, Vyacheslau Frantsavich (Vyacheslav Frantsevich): Chairman of the Council of Ministers of Byelorussia; b. 10 June 1936. *Career:* a member of the Communist Party Central Committee, he was elected Chairman of the Council of Ministers (Prime Minister) in April 1990. He had acquired a reputation as an unorthodox, but successful, economic reformer. Following the discrediting of the republican Communist leadership after the Moscow coup attempt of August 1991, he stood as a candidate for the post of Chairman of the Supreme Soviet (president) of Byelorussia. He withdrew 'in the cause of unity', in favour of Stanislau Shushkevich (q.v.). *Address:* Council of Ministers, Byelorussia, 220010 Minsk.

KELAM, Tunne: Estonian politician. *Career:* a prominent member of the Estonian National Independence Party, he favoured the election of an alternative assembly to the Supreme Soviet, based on the citizenship of independent Estonia. When this Congress of Estonia was elected, therefore, in March 1990, he was elected its leader. Although more right-of-centre and radical than the ruling Supreme Council (the renamed Supreme Soviet), the Congress and its executive Committee of Estonia were prepared to accept its interim authority. In August 1991, with Estonian independence fully

established, it was agreed to form a Constituent Assembly, to which the Congress nominated one-half of the members. *Address:* Congress of Estonia, Endla 6-4, 200001 Tallinn, Estonia.

KENZHAYEV, Safarali: Chairman of the Supreme Council of Tadzhikistan. *Career:* a Communist member of the Supreme Soviet, he was elected Chairman of the Supreme Soviet (parliamentary speaker) in September 1991. His election was part of the conservative backlash against the banning of the republican Communist Party (renamed the Socialist Party of Tadzhikistan), in the aftermath of the August coup attempt in Moscow. In January 1992 the Supreme Soviet was renamed the Supreme Council and he was re-elected Chairman. *Address:* Supreme Soviet, Tadzhikistan, Dushanbe.

KHASBULATOV, Ruslan Imranovich: Chairman of the Russian Supreme Soviet; ethnic Chechen. *Career:* a member of the parliament of the Russian Federation, he was elected for the constituency of Grozny, in the Chechen-Ingush Autonomous Republic (which declared its independence in October 1991). He was a member of the Democratic Russian group and a supporter of President Boris Yeltsin (q.v.). He replaced Yeltsin in the office of Chairman of the Supreme Soviet, in July 1991, after the elections for an executive President. He had previously been First Deputy Chairman (hence, deputy republican head of state) and was only Acting Chairman until October, when the deputies finally agreed on a permanent successor. In January 1992 he was reported to be expressing opposition to the consequences of the dramatic price rises of that month. *Address:* Supreme Soviet, Russian Federation, Moscow, White House.

KHAYEYEV, Izatullo Khayeyevich: Prime Minister of Tadzhikistan; b. 1936. *Career:* a senior Communist, he was premier between January 1986 and December 1990, his Government having survived an attempt to oust it, in February 1990, by senior officials and nationalist leaders. He was recalled to office in September 1991, as part of the reorganization of government after the Moscow coup attempt of August. *Address:* Council of Ministers, Tadzhikistan, Dushanbe.

KITOVANI, Tengiz: Georgian military leader, artist and sculptor. *Career:* the commander of Georgia's National Guard, he was formerly a nationalist supporter of President Zviad Gamsakhurdia (q.v.). In September 1991 he led a considerable number of his troops in refusing to acknowledge the attempted subordination of his command to the Ministry of Internal Affairs. By December he was heading the opposition military forces, which were now engaged in civil war with the presidential loyalists. He and Dzhaba Ioseliani (q.v.) were joint heads of the Military Council, which the rebels announced had assumed power, in January 1992, declaring the President deposed and his office abolished. *Address:* Georgia, Tbilisi.

KLAUS, Dr Václav: Czechoslovak Deputy Prime Minister, in the Federal Government, and Minister of the Economy; b. 1941, in Prague. *Career:* he worked at the Economic Institute of the Czechoslovak Academy of Sciences during the 1960s, but was dismissed in 1970. From 1970–88 he was employed at the Czechoslovak State Bank, and then worked briefly for the Academy of Sciences again, at the Prognostic Institute. He was a leading member of Civic Forum and became Minister of Finance, in December 1989. He was reappointed in June 1990, after the elections. The leader of Civic Forum, he became leader of the conservative Civic Democratic Party when the original organization split in 1991. He was made a Deputy Prime Minister and Minister of the Economy in mid-1991. *Address:* Nábř. kpt. Jaroše 1000, 170 32 Prague 7, Czechoslovakia.

KLJUIĆ, Stjepan: Yugoslav politician, member of the State Presidency of Bosnia-Herzegovina; b. in Bosnia-Herzegovina; ethnic Croat. *Career:* the leader of the Croatian Democratic Union in the Republic, he is associated with the Croatian President's party. At the elections of December 1990 it became the third-largest party in the republican Assembly, and the acknowledged representative of the Croats of Bosnia-Herzegovina. He was directly elected to the seven-member State Presidency in the same month. Although in favour of retaining the ethnic balance in the Republic by consensus and the maintenance of its identity, during 1991 he was forced to lead his community into closer alliance with the Muslims, against the Serb community. However, he has also been accused of negotiating the cantonization or the division of the Republic between Serbia and Croatia. *Address:* Yugoslavia, Bosnia-Herzegovina, 71000 Sarajevo, trg Dure Pucara bb.

KLJUSEV, Dr Nikola: Yugoslav academic and economist, Premier of Macedonia; b. in Macedonia. *Career:* a retired economics lecturer, he was politically unaffiliated when nominated to head a Macedonian Government of 'experts', in March 1991. He declared that his Government would concentrate on economic matters and, although in favour of a 'renewed' federation (for economic reasons), most of the political initiative in Macedonia has been led by the President, Kiro Gligorov (q.v.). *Address:* Office of the Macedonian Executive Council, Yugoslavia, Macedonia, 91000 Skopje, Dame Grueva 6.

KOSTIĆ, Dr Branko: Vice-President of the Yugoslav Collective State Presidency and its member for Montenegro; b. 1939, in Rvaši, Montenegro. *Career:* he joined the Communist Party in 1957. He was a Party functionary until he was elected President of the Presidency of Montenegro, in March 1989, following the resignation of the previous leadership. He failed to secure the Party's nomination for direct elections to the Presidency, in 1990, but, in March 1991, became the Republic's member on the federal State Presidency. He was considered strongly pro-Serb and, although he was in line to become Vice-President of the State Presidency, in May, he participated in blocking the election of Stjepan Mesić (Croatia) as President. At the end of June, after the outbreak of civil war, it was eventually agreed to elect Mesić and Kostić to the posts of President and Vice-President, respectively, of the collective body. Nevertheless, its normal functioning continued to be interrupted by the boycott of some of the members. From October, however, the 'Serbian bloc' of members, chaired by Vice-President Branko Kostić, functioned as a 'rump' Presidency. *Address:* Office of the Federal Presidency, Yugoslavia, 11070 Belgrade.

KOSTIĆ, Jugoslav: Yugoslav Collective State Presidency member for Vojvodina (Republic of Serbia), President of the State Presidency of Vojvodina; b. 1938, in Vojvodina; ethnic Serb. *Career:* an orthodox Communist and supporter of Slobodan Milošević of Serbia, he was made President of the Presidency of Vojvodina, in April 1989, after two months as an ordinary member. He was re-elected in December 1989 and acquiesced in the Serbian reduction of his Province's autonomy. In February 1991 he was nominated as the member for Vojvodina of the federal State Presidency. He loyally supported the Serbian side in the various constitutional disputes of 1991 and, from October, participated in the 'rump' federal Presidency. *Address:* State Presidency of Vojvodina, Yugoslavia, Serbia, Novi Sad.

KOZYREV, Andrey Vladimirovich: Russian Minister of Foreign Affairs; b. 1951, in Brussels, Belgium; ethnic Russian; m., with one d. *Education:* graduate of the Moscow State Institute of International Relations (1974); speaks English, French and Portuguese. *Career:* before studying for his degree, he worked at the Kommunar factory in Moscow. After graduating, he worked in the USSR Ministry of External Affairs and, in 1991, he was appointed head of the Dept of International Organizations. A member of the radical 'Young Turks' (*Mladoturki*) group of Russian politicians, in October 1990 Boris Yeltsin (q.v.) appointed him Foreign Minister of the newly assertive Russian Federation. *Address:* Ministry of Foreign Affairs, Russian Federation, Moscow.

KRAJIŠNIK, Momčilo: Yugoslav politician, President of the Assembly of Bosnia-Herzegovina; b. in Bosnia-Herzegovina; ethnic Serb. *Career:* a member of the nationalist Serb Democratic Party, he was elected as a deputy to the republican Assembly in December 1990. Following the coalition agreement between the three main parties, the SDP was allowed to

nominate its candidate for parliamentary speaker, and Krajišnik was duly elected. On 14 October 1991 he attempted to prevent the Muslim and Croat deputies from declaring the Republic's sovereignty by ending the parliamentary session. He was subsequently elected speaker of the unilaterally proclaimed 'Assembly of the Serb Nation', which declared its adherence to the Yugoslav federation. *Address:* Yugoslavia, Bosnia-Herzegovina, 71000 Sarajevo, trg Dure Pucara bb.

KRAVCHUK, Leonid Makarovich (Makarovych): President of Ukraine; b. 10 Jan. 1934. *Career:* a CPSU member since 1958, he was the Second Secretary of the Communist Party of the Ukraine when elected Chairman of the Ukrainian Supreme Soviet, in July 1990. Although a Communist, he won support from his Ukrainian nationalism and, against a divided opposition, he was elected President of Ukraine, with 63% of the votes cast, on 1 December 1991. On the same day overwhelming support for Ukrainian independence was expressed in a republican referendum. Kravchuk did agree to the formation of the Commonwealth of Independent States (originally with the Russian and Byelorussian leaders), but maintained an independent stance against Russian domination of the new association. *Address:* Office of the President of the Republic, Ukraine, Kiev.

KUČAN, Milan: Yugoslav politician, President of the Presidency of Slovenia; b. 14 January 1941, in Krizevci, Slovenia. *Education:* he graduated in law from Ljubljana University (1963). *Career:* he was president of the official Communist youth organization, the Slovene Socialist Youth League, 1968–69, and a member of its secretariat, 1969–73. He worked as secretary of the Socialist Alliance for Slovenia, 1973–78, and was President of the Slovene National Assembly, 1978–82. In 1986 he was made leader of the League of Communists of Slovenia. As with other Communists who espoused nationalist causes, he retained some popularity and, in the republican presidential elections of April 1990, he was elected President of the five-member State Presidency in a direct, popular ballot, despite the opposition parties winning the parliamentary contest. With the failure of attempts to reform the Yugoslav federation, he became head of state of an independent Slovenia, during 1991. *Address:* Slovenia, 61000 Ljubljana, Erjavčeva st. 17.

KUROŃ, Jacek: Polish politician and historian; b. 3 March 1934, in Lvov, Ukraine (then part of Poland); ethnic Polish; m. Grażyna Kuroń (deceased); one s. *Education:* at Warsaw University. *Career:* a member of the Polish United Workers' Party, 1953 and 1956–64, he was a teacher at the Fine Arts Lycée in Warsaw from 1957. He was arrested and sentenced to three years' imprisonment, in 1964, and was again charged in 1968. A prominent dissident activist, he was a founder-member of the Committee to Safeguard Workers' Rights. In 1980 he became a member of, and adviser to, Solidarity. He was imprisoned once again, 1981–84. In 1988–1990 he was Chairman of Solidarity and, 1989–91, Minister of Labour. *Address:* Warsaw, Poland.

KUZNETSOV, German Serapionovich: Vice-President of Kyrgyzstan; b. 1948. *Career:* a Communist Party official, he rose to become Second Secretary of the Frunze (now Bishkek) City Committee. A reformist, he was an ally and deputy of President Askar Akayev (q.v.) and was himself elected Vice-President of the Republic (by direct popular election in October 1991). He resigned from the CPSU following the Moscow coup attempt of August 1991 and formed his own moderate, democratic party, called National Unity. *Address:* Office of the Vice-President of the Republic, Kyrgyzstan, Bishkek.

LANDSBERGIS, Vytautas: Chairman of the Supreme Council of Lithuania; b. 1932, in Kaunas. *Education:* he was trained as a musicologist at the Vilnius Conservatoire. *Career:* he was a founding member and first leader of Sąjūdis, the nationalist opposition movement. He secured its position against the still-popular Communist leadership, as the best vehicle for achieving independence from the USSR. Following the movement's overwhelming victory in the elections of February 1990, the new Supreme Soviet (renamed the Supreme Council) elected him its Chairman, the *de facto* republican president, on 11 March 1990. The same day the Supreme Council reclaimed Lithuania's independence, which was only recognized by Iceland, until August 1991. On 4 September 1991 the USSR State Council recognized Lithuanian independence and the country (with the other Baltic states) became members of the UN on 17 September. *Address:* Gedimino pr. 53, 232026 Vilnius, Lithuania.

LYUBACHIVSKY, Cardinal Myroslav Ivan: Ukrainian religious leader. *Career:* a Uniate or Greek Catholic, he fled Ukraine in 1939, living in exile in Rome and the USA, of which he became a citizen. Pope John Paul II made him a Cardinal and the head of the Ukrainian Uniates (the most numerous of the Roman Catholics of the former USSR). In March 1991, as the Cardinal Archbishop of Lvov, in Western Ukraine, he returned to his homeland and, in June, announced that he would take up permanent residence in Lvov. Soon after this, the authorities granted legal recognition to the Uniates. *Address:* St George's Cathedral, Ukraine, Lvov.

MANOLESCU, Nicolae: Romanian politician and author; b. 27 Nov. 1939, in Rîmnicu Vîlcea. *Education:* graduated in philosophy from Bucharest University. *Career:* he worked as a journalist, historian, academic. He became a politician and leader of the Civic Alliance. In 1991 he was elected President of the electoral coalition, the Democratic Convention, which opposed the ruling National Salvation Front. *Address:* Civic Alliance, Romania, Bucharest.

MARKOVIĆ, Ante: Yugoslav politician, former President of the Yugoslav Federal Executive Council; b. in 1924, in Konjić, Croatia; ethnic Croat. *Education:* he graduated from Zagreb University after the Second World War. *Career:* in 1941 he joined Tito's Partisans. He worked in the Rade Končar engineering factory, Zagreb, after leaving university, and was director-general of the factory, 1961–86. A Communist, he was Premier of Croatia, 1982–86, and was made President of the republican Presidency in May 1986. In March 1989 he was made President of the Federal Executive Council (Yugoslav Prime Minister). He advocated the introduction of liberal economic policies and was a strong supporter of the multi-party system. He established the Alliance of Yugoslav Reform Forces, which gained federal and republican representation. He was a supporter of the federation, but was considered reluctant to countenance Serbian domination. Despite his international support, and with civil war rendering his attempted economic reforms useless, he had virtually been ousted from power by November 1991. Moreover, Croatia had ordered the recall of all its citizens from federal institutions and he resigned his post. In January 1992 he was invited to the mixed-race Republic of Bosnia-Herzegovina, but was reported to be remaining in Zagreb (there were reports that he was under house arrest). *Address:* c/o Alliance of Reform Forces, 11070 Belgrade.

MAXIM, His Holiness Patriarch: Head of the Bulgarian Orthodox Church, Chairman of the Bulgarian Patriarchy; b. 29 April 1914, in Oreshak village, Lovech region. *Education:* graduate of Sofia Academy of Theology. *Career:* originally Marin Naydenov Minkov, he graduated in 1935 and served the Church in Ruse and Lovech. He became a monk in 1941, when he took the name of Maxim; in 1947 he was appointed Archimandrite and Coadjutor in the Ruse diocese; in 1950–55 he represented the Bulgarian Church in Moscow; in 1955 he became Secretary-General of the Holy Synod and was ordained bishop in 1956; he became Bishop of Lovech in 1960; in 1971 he was elected Bishop of Sofia and Patriarch of Bulgaria. *Address:* Bulgaria, 1090 Sofia, Oborishte str. 4.

MAZOWIECKI, Tadeusz: Polish politician and lawyer; b. 18 April 1927, in Płock. *Education:* he graduated in law. *Career:* Chairman of the Academy Publishing Co-operative, in Warsaw (1947–48), he wrote for *PAX* until his suspension in 1955. He was co-founder and editor-in-chief of the Roman Catholic monthly, *Więź* (1968–). As a deputy in the Sejm (1961–72) he fought for democratization. An adviser to Solidarity, from 1980, he was also editor of the Solidarity weekly *Tygodnik Solidarność*. He was interned from 1981–82. From 1989–90 he

was Prime Minister, and became leader of the Democratic Union. He is known as an intellectual and a member of the liberal centre of the political spectrum. *Address:* Al. Jerozolimskie 30, 00-024 Warsaw, Poland.

MEČIAR, Vladimir: Czechoslovak politician; b. 1942, in Zvolen, Slovakia. *Education:* graduated in law from Comenius University, Bratislava (1973). *Career:* from 1959 he spent several years working in the Communist youth movement. In 1969 he was accused of supporting the reformists. He was expelled from the Communist Party of Czechoslovakia in 1970. While studying law he worked as a welder in Dubnica. He then worked as an enterprise lawyer, until November 1989, when he became Minister of the Interior and the Environment in the new Government of Slovakia. He became Premier after the elections of June 1990, but split from the ruling Public Against Violence movement (Slovakia's counterpart of Civic Forum) to found the Movement for a Democratic Slovakia (MDS), in March 1991. On 23 April 1991, therefore, he was dismissed by the Slovak National Council (republican assembly). *Address:* Movement for a Democratic Slovakia, Bratislava, Czechoslovakia.

MESIĆ, Stjepan (Stipe): Yugoslav (Croatian) politician, former President of the Yugoslav Collective State Presidency and its member for Croatia; b. in Croatia; ethnic Croat. *Career:* a member of the Croatian Democratic Union, which won the republican elections in Croatia, he was then made Premier (Prime Minister) of the Republic, in May 1990. In August he was elected as the Croatian member of the federal State Presidency and, consequently, its Vice-President. An anti-Communist and Croat nationalist, he was also one of the Presidency members who refused to vote for the Serbian request for a state of emergency, in March 1991. The Serbian-dominated establishment, therefore, refused to countenance what should have been the automatic election of the Croatian member as President of the federal Presidency, in May. Following the declarations of 'dissociation' by Croatia and Slovenia, and an EC-negotiated cease-fire at the start of the civil war, he was elected Yugoslav President, at the end of June 1991 (the first non-Communist President). However, the Presidency was increasingly revealed as too divided to function effectively, and the armed forces were reluctant to obey the orders of a Croat who supported his Republic's attempted secession. In October the 'Serbian bloc' of Presidency members began to meet without Mesić or the members for Bosnia-Herzegovina, Macedonia or Slovenia. Mesić's position was rendered more ambiguous by Croatia's recall of its citizens from federal institutions. On 5 December he formally resigned his federal post and was considered likely to pursue a political career in Croatia, where he was one of the most popular politicians. *Address:* c/o Government of Croatia, Croatia, 41000 Zagreb, Opatička 2.

MIKLOŠKO, Jozef: Czechoslovak Deputy Prime Minister, in the Federal Government. *Career:* an ethnic Slovak, he is a leading member of the Christian Democratic Movement and its only representative in the Government formed in 1990. In the Government he is responsible for human rights. *Address:* Office of the Federal Government, Nábř. kpt. Jaroše 4, 125 09 Prague 1, Czechoslovakia.

MILOŠEVIĆ, Slobodan: Yugoslav politician, President of Serbia; b. 20 August 1941, in Požarevac, Serbia. *Education:* he graduated in law, from Belgrade University (1964). *Career:* a conservative Communist, he worked in local government until 1969, when he became deputy director and then, in 1973, director-general of Tehnogas Enterprises. He was leader of the Belgrade Communists, until 1986, when he was made leader of the League of Communists of Serbia. He initiated an 'anti-bureaucratic revolution' and espoused nationalist rhetoric, which maintained the popularity of the ruling party (subsequently renamed the Socialist Party of Serbia). He helped engineer constitutional changes which gradually brought Kosovo (now Kosovo-Metohija) and Vojvodina under Serbian control, in 1988–90. In May 1989 he was made President of the republican State Presidency and was re-elected, in a direct ballot, in December 1989, and to the new post of sole, executive

President, in December 1990 (again by direct ballot). He was accused of orchestrating demonstrations in other Republics, in the late 1980s, which secured sympathetic Communist leaderships, and, in 1991, of being in league with the federal armed forces and the insurgent Serbs of Croatia and Bosnia-Herzegovina. His administration was criticized during opposition demonstrations in 1991 and, although his nationalism was popular, the war in Croatia was not strongly supported by the Serbian population. At the end of 1991, under pressure from EC economic sanctions against his Republic, he agreed to a UN-mediated peace plan. *Address:* Yugoslavia, 11000 Belgrade, Andricev venac 1.

MIRSAIDOV, Shukurulla Rakhmatovich: Vice-President of Uzbekistan; b. 1938. *Career:* a Communist official, he worked as an economic planner in Uzbekistan, for 25 years. In the 1980s he was Chairman of the Soviet (mayor) of Tashkent for five years, and was made a deputy premier of the republican Government in 1989. He became Chairman of the Council of Ministers in March 1990 and, in November, Vice-President of the Republic. The latter office was abolished in January 1992, and he refused a further post. *Address:* Office of the Vice-President of the Republic, Uzbekistan, Tashkent.

MIRZOYEV, Akbar: Chairman of the Cabinet of Ministers (Prime Minister) of Tadzhikistan. *Career:* formerly head of the Kulyab Oblast administration, he was appointed to the premiership, in January 1992, upon the re-creation of the post. *Address:* Cabinet of Ministers, Tadzhikistan, Dushanbe.

MOŠANU, Alexandru: Chairman of the Parliament of Moldavia; b. 1932. *Career:* an eminent historian, he was elected to the Supreme Soviet (renamed Parliament in May 1991) of Moldavia as a Communist. In the 1990 elections he was, however, backed by the nationalist Popular Front, which was forbidden from taking part itself. In September he succeeded Mircea Snegur (q.v.) as Chairman of the Supreme Soviet, which was now solely to perform the functions of a parliamentary speaker, Snegur having assumed the new post of executive President. *Address:* Parliament, Moldavia, Kishinev.

MURADOV, Sakhat Nepesovich: Chairman of the Supreme Soviet of Turkmenistan. *Career:* a conservative Communist, he was head of the department responsible for science and education in the Central Committee of the Turkmen Communist Party, 1968–71. He was a minister for education from 1979 and a full member of the Central Committee from 1981. As deputy to Saparmuryad Niyazov (q.v.), he replaced him as Chairman of the Supreme Soviet, in November 1990, when the latter was elected to the post of executive President of the Republic. *Address:* Supreme Soviet, Turkmenistan, Ashkhabad.

MURAVSCHI, Valeriu: Prime Minister of Moldavia. *Career:* an economist and member of the Popular Front, he was appointed Minister of Finance in June 1990 and was also a deputy premier from March 1991. He became Prime Minister at the end of May 1991, his predecessor having been ousted after allegations of corruption. *Address:* Council of Ministers, Moldavia, Kishinev.

MUTALIBOV, Ayaz Niyazi ogly: President of Azerbaidzhan; b. 12 May 1938. *Career:* a member of the CPSU since 1963, in January 1990 he was appointed First Secretary of the Azerbaidzhan Communist Party Central Committee, in July 1990 a member of the CPSU Politburo and, in May 1990, Chairman of the Supreme Soviet (President) of Azerbaidzhan. He resigned as First Secretary following the Moscow coup attempt of August 1991, although there were reports that he had initially reacted favourably to the news. In September 1991 there were direct elections to the post of President of the Republic, and Mutalibov was elected unopposed. *Address:* Office of the President, Azerbaidzhan, Baku.

MUTALOV, Abdulkhashim: Prime Minister of Uzbekistan; b. 1947. *Career:* a Communist Party official, he was Minister of Grain and a Deputy Chairman of the Council of Ministers, under the President. On 13 January 1992 the Supreme Soviet

elected him to the new post of premier. *Address:* Council of Ministers, Uzbekistan, Tashkent.

NABIYEV, Rakhmon (Rakhman) Nabiyevich: President of Tadzhikistan; b. 1930. *Education:* graduate of the Tashkent Institute of Irrigation and Mechanized Agriculture (1954). *Career:* trained as an agricultural engineer, he began to rise in the Party and state hierarchy in 1960. He was premier of Tadzhikistan between 1972 and 1982, until he became First Secretary of the republican Communist Party (to 1985). He contested the elections for the republican presidency, in November 1990, but did not achieve that post until after the discrediting of the Tadzhikistan Communist leadership following the coup attempt of August 1991. He acted as President from September until early October, as a compromise candidate, who could retain moderate support for the Communists. He was elected to the office, with 54% of the votes cast, in November. *Address:* Government House, Tadzhikistan, Dushanbe.

NADJER, Zdzisław: Polish politician and author; b. 31 Oct. 1930, in Warsaw; m., with one s. *Education:* studied at Warsaw University and the University of Oxford (United Kingdom). *Career:* an academic, he spent most of his professional life out of Poland. In 1982 he became head of Radio Free Europe's Polish Service; there was martial law in Poland and he was sentenced to death, in his absence, for this employment. The sentence was formally revoked in 1989, when he returned to Poland and supported Solidarity in the 1989 national and the 1990 local elections. In 1991 he was elected Chairman of the electoral wing of Solidarity. *Address:* Office of the Chairman, Poland, 00-902 Warsaw, Al. Ujazdowskie 13.

NAGY, Dr Ferenc Jószef: Hungarian politician and agronomist; b. 1923, in Kisharsány, Baranya. *Education:* trained as an agricultural engineer at the People's College of Pécs. *Career:* he was a farmer until 1990. In April 1990 he was elected Chairman of the revived, agrarian Independent Smallholders' Party. In May he was made Minister of Agriculture, but he left the Government at the beginning of 1991. *Address:* Hungary, 1126 Budapest, Szoboszlai u. 2–4.

NANO, Fatos: Albanian politician; b. 1951. *Career:* an economist and a reformist Communist, he became a member of the Government in January 1991, when the ruling Party was under pressure to satisfy popular demands. In March he was appointed to lead a provisional Council of Ministers, which was confirmed in office by the Communist-dominated Assembly, which was elected in April. However, he was forced to resign in June, but, later that month, became President of the newly renamed Socialist Party of Albania (the former Communists), which remained the largest party. *Address:* Partia Socialiste e Shqipërisë, Albania, Tirana.

NAŠTASE, Adrian: Romanian Foreign Minister; b. 1950, in Bucharest. *Education:* graduated in law from Bucharest University (1973) and then studied for a doctorate in international law (1978). *Career:* he expressed some dissent under President Nicolae Ceaușescu, in December 1989 becoming a member of the National Salvation Front, for whom he was elected to parliament. He is Vice-President of the Romanian Association of International Law and International Relations and holds associate membership of the International Institute for Human Rights (Strasbourg, France). He became Minister of Foreign Affairs after the elections, in May 1990. *Address:* Ministry of Foreign Affairs, Romania, Bucharest, Piața Victoriei 1.

NATADZE, Nodar: Georgian politician; b. 1929. *Career:* a philologist and department head at the Institute of Philosophy of the Georgian Academy of Sciences, he became leader of the Georgian Popular Front in 1989. A political moderate he was an unsuccessful candidate in the presidential elections of 1991, against Zviad Gamsakhurdia (q.v.), whose democratic credentials he expressed anxiety about. He was a leading member of the rebel opposition in the civil war which broke out in December 1991.

NAZARBAYEV, Nursultan Abishevich: President of Kazakhstan; b. 6 July 1940. *Career:* he joined the CPSU in 1962, while working at the Karaganda Metallurgical Combine and, in 1969, began work with the Komsomol in Temirtau. He rose rapidly in the Kazakh Party and state apparatus, in 1984 becoming the Chairman of the Kazakh Council of Ministers. In June 1989 he replaced Gennady Kolbin, the ethnic Russian whose appointment in 1986 had caused riots, as First Secretary of the Kazakh Communist Party and he was elected as a deputy to the All-Union Supreme Soviet. In April 1990 the Kazakh Supreme Soviet elected him to the new post of executive President. In July 1990 he became a member of the CPSU Politburo and an increasingly important politician outside Kazakhstan. Although he promoted Mikhail Gorbachev's (q.v.) concept of a new Treaty of Union he stressed that Kazakhstan's declaration of sovereignty must be implemented. A political moderate, by 1990 he was convinced of the need for the introduction of a market economy, but only in the context of a Union. However, he was prepared to agree to the creation of the Commonwealth of Independent States, despite his objections at not having been invited to be an original signatory of the Minsk Agreement, in December 1991. *Address:* Government House, Kazakhstan, Alma-Ata.

NIYAZOV, Saparmuryad Atayevich: President of Turkmenistan; b. 19 Feb. 1940. *Career:* he joined the Communist Party in 1962, heading the Ashkhabad organization until 1984, when he went to the central CPSU headquarters in Moscow. In 1985 he returned to Turkmenia (now Turkmenistan) as premier and, subsequently, Party leader. He was elected Chairman of the Supreme Soviet (*de facto* head of state), in January 1990, and was returned unopposed as a directly elected President in October. A conservative Communist, he did not condemn or condone the coup attempt of August 1991 and retained the Communists as the ruling party (although the name was changed to the Democrat Party). Only after this were opposition parties permitted to register in Turkmenistan, which remained the least reformed of the former Soviet Republics and had been the one least interested in independence. *Address:* Office of the President, Turkmenistan, Ashkhabad.

OŁSZEWSKI, Jan: Prime Minister of Poland; b. 20 August 1930, in Warsaw. *Education:* graduated in law from Warsaw University (1953). *Career:* he had served in the Home Army during the Warsaw Uprising. As a lawyer, he defended many political activists. From the early 1980s he acted as adviser to Solidarity and took part in its negotiations with the Communist Government. In December 1990 he was asked to form a coalition administration, but failed to do so. As a member of the Centre Alliance, despite the reluctance of President Wałęsa (q.v.) to appoint him, he was asked to be Prime Minister, in December 1991, and succeeded in forming a coalition Government. *Address:* Urząd Rady Ministrów, Poland, 00-583 Warsaw, Al. Ujazdowskie 1/3.

OTA, Abdulla: Uzbekistan politician. *Career:* he is leader of the Islamic Renaissance Party (originally an all-Union party) in Uzbekistan. It held a founding Congress in Tashkent, in January 1991, but was subsequently declared outlawed. It is, however, believed to be one of the most significant opposition groups in the Republic.

PASHKO, Gramoz: Albanian politician. *Career:* the son of a Communist minister, he was Professor of Economics at Tirana University. A leader of the main opposition Democratic Party, he is the author of their economic policy proposals. He was a Deputy Prime Minister in the coalition Bufi Government of 1991 and opposed the Democratic Party's withdrawal from it, in December. He was one of the leaders of the more moderate wing of the party. *Address:* Partia Demokratike të Shqipërisë, Albania, Tirana.

PAZNYAK, Zenyon: Byelorussian politician. *Career:* an anti-Communist dissident, he was a founder member of the Byelorussian Popular Front (BPF), formed in October 1988. He was formally elected its leader at the founding Congress, in Vilnius (Lithuania), in June 1989. The BPF was forbidden to participate in elections to the republican Supreme Soviet, in March 1990, but sponsored candidates in coalition with other groups, known as the Byelorussian Democratic Bloc. Paznyak

was elected in Minsk. *Address:* Byelorussian Popular Front—Rebirth (Byelarusky Narodny Front 'Adradzhenye'), Byelorussia, 220040 Minsk, POB 208.

PELIVAN, Jure: Yugoslav politician, Premier of Bosnia-Herzegovina; b. in Bosnia-Herzegovina; ethnic Croat. *Career:* he was a member of the Croatian Democratic Union, which was the third-largest party in the republican Assembly after the elections of 1990. Later in December the three main nationalist parties agreed upon a coalition arrangement and the CDU nominated Pelivan as the republican head of government. *Address:* Office of the Executive Council of Bosnia-Herzegovina, Yugoslavia, Bosnia-Herzegovina, 71000 Sarajevo, vojvode Putnika 3.

PETERLE, Lozje: Yugoslav politician, Premier (Prime Minister) of Slovenia; b. 1948, in Slovenia. *Education:* he graduated as an economist. *Career:* he was leader of the Slovenian Christian Democrats, which emerged as the largest party in the victorious DEMOS coalition after the republican general elections of April 1990. As such he became Premier or Prime Minister of the Government. He co-ordinated the policy of gradual secession, or 'dissociation', of Slovenia from the Yugoslav federation. His party is conservative and Roman Catholic. *Address:* Office of the Executive Council, Slovenia, 61000 Ljubljana, Prešemova st. 8.

PETKOV, Prof. Dr Krustyo: Bulgarian trade union leader; b. 18 November 1943, in Dimovo, Vidin region; m., with two c. *Education:* educated as an economist, he has a doctorate. *Career:* an academic, who was a professor of labour sociology, he was involved in the official trade union movement of Communist Bulgaria. He led the Communist-dominated Bulgarian Professional Union in its renunciation of any political affiliations and, in February 1990, its transformation into the Confederation of Independent Trade Unions in Bulgaria, of which he became Chairman. It remained the largest trade union body in the country. *Address:* Bulgaria, Sofia 1, pl. Makedonia.

PIRNAT, Dr Rajko: Yugoslav politician, Slovenian Minister of Justice and Administration; b. 1951, in Slovenia. *Career:* a lawyer by profession, he was a deputy leader of the first Slovenian opposition party, the Slovenian Democratic Union (SDU). When it and its DEMOS coalition partners achieved office, after the 1990 elections, he was made Minister of Justice and Administration. The SDU, as the first opposition to the Communists, contained many different opinions and its eventual split was probably inevitable. Pirnat, a popular politician, was leader of the more right-wing, populist faction, which formed a majority, and, in October 1991, he split with the SDU leader, Dimitrij Rupel, and became leader of the Slovenian Democratic Union-National Democratic Party (still within DEMOS). *Address:* Ministry of Justice and Administration, Slovenia, 61000 Ljubljana, Županičeva st. 3.

PITHART, Petr: Czechoslovak politician, Premier of the Czech Republic; b. 2 January 1941, in Kladno. *Education:* at Charles University, Prague. *Career:* in the 1960s he lectured in law at Charles University, before becoming editor of *Literarni Noviny*. From 1970 he could take only menial jobs, because of the repression after the events of 1968. He was a signatory of Charter 77. In November 1989 he became spokesman for Civic Forum's co-ordination centre and, on February 1990, he was made Premier of the Czech Lands. He was re-elected, following the June 1990 elections. *Address:* Office of the Premier, Lazarska 7, 113 48 Prague, Czechoslovakia.

PLYUSHCH, Ivan: Chairman of the Supreme Soviet of Ukraine. *Career:* previously the First Deputy Chairman of the Supreme Soviet, he was elected Chairman on 5 December 1991. This post, which was previously the *de facto* republican head of state, had been vacated by Leonid Kravchuk (q.v.), who had been elected executive President of the now-independent Republic. Plyushch succeeded to the functions of a parliamentary speaker. *Address:* Supreme Soviet, Ukraine, Kiev.

POPOV, Gavriil Kharitonovich: Russian politician and economist; b. 1936, in Moscow; ethnic Greek. *Education:* he studied economics at Moscow State University. *Career:* he joined the CPSU in 1959 and was an economist and academic. In 1988 he also served as editor-in-chief of *Voprosy Ekonomiki*. He acted as Chairman of the Soviet Greek Society. In 1989 he was elected to the Congress of People's Deputies and to the Moscow City Soviet (Council), of which he became Chairman (that is, mayor of Moscow). A radical reformer and a prominent member of the democratic movement, he resigned from the CPSU in July 1990 and was a strong supporter of Boris Yeltsin (q.v.). In December 1991 he threatened to resign, in protest at obstacles to his reforms, but he was persuaded to remain in office. *Address:* Moscow City Council, Russian Federation, Moscow.

PUČNIK, Dr Jože: Yugoslav (Slovenian) politician; b. in Slovenia. *Career:* he spent some 20 years in exile in the Federal Republic of Germany, because of his political views. With the disintegration of the Communist system, opposition parties began to be formed in Slovenia, in 1989. In February the Social Democratic Party of Slovenia (SDPS), of which he was elected leader, was formed by protesting workers. Later in the year the SDPS and five other opposition parties formed a coalition, the Democratic Opposition of Slovenia (DEMOS). Pučnik was elected leader of DEMOS, but he failed to win the presidential elections of April 1990 and did not then hold any state or government office. This partly accounts for the weak presence of the SDPS in the ruling coalition, but he became important in easing the increasingly strained relations between the coalition partners. However in December 1991, DEMOS agreed to dissolve itself. *Address:* Slovenia, Šubičeva st. 4.

PULATOV, Abdul Rahmid: Ukbekistan politician. *Career:* an academic and a nationalist, he is leader of the main opposition group in Uzbekistan, the Popular Front, Birlik (Unity). His organization is registered as a movement and not as a political party, to limit its ability to participate in elections. *Address:* c/o Union of Writers, Uzbekistan, 700000 Tashkent, ul. Pushkina 1.

ROMAN, Petre: Romanian politician; b. 22 July 1946, in Bucharest; m., with two c. *Education:* at Bucharest Polytechnic, and then in Toulouse (France), where he completed his doctorate in 1974. *Career:* the son of prominent members of the Communist nomenklatura, he became a professor and head of the Department of Hydraulics at Bucharest Polytechnic. He became involved in the 1989 Revolution, despite his membership of the Romanian Communist Party. He was nominated as Prime Minister by the National Salvation Front (NSF), on 26 December 1989. He resigned on 26 September 1991, following protests from striking coal-miners, but remained the leader of the ruling NSF, which supported the Government of Prime Minister Theodor Stolojan (q.v.). *Address:* Romania, Bucharest.

RUGOVA, Dr Ibrahim: Yugoslav (Serbian/Kosovar) politician and writer; b. in Kosovo (now Kosovo-Metohija), Republic of Serbia; ethnic Albanian. *Career:* a prominent dissident writer, who has consistently championed the rights of the Kosovar (Albanian) population. In 1990 he founded and became leader of the Democratic Alliance of Kosovo, which became the mass party of the ethnic Albanians by its effective take-over of the provincial Socialist Alliance of Working People. He is the most prominent politician in the ethnic Albanian community and led the boycott of the 1990 constitutional referendum and elections. He supports the creation of Kosovo-Metohija as the ethnic Albanian 'home' Republic, in the Yugoslav federation, although union with Albania has considerable support in the province and, at the end of September 1991, Rugova was one of the Kosovar leaders to attend the opening of the Albanian parliament in Tirana. *Address:* KDA, Yugoslavia, Kosovo-Metohija, Priština.

RUPEL, Dr Dimitrij: Yugoslav politician, Slovenian Minister of Foreign Affairs; b. 1946, in Slovenia. *Career:* a doctor of sociology, he became the leader of the Slovenian Democratic Union, which was founded in 1989 as the first opposition party to the Communists since the Second World War. Following the victory of the DEMOS opposition coalition, in the elections of 1990, he was made Minister of Foreign Affairs, although he frequently clashed with Prime Minister Peterle. In October

1991 the disparate elements of the original party split into two factions. The minority, centrist faction remained loyal to Rupel, who was subsequently elected leader of the a new party, the Democratic Party of Slovenia (still within DEMOS). *Address:* Ministry of Foreign Affairs, Slovenia, 61000 Ljubljana, Gregorčičeva st. 25.

RUTSKOY, Col Aleksandr Vladimirovich: Vice-President of the Russian Federation; b. 1947. *Career:* a soldier by profession, he was a fighter-bomber commander and fought in the Afghan war. A moderate Communist, Boris Yeltsin (q.v.) persuaded him to stand for election as the Vice-President of the Russian Federation, in the June 1991 presidential elections. This was to ensure some Communist support in the Supreme Soviet. He opposed the coup attempt of August 1991 and, in October, the party of which he was leader, Communists for Democracy, changed its name to the People's Party of Free Russia. As part of Yeltsin's reorganization of the Russian Government, in November 1991, Rutskoy was appointed head of a Centre for the Operational Supervision of the Progress of Reforms. Particularly after December, however, he came into increasing conflict with President Yeltsin, over political and economic policies. *Address:* Office of the Vice-President, Russian Federation, Moscow, White House.

RÜÜTEL, Arnold Fyodorovich: Chairman of the Supreme Council of Estonia; b. 1928, in Estonia. *Education:* he was trained as an agronomist at the Estonian Agricultural Academy. *Career:* he became a member of the Communist Party in 1964, while working as an agronomist. In 1979 he became First Deputy Chairman of the Estonian Council of Ministers, before becoming Chairman of the Presidium of the Supreme Soviet (republican head of state), in 1983. In 1988–89 he expressed his sympathies with the Estonian nationalists and was not only re-elected to parliament, in March 1990, but also to his former post, now redesignated the Chairman of the Supreme Soviet (subsequently renamed the Supreme Council). By October 1991, however, his attempts to encourage the creation of an executive presidency were meeting increasing resistance. In that month the Constituent Assembly (formed in August, when Estonia fully reclaimed its independence) decided to render the post of head of state purely ceremonial. *Address:* Supreme Council, Lossi plats 1a, 200100 Tallinn, Estonia.

RYCHETSKÝ, Pavel: Czechoslovak Deputy Prime Minister, in the Federal Government. *Career:* as someone without declared political affiliations, he was made Deputy Prime Minister, in June 1990. Since then, however, he has become Deputy Chairman of the Civic Movement, one of the successors of Civic Forum, the original anti-Communist movement. In the Federal Government, he is responsible for legislative affairs. *Address:* Office of the Federal Government, Nábř. kpt. Jaroše 4, 125 09 Prague 1, Czechoslovakia.

ŠABATA, Jaroslav: Czechoslovak politician, Minister of International Relations and Contacts with the Federal and Slovak Governments for the Czech Republic; b. 2 November 1927, in Dolenice. *Education:* studied philosophy and psychology at Brno University. *Career:* he worked as Professor of Psychology at Brno University, 1964–68 and as a lecturer in social sciences, in 1969. From 1968 he was a member of the regional and central committees of the Communist Party of Czechoslovakia, but was expelled from the Party, in October 1969, for his pro-reformist views. He was imprisoned for subversion, in 1971, and again in 1978–80, on the latter occasion following an interview with a western newspaper. He was a signatory of Charter 77, and its spokesman in 1978, and 1981–82. He has published writings in *samizdat* and foreign journals. *Address:* Ministry of International Relations and Contacts with the Federal and Slovak Governments, Prague, Czechoslovakia.

SAVISAAR, Edgar: Estonian politician; b. 1949, in Estonia. *Career:* an economist by training, he was a Communist (until January 1990), but also became a leader of the Estonian Popular Front, which was founded in April 1988. From July 1989 he was a deputy premier in the Estonian Government and, upon the 1990 electoral victory of the Front, he was appointed to lead the Council of Ministers. He enjoyed good relations with the rival Congress of Estonia, which rejected the validity of the existing institutions, but were prepared to accept the Government's interim authority. He supported the creation of the Constituent Assembly, in August 1991. In January 1992, despite the hitherto relatively strong performance of the Estonian economy, he was obliged to ask for emergency powers because of the increasing shortage of supplies. However, at the end of the month, he resigned as Prime Minister. *Address:* Uus 28, 2001001 Tallinn, Estonia.

SELIMOVSKI, Hadži Jakub Effendi: Reis-ul-ulema of the Islamic Community of Yugoslavia; b. 1946, in Kičevo, Macedonia; ethnic Muslim. *Education:* educated in Sarajevo and Cairo, he speaks Macedonian, Serbo-Croat, Albanian, Turkish and Arabic. *Career:* a reformist, he provisionally replaced his predecessor as head (Reis-ul-ulema) of the Islamic Religious Community of Yugoslavia, after the latter was forced out of office by those opposed to the Communist regime. In March 1991 he was formally elected to the post, for an eight-year term. There were four candidates and Selimovski won 67 of the 96 votes in a secret ballot. Since the office of Reis-ul-ulema was first created, in 1882, he was the first to be democratically elected and the first holder of it not to be from Bosnia-Herzegovina. He has denied accusations of attempting to create a Muslim republic, and argues for the retention of a federation and the preservation of the IRC. *Address:* Rijaset Islamske Zajednice, Yugoslavia, Bosnia-Herzegovina, 71000 Sarajevo, Save Kovačevića 2.

ŠEPAROVIĆ, Dr Zvonimir: Yugoslav politician, Croatian Minister of Foreign Relations; b. 14 Sept. 1928, in Blato, Korčula, Croatia. *Education:* graduated and gained a doctorate in law, from the University of Zagreb. *Career:* he was a journalist before practising law, becoming a judge in 1966, and then a professor of law from 1975 (part-time since 1961). He became President of the University of Zagreb, 1989–91, and the Croatian Minister of Foreign Affairs in the administrations appointed by President Franjo Tudjman. He is politically unaffiliated. *Address:* Croatia, 41000 Zagreb, Visoka 22.

ŠEŠOK, Dušan: Slovenian Minister of Finance; b. 1953, in Slovenia. *Career:* he is a graduate economist, without party affiliation. He became Minister of Finance in April 1990 and organized the monetary independence of Slovenia, particularly during 1991. In October the new Slovenian currency, the tolar, was successfully introduced. *Address:* Ministry of Finance, Slovenia, 61000 Ljubljana, Župančičeva st. 3.

SHAPOSHNIKOV, Air Marshal Yevgeny I.: Acting Commander-in-Chief of the Armed Forces of the Commonwealth of Independent States; b. 1942; m., with two d. and one s.; ethnic Russian. *Career:* he worked his way up the ranks of the Soviet Red Army, becoming head of the Soviet Air Force in Germany, 1987–88, and then First Deputy Commander of the All-Union Soviet Air Force. He became Commander in July 1990 and, after the Moscow coup attempt of August 1991, which he opposed from the start, he was appointed the USSR Minister of Defence and head of the Soviet armed forces. He was considered a pragmatist, who believed in the concept of 'defence sufficiency', and was a long-standing critic of senior officers and the lack of discipline, control and initiative in the armed forces. He was forceful in advocating a unified command structure for the new Commonwealth of Independent States (CIS), formed in December 1991, and was backed by the Russian President, Boris Yeltsin (q.v.). He was made interim Commander-in-Chief of the CIS armed forces at the end of December.

SHERIMKULOV, Medetkan: Chairman of the Supreme Soviet of Kyrgyzstan. *Career:* he was elected to be the republican parliamentary speaker, in December 1990, following the resignation of Absamat Masaliyev, who had failed to be elected to the new post of executive President. He was then also replaced as speaker, by Sherimkulov, a reformist ally of the new President, Askar Akayev (q.v.). Sherimkulov resigned from the CPSU following the Moscow coup attempt of August 1991. *Address:* Supreme Soviet, Kyrgyzstan, Bishkek.

SHEVARDNADZE, Eduard: Georgian/Soviet politician and former USSR Foreign Minister; b. 1928, in Georgia; ethnic Georgian. *Career:* he was a Komsomol official, becoming its leader in 1957. In 1961 he joined the hierarchy of the Communist Party. He soon became a minister of the republican government and, in 1971, Georgian Party leader. He campaigned against corruption, but also gained a reputation for being harsh with dissidents and nationalists. In 1978 he became a candidate member of the CPSU Politburo and, in July 1985, a full member (the first Georgian to be so since the death of Stalin). At the same time, as a close colleague of Mikhail Gorbachev (q.v.), he was appointed Soviet Foreign Minister. His and Gorbachev's 'new thinking' in foreign policy caused dramatic changes in international politics, but, in December 1990, he resigned, warning of the approach of 'dictatorship'. In 1991 he was a founder and leader of an all-Union democratic opposition party and was briefly Soviet Foreign Minister again at the end of the year. His political future was uncertain with the demise of the USSR in December, but, in January 1992, there were reports that he might return to Georgia. *Address:* Russian Federation, Moscow.

SHOKHIN, Aleksandr: a Deputy Chairman of the Russian Council of Ministers, responsible for social policy, and Minister of Labour. *Career:* he was appointed a Deputy Chairman of the Russian Government, under Boris Yeltsin (q.v.), in November 1991, and made responsible for the co-ordination of five ministries involved in social welfare. *Address:* Ministry of Labour, Russian Federation, Moscow.

SHUSHKEVICH, Stanislau Stanislavavich: Chairman of the Supreme Soviet (President) of Byelorussia; b. 1934. *Career:* he was the son of a poet, who died in Stalin's camps, but managed to achieve a university education, where he trained as a physicist. He only became involved in politics after 1986, when he established a reputation as a critic of the misconduct and negligence of the authorities in the aftermath of the Chernobyl nuclear accident. He was elected to the republican Supreme Soviet with the backing of the opposition Byelorussian Popular Front, in March 1990. After his election as the First Deputy Chairman of the Supreme Soviet, he was revealed as a more cautious reformist than initially thought. Thus, in December 1990, he did not carry out his threat to resign from the Communist Party if it did not introduce democratic reforms, which it did not do. He resigned from the Party only after the failure of the Moscow coup attempt, in August 1991. However, he gained credit as a nationalist and a supporter of attempts to revive the Byelorussian language. On 18 September, after several rounds of voting, he was elected to be the Byelorussian leader. He was one of the original signatories of the Commonwealth of Independent States, which was to be based in Minsk. *Address:* Office of the Presidium of the Supreme Soviet, Byelorussia, 220010 Minsk, Dom Urada.

SIGUA, Tengiz Ippolitovich: Georgian politician; b. 9 Nov. 1939. *Career:* an engineer and director of the Metallurgy Institute of the Georgian Academy of Sciences, he was a leading member of the Round Table-Free Georgia alliance, which won the 1990 elections. His nationalist sympathies were attested by his chairmanship of the All-Georgia Rusteveli Society. He was appointed head of government by Zviad Gamsakhurdia (q.v.), Chairman of the Supreme Soviet (later President) of Georgia, in November 1990. He resigned from the Government in August 1991, joining the opposition, which was soon involved in armed rebellion. By December there was civil war and Sigua was prominent in the coalition of opposition forces. At the beginning of January 1992 the opposition declared the President deposed, his office abolished and the parliament dissolved. Power was assumed by a Military Council, which appointed Sigua Prime Minister and ordered new elections to be arranged. *Address:* Government of Georgia, Georgia, Tbilisi.

SILAYEV, Ivan Stepanovich: Russian politician; b. 21 October 1930. *Education:* Kazan Aviation Institute. *Career:* he began work in the Gorky Aviation Works, as an engineer, rising to be plant director. In 1974 he was appointed USSR Deputy Minister of the Aviation Industry. Between 1980 and

1985 he was a full Minister of the Aviation Industry and was then promoted to Vice-Chairman of the Council of Ministers. He was elected Chairman of the Russian Council of Ministers, in June 1990, but only acquiring the support of Boris Yeltsin (q.v.) after he had defeated Yeltsin's favoured candidate in a first round of voting. Although more cautious in his approach to reform than Yeltsin, he supported Yeltsin in his attempt to provide the Russian Federation with real power. In September 1991 he resigned the premiership, in favour of his duties on an all-Union economic co-ordination committee. In January 1992 he was appointed Russian Permanent Representative to the EC. *Address:* Supreme Soviet, Russian Federation, Moscow.

SKUBISZEWSKI, Prof. Krzysztof: Polish Minister of Foreign Affairs; b. 8 October 1926, in Poznań. *Education:* he studied at Poznań University, at the University of Nancy (France) and at Harvard University (USA). *Career:* a lawyer by training, he was a staff member at Poznań University, 1948–73, and was then at the Polish Academy of Sciences, Warsaw. He taught at many universities in the West, as a visiting lecturer. He was appointed Minister of Foreign Affairs in 1989 and was considered popular, because of his efforts to maintain Polish independence and to promote good relations with Germany and the USSR and its successor states. His appointment was again confirmed for the new Government formed in December 1991. *Address:* Ministry of Foreign Affairs, Al. I. Armii Wojska Polskiego 23, 00-580 Warsaw, Poland.

SNEGUR, Mircea Ion: President of Moldavia; b. 1939. *Career:* an agronomist by profession, he became a Communist official in the 1980s, but was also a nationalist, strongly supported by the Popular Front. He was elected the republican leader, Chairman of the Presidium of the Supreme Soviet, in July 1989, and re-elected, as Chairman of the Supreme Soviet, in April 1990. In September he was elected unopposed to the new post of executive President. He advocated the sovereignty and economic independence of Moldavia, but repudiated any unification with Romania, particularly in attempting to allay the fears of the secessionist ethnic Russians and Gagauz. *Address:* Office of the President, Moldavia, Kishinev.

SOBCHAK, Anatoly Aleksandrovich: Russian politician; b. 1937, in Leningrad (now St Petersburg). *Education:* graduated as a lawyer from Leningrad University. *Career:* a former law professor, in 1989 he was elected as a radical People's Deputies to the Soviet parliament. His intellect and political style gained him one of the most formidable reputations among the reformists in the Supreme Soviet of the USSR. He was a founder member of the Inter-Regional Group of Soviet deputies and a prominent member of the democratic movement. In May 1990 he was elected head of the Leningrad City Soviet or Council (that is, mayor); in 1991 a referendum in the city endorsed a proposal, which he supported, to change the name from Leningrad back to St Petersburg. During the coup attempt of August 1991 he was prominent in rallying his city against the putschists. *Address:* St Petersburg City Council, Russian Federation, St Petersburg.

SPIROIU, Lt-Gen. Constantin Nicolae: Romanian Minister of National Defence. *Career:* a career officer, he joined the National Salvation Front at the time of the 1989 Revolution, and was appointed to the Government in June 1990. *Address:* Ministry of National Defence, Romania, Bucharest, Intrarea Drumul Taberei 9.

STANKEVICH, Sergey: Russian politician and historian; b. 1954, in Moscow district. *Education:* he was educated at the Lenin Pedagogical Institute, Moscow. *Career:* before entering politics he was a senior researcher at the Institute of World History, in Moscow, where he studied foreign political systems and parliaments. In 1989 he was elected to the Congress of People's Deputies and to the Supreme Soviet, where he was to become co-chairman of the radical Inter-Regional Group of deputies. He made himself known in the Supreme Soviet for his reformist views and for his criticism of President Mikhail Gorbachev's (q.v.) increasing powers. In March 1990 he was elected to the Moscow City Soviet (Council) and was quickly elevated to the office of deputy mayor. He left the CPSU at the Congress of July 1990, together with Boris Yeltsin (q.v.). He became a leading member of the Democratic Russia coalition and an adviser to Boris Yeltsin. *Address:* Moscow City Council, Russian Federation, Moscow, ul. Tverskaya.

STARAVOYTOVA, Galina: Russian politician and ethnographer. *Career:* a respected academic ethnographer, she used her background to join the 1988 campaign for the return of Nagorny Karabakh to Armenia. She was elected to the Supreme Soviet of the USSR, from an Armenian constituency, and made an impact with her outspoken criticism of the Government and of President Mikhail Gorbachev (q.v.). She became a co-chairman of the Inter-Regional Group of radical deputies. In 1990 she was elected to the Russian Federation Supreme Soviet, from a Leningrad (now St Petersburg) constituency and acted as an adviser to President Boris Yeltsin (q.v.) on ethnic affairs. *Address:* Supreme Soviet of the Russian Federation, Russian Federation, Moscow.

STEPONAVIČIUS, Archbishop Julijonas: Lithuanian religious leader. *Career:* leader of the largest single group of Roman Catholic (Latin Rite) adherents in the former USSR, the Metropolitan See of Vilnius remained at the head of the only intact Roman Catholic Church hierarchy under Communist rule. *Address:* Lithuania, 232001 Vilnius, Šv. Mikalojaus gatvé 16.

STOLOJAN, Theodor: Prime Minister of Romania; b. 24 Oct. 1943; m., with two c. *Education:* graduate (1966) and doctor (1980) of the Bucharest Institute of Economics. *Career:* he worked as an economist in the food industry and then, for almost 20 years, in the state administration. After the Revolution of December 1989 he was appointed First Deputy Minister of Finance. He remained a financial minister under Petre Roman until April 1991, when he resigned, reportedly because he considered that economic reform was being implemented too slowly. Between May and October he was Chairman of the National Agency for Privatization. On 3 October 1991 President Iliescu designated him for the office of Prime Minister and he formed a Government, which was supported by the National Salvation Front. *Address:* Council of Ministers, Romania, Bucharest.

SURANYI, Dr György: President of the National Bank of Hungary. *Career:* he has been prominent in adjusting Hungarian financial arrangements to the international system. *Address:* 1850 Budapest, Szabadság tér 8–9.

SZABAD, Dr György: President of the Hungarian National Assembly; b. Aug. 1924, in Arad, Romania; ethnic Hungarian; m., with one d. *Education:* studied at the Loránd Eötvös University, Budapest. *Career:* an historian, he worked in a forced labour camp (1944) before returning to an academic career. He became a professor in 1970, his career having been impeded by his involvement in the 1956 Uprising. In 1989 he was a founding member of the Hungarian Democratic Forum and was elected to be President (speaker) of the National Assembly in April 1990. *Address:* National Assembly, Hungary, 1055 Budapest, Kossuth Lájos tér. 1–3.

TEOCTIST, His Holiness Patriarch: Head of the Romanian Orthodox Church, Patriarch of the Metropolitan of Wallachia and Dobrogea and Archbishop of Bucharest; b. 1915. *Career:* born Teoctist Arăpaşu, he was made Bishop of the Romanian Missionary Diocese in the USA, in 1963, but failed to attain a residency permit. In March 1973 he was made Archbishop of Craiova, Metropolitan of Oltenia-Craiova, and later Metropolitan of Moldavia and Suceava. In October 1977 he was appointed Archbishop of Iaşi. In 1986 he was elected Patriarch of the Romanian Orthodox Church. After the Revolution of December 1989 he offered his resignation, but any likely successor was considered as tainted by association with the previous regime as he was, and he was reinstated. *Address:* Romania, 70666 Bucharest, Str. Antim 29.

TERESHCHENKO, Sergei Aleksandrovich: Prime Minister of Kazakhstan. *Career:* he was a supporter of President Nursultan Nazarbayev (q.v.). His appointment to the premiership was part of the government reorganization occasioned by constitutional reforms (such as presidential elections in December 1991) and the discrediting of the Communist establishment after the August 1991 coup attempt. *Address:* Cabinet of Ministers, Kazakhstan, Alma-Ata.

TER-PETROSYAN, Levon Akopovich: President of Armenia; b. 9 Jan. 1945. *Career:* a radical nationalist, he was a member of the Karabakh Committee and was in prison, December 1988–May 1989. He was leader of the Armenian Pan-National Movement and, in August 1990, was elected Chairman of the Supreme Soviet (*de facto* head of state). He was confirmed in office by an overwhelming victory in direct elections for the post of executive President of the Republic, in October 1991. *Address:* Office of the President of the Republic, Armenia, Yerevan.

TŐKES, László: Romanian religious leader; b. 1937, in Transylvania; ethnic Hungarian. *Career:* the son of a minister in the Calvinist Reformed Church, he too became a pastor. He was a vociferous critic of the Ceauşescu regime, and championed the rights of the ethnic Hungarian minority and human rights generally. It was the authorities' attempt to arrest him that was the catalyst for the December Revolution of 1989. He was subsequently made Bishop of Oradea for the Reformed Church. Although he was appointed as a member of the Provisional National Unity Council, he became increasingly critical of the ruling National Salvation Front. By January 1992, however, there was serious concern for his life, following a series of death threats. *Address:* Romania, 3700 Oradea, Str. Craiovei 1.

TOLGYESSY, Peter: Hungarian politician; b. 1956. *Career:* a lawyer who specialized in constitutional law, he had a major role in the round-table negotiations, in 1989. On 24 November 1991 he was elected Chairman of the Alliance of Free Democrats, the main opposition party, in succession to János Kis. *Address:* Alliance of Free Democrats, Hungary, 1051 Budapest, Mérleg u. 5.

TUDJMAN, Dr Franjo: Yugoslav politician and historian, President of Croatia; b. 14 May 1922, in Veliko Trgovišće, northern Croatia. *Education:* he studied at the Higher Military Academy in Belgrade, after the Second World War, and, in 1965, he gained a doctorate in history, at the University of Zagreb. *Career:* he joined Tito's Partisans, in 1941, and, after attending the military academy, he worked in the Ministry of Defence and for the Yugoslav People's Army. He attained the rank of major-general and then left the military to pursue his academic interests in history. He was a professor of history at Zagreb University, from 1963, but was dismissed for his nationalist tendencies, in 1967, and expelled from the League of Communists. Following the *Maspok* movement, he was imprisoned in 1972–74. His dissident activities earned him a prison sentence again, in 1981–84. In 1989 he founded the Croatian Democratic Union, which won the elections to the Croatian Assembly, in 1990. On 30 May the Assembly elected him President of Croatia. He led Croatia towards independence, the moves towards which were formally begun on 25 June 1991, and in the civil war which began that year. Sometimes accused of being too right-wing, he was under pressure from both the moderates and the extreme nationalists, with a policy dependent upon foreign support, which was slow in being realized. *Address:* Office of the President, Croatia, 41000 Zagreb, Banski Dvori.

TUPURKOVSKI, Vasil: Yugoslav (Macedonian) politician, former Yugoslav Collective State Presidency member for Macedonia; b. 1951, in Skopje, Macedonia. *Education:* he gained a doctorate in law (1976). *Career:* a professor of international law, at Skopje University, he joined the League of Communists in 1972. In 1986 he became a member of the presidium of the Central Committee of the federal Party. At a direct, popular election, in 1989, he became the member for Macedonia on the federal State Presidency. During 1991 he generally supported Croatia and Slovenia, although Macedonia tended to favour a continued federation. In early January 1992 he resigned from the Presidency, becoming President Kiro Gligorov's (q.v.) special representative. *Address:* Government of Macedonia, Yugoslavia, Macedonia, 91000 Skopje, Dame Grueva.

TURADZHONZODA, Hajji Akbar: Tadzhikistan religious leader. *Career:* although the Communist regime courted the official Muslim hierarchy, as Kazi (religious leader of Islam in the Republic), he became associated with the opposition. His Kaziat Party is allied with the banned Islamic Renaissance Party and the Sufi spiritualists, and their opposition is inspired by the Afghan mujaheddin. *Address:* Office of the Chief Kazi, Tadzhikistan, Dushanbe.

VAGNORIUS, Gediminas: Prime Minister of Lithuania. *Career:* a prominent member of Sajūdis, the nationalist movement that had won the 1990 elections, he became the head of government upon the resignation of Kazimiere Prunskiene, in January 1991. The Supreme Council had refused to support her Government's proposed price rises, and he replaced her as head of government, amid increasing pressure from the Soviet authorities. In September 1991, however, Lithuania finally achieved recognition of its independent state. *Address:* tumo-Vaizganto 2, 232039 Vilnius, Lithuania.

VAZGEN I, His Holiness Supreme Patriarch: Catholicos of All Armenians, Head of the Armenian Apostolic Church; b. 1908, in Romania. *Career:* born L. K. Baldzhian, he was ordained a priest in Romania and later appointed head of the Armenian Church in Romania and Bulgaria. He was elected Catholicos of All Armenia in 1955. From the mid-1980s he became active in attempting to find a peaceful solution to the dispute over Nagorny Karabakh. *Address:* Residence of the Catholicos of Armenia, Armenia, Echmiadzin.

VIDENOV, Zhan: Bulgarian politician; b. 1959; m. *Education:* graduate of the Moscow Institute of International Relations (speaks Russian, English and Arabic). *Career:* he began his Communist Party career as a Young Communist and worked as a specialist in foreign economic relations. A known conservative hard-liner of the Bulgarian Socialist Party (BSP—former Communists), he was first elected as a deputy in June 1990, in Plovdiv city. In December 1991 he was elected Chairman of the Supreme Council (leader) of the BSP, as the favoured successor of Aleksandur Lilov. *Address:* Bulgaria, 1000 Sofia, pl. Aleksandur Battenberg.

VULCHEV, Prof. Todor: Pres. of the National Bank of Bulgaria; b. 28 October 1922; m., with two c. *Education:* graduated from the National and World Economy Institute of Sofia University. *Career:* he worked mainly at the Bulgarian Academy of Sciences, until being appointed head of the National Bank in 1990. *Address:* Bulgaria, 1000 Sofia, pl. Aleksandur Battenberg 2.

WAŁĘSA, Lech: President of Poland; b. 29 September 1943, in Popowo, in the Włocławek district; m. (Danuta Wałęsa, 1969), with four s. and four d. *Career:* worked as an electrician for a collective farm, fulfilling his two years military service, in 1963–65. In 1967 he began work at the Lenin Shipyard, in Gdansk. By December 1970 he was the head of a strike committee; six years later he was dismissed for his protests about working conditions, voiced at a union meeting. Having then found work repairing machinery, in 1979 he again lost his job, for commemorating the 1970 strike. In August 1980 he joined strikers at the Lenin Shipyard and became head of their 'inter-factory' committee. His success in negotiations with the Government led to the signing of the 'Gdańsk accords', which permitted free trade unions and the right to strike. By 1981 Wałęsa was Chairman of the Solidarity union and movement, which was banned under the martial law introduced in December. He was arrested and interned, in 1981–82, but was involved in subsequent negotiations with the Government, in 1988, which resulted in the lifting of the ban on Solidarity and the prospect of democratic reform. He headed the coalition which defeated Communist rule in the legislative elections of 1989, and was elected President in December 1990. He resigned as leader of Solidarity. As President he acquired a reputation for attempting to dominate government policy, which was more popular when there was still a Communist-dominated parliament, but less so after the elections of 1991. *Address:* Office of the President, Belvedere Palace, Warsaw, Poland.

YELTSIN, Boris Nikolayevich: President of the Russian Federation; b. 1 Feb. 1931, in Sverdlovsk (now Yekaterinburg). *Education:* he graduated from the Urals Polytechnic Institute. *Career:* after several years spent working for construction companies, he began full-time Communist Party work in 1968. He gained a reputation outside Sverdlovsk district, where he was appointed First Secretary in 1976. When Gorbachev came to power, in 1985, he was appointed First Secretary of the Moscow Party Committee. He became outspoken in his commitment to reform and an end to corruption in the Party. His criticism of the slow pace of reform led, in 1987, to his dismissal from his post and from the Politburo and a demotion to a post in the State Construction Committee. In 1989, however, he stood in the elections to the Congress of People's Deputies and won over 90% of the vote in the Moscow constituency. He continued to demand faster reforms and the dismissal of conservative Communists, such as Yegor Ligachev. In 1990 he was elected to the RSFSR (now Russian Federation) Supreme Soviet and, by a narrow margin, was elected its Chairman. His criticisms of Mikhail Gorbachev (q.v.) and the all-Union Government continued, but his attempts to implement reforms in the RSFSR more radical than those proposed by Gorbachev were hindered by his lack of real power. In early 1991 he was granted executive powers by the Supreme Soviet, pending direct elections to an executive presidency of the Russian Federation, in June. He won these elections with a convincing mandate and further secured his authority by his leadership against the coup attempt of August 1991. He was an original signatory of the Minsk Agreement, which established the Commonwealth of Independent States. This move, in December 1991, ensured the demise of the USSR, of which his Russian Federation became the internationally recognized successor state. *Address:* Office of the President, Russian Federation, Moscow, Kremlin.

YULDASHEV, Shavkat Mukhitdinovich: Chairman of the Supreme Soviet of Ukbekistan. *Career:* he succeeded to the post in 1991. *Address:* Supreme Soviet, Uzbekistan, Tashkent.

ZHELEV, Dr Zheliu: President of Bulgaria; b. 3 March 1935, in Vesselinovo village, Shumen district; m., with two c. *Education:* doctorate in philosophy from the University of Sofia. *Career:* in 1965 he was expelled from the Communist Party for an anti-Leninist doctoral thesis (the thesis was not accepted until 1975), after which he was unemployed until 1972, when he began work as a sociologist. He achieved further notoriety in 1982, when his book, *Fascism*, on the nature of totalitarianism, was banned. In the late 1980s, as a prominent dissident, he was one of the founders of the Club for the Support of Glasnost and Perestroika. In December 1989 he became leader of the opposition coalition, the Union of Democratic Forces. He resigned form this post in August 1990, when he was elected President of the Republic; in January 1992 he was re-elected in Bulgaria's first free presidential elections. *Address:* Bulgaria, 1000 Sofia, 2 Blvd Dondukov.

ZORKIN, Prof. Valery Dimitriyevich: Chairman of the Constitutional Court of the Russian Federation. *Career:* a doctor of juridical science and a professor at the Dept of State and Law, MVD Higher Judicial Correspondence School, he was a member of the Russian federation Supreme Soviet's Constitutional Committee. In October 1991 his appointment as chairman of the newly formed Russian Constitutional Court was confirmed by the Supreme Soviet. *Address:* Russian Constitutional Court, Russian Federation, Moscow.